CollegeBoard

THE COLLEGE BOARD
Book of
Majors
SECOND EDITION

THE COLLEGE BOARD

Book of Majors

SECOND EDITION

The College Board, New York

The College Board: connecting students to college success™

The College Board is a not-for-profit membership association whose mission is to connect students to college success and opportunity. Founded in 1900, the association is composed of more than 5,000 schools, colleges, universities, and other educational organizations. Each year, the College Board serves seven million students and their parents, 23,000 high schools, and 3,500 colleges through major programs and services in college admissions, guidance, assessment, financial aid, enrollment, and teaching and learning. Among its best-known programs are the SAT®, the PSAT/NMSQT®, and the Advanced Placement Program® (AP®). The College Board is committed to the principles of excellence and equity, and that commitment is embodied in all of its programs, services, activities, and concerns.

For further information, visit www.collegeboard.com.

Copies of this book may be ordered from College Board Publications, P.O. Box 869010, Plano, Texas 75074, or online at www.collegeboard.com. The price is $24.95.

Editorial inquiries concerning this book should be directed to College Planning Services, The College Board, 45 Columbus Avenue, New York, NY 10023-6992.

In all of its book publishing activities the College Board endeavors to present the works of authors who are well qualified to write with authority on the subject at hand, and to present accurate and timely information. However, the opinions, interpretations, and conclusions of the authors are their own and do not necessarily represent those of the College Board; nothing contained herein should be assumed to represent an official position of the College Board or any of its members.

Library of Congress Control Number: 2006903733

ISBN-10: 0-87447-765-4
ISBN-13: 978-0-87447-765-8

Printed in the United States of America

Dear Friends,

The College Board is dedicated to connecting students to college success and opportunity. We believe in the principles of excellence and equity in education and try to promote them in all that we do. With *The College Board Book of Majors*, we hope to put an authoritative source of college information at your fingertips to help connect you to a college education.

College is a dream worth working hard to achieve. I've been a businessman, a governor, and now, the president of the College Board, but nothing makes me prouder than to say that I am a college graduate. With perseverance, anyone who desires a college education can attain one. College Board publications can help you get there.

My best wishes on your journey to success.

Gaston Caperton
President, The College Board

Contents

Part II: Brief Descriptions of Majors

Brief descriptions of 900 majors 567

Part III: College Listings

Preface

The *College Board Book of Majors* is the only book of its kind that provides a complete, all-in-one source for what students exploring majors need to know: what the majors are about, *and* where they can be studied.

The 193 majors profiled in Part I of this book are primarily undergraduate programs, taught at the associate or bachelor's degree level. These majors represent not only those that are most widely offered, but also those that students most often express interest in.

Each profile of a major is compiled from detailed questionnaires submitted by college professors teaching in the field. Where appropriate, information from secondary sources—including professional and academic associations, national newspapers, and the federal Department of Labor's *Occupational Outlook Handbook* was also used. Additional insights are included from college students enrolled in these majors, who were interviewed for MyRoad™, the College Board's online college planning and guidance tool.

In Part II of this book are brief descriptions of more than 900 majors contained in the *Classification of Instructional Programs: 2000 Edition* (*CIP* for short), developed by the National Center for Educational Statistics for the U.S. Department of Education.

In Part III, those 900 majors are listed alphabetically, with the colleges and graduate schools that offer them presented state by state. Each college listing also indicates at which degree level or levels the major can be studied (certificate, associate, bachelor's, master's, doctorate, or first-professional). Following these are 31 special academic programs, similarly arranged alphabetically, with state-by-state listings of the colleges offering them.

What's New in the Second Edition

This second edition has been revised and expanded to reflect trends over the last two years. Part I now profiles five preprofessional advising programs (such as prelaw and premedicine) which, while not technically majors, are of great interest to students. Additionally, eight more popular majors are profiled, including construction management, Japanese, two new computer-related majors, Chicano studies, environmental design and historic preservation.

Each profile in Part I that has been carried over from the first edition has been reviewed by a college professor and the editors, with special emphasis on the latest career trends. The contact information that appears in the "For more info" section of each profile has also been verified and updated.

About the College Data

In addition, the data in the college listings have been completely updated. These data were provided by the schools themselves in the College Board's Annual Survey of Colleges, conducted in the spring of 2006. Colleges reported their programs of majors according to the *CIP* (even though the names they give majors may differ slightly from the *CIP* titles).

The information provided by the colleges was verified by a staff of editors to ensure that the data are as complete and accurate as possible. However, program changes occur, and readers are urged to contact colleges directly to confirm facts related to their major of choice.

To be eligible for inclusion, a college must be accredited by a national or regional accrediting association recognized by the U.S. Department of Education. Graduate programs are listed only for those schools that also have undergraduate programs. A complete list of the colleges appearing in this book can be found at the back, along with an alphabetical index of every major profiled in Part I and/or listed in Part III.

Acknowledgements

Many people helped with the creation and publication of this book, and it is a pleasure to acknowledge them here:

First of all, thanks are due to Renee Gernand, whose efforts, assistance, and guidance were essential to the successful completion of this book. Thanks also to Bonnie Schullenberger, for her help with locating professors and coordinating the questionnaires, and Svea Vocke, who assisted with editing the original profiles of majors. "What to know about majors" and the introductions to the major categories in Part I were written by Barbara Kram. Kevin Troy and Erica Lies provided editorial assistance throughout all phases of development and production; Susan Joseph did the copyediting. The enormous task of collecting and verifying the college information in Part III of this book was conducted by Stan Bernstein and the editorial staff of the Annual Survey of Colleges, under the direction of Shauna Morrison, and with the assistance of Lesley McBain and Cathy Serico. Thanks to everyone in Creative Services who, under the direction of Kathryn Diminnie, brought the book to press; and to John Mullen, Cathy Harlem, and the staff at Thomas Tech Solutions, Inc., who provide the technological savvy that helps us turn our databases into books.

The professors, who made gifts of their knowledge, insights, and enthusiasm for their subjects, are individually acknowledged in the list of contributors beginning on the following page. It is a privilege to forward those gifts along to the students who, we all hope, will find guidance in this book.

Tom Vanderberg
Editor, Database Publications
The College Board

List of contributors

Agriculture

Arthur Cameron
Professor of Horticulture
Michigan State University

Stephanie Doores
Associate Professor of Food Science
Penn State University Park

Lee A. Edgerton
Director of Undergraduate Studies, Department of
    Animal Sciences
University of Kentucky

Donald W. Larson
Professor, Department of Agricultural, Environmental,
    and Development Economics
Ohio State University

Kenneth L. Larson
Professor Emeritus, Department of Agronomy
Iowa State University

Murray H. Milford
Professor Emeritus, Department of Soil and Crop
    Sciences
Texas A&M University

M. Edward Rister
Professor of Agricultural Economics
Texas A&M University

H. Jerry Schurink
Director of Equine Studies and IHSA Team Coach
University of Massachusetts Amherst

Douglas L. Young
Professor, College of Agricultural, Human and Natural
    Resource Sciences
Washington State University

Architecture

Michael Bednar
Associate Professor of Architecture
University of Virginia

Philip N. Pregill
Professor and Chair, Landscape Architecture
California State University: Pomona

Alfred D. Price
Associate Professor, Department of Urban and Regional
    Planning
State University of New York at Buffalo

John B. Wright
Professor of Geography and Planning
New Mexico State University

Area, ethnic, and gender studies

Lynne S. Abel
Associate Dean for Undergraduate Education, College of
    Arts and Sciences
Cornell University

Sandra Lipsitz Bem
Professor of Psychology
Cornell University

Bernard Haykel
Associate Professor of Middle Eastern and Islamic
    Studies
New York University

Eleuteria Hernández
Student Affairs Officer, Department of Chicana/o
    Studies
University of California: Los Angeles

Daniel Horowitz
Professor of American Studies
Smith College

Theresa Chang-whei Jen
Professor and Director, East Asian Studies
Lauder Institute, Wharton School, University of
    Pennsylvania

Reynaldo F. Macías
Professor of Chicana/o Studies, Education & Applied
    Linguistics
University of California: Los Angeles

R. Baxter Miller
Professor of English and Director, Institute for African
    American Studies
University of Georgia

Peter W. Rees
Associate Professor of Geography and Former Director,
    Latin American Studies Program
University of Delaware

Kathryn W. Shanley
Associate Professor and Chair of Native American
    Studies
University of Montana

Biological sciences

Austin E. Brooks
Treves Professor of Biology
Wabash College

William H. Coleman
Professor of Biology
University of Hartford

Carter Denniston
Professor, Genetics and Medical Genetics
University of Wisconsin–Madison

Robert S. Greene
Professor of Biology
Niagara University

Eileen Gregory
Professor of Biology
Rollins College

Kenneth F. Haynes
Professor, Department of Entomology
University of Kentucky

Donald L. Lovett
Associate Professor, Department of Biology
The College of New Jersey

Douglas Meikle
Professor and Chair, Department of Zoology
Miami University

Amanda Norvell
Assistant Professor, Department of Biology
The College of New Jersey

C.O. Patterson
Associate Professor, Department of Biology and
    Molecular and Environmental Plant Sciences
Texas A&M University

Gregory M. Raner
Associate Professor, Chemistry and Biochemistry
University of North Carolina at Greensboro

Dean E. Wendt
Assistant Professor, Biological Sciences Department and
    Center for Coastal Marine Science
California Polytechnic State University

Business

Gedas Adomavicius
Assistant Professor, Carlson School of Management
University of Minnesota

Stephen J. Brown
David S. Loeb Professor of Finance
Stern School of Business, New York University

Peter Bycio
Professor, Department of Management and
    Entrepreneurship
Williams College of Business, Xavier University

Wayne F. Cascio
U.S. Bank Term Professor of Management
University of Colorado at Denver

Diane Kaufman Fredette
Chair and Professor, Construction Management
    Program, School of Architecture
Pratt Institute

Lorin M. Hitt
Alberto Vitale Term Associate Professor of Operations
    and Information Management
The Wharton School, University of Pennsylvania

Susan Ivancevich
Associate Professor of Accounting
University of North Carolina at Wilmington

Carol A. B. Jordan
Eminent Scholar of Risk Management and Insurance
Troy State University

Ann-Mary Kapusta
Associate Dean, McDonough School of Business
Georgetown University

Mark Lee Levine
Professor, Burns School of Real Estate and Construction
    Management
University of Denver

Debbie Thorne McAlister
Chair, Department of Marketing
Texas State University: San Marcos

Charles J. Metelka
Professor, Department of Hospitality and Tourism
University of Wisconsin–Stout

Patricia Rigia
Professor and Director, Fashion Merchandising Division,
    School of Business
University of Bridgeport

Stephen Spinelli, Jr.
Vice Provost for Entrepreneurship and Global
    Management
Babson College

Communications

Thomas A. Bowers
James L. Knight Professor and Interim Dean, School of
    Journalism and Mass Communication
University of North Carolina at Chapel Hill

John Doolittle
Associate Director, Center for Teaching Excellence, and
    Associate Professor
American University

Bruce E. Gronbeck
A. Craig Baird Distinguished Professor of Public Address
University of Iowa

Joel A. Kline
Assistant Professor of Business and Economics and
    Director, Digital Communications Program
Lebanon Valley College

Patsy G. Watkins
Associate Professor and Chair, Lemke Department of
    Journalism
University of Arkansas

Computer and information sciences

Sampath Kannan
Associate Dean of Engineering
University of Pennsylvania

Anne Marchant
Associate Professor, Applied Information Department
George Mason University

Kathryn M. Stewart
Chair, Computer Technology
Tallahassee Community College

Murray Turoff
Distinguished Professor, Information Systems
    Department
New Jersey Institute of Technology

Education

Mary C. Clement
Associate Professor of Teacher Education
Berry College

Jeannine P. Jones
Professor of Middle Grades Education
University of North Carolina at Charlotte

Dawn Eddy Molloy
Faculty Research Associate
University of Maryland

Lynda M. Nilges
Associate Professor, Department of Physical Education
University of South Carolina

Susan J. Olson
Professor and Chair, Department of Educational
    Foundations and Leadership
The University of Akron

Engineering

Stanley M. Barnett
Professor of Chemical Engineering and Pharmaceutics
University of Rhode Island

Roger H. Compton
Dean and Professor of Engineering
Webb Institute

Lyle. D. Feisel
Dean Emeritus, Watson School of Engineering and
    Applied Science
State University of New York at Binghamton

Audeen W. Fentiman
Chair, Nuclear Engineering Program
Ohio State University

Stephan Grilli
Chair and Professor of Ocean Engineering
University of Rhode Island

Edward A. Hiler
Vice Chancellor and Dean of Agriculture and Life
    Sciences Emeritus
Texas A&M University

Keith D. Hjelmstad
Associate Dean of Engineering and Professor of Civil
    Engineering
University of Illinois at Urbana-Champaign

Charles A. Kliche
Professor, Mining Engineering and Management
    Department
South Dakota School of Mines and Technology

C. Patrick Koelling
Associate Professor, Grado Department of Industrial and
    Systems Engineering
Virginia Polytechnic Institute and State University

Alan Lawley
A.W. Grosvenor Professor of Materials Engineering
    Emeritus
Drexel University

Brian A. Rock
Associate Professor of Architectural Engineering
University of Kansas

Malcolm L. Spaulding
Professor of Ocean Engineering
University of Rhode Island

Alfred G. Striz
Professor and L. A. Comp Chair in Engineering
University of Oklahoma

Calvin L. White
Professor of Materials Science and Engineering
Michigan Technological University

Frank H. Young
Professor Emeritus of Computer Science and Software
    Engineering
Rose-Hulman Institute of Technology

Engineering technology

Harold L. Broberg
Associate Dean of Engineering, Technology, and
    Computer Science
Indiana University–Purdue University Fort Wayne

Pierre Catala
Senior Lecturer Emeritus
Texas A&M University

Paul Clarke
Lead Instructor, Drafting and Engineering Technology
MiraCosta College

Thomas M. Hall, Jr.
Professor and Head, Department of Engineering
    Technology
Northwestern State University

James Kamm
Professor of Mechanical Engineering Technology
University of Toledo

Mark R. Steinle
Professor, Department of Trades and Technology
Casper College

Indrajith Wijayratne
Associate Professor of Surveying
Michigan Technological University

English language and literature

Jonathan Fink
Creative Writing Fellow in Poetry
Emory University

David A. McMurrey
Program Chair, Technical Communications
Austin Community College

Brett C. Millier
Reginald L. Cook Professor of American Literature
Middlebury College

James G. Taaffe
Professor of English
University of Alabama

Family and consumer sciences

Eva L. Essa
Professor of Human Development and Family Studies
University of Nevada: Reno

Sally L. Fortenberry
Associate Professor and Internship Coordinator,
    Department of Design, Merchandising and Textiles
Texas Christian University

Bonita A. Glatz
Professor of Food Science and Human Nutrition
Iowa State University

Penny A. Ralston
Professor and Dean, College of Human Sciences
Florida State University, Tallahassee

Paul Sorgule
Dean of Culinary Arts and Hospitality
Paul Smith's College

Anne L. Sweaney
Professor and Head, Housing and Consumer Economics,
    College of Family and Consumer Sciences
University of Georgia

Health

Debra L. Agard
Clinical Assistant Professor, Department of Pharmacy
    Practice
University of Illinois at Chicago College of Pharmacy

Marcia A. Armstrong
Director, Medical/Laboratory Technology and
    Phlebotomy Programs
University of Hawaii: Kapiolani Community College

Paula Owens Ashby
Assistant Director of Academic Services and Chief
    Health Professions Advisor
University of Maryland: Baltimore County

Jean E. Bartels
Chair and Professor of Nursing
Georgia Southern University

Georgine W. Bills
Program Director, Respiratory Therapy
Weber State University

Stan S. Cooke
Professor and Head of Department of Communication
    Disorders
Western Kentucky University

Susan S. Deusinger
Director, Program in Physical Therapy
Washington University School of Medicine

Anne E. Dickerson
Professor and Chair, Department of Occupational
    Therapy
East Carolina University

Leonard H. Friedman
Associate Professor of Public Health
Oregon State University

Paul N. Gonzales
Director, Radiologic Technology Program
Fresno City College

Rosann M. Ippolito
Associate Director, Physician Assistant Program
Northeastern University

Mary Anne Marsh
Chair, Department of Nursing
Dickinson University

Connie L. Peterson
Assistant Professor
James Madison University

Professor Nicholas G. Popovich
Head, Department of Pharmacy Administration
University of Illinois at Chicago College of Pharmacy

Susan H. Stadler
Director, Veterinary Technician Program
Lehigh Carbon and Northampton Community College

Annmary E. Thomas
Assistant Professor, Emergency Medical Services
    Program
Drexel University

Olivia Bennett Wood
Associate Professor and Director, Didactic Program in
    Dietetics
Purdue University

Nancy C. Zinser
Professor and Chair, Dental Health Services
Palm Beach Community College

Humanities

D. Terence Langendoen
Professor Emeritus, Department of Linguistics
University of Arizona

Richard T. Lee
Brownell Professor of Philosophy
Trinity College

Michael D. Richards
Samford Professor of History
Sweet Briar College

Kenneth S. Rothwell, Jr.
Associate Professor and Chair, Department of Classics
University of Massachusetts Boston

Tobin Siebers
Professor and Director, Program in Comparative
    Literature
University of Michigan

Joseph Ugoretz
Professor of English and Director of Teaching and
    Learning with Technology
Borough of Manhattan Community College

Languages

Theresa A. Antes
Assistant Professor of French and Linguistics
University of Florida

Scott Cook
Associate Professor of Chinese
Grinnell College

Michael Fishbein
Lecturer in Arabic
University of California: Los Angeles

Melissa Frazier
Professor of Russian Language and Literature
Sarah Lawrence College

H. Mack Horton
Professor of Japanese Literature
University of California, Berkeley

Mike Kemp
Professor, Department of ASL and Deaf Studies
Gallaudet University

María Negroni
Assistant Professor
Sarah Lawrence College

Robert E. Proctor
Joanne Toor Cummings '50 Professor of Italian
Connecticut College

Heidi Thomann Tewarson
Professor and Chair, Department of German Language
    and Literature
Oberlin College

Legal studies

Diane Curtis
Prelaw Advisor
University of Massachusetts Amherst

Jeffrey J. Davis
Assistant Professor of Political Science
University of Maryland, Baltimore County

Lenore M. Molee
Associate Professor and Deputy Chair, Department of
    Legal Studies
Montclair State University

Mathematics

James Alexander
Chair, Department of Mathematics
Case Western Reserve University

David M. Bressoud
DeWitt Wallace Professor of Mathematics
Macalester College

Michele Marini
Undergraduate Administrator, Department of Statistics
Virginia Polytechnic Institute and State University

Multi/interdisciplinary studies

Stephen M. Buhler
Professor of English
University of Nebraska-Lincoln

Joseph F. Cimini
Associate Professor, Department of Sociology &
    Criminal Justice
University of Scranton

Caroline Higgins
Professor of History and Convener, Peace and Global
    Studies
Earlham College

Richard S. Lewis
Associate Professor of Psychology and Neuroscience
Pomona College

Ann Milkovich McKee
Assistant Professor and Director, Undergraduate Historic
    Preservation
Goucher College

Eve Walsh Stoddard
Professor of English and Chair, Global Studies
    Department
St. Lawrence University

Natural resources and conservation

Eric M. Hallerman
Professor and Associate Head, Department of Fisheries
    and Wildlife Sciences
Virginia Polytechnic Institute and State University

David H. Hirth
Associate Professor and Chair, Wildlife and Fisheries
    Biology Program
University of Vermont

Steven E. Jungst
Professor, Department of Forestry
Iowa State University

David K. Loomis
Associate Professor, Human Dimensions Research Unit,
    Department of Natural Resources Conservation
University of Massachusetts Amherst

Michael Maniates
Associate Professor of Environmental Science and
    Political Science
Allegheny College

David E. Smith
Professor, Department of Environmental Sciences
University of Virginia

Parks and recreation

Lowell Caneday
Professor of Leisure Studies
Oklahoma State University

Stephen W. Jefferson
Chief Undergraduate Adviser and Undergraduate
    Program Director, Sport Management Program
University of Massachusetts Amherst

Physical sciences

Neta A. Bahcall
Professor of Astrophysics
Princeton University

Dave Esser
Professor and Program Coordinator, Department of
    Aeronautical Science
Embry-Riddle Aeronautical University

Richard G. French
Professor and Chair, Astronomy Department, and
    Director, Whitin Observatory
Wellesley College

Ronald E. Johnson
University Professor and Associate Professor of
    Oceanography
Old Dominion University

Stanley T. Jones
Professor and Chair, Department of Physics &
    Astronomy
University of Alabama

James P. Koermer
Professor of Meteorology
Plymouth State University

Jonathan W. Peterson
Associate Professor of Geology and Environmental
    Science
Hope College

James N. Spencer
William G. and Elizabeth R. Simeral Professor of
    Chemistry
Franklin & Marshall College

Protective services

Dennis R. Longmire
Professor, College of Criminal Justice
Sam Houston State University

Frank Vozzo
Associate Professor of Forensic Science
Russell Sage College for Women

Thomas J. Woodford
Associate Professor and Department Head, Fire
    Protection and Safety Technology
Oklahoma State University

Public administration

Danny L. Balfour
Professor and Director, School of Public and Nonprofit
    Administration
Grand Valley State University

Tuesday L. Cooper
Associate Dean, School of Education, Professional
    Studies, and the Graduate Division
Eastern Connecticut State University

Irene Queiro-Tajalli
Professor and Executive Director of Undergraduate
    Education, School of Social Work
Indiana University–Purdue University Indianapolis

Religion and theology

Kamran S. Aghaie
Assistant Professor of Islamic Studies
University of Texas at Austin

Sandra Billy
Director, Center for Sacred Music
Virginia Wesleyan College

Shmuel Bolozky
Professor of Hebrew
University of Massachusetts Amherst

John A. Grim
Professor of Religion
Bucknell University

Andrew E. Hill
Professor of Old Testament
Wheaton College (IL)

Richard B. Pilgrim
Associate Professor and Chair, Department of Religion
Syracuse University

Shelley Shepherd
Preministerial studies advisor
Southern Methodist University

David G. Truemper
Professor and Chair of Theology
Valparaiso University

Social sciences

David L. Browman
Chairman, Interdisciplinary Program in Archaeology
Washington University in St. Louis

Gregory A. Elmes
Professor of Geography, Department of Geology and
    Geography
West Virginia University

Jacqueline Johnson
Assistant Professor, Sociology
Fordham University

Andrew A. Latham
Associate Professor of Political Science and Associate
    Director, Center for Scholarship and Teaching
Macalester College

Robert Mandel
Professor and Chair, International Affairs Department
Lewis and Clark College

Lee McCann
Professor of Psychology
University of Wisconsin-Oshkosh

Baron Perlman
Professor of Psychology
University of Wisconsin-Oshkosh

John J. Siegfried
Professor of Economics
Vanderbilt University

Visual and performing arts

Chrystelle Trump Bond
Professor of Dance and Founding Chair, Dance
    Department
Goucher College

Lilly Ann Boruszkowski
Associate Professor
Southern Illinois University Carbondale

David B. Brownlee
Professor of the History of Art
University of Pennsylvania

Jo Anne Caputo
Professor
Cleveland Institute of Music

Meredith Davis
Professor of Graphic Design
North Carolina State University College of Design

Bevin Engman
Associate Professor of Art
Colby College

David B. Greene
Director of the Arts Studies Program
North Carolina State University

Janine King
Associate Professor and Chair, Department of Interior
    Design
University of Florida

Anthony J. LaMagra
Professor and Director of Music Emeritus
Manhattanville College

Judy Lochhead
Professor and Chair, Department of Music
State University of New York at Stony Brook

Ronald Naversen
Professor of Scenic Design
Southern Illinois University Carbondale

Fred Niles
Professor and Chair, Department of Visual Arts
University of Dayton

Donald Poynter
Animation Instructor
School of Visual Arts

Mary Stephens
Department Chair for Fashion Design
Fashion Institute of Design and Merchandising

Diane Timmerman
Associate Professor of Theatre
Butler University

Allen Winold
Professor Emeritus of Music
Indiana University Bloomington

How to use this book

Find a major, find a college

If you are thinking about college majors, this book offers a lot of help.

If you have no idea what you want to study in college, it can help you discover majors that might appeal to you.

If there are several majors that interest you, it can help you make an informed choice.

If you already know what you want to major in, it can help you prepare for the program by letting you know what to expect. (Or it might present a completely different but more attractive option you never knew existed—which just might be the best help of all.)

But choosing a major is only half the job—you also have to find a college that offers it, at the degree level that is right for you, and in a place where you want, or need, to be. This book helps you do that, too. (The description of Part II below will tell you how.)

Part I: Full Descriptions of Majors

According to the U.S. Department of Education's *Classification of Instructional Programs: 2000 Edition* (CIP), there are over 900 fields of study—majors, that is. Part I describes 193 of these in full detail; all are briefly described in Part II.

Major categories

The 193 profiled majors are grouped into 26 broad categories, arranged alphabetically. Each category begins with a short write-up about the field of study as a whole, to guide your exploration of the majors and the colleges that offer them. You'll get a feel for the different ways colleges approach the majors, insights from professors, and guidance on questions to ask as you explore the majors in the group.

The category introductions are just a starting point. You'll want to read all the details in the individual profiles of the majors that interest you.

The profiles

Each profile is based on information gathered from college professors teaching in the field. The major is described as it is generally taught at colleges across the United States, not just at a particular school. Throughout, the term *college* refers to any institution of higher education—two-year college, four-year college, university, technical school, professional school, and so on.

How did we pick the majors to profile? First, we looked at the majors that high school students (1.5 million of them) said they were most interested in when they completed a brief questionnaire on their SAT registration forms. Then we examined which majors are most widely offered at colleges across the country, to be sure a broad spectrum was represented. And we added a few that we believe are noteworthy or up-and-coming (like Japanese and construction management), even if they are not among the most popular or the most available.

Almost all the profiled majors are for undergraduate study, either at the two-year associate degree level or in a four-year bachelor's degree program. For the few majors that are available only as graduate programs (physical therapy, for instance), we've described the undergraduate course of study that will prepare you for grad school. We also describe preprofessional programs (such as prelaw and premedicine) that are technically not majors.

The following headings correspond to what you will find in the profiles.

Name of major: This is the generic name of the major that is most often used and most widely recognized. You are likely to see variations in individual college catalogs, but they should be similar to the name shown here.

Also known as: Colleges don't always agree on what to call a major; alternative names that you might come across are listed here.

What it's about: This paragraph gives you a quick idea of the subject area the major covers and the careers it prepares you for.

Is this for you? This section should help you select a major according to what you like to do or to study, what you are good at, and what your personal qualities are. We've listed some characteristics common to students who have succeeded in the major. They are not requirements, and you certainly don't have to match them all, or even any of them; your interest in a particular field may be based on something totally different and be just as valid.

Recommended high school prep: The course units recommended here refer to years of study in a four-year high school. "Math 3" refers to Algebra I, geometry, and Algebra II; "lab science 3" includes earth science, biology, and either chemistry or physics, each with a lab component. "Social studies 3" includes U.S. history, world history, and either geography or government/economics.

The recommended courses tend to be similar for all majors, because a well-rounded high school curriculum, with courses in English, math, science, social studies, and a foreign language, is generally required for admission to most colleges, regardless of major. The recommendations will differ with respect to additional units or elective courses that can help you prepare for a particular major. But these are suggestions only; your high school may not teach some of the courses mentioned here.

What if you don't know what you want to major in? Preserve your options by taking the most rigorous courses you can. The College Board recommends four years of English, four years of math (including Algebra I, Algebra II, Geometry, and pre-Calculus or Calculus), a minimum of two years of lab science (some colleges require more), three years of social science and history, and at least two years of the same foreign language. Your school counselor will have the best advice as to whether your choice of high school courses will support your college goals.

Did you know...? Included here are important aspects or interesting facts about the major, or the careers it may lead to, that many students entering the major are not aware of.

Typical courses in the major: This list is a sampling of courses commonly offered in the major, in roughly the order of sequence they are taken. Some colleges offer fewer courses than these and some more, and course titles may vary.

Concentrations: You can sometimes concentrate your studies, or specialize, in a certain area within your major. The concentrations listed here are not available at all colleges. Concentrations that are generally not available until grad school are listed separately.

What the study of this major is like: This section tells you what you'll actually study in a major, and how the major is generally taught and learned. We've described differences in emphasis, requirements, and philosophies among colleges that offer the major, to help you evaluate the program at the colleges you are considering. You will also get a sense of what your academic lifestyle will be like, and what challenges to expect.

Other majors you might like: This section lists majors that are related by subject matter, approach, or the interests and characteristics of the students who study them. Some of the related fields are obvious, but some may surprise you; they are included to help you cover all the bases, or perhaps to suggest an option you may not have known about. Majors in **bold type** are fully profiled in this book. Those in regular type are described in Part II.

Questions to ask colleges: These questions are designed to help you find colleges that have strong programs for your major, or that approach the subject area in a way that is compatible with your goals and interests. Good for college visits, interviews, or an email to the Web sites of the colleges you are considering.

Career options and trends: This section lists job titles in careers the major may lead to—an asterisk indicates a type of job that graduates most often pursue. Also described are any additional education, certification, or licensure requirements for the careers listed, plus trends occurring or likely to occur in careers related to the major.

Insider's viewpoint: We asked professors to tell something about what appeals to them about the major. We also asked college students actually enrolled in the major to give some pointers or insights, or to describe their experiences as a major in class, internships, or field studies. [The student perspectives are taken from MyRoad, the College Board's online college and career planning guidance resource.]

For more info: Contact information is provided here for associations (educational and business) that you should investigate to explore further the major and/or related careers. Most of these associations have robust sections for students, although sometimes you have to drill down to find them.

Part II: Brief Descriptions of Majors

Adapted from the U.S. Department of Education's *Classification of Instructional Programs: 2000 Edition (CIP)*, these descriptions cover the whole spectrum of majors offered by colleges throughout the United States, and are included to supplement the college listings in Part III. Each description indicates the scope of the major and, where appropriate, the jobs for which you are prepared. Some of these majors are only available at the graduate degree level.

Part III: College Listings

Colleges Listed by Major and State

Here you will find the colleges that offer the major (or majors) you are interested in. The majors are presented alphabetically, and under each major is a state-by-state list of the colleges that teach it. Some colleges listed here do not offer majors in the traditional sense but provide in-depth specialization that is very similar to the course work usually required for a degree.

A lot more majors are listed here than are profiled in Part I. There are over 900, in fact—all the undergraduate majors and graduate programs offered by the schools responding to the College Board's Annual Survey of Colleges. The names of the majors conform to the *CIP*, but individual colleges may use different names in their course catalogs.

Levels of study

Are you looking for a two-year program or a four-year program? Going on to graduate school? Thinking about beefing up your credentials with a certificate in your career area? Then you need to know that the colleges offering the major you want also offer it at the right level of study for you.

In the list of colleges by major, the different degree levels offered for each major are designated by the following letters found after the college name:

C   Certificate or diploma
A   Associate degree
B   Bachelor's degree
T   Teacher certification
M   Master's degree
D   Doctorate
F   First-professional degree

Certificate or diploma. Certificates are awarded to students who complete nondegree programs, which usually take one year or less and are most frequently offered in technical and vocational fields of study. Entry requirements for the programs may vary; for some you might need only a high school diploma or equivalent, while for others (accounting, for example) you might have to have some college under your belt.

Associate degree. The degrees most frequently earned at this level are the associate of arts (A.A.) (in the context of academic degrees, arts refers to the humanities, not to painting and drawing) and the associate of science (A.S.). The associate in applied science (A.A.S.) is also used for technological or vocational fields. Usually two years in length, associate degree programs are most often found at community colleges and technical schools, but they are also offered at many four-year colleges. Associate degrees in transfer programs are designed to provide the first two years of a four-year bachelor's degree at most colleges.

Bachelor's degree. Programs in which you earn a bachelor's (sometimes called a baccalaureate) degree usually take four years, but some programs can be completed in three years and some take five. The bachelor of arts (B.A.) and the bachelor of science (B.S.) are the most common; both include general education courses, a major, and electives. Some programs offer specialized degrees, such as the bachelor of fine arts (B.F.A.) or bachelor of architecture (B.Arch.). There are no absolute, or universally accepted, differences between the degrees, and colleges may vary in whether they give an arts or a science degree to graduates in a particular program.

Teacher certification. Each state sets its own certification standards, and all colleges that prepare teachers are accredited by the state in which they are located. Students must meet both bachelor's degree requirements and state certification requirements. Most states require candidates to pass an examination in the field they plan to teach.

Master's degree. Master of arts (M.A.) and master of science (M.S.) programs are graduate degrees in the liberal arts and sciences, intended for students with B.A. or B.S. degrees,

and usually take one or two years to complete. Among other master's degree programs are the master of business administration (MBA), the master of library science (M.L.S.), and the master of social work (M.S.W.) In some fields, such as law and medicine, the master's degree follows the first-professional degree (J.D., M.D.).

Doctorate. The most common type of doctorate is the doctor of philosophy (Ph.D.), awarded in most of the humanities, the arts, and the sciences. Examples of other programs are the doctor of education (Ed.D.) and the doctor of public health (D.P.H.). Doctoral programs usually consist of course work and independent research culminating in a dissertation or other formal presentation of the results of independent study. Length of study varies widely, and is usually self-determined.

First-professional degree. These programs provide the academic prerequisites to become licensed in a recognized profession, such as medicine, law, or veterinary medicine. At least two years of prior college-level study are required for entrance into the program, and the total registered time of study must equal six academic years. First-professional degrees are awarded in the following fields:

Chiropractic	D.C., D.C.M.
Dentistry	D.D.S., D.M.D.
Divinity/Ministry	D.D., M.Div.
Law	L.L.B., J.D.
Medicine	M.D.
Optometry	O.D.
Osteopathic medicine	D.O.
Pharmacy	Pharm.D.
Podiatry	Pod.D., D.P., D.P.M.
Rabbinical/Talmudic studies	M.H.L., Rav.
Veterinary medicine	D.V.M.

Special academic programs

In addition to majors, minors, and concentrations, many colleges offer other ways to enhance, focus, or further shape your undergraduate education. For each of the following programs, there is a state-by-state listing of colleges that offer them.

Combined bachelor's graduate program. In this program, you study at both the undergraduate and the graduate levels. Usually, you can earn a bachelor's degree and a master's or a first-professional degree in less time than if you pursued the two degrees separately.

Double major. Colleges listed here allow you to complete the requirements of two majors at the same time.

External degree. If you want or need to earn a college degree with minimal or no classroom attendance, an external degree program allows you to do so through independent study, distance learning, proficiency exams, and demonstrated personal experience.

Semester at sea. You spend a semester on a research vessel, doing field work in the marine sciences and taking academic course work.

Student-designed major. This program allows you to create for yourself a major that is not formally offered by the college. You develop your major, which is likely to be nontraditional and interdisciplinary, with the approval of a college officer or a committee.

Teacher certification. Colleges that have certification programs can prepare you to meet state requirements for teaching in elementary and secondary schools. [See a more detailed explanation of teacher certification in "Levels of Study" above.]

United Nations semester. The colleges listed here let you take courses at a college in the New York City area while you participate in an internship program at the United Nations.

Urban semester. You spend a semester in a major city, such as New York, Chicago, Los Angeles, or Houston, experiencing life in an urban center while pursuing course work, seminars, and/or internships related to your major.

Washington semester. You take an internship program with a government agency or department in the Washington, D.C., metro area. You can earn field service credit for your work and may also take courses at area colleges.

Colleges in this book

Every college that appears in this book is listed here, state by state, with its Web site address if it was provided; otherwise with its street address.

Alphabetical index of majors

A page reference in bold indicates a full profile of the major begins on that page. Otherwise, the page references are to the "Colleges listed by major" in Part III.

What to know about majors

What is a major?

Your college major is the subject that you will take the most courses in and learn most about. It's the area of study that your degree will be in, after you complete the required courses.

As an undergraduate, you will most likely work toward a two-year Associate of Arts (A.A.) or Associate of Science (A.S.) degree, or a four-year Bachelor of Arts (B.A.), Bachelor of Science (B.S.), or Bachelor of Fine Arts (B.F.A.) degree.

Whatever your major, you'll probably take up to half your courses in the liberal arts, to fulfill what's known as "general education" or "core" requirements. This group of subjects includes the humanities, such as literature, the fine arts (such as music and art), philosophy, and history; foreign languages; the social sciences (like anthropology, psychology, economics, political science, and sociology); math; and the biological sciences (such as zoology) and the physical sciences (for example, astronomy, chemistry, geology, and physics). Most students take these general education requirements in the first two years of a four-year program. Many two-year colleges also have liberal arts requirements.

Why so much work outside your major? Colleges want to make sure that you have a well-rounded education—that you become familiar with a wide variety of subjects. If you're an English major, for example, you're likely to benefit more from your literature courses if you also explore, say, psychology and history. If you're a math major, you'll need to be able to communicate your ideas. Think of general education as a foundation of knowledge to support your major studies. The liberal arts expose you to new ideas, and open your mind to many ways of thinking and understanding the world.

How to choose a major

You may have no idea, at the moment, what you want to study in college. A good way to zero in on a major is to think of what interests you and what you are good at. Examine your academic strengths and the subjects that inspire you to learn. Which are your favorite classes in high school? Where did you get the best grades?

What activities do you enjoy, either in or outside school? Are you a whiz at creating cartoons on the computer? Does teaching a younger sibling to cook give you pleasure? Do you love working with your hands or being outdoors? Maybe you're a political junkie who can't get enough current events. Or do you make sense of the world by learning about the past? Any of these skills and interests might suggest a major (for instance, animation, chef training, forestry, journalism, archaeology).

For many students, hobbies and extracurricular activities are as important as class work. If that's you, then maybe your major will relate to your experience in community or volunteer work, religious activities, camping or Scouting, sports or the arts.

What are your values and your vision of the future? What do you see yourself doing for a living? Do you plan to go on to graduate or professional school? Do you want to make sure that you are financially comfortable above all else? Maybe you see yourself as a leader and a motivator of others. Can you picture yourself doing scientific research or working in health care? Do you like to work outdoors? Are you an artist? Have you always wanted to be a teacher? Think about what matters to you and how your priorities may affect your choice of a major.

Then, look around and ask yourself how the world affects you. Are there careers, like nursing, that have a shortage of professionals, so that a degree in the subject should be a passport to a good job? Are you worried that, in a global economy, many jobs may be shipped overseas? If so, you may want to choose a major based on the likely needs of the job market. (You can go to www.bls.gov/oco for more information.)

Look inside yourself and look outside at other forces in your life. Before you know it, you'll start to make some choices about what to study.

When to decide on your major

Many first-year college students are undecided about their majors, and there's nothing wrong with needing more time to make a decision. Most four-year colleges expect you to declare (choose) your major at the end of your second year or at the beginning of your third year. That gives you time to take courses, including the liberal arts requirements, in a number of fields before you settle on a major.

During your first two years as an undergraduate, you can usually take some electives—nonrequired courses that interest you. If you have not yet decided on a major, you can use your electives to sample several areas of study—for instance, you might take introductory courses in two or three fields that you are considering as a major. Whether you choose electives as a way to test-drive a major or simply to learn more about a subject that appeals to you, electives will give you the opportunity to explore new ideas.

For some degrees, however, you will want to declare a major as soon as possible. That's because some majors have requirements that you'll have to meet in your first year or two of college. An example is nursing: you may have to qualify for the major by achieving a certain grade-point average in prerequisite courses before being admitted to the college's nursing program. Another example is an education major: you may need certain grades in liberal arts courses in order to qualify for a teaching program. Being accepted by a college doesn't guarantee that you'll get into the program you want at the college. Before you begin your first year, find out what's required, so you can work out your education plan.

Applied and academic majors

You can divide majors into two big groups. One group consists of the *applied majors*. These programs prepare you for a specific career by giving you the knowledge and skills you'll need in a particular line of work. When you go to work in that field, you'll put into action the information and skills you learned in college. Some examples are food science, landscape architecture, finance, real estate, journalism, special education, electrical engineering technology, nursing, veterinary technology, and forensic science. Applied majors also prepare you for the special licensing or certifications you'll need in jobs like accounting, teaching, occupational therapy, and social work.

The other big group covers the *academic majors*. Many of these majors are in the arts and sciences and include the humanities, science, and math. The academic majors don't necessarily lead to specific careers, though. They prepare you for graduate studies or for professions in which a wide range of skills and creative talents are valued—the ability to communicate, to understanding people, to read, to think about the world, or to work with numbers. Some examples of academic majors are African-American studies and Latin American studies, English, history, mathematics, chemistry, economics, and communications. (Colleges don't always agree on which majors fall into the liberal arts category. You'll find both applied and academic majors in this book.)

Applied and academic majors each have advantages and disadvantages. For the academic majors, the downside is that you will enter the job market without specific job training; you might have to settle for a lower starting salary. On the plus side, your academic training enables you to understand texts, express yourself verbally, and analyze and solve problems. Employers value these skills because they help you adapt to change. Academic majors also prepare you for graduate school in many fields. In graduate school, you can continue your education as you work toward a master's degree (M.A. or M.S.) or, maybe a doctorate degree (Ph.D.) or first-professional degree (law degree, medical degree).

The applied majors are popular choices because students can target their college work to launch a career. But by committing to a particular field, you will probably have fewer options, and you'll have to worry about job cycles and economic slumps in your field, or the possibility that your education and training will become out of date.

The right major at the right college

Which comes first, your choice of a major or your choice of a college? You should have some idea of what you want to study as you search for colleges because you'll want a school with a strong program in that area. Look for colleges that offer the majors you like and the related majors, too (they are listed with the majors profiled in this book). If you choose a college that teaches several majors that appeal to you, you'll be less likely to have to transfer to another college if, for any reason, you change your major.

Is a two-year or a four-year college right for you? Many two-year colleges, usually called community colleges, offer excellent training for a variety of careers, such as engineering technology, business administration, and support services in health care.

Another option is to earn a two-year associate degree in a transfer program. You'll study the equivalent of the first two years of a bachelor's degree program, and then transfer the credits when you apply to and are accepted by a four-year college. But be sure to find out which courses will be accepted for credit at the four-year college you would apply to.

As you start thinking about majors, it's good to know how colleges work. For instance, many small, private colleges are known for their liberal arts offerings. Larger universities often emphasize graduate programs. Most big-name schools, including state universities, are made up of several colleges. Sometimes it's clear what an undergraduate college or school in a university system, such as the college of agriculture or the school of nursing, has to offer. But sometimes the name of a college doesn't provide many clues. For instance, the college of arts and sciences and the school of business administration, in the same university system, might both offer a major in economics. But the course requirements might differ, and so might the admission requirements. As you look for a major, do some research on colleges. You can find more information on official college Web sites (their Internet addresses usually end in .edu).

When you scout about for the right college, you'll probably read books, magazines, and Web sites that rank the most competitive schools—that is, label one college as the best, another as the next best, and so on. Keep in mind, though, that rankings can't convey many of the features of a college, and that a listing may be based on factors that are not very important to you. So before examining a ranking, try to find out what the ratings were based on.

Your choice of college depends on what's right for you, and only you can come up with the college list that really matters. To help find colleges with good programs in the majors of interest to you, check out "Questions to ask colleges" in the major profiles in this book.

Concentrations, minors, double majors, and special programs

When you get to college, you may have even more options besides the choice of major. For example, you might select a concentration that allows you to specialize in a topic within your major, by taking a cluster of courses in the subject area. If you major in history, for instance, you might concentrate on Europe during the Middle Ages; or as a studio arts major, you might concentrate on painting. The availability of a concentration will vary from major to major and from college to college. Occasionally, a concentration may be required. In music performance, for example, you may have to choose a particular instrument that you'll concentrate on. Concentrations are less common in smaller colleges, and some programs offer concentrations only in graduate school.

Another option is to add a minor to your major. A minor is course work in which you explore another field, but not as widely or as deeply as for your major. You might minor in a subject that complements, or adds strength to, your major, such as a minor in business administration with a major in public relations, or an Arabic-language minor with a major in international relations. Then again, you could minor in a subject that's not related to your major, to give your brain a break from the type of work you do in your major courses. For example, computer science majors might enjoy studying creative writing, too.

Some colleges let you take a double major in related or even unrelated fields. In a double major, you complete two majors at the same time. For example, you could major in art history and in fine/studio arts, or in anthropology and Native American studies. You can even combine an academic and an applied major—for example, majoring in linguistics and in computer science. Double majors aren't for everyone, because college is tough enough without taking required courses for two majors. But it's something to think about if you can handle the workload and want to boost your academic résumé.

Another option to consider is a combined bachelor's and graduate degree. For many of these joint degrees, you are accepted into both programs when you apply to college. That way, you won't have to apply to grad school after you finish your undergraduate degree. These special programs (listed in Part III of this book) often include three years of study for a bachelor's degree, and then you begin the graduate program in your fourth year. The advantage is that you can complete both degrees in less time than it would take to earn the two degrees in the traditional way (often saving a year). As an example, you could earn a bachelor's degree in biology plus a master's in physical therapy in six years. Some schools of education offer five-year programs combining a bachelor's in education and a Master of Teaching degree.

Even if you know what major you want, adding concentrations, minors, or double majors, or entering combined programs, expands your choices of what to study in college. And here's another option: at some colleges you can create your own major or work with a professor on an independent project.

Preprofessional programs

Sometimes college is a stepping stone to... more college. That's not a bad thing. The more education people have, the lower their unemployment and the higher their earnings. Also, lawyers, doctors, and other health care professionals, including pharmacists, dentists, and physical therapists, must have professional degrees. Many members of the clergy and business executives also earn advanced degrees.

To prepare you for advanced studies, some colleges offer preprofessional programs. These are advisory programs, or "tracks," that lead you through a group of requirements that you can fulfill in almost any major.

Take law school, for example. More students earn law degrees than any other professional degree. In law school, the emphasis is on the writing, reading, and understanding of documents and texts. These skills are needed in nearly every undergraduate college course. So if you intend to apply to law school, you have a wide choice of undergrad majors, including history, political science, English, philosophy, criminal justice, the sciences, math, engineering, and a foreign language.

Medical schools do not insist that applicants have specific undergraduate majors, either. However, it's no surprise that most med school applicants major in the biological sciences. Others study the physical or social sciences, or one of the liberal arts. Med school applicants are typically required to have taken five year-long courses in math and science, as well as some general education courses. The requirements, and the number of credits and labs they include, are spelled out by the college in its pre-med program.

The best thing you can do, if you plan to go to law school or medical school or to graduate programs, is to get excellent grades in your undergraduate work. You'll also need to prepare for the appropriate professional school or grad school entrance exam.

Switching majors

Many students switch majors in college. This can be risky depending upon how far along you are in your college career, because you may have to spend more time than you'd planned, and more money, to finish your degree. But your original major might not be right for you, or an elective course might spark within you a passion for another field of study. Many options are open to you, even after you enroll in college.

If you find yourself in a major that you want to change, be sure to check with your college academic adviser. Like a high school counselor who can give you guidance, a college academic adviser can help you sort through electives, choose a major, change your major, and steer you toward completion of your degree.

Planning for now and for later

You don't have to feel overwhelmed by the choice of a major and of a college. Having a lot of choices can only benefit you. Think about your interests and talents while you read about the majors. Once you narrow the selection to a few majors you like, do some research on college programs in those majors (you might also ask about the credentials, or qualifications, of faculty members, and about the availability of libraries, computers, and labs).

You can also visit the Web sites of professional associations for specific careers and of leading employers of graduates in a particular major (employers may include corporations, small businesses, nonprofit organizations, and various levels of government). A look at the job descriptions and career opportunities will give you an idea of the educational requirements that employers expect. Web sites for professional associations are included in the descriptions of majors in this book.

Thinking about a career as you are deciding on a major and a college is understandable, but try to remain flexible. The world is changing so rapidly that the jobs in demand when you declare a major may be different after you graduate. That's just one good reason to choose a major that fits the person you are. Do that, and success will follow.

All about MyRoad™

If you take the PSAT/NMSQT® as a sopho-more or junior, you will get free access to MyRoad™, an easy-to-use, interactive Web site designed to help you explore majors, colleges, and careers. MyRoad combines the College Board's popular college search tools with on-line self-assessments and in-depth information about majors and careers. With this unique, per-sonalized tool, planning your future is fun.

Using MyRoad

One way to get started is to learn more about your personality type through MyRoad's research-validated personal assessment survey. Your results will include a list of suggested ma-jors and careers. You can also take an informal QuickStart survey to create a list of possible majors and careers based on your interests.

Explore majors and careers

In the Explore Majors area of the MyRoad Web site, you will find in-depth articles on 67 aca-demic fields, covering 175 majors. You'll find out which high school courses and other activ-ities will help you prepare. You'll also get in-sights from college students who have already taken the major you're considering. Finally, the Career Spiderweb connects each major to the world of work.

The Research Careers area has information on over 450 different occupations. You'll learn about the educational requirements, future, and compensation of each line of work. What's more, you'll find interviews with professionals who'll describe the joys and challenges of their work and what a typical day on the job is like.

Plan your future

On MyRoad, you can create your own per-sonal plan. My Plan is an online portfolio where you'll keep track of your interests and college application essays. It's also a great place to keep a record of your high school years, with space for your classes, grades, and other accomplishments. You can even use Resume Builder to create custom resumes on the fly.

For a completely different approach, try MyRoad's online magazine, *Insights*. Follow the adventures of current high school and college students in their Road Journals. Click on Men-tor's Corner to read interviews with profes-sionals at the top of their fields. Read about groundbreaking college programs in Campus View. Or turn to the Resource Library for ad-vice on everything from studying to searching for and applying to colleges.

Are you ready to get started on MyRoad?

If you are still in high school, your PSAT/NMSQT score report includes a personalized access code. You can use this code and your e-mail address to set up a MyRoad account. For instructions on how to do so, visit www.collegeboard.com, click on "PSAT," then click on "MyRoad."

If you have already gone on to college, you can purchase an individual sub-scription to MyRoad. To learn more, visit www.myroad.com.

Glossary

Academic adviser. A professor assigned to help students choose appropriate courses each semester. Many students consult their adviser for help in selecting a major. At some schools, when a student declares a major, he or she is assigned an adviser who teaches in the student's chosen field of study.

Academic year. A measure of the academic work that a student is expected to accomplish. Each college defines its own academic year, but federal regulations set minimum standards. Every program must have a defined academic year that contains a minimum of 30 weeks of instructional time. For undergraduate programs, a full-time enrolled student is expected to complete at least 24 semester or trimester hours, 36 quarter hours, or 900 clock hours over the 30-week period.

Accelerated program. A college program of study completed in less time than is usually required, most often by attending classes in summer or by taking extra courses during the regular academic term. Completion of a bachelor's degree program in three years is an example of acceleration.

Accreditation. A process that determines whether a college meets acceptable standards in its programs, facilities, and services. Some programs, such as the journalism and nursing programs, may be accredited by professional organizations. The descriptions of majors discuss program accreditation if it is significant in the field.

ACT Assessment. The group of tests from ACT, Inc., formerly known as the American College Testing Program, given at specific locations in the United States and other countries on specified dates throughout the year. The program includes tests in English, reading, mathematics, and science reasoning.

Adjunct professor. A member of the faculty who is not on the track for tenure and may teach part-time or full-time. Some colleges may refer to adjuncts as "lecturers" or "visiting professors." See also *professor* and *teaching assistant*.

Advanced placement. Admission or assignment of a first-year student to an advanced course in a subject, on the basis of evidence that the student has completed the equivalent of the college's first-year course in that subject.

Advanced Placement Program® (AP®). A program of the College Board that provides high schools with course descriptions of college subjects and with Advanced Placement examinations in those subjects. The AP program offers 37 exams in 22 subject areas. High schools offer the courses and administer the examinations to interested students, who are then eligible for *advanced placement*, college credit, or both, if their grades are satisfactory. Most colleges in the United States accept qualifying AP exam grades for credit, advanced standing, or both.

Adviser. See *academic adviser*.

Applied study. The practice of putting theoretical knowledge to practical use, as in the use of engineering principles to design machinery.

Area studies. A program of study that focuses on the history, geography, economics, politics, and culture of a region of the world—for example, Latin America, Eastern Europe.

Articulation agreement. An agreement between two colleges to facilitate the transfer of students from one college to the other without duplication of course work.

Associate degree. A degree granted by a college or university after the satisfactory completion of a two-year, full-time program of study or its part-time equivalent. In general, the Associate of Arts (A.A.) or Associate of Science (A.S.) degree is granted after students complete a program similar to the first two years of a four-year college curriculum. The Associate in Applied Science (A.A.S.) is awarded by many colleges on completion of technological or vocational programs of study.

Audit. To attend a course without getting credit for it.

Bachelor's, or baccalaureate, degree. A degree received after the completion of a four- or five-year, full-time program of study (or its part-time equivalent) at a college or university. The Bachelor of Arts (B.A.) and Bachelor of Science (B.S.) are the most common baccalaureates. There is no absolute difference between the degrees, and policies concerning their award vary from college to college.

Calendar. The system by which a college divides its year into shorter periods for providing instruction and for awarding credit. The most common systems are those based on the *semester*, the trimester, the *quarter*, and the *4-1-4 calendar*.

Candidates Reply Date Agreement (CRDA). A College Board-sponsored agreement under which applicants offered admission as first-year students do not have to notify the college of their decision to attend (or to accept an offer of financial aid) before May 1 of the year the applicants are accepted. The agreement gives applicants time to hear from all the colleges to which they have applied, before making a commitment to any of them.

Capstone course. A senior-year course in which students use information and skills learned in previous course work to address a topic, issue, or set of problems.

Carnegie unit. A unit of credit given for successful completion of one year's study of a college preparatory or academic subject in high school. Some colleges refer to Carnegie units as academic units. The name comes from the Carnegie Foundation for the Advancement of Teaching.

Case study. A means of learning by studying a specific example. For instance, students of hotel management might observe the work of an actual hotel to learn how to conduct a marketing survey, hire and train staff, and advertise.

CB code. A College Board code number that students use to designate which colleges or scholarship programs are to receive their SAT score reports.

Certificate. An award for completing a particular program or course of study, usually given by two-year colleges or vocational or technical schools for non-degree programs of a year or less.

College. The generic term for an institution of higher learning; also a term used to designate divisions within a university. A university may consist of various colleges: of arts and sciences, of engineering, of music, of agriculture, of architecture, and more. When a university is divided into colleges, students usually have to apply for admission to a specific college. Colleges in a university usually have their own requirements. For example, the college of arts and science may require two units of a foreign language, and the college of music may require an audition.

College calendar. See *calendar*.

College-Level Examination Program® (**CLEP®**). A series of examinations in undergraduate courses that gives students of any age the opportunity to demonstrate college-level achievement and, as a result, be able to reduce the time and money needed to complete a degree. The examinations, sponsored by the College Board, are administered at colleges year-round. All CLEP exams are delivered on computer, providing test-takers instant score results.

College preparatory subjects. Areas of study required for admission to, or recommended as preparation for, college. College prep subjects usually include English, history and social studies, foreign languages, mathematics, science, and the arts.

Combined bachelor's/graduate degree. A program in which students complete a bachelor's degree and a master's degree or first-professional degree in less than the usual amount of time. In most programs, students apply to undergraduate study and begin the graduate program in their fourth year of college. Graduates of the program are awarded both bachelor's and graduate degrees. At some colleges, this option is called a joint degree program.

Combined liberal arts/career program. A program in which a student typically completes three years of study in a liberal arts field and then two years of professional or technical study (for example, engineering). Graduates of the program are awarded a Bachelor of Arts degree and a Bachelor of Science degree. The combination is also referred to as a 3-2 program.

Community/junior college. A college offering a two-year program rather than a four-year program. A community college usually offers vocational programs as well as the first two years of a four-year program. Students in the vocational program usually go directly to work after graduation, while students in the academic program generally transfer to a four-year institution.

Concentration. A specialized branch of study within a *major*. For example, students majoring in psychology might choose a concentration in personality and social psychology; in fulfilling the requirements of the major, they would select courses focusing on personality and social psychology. In some programs, a concentration consists of a few courses in the area of specialty; in others, students may take 30 to 40 credits in their chosen area. A concentration may help students prepare for graduate study.

Cooperative education. A program in which students divide their time between traditional academic study and employment in business, industry, or government. Students are typically paid for their work. Under a cooperative plan, students normally need five years to earn a bachelor's degree, but graduates have the advantage of about a year's work experience in addition to their studies.

Core curriculum. A group of courses, in varied areas of the arts and sciences, designated by a college as one of the requirements for a degree. See *general education requirements*.

Course load. The number of class hours the student is permitted to schedule, in a given semester or quarter. It is usually 16–18 hours on a semester calendar, and 15–16 hours on a quarter calendar.

Credit by examination. Academic credit granted by a college to entering students who have demonstrated proficiency in college-level studies through examinations such as those sponsored by the College Board's *Advanced Placement Program*® and *College Level Examination Program*®. This plan is a means of cutting college costs by reducing the number of courses needed for a degree.

Credit hour. A unit of measure representing an hour (50 minutes) of instruction over a 15-week period in a semester or trimester system, or a 10-week period in a quarter system. It is applied toward the total number of hours for completing the requirements of a degree, diploma, certificate, or other award.

Curriculum. A set or program of courses. Students complete a certain curriculum, often consisting of liberal arts courses, electives, and courses in their major, to earn their degree.

Department. A group of related programs of study within a college. The Romance languages department, for example, may include programs in French, Italian, and Spanish. Some colleges have only a few departments, and some have a wide variety. Most departments offer several majors. A biology department might offer majors in marine biology, in microbiology, and in botany, for example.

Discipline. An academic area of study. Literature, history, social science, natural science, mathematics, the arts, and foreign language are disciplines; each takes a certain approach to knowledge

Discussion section. A supplement to a large lecture course in which students meet with either the professor or a teaching assistant, usually once a week, to discuss the lectures and assigned reading.

Distance learning. An option for earning course credit off campus, via cable television, Internet, satellite classes, videotapes, correspondence courses, or other means.

Doctoral degree. See *graduate degree*.

Double major. Any program in which a student completes the requirements of two majors at the same time.

Dual enrollment. The practice in which students, while still in high school, take college courses.

Elective. A course, not required for one's chosen major, that is selected to fulfill credit hours required for graduation.

ESL program. One of the special study options offered on many campuses to help students for whom English is not their native language improve their language skills.

Ethnic studies. A group of courses that focus on the culture, society, literature, and history of an ethnic group such as African Americans or Hispanic Americans.

Exchange student program. Any arrangement that permits a student to study for a semester or more at another college in the United States without extending the amount of time required for a degree.

External degree program. A system of study in which a student earns credit toward a degree through independent study, college courses, proficiency examinations, and personal experience. External degree colleges generally have no campus or classroom facilities.

Field of study. See *major*.

Fieldwork. Study that takes place outside the classroom and provides students with hands-on experience in their major. Geology majors may spend time in a ravine studying rock formations; major in food science may spend time in a hospital kitchen.

First-professional degree. A degree granted on completion of academic requirements to become licensed in a recognized profession. The programs of study require at least two years of college work for entrance, and at least six years of college work for completion.

4-1-4 calendar. A variation of the semester calendar system that consists of two terms of about 16 weeks each, separated by a one-month intersession used for intensive short courses, independent study, off-campus work, or other types of instruction.

Full-time student. An enrolled student who is carrying a full-time academic workload (other than correspondence courses). What makes up a full-time workload is determined by the institution and is applicable to all students enrolled in a program.

General Educational Development (GED). A series of five tests that individuals who did not complete high school may take through their state education system, to qualify for a high school equivalency certificate. The tests cover correctness and effectiveness of expression, interpretation of reading materials in the natural sciences and the social sciences, interpretation of literary materials, and general mathematics ability. Many colleges accept satisfactory GED test results in lieu of high school graduation. Some colleges require home-schooled students to take the GED.

General education requirements. Courses that give undergraduates background in the primary academic disciplines: natural sciences, social sciences, mathematics, literature and language, and fine arts. Most colleges have general education requirements; students usually take the courses in their first and second years, as a way to sample a wide range of courses before choosing a major. Students generally select from a variety of appropriate courses and take, for example, one course in each of the primary disciplines. At some colleges, general education courses are referred to as the core curriculum; at others, a few courses within the general education requirements are core courses that all students must take.

Grade-point average or ratio (GPA). A system used by many schools for evaluating the overall scholastic performance of students. Grade points are usually determined by first multiplying the number of hours given for a course by the numerical value of the grade, and then dividing the sum of all grade points by the total number of hours carried. The most common system of numerical values for grades is: A = 4, B = 3, C = 2, D = 1, and E or F = 0.

The GPA is also called a quality-point average ratio.

Graduate degree. A degree (sometimes called a postgraduate degree) pursued after a student has earned a bachelor's degree. The master's degree, which requires one to three years of study, is usually the degree earned after the bachelor's. The doctoral degree requires further study. *First- professional degrees* are also graduate degrees.

Honors program. A plan designed to encourage superior students to take a more challenging program in their major than is required. Students who meet the stringent requirements of an honors program are usually granted degrees *cum laude*, which means "with honors" in Latin.

Humanities. The branches of learning that usually include art, the classics, dramatic art, English, general and comparative literature, journalism, music, philosophy, and religion. Many colleges divide their offerings into three divisions: humanities, social sciences, and natural sciences.

Independent study. Academic work chosen or designed by the student, with the approval of the department concerned, and pursued under an instructor's supervision. The work is usually undertaken outside the regular classroom structure.

Interdisciplinary major. See *multidisciplinary major.*

International Baccalaureate (IB). A comprehensive and rigorous two-year curriculum (usually taken in the final two years of high school) that is similar to the last year of secondary school in Europe. Some colleges award credit or advanced placement to students who have completed an IB program.

Internship. A short-term, supervised work experience, usually related to a student's major field, for which the student earns academic credit. The work can be full- or part-time, on or off campus, paid or unpaid. *Student teaching* and apprenticeships are examples.

Junior college. See *community college.*

Laboratory course. A course, usually supplemented by lectures, in which students perform scientific experiments under the supervision of a professor or a teaching assistant.

Land-grant university. One of the universities established by the federal government in 1862. The institutions were intended to educate the agricultural workforce the country needed. Many are now large universities teaching a wide range of subjects, but they still offer numerous agriculture-related majors.

Lecture course. A midsize or large course, in which the instructor speaks from prepared notes on a topic relating to the assigned reading or laboratory work. Lectures are usually supplemented by discussion sections or laboratories.

Liberal arts. The study of the humanities (literature, the arts, and philosophy), history, foreign languages, social sciences, mathematics, and natural sciences. The liberal arts and humanities stress the development of general knowledge and reasoning ability rather than specific skills.

Liberal arts/career combination. See *combined liberal arts/career program.*

Licensure. The procedure in which graduates pass one or several examinations and are awarded a license to practice a profession. For example, an accounting major must take a licensing exam after graduation to become a certified public accountant (CPA). Some of the majors described in this book prepare students to take licensing examinations after earning their bachelor's degree.

Lower-division courses. Courses that students are expected to take in their first two years of college. These courses lay the foundation for further study in the subject area.

Major. The field of study in which students concentrate, or specialize, during their undergraduate study. At most colleges, students take a third to a half of their course work in the major; the rest is devoted to liberal arts requirements and electives. In academic majors, students generally take a third of their courses in their academic field, which they usually must choose by the beginning of their junior year. In career-related, or applied, programs, such as nursing and engineering, students may take up to half their courses in their major. See *concentration* and *minor*.

Master's degree. See *graduate degree*.

Matriculation. The process in which a student is accepted, pays fees, and enrolls in classes, officially becoming a student at the college. This term is applied only to first-year students or to transfer students' first enrollment.

Minor. Course work that is not as extensive as that in a major but gives students some specialized knowledge of a second field. Students may choose a minor in the department of their major (for example, a major in comparative literature with a minor in German literature), or in a different department (for example, a biology major with a minor in philosophy). College catalogs describe the requirements for minors.

Multidisciplinary major. A major that uses the perspectives of many disciplines, or academic subjects, simultaneously, to explore problems, events, or situations. For example, women's studies uses anthropology, history, sociology, literature, and psychology to examine women in various times and cultures.

MyRoad. The College Board's premier Internet guidance solution, part of collegeboard.com. MyRoad is a personalized, comprehensive system that helps students research college majors, colleges, and careers. The program incorporates a validated assessment, the ORA Personality Profiler. It also provides complete guidance solutions for schools, including a secure environment for counselors called Counselor's Corner, where professionals can follow students' progress and interests.

Pass/fail course. A course in which a student's achievement is noted only as either passing or failing. In some cases, the course may be offered only as a pass/fail course. In others, a student, with the instructor's permission, may take a regular course on a pass/fail basis.

Placement test. A battery of tests designed to assess a student's aptitude and level of achievement in various academic areas so that he or she can select the most appropriate courses.

Postgraduate degree. See *graduate degree*.

Practicum. A course, usually taken in the third or fourth year of college, in which classroom learning is put into practice in a clinic (for students in medical fields) or in a classroom (for education majors). Students are supervised by a working professional during this phase of their education.

Preprofessional program. An advising program and recommended course of study for undergraduate students intending to pursue a *first-professional degree* after college. Although there is no prescribed *major* for entrance to professional school, students planning for a career in law, ministry, or a medical profession need to take an undergraduate program that lays the groundwork for their training. Premed students, for example, must complete certain science courses. Preprofessional advisors help students plan their undergraduate studies and to prepare for admission to professional school.

Prerequisite. A course that must be taken as preparation for more advanced course work in a particular field. For example, introductory calculus would be a prerequisite for differential mathematics. College catalogs usually indicate whether a course has a prerequisite.

Private college or university. An institution of higher education not supported by public funds. Private colleges may be independent or church-affiliated.

Probation. At most colleges, disciplinary action for students whose grade point average is below "C." If the average is not raised to a certain level, the students are asked to withdraw.

Professor. A member of the faculty at a college or university who either has tenure or is on the "track" for tenure. See also *adjunct professor* and *teaching assistant*.

Program. See *major*; see also *honors program*.

Proprietary college. A private institution operated by its owners as a profit-making enterprise.

PSAT/NMSQT® (Preliminary SAT/National Merit Scholarship Qualifying Test). A shorter version of the SAT I with an additional writing skills section as well as a diagnostic component providing skills feedback. Administered by high schools to sophomores and juniors each October, the PSAT/NMSQT aids high schools in the early guidance of students planning for college and serves as the qualifying test for scholarships awarded by the National Merit Scholarship Corporation.

Public college/university. An institution of higher education supported by taxes and other public revenue.

Quarter. An academic *calendar* period of about 12 weeks. Four quarters make up an academic year, but at colleges using the quarter system, students make normal progress by attending three quarters each year. In some colleges, students can accelerate their progress by attending all four quarters in one or more years.

Remedial course. A noncredit course taken to help the student with a weak background in a particular area. Remedial courses are taken to prepare the student for a credit course in that subject.

Reserve Officers' Training Corps (ROTC). Programs conducted by some colleges in cooperation with the U.S. Air Force, Army, and Navy. Naval ROTC includes the Marine Corps (the Coast Guard and the Merchant Marine do not sponsor ROTC programs). Local recruiting offices of the military services themselves can supply detailed information about these programs, as can participating colleges.

SAT Reasoning Test (SAT®). The College Board's test of developed critical reading, writing, and mathematical reasoning abilities, given on specified dates throughout the year at test centers in the United States and other countries. The SAT is required by many colleges and sponsors of financial aid programs.

SAT Subject Tests®. College Board tests in specific subjects, given at test centers in the United States and other countries on specified dates throughout the year. These tests are used by colleges for help both in evaluating applicants for admission and in determining course placement and exemption of enrolled first-year students.

School. One name for a subdivision of a university. For example, the administrative unit that offers nursing courses may be called the "college of nursing" at one institution, and the "school of nursing" at another.

Semester. On a college's *calendar*, a period of about 15 weeks. Colleges on a semester system offer two periods of instruction, fall and spring, a year; there may also be a summer session (usually a shorter, more concentrated period of time).

Semester at sea. A program for credit, usually for students majoring in oceanography, marine biology, or related fields, in which students live for part of a semester on a ship, usually a research vessel. Academic courses are generally taken in conjunction with the sea experience or at other times during the semester.

Seminar. A course, with a small enrollment, that focuses on a specific topic. Class discussions, student presentations, and student writing are usually emphasized over lectures and exams.

Short course. A course, generally a *seminar*, offered during the middle term at colleges on a *4-1-4 calendar*, or sometimes offered as a one-credit class during a regular term. Students often take short courses, which usually focus on limited topics of general interest, on a *pass/ fail* basis.

Specialization. See *concentration*.

Student-designed major. An academic program that allows a student to construct a major that the college does not formally offer. Often nontraditional and *multidisciplinary*, the major is developed with the approval of a college officer or committee.

Student teaching. A program in which education majors, in their fourth year, teach in a local school, under the supervision of a licensed teacher.

Studio course. A course in which students create works of art, under the guidance of an instructor, rather than receive information through lectures. Studio courses are an important component of some visual and performing arts majors.

Study abroad. An arrangement by which a student completes part of the college program—typically the third year but sometimes only a semester or a summer—studying in another country. A college may operate a campus abroad, or it may have a cooperative agreement with another U.S. college or with an institution in the host country.

Teacher certification. A college program designed to prepare students to meet the requirements for certification as teachers in elementary and secondary schools.

Teaching assistant. A graduate student who aids a professor by grading papers, leading discussion sections, and/or supervising labs.

Tenure. Permanent appointment to the faculty of a college. Professors who have tenure cannot be dismissed from the faculty except for gross misconduct.

Term. The shorter period into which colleges divide the school year. Some colleges are on the *semester* system, in which students complete two semesters, or terms, each year. Others are on the *quarter* system, in which they attend three quarters each year. Many colleges offer a summer term, so that students can attend college year-round and thus receive their degree more quickly, or can finish incomplete credits. See also *calendar*.

Terminal degree. The highest degree that can be earned in a particular field. For most faculty members, it is the doctoral degree. In certain fields, however, a master's degree is the highest level.

Terminal program. An education program designed to prepare students for immediate employment. The program can usually be completed in less than four years beyond high school and is available in most community colleges and vocational-technical institutes.

Thesis. A long research paper written as a requirement for a degree. At some colleges, departments may require an undergraduate thesis for a bachelor's degree. At others, an undergraduate thesis may be required of students only in certain programs. Theses are usually written under the supervision of a faculty adviser over a semester or an entire academic year.

3-2 program. See *combined liberal arts/ career program*.

Transcript. A copy of a student's official academic record, listing all courses taken and grades achieved.

Transfer program. An education program in a two-year college (or four-year college that offers associate degrees), designed primarily for students who plan to continue their studies in a four-year college. *See also community/ junior college*.

Transfer student. A student who attends a college—typically for a period ranging from a single term up to three years—and then is accepted by and enrolls in another college. A transfer student may receive credit for all or some of the courses successfully completed before the transfer.

Trimester. An academic *calendar* period of about 15 weeks. Three trimesters make up one year. Students normally progress by attending two of the trimesters each year and in some colleges can accelerate their progress by attending all three trimesters in one or more years.

Two-year upper-division college. A college offering bachelor's degree programs that begin with the third year. An entering student must have completed the first and second years at another college.

Undergraduate. A student in the first, second, third, or fourth year of an academic program, as differentiated from a graduate student, who has earned a bachelor's degree and is pursuing a master's, doctoral, or professional degree.

United Nations semester. A program for credit in which students generally take courses at a college in the New York City metropolitan area while participating in an internship program at the United Nations.

Upper division. The third and fourth years of study. Some colleges offer only upper-division study—students must have completed the first and second years (lower division) at other institutions before entering the upper-division institution to earn their bachelor's degree.

Upper-division courses. Courses taken during the third and fourth years of study. Often numbered 300, 400, or 500, these courses build on the foundation of knowledge gained during the first two years and provide an in-depth exploration of the topic.

Urban semester. A program for credit in which students of diverse majors spend a semester in a major city, such as New York, Philadelphia, Chicago, Denver, or San Francisco, experiencing the complexities of an urban center through course work, seminars, and/or *internship* related to their major.

Virtual university. A degree-granting, accredited institution in which all courses are delivered by *distance learning*, with no physical campus.

Washington semester. A program in which students participate in an *internship* program with a government agency or department in the Washington, D.C., metropolitan area. Students earn field service credit for their work and frequently take courses at area colleges.

Weekend college. A program that allows students to take a complete academic course by attending classes only on weekends. The program, generally restricted to a few areas of study at a college, requires more than the traditional number of years to complete.

Part I: Full Descriptions of Majors

Part I: Full Descriptions of Majors

About Part I

Here you will find in-depth descriptions of 188 undergraduate majors, plus 5 preprofessional programs. These profiles are grouped into 26 broad categories. See the Table of Contents for a complete listing.

The headings below correspond to what you will find in the profiles. For more on how to interpret the profiles, read "How to Use This Book" on pages 11 to 15.

Name of major: This is the generic name of the major that is most often used by colleges.

Also known as: Alternative names that you might come across are listed here.

What it's about: This gives you a quick idea of the subject area the major covers and the careers it prepares you for.

Is this for you? This section should help you select a major according to what you like to do or to study, what you are good at, and what your personal qualities are.

Recommended high school prep: The course units recommended here refer to years of study in a four-year high school.

Did you know ...? Included here are important aspects or interesting facts about the major that many students entering the major are not aware of.

Typical courses in the major: This list is a sampling of courses commonly offered in the major, in roughly the order of sequence they are taken.

Concentrations: You can sometimes concentrate your studies in a certain area within your major. The concentrations listed here are not available at all colleges.

What the study of this major is like: This section tells you what you'll actually study in a major, and how the major is generally taught and learned.

Other majors you might like: Some of these will be obvious, but some may surprise you. We encourage you to consider them with an open mind. Majors in **bold type** are fully profiled in this book. Those in regular type are briefly described in Part II.

Questions to ask colleges: Good for college visits, interviews, or an email to the Web sites of the colleges you are considering.

Career options and trends: This section lists job titles in careers the major may lead to—an asterisk indicates a type of job that graduates most often pursue. Also described are any additional education, certification, or licensure requirements for the careers listed, plus trends occurring or likely to occur in careers related to the major.

Insider's viewpoint: We asked professors and students to give some insight or describe what appeals to them about the major.

For more info: Contact information is provided here for associations (educational and business) that you should investigate to explore further the major and/or related careers.

Agriculture

Agriculture is an ancient practice that has become a cutting-edge science and industry. It's all about the production of crops, livestock, feed, and fiber. People need agriculture for the basics like food and clothing.

"The things that we do have a major impact on everyone—everyone must eat," says Bonita A. Glatz, a food science professor at Iowa State University.

Farmers and ranchers have gotten pretty good at growing and raising crops and food. The big push in agriculture now is to increase the quality and quantity of plant and animal products. Things are really getting technical. In many majors, agricultural study is a type of applied biology or applied chemistry. It's a science. So if you study agriculture in a four-year program, you're likely to get a solid science background followed by an in-depth exploration of chemistry, biochemistry, genetics, pathology (study of diseases), meteorology (weather), economics, or education.

Is agriculture for you? People who study and work in farming represent a wide variety of skills and interests. If you care about people, animals, or planet Earth, you might consider an agriculture major. Do you have a passion for vegetable gardening or horseback riding? Maybe you love nature, plants, or the outdoors. Perhaps you want to protect the environment or help developing countries that are struggling with poverty and malnutrition. Many students bring experience in farming and ranching with them to college. During college, they gain an interest in economics and business or a particular branch of agriscience. You don't have to come from a farming background or plan to work on a farm to be an ag major. But you will need quantitative skills—math and statistics—to study this field.

What about job prospects? We all need agricultural products, but the industry is so efficient that we don't need as many farms and traditional farm jobs as we did in the past. Farms are merging so that we have fewer and larger farms now. Agriculture is big business. That means a smaller number of jobs for farmers and ranchers. On the other hand, the business of farming and the global scale of food distribution expand the role of other things like agribusiness and agricultural economics. In fact, students in these two majors will take many of the same classes. The difference is that agribusiness students will probably have a career path toward management in a food company. Agricultural economics is more analytical and good preparation for either research or business. Your choice of major and level of degree affect your job prospects.

What's hot in the field

If you're thinking that agriculture is just plants and soil, no way. Computers, telecommunications, and other high-tech tools play a huge role. "Precision agriculture guided by geographic information systems, satellite guidance, and computer-equipped tractors increases production and conserves natural resources," explains Professor Douglas L. Young of Washington State University.

What else is happening? You've probably seen news stories about environmental regulations or about real estate development in what were once rural areas. These trends may require agriculture students to learn more about the environment and resource economics. Sustainable and organic agriculture are also big issues. Another new area of study is the economics of biotechnology. The job picture is also bright for students in food science, partly because people's tastes change and consumers are learning more about nutrition, health, and wellness. And don't forget food safety and bioterrorism. They couldn't be more important. Other hot jobs are in plant breeding and genetics, financial management, information systems, and teaching.

From field to table, from the plant to the planet, agriculture requires more knowledge and education than ever before. Today's agricultural professionals have business, economic, scientific, and technical skills and expertise.

It's no surprise that during graduate-level studies, students focus on a very specific area. For example, in agronomy, grad students zoom in on things like crop production and physiology; or soil sciences including soil chemistry, microbiology, and biochemistry. If you're interested in a business track, keep in mind that nearly all agribusiness professions require advanced degrees; grad studies veer toward agricultural marketing or agricultural trade.

But not all colleges and universities define majors in the same way. Colleges vary in the areas of study they emphasize. The differences could stem from the regional climate and its specific crop or soil suitability, or even a college's size and priorities. In college catalogs and on the Internet, look under agricultural sciences, biological sciences, environmental sciences, and natural resources. And be sure to go to the Web sites of the land-grant universities and the big state schools, which dominate agricultural education. Another section in this book related to agriculture is Natural resources and conservation. There you'll find majors in forestry, fisheries, and environmental studies. Here are some Web sites to get you started thinking about your future in agriculture: the U.S. Department of Agriculture (www.usda.gov), the U.S. Food and Drug Administration (www.fda.gov), the National Future Farmers of America Organization (www.ffa.org), and the American Farm Bureau (www.fb.com).

Agricultural business

Also known as:

Agribusiness

What it's about:

Agricultural business deals with the management, marketing, and financing of food and fiber, "from the field to the table." You study principles from agricultural sciences, economics, business, and statistics in preparation for a career in agribusiness, farming, natural resources, government, and related areas.

Is this for you?

You might like this major if you also like: 4-H projects and competitions; debating; organizing or leading a club or other group activity; solving problems; sports. A concern for the problems of developing countries that are struggling with poverty and malnutrition might also lead you to this major.

Consider this major if you are good at: attention to detail; critical reading/thinking; leadership; organizing; persuading/influencing; quantitative analysis; teamwork *...or have...* initiative; verbal skills; writing skills.

Recommended high school prep:

English 4, math 3 (including precalculus), lab science 3 (including biology and chemistry), social studies 3, and a foreign language 2–3. If available, take a computer course covering basic office applications and spreadsheets.

Did you know...

...that to be successful in agricultural business, you must know math and statistics? Many students are surprised by the idea, as well as by the need for excellent writing and speaking skills.

Typical courses in this major:

Introduction to agribusiness
Managerial accounting
Economics (micro and macro)
Statistics
Farming technologies
Production management
Farm and ranch management
Human resources management
Agricultural marketing
International trade
Agricultural finance
Farm management laboratory
Agricultural history and law
Agricultural policy
Business/environmental law
Management information systems

Concentrations:

In college: agricultural economics; agricultural marketing; farm and ranch management; agricultural finance; environmental economics; crop or animal production; international agriculture and trade.

If you go on to grad school: econometrics; agricultural policy; rural and community economic development.

What the study of this major is like:

The agricultural business major prepares you to apply business and economic principles to the production and marketing of food and other agricultural products and to the management of natural resources. In order to make economically and environmentally sound decisions in this field, you need to understand accounting, economics, finance, labor, marketing, management, and public policy, as you analyze and deal with business and environmental risk; identify and respond to changes in the demand for food products and services; and improve profitability.

You learn principles associated with best practices for product development, profit maximization, and investment planning. You become familiar with accounting tools like balance sheets, income statements, and cash flow statements. You are taught to use quantitative tools such as statistics, accounting methods, computer programs, and investment analysis to solve management and planning problems.

You also learn the importance of risk management in an industry in which prices can zigzag (because of the uncertainties of worldwide markets) and production is at the mercy of weather, pests, and natural disasters. To thrive despite the risks, you must make smart use of futures markets, insurance, contracting, machinery maintenance, emerging technologies, and labor management. You also take supporting courses in data analysis, international studies, biological sciences, social sciences, and written and oral communication. A number of agribusinesses offer internships that give you a chance to get some real business experience.

Many majors are challenged by such requirements as calculus and courses in the humanities and social sciences. Third- and fourth-year team and individual projects—which can sometimes conflict with off-campus employment or other activities—require long hours of work. But problem-centered assignments help you build a solid foundation for future employment.

Leading agricultural colleges may emphasize agribusiness, marketing, farm/ranch management, technology, natural resource economics, or statistics/ econometrics, but most colleges offer courses in all these areas. If you are interested in other areas, such as international agricultural development or rural development, explore the catalogs or Web sites of various programs to see what they offer. If you want to combine an agribusiness degree with another field (for instance, wine grape production), examine course offerings and prerequisites in departments such as crop and soil sciences. The agricultural business major is also offered at the two-year associate degree level; the program is generally geared for transfer into a four-year agribusiness program.

Other majors you might like:
Economics
Business administration and management
Accounting
Agronomy and crop science

Animal sciences
Forest resources production
Range science
Agricultural and biological engineering
Geography
Farm and ranch management
International business
Aquaculture

Questions to ask colleges:
Does the program feature the latest technologies being applied to agricultural production?

What ties do the faculty members have to the industry? Are undergrads given assistance in finding internships?

Where have recent graduates gone to work?

Career options and trends:
Agribusiness manager or marketer*; farmer or rancher*; loan officer*; government agency employee; production supervisor; financial analyst; commodity merchandiser.

The long-term trend toward consolidation into fewer and larger farms is projected to continue, further reducing the number of jobs for farmers and ranchers but increasing employment opportunities for agricultural managers. Most graduates obtain jobs in business and industry. There is demand for managers and specialists trained in accounting, credit analysis, marketing, and international trade. Job prospects are generally good, especially if you are willing to relocate.

For more info:
United Agribusiness League
54 Corporate Park
Irvine, CA 92606-5105
(800) 223-4590
www.ual.org

Agricultural economics

What it's about:

The agricultural economics major teaches you to understand agriculture from both the national and the international perspective. You apply economic principles to the study of agricultural trends, productivity, investment, and the use and conservation of natural resources.

Is this for you?

You might like this major if you also like: social studies; math; business; government; working with numbers; looking at the big picture; environmental issues.

Consider this major if you are good at: critical reading/thinking; leadership; math; persuading/influencing; quantitative analysis; teamwork *...or have...* initiative; verbal skills; writing skills.

Recommended high school prep:

English 4, math 4 (including precalculus), lab science 3, social studies 3, and a foreign language 3. If possible, take courses in computer science, economics, and statistics. A foreign language is especially helpful because agricultural markets are increasingly global.

Did you know...

...that most graduates in this major, contrary to popular belief, do not farm? While nearly 20 percent of all jobs in the United States are in the food and fiber industries, fewer than 3 percent of the employees in those industries actually work on a farm.

Typical courses in this major:

Accounting
Economics (micro and macro)
Statistics
Quantative methods in agricultural economics
Agricultural marketing and sales
Agricultural price analysis
Agribusiness management
Agricultural cooperatives
Agricultural finance
Agricultural policy
Commodity futures markets
International trade and finance
Agricultural and business law
Environmental resources development
Rural economic development
Professional career development

Concentrations:

Farm and ranch management; marketing; finance; environmental economics; rural development; international economic development.

What the study of this major is like:

Economics is the study of the way societies use available resources to meet people's needs. Since farming is the largest user of the earth's resources, agricultural economics is a wide-ranging field. You are most likely to benefit from the major if you have a broad educational background. Your general education courses may include English, speech, data analysis, chemistry, physics, economics, the natural and social sciences, history, literature, and the arts.

Many of the courses offered in this major are the same as in the agricultural business major, and sometimes it's hard to distinguish the two. Both majors cover economic principles, technical agricultural sciences, and business management tools. Whereas the agricultural business major provides management, operational, and production skills for business careers in the industry, agricultural economics focuses analytically on a broader range of issues to prepare you for graduate study or for careers in research and public policy as well as in business. You explore the relationship between agriculture and other sectors of the economy; you evaluate responses to economic problems created by the changing agricultural environment. You learn quantitative problem solving and qualitative reasoning, as well as how to make ethical judgments.

You also take upper-level electives in your chosen concentration, which may focus on public policy and regional development issues; natural resource allocation and environmental issues; management and production; or international trade. In many programs, a capstone project teaches you to debate concepts and integrate them into a wider perspective. Some colleges require you to do an internship or declare a minor. You may be able to earn college credit by participating in a study-abroad program.

Typically, you need good preparation in math and science to succeed in this major. Joining a student chapter of a national agricultural association will help you to learn more about the field, make valuable career contacts, and find internships and job opportunities.

Programs are typically found in colleges of agriculture at land-grant universities. Some smaller, four-year private and public colleges offer a similar major, particularly in regions where agriculture is a significant industry. Admission and course requirements differ slightly among colleges. Some colleges combine agricultural business and agricultural economics into one program. There may also be differences in the areas of concentration offered.

Other majors you might like:
Agricultural business
Farm and ranch management
Agricultural education services
Environmental studies
Finance
Development economics
Mathematics
Statistics
Management information systems
Global studies
Public policy analysis
International business

Questions to ask colleges:
How much emphasis is placed on math and quantitative analysis?

How does the agricultural economics program differ from the agribusiness major? Are courses in the agricultural technical sciences included?

Is a senior capstone project required? What sort of projects have recent graduates submitted?

Career options and trends:
Agricultural statistician; agricultural consultant; government agency employee (e.g., USDA); financial analyst; bank manager or loan officer; sales representative; natural resources manager; public policy analyst; commodities broker, trader, or merchandiser.

The food and fiber industries are changing rapidly, because of corporate mergers and consolidations, the increasing reliance on telecommunications, and the growth of global trade and competition. As a result, companies want educated, productive, and flexible employees who can adapt in a rapidly shifting world market.

Demand for economists in general remains fairly constant, in good times and bad. Opportunities for agricultural economists in particular are increasing, as is the diversity, globalization, and high-tech nature of the profession.

Insider's viewpoint:
"I have enjoyed almost all the classes that are offered through this major, especially those dealing with commodities, farm planning, and managerial and decision-making economics. All of these classes deal with real-world situations; they are not all just about theories and concepts."

—Christopher, senior, University of Wisconsin

For more info:
American Agricultural Economics Association
415 South Duff Ave., Suite C
Ames, IA 50010-6600
(515) 233-3202
www.aaea.org

Agronomy and crop science

What it's about:

This major provides the theoretical and practical knowledge needed for the efficient and sustainable production of food, fuel, feed, and fiber. You will gain a broad understanding of the diversity of, and relationships among, plants, soils, and climates. You will also explore the ethical, cultural, and environmental issues facing professionals in agriculture and natural resources.

Is this for you?

You might like this major if you also like: 4-H or FFA (Future Farmers of America) projects and competitions; Boy/Girl Scouts; science and math; the Weather Channel; gardening; outdoor activities; collecting or observing insects; seed collecting; issues relating to world hunger and the environment.

Consider this major if you are good at: attention to detail; critical reading/thinking; leadership; organizing; quantitative analysis; research; teamwork ...*or have...* initiative; manual dexterity; verbal skills.

Recommended high school prep:

English 4, math 3 (including precalculus), lab science 4 (including biology, physics, and chemistry), social studies 3, and a foreign language 2–3. Take as much math and science as you can, and a computer science course if available. Courses that help you develop good writing and oral communication skills are also important.

Did you know...

...that a farm background is not essential for a major in agronomy?

Typical courses in this major:

Plant pathology
Entomology
Pest management
Fertilizers
Weed science
Environmental science
World food issues
Sustainable agriculture
Genetics
Weather and climate
Seed science and technology
Global climate change
Plant breeding
Crop management and production
Soil ecology
Statistics

Concentrations:

In college: crop and soil management; agricultural chemicals; pest management; seed production and technology; soil conservation; turfgrass management; climatology; biotechnology.

If you go on to grad school: agricultural meteorology; crop production and physiology, with specializations in seed science and weed science; plant breeding; and soil science, with specializations in soil chemistry, physics, morphology, genesis, biology, fertility, and management.

What the study of this major is like:

Agronomists work to provide consumers with a sufficient supply of food; to help producers increase profitability and efficiency; and to protect the environment. As an agronomy and crop science major, you learn how the plant and soil sciences are used in the production of abundant, high-quality food, fuel, feed, and fiber. Crop and plant sciences relate primarily to the genetics, breeding, physiology, and management of crops. Soil science covers the physics, chemistry, origin, microbiology, fertility, and management of soil, as well as other uses for soil, such as in road construction, waterways, and waste disposal systems. Majors also study weather and climate.

You generally begin with courses in soil science, crop production, botany or biology, geology, chemistry, English, and statistics. In addition, you study the physical and social sciences, communications, economics, and math. Agronomy students are encouraged to take at least one course in plant pathology, entomology, weed science, and soil fertility/plant nutrition. As you learn more about the discipline, you may develop specific interests in crop science, soil science, or climatology. You can generally double-major (or minor) in agronomy/crop science and agribusiness, agricultural journalism, animal science, environmental sciences, or extension education.

Core courses (natural sciences, math, English, and social sciences) are usually taught in a lecture/lab format. Upper-level agronomy and crop science courses focus on problem solving, real-life situations, and professional competency. Integrated into the instruction is an emphasis on teamwork, leadership, communication, critical analysis, and management skills, as well as sustainability principles and ethical values.

Your course work is often supplemented by field trips or industrial tours; visiting professors may give seminars on agronomy issues. Majors can participate in regional and national contests with crop and soil judging teams. You are also encouraged to seek internships and summer/part-time employment in government agencies, agricultural businesses (seed, fertilizer, agricultural chemicals), conservation centers, integrated pest management, land appraisal, or other areas relating to food, fuel, feed, and fiber production and marketing. You can generally earn academic credit for such work.

Colleges may vary in their emphasis on the role of science in response to world hunger and pollution. If you plan to go on to grad school, you generally need to complete an undergraduate program that stresses agronomic, biological, mathematical, and physical sciences.

Other majors you might like:
Forestry
Horticulture
Plant sciences
Atmospheric science
Plant protection/pest management
Range science
Soil science

Biochemistry
Agricultural and biological engineering
Botany
Turf management
Agricultural education services

Questions to ask colleges:
Are internships and summer work opportunities available? When you evaluate a curriculum, you should take into account the availability of internships and exchange programs that provide work in the profession and study-abroad experiences.

Does the program provide learning experiences at a working farm or in a campus greenhouse?

Does the program include courses covering leadership qualities and skills, especially in communications, ethics, and decision-making?

Career options and trends:
Agricultural business manager*; plant breeder; seed production specialist*; environmental and natural resources manager; farm manager; government agency employee*; range management specialist; crop and soil management specialist; soil conservationist and surveyor*.

Agronomy is increasingly international—you should expect to travel during your career. The "green revolution" occurring in developing countries calls for expertise in seed physiology, soil science, and plant breeding, to counter the effects of pests, disease, and drought. The role of genetic engineering will increase in importance as well, and you should expect a greater emphasis on bioterrorism and food management and safety practices.

For more info:
American Society of Agronomy
677 South Segoe Rd.
Madison, WI 53711-1086
(608) 273-8080
www.agronomy.org

Animal sciences

What it's about:
The animal sciences major deals with the breeding, raising, and management of livestock and poultry, and the foods and products obtained from them. The care and welfare of companion or captive animals may also be covered.

Is this for you?
You might like this major if you also like: working with large animals; biology; Animal Planet; working outdoors; physical challenges; 4H groups; farmwork.

Consider this major if you are good at: attention to detail; caring/nurturing; critical reading/thinking; math; organizing; quantitative analysis ...*or have...* initiative; patience; physical stamina; writing skills.

Recommended high school prep:
English 4, math 4 (including precalculus or calculus), lab science 4, social studies 3, and a foreign language 2–3. If available, take an advanced biology course.

Did you know...
...that this major is not for the squeamish? You have to be willing to get up close and personal with the animals, and not mind the aroma—or maybe even like it.

Typical courses in this major:
Animal behavior
Animal biology
Animal evaluation
Nutrition
Livestock management
Poultry science
Dairy science
Endocrinology
Genetics
Growth and development
Lactation
Livestock marketing
Reproductive physiology
Artificial insemination practices
Companion animal management
Meat science and processing

Concentrations:
In college: reproductive physiology; genetics and breeding; endocrinology; animal nutrition; animal behavior.

If you go on to grad school: reproductive physiology; genetics and breeding; endocrinology; animal behavior.

What the study of this major is like:
Like most science majors, you will spend at least 40 percent of your time in courses in the humanities, social sciences, natural sciences, and math—typically during your first two years. A solid foundation in the biological and physical sciences will help you get the most from the animal science courses you will take in your third and fourth years.

Biological concepts and animal science terminology are usually presented in lectures; you then get hands-on experience in class demonstrations and labs. You will also be encouraged (in some programs, required) to gain practice outside the classroom, by participating in an internship, research project, livestock judging competition, or extension work.

Because animal agriculture is a process that depends on cooperation among professionals and technicians, your courses will probably include teamwork activities. In fact, communication skills are essential in this discipline. You will also benefit from sharpening your understanding of math and chemistry. Most students who transfer out of animal sciences do so because they are having difficulty with one or both of these subjects.

Most colleges offer several options in the major: a production track, business/management track, science track, or preveterinary track. Colleges in regions with a livestock industry may focus on production systems and offer plenty of hands-on training. Colleges with strong research programs may emphasize the biology of animal growth and reproduction, biotechnology, and genetics. Some programs stress compatibility with the preprofessional requirements of veterinary medicine and human medicine, as well as with grad school requirements. A business option will emphasize agricultural economics.

If a species is prominent in the area around a college, its presence will likely be reflected in the expertise of the faculty and the courses offered. You can strengthen your ability to observe similarities and differences if you study not only the commonly found species but others as well.

Other majors you might like:

Zoology
Livestock management
Wildlife and wilderness management
Veterinary technology
Biochemistry
Aquaculture
Dairy science
Entomology
Food science
Microbiology
Poultry science
Agricultural and biological engineering

Questions to ask colleges:

Does the program have adequate resources, including labs and animal facilities, to provide practice in the animal handling skills you will need professionally? Access to facilities in which you can study meat, dairy, and other food processing and testing is also desirable.

Are there opportunities to participate with faculty members in their research programs? Such experiences are essential if you wish to go on to a graduate or professional program.

Career options and trends:

Livestock production manager*; artificial breeding technician; research technician; vocational agriculture teacher; sales representative for agricultural supplier*; extension agent; farm or ranch manager; veterinarian*.

For certain positions, such as consulting work, it may be desirable or necessary to be certified by ARPAS (American Registry of Professional Animal Scientists). To become a veterinarian, you must obtain a doctorate of veterinarian medicine (D.V.M.) and pass a licensing exam.

An understanding of environmental issues associated with animal production; concerns about animal welfare; and a sense of the ethical issues associated with animal product development are increasingly important to animal scientists. Global issues, such as growing populations, decreasing arable land, and climate change, will create opportunities for innovative professionals.

Insider's viewpoint:

"I liked being able to apply to real life the knowledge I gained through my classes. It's enjoyable to consult with a farmer on the best way to manage his dairy cattle, or to help a horse owner formulate a diet for her dressage horse."

—Kristen, senior, University of Maryland

For more info:

American Society for Animal Science (ASAS)
1111 North Dunlap Ave.
Savoy, IL 61874
(217) 356-9050
www.asas.org

Equestrian studies

Also known as:
Equine studies

What it's about:
This major deals with horses and horsemanship (in Latin, *equus* means "horse"). You learn the scientific principles needed for the care, breeding, and conditioning of horses; the business principles needed for managing horse-related enterprises and facilities; and the equitation and training skills needed for teaching horseback riding and for training horses.

Is this for you?
You might like this major if you also like: horses and horseback riding; working outdoors; sports and competition; tutoring; business activities; taking care of animals.

Consider this major if you are good at: attention to detail; caring/nurturing; coaching; counseling; memorizing; organizing ...*or have...* a sense of responsibility to your work; initiative; patience; physical stamina.

Recommended high school prep:
English 4, math 3, lab science 3, social studies 3, and a foreign language 2–3. If available, take anatomy and physiology.

Typical courses in this major:
Equine anatomy and physiology
Equine nutrition
Equine breed types and selection
Stable management
Equine lameness and disease
Stud farm management
Equine breeding lab
Equine business management
Equine health management
Management of equine events
Equine breaking and training
Equitation (riding) classes
Care and prevention of athletic injuries
Teaching horsemanship
Entrepreneurship

Concentrations:
Equine business management.

What the study of this major is like:
As an equestrian studies major, you learn to understand the horse and its role in society today. If you have little familiarity with horses, you take handling and riding courses and gain practice in caring for horses and horse tackle. If you are more experienced, you are taught how to break and train horses, instruct riders, and ride at an advanced level (such as dressage and jumping). To learn how to live and work responsibly with horses, all majors study the animal's history and its health and safety needs. Most likely, you will also explore various horse-related enterprises, such as feed sales, racing, breeding, and equine publications.

In general, programs allow students at all levels to be stimulated by their course work. You typically begin with general science courses (for example, biology and chemistry) and then specialize, taking courses in anatomy and physiology, equine breeds, and types and selection. In higher-level courses, such as a breeding lab, you apply what you learn. Equitation courses (involving actual horseback riding) are also taught at beginning, intermediate, and advanced levels.

Many programs offer a two-year associate of science or applied science degree. You can usually choose one of three tracks—equestrian, equine science, or equine business management. In the equestrian track, you concentrate on horsemanship, teaching, and training skills, as you prepare to enter the field of horse training and riding instruction. The science and business tracks generally prepare you to transfer to a four-year program.

In a four-year program, a concentration in science and preveterinary courses focuses on biology, chemistry, math, and equine health and breeding and usually leads to a Bachelor of Science degree. An equine management track includes business subjects and stresses industry-oriented courses, such as stable or stud farm management, equine economics, and equine marketing. At some colleges, equestrian studies (or equine science) is offered only as a concentration in an animal sciences program.

Other majors you might like:

Animal sciences
Physical education
Horse husbandry/equine science
Veterinary technology
Wildlife and wilderness management
Sports and fitness administration
Athletic training
Biology
Zoology
Entrepreneurial studies

Questions to ask colleges:

What are the graduates of the equine degree program doing in the industry now? The answer should indicate whether the program is a strong one.

Career options and trends:

Horse care technician; assistant manager/trainer; farrier (individual who shoes horses); riding instructor; equine massage therapist; veterinarian; biomedical technician; nutritional consultant; pharmaceutical representative.

Jobs as a professional horse trainer are very hard to come by; graduates might find positions as assistant trainers at best, or, more probably, as managers, assistant managers, and grooms. Graduates with a solid science background can investigate alternative career opportunities in the biomedical field and in the pharmaceutical and nutritional industries.

Today, horses represent a larger financial commitment than in years past. As a result, employers in the industry look for better-educated, more qualified personnel than previously.

Insider's viewpoint:

"I look at every student and every horse similarly. Each is an individual that needs support and the freedom of self-expression in order to grow and realize his or her full potential."

—H. Jerry Schurink, Director of Equine Studies, University of Massachusetts Amherst

For more info:

United States Pony Clubs, Inc.
4041 Iron Works Parkway
Lexington, KY 40511
(859) 254-7669
www.ponyclub.org

Farm and ranch management

What it's about:

By combining courses in economics, business administration, and agriculture, this major prepares students to manage a farm, a ranch, and other rural businesses and to do commercial and professional work related to agriculture.

Is this for you?

You might like this major if you also like: working outdoors; using equipment; rural communities; team sports; animals.

Consider this major if you are good at: attention to detail; critical reading/thinking; organizing; quantitative analysis; research; teamwork *...or have...* initiative; manual dexterity; mechanical facility; physical stamina.

Recommended high school prep:

English 4, math 3, lab science 3, social studies 3, and a foreign language 2-3. Three years of vocational agriculture is recommended, if available; as well as two years of computers and speech, and an accounting course.

Typical courses in this major:

Introduction to agricultural economics
Microeconomic theory
Marketing agricultural products
Principles of farm and ranch management
Equipment operation and maintenance
Financial management in agriculture
Business records
Animal health and nutrition
Feedlot management
Livestock production
Advanced farm and ranch management
Agricultural price analysis
Agricultural commodity futures
Agricultural policy
Macroeconomics of agriculture
Rural entrepreneurship

Concentrations:

Crop production; animal husbandry; agricultural mechanization; agricultural marketing.

What the study of this major is like:

Your course work in this major provides a foundation in accounting, finance, marketing, management, economics, and technical production and/or processing. You use computer applications to integrate what you learn into a comprehensive set of entrepreneurial skills. Although you will be expected to study subjects in a number of academic and technical disciplines, you will have flexibility when it comes to identifying your specialty field.

At some colleges, the program emphasizes accounting and a traditional farm and ranch management–oriented curriculum. At others, more attention is placed on technical applications; some colleges may relax their focus and teach general rural entrepreneurship. And while some cover a variety of business, economic, and technical subjects, others stress the application of those subjects to a comprehensive business plan. Programs may also vary in the extent to which they explore risk management.

This major provides opportunities for you to learn and apply business and economic principles, concepts, and tools to a broad spectrum of rural management areas. Career opportunities include the operation of your own farm, ranch, or other rural business; professional farm and ranch management; and agricultural real estate appraisal. During college, you can benefit from interning with a rural lending institution or business.

Other majors you might like:

Range science
Agronomy and crop science
Veterinary technology
Animal breeding
Dairy science

Agricultural and biological engineering
Mining and mineral engineering
Entomology
Heavy equipment maintenance
Operations management
Turf management
Entrepreneurial studies

Questions to ask colleges:

What are the experiences and interests of faculty members who teach the core courses?

What computer resources are available, and how are they used in the curriculum?

How are "real-world" professionals involved in the program? People employed in rural management can help prepare you for challenges you may face in your career.

Career options and trends:

Farmer*; rancher*; business owner or manager*; farm/ranch appraiser; rural loan officer*; consultant; farm machinery company representative.

The number of entry-level jobs in farming and ranching is declining; farm/ranch consolidation, increased agricultural productivity, and the high cost of starting a farm or ranch are all contributing factors. However, if you are good at integrating business, economics, and technical expertise, you may be able to take advantage of other types of rural entrepreneurial opportunities that are increasing. A growing number of small-scale farmers have found success in "niche" (closely targeted) markets, organic farming, farmers' markets, and agricultural and marketing cooperatives. In fact, organic farming, while still a small part of the overall U.S. food supply, is the fastest-growing sector in agriculture.

For more info:

National FFA Organization (Future Farmers of
   America)
P.O. Box 68960
6060 FFA Drive
Indianapolis, IN 46268-0960
(317) 802-6060
www.ffa.org

Food science

What it's about:

In the food science major, you integrate and apply your knowledge of chemistry, biology, nutrition, and engineering as you learn to preserve, process, package, and distribute foods that are wholesome, affordable, and safe to eat.

Is this for you?

You might like this major if you also like: science and math; cooking; hands-on learning; working individually or in teams; applying scientific principles to real-world problems.

Consider this major if you are good at: attention to detail; critical reading/thinking; quantitative analysis; research; teamwork ...*or have...* initiative; lab skills; manual dexterity; verbal skills.

Recommended high school prep:

English 4, math 4 (including precalculus), lab science 4 (including chemistry, biology, and physics), social studies 3, and a foreign language 2–3. Chemistry is essential; courses in health and nutrition are helpful if available.

Typical courses in this major:

Introduction to food science
Agricultural economics
Food chemistry
Food microbiology
Food engineering
Packaging and distribution
Nutrition
Dairy foods processing
Plant foods processing
Meat processing
Food laws and regulations
Sensory analysis
Food quality control and management
Unit operations

Concentrations:

Food chemistry; food-processing technology; packaging; safety and quality assurance; sensory evaluation; food microbiology; food engineering; nutrition.

What the study of this major is like:

Food science is an interdisciplinary program. It brings together principles from the natural sciences, the social sciences, engineering, and business to shed light on the nature and characteristics of food and the nutritional needs of people of various ages, cultures, and lifestyles.

The first two years of a typical food science program consist of required core courses in general chemistry, organic chemistry, and biochemistry; biology; general microbiology; physics; calculus; statistics; human nutrition; communications; and humanities. Most courses have a practical, hands-on laboratory work or project assignment in which you put into practice the facts and concepts you've learned in the classroom.

The course of study is rigorous, but it lays a solid foundation for the food science courses you take in the third and fourth years. Because scientists, technicians, producers, and business people work together in the food industry, you need to develop good communication skills and to understand the differing perspectives these individuals represent.

In upper-level courses, you learn and apply technology to the sanitary processing, preservation, storage, and marketing of foods. You become skilled at using food science instruments and processing equipment. You also receive extensive training in laboratory techniques. Internships with industry or government agencies provide valuable experience.

Special emphasis may vary among colleges, depending on the particular strengths of the faculty members or the needs of local industry. Programs that stress basic science, as it applies to food and food ingredients, focus on food microbiology, food chemistry, or food engineering. Other programs are more commodity-oriented; they focus on dairy processing, meat processing, or plant processing. You may be encouraged to take a minor concentration in food marketing, consumer education, nutrition, business, or economics.

Other majors you might like:
Food and nutrition studies
Dietetics
Agricultural and biological engineering
Animal sciences
Dairy science
Plant sciences
Agricultural business
Microbiology
Chemical engineering
Biotechnology
Restaurant/food services management
Culinary arts and chef training

Career options and trends:
Food technologist; research and development scientist; quality assurance manager; food inspector; process engineer; packaging technologist.

A graduate degree (master's or doctorate) is required for a position as a research scientist or extension food technologist.

Employment can be found with manufacturers of retail food products, as well as with companies that supply food ingredients, processing equipment, and packaging materials, or are involved in institutional food service. Positions are also available in various government agencies and in independent testing laboratories. Prospects are generally good in this field, even during economic downturns.

For more info:
Institute of Food Technologists (IFT)
525 West Van Buren, Suite 1000
Chicago, IL 60607
(312) 782-8424
www.ift.org

Horticulture

What it's about:

Horticulture is a diverse field that includes plant biology, physical sciences, systems management, and the arts. Horticulturists study fruits, vegetables, herbs, trees, shrubs, flowers, and ornamental perennials and annuals, as well as the operation and management of field and greenhouse production, and the design and construction of gardens and landscapes.

Is this for you?

You might like this major if you also like: being outdoors; working with your hands; the arts; science; gardening clubs; arboretums; the environment.

Consider this major if you are good at: attention to detail; caring/nurturing; creativity; critical reading/thinking; math; memorizing; organizing; spatial thinking/analysis; teamwork *...or have...* manual dexterity.

Recommended high school prep:

English 4, math 3, lab science 3 (including biology, chemistry, and physics), social studies 3, visual arts 1, and a foreign language 2-3.

Typical courses in this major:

Plant biology
Plant propagation
Plant taxonomy and identification
Soil science and plant nutrition
Plant genetics
Greenhouse management
Floriculture production
Vegetable production
Nursery management
Organic and sustainable plant production
Fruit production
Viticulture (grapes and wine making)
Plant physiology
Landscape design
Plant pathology
Entomology

Concentrations:

In college: floriculture; ornamental horticulture; field crops; nursery management; greenhouse operations; landscape design; fruit crops.

If you go on to grad school: plant breeding and genetics; plant pathology; environmental plant physiology; horticulture management.

What the study of this major is like:

As a horticulture major, you study the biological and physical sciences as they relate to plants and plant growth (the effects of temperature, light, moisture, and nutrition) and to the environment. You will probably be required to take general and organic chemistry, and math at least through trigonometry. You should also expect to take a computer systems course.

Because many graduates eventually take on managerial positions, curricula often include horticultural business management and economics. You are encouraged to develop problem-solving and quantitative reasoning skills. To help you learn the techniques of sustaining production systems, your course work combines principles of biological sciences, ecology, and horticultural technology. You usually concentrate in one of the following:

General horticulture is the study of crops, including fruits, vegetables, and herbs.

Landscape design and construction trains you in plant materials, irrigation control, and other aspects of landscape maintenance.

Floriculture examines the production, marketing, and use of cut flowers and potted plants. You learn about greenhouse construction; plant breeding, nutrition, disease, and insect pests; effects of the environment on plant growth; floral design; and interior plantscaping.

Olericulture/vegetable science covers the production and marketing of vegetables and herbs. You explore greenhouse, field, organic, and inorganic production techniques; plant breeding, nutrition, disease, and insect pests; and related human health issues.

Environmental horticulture teaches you about urban and natural landscapes. You learn how native plants are selected, produced, and installed to restore disturbed habitats. The habitats you cover are often determined by local needs.

Ornamental horticulture studies landscape and greenhouse crops, including trees, shrubs, potted plants, and foliage plants.

Greenhouse operations is the study of the construction and operations of greenhouses, with an emphasis on producing ornamental and vegetable crops.

Nursery operations focuses on the outdoor or protected production of ornamentals, perennials, fruit trees, and other crops.

Turfgrass management explores the production, marketing, installation, and maintenance of grasses used in golf courses, athletic fields, parks, and commercial and residential landscapes.

Although you learn horticultural basics in the classroom, your training involves plenty of hands-on work, such as greenhouse production or landscape design. In most programs, you get to know your professors and interact with students of diverse interests and ages. Horticulture clubs are often an important part of your academic (and perhaps social) life.

Generally, research horticulture is conducted at land-grant universities, which usually have good facilities and strong programs. The most significant differences among programs relate to the fact that horticulture generally focuses on crops specific to a state or a region. For example, you would not go to Minnesota to study banana production!

Other majors you might like:
Botany
Plant sciences
Forestry
Entomology

Natural resource conservation
Landscaping/groundskeeping
Turf management
Agricultural and biological engineering
Landscape architecture
Fine/studio arts

Questions to ask colleges:
Does the program utilize teaching greenhouses and field plots?

Which areas of specialization are available? If, like most entering students, you don't know which area of horticulture to pursue, you should look for a strong program that offers a range of possibilities.

Career options and trends:
Plant production manager; manager of garden center or retail florist; golf course or resort landscape manager; fruit or vegetable grower; greenhouse grower; nursery manager; landscape designer; organic producer; viticulturalist (wine grower); research technician.

While the number of people involved in agriculture in the United States is still on the decline, the consumer plant industry remains strong, and opportunities exist in landscaping, ornamentals, organic production, health aspects of plants, and greenhouse operations. More efficient production often means more sophisticated techniques, so there is a market for well-trained, motivated, creative professionals. In an exciting trend, horticulture and education join forces to set up "children's gardens" as an imaginative method of teaching and learning.

For more info:
American Society for Horticulture Science (ASHS)
113 South West St.
Suite 200
Alexandria, VA 22314-2851
(703) 836-4606
www.ashs.org

Soil science

What it's about:

Soil science applies principles of biology, chemistry, mathematics, geology, and physics to one of the most important and dynamic natural resources—often abused, sometimes reclaimable, and only slowly renewable. Soil science majors examine the nature and properties of soils and gain the skills needed for wise use, conservation, and management of this resource.

Is this for you?

You might like this major if you also like: nature and the outdoors; working with your hands; science and math; solving complex and multi-faceted problems; farming; gardening; environmental issues.

Consider this major if you are good at: attention to detail; critical reading/thinking; organizing; quantitative analysis; spatial thinking/analysis *...or have...* initiative; manual dexterity; verbal skills.

Recommended high school prep:

English 4, math 4 (including precalculus), lab science 4 (including earth science, biology, physics, and chemistry), social studies 3, and a foreign language 2-3. If they are available, take a computer science course and an environmental science course.

Did you know...

...that soil is not just dirt, but a complex, varied ecosystem that makes up as much as one third of our environment? Critical for life, this natural resource is often taken for granted; but after years of being studied and put to a variety of uses, soils still hold many secrets for scientists to unlock.

Typical courses in this major:

General and organic chemistry
Quantitative soil analysis
Meteorology
Geology
Soil chemistry
Soil morphology, genesis, and taxonomy
Soils and land use
Soil fertility
Environmental soil management
Soil microbiology
Agronomic crop science
Soil contaminants
Plant and soil water relations
Soil physics
Introductory plant pathology
Hydrogeology

Concentrations:

Generally, none in college; but if you go on to grad school: soil microbiology; soil chemistry; soil mineralogy; soil physics; soil conservation; soil management; soil fertility; forest soils; land reclamation.

What the study of this major is like:

Soil scientists have prime responsibility for determining the distribution of soils on the landscape, assessing their characteristics, and predicting their suitability for different purposes. Professionals also help promote practices that will conserve or reclaim soils. Majors learn to describe soils in the field, recognize their uses and limitations, and make recommendations for erosion control, reclamation practices, water movement, and soil improvement.

Soil science is sometimes a concentration within agronomy and crop science; geology and earth science; environmental science; or natural resources and conservation majors. Whether you major or concentrate in soil science, you need a solid foundation in chemistry, biology, physics, and mathematics, along with courses in the humanities and the social sciences. Courses in geology, geography, economics, plant sciences, statistics, nutrition, and genetics are often recommended or required.

In your first and second years, you may be discouraged by the emphasis on university core and basic science courses—soils are hardly mentioned. But if you master the basics, you will likely be rewarded later: in upper-level, soil-oriented courses, you will be expected to apply what you've learned earlier. Because many courses are in lecture-laboratory format, you will spend more hours a week in class/lab than students who take only lecture classes. On the other hand, you generally learn more through hands-on experimentation and probably have to spend less out-of-class time reading and writing.

You are usually encouraged (if not required) to do summer internships and/or part-time work with field soil scientists. Many organizations that employ graduates—such as contractors, mining companies, government agencies, power companies, and landscaping firms—also offer summer internship opportunities.

Relatively few colleges, other than the land-grant state universities, offer the number of credit hours in soil science needed for certification or licensure as a soil scientist. Among those that do, some may emphasize agronomic applications, and others may focus on environmental aspects; but generally there are few differences. Look for a program that is strong not only in soil science but also in the basic sciences.

Other majors you might like:
Horticulture
Environmental science
Natural resources and conservation
Agronomy and crop science
Landscape architecture
Microbiology
Range science
Agricultural and biological engineering
Botany
Farm and ranch management
Geology/earth science
Biochemistry

Questions to ask colleges:
Does the program have a soil judging team? This competitive activity helps you solidify your understanding of soil morphology, classification, interpretations, and landscape distribution, and provides a way to meet other people in the field.

Are the teaching labs well equipped for soil analysis? Are agricultural research stations, as well as farm, forest, and/or range lands, close by and accessible?

Career options and trends:
Soil surveyor*; researcher; field soil scientist with federal or state agricultural or environmental agency, or with private industry*; environmental consultant; soil chemistry consultant; hazardous waste specialist.

Several states require certification or licensing in order to practice as a professional soil scientist. Requirements vary but usually involve taking a certification exam and three to five years of experience.

Soil scientists find more jobs in nonagricultural areas than agricultural. Traditionally, most jobs were in government agencies, but opportunities have been growing in the private sector, especially in environmentally related fields. Overall, the number of job opportunities outpaces the number of graduates in this field.

Insider's viewpoint:
"I interned with a field soil scientist to run soil transects and update the soil surveys in Delaware. I worked outside almost every day in the summer, investigating the different soils in the lower part of Delaware, and scientifically classifying these soils so that they can be mapped and correlated."

—Kristin, sophomore, University of Delaware

For more info:
The Soil Science Society of America (SSSA)
677 South Segoe Rd.
Madison, WI 53711
(608) 273-8080
www.soils.org

Soil science education home page:
http://soil.gsfc.nasa.gov

Architecture

In the fall of 1980, a professor gave his architecture class an assignment: to enter a national design competition for a memorial honoring those who had served in the Vietnam War. You may already know the rest. One student's vision was chosen unanimously by the experts and was built on the National Mall in Washington, D.C. The Vietnam Veterans Memorial was designed by a Yale University undergraduate, Maya Lin.

Of course, very few people start their careers so successfully. Lin created an inspiring physical environment in an urban park by integrating architectural and landscape design. What was once an ordinary space became a national treasure.

"Students who want to understand the connections between people and the environment and want to do something to improve the world" should consider majoring in architecture, suggests Professor John B. Wright of New Mexico State University.

"It is thrilling to recognize that the physical shape of our destiny is in our own hands," says Alfred D. Price, School of Architecture and Planning, State University of New York at Buffalo. "Good environmental design, sound planning, engaging architecture, responsible landscape design can, do, and will make a difference."

To learn architecture, you study many things: humanities, math, natural sciences, architectural history, graphics, design, photography, economic development, environmental planning, geography, and more.

You don't have to be a great artist to be an architect, but design is a big part of the program. Some schools are based more in studio art and creative expression, while other colleges take the engineering angle to solve problems through analysis. In between are colleges that do both.

"The median approach is one that integrates creative artistic responses with methodical analysis, the art and science of design, the poetic and the practical," notes Professor Michael Bednar of the University of Virginia. "The best way to assess the design philosophy is by speaking with faculty and students. Viewing student work is another useful means of assessing a school's design direction."

Still another helpful guide is the college's list of required courses for majors in architecture, planning, landscape, or environmental design. That list will tell you what's covered in the degree program. Keep in mind that some bachelor's degree programs take five years. On the graduate level, concentrations include ecological planning, urban design, land use, building conservation, transportation, universal design, and community development. Among the emerging fields of study are environmental and sustainable architecture.

Your model campus

Okay, let's get real. You probably won't be designing a national memorial anytime soon. But you can plan your studies and prepare for work in the highly professional field of architecture. Some architects work for government or nonprofit organizations; some are employees of contractors, real estate developers, or engineering firms; many are independent professionals who are hired as consultants. Specific jobs include architect, landscape architect, neighborhood and community planner, industrial designer, conservator, graphic designer, and other careers. City planners and rural planners are in great demand lately for their expertise in land use.

Look for architecture and related majors in schools of architecture, colleges of environmental design, colleges of arts and sciences or natural resource management; and departments of geography, landscape architecture, and public administration. You might even look at schools of engineering for some city planning studies.

And while you're comparing colleges, ask about the design studios. After all, you'll be spending plenty of time there working on projects.

"Students spend long hours individually designing their projects and making drawings and models to express their design intentions," explains Bednar. "Drawings are in all media from informal sketches to formal presentations."

Ask how often the design studios meet and if you can get into the studio after class. Are the studios equipped with state-of-the-art computer hardware and specialized software? What are the other facilities and libraries like?

The faculty's credentials may be an attraction at a particular college. Are professors accomplished, practicing architects? If so, what do their designs look like? Has the work of students in the department been recognized nationally in recent years as outstanding?

Do you have particular interests such as the environment, urban planning, historical preservation, or high-tech design? If so, look for colleges with those priorities. And see if the program is accredited. One accreditation to look for is by the National Architectural Accrediting Board.

And don't forget to think about your degree options. What is the first degree you'll earn? Is it an accredited professional degree or a preprofessional degree that will qualify you to apply to grad school? Will your undergrad program take four or five years? For each type of degree, you'll want to find out about the requirements and the career options.

Important sources of information include the American Institute of Architects at www.aia.org; the Association of Collegiate Schools of Architecture at www.acsa-arch.org; the American Planning Association at www.planning.org; and the American Society of Landscape Architects at www.asla.org.

One last thing: be ready for a pretty competitive field if you choose to study an architectural major. Maya Lin only got a B in that class!

Architecture

What it's about:

Architecture majors prepare for the professional practice of architecture by learning how to design buildings and other aspects of the built environment. The course of study includes architectural drawing, design, history, and theory; project and site planning; construction methods and technology; professional responsibilities and standards; and related cultural, social, economic, and environmental issues.

Is this for you?

You might like this major if you also like: drawing; photography; making models; crafts of all kinds; science; art; history; cities; landscapes.

Consider this major if you are good at: creativity; critical reading/thinking; organizing; persuading/influencing; quantitative analysis; sketching ideas; spatial thinking/analysis *...or have...* initiative; manual dexterity; visual sensitivity.

Recommended high school prep:

English 4, math 4 (including precalculus), lab science 4 (including physics), social studies 4, visual arts 1, and a foreign language 3–4. If they are available, courses in environmental science, drafting/technical drawing, and computer science are also recommended.

Did you know...

...that artistic talent is not essential to be successful in this major?

Typical courses in this major:

Architectural history
Architectural graphics
Design fundamentals
Architectural design
Architectural theory
Construction materials and methods
Structural design
Environmental controls
Site design
Engineering mechanics
Computer-aided design (CAD)
Construction economics

Concentrations:

Generally, none in college; but if you go on to grad school: historic preservation; urban design; environmental design; architectural engineering.

What the study of this major is like:

The architecture major combines courses in the liberal arts and sciences with architecture. Along with technical and design skills, architects must understand the culture they work in (humanities), the physical world (physical sciences), and human relations (social sciences). They must also be familiar with the history of art and architecture.

After two years of liberal arts, you begin studying architecture by taking courses in visual and graphic skills. Courses in history and theory of architecture teach you how the built environment was formed, and the role of related disciplines.

The most important courses in every architecture program are the design studio courses. In beginning studios, you learn to design objects, furniture, and rooms. Intermediate studios stress the design of small buildings, such as museums, libraries, and schools. In your final year, you design larger buildings for urban areas.

In the studio, you work on a series of projects. Your instructor assigns a project, outlines expectations, and provides resources. As you develop your design, you benefit from group feedback from fellow students. The project itself, which includes drawings and models you've created in various media, will be evaluated by faculty members for its strengths and weaknesses. Studio work can also include field trips, documentation, photography, interviews, research, model making, and graphic analysis. Your work is supported by classes in construction technology, computer graphics, and design theory.

Be ready to spend long hours on your projects. The studio is both a supportive and a competitive environment—design work is stimulating, spontaneous, and often difficult. To be successful, you need to be resourceful and to have good critical-thinking and time management skills.

Although a four-year undergraduate degree in architecture is a significant part of your education, it does not qualify you to become a professional architect. To become licensed, you must do one to three more years of study, complete a three-year paid internship, and pass an examination. A degree from a college approved by the National Architectural Accrediting Board (NAAB) satisfies all states' educational requirements, but you must still pass the exam mandated by the state where you will practice.

Programs can take different approaches to architectural design. In one approach, based in studio art, you are encouraged to express yourself creatively. In an opposite, engineering-oriented approach, you analyze the needs of a project and evaluate various solutions. Balanced programs, which emphasize both the art and the science of design, combine artistic responses and methodical analysis. But even balanced programs can vary: some may use historical models; others may draw on cultural philosophies; still others may favor social or environmental ethics. You may have difficulty telling how a college approaches architectural design if the focus is not clearly stated in the catalog. The best way to find out is to speak with faculty members and students and to view student work.

Other majors you might like:
Civil engineering
Architectural history /criticism
Historic preservation
Real estate
Environmental design
Industrial design
Drafting and design technology
Housing and human environments
Physics

Interior design
Construction management
Marine engineering /naval architecture

Questions to ask colleges:
How are the design studios set up?

How often do they meet and how many students are in each section?

Is the studio space you are assigned available to you exclusively, 24/7?

What role do computers play in the studio process?

Do the faculty members practice architecture?

What kind of buildings have they designed?

Career options and trends:
Architect; urban planner; landscape architect; architectural historian; graphic designer; industrial designer; construction manager.

Recently, more architects are working for contractors or real estate developers as employees than as independent professionals that are hired as consultants. Many also work for public agencies or for corporations as in-house architects. Overall, employment of architects is strongly tied to activity in the construction industry, where strong growth is expected to come from increasing demand for both commercial and residential space.

Insider's viewpoint:
"The combination of the poetic and the practical, the art and the science, is what has always attracted me to this field. An architect needs to use both sides of the brain simultaneously to produce good architectural design."

—Professor Michael Bednar, University of Virginia

For more info:
Association of Collegiate Schools of Architecture
1735 New York Ave., N.W.
Washington, DC 20006-5292
(202) 785-2324
www.acsa-arch.org

Environmental design

What it's about:
This major will prepare you to design public and private spaces, indoor and outdoor, in a way that shapes, restores, preserves, and sustains both the built and the natural environments. It can also ready you for professional practice as an environmental designer or architect.

Is this for you?
You might like this major if you also like: drawing; nature study; natural and physical sciences; joining volunteer activities; model-building; computers; crafts; photography; cities; landscapes. Most students in this major share a passionate concern both for the environment and for people.

Consider this major if you are good at: attention to detail; creativity; critical reading/thinking; math; organizing; spatial thinking/analysis; teamwork *...or have...* manual dexterity; patience; writing skills.

Recommended high school prep:
English 4, math 4 (including precalculus), lab science 4 (including biology, chemistry, and physics), social studies 4, visual arts 1, and a foreign language 3-4. Drawing (freehand) is important. A course in computer-aided drafting is helpful, since much of your college course work will use that technique, but it's not required.

Typical courses in this major:
Architectural and landscape drawing
Behavior and environment
Materials and methods
Construction technology
Environmental control systems
Urban history
Computer-aided design
Landscape design
Community planning
Architectural history
Landscape ecology
Law and urban land use
Site systems and engineering
Geographical information systems (GIS)
Restoration and reclamation ecology
Facilities planning and design

Concentrations:
Landscape and horticultural design; urban planning and design; facilities planning; designing for universal access; designing for special populations (elderly, physically-challenged, etc.).

What the study of this major is like:
In this major, you study the various aspects of the environment from a design point of view. You learn to consider the built, natural, and human components of space and place holistically. Your goal will be to create designs for structures and spaces that harmonize these components, while meeting the requirements of function, environmental safety, and ecological sustainability.

For this reason environmental design is an interdisciplinary major that combines creative concepts in architecture, landscape, interiors, and environmental graphics (signs and information boards) with courses covering social science, health science, environmental science, and physical science.

These topics are taught through a combination of lecture courses, research seminars, field assignments, and studio workshops. In your first two years of study, you'll fulfill your college's general education requirements in the liberal arts and sciences, along with required introductory and foundation courses in environmental design. In your third and fourth years you will spend almost all your time on upper-level elective courses within a concentration of your choice, such as urban and regional planning or landscape design.

What's most distinctive about this major are the studio or workshop courses. They require a far greater time commitment than usual—for both class work and projects outside class. Especially in your third and fourth years, you'll understand why design students are known for burning the midnight oil.

Workshops and internships introduce you to real-world exercises in planning and design. You might work with a local public, private, or nonprofit organization to analyze the economic, social, political, and design issues involved in a community planning or development project. Or you might work hands-on in a machine and assembly shop, learning about construction methods and materials.

In the studio, you'll learn that for any given problem, there is no single solution, as there is in math or chemistry. Designers continually revise their concepts, each time seeking to refine and improve their ideas. Critical-thinking skills, good judgment, and the capacity for reflection and healthy self-criticism are key to success.

An environmental design program can usually be distinguished from ones taught at other colleges by its primary focus. Some programs emphasize traditional physical design; others feature research-based design for special-needs populations; still others stress community-based approaches to planning.

Programs that highlight physical design are usually found in schools of architecture, interior design, landscape design, or possibly engineering (for industrial or product design). Programs at colleges that are more research-oriented will have formal research centers that are doing important new work, and that work should be described on their websites. Programs that are geared toward planning and policy (which are most common) are closely allied with departments of city/urban/regional planning.

Other majors you might like:
Landscape architecture
Interior design
Urban studies
Parks, recreation, and leisure studies
Environmental studies
Historic preservation
Industrial design
Geology/earth science
Construction management

Land use planning
Housing and human environments
Drafting and design technology

Questions to ask colleges:
Are there specialized, dedicated computing facilities for environmental design majors, or is access shared with all other students at the campus computing center?

Are the program's design studios equipped with state-of-the-art hardware and software?

Does the program use faculty members or administrative staff as academic advisers for undergraduates?

Has any student work received national recognition in recent years?

Career options and trends:
City or community planner*; neighborhood housing specialist; architect; interior designer; landscape architect; construction manager*; facilities planner/manager*; real estate developer.

All architects must be licensed, as must most landscape architects and interior designers, depending on the state in which they intend to practice.

Because there are relatively few graduates in this field, employment prospects are good. However, demand for designers and planners is greatest where populations are growing, so it might be necessary to relocate in order to find a job. In recent years, the employment opportunities have been most notable in the South, the West, and the Southwest.

For more info:
Environmental Design Research Association
    (EDRA)
Post Office Box 7146
Edmond, OK 73083-7146
(405) 330-4863
www.edra.org

Landscape architecture

What it's about:

Landscape architecture explores contemporary issues related to the design, planning, and management of the constructed landscape. You learn fundamental techniques of site design and planning and receive studio training in advanced areas such as urban and regional landscape design and planning.

Is this for you?

You might like this major if you also like: tackling environmental concerns; environmental art; gardening; arboretums; outdoor activities; drawing and graphic expression.

Consider this major if you are good at: active listening; attention to detail; creativity; critical reading/thinking; organizing; quantitative analysis; spatial thinking/analysis; teamwork *...or have...* initiative; verbal skills.

Recommended high school prep:

English 4, math 3, lab science 4 (including physics), social studies 3, and a foreign language 2. If possible, take a year of computer drafting, one to two years of art, and a business course.

Did you know...

...that landscape architecture can range from designing a skateboard park to an entire wilderness area? It's not just about the trees and shrubs around buildings.

Typical courses in this major:

Fundamentals of design
Computer-aided drafting (CAD)
Landscape planning
Landscape design
Landscape technology
Graphic communications
Applied ecology
Landscape construction
Plant materials
Plant identification
Plane surveying
Landscape architectural history
Landscape architectural theory

Concentrations:

Landscape restoration; landscape technology; ecological planning.

What the study of this major is like:

Landscape architects plan, design, and manage outdoor settings, such as parks and areas around buildings, to make these displays useful, beautiful, and in harmony with nature. As a landscape architecture major, you work with the land: drawing, painting, and mapping it; describing it; examining and analyzing it; and imagining what it might become in the future. You learn about the complex ecology of natural landscapes and the even more complex human ecology of urban landscapes.

Landscape architecture is a studio-based program that requires you to become thoroughly familiar with the ways in which natural vistas can be created or changed. First you learn traditional techniques of site planning and design, including drawing and computer graphics, and the principles and vocabulary of design. In addition to the studio curriculum, you take courses in graphic communications, history and theory, materials, and professional practice. You study ecological systems, learn to identify and work with a broad range of locally grown plants, and analyze the relationships between social and political institutions, on the one hand, and the land, on the other.

Later you study advanced techniques that include urban design, landscape technology, and regional planning and analysis. Building on your foundations, you shape increasingly complex landscapes and develop detailed drawings, specifications, and other means of bringing your plans to life. In a typical studio course in your third or fourth year, you might design a park, a public garden, or a plaza; plan a site for an apartment house or a sports arena; or develop a management program for a natural reserve. In construction courses, you learn how to produce the detailed drawings for projects like these.

As a major, you might join college organizations devoted to environmental issues, urban design, and regional landscape awareness. You can often find volunteer opportunities that include mentoring high school students about landscape architecture. Some students participate in community planning groups. At the conclusion of a four- or five-year program, you should be qualified to enter the profession, with a private firm or a public agency.

Landscape architecture departments differ a great deal in the approach they take to the major. Some programs focus on physical design, while others concentrate on sustainability and regeneration (to protect natural settings and to ensure their survival). Still other programs stress both physical design and ecological issues. Geographic and social distinctions may also influence the focus of a particular program. Programs at colleges in cities are more likely to devote themselves to urban landscape design than programs in suburban or rural areas. Another reason for differences in programs is that some colleges encourage faculty members to conduct research, whereas in other programs, instructors spend more time in professional practice. Finally, some programs are based on a four-year curriculum and award a Bachelor of Science in Landscape Architecture (B.S.L.A.), while others offer a five-year degree, the Bachelor of Landscape Architecture (B.L.A.), which requires you to complete additional studio and lecture courses.

Other majors you might like:
Environmental design
Environmental studies
Landscaping/groundskeeping
Horticulture
Land use planning
Mining and mineral engineering
Urban forestry
Graphic design
Parks/recreational/leisure facilities management
Environmental engineering

Botany
Turf management

Questions to ask colleges:
Does the program offer a degree in four years or in five years? What is the academic focus of the program? What are the professional and academic activities of the faculty members?

Career options and trends:
Landscape architect; landscape construction manager; political advocate; urban planner; environmental agency manager; natural resource manager.

Most states require landscape architects to be licensed or registered, based on the Landscape Architect Registration Examination (LARE) and one to four years work experience. Some states also require an additional state-specific exam focusing on local laws and environments.

Most graduates of landscape architecture programs work in private consulting firms as designers, planners, or managers. Landscape architects can also work in city planning, recreation, and parks departments at the local level and in land management agencies such as the National Park Service, National Forest Service, and Bureau of Land Management at the federal level. In addition, the training you receive in landscape architecture provides a foundation for other careers related to shaping the environment, such as landscape restoration.

Employment prospects are projected to be strong. Demand for landscape architects will be driven by growth in development, the need to comply with environmental regulations and security requirements, and continued efforts to restore and preserve lands, wetlands, and ecosystems.

For more info:
American Society of Landscape Architects (ASLA)
636 Eye Street, N.W.
Washington, DC 20001-3736
(202) 898-2444
www.asla.org

Urban, community, and regional planning

What it's about:

The urban, community, and regional planning major focuses on creating livable, responsibly financed, and environmentally healthy communities. You learn about transportation, economic development, housing, land-use regulations, infrastructure management, and preservation of parks and other open spaces. Planners shape surroundings that are appropriate to the needs of urban, suburban, or rural residents.

Is this for you?

You might like this major if you also like: the outdoors; maps; architecture; history; working with people; exploring cities and small towns; environmental and social causes; community service activities.

Consider this major if you are good at: attention to detail; creativity; organizing; persuading/influencing; spatial thinking/analysis; teamwork ...*or have...* initiative; patience; verbal skills; writing skills.

Recommended high school prep:

English 4, math 3, lab science 3, social studies 3, and a foreign language 3–4. If possible, also take classes in geography, environmental issues, statistics, and computer applications.

Typical courses in this major:

Planning theories
Planning practice
Regional studies
Technology of urban life
History of cities
Urban and landscape design
Social issues
Land use regulation and law
Transportation planning
Economic development
Community development
Housing
Environmental planning
Geographic information systems (GIS)
Cartography
Field/design project

Concentrations:

Generally, none in college; but if you go on to grad school: land use regulation; transportation planning; urban design; community development (including housing, economic development, and social issues).

What the study of this major is like:

To create a livable community, planners must reduce conflicts between competing interests (real estate developers and residents, for example) and ensure that the development is fiscally, structurally, and environmentally sound. As an urban, community, and regional planning major, you explore such topics as physical and environmental geography, urban studies, transportation, land use and real estate law, community development and economic development, mapping, statistics, economics, history, political science, and human geography.

In this major, courses are mostly in lecture format, although there are some design classes. Your course work will cover a range of tools and techniques—from computer modeling to group decision-making; from statistical programming to brainstorming and values clarification. You will often work in groups, addressing difficult questions as a team: Can a community learn to recycle, conserve resources, and protect wildlife? Are a community's transportation systems appropriate for conditions anticipated in the next hundred years? How can a city upgrade the standard of living of its low-income residents? How can conflicts be resolved between developers and architectural preservation groups? How can volunteer groups, corporations, and governments work together to solve problems? Together with your team, you may visit project sites and tour development areas.

Generally, majors do internships with public planning agencies, nonprofit groups, or private businesses. Independent projects (usually research papers) are also common. Students often have the most trouble with "spatial thinking"—understanding how the landscape is structured and how communities function. After a few required courses, though, most students catch on. Group projects and small classes tend to create a friendly, supportive environment.

Planning programs may be housed in departments of geography, landscape architecture, or public administration, or in their own department. Planning programs tend to break down into three areas of concentration: urban, rural/regional, and environmental. Although all programs focus on land use regulations, the first two approaches emphasize distinct types of communities, and environmental planning deals with issues like pollution, environmental impact statements, cleanup of toxic waste sites, and natural hazards such as flooding and earthquakes. Because planning overlaps with many other fields, you may double-major in planning and another subject, or minor in a related field.

Planning is a hands-on major—you learn to analyze a situation, to imagine a better one, and to determine how to bridge the gap. Planning offers you a career in which you can conserve nature and help build a better world.

Other majors you might like:
Civil engineering
Urban forestry
Environmental studies
Landscape architecture
Land use planning
Historic preservation
Housing and human environments
Environmental design
Public administration
Urban studies
Political science
Sociology

Career options and trends:
Land use planner; geographic information systems director; transportation planner; grant writer; housing coordinator; parks/open space planner; architect; cartographer.

Planners also find work in local government agencies dealing with zoning and community/economic development; fish and game agencies; and parks, transportation, and environment departments; in federal agencies such as the Forest Service, Environmental Protection Agency, Defense Mapping Agency, Housing and Urban Development, and Natural Resources Conservation Service; in environmental consulting companies, engineering firms, real estate companies, land development companies, and surveyors' offices; and in nonprofit groups such as the Nature Conservancy, Trust for Public Lands, and American Farmland Trust.

With cities and rural areas growing in all regions of the country, there is a high demand for planners in the United States. The recent devastation caused by Gulf Coast hurricanes is expected to further spur demand for planners who can help communities prepare for both natural and man-made disasters.

Insider's viewpoint:
"All-time famous misperception about the major: planning equals architecture. Planning is a very political field, and the department recognizes this in its courses. If you don't like politics, you might not like planning."

—Kacey, senior, Cornell University

For more info:
American Planning Association (APA)
1776 Massachusetts Ave., N.W.
Washington, DC 20036-1904
(202) 872-0611
www.planning.org

Area, ethnic, and gender studies

At first glance, these majors seem to be devoted to the interests of a minority of people. Not so. These studies embrace the vast majority of the world's population.

"The primary objective of the curriculum, regardless of race or color, is education for positive and productive citizenship," says R. Baxter Miller of the University of Georgia's Institute for African American Studies. "One would see oneself as a thoughtful and creative agent of cultural transformation and change—a guardian of the true implementation of American democracy."

From the studies of indigenous peoples to those from faraway lands, these majors help students understand other cultures and their own.

"Most students don't realize the inextricable connections between the Middle East with our own Western history and traditions—we are in fact part of the same civilizational unit," says Professor Bernard Haykel of New York University. "By engaging in Middle Eastern studies, one acquires an entirely novel way of looking at one's own identity and develops a much broader understanding of the world we live in."

In some majors, such as Latin American studies, language is central. "To me the most important aspect of this field is the opportunity to learn about and communicate with a variety of peoples and cultures," says Professor César G. López of Scripps College.

The women's studies major cuts across many cultures. Women hold up half the sky, as the Chinese proverb goes. The major explores gender, sexuality, power, inequality, racism, class issues, oppression, and the connection between these topics.

The area, ethnic, and gender studies majors cover everything imaginable—history, culture, language, literature, anthropology, political science, religion, the arts—you name it. If these subjects appeal to you, you might check other sections in this book: Humanities, Languages, Multi/interdisciplinary studies, Religion and theology, Social sciences, and Visual and performing arts.

"The American studies major enables students to understand the world around them from a variety of perspectives," says Daniel Horowitz of Smith College. "It enables students to understand how the nation's history, literature, arts, politics, and society illuminate their nation's experiences."

The culture of work

Okay, let's look at these studies from the shameless, self-serving, capitalistic perspective of what they can do for you. Fortunately, many of the subjects taught in area and ethnic majors translate to valuable job skills. For example, "area studies" means just what it sounds like, the study of a particular region of the world. Such majors are great preparation for jobs with companies that do business in the region being studied. It's a big plus in today's multicultural workplaces and in the expanding global markets, especially Asia.

If you speak an Asian language, Arabic, or Spanish, you automatically have a marketable skill. "Spanish is today the second language in the United States after English," says López. "There is a big demand for teachers at all levels. In some states, the knowledge of Spanish is necessary for medical personnel (especially pediatricians), lawyers, and social workers."

Clearly, Middle Eastern experts are also in demand. "In the post-September 11th world, and because of the political and economic turbulence in the Middle East, the United States, at the level of the public and private sectors, will be intensely engaged in the region for years if not decades to come," says Haykel. "Persons with language and other skills pertaining to the Middle East will easily find gainful and rewarding employment."

In addition to language, critical thinking and human understanding are aspects of these majors that are essential in professions including communications, law, teaching, public service, social services, labor relations, business, counseling, Foreign Service/diplomacy, and humanitarian work.

When choosing a school, look for colleges of arts and sciences or liberal arts, and divisions of humanities or social sciences. While you're at it, see how the college balances the humanities and the social sciences. Is the curriculum mostly language-based or does it focus more on history and political science? If the emphasis is on history, the courses may concentrate on a time period, such as the Middle Ages or the present. If the focus is on language, look into the quality of the school's language labs. Also, what are the library holdings to support your studies and research? Will you be studying abroad as a requirement or as an elective?

Ethnic and gender majors are so broad that no one college can cover them all. Check the core requirements to get a feel for the program. Do the courses build on one another? Is the major supported with its own department? How many full-time faculty members are in the department? Are they prominent, published scholars? Do the professors teach undergraduates?

Oddly, no matter which of these diverse majors you may choose, your studies will be influenced by a dead white guy, Socrates. The Greek philosopher's method of teaching was to ask the class questions. Students learned through participation and conversation, and that's how these majors are often taught. The technique makes the quality of the faculty even more important.

African-American studies

Also known as:
Black studies

What it's about:
The major in African-American studies includes the history, politics, traditions, literature, art, and lives of North American peoples of African descent. Traditional assumptions about race are tested and examined to help students make enlightened choices for themselves and their society. The primary objective of this major is to prepare all students, regardless of race or color, for positive, productive citizenship.

Is this for you?
You might like this major if you also like: community involvement; reading; debating; travel; foreign languages; sports; music; dance; theater; politics.

Consider this major if you are good at: caring/nurturing; creativity; critical reading/thinking; leadership; persuading/influencing ...*or have...* initiative; verbal skills; writing skills.

Recommended high school prep:
English 4, math 3, lab science 3, social studies 4, and a foreign language 2–3. Courses in government, economics, music, and art are also recommended.

Did you know...
...that in business and government, there is an increasing demand for graduates trained in multiculturalism? In a society in which power is distributed unequally, multiculturalists can mediate disputes, in the workplace and elsewhere, between individuals or communities of different ethnic or racial backgrounds.

Typical courses in this major:
American history to 1865
African-American politics
History and cultures of Africa
Multiculturalism in modern America
Modern African-American experience
Caribbean history and society
Christianity and colonialism in Africa
African-American religions
African-American society
African-American folklore
African-American poetry
Modern African literature
African-American music
Women in African-American cinema
Seminar in race and ethnicity

Concentrations:
In college: African-American history; African-American language, literature, and art; social and political inquiry.

If you go on to grad school: African-American literature; African-Hispanic literature; African-American drama; African-American psychology, African-American sociology, African-American religions.

What the study of this major is like:
African-American studies is an interdisciplinary major in the liberal arts and social sciences. You learn through a Socratic method that takes place within a human laboratory of constant challenges. Learning reveals a discrepancy between tradition and dissent in American life; a vitality of diversity in redefining the ideal of freedom. Majors develop the ability to communicate highly charged cultural and emotional issues into well-reasoned proposals subject to logical debate and resolution.

Your introductory courses examine the history of African-Americans, prepare you for interdisciplinary work, and place black history in the context of world history. You examine the works of anthropologists, economists, political scientists, psychologists, theologians, and sociologists. In most introductory courses, you also study music, dance, and the arts of African-Americans.

Throughout the program, the emphasis is on how people of color see themselves and how others see them. You examine the heritage of slavery from the perspectives of both the slaveholder and the slave: you are asked to reconcile opposing viewpoints, sort out the emotions and motivations of whites and blacks alike, explore your own feelings about race, and reach a balanced conclusion about the effects of slavery on whites and blacks today.

Advanced courses, which build on this introduction, provide in-depth analysis and allow you to develop a concentration reflecting your interests.

Courses in art and literature cover such topics as slave and folk songs of the mid-nineteenth century; the Harlem Renaissance of the 1920s; contemporary rap; the poetry of Langston Hughes, Margaret Walker, Gwendolyn Brooks, Sonia Sanchez, and Amiri Baraka; and the stories, novels, and other works of Frances Harper, Richard Wright, Jean Toomer, Ralph Ellison, James Baldwin, Alice Walker, and Toni Morrison.

Courses taught from a historical, sociological, and political viewpoint explore the impact of social class, status, and power relations on African-Americans, as members of the current social structure and as descendants of the African diaspora (forced migration). After studying such issues as the civil rights movement, affirmative action, the role of African-American women, and urban families, you examine ways of turning theory into public policy. Most programs require you to take one or two courses in the history and cultures of the African continent.

Programs can usually be distinguished by the emphasis they give to politics, humanities, and the social sciences. One program may stress the formulation of public policy, whereas another focuses on theory. One may take a somewhat radical approach; another, a more traditional one. Some may emphasize arts, literature, and drama; others may focus on social and multicultural issues; still others may be stronger in history. You can probably learn about a program's orientation by speaking with graduates and faculty members.

Other majors you might like:
African studies
Latin American studies
Chicano studies
Jazz studies
American literature
Intercultural /diversity studies
Islamic studies
Caribbean studies
Women's studies
Urban studies
Anthropology
Sociology

Questions to ask colleges:
How do faculty members and majors interact in and out of class? Which events and activities help majors bond as a unified group?

Which outstanding graduates in the discipline have come out of the program in the last decade or so?

Career options and trends:
African-American studies prepares students for careers in education, social service, public administration, business, and a range of other areas. It is also excellent preparation for graduate or professional study in law, business, religion, medicine, or social work.

As the population becomes more diverse, multiculturalists, who can explain reasons behind conflicts, help create bonds among employees, and strengthen the body politic by promoting education and equality, will be of increasing value to society.

Insider's viewpoint:
"It's only in my ethnic studies classes that I've learned about the Civil Rights movement, the brown power movement, the women's rights movement, and gay liberation. This is all stuff that the departments called history don't teach."

—Ronald, senior, University of California: Berkeley

For more info:

National Council for Black Studies
Georgia State University
P.O. Box 4109
Atlanta, GA 30302-4109
(404) 463-9483
www.ncbsonline.org

Association for the Study of African American Life
    and History
Howard University, C. B. Powell Building
525 Bryant St., Suite C142
Washington, DC 20059
(202) 865-0053
www.asalh.org

American studies

What it's about:

The American studies major uses a wide variety of materials and approaches to give you a comprehensive understanding of American society and values. As an interdisciplinary program, it integrates courses in American history, literature, popular culture, and contemporary social concerns.

Is this for you?

You might like this major if you also like: the History Channel; movies; talk radio; studying media and popular culture; biographies; debating; antiquing; traveling and sight-seeing; learning about people who are different from you.

Consider this major if you are good at: creativity; critical reading/thinking; research ...*or have...* curiosity; initiative; self-motivation; sense of adventure; verbal skills; writing skills.

Recommended high school prep:

English 4, math 3, lab science 3, social studies 4, and a foreign language 3.

Did you know...

...that, in this major, you often analyze forms of cultural expression, such as songs, novels, magazines, and movies?

Typical courses in this major:

American civilization
Women in American society
American literature
American film
The American wilderness
American art and architecture
American folklore
Ethnicity in America
American regional cultures
Religion in America
American music
American popular culture
American eras
Contemporary America
American political culture
Native American cultures

Concentrations:

In college: ethnic studies (including a focus on specific groups); media studies; popular culture studies; gender and/or gay and lesbian studies.

If you go on to grad school: American literature; American history; cultural theory.

What the study of this major is like:

American studies is an interdisciplinary major that relies on a number of approaches to study the United States. Although history and literature were once the focus of the field, the major now also draws on such disciplines as sociology, anthropology, political science, African-American studies, film studies, women's studies, theater criticism, and music. By analyzing the United States in terms of, for example, region, ethnicity, gender, and class, you learn to understand the world around you from a variety of perspectives, including that of transnationalism, the ways in which people and ideas cross national borders. While programs vary according to faculty strengths and college requirements, all have a common aim: to explore American society and values, past and present.

Among the typical core courses are those focusing on a chronological period (the 1890s; the 1960s), a topic (the West; individualism and community), or a scholarly approach (literary criticism; cultural analysis). In your first and second years, you usually take survey courses that trace American society from colonization to the present. Topics in the first semester may include immigration (history), the rise of American architecture (art), and the evolution of colonial politics (political science), all as part of the study of pre-Revolutionary society. In the next semester, you may focus on family life and urbanization (sociology), the rise of advertising (history), and the origins of American realism in the 1880s and 1890s (art and literature).

During your third and fourth years, you are likely to concentrate on a few subjects. You consult with a faculty adviser and develop an area of interest. In history and literature (a popular concentration), for instance, your course work might include political history, modern literature, and film. To explore American pluralism (the nation's diverse population), you can enroll in courses on ethnic studies, sociology, religion, and history. Majors are usually stimulated by this interdisciplinary approach—you may gain a greater appreciation of literature, art, and film by studying the country's political and economic development.

American studies programs usually include fourth-year seminars (or capstone courses), which build on your previous work. Although these seminars vary from one program to the next, most use in-depth readings to examine the development of American society and culture. In some programs, you can also pursue a special research project.

The interdisciplinary focus of American studies encourages you to spend a good deal of time with other undergrads and with faculty members. Instructors are usually easy to talk to, and classes tend to be relatively small. Thus, the strong bond with other students you are likely to develop should make the program as enjoyable as it is useful.

Other majors you might like:
American literature
Political science
Sociology
Art history
Anthropology
African-American studies
Women's studies
Latin American studies
Geography
Native American studies
Chicano studies

Questions to ask colleges:
What are the core requirements in the program? Most strong programs have core courses that bring together the diverse fields the major draws from. Also, it is good to have some flexibility when choosing your courses.

Are the primary loyalties of the faculty members (as teachers, advisers, and program developers) to American studies rather than to other fields?

How extensive are offerings in American history, American literature, fine arts, film studies, African-American studies, Hispanic-American studies, sociology, women's studies, and American government?

Career options and trends:
High school teacher; writer; journalist; literary or media critic; political consultant.

Many graduates with American studies degrees are employed in helping professions (such as social service), museums, historical societies, and communications. Communications fields such as the media, Internet, advertising, television, and film attract graduates who can interpret American culture from a variety of perspectives. With graduate or professional training, majors can pursue careers in higher education (college teaching), museum administration, law, medicine, public policy, and business.

Insider's viewpoint:
"I don't know how many times I've heard people say, 'Oh, what's American studies? The study of America?' A lot of people think it's a basket-weaving discipline, but I've gotten a lot of calls from potential employers who didn't care what I studied, they just cared that I studied it well."

—Michael, senior, University of Colorado

For more info:
American Studies Association (ASA)
1120 19th St., N.W.
Suite 301
Washington, DC 20036
(202) 467-4783
www.georgetown.edu/crossroads

Asian studies

What it's about:

The major in Asian studies is designed to provide a background in Asian languages and cultures. Programs may concentrate on one area of Asia (Japan, China, Korea, Southeast Asia, or South Asia) or focus on a comparative study of the entire region. Students usually study an Asian language and take a range of social science and humanities courses to gain insight into Asian societies, history, politics, and economics.

Is this for you?

You might like this major if you also like: exploring other cultures and societies; travel; new experiences; learning a foreign language; art; literature; mythology; learning about philosophies and religions.

Consider this major if you are good at: attention to detail; memorizing; research *...or have...* curiosity; verbal skills; writing skills.

Recommended high school prep:

English 4, math 3, lab science 3, social studies 4, and a foreign language 4.

Typical courses in this major:

Asian language (I, II)
Religions of India
Buddhist thought and values
Introduction to Asian art
Classical Asian civilizations: China and Japan
Asian politics and economic development
Masterpieces of Asian literature
Political philosophy in Southeast Asia
Japanese art and culture
Chinese calligraphy
Modern Japan
The Chinese-American experience
Political power in contemporary China
Premodern Japanese literature
Music of Asia
Tibetan civilization

Concentrations:

An Asian language; East Asian literature; South Asian literature; politics and history; anthropology; geography; art history.

What the study of this major is like:

In the major in Asian studies, you study the languages, cultures, religions, societies, politics, and economic characteristics of all of Asia or one of its primary subdivisions: Japan, China, Southeast Asia, or South Asia. The program usually includes interdisciplinary courses that survey a wide range of topics in the social sciences and humanities, providing you with an historical and contemporary overview of the region. With this background, you choose additional courses in fields such as history, anthropology, political science, art history, literature, and religion.

Programs may cover traditional aspects of Asian culture, the impact of the prominent religions (Hinduism, Buddhism, Islam, Taoism, and Shinto), the history of art (architecture, music, literature, and film), the role of women, and interaction with the West.

Central to any program is the study of an Asian language (for example, Chinese, Japanese, Korean, Thai, Hindi). All programs require at least two semesters (most require four) of language study. Learning the language will enrich your appreciation of the cultures of Asia. Intensive summer programs in the United States and Asia, together with one-year programs in Asia, enable you to obtain additional language training and practice. Many Asian studies programs encourage students to spend a summer or a year in Asia. The experience can be very rewarding.

In general, work in Asian studies builds a feeling of solidarity among fellow majors. In addition, faculty members, who share a commitment to increasing your knowledge about and contacts with Asia, tend to be accessible and supportive. With more than half the world's population and the fastest-growing economies, Asia is, and will probably continue to be, a dominant force in the twenty-first century. Asian studies majors are likely to find opportunities to help foster understanding and to enhance communications between Asian and Western societies.

Other majors you might like:
Asian-American studies
Chinese
Linguistics
Anthropology
Archaeology
Geography
Global studies
Religious studies
Islamic studies
International business
International relations
Art history

Career options and trends:
International trade consultant; importer/exporter; journalist; Foreign Service officer; ESL teacher.

Graduates in Asian studies often pursue careers in education, government, journalism, communications, international business, the travel industry, and international law. Teachers with special knowledge of Asia are needed at graduate, undergraduate, and secondary levels. There are positions in government agencies (State Department, development agencies, CIA) and in private foundations and international agencies. Businesses, particularly banks, seek Asia specialists to work overseas; international law firms also provide opportunities for Asia generalists and specialists. As is usually the case, the more language training you have, the more job opportunities will be available to you.

Insider's viewpoint:
"I like interesting stories, so Asian history, culture, and politics really fascinate me. There is so much that has happened in Asia in the past fifty years, not to mention the wealth of history that dates back as far or farther than some of the more widely recognized cultures."

—Min, class of 2000, University of California: Berkeley

For more info:
Association for Asian Studies
1021 East Huron St.
Ann Arbor, MI 48104
(734) 665-2490
www.aasianst.org

Chicano studies

Also known as:
Mexican American studies

What it's about:
This major is an interdisciplinary, comparative exploration of the history, sociology, politics, culture, and economics of Mexican-origin communities in the United States, studied within a regional, national, and global context. The field also examines other Latino and indigenous populations of the Americas, and the ways they influence Chicano communities.

Is this for you?
You might like this major if you also like: community involvement; reading; talking about social justice issues; music, dance, theater, and art; Chicano/Latino culture; languages. Students who see themselves heading for the "helping professions" or wish to give back to their communities are often attracted to this major.

Consider this major if you are good at: attention to detail; creativity; critical reading/thinking; leadership; organizing; research ...*or have...* initiative; patience; verbal skills; writing skills.

Recommended high school prep:
English 4, math 3, lab science 3, social studies 4 (including history and geography), and a foreign language 3–4. If available, economics and sociology are also recommended.

Did you know...
...that Chicano studies is not an "identity, feel-good" major for Chicanos only? While it may be particularly advantageous for Mexican-American and other *raza* students to learn about their history and cultures, non-Latinos can also benefit from exploring one of the fastest-growing populations in the United States.

Typical courses in this major:
History of Chicano Los Angeles
Recent Chicano literature
Farmworker movements, social justice, and AFL-CIO
Chicano folklore and oral tradition
Contemporary Chicano theater
Music of Latin America
Chicana feminism
Barrio popular culture
Immigration and Latino identity
Border consciousness
The Mexican mural
Health in Chicano/Latino populations
Mexican Americans and U.S. education
U.S.–Mexico relations
Bilingual writing workshop
Interracial dynamics in American society

Concentrations:
Generally, none in college; but if you go on to grad school: Barrio, community and urban studies; Chicano languages and literature; political, economic, and social issues; Chicano/Latino history and culture; Chicano/Latino music, art, theater.

What the study of this major is like:
Topics in this major cover a wide range of issues. You'll study both the history of Mexican-origin peoples and the conditions in which they are living today—primarily in the United States but also across North America and around the world.

You'll explore this group from within, by looking at its literature, art, music, theater, oral history, and folklore. And you'll also explore the group from an external focus, by looking at the way the U.S. society and government has treated Chicanos over time. During this exploration you'll compare how the experience of Chicanos is similar to or different from the experiences of other groups in the United States and elsewhere in the world.

In Chicano studies, majors analyze the world with an eye toward social justice, and the scholarship emphasizes social change, social ethics, and equity. The program focuses on the real world; a service learning component, included in many of your courses, involves interaction with the Chicano community. Even as an undergraduate, you'll have an opportunity to engage in research training.

Some students are challenged by the breadth of the field and its interdisciplinary nature—they may have difficulty synthesizing the various perspectives. And this major does not shirk the hard issues—the focus on inequality, stereotypes, and discrimination can be unsettling at first.

Most programs encourage students to be scholar-activists (in the sense of being civically engaged); as a result, extracurricular activities, volunteerism, and commitment to the community are emphasized. Many programs also expect students to participate in academic advising and governance, as part of their responsibility for their own education and development, by taking part in departmental committees and student senates, or by designing student-initiated courses.

Where this major is housed within a college (under social sciences, humanities, or the arts) can affect the content and curriculum of the program. The geographic location of the college itself is also important to consider—having access to large concentrations of Chicanos in Los Angeles, for example, as opposed to smaller communities elsewhere, can make a difference in the service learning and civic engagement aspects of the program. At some colleges, courses might be taught in English, Spanish, or bilingually, and some programs require a Spanish (or Mexican-indigenous) language competency.

Other majors you might like:
Anthropology
Sociology
Urban, community, and regional planning
Intercultural/diversity studies
ESL teacher education
Latino studies
Journalism
Caribbean studies

Latin American studies
Native American studies
Labor studies
Geography

Questions to ask colleges:
How many students take this major?

How often are required courses offered?

Will I meet with a faculty adviser or a counselor? How often is this person available?

Are classes normally large or small?

Career options and trends:
Chicano studies (like most liberal arts majors) is not "vocational" preparation for an occupation. It is as useful in the job market as most other liberal arts majors (history, English, etc.). Since most Chicano studies majors are bilingual and biliterate, however, they are attractive job candidates in many fields, especially business, education, and government. Majors often go on to graduate or professional school to prepare for careers in law, health and medicine, teaching, and social work.

Insider's viewpoint:
"I love this major because for the first time in my life I feel empowered. I love learning about my own history, but at the same time learning about others who have also been marginalized and the struggles they face."

—Robert, senior, University of California: Los Angeles

For more info:
National Association for Chicana and Chicano Studies (NACCS)
P.O. Box 720052
San Jose, CA 95172-0052
www.naccs.org

Mujeres Activas en Letras y Cambio Social
http://malcs.net

European studies

What it's about:

European studies is an interdisciplinary major for students who want to increase their understanding of the languages, cultures, societies, history, and economics of the peoples of Europe and European civilization, from antiquity to the present.

Is this for you?

You might like this major if you also like: learning a foreign language; reading; travel; exploring different cultures; history; politics; current events; art; music; philosophical discussions.

Consider this major if you are good at: critical reading/thinking; languages; research *...or have...* initiative; verbal skills; writing skills.

Recommended high school prep:

English 4, math 3, lab science 3, social studies 4, and a foreign language 4. Courses in music, art, government, and economics are also recommended.

Typical courses in this major:

Greece and Rome
Cities of Europe
Medieval Europe
United States and the European Economic Union
Post-Communist Russia
Baroque art
Indo-European comparative mythology
European cinema
Folk music of Eastern Europe
Irish nationalism
Modern Britain
Women in Italian culture
The Mediterranean world, past and present
Don Quixote
Dante's *Divine Comedy*
The Third Reich and the Holocaust

Concentrations:

Comparative literature; international relations; government and politics; history and culture of a particular country (for instance, Italian studies, Russian studies), region (Mediterranean, Scandinavian), or historical period (the Renaissance, Europe since 1945).

What the study of this major is like:

The study of European civilization—past and present—is a vast interdisciplinary undertaking. It covers several millennia of political, social, and economic history; the development of art, music, religions, philosophy, and literatures in more than a dozen languages; monumental contributions to science, mathematics, and technology; and the study, often comparative, of politics, religion, philosophy, and the arts in present-day Europe. If you find a wide variety of topics and disciplines to choose from liberating rather than overwhelming, then this major might be a good choice.

Usually you are introduced to this wealth of material in one of two ways: in a survey course in European civilization, or in a course that deals with a particular era of European history (the Renaissance, the Age of Reason, the Romantic period) or with the culture of a single country in modern Europe (France, Germany, Spain). Occasionally, both approaches are used. You also begin to fulfill the language requirement—most programs expect you to take a language (other than English) through the intermediate level.

Within a framework that ensures that you acquire both a historical and a contemporary perspective, you are given wide latitude to work out the rest of your studies. In other words, you will mostly design the major yourself, to fit your own interests, talents, and background.

For example, if you have studied Latin and have an interest in the medieval period, you might take further work in Latin and courses in the history, philosophy, theology, and literature of the Middle Ages. Or if you know some German and enjoy reading about Germany today, you can, after basic work in economics and comparative politics, focus on the challenges of reunification. Perhaps you have learned Polish at home; after preparation in history and comparative politics, you might concentrate on Poland's transition from a socialist country under the former Soviet Union to a democracy. As another example, if examining the relationships between music, painting, and literature in early-twentieth-century Europe appeals to you, why not obtain the needed background in music and art history and complete the major with appropriate courses in the humanities?

European studies programs may recommend, or even require, that you spend a semester or a year (usually the third year) in Europe. Living and studying in Europe and using a language other than English (except in the United Kingdom and Ireland) can be an extraordinary experience. Colleges that do not have a study-abroad program usually honor work taken under the auspices of another institution. Or you can enroll at a European university whose credits will transfer to your college at home.

You may be required, in your final year, to complete a capstone project related to your area of concentration. Most likely, you will do a research paper or thesis, based on independent study or on participation in a seminar.

Other majors you might like:

International business

Linguistics

Anthropology

History

Geography

Global studies

Tourism/travel management

Journalism

Architectural history/criticism

Classics

Medieval and Renaissance studies

Art history

Questions to ask colleges:

Does the program include a study-abroad semester or year with an affiliated European university? Are the costs comparable to those for your college at home? Do students remain registered while abroad, and do all credits earned overseas count toward the major and general degree requirements?

Is there an adviser to help students design their areas of concentration?

Can students "test out" of the language requirement? Can the language requirement be fulfilled by study abroad in a university in which the instruction is not in English?

Career options and trends:

The European studies major is not designed to lead to any particular profession, but rather to prepare you for a wide variety of careers. Government service, international business and finance, travel and tourism, journalism, law, management, public relations, teaching—are all possible career paths. Many of these careers require graduate or professional study, for which the major is a strong foundation.

For more info:

Council for European Studies

Columbia University /1203A International Affairs
   Building, MC 3310

420 West 118th St.

New York, NY 10027

(212) 854-4172

www.europanet.org

Latin American studies

What it's about:

Latin American studies is an interdisciplinary major that provides you with comprehensive training in the Spanish and Portuguese languages, as well as Latin American literature, history, politics, geography, anthropology, art and music, and economics.

Is this for you?

You might like this major if you also like: traveling; Hispanic culture; history; learning about international politics and trade; discovering connections across subject areas; languages.

Consider this major if you are good at: attention to detail; creativity; critical reading/thinking; leadership; learning languages; organizing; spatial thinking/analysis; teamwork *...or have...* initiative; verbal skills; writing skills.

Recommended high school prep:

English 4, math 3, lab science 3, social studies 4 (including history and geography), and a foreign language 3–4. If they are available, economics and sociology are also recommended.

Did you know...

...that the most widely spoken indigenous language in the Americas is Kechwa (also spelled Quechua), the language of the Incas? About a quarter of the population of Peru still speaks Kechwa, and for many it is the only language they speak.

Typical courses in this major:

Introduction to Latin American studies
Latin American history
Latin American economics
Latin American geography
Latin American art
Latin American anthropology
Latin American literature
Current Latin American politics
High civilizations of the Americas
Peoples and cultures of modern Latin America
Latin American environmental issues
Colonial rule in Latin America
Revolutionary change in Latin America
The United States and Latin America

Concentrations:

Economics; history; political science; Spanish literature; Portuguese literature; geography; sociology; anthropology; international business; particular geographic areas.

What the study of this major is like:

As a Latin American studies major, you examine the diverse area in the Western Hemisphere that stretches from Mexico to the southern tip of Chile and Argentina. Some programs also include the islands of the Caribbean. You focus on the region's evolution and its relationship to other parts of the world, particularly the United States. Because the major is interdisciplinary, it makes use of courses and faculty members from a number of departments. For example, by taking courses offered by the departments of art history, political science, and ecology, you look at Latin America from artistic, political, and environmental perspectives.

All Latin American studies majors begin with a core of social sciences, natural sciences, and humanities requirements (such as math and English composition), along with courses specific to Latin America. After getting an overview of the region, you choose a concentration—usually from such disciplines as anthropology, political science, sociology, history, geography, business, agriculture, journalism, art history, government, ecology, Portuguese, or Spanish.

Some programs require you to take your concentration in one department (for example, Mexican history within the history department). At other colleges, concentrations may cut across departments (such as a Latin American business and economics concentration that draws from business and economics departments).

Most likely, you will be required to take at least two years of either Spanish or Portuguese—the chief languages of Latin America (Portuguese is the language of the continent's largest nation, Brazil). Languages such as Kechwa, Kaqchikel Maya (still spoken in Guatemala), and Haitian Creole (a mixture of European and Native languages) may also be available. You are encouraged to study for a summer, semester, or year in Latin America, in a program sponsored by your own or another college. Some students double-major—in Latin American studies and, for example, geography, economics, history, or political science.

Your courses vary in size, and language courses are generally small. The major typically attracts U.S. and foreign students, from both Hispanic and Anglo cultures, and you can expect to interact with a diverse group of people. In many programs, Portuguese is not stressed as much as Spanish. Also, some programs have a strong emphasis on literature and culture, while others focus on politics and international economics.

Other majors you might like:

Chicano studies
Spanish
Portuguese
International economics
Women's studies
History
Geography
International business
Anthropology
Caribbean studies
International relations
Sociology

Questions to ask colleges:

Is the program balanced across all subject areas, from the arts to social studies? Is the program geographically balanced, or is more emphasis given to certain countries or regions?

Does the program offer opportunities for students to study in Latin America?

Career options and trends:

International business manager/consultant; export-import manager; translator/interpreter; journalist; Foreign Service officer.

Careers in the Foreign Service are usually open only to U.S. citizens.

Graduates also pursue careers in government (CIA, State Department, or developmental agencies), non-governmental organizations (NGOs), teaching (such as teaching English in Latin America), international business (especially marketing and banking), social work (especially with agencies that work in Latin America), the travel industry, or law. Diplomatic service may require additional specialized training; translators and teachers usually need certification. Some graduates participate in the Peace Corps before beginning a career.

The presence of substantial numbers of recent immigrants from Latin America in many parts of the United States is likely to generate additional jobs—particularly in education, health care, social services, translation, journalism, and government—for those with a Latin American studies background.

Insider's viewpoint:

"I find myself easily bored by routine things. I can't imagine sitting through class after class of one discipline, like you have to do in English or business. In Latin American studies, your classes come from all different majors: language, government, history, economics, anthropology."

—Jennie, senior, University of Texas at Austin

For more info:

Latin American Studies Association (LASA)
University of Pittsburgh
946 William Pitt Union
Pittsburgh, PA 15260
(412) 648-7929
http://lasa.international.pitt.edu

Native American studies

What it's about:

The Native American studies major provides an overview of tribes that are indigenous to the United States (including Alaska) and a history of cross-cultural relations from first contact with Europeans up to the present. You study tribal literatures, art, dance, song, religious traditions, philosophies, educational institutions, political and economic structures, and ecological perspectives.

Is this for you?

You might like this major if you also like: tackling social justice and/or environmental issues; Native American culture; non-traditional religions; mythology; other cultures.

Consider this major if you are good at: creativity; critical reading/thinking; persuading/influencing; research; teamwork *...or have...* initiative; verbal skills; writing skills.

Recommended high school prep:

English 4, math 3, lab science 3, social studies 4, and a foreign language 3–4.

Typical courses in this major:

Cultures of Native North America and Alaska
Tribal governments
Contemporary issues in Native American studies
Oral and written traditions of Native Americans
Native American health and healing
Native American religion and philosophy
Native American arts
Contemporary indigenous issues and literatures
Native American history until 1865
Ecological perspectives of Native Americans
Sociology of Native Americans
Native Americans and film
Research and methods in Native American studies
Gender issues in Native American studies
Indigenous worldview perspectives
Native language study/linguistics

Concentrations:

Concentrations can be based on discipline, e.g., anthropology, political science, sociology, literature, or history; or on a particular region, e.g., North America, Mexico, Central America, or South America.

What the study of this major is like:

As a major in Native American studies, you must first catch up on any significant history you may not have covered in high school—in particular, the treatment of Native American tribal cultures by Europeans settling the Americas. Because your studies will include information not often presented in mainstream education and media, your first courses in the major may leave you feeling both dismayed and inspired. You will learn Native perspectives on a range of subjects, including the treaty-making process through which European Americans obtained access to and/or ownership of land and resources. In upper-level courses, you delve more deeply into art, literature, government, and religion; regions such as Alaska and the Southwest; and historical development, such as U.S.–Native contact before 1865.

Most faculty members who teach Native American studies have degrees in a subject such as history, anthropology, or English, but they draw from a variety of disciplines to develop their courses. For example, a course on present-day issues might incorporate writing by Native Americans (literary studies), as-told-to autobiographies (anthropology or literature), tribal arts and crafts (contemporary or historical art), sociological information (sociology), tribal newspapers (journalism), historical documents (history), court cases (law), or archaeological study (archaeology). Thus, because of the variety of academic approaches and cultural perspectives, the Native American studies classroom experience can be varied and exciting.

You may have a few large historical-overview courses, but most classes will be small groups that foster discussion and encourage you to sharpen your researching and writing abilities. Your two biggest challenges will be to deepen your cross-cultural understanding and to enhance your communication skills. Although much of your course work will consist of research and writing, you might also do projects, field studies, or interviews that take you off campus. And Native American elders, community activists, artists, scholars, and other visiting speakers may give on-campus talks that enrich your studies.

Native American studies programs tend to focus on the regions in which the college resides; for example, colleges in the Southwest are likely to have specialized courses on the Native American cultures and languages of Arizona and New Mexico, and on the connections between these tribal groups and those of Mexico and Latin America. Programs often have a disciplinary emphasis or strong link to another academic department, such as anthropology, social work, or history. These bonds exist because many Native American studies programs have grown out of traditional academic departments. Some programs are known for a particular strength; one college, for example, might support a project on Native voices and the media, while another offers a joint master's degree in Native American studies and law.

Native American studies can offer fresh perspectives that may give you a sense of purpose. Majors often strive to make a difference; they learn all they can about indigenous thought, traditions, values, and contributions to the global community. Their goal is to help Native Americans retain land and resources and revitalize cultural practices and beliefs.

Other majors you might like:
American history (U.S.)
Anthropology
Environmental studies
Linguistics
Latin American studies
Chicano studies
Musicology/ethnomusicology
Archaeology
Historic preservation
Sociology

Social work
Community health services

Questions to ask colleges:
Does the program cover Latin America, Alaska, or Canada, or does it focus on the United States, particularly on the lower 48 states? Although each type of program has merits, you should consider whether your interests fit a program's emphases.

Career options and trends:
Teacher*; park ranger; government officer (e.g., Indian Health Service, Bureau of Indian Affairs)*; lawyer (American Indian law); social worker*.

A state certificate or license is required for teaching in public schools. A law degree and license are required for practicing American Indian law off-reservation. Civil service exams are needed for most government employment.

Native American studies majors also pursue careers in environmental monitoring, business, Native American cultural preservation, tourism, tribal and nontribal criminal justice, health professions, and Native language preservation.

States are increasing their requirements for certification in Native American studies. Businesses are demanding an understanding of cultural diversity from employees, and social service and law enforcement agencies are looking for culturally appropriate ways to approach the populations they serve. These developments should increase employment opportunities for graduates with in-depth knowledge of Native American issues and traditions.

For more info:
American Indian Higher Education Consortium
121 Oronoco St.
Alexandria, VA 22314
(703) 838-0400
www.aihec.org

Near and Middle Eastern studies

What it's about:

Near and Middle Eastern studies focuses on a vast, culturally diverse geographic area that extends from North Africa to Central Asia. Using interdisciplinary and comparative approaches, you study the cultures and languages of the region. In addition, you examine the area's history, from antiquity to the present day, with particular focus on the period after the emergence of Islam.

Is this for you?

You might like this major if you also like: the History Channel; travel; adventure; languages; politics; reading about international events and military affairs; learning about other religions and cultures; languages written in unfamiliar alphabets.

Consider this major if you are good at: attention to detail; critical reading/thinking; memorizing; research ...*or have...* curiosity; patience; verbal skills; writing skills.

Recommended high school prep:

English 4, math 3, lab science 3, social studies 3, and a foreign language 2–3. You are not expected to have studied the region in high school, but it is helpful if you can study a Near and Middle Eastern language. Other useful languages (especially if you intend to go to grad school in the field) are German and French.

Did you know...

...that some of the languages of the Middle East—Persian for instance—are among the easiest to learn? Arabic, on the other hand, is among the more difficult.

Typical courses in this major:

Arabic
Arabic literature in translation
Modern Near and Middle Eastern history
Near and Middle Eastern politics
Turkish
Islamic history and civilization
Islamic religion
People of the Near and Middle East
Hebrew
Persian
Islam and politics
Christianity, Judaism, and Islam
The United States and the Near and Middle East
Colonialism, imperialism, and nationalism
Palestine, Zionism, and Israel
Art in the Islamic world

Concentrations:

Geographic areas; area languages (Arabic, Turkish, Persian, Hebrew, etc.); area literature; disciplines with Near and Middle Eastern focus (such as Turkish history).

What the study of this major is like:

In a typical program, you take an introductory survey course covering the geography, history, and religious traditions of Asia Minor, Southwestern Asia, the Arabian Peninsula, and North Africa. In your second year, you take one or two specialized courses in history, political science, anthropology, religion, or literature translation. You should begin language study early enough to complete at least three years of Arabic and two years of Turkish, Persian (also known as Farsi, the language of Iran), or Hebrew. (At some colleges, you can take other languages, such as Armenian, Kurdish, or Berber.) If Middle Eastern language courses are not offered, try to take them at a neighboring college or as independent study, particularly if you plan to apply to grad school in the field.

You'll study languages in small classes, with professors who are generally native speakers. Learning a language will probably take at least four semesters of intensive daily study. Once you learn to decipher an unfamiliar alphabet and master the grammar, you may feel exhilarated to be able to read the works of contemporary as well as medieval authors from the Near and Middle East.

While studying a language, you attend lecture courses and seminars (in English) that address history, literature, politics, and other aspects of the region. Seminars usually have only about 10 to 20 students, and all of them are expected to take part in class discussion. In general, majors passionately debate current events; they readily observe links between the past and the present. Many majors spend a semester or a year abroad at a university (for example, the American University of Beirut, American University of Cairo, and Hebrew University of Jerusalem).

Near and Middle Eastern studies programs are differentiated mainly in two ways. First, programs concentrate either on the classical and medieval periods or on the modern period. Second, programs have either a language-and-literature approach or a discipline-based approach (historical, anthropological, political, philosophical, for example). Programs that stress the classical and medieval tend also to emphasize languages and literatures; the modern-oriented programs tend to take the discipline-based (or even multidisciplinary) approach. Some programs have a good mix of the medieval and the modern, and they include, as well, languages, literature and discipline-based studies.

Other majors you might like:
Arabic
History
Journalism
Linguistics
Archaeology
Art history
Islamic studies
Peace and conflict studies
Religious studies
Judaic studies
Ancient Near Eastern/Biblical languages
International relations

Questions to ask colleges:
What is the program's definition of Near and Middle Eastern studies? For example, a major may not fit the needs of students interested in contemporary issues and politics. Such students may be better served by majoring in history or political science and taking a Near and Middle Eastern language on the side.

Career options and trends:
Foreign Service Officer; international business or trade consultant; teacher; college professor; translator/interpreter; intelligence analyst; journalist; social worker.

Careers in the Foreign Service are usually open only to U.S. citizens.

Because of the political and economic turbulence in the Near and Middle East, the United States (including both the public and the private sector) will be intensely engaged in the region for years to come. People with language and other skills pertaining to the region should have a relatively easy time finding rewarding jobs.

Insider's viewpoint:
"Not only are there many areas of Middle Eastern history yet to be discovered (e.g., unknown and unedited medieval manuscripts), but what I teach and write about the Middle East has real contemporary relevance."

—Professor Bernard Haykel, New York University

For more info:
Middle East Studies Association (MESA)
University of Arizona
1219 North Santa Rita Ave.
Tucson, AZ 85721
(520) 621-5850
http://fp.arizona.edu/mesassoc

Women's studies

Also known as:
Feminist, gender, and sexuality studies

What it's about:
Women's studies is an interdisciplinary major that examines the connections between gender, sexuality, power, and inequality. You study such issues as oppression of women and sexual minorities; class exploitation; racism; and women's cultural and historical roles, both in the U.S. and around the world.

Is this for you?
You might like this major if you also like: thinking about the differences between men and women; seeing connections between ideas, people, and systems; thinking about issues in a comprehensive way.

Consider this major if you are good at: critical reading/thinking; organizing; persuading/influencing; research; teamwork ...*or have...* tolerance for ambiguity; writing skills.

Recommended high school prep:
English 4, math 4, lab science 3, social studies 4, and a foreign language 3. If it is available, take statistics.

Typical courses in this major:
Women's history
Women in the economy
Women and literature
Gender, race, and class
Biological basis of sex differences
Feminism, state, and public policy
Feminist theories
Gender and colonization
Gender and language
Gender and sexuality in cross-cultural perspective
Gender inequality
Global perspectives on gender
Gender, sexuality, and law
History of sexuality
Women in cinema
Sociology of marriage

Concentrations:
Race, class, and ethnicity in the United States; lesbian, bisexual, gay, and transgender studies; global perspectives; feminist theory; women's history; movements, institutions, and social policy; gender, science, and health; women's art and literature.

What the study of this major is like:
If you are curious about gender and sexuality issues, women's studies is a good major to choose. It seeks to understand what it means now, and has meant in the past, to be a woman. You examine differences among women themselves, as well as the concept and uses of gender—that is, the changing definitions that societies attach to being women and men. Because gender can reflect and determine differences in power and opportunity, majors learn to analyze economic and social systems, ask searching questions about equality, and discuss ways in which society can be transformed. In addition, you explore the political and cultural effects of race, class, age, nationality, sexual identity, and ethnicity.

Women's studies began in the late 1960s as an attempt to make up for the lack of information, in most college courses, about women. What started as an effort to fill in the gaps has become a comprehensive analysis of the role of women in all areas of life. Besides supplying research about women, the major questions accepted beliefs and unexamined norms. Almost every discipline in the arts, humanities, and social sciences contributes to women's studies. For many majors in the field, women's studies becomes a window on the rest of the world.

A typical program includes courses offered within women's studies as well as courses offered by other departments. You will probably take an introductory women's studies course; a series of electives in the humanities, social sciences, and, where possible, natural sciences. A capstone experience is usually required in the form of a fourth-year seminar, fieldwork or internship project, or independent study. Many programs also require courses in feminist theory as well as in race, ethnicity, or non-Western culture.

Over the years, the major has concerned itself not only with *what* is taught but also *how* the material is taught. Classes seek to foster dialogue and to create a safe arena in which to debate. Course work often includes various methods of presentation, group activities, self-defined papers and projects, and invitations to tie theory to your own experience. Most programs offer the flexibility to tailor your program to meet your needs and interests. Many students double-major in a traditional liberal arts discipline and in women's studies.

Colleges may vary in their name for the major—the most common are gender and sexuality studies, feminist studies, and women's studies—and the differences in the name may signal variations in emphases. Because the field is wide-ranging, most programs cannot cover everything. Therefore, you should read course catalogs to find out which aspects individual programs emphasize.

Other majors you might like:
African-American studies
European studies
Native American studies
Latin American studies
American literature
Anthropology
Comparative literature
Psychology
Sociology
Human development and family studies
History
Gay/lesbian studies

Questions to ask colleges:
Are the faculty members permanent, full-time professors? What are some faculty research projects? Do the courses build on and connect to one another? Are they offered regularly?

What research opportunities are available to undergraduates?

You should make sure that the college supports women's studies as a serious field of inquiry.

Career options and trends:
Some women's studies graduates go on to activist careers in social and political issues or social services. Others find jobs in education (all levels), business, public policy and administration, health services, communications, and film, and (with appropriate graduate degrees) in college teaching, research, law, and medicine.

Insider's viewpoint:
"The way I understand women's studies, it's a critique of traditional disciplines and so it was a way of looking at things I'd seen my entire life from a different viewpoint."

—Paulette, senior, Oberlin College

For more info:
National Women's Studies Association (NWSA)
University of Maryland
7100 Baltimore Blvd., Suite 502
College Park, MD 20740
(301) 403-0524
www.nwsa.org

Biological sciences

The biological sciences are no less than the study of life itself. Biologists often see the big picture by looking through a microscope.

Studies focus on animals, plants, and microbes, all on the levels of molecules and cells; organs, such as the heart; organisms (individuals of a species); populations (such as migrating birds); and environments, such as rain forests. Some biologists research particular life forms. Botanists study plants, marine biologists investigate sea life, and entomologists look into the world of insects.

Professors talk about the many fields of biology as explorations into the frontiers of biochemistry, biotechnology, and the rapidly growing areas of genetics and molecular and cellular biology.

"The complexity of living organisms represents an ideal outlet for satisfying the need to discover," says biochemist Gregory M. Raner of the University of North Carolina at Greensboro.

"Molecular biology is for people who are constantly asking why," notes Eileen Gregory of Rollins College. And according to the botanist C. O. Patterson of Texas A&M University, "New discoveries and invention of new techniques have generated an explosion of understanding and interest in this field."

Many scientific journeys in biological and medical research are aimed at improving health through vaccines, medicines, and cures for cancer, heart disease, AIDS, Alzheimer's, and other diseases. Some researchers venture into realms of genetic engineering, immune system therapies, and stem cell research. These emerging fields are reflected in new majors, which include bioengineering, genomics, biostatistics, and molecular modeling.

The life sciences prepare you to work in any number of professions—as a clinician, research assistant or technician, or scientist. Biotech labs, pharmaceutical companies, hospitals, and medical testing firms all hire biologists, as does the government, which has increased funding for research.

Employment growth in the biological sciences is slowing somewhat. However, scientists are needed to put new discoveries to use, such as fighting disease with gene therapies. Naturally, the more education, training, and experience you have, the better the job you're likely to get. For instance, a four-year Bachelor of Science degree is a must for most nonresearch jobs in the life sciences. Researchers usually need even more education. A master's degree is okay for some researchers but a doctorate (Ph.D.) is required in the competition for other research jobs. No matter what level you study, professors say, you'll need to know chemistry as well as biology from the get-go.

Colleges great and small

When you compare biology programs, keep in mind the size of the colleges. While smaller colleges provide a solid foundation in the biological sciences, many of the newer majors are offered only at large universities. Also, larger universities have more funding for research. On the other hand, small colleges often pride themselves on the quality of their teaching. Find out if the college's faculty members are active in research and have published their work. Ask, too, whether undergrads can do research, in the college or on an internship. It's valuable experience, especially if you plan to go for a graduate degree and need an edge by getting hands-on experience.

"One of the most important things a graduate admission committee looks for is a good letter of recommendation from a respected researcher in whose laboratory you have participated," suggests Carter Denniston, professor of genetics at the University of Wisconsin, Madison.

You can study practically any area in biology in graduate school, including hot topics like microbial, plant, and animal genetics. Genetics is now central to biology, providing "general concepts and techniques for the study of inheritance, development, disease, and evolution in all living organisms and viruses," Denniston says.

You may find that molecular biology, virology, or another course you want is offered only at the graduate level—it all depends on the college. Some examples of graduate programs are bacterial physiology, pharmacogenetics, community and evolutionary ecology, environmental or conservation biology, toxicology, immunology, and neurobiology.

When you study biology, expect to do class work, fieldwork, and especially laboratory work. You'll spend a lot of quality time in the lab. So, if possible, compare the labs and equipment, as well as courses and faculty members, in the colleges you may apply to. Find out if your studies will cover a range of biology topics or zero in on one aspect of the life sciences, such as molecular or cellular biology or biochemistry. The course list will give you an idea of what the college stresses. And remember, some colleges are geared for premed students—those who plan to become doctors.

When searching for colleges with bio programs, look for colleges or divisions of arts and sciences, biological sciences, colleges of medicine, natural science and mathematics, health sciences, or applied science and technology.

Your career as a researcher begins now. Start your college search by reading about the majors in this section and visiting the American Instititute of Biological Sciences's Web site (www.aibs.org). For information about other majors related to the life sciences, go to the sections on Agriculture, Health, and Natural resources and conservation.

Biochemistry

What it's about:

Biochemistry majors study the principles that enable living things to function as they do. Combining knowledge of chemical structure and of the behavior of molecules with a "big picture" view of biological processes helps you understand how "life" occurs at its most basic level.

Is this for you?

You might like this major if you also like: all areas of science; all varieties of living things; new technologies; mysteries (novels, movies, computer games) and puzzles; finding out how things work; seeking answers to fundamental questions about nature and living things.

Consider this major if you are good at: attention to detail; creativity; critical reading/thinking; math; memorizing; quantitative analysis; research; spatial thinking/analysis; teamwork *...or have...* initiative; manual dexterity.

Recommended high school prep:

English 4, math 4 (including precalculus or trigonometry), lab science 4 (biology, chemistry, physics, earth science), social studies 3, and a foreign language 2–3. Take as many advanced or honors-level science courses as you can. Any computer courses would also be useful.

Did you know...

...that many students in this major find biochemistry easier to learn than the more traditional branches of science? This is because you study the basic principles in a familiar context: the world of living organisms. In fact, many students do better with chemistry and physics when the material is linked to principles of biology.

Typical courses in this major:

Analytic chemistry
Organic chemistry
Calculus
Physics
Microbiology
Physical chemistry
Biochemistry
Quantitative analysis
Cell biology
Genetics
Inorganic chemistry
Physiology
Immunology
Physical biochemistry

Concentrations:

Biotechnology; toxicology; pharmacology; cell biology; immunology; neurochemistry; genetics; hematology; bacteriology.

What the study of this major is like:

Biochemists, who study the chemistry of organisms, relate the principles of chemistry to the functions of living systems. Biochemistry majors learn how to recognize the chemical nature of biological molecules by taking many of the core courses needed for a chemistry degree. You will also take courses that introduce you to human metabolism; DNA replication (how cells reproduce themselves) and the conversion of genetic information into functional cell components; human and mammalian physiology; and real-world applications of biotechnology.

Many people define biochemistry too narrowly; they think that it is simply a fifth division of chemistry, along with physical, inorganic, organic, and analytical. In reality, biochemistry includes all of the traditional divisions of chemistry and extends beyond the physical sciences into the life sciences and medicine as well.

Most courses in biochemistry are in lecture format and may include laboratory work. In many courses, you'll have plenty of homework, especially problem sets to complete and daily reading assignments. Most programs strongly encourage you to do some type of research. You may also be required to give oral presentations. Usually the biggest challenges students face is scheduling their courses and managing their time. Students sometimes take light course loads early on, not realizing that they are simply shifting the weight of their work to their third or fourth year, when courses become more challenging and time-consuming. You can help balance your workload by developing and sticking to a study plan.

There are many different approaches to the study of biochemistry. At some colleges the program emphasizes the chemical nature of biological systems. These programs are usually in departments of chemistry or physical science. Biochemistry programs in life science or medical departments may focus on physiology or molecular and cellular biology. Probably the best way to determine the emphasis of a program is to examine the required courses for the major. A program that does not require physical or inorganic chemistry would be likely to emphasize the biological aspects of biochemistry, with less attention to the chemistry of biomolecules. In contrast, a stress on chemistry might indicate a commitment to the fundamental aspects of biological interactions.

Other majors you might like:
Cell biology and histology
Microbiology
Molecular biology
Clinical nutrition
Neuroscience
Pharmacy
Chemistry
Biotechnology
Clinical/medical laboratory technology
Biomedical engineering
Chemical engineering
Forensic science

Career options and trends:
College professor*; physician*; research technician; research scientist*; science teacher.

Graduate or professional school after college is required for careers in medicine and scientific research. To teach in college you will need at least a master's degree and preferably a Ph.D. Additional credits in education and certification are usually needed for teaching in high school as well.

A major in biochemistry is a logical choice to prepare for medical, dental, or veterinary school, or for health and agricultural careers in such areas as toxicology, biomedical engineering, clinical chemistry, plant pathology, and animal sciences. Industries that may employ biochemistry majors include biotechnology, pharmaceutical, and medical testing and diagnostic firms. Biochemistry majors who also obtain a certificate in specialized lab training (DNA sequencing, in vitro cell biology, genetic engineering, for example) will improve their prospects.

For more info:
American Society of Biochemistry and Molecular Biology
9650 Rockville Pike
Bethesda, MD 20814
(301) 634-7145
www.asbmb.org

Biology

Also known as:

Life science

What it's about:

Biology is the study of the structure, function, heredity, and evolution of all living things—microorganisms, fungi, plants, and animals. These life forms are studied at the levels of molecule, cell, organism, and population. Through lab work and fieldwork, you acquire a basic understanding of organisms, their habitats, and the processes that govern their life activities.

Is this for you?

You might like this major if you also like: pets; wildlife; gardening; wellness/fitness activities; environmental issues; outdoor activities (hiking, canoeing, rock climbing, etc.); zoos; insects.

Consider this major if you are good at: attention to detail; creativity; critical reading/thinking; memorizing; organizing; quantitative analysis; research; teamwork ...*or have...* critical observation; manual dexterity; patience.

Recommended high school prep:

English 4; math 4 (including trigonometry and precalculus); lab science 4 (including earth science, biology, chemistry, and physics); social studies 2; a foreign language 2–3; and a computer applications course. Because biology is increasingly quantitative, a strong foundation in the physical sciences and math is essential.

Did you know...

...that mathematics is becoming increasingly important in biological research and innovation? If you are strong in both areas you will be in a good position for 21st century jobs.

Typical courses in this major:

Genetics
Cell biology
Microbiology
Molecular biology
Developmental biology
Immunology
Animal or plant physiology
Comparative anatomy and embryology
Animal behavior
Plant biology
Invertebrate biology
Parasitology
Aquatic biology
Environmental biology
Ecology
Evolution

Concentrations:

In college: biochemistry; botany; environmental science; microbiology; molecular biology; neuroscience; zoology.

If you go on to grad school: anatomy; behavioral biology; bioinformatics, cell biology; developmental biology; evolutionary biology; genetics; immunology; limnology; mycology; ornithology; paleontology; parasitology; pharmacology; physiology (animal and plant); systematics (animal and plant).

What the study of this major is like:

As a biology major, you'll focus on the way organisms solve the problems they face in their environments. In addition, you'll seek answers to the question most biology programs ask: How have ecological and hereditary factors contributed to the evolution of plants, animals, and microbes?

Generally, biology courses are taught through a combination of lectures and coordinated labs. Some professors provide opportunities for collaborative activities and online assignments as well. In the lab, hands-on experiences include observational exercises and open-ended experiments; for both types of work, you analyze data and then write reports.

After the intro courses, which stress the primary concepts, processes, and vocabulary of biology, you'll examine many of the subjects in greater depth. In cell biology and physiology, for instance, you analyze the link between the structure and function of cells—how they divide and then differentiate (take on new forms and new tasks). You'll observe cells through the microscope and do data-gathering experiments on different kinds of cells.

In genetics, you identify the molecular and cellular aspects of heredity in animals and in plants. You may also cover topics such as human hereditary disorders and DNA technology. Labs usually require you to work independently on fruit flies, molds, bacteria, and viruses. In ecology, you study the relation of plants and animals to their environment. Most likely, you'll follow up fieldwork with data analysis based on varied computational and statistical methods.

Courses beyond the intro level may include botany and more-specialized courses in seed plants, algae, fungi; invertebrate zoology and more-specialized classes in entomology (insects), protozoology (amoebas and other one-celled forms); and vertebrate zoology and more-specialized courses in ornithology (birds), ichthyology (fish), and so on.

Again, as you observe the relationship between function and structure, you'll consider how evolution has led to the diversity of the animal and plant kingdoms. In labs, you dissect fresh and preserved material, and sometimes apply culture techniques. Microbiology concentrates on the structure, function, genetics, and ecology of bacteria and viruses. Molecular biology and biochemistry are concerned with the substances that help regulate living systems. In these and other advanced courses, you read, analyze, and discuss current biology literature and often conduct independent research. Some advanced courses offer extended fieldwork.

The greatest challenge for biology majors is to deal with the large amount of information you must learn. Also, in most semesters you have to take two or even three lab courses. The most successful majors keep up-to-date with their assignments and learn to manage their time effectively. An upside of the workload, though, is that you often do lab projects with a partner or a small team of students, so you have the benefit of a support group and a chance to develop friendships with other majors.

Although most biology programs cover all aspects of the field, programs may emphasize different areas of biology. For example, one department might focus on cellular and molecular biology, while another emphasizes the organism or environmental studies. Some programs feature extended field trips to unique habitats, such as rain forests, mountains, or deserts. Another difference among programs is the amount of emphasis placed on undergrad research. Requirements for the major may also vary from college to college, particularly in the number of chemistry, physics, and math courses you must complete before you graduate.

Other majors you might like:
Agronomy and crop science
Environmental science
Wildlife and wilderness management
Forestry
Horticulture
Veterinary technology
Marine biology
Anthropology
Biomedical engineering
Entomology
Zoology
Biotechnology

Questions to ask colleges:
Are there opportunities for independent study and research?

Are the lab facilities up-to-date and sufficient for the number of students in the program?

Is this primarily a premed program, or do many of the graduates go on to pursue the science of biology in grad school and industry?

Career options and trends:
Teacher*; naturalist; industrial or university researcher*; lab technician; state or federal government biologist; health care professional (physician, dentist, vet, nurse)*; health care administrator; sales/marketing representative (pharmaceutical/biotech).

You will need to go on to graduate or professional school for a career in research or medicine, or to teach at the college level. Additional education credits and certification is usually needed to teach in high school as well.

According to the Bureau of Labor Statistics, slightly more than half of all biologists work for federal, state, and local government agencies (environmental, agricultural, health), and most of the others work in the pharmaceutical and biotech industries. Job growth in the biotech field continues to be strong—even after a fast-paced start—but that may slow down as the industry matures. Biologists with diverse knowledge and training, particularly in math and computer science, will enjoy the best prospects and demand.

Insider's viewpoint:

"I'm not premed, but a lot of people in my classes are. They're really, really competitive. For me, I'm taking the class because it's interesting to me, but for them, they have to get 100 percent on everything, so the curve is really high."

—Romi, sophomore, University of California: Los Angeles

For more info:

American Institute of Biological Sciences (AIBS)
1444 I St., N.W.
Suite 200
Washington, DC 20005
(202) 628-1500
www.aibs.org

Biotechnology

What it's about:

The biotechnology major combines the molecular life sciences and engineering. You learn how to use living cells, cellular and molecular processes, and genetic information to solve problems and to create new products.

Is this for you?

You might like this major if you also like: science and technology (a lot); science fairs; putting theory to practical use; building things; running your own business; working with people.

Consider this major if you are good at: attention to detail; creativity; critical reading/thinking; organizing; quantitative analysis; research; teamwork *...or have...* initiative; patience; verbal skills.

Recommended high school prep:

English 4, math 4 (including precalculus), lab science 4, social studies 3, and a foreign language 2–3. Take computer science if offered. If possible, participate in a summer research program for high school students, available at many research institutes (such as Roswell Park Cancer Institute Summer High School Research Program).

Did you know...

...that biotechnology involves nanotechnology—working with materials (genes and DNA) that are invisible without powerful microscopes?

...that biotechnology is one of the oldest technologies? Humankind has been using the biological processes of microorganisms—such as yeast—for over 6,000 years. On the other hand, 70 percent of all biotechnologically produced medicines now on the market were approved since the early 1990s.

Typical courses in this major:

General biology I & II
Cell biology
Cell physiology
Microbiology
Developmental biology
Organic chemistry
Biochemistry
Immunology
Virology
Tissue culture methods
Bioanalytical techniques
Plant biotechnology
Genetic engineering
Genomics (gene function)
Bioinformatics
Proteinomics

Concentrations:

Bioinformatics; genomics; protenomics; toxicogenomics; pharmacogenomics; bioprocess; molecular modeling; computational chemistry.

What the study of this major is like:

In biotechnology, which combines molecular life sciences and engineering, you use living matter to develop products and services in agriculture (plant growth hormones, food additives), health care (vaccines, improved medicines and vitamins), the environment (detoxification of chemicals), and other areas. The study of biotechnology has greatly expanded with the sequencing of the human genome, as well as many other genomes. In fact, all of life's processes are now open to study—from the human to the bacterial.

As a biotechnology major, you learn to use several technologies to explore organisms: genetic engineering (changing gene characteristics for a specific purpose); bioprocessing (using separating and purifying techniques); immunobiochemistry; protein engineering; and biocatalysis (using enzymes to produce a biochemical reaction). In fact, biotechnologists need all the tools of the biochemist, the molecular biologist, the immunologist, and even the engineer, to prepare a product or an application on a large scale for the marketplace.

Because biotechnology course work covers all the life sciences (including areas such as exobiology and nuclear transfer cell therapy), you are likely to find subjects that interest you. The major is taught in both lecture and lecture/lab formats. In some classes, you may work on research projects with faculty members—an experience worth seeking out. You might also be required to complete independent research. An individual research project in biotechnology at the undergraduate level is a big undertaking. But producing an original contribution will give you a taste of what science has to offer—a chance to do something unique.

You can find biotechnology offered at the four-year bachelor's degree level, the two-year associate degree level, and even as a ten-week certificate program. Community colleges across the country have been increasing their offerings in this field in order to match growth in the industry, particularly in the areas of medical, pharmaceutical, and agricultural manufacturing.

Differences among biotechnology programs occur because of differences in the size of the institutions and the funding available for the undergraduate program. At well-funded institutions, the program may be good, but teaching may be less valued than research. At small institutions, teaching is often the primary concern, but funding may be nonexistent. If there's a balance between size and funding, faculty members can be active in research but still have the time and interest to help undergraduates.

Other majors you might like:
Agricultural and biological engineering
Microbiology
Biochemistry
Molecular biology
Biological/physical sciences
Forest technology
Chemical engineering
Biomedical technology
Biomedical engineering
Clinical/medical laboratory technology
Environmental engineering
Bioinformatics

Career options and trends:
Biomedical researcher*; biochemical development engineer; environmental health and safety specialist; pharmaceutical product development researcher or engineer*; forensic scientist; medical diagnostician; biotechnology industry researcher, engineer or manager*; quality control analyst or engineer; regulatory affairs specialist.

The biotechnology field is large and growing, so job opportunities will be strong in the foreseeable future. The fastest employment growth is projected to occur in the pharmaceutical and medical manufacturing industry and in firms providing research and testing services.

Insider's viewpoint:
"I'm doing independent research with a professor in the med school, and I'm working directly under the president of a biotech company, helping him with scientific literature research. These experiences help me tremendously; I learned how to network and overcame the fear of talking to professors. In addition, there's the research experience itself. It's very hard-core and takes a lot of endurance, patience, and stamina. Being single-minded is key."

—Clare, senior, University of California: Davis

For more info:
Biotechnology Industry Organization (BIO)
1225 Eye Street, N.W.
Suite 400
Washington, DC 20005
(202) 962-9200
www.bio.org

National Center for Biotechnology Information
National Library of Medicine
Building 38A
Bethesda, MD 20894
(301) 496-2475
www.ncbi.nlm.nih.gov

Botany

Also known as:

Plant biology

What it's about:

Majors in botany study all aspects of plant life, which ranges from the smallest to the largest organisms on earth. Courses teach both microscopic and field investigation techniques.

Is this for you?

You might like this major if you also like: discovering new things, observing nature, gardening, hiking, working and playing outdoors, natural history.

Consider this major if you are good at: attention to detail; creativity; logical reasoning; quantitative analysis; research; teamwork *...or have...* manual dexterity; observation skills; patience.

Recommended high school prep:

English 4, math 4 (including precalculus and statistics), lab science 4 (including biology, chemistry and physics), social studies 3, and a foreign language 2–3.

Typical courses in this major:

General biology
Biochemistry
Microbiology
Genetics
Plant anatomy and physiology
Field ecology
Plant evolution
Photosynthesis
Plant taxonomy and systematics
Mycology (fungi)
Pteridophytes (ferns)
Phycology (algae)
Lichens and bryophytes
Vascular plant morphology
Paleobotony

Concentrations:

In college: plant physiology; plant ecology; plant genetics.

If you go on to grad school: paleobotany; plant genomics; plant development and hormonal regulation; plant cell biology; plant systematics; community and evolutionary ecology.

What the study of this major is like:

Although people have been studying plants for thousands of years, discoveries made and techniques developed in the last few decades have generated an explosion of interest in botany. This is indeed an exciting time in the plant sciences.

Introductory courses in botany (first- and second-year courses) usually have both lecture and lab components. In courses that include fieldwork, you study organisms in their natural habitats, where you may observe interesting examples of anatomical and physiological adaptations to features of the environment. While even a handheld lens can provide vital information about many species, most botanical studies rely on sophisticated tools. That's why it's useful to take as many courses as possible that offer hands-on experience with a range of equipment and techniques.

In cell biology courses, you will study the biochemical pathways that maintain and promote life through each of the cell's parts. In plant anatomy and plant physiology, you will explore the unique nature of plants: how cells are organized; how organs are formed and function; and how growth, development, and reproduction processes are coordinated. Plant ecology focuses on the way individual plants integrate into communities of organisms and the way plants respond to their environment—for example, how plants coexist with animals that eat them or how plants use animals to help them pollinate and reproduce.

The diversity of plants is so great that you may, at first, feel overwhelmed by the amount of information available. But as you examine plants more closely, you will see that most of the basic features of plants are the same for nearly all species. Rather than try to learn every detail about every kind of plant, you can begin to focus on one plant group.

Some colleges stress ecology and the evolution of plants, while others emphasize molecular and ultra-structural studies. At many colleges, you must complete a set of core courses in biology before beginning specialized botany courses; on other campuses, you may take botany courses in your first year.

Because botanists spend a lot of time in the lab or in the field, they tend to dress comfortably and informally. Likewise, they often have laid-back attitudes. Nevertheless, they work hard, both physically and intellectually. Some botanists visit unexplored regions looking for new species, even putting themselves in danger in the search. Others rarely stray outside their lab, although they may put in 16-hour days carrying out complex experiments. Because plants function on their own schedules, without regard for human convenience, botanists usually plan their days (and nights) to meet the needs of their research organisms. So a botanist may be in the lab at 3:00 a.m. to observe the unfurling of a flower bud, the division of a growing cell, the opening and closing of stomata—but the thrill of discovery makes any loss of sleep worth while.

Other majors you might like:
Horticulture
Genetics
Ecology
Plant pathology
Agricultural and biological engineering
Wood science/paper/pulp technology
Agronomy and crop science
Range science
Landscape architecture
Herbalism
Floriculture
Forestry

Questions to ask colleges:
Is there access to a nearby nature reserve or other protected, undisturbed area? For plant ecology studies, this would be very valuable.

Is there a well-equipped herbarium on campus? It would be useful for taxonomic and systematics work. For most areas of research in botany, modern, fully equipped labs are essential.

Career options and trends:
Laboratory technician; manager of a nature conservancy or environmentally protected area; technical artist, illustrator, or photographer; curator of a museum, herbarium, or arboretum; pharmaceutical researcher or investigator; plant breeder.

Employment opportunities are generally good, with higher salaries closely linked to advanced education and training and/or experience. The two areas showing most rapid expansion are the molecular biology of plants, and field studies of protected or endangered plant species.

Insider's viewpoint:
"Think about botany in relation to horticulture and decide if the science of plants sounds interesting or if the growing of plants is more interesting to you. I, myself, love both but I really wanted to learn the science."

—Deborah, senior, University of Wisconsin

For more info:
American Society of Plant Biologists (ASPB)
15501 Monona Drive
Rockville, MD 20855-2768
(301) 251-0560
www.aspb.org

Botanical Society of America (BSA)
P.O. Box 299
St. Louis, MO 63166-0299
(314) 577-9566
www.botany.org

Cell biology and histology

What it's about:

Cell biology emphasizes the cell as the basic unit for examining characteristics common to all living organisms. Histology is the study of how cells are organized into functional units called tissues, and how tissues are organized into organs.

Is this for you?

You might like this major if you also like: microscopes and lab work; math and science, especially biology and chemistry.

Consider this major if you are good at: attention to detail; creativity; critical reading/thinking; math; organizing; quantitative analysis; research *...or have...* initiative; manual dexterity; patience.

Recommended high school prep:

English 4, math 3, lab science 4 (including biology, chemistry and physics), social studies 3, and a foreign language 2–3. Take as many advanced or honors science courses as possible.

Typical courses in this major:

Physics
Calculus
Organic chemistry
Cell biology
Molecular biology
Genetics
Biochemistry
Cell physiology
Immunology
Developmental biology
Neurobiology
Structural biology
Virology
Histology/microanatomy
Microscopy/microtechnique
Electron microscopy

Concentrations:

Generally, none available.

What the study of this major is like:

Cell biology is often offered as a concentration within the broad-based major in biology; in some cases it is offered as a major in cellular and molecular biology. Histology, also called microscopic anatomy, may be included under histotechnology, cytotechnology, microtechnique, or even microscopy. Histology is usually taught as a course within a major or as a separate associate's degree or certification program.

In cell biology, the focus is on the cell as the basic unit of life. You will explore the fundamental processes that are common to all living cells, and investigate the unique characteristics and processes of more specialized cell types such as lymphocytes and neurons. Additionally, you should acquire a broad, general foundation in biology, chemistry, and physics.

Most of your classes will involve lectures. However, as is usual for science classes, most of your learning will take place in the lab. In cell biology laboratory sections, you will take part in various aspects of research. You may also have the opportunity to participate in research on your own, either on an independent-study project mentored by faculty members or on an internship.

Since cellular biology and molecular biology are two rapidly growing areas in biology, the amount of information you will have to deal with can be overwhelming. You'll find that the work requires both attention to detail and the ability to appreciate and comprehend broad concepts. As a biologist, you should be ready to take initiative and to work cooperatively with others. Although you will often study alone, you will sometimes work in pairs or in small groups in the lab. Because of the emphasis on real-life learning, many laboratory experiments cannot be completed within a typical laboratory period (3 hours). Therefore, you can expect to work outside of class, either alone or in small groups. Keep in mind, too, that much of the laboratory learning may at first seem repetitious; but this valuable experience will help you master the hands-on research skills you'll need.

In some colleges, the biology degree offers a broad exposure to the hierarchy of living things, spanning molecules, cells, organisms, ecologies, and ecosystems. In other colleges, the biology major focuses on molecular, cellular, or biochemical processes. If you select a broad-based program, it is possible that you may discover a field that interests you more than the one you initially selected. In a narrower program, you might have fewer options if you decide to make a change. With a strong background in basic biology, however, you can take supplemental courses in graduate school to keep yourself competitive with students coming from more specialized undergraduate programs.

Other majors you might like:
Molecular biology
Microbiology
Biochemistry
Chemistry
Zoology
Botany
Genetics
Biomedical engineering
Chemical engineering
Biomedical technology
Biotechnology
Clinical/medical laboratory technology

Questions to ask colleges:
What is the laboratory enrollment size? Do full-time faculty members, teaching assistants, or adjunct instructors teach laboratory courses? What type of access do undergraduates have to laboratory equipment?

Career options and trends:
Research scientist; physician or health care professional; research assistant or technician; regulatory compliance officer; college professor.

For work as a research technician, certain laboratories require certification in areas such as histotechnology.

Cell biology is a fast-moving field, so it is hard to predict trends. Today's discoveries may become tomorrow's ordinary tools and techniques.

For more info:
American Society for Cell Biology (ASCB)
8120 Woodmont Ave.
Suite 750
Bethesda, MD 20814-2762
(301) 347-9300
www.ascb.org

Entomology

Also known as:
Insect biology

What it's about:
Entomology deals with the biology and economic importance of insects and their relatives. If you are interested in understanding the diversity of insects in all their habitats, or their impact on human health and resources, you may find this major a better match than the broader life sciences majors.

Is this for you?
You might like this major if you also like: bugs, of course; nature and the environment; farming and agriculture; lab sciences.

Consider this major if you are good at: attention to detail; critical reading/thinking; organizing; quantitative analysis; research; teamwork *...or have...* curiousity; initiative; verbal skills.

Recommended high school prep:
English 4, math 4, lab science 4, social studies 3, and a foreign language 2–3. Take a course in computer science or computer applications if one is available.

Did you know...
...that not many students major in this subject? Those who do, therefore, have more opportunity for one-on-one interactions with their advisers and professors.

...that over a million different species of insects have been identified so far? Some experts believe that there may be another 30 million species yet to be discovered.

Typical courses in this major:
General biology
Microbiology
Chemistry
General entomology
Insect physiology
Insect taxonomy and systematics
Field crop insects
Horticultural entomology
Livestock entomology
Insect behavior
Aquatic entomology
Beekeeping
Agricultural entomology (pest management)
Medical entomology
Forest entomology
Urban entomology

Concentrations:
Generally, none in college; but if you go on to grad school: evolution and behavior; molecular entomology; pest management.

What the study of this major is like:
Entomology evolved into a field of its own because of the enormous impact insects have on humans. Some entomologists teach farmers how to use efficient, environmentally safe methods of pest control. Others work in forest management or in ornamental plant industries to protect trees from destructive bugs. Still others, employed by public health agencies, help ranchers deal with insects that plague livestock. Entomologists also conduct basic research in ecology, physiology, toxicology, genetics, and biotechnology, since insects can serve as test organisms for the examination of principles common to all animal life.

Before you begin study in entomology, you take introductory courses in plant and animal biology and in chemistry (including organic chemistry). Because entomology is a biological science, you will be taking biology courses throughout your undergraduate studies. From a general entomology course you progress to advanced classes in the morphology, taxonomy, physiology, ecology, and behavior of insects. Other advanced courses may deal with the importance of insects to human health and welfare (for example, pest management or medical entomology). Elective courses include plant physiology, plant pathology, nematology (nematodes or roundworms), microbiology, parasitology, agricultural engineering, agronomy, sociology, and economics.

Laboratories are an important part of many entomology courses. In some courses, you may even be required to collect insects. You will probably be encouraged to conduct an independent research project under the supervision of a professor. The electives you choose should reflect your educational and career objectives. If, after college, you plan to go directly into pest management, you should take courses in other agricultural sciences, such as weed science or plant pathology. If, on the other hand, you would like to go to graduate school, take advanced courses in biology and entomology that relate to your interests.

Entomology is not generally offered as an undergraduate major except in large public research universities and land grant colleges. Some programs may focus more on pest management (usually in agricultural departments); others emphasize basic science. Those that are comprehensive in both areas may allow you to design a curriculum that meets your needs.

Other majors you might like:
Plant protection/pest management
Environmental science
Ecology
Zoology
Agricultural and biological engineering
Agronomy and crop science
Wildlife biology
Animal sciences
Aquatic biology/limnology

Questions to ask colleges:
What are the opportunities for independent research?

How flexible is the major in meeting my career objectives (for example, pest management or basic science)?

Do graduates get jobs that relate to their major in entomology?

Career options and trends:
Urban or agricultural pest management specialist*; government research technician or scientist; university research technician*; industry researcher; industry technical or sales representative; university extension agent.

Entry-level positions in industry and government may be obtained with a bachelor's degree, but a graduate degree is required for most research and upper-level jobs.

For more info:
Entomological Society of America
10001 Derekwood Lane
Suite 100
Lanham, MD 20706-3115
(301) 731-4535
www.entsoc.org

Genetics

What it's about:

Genetics began when an Austrian monk examined the heredity of simple traits in peas. It now serves as the framework for the biological sciences, by providing concepts and techniques for studying inheritance, development, disease, and evolution in all living organisms and viruses. As a major in genetics, you gain a solid background from which you can specialize in most areas of biology.

Is this for you?

You might like this major if you also like: science and technology; finding out how things work; solving puzzles; natural and human history; research; learning about medicine and evolution.

Consider this major if you are good at: attention to detail; creativity; critical reading/thinking; math; quantitative analysis; research ...*or have...* manual dexterity; mechanical facility; patience; writing skills.

Recommended high school prep:

English 4, math 4 (including calculus), lab science 4 (including biology, physics, and chemistry), social studies 3, and a foreign language 2–3. Be sure to take all available computer science courses.

Typical courses in this major:

Calculus
Organic chemistry
Inorganic chemistry
Biochemistry
Statistics
Physics
General biology
Principles of genetics
Advanced genetics
Human genetics
Molecular genetics
Quantitative genetics and breeding
Evolutionary genetics
Population genetics
Developmental genetics
Genetic data analysis

Concentrations:

Generally, none in college; but if you go on to grad school: human genetics; plant genetics; animal genetics; microbial genetics; viral genetics; developmental genetics; population genetics; cytology; quantitative genetics; behavioral genetics.

What the study of this major is like:

Genetics majors usually begin with a solid grounding in chemistry, biochemistry, and general biology. Math and statistics requirements vary from college to college. Within the major, your work can be diverse, including courses in classical genetics, molecular biology, plant and animal genetics, population genetics, cytology, human genetics, microbial genetics (bacteria and viruses), behavioral genetics, and specialized courses related to model organisms (such as maize, roundworms, or mice) or to laboratory skills such as molecular genetics techniques.

Some colleges do not have the undergraduate major "genetics," but they offer similar courses under "molecular biology." Most programs contain a mix of lecture, laboratory, and independent research opportunities; in addition, some programs have a capstone course in which you read original research papers and discuss them. To be a successful major, you should be committed to genetics and have good study habits. Some students find genetics challenging because it is a research-oriented major. If you don't like research (many people don't), then genetics is probably not for you. But if you love working in the lab at all hours, you should do well.

If you plan on going for a Ph.D. in genetics or another biological science, pick a college that offers quality undergraduate research opportunities. A graduate admissions committee will probably expect you to supply a letter of recommendation from a respected researcher in whose laboratory you worked.

Genetics is a good undergraduate major for students heading for medical school, veterinary school, and most other graduate programs in biology. On the other hand, you don't have to major in genetics to get into a graduate program in the field. Graduate programs accept majors in biochemistry, bacteriology, biology, zoology, botany, and other biological sciences.

Other majors you might like:

Biomedical engineering
Agricultural and biological engineering
Botany
Zoology
Genetic counseling
Biotechnology
Forensic science
Animal breeding
Biomedical technology
Biochemistry
Molecular biology

Career options and trends:

Genetics counselor*; medical or veterinary doctor*; genetics researcher or investigator*; lab bench scientist or technician, or lab manager; science writer; executive, manager, or sales rep in the biotechnology industry; clinical and medical geneticist.

A degree from a professional school and licensing are required for those wishing to become physicians or veterinarians, and most jobs in genetic research require a Ph.D.

The biotechnology industry has a number of career opportunities for students with just a baccalaureate. The aggressive growth that occurred in that industry in the 1990s has slowed somewhat but is still going strong, and is expected to remain strong for the foreseeable future. There is also an increasing need for people with a solid background in both genetics and communications.

For more info:

Genetics Society of America (GSA)
9650 Rockville Pike
Bethesda, MD 20814-3998
(301) 634-7300
www.genetics-gsa.org

Marine biology

What it's about:

Students in marine biology explore the diversity of sea life, the functioning of marine ecosystems, and the chemical and physical nature of the oceans. As a marine biology major, you will gain a broad understanding of the processes that control life in underwater environments.

Is this for you?

You might like this major if you also like: the sea and shore; boats and boating; water sports; aquariums; the outdoors; nature; travel; science and technology.

Consider this major if you are good at: attention to detail; creativity; critical reading/thinking; leadership; math; quantitative analysis; research; spatial thinking/analysis; teamwork *...or have...* communication skills; initiative.

Recommended high school prep:

English 4, math 4 (including precalculus), lab science 4 (including earth science, chemistry and physics, and field biology if available), social studies 3, and a foreign language 2–3. You will need calculus and computer skills in college. The ability to communicate well, in writing and in speaking, is important in this field, so don't neglect your English courses. If possible, participate in a summer internship program at an aquarium or a research center.

Did you know...

...that marine biology covers more than fish and sea mammals? You study everything from the microscopic, single-cell plants that float in the oceans, to ecosystems like coral reefs, kelp forests, and the intertidal zone (at the edge of the sea where tides ebb and flow) and widely differing environments, such as hydrothermal vents miles below the ocean's surface and the frigid waters of the Antarctic Ocean.

...that this major requires a sound training in chemistry? Chemistry is important in understanding the building blocks of life, such as DNA and proteins, and the way the biological world affects and is affected by the physical world undersea.

Typical courses in this major:

Chemical oceanography
Physical oceanography
Ichthyology
Invertebrate biology
Marine botany
Deep-sea biology
Fisheries biology
Limnology (freshwater environments)
Marine ecology
Marine mammals
Aquaculture
Coastal ornithology
Marine policy
Plankton biology
Phycology (algae)
Computer modeling

Concentrations:

Generally, none in college; but if you go on to grad school: vertebrates; invertebrates; coastal ecology; coral reef ecology; fisheries biology; marine mammals.

What the study of this major is like:

Marine biologists study the ocean as a system—how underwater species relate to one another as food and prey and how various species depend on the ocean's physics and chemistry. As a major, you will have in-depth exposure to this complex ecosystem and will gain insight into environmental problems, such as the consequences of global climate changes and ocean pollution. And you will examine the consequences of humankind's reliance on the seas.

Courses cover the form, structure, development, evolution, physiology, biochemistry, and genetics of marine systems, including fisheries. Emphasis is placed on the spatial and regional distributions of species—for example, whether they inhabit coastal or open ocean, cold or warm water, deep or shallow water. You may study why certain species are endangered and how they can be protected, or you can pursue special interests, such as the economics of harvesting marine organisms for food and energy.

During the first two years, majors take basic courses including math, chemistry, physics, and biology. You may also take a first-year survey, with field trips, of marine environments. In your second year, you might conduct laboratory examinations of the ecology, physiology, and behavior of marine organisms. Upper-level work focuses on the chemical and physical characteristics of the ocean. In addition, you will probably take courses in conservation, marine resources, and policy (coastal law, pollution, economic resources of the ocean).

The coursework is generally a mix of lectures, laboratory activities, and, especially in the third and fourth years, fieldwork. Many students do summer internships or research outside college, and a senior thesis—an independent research project, conducted under faculty supervision and summarized in a written report—is often required.

A frequent challenge for majors is to develop a coordinated path through the field. Marine biology is not a distinct area of study; rather, it draws heavily on other disciplines such as biology, chemistry, and physics. Avoid taking just a collection of survey courses from various areas of science. Instead, try to explore one field of marine biology in depth. Also, majors often spend a lot of time on fieldwork. But although they work hard, they generally enjoy what they do.

Because marine biology is such a broad area, different programs have different emphases. For example, professors at some colleges may concentrate on open-ocean rather than near-shore species; at other colleges, faculty members may have expertise in marine mammals and know little about fisheries. Some colleges offer a biological concentration within a broader oceanography major. Take a look at course catalogs, which should reflect colleges' emphases.

Other majors you might like:
Oceanography
Aquaculture
Ecology
Environmental biology
Ocean engineering
Environmental science
Aquatic biology/limnology
Zoology
Marine engineering/naval architecture
Water, wetlands, and marine management
Fishing and fisheries

Questions to ask colleges:
In which area of marine biology do faculty members have the most expertise?

Which types of marine field research or internships are available to undergraduates?

Career options and trends:
Government resource manager*; science teacher; fisheries biologist; laboratory research technician*; environmental consultant*; staff member at a museum or aquarium.

The job market is tight in this field. A strong math background and computer skills will give you a competitive edge, especially in the fisheries industry. Most research and academic positions will require a graduate degree.

Insider's viewpoint:
"A misconception is that fieldwork, such as scuba diving and cruises, is all fun and games. Taking a midnight dive—and my fifth dive of the day—in the pouring rain or being seasick is not fun."

—Amy, senior, University of San Diego

For more info:
American Fisheries Society (AFS)
5410 Grosvenor Lane
Bethesda, MD 20814
(301) 897-8616
www.fisheries.org

Microbiology

What it's about:

The microbiology major focuses on the biology of microscopic organisms, such as bacteria, algae, and fungi. Your goal is to understand the function of microbes in agriculture, medicine, ecology, and biotechnology. You will also receive training in sterile procedures; the identification, enumeration, and growth of microorganisms; the evaluation of antimicrobials and antibiotics; and the practice of microbial genetics.

Is this for you?

You might like this major if you also like: science projects; gardening; environmental causes; microscopes; caring for people; keeping things organized.

Consider this major if you are good at: attention to detail; creativity; critical reading/thinking; organizing; quantitative analysis; research; spatial thinking/analysis; teamwork *...or have...* manual dexterity.

Recommended high school prep:

English 4 (a writing course would be helpful), math 4 (including precalculus or calculus), lab science 4 (including chemistry and physics), social studies 3, and a foreign language 2–3. If possible, take a course in statistics and in computer science.

Did you know...

...that the study of microorganisms is not just about germs and disease? Oil prospecting, soil use and management, agriculture, development of nanosystems, genetic engineering, uses and misuses of microbes in military activities, and monitoring for microbes are just some of the many applications.

Typical courses in this major:

General biology I, II
Organic chemistry
Inorganic chemistry
Cell biology
Genetics
Bacteriology
Biochemistry
Microbial ecology
Bioinformatics/computational biology
Advanced microbiology
Bacterial physiology
Medical bacteriology
Immunology
Virology
Recombinant DNA techniques
Mycology and parasitology

Concentrations:

Generally, none in college; but if you go on to grad school: bacteriology; virology; mycology (fungi); phycology (algae); microbial physiology; genetics; biotechnology.

What the study of this major is like:

As a microbiology major, you will probably begin by familiarizing yourself with microscopes. You'll get an overview of the diversity, structure, function, growth, reproduction, genetics, physiology, preservation, and control of microorganisms. You'll then learn to grow and catalog a wide variety of microorganisms, including bacteria, algae, fungi, protozoa, and viruses. When you progress to biochemistry and molecular genetics, the work becomes more abstract. In labs and lectures, you use critical-thinking skills to prepare and conduct experiments. As you advance, your work focuses on bacterial mutants, the documentation of agents (including viruses, which are not usually seen directly), and measurements with biochemical tools.

Microbiology majors develop laboratory procedures that enable them to study a type or a group of microorganisms. Students sometimes have trouble attending to the many important details and thoroughly applying sterile procedures and techniques. You must work well in a group, even if you are doing an individual research project. Majors have to cooperate in order to maintain and use shared equipment and materials safely, often under sterile conditions. Sometimes you need to develop new skills for a particular project, such as the ability to search gene databases. For most investigations, you'll need to understand the molecular biology and biochemistry of both hosts and parasites. To be successful in this field, you should be willing to learn unfamiliar methodologies and adapt to unexpected situations.

Some colleges emphasize a premedical curriculum in biology, and give less attention to other biological sciences. In such programs you may be limited to broader applications in microbiology. Other colleges emphasize environmental science or molecular biology rather than a more integrated approach to the diverse areas within microbiology. Most small colleges offer solid foundations in the biological sciences, teaching concepts (such as the theories behind evolution, genetics, respiration, photosynthesis, and biochemistry) as well as technical skills. Conceptual skills are useful because the field of microbiology is changing rapidly, and certain technologies and methods might one day be out-of-date.

Other majors you might like:
Clinical/medical laboratory technology
Biotechnology
Biomedical engineering
Cell biology and histology
Zoology
Genetics
Biochemistry
Entomology
Chemistry
Soil science
Ecology
Agricultural and biological engineering

Questions to ask colleges:
Do undergraduates learn lab techniques and practical skills that would qualify them for entry into the job market? Where do most majors go after graduation—medical school, graduate school, or employment?

Career options and trends:
Physician*; veterinarian; high school and college teacher; research technician*; environmental scientist; hospital administrator; biotechnologist*; health care professional (respiratory therapist, phlebotomist, etc.); government agency microbiologist.

Graduates with a degree in microbiology find positions in health care and in the biotechnology, agricultural, food, and pharmaceutical industries. Job opportunities are projected to grow faster in this field than in the biological field as a whole. Job growth is coming back strong in the biotechnology industry, especially in the areas of pharmaceutical and medical manufacturing. Health care is a particularly strong field even in tight job markets.

Insider's viewpoint:
"I had a misconception of what people do in labs. I thought you just go there and do your experiments. In fact it's far more involved. You think about the experiments, you talk to your instructor, you talk to other students who work with you, and you go to conferences. It's a very different culture. You're not completely isolated."

—Julio, senior, San Francisco State University

For more info:
American Society for Microbiology (ASM)
1752 N St., N.W.
Washington, DC 20036
(202) 737-3600
www.asm.org

Molecular biology

Also known as:
Cell and molecular biology

What it's about:
As a major in molecular biology, you investigate the basic mechanisms of life by studying the macromolecules—proteins, for example—essential to living organisms. Using chemical analysis, you explore metabolism, gene function and regulation, cell differentiation, and development. Special emphasis is placed on the role of proteins and nucleic acids in cellular processes.

Is this for you?
You might like this major if you also like: science clubs and projects; new technology; thinking creatively and abstractly; exploring the inner workings of things. Molecular biology is for people who are constantly asking "Why?" and are not satisfied until something is completely explained.

Consider this major if you are good at: attention to detail; critical reading/thinking; math; quantitative analysis; research; spatial thinking/analysis; teamwork *...or have...* initiative; manual dexterity; perseverance.

Recommended high school prep:
English 4, math 4 (including calculus and statistics), lab science 4 (including biology, chemistry, and physics), social studies 3, and a foreign language 2-3. Take as many advanced science courses as possible, and a course in computer science if available.

Did you know...
...that you must have an understanding of chemistry when you study living organisms? The ability to apply chemical principles to the function and structure of cells is the basis of molecular biology.

Typical courses in this major:
General biology (I, II)
General chemistry (I, II)
Organic chemistry (I, II)
General physics (I, II)
Cellular biology
General molecular biology
General microbiology
Biochemistry
Plant molecular biology
Molecular genetics
Biostatistics
Endocrinology
Nucleic acid chemistry
Developmental biology
Protein isolation and characterization (lab)
Writing in molecular biology

Concentrations:
Generally, none in college; but if you go on to grad school: bioinformatics; structural biology; computational biology; molecular medicine; functional genomics; molecular genetics; pharmacogenetics.

What the study of this major is like:
As a molecular biology major, you focus on subcellular components. You'll investigate cellular mechanisms (including cell metabolism and genetics) and learn to apply principles of chemistry to biological systems.

Most likely, you'll begin with an introduction to the essential macromolecules, especially the structure and function of proteins and nucleic acids. Then you'll conduct an in-depth study of DNA replication and function. You also focus on protein biosynthesis and enzyme regulation. In the required biochemistry courses, you cover metabolic pathways for energy and precursor production.

Cellular biology courses combine molecular and biochemical information to describe the production of cellular material. Because successful molecular biologists need well-developed analytical skills, most majors enroll in biostatistics and quantitative analysis courses. You are also expected to have strong computer skills. If you don't have experience with database searches, spreadsheets, and presentation software, you should take technology courses in your early college years.

Advanced courses focus on the interaction of specific proteins and the role of DNA in the regulation of cellular processes. In biotechnology courses, you begin to apply these principles to real-world problems. In bioinformatics and computational biology, you'll learn to use information obtained from genome sequencing. Besides lectures and seminars, most courses have labs in which you practice basic research techniques, including DNA and protein isolation, purification, and manipulation. Advanced courses generally require you to do an independent research project.

Majors spend a considerable amount of time working independently in the lab. The field of molecular biology depends on experimentation, so you must develop excellent laboratory skills and good hand-eye coordination. You spend additional out-of-class time reading journals and writing scientific reports. Although you need to be creative, you also have to develop an organized approach to problem solving, be able to memorize technical terms, and do complex data analysis and application. Most students in molecular biology study and work in groups; teamwork is essential to success. In addition to lightening individual workloads, study groups provide a strong support system.

Other majors you might like:
Biochemistry
Cell biology and histology
Agricultural and biological engineering
Biomedical engineering
Neuroscience
Microbiology
Genetics
Clinical/medical laboratory technology
Biomedical technology
Physics
Chemistry
Forensic science

Questions to ask colleges:
What is the primary focus of the program? At some colleges, the program may emphasize one aspect of biology (such as genetics) or a particular group of organisms; while other colleges may focus on the chemistry/biochemistry aspects. You may also have to choose between a biotech track and a preprofessional (premed) track.

Which lab equipment is available for undergraduates? Because the field of molecular biology is highly dependent on experimentation, undergrads must develop excellent lab skills.

Career options and trends:
University researcher/professor; medical or pharmaceutical researcher*; forensic scientist; health professional (such as physician, nurse)*; genetic counselor; high school teacher; agricultural researcher; laboratory technician*; public health officer.

Research positions may require a graduate degree.

Recent technological developments, such as genome sequencing and DNA arrays, have significantly increased the role of molecular biology research in the field.

For more info:
American Society for Biochemistry and Molecular Biology (ASBMB)
9650 Rockville Pike
Bethesda, MD 20814-3996
(301) 634-7145
www.asbmb.org

Zoology

Also known as:
Animal biology

What it's about:
Zoology majors study animals—their origin, cell structure, genetics, physiology, behavior, ecology, and life processes. They also receive training in molecular biology techniques, quantitative field sampling, and statistical analysis.

Is this for you?
You might like this major if you also like: all creatures great and small; natural history museums; the outdoors; lab work and fieldwork; identifying animals; bird watching; anatomy; environmental issues.

Consider this major if you are good at: attention to detail; critical reading/thinking; memorizing; organizing; quantitative analysis *...or have...* communication skills; initiative; manual dexterity; patience.

Recommended high school prep:
English 4, math 4 (including precalculus or calculus), lab science 4, social studies 3, and a foreign language 2–3. If they are available, take additional science courses in anatomy, physiology, or genetics.

Did you know...
...that the proper pronunciation of this major is "zo" (like "no") -ology, not "zoo" -ology? The word "zoo" is actually a mispronounced abbreviation for "zoological park."

Typical courses in this major:
Animal behavior
Animal physiology
Comparative anatomy
Ecology
Endocrinology
Genetics
Entomology (insects)
Evolutionary biology
Herpetology (reptiles and amphibians)
Invertebrate biology
Limnology (ponds and lakes)
Mammalogy
Ornithology
Parasitology
Primatology
Vertebrate zoology

Concentrations:
In college: Conservation or environmental biology; ecology and evolution; entomology; marine biology; neurobiology; physiology.

If you go on to grad school: anatomy and histology; ornithology (the study of birds); herpetology; developmental zoology; endocrinology; invertebrate zoology; parasitology; population biology.

What the study of this major is like:
As a zoology major, you explore how animals function. You study the way an organism acquires energy and material for growth and reproduction, and examine animals' interaction with their own kind as well as with other living and nonliving things. You also consider how animals have evolved.

In your first year, you will probably enroll in introductory courses in both biology and chemistry. Biology courses cover the significant concepts, from molecular biology to ecosystem ecology. In your second and third years, you take focused core courses, such as anatomy, cell biology, ecology, evolution, genetics, and physiology. Zoology majors usually study at least two years of chemistry, a year of physics, and some advanced math such as calculus. In your third and fourth years, you select upper-level electives specific to zoology.

In most zoology courses, you study the basic concepts in lectures; then, in a lab or field setting, you are introduced to data collection and techniques of analysis. Zoology majors usually spend about the same amount of time in lectures and in labs. After the first year, many majors do independent research projects with faculty members or sometimes with graduate students. Most first-year majors face serious challenges, especially in the first semester. Introductory biology and chemistry are generally taught in greater depth and more rigorously than in high school. If you do not complete the assignments on time, you may find it difficult to keep up with the work as the semester progresses. You need to call on your self-discipline in lectures, the laboratory or fieldwork, and no-nonsense studying.

Course offerings tend to mirror the research activities of the faculty. Different zoology departments may emphasize one area of biology or zoology over others. For example, some departments focus on molecular and cell biology and feature courses that explore how the parts of organisms (such as molecules and tissues) function. Other departments may stress whole organisms and populations and offer courses in ecology, environmental biology, and taxonomic groups (entomology, invertebrate zoology, ornithology, for example). Because most high school biology classes take only a brief look at the diversity of the animal kingdom, your interests may change in college as you encounter new areas of study. A department with a well-balanced curriculum that offers a wide variety of courses may give you the most options.

Other majors you might like:
Anthropology
Biology teacher education
Ecology
Evolutionary biology
Microbiology
Wildlife and wilderness management
Animal sciences
Livestock management
Marine biology
Veterinary technology
Entomology
Aquatic biology/limnology

Questions to ask colleges:
Is the major broad-based or does it concentrate on one particular area of zoological study?

What percentage of zoology majors are admitted into medical and other professional schools?

Which facilities are unique to the zoology program (such as a breeding facility), and which facilities are shared with other biological programs (electron microscope, computers)?

Career options and trends:
Health care professional; park ranger or guide; research assistant; teacher or college professor; environmental consultant; staff member at an aquarium, zoo, or animal park; veterinarian or veterinarian technician.

The best prospects are in the health care, biomedical, and environmental industries. A graduate or professional degree is necessary for most research, academic, and medical positions. A doctorate is generally required for work as a zoologist. Summer employment in a medical, environmental, or other career area is increasingly expected of job applicants.

For more info:
American Institute of Biological Sciences (AIBS)
1444 Eye St., N.W.
Suite 200
Washington, DC 20005
(202) 628-1500
www.aibs.org

Business

"The chief business of the American people *is* business," President Calvin Coolidge said. "They are profoundly concerned with producing, buying, selling, investing and prospering in the world." It's no wonder that business is by far the most widely chosen undergraduate major. More than one in five bachelor's degrees is earned in business. And one-quarter of all master's degrees are in business—second only to education.

Do you have what it takes to succeed in business? Business abilities cover a wide range of talent—"people skills" and communication, technical expertise, math and analytical skills, leadership, teamwork, and creativity— as well as commitment to integrity.

The main subject areas in business are topics that everyone should know something about.

"Knowledge of finance is an essential life skill," says Stephen J. Brown of the Stern School of Business, New York University.

"The same management concepts that ensure that the resources of a business organization are used effectively and efficiently can and should be applied to the choices one makes in life generally," observes Peter Bycio, Williams College of Business, Xavier University.

No matter what you're interested in, a knowledge of business can enhance your career.

"Entrepreneurship is applicable to any number of other careers," says Stephen Spinelli, Jr. of Babson College. "If someone has a passion for theater, studying business can help that person create, grow, and manage a theater company. Engineers, doctors, and lawyers need entrepreneurial skills to grow and succeed. The list goes on and on."

One way to think about business studies is to group them into functions, like finance, accounting, and marketing. Some majors cut across these functions. For instance, if you study business management or management information systems, you'll need to know about all aspects of operations and administration. Still other business majors, such as real estate, insurance, fashion merchandising, hospitality, and construction management, take you into specific industries or professions.

If you study business, you'll learn more than how to use a spreadsheet. Understanding human behavior is so important that many business programs contain courses in sociology, psychology, and the humanities.

Trends in business may also affect what you'll study. Current economic forces include globalization of companies and markets, a shift from manufacturing to service industries, corporate mergers, rapid developments in technology, changes in government regulations, price pressures, and shifting demographics. These trends have resulted in the recent creation of such business majors and courses as risk management, information management, e-commerce, supply chain management, and entrepreneurship. "We live in a world in which *change* may be the only constant," says Professor Diane Kaufman Fredette of Pratt Institute. "Given this trend, *managing change* has become an increasingly critical skill for construction managers."

On the undergraduate level, colleges have different philosophies of teaching business. Some colleges focus on quantitative, analytical, and technological aspects of business, while others emphasize strategy and management. Some programs get you ready to apply to grad school by teaching all about business theory. Other schools, taking a more practical, hands-on approach, prepare you for a business career with your bachelor's degree. Sometimes bachelor's and master's degrees are combined in a five-year program. A two-year degree is what you need for some jobs in hospitality and fashion merchandising.

Is grad school for you?

Each year, more than 100,000 students get master's degrees in business administration. That's a lot of competition for top jobs. Is the MBA a one-way ticket to a corner office? Not necessarily, but a survey of MBA students by the Graduate Management Admission Council shows that 65 percent of the class of 2005 rated the value of their degree as outstanding or excellent. Overall, managers who plan and direct the activities of business (as well as government and other organizations) can expect to see their employment opportunities increase by 2.2 million jobs, or 14.4 percent by 2014, according to the U.S. Department of Labor.

What do grad students in business actually study? It all depends on the major. Graduate tracks might include quality management; franchise, distributorship, and license ownership; corporate or international finance; investment banking; compensation and labor relations; information technology and systems; marketing research; and accounting information systems.

In the meantime, think about where you might go as an undergrad. Often, the location of the college dictates its business offerings. If the school is in an urban area and you're studying finance, for example, the program may prep you to work in financial services, which have offices in the city, rather than in financial management in suburban businesses.

Here are a few things to ask at all business-degree levels when comparing colleges: How long has the major been offered? Who are the faculty members? Are they full-time professors, or adjunct (part-time) professors (who are business professionals), or a combination? It's good to learn from the experts, but if they're on campus only a few hours a week, can you contact them easily? Are courses lecture-oriented, project-oriented, or action-oriented, and do you have a preference? How is technology used in class?

What kinds of resources do students have? Seed funding? Business-plan competitions? Internships? Access to industry experts? Do student organizations have chapters on campus? What kind of job placement assistance and career counseling will you get after you graduate? What career paths do most graduates follow? Which employers interview business majors on campus?

Make it your business to find out about colleges that offer these majors. They include schools of business, management, commerce, business administration, and arts and sciences.

Accounting

What it's about:

Accounting is known as the language of business. The major prepares you to gather, record, analyze, interpret, and communicate financial information about an individual's or an organization's performance and risks. You study such topics as financial statement preparation and analysis, risk assessment and control, management decision-making, tax preparation and planning, management of accounting information systems, auditing, and fraud.

Is this for you?

You might like this major if you also like: computers; leadership roles; working with numbers; interacting and working with people; seeing both the details and the "big picture" when analyzing situations.

Consider this major if you are good at: attention to detail; critical reading/thinking; leadership; organizing; quantitative analysis; teamwork ...*or have...* people skills; verbal skills; writing skills.

Recommended high school prep:

English 4 (including writing), math 3 (including trigonometry), lab science 3, social studies 3, and a foreign language 2–3. If possible, also take communications, speech, and computer courses.

Did you know...

...that accounting is not just about crunching numbers? Communication and critical-thinking skills are essential for success in the profession, because accountants spend most of their time advising, analyzing, communicating, and managing. The profession is often viewed as the fast track to upper-level management positions like controller, chief financial officer (CFO), or chief executive officer (CEO).

Typical courses in this major:

Introductory accounting
Intermediate accounting
Advanced accounting
Auditing
Cost accounting
Taxation
International accounting
Accounting information systems
Government and not-for-profit accounting
Financial statement analysis

Concentrations:

Generally, none in college; but if you go on to grad school: financial accounting; accounting information systems; cost accounting; managerial accounting; forensic accounting.

What the study of this major is like:

Accounting is a popular major available at most colleges, often housed in a school of business or management. Otherwise, accounting may be offered as part of a program in the liberal arts or sciences, usually in the economics or social sciences department. The accounting major includes both technical and application-based course work. The technical nature of some courses makes them well suited to the lecture format, which is often supplemented with interactive learning tools such as case analyses, computer simulations, and research projects. Many courses are taught as seminars, with plenty of student participation; some courses include hands-on, real-world experience.

Undergraduate concentrations are rare. You take courses in economics and finance, business law, business organization and management, marketing, and computer information sciences. You learn to measure costs, compile data, and determine how the data affect efficiency and profitability. After your introductory accounting courses, you study financial statements and how they are used to make business decisions. You also study such topics as risk assurance, e-commerce accounting and control, fraud investigation, internal auditing, and ethics.

One of the more challenging areas you may face as a major is financial accounting. Many students find it difficult at first—comprehending it can be like solving a complex puzzle. But once you master the subject, its framework and logic become second nature.

In addition to your accounting curriculum, you are usually required to take a range of liberal arts and science courses. Especially important are those in history and foreign languages (finance has become global). Because good communication is vital to the profession, you will also benefit from classes that sharpen your writing, speaking, and problem-solving skills.

In some accounting programs, you focus on theory. Other programs take an applied approach that stresses the skills you will need as an accountant. Some programs also have a niche emphasis, such as internal auditing or accounting information systems. Although some programs still have separate undergraduate and master's degrees, others offer a five-year program—a bachelor's and a master's are awarded jointly at graduation. These programs have become more popular with the phasing in of the rule requiring students who want to become a certified public accountant (CPA) to complete 150 credit hours of course work.

The accounting major prepares you for careers in public or managerial accounting. Public accountants work with auditing firms to produce credible financial reports; managerial accountants work with management to monitor an organization's financial health. Managerial accountants often need special knowledge about taxes, budgeting, and investing. While often helpful, a CPA designation is not essential for internal auditing, corporate accounting, and government accounting.

Other majors you might like:
Finance
Management information systems
Accounting technology/bookkeeping
Information systems
Statistics
Economics
Insurance
Public administration
Real estate
International business
Marketing
Theater arts management

Questions to ask colleges:
Does the program encourage internships?

Is course work primarily applied (analysis-based) or conceptual (theory-based)?

Are bachelor's and master's degrees offered in separate programs or in a unified, five-year program?

Career options and trends:
Auditor*; tax accountant/adviser*; risk assurance/information technology consultant*; corporate accountant*; financial planner; fraud examiner; government investigator (IRS, FBI).

To become a CPA, you must pass the national CPA exam, and also meet the certification requirements of the state where you want to practice; most states require a period of professional work experience and the equivalent of five years of college (150 credit hours).

The job outlook for accountants is very good. Large-scale business scandals have put accounting, auditing, and fraud investigations in the spotlight, and resulting legislation has significantly changed accounting practices both inside and outside of organizations. CFOs and CEOs must now sign off on financial statements, and auditors have greater responsibilities and tighter rules governing their behavior. Thus the demand for well-qualified accounting professionals should remain high.

For more info:
American Accounting Association (AAA)
5717 Bessie Drive
Sarasota, FL 34233-2399
(941) 921-7747
www.aaahq.org

American Institute of Certified Public Accountants
1211 Sixth Ave.
New York, NY 10036-8775
(212) 596-6200
www.aicpa.org

Business administration and management

What it's about:

This major teaches you how to plan, organize, lead, and control the human, financial, and physical resources of an organization to achieve business goals. As a manager, you will be expected to meet the many demands of your employer, your organization's internal and external customers, and society in general.

Is this for you?

You might like this major if you also like: working with people; starting and running a business; the *Wall Street Journal*; debating; organizing or leading a club or group activity; solving problems; taking risks; competing; sports; helping others to succeed.

Consider this major if you are good at: attention to detail; critical reading/thinking; leadership; organizing; persuading/influencing; quantitative analysis; teamwork ...*or have...* initiative; verbal skills.

Recommended high school prep:

English 4, math 4 (including precalculus), lab science 3, social studies 3, and a foreign language 2–3. If available, take calculus and a computer course covering basic office applications and spreadsheets.

Did you know...

...that this is by far the most popular major? That means you'll have lots of company—and a wide choice of colleges that offer this major.

...that math skills are important for a business degree? Quantitative analysis is required for several areas of business, such as accounting, finance, and business statistics.

Typical courses in this major:

Accounting I, II
Business law
Economics
International trade and business
Business finance
Human resources
Managing information technology
Managerial communication
Principles of marketing
Business statistics
Production management
Operations management
Organizational design and development
Leadership
Quality planning and improvement
Strategic formulation and implementation

Concentrations:

Accounting; entrepreneurship; finance; international business; leadership; marketing; organizational behavior; production operations management.

What the study of this major is like:

Few people can avoid management. One day, you will probably either be a manager or work for one. The business management and administration major prepares you to serve as an effective, responsible manager in business, government, or nonprofit sectors. Managers have both the opportunity and the duty to make a difference: receiving good service can reflect good management; an employee's unethical behavior can reflect poor management; and good managers make sure that organizations generate value for their stakeholders on a sustained basis.

In the major, you typically learn how to achieve goals by planning (defining goals and deciding how to achieve them), organizing (deciding what resources need to go where to best support the plan), leading (influencing people to work toward accomplishing goals), and controlling (monitoring progress toward achieving goals and adjusting initial plans as needed). You study how managers respond to the complex, ever-changing expectations of employees, bosses, customers, governments, the legal community, and society as a whole. Majors begin with basic courses in accounting, marketing, and finance. You then take specialized courses, such as organizational behavior, human resources management, supervisory skills, and international management. In your fourth year, you usually take a capstone course in business strategy or business policy; applying what you have learned, you explore the way an organization interacts with the outside world and operates internally.

Most management programs offer internships, usually for a semester, to help you gain experience, learn about possible careers, and relate classroom learning to the workplace. Most internships award academic credit and require you to submit material to be graded. Some internships can lead to future job opportunities. Many colleges offer a semester-abroad program that lets you practice your management skills in another country. Because the policies and practices of employees, customers, organizations, and their competitors can reflect—positively or negatively—on the society in which they are located, managers must understand the cultural expectations of their host country.

Nevertheless, the objective of the major is to prepare you to lead others in an organization. Most management courses stimulate your persuasive and creative abilities—memorizing facts is generally not top priority. Courses are typically taught through lectures, videos, case studies, and, perhaps, role-playing. Professors use case studies to develop your problem-solving and analytical skills, to teach you to defend ideas logically, and to push you to challenge the ideas of others. You analyze actual business problems, develop realistic responses, and present your recommendations to professors and classmates. Working managers are often brought in to share their experiences. You use computers for spreadsheet programs, databases, and other programs that help you conduct statistical analysis, prepare financial projections, and do marketing research. If you choose this major, you should be ready to work hard.

Although most agree on a definition of general management, different colleges may have different emphases. Some programs take a quantitative approach and focus on decision-making techniques. Other programs may emphasize a management function such as leadership or an area of general management—for example, human resource management or organizational behavior. Differences among programs are also reflected in their readiness to adapt to changes in the field. For example, supply chain management, project management, and entrepreneurship are emerging topics. Some programs will be relatively conservative in their approach to such topics, offering only a course or two at first, while others may develop new concentrations or even new majors.

Other majors you might like:
Agribusiness operations
Entrepreneurial studies
Marketing
International business
Construction management
Hospitality administration and management
Music management
Parks/recreational/leisure facilities management
E-commerce
Public administration
Economics
Nonprofit/public organization management

Questions to ask colleges:
Is the program accredited by the Association to Advance Collegiate Schools of Business? If so, the program has been examined for quality from a number of perspectives.

Are there internships or co-op programs available in this major?

Do companies recruit on campus?

Career options and trends:
Management trainee or assistant manager*; sales or account representative*; corporate executive; management consultant; franchise or small business owner; human resources specialist; systems analyst; financial analyst; venture capitalist.

The job outlook mirrors the economic times, but organizations are always looking for good managers. As the world of business grows more complex, risky, and global in scope, the need for professional managers increases. Job growth is particularly expected within management consulting firms specializing in information technology, health care, and marketing.

An MBA is usually essential if you want to climb the corporate ladder; but many well-known companies will help you obtain this advanced degree while you're working.

Insider's viewpoint:

"Some classes, like accounting or information systems, are a much bigger time commitment. But I would estimate that on average, I spend about four hours per class per week on homework. However, that doesn't include the group projects, which take much more time. Business-school classes have many more group projects than any other classes I've taken."

—Dan, junior, University of Washington

For more info:

Association to Advance Collegiate Schools of
  Business (AACSB)
777 South Harbor Island Blvd.
Suite 750
Tampa, FL 33602-5730
(813) 769-6500
www.aacsb.edu

American Management Association (AMA)
1601 Broadway
New York, NY 10019
(800) 262-9699
www.amanet.org

Construction management

What it's about:

Construction management is the art of orchestrating all the components necessary to complete a building project within budget and on time. This major combines courses in business management, technology, and the liberal arts to provide the practical knowledge and critical thinking skills that a leadership role in construction requires.

Is this for you?

You might like this major if you also like: the outdoors; running a group project; working in teams; taking responsibility; working with your hands; achieving goals and results; watching construction sites.

Consider this major if you are good at: attention to detail; leadership; multi-tasking; organizing; persuading/influencing; quantitative analysis; spatial thinking/analysis; teamwork *...or have...* mechanical facility; verbal skills.

Recommended high school prep:

English 4, math 3 (including trigonometry), lab science 3, social studies 3, industrial arts 2, and a foreign language 2. Spanish is recommended because it is spoken by many workers in the construction industry. If available, courses in business, accounting, and computer-aided drafting (CAD) are also helpful.

Did you know...

...that the ability to think in three dimensions is essential in this field? Before giving instructions or solving problems, construction managers often have to visualize how a structure should take shape.

Typical courses in this major:

Principles of management
Principles of accounting
Labor relations
Business law and ethics
Project scheduling
Construction estimating
Blueprint reading
Specifications
Construction materials
Structural methods
Mechanical and electrical systems
Environmental compliance
Project budgeting and cost management
Construction law, codes, and regulations
Site logistics
Safety management

Concentrations:

Construction technology; safety management; planning and logistics.

What the study of this major is like:

Construction management is both an on-site job (making sure that the project is going smoothly and according to plan) and a desk job (dealing with bids, contracts, insurance, and other paperwork). A successful manager has expertise in three areas: construction, management, and people skills.

This major helps you develop this expertise by blending business management training with technical know-how. Course work covers creative problem solving, emerging technologies, best practices, and ethical principles. The goal is to prepare you to become a professional manager who can combine business acumen with an awareness of the diverse interests of the developer, contractor, owner, architect, and engineer.

Beginning with basic studies of blueprints and drawings, construction materials and techniques, you progress to an understanding of more complex components such as site logistics, specifications, cost estimating, and design, mechanical, structural, electrical, and legal issues. You learn to consider construction drawings as a picture not only of the planned structure but also of the complex process involving five dimensions—which include time and money, referred to as "schedule" and "budget."

Crunching numbers may not sound much like construction work, but nothing gets built before a budget is in place. That's why courses in estimating and accounting are usually required. You'll learn, step by step, how to figure the costs for everything from building materials to labor. You'll practice looking for clues in floor plans, and you'll get a handle on competitive bidding.

Many students enjoy the technical and graphic aspects of the major but find that writing skills do not come as easily. To help bring these skills together, most programs require a capstone project in the final year. For that you research a topic of your own interest and present a professional quality report to be reviewed by faculty or invited professionals.

Most programs include practical exposure to the profession. Lectures and lab courses are supplemented by opportunities for internships in which you do hands-on work under the guidance of a mentor. Actual construction experience is as essential as a degree when it comes to finding a job after graduation.

While construction management can be considered a business major, it is usually housed in a school or department of technology, engineering, or architecture. The emphasis on business management skills may vary depending on the overall strength of the college's business program. Architecturally based programs usually focus on design and on a team approach to problem solving.

This major is offered at both the associate degree and the bachelor's degree level. Four-year programs include more business management skills and liberal arts requirements. Two-year programs usually concentrate on construction technology.

Other majors you might like:
Civil engineering
Construction technology
Architectural engineering
Land use planning
Operations management
Real estate
Surveying technology
Geology/earth science
Mining and mineral engineering
Historic preservation
Heavy/earthmoving equipment operation
Architecture

Questions to ask colleges:
Is the program accredited by the American Council for Construction Education (ACCE)?

Do the professors incorporate their field experience into their classroom instruction?

What kinds of hands-on experiences are provided? Is there an internship program?

Career options and trends:
Construction manager; general contractor; site inspector; cost estimator; specifications writer; contract administrator.

According to the Bureau of Labor Statistics, excellent employment opportunities for construction managers are expected through 2014. However, employment can be sensitive to the short-term nature of many projects and to cyclical fluctuations in the industry. Prospects will be best for those with a bachelor's degree and construction work experience gained through internships and summer jobs. Large construction companies usually look for a master's degree when hiring managers.

For more info:
American Council for Construction Education
1717 N. Loop 1604 E.
San Antonio, TX 78232
(210) 495-6161
www.acce-hq.org

Construction Management Association of America
7918 Jones Branch Drive, Suite 540
McLean, VA 22102
(703) 356-2622
www.cmaanet.org

E-commerce

Also known as:
Digital business strategy

What it's about:
This major focuses on how to use marketing concepts, business strategies, economics, and computer science to develop new businesses, or to transform an existing business, through the use of the Internet and related information technology.

Is this for you?
You might like this major if you also like: computers; the Internet; starting or running a business venture; new technology; taking risks; science fiction; advertisements; buying and selling.

Consider this major if you are good at: attention to detail; creativity; leadership; math; organizing; persuading/influencing; quantitative analysis; research *...or have...* computer skills; initiative.

Recommended high school prep:
English 4, math 3, lab science 3, social studies 3, and a foreign language 2–3. If available, take a computer science course and an economics course that covers microeconomics.

Did you know...
...that e-commerce is not solely about technology, but rather the linking of technology and new business approaches? So you don't have to be a computer geek to do well in this major.

...that most of the interesting applications of e-commerce are likely to be in established businesses rather than in start-up ventures? This makes the long-term prospects of an e-commerce-related career more stable and broadens the types of job opportunities available.

Typical courses in this major:
Management information systems
Introduction to e-business
E-commerce marketing
E-commerce strategy
Law of electronic commerce
Strategic management
Entrepreneurial management
Venture capital
New venture initiation
Business application development (programming)
Internet technology
Computer networking and communications
Systems analysis and design
World Wide Web design
Business transformation/reengineering

Concentrations:
Business to consumer (B2C) e-commerce; business to business (B2B) e-commerce; electronic marketing; business strategies; computer/electronic technology.

What the study of this major is like:
Although business-to-business e-commerce has been receiving a lot of attention, e-commerce as a discipline, or academic subject, is still in its infancy. New technologies and creative individuals are continually remaking e-commerce and keeping it interesting. How many other disciplines transform themselves so extensively every few years? Another factor that makes e-commerce exciting is that you can apply your ideas quickly; you may have the satisfaction of producing immediate results.

The e-commerce major usually begins with a combination of general courses in technology and management fundamentals. Next, you take courses focusing on how e-commerce can be used in creating businesses or improving the performance of existing businesses. In many of your courses, you'll examine recent developments in electronics, such as wireless communications, and then identify opportunities to apply the new tools. You may also focus on finding technological solutions to classic business problems—for instance, figuring out how computers can help deliver customized products more efficiently. Because much of your work involves exploring ways to apply technology, you will probably spend considerable time brainstorming with others on team projects.

The biggest difference among programs is whether they emphasize technology or business. Almost all programs have a mix of the two areas, but the number of technology or business offerings can vary dramatically. Some programs focus almost entirely on technology. In these programs, courses usually deal with computer programming, network technology, and the development of World Wide Web content. Other programs focus on management issues, such as marketing, business case analyses, business plan development, or business strategies made possible by the Internet. In still other programs, you cannot take e-commerce as a stand-alone major; you must combine it with a major in computer science, management, marketing, or information technology.

Other majors you might like:
Marketing
Business administration and management
Information technology
Electrical and communications engineering
Economics
Digital media
Entrepreneurial studies
Management information systems
Web/multimedia management
Advertising
Computer engineering
Consumer merchandising

Questions to ask colleges:
Does the program focus primarily on the technological aspects or the business aspects of e-commerce?

Are the courses staffed with regular faculty members or with outside professionals and visiting professors? Are the faculty members engaged in the field? How do they keep current with fast-changing developments?

What computer facilities are available for students?

Career options and trends:
Web developer*; Internet business developer (analyst or manager); network engineer; product manager/marketing manager; business alliance manager; technology analyst*; venture capitalist/fund manager; investment banking analyst; market analyst*; Internet applications designer.

The long-term employment prospects for e-commerce and related professions are very strong. The Bureau of Labor Statistics describes the growth of e-commerce as "explosive" and notes that the expansion of the wireless Internet will spur the need for managers with both business savvy and technical proficiency. Technology constantly improves, and each advance presents new business opportunities.

Insider's viewpoint:
"It's exciting to be in a field where things thought to be impossible only a decade before become commonplace."

—Professor Lorin Hitt, Wharton School of Business

For more info:
Association for Computing Machinery (ACM)
1515 Broadway
17th Fl.
New York, NY 10036-5701
(800) 342-6626
www.acm.org

Entrepreneurial studies

Also known as:
Enterprise management

What it's about:
The entrepreneurial studies major teaches you how to recognize, evaluate, and respond to new business opportunities. You learn to use management skills to set up and run your own business or franchise, or to apply your creativity and energy to increase the productivity of an existing business.

Is this for you?
You might like this major if you also like: thinking of better ways to do things; learning new ideas, exploring new places, and meeting new people; starting or running a business; puzzles; sports; competition; taking charge of a group activity; taking risks.

Consider this major if you are good at: creativity; critical reading/thinking; leadership; organizing; persuading/influencing; teamwork *...or have...* initiative; perseverance; self-confidence; verbal skills.

Recommended high school prep:
English 4, math 3, lab science 3, social studies 3, and a foreign language 2-3. If available, take a business course, an economics course, and statistics.

Did you know...
...that entrepreneurship is about more than creating a new business? There are opportunities to apply entrepreneurial thinking to the corporate world, socially focused projects, venture capital financing, and a host of other possibilities.

...that in this major, risk and failure are rewarded? Because many businesses disappear within the first five years of operation, most entrepreneurship professors expect students to explore risky ideas that have a greater than 50 percent chance of failing. If an opportunity is worth taking, most likely it will be risky (otherwise, someone would have already taken it).

Typical courses in this major:
Foundations of entrepreneurship
Living the entrepreneurial experience
New ventures and the business plan
Entrepreneurial finance
Managing a growing business
Family business
Social enterprise management
Investor relations and funding
Business and tax planning
Entrepreneurial marketing
New product design and development

Concentrations:
New-venture creation; entrepreneurial finance; corporate entrepreneurship; family-controlled enterprise management; franchise, distributorship, and license ownership; entrepreneurial economics.

What the study of this major is like:
Entrepreneurial studies is the liberal arts major of business school. To be successful as an entrepreneurial major, you need to be able to see the "big picture" and still remain focused enough to take action. You can apply entrepreneurial thinking to almost any field of study—from liberal arts and social sciences to mathematics and physics—and to a variety of careers. If you have a passion for, say, theater, you can use what you learn in entrepreneurial studies to help you create, grow, and manage a drama company. An engineer with an entrepreneurial studies degree can develop innovations that are not just new, but that people will want and buy. Doctors and lawyers who work on their own can use entrepreneurial skills to make their private practices develop and thrive. Business executives can use their entrepreneurial skills to capitalize on opportunities from within their companies. This major prepares you not only for a career but also for life.

Almost all entrepreneurship programs require you to complete a core of business courses. Most programs also offer courses in developing a business plan and in entrepreneurial finance. Good programs blend academic exercises such as case studies and class discussion with hands-on experience creating an enterprise or working with an existing organization. They also provide a variety of specialty paths that may include social entrepreneurship, management of a growing business, and family-controlled enterprises.

The challenges you will face depend on the rigor of the program you attend. Students in strong programs often have to deal with real-world experiences that are outside the bounds of traditional academic activities—for instance, handling professional vendors or actual customers. In general, entrepreneurship can be emotionally demanding because you must make a personal commitment, to your stakeholders (investors, employees, your family, society), that you will create value or improve social conditions. And you don't commit to try—you commit to *do*.

The most obvious difference among programs is how much the sponsoring school or college focuses on entrepreneurship. The programs generally evolve as follows: first, a handful of entrepreneurs and management professors teach a course or two on new-venture creation; then a division of professors teach a number of concentrations in the discipline (such as new ventures or financing) with little interaction with other departments; finally, the college (or school of business) reshapes it curriculum, teaching business in the context of entrepreneurship.

Other majors you might like:
E-commerce
Business administration and management
Franchise operations
Marketing
Consumer economics
Farm and ranch management
Real estate
Small business administration/management
Arts management
Economics

Development economics
Finance

Questions to ask colleges:
How many full-time faculty members teach and research entrepreneurship as their principal endeavor? Do any of the professors have real-world experience or background as entrepreneurs?

How long has the major been offered at this college?

Which career path do graduates from the college generally follow: start-up? industry? finance?

Which kinds of resources are available for students (such as incubator space, seed funding, business plan competitions, access to industry experts and sources of funding)?

Career options and trends:
Business owner/new-venture creator*; investment banker; consultant*; sales and marketing professional*; venture capitalist; operations manager.

Entrepreneurship remains strong in both good and bad economic periods. When the economy is strong, entrepreneurs find an abundance of opportunity, and companies and consumers have more money to spend on the emerging products and services that entrepreneurs provide. When the economy is weak and jobs are scarce, entrepreneurs will spend their time creating a job rather than looking for one.

For more info:
Junior Achievement Inc.
One Education Way
Colorado Springs, CO 80906
(719) 540-8000
www.ja.org

National Foundation for Teaching
    Entrepreneurship (NFTE)
120 Wall St.
29th Fl.
New York, NY 10005
(800) 367-6383
www.nfte.com

Fashion merchandising

What it's about:

The major in fashion merchandising introduces you to all areas of the industry, including design, product development, textiles, buying, marketing, advertising, importing and exporting, sales, and retail management. You learn how to identify and acquire the fashions that customers want, and to sell those fashions.

Is this for you?

You might like this major if you also like: shopping at secondhand stores, consignment shops, and tag sales; fashion magazines; art and photography; travel; interesting people; learning about different cultures; clothes, fabrics, and fashion accessories; cosmetics; keeping up with trends; thinking creatively.

Consider this major if you are good at: attention to detail; creativity; critical reading/thinking; leadership; organizing; stress management; teamwork ...*or have...* an eye for color and design; initiative; verbal skills; writing skills.

Recommended high school prep:

English 4, math 3, lab science 3, social studies 3, and a foreign language 3–4. Courses in art, art history, and business are also recommended. Because the fashion industry operates in the global marketplace, a foreign language is highly desirable.

Typical courses in this major:

History of fashion
Textiles
Sales
Advertising
Marketing
Fashion buying
Merchandising accounting
Fashion show
Consumer behavior
Retail management
International fashion marketing
Mass marketing
Product pevelopment
Computer-aided design (CAD)

Concentrations:

In college: fashion buying; textiles; marketing and advertising; visual merchandising; retail management; apparel production.

If you go on to grad school: production; supply chain management.

What the study of this major is like:

The fashion merchandising major prepares you for a wide variety of career opportunities in the business of marketing and distributing fashion products. Fashion merchandising is an exciting field, reflecting a fast-paced global industry that shapes worldwide trends. The glitz of fashion shows and fashion magazines is the result of creative and analytical thinking, market research, and hard work.

You can learn to manage a retail firm, buy goods for a firm, or work with designers in planning an apparel manufacturer's fashion message. To acquire the communication, analytic, and computer skills necessary to succeed in this competitive industry, you will probably begin with courses in writing, speech, mathematics, history, social science, and natural science. During your first and second years, you take courses such as fashion analysis and textiles, which provide an introduction to the field. In advanced courses, you learn to organize and operate a retail clothing business; to plan, promote, and manage merchandise inventories; and to calculate retail figures for a profitable business. You may also study historical and multicultural costumes—you can later draw on this interesting subject to develop special promotions or store events.

Fashion merchandising programs can lead to either two-year (associate) or four-year (bachelor's) degrees. Associate degree programs generally include courses on the fashion industry, textiles, buying, advertising, sales, and retail management. Sometimes students who have earned a bachelor's degree in another field obtain an associate degree in fashion merchandising. Bachelor's programs in fashion merchandising include traditional liberal arts courses and professional courses in product development, importing and exporting, marketing textiles, product design, retail management, and business law. At some colleges, you can minor in marketing, textiles, and design. Many programs offer field experiences for college credit. Associate degree programs generally offer one opportunity for an industry internship. In bachelor's programs, you may be able to take more than one internship, as well as to study abroad for a semester.

The program is a combination of traditional academic courses and less traditional fashion merchandising courses. The academic courses, which are generally lectures and discussions or laboratory sessions, usually require tests and papers. The fashion merchandising classes generally include lots of hands-on work. Most faculty members and academic advisers have extensive industry experience and do not teach only from textbooks. Fashion merchandising courses are often enriched by field trips and guest speakers. Some programs offer study tours of major U.S. fashion markets (such as New York, Dallas, and Los Angeles) or of European fashion centers. In advanced courses, you are assigned group projects to help you become an effective team player. Many fashion merchandising majors hold jobs while carrying a full-time class load.

Some colleges offer only associate degree programs; some offer only bachelor's degree programs; and some offer both. Certain colleges allow you to move from an associate degree directly into the bachelor's program with no loss of credit. Other associate degree programs provide credit transfer arrangements with four-year colleges.

Other majors you might like:

Marketing
Retailing
Hospitality administration and management
Fiber/textile arts

Fashion and apparel design
Commercial/advertising art
Photography
Anthropology
Psychology
Clothing, apparel and textile studies
Family and consumer sciences
Cosmetic services

Questions to ask colleges:

Do faculty members keep current in their field by continuing to work in the industry? Do they maintain contacts in the field?

Is help available for students looking for internships? Is there a cooperative education program? Students who make contacts in the industry and do networking are likely to receive job offers before graduation.

Career options and trends:

Fashion designer; buyer*; fashion marketing executive*; showroom account executive*; fashion editor; textile designer*; import/export specialist; fashion advertising director; visual merchandiser*; merchandise manager.

Many majors think that the only careers open to them are fashion design and retail buying. However, a survey has identified 31 additional fashion careers, including computer-assisted apparel design; color forecasting; storyboard design; catalog production; mall management; private label development; Web-based retailing; online direct marketing; and fashion consulting. Experience on the job and good networking skills should lead to promotions and future job offers.

For more info:

International Textile and Apparel Association
    (ITAA)
P.O. Box 1360
Monument, CO 80132
(719) 488-3716
www.itaaonline.org

Finance

What it's about:

The finance major provides you with a general understanding of financial decision-making and an insight into the way financial markets perform. Emphasis is on the financial management function in firms and not-for-profit organizations, the valuation of financial securities, and the appropriate management of financial risk.

Is this for you?

You might like this major if you also like: family business discussions; the *Wall Street Journal*; doing research; following the stock market; investment clubs.

Consider this major if you are good at: attention to detail; creativity; critical reading/thinking; math; quantitative analysis; research; teamwork *...or have...* mental stamina; writing skills.

Recommended high school prep:

English 4, math 4 (including precalculus), lab science 3, social studies 3, and a foreign language 2–3. If possible, take computer science, economics, and statistics courses. Calculus is also helpful, although not required.

Did you know...

...that even though this major deals with money, you should not count on getting rich quick? Most entry-level positions open to undergraduate finance majors involve hard work and long hours. Students who have become successful have usually exerted considerable effort early on in their career.

...that even bright, well-motivated students often think that finance is a difficult major and that the language of finance is incomprehensible? Most majors quickly learn, however, that the subject matter is made up of simple, straightforward concepts.

Typical courses in this major:

Financial management
Financial institutions and markets
Corporate finance
Futures and options
Portfolio analysis
International finance
Investment banking
Real estate finance
Risk and insurance
Working capital management
Bank management
Investments
Accounting
Economics

Concentrations:

Corporate finance; real estate finance; investment banking.

What the study of this major is like:

In many business schools, finance classes are offered only to students in their second year or higher; because of the technical nature of the material, you'll need to have mastered a number of foundation courses. During your first two years, your general education requirements usually include mathematics, humanities, natural sciences, and social sciences courses. Most programs also require three to six credits each of economics, statistics, and accounting.

After completing the prerequisites, majors take introductory courses in finance and other functional areas of business, such as accounting, management, marketing, and management of information systems (MIS). Usually you must also take one or more courses in financial management/corporate finance and in financial institutions and markets, most of them taught in a large lecture format.

Your first finance course will probably focus on corporate financial analysis, as well as on valuation principles for financial assets such as stocks and bonds. Emphasis is on the tools of analysis, including the evaluation of financial statements and the time value of money calculations. Subsequent classes cover investments and portfolio managements, corporate finance, banking and financial institutions, and international finance. Then you're likely to take smaller classes or seminars on a variety of finance subspecialties that interest you. Because of the critical relation of economics and accounting to finance, most finance programs require at least 12 to 15 semester hours of course work in both economics and accounting.

Many finance courses require the use of computers for problem solving, to improve your facility with spreadsheet programs, statistical and financial analysis, financial forecasting, and the preparation of financial reports. Electives may be in statistics, economics, accounting, computer applications, and communications.

Most of your classes will demand a level of familiarity and comfort with quantitative analysis. This subject area may well be your biggest challenge. The style of teaching varies according to subspecialty. Most advanced corporate finance and financial management courses are taught by means of case analysis; you are presented with a situation and, either individually or as a group, you prepare a presentation. Some areas (particularly derivative securities and futures and options classes) are math-oriented; if you have not covered precalculus or other advanced math in high school, you may have to play catch-up.

Programs typically differ on whether they emphasize financial markets, investment and financial management, or corporate finance. The split will often reflect the college's evaluation of job opportunities in the locality. For example, colleges close to financial centers may stress financial markets and investments, on the assumption that many graduates will head for the financial services sector. Colleges in other regions may emphasize financial management, on the assumption that most graduates will seek employment in the finance departments of nearby corporations.

Other majors you might like:

Accounting
Actuarial science
Banking/financial services
Business administration and management
Economics
Financial planning
International finance
Investments/securities
Insurance
Management science
Real estate
Credit management

Questions to ask colleges:

What is the emphasis of the program? If you want to work in a corporate setting, a program that focuses on financial management would seem appropriate. If you'd rather work in the financial services sector, then you might prefer a program featuring the financial markets and investments.

Career options and trends:

Stockbroker; security sales representative; financial analyst; investment banker; commercial banker; portfolio or mutual fund manager; financial planner.

To be a stockbroker or to engage in securities sales and trading, you must pass the general securities registered representative examination (Series 7), administered by the National Association of Security Dealers (NASD). Portfolio managers and other investment management professionals typically acquire the postgraduate chartered financial analysts (CFA) certification, administered by the Association for Investment Management and Research (AIMR). Certification requirements for other positions vary on a state-by-state basis.

Employment in the financial services sector is necessarily cyclical, although less so at the undergraduate than at the graduate (MBA) level. Demand for financial analysts in a corporate setting is more stable. A sound training in finance is considered useful for any general management position.

Banks often employ finance majors in a variety of areas, from corporate lending to trust operations. Corporations hire graduates as financial managers, as financial controllers, or in international financial operations. Brokerage and investment banking firms offer opportunities as account executives or financial consultants for clients. Insurance companies and real estate developers also offer entry-level opportunities.

Insider's viewpoint:

"I like to think of this field as 'advanced common sense.'"

—Professor Stephen J. Brown, Stern School of Business, New York University

For more info:

National Association of Security Dealers (NASD)
One Liberty Plaza
New York, NY 10006
(212) 858-4000
www.nasdr.com

Financial Management Association International
University of South Florida College of Business
   Administration
4202 East Fowler Ave., BSN 3331
Tampa, FL 33620-5500
(813) 974-2084
www.fma.org

Hospitality administration and management

Also known as:

Hotel, restaurant, and tourism management

What it's about:

Hospitality management is a career-oriented program focusing on anticipating and satisfying the needs of the traveling visitor/guest. It prepares you for professions in the travel, lodging, food service, and recreation industries.

Is this for you?

You might like this major if you also like: travel; meeting new people; cooking; giving parties; working with people; sports; learning about different cultures; socializing in large groups; leadership roles.

Consider this major if you are good at: attention to detail; creativity; critical reading/thinking; leadership; math; teamwork *...or have...* initiative; verbal skills; writing skills.

Recommended high school prep:

English 4, math 3, lab science 3, social studies 3, and a foreign language 3–4. Courses covering accounting and geography would also be helpful. The Hospitality Business Alliance (www.nraef.org) has spearheaded the School to Career Partnership of hotels, restaurants, high schools, and colleges. High school students can earn credits that are transferable to two- and four-year colleges.

Did you know...

...that the hospitality and tourism industry is one of the top three employers in the U.S., and is estimated to be the largest industry in the world? Whether for a business conference, a rock concert, or a family wedding, the industry can provide the transportation, accommodations, meals, sound systems, security—whatever is needed to make the event happen.

Typical courses in this major:

Introduction to tourism
Management principles
Marketing
Employee labor relations
Facilities design
Lodging administration
Resort operations
Hospitality law
Hospitality finance/accounting
Geography of tourism
Festival and event management
Food service operations

Concentrations:

Casino management; community economic development; time-share management; hotel/motel management; club management; restaurant management; tourism and service management.

What the study of this major is like:

Hospitality is serious business, a fact that is often overshadowed by media images of a carefree vacation destination. The major requires a wide variety of business courses. In addition, you can expect hands-on experiences, including restaurant operation, front-office management, and housekeeping supervision. The program usually requires co-op service or an internship (which may be paid); study abroad opportunities are especially valuable in this major.

Often the faculty members have industry experience in addition to academic credentials. Moreover, there are generally several active student associations that arrange industry speakers, on-site facility visits, and fund-raisers to finance these activities.

When comparing programs, remember that there is no one best format. Colleges may take advantage of their closeness to large hotels, casinos, small resorts, or other establishments that attract business travelers and international visitors. Majors housed in a college of business tend to offer modified versions of traditional business courses. An emphasis on food and beverage operations is also a feature at some colleges. Customer/guest contact is the cornerstone of any variation of the major.

The hospitality industry thrives on outgoing, creative people. There is no routine day. The industry strives to produce satisfied guests by customizing their experience, and in a well-managed facility, employees know how to to meet the challenge. The ability to pay attention to detail is also required. A hospitality property rarely has a second chance to make a good impression. It is also a well-recognized reality that students in this major will have to adjust to the fact that they will be working while almost everyone else around them is playing! Finally, expect to travel.

Other majors you might like:
Geography
Tourism/travel management
Hotel/motel administration/management
Resort management
Interior design
Restaurant/catering management
Landscape architecture
Culinary arts and chef training
Security services management
Sports and fitness administration
Parks, recreation, and leisure studies
International business

Questions to ask colleges:
Do the faculty members have industry experience?

To what extent has the college invested in the excellence of the major by providing course-linked restaurant laboratories, design labs, computer simulations, and, in some cases, hotel facilities operated by students?

Career options and trends:
Restaurant manager; hotel/resort manager; club manager; convention and visitor's bureau director; supplier salesperson; convention and meeting planner; festival and event organizer; caterer; state tourism department employee.

This industry is sensitive to the business cycle, but opportunities always exist if you are willing to travel or relocate. Technological advancements in the form of "virtual meetings" and "virtual vacations" will have an impact on the industry (a simulation of a vacation destination may serve as an ideal preparation for an actual visit), and people who can manage that technology will be in demand. Security is a major concern and represents a rapidly growing career opportunity. However, travel agents have been hit hard by the move toward self-service, computerized travel planning.

Insider's viewpoint:
"We're doing a design-your-own-resort project, and you have to go into what type of people you want to come, what type of buildings you want to have, and where you're going to put everything. Our teacher wants us to get a realistic view of how difficult and expensive it is to develop a resort."

—Jennifer, senior, San Francisco State University

For more info:
American Hotel & Lodging Association (AHLA)
1201 New York Ave., N.W.
Suite 600
Washington, DC 20005-3931
(202) 289-3100
www.ahla.com

National Restaurant Association
1200 17th St., N.W.
Washington, DC 20036-3097
(202) 331-5900
www.restaurant.org

Human resources management

Also known as:
Personnel management

What it's about:
Majors in human resources (HR) management study employment-related issues that affect men and women at work. You study topics such as recruitment, staffing, training, performance management, compensation, labor relations, and health and safety, in order to support the goals and strategies of business organizations.

Is this for you?
You might like this major if you also like: working with people; working with numbers; serving people; helping people reach their goals; team sports; clubs; tutoring; camp counseling.

Consider this major if you are good at: counseling; listening; negotiating; organizing; quantitative analysis; teamwork *...or have...* patience; verbal skills.

Recommended high school prep:
English 4, math 3, lab science 3, social studies 3, and a foreign language 2–3. If available, the following courses would also be helpful: statistics, psychology, geography, speech, computer applications, accounting, and business.

Typical courses in this major:
Organizational behavior
Managing individuals and teams
Recruitment and staffing
Occupational safety and health
Employment law
Statistics
Compensation and benefits
Training and development
Performance management
Employee and labor relations
International human resources management

Concentrations:
Generally, none in college; but if you go on to grad school: compensation; labor relations.

What the study of this major is like:
This major prepares you to work with employees in business and nonprofit organizations. The field of human resources management is exciting because it is continually evolving. Frequent developments in the law, in judicial rulings, in technology (for example, the Internet), and in research in many specialty areas of the field require that HR professionals constantly "reinvent" themselves.

As a major, you begin with a sound foundation in the humanities, fine arts, mathematics, and social sciences, including philosophy, psychology, and sociology. In your third and fourth years, you mix business administration and HR management course work. Business administration courses include marketing, finance, accounting, statistics, information systems, and organizational behavior. Human resources management courses include the following:

Employment law. Your study of laws dealing with civil rights, pay, benefits, and health and safety, as well as important court rulings on employment relationships, will help you advise employees of their rights and obligations at work.

Recruitment and staffing. You learn how to attract potential employees and how to decide which ones to hire. Tools in decision-making include interviews, psychological and performance tests, reference checking, and screening devices to identify the most-qualified candidates.

Training and development. You learn how to create and evaluate programs designed to enhance the skills and productivity of individuals and teams.

Compensation and benefits. You focus on designing and putting in place improved systems of pay, benefits, and incentives. Key topics include social security, unemployment and workers' compensation programs, pensions, and life and health insurance.

Employee and labor relations. You examine the history and legal framework of labor-management relations, including collective bargaining, strikes, and dispute-resolution mechanisms (such as arbitration) in union and nonunion companies.

International human resources management. You examine the role of HR management in international business.

The chief difference among programs is in their emphasis on quantitative (numbers-oriented) study. For example, engineering colleges that offer the HR management major tend to require a background in mathematics. A familiarity with statistics can be a big help in courses like compensation and benefits. Staffing can also be highly quantitative, especially if professors assign readings in the research literature. Liberal arts colleges generally require fewer math courses.

Other majors you might like:
Human services
Occupational therapy
Occupational health/industrial hygiene
Industrial engineering
Psychology
Sociology
Labor/industrial relations
Counselor education
Family/community services
Hospitality administration and management
Medical records administration
Human resources development

Questions to ask colleges:
Is there an active student association chapter for HR majors on campus? Is there a professional association chapter nearby? If so, students can work as administrative aides and attend the meetings, make connections with people who have similar interests, and hear invited speakers discuss cutting-edge issues in the field.

Career options and trends:
Human resources manager; management consultant; compensation consultant; labor lawyer; office manager; pension manager; recruiter.

Many HR responsibilities are outsourced (the work is contracted to be done outside the organization), especially such tasks as benefits administration and claims processing. To remain relevant and in demand, professionals in the field need to build HR systems that "fit" the business strategy of their organization. Doing so will demonstrate the value of their services in quantifiable terms.

For more info:
Society for Human Resource Management (SHRM)
1800 Duke St.
Alexandria, VA 22314
(800) 283-7476
www.shrm.org

American Society for Training and Development (ASTD)
1640 King St., Box 1443
Alexandria, VA 22313-2043
(703) 683-8100
www.astd.org

Insurance

Also known as:

Risk management

What it's about:

As an insurance major, you learn how to help people and businesses manage risk, recover from losses, and plan for the future. You study the legal principles underlying insurance; the types of insurance (including liability, life, property); employee benefits and pension plans; the role of insurance in financial planning; risk assessment and loss evaluation; the preparation of insurance contracts (underwriting); and the way insurance companies operate.

Is this for you?

Consider this major if you are good at: attention to detail; building relationships; communicating; leadership; math; quantitative analysis; teamwork *...or have...* initiative; writing skills.

Recommended high school prep:

English 4, math 3–4, lab science 3, social studies 3, and a foreign language 3. If possible, take courses in statistics and computer applications. Courses in accounting and economics, if available, are also recommended.

Did you know...

...that insurance is an important part of business planning and creation? Many people think a career in insurance involves only selling policies and adjusting claims. But in a global economy, risk management is vital to the economies of all nations.

Typical courses in this major:

Principles of insurance
Property and liability insurance
Personal insurance
Insurance operations
Corporate risk management
Insurance accounting
Surplus lines and reinsurance
Life and health insurance
Employee benefits
Estate planning
Financial planning
Ethics of insurance

Concentrations:

Risk management; property and casualty insurance; employee benefit planning; estate planning; financial planning.

What the study of this major is like:

Individuals, families, and businesses invest in insurance to protect and provide for themselves if, one day, their situation changes or disaster strikes. Because people and businesses are increasingly looking to shield themselves from liability lawsuits (in which they may be held responsible, or liable, for harm to another) and losses resulting from serious illness, theft, or death in the family, job prospects in the insurance field continue to grow.

As an insurance professional, you will need to be a "people person" and, in particular, be successful at relationship building. You should enjoy challenges, problem solving, and multitasking. And because every insurance contract represents an act of "utmost good faith," you must also have a sense of integrity and responsibility.

In your first two years of study, you typically concentrate on the liberal arts (English, history, and sociology, for example). A core of business courses (such as accounting, economics, and management information systems) either overlaps with or follows your liberal arts courses. You usually take specialized insurance courses in your third and fourth years. These courses may focus on property loss and legal liability, as well as on employee-related plans dealing with health, disability, and retirement.

In many courses, you'll explore methods of minimizing the impact of such problems (risk management); then you'll analyze how well these methods work.

Because insurance providers are regulated by the government, you need to become thoroughly familiar with the laws and rules that apply. You learn how to assess the risks taken by profit-seeking and nonprofit organizations—and how to respond to disaster. In classes on contracts, there is a lot of required reading. You also need to develop critical-thinking skills—the skills insurance underwriters and risk managers use in assessing potential losses to which organizations may be exposed.

Courses in the major build on and relate to each other, so as you progress through your studies, you'll be applying what you learned in previous courses. Many programs encourage or require you to do internships that make use of the material you've studied in class. Internships are a good way to interact with industry professionals before you graduate.

Some programs, especially those preparing you for graduate school, are highly theoretical in their approach to insurance. Other programs take a more practical approach, teaching you the knowledge and skills you need if you plan to enter the workplace with a bachelor's degree. Some colleges incorporate the insurance major into their finance programs.

Other majors you might like:
Actuarial science
Fire protection and safety technology
Finance
Real estate
Accounting
Financial planning
Statistics
Economics
Human resources management
Security services management
Entrepreneurial studies
Medical insurance specialist

Career options and trends:
Commercial lines underwriter*; property risk analyst*; liability risk analyst*; claims adjuster*; risk

manager; broker/agent; financial planner; actuarial trainee; reinsurance intermediary or reinsurance underwriter.

Insurance executives report that one of their most critical problems is to find enough entry-level candidates educated in the professional areas discussed here.

For more info:
American Institute for CPCU/Insurance Institute
   of America
720 Providence Rd.
P.O. Box 3016
Malvern, PA 19355-0716
(800) 644-2101
www.aicpcu.org

American Risk and Insurance Association
716 Providence Rd.
Malvern, PA 19355-3402
(610) 640-1997
www.aria.org

International business

What it's about:

This major prepares you to think globally and manage complexity in an international environment and in cultures other than your own. While learning basic business management techniques and practices, you study how business is conducted in and between nations and how it is affected by the financial systems, government policies, cultural differences, management styles, and other factors that apply.

Is this for you?

You might like this major if you also like: travel; new ideas, people, and places; adventure; unusual challenges; leadership roles.

Consider this major if you are good at: creativity; critical reading/thinking; leadership; teamwork ...*or have...* cross-cultural sensitivity; initiative; patience; self-confidence; verbal skills; writing skills.

Recommended high school prep:

English 4, math 4 (including precalculus), lab science 3, social studies 3, and a foreign language 4. If possible, take calculus.

Did you know...

...that your first position will likely be a domestic, not an overseas, assignment? Within two years after graduation, you probably will not be overlooking the Eiffel Tower but will be employed stateside, working for either a domestic or a foreign multinational corporation, a bank with international operations, or perhaps an international organization such as the United Nations or the World Bank.

Typical courses in this major:

International finance
Derivatives and financial markets
International marketing
Intercultural communication
Global logistics
International operations
Advanced seminar in international business
Economics
Accounting
Management
Business in specific regions

Concentrations:

In college: international economics and trade; marketing; finance.

If you go on to grad school: developing nations; public policy; banking and finance in different regions of the world; business–government relations; international security.

What the study of this major is like:

The international business major provides you with a solid foundation in accounting, marketing, finance, and management. It includes courses that train you to analyze information about overseas businesses and that encourage you to think globally when making work-related decisions. Business environments vary from country to country, and it is increasingly important for managers to understand the causes and consequences of the differences.

As a major, you begin with basic business courses and then advance to ones with an international focus. These courses may examine how money and capital (equipment and other goods) move within and between countries; how technology is transferred between nations; and what management skills are practiced abroad. You analyze the international economic scene, study competition and interdependence, and assess cultural distinctions among nations. You may learn how to market goods and services from the United States and to evaluate the strength of overseas investments. Because an understanding of politics and government is essential to the practice of international business, you should take electives in these areas.

Most programs require you to master a foreign language. Many international business majors gain experience by studying abroad for a semester, a summer, or even a year. Sometimes there are opportunities to visit foreign companies and meet with managers working in U.S. companies.

Although some students think that the international business major is less difficult than other business majors, they soon discover it's not the case. In this major, you are expected to take a variety of demanding courses, such as international marketing, international finance, international management, and international operations. The combination of international business and another major, such as finance or marketing, can be especially challenging.

When comparing programs at different colleges, you'll find that some take an interdisciplinary approach, stressing a wide range of knowledge, with extensive offerings in the liberal arts as well as business; while others may emphasize specific areas of business, such as the ethical dilemmas you may encounter as you do international work.

Other majors you might like:
Accounting
Finance
International relations
Marketing
Tourism/travel management
Global studies
Comparative literature
International marketing
Foreign languages/literatures
Latin American studies
Asian studies
Development economics

Questions to ask colleges:
Do most of the students select international business as a solo major or as a double major?

What is the career track of the most recent graduates?

Is there a study-abroad requirement? How is it financed?

Is there a language requirement?

Are there internship opportunities with an international focus?

Career options and trends:
Derivatives trader; investment banker*; management consultant*; real estate developer; government employee; financial analyst*; brand manager; import/export manager.

Because almost all business has become global, qualified managers with an international perspective are increasingly in demand. In many quarters, in fact, graduates are assumed to have a global view of the world. Now more than ever, with the world a less certain place and with the growing volatility of the economy, business leaders who can operate effectively in a variety of cultural environments are needed.

Insider's viewpoint:
"It is exciting to see a student from Kansas form a worldview, or a student from New Jersey who had never traveled beyond the East Coast corridor discover that, contrary to her prior beliefs, the United States is not the center of the universe."

—Professor Ann-Mary Kapusta, Georgetown University

For more info:
AIESEC International
Teilingerstraat 126
3032-AW
Rotterdam, the Netherlands
+31 10 443 4383
www.aiesec.org

Washington International Trade Association (WITA)
1300 Pennsylvania Ave., N.W.
Suite 350
Washington, DC 20004
(202) 312-1600
www.wita.org

Management information systems

Also known as:
Information technology

What it's about:
In this major, you learn how to apply information technology to solve business problems. MIS prepares you to understand the function of information technologies and systems in business organizations, and it provides the knowledge and skills you will need when you analyze, design, develop, and manage information systems.

Is this for you?
You might like this major if you also like: team sports; computers and electronics; solving problems; working with people; reading; tutoring.

Consider this major if you are good at: attention to detail; creativity; critical reading/thinking; leadership; math; organizing; research; teamwork *...or have...* communication skills; initiative.

Recommended high school prep:
English 4, math 4 (including precalculus), lab science 3, social studies 3, and a foreign language 2–3. If available, take calculus, a writing course, a business or economics course, and an introductory computer science course.

Did you know...
...that computers and technology are not the sole focus of this major? The functional areas of business (operations, finance, accounting, marketing, etc.) and the information itself, as well as the people who will use the information, are primary concerns you must deal with.

Typical courses in this major:
Programming for systems development
Systems analysis and design
Database design
Database management and administration
Networks and telecommunication
Financial information systems
E-commerce
Information services management
Emerging technologies
Advanced software development
Data warehousing
Decision support technologies
Project management and practice

Concentrations:
Information systems design and development; information technology infrastructure; information services management; e-commerce; software development; information technology (IT) strategy.

What the study of this major is like:
As a management information systems major, you must be comfortable with all types of computers, software, and communications (such as phone systems). You study the design, development, and maintenance of information support systems; the ways in which they support business processes and managerial decision making; managerial approaches to effective systems development; and emerging technologies used by information systems. You learn critical-thinking and problem-solving skills so you can handle changing situations and apply the right technology to problems as they arise.

Because you'll be working in organizations and businesses, you must also learn how they operate, by studying finance, human resources, marketing, and accounting. In addition, you are often encouraged to take courses in sociology and psychology and to sharpen your communication skills (writing, speaking, and listening). By understanding human behavior and perfecting your "people skills," you learn how to be a successful link between technology and the people who use it.

Management information systems courses are taught in a variety of ways, including lectures. In labs you can use various software packages to help you with your course work: readings, quizzes, homework assignments, midterm and final examinations, individual and group projects, and term papers. Students interested in research may have opportunities to work on an independent project under the supervision of a faculty member.

When searching for an MIS job, you should have some experience in a business setting. Many programs offer local internships to give you hands-on experience, which is particularly useful for systems analysis (which emphasizes analyzing business processes) and consulting (in which you may work with several industries).

Management information systems programs may emphasize different aspects of the curriculum. For example, some programs may focus on technology-related topics, while other programs may cover more managerial topics. You can usually determine a program's focus by looking at its course offerings.

Other majors you might like:
Business communications
E-commerce
Organizational behavior studies
Software engineering
Management science
Computer engineering technology
Digital media
Organizational communication
Information technology
Computer science
Medical informatics
Computer networking and telecommunications

Questions to ask colleges:
How many classes make use of computer labs (or other advanced facilities) as part of the course work? Practical experience is essential in this field.

Are the faculty members actively involved in research or the local business community? It's important for the faculty and the curriculum to keep up with the rapid change in this field.

Is the equipment in the computer labs kept current with changing technology and maintained with good tech support? Students should learn in a

technical environment similar to the one they will work in professionally, so a fairly rapid upgrade/replacement cycle is necessary.

What sort of network access is available? Are the classrooms connected to the Internet and campus networks, either by "port per seat" or wireless networking?

Career options and trends:
Systems analyst/designer*; software developer (programmer)*; database administrator*; consultant; project manager; chief information officer (CIO); researcher.

Job opportunities are generally excellent for students with MIS knowledge and good business sense. Heightened concern over "cyber security" is also spurring demand for managers proficient in computer security issues; in fact, such knowledge is almost a prerequisite.

Students who have very specific interests and career goals ("information security analyst for medical information systems," for example) usually have excellent opportunities for specialization after they graduate. In addition, the job market rewards students who double-major and match MIS with finance, marketing, operations, or accounting.

For more info:
Association for Information Systems (AIS)
P.O. Box 2712
Atlanta, GA 30301-2712
(404) 651-0348
www.aisnet.org

Association of Computing Machinery (ACM)
1515 Broadway
New York, NY 10036-5701
(800) 342-6626
www.acm.org

Marketing

What it's about:

Marketing is concerned with the process of developing customer relationships, uncovering business opportunities, and delivering products and services to buyers. Marketing majors learn to analyze customers and their needs, and to make decisions about product design and quality, pricing, advertising, selling, and distribution.

Is this for you?

You might like this major if you also like: buying and selling; looking at quality TV commercials, magazine ads, and store window displays; working in teams; involvement with student groups; volunteerism; part-time work; thinking about what motivates people; shopping.

Consider this major if you are good at: creativity; critical reading/thinking; leadership; persuading/influencing; quantitative analysis; research; teamwork *...or have...* initiative; verbal skills; writing skills.

Recommended high school prep:

English 4, math 3, lab science 3, social studies 3, and a foreign language 2–3. If available, take computer classes that teach word processing and spreadsheet applications.

Did you know...

...that marketing isn't just about advertising and sales? Actually, it is much broader and more strategic in focus, requiring a strong understanding of accounting, economics, finance, management, information technology, and other areas.

Typical courses in this major:

Principles of marketing
Retailing
Professional selling
Sales management
Consumer behavior
Marketing communications/promotion
E-commerce/Internet marketing
Services marketing
Product development and management
International marketing
Marketing research
Marketing management
Marketing strategy
Advertising principles

Concentrations:

Generally, none in college; but if you go on to grad school: market research; e-commerce; advertising management; product management.

What the study of this major is like:

Marketing focuses on important business measures that have a central role in company performance and success, such as customer satisfaction, sales revenue, and market share. As a major in marketing, you will explore the role of marketing in business performance and examine the functions of marketing professionals.

Questions you will ask include these: How does marketing affect society, and how does society affect marketing? In which ways is research important to marketing? On what basis do consumers and industrial buyers make purchasing decisions? How are products developed, priced, and distributed? How do organizations communicate with prospective customers through advertising, personal selling, and publicity? What are the steps involved in developing, conducting, and evaluating marketing strategies? What impact do international environments have on marketing?

Marketing is an intellectually stimulating and demanding subject. Analytical, creative, and communication skills are important to success in the profession. As a marketing major, you will spend about half your time doing course work in the liberal arts. You must also take a number of business courses, including economics, statistics, accounting, finance, computer information systems, and management.

These courses may challenge you, but they are fundamental for exploring the field. For instance, you'll familiarize yourself with the two primary types of marketing. In business-to-business (B2B) marketing, products such as computers, copying machines, steel, and chemicals are sold to other businesses. In business-to-consumer (B2C) marketing, in contrast, individuals buy products (called, appropriately, "consumer products") such as appliances, cars, packaged goods (food, soap), and services such as insurance and banking. Courses in marketing principles and marketing management teach you to develop and implement plans to market products and services.

Other courses specialize in a single aspect of marketing management. Market research—usually required of all majors—teaches you to use surveys, experiments, test markets, and other techniques to obtain the information you need in making effective marketing decisions. In advertising management, you study the development, testing, execution, and monitoring of advertising campaigns. (Marketing majors are usually not involved in the creative aspects of advertising—design and production.) Courses in sales management focus on the psychology of effective selling and the recruiting, selecting, organizing, training, and motivating of salespeople. In marketing channels courses, you learn about the institutions (retailers, wholesalers, industrial distributors) that work as intermediaries between manufacturers and buyers.

Most marketing courses combine lecture with discussion. Majors usually complete a number of team and individual projects that involve research, analysis, critical thinking, creativity, information technology, writing skills, and oral presentations.

Strong marketing programs focus on ideas and theories while providing you with experiences and teaching you skills that can be easily applied in the workplace. Differences in programs may involve the relative emphasis on project-oriented, hands-on courses; the availability and use of technology; the availability of internships and student competitions; and the degree to which quantitative (math-related) skills are woven into the curriculum. Location, potential employers, and faculty members may add unique aspects to a program.

Other majors you might like:
Advertising
Communications
Fashion merchandising
Selling/sales operations
Family and consumer sciences
Economics
Public relations
Sociology
Political communications
Tourism promotion
Business statistics
Psychology

Career options and trends:
Sales representative*; sales manager; advertising and integrated marketing communications manager*; retail manager*; entrepreneur/business owner; product manager; marketing researcher; marketing consultant; customer service manager.

The broad nature of marketing directly relates to the positive job outlook. Since marketing is used in business, nonprofits, and government agencies, there are many job opportunities. Marketers are generally paid well, and the field is especially lucrative for those who earn commissions or bonuses based on performance.

For more info:
American Marketing Association (AMA)
311 South Wacker Drive, Suite 5800
Chicago, IL 60606
(800) AMA-1150
www.marketingpower.com

Real estate

What it's about:

The real estate major provides you with an understanding of the economic and social principles that affect how real property—buildings and land—is developed, financed, operated, and traded.

Is this for you?

You might like this major if you also like: working independently; making decisions; interacting with people; building things; travel; buying and selling; playing Monopoly.

Consider this major if you are good at: caring/ nurturing; critical reading/thinking; negotiating; organizing; persuading/influencing; teamwork *...or have...* initiative; patience; verbal skills; writing skills.

Recommended high school prep:

English 4, math 3, lab science 3, social studies 3, a foreign language 2–3. If they are available, take a course in statistics and a course that teaches business fundamentals and/or general legal principles.

Did you know...

...that real estate is not simply about building, buying, or selling a home? Professionals who handle appraisals, valuation, investments, and similar activities for multimillion dollar projects around the world need sophisticated training. Think about it— all businesses must operate at some physical location that they either lease or own. In either case, someone must develop the property, and someone must handle the financial transactions.

Typical courses in this major:

Real estate principles and practices
Real estate law
Financing
Appraising
Real estate investments
Residential real estate
Commercial real estate
Taxation
International real estate
Computer applications for real estate analysis
Global perspectives in real estate
Management of income properties
Real estate securities and syndications
Real estate practicums (practical applications)

Concentrations:

Real property development; construction management; real estate finance and mortgage lending; international real estate; real estate law; real estate asset management; appraising; market analysis; and a combination of real estate and almost any other professional subject offered by a typical college of business.

What the study of this major is like:

In real estate, which is an interdisciplinary field, you study various areas of business and you learn to communicate well, both in speaking and in writing. As a major, you probably won't take real estate courses until after you complete course work in the liberal arts and introductory business courses such as accounting, economics, and statistics. Then you take an introductory course covering the language of real estate, ethics, brokerage (the buying and selling of real estate), appraisal (the valuation of real estate), contracts, and property management.

In higher-level courses, you learn about the law of property ownership, transfer, and land-use control; methods of financing property purchases and sales; the effect of tax laws on real estate investments; management of office buildings and apartment buildings; and marketing techniques. In addition, you gain development and redevelopment skills, including ways of salvaging abandoned properties. You might also have the opportunity to do a residential or commercial practicum, managing the construction or development of an actual piece of property.

Real estate classes typically follow a lecture-discussion format and use case studies and computer software as problem-solving tools. Some programs in real estate focus on physical elements (sites and structures) and have studio courses to teach physical planning and construction. Other programs concentrate on theory. Try to determine which type of program interests you the most. You might be attracted to theory-oriented programs if you are considering a job in planning or government. If you want to go into the real estate business, look for programs that emphasize real-world interaction between the real estate and business communities.

The real estate field, which is constantly changing, is a challenging area. To creatively meet the needs of owners, landlords, tenants, purchasers, financiers, and others involved in property transfers, real estate professionals must understand the many aspects of the business and work well with a variety of individuals and representatives. For example, you might have to locate a site for an office building; determine how to finance the transaction; figure out a tax-saving strategy; and work with teams of attorneys, accountants, and other professionals. Successful real estate professionals need initiative, patience, and stamina to see projects through; various technical skills; and an ability to see the "big picture" of a real estate deal.

Although many graduates work in established sectors of the industry, others establish their own businesses or manage their own investments. In addition to financial rewards, the real estate field can give you the chance to set your own flexible schedule.

Other majors you might like:
Construction management
Finance
Building/property maintenance
Urban, community, and regional planning
International business
Environmental studies
Landscape architecture
Architecture
Construction technology
Surveying technology

Housing and human environments
Historic preservation

Questions to ask colleges:
How well are the computer applications used in this major kept up-to-date with advances in technology in the current real estate market?

Can students combine a real estate major with another, such as accounting, finance, international business, or entrepreneurial studies?

What are the research opportunities, internships, or other ways for students to interact with faculty members and the real estate community as a way to gain practical experience?

Career options and trends:
Real estate broker or sales agent; appraiser; consultant; mortgage banker; financial analyst; developer; tax assessor; real estate asset manager.

In order to work as a real estate sales agent or broker, you must pass a state real estate licensing exam.

Opportunities in the real estate field can be found in global and international real estate, REITs (real estate investment trusts), corporate positions, investment houses, financial and tax planning organizations, low-income housing, and government agencies dealing with housing, building regulation, and property management.

The real estate field tends to be cyclical. Swings in the economy, especially interest rates, affect agents and brokers the most. However, there are a wide variety of employment opportunities in the industry. After all, everyone needs a place to live, and a place to work. With or without cycles, this fact won't change.

For more info:
National Association of Realtors (NAR)
430 North Michigan Ave.
Chicago, IL 60611-4087
www.realtor.org

Communications

When you are reading a newspaper, you're probably aware that reporters, photographers, and editors work on it, along with Web designers for the online version. But a news organization is also a business. Many professionals focus on the advertising and business operations.

"Advertising pays the bills and some see it growing in influence on the news product," observes Patsy G. Watkins of the University of Arkansas's journalism department.

A major in communications—which might be in advertising, digital media, journalism, pubic relations, radio and television, or in communications itself—is a gateway to jobs on the content and business sides of broadcasting, telecommunications, and other media and sectors. You might become a writer, designer, producer, or announcer; or you might work in sales, management, human resources, the legal department, or research.

"Most students began their post-baccalaureate work, not in the communications field but in general business and industry, usually sales," says Professor Bruce E. Gronbeck of the University of Iowa.

"Students considering radio and TV don't realize how satisfying it is to work in less visible positions which are crucial to the success of any media production," says Professor John Doolittle of American University. "News producers, radio sales staff, video shooters, and Web designers are in very demanding and rewarding jobs."

"Understanding business and the needs of the commercial world is integral to succeeding in the field," adds Professor Joel A. Kline of Lebanon Valley College. "Opportunities are also found in public relations and the government."

New jobs in communications are linked to the latest technologies. Emerging majors on campus get students up-to-date on computer-assisted, electronic, and interactive communications; visual journalism and video graphics; strategic communications; health communications; human interface design; new media; multimedia arts; and Internet advertising and marketing. Many media are coming together so students will have to be familiar with a variety of methods of communication.

"To communicate requires writing skills, visual skills, and technological skills. When students master these perspectives, they can enter many different fields," Kline says.

Get the story on colleges

To choose a college, do some investigative reporting. Get out your notebook or video camera, burn some shoe leather, check the library, read guidebooks; if possible, visit colleges and talk to people who may be helpful. Or send e-mails instead (look on a college's Web site for details). Either way, get the scoop about colleges, including schools of journalism, communications, mass communications, media studies, business, humanities, social sciences, liberal arts, and arts and sciences.

Colleges have many different ways of covering communications.

"The single most important dividing line is between programs that are practically oriented and those that are built around a liberal arts philosophy," explains Gronbeck. "Some colleges offer professionally oriented courses, believing that students are completing a business-type degree aimed at the communication industries. Others are constructed around the philosophy that 'communication' is such a general notion that training should be focused on the analytical and speaking/writing skills that students can bring to any entry-level position."

If you did a TV series on choosing a college, it would have five episodes: Faculty, Courses, Facilities, Internships, and Jobs. Here are some ideas for your script.

Episode One: Faculty. Are they experienced professionals? What are the backgrounds of instructors teaching the courses? Are professors easy to meet with outside class?

Episode Two: Courses. When must you declare your major and what are the required courses? Is the focus on technical skills or creative and thinking skills?

Episode Three: Facilities. What's in the computer lab? How new is the broadcast equipment like cameras and editing platforms? How often is the hardware and software updated? How much access will you have to the studios and labs? Can you work for the campus newspaper, radio or TV station, or other publications and outlets? Are they run by the faculty or independently?

Episode Four: Internships. What kinds of internship programs are offered and what are the typical assignments? Will the college help you land an internship at a broadcast or other outlet (on or off campus)? Is the campus near a city with lots of communications opportunities? Will you put together a portfolio or reel of your projects to show your talents to future employers? (At this point in your script, cut to an interview with an expert like advertising maven Thomas A. Bowers, University of North Carolina at Chapel Hill.) "Potential employers will ask for samples of work the student did on campus publications or at internships. Having such experience is absolutely essential."

Episode Five: Jobs. Will you get help finding a job after graduation? Where are graduates working now and what kinds of work are they doing? How many go on to law school or graduate work in communication studies? (Show a graphic here of the top five careers for graduates, then cut to Watkins.) "A variety of career opportunities are available for people with skills in researching, writing, and presenting information clearly."

Fade to black and roll credits.

Advertising

What it's about:

Advertising majors learn to create and distribute paid messages in communication media in order to persuade people to accept an idea, change attitudes, or to take action. Your studies include analysis of customers, markets, and media, as well as advertising's history, regulation, and social and economic effects.

Is this for you?

You might like this major if you also like: writing; art and design; being curious about a wide variety of subjects; keeping up on current trends and current events.

Consider this major if you are good at: active listening; attention to detail; creativity; critical reading/thinking; quantitative analysis; spatial thinking/analysis; teamwork *...or have...* initiative; verbal skills; writing skills.

Recommended high school prep:

English 4, math 3, lab science 3, social studies 3, and a foreign language 2–3. Courses in art, business, and computer applications are also recommended.

Did you know...

...that most advertising agencies hire copywriters and art directors who have attended portfolio-preparation schools that offer specialized, advanced training to college graduates? Such preparation has become essential for creative positions.

...that creativity in advertising is not limited to copywriting and design? Creativity—the approach to a familiar problem from a fresh perspective—is important, as well, in media planning, research, and account development.

Typical courses in this major:

Principles of advertising
Copywriting
Advertising design
Media planning
Advertising campaigns
Advertising management
New media and Internet design
Creative strategy
Market research
Account planning
Advertising sales
Retail advertising
Consumer behavior
Social and economic aspects of advertising
Mass media law
Marketing

Concentrations:

Copywriting; design; account management.

What the study of this major is like:

Advertising programs are usually found in schools of journalism and mass communications and are influenced by the strong liberal arts emphasis in such institutions. Don't be surprised to find out that you will probably be required to choose two-thirds of your courses from outside the major. A typical major consists of four or five advertising courses; a few courses in news writing, mass media law, and ethics; and many liberal arts courses. You are advised or required to take at least one course in marketing, usually taught in a school of business.

Advertising courses are a mix of theory and practical experience. You are introduced to concepts and principles that you will use when you develop advertising campaigns. In most courses, you will be expected to make oral presentations, an essential part of advertising. Because much of the work in advertising is done by teams of people, advertising courses typically require group projects. All advertising courses stress clear, concise writing.

Courses in the major cover such areas as copywriting, in which you learn to create the text of your ads; media planning, in which you decide where your ads will appear (TV, magazine, and so on); and research, in which you explore ways to conduct surveys and other analyses of your "targets": those whom the ads are intended to persuade. Advertising art and design is usually not a big part of this major at most colleges. If you have artistic talent and intend to pursue a career in advertising art, you should consider majoring in commercial art or graphic design instead.

You should be prepared to balance several responsibilities and assignments at one time. In addition, you may be frustrated occasionally by the difficulty of arranging project meetings with group members who are equally time-pressed (this is actually good preparation for the real world). Courses in research or in media planning require some quantitative analysis, so you might have to brush up your math skills.

It may be difficult to land a full-time job after graduation without some experience. Opportunities to get experience include internships at an advertising agency, newspaper, or broadcasting station, and part-time jobs with a campus newspaper or radio station. Colleges in or near cities can usually offer more internship and employment opportunities than rural colleges can. Although studying advertising in an accredited program is not essential for employment in the profession, the major can help open doors for you. Because of its stress on broad knowledge, critical analysis, and communication skills, it can be valuable preparation for other careers as well.

Other majors you might like:
Journalism
Broadcast journalism
Marketing
Commercial/advertising art
Public relations
Business administration and management
Communications
English
Graphic design
Photojournalism
Fashion merchandising
Web page/multimedia design

Questions to ask colleges:
What is the professional experience of the professors? In a strong program, at least some of the professors have worked as professionals in advertising.

What are the opportunities for internships and other hands-on experience? Potential employers often ask for samples of work you did for campus media organizations or on internships.

Career options and trends:
Copywriter*; media planner*; account executive*; advertising salesperson; account planner.

After graduate study, you may pursue work as an advertising research specialist.

When businesses suffer, advertising budgets often take the first hit. However, advertisers are just beginning to successfully harness the power of the Internet. If you understand how the various forms of media are evolving and can apply that understanding, you will be at an advantage.

Insider's viewpoint:
"I love the fact that our knowledge of human behavior will never be complete and that even the best advertising campaigns will not always be successful. Long live the independent-minded consumer!"

—Professor Thomas A. Bowers, University of North Carolina at Chapel Hill

For more info:
Accrediting Council on Education in Journalism and Mass Communications (ACEJMC)
Stauffer-Flint Hall, University of Kansas
1435 Jayhawk Blvd.
Lawrence, KS 66045-7575
(785) 864-3973
www.ku.edu/~acejmc

Communications

What it's about:

In the communications major, you examine the many ways in which information and ideas are exchanged in modern society. You may study the history of political and religious speeches; write reviews of TV programs and films; explore the sociology of interpersonal and group dynamics; evaluate the impact of the media on individuals and society; and inquire into the ethics of communication.

Is this for you?

You might like this major if you also like: group discussions; writing; tutoring or camp counseling; volunteering for political/service organizations; the Internet; movies, radio, and television; student government; making presentations; working on the school newspaper or yearbook.

Consider this major if you are good at: active listening; caring/nurturing; creativity; critical reading/thinking; leadership; spatial thinking/analysis; teamwork *...or have...* verbal skills; writing skills.

Recommended high school prep:

English 4, math 3, lab science 3, social studies 3, and a foreign language 2–3. If possible, take courses in speech, journalism, debate, and theater. It is also valuable to work on the yearbook or newspapers; at a radio station; as a DJ at dances; or with political, service, or outreach organizations.

Did you know...

...that after college, most majors begin working in business and industry—usually in sales? Communications is one of the most popular gateways into a wide variety of jobs in business and industry.

Typical courses in this major:

History of public address
Interpersonal communications
Organizational communications
Communications theory
Advertising
Media criticism
Interviewing
Radio/TV/film production
Public relations
Public speaking
Argumentation
Mass media and society
Group communications
Persuasion
Broadcast journalism
Ethical and legal foundations of media practices

Concentrations:

In college: speech communications; journalism; advertising; public relations; political communications; broadcasting; film studies; media studies; theater arts.

If you go on to grad school: rhetorical studies; communications technologies; new media/technologies; computer-assisted communications.

What the study of this major is like:

The study of communication is as old as the writings of the ancient Greeks on rhetoric and politics. Today, social and electronic communications are explored from historical, critical, theoretical, ethical, and sociological perspectives.

The communications major blends practical training with a liberal arts education. To fulfill humanities requirements, you will probably select courses in history, communications theory, media criticism, social science, and public policy. Most courses in communications include both theory and practice. For example, you will be expected to analyze situations and then communicate your conclusions through speaking, writing, negotiating, listening, or producing.

Typically, you begin the major with either an introductory course or communication skills courses (public speaking, reporting, radio production). Large lecture classes are supplemented by small discussion sections. In performance and production courses, which are usually small, you present oral or media work for evaluation. Media production courses train you in preproduction (planning and writing), production (shooting), and postproduction (editing). Some colleges have up-to-date studios, whereas others send you to work in the field. In courses in public speaking, interviewing, group communications, and argumentation, you learn to prepare and deliver messages and to listen carefully to what others have to say.

Third- and fourth-year courses generally emphasize theory and research, history and criticism, and advanced practical work. You may read and discuss videotapes of presidential speeches, First Amendment court cases, or other documents that call on your critical-thinking skills. You are graded on your mastery of the readings, your contributions to class discussions, and your ability to analyze what you have read and observed.

Internships are a popular feature of many programs: you may spend a few hours a week or an entire semester getting on-the-job experience in a workplace that interests you, such as a radio station, an advertising firm, an insurance agency, a cable TV company, or a customer relations department. You may also spend a semester abroad studying the politics, theater, mass media, or cinema of another culture.

The biggest difficulty in choosing a college or a program is to sort through the many communications programs that are available. Some may focus on speech; media studies; dramatic or theater arts; broadcasting, film, or multimedia arts; humanities or social sciences; or print or electronic journalism. Some programs may also stress speech disorders, pathology, or audiology.

The most important distinction to consider is whether a program focuses on practical applications or is based on a liberal arts philosophy. Programs that emphasize skills and a professionally oriented curriculum offer a business-type degree aimed at the communications industries, such as journalism, sales, and health services. Other programs stress the analytical, speaking, and writing skills useful for a wide variety of entry-level positions. Some programs also encourage you to take elective courses outside the major, to give your studies a particular focus. For example, you might take electives in social work to prepare for a career in the service industries, or political science electives if you plan to work for the government.

Other majors you might like:
Journalism
Business communications
Media studies
Design/visual communications
Multimedia
Graphic design
Photography
English
Drama and theater arts
Technical and business writing
Speech/rhetorical studies
Web page/multimedia design

Questions to ask colleges:

What are the five most frequent careers graduates pursue? How many majors each year go on to law school, an MBA program, or graduate work in communications?

Is there an internship program? If so, what are some typical assignments?

Does the college have the up-to-date electronic equipment that prepares students for the communications technologies they'll be using on the job?

Career options and trends:

Sales associate*; staff worker in political, governmental, or social service organizations*; business/industry management trainer*; communications research specialist; communications consultant.

Communications majors also go on to careers in law, management, human resources, the broadcasting industry (radio, TV, cable), the telecommunications industry, research, public advocacy, and agencies of the municipal, state, and national governments.

Because this major often leads to careers in business and sales, graduates usually find work quickly. Entry-level positions in radio, television, and cable operations are still obtainable, mostly because of turnover. Entering the film industry remains difficult. Social service positions are relatively stable.

Insider's viewpoint:

"We had to research the court system and the communication theory that was tied to it. We looked at footage from the Rodney King case, and 'Court TV' and 'Judge Judy.' Bringing all of these elements together, deciding what was most important, and then arguing our conclusion took a lot of critical thought."

—Molly, senior, University of Colorado

For more info:

National Communication Association (NCA)
1765 N St., N.W.
Washington, DC 20036
(202) 464-4622
www.natcom.org

Digital media

Also known as:
New media design and studies
Interactive media

What it's about:
Digital media is an interdisciplinary major that combines new communication technology with art, business, English, and computer science. A degree in digital media prepares you to develop and manage digital communications media for a wide range of applications.

Is this for you?
You might like this major if you also like: writing; Web site design; art; business; computers; explaining ideas with writing and graphics.

Consider this major if you are good at: attention to detail; creativity; critical reading/thinking; organizing; quantitative analysis; spatial thinking/analysis; teamwork *...or have...* initiative; mechanical facility; writing skills.

Recommended high school prep:
English 4, math 3, lab science 3, social studies 3, and a foreign language 2–3. If possible, take a journalism or writing course, as well as an intro to computer science or programming course, a Web site design course, and a computer graphics course.

Did you know...
...that you don't need a strong art background in order to succeed in this major? Since digital media is interdisciplinary, almost anyone with an interest in technology can find an enjoyable area of concentration.

Typical courses in this major:
Introduction to computer programming
Fundamentals of networks and databases
Two-dimensional design
Multimedia design
Writing for digital media
E-commerce
Information law and ethics
Introduction to digital design
Project management seminar
Web site management
Senior project

Concentrations:
In college: design; art history; e-commerce and e-business; programming and network infrastructure; writing for digital media; teaching technology.

If you go on to grad school: multimedia design; educational instructional design.

What the study of this major is like:
Digital media blends theoretical and applied concepts. The major requires you to develop skills in many different areas, some of which will be new to you when you begin college. Few high school students are familiar with the complete digital media field, including the computer programming, graphics, business, and writing topics that most colleges teach in this major.

Early on in your first semester, you should be ready to do a lot of reading in your studies. Although a digital media program has many hands-on applications, the theory behind the field comes from your readings. Most programs teach only basic math; they focus, instead, on creative projects. Because you take fewer math courses than computer science and engineering majors, the digital media course load is generally more manageable.

You do much of the creative work—writing, art, and media programming—in a computer lab. Here you transform an idea into a completed project. Other ways of approaching digital media, such as from business, law, and ethics perspectives, are usually presented in a lecture or discussion format. Students are sometimes stressed by the amount of creative projects they are expected to complete in a semester. Developing texts, graphics, and media programs for several courses can be a strain, especially for students who are not used to using computers as instruments for stimulating the imagination.

Because digital media is an emerging field, the content of majors varies among colleges. Many colleges teach only visual and written components; they focus on the design of a communication instead of its technology or commercial elements. Some colleges combine technology and commercial elements into a program that stresses business technology. Other schools do not treat the program as interdisciplinary and offer it from the art department, with an emphasis on graphic design.

Other majors you might like:
Web page/multimedia design
Graphic design
Web/multimedia management
Information technology
Business communications
Media studies
E-commerce
Public relations
Technical and business writing
Management information systems
Animation

Questions to ask colleges:
Do the program's faculty members have both academic and applied experience in the field? A mixture of academic researchers, consultants, and practitioners ensures that you learn about a wide variety of digital media.

Does the program seek to develop students' creative and critical-thinking skills or only to develop software competency?

Career options and trends:
Multimedia designer; information architect; Web site content manager; e-business analyst; graphic artist; public relations manager; technology support specialist; sales and marketing specialist; Webmaster; e-business manager.

Some technology positions need network or application certifications that are relevant to the type of products the company uses or installs.

There is demand for digital media specialists in all areas where communication is a primary function—marketing, public relations, advertising, government, education, the arts—but to be successful requires an understanding of the needs of business and the commercial world.

For more info:
Information Technology Association of America
  (ITAA)
1401 Wilson Blvd.
Suite 1100
Arlington, VA 22209
(703) 522-5055
www.itaa.org
Internet Society (ISOC)
1775 Wiehle Ave.
Suite 102
Reston, VA 20190-5108
(703) 326-9880
www.isoc.org

Journalism

What it's about:

Beginning with a broad introduction to the liberal arts and sciences, journalism majors learn how to find information and how to communicate their findings through writing, speech, and other forms of expression, such as graphics, video, and still photography. You also practice the skills you'll need for working with a newspaper, radio and TV station, advertising or public relations agency, and Web media.

Is this for you?

You might like this major if you also like: reading and writing; being in the know; current events; history; politics; photography; Web surfing; sports; movies; digging for facts; research; adventure; working independently or in groups.

Consider this major if you are good at: attention to detail; creativity; critical reading/thinking; meeting deadlines; organizing; research ...*or have...* curiosity; initiative; perseverance; verbal skills; writing skills.

Recommended high school prep:

English 4, math 3, lab science 3, social studies 4, and a foreign language 3-4. Being active on your high school media—newspaper, yearbook, literary magazine, and/or, if available, television and radio—is also recommended. But many students enter college with little or no high school journalism experience and do very well.

Did you know...

...that there is a strong emphasis on writing skills in this major? You will be required to write, write, write—whether for print news, broadcast news, or advertising and public relations.

...that to succeed in this major, you must do more than merely go to class? You have to connect personally with faculty members, seek out mentors (instructors or others who give you guidance and support), make professional contacts, and get real-world experience through school media and internships.

Typical courses in this major:

News reporting methods and techniques
Copyediting
Magazine writing
Photojournalism
Writing for the Web
Feature writing
Public affairs reporting
Broadcast news
Media law
Ethics
Newspaper management
Digital media
The documentary
Sports writing and reporting
Political reporting
Media campaigns

Concentrations:

In college: broadcast journalism; print journalism; public relations; newmedia technology; photojournalism.

If you go on to grad school: specialized reporting (such as political, financial, international, agricultural); investigative reporting; documentary studies.

What the study of this major is like:

Students who plan to enroll in a journalism program often say they have so many interests they can't decide on a major—they want to major in everything. As a journalism major, in fact, you'll have the chance to explore many subjects. You may even be able to make a difference in people's lives—for example, by reporting about someone unfairly convicted of a crime, or by developing a promotional campaign for a nonprofit agency.

Majors typically take many courses in the liberal arts and sciences, to gain a broad understanding of history, geography, political science, economics, literature, and the natural sciences. This comprehensive background will help you understand the context of the information you will, as a journalist, gather and report.

Overall, your course work emphasizes writing, reporting, and technology skills, as well as professional practices and values. Assignments develop your ability to express yourself using language, computers, software, and recording equipment. You also take courses in media law, ethics, and the fundamentals of journalism (emphasizing the *Associated Press Stylebook*.) Most journalism programs arrange for you to intern with a professional media organization.

Typically, about 60 percent of your courses will cover skills and 40 percent will be "topical" courses, devoted to a particular subject. Skills course work is heavily hands-on, with a great deal of personal instruction. The main challenges you are likely to face are heavy writing assignments and the emphasis on meeting deadlines. Journalism course work is very much project-based—you will probably have assignments in most of your courses, every semester. Frequently, course projects involve helping local community groups to develop ad campaigns or publications. You are also encouraged to participate in one or more of the college media outlets: you might report for a student newspaper, magazine, or radio station.

Electives you can choose might include sports journalism; government and the media; electronic publishing; Web design; computer-assisted reporting; television documentary studies; gender and the media; television and society; visual literacy; business reporting; and the presidency and the press.

At some colleges, you can't become a journalism major until you have completed a certain number of credits, and you can't join a student media organization until a specified point in your academic progress. Other schools admit you as a major in your first year and encourage you to join student media organizations from day one. Generally, the policy depends on the size of the school; larger schools tend to be more restrictive.

And in some journalism programs, you will be trained to work in the most important types of media—print, broadcast, and the Internet—rather than specialize in one of these areas. This curriculum follows what is called the "convergence" approach. Other programs have specialty divisions, but you can also choose to develop skills in a second area of journalism. For example, a still photojournalist may also learn video shooting and editing.

Other majors you might like:
History
Radio and television
Communications technology
Community organization/advocacy
Public relations
Political science
Agricultural communications
Peace studies
Marketing
International relations
Media studies
Global studies

Questions to ask colleges:
What student media are available? How and when can a student join the college newspaper, radio station, or other type of media? Is there faculty supervision, or are the media outlets independent?

Is there an internship program? Is an internship required? Are students assisted in finding internships?

Are students and student organizations encouraged to enter regional and national competitions?

Career options and trends:
Print or online news reporter, editor, or photographer*; broadcast reporter, producer, or anchor*; advertising copywriter*; public relations manager*; magazine or Web editor; freelance writer (magazine, Web, newsletter); photojournalist; news outlet manager; Web designer.

There is stiff competition for reporting jobs at large newspapers, broadcast stations, and national magazines, so most entry-level positions are in small-town or suburban media. Large newspapers and broadcasters require 3 to 5 years of postgraduate experience and usually prefer job applicants who have a degree and/or experience in a specific subject area, such as economics, business, science, or politics.

While job prospects for newspaper journalists is expected to decline, some growth is projected in broadcast journalism, and strong growth is predicted for employment in online media. Recent surveys of journalism graduates indicate that the best-paid entry-level jobs are with Internet organizations.

Insider's viewpoint:

"We came into class one morning, and the professor gave us the topic for a newspaper story and said we had an hour and a half to complete it. We had to run around campus gathering information and opinions, which is difficult at 8:30 a.m. because no one is awake yet. It was good experience, though."

—Courtney, senior, SUNY Binghamton

For more info:

American Society of Newspaper Editors (ASNE)
11690B Sunrise Valley Drive
Reston, VA 20191-1409
(703) 453-1122
www.asne.org

Public relations

Also known as:
Image management
Organizational communication

What it's about:
Public relations majors examine how to manage the public image and communications of an organization or individual (such as an entertainer or a political candidate). You learn how to shape the appropriate message, and you'll explore the best ways to get your message across. You also master technical and managerial skills, such as writing and producing printed and visual materials; and study strategic planning and problem solving.

Is this for you?
You might like this major if you also like: writing; public speaking; planning parties, club activities, or fund-raising events; team sports; working on the school newspaper.

Consider this major if you are good at: creativity; critical reading/thinking; organizing; persuading/influencing; research; teamwork ...*or have...* "people skills"; initiative; verbal skills; writing skills.

Recommended high school prep:
English 4, math 3, lab science 3, social studies 4, and a foreign language 3–4. If available, take a journalism course, a business course, and a computer applications course.

Did you know...
...that this field involves technical and analytical skills, not just communication skills? Some students think that public relations is a "soft" business major; but the job of a PR professional is not only about managing image and message, but also about showing how the results of these efforts affect the bottom line. To do this effectively requires familiarity with statistics, research methods, finance, and communications technologies.

Typical courses in this major:
Fundamentals of public relations
Writing for mass media
Writing for the Web
Media planning
Principles of advertising
Public relations research
Public relations writing
Speech writing
Media law and ethics
Media campaigns
Visual communications and graphic design
Video production
Image management
Crisis management
Case studies in public relations management

Concentrations:
Corporate public relations; consumer relations; employee relations; public affairs; nonprofit public relations; financial or investor relations; publicity and media relations; international public relations.

What the study of this major is like:
Public relations courses address three aspects of professional work. One group of courses—writing, graphic design, and video production—focuses on the techniques you'll need in publicizing a client's message: the how of communication.

The second group of courses—social sciences, humanities, natural sciences, mathematics, foreign language, business, and fine arts—provides an understanding of the social and cultural environment: the what of communications.

The third group of courses, which explore why clients communicate with the public, includes public opinion, research methods, strategic planning, problem solving, and ethics. You learn how to obtain and evaluate feedback from the public and how to incorporate the information into business strategies.

Most public relations programs are offered by schools or departments of journalism or mass communications. Sometimes the major is in a department of speech or communications, where it may be called organizational communications. Wherever the major is housed, you take about 25 percent of your courses in public relations, primarily in writing and other skills and in methods of planning, developing, and implementing public relations campaigns (or projects). The rest of the courses are usually in the liberal arts and sciences.

Majors are encouraged to complete a minor or to take most of their electives in business (including accounting, finance, and marketing), especially if they plan to do public relations work for a corporation or for a firm that represents corporate clients.

A highlight of the major is an internship, which may be required, during the academic year or in the summer. On-the-job experiences allow you to apply, in the real world, the principles and techniques you learned in the classroom. When looking for that first job after graduation, you'll need a portfolio of articles, scripts, presentations, or other work that illustrates your ability. Writing for your college TV or radio station or student newspaper is another excellent way to gain experience and material for your portfolio.

Many public relations courses are taught in a laboratory format; you complete in-class writing, editing, and production assignments. Other courses use the case study approach, in which you evaluate an actual or hypothetical public relations presentation. This type of exercise helps you develop skills in problem solving and critical analysis. In-class discussion and debate give you the opportunity to express and defend your opinions. You will most likely be required to participate in a capstone project, in which you plan, develop, implement, and evaluate a public relations campaign, working alone or in a group organized along the lines typically encountered in the working world.

Other majors you might like:
Advertising
Journalism
Marketing

Music management
Public administration
Community organization/advocacy
Human resources management
Media studies
Graphic design
Organizational behavior studies
Hospitality administration and management
Science, technology, and society

Questions to ask colleges:
Is the program accredited by the Association for Education in Journalism and Mass Communication?

How does the program include technical and research skills in the curriculum?

Career options and trends:
Public relations manager; corporate communications manager; publicist; media relations specialist; event planner; speech writer; public opinion researcher; public relations agency representative; promoter; nonprofit or educational fund-raiser.

Over the next decade or so, employment opportunities in the public relations field are expected to grow much faster than in many other professions. Nevertheless, there will be stiff competition for entry-level jobs because the major is so popular. In fact, there is currently a shortage of public relations instructors around the country. Prospects will be best for graduates who combine their public relations degree with business courses and who have internship or related work experience.

For more info:
Public Relations Society of America (PRSA)
33 Maiden Lane
New York, NY 10038
(212) 460-1400
www.prsa.org

Radio and television

What it's about:

The radio and television major prepares you for a career in all areas of these two types of media, including writing, editing, production, performance, and sales. In addition, you develop an understanding of the history, structure, regulation, and functions of the electronic media and explore the ethical issues you may encounter when you deal with radio and TV audiences.

Is this for you?

You might like this major if you also like: telling or writing stories; knowing about everyday events and issues; expressing your ideas and opinions; technology; taking pictures or making videos.

Consider this major if you are good at: active listening; attention to detail; creativity; critical reading/thinking; organizing; teamwork *...or have...* initiative; verbal skills; writing skills.

Recommended high school prep:

English 4, math 3, lab science 3, social studies 3, and a foreign language 2–3. If possible, participate in student media activities such as radio and TV stations, newspapers, and yearbooks.

Did you know...

...that you don't have to be "on the air" to have a satisfying job in radio or television? Most news producers, radio sales staff, video shooters, and Web designers have demanding but rewarding careers. You are also more likely to find a job behind the scenes.

Typical courses in this major:

Introduction to mass communication
History of broadcasting
Writing for the electronic media
Fundamentals of video production
Radio/television news producing
Mass media and society
New communications technology
Media law and regulation
On-air performance
Interactive media
Sound design/production
Studio television production
Marketing and sales

Concentrations:

In college: television production; radio production; broadcast news; media management; media studies; integrated media/multimedia/new media; audio recording; media sales; media promotion.

If you go on to grad school: telecommunications policy; audience studies; law and policy; media and society; international communication; screenwriting.

What the study of this major is like:

In this major, you quickly discover that radio and television production requires teamwork. You must learn to cooperate with others on the job and to be both a follower and a leader. Any glamour that the mass media might have had for you can swiftly fade when you are faced with deadlines, difficult-to-meet standards for scripts, and technical problems. Opportunities to practice and polish your writing, performance, and other creative skills make your training both demanding and satisfying.

In a four-year program, about 50 percent of your courses are in the liberal arts—history, literature, social sciences, and natural sciences—and most of these are taken in your first two years. An introductory course in mass media provides an overview of the social, political, economic, and historical factors that affect all media in our society. Elective courses in the major allow you to focus on one media or the other, or to concentrate on certain aspects of the industry.

In addition to lecture classes, you receive hands-on experience in lab courses and field assignments. This training can include working in a production studio, interviewing people outside of class, or using specialized communication gear such as audio and video recorders, editing equipment, and lighting. Two-year programs are usually more technically oriented, or designed for specific occupations in the industry.

Colleges near large cities usually offer numerous opportunities for internships and part-time employment during the academic year. On the other hand, newspapers and radio stations in rural or suburban communities may allow you to do the kind of work that students in metropolitan areas would not be permitted to do. Student-run radio and television organizations can provide you with excellent outside-of-class opportunities. Colleges with a tradition of media-related programs, such as journalism, advertising, and the arts, are likely to emphasize those areas in their radio and television offerings.

Other majors you might like:
Journalism
Film/cinema studies
Electrical and communications engineering
Drama and theater arts
Business communications
Recording arts
Photographic/film/video technology
Cinematography and film/video production
Media studies
Broadcast journalism
Photojournalism
Telecommunications technology

Questions to ask colleges:
What kinds of equipment are available? Is the equipment updated as necessary, and adequate to meet the needs of everyone in the program?

What kind of jobs do graduates of the program typically obtain?

Career options and trends:
Producer*; news reporter*; station manager; production assistant*; camera operator; disk jockey; Web master; sales executive; entertainment lawyer.

Mergers, new technology, and the growth of alternative media sources are reshaping the radio and TV industries. Corporate media "families" may now

include cable and/or broadcast TV stations, film studios, radio stations, newspapers, magazines, and Internet companies. If you have skills and experience that can be applied in two or more of these areas, such as the ability to write for both TV news and the Web, you may have a better chance of getting a job with a media company. Camera operators and editors are projected to have the best job prospects through 2014.

For more info:
International Radio and Television Society (IRTS)
420 Lexington Ave., Suite 1601
New York, NY 10170
(212) 867-6650
www.irts.org

National Broadcasting Society, Alpha Epsilon Rho
   (NBS, AERho)
P.O. Box 4206
Chesterfield, MO 63006
(866) 272-3746
www.nbs-aerho.org

Computer and information sciences

Entire university departments are devoted to this one invention. It has spawned multi-billion-dollar businesses and become an indispensable tool in nearly all fields of endeavor. Computers are certainly worth knowing about.

Perhaps because of news accounts of computer jobs going overseas, the number of incoming college freshman planning to major in computer science plummeted more than 60 percent between 2000 and 2004, according to the Computing Research Association. But despite global competition, more IT jobs are available in the United States today than at the height of the dot com boom, reports the Association for Computing Machinery.

The demand for workers should far exceed supply—in fact, computer occupations are expected to be among the fastest-growing fields in the United States. Employment in information systems design and related services is expected to grow 40 percent in the decade ending in 2014. Computer and mathematical science occupations, projected to add 967,000 jobs, are among the fastest-growing professions. The trend toward off-shoring does adversely affect programmers and support specialists, but integrating and designing systems still needs to be done on site.

"One thing I can say for sure is people with a good computer science education in the next 15 years will have tons and tons of opportunities to choose from," Microsoft Chairman Bill Gates told students at the University of Michigan in 2005. "If there's a great field to go into, this is it."

If you're leaning toward a computer major, you probably already have a good deal of experience using computers for e-mail and surfing the Web, doing homework, and gaming. Maybe you've used graphics, animation, or multimedia systems. People probably come to you for help with their computers. You may also enjoy doing math and puzzles and building mechanical, electrical, or electronic gadgets.

But how do you turn your familiarity with computing into a challenging and rewarding college education and career? First, get to know how computer science is taught and which areas of the field attract your interest.

Computer science provides a foundation in the theory and design of computer systems. The information sciences majors add an understanding of the way people use the technologies. After all, an information system includes not just the computers, programs, and networks but also the way individuals, organizations, and society use these powerful tools.

"One can view the world of computing as a continuum," explains Anne Marchant, Department of Applied Information Technology, George Mason University. "At one end, you have fields like computer science and electrical engineering that focus on the development of hardware and software. At the other end, you have fields like information science ... and management information systems. Information technology is in the middle. Practitioners in the field of IT integrate technologies to build and administer information infrastructure."

Since computers influence just about every profession, you may also be interested in other chapters in this book that discuss majors including management information systems, digital media, electrical and communications engineering, computer engineering technology, drafting and design technology, graphic design, and animation. Computer sciences are also applied to emerging areas of study such as bioinformatics, computer forensics, mobile/wireless computing, digital media design, and cognitive science.

The program for you

When you enter the workplace as a college grad, you'll need the latest skills and knowledge of sophisticated software, the Internet, networking and wireless technologies and a variety of programming tools and languages in order to make computers work for people.

Problem solving is a mission for computer programmers, according to Kate Stewart, Department of Technology and Professional Programs, Tallahassee Community College. "Students who truly enjoy the challenge of creating software that serves a user's needs are passionate and addicted to the process of design and development."

When you are comparing colleges, look for adequate lab facilities and a wide selection of courses. See if you'have access, from your home or dormitory, to the Internet and the computer networks you'll need. Will you have to invest in hardware and software? Find out if research or internship opportunities are open to you. Also, be aware that colleges stress different aspects of computer sciences. Some colleges may be more theoretical, others more hands-on or business oriented. If possible, conduct some research on faculty members to see what they've published. Are their priorities similar to yours?

"Each orientation has its strength, and the student should consider his or her overall goal—graduate school or employment. The student should also consider the industry needs of the geographic area he or she hopes to reside in," Stewart suggests.

Some concentrations in undergraduate majors include computer systems, database management, programming, robotics, interface design, systems analysis, information systems management, multimedia, data communications and networking, e-commerce, and Web development.

Learning never ends in these cutting-edge fields. Advanced and graduate studies include computer architecture, compilers, operating systems, programming languages, networks and security; advanced database applications, knowledge systems, artificial intelligence, medical or biological informatics; data mining, software engineering; algorithm analysis, programming languages, and artificial intelligence.

Look for these majors in colleges of computing, engineering, information technology, applied sciences, liberal arts and sciences, and in business schools. Also check colleges of engineering, because some programs combine electrical and computer engineering.

For more information, visit the Association for Computing Machinery (www.acm.org), the Institute of Electrical and Electronics Engineers (www.ieee.org), the Society for Industrial and Applied Mathematics (www.siam.org), and the Association for Information Systems (www.aisnet.org and www.isworld.org).

Computer programming

What it's about:

Computer programming majors learn how to write various programming languages used for software development and operating systems. Topics covered include software installation and maintenance, program customization and linking, debugging, and prototype testing.

Is this for you?

You might like this major if you also like: puzzles and brain teasers; computer games; learning new technology; figuring out creative solutions to challenging problems.

Consider this major if you are good at: attention to detail; creativity; critical reading/thinking; math; organizing; teamwork *...or have...* listening skills; patience; verbal skills; writing skills.

Recommended high school prep:

English 4, math 3, lab science 3 (including physics), social studies 3, and a foreign language 2–3. Take as many computer courses as you can. Courses that cover business and communication are also helpful.

Did you know...

...that the core of computer programming is to figure out how to meet users' needs, not just to know how the computer works? That's why communication skills are important.

Typical courses in this major:

Computer literacy
Introduction to computer technology
Business communications
Operating systems
Networking essentials
C++ programming
Java programming
Object oriented programming
Visual basic programming
Database design
Database systems
Multimedia applications
Web page development
Scripting languages
Network security

Concentrations:

Generally, none available.

What the study of this major is like:

In this major you learn how to talk to computers—using programming languages to tell a computer how to do what you want it to. If you are interested in a higher-level study of the theory and design of computer systems, consider a major in computer science. But if you want to dive right into coding, this could be the major for you.

Course work in computer programming gives you an understanding of software design and development strategies; basic hardware principles; elementary network concepts; database design and implementation techniques; and a combination of Web, multimedia, and security concepts. Most of these topics are taught through a combination of lectures and lab work. Lectures cover techniques, strategies, vocabulary, and concepts. The lab time allows you to put into practice what you've learned.

It's not rote learning. Because a successful computer programmer must have the ability to analyze a user's needs and then develop an efficient piece of software that meets those needs, the program's emphasis is on building strong problem-solving and communication skills. Stress is also placed on cultivating habits of patience and attention to detail.

You will probably spend a lot of time outside of class acquiring these skills and habits. Each programming language and/or topic may present specific challenges. As might be expected, many students find that they are stronger in some areas than in others—for example, they have an easier time understanding hardware than programming concepts, or they have particular difficulty anticipating how changes in code will affect outcomes. In the beginning, some assignments will drive you nuts.

But if you are prepared at the outset to dedicate the extra time and effort required to patiently think about, design, implement, and debug your work, you should find that the rewards outweigh the frustrations. The satisfaction you get when a project is completed and functioning properly is addictive—as you encounter each assignment, problem solving becomes a mission. But there's no getting around the fact that this is a rigorous major. It takes practice, patience, and dedication.

This major is offered mostly at two-year (community) colleges and technical schools. If you come across a four-year program, it's most likely a higher-level computer science major. Colleges use many different names for their computer majors, so go by the description in the course catalogue, not the name.

As you explore colleges, you will notice that the major can vary widely in focus. At some schools, the concentration is on software (mostly programming); at others, the emphasis is on Web page design and management. Some majors are geared toward industry-recognized certifications (Cisco or Microsoft, for example); others are applications oriented (computer graphics, data entry, etc.); still others deal mostly with systems and networking. Examine the descriptions closely to see which programs best match your goals.

And as you think about your goals, remember that programmers can never stop learning; to stay employable, you'll have to keep up with the state of the art.

Other majors you might like:
Information technology
Mathematics
Computer engineering technology
Information systems
Computer science
Medical office computer specialist
Animation
Computer graphics

Database design/management
Management science information systems

Career options and trends:
Computer programmer*; web developer/administrator*; database administrator; network administrator; help desk operator; PC support/technician; network support/technician*.

Industry-recognized vendor certifications, such as those offered by Cisco, Microsoft, CompTia, or C-Tech, are good credentials to take into the job market. Learning a variety of programming languages and tools for networking, database management, and Internet applications will also increase your chances of landing a job.

While job prospects are good, basic or routine programming jobs are being shifted to countries with educated workers and low wages, like India and China. For future job security, combine your technical savvy with knowledge of some other business or scientific field, so you'll know both how to use programming tools and how to apply them to a specific goal.

For more info:
Association for Computing Machinery (ACM)
1515 Broadway
New York, NY 10036
(800) 342-6626
www.acm.org

Institute of Electrical and Electronics Engineers
    (IEEE)
445 Hoes Lane
Piscataway, NJ 08854
(732) 981-0060
www.ieee.org

Computer science

What it's about:

The computer science major trains you in the theory and design of computing systems and software, as well as in important application areas. Your course work balances the need to keep up-to-date with the latest technology with the need to acquire a conceptual foundation that will last throughout your career.

Is this for you?

You might like this major if you also like: mathematical and logical puzzles; using programming to solve real-world problems or explore mathematics; giving precise and elegant explanations for how things work; building mechanical or electronic gadgets.

Consider this major if you are good at: active listening; attention to detail; creativity; critical reading/thinking; math; quantitative analysis; research; teamwork ...*or have...* mental stamina; writing skills.

Recommended high school prep:

English 4, math 4 (including precalculus), lab science 3, social studies 3, and a foreign language 2–3. If possible, take discrete mathematics, calculus, a computer science course, and physics (covering electricity and magnetism).

Did you know...

...that companies like Microsoft have more jobs for computer-science graduates with bachelor's degrees than they can fill? But while high-end computer jobs in the United States may be abundant, the Commerce Department confirms that the outsourcing of low-end, routine jobs is on the rise.

...that mathematical ability and logical thinking are the core skills you need for this major? You don't need to learn programming in high school. In fact, many students come to college thinking they know how to program, only to find that they have to relearn the subject from a more analytical perspective.

...that there are many interdisciplinary areas of study within the computer science major? Cognitive science connects computer science and psychology, linguistics, philosophy, and neuroscience. Bioinformatics and computational biology combine computer science and biology. Digital media design links computer science to the fine arts and communications.

Typical courses in this major:

Introduction to program design
Data structures
Computer system organization
Mathematics for computer science
Automata and formal language theory
Algorithms
Digital system design
Operating systems
Software engineering
Compilers
Principles of database design
Computer graphics
Artificial intelligence
Robotics

Concentrations:

In college: theoretical computer science; computer systems; artificial intelligence; databases; graphics; robotics; computational biology; computational linguistics; multimedia.

If you go on to grad school: computer architecture; compilers; operating systems; programming languages; networks and security; robotics and computer vision; natural language processing; algorithms and complexity; bioinformatics.

What the study of this major is like:

In this major you study many abstract concepts, and examine fundamental notions such as mathematical proof, knowledge, computability, and randomness in a new light. But computer science, of course, also focuses on the computer.

Because using a computer to communicate requires precision, you must learn to use precise programming languages. During your core training, you'll be asked to think about many questions: Why are programming languages designed the way they are? How do you translate a real-world problem into a carefully worded set of instructions—a program—that a computer can execute (or follow) to produce the solution? What goes on inside a computer when a program is being executed? How is the computer constructed to enable it to function? What impact do computers and programs have on a variety of fields?

Computer science programs vary in the amount of core training they provide. A solid foundation will help you solve problems in application areas. Some programs focus on skills that are immediately applicable, while others emphasize abstract, conceptual ideas to ensure that what you learn will be able to help you to adapt to rapid changes in technology. In addition, some programs assume that students have pretty sophisticated backgrounds in math and logic. In other programs, students aren't necessarily expected to have such in-depth, high-level preparation.

Designing and analyzing computer programs requires a mathematical creativity that you may find challenging. Furthermore, you will encounter a multitude of programming environments and languages and may struggle to master them. Projects and assignments typically require long hours of work. On the whole, the computer science major is intellectually demanding, but the field is young and full of possibilities. Once you acquire a mathematical and logical foundation, you can quickly reach the point where you are conceiving and evaluating ideas on your own. If you are attracted to abstract thinking as well as to practicality, computer science can offer you the best of both worlds.

Other majors you might like:
Computer engineering
Electrical and communications engineering
Computer hardware engineering
Computational mathematics
Cognitive science
Software engineering
Systems engineering

Robotics technology
Information technology
Computer engineering technology
Computer graphics
Digital media

Questions to ask colleges:
Does the computer science program include aspects of electrical engineering? If you are interested in the circuitry of computers, examine a school's course list carefully. Because schools may differ in the way they divide the content of electrical engineering and computer science, the circuitry of computers is not taught in all computer science departments.

Career options and trends:
Senior programmer*; systems analyst*; network administrator; database manager; software developer*; financial analyst*.

Job prospects are generally excellent. There are minor fluctuations in the market and small ups and downs in the salaries for entry-level jobs. But the shortage of students choosing this field will increase demand for those that do.

Insider's viewpoint:
"Networking and Graphics are my favorite classes. Networking is the backbone for communications nowadays, and there is much to be done to increase security, speed, and availability. Graphics is simply fun. In my Graphics class, we created a video game, a flight simulator, and a ray tracer that produces highly realistic pictures."

—Amy, senior, University of Maryland

For more info:
Association of Computing Machinery (ACM)
1515 Broadway
17th Floor
New York, NY 10036-5701
(800) 342-6626
www.acm.org

Information systems

Also known as:
Information science

What it's about:
Information systems is about bringing computers and people together. Majors learn how to conceive, design, and implement computer applications, systems, and information technology (IT) that meet the specific needs of individuals, businesses, and many other types of organizations.

Is this for you?
You might like this major if you also like: using computers to solve problems or accomplish tasks; showing others how to use computers; having your own Web site; playing computer games; working on team projects; tutoring. If you enjoy working both with computers and with people, this major could be a good choice.

Consider this major if you are good at: attention to detail; communicating; critical reading/thinking; math; organizing; teamwork *...or have...* initiative; listening skills; writing skills.

Recommended high school prep:
English 4, math 4 (including precalculus), lab science 4 (including physics), social studies 3, and a foreign language 2–3. If available, take courses that cover computer science and applications, psychology or sociology, speech, and writing.

Did you know...
...that in this major, you learn the same technology skills as a computer science major, but you must also develop good communication skills? An ability to communicate well with nontechnical users and to write specifications accurately is essential for students in this field.

Typical courses in this major:
Introduction to programming
Introduction to data structures
Operating systems
Systems analysis
Information retrieval and data mining
Object-oriented programming
Web development and e-commerce
Human and computer interaction
Principles of database design
Database applications
Multimedia systems
Computer graphics
Simulation and modeling
Game design
Decision support systems
Advanced information systems

Concentrations:
In college: computer interface design; systems analysis and design; decision support systems; information systems management; multimedia, visualization, and graphics; data communications and networking; management information systems; e-commerce and Web development.

If you go on to grad school: networking and security; advanced database applications; information systems assurance (IS auditing and security); computer-mediated communications; knowledge systems; artificial intelligence and expert systems; medical or biological informatics.

What the study of this major is like:
This major prepares you to bring computers and people together to solve problems. Computers are fast and logical; people are slower and intuitive, but also creative and insightful. To develop useful information systems and computer applications for business, government, science, and society, you need to understand both the benefits and the dangers that can occur when humans interact with computers. You must learn how humans solve problems, as well as how organizational processes work.

Generally, about half your course work is devoted to general education—math, science, speech, writing, social sciences, humanities, and electives, most of which you complete during your first two years. The work is geared to help you explore the way people solve problems and the way group and organizational processes function. What you learn can be translated into the design and implementation of computer systems and applications.

The technical skills you'll learn are similar to those taught in the computer science major. Although computer studies begin in your first year, you take most computer courses in your third and fourth years. Core requirements are generally spread evenly over the following areas:

Computer and programming concepts. Basic information and skills you'll use for developing computer hardware, computer operating systems, and computer programs.

Data and file structures. Basic ideas and techniques you'll use in creating the logical and physical structures of data and files.

Database management. Instruction that enables you to design, construct, and use database systems.

Data communications. Basic ideas, terms, design, and applications you'll need for developing data communications and networks.

Systems analysis and design. Tools and techniques you'll use in analyzing and developing computer-based systems.

In the lab, you'll be taught a variety of computer languages and systems. You are usually required to learn at least one high-level computer language well enough so that you can create programs in it. Electives and advanced courses may be offered in interface design, multimedia systems, expert systems, e-commerce and Internet applications, and computer-aided modeling and systems engineering.

The field of information systems is rapidly evolving; new material is constantly being developed. Among the essential things you learn as a major is how to master the professional literature and how to keep up with new developments.

Leading information systems programs are accredited by the Computing Sciences Accreditation Board (CSAB). Ideally, a program should encourage

you to pursue an area of concentration but not to overemphasize that area (that is, not to take more than about five courses in one application). In fact, most courses should concentrate on concepts of system design and evaluation that cut across application areas—that can be useful in any number of situations.

Other majors you might like:
Computer science
Behavioral sciences
Communications
Web page/multimedia design
Information technology
E-commerce
Management information systems
Mathematics
Digital media
Electrical and communications engineering
Software engineering
Computer education

Questions to ask colleges:
Are faculty members actively engaged in research? This is an important indicator of a good program. If instructors are doing research in areas that interest you, that's another good sign.

Are faculty members using the Web and group communications to extend discussions outside the classroom? If they are not, perhaps they are somewhat behind the times.

What types of computer networks are available on campus? Can the computer facilities be accessed from off-campus over the Internet? Are majors required to have their own laptops or other equipment?

Is this program accredited by the Computer Science Accreditation Board (CSAB)?

Career options and trends:
Systems analyst*; trainer/consultant; database administrator; information systems manager*; applications programmer.

Fear about computer jobs being outsourced overseas is discouraging many students from entering this field, but that fear is unjustified—more jobs are being created state-side than there are applicants to fill them. Projections indicate that computer applications development will continue to be the fastest-growing segment of the computer industry. Because of the rapid evolution of technology, however, you will have to continually upgrade your skills throughout your career in order to remain employable.

Insider's viewpoint:

"We study a lot about design issues, figuring out what users find attractive, what they think is the easiest to read on Web pages, things of that sort. We're learning how to make things simpler, more accessible, because people in the computer industry have a tendency to make things hard."

—Erin, junior, Florida State University

For more info:

Association for Information Systems (AIS)
P.O. Box 2712
Atlanta, GA 30301-2712
(404) 651-0348
www.aisnet.org

Association for Computing Machinery (ACM)
1515 Broadway
New York, NY 10036
(800) 342-6626
www.acm.org

Information technology

What it's about:

As an information technology (IT) major, you'll study the ways in which information and computing systems support business, research, and communications needs.

Is this for you?

You might like this major if you also like: using computers to solve real-world problems; experimenting with computer hardware and software; playing computer games; being online.

Consider this major if you are good at: attention to detail; creativity; critical reading/thinking; math; organizing; research; teamwork *...or have...* patience; verbal skills; writing skills.

Recommended high school prep:

English 4, math 4 (including precalculus), lab science 4 (including physics), social studies 3, and a foreign language 2–3. If available, take courses that cover computer science and applications, Java programming, psychology or sociology, and business.

Did you know...

...that there are more IT jobs now than at the height of the dot-com boom? A recent report by the Association for Computing Machinery found that the 2 to 3 percent of IT jobs that are outsourced overseas each year are more than made up for by new jobs created in the U.S.

Typical courses in this major:

Fundamentals of programming
Computer systems and architecture
Database management
Web development
Information security
Introduction to computer science
Problem solving and algorithm design
Networking
Telecommunication
IT ethics and social issues
Probability and statistics
Discrete mathematics
Technical writing
Speech communication
Human and computer interaction
Systems analysis and design

Concentrations:

In college: Web development; networking; database management; digital communications; applications development.

If you go on to grad school: information security; data mining; computer forensics; medical information systems.

What the study of this major is like:

Sometimes it's difficult to figure out how the IT major differs from other computer majors. It might help to imagine all the computer fields arranged along a line.

At one end are fields like computer science and computer engineering, which focus on the development of hardware and software. At the other end are topics like information systems, which explores the ways computers and people work together, and management information systems, which examines the application of computers to specific business processes, such as accounting or inventory control.

IT is in the middle, where technologies and concepts from both ends are integrated to build and administer an information infrastructure—systems, networks, applications, hardware, and software.

As a result, IT majors develop a breadth of knowledge through introductory courses in a range of subjects, including Web development, database management, networking, information security, programming, and human-computer interaction. They then acquire in-depth understanding by concentrating elective courses on a particular area.

For example, you may decide to specialize in Web development and take classes such as Web page design and database development for the Web. Or you may be drawn to digital communications and take classes in telecommunications networks.

Courses in discrete mathematics and probability and statistics are usually required. You won't need to take as much math as in other computer or engineering majors, but the work can still be challenging. Most programs also require supporting courses in natural science, business, speech, and writing. You will be encouraged to minor in a related field such as business, visual arts, or communication.

Classes usually combine lectures, hands-on lab experience, projects, presentations, and online applications. Teamwork is emphasized, along with writing, research, and presentation skills. In most four-year programs, you'll be expected to do a senior project in which you will collaborate with other students to solve an IT problem. This learning approach mirrors the real world of IT.

The academic lifestyle of an IT major is fast paced and energized. Most likely you'll be taught by instructors from the industry, who bring real-world experience to the classroom and are up-to-date on the latest developments.

A good IT program should offer a balance between theory and applied skills. You'll want to see plenty of hands-on lab experience, but not so much that you'll be acquiring only technical skills or short-term (vendor-specific) knowledge. Programs administered by schools of business may include more courses in finance, accounting, marketing, and management, while majors that have evolved from computer science departments may require more math and programming.

IT is available in many two-year programs at community colleges, where you can get a good grounding in the field. If you go that route, though, you should think about continuing on to a four-year program at some point—you'll have better career prospects with a bachelor's degree.

Other majors you might like:
Management information systems
Computer engineering technology

Systems engineering
Bioinformatics
Information systems
Software engineering
Library science
Communications
Applied mathematics
Medical office computer specialist
Behavioral sciences
E-commerce

Questions to ask colleges:
Are professors working in the field, applying the latest trends in information technology?

Will the college help me find an internship?

Is the program recognized by the Accreditation Board for Engineering and Technology (ABET)?

Career options and trends:
IT project manager; tech support; network administrator; Web developer; Web site administrator; information security analyst; database administrator; applications developer; software tester.

Job growth for IT professionals is predicted to remain strong through 2014. Businesses continue to depend heavily on networks and are particularly concerned about cyber-security. Some IT jobs (such as routine programming and customer support) are being outsourced overseas, but jobs that require on-site support or are security related will remain domestic. Job prospects are also better for those who can combine IT with other areas of business, such as e-commerce or supply chain management.

Women students are often attracted to IT because of the opportunities for collaborative work, particularly in health-related fields and in government.

For more info:
Association for Computing Machinery (ACM)
1515 Broadway
New York, NY 10036
(800) 342-6626
www.acm.org

Education

To be an educator, you have to be educated. It makes sense that education is the field with the most graduate degrees awarded, both masters' and doctorates. It's second only to business in the number of all degrees earned.

Teaching is something you should know about already. You've seen teachers in action for many years now. You can probably think of a teacher who has influenced your vision of the future.

"This is truly a career where you can influence the hearts and minds of young teenagers, ensuring them a healthier and more productive adulthood," says Jeanneine Jones, a professor of middle school education at the University of North Carolina at Charlotte. "Students touch my life and I touch theirs; they teach me and I teach them. It's a wonderful relationship built on mutual respect and pervasive caring."

You may be wondering why a middle school teacher like Jones is working at a college. She became a university instructor so she can pass on her skills and knowledge to the next generation of teachers. To become a teacher isn't easy. To begin with, you have to prove that you're a good student in your first year or two of college. Then you may qualify to enter an education program. There you learn two big things—the subject you'll be teaching and how to teach it. You'll also have to work as a student teacher for a semester, under the watchful eye of an experienced educator. That's similar to the way doctors learn—by working for real. Finally, teachers take a test to get certified. Many states require another test to show that you know the subject(s) you'll be teaching.

Education is a hot topic lately. Things are changing: the government spends a lot of money on education, and public schools are under pressure to prove that kids are learning.

Teaching may not be a breeze, but it can make you walk on air. "The sense of accomplishment that I feel after teaching a class is as good as climbing to the top of a mountain," says Professor Mary C. Clement of Berry College. "I feel that I have won the lottery when students 'get' the lesson presented and when something that they learned in my class helps them to attain success."

Making the Grade

In a way, you have already begun your teaching career by working hard in school to master a number of academic subjects.

"Studying to be a teacher involves learning the subject you plan to teach extremely well, so students must be prepared to complete a major or the equivalent if they are going to teach a subject like math, English, French, history, or physics," Clement advises.

Why not talk to some of your teachers about their college years and how they chose their schools? They may tell you that some universities have separate divisions of education, while others offer the education major as part of studies like arts or sciences.

When comparing education programs, you'll find that some emphasize teaching reading and literacy and that colleges use technology in different ways. However, the standards for a major are mostly set by the state in which the college is located. When you finish your bachelor's degree, you'll need to be certified in the state where you'll teach. Specific certifications go with particular types of teaching, like early childhood, elementary, middle school, secondary (high) school, special education, and physical education. In general, look for a program that's been approved by the National Council for Accreditation of Teacher Education (www.ncate.org). And be sure to ask the college about the percentage of its grads who become certified.

Of course, teaching isn't the only career that educators pursue. Other jobs include administrator (like your principal), school counselor, school psychologist, curriculum director, and education researcher; or you might be interested in becoming a corporate trainer to use your teaching skills in the business world.

Employment prospects are good, partly because many teachers are expected to retire soon. Also, as states and schools try to improve education and boost course requirements for students, more and better-qualified teachers are needed. Teaching jobs are likely to increase at all grade levels through 2012. Job opportunities vary, of course, depending on the region and the subject. Teachers of foreign languages, math and science, and bilingual education are especially in demand.

Teachers often go to grad school to obtain certifications and credentials such as an "endorsement," which allows you to teach a particular subject, like reading. Other grad students in education focus on advanced work in their subjects so that they become experts in their field who can inspire and enlighten students.

"It is my philosophy that teachers are not just subject matter experts, but dispensers of hope for students of all ages," offers Clement.

With any luck, you've had a teacher like that. With hard work and dedication, you may become one.

Early childhood education

What it's about:

This major prepares you to teach infants and children through age eight, in all subjects through grade 3. You receive practicum/internship experience with small children in a variety of settings, such as day care, before- and after-school programs, pre-K (kindergarten) programs, early start, and K through grade 3 classrooms.

Is this for you?

You might like this major if you also like: working with very young children; watching them grow and change; volunteer or part-time work at day care or community centers; crafts; games; puppet shows; team sports; being creative; tutoring.

Consider this major if you are good at: active listening; caring/nurturing; coaching; communicating; critical reading/thinking; empathizing with children's thoughts and feelings; teamwork *...or have...* an open mind; manual dexterity; patience; physical stamina.

Recommended high school prep:

English 4, math 3, lab science 3, social studies 3, and a foreign language 2–3. In addition, take a course in family and consumer science (home economics), especially if there is a child development component; and courses in psychology and sociology, if available.

Did you know...

...that early childhood is perhaps the most flexible field in education, with numerous areas in which to gain expertise? In fact, with just a few additional courses, you can pick up credentials in special education, child development, or literacy for early childhood along with your major, thus increasing your career possibilities.

Typical courses in this major:

Child development and learning
Parent–child relations
Curriculum methods in early education
Early childhood children's literature
Music methods
Arts and the child
Early childhood language arts
Early childhood mathematics
Social development and play
Educational psychology
Classroom management and behavior
Instructional resources and technology
Professional issues or foundations of education
Inclusion methods for special-needs students
Diversity of learners methods
Early childhood health and physical education

Concentrations:

Generally, none available.

What the study of this major is like:

Most early childhood education programs require a broad, general background in education; a core of professional courses that include education basics, knowledge of curriculum, and teaching methods; and opportunities to observe and student-teach in a variety of settings and at a variety of age and grade levels.

Because the early childhood curriculum focuses on a variety of subjects, you should take general education courses similar to those required in colleges of liberal arts and sciences. Your goal is to learn communication, critical-thinking, and problem-solving skills while you study the humanities, math, biological and physical sciences, social sciences, history, health, and physical education. You may be expected to complete a minor, or concentration, in one of the general education areas. If so, general education courses would make up between two-thirds and three-fourths of your undergraduate course work.

In professional education courses, you study the history and philosophy of early childhood education as well as early childhood growth and development. You also explore curriculum and classroom organization, by planning, putting into practice, and evaluating a program appropriate for young children. Since preschoolers learn through play, you learn how to introduce language arts, social skills, and basic math and science concepts through play and other hands-on activities. In addition, you learn how to introduce academics at the kindergarten and early primary grade levels. You may also take courses on teaching special-needs children in the regular classroom.

Your professional education includes fieldwork, called practicums, in which you observe and participate in programs for young children in settings such as elementary schools, child care centers, and Head Start programs. You conclude with student teaching or an internship, as you take on increasing responsibility for a class. Most programs require you to do a semester of student teaching in pre-K through grade 3 settings, or perhaps several student-teaching assignments at different age or grade levels.

As an early childhood education major, you will probably be taught in lectures, small-group interactive projects, discussions, demonstrations, and presentations. You may take part in distance-learning through video segments and hear expert speakers. In your third and fourth years, you will spend a great deal of (unpaid) time working with children in schools; keep that point in mind if you plan to hold a job during college. While you are student-teaching (also unpaid), you will have no time for a job, so plan to save money for that final semester.

Early childhood programs may emphasize different teaching philosophies. Many programs include all models and theories, and let you pick the approach that best suits you. Others may focus on one model, such as the Bank Street or the Montessori approach. In general, most quality programs follow standards set by the National Association for the Education of Young Children (NAEYC).

In all states, to be licensed to teach pre-K–3, you must have a four-year degree. Some states do not offer the early childhood teaching certificate but provide instead a "kindergarten endorsement" on an elementary teaching certificate. In these states, early childhood education may be a minor offered to elementary education majors. Some institutions offer teacher certification for early childhood education only at the graduate level. Many states are moving to requiring a master's degree or the equivalent for continued teacher certification. If you think you may relocate, check to see if the state you are moving to will honor the degree you plan to pursue.

Other majors you might like:
Elementary education
Middle school education
Special education
Teacher assistance
Communication disorders
Sociology
Human development and family studies
Behavioral sciences
Psychology
Social work
Child development
Child care management

Questions to ask colleges:
Where do students complete their fieldwork, practicum, internship, and student teaching? When do these projects occur in the program? How many hours are required? What kind of support do students receive in the assignments? What choices, if any, do students have in these placements? Are the settings rural, urban, suburban, metropolitan, or a mix?

What are the prerequisites for full admission into the early childhood major (e.g., required courses, GPA, cutoff scores on the SAT, ACT, or PRAXIS I exams)? Do I need a background check?

Career options and trends:
Teacher assistant or aide; pre-school teacher*; kindergarten teacher*; child care administrator; family service coordinator.

An associate degree is usually required for teacher aides or teacher paraprofessionals to work in public school classrooms. These persons may work with small children as well as older children with disabilities.

Center directors often have a master's degree, but it is not a requirement.

In general, the shortage of early childhood/elementary education teachers is less severe than for teachers of older students. However, the South (Florida, Georgia, and the Carolinas) and the West (Arizona, Texas, Nevada, and California) have a higher demand for early education teachers because of their increasing numbers of young children. Job prospects continue to be better in urban and isolated rural areas. In many regions, teachers who are willing to relocate and who hold more than one license/certification, such as in early childhood and special education or ESL (English as a second language), will have an advantage.

For more info:
National Association for the Education of Young
    Children (NAEYC)
1313 L St., N.W.
Washington, DC 20005
(800) 424-2460
www.naeyc.org

Elementary education

What it's about:

Elementary education majors prepare to teach children in the elementary grades, which can range from K (kindergarten) through 8, depending on the school system. In addition to learning how to teach specific subjects, such as reading and math, you study the way children develop socially and intellectually, and you get hands-on professional experience in teaching and learning.

Is this for you?

You might like this major if you also like: working with children; tutoring; team sports; volunteer or community service; public speaking; problem solving.

Consider this major if you are good at: active listening; communicating; creativity; critical reading/ thinking; organizing; persuading/influencing *...or have...* enthusiasm; flexibility; patience; physical stamina.

Recommended high school prep:

English 4, math 3, lab science 3, social studies 3, and a foreign language 2–3. Take any computer science or applications courses available. Four years of Spanish is highly recommended, because fluency in that language would be a great asset for a teacher.

Typical courses in this major:

Child development and learning
History and philosophy of education
Curriculum methods in elementary education
Teaching language arts
Teaching mathematics
Teaching science
Teaching social studies
Reading fundamentals
Educational psychology
Classroom management and behavior
Educational assessment and measurement
Instructional resources and technology
Special education needs and issues
Schooling in a culturally diverse society

Concentrations:

Generally, none available.

What the study of this major is like:

Almost all elementary education programs offer a liberal arts foundation, a professional education core that includes course work in teaching methods, and a variety of student-teaching experiences in elementary school settings. The goal is to prepare you for state certification to teach in the elementary grades. States have different rules, and there may be special requirements for teaching kindergarten through third grade (K–3) or grades 6–8. In addition to completing the elementary education major, many states require students to pass tests in subject matter, communications, and knowledge of methods, in order to be certified. Some states also require a second major in a particular subject area (e.g., language arts) or specialty (e.g., reading).

Most elementary school teachers instruct one class in several subjects, using a wide range of tools, such as games, music, artwork, films, books, and computers. Therefore, you should probably take between 50 and 60 percent of your course work in the humanities, social sciences, natural sciences, technology, and mathematics—mostly during your first two years. Generally, you do not become fully admitted into the major until your second year, after you meet certain requirements. They vary among colleges, so be sure to find out what they are before you enroll in a program.

In methods courses, you focus on ways to instruct children, and you develop your capacity to solve problems that may arise as you introduce reading, language arts, mathematics, science, and social studies to young children. You also gain practice in planning lessons, evaluating learning, and managing the classroom. Some elementary education majors can minor in early childhood or special education.

Throughout the major, practical experiences in schools are typically interwoven with classroom studies. As you observe, assist, and teach elementary children, what you've learned in your classes becomes more meaningful and more useful. Student teaching, which normally occurs in your last semester, is often the high point of the elementary education major. This experience, under the supervision of both college and school instructors, gives you a big boost in your goal of becoming a teacher.

Other majors you might like:

Early childhood education
Middle school education
Special education
Teacher assistance
Reading teacher education
Communications
Family/consumer sciences education
Behavioral sciences
Psychology
Social work
Child development
Sociology

Questions to ask colleges:

Is the program accredited by the National Council for Accreditation of Teacher Education?

Career options and trends:

Besides teaching in the elementary schools, majors who pursue appropriate graduate training can become school administrators, educational researchers, curriculum specialists, reading specialists, or school counselors.

Currently there is no shortage of elementary school teachers, and enrollment of elementary school children is projected to rise slowly overall; but these factors will vary by region. Fast-growing states in the South and West—particularly California, Texas, Georgia, Idaho, Hawaii, Alaska, and New Mexico—will experience the largest enrollment increases. Minority teachers and teachers who are bilingual in Spanish are in short supply, and demand for these will grow with the rising enrollment of minority and Spanish-speaking children.

While certification requirements vary by state, all states require a bachelor's degree and completion of an approved teacher education program with a prescribed number of subject and education credits as well as supervised student teaching. About one-third of the states also require technology training, and some require specific minimum grade point averages as well.

Insider's viewpoint:

"Most of the assignments focus on analyzing classroom practices—tell why you like it, how you'd change it. Then you plan your own lessons and implement those plans."

—Kau'i, senior, University of Hawaii

For more info:

National Association for the Education of Young Children (NAEYC)
1313 L St., N.W.
Washington, DC 20005
(800) 424-2460
www.naeyc.org

Middle school education

Also known as:
Junior high education

What it's about:
This major prepares you for an entry-level license or certification to teach specific content areas (such as language arts, mathematics, social studies, or science) in middle school, intermediate school, or junior high school, which may include grades 4–9, depending on the school system.

Is this for you?
You might like this major if you also like: community service; working with youth; reading; writing; public speaking; tutoring; coaching; helping friends and others with their problems; leadership roles in high school.

Consider this major if you are good at: caring/ nurturing; counseling; critical reading/thinking; leadership; organizing; persuading/influencing; teamwork ...*or have...* patience; physical stamina; verbal skills.

Recommended high school prep:
English 4, math 3, lab science 3, social studies 3, and a foreign language 2–3. Course work that helps you develop your reading and communication skills is essential.

Did you know...
...that elementary school teachers teach children, and high school teachers teach content, but middle school teachers teach content to children?

...that the middle school years are commonly labeled the turning point in the life span? Middle school teachers can have a real impact on young people, encouraging them to become healthy, productive adults.

Typical courses in this major:
Introduction to middle school education
Early adolescent learners
Classroom management
Specific subject curriculum
Content methods
Philosophy of middle grades education
Curriculum of middle grades education
Reading and writing across subject areas
Research and analysis of middle grades education
Health and safety issues in middle schools
Instructional design and technology
Teaching students with special needs
Schooling in a culturally diverse society

Concentrations:
Specific content areas, such as science, math, language arts, social studies, and music.

What the study of this major is like:
As a middle school education major, you have the opportunity to make a real difference in the life of young adults. Although early adolescents are often portrayed as defiant and confused, people who work with middle school students generally agree that they are sensitive, stimulating, motivated, and eager to contribute to the world around them.

Majors study the developmental and learning styles of the 10- to 15-year-old and examine the ways in which students can be given structure and guidance, as well as a sense of independence and personal responsibility. You will also take about six to eight courses in one or two subject areas, such as language arts, mathematics, social studies, and science. As a whole, the program prepares you to enter a school knowing what to teach, how to teach, and the needs of your audience.

Although courses contain some lectures, they feature hands-on work experiences, called practicums or clinical hours, in local public and private schools. These are included in the course assignments and are a critical part of your workload.

They are designed to help you transfer campus discussions and studies into successful classroom applications.

These experiences culminate in a full semester of student teaching in your last year. It will enable you to master the material you've been studying and to practice your presentation of it under the supervision of both college and middle school instructors. Perhaps even more important, your student-teaching semester will help you deal with the frustrations often associated with teaching, including enforcing classroom discipline, managing your time, and motivating unresponsive students.

While colleges vary, all strong programs should require the study of at least one content area. They should also communicate an in-depth understanding of adolescent development and middle school philosophy. Courses should cover lesson plan design, effective teacher behavior, and classroom management. Finally, you should be given opportunities to apply your course work in local schools and related community programs, especially in a challenging, well-supported student-teaching semester.

Other majors you might like:
Child development
Secondary education
Special education
ESL teacher education
Bilingual/bicultural education
Human development and family studies
Native American education
Liberal arts and sciences
Juvenile corrections
Youth ministry
Social work
Psychology

Questions to ask colleges:
Does this college have a clearly identified middle school program, which includes a professor to coordinate it? Do core faculty members have experience teaching in grades 6–8?

Does the surrounding region have strong middle schools for student-teaching work?

Career options and trends:
Middle school teacher*; secondary school teacher*; elementary school teacher; school counselor; school administrator*.

An additional, but related, license or certification is required for teaching at the elementary or secondary school level. An advanced degree is necessary for positions as a school counselor, administrator, or supervisor.

This area of education is one of the most marketable in the country, but demand will vary by region and subject specialty. Currently, those most in demand are qualified to teach mathematics, science (especially chemistry and physics), bilingual education, foreign languages, and computer science.

Insider's viewpoint:
"Once I really, really know these children, they emerge as stimulating, and stimulated, young adults who are sensitive, capable, and productive citizens. They touch my life and I touch theirs, they teach me and I teach them. It's a wonderful relationship built on mutual respect and caring."

—Professor Jeanneine P. Jones, University of North Carolina at Charlotte

For more info:
National Middle School Association (NMSA)
4151 Executive Parkway
Suite 300
Westerville, OH 43081
(800) 528-6672
www.nmsa.org

Physical education

What it's about:

Physical education majors prepare to teach physical education (PE) or to coach sports in public or private schools, kindergarten through twelfth grade (K–12).

Is this for you?

You might like this major if you also like: helping people; sports and competition; physical exercise; good health habits; coaching; tutoring; a sense of humor.

Consider this major if you are good at: caring/nurturing; coaching; critical reading/thinking; leadership; persuading/influencing; sports, gymnastics, or dance; teamwork *...or have...* patience; physical stamina; verbal skills; writing skills.

Recommended high school prep:

English 4, math 3, lab science 3, social studies 3, and a foreign language 2–3. If possible, take extra physical education credits to enhance your skills, or serve as a physical education assistant in addition to participating in team sports. Knowledge of or fluency in a foreign language (especially Spanish) will make you more marketable.

Did you know...

...that this is not the easy major many people think it is! Learning to teach physical education means more than playing games. You must love sports and also enjoy teaching a variety of subjects to children and adolescents. In addition, you will be expected to continue your educational and professional development throughout your career.

Typical courses in this major:

Biology
Physics
Anatomy and physiology
Human growth and development
Motor learning and development
Observation and analysis of motor skills
Physical education teaching methods
Methods for teaching lifetime fitness
Physical education curriculum
Multicultural education
Educational psychology
History and philosophy of physical education
Tests and measures in physical education
Administration of physical education programs
Adapted physical education
Coaching effectiveness

Concentrations:

Elementary school physical education; secondary school physical education; adapted physical education; athletic coaching.

What the study of this major is like:

If you want to become a physical education teacher, you should generally enjoy many types of sports and exercise. Since few children and adolescents are elite athletes, knowing how to work with students at all skill levels is essential. Another plus is to feel comfortable speaking to groups and to be a skillful communicator. In addition, you should be warm and caring in your approach to young people. Good physical education teachers are role models of active, healthy lifestyles.

As a PE major, you take general education courses during your first two years. Then you enroll in science courses that focus on how the human body is affected by exercise and sports and how performance can be improved. Other courses include child development, psychology, and curriculum and instruction, and you'll have opportunities to work with children in supervised field settings. Although you will probably be required to take part in numerous recreational activities and sports, don't expect to get much academic credit. At the end of most programs, you'll do student teaching.

Many majors are challenged by the lab sciences that are often required (for example, anatomy and physiology and biology). In your third and fourth years, you typically take practicum courses, which give you extensive teaching practice in local schools. You'll learn to teach such subjects as sport skills, gymnastics, dance, lifetime activities, and fitness to diverse students in a range of settings. Practicum courses can be nerve-racking, though, because you teach real kids in real schools. After practicums, you usually do your student teaching. During this semester-long assignment, you gradually assume the full responsibilities of a teacher. Student teaching is often challenging, as you experience both the difficulties and the rewards of the profession.

Requirements for teaching certification vary from state to state. But programs that are approved by the National Council for Accreditation of Teacher Education (NCATE) meet the standards that ensure effective teaching preparation. In many states, to obtain a teaching certificate, you also need to earn acceptable scores on competency exams (for example, the PRAXIS I and II), and some physical education programs require you to pass competency exams in order to graduate. Most physical education programs will qualify you to be certified to teach K-12. However, in some programs you can major in elementary school physical education or secondary school physical education. If you enjoy working with young children, for example, you might seek out a program that specializes in elementary physical education.

Other majors you might like:
Athletic training
Exercise sciences
Sports and fitness administration
Parks, recreation, and leisure studies
Health teacher education
Physical therapy
Occupational therapy
Biology
Food and nutrition studies
Dance therapy
Recreational therapy
Community health services

Questions to ask colleges:
How much hands-on teaching experience is given in an actual school setting? Good programs should provide ample practical experience leading up to student teaching.

Is the program NCATE accredited?

Career options and trends:
Physical education teacher (K–12)*; recreation supervisor (community or private setting); aerobic dance instructor; physical trainer.

The demand for physical education teachers across the United States is not as high as it is for teachers in areas such as math and science, bilingual education, and special education. However, some districts (especially urban and rural) need teachers in all subject areas, including physical education.

Obtaining a minor in another teaching area or athletic coaching can really improve your career prospects. A physical education teacher who is dual certified (can teach physical education and an academic subject, or can teach physical education and coach a sport) is much more marketable. Increasing awareness of the growing problem of childhood obesity should also increase demand for PE teachers who can help combat this problem.

For more info:
American Alliance for Health, Physical Education, Recreation and Dance (AAHPERD)
1990 Association Drive
Reston, VA 20191-1598
www.aahperd.org

Secondary education

Also known as:
High school teacher education

What it's about:
This major prepares you to be a high school teacher. You learn the curriculum and methods of teaching a specific subject (math, science, English, history, foreign language, and so forth), organization and management of a classroom, needs of diverse learners, and the role of high schools in today's society.

Is this for you?
You might like this major if you also like: Scouting; 4-H; extracurricular activities; sports; coaching; tutoring; working at summer camps; leading, not following. Idealism is a good attribute for teachers.

Consider this major if you are good at: caring/nurturing; creativity; organizing; persuading/influencing *...or have...* initiative; patience; verbal skills; writing skills.

Recommended high school prep:
English 4, math 3, lab science 3, social studies 3, and a foreign language 2–3. Take a course in psychology, if one is offered. You should take a four-year sequence in the subject you plan to teach; if advanced or honors courses in that subject are available, taking those is highly recommended.

Did you know...
...that majoring in education as an undergraduate is generally the quickest way to become a teacher? If you decide after college to become a teacher, you will probably need to return to college for two more years.

...that in many states, you may have to undergo a criminal background check and be fingerprinted before observing or student-teaching in a public school district?

Typical courses in this major:
Introduction to secondary education
Issues and trends in secondary education
Adolescent behavior and development
Educational psychology
History and foundations of education
Educational technology
Specific subject curriculum
Specific subject instructional methods
Classroom management
Diversity/multicultural education
Teaching students with special needs
Testing in the classroom

Concentrations:
Generally, none available.

What the study of this major is like:
The secondary education major provides a foundation in the arts and sciences, in-depth study in a particular subject, and courses in teaching procedures. To achieve their goals, most students take a double major or the equivalent.

In introductory courses, which may include visits to schools to observe and interview teachers, you will explore the conditions of today's schools, the diversity of students, and the role of schools in today's society. Educational psychology courses focus on the way children and teenagers learn and provide strategies for motivating learners and for meeting the needs of all students, including those with disabilities, language deficiencies, and emotional problems. You will also take at least one special education course.

In content-based course work, you learn *what* to teach; how to prepare lesson plans, unit plans, and tests; and how to meet state and national teaching standards. In methods courses, you learn *how* to teach. For these upper-level courses, you may spend three to five hours a week in local schools before you begin student teaching.

A course in classroom management provides strategies for organizing time, space, and materials, as well as guidelines for creating a management style that suits your needs. In other courses you gain practice in giving lectures, doing demonstrations, running audio/visual equipment, and maintaining classroom discipline. Future science teachers learn how to supervise laboratory work; students interested in vocational education learn how to give students hands-on experience with tools and equipment.

Your final activity as a major is a semester of student teaching—working with a teacher, every school day for the entire day. You still pay full tuition and fees during student teaching, and you are not paid by the school district. You may also have to travel a considerable distance from campus, and it is difficult to hold a part-time job while you student-teach. Graduates say that this semester is the most challenging, but often the most useful, time of their college years.

At some colleges, you are required to double-major in the subject area you plan to teach; at others you major in your subject area and minor in secondary education or a teacher certification program. Many colleges gear their programs to the certification requirements of the state in which they are located; keep this point in mind when you are considering where to apply to college.

Other majors you might like:
Middle school education
Special education
ESL teacher education
Liberal arts and sciences
Agricultural education services
Human resources management
Juvenile corrections
Psychology
Social work
Sociology

Questions to ask colleges:
Is the program accredited by both the state body for teacher certification and by the National Council for Accreditation in Teacher Education (NCATE)?

How are student-teaching placements made? Are they assigned or do students have a choice? For how long is the full-time student-teaching placement, and how far away from campus may it be located?

Does this teacher education program require minimum exam scores for admission? Since some states require candidates to have a certain ACT, SAT, or PRAXIS I score in order to be granted a teaching license, many colleges now require such scores for admission to the major.

Career options and trends:
High school teacher*; school principal or assistant*; school superintendent or assistant; curriculum director; school counselor; educational writer; program director in Scouting, 4-H, youth programs, churches, or other organizations.

Although states have different certification requirements, most require you to have a bachelor's degree (and in some states, an additional year or a master's degree) in a program accredited by the state and by either the Teacher Education Accreditation Council (TEAC) or NCATE; to complete a major (or the equivalent) in your chosen subject area(s); and to pass a state exam, the Praxis II exam, or another test.

Additional licensing or certification and an advanced degree are necessary for a position as a principal, superintendent, or other upper-level administrator.

The acute shortage of math and science high school teachers in many parts of the United States is being called the "silent crisis." Shortages also exist for foreign languages, bilingual education, and special education. Teachers who earn certification in more than one subject are highly employable, and so are teachers who choose to work in non-English-speaking or disadvantaged communities. Graduates with ESL training are also in demand.

For more info:
Recruiting New Teachers, Inc. (RNT)
385 Concord Ave., Suite #103
Belmont, MA 02478
(617) 489-6000
www.rnt.org

Special education

What it's about:

The special education major prepares you to meet the educational, social, emotional, and vocational needs of infants, children, and youth with disabilities. Your professional preparation includes specialized course work, field experiences with children with disabilities, and student teaching.

Is this for you?

You might like this major if you also like: helping people, especially people who appear to be different; working with people one-on-one; multitasking.

Consider this major if you are good at: caring/nurturing; coaching; counseling; critical reading/thinking; leadership; organizing; teamwork ...*or have...* initiative; patience; verbal skills.

Recommended high school prep:

English 4, math 3, lab science 3, social studies 3, and a foreign language 2–3.

Did you know...

...that, because special education serves a wide range of students, special educators work in many settings, both in and out of schools? Besides schools, settings include hospitals, private practice environments, health care centers, and correctional facilities.

...that many states and the federal government offer scholarships and loan forgiveness to students entering the special education field?

Typical courses in this major:

Introduction to psychology
Introduction to sociology
Statistics
Human development
Introduction to special education
Educational assessment
Behavior management
Curriculum and instruction
Speech/language development
Content area courses (e.g., reading, math)
Computers/technology for teachers
Educational policy and law
Integrated fieldwork
Student teaching

Concentrations:

In college: early childhood, elementary, or secondary special education; learning disabilities; mental retardation; autism; deaf/hard of hearing; visual impairments; severe/profound disabilities; emotional/behavioral disorders.

If you go on to grad school: policy studies; vocational training; transition to adult services; educational administration.

What the study of this major is like:

Special education refers to instruction that is specifically designed to meet the needs of infants, children, and youth with disabilities; special education services cover infants through 21-year-olds. To become a special education professional, you must develop skills in educational assessment and instruction for students with disabilities and in working with their families. Your course work usually includes lectures and field placement, or hands-on activities, such as assisting in a special education classroom.

In your first and second years as a major, you will probably take introductory and core courses in education, psychology, and child development, along with general studies. In your third year, you explore the types of disabilities you are likely to encounter in your work. In addition, you observe classrooms and obtain supervised field placement experience.

In field placements, you receive hands-on experience working with children with disabilities in a special education setting, such as a regular classroom, resource room, self-contained classroom, vocational-technical school, or institution. During your first field placement experiences, you spend most of your time observing the teacher with whom you are placed; but as you progress, you gradually assume greater responsibility. In your fourth year, you take advanced courses in special education, along with electives, and do student teaching. By then, you will do most, if not all, of the teaching.

Being a special education teacher often means being an "educational manager"—the person who coordinates all the education and training a child receives. Many students with disabilities require the services of several professionals (such as school psychologists, speech therapists, occupational therapists). As a special educator, you need to know what role these professionals will play in a student's education and how their work relates to yours. In fact, you and the other service providers will function as a multidisciplinary team—each contributing professional and personal skills for the benefit of the child.

Several features distinguish special education programs. First, colleges vary in their approach to special education. For example, some colleges offer dual programs in elementary and special education, with less emphasis on special education than in a program focusing on that field alone. Further, some programs offer a generalized treatment of special education, while in others you can specialize by age level or type of disability. While some programs take four years to complete, others take five; some offer graduate credits and/or degrees in conjunction with the bachelor's program. Colleges also differ in the amount of required field experiences. Finally, special education programs may be distinguished by their philosophies. Programs may differ according to their emphasis on inclusion of individuals with disabilities in community settings and on using research to inform your teaching.

Majors are expected to demonstrate professional behavior from the first semester they are placed in classrooms. Professional behavior includes punctuality, time management, and the ability to interact as an adult with students, school staff, and students' parents. Opportunities to establish a network of potential job contacts begin the day you start your field placement. A career in special education is rewarding, exciting, and intellectually challenging.

Other majors you might like:
Communication disorders
Child development
Audiology/speech pathology
Education of learning disabled
Education of physically handicapped
Early childhood education
American Sign Language (ASL)
Art therapy
Occupational therapy
Physical therapy
Recreational therapy
Human development and family studies

Questions to ask colleges:
How much and which types of fieldwork are required? Where are students placed and who supervises field placements? What ages or disability types are students being prepared to teach?

Does the special education program have a more selective admissions process than other divisions of the college?

Which certification do students earn? Is certification transferable to other states?

Is the program focused on special education, or is training split between general and special education? Does the program provide graduate credits?

Career options and trends:
Special education teacher*; special education instructional assistant; special education advocate; educational administrator*; parent educator; psychologist; lobbyist; policy analyst; educational researcher.

The special education major prepares you to work in a school or institutional setting. With graduate study, students often pursue careers as administrators of special education. Advanced training may also lead to a career as a speech/language pathologist, audiologist, physical therapist, occupational therapist, school psychologist, school counselor, evaluation specialist, teacher trainer, parent/community coordinator, rehabilitation counselor, vocational/special needs teacher, or adaptive physical education instructor. A state certificate or license is required for teaching in public elementary and secondary schools.

Job opportunities in special education are excellent. All areas of special education are in the process of evolving, especially at the early childhood and secondary/transition levels. All regions of the country are experiencing shortages of special education teachers, and long-term projections indicate that the shortages will continue.

Insider's viewpoint:

"It is exciting to be in a profession that continually offers intellectual challenges, while serving individuals who have historically been relegated to the fringe of society."

—Dawn Eddy Molloy, University of Maryland

For more info:
American Association of Colleges for Teacher
    Education (AACTE)
1307 New York Ave., N.W.
Suite 300
Washington, DC 20005
(202) 293-2450
www.aacte.org

Engineering

Have you ever wondered how a DVD works? Or what makes a metal magnetic? Do you enjoy brain teasers? Can you twist a wire hanger into something useful? Do you secretly love the math story problems that other students dread? You, my friend, might be an engineer.

But it's not enough to be mechanically inclined or have the ability to visualize in 3-D. To become an engineer takes an awful lot of work.

"Realize that engineering is not a 'party' major. You will have to work harder than your friends, but the rewards and satisfaction are worth it," says Lyle D. Feisel, retired dean of the State University of New York at Binghamton.

Engineers design systems, components, and processes to make life better. Whenever a plane takes off, a computer boots up, the lights go on, a car is driven, a building constructed, a medical device used, a phone call made, a photo taken, or a product sold, it all comes down to engineering. When engineers show up for work, they may do research, development, production, construction, operations, quality improvement, management, technical sales, consulting, or teaching. Jobs in the field and studies of engineering cover materials, mining and metals, manufacturing, marine engineering, and mechanics—and those are just the ones that start with "m."

Anyone who goes into engineering can look forward to lifelong learning about leading-edge science—nuclear and alternative energy, information technologies, integrated circuits, aerospace and defense, global positioning systems, genetic research.

Colleges offer more than 30 engineering majors. The most common majors offered are electrical, mechanical, civil, chemical, and computer engineering. More than half of engineers find work in these areas. Some new majors include architectural engineering, biochemical engineering, robotics, environmental engineering, manufacturing engineering, nanotechnology, biomaterials, and energy management technology.

Did you know that engineers earn some of the highest salaries for people with a bachelor's degree? But apparently money is not the only consideration, because fewer students are choosing engineering, and so overall opportunities are expected to be good. Of course, jobs depend on how the economy is doing. Are businesses and the government spending money on research, technology, and projects such as highway reconstruction? The good news is that, even if the economy is slow, many engineering efforts—like building a bridge—are based on long-term plans that will continue through lean times.

Where will you go?

When picking a school, look for a college of engineering. Duh. You'll see that many undergraduate programs look alike because standards are in place. If a program is good enough, it is "ABET-accredited" by the Accreditation Board for Engineering and Technology.

How do colleges differ? Mostly in their approach. Some schools are more hands-on and mechanical, giving you a sort of job training through work in laboratories. Other colleges focus on theoretical concepts and abstract mathematical modeling to prepare you for graduate school. Graduate tracks include math, basic science, engineering sciences, design, and research. Some specific graduate areas are wireless engineering, hydrosystems, biochemical or pharmaceutical engineering, and software user interface design.

It's important to find out if the school is a research college that attracts talented professors. Also judge the quality of facilities like the design, computing, and testing laboratories and the libraries. Other factors to look at are admissions criteria, location, tuition and fees, and financial aid. How about work-study programs, part-time employment on campus, internships, or cooperative work to help finance your engineering education? It's okay to ask what recent graduates are doing. Have they gone on to grad school? Or have they taken jobs? If so, where? What percent of recent graduates got hired right away?

The one thing that will always come up is the need for strong math and science preparation on your part. Once you're at college, expect heavy math, statistics, basic science, and lab work for the first two years, followed by applied science and engineering courses later.

"Engineers are problem solvers, but many engineering students become disillusioned early in their studies because they fail to see the applicability of the abstract mathematical principles they encounter in their freshmen and sophomore years," warns Edward A. Hiler, a dean at Texas A&M University. "Perseverance is necessary, and is well rewarded later in college and in their careers."

Only about one-third of engineering graduates finish their degree in four years. Most students take nine or more semesters to graduate. Studies often finish with a capstone course. That's a real-world project putting together everything you've learned. Ask the college about the types of projects students have done in the past.

Keep in mind that when you look up engineering majors in college catalogs and on the Internet, you might see some combinations and hybrids. Aerospace engineering and aviation might be called aeronautics. Industrial engineering is also known as industrial and systems engineering. Think it through.

Read more about the particular engineering majors in this section and about the field in general by going to the Junior Engineering Technical Society (www.jets.org), American Society for Engineering Education (www.asee.org), and the Accreditation Board for Engineering and Technology (www.abet.org).

Aeronautical/aerospace engineering

What it's about:

As an aeronautical/aerospace engineering major, you study the design and development of high-speed transportation vehicles such as aircraft, spacecraft, missiles, launch vehicles, deep space probes, dirigibles, hang gliders, unmanned aerial vehicles (UAVs), and space habitats. In addition, you examine the physics of the flow of air, water, and plasma around these vehicles.

Is this for you?

You might like this major if you also like: anything to do with aircraft, spacecraft, or space exploration; model aircraft building; flying; hang gliding; physics; astronomy; science fiction; computer programming; designing things; problem solving. If you instinctively look up when you hear an airplane, you know you have the aerospace bug.

Consider this major if you are good at: attention to detail; creativity; critical reading/thinking; leadership; math; organizing; quantitative analysis; spatial thinking/analysis; teamwork *...or have...* imagination; initiative.

Recommended high school prep:

English 4, math 4 (including precalculus), lab science 4, social studies 3, and a foreign language 2–3. If you must choose, take physics and chemistry over biology or earth science. Also, if possible, take a year of computer literacy, a computer programming course, and calculus.

Typical courses in this major:

Introduction to aerospace engineering
Thermodynamics
Strength of materials (with lab)
Aerodynamics (with lab)
Aerospace structures
Flight mechanics
Control systems
Aerospace propulsion
Flight controls
Space science and systems
Aerospace vehicle design
Robotics lab
Intelligent systems
Space mission design
Systems engineering
Computer-aided design (CAD)

Concentrations:

In college: aerodynamics; aerospace structures; propulsion; controls; aerospace vehicle design; intelligent systems; space science and systems.

If you go on to grad school: theoretical mechanics; heat transfer; numerical modeling.

What the study of this major is like:

For all engineers, the academic program usually consists of two years of science and engineering basics, followed by two years of specialty courses. In the aeronautical/aerospace engineering major, most of your general education electives and required courses (such as English, history, and social science) are taught in the lecture format, but some of the science courses also have labs. You will probably be required to take four semesters of calculus and analytic geometry, one semester of chemistry, two semesters of physics, one semester of differential equations, and courses in computer programming and in numerical methods.

Most likely, your engineering studies will begin with an overview course, often containing team projects and reports. You then take statics/dynamics, thermodynamics, electrical science, and materials science, courses that are normally taught as lectures, with homework and exams, and sometimes project reports. Advanced general engineering courses, such as computer programming, graphics, strength of materials, and controls, are also taught as lectures, but they often have lab sessions in which you work with a team on experimental or computer projects and on written reports. Most programs also require a fourth-year capstone course featuring a team experimental or vehicle design project.

You can probably specialize in either aeronautics (aircraft) or astronautics (spacecraft) at the undergraduate level. Although most programs cover both areas, usually with less emphasis on space, some colleges offer only one or the other. Aerospace courses, such as propulsion, flight mechanics, avionics, and vehicle/system design, have varied formats, but they often contain open-ended design projects (including reports) that you can do on your own or with a team. Technical and experimental electives—such as CAD, FEM (finite element method), courses from other engineering departments, and aerospace-specific courses such as space mission design and robotics lab—have varied formats featuring lectures, lab experiments, or design work.

As an aeronautical/aerospace engineering major, you need to sharpen your ability to visualize in three dimensions, in order to understand complex physical systems. The required work, as you would expect, is harder than in high school. New college students are not always good at budgeting their time, or at studying on their own; developing these skills in high school will give you a leg up. You must also learn how to work with a team. The demands of this major (including project reports and computer projects) leave little time for extracurricular activities. But if you have the time, you can usually join a technical society or a design/build/fly team. Tech societies often organize trips to aerospace companies or professional conferences.

There are four types of aeronautical/aerospace engineering programs approved by the Accreditation Board for Engineering and Technology (ABET): aeronautical engineering programs with a brief introduction to space; space programs with a short introduction to aeronautical engineering; aeronautics and astronautics programs that cover the two areas more or less equally; and aerospace options in fields such as mechanical engineering and engineering mechanics. Accredited programs regularly undergo standardized outside review. On the other hand, some of the best programs in the United States do not seek accreditation. Programs may also differ in their emphasis. Some colleges stress open-ended problems (design) rather than questions with specific answers (analysis). Some programs may include more hands-on experiences, and others, more computer simulations. Even standard aeronautical/aerospace engineering programs may sometimes set a particular emphasis, such as on intelligent systems, information technology, or space telecommunications.

Other majors you might like:
Aeronautics and aviation science
Aeronautical/aerospace engineering technology
Mechanical engineering technology
Astronomy
Astrophysics
Atmospheric sciences
Physics
Instrumentation technology
Marine engineering/naval architecture
Aviation management
Materials science
Nuclear engineering

Questions to ask colleges:
Which of the four ABET accredited aeronautical/aerospace engineering programs does this college offer?

Which facilities (such as wind tunnels, computer labs, and design labs) are available? What designing, building, and flying opportunities exist on a regular basis?

Career options and trends:
Design engineer*; project engineer*; fighter pilot; flight test engineer; research engineer.

Majors usually enter the aerospace industry, which loosely includes the prime aerospace contractors and their chief suppliers, the propulsion industry, academia, NASA, the Federal Aviation Administration, Department of Defense research and development (R&D), other government agencies, and the airlines (to be a pilot, you need rigorous training and licensing). Careers fall into the following areas: R&D, manufacturing, maintenance, marketing/planning, and computer applications technology.

Engineers generally work in groups devoted to specific disciplines, such as systems engineering, structures, aerodynamics, controls, and human factors.

The aeronautical/aerospace engineering industry tends to be cyclical but is projected to grow over the next decade or so: increased defense spending and the need to replace much of the commercial fleet with "next-generation" aircraft are creating job opportunities for graduates. The aerospace industry is distributed across the country, from the West Coast (Seattle, Los Angeles) to the Midwest (St. Louis and Forth Worth) and the South (Atlanta). Workplaces are normally in or near large cities and cultural centers.

Insider's viewpoint:

"I like building things that fly. I also like the fact that aero/astro is a combination of mechanical engineering, electrical engineering, and physics. I'm excited by the cutting edge stuff we do, the hands-on work."

—Stuart, senior, Massachusetts Institute of Technology

For more info:

American Institute of Aeronautics and Astronautics (AIAA)
1801 Alexander Bell Dr.
Suite 500
Reston, VA 20191-4344
(800) 639-2422
www.aiaa.org

NASA/Educational Programs
300 E St., S.W.
Washington, DC 20546
(202) 358-1110
www.nasa.gov

Agricultural and biological engineering

Also known as:
Bioengineering

Biosystems engineering

What it's about:
Majors in agricultural and biological engineering learn to apply principles from the physical, biological, and engineering sciences to come up with improved methods of producing food, fiber, timber, and renewable energy sources; to preserve environmental quality; to tackle problems affecting plant and animal systems; and to develop products from biological resources.

Is this for you?
You might like this major if you also like: farming and agriculture; working on machinery and equipment; the outdoors; biology, chemistry, and math; scientific research; computers. If you are drawn to engineering, but would also like to do something about world hunger and environmental pollution, this major might be a good choice for you.

Consider this major if you are good at: creativity; critical reading/thinking; leadership; math; quantitative analysis; spatial thinking/analysis; teamwork *...or have...* a social conscience; initiative; mechanical facility; verbal skills.

Recommended high school prep:
English 4, math 4 (including trigonometry and pre-calculus), lab science 4 (including biology, chemistry and physics), social studies 3, and a foreign language 2–3. Try to take as many math and science courses as possible, including life sciences, and if they are available, courses in calculus and computer science. You should also take courses in writing and speech, because all engineers must be able to communicate effectively.

Typical courses in this major:
Agricultural engineering design

Biochemistry

Water resources engineering

Power and machinery

Engineering properties of biological materials

Biological and agricultural energy systems

Soil science

Instrumentation and measurement

Transport processes

Bioenvironmental systems design

Hydrology

Food process engineering

Biosystems engineering

Electrical energy applications

Engineering mechanics

Fluid mechanics

Concentrations:
Agricultural process engineering; environmental and natural resources engineering; machine systems design; bioenvironmental controls; biomaterials systems; soil and water resources; food engineering; biochemical engineering.

What the study of this major is like:
The agricultural and biological engineering major, which focuses on theory, analysis, and design, includes supplementary lab work and project development. In core courses, you explore the nature of biological materials and study hydraulic systems, irrigation, agricultural machinery design, and erosion control. You take math, including calculus and differential equations; science, including biology, chemistry, physics, biochemistry, materials science, and plant and animal physiology; and basic engineering courses. In addition, you study the humanities and social sciences, and perhaps computer programming and numerical analysis. To enhance your ability to work with others, you sharpen your oral and written communication skills.

Some students become disillusioned because they don't see how the abstract mathematical principles they encounter in their first and second years apply to the major. But self-discipline, commitment, and perseverance pay off in the third and fourth years, when you explore practical applications in the upper-level courses.

Majors can generally concentrate in several areas, such as food engineering (which focuses on production, nutrition, packaging, factory design, and preservation); soil and water engineering (irrigation, soil science, drainage and hydraulic structure design, and erosion control); or machine design (various topics, such as the automation of animal feeding for large-scale farming). Many colleges offer cooperative education programs that provide opportunities for full-time employment during alternating academic terms. You will probably be eligible for these programs after completing the basic engineering course work. Most colleges include a capstone design course integrating concepts from previous courses.

Agricultural and biological engineering programs may vary in the emphasis they place on different areas of the field. For example, programs may stress natural resource and environmental engineering, food systems engineering, machinery systems engineering, or biological systems engineering. In addition, some programs prefer a hands-on, practical approach, while others focus on the theories behind agricultural and biological engineering.

Other majors you might like:
Aquaculture
Biomedical engineering
Forest engineering
Environmental engineering
Biomedical technology
Food science
Agronomy and crop science
Agricultural equipment technology
Environmental science
Biotechnology
Biochemistry
Genetics

Career options and trends:
Environmental engineer; design engineer; project engineer; product development engineer; soil and water conservationist; irrigation engineer; bioengineer; food engineer.

As the world's population grows and our global ecosystem becomes more fragile, the contributions of agricultural and biological engineers will be increasingly important to society. Technological developments in the biological sciences require engineers to design equipment and processes that make use of these advances. Career opportunities are also available in such related fields as medicine, pharmacy, and bioinstrumentation.

For more info:
American Society of Agricultural and Biological
  Engineers (ASABE)
2950 Niles Rd.
St. Joseph, MI 49085
(269)429-0300
www.asabe.org

Architectural engineering

What it's about:

Architectural engineering combines architecture and engineering to focus on the links between design and construction. Professionals in this discipline work with both architects and other engineers to ensure the timely, effective design and construction of buildings and other structures and systems.

Is this for you?

You might like this major if you also like: building things; discovering how things work; drawing; model making; working with your hands; working in teams; art; history; studying different architectural styles. If you are interested in architecture and have excellent math and science abilities, architectural engineering may be a good major for you.

Consider this major if you are good at: attention to detail; creativity; designing and drafting; math; quantitative analysis; spatial thinking/analysis; teamwork *...or have...* patience; verbal skills; writing skills.

Recommended high school prep:

English 4, math 4 (including calculus or precalculus), lab science 4 (including physics and chemistry), social studies 3, and a foreign language 2–3. Take as many math, science, and English courses as possible. High school physics and chemistry are essential, but geology, biology, and environmental science are also relevant. Courses in computer skills, freehand drawing, CAD, and speech, if available, are good preparation, too.

Typical courses in this major:

Architectural design fundamentals
Thermal/fluid sciences
Energy conservation in buildings
Architectural history
Soil mechanics
Seismic analysis and design
Construction materials and methods
Architectural graphics
Steel and reinforced concrete design
Computer-aided design (CAD)
Lighting and power systems
Fire protection and plumbing design
Environmental systems design
Structural analysis
Construction finance and economics
Specifications and contracts

Concentrations:

Heating, ventilating, and air-conditioning (HVAC) systems; plumbing, piping, and fire protection; energy conservation and solar energy; electrical, lighting, communications, and control systems; structures; construction; acoustics; facility management.

What the study of this major is like:

Historically, architecture at most universities was housed in engineering schools, and architectural engineers were generally viewed as architects with a technical background. But in the late 1970s, many architecture programs, seeing themselves as more artistic than scientific, separated from engineering to form their own schools. Architectural engineering then redefined itself as a hybrid engineering discipline, focused on the analysis, design, and construction of building systems—functions that had once been part of architecture and civil, mechanical, and electrical engineering. But because architectural engineers still receive some architectural training, they are valuable links between architects and traditional engineers working on construction projects.

Both architecture and engineering are challenging fields that require dedication, passion, and stamina. If you are trying to decide between the two majors, architectural engineering might be a good solution. Typically, architectural engineering programs have competitive admissions standards. Therefore, you should take as many rigorous courses in high school as you can.

Even if you had introductory calculus in high school, you will probably be required to take engineering calculus courses in college. Majors typically complete four courses in advanced math, two in physics, one in chemistry, two in English, and several humanities electives. You can also expect to take a series of courses in structures—including statics, dynamics, strength of materials, and steel/concrete design—and some courses in mechanical and electrical systems and basic engineering sciences, such as circuits, thermodynamics, and fluid mechanics. While requirements may vary, most programs include at least one year's worth of architectural design and architectural history courses.

Course work includes lecture classes, lab sessions, and both independent and team projects. Because your work will be challenging, you must become excellent at time management and develop superior study skills. Summer internships are beneficial for obtaining that first full-time, post-graduation position.

All the programs approved by the Accreditation Board for Engineering and Technology (ABET) have similar basic requirements, usually covered in the first two years. However, colleges may differ in their emphasis on architecture, science, or engineering. If you are interested in design, you might choose a program that stresses architectural content, but if you are scientifically inclined, you may want to focus on engineering. Also, some programs include many electives that allow concentrations, whereas other programs are not as flexible. Architectural engineering courses are generally offered through a number of departments, so you may encounter a variety of philosophies and teaching styles.

Training to be a good architectural engineer is hard work. But careers in the field are often intellectually (and financially) rewarding—and you'll appreciate seeing your designs actually built!

Other majors you might like:
Drafting and design technology
Civil engineering
Structural engineering
Construction engineering
Marine engineering/naval architecture

Physics
Construction technology
Fire protection/safety technology
Heating/air conditioning/refrigeration technology
Urban, community, and regional planning
Environmental design
Architectural history/criticism

Questions to ask colleges:
How long will it take to earn a degree? Most bachelor's degree programs take four years, but a few take five years.

Is the program accredited by ABET? Most architectural engineers seek professional registration after graduation, and a degree from an accredited program is required.

Do undergraduates have open access to up-to-date design, computing, and testing laboratories? Are the facilities dedicated to the architectural engineering program, or are they shared with other engineering majors? Are design studios set aside for senior projects?

Career options and trends:
Consulting engineer*; analytical or design engineer*; architect*; engineering manager; construction manager.

Architectural education has become less technical and other engineering fields have become more general. As a result, architectural engineers are in demand because of the unique combination of design and analytical skills they possess. Graduates with concentrations in mechanical and electrical systems are in higher demand than grads with concentrations in construction and structural areas, who face competition from civil and construction engineers. Many architectural engineers move swiftly from design positions to project management and administration. Some soon start their own firms.

For more info:
Architectural Engineering Institute (AEI)
1801 Alexander Bell Dr.
Reston, VA 20191-4400
(800) 548-2723
www.aeinstitute.org

Chemical engineering

What it's about:

Through the study of math and the natural sciences, chemical engineering majors learn to develop products for businesses, government, and consumers; they also look for solutions to regional or global problems, such as pollution. Like most engineers, chemical engineers turn technological advances in the lab into useful materials and services beyond the university walls.

Is this for you?

You might like this major if you also like: science and math (of course); exploring the basic nature of things; lab work and technology.

Consider this major if you are good at: attention to detail; creativity; critical reading/thinking; math; memorizing; organizing; quantitative analysis; teamwork *...or have...* initiative; writing skills.

Recommended high school prep:

English 4, math 4 (including calculus or precalculus), lab science 4 (including biology, chemistry and physics), social studies 3, and a foreign language 2–3. If possible, take other advanced mathematics or science courses.

Did you know...

...that Frank Capra, the director of *It's a Wonderful Life*, earned a chemical engineering degree at Stanford?

Typical courses in this major:

General chemistry
Organic chemistry
Physical chemistry
Physics
Calculus
Differential equations
Computer programming
Statistics
Microbiology
Materials engineering
Energy and material balances
Thermodynamics
Heat mass and momentum transfer
Chemical and biological reaction engineering
Engineering economics
Chemical and pharmaceutical plant design

Concentrations:

Biochemical engineering; biomolecular engineering; biomedical engineering; environmental engineering; materials engineering; thin films and surface science; pharmaceutical engineering.

What the study of this major is like:

Chemical engineers convert the discoveries that physical or biological scientists make in the laboratory into products used by industry, the military, and ordinary consumers. In addition, they play an important role in the new areas of biotechnology (the development of medical treatments), nanotechnology (the science of miniaturization), and information technology. As a chemical engineering major, you are trained to design and develop many of the processes and products necessary for modern industrial society, including antibiotics and other medicines, natural and synthetic fibers, semiconductors, fuel cells, synthetic fuels, petroleum-based fuels and hydrogen, body parts and organ substitutes, and environmental pollution prevention and cleanup. In your work, the primary goal is to create products and processes that are safe and economical.

Chemical engineering programs in the United States are approved by the Accreditation Board for Engineering and Technology (ABET), in cooperation with the American Institute of Chemical Engineers (AIChE). These programs begin with courses in the natural sciences, math, and computer programming. In most programs, you will also be required to study speech and writing as well as the humanities and social sciences. Programs may vary in their focus; they may emphasize materials engineering, bioengineering, environmental concerns, modeling and computer applications, or some or all these areas. Physics and biochemistry or biophysics courses may be included as electives.

One of the most important courses you take as a major is energy and material balances—the basis for the design and evaluation of biological, chemical, energy, and environmental processes. Thermodynamics teaches you to determine the energy efficiency of chemical and biological processes, including those in the human body. In other courses, you learn about the economics of alternative designs, life-cycle analysis, and mathematical analysis by computer simulation. You'll need to get a good background in mathematics to do, for example, rigorous analyses of chemical plant processes. In a capstone course, you may design an entire process for the production of chemicals, fuels, electronic devices, or drinking water from the oceans; or you may design devices for kidney dialysis or blood oxygenators.

Other majors you might like:
Biotechnology
Biochemistry
Agricultural and biological engineering
Biomedical engineering
Materials engineering
Polymer/plastics engineering
Metallurgical engineering
Soil science
Environmental engineering
Chemical technology
Forensic science
Clinical/medical laboratory technology

Questions to ask colleges:
Does the college help students find internships while in school, and jobs after graduating?

Ask to see the facilities, particularly the computer rooms and student work areas. You should also ask for a list of graduate schools, companies, and government agencies that the previous 100–200 graduates enrolled in or were offered jobs by.

Career options and trends:
Consulting engineer; product designer/engineer; research and development engineer; production engineer or plant manager; sales representative; environmental engineer.

Careers are readily available in the environmental, pharmaceutical, materials, fuel, and specialty chemical industries. Positions in the alternative energy and biotechnology fields are rapidly expanding. Engineering positions will require state certification in addition to the required degrees.

Insider's viewpoint:
"Go to class and get involved; just get through those first two years and you're golden."

—Travis, senior, Penn State

For more info:
American Institute of Chemical Engineers (AIChE)
3 Park Ave.
New York, NY 10016-5991
(212) 591-8100
www.aiche.org

Civil engineering

What it's about:

Civil engineering majors learn to apply the principles of science and math to the planning, construction, and maintenance of facilities, both public and private, that are essential to industrialized society. Civil engineers work on buildings; on such large-scale projects as bridges, dams, highways, environmental control systems, and water purification systems; and on other structures in both the urban and rural environments.

Is this for you?

You might like this major if you also like: learning how things work (building things, taking things apart); thinking big; brain teaser puzzles; math and science; achieving practical results; outdoor activities; watching construction sites. If you like to solve problems by dividing them up into logical parts (divide and conquer), then civil engineering might be a good choice. Projects tend to be large in scope, and you should have the patience for complexity and long-term commitments.

Consider this major if you are good at: attention to detail; math; organizing; quantitative analysis; research; spatial thinking/analysis; teamwork ...*or have...* initiative; interpersonal skills; mechanical facility; verbal skills.

Recommended high school prep:

English 4, math 4 (including trigonometry, geometry, and calculus or precalculus), lab science 3–4 (including chemistry and physics), social studies 3, and a foreign language 2–3. Courses in computer applications, business, and economics are also helpful.

Typical courses in this major:

Engineering graphics
Structural analysis and design
Soil mechanics
Statics
Dynamics
Strength of materials
Surveying
Environmental engineering
Construction materials
Fluid mechanics
Water resources
Engineering economics
Transportation engineering
Geotechnical engineering
Construction management
Hydraulics and hydrology

Concentrations:

Structural engineering; geotechnical engineering; environmental engineering; construction; transportation engineering; hydrosystems (hydraulics, hydrology, water resources).

What the study of this major is like:

Civil engineers plan, analyze, design, and erect structures (such as buildings, bridges) and systems (transportation, water supply). Civil engineering is often called "the people-serving profession" because many of its projects serve the public good. To tackle complex problems, civil engineers use principles of math and science, as well as their creativity. Civil engineering works are generally large-scale, one-of-a-kind projects, usually requiring cooperation among professionals from a variety of disciplines.

Differences among civil engineering programs are minimal because of the requirements established by the Accreditation Board for Engineering and Technology (ABET). Programs include a broad range of courses in mathematics (especially calculus and differential equations); basic sciences (chemistry, physics, and possibly geology or biology); engineering sciences; engineering design; and the humanities and social sciences. In addition, programs may include courses in computers, English composition, speech, report writing, engineering economics, and statistics.

You can expect to take most professional courses during your last two years of study. In civil engineering, probably more than in any other engineering field, you can concentrate in a number of areas. Some typical concentrations include the following:

Structural engineering. The planning and design of large structures, including bridges, buildings, towers, dams, offshore drilling, and exploration facilities.

Environmental engineering. The planning and design of facilities for water purification; control of air and water pollution; solid water management; and disposal of hazardous materials.

Geotechnical engineering. The analysis and design of foundations and retaining walls; the development of excavation and construction techniques for tunnels, dams, and storage systems for hazardous materials.

Hydrosystems. The analysis and design of dams, floodwalls, pumping stations, aqueducts, canals, harbor and coastal facilities, irrigation and drainage systems, and navigable waterways.

Transportation engineering. The analysis and design of facilities for highways, airports, railways, aerospace systems, and pipelines.

Most courses are taught in lecture format, but some have lab components. In most technical courses, you learn primarily by solving "story problems": scenarios are described to the class, and you must determine which theories are applicable, which information is superfluous, which information is missing, and so on. Later courses often have open-ended problems, possibly involving teamwork or research. Like all engineering majors, this one is very demanding. Because many of your courses build on one another, you need to keep up with your studies.

Other majors you might like:

Mechanical engineering
Civil engineering technology
Industrial engineering
Materials science
Architecture
Architectural engineering
Construction management

Ocean engineering
Physics
Urban, community, and regional planning
Geology/earth science
Surveying technology

Questions to ask colleges:

Is there a student chapter of the American Society of Civil Engineers (ASCE) on campus?

Does the college offer a five-year combined bachelor's/master's degree program? (More than one-third of civil engineering graduates go on to earn a master's degree.)

Does the college offer a five-year cooperative study program in which you alternate periods of study with related employment?

Career options and trends:

Consulting engineer*; city engineer or official at a state or federal agency (e.g., EPA, Department of Transportation)*; construction engineer; researcher in a government laboratory, forensic engineering firm, or university.

Civil Engineers often need a professional engineer's (PE) license to practice. In some states, structural engineering (SE) has a separate licensure. Increasingly, a master's degree is required for entry-level positions or advancement.

Since many civil engineering projects are large in scope, they create numerous jobs that last a long time. As a result, employment may remain strong for some time after an economic downturn. Thus, hiring trends in civil engineering may lag behind national trends.

Insider's viewpoint:

"I love civil engineering because it is a field with a fascinating balance between the certainty of science and uncertainty of the natural environment."

—Professor Keith Hjelmstad, University of Illinois

For more info:

American Society of Civil Engineers (ASCE)
1801 Alexander Bell Drive
Reston, VA 20191-4400
(800) 548-2723
(www.asce.org)

Electrical and communications engineering

Also known as:
Electrical and computer engineering

What it's about:
Electrical and communications engineering deals with the design, manufacture, and operation of the range of devices and systems that depend on electricity—from wireless telephones to giant power generators. You examine superconductors, wave propagation, energy storage, fiber optics, reception, and amplification, from both a theoretical and an applied perspective.

Is this for you?
You might like this major if you also like: tinkering (putting things together, taking them apart, making them work); music; ham radio; computers.

Consider this major if you are good at: attention to detail; creativity; math; organizing; quantitative analysis; spatial thinking/analysis; teamwork; vsualization ...*or have...* initiative; writing skills.

Recommended high school prep:
English 4, math 4 (including precalculus or calculus), lab science 3-4 (including physics), social studies 3, and a foreign language 2-3. Advanced or honors courses in math and physics are recommended, as well as courses in computer applications and writing.

Did you know...
...that more engineers are employed in electrical engineering than in any other branch of engineering? According to the U.S. Bureau of Labor Statistics, nearly one-third work in California, Texas, New York, and New Jersey, where many large electronics firms are located.

Typical courses in this major:
Electric circuits and systems
Electromagnetics
Control systems
Electromechanical energy conversion
Digital circuits
Materials science
Microwaves and high-speed circuits
Signal processing
Semiconductor electronics
Instrumentation
Microprocessor systems
Fields, matter, and waves
Communications systems
Physics of electronic devices
Fiber optics and photonics
Electrical engineering practicum

Concentrations:
In college: communications systems; electric power; electronic design; electromagnetics; computer systems; digital systems; control systems; telecommunications.

If you go on to grad school: physical electronics; bioengineering; wireless engineering; electronics packaging; photonics; microwave engineering.

What the study of this major is like:
Most electrical and communications engineering programs begin with an introduction to the design process that stresses engineering fundamentals and suggests some of the careers you might pursue after graduation. You also start with mathematics, physics, and some chemistry courses that are the basis for many engineering courses you will take later on.

Your other courses cover engineering science and design, humanities, social sciences, and electives that correspond to your concentration. In humanities and social sciences courses, you see how the work that engineers do impacts society. You will probably participate in a significant design project in your fourth year, or perhaps earlier. Most students find the experience rewarding because it brings together what you've learned in various courses and helps you understand what engineering can accomplish. These projects, which are usually team efforts and may involve professional engineers and instructors, often require a written report and perhaps several oral presentations.

You learn by attending lectures and by working on computers, but especially by doing homework. Working through your homework problems and making sure you understand the concepts they illustrate is essential. Most engineering students do homework in small groups, but you should find out what your professors' policies are—sometimes instructors prefer that you work independently. You'll also take a number of lab courses, in which you explore abstract principles you learn in the classroom. Labs also provide opportunities to develop teamwork skills and your ability to write clear technical reports.

Your education does not necessarily take place entirely on campus. You will probably take a number of field trips to engineering labs and factories. You may also work as an engineering summer intern—an invaluable experience that can help when you seek your first job. In addition, many international programs allow engineering students to work or study abroad while earning academic credit.

Although there is much similarity among programs, there are also variations in coverage or emphasis. Some programs stress computer engineering; others may have more courses in digital communication technology and information science. All programs prepare graduates for entry into the profession, but some devote more attention to preparing students for graduate school. Graduates from these programs, which tend to emphasize theory over application, may need more on-the-job training before they can work independently in industry.

The ABET (Accreditation Board for Engineering and Technology) standards for approving engineering programs in the United States require that programs clearly state their objectives. These goals (published in college catalogs) might help you clarify a program's focus to see if it fits your interests. As in all areas of engineering, your education never really ends, because of the need to keep up with the rapid advances in electrical and communications technology.

Other majors you might like:
Mechanical engineering
Engineering physics
Systems engineering
Metallurgical engineering
Software engineering
Electrical engineering technologies
Rehabilitation engineering/assistive technology
Computer science
Physics
Neuroscience
Electrical drafting/CAD/CADD
Computer engineering technology

Questions to ask colleges:
Is computer engineering considered part of the electrical engineering major, or a separate major?

Are co-op educational experiences available?

How do you prepare graduates to work in an industry where outsourcing of engineering services is a growing trend?

Career options and trends:
Production engineer*; design engineer; engineering manager; systems analyst; consulting engineer*; field engineer; research engineer.

Licensure (or registration) as a professional engineer (PE) is often required of engineers working in the public sector (for instance, for power companies and government agencies) but not of engineers working for private firms. Although some electrical engineers (EEs) are licensed, most are not.

Job prospects are likely to be favorable, especially for graduates who have had engineering intern experience. Consulting engineering firms are expected to generate the fastest job growth. Because most products today involve electricity and electronics, EEs are found in almost every industry at every level, doing all kinds of work—from designing integrated circuits to performing instrumentation on a ship in the Antarctic Ocean.

"In my first class, my partner and I designed the logic for a small, battery-powered vehicle to follow a path on the ground set by white tape. We used sensors on the vehicle to follow the tape and then send the correct signals to the motors and wheels. If anyone had told me before that I would be doing this my first semester, I probably would not have believed them."

—Ray, junior, University of Illinois at Urbana–Champaign

For more info:

The Institute of Electrical and Electronics
   Engineers (IEEE)
445 Hoes Lane
Piscataway, NJ 08854
(732) 981-0060
www.ieee.org

Association for Computer Machinery (ACM)
1515 Broadway
New York, NY 10036-5701
(800) 342-6626
www.acm.org

Industrial engineering

What it's about:

Industrial engineering is the most "people-oriented" of the engineering fields. As a major, you learn to plan, design, and implement complex systems for industry that take into account the needs and capabilities of individuals and groups, as well as the availability of information, equipment, and materials. Industrial engineers (IEs) find ways to increase both productivity and customer satisfaction in all kinds of organizations, from hospitals to steel foundries, and they are the only engineers educated as quality and productivity improvement professionals.

Is this for you?

You might like this major if you also like: helping people; working in teams; math and science; figuring out how to do things more easily; working with numbers; debating; solving puzzles and brain teasers.

Consider this major if you are good at: attention to detail; communicating ideas; creativity; critical reading/thinking; leadership; math; organizing; persuading/influencing; quantitative analysis ...*or have...* initiative; listening skills.

Recommended high school prep:

English 4, math 4 (up to precalculus), lab science 4 (including biology, chemistry and physics), social studies 3, and a foreign language 2–3. English is important because industrial engineers must effectively communicate the ideas and procedures they develop. If available, courses in speech, psychology, and economics are also helpful.

Did you know...

...that industrial engineers are more widely distributed among manufacturing businesses than any other type of engineer? And IEs also work in unexpected places, like Disney World and other theme parks.

Typical courses in this major:

Production planning and control
Operations research
Quality control
Supply chain logistics
Human factors
Ergonomics
Facilities planning and design
Discrete event computer simulation
Engineering management
Engineering economics
Probability and statistics
Materials handling and control
Computer modeling
Information systems
Robotics
Safety management

Concentrations:

Generally, none in college; but if you go on to grad school: manufacturing; operations research; ergonomics; management systems.

What the study of this major is like:

While other engineers produce things, industrial engineers create or improve the systems and procedures used in making or doing things. The work that IEs do has been around a long time, and the profession has been recognized since the 1920s. In the early 1900s, two of industrial engineering's founders, Frank and Lillian Gilbreth, helped determine the "one best way" for hospitals to perform surgery and train doctors, nurses, and technicians. As a result, operating times dropped drastically and survival rates increased. Today, IEs serve as integration engineers, focusing on the way the numerous components of industrial or service systems work as a unit. In figuring out how to improve a procedure, IEs seek to reduce or eliminate the many areas of waste, especially of time, money, materials, and energy.

IEs concern themselves with the design of workplaces, ergonomic and safety studies, and productivity. They design factories (workstations, automated procedures, and robotics; material handling systems; and control systems) and determine the "best way" to manufacture goods. But the word "industrial" refers to more than just manufacturing; today, IEs work in (or with) providers of health care, lodging, and food service; in defense and government; and in such businesses as transportation and communications. A typical task might involve getting a package from San Francisco to Düsseldorf overnight.

Your first two years as a major are similar to those of most engineering students. You take courses in math, the physical sciences, and engineering sciences such as statics, thermodynamics, and electrical circuits. These two years can be intellectually challenging, and you may wonder whether you'll ever get to your chosen field of study, industrial engineering; perseverance and patience will pay off. In your third and fourth years, you explore topical areas of the major and take supporting math and statistics courses. Here, most students begin to identify their fields of interest.

You can expect to receive a diverse education in computer systems, design, and management, as well as in the physical and social sciences, including economics. Because IEs focus on organizations and the people in them, you will need to take arts and humanities courses. Your schedule will be full, with little room for electives.

Among different industrial engineering programs, requirements are similar and philosophies are fundamentally the same. Most programs stress manufacturing, operations research (applying mathematical modeling and analysis to problems), or "general" industrial engineering, which covers all or most topical areas. A few undergraduate programs have an in-depth focus on safety management, logistics, quality control, or human factors.

Other majors you might like:
Systems engineering
Business administration and management
Management science
Materials engineering
Industrial technology
Information systems
Psychology
Occupational safety/health technology
Management information systems
Human resources management
Economics
Organizational behavior studies

Questions to ask colleges:
How extensive and state-of-the-art are the computer lab facilities, and how accessible are they to undergrads? For industrial engineering majors, the computing equipment is essential because of the specialized (and often expensive) software they use.

Which types of research projects are under way? The answer will provide insight into the interests and strengths of the faculty.

Career options and trends:
Consulting industrial engineer*; manufacturing/production supervisor*; plant manager or chief operating officer; quality engineer; safety engineer; systems engineer; materials manager; operations analyst*; process engineer.

The declining role of manufacturing in the U.S. economy will affect job prospects for industrial engineers (although opportunities may increase overseas). At the same time, demand for IEs is increasing in service industries, such as banking and insurance; health care; transportation and distribution; environmental protection; and information processing.

Because of their people skills and their ability to see the "big picture" and to take a systemwide view of problems and opportunities, many IEs move into management positions.

For more info:
Institute of Industrial Engineers (IIE)
3577 Parkway Lane, Suite 200
Norcross, GA 30092
(800) 494-0460
www.iienet.org

Marine engineering/naval architecture

What it's about:

Marine engineers and naval architects design, build, operate, and maintain a wide variety of oceangoing vehicles, from recreational boats to ships at sea. Marine engineering concentrates on ship machinery, including propulsion, electrical, mechanical, and control systems. Naval architecture focuses on ship design, including hull shape, structure, power requirements, and performance.

Is this for you?

You might like this major if you also like: anything to do with ships and the sea; boating; competitive sailing; working with machinery; drawing, drafting, and design; model ship building; radio-controlled boat building; math and science.

Consider this major if you are good at: attention to detail; creativity; critical reading/thinking; making decisions; math; quantitative analysis; spatial thinking/analysis *...or have...* communication skills; initiative; mechanical facility; patience.

Recommended high school prep:

English 4, math 4 (including trigonometry and calculus), lab science 3–4 (including chemistry and physics), social studies 3, and a foreign language 2–3. Take as much math and science as you can. Courses that prepare you to communicate well are also important. Knowledge of a foreign language would be useful, as the maritime industry is, by its nature, global. If possible, take courses in spreadsheet applications, manual graphics, and computer-assisted design (CAD).

Typical courses in this major:

Foundations of ship design
Hullform and hydrostatics
Intact and damaged stability
Ship structures
Resistance and powering
Seakeeping and maneuvering
Ship production
Marine power systems
Solid mechanics
Thermodynamics
Marine hydrodynamics
Marine electronics
Marine dynamics
Sailing craft design
Small craft design

Concentrations:

Generally, none in college; but if you go on to grad school: structural analysis; hydrodynamics; autonomous vehicles; maritime business; marine power systems; sailing yachts; energy conversion; nuclear propulsion; control systems; robotics.

What the study of this major is like:

Marine engineering and naval architecture has wide-ranging applications to ships and boats, from tankers to trawlers, submarines to sailboats, military ships to personal watercraft. It encompasses a variety of engineering challenges, including stability, seakeeping, engine selection, space utilization, structural design, model testing, propeller design, high-speed submarine dynamics, and historical ship performance.

The major usually stresses general technical content and design. Programs tend to be more applied than theoretical, although both facets are covered. Hands-on lab experiences are essential. As part of a long tradition, you take capstone courses in ship design. Field trips and practical work experience are also highly useful and instructive.

As a major, you will face challenges typical of any engineering program. Some students have a hard time with the spatial visualization of complex three-dimensional shapes. In addition, you may have to develop the ingenuity and patience needed in tackling the open-ended engineering problems that are often solved through repetitive trials. You should be prepared to spend plenty of time on your course work, especially on design courses. At the end of the program, you will be rewarded with comprehensive knowledge and a confidence in your ability to do the work. You will understand "the big picture" of the engineering and design of ships.

Although entry requirements are uniform, the various marine engineering and naval architecture programs reflect the expertise and interests of the teaching faculty. Some programs emphasize the analysis of marine vehicles; some, the design of marine vehicles; others, a particular category of ships or boats; and still others, a combination of these fields. In some programs, industry experience is incorporated into the curriculum. Also, some institutions consider their marine engineering and naval architecture programs to be subsets of larger engineering programs.

Other majors you might like:
Ocean engineering
Marine science/Merchant Marine
Electrical and communications engineering
Nuclear engineering
Oceanography
Mechanical engineering
Fishing and fisheries
Military technologies
Aircraft powerplant technology
Marine maintenance/fitter/ship repair
Drafting and design technology

Questions to ask colleges:
Do majors have access to a marine towing tank as an integral part of their academic program? Other facilities to inquire about: model basin, gravity wave tank, propeller tunnel, CAD computer laboratories.

How is the curriculum split between marine engineering and naval architecture studies? Does the school's marine engineering curriculum emphasize design or ship operations?

Is there a summer internship program in the marine industry?

Career options and trends:
Naval architect*; marine engineer*; yacht designer; naval officer; ship's officer (Merchant Marine); shipyard engineer.

Majors in marine engineering and naval architecture also pursue careers in ship operations and marine commerce. After additional professional or graduate study, you may find work in admiralty law or research. It is not necessary to be registered as a professional engineer (PE) to obtain employment, but it is a respected credential. Registration requirements vary, but they generally involve two examinations and a period of work experience.

For the near future, the job market in the marine transportation industry is projected to be tight. Ship design, building, and operations have become an increasingly international business. As a result of global events and technological advances, significant changes are occurring in military ship design. Commercial goods will continue to travel by ships. The recreational boat industry in the United States is cyclical, but is currently growing.

For more info:
Society of Naval Architects and Marine Engineers (SNAME)
601 Pavonia Ave.
Jersey City, NJ 07306
(800)798-2188
www.sname.org

American Society of Naval Engineers (ASNE)
1452 Duke St.
Alexandria, VA 22314-3458
(703) 836-6727
www.navalengineers.org

Materials engineering

Also known as:
Materials science and engineering

What it's about:
This major focuses on the materials used by all engineers: ceramics, metals, polymers, and combinations of these (composites). The major provides a rigorous exposure to the principles governing the fabrication, properties, and applications of these materials. Because a primary task of engineers is to create various types of products from a wide variety of ingredients, the study of materials is a gateway to almost any engineering field or project.

Is this for you?
You might like this major if you also like: chemistry, physics, and math; exploring the nature of things. Are you fascinated by the architecture of materials at the atomic and molecular levels? Do you wonder what things are made of—for example, computers, milk cartons, DVD players? Have you asked yourself, "Why are some plastics hard, while others are soft?" Would you rather work on a range of engineering projects than be limited to a particular field? If your answer is yes, read on.

Consider this major if you are good at: attention to detail; creativity; critical reading/thinking; math; organizing; quantitative analysis; spatial thinking/analysis; teamwork *...or have...* initiative; manual dexterity; writing skills.

Recommended high school prep:
English 4, math 4 (including precalculus), lab science 4 (including chemistry and physics), social studies 3, and a foreign language 2–3. If it is available, take a course that covers both integral and differential calculus. Courses that help you develop writing and speaking skills are essential in engineering.

Did you know...
...there are such things as "magnetic liquids" (magneto-rheological fluids), that you can morph from a fluid to a solid simply by moving your hand through them, and "memory metal" (Nitinol), which, after being bent and twisted, returns to its original shape with a blast of hot air? The discovery of materials like these, and the development of applications for them, is the fun part of materials engineering.

Typical courses in this major:
Introduction to materials
Thermodynamics of materials
Kinetics of materials
Physical metallurgy
Processing and properties of ceramics
Composites
Fundamentals of polymers
Polymer processing
Mechanical behavior of solids
Materials engineering design
Materials characterization laboratory
Engineering computational laboratory
Degradation of materials
Failure analysis
Phase equilibria
Senior design project

Concentrations:
In college: biomaterials; ceramic materials; composites; electronic materials; metals and alloys; nanomaterials; polymeric materials.

If you go on to grad school: materials processing; process and microsection modeling; smart materials.

What the study of this major is like:
Materials are a common denominator among all branches of engineering because, without them, engineers cannot work. When designing systems,

other engineers (civil, chemical, electrical, mechanical) frequently collaborate with materials engineers to select the most appropriate materials. Materials engineering can be done at the atomic level (as in fiber reinforcement to make a graphite fishing rod) or at the macroscopic level (as in the manufacture of appliances, cars, and bridges). In fact, everything we see and use—from skyscrapers to computers—is made of materials derived from the earth. As a major, you learn to develop materials to meet specific needs.

Programs normally include math, communications, computer science, natural sciences (especially chemistry and physics), humanities, social sciences, engineering science, and engineering design courses. As a major, you study the physical and chemical properties of materials, transport phenomena, strength of materials, and tools for structural and chemical characterization. You use differential and integral calculus to solve equations governing the behavior of solids. In design courses, you gain practice in devising materials, components, systems, or processes to meet particular objectives. In various courses you will employ a variety of tools (such as electron microscopes, and software for modeling the behavior of materials and components) and ways of processing material (such as microgravity processing).

Typically, materials engineering classes are small (about 20 students), allowing for close interaction between students and faculty members. You learn primarily through lectures, presentations, and hands-on laboratories. You are encouraged to develop your oral and writing skills. Because much of the subject matter is conceptual, you must learn how to visualize solid materials in three dimensions.

Course requirements are similar at most colleges. All programs focus on the relation, in solids, of processing, microstructure, and property. Some colleges may stress mechanics of materials, thermodynamics, or kinetics. Other programs emphasize a particular material, such as ceramics or polymers. Differences in approach generally reflect faculty members' interest and expertise.

This major is often referred to as a science as well as an engineering discipline, because much of the science (chemistry and physics) of engineering materials is still being developed. You will find that most programs have a high ratio of graduate research students to undergraduate majors. This usually results in many opportunities for undergraduates to take part in important research on new materials, such as carbon nano tubes, for example.

Other majors you might like:

Materials science
Ceramic sciences/engineering
Polymer/plastics engineering
Metallurgical engineering
Mining and mineral engineering
Physics
Chemical engineering
Agricultural and biological engineering
Biotechnology
Manufacturing engineering
Industrial engineering
Hazardous materials technology

Questions to ask colleges:

Is the program accredited by the Accreditation Board for Engineering and Technology (ABET)?

Are faculty members engaged in research?

Is there a graduate program in materials science or engineering on campus? Are there opportunities for undergraduates to join in research, or to pursue independent study projects?

What types of lab facilities and equipment (such as electron microscopes) do undergrads have access to?

Career options and trends:

Applications engineer*; production engineer; metallurgist; polymer engineer*; industrial research and development staff member*; technical writer.

There is a continuing demand for undergraduates majoring in materials engineering. Every year, fewer than 1,000 students receive bachelor's degrees in this discipline. For this reason and because of the interdisciplinary nature of the field, there are a wide variety of job opportunities. Salaries are competitive with those in other fields of engineering.

Insider's viewpoint:

"It's a lot of fun; you get to break a lot of things. With materials you really get to delve into the nitty-gritty. Instead of mechanical engineers who look at how they can build a structure and how all the forces will act on the structure, we look at the little parts inside, what makes that structure."

—Tom, junior, Case Western Reserve University

For more info:

Materials Research Society (MRS)
506 Keystone Drive
Warrendale, PA 15086-7573
(724) 779-3003
www.mrs.org

The Minerals, Metals, and Materials Society (TMS)
184 Thorn Hill Rd.
Warrendale, PA 15086-7514
(724) 776-9000
www.tms.org

The Materials Information Society (ASM
  International)
9639 Kinsman Road
Materials Park, OH 44073-0002
(800) 336-5152
www.asminternational.org

Mechanical engineering

What it's about:

Mechanical engineering deals with the forces and energy at work in thermal and mechanical (solid and fluid) systems. You learn the engineering principles underlying the generation, transmission, and utilization of these energies, and the design, production, and application of mechanical devices and systems.

Is this for you?

You might like this major if you also like: mechanical devices; learning how things work; computers; cars; solving problems; math and science.

Consider this major if you are good at: attention to detail; creativity; organizing; quantitative analysis; research; spatial thinking/analysis *...or have...* manual dexterity; mechanical facility; verbal skills; writing skills.

Recommended high school prep:

English 4, math 4 (including precalculus), laboratory science 4 (including chemistry and physics), social studies 2, a foreign language 2–3. If it is available, take a computer science course.

Typical courses in this major:

Statics
Dynamics
Circuit analysis
Engineering graphics
Mechanical design fundamentals
Computer modeling
Mechanical vibrations
Solid mechanics
Energy systems
Mechanical systems
Fluid mechanics
Automatic controls
Thermodynamics
Materials science
Manufacturing systems
Heat transfer

Concentrations:

Automatic controls; energy systems; materials engineering, design, manufacturing systems; thermal systems; automotive engineering.

What the study of this major is like:

In mechanical engineering, you focus on mechanics (fluids and solids) and heat as forms of energy. You learn about the forces and motions that affect mechanical performance. Before you build a device, you use math to determine what the machine will do. You learn to model—to visualize a piece of equipment and to convey to others what it would do. And you learn what's involved in manufacturing the machinery you design—for example, a vehicle, an acoustic system, an engine.

All engineering disciplines start out the same way: with courses in math (calculus through differential equations) and numerical analysis; natural science (chemistry, physics, and perhaps biology or materials science); humanities and social science; and basic engineering science. In your second year, you will be introduced to mechanical engineering, in courses that include the design of thermal and mechanical systems. Training in engineering design, which is now largely computer-based, involves modeling, simulation, analysis, and synthesis.

Programs generally emphasize theory and analysis as well as design, with appropriate supporting labs and project work in such areas as these:

Engineering mechanics. Static and dynamic forces within and on structures; equivalent force systems; dynamics; stresses and strains; and strength of materials.

Materials. Properties of materials; physical metallurgy; and metallic and other materials including polymers, ceramics, and composites.

Electrical systems. Electrical circuits; direct and alternating current; electrical machinery; digital and analog electronic devices; circuits; and control systems.

Thermal systems. Fluid mechanics; thermodynamics; combustion; refrigeration; heat transfer; energy systems; and internal combustion engines.

Mechanical systems. Kinematics and mechanisms; modeling of multicomponent systems; control of mechanical systems; vibrations; component design and analysis; machine design; and dynamics of machinery.

Manufacturing systems. Modern manufacturing systems; robotics; computer-aided manufacturing systems; artificial intelligence; and computers integrated in manufacturing.

Specialty course work or technical electives typically include in-depth study of acoustics and noise control; advanced control system design; applied solar energy; automotive engineering; biomechanics and biomedical engineering; biotechnology; computer-aided design; composite materials; direct energy conversion; energy conservation; energy system analysis; environmental control systems; gas dynamics; heating, ventilating, and air conditioning; nondestructive testing; numerical modeling and simulation; packaging engineering; propulsion systems; polymer processing; robotics; and turbomachinery.

Because computers are used in the solution of many engineering problems, the major includes a great deal of programming and numerical analysis.

Many colleges offer cooperative education programs, which provide opportunities for full-time employment during alternating academic terms. Such programs are generally available after you have completed the basic engineering course work.

Other majors you might like:
Mechanical engineering technology
Aeronautical/aerospace engineering
Nuclear engineering
Robotics technology
Marine engineering/naval architecture
Electrical and communications engineering
Physics
Industrial engineering

Materials engineering
Drafting and design technology

Career options and trends:
Consulting engineer; industrial engineer; plastics fabrication engineer; safety engineer; test engineer; automotive engineer; manufacturing engineer; design engineer; research and development engineer.

Mechanical engineers are engaged in a wide range of careers in industry, business, government, and universities. They interact with people and machines in research, design, development, testing, manufacturing, operations, marketing, sales, and management. Continued demand for graduates trained in mechanical and materials engineering is projected for the near future.

Insider's viewpoint:
"There is a lot of freedom in a mechanical engineering major. I feel like I'm learning a thought process as opposed to a trade, and this thought process is more powerful than anything you could memorize from a book."

—Alison, junior, Colorado State University

For more info:
American Society of Mechanical Engineers (ASME)
3 Park Avenue
New York, NY 10016-5990
(800) 843-2763
www.asme.org

Metallurgical engineering

What it's about:

In this major, you study the structure, properties, and performance of metals and alloys. Metallurgical engineering is a distinct discipline, although it is closely related to the more inclusive fields of materials science and materials engineering, which address similar relationships in all classes of materials (such as metals, ceramics, polymers, and fabrics).

Is this for you?

You might like this major if you also like: chemistry, physics, and math; exploring the nature of things. Have you ever asked yourself, "Why is glass transparent and steel shiny? Why do some steels rust and others don't? What makes some metals magnetic and other not?" If so, this major might interest you.

Consider this major if you are good at: attention to detail; creativity; critical reading/thinking; math; organizing data; quantitative analysis; spatial thinking/analysis; teamwork ...*or have...* initiative; patience; writing skills.

Recommended high school prep:

English 4, math 4 (including trigonometry and calculus or precalculus), lab science 3–4 (including chemistry and physics), social studies 3, and a foreign language 2–3.

Did you know...

...that most high school students considering metallurgical engineering envision a career in a steel mill or foundry? Such careers are actually in the minority. Many metallurgical engineers work in the aerospace industry, processing exotic alloys; in the microelectronics industry, contributing to advances in electro-optical materials; or in the biomedical industry, developing implants and biomedical sensors.

Typical courses in this major:

Structure and properties of materials
Mechanics of materials
Mechanical behavior of solids
Metallurgical thermodynamics
Physical metallurgy
Chemical metallurgy
Extractive metallurgy
Processing and properties of metals
Transport phenomena in metallurgy
Casting and solidification processing
Metallurgic engineering design
Degradation of materials
Engineering economics
Senior design project

Concentrations:

In college: physical metallurgy; extractive metallurgy.

If you go on to grad school: programs may focus on a specific alloy, processing technique, or application.

What the study of this major is like:

Although metallurgical engineering builds on a tradition of metalworking that is thousands of years old, it is sufficiently complex that materials and processes are continuously being discovered. Until fairly recently, high-temperature superconductivity, amorphous metals, buckyballs, and carbon nanotubes were unknown. Yet, if you consider the many elements on the periodic table, the ways in which they can be combined, and the possibilities for processing them to achieve novel structures, you will realize that the universe of achievable materials has barely been explored.

As an undergraduate in a program approved by ABET (Accreditation Board for Engineering and Technology), you must complete two years of math (including calculus and differential equations) and at least a year of both chemistry and physics. Majors typically take at least 48 semester credits of engineering-related courses, divided between general engineering courses (such as statics, design, and programming) and metallurgical core courses.

The core courses stress the relationships among the structure, properties, processing, and performance of metals and alloys. You study the structure of a metal on scales ranging from the bonding between individual atoms to the interaction of macroscopically visible components in engineered composites (such as fibers and particles). You use advanced techniques including optical and electron microscopy; X-ray diffraction; mechanical testing; thermal analysis; and electrical, magnetic, and optical characterization of materials.

Other courses cover the mechanical, chemical, and physical properties of alloys. Typically, you are required to take at least one course on mechanical properties and one course on physical properties (electrical, magnetic, optical). Often courses on electrochemical behavior of material (such as corrosion) are also required.

You study processing in courses that range from the thermodynamics of materials and the kinetic processes that govern movement of atoms and molecules, to the applied aspects of materials processing, such as sintering, casting, or vapor deposition of metals and alloys.

The desired performance of metals and alloys is governed by their properties, as well as factors such as cost, availability, and recyclability. Performance is usually incorporated into a number of courses and then emphasized in a major design project—which you probably undertake during your last year—that integrates knowledge and skills from earlier courses.

Most departments are relatively small and informal. Depending on the college, classes have from 10 to 50 students. Because metallurgical engineering depends on the application of advanced experimental techniques, you may take more lab classes than students in other engineering majors. Most majors get to know faculty members and fellow students, and many programs have student societies that help you become integrated into the profession before you graduate.

There are significant differences in emphasis among various departments across the United States. Some programs focus exclusively on metals; some include other classes of materials (ceramics, composites, and so on.). While some programs emphasize extractive processing of commodity metals, others concentrate on physical metallurgy and the application of engineering alloys. A careful examination of third- and fourth-year core and elective courses gives you a good indication of a program's emphasis.

Other majors you might like:

Materials engineering
Ceramic sciences/engineering
Chemical engineering
Electrical and communications engineering
Materials science
Chemistry
Physics
Metallurgical technology
Electrical engineering technology

Career options and trends:

Industrial metallurgist*; industrial researcher; research scientist at a university; quality control specialist; production engineer; production supervisor.

Because metallurgical and materials engineers work in all segments of the manufacturing economy, employment prospects for graduates tend to be less affected by downturns in a single industry than are some other engineering disciplines. Demand for metallurgical and materials engineers will likely be sustained by the need for fuel-efficient transportation; by advances in biomaterials, computers, and information technology; and by increased spending on national defense.

For more info:

The Minerals, Metals, and Materials Society (TMS)
184 Thorn Hill Rd.
Warrendale, PA 15086
(724) 776-9000
www.tms.org

Mining and mineral engineering

Also known as:
Natural resources engineering

What it's about:
Mining engineering is the application of scientific principles to the discovery, appraisal, and extraction of minerals from the earth and the sea. The engineer may work in underground mines or mines on the Earth's surface, overseeing the recovery of mineral resources from the natural environment; processing the extracted materials; ensuring safety; and restoring the land.

Is this for you?
You might like this major if you also like: rocks and rock collecting; fossil collecting; working outdoors rather than in an office; camping, fishing, hiking; the prospect of working with large, complex equipment.

Consider this major if you are good at: leadership; math; quantitative analysis; spatial thinking/analysis; teamwork *...or have...* initiative; mechanical facility; patience; verbal skills; writing skills.

Recommended high school prep:
English 4, math 4 (including trigonometry, calculus or precalculus), lab science 3–4 (including chemistry and physics), social studies 3, and a foreign language 2–3. Courses in written and oral communication are also important.

Did you know...
...that according to the U.S. Bureau of Mines, for every American, every year, the equivalent of 40,000 pounds of new minerals, and energy equal to that produced by 30,000 pounds of coal, are harvested? With so much demand for extraction, mining engineers can choose to work in diverse environments, in many areas of the world. So if you're looking for a well-paid career with opportunities for advancement, then mining engineering could be a good major for you.

Typical courses in this major:
Physical geology
Structural geology
Engineering mechanics
Fluid mechanics
Thermodynamics
Ore and mineral deposits
Petrology
Mineral economics
Mining methods
Mine surveying
Mine planning and design
Ground control and rock mechanics
Rock blasting and fragmentation
Mineral or coal processing
Environmental reclamation
Mine health and safety

Concentrations:
In college: surface mining; underground mining; hard-rock mining; soft-rock (coal, phosphate, clays) mining; placer mining; quarry and industrial-minerals mining.

If you go on to grad school: rock mechanics; rock slope engineering; mine planning and design; geostatistical techniques; explosives engineering; mine health and safety; mine environment and reclamation; mine management.

What the study of this major is like:
Mining and mineral engineering is more hands-on than many other engineering fields. Like other areas of engineering, though, it is a highly technical field. These days, mining operations routinely use technologies such as global positioning, radio telemetry of data, satellite communications, computer-aided design, automation, and robotics. The equipment gets bigger and better; the industry's health and safety record continues to improve; and the productivity of miners in the United States (and, generally, worldwide) keeps increasing.

Mining engineers spend a considerable portion of their time out in the field. Accordingly, most majors consider themselves outdoorsy types. Often, students in the major started out in another science or engineering discipline. They took a summer internship at a mine operation, enjoyed the experience, and changed majors after returning to college in the fall.

Your course work generally includes math and science, basic engineering, mining engineering, geology, and the humanities and social sciences. Many courses, especially in mining and geology, are taught as a combination of lectures and laboratory experience. On the whole, though, most courses are still conducted as lectures. The greatest challenge most students encounter is to complete some of the other required engineering courses—for example, an electrical engineering course. Most programs in the United States are small, compared with better-known programs such as mechanical engineering. Therefore, students normally work in small groups with their instructors. Teamwork is emphasized; you'll get to know your colleagues and professors well.

Many of the eastern colleges offering degrees in mineral engineering specialize in coal mining, whereas western colleges tend to specialize in hard-rock mining. Graduates of eastern colleges most often find work in the coalfields of the eastern and central states, whereas their counterparts in western colleges usually find jobs in the central and western part of the country. Although some colleges have a practical orientation, a few emphasize undergrad research and the utilization of research conducted by faculty members and graduate students. Some programs have started offering specializations in areas such as quarry mining, underground construction, and management.

Other majors you might like:
Structural engineering
Geotechnical engineering
Environmental engineering
Natural resources and conservation
Mining technology
Surveying technology
Geology/earth science
Range science

Heavy/earthmoving equipment operation
Ocean engineering
Petroleum engineering
Geography

Questions to ask colleges:
Does the program specialize in a particular area of mining engineering?

Are summer internships or co-op education programs available?

Are field trips part of the curriculum, so that students can visit mines and gain real-world experience?

Career options and trends:
Mine engineer*; construction engineer*; mine manager*; environmental engineer; sales/technical representative.

In the mid-1980s, the industry suffered a severe downturn, and the number of students entering this field dropped precipitously. Now the industry is stable, but in the United States, only about 125 students graduate each year with a degree in mining engineering. Recent studies have concluded that over 300 new graduates per year will be needed just to keep up with retirements. Starting salaries are expected to rise dramatically with this increase in demand.

Globalization is another trend affecting this field. Mining engineers frequently find opportunities overseas to introduce advances in technology or to assist in the development of the mining economy.

Insider's viewpoint:
"Mining engineering is as much of a lifestyle choice as a career choice."

—Professor Charles Kliche, South Dakota School of Mines and Technology

For more info:
Society for Mining, Metallurgy, and Exploration (SME)
8307 Shaffer Parkway
Littleton, CO 80127-4102
(800) 763-3132
www.smenet.org

Nuclear engineering

Also known as:
Radiological engineering

What it's about:
Nuclear engineering focuses on the application of radioactive materials and radiation to meet many of society's needs. The generation of electricity by nuclear power plants typically receives the most attention, but other applications include nuclear medicine, space power, environmental research, and the use of radiation in industrial processes and research.

Is this for you?
You might like this major if you also like: math and science, especially physics; science fairs; science fiction; working in teams; building things.

Consider this major if you are good at: attention to detail; creativity; math; quantitative analysis; spatial thinking/analysis; teamwork *...or have...* initiative; persistence; verbal skills; writing skills.

Recommended high school prep:
English 4, math 4 (including precalculus or calculus), lab science 3-4 (including chemistry and physics), social studies 3, and a foreign language 2-3. If available, courses in computer programming and technical writing would be valuable.

Did you know...
...that every year, two million nuclear medical procedures are performed in the United States? These procedures include cancer radiation treatments, nuclear magnetic resonance imaging (MRI), gamma knife surgery, boron neutron capture therapy, brain scans, and other applications to diagnose disease.

...that before its nuclear properties were discovered, uranium was used for coloring glass?

Typical courses in this major:
Introduction to nuclear science and engineering
Nuclear reactor theory
Nuclear fuel cycle
Radiation safety
Thermal hydraulics for nuclear plants
Radiation interactions with matter
Materials for nuclear applications
Radiation detection
Radiation shielding
Nuclear power systems
Nuclear engineering design
Engineering ethics

Concentrations:
In college: health physics; radiation protection.

If you go on to grad school: nuclear power; nuclear fusion; nuclear medicine; radioactive waste management; instrumentation and control; probabilistic safety assessment; nuclear reactor theory.

What the study of this major is like:
Nuclear engineers can work with radioactive materials and radiation in a variety of ways. Some are employed at large commercial power plants that produce electricity, while others work on smaller nuclear reactors that generate power for naval vessels, spacecraft, or equipment operating at remote locations. Some nuclear engineers focus on medical applications; others devote their efforts to radioactive waste disposal and environmental restoration of sites that have been contaminated.

As a nuclear engineering major, you will be introduced to these and other applications of radiation and radioactive materials. Primarily, though, you will learn the fundamentals that are essential for nuclear engineers preparing themselves for a number of possible careers. In your courses, more than likely, you will explore the nature of radiation and radioactive decay; naturally occurring radioactive materials; the detection of radiation; its interaction with matter (its effects on humans and other living things, as well as on materials in the power plant); the principles of radiation protection; the fuel cycle; and the environmental impact of nuclear facilities. At most colleges, courses contain some material that engineering students often consider to be soft science. But these topics (including ethics, economics, and regulation of nuclear facilities) are critical to professionals in the discipline.

Most of your courses are taught as lectures; you'll have a variety of out-of-class assignments, such as finding solutions to problems, developing or applying computer models to analyze reactors or other nuclear systems, and working on team research or design projects. Several courses have a laboratory component, in which you work with detection equipment and perhaps with a research reactor or a simulator (if your college has such equipment). Lab experiments are generally done in teams. You frequently spend one or more terms as a co-op or intern, working at a nuclear facility and learning firsthand what nuclear engineers do. Positions as co-ops, interns, or assistants on faculty research projects provide excellent opportunities to apply the theoretical material you learned.

A unique challenge students face is the public's ignorance about—and sometimes fear of—radiation, nuclear power, nuclear waste, and related topics. Professionals in this field need to educate themselves about the industry and learn to talk about it with laymen, in language they can understand. Most nuclear engineers belong to a professional organization, such as the American Nuclear Society. Nuclear engineering students are generally encouraged to begin participating in the ANS while they are still in college.

There are several areas in which nuclear engineering programs may vary among colleges. Some focus on nuclear power engineering; some focus on radiological engineering/health physics; and some include both subjects. At some colleges, the curriculum emphasizes theory, whereas others offer a good deal of practical application, including visits to nuclear facilities or hands-on lab courses. The curriculum may be geared toward students going on to graduate school, toward those who plan to work in the industry after completing a Bachelor of Science degree, or it may combine the two orientations.

Other majors you might like:

Radiation protection/health physics technology
Nuclear engineering technology
Hazardous materials technology
Applied math
Environmental engineering
Marine engineering/naval architecture
Nuclear medical technology
Nuclear power technology
Physics
Astrophysics
Medical radiologic technology/radiation therapy
Radiologic technology/medical imaging

Questions to ask colleges:

What are the primary research areas of the nuclear engineering faculty members? Are undergraduate students encouraged to become involved in research?

What opportunities are available for co-op or intern positions in the nuclear industry, and what co-op and/or intern positions have recent students in the program held?

What lab facilities do undergrads have an opportunity to use?

Career options and trends:

Health physicist; radiation safety officer; nuclear reactor operator*; nuclear equipment design engineer; consulting engineer*; researcher at a national laboratory; government employee (U.S. Navy or Department of Energy)*; instrumentation design specialist; radioactive waste manager or environmental restoration specialist.

Approximately a third of the nuclear workforce is expected to retire in the next decade, and a shortage of new engineers is projected. While no commercial nuclear power plants are currently under construction in the United States, nuclear engineers will be needed to operate existing plants; they will also be needed in the areas of nuclear medicine technology, national defense, fusion research, waste management, and regulatory compliance. Salaries of nuclear engineers are among the highest for all engineers.

An exciting development in the nuclear industry is the worldwide effort to design a generation of nuclear power plants that are safer, more efficient, and more economical than existing plants. In addition to generating electricity, some of these plants are being designed to produce hydrogen to support the "hydrogen economy," desalinate water, provide industrial process heat, and burn nuclear waste.

Insider's viewpoint:

"I purchased a book from the bookstore with the misleading title 'Introductory Nuclear Engineering.' I managed to read up to chapter 3 until it made no sense whatsoever. In high school, I took physics, chemistry, anatomy, and math up to precalculus. These courses were necessary to even understand the first three chapters of that book."

—Robert, junior, University of Tennessee: Knoxville

For more info:

American Nuclear Society (ANS)
555 North Kensington Ave.
La Grange Park, IL 60526
(708) 352-6611
www.ans.org

Nuclear Energy Institute (NEI)
1776 I St., N.W.
Suite 400
Washington, DC 20006-3708
(202) 739-8000
www.nei.org

Ocean engineering

Also known as:

Coastal engineering

What it's about:

Ocean engineers apply a variety of engineering disciplines to develop systems that operate in ocean and coastal waters. The profession includes such project areas as the construction and maintenance of facilities such as ports, harbors, and dikes; ocean drilling, dredging and salvage operations; underwater construction; and management of the ocean environment. This field should not be confused with marine engineering, which focuses primarily on the mechanics and operation of seagoing vessels.

Is this for you?

You might like this major if you also like: water sports (boating, diving, sailing, swimming, rowing, and surfing); math, science, and technology; designing and building things; the coastal and offshore environments.

Consider this major if you are good at: attention to detail; creativity; critical reading/thinking; math; quantitative analysis; research; spatial thinking/analysis; teamwork *...or have...* initiative; mechanical facility; verbal skills.

Recommended high school prep:

English 4, math 4 (including precalculus), lab science 4 (earth science, biology, chemistry and physics), social studies 3, and a foreign language 2–3. If available, advanced or honors courses in math and physics are recommended. Since ocean engineering is, by its nature, a global discipline, facility with a foreign language can be valuable.

Typical courses in this major:

Marine structures
Coastal structures
Oceanography
Marine hydrodynamics
Mechanics of materials
Diving technology
Passive and active circuits
Fluid mechanics
Ocean measurements and instrumentation
Fundamentals of ocean mechanics
Wave mechanics and littoral (seashore) processes
Underwater acoustics
Engineering materials
Marine geomechanics
Ocean resources engineering
Nearshore environmental engineering

Concentrations:

Generally, none in college; but if you go on to grad school: ocean instrumentation and seafloor mapping; underwater acoustics; marine hydrodynamics and water wave mechanics; environmental engineering; marine geomechanics; coastal and offshore structures.

What the study of this major is like:

During your first two years as an ocean engineering major, you focus primarily on mathematics, chemistry, physics, and engineering fundamentals. You will probably take courses in calculus and analytic geometry; differential equations; statics/mechanics; electrical engineering; and engineering economics. Other general education requirements may be distributed throughout the curriculum. Electives, which will fill most of your third and fourth years, may include these:

Ocean acoustics. Sound is often the only way to sense the underwater environment or to transmit information underwater. You study the influence of water properties on sound speed and refraction; sonar systems; and sounds generated by ships and marine life.

Hydrodynamics. This field covers the behavior of water; floating and submerged objects; lift and drag forces; wave forces on beaches, vessels, and off-shore platforms; and basic seakeeping.

Ocean measurements. You explore the principles of sensors, measurement, and electronics as applied to the ocean environment. You may also study seafloor mapping and underwater acoustics.

Ocean resources engineering. Here you examine systems to develop the energy, mineral, and living resources of the sea; the use of the ocean for waste disposal; and related environmental and economic issues.

Marine geomechanics. This focuses on the behavior of the seabed and sediments, dredging, cables and pipelines, and foundations for offshore and coastal structures.

Coastal engineering. Topics include ports and harbors, inlets, and barrier islands; nearshore environmental engineering; beach dynamics; flood hazards; and coastal structures such as piers.

Your fourth year will be dominated by a capstone project, in which you apply the knowledge and skills you've learned to a real-world design problem. It is usually a group project involving analysis, data collection, design, and a final presentation and report, and may also include scale-modeling, construction, and testing.

Programs are generally rigorous and comprehensive, requiring hardworking and dedicated students. Courses are typically taught as lectures, some with associated lab work and experimental projects. There is usually a great deal of fieldwork required, which most students enjoy. You may also take hands-on courses that focus on designing and building a system or structure, such as an autonomous underwater vehicle (AUV). Ocean engineering courses are sometimes supplemented by classes offered by other departments of engineering (chemical, civil, environmental, electrical, and/or mechanical), math, computer science, and grad schools of oceanography. Programs may be approved by the Accreditation Board for Engineering and Technology (ABET).

Other majors you might like:
Oceanography
Marine engineering/naval architecture
Environmental engineering
Marine biology
Marine science/Merchant Marine
Civil engineering
Water, wetlands, and marine management
Environmental science
Construction technology
Geology/earth science
Physics
Geography

Questions to ask colleges:
Are offshore or shoreline field experiences offered? What laboratory and experimental facilities are available? The extent of hands-on learning opportunities is a good indication of the strength of the program.

Career options and trends:
Coastal engineer*; civil engineer; underwater acoustician*; geotechnical engineer*; offshore engineer; marine engineer.

Job opportunities remain strong in the fields of coastal engineering; environmental engineering and pollution control; ocean instrumentation; dredging engineering; acoustics; ocean systems; and consulting. As nations increasingly rely on the oceans to meet the growing demand for resources, ocean engineers will be needed to meet these demands effectively and wisely.

For more info:
Marine Technology Society (MTS)
5565 Sterrett Place
Suite 108
Columbia, MD 21044
(410) 884-5330
www.mtsociety.org

Association of Coastal Engineers
c/o Patricia Ehrman, Executive Secretary
2770 Northwest 43rd St., Suite B
Gainesville, FL 32606
www.coastalengineers.org

Software engineering

What it's about:

As a software engineering major, you study the techniques used in constructing large, complex software systems. The discipline covers the analysis, specification, design, construction, testing, and maintenance of software systems. Software engineers build systems that empower users, increasing their capabilities and improving the way they work.

Is this for you?

You might like this major if you also like: solving puzzles and complex problems; abstract thinking; planning and organizing activities and events; explaining things; working in groups.

Consider this major if you are good at: attention to detail; creativity; critical reading/thinking; giving directions; logical reasoning; organizing; teamwork *...or have...* math skills; writing skills.

Recommended high school prep:

English 4, math 4 (including calculus or precalculus), lab science 3–4, social studies 3, and a foreign language 2–3. If possible, take advanced or additional classes in discrete mathematics, computer science, and writing.

Did you know...

...that software engineers don't have to be passionate, compulsive programmers? Many students who major in one of the computing fields never did computer programming in high school.

Typical courses in this major:

Fundamentals of software development
Introduction to computer science
Systems analysis
Programming language concepts
Discrete mathematics
Statistics
Software architecture and design
Software construction and evolution
Software requirements and specification
Database systems
Operating systems
Software testing and quality assurance
Software project management
Senior project/capstone experience

Concentrations:

In college: commercial applications; computer engineering; scientific computing; embedded systems.

If you go on to grad school: systems analysis; software development methodologies; software testing and quality assurance; software project management; software reengineering and evolution; user interface design; software metrics.

What the study of this major is like:

Software engineers do much more than program computers; they use their talents to help nonexperts benefit from the computer in their daily activities. They also create tools that enable computer users to work efficiently, economically, and effectively.

Most students don't realize that software engineering uses concepts from engineering, computer science, and mathematics, as well as from management, psychology, economics, politics, art, sociology, and language arts. To be successful in the discipline, you need good writing and oral presentation skills and the ability to use mathematical thinking (abstraction, logical reasoning), to work effectively in teams, and to understand computer programming. In addition, you must be able to learn new practices and procedures quickly, so that you can apply them soon after they are introduced.

In your first two years as a major, you take basic courses in computer science and math (including calculus and discrete mathematics) and other general education courses. Your last two years will focus on software engineering and related areas. Most programs have a capstone course in which you complete a software development project. The project requires you to put into practice what you have learned in previous courses, as a means of preparing you for a professional career. Courses in computer science and software engineering often involve group projects. Some courses have scheduled laboratories, but you can often do lab work at other times as well. If you delay your group project and lab assignments until just before the deadline, the result may be poor-quality work—and you will probably learn less as you play last-minute catch-up.

The earliest undergrad programs in software engineering date from the 1990s, and many colleges have not yet developed separate software engineering programs. Colleges may still offer numerous software engineering courses, however, provided by computer science, computer engineering, and/or electrical engineering programs. Software engineering, computer engineering, and computer science are not completely separate fields; they have significant amounts of overlap. Software engineering programs that are housed in electrical and computer engineering departments tend to focus on hardware issues. On the other hand, software engineering programs in departments of computer science (or math and computer science) tend to emphasize software, and their orientation is likely to be theoretical and mathematical.

As you study college catalogs, be aware that similarly named programs may actually contain different content—and programs with different names may, in fact, be very similar. Variation is to be expected in a field as new as software engineering.

Other majors you might like:
Computer science
Computer engineering
Digital media
Electrical and communications engineering
Management information systems
Computer programming
Animation
Artificial intelligence/robotics
E-commerce
Computer engineering technology
Bioinformatics
Applied mathematics

Questions to ask colleges:
What is the nature of the capstone course? What kinds of projects have been done in the past?

How good is the campus computer network? Are appropriate software tools available for software engineering students?

Do faculty members have experience building large software systems?

Are there any opportunities for summer internships or co-op work experiences? Are there opportunities for students to use their technical skills in campus jobs?

Career options and trends:
Software engineer*; software developer*; software or systems analyst*; senior programmer; systems programmer; database administrator.

Jobs in all computing fields are increasing much faster than in most other fields, and software engineering opportunities are expected to grow rapidly in the near future. There is an important warning about entry-level jobs in computing fields: change in the computer industry is constant and rapid. A job you may want to prepare for as you begin college will probably be completely different by the time you graduate. Therefore, computer majors must be prepared for a life of constant learning. Their studies will not stop when their formal education ends.

For more info:
Association of Computing Machinery (ACM)
1515 Broadway
New York, NY 10036-5701
(800) 342-6626
www.acm.org

Institute of Electrical and Electronics Engineers
 Computer Society (IEEE-CS)
1730 Massachusetts Ave., N.W.
Washington, DC 20036-1992
(202) 371-0101
www.computer.org

Engineering technology

What's the difference between engineering (covered in the previous section) and engineering technology? To begin with, engineering programs always lead to bachelor's degrees and, often, graduate degrees. Engineering technology programs can lead to either an associate degree or a bachelor's degree (currently, most students earn associate degrees). Second, engineering is more theoretical and employs higher-level math and physics, to prepare you for a career in product design or systems research. Engineering technology gives you more practical experience with the installation, maintenance, and operation of components and instruments.

Let's look at a specific example from this section: telecommunications technology. "While engineering programs typically prepare you for equipment design, graduate school and research, telecommunications technology programs are usually oriented toward using existing equipment for system and network design," explains Professor Pierre Catala of Texas A&M University. "Telecom engineering technicians maintain all the networks and sophisticated gear that make the World Wide Web, satellite and space probe transmissions, and e-commerce possible."

In this case, the associate degree (technician) programs in engineering technology usually deal with the testing, operation, initial software configuration, and maintenance of telecommunications equipment. Bachelor's degree (technologist) programs in engineering technology expand into design, implementation, configuration, and management of telecommunications networks.

"Engineering technologists bridge the gap between technicians and engineers with an understanding of both operations and design," says Thomas M. Hall, Jr. a professor at Northwestern State University. "Engineering technology graduates solve the problems of today, while research engineers solve the problems of tomorrow."

Mechanical engineering technologists are another example. "Now that mechanical engineering technology and other branches of engineering technology are offered as four-year Bachelor of Science programs, the industry has begun to accept engineering technology graduates as full engineers," suggests Professor James Kamm, University of Toledo.

The same level of application-related education and training goes into other engineering technologies—computer, electrical, construction, drafting, and surveying.

"Electrical engineering technology programs apply math and science to the real world," Hall says of his specialty.

With these majors, you can make an immediate impact working in manufacturing, field service, systems engineering, and applied design. Jobs include technicians, salespeople, network administrators, support specialists, drafters, designers, computer-aided design (CAD) operators, project managers, field supervisors, and inspectors.

The employment outlook depends on the specific industry. For instance, jobs are continually being generated in mechanical engineering and computing. However, signals are mixed in telecommunications because it's a growth industry, but not for equipment installers and repairers. Meanwhile, business is booming in construction, and many surveying opportunities are on the horizon. For the best job prospects in electrical fields, get well grounded in the basics and keep current with the latest technologies.

A bachelor's degree in one of the engineering technologies improves your chances. So do professional licenses and certifications.

Design for learning

If you choose one of these college majors, you won't have your nose in a book all day. "The hallmark of any engineering technology program is the extensive laboratory experience," says Hall. In addition to labs and class, some colleges offer field experience, and cooperative educational (co-op) programs, in which you combine your academic studies with on-the-job training.

When comparing colleges, get a feel for how much they stress fundamentals compared to the latest gizmos. You want to learn the state-of-the-art technology, but you'll also need to know the principles, because technologies are changing. The newest tracks include wireless communications, 3-D modeling and animation, geographic information systems, and environmental and energy management technologies.

Think about whether you're going for a two-year associate degree or a four-year bachelor's degree. The associate degree is for technical training, current technologies and hands-on, nuts-and-bolts preparation for an entry-level job. A bachelor's degree in engineering technology, like an engineering degree, means more math and science, to help you analyze complex problems. Some programs also delve into the business or management side. The B.S. degree can be a launching pad to graduate work in geomatics (three-dimensional computerized mapping), engineering economics, network engineering, and management information systems.

Here are some things to think about or to ask people: What is the college's philosophy and approach? Does the college see its role as preparing talent for local industry? If so, which companies are they and what kind of jobs are likely? What is the background of some of the professors? If they're from industry, the courses will probably be more practical; if the faculty members have academic backgrounds, the courses will be more theoretical and scientific.

Ask if the program is approved by the leading commission in the field, like the Accreditation Board for Engineering and Technology for some specialties. How large are the lab classes and what type of equipment is used? Is it the kind used in industry? Is the program equipped to teach how computers interface with engineering technology? What is the seating capacity of the lab facilities?

In most other majors, you want to know the ratio of students to faculty members, but in these majors you may also want to ask about the ratio of students to computers.

Computer engineering technology

What it's about:

The computer engineering technology major will prepare you for a career in a number of fields: computer networking, telecommunications, computer electronics, programming, wireless and data communications and networks, embedded system design, and robotics. Offered at both the associate and bachelor's degree levels, this major is designed to meet the needs of technically inclined students who prefer hands-on teaching and learning to the more theoretical, mathematics-oriented computer science and engineering disciplines.

Is this for you?

You might like this major if you also like: working and playing with computer hardware and software; electronics; math and science; figuring out why things work the way they do; mathematical and logical puzzles; solving complex problems.

Consider this major if you are good at: attention to detail; critical reading/thinking; math; memorizing; organizing; quantitative analysis; teamwork ...*or have...* initiative; patience.

Recommended high school prep:

English 4, math 3–4, lab science 3 (including physics), social studies 3, and a foreign language 2–3. Precalculus, computer-aided design (CAD), and other computer programming and applications courses are also recommended, although not required.

Typical courses in this major:

Basic electricity and electronics
Digital systems and microprocessors
Object-oriented software development
Programming fundamentals I, II
Operating systems
Digital/communications
Computer architecture
Assembly language applications
Electronics computer-aided design
Data structures and file processing
Digital testing techniques
Wide-area networking
Local-area networking
Systems administration
Technical writing and communications

Concentrations:

Local-area and wide-area networking (LAN/WAN); systems administration; communications systems; microprocessors; programming languages; software engineering; hardware engineering; industrial automation systems; robotics.

What the study of this major is like:

This major provides you with practical training and skills in courses covering hardware and software, electronics, programming, and supporting topics. Most programs in computer engineering technology focus on both the hardware and the software aspects of the applications, including the interfacing of computers and systems; in contrast, most electrical engineering technology programs concentrate primarily on hardware and secondarily on related software.

Hands-on training in applications and equipment is the primary teaching method, but you'll also learn theoretical aspects to help you adapt to new technology in the future. You begin with the basics of electricity and electronics, including analog and digital circuit analysis. Then you'll be introduced to the fundamentals of microprocessors and operating systems; programming; and applications that use word processors, spreadsheets, and high-level and low-level computer languages.

Other required courses zero in on mathematical and communication skills, and you'll learn enough about the industrial and business environment to perform effectively on the job. In labs, you work on a variety of microprocessor systems and devices, as you gain experience in installing, diagnosing, operating, and servicing computer systems and related equipment.

Upper-level courses, in which you get an in-depth look at the hardware and software used in industry and business, are usually wide ranging enough to allow for specialization. Topics include networking technology and security; advanced programming; digital testing technology; data communications; hardware description languages; embedded system design; industrial instrumentation; and industrial automation systems.

Because many areas of computer application are important in industry and business, colleges vary in the aspects of the major that they emphasize. For instance, some programs may focus on computer-use topics such as programming, Internet technology, and database systems, while others may stress technical applications such as industrial networking, Web-based control, electronic devices, Web services, and other aspects of enterprise networking.

Two-year associate degree programs are more likely to focus on specific occupations or systems than are programs designed for a four-year bachelor's degree. In bachelor's programs, you'll study more math (in particular, differential equations, sets and logic, and calculus), alongside courses in the humanities and sciences. Coupled with business electives, a four-year degree will generally increase your employment options. Many students begin in the less-costly two-year program and then transfer into the last two years of a bachelor's program, usually with enough job skills to work as they continue their education.

In computer engineering technology, lifelong learning really counts—you have no choice but to continue your education if you want to remain employable. Technological advances come so rapidly that even people with good jobs have to keep their skills up-to-date. After all, employers are often looking to put the latest technologies to profitable use. Continuing education opportunities are plentiful, however, and many employers will help you take advantage of them.

Other majors you might like:
Computer science
Software engineering
Digital media
Electrical and communications engineering
Management information systems
Computer programming
Computational mathematics
Robotics technology
E-commerce
Information technology
Recording arts
Applied mathematics

Questions to ask colleges:
How often are the lab facilities upgraded with the latest hardware and software? Be sure that the new equipment includes various operating systems in the Microsoft, Apple, and Unix/Linux categories.

Is the program approved by the Technology Accreditation Commission of the Accreditation Board for Engineering and Technology (TAC/ABET)?

Are co-op education and internships available? If so, take advantage of them. Real-world experience will greatly enhance your employment opportunities.

How successful have graduates been in getting jobs in the specialty areas emphasized by the college?

Career options and trends:
Systems analyst; consulting engineer*; network administrator*; database administrator; systems administrator; software engineer (applications or systems); support specialist*.

Certification in a particular application, program language (such as JAVA), or system (Linux) may be of value to employers using them. Some vendors and software firms may require certification if you will be working with their products.

The job titles listed above are among the fastest-growing careers, according to the U.S. Bureau of Labor Statistics, which also projects computer and data processing services to be the most rapidly growing industry in the economy. The employment outlook is favorable for graduates who can set up and maintain computer networks, information and Internet technology, and computer-based electronic systems.

However, computer support, like many technical fields, is becoming increasingly competitive internationally. As a result of the expanding knowledge economy, countries in Eastern Europe and Asia are producing labor pools of relatively low-cost, highly trained computer specialists; and because of the Internet, many computer support positions are being outsourced overseas.

But don't let that spook you—job creation is outpacing job destruction in this field, and you can prepare yourself for the competition by obtaining a broad-based education, developing interpersonal and business skills, and remaining alert to the areas of greatest demand, such as e-commerce and communications security.

For more info:
Institute of Electrical and Electronics Engineers
   (IEEE)
445 Hoes Lane
Piscataway, NJ 08855
(732) 981-1686
www.ieee.org

Association for Computer Machinery (ACM)
1515 Broadway
New York, NY 10036-5701
(800) 342-6626
www.acm.org

Construction technology

What it's about:

The construction technology major provides practical training and broad-based education in general, structural, and construction engineering principles; in planning and design; and in construction management.

Is this for you?

You might like this major if you also like: working in groups or teams; working with your hands; carpentry; the outdoors; achieving goals and results; watching construction sites.

Consider this major if you are good at: attention to detail; coaching; critical reading/thinking; leadership; math; organizing; persuading/influencing; spatial thinking/analysis; teamwork *...or have...* initiative; mechanical facility.

Recommended high school prep:

English 4, math 3 (including trigonometry), lab science 3 (including physics and chemistry), social studies 3, industrial arts 2, and a foreign language 2. If they are available, take courses in computer-aided drafting (CAD) or mechanical drawing.

Did you know...

...that the construction industry is the second-largest employer in the United States, after the federal government?

Typical courses in this major:

Planning and scheduling
Safety, security, and environmental impact
Blueprint reading
Site surveying, planning, and design
Cost estimating
Architecture and urban form
Construction practices and methods
Computer-integrated construction (CIC)
Electrical systems
Groundwater hydrology
Soils and foundations
Construction materials and systems
Reinforced concrete design
Materials handling
Structural steel design
Technical report writing

Concentrations:

Structural design; construction management; construction engineering.

What the study of this major is like:

This major will provide you with a breadth of training, from management to carpentry, business law to asphalt paving. While the particular emphasis may vary, all programs feature hands-on, practical learning experiences in labs or in the field, in conjunction with classroom lectures.

You are encouraged to apply your skills through cooperative (co-op) experiences and independent studies. Most lecture classes use demonstrations and video aids, and in the labs you are introduced to construction methods and problems, which you work on either through simulations or with actual materials and equipment. Concepts and training come together in field experiences on construction sites.

Construction technology is usually taught in one of two ways. In one, the program follows the traditional engineering track: you apply mathematical theories and equations to explain abstract engineering principles. Courses cover such topics as statics, applied thermodynamics, and fluid mechanics. The other method is to pattern the curriculum after business management courses, with emphasis on lectures, reading, and case studies. Programs feature course content in contract management, plans and specifications, estimation of costs, building codes, labor relations, team dynamics, project management, and environmental and land-use concerns. In programs that are geared toward construction management, most students earn a four-year Bachelor of Science degree.

Either approach will give you sufficient technical training to be familiar with the methods used in residential, commercial, industrial, and public-works construction. Architectural drafting and computer-aided design (CAD), blueprint reading, and the basics of surveying are also likely to be core requirements.

In a two-year associate degree program, which focuses on the technical aspects of construction, you will study the basics of structural design, construction methods and practices, and project management. Bachelor's degree programs include courses in mathematics, natural sciences, business, humanities, social sciences, and written and oral communications. In upper-level course work, you concentrate on advanced engineering, design, and management principles.

A valuable part of a strong construction technology program is co-op educational experience: you combine your academic studies with paid, on-the-job training, either during regular semesters or over the summer. Independent study opportunities—which are often available through student chapters of professional organizations such as the Associated Builders and Contractors, the Associated General Contractors of America, and the National Society of Professional Engineers—are another way to supplement your classroom and lab training.

Other majors you might like:
Civil engineering
Construction management
Structural engineering
Architectural engineering technology
Drafting and design technology
Historic preservation
Housing and human environments
Surveying technology
Heating/air conditioning/refrigeration technology
Heavy/earthmoving equipment operation
Parks, recreation, and leisure studies
Theater design and technology

Questions to ask colleges:
Do the lab facilities have enough computers and construction equipment to offer adequate training in the wide range of problems this program explores, such as soil analysis, materials testing, CAD, surveying?

Is the program approved by the Technology Accreditation Commission of the Accreditation Board for Engineering and Technology (TAC/ABET)?

Career options and trends:
Field engineer; job expeditor; project manager; field supervisor; site inspector; scheduler; contract administrator; estimator; designer.

Excellent employment opportunities are forecast in the construction industry, because of a shortage of professionals who can handle the increasing complexity of projects, technology, and regulatory standards, and because of the need to replace much of the country's aging infrastructure. Job prospects will be best for graduates with a bachelor's degree and previous construction work experience.

For more info:
Associated Builders and Contractors (ABC)
4250 Fairfax Drive, 9th Fl.
Arlington, VA 22203
(703) 812-2000
www.abc.org

National Association of Women in Construction (NAWIC)
327 South Adams St.
Fort Worth, TX 76104
(800) 552-3506
www.nawic.org

Drafting and design technology

Also known as:

Computer Aided Drafting and Design (CADD)

Technical drawing and design

What it's about:

The major in drafting and design technology, which can lead to either an associate degree or a bachelor's degree, prepares you for a career in industry or in another design-related field. You learn how to make drawings, plans, and computer-aided drafting (CAD) models and simulations that will be used in constructing a building, manufacturing a product, or developing a creative project such as marketing materials.

Is this for you?

You might like this major if you also like: learning new tricks on the computer; being precise; working independently as well as in groups; contributing to large projects; drawing; making models; planning how things fit together.

Consider this major if you are good at: attention to detail; concentrating; creativity; critical reading/thinking; math; organizing; spatial thinking/analysis ...*or have*... manual dexterity; mechanical facility; patience.

Recommended high school prep:

English 4, math 3, lab science 3 (including physics), social studies 3, industrial arts 2, and a foreign language 2–3. If they are available, take courses in computer-aided drafting or mechanical drawing, computer applications, and a fine arts drawing class.

Did you know...

...that in this major, you learn another language—a graphic language? Known as the "the language of industry," drafting is a universal method of communication that is understood by technicians, engineers, designers, and architects all over the world.

Typical courses in this major:

Blueprint reading

Technical drawing

Computer-aided drafting (CAD) I, II

Engineering design graphics

Construction materials

Manufacturing processes

Solid modeling

Machine drafting

Architectural drafting

Business and technical writing

Geometric dimensioning and tolerancing

Descriptive geometry

Building codes

Architectural delineation

Electromechanical design

Product design

Concentrations:

Product design; architectural drafting.

What the study of this major is like:

Drafters and designers are important links between great ideas and actual products, buildings, processes, or services. As a drafting and design technology major, you study idea generation and sketching, product specification, working and assembly drawings, product realization and construction, and manufacturing processes and materials.

Few disciplines have been changed more by computers than drafting and design. You may be taught basic drafting on the drawing board, but you will certainly be trained to use computer-aided-drafting software and solid modeling software. "CAD" no longer refers just to drawing—it is now the first step in the programming of automated production equipment. Also, CAD is the principal ingredient in the trend away from making prototypes of products the old-fashioned way, by hand. More and more engineers are creating prototypes on modeling software and then testing them through computer simulation.

In most drafting and design courses the instructor will introduce a concept through a lecture and demonstration; then students complete an assignment to reinforce the concept. In a final project, you will show what you've learned: you'll develop an idea of your own choosing into a usable design. Your project and other work may be included in a portfolio that will be helpful during your job search.

What are the challenges? The ability to see an object in three dimensions is a skill that most majors must learn—it rarely comes naturally. Majors who are not familiar with computers may also have difficulty mastering CAD software while also learning the basics of computer operating systems.

The major is usually offered at two-year technical and community colleges. Programs may have different philosophies, requirements, and emphases. Philosophically, they may differ in the importance they place on teaching the fundamentals versus introducing students to the latest technology. Some colleges emphasize a theoretical, scientific orientation, while others focus on the "nuts and bolts" essentials that are needed for real-world jobs. Finally, programs may differ in the emphasis they place on certain industries. Community colleges in particular often reflect the local industries they serve. This emphasis can be seen in the types of courses and CAD software the program offers.

Other majors you might like:
Graphic design
Architectural technology
Surveying technology
Architectural engineering technology
Mechanical engineering technology
Industrial design
Medical illustrating
Digital media
Animation
Cartography
Computer science
Geology/earth science

Questions to ask colleges:
What types of computer software and hardware are used in the courses? Are they up-to-date? Is the software widely used in key industries? Is it used in the industry or geographic location you are considering?

What is the seating capacity of the lab facilities? Are the computers connected to a campus network? Are open labs available for homework and projects? What is the student-to-computer ratio?

Career options and trends:
CAD operator*; drafter or designer*; engineering technician; design engineer; CAD systems manager; technical illustrator.

Engineering positions such as design engineer usually require a four-year degree, although some designers earn these positions through progressive work experience. Design engineers doing work for government agencies may need to be registered as a professional engineer in the state in which they are working.

The job outlook for drafting technicians is generally strong. The number of industries and fields in which CAD is used continues to expand, as does the use of technical drawings and models in the production process. CAD modeling is also being used by marketing professionals for product packaging and promotion. Students who gain a strong understanding of the fundamentals and then keep up-to-date with the latest technology will be most likely to advance in their careers.

Insider's viewpoint:
"Drafting is a great field because of the opportunities it offers my students. What other field allows you to complete a degree or certificate program in two years or less, get a good-paying job, and continue your education while being paid for the valuable experience you are gaining?"

—Professor Paul Clarke, MiraCosta College

For more info:
American Design and Drafting Association (ADDA)
105 East Main St.
Newbern, TN 38059
(731) 627-0802
www.adda.org

Electrical engineering technology

Also known as:

Electrical and computer engineering technology

What it's about:

This major gives you practical training in a wide-ranging field of electrical engineering, including electronics, computers, communications, automatic controls, robotics, instrumentation, power systems, and computer-aided design (CAD). At the associate degree level, the focus is on operation, repair, and maintenance. At the bachelor's degree level, you also study the analysis, design, and development of electrical and electronic devices, systems, and processes.

Is this for you?

You might like this major if you also like: anything that involves math, science, electronics, and computers; tinkering and kit building; figuring out why things work the way they do.

Consider this major if you are good at: attention to detail; critical reading/thinking; math; organizing; quantitative analysis; spatial thinking/analysis; teamwork *...or have...* initiative; mechanical facility; patience.

Recommended high school prep:

English 4, math 3–4, lab science 3 (including physics), social studies 3, and a foreign language 2–3. Precalculus, calculus, computer-aided drafting, and other computer programming and applications courses are also recommended, although they are not required.

Did you know...

...that employers often prefer to hire engineering technologists rather than traditional engineers for positions in manufacturing, field service, systems engineering, and applied design? That's because engineering technologists combine an understanding of theory and design with hands-on operational experience.

Typical courses in this major:

Fundamentals of electricity
Control systems
Statics
Analog and digital electronics
Electronic system drafting (CAD)
Telecommunications systems
Electrical power and machines
Project management
Optical technology
Laser technology
Robotics
Data communications and computer networks
Technical writing
Transmission networks
Industrial electronics
Capstone project

Concentrations:

Electronics; electrical power and machinery; digital systems; computers and microprocessor systems; instrumentation; automation and control systems; telecommunications; information technology; electrical computer-aided drafting (CAD).

What the study of this major is like:

Students in electrical engineering technology (EET) programs like to build things, fix things, and make things work—or make them work better. They like to get their hands on the systems and the lab equipment. EET programs provide exactly that experience for you. The hallmark of any engineering technology program is the extensive laboratory experience—and EET is no exception.

EET programs apply math and science to the real world. Technical courses usually begin in your first year, along with general education courses in math, science, and the humanities. Sometimes students are surprised, and challenged, by the nontechnical course requirements; but employers expect EET graduates to acquire more than technical savvy. To prepare for a good job, you'll need to sharpen your skills in oral and written communication, teamwork, and project management; develop professional, ethical, and social responsibility; and be aware of contemporary issues.

In a bachelor's program, you are introduced to design concepts; and some courses stress calculus applications. Your first two years will lay a foundation in mathematics, chemistry, physics, and computer applications. In the third and fourth years, courses take an in-depth, technical approach and allow for specialization. You use software programs to simulate and design electrical systems and circuits, and to analyze complex problems.

Two-year associate degree programs provide technical training in circuit analysis, electronics, digital logic, microprocessors, communications, and control systems, with an emphasis on specific applications. The goal is to prepare you for entry-level employment as a technician.

The best students in EET programs learn, work, and play together. Often, student chapters of professional organizations, such as the Institute of Electrical and Electronics Engineers (IEEE) and the Instrumentation, Systems and Automation Society (ISA), offer a variety of programs and opportunities for students.

The field of EET is very broad. Typically, colleges with EET programs design a curriculum that is appropriate for both graduates and employers in the region. While all programs may touch on a range of topics, many emphasize one or more areas, such as robotics or industrial automated systems. In these areas of concentration, you get in-depth training and develop expertise; but be sure, when you are selecting a college, that its program matches your own interests.

Programs at various colleges can differ in other ways as well. Some rely heavily on the traditional classroom and laboratory settings; others make extensive use of field experience, co-op programs, or internships. In most programs, you will study with faculty members who have broad industrial experience. But in colleges that concentrate on theory and design, faculty members tend to have academic backgrounds.

Other majors you might like:

Computer engineering technology
Robotics technology
Applied mathematics
Telecommunications technology
Instrumentation technology
Electrocardiograph technology
Information technology
Laser/optical technology
Electrical drafting/CAD/CADD
Electrician
Avionics maintenance/technology
Radio and television

Questions to ask colleges:

Is the program approved by the Accreditation Board for Engineering and Technology (ABET)?

Does the program emphasize any particular areas within the broad field of EET?

Career options and trends:

Electrical/electronic technician; electrical engineering technologist; field service technician; systems technologist; communications engineer; design engineer; manufacturing process technologist; technical assistant; technical salesperson; technical writer.

According to the U.S. Bureau of Labor Statistics, employment for electrical engineering technologists is expected to grow at a moderate rate for the near future; job increases will be fueled by a demand for more sophisticated electrical and electronic products, controls, and processes. Most jobs are in electronic machinery and equipment manufacturing, instrumentation, and service industries.

For more info:

Institute of Electrical and Electronics Engineers
   (IEEE)
445 Hoes Lane
Piscataway, NJ 08855
(732) 981-0060
www.ieee.org

Mechanical engineering technology

What it's about:

As a major in mechanical engineering technology, you will learn to apply engineering principles and technical skills to the design and development of a wide variety of projects involving mechanical systems and the products that they create.

Is this for you?

You might like this major if you also like: achieving practical results; working on something different every day; math and science.

Consider this major if you are good at: attention to detail; creativity; critical reading/thinking; math; quantitative analysis; spatial thinking/analysis *...or have...* initiative; mechanical facility; patience; writing skills.

Recommended high school prep:

English 4, math 3, lab science 3 (including physics), social studies 3, and a foreign language 2–3. Your math classes should cover algebra and precalculus, and a class in computer-aided drafting or mechanical drawing would also be helpful.

Did you know...

...that math skills, rather than mechanical ability, are the most important indicator of success in this major? While high school calculus is not required, algebra and geometry are essential.

Typical courses in this major:

Fundamentals of mechanics
Computer-aided design (CAD)
Statics
Strength of materials
Thermodynamics
Fluid mechanics
Electrical circuits
Electromechanical control systems
Heating, ventilation, and air conditioning systems
Manufacturing processes
Stress and vibration analysis
Dynamics of systems
Machine design
Technical communications
Mechanical measurement and devices
Quality control systems

Concentrations:

In college: computer-aided design (CAD); thermodynamics; fluid mechanics; control systems; computer-controlled automation; materials science; machine design.

If you go on to grad school: engineering management; engineering economics.

What the study of this major is like:

Many people believe, incorrectly, that students who major in mechanical engineering technology must be amateur mechanics who love to work on, or under, cars. Although some majors do become automotive engineers or technicians, many others find good jobs as energy conservation engineers, plant managers, technical sales representatives, technical writers, robotics experts, and designers of alternative energy systems.

What's more, mechanical engineering technicians (METs) are no longer thought of simply as workers who simply assist mechanical engineers. Now that mechanical engineering technology and other branches of engineering technology are offered as four-year Bachelor's of Science programs, the industry has begun to accept graduates as full engineers. In fact, METs and mechanical engineers (MEs) often compete for the same jobs. Although MEs are more likely to get the jobs requiring a strong science background (for example, working with NASA or other research facilities), METs and MEs are usually considered equally qualified for a wide variety of jobs. There is even a procedure for METs to become registered as Professional Engineers (PEs).

The biggest difference between MEs and METs is in their education. MEs take more courses that require abstract thinking and heavy calculus loads; METs, on the other hand, take mostly applied, or practical, courses, with less calculus. At the undergraduate level, MEs prepare themselves for graduate school and employment as researchers, while METs are trained to get an engineering job—their only graduate school possibilities are in management or business. But the skills in design, application, and troubleshooting that METs and other engineering technology majors learn provide a significant career boost.

The mechanical engineering technology curriculum is diverse. You begin with physics; in your examination of machines, you'll observe the forces that are applied to mechanical devices and the forces that they generate. You'll learn, too, how engineers predict the way these forces are transmitted, multiplied, and/or reduced. You'll also study fluid mechanics: some machine systems rely on fluids to transmit either power or control. On the other hand, some fluid systems depend on machines, such as pumps, to distribute liquids (think of soup on an assembly line being poured into cans). In your class on thermodynamics, the science of heat, you'll concentrate on energy—how to make it work, how to use it more efficiently, how to find it in unexpected places (the sources of alternative energies). You study heat in automobile engines as well as in electric power plants. You also learn graphic arts by taking courses in computer-aided design (CAD) in both two- and three-dimensional formats.

Two-thirds of your courses deal primarily with problem solving—in the type of problem solving that engineers call "design," you'll use equations to determine important properties of a situation. For this work, you'll need a solid understanding of mathematics (including some calculus applications), as well as good critical-thinking skills, so that you can apply the math logically. You also take courses that develop your mechanical skills, usually by doing laboratory activities. Because, in some cases, laboratories simulate work environments, you'll have the chance to become familiar with instruments and equipment used in industry. Some equipment is based on cutting-edge technology, but most of the equipment in engineering labs is traditional, even timeless, such as pressure gauges, thermometers, material testers, and machine tools (metal cutting machines). Most programs end with a senior capstone design project.

Other majors you might like:
Biomedical technology
Robotics technology
Industrial technology
Aeronautical/aerospace engineering technology
Automotive engineering technology
Agricultural equipment technology
Drafting and design technology
Heavy equipment maintenance
Machine tool technology
Manufacturing technologies
Technical and business writing

Questions to ask colleges:
Is the program approved by the Accreditation Board for Engineering Technology (ABET)? If so, it will probably require an advanced level of calculus and have advanced courses that focus on abstract engineering, rather than on specific types of jobs in industry.

Career options and trends:
Plant manager; consulting engineer; manufacturing engineer; design engineer; sales engineer.

Consulting engineers typically are certified as Professional Engineers (PEs) by the state they work in. When you know where you'll be working, you should find out how a graduate of an engineering technology program becomes a PE in that state, since rules may differ from state to state.

Mechanical engineers and technicians are typically the most sought after of all the engineering disciplines, and entry-level salaries are good. Many graduates begin their careers performing CAD functions. Once they learn the product or service, they take on more responsibility for its actual design. Employment opportunities follow the national economy; sometimes jobs are more difficult to find or starting salaries are lower than normal, but graduates can almost always find a job.

Insider's viewpoint:

"A career in mechanical engineering technology is full of options—it allows you to go to the community of your choice, anywhere in the United States, anywhere in the world, and find a good-paying and respected job; and it allows you to choose whether you want to travel or work a 9-to-5 job, carry tools or carry a laptop, or spend your days dealing with dozens of people or work in solitude in your own office."

—Professor James Kamm, University of Toledo

For more info:
American Society of Mechanical Engineers (ASME)
3 Park Ave.
New York, NY 10016-5990
(800) 843-2763
www.asme.org

Surveying technology

Also known as:
Geomatics engineering

What it's about:
Using specialized equipment and techniques, surveying technology majors learn how to measure the physical features of the earth. You gather data to determine land boundaries, locate existing and proposed engineering structures, make topographic maps of the earth's surface, and perform computations and computer-assisted drafting.

Is this for you?
You might like this major if you also like: drafting; drawing; working outdoors; geography and maps; solving practical problems; working with precision and detail.

Consider this major if you are good at: attention to detail; math; organizing; research; spatial thinking/analysis; teamwork *...or have...* communication skills; initiative; manual dexterity; physical stamina.

Recommended high school prep:
English 4, math 3, lab science 3 (including physics), social studies 3, and a foreign language 2–3. Math courses should cover algebra, geometry, trigonometry, and perhaps precalculus. If possible, also take courses in drafting and computer science or computer applications.

Did you know...
...that surveyors can map in three dimensions? They use the computerized technology known as geomatics, which processes information received from satellites and from sensors and imaging systems in the air, sea, and ground. Geomatic surveying is important for the building and monitoring of large engineering projects.

Typical courses in this major:
Calculus and analytic geometry
Basic statistics
Physics
Surveying fundamentals
Advanced surveying
Engineering and construction surveying
Measurement error analysis and adjustment
Geodetic datums and coordinate systems
Photogrammetry
Land information systems
Real estate law
Boundary surveying principles
Technical writing
Soil mechanics
Statics and strength of materials
Hydrology and drainage

Concentrations:
In college: geodetic (large-area) surveying; mine surveying; hydrographic surveying; cartography; photogrammetry (aerial surveying); geographic information science.

If you go on to grad school: geomatics (three-dimensional computerized mapping); geodesy; remote sensing.

What the study of this major is like:
In this major, you study the technologies used in making accurate measurements on earth. These measurements include distances, directions, and elevations that can be calculated directly or indirectly with optical or electromechanical instruments. The most recognizable device is the tripod-mounted *theodolite*, which measures horizontal and vertical angles. You will also learn to gather measurements by using tools such as aerial photographs, global positioning system (GPS) satellites, geographic information systems (GIS), and satellite remote sensing imagery. In addition to taking measurements, you'll acquire skills in analyzing the information you collect and in making conclusions and recommendations.

Courses are laboratory-oriented. In outdoor lab work, you explore different surveying techniques and gain practice in using the equipment. In indoor labs, you use specialized software to do survey computations and related drafting. Because most survey technology programs have small enrollments, students often become a closely knit group whose members help each other. In most schools, organizations representing students in the major are affiliated with state or national professional surveying organizations.

This major is offered at either the associate (two-year) or the bachelor's (four-year) degree level, depending on the college. Many programs prepare students to obtain state licensure for professional practice. These programs usually consist of courses on boundary determination, land development, and related state and federal statutes. Programs at some colleges may emphasize engineering and construction surveying, while other programs may stress mapping and the management of geographic information. Although a bachelor's degree from any accredited surveying technology program will make you eligible to apply to graduate school, an undergraduate program that gives you a strong grounding in math may better prepare you for graduate studies.

After graduation, your work location and responsibilities may change as you progress in your career. Early on, you will probably work mostly outdoors, performing different types of surveys. Senior surveyors usually become partners in surveying/engineering companies and hold management positions.

There are several career tracks open to you, in addition to assisting professional surveyors as a technician. *Photogrammetrists* prepare detailed maps of remote or inaccessible areas, using aerial photographs and other imaging systems. *Geodetic surveyors* measure large areas of the earth's surface, using technology such as satellite remote sensing. *Geophysical surveyors* map prospecting sites for subsurface exploration. *Hydrographic surveyors* survey harbors, rivers, and other bodies of water to determine depths, shorelines, bottom topography, and other nautical features.

In most states, to become a professional land surveyor, you must have a license or registration. Requirements vary but generally include the completion of a two-part examination, conducted by the National Committee of Examiners for Engineering and Surveying, and a period of apprenticeship. An increasing number of states also require a bachelor's degree. Licensure is not required unless your practice includes work related to property boundaries. Certification as a survey technician is available through national professional societies.

Other majors you might like:
Cartography
Civil engineering
Drafting and design technology
Real estate
Forest engineering
Landscape architecture
Geology/earth science
Geography
Construction management
Land use planning
Mining and mineral engineering
Instrumentation technology

Questions to ask colleges:
Does the program offer an associate degree, a bachelor's degree, or both?

Is the program accredited? Most programs in this major are approved under one of three commissions of the Accreditation Board for Engineering and Technology (ABET): the Engineering Accreditation Commission, the Applied Science Accreditation Commission, or the Technology Accreditation Commission.

What surveying equipment is available for laboratory work? Are students trained in the latest surveying technologies?

Are the students required to purchase any supplies other than textbooks?

Career options and trends:
Surveying technician*; drafting technician; photogrammetric technician; professional land surveyor*; GIS manager; consultant.

Job prospects for surveying technicians are likely to increase faster than average over the next decade or so. Opportunities will be greatest for those who have a bachelor's degree and proficiency in advanced technologies such as GPS and GIS. Continued growth in construction, which is also projected, should create demand for surveyors to lay out projects and to define areas in need of environmental protection.

Insider's viewpoint:

"Being a person who loves the outdoors, I prefer surveying to any other engineering related field."

—Professor Indrajith Wijayratne, Michigan Technological University

For more info:

American Congress on Surveying and Mapping
    (ACSM)
6 Montgomery Village Ave.
Suite 403
Gaithersburg, MD 20879
(240) 632-9716
www.acsm.net

American Society of Photogrammetry and Remote
    Sensing (ASPRS)
5410 Grosvenor Lane
Suite 210
Bethesda, MD 20814-2160
(301) 493-0290
www.asprs.org

Telecommunications technology

What it's about:

In the telecommunications technology major, students are trained in the installation, management, operation, and maintenance of telecommunications equipment and systems, such as those used in telephone, data, Internet, and wireless networks. Graduates of associate degree (technician) programs typically handle the testing, operation, initial software configuration, and maintenance of telecommunications equipment. Bachelor's degree (technologist) programs, in contrast, prepare you to design, implement, configure, and manage telecommunications networks.

Is this for you?

You might like this major if you also like: amateur or ham radio; working and playing with computers; connecting systems (computers, home entertainment systems); electronics.

Consider this major if you are good at: attention to detail; creativity; critical reading/thinking; math; memorizing; organizing; teamwork *...or have...* initiative; patience; verbal skills; writing skills.

Recommended high school prep:

English 4, math 3–4 (trigonometry and precalculus), lab science 3, social studies 3, and a foreign language 2–3. If they are available, take courses in computer office applications (word processing, spreadsheets, and databases) and introductory computer programming.

Did you know...

...that telecommunications covers a lot more than just communicating by phone, cell, or instant messaging? Telecom engineering technicians maintain all the networks and sophisticated gear that make the World Wide Web, satellite and space probe transmissions, and e-commerce possible. These networks form the fabric of the global economy.

Typical courses in this major:

Communication systems
Electrical circuits and systems
Data communications
Telephony
Digital transmission
Central offices
Local-area networks and wide-area networks
Internet protocols (IP) for data and voice
Fiber optics
Telecom testing techniques
Wireless systems
Radio frequency design
Network planning and design
Satellite networks
Microwave link design
Network management

Concentrations:

In college: data communications; local-area networks (LAN); wide-area networks (WAN); telephony (transmission and switching); wireless systems (wireless LAN, microwave links, satellites); fiber optics.

If you go on to grad school: network engineering; traffic engineering; telecom regulations; international telecommunications; management of information systems (MIS).

What the study of this major is like:

Telecommunications technology professionals design, install, manage, operate, and maintain the equipment and systems (such as telephone, data, Internet, and wireless networks) that make possible today's fast-paced exchange of information. Telecom technicians and technologists work to create the right balance between sophistication and cost effectiveness while setting up networks and ensuring that they function properly.

To become an engineering technologist, you must complete a four-year bachelor's degree program that prepares you to design, implement/configure, and manage telecommunications networks. Two-year associate degree programs, which train you to become a technician, typically cover the testing, operation, initial software configuration, and maintenance of telecommunications equipment.

As a major, you learn to design both local and long distance telecommunications networks (LANs and WANs). You also learn the principles of cellular telephone networks and receive a strong foundation in LAN administration.

Although the major is mostly system- or network-oriented, you generally take additional electronics and computers courses that cover basic electricity, solid-state fundamentals, digital concepts, and microprocessors. You learn about central office switching, analog and digital carrier circuits, broadband design and analysis, fiber optics, coaxial and twisted pair splicing, outside plant construction, and specific computer applications. And because communication skills are important, development of your writing and speaking abilities is an essential part of your training.

You are taught through lectures, videotapes, and presentations from industry visitors. Almost all your courses have accompanying labs, in which you get hands-on experience, working with a variety of tools and electronic testing equipment. Starting in your second year, you work on many team projects. To prepare you for the industry, you write reports and term papers and give oral presentations to other students. In addition, you can join a telecom student society—the field trips and other interesting activities that such groups usually sponsor are good opportunities for you to meet industry professionals.

While most electrical engineering programs prepare you for graduate school, research, or a job designing new equipment, telecommunications technology programs train students to use existing equipment for system and network design. Telecom technology programs also have fewer math requirements but a much greater emphasis on hands-on experience. Some four-year programs focus on the business or management side of telecommunications.

Other majors you might like:

Electrical engineering technology
Radio and television
Recording arts
Information technology
Computer engineering technology
Communications
Electrical drafting/CAD/CADD
Communications systems installation/repair
Digital media
Medical records technology
Technical and business writing
Management information systems

Questions to ask colleges:

How large are the lab classes? What types of equipment are used? The ability to learn on up-to-date, accessible, "real-industry" equipment is an important factor in selecting a program.

How "wired"—and wireless—is the campus? How many types of network technologies are available?

Career options and trends:

Design engineer; network developer*; network administrator*; network applications support specialist; test engineer; radio frequency (RF) engineer*; sales engineer; facilities engineer; telecom manager.

The recent past has been a difficult time for the telecom industry, but a turnaround is underway. While employment prospects for equipment installers and repairers are expected to decline through 2014, the need for telecommunications has not disappeared and, in fact, will continue to grow, especially in the wireless and Internet areas. The rapid pace of change and technological development in this industry should create a demand for college-educated technologists with the training, knowledge, and skills to oversee these changes.

For more info:

IEEE Communications Society
3 Park Ave., 17th Fl.
New York, NY 10016
(212) 705-8900
www.comsoc.org

English language and literature

English is a major major, to borrow from Joseph Heller. More bachelor's degrees are earned in English than in any of the other liberal arts.

The English language dates back to Anglo-Saxon, yet it's perfectly suited to the digital age. English lends itself well to computer and multimedia communications because it's dense in meaning and conveys more ideas in less time and space than many other tongues do. The spread of American culture and business internationally has also popularized the language.

To study English is to grasp its Germanic roots and shake loose its literary leaves, from *Beowulf* to Weblogs. Students who choose to study English must be ready to read as many as 500 pages each week.

"One of the most important interests or activities for a creative writer is engaged reading—to try and understand how a text influences a reader's emotions or intellect," explains Jonathan Fink, a poet who teaches at Emory University.

Fortunately, if you like high school English, you're probably already an avid reader and a skilled writer. These talents aren't just for budding novelists, either. Corporations, nonprofit organizations, and government agencies all need good writers to take advantage of online communications, desktop publishing, and video editing tools.

"The discipline's emphasis on analytical skills and on careful writing prepares students for a variety of professions and occupations far beyond the world of teaching," says Professor James G. Taaffe of the University of Alabama.

English majors go on to journalism, publishing, advertising, technical writing, management, law, and other careers. Graduate students specialize in genres, or types of literature, such as fiction, poetry, children's books, sci fi, and even hypertext—interactive fiction online. Other graduate areas include linguistics, film, and drama. Some grad students latch on to a specific historical period—say, nineteenth-century American literature. Multicultural literature, which might focus on works by African Americans or by women, is an emerging area these days. (See the section on Area, ethnic, and gender studies for related majors.)

"For a student, the number of possibilities for graduate study is encouraging; for a graduate, the competition for employment in creative writing can be daunting," cautions Fink. College English teaching positions are also hard to come by, so be flexible in planning a career using your English smarts. Technical or business writing may be an outlet if you're a good communicator with an interest in technology and multimedia.

"Increasingly, even liberal arts majors such as those in American literature are asked to have high-level technical skills," notes Professor Brett C. Millier of Middlebury College. "Many careers, ranging from magazine editing to investment banking, require strong research skills."

Read Up on Colleges

Look for these majors in colleges of arts and sciences or arts and letters, and in departments and schools of English, liberal arts, and humanities.

When comparing colleges, you should do some reading, research, and critical analysis of your own. You'll notice that two-year colleges usually prepare students for the workplace and technical communications jobs. If that's your goal, find out if you'll be ready for an entry-level job when you get your associate degree. Also for technical writers, scope out the software at the college and find out how widely it's used in the real world. See if the college has partnerships and internships with industry to get your foot in the door.

Most English majors go to four-year colleges, which have an academic slant.

"Inquire about whether the department is committed to a cultural studies approach or whether its focus is on critical theory," Taaffe advises. Cultural studies requires intense reading of literature to put it into a social or historical context. In critical theory, instead of reading and interpreting a work, you explore what other people, especially writers over the years, have said about it.

Other points to consider: Check out the college library, its books and journals. Is the library catalog online? Will you have access to the *Oxford English Dictionary* (*OED* to you), which traces how words have been used over the centuries? You'll certainly want a computer with a word processor in the library, labs, and dorm.

The faculty is most important. You want class time with the top profs. How many lower-division and upper-division courses are taught by graduate students instead? Are any of the leading professors called "emeritus"? That means they don't teach anymore.

Will you have the chance to work on a literary journal or publications? Does the university often host visiting writers on campus? Are other literary or cultural opportunities nearby?

If American lit is your passion, ask if it's a department of its own. How many courses are offered and in what depth? Are they huge lectures or smaller seminars? Keep in mind that you'll read modern writers, but even as an American literature major, you'll curl up with the masters of English literature—including Chaucer, Shakespeare, and Milton—during your college years.

American literature

What it's about:

As an American literature major, you study the principal literary movements and the fiction, nonfiction, poetry, and drama of the United States. You examine how American literature has developed historically and learn about the intellectual, economic, geographic, and social forces that have shaped U.S. culture.

Is this for you?

You might like this major if you also like: reading; expository and critical writing; contemporary literature; literature in its cultural and historical context; creative writing.

Consider this major if you are good at: active listening; attention to detail; creativity; critical reading/thinking; research *...or have...* initiative; verbal skills; writing skills.

Recommended high school prep:

English 4, math 3, lab science 3, social studies 3, and a foreign language 2–3.

Did you know...

...that even American literature majors should take Chaucer, Shakespeare, and Milton?

Typical courses in this major:

Survey of American literature
The American novel
American drama
Native American literature
Melville
Faulkner
The American Renaissance
American poetry
African-American literature
Literature by American women
American autobiography
American poetry
Senior seminar

Concentrations:

In college: comparative studies; creative writing.

If you go on to grad school: a particular historical era (e.g., 18th, 19th, 20th centuries); a particular genre (e.g., fiction, poetry).

What the study of this major is like:

Although American literature is comparatively young, its writings are rich and varied. The tradition began in the oral songs and tales of Native Americans and continued in the literature of European exploration and settlement, through the seventeenth century. In New England, the Puritans developed a prolific literary culture that included histories, biographies, poetry, and sermons. The Puritan influence was transformed, in the mid-nineteenth century, by Nathaniel Hawthorne, Ralph Waldo Emerson, Henry Thoreau, Emily Dickinson, and Harriet Beecher Stowe. Although New England dominated American writing until the Civil War, authors elsewhere in the North (Benjamin Franklin, James Fenimore Cooper, Herman Melville, and Walt Whitman) and in the South (William Byrd, Thomas Jefferson, and Edgar Allan Poe) created a distinctive, significant literature. Other lively, often subversive traditions flourished: fugitive slave narratives, Native American protest speeches, folk songs, and frontier humor.

Since the Civil War, American literature has undergone a cultural explosion. As an American literature major, you will follow the development of this legacy, by exploring the rise of realism in fiction (William Dean Howells, Henry James, Stephen Crane, Edith Wharton, Theodore Dreiser); the growth of midwestern, western, and southern regionalism (Willa Cather, Sherwood Anderson, Frank Norris, John Steinbeck, Flannery O'Connor, Eudora Welty); America's leadership in international modernism in poetry (Ezra Pound, T. S. Eliot, Marianne Moore, Wallace Stevens, William Carlos Williams); the modernist novels of Ernest Hemingway, F. Scott

Fitzgerald, William Faulkner; the emergence of major dramatists (Eugene O'Neill, Arthur Miller, Tennessee Williams); the prominence of African-American literature (Langston Hughes, Zora Neale Hurston, Richard Wright, Ralph Ellison, James Baldwin); the self-conscious affirmations of post-World War II fiction (Saul Bellow, Vladimir Nabokov, Norman Mailer, John Updike); the grimness of post-World War II poetry (Robert Lowell, John Berryman, Elizabeth Bishop, Sylvia Plath); the revolt of the Beat Generation (Jack Kerouac). The course work also highlights the achievements in Native American writings in English (N. Scott Momaday, Leslie Silko, James Welch, Louise Erdrich); literature by and for women (Adrienne Rich, Ann Beattie, Joan Didion, Toni Morrison); and a powerful array of ethnic literatures.

If you major in American literature, you will probably take an introduction-to-literature course and then three or four courses covering (in historical order) the literary traditions of the United States. You may then take a seminar or two on a single author, and you elect your concentration—usually either comparative studies or creative writing. You also take several electives—in American poetry, or African-American literature, for example—in preparation for advanced study in your fourth year. Fourth-year work usually consists of a seminar or two, a comprehensive exam, and, if you are eligible, an honors thesis.

American literature is studied today basically as it has always been studied. While computers help you write papers more easily and have easier access to resource materials, you still do the important work by reading a book and your professor still lectures in front of a chalkboard. Your academic routine will be generally low-tech, quiet, and relatively solitary. You must read a great deal—sometimes 400 or 500 pages in a week—and typically write several papers for each course.

Not many colleges offer an American literature major, so most students study American literature within the context of an English major. English departments may vary as to how many courses in American literature are offered, and there may be gaps in historical sequence. Departments may also vary in their course offerings in emerging fields such as ethnic American literatures, or reject the idea of "cultural studies" of literature altogether.

Other majors you might like:
English
American studies
African-American studies
Publishing
Native American studies
American history (U.S.)
Media studies
English literature (British)
Comparative literature
Political science
Women's studies
Creative writing

Questions to ask colleges:
Is American literature taught within an English department or on its own? If it is taught within an English department, how many courses in the field are offered in a typical year, and how much depth can students achieve?

How big are the courses—are they all large lecture courses, or are there also medium-size courses and seminars? Are there courses in emerging fields like African-American literature or ethnic American literatures?

Career options and trends:
High school teacher; journalist; editor; college professor.

American literature majors do well in a variety of fields because careers ranging from magazine editing to investment banking often require strong research skills.

For more info:
American Studies Association (ASA)
1120 19th St., N.W.
Suite 301
Washington, DC 20036
(202) 467-4783
www.theasa.net

Creative writing

What it's about:

As a creative writing major, you study the creation and construction of poetry, fiction, drama, nonfiction, and screenwriting. You examine the works of established writers and develop your own original work (poems, stories, dramas, etc.), and submit your work to professors and peers for discussion and analysis.

Is this for you?

You might like this major if you also like: reading; drama; poetry; fiction; film; language; self-expression; the subtle meanings of words and sentences. Creative writing majors find pleasure in weighing, balancing, and selecting words for their ability to convey meaning through image, tone, rhythm, and scene.

Consider this major if you are good at: attention to detail; creativity; critical reading/thinking; organizing; persuading/influencing *...or have...* emotional stamina/endurance; initiative; patience; perception; verbal skills; writing skills.

Recommended high school prep:

English 4, math 3, lab science 3, social studies 4, and a foreign language 4. If available, take courses that encourage you to write and to think about how art is constructed. Also, activities such as working on a student literary journal or newspaper are recommended.

Typical courses in this major:

Introduction to creative writing
Poetry writing
Fiction writing
Journalism
Composition
Playwriting
Screenwriting
Argumentation
Advanced creative writing
Expository writing
Memoir/creative non-fiction writing
Topics in English composition

Concentrations:

Poetry; fiction; playwriting; screenwriting; creative nonfiction.

What the study of this major is like:

The creative writing major closely resembles the English major. Much of the course work is similar, and you study works of drama, prose, and poetry, as well as composition. But in creative writing, you develop your own literary voice in workshops that are taught by practicing writers who know first-hand the challenges and struggles of the writing process.

In general, your course work is divided among writing workshops, literature courses, and liberal arts requirements in the sciences, mathematics, and other humanities. In most programs, your writing samples and performance in writing courses is examined before you are admitted into the workshops.

Most introductory creative writing courses combine several forms of writing. Similar to survey courses in the arts, an introductory course in creative writing usually encourages you to write fiction, poetry, and, often, drama. You will also examine the history of several forms of writing and analyze the works of contemporary authors.

"Forms" courses are similar to a traditional literature course, but with a focus on an aspect of writing not usually covered in core courses. The topics may range from contemporary short story or memoir to an examination of the struggles involved in revision. Most upper-level courses are divided by genre, which allows you to focus more in-depth on your own poetry, fiction, or drama. You will also probably be required to submit a thesis project—usually a collection of poems, stories, or essays.

Upper-level workshops also focus on a particular form. In essay writing, you study techniques of analysis and persuasion, explore the relation between voice and purpose, and learn how to design an argument. In poetry writing, you experiment with meter, image, tone, and organization. In fiction courses, you may focus on characterization, narrative, scene, dialogue, or plot. In most courses, members of the class analyze each other's work with guidance from the instructor. Because writing is such a solitary endeavor, most students consider this feedback to be the most valued aspect of the major.

Being a creative writing major requires maturity, patience, and determination. The challenges you are likely to face are generally those that all writers encounter: Where do I get ideas? How can I overcome writer's block? How can I choose the most appropriate way to express my ideas? You will also need to set writing and revision schedules for yourself; this task can be hard, because the amount of time creative work takes is often unpredictable. Unlike majors that have clearly mapped out paths to success, creative writing challenges you not only to follow the guidance of professionals, but also to rely heavily on your own initiative and conviction.

Creative writing may be offered as an independent major, as a concentration in the English major, or as an independent minor. Because content and approach vary widely in creative writing programs, you should examine the writing of professors at the colleges you are considering. Look for writers whose work addresses some of your own interests and concerns.

Other majors you might like:
English
Drama and theater arts
Journalism
Publishing
Comparative literature
Advertising
Philosophy
Psychology
Business communications
Radio and television
Fine/studio arts
Technical and business writing

Questions to ask colleges:
Does the college have a visiting-writers program that invites authors to campus?

What opportunities are there for students to become involved in literary journals or readings?

How many creative writing majors does the college currently enroll?

Career options and trends:
Freelance writer; copywriter for advertising or marketing; editor; content manager for Web site or other electronic publishing venue.

Not many authors make a living from their writing. Creative writing majors do find employment, however, in related fields like teaching, advertising, journalism, television, radio, film, and publishing; or, they ply their language skills in graduate programs in law, medicine or business. Most university-level teaching positions require an advanced degree.

Recently, there has been an increase in the number of graduate creative writing programs. For a student, the increased possibilities for graduate study are encouraging; for a graduate, the competition for employment in the field of creative writing can be daunting.

Insider's viewpoint:
"The longer I struggle with the creation and motivation of my invented characters, the more I am able to translate that empathy to individuals I encounter in 'real' life."

—Professor Jonathan Fink, Emory University

For more info:
Associated Writing Programs
George Mason University
Mail Stop 1E3
Fairfax, VA 22030
(703) 993-4301
www.awpwriter.org

Poets & Writers, Inc.
72 Spring St.
Suite 301
New York, NY 10012
(212) 226-3586
www.pw.org

English

What it's about:

English majors read, discuss, and write about literature. Literary works include poetry, prose, and drama but may also be drawn from film, journalism, and television. Study focuses on the critical, historical, linguistic, and cultural contexts of these works. In addition, you practice your own writing, developing your language-use and composition skills.

Is this for you?

You might like this major if you also like: reading; writing; discussion; languages; film; music; theater; dance; working independently.

Consider this major if you are good at: attention to detail; creativity; critical reading/thinking; persuading/influencing; research *...or have...* initiative; patience; verbal skills; writing skills.

Recommended high school prep:

English 4, math 3, lab science 3, social studies 3, and foreign language 3.

Did you know...

...that the major requires a lot of library research, as well as reading and writing assignments? Even if you are an avid reader, you must plan your time carefully in order to complete your work.

...that the study of English literature covers not just the text of a work but also its context—how, when, and why it was produced, as well as how it has influenced generations of readers?

Typical courses in this major:

Survey of English literature
Chaucer
Shakespeare
Milton
History of the English language
Medieval literature
Victorian literature
The Romantics
Modern English grammar
English drama
American literature
Continental literature
Critical theory
New voices in literature
Poetry
The modern short story

Concentrations:

Creative writing; critical theory; drama; film; linguistics; ethnic literatures; literature of a particular period.

What the study of this major is like:

An almost universal first-year requirement of this major is a semester- or year-long chronological (or thematic) survey of English and American literature, which lays the groundwork for further courses in particular genres or literary time periods. Classes are usually small, and you are expected to contribute to class discussion and to write term papers—usually two per course.

Upper-level courses present a more formal study of literature. You learn how to read critically, how to determine the contexts of literature, and how literature creates and reflects the culture from which it springs. In addition, you study point of view, explication, tone, irony, metaphor, image, structure, and allusion. You also explore the ways in which texts affect audiences' beliefs and emotions, and the ways in which literature sheds light on our lives.

Besides the core courses, most programs offer a broad selection of electives focusing on genre study, critical theory, individual authors, and other topics. Courses in writing encourage you to practice the techniques you learn by reading the works of others. You'll become increasingly sensitive to the subtleties of language and to the influences of what you read and hear. In both literature and writing courses, you will examine the logic of an argument, the ways experiences are organized, and reactions to psychological and emotional persuasion. Your studies may conclude with a seminar on a particular theme or subject approached from a variety of directions. And there will likely be a lengthy term project for that seminar.

In addition to classes, most programs provide opportunities to attend readings presented by guest speakers, topical seminars, and more formal lectures given by faculty members. It is also common for English majors with similar interests to meet informally outside of class (usually at the local watering hole) to discuss their work and to exchange ideas and opinions.

Other majors you might like:
Communications
Drama and theater arts
Chicano studies
African-American studies
Comparative literature
Public relations
Medieval and Renaissance studies
Film/cinema studies
English teacher education
History
Philosophy
Classics

Questions to ask colleges:
What are typical class sizes? Which classes have prerequisites? English classes are popular and often, especially at larger colleges, getting into classes is competitive. If you see a course in the catalog that you must take, be sure to ask about it, so you know you have at least a chance of being enrolled.

Does the college offer both U.S. and foreign library catalogs online? Does it offer access to the *Oxford English Dictionary* and *Early English Books Online*? You might research the college's holdings of books and journals to see what is available in the library and online.

Career options and trends:
Elementary, middle, or high school teacher; college professor; editor; journalist; technical writer.

The English major also prepares you for a career in publishing, radio and television broadcasting, social work, and management. With graduate or professional study, you can pursue a career in law, medicine, or other field.

A state certificate or license is required for teaching in public schools. College-level teaching positions in English are few and difficult to obtain.

Insider's viewpoint:
"Have an idea of where you want to go with the major. Many people choose English because they don't know what else to do or they think it's easy. Having a career goal, like journalism in my case, helps a lot."

—Courtney, senior, SUNY Binghamton

For more info:
Modern Language Association (MLA)
26 Broadway
3rd Floor
New York, NY 10004-1789
(646) 576-5000
www.mla.org

Technical and business writing

Also known as:
Professional writing

What it's about:
As a technical and business writing major, you learn how to adapt technical information to specific audiences and types of media (text, images, animation, audio, video). You also learn to manage the technical communication process—the steps you go through before, during, and after you write.

Is this for you?
You might like this major if you also like: working with computers; science and technology; reading; tutoring; working with different types of people; being precise; expressing yourself in writing and in person.

Consider this major if you are good at: attention to detail; concentrating; creativity; critical reading/thinking; organizing; research; teamwork ...*or have...* initiative; verbal skills; writing skills.

Recommended high school prep:
English 4, math 3, lab science 3, social studies 3, and a foreign language 2–3. Courses in business and computer science or applications are also recommended.

Did you know...
...that you don't need technical expertise to go into technical and business writing? The "technical" part of the major isn't nearly as scary as some students think. And the major doesn't deal just with computers. What is most important is the ability to work with many different people and to communicate clearly and carefully.

Typical courses in this major:
Foundations in technical communications
Technical editing
Software documentation
Product documentation
Correspondence and report writing
Graphics for technical communications
Documentation process and management
Writing grant proposals
Web authoring
Science writing
Business writing
Multimedia for training and tutorials
Usability testing for technical communications
Internationalizing/localizing documentation

Concentrations:
Internet publishing; scientific writing; business writing; writing for the arts.

What the study of this major is like:
In this major you learn how to translate technical texts into "ordinary" language so that people with no special training can understand them. You also learn how to manage the overall process of technical communications—in particular, determining what type of work you are expected to create (such as a draft copy) and when you need to deliver the completed project. In addition, you gain practice in tracking and reviewing your work, and in writing up your decisions as documentation plans and proposals.

Courses on the internationalization and the localization of information focus on ways to make information understandable to a broad audience or to a specific audience. In other courses you study editing and usability testing, as well as financial, legal, and ethical issues. Most programs include a research component where you learn how to gather information from print and electronic sources, conduct interviews, and design surveys and questionnaires.

The curriculum also introduces you to "visual writing"—the use of layout and design, tables and graphs, illustrations, and other ways to highlight and structure text. By the time you graduate, you will have experience with desktop publishing, image editing, graphics, multimedia, and other types of software.

Your studies generally prepare you for entry-level technical communications jobs. Four-year programs may concentrate on theory and research, along with general education courses in the sciences and humanities. Two-year programs at community colleges and technical schools focus more on training you for entry into the workforce.

Other majors you might like:
Desktop publishing
Information systems
Web page/multimedia design
Creative writing
Management information systems
Public relations
Design/visual communications
Drafting and design technology
Digital media
Business communications
Computer graphics
Medical records administration

Questions to ask colleges:
Is there an open lab where majors can use publishing software? Which software programs does the program make available, and how often are they upgraded? Are software applications used in various industries featured in the courses?

Does the program have partnerships and internships with local businesses?

Career options and trends:
Workplace technical communicator*; software documentation writer; Web site editor/writer; information architect; product planner; marketing technical communicator.

The role of the technical communicator may evolve as businesses look for ways to manage content most effectively—that is, to enable one text to be published in different media forms. Also, the profession may join forces with related areas such as quality assurance and technical support.

For more info:
Society for Technical Communication (STC)
901 North Stewart St.
Suite 904
Arlington, VA 22203-1822
(703) 522-4114
www.stc.org

Association for Computing Machinery (ACM)
1515 Broadway
New York, NY 10036
(800) 342-6626
www.acm.org

Family and consumer sciences

People who study and work in the family and consumer sciences home in on living.

"A general major addresses the study of individuals, families, and communities to understand people's basic needs of food, clothing, shelter, and relationships—and to seek solutions to problems," says Professor Penny A. Ralston of Florida State University.

On the undergraduate and graduate levels, students specialize in the social and behavioral sciences, like child development and family relations, and in such fields as consumer economics, apparel design and merchandising, housing and living environments, and applied sciences in food, nutrition, and textiles. Those who choose family and consumer sciences tend to be creative, analytical, and caring. "The desire to help others and the opportunity to make a difference in people's lives" lead students to these majors, according to Professor Anne L. Sweaney of the University of Georgia.

Colleges have dozens of names for this category. The old name, "home economics," just doesn't cut it anymore. Instead, new and dynamic fields of family and consumer sciences are taught in schools, colleges, and departments of human sciences, human ecology, human resources, humanities and social science, business management, professional studies, arts and sciences, applied sciences, applied technology, or even education.

The majors differ at each college, so be sure to do your homework if you're planning to go into housing, human and family studies, apparel and textiles, or culinary arts. Find out if the program focuses on the industrial or the creative aspects of the field. In housing majors, for instance, the industrial approach emphasizes business functions like residential property management, while creative programs stress space design and planning. Culinary arts or apparel studies might also focus on one approach or the other.

Finding your college home

When choosing a college, see how many credits you'll take in general education courses in comparison with specific courses in your major. The issue here is, does the college mostly look at the "big picture" or does the program plunge into the occupation in a practical way?

"At some, especially larger, institutions, there may be more opportunity to specialize in one area of the major, while other colleges may treat the major in a more integrated and holistic manner, with broad, contextual courses," explains Professor Eva L. Essa of the University of Nevada, Reno.

Talk to an adviser on campus about what's important at that college. How much of your work will be in the classroom, and how much hands-on experience will you get? If you major in housing and human environments, will you work in the housing industry or do service work in the community to learn problem solving? Can you do an internship at a preschool if you're majoring in family studies, or at a restaurant if you're majoring in culinary arts? Will the college help you find the position? Will you be paid?

"Culinary arts programs will require students to complete internships in the field," says Paul Sorgule, a dean at Paul Smith's College. "These 'real-life' experiences can be a gateway to a permanent job after graduation."

Also ask how much real-world experience the faculty members have. As Sorgule puts it, "Not all chefs make the best teachers, but no teacher can be effective teaching the culinary arts without the experience to back up theory." That's good advice in many areas of study.

You might also find out what other courses you will take in college. Perhaps physical sciences to learn about foods or textiles? How about a foreign language as an academic and professional enhancement? For that matter, you might want to take courses at other parts of the university to learn topics from other colleges or departments. Ask if that's okay.

Other questions for colleges: What types of careers do their graduates pursue? What is the employment rate for graduates with the major you want?

Job prospects will differ depending on your major. For example, the apparel industry can go up or down with the economy and is extremely competitive. Production has moved overseas, where wages are low. Culinary and housing professionals enjoy fields with high employment even in shaky economic times. In addition to private industry, many of these fields of study can lead to work in the public sector and steady government jobs for teachers and social workers.

Family and consumer sciences are also great preparation for further studies in and outside of the field. Graduate students might specialize in adult development and the aging population. In apparel, graduate programs include textile engineering and retail marketing; housing grads might choose real estate or city and regional planning.

Two good general Web sites are those of the American Association of Family and Consumer Sciences (www.aafcs.org), and the National Council on Family Relations (www.ncfr.org). Also read about related majors in this book, including fashion merchandising and hospitality administration and management in the Business section, food science in the Agriculture section, and the majors in the section on Public administration.

Clothing, apparel and textile studies

What it's about:

The apparel and textiles major includes the design, production, marketing, and use of garments, fabrics, and fibers. You learn about technology applications, manufacturing systems, product development, buying, promotional techniques, clothing and material design and customization, and quality control in the apparel and textiles industries.

Is this for you?

You might like this major if you also like: combining colors, fabrics, and shapes; using your imagination; sewing; drawing; sketching; shopping; history; fashion magazines; predicting trends.

Consider this major if you are good at: creativity; critical reading/thinking; leadership; math; persuading/influencing; quantitative analysis; research; teamwork *...or have...* initiative.

Recommended high school prep:

English 4, math 2, lab science 2, social studies 3, and a foreign language 3. If possible, take courses in computer/graphic arts, photography, business, accounting, and family and consumer studies (for example, fashion design).

Did you know...

...that this major requires you to have a working knowledge of computer applications such as Excel, Access, and PowerPoint? Knowledge of creative software, such as PhotoShop and Publisher, is also helpful.

Typical courses in this major:

Textile fundamentals
Apparel design
Sociology of clothing
Clothing construction
Mass production of apparel
Figure and fashion illustration
Promotion and marketing principles
Historic textiles and costumes
Textiles in non-apparel uses
Tailoring
Product development
Advanced textile testing and analysis
Computer-aided design
Merchandise buying and management
Contemporary fashion designers
Textile and apparel economics

Concentrations:

In college: buying; product development; textile production; apparel design and production; fashion promotion and marketing; interior merchandising.

If you go on to grad school: retail marketing; costume design; textile design; textile science; historic costume and textiles; curating and preservation; textile economics.

What the study of this major is like:

This major is typically taught in laboratory, studio, and lecture settings. In most classes you apply what you learn by completing projects or papers. You will probably be expected to make presentations to the class, so good oral communications are an asset. Your work may occasionally be evaluated by industry professionals. Especially in senior-level courses, you will apply critical-thinking skills in analytical and persuasive writing. Many classes invite guest speakers to discuss up-to-date trends and requirements of the industry.

Understanding consumer behavior, likes, and wants will contribute to your potential success in this field. Therefore, many colleges require internships in which you earn credit while getting firsthand experience in the industry. You can also participate in field trips or off-campus study programs in manufacturing and fashion centers, including retail stores, design houses, textiles factories, museums, and historic sites in areas such as New York, Dallas, and Europe.

This major may be offered in a college of arts and sciences or in a college of family and consumer sciences (formerly home economics), and may lead either to a Bachelor of Science degree (with an emphasis on physical science) or a Bachelor of Arts (humanities). In some Bachelor of Science programs, you take chemistry to fulfill the science requirement. Bachelor of Arts programs usually require fewer core courses and more general education courses. Colleges that focus on retailing do not offer creative courses as part of the major. Programs in other colleges may focus on design, product development, or textiles. Many colleges require you to take two semesters of foreign language and at least one semester of economics, and to be proficient in computer systems.

Apparel and textiles majors tend to be outgoing and self-motivated. Most colleges host an industry-related organization like Fashion Group International. Depending on the campus, you might participate in the Student Marketing Association, Student Retail Federation, or the Advertising and Public Relations Club. Majors who are active in the community or have a part-time job may conduct fashion shows for fund-raisers, organize clothing drives, or set up programs to recycle textiles, apparel, and shoes.

Other majors you might like:
Fashion and apparel design
Textile science
Fashion merchandising
Textile sciences/engineering
Retailing
Marketing
Family and consumer sciences
Advertising
Fiber/textile arts
Theater design and technology
Interior design

Questions to ask colleges:
In what ways do faculty members and students become involved in related local industries? How many faculty members have had industry experience? How frequently do industry professionals serve as guest speakers in classes?

What types of off-campus study programs are available? Does the program require an internship prior to graduation? Are students assisted in obtaining these internships?

What types of careers do graduates in this major pursue after graduation? Where do most graduates relocate to for their first industry job?

Career options and trends:
Buyer; product developer; product manager; market researcher; fashion coordinator; fashion reporter; fashion or textile designer; pattern maker; visual merchandising manager.

The apparel and textiles major can prepare you to work as a merchandise coordinator with a national-brand wholesale firm; an in-store sales associate or manager with a major retailer; a production assistant with a manufacturing firm; an educational representative for a fabric, pattern, sewing machine, or notions firm; a textile and apparel advertiser and promoter; or a quality control analyst. With specialized training, you may work as a textile chemist, textile engineer, or museum costume curator.

The apparel and textiles industries are strongly affected by the national economy and consumer spending. In good times, the industry expands so rapidly that firms have a difficult time hiring enough people; but when the economy suffers, the industry may not hire entry-level employees and may even close stores. Be aware that most of the labor-intensive activities (especially apparel manufacturing) have moved to developing countries, where wages are significantly lower.

For more info:
International Textile and Apparel Association
   (ITAA)
P.O. Box 1360
Monument, CO 80132-1360
(719) 488-3716
www.itaaonline.org

Fashion Group International, Inc. (FGI)
8 W. 40th St.
7th Floor
New York, NY 10018
212-302-5511
www.fgi.org

Culinary arts and chef training

What it's about:

Culinary arts and chef training programs prepare you for a career in the food service industry as a chef, executive chef, pastry chef, restaurant manager, food and beverage director, food service director, or restaurateur. Chefs today are managers of people, products, and facilities. They have a responsibility to provide quality food and experiences in a safe, sanitary environment.

Is this for you?

You might like this major if you also like: cooking and presenting different kinds of food; serving others; people of diverse backgrounds; expressing yourself in artistic ways; travel; creating something and receiving immediate feedback.

Consider this major if you are good at: coaching; counseling; leadership; multi-tasking; organizing; spatial thinking/analysis; teamwork *...or have...* initiative; manual dexterity; physical stamina.

Recommended high school prep:

English 4, math 3, lab science 3, social studies 3, and a foreign language 2–3. If possible, also take a basic computer applications course.

Did you know...

...there is much more to this major than cooking? Being a professional cook is a hands-on career, but chefs need a strong foundation in math applications, problem resolution, decision making, human resources management, team building, and critical-thinking skills.

Typical courses in this major:

Professional cooking
Foundations of baking
International cooking
Advanced cooking
Banquets and catering
Garde-manger (cold food preparation)
Fabrication and charcuterie
Nutrition
Food science
Restaurant management
Food service sanitation
Menu planning and purchasing
Food and beverage control
Human resources management

Concentrations:

Pastry arts; baking.

What the study of this major is like:

Training to be a chef requires discipline. The field demands a strong work ethic; empathy; a dedication to excellence; and self-assessment, organizational, multitasking, and timing abilities. A successful chef is good at following through on projects, always aware that the job must get done.

Like many academic programs, programs in culinary arts require dedication to research, reading, writing, and computation. However, as a chef-in-training, you must work long hours, under the critical eye of instructors and the dining public. Most colleges insist you follow the conservative uniform and grooming standards of the industry. In chef training programs, you work with others, performing as part of a team, and you are evaluated and receive critiques as a group member. At most colleges you will spend 15–40 hours a week in the kitchen (depending on the semester), beginning as early as 5 a.m. and often working into the evening. At the same time, you must complete assignments for courses in cooking, liberal arts, and management.

Training programs include internships that can be anywhere in the country. Traditionally, internships are paid positions, although some are not. Most students use these real-world experiences as a way to obtain permanent jobs after graduation.

Many colleges offer degrees in culinary arts and related services. As you investigate the schools you are considering, keep in mind their philosophies and methodologies. Most programs require hands-on experience, although some emphasize it more strongly than others. In some programs, general education courses are optional. Other programs include both cooking and liberal arts courses.

Recently, some colleges have started offering bachelor's degrees in culinary arts. Besides stressing the technical skills that can make you a successful chef, they encourage you to be a decision maker, team builder, manager, and leader.

If you think you'd like to be a chef, you should pursue a balanced education. A chef must understand the finances of an operation, be well read and able to design restaurant menus that match a profiled guest, know how environments affect human behavior, and be a good communicator.

Other majors you might like:
Restaurant/food services management
Food and nutrition studies
Food science
Dietetics
Hospitality administration and management
Baking/pastry arts
Nutrition sciences
Human resources management
Italian studies
Entrepreneurial studies

Questions to ask colleges:
Which types of industry experience does the faculty have? Not all chefs make good teachers, but it is hard to be an effective teacher in the culinary arts without some experience to back up the theory.

Is the program accredited by the American Culinary Federation? How current are the facilities?

Career options and trends:
Cook; sous chef; executive chef; food and beverage director; restaurant manager; restaurateur.

Increasingly, serious chefs are seeking certification through the American Culinary Federation as chef de cuisine, executive chef, pastry chef, or master

chef. A certificate in sanitation from the National Restaurant Association is also useful.

Since dining out has become essential to the American lifestyle, the culinary business continues to grow, even during tough economic times. In fact, 2005 was the 14th consecutive year of growth in the restaurant industry.

A bachelor's degree will soon become the standard for positions at the chef level, and within a decade or so, a master's degree may be necessary. The major companies are winning the battle for customers, so even though 80 percent of the restaurants in the United States are privately owned, restaurant chains have the ability and cash flow to reward their employees. The chains are therefore likely to offer the most career opportunities.

Insider's viewpoint:
"Chefs are designers of experiences that are the basis for building relationships, mending disagreements, creating partnerships, confirming friendships, celebrating accomplishments, and recognizing personal and professional achievements."

—Paul Sorgule, Paul Smith's College

For more info:
American Culinary Federation (ACF)
180 Center Place Way
St. Augustine, FL 32095
(800) 624-9458
www.acfchefs.org

National Restaurant Association
1200 17th St., N.W.
Washington, DC 20036
(202) 331-5900
www.restaurant.org

Family and consumer sciences

Also known as:

Human sciences

Home economics

What it's about:

The major in family and consumer sciences focuses on individuals, families, and communities from ecological and interdisciplinary perspectives. The purpose of the major is to help you understand the problems they face—especially those related to the basic needs of food, clothing, shelter, and relationships—and to seek solutions.

Is this for you?

You might like this major if you also like: children and families; community service; leadership roles; helping people make decisions and solve problems.

Consider this major if you are good at: active listening; caring/nurturing; critical reading/thinking; leadership; research; teamwork *...or have...* initiative; verbal skills; writing skills.

Recommended high school prep:

English 4, math 3, lab science 4 (including biology and chemistry), social studies 3, and a foreign language 2–3. If possible, take at least one year of family and consumer sciences.

Did you know...

...that you need a background in chemistry to do well in courses like food science, nutrition, and textiles, which are usually included in the major?

Typical courses in this major:

Personal and family financial management

Child development

Family relations

Consumer economics

Housing and interior design

Food science

Fundamentals of nutrition

Nutrition in the life cycle

Community nutrition

Apparel production and analysis

Consumer textiles

Human development

Concentrations:

Child development; family relations; consumer economics (including personal finance); apparel design; fashion merchandising; textiles; housing and interiors; food and nutrition; family and consumer science education.

What the study of this major is like:

The family and consumer sciences major is the interdisciplinary study of factors that can affect the well-being of people of all ages. As you explore a range of subjects—from social and behavioral sciences, such as child development and family relations, to applied sciences, such as food science, nutrition, and textiles—you must be open to different approaches to understanding individuals, families, and communities.

The major begins with course work in the liberal arts. You then choose courses in areas such as family studies, housing, clothing and textiles, food science and nutrition, and personal/family finances and resource management.

The information you learn will be applied to individual and family concerns. For example, you might translate a family's nutritional problems into strategies for selecting better diets, or you may determine how children's developmental needs can be met in different settings, such as child care and community centers. For your last year, you will select a practicum, or internship, that will provide both the work experience and the contacts needed in any job search. Some programs offer opportunities for international or cross-cultural internships.

At large institutions the program may be located in divisions of human ecology, human sciences, or family and consumer sciences. Generally, the number of required courses depends on the size of the program. Larger programs usually provide more flexibility, so that you can focus on an area of your choice.

Family and consumer sciences majors gain not only an in-depth appreciation of the subject matter but also a broad understanding of the environments in which consumers and families live, work, and, sometimes, struggle. As a graduate, you'll have a variety of career options, particularly if you choose to specialize. Course work and internships or other supervised practical experiences prepare you for professional roles in business, government, education, and human services.

Other majors you might like:

Human services
Psychology
Environmental design
Culinary arts and chef training
Dietetics
Gerontology
Fashion and apparel design
Interior design
Business administration and management
Community health services
Sociology
Youth services

Questions to ask colleges:

How much access do majors have to advisers? Students pursuing the general major in family and consumer sciences often look for a flexible program. You'll need appropriate guidance on how to handle practicums, internships, honors, and undergraduate research.

Career options and trends:

High school teacher; child care professional; family services professional; community agency administrator; sales representative; product designer; financial planner.

With appropriate course work, you can become certified as a family life educator and, with an examination, as a family and consumer sciences professional.

In the light of increasing globalization, family and consumer sciences majors should consider international opportunities, including study abroad. The experience can lead to jobs with national or international health organizations and strengthen your credentials for human service and education positions. Also, there is a critical shortage of secondary school teachers in this field. With additional coursework, you can become certified to teach.

For more info:

American Association of Family and Consumer Sciences (AAFCS)
400 N. Columbus St.
Suite 202
Alexandria, VA 22314
(703) 706-4600
www.aafcs.org

National Council on Family Relations (NCFR)
3989 Central Ave., N.E.
#550
Minneapolis, MN 55421
(888) 781-9331
www.ncfr.org

Food and nutrition studies

What it's about:

The food and nutrition studies major covers the processing and preparation of food before it is eaten (food science) and the role of nutrients in human metabolism (nutrition). You study food safety, quality, and nutritional content; food product and recipe development; the planning of diets to maintain wellness and nutrition counseling.

Is this for you?

You might like this major if you also like: cooking, tasting, and experimenting with recipes; sports and exercise; helping others; science (especially biology and chemistry) and math; knowing what you eat and how it is made; working with others to tackle problems.

Consider this major if you are good at: attention to detail; caring/nurturing; critical reading/thinking; leadership; math; organizing; teamwork *...or have...* initiative; verbal skills; writing skills.

Recommended high school prep:

English 4, math 3 (including trigonometry and pre-calculus), lab science 4 (including biology, chemistry, and physics), social studies 3, and a foreign language 2–3. If possible, also take speech.

Did you know...

...the differences between the food and nutrition studies major, the food science major, and the dietetics major? Food science primarily focuses on food production and safety—what happens before it gets into your kitchen. Dietetics programs prepare you to become a licensed health professional as either a registered dietician (RD) or a dietician technician (DTR). Food and nutrition studies spans much of what is covered in both, with a broader, interdisciplinary approach to healthy eating and living.

...that this major requires strong science and math skills? The basic courses are the same as those taken by biology or chemistry majors. Food and nutrition studies can be thought of as an applied biology or an applied chemistry major, with the focus on food, nutrition, and human health.

Typical courses in this major:

Biology
Biochemistry
Microbiology
Physiology
Chemistry
Physics
Mathematics
Statistics
Nutrition
Community nutrition
Food chemistry
Food microbiology
Food preparation
Food product development
Food processing
Sensory evaluation

Concentrations:

In college: consumer-related issues; food processing; food product development; food safety; wellness studies; clinical nutrition; community nutrition; pre-health professional track for entry into graduate or medical school.

If you go on to grad school: food chemistry; food microbiology; sensory and quality evaluation; nutritional biochemistry; nutritional toxicology.

What the study of this major is like:

The food and nutrition studies major is usually found at large universities in schools of home economics, agriculture, human ecology, family and consumer sciences, health and human services, or applied sciences. At some institutions, food science and nutrition are separate majors; at others, they are one major and you may specialize in either food science or nutrition. The breadth of the major can vary from narrow, emphasizing only food science, nutrition, or dietetics, to broad, covering many aspects of food and nutrition studies.

In your first two years, you take courses such as chemistry, biochemistry, physiology, and microbiology, often in large lecture classes that break into smaller discussion and laboratory sections. The science and math requirements are similar to most other science- or health-related majors. If you plan to focus on dietetics or nutrition education (working with individuals and families to promote health), you also take courses in education and communication. To prepare for work in the business world, you should take business administration, marketing, computers, and public relations courses. Courses in sociology and psychology are also helpful.

You'll likely enroll in an introductory nutrition or food science course during your first two years, but you probably won't take many courses in the major until you have completed the basic science courses. In the beginning, you may feel lost in large lecture classes. Because these courses are prerequisites for the major rather than part of it, you may wonder about their relevance; but you'll soon see how they relates to your career goals.

You may usually concentrate on either food science or nutrition or both. In food science, you learn about food preparation, processing, packaging, storage, and distribution. You also learn what makes food pleasing to our sense of sight, smell, and taste. In nutrition courses, you study food selection, preparation, consumption, and digestion. You take courses in food chemistry and in basic and advanced nutrition. Although emphasis is placed on the chemistry of these processes, you also study the psychological and behavioral aspects of eating.

In addition to lectures, most courses have laboratory work, to provide you with hands-on experience in, for example, identifying microorganisms in foods. In laboratory sessions, you often work in teams to conduct short-term experiments and independent projects. Upper-level class sizes are usually small. Courses may be taught as lectures or as

discussion sections on subjects such as community nutrition, assessment methods, and nutrition and disease. Individual and team projects are often included.

Summer jobs or internships provide real-world experiences that relate to academic course work. You can also work with faculty members on research projects during the academic year; these experiences are valuable when you apply for jobs or acceptance into graduate school or internship programs. The Institute of Food Technologists and the American Dietetic Association approve or accredit undergraduate programs, but some colleges offer nonaccredited programs instead. The level of science courses required for the major varies and is usually lower in nonaccredited programs. The laboratory facilities also vary from one college to another.

Technology has drastically changed the way food is grown, harvested, packaged, transported, and sold. Our understanding of the relation of nutrition to health, especially in the causes and treatment of chronic diseases, has greatly increased and an enormous variety of products are available from all over the world. At the same time, fad diets, eating disorders, substance abuse, and nutrient-drug interactions threaten health and well-being. Careers in food and nutrition studies provide many opportunities for making important contributions to our world.

Other majors you might like:

Food science
Chemistry
Dietetics
Culinary arts and chef training
Nutrition sciences
Sports and fitness administration
Food service
Institutional food production
Pharmacy
Restaurant/food services management
Hospitality administration and management

Career options and trends:

Food purchasing manager; test kitchen/recipe developer*; product researcher/developer; dietitian*; nutrition counselor*; community nutritionist; food editor (for newspaper or magazine); inspector for the Food and Drug Administration or the Department of Agriculture.

To become a registered dietitian (RD), you must complete a prescribed set of undergraduate courses and a supervised internship program and take the registered dietitian's examination (see the description for the dietetics major in the section on Health).

The food industry itself, and the demand for all types of industry professionals, remain quite stable; population growth and the marketability of new food products provide more job opportunities. Because of current concerns, food safety specialists should have no trouble finding work. Also with the increasing interest in nutrition, the development of enhanced foods, and the emergence of wellness programs, the demand for nutritionists and dietitians is likely to continue.

Insider's viewpoint:
"Ever since I became a nutrition major, I am eating better, exercising more, and basically living a healthier lifestyle. I honestly believe that this lifestyle has aided me in my studying and my overall college performance."

—Kate, senior, Rutgers University

For more info:
Institute of Food Technologists (IFT)
525 West Van Buren, Suite 1000
Chicago, IL 60607
(312) 782-8448
www.ift.org

American Society for Nutritional Sciences (ASNS)
9650 Rockville Pike
Suite 4500
Bethesda, MD 20814
(301) 634-7050
www.asns.org

Housing and human environments

What it's about:

As a housing and human environments major, you study various aspects of housing, including needs assessment, financing, legislation, equipment, energy conservation, and housing alternatives. Your goal is to gain an in-depth understanding of housing as a product, an environment, a service, and a process for sheltering a diverse, changing population adequately, accessibly, and affordably.

Is this for you?

You might like this major if you also like: helping others; community or volunteer service; interior design; working on team projects.

Consider this major if you are good at: caring/nurturing; critical reading/thinking; leadership; persuading/influencing; research ...*or have...* initiative; patience; verbal skills; writing skills.

Recommended high school prep:

English 4, math 3, lab science 3, social studies 3, and a foreign language 2–3.

Typical courses in this major:

Housing in contemporary society
Advanced housing theories
Housing alternatives
Housing policy
Housing counseling
Household technology and systems
Family demographics and policy
Interiors and furnishings
Kitchen and bath design
Real estate
State and local developments
Special needs housing
Family resource management
Property management
Principles of family finance

Concentrations:

Property management; public policy; interiors.

What the study of this major is like:

All housing and human environment majors receive a background in liberal arts, mathematics, natural sciences, and social studies before choosing a concentration. You study housing issues (safety, types of dwellings, ownership) and learn how housing policies, particularly financial programs, government regulation, and taxation, affect families. You also study factors influencing family well being, such as poverty and access to health care, education, and other public services. You might examine consumer legislation and lobbying efforts by housing advocates. Economics and other business courses are often required.

Most programs emphasize learning through experience. You can often do an internship in your area of interest and earn a limited amount of course credit (and sometimes pay) for your work. A positive internship may even lead to a job offer. Another advantage is the mentoring you receive from your field supervisor—a relationship that may last beyond your internship. Guest speakers, field trips, and community service projects can also enhance your studies. For example, students in one program worked with AARP to publicize predatory lending practices. They delivered literature to senior citizens who were at risk of being targeted by dishonest lenders.

Every housing and human environments program is unique. Some focus on space planning and design, with courses in environmental or interior design, and in preparation for kitchen and bath certification. In others, where there is emphasis on the residential property management industry, you use your academic experience to tackle real-life problems that may occur among residents of multifamily dwellings. Still other programs focus on the socioeconomic and policy aspects of housing, where you take additional courses in political science or economics. Before you decide on a program, study the catalogs from different colleges to make sure your interests match a program's strengths.

This major provides you with opportunities to work in both public and private housing arenas. You will be able to apply what you learn in your personal as well as your professional life. Students seeking degrees in housing can be creative in designing programs and career paths to match their interests and abilities, but they all share the desire to help shape the present and future accommodations of our society.

Other majors you might like:
Real estate
Home furnishings
Construction technology
Social work
Historic preservation
Public administration
Urban, community, and regional planning
Construction management
Interior design
Sociology
Civil engineering

Questions to ask colleges:
Are there opportunities to take courses in other majors such as real estate, social work, journalism, and computer science?

What opportunities are there for students to work on service projects in the community, such as Habitat for Humanity, homeless shelters, or homebuilder shows? What kinds of internships are available?

Career options and trends:
Commercial real estate broker*; residential property manager*; construction project manager; residential home loan officer; area housing administrator*; housing counselor; mortgage originator; homebuilder; banking officer; research analyst.

Housing majors find jobs with real estate companies, state and federal agencies, public utilities, historic preservation firms, financial/mortgage institutions, and trade organizations.

Strong housing starts and low interest rates have kept the housing market active. As the population ages, there are many employment possibilities involving housing for older adults. Also, as the housing stock itself ages, many consumers are remodeling. These factors are providing good career opportunities for graduates of housing programs.

For more info:
Housing Education and Research Association (HERA)
Montana State University Extension Service
P.O. Box 173580
Bozeman, MT 59717-3580
(406) 994-3451
www.housingeducators.org

National Apartment Association (NAA)
201 North Union St.
Suite 200
Alexandria, VA 22314
(703) 518-6141
www.naahq.org

Human development and family studies

Also known as:
Human ecology

What it's about:
The human development and family studies major prepares you to investigate how individuals interact as members of a family and how individuals and families interact with the larger social and economic community. You also study the impact of life cycle changes on individuals, families, and societies.

Is this for you?
You might like this major if you also like: taking care of children or the elderly; learning family histories; helping people work out their problems.

Consider this major if you are good at: caring/nurturing; counseling; critical reading/thinking; leadership; organizing; teamwork *...or have...* initiative; verbal skills; writing skills.

Recommended high school prep:
English 4, math 3, lab science 3, social studies 3, and a foreign language 2–3. If possible, take courses in economics, sociology, and psychology.

Typical courses in this major:
Lifespan human development
Child guidance and parenting
Family finance
Communications in human development
Early childhood education
Human sexuality
Administration of child and family services
Family education and intervention programs
Child socialization
Family interaction
Death and dying: a family and lifespan perspective
Children and families in a multiethnic society
Work and family systems
Families and public policy
Contemporary family issues
Issues in family health

Concentrations:
In college: early childhood education; child development; adolescent development; adult development and aging; family studies; consumer education; family resource management.

If you go on to grad school: consumer economics; work and family studies; financial planning and counseling; marriage and family therapy.

What the study of this major is like:
If you major in human development and family studies, you explore the biological, psychological, and sociological development of individuals and families. Courses are designed to help you learn about people in various contexts (including communities and society) and to study them within appropriate theoretical frameworks. Theory and research are coordinated with supervised field experiences.

Generally, you take two introductory courses: one in lifespan development, which covers both continuity and change in individuals from conception to death; the other in the study of families. More advanced courses dealing with such subjects as death and dying and family interaction deepen your understanding. Other courses, such as family education and intervention programs, and the administration of child and family services, have a more practical purpose. Still others, on research and communication, are focused on auxiliary skills.

Professors in human development and family studies use a wide variety of teaching methods, including lecture, discussion, Web-based instruction, field study, and community internship. You are expected to build on and integrate the information and skills you learn as you progress in the program, and to develop your analytical skills and demonstrate good written and oral communication abilities. Most courses include written assignments, essay exams, and opportunities for discussion. An important element in most programs is the fourth-year internship, which is customized to help you consolidate your learning in a semester-long community-based experience.

At some institutions, especially the larger ones, you will probably have greater opportunity to focus your studies on a particular area. These colleges may concentrate on a specialized area such as infant development or family communication and, as a result, offer fewer courses that explore topics from a wider social perspective. Other colleges have a more integrated, holistic approach to human development and family studies, offering a broader, more comprehensive program.

Other majors you might like:
Psychology
Sociology
Early childhood education
Gerontology
Funeral services/mortuary science
Child care management
Occupational therapy
Adult development/aging
Child development
Food and nutrition studies
Work/family studies
Social work

Questions to ask colleges:
How available are supervised practicum sites, such as an infant program, a preschool, or a family-counseling center, where hands-on involvement and observation are carried out?

How many credits are required in general education, in the major, and in elective courses? How accessible and supportive is student advisement? To what extent do students have opportunities to design courses of study to meet their individual interests?

Career options and trends:
Counselor*; early childhood educator*; child care or youth program administrator*; human services agency administrator*; family life educator; family or consumer advocate; child care curriculum coordinator; senior center coordinator; family financial planner.

Human development and family studies majors also find work in child care licensing, Child Life programs, parent education, and human resources.

With a graduate degree, you can pursue counseling certification as a Marriage and Family Therapist (MFT). If you plan to work in parent education or as a family life educator, you will need to fulfill additional requirements and become a Certified Family Life Educator (CFLE).

The job outlook is good. Human service and teaching fields continue to need well-trained individuals.

For more info:
National Council on Family Relations (NCFR)
3989 Central Ave., N.E.
Suite 550
Minneapolis, MN 55421
(888) 781-9331
www.ncfr.org

Health

If you're looking for a major that leads to job security and satisfaction, you've come to the right place. Health care is a growth industry. About 19 percent of all new jobs created by 2014 are expected to be in the health field. Hospitals, home health care services, doctors' offices, and other providers are likely to add 3.6 million jobs—more than any other industry—as the need for health care increases because people are living longer. Not only that, but fewer students are getting bachelor's degrees in health professions and related sciences lately.

"Today's growing health care system has created unlimited employment opportunities for nurses in practice, education, and research," says Professor Jean E. Bartels of Georgia Southern University School of Nursing.

"This is an industry that truly combines high tech with high touch," notes Leonard H. Friedman of the Department of Public Health, Oregon State University. "I can think of no professional activity that is more important, worthwhile, or ultimately satisfying."

How will you prepare for a demanding and in-demand career as a clinician, therapist, technician, or other health professional? Look for colleges that specialize in health education. They include schools or divisions of medicine or allied health; nursing schools; colleges of pharmacy, health sciences or services, health occupations, or health professions; and schools of arts and sciences, professional studies, human environmental sciences, health and human sciences, or medical sciences.

The names of the colleges may vary, but the health studies in each field—respiratory therapy, for example—should be very much alike. That's because of groups like CoARC, ARC-PA, AUPHA, and CAPTE. What's with the alphabet soup? Those letters stand for the names of accrediting groups. For instance, more than 130 physician assistant programs nationwide have gotten a professional OK from the Accreditation Review Commission on Education for the Physician Assistant (but you can call it ARC-PA for short). Having standardized courses means that college programs cover similar material to prepare students for professional certification or licensing. Accreditation is the stamp of approval that you'll want your college to have.

Do you want to be a doctor, dentist, or veterinarian? Each field requires specific preprofessional undergraduate courses even though the fields aren't actually majors. That's right—you may know what you want to be but not know what to major in as an undergraduate! For example, premedical studies is a program of prerequisite courses for entrance into medical school. But premed students still have to pick an academic major, and most choose a science such as biology. A preprofessional adviser at college will help you choose a major, prepare for the graduate school entrance examination, arrange the interview, get letters of recommendation, and find volunteer or paid clinical, research, and community service opportunities.

Look for colleges with a strong record of placing students into medical, dental, or veterinary school. For other health studies, ask how long the program has had its gold star from the group that oversees education and training in the profession. (See the individual majors in this section for accrediting bodies.) Also, is it a full accreditation or just something pending? Is the college itself accredited or only the particular program?

Get a complete history

Even with standards in place to nail down core skills and knowledge, programs can differ. Some may take a clinical, practical, hands-on approach to teaching, while others are geared toward theory or research. Some go past the basics into cutting-edge science.

Ask about the three main types of studies you'll do: class/lecture, lab, and clinical internships. Find out about the credentials and experience of the faculty members. What is the ratio of students to teachers? Will the top professors actually do the teaching, or are most courses taught by grad students? Will you be able to do research? Are the labs and equipment up-to-date? What kind of fieldwork or clinical experience is the college set up to give you? Will you work in a hospital? Is it near campus? Will you need to take a licensing exam to work in your professional area? What percent of grads pass that exam?

Also, find out if you're looking at a two-year or a four-year degree program. Different levels of degrees prepare you for different types of work. A dental hygiene or laboratory technician program typically takes two years. Radiologic technicians need an associate degree but can add a bachelor's degree to learn a particular type of medical imaging technology. Veterinary technicians typically have two-year associate degrees.

Nurses at the baccalaureate level are qualified to work in nearly all health care settings, while two-year degrees prepare entry-level LPNs—licensed practical nurses—with lesser responsibilities that vary from state to state.

Is graduate school for you? Physicians, dentists, and veterinarians aren't the only health care professionals with advanced degrees. Pharmacy is a six-year doctoral (Pharm.D.) program starting with two years of preprofessional requirements. You'll need to go beyond a four-year degree for physical therapy programs; the doctorate is becoming the degree of choice to work in that field. Occupational therapists must also have at least a master's degree. Some nurses study at the graduate level to learn clinical specialties like neonatal (newborn) acute care.

If you're interested in health care but don't want to be a clinician or provide direct patient care, you might go into health care administration or work as a clinical or medical lab technician.

In many health specialties, you'll need continuing professional education to keep up with new technologies and therapies. State licenses may require it. If you want the career benefits of working in health care, your education is only just beginning.

Athletic training

Also known as:

Sports medicine

What it's about:

This major prepares you to become a certified athletic trainer (ATC), a health care professional who knows how to prevent, evaluate, and treat the injuries and related illnesses sustained by physically active people.

Is this for you?

You might like this major if you also like: helping people; sports and competition; problem solving; science and medicine; physical exercise; working with people; tutoring.

Consider this major if you are good at: caring/nurturing; organizing; persuading/influencing; teamwork *...or have...* a sense of humor; initiative; manual dexterity; physical stamina; verbal skills; writing skills.

Recommended high school prep:

English 4, math 3, lab science 4 (take all possible lab sciences), social studies 3, and a foreign language 2–3 (Greek or Latin would help with medical terminology). If available, take a course in anatomy or physiology, and try to obtain First Aid and CPR certification. If possible, work as a team manager, attend summer athletic training camps, or volunteer in sports medicine clinics.

Did you know...

...that more than 60 percent of certified athletic trainers have a master's degree or higher? While the minimum degree needed for many jobs is a bachelor's, you'll significantly improve your career prospects if you have one to two years of graduate school.

Typical courses in this major:

Prevention and care of athletic injuries

Assessment of extemity injuries

Assessment of illnesses

General medical conditions and disabilities

First Aid and emergency care

Therapeutic modalities

Therapeutic exercise and rehabilitation techniques

Human anatomy

Human physiology

Exercise physiology

Kinesiology or biomechanics

Nutrition

Strength and reconditioning

Pharmacology

Pathology

Psychosocial intervention

Concentrations:

Generally, none in college; but if you go on to grad school: health promotion; exercise physiology; biomechanics; exercise psychology; physical education teaching certification; anatomy.

What the study of this major is like:

As an athletic training major, you study academic and clinical sciences. You'll be trained to watch for injuries that may occur in the gym or on the field and to determine, through examination, whether an injury requires First Aid and whether a doctor or an ambulance should be called. You'll also prepare yourself to become a member of a health care team, so that (under a physician's direction), you can administer treatment: whirlpool baths, ultrasound, electrical stimulation, taping, splints, and exercise.

As you work with coaches, physicians, administrators, and athletes, you develop leadership and communication skills. When you complete the program and pass the required exam, you qualify for national certification—the entry-level standard for this profession.

Your first year or two of courses include general studies in the humanities, basic sciences (anatomy, physiology, and chemistry), and an introduction to athletic training. You also learn more about the profession and the major. In some colleges, you must then be accepted into the program. As a major, you are required to complete a minimum of four semesters of clinical experience, in addition to your course work. You'll probably receive at least 800 hours of directed clinical experience, usually in a range of sports: contact and noncontact; male and female; team and individual. Clinical settings are both on- and off-campus, or perhaps in sports medicine clinics in hospitals or private settings.

Most courses include both lecture and laboratory sessions. In lab and clinical courses, you develop practical application (psychomotor) skills and apply them in real-world situations. The biggest challenge most majors face involves time management. Your day might consist of classes during the morning, clinical work for several hours every afternoon, perhaps a class in the evening, and even sports competitions on weekends. You'll have to devote a lot of time to clinical work, but you won't want to neglect your other course assignments. Probably most important, you are responsible for keeping sensitive medical information confidential, and you must always act professionally.

The biggest difference among programs often depends on the orientation of the department that runs the major. Programs in a sports or exercise science department tend to require more science-based courses; those housed in departments of kinesiology or physical education may require more courses in sports training; and programs in a health science or health education department may stress such areas as prevention of injuries. Philosophical differences among programs show up in the way students are selected and assigned to clinical experiences. In some programs, you begin clinical education during your first semester, while other programs require one or two years of courses and observation before you are admitted to the major and begin your clinical education. In addition, some programs offer many off-campus opportunities in sports medicine clinics and at local high schools, while others provide clinical opportunities only on campus.

Other majors you might like:
Physical therapy
Recreational therapy
Sports and fitness administration
Psychology
Occupational therapy
Exercise sciences
Physical education
Health/physical fitness
Emergency medical technology (EMT paramedic)
Physician assistant
Parks, recreation, and leisure studies
Hospitality administration and management

Questions to ask colleges:
Is this program accredited by the Commission on Accreditation of Allied Health Education Programs (CAAHEP)? Only graduates of an accredited program are eligible to take the national certification exam.

What is the application process to be formally accepted into the major?

What is the school's passing rate on the National Athletic Trainers Association Board of Certification exam?

Where are some of the graduates employed—in which settings, in which schools, and with which teams?

Where are clinical rotations completed?

Career options and trends:
High school athletic trainer*; college athletic trainer*; clinical athletic trainer (sports medicine clinic or hospital); industrial athletic trainer; professional sports athletic trainer; medical sales representative; personal trainer.

Although there is opportunity for employment in a wide variety of settings, the job outlook is very competitive. Many high schools require a teaching license in addition to the athletic training certification. Sports medicine clinics were once a primary source for entry-level employment, but this market has become saturated. High-profile colleges and universities, as well as professional sports, have limited turnover; but colleges and universities are creating additional positions, and currently provide the most opportunities.

Insider's viewpoint:
"This is a great major for people who love the human sciences because you get just enough of basic science but you are not inundated with chemical formulas and learning why starfish are in phylum Echinodermata."

—Caleb, sophomore, University of Southern California

For more info:
National Athletic Trainers' Association (NATA)
2952 Stemmons Freeway
Dallas, TX 75247-6916
(214) 637-6282
www.nata.org

Commission on Accreditation of Allied Health
    Education Programs (CAAHEP)
35 East Wacker Drive
Suite 1970
Chicago, IL 60601-2208
(312) 553-9355
www.caahep.org

Clinical/medical laboratory technology

What it's about:

Clinical/medical lab technicians examine blood and other body fluids to search for clues in the diagnosis of various diseases. In this major, you are trained to perform general tests in all medical laboratory areas, such as blood banking and hematology; clinical chemistry; urinalysis; immunology; and medical microbiology.

Is this for you?

You might like this major if you also like: solving problems; challenges; puzzles; computers; science and technology; knowing why and how things work; working with precision and accuracy.

Consider this major if you are good at: attention to detail; critical reading/thinking; organizing; quantitative analysis; spatial thinking/analysis; teamwork *...or have...* manual dexterity; mechanical facility; patience; verbal skills.

Recommended high school prep:

English 4, math 3, lab science 3 (biology, chemistry, physics), social studies 3, and a foreign language 2–3. Take computer technology and advanced chemistry if available.

Did you know...

...that 70 to 80 percent of all medical decisions are based on laboratory data? The practice of medicine would be impossible without the tests performed by clinical/medical laboratory technicians.

...that the ability to communicate well, both in writing and in speaking, is important in this field? Technical skills alone do not get the job done—results must be communicated accurately and completely.

Typical courses in this major:

Introduction to the clinical laboratory
Clinical chemistry
Hematology
Immunology
Immunohematology
Microbiology
Quality assessment
Anatomy and physiology
College algebra
General chemistry and lab
English composition
Urinalysis/body fluids
Clinical internship

Concentrations:

In college: clinical chemistry; hematology; immunology; clinical microbiology; urinalysis.

If you go on to grad school: clinical/laboratory facilities management; molecular diagnostics.

What the study of this major is like:

A career in clinical/medical laboratory technology is an excellent choice if you want to work in health care, but not directly with patients. As a clinical/medical laboratory technician, you apply your knowledge of, and skills in, the basic sciences to testing in such settings as health care, research, industry, or government agencies.

Laboratory technicians work with medical teams of pathologists, other specialists, and scientists to determine the absence, presence, extent, or cause of disease, and to provide data for evaluating the effectiveness of treatment. The field offers opportunities to learn and grow. As procedures are developed to detect both old and new diseases, the laboratory remains in the forefront of medicine. In addition to an array of precision instruments and electronic equipment, successful laboratories need well-trained, responsible staff.

The clinical/medical laboratory technology major is offered as both a two-year associate degree and a four-year bachelor's degree. This major may be found in departments of biology, chemistry, natural sciences, or life sciences, and in schools of health professions, allied health and/or nursing, or medicine.

Because classes are usually small and labs generally have fewer than 18 students, teamwork and group learning are encouraged. To gain a sound foundation for your clinical studies, you are likely to begin with a number of science courses. You'll take courses in anatomy and/or physiology, genetics, and microbiology, and perhaps advanced cell physiology. In chemistry courses, you'll focus on inorganic and organic compounds and biochemistry. Algebra and statistics may also be also required; courses in chemical analysis and computer science are useful. Many students find the large amount of information presented in a two-year program a bit overwhelming, especially if they have not been full-time college students before entering the program.

In this major, the emphasis is on laboratory practice. Unlike traditional science majors, in which the lab work illustrates theories you learn in the classroom, clinical/medical laboratory technology uses theory to support the lab work. You learn by doing, in order to understand the theoretical and clinical significance of lab procedures. In most programs you spend the equivalent of one semester learning the theory, procedures, equipment, and practices of clinical laboratory science in a working laboratory. During this time, you learn to test body fluids and tissues and practice what you learn in class. Most majors find laboratory work the most exciting and interesting part of the program.

To be eligible for national certification exams, you should attend an accredited program—one that meets the standards set by the National Accrediting Agency for Clinical Laboratory Science (NAACLS). Programs at different colleges may meet the standards in different ways—for example, by teaching courses in a different order, making use of online programs or courses, or varying the required clinical internship from none to several hundred hours.

Other majors you might like:
Chemistry
Biochemistry
Biomedical technology

Molecular biology
Cytotechnology
Microbiology
Forensic science
Phlebotomy
Biotechnology
Dental laboratory technology
Clinical laboratory science
Radiologic technology/medical imaging

Questions to ask colleges:
Is the program accredited?

Are the lab facilities dedicated to this major?

In a two-year program, is there an articulation agreement with a four-year college to accept transfer credit for these courses?

Is space guaranteed in the clinical facility for the internship?

Career options and trends:
Clinical/medical laboratory technologist*; microbiologist*; laboratory director; forensic analyst; biotechnician; research technician; technical/marketing sales representative.

Clinical/medical laboratory technicians work in a variety of practice settings, such as hospitals, for-profit laboratories, clinics, nursing homes, public health facilities, business, and industry. Supervisory or management positions usually require Clinical Laboratory Scientist (CLS) certification.

The long-term employment for medical laboratory technicians looks bright. According to the Bureau of Labor Statistics, there will be a shortage in this field over the next decade or so, with nearly twice the number of positions as graduates to fill them.

For more info:
American Society for Clinical Laboratory Science (ASCLS)
6701 Democracy Blvd., Suite 300
Bethesda, MD 20817-1574
(301) 657-2768
www.ascls.org

Communication disorders

What it's about:

At the undergraduate level, this major is primarily a preprofessional program designed to give training in the identification and treatment of human communication disorders, in preparation for professional training in a master's degree program in either speech-language pathology or audiology. You learn about the normal processes of human communication and the problems that may occur, including disorders of articulation, language, hearing, cognition, swallowing, and voice.

Is this for you?

You might like this major if you also like: helping people; problem solving; using technology; working with children; working with older adults.

Consider this major if you are good at: attention to detail; caring/nurturing; counseling; creativity; math; persuading/influencing *...or have...* initiative; patience; verbal skills; writing skills.

Recommended high school prep:

English 4, math 3, lab science 3, social studies 3, and a foreign language 2–3. Take anatomy and psychology if they are available.

Typical courses in this major:

Survey of communication disorders
Phonetics
Normal speech and language development
Audiology
Anatomy and physiology
Articulation disorders
Language disorders
Aural rehabilitation
Diagnostics
Augmentative communication

Concentrations:

In college: childhood speech; language disorders.

If you go on to grad school: speech-language pathology; audiology; adult and neurological communication disorders; childhood and developmental communication disorders.

What the study of this major is like:

The major in communication disorders emphasizes both normal and abnormal growth and development. Professionals (such as speech-language pathologists and speech, language, and hearing scientists) deal with infants, children, adolescents, adults, and the elderly, in schools, hospitals, businesses, private practice, universities, research laboratories, and government agencies.

The undergraduate major prepares you for professional study at the master's degree level. As a major, you explore normal and defective hearing and speech, and then learn to identify and evaluate communication disorders and available treatment. The typical program is sequential—courses are based on the knowledge and skills you developed in previous course work.

In introductory courses, you study normal voice, speech, and language processes and the symptoms of disorders. Taking anatomy and physiology teaches you how people produce and perceive speech. You will read research reports on speech disorders, in order to apply findings to treatment programs and to determine what further research should be done. You may study stuttering, aphasia, and other common disorders.

While you pursue your major, you complete requirements in academic areas that support the core courses, including biology and physical sciences, behavioral and social sciences, and other liberal arts and sciences course work. Majors usually get clinical experience by working (under close supervision) in the college speech and hearing clinic with children and adults.

Although most courses follow the lecture format, you may also work with interactive computer instruction. Academic standards for the major are high, because the majority of students will continue on to a master's program. In fact, most states require an advanced degree for certification in this field. To be successful in this major, you need a strong background in math, science, and writing. Anatomy and neurology require a lot of memorization, and you may have difficulty managing your time as a result of heavy clinical requirements. But students in this major tend to bond into closely knit groups and assist each other through the program.

Other majors you might like:
Child development
Psychology
Gerontology
Special education
Education of speech impaired
Linguistics
Audiology/speech pathology
American Sign Language (ASL)
Anthropology
Speech teacher education
Education of deaf/hearing impaired
Speech/rhetorical studies

Questions to ask colleges:
What are the academic requirements for admission into the major, both at the undergraduate and at the graduate level? Are students admitted into the program as freshmen, or must they qualify for admission after their first or second year in college?

Is a combined bachelor's/graduate degree program available?

Is the undergraduate program broad-based, or is it geared toward either childhood disorders or adult disorders?

Career options and trends:
School speech/language therapist*; speech pathologist*; audiologist; speech scientist.

The American Speech–Language–Hearing Association (ASHA) sets standards for national certification in speech-language pathology or audiology (check their Web site for updates). Currently, this certificate requires a master's degree, passing a national exam, and at least 36 weeks of supervised professional employment in the field. State teacher certification is required for teaching students with speech and language disabilities in the public school system. Most states also have professional license requirements for speech pathologists employed in a health care setting.

This field is ranked among the top 30 of the 700 fastest-growing professions. Factors contributing to this demand are the increasing population of older Americans and the need for therapists to work with non-native speakers of English.

Insider's viewpoint:
"We're required to have a lot of clinical hours, and we have to get them in a lot of different areas, including adults and children, diagnostics, and treatment. So it's the fun part and it's also the hard part, to make sure you get all those hours in."

—Cara, graduate student, University of Pittsburgh

For more info:
American Speech–Language–Hearing Association (ASHA)
10801 Rockville Pike
Rockville, MD 20852
(800) 498-2071
www.asha.org

Dental hygiene

What it's about:

As a major in dental hygiene, you obtain the knowledge and clinical skills needed to prevent and treat oral diseases in order to protect teeth and gums—and to preserve patients' general health. Courses in basic and dental sciences, as well as clinical training in patient care, prepare you to become a licensed dental hygienist.

Is this for you?

You might like this major if you also like: working with your hands; routines and schedules; working with people; detail-oriented activities; crafts.

Consider this major if you are good at: caring/nurturing; counseling; following directions; multitasking; organizing; teamwork *...or have...* manual dexterity; mechanical facility; patience; verbal skills.

Recommended high school prep:

English 4, math 3, lab science 3 (including chemistry), social studies 3, and a foreign language 2–3. Take a basic computer/keyboarding course and a health course, if available.

Did you know...

...that while an associate degree in dental hygiene is offered at many two-year colleges, it may actually take longer than two years to complete? That's because most schools require you to take prerequisite courses before admission into the program.

Typical courses in this major:

Pharmacology
Histology
Pathology
Radiology
Microbiology
Chemistry
Dental anatomy
Preventive dentistry
Dental materials
Dental hygiene techniques
Nutrition
Office emergencies
Office management
Introduction to clinic procedures

Concentrations:

Generally, none available.

What the study of this major is like:

Registered dental hygienists are licensed health care professionals. To become licensed, you must graduate from an accredited dental hygiene program and pass state and national exams.

The primary responsibility of dental hygienists is to assist patients in maintaining oral and dental health. Majors in dental hygiene are therefore required to master a wide range of skills related to health and patient education. Although training differs among states, you are usually taught to perform patient assessments (including medical histories; blood pressure testing; head, neck, and mouth examinations; and oral cancer screenings); remove deposits from the teeth (oral prophylaxis); use agents such as fluoride to help prevent decay; work with dental X rays; and advise patients on maintaining healthy lifestyles.

You first take anatomy, physiology, and pathology to explore the functions of the human body, the process of disease, and the biological and physiological basis of health. Courses in dental hygiene sciences provide the foundation for dental hygiene care and clinical practice. Learning takes place in the classroom, in laboratories, and in clinical experiences. In your first year, you develop skills by practicing on models and then, under professional supervision, by treating patients. Your course work emphasizes providing dental hygiene services to diverse groups of patients in clinical settings. Because much of a dental hygienist's time is spent interacting one-on-one with patients, you take courses in psychology, speech, sociology, and patient management to develop strong communications and interpersonal skills.

Dental hygiene programs are full-time courses of study. Course material must be covered in a certain sequence, because new courses build on past work. Throughout your clinical experience, you will continue to apply what you've learned in your courses. Outside experiences may include visits to patients in public health clinics, hospitals, child care centers, nursing homes, and correctional facilities. You may also participate in health fairs, health education presentations, and elementary school activities. Some programs send you to work in dental offices in the community to gain real-world experience.

Dental hygiene programs may be located in community colleges or four-year institutions. Some programs are affiliated with dental schools. In the two-year associate degree program, the curriculum should be accredited by the American Dental Association (ADA). The associate degree is the minimum required for entry-level certification. Bachelor's or master's degree programs prepare you to work in industry, education, or research. If you have dental assisting experience or are a graduate of an ADA-accredited dental-assisting program, some colleges give you transfer credit for your experience, so that you do not have to repeat material you have already covered.

Other majors you might like:
Clinical/medical laboratory technology
Dental laboratory technology
Physical therapy
Makeup artist
Public health education
Ophthalmic technology
Physician assistant
Radiologic technology/medical imaging
Medical records technology
Dietetics
Social work
American Sign Language (ASL)

Questions to ask colleges:
Is the program accredited by the ADA? If not, your degree will not be recognized by state licensing bodies and you will not be eligible to take the national board exam.

Which courses must be taken before entry into the program?

Where is the clinical component performed? Most programs have on-site clinical facilities, but some may require travel to nearby locations.

Career options and trends:
Dental hygiene practitioner*; clinical instructor; clinical researcher.

In order to become a registered dental hygienist and obtain a state license, you must pass a national written examination, and a state or regional clinical examination.

Most dental hygienists work in private dental offices, but many work in clinics, schools, nursing homes, hospitals, universities, managed health care organizations, and correctional institutions. As health care expands to include dental professionals as part of an interdisciplinary team, practice settings available to dental hygienists will also expand.

For more info:
American Dental Hygienists' Association (ADHA)
444 North Michigan Ave., Suite 3400
Chicago, IL 60611
(312) 440-8900
www.adha.org

Dietetics

What it's about:

Dietetics prepares you to provide for the nutritional needs of people in conditions of both wellness and ill health. Your studies include the basic sciences, nutrition and food science, principles of management, and behavioral and social sciences. Bachelor degree programs prepare you to become a registered dietitian (RD), and associate degree programs prepare you to be a dietitian technician (DTR).

Is this for you?

You might like this major if you also like: cooking and eating; watching cooking shows on TV; reading about nutrition and health in magazines; science fairs and projects; sports; health and fitness activities; helping people.

Consider this major if you are good at: attention to detail; caring/nurturing; counseling; critical reading/thinking; science; teamwork *...or have...* initiative; verbal skills.

Recommended high school prep:

English 4, math 3, lab science 4 (including chemistry and physics), social studies 3, and a foreign language 2–3. If possible, take advanced biology and chemistry; courses on health, foods, and nutrition are also recommended.

Did you know...

...that this is a great major for entrepreneurs? The food industry is the fourth largest in the world. Almost any food- or health-related setting needs dietitians, and nutrition is essential to health, from birth to old age.

Typical courses in this major:

Organic chemistry
Biochemistry
Anatomy and physiology
Microbiology
Food science
Food chemistry
Basic nutrition
Advanced nutrition and metabolism
Medical nutrition therapy
Maternal and child nutrition
Geriatric nutrition
Public health *or* Community nutrition
Quantity food production and procurement
Diet selection and management

Concentrations:

Clinical nutrition; health and fitness; institutional food management.

What the study of this major is like:

All dietetics programs must be approved by the Commission on Accreditation for Dietetics Education (CADE). To become a registered dietitian, you must complete an accredited program and earn at least a four-year Bachelor of Science degree. Your course work includes biochemistry, microbiology, and anatomy, as well as industry-related subjects such as culinary arts, food service systems management, and food and nutrition sciences. In courses like communications, computer science, and sociology, you learn the necessary business skills and "people skills."

You must also complete a supervised practice program in dietetics (typically 6 to 12 months)—either while you're in college or afterward—and pass an exam administered nationally by the Commission on Dietetic Registration (CDR). Programs that combine your degree work and the practice program are called coordinated programs in dietetics (CPD). Programs that postpone the supervised practice work until after you graduate are called didactic programs in dietetics (DPD). You should choose which program is best for you before you enroll.

If you plan to become a dietitian technician, you must complete a CADE-accredited dietetics program while you earn at least a two-year associate degree. You take courses in food and nutrition, food service systems management, and general science, together with at least 450 hours of supervised practice in a health care facility or food service organization. After you graduate, you must pass the CDR's nationally administered registration examination. If you think you might later want to become an RD, check with the dietitian program you are considering to see if it has formal arrangements (known as an articulation agreement) with CPD and DPD programs to accept some or all of your credits. Otherwise, check directly with the CPD or DPD programs you are considering to see if your courses will receive transfer credit.

Course work in the dietetics major includes lecture, labs, individual and group projects, and required practical experience and/or summer internships. In courses with labs, you'll be kept very busy, so you must organize your time efficiently. Programs may differ in aspects of the curriculum that work best for faculty members. For example, a program in a research-based university may emphasize science, whereas in a small college, it may stress food service systems management. As a result, some programs may be more academically challenging than others, and some may offer opportunities beyond the basic requirements. To find out about a program's emphasis, look at the catalog. Faculty members' areas of expertise will be reflected in the courses they teach.

Sometimes people confuse registered dietitians, dietitian technicians, and nutritionists. Although in some states you need to be licensed to call yourself a nutritionist, the definition often varies. In every state, however, only professionals who are certified by the Commission on Dietetic Registration (CDR) can legally use the titles "registered dietitian" and "dietitian technician."

Other majors you might like:
Culinary arts and chef training
Food and nutrition studies
Pharmacy
Sports and fitness administration
Physician assistant
Occupational therapy
Restaurant/food services management
Hospitality administration and management
Nutrition sciences
Public health education
Gerontology
Food science

Questions to ask colleges:
Does the program help identify opportunities for summer jobs and entry-level job?

What percent of the program's graduates pass the certification examination to become an RD?

What is the acceptance rate of graduates into dietetic practice programs?

Career options and trends:
Registered dietitian (RD) in clinical, administrative, or private practice*; registered dietitian technician (DTR) working in a school or health care facility*; restaurant manager; extension educator; research dietitian; chef; food industry representative.

According to the National Bureau of Labor Statistics, job prospects for dietitians will likely increase, especially in home health care and social services. Employment in hospitals is expected to show little change over the next decade or so because of anticipated slow growth and reduced length of patients' hospital stays. Faster growth, however, is anticipated in nursing homes, residential care facilities, and physician clinics.

While job prospects are good for all dietetics majors, the best and most plentiful jobs go to graduates who are RDs.

For more info:
American Dietetic Association
120 South Riverside Plaza, Suite 2000
Chicago, IL 60606
(800) 877-1600
www.eatright.org

Emergency medical technology (EMT paramedic)

Also known as:
Emergency medical services (EMS)

What it's about:
In this major, you develop the problem-solving, critical-thinking, and management skills necessary to function independently in prehospital settings. You learn how to recognize, assess, and manage medical emergencies; to supervise ambulance personnel; and to carry out medical interventions, from basic responses such as bandaging to high-level techniques such as administering medication, providing cardiac care, and performing advanced airway measures.

Is this for you?
You might like this major if you also like: working with all types of people; helping people in times of crisis; fast action; sports; technology, science, and medicine; taking command.

Consider this major if you are good at: attention to detail; caring/nurturing; critical reading/thinking; organizing; persuading/influencing; teamwork; thinking on your feet *...or have...* initiative; patience; self-confidence; verbal skills.

Recommended high school prep:
English 4, math 3, lab science 3–4 (biology and chemistry most important), social studies 3, and a foreign language 2–3. If available, take a course on anatomy or physiology; and try to obtain First Aid and CPR certification.

Did you know...
...that being a paramedic requires more responsibility than putting people into the back of an ambulance and driving them to the hospital? The job involves interacting with other community organizations, family members, and hospital personnel. In many communities, you are crossed-trained with other public safety responders, such as police officers and firefighters.

Typical courses in this major:
Anatomy and physiology
College math
Pathophysiology
Pharmacology
Bioterrorism
Medical and trauma assessment
Emergency care analysis and intervention
Communications and computer operations
Crisis scene management
Accounting and budgeting
Advanced cardiac life support
Prehospital field techniques
Vehicle rescue
Equipment operation and maintenance
Prehospital trauma life support
Professional standards

Concentrations:
In college: pharmacology; trauma assessment; anatomy and physiology; emergency care and analysis.

If you go on to grad school: emergency management; ambulatory care.

What the study of this major is like:
Emergency medical services (EMS) providers help people in life- or health-threatening situations. The most highly trained prehospital EMS providers are EMT (emergency medical technician) paramedics, who care for patients on site and then help get them to hospitals. As workers or volunteers for ambulance services, fire departments, hospitals, and government-based services, EMTs may be called in to help someone suffering from a broken toe one hour, and someone else having a massive heart attack the next.

If you major in emergency medical technology, you usually take courses such as anatomy and physiology, disease process, pharmacology, cardiology, medical and trauma assessment, hazardous material, bioterrorism, and vehicle rescue. Liberal arts courses teach you how to communicate and work with patients and with other health professionals. Courses are taught in a number of ways, ranging from lecture format to Web-based scenario practice. In classrooms and labs, you learn and practice skills such as intravenous (IV) insertion, intubations, and defibrillation.

In addition to course work, you do clinical rotations in hospitals and with paramedic units. During clinical rotations, you gain experience in making decisions, assessing patients' condition, and providing appropriate treatment—always under close supervision. Because paramedics must be familiar with all types of injury and illness, your clinical rotations cover a range of patients, including adult, pediatric, and geriatric patients, as well as a wide variety of conditions, including chest pain, respiratory distress, broken bones, and spinal cord injuries. You may work in a cardiac intensive care unit, an operating room, an emergency department, a trauma unit, a burn unit, or a behavioral unit.

In your paramedic unit rotation, you work in the field, answering calls with a qualified instructor. You learn how to care for patients under often-difficult conditions. Some programs require one paramedic field rotation, whereas others call for two—one in a suburban ambulance and one in an urban ambulance. Most EMT majors are enrolled full-time, and some find it hard to balance study time with clinical rotations and course work. Still, most majors find, in the end, that being well trained to help others is worth the effort they have put into studying.

Emergency medical technology programs are found in colleges, EMT academies, and hospitals. Most are similar, emphasizing critical-thinking, problem-solving, and clinical skills. Some programs provide training in entry-level management. Others focus on paramedic studies and do not include management or education courses. The majority of programs offer a two-year associate degree or certificate program; but if you plan to move up quickly into management or supervisory roles, you should consider pursuing a four-year Bachelor of Science degree.

Other majors you might like:

Physician assistant

Nursing (RN)

Special education

Athletic training

Community health/preventative medicine

Respiratory therapy

Occupational safety/health technology

Forensic science

Hazardous materials technology

Fire protection and safety technology

Paralegal studies

Social work

Questions to ask colleges:

Where are the clinical rotations done (for instance, in trauma centers or in a local hospital)? Where are the prehospital rotations done?

What system is used to track and record the required number of student-patient contacts necessary for certification?

Are graduates of the program eligible to sit for the National Registry Examination for paramedics?

Career options and trends:

Paramedic*; emergency room technician; fire fighter; police officer; occupation health officer; state office of EMS employee; Federal Emergency Management Agency (FEMA) employee; infection control officer; EMS coordinator; EMS supervisor.

Most states require certification through the National Registry Examination for Paramedics, which makes it easier to relocate from state to state. Municipal or federal employment usually requires you to take a civil service exam as well.

EMS employment is expected to have higher than average growth through the year 2014.

For more info:

National Association of Emergency Medical Technicians (NAEMT)
P.O. Box 1400
Clinton, MS 39060-1400
(800) 34-NAEMT
www.naemt.com

Health care administration

What it's about:

The health care administration major prepares you to manage the business activities of a wide variety of organizations that make up the health care delivery system, such as hospitals, clinics, nursing homes, insurance companies, and public health agencies.

Is this for you?

You might like this major if you also like: organizing or leading a club or group activity; solving problems; team sports; working with different types of people; starting and running a business; debating; health and science issues; community service projects.

Consider this major if you are good at: active listening; attention to detail; leadership; organizing; persuading/influencing; quantitative analysis; teamwork *...or have...* initiative; verbal skills; writing skills.

Recommended high school prep:

English 4, math 3, lab science 4, social studies 3, and a foreign language 2–3. While not a specific requirement, evidence of leadership either in high school or in the community is desirable. Additionally, a course in public speaking would be helpful.

Did you know...

...that the majority of undergraduates pursuing health administration are women?

Typical courses in this major:

Introduction to health care
Organizational behavior
Statistics
Epidemiology
Health policy
Ethics
Strategic planning
Marketing health care
Economics of health care
Accounting
Management information systems
Public health
Health law
Health care management
Financial management
Human resources management

Concentrations:

Long-term health care; health information systems; physician practice management.

What the study of this major is like:

If you want to work in health care delivery but do not want to become a clinician, health care administration is the perfect major. You will learn how to make health care available to individuals and how to manage organizations such as nursing homes, clinics, welfare departments, rehabilitation centers, and hospitals. The program teaches you to manage finances, deal with personnel, understand and comply with the laws that affect health care delivery, and oversee other aspects of administration.

Health care administration is a "people business." As a health care administrator, you'll spend most of your time dealing with physicians, nurses, patients and their families, payers, regulators, government agencies, and media representatives. Although majors must be organized and willing to work hard, the most important quality health care administrators need is good interpersonal skills. To be successful, you should feel comfortable working with diverse groups of people; communicate well (writing, speaking, and listening); be able to assume a leadership role when necessary; accept criticism without taking it personally; juggle multiple demands; take into account information from a variety of sources when making decisions; and be ready to improve your organization.

Majors take courses in three broad areas--liberal arts, general management, and health services management. In liberal arts courses, you study communications (especially public speaking), mathematics (especially statistics), critical thinking, and social context (including philosophy, sociology, psychology, political science, and economics). For general management, you examine theories of management, the functional areas of management (such as accounting, computer applications, human resource management, marketing, and strategic management courses), and leadership skills. Health services management courses cover health and disease, health services organization and delivery, financial management, law and government regulation, and health policy.

Health services management courses begin in your third year. Your classes will primarily be lecture/discussion. Many courses use the case method: groups of students examine a question or a problem and come up with a number of solutions. Most programs require a supervised, field-based internship (in the summer or for a semester). Additional practicum experience is highly recommended. Experience in either paid or volunteer positions can make all the difference when you begin your job search.

There are two challenges that most majors face. The first is time management—courses (particularly at the upper level) are intense and require numerous papers and extensive reading. The second challenge is public speaking—an essential skill for health care professionals. In upper-level courses, you often work to overcome both challenges by participating in study groups.

Programs may have different emphases, depending on where they are housed. For example, programs in business schools stress finance and similar subjects, whereas programs in schools of public health or health sciences stress subjects like community response to infectious diseases. As a major, you should seek out courses that balance your studies. If your program has a business focus, be sure to enroll in courses in public health; similarly, if the program is in a health sciences/public health school, you should think about minoring in business.

Other majors you might like:

Business administration and management
Occupational health/industrial hygiene
Insurance
Funeral services/mortuary science
Health services administration
Biotechnology
Psychology
Public administration
Human services
Social work
Community health services
Management information systems

Questions to ask colleges:

Is the program a certified member or candidate member of the Association of University Programs in Health Administration? Certification by AUPHA indicates that the program has met national standards in facilities, program support, curriculum, and outcomes measures.

Are student chapters of health care professional organizations available on campus? These clubs give students valuable leadership and networking opportunities.

Career options and trends:

Health plan administrator; health policy analyst; hospital or health system management*; nurse management; nursing home administrator*; physician group practice administrator*; public health administrator; pharmaceutical sales representative.

State licensure is usually required to run a skilled-care nursing home. Administrators of public health departments or agencies typically have a clinical background either in nursing, social work, or equivalent field of practice.

As the population ages, the demand for health care services, and professionals to manage them, will continue to grow. The most significant trend for likely employment is in the areas of long-term care and physician group-practice management. The increasing number of acute care hospitals is also opening up employment opportunities. But keep in mind that to move up from an entry-level management position, you'll probably need a master's degree and at least five years' experience.

For more info:

Association of University Programs in Health
    Administration (AUPHA)
2000 14th St. North
Suite 780
Arlington, VA 22201
(703) 894-0940
www.aupha.org

American College of Healthcare Executives
    (ACHE)
One North Franklin, Suite 1700
Chicago, IL 60606
(312) 424-2800
www.ache.org

Medical Group Management Association (MGMA)
104 Inverness Terrace East
Englewood, CO 80112
(303) 799-1111
www.mgma.org

Licensed practical nursing

Also known as:
Vocational nursing

What it's about:
The practical nursing major is a one- or two-year program that prepares you to assist registered nurses and physicians in providing general nursing care. After you graduate, you will be eligible to take the National Council Licensing Examination for Practical Nurses (NCLEX-PN). Passing the exam allows you to be certified by a state board of nursing as a licensed practical/vocational nurse (LP/VN).

Is this for you?
You might like this major if you also like: working with others; caring for peoples' physical, psychological, and emotional needs; physical and social sciences; learning about the human body.

Consider this major if you are good at: caring/nurturing; communicating; critical reading/thinking; making decisions; math; organizing; teamwork ...*or have...* manual dexterity; patience; physical stamina; positive attitude.

Recommended high school prep:
English 4, math 3, lab science 3 (including biology and chemistry), social studies 3, and a foreign language 2–3.

Typical courses in this major:
Nursing (lecture and clinical courses)
Nutrition
Pharmacology
English composition
Chemistry
Anatomy and physiology
Microbiology
Psychology
Developmental psychology
Sociology

Concentrations:
Generally, none available.

What the study of this major is like:
Licensed practical nurses (LPNs)—also called licensed vocational nurses (LVNs) in some states—play an essential part in hospital care: monitoring patients' condition and reporting changes to nurses and physicians; taking temperature and blood pressure; helping patients do rehabilitative exercises; giving medications; bathing patients; changing bandages; and collecting laboratory samples. With the growing shortage of registered nurses (RNs) throughout the world, the role of the LPN continues to evolve. For example, intravenous (IV) therapy for patients used to be provided only by RNs. In some states, certified LPNs can now perform IV therapy.

The major includes general education, science, and nursing courses. Behavioral and social science courses stress the elements of human behavior, growth and development, interpersonal relationships, and cultural diversity. Nursing courses generally cover the nursing process, basic and advanced nursing skills, communication, disease, medications, dosage calculations, lab tests, treatments, ethics, legal/professional issues, and patient care from birth to death.

Behavioral and social science courses are typically in lecture format. Nursing and natural science courses include both lecture and laboratory/clinical experiences. Your initial lab courses allow you to safely practice your nursing skills. Before working with patients, you need to become knowledgeable, competent, and confident. You then move out into the real world for your clinical practice work, where you are supervised as you care for patients in acute care or long-term care facilities.

The most likely challenge you may face is to recognize how difficult the work can be and to devote the necessary time and effort to it. To participate actively in class, you must prepare the required class presentations and written work. Many programs expect you to maintain a minimum grade point average. After you graduate, you must complete a national exam.

To become an LPN, you can pursue either a one-year vocational program at a technical school or a two-year associate degree at a college. As you compare programs, consider your career plans. If you see yourself as a bedside nurse working under the supervision of a registered nurse, doctor, or dentist, then a one-year vocational program is enough. On the other hand, if you think you might want to advance further in nursing, you should start with an accredited two-year program where you can transfer credits to other programs. Because nursing courses vary among colleges, it may be hard to transfer—so if you need to transfer, meet with the director of the new program and provide a description of the courses you have completed. Try to get credit for what you have learned.

Other majors you might like:
Nursing (RN)
Dietetics
Physician assistant
Psychology
Dental hygiene
Physical therapy
Art therapy
Gerontology
Medical office administration
Human development and family studies
American Sign Language (ASL)
Emergency medical technology (EMT paramedic)

Questions to ask colleges:
Is the nursing program approved by the state board of nursing?

What are the admission, curriculum, progression, and graduation requirements? You should find out before you enroll, so you won't have any surprises later.

What percent of the school's graduating nurses pass the NCLEX-PN?

Career options and trends:
Specialty certification is available to LPNs in areas such as long-term care, pharmacology, I.V. therapy, and gerontology. To advance to higher levels of nursing—to become, say, a registered nurse or a certified nurse specialist in pediatrics, you will most likely need a bachelor's or master's degree, work experience in the particular area of nursing, and a passing grade on a certification exam.

Employment prospects for LPNs are excellent because of a severe shortage of nurses worldwide. The majority of LPNs work in hospitals, clinics, long-term-care and nursing home facilities; but other employment opportunities are available in rehabilitation centers, public health agencies, industrial/occupational health offices, private doctor's offices, and schools. Employment growth is expected in the areas of community and home health nursing, because insurance companies are mandating shorter hospital stays, and more patients will require nurses to aid recovery at home.

Insider's viewpoint:
"Nursing is not just medication administration; you are there for the patients when they are throwing up or have diarrhea. One must think about those things as well: can you handle that?"

—Josette, A.S. candidate, Riverside Community College

For more info:
National Federation of Licensed Practical Nurses (NFLPN)
605 Poole Drive
Garner, NC 27529
(919) 779-0046
www.nflpn.org

National Association for Practical Nurse Education & Service (NAPNES)
PO Box 25647
Alexandria, VA 22313
(703) 933-1003
www.napnes.org

Nursing (RN)

What it's about:

This major prepares students to be frontline providers of health care. Registered nurses design, manage, and coordinate care for individuals, families, groups, communities, and larger populations. Nursing students learn how to attend to the sick and the injured; how to rehabilitate, counsel, and educate patients; and how to work as part of a health care team in many settings.

Is this for you?

You might like this major if you also like: caregiving; volunteer work; making a difference in people's lives; science; autonomy and independence; a fast pace; working in groups; challenges.

Consider this major if you are good at: active listening; caring/nurturing; critical reading/thinking; leadership; math; organizing; problem solving; teamwork ...*or have...* initiative; patience; verbal skills.

Recommended high school prep:

English 4, math 4 (including precalculus, calculus, or statistics), lab science 3 (including biology and chemistry), social studies 3, and a foreign language 2-3. If available, courses in psychology, growth and development, nutrition and health are recommended, as are speech and writing courses. A computer applications course would also be helpful.

Did you know...

...that nurses aren't just doctors' helpers? Nurses are independent primary health care providers, whose responsibilities range from directly treating patients to developing and supervising complex nursing care systems. In the United States, RNs—who outnumber physicians by more than four to one—are involved in just about every type of health care service.

Typical courses in this major:

Psychology
Anatomy and physiology
Microbiology
Chemistry
Nutrition
Fundamentals of practice in nursing
Pharmacology
Physical assessment
Nursing leadership
Sociology
Mental health
Environmental and occupational health
Adult, pediatric, and geriatric care
Maternal/child and neonatal care
Medical and surgical care
Home health care

Concentrations:

Generally, none in college; but if you go on to grad school: family primary care; women's health; pediatrics; adult primary care; geriatrics; neonatal acute care; adult acute care.

What the study of this major is like:

Generally, you take courses in English, social sciences, the humanities, and the natural sciences during your first two years as a major. In your nursing program, you apply your education in liberal arts and sciences to learn the principles of nursing theory. You evaluate research to determine its benefit to nursing practice; examine nurse–client relationships and the organization of health care delivery; study ethical and practical issues related to terminal illness and death; and examine ways of providing health promotion services and illness care to culturally diverse communities.

Some programs require a fourth-year internship in which you receive academic credit while gaining clinical experience. You may work (under supervision) in hospitals, long-term care facilities, schools, community health organizations, mental health/psychiatric institutions, and other settings. There may also be opportunities for paid summer work experience.

You do not specialize at the undergraduate level. Graduates of nursing programs are generalists, able to assume roles in acute care, long-term care, and community-based facilities. After completing your undergraduate degree, you must pass the National Council Licensing Examination for Registered Nurses (NCLEX-RN) in order to work in the field.

Perhaps the biggest surprise for beginning students in nursing is the intensity and rigor of the subject matter and clinical practice requirements. Because nurses, who often work independently, must be responsible and accountable, they are expected to master a great deal of specialized (often technical) knowledge and theory.

Being a nursing major requires time management and a commitment to long hours of both course work and clinical practice. Usually you will need to study for several hours for every hour of class time. Clinical practice generally involves 16 hours a week of work in a variety of health care settings. Before and after clinical practice, you develop case studies, care plans, and education projects related to your client population. Also, early in your studies, you must begin preparation for the NCLEX-RN exam.

Programs can grant an associate degree in nursing (A.D.N.) or a Bachelor of Science degree in nursing (B.S.N.). For an A.D.N. (usually from a community college), you complete the program in two to three years and are prepared for entry-level registered nurse practice at the bedside.

The four-year B.S.N. prepares you to work in the full range of health care settings, including hospitals; critical care, long-term care, rehabilitation, outpatient care, public health, community health, and mental health facilities; private homes; and neighborhood clinics. It also prepares you for graduate work. In addition to the liberal arts and sciences courses, B.S.N. programs feature more in-depth nursing courses, including theory, research, pharmacology, pathophysiology, physical assessment, and nutrition. You also receive training in specific areas such as community and public health nursing, medical-surgical nursing, maternal-child nursing, pediatric nursing, mental health nursing, and nursing leadership and management.

Other majors you might like:
Education of physically handicapped
Human services
Communication disorders
Psychology
Licensed practical nursing
Physical therapy
Music therapy
Gerontology
Food and nutrition studies
Human development and family studies
American Sign Language (ASL)
Emergency medical technology (EMT paramedic)

Questions to ask colleges:
Is the program accredited by the Commission on Collegiate Nursing Education (CCNE) or the National League for Nursing Accrediting Commission (NLNAC)?

What is the NCLEX-RN passing rate for graduates?

What types of laboratories are available for the program, and how well equipped are they?

What are the types and locations of clinical sites used for student practice opportunities?

Career options and trends:
Advanced nurse practitioner*; nurse educator*; clinical nurse specialist; nurse anesthetist; nurse midwife; nurse researcher; nurse administrator*.

For advanced or specialty practice, a bachelor's or master's degree and certification based on examination and clinical practice requirements are essential.

The United States is in the midst of a national nursing shortage that is projected to intensify as the population ages and the demand for new health care services and technologies increases. It is anticipated that by the year 2020, there will be a severe shortage (more than 800,000 RNs) in the number of nurses needed in the nation's health care system.

Insider's viewpoint:
"Put on your seat belt; you are in for a wild ride. You will feel emotions you have never felt before."

—Jenn, class of 2000, Golden West College

For more info:

American Association of Colleges of Nursing
    (AACN)
One Dupont Circle, N.W.
Suite 530
Washington, DC 20036
(202) 463-6930
www.aacn.nche.edu

National Student Nurse Association (NSNA)
45 Main St., Suite 606
Brooklyn, NY 11201
(718) 210-0705
www.nsna.org

American Nurses Association (ANA)
8515 Georgia Ave.
Suite 400
Silver Spring, MD 20910
(800) 274-4262
www.ana.org

Occupational therapy

What it's about:

Occupational therapy is the use of "occupation" (work, self-care, and play/leisure) to help people who are affected by developmental, psychosocial, or physical problems to achieve or regain independent function, enhance development, and prevent injury. You must have a master's degree or higher in order to be certified as an occupational therapist. In college you take the prerequisite courses needed to be admitted into the graduate program.

Is this for you?

You might pursue this program if you like: working with individuals from diverse backgrounds; hobbies, activities, or interests involving fine hand (motor) skills; solving problems or puzzles in creative ways, even when there are no right or wrong answers; technology; physical activity; working in groups.

Consider this program if you are good at: active listening; caring/nurturing; counseling; creativity; critical reading/thinking; organizing; teamwork *...or have...* initiative; manual dexterity; verbal skills; writing skills.

Recommended high school prep:

English 4, math 3–4, lab science 3 (including biology, chemistry, and physics), social studies 3, and a foreign language 2–3. Courses in the arts, music, and, if available, psychology or human behavior would be helpful.

Did you know...

...that creativity and problem solving are important in this profession? After you learn the knowledge and skills to be an OT, you must be able to apply them to the unique situations and individuals you encounter in the various areas of practice that make up the profession.

Typical courses in this program:

Biology
English composition
Anatomy and physiology
General psychology
Developmental (life-span) psychology
Human development
Ergonomics
Statistics
Sociology
Anthropology
Mechanical physics
Kinesiology
Neuroscience
Gerontology
Leadership and management
Research methods

Concentrations:

Generally, none in college; but if you go on to grad school: occupational science; psychiatric disabilities; physical disabilities; pediatrics; rehabilitation technology.

What the program is like:

Occupational therapists help people who may have conditions that make it hard for them to function. These conditions may include developmental problems (such as learning disabilities), psychosocial issues (eating disorders), physical problems (arthritis or repetitive stress injury), the aging process (difficulty seeing or hearing), poverty, or cultural differences. OTs start by considering people's surroundings, evaluating their performance of everyday tasks, and assessing their personal goals. Then they use various activities to help the clients function with greater independence and to make the most of their abilities. Finally, OTs determine how well the therapy has worked.

To become an OT, you must pass the National Board for Certification in Occupational Therapy examination (NBCOT). Those who pass the exam are awarded the title "Occupational Therapist Registered" (OTR), and are eligible for state licensure.

As of January 1, 2007, in order to qualify for the exam, you must graduate from an accredited graduate program in OT, at either the master's or doctorate degree level. In college, this major is now primarily a preprofessional program made up of prerequisite courses that will prepare you for admission into a graduate program in OT.

These prerequisite courses generally include one year (two semesters) of anatomy and physiology, English, statistics, and sociology, and usually three semesters of general and developmental psychology. In addition, most graduate programs require you to be certified in CPR (cardiopulmonary resuscitation) and to have at least 50 hours of volunteer experience working with a licensed OTR. A course in mechanical physics (related to movement and/or principles of movement) is often recommended, although not required.

You can major in anything you want in college so long as you take the prerequisite courses, but the most popular majors are biology, psychology, sociology, anthropology, liberal arts, and anatomy. Quite a few colleges offer a combined bachelor's/master's program that allows you to enter as a college freshman, and continue straight through to the OT graduate degree in five years.

Once you get into the graduate program, the curriculum includes the study of normal maturation, development, and function; the effect of diseases, trauma, and aging; and the varied ways in which therapists can help people whose ability to do normal activities is threatened or impaired. Programs generally consist of lecture courses; lab courses, in which you practice and analyze skills; and fieldwork training in clinical settings.

In courses on occupational therapy theory and practice, you do closely supervised fieldwork, where you observe and then treat clients in hospitals, schools, or other facilities. As you advance in the program this fieldwork becomes full-time, for a minimum of 24 weeks; also under the supervision of a qualified occupational therapist.

Fieldwork is the most demanding part of your studies because you must apply, in a real-world setting, what you've learned in class and the lab. However, students typically enjoy fieldwork immensely, and their enthusiasm helps them complete the program.

Other majors you might like:
Physical therapy
Gerontology
Child development
Art, dance, or music therapy
Psychology
Special education
Athletic training
Recreational therapy
Human services
Exercise sciences
Human resources management
Biomedical engineering

Questions to ask colleges:
Is the program approved by the Accreditation Council for Occupational Therapy Education?

Is there a combined bachelor's/graduate degree option? If so, what are the requirements to move on into the graduate part of the program?

What kinds of internships or volunteer experiences working with OTs are available?

Career options and trends:
Occupational therapist*; researcher; industrial ergonomist; instructor; master clinician; health care administrator.

In addition to requiring successful completion of the NBCOT exam, most states have licensing standards. Practitioners must also renew their certification every three years.

Job prospects are excellent—as society ages, occupational therapists will be more in demand. Because the profession has been underutilized, many areas of practice have yet to be developed. In addition to hospitals, schools, rehabilitation centers, and long-term-care facilities, emerging areas of practice include evaluation, rehabilitation, and training for driving skills; consultation on accessibility design and home modification; ergonomics and workplace modification; assistive device development;

services for those with impaired vision; and private practice in community health services.

For more info:

American Occupational Therapy Association
  (AOTA)
4720 Montgomery Lane
P.O. Box 31220
Bethesda, MD 20824-1220
(800) 377-8555
www.aota.org

National Board for Certification in Occupational
  Therapy (NBCOT)
800 South Frederick Ave., Suite 200
Gaithersburg, MD 20877-4150
(301) 990-7979
www.nbcot.org

Pharmacy

What it's about:

Pharmacists apply a knowledge of medicines to patient needs. As a pharmacy student, you learn how to counsel patients, dispense drugs, monitor drug therapy, minimize side effects, and work with physicians, nurses, and other health care professionals. Pharmacy is no longer an undergraduate major. The entry-level degree is now the Doctor of Pharmacy (Pharm.D.) first-professional degree, a four-year program that usually follows two years of college-level prepharmacy courses.

Is this for you?

You might pursue this program if you like: chemistry; community service activities; meeting different kinds of people; helping people; learning; reading; being independent.

Consider this program if you are good at: attention to detail; counseling; critical reading/thinking; multitasking; organizing; quantitative analysis; teamwork *...or have...* initiative; verbal skills; writing skills.

Recommended high school prep:

English 4, math 4 (including precalculus), lab science 4 (including biology, chemistry and physics), social studies 3, and a foreign language 2–3. Courses that develop communications skills (writing and speech) are also important. Latin can be helpful, but is not necessary. Computer skills are essential.

Did you know...

...that pharmacists do much more than fill prescriptions? While about half of all pharmacists work in community pharmacies, many others are employed as clinical education specialists, researchers, government agency employees (e.g., in the Food and Drug Administration), or work in the pharmaceutical industry as scientists, consultants, product development managers, or marketing reps.

Typical courses in this program:

Physiology
Pathophysiology
Biochemistry
Microbiology
Molecular biology
Pharmaceutics
Pharmacology/medicinal chemistry
Immunology
Nonprescription medications and self-care
Dietary supplements and herbal medicines
Biostatistics
Professional communication
Pharmaceutical care
Pharmacy law and ethics
Health systems management
Physical assessment

Concentrations:

Generally, none available.

What the program is like:

Typically, the pharmacy (Pharm.D.) major is a six-year doctorate program that requires two undergraduate years of prepharmacy courses, followed by four academic years (or three calendar years in an accelerated program, with summer semesters) of professional education. The prepharmacy curriculum usually includes courses in writing and speech, biology, general chemistry, organic chemistry, microbiology, calculus, human anatomy and physiology, social and behavioral sciences, economics, English, and humanities. Some prepharmacy programs also require physics courses and computer competency.

But you do not have to do prepharmacy training in order to be accepted into the professional pharmacy program; you must simply complete the prerequisite courses in college. For example, many pharmacy applicants are chemistry, biochemistry, or biology majors, and their pharmacy prerequisites are usually covered by courses they took to complete their major. Be aware that admissions requirements may vary greatly among professional pharmacy programs. To be considered for admission in about half the programs, you must submit Pharmacy College Admission Test (PCAT) scores.

At the graduate level, you focus on the physiology and biochemistry of the body, and on appropriate medication therapy, to diagnose, treat, or prevent disease. In medicinal chemistry (biochemistry of medicinals, immunology, biotechnology) and pharmacology courses, you study the effects of various classes of medications on the body. In courses on pharmaceutics/drug delivery systems, you learn how drugs are administered to, absorbed into, and eliminated from the body. Pharmacotherapy focuses on choosing and implementing medication therapies, including patient evaluation and counseling; risk assessment; prescribing, preparing, and dispensing; symptom management; and evaluation of results. In pathophysiology courses, you examine the way disease affects the body; pharmacokinetics explores the body's reactions to medications over time, as well as the measurement of blood levels to determine dosage; and in pharmacognosy, you study drugs derived from plants or animals.

You'll be trained to dispense medication safely and to educate patients about their prescription and nonprescription (over-the-counter) therapy. Further, you learn to work with, and advise, physicians on medication selection. You also take courses in pharmacy management, pharmacy law, pharmacoeconomics, managed care, and pharmaceutical marketing.

Most programs have three years of classroom instruction involving lectures, discussion sessions, laboratories, and practice-related activities followed by one year of structured, real-life learning (clerkship rotations). During your clerkship rotation, you apply what you have learned, completing 1,500 hours or more of hands-on practice in hospitals, clinics, community pharmacies, or other medical settings.

Some colleges offer a bachelor's degree in pharmaceutical sciences or pharmacology, which can prepare you for a career in the pharmaceutical industry or for graduate study or medical school; but such a degree will not make you eligible for licensure as a pharmacist. Another option is the two-year associate degree (or diploma or certificate, depending on the program) that trains you to become a pharmacy technician. Pharmacy technicians work under the close supervision of pharmacists, performing technical tasks such as stocking, packaging, and pricing medications, and maintaining records and inventories of prescriptions, medications, and supplies.

Other majors you might like:
Biochemistry
Clinical/medical laboratory technology
Chemistry
Substance abuse counseling
Health care administration
Pharmacy assistant
Public heath
Community health/preventative medicine
Microbiology
Medical records administration
Small business administration/management
Dietetics

Questions to ask colleges:
Does the college offer a six-year prepharmacy/Pharm.D. program for entering students? If so, what are the requirements (such as GPA) for continuing on into the professional program? What percentage of the prepharm students continue? If a state school, do in-state students get preference?

Are students required to take the PCAT before admission into the Pharm.D. program? If so, what is the score range for admission?

Do students get help in obtaining summer internship opportunities?

What is the range of clerkship opportunities available during the last professional year? How does the college assign students to these clerkships, and do students often have to relocate to attend them?

Career options and trends:
Community pharmacist*; hospital staff pharmacist*; long-term care facility pharmacist; managed care pharmacist; public health service pharmacist; clinical specialist; clinical drug researcher; quality control supervisor.

Every state requires a license to practice pharmacy. To qualify, you must serve an internship period and pass a national board exam and a state exam. Continuing education is required for license renewal.

Some positions in research, clinical pharmacy, teaching, or other specialty area may require an advanced graduate degree (master's or Ph.D.), and/or further training in a residency program or fellowship.

The job outlook is very positive, with good employment opportunities projected for the near future. Also, fewer Pharm.D. degrees are expected to be granted than the number of jobs created. The retail sector will be influenced by such trends as automated dispensing and wider use of pharmacy technicians to meet the growing demand at lower cost; expansion of chain drugstores and of mail order firms; and increased involvement by managed care and Medicare.

For more info:
American Association of Colleges of Pharmacy
  (AACP)
1426 Prince St.
Alexandria, VA 22314
(703) 739-2330
www.aacp.org

Physical therapy

What it's about:

Physical therapists (PTs) are licensed health care professionals who work to prevent, diagnose, and treat conditions that affect a person's movement and functional independence. Although you have to go to graduate school to earn a degree in physical therapy, a variety of undergraduate majors can prepare you for a professional PT program.

Is this for you?

You might pursue this program if you like: helping people; sports and exercise; dance; gymnastics; science and technology; learning and discovery; problem solving; understanding other people's perspectives; seeking and using feedback.

Consider this program if you are good at: active listening; caring/nurturing; creativity; critical reading/thinking; organizing; persuading/influencing *...or have...* initiative; patience; physical stamina; verbal skills.

Recommended high school prep:

English 4, math 3, lab science 3 (including biology and chemistry), social studies 3, and a foreign language 2–3. In addition, it may be helpful to participate in a job-shadowing program at a local hospital.

Did you know...

...that physical therapists have considerable flexibility in their career paths? You can serve as a clinician, teacher, researcher, consultant, administrator, or in some combination of these roles. Also, both full-time and part-time opportunities exist in physical therapy, so that you can pursue other personal and professional goals if you wish.

Typical courses in this program:

Biology
Human development
Anatomy
Physiology
Physics
General (inorganic) chemistry
Mathematics
Statistics
Psychology
Sociology
Ethics
Neuroanatomy
Orthopedics
Health policy
Physical therapy exercise
Kinesiology

Concentrations:

Generally, none available.

What the program is like:

Physical therapy is a rapidly evolving field of study. Since January 1, 2002, the Commission on Accreditation in Physical Therapy Education only approves PT programs at the master's degree level or above. To become a physical therapist, you must complete the prerequisites in college and then take a full-time, three-year, graduate-level program. Some colleges offer "3 + 3" programs, which enable you to complete both college and graduate work in six years.

Currently, the professional degree in physical therapy is either a master's degree (M.S.P.T. or M.P.T.) or the recently established Doctorate in Physical Therapy (D.P.T.). The D.P.T. emerged in response to a significant shift in the roles and responsibilities of the physical therapist; PT education now requires a depth and breadth like that in other professional health care fields, such as medicine, dentistry, and optometry. A large number of professional programs have either converted to the D.P.T. degree, or have indicated an intention to do so.

Although various undergraduate majors, including biology, psychology, chemistry, or engineering, may help you get into a professional physical therapy program, you must be interested in movement as a primary component of health, and be committed to the study and application of the science of movement in the context of health care. As an undergraduate, you should take courses in the natural sciences, social sciences, and humanities, as well as in quantitative and analytical fields. A broad liberal arts education will help you hone your interpersonal skills, think critically, provide evidence-based care, and learn how to serve diverse populations.

Prerequisite course work for admission to professional programs can include anatomy, kinesiology, athletic training, exercise science, neuropsychology, social psychology, human development, physiology, physical education, and special education. Many graduate PT programs also require computer literacy, certification in CPR, and competence in medical terminology (a knowledge of Latin and Greek roots). Many also require a certain number of hours of volunteer clinical experience. You should plan each semester in college to be sure that you fulfill all the requirements for admission to grad school.

What can you look forward to in grad school? Most programs begin with basic science courses such as anatomy (generally dissection-based), neuroscience and motor control, exercise physiology and pathophysiology, and the psychosocial aspects of health and disability. You then apply what you learn to clinical practice, through guided clinical experiences. The core of your curriculum involves studying clinical sciences in neurology, cardiology, pediatrics, and orthopedics and acquiring patient management skills that you can use in diagnosing problems, planning interventions, and assessing results. Your clinical competence will be judged by a variety of clinical internships that you must complete.

Other majors you might like:
Psychology
Biomedical engineering
Anthropology
Exercise sciences
Occupational therapy
Nursing (RN)
Athletic training

Sports and fitness administration
Dance therapy
Social work
Dietetics
Respiratory therapy

Questions to ask colleges:
Does the college offer a combined pre-PT/ graduate program? If so, what are the requirements for admission and for continuing on into the professional program?

How are students advised about, and assisted in, meeting prerequisites for grad school?

What are the opportunities for volunteer experience in physical therapy settings?

Career options and trends:
Clinician; private practitioner; clinical administrator; clinical educator.

Physical therapists work in hospitals, extended-care facilities, home health agencies, public and private schools, industry, programs for people with developmental disabilities, and private clinics.

All states require physical therapists to pass a licensure exam before they can practice, after graduating from an accredited PT educational program. A number of states require continuing education to maintain licensure.

Physical therapy is now about prevention as well as rehabilitation. Clients include individuals in good health, as well as those at acute stages of illness; in schools and fitness facilities as well as in hospitals and nursing homes; and of both young and old ages. Therefore, the job outlook is excellent; health care, health promotion, and prevention opportunities abound.

For more info:
American Physical Therapy Association (APTA)
1111 N. Fairfax St.
Alexandria, VA 22314
(800) 999-2782
www.apta.org

Physician assistant

What it's about:

Physician assistants (PAs) are licensed to practice medicine under the supervision of a doctor. Working as part of a health care team, PAs take medical histories, examine and treat patients, order and interpret laboratory tests and X-rays, make diagnoses, and prescribe medications.

Is this for you?

You might like this major if you also like: working both independently and as part of a team; taking responsibility; solving problems for others; volunteer work in hospitals or clinics.

Consider this major if you are good at: active listening; attention to detail; caring/nurturing; critical reading/thinking; handling emergencies; leadership; organizing; teamwork; time management *...or have...* initiative; self-confidence; verbal skills.

Recommended high school prep:

English 4, math 3–4 (statistics would be helpful), lab science 3–4 (biology and chemistry most important), social studies 3, and a foreign language 2–3.

Did you know...

...that in some programs, PA majors attend many of the same classes as medical students? PA education and physician education differ not so much in the curriculum but in the amount of training.

...that PAs often work autonomously? In rural or inner-city clinics, where a physician may be available only one or two days a week, PAs may be the principal care providers; they consult with the supervising physician as needed. PAs also make house calls and go to hospitals and nursing homes to check on patients and report back to the physician.

Typical courses in this major:

Anatomy
History taking and physical diagnosis
Pharmacology
Microbiology
Behavioral sciences
Clinical medicine
Obstetrics and gynecology
Pediatrics
Geriatrics
Psychiatry
Surgery
Critical care
Medical laboratory sciences
Radiology
Health care delivery
Ethics

Concentrations:

Generally, none available.

What the study of this major is like:

All states require that new PAs complete a program approved by the Accreditation Review Commission on Education for the Physician Assistant, Inc. (ARC-PA). PA programs are located within sponsoring institutions such as universities, four-year colleges, community colleges, and hospitals. The credential offered by a program (certificate, associate degree, bachelor's degree, or master's degree) depends on the institution; more than half award a master's degree, and most PA graduates earn at least a bachelor's. No matter what degree is granted, every accredited PA program must meet the standards established by the ARC-PA, by offering courses in the basic medical sciences, behavioral and social sciences, clinical sciences, health policy, and professional practice, as well as supervised clinical practice. The average length of PA training is 26 months.

For admission, many PA programs require you to have completed at least two years of college and participated in some health care work. Many applicants enter PA programs from other health care professions, such as nursing and emergency medical technology. Prerequisites (including health care experience, courses, degree, and test scores) and application deadlines vary, so be sure to research PA programs well in advance.

In general, PA education includes one year of classroom studies followed by a year of supervised clinical experience (rotations) in health care institutions. You take courses in anatomy, microbiology, clinical medicine, clinical pharmacology, physical diagnosis, medical ethics, geriatric and home health care, biochemistry, pathology, and disease prevention. In addition to lectures, there are many opportunities for you to learn in small groups and refine your clinical skills under faculty supervision. During your second year, you spend at least 40 hours a week at your clinical rotation sites, including internal medicine, family medicine, emergency medicine, obstetrics and gynecology, pediatrics, general surgery, and psychiatry.

After completing the PA program, you must pass the national exam administered by the National Commission on Certification of Physician Assistants (NCCPA). In addition to national certification, you must then be licensed or registered by the state in which you practice. The profession is committed to lifelong learning, and PAs must recertify by examination every six years and complete 100 hours of continuing medical education every two years.

Other majors you might like:
Optometric assistant
Licensed practical nursing
Radiologic technology/medical imaging
Athletic training
Funeral services/mortuary science
Respiratory therapy
Medical records administration
Medical illustration
Forensic science
Biology
Biomedical engineering

Questions to ask colleges:
How much heath care experience is required for admission to the PA program? Which types of experiences qualify?

Does the program participate in the Central Application Service for Physician Assistants (CASPA)? This service collects and authenticates applicant materials for distribution to participating programs.

What is the first-time pass rate for recent graduates taking the Physician Assistants National Certifying Examination?

Career options and trends:
Many PAs work in primary care areas, such as internal medicine, pediatrics, and family medicine. Others work in specialty areas, such as general and thoracic surgery, emergency medicine, orthopedics, and geriatrics. PAs specializing in surgery provide pre- and postoperative care, and may work as assistants during major surgery.

Employment opportunities are excellent and projected to grow at an above-average pace, because of the nation's expanding health care needs and efforts to contain costs. Demand for PAs will be high in areas and settings where there is a shortage of physicians, such as rural and inner-city clinics. Technology that allows interactive consultations with off-site doctors ("telemedicine") will also increase the role of PAs.

For more info:
Physician Assistant Education Association (PAEA)
950 North Washington St.
Alexandria, VA 22314-1552
(703) 548-5538
www.apap.org

Predental

What it's about:

Predental studies consists of the courses you need to take in college in order to get into dental school. It's not a major by itself, so you have to choose a major in addition to completing the predental requirements. Predental programs also provide guidance to help you prepare for dental school.

Is this for you?

You might pursue this program if you like: helping people of all kinds; science and technology; working with your hands; arts and crafts; model making; playing a musical instrument; problem solving.

Consider this program if you are good at: attention to detail; caring/nurturing; creativity; critical reading/thinking; math; memorizing *...or have...* integrity; manual dexterity; motivation; verbal skills.

Recommended high school prep:

English 4, math 4 (including precalculus and calculus), lab science 4 (including biology, chemistry, and physics), social studies 4 (including economics), and a foreign language 3–4 (Spanish recommended). If available, courses in psychology, speech communication, business, and computer science are also recommended.

Did you know...

...that cleaning and filling teeth are just a few of the jobs a dentist performs? Since many medical conditions that affect the whole body are revealed in the mouth, dentists are on the forefront of the early detection of disease.

Typical courses in this program:

Inorganic (general) chemistry
Organic chemistry
Biology
Zoology
Biochemistry
Physics
Calculus
College mathematics
English
Psychology
Cell biology
Genetics
Anatomy and physiology
Speech communication
Computer science
Sculpture

Concentrations:

Generally, none available.

What the program is like:

Sometimes students are surprised to learn that taking part in studio arts or playing a musical instrument is good preparation for a career in dentistry. But it makes sense—dentists must be able to visualize three-dimensional objects from diagrams, have good eye-hand coordination, and perform detailed tasks in very small spaces. Perhaps you didn't realize that it takes some artistic ability to give people beautiful smiles.

In a predental program, however, science rather than the sculptural arts will occupy most of your time. You must take two semesters each of biology, general chemistry, organic chemistry, and physics. Many dental schools also expect you to take calculus and biochemistry. Courses in English and perhaps psychology are in the mix too. On top of all that, you will have to fulfill the requirements for the major you select.

Most students choose a science major, since the courses dovetail with the predental requirements. However, you don't have to follow that path if you don't want to. Many predental students select a nonscience major, and dental school admissions offices are satisfied with that option; in fact, they like to accept students from a variety of academic backgrounds, as long as the applicants excelled in their science courses. Choosing a nonscience major, though, may create some course-scheduling conflicts that might make it difficult to graduate in four years. The trick is to keep your goal in mind, but also to follow your bliss—you'll do best in a major you like.

Your predental adviser will play a critical role in helping you navigate your undergraduate career. He or she will assist you in planning your course work, choosing a major, coping with difficulties that may arise, and finding internships or community service opportunities. You will appreciate your adviser's help most during the process of applying to dental school: evaluating your prospects, lining up interviews and letters of recommendations, and preparing for the Dental Admission Test (DAT).

What you do outside class is another important aspect of a predental program. It's a definite plus to get related experience, such as "job-shadowing" a dentist or volunteering in a dental office. Many communities have Healthcare for the Homeless organizations, which provide oral care to people who are unable to visit a dentist; these groups often use student volunteers. Successful dental school candidates usually devote 15–20 hours a week to such activities during the school year and 40–50 hours a week over the summer.

Just how hard is it to get into dental school? Nationally, the mean GPA of successful dental school applicants is in the 3.1–3.2 range. The percentage of students who are accepted depends on the number of applicants per year, but is usually between 40 and 60 percent. Most dental schools are state institutions that give preference to residents of their state.

Here's something to consider: more than half the dental schools in the United States cooperate with colleges to offer joint programs that enable you to achieve both a bachelor's degree and a dental degree in less time than if you pursued the two programs separately. If you are interested, look at the latest edition of the *Official Guide to Dental Schools,* published by the American Dental Education Association.

Other majors you might like:

Biology
Biochemistry
Chemistry
Dental laboratory technology
Biomedical technology
Entrepreneurial studies
Anthropology
Occupational therapy
Communication disorders
Medical office administration
Forensic science

Questions to ask colleges:

How many predental and premedical students does the institution have? (The premedical and predental populations are often considered as one.)

How many predental students get into dental school after one application? After two or more applications?

Is the predental adviser easily accessible, particularly when students apply to dental school?

Is there help to obtain dentistry-related internship or volunteer experiences, during both the school year and school breaks?

Does the college have a combined bachelor's/D.D.S. program or other special relationship with dental schools?

Is there a DAT prep course available on campus?

Career options and trends:

Dentist*; oral surgeon*; orthodontist; dental or medical laboratory technician.

During dental school you must pass Parts I and II of the National Board Dental Examination. After dental school you will have to become fully licensed in the state(s) in which you want to practice. Like most licensed professionals, dentists are required to complete a certain amount of continuing education credits each year.

The demand for dentists is strong and growing, because the population is increasing and improved public oral hygiene has enabled people to keep their teeth longer! Also, many dentists who were educated in the 1960's and '70's will be retiring soon.

For more info:

American Dental Education Association (ADEA)
1400 K St., N.W., Suite 1100
Washington, DC 20005
(202) 289-7201
www.adea.org

American Student Dental Association (ASDA)
211 E. Chicago Ave., Suite 1160
Chicago, IL 60611-2678
(800) 621-8099 ext. 2795
www.asdanet.org

Premedicine

What it's about:

If you want to be a medical doctor, osteopathic doctor, or podiatrist, you must go to medical school, and that means you have to take certain courses in college. Premedicine is not itself a major—just those prerequisite courses. It' also an advising program to help you get into medical school.

Is this for you?

You might pursue this program if you like: helping people; science and technology; anatomy; learning and discovery; problem solving; *ER*. You will spend many years studying and training to become a doctor, so a desire to heal and prevent disease must be a strong motivator.

Consider this program if you are good at: attention to detail; counseling; critical reading/thinking; math; memorizing *...or have...* compassion; initiative; integrity; motivation; verbal skills.

Recommended high school prep:

English 4, math 4 (including precalculus and calculus), lab science 4 (including biology, chemistry, and physics), social studies 4, and a foreign language 3–4 (Spanish recommended). If available, courses in psychology, statistics, and computer science are also recommended. It is also advisable to do volunteer work at a local hospital or other health facility.

Did you know...

...that you don't need a 4.0 to get into medical school? You should be an excellent student, but medical schools look at applicants as more than the sum of their grade point averages and MCAT test scores.

...that some colleges offer a seven-year program that combines undergraduate and medical studies and culminates in an M.D.?

Typical courses in this program:

Inorganic chemistry
Biology
Calculus
Organic chemistry
Physics
Psychology
Cell Biology
Genetics
Sociology
English
Statistics
Biochemistry
Computer science
Bioethics
Neuroscience
Medicinal chemistry

Concentrations:

Generally, none available.

What the program is like:

"Declaring" premed may be as simple as checking off a box on your college application or filling out a form during orientation. In any event, you should contact the premed adviser at your college as soon as you enroll.

The adviser's role is critical to your success in college. He or she will help you plan your premedical course work, choose a major, overcome any academic difficulties, and find internships or community service opportunities. You will also receive help applying to med school, preparing for the Medical College Application Test (MCAT), securing and sending letters of recommendation, preparing for interviews, and making a successful transition to medical school.

The premed science requirements include a full year (two semesters) each of general chemistry, biology, organic chemistry, and physics. Some medical schools also require either one or two semesters of calculus. Other courses that, although not required, will help you prepare for the MCAT and medical school are cell biology, biochemistry, genetics, molecular biology, and physiology. Because there is a two- to three-year sequence in the required science courses, you should take general chemistry and biology in your first year, no matter what you decide to major in.

It is important to know that premed is not just about science. Medical schools look for well-rounded students who possess a broad background in the humanities and social sciences. For example, English courses will provide an opportunity to sharpen your writing skills, a philosophy course will help you develop critical thinking skills and a moral compass, and psychology courses can help you understand the connection between mind and body. At most colleges you can usually fulfill the nonscience premed requirements by taking courses in the core liberal arts program.

Because the premed requirements emphasize science, the field in which their interests lie, most premed students choose a science major—but about 15 to 20 percent do not. Not only can students pursue a nonscience major, but most medical schools, seeking diversity, look with favor on applicants who take this route. If you are considering a nonscience major, however, you should realize that you must excel in the science courses you do take and that because of scheduling conflicts between premed and major-course requirements, you may not be able to graduate in four years.

During college you will need to pace yourself. Avoid taking more than two science and/or math courses per semester, and if you want to enter med school right after college, plan to complete your science/math requirements by the end of your third year, so that you can take the MCAT and then apply to med school during your fourth year. In addition, to be competitive you should consider taking honors and independent-study courses. Your premed advisor will help you juggle this challenging course load.

A premed program is not just about schoolwork, either. A successful premed student usually spends an average of 15–20 hours per week in extracurricular activities (clinical, research, or community service work) during the academic year, and 40–50 hours per week during school breaks. When selecting colleges, look to see if opportunities for such experiences are easily available nearby, and if you will receive help in obtaining them.

Other majors you might like:
Biology
Biochemistry
Chemistry
Music therapy
Physician assistant
Biomedical engineering
Psychology
Sociology
Anthropology
Health care administration
Emergency medical technology (EMT paramedic)
Neuroscience

Questions to ask colleges:
How many premed students are there at this college? How many are accepted into medical school?

Is the premed adviser easily accessible, particularly when students apply for medical school?

Is assistance available to obtain clinical, research, and community service experience during the school year and school breaks?

Is there an MCAT prep course available on campus?

Career options and trends:
Medical doctor*; osteopathic doctor*; podiatrist; physician assistant; physician/scientist*; optometrist; physical therapist; pharmacist; radiologist.

Medical school graduates must complete the United States Medical Licensing Examination (USMLE), Parts I–III. Physicians must be licensed in each state in which they want to practice; there are some interstate and regional agreements between and among states. In addition, in order to maintain their licenses, physicians must complete a certain amount of continuing medical education (CME) credits each year.

There is a particular need for general practitioners, geriatricians, psychiatrists, and podiatrists. In addition, because of a growing interest among patients in alternative cures and treatments, there is expected to be an increased demand for naturopathic physicians.

For more info:

Association of American Medical Colleges (AAMC)
2450 N Street, N.W.
Washington, DC 20037
www.aamc.org

The Student Doctor Network
26922 Oso Parkway #380
Mission Viejo, CA 92691
www.studentdoctor.net

Preveterinary

What it's about:

If you love animals and are good at science, you might be thinking you want to go to veterinary medical school after college. Because there are only twenty-eight vet schools in the United States, however, being accepted is a challenge. A program in preveterinary studies will help you become a competitive candidate by guiding you through the college courses and extracurricular experience that vet schools require. But keep in mind that prevet studies is not itself a major—you'll still have to pick one.

Is this for you?

You might pursue this program if you like: all creatures great and small; people too; science and nature; volunteering at the local shelter or animal rescue center. Prevet students have a passion for animals, both sick and well, and the people who own them.

Consider this program if you are good at: attention to detail; caring/nurturing; critical reading/ thinking; math; memorizing *...or have...* integrity; mechanical facility; motivation; patience; verbal skills.

Recommended high school prep:

English 4, math 4 (including precalculus and calculus), lab science 4 (including biology, chemistry, and physics), social studies 4, and a foreign language 3–4 (Spanish recommended). If available, courses in psychology, statistics, speech, and computer science are also recommended. It is strongly suggested that you have experience working with animals.

Did you know...

...that veterinary school is actually more competitive than medical school? That's because there are very few veterinary schools and many applicants. The prevet science requirements are the same as for premed, plus additional courses such as zoology, microbiology, or animal science. But don't be discouraged—you should be able to reach your goal if you have faith in yourself and stay focused.

Typical courses in this program:

Inorganic (general) chemistry
Organic chemistry
Biology
Biochemistry
Zoology
Physics
Calculus
Speech communication
Statistics
English
Animal science
Genetics
Comparative anatomy
Microbiology
Animal nutrition
Business management

Concentrations:

Generally, none available.

What the program is like:

The preveterinary curriculum usually includes courses in biochemistry, biology, general chemistry, organic chemistry, physics, and English. Some veterinary schools require additional course work in microbiology, biochemistry, nutrition, or animal science. You may also be expected to take courses in the humanities and social sciences.

Nonscience courses are important because veterinary schools prefer well-rounded students. What is more, these courses help you develop the skills you'll need as a vet. For example, courses in psychology can help you understand the behavior of animals as well as that of their owners; business courses will be valuable if you, like most vets, run your own practice.

In addition to academics, you will need to acquire hands-on experience working with both small and large animals under the eye of a veterinarian. Practical experience might involve breeding, rearing, feeding, and showing various kinds of animals, including pets, livestock, laboratory animals, zoo animals, or wildlife. Some vet schools set a minimum number of hours for such work, usually 200, but successful applicants usually have much more than that.

At most colleges, preveterinary studies is not a major; it's an advising program—and the prevet adviser at your college will be a very important to you. You'll get assistance in selecting and scheduling courses, choosing a major, dealing with difficulties that may crop up, and finding internships and other extracurricular opportunities. Your adviser will also be a big help when you apply to veterinarian school.

You might wonder whether you can pursue a prevet program while taking a nonscience major. Yes, it is possible; but because veterinary schools require their students to become familiar with so many different species, a solid science background is strongly recommended. Students with a nonscience interest are usually encouraged to have a science major but a nonscience minor. If you are still committed to a nonscience major, go for it—but you might need more than four years to finish college.

A recent change in the application process is the elimination of the Veterinary College Admission Test (VCAT); now, vet schools accept either the Graduate Record Exam (GRE) or the Medical College Admission Test (MCAT).

About a third of the twenty-eight accredited vet schools in the United States offer joint programs with undergraduate colleges, ranging in length from six to eight years. Admission to these highly competitive programs is open to excellent students who, as high school seniors, are committed to pursuing a career as a veterinarian. If you are interested, review the latest edition of *Veterinary Medical School Admissions Requirements*, available from Purdue University Press.

Because managing the work load while maintaining academic excellence in all your courses is a challenge, you must be highly motivated and committed to your goal of becoming a veterinarian. Success also requires a four-year plan at the outset that allows you to fulfill all the requirements at a pace you can handle. But remember—college offers a wonderful opportunity to grow as a person and should not be a total grind. Your prevet adviser can help you achieve the right balance.

Other majors you might like:

Animal sciences
Biology
Zoology
Anthropology
Biochemistry
Chemistry
Wildlife and wilderness management
Agricultural and biological engineering
Genetics
Veterinary technology
Wildlife biology
Equestrian studies

Questions to ask colleges:

How many prevet students does the college have, as opposed to other pre–health profession students?

How many students are accepted into vet school after one application? After two or more applications?

Is there a knowledgeable prevet adviser who is easily accessible, particularly when students apply to vet school?

What kind of opportunities are available to gain practical experience working with animals, and where are these opportunities located?

Does the college have a combined D.V.M. program or other special relationship with vet schools?

Career options and trends:

About 75 percent of veterinarians today work in private practice. The rest are employed in a variety of areas, such as teaching at colleges and universities; conducting biomedical research in the public or private sector; or working for local, state, or federal agencies, departments of agriculture, and public health services that regulate or protect animals as well as people. Practice settings may also include race tracks, zoos, animal shelters, aquariums, and wildlife management facilities.

After graduating from veterinary school, you will have to meet the licensure requirements of the state(s) where you want to practice. In addition, like most licensed professionals, you must complete a certain amount of continuing education credits each year.

For more info:

Association of American Veterinary Medical
    Colleges
1101 Vermont Ave., N.W., Suite 101
Washington, DC 20005
www.aavmc.org

American Veterinary Medical Association
1932 N. Meacham Rd., Suite 100
Schaumburg, IL 60173-43660
www.avma.org

Radiologic technology/medical imaging

Also known as:
X ray technology

What it's about:
Radiologic technologists, also called radiographers, use X ray equipment to perform diagnostic imaging examinations of internal parts of the body. Experienced radiographers may perform more complex imaging procedures, such as computed tomography (CT) scans and magnetic resonance imaging (MRI).

Is this for you?
You might like this major if you also like: science and technology; art and photography (radiologic technology is said to be a combination of science and art); medical illustrations; working in teams; thinking about what's inside the human body.

Consider this major if you are good at: attention to detail; caring/nurturing; creativity; critical reading/thinking; organizing; quantitative analysis; spatial thinking/analysis; teamwork *...or have...* initiative; manual dexterity; writing skills.

Recommended high school prep:
English 4, math 3, lab science 3 (including biology and physics), social studies 3, and a foreign language 2–3. Participating in a job-shadowing program in radiologic technology at a local hospital would be most helpful, and you will need CPR certification before you begin your clinical courses in college.

Did you know...
...that radiologic technology is not always neat and clean? Occasionally a technologist must perform unpleasant examinations, and sometimes physical stamina is required for lifting patients and positioning them properly.

...that radiation is natural? Each year, you are exposed to an amount of naturally occurring "background radiation" from the atmosphere, the Earth's crust, and cosmic rays, that is 50 times stronger than a typical dental X ray.

Typical courses in this major:
Radiologic physics
Radiographic positioning
Imaging equipment
Medical terminology
Human anatomy and physiology
Radiographic exposure
Radiobiology and protection
Radiographic pathology
Clinical practice
Cross-sectional anatomy
Health law and ethics
Principles of radiation exposure

Concentrations:
Radiation biology; fluoroscopy; and anatomical positioning.

What the study of this major is like:
Radiographers take X rays of parts of the body to create films that are used in diagnosing medical conditions. Closely following physicians' instructions and radiation-use regulations, radiographers prepare, position, and protect patients (for example, by using lead shields); position and operate radiographic equipment; and develop the film. In addition, they may help to decide which types of equipment to buy; maintain equipment; keep patient records; and manage an office or department.

If you choose to study radiologic technology/medical imaging, you can pursue a certificate, an associate degree, or a bachelor's degree. There are more two-year associate degree programs than four-year bachelor's programs, and some hospitals offer certificate programs. Most formal training programs are accredited by the Joint Review Committee on Education in Radiologic Technology (JRCERT) and have similar requirements in anatomy, physiology, algebra, and physical science. Bachelor's degree programs offer more concentrations in specialty areas, such as radiation therapy, nuclear medicine, ultrasound, CT scan, or MRI, than are available in associate degree programs.

As a major in radiologic technology/medical imaging, you split your time among classroom lectures, laboratory activities, and clinical internship work. You must fulfill both general requirements (such as English, algebra, psychology, political science, sociology, and speech courses) and radiologic-specific course work. For the major, you study anatomy, physiology, biology, pathology, physics, radiation safety, patient care procedures, principles of imaging, medical ethics, and medical terminology. You learn to use computers and operate highly advanced medical equipment.

You must also develop your communication skills in order to work with patients and with other health care professionals as part of an effective team. In laboratories, you apply what you learn in the classroom, experimenting with patient positioning and X ray equipment. During hands-on clinical training, you work in actual radiology departments with physicians, nurses, and radiographers, again practicing what you learned in the classroom and laboratory.

Other majors you might like:
Laser/optical technology
Clinical/medical laboratory technology
Respiratory therapy
Electrical engineering technology
Computer science
Nuclear medical technology
Photographic/film/video technology
Physician assistant
Ophthalmic technology
Neuroscience
Animation
Radiation protection/health physics technology

Career options and trends:
There is an acute shortage of radiologic technologists that is expected to continue. As the population ages, the demand for diagnostic imaging will likely increase. This situation should not only guarantee employment but also generate improved compensation and working conditions.

In addition to becoming a staff X ray technician, you can—with on-the-job training, home study, and continuing education—go into a specialty area of radiography, such as heart catheterization; CT or MRI; ultrasound; mammography; nuclear medicine; radiation therapy; commercial sales; equipment repair; radiation health physics; education; or administration.

Although most jobs are found in hospitals, greater employment growth is projected in doctors' offices, clinics, and diagnostic imaging centers, because of the strong shift toward outpatient care. Radiologic technologists who are qualified for more than one type of diagnostic imaging technology, such as radiography and sonography or nuclear medicine, will be the most sought after.

Depending on where you work, you may have to be certified, registered, or licensed; and the differences between these credentials can be confusing. Certification is awarded by the American Registry of Radiologic Technologists (ARRT) to those who complete the required education and training and pass the national exam. Certification qualifies you to practice anywhere in the U.S. and is generally required for employment. Registration, which is voluntary but preferred by many employers, is an annual renewal of the certificate; it indicates that you have complied with ARRT's continuing education requirements. Licensing is required by most states in order to practice. Each state administers its own licensing process, but most require only ARRT certification and a fee.

For more info:
American Society of Radiologic Technologist (ASRT)
15000 Central Ave., S.E.
Albuquerque, NM 87123-3917
(800) 444-2778
www.asrt.org

Respiratory therapy

What it's about:

This major trains you to work with physicians, nurses, and other health care professionals in the diagnosis, treatment, and rehabilitation of patients whose heart, circulation, or lungs are functioning abnormally. Working mostly in hospitals, respiratory therapists manage the ventilation of critically ill patients, or provide immediate and long-term care to patients with breathing disorders.

Is this for you?

You might like this major if you also like: helping people; working with technology; science.

Consider this major if you are good at: attention to detail; critical reading/thinking; math; organizing; persuading/influencing; teamwork *...or have...* initiative; manual dexterity; mechanical facility; verbal skills.

Recommended high school prep:

English 4, math 3, lab science 3 (including biology, physics, and chemistry), social studies 3, and a foreign language 2–3. If they are available, take courses in health, sociology, psychology, interpersonal communications, and computer skills.

Typical courses in this major:

Human anatomy and physiology
Medical terminology
Cardiopulmonary pathophysiology
Pharmacology
Respiratory therapy procedures
Physical assessment
Mechanical ventilation
Neonatal and pediatric care
Critical care
Home care
Pulmonary function testing
Sleep disorders and their treatment
Microbiology
Pulmonary rehabilitation
Pulmonary diagnostics

Concentrations:

In college: neonatal/pediatric respiratory care; adult critical care; home care/extended care; polysomnography (sleep disorders, sleep medicine); cardiovascular technology; and pulmonary function testing.

If you go on to grad school: perfusion technology; extracorporeal circulation; health education; management/administration.

What the study of this major is like:

Respiratory therapists typically treat patients of all ages on all floors, in the emergency room, in clinics—in short, all over the hospital. They may attend to premature newborns; heart attack, stroke, drowning, or shock victims; and older patients with chronic diseases such as emphysema or asthma.

Respiratory therapists often deal with high-stress situations, working in intensive care units and participating in all cardiac resuscitations ("Code Blue"). They work with a variety of medical professionals and assist with other cardiac procedures such as pacemaker insertions, cardiac catheterization, and cardioversion. Besides hospitals, respiratory therapists can be employed in patients' homes, long-term-care facilities, diagnostic labs, and rehabilitation and educational facilities. And although sleep disorders have only recently become widely known, over half the professional staff in sleep labs now are respiratory therapists.

As a respiratory therapy major, you must fulfill general education requirements, including college algebra, chemistry, physics, English, computer and information literacy, communications, and social science (psychology or sociology). In the major, you take courses in anatomy, physiology, microbiology, pharmacology, diseases of the heart and lungs, and medical terminology, as well as technical courses that deal with procedures and clinical tests.

After examining the way the heart and lungs function, learning how to evaluate their condition, and determining which injuries, diseases, and disorders can seriously threaten cardiopulmonary (heart and lung) function, you are taught how to treat patients who have problems with their breathing and circulation. You gain practice in administering medications and using techniques and equipment (gases, humidity, equipment function and sterilization, arterial puncture and blood gas analysis, expansion therapies) to improve oxygen delivery to vital organs. You also spend time in hospitals applying what you have learned and providing patient care under supervision.

The program features lectures, laboratory work, and clinical practice. You learn theory in class, have hands-on experience with equipment in a laboratory setting, and then practice direct patient care under the supervision of faculty. Observing and caring for critically ill patients can be stressful and requires maturity. You will also have to adapt to the rigorous course work and the hours you must spend in the laboratory and clinical settings. You will be doing patient care during actual shifts, which are usually 12 hours long and may include afternoons and nights. You should therefore plan to attend classes, labs, and clinical courses full-time. As a result, you may not be able to have a job in addition; try to save money for your education before you enroll.

Respiratory therapy programs vary in length as well as in the degree or credential that graduates earn. Some programs offer two-year associate or four-year bachelor's degrees, preparing you for a career as a registered respiratory therapist (RRT). Shorter programs offer certificates and prepare you for work as an entry-level certified respiratory therapist (CRT).

Other majors you might like:
Cardiovascular technology
Physician assistant
Occupational therapy
Renal/dialysis technology
Clinical/medical laboratory technology
Licensed practical nursing
Gerontology
Biomedical technology
Social work
Recreational therapy
Radiologic technology/medical imaging

Questions to ask colleges:
Is the program approved by the Committee on Accreditation for Respiratory Care (CoARC)?

How many hospitals are used for clinical training, and where are they located?

After completing the program, are students eligible to take the National Registration Exam offered by the National Board for Respiratory Care (NBRC)? What is the first-time pass rate for recent graduates?

Career options and trends:
Respiratory therapist*; advanced-practice respiratory therapist; polysomnography technologist (sleep tech); cardiac ultrasound technician; perfusionist (operates bypass during heart surgery).

You must pass the NBRC examination to become a certified respiratory therapist, which allows you to practice as a CRT in every state that requires a license.

Respiratory therapists are employed in acute care hospitals, long-term care facilities, home health care, equipment and pharmaceutical sales, education, sleep laboratories, and health promotion. Employment forecasts for RTs indicate a continuing need for more therapists for the next decade or so. Therapists with cardiopulmonary care skills, or experience working with newborns and infants, will be especially in demand.

For more info:
American Association for Respiratory Care (AARC)
9425 N. MacArthur Blvd.
Suite 100
Irving, TX 75063
(972) 243-2272
www.aarc.org

Veterinary technology

Also known as:
Animal health technology

What it's about:
This major prepares you to work under the supervision of veterinarians, zoologists, and lab specialists to provide animal care and clinical assistance. Veterinary technicians (VTs) serve as receptionists, practice managers, radiologic/imaging technicians, medical and surgical nurses, anesthetists, pharmacy and laboratory technicians, animal behavior educators, and client liaisons.

Is this for you?
You might like this major if you also like: animal or pet training; the sciences; volunteering at the local shelter; 4H groups; farmwork; getting involved in animal welfare issues; meeting people; talking about animals.

Consider this major if you are good at: attention to detail; caring/nurturing; critical reading/thinking; organizing; problem solving; teamwork *...or have...* initiative; patience; verbal skills.

Recommended high school prep:
English 4, math 3, lab science 4, social studies 3, and a foreign language 2–3. If your high school offers an advanced science track, try to take one or more of the following: anatomy and physiology, microbiology, nutrition, and genetics.

Did you know...
...that veterinary technicians spend a great deal of their time working not only with animals but with people? Students who find satisfaction in this field possess good "people skills" and can function well as team players.

Typical courses in this major:
Animal anatomy and physiology
Parasitology
Clinical laboratory techniques
Animal nutrition
Large animal clinical procedures
Small animal clinical procedures
Veterinary pharmacology and anesthesia
Animal disease
Veterinary radiology and surgical nursing
Lab animal science and exotics
Externship/internship

Concentrations:
Generally, none available.

What the study of this major is like:
VTs perform a wide range of activities, doing everything veterinarians do expect making diagnoses, performing surgery, and prescribing medicine. VTs assist veterinarians with client appointments, client education, and management of the practice. They work as medical and surgical animal nurses, animal physical therapists, animal dental hygienists (cleaning teeth), and diagnostic laboratory technicians (working with laboratory specimens). In laboratory animal medicine, VTs do experimental procedures, keep records, analyze data, write reports, and take care of animals. In the pet food industry, VTs work in sales, marketing, and research.

As a veterinary technology major, you would probably earn a two-year associate degree in applied science. Introduction to veterinary technology courses usually cover office procedures, vocational opportunities, regulatory issues, and client communication. In addition to other core courses, most programs require general education courses, in English, applied mathematics (algebra, statistics), social science, humanities, and biological science (microbiology). To be successful in this career, you need to do well in science. You should also develop computer and communication skills, as well as critical-thinking skills, such as patient assessment, and decision-making abilities.

In all programs, you must work as a student intern/extern for a minimum of 240 hours at specific types of veterinary sites. This experience allows you to explore various vocational opportunities (such as jobs in companion animal and large-animal care, and in biomedical research) and to develop the skills you learned during your early training. In your intern/externship, you are also exposed to specialized clinical areas such as cardiology, emergency medicine, and exotic animals.

Veterinary technology programs are career-oriented; if you complete the curriculum, you should be ready to work in a veterinary facility. Most programs incorporate traditional lecture format, computer self-study, guest speakers, "wet labs" (for hands-on work such as dentistry), and scheduled and open laboratory time. You also have opportunities to work with a variety of species and are usually responsible for caring for the animals housed on campus.

Programs accredited by the American Veterinary Medical Association Committee on Veterinary Technician Education and Activities (AVMA CVTEA) have a required content, to ensure that you are properly prepared for a career. But programs may vary. Some provide additional instruction in laboratory animal science and medicine, clinical diagnostic techniques, or large-animal or exotic species care. Programs may incorporate distance learning or online training into their curriculum or vary their scheduling (offering day and/or night courses). Some programs prepare you to become a veterinary assistant (VA); but take note that VAs do *not* receive an equivalent form of training as VTs.

Other majors you might like:
Biology
Animal sciences
Wildlife and wilderness management
Animal breeding
Equestrian studies
Dairy science
Zoology
Genetic
Biotechnology
Wildlife biology

Questions to ask colleges:
Is the program accredited by the American Veterinary Medical Association (AVMA)?

How many courses provide hands-on experience with animals, and which species of animals will students work with?

What kind of veterinary sites are offered to students for their externship experience, and where are they located?

Career options and trends:
Many states provide licensure for veterinary technicians. The terminology will vary (certified, registered, licensed), as will the requirements. Most states require that you graduate from an accredited program and pass the National Veterinary Technician Board Examination.

Job prospects in this field are excellent, as there is currently a shortage of formally trained veterinary technicians, and demand is projected to increase in all veterinary practice areas and industrial fields.

Some of the areas in which graduates find job opportunities are small-animal and large-animal veterinary clinics; companion animal practice; pet food and pharmaceutical companies (technical research assistance or sales); laboratory animal research; animal diagnostic laboratories; zoos and wildlife centers; wildlife rehabilitation; and government regulatory agencies. Research and academic institutions usually require a bachelor's degree.

For more info:
National Association of Veterinary Technicians in America (NAVTA)
P.O. Box 224
Battle Ground, IN 47920
(765) 742-2216
www.navta.net

Humanities

In the humanities, it's not so much *what* you know as *how* you know it. In these liberal arts majors, you'll learn how to learn by honing skills in research, reading, writing, and thinking.

"Liberal arts is a major for students who enjoy learning, who want to spend their college time getting an education and exploring new ideas, rather than strictly preparing for a specific career," says Professor Joseph Ugoretz, Manhattan Community College.

What are the humanities? You could write a whole term paper on that question. They cover history, philosophy, comparative literature, the classics, linguistics, and many other subjects, including the liberal arts. Perhaps in keeping with the spirit of these studies, their exact definition is open to interpretation.

When you search for colleges offering humanities majors, look for schools and divisions of arts and sciences, arts and letters, liberal arts, general studies, literature, science, and social sciences. Other sections in this book include related majors in Languages, English language and literature, Social sciences, and Religion and theology.

By now you may be worried that studying the humanities is like trying to nail Jell-O to the wall. But it's not. The fact is that more associate degrees are awarded in the humanities than any other major by far. And a college degree is something you really *can* hang on the wall!

It turns out that the humanities provide a wealth of understanding that can transfer to many other studies and careers. Liberal arts majors are able to "take advantage of openings in the job market that may be closed to others who are less broadly prepared," Ugoretz points out.

Many humanities students go on to advanced degrees and pursue careers in law, medicine, business, and teaching. History and the classics are two majors that often lead to a Master of Arts in Teaching degree.

Cross training for the mind

Some humanities, such as liberal arts, allow students to find themselves academically. (Examples of new liberal arts programs include multimedia design and writing for the Internet.) Other humanities majors are specialized. Linguistics, which teaches us how language works, is also a good place to sharpen your computer programming skills. "Linguistic training is excellent preparation for employment in high-tech industry, particularly when combined with computer science or information science training," says Professor D. Terence Langendoen of the University of Arizona, Tucson. The humanities sometimes merge with each other and with other fields to create new areas of thought. For example, philosophy and computer science together give rise to the study of artificial intelligence. Linguistics and philosophy combine to become cognitive sciences. Whew! You won't find gut courses here.

Even though the humanities cover a lot of ground, colleges pretty much take the same approach to these majors. That means if you transfer from one college to another, your humanities credits will likely be accepted. But check to make sure the credits from your first college will go toward your degree at the second one, especially if you transfer from a two-year to a four-year college.

When choosing a college, always consider the faculty factor. Who teaches the undergrad classes? Is it the regular faculty (that's who you want) or graduate students (who may be less able to inspire you)?

"The best way to find out about a particular department's undergraduate curriculum is to talk to a current student, a recent graduate, or one of the faculty members," says Professor Richard T. Lee of Trinity College. "Even an e-mail correspondence with a faculty member will give the student some feel for the program."

Another issue: Does the major you want have its own department? That's a sure sign it's an important curriculum at the college. Also ask about class size. Will you have the opportunity to take small classes and seminars with fewer than 20 students?

Essential to these majors are the college's library, archives, and databases, to give you access to the storehouse of knowledge that the humanities encompass.

You may want the freedom to explore other subjects and courses, so find out how many electives you can take. If it's a big university, can you take courses at other colleges in the university system? If it's a small college, are any of the top profs planning a leave of absence or sabbatical during the time you plan to attend?

Speaking of leave of absence, you may want one yourself. To strengthen skills and enhance experience, humanities majors often take time to study abroad. See if the college has a strong program.

In a world that's changing rapidly, nobody knows exactly what skills and knowledge will be needed down the road. The humanities provide a kind of cross training for the mind that can prepare you for more specialized studies and career development later. Knowing how to know may be one of the most sought-after abilities in the workplace of the future.

Classics

Also known as:
Greek and Latin

What it's about:
Classics is the study of the language, literature, and civilization of the ancient Greco-Roman world, including both ancient Greek and Latin. Course work usually involves reading classical texts in these two languages (with discussion in English); but in some programs, the readings may be in English translation.

Is this for you?
You might like this major if you also like: the History Channel; archaeology; languages; debate; computer programming; music; theater.

Consider this major if you are good at: attention to detail; creativity; critical reading/thinking; memorizing; organizing; research *...or have...* initiative; linguistic ability; patience; verbal skills.

Recommended high school prep:
English 4, math 3, lab science 3, social studies 4, and a foreign language 4. If possible, take Latin. French, Italian, and German are also useful.

Did you know...
...that classics can appeal to both "techie" students and "fuzzy" students (those who like art, literature, and philosophy)? To master Latin and Greek, you develop the same kind of mental discipline that is typical of physicists or computer programmers. Some computer companies, in fact, hire classicists because they, like programmers, insist on obeying the language rules. Classicists even distinguished themselves as code breakers in World War II.

...that classics is a leader in the use of computer technology in the humanities? Because the discipline is based on intensive study of a set of texts, databases were developed to help classicists analyze these works. These databases are now part of the regular research tools for students and professionals.

Typical courses in this major:
Elementary Greek
Intermediate Greek (Plato, Homer)
Elementary Latin
Intermediate Latin (Caesar, Ovid)
Ancient philosophy
Classical art and archaeology
Greek and Roman civilization
Attic Greek
Classical mythology
Tragedy and comedy
Elegiac poetry
Lyric poetry
Epic and lyric: Virgil and Horace
Livy and Tacitus
Herodotus

Concentrations:
In college: classics and philosophy; classics and archaeology; classics and religion; classics and ancient history; classics and art.

If you go on to grad school: Greek literature (in ancient Greek); Latin literature (in Latin); Latin teacher education.

What the study of this major is like:
"Classics" refers to the literature of the ancient Greeks and Romans. Its themes, forms, and images have inspired generations of readers and writers. In the classics major, you learn Latin, Greek, or both and, in the process, learn about language itself. You explore different methods of interpreting literature—methods that consider audience, context, transmission of the text, and modern theory. You also gain practice in distinguishing between reliable and unreliable sources and in using evidence to understand others' arguments and to create your own. These skills are useful in any career.

You will almost certainly study the oldest surviving classical text (and one of the oldest texts of Western literature): Homer's *Iliad.* Homer probably composed this epic in the ninth century B.C., but he incorporated songs and themes from far earlier times. Homer reveals a society just beginning to develop the intellectual, cultural, and political life of the Greek city-state.

You are introduced to the more lyrical works of later Greek poets, such as Sappho and Pindar. Aeschylus, Sophocles, and Euripides created tragedies, and Aristophanes wrote comedies for democratic Athens. Their plays are still powerful, beautiful, and funny. The works of other Greek writers—Herodotus, Thucydides, Plato, Aristotle, and Demosthenes—were devoted to history, philosophy, rhetoric, and literary theory. As a classics major, you'll consider the questions about human existence, knowledge, politics, ethics, and beauty that these writers asked and that still interest us today.

Latin literature begins with the lively comedies of Plautus in the third century B.C., when Rome was already a great power. Your reading of Latin works includes the comedies of Terence, the philosophical poetry of Lucretius, the love poetry of Catullus, Caesar's accounts of his conquest of Gaul (roughly, modern France), and the orations of Cicero; these works all are part of the turbulent culture of the late Roman Republic.

In the early years of the empire founded by Augustus in 29 B.C., the great Latin writers flourished: the poets Virgil, Horace, and Ovid; the satirist and poet Juvenal; the historians Livy and Tacitus; and the statesman and playwright Seneca. In addition to their works (and despite Horace's conviction that poetry is the most enduring of all monuments), you'll examine the practical Roman creations: architectural and civil engineering works, legal codes, and principles of governing. Like the literature, these achievements have shaped Western society.

In classics departments, classes are often small, so you should have regular contact with faculty members. Individual professors may offer different approaches. Some might emphasize the learning of the languages, whereas others may stress literary interpretation or the analysis of the social and intellectual contexts of the written works. It's helpful to have both sides represented in a department.

Although students often expect classics majors to be stuffy and conservative, most of them aren't. Qualities typical of classics majors are intellectual curiosity about the ancient world, a willingness to accept the challenge of learning no-longer-spoken languages, and an urge to do something unconventional. Most classics majors take their academic work (but not necessarily themselves) seriously; learning Greek and Latin can be difficult. You will probably spend most of your time working alone, although students occasionally work together outside class—for example, upper-level students sometimes tutor lower-level students. Indeed, majors tend to have a shared feeling of enthusiasm and commitment. Beyond acting as curators of a great literary tradition, they discover new meaning in the works of the ancient Greeks and Romans, so that the classic texts remain alive and relevant.

Other majors you might like:
Comparative literature
Medieval and Renaissance studies
History
Philosophy
Archaeology
Linguistics
Liberal arts and sciences
Judaic studies
Ancient studies
Ancient Near Eastern/Biblical languages
Architectural history and criticism
Speech/rhetorical studies

Questions to ask colleges:
Do students have access to databases such as the *Thesaurus Linguae Graecae* and the L'Année philologique Web site?

Career options and trends:
A recent survey of business recruitment officers shows that employers appreciate the intellectual stamina, communication and analytical skills, ability to handle complex information, and broad perspective that Classics majors bring to the

workplace. Classics majors pursue careers in law, medicine, journalism, education, finance and banking, marketing, management, government, computer programming, publishing, speechwriting, TV production, and the ministry.

Since the 1990s, Latin-class enrollments have increased by well over 50 percent, and so has the demand for high school Latin teachers.

Insider's viewpoint:

"What most appeals to me is the intellectual challenge of tackling a text written in a complicated, long-dead language, and the thrill of discovery in decoding it. Every time I meet with my Greek and Latin students it is to unravel something that was written over two thousand years ago."

—Professor Kenneth S. Rothwell Jr., University of Massachusetts Boston

For more info:

American Philological Association (APA)
292 Logan Hall, University of Pennsylvania
249 S. 36th St.
Philadelphia, PA 19104-6304
(215) 898-4975
www.apaclassics.org/

National Committee for Latin and Greek (NCLG)
www.promotelatin.org

American Classical League (ACL)
Miami University
Oxford, OH 45056
(513) 529-7741
www.aclclassics.org/

Comparative literature

What it's about:

As a comparative literature major, you study the literature of different countries, cultures, and languages. You explore poetry, prose, and drama and consider the relation of literature to other arts and other fields of study. The major requires you to study at least two bodies of literature (one of which may be English) in their original languages.

Is this for you?

You might like this major if you also like: travel; literature; art; foreign languages; different cultures; debating; philosophy.

Consider this major if you are good at: active listening; attention to detail; creativity; critical reading/thinking; research ...*or have...* initiative; linguistic ability; verbal skills; writing skills.

Recommended high school prep:

English 4, math 3, lab science 3, social studies 4, and a foreign language 4 (one language). If possible, take a year of world literature and all available world history courses.

Typical courses in this major:

Great books of Western culture
Medieval epic
Tragedy
Romanticism
Baroque and Neoclassicism
Proust, Mann, and Joyce
History and the novel
The novel of the self
Myths and legends
Literature of China and Japan
Literature of the Americas
Gender and interpretation
Narrative technique

Concentrations:

Literature of a particular nation or culture.

What the study of this major is like:

Comparative literature majors study subjects that cross national, historical, and language boundaries. Topics include literary movements (for example, Romanticism), literary periods (the Renaissance), literary forms (the novel), literary issues (the treatment of science and technology), and literary theory and criticism. You'll study at least two bodies of literature (American students usually choose English or American literature as one of the fields) and at least one foreign language.

Then you'll focus on comparisons and contrasts between the two cultures and their literature. You may also explore the connections between literature and other artistic fields, such as painting, photography, film, or sculpture, or between literature and other academic areas, such as anthropology, psychology, or history. The field is strongly interdisciplinary, and the possibilities for comparative study are nearly endless. And if you'd enjoy reading works of literature from as many societies as you can, this is the major for you.

Most programs require one or more courses that introduce you to comparative analysis and to new approaches to reading. You may focus on the text alone; or on the society and the times in which it was written; or on the link between the text, its author, and its readers. Which traditions did an author draw upon? What influences can be seen underlying a poem, play, or novel?

In advanced courses you may read works in the language in which they were written. Most colleges offer the study of English, French, Spanish, German, Latin, and Greek language and literature; others offer Russian, Japanese, Chinese, Arabic, Polish, or others. Because you study these bodies of literature in their own language departments, you come across a variety of critical approaches. Many programs also require a capstone project—such as researching and writing a fourth-year thesis.

Comparative literature departments and classes are usually small, and tend to identify with a particular literary theory, interpretative tradition, and attitude toward language study. The major requires a lot of reading and writing, sometimes in a foreign language. Also, you should be ready, willing, and able to see the world from a perspective that differs from the one you are familiar with. Therefore, study abroad can be an exciting and important part of your college work. By graduation, most students have developed a powerful connection to at least one other culture—its literature, art, and unique view of life.

Other majors you might like:

Anthropology
Medieval and Renaissance studies
Area, ethnic, and gender studies
Linguistics
English
Philosophy
Film/cinema studies
Global studies
Art history
International business
Creative writing
Religious studies

Questions to ask colleges:

Are the professors full-time comparative literature faculty members or are they borrowed from other departments?

Is a senior thesis required? If so, do students receive help from comparative literature faculty members?

Does the department have a club for majors? Do majors help plan events (such as speakers and readings)?

Career options and trends:

Comparative literature majors pursue jobs in journalism, business, cultural institutions, education, publishing, law, government, radio, television, and film. Graduate or professional school is also a popular option. Prospects are best for majors who have mastered another language.

Insider's viewpoint:

"In comparative literature the implicit nationalism of most programs of literary study is rare. Comparatists like to ride the fence, so to speak, which means that you have an investment in more than one place."

—Professor Tobin Siebers, University of Michigan

For more info:

American Comparative Literature Association (ACLA)
University of Texas
1 University Station B5003
Austin, TX 78712-0196
(512) 471-8020
www.acla.org

History

What it's about:

History is the study of the record of past human experience. Working with written, oral, visual, and artifacts, history majors examine the causes, contexts, and chronologies of historical events to understand how human experiences have both remained the same and changed over time.

Is this for you?

You might like this major if you also like: reenactments; the History Channel; model building; museums; historical novels; collecting stamps, coins, etc.; other cultures and other times; genealogy and family history.

Consider this major if you are good at: attention to detail; critical reading/thinking; organizing; persuading/influencing; research *...or have...* curiosity; initiative; patience; verbal skills; writing skills.

Recommended high school prep:

English 4, math 3, lab science 3, social studies 4, and a foreign language 4. If possible, take a year of both European and American history. One year of civics or government would also be beneficial.

Did you know...

...that the study of history is not confined to just books and documents? For example, to research the history of the blues, you might include such sources as posters, music recordings, photographs, oral histories, newspaper clippings, and business contracts.

Typical courses in this major:

Survey of European history
Western civilization
Ancient Greece
Tudor and Stuart England
Precolonial Africa
U.S. constitutional history
Modern Latin America
Renaissance and Reformation
French Revolution
East Asian civilization
Ancient Rome
Modern England
American history
U.S. economic history
Medieval history
Historical research

Concentrations:

Geographical regions (for example, European civilization, Russian history); time periods (medieval and early modern studies); themes (law and society, environmental history).

What the study of this major is like:

As a history major, you examine the causes, contexts, and narratives of past events. Historians now study a wide range of subjects, but most historians work with either political or social history. Although historians employ their own methods, they also make use of those of many other disciplines. Some "studies" majors include history; for instance, American studies generally has a literary or historical emphasis, whereas Russian/Slavic studies tends to focus on political science or international relations.

Courses usually focus on time periods, nations, geographic areas, historical perspectives, and themes, often in combination (for example, civil rights in the United States, or women in nineteenth-century Europe). Your course work helps you to understand the purposes, principles, and methods of the study of history, and to grasp both the particulars and the universals of societies past and present. You also explore questions of judgment and interpretation.

There are prerequisites for advanced work, but you do not necessarily have to take courses in a fixed, chronological order. You devise a program that meets your interests and also fulfills requirements found in most colleges: one or two introductory courses, one or more courses that acquaint you with cultures and histories other than your own, a course in historical methods, and a research seminar.

Some programs offer an introductory course that teaches the basics of history while featuring a particular topic, such as immigration in American history. Other lower-level courses may cover the history of Europe, the United States, and, perhaps, the non-Western world. Upper-level courses are usually seminars in areas you find most interesting. There is generally a capstone course that may explore great historical writing, the different genres of the subject, or the construction of chronologies from the raw materials of human experience.

As a major, you read extensively and develop writing skills through essay exams, book reviews, and research papers (you must become familiar with computer-aided research, especially if your research project has a social science focus). Because history majors often do archival research and interviewing, and your classes rely on lectures and discussion, you'll need to sharpen your listening and speaking skills.

The main challenge you will face as a major is to find source material for your research studies. At first, you'll interpret documents presented to you. Eventually, though, you must choose a question you want to answer (such as, what was the route of the Underground Railroad?) and then decide how to locate the books and other sources that will help you come up with an answer. With the encouragement of instructors and others in the field, you should quickly become an independent historian.

Other majors you might like:
Classics
Medieval and Renaissance studies
European studies
Asian studies
Art history
Anthropology
International relations
Political science
Archaeology
African-American studies

Public history/archives
Journalism

Questions to ask colleges:
Is the curriculum heavily focused on European and American history, or are there courses on the non-Atlantic world?

What are the library's strengths and weaknesses? Which journals does the library subscribe to and which archives (if any) does it control? Does the library make online databases available and offer online access to journals?

What kinds of connections does the department have with local historical societies, museums, historical sites, or the history departments of other colleges in the area?

Career options and trends:
College professor; high school teacher*; lawyer; museum curator or archivist*; journalist.

History majors learn how to locate, synthesize, and present information—valuable training for almost any career. Graduate and professional schools also value the education history majors receive. Few majors actually become historians—and college level teaching positions are extremely competitive—but employment options are many and varied, including government service, business, teaching in elementary and secondary schools, law, medicine, and other professions.

Insider's viewpoint:
"I used to read every book I could get my hands on about the Holocaust, about sixteenth-century France. If you think about it, every novel you read, if it's not set in the present, is a historical novel. Studying history is an extension of that love of literature; it's like watching a very long movie."

—Emily, sophomore, Northwestern University

For more info:
American Historical Association (AHA)
400 A St., S.E.
Washington, DC 20003-3889
(202) 544-2422
www.historians.org

Liberal arts and sciences

What it's about:

The liberal arts and sciences major provides you with a well-rounded education in the sciences, humanities, mathematics, and languages. You gain the ability to reason critically, communicate effectively, and understand relationships across broad fields of knowledge. This generalist background prepares you for a wide range of endeavors rather than for a specific career.

Is this for you?

You might like this major if you also like: reading; writing; discussing new ideas; arguing; reasoning.

Consider this major if you are good at: creativity; critical reading/thinking; persuading/influencing; quantitative analysis; teamwork *...or have...* initiative; patience; verbal skills; writing skills.

Recommended high school prep:

English 4, math 3, lab science 3, social studies 3, art 1, and a foreign language 3.

Did you know...

...that liberal arts and sciences is not just another term for "undecided"? Choosing this major is a decision to prepare for a world in which new and unexpected careers are invented every day.

Typical courses in this major:

English literature
Biological concepts
Environmental science
American history since 1865
World religions
Philosophy
Psychology
Sociology
Fundamentals of economics
Cultural anthropology
Philosophy
Probability and statistics
Foreign language I, II
Communications
Music history
Art history

Concentrations:

A wide range is available; among them are gender studies, multicultural studies, social sciences, literature and linguistics, natural sciences.

What the study of this major is like:

If you enjoy learning and want to spend your college years exploring new ideas rather than preparing for a specific career, you might consider majoring in liberal arts. The liberal arts program is typically offered only as an undergraduate major. Most liberal arts courses include a great deal of reading, writing, and discussion, and classes tend to be small.

As a liberal arts major, you will be required to study a wide range of subjects, some of which may be new to you or may be in areas in which you have not excelled in the past. Even though you might prefer studying literature, you will have to take classes in history and mathematics. Science lovers will have to take classes in poetry and music.

Most liberal arts programs have a required "core"—meaning you must take at least an introductory course in each of certain designated areas (although you usually have a choice of courses in each area). The areas include the fine arts (such as art history, music, drama); social sciences (economics, sociology, history); natural sciences (chemistry, biology); mathematics; humanities (literature, philosophy); and a foreign language. Some programs also require a semester of study abroad, or some other cross-cultural experience.

In addition to a core of required courses, you will likely be offered a wide range of electives from a wide range of subjects. You might find this freedom to choose very liberating; or you might find it confusing or intimidating. In either case, you would be wise to ask your academic adviser for help in designing a course of study that is relevant to your talents and interests.

Because the liberal arts program includes basic college subjects, you will meet students from many disciplines and be exposed to the perspectives of many academic areas. For the liberal arts major, college is an opportunity to discover and refine goals rather than to work single-mindedly on a predetermined regimen. This major allows you to be flexible with your schedule and to follow specific interests over several semesters in various related courses. Although your reading and writing assignments tend to be heavy, the variety of the subject matter keeps your work fresh and interesting. You will have opportunities to see connections between different subjects and to broaden and deepen your learning.

As a survey of college subjects, the major tends not to vary much, in emphases, requirements, and philosophies, from one college to another. The similarity will come in handy if you should want to transfer to another institution. At the two-year or community college level, students intending to continue on to a four-year college usually prefer this major. Generally, most of your liberal arts credits will be accepted at other colleges, and you will be well prepared for upper-level courses.

Other majors you might like:
Humanities
Journalism
English
American studies
Mathematics
Natural sciences
Communications
Global studies
Environmental studies
Women's studies
Classics
Philosophy

Questions to ask colleges:
Is this major housed in its own department, or is it pulled together from different departments?

How easy is it to transfer to other majors?

Are students eligible to take classes at other colleges while they are enrolled in the program? Is there a study-abroad program?

Career options and trends:
Teacher*; lawyer*; doctor; journalist*; filmmaker.

Career paths for liberal arts and science majors are wide open: they include journalism, teaching, business and industry, sales, social work, government, film, entrepreneurship—almost any area of human endeavor. The major is also an excellent foundation for an advanced or professional degree leading to careers in law, medicine, engineering, or teaching.

For liberal arts majors, the job outlook is positive, even in difficult times. Because the curriculum is flexible in terms of career preparation, graduates can take advantage of openings in the job market (including jobs that don't even exist yet) that may be closed to others who are less broadly prepared.

For more info:
American Academy for Liberal Education
1050 17th St., N.W.
Suite 400
Washington, DC 20036
(202) 452-8611
www.aale.org

Linguistics

What it's about:

As a linguistics major, you learn what makes human languages special: how they are spoken, written, and understood. You'll also examine many of the world's languages—how they are related and how they have changed over time—as well as methods of analyzing languages for their characteristic and distinctive properties.

Is this for you?

You might like this major if you also like: learning new languages; traveling; exploring other cultures; your own heritage culture; crossword puzzles and word games like Scrabble; figuring out where people come from by their accent; word origins.

Consider this major if you are good at: active listening; attention to detail; creativity; critical reading/thinking; organizing; research ...*or have...* initiative; patience; verbal skills.

Recommended high school prep:

English 4, math 3, lab science 3, social studies 3, and a foreign language 4. It may be helpful to divide your foreign language studies between two languages. If possible, take a year of computer programming.

Did you know...

...that there are more than 5,000 languages spoken in the world today and that many of them are threatened with extinction before the end of this century? Linguists are leading the efforts to document these languages and to help their speakers preserve them, in written and oral form, for future generations.

...that linguistic training is excellent preparation for employment in high-tech industry, particularly when combined with training in computer science or information science? Linguistics also prepares you for further study in any area in which knowledge of how language works is useful.

Typical courses in this major:

Introduction to linguistics
Phonetics
Phonology
Syntax
Semantics
Morphology
Dialectology
Languages of the world
Language and mind
Language and society
Historical linguistics
Writing systems
Structure of a particular language
Psycholinguistics

Concentrations:

In college: a language or group of languages, e.g., Germanic languages (such as English, German, Dutch); Romance languages (Spanish, Portuguese, French, Italian); Semitic languages; or East Asian languages. However, few undergraduate linguistics programs are large enough to support concentrations.

If you go on to grad school: phonetics/phonology; morphology/syntax; semantics; typology; psycholinguistics; sociolinguistics; computational linguistics; historical linguistics; structure of a language or group of languages.

What the study of this major is like:

Linguistics focuses on the similarities among the world's languages, as well as on the unique characteristics of individual languages, in order to understand those traits and the people who speak the languages. The major usually begins with an introductory course, followed by courses in phonetics and phonology (the study of speech sounds), morphology (the structure and function of words), syntax (the way words combine to form phrases or sentences), and semantics (meaning and use of words).

In addition, the major may include the study of specific languages, or families of languages, and the communities or societies that speak them. You might undertake comparative and historical studies of both well-known and little known languages and dialects. You might explore how children acquire language; how people produce and comprehend written, spoken, and signed language; how language disorders are diagnosed and treated; how languages can be taught most effectively; how the use of particular languages and dialects has been fostered (or discouraged) by government policy; and how computers can be programmed to recognize and produce language.

Most students find linguistics intellectually challenging—in a word, hard. In introductory courses, you will most likely be given samples from languages you don't know and be asked to describe the languages. Once you get the hang of it, you will probably enjoy such exercises and be ready for the next stage of training, in which you'll explore linguistic theories and their explanation of observed data. At first, this approach may be frustrating, because you won't understand how the theories work. But once you feel comfortable doing a linguistic experiment, you might begin a project for an advanced course or an undergraduate thesis. You may, in fact, find yourself working on cutting-edge studies while still an undergraduate.

There are two major approaches to the study of human language: formal and functional. Formal study emphasizes the structure of languages and requires good data-handling and reasoning skills. Functional study emphasizes the use of language and may involve laboratory or field research and statistics. Most linguistics programs stress one or the other of these approaches. A few (mostly larger) departments combine them successfully.

Other majors you might like:
Native American studies
Anthropology
Classics
Speech/rhetorical studies
Communications
Computer science
Foreign language teacher education
Language interpretation/translation

Philosophy
Psychology
Communication disorders
American Sign Language (ASL)

Questions to ask colleges:
Is the major offered by a linguistics department, by another department that includes linguistics, or as an interdisciplinary program? Are courses in the core areas of linguistics (phonology, syntax, semantics) regularly offered?

Is there a strong study-abroad program that enables students to learn a language or strengthen skills in one they already know?

Can students do independent research with a faculty member in linguistics, work in a linguistics lab, or do an industry internship (for example, in computational linguistics) as part of the undergraduate degree?

Career options and trends:
High school language teacher*; college professor*; translator; consultant.

The linguistics major can also prepare you for jobs in international business, government service, public relations, software design, marketing, publishing, advertising, English as a second language (ESL) teaching and research, health-related professions (speech pathology and language disorders), industrial research and development (speech recognition, text analysis and interpretation, electronic dictionary preparation, artificial intelligence, and speech synthesis), and law. Some of these fields require graduate study.

Linguists are playing a prominent role in high-tech industry, primarily in information retrieval and analysis and in speech technology. The bursting of the high-tech bubble a few years ago temporarily restricted career opportunities in these areas, but they are expanding once again because of the ongoing need for improved speech, language, and information technologies. Good language teachers are always needed in the United States and overseas (especially English teachers), as are speech and language therapists.

Philosophy

What it's about:

Philosophy is the study of the fundamental questions about the nature of being, knowledge, right and wrong, and our place in the physical world. You explore the key philosophical texts and traditions, and examine the nature of argument and reasoning. You'll also consider the ways philosophy affects other fields of inquiry, such as physics, religion, and computer science.

Is this for you?

You might like this major if you also like: puzzles and games; thinking about what life is about; debate and argument; science fiction or other imaginative literature; thinking differently from the way other people do.

Consider this major if you are good at: attention to detail; creativity; critical reading/thinking; organizing *...or have...* patience; verbal skills; writing skills.

Recommended high school prep:

English 4, math 3, lab science 3, social studies 4, and a foreign language 3-4. If possible, take a course in philosophy or a humanities course that includes philosophical works. Any course that requires a lot of reading will also be beneficial.

Did you know...

...that it is a rare and valuable ability to know what an argument is? Employers are often grateful to find someone who can write clear prose and think logically.

Typical courses in this major:

Problems of philosophy
History of philosophy
Ethics
Political theory
Logic
Epistemology
Philosophy of religion

Aristotle
Kant
Aesthetics
Metaphysics
Theory of knowledge
Philosophy of science
Plato
Locke
Hegel

Concentrations:

In college: history of philosophy; ethics; logic.

If you go on to grad school: epistemology; metaphysics.

What the study of this major is like:

Philosophy majors participate in a tradition of thought as old as civilization and as new as artificial intelligence. Philosophy is the most general field of study. Every religious or moral belief, every detail from science—even ordinary information—can be viewed as subject matter. Philosophy majors are encouraged to contemplate the universe, both human and nonhuman. At the same time, they are trained to become disciplined, imaginative thinkers who can persuasively support their positions.

Many questions that philosophers ask are often asked by children: How did the world begin? Do animals have their own language? Could I be someone else? Part of the fascination of philosophy is that it can reveal the complexity and subtlety of simple matters. On the other hand, philosophy tries to expose the muddled thinking we read and hear every day.

Beginning courses in philosophy are designed for students with little background, because few high schools teach philosophy. Most college programs have introductory courses in philosophical problems, which may include such topics as ethics (moral conduct), metaphysics (the nature of reality), logic, epistemology (the study of knowledge), and aesthetics (the nature of art). Another introductory course surveys the history of philosophy beginning with the Greeks, and usually takes one or two years to complete.

As you progress through the major, you will read works by Plato, Aristotle, Aquinas, Descartes, Hume, Kant, Hegel, Wittgenstein, John Dewey, and other important writers on such issues as the nature of consciousness, "truth," and social justice. Increasingly, though, you will be expected to think from a philosophical perspective on your own. A substantial paper or thesis is usually required in your senior year.

Philosophy can present you with ideas that may at first seem overly abstract, incomprehensible, or pure fantasy. You may also have trouble seeing the connection between the philosophical concepts you study and the issues that matter in your daily life. In addition, philosophy courses seldom begin with easy material and then progress to the more difficult. Philosophers circle back on questions again and again. When studying philosophy, you can expect to progress from confusion to some clarity, but not from one small but clear concept to another well-defined concept. This situation frustrates some students and excites others.

Most philosophy departments at large universities are strong in certain areas of philosophy, such as ethics and moral philosophy, philosophy of language, history of philosophy, or political philosophy. Some departments focus on the sciences, some on the humanities, and a few take a religious approach. Departments at colleges that do not have graduate programs tend not to be specialized. Most departments, however, offer undergraduates a full range of courses. You can generally assume that the more professors in the department, the greater the variety of subjects taught.

Other majors you might like:
English
Religious studies
Political science
History
Mathematics
Music, general
Physics
Classics
European studies
Asian studies
Legal studies
Theology

Questions to ask colleges:
Is there an opportunity to take small classes (under 20 students) and seminars? Is there a philosophy club? Do students have any role in the department's activities, such as helping to select outside speakers?

Career options and trends:
Philosophy majors find their training useful in a variety of fields. The analytic skills developed in college are easily transferable to a number of professional areas. Students of philosophy tend to have the flexibility and capacity for growth that employers find valuable. Many graduates accept jobs in business, journalism, computer science, public administration, teaching, publishing, and public relations.

Teaching positions at the college level are very competitive and require a Ph.D.

Insider's viewpoint:
"Philosophy unites living and thinking in a way that few other disciplines do. It is a matter of giving yourself over to a life of questioning and searching, with no holds barred. It rewards honesty, courage, and curiosity. Philosophy at its best is not a way to make a living, but a way to be alive."

—Professor Richard T. Lee, Trinity College

For more info:
The American Philosophical Association (APA)
University of Delaware
31 Amstel Ave.
Newark, DE 19716-4797
(302) 831-1112
www.udel.edu/apa

Languages

People don't realize that the United States has no official language. There's a movement afoot to give English the nod (and English has its own section in this book). But what about the 28 million Americans who speak Spanish at home? Or the 7 million who speak Asian tongues? Knowing more than one language is a valuable skill in business, government, and the nonprofit sectors here and around the world.

"More students would consider language majors if they knew how important proficiency in a foreign language is in the workplace today," says Professor Theresa A. Antes, University of Florida, Gainesville. "Many employers will hire an applicant who is proficient in a foreign language over one who is not."

Language skills are growing in importance because of Internet communications, global business, the integration of the European Union, unrest in the Middle East, and the emergence of China as a participant in international affairs and commerce.

Regarding China, Professor Scott Cook of Grinnell College says, "Students may not realize just how important China is in the world and how many job opportunities a Chinese degree may open up for them."

The significance of Arabic is not in doubt, with the Middle East so prominent in the news. "Knowledge of Arabic is indispensable for a firsthand acquaintance with events in the region," says Professor Michael Fishbein, University of California: Los Angeles.

The world is your oyster (and your ostra, Auster, huître, ostrica) if you master languages. Consider these pearls of opportunity: employment in international relations, diplomacy, intelligence gathering, journalism, law, medicine, tourism, and the arts; jobs as translators/interpreters, Foreign Service specialists, and environmental specialists; and positions in a nongovernmental organization, the computer industry, and international banking and business.

"It used to be assumed that all students pursued a degree in French in order to teach at the high school level, but demands of the global economy have changed that scenario," Antes says.

La Dolce Vita

Studying a language requires much more than memorizing vocabulary and learning grammar rules. And the rewards go beyond career enhancement.

"Learning to speak Italian enables one to combine good employment with fine living," notes Professor Robert E. Proctor, Connecticut College. "There's always something new to discover," he says of Italy.

"Once you take Russia as your focus," observes Professor Melissa Frazier of Sarah Lawrence College, "concepts like 'East' and 'West,' 'Europe' and 'Asia' become more tentative, and your understanding of the world around you much more complicated and also much more interesting."

Japanese is a subject of inexhaustible riches, according to H. Mack Horton, University of California, Berkeley. Sure, Japan is the world's second-largest economy, but he's talking about intellectual enrichment. "The Japanese major is a gold mine for anyone with an abiding curiosity about the human condition," he says.

Just as languages differ, so do college programs. At some colleges, you'll choose between studying the language/linguistics, or the literature/culture, of the countries where the language is spoken. By the way, there are also separate majors called area studies, which emphasize the history, culture, politics, and economics of a region rather than its language and literature. As an example, German (language/literature) is a different major from German studies. It's good if colleges offer both types. (See the chapter on Area, ethnic, and gender studies.)

Many graduate programs combine language studies with studies of other things, such as the arts, political science, religious studies, sociology, and economics. Graduate tracks in literature may concentrate on a particular period—classical or modern—or on a genre, such as poetry or drama. (Some colleges teach literature in translation, so find out if you'll be reading works in the original language.)

Here are some questions to ask: What are the possibilities for study abroad? Are the study-abroad programs offered through the university, so you can be sure credits will be transferred? Are tuition and fees the same as those for courses on campus?

How many faculty members are native speakers? What are their specializations? If you want to learn a particular dialect, make sure a faculty member teaches it. How big are the classes? To master a language, you'll want the chance to speak in class.

In choosing a college, look for facilities that include a library with computers and databases. Are computers set up to access the Web and handle word processing in the language? How good is the library's collection? What about language labs? Does the college receive news and other TV programming in the language?

Will your college experience include social opportunities to meet and converse with others who speak the language in dorms or the cafeteria? Is a community of native speakers nearby? Are activities and lectures offered to promote studies on and off campus?

Resources for more information include the Association for Asian Studies, at www.aasianst.org; Modern Language Association, at www.mla.org; American Council on the Teaching of Foreign Languages, at www.actfl.org; Association of Professional Schools of International Affairs, at www.apsia.org; and National Foreign Affairs Training Center (Foreign Service Institute), at www.state.gov.

This section also covers American Sign Language. For more information about the classics and linguistics majors, turn to the Humanities chapter.

American Sign Language (ASL)

What it's about:

American Sign Language (ASL) is a visual language used by the Deaf community in the United States and Canada. In this major you learn how to sign, and study the literature, grammar, and history of this language and its use among members of the Deaf community in North America.

Is this for you?

You might like this major if you also like: taking risks; interacting with people from different cultures and with different points of view; helping others; breaking down barriers.

Consider this major if you are good at: critical reading/thinking; memorizing; spatial thinking/ analysis ...*or have...* cultural sensitivity; initiative; manual dexterity; patience; physical stamina; verbal skills.

Recommended high school prep:

English 4, math 3, lab science 3, social studies 3, and a foreign language 3–4.

Did you know...

...that ASL is not based on English? Its syntax has more in common with Japanese, and is also completely different from British Sign Language.

...that there are cross-cultural issues you might not be aware of? Deaf Culture is a distinct group that has its own language and customs. Students who hear can sometimes cross invisible cultural lines without realizing it.

Typical courses in this major:

Comparative analysis of ASL and English
ASL literature
ASL classifiers
ASL incorporated numbers and fingerspelling
Introduction to methods of teaching ASL
Introduction to Deaf studies
Deaf Culture
History of the Deaf community
Communication in gestures
Senior thesis/seminar

Concentrations:

In college: ASL teacher education; ASL interpretation.

If you go on to grad school: ASL linguistics; Deaf studies with an emphasis on ASL.

What the study of this major is like:

When you begin learning American Sign Language, you can expect to be fascinated by it. Language acquisition research shows that picking up the basics of ASL shouldn't take you a long time. But although you may at first think that ASL is easy, you will probably realize, soon enough, that mastering the language can be a challenging, sometimes tedious experience.

ASL does not "mime" spoken English and is not structured like English at all. ASL has its own rules for the creation of words, phonetics, and grammar quite unlike those for spoken languages. ASL also involves more than hand gestures—facial movements are also part of the grammatical structure, and meaning is also derived from the signer's use of the surrounding space.

You may also have difficulty communicating with Deaf people because they sign quickly; for many, ASL is their native language. And after you become proficient in ASL, you may still feel stalled in your ability to interact with members of the Deaf community. But if you persevere and don't let yourself be discouraged by the frustrations of being unable to understand them at times and of occasionally being rejected, you will eventually qualify as a skilled interpreter.

Some colleges offer courses in Signed English, in the belief that this form of communication can enhance Deaf children's English literacy skills. This practice is not widely accepted in the Deaf community, however.

If you think you may want to become an ASL teacher, keep in mind that while this is not impossible, such training is intended, primarily, for Deaf students. ASL-trained people who hear can more easily find jobs as general teachers of the Deaf, ASL interpreters, or counselors.

Other majors you might like:
Communication disorders
Education of Deaf/hearing impaired
Special education
Audiology/hearing sciences
Linguistics
Sign language interpretation
Anthropology
Human services
Foreign languages/literatures
Audiology/speech pathology
Child development

Questions to ask colleges:
Are there Deaf teachers? Are there adequate ASL labs?

Does the program provide interaction with the local Deaf community? Is there group support for students who are new to Deaf Culture and may experience culture shock?

Career options and trends:
ASL interpreter; high school teacher; ASL specialist.

The American Sign Language Teachers Association offers three levels of certification: Provisional, Qualified, and Professional. ASL interpreters earn certifications from the Registry of Interpreters for the Deaf or from the National Association of the Deaf.

Legislators have recently passed laws that incorporate ASL into foreign language curriculums. The change in status is increasing the demand for ASL high school teachers all over the United States.

In metropolitan areas, the job market for ASL interpreting is both very hot and very competitive. The hourly rates are excellent, but freelance interpreters receive no fringe benefits, such as health insurance, retirement, pensions, or workers' compensation.

Insider's viewpoint:
"I enjoy watching my students acquiring the language. They appear to be intimidated on the first day of classes but by the end, they are animated with the use of their faces, hands, and bodies when they communicate."

—Professor Mike Kemp, Gallaudet University

For more info:
American Sign Language Teachers Association (ASLTA)
P.O. Box 92445
Rochester, NY 14692-9998
www.aslta.org

National Association of the Deaf (NAD)
8630 Fenton St.
Suite 820
Silver Spring, MD 20910
(301) 587-1788
www.nad.org

Arabic

What it's about:

Arabic majors learn to understand, read, and speak Modern Standard Arabic; read and analyze the key works of classical and modern Arabic literature; and study Islam and Middle Eastern history.

Is this for you?

You might like this major if you also like: learning languages; Arabic and Islamic culture; history; travel; religious issues and thought.

Consider this major if you are good at: attention to detail; critical reading/thinking; memorizing; organizing; research *...or have...* linguistic ability; patience; verbal skills; writing skills.

Recommended high school prep:

English 4, math 3, lab science 3, social studies 4, and a foreign language 3–4. If possible, take Arabic. Otherwise, take another language with a case system (where nouns and adjectives are inflected depending upon the grammar of the sentence), such as German, Russian, or Latin. World history, comparative religion, and literature courses are also helpful.

Did you know...

...that Arabic is the classical language of Islamic civilization and is the language preferred for religious expression by Muslims everywhere, whether or not their native language is Arabic? Much of classical Arabic literature also covers history, biography, travel literature, poetry, and philosophy from a non-religious perspective.

Typical courses in this major:

Literary Arabic
Islamic texts
Classical Arabic texts
Philosophical and Kalam texts
Modern Arabic literature
Arabic media
Shi'ia in Islamic history
Contemporary Islamic thought
History of the Arabs
Spoken Egyptian Arabic
Spoken Moroccan Arabic
Western Islamic art
Survey of the Middle East from 500 to the present
Islamic civilization: premodern Islam
Islamic civilization: Islam and the modern world

Concentrations:

Generally, none in college; but if you go on to grad school: classical Arabic literature; Islamic texts; modern Arabic literature.

What the study of this major is like:

If you major in Arabic, you can expect to devote plenty of time to learning the language. According to the U.S. Foreign Service, Arabic, along with Chinese and Japanese, is among the languages that adults have most trouble learning. Arabic has a complicated phonetic system and grammar, as well as a system of usage that is not even remotely related to English. In addition, the formal Modern Standard Arabic is very different from informal, colloquial Arabic. Students often feel that they are learning two languages at the same time, so be prepared to work hard and to persevere.

To become proficient in listening to, speaking, reading, and writing Arabic, you'll have to study long hours outside class, completing homework assignments, reading and preparing texts for discussion, researching topics for reports and papers, and reviewing. Arabic courses may use videotapes and CDs, in addition to textbooks. You should gain as much exposure to the language as possible; for example, you can use the Web to access Arabic newspapers and radio broadcasts. An exciting development in recent years is the availability of up-to-the-minute journalism in Arabic online.

Undergraduate Arabic courses usually include language, literature, culture, history, and Islamics (the study of the religion). You should plan to spend at least one summer in an Arabic-speaking country, or possibly in a semester- or year-abroad program. Most American institutions have adopted the proficiency method of language teaching. In other words, Arabic is no longer taught purely as a classical language, with stress on grammar and translation. So even if you are interested primarily in modern or classical literature, you'll be expected to learn to pronounce the language correctly and to acquire a reasonable fluency in speaking.

Because only a few students major in Arabic, you'll have more opportunities to receive individual attention from faculty members than you would in most other majors. You will also have ample opportunity to meet other Arabic majors. Friendships often form across cultural borders: for example, between Muslim and Christian students or between students with a Middle Eastern background and those of European or African origin.

Other majors you might like:
Near and Middle Eastern studies
Linguistics
Ancient Near Eastern/Biblical languages
History
Religious studies
Art history
Musicology/ethnomusicology
Political science
Classics
Islamic studies
Judaic studies
International relations

Questions to ask colleges:
Does the program have a special focus? One program may emphasize modern literature, another linguistics, or Islamic thought. Look for a program that will satisfy your own interests.

Is the library committed to keeping the Arabic and Middle Eastern collections up-to-date? Library resources are extremely important for the study of Arabic.

Do computers have access to the Web in Arabic, and can they handle Arabic word processing?

Career options and trends:
College professor*; translator/interpreter*; Foreign Service Officer*; journalist.

Jobs in the U.S. Foreign Service are usually open only to U.S. citizens. To become a FSO, you must pass the Foreign Service Examination.

In the light of recent world events, there has been an increased interest in Arabic. More jobs are available in intelligence, translation, and journalism for people with expertise in Arabic and the Middle East. More universities are establishing Arabic programs and are hiring faculty members in the field. Arabic is obviously required for Islamic clergy, but it is also very useful for Christian clergy serving Eastern Orthodox, Catholic, or Protestant congregations of Arabic ethnic origin.

For more info:
American Association of Teachers of Arabic (AATA)
College of William and Mary
P.O. Box 8795
Williamsburg, VA 23187-8795
(757) 221-3145
www.wm.edu/aata

Middle East Studies Association of North America
University of Arizona
1219 North Santa Rita Ave.
Tuscon, AZ 85721
(520) 621-5850
www.mesana.org

Chinese

What it's about:

The Chinese major prepares you to interact with and understand the modern Chinese world, while introducing you to China's long and rich cultural tradition. It typically combines three to four years of language study (modern Mandarin) with courses in literature, philosophy, history, and other fields.

Is this for you?

You might like this major if you also like: Chinese culture; studying languages; history; travel; different ways of thinking about the world.

Consider this major if you are good at: attention to detail; creativity; critical reading/thinking; memorizing *...or have...* initiative; linguistic ability; patience; persistence; verbal skills; writing skills.

Recommended high school prep:

English 4, math 3, lab science 3, social studies 4, and a foreign language 4. Be sure to take as much foreign language as possible; Chinese is preferable but in no way required. World history courses are also recommended.

Did you know...

...that you don't need to know any Chinese before you begin college? If you have solid study habits, the language, as difficult as it may be, is highly learnable.

Typical courses in this major:

Elementary Chinese
Intermediate Chinese
Advanced Chinese
Advanced classical Chinese
Traditional Chinese literature
Modern Chinese fiction
Modern Chinese film
Modern Chinese theater
Chinese philosophy
Chinese religion
Chinese history
East Asian civilization
Chinese linguistics
Chinese gender and women's studies
Chinese music
Chinese art

Concentrations:

Chinese language; Chinese literature; Chinese calligraphy.

What the study of this major is like:

For English speakers, Chinese is easy to learn, but difficult to master. Once you learn the four tones and basic vocabulary, speaking the language should not be hard, because the grammar is user-friendly.

If you major in Chinese, be ready to immerse yourself in the language. Language courses typically meet five days a week and are often conducted in Chinese only. The classes may consist of alternating grammar and drill sessions. You learn to speak, listen, read, and write Chinese. In your first year or two, greater emphasis is placed on speaking and listening. Most language programs introduce Chinese written characters almost immediately, although some instructors wait until you establish a solid foundation in the spoken language.

By your third year, the emphasis will likely shift, to take in more written materials, such as newspaper articles and fairly simple literature. Your fourth-year courses usually include advanced literature and perhaps a course in classical Chinese. Although classical Chinese is grammatically different from modern Chinese, learning it will increase your understanding of Chinese as a whole. Language courses are supplemented by English-taught courses in literature, philosophy, and history. Such courses typically focus on lecture and discussion and require written papers in English.

As a Chinese major, you should expect a demanding workload, especially in the language courses, although your studies should be enjoyable if you are well prepared. Your greatest challenge will be to get off to a good start—to develop solid study habits and establish a strong foundation for future language study. You should advance quickly in your first year; but in your second year, your progress, though no less real, may be less noticeable. In your second year you focus on memorization and the acquisition of characters and vocabulary, which can be frustrating if you have not mentally prepared yourself for it. After the second year, students generally feel more confident as they begin to gain mastery of the language. For real fluency, you should study in a Chinese-speaking community or country for at least a semester, preferably a year.

The Chinese major may be housed in departments that teach only modern languages, teach East Asian languages and culture, teach East Asian languages and literature, teach comparative literature, teach linguistics, or offer second-language education, including bilingual education. The biggest difference among Chinese programs is the balance between courses in language study and in area studies (for example, the literature, religion, and history of a region). Often, if a program requires only two years of language study but offers a number of courses in area studies, the reason is not a matter of philosophy but rather of necessity. The program may not have enough professors to offer more than two or three years of Chinese. You would then take area studies courses from faculty members in other departments.

Other majors you might like:
Asian studies
Linguistics
Asian-American studies
Comparative literature
Foreign language teacher education
Philosophy
History
Chinese studies
East Asian studies
International relations
East Asian languages
Art history

Questions to ask colleges:
How many years of Chinese are offered on campus? A small liberal arts college that offers three or four years of the language should be considered to have, for its size, a substantial program.

How many other departments offer China-related courses? How many hours a week do language courses meet? A college that offers less than five hours per week at the first- and second-year levels is cutting corners.

How large is the Chinese community on campus? What kinds of activities promote Chinese studies on campus, including guest lecturers, Chinese tables, Chinese houses, or Lunar New Year celebrations?

Career options and trends:
Chinese language teacher*; ESL teacher; Foreign Service Officer; administrator or analyst for an international NGO (nongovermental organization); translator/interpreter; journalist.

An increasing number of Chinese language majors are hired by firms dealing with overseas markets. Various branches of government and international organizations need experts in Chinese languages and culture. The Foreign Service is usually open only to U.S. citizens who pass an exam.

As China prospers economically and grows in political importance, job opportunities related to China continue to increase. However, fluency in Chinese alone may not get you a foot in the door; you also need training in another field—for instance, if you want to do business in China, you should take economics courses, and preferably pursue an MBA degree later on. College faculty positions in Chinese are not easy to come by, so you should not consider seeking a doctorate in Chinese unless you have a deep commitment to the field.

For more info:
Association for Asian Studies (AAS)
1021 East Huron St.
Ann Arbor, MI 48104
(734) 665-2490
www.aasianst.org

French

What it's about:

Majors in French study the language, literature, and culture of France and other areas of the French-speaking world.

Is this for you?

You might like this major if you also like: French culture; studying languages; literature; art; traveling.

Consider this major if you are good at: active listening; attention to detail; critical reading/thinking; memorizing ...*or have...* linguistic ability; perseverance; verbal skills; writing skills.

Recommended high school prep:

English 4, math 3, lab science 3, social studies 4 (including European and world history), and French 4. If possible, also take a second foreign language; Spanish, Italian, and Latin are especially recommended.

Did you know...

...that there are many career opportunities available to French majors besides teaching? In addition to language and literature classes, you can often choose among topics such as French for business, French for medicine, cultural studies, or film studies to expand your options in the global economy.

...that, in many programs, the courses in elementary French are considered prerequisites and do not count toward your major? So if you can, take at least two years of high school French; then you can begin studying at the intermediate level in college.

Typical courses in this major:

French composition
French conversation
French grammar
Stylistics
French literature
French phonetics
Structure of French
French theater
Realism and naturalism
Twentieth-century poetry

Concentrations:

French literature and culture; French language and linguistics; foreign language education.

What the study of this major is like:

As a French major, you study the language, literature, and culture of the people of France and other French-speaking regions. Traditionally, Parisian French (the language spoken in France's capital) and the culture of France have dominated the major. But since World War II, the French major has broadened to include the language and cultures of nations formerly under French control, such as Algeria, the Ivory Coast, Lebanon, and Indochina (now Southeast Asia). The widened perspective reflects the importance of French, which has been an international language (one used in diplomacy and global trade) since the eighteenth century.

Most programs provide a combination of language and literature courses. While you work on fluency and accuracy in language courses, you learn about the culture by studying various French texts. In a series of grammar, composition, and conversation courses, you read, listen to, speak, and write French. In literature courses you may examine the classics: the theater of Molière, Corneille, and Racine; the poetry of the Renaissance; the novels of Flaubert. You may also view films or read newspapers, magazines, and technical reports.

To succeed as a French major, you must be willing to spend a good deal of time outside class memorizing word forms, listening to cassettes, working with multimedia materials, and doing other language-learning activities. In fact, you'll probably spend twice as much time preparing for class as you spend in class. Although many French majors have been exposed to the language before college, you can begin studying French in your first year and start your course work for your major in your third year. Generally, you must complete at least 12 semester-length courses in upper-level French.

Many students learning a foreign language in the United States face the challenge of working in a sort of intellectual vacuum. You're most likely to succeed in the French major if you seek out opportunities to practice the language with native speakers, attend French club meetings, eat dinner at a French table, or even live in a language house.

At many colleges, study abroad is strongly encouraged, in either a summer program or your third year. Many French departments also sponsor film series, lectures, theatrical performances, and informal social gatherings where you can speak and hear French. Keep in mind that you'll usually have to look for such opportunities yourself. Although they are essential for gaining proficiency in French, they are not necessarily required.

If you want to teach French in elementary or high school, the Bachelor of Science in Education is the logical choice; for all other careers or if you wish to go on to grad school, the Bachelor of Arts probably makes sense.

Other majors you might like:
Comparative literature
Linguistics
International relations
Latin
Business
Art history
History
French teacher education
Romance languages
European studies
European history
French studies

Questions to ask colleges:
How many faculty members are native or near-native speakers? When do students have contact with native speakers?

What is the variety of specializations among the faculty members? Is there one literature specialist who teaches all courses, or are there several, who specialize in different centuries or genres? Is there a linguist on the faculty?

Career options and trends:
High school teacher*; Foreign Service Officer*; interpreter/translator.

French majors also go on to jobs in tourism, international relations, the computer industry, international business, journalism, and publishing. With appropriate graduate degrees, you can work in research, law, diplomacy, banking, and marketing. A state certificate or license is required for teaching in public elementary and secondary schools. Translation work usually requires that you get specially certified.

Many states are predicting a shortage of high school French teachers in the near future, due to the expected retirement of older teachers. To a lesser extent, a shortage of college faculty members is also expected. The computer industry has provided numerous jobs for linguists and translators, and this trend will probably continue.

For more info:
Modern Language Association (MLA)
26 Broadway, 3rd Fl.
New York, NY 10004-1789
(646) 576-5000
www.mla.org

American Association of Teachers of French
Southern Illinois University
Mailcode 4510
Carbondale, IL 62901-4510
(618) 453-5731
www.frenchteachers.org

German

What it's about:

This major primarily teaches the language and literature of Germany, Austria, and much of Switzerland. By examining genres, literary movements, and individual authors and themes, you expand your capacity for literary analysis and appreciation.

Is this for you?

You might like this major if you also like: German culture and heritage; languages; travel; history; philosophy; literature; music; art; architecture; science.

Consider this major if you are good at: attention to detail; creativity; critical reading/thinking; memorizing; organizing *...or have...* initiative; patience; perseverance; verbal skills; writing skills.

Recommended high school prep:

English 4, math 3, lab science 3, social studies 4, and foreign language 4. If possible, social studies should include both European history and art history. Language should be German, and a year of Latin is useful. One year of classical music (orchestra, lessons) is also recommended.

Did you know...

...that beginning and intermediate language courses often do not count toward your major?

...that in almost every German department, there are opportunities, including stipends, for study abroad?

...that German is often required for graduate study in fields such as art, music history, and philosophy?

Typical courses in this major:

Introduction to German literature I, II
Conversation and composition
German history and thought
The age of Goethe
Romanticism
Realism
Fin-de-siècle Vienna
Thomas Mann
Franz Kafka
German drama
German women writers
Jewish contributions to German culture
Postwar literature
Migration literature
German film
Modern German literature

Concentrations:

German literature of a particular period; German cinema; German area studies; Germanic linguistics; German intellectual history.

What the study of this major is like:

If you major in German language and literature, you must first concentrate on the language. You need a good knowledge of grammar in order to write properly, so, even if you know how to speak German and have a wide vocabulary, be prepared to polish your skills. You then use the language to explore increasingly complex texts in courses that are taught in German and tend to have small enrollments.

Like other literature majors, German language and literature includes the study of literary theory. You are introduced not only to classical German literature but also to recent works. You read eighteenth- and nineteenth-century authors such as Goethe, Schiller, and Heine, and major figures from the early twentieth century such as Kafka, Rilke, Dürrenmatt, and Brecht. You also read contemporary writers such as Frisch, Sebald, Böll, and Grass. Many German departments teach the literature and film of postwar divided Germany (1945–89) or of recent immigrants (for example, Italian, Turkish). You thus explore questions of multiculturalism and diversity as they are emerging in Europe today.

Some colleges offer a German studies major—a more interdisciplinary approach that emphasizes cultural expressions other than literature, such as music, art, film, philosophy, science, and history. German studies may cover anything from the works of great philosophers such as Kant, Hegel, Nietzsche, and Marx to the role of women in contemporary German culture.

The major typically includes time abroad, in either academic or work programs. Generally, colleges that have their own programs abroad offer courses taught by special staff; students live in dormitories, apartments, or local homes. Most of the stronger junior-year-abroad programs accept students from various institutions. Colleges without their own programs generally permit, or even encourage, qualified students to attend them. Many American colleges and other organizations can help you find vacation employment in German-speaking countries, to strengthen your command of the language and appreciation of the culture.

Other majors you might like:
Comparative literature
Linguistics
European studies
Music, general
Philosophy
History
Political science
German studies
Germanic languages
German teacher education

Questions to ask colleges:
Does the program teach literary works primarily in the original German or in translation? How will previous language training be credited?

Is there a German house or dormitory on campus that students can live in? Which types of study-abroad programs does the program offer? Does the program provide stipends?

Career options and trends:
College professor*; high school teacher*; interpreter/translator*; international lawyer.

German majors tend to pursue a rich variety of careers. Many enter jobs in government, business, library and information science, tourism, or journalism. With appropriate professional study, you can pursue a career in law or medicine. A mastery of German is valuable in almost any academic field, as well as in international business and diplomacy. A graduate degree is usually necessary for obtaining a job in a German field. An additional state certificate or license is required for teaching in public elementary and secondary schools.

Insider's viewpoint:
"I took a class with a professor who made me realize that German was a new way in which I could communicate my life experiences and emotions. A lot of German literature tends to be highly emotionally charged, and it takes a strong person to deal with it."

—Sabrina, junior, Oberlin College

For more info:
Modern Language Association (MLA)
26 Broadway, 3rd Fl.
New York, NY 10004-1789
(646) 576-5000
www.mla.org

American Association of Teachers of German (AATG)
112 Haddontowne Court, #104
Cherry Hill, NJ 08034-3668
(856) 795-5553
www.aatg.org

Italian

What it's about:

As an Italian major, you study the language and literature of Italy, usually in the broader context of Italy's culture, history, and society.

Is this for you?

You might like this major if you also like: Italian culture and heritage; Romance languages; traveling; art; history; nature; food; architecture; music; film.

Consider this major if you are good at: active listening; caring/nurturing; critical reading/thinking; leadership; memorizing *...or have...* initiative; patience; verbal skills; writing skills.

Recommended high school prep:

English 4, math 3, lab science 3, social studies 4 (including European history and art history), and a foreign language 4. If possible, take Latin. If Latin is not available, take French or Italian.

Typical courses in this major:

Elementary Italian
Intermediate Italian
Advanced Italian
Italian composition and conversation
Masterworks of Italian literature
Dante's *Divine Comedy*
Twentieth-century literature
Italian theater
Italian civilization
Renaissance literature
Nineteenth-century literature
Italian cinema

Concentrations:

Italian language and literature; Italian culture and society; Italian and linguistics.

What the study of this major is like:

If you don't know the language, you begin with elementary Italian, a two-semester course in which you study basic grammar and learn to listen to, speak, read, and write Italian. After this course (or if you know basic Italian before entering college), you take intermediate Italian, a two-semester course usually taught in Italian, in which you review grammar and practice listening, speaking, reading, and writing.

Most intermediate courses include poetry and prose, and introduce you to Italian history, culture, and contemporary Italian society. Intermediate Italian also prepares you for a possible third year abroad, which all language majors are encouraged to pursue. Most study-abroad programs require two years of college Italian because the courses are taught entirely in Italian. In advanced Italian, which emphasizes conversation and composition, you discuss and write about historical and contemporary aspects of Italian culture and civilization.

Italy's greatest poet is Dante Alighieri, author of *The Divine Comedy*, a work in three parts that profoundly influenced the development of modern Italian. You are usually required to read either part or all of this poem in the original language. Most programs in Italian also include study of Italian Renaissance literature, especially the writings of Boccaccio and Petrarch, sometimes the epic poems of Ariosto and Tasso, and often the writings of Machiavelli and Galileo. Most colleges expect majors to explore the works of nineteenth-century Romantic writers, such as the novelist Alessandro Manzoni, author of *I promessi sposi* (*The Betrothed*).

Twentieth-century literature, a popular course among majors, includes the best Italian fiction writers of our time—Pirandello, D'Annunzio, Moravia, Pasolini, Ginsburg, and Calvino—and the poets Montale, Ungaretti, Saba, and Quasimodo. At some colleges you can take a course in masterworks of Italian literature, an in-depth examination of one or more great writers, or a survey course on writers from Dante to the present. In many programs, films are shown in the contemporary literature course; or a course in Italian cinema may be offered, devoted to the works of such famous directors as De Sica, Visconti, Fellini, Antonioni, Pasolini, and Bertolucci. You may also have one or more required courses in Italian opera.

Learning a language is like playing a musical instrument; you have to practice every day. Most students find that reading serious literature in Italian is a challenge, because building a vocabulary takes time and effort. But the more time you spend reading Italian, the sooner you will be able to read effortlessly. Colleges may offer different literature and cultural courses, depending on the interests of the faculty members, and may vary in the way they teach these subjects. Approaches can range from a textual and linguistic analysis, to a cultural and historical orientation, to interpretations of the text based on recent theories of art and literature, such as feminist literary theory.

Other majors you might like:
Linguistics
Romance languages
Classics
Art history
Comparative literature
Latin
Medieval and Renaissance studies
Culinary arts and chef training
Spanish
Italian studies
Music, general
European studies

Questions to ask colleges:
Who teaches the Italian language courses? Some colleges believe that teaching language and teaching literature and culture are separate specializations that require different instructors. Other colleges adopt a liberal arts approach that encourages each faculty member to teach all areas of Italian, from elementary language to Dante, and to introduce students to culture and literature when they teach language courses.

Career options and trends:
College professor*; high school teacher; art historian; interpreter/translator.

Italian majors also go on to careers in music, film, the arts, research, government, NGOs (nongovernmental organizations), diplomacy, law, fashion design, tourism, international politics, or international business. Graduate study is required for some of these careers.

Italy is "in." New York and Los Angeles are filled with upscale Italian restaurants. College students want to study in Italy; their parents want to vacation there. College enrollments in Italian courses continue to rise. More high schools are offering Italian. The need for people fluent in both English and Italian is growing.

For more info:
National Italian American Foundation (NIAF)
1860 19th St., N.W.
Washington, DC 20009
(202) 387-0600
www.niaf.org

American Association of Teachers of Italian (AATI)
www.italianstudies.org/aati/

Japanese

What it's about:

This major focuses on Japanese spoken and written language, often in both premodern and modern forms. Students are generally exposed to Japanese literature through reading primary texts in either the original or in English translation, as well as through secondary sources.

Is this for you?

You might like this major if you also like: Japanese culture; learning difficult languages; travel; anime and *manga*; word games; poetry; calligraphy; interacting with different cultures.

Consider this major if you are good at: attention to detail; critical reading/thinking; memorizing; research ...*or have...* Linguistic ability; Motivation; Self Discipline; patience; verbal skills; writing skills.

Recommended high school prep:

English 4, math 3, lab science 3, social studies 4, and a foreign language 4. Be sure to take as much foreign language as possible; Japanese is preferable but not required. World history courses and classes involving writing and research are also recommended.

Did you know...

...that the Japanese use several different writing systems? In earlier times, there was even one form of writing for men and another for women.

Typical courses in this major:

Elementary Japanese
Intermediate Japanese
Advanced Japanese
Reading Japanese—newspapers and periodicals
East Asian cultures
Survey of Japanese literature in translation
Introduction to Classical Japanese
Introduction to Japanese linguistics
Readings in modern Japanese literature
Japanese history
The world of premodern Japan
The Tale of Genji
Japanese theater: ghosts, masks and actors
Religion and philosophy in premodern Japan
Japanese cinema
Writers and thinkers: modern Japan in the world

Concentrations:

Generally, none in college; but if you go on to grad school: Premodern literature, modern literature, linguistics.

What the study of this major is like:

This major is for those who really like to challenge themselves. Modern Japanese is one of the most difficult languages to learn. Its grammar is the reverse of that of English, and its writing system is very complex, involving two different syllabary sets (*hiragana* and *katakana*) and between two thousand and three thousand characters (*kanji*), most with at least two different readings. Despite its difficulty, though, Japanese has become a highly popular language major.

Unless you have had experience speaking Japanese, you will spend the first year acquiring the basics of the grammar and writing system. In many colleges, lecture courses are taught in English and may meet once or twice a week; they are coupled with smaller practice or recitation classes, conducted in Japanese and meeting daily.

Often beginning Japanese courses focus on the everyday side of the language. You might learn how to talk about weather, food, shopping, or school, and how to read menus, street maps, signs, and letters to and from friends. You may even have an opportunity to send e-mail in Japanese. Since Japanese majors often go on to work in business, practical details like these are important.

During the first and perhaps second year, you will probably also take one or two literature survey courses in English translation, which will involve considerable reading, class discussion, quizzes and exams, and papers of varying length.

In the third and fourth years, you will spend more time with electives in your areas of interest, such as modern literature, drama, film, or courses built around specific themes or questions, such as love in classical and modern Japan, the life of the pre-modern warrior, and representations of gender in literature.

If Japanese is offered within a broader major in Asian or East Asian studies, as it is at many smaller colleges, the language requirement is often only two years. Courses relating to other Asian countries may be required as well.

You are unlikely to learn enough, even after two or three years of courses in the language, to read Japanese high school texts or newspapers easily, much less to work in business or as a translator. A year of study in Japan is extremely helpful for attaining conversational fluency. Keep in mind, however, that the university experience in Japan is very different from that in the United States; the academic year starts in April, and your credits may not all transfer.

Other majors you might like:
Asian studies
Linguistics
International relations
Comparative literature
International business
Asian-American studies
Anthropology
East Asian studies
Animation
Global studies
Geography

Questions to ask colleges:
How many full-time professors does the program have?

How many years of Japanese-language courses does the program offer?

Does the program offer a study-abroad or exchange program, or access to Japanese television and other media?

Career options and trends:
Japanese-language teacher*; ESL teacher; interpreter or translator; journalist; Foreign Service officer*.

Knowledge of Japanese is an asset for almost any career path. There is significant demand for people with good Japanese-language ability and knowledge of Japanese culture in the areas of international business and the travel industry, and those who possess a Ph.D. have a much better chance of obtaining a faculty position in a college or university than is true for other fields.

Japanese companies, either in Japan or elsewhere, often hire non-Japanese with good language ability for translation, writing, or research duties, although the growth potential in such positions may be limited.

Insider's viewpoint:
"There is so much to read, and so few people outside Japan who can read it; you can go into the library and peruse ancient Japanese works that may not have been read by anyone else at the university."

—Professor H. Mack Horton, University of California: Berkeley

For more info:
Association for Asian Studies (AAS)
1021 E. Huron St.
Ann Arbor, MI 48104
(734) 665-2490
www.aasianst.org

Russian

What it's about:

In this major, you learn the Russian language and investigate the Russian-speaking world. You learn oral and written communication, and you explore the historical, geographic, and cultural factors that have contributed to the development of the Russian language.

Is this for you?

You might like this major if you also like: Russian literature; international politics; Russian culture; Russian/world film, dance, theater, and music.

Consider this major if you are good at: attention to detail; creativity; critical reading/thinking; learning languages; memorizing *...or have...* initiative; patience; persistence; verbal skills; writing skills.

Recommended high school prep:

English 4, math 3, lab science 3, social studies 3 (including a year of world history), and a foreign language 4. Although any language experience is helpful, another inflected language (for example, Latin or German, whose nouns change form for gender) can be especially useful.

Did you know...

...that many opportunities exist for study abroad in Russia? There are now excellent programs in a variety of Russian locations.

Typical courses in this major:

Elementary Russian
Intermediate Russian
Advanced Russian
Russian theater and drama
The Russian short story
The Russian novel
Phonetics and intonation
Conversation and composition
Survey of Russian literature
Alexander Pushkin
Nikolai Gogol
Doestoyevsky and Tolstoy
Anton Chekhov

Concentrations:

In college: Russian literature; Russian language.

If you go on to grad school: Slavic literatures/languages/linguistics (such as Russian); non-Slavic Eurasian literature/language/linguistics (focusing on the Caucasus, Central Asia, and other areas); folklore; drama; literary theory; specific literary genres or periods.

What the study of this major is like:

Russian, the language of one of the world's greatest bodies of literature, is valuable in international relations, business, and science. Russian majors study the language and read the literature; you may also study Russian culture and civilization, Russian and European history, and related disciplines.

The Russian major usually requires three to four years of language study, or an equivalent combination of language study and advanced literature/culture courses in the original Russian, survey courses in Russian literature/culture in translation, or Russian-related courses in other departments. Lecture and seminar courses in Russian departments offer you the opportunity to read the classics of Russian literature, but they have also become increasingly interdisciplinary, incorporating, for example, the study of film, contemporary society, or intellectual history. Russian literature today is not studied in geographic isolation, and many departments offer you the option of studying the language, literature, and cultures of other eastern European, central European, and Eurasian countries. You can sometimes count courses in other literature programs toward your major.

During your first two years, you are usually required to take at least 5–6 hours a week of language classes and labs. Some colleges offer intensive language courses, which require 8–12 hours a week. In upper-level language courses, you learn to communicate effectively with Russian speakers on a variety of topics. The choice of courses at the advanced level depends on the department and the strength of its program. Several offerings allow you to pursue your own interests. During your fourth year, you may participate in a seminar on a literary topic.

As a major, you spend a significant amount of time studying a language that most English speakers don't find easy. Fortunately, your classes are likely to be small and your teachers and classmates a quirky, interesting, and highly motivated bunch. All Russian majors should seriously consider the option of studying for a summer, a semester, or, best of all, a year abroad. Although the culture shock can at first be extreme, students often find that their time in Russia is the most personally and intellectually rewarding experience of their college career.

Other majors you might like:

Linguistics
Comparative literature
History
Political science
Geography
Anthropology
International relations
International business
Russian/Slavic studies
Slavic languages
Central/Middle/Eastern European studies

Questions to ask colleges:

Are there student- or department-sponsored activities, such as Russian tables and Russian clubs, lectures, film screenings, musical gatherings, or dinners? Most good Russian departments have enthusiastic students looking for opportunities to satisfy, outside the classroom, their love of things Russian.

Career options and trends:

High school teacher; college professor; Foreign Service Officer; interpreter/translator.

Russian majors also enter the fields of international law, international business, not-for-profit work, health care, social work, environmental affairs, and journalism. Although strong language skills are most important for Russian majors looking for work in these areas, some employers may want you to have at least a master's degree. Translating work usually requires that you get specially certified. Careers in the Foreign Service are usually open only to U.S. citizens.

Politics always plays a role for Americans looking for work related to Russia, no matter how apolitical that work may seem. In the post-Soviet world, visa regulations, laws of international business, and the degree of U.S. involvement in the region are in a state of uncertainty and will remain so for some time. If you are looking for work in or with Russia, you should keep up-to-date on current events. A focus on Eurasia is of increasing importance for all jobs.

Insider's viewpoint:

"For me the defining marker of Russian-ness is the question 'what is Russia?'—a question that Russians are still trying to answer in a post-Soviet, postmodern world. The endlessly creative ways Russian writers have tried to resolve the issue of their own identity is fascinating for me as a literary scholar."

—Professor Melissa Frazier, Sarah Lawrence College

For more info:

American Association of Teachers of Slavic and
   Eastern European Languages (AATSEEL)
P.O. Box 7039
Berkley, CA 94707-2306
(510) 526-6614
www.aatseel.org

American Association for the Advancement of
   Slavic Studies (AAASS)
Harvard University
8 Story St., 3rd Fl., Box 14
Cambridge, MA 02138
(617) 495-0677
www.fas.harvard.edu/~aaass/

Spanish

What it's about:

As a Spanish major, you learn the Spanish language and explore the literature and culture of Spain, Latin America, and the Latino communities living in the United States.

Is this for you?

You might like this major if you also like: Spanish culture and heritage; community service; travel; politics; history; languages; reading.

Consider this major if you are good at: attention to detail; creativity; critical reading/thinking; memorizing; persuading/influencing; teamwork *...or have...* patience; verbal skills; writing skills.

Recommended high school prep:

English 4, math 3, lab science 3, social studies 4, and a foreign language 4. Studying Spanish is, of course, useful, but any other Romance language (such as Italian, French, or Latin) is also highly recommended. If possible, take a year of Latin American history.

Did you know...

...that Spanish is the official language of more countries than any other language except English? Depending on the methodology used, Spanish is also ranked as either the second or third most spoken language on earth. It is unlikely to ever catch number one, however—Mandarin Chinese.

Typical courses in this major:

Elementary Spanish
Intermediate Spanish
Advanced Spanish
Spanish literature in translation
Culture and civilization
Business Spanish
Latin American novels
Applied linguistics
Spanish Renaissance
Miguel de Cervantes
Phonetics
Latin American literature in translation
Iberian peninsular literature

Concentrations:

Spanish literature; Latin American literature; Spanish and Portuguese literature; language teaching; international trade; translation.

What the study of this major is like:

During your first and second years in college, your primary focus is on learning and using the Spanish language. Almost all of your classes are conducted in Spanish, so you can hone your basic skills (speaking, listening, reading, writing) rapidly.

During your third and fourth years, you work on advanced speaking and writing skills, learning phonetics and doing creative writing in Spanish. You also study literature, usually that of both Spain and Latin America. The broad range of Spanish-language literature may include the medieval epic *El Cid* and the literature written when Christians, Jews, and Moors shared the Iberian Peninsula; the early Renaissance Spanish classic *La Celestina*; the picaresque novel *Lazarillo de Tormes*; the writings of the mystics; the great Spanish dramatists of the Golden Age (Lope de Vega, Tirso de Molina, Calderón de la Barca); the baroque masterpiece *Don Quixote*; and neoclassical, Romantic, realist, and modernist works. The literature of Latin America includes such authors as Borges, García Márques, Fuentes, and Vargas Llosa. You may also watch films produced in Spanish-speaking regions.

In general, you will be asked to do research and write papers on different topics. Oral practice is important when learning a language. This is accomplished outside of class by working in language labs, meeting with language assistants, doing field or community work, attending lectures and poetry readings in Spanish, or even participating in the construction or maintenance of a Spanish Web site.

Many Spanish departments have different styles and philosophies. Individual faculty members also vary in their approaches to teaching. Some stress grammar over oral communication or, when teaching literature, the social and intellectual context of a work over the literary aspects. The program may offer courses in teaching methods and applied linguistics, often in collaboration with the school of education. Many programs—responding to the number of students looking to use Spanish in their careers—offer business Spanish and medical Spanish, as well as courses in the history and culture of Spain and Latin America (independent of courses offered by the history department).

The biggest challenge you will encounter is to immerse yourself in the Spanish language without falling back on English when you don't know how to express your ideas. Almost all programs encourage you to spend a semester, a summer, or a year of study—often during your third year—in a Spanish-speaking country. The lifestyle of the Spanish major is one of its most appealing features. Latin culture offers good food, music, literature, and social life—and it usually influences class dynamics. Students tend to work in groups and find it rewarding as a way to relax and make friends.

Other majors you might like:
Comparative literature
Linguistics
Language interpretation/translation
ESL teacher education
European studies
Spanish/Iberian studies
Latin American studies
History
Linguistics
Chicano studies
Spanish teacher education
International business

Questions to ask colleges:
Does the program recognize the varieties of the language as spoken throughout the Spanish-speaking world, or does it focus only upon how Spanish is spoken in Spain?

Does the library provide access to computers and databases? How extensive is the library's catalog in the field?

Career options and trends:
College professor; interpreter/translator; high school teacher; ESL teacher.

Spanish majors can also find jobs in business, banking, social services, government, and international organizations. A state certificate or license is required for teaching in public elementary and secondary schools. Translating work usually requires that you get specially certified. With appropriate advanced degrees, you may also work in medicine, law, and other professions, where you will be especially valued in bilingual Spanish/English-speaking communities.

For more info:
Modern Language Association (MLA)
26 Broadway, 3rd Fl.
New York, NY 10004-1789
(646) 576-5000
www.mla.org

Latin American Studies Association (LASA)
University of Pittsburgh
946 William Pitt Union
Pittsburgh, PA 15260
(412) 648-7929
lasa.international.pitt.edu

Legal studies

Sometimes you have to know what something isn't before you can know what it is.

The programs in this chapter will not qualify you to take the bar exam and become a lawyer. To do that, you must go to law school to get a graduate degree called a juris doctor (J.D.), or doctor of jurisprudence (in simpler terms, doctor of law).

If you want to be an attorney, you can take nearly any undergraduate major, not just the ones in this chapter. That's true even if you take prelaw. "Students interested in legal careers major in every possible field. There is no required course of study for admission to law school," says Diane Curtis, prelaw adviser at the University of Massachusetts, Amherst.

"Prelaw is not a major or a specific course of study," Curtis explains. "At the overwhelming majority of colleges and universities, it is an advising program designed to assist students to explore future legal careers, and to help with the law school application process."

Okay. Now that you know what this chapter isn't, let's move on to what is. (See? You are thinking like a lawyer already.)

Whether you choose a prelaw program or not, if you are planning on going to law school, you must be prepared to take the most challenging undergraduate courses from the toughest professors and get good grades. "In your undergraduate classes, you need to acquire the core knowledge and skills upon which your legal education will be built," Curtis says. "Since law deals with a wide variety of human conflicts, the more you know about the diversity of human experience, the better prepared you will be to study law."

Legal studies is a major by itself, and can lead to any number of careers—lawyer, professor, teacher; legal assistant, paralegal, librarian, mediator, arbitrator; a job in the courts, or in other areas of government or politics; police or corrections work; business.

Is legal studies the right field for you? Students who gravitate toward the program tend to have leadership potential; analytical, problem-solving, and quantitative skills; a talent for persuasion or counseling; a powerful memory; research abilities; and a gift for communicating. Interests often include history, current events, politics, debating, student government, community service, and social justice.

"Legal studies is a fascinating field because...virtually every aspect of our lives is touched in some way by the law, and a knowledge and awareness of the legal system is beneficial regardless of the career path a student might take," says Jeffrey J. Davis, assistant professor of political science at the University of Maryland.

The Paper Chase

To find legal studies majors, look at a college's school of government or political science, or sociology department. For paralegal studies, check out colleges of arts and science or business and management.

Programs differ. Those geared toward training students to become paralegal and legal assistants offer more practice- and skills-oriented courses than programs that prepare you for law school, other graduate school, or for careers in government or business. Ask yourself if you're more likely to succeed in rigorous academic and theoretical courses or in hands-on training for law-related work. If you're considering a paralegal or legal assistant program, see if it's approved by the American Bar Association. Whether it's a two-year or four-year paralegal or legal assistant program, expect to study areas and foundations of the law in a very demanding environment requiring loads of reading and writing.

You may be bound for law school or for a legal career straight out of college. In either case, be sure to research the institution. Do your due diligence. Find out if the college's faculty members or advisers have law degrees themselves. Have they actually practiced law? Does the college arrange for graduates to have internships with attorneys and/or judges? Are participatory activities available, such as mock trial, moot court, or debate team?

For prelaw programs, it's a good idea to register with a prelaw adviser as early as possible in your college career, to get on track academically. Your adviser can also help you explore the different legal specialties and work environments. (A few examples: litigating criminal cases in court, doing corporate law at a big firm, devoting yourself to government service.) Ask what percentage of students who see an adviser gain admission to one or more law schools. See whether advisers will help you after you graduate. Is an LSAT prep course offered? Does the school have a network of attorney-alumni that undergraduates can contact? (Note that some institutions compress B.A. and J.D. curriculums into a joint six-year program.)

While there will always be a need for lawyers, competition for openings is keen because of the large number of students graduating from law school each year (about 40,000). For paralegals and legal assistants, job opportunities are projected to grow rapidly as employers try to reduce costs by hiring paralegals to perform tasks formerly done by lawyers.

For more information, go to the American Bar Association (www.abanet.org). Who knows? You may become a member of that organization one day.

Legal studies

What it's about:

This major examines the law and legal issues from the perspectives of the social sciences and the humanities. Taking a theoretical rather than a practical approach, students explore the origins, evolution, function, and effects of the law as a social phenomenon. Legal studies is not a prelaw program, and this major will not qualify you to take the bar examination or to work as a lawyer. If your goal is to become an attorney, you must attend law school after college.

Is this for you?

You might like this major if you also like: history; philosophy; current events; politics; debating; student government; community service activities; issues relating to social justice; reading and writing.

Consider this major if you are good at: attention to detail; counseling; creativity; critical reading/thinking; leadership; persuading/influencing; research *...or have...* initiative; verbal skills; writing skills.

Recommended high school prep:

English 4, math 3, lab science 2, social studies 4, and a foreign language 3–4. Other recommended courses include business law, philosophy, sociology, psychology, statistics, and comparative government and politics.

Did you know...

...that while legal studies is a good prelaw major, it won't increase your chances of getting into law school? Law schools don't favor any specific college major.

...that combining a science or technology major with a major or minor in legal studies is a good marriage for the career-minded? The areas are increasingly intertwined, in both law and business.

Typical courses in this major:

American politics and government
Philosophy of law
Civil rights and liberties
Legal and judicial process
Legal reasoning
Constitutional law
Law, crime, and social justice
International law
Comparative law
Business law
Legal history
Environmental law
Law and literature
Legal ethics
Legal research and writing
Women and the law

Concentrations:

Criminal justice; government and politics; international and comparative law; business and commercial law.

What the study of this major is like:

Shortly after the September 11, 2001, terrorist attacks, President George W. Bush signed the Patriot Act. This law made it easier for the government to guard against terrorist activity by allowing such tactics as searches without notice. But many people believe that the measure endangers the civil rights and civil liberties of both citizens and immigrants.

Does it make sense to trade in some civil rights for greater protection against terrorism? Will the government's greater access to our private lives make us safer? As a legal studies major, you'll take an in-depth look at these and other important issues.

While legal studies is not a prelaw program, it is a good major for prelaw students because it will help you to develop your ability to think clearly and to analyze arguments critically. It is also an excellent major if you are leaning toward a career in public service or planning to study business or the social sciences in grad school.

The major is academically rigorous. It requires excellent reading comprehension skills and sharp analytical ability. Reading and writing assignments can be substantial. You should be ready to engage in intense discussion of thorny legal problems, study actual court cases, do computer research using legal databases, and write a senior thesis.

Course work, which is usually interdisciplinary, focuses on the legal process, legal institutions, and how they operate in society. For example, you might examine crime and punishment from the viewpoint of psychology, philosophy, and anthropology, or use legal doctrines to study international business models in a globalized economy. A course in comparative law will expose you to systems that differ from those in the United States, such as European civil law or Islamic Sharia. Legal studies is based on the idea that an understanding of the foundations of law and justice requires the application of a broad range of academic disciplines, as well as a critical analysis of human behavior and institutions.

In most programs you will have a chance to participate in moot courts (arguing an artificial appeal), mock trials (playing a role in an artificial trial) and to serve internships with judges, private lawyers, prosecutors, defense attorneys, or in government offices. This aspect of the major can give you a close perspective on a legal career prior to deciding on law school.

At some colleges this major emphasizes training for the paralegal and legal assistant professions. These programs, which may be available at the two-year, or associate degree, level, often provide practice-oriented courses in specific areas of law, such as real estate or contracts. Generally, four-year colleges that house the major prepare students for law school, for graduate school, or for careers in government and business. These programs offer courses in a variety of disciplines, and are usually more rigorous academically and more theoretical.

Other majors you might like:
Political science
Criminology

Sociology
History
Public policy analysis
Environmental studies
International relations
Labor studies
Behavioral sciences
Peace studies
Criminal justice and law enforcement
Public administration

Questions to ask colleges:

Do any of the faculty members have law degrees, and have they actually practiced law?

Does the school assist with internships with lawyers and/or judges in the area?

Is there a mock trial, moot court, or debate team?

Is there an active legal studies club?

Career options and trends:

Lawyer*; government official*; paralegal; public interest advocate; business executive; law enforcement officer; journalist.

To practice law, you must go to law school, pass a bar exam, and be certified by the bar of the state in which you will practice.

As a liberal arts program, legal studies can prepare you for a variety of careers in business and public service, as well as in the law. The major will also qualify you to apply to graduate school in the humanities and social sciences, or to professional school in teaching, public policy, business and health administration, and social work.

For more info:

American Bar Association
321 N. Clark St.
Chicago, IL 60610
(800) 285-2221
www.abanet.org

Paralegal studies

What it's about:

This major prepares you to conduct legal research; draft legal documents; and perform investigatory, record-keeping, and other administrative duties under the supervision of an attorney or a court officer. Paralegal education is not the equivalent of law school training and does not qualify you for, or make you eligible to take, a bar examination.

Is this for you?

You might like this major if you also like: public speaking; Mock Trial competitions; debate; student government; politics; public service; reading; research; social justice issues.

Consider this major if you are good at: attention to detail; critical reading/thinking; leadership; organizing; research; teamwork *...or have...* initiative; patience; verbal skills; writing skills.

Recommended high school prep:

English 4, math 3, lab science 3, social studies 3, and a foreign language 2–3. If possible, take an introductory law or political science course.

Did you know...

...that the paralegal profession is one of the five fastest growing career fields in the United States? Today, paralegals perform much of the work that was once done by lawyers. As a result, paralegals have a great deal of responsibility and play an essential role in providing legal services to the public. Some paralegals even represent clients before local, state, and national administrative agencies.

Typical courses in this major:

Litigation/civil procedure
Criminal law and procedure
Computerized research
Legal writing
Real estate law
Business law
Wills, trusts, and probate law
Family law
Immigration law
Intellectual property law
Evidence
Ethics
Personal injury/tort law
Environmental law
Alternative dispute resolution
Elder law

Concentrations:

Generally, none available.

What the study of this major is like:

As a paralegal studies major, you learn practical, job-related skills along with the underlying legal theory. You study substantive law (the particular disciplines, or areas, you can practice) and procedural law (how you practice—such as rules of evidence and pre-trial paper work). Legal research and writing are essential parts of the curriculum and often are the most challenging elements for students. Your course work also stresses communication skills (oral, nonverbal, and interpersonal), computational and organizational skills, an ability to think critically, and an appreciation of legal ethics. You use computer-based resources to help you with your work.

You are encouraged to learn through hands-on work; therefore, internships, practicums, or clinical experience are highly recommended and sometimes required. Internships and similar experiences give you the chance to obtain firsthand knowledge about the practice of law and may even lead to a full-time position after graduation. Most paralegal programs have active student organizations, which build camaraderie among participants by organizing law-related events on or near the campus.

This major is offered at two-year, community and junior colleges; four-year colleges; and business and proprietary schools devoted solely to providing this training. Because there is no uniformly accepted educational standard for entry into the paralegal field, content, length, and admissions requirements vary among colleges.

The American Bar Association approves paralegal education programs that meet its guidelines. Although seeking ABA approval is voluntary on the part of the college, the bar association's standards are rigorous and, therefore, helpful in evaluating a program. However, there are some quality programs that have chosen not to seek ABA approval. A complete listing of paralegal education programs approved by the ABA is found on its Web site (www.abanet.org). Additionally, the American Association for Paralegal Education (AAPE) has a set of minimum program requirements that must be adhered to by member institutions and can be found on the AAPE website.

When deciding among programs, you may also want to consider local or regional standards, particularly with regard to future job opportunities. Check with your local or regional paralegal associations for additional information about educational standards for paralegals in your area.

Other majors you might like:
Criminal justice and law enforcement
Political science
Sociology
Office management
Physician assistant
Technical and business writing
Real estate
Social work
Insurance
Criminology
Legal studies
Labor studies

Questions to ask colleges:
Is the paralegal studies program approved by the American Bar Association? Is the institution a member of the American Association for Paralegal Education and therefore guided by its requirements?

Are faculty members practicing attorneys and/or paralegals?

Do students have access to the resources they need to do legal research (such as a law library)?

Are students taught how to use computerized legal research systems (WESTLAW or Lexis-Nexis)?

Career options and trends:
The Bureau of Labor Statistics projects strong growth in this field. Graduates also pursue careers as private investigators, law librarians, human resources personnel, court personnel, mediators, arbitrators, special advocates, estate and trust officers, real estate professionals, insurance agents, risk managers, contract managers, legal administrators, corporate compliance officers, and government workers.

Although there is no mandatory certification of paralegals, voluntary certification is sponsored by the two paralegal professional associations. The National Association of Legal Assistants sponsors a national certification exam, several state-specific exams, and certification for specialty areas of law. The National Federation of Paralegal Associations offers the Paralegal Advanced Competency Examination (PACE).

Many states, through the legislature, court system, or bar association, have issued ethics opinions dealing with a paralegal's use of title, the scope of duties, the unauthorized practice of law, and how clients may be billed for paralegal services. You should examine and review these opinions prior to obtaining employment as a paralegal.

For more info:
National Association of Legal Assistants (NALA)
1516 South Boston Ave., Suite 200
Tulsa, OK 74119
(918) 587-6828
www.nala.org

American Association for Paralegal Education
   (AAfPE)
19 Mantua Road
Mt. Royal, NJ 08061
(856) 423-2829
www.aafpe.org

Prelaw

What it's about:

Prelaw is not a major or a prescribed course of study, and it is not a requirement for law school. Rather, it is an advising program designed to help you prepare for law school while in college, explore future legal careers, and manage the law school application process. You must obtain a bachelor's degree to apply to law school, but you can major in anything you want.

Is this for you?

You might pursue this program if you like: history; philosophy; current events; politics; debating; student government; community service activities; social justice issues; problem solving; reading and writing. The law plays a role in almost every field—from sports to music to banking—and many potential law students have a wide variety of hobbies and interests.

Consider this program if you are good at: attention to detail; critical reading/thinking; leadership; organizing; persuading/influencing; research *...or have...* initiative; intellectual curiousity; verbal skills; writing skills.

Recommended high school prep:

English 4, math 3, lab science 2, social studies 4 (including economics and government, if available), and a foreign language 3–4. Other recommended courses include philosophy, sociology, psychology, statistics, and speech.

Did you know...

...that only one-third of law school applicants come directly from college? Many law schools like to see applicants that have gained some work experience after college.

Typical courses in this program:

Principles of economics
English composition
U.S. history to 1865
U.S. history from 1865 to present
Western philosophy
Introduction to psychology
Ethics
Logic
Social anthropology
Law and literature
American government and politics
Scientific methods
Computer science
English literature
Principles of accounting
Expository writing

Concentrations:

Generally, none available.

What the program is like:

Because "prelaw" is not a major but an advising program, there are no admission requirements—just register with the prelaw adviser as early as you can. You will still have to pick a college major before the end of your second year.

While many prelaw students choose majors that are considered traditional preparation for law school, such as English, history, political science, legal studies, economics, or business, none of these disciplines are preferred by law schools. You can major in art, music, math, computer science, a foreign language—anything that will lead to a bachelor's degree. What matters is that you take courses that will help you develop the skills law schools are looking for and that will help you do well on the Law School Admission Test (LSAT).

Just what are those skills? According to the American Bar Association (ABA), a likely candidate for law school is good at critical thinking and reading; writing, speaking, and listening; research; and task management and organization. Law schools also look for applicants who value service and justice and who have an understanding of the historical, cultural, and political influences on society; of human behavior and sociology; and of basic math and science.

Your prelaw adviser will assist you in selecting courses and extracurricular activities that can give you the grounding you need. A useful approach is to choose challenging courses from demanding professors. Get as much practice as you can in critical thinking and writing. Seek out courses in which you will be expected to write several papers and will receive detailed feedback. Literature courses offer practice in close reading, and a course in logic is often recommended for reasoning and analysis.

If you like math or science, you might want to consider a major in one of those areas. Scientific or technical knowledge can make you marketable in specialized fields such as patent law or environmental law.

In evaluating an applicant's extracurricular activities or internships, law school admissions committees are flexible. Still, they favor activities that indicate a candidate's sense of service and justice and that helps reveal his or her interests and experiences. While a law-related internship will not give you an edge, it is an excellent way to see what lawyers do and to determine if their work is what you would enjoy doing.

If you choose prelaw, be prepared to take your college work seriously. Admission to law school is competitive, so aim for an above-average GPA—3.5 and higher is preferable, although 3.0 to 3.5 is still acceptable, if coupled with a good LSAT score. Other factors such as letters of recommendation and extracurricular activities are relatively minor compared with the GPA and the LSAT score. The higher these numbers are, the more options you will have when choosing law schools.

But don't worry about law school right now. Enjoy college, and be open to the ideas and options you will discover there. There will be plenty of time to focus on a legal career later. Major in what interests you—you will do better in classes that excite and challenge you.

Other majors you might like:
Accounting
English
Journalism
Environmental studies
Women's studies
Liberal arts and sciences
Peace and conflict studies
Philosophy
Criminal justice and law enforcement
Political science
Real estate
History

Questions to ask colleges:
How much individual attention is the prelaw adviser able to give each student? What kinds of services are offered?

What kind of resources does the school offer to students seeking law-related internships?

Does the school have a network of attorneys who graduated from the college that undergraduates can contact?

Do you offer LSAT preparation courses?

Career options and trends:
Private practice lawyer*; government attorney*; corporate attorney*; paralegal; legislative aid; journalist; business executive; public interest lawyer; public official; legal editor.

Prelaw advising helps prepare the student for law school, not for a career. To become a practicing attorney, you must obtain a J.D. degree from a law school, pass a state bar exam, and be admitted to the bar in a specific jurisdiction (state or federal). But there are many law-related careers that do not require admission to the bar.

There will always be a need for lawyers, regardless of how business is doing. The general economy often has an impact on first-year attorneys' salaries but not on job availability overall. Certain areas of practice, such as real estate, are more likely than others to be affected by economic cycles.

Insider's viewpoint:
"I was an English major in college, and I think that major—or any that requires a great deal of careful

reading and analytical writing—is useful if not essential preparation for law school."

—Sara, J.D. candidate, Columbia University

For more info:
American Bar Association
321 North Clark Street
Chicago, IL 60610
(800) 285-2221
www.abanet.org

The Council on Legal Education Opportunities
740 15th St., NW
9th Floor
Washington, DC 20005
(866) 886-4343
www.cleoscholars.com

Mathematics

Is the probability high that you will study mathematics? If so, you may be interested to know that the number of students getting bachelor's degrees in math is way down. In 2001, 24 percent fewer scrolls were awarded in math than in 1990, the biggest slump of any major in the last decade. But the silver lining may be that by studying math, you can rise above other students and job seekers.

"There is a steady, strong demand for math majors," says Professor David M. Bressoud of Macalester College. "Many employers (as well as graduate schools in professions such as law and medicine) will give preferential treatment to graduates with a degree in math."

Then why don't more students major in math? The work is intense. But students don't realize it's also very creative.

"Mathematics is not just learning a bunch of formulas," says Professor James Alexander of Case Western Reserve University. "Mathematics ranges from the purely theoretical studies to highly integrated with engineering and the physical and social sciences; and many majors, including applied mathematics, are available."

Professor Bressoud points out, "Mathematics is about understanding basic, abstract structures to discover progressively deeper and more refined patterns that give profound insights into the workings of the world around us."

And don't forget statistics. Virginia Tech's Michele Marini calls statistics "an undiscovered gem of a major."

As a likely math student, you'll choose from many colleges offering mathematics, applied mathematics, statistics, and related programs. Look for these majors in colleges, divisions, or schools of sciences, mathematical sciences, physical sciences, engineering, arts and sciences, and humanities.

You'll want a college that shares your interests. For instance, some colleges put more emphasis on applied mathematics to prepare you for the workplace, while other programs stress advanced topics in analysis, algebra, geometry, and related areas—rigorous preparation for grad school. Graduate tracks include statistics, applied mathematics, computational mathematics, algebra, number theory, analysis, logic, geometry, and topology (the bending and stretching of geometric forms). Other advanced studies cover computing/information science, operations research, and control theory; or industrial statistics, environmental statistics, and bioinformatics (computerized health and medical stats).

When comparing colleges, ask if computers are used in the classroom or if it's mostly "chalk and talk," as instructors like to call their lectures. Is statistics required for nonstatistics majors? How often are key courses like modern algebra taught? Do students enter math competitions? Or help the faculty members with research? Have any students been published as co-writers? What kind of capstone or senior project is required?

Also ask how many students go on to graduate school. How successful are students at getting jobs after graduation? What kinds of jobs are they getting?

Career permutations and combinations

You'll find that the job outlook is good for students with a math education.

"The study of mathematics is excellent preparation for a host of employment opportunities in business, finance, insurance, communications, electronics, scientific research of any type, and any field that has challenging problems to solve," Bressoud says. "Mathematics lies behind the models of the physical world that are used in predicting weather or in understanding subatomic particles. It lies at the root of economics as well as ecology. It provides the tools for analyzing medical, sociological, or psychological research. It explains electricity and magnetism, radio waves, and quantum tunneling, as well as the hidden patterns of business cycles."

If you major in applied math, you'll be preparing for a career in which you use your math skills in a particular industry or for a particular purpose.

"The Bachelor of Science degree in applied mathematics includes a solid foundation in mathematics as well as a professional core that is specific to computing and information science, operations research, systems engineering, control theory, and statistics," explains Alexander.

If you're going for applied math, see if you can shave college time through a five-year integrated program leading to a Bachelor of Science degree in math and a master's degree in your specialty.

Your math and statistics skills can be used in almost any type of business or research effort.

"I can work on a psychological problem one week, work on U.S. census data the next, and then work on health issues," says Marini.

"The importance of a math background is the ability to think abstractly and conceptually. This is especially important because technology changes rapidly and more specialized skills are likely to be outmoded soon," Alexander notes.

Careers in math include all sorts—engineering, business, and management consulting; high school or college teaching; working for a government agency; as a financial analyst; or as an actuary in the insurance industry. An advanced degree is an enhancement in nearly all math work.

For more information, visit the Mathematical Association of America (www.maa.org), the American Mathematical Society (www.ams.org), the American Statistical Association (www.amstat.org), and the Society for Industrial and Applied Mathematics (www.siam.org).

In this book, see also the sections on Computer and information sciences, Engineering, and Multi/interdisciplinary studies.

Applied mathematics

What it's about:

In the applied mathematics major, you receive a solid grounding in mathematics as well as professional training in your chosen area of application. Possible application areas are computing and information science, operations research, systems engineering, control theory, and statistics.

Is this for you?

You might like this major if you also like: seeing how math explains natural phenomena; understanding the theory behind the way computers and other mechanical things work.

Consider this major if you are good at: attention to detail; creativity; critical reading/thinking; math; organizing; quantitative analysis; teamwork *...or have...* initiative; patience; writing skills.

Recommended high school prep:

English 4, math 4, lab science 3, social studies 3, and a foreign language 2–3. Try to take as many mathematics classes as possible. Also, if available, take courses in computer programming and statistics.

Did you know...

...that you can become an applied mathematics major if you have an interest in math and in an application such as engineering—you don't necessarily have to decide between your two interests?

Typical courses in this major:

Calculus
Differential equations
Linear algebra
Discrete mathematics
Numerical analysis
Physics
Computer science
Probability theory
Logic design and computer architecture
Systems design
Signals, systems, and control engineering
Optimization theory and technique
Data analysis and linear models
Multivariate analysis and data mining
Theoretical statistics
Time series

Concentrations:

In college: computing/information science; systems engineering; statistics.

If you go on to grad school: operations research; control theory.

What the study of this major is like:

As an applied mathematics major, you have two homes. You spend plenty of time studying math—in your third and fourth year, you will most likely take at least two math courses per semester. In addition, you'll enroll in classes in the application area you choose. By searching for connections between math and its applications, you combine knowledge from your two bases. In a kind of conceptual loop, you apply abstract principles of math to your area of interest, and then translate functions of that application back into more general mathematics. For example, in a control theory course, you learn how to construct a feedback mechanism, such as a robot. In a math course, you explore the math behind the mechanism. Your task is to discover the link between what you've learned in the two courses.

The material in math courses and in many applications courses is presented in lecture formats. You are expected to spend considerable time outside class getting comfortable with the material. Some applications courses may involve laboratories or computer programming.

Although a Bachelor of Science degree prepares you to start a career, many professionals return for more specialized training by pursuing a master's degree. Some colleges offer a five-year integrated program leading to a Bachelor of Science degree in applied mathematics and a Master of Science degree in your chosen application area or in applied mathematics. Colleges may also have different mathematics requirements. No matter which technical field you go into, a strong mathematical background—one that teaches you to think abstractly and conceptually—is essential. Because technology changes so rapidly, specific engineering skills can soon become out-of-date. If you have a good grounding in math, though, you should be able to adapt to advances in technology.

Other majors you might like:

Computer science
Management information systems
Aeronautical/aerospace engineering
Statistics
Systems engineering
Management science
Astrophysics
Mathematics/computer science
Computational mathematics
Information systems
Economics

Questions to ask colleges:

How are the different majors offered in the math department distinguished? Do they contain distinctly different content?

How well do relevant departments (such as physics and engineering) cooperate? Are there adequate facilities, particularly in the applications areas, for course work and research?

How easy is it to switch majors? There are many exciting disciplines in and around applied mathematics, so your course work may spark new interests.

Career options and trends:

Engineer*; statistician*; actuary; management consultant; financial mathematical analyst.

Demand is always strong for people who are strong in math. Traditionally, jobs requiring a math background have been found primarily in the technical and engineering fields; but going forward the best career prospects are for those who can apply math to the life and medical sciences.

Insider's viewpoint:

"As a mathematician, I'm excited about being able to bring my knowledge to bear on other areas of knowledge. I love having problems brought to me by researchers from a wide variety of disciplines, from science and engineering to social science and medicine."

—Professor James Alexander, Case Western Reserve University

For more info:

Society for Industrial and Applied Mathematics (SIAM)
3600 University City Science Center
Philadelphia, PA 19104
(215) 382-9800
www.siam.org

Mathematical Association of America (MAA)
1529 18th St., N.W.
Washington, DC 20036
(800) 741-9415
www.maa.org

Mathematics

What it's about:

Math majors develop the ability to explore, conjecture, and reason logically, as well as to use mathematical methods to solve problems. Mathematics is both a discipline and a tool used extensively in the sciences, medicine, engineering, and industry.

Is this for you?

You might like this major if you also like: music, especially composition; art, especially as it relates to shape, balance, and design; playing with abstractions; intellectual challenges; solving puzzles; philosophy; writing that is succinct and precise.

Consider this major if you are good at: attention to detail; creativity; critical reading/thinking; math; organizing; quantitative analysis; spatial thinking/analysis *...or have...* initiative; patience.

Recommended high school prep:

English 4, math 4 (including precalculus and trigonometry), lab science 4 (including physics), social studies 3, and a foreign language 2–3. Calculus and statistics would be helpful, but are not required.

Did you know...

...that high-level math is not about memorizing procedures? It is about understanding basic, abstract structures to discover deeper, more refined patterns that give insights into the workings of the world around us. Like music, math is the creative exploration of possibilities within prescribed rules and parameters.

Typical courses in this major:

Single-variable calculus
Multivariable calculus
Elementary statistics
Discrete mathematics
Linear algebra
Differential equations
Modern algebra
Modeling
Combinatorics
Number theory
Modern geometry
Topology
Complex analysis

Concentrations:

In college: statistics; applied mathematics; discrete mathematics; computational mathematics.

If you go on to grad school: number theory; functional analysis; geometric analysis; topology; logic.

What the study of this major is like:

Mathematics deals with how basic patterns and processes can be turned into abstract representations. As a math major, you work with increasingly abstract concepts in analytic, algebraic, and geometric math.

Analysis (the mathematics of dynamic change) begins with calculus. Calculus was developed in the seventeenth century to analyze changes in physical quantities—for example, the minimum distance between two planets or the maximum profit of a business enterprise. Through calculus, you can determine the lengths of curves and the volumes of solids, or investigate the acceleration of moving objects. Analysis continues with differential equations, in which you use the knowledge of the way things interact to predict their future state. Real analysis, complex analysis, and functional analysis provide tools that deal with unexpected phenomena.

Modern algebra involves integers, counting problems, and symmetries. It begins with linear algebra (probably the most useful undergrad course) and continues with combinatorics and number theory. You also study structures known as groups, rings, and fields, in order to explore such questions as "is pi rational?"

Discrete mathematics and combinatorics consider the finite nature of certain problems—for instance, in how many ways can a fixed number of vehicles visit multiple locations, and which schedule would be the least costly? Modern geometry and topology study the world of transformations and explore the deeper meaning of concepts such as shape, area, and distance.

Traditionally, math has been taught entirely through lectures, but this approach is changing. Many math courses now make use of computers; you do projects that help you explore a topic in depth; and in written assignments, you clarify difficult concepts. In addition, lectures themselves have changed. Today, many professors understand the importance of describing how particular mathematical concepts came about and of showing how mathematical insights can be applied outside the classroom.

Majoring in mathematics can be an intense experience. There are always new ideas to be mastered. Learning how to rely on precise definition, how to tackle an unfamiliar problem, and how to construct a proof is sometimes difficult. Many math majors find it helpful to form supportive study groups, in which participants share their struggles and insights. Activities such as annual CO-MAP modeling competitions are built on teamwork; good mathematics programs build strong camaraderie among majors.

Some colleges emphasize applied math or allow you to take an applied mathematics track. These programs typically replace advanced courses in analysis, algebra, and geometry with advanced work in statistics, operations research, and modeling. It is usually a less intense major that can be excellent preparation for the workplace.

Other majors you might like:
Engineering
Economics
Physics
Computer science
Accounting
Finance
Business statistics
Actuarial science
Mathematics teacher education
Information systems
Music theory and composition
Philosophy

Questions to ask colleges:
How does the program incorporate computers into math classes? Is there an emphasis on writing?

In which competitions do math students participate?

Do any of the faculty members use students to help with their research? Have any instructors published a joint paper with a student?

Is a capstone project or fourth-year thesis required?

Career options and trends:
Operations researcher*; business consultant; high school teacher*; statistician*; financial or securities analyst; college professor; actuary.

There is a steady, strong demand for math majors. Many employers (as well as graduate schools in professions such as law and medicine) will give preferential treatment to graduates with a degree in math. The study of mathematics is excellent preparation for a host of employment opportunities in business, finance, insurance, communications, electronics, scientific research of any type, and any field that has challenging problems to solve.

Insider's viewpoint:
"Be careful; it's a difficult field. All the classes I'd ever taken before were 'standard' math, very real-world-based math, application-based math, which is a far cry from the abstract reality of a math major's world."

—John, sophomore, Case Western Reserve University

For more info:
The Mathematical Association of America (MAA)
1529 18th St., N.W.
Washington, DC 20036
(800) 741-9415
www.maa.org

Statistics

What it's about:

Statistics is the practical science of dealing with data—information in the form of numbers, often from many sources. In this major, you study the most efficient ways to collect data and to analyze and interpret it. Statistics, which forms the backbone of all research methods, includes the study of experimental design, regression analysis (the relationships between measurements), probability, and sampling theory.

Is this for you?

You might like this major if you also like: math; quantitative problems; figuring out how things work and how to make them work better; dealing with numbers; puzzles.

Consider this major if you are good at: active listening; attention to detail; critical reading/thinking; math; quantitative analysis; research; teamwork ...*or have...* patience; writing skills.

Recommended high school prep:

English 4, math 4 (including calculus), lab science 3, social studies 3, and a foreign language 2–3. If possible, take statistics.

Did you know...

...that statistics includes much more than just tallying batting averages or shooting percentages? Using statistics, you can perform a wide range of tasks, such as deciding which people should fill out a certain survey or ensuring that a medication up for approval works better than medicines currently on the market.

...that statisticians are in high demand and are often well paid? Think of an area of study that interests you. You can usually find statisticians giving work-related advice to professionals in that field.

Typical courses in this major:

Statistical methods I, II
Statistical theory I, II
Experimental design and analysis of variance
Regression analysis
Statistical computing
Sample survey theory
Applied time series analysis
Technical writing
Probability
Statistical quality control
Calculus

Concentrations:

In college: actuarial science.

If you go on to grad school: industrial statistics; environmental statistics; bioinformatics.

What the study of this major is like:

Statistics is the science of handling data in the most effective way. It's not just a branch of mathematics, but a separate discipline that uses a great deal of math and relies heavily on computers. Most statistics departments are in colleges of liberal arts and sciences, but several are in business colleges and a few are in colleges of engineering or agriculture. Combined departments of mathematics and statistics also exist, primarily in small- to medium-size institutions.

If you want to complete an undergraduate degree (B.S.) in statistics, be prepared to take a fairly vigorous math curriculum. In your first year, you concentrate on general courses and mathematics, including a year of calculus. Introductory courses in statistics and computers most often begin in the second year, after you have developed sufficient math skills. In your third year, statistics becomes the dominant part of your studies.

Courses in the applied techniques of describing and analyzing data to extract information require strong skills in algebra and computing. For courses focusing on probability and the mathematical theory of statistics, you'll need to sharpen your abilities in calculus and in logic. In courses that deal with the preparation of sample surveys, small groups of students design a study, collect and analyze the data, and present a report of the results. If you plan on going to graduate school, you should study advanced calculus.

To be a successful statistician, you must understand both the theory and the application of statistics. In an important application, statisticians routinely advise scientists and researchers in business, government, nonprofit organizations, and industry on how to handle data in a wide variety of projects. The work that statisticians do demands not only mathematical tools but also communication, teamwork, and technical writing skills, as well as familiarity with the concepts and terminology of the business or organization they're assisting. In fact, statisticians must rely on the business executives or professionals in these organizations to supply the data they'll be examining. Therefore, courses in the natural sciences, humanities, and social sciences are essential. You are strongly encouraged to strengthen your oral and written communication skills by taking writing and speech courses or participating in related extracurricular activities.

Statistics programs that emphasize actuarial science tend to focus on preparing you for actuarial exams. Other programs concentrate on a particular discipline. For example, biostatistics is more likely to be taught in a college that has a medical education program. In still other programs, geared to preparing students to pursue advanced degrees, the math curriculum is usually much more rigorous.

Other majors you might like:
Accounting
Information systems
Genetics
Economics
Systems science/theory
Econometrics/quantitative economics
Computational mathematics
Actuarial science
Applied mathematics
Systems engineering
Operations research
Business statistics

Career options and trends:
Actuary; data analyst*; statistician*; statistical analyst*; statistical programmer; professor*; project statistician.

Statisticians work in a wide variety of areas, including manufacturing, pharmaceuticals, insurance, government agencies, consulting firms, and agricultural research. Statistics majors also find jobs in actuarial science, statistical programming, operations research, and mathematical analysis. A graduate degree can increase your career opportunities.

Most high school students haven't heard of statistics and thus don't consider it as a major; this situation seems unlikely to change. Therefore, there are always more jobs available than there are college graduates to fill the positions.

Insider's viewpoint:
"I can work on a psychological problem one week, work on U.S. census data the next, and then work on health issues in an animal species. I have the constant opportunity to learn new things about subjects that I have no formal education in."

—Michele Marini, Instructor, Virginia Tech

For more info:
American Statistical Association (ASA)
1429 Duke St.
Alexandria, VA 22314-3415
(888) 231-3473
www.amstat.org

Multi/interdisciplinary studies

If you've ever written a college application essay, you've probably tried to tap your knowledge and experience in many areas in order to answer an interesting or important question. That's what multi/interdisciplinary studies are like. These majors take more than one path of learning to arrive at understanding.

The world is not just black and white. To get the flavor of multi/interdisciplinary studies, don't think chocolate or vanilla. Think swirl or twist. By mixing areas of study, we can effectively answer questions like these: Why do we think and behave the way we do? How does the mind relate to the body? Can we ever live in peace? If you want that broad perspective, you need to study the finer points of more than one subject. Each of these majors covers many topics and the majors are very different from one another. In this chapter you'll flash back to the fall of Rome and glimpse the future frontiers of science.

Multi/interdisciplinary fields include Medieval and Renaissance studies, neuroscience, gerontology, global studies, and peace studies. Gerontology, for example, looks at aging from many angles—biological, behavioral, and social.

"Almost every aspect of the human aging process impacts on most academic disciplines—arts and sciences, business administration, education, government, law, medicine, mental health, nursing, public health, public relations, and communication," says Professor Joseph F. Cimini, University of Scranton.

Global studies also casts a wide net. "The global studies major is based on new approaches to knowledge and combining political economy and cultural studies with comparative regional studies," explains Professor Eve Walsh Stoddard of St. Lawrence University. "It emphasizes the interconnections and interactions, as opposed to studying discrete, separate topics."

The same goes for neuroscience, which combines studies of the nervous system and behavior. Neuroscience is found within other sciences such as biology, chemistry, physics, and psychology, but also in mathematics, computer science, philosophy, economics, and cognitive science. "Neuroscience has a huge impact in many areas of science and beyond," says Professor Richard Lewis, Pomona College.

A glimpse at graduate studies in just three majors suggests how relevant multi/interdisciplinary studies can be. In gerontology, graduate tracks include elder law, geriatric nursing, personal care/assisted living, and retirement planning. In global studies, graduates might specialize in peace and conflict studies, international relations, or environmental issues. In neuroscience, graduate studies include behavioral or cognitive functions of the nervous system.

No easy questions

You can probably picture the reaction at the Thanksgiving table when you come home from college and tell everyone you're considering a multi/interdisciplinary major. "Huh?" they may ask. If that happens, calmly explain the importance of knowing about more than one thing—and that these majors combine various in-depth studies to meet a new need, like caring for a growing population of old people, or understanding a complex problem like war.

At that point, the focus should shift to the turkey. But if anyone's still listening, tell them how you carefully chose your college and your major.

Why would you choose an interdisciplinary major? Maybe you enjoy making connections between cultures or exploring the unknown. Perhaps you have good interpersonal skills, like to solve problems, are socially or politically active, or love to volunteer. Those are the types of students who are interested in these majors.

To pinpoint your multidisciplinary or interdisciplinary major requires a lot of legwork. You'll need to find out as much as you can about the major and how it fits into the college's courses. What is the history of the major at the college? What is the expertise of the faculty members? Is your major supported by related activities, speakers, or conferences? What exactly will your degree be in? Can you declare a double major, a minor, or a concentration in another subject? How about an independent study or self-guided learning in something that you're passionate about? What are graduates doing—going to professional or grad school, teaching, or pursuing business careers? What opportunities exist for off-campus and experiential study?

Just as there are no easy answers when you study these diverse fields, there are no easy questions when looking at colleges that offer them. You'll need to know if study abroad is required. If so, what are the costs and are they greater than studying on campus? Can your financial aid be applied toward study abroad? In a major that fuses two or more fields, is one stressed more than the other? Which department is the major under? Does the college offer career help, field experience, research opportunities, or a mentoring program to get real-world skills or find a job?

Students interested in these combined majors should look for colleges of arts and sciences, liberal arts, social sciences, or professional studies; schools of humanities; and divisions of interdisciplinary majors or life sciences. In this book, also read the sections on Area, ethnic, and gender studies; the Humanities; and the Social sciences.

Gerontology

Also known as:
Elder studies

What it's about:
Gerontology majors study the processes of aging and the resulting biological, behavioral, and social changes that affect older people's lives. The practical application of gerontology involves providing services to older adults and their families.

Is this for you?
You might like this major if you also like: helping people; community service activities; family relationships; interacting with older adults.

Consider this major if you are good at: caring/ nurturing; counseling; creativity; critical reading/ thinking; organizing ...or have... a sense of justice; initiative; interpersonal skills; patience; verbal skills; writing skills.

Recommended high school prep:
English 4, math 3, lab science 3, social studies 3, and a foreign language 2–3. If possible, take a service-learning class—one that combines community service experience with learning.

Did you know...
...that according to estimates, by the year 2030 there will be about 72 million older persons in the United States, more than twice as many as there were in 1997?

Typical courses in this major:
Social problems of aging
Aging around the world
Aging and the life cycle
Aging and human behavior
Aging and the community
Health and aging
Crime and aging
Social policy and aging
Aging and death
Special topics in gerontology
Psychology of aging
Housing needs of older adults
Physical activity programs
Services for older adults
Food for the elderly

Concentrations:
In college: health care; human services; long-term-care administration; social work.

If you go on to grad school: elder law; community advocacy; estate and financial planning; geriatric nursing; human development; nursing home administration; personal care/assisted living; recreation/ leisure; retirement planning.

What the study of this major is like:
The gerontology major prepares you to understand the process of aging and to work for organizations that serve older adults (such as Area Agencies on Aging; family services; long-term-care facilities; federal, state, and local government agencies; retirement communities; and business and industry institutions). If you plan to pursue a career administering or developing programs for a government agency, you should take courses in finance and accounting, and, probably, program planning and evaluation. In addition, oral and written communications skills and computer literacy are essential.

In this major, your course work will include both the liberal arts and preparation for an entry-level practice in human services or advanced work in gerontology/aging studies, social work, public administration, social welfare, or related fields. Your courses in the major are interdisciplinary and cover topics that explore what it is like to grow old, how an individual typically progresses through the life cycle, and what an aging population means to society.

In courses on the aging process, you examine, first, the physical and intellectual changes that occur from middle age to the end of life, including intellectual stability and Alzheimer's disease. Later courses deal with the influence of family and community on older people's quality of life; topics include the changing role that families play, ways in which members of minority and ethnic groups experience aging, and influences of social class on aging. Your third area of study will focus on the laws, programs, and institutions that help or hinder the process of aging in the United States and other countries. You examine programs such as Social Security, Medicare, and Medicaid, and the ways in which government influences private programs through tax incentives and regulation.

Some gerontology programs emphasize research and statistics. Others stress theory. Still others may focus on casework. The traditions of the college, as well as any religious affiliation, will likely determine the orientation of its gerontology program.

The gerontology major is not more, and not less, challenging than most social science programs. The subject matter is generally taught in lecture courses, with opportunities for service learning, internships, special-topic courses, guided independent study, and faculty-student research projects. As a major, you will probably spend substantial time volunteering or interning in both profit-making and not-for-profit agencies that provide services for the elderly in areas like housing, health, mental health, transportation, education, recreation, and social work. For example, you may visit senior citizen centers, volunteer in nursing homes, work part-time in retirement communities, or have field experiences in a government program.

Other majors you might like:
Urban, community, and regional planning
Human development and family studies
Exercise sciences
Health care administration
Human services
Nursing (RN)
Occupational therapy
Physical therapy
Psychology
Social work

Anthropology
Women's studies

Questions to ask colleges:
Are guided independent-study courses, community-service learning experiences, and internships available?

Can students declare double majors, a minor, or a concentration?

What library and electronic media resources support gerontology study?

How successful are graduates of the program in graduate and professional schools, as well as in careers?

Career options and trends:
Research gerontologist; geriatric physician; elder law attorney*; gerontology research assistant; long-term care administrator*; advocate for older adults; long-term care caseworker*; area agency on aging staff member*.

Additional employment possibilities for gerontology graduates include program development positions in recreation, education, and social services; administration of nursing homes, housing projects, and government programs; and service roles in multipurpose senior citizen centers, mental health agencies, and human resources departments of corporations and not-for-profit organizations.

Employment prospects are excellent in this field. An aging population with increasing life spans ensures continued demand for professionals knowledgeable in gerontology and elder care issues.

For more info:
Gerontological Society of America (GSA)
1030 15th St., N.W.
Washington, DC 20005
(202) 842-1275
www.geron.org

Association for Gerontology in Higher Education
1030 15th St., N.W.
Suite 240
Washington, DC 20005
(202) 289-9806
www.aghe.org

Global studies

What it's about:

Global studies is an interdisciplinary major that combines politics, economics, and cultural studies with comparative regional studies. You learn to view individuals, communities, states, economies, cultures, and ecologies in larger, internationally oriented contexts.

Is this for you?

You might like this major if you also like: current events; politics; international popular culture; world music; other cultures; travel; geography; history; peace and/or social justice movements.

Consider this major if you are good at: creativity; critical reading/thinking; leadership; research; spatial thinking/analysis *...or have...* initiative; verbal skills; writing skills.

Recommended high school prep:

English 4, math 3, lab science 3, social studies 4, and a foreign language 4. If possible, take courses in world history, economics, statistics, and world geography.

Typical courses in this major:

Introduction to global studies
Introduction to international relations
Introduction to anthropology
Modern world history
The international economy
The global environment
Ethnic conflict and nationalism
Comparative education
Topics in world literature
Global women's issues
Global social movements
Global climate change
Cultural geography
Intercultural studies
Regional perspectives

Concentrations:

Peace and conflict studies; international relations; international economics; gender issues; environmental issues; media and communications; specific regions.

What the study of this major is like:

The global studies major can be challenging, because the field is immense and it requires you to think in ways you might not be accustomed to. Your global studies course work combines aspects of history, economics, geography, and culture. As a major, you will move back and forth between two perspectives: the big-picture approach, in which you examine world systems and world history, and the case studies approach, in which you take an in-depth look at specific regions or nations.

Topics you'll consider include mass migrations, the effects of colonialism, and questions of cultural influence—for instance, can globalization be labeled a synonym for Americanization? Your courses will be taught in lecture or discussion format; students usually do research projects on areas they want to pursue. Language study and experiential learning (such as study-abroad) are important. You will also benefit from reading, and watching, the news and checking the Internet for alternative perspectives.

The global studies major may differ from college to college. Some colleges require you to study abroad and to learn the language of your host area; some have a capstone fourth-year independent project; and some allow you to design the focus of your major. Although certain programs have their own core courses and may have dedicated full-time faculty members, programs in other colleges may be a collection of courses from various departments, sometimes coordinated by only one faculty member.

Some colleges offer a broad range of international courses; others have a smaller number, perhaps restricted to fewer regions of the world. In some colleges, the cost of study abroad is the same as on-campus study; in others, you cannot take all your financial aid with you when you study abroad. Also, the types of concentrations offered can vary among colleges.

Other majors you might like:
International business
Peace and conflict studies
Geography
Sociology
Anthropology
Religious studies
Intercultural/diversity studies
International relations
Women's studies
Journalism
Economics
Linguistics

Questions to ask colleges:
What kinds of study-abroad opportunities are offered? For example, a strong global studies program should offer both on-campus studies of, and off-campus opportunities in, the developing countries outside Europe. Also, look for colleges that make it affordable to study abroad.

Does the program cover a range of topics? Most global studies programs include the social science disciplines (sociology, anthropology, politics, history, economics) within an international framework. But does the program also touch on the arts, communications, and ecology and climate?

Career options and trends:
High school teacher*; international NGO (nongovernmental organization) worker*; Peace Corps volunteer; government/State Department worker*.

Global studies majors also go on to work in international business and international banking. A state certificate or license is required for teaching in secondary public schools. Working for the State Department usually requires language proficiency.

As political, social, economic, and environmental concerns continue to bring the world closer to us, job opportunities in the global studies field continue to grow. These days, it is crucial that you strengthen your qualifications by living abroad or learning to speak a second language.

For more info:
Global Studies Association (GSA)
Oxford Brookes University
Headington
Oxford, UK OX 013P
+44 (0) 18 65 483 752
www.globalstudiesassociation.org

International Studies Association (ISA)
324 Social Sciences
University of Arizona
Tuscon, AZ 85721
(520) 621-7715
www.isanet.org

Social Science Research Center (SSRC)
810 Seventh Ave.
New York, NY 10019
(212) 377-2700
www.ssrc.org

Historic preservation

What it's about:

Majoring in historic preservation will teach you the theories and practices of preserving historically significant buildings, structures, and landscapes for future generations. You'll study the history of architecture, the principles of conservation and restoration, and the tools and techniques used in documenting, maintaining, and protecting cultural resources.

Is this for you?

You might like this major if you also like: exploring old buildings; antiquing; storytelling; detective work; reading about history and other cultures; travel; photography; visiting museums and historic sites.

Consider this major if you are good at: attention to detail; creativity; critical reading/thinking; leadership; research; spatial thinking/analysis; teamwork ...*or have...* initiative; verbal skills; writing skills.

Recommended high school prep:

English 4, math 3, lab science 4 (including physics), social studies 4, visual arts 2, and a foreign language 3–4. History courses offer the best preparation for this major. If they are available, courses in art history, photography, drafting/technical drawing, and speech communication are also recommended.

Typical courses in this major:

Foundations of architecture
Architectural history
American architecture
Documentation and recording
History and theory of preservation
Preservation planning and policy
Material resources of preindustrial America
Preservation law and finance
Landscape preservation
Researching historic structures and sites
Technology and materials for building conservation
Designing for an existing context
Exterior and interior rehabilitation
Social and cultural landscapes
Codes and requirements
Site development, interpretation, and management

Concentrations:

Building conservation; landscape preservation; documentation and research; preservation planning; site management.

What the study of this major is like:

This major trains students to be the stewards of America's historic buildings, structures, and landscapes. The program, which involves a mix of lectures and hands-on experience, presents the theory and history of preservation and the tools and techniques used in documenting, maintaining, and protecting cultural resources.

You'll learn the nuts and bolts of the profession—investigation of the history of a building using local records and archives, analysis of its construction and style, and examination of physical evidence. By pulling all the information together, you'll be able to determine the significance of the structure. And you'll come to understand how preserving historic buildings and sites provides the community with a renewed appreciation of its heritage.

Your classes will cover a wide range of subjects, such as landscape architecture and urban planning, architectural history, conservation techniques, public relations, as well as land-use, real-estate, and tax policies. Then in individual and group projects, these interrelated topics will be applied to specific buildings, sites, structures, and objects as well as to the community as a whole.

The fieldwork is what distinguishes the historic preservation major. You deal directly with old stones, timbers, and documents. Some colleges have specialized laboratories for this work; most programs team with local or regional historic sites and agencies to supplement their on-campus facilities and to provide extended learning opportunities for their students.

All programs have similar core requirements that include courses on preservation theory and philosophy, architectural history, documentation techniques, and public policy principles. Programs differ in the amount of emphasis given to fieldwork and in the types and variety of elective courses and internship opportunities offered. The specific nature of each program usually depends on which academic department the historic preservation major is housed in and where the college itself is located.

Programs housed in schools of architecture tend to be more technically oriented—they emphasize the built environment through documentation and technology courses and through projects in adaptive use and design. Programs housed in planning departments focus more on public policy. If the major is in the history department, the emphasis will be on general research using documentation from the past. And the location of the college itself largely determines the types of internships and on-site fieldwork available. As might be expected, smaller communities have a feel and an influence that differ from those of urban areas.

One of the biggest challenges of this rewarding major is the research component. You'll use a variety of research techniques, including nontraditional primary sources such as the building itself. Time management is very important, because many projects require you to be self-motivated and self-directed. A keen sense of curiosity and a good dose of patience will serve you well as you work beyond the classroom and in your future career.

Other majors you might like:
American studies
Archaeology
Housing and human environments
Art history
Architectural history/criticism
Geography
Cultural resource management
History

Architectural engineering
Museum studies
Urban, community, and regional planning
Public policy analysis

Questions to ask colleges:
Are internships or fieldwork required for this major? What types are available, and how does the college help students obtain them?

Is the college connected to local preservation organizations, agencies, and historic sites?

What types of jobs have graduates of the program obtained?

Career options and trends:
Historic preservation consultant; cultural resource manager; historic site manager or curator; urban planner.

Planners and developers have come to realize that it is often more economical to restore than to build anew. Because of the growing trend to adapt and reuse historic buildings by modifying and repurposing the interiors, a greater number of skilled professionals with formal preservation training will be needed.

For more info:
National Trust for Historic Preservation
1785 Massachusetts Ave., N.W.
Washington, DC 20036-2117
(800) 944-6847
www.nationaltrust.org

National Council for Preservation Education
www.uvm.edu/histpres/ncpe

Medieval and Renaissance studies

What it's about:

Medieval and Renaissance studies explores the ideas, achievements, and practices of the period A.D. 500–1660. These eras comprise the heart of most modern cultures of the West and Near East, affecting current literature, philosophy, art, history, religion, and politics.

Is this for you?

You might like this major if you also like: the History Channel; drama; music; Renaissance fairs; foreign languages and cultures; Shakespeare; painting; sculpture; architecture; discovering the origins of social attitudes and practices.

Consider this major if you are good at: attention to detail; creativity; critical reading/thinking; organizing; research; spatial thinking/analysis *...or have...* initiative; writing skills.

Recommended high school prep:

English 4, math 3, lab science 3, social studies 4, and a foreign language 3–4. If possible, take at least one European history class as well as an art history, music history, or theater history class.

Did you know...

...that this major offers you opportunities to do focused, original research based on your own interests? You might be drawn to examples of devout worship or bawdy storytelling. You may concentrate on a specific author or artist, and then study the society in which he or she worked. Or you might consider the social forces that shaped the hospital, the parliament, and the organization of work according to clock time; study the evolution of jury trials or the idea of human rights; or trace the spread of ideas after the printing press was invented.

Typical courses in this major:

The great cathedrals
Medieval art
Leonardo da Vinci
Classical drama
Dante and medieval theology
Religion of late antiquity
Arthurian legend
Science and Islam
Chaucer/Shakespeare/Milton
Age of the Baroque
Judaism in the Middle Ages
The Italian Renaissance
England: Reformation to revolution
Spanish medieval literature
Music and the Church
Medieval philosophy

Concentrations:

In college: a particular author, artist, nation, monarch (e.g., Elizabeth I), or cultural practice.

If you go on to grad school: the medieval period; the Renaissance; a particular religious tradition, philosophic tradition, or art form.

What the study of this major is like:

If you major in medieval and Renaissance studies, you will analyze the historical and cultural features of the sixth through seventeenth centuries in Europe and the Middle East; be able to read at least one relevant language; become familiar with the primary artistic, intellectual, and social developments of the period; and recognize medieval and Renaissance contributions to modern thought and culture.

In this major, you should take a variety of courses in a number of academic areas: architecture, art history, classics, religious studies, English, history, modern languages, music, philosophy, and theater arts, among others. Although some courses may be in lecture format, most are seminars highlighting student discussion, independent research, and presentations (as individuals and in groups). Several courses may be devoted to interdisciplinary topics, such as the medieval or Renaissance city, the iconographic tradition, Shakespeare's world, encounters with Islam, and voice and verse. Because many central documents of the period were written in languages other than English, a reading knowledge of Latin, French, German, Spanish, or Italian—whichever suits your interests—is generally required.

Many programs have a strong focus on either English or history; others emphasize England or Europe; still others stress the Renaissance to the near-exclusion of the Middle Ages. Sometimes the focus of a program is evident in the basic course offerings or in specially presented topics or seminars. At other times, the focus is apparent only when you look into the faculty's research interests. If certain aspects of the major appeal to you, check into the emphases of the colleges you are considering to make sure you don't end up feeling frustrated or restricted.

Student and faculty gatherings are often an excellent source of information and community for medieval and Renaissance studies majors. At such meetings, you can hear about the latest research and get to know both professors and other students with similar interests. Many programs encourage you and your classmates to attend local stage and musical performances, museum exhibits, lectures, and conferences. As a medieval and Renaissance studies major, you can look forward to having stimulating exchanges with students and faculty members and to making genuine academic discoveries.

Other majors you might like:
English
History
Art history
Archaeology
Classics
Philosophy
Architectural history/criticism
Comparative literature
European studies
Religious studies
Italian studies
Drama and theater arts

Questions to ask colleges:

How many departments contribute to the medieval and Renaissance studies faculty? Is there an undergraduate research program? Is an undergraduate thesis required or encouraged? Which relevant study resources or activities are available on campus? Is there a larger academic community (such as a related graduate program) that undergraduate majors can easily access?

Career options and trends:

A degree in Medieval and Renaissance studies, like all liberal arts degrees, gives you a well-rounded education rather than training for a particular career. The degree is excellent preparation for graduate or professional school, and for careers in law, medicine, businesses, the arts, journalism, museology, and teaching.

For more info:

Medieval Academy of America (MAA)
104 Mount Auburn St., 5th Fl.
Cambridge, MA 02138
(617) 491-1622
www.medievalacademy.org

Renaissance Society of America (RSA)
City University of New York
365 Fifth Ave., Room 5400
New York, NY 10016-4309
(212) 817-2130
www.rsa.org

Neuroscience

Also known as:
Psychobiology

What it's about:
Neuroscience is the interdisciplinary study of the nervous system and behavior. It covers issues such as the molecular and cellular basis of neuronal function, nervous system structure, systems of neurons as processors of information, the representation of functions in the brain, the evolutionary development of the nervous system, neural correlates of behavior, and mechanisms of nervous system disorders. The neuroscience major prepares you for graduate study in neuroscience or a related field and for careers requiring a solid foundation in science.

Is this for you?
You might like this major if you also like: thinking about how we think; anatomy; computers; science; exploring the unknown; probability-based reasoning; complex problems.

Consider this major if you are good at: attention to detail; creativity; critical reading/thinking; math; quantitative analysis; research; teamwork *...or have...* manual dexterity; mechanical facility; verbal skills.

Recommended high school prep:
English 4, math 4 (including precalculus), lab science 4 (including biology, chemistry, and physics), social studies 4, and a foreign language 3–4. Your courses in English and social studies are just as important as your math and science courses.

Did you know...
...that areas of neuroscience are found not only in traditional science fields, such as biology, chemistry, physics, and psychology, but also in mathematics, computer science, philosophy, economics, and cognitive science?

...that the curriculum for neuroscience at most colleges parallels a pre-med program?

Typical courses in this major:
General chemistry
Organic chemistry
General biology
Calculus
Statistics
Physics
Introductory psychology
Introductory neuroscience
Neurobiology
Behavioral neuroscience
Cognitive neuroscience
Systems neuroscience
Neuropharmacology
Sensory neuroscience
Developmental neuroscience

Concentrations:
Neurobiology; comparative and evolutionary neuroscience; systems neuroscience; behavioral neuroscience; social neuroscience; cognitive neuroscience; computational neuroscience.

What the study of this major is like:
Neuroscience addresses interesting questions. How do we think? Why do we behave the way we do? What is the relationship between the mind and the brain? How does the brain give rise to consciousness? How do nature and nurture influence our behavior? But neuroscientists seek answers to these questions in the lab sciences.

You shouldn't think of becoming a neuroscience major unless you enjoy laboratory research approaches to exploring these issues. Like other life sciences majors, neuroscience students spend many hours in labs. All neuroscience programs will expect you to obtain a firm grounding in the basics, including biology, chemistry, physics, math, psychology, and statistics. Some students may be frustrated by taking so many courses that do not deal specifically with the major. But your understanding of the nervous system will depend on your familiarity with scientific fundamentals.

Neuroscience may be the broadest major that exists. It is based in the life sciences but has connections to the social sciences and humanities. To date, there is no agreed-on sense of what is essential for the neuroscience curriculum. Each program differs in some ways from all the others. At each school that offers the major, the nature of the program is determined by the faculty members who teach the courses. Few colleges have hired instructors specifically to develop undergraduate programs in neuroscience. Instead, professors develop departmental majors such as biology and psychology. Therefore, the major depends on which areas of neuroscience are valued in the departments that contribute faculty members to the program. Look carefully at course offerings to see if the courses in the major match your interests.

Neuroscience is in an exciting phase because techniques have been developed that provide new ways to explore the brain. The human brain is the most complex phenomenon in nature. Answers to many neuroscientists' questions are beginning to surface, but much remains unknown. If you expect final answers, you will be frustrated by the brain's complexity. If you are excited by a sense of discovery, then you should do well in neuroscience.

Other majors you might like:
Molecular biology
Psychology
Behavioral sciences
Chemistry
Philosophy
Biopsychology
Information systems
Neurobiology/physiology
Biomedical engineering
Robotics technology
Biological/physical sciences
Electroencephalograph technology

Questions to ask colleges:
What are the areas of faculty expertise?

Will students get a background in molecular and cellular aspects of neuroscience? Will students get training in neuroanatomy, neuropharmacology, neurophysiology, and neurochemistry?

How much emphasis is placed on behavior? How much emphasis is placed on cognitive neuroscience, social neuroscience, computational neuroscience, and comparative and evolutionary neuroscience?

Career options and trends:
Physician*; college professor/researcher*; high school teacher; science writer; research technician (e.g., with a drug company or research lab); electroneurodiagnostic technician.

Neuroscience is becoming an important area within the sciences. Medical and academic prospects are relatively good in this field. Increasingly, universities are hiring in this area, especially in fields that have not had neuroscience representation, such as computer science, mathematics, and cognitive science.

Insider's viewpoint:
"I enjoy learning about the human brain and all of the bodily and spiritual connections to it, to help understand people around me as well as myself. Being able to spout off about the brain is also great at parties."

—Candace, class of 1998, University of Rochester

For more info:
Society for Neuroscience (SfN)
1121 14th St., N.W.
Suite 1010
Washington, DC 20005
(202) 962-4000
www.sfn.org

Peace and conflict studies

What it's about:

As a peace and conflict studies major, you explore strategies for constructing a just and peaceful world. You study issues of war, sexism, racism, and poverty; nonviolent social change; and conflict resolution. The approach is both theoretical and experience-based.

Is this for you?

You might like this major if you also like: social and political activism; service-related activities; volunteer activities; creative writing; theater; art; community building; human rights issues.

Consider this major if you are good at: caring/nurturing; creativity; critical reading/thinking; leadership; organizing; persuading/influencing; teamwork *...or have...* initiative; people skills; verbal skills; writing skills.

Recommended high school prep:

English 4, math 3, lab science 3, social studies 4, and a foreign language 4.

Did you know...

...that peace and conflict studies is less about mastering material and more about learning a process of action and reflection? There is a substantial hands-on component to this major. Most students complete internships in the United States and abroad.

Typical courses in this major:

Theory and practice of nonviolence
History of nonviolence
The global political economy
Introduction to international relations
Philosophical inquiry: peace and justice
Contemporary social theory
Postcolonial theory
Conflict resolution
Methods of peacemaking
Philosophy of social science
International law
Theories of international relations
Issues before the United Nations
Marxism
Urban political economy
Feminism, ecology, and peace

Concentrations:

Interpersonal and intergroup conflict resolution; international war and peace; social, economic, and/or environmental justice.

What the study of this major is like:

As a peace and conflict studies major, you spend part of your time in class, learning theory and history, and part of your time in lab situations—in settings (such as internships) where you can develop peacemaking skills and put them to good use. Many courses require you to write papers and present oral reports based on group projects. You become accustomed to analyzing problems locally and globally.

Peace and conflict studies may be a program on its own or an interdepartmental major including courses from different departments. Many programs have been influenced by the traditional peace churches (Quakers, Mennonites, Church of the Brethren) or by Catholic social thought, although some are not affiliated with any religion.

Some programs are global in scope; others tend to focus on the United States. In either case you will be encouraged to explore a non-western culture and issues of human diversity. Some programs also require proficiency in a foreign language equivalent to two years of college-level study. Internships and hands-on learning are encouraged more on some campuses than on others; some programs even offer their own international, off-campus study programs.

Most peace and conflict studies majors take their education very seriously. You will have significant interaction with faculty members who serve as teachers and mentors both in and out of the classroom. Majors frequently make friends they keep long after graduation.

Other majors you might like:
International relations
Women's studies
Gay/lesbian studies
Environmental studies
Religious studies
Philosophy
Criminal justice and law enforcement
Labor/industrial relations
Legal studies
Intercultural/diversity studies
Political science
Near and Middle Eastern studies

Questions to ask colleges:
Does the program sponsor peace-related activities, speakers, conferences, and so on?

How many faculty members participate in the program?

Do the students have a say in the design of their education? What opportunities are there for off-campus and experience-based study?

Have graduates found work in peace and justice efforts?

Career options and trends:
College professor*; nongovernmental organization (NGO) worker*; lawyer*; minister or other member of the clergy*; government worker; public relations manager; international business consultant; human resources manager.

Peace and conflict studies majors also enter graduate and professional schools to become doctors, lawyers, teachers, and caregivers. Many people who eventually teach peace and conflict studies do not pursue graduate training in the field. Instead, they specialize in a discipline that lends itself to a peace perspective, such as sociology, economics, political science, history, or philosophy.

In the United States, mediation and conflict resolution are becoming increasingly promising fields. Also, a peace and conflict studies degree can be useful for positions in a wide range of nongovernmental organizations.

For more info:
Peace and Justice Studies Association (PJSA)
University of San Francisco
2130 Fulton Street, 5th Floor
San Francisco, CA 94117-1080
(415) 422-5238
www.peacejusticestudies.org

Natural resources and conservation

If you are considering the majors in this section, you probably already know about disappearing forests, threats to wildlife habitats, and other ways that humans hurt the environment. The good news is that, by learning about natural resources and conservation, you should be able to do something about these problems. "Students for whom environmental studies is the right major are those who take pleasure in making a difference," says Professor Michael Maniates of Allegheny College. "They have compelling interest in environmental issues and deep-felt concern about current patterns of assault on the environment and what this means for future generations."

If you the love the outdoors, enjoy camping trips or Scouting, or have a passion for bird watching, these majors may be right for you.

Many areas of study, including programs that mix several subjects, fall under this category. "Environmental science zips together a working knowledge of physics, chemistry, and biology," says Professor David E. Smith, University of Virginia. "Environmental *science* programs focus on the natural sciences, whereas environmental *studies* also emphasizes the social sciences as they relate to environmental issues."

Why should you study the social sciences if your interest is in the environment? "Many students enter natural resource and conservation programs in the belief or expectation that they will not be dealing with political, economic, or social areas of study," says Professor David K. Loomis, University of Massachusetts. "Managing natural resources is in many ways accomplished by managing people. There is no distinct separation between society and our natural resources."

As a professional in these fields (and forests, wetlands, and waterways!), you will spend a great deal of time working with the public. In fact, public awareness of the urgency to protect the environment increases funding and jobs in conservation. It's weird, but a healthy job outlook stems in part from an unhealthy environmental outlook.

"Americans are concerned about the environment, and this awareness has created a stable need for environmental professionals in both the government and private sector," Smith says.

Fields, forests, and fisheries

Careers in natural resources management and conservation include research, teaching, consulting, law, journalism, policymaking, government regulation, and advocacy. Some new areas of study and work include conservation biology and watershed management. Okay, now, get out the bug spray and consider these specific jobs: environmental consulting, engineering, and policy analysis; community recycling and energy-conservation projects; research in health risks from pollutants; or working as an outdoor educator, field naturalist, forester, or park ranger; endangered species officer; fisheries biologist, manager, or ecologist. To get a job in wildlife work, such as wildlife biologist or operations officer, you'll face more competition.

When you compare colleges, you'll see that they differ in the way they achieve balance between the scientific and the human pieces of the environmental puzzle.

"This difference is fine and welcome, so long as the program incorporates significant insight from other disciplines and features courses and projects that allow students to effectively combine the skills and ideas they're learning from different fields," advises Maniates.

The issues of accreditation and certification are also huge. That's because some jobs in conservation require specific credentials, like state certifications. See whether your area of interest has certifications and find out if the college degree comes with a certification or a way to earn it. Accreditation is different from certification: certification is for you, while accreditation is for the college. Look for college programs accredited by the professional association for your specialty.

Here are some other questions for colleges: What's the most important course in the program? The answer should reveal that college's priorities. Is your major a full-fledged degree area or just a concentration under another major—like wildlife under zoology?

Are internships available for what you're studying? Are the laboratories up-to-date? Will you get field experience? Are good field sites near the university? The location of the college may suggest a strong program—for instance, in fisheries or regional forestry. Also ask about the variety of classes open to you and how many electives you can take. Explore where students go after graduation. But most of all, read the catalog descriptions of the faculty members.

"College and university programs are only as good as their faculties," Smith emphasizes. "The faculty should be fully engaged in all aspects of scholarship, both teaching and research." Look for opportunities to do supervised research and independent study in a topic that's important to you, especially if you're planning to go to grad school. Graduate studies include environmental policy and law; land use, sprawl, and urban planning; water, wetlands, and marine resources management; forest management/resources and wood science; and fisheries science and management.

For information, go to the Environmental Careers Organization (www.eco.org), and the Ecological Society of America (www.esa.org). Read about related majors in the sections on Agriculture; Parks and recreation; and the Physical sciences.

Environmental science

What it's about:

The interdisciplinary field of environmental science spotlights two concerns: the interaction of the physical and biological processes that shape our natural environment, and the application of scientific methods and research to environmental problems.

Is this for you?

You might like this major if you also like: complex puzzles; exploring the outdoors; using computers; taking a journey to an unknown destination; working on real-world problems; learning how the environment works.

Consider this major if you are good at: attention to detail; creativity; critical reading/thinking; math; organizing; quantitative analysis; research; teamwork *...or have...* initiative; patience; writing skills.

Recommended high school prep:

English 4, math 4 (including precalculus), lab science 4 (earth science, biology, chemistry, physics), social studies 3, and a foreign language 2–3. If they are available, take courses in environmental studies or sciences, ecology, computer applications, and calculus or statistics.

Did you know...

...how important a background in the physical sciences and the life sciences is in this field? If you were investigating the oxygen concentration in a lake or the impact of acid rain on a forest, you would have to evaluate both the physical and the biological processes, and their interaction, to show how the environment works.

Typical courses in this major:

Environmental modeling and methodology
Physical geology
Fundamentals of ecology
Hydrology and water resources
Atmosphere and weather
Population and the environment
Geographic information systems (GIS)
Remote sensing
Global biogeochemistry cycles
Climatological analysis
Biochemistry
Coastal processes
Management of forest ecosystems
Environmental impact assessment
Waste management systems
Marine biology/ecology

Concentrations:

Environmental biology; environmental chemistry; environmental geology; environmental physics; aquatic ecology; terrestrial ecology; environmental health; environmental protection; natural resource management.

What the study of this major is like:

Because problems that affect the environment are complex, environmental science requires an imaginative approach that includes a working knowledge of physics, chemistry, and biology. As a major, you will probably be expected to gain a clear understanding of a wide range of physical and biological processes. For example, you may be required to take classes that deal with the water cycle and its effect on sediments and rocks. You will also study atmospheric science, geoscience, ecology, environmental chemistry, hydrology, and land and resource analysis. When you complete the required subjects, you should be ready to construct a course of study that emphasizes your own strengths and interests.

Fieldwork, which is often an important part of your education, can offer intellectual challenges and the sort of real-world risks that laboratory research can't provide. You may have additional opportunities to do supervised research in which you work closely with faculty members in the field or the laboratory. Paid summer research internships or fellowships at research sites throughout the country are also available; these opportunities supplement your academic course work. For a variety of reasons, environmental science is collaborative; many individuals contribute their special talents as they work in research or investigative groups to solve problems. Therefore, you should develop your communication skills (writing, reading, speaking, listening) and learn the terminology, or distinct vocabulary, of the profession.

Computer skills are also essential; a strong program will provide experience with data analysis, digital mapping, remote sensing, and geographic information systems (GIS). The opportunity to conduct professional-level research in a senior capstone project is another indicator of a good program.

People sometimes confuse environmental science and environmental studies, but these programs differ in key ways. In general, environmental science focuses on the natural sciences (chemistry, biology, physics) as they relate to the environment, whereas environmental studies emphasizes the social sciences (such as economics, policy, or law) as they relate to environmental issues. Environmental science majors study the natural sciences on a deeper level, while environmental studies majors gain additional opportunities through their exposure to the social sciences. Be sure to investigate the programs that interest you to see that you understand the goals and requirements of each.

Other majors you might like:
Environmental engineering
Petroleum engineering
Ecology
Natural sciences
Soil science
Hazardous materials technology
Hydrology/water resources science
Geology/earth science
Geography
Atmospheric science
Oceanography
Environmental health

Questions to ask colleges:
Are the faculty members in this program engaged in both teaching and research? Professors who are active in research can, and do, incorporate aspects of their research into their teaching.

Are undergraduates given opportunities to participate in supervised research and/or independent study? These activities are valuable regardless of which career path you take after graduation.

Career options and trends:
Researcher; college professor or high school teacher; environmental consultant; environmental lawyer; resource manager in industry; regulatory compliance specialist; state or federal government regulator; staff member of an advocacy group.

A master's degree is required for most entry-level research and teaching positions, and a Ph.D. is usually necessary for high-level research.

Job prospects are generally very good in the government, academic, and private sectors for students with undergraduate and graduate degrees, although a master's degree is usually preferred. Because of increasing pressures on the environment from expanding populations and economic development, demand for environmental scientists in both government and industry is projected to grow, both in the United States and abroad. Opportunities should be especially strong in companies that provide regulatory compliance services.

Coupling a major in environmental science with a minor in business, public administration, or health will also improve your job prospects.

For more info:
Ecological Society of America (ESA)
1707 H St., N.W.
Suite 400
Washington, DC 20006
202-833-8773
www.esa.org

Environmental Careers Organization
30 Winter St.
Boston, MA 02108-4720
(617) 426-4375
www.eco.org

Environmental studies

What it's about:

Environmental studies integrates insights and tools from natural and engineering sciences, social sciences, and humanities to explore the effects of human activities on the natural world. In this major, you identify environmental problems, analyze their causes, and learn how to develop a range of solutions.

Is this for you?

You might like this major if you also like: community service; environmental causes; the outdoors; camping trips; Scouting; fishing; hunting; bird watching; working on problems without easy answers; making the world a better place.

Consider this major if you are good at: advocating; attention to detail; creativity; critical reading/ thinking; organizing; quantitative analysis; teamwork ...*or have...* curiosity; initiative; writing skills.

Recommended high school prep:

English 4, math 3, lab science 3 (earth science, biology, chemistry), social studies 3, and a foreign language 2–3. If it is available, take a course in environmental science/studies or ecology.

Did you know...

...that most undergraduates majoring in environmental studies are women?

Typical courses in this major:

Introduction to environmental studies
Ecology
Conservation biology
Environmental chemistry
Geology
Environmental politics
Environmental philosophy and ethics
Environmental and ecological economics
Tools of environmental analysis
Wildlife management
Land use planning
Environmental education
Environmental history
Environmental health
Energy technologies, supply, and policy

Concentrations:

Environmental policy and law; terrestrial ecosystems; aquatic ecosystems; conservation biology and biodiversity; environmental education; environmental ethics and philosophy; environmental preservation; land use and urban planning; energy production and conservation.

What the study of this major is like:

The rapidly growing interest in environmental studies as an undergraduate major results from an increasing awareness of the human impact on the environment. Environmental studies differs from environmental science and environmental engineering in its greater emphasis on the social sciences and humanities. As an environmental studies major, you enroll in a number of academic subjects to examine the causes of, and possible solutions to, environmental problems.

Programs can differ greatly from college to college. Typically, you begin by taking introductory courses in the natural sciences and the social sciences, with at least half your courses in biology, chemistry, and geology. If you have a strong interest in natural science, you might combine a concentration in science with courses in environmental studies.

Many programs offer courses and projects that allow you to integrate, or combine, what you learn from different fields. Some may focus on the natural sciences, while others offer advanced courses in the social sciences, environmental economics, and environmental history. Economic analysis is often the basis of solutions to problems such as pollution and resource depletion (overuse). Classes in environmental politics will help you understand the context in which policies and programs are created and carried out. Some programs also cover environmental issues in foreign countries—for example, the erosion of beaches in the Caribbean islands—and global concerns like the greenhouse effect. In programs that include humanities, you are encouraged to take courses in environmental philosophy and ethics as well as in art, religion, and literature, as a way of examining the links between human activity and the environment.

Programs in environmental studies tend to argue that human society is undermining the ecological foundations of life and that we must fundamentally change behavior if we are to prosper as a species—we must go beyond recycling or planting trees in order to tackle looming environmental threats. For some students, this claim can be unsettling. Most programs value your ability to think critically about problems and to develop innovative solutions, but a problem-solving emphasis is likely to make certain demands on you. Instead of learning facts about specific environmental problems, you are encouraged to analyze them, because the environmental challenges we will face in twenty years will probably differ significantly from the ones that confront us today.

In environmental studies, your course work is often rewarding and eye-opening. You can get hands-on experience in responding to environmental threats through fieldwork, service-learning programs, and internships. However, careers in the field increasingly require technical training at advanced levels, usually graduate work. The liberal arts education in environmental studies does not replace specialized training, but it provides excellent preparation for such training.

Other majors you might like:
Geography
Political science
Economics
Environmental engineering
Global studies
Geology/earth science
Forestry
Urban, community, and regional planning
Journalism
Ecology

Environmental health
Wildlife and wilderness management

Questions to ask colleges:
In which courses do you apply ideas from various fields to resolve environmental problems? Some programs ask you to take a variety of courses from different disciplines but offer few opportunities to integrate, or tie together, what you've learned.

What internships are available? How well do these internships complement, or enrich, the course offerings?

Has the number of students majoring in the program grown over the past few years and, if so, are faculty members being brought in to accommodate the increased interest?

Are there faculty members whose primary responsibility is teaching and advising environmental studies students? Sometimes the program's professors are "on loan" from other programs, which may hold first claim to the instructors' time.

What is the most important course in the curriculum? The answer will tell you about the focus of the program. Compare that focus with your own interests.

Where are recent graduates of the program working? If they have landed jobs that sound interesting, that's a good sign.

Career options and trends:
Environmental consultant*; environmental lobbyist; environmental engineer; park naturalist; specialist in environmental communications; specialist in regulations compliance; environmental educator.

As environmental problems are becoming more of a concern throughout the world, the job market is expanding. Career opportunities exist in toxic waste disposal, management of environmental organizations, journalism, community recycling and energy conservation, and environmental and economic development in nonindustrial countries. With appropriate graduate work, you can pursue a career in air or water quality planning, solid waste planning, land use planning, fisheries and wildlife management, policy analysis, environmental law, laboratory research, or resource economics.

Insider's viewpoint:

"I love the excitement of working directly on problems that scare us all at least a little bit. It's hard, as a professor or as a student, to be bored by the subject: the issues are too large, the stakes too high, the rewards too great."

—Professor Michael Maniates, Allegheny College

For more info:

Environmental Careers Organization (ECO)
30 Winter St., 6th Floor
Boston, MA 02108-4720
(617) 426-4375
www.eco.org

National Wildlife Federation
11100 Wildlife Center Drive
Reston, VA 20190-5362
(800) 822-9919
www.nwf.org

Association for the Study of Literature and
    Environment (ASLE)
www.asle.umn.edu

Fishing and fisheries

What it's about:

The major in fisheries explores the biology and ecology of fishes and other aquatic species; the bodies of water that are their habitats; and the human use, management, and production of aquatic species. Courses cover both basic science and applied aspects of commercial and recreational fishing activities.

Is this for you?

You might like this major if you also like: fishing, boating, or hiking; working with your hands as well as your mind; keeping an aquarium or raising live animals; learning about living creatures and natural ecosystems.

Consider this major if you are good at: attention to detail; creativity; critical reading/thinking; problem solving; quantitative analysis; spatial thinking/analysis; teamwork *...or have...* initiative; mechanical facility; verbal skills.

Recommended high school prep:

English 4, math 3, lab science 3, social studies 3, and a foreign language 2-3. Courses in advanced biology, environmental science, precalculus, and computer literacy are also recommended.

Typical courses in this major:

Evolutionary biology
Genetics
Fisheries techniques
Ichthyology
Fish ecology
Limnology
Aquatic animal nutrition
Economics
Aquatic entomology
Freshwater ecology
Statistics
Policies, laws, and regulations
Principles of aquaculture
Fisheries management

Concentrations:

Fisheries management; fisheries science; aquaculture.

What the study of this major is like:

Fisheries management is a science-based field that requires you to understand and apply principles of biology, ecology, statistics, and social sciences. Professionals who work in fisheries management do not simply sample, assess, and stock fish populations; they also improve habitats for certain species to protect biodiversity (for example, helping endangered species recover) and interact with the public. Fisheries managers must also be able to communicate technical information in person and in writing.

You begin your studies by establishing a strong foundation in fields such as biology, chemistry, mathematics, and English. You will also probably take an introductory course in natural resources management in your first year. Your second-year studies generally include plant and evolutionary biology, physical sciences, and social sciences, along with an introduction to principles of fisheries and wildlife management. Through your first two years, the prime method of instruction is lectures, supplemented by laboratories in biology and chemistry and some fieldwork in natural resources management. Many majors tend to feel most challenged by course work in chemistry and calculus.

In your third and fourth years, course content becomes more fisheries-oriented; fieldwork and hands-on learning is more important. Your third year generally includes foundation courses, such as field techniques, ichthyology (the study of fishes), and fish ecology. The fourth year usually features such key courses as freshwater ecology, human dimensions of fisheries and wildlife management, aquaculture, and a capstone course in fisheries management. The capstone course generally combines everything you have learned; groups of students devise action plans for solving real-world problems in fisheries management. In your third and fourth years, classes are smaller and you have more opportunities to interact personally with your professors and with other majors. In fact, majors typically study in groups and socialize after hours. Many of them enroll in the local chapter of a professional society and begin to feel part of the profession.

You will be encouraged to learn from practical experience by volunteering to help graduate students with fieldwork or laboratory work, by participating in internships in fisheries management agencies or nongovernmental organizations, or by conducting independent research projects. In these activities, you can identify and explore areas of technical specialization. You can also establish professional contacts that may prove helpful if you look for an entry-level position after graduation. Of students graduating with bachelor's degrees, roughly one-quarter move on to graduate studies and three-quarters obtain entry-level jobs in the field.

Some of the programs emphasize fisheries science, which encourage you to solve management problems by understanding fish ecology. Science-based programs are essential if you are considering going to graduate school and pursuing a challenging career in fisheries science. Other programs stress instruction in practical fisheries management and aim to produce entry-level managers for state or federal fisheries management agencies. Programs may also differ in the amount of hands-on learning available and in the opportunities for participation in research and internships. Often, universities with graduate programs in fisheries offer more opportunities for learning outside formal classes.

Other majors you might like:
Aquaculture
Marine biology
Ocean engineering
Parks, recreation, and leisure studies
Zoology
Aquatic biology/limnology

Marine engineering/naval architecture
Marine science/Merchant Marine
Underwater diving
Oceanography
Natural resources management/policy
Water, wetlands, and marine management

Questions to ask colleges:
What sorts of facilities are offered? Do they include laboratories, experimental ponds, raceways (canals), and aquaria, as well as access to nearby streams, rivers, or reservoirs?

Are there opportunities for doing hands-on learning and for gaining practical research experience? Is there a graduate program, so that undergraduates can learn by helping graduate students with their research? Are undergraduates encouraged to undertake independent research projects?

Career options and trends:
Fisheries manager*; conservation officer; fish ecologist; fish culturist*; endangered species management officer; environmental consultant; fisheries research scientist; fisheries and wildlife journalist.

Many state and federal fisheries management agencies require their employees to become certified fisheries scientists under the program administered by the American Fisheries Society. Certification requires formal education and professional experience. Although entry-level jobs can be obtained with a bachelor's degree, an advanced degree will lead to a more rewarding career.

Not all jobs focus on management of sport and commercial fisheries, and many address recovery of endangered species, public education, development of public policy, and other areas. Most jobs in fisheries combine physical work outdoors with intellectual engagement—the talents, skills, and energies of fisheries managers seldom go unused.

Private-sector employment has grown in response to our increased awareness of environmental issues. Fisheries professionals are employed by environmental consulting firms, forest products companies, public utilities, and conservation groups. Aquaculturists can work in both public agencies and private firms.

Employment of captains and crews in the fishing industry is declining, because of foreign competition, stock depletion, and habitat destruction. The good news is that these same factors should spur demand for professionals trained in fisheries science and management.

Insider's viewpoint:

"Fisheries management is maturing as a field of applied science, and it is exciting to witness and participate in its application. For example, during my own career, I have witnessed the restoration of Great Lakes fisheries, the rise of aquaculture, and the emergence of conservation science and management. Many are the days that I smile inwardly and think, 'I get paid to do what I love.'"

—Professor Eric Hallerman, Virginia Polytechnic Institute and State University

For more info:

American Fisheries Society (AFS)
5410 Grosvenor Lane
Bethesda, MD 20814
(301) 897-8616
www.fisheries.org

World Aquaculture Society
143 J. M. Parker Coliseum
Baton Rouge, LA 70806
(225) 578-3137
www.was.org

Forestry

What it's about:

This major deals with the management, conservation, and preservation of forest ecosystems. Integrating what you learn in the physical, biological, and social sciences helps you appreciate the numerous benefits and resources of forests, including wood and fiber products, biodiversity, recreation, water, wilderness, and wildlife.

Is this for you?

You might like this major if you also like: the great outdoors; math and science; maps; geography; arboretums; building things; working with people; helping others accomplish their goals.

Consider this major if you are good at: critical reading/thinking; leadership; managing people; organizing; quantitative analysis; teamwork *...or have...* initiative; patience; verbal skills.

Recommended high school prep:

English 4, math 4 (including pre-calculus), lab science 4 (earth science, biology, chemistry, and physics), social studies 3, and a foreign language 2–3. If they are available, courses in statistics, environmental science or ecology, and computer applications are also recommended. Many agencies, such as county conservation boards, state and national parks, and the U.S. Forest Service, provide summer employment opportunities in forestry.

Did you know...

That the amount of forest land in the United States is down only about one-third from what it was when the Pilgrims landed, and is about the same as it was a century ago? Because of forest management policies, forest growth exceeds harvesting by 33 percent each year—a reassuring statistic, because, for every individual in the United States, the equivalent of a full-grown tree is turned into wood and paper each year.

Typical courses in this major:

Botany
Forest soils
Forest management and policy
Forest measurements
Forest economics
Silviculture
Forest ecology
Forest growth and yield
Wildlife management
Resource allocation
Aerial photo interpretation
Geographic information systems (GIS)
Harvesting and production technology
Hydrology
Wood science
Composite products

Concentrations:

In college: forest resource management; urban forestry; wood products; wood science; fire management.

If you go on to grad school: forest biology; forest economics; forest biometry; forest ecology.

What the study of this major is like:

Forestry programs begin with general course work in English, mathematics, chemistry, physics, speech, and statistics. In your first year, you generally take introductory forestry courses and do field studies conducted by forestry faculty members. Because forestry is a broad field, you typically have to choose an area of concentration. You may pick your concentration as early as your first year or as late as the end of your second year. You then begin course work in your chosen area. Nonforestry courses, such as business management, industrial engineering, and technical report writing, help you prepare for work in the field.

Many aspects of a forestry education are hands-on. Some courses are taught in the field so that you can experience for yourself the complexities of the forest and apply theories learned in the classroom to real situations. Most problems encountered in forestry represent new challenges, arising from new circumstances, and your task may be to come up with appropriate solutions. Therefore, critical thinking, analysis, and problem-solving skills are essential.

In laboratory sessions, you do statistical analysis of data collected in the field and study biological relationships among different species of trees, as well as between trees and other living organisms in the forest. You are encouraged to use your summers to work in forestry-related jobs. Many programs offer credit for these experiences, most of which are paid jobs in private industry; with county, state, or federal government agencies; or with other resource management agencies. Working in the field improves your understanding of forestry and your chances of finding a permanent job after graduation. You should also become active in professional organizations so you can practice the teamwork and leadership skills that are central to a successful forestry career.

There are four main types of forestry programs. Some programs train students to be forestry technicians and usually grant two-year degrees that allow graduates to work in field jobs related to forestry. Other programs prepare you for both field and supervisory work, such as being a district ranger, forest supervisor, regional forester, or chief forester with the U.S. Forest Service; a consulting forester; or a forester with a state department of natural resources. These are usually four-year Bachelor of Science programs. Other programs prepare you to work in wood science, with either a B.S. degree or an advanced degree. Still other programs are intended primarily for graduate students. And some forestry programs offer a combination of the four options. In addition, some programs focus on forestry in a particular region of the United States, while others offer a generic, broad-ranging approach.

Other majors you might like:

Botany
Wildlife and wilderness management
Forest resources production

Surveying technology
Landscape architecture
Horticulture
Environmental studies
Ecology
Land use planning
Wood science/pulp/paper technology
Entomology
Forest engineering

Questions to ask colleges:

Is the program accredited by the Society of American Foresters or the Society of Wood Science and Technology? If it is, then you know that the curriculum is reviewed periodically by an outside team of professionals, and that it meets accepted standards.

What types of field laboratory experiences are offered, and in what types of environments? What forestry-related facilities (research labs, habitats, remote sensing equipment, greenhouses, preserves) are on or near campus?

Career options and trends:

Forester with the U. S. Forest Service or state agency*; park ranger*; urban forester; industrial forester or timber manager*; arborist; wood product sales; consulting forester.

Generally, not much job growth is projected in the forestry field, and overall employment is expected to decline in the timber industry. Nevertheless, there is increasing demand for graduates in the areas of wood science, urban and community forestry, and natural resource conservation or interpretation. The growing public demand for protection and responsible management of forest resources should create opportunities in research, testing, and compliance services.

For more info:

Society of American Foresters (SAF)
5400 Grosvenor Lane
Bethesda, MD 20814-2198
(301) 897-8720
www.safnet.org

Society of Wood Science and Technology (SWST)
www.swst.org

Natural resources and conservation

What it's about:

Natural resources and conservation is a broad, interdisciplinary field of study that addresses the management, protection, use, restoration, and enjoyment of the Earth's resources. Training is provided in a number of academic areas, including biology and other natural sciences, social sciences, economics, and environmental studies.

Is this for you?

You might like this major if you also like: outdoor activities such as camping, fishing, hunting, hiking, and canoeing; traveling; photography; debating; getting involved in environmental causes; politics; business and economics; leading or organizing school activities.

Consider this major if you are good at: creativity; critical reading/thinking; integrative thinking; leadership; quantitative analysis; research; teamwork ...*or have...* initiative; verbal skills; writing skills.

Recommended high school prep:

English 4, math 3, lab science 3, social studies 4, and a foreign language 2–3. If they are available, courses in environmental studies, economics, and computer applications are also recommended.

Did you know...

...that the management of natural resources is in many ways accomplished by the management of people? There is no distinct separation between society and the natural world. Many students begin this major expecting an in-depth examination of the environment. They soon learn, however, that they must also take courses in the social sciences, and that as professionals they will spend a great deal of time working with the public.

...that much of the work in this field is done indoors? This is especially true as you advance in your career.

Typical courses in this major:

Biology
Ecology
Chemistry
Plant and animal identification
Economics
Human dimensions
Natural resources management
Environmental policy
Conservation law
Wildlife and fisheries conservation
Geographic information systems (GIS)
Measurements and sampling techniques
Environmental communication
Soils and land use
Politics and ecology
Ecotourism

Concentrations:

Natural resources policy; outdoor recreation; resources management; environmental law and policy; environmental education; wildlife rehabilitation; wetlands restoration; coastal zone management.

What the study of this major is like:

Historically, professionals working in the natural resources and conservation field focused on specific academic areas, or disciplines, such as forestry or wildlife biology. Today, leading programs combine a range of courses; as a result, all majors become familiar with several fields, including forestry, wildlife, fisheries, physical sciences (such as chemistry), and social sciences (economics and political science). In addition, you take writing and, often, public speaking courses. Majors learn to integrate, or link, many disciplines and apply them to natural resource issues.

Many natural resources and conservation courses are taught in the traditional lecture and discussion format. Other courses focus on fieldwork, such as plant or animal identification and sampling techniques. Some courses combine the two, with a lecture/discussion session followed by fieldwork. An increasing number of courses require group projects, designed to prepare you for the type of work you may do after you graduate.

Natural resources and conservation programs vary a great deal in their emphases, degree requirements, and philosophies. Some programs have well-defined requirements that offer little flexibility, while others can accommodate almost any reasonable curriculum you want to pursue. At the same time, accreditation (offered by the Society of American Foresters) and individual certification (offered by SAF, the American Fisheries Society, and The Wildlife Society) ensure that all programs follow professional guidelines. All programs that are accredited must meet the same standards of quality and course requirements.

Some programs place more emphasis on either the biophysical or the socioeconomic aspects of natural resources and conservation. The combination of disciplines available at a college can also create differences among programs. For example, some programs cover only forestry or wildlife conservation. Even though such programs might be of high quality, your study and career options are somewhat limited. Other colleges have larger, integrated programs that offer you more possibilities. For instance, a college might combine wildlife and fisheries conservation, forestry, and natural resource studies into a single program.

Other majors you might like:
Biology
Economics
Geography
Geology/earth science
Political science
Oceanography
Range science
Agronomy and crop science
Natural resources management/policy
Ecology
Agricultural and biological engineering
Mining and mineral engineering

Questions to ask colleges:
Which field experiences or other opportunities for hands-on learning are offered to undergraduates? Where do the activities take place? Is there access to nearby nature preserves, field stations, or research centers?

How flexible is the program regarding electives—can students design a course of study that reflects their interests?

Is the program accredited? What certification requirements can be fulfilled through this program?

Career options and trends:
Wildlife biologist; fisheries manager; forester; park ranger; conservation law enforcement officer; natural resources manager; government agency employee (EPA, state conservation department, etc.); natural resources policy analyst; environmental lawyer; environmental educator.

The various professional disciplines in this field have different certification requirements. You should investigate the certification options and their importance in the area of natural resources you are most interested in. Also, many careers in the discipline require graduate study.

While the rate of job growth has slowed recently, job trends remain promising. The broad nature of this field provides a variety of career options in both government and industry. Most students with a bachelor's degree will find employment, but prospects are better if you have a master's degree or higher. Also, many employees in public natural resources management agencies are reaching retirement age. As with any occupation, there are times of greater or lesser demand, but highly motivated, well-trained graduates should be able to find employment.

Insider's viewpoint:
"Economics and policy are an integral part of natural resources management; these 'practical' concerns are necessary to be able to effectively deal with natural resources in today's society. If you're not cut out for the economics, look somewhere else for a major."

—Zeb, senior, University of Delaware

For more info:
Society of American Foresters (SAF)
5400 Grosvenor Lane
Bethesda, MD 20814-2198
(301) 897-8720
www.safnet.org

The Wildlife Society (TWS)
5410 Grosvenor Lane
Suite 200
Bethesda, MD 20814
(301) 897-9770
www.wildlife.org

The Environmental Careers Organization (ECO)
30 Winter St., 6th floor
Boston, MA 02108-4720
(617) 426-4375
www.eco.org

Wildlife and wilderness management

Also known as:
Conservation biology

What it's about:
Wildlife and wilderness management is an area of applied ecology that deals with the conservation of animal populations, ranging from those that are regularly hunted to those that are considered endangered, and the habitats in which these animals are found.

Is this for you?
You might like this major if you also like: outdoor activities such as hiking, camping, fishing, and hunting; science; Scouting; caring for animals; bird watching; natural history museums; zoos; travel; learning about the natural world.

Consider this major if you are good at: attention to detail; creativity; critical reading/thinking; leadership; organizing; quantitative analysis; teamwork *...or have...* initiative; physical stamina; verbal skills; writing skills.

Recommended high school prep:
English 4, math 3, lab science 4, social studies 3, and a foreign language 2–3. Any course in environmental studies is recommended, if available. Advanced biology would also be a plus, but is not required.

Did you know...
...that this is the best major at most universities for students who have a strong interest in field-oriented ecology? Biology programs typically cater to premed students and emphasize "skin-in" biology. Wildlife programs attract students interested in animal populations and emphasize "skin-out" biology.

Typical courses in this major:
Biology
Anatomy
Chemistry, general and organic
Statistics
Principles of wildlife management
Terrestrial wildlife ecology
Wetlands wildlife ecology
Field methods for wildlife management
Ornithology (study of birds)
Mammalogy
Entomology (study of insects)
Conservation biology
Genetics
Behavioral ecology
Systematic botany
Conservation law and policy

Concentrations:
Wildlife biology; wildlife conservation; habitat management; wetlands conservation.

What the study of this major is like:
Wildlife and wilderness management programs began as game management programs in the 1950s. Back then, people thought game species (mostly birds and mammals) were the only wildlife that needed to be managed. But human population growth inevitably affects animal populations by loss or change of habitat, reduction of food supply, presence of pollutants, and other human-related factors. In recent years, more and more rare and endangered species have been added to the list of wildlife in need of active management.

Wildlife professionals have come to realize that many species that are neither hunted nor endangered are also in need of our attention. Examples include declining populations of amphibians, birds of prey, and neotropical migrant birds; they could all become endangered if they do not receive immediate assistance. As a result of changes in attitudes toward the natural world, many wildlife and wilderness programs study a much broader array of species, and teach the skills needed to protect them, than those traditionally covered in game management programs.

As a wildlife major, you study both resource management and biology. Most of your courses are in biology, but you must also take chemistry, mathematics (through elementary calculus), and statistics. Anatomy and vertebrate zoology courses, such as ornithology and mammalogy, are important, too. Because wildlife biologists must be able to identify plants, at least one plant taxonomy course is generally required. Most other courses in a wildlife and wilderness management program are field-oriented and deal with ecology.

You will probably have to take several lab courses each semester in order to graduate in four years. Most lab courses (beyond introductory biology and chemistry) are strongly field oriented. Wildlife and wilderness management deals with animals living in natural environments; you must therefore be prepared to work with animal populations and their habitats. In the field, you gain experience in identifying birds and mammals, estimating their populations, and analyzing their habitats—you acquire firsthand knowledge of how and where the animals that you study in the classroom live. At many colleges, summer courses give you an opportunity to work full-time on field projects.

If you are comparing wildlife and wilderness management programs, look carefully at the courses offered to see whether programs you are considering favor traditional game management, or whether their courses reflect a broader, more modern conservation-biology focus.

Other majors you might like:

Forestry
Zoology
Botany
Entomology
Range science
Veterinary technology
Animal sciences
Biology
Natural sciences
Land use planning
Wildlife biology
Ecology

Questions to ask colleges:

Is the wildlife program a full major, or just a concentration within another major, such as zoology or forestry?

Does the school offer (or require) a broad array of natural resources management courses beyond those in the wildlife major?

What opportunities are there to do course-related field experience or to become involved in graduate student or faculty research? Are there good field sites near the campus? Is there a study-abroad program in this major?

Do the courses required for the major satisfy The Wildlife Society's standards for certification?

Career options and trends:

Wildlife biologist; research biologist; environmental educator; environmental consultant; university professor; park or field naturalist; conservation biologist; wildlife manager.

The job outlook continues to be very competitive. Students hoping to enter this field should complete at least a four-year Bachelor's of Science degree. Field experience gained through internships and temporary jobs remains an important way to obtain a permanent job. A graduate program leading to a Master's of Science degree can enhance your marketability for full-time employment and for advancement in the field.

Insider's viewpoint:

"A challenge of the major is low pay. It's also a really competitive field. There are a lot of people wanting to go into it."

—Chad, junior, Oregon State University

For more info:

The Wildlife Society (TWS)
5410 Grosvenor Lane
Suite 200
Bethesda, MD 20814-2197
(301) 897-9770
www.wildlife.org

Parks and recreation

If you choose to study parks and recreation, you will become something of an expert in leisure, and that may mean you'll get teased a bit.

"Students in this major should expect some 'razzing' regarding their chosen major," admits Professor Lowell Caneday of Oklahoma State University.

But you may end up laughing all the way to the bank, because several mega-trends suggest that working at playing will be a hot job market in the future. Employment in recreation, parks, and leisure services has been going up for many years. One reason is that many people in developed countries like the United States have the time and money to enjoy recreational activities. Also, folks are living longer, more active lives. Students are getting the idea and majoring in recreation and sports. This category has grown more than any other in the last decade, when you count bachelor's degrees.

Hmmm, let's see.... A popular group of majors. A growing market segment. A college career devoted to studying what people do for fun. Sounds like a slam dunk. But these majors aren't just a walk in the park or a day at the beach. College is college, and you will have to buckle down.

The foundations for academic preparation in recreation, park, and leisure studies include behavioral sciences: human growth and development, normal and abnormal psychology, cultural and environmental sociology, learning and leadership theory, motivation and consumer behavior.

People in this field run programs and supervise and administer activities in many settings: state and national parks, campus recreational programs, hospitals, long-term-care facilities, youth service agencies, military recreational facilities, forest recreation, commercial settings, church outings, corporate and employee recreational destinations, resorts and cruise ships, and camps.

Graduate students dive into topics like leisure services management and therapeutic recreation, or follow business tracks in commercial recreation and tourism management.

Fans know that sports management is also big. Even if you can't swish a trey, you can become a pro at sports marketing, sports and the law, sports finance and business, college sports, events management, and labor relations.

Sports management "is concerned with the operation of many types of sports organizations, ranging from professional teams and leagues to national and international amateur sports organizations, federations, conferences, and associations," says Professor Stephen W. Jefferson, University of Massachusetts. Sports management is linked to professions including broadcasting, community relations, finance and accounting, law, licensing, and merchandising.

A park-like campus

Start your college search by looking at divisions and schools of education, physical education, and recreation; health and human services; arts and sciences; forestry and natural resources; and yes, business. Where the college stands in its approach to these majors may depend on where it sits.

"Since these programs may be found in a wide variety of academic units or divisions on college campuses, differences between programs can be expected depending upon the 'academic home,'" says Caneday. "Programs housed in education or human services divisions focus on human behavior, whereas programs offered by forestry or natural resources divisions emphasize the natural environment. Programs in business divisions will likely stress management, economics, finance, and business practices."

Compare schools by considering whether the program plays an important role in the college's family of offerings or is just an add-on to a department devoted to other majors. Does the college have diverse courses such as program design in leisure services; natural resource recreation; sport marketing, management, and law?

Is the program accredited? If so, it has passed an external review by the likes of the National Recreation and Park Association (www.nrpa.org), the American Association for Leisure and Recreation (www.aahperd.org/aalr), or other recognized body. Parks and recreation programs that are accredited must teach conceptual foundations, professional practices and service delivery, programming strategies, assessment, planning, evaluation, management, and legislative and legal issues. Accredited programs also offer field experience. There's more than one type of accreditation, so ask which kind the college has.

In addition to accreditation, you will need to be certified for some jobs in therapeutic recreation, so ask what the pass rate is for recent grads on their national certification examinations. (See, these majors aren't so easy after all.)

Other questions: What is the placement rate of graduates, and where are they finding jobs? What research are faculty members doing, and are undergraduates helping? Will regular faculty members teach your classes or will graduate assistants? You want the veterans, not the rookies.

In sports management programs particularly, find out if the college has a good network of graduates that gives you a chance to rub elbows with professionals, do networking, and find internships. An internship might be a tryout for a great job.

"A major in recreation, park, and leisure studies provides the foundation to work in a career focusing on improving the quality of life for all," Caneday observes.

That would certainly make the teasing worthwhile.

Parks, recreation, and leisure studies

Also known as:

Leisure sciences

What it's about:

This major focuses on the environments, behaviors, and experiences of people during recreation. You examine people's motivations for choosing a pastime, investigate the effects of their behaviors, and develop skills to manage a variety of recreation and leisure services, enterprises, and organizations.

Is this for you?

You might like this major if you also like: working with different types and ages of people; voluntary service programs such as Scouting, 4-H, YM/YWCA; sports; games that require physical and social interaction; leading or organizing group activities.

Consider this major if you are good at: active listening; caring/nurturing; counseling; creativity; leadership; organizing; persuading/influencing ...*or have...* initiative; verbal skills; writing skills.

Recommended high school prep:

English 4, math 3, lab science 3, social studies 3, and a foreign language 2–3. If possible, also take courses in writing, computer applications, communications (speech, drama, or debate), psychology, and sociology.

Did you know...

...that jobs related to parks, recreation, and leisure are among the fastest-growing areas of employment according to the United States Department of Labor? In addition, a career in this field is identified as one of the top ten most satisfying jobs among working people surveyed.

Typical courses in this major:

Introduction to parks, recreation, and leisure
History of leisure
Philosophy of leisure
Recreation for special populations
Recreation leadership
Program and event planning
Area and facility design
Computer applications in leisure services
Evaluation of leisure services
Administration of leisure services
Legal issues in leisure services
Marketing recreation enterprises
Outdoor recreation
Commercial recreation

Concentrations:

Leisure services management; therapeutic recreation; natural resources recreation; tourism; program management; commercial recreation.

What the study of this major is like:

"Leisure" is actually a complex, multifaceted concept that differs from person to person. As a major in parks, recreation, and leisure studies, you encounter many different aspects and applications, from the operation of community leisure services to the provision of therapeutic recreation. Your studies are generally built upon behavioral science courses, such as human growth and development, normal and abnormal psychology, cultural and environmental sociology, learning and leadership theory, and motivation and consumer behavior.

Professors may employ a variety of teaching techniques and learning styles. Most classes feature lectures supported by appropriate technology, questioning, and group interaction; in many classes, you'll do laboratory work, or applied experiences, in which you organize, deliver, and evaluate leisure services for specific populations. In fact, all accredited programs in the major require one or more fieldwork activities, either as part of your regular courses, as internships for credit, or as employment or voluntary service.

Parks, recreation, and leisure studies has been identified as a "discovery" major, meaning most students learn about it only after arriving at college; so you may find second- or third-year students beginning the major with you. The two biggest challenges of the major are, first, the combination of theory, applied learning, and service delivery experience that is necessary to develop a complete perspective; and second, time management. Don't be surprised by how demanding this major can be.

Programs in parks, recreation, and leisure studies may be found in a variety of academic divisions. Therefore, differences between programs may depend upon a program's academic home. Programs housed in education or human services divisions focus more on human behavior, whereas programs offered by forestry or natural resources divisions emphasize the natural environment. Programs in business divisions will likely stress management, economics, finance, and business practices.

Besides fieldwork, the accreditation standards require all students to learn conceptual foundations; professional and service delivery practices; programming and assessment strategies; planning; and evaluation, management, legislative, and legal issues. Concentrations can prepare you for service in therapeutic recreation, park and recreation management, not-for-profit management, military recreation, correctional leisure services, natural resources recreation, sports management, tourism management, and other specialties.

Other majors you might like:

Landscape architecture
Physical education
Tourism/travel management
Recreational therapy
Occupational therapy
Hospitality administration and management
Gerontology
Forestry
Athletic training
Sports and fitness administration
Exercise sciences
Family/community services

Questions to ask colleges:

Is the program accredited by The National Recreation and Park Association (NRPA) and the American Association for Leisure and Recreation (AALR)? If you are interested in a specific concentration, be sure to ask if that aspect of the program is also accredited.

Where do students complete their internships? What additional field experience is expected or required of students? What is the "pass rate" for recent graduates on the national certification exams?

Career options and trends:

Activities director (sports, aquatics, outdoor pursuits, etc.); program supervisor; department administrator; facilities manager; park ranger; certified therapeutic recreation specialist.

Majors find jobs in campus recreation, hospitals, long-term-care facilities, YM/YWCAs and other youth service agencies, commercial outfitters, corporate recreation services, resorts and cruise ships, camps, and similar areas.

Most public park and recreation agencies will expect you to have the certified park and recreation professional (CPRP) credential offered by the NRPA. Numerous skill-based certifications, in such areas as first aid, aquatic facility management, challenge-course programming, and outdoor/environmental education, may also be required.

Trends that are fueling employment growth include increasing affluence within a growing population; longer and more energetic retirement lives; expanding leisure opportunities through technology; and increased expectations of populations that have been underserved in the past. These trends are likely to continue well into this century.

For more info:

National Recreation and Park Association (NRPA)
22377 Belmont Ridge Rd.
Ashburn, VA 20148
(703) 858-0784
www.nrpa.org

Sports and fitness administration

What it's about:

The sports and fitness administration major prepares you to apply the principles of business, coaching, and physical education to the management of athletic programs, sports teams, fitness facilities and health clubs, and sport recreation.

Is this for you?

You might like this major if you also like: mathematical and logical puzzles; playing sports; managing fantasy league sports teams; attending sports events; interacting with athletes; tracking sports statistics.

Consider this major if you are good at: attention to detail; coaching; critical reading/thinking; leadership; math; teamwork *...or have...* initiative; patience; verbal skills; writing skills.

Recommended high school prep:

English 4 (including a writing course), math 4 (including precalculus), lab science 3, social studies 3, and a foreign language 2–3. If possible, take an economics course and any business courses that are offered.

Did you know...

...that successfully managing athletes, sports teams, or sports facilities involves a lot of math, logic, and other business skills?

Typical courses in this major:

History of sports
Sociology of sports
Kinesiology (exercise science)
Human anatomy and physiology
Sports and fitness marketing
Sports communications
Sports finance
Sports law
Athletic program management
Fitness program management
Labor relations and professional sports
Facilities management
Media relations
Economics of sports
Community relations
Principles of coaching

Concentrations:

In college: professional sports; sports communication; sports broadcasting; fitness management; recreation and tourism; sports marketing; sports finance; sport agency; facilities and event management.

If you go on to grad school: social-historical foundations of modern sports; sports economics; sports organizational behavior and development; sports management policy; labor relations.

What the study of this major is like:

Sports are fun and exciting, but sports are also a business. Whatever aspect of sports and fitness administration you pursue, you will most likely need a solid business foundation. In most sports and fitness administration programs, you take courses in accounting, finance, management, economics, and marketing (and perhaps computer science and precalculus) before you begin sports-specific business courses.

Within the major, you generally take three types of courses. The first type is devoted to theory—the sociology, psychology, physiology, and history of sports. The second explores the fundamentals of business and management. The third type involves the application of management theory to specific aspects of the sports and fitness industry, such as marketing and public relations; sports law; business operations for sports, health, and fitness organizations; the organization of and management of events; media relations; broadcasting; and college athletics.

Because sports management is relatively difficult to break into, most programs include a fieldwork component or encourage you to get hands-on experience and to make valuable connections through internships. The types of internships offered by programs vary. Some colleges have connections to sport industries or are located near sports or broadcasting facilities that are willing to hire interns. You may also be able to work in facilities on campus or at college-sponsored events.

In addition, programs at different colleges may have different emphases. Some programs focus on college athletics—how to create and nurture competitive teams, meet budgets, and maybe even coach. In programs that focus on spectator sports, you learn how to attract and satisfy fans. Programs that stress participant sports and fitness teach you how to find and manage individual athletes, or how to manage and operate health clubs and spas. Fitness-oriented programs will stress health related courses such as anatomy and physiology, nutrition, injury prevention, and physical training.

Other majors you might like:

Athletic training
Physical education
Public relations
Business administration and management
Marketing
Radio and television
Physical therapy
Entrepreneurial studies
Equestrian studies
Fishing and fisheries
Hospitality administration and management
Tourism/travel management

Questions to ask colleges:

Are there adequate facilities for students to do hands-on activities as part of their course work? For example, are there places where students participate in selling tickets, running events, or marketing? The answers should help you determine the quality of the program.

Is the sports and fitness program offered as its own major or is it simply a minor (sometimes offered through a business school) or a concentration in some other field? The answer to this question can give you an idea of the size of the program as well as the college's commitment to it.

Does the cu
that might le
so, are a wid
cluding position.
ment, events mana,
marketing? Check to .
ment opportunities mat.

Does the program have a s
Often a good alumni networ
ternship opportunities and job o

Career options and trends:

Athletic director; health club manager; sports broadcaster; promoter; sports agent or scout; fitness program coordinator; general manager.

Sports managers are concerned with the operation of many types of organizations: professional teams and leagues, college athletic departments and conference offices, and national and international amateur sports organizations. Sports and fitness administration graduates also serve the sport industry through club and facilities management, marketing and event promotion, and sports clothing and equipment sales and distribution.

Job prospects are generally excellent—the sports and fitness industry is strong and growing. There are minor fluctuations from year to year and small ups and downs in salaries for entry-level jobs, but even in tighter markets, sports fitness and administration majors who have initiative are in demand.

For more info:

North American Society for Sport Management (NASSM)
NASSM Business Office, West Gym 014
Slippery Rock University
Slippery Rock, PA 16057
(724) 738-4812
www.nassm.com

American Alliance for Health, Physical Education, Recreation and Dance (AAHPERD)
1900 Association Drive
Reston, VA 20191-1598
(800) 213- 7193
www.aahperd.org

Physical sciences

If someone asked you why the sky is blue, would you tell them about wavelengths? If so, you know something about the laws of nature, and that's what the physical sciences are all about. Areas of study in this group include aeronautics and aviation science, astronomy, astrophysics, atmospheric science, chemistry, geology (earth science), oceanography, and physics. The most popular major is chemistry, where students earn more than half of all bachelor's degrees in the physical sciences.

"Chemistry is the entry point for many careers in science. Almost every interesting question has chemistry at its base," says Professor James N. Spencer, Franklin and Marshall College. "As we learn about life processes, drug action, synthetic fuels, and behavior, the more evident it is that chemical processes are vitally important to understanding."

Physics is another top major and a foundation for many of these studies. It covers the principles of mechanics (forces, energy, and the basic laws of motion), electricity and magnetism, quantum mechanics, and thermodynamics (the theory of heat).

"Physics courses will study phenomena as diverse as the structure and evolution of the universe, and the fundamental particles from which all matter is made," according to Professor Stanley T. Jones of the University of Alabama. "Students will learn about the nature of light, atomic structure, and the properties of solids, including the semiconductors that have revolutionized our world."

The physical sciences are exciting and exacting. How deep is the ocean? What will tomorrow's weather be? When did the world begin? Better get out your calculator to answer physical science questions.

"You are usually required to complete an introduction to probability and statistics course, and mathematics through first-year calculus," says Ronald E. Johnson, professor of oceanography at Old Dominion University. "You then apply this knowledge at increasingly complex levels."

The climate is the same in atmospheric science. "Most students don't realize that meteorology is an applied physical science that is mathematically intensive and challenging. It involves developing sophisticated quantitative and conceptual skills. Mathematics is heavily used," says Professor James P. Koermer, Plymouth State College.

"Astronomy is a quantitative physical science, and upper-level astronomy courses usually require substantial preparation in physics and mathematics," adds Professor Richard G. French of Wellesley College. "I love being able to reach into the toolkit of mathematics and physics to help untangle the mysterious objects that we see."

Make a quantum leap

You've worked hard in high school and studied all the math offered. Soon you'll be ready for the next level: choosing a college with a great physical sciences program. Look for these majors in colleges of arts and sciences or engineering, and schools or divisions of science. For aeronautics, look for schools of aviation or transportation.

Here are a few things to consider: Find out if you need to come in with stellar math skills or if the college will help you catch up. Ask if your major is in the physical sciences department or has its own department. The setup may affect the course sequence and which courses you can take. "A wide range of courses offered on a reasonable time schedule is a good indication of a quality program," Johnson says.

Every college is different, just as every student is different. Some departments put more emphasis on lab work than others. Ask if introductory courses have a lab component. Some colleges require undergrads to do a research project. Ask if you'll have the chance to do research with faculty members or if you'll work independently. See what recent projects students have done.

Try to get an idea of the college's approach. Is the program more about applying the science or learning it in an academic sense? "Some colleges may emphasize work in observational astronomy more than theoretical astrophysics, some may do the reverse. A good, balanced program is best," suggests Professor Neta A. Bahcall, Princeton University. "Evaluate the quality of the program—the faculty, facilities, teaching and research programs, as well as the mentorship available."

As for the faculty, how many professors have advanced degrees and will those professors be your teachers (or will your instructors be grad students)? Have a look at the faculty members' publications to see what they're researching. Find out if you'll be studying hot new majors like nanotechnology or environmental aspects of the physical sciences.

Also ask about the quality of the laboratories, computers, and other equipment. How much access will you have to the best stuff, like the most powerful telescope on or near campus? Will you go on expeditions like coastal field exercises in oceanography?

What are former students doing? Are graduates successful at landing jobs in government and industry? Jobs in the physical sciences include scientist, researcher, teacher or professor, policymaker, writer, data analyst, software developer, pilot, astronaut, broadcaster, and medical doctor. Be sure to explore your graduate school options for advanced sciences. (See the majors in this section for examples of graduate studies.)

Aeronautics and aviation science

Also known as:
Air transportation
Airline/commercial pilot

What it's about:
The aviation science major prepares you for a career as a flight crew member on commercial aircraft, a corporate pilot, or other type of pilot. In your training to become an aviation professional, you will be encouraged to develop your mathematical and problem-solving skills. Emphasis is placed on crew resource management, safety, and the principles involved in aircraft operations.

Is this for you?
You might like this major if you also like: flying; travel; mathematical and logical puzzles; working with machinery; interacting with people; looking up at every airplane that flies over.

Consider this major if you are good at: attention to detail; leadership; math; memorizing; spatial thinking/analysis; teamwork *...or have...* manual dexterity; mental stamina; verbal skills.

Recommended high school prep:
English 4, math 4 (including precalculus), lab science 3 (including a physics course that covers electricity and magnetism), social studies 3, and a foreign language 2–3. It is not necessary to have flight experience.

Did you know...
...that this major covers a variety of subjects? Math and physics are obviously important, but your course work will also help you acquire problem-solving and communication skills, as well as good judgment.

...that an increasing number of men and women enter professional flying careers directly out of college, without military training?

Typical courses in this major:
Aeronautics
Flight instruction
Meteorology
Aerodynamics
Aircraft performance
Aircraft engines
High speed, long range navigation
Aircraft systems and components
Flight physiology
Crew resource management
Jet transport systems
Flight safety
Flight technique analysis
Turbojet techniques and crew procedure
Electronic navigation and flight control systems
International flight operations

Concentrations:
In college: airline pilot; corporate pilot; law enforcement aviation; agricultural aviation; military pilot (ROTC).

If you go on to grad school: aviation education technology; aviation management; aviation/aerospace operations; safety systems; human factors in aviation systems; space studies.

What the study of this major is like:
As an aviation science major, you combine flight training and academic studies, preparing for a career as a professional flight crew member on a jet transport aircraft, a corporate pilot, or a military pilot. Generally, you spend your first two years learning basic physics, mathematics, and communications skills, as well as fundamental aeronautics. You study how aircraft are designed and how they work, including the function of flight systems and controls and of navigation systems. You also study the procedures and government regulations for flight crew operations, radio communications, air safety, air traffic, and navigation.

In your third and fourth years, you take advanced training courses and study high-level aeronautical science. With the aid of both aircraft trainers and simulator trainers, you practice flying, navigating, and operating aircraft. These exercises help you sharpen your abilities to react quickly and effectively, by analyzing situations and solving problems. As in all flight-related courses, the paramount emphasis is on safety.

In addition to flight training, some programs offer courses in the human factors of aviation, which may include cockpit resource management, aviation psychology, and aviation accident investigation and analysis. In conjunction with courses in business, economics, communications, and management, you are prepared for a variety of careers in the aviation industry besides flying.

Depending on the strength of the program, by the time you graduate you may be qualified to take commercial and airline crew examinations given by the Federal Aviation Administration, or you may have already earned FAA certification as an instrument-rated commercial pilot.

Other majors you might like:
Aviation management
Aeronautical/aerospace engineering
Atmospheric science
Physics
Transportation management
Geography
Air traffic control
Aircraft powerplant technology
Avionics maintenance/technology
Military technologies

Questions to ask colleges:
Are faculty members experienced in the aviation industry? Professionally experienced instructors can do more than teach you about aircraft and how to fly them; they can also give you valuable insights into the aviation industry.

Which FAA certifications (private pilot, multi-engine, commercial, and others) and ratings do students qualify for at the completion of their training? How much of the costs of obtaining the certifications are covered by tuition?

How many and which types of aircraft and simulators are available for student flight training? You will need sufficient access to appropriate, well-maintained aircraft and adequate simulator time.

Is the program accredited by the Council on Aviation Accreditation (CAA)?

Career options and trends:
Passenger airline pilot*; corporate pilot*; military pilot*; aircraft dispatcher; flight instructor; natural resources pilot; firefighting pilot; law enforcement pilot; aerial applicator.

All pilots who are paid to transport passengers or cargo must have a commercial pilot's license with an instrument rating issued by the FAA, which requires a minimum of 250 hours of flight experience. Requirements for the airlines are much higher. You must have an airline transport pilot's license (minimum of 1,500 hours); obtain night, instrument, and multiengine ratings; and pass FAA written and flight examinations. Depending on the airline, you may have to be certified for specific types of aircraft and pass psychological and aptitude tests.

Jobs in the airline industry are closely tied to the economy. During times of recession, as well as decreased air travel for other reasons, airlines will be forced to lay off flight crews, normally for a few months only. Competition for jobs is expected to be strong, even with a projected growth in passenger travel and the approaching retirement age of a considerable number of pilots. The fastest growth should occur among regional commuter airlines.

Although more pilots with civilian rather than military training are entering the airline profession, military pilots continue to have a competitive advantage because they usually have more flight experience in sophisticated equipment.

Insider's viewpoint:
"Aviation allows one to meet individuals from many cultures, and get paid to have a god's-eye view of humanity below."

—Professor David Esser, Embry-Riddle Aeronautical University

For more info:

Council on Aviation Accreditation (CAA)
3410 Skyway Drive
Auburn, AL 36830-6444
(334) 844-2431
www.caaaccreditation.org/intro.html

Federal Aviation Administration (FAA)
800 Independence Ave., S.W.
Washington, DC 20591
www.faa.gov

Women in Aviation, International (WAI)
3647 State Route 503 South
West Alexandria, OH 45381
(937) 839-4647
www.wai.org

Astronomy

What it's about:

Astronomy majors study the universe beyond our atmosphere, beginning with the underlying physical principles. You observe and investigate the planets, stars, and galaxies, as you learn methods of inquiry such as optical astronomy, radio astronomy, and theoretical astronomy.

Is this for you?

You might like this major if you also like: observing the changing patterns in the sky—the constellations, phases of the moon, and eclipses; news about space exploration and technology; science museums; computers; taking things apart and putting them back together to see how they work.

Consider this major if you are good at: attention to detail; creativity; critical reading/thinking; math; quantitative analysis; research; spatial thinking/analysis; teamwork ...*or have...* initiative; patience.

Recommended high school prep:

English 4, math 4 (including precalculus or calculus), lab science 4 (including physics), social studies 3, and a foreign language 2–3. If possible, take an introduction to computer science course and a writing course. Also, take as many advanced science courses as you can.

Did you know...

...that astronomers spend only a small part of their time looking through telescopes? In fact, astronomers spend most of their time analyzing data with computers. Most people think that astronomy is about stargazing, but it is actually a quantitative science with plenty of math and physics.

Typical courses in this major:

Stars, galaxies, and cosmology
Planetary astronomy
Observational astronomical techniques
Planetary geology
Archaeoastronomy and the history of astronomy
Computer science
Multiwavelength astronomy
Calculus
Quantum physics
Planetary physics
Galactic astronomy
Extragalactic astronomy and cosmology
Stellar structure and evolution
Astrophysical techniques
Observational radio astronomy
Observational optical astronomy

Concentrations:

In college: observational astronomy; planetary science; extragalactic astronomy and cosmology; multiwavelength astronomy.

If you go on to grad school: radio astronomy; interstellar processes; planetary physics; stars and stellar structure; dynamical astronomy; galactic structure; astronomical instrumentation.

What the study of this major is like:

Students of astronomy examine the key components of the universe, such as the stars and planets, and the physical and mathematical laws that govern them. In cosmology, you analyze current theories about the origins and future of the universe; planetary astronomy describes the surfaces and makeup of the planets and moons in the solar system. Usually, the solar system and stars, galaxies, and cosmology are covered in two separate courses. Most likely, you'll attend weekly laboratory sessions in which you study such topics as the constellations and the motions of the sky, the properties of gravity and of light, and the operation of telescopes.

Once you complete the survey courses, the pace quickens. If you are serious about majoring in astronomy, you should plan your program of study to ensure that you take the required upper-level courses in physics and mathematics. Typically, these courses are the equivalent of a major in physics and a minor in math.

Most astronomy departments offer at least one course in astrophysics; as the theoretical side of astronomy, it explores the formation and evolution of stars, galaxies, and the universe itself. Many students find this investigation to be challenging, because it requires fluency in the language of math and physics. To learn why a star shines, for example, you need a basic understanding of mechanics, electricity and magnetism, thermodynamics and statistical mechanics, quantum mechanics, special relativity, and nuclear physics.

Most astronomy departments offer upper-level courses in observation through telescopes. You may have opportunities to carry out independent projects, typically using a digital (CCD) camera and requiring computer analysis of the observations. Even on research projects, you can often get by with relatively small telescopes. For a taste of professional astronomy, you may be able to do research, during the summer, at national observatories, or at some universities and colleges.

Departments with a strong physics orientation might emphasize astrophysics rather than observational techniques; those with strong connections to a research observatory might stress the development of instrumentation and hands-on astronomy. At some colleges, planetary astronomy is offered in coordination with the departments of geology and/or atmospheric science. Some departments offer two tracks in the astronomy program: one leads to broad, general knowledge of the field; the other, which includes intensive work in physics and mathematics, prepares you for graduate study.

Other majors you might like:
Astrophysics
Planetary sciences
Atmospheric sciences
Computer science
Geology/earth science
Physics
Aeronautical/aerospace engineering
Mathematics
Aeronautics and aviation science

Questions to ask colleges:
What observing facilities are available on or near campus? Can undergraduates use the largest telescope? Is there a digital camera on the telescope? Are there computers that can be used to analyze the observations?

What opportunities are available for undergraduates to participate in research during the academic year or over the summer? Are there opportunities for independent study? What are some recent projects by astronomy majors? Is there an astronomy club?

Career options and trends:
Most astronomers working in the field do research at universities, observatories, or laboratories, or teach at the high school or college level. A small number work in planetariums and science museums. An advanced degree is required.

The major in astronomy provides excellent preparation for careers in fields other than the physical sciences. Astronomy majors have become engineers, neurosurgeons, trial lawyers, insurance executives, and business leaders.

Insider's viewpoint:
"There's a lot of acronyms, special terminology for things. There's a lot of data: when people give talks they list names of stars, not "Rigel" or the sun, but they'll give the names and numbers. It takes a few years of experience to comprehend those."

—David, junior, University of Texas at Austin

For more info:
American Astronomical Society (AAS)
2000 Florida Ave., N.W.
Suite 400
Washington, DC 20009-1231
(202) 328-2010
www.aas.org

American Association of Variable Star Observers
25 Birch St.
Cambridge, MA 02138
(617) 354-0484
www.aavso.org

Astrophysics

What it's about:

Astrophysics, which focuses on the theoretical side of astronomy, presents the basic physical laws of the formation, evolution, and behavior of stars, galaxies, and the universe itself.

Is this for you?

You might like this major if you also like: using a telescope; math; computers; science fiction; abstract thinking; logical solutions; working through complex problems.

Consider this major if you are good at: attention to detail; creativity; critical reading/thinking; math; quantitative analysis; research; spatial thinking/analysis *...or have...* imagination; initiative.

Recommended high school prep:

English 4, math 4 (including precalculus or calculus), lab science 4 (earth science, biology, chemistry, and physics), social studies 3, and a foreign language 2–3. Take as much advanced math and science as you can. Courses in language arts and computer skills are also important.

Did you know...

...the difference between astrophysics and astronomy? Some people in the field say there isn't any, because all astronomers use physics to understand their findings. Basically, astronomy places greater emphasis on observing, measuring, and gathering data about celestial bodies and phenomena, while astrophysics concentrates on the physical processes of outer space and the origin and future of the universe.

Typical courses in this major:

Principles of astrophysics
Waves and particles
Quantum mechanics
Differential equations
Stars and star formation
Topics in modern astronomy
Galactic astronomy
Extragalactic astronomy
Cosmology
The early universe
Plasma astrophysics
The interstellar medium
High-energy astrophysics
General relativity

Concentrations:

Theoretical astrophysics; observational astronomy; cosmology; high-energy astrophysics.

What the study of this major is like:

Astrophysics is a rigorous major, with plenty of physics and mathematics (much like the physics major itself), especially in your first two years. You typically take courses in upper-level astronomy, astrophysics, physics, and math; you also do independent research projects in observational or theoretical astrophysics. Your course work generally includes topics such as stars and stellar evolution, galaxies and extragalactic astronomy, cosmology, relativity, and the physics of space plasma.

You should be prepared to spend time in an observational astronomy lab and perhaps to research and write a senior thesis. Most programs place a great deal of emphasis on both independent and collaborative research. Independent projects can cover any research topic in the field, from planets to the Big Bang. You use computers for all projects, including data analyses, investigation through telescopes, and theoretical modeling of the universe. If you are interested in the solar system, you should probably take additional geology courses.

Some colleges do not distinguish between astrophysics and astronomy; others design the astrophysics major primarily as a stepping-stone to graduate study in the field and offer astronomy as a less rigorous science major for liberal arts students. If you see yourself working with equations more than with telescopes to unlock the secrets of the universe, then a strong astrophysics program might be for you.

Other majors you might like:

Physics
Aeronautical/aerospace engineering
Astronomy
Planetary sciences
Geology/earth science
Geophysics//seismology
Nuclear engineering
Mathematics
Computer science
Aeronautical/aerospace engineering technology
Philosophy

Questions to ask colleges:

What opportunities are there for undergrads to work individually with faculty members on research projects?

Such opportunities are desirable for any science major, but they are particularly important for astrophysics majors because research is fundamental to the field.

Is the department of astronomy and astrophysics separate from the physics department?

Are the physics courses that are needed to fulfill requirements offered on a regular basis?

How much time do undergraduates get at either on-campus or off-campus observatories?

Career options and trends:

Professor*; researcher*; science teacher; software developer.

Most jobs are in basic research and development, and in college-level teaching; a doctoral degree is the usual educational requirement for these positions. A bachelor's or master's degree is sufficient for some jobs in applied research and development and in teaching at the high school level. A degree in astrophysics also prepares you for a wide variety of technical careers in industry, especially the computer science, space, and aeronautical fields.

Insider's viewpoint:

"It's very demanding, very time-consuming. The physics and math are really hard. It's a lot of late nights, problem sets, and labs. But I think it's worth it; it's so interesting. I don't want to go to college and not be challenged."

—Allison, sophomore, Harvard University

For more info:

American Astronomical Society (AAS)
2000 Florida Ave., N.W., Suite 400
Washington, DC 20009
(202) 328-2010
www.aas.org

Atmospheric science

Also known as:
Meteorology

What it's about:
In the atmospheric science major, you gain a broad understanding of the Earth's atmosphere, including its composition, structure, processes, and weather systems. Most programs are highly interdisciplinary and rely heavily on math, physics, and chemistry to develop the underlying theories and principles governing atmospheric behavior.

Is this for you?
You might like this major if you also like: the outdoors; computers; aviation; sailing; scientific inquiry and analysis; the Weather Channel; dealing with changing situations.

Consider this major if you are good at: attention to detail; critical reading/thinking; math; organizing; quantitative analysis; spatial thinking/analysis; teamwork *...or have...* a strong work ethic; initiative; patience.

Recommended high school prep:
English 4, math 4, lab science 4 (earth science, biology, chemistry, and physics), social studies 3, and a foreign language 2–3. If it is available, calculus is recommended, as are courses in communications, environmental science, and computer applications.

Did you know...
...that this major is not only about weather maps and TV forecasting? It is an applied physical science that requires you to develop sophisticated skills in math and in abstract thinking. Atmospheric science is essential in such fields as air pollution control, agriculture, air and sea transportation, defense, and the study of trends in the earth's climate, including global warming, droughts, or ozone depletion.

Typical courses in this major:
Climatology
Atmospheric thermodynamics
Observations and instrumentation
Weather communications
Weather analysis and forecasting
Atmospheric dynamics
Air pollution
Mesoscale meteorology
Micrometeorology
Tropical meteorology
Radar meteorology
Remote sensing systems
Stormwater hydrology
Atmospheric boundary layer
Biosphere and carbon cycle

Concentrations:
In college: broadcast meteorology; climatology; mesoscale meteorology; synoptic meteorology; air quality and pollution.

If you go on to grad school: atmospheric physics and dynamics; atmospheric modeling; air chemistry; climate change; cloud physics; tropical meteorology; paleoclimatology; remote sensing; satellite meteorology.

What the study of this major is like:
The major in atmospheric science builds on a core of mathematics, physics, and chemistry. (In fact, you might be required to take enough math courses to earn a math minor.) Your first two years generally include math every semester, a two-semester sequence in chemistry, and a two-semester sequence in physics. In some colleges, you take descriptive, introductory-level meteorology courses during your first few semesters. Other programs may hold off on meteorology until you complete the required math and science courses. In your third and fourth years, you apply math, physics, and chemistry to

gain a scientific understanding of how the atmosphere works. Most weather analysis and forecasting courses are offered at this level. Many programs also offer internships, practicums, and research opportunities.

Although some meteorology courses are primarily in a lecture format, most of them usually have associated laboratories. As with other science and engineering majors, you can expect to spend more time in classes than students in nonscience disciplines, because of longer laboratory courses. Nonscience majors may spend 15 hours per week in class; science and/or engineering majors probably spend closer to 20 hours.

At first, many students are challenged by the math and chemistry requirements, especially if their backgrounds are weak in these areas. Perhaps the biggest hurdle to clear, though, is calculus-based physics, which is the most time-consuming course many students have taken. A solid understanding of physics takes patience and commitment—you should expect to do a great deal of work in this area. But once these potential stumbling blocks have been passed, most students can complete a meteorology program if they remain focused and continue to work hard.

A few colleges emphasize a particular area of atmospheric science, such as weather analysis and forecasting, theoretical meteorology, physical meteorology, or climatology. If you are interested in becoming a weather forecaster, choose a college that emphasizes weather analysis and instrumentation. If you might like to become a broadcast meteorologist for radio or TV, look for programs that will help you develop strong communication skills, with courses in speech, journalism, and related areas.

Other majors you might like:
Chemistry
Geology/earth science
Aeronautics and aviation science
Oceanography
Geography
Agronomy and crop science
Instrumentation technology
Environmental science

Aeronautical/aerospace engineering
Radio and television

Questions to ask colleges:
Does the program meet the minimum guidelines established by the American Meteorological Society? Do graduates possess the minimum requirements needed for entry-level forecasters with the National Weather Service?

Does the program have reliable access to real-time weather data? Does the program support weather visualization tools to access these data? If you are interested in broadcasting, you should also ask if the program has access to studio facilities.

Does the program have any student organizations, such as a student chapter of the American Meteorological Society or the National Weather Association?

Career options and trends:
Operational meteorologist*; certified consulting meteorologist (CCM); broadcast meteorologist*; researcher*; forensic meteorologist.

To be a CCM, you must be certified by the American Meteorological Society (AMS), which requires at least a B.S. degree, experience, a passing grade on AMS exams, and professional references.

Most atmospheric scientists work as weather forecasters, known professionally as operational meteorologists. As long as you are willing to relocate and be flexible, entry-level jobs in forecasting are generally available. A master's degree will improve your job prospects and chances for advancement; it is usually required for positions involving research and development.

The federal government is the largest employer of atmospheric scientists, but hiring in the public sector is expected to decline. This situation should be offset by increased opportunities in private industry, spurred by continuing improvements in weather forecasting. Demand is projected to grow for consulting firms that can give weather-sensitive industries more detailed and closely targeted information than the National Weather Service.

Insider's viewpoint:

"It's frustrating being a meteorology major and someone asking you 'What's the weather going to be like tomorrow?' and you have to say 'I don't know.' You have to pay your dues, but in the end you come out with a real good understanding of the atmosphere."

—Haddie, senior, University of Wisconsin–Madison

For more info:

American Meteorological Society (AMS)
45 Beacon St.
Boston, MA 02108-3693
(617) 227-2425
www.ametsoc.org

National Weather Association (NWA)
1697 Capri Way
Charlottesville, VA 22911-3534
(434) 296-9966
www.nwas.org

Chemistry

What it's about:

Majors in chemistry study the composition, structure, and properties of matter, as well as the reactions that transform one form of matter into another. Because it is an experimental science, students learn to design and perform the investigations that will lead to a better understanding of the physical world.

Is this for you?

You might like this major if you also like: solving problems; lab experiments; taking things apart; working independently; using math; questioning why things are the way they are.

Consider this major if you are good at: attention to detail; critical reading/thinking; math; quantitative analysis; research; teamwork *...or have...* curiosity; initiative; perserverance; writing skills.

Recommended high school prep:

English 4, math 4 (including precalculus or calculus), lab science 4 (earth science, biology, chemistry and physics), social studies 3, and a foreign language 2–3. If it is available, also take a computer science course.

Did you know...

...that the chemistry major provides preparation for many careers, even outside science? The thorough grounding in math, critical thinking, and computers that the major offers can qualify you for work in areas you might not have expected, such as banking, business, and law.

Typical courses in this major:

General chemistry
Inorganic chemistry
Organic chemistry
Physical chemistry
Analytical chemistry
Biochemistry
Thermodynamics
Quantitative analysis
Instrumental analysis
Environmental chemistry
Spectroscopy and crystallography
Biochemistry
Polymer and materials chemistry

Concentrations:

In college: analytical chemistry; inorganic chemistry; organic chemistry; physical chemistry.

If you go on to grad school: physical and theoretical chemistry; polymer chemistry; materials chemistry; forensic chemistry; medicinal chemistry; environmental chemistry.

What the study of this major is like:

Chemists provide the expertise to create products you encounter every day, such as medicines, fabrics, and synthetic materials. As a major, for example, you learn ways to control the chemical reactions that produce ceramics, semiconductors, insulators, polymers with unusual properties, and molecules essential for life. In your examination of atoms bonding to form molecules, you observe how the properties of substances depend on which atoms are combined, and how.

Chemistry has traditionally been divided into four areas: organic, inorganic, physical, and analytical. Organic chemistry is the study of carbon compounds, whereas inorganic chemistry is the study of all other elements. Physical chemists investigate the structure and properties of matter, and analytical chemists devise the procedures used in identifying and measuring the individual components of complex mixtures.

Chemistry majors usually take a core curriculum that includes courses in all four areas before they concentrate in one area. Your concentration may require you to take advanced courses that explore the methods for synthesizing natural products; that introduce you to the instruments and techniques used in analyzing unknown compounds; or that show you how to use lasers to study a molecular collision. You will also be expected to take courses in math, physics, and, probably, biology.

All chemistry majors spend a great deal of time performing experiments in the laboratory. The lab experience teaches you to observe the world around you, to draw conclusions from these observations, and to challenge currently accepted beliefs. A typical week's classes consist of about three 50-minute classroom sessions and a two- to four-hour lab. Advanced students take independent study courses, in which they work with a professor on a research project. There is generally little time for electives. On top of lecture classes and lab work, you should expect to work on daily problem sets and put in considerable time studying and writing reports.

Some colleges award Bachelor of Arts degrees in chemistry; others award Bachelor of Science degrees; still others offer both. But regardless of which degree is offered, most chemistry programs emphasize critical-thinking and laboratory skills. The American Chemical Society specifies the course requirements that enable a bachelor's degree program to qualify graduates for ACS certification, which most employers look for.

Other majors you might like:

Atmospheric science

Environmental science

Clinical/medical laboratory technology

Soil science

Chemical engineering

Materials engineering

Biochemistry

Molecular biology

Chemical technology

Forensic science

Pharmacy

Chemistry teacher education

Questions to ask colleges:

Are research opportunities and equipment available for all students? Doing worthwhile research is especially important if you intend to go on to grad school.

What do most chemistry majors do after obtaining their degree—go to medical school or graduate school, or go into industry? If one area predominates, it may reflect a particular emphasis in the program.

Does the program qualify graduates for ACS certification?

Career options and trends:

Industrial or pharmaceutical research chemist*; physician, pharmacist, or other medical professional*; pharmaceutical sales representative; high school chemistry teacher*; chemical lab technician; food scientist; government inspector (for FDA or EPA); crime lab analyst or forensic chemist; occupational safety specialist; environmental consultant.

Unemployment remains low in chemistry-related fields. More than half of all chemists work in the manufacturing industry, where job opportunities are expected to be most plentiful in pharmaceuticals and biotechnology. Research and testing firms will probably experience healthy growth as they are contracted, by a wide variety of businesses, to do specialized research formerly done by in-house chemists. Another area of opportunity is environmental research and regulatory compliance. Chemists with a master's or doctorate degree will be in most demand.

Insider's viewpoint:

"I really enjoyed organic chemistry, despite the many horror stories I heard beforehand. There is a certain thought process that goes along with orgo and once that process is understood, it becomes logical. Understanding why reactions go the way they do simplifies many problems."

—Christina, junior, University of California: Davis

For more info:

American Chemical Society (ACS)
1155 16th St., N.W.
Washington, DC 20036
(202) 872-4600
www.chemistry.org

Geology/earth science

What it's about:

Geology/earth science is the study of the earth and the forces that act on it. Topics include the history and formation of planet Earth; the behavior of the solids, liquids, and gases that it is composed of; and the interaction between the biosphere—the living things that call the earth their home—and the planet's inorganic, or nonliving, substances.

Is this for you?

You might like this major if you also like: the outdoors; history; archaeology; gems; dinosaurs; rock climbing; hiking and camping; collecting; environmental issues; a broad range of scientific inquiry, from the unimaginably big to the very small.

Consider this major if you are good at: attention to detail; creativity; critical reading/thinking; math; quantitative analysis; spatial thinking/analysis; teamwork ...*or have...* initiative; patience; physical stamina; verbal skills; writing skills.

Recommended high school prep:

English 4, math 4 (including precalculus), lab science 4 (earth science, biology, chemistry, and physics), social studies 3, and a foreign language 2–3. Courses in computer science or applications are recommended, if available; and you will benefit if you can obtain a basic understanding of geographic information systems, either in school or on your own.

Did you know...

...that geology isn't just about rocks—it is a scientific discipline closely linked to chemistry, biology, and physics? It is not a place to avoid these other sciences, but rather a place to apply them. The field is becoming increasingly quantitative, so math skills are a definite advantage.

Typical courses in this major:

Physical geology
Historical geology
Paleontology
Structural geology
Mineralogy
Petrology
Surficial geology
Geophysics
Geochemistry
Hydrogeology
Field geology
Stratigraphy and sedimentation
Geologic hazards
Tectonics
Geographical information systems
Earth resources

Concentrations:

In college: geochemistry; geophysics; environmental geology.

If you go on to grad school: paleontology; petrology; petroleum geology; mineralogy; hydrology; tectonics; paleomagnetics; structural geology and tectonics; geological engineering; geochronology.

What the study of this major is like:

Geology/earth science students first take introductory courses in physical and/or historical geology that teach you basics: rock, mineral, and fossil identification; landform evolution; plate tectonics; and the geological time scale. Topical courses, such as environmental geology, planetary geology, or oceanography, may also serve as introductions to the major. Most introductory courses and upper-level courses have weekly three- to four-hour laboratories or field trips of various lengths. To learn other essential geology/earth science tools, you take yearlong courses in chemistry, physics, mathematics, and biology.

Upper-level courses are often arranged in sequence: you take courses in a specific order so that you learn the skills and knowledge needed to continue. For instance, a semester or year of mineralogy provides the analytic skills (such as the use of the petrographic microscope) essential for later courses in petrology. Paleontology, sedimentation, and stratigraphy often form a sequence covering the origin of sedimentary rocks and the fossil organisms they may contain. Geomorphology and glacial geology courses focus on processes that shape the earth's surface. Courses in resources—energy, minerals, and water—examine their origin, as well as the exploration, recovery, and use of these essential commodities.

A unique aspect of geology/earth science is its emphasis on the history of the earth—a recurring theme of many courses in the major. Another trademark is its reliance on fieldwork. Because the field is to a geologist what the library is to a historian, most geology/earth science courses include fieldwork as well as lab work. Some undergraduate departments require a semester-long or summer course in field geology, and most graduate departments require such a course for admission. Many summer courses, which average four to five weeks and are based at permanent facilities in the western states, offer intensive training in geological mapping and in preparing reports. After completing the third year and a field course, the best-qualified majors may be able to find summer jobs as geological field assistants or interns in industry or government.

Visualizing in three dimensions, and comprehending the large scale of many geological phenomena, can be challenging at first. And although geologists are typically not regimented in their activities, you cannot afford to be undisciplined. Because deadlines in geology/earth science courses are usually farther apart than in many other majors, you must figure out a long-term time management plan.

The main philosophical differences among programs are in applied rather than purely academic geological science. If you are interested in using your geological training to tackle concrete problems, you will probably be more comfortable in a department that focuses on hydrogeology, petroleum geology, environmental geology, and exploration seismology. Such departments have more of an engineering perspective, and may even have a geological engineer or civil engineer on staff. In more academically focused departments, faculty members include petrologists, mineralogists, paleontologists, and tectonists.

Other majors you might like:
Atmospheric science
Geography
Oceanography
Soil science
Surveying technology
Environmental science
Mining and mineral engineering
Planetary sciences
Geological engineering
Petroleum engineering
Landscape architecture
Science teacher education

Questions to ask colleges:
Are field trips and field instruction built into most, if not all, of the courses?

How many geology majors take chemistry, biology, physics, or math beyond the minimum requirements?

How accessible are facilities and instrumentation housed in other departments, like chemistry, for use by geology majors?

Do any of the faculty members have experience working as professional geologists outside the academic setting (e.g., industry)?

Career options and trends:
Earth science teacher*; engineering geologist; environmental hydrologist*; petroleum geologist; government agency staff geologist; researcher*.

A Ph.D. degree is required for most research positions in colleges and universities and in government.

The petroleum industry is a cyclical business, but over the long term, there will be opportunities in the energy sector, especially for those willing to work overseas. In other industries, the need to comply with environmental regulations will create opportunities for environmental geoscientists, especially hydrologists and engineering geologists.

Oceanography

What it's about:

Oceanography majors study the oceans—their origins; movement; and biological, chemical, geological, and physical components. As an interdisciplinary science, oceanography draws on the natural sciences to increase our understanding of the ocean environments of planet Earth.

Is this for you?

You might like this major if you also like: the coast and the sea; science and math; exploring the unknown; water sports such as boating, diving, surfing, sailing; travel; environmental issues; asking questions such as "how did that bottle get to our beach?".

Consider this major if you are good at: attention to detail; creativity; critical reading/thinking; math; quantitative analysis; research; teamwork *...or have...* initiative; writing skills.

Recommended high school prep:

English 4, math 4 (including precalculus or calculus), lab science 4 (earth science, biology, chemistry, and physics), social studies 3, and a foreign language 2–3. Courses in writing, computer science, and environmental science are also recommended, if available.

Typical courses in this major:

Physical oceanography
Chemical oceanography
Geological oceanography
Biological oceanography
Waves and tides
Fluid mechanics
Meteorology
Marine ecology
Environmental physiology of marine animals
Sedimentology
Marine pollution
Barrier islands and coastal lagoons
Oceanic and atmospheric processes
Polar oceanography
Estuarine oceanography
Sampling techniques and field studies

Concentrations:

Biological oceanography; chemical oceanography; geological oceanography; physical oceanography; marine resource management.

What the study of this major is like:

Scientists know more about the surface of the moon than they do about the depths of the oceans. Oceanography is an interdisciplinary science that makes use of principles of biology, chemistry, geology, physics, geophysics, mathematics, botany, zoology, meteorology, and geography.

You begin the major by taking math, physics, biology, geology, and chemistry. Usually you must complete an introduction to probability and statistics course, and mathematics through first-year calculus. (In some programs, an earth science education track requires only precalculus.) As you study oceanography at increasingly complex levels, you explore the methods and instruments of research and do fieldwork, collecting data to analyze and interpret.

In your third year, you will probably choose to concentrate in biological, chemical, geological, or physical oceanography. In biological oceanography, you study the distribution, abundance, and production of plants, animals, and nutrients in the oceanic ecosystem; the emphasis is on the investigation of bacteria, phytoplankton, zooplankton, and other organisms living at the bottom of the sea.

Chemical oceanography examines the complex chemistry, distribution, and cycling of dissolved substances, nutrients, and gases in seawater, especially the mechanisms that control these elements and compounds. Geological oceanography focuses on marine sediments, examines the theory of ocean basin formation, and surveys shoreline formation. In physical oceanography, you observe and predict the seas' motion, from small tidal changes to the giant circular currents. Important areas of research include the distribution of physical properties (temperature, salinity, sea ice), and air-sea interaction, with its effect on climate.

In accompanying laboratories, you apply lecture and reading material in a practical setting. By your fourth year, you are ready to do solid fieldwork and to assist faculty members in their research. Most programs finish with a yearlong capstone field study course in ocean and earth science.

Some oceanography majors have trouble completing the math requirements. It helps if you focus on math in high school and in your first two years of college—especially if you are thinking of concentrating in physical oceanography. It is also important to complete your introductory science courses during your first two years. Because oceanography is an integrated field, most of your concentration courses will include material from biology, chemistry, geology, and physics. And since oceanography requires a lot of fieldwork, you should learn, early on, how to translate the theoretical material in textbooks to the practical activities in the lab. Another recommendation is to do volunteer work on faculty research projects, both in the lab and in the field. Many majors experience field exercises, aboard a research ship bound for distant seas—a highlight of their college career.

Other majors you might like:
Marine biology
Ocean engineering
Fishing and fisheries
Marine engineering/naval architecture
Water, wetlands, and marine management
Geology/earth science
Atmospheric science
Environmental science
Geography
Aquaculture
Marine science/Merchant Marine
Underwater diving

Questions to ask colleges:
What types of offshore or coastal field exercises are offered to undergraduates? Are research opportunities with faculty members also available?

Does the program emphasize a particular concentration within oceanography? Some colleges stress physical oceanography, others take a biological or environmental slant, and some integrate oceanography and atmospheric science. A wide range of courses offered on a reasonable schedule indicates a quality program.

Career options and trends:
Middle school or high school earth science teacher; government, faculty, or industry researcher; government agency staff oceanographer (U.S. Geological Survey, National Oceanographic and Atmospheric Administration, state environmental protection agencies); marine technician.

The largest employers of oceanographers, besides colleges and universities, are the federal and state governments. Careers in private industry are also available, primarily in engineering, geology, geophysics, environmental quality, marine policy, and marine fisheries. More students are entering this field than in the past, so competition is increasing, especially for biological oceanographers. Most jobs require an advanced degree. There is strong demand, however, for qualified earth science teachers in middle and high schools.

Insider's viewpoint:
"I went on a research cruise with Scripps (Institution of Oceanography) with kids from across the country. We sailed to Samoa for the quarter, dredging the bottom of the ocean to pick up volcanic rocks in hope of dating these submarine volcanoes. I worked the night shift, and even though there were hardships, I found that it pushed me."

—Teresa, junior, University of California: Los Angeles

For more info:
The Oceanography Society
P. O. Box 1931
Rockville, MD 20849-1931
www.tos.org

Physics

What it's about:

Physics is the study of the basic laws of nature, including mechanics, sound, electricity and magnetism, optics, heat, and quantum theory. You explore matter and systems, and the particles within them to see how they exchange energy and momentum with their surroundings, exert forces on one another, and move under the influences of these forces.

Is this for you?

You might like this major if you also like: math; computers; electronics; tinkering with things to see how they work; learning about the natural world; abstract thinking; logical solutions; solving puzzles.

Consider this major if you are good at: attention to detail; creativity; critical reading/thinking; math; organizing; quantitative analysis; spatial thinking/analysis *...or have...* imagination; manual dexterity; mechanical facility; patience.

Recommended high school prep:

English 4, math 4 (including precalculus or calculus), lab science 4, social studies 3, and a foreign language 2–3. Take as many advanced science courses as possible, but don't neglect language arts and social studies.

Did you know...

...that a lot of math is required in this major? Your math courses will probably include calculus, linear algebra, differential equations, complex variables, and statistics.

Typical courses in this major:

Modern physics
Classical mechanics
Electricity and magnetism
Thermodynamics
Statistical mechanics
Quantum mechanics
Computational physics
Advanced laboratory
Solid-state physics
Electronics
Nuclear physics
Wave motion
Particle physics
Optics
Acoustics

Concentrations:

In college: applied physics; biophysics; computational physics.

If you go on to grad school: atomic/molecular physics; elementary particle physics; nuclear physics; condensed matter; optics; plasma physics; solid-state physics; astrophysics.

What the study of this major is like:

Physics courses examine phenomena as different as the structure and evolution of the universe, on the one hand, and the fundamental particles from which all matter is made, on the other. As a major, you begin with courses that introduce you to the principles of physics: mechanics (forces, energy, and the laws of motion); electricity and magnetism (the emission of electromagnetic radiation by charged particles); quantum mechanics (the particle nature of electromagnetic waves, the wave nature of particles, energy levels, and the effect of the uncertainties of nature on particle behavior); and probably thermodynamics (the theory of heat). These courses emphasize the logical, mathematical structure of the principles of nature, as well as important applications of these principles. For example, you learn about the nature of light, atomic structure, and the properties of solids, including the semiconductors that have revolutionized our world. As you advance in the major, the math becomes more complex, so strong computation skills are imperative.

Physics courses stress problem-solving skills. You will be assigned homework sets consisting of increasingly difficult problems. Most courses are taught in lecture format, but there are several laboratory courses as well. Physics is an experimental science, and your course work will show the relation between experiments and the theories derived from them. Because some of the advanced material is conceptually and mathematically challenging, physics majors often work together. Collaborating with others is one of the highlights of physics study. In the end, of course, you must be able to work on your own, on exams and certain assignments. As a physics major, your goal is to become an independent thinker, a problem solver, and a researcher.

The main challenge most physics majors face is the conceptual complexity of the subject. You will have to visualize abstract concepts, some of which may not immediately make sense. Although the task can be hard, understanding a difficult concept can give you great satisfaction. Another challenge you may encounter is to find solutions to complicated problems. Simply selecting a formula won't help; you must comprehend the principles at work and determine a strategy for unraveling the puzzle. Solutions often require lengthy mathematical computations.

Most physics departments have an undergraduate organization that encourages you to take part in the life of the department. In the departments, interaction between faculty members and students is generally high. You can often participate in independent research with faculty members. Although most physics programs have similar curricula, the sequence of courses might differ—for example, some programs introduce the modern fields of physics (relativity, quantum theory) earlier on than in other programs. In many programs, the introductory courses are taught with combined lectures and labs. But some programs place more emphasis on laboratory work than others do. There may also be variations among departments in the use of technology in instruction. And in some programs, you must complete a research project as part of your degree requirements.

Other majors you might like:

Architecture
Mathematics
Astrophysics
Philosophy
Computer science
Engineering physics
Civil engineering
Aeronautical/aerospace engineering
Nuclear engineering
Radiologic technology/medical imaging
Technical and business writing
Nuclear medical technology

Questions to ask colleges:

Are the physics courses listed in the course catalog offered on a regular basis? Often they are not, so you should find out which courses will actually be available to you in your third and fourth years.

What are the opportunities for undergraduate research? This is an important consideration if you intend to go on to grad school.

How accessible are the computers in the physics labs and outside of class?

Is there an active SPS (Society of Physics Students) chapter on campus?

Career options and trends:

Researcher*; engineer*; high school teacher; professor; laboratory technician; computer programmer*; financial analyst.

Certification in education is required for teaching in public high schools; a Ph.D. is essential for teaching in college.

Most physicists work in research and development, in industry, government, or academia. A Ph.D. is generally required for basic research, but with a master's degree, you can get an entry-level position in manufacturing and applied research and development.

Nanotechnology is becoming an important field. In this discipline, physicists, chemists, and engineers explore the properties and applications of materials of increasingly small size ("nano" means "one-billionth"). In fact, physics in general is growing more interdisciplinary, as it overlaps with chemistry, engineering, biology, and other fields.

Students who double-major in physics and engineering or business, or pursue these areas in grad school, have greater job options. But a bachelor's degree in physics can open doors in many fields that value analytical skills. There is a strong demand for high school physics teachers.

Insider's viewpoint:

"Being a woman in physics now is not as weird because you learn to adapt to the culture. I just went to the CERN laboratories in Switzerland, and out of the eight people who were invited, I was the only woman. You just get used to that."

—Sarah, senior, Columbia University

For more info:

American Institute of Physics (AIP)
One Physics Ellipse
College Park, MD 20740-3845
301-209-3100
www.aip.org

PhysLink.com
5318 East Second St., #530
Long Beach, CA 90803
www.physlink.com

Protective services

Working in the protective services is not exactly like what you see on some TV crime dramas. The detective doesn't crack the case alone. Several professionals each have a well-defined role in collecting and examining evidence and bringing the bad guys to justice. It may not be as glamorous as it seems, but the contributions of professionals in protective services are just as essential as the TV shows depict.

"Both crime prevention and justice delivery are important matters for society at large," says Professor Dennis R. Longmire, Sam Houston State University. "Being able to engage in studies related to these important issues is both fulfilling and exciting."

Criminal justice professionals work in a wide variety of settings, in both industry and government. Most work for federal, state, or local government, but some private firms, such as security companies or correctional service providers, receive government contracts for certain types of work.

What types of jobs are we talking about here? Criminal justice majors go on to become police officers, security officers, probation officers, parole officers, and other law enforcement agents. Forensic science majors, who learn to analyze evidence, work as evidence technicians, fingerprint analysts, firearms experts, and as scientists like chemists, DNA or dental experts, anthropologists, pathologists, and psychiatrists. Of course, the fire service is another important branch of public safety. Professionals in those ranks include fire protection consultants; fire marshals or inspectors; environmental, health, and safety experts; and loss control personnel, who often work in the insurance business.

For better or worse, many jobs are available in occupations that protect people and property. "Crime is a 'growth industry,'" Longmire says. "Any of the careers associated with it continue to experience increased demands for new and highly qualified workers."

Law enforcement and corrections agencies are regularly looking for police recruits and officers. If you want to be among the Finest, as the police are rightly known, or the Bravest—the firefighters—it helps to go to college. In many communities, you need a college degree to become a police officer.

"The field of criminal justice continues to become increasingly professionalized. What this means is that positions that were once filled by workers who only held high school degrees now require college-level workers who can exercise increasingly complex and demanding discretion," Longmire explains.

Several national trends contribute to the growing importance of these fields. Mandatory minimum prison sentences have swelled the prison population and created the need for workers in corrections agencies and industries. Other laws have increased the use of DNA and fingerprints, so hiring is also taking place in forensic sciences. The reorganization of federal agencies into the Department of Homeland Security keeps the job market strong.

"There will always be demand for scientists in crime labs, police, and security agencies," predicts Professor Frank Vozzo of Russell Sage College.

First and second degrees

These majors reside in many types of colleges, and in divisions and departments within colleges. Look for criminal justice, public administration, social sciences, natural sciences, applied arts and sciences, applied arts and technology, behavioral science, anthropology, engineering, and engineering technologies.

You'll notice that protective services majors are multidisciplinary—they require you to study many subjects to understand complex topics like criminal behavior or the way the justice system works. For instance, the criminal justice major mixes sociology, psychology, and public administration, and colleges strike different balances among those fields. Forensics combines science and the law with varying emphasis on each. The fire and safety programs may differ in whether they stress practical skills or theoretical studies.

Read up on the colleges of interest and their programs and ask some questions about finding work with an associate, bachelor's, or graduate (master's, doctorate, or law) degree. Look for schools that offer internship programs in agencies for your field. Ask about the professional and academic credentials of the faculty members. You can learn a lot from a former cop as an instructor, but you really need professors who are also highly educated and keep current with the latest trends and techniques in law enforcement and forensic sciences. Like the faculty, the college labs need to be up-to-date. Also find out if the program is accredited and if you will need professional certification.

Graduate tracks in criminal justice include criminological theory, private and public security, and criminal justice administration or management. Graduates in forensics specialize in administration, analytical chemistry, forensic toxicology (poisons), molecular biology, genetics or serology (blood) as they relate to forensics. In the fire service, grads may become professionals in industrial hygiene or in computer fire modeling.

Some of the newest majors in these fields include victim studies, international security studies, terrorism and security analysis, bioinformatics (clinical databases), and fire and emergency management.

"The field of criminal justice is filled with exciting and important issues that are constantly changing," says Longmire.

That's not just on TV, but in real life.

Criminal justice and law enforcement

What it's about:

The major in criminal justice and law enforcement administration focuses on how society responds to criminal behavior. Areas of study include policing, the courts, and the sentencing of both adult and juvenile violators. Don't confuse this major with criminology, which is primarily concerned with the sociopathic and psychological bases of criminal behavior.

Is this for you?

You might like this major if you also like: working with people; helping others; membership in religious or community groups; "service" activities; public speaking; debating; mystery games; crime stories.

Consider this major if you are good at: attention to detail; counseling; leadership; organizing; persuading/influencing; problem solving; teamwork *...or have...* composure during crises; initiative; patience; verbal skills; writing skills.

Recommended high school prep:

English 4, math 3, lab science 3, social studies 3, and a foreign language 2–3. If they are available, take courses in psychology and philosophy.

Did you know...

...that criminal justice professionals are primarily involved in the delivery of human services to their communities? Many courses you will take draw from psychology, social work, and public-service-related disciplines.

...that criminal justice professionals work in both the public and the private sectors? While most of them work for government agencies (federal, state, and local), some are employed by private security agencies, as well as by private correctional agencies that contract with the government. Criminal justice positions are also available in all branches of the military.

Typical courses in this major:

Introduction to the criminal justice system
Legal aspects of law enforcement
Criminology
Courts and criminal procedure
Fundamentals of criminal law
Human behavior
Comparative criminal justice systems
Law and society
White-collar crime
Research methods
Criminal profiles
Forensic sciences
Correctional systems and practices
Police systems and practices
Criminal investigation
Professionalism and ethics

Concentrations:

In college: law enforcement; forensic studies; corrections.

If you go on to grad school: criminological theory; private and public security; criminal justice administration; criminal justice management; research methods and statistics.

What the study of this major is like:

Course work in criminal justice includes the behavioral sciences, especially sociology, psychology, and social work. You examine theories about the causes of crime, as well as ways to organize public agencies for both crime prevention and crime control. Courses in research methods and criminal statistics are often required. In most programs, you can concentrate in either law enforcement (policing) or corrections (including probation, prisons, and parole), but you must still take courses on a wide variety of subjects related to the administration of justice. All programs emphasize effective communication skills: the ability to speak well is essential, because there is extensive public contact in the criminal justice profession; you must know how to write well because written reports are an integral part of the work.

Since the discipline of criminal justice is actually a blend of sociology, psychology, and public administration, colleges may vary in the emphasis they place on these areas. Programs that developed out of sociology tend to stress theories of crime causation that focus on the problems that plague society. In contrast, programs that emerged from psychology tend to see crime primarily in terms of individual background, motivation, and behavior. And degree programs that evolved out of public administration are usually more interested in issues of law enforcement than in crime causation itself.

All programs require students to explore the constitutional and legal aspects of the administration of justice. However, some colleges place less emphasis on these courses than others. Those that do so tend to focus on the scientific study of crime causation and require students to take more courses in research methods and in statistics.

In general, courses involve classroom lectures, supplemented by out-of-class reading and other homework assignments. Many programs deliver some of their course work online, and some even offer complete degree programs through nontraditional, Web-based methods. Many programs will also allow you to accumulate academic credit through internships with criminal justice agencies, in which you work under the supervision of a professor as well as a criminal justice professional. Some programs provide the opportunity to travel to foreign countries to examine the cross-cultural and international issues facing criminal justice professionals around the world.

Other majors you might like:
Criminology
Corrections
Police science
Legal studies
Psychology
Security/loss prevention
Public administration
Forensic science
Human services
Juvenile corrections
Sociology
Security services management

Questions to ask colleges:
Does the program place students in internships with appropriate public or private agencies? Wide-ranging experience in such agencies can help graduates seeking jobs in those agencies or similar organizations.

What are the academic and professional backgrounds of the faculty members? Some programs employ former law enforcement personnel who have had little or no academic training. Their teaching style often relies on the telling of "war stories." These instructors may be interesting, but they may not provide the most current and useful information in the field.

Career options and trends:
Police officer*; security officer; probation officer*; parole officer*; correctional counselor; federal law enforcement agent (FBI, Secret Service, etc.).

Special certification is usually required for positions involving "special-needs offenders," such as youthful, drug- and alcohol-addicted, and mentally challenged violators of the law. Often, your college course work can be counted as partial credit toward such certification.

The field of criminal justice has become increasingly professionalized—college degrees are required where high school diplomas would once have been enough. It is also becoming more globalized, as professionals from all over the world cooperate on significant issues and cases. Job applicants who are bilingual or multilingual have a competitive edge.

Insider's viewpoint:
"My particular interest in the discipline is driven by the realization that issues associated with law enforcement and criminal justice are also associated with human rights and basic freedoms."

—Professor Dennis R. Longmire, Sam Houston State University

For more info:
Academy of Criminal Justice Sciences (ACJS)
P.O. Box 960
Greenbelt, MD 20768
(800) 757-2257
www.acjs.org

American Correctional Association (ACA)
206 North Washington St., Suite 200
Alexandria, VA 22314
(703) 224-0000
www.aca.org

American Probation and Parole Association (APPA)
2760 Research Park Drive
Lexington, KY 40511-8410
(859) 244-8203
www.appa-net.org

Fire protection and safety technology

What it's about:

In this major, you learn to evaluate and reduce potential loss of property and life in the workplace and other settings. You explore three of the most likely threats to safety: fire, accidents, and exposure to hazardous materials.

Is this for you?

You might like this major if you also like: volunteer work; firefighting; change; working with people; helping others.

Consider this major if you are good at: attention to detail; creativity; critical reading/thinking; leadership; organizing; persuading/influencing; quantitative analysis *...or have...* initiative; mechanical facility; verbal skills.

Recommended high school prep:

English 4, math 4 (including precalculus or calculus), lab science 4 (including chemistry and physics), social studies 3, and a foreign language 2–3. Courses in computer applications and drafting are also recommended.

Did you know...

...that professionals in fire protection and safety technology are dedicated to protecting people in all types of employment from many kinds of hazards? The major is not limited to firefighting and fire service organizations.

...that there is a big demand for the services of loss control professionals? The opportunities for women and minorities are at an all-time high, and graduates are enjoying record placement rates of nearly 100 percent.

Typical courses in this major:

Fire safety and hazards recognition
Fire suppression and detection systems
Introduction to occupational safety techniques
Studies in loss control
Fire protection management
Design and analysis of sprinkler systems
Elements of industrial hygiene
Fire protection hydraulics and water supply
Industrial safety organization
Structural designs for fire and life safety
Human factors in accident prevention
Fire dynamics
Building electrical systems
Issues in local government and fire services
Disaster and fire defense planning
Hazardous materials management

Concentrations:

In college: fire protection systems; code compliance; fire dynamics and behavior; fire investigation; industrial safety; industrial hygiene.

If you go on to grad school: computer fire modeling.

What the study of this major is like:

Programs in fire protection and safety technology prepare you for a career in loss control. The profession is divided into three areas: loss from fire; loss from physical accidents; and loss from environmental exposure. As a major, you learn to predict threats to safety in the workplace and to take steps to prevent them—for example, by designing efficient evacuation routes; by identifying objects that could injure workers; and by controlling the use of toxic materials in factories.

The curriculum introduces you immediately to issues in fire protection and safety. Therefore, you can measure your interest in a fire protection and safety technology career early on in your studies. The program includes many courses in math and in the physical sciences. Two semesters of calculus are required, as well as two semesters of chemistry and one semester of physics. Computers are an essential tool in most courses. If you know that you want to pursue this major, you should try to take classes in high school that will prepare you for college-level math and science.

Some programs include plenty of hands-on work; you do numerous lab exercises to reinforce the facts and ideas that are taught in lectures. You might be expected to take at least two or three afternoon lab sessions each semester. Industry internships are frequently encouraged, because they provide valuable experience and let you apply, in a real-world setting, what you've learned.

A number of programs gear their curriculum toward careers in the fire service. The emphasis of these programs is on practical application—you put into use the techniques you've studied, but you may or may not learn the theories behind the techniques. Courses designed specifically for fire protection may not be easily transferred to more general programs. Therefore, you should be committed to a career in fire safety if you enroll in such a program.

Other majors you might like:
Architectural engineering
Industrial engineering
Fire services administration
Occupational safety/health technology
Firefighting/fire science
Security/loss prevention
Insurance
Civil engineering
Hazardous materials technology
Construction technology
Building inspection

Questions to ask colleges:
Is the program approved by an outside professional organization, such as the International Fire Service Accreditation Congress (IFSAC) or the Technology Accreditation Commission of the Accreditation Board for Engineering and Technology (ABET/TAC)? These organizations have set standards that can help you judge the quality of a program.

Does the college support internships and co-ops? Internships are especially valuable in the broad field of fire protection and safety.

Are there enough lab facilities available? Are the faculty members and students dedicated to safety?

You may be able to get an indication of the program's commitment to safety by observing the college's own facilities.

Career options and trends:
Fire protection consultant*; environment, health, and safety engineer*; building code official/plans examiner; loss control consultant (for insurance companies)*; industrial safety engineer; deputy fire marshal/inspector.

You can become certified as a certified fire protection specialist (CFPS), an associate safety professional (ASP), a certified safety professional (CSP), or an engineer-in-training/professional engineer (EIT/PE). You can also become state-licensed as a fire prevention officer.

Fire protection engineering activities are indirectly tied to the construction industry. Upturns in construction have a significant, positive impact on job opportunities. The effects of downturns are less dramatic; because of code requirements, structures must be maintained and retrofitted as necessary. Recent emphasis on homeland security is predicted to create substantial growth in the fire protection field.

The field of safety is more closely linked to manufacturing and industrial activities, which are subject to shifts in the global economy. Homeland security concerns are expected to increase activities in safety, security, and environmental monitoring.

Insider's viewpoint:
"Testing the response of materials and structures to the assault of fire is dramatic and interesting, and protecting firefighters and occupants from the effects of fire is challenging and rewarding."

—Professor Thomas J. Woodford, Oklahoma State University

For more info:
International Fire Service Accreditation Congress (IFSAC)
1700 West Tyler
Oklahoma State University
Stillwater, OK 74078-8075
(405) 744-8303
www.ifsac.org

Forensic science

What it's about:

Forensic science is an interdisciplinary major that applies knowledge of the natural sciences, the criminal justice system, and the law to the analysis and evaluation of evidence gathered from a crime or accident scene.

Is this for you?

You might like this major if you also like: science clubs; chemistry; computers; lab experiments; amateur sleuthing; detective stories and police shows; working with precision instruments.

Consider this major if you are good at: attention to detail; math; organizing; quantitative analysis; spatial thinking/analysis; teamwork *...or have...* manual dexterity; observational skills; patience; writing skills.

Recommended high school prep:

English 4, math 4 (including precalculus), lab science 4 (including biology, chemistry, and physics), social studies 3, and a foreign language 2–3.

Did you know...

...that forensic scientists, evidence technicians, crime scene investigators, and detectives are separate people who have taken separate career paths? TV shows can give the impression that one person does it all, from discovering trace evidence to cracking the case—but most forensic science takes place in the field or in the lab, as one part of an investigatory team process.

Typical courses in this major:

Introduction to criminal justice
Analytical chemistry
Human anatomy
Instrumental analysis
Genetics
Microbiology
Molecular biology
Criminal evidence and procedure
Criminalisitics
Crime scene investigation
Statistics
Care and preservation of evidence
Fire investigation
Toxicology
Forensic anthropology
Forensic entomology

Concentrations:

In college: toxicology; forensic anthropology; crime scene investigation; forensic chemistry; trace evidence; accident and fire investigation.

If you go on to grad school: criminalistics; forensic science administration; analytical chemistry; forensic molecular biology; forensic engineering; forensic entomology; forensic DNA/serology.

What the study of this major is like:

Although trace evidence may be tiny, it is often enough to establish the particulars of a crime and lead to its solution. The forensic science major teaches you how to use scientific analysis to tie pieces of evidence to particular sources. Because analytical techniques are constantly improving, forensic scientists can more easily protect the innocent and bring the guilty to justice. In fact, investigators can often crack cases that have gone unsolved for decades.

Your first two years in the Bachelor of Science program are typically like those of a chemistry major or a premed student. You take challenging courses in biology, general and inorganic chemistry, and physics, as well as college-level statistics and calculus. Since the chemistry, biology, and math courses have sequencing requirements, you must begin them in your first semester. You will also take introductory courses in criminal justice, the social sciences, and psychology.

In your third and fourth years, you enroll in specialized lab courses, taught by or in association with forensic scientists, where you apply the scientific principles and techniques from your earlier courses to forensics. These later courses, which sometimes include independent work (such as research projects or internships), provide you with professional skills and career information. In your final year, you usually participate in a field practicum and a capstone seminar project. Although the forensic science major prepares you for direct employment as a laboratory technician, you are generally encouraged to go on to graduate school for further specialization.

Most forensic science programs have developed from existing programs in criminal justice or the natural sciences. There is considerable variation as to which areas they cover in depth. The oldest and largest programs may offer a variety of concentrations, while newer and smaller programs generally focus on one or two of the following subdisciplines:

Forensic biology, which deals with the analysis of blood and other body fluids, physical wounds, and body positions; DNA analysis; forensic chemistry, which examines trace evidence such as hairs, fibers, paint, soil; forensic anthropology, which is concerned with skeletal remains; forensic entomology, which uses insect activity in decomposing bodies to determine place and time of death; forensic toxicology, which analyzes specimens of blood, urine, or tissue for drugs, alcohol, or poison. There are other specializations in such areas as computer crime, fingerprints, firearms and explosives, and footprint, tool, and tire impressions.

Two-year or certificate programs in forensic science prepare you for careers as crime scene or evidence technicians. Training may include the collection and preservation of evidence; crime scene photography; latent fingerprint processing; and/or composite drawing. Many of these positions require you to pass a certification exam given by the International Association for Identification (IAI). Not all jurisdictions use civilian technicians for these functions, so be sure to check the rules where you intend to work.

Other majors you might like:
Criminology
Psychology
Microbiology
Biochemistry
Anthropology
Criminal justice and law enforcement
Police science
Chemistry
Materials science
Biotechnology
Emergency medical technology (EMT paramedic)
Clinical/medical laboratory technology

Questions to ask colleges:
Are internships available in crime labs or related facilities?

What opportunities do undergraduates have for field research or other hands-on training?

Career options and trends:
Forensic lab technician*; crime scene investigator*; latent fingerprint analyst; forensic engineer; forensic chemist*; forensic DNA analyst*; law enforcement officer.

In some states, only uniformed law enforcement officers investigate crime scenes. Forensic pathologists, psychiatrists, and medical examiners are licensed physicians.

Demand for forensic science professionals is projected to increase because of new technologies in the field, the needs of homeland security, and legislation requiring DNA and fingerprint sampling from members of certain groups. Prospects are best for those who have a strong background in the basic sciences (especially chemistry) and who are willing to relocate.

Insider's viewpoint:
"Don't major in forensic science as an undergrad. Get a strong science background first. Make sure this is what you want to do. Nothing is worse than getting into a field after two or more years of

higher learning and discovering it isn't your cup of tea."

—Elizabeth, M.S. candidate, John Jay College of Criminal Justice

For more info:
American Academy of Forensic Sciences (AAFS)
410 North 21st St.
Suite 203
Colorado Springs, CO 80904
(719) 636-1100
www.aafs.org

International Association for Identification (IAI)
2535 Pilot Knob Road
Suite 117
Mendota Heights, MN 55120-1120
(651) 681-8566
www.theiai.org

Public administration

What is public administration? Let's break it down. "Public" refers to the public sector, and that means government. "Administration" means the management of a program or an agency. So public administrators manage government programs, right? Well, that's true, but it's not the whole story. Public administration isn't just for your class treasurer. These majors also prepare students for work in nonprofit organizations and for the private (business) sector. That's because more and more, the government is outsourcing—hiring outside companies to do government work.

Why does public administration have a whole chapter in this book? Because it is the largest category of civilian jobs in the federal government. And then there are the state, county, and local government employees, like those in public welfare agencies. But it's not the quantity, it's the quality of work that counts. Public administrators run the most critical services for the most vulnerable citizens.

"Public administration is a great field for those who want to make a difference in society," says Professor Danny Lee Balfour of Grand Valley State University.

What do public administrators do? In addition to providing direct service to individuals, they have management and supervisory responsibilities, in areas like human resources management, budgeting, and policy and planning. They might also do economic development, labor relations, and court administration—almost anything requiring organizational and time management skills and a concern for people.

"Students should be passionate about improving the human condition and see in themselves a sense of compassion, integrity, creativity, extreme patience, and responsibility," suggests Professor Tuesday L. Cooper of Springfield College (MA).

In human services agencies, professionals and paraprofessionals help individuals and families become self-sufficient. Jobs include drug and alcohol counselors, probation officers, and child abuse workers. Social work is another big part of public service, even bigger than you may think.

"Unfortunately, many students equate social work only with public assistance, and their vision of a social worker is that of a case worker," says Professor Irene Queiro-Tajalli, Indiana University-Purdue University Indianapolis. "Students need to realize the wide range of employment opportunities after graduation."

As you may know, many states and the federal government have had budget problems lately. In some cases, this has led to a reduction in the public workforce or to a hiring slowdown. On the plus side, the work that public administrators do is often essential and can't be cut because it helps people get the necessities of life. The job outlook for new graduates is buoyed by an expected wave of retirement of older government workers.

Know your goals

When you look for colleges, you'll find the public administration program in schools or divisions of social science, professional studies, health studies, anthropology, sociology, social work, and public affairs.

Some public administration programs are geared toward getting you ready to work at a specific level of government—local, state, or federal. If it's local government, for instance, you'll learn skills for community development and city management. It's good to know ahead of time what level of government you're interested in. It would also be great if you had a preference for direct service (one-to-one contact like social work) or management and supervisory work.

You may not be able to make all these decisions yet. But give some thought to what type of degree you're after, because you can pursue a public administration major (and later a career) at any degree level. If it's a certificate program, find out if your course work would be eligible for transfer credits toward a college degree later.

Think about style as well as substance: What is your learning style? You may want to get both theory (book learning) and practice (getting out there and doing it!). Also, find the class size and faculty-to-student ratio that works for you. Ask if you'll do an internship or community service project before graduation. If you're juggling many responsibilities, see if classes are offered in the day and in the evening. How about online?

For studies leading to social work, you want a program accredited by the Council on Social Work Education. Most accredited programs cover topics like human behavior and social policy, and there isn't a huge difference among colleges. However, the location of the college and the needs of its surrounding community may guide the way the college prepares students to help people.

Graduate studies in social work may be organized in several different ways: by who is served (individuals, families, communities); by fields of work, such as child welfare, aging, and mental health; or by particular social problems, such as poverty and homelessness. In other areas of public administration, specialties in graduate school include management and leadership, nonprofit administration, criminal justice, urban or regional affairs, and community health.

Find out more from the National Association of Schools of Public Affairs and Administration (www.naspaa.org), the American Society for Public Administration (www.aspanet.org), and the International City/County Management Association (www.icma.org).

Human services

What it's about:

The human service major prepares you to become an aide to a professional or to practice as a professional who helps individuals, families, or communities become self-sufficient. You learn about social service delivery systems and explore the reasons why many people are unable to obtain or hold on to the basic necessities of life.

Is this for you?

You might like this major if you also like: helping people from different backgrounds; improving people's lives; volunteering in your community; working both independently and in groups.

Consider this major if you are good at: caring/nurturing; counseling; creativity; critical reading/thinking; organizing; teamwork *...or have...* initiative; patience; social skills; verbal skills; writing skills.

Recommended high school prep:

English 4, math 3, lab science 3, social studies 3, and a foreign language 3–4. If possible, take courses in speech and computer literacy. Community volunteering experience is also helpful.

Did you know...

...that being able to speak a foreign language is particularly useful in the human services field? As immigration to the United States increases, social service professionals who can communicate with non-English-speaking populations are in great demand.

Typical courses in this major:

Group dynamics/process
Intake and referral
Introduction to counseling
Introduction to criminal justice
Local, state, and federal government
Multiculturalism
Social problems
Introduction to psychology
Ethics and the law
Introduction to sociology
Human services agencies and organizations
Organizational behavior
Human development
Legal issues in human services
Medical aspects of human services
Adult development

Concentrations:

In college: criminal justice; addiction studies (drug and alcohol); counseling; youth development; advocacy; human services management.

If you go on to grad school: organizing human services; human services management and leadership; community organization.

What the study of this major is like:

As a human services major, you study a range of topics. You will most likely examine the history of the human services delivery systems in the United States; counseling and service theories; and the various philosophical approaches to the human condition, team work, and social problems. Most courses are lecture based and often feature case studies, group work, games, and class discussion. Well-rounded programs provide you with the opportunity to participate in (and often require) internships, community service learning, or practicums. Strong bachelor's degree programs will also require course requirements outside the human services major.

Generally, the challenges you encounter involve managing your time, being organized, and working effectively in groups. As in any major, expect to spend a lot of time studying. But you may be asked to apply your newly learned skills and theories earlier in your academic career than your colleagues in other majors.

Because of the range of content and skills taught in human services, the major can be housed in various departments. You can also study human services at a variety of institutions that offer certification or degree options. Before you pick a program, you should think about the level of education you plan to attain. Courses in certificate programs might not be transferable if you later wish to earn a bachelor's degree. In addition, some programs focus on direct service (one-to-one contact) and others focus on human services management (supervisory skills). You should probably look for a program that offers a variety of courses, so that you can explore many tracks within the profession. You don't need to choose your area of specialization before you enter college.

Other majors you might like:
Criminal justice and law enforcement
Urban, community, and regional planning
Public policy analysis
Family/community services
Human development and family studies
Gerontology
Community organization/advocacy
Community health services
Health care administration
Substance abuse counseling
Anthropology
Behavioral sciences

Questions to ask colleges:
What are the different types of internship or community service learning experiences available? Is the program affiliated or in partnership with local organizations?

Career options and trends:
Residential counselor; drug/alcohol counselor; case manager; probation/parole officer; client advocate; child abuse worker; mental health worker; youth worker; rehabilitation case worker; social service worker.

Certification requirements for different careers vary from state to state. For example, some states require drug and alcohol counselors to have state certification in addition to a college degree. Most human services professions have a continuing education requirement.

The aging baby boomer population is creating a demand for human services workers and professionals skilled in working with older people. The restorative justice field (in which members of the community are brought into the criminal justice process, such as sentencing and rehabilitation) is also expected to continue growing. In another trend, most states are funding drug treatment and counseling through departments of corrections, rather than the traditional human services areas. This development will further integrate the fields of human services and criminal justice.

For more info:
National Organization for Human Services (NOHS)
5601 Brodie Lane
Suite 620-215
Austin, TX 78745
www.nohse.com

Council for Standards in Human Service
    Education (CSHSE)
www.cshse.org

Public administration

Also known as:
Public affairs

What it's about:
Public administration majors study the management of public and nonprofit organizations and the many aspects of public service and governance. Topics include political issues, group dynamics, public policy, health care delivery, economic development, human resources management, philanthropy, voluntarism, budgeting, public finance, information technologies, and neighborhood analysis.

Is this for you?
You might like this major if you also like: community service; student government; Boy or Girl Scouts; joining clubs or teams; environmental issues; organizing group activities.

Consider this major if you are good at: critical reading/thinking; leadership; organizing events; persuading/influencing; solving problems; teamwork *...or have...* initiative; patience; verbal skills; writing skills.

Recommended high school prep:
English 4, math 3, lab science 3, social studies 4 (including government and economics), and a foreign language 2-3. A business course is also recommended.

Typical courses in this major:
Introduction to public administration
Public budgeting and financial administration
Public human resources administration
Public policy and policy processes
Local politics and administration
Introduction to nonprofit management
Developing nonprofit resources
Volunteerism and the nonprofit sector
Public sector information technology
Grant writing
Organization theory
Community analysis
Economic development
Structure of state government
Public service ethics

Concentrations:
Public finance; economic development; community development; health administration; human resources; environmental policy; nonprofit administration; urban/regional affairs.

What the study of this major is like:
In this major you explore the ways that public administration professionals achieve managerial efficiency, program effectiveness, legal accountability, client-driven responsiveness, political representation, and organizational reform. You acquire practical skills, including analyzing agency budgets, supervising staff, designing Web pages and evaluation surveys, and writing grant proposals. You learn to recognize the moral, social, political, economic, and technical issues to consider as you design and lead programs in the public interest.

Upper-level courses deal with budgets, accounting, and financial management, as well as with specific executive and personal skills such as strategic planning, leadership, and ethical sensitivity. Majors are strongly encouraged to take a broad range of liberal arts courses, including English, history, communications, economics, political science, psychology, and sociology.

Courses frequently use case studies, simulations, and other activities to provide a sense of what real-world public administration is all about. Most programs require you do an internship, perhaps in Washington, D.C., or in a state capital, to gain experience in public or nonprofit agencies. At some institutions, cooperative programs allow you to alternate semesters (first studying in the classroom, then working in a government agency).

Programs at different colleges may vary in their organization, approach to public policy, or the level of government they emphasize. For example, some programs focus on local politics, economic and community development, and city management. Other programs prepare you for a career in state government or in the federal government. A few programs specialize in environmental policy, international development, regulatory policies, social policy, or other areas. A growing number of programs provide courses in nonprofit administration, including grant writing, volunteer management, fund-raising, and philanthropy.

A bachelor's degree opens doors to a variety of public service careers with government agencies, nonprofit organizations, and private sector firms. It also offers a good background for many graduate programs. You can enhance your marketability by taking part in paid or volunteer internships; gaining valuable skills in information technology, public relations, or planning; joining professional organizations; and developing your oral, written, and visual communication skills. The most successful students combine classroom study with real-world experience, and they network, or make contact, with professionals in the field. Increasingly, international study is playing an important role in public affairs, and you are encouraged to participate in study-abroad programs.

Other majors you might like:
Political science
Public policy analysis
Urban, community, and regional planning
Parks, recreation, and leisure studies
Business administration and management
Public relations
Economics
Civil engineering
Urban studies
Sociology
Health care administration
Environmental studies

Questions to ask colleges:
Does the program require or provide internship opportunities?

How active is the program in the field's professional associations?

Does the program specialize in particular areas? If so, which ones? Does the program focus on a level of government (local, state, or federal), or include nonprofit administration?

Career options and trends:
City manager; assistant city manager*; budget/financial officer; human resource manager; policy analyst; grant coordinator; program evaluator; volunteer coordinator; neighborhood planner; economic development coordinator.

The retirement of the baby boom generation should open up job opportunities, even at the coveted federal level. For example, the Office of Personnel Management projects that 282,000 of the executive branch's full-time civilian employees will leave within a few years.

Nonprofit organizations (neighborhood associations, religious organizations, schools, chambers of commerce, etc.) provide a good employment entry point because they offer many volunteer and internship positions through which you can acquire experience.

Insider's viewpoint:
"Public policy studies how to do things, how to use what we have to make a world. In many cases, we even try to be fair. It has amazed me to learn that there is a science, a precision, a balancing to be addressed with the precision and discipline of an artist."

—Kobi, senior, Columbia University

For more info:
American Society for Public Administration (ASPA)
1301 Pennsylvania Ave., N.W.
Suite 840
Washington, DC 20004
(202) 393-7878
www.aspanet.org

Social work

What it's about:

The social work major is a professional degree program that provides the knowledge, values, and skills needed for generalist social work practice. You learn to help individuals, families, groups, and communities prevent and respond to social problems. As a practicing social worker, you modify harmful social conditions, promote social and economic well being, and increase opportunities for people to live fulfilling, dignified lives.

Is this for you?

You might like this major if you also like: helping people in need; diversity; being a "people person"; working for social and economic justice.

Consider this major if you are good at: caring/nurturing; counseling; creativity; critical reading/thinking; leadership; organizing; teamwork *...or have...* initiative; respect for others; verbal skills; writing skills.

Recommended high school prep:

English 4, math 3, lab science 3, social studies 4, and a foreign language 2–3. If you can, take classes in computer science and anthropology. Spanish is a useful language to learn because of the changing makeup of the U.S. population. Volunteer work or community service activities are strongly recommended.

Did you know...

...that social work covers more than just administering public assistance? Many students' idea of a social worker is that of a caseworker. Ironically, few caseworkers are trained social workers.

Typical courses in this major:

Human behavior and social environment
Introduction to psychology
Introduction to sociology
Social work research
Social work practice
Social policy and services
Values and ethics
Diversity
Modern social problems
Populations-at-risk
Social and economic justice
Community resources
Field internship

Concentrations:

Generally, none in college; but if you go on to grad school: child welfare; family welfare; aging; health; addictions; working with individuals, groups, families, or communities; poverty, homelessness, and other social problems; social administration; social work research.

What the study of this major is like:

As a social work major, you gain a foundation in the liberal arts, with an emphasis on the social sciences. In your first two years of college, you generally take sociology, political science, economics, psychology, and human biology. In your third and fourth years, you take most of your social work courses, learning how to conduct a generalist social work practice.

In courses in social welfare policy and services, which describe the laws, programs, and benefits available to meet human needs, you consider the way social programs are developed and changed. Research courses teach basic methods and stress the evaluation of social welfare programs. At most colleges, the major emphasizes the understanding and acceptance of diversity in ethnicity, race, culture, gender, and sexual orientation.

Typically, social work professors use a variety of approaches in their courses: lectures, teamwork, role-playing, research projects, field trips, and skill-building exercises. An attractive feature of the major is the combination of theory and hands-on experience. Your most important educational experience is a supervised practicum (field internship), most likely in a social service agency. All undergraduates earning a Bachelor's of Social Work (B.S.W.) must complete at least 400 hours of field experience under the supervision of a qualified social worker.

Early in your studies, you may have difficulty applying theoretical concepts to practical situations. Programs handle this challenge by closely supervising students as they complete their internships. You may also be troubled by differences between your personal values and those of the profession. In response, most programs encourage you to examine your values as well as those of social workers and society.

In many states, you must graduate from a program accredited by the Council on Social Work Education (CSWE) in order to be licensed and certified. Because of these standards, undergraduate social work programs tend to be very similar. Differences may exist in the number of courses offered, but the choices you have are usually based more on program resources or regional mission than on program philosophies.

The sense of calling and commitment that can lead you to choose social work as a profession may generate a spirit of camaraderie and dedication among students. Although healthy competition is part of academic life, social work students often develop projects cooperatively, make group presentations, and form long-lasting professional relationships. In recent years many nontraditional and older students have found social work an attractive choice for a major and a career.

Other majors you might like:
Sociology
Psychology
Native American studies
American Sign Language (ASL)
Funeral services/mortuary science
Human development and family studies
Community health services
Gerontology
Youth ministry

Emergency medical technology (EMT paramedic)
Nursing (RN)
Occupational therapy

Questions to ask colleges:
Is the program accredited by the CSWE?

Which types of agencies are available for students looking to fulfill their practicum requirements?

Career options and trends:
Generalist social work practitioner; clinician; administrator; case manager; social planner; researcher.

A bachelor's degree prepares you for generalist social work in a wide range of settings, such as child welfare and public welfare agencies, hospitals and other health care facilities, schools, developmental disabilities services, services for the aged, the juvenile and criminal justice systems, industry, and business. A master's degree is required for jobs involving supervision, administration, or complex research.

All states license or regulate social workers, but regulations and procedures vary from state to state. For more information, visit the Association of Social Work Boards Web site at www.aswb.org.

Insider's viewpoint:
"When my adviser suggested I take the introductory social work class I didn't want to because I never heard anything positive about it; I associated it with child protection services and doing the dirty work. But that was before my favorite professor introduced me to macro social work and the public policy side of it: legislation, community development and economic revitalization, that sort of thing."

—Melissa, junior, Michigan State University

For more info:
National Association of Social Workers (NASW)
750 First St., N.E.
Suite 700
Washington, DC 20002-4241
(202) 408-8600
www.naswdc.org

Religion and theology

The study of religion is not what you may think. It's not necessarily faith-based, or a form of worship. And it isn't always preparation for the clergy. Instead, the majors in this group often approach religion as an academic subject.

"The study of religion in the academic context is not the same as in some religious context (church, synagogue, mosque)," says Professor Richard B. Pilgrim of Syracuse University.

"Once students realize that the study of religion does not favor or teach about a religion in order to convert or train a person in that tradition, then religion as an academic discipline begins," explains Professor John A. Grim, Bucknell University.

The academic approach to religion includes studies of civilization and society, history, language and texts, culture, music, and many other subjects.

Theology is just one of the majors in the universe of religion studies. "Theology" literally means "the study of God." This major often concentrates on a particular faith, and may have liturgical (worship) and counseling components to prepare students for graduate work in the ministry, among other careers.

"A major in theology typically includes courses in biblical studies, history of the church, history of Christian thought, ethics, and the moral life. It is also likely to include study of world religions," says Professor David G. Truemper of Valparaiso University.

Religion and theology majors are all about the big picture.

"The study of religion is only one aspect of Judaic studies," says Professor Shmuel Bolozky, University of Massachusetts. "It is also the study of the Jewish people, its role in civilization, and its interaction with the other members of society."

For its part, Islamic studies "involves a great deal of reading, researching, and writing," says Professor Kamran S. Aghaie, University of Texas at Austin. "It entails expanding one's perspective on the world and understanding different cultures."

Your Higher Education

Studying religion as part of a liberal arts education is a way to obtain skills in research, reading, writing, and thinking that are needed in graduate school and in almost any career. When you look for an institution offering religion majors, consider colleges of liberal arts or humanities or arts and sciences, divinity schools, and schools of religion or theology.

How religion is taught depends on the college. Some colleges have been set up by a particular religion, so they are faith-based. If you are preparing for the ministry, consider a religion-affiliated university with a preministry program to guide you toward a major and graduate studies. "Through advising, internship experiences, and well-chosen curricula across the disciplines in courses from biblical literature to psychology to ethics, interested men and women can determine what types of ministry suits them," says Shelley Shepherd, preministerial studies adviser at Southern Methodist University.

At other colleges, including state universities, the approach is not religious but secular. Be sure you are entering the type of program you want and double-check that any state aid you will receive applies if you study religion. It may not.

Professor Pilgrim explains the primary distinction between religious and nonreligious colleges: "The difference is between private, parochial schools where religious indoctrination or advocacy may be the main thrust in a religion or theology major, and private or public colleges or universities where religious studies is clearly an academic, scholarly enterprise," he says. "It's not always easy to tell one from the other, but prospective students need to check closely about this."

Some programs are devoted to a particular tradition, like Buddhism, Christianity, Islam, or Judaism, or to an aspect of a tradition, like the Bible or Islamic law. Other programs specialize in theoretical approaches (such as ethics, psychology, philosophy, anthropology).

"A prospective student should look for balance across approaches and cultural traditions in a religion department. Look for courses in ethics, philosophy of religion, religion and ecology, or popular religion," Grim suggests. "A basic perspective is to look for courses in Judaism, Christianity, Islam, Buddhism, Hinduism, Confucianism, or Taoism to get a sense of the commitment of the department to teaching the full spectrum of cultural religious expressions."

Whatever your likely major, check out the courses and faculty members to see if their focus matches your interests. You can reach out to educators at the college. Ask how the school can help you connect personal religious faith with intellectual and academic work. How does the program help you relate to people of other faiths? Will your studies have a global dimension? Is there a religious community nearby to provide support and stimulation? Does the college have resources such as online library subscriptions, translations, and a language lab? Are grants and scholarships available? How about an internship, mission, or social service, if such an opportunity is right for you?

In choosing a college, think about your future. Most religion students are probably planning to work in education, law, business, medicine, social activism, or social service. If you envision a career in the clergy, or plan on graduate studies, see the individual majors in this section for graduate tracks. A good general resource is the American Academy of Religion, at www.aarweb.org.

Bible studies

What it's about:

As a Bible studies major, you explore the literature of the Bible, including the historical and cultural setting of the biblical world. Emphasis is placed on the content, concepts, and theological teachings of the Bible, as well as on ways to interpret biblical literature. Some programs may require you to study Greek and Hebrew.

Is this for you?

You might like this major if you also like: archaeology; history; volunteering and service activities; exploring your spirituality; reading the Bible and biblical literature.

Consider this major if you are good at: attention to detail; caring/nurturing; creativity; critical reading/thinking; organizing; research *...or have...* patience; verbal skills; writing skills.

Recommended high school prep:

English 4, math 3, lab science 3, social studies 4, and a foreign language 3. If possible, take classes in ancient history, anthropology, classical Greek, Latin, philosophy, or world religions.

Did you know...

...that this major is much broader than you might think? It covers the rich heritage of Hebrew and Judeo-Christian religious traditions, often emphasizing interdisciplinary study. Majoring in Bible studies can lead to job opportunities for both women and men.

Typical courses in this major:

New Testament overview
Old Testament overview
Christian doctrine and systematic theology
Church history and historical theology
Biblical interpretation and hermeneutics
History of Greece
History of Rome
History of the ancient Near East
Biblical archaeology
Biblical criticism
Christian ethics
Literature of the Bible
Geography of the Bible
Contemporary social concerns
Global Christianity
Key figures in biblical or Church history

Concentrations:

In college: Church history; New Testament; Old Testament.

If you go on to grad school: apologetics; biblical criticism; biblical interpretation; biblical theology; Christian/spiritual formation; classical dogmatics; early Christianity; evangelism/missions; religion in America; systematic theology.

What the study of this major is like:

Bible studies majors encounter broad and diverse subject matter. Course work may cover biblical history, biblical literature and methods for interpreting it, key characters in the Bible, important eras and figures in Church history, historical or systematic theology and ethics, the original languages of the Bible, the culture of the biblical world, the contribution of archaeology to biblical studies, and world religions.

Bible studies is taught and learned in many ways, and classes may vary in size. Your classes may feature lectures, discussion, seminars, research, writing, oral and written examinations, special projects, and student presentations. Other learning opportunities may include independent or guided study with a small group of students (directed by a faculty member); special lectures, symposiums, and conferences conducted by guest speakers; study-abroad programs; off-campus internships and social service projects; and language lab instruction in Greek or Hebrew.

The reading, research, and writing demanded by your course work will require time management, good study habits, and personal discipline. Challenges specific to the Bible studies major include mastering the subject matter; the interdisciplinary nature of the major; and the diversity of Christian thought and teaching that has emerged from Roman Catholic, Orthodox, and Protestant traditions over many centuries. You must also balance your intellectual pursuits, on the one hand, with your spiritual and religious needs and your desire to serve, on the other.

Bible studies programs may differ in their requirements. Some may emphasize the biblical languages of Greek and Hebrew. Others may require an internship or a missions or social service component. There is considerable variation in how much emphasis is given to liberal arts or interdisciplinary studies. Programs also differ in their selection of reading strategies and their choice of interpretive approaches to biblical and religious literature.

Differences in emphases and philosophies stem from several factors. The weight given to matters of history, literature, and theology often reflects the specialized training of the faculty members. Another consideration is whether the educational institution is a state-supported, public college or a private institution linked to a particular Christian denomination or other religious group. Keep in mind that each of the three branches of the Christian tradition (Roman Catholic, Orthodox, and Protestant) sustains college programs in Bible studies committed to its own historical and theological traditions—traditions that, in turn, are based on doctrines and beliefs, biblical teachings, worship practices, and the religious body's purpose in providing theological education.

Other majors you might like:
Anthropology
Archaeology
Youth ministry
Ancient studies
Preministerial studies
Sociology
Sacred music
Christian studies

Ancient Near Eastern/biblical languages
Missionary studies
Philosophy

Questions to ask colleges:
Does the major require biblical languages (Greek or Hebrew)?

Are faculty members involved in the ministry of the church, in social services, or in missions?

At what kinds of academic institutions (research universities, seminaries, or professional schools) did faculty members study or work?

Career options and trends:
Christian education director; youth minister; clergy member; chaplain (military, hospitals, prisons, retirement/nursing homes); college professor.

Many church denominations require those entering the clergy to be ordained. Most states require licensing for clergy conducting religious rites with civil implications, such as marriages, funerals, and burials, and some types of counseling.

Bible studies majors also pursue careers in church ministry, campus ministries, social service organizations, counseling ministries, home or overseas missions, religious education, religious publishing, religious administration, journalism, business, or law.

Insider's viewpoint:
"Jewish tradition has an expression for the love of the Hebrew Scriptures known as *simchah Torah* or 'the joy of Torah.' My passion for the study of the Bible was sparked by a professor who taught courses in Hebrew language and Old Testament studies with this sense of joy."

—Professor Andrew E. Hill, Wheaton College (IL)

For more info:
Council for Christian Colleges and Universities (C.C.C.U.)
321 Eighth Street, N.E.
Washington, DC 20002
(202) 546-8713
www.cccu.org

Islamic studies

What it's about:

As an Islamic studies major, you explore the history, culture, and interpretation of the Islamic faith. You may also be required to study Arabic, Persian, Turkish, or Urdu for the equivalent of two years.

Is this for you?

You might like this major if you also like: learning about Islamic culture and heritage; religious customs and writings; foreign languages and cultures; history; philosophy; understanding world events; community service activities.

Consider this major if you are good at: attention to detail; critical reading/thinking; leadership; organizing; persuading/influencing; research *...or have...* an open mind; initiative; verbal skills; writing skills.

Recommended high school prep:

English 4, math 3, lab science 3, social studies 3, and a foreign language 2–3. If possible, take courses in the Arabic, Turkish, Persian, or Urdu language.

Did you know...

...that Islam is the fastest-growing religion in the United States?

...that most Muslims do not live in the Middle East and are not Arabs? Arabs make up less than 15 percent of the Muslim population. The nation with the largest Muslim population is Indonesia.

Typical courses in this major:

Prophet of Islam
The Qur'an
Islamic sciences
Sufism
Shi'ite Islam
Popular Islam
Modern political Islam
Islamic revolution of Iran
Women in Islam
Islamic art
Islamic architecture
Islamic law
Islamic theology
Islamic philosophy
Hadith
Muslim intellectual history

Concentrations:

Women and gender issues; Islam in America; Islamic art and architecture; Islam in South Asia (India and Pakistan); Islam in Iran; Sufism; Islamic law; modern political Islam and fundamentalism; Shi'ite Islam; popular Islam; Islamic theology and philosophy; Islamic history.

What the study of this major is like:

The Islamic studies major focuses on the diversity of Islamic society and culture found in many geographic areas, time periods, and branches of the faith (including Sunni, Shi'ia, and Ahmadiyya). Your studies begin in sixth-century Arabia with the teachings of the Prophet Muhammad and include interpretations and additions made by Islamic teachers and scholars over the centuries.

You learn about Islamic scripture, principally the Qur'an, and other texts (Hadith, Sirah, Sunnah, Tafsir) that interpret, describe, or illustrate the Qur'an and the life and teachings of the Prophet. In addition, you examine the mystical beliefs of Sufism, modern Islamic politics, gender issues in Islam, Islamic sciences, Islamic law, Islamic art, and Islamic architecture.

As an Islamic studies major, you are required to do a great deal of reading, researching, and writing. Some colleges teach Islam as a component of U.S. foreign policy studies. Others include Islamic studies in the context of comparative religions. In most colleges, though, Islam is taught from an "area studies" perspective; the focus is on culture and history rather than on religion. In all programs, you develop an understanding of different societies and expand your perspective on the world.

Other majors you might like:
Near and Middle Eastern studies
Religious studies
Arabic
Iranian/Persian languages
Asian studies
Anthropology
History
South Asian studies
Sociology
Peace and conflict studies
Medieval and Renaissance studies
Judaic studies

Questions to ask colleges:
Which approaches to Islam does the program offer? Which specialties are the strongest?

Career options and trends:
College professor; teacher; journalist; Foreign Service Officer.

Majors in Islamic studies often go on to study at professional or graduate schools to prepare for careers in the clergy, law, medicine, or social work. They also find employment in the government; in nongovernmental organizations dealing with the Muslim world; and in business, education, and publishing.

Opportunities in all areas of Islamic studies have dramatically increased, especially positions in higher education (as college professors), research, government, and think tanks. For most jobs in the field, competence in an Islamic language is highly desirable.

For more info:
Middle Eastern Studies Associations of North
   America
University of Arizona
1219 North Santa Rita Ave.
Tuscon, AZ 85721
(520) 621-5850
www.mesana.org

Judaic studies

Also known as:
Jewish studies

What it's about:
This major explores the culture and religion of the Jewish people over the course of its 3,500-year history, in both their ancestral land and the lands of dispersion (migration to Europe, North America, and Israel). Your studies are wide-ranging, including the Jewish religion, heritage, philosophy, and intellectual history; Hebrew and Yiddish languages and literature; anti-Semitism; Jewish-Gentile (non-Jewish) relations; the Holocaust; Zionism; and the State of Israel.

Is this for you?
You might like this major if you also like: foreign cultures and languages; the Bible and religion; learning about Jewish heritage; community service activities.

Consider this major if you are good at: attention to detail; creativity; critical reading/thinking; leadership; research; teamwork ...*or have...* initiative; verbal skills; writing skills.

Recommended high school prep:
English 4, math 3, lab science 3, social studies 4, and a foreign language 4. Hebrew is recommended if available, although it is not a prerequisite; knowledge of any other foreign language will help you learn Hebrew in college.

Did you know...
...that the study of religion is only one aspect of Judaic studies? The major also includes the history of the Jewish people, their role in civilization, and their interaction with other cultures. Because Jewish studies is interdisciplinary, you can explore areas suited to your interests and goals.

Typical courses in this major:
Elementary, intermediate, and advanced Hebrew
Biblical Hebrew
Ancient Israel and the ancient Near East
Judaism in the Middle Ages
Jewish law and society
Family and sexuality in Judaism
Women in Jewish history
Modern Jewish history
Anti-Semitism in historical perspective
The Jews of Eastern Europe
Yiddish language and culture
The Holocaust
Jewish culture in America
Zionism and Israel
Hebrew/Israeli literature in translation
Jewish mysticism

Concentrations:
In college: Jewish civilization in the ancient Near East; Rabbinical Hebrew and medieval Judaism; Jewish literature; modern Jewish religion and philosophy; Holocaust studies.

If you go on to grad school: ancient Jewish texts in related languages (Hebrew, Aramaic, Akkadian); Mishna/Talmud; medieval texts; modern Rabbinical writing; Jewish history of a particular period; Zionism and Israel studies; modern Hebrew language and literature.

What the study of this major is like:
This major allows Jewish students to explore their culture in an objective, academic setting, and it gives non-Jewish students the opportunity to broaden their understanding of Judaism, a central foundation of Western civilization, Christianity, and Islam. It is a demanding course of study; you must be willing to work hard in reading and analyzing classical texts, and in most programs you are required to obtain proficiency in the Hebrew language.

Areas covered include archaeology, Biblical times, Christian Europe, and the Islamic world. In-depth study is available in Rabbinical Hebrew and medieval Judaism, including the Mishna/Talmud and medieval Jewish philosophy. Of special interest is the modern period—the beginnings of secularization, the origins of Reform and Conservative Judaism, and the development of modern anti-Semitism, leading to the Holocaust. Examination of the State of Israel focuses on the gathering of exiles; the revival of Hebrew; the status of the Palestinians; and the historical, social, and political forces that have shaped the struggle to maintain a democracy in the Middle East.

Most classes are conducted as seminars, with plenty of outside reading and directed group discussion. A frequent attribute of programs is a close relationship between students and their professors and classmates. Majors tend to study in groups, and work together on projects. Advanced Hebrew language students often tutor beginning students (for practicum credit), an activity that fosters group interaction and friendships.

Study abroad is an important aspect of the major. Most overseas study takes place in Israel; however, travel advisories in times of conflict may require colleges to offer alternative locations, such as Prague or other European cities with strong Jewish communities. Internships in Jewish community centers, museums, synagogues, and Hillel (a prominent Jewish student organization) are also encouraged, or even required.

One significant difference among programs concerns the importance placed on achieving proficiency in Hebrew. Some departments insist that students who cannot read Hebrew documents in the original language cannot gain a genuine understanding of Jewish culture. Other programs believe that what really matters is the content, and reliable translations are sufficient. If you might want to continue your Judaic studies in graduate school, however, you will need at least intermediate-level skills in Hebrew or other Semitic language (such as Arabic or Aramaic).

Other majors you might like:
Religious studies
History
Philosophy

Archaeology
Anthropology
Hebrew
Near and Middle Eastern studies
Ancient Near Eastern/Biblical languages
Talmudic studies
Islamic studies
Linguistics
Sociology

Questions to ask colleges:
What resources does the library have in Judaic studies? Do they include online resources, educational DVDs, Israeli publications, and so on? Does the Judaica collection include both Yiddish and Hebrew texts? Is there access to Jewish music and film?

Is there a language lab, and are there computer-assisted instructional materials for Hebrew?

Are there Judaica-related extracurricular activities on or near campus?

Career options and trends:
College professor*; teacher*; Rabbi*; director of religious education; journalist; community center administrator.

A teaching certificate is required for teaching in public school, but not necessarily for Hebrew day schools or religious schools.

Judaic studies can lead to careers in business, education, government service, social work, and other careers that require a liberal arts education. It is also sound preparation for a range of graduate or professional programs, such as law, medicine, Jewish scholarship, the rabbinate, or the cantorate.

Insider's viewpoint:
"Hebrew is a fascinating language, as all Semitic languages are, because of its special mechanisms for word formation, but also because of its revival as a spoken language in the last century. I love reading Hebrew texts, and enjoy imparting their internal beauty to my students."

—Professor Shmuel Bolozky, University of Massachusetts Amherst

For more info:

Association for Jewish Studies (AJS)
Center for Jewish History
15 West 16th St.
New York, NY 10011-6301
(917) 606-8249
www.ajsnet.org

American Academy for Jewish Research (AAJR)
420 Walnut St.
Philadelphia, PA 19106
(215) 238-1290
www.aajr.org

National Association of Professors of Hebrew
1346 Van Hise Hall
University of Wisconsin–Madison
Madison, WI 53706
(608) 262-3204
http://polyglot.lss.wisc.edu/naph/

Preministerial studies

What it's about:

A preministerial studies program will help you prepare to become an ordained Christian minister, priest, or other religious leader. At most colleges it is not a major but an advising program; students planning to enter a seminary, divinity school, or full-time ministerial work after college may pursue any major they choose.

Is this for you?

You might pursue this program if you like: Bible study; public speaking; reflecting on spiritual issues and discussing them with others; being a friend to turn to; taking an active role in the church community. A true calling to the ministry is sometimes clear and sometimes not; but a deep religious faith and empathy for others are often found among those who are called.

Consider this program if you are good at: caring/nurturing; counseling; creativity; leadership; organizing ...*or have...* Compassion; patience; verbal skills; writing skills.

Recommended high school prep:

English 4, math 3, lab science 3, social studies 4, and a foreign language 2–3. If available, a year of Latin or Greek would be helpful, and courses in psychology, philosophy, speech, and world religions are also recommended.

Typical courses in this program:

New Testament
Western philosophy
Old Testament/Hebrew Bible
Church history
World religions
Christian ethics
Sociology
Introductory psychology
Advanced Bible study
Expository writing
Homiletics (preaching)
Church organization and management
Evangelism
Dynamics of intercultural communication
Western civilization
Liturgical theology and practice

Concentrations:

Generally, none available.

What the program is like:

Many preministerial programs are nondenominational, with no sectarian or religious requirements for admission. Most, however, are typically offered at colleges affiliated with a particular religion and focus on the history, rituals, traditions, and beliefs of that denomination. Each faith usually sets its own requirements for becoming a minister. Some religions require a graduate degree from a seminary or divinity school, while others do not; so where and how a candidate is educated varies from one faith to the next.

But common to all preministerial programs is the role of the adviser, who will help you to choose a major in line with your interests and to select courses that will prepare you for the ministry or for admission to divinity school or other graduate program—and who will, in addition, discuss with you how best to use your skills in the community. Although your adviser will assist primarily in the academic aspects of your education, he or she will be sensitive to your unique concerns as you contemplate a career in ministry.

In a typical preministerial program, the courses provide you with a strong background in biblical literature, as well as a look at the cultures that produced the sacred texts. A balanced curriculum that emphasizes the liberal arts will give you the well-rounded education you'll need as you prepare for the variety of challenges you will face as a minister. If you decide to go on to the graduate level, you will have the skills necessary there as well: how to make use of the library, do research, and write effectively.

Some preministerial programs are very flexible about what courses you can select, while other programs have specific requirements, which may include vocational experience courses and courses in cross-cultural understanding. Usually, programs with specific requirements are geared to a particular faith or tradition; so check out a school's affiliation and direction before you apply.

In addition to academic pursuits, you'll do one or more internships, practicing what you've been learning about the ministry. This experience can take a number of forms: you might visit congregation members' homes, work with young people at a Christian summer camp, teach Bible lessons, give sermons, or play sacred music.

You should also attend lectures and seminars and talk with clergy to familiarize yourself with current issues. A useful pursuit is to engage in volunteer work in the community, that will expose you to real-world problems such as poverty, homelessness, and substance abuse.

Preministerial programs are not abundant and are more likely to be found at religiously affiliated universities and colleges. It is not essential to come from a preministerial program in order to get into graduate school or enter the ministry. But a good preministerial program will give you the time to broaden your understanding, to participate in a multitude of experiences, and to determine who you are and what really matters to you.

Other majors you might like:
Religious studies
Bible studies
Judaic studies
Pastoral counseling
Philosophy
History
Sacred music
Social work
Psychology
Peace and conflict studies
Religious education
Youth ministry

Questions to ask colleges:
May I choose any major if I wish to pursue a preministerial studies path, or are there specific disciplines I must choose from?

Is there a faculty member or adviser to help students navigate the program and assist them in obtaining related internship or vocational experiences?

If the program is nondenominational, is there a club or other student organization on campus for my specific faith?

Career options and trends:
Minister; priest; religious education coordinator; theology professor; military chaplain; missionary.

Usually ministers, priests, and chaplains must go through a candidacy and ordination process through a church conference or diocese before they may become a minister. In some Christian denominations, students who wish to start the process toward ordination must secure the blessing of a bishop or other church authority well in advance of beginning a graduate program.

Fewer young people are entering the ministry as a first career these days. Job prospects are good, especially for those who have a graduate degree, or are willing to accept part-time positions or to work in rural areas. In some Christian denominations, you may have to relocate at the discretion of a bishop.

For more info:
Association for Biblical Higher Education
5575 S. Semoran Blvd., Suite 26
Orlando, FL 32822-1781
(407) 207-0808
www.abhe.org

Association of Theological Schools (ATS)
10 Summit Park Drive
Pittsburgh, PA 15275-1103
(412) 788-6505
www.ats.edu

Religious studies

Also known as:
Comparative religion

What it's about:
In the religious studies major, you become familiar with many of the world's spiritual traditions, and learn to use a range of approaches—historical, textual, psychological, philosophical, sociological, and anthropological—to examine the variety of religious experience.

Is this for you?
You might like this major if you also like: philosophy; literature; the arts; other cultures, past and present; mythology; languages; thinking about religious themes and motivations.

Consider this major if you are good at: caring/nurturing; creativity; critical reading/thinking; memorizing; research; teamwork *...or have...* an open mind; patience; writing skills.

Recommended high school prep:
English 4, math 3, lab science 3, social studies 4, and a foreign language 3–4. Take as many history courses as possible, including art history.

Did you know...
...that most religious studies majors do not intend to pursue careers as priests, imams, or rabbis? This major is mostly taught as an interdisciplinary liberal arts field that prepares you for many different career paths.

Typical courses in this major:
Introduction to religion
Judaism
Hinduism
Christianity
Buddhism
Islam
Religions of China
American religions
Existentialist theology
Religions of Japan
Religion and moral issues
Critiques of religion
Pilgrimage
Mysticism
New religious movements
Philosophy of religion

Concentrations:
In college: particular religions; groups of religions (for example, Asian); historical periods; cultural studies (Christianity in the Americas); comparative religions.

If you go on to grad school: psychology of religion; religious anthropology; ritual studies; language and scriptural studies (such as the Torah and Hebrew, the Sanskrit scriptures of Hinduism, or Taoist classics in Chinese); religion and science.

What the study of this major is like:
The study of religion includes many cultures and traditions. You learn the difference between *participating in* a religious tradition—its stories, rituals, symbols, beliefs, social and institutional structures, and customs—and *understanding* that tradition, regardless of whether or not you participate in it. By studying religion independently of participants' beliefs, you learn to think critically and imaginatively.

Your course work teaches you a variety of methods and approaches, including historical investigation, psychological inquiry, social analysis, anthropological and ethnological investigation, feminist criticism, and linguistic analysis. As you examine a range of religions, you begin to recognize and appreciate their similarities and differences.

Generally, you are not expected to enter college with a background in religion. The major typically begins with introductory courses that familiarize you with the basic elements of religion, such as myth, ritual, scripture, and symbols. You can usually choose from among courses in several areas: the Western traditions of Judaism, Christianity, and Islam; the Asian traditions of Hinduism, Jainism, Sikhism, Buddhism, Confucianism, and Taoism; theoretical and philosophical approaches to the study of religion; and, occasionally, on indigenous traditions (for instance, the religious practices of Native American cultures).

Most programs require an entry-level course in at least two traditions and recommend that you take courses in both Western and non-Western traditions. At least one of your courses will examine theoretical approaches. In some programs, languages associated with religious traditions may be offered. Although you are not usually required to take a foreign language, such training is helpful, especially if you intend to continue religious studies in grad school.

Your course work examines key questions on such topics as ecology, science, gender relations, cultural and historical conflicts, the emergence of the universe, and conscious awareness. You explore the development of religious traditions over time, as well as the creativity that keeps religions relevant today. Areas that may prove difficult to deal with include unfamiliar worldviews and practices, and abstract theological and philosophical ideas. But learning to recognize other religious points of view will challenge, contradict, and then deepen your understanding.

Programs at different colleges may vary in their emphases. For example, some specialize in theoretical approaches, such as ethics, philosophy, or anthropology, while others may focus on a particular religion or an aspect of a religion (such as biblical studies or Islamic law/Shari'ah). Look for balance across approaches and traditions—for a good indication, look for courses in both Eastern and Western faiths. Also, some private colleges teach religious studies from a faith-based, rather than an academic, point of view. It is not always easy to tell, so if you have a preference, be sure to check.

Other majors you might like:
Anthropology
Peace and conflict studies

Theology
Near and Middle Eastern studies
Medieval and Renaissance studies
History
Archaeology
Philosophy
Psychology
Sociology
Global studies

Questions to ask colleges:
Which religious traditions are taught? Do course descriptions mention women, ritual, or indigenous peoples? Are topics such as the psychology of religion or science and religion covered in the curriculum?

Career options and trends:
High school teacher; college professor; social worker; journalist.

Majors in religious studies also go on to work in business, law, medicine, counseling, management, psychology, academic research, and religious vocations. Careers in many of these disciplines require graduate or professional study.

Insider's viewpoint:
"I wrote a paper on the anthropology of religious war. It really helped me see that, wow, maybe I can do this sort of thing and maybe it can be useful. I see a great need to make religious studies practical."

—Andy, junior, Cornell University

For more info:
American Academy of Religion (AAR)
825 Houston Mill Rd., N.E.
Suite 300
Atlanta, GA 30329
(404) 727-3049
www.aarweb.org

Council of Societies for the Study of Religion
www.cssr.org

Sacred music

Also known as:
Religious music
Pastoral music

What it's about:
The sacred music major provides a broad base of information about music history, music theory, and performance skills as preparation for careers as minister of music, organist, or choir director in a place of worship. You develop a repertory of sacred music, grounded in both historical and contemporary forms of expression.

Is this for you?
You might like this major if you also like: singing; chorus; expressing your faith through music; playing an instrument; participating in worship-related activities; leading group activities; tutoring.

Consider this major if you are good at: caring/nurturing; coaching; creativity; leadership; musicianship; organizing; persuading/influencing; teamwork *...or have...* patience; verbal skills.

Recommended high school prep:
English 4, math 3, lab science 3, social studies 3, music 1–2, and a foreign language 2–3. Participation in high school chorus (2 or 3 years) is highly recommended. Basic keyboarding skills (piano or organ) are also expected.

Did you know...
...that success in this field requires more than just musical ability? Certainly a passion for sacred music is essential; but enthusiasm and a desire to work with people can be as important as musical skills.

Typical courses in this major:
Music theory
Music history
Composition
Choral conducting
Choir training methods
Sight singing
Sacred music history
Choral literature
Hymnology
Children's choir leadership
Church music administration
Applied voice, piano, or organ
College choir, vocal, or instrumental ensemble

Concentrations:
Organ studies; conducting; worship leadership.

What the study of this major is like:
Throughout history, musicians have worked alongside the clergy to lead others in worship and praise. Many consider expressing faith through music to be one of the highest forms of worship. The sacred music major helps you develop the skills you need to be successful in the profession.

Besides training in music, professionals in sacred music need skills in areas such as arts management, program planning and organization, community building, and talent development. As a professional, you are responsible for bringing the music of the religious institution to life, developing musical resources, and guiding the congregation in praise and worship. The exploration of contemporary worship music, such as music from world cultures, keeps the profession fresh.

As a major, you study basic musicianship. Theory courses review the mechanics of music (such as rhythmic and pitch notation, key signatures, triads, and scales) and explore composition (harmonic activity and structure). In sacred music history courses, you examine the development of music in worship (in the West and in traditional Asian and African cultures), liturgy, the historical significance of the sections of a worship service, and the primary works of sacred music.

Because most majors plan to be musical leaders in congregations, programs include performance and ensemble participation, conducting, choir training, and choral literature. You also study hymnology (the history and techniques of congregational singing); administrative skills; and applied instruction in voice, piano, or organ. Organ instruction is highly recommended, and some proficiency at the piano is generally expected. In addition, you may have opportunities to conduct children's and/or handbell choirs.

Because musicians serving congregations often function as performers, most programs encourage majors to participate in third-year and fourth-year solo recitals. In addition, you can attend concerts and recitals by ensembles, faculty members, and visiting artists, and perhaps intern in local houses of worship. Some programs offer workshops and conferences (on weekends or during the summer) that teach current trends and special aspects of the profession.

The sacred music program presents challenges beyond those of performance. Unlike other music programs, you are faced with questions about music's role in worship, its historical significance to modern liturgy, its place in contemporary society, and its function as "performance" or "offering." Also, at large conservatory programs, sacred music majors often find they are less respected than students majoring in performance or education. This can dishearten students who work just as hard as their peers in other concentrations do.

As a sacred music major, you earn either a Bachelor of Arts degree, which denotes a music specialty within a broad liberal arts program, or a Bachelor of Music degree, which focuses on performance and professional training. At a faith-based college, religious training may be just as important as musical training. At a music conservatory, the focus is on scholarly work and performance, and music study is offered at a more demanding level. You are expected to enter the program with considerable musical ability and to show achievement in performances throughout your college career. If the university is state-supported, certain sacred music courses may not be offered.

Other majors you might like:
Conducting
Piano/organ
Youth ministry
Music pedagogy
Music teacher education
Music history/literature
Recording arts
Music theory and composition
Voice/opera
Music management
Religious studies

Questions to ask colleges:
Are internships or other practical experiences available at local places of worship?

Does the program offer special campus activities, such as workshops/seminars/conferences related to sacred music, led by respected practitioners?

Is there ample access to organ or piano instruments for practice and rehearsals?

Career options and trends:
Choir director; organist in house of worship*; director of music ministries*; children's choir director; handbell choir director; parochial school music teacher.

Two issues present challenging opportunities for newcomers to the field: global music and contemporary worship music. Due to our growing appreciation of other cultures, the sacred music professional needs to be aware of the contributions and performance styles of other societies. Additionally, many mainstream denominations are including contemporary styles of worship, requiring the ability to blend praise choruses with traditional hymns or to incorporate instruments such as keyboards, guitar, and percussion into the worship service.

For more info:
National Association of Pastoral Musicians (NPM)
962 Wayne Ave.
Suite 210
Silver Spring, MD 20910-4461
(240) 247-3000
www.npm.org

Theology

What it's about:

Theology is the academic study of the beliefs and practices of a particular religion or religious community. You gain an understanding of its faith and practices by studying its history, literature, ethics, doctrines, and present-day situation. This major may also include a comparative study of world religions and practical courses in counseling, homiletics (preaching), and worship services.

Is this for you?

You might like this major if you also like: thinking about philosophical and spiritual matters; ritual and liturgy; music or drama; helping others; community activities.

Consider this major if you are good at: caring/nurturing; counseling; creativity; critical reading/thinking; leadership; research ...*or have...* initiative; patience; verbal skills; writing skills.

Recommended high school prep:

English 4, math 3, lab science 3, social studies 4, and a foreign language 2–3. If available, courses in psychology, sociology, and world literature are also recommended.

Did you know...

...that the study of theology can be both intellectually and spiritually demanding? It requires reflection on the relationship (even tension) between personal faith and critical thinking on fundamental religious questions.

Typical courses in this major:

Introduction to theology
The Old Testament
The New Testament
History of Christian thought
The early church
Medieval thought
The Reformation era
Biblical interpretation and hermeneutics
Studies in the Gospels
Studies in the Epistles
Christian doctrine
Liturgical theology and practice
Ethics
Systematic theology
Church history
World religions

Concentrations:

In college: biblical studies; history of religions; youth and family ministry; religious education; church history.

If you go on to grad school: theology and ministry; Hebrew Bible; New Testament/Christian origins; pastoral theology; liturgical studies.

What the study of this major is like:

Theological studies can be a rich and diverse major. It may be found in departments of theology, religion, philosophy and religion, or Bible studies. In most colleges, theology is taught not just as the beliefs of a particular religious community, but in a more all-encompassing spirit—that is, you learn about the theologies of your community, other communities, and the broader non-Christian world.

As a major, you explore the issues of justice, mercy, and the power attributed to God, and meditate on the problem of evil, suffering, and death in a world ruled by God. In Christian theology, you read the Bible, if possible in the original languages. By studying various religions, you learn how their followers perceive the moral life, and you evaluate the effect of faith on practical matters of worship and ethics.

Other Bible-oriented courses may examine how the books of the Bible came to be considered by Jews and Christians as sacred. Taking note of parables and metaphors in secular, or nonreligious, literature highlights the similarities and differences between the Bible and other literary works.

In church history courses, topics include the development of spirituality and worship; the relationship between religious institutions and civil governments and secular society; the impact of believers on culture and politics; and the way social and political environments affect the church. In ethics, you study the personal and social teachings of the living faith, including the challenges of medical and economic technology, and consider the ways in which believers can participate in social action and political life.

Your college experience will include a lot of reading and reflection, intense and wide-ranging conversations with other students, and exploratory visits to worshiping communities from other traditions. You typically learn through a combination of reading, lecture, discussion, and, sometimes, formal debate. Fieldwork, internships, and practicums are regular features of theological studies programs, and service learning is becoming increasingly popular.

Between your third and fourth years, you are likely to do an internship. Practical/ministerial studies also include clinical experience and frank self-reflection. The biggest challenge you may face is to take an objective look at beliefs and ideas you may have accepted unquestioningly; students are often afraid of asking hard-driving questions about their faith.

Some colleges encourage this no-holds-barred inquiry into the faith, on the basis that critical questioning (when supported by a community of believing scholars) can deepen and strengthen your faith by helping you become mature and reflective. Other colleges focus on instilling faith and strengthening your conviction, contending that careful teaching of the faith can make you a mature believer, without causing you stress by questioning your basic convictions.

Other majors you might like:
Bible studies
Religious studies
Human services
Youth ministry
Preministerial studies
Philosophy
Religious education
Social work
Anthropology
Legal studies
Peace and conflict studies

Questions to ask colleges:
How does the program help students relate to persons of other faiths in a pluralistic society?

Is there a community of faith that can provide support and stimulation?

Career options and trends:
Priest or minister; teacher; youth minister; director of religious education; journalist; social worker; parish administrator; vocational counselor.

Like other liberal arts majors, theology prepares you for a variety of careers in education, business, government, public affairs, and social work. A theology degree is excellent preparation for graduate study in divinity, which enables you to work in pastoral positions. Most mainline Christian church bodies are suffering from severe shortages in pastoral and other ministry positions.

For more info:
American Academy of Religion (AAR)
825 Houston Mill Rd., N.E.
Suite 300
Atlanta, GA 30329-4246
(404) 727-3049
www.aarweb.org

Association of Theological Schools (ATS)
10 Summit Park Drive
Pittsburgh, PA 15275-1103
(412) 788-6505
www.ats.edu

Social sciences

Social sciences are the most popular academic majors in American four-year colleges and second only to business among all categories of majors chosen. More than 175,000 bachelor's degrees are given in the social sciences each year, including nearly 75,000 in psychology alone. It seems we can never know enough about our fellow human beings.

These majors cover the world inside and out, from archaeological digs that investigate the beginnings of humankind, to satellite global positioning systems that pinpoint where we are today. (You'll study GPS in the geography major.) Anthropology explores our origins, cultures, and evolution from prehistory to the present. Sociology, the study of groups of people, covers places, spaces, and races. Psychologists probe the way we behave and think. Economists track resources. Political scientists gauge power. And experts in international relations tackle global conflicts, poverty, oppression, and the flip side—peace, wealth, and freedom.

"I love this field because it addresses the 'big' issues, problems and challenges that confront humanity today to provide tools and insights that can help us create a more just, humane, and peaceful world," says Professor Andrew A. Latham of Macalester College.

These majors touch on many fields, and the knowledge and skills you'll learn can be applied later along many career paths.

"Economics graduates find jobs in education, government, industry, public policy, and planning. Many become business managers," says Professor John J. Siegfried, Vanderbilt University. "The field is also excellent preparation for law school, business school, and, more recently, medical school. Many students with a B.A. or a B.S. degree enter general management training in large corporations. Others start out in sales or analyst positions."

As is often the case, jobs are harder to get for students with just a bachelor's degree, if the economy is slow. But because the social sciences make students think, use numbers intelligently, write well, and understand people, these majors are good overall training for the workplace.

"More students would consider international relations if they knew how valuable this major is as a flexible basis for future careers," notes Professor Robert Mandel, Lewis and Clark College, of his department, whose grads are likely to be in demand in today's global workplace.

"For political science majors," Latham says, "developing the intellectual tools necessary to understand politics equips students with some of the skills required for leadership in their chosen field."

Mixing art and science

These majors cover a lot of bases, so, in addition to schools of social sciences, look into colleges of humanities, liberal arts, arts and sciences, arts and letters, behavioral sciences, life sciences, and education, as well as preprofessional divisions. For economics, be sure to check out business programs.

But wait, are social sciences really humanities or are they really sciences?

"The study of political science can be both 'scientific' and 'humanistic,'" Latham explains. "Some schools favor methods that are more scientific or quantitative, some more humanistic or qualitative."

Another example of this blend is in geography. "Two main specializations within geography are physical geography and human geography," says Professor Gregory A. Elmes of West Virginia University. "Purely physical geography is akin to the natural sciences with emphasis on theory, laws, and experimental evidence. Within human geography are the more conventional systematic elements, such as cultural, economic, and urban studies."

When choosing a college program, ask if it's more about humankind or research, the people or the numbers. Are you mostly theorizing about the subject or analyzing it? Or both? Some majors, including psychology, can lead to either a Bachelor of Arts or a Bachelor of Science degree.

Ask colleges which electives you should take with your major, like history with international relations. How much math will you need to know? What are the degree requirements and what special courses can you take? Do most students in the major finish their degree in four years?

Learn the strengths of the faculty members. Do they know about other fields so they can help you draw connections to other disciplines? Are full professors teaching undergraduates? Do the profs also teach the labs and offer advising? What kind of research are the faculty members doing? Will you get a chance to do research with them? How big are the classes? Are libraries, book collections, journals, and computers and software adequate and up-to-date?

Are scholarships and internships available for undergrads? What kinds of jobs do grad students often get? Find out if your major has a graduate program, where you could go for a master's or a Ph.D. (See the individual majors in this section for graduate concentrations, careers, and sources of information.)

Also in this book, read about related majors in the sections on Area, ethnic, and gender studies; Business; Education; Engineering technology; Family and consumer sciences; Humanities; Multi/interdisciplinary studies; Natural resources and conservation; and Public administration. You see, the social sciences are everywhere.

Anthropology

What it's about:

Anthropology is the study of people—their origins, physical nature, and social behavior. Anthropology majors explore human cultural and biological evolution and the way all peoples, from prehistoric times to today, adapt to their environment; form families, clans, tribes, and nations; regulate behavior through laws and government; worship and celebrate; communicate; educate their young; and adapt to change.

Is this for you?

You might like this major if you also like: traveling; learning about different peoples and cultures; *National Geographic*; reading; history; geography.

Consider this major if you are good at: attention to detail; foreign languages; observing; research *...or have...* initiative; verbal skills; writing skills.

Recommended high school prep:

English 4, math 3, lab science 3 (including biology), social studies 4, and a foreign language 3-4. If available, courses in sociology and government are also recommended.

Typical courses in this major:

Biological anthropology
Introduction to archaeology
Cultural anthropology
Primate behavior
Archaeological field methods
Religion and culture
Music and culture
Language and culture
Mythology
Human origins and evolution
Culture and personality
Native American cultures
Forensic anthropology
Human population genetics
Old World prehistory
Peoples and cultures of Africa, Asia, etc.

Concentrations:

Archaeology; physical/biological anthropology; linguistic anthropology; cultural anthropology; urban anthropology; applied anthropology; cultural resource management.

What the study of this major is like:

Majors in anthropology focus on the similarities and differences between human beings and other primates, as well as on the similarities and differences among human populations. Anthropologists are interested in all aspects of what it means to be human.

You learn how people in different parts of the world live their lives and adapt to their environments. Most programs require courses in each of the four main subdivisions of anthropology: physical anthropology, cultural anthropology, linguistic anthropology, and archaeology. Elective courses allow you to follow your interests—a specific country or cultural unit, such as Japan or Mexico, or a topic, such as political systems, child-rearing practices, music, or art.

Physical anthropology (also known as biological anthropology) investigates when and where human beings first appeared; you may even handle stone tools, skeletal materials, and plaster casts of the remains of people who lived many centuries ago. You may spend time in a local zoo observing chimpanzees and other primates to compare their actions with human behavior. In addition, you'll examine genetic evidence, as you trace human biological origins and evolutionary development.

Cultural anthropology explores specific cultures or concentrates on aspects shared by all cultures—religion, politics, law, or ecology. Cultural anthropologists study the diversity found in contemporary societies, from the few remaining peoples who hunt and gather roots and berries to those who shop in supermarkets and live in metropolitan areas such as Tokyo, New York, and London.

In linguistic anthropology, you examine the relationship of language to other aspects of culture. For instance, you study methods of communication—including body language, dialects, jargon, and slang; you observe how the language people use reflects their perception of and interaction with the world around them.

Archaeology, which deals with excavating, analyzing, and interpreting physical and cultural remains, is increasingly studied as an independent major or graduate program. Most anthropology programs offer introductory courses and opportunities to study field methods during a summer session.

Some programs encourage students to apply what they learn to contemporary problems facing the United States or other industrial societies; this approach is usually called applied anthropology.

As a rule, instructors will have spent a year or more living and studying among the peoples they are teaching about; the firsthand experience of living for extended periods in other cultures is an important part of anthropological training. In fact, fieldwork in other cultures sets anthropology apart from other social sciences and usually results in engaging lectures.

Most colleges offer courses in the four main subdivisions of anthropology, but few have courses in all the specialized subjects or include all regions of the world with equal thoroughness. If you are interested in a specific society, such as Japan, or a specific topic, such as legal anthropology, you should read course catalogs carefully to see if a particular program covers the topics you want.

Other majors you might like:
Archaeology
Sociology
Linguistics
Classics
Genetics
Geography
History
Psychology
Native American studies
Human development and family studies

Religious studies
Urban studies

Questions to ask colleges:
Are majors encouraged to spend a semester or term abroad? The opportunity to relate what you have learned in your anthropology courses to your own experiences with another culture is the best way to grasp the theories and methods of anthropology. Some programs consider fieldwork so important that they make a term abroad a requirement.

Career options and trends:
Social worker; genetic counselor; field archaeologist; teacher of English as a second language (ESL); cultural artifact specialist; educator; national/state park interpreter; environmental impact assessment researcher; travel agent/guide/consultant; museum administrator or technician.

Some occupations, such as field archaeologist, genetic counselor, and museum technician, may require additional specialized training and experience; graduate study is usually required for research, social work, and teaching.

Anthropology provides good preparation for a wide variety of jobs—in government, business, social services, the news media, museums, and education—that require an understanding of cultural and national differences and the ability to work with people from a variety of backgrounds.

Insider's viewpoint:
"Come prepared to think. This isn't a major for people who like to sit back and listen to others talk. Also, you need an open mind to study anthropology, because part of what you have to learn is that the way other people think is no less developed, no less 'right,' than the way you think."

—Chris, senior, Williams College

For more info:
American Anthropological Association (AAA)
2200 Wilson Blvd.
Suite 600
Arlington, VA 22201
(703) 528-1902
www.aaanet.org

Archaeology

What it's about:

Archaeology majors investigate extinct societies and the history of living societies. By excavating, analyzing, and interpreting cultural remains, you reconstruct lifeways and study why and how human cultures have changed over the last 2.5 million years.

Is this for you?

You might like this major if you also like: Scouting; collecting; detecting; discovery; history; mummies; ancient civilizations.

Consider this major if you are good at: attention to detail; creativity; critical reading/thinking; organizing; research; spatial thinking/analysis *...or have...* curiosity/thirst for knowledge; initiative; patience; writing skills.

Recommended high school prep:

English 4, math 3, lab science 3, social studies 3, and a foreign language 3–4. Computer skills and an additional language are useful but not mandatory.

Did you know...

...that archaeological "digs," or investigations, require systematic, detailed, and often physically demanding data collection? While there is excitement in discovery, the process can be slow and somewhat tedious, often based upon minute and fragmentary evidence.

Typical courses in this major:

Introduction to archaeological theory and methods
Survey of world prehistory
Greco-Roman studies
Egyptology
Chinese dynastic history
Paleolithic cultures
Origins of New World civilizations
Sub-Saharan African cultures
Asian cultures outside of China
Origins of Australian and Polynesian cultures
European pre-Greco-Roman cultures
Field excavation
Zooarchaeology
Paleoethnobotany
GIS (Geographic Information Systems)
Forensic archaeology

Concentrations:

In college: classical archaeology; anthropological archaeology.

If you go on to grad school: maritime archaeology; zooarchaeology; paleoethnobotany; environmental archaeology; forensic archaeology; cultural resources management; GIS (Geographic Information Systems) and spatial analysis; rock art analyses; and regional studies, such as Egyptology, Hittite archaeology, Mayan archaeology.

What the study of this major is like:

First- and second-year archaeology courses are survey lectures that provide the tools to get you involved in the more interesting aspects of the discipline. For example, you need to learn where and when a culture existed before you go out into the field and study it. Your third- and fourth-year courses, usually seminars of about 5 to 15 students, focus on specific issues, areas, and problems of anthropological or classical archaeology.

For anthropological archaeology, you take lab courses ranging from the preliminary analyses of excavation materials to advanced labs in specialty fields, such as zooarchaeology (the analysis of animal remains); geoarchaeology (the use of geologic methods to interpret an excavation site); paleoethnobotany (the analysis of plant remains); forensic archaeology (the recovery of buried criminal evidence); spatial analysis (use of GIS technology); or historical archaeology (the archaeologic record of historic events).

If you concentrate in classical archaeology, your work shifts to literature-and-language studies and intensive investigation of Greek, Roman, Egyptian, or Chinese cultures. In both trajectories, students often prepare an honors thesis, the product of an independent study.

Most students participate in one or more semester-abroad excavation projects, which sometimes take place during the summer. There are many possibilities; selecting the one best for you is often a challenge. For some, the issue is cost; to attend a field school, you must pay for room and board, transportation, and perhaps tuition. Also, if you need to work during the summer to help pay for school, field projects can interfere. Another consideration is the type of data you need to collect. Although the field school is a good place to do research for an honors thesis, you may have trouble knowing which kind of data your project requires. Your college advisers should provide you with suggestions.

Archaeology professors are often working on their own field research projects, so you may be able to help with the analysis of earlier excavations or participate in the excavations on a current project. If you develop an interest in a geographic area or an ancient culture other than those your instructors are pursuing, you might work on a project with some of their colleagues. Also, colleges with a grad program may allow you to work with master's or doctorate degree students on their research projects. Advanced students often make good mentors.

Working together in the field and on thesis projects can be fun and exciting. Students often develop a strong camaraderie and pick up on each other's enthusiasm. Most programs offer colloquiums, in which students meet to hear an undergrad, grad student, faculty member, or distinguished visitor give an informal presentation on work in progress.

Other majors you might like:
Art history
Anthropology
Geology/earth science
Classics
Environmental studies
Architectural history/criticism

History
Historic preservation
Bible studies
Medieval and Renaissance studies
Ancient studies
Classical/ancient Mediterranean/Near Eastern
   studies

Questions to ask colleges:
Does the program offer undergrad concentrations in classical and/or anthropological archaeology? Learning about both approaches provides you with a broader grasp of archaeology and may offer you more graduate and post-graduate opportunities.

Does the college have a grad program in archaeology? What kinds of archaeological labs are available? Are there opportunities for students to go on excavation projects? The presence of a grad program usually indicates a stronger program for undergraduates, with more facilities and field opportunities.

Where do the faculty members conduct their field research? If you are already interested in a particular region, you should go to a college that will allow you to work in that area.

Career options and trends:
College professor; museum curator; cultural resource management specialist; state or federal government archaeologist; park ranger.

If you go into cultural resource management or, to a lesser extent, other archaeological fields, you are strongly encouraged to meet the training and certification requirements of the Register of Professional Archaeologists (www.rpanet.org).

Less than half of all archaeologists work in traditional areas such as teaching and museums. The majority now work for state or federal government agencies or in the private sector. Probably as many as two-thirds of all archaeologists hold positions that did not exist a generation ago.

Insider's viewpoint:
"I thrill to the excitement of discovery, finding the first known example of geophagy (the practice of eating earth when food is scarce) in the Andes, discovering evidence for a new trade route, pulling

the disparate pieces of the puzzle together and figuring out the lifeways of past human cultures."

—Professor David L. Browman, Washington University in St. Louis

For more info:
Society for American Archaeology (SAA)
900 Second St., N.E.
Suite #12
Washington, DC 20002-3557
(202) 789-8200
www.saa.org

Society for Historical Archaeology (SHA)
15245 Shady Grove Road
Suite 130
Rockville, MD 20850
(301)-990-2454
www.sha.org

Economics

What it's about:

The economics major provides a framework for analyzing issues such as inflation, unemployment, monopoly, and economic growth. You learn how economic systems function to provide goods and services. As you study theory, policy, and trends, you explore ways to deal with the economic problems that confront individuals, businesses, and nations.

Is this for you?

You might like this major if you also like: Thinking about issues such as wealth, poverty, discrimination, the environment, and trends in the global economy; working with numbers; reading about current events in newspapers and news magazines; investment clubs.

Consider this major if you are good at: attention to detail; logical reasoning; math; organizing; quantitative analysis *...or have...* initiative; writing skills.

Recommended high school prep:

English 4, math 4, lab science 3 (including physics), social studies 4 (including American/U.S. history, world history, government/civics, and economics), and a foreign language 2–3. If possible, take a computer science course.

Did you know...

...that economics is concerned with choices people make in all areas of their lives, not just choices related to financial matters?

Typical courses in this major:

Principles of microeconomics
Principles of macroeconomics
Economic statistics
Money and banking
Business and government
International trade
International finance
Urban economics
Environmental economics
Labor economics
Public economics
Industrial organization
Economic history
Poverty and discrimination
Health economics
Law and economics

Concentrations:

Generally, none in college; but if you go on to grad school: microeconomic theory; macroeconomic theory; econometrics; labor economics; monetary economics; industrial organization; public economics; international economics; economic history; economic development.

What the study of this major is like:

Economics is about choices and change. By investigating how people make decisions, economists can predict how people will react to change. Economics can help people to understand the causes of economic problems and to devise ways to avoid them. It is a practical discipline that plays an important role in the formulation of policies on such issues as taxation, international trade, health care, the environment, and the rate of inflation.

If you like rigorous analysis and problem solving, economics can be intellectually appealing. It uses simplified models to explain and predict economic behavior in a complicated, disorderly world. For example, when the interest rate goes down, what happens to mortgage rates and to the cost of new cars? Economics emphasizes insights derived from observation. It teaches you to isolate the most important facts and to focus on their implications.

As a major, you will probably begin with introductory and intermediate microeconomics (the study of individual firms, consumers, and workers) and macroeconomics (the study of economy-wide income, employment, and prices), and an economic statistics course. Later, in electives—such as international trade and finance, environmental economics, labor, public finance, or comparative economic systems—you see how basic principles come to bear in specific applied fields. Your standard tools of analysis are graphs and algebra. Most of your classes will be taught as lectures, and you can expect to do plenty of problem sets.

Some programs focus on theoretical analysis; others favor data analysis. Programs may also vary in their definition of economic practice. According to some professionals, an economist's main job is to model the economy as it might be—to develop theories that predict the consequences of policies. Other economists see their job as collecting data that describe the economy as it is. Still others examine the social, cultural, and political factors that influence the economy.

Although few economics departments have enough staff to offer courses in all the applied fields, most programs emphasize universal, fundamental principles. However, if you are interested in applying economics to a particular problem, be sure to choose a college that has the courses you'll need.

Other majors you might like:
Agricultural economics
Business administration and management
Accounting
Applied mathematics
Business/managerial economics
Finance
Psychology
Entrepreneurial studies
Statistics
Econometrics/quantitative economics
International business
International relations

Questions to ask colleges:
How much math do you need to succeed in the major? Is it enough to do well in algebra, or is calculus or even more advanced math necessary? The answers can help you plan what courses to take in both high school and college.

Is there a capstone experience such as a senior seminar, thesis, or independent-study project?

Career options and trends:
Business economist; economic consultant; government economist; investment banker; market researcher.

Graduates also find jobs in education, industry, public policy, and planning. In addition, the field is excellent preparation for law school, business school, and, recently, medical school. Many students with a B.A. or B.S. degree in economics enter training programs in large corporations and may become business managers. Others start out in sales or analyst positions.

Insider's viewpoint:
"It's hard to understand and accept the fact that there are economic theories that support either conservative or liberal policies and that, although these theories contradict each other, they are both viable."

—David, senior, Cornell University

For more info:
National Council on Economic Education (NCEE)
1140 Ave. of the Americas
New York, NY 10036
(800) 338-1192
www.ncee.net

Geography

What it's about:

Geography is the science of space and place on the earth's surface. You examine how people, regions, and environments interact to create and sustain the world in which we live. Using a multidisciplinary approach, you study local, regional, and global geography.

Is this for you?

You might like this major if you also like: maps; current affairs; *National Geographic*; travel; backpacking; biking; environmental issues; Model UN; computer graphics; other people and cultures.

Consider this major if you are good at: Integrating information from different sources; attention to detail; creativity; critical reading/thinking; research; spatial thinking/analysis *...or have...* graphical skills; initiative; verbal skills; writing skills.

Recommended high school prep:

English 4, math 3, lab science 3, social studies 4, and a foreign language 2–3. If they are available, also take ecology and AP human geography.

Typical courses in this major:

Human geography
Physical geography
Urban geography
World regional geography
Cultural geography
Economic geography
Remote sensing
Political geography
Cartography
Natural resources
Energy and the environment
Urban and regional planning
Weather and climate
Social geography
Geographic Information Systems (GIS)
Human-environmental relations

Concentrations:

In college: physical geography; environmental geography; human geography; spatial skills (tools and techniques); regional or area studies.

If you go on to grad school: human-environment relations; geographic information science; environmental geoscience; atmospheric and climatic studies; geomorphology; urban and regional systems; development studies.

What the study of this major is like:

Geography includes much more than the memorization of place names, capitals, and longest rivers. It investigates the way people from a variety of localities relate to their environment and the way their surroundings shape their lives. As a major, you gain a broad understanding of the way humans have adapted to, changed, and organized their physical environments. Geography draws from related fields, such as anthropology, economics, political science, and biology.

Two main specializations in the major are physical geography and human geography—and discussions often focus on their overlap. Physical geographers study climates, landforms, vegetation, soils, and water. In human geography, the emphasis is on people's perception, use, and modification of space, as individuals and communities create and sustain the places they call home. Topics the two groups examine include the effects, on both human activity and the natural world, of global warming, desertification, deforestation, loss of biodiversity, groundwater pollution, fire, and flooding.

The major begins with first-year courses that introduce you to facts, ideas, and tools. Besides human geography and physical geography, you take statistics, regional geography (such as courses on Africa or North America), and skills (such as cartography or remote sensing). Then you can concentrate in an area such as environmental geography, geographic education, or geographic information processing.

You may be required to complete an independent research project—a capstone experience that pulls together numerous topics and skills. Sometimes you can meet the requirement by participating in a field course. You should also take courses in other departments that relate to your concentration.

Because geography is not usually emphasized in high school, few students begin college as geography majors. Many pick this major in their second or third year of college, so your classmates are often a mixture of upper- and lower-division students. Your course work includes a rich mixture of lectures, lab, and library and field research. As you progress, you spend more time in specialized computer labs for cartography, GIS, and remote sensing; and in labs for physical geography (soils, geomorphology, and fluvial and glacial processes).

Frequently, the best place to learn is in the field. For example, you can spend a semester collecting, analyzing, and presenting local data, or you can study overseas. Often, the hardest part of being a geography major is integrating varied subject matter and approaches. In particular, you need to appreciate the perspectives of both the natural and the social sciences.

Because of geography's roots in both the natural sciences and the humanities, programs are offered in a wide variety of divisions and schools. Undergrad programs are often influenced by the emphasis and philosophy of connected graduate programs. Some programs rely heavily on graduate teaching assistants and part-time faculty members. Many specialized courses—such as medical geography; social and physical planning; population and demographics; and race, ethnicity, and class—are based on the research interests of faculty members. But the most noticeable differences are among programs that stress either physical or human geography. Some colleges have successfully bridged the two by focusing on human-environment relations.

Other majors you might like:
Cartography
Environmental engineering
Urban, community, and regional planning
Global studies
Mining and mineral engineering
Landscape architecture
International relations
Area/ethnic/cultural studies
Wildlife and wilderness management
Surveying technology
Natural resources and conservation
Geology/earth science

Questions to ask colleges:
Are there labs for GIS, remote sensing, and cartography? Which software packages are available? How many computer seats are dedicated to geography majors?

Are there certificate programs in GIS, remote sensing, or applied geography? Where and how large is the library/map collection? Which digital data sources are available (for example, population census and aerial photographs)?

What field trips are required or recommended for graduation?

Career options and trends:
Cartographer; GIS manager; economic development analyst; energy analyst; environmental engineer; engineer in photogrammetry (aerial surveying); land use planner; land surveyor; remote sensing specialist; water resources planner.

Engineering jobs such as surveying require certification. Increasingly, certification is a requirement for GIS-related jobs. Planning jobs are available to geographers without specific qualifications, but a master's degree or equivalent in planning is strongly recommended.

The hottest job market in the field is for graduates with experience in geographic information systems and remote sensing.

Insider's viewpoint:
"I do everything from calculus to paper writing to map analysis. There is incredible variety in the work involved in my major and that's one of the things I love about it. Things stay interesting."

—Carolyn, senior, Arizona State University

For more info:

Association of American Geographers (AAG)
1710 16th St., N.W.
Washington, DC 20009-3198
(202) 234-1450
www.aag.org

National Geographic Society (NGS)
1145 17th St. N.W.
Washington, DC 20036-4688
(800) 647-5463
www.nationalgeographic.com

University Consortium for Geographic
   Information Science (UCGIS)
P.O. Box 15079
Alexandria, VA 22309
(703) 799-6698
www.ucgis.org

International relations

What it's about:

International relations is the study of the causes, consequences, and efforts to resolve global patterns of conflict and peace, poverty and wealth, and freedom and oppression. As a major, you examine nations and international organizations to understand political, economic, military, and cultural interactions on the international level.

Is this for you?

You might like this major if you also like: world history; travel; maps; flags; "big picture" issues; stamp collecting; languages; politics.

Consider this major if you are good at: attention to detail; creativity; critical reading/thinking; leadership; persuading/influencing ...*or have...* initiative; patience; verbal skills; writing skills.

Recommended high school prep:

English 4, math 3, lab science 3, social studies 4 (especially world history), and a foreign language 4.

Typical courses in this major:

U.S. foreign policy
International organizations
International law
African politics
Latin American politics
European politics
Russian and East European politics
Northeast Asian politics
South Asian politics
Middle East politics
Global environmental issues
International relations theory
National security
International conflict
International political economy
Global human rights issues

Concentrations:

International law and organization; international business; human rights; international political economy; national security; international environmental issues; transnational studies; comparative and regional perspectives; U.S. foreign policy.

What the study of this major is like:

This major draws from many disciplines, such as political science, economics, history, sociology, and foreign languages.

You typically begin with an introduction to international relations (usually offered by the political science department), intro courses in micro- and macroeconomics, one or two courses in world history, and a course in sociology or anthropology. Generally, in your third and fourth years you take courses in U. S. foreign policy, international organizations (especially the United Nations), regional issues, diplomacy, national security, and in economics, law, the environment, and human rights, all from a global perspective.

Courses typically incorporate insights from several disciplines and focus on significant current issues. Other requirements may include a seminar in your area of concentration, as well as proficiency in a related foreign language. International travel is recommended to deepen your understanding of other societies.

Although much of the material is presented in lectures, you listen to, and may participate in, serious debate on how the theories of international relations can be most effectively applied. Global discussions, such as those at regional conferences, frequently involve controversial topics. In most colleges, therefore, you will encounter a wide variety of viewpoints on international issues. Exams generally stress interpretive essays rather than single-answer questions. In addition, you will be expected to write papers that combine solid research with independent thinking.

Many majors are overwhelmed, at first, by the broad scope of international relations and the rapidly changing state of world affairs. Because the discipline does not have a fixed body of absolute truths, you must make full use of your critical-thinking and analytical skills. You should expect ongoing challenge and a constant questioning of your views.

There are several differences in the way the major is taught. Often, the program is a multidisciplinary subject of study administered by a committee of professors from various departments. There are few actual departments of international relations, because most professors who teach the subject hold positions in political science, history, or economics departments. Programs may also vary in emphases. While most programs focus on political science, history, and economics, some emphasize language and literature. In addition, a few colleges stress the worldview of the United States, while most attempt to represent a more global perspective.

Some programs may require you to specialize in a global region, although most permit you to be a generalist with a functional, rather than a geographic, specialty (such as business/economics, security/conflict, or human rights). In other programs, the focus is almost entirely on sovereign states. Still others examine transnational and subnational forces (such as humanitarian organizations, terrorist groups, multinational corporations, and separatist groups like the Basques, the Tibetans, and the Tamils). A program may emphasize concepts and theories or practical cases in world affairs. Some programs cover most of the twentieth century, while others focus on recent issues.

Other majors you might like:
International business
Political science
History
European studies
Geography
Global studies
Comparative literature
Asian studies
Islamic studies
Peace and conflict studies
Linguistics
Journalism

Questions to ask colleges:
Do students in the program pursue internships for undergraduate credit? How are overseas programs integrated into the major?

Career options and trends:
Graduates in international relations are usually eligible for entry-level positions in the federal Civil Service (especially the departments of State, Defense, Agriculture, and Treasury). Many graduates take positions with members of Congress, congressional committees, or the CIA. Other options are United Nations work, international journalism, paralegal positions with law firms and public service legal agencies; jobs in banks and other firms doing international business; and positions with humanitarian organizations such as Amnesty International. A graduate degree in international relations enhances your career options, especially in the Foreign Service and international business.

Graduates with international relations training are in high demand. Globalization is accelerating, and many jobs now have an international component. People who have cultural sensibilities and understand international political, economic, and military issues are much needed.

Insider's viewpoint:
"I just like the fact that the news is part of my major. What I learn in class I can apply to what I read in the news or on the Internet or see on TV. I like having a sense of what's outside the bubble of my university and the United States."

—Sean, senior, Baylor University

For more info:
International Studies Association (I.S.A.)
324 Social Sciences Building
University of Arizona
Tuscon, AZ 85721
(520) 621-7715
www.isanet.org

Political science

Also known as:
Government

What it's about:
As a political science major, you explore the origins, historical development, and functions of government and political power. You study the ways in which electoral, legislative, judicial, and administrative structures vary among countries; the reasons why governments change, fall, and engage in wars; and the behavior of public officials and other citizens who take part in politics.

Is this for you?
You might like this major if you also like: history; current events; politics; debating; student government; *The West Wing;* community service activities; issues relating to social justice.

Consider this major if you are good at: critical reading/thinking; leadership; quantitative analysis; research; teamwork *...or have...* initiative; verbal skills; writing skills.

Recommended high school prep:
English 4, math 4, lab science 2, social studies 4, and a foreign language 3-4.

Typical courses in this major:
U.S. government
Judicial processes
U.S. foreign policy
Public policy analysis
International law
Global issues
Political action groups
Comparative politics
Political theory
American political campaigns and elections
Politics of developing areas
Politics of ecological crisis
U.S. intelligence and policymaking
Contemporary political ideologies
Ethnic and racial politics
U.S. political thought

Concentrations:
U.S. politics; international relations; comparative politics; political theory.

What the study of this major is like:
The political science and government major deals with a range of domestic and international issues, including civil rights, health care, war and peace, economic development, democracy, the environment, and the role of race, ethnicity, and gender in political life.

You might begin the major with an intro course in political science or, more likely, with an intro to one or more subfields (for example, international relations). In addition, you'll probably take intro theory courses and a class on analytical methods and databased research. Intermediate and advanced courses may cover such topics as international security and global political economy, and U.S. institutions and constitutional law.

Most programs require you to minor in a related field, such as history, sociology, economics, or anthropology. You examine such issues as the principles of human behavior that underlie political activity, the actions of citizens, politicians, and public officials; overall social and economic structures and processes; the origins and development of individual political systems; and the physical and social geography in which governments exist and politics takes place. In some colleges, you study these and other subjects through the core curriculum. If there is no core curriculum, you should choose electives that cover these areas.

Many programs now require majors to complete a capstone project—usually a substantial piece of research in which you integrate the knowledge and skills you have learned, as you investigate questions that interest you. Designing a research project and writing a paper based on your research can be very rewarding.

Your classes may be in either a traditional (lectures) or an active (seminars, problem-based learning) format. You learn both individually and, especially in upper-division courses, in teams. College courses generally take an analytical approach, rather than the historical and current-events approach that students may be accustomed to in high school courses. Even at large colleges, courses above the intro level usually have relatively few students and provide opportunities for discussion among students and instructors.

Most programs offer academic and practical experience outside the classroom—for example, internships in public offices (such as those of state legislative committees, public defenders, and county attorneys) or in administrative agencies. You may spend a "Washington semester" working and studying in the nation's capital. Political science departments often participate in the college's study-abroad programs. Political science clubs and campus political organizations can also enhance the intellectual and social life of majors.

Political science programs differ widely; you should examine the description of the major at colleges you may apply to. Some colleges are more liberal, others more conservative. Some favor scientific or quantitative (math-based) approaches; others choose a humanistic or qualitative perspective.

Other majors you might like:
International relations
History
Criminal justice and law enforcement
Public administration
Public relations
American studies
Urban, community, and regional planning
Legal studies
Journalism
Peace and conflict studies
Urban studies
Military technologies

Career options and trends:
The study of political science and government can lead to careers in a wide range of fields including business, journalism, government service, public administration, nongovernmental organizations (NGOs), law, teaching, the Foreign Service, and the diplomatic corps.

Insider's viewpoint:
"A special commitment to understanding history and current events is helpful. More importantly, perhaps, political science majors should feel comfortable engaging with others on these issues, occasionally in heated debates. I love doing that."

—Brian, junior, Columbia University

For more info:
American Political Science Association (APSA)
1527 New Hampshire Ave., N.W.
Washington, DC 20036
(202) 483-2512
www.apsanet.org

Psychology

What it's about:

Psychology majors study the behavior and mental (emotional, learning, and thought) processes of animals and humans. You learn psychological principles, facts, and theories about individuals and groups, using experimental, observational, and case study methods.

Is this for you?

You might like this major if you also like: observing how animals and people act and respond; science; helping others; working with children or the elderly; working with numbers.

Consider this major if you are good at: critical reading/thinking; math; memorizing; research *...or have...* empathy; initiative; motivation; people skills; writing skills.

Recommended high school prep:

English 4, math 4 (including trigonometry or pre-calculus), lab science 4 (including advanced biology or chemistry), social studies 3, and a foreign language 2–3. If possible, take computer science and statistics courses and a year of psychology. Participating in community service is also beneficial.

Did you know...

...that in psychology, animals are studied both to examine their behavior and to provide insights into human behavior?

...that this major requires you to learn scientific and statistical methods? Many students are surprised by this but then find it to be not that difficult.

...that for almost all work done as a professional psychologist, you need a graduate or professional degree?

Typical courses in this major:

Abnormal psychology
Social psychology
Personality development
Learning and memory
History of psychology
Tests and measurement
Cognitive psychology
Statistics
Child psychology
Perception
Physiological psychology
Experimental psychology
Industrial/organizational psychology
Developmental psychology
Research methods in psychology
Cross-cultural psychology

Concentrations:

In college: methodology/research; applied psychology; clinical psychology; child psychology; social psychology.

If you go on to grad school: ecological psychology; personality; sensation and perception; animal behavior; industrial and organizational psychology; sports psychology; forensic psychology.

What the study of this major is like:

The psychology major most often begins with a required one-semester intro course; continues with several other required core courses, such as in research methods, statistics, and experimental psychology; and concludes with a fourth-year capstone experience—perhaps a research seminar.

Most departments divide the major into concentrations—such as developmental psychology (which may include infant and child psychology, adolescence, gerontology, and the life span) and experimental psychology (learning, sensation and perception, and biological psychology)—and require you to take courses from each area. In addition, you can usually choose from a range of electives. You earn either a Bachelor of Science degree (which requires more math and science) or a Bachelor of

Arts degree (requiring more humanities and a foreign language); otherwise, there may be little difference in course work between the two degrees.

The subject matter of psychology is diverse. An intro course may cover the basics of motivation, perception, learning, memory, social psychology, developmental psychology, abnormal psychology, counseling psychology, and language—topics that may also be covered, in depth, in intermediate and advanced courses. In undergraduate counseling psychology, you learn about psychotherapy. Clinical psychology adds psychological assessment (testing) and program evaluation and research skills.

Some courses feature lecture and discussion, and some have research components. Labs may involve working with sophisticated equipment, or with a rat, pigeon, or other animal colony. Doing research allows you to learn scientific methods and to differentiate between commonsense notions and research-based findings. In individual and group research, you may investigate attitudes and beliefs through questionnaires; observe people in social situations; or explore differences in responses between experimental groups and control groups.

The challenges you may face include mastering statistics and becoming familiar with the methods of scientific inquiry. Learning the terminology and basic concepts of psychology will probably require some no-nonsense studying. Presenting research at a forum or conference can be a rewarding, if intimidating, experience.

Departments may vary in whether they emphasize psychology as a liberal arts or as a preprofessional program. At some colleges, the emphasis is on pure research. At others, which stress the practical application of research, there may be more opportunities to do internships in the mental health/human service and industrial/organizational areas.

Other majors you might like:
Mental health services technology
Behavioral sciences
Gerontology
Industrial engineering
Neuroscience
Human development and family studies
Criminology

Sociology
Child development
Anthropology
Human resources management
Religious studies

Questions to ask colleges:
Can students take courses that give them experience with professional or applied psychology, such as counseling or industrial/organizational work? Which courses allow students to participate in labs and/or field research?

Do faculty members help students determine if they should go on to grad school? Ideally, full-time instructors are available as advisers throughout your undergraduate education.

Career options and trends:
Social worker; school psychologist; clinical psychologist; lawyer; counseling psychologist; physician (internist, psychiatrist, or other specialist); health care administrator; psychotherapist.

Psychology majors also pursue careers in a wide variety of public, private, profit, nonprofit, business, and service organizations, working in administration/management, community relations, program development, research, human resources, public relations, military service, advertising, market research, retail, and sales.

Jobs in health care administration, social work, industrial/organizational psychology, and medicine (including psychiatry) require graduate or professional degrees. Positions in school psychology, clinical psychology, and human services/mental health work at either the master's or the doctorate level often require state certification or licensure, and sometimes a one-year internship. Physicians must pass the state board exams to be licensed to practice in a particular state.

Many graduate programs that teach clinical skills (such as psychotherapy, assessment, and program evaluation) are discontinuing such training at the master's level; the doctorate is becoming the entry-level degree of choice.

Insider's viewpoint:

"Don't base your decision to major in psychology on Psych 101 because it is pretty broad and boring. I found classes in social, abnormal, and adolescent psychology to be the most interesting."

—Alison, senior, University of Virginia

For more info:

American Psychological Association (APA)
750 First St., N.E.
Washington, DC 20002-4242
(800) 374-2721
www.apa.org

American Psychological Society (APS)
1010 Vermont Ave., N.W.
Washington, DC 20005-4907
(202) 783-2077
www.psychologicalscience.org

Sociology

What it's about:

Sociology is the study of society and social behavior. By studying how individuals act in small and large groups, as well as how such groups are formed and function, you explore social problems and public policy. You investigate a range of topics, including the intimacies of family relationships; the demographics of urban and rural spaces; and the consequences of race, gender, and class divisions across societies.

Is this for you?

You might like this major if you also like: observing human behavior; reading; research; writing; community service activities; debating; computers; politics; exploring different perspectives on social issues such as gender and race.

Consider this major if you are good at: attention to detail; creativity; critical reading/thinking; organizing; quantitative analysis; research; teamwork *...or have...* initiative; patience; writing skills.

Recommended high school prep:

English 4, math 3, lab science 3, social studies 3, and a foreign language 2–3.

Did you know...

...how much scientific research is involved in sociology? Sociologists follow strict guidelines for the collection and analysis of information, including quantitative methods used for conducting surveys, qualitative methods used for interviews and observations, analytical procedures used for coding and interpreting field notes, and statistical procedures used to analyze data.

Typical courses in this major:

Introduction to sociology
Sociological theory
Research methods
Social stratification
Deviance
Socially complex organizations
Minority groups
Juvenile delinquency
Social problems
Gender roles
Social psychology
Sociology of education
Sociology of the family

Concentrations:

In college: racial and ethnic minorities; sex and gender; criminology and delinquency; family sociology; work and occupations; urban or rural affairs; stratification.

If you go on to grad school: demography; methodology; education; social movements; gerontology; medical sociology.

What the study of this major is like:

Course work ranges from case studies of the relationships among individuals in particular social settings, to scrutiny of governments and economic systems across time. Intro courses ask questions such as "How are rules of normality established? How do these rules change? How do social institutions (such as the family) influence our choices, our perceptions of reality, and our plans for the future?" To answer these questions, you may explore the issues from several perspectives (often drawn from disciplines such as history, economics, and political science) as you make progress in your studies.

Sociology is taught mostly through lectures, supplemented by presentations, films, guest speakers, and independent research. Required courses usually include introductory sociology, research methods, theory, and statistics. Probably you'll take courses in such related areas as geography, political science, religion, and economics. Many courses deal with social policy. For example, a course on social stratification (that is, how societies are divided up) may include discussion of policies designed to reduce inequality.

Most programs require you to learn the theories and research methods that prepare you for independent projects. You'll gain practice in using academic journals, computerized databases, and other materials available at most college libraries; or you might gather and analyze data yourself, through surveys, interviews, and observations. In many programs, you will have the opportunity to do an internship at a social service agency, where you can apply what you have learned in the classroom.

There are some challenges. First, the field is so wide that you may have difficulty narrowing your interests to a specific research topic. Second, the scientific method of conducting research, especially the emphasis on statistical analysis, can cause trouble for some students. But students who master data analysis are usually rewarded. Statistics makes their research work much more efficient, and many jobs that majors take after graduation require data analysis. Finally, there is a fair amount of reading, writing, studying terminology, and evaluating different perspectives and theories that are sometimes difficult. The independent research project that some colleges require takes time, initiative, patience, and, often, creativity. Despite the academic demands of this major, though, students rarely complain that the readings are uninteresting.

Programs may vary in the number of courses required for the major. Across colleges, concentrations may also vary according to faculty members' expertise, and areas of concentration may change as new topics emerge. You can get a feel for the differences among programs by comparing courses required and concentrations offered and by looking at the types of research the professors are doing.

Other majors you might like:

African-American studies

Political science

Anthropology

Community organization/advocacy

Criminal justice and law enforcement

Chicano studies

Media studies

Parks, recreation, and leisure studies

Human development and family studies

Social work

Urban, community, and regional planning

Gay/lesbian studies

Career options and trends:

The sociology major can lead to careers in marketing, consumer research, advertising, insurance, human resources, teaching, nonprofit organizations, community development agencies, environmental groups, criminal justice (probation or parole officers), government research (in local, state, and federal agencies), law, urban planning, Foreign Service, and industrial sociology. Advanced degrees are required for work as college professors, lawyers, demographers, policy analysts, and research institute managers.

Insider's viewpoint:

"I've heard many people say statistics don't mean anything, they're just numbers, but to me they represent what goes on. When I took statistics in my first semester, I didn't understand why I had to, but in a lot of the classes it's 'ninety percent of these people...' or 'ninety-seven percent of kids...'"

—Liz, senior, San Jose State University

For more info:

American Sociological Association (ASA)
1307 New York Ave., N.W.
Suite 700
Washington, DC 20005
(202) 383-9005
www.asanet.org

Visual and performing arts

If you turned to this chapter first, you probably think of the arts as more than just entertainment or pretty pictures. You are not alone. The arts are popular majors for students who might like to pursue a career in painting, acting, dance, or other creative or expressive fields. The performing arts differ from the visual arts, so let's start with the performing arts.

If you're a singer, actor, dancer, or musician, you may already know that the intense competition for performance work limits jobs to the most accomplished artists in a given field.

"Very few performance majors are ever able to make a living through music performance alone," says Professor Sandra Billy of the Center for Sacred Music at Virginia Wesleyan College. (See the Religion and theology section for sacred music.)

Fortunately, you can break the stereotype of the starving artist. Many doors are open to trained artists. For instance, dancers and choreographers (who create dances) may not be able to break through the competition barrier, but dance teachers are needed. Arts management is another professional outlet.

"Despite limited job opportunities, there is always room for those who are highly talented and well prepared," says Jo Anne Caputo, a member of the faculty at the Cleveland Institute of Music.

You can parlay your talent and training in the arts into a rewarding career. Take another example. Theater majors are known for their ability to get ideas across. That skill is important in many professions—law, advertising, business, teaching, and even politics. President Ronald Reagan and California governor Arnold Schwarzenegger worked as movie actors before running for public office.

"Fine arts are excellent preparation for any field requiring careful thinking, synthesis, accurate observation and expression, not just art-related positions," assures Professor David B. Greene of North Carolina State University.

In the visual arts, a similar dynamic is at play, because few people earn their living from gallery exhibits and sales of their artwork. But visual and design skills can be transferred to jobs like interior and fashion design; photography; and graphic design for print, video, and the Internet. Many new college programs, including digital, multimedia, interactive, and Web design and production, apply computer technologies to the visual arts. Composers of music use computers and digital musical instruments in their craft, leading to valuable workplace skills.

If you can use digital technologies or think visually, you have prized talents in a media-driven world. "In a knowledge economy, those who make information comprehensible are valued," explains Professor Meredith Davis of North Carolina State University.

The education landscape

If someone did a painting depicting all of the country's college art programs, it would look like a Pollock, not a Mondrian. "This is a complicated educational landscape...with wildly different degree offerings," cautions Professor Davis.

Choose wisely if you plan to study the arts in college. Especially if you're interested in the fine arts, ask yourself how competitive a school you really want. "Some performance students prefer and thrive in a hyper-competitive environment. Others may prefer a less intense, more nurturing setting. It is important to find the right fit," Caputo advises.

Here are some other things to think about in choosing visual or performing arts programs: Should you study near a city with lots of concerts and galleries? Does the college have its own collection, facilities, image archive, rehearsal instruments, and studios? Do you have to audition or submit a portfolio of your artwork to be accepted?

Are you going for a B.A. degree or a B.F.A (Bachelor of Fine Arts)? The B.A. is a broader approach to art. The B.F.A. gets you ready for a career in a specific art form and might require an audition or portfolio to get into college.

If you're headed for a teaching career, you'll want a higher degree. Graduate studies in the various arts focus on recording and studio production techniques, animation, creative art therapy, and performance art, to name a few. Fine arts grad students may study a particular period, region, or medium.

Also try to get an idea of the daily life of an arts major. How many hours per week will you be taking lessons or working in a studio or at a computer? Is instruction included in your tuition? Will you set your own schedule or are rehearsals preset? How crowded are studios or computer stations? Are they open late? Look at the studios, concert halls, galleries, and design technologies on campus. Nice digs mean the school is committed to the arts.

The faculty is most important, especially in the performing arts, where students are guided by mentors. Your choice of a college may hinge on the availability of a master teacher.

In your search, you'll run across art programs in colleges of arts and sciences, liberal arts, mass communications, fine and performing arts, schools of design, schools or conservatories of music, and so on. A good Web site to get you going is www.arts-accredit.org. If you don't have a computer, ask your school counselor or local librarian to help you compare colleges and programs. Also see the Communications section for some related majors.

Animation

What it's about:

Animation majors learn a broad range of animation techniques, both traditional and contemporary. Your training covers a broad range of drawing, sound, acting, film, and storytelling skills, along with current software applications.

Is this for you?

You might like this major if you also like: filmmaking; photography; reading and writing stories; drama clubs; art clubs.

Consider this major if you are good at: attention to detail; creativity; critical reading/thinking; organizing; spatial thinking/analysis; teamwork ...*or have...* imagination; mechanical facility.

Recommended high school prep:

English 4, math 3, lab science 3, social studies 3, and a foreign language 2–3. Take as many courses in art (including studio art and art history) and computer applications as you can. A strong background in language arts (literature and writing) is also recommended.

Did you know...

...that traditional art skills are still the most important quality that successful animators have? If you have these skills, you will have an edge over those who don't. Specific knowledge of software is not essential; you will learn computer techniques in the major.

...that an interest in literature and storytelling is also important? Knowing what makes a good story is just as significant as having technical skills.

Typical courses in this major:

Figure and animal drawing
Color theory
Storyboard and narrative
Screenwriting for animators
Acting for animators
History of animation
Character animation techniques
Stop-motion techniques
Experimental animation techniques
Layout and background design
Digital ink and paint
Special effects
Sound design
Digital compositing
Digital character modeling
3-D computer animation

Concentrations:

Computer animation; character animation; stop-motion animation; special effects.

What the study of this major is like:

Do you enjoy telling stories? Do you love to draw? Do you visualize the characters and settings in some of the works you read? If so, animation might be a good major for you. The field of animation offers many ways to use your imagination, including writing stories, designing characters, and re-creating the worlds that the characters inhabit.

As an animation major, you'll first receive a firm grounding in the principles of art, and you'll explore a variety of ways to develop and tell stories. You then learn the techniques (practical as well as creative) of cinema and how to apply these techniques to both traditional and computer-assisted filmmaking.

As you advance in the program, you are introduced to various animation software packages (for example, 3D Studio Max and Maya for three-dimensional modeling and animation; Flash, Photoshop, and After Effects for compositing; Toonz for digital ink and paint). These and other software systems become part of your toolkit as you gain experience in making your own films. You'll finish with a fourth-year thesis film.

Your courses consist of lectures and demonstrations, accompanied by many hours of practice in and out of the classroom. Early in the program, you concentrate on drawing, a skill that will help you master the more advanced techniques taught later on. Ideally, animation programs challenge you to enlarge your visual vocabulary and storytelling abilities. To do so, you should have a passion for your studies and a willingness to work long hours outside of class—qualities that will serve you well in the professional world.

All strong animation programs emphasize a solid foundation in art while also teaching skills and techniques that are in demand in the real world. Because there are a number of specializations within the animation business (for example, storyboard artist, character designer, and 3-D modeler), programs may differ in the concentrations they offer.

As you progress through the major, your assignments will become more complex and instructors will review your work periodically to see how well you are integrating the skills you have learned with your creative ideas. At some colleges, passing these reviews is a requirement for continuing in the major. Your final project, the thesis film, along with a portfolio, will serve as your "résumé" in the industry.

Other majors you might like:
Computer graphics
Cinematography and film/video production
Illustration
Graphic design
Digital media
Photographic/film/video technology
Make-up artist
Computer engineering technology
Drafting and design technology
Arts management
Web page/multimedia design
Radio and television

Questions to ask colleges:
What is the student-to-instructor ratio? Are the instructors currently working in the animation industry? In a good program, you will receive close instruction from faculty members who are familiar with the latest technology and have helpful contacts in the industry.

Are there adequate studio facilities, and are they available around the clock, so that students have a chance to complete assignments? Do the hardware and software capabilities keep current with the industry?

Are internships or apprenticeships in the animation business part of curriculum?

Career options and trends:
Art director/production designer*; storyboard/concept artist*; background/layout designer; character designer; 3-D animator (computer)*; 2-D animator; stop-motion animator; game designer; production coordinator.

Jobs are increasingly freelance in nature, with staff hired from project to project. Some portions of productions are being outsourced overseas. Developing multiple skills will give you a competitive advantage, particularly during economic downturns. In addition to film, television, advertising, and advertising productions, there are opportunities in the creation of computer games and in Web design.

For more info:
International Animated Film Association (ASIFA)
ASIFA WASHINGTON
P.O. Box 3115
Silver Spring, MD 20918
(301) 681-2712
http://asifa.net/washington/

Animation World Network (AWN)
6525 Sunset Blvd.
Garden Suite 10
Hollywood, CA 90028
(323) 606-4200
www.awn.com

StopMotionAnimation.com
www.stopmotionanimation.com

Art history

What it's about:

Art history majors study how works of art were created, how they were interpreted by their first audiences, and what they mean to us now. Through visual analysis and extensive reading and writing, majors achieve an understanding of the context of art—time, place, culture, influences, and traditions—and develop the ability to describe art and its meaning to others.

Is this for you?

You might like this major if you also like: visual arts and architecture; antiquing; museums and galleries; travel; model making; reading about history and other cultures; finding connections and relationships between things.

Consider this major if you are good at: active listening; attention to detail; creativity; critical reading/thinking; research; spatial thinking/analysis *...or have...* initiative; verbal skills; writing skills.

Recommended high school prep:

English 4, math 3, lab science 3, social studies 4, art 2, music 1, and a foreign language 3–4. English and social studies courses that teach writing, speech, critical analysis, and research skills are essential, and studio art classes give valuable insight.

Did you know...

...that while the study of art history is similar in many ways to the study of literature or other cultural fields, it is unique in that you rely primarily on visual perception and on your ability to translate a nonverbal language into a verbal one?

Typical courses in this major:

Art and civilization before 1400
Asian art and temple architecture
Greek and Roman art
Egyptian art and architecture
Medieval art and architecture
The Renaissance
Michelangelo
European Baroque
Early modern architecture
Impressionism and Postimpressionism
Picasso
Postmodernism
Abstract expressionism
American art
History of photography
Introduction to museology

Concentrations:

In college: a historical period, such as ancient, medieval, or modern; a medium, such as painting, architecture, or sculpture; or the arts of a specific culture, such as America, Byzantium, or Polynesia.

If you go on to grad school: a particular artist or movement; museology and curatorship.

What the study of this major is like:

This major teaches you to differentiate among artworks by their style, materials, workmanship, and other characteristics. You can then identify (and seek to understand) the artists, cultures, and/or periods that produced the works. In addition, you consider how individual works of art and groups of works may express or symbolize ideas or emotions. Like archaeologists and anthropologists examining artifacts, you explore what a work of art reveals about a society's culture, rituals, and other aspects of civilization. Often you discover that the art's original value and meaning resulted from its connection to specific religious, political, or social practices.

In your first and second years, you generally take introductory art history courses, along with liberal arts courses in science, English, math, and history. Because art varies widely among societies (both past and present), art is often studied in association with a particular time and place (for example, Renaissance art, East African art). Thus the study of art generally includes some account of the religious, political, economic, literary, and intellectual history of the culture in which a work was created. You will read about art patrons, critics, and viewers, as well as artists. Frequent field trips to local museums augment classroom slide presentations.

After the introductory courses, you take smaller lecture courses that explore art in more detail. Seminars help you develop and refine advanced skills in research and presentation. In your fourth year, you usually have the option of writing a thesis under the direction of a faculty member. Many art history majors also take courses in areas related to their particular interests, such as history, anthropology, or literature. In addition, many study two or more years of a foreign language as a way of understanding other cultures.

Art history majors usually enjoy the benefits of working in a relatively small department where your needs can be dealt with individually. Study-abroad programs are common, and you should have opportunities to participate in internships at museums, galleries, and historic sites. Keep in mind, however, that while internships in museums are attractive, many involve work in education departments that may be isolated from the museum's curatorial activity. Smaller museums often offer more interesting opportunities. Commercial galleries may hire some summer staff, although summer is generally their slow period.

Other majors you might like:
Museum studies
Architecture
Architectural history/criticism
Anthropology
Classics
Comparative literature
Area studies (European, Asian, etc.)
Historic preservation
Medieval and Renaissance studies
Archaeology
Arts management
Music history/literature

Questions to ask colleges:
What is the extent of the visual media collection (slides, digitized images, etc.)?

What opportunities are there to study original works of art in a university collection or nearby museum?

Career options and trends:
Teacher (college or high school); museum curator*; museum management/staff (education, installation, registrar, etc.)*; commercial gallery operator/assistant*; art editor; art appraiser.

Art history majors graduate with a liberal arts degree that has trained them in observation, analysis, and communication. This preparation may qualify you for many jobs in business and government. A master's degree is generally required for employment in museums, archives, auction houses, and galleries, and for teaching in high school; a Ph.D. is essential for positions as museum curators and directors, and as instructors at the college level. Art conservation usually requires specialized training and knowledge of chemistry.

Insider's viewpoint:
"It's fairly important to study a foreign language, especially if you want to go to grad school. I've been taking Italian, so I chose to concentrate on late-medieval and early-Renaissance art; I wanted to read primary documents in the original."

—Dilip, senior, Northwestern University

For more info:
College Art Association (CAA)
275 Seventh Ave.
New York, NY 10001
(212) 691-1051
www.collegeart.org

Cinematography and film/video production

What it's about:

This major prepares you to work in all aspects of film and/or video production, including producing, media writing, production management, directing, lighting, cinematography and/or videography, editing, and sound recording and mixing. The major also provides a strong foundation in media literacy, history, and theory.

Is this for you?

You might like this major if you also like: movies and television; taking photographs and making videos; reading; storytelling and creative writing; painting and drawing; the theater and stagecraft; working with computers; using technology creatively. If you like to make things and can think in visual terms, this field may be for you.

Consider this major if you are good at: attention to detail; creativity; critical reading/thinking; organizing; spatial thinking/analysis; teamwork ...*or have...* discipline; initiative; mechanical facility; verbal skills; writing skills.

Recommended high school prep:

English 4, math 3, lab science 3, social studies 3, and a foreign language 2–3. Take as many art courses as possible, especially those covering photography and media; theater and drama; and computer courses. If these subjects are not available in high school, extracurricular or community activities in these areas are highly recommended.

Did you know...

...that the digital revolution in this field has made skills in math, science, and computers increasingly important? Writing skills and social, cultural, and media literacy are also necessary—if you want to make meaningful films, you need something meaningful to say.

Typical courses in this major:

Introduction to film and video production
Advanced film and video production
Studio television production
Directing
Cinematography and/or videography
Digital editing
Screenwriting
Sound design/production
Animation and special effects
Production management
Lighting
Television programming
Media and society
Visual literacy and communication
Film history
Film, video, and television genres

Concentrations:

Directing; producing; editing; screenwriting; sound; cinematography/videography; animation; narrative production; documentary production; alternative/experimental production.

What the study of this major is like:

Terms used in film and/or video production can be confusing. Although "film" programs traditionally use motion picture cameras and celluloid (film) to capture images, they are increasingly incorporating digital video. "Video" generally refers to single-camera production using either analog or digital videotape, and is similar to filmmaking in the way its production is organized.

Most programs in cinematography/film/video provide a mix of media studies and production courses. In media studies, you explore film and video history, theory, and analysis. You learn the language, theories, and politics of using images and sound to communicate. Because media making is a social and cultural practice that overlaps with many other disciplines, most programs require a foundation in liberal arts. In production courses, you are taught basic techniques: the creative use of lenses, lighting, cameras, and film stock; the theory and practice of editing; and the art and technology of sound design and recording. Once you master the basics, you move on to intermediate and advanced production work. In many programs, your studies culminate in a thesis project, which often becomes part of a demo reel—a viewable collection of your work—that can help you in your job search.

Programs may offer concentrations in one or more areas, such as editing or cinematography. In all programs, you can expect to work as a crew member on other students' projects. By crewing for other students, you can focus in one area of production or expand your skills in several areas. For example, if you are interested in sound design, you can volunteer to record and mix students' projects. You should seek as much practical production experience as possible because anything you work on can be included in your demo reel.

In media studies, most courses consist of both lectures and screenings, and assignments include writing research papers. Typical production courses require two two-hour lectures and one two-hour lab per week. Labs, which have fewer students than lectures do, involve hands-on learning and the screening of student projects. You generally shoot required projects outside of class.

The cinematography and film/video production major is time-intensive. You often work on projects during the evenings and on weekends. Because you're most likely to get a job through skill and experience, you should take advantage of all on- and off-campus opportunities, such as volunteering at a public TV station, and also seek internships or media jobs in the summer. Students sometimes earn course credit for participation in extracurricular activities.

This major can be costly, because you will probably have to buy some of the gear. While all programs provide major equipment, most expect you to purchase your own light meter, computer hard drive, and film/tape stock, and to pay for film lab services. But there is always a market for used equipment, and you can often purchase items at reduced cost from graduating majors.

Some cinematography/film/video programs emphasize production for "the industry," while others focus on film/video as an art form. Commercially oriented programs use Hollywood production techniques and tend to stress narrative fiction or broadcast news; little attention is given to avant-garde work. An arts-oriented program, in contrast, challenges you to explore your own vision and may also emphasize experimental or documentary production. Most programs strive for a balance. Some programs emphasize individual production and require you to write, direct, and edit your own projects. Other programs operate on a crew-oriented basis: only a few student projects are picked for production, and the other students crew on these films.

Other majors you might like:
Radio and television
Photography
Digital media
Web/multimedia management
Playwriting/screenwriting
Media studies
Computer graphics
Theater design and technology
Animation
Photographic/film/video technology
Instructional media
Laser/optical technology

Questions to ask colleges:
What equipment does the department provide, and how available is the equipment? Are editing and sound labs open on evenings and weekends? Does the department have a television studio/sound stage?

When do students start doing actual production? (Some programs introduce students to production in the first or second year; others wait until the third year.) Do the students own the rights to the productions they produce? Who funds the productions? Does the college provide film stock, or tape, or lab services?

Does the department sponsor a film or video festival?

Career options and trends:

Independent film/videomaking*; camera operator, director of photography*; sound editor, designer, mixer; apprentice or assistant editor; production assistant*; producer; director or assistant director; production manager; screenwriter.

Employment in the industry depends on ability, as evidenced in a demo reel, or in previous jobs or internships, rather than on a college degree. However, college training is often the best way to acquire job-qualifying skills, contacts, hands-on experience, and a demo reel. Technical positions other than entry-level ones may require membership in a union or guild.

The job market in film/video is competitive. There are far more job seekers than positions, but that should not discourage you from pursing this major. Students who commit to the profession, who excel in their production skills, who develop a good work ethic, and who are attentive and enthusiastic do get jobs. Moreover, the field as a whole is projected to grow as the entertainment market expands and computers and the Internet provide opportunities for interactive productions.

Many graduates do not hold full-time or staff jobs but work freelance; but even those who work on a television series can have months of downtime each year.

Insider's viewpoint:

"The hardest classes are critical studies in film. You've got to know the film terminology and be able to pull apart scenes and read into them. That's a little bit hard, reading what's going on behind what you see on the screen."

—Anthony, junior, San Francisco State University

For more info:

American Film Institute (AFI)
2021 North Western Ave.
Los Angeles, CA 90027
(323) 856-7600
www.afi.com

University Film and Video Association (UFVA)
1325 South Oak St.
Champaign, IL 61820-6903
(866) 244-0626
www.ufva.org

Dance

What it's about:

Dance majors learn to use their bodies in motion as instruments of artistic expression. As a major, you receive intensive training in the art of dance, in a liberal arts context, to prepare you for a career as a dancer or a choreographer. You'll study dance from several perspectives: technical, choreographic, aesthetic, historical, anatomical, cultural, anthropological, psychological, and therapeutic.

Is this for you?

You might like this major if you also like: dance; music; theater; learning about different cultures. Dance students have a passion for this art form; dance is a part of their daily lives.

Consider this major if you are good at: active listening; attention to detail; creativity; critical reading/thinking; memorizing; organizing; spatial thinking/analysis; teamwork *...or have...* perseverance; physical stamina; self-discipline.

Recommended high school prep:

English 4, math 3, lab science 3, social studies 3, and a foreign language 2–3. Your dance training should consist of ballet and modern dance, with integrated dance history and anatomy components, and courses in dance composition and motif description.

Did you know...

...that there are significant differences between a Bachelor of Arts degree in dance, in which you study dance in a liberal arts context, and a Bachelor of Fine Arts degree, in which you train for a professional career as a dancer? Since many dancers stop performing by their late thirties, these differences are important: with a B.A. rather than an B.F.A., you may have an easier time getting a job after you retire from dancing.

Typical courses in this major:

Dance technique (ballet, modern, and jazz)
Principles of choreography
Improvisation
Dance appreciation
Dance composition
Technical production for dance
Music for dance
Dance history
Motif description and labanotation
Anatomy and kinesiology for dance
Dance theory, philosophy, and criticism
Historic dances (Renaissance, Baroque, Ragtime)
The teaching of dance

Concentrations:

In college: technique and performance; choreography; dance education; dance history and criticism; dance therapy.

If you go on to grad school: dance kinesiology; dance and technology; labanotation (for scoring music and dance) and labanalysis (movement analysis)—terms named for Rudolf Laban, a dance theorist.

What the study of this major is like:

To pursue a B.F.A. degree in dance, you will take a number of studio courses in technique, choreography, partnering, company repertoire, mainstage performances, and notation—a curriculum that trains students to become performing and creative artists. In contrast, a B.A. degree in dance, which emphasizes courses in liberal arts subjects such as English, history, literature, and music, can prepare you for a career as a performing and creative artist *and* as a dance educator, administrator, historian, or critic. The B.A. is usually stronger preparation if you plan to go on to grad school or simply want to have more career options.

For a B.A. in dance, you take a minimum of 12 required credit hours in ballet, modern, and jazz dance technique courses. In-depth training in technique is essential, but a breadth of experience is also important. Technique courses may include other kinds of dance, such as ethnic, folk, social, tap, historic, or character dance.

Course work in anatomy and kinesiology (the anatomical study of movement) will enhance your technical skills by teaching you how the body moves and how to avoid injury. Courses in rhythmic analysis, percussion accompaniment, and music resources sharpen your sensitivity to rhythm and help you find or create appropriate accompaniment for your choreography. In dance notation courses, you analyze movement and record it, and read movement scores. In a course on dance philosophy, you may learn principles of aesthetics that you can apply to choreography. And when you study dance history, you'll be encouraged to develop an appreciation for dance as an innate (inborn) and universal form of human expression.

Dance majors should expect to choreograph throughout college—at first, simple dance studies and improvisations; then, later, at least one fully staged work. You learn to design costumes, to light dances, and to help produce concerts. You also learn to work cooperatively with others, to direct, to evaluate choreography (including your own), and to accept and benefit from criticism. And you perform! Some performances are informal presentations for teachers and classmates; others are theater productions before the public. If possible, take advantage of courses on teaching methods. Although many professional dancers may not plan to teach, almost all eventually do.

Daily classes in dance technique, rehearsals, and performances will cut deeply into your study time for academic subjects. To be a successful dance major, you need to have time management and stress management skills, the ability to focus clearly on the task at hand, and a commitment to produce quality work under deadline pressure.

At some colleges, the dance major is housed in the department of physical education rather than a department of fine arts, dance, or theater. Such programs usually emphasize kinesiology, physiology of exercise, health science, nutrition, and physical therapy.

Other majors you might like:
Anthropology
Sociology
Physical therapy
Dance therapy
Physical education
Theater arts management
American Sign Language (ASL)
Athletic training
Fine/studio arts
Drama and theater arts
Communications
Creative writing

Questions to ask colleges:
May both dance majors and nonmajors participate in the technical dance courses?

How many and what kinds of performance opportunities are offered each semester?

What is the audition policy? Do students have to audition for entrance into the dance major, for placement in technique classes, for opportunities to perform their own choreography or to select dancers for their own choreography, to perform in someone else's choreography, or to be in the dance company?

How many hours per week are devoted to technical instruction?

Are students able to control their own rehearsal schedule or is it predetermined?

Career options and trends:
Professional dancer and/or choreographer; dance teacher; dance critic; dance scientist/kinesiologist/physical therapist; dance historian/reconstructor; dance arts administrator; dance therapist.

Certification is required for teaching, and physical therapists and dance therapists are licensed health professionals with graduate degrees in their fields.

The field is overcrowded with professional dancers and choreographers—only the most talented find regular employment. Many performance opportunities depend on funding from public and private organizations; such support is not expected to keep up with rising production costs. On the other hand, there is a great need for dance educators in public and private elementary and secondary schools. There are few positions in dance criticism or dance therapy; but opportunities are expanding in the fields of dance/arts administration, dance science, dance history and reconstruction, and dance kinesiology (which usually require a master's degree).

Insider's viewpoint:
"If you're constantly comparing yourself to others, you won't get anywhere. And don't always stand in the back corner of your class; have enough confidence in yourself to stand in the front."

—Nicole, sophomore, University of Wisconsin

For more info:
National Dance Association (NDA)
American Alliance for Health, Physical Education, Recreation and Dance
1900 Association Drive
Reston, VA 20191-1598
(800) 213-7193
www.aahperd.org

Drama and theater arts

What it's about:

The major in drama and theater arts covers many aspects of staged plays, including theater history, literature, and criticism; acting and directing; lighting, scenery, and costume design; stage management; playwriting; and arts administration. You may specialize in one area while you obtain a broad foundation in many of the other areas.

Is this for you?

You might like this major if you also like: school and community drama clubs; speech and debate; music and art; expressing ideas and feelings; collaborating with others. Because theater encompasses many areas, a variety of personality types enjoy this major.

Consider this major if you are good at: creativity; critical reading/thinking; leadership; organizing; persuading/influencing; teamwork *...or have...* initiative; physical stamina; verbal skills; writing skills.

Recommended high school prep:

English 4, math 3, lab science 3, social studies 4, and a foreign language 2–3. In addition to any drama/theater courses available, take courses covering Shakespeare and dramatic literature, art history, music appreciation, art studio, and industrial arts (woodworking, drafting, etc.). Participation in theater, dance, or musical activities is a must.

Did you know...

...that theatrical skills are practical as well as creative? Dramatic projects must be produced within the boundaries of time, money, and labor constraints. Theater majors learn to think creatively, speak well, motivate a group, sell an idea, and get a job done on time—achievements that look good on a résumé for almost any job.

Typical courses in this major:
Introduction to theater
Theater design
Theater history
Dramatic literature
Play analysis
Acting
Directing
Production laboratory
Stagecraft
Production fundamentals
Voice for the actor
Shakespeare
Lighting design
Costume design
Scenic design
Musical theater

Concentrations:

In college: acting; directing; theater studies (history, literature, criticism); lighting design; costume design; scenic design; stage management; theater technology; production management.

If you go on to grad school: playwriting; dramaturgy.

What the study of this major is like:

The first thing to decide is whether to pursue a Bachelor of Arts or a Bachelor of Fine Arts degree. In a B.A. program, you gain a broader education, but may have difficulty competing with B.F.A. graduates in the professional world. But although the B.F.A. prepares you more rigorously for a theatrical profession, you may be less able to explore other areas of interest while you're in college.

You can generally choose from a wide variety of theater-related courses. In dramatic art courses, you study dramatic style and structure, theories of criticism, and the functions of theater artists, technicians, and managers. Theater history and dramatic literature courses cover Western theater from ancient Greece to the twentieth century. In directing courses, you learn how to analyze a script's style, form, and action, with the goal of translating the text into a staged production.

Introductory acting courses teach the fundamentals of relaxation, trust, sensory awareness, group interaction, and reaction and response. Improvisations, group exercises, and monologues are usually included. In advanced acting courses, you generally do scene work of increasing complexity in various classical and contemporary styles.

In courses in speech and voice, you practice phrasing, dialect, and breath control. Stage movement (sometimes taught as dance) develops relaxation and expressiveness. Theater history and criticism courses, often taught as lectures, involve considerable reading, discussion, and paper writing. Design and production courses are typically more hands-on; usually the lecture portion is coordinated with a laboratory session in which you work with tools and materials. For a concentration in arts administration, you study business and public relations/communications, in addition to taking theater courses.

Theater students and faculty members are typically opinionated and creative; class discussions and projects can be high-spirited. To add to the excitement, you may study, in a single day, contemporary theater in an acting course, fencing in a stage movement course, Shakespeare in a voice course, and end by rehearsing a performance art piece.

But the wide range of work is not only a blessing; if you do not have good organizational skills and time management skills, it can also be a curse. The greatest challenge that majors face is being committed to too many production projects. You must be able to withstand the rigors of nightly rehearsals, while still participating fully in your classes. Developing time management skills and the ability to take care of yourself (proper eating and sleeping) may be the most important thing you can do to ensure success as a drama and theater arts major.

The presence of a graduate theater program at an institution may have both advantages and disadvantages. Faculty members connected with a graduate program tend to be more high-powered, and production standards tend to be more professional. On the other hand, the graduate program may overshadow the undergraduate program.

The size of a program may also make a big difference: larger programs may offer a greater variety of courses and more chances to act, direct, and design, whereas at smaller colleges, there may be more production opportunities.

Other majors you might like:
Theater design and technology
Fashion and apparel design
Film/cinema studies
Cinematography and film/video production
Art history
Music management
Theater arts management
Communications
Radio and television
Digital media
Make-up artist
English

Questions to ask colleges:
What is the policy on crew hours and rehearsals? Sometimes working on a crew or attending rehearsal is tied to course work, sometimes to a non-credit requirement. There should be guidelines for time spent rehearsing and building a production.

Does the department provide assistance in obtaining internships and summer work?

Is there ample space for students to practice acting and directing? At least two performance sites are desirable.

Career options and trends:
Actor, director, technician, or designer*; drama teacher; business manager, marketer, or publicist for theater*; arts educator at regional theaters*.

Competition for jobs is fierce in the performance segment of the industry. Versatility is one way to expand your career possibilities. Although technicians and arts administrators usually find more work than actors, directors, and designers, all theater students should be able to multitask. For example, touring companies might hire actors who have the technical skills to set up and strike, or take down, a set. Regional theaters may hire graduates to teach in their educational programs or to participate in workshops or other short-term projects.

Taking jobs in related areas can often open doors for future work in your specialty.

Insider's viewpoint:

"Some of the best theater I have witnessed has been in scene work for acting classes. Also, rarely produced classics, new plays, large cast shows, and alternative performance art pieces are often found on university stages, rather than in the commercial or regional theater that can't take the risk."

—Professor Diane Timmerman, Butler University

For more info:
University/Resident Theater Association
1560 Broadway, Suite 712
New York, NY 10036
(212) 221-1130
www.urta.com

Fashion and apparel design

What it's about:

This major prepares you for a career as a designer of commercial fashions, clothing, and accessories. You are trained in all aspects of fashion design, including sketching, creative design, computer applications, draping, and flat pattern drafting. You also learn how to communicate design ideas through storyboards and fashion shows, and how to work effectively in a diversified, global industry.

Is this for you?

You might like this major if you also like: drawing; sewing; decorating; museums; pop culture; travel; fabrics; shopping; fashion magazines; art and photography; keeping up with trends.

Consider this major if you are good at: attention to detail; creativity; math; organizing; persuading/influencing; quantitative analysis; spatial thinking/analysis; teamwork *...or have...* manual dexterity; patience.

Recommended high school prep:

English 4, math 3, lab science 3, social studies 3, visual arts 2–3, and a foreign language 2–3. Also recommended, if they are available: vocational and family/home economics courses covering sewing, textiles, and apparel; drafting and design; and computer applications.

Did you know...

...that in this major, you need to feel comfortable with math? That's because you must have technical and analytical skills to design a garment from sketch to pattern to construction and finishing of the garment.

Typical courses in this major:

Fashion sketching
History of costume
Creative design theory and elements
Color and design theory
Computer-aided design
Computer pattern drafting
Computer grading, marking, and cutting
Draping
Industrial sewing techniques
Garment construction
Accessory design
Fashion industry survey
Collection development
Fashion show production
Professional practices
Portfolio development

Concentrations:

Film and TV costume design; theater costume design; footwear design.

What the study of this major is like:

The fashion and apparel design major is generally hands-on, immersing you in a working environment from day one. From sketching to pattern making, you explore the many areas of design, under the instruction of industry professionals.

In your lower-level courses, you are introduced to figure-sketching techniques and to pattern drafting. In later courses, you explore such topics as color and design theory; textiles; and industry practices, including fashion groups, storyboards, and the development of collections. In computer-aided design (CAD) work, you learn how to design garments and construct patterns using techniques that are widespread throughout the industry. Most programs require a capstone course in which you develop a complete collection. This is the final course you take, and it prepares you to begin interviewing for jobs. You should leave the program with a comprehensive portfolio and real-world experience.

Expect to work hard; majors sometimes have to pull all-nighters to complete their projects. Fashion and apparel design is a highly technical industry that requires attention to detail and patience.

Measurements must be exact, sketches must be proportional, and patterns must be cut precisely. Majors often find that the technical requirements are the most challenging. But programs are developed with these challenges in mind, and you generally have step-by-step guidance.

You will find many two-year fashion design programs leading to an associate degree, and some four-year programs leading to a bachelor's degree. The fashion design curriculum is similar in the two programs, but the first two years of B.A. programs provide a broad liberal arts background.

Programs can also be categorized by type of approach: training-based and theory-based. Elements of both types are essential for success in the industry. In the training approach, you have more opportunity to practice the skills you study in the classroom. As you construct garments from start to finish, you absorb the nuances of design, discover and solve problems, and perfect your technique. A theory-based education, in contrast, gives you a broader understanding of the industry as a whole—its history and its future.

Other majors you might like:

Commercial/advertising art
Fashion merchandising
Marketing
Fiber/textile arts
Advertising
Interior design
Metal/jewelry arts
Theater design and technology
Anthropology
Family and consumer sciences
Apparel/textile marketing
Entrepreneurial studies

Questions to ask colleges:

What ties does the college have to the fashion industry? Are the instructors industry professionals?

Does the college use the latest industry technology? How accessible are computers, and design and production facilities, after class?

If this is a four-year bachelor's degree program, are students admitted into the major at the outset, or do they have to meet requirements (such as a portfolio or high academic standing) at the end of the second year in order to continue?

Career options and trends:

Designer or assistant designer; pattern maker; grader; visual merchandiser; textile designer; technical designer; illustrator; stylist; costume designer.

As the fashion industry incorporates computer technology into every aspect of design, traditional ways of creating garments are being revolutionized. Majors in fashion should become proficient in as many of the software programs used in the fashion industry as possible. Since two-thirds of salaried fashion designers work in either New York or California, a willingness to relocate may be necessary.

As in all design fields, fashion majors face a lot of competition. Demand for designers should remain strong, however, because style-conscious consumers will always want something new to wear.

For more info:

Fashion Group International
8 W. 40th St., 7th Floor
New York, NY 10018
(212) 302-5511
www.fgi.org

Fine/studio arts

Also known as:
Visual arts

What it's about:
Students majoring in the fine and studio arts learn to create images, objects, and environments using a variety of techniques and media. As you work on a number of structured assignments and independent studio projects, you sharpen your visual understanding and enhance your critical-thinking skills. Most likely, you will begin with an introduction to design and then choose a medium, such as photography or ceramics, for focused study.

Is this for you?
You might like this major if you also like: handicrafts, especially sewing, woodworking, model building, or pottery; riddles and metaphors; cooking; museums and galleries; drawing and painting; manipulating digital images; working independently; taking risks.

Consider this major if you are good at: attention to detail; creativity; critical reading/thinking; relational thinking; research; spatial thinking/analysis *...or have...* manual dexterity; patience; persistence; verbal skills.

Recommended high school prep:
English 4, math 2, lab science 2, social studies 4, and a foreign language 3. If possible, take a variety of visual and performing arts classes, including as many object- and figure-drawing classes as you can. Some colleges will require a portfolio of your artwork for admission.

Did you know...
...that you don't need to think of yourself as "artistic" or "really creative" to major in art? Art can be taught; it need not be regarded as a mysterious gift that only a few possess. To be successful in this major, you should have a strong interest in studio art and a commitment to learning.

...that this major is work-intensive, with plenty of outside projects? Studio projects take more time to complete than regular academic assignments. To do well, you need to be disciplined, patient, attentive to detail, and good at managing your time.

Typical courses in this major:
Two- or three-dimensional basic design
Drawing
Art history
Painting
Jewelry
Illustration
Sculpture
Book arts
Digital imaging
Printmaking
Graphic design
Ceramics
Industrial design
Textile and fiber arts
Photography
Art theory

Concentrations:
In college: drawing; sculpture; printmaking; graphic design; illustration; painting; photography; book arts; textile and fiber arts; ceramics; animation; glass blowing; architecture; jewelry and metalsmithing; industrial design; film and video.

If you go on to grad school: historic preservation; performance art; art conservation; environmental works; art history; museum studies; landscape architecture; time-based media; city planning; urban design.

What the study of this major is like:
Art classes in this major take place in studios outfitted with the equipment you'll need for a particular medium, such as charcoal drawing or woodworking. Your instructors are practicing, exhibiting artists and designers. In most programs, a

basic design course is a prerequisite for upper-level courses. You will probably be required to take a series of art history courses as well, although some colleges emphasize art history more than others. By designing and producing artworks of your own and by studying the work of others, you learn to understand the ideas, values, motives, and vocabulary of artists, and you develop an appreciation of the way art was, and is, created and the important social and cultural role it plays.

Art schools offer a Bachelor of Fine Arts degree, while liberal arts colleges usually offer a Bachelor of Arts. Both degrees have their strengths. A B.F.A. program allows you to become immersed in art. Classes tend to be three or four hours long. After completing foundation courses in your first two years, you focus on your concentration (for example, painting, sculpture) for two or three years before graduating. In contrast, a B.A. program allows you to maintain a focus on art but also explore other serious interests—which are likely to serve as inspiration for the images and objects you will create. B.A. classes are generally shorter, around two hours. When you graduate, you might have done only one or two years of independent work (less than in the B.F.A. program), but you have benefited from an exposure to a multitude of issues and ideas.

Not all studio programs offer the same choices of media. Even in a single medium like painting, the philosophy of programs can differ greatly. Some colleges stress conceptual or contemporary references to shape the curriculum. Others might emphasize the traditional materials and techniques. It may be useful to review images of student and faculty work, which are often available on a college's Web site.

As a major, you balance structured, in-class assignments with independent, outside work. Instead of term papers and exams, you receive feedback through individual and group critiques and portfolio reviews, in which you learn to take and give criticism. You are encouraged to read art magazines and be aware of current exhibitions in galleries and museums. A good student learns to work steadily throughout the semester. In the studio,

don't expect to cram to make up for lost time; creativity cannot be rushed. You spend long hours and many late nights working. In effect, the studio becomes your second home and part of your social life.

While in the program, you can seek employment in galleries, studio apprenticeships to artists, and internships in architecture firms or museums. Both the B.A. and B.F.A. prepare you for continuing work toward a Master of Arts or Master of Fine Arts. The major also provides preparation for a fulfilling career as a practicing artist or commercial designer.

Other majors you might like:
Arts management
Museum studies
Medical illustrating
Film/cinema studies
Theater design and technology
Architecture
Art therapy
Drafting and design technology
Commercial/advertising art
Graphic design
Classics
Medieval and Renaissance studies

Questions to ask colleges:
How crowded are the studios? How late are they open? What security is offered for late-night work? Is there an accessible collection of art (on slides or elsewhere)? How extensive is the library's collection of art and art history books? The availability and condition of resources and facilities often reflect the institution's commitment to teaching the arts.

How many students go on to graduate school or related professional opportunities? Art is highly competitive, and the number of students who continue on in the field may point to the seriousness and success of the program.

Career options and trends:
Art teacher*; commercial artist; museum curator; architect; gallery preparator*; art therapist; studio artist; art editor or critic; art restorer/conservator; art director or administrator*.

A master's degree is generally required for employment in museums and galleries, and a Ph.D. (usually in art history) is required for positions as museum curators and directors. A master's in art education is the usual requirement for teaching in high school, and a master of fine arts (M.F.A.) for teaching at the college level. Art restoration and conservation usually requires specialized training and knowledge of chemistry.

Making a living solely from producing art is extremely difficult; most working artists have a sideline. One source of employment is the growing number of city and county arts councils that need staff for a variety of positions, including management and teaching; art therapy is also a growing field, but it requires further specialized education.

The interface between computers and art is the most important trend, for both creating art and teaching art. Illustrators are especially impacted by technology, with outsourcing jobs overseas a growing trend.

Insider's viewpoint:

"Majoring in visual arts was never an easy way out. I spent more time and effort on my painting projects than some people in premed spent studying. And in the end, I believe I learned more than any academic major could have taught me: how to see the world I live in and express it to others."

—James, class of 2002, Fordham University

For more info:

College Art Association (CAA)
275 Seventh Ave.
New York, NY 10001
(212) 691-1051
www.collegeart.org

Graphic design

What it's about:

The graphic design major is about visual communication—how it is created and how it is perceived. Graphic designers plan and create print, film, and electronic communications composed of images and typography; their work ranges from books to multimedia programs, CD covers to film titles, logos to Web sites.

Is this for you?

You might like this major if you also like: books, magazines, and comics; graphic novels; coming up with practical solutions; working on the school newspaper, yearbook, or literary and arts magazines; drawing; color; working with different types of people; computers; craftsmanship.

Consider this major if you are good at: Communicating; attention to detail; creativity; critical reading/thinking; organizing; persuading/influencing; spatial thinking/analysis *...or have...* curiosity; imagination; patience; writing skills.

Recommended high school prep:

English 4, math 3, lab science 3, social studies 3, and a foreign language 2–3. Many colleges require a portfolio (examples of your work), and your high school art classes can help you prepare one. Many colleges also offer summer or Saturday design camps, where you can develop your portfolio and get a taste of college-level instruction in design.

Did you know...

...that historically, the graphic design profession arose from the typesetting and printing trades? Practitioners came into the field through apprenticeships, without a formal education in design. Today, the complexity of contemporary communications requires graphic designers to have a deeper knowledge of how visual information works.

...that this major is about design more than computers? While graphic designers use computers extensively, knowledge of computers and software applications is not the same as knowledge of design.

Typical courses in this major:

Design analysis and theory
Typography
2-D and 3-D graphics
Factors of human perception
Packaging and display
Technical and professional writing
Drawing and illustration
Photography
Web page design
History of visual communications
Text and images
Identity and symbols
Digital imagery
Multimedia design
Motion graphics
Advertising design

Concentrations:

Advertising; multimedia; computer graphics; motion graphics (film titles and animation); Web design; identity or symbol design; information design (charts and graphs); publications; packaging; environmental graphics (signs and signage systems).

What the study of this major is like:

Graphic design programs vary widely from college to college, and a course title in a catalog does not necessarily describe the course content. But regardless of content distribution or course names, the graphic design major should prepare you to solve design problems; understand audiences; handle tools and technology (including offset printing, photography, and interactive media); apply concepts such as visual organization, information hierarchy, symbolic representation, and aesthetics; understand design history, theory, and criticism from a variety of perspectives (including art history, linguistics, and communication and information theory); and know basic business practices (such as organizing design projects and working productively with teams).

If you expect to go into advertising, you should enroll in a program that includes additional course work in marketing, audience and/or user evaluation, art direction, copywriting, and communications theory. If you want to work in time-based or interactive media, select programs with additional courses in storyboarding, computer scripting, sound editing, and interface design. For a career in planning and strategy development, seek programs that teach team problem solving; systems analysis; writing for business; and the application of management, communications, and information theories.

As a graphic design major, you learn primarily by completing hands-on projects in classes of 15–25 students. Design majors work long hours and must be self-motivated. Assignments are usually open-ended, with many right answers; they require you to think through different approaches and a variety of solutions. Your work is then evaluated by your classmates and instructors, based on how well you fulfilled the requirement of the assignment and on whether you showed an understanding of the audience and the context for which the item was intended. This approach is frequently used in all design and studio courses, and you have to learn not to take the criticism personally.

Exhibitions, auctions of visual work, costume balls, and design competitions are extracurricular activities in most colleges. Most design programs have some affiliation with the graphic design profession through clubs, portfolio reviews, field trips, internships, sponsored projects, or conferences. Generally, design programs have strong networks of graduates who can help you make the transition from college to work.

According to the accreditation requirements of the National Association of Schools of Art and Design, a Bachelor of Fine Arts degree in graphic design requires at least 65 percent of your courses to be studio art and design instruction, with at least 25 percent of those courses to be specifically related to graphic design. The B.F.A. is considered to be the professional degree for graphic design practice. In Bachelor of Arts or Bachelor of Science programs (B.A., B.S.), you will find a higher percentage of general education/liberal arts courses, and a smaller percentage of graphic design courses as part of the total art and design requirements. Two-year associate degree programs prepare you for technical support positions in the field and for transfer to four-year programs in design.

Other majors you might like:
Animation
Computer graphics
Information systems
Digital media
Drafting and design technology
Illustration
Industrial design
Communications
Advertising
Desktop publishing
Web page/multimedia design
Instructional media

Questions to ask colleges:
What studio, computer resources, and lab facilities are provided and how many hours do students have access to them? Are there any lab fees?

Is there a graphic design slide collection? What other library resources support graphic design majors?

Do students have to buy their own computer equipment? Does the college provide technical assistance for student-owned computers and/or software? Are printers, scanners, digital cameras, video and sound equipment, or other peripherals available for student use?

Career options and trends:
Art director*; graphic designer in design group or studio*; interactive/multimedia designer*; Web designer*; illustrator; exhibition designer; advertising agent; package designer; design strategist/planner; print production pre-press designer.

In a knowledge-based economy, those who make information comprehensible are valued. Success in the field of graphic design depends on talent, education, and work ethic, and students who graduate at the top of their class find jobs. Rapid technological change has created specializations in the field; as a result, specialists are in demand and more graphic designers are likely to obtain a graduate degree.

Increasingly, basic layout and design work is being outsourced to design firms overseas. Higher-level graphic design jobs that focus on "strategic design"—developing communication strategies for clients and firms—require proximity and will remain in the United States. Graphic designers with skills in Web site design and animation will have the best opportunities, as will those with knowledge or experience in marketing and business.

For more info:
American Institute of Graphic Arts (AIGA)
164 Fifth Ave.
New York, NY 10010
(212) 807-1990
www.aiga.org

The National Association of Schools of Art and
    Design (NASAD)
11250 Roger Bacon Drive
Suite 21
Reston, VA 20190-5248
(703) 437-0700
www.arts-accredit.org

Interior design

What it's about:

This major provides academic preparation for professional practice as an interior designer. You learn how to create indoor environments that are both beautiful and functional: they are intended to improve the quality of life, increase productivity, and protect the health and safety of the public.

Is this for you?

You might like this major if you also like: tours of museums and historical buildings; art; theater; math; debate; community service; working with people; making things; learning about different cultures; travel.

Consider this major if you are good at: attention to detail; creativity; critical reading/thinking; math; organizing; research; spatial thinking/analysis; teamwork *...or have...* initiative; verbal skills.

Recommended high school prep:

English 4, math 3, lab science 3, social studies 3, and a foreign language 2–3. Art and art history courses, if offered, are highly recommended. A course in computer-aided design (CAD) would be good but it is not a prerequisite. Taking part in theater or music activities can teach you disciplines and skills used by successful interior design students.

Did you know...

...that there is a difference between interior design and interior decorating? While both fields are concerned with aesthetics, decorators work only with surface adornment; they work with paint, fabric, furnishings, lighting, and other materials. Interior designers are professional space planners, who ensure that interiors meet code requirements and the practical, technical, and functional needs of a wide range of clients—commercial, industrial, and residential—in such facilities as hospitals, schools, hotels, and apartment complexes.

...that interior design is subject to government regulation? Almost half the states and the District of Columbia require interior designers to be licensed or registered after passing the National Council for Interior Design's qualification examination.

Typical courses in this major:

Principles of interior design
History of interiors and decorative arts
Drawing and design in two and three dimensions
Computer-aided design
Interior materials and finishes
Construction documents and specifications
Codes, public health, and safety
Residential interiors
Furniture design
Textiles
Acoustics and interior design
Lighting design and building systems
Environmental control systems
Interiors for special populations
Professional practice
Portfolio preparation

Concentrations:

In college: lighting design; furniture design; exhibition design; acoustics; fabric design.

If you go on to grad school: historic preservation; workplace design; institutional facilities; interior environmental health; construction management.

What the study of this major is like:

Interior design majors study all aspects of the built environment: scale, proportion, arrangement, light sources, acoustics, temperature, textures, colors, and materials. Because interior design projects are complex, you learn to employ a systematic process; you balance the client's needs and resources, on the one hand, with the goal of creating safe, attractive, and practical interiors, on the other.

To design successful interior environments, you must be trained in building construction, materials

549

specification, lighting techniques, technical drawing, and business practices. You learn to analyze problem areas; develop detailed design solutions; and organize and oversee the project to completion. You must be familiar with building codes and fire regulations. And because interior designers usually function as members of a team rather than as individual designers, you need to be able to work well with other professionals.

Programs usually consist of a series of design courses that culminate in a senior thesis. Generally, studio courses use a hands-on approach: the professor presents a problem and you work on a solution, discussing and evaluating your progress with the instructor. As you advance through the program, you will be expected to demonstrate increasing skill in tackling such problems.

Undergraduate majors receive a generalized education in interior design. Nevertheless, some programs may emphasize architecture or environmental design, whereas others stress fine arts or family and consumer science. Programs with an architectural focus generally concentrate on three-dimensional design, construction practices, and large-scale commercial projects. These programs tend to prepare you for work in large architectural and interior design firms. Programs that concentrate on fine arts or family and consumer sciences usually focus on the decorative aspects of the field—fixtures and furniture, selection and layout, and coordination of finishes. Also some programs feature residential design, while others highlight commercial and/or institutional design. However, standards ensure that all accredited programs prepare you for entry-level professional work in either residential or commercial/institutional design.

Other majors you might like:
Housing and human environments
Environmental design
Industrial design
Architectural history/criticism
Furniture design/manufacturing
Fashion and apparel design
Psychology
Anthropology
Theater design and technology
Drafting and design technology

Hotel/motel administration/management
Art history

Questions to ask colleges:
Is the program accredited by the Foundation of Interior Design Education and Research (FIDER)? Most states that license interior designers require graduation from a FIDER-accredited program.

Are students given their own desks in the studio for the entire semester? "Cold studios" are those in which students are given work spaces for the term; "hot studios" are more like typical classrooms with drawing tables. Colleges with cold studios generally have stronger design programs.

Are the computer laboratories accessible most hours of the day? Do they provide access plotters and printers? Gaining proficiency in computer-aided design applications is essential.

Career options and trends:
Interior designer*; furniture designer; lighting designer; facilities manager; real estate broker; trade show exhibit designer; product representative.

Interior designers work for interior design firms, architectural firms, department and home furnishing stores, theme parks and resorts, and hotel and restaurant chains. Some designers do freelance work full-time, part-time, or in addition to a salaried job. Beginning designers usually receive on-the-job training and normally need one to three years of apprenticeship before they advance to higher-level positions.

Ergonomics and "green design" are trends to watch. Ergonomic design is important for an aging population and workplace safety, and concerns for environmental quality and the needs of people with allergies and asthma are driving demand for green design.

For more info:
American Society of Interior Designers (ASID)
608 Massachusetts Ave., N.E.
Washington, DC 20002-6006
(202) 546-3480
www.asid.org

Music, general

What it's about:

This liberal arts major is for those who want a generalist approach, rather than a career-specific orientation, to the subject. You study music from various perspectives: the historical development of musical styles; ear training and musicianship; the structures and theory of music; composition; music technologies; performance instruction; and music teaching.

Is this for you?

You might like this major if you also like: playing, listening, and learning about music, of course; math; travel; working independently as well as in groups; using computers. Mere enjoyment of music is not enough for success in this major —you must have a real commitment and well-developed musical skills.

Consider this major if you are good at: attention to detail; concentration; creativity; critical reading/thinking; memorizing; quantitative analysis; spatial thinking/analysis ...*or have...* patience; perseverance; physical stamina; self-discipline; verbal skills.

Recommended high school prep:

English 4, math 3, lab science 3, social studies 3, music 4, and a foreign language 3. Courses in music theory, music history, individual lessons on an instrument or in voice, and participation in performance ensembles (orchestra, band, jazz, chamber music) are highly recommended, whether available inside or outside high school. No matter what instrument you play or even if you don't intend to perform, all college music majors are expected to have basic knowledge of piano (keyboard). Even six months of lessons will help—a year is better.

Did you know...

...that this major isn't just about playing music? In some ways it is more demanding than many other majors, because you have to be both academic and musical.

Typical courses in this major:

Music history
Ethnomusicology
Music theory
Ear training and/or musicianship
Composition
Conducting
Orchestration
Keyboard competence
Sight singing
Lyric diction
Chamber ensemble
Wind ensemble
Chorus
Tonal counterpoint
Computer and electronic music
Jazz studies

Concentrations:

History or musicology; ethnomusicology; performance; conducting; theory; composition; music education.

What the study of this major is like:

Most music programs require at least four courses in music history, in which you study the musical styles and genres of different periods, as well as the most important composers. You may do advanced work in the music of a period or of a composer; the extent of change in music from one period to the next; and the connection between music and the society in which it was created. More and more colleges are teaching music produced outside Europe and North America—for example, traditional Chinese music and music of the West African coast.

Music theory courses assume that you are familiar with the fundamentals of music (rhythmic and pitch notation, key signatures, and scales). In a minimum of four theory courses, you learn the principles of four-part music. You then practice these principles in weekly writing exercises. Theory courses also teach methods of analyzing music in depth. You may do advanced work in counterpoint, analysis, or the history of music theory; or begin work in composition. In composition courses, you may use computer programs to synthesize music electronically.

The music major almost always includes work in basic musicianship—piano, sight singing, score reading, keyboard harmony, and melodic and harmonic dictation. All programs provide you with opportunities to perform in ensembles, and many require you to do so. Individual voice and instrumental lessons, as well as conducting courses, are available at many colleges. Some programs offer a music performance degree, which involves much more performance work (for example, in voice, violin, trumpet, or percussion). These programs often lead to the Bachelor of Music degree rather than to a liberal arts degree with a music major.

Instruction style may vary according to the aspect of music you are studying. Your courses may be research-oriented or lab-oriented, or you may work mostly one-on-one with your professors. The music major can be demanding, because it requires you to take numerous courses and spend many hours studying and rehearsing, both in and out of the classroom. But majors generally have a strong sense of community and of working toward a common goal. Because colleges sponsor recitals and concerts by faculty members and guest artists, students frequently meet and talk extensively with professional performers and also participate in the management of these concerts. Many colleges offer music majors the opportunity to present their own recitals when they are in their fourth year.

Colleges vary widely in their approach to the study of music. Some schools are conservatories that emphasize performance and composition. Other colleges focus on the historical and theoretical study of music. Still others seek a balance between practice and theory.

Other majors you might like:
Music management
Sacred music
Music history/literature
Music teacher education
Music therapy

Radio and television
Recording arts
Musical instrument fabrication/repair
Computer science
Electrical and communications engineering
Mathematics
Digital media

Questions to ask colleges:
Are auditions required for admission into or placement in the major? In many programs, candidates must be able to sing in tune and also take a written music exam.

What practice facilities are available and during what hours? Is digital recording equipment available?

What are the performance opportunities? What kinds of ensembles are available?

To what extent is non-Western music taught?

Career options and trends:
Professional or studio musician; composer; music teacher; recording engineer or mixer; art administrator; music publishing editor; film music editor; music therapist; music store manager; music software developer.

To become a music therapist or to teach in public schools, you must obtain certification and meet specific education requirements.

A general music major does not directly lead to careers in the profession, but like all liberal arts majors, it provides a broad, flexible foundation for a variety of occupations or for graduate school. Students at the top of their class who are willing to relocate may obtain music-related jobs after graduation, but the music industry is very competitive.

For more info:
College Music Society (CMS)
312 East Pine St.
Missoula, MT 59802
(406) 721-9616
www.music.org

Music management

What it's about:

This major provides a broad understanding of the fields of music and management. You take courses in music history, theory, and performance. In addition, you explore the methods, concepts, and principles of management, with specific focus on the music business.

Is this for you?

You might like this major if you also like: starting or running a business venture; managing or performing in a band; organizing or leading a club or group activity; solving problems; taking risks; competing; sports; helping others to succeed.

Consider this major if you are good at: attention to detail; critical reading/thinking; leadership; organizing; persuading/influencing; teamwork *...or have...* initiative; verbal skills; writing skills.

Recommended high school prep:

English 4, math 3, lab science 3, social studies 3, music 3–4, and a foreign language 3. If they are available, these are also recommended: statistics, computer applications, economics, accounting, business, psychology, and participation in music performance such as band or orchestra.

Typical courses in this major:

Introduction to the music business
Music publishing and copyright law
Recording and broadcast industries
Contracts and other legal issues
Accounting
Economics
Introduction to marketing
Fundamentals of management
Computer applications
Music history
Basic music theory and ear training
International marketing
Concert and tour promotion
Business statistics
Music technology
Recording techniques

Concentrations:

In college: recording and studio production techniques; marketing and merchandising; arts management.

If you go on to grad school: international marketing.

What the study of this major is like:

The music management major prepares you to enter the music business world. You learn about issues such as patronage, copyright laws, and musicians' union regulations, as well as fund-raising, grant-proposal writing, and advertising techniques.

There are two main approaches to the music management major. Some colleges focus on business or management, expecting you to learn only a minimal amount about music. In these programs, you generally take a core of courses that teach methods, concepts, and principles of music management and business. A number of other programs have strong offerings in music, with only a smattering of business and management courses. Industry experts have come to demand a greater balance between the two aspects of the major. Ideally, you should choose a program that provides maximum opportunities to study both music and business/management.

For a comprehensive or music-oriented program, you may be asked to demonstrate (through an audition) the ability to play an instrument or sing, and to take a music theory placement examination. To prepare yourself, you'll need some previous music training. Such colleges also require you to enroll in a sequence of music history and theory courses, in addition to the business and management courses. In all programs, you must participate in activities promoting music and art on campus and in the surrounding community (such as campus concerts and local civic organizations) to test out the concepts and strategies you study in class. Additionally, most colleges expect you to take 30–40 percent of your total course work in humanities, mathematics, and the sciences, to ensure that you receive a well-rounded education.

Upper-level courses often require at least two internships at off-campus establishments. These internships, often in cooperation with recording studios, music publishing houses, arts organizations, symphony orchestras, or television studios, provide a unique way for you to explore the professional field under the guidance of college mentors. The biggest challenge most students encounter involves time management—balancing the development of academic skills with practical fieldwork. You also need to cultivate good "people skills."

Other majors you might like:
Radio and television
Recording arts
Musicology/ethnomusicology
Jazz studies
Public relations
Business administration and management
Hospitality administration and management
Web/multimedia management
Information systems
Theater arts management
Music history/literature
Entrepreneurial studies

Questions to ask colleges:
Are there opportunities on campus to gain experience in promoting concerts and other arts events?

Does the college have a recording studio, or a radio and/or television station, and opportunities to develop skills in audio and video work?

What connections do the faculty members and the department have with the music industry?

Career options and trends:
Business manager*; recording industry promoter or producer*; orchestra manager; booking agent; artist representative or manager; music publishing executive or editor*; television and radio promoter*;

A&R (artist and repertoire) administrator or coordinator; studio production manager; entertainment lawyer.

The field is becoming highly international, so knowledge of a foreign language (such as Spanish, French, or Japanese) is a big plus. Also, knowledge of digital technology and intellectual property rights is essential. As in all art-related fields, there is plenty of competition, but the business end of music is varied enough to provide greater opportunity. Internship experience, which is expected of job applicants in all music-related businesses, is an invaluable way to develop networking contacts and, sometimes, to receive job offers.

For more info:
American Society of Composers, Authors, and
　　Publishers (ASCAP)
One Lincoln Plaza
New York, NY 10023
(212) 621-6000
www.ascap.com

American Federation of Musicians
1501 Broadway
Suite 600
New York City, NY 10036
(212) 869-1330
www.afm.org

Music performance

Also known as:

Applied music

What it's about:

The music performance major allows you to achieve a high level of technical proficiency and musical sensitivity. You are trained to play a musical instrument or to sing professionally, both as a solo and ensemble performer.

Is this for you?

You might like this major if you also like: communicating through music; listening to music; performing outside school; reading music biographies. If you have strong encouragement from your music teachers, confidence in your abilities, and a commitment to succeed, you might consider this major.

Consider this major if you are good at: attention to detail; creativity; math; memorizing; organizing; teamwork *...or have...* aural skills; physical stamina; self-discipline.

Recommended high school prep:

English 4, math 3-4, lab science 3, social studies 3, music 3-4, and a foreign language 2-3. While not required, music courses covering large ensembles, small ensembles, solo performance, music theory, and music history are recommended. Regardless of your specific training (voice or instrument), you will be expected to have basic knowledge of the piano keyboard.

Did you know...

...that most auditions require you to sing? No matter what your instrument, you are expected to be able to use your voice intelligently and in tune.

Typical courses in this major:

Music theory
Aural skills
Music history
Individual instruction
Computer and/or electronic music
Vocal diction
Percussion
Strings
Brass
Woodwinds
Introduction to music literature
Accompanying
Instrumental ensemble
Vocal ensemble
Fundamentals of conducting
Pedagogy of the piano/voice/etc.

Concentrations:

Voice; piano; organ; individual orchestra or band instruments; jazz studies; early music; instrumental pedagogy; conducting.

What the study of this major is like:

Most music performance majors have already taken part in musical activities in high school, except perhaps for singers, whose "instruments" are not available until their voices mature. Most programs test new students to determine their background and skills. Tests may include an audition and both a written and an oral exam. If you lack necessary skills, you may have to enroll in catch-up courses.

In addition to performance work and related instruction, the major includes core courses in music theory, literature, and history. Traditionally, you attend weekly private lessons in your chosen instrument (or in voice) with your concentration instructor. You also participate in master classes, studio recitals, and solo recitals. Instrumentalists take part in chamber music coaching and performances; vocalists take part in opera coaching, workshops, and performances; and all students participate in rehearsals and large-ensemble performances.

In music theory and aural skills courses, you study harmony, rhythm, counterpoint, sight singing, ear training, melodic and harmonic dictation, improvisation, and analysis of musical structure. Mastering theory and aural skills helps you understand the way a piece of music is put together. In music history and literature courses, you will survey music through the ages and explore books and documents related to your concentration. Other courses may cover repertoire, music education, conducting, composition, and jazz studies.

Voice concentrates may need to take Italian, German, Russian, and/or French, the languages of many operas. Nonpiano concentrates must take an introduction to keyboard harmony. And almost all performance programs require you to do 25–50 percent of your course work in the liberal arts. Therefore, you must come to college with the same study skills, writing skills, and academic background as liberal arts majors.

For performance majors, time is precious; large blocks of it (besides the hours you spend in classes and studying) must be set aside for solitary practice. When you are not practicing and studying, you often perform both on and off campus and participate in competitions—leaving you very little free time. Your social life will probably center on a small group of friends who share your goals and serve as a support group.

Among various colleges, striking differences may exist in mission and atmosphere. For example, a single-purpose conservatory that enrolls top students will differ significantly from a four-year liberal arts college. Professionally oriented performance schools sometimes foster intense competition. Whereas some students thrive in such an environment, others prefer a less intense, more nurturing educational setting. You should examine your options carefully to find the right fit.

Other majors you might like:
Music management
Sacred music
Music theory and composition
Music teacher education
Music therapy
Radio and television
Recording arts
Jazz studies

Computer science
Electrical and communications engineering
Mathematics
Voice/opera

Questions to ask colleges:
What is the ratio of students to practice rooms?

How many hours of private instruction do students receive each week in their major? Can incoming students meet with the instructor to whom they will be assigned?

How will this program and the faculty members help undergraduates make the transition from student to professional life?

Career options and trends:
Orchestral musician; solo musician; ensemble musician (string quartet, jazz trio, etc.); church musician; orchestra or opera company manager; music technician/producer; music teacher (private); music teacher (public school or college); music therapist.

Performing arts are risky career choices, because they are competitive and compensation for artists is notoriously low. The recording industry is reporting a downturn in sales and earnings, and symphony orchestras and opera companies are facing decreased contributions, endowment income, and ticket sales.

Longer term, the pendulum will swing the other way and conditions should improve all around. All signs point to a future with plenty of audience for the work of performers. Teaching music shows promise, as there has been no falloff in the desire to study music. The American String Teachers Association (ASTA) projects a need for 5,000 string teachers over the next several years.

For more info:
College Music Society (CMS)
312 East Pine St.
Missoula, MT 59802
(406) 721-9616
www.music.org

National Association of Schools of Music
http://nasm.arts-accredit.org

Music theory and composition

What it's about:

This major consists of two related areas of study—music theory is the study of the materials, processes, and structures of music; music composition is the art of writing music. In some institutions, the two are combined into a single major; in other institutions, they are separate.

Is this for you?

You might like this major if you also like: computer science; psychology; mathematics; audio recording; languages; art; drama.

Consider this major if you are good at: attention to detail; creativity; critical reading/thinking; organizing; quantitative analysis ...*or have...* aural perception; initiative; patience; writing skills.

Recommended high school prep:

English 4, math 3–4, lab science 3, social studies 3, and a foreign language 2–3. Most colleges do not require or recommend any specific music courses at the high school level. But you must have a thorough knowledge of the fundamentals (intervals, scales, chords in treble and bass clef; simple rhythmic and metric notation) and skill in basic ear training (intervals, scales, triads; dictation of simple rhythmic, melodic, and harmonic examples). An ability to play a keyboard instrument is recommended. Courses that cover math, psychology, and computer science can be good background for music theory.

Typical courses in this major:

Aural skills
Music history
Schenkerian analysis
Analysis of twentieth-century music
Atonal music
Operatic literature
Symphonic literature
Composition seminar
Psychology of music
Music technology
Diction and song literature
Counterpoint
Piano pedagogy
Orchestration
Computer-assisted music notation
Senior thesis project

Concentrations:

Generally, none available.

What the study of this major is like:

As a music theory and composition major, you learn to understand and describe the forces that shape music. The discipline of music theory can be compared with subjects such as linguistics and psychology: you explore the principles that help determine the results, whether in music or in human behavior and language. Studying music composition is similar to studying creative writing: you combine knowledge of the principles and techniques with imagination to produce a work of art.

In beginning theory courses, you will read works on the topic by leading scholars (for example, Rameau, Schenker, Forte). When you first take composition, you may study under the guidance of a master teacher, who sets tasks or goals for you and then analyzes your work and suggests possible improvements. For both theory and music composition, you typically examine the literature—including scholarly writings and original scores—and enhance your musical skills. Advanced theory courses teach you how to formulate and test your own ideas through research; advanced composition courses usually offer you more opportunities for creative expression.

Musical skills courses include ear training and sight singing, and training in voice or in your instrument. Like all music majors, you will participate in a student ensemble, band, choir, or other group. You cannot become a good theorist or composer without also becoming a good musician.

Although some programs combine music theory and composition in a single major, other programs address them separately. But differences among individual professors of music theory and of composition are usually more significant than differences among programs. To figure out which program is probably best for you, you should talk to professors about their teaching style and expectations.

Other majors you might like:
Music performance
Jazz studies
Music history/literature
Musicology/ethnomusicology
Music management
Creative writing
Mathematics
Linguistics
Computer science
Conducting

Questions to ask colleges:
Is the program accredited by the National Association of Schools of Music?

What opportunities does the program offer in music pedagogy?

Is electronic or computer music part of the curriculum?

Are there any audition requirements?

Career options and trends:
A bachelor's degree in this major does not prepare students for specific careers, except possibly as a private teacher, performer, or composer. Teaching in elementary, middle, and high school requires a music education degree and state certification, and teaching at the college level usually requires a doctorate degree.

For more info:
College Music Society (CMS)
312 East Pine St.
Missoula, MT 59802
(406) 721-9616
www.music.org

Society for Music Theory
University of Chicago
1010 East 59th St.
Chicago, IL 60637
(773) 834-3821
www.societymusictheory.org

Photography

What it's about:

The major in photography is for students interested in the art of communicating information, ideas, moods, and feelings through photographic images. You gain a broad background in both the technical and the aesthetic aspects of photography.

Is this for you?

You might like this major if you also like: nature studies; art and art classes; science and technology; working with equipment and chemicals; the school newspaper, yearbook, or photography club; working independently.

Consider this major if you are good at: attention to detail; creativity; organizing; spatial thinking/analysis; visualizing ideas or images *...or have...* initiative; mechanical facility; patience; verbal skills; writing skills.

Recommended high school prep:

English 4, math 3, lab science 3 (including chemistry and physics), social studies 3, visual arts 3–4, and a foreign language 2–3. If available, a journalism course would be helpful, and computer applications courses are recommended.

Did you know...

...that often the same type of preparatory courses are required for photography as for other art disciplines—drawing, two-dimensional and three-dimensional design, and color theory?

Typical courses in this major:

Elementary photography
History of photography
Two-dimensional design
Black-and-white photography
Color photography
Digital photography
Materials and processes
Commercial and/or industrial photography
Portraiture
Photo editing
Studio photography
Photojournalism
Advanced photographic techniques
Lighting techniques
Biomedical and forensic practicum
Portfolio preparation

Concentrations:

In college: fine art photography; digital imaging; portraiture; biomedical photographic illustration; commercial photography; fashion photography; photojournalism.

If you go on to grad school: most graduate photography programs concentrate on fine art applications, and many are self-directed.

What the study of this major is like:

As a photography major, you begin by exploring the fundamentals of design, form, color, and composition. You learn about the nature of light and analyze how three-dimensional space is changed into two-dimensional images. In an introductory course, you study camera operation and controls (such as focus, shutter speed, and aperture setting) and their effects on photographic images; you also learn about types of cameras: digital, 35 mm, medium format, and large format field cameras that produce single negatives. You discuss contemporary issues in photography, as well as photographic history. Critiques (in which you evaluate the strengths and weaknesses of a photograph) are an essential part of your learning process.

In lower-level photography courses, your assignments center on depicting specific ideas or situations. As you progress through the major, you concentrate more on your own ideas of what to depict. You create portfolios (a group of photographs on a theme) and study many approaches to photography, such as studio techniques, color, digital applications, and alternative processes. Taking courses in other arts, such as drawing, sculpture, and painting, can enrich your work. If you are interested in documentary photography or photojournalism, you might take courses in journalism, English, and anthropology. Throughout your studies, you evaluate your strengths and interests in relation to a possible career. A final portfolio that showcases your work is the capstone to almost every degree program.

Most photography programs try to balance the technical and the creative aspects of the art. Programs often specialize in one or two areas of photography; fine arts and journalism are the most common. (Such courses may also be offered in conjunction with broader art or journalism programs.)

The biggest issue facing photography programs is the tension between traditional, "wet" darkroom practice and digital processes, so be aware of the technical practices of the programs you consider. Also, some colleges emphasize the practical, commercial aspects of photography; these programs train you to concentrate on meeting the demands of clients. Other programs, which are based in the fine arts, encourage you to express your personal point of view. Degree programs can range from two-year associate degrees to four-year Bachelor of Arts, Bachelor of Science, or Bachelor of Fine Arts degrees, each with its own emphasis.

Other majors you might like:
Cinematography and film/video production
Journalism
Graphic design
Advertising
Physics
Fashion merchandising
Entrepreneurial studies
Photographic/film/video technology
Radiologic technology/medical imaging
Surveying technology
Computer graphics
Digital media

Questions to ask colleges:
Does the program offer training in digital technologies?

What equipment must students provide on their own, and what equipment is available for student checkout?

Is there sufficient darkroom space and access time? How many majors and nonmajors share darkroom facilities?

Career options and trends:
Photojournalist; fine art photographer; freelance photographer; commercial or industrial photographer; technical or medical photographer; digital image technician; wedding photographer; portrait photographer; animator; manager of a photo lab.

Most photographers are either working freelance or running their own businesses and studios; salaried jobs are increasingly hard to find. Competition is keen, especially for photojournalists and commercial photographers. Fine arts photographers face the same challenge as other artists: how to attract audiences who favor their particular type of work. In all areas, good business sense, creative talent, and technological savvy are necessary ingredients for success.

Insider's viewpoint:
"I like isolating segments of the environment through the frame of the camera's viewfinder. I tend to see my surroundings in a series of still images—like the stop-action aspect of a movie."

—Professor Fred Niles, University of Dayton

For more info:
Student Photographic Society
229 Peachtree St., N.E.
Suite 2200
Atlanta, GA 30303
(800) 339-5451
www.studentphoto.com

Society of Photographic Education (SPE)
126 Peabody Hall
Miami University
Oxford, OH 45056
(513) 529-8328
www.spenational.org

Theater design and technology

Also known as:
Technical theater

What it's about:
This major covers the design and production of costumes, lighting, scenery, and sound for theater, opera, and dance. Typically housed in a theater or a performing arts department, the program enables students to specialize in one or more of these areas while they gain a broad foundation in the related disciplines of acting, directing, and theater history and theory.

Is this for you?
You might like this major if you also like: building things; working with your hands; decorating; art and literature; music; photography; working collaboratively with people; organizing events; solving problems. If you enjoy plays, movies, museums, and theme parks and would like to know how these attractions are produced, you might consider working behind the scenes in theater.

Consider this major if you are good at: attention to detail; creativity; critical reading/thinking; organizing; spatial thinking/analysis; teamwork *...or have...* initiative; manual dexterity; mechanical facility; patience; verbal skills.

Recommended high school prep:
English 4, math 3, lab science 3, social studies 3, foreign language 2–3, music 1–2, and visual arts 1–2. Courses that cover music appreciation, design (computer-aided if possible), and dramatic arts and literature are recommended, as is participation in extracurricular activities such as drama, art, and music clubs, and community organizations or summer theater companies. Industrial and/or vocational arts classes in woodworking, metalworking, drafting, and sewing are also helpful.

Did you know...
...that even though they work behind the scenes, majors in theater design and technology are often required to take performance classes such as acting or dance, and courses in theater history and theory? That's because the technician's job is to enhance the work of performers and directors, so an understanding of their craft is necessary.

Typical courses in this major:
Introduction to theater
Mechanical drafting
Scenographic techniques
Computer applications for theater
Sound
Stage management
Costume design and construction
Makeup for the stage
Lighting
Scene design and construction
Theater history
Theater graphics
Play analysis
Acting and performance courses
Art and art history courses
Portfolio development and presentation

Concentrations:
Lighting design; costume design (including makeup); scene design; technical direction; sound design; stage management.

What the study of this major is like:
This major is generally divided into design and production courses. The design component includes introductory and advanced courses in costume, lighting, scenery, and sound design. You'll study script analysis, historical research, fundamentals of visual art, drawing, rendering, and design presentation. In the production courses, you'll learn how to pattern, drape, and fit costumes on an actor's body; construct, paint, and prop scenery; rig,

hang, and focus lighting equipment; record sound effects; and place microphones or speakers for sound reinforcement. Introductory courses in these subjects teach basic vocabulary, tool usage, and procedures for design production. Some departments offer specialty courses in period styles in clothing and architecture; drawing and painting techniques; and advanced crafts, such as millinery, fabric dyeing and modification, makeup, wig construction, scene painting, properties design and construction, model making, and structural engineering for scenery.

Many production courses consist of a lecture class that addresses theory and laboratory sessions in which you have the opportunity to practice what you learn. Labs often provide the labor to implement your designs for department plays. Faculty members evaluate each assignment to determine if you are ready for projects that are more challenging. Ideally, you progress through the program by taking more advanced classes and assuming greater responsibilities in the design and production of plays. Because you'll often have to spend hours doing work outside your course requirements, you should be prepared to balance your academic and production commitments.

Most theater design and technology programs offer either a Bachelor of Arts or a Bachelor of Fine Arts degree. The B.A. program provides a liberal arts education that gives you an understanding of the world that the theater attempts to reflect; the program also prepares you for jobs you can take while pursuing the goal of working full-time in theater. The B.F.A. program trains you for a professional career in theater by offering more specialized, intensive course work. Most B.F.A. programs require auditions and/or interviews for admission and yearly performance evaluations to remain in the program. A few universities offer Bachelor of Science (B.S.) degrees in theater, which have stronger science and technology components than B.A. programs. A few junior and community colleges offer a two-year associate of arts (A.A.) degree in theater design and technology.

Other majors you might like:
Radio and television
Cinematography and film/video production
Architecture
Interior design
Theater history/criticism
Theater arts management
Fashion and apparel design
Structural engineering
Construction technology
Resort management
Interior design
Museum studies

Questions to ask colleges:
Is the program accredited by the National Association of Schools of Theater (NAST)?

Is there also a graduate program at this college? The presence of a graduate program has both advantages and disadvantages for undergrads—usually the quality of productions is high, but undergraduates may have to compete with grad students for the best design and production opportunities.

How many productions are offered per season and/or academic year? What types of theatrical works are produced (period plays, musicals, opera, dance)?

Do student designers and technicians have to audition and/or interview for positions on a production?

Career options and trends:
Regional/professional theater designer (costume, scenery, lighting, sound)*; theater technician (carpenter, scene painter, tailor or seamster, cutter/draper, electrician, sound engineer)*; technical director/production manager; art director/production designer for film and television; college or high school teacher in theater*.

The skills learned in this major are also useful in designing and working in theme parks, film, television, special effects, concerts, circuses, interior design, store and window display, apparel design, museum display and exhibition design, cruise ship tours, party design, parade and float design, architecture, and any business requiring the creation of an environment (such as multimedia and Internet) that people can view and interact with.

A bachelor's degree in Education and/or state certification is necessary to teach theater on a high school level. An advanced degree (MFA or Ph.D.) is mandatory for teaching at the college level. Technicians who have gained production experience can often find entry-level jobs with a bachelor's degree, but designers usually need to attend grad school for additional training.

Because theater is both an art and a business, it is subject to the ups and downs of local, state, and national economics and to trends in political ideology. While theater technicians enjoy more job security than actors, directors, and playwrights, they still must look for seasonal jobs at a variety of theaters.

Insider's viewpoint:

"If you're passionate about something you might as well go out and do it. Even if you're not famous or rich at least you'll be happy instead of being stuck in a cubicle. I'd rather be happy doing what I love, which is theater, than in a different job and making money."

—Emily, senior, San Jose State University

For more info:

Educational Theater Association (ETA)
2343 Auburn Ave.
Cincinnati, OH 45219
(513) 421-3900
www.edta.org

Part II: Brief Descriptions of Majors

About Part II

There are far more fields of study available at U.S. colleges and universities than are fully described in Part I of this book. To give you an idea of what they are about, Part II includes brief descriptions of the more than 900 majors recognized by the U.S. Department of Education and offered among the nation's undergraduate colleges, graduate schools, and first-professional schools.

Use the brief descriptions of majors in this Part in conjunction with Part III. They will help you get a better idea of what the colleges listed there are offering. These brief descriptions indicate the scope of the major and, where appropriate, the job or career for which it prepares you.

You won't find all of these majors at every institution. Some are very specialized fields, which are offered only by a few colleges. Some are vocational or technical in nature, and only offered by community colleges, technical institutes, or other two-year institutions. And some are only available as graduate degree programs.

Some of these briefly-described majors are mentioned in the "related majors" section of the full descriptions of majors that appear in Part I. All of these majors are listed in Part III of this book, showing which colleges and universities offer degrees for each major, and at what degree level.

If you think one of these majors sounds interesting, but you can't find a college listed in Part III that offers it at the degree level that's appropriate for you, keep in mind that there might still be ways you can study the subject in college. One way is to go to a college that offers a major in a related, broader field, and then concentrate or minor in your preferred subject. If you do this, you will then be well-prepared for a career or graduate study that focuses on the specialization you've chosen.

Brief descriptions of 900 majors

Accounting. Includes instruction in various types of accounting, legal considerations, auditing, report procedures, planning and consulting, research methods, and professional standards and ethics.

Accounting technology/bookkeeping. Prepares students to provide technical administrative support to financial management personnel.

Accounting/business management. A combined program in accounting and business management.

Accounting/computer science. A program that combines accounting with computer science and/or computer studies.

Accounting/finance. An integrated program that trains individuals to function as accountants and financial managers.

Acoustics. Investigates the properties and behavior of sound waves under different conditions.

Acting. Prepares students to impart ideas and feelings through naturalistic and believable behavior in imaginary circumstances.

Actuarial science. Highlights the mathematical and statistical analysis of risk and its applications to insurance and other business management problems.

Acupuncture. Readies individuals to practice pulse diagnosis, acupuncture point selection, and needle insertion to treat health imbalances.

Administrative/secretarial services. Describes the duties of administrative assistants and/or secretaries and stenographers.

Adult development/aging. Investigates aging populations and the needs of older individuals in family and institutional settings.

Adult health nursing. Informs registered nurses how to provide general care for adult patients.

Adult literacy instruction. Prepares students to serve as instructors and mentors for adults in literacy programs in school, institutional, community, and private settings.

Adult/continuing education. Prepares students to instruct adult students in various types of educational programs.

Adult/continuing education administration. Readies individuals to serve the basic educational needs of undereducated adults or the needs of adults seeking further instruction.

Advertising. Focuses on commercial messages intended to promote and sell ideas, products, and services.

Aeronautical/aerospace engineering. Highlights the design, development, and operational evaluation of aircraft, space vehicles, and their systems.

Aeronautical/aerospace engineering technology. Covers the development, manufacturing, and testing of aircraft, spacecraft, and their systems.

Aeronautics and aviation science. The study of aviation, including in-flight and ground support operations.

Aesthetician/skin care. Prepares individuals to cleanse, depilate, massage, and beautify the human body.

African languages. Focuses on one or more of the languages originating in Africa.

African studies. Explores the history, society, politics, culture, and economics of Africa.

African-American studies. Investigates the history, sociology, politics, culture, and economics of the North American peoples descended from Africa.

Agribusiness operations. Investigates the management of agricultural businesses and agriculturally related operations within diversified corporations.

Agricultural and biological engineering. The study of systems used to produce, process, and store agricultural products; and the improvement of agricultural methods and biological systems.

Agricultural business. Focuses on the organization, operation, and management of agricultural enterprises.

Agricultural business technology. Explores the operation of agricultural office equipment, software, and information systems.

Agricultural communications. Prepares students to apply journalistic, communication, and broadcasting principles to develop, produce, and transmit agricultural information.

Agricultural economics. The analysis of resource allocation, productivity, investments, and trends in the agricultural sector.

Agricultural education services. Features the provision of referral, consulting, technical assistance, and educational services to gardeners, farmers, ranchers, and agribusinesses.

Agricultural equipment technology. Provides instruction in the maintenance and repair of specialized farm, ranch, and agribusiness power equipment and vehicles.

Agricultural mechanization. Readies students to sell, select, and service agricultural or agribusiness technical equipment and facilities, including computers, power units, machinery, and utilities.

Agricultural power machinery operation. Highlights the operation of specialized farm, ranch, and agribusiness power equipment.

Agricultural production. Focuses on the general planning, economics, and use of facilities, natural resources, labor, and capital to produce plant and animal products.

Agricultural supplies. Highlights the purchasing, marketing, and selling of agricultural products.

Agricultural teacher education. Prepares students to teach vocational agricultural programs at various educational levels.

Agricultural/food products processing. Readies individuals to receive, inspect, process, and package agricultural products for human consumption, animal or plant food, or other products.

Agriculture, general. The study of agricultural research and production.

Agronomy and crop science. The study of the chemical, physical, and biological relationships of crops and soils.

Air traffic control. Prepares students to manage and control air traffic, usually with additional training at the FAA Flight Control Center in a cooperative education program.

Aircraft maintenance/technology. Prepares individuals to repair all aircraft components other than engines, propellers, avionics, and instruments.

Aircraft powerplant technology. Prepares students to repair, service, and maintain all types of aircraft power plant and related systems.

Airline/commercial pilot. Focuses on the flying and/or navigation of commercial fixed-wing aircraft.

Algebra/number theory. Prepares students to express quantities by means of symbols, vectors, matrices, equations, and integer properties.

Alternative fuel vehicle technology. Describes the maintenance of alternative fuel vehicles and the conversion of standard vehicles to AFV status.

American government/politics. Features the political institutions of the United States.

American history (U.S.). Focuses on the development of American society, culture, and institutions from the Pre-Columbian period to the present.

American literature. Features the literature of the United States from the colonial era to the present.

American Sign Language (ASL). Focuses on American Sign Language as a medium of communication for deaf individuals and Deaf culture.

American studies. The study of the history, society, politics, culture, and economics of the United States.

Analysis/functional analysis. Defines the properties of equations, multivariate solutions, functions, and dynamic systems.

Analytical chemistry. Prepares students to analyze and describe the composition of matter.

Anatomy. Highlights organs, tissues, and whole bodies together with their cellular and structural components.

Ancient Greek. Highlights the Greek language and literature from its origins through the fall of the Byzantine Empire, as a secular and/or theological subject.

Ancient Near Eastern/Biblical languages. The study of the extinct Semitic and/or Non-Semitic languages spoken in the ancient Near East, including those used to write historical Jewish and Christian religious texts.

Ancient studies. Focuses on Western and non-Western cultures and related topics in the periods of prehistory and antiquity.

Anesthesiologist assistant. Trains students to assist anesthesiologists and nurses in developing and implementing patient anesthesia care plans.

Animal behavior/ethology. Highlights the psychological and neurological processes of animals.

Animal breeding. Applies the principles of genetics and genetic engineering to the improvement of agricultural animal health and the development of new animal breeds.

Animal genetics. Features animal genetics from the experimental, comparative, veterinary, and medical viewpoints.

Animal health. Investigates the prevention and control of diseases in agricultural animals.

Animal husbandry. Features the selection, breeding, care, processing, and marketing of livestock and small farm animals.

Animal nutrition. Focuses on nutrition as related to animal health, and on the production of improved animal products.

Animal physiology. The study of internal function, development, and dynamics within animal species, with comparative applications to humans.

Animal sciences. Studies the scientific principles underlying the breeding and husbandry of agricultural animals; and the production and distribution of agricultural animal products.

Animal training. Prepares individuals to teach and exercise animals for leisure, sport, show, and professional purposes.

Animation. Prepares individuals to communicate simulated real-world content through the manipulation of film, video, photographs, digital copy, and soundtracks.

Anthropology. Describes human beings, their antecedents, and their cultural behavior and institutions in comparative perspective.

Apparel/accessories marketing. Prepares students to perform operations connected with the distribution and sale of apparel and accessories.

Apparel/textile manufacture. A program that focuses on the design, development, and production of textile products and related processes.

Apparel/textile marketing. Trains students to apply marketing research and management to the products of the apparel and textile industries.

Appliance installation and repair. Readies students to mend, install, and fix major gas, electric, and microwave appliances.

Applied economics. Applies economics to the study of particular industries, activities, or the exploitation of particular resources.

Applied mathematics. Uses mathematics to find solutions to functional problems in fields such as engineering, computing and information science, and the applied sciences.

Aquaculture. Prepares students to culture, propagate, harvest, and market domesticated fish, shellfish, and marine plants.

Aquatic biology/limnology. Highlights the ecology and behavior of microbes, plants, and animals inhabiting inland fresh waters.

Arabic. The study of the language, literature, and culture of Arabic-speaking peoples.

Archaeology. Explores societies via the excavation, analysis, and interpretation of their artifactual and human remains.

Architectural drafting/CAD/CADD. Highlights the technical skills used to develop working drawings and electronic simulations for architectural and related construction projects.

Architectural engineering. Features the mathematical and scientific principles applied to the design and development of materials, systems, and methods used to construct buildings for human habitation or other purposes.

Architectural engineering technology. Prepares students to support architects, engineers, and planners engaged in designing and developing buildings and urban complexes.

Architectural history/criticism. Studies the aesthetic, technical, and social development of the built environment and the architectural profession from ancient times to the present.

Architectural technology. Prepares students to assist architects in developing plans and documentation, and in performing office services.

Architecture. Prepares students for the professional practice of architecture, with instruction in architectural design, history, and theory; building structures; site planning; and construction.

Art. An introductory study and appreciation of the visual arts.

Art history. Studies the historical development of art as social and intellectual phenomenon, the analysis of art, and art conservation.

Art teacher education. Readies individuals to provide art and art appreciation programs at various educational levels.

Art therapy. Describes the use of art media to assess, treat, and rehabilitate individuals with physical, emotional, developmental, or mental disorders.

Artificial intelligence/robotics. Focuses on the simulation by computers of human learning and reasoning, and of human motor control and motions by computer-driven machinery.

Arts management. Trains individuals to organize and manage art organizations and facilities.

Asian bodywork therapy. Readies students to provide relief and improved health through the traditional bodywork therapies of Asia.

Asian history. Examines the development of the societies, cultures, and institutions of the Asian continent from their origins to the present.

Asian studies. Studies the history, society, politics, culture, and economics of the Asian continent.

Asian-American studies. Describes the history, sociology, politics, culture, and economics of Asian population groups who have immigrated to the United States and Canada.

Astronomy. Focuses on the planetary, galactic, and stellar phenomena occurring in outer space.

Astrophysics. The theoretical study of the physical laws underlying the formation, evolution, and behavior of stars, galaxies, and the universe.

Athletic training. Instructs students on the prevention, evaluation, and treatment of sports injuries.

Atmospheric physics/dynamics. Features the processes governing the behavior of atmospheric, terrestrial, and solar phenomena.

Atmospheric science. Investigates the earth's atmosphere and its effect on terrestrial weather, and on related environment and climate problems.

Atomic/molecular physics. Investigates the behavior of matter-energy phenomena at the atomic and molecular levels.

Auctioneering. Trains individuals for careers as auctioneers and auction managers and for meeting state licensing requirements.

Audiology/hearing sciences. Trains students to diagnose hearing loss, advise patients on how to use their remaining hearing, and select and fit hearing aids.

Audiology/speech pathology. An integrated program that prepares individuals as audiologists and speech-language pathologists.

Auditing. Prepares individuals to evaluate organizational financial and operational activities, ensure regulatory compliance, safeguard assets, and promote resource allocation.

Australian/Oceanic/Pacific languages. Focuses on the languages spoken by the Melanesian, Micronesian, and Polynesian peoples.

Auto body repair. Prepares individuals to repair, reconstruct, and finish automobile bodies, fenders, and external features.

Automotive engineering technology. Trains students in the development, manufacture, and testing of self-propelled ground vehicles and their systems.

Automotive technology. Describes the servicing and maintenance of all types of automobiles.

Aviation management. Emphasizes the management of aviation industry operations and services.

Avionics maintenance/technology. Trains individuals to maintain aircraft operating, control, and electronic systems.

Bacteriology. Features bacteria that are significant factors in causing human disease.

Baking/pastry arts. Describes bread and pastry making, decorating, marketing, counter display, and service.

Ballet. Trains individuals to express ideas and feelings through interpretation of classical dance choreography.

Banking/financial services. Describes a variety of customer services in banks, insurance agencies, and savings and loan companies.

Barbering. Focuses on facial shaving, hair cutting, styling art, facial and scalp massage, hairpiece fitting, equipment operation, and safety.

Bartending. Readies students to mix beverages and manage bars, lounges, and beverage services operations.

Behavioral sciences. Studies problems of human individual and social growth and behavior.

Bible studies. The study of the Christian and/or Jewish Bible, with an emphasis on interpreting the messages contained therein.

Bilingual/bicultural education. Focuses on the design and provision of teaching to bilingual/bicultural children or adults.

Biochemistry. Focuses on living systems, their chemical substances and pathways, and information transfer systems.

Biochemistry/biophysics and molecular biology. An integrated program focusing on the structure, function, and behavior of biological systems at molecular levels and their influence on biological activity.

Bioethics/medical ethics. A course of study that analyzes health care issues, clinical decision-making, and research procedures.

Bioinformatics. Applies computer-based technologies to biological, biomedical, and biotechnological research.

Biological immunology. Describes the biological origination and development of disease and host responses to disease.

Biological/physical sciences. A program that is either a general synthesis of the biological and physical sciences, or a specialization that draws from the biological and physical sciences.

Biology. Introductory study of living organisms and their relations to their natural environments.

Biology lab technology. Prepares students to apply scientific principles and skills in support of biologists in research, industrial, and government settings.

Biology teacher education. Trains individuals to teach biology at various educational levels.

Biomedical engineering. Studies the design and development of biological and health systems and products such as integrated biological systems, medical information systems, and artificial organs and prostheses.

Biomedical sciences. The scientific study of biological issues related to health and medicine.

Biomedical technology. Readies students to support engineers engaged in developing biological or medical systems and products.

Biometrics. Applies various computational methods to the study of problems in the biological sciences and related fields in agriculture and natural resources.

Biophysics. Applies the principles of physics to the workings of biological processes and assemblies.

Biopsychology. Highlights linkages between biochemical and biophysical activity to central nervous system functioning.

Biostatistics. Prepares students to apply statistics to biomedical research and clinical, health, and industrial issues related to humans.

Biotechnology. Combines biological sciences, biochemistry, and genetics with engineering principles to prepare new agricultural, environmental, clinical, and industrial products.

Boilermaking. Trains individuals to make and repair steam boiler components.

Botany. The study of plants, related organisms, and plant habitats and ecosystem relations.

Broadcast journalism. Prepares students to report, produce, and deliver news via radio, television, and video/film media.

Buddhist studies. Explores the Buddhist faith; along with its intellectual, cultural, social, and ritual developments.

Building inspection. The study of industrial, labor, and governmental standards to the oversight of construction projects and the maintenance of completed buildings.

Building/property maintenance. Prepares individuals to keep a building functioning and service a variety of structures.

Business administration and management. Prepares students to plan, organize, direct, and control the functions of a firm or organization.

Business communications. Prepares students to function in an organization as a composer, editor, and proofreader of business communications.

Business machine repair. Prepares individuals to install and maintain a variety of office machinery.

Business statistics. Features the description, analysis, and forecasting of business data.

Business teacher education. Prepares individuals to teach vocational business programs.

Business/commerce. The general study of business, business organization, and accounting as used in profit-making and nonprofit public and private institutions and agencies.

Business/managerial economics. The application of economic principles to the analysis of the organization and operation of business enterprises.

Cabinetmaking/millwright. Prepares students to set up, operate, and repair woodworking machinery, and to design and fabricate wooden items.

CAD/CADD drafting/design technology. Prepares individuals to create graphic representations and simulations in support of engineering projects.

Canadian government/politics. Explores Canadian political institutions and behavior.

Canadian history. The study of the development of the society, culture, and institutions of Canada from its origins to the present.

Canadian literature. Focuses on Canadian literature from its origins to the present.

Canadian studies. Describes the history, society, politics, culture, and economics of the Canadian people.

Cardiopulmonary technology. Readies individuals, under the supervision of physicians and nurses, to perform cardiovascular and pulmonary procedures.

Cardiovascular science. Highlights the heart, vascular system, and blood, and the disorders associated with the cardiovascular system.

Cardiovascular technology. Describes cardiovascular testing procedures used to aid in diagnoses and treatments.

Caribbean studies. Explores the history, society, politics, culture, and economics of the major islands and archipelagoes of the Caribbean Sea.

Carpentry. Prepares students to lay out, fabricate, install, and repair wooden structures and fixtures using hand and power tools.

Cartography. Describes mapmaking through the use of mathematical and computer techniques.

Cell biology and histology. Features the structure, function, and regulation of cells as individual units and as components of tissues and organs.

Cell physiology. Features the physiological processes, communications, and behavior of cells in the context of whole organisms.

Cellular/anatomical biology. Integrates the study of cell structure and function within the context of anatomical systems.

Cellular/molecular biology. Integrates the study of cells, cellular systems, and the molecular basis of cell structure and function.

Celtic languages. A program that focuses on the historical and modern languages spoken by the Celtic peoples of the British Isles, Continental Europe, and Asia Minor.

Central Asian studies. Focuses on the history, society, politics, culture, and economics of Inner/Central Asia, including the inhabitants of the Caspian, Amur, Tien Shan, Baikal, Gobi, Siberian, and Manchurian regions and the historical Silk Road.

Central/Middle/Eastern European studies. Highlights the Balkans, Belarus, Czech Republic, Hungary, Poland, Romania, Russia, Slovakia, and the Ukraine.

Ceramic sciences/engineering. Prepares students to design, develop, and evaluate inorganic nonmetallic materials.

Ceramics. Studies the production of artwork out of clay and similar materials.

Chemical engineering. The study of the design and development of systems employing chemical processes and the analysis of chemical problems such as corrosion, pollution, and energy loss.

Chemical physics. Combines the disciplines of physical chemistry and atomic/molecular physics to study structural phenomena.

Chemical technology. Prepares students to aid chemical and biochemical research and industrial operations.

Chemistry. Investigates the composition and behavior of matter, the processes of chemical change, and the laboratory simulation of these phenomena.

Chemistry teacher education. Prepares individuals to teach chemistry.

Child care management. Prepares individuals to plan, design, and manage child care facilities that meet children's developmental needs in a safe environment.

Child care service. Includes instruction in child development, nutrition, recreation, activities supervision, child abuse prevention, and parent-child relationships.

Child development. Features the intellectual, social, emotional, and biological development of children and the planning of related human services.

Chinese. Features the Chinese language and its associated dialects and literature.

Chinese studies. Investigates the history, society, politics, culture, and economics of present-day China.

Chiropractic (D.C.). Readies students to apply noninvasive treatments and spinal adjustments to alleviate problems caused by vertebral misalignments.

Chiropractic assistant. Prepares students to assist chiropractors by providing patient management, examinations, and treatment services.

Christian studies. Features the teachings of Jesus Christ and the subsequent movements and institutions based on Christianity.

Cinematography and film/video production. Prepares students to communicate dramatic information, ideas, moods, and feelings through the creation and production of films and videos.

Civil engineering. Studies the design, development, and evaluation of public facilities, including structural, load-bearing, transportation, water resource, and material control systems.

Civil engineering drafting/CAD/CADD. Features the technical skills necessary to develop working drawings and electronic simulations in support of civil engineers and geological engineers.

Civil engineering technology. Trains individuals in the practical application of the design and execution of public works projects.

Classical/ancient Mediterranean/Near Eastern studies. Explores the cultures, environment, and history of the ancient Near East, Europe, and Mediterranean basin from the perspectives of the humanities, social sciences, and archaeology.

Classics. Focuses on the Greek and Latin languages and literatures.

Clinical child psychology. Emphasizes the developmental processes of children and associated disorders.

Clinical laboratory science. Readies students to conduct medical tests and research, manage laboratories, and consult with physicians and researchers.

Clinical nurse specialist. Trains registered nurses to deliver direct patient care in clinical settings.

Clinical nutrition. Readies students to manage nutrition programs as part of clinical therapies, and oversee health care facility food services.

Clinical pastoral counseling. Prepares clergy and other counseling professionals to respond to the emotional and spiritual needs of patients and families in emergency or dibilitating health care situations.

Clinical psychology. Describes the analysis, diagnosis, and clinical treatment of psychological disorders and behavioral pathologies.

Clinical/medical laboratory assistant. Prepares students to assist laboratory teams by performing tests, phlebotomy, and other duties.

Clinical/medical laboratory technology. Trains individuals to engage in various medical laboratory procedures and tests and to record and analyze data.

Clinical/medical social work. Describes the professional practice of social work in hospitals and other health care facilities and organizations.

Clothing, apparel and textile studies. Highlights the development, distribution, and use of textile products in terms of the consumer's needs.

Cognitive psychology/psycholinguistics. Studies the processes of learning, thinking, and associated information systems.

Cognitive science. An interdisciplinary study of the mind and the nature of intelligence.

College student counseling. Studies the provision of counseling and administrative services to students in postsecondary educational institutions and adult education facilities.

Commercial fishing. Prepares students to function as commercial fishermen or fishing operations supervisors.

Commercial photography. Focuses on artistic techniques for communicating ideas and information to business and consumer audiences, and recording events and people, by way of digital, film, still, and video images.

Commercial/advertising art. Prepares students to communicate ideas and information to business and consumer audiences via illustrations and other media.

Communication disorders. The study of speech, language, hearing, and cognitive communication problems caused by disease, injury, or disability.

Communications. Explores human communication in a variety of formats, media, and contexts.

Communications systems installation/repair. Prepares students to assemble, operate, and fix one- and two-way communications equipment.

Communications technology. Prepares individuals to function within communications industries.

Community health services. Readies students to link health care and related social services with affected recipient communities.

Community health/preventative medicine. Prepares individuals to plan and manage health services in local community settings.

Community organization/advocacy. Prepares individuals to provide services to communities, organize communities for social action, and serve as community liaisons to public agencies.

Community psychology. Trains students to analyze social problems and implement intervention strategies for addressing these problems.

Community/junior college administration. Focuses on administration at community and junior colleges and related postsecondary systems.

Comparative literature. The study of the literatures of different societies and linguistic groups from a comparative perspective.

Comparative psychology. Focuses on the behavior of group members and the relationship of those behaviors to the group's evolutionary origins.

Comparative/international education. Compares educational practices and institutions within different countries, states, and societies.

Computational mathematics. Prepares students to apply mathematics to the theory, architecture, and design of computers, computational techniques, and algorithms.

Computer education. A program that prepares individuals to teach computer education programs.

Computer engineering. Prepares individuals to design and develop computer systems and to analyze specific problems related to computer applications.

Computer engineering technology. Provides practical training in the design, development, and maintenance of computer systems, networks, and installations.

Computer graphics. Studies the software and hardware used to represent, display, and manipulate topological, two-, and three-dimensional objects on a computer screen.

Computer hardware engineering. Readies students to design, develop, and evaluate computer hardware.

Computer hardware technology. Highlights the design of computer hardware and peripheral systems.

Computer installation and repair. Describes the application of technical skills to install and maintain computers.

Computer networking/telecommunications. Analyzes the management of linked computer systems, peripherals, and software to maximize efficiency and productivity.

Computer programming, general. Studies the writing and implementation of programs to drive operating systems and other applications, including instruction in software design, installation, and maintenance.

Computer programming, specific applications. Prepares individuals to devise customized solutions for problems presented by individual software users.

Computer science. Focuses on computers, computing problems and solutions, and the design of computer systems and user interfaces.

Computer software technology. Prepares students to aid in developing, implementing, and evaluating computer software and program applications.

Computer systems analysis. Trains students to design and implement large-scale computer applications and networking systems.

Computer systems technology. Includes instruction in basic computer design and architecture, programming, maintenance and inspection, and problem diagnosis and repair.

Computer typography. Prepares students to execute page formats, layouts, and text composition; and to make typographical selections using computer programs.

Computer/information sciences, general. Focuses on computing, computer science, and information science as part of an interdisciplinary program.

Computer/systems security. Readies students to assess the security needs of computer systems, recommend solutions, and manage security devices and procedures.

Concrete finishing. Trains individuals to prepare, construct, and finish buildings using masonry mixtures.

Conducting. Prepares students to lead bands, choirs, orchestras, and other ensembles in performance.

Conservation biology. Specifies conservation issues that result from advancing human social, economic, and industrial pressures.

Construction engineering. Studies the planning, design, and building of facilities and structures, including structural principles, site analysis, geology, materials, contracting, project management, and graphic communications.

Construction management. Readies students to coordinate the construction process from concept development through project completion on a timely and economical basis.

Construction site management. Prepares students to supervise, manage, and inspect construction sites and buildings.

Construction technology. Provides practical training in the planning, design, execution, and management of construction projects.

Construction trades. Focuses on the building, inspecting, and maintenance of structures.

Consumer economics. Prepares students to apply economic theories to consumer behavior and individual and family consumption of goods and services.

Consumer merchandising. Highlights product and service promotion from the consumer's perspective.

Consumer services/advocacy. Features the techniques needed to protect consumers from unsafe, unreliable, and/or unhealthy products and services.

Correctional facilities administration. Trains students to provide management services for institutional facilities that house and rehabilitate prisoners.

Corrections. The study of correctional science in preparation for becoming a corrections officer in an incarceration facility.

Cosmetic services. Trains students for licensed practice in hair cutting and styling, cosmetic preparations, manicures and pedicures, and facial treatments.

Cosmetology. Prepares grooming technicians to teach their specializations in schools of cosmetology and barbering.

Counseling psychology. Highlights the provision of therapeutic services to individuals and groups experiencing psychological problems and symptoms.

Counselor education. Prepares individuals to support student development and to organize guidance services within educational institutions.

Court reporting. Readies students to record examinations, testimony, judicial orders, and other proceedings via print or electronic methods.

Crafts/folkart/artisanry. Features the aesthetics and techniques for designing objects in the handcraft or folk art traditions.

Creative writing. Describes the composition of literary forms such as the short story, poetry, and the novel.

Credit management. Includes instruction in how to perform credit, collateral, and loan processing operations.

Criminal justice and law enforcement. Prepares students to apply theories and practices of criminal justice to the management of criminal justice agencies, including police departments and private protection services.

Criminal justice studies. Focuses on the criminal justice system, its components and processes, and its legal and public policy contexts.

Criminalistics/criminal science. Highlights the reconstruction of crimes and the analysis of physical evidence.

Criminology. Highlights crime as a sociopathological phenomenon, the behavior of criminals, and the social institutions developed to respond to crime.

Critical care nursing. Readies students to provide specialized care to patients with life-threatening problems.

Crop production. Prepares individuals to cultivate grain, fiber, forage, oilseed, fruits and nuts, vegetables, and other domesticated plant products.

Culinary arts and chef training. Prepares students to provide professional chef and related cooking services, with instruction in various cuisines, recipe and menu planning, cooking techniques, kitchen supervision, food supply management, and food presentation.

Culinary arts/related services. The general study of cooking and related culinary arts, including food preparation, cooking techniques, equipment operation, sanitation and safety, and food service management.

Cultural resource management. Readies students to preserve and protect cultural heritage sites and artifacts.

Curriculum/instruction. Includes instruction in curriculum theory, design, planning, and evaluation, as well as instructional material design and evaluation.

Customer service management. Prepares students to monitor customer service performance and manage frontline customer support services.

Cytogenetics/clinical genetics technology. Readies students to analyze human chromosomes for the research and diagnosis of genetic diseases, organ transplants, and cancer treatments.

Cytotechnology. Explores the change in body cells that may indicate the early development of cancers and other diseases.

Czech. Explores the languages, literatures, and cultures of the Czech people.

Dairy husbandry. Prepares students to manage the selection and care of dairy animals and associated dairy farm facilities.

Dairy science. Prepares students to produce and manage dairy animals and products.

Dance. Explores the cultural effects of dance and prepares students to perform in one or more of the dance disciplines.

Dance therapy. A course of study that applies creative dance movement to promote client rehabilitation and physical, emotional, and mental health.

Danish. Features the Danish language as used in Denmark and Greenland.

Data entry/applications. Prepares individuals to perform basic data and text entry using varied software products.

Data processing technology. Describes the use of computers and software packages for text processing, number processing, graphics, and database management.

Database design/management. Prepares individuals to design and manage databases, including the linking of data sets to create complex searchable databases and the use of analytical search tools.

Demography/population studies. Emphasizes population models, population phenomena, and related problems of social structure and behavior.

Dental assistant. Focuses on the provision of patient care, the preparation for procedures, and the completion of office functions under the supervision of dental professionals.

Dental clinical services. Generally prepares dentists in one or more of the oral sciences and advanced/graduate dentistry specialties.

Dental hygiene. Prepares individuals to clean teeth, provide oral health education, identify oral pathologies, and manage dental hygiene practices.

Dental laboratory technology. Trains students, under the supervision of dentists, to design and construct dental prostheses.

Dentistry (D.D.S., D.M.D.). Prepares students for the professional practice of dentistry, including the evaluation, diagnosis, prevention, and treatment of diseases, disorders, and conditions of the teeth and mouth.

Design/visual communications. Focuses on effectively communicating ideas and information, and packaging products, to business and consumer audiences.

Desktop publishing. Trains students to design the layout and typography of printed and electronic graphic and textual products.

Development economics. Defines economic development and its application to the problems of specific countries and regions.

Developmental biology/embryology. The scientific study of the development and growth of animals and human beings from fertilization to birth.

Developmental/child psychology. The study of the psychological growth and development of individuals from infancy through adulthood.

Diagnostic medical sonography. Features the utilization of medical ultrasound techniques to gather data used to diagnose a variety of conditions and diseases.

Diesel mechanics. Trains individuals to maintain diesel engines in vehicles, as well as stationary diesel engines in electrical generators.

Dietetic technician. Prepares individuals to implement nutritional and dietetic plans and to provide direct client services as certified dietitian technicians.

Dietetics. A program that trains students to design and manage effective nutrition programs in a variety of settings as a registered dietitian.

Dietician assistant. Trains students to assist in planning, preparing, and serving meals to individuals with specific dietary needs.

Digital media. Studies the development, use, and regulation of electronic communication technologies using computer applications.

Directing/theatrical production. Readies individuals to manage the planning, design, preparation, and production of theatrical entertainment programs.

Divinity/ministry (B.Div., M.Div.). Prepares individuals for ordination as ministers or priests in any of the Christian religious traditions.

Dog/pet/animal grooming. Studies the provision of cosmetic services for pets, show animals, work animals, and animal athletes.

Drafting and design technology. Features the application of technical skills to create working drawings and computer simulations for a variety of applications.

Drama and theater arts. Focuses on the general study of dramatic works and their performance.

Drama/dance teacher education. A program that prepares students to teach components of drama and/or dance.

Drawing. Highlights the expression of emotions, ideas, or inner visions through lines made on a surface.

Driver/safety education. The study of driver and safety education curricula.

Drywall installation. Describes how to install, tape, and plaster drywall installations in interior and exterior construction jobs.

Dutch/Flemish. Highlights the Dutch language as used in the Netherlands, Flemish-speaking Belgium, and Suriname.

E-commerce. Trains individuals to manage, supervise, and market electronic operations, products, and services provided on the Internet.

Early childhood education. Readies individuals to teach all relevant subject matter to students ranging in age from infancy through eight years.

Early childhood special education. A program that specifies teaching infants and preschool age children with special learning needs.

East Asian languages. Highlights one or more of the Sino-Tibetan, Japanese, and Korean languages of East Asia.

East Asian studies. Focuses on the history, society, politics, culture, and economics of China, Korea, Mongolia, Taiwan, Tibet, and related borderlands and island groups.

Ecology. Prepares students to relate small-scale biological systems, such as organisms, to complex and whole systems, and to the physical environment.

Econometrics/quantitative economics. Prepares students for the mathematical and statistical analysis of economic phenomena.

Economics. Covers the production, conservation, and allocation of resources, together with the organizational systems related to these processes.

Education of autistic. Prepares students to plan and implement educational services for children or adults who are autistic.

Education of blind/visually handicapped. Readies individuals to provide services for children or adults with visual disabilities.

Education of brain injured. Highlights educational services for students who are recovering from brain injuries that affect their cognitive, perceptive, and motor functions.

Education of Deaf/hearing impaired. Prepares students to provide educational services to Deaf and hard of hearing students at various grade levels.

Education of developmentally delayed. Readies individuals to provide educational services for students who exhibit slow social, physical, cognitive, or emotional growth patterns.

Education of emotionally handicapped. Readies students to provide educational services for individuals affected by emotional conditions.

Education of gifted/talented. Studies the provision of educational services and opportunities to individuals exhibiting exceptional intellectual or artistic talent, maturity, or social leadership skills.

Education of learning disabled. Characterizes various learning disabilities and the programs designed to address them.

Education of mentally handicapped. Characterizes mental disabilities that adversely affect educational performance and the programs designed to address them.

Education of multiple handicapped. Prepares students to design and provide educational services for individuals with multiple disabilities.

Education of physically handicapped. Describes orthopedic and other physical health impairments that affect students and their educational performance.

Education of speech impaired. Describes the design and provision of educational services for children or adults with speech impairments.

Education, general. Covers learning and teaching, educational psychology, educational activities, and the social foundations of education.

Educational assessment/testing. Prepares students to design, implement, and evaluate tests, and to assess teaching tools, strategies, and curricula.

Educational evaluation/research. Highlights procedures for generating information about educational programs, personnel and methods, and the analysis of such information for planning purposes.

Educational leadership/adminstration. The description of techniques for administering a wide variety of schools, to prepare individuals as general administrators and supervisors.

Educational psychology. Studies learning environments, their effects on behavior, and the effects of nonschool experience on the educational process.

Educational statistics/research methods. The application of statistics to the analysis of educational research problems, and the development of technical designs for research studies.

Educational superintendency. Prepares students to lead and manage multi-school educational systems and school districts.

Educational supervision. Includes instruction in staffing and organization, personnel relations, and administrative duties at the school building, facility, or staff level.

Electrical and communications engineering. Trains students to design, develop, and evaluate electrical, electronic, and related communications systems.

Electrical drafting/CAD/CADD. Readies students to design working schematics and representations in support of electrical/electronic engineers and computer engineers.

Electrical engineering technology. Includes instruction in electrical circuitry, prototype testing, systems analysis and maintenance, instrument calibration, and report preparation.

Electrician. Prepares students to install, operate, maintain, and repair electric systems, as well as DC and AC motors, controls, and electrical distribution panels.

Electrocardiograph technology. Readies individuals to administer EKG and ECG examinations, and to report results to the treatment team.

Electroencephalograph technology. Prepares students, under the supervision of a physician, to study and record electrical activity in the brain and nervous system.

Electrolysis. Describes the process of hair removal from the human scalp, face, and body using specialized needle probes.

Electromechanical technology. Prepares individuals to support engineers engaged in developing and testing automated, servomechanical, and other electromechanical systems.

Electronics/electrical equipment repair. The study of the operation, maintenance, and repair of electrical and electronic equipment.

Elementary education. Readies individuals to teach subject matter to students in grades kindergarten through grade eight.

Elementary/middle school administration. Prepares individuals to serve as principals and masters of elementary and middle schools.

Emergency care attendant (EMT ambulance). Readies individuals to assist EMTs to transport patients and operate emergency vehicles and equipment.

Emergency medical technology (EMT paramedic). Prepares students to recognize, assess, and manage medical emergencies in prehospital settings, and to supervise ambulance personnel.

Endocrinology. Covers the development and secretion of protein compounds by cells and glands, and the role of endocrine substances in bodily processes.

Energy systems technology. Readies students to support engineers engaged in the development of energy-efficient systems or monitoring energy use.

Engine machinist. Focuses on the construction of automotive and commercial vehicle engines.

Engineering mechanics. Investigates the behavior of structures, forces, and materials in engineering problems.

Engineering physics. Prepares individuals to apply the principles of physics to the analysis of engineering problems.

Engineering science. Focuses on the general application of various mathematical and scientific principles to the analysis and evaluation of engineering problems.

Engineering technology, general. A program that readies individuals to apply basic engineering principles and technical skills in support of engineers engaged in a wide variety of projects.

Engineering, general. Prepares individuals to solve a wide variety of practical problems in industry, social organizations, and commerce.

Engineering/industrial management. Covers the planning and operational management of industrial and manufacturing operations.

English composition. Investigates English vocabulary, grammar, morphology, syntax, and semantics, and the techniques used to express ideas in written forms.

English literature. Explores the English language, including its history and structure, and the literature and culture of English-speaking peoples.

English literature (British). Studies the literature of the English speaking peoples of Britain and the British Commonwealth from the origins of the English language to the present.

English teacher education. Studies the teaching of English grammar, composition, and literature programs.

Entomology. The scientific study of insects.

Entrepreneurial studies. Prepares students to perform development, marketing, and management functions associated with owning a business, and to recognize, evaluate, and respond to new business opportunities.

Environmental biology. Focuses on living populations in relation to changing environmental processes.

Environmental design. Prepares students to design total environments and living systems, both indoor and outdoor.

Environmental engineering. Studies the design, development, and evaluation of environmental systems, including pollution control, waste and hazardous material disposal, health and safety protection, and conservation.

Environmental engineering technology. Investigates the development and use of indoor and outdoor environmental pollution control systems.

Environmental health. The study of environmental factors affecting human health.

Environmental psychology. Investigates ways in which to improve the behavioral interactions between human beings and the environment.

Environmental science. Applies various scientific principles to the study of the physical environment and the solution of environmental problems.

Environmental studies. Studies environment-related issues using a combination of scientific, social, or humanistic approaches.

Environmental toxicology. Focuses on the effects of exposure to toxic chemicals, pollutants, and biohazards, the management of environmental toxins, and the development of protective measures.

Epidemiology. Studies the distribution and prevention of disease across populations.

Equestrian studies. Focuses on the horse, horsemanship, and related businesses, facilities, and equipment, and the training of horses and riders.

ESL teacher education. Studies the principles and practice of teaching English to students who are not proficient in the language or who do not speak, read, or write English.

Ethics. Investigates the theory of moral good and its application to various theoretical and practical problems.

European history. Studies the development of European society, culture, and institutions from its origins to the present.

European studies. Focuses on the history, society, politics, culture, and economics of the European continent.

Evolutionary biology. Describes the emergence and changes of organisms and species over time.

Executive assistant. Trains individuals to function as special assistants and/or personal secretaries for business executives and top management.

Exercise physiology. Explores the processes involved in physical or motor activity.

Exercise sciences. Focuses on the anatomy, physiology, biochemistry, and biophysics of human movement, and applications to exercise and therapeutic rehabilitation.

Experimental psychology. Investigates behavior under experimental conditions and analyzes controlled behavioral responses.

Facial treatment. Studies massage and treatment of the face, scalp, and neck.

Facilities/event planning. Prepares students to become facility and event managers and workplace consultants.

Family and consumer sciences. Studies family, work, and community settings and how people relate to their physical, social, emotional, and intellectual environments.

Family practice nurse/nurse practitioner. Readies registered nurses to provide independent general care for family groups and individuals.

Family psychology. Readies students to provide therapeutic, evaluative, and research services to families and individuals in the family unit context.

Family resource management studies. Includes instruction in financial goal-setting and management, preventing and resolving financial difficulties, and the use of relevant public resources.

Family systems. Highlights the family in its development and its significance as a system that impacts individuals and society.

Family/community services. Focuses on the development and implementation of support services for individuals, families, and localities.

Family/consumer business sciences. Investigates the relationship between the economy and the consuming individual and family.

Family/consumer sciences education. Readies students to teach vocational home economics programs.

Farm and ranch management. Prepares individuals to manage farms, ranches, or similar enterprises.

Fashion and apparel design. Trains students to design commercial fashions, apparel, and accessories, and to manage fashion development projects.

Fashion merchandising. Readies students to promote fashion product lines/brands and to organize promotional campaigns to attract retailer interest, wholesale purchasing, and supply contracts.

Fashion/fabric consultant. Readies individuals to assist in fashion selection, style coordination, sales, fabric selection, clothing specifications, and purchasing.

Fiber/textile arts. Readies students to construct designs from woven or nonwoven fabrics and fibrous materials.

Filipino/Tagalog. Emphasizes the modern Filipino/Tagalog language as used in the Philippines.

Film/cinema studies. The study of film/video arts, as well as the basic principles of filmmaking and film production.

Finance. Readies students to plan, manage, and analyze the financial aspects and performance of business enterprises or banking institutions.

Financial planning. Prepares individuals to plan and manage the financial interests and growth of individuals and institutions.

Fine/studio arts. Prepares individuals to function as creative artists in the visual and plastic media.

Fire protection and safety technology. Studies the application of fire prevention and control skills to loss limitation, substance removal, and fire investigations.

Fire services administration. Prepares students to structure, manage, direct, and control fire departments, prevention services, and inspection and investigation offices.

Firefighting/fire science. Readies individuals to perform the duties of firefighters.

Fishing and fisheries. The scientific study of the husbandry and production of fish and shellfish populations for commercial and recreational purposes, and the management of fishing and related product processing.

Flight attendant. Readies students to perform a variety of personal services conducive to the safety and comfort of airline passengers during flight.

Flight instructor. Prepares individuals to train pilots and flight crews to fly and/or operate commercial, corporate, agricultural, public service, or rescue aircraft.

Floriculture. Explores the operation and management of florist enterprises, supply and delivery services, and flower catering services.

Food and nutrition studies. A general program that focuses on the role of foods and nutrition in human health and wellness.

Food preparation. Trains students to serve as kitchen support staff and food preparation workers.

Food science. Studies the conversion of raw agricultural products into processed forms suitable for human consumption.

Food service. Includes instruction in table and counter services, dining room operations, personnel supervision, safety, and sanitation.

Food technology/processing. Describes the manufacturing, packaging, storage, and distribution technologies and processes for food products.

Foreign language teacher education. Instructs individuals how to teach foreign languages other than French, German, or Spanish.

Foreign languages, general. A program that studies multiple foreign languages at the basic/elementary level.

Forensic psychology. Prepares individuals to apply clinical, counseling, and neuropsychological skills to criminal investigations.

Forensic science. Trains students to apply physical, biomedical, and social sciences to analyze physical evidence, human testimony, and criminal suspects.

Forest engineering. Highlights the mechanical devices and processes used for efficient forest management, timber production, and related systems.

Forest management. Prepares individuals for the management and administration of forest lands and related resources.

Forest resources production. Prepares students to perform technical and managerial functions as they relate to the production, harvesting, and processing of forest resources.

Forest sciences/biology. The study of environmental factors affecting forests and the growth and management of forest resources.

Forest technology. Readies individuals to assist foresters in the management and production of forest resources.

Forestry. Features the management and development of forest areas for economic, recreational, and ecological purposes.

Franchise operations. Trains individuals to manage and operate franchises.

French. The study of the language and literature of French-speaking peoples, including related dialects and creoles.

French studies. Describes the history, society, politics, culture, and economics of France.

French teacher education. Describes how to teach French language programs.

Funeral direction. Prepares individuals for professional licensure as managers of funeral homes and cemeteries.

Funeral services/mortuary science. Describes the basic elements of mortuary science, the funeral service business, and counseling.

Furniture design/manufacturing. Readies individuals to design furniture projects; assemble, finish, and repair furniture articles; and use hand and power tools.

Gay/lesbian studies. The study of homosexuality and the public policies and legal issues surrounding the gay and lesbian community.

Gene therapy. Describes the treatment of diseases and inherited abnormalities through the modification of gene expression.

Genetic counseling. Readies students to counsel patients and families concerning inherited genetic disorders and diseases.

Genetics. The study of biological inheritance, development, disease, and evolution in all living organisms and viruses.

Geochemistry. Investigates the properties and behavior of the substances forming, and formed by, geomorphological processes of the earth and other planets.

Geography. Highlights the spatial distribution and interrelationships of people, natural resources, and plant and animal life.

Geography teacher education. Describes teaching geography at various grade levels.

Geological engineering. Prepares students to apply geological analysis to engineering problems, such as environmental recovery sites, or the geological forces acting upon structures.

Geology/earth science. The scientific study of the earth, the forces acting upon it, and the behavior of the solids, liquids, and gases comprising it.

Geophysics/seismology. The scientific study of the physics of solids and its application to the study of the earth.

Geotechnical engineering. Explores the systems used to manipulate and control surface and subsurface features at or incorporated into structural sites.

German. Highlights the German language as used in Austria, Germany, and Switzerland.

German studies. Focuses on the history, society, politics, culture, and economics of the Germanic peoples.

German teacher education. Prepares students to teach German language programs at various educational levels.

Germanic languages. A general program that focuses on one or more of the Germanic languages of Western, Central, and Northern Europe.

Gerontology. Investigates the aging process and aged human populations.

Geropsychology. Investigates the psychology of aging populations, with reference to growth and decline across the life span.

Glazier. Readies individuals to install and repair fixtures, sheets, windows, and skylights made of glass or Plexiglas.

Global studies. Investigates global and international issues from the perspective of the social sciences and social services.

Graphic communications. Provides technical training in the manufacture, distribution, or transmission of graphic communications, including prepress, press, and postpress operations.

Graphic design. Readies students to use artistic and computer techniques to convey technical and commercial concepts through images and typography.

Graphic/printing production. Prepares students to apply technical knowledge to perform a variety of commercial and industrial graphic communications jobs.

Greenhouse operations. Investigates the production and storage of plant species in controlled indoor environments for sale or research purposes.

Gunsmithing. Highlights the making and modification of firearms.

Hair styling. Readies individuals to shampoo, style, and set hair, and apply hair cosmetics and wigs.

Hazardous materials technology. Focuses on basic engineering principles to aid in identifying and disposing of hazardous materials.

Health aide. Readies individuals to provide supervised care to patients, and/or perform maintenance and general assistance in health care facilities.

Health care administration. Readies individuals to develop, plan, and manage health care operations and services within health care facilities.

Health communications. Explores how people understand health and illness and the media's role in shaping health care messages.

Health management/clinical assistant. Prepares students to perform office services and clinical specialties under the supervision of physicians, nurses, or other health care professionals.

Health occupations teacher education. Trains students to teach specific vocational health occupations programs.

Health physics/radiologic health. A program of study that applies nuclear science and engineering physics to diagnostic, treatment, and therapeutic processes, and to public health protection.

Health services. Prepares for entry into specialized training programs or for concentrations in the allied health area.

Health services administration. Readies students to plan and manage health services delivery systems in the public and private sectors.

Health teacher education. Prepares individuals to educate students about health-related topics.

Health unit coordinator. Readies individuals to perform administrative and reception duties in a patient care unit.

Health unit manager. Prepares students to supervise and coordinate the operations of patient care units.

Health/medical psychology. Studies health, illness, and recovery, from the perspective that these phenomena arise from a combination of physical, behavioral, and social conditions.

Health/physical fitness. Readies students to promote physical fitness and athletic prowess, and to accomplish related research and service goals.

Heating/air conditioning/refrigeration maintenance. Describes the maintenance of heating, air conditioning, and refrigeration systems.

Heating/air conditioning/refrigeration technology. Focuses on the development and installation of air conditioning, refrigeration, and heating systems.

Heavy equipment maintenance. Trains individuals to repair and overhaul heavy equipment.

Heavy/earthmoving equipment operation. Trains students to operate and maintain heavy construction equipment involved in digging, sloping, grading, stripping, backfilling, clearing, and excavating.

Hebrew. Explores the Hebrew language in either premodern or modern forms.

Hematology technology. Readies students, under the supervision of a laboratory scientist or physician, to perform tests and analyze blood samples.

Herbalism. A program that utilizes herbal medicines to prevent and cure illnesses and temporary physical disorders.

Higher education administration. Prepares students to become administrators in four-year colleges, universities, and higher education systems.

Hindu studies. A program that defines the philosophies, religious history, and cultural and social manifestations of Hinduism.

Hispanic-American/Latino/Chicano studies. The study of the Hispanic-American immigrant populations within the United States and Canada.

Histologic assistant. Readies individuals to process tissue samples and perform routine histologic procedures and tests.

Histologic technology. Trains students to identify tissue and cell components and relate these findings to physiological functions and to the detection and diagnoses of diseases.

Historic preservation. Studies the process of saving and restoring old structures for contemporary use.

History. The study and interpretation of the past.

History of science/technology. Describes the historical evolution of scientific theories and science applications and technologies.

History teacher education. Prepares students how to teach history programs at various educational levels.

Holocaust studies. Investigates acts of genocide in human history with particular reference to twentieth-century genocides.

Home furnishings. Includes instruction in selecting, purchasing, designing, and decorating home furnishings; floral design; accessory construction; textiles; and upholstery.

Home health attendant. Highlights the provision of support services for homebound disabled, recovering, or elderly people.

Horse husbandry/equine science. Trains students in the care and maintenance of horses and of horse farms, stables, and tracks.

Horticultural science. Focuses on the scientific principles related to the cultivation of garden and ornamental plants, including fruits, vegetables, flowers, and landscape and nursery plants.

Horticulture. Describes the production of domesticated plants, shrubs, flowers, trees, and groundcover, and the management of horticultural services.

Hospital/health care facilities administration. Prepares students to administer hospitals, clinics, nursing homes, and other health care facilities.

Hospitality administration and management. Prepares students to serve as general managers of hospitality operations in the travel, lodging, food service, and recreation industries.

Hospitality/recreation marketing. Focuses on the provision of marketing services in the hospitality and leisure fields.

Hotel/motel administration/management. Prepares individuals to oversee operations and facilities that provide lodging services to travelers.

Housing and human environments. The study of the behavioral, social, economic, functional, and aesthetic aspects of housing, interiors, and other environments.

Human development and family studies. Studies human development and behavioral characteristics of the individual within the context of the family.

Human nutrition. Highlights the relationships between food consumption and human development and health.

Human resources development. Readies students to manage and evaluate programs to improve individual productivity, employability and job satisfaction, and organizational effectiveness.

Human resources management. Prepares students to manage the development of personnel in organizations, including recruitment, staffing, training, performance management, compensation, labor relations, and health and safety.

Human sciences communication. Focuses on communication of human sciences subject matter to various audiences through print and non-print media.

Human services. Explores the provision of human and social services to individuals and communities.

Human/medical genetics. Describes human genetics as they relate to diagnosis, genetic engineering and therapy, transplantation, and diseases and their defense.

Humanities. Combined studies in the humanities, emphasizing languages, literatures, art, music, philosophy, and religion.

Hydraulics technology. Includes instruction in hydraulics principles, pipeline and pumping systems, operational testing, and inspection and maintenance procedures.

Hydrology/water resources science. The study of the circulation, distribution, chemical and physical properties, and environmental interaction of surface and subsurface waters.

Illustration. Highlights artistic techniques to portray the concepts of authors and designers to specifications.

Industrial design. Readies individuals to convey information through forms, shapes, and packaging for manufactured products.

Industrial electronics technology. Trains individuals to assemble, manage, and service industrial electrical/electronic equipment.

Industrial engineering. Prepares students to design systems for managing industrial production processes.

Industrial equipment maintenance/repair. Readies students to fix and sustain the operation of industrial machinery and equipment.

Industrial radiologic technology. Focuses on the operation of industrial and research testing equipment using radioisotopes.

Industrial safety technology. Prepares students to implement and enforce industrial safety standards.

Industrial technology. Includes instruction in organizational behavior, industrial planning, computer applications, and report and presentation preparation.

Industrial/organizational psychology. Examines individual and group behavior in industrial and organizational settings.

Information resources management. Prepares students to plan, manage, and evaluate information services in organizations.

Information systems. Focuses on the theory and process of information collection, transmission, and utilization in traditional and electronic forms.

Information technology. Highlights the design of technological information systems as solutions to business, research, and communications support needs.

Inorganic chemistry. Covers elements and their compounds, other than the hydrocarbons and their derivatives.

Institutional food production. Focuses on the management of food service operations in institutional settings.

Institutional food service. Provides instruction in the production and service used in institutional food establishments.

Instructional media. Focuses on the techniques of creating instructional products and educational resources in various media formats.

Instrumentation technology. Readies students to apply basic engineering principles in support of engineers engaged in developing measurement systems and procedures.

Insurance. Trains individuals to manage risk in organizational settings and provide insurance and risk-aversion services to businesses and individuals.

Intercultural/diversity studies. Examines the social relations between and among majority and minority groups, and ways to promote cooperation, tolerance, and management of diversity issues.

Interior architecture. Prepares students to apply architectural principles in the design of structural interiors for living, working, and leisure purposes.

Interior design. Readies individuals to plan, design, equip, and furnish interior spaces.

International agriculture. Studies the problems of global food production and distribution, and the agricultural systems of other countries.

International business. Trains individuals to oversee international business operations.

International economics. Prepares individuals to analyze international commercial behavior and trade policy.

International finance. Trains students to manage international financial operations and related currency transactions.

International marketing. Readies students to perform marketing techniques for enterprises engaged in exporting or importing goods and services in world markets.

International public health. Focuses on public health problems in poor and developing countries and regions.

International relations. The study of international politics and institutions, and the conduct of diplomacy and foreign policy.

Investments/securities. A program that prepares students to oversee assets placed in capital markets.

Iranian/Persian languages. A program that focuses on the languages used in ancient, medieval, and modern Iran.

Ironworking. Readies individuals to make and install ornamental and reinforcing metal structures and supports.

Islamic studies. The study of the history, culture, and interpretation of the Islamic faith.

Italian. Explores the Italian language and its applications in varied settings.

Italian studies. Highlights the history, society, politics, culture, and economics of modern Italy.

Japanese. The study of Japanese literature, language, and dialects.

Japanese studies. Features the history, society, politics, culture, and economics of Japan.

Jazz studies. Studies the performance and composition of jazz.

Journalism. Focuses on gathering, processing, and delivering news.

Judaic studies. Focuses on the history, culture, and religion of the Jewish people.

Juvenile corrections. Studies the provision of correction services to underage populations.

Kindergarten/preschool education. Trains individuals to instruct students ranging in age from three to six years, in settings prior to beginning regular elementary school.

Kinesiotherapy. Readies individuals to treat the effects of disease, injury, and congenital disorders through exercise and education.

Knowledge management. The study of knowledge management in government agencies and corporations for the purpose of supporting stated goals and objectives.

Korean. The study of Korean literature, language, and dialects.

Korean studies. Examines the history, society, politics, culture, and economics of Korea.

Labor studies. Highlights work, labor organization, policy, and movements from the perspective of the social sciences and history.

Labor/industrial relations. The study of employee-management interactions and the management of issues regarding working conditions and worker benefit packages.

LAN/WAN management. A program that prepares students to oversee and regulate computer systems and performance requirements of an entire network of satellite users, including local and wide area networks.

Land use planning. Focuses on how land can be preserved, developed, and used for maximum social, economic, and environmental benefit.

Landscape architecture. Prepares students for the professional practice of landscape architecture, with instruction in geology and hydrology; soils, groundcovers, and horticultural elements; site planning; and landscape design.

Landscaping/groundskeeping. Describes the maintenance of ornamental and recreational plants and related conceptual designs.

Language interpretation/translation. Highlights the interpretation and/or translation of documents and data files, either from English or (Canadian) French into another language or vice versa.

Laser/optical technology. Readies individuals to support engineers in the development and use of lasers and other optical instruments for commercial or research purposes.

Latin. Features the Latin language and literature and its current ecclesiastical usage.

Latin American studies. Features the history, society, politics, culture, and economics of the North and South American continents outside Canada and the United States.

Latin teacher education. A program that prepares individuals to teach Latin at various grade levels.

Law (J.D.). Preparation for the independent practice of law, taking bar examinations, and advanced research in jurisprudence.

Legal administrative assistance. Instruction includes legal terminology, research, and documentation; software applications; and office procedures.

Legal studies. Applies the social sciences and humanities to the study of law and legal issues.

Liberal arts and sciences. A program that is a structured combination of the arts, sciences, and humanities, emphasizing breadth of study.

Library assistance. Includes instruction in library operation and services; acquisition, storage, and display systems; and material retrieval.

Library science. Prepares individuals for professional service as librarians and information consultants.

Licensed midwifery. Readies individuals to provide for prenatal, natural birth, and immediate postpartum care to pregnant women.

Licensed practical nursing. Prepares students, under the direction of a registered nurse, physician, or dentist, to assist in providing general nursing care.

Lineworker. Describes how to install, operate, maintain, and repair electric power cables; erect and construct pole and tower lines; and install underground cables.

Linguistics. The study of language, language development, and the relationships among languages and language groups.

Livestock management. Readies individuals to produce and manage livestock animals and the production and handling of meat and other products.

Locksmithing. Trains students to open locks, make keys, enter and change lock and safe combinations, and install and repair safes.

Logic. The systematic study of valid inference, argument, and sound reasoning.

Logistics/materials management. Prepares individuals to coordinate all logistical functions within an enterprise, such as acquisitions, receiving and handling, storage, allocation of resources, quality control, and shipping.

Machine shop technology. Trains students to make and modify metal parts used in manufacturing, repair, or design activities.

Machine tool technology. Prepares individuals to manufacture, assemble, test, and repair parts, mechanisms, and machines.

Make-up artist. Prepares students to apply cosmetics and perform specialized makeovers including wig work, masking, and related costuming for professional, artistic, security, or leisure purposes.

Management information systems. Readies individuals to manage data systems for processing and retrieving internal business information, to select systems, and to train personnel.

Management science. Highlights the application of mathematical modeling, programming, forecasting, and operations techniques to the analysis of business organization and performance problems.

Manicurist. Readies students to shape fingernails and toenails, remove unwanted skin, and apply polish and cosmetics to nails.

Manufacturing engineering. Includes instruction in the design, development, and implementation of manufacturing systems.

Manufacturing technologies. Covers the basic engineering principles used to identify and resolve production problems in the manufacturing process.

Marine biology. Emphasizes marine organisms and their interactions with the physical environment.

Marine engineering/naval architecture. Prepares individuals to design vessels operating on or under the water, and to analyze related engineering problems.

Marine maintenance/fitter/ship repair. Prepares students to repair vessel components and mechanical devices, maintain sails, and repair and balance propeller and drive shafts.

Marine science/Merchant Marine. Prepares individuals to serve as captains, executive officers, engineers, and ranking mates on commercially licensed vessels.

Marketing. Prepares students to manage the development of consumer audiences and the delivery of products from producers to consumers.

Marketing research. A program that readies individuals to describe consumer behavior patterns and market environments to marketing managers.

Marriage/family therapy. Trains individuals to diagnose mental and emotional disorders within marriages and family systems, and to apply short- and long-term therapeutic strategies.

Masonry. Focuses on the laying or setting of brick, concrete block, hard tile, and marble, using hand tools.

Massage therapy. Prepares individuals to apply manual techniques for manipulating skin, muscles, and connective tissues.

Materials engineering. Focuses on the design, development and evaluation of materials used in manufacturing, the synthesis of new materials, and the analysis of materials requirements.

Materials science. Focuses on the analysis and evaluation of the characteristics and behavior of solids.

Maternal/child health. Emphasizes public health issues affecting women, children, and families.

Maternal/child health nursing. Informs registered nurses how to provide prenatal care to pregnant women and to mothers and their newborn infants.

Mathematical statistics/probability. Focuses on the mathematical theory underlying the use of statistical methods.

Mathematics. A general program that analyzes quantities, magnitudes, forms, and their relationships, using symbolic logic and language.

Mathematics teacher education. Prepares individuals to teach mathematical subjects.

Mathematics/computer science. A program with a general synthesis of mathematics and computer science, or a specialization that draws from mathematics and computer science.

Mechanical drafting/CAD/CADD. Trains individuals to prepare working drawings and electronic simulations in support of mechanical and industrial engineers.

Mechanical engineering. Focuses on the design and development of mechanical devices and systems, including physical systems used in manufacturing; engines; power units; hydraulics; and the integration of computers and remote control with operating systems.

Mechanical engineering technology. Provides practical training in the design, development, and implementation of engineering projects involving mechanical systems.

Mechanics/repairers, general. Emphasizes the application of technical skills in the adjustment, maintenance, part replacement, and repair of tools, equipment, and machines.

Media studies. Analyzes the criticism of media, how people understand media, and the roles of media in transforming culture.

Medical administrative assistant. Prepares students to provide administrative assistance to physicians and other health professionals.

Medical claims examiner. Readies students to investigate, analyze, and evaluate medical/health insurance claims.

Medical illustrating. Focuses on the creation of visual materials to facilitate educational, research, and clinical purposes.

Medical informatics. Prepares individuals to apply computer science to medical research and clinical support, and to develop advanced imaging, database, and decision systems.

Medical insurance coding specialist. Trains students to conduct data entry, classification, and record-keeping procedures related to medical insurance documentation.

Medical insurance specialist. Covers the management of insurance operations in a medical office, facility, or organization.

Medical office administration. Focuses on the management of business functions in a medical or clinical office.

Medical office assistant. Trains individuals to perform routine administrative duties in a medical, clinical, or health care facility office.

Medical office computer specialist. Readies individuals to install, maintain, and upgrade medical software and associated hardware.

Medical radiologic technology/radiation therapy. Readies students to administer prescribed radiation treatments, manage patients, and maintain pertinent records.

Medical receptionist. Readies students to provide customer service, visitor reception, and patient services.

Medical records administration. Readies individuals to plan, design, and manage systems, processes, and facilities used to collect, store, analyze, and transmit medical records and related information.

Medical records technology. Trains individuals to classify, construct, and secure medical records under the supervision of health information administrators.

Medical scientist. Prepares graduated physicians as research scientists in various areas.

Medical staff services technology. Prepares individuals to provide personnel management, credentialing, and accreditation compliance services for health care facilities and organizations.

Medical transcription. Prepares students to execute verbatim medical minutes, reports, and orders.

Medical/clinical assistant. Readies students to support physicians by providing assistance during patient consultations and examinations.

Medication aide. Prepares students to administer prescribed medications, report patient reactions, and perform emergency and recording duties.

Medicinal/pharmaceutical chemistry. Explores the properties of compounds intended for medicinal applications, and the development of related research methods and clinical trial procedures.

Medicine (M.D.). Prepares individuals for the independent professional practice of medicine as licensed physicians.

Medieval and Renaissance studies. Explores the medieval and Renaissance periods in Europe from the perspective of the humanities and social sciences.

Medium/heavy vehicle technology. Highlights the specialized maintenance of commercial and industrial vehicles, such as trucks and buses.

Mental health counseling. Trains students to evaluate, refer, and counsel people to prevent or mediate personal conflicts and emotional crises.

Mental health services technology. Prepares individuals to assist psychiatrists, psychologists, and nurses in patient care and treatment.

Merchandising/buying operations. Prepares students to function as professional buyers of resale products and product lines for stores, chains, and other retail enterprises.

Metal building assembly. Highlights the construction of metal structures using prefabricated framing and siding components.

Metal/jewelry arts. Trains individuals to fashion artwork from gems and other stones and precious metals.

Metallurgical engineering. Covers the metal components of structural, power, transmission, and moving systems, and the analysis of engineering problems.

Metallurgical technology. Trains students to support metallurgists engaged in developing and using industrial metals and manufacturing processes.

Meteorology. Readies students to predict atmospheric motion and climate change.

Microbiology. The study of small organisms, including bacteria and viruses, as distinguished from the cellular material of larger organisms.

Middle school education. Trains individuals to guide students in the middle, intermediate, or junior high grades.

Military technologies. Prepares individuals for various responsibilities in the armed services and related national security organizations.

Mining and mineral engineering. Studies the evaluation of mineral extraction and refining systems, including open shaft mines and prospecting equipment.

Mining technology. Prepares individuals to support engineers engaged in the development and operation of mines and related mineral processing facilities.

Missionary studies. The theory and practice of religious outreach, social service, and proselytization.

Modern Greek. A program that focuses on the development and use of the Greek language.

Molecular biochemistry. Describes the chemical processes of living organisms at the molecular level.

Molecular biology. Investigates the structure and function of biological macromolecules, with emphasis on proteins and nucleic acids, and processes such as metabolism, gene function and regulation, differentiation, and development.

Molecular biophysics. Applies physics principles to the study of living cells and organisms at the molecular level.

Molecular genetics. Covers the molecular structure and processes that regulate gene expression, information transfer, replication, and stability.

Molecular pharmacology. Highlights characteristics of drugs at the molecular level and their interaction with, and effects on, microbiological structures and processes.

Molecular physiology. Focuses on the scientific study of biochemical communications and processes at the subcellular level.

Molecular toxicology. Describes the interaction of toxic agents with biological systems at the molecular and cellular levels.

Montessori teacher education. Highlights the pedagogical principles and methods developed by Maria Montessori and her followers.

Mortuary science/embalming. Prepares students for licensure as embalmers and morticians, with instruction in embalming, restorative art, laws and regulations, and special services.

Motorcycle maintenance. Prepares students to fix motorcycles and other similarly powered vehicles.

Movement therapy. Prepares individuals to promote body awareness and optimal mental and physical functioning.

Multicultural education. Highlights the design and implementation of instructional and advising services for culturally diverse learning populations.

Multimedia. Prepares students to display ideas in either two or three dimensions, through the simultaneous use of a variety of materials and media.

Museum studies. Prepares individuals to develop, conserve, and retrieve artifacts, exhibits, and collections in museums and galleries.

Music history/literature. Highlights the evolution of music, the development of musical instruments, and the analysis and criticism of musical literature.

Music management. Explores the organization and management of music operations, facilities, personnel, bands, ensembles, and individual artists.

Music pedagogy. Studies the provision of musical instruction and tutoring to clients in private and institutional settings.

Music performance. Prepares individuals to master musical instruments or to sing, and to become solo and/or ensemble performers.

Music teacher education. Prepares individuals to teach music and music appreciation.

Music theory and composition. The study of the structures and processes of music, and the art of writing and arranging music.

Music therapy. Highlights the utilization of music to address patients' physical, psychological, cognitive, emotional, and social needs.

Music, general. An introductory study and appreciation of music and the performing arts.

Musical instrument fabrication/repair. Describes the fabrication, repair, maintenance, and tuning of musical instruments.

Musicology/ethnomusicology. The study of the forms, methods, and functions of music in Western and non-Western societies and cultures.

Mycology. The study of various fungi and their relationship to diseases in plants, animals, and humans, as well as to useful drug products.

Native American education. Prepares individuals to provide teaching and administrative services to American Indian, Alaska Native, and Hawaiian Native students that attend Tribal/First Nation schools.

Native American languages. A program that focuses on the languages native to the Western Hemisphere, with an emphasis on American Indian languages and literatures.

Native American studies. Highlights the history, sociology, politics, culture, and economics of the American Indian, Aleut, Inuit, and Hawaiian peoples.

Natural resource economics. Applies economic concepts and methods to the analysis of issues such as pollution, land use planning, waste disposal, and conservation policies.

Natural resources and conservation. Focuses on the natural environment and its conservation, use, and improvement.

Natural resources management/policy. Readies students to plan, manage, and evaluate programs to protect and regulate natural habitats and resources.

Natural sciences. A combined or undifferentiated focus on one or more of the physical and biological sciences.

Naturopathic medicine. Describes an approach that combines medical knowledge with noninvasive therapies and emphasizes disease prevention, wellness, and self-healing.

Near and Middle Eastern studies. Covers the history, society, politics, culture, and economics of North Africa, Southwestern Asia, Asia Minor, and the Arabian Peninsula.

Neuroanatomy. Focuses on the scientific study of the structure and function of the brain and central nervous system.

Neurobiology/physiology. Describes the neural functions and control of physiological systems in animals and humans.

Neuroscience. Investigates the molecular, structural, cognitive, and behavioral aspects of the brain and nervous system.

Nonprofit/public organization management. Readies individuals to manage the business affairs of foundations, educational institutions, associations, public agencies, or governmental operations.

Norwegian. The study of the language and related dialects of the Norwegian-speaking peoples.

Nuclear engineering. Focuses on systems for controlling and manipulating nuclear energy and the analysis of related engineering problems.

Nuclear engineering technology. Readies individuals to support engineers operating nuclear facilities and engaged in nuclear applications and safety procedures.

Nuclear medical technology. Features the employment of nuclides in evaluations and therapeutic applications, while monitoring for patient health and safety.

Nuclear physics. The scientific study of the properties and behavior of atomic nuclei.

Nuclear power technology. Readies individuals to support engineers in the running of nuclear reactors, and in nuclear materials processing and disposal.

Nurse anesthetist. Teaches registered nurses how to administer anesthetics and provide care for patients before, during, and after anesthesia.

Nurse midwifery. Readies registered nurses to independently deliver babies and treat mothers in the prenatal, delivery, and post-delivery periods.

Nursery operations. Studies the management of plant farms, nurseries, and facilities that develop domesticated plant products for propagation, harvesting, and transplantation.

Nursing (RN). Provides instruction in the knowledge, techniques, and procedures for promoting health and providing care for the sick and disabled, and preparation for licensure as a registered nurse.

Nursing administration. Prepares registered nurses to manage nursing personnel and services in hospitals and other health agencies.

Nursing assistant. Readies individuals, under the training and supervision of a registered nurse or licensed practical nurse, to provide nursing-related services to patients.

Nursing science. The study of clinical practices, research methodologies, and the administration of complex nursing services.

Nutrition sciences. Focuses on the utilization of food for human growth and metabolism in both normal and dysfunctional states.

Occupational health/industrial hygiene. Trains students to monitor and evaluate health and related safety standards in the workplace.

Occupational safety/health technology. Features the maintenance of job-related health and safety standards.

Occupational therapy. Prepares students to maximize patient independence and health through a mix of skills, motivation, environmental adaptations, and assistive technologies.

Occupational therapy assistant. Focuses on aiding occupational therapists by providing assistance during examinations and treatments and by keeping patient records.

Occupational/environmental health nursing. A program that prepares registered nurses to deliver nursing services to worker populations in clinical settings and at job sites.

Ocean engineering. Describes how to plan, design, and evaluate systems that monitor, control, and operate within coastal and ocean environments.

Oceanography. Features the chemical components, mechanisms, and movement of ocean waters and their interactions with terrestrial and atmospheric phenomena.

Office management. A program that prepares students to supervise and manage the operations and personnel of business offices and management-level divisions.

Office technology/data entry. Readies students to support businesses by using computer equipment for administrative purposes.

Office/clerical services. Prepares individuals, under the supervision of office managers, administrative assistants, and secretaries, to provide administrative support.

Oncology. Features the genetics, onset, and composition of cancer cells, as well as cancer behaviors and treatments.

Operations management. Readies students to direct the development, production, and manufacturing functions of an organization.

Operations research. Focuses on the development and application of simulation models to solve problems involving operational systems that are subject to human intervention.

Ophthalmic laboratory technology. Prepares individuals, under the supervision of an ophthalmologist or optometrist, to make corrective lenses and eyewear.

Ophthalmic technology. Prepares students to aid ophthalmologists and optometrists in examining and treating patients with vision disorders and eye diseases.

Opticianry/ophthalmic dispensing. Trains students to fit corrective eyewear, assist patients in selecting appropriate frames, and prepare work orders for ophthalmic technicians.

Optics. Covers light energy and its structure, properties, and behavior under different conditions.

Optometric assistant. Readies individuals to assist in providing patient care, administer examinations and treatments, and perform office functions.

Optometry (O.D.). Prepares individuals for the professional practice of optometry, focusing on the techniques for examining, diagnosing, and treating conditions of the human eye.

Organic chemistry. Investigates the properties and behavior of hydrocarbon compounds and their derivatives.

Organizational behavior studies. Focuses on the scientific study of the behavior and motivations of individuals functioning in organized groups and its application to business and industrial settings.

Organizational communication. Includes instruction in group relations within organizations; decision-making and conflict management; symbolic messages; and human interaction with computer technology.

Ornamental horticulture. Prepares students to breed, grow, and utilize ornamental plant varieties for commercial and aesthetic purposes.

Orthotics/prosthetics. Features the techniques used to design and fit orthoses and prostheses for patients with disabling conditions or limb deformity.

Osteopathic medicine (D.O.). A program that prepares individuals for the professional practice of osteopathic medicine, involving a combination of traditional medicine with principles of holistic medicine and the relationship of the musculoskeletal system to general health.

Pacific area/rim studies. Describes the history, society, politics, culture, and economics of Australia, New Zealand, and the Pacific Islands.

Painting. Readies individuals to impart ideas through the application of paints and chemical color substances to canvases.

Painting/wall covering. Prepares students to finish structural surfaces by applying protective or decorative coating materials, such as paint and wallpaper.

Paleontology. Features the reconstruction and analysis of ancient and extinct lifeforms, ecosystems, and geologic processes.

Paralegal studies. Prepares students to perform research, drafting, investigatory, record-keeping, and administrative functions under the supervision of an attorney or court.

Parasitology. Focuses on organisms that live on or within host organisms, and the role of parasites in causing injury, disease, and environmental damage.

Parks, recreation, and leisure studies. Investigates the practices involved in the provision of recreational facilities and services to the general public.

Parks/recreational/leisure facilities management. Prepares students to develop and manage park facilities and other recreational and leisure facilities.

Particle physics. Studies the basic elements of subatomic matter and energy, and the forces governing their fundamental processes.

Pastoral counseling. Prepares ordained clergy to provide nonclinical pastoral counseling.

Pathology assistant. Trains individuals to help pathologists by performing autopsies, obtaining and preparing surgical specimens, and writing autopsy reports.

Pathology, human/animal. The scientific study of tissue injury and disease, including death and disease infestation and transfer.

Peace and conflict studies. Emphasizes the origins, resolution, and prevention of international and inter-group conflicts.

Pediatric nursing. Prepares registered nurses to provide care for children from infancy through adolescence.

Perfusion technology. Trains individuals to operate equipment that supports or replaces a patient's own respiratory or circulatory system.

Personal/culinary services. Focuses on professional services related to cosmetology, funeral services, and food service.

Personal/financial services marketing. Prepares students to perform marketing and operational tasks associated with the provision of personal and financial services.

Personality psychology. Focuses on characteristics that set the individual apart from other individuals and on how others respond to that individual.

Petroleum engineering. Readies students to develop systems for locating, extracting, processing, and refining crude oil and natural gas.

Petroleum technology. Readies individuals to implement the development and operation of oil and natural gas extraction and processing facilities.

Pharmacology. Emphasizes the interactions of drugs on organisms and their various uses.

Pharmacology/toxicology. The study of pharmacological and toxicological issues in biology and the biomedical sciences.

Pharmacy. A first-professional program that prepares students to prepare and dispense medications, monitor drug therapy, manage pharmacy practices, and counsel patients as professional pharmacists.

Pharmacy assistant. Prepares students, under the supervision of pharmacists, to prepare medications, provide medications to patients, and to manage pharmacy business and clinical operations.

Philosophy. Focuses on ideas and their structure, including arguments and investigations about abstract and real phenomena.

Phlebotomy. Trains students to draw blood samples from patients using a variety of intrusive procedures.

Photographic/film/video technology. Readies students to operate and maintain camera and lighting equipment; and produce finished still, video, and film products.

Photography. Describes the creation of images on photographic film, plates, and digital images.

Photojournalism. Describes the use of still and motion photography in journalism.

Physical anthropology. Studies the adaptations, variability, and evolution of human beings and their living and fossil relatives.

Physical education. Readies students to coach sports and/or teach physical education programs.

Physical sciences. The study of the topics, concepts, processes, and interrelationships of physical phenomena.

Physical therapy. Readies individuals to alleviate physical and functional impairments and limitations caused by injury or disease through the use of therapeutic interventions.

Physical therapy assistant. Trains individuals to support physical therapists by providing assistance during patient examinations, treatment, and monitoring.

Physical/theoretical chemistry. Investigates the properties of matter and the relation of force to the chemical structure and behavior of molecules.

Physician assistant. Prepares students, under the supervision of a physician, to practice medicine.

Physics. The study of matter and energy, and the formulation and testing of the laws governing their behavior.

Physics teacher education. Focuses on the teaching of physics curricula.

Physiology. The study of the functions, processes, and interactions of cells, tissues, and organs, such as respiration, circulation, digestion, sensory perception, and reproduction.

Piano/organ. Readies students to develop the skills necessary to master the piano or organ, and to perform art as solo, ensemble, and/or accompanist performers.

Pipefitting. Focuses on the design, installation, and testing of piping systems and automatic fire and exposure protections systems.

Planetary sciences. The scientific study of planets, small objects, and related gravitational systems.

Plant breeding. Applies genetics and genetic engineering to the improvement of agricultural plant health and populations and the development of new plant varieties.

Plant genetics. Highlights the relation of botanical research, comparative genetics, ecology, and evolutionary studies to the genetics of plants and fungi.

Plant molecular biology. Explores molecular structures, functions, and processes specific to plants and plant substances.

Plant pathology. Highlights plant diseases, plant health, and the development of disease control mechanisms.

Plant physiology. Investigates the internal workings and systems of plants, plant-environment interaction, and plant life cycles and processes.

Plant protection/pest management. Prepares students to control animal and weed infestation of domesticated plant populations and crops; prevent/reduce economic loss; and control environmental pollution related to pest control measures.

Plant sciences. Highlights the breeding, cultivation, and production of plants and the processing and distribution of agricultural plant products.

Plasma/high-temperature physics. Highlights the properties and behavior of matter at high temperatures.

Plastics engineering technology. Includes instruction in the use of industrial polymers, plastics manufacturing and equipment, and design and operational testing procedures.

Platemaker/imager. Readies students to prepare film, digital data, and surfaces to reproduce printed or graphic images.

Playwriting/screenwriting. Describes the composition of written works for the theater and/or film.

Plumbing. Trains students to install and maintain piping fixtures and systems in home and business environments.

Podiatry . Prepares individuals for the professional practice of podiatry, focusing on the prevention, diagnosis, and treatment of diseases and injuries to the foot and lower extremities.

Police science. Prepares individuals to perform the duties of police and public security officers.

Polish. Highlights the Polish language and its use in literature.

Polish studies. Covers the history, society, politics, culture, and economics of Poland.

Political communications. Focuses on human and media communication in the political process and readies individuals to function as members of political and public affairs organizations, political campaign staffs, and related media entities.

Political science. A general program that focuses on the study of political institutions and behavior.

Polymer chemistry. The study of synthesized macromolecules and their interactions with other substances.

Polymer/plastics engineering. Studies the design and development of synthesized macromolecular compounds and their application to specific engineering uses.

Population biology. Investigates the natural history, life cycle behavior, and ecosystem dynamics of single- and multi-species communities and the causes of diversity among such populations.

Portuguese. Focuses on the Portuguese language and related dialects.

Poultry science. Prepares students for the production and management of poultry animals and products.

Power/electrical transmission. Features the installation of indoor and outdoor residential, commercial, and industrial electrical systems and associated power transmission lines.

Precision production trades, general. A program that prepares individuals to apply technical knowledge in creating products using precision crafting and technical illustration.

Predental. Prepares individuals for admission to a first-professional program in dentistry.

Prelaw. A four-year program, in virtually any major, that prepares individuals for admission to a first-professional law program.

Premedicine. Readies students for admission to a first-professional program in medicine, osteopathic medicine, or podiatric medicine.

Preministerial studies. Readies students to enter a seminary or other religious ordination program, or a related religious vocation.

Prenursing. Prepares individuals for admission to professional study in nursing.

Preoperative/surgical nursing. Readies registered nurses to provide care to surgery patients and to provide tableside assistance to surgeons.

Prepharmacy. Prepares individuals for admission to a first-professional program in pharmacy.

Preveterinary. Readies students for admission to a first-professional program in veterinary medicine.

Printing management. Analyzes the application of managerial skills to printing operations from design through finished product.

Printing press operator. The application of technical skills to set up, operate, and maintain printing presses.

Printmaking. Prepares individuals to render art concepts onto surfaces and transfer images, via ink or dyes, onto paper or fabric.

Psychiatric nursing. Describes the provision of nursing care to patients with mental, emotional, or behavioral disorders.

Psychoanalysis. Readies individuals to provide psychoanalytic counseling to individuals and groups.

Psychobiology/physiological psychology. Covers the biological bases of psychological functioning and their application to experimental and therapeutic research.

Psychology. The study of individual and collective behavior, the bases of behavior, and the analysis and treatment of behavior problems and disorders.

Psychology teacher education. A program that prepares students to teach general psychology at the secondary school level.

Psychometrics/quantitative psychology. Explores psychological test construction and validation procedures; problems associated with behavior measurement; and quantitative methods used in research design.

Psychopharmacology. Describes the behavioral effects of drugs, nutrients, and chemicals in laboratory and clinical settings.

Public administration. Trains students to serve as managers in the executive arm of local, state, and federal government.

Public finance. Readies individuals to tend to the financial assets and budgets of public sector organizations.

Public health. Prepares individuals to plan, manage, and evaluate public health care services.

Public health education. A program of study that promotes preventive health measures and the education of targeted populations on health issues.

Public health nursing. Prepares individuals, under the supervision of a public health agency, to provide nursing services for groups or communities.

Public history/archives. A program that applies history and administrative skills to the recording of public events and the management of related historical resources.

Public policy analysis. The study of public policy issues and decision processes.

Public relations. Prepares students to manage the media image of an organization and communicate with clients and the general public.

Publishing. Describes the creation, publishing, and distribution of print and electronic books and other text products.

Purchasing/procurement/contracts. Readies individuals to manage the process of contracting goods and services for an organization.

Quality control technology. Highlights the maintenance of manufacturing and construction standards.

Rabbinical studies (M.H.L., Rav.). A program that prepares individuals for ordination as rabbis.

Radiation biology. Emphasizes the effects of radiation on organisms and biological systems.

Radiation protection/health physics technology. Prepares students to monitor and control radiation exposure and implement preventive measures in health care, work, and natural environments.

Radio and television. Studies the planning, production, and distribution of audio and video programs, and prepares students to function as staff, producers, directors, and managers of radio and television shows.

Radio/television broadcasting. Prepares students to apply technical knowledge to the production of radio and television programs.

Radiologic technology/medical imaging. Focuses on the provision of x-ray and other medical imaging services to patients and health care professionals.

Range science. Studies rangelands, arid regions, and grasslands, and the principles of managing such resources for maximum benefit and environmental balance.

Reading teacher education. Describes how to diagnose reading difficulties and teach reading programs.

Real estate. Prepares individuals to develop, buy, sell, appraise, and manage real property.

Receptionist. Prepares students to perform front-line public relations duties for a business, organization, or answering service.

Recording arts. Prepares individuals to produce sound recordings as finished products or as components of other media productions.

Recreational therapy. Trains students to organize and direct recreational activities designed to promote health for patients who suffer from disabling conditions.

Regional studies. The study of the defined geographic subregions and subcultures within countries and societies.

Religious education. Prepares individuals to provide religious educational services to members of faith communities.

Religious studies. Explores the nature of religious beliefs and specific religious and quasi-religious systems.

Renal/dialysis technology. Trains individuals to administer hemodialysis treatments to patients with renal failure.

Reproductive biology. The study of reproductive processes in animals and human beings.

Resort management. Emphasizes the planning, management, and marketing of comprehensive vacation facilities, services, and products.

Respiratory therapy. Trains individuals to manage the ventilation of critically ill patients, provide respiratory care to patients with breathing disorders, and consult with other health care team members.

Respiratory therapy assistant. Highlights the administration of general respiratory care procedures under the supervision of respiratory therapists.

Restaurant/catering management. Readies individuals to plan, supervise, and manage food and beverage service operations, restaurant facilities, and catering services.

Restaurant/food services management. Trains students to manage restaurants, food services in hospitality establishments, chains and franchises, and restaurant suppliers.

Retailing. Readies individuals to perform operations associated with retail sales in a variety of settings.

Robotics technology. Prepares individuals to aid engineers and other professionals engaged in developing and using robots.

Romance languages. A general curriculum that focuses on the Romance languages of Western, Central, and Southern Europe.

Roofing. Readies individuals to prepare, install, and maintain exterior roofing materials and roofs.

Russian. The study of the languages, literatures, and cultures of Russian-speaking peoples.

Russian/Slavic studies. Focuses on the history, society, politics, culture, and economics of the Russian Federation.

Sacred music. Highlights the history, theory, composition, and performance of music for religious or sacred purposes.

Sales/distribution. Studies the process and techniques of direct wholesale and retail buying and selling operations and introduces individuals to related careers.

Sales/marketing education. Investigates the teaching of vocational sales, marketing, and distributive operations education programs.

Salon management. Trains individuals to manage beauty parlors, shops, and specialized salons.

Sanskrit/classical Indian languages. The study of Sanskrit and related ancient and classical Indo-Aryan languages.

Scandinavian languages. A program that characterizes one or more of the languages, literatures, and linguistics of the Scandinavian peoples.

Scandinavian studies. Studies the history, society, politics, culture, and economics of Denmark, Finland, Greenland, Iceland, Norway, and Sweden.

School librarian education. Prepares students to serve as librarians and media specialists in elementary and secondary schools.

School psychology. Prepares individuals to treat and diagnose student behavioral problems.

Science teacher education. Prepares students to teach general science subjects or a combination of biology and physical science.

Science, technology, and society. Covers the relationship, ramifications, and ethical dimensions of science and technology to public policy.

Sculpture. Features the use of clay, plaster, wood, stone, and metal to create three-dimensional works of art.

Secondary education. Readies individuals to teach a comprehensive curriculum or specific subject matter to students at the secondary school level.

Secondary school administration. Prepares individuals to serve as principals and masters of junior high, secondary, or senior high schools.

Security services management. Readies individuals to plan, manage, and supervise services providing private security protection for people and property.

Security system installation/repair/inspection. Prepares individuals to install and repair household, business, and industrial security devices.

Security/loss prevention. Focuses on the performance of routine inspection, patrol, and crime prevention services for private clients.

Selling/sales operations. Prepares individuals in the direct promotion of products and services to potential customers, and to function as sales representatives and managers.

Semitic languages. Focuses on the Semitic languages of Western Asia, North Africa, and Europe.

Sheet metal technology. Focuses on the forming, shaping, bending, and folding of metal, including the creation of new products, using hand tools and machines.

Shoe/leather repair. Readies students to replace, mend, refinish, and dye leather goods and footwear.

Sign language interpretation. Prepares students to be simultaneous interpreters of American Sign Language and other sign language systems, both one-way and two-way.

Slavic languages. A general program that focuses on one or more of the Slavic languages of Central and Eastern Europe.

Slavic studies. Analyzes the history, society, politics, culture, and economics of the Slavic peoples.

Slovak. The study of the Slovak language, dialects, and literature.

Small business administration/management. A program that prepares individuals to develop and manage independent small businesses.

Small engine mechanics. Readies students to service small internal-combustion engines used on portable power equipment.

Social psychology. Explores individual behavior in group contexts, group behavior, and associated phenomena.

Social science teacher education. Studies the teaching of specific social science subjects and programs.

Social sciences. The study of human social behavior and institutions using any of the methodologies common to the social sciences and/or history.

Social studies teacher education. Prepares students to teach general social studies programs.

Social work. Studies the provision of basic support services for vulnerable individuals and groups.

Social/philosophical foundations of education. Studies education as a social and cultural institution, and the educational process as an object of humanistic inquiry.

Sociology. The systematic study of human social institutions and social relationships.

Software engineering. Prepares individuals to design, implement, validate, and maintain computer software systems using a variety of computer languages.

Soil science. The scientific classification of soils and soil properties, and the study of their relationship to agricultural crops.

Solar energy technology. Highlights the development of solar-powered energy systems.

Solid-state/low-temperature physics. Focuses on solids and related states of matter at low energy levels, including liquids and dense gases.

Somatic bodywork. A course of study that encourages physical and emotional balance through the provision of skilled touch principles and techniques.

South Asian languages. Features one or more of the languages, literatures, and linguistics of the peoples speaking the languages of the Indian subcontinent.

South Asian studies. Analyzes the history, society, politics, culture, and economics of Afghanistan, India, the Maldives, Burma, Pakistan, and Sri Lanka.

Southeast Asian languages. Focuses on one or more of the modern or historical languages spoken or originating in mainland Southeast Asia.

Southeast Asian studies. Covers the history, society, politics, culture, and economics of the peoples of Southeast Asia, defined as Brunei, Cambodia, Indonesia, Laos, Malaysia, The Philippines, Singapore, Thailand, and Viet Nam.

Spanish. Features the language, literature, and culture of Spanish-speaking peoples.

Spanish teacher education. Readies individuals to teach the language, literature, and culture of Spanish-speaking peoples.

Spanish/Iberian studies. Analyzes the history, society, politics, culture, and economics of the peoples of the Iberian Peninsula.

Special education. Describes the design and provision of educational services to children or adults with special learning needs.

Special education administration. Highlights the planning, supervision, and management of programs for exceptional students and their parents.

Special products marketing. Trains individuals to execute marketing and sales operations connected with the promotion of special products, including floristry, food, and home and office products.

Speech pathology. Readies individuals to evaluate patients' speaking capabilities and develop rehabilitative solutions in consultation with related professionals.

Speech teacher education. Prepares students to teach speech and language arts at various educational levels.

Speech/rhetorical studies. Studies interpersonal communication from the scientific/behavioral and humanistic perspectives.

Sports and fitness administration. Highlights the organization, administration, and management of athletic programs and teams, fitness/rehabilitation facilities, and sport recreation services.

Statistics. A study of the theory and proofs that form the basis of probability and inference, and of the methods of collecting, analyzing, and interpreting data.

Structural biology. The scientific study of molecular components and how they are organized into cells and tissues.

Structural engineering. Studies the design, analysis, and structural problems of load-bearing structures such as roads, bridges, and dams.

Substance abuse counseling. Focuses on intervention techniques and therapeutic services for persons suffering from addiction.

Surgical technology. Prepares students to maintain, monitor, and enforce the sterile field and aseptic technique by surgical personnel.

Surveying engineering. Readies individuals to determine the location, elevations, and alignment of natural and man-made topographic features.

Surveying technology. Trains students to determine, plan, and position land tracts and water boundaries, and to prepare related maps, charts, and reports.

Swedish. Focuses on the Swedish language as used in Sweden and Finland.

System administration. Trains individuals to control the system configurations and manage the computer operations of a specific site or network hub.

Systematic biology. Features the patterns of origin, maintenance, diversification, distribution, and extinction of species.

Systems engineering. Trains individuals to design, develop, and evaluate total systems solutions to a wide variety of engineering problems.

Systems science/theory. Focuses on the solution of complex problems using data from the natural, social, technological, behavioral, and life sciences.

Talmudic studies. Prepares students for advanced Talmudic scholarship and entry to ordination programs and conventional graduate and professional schools.

Taxation. Prepares students to provide tax advice and management services to individuals and corporations.

Taxidermy. Trains individuals to reproduce life-like representations of living animals for permanent display and to manage taxidermy businesses.

Teacher assistance. Readies individuals to assist teachers in regular classroom settings or instruct and supervise special student populations.

Teacher education, multiple levels. Prepares individuals to teach students at more than one educational level.

Technical and business writing. The study of the methods and skills needed for writing and editing scientific, technical, and business papers.

Technology/industrial arts education. Trains students to teach technology education/industrial arts programs at various levels.

Telecommunications technology. Focuses on the design and implementation of telecommunications systems.

Textile science. Investigates the properties and processing of fibers, yarns, whole fabrics, dyes, and finishes.

Textile sciences/engineering. Focuses on systems that test and manufacture fiber products and the development of new and improved fibers, textiles, and their uses.

Theater arts management. Trains students to manage theaters and production companies.

Theater design and technology. Prepares students to communicate dramatic information, ideas, moods, and feelings through technical theater methods, including set design, lighting, sound, scene painting, costumes, and computer applications.

Theater history/criticism. Studies the literature, history, and analysis of theatrical productions and theater methods and organization.

Theological studies. The study of the beliefs and doctrines of a particular religious faith from the point of view of that faith.

Theoretical/mathematical physics. Prepares individuals to formulate and evaluate the physical laws governing matter-energy phenomena and to analyze experimental designs and results.

Tibetan studies. Describes the history, society, politics, culture, and economics of Tibet.

Tool and die technology. Prepares individuals to operate tools and make instruments used to form metal parts.

Tourism promotion. Trains students to perform marketing and sales operations connected with the promotion of tourism in a variety of settings.

Tourism/travel management. Readies individuals to manage travel-related enterprises and conventions and/or tour services.

Tourism/travel services. Features the provision of retail services to hotel and motel clients and customers in a variety of settings.

Toxicology. The study of toxic substances; their interaction with organisms; and their prevention, management, and counteraction.

Trade/industrial education. Prepares students to teach specific vocational trades and industries programs.

Traditional Chinese medicine/herbology. Highlights the use of natural products and prescribed medical formulae to treat health imbalances as defined in the Nei Ching Su Wen and other authorities.

Transportation. A program that prepares individuals to apply technical skills to perform services that facilitate the movement of people or materials.

Transportation management. Readies students to coordinate physical transportation operations, networks, and systems.

Transportation/highway engineering. Focuses on the development of systems for the physical movement of people, materials, and information.

Truck/bus/commercial vehicle operation. Trains individuals to drive trucks and buses, delivery vehicles, and for-hire vehicles.

Turf management. Readies individuals to develop, plant, and manage grassed areas and produce and store turf used for transplantation.

Turkish. A program that focuses on the Turkish language in either or both of its premodern and modern variants.

Ukrainian. Focuses on the Ukrainian language and its applications in varied settings.

Underwater diving. Prepares students to function as professional deep-water or scuba divers, diving instructors, or support personnel.

Upholstery. Highlights the installation of springs, padding, covering, and finishing on furniture, seats, caskets, mattresses, and bedsprings.

Urban education. Describes issues specific to the educational needs of populations located in metropolitan areas and inner cities.

Urban forestry. Studies the development, care, and maintenance of trees and forested areas that are within or near areas of dense human habitation.

Urban studies. Emphasizes urban institutions and the forces influencing urban social and political life.

Urban, community, and regional planning. The application of planning, analysis, and architecture to the development and improvement of urban areas.

Vehicle emissions inspection/maintenance. Prepares individuals to test and service all vehicle emission systems in accordance with relevant laws and regulations.

Vehicle parts/accessories marketing. Prepares individuals to distribute and sell replacement parts and other supplies in the automotive, marine, and aviation industries.

Vendor/product certification. Prepares students to fulfill requirements set by vendors for professional qualification to install, customize, and maintain specific software products and/or processes.

Veterinary medicine (D.V.M.). Trains students for the professional practice of veterinary medicine, involving the diagnosis, treatment, and management of animal health care.

Veterinary technology. Prepares students, under the supervision of veterinarians, to provide animal health care, clinical assistance, and owner communication.

Violin/viola/guitar/stringed instruments. Prepares students to master a stringed instrument.

Virology. Examines viruses that inhabit living cells in parasitical relationships and their role in causing disease.

Vision science. The study of vision, visual processes, clinical research, and forms of treatment.

Visual/performing arts. Highlights the visual and performing arts, and prepares individuals in any of the visual artistic media or performing disciplines.

Vocational rehabilitation counseling. Prepares students to counsel disabled individuals in order for them to have fulfilling and productive lives.

Vocational/technical education. Readies individuals to teach vocational technical education programs to students.

Voice/opera. Trains students to master the human voice and to perform in concerts, choirs, operas, or other forms of singing.

Waldorf/Steiner teacher education. Features the pedagogical principles and methods developed by Rudolf Steiner and his followers.

Warehousing/inventory management. Readies individuals to support warehouse operations, inventory control, parts identification, and counter services for customers.

Watch/jewelrymaking. Readies individuals to mend and maintain time-measuring devices and jewelry items.

Water quality/treatment/recycling technology. Prepares individuals to implement engineering designs for origination and use of water storage, water-power, and wastewater treatment systems.

Water resource engineering. Describes systems for collecting, storing, moving, conserving, and controlling surface- and groundwater.

Water, wetlands, and marine management. Investigates the development, conservation, and management of freshwater and saltwater environments.

Web page/multimedia design. Readies students to produce and publish documents, images, graphics, sound, and multimedia projects on the World Wide Web.

Web/multimedia management. Covers the development and maintenance of Web servers and Web pages at Web sites.

Welding technology. A program that prepares individuals to apply technical knowledge and skills to join or cut metal surfaces.

Well drilling. Readies individuals to operate well-drilling equipment; locate, drill, and construct wells; and test and monitor wells.

Western European studies. Covers the history, society, politics, culture, and economics of historical Western Europe.

Wildlife and wilderness management. Describes the conservation and management of wildlife and wilderness areas, and the management of wildlife reservations and zoological facilities.

Wildlife biology. A program that applies biological principles to the study of vertebrate wildlife and habitats in remote and urban areas.

Women's studies. Focuses on the history, sociology, politics, culture, and economics of women and the development of modern feminism.

Wood science/pulp/paper technology. Describes the properties and behavior of wood and the development of processes for converting wood into paper and other products.

Woodworking. Trains students to shape, mark, saw, carve, sand, and repair wooden products, and to use a variety of hand and power tools.

Word processing. Highlights typing, table construction, and document formatting on personal computers.

Work/family studies. Focuses on family and consumer science concepts and the various career paths open to interested students.

Yoga teacher/therapy. Trains students to provide spiritual and physical Yoga therapy in private, institutional, and clinical settings.

Youth ministry. Studies the provision of spiritual counseling and leadership services to children, adolescents, and young adults.

Youth services. Readies students to plan, manage, and implement social services for children, youth, and families.

Zoology. Emphasizes the anatomy, structure, and behavior of animals.

Part III: College Listings

About Part III

Once you have an idea of what you might want to study, you can use this Part to find colleges that offer the majors or academic programs you are interested in.

Colleges listed by major

All of the majors that are fully or briefly described in this book (over 900 in all) are presented here alphabetically, and under each is a state-by-state list of the colleges that teach it. After the college name you'll find letter symbols that designate the different degree levels at which the major is offered by that college:

C Certificate or diploma
A Associate degree
B Bachelor's degree
T Teacher certification
M Master's degree
D Doctorate
F First-professional degree

Certificate or diploma. Certificates are awarded to students who complete nondegree programs, which usually take one year or less and are most frequently offered in technical and vocational fields of study.

Associate degree. Usually two years in length, associate degree programs are most often found at community colleges and technical schools, but they are also offered at many four-year colleges.

Bachelor's degree. Programs in which you earn a bachelor's degree usually take four years, but some programs can be completed in three years and some take five.

Teacher certification. Each state sets its own certification standards, and all colleges that prepare teachers are accredited by the state in which they are located. Students must meet both bachelor's degree requirements and state certification requirements. Most states require candidates to pass an examination in the field they plan to teach.

Master's degree. Master of arts (M.A.) and master of science (M.S.) programs are graduate degrees in the liberal arts and sciences, intended for students with B.A. or B.S. degrees, and usually take one or two years to complete. Among other master's degree programs are the master of business administration (MBA), the master of library science (M.L.S.), and the master of social work (M.S.W.) In some fields, such as law and medicine, the master's degree follows the first-professional degree (J.D., M.D.).

Doctorate. Doctoral programs usually consist of course work and independent research culminating in a dissertation or other formal presentation of the results of independent study. Length of study varies widely, and is usually self-determined.

First-professional degree. These programs provide the academic prerequisites to become licensed in a recognized profession, such as medicine, law, or veterinary medicine. At least two years of prior college-level study are required for entrance into the program, and the total registered time of study must equal six academic years.

Special academic programs

In addition to majors, minors, and concentrations, many colleges offer other ways to enhance, focus, or further shape your undergraduate education. For each of the more common and popular programs, there is a state-by-state listing of colleges that offer it, beginning on page 1243.

Colleges listed by major

Accounting

Alabama

Alabama Agricultural and Mechanical University *B*
Alabama Southern Community College *A*
Alabama State University *B, M*
Athens State University *B*
Auburn University *B, M*
Auburn University at Montgomery *B*
Birmingham-Southern College *B*
Bishop State Community College *A*
Calhoun Community College *A*
Chattahoochee Valley Community College *A*
Faulkner University *B*
Huntingdon College *B*
J. F. Drake State Technical College *C, A*
Jacksonville State University *B*
Lawson State Community College *A*
Miles College *B*
Northeast Alabama Community College *A*
Oakwood College *A, B*
Samford University *B, M*
South University *A*
Southern Union State Community College *A*
Spring Hill College *B, M*
Talladega College *B*
Troy University *B*
Tuskegee University *B*
University of Alabama *B, M, D*
University of Alabama
  Birmingham *B, M*
  Huntsville *B, M*
University of Mobile *B*
University of Montevallo *B*
University of North Alabama *B*
University of South Alabama *B, M*
University of West Alabama *B*
Virginia College *C, A, B*
Wallace State Community College at Hanceville *A*

Alaska

Charter College *C, A*
University of Alaska
  Anchorage *A, B*
  Fairbanks *B*
  Southeast *C, B*

Arizona

Arizona Institute of Business and Technology
  International Institute of the Americas: Mesa *A*
Arizona State University *B, M*
Arizona State University West *B*
Central Arizona College *C, A*
Chandler-Gilbert Community College
  Pecos *A*
Chaparral College *A, B*
Coconino County Community College *C*
DeVry University
  Phoenix *M*
Everest College *C, A*
Gateway Community College *C, A*
Grand Canyon University *B*

International Institute of the Americas
  Phoenix *C, A*
  Tucson *C, A*
International Institute of the Americas: West Valley *C, A*
Lamson College *A*
Mesa Community College *A*
Mohave Community College *C*
Northern Arizona University *C, B*
Northland Pioneer College *C, A*
Paradise Valley Community College *C, A*
Phoenix College *A*
Pima Community College *C, A*
Prescott College *B*
Rio Salado College *C, A*
Scottsdale Community College *C, A*
University of Arizona *B, M*
University of Phoenix *B, M*
Western International University *B, M*
Yavapai College *C, A*

Arkansas

Arkansas Northeastern College *C*
Arkansas State University *B, M*
Arkansas State University
  Beebe *C*
Arkansas Tech University *B*
Black River Technical College *A*
Harding University *B*
Henderson State University *B*
Hendrix College *B, M*
John Brown University *B*
Lyon College *B*
National Park Community College *A*
North Arkansas College *C*
Northwest Arkansas Community College *C*
Ouachita Baptist University *B*
Ouachita Technical College *C*
Pulaski Technical College *C*
South Arkansas Community College *C*
Southeast Arkansas College *C*
Southern Arkansas University *B*
University of Arkansas *B, M*
University of Arkansas
  Community College at Batesville *A*
  Fort Smith *B*
  Little Rock *B*
  Monticello *B*
  Pine Bluff *B*
University of Central Arkansas *B, M*
University of the Ozarks *B*

California

Allan Hancock College *C, A*
American River College *C, A*
Azusa Pacific University *B*
Bakersfield College *A*
Barstow College *C, A*
Biola University *B*
Butte College *C, A*
CEI College
  Maric College: Panorama City *A*
Cabrillo College *C, A*
California Lutheran University *B*
California State Polytechnic University: Pomona *B*
California State University
  Chico *B, M*
  Dominguez Hills *B*
  East Bay *B, M*
  Fresno *B*

Fullerton *B, M*
Long Beach *B*
Los Angeles *M*
Northridge *M*
Sacramento *B*
San Bernardino *B, M*
Canada College *C, A*
Cerritos Community College *A*
Chabot College *A*
Chaffey College *C, A*
Chapman University *B*
Citrus College *C*
City College of San Francisco *C, A*
Claremont McKenna College *B*
Coastline Community College *C, A*
College of Alameda *A*
College of Marin: Kentfield *A*
College of San Mateo *C, A*
College of the Canyons *C, A*
College of the Desert *C*
College of the Sequoias *C, A*
College of the Siskiyous *C, A*
Columbia College *C*
Copper Mountain College *C*
Cosumnes River College *C, A*
Crafton Hills College *C*
Cuyamaca College *C, A*
Cypress College *C, A*
De Anza College *C, A*
Diablo Valley College *C*
East Los Angeles College *A*
Empire College *C, A*
Evergreen Valley College *C*
Foothill College *C, A*
Fresno City College *C, A*
Fresno Pacific University *B*
Fullerton College *C, A*
Gavilan Community College *C*
Glendale Community College *C, A*
Golden Gate University *C, B, M*
Golden West College *C, A*
Heald College
  Fresno *C, A*
  Rancho Cordova *C, A*
  Roseville *C, A*
  Salinas *A*
  San Jose *C, A*
  Stockton *C, A*
Humphreys College *A, B*
Institute of Computer Technology *C*
Irvine Valley College *C, A*
La Sierra University *B, M*
Lake Tahoe Community College *C, A*
Laney College *C, A*
Las Positas College *C*
Lassen College *A*
Lincoln University *B*
Long Beach City College *C, A*
Los Angeles City College *A*
Los Angeles Harbor College *C, A*
Los Angeles Mission College *A*
Los Angeles Pierce College *C, A*
Los Angeles Southwest College *A*
Los Angeles Trade and Technical College *C, A*
Los Angeles Valley College *C*
Los Medanos College *C, A*
Loyola Marymount University *B*
MTI College *C*
Master's College *B*
Mendocino College *C, A*
Merced College *C, A*
MiraCosta College *C, A*

Mission College *A*
Modesto Junior College *C, A*
Monterey Peninsula College *C, A*
Moorpark College *C, A*
Mount St. Mary's College *A, B*
Mount San Antonio College *C, A*
Napa Valley College *A*
National University *C, B, M*
Ohlone College *C, A*
Orange Coast College *C, A*
Pacific States University *C, B, M*
Pacific Union College *B*
Palo Verde College *C, A*
Palomar College *C, A*
Pasadena City College *C, A*
Pepperdine University *B*
Point Loma Nazarene University *B*
Reedley College *C, A*
Rio Hondo College *A*
Riverside Community College *C, A*
Sacramento City College *C, A*
Saddleback College *C, A*
St. Mary's College of California *B*
San Bernardino Valley College *C, A*
San Diego City College *C, A*
San Diego Mesa College *C, A*
San Diego Miramar College *A*
San Diego State University *B, M*
San Francisco State University *B, M*
San Joaquin Delta College *A*
San Jose City College *C, A*
San Jose State University *B, M*
Santa Ana College *C, A*
Santa Barbara City College *C, A*
Santa Clara University *B*
Santa Monica College *A*
Santa Rosa Junior College *C*
Santiago Canyon College *A*
Shasta College *A*
Sierra College *C, A*
Skyline College *C, A*
Solano Community College *C, A*
Southwestern College *C, A*
Taft College *C, A*
University of California
  Santa Cruz *B*
University of La Verne *B*
University of Redlands *B*
University of San Diego *B, M*
University of San Francisco *B*
University of Southern California *B, M, D*
Vanguard University of Southern California *B*
Ventura College *C, A*
West Hills Community College *C, A*
West Los Angeles College *C, A*
West Valley College *A*
Woodbury University *B*
Yuba Community College District *C, A*

Colorado

Adams State College *B*
Aims Community College *A*
Blair College *A*
Colorado Mountain College
  Alpine Campus *C, A*
  Spring Valley Campus *C, A*
  Timberline Campus *C, A*
Colorado State University
  Pueblo *B*
Community College of Aurora *C, A*

Community College of Denver *C, A*
Fort Lewis College *B*
Front Range Community College *C, A*
Johnson & Wales University *A, B*
Mesa State College *B*
Metropolitan State College of
 Denver *B*
Morgan Community College *A*
National American University
 Denver *A, B*
Northeastern Junior College *A*
Parks College *A*
Parks College:Aurora *A*
Pueblo Community College *A*
Red Rocks Community College *C, A*
Regis University *B*
Trinidad State Junior College *A*
University of Colorado
 Boulder *B, M*
 Colorado Springs *B*
 Denver and Health Sciences
 Center *M*
University of Denver *B, M*
Western State College of Colorado *B*
Westwood College of Technology *B*

Connecticut

Albertus Magnus College *B*
Briarwood College *A*
Capital Community College *C, A*
Central Connecticut State
 University *B*
Eastern Connecticut State
 University *B, M*
Fairfield University *B*
Gateway Community College *A*
Gibbs College *C*
Housatonic Community College *A*
Manchester Community College *C, A*
Middlesex Community College *A*
Northwestern Connecticut
 Community College *A*
Norwalk Community College *A*
Post University *A, B*
Quinebaug Valley Community
 College *A*
Quinnipiac University *B, M*
Sacred Heart University *B*
Southern Connecticut State
 University *B*
Three Rivers Community College *C, A*
Tunxis Community College *C, A*
University of Bridgeport *B, M*
University of Connecticut *B, M*
University of Hartford *B, M*
University of New Haven *B*
Western Connecticut State
 University *B*

Delaware

Delaware State University *B*
Delaware Technical and Community
 College
 Owens Campus *C, A*
 Stanton/Wilmington Campus *C, A*
 Terry Campus *C, A*
Goldey-Beacom College *A, B*
University of Delaware *B, M*
Wesley College *B*
Wilmington College *B*

District of Columbia

American University *B*
Catholic University of America *B, M*
Gallaudet University *B*
George Washington
 University *B, M, D*
Georgetown University *B*
Howard University *B*
Southeastern University *A, B, M*
Strayer University *C, A, B, M*
University of the District of
 Columbia *B*

Florida

Barry University *B*
Bethune-Cookman College *B*
Brevard Community College *C*
Broward Community College *C, A*
Central Florida Community
 College *C, A*
Clearwater Christian College *B*
Daytona Beach Community
 College *C, A*
DeVry University
 Miramar *M*
 Orlando *M*
Edison College *C, A*
Edward Waters College *B*
Flagler College *B*
Florida Agricultural and Mechanical
 University *B*
Florida Atlantic University *B, M*
Florida Community College at
 Jacksonville *A*
Florida Gulf Coast University *B, M*
Florida Institute of Technology *B, M*
Florida International University *B, M*
Florida Memorial University *B*
Florida Metropolitan University
 Brandon Campus *A, B*
 Melbourne Campus *A, B*
 Orlando College North *A, B*
 Pinellas *A, B*
 Pompano Beach *A, B*
 Tampa College *A, B*
 Tampa College Lakeland *B*
Florida Metropolitan University:
 Jacksonville *C, A, B*
Florida National College *A*
Florida Southern College *B, M*
Florida State University *B, M, D*
Gulf Coast Community College *C, A*
Hillsborough Community
 College *C, A*
Indian River Community College *C, A*
International College *A, B*
Jacksonville University *B*
Johnson & Wales University *A, B*
Jones College *A, B*
Lake City Community College *C*
Lynn University *B*
Manatee Community College *C, A*
Miami Dade College *C, A*
Northwood University
 Florida Campus *A, B*
Nova Southeastern University *B, M*
Okaloosa-Walton College *C, A*
Palm Beach Community College *A*
Pensacola Junior College *C, A*
Polk Community College *A*
St. Johns River Community College *A*
St. Leo University *B*
St. Thomas University *B, M*
Santa Fe Community College *C, A*
South Florida Community
 College *C, A*
South University:West Palm Beach
 Campus *A*
Southeastern College of the
 Assemblies of God *B*
Southwest Florida College *C, A*
Southwest Florida College
 Tampa *A*
Stetson University *B, M*
Tallahassee Community College *A*
University of Central Florida *B, M*
University of Florida *B, M*
University of Miami *C, B, M*
University of North Florida *B, M*
University of South Florida *B, M*
University of Tampa *B*
University of West Florida *B, M*
Valencia Community College *A*
Warner Southern College *B*
Webber International
 University *A, B, M*
Webster College: Holiday *A*

Georgia

Abraham Baldwin Agricultural
 College *A*
Albany State University *B*
Augusta State University *B*
Augusta Technical Institute *C, A*
Bainbridge College *A*
Berry College *B*
Brenau University *B*
Brewton-Parker College *B*
Brown Mackie College:Atlanta *A*
Chattahoochee Technical College *C, A*
Clark Atlanta University *B, M*
Clayton State University *B*
Coastal Georgia Community
 College *A*
Columbus State University *B*
Columbus Technical College *C, A*
Darton College *C, A*
DeKalb Technical College *C, A*
DeVry University
 Decatur *M*
Emory University *B*
Fort Valley State University *B*
Gainesville State College *A*
Georgia College and State
 University *B, M*
Georgia Southern University *B, M*
Georgia Southwestern State
 University *B*
Georgia State University *B, M, D*
Griffin Technical College *A*
Gwinnett College *C*
Gwinnett Technical College *C, A*
Kennesaw State University *B, M*
LaGrange College *B*
Middle Georgia College *A*
North Georgia College & State
 University *B*
Northwestern Technical College *C, A*
Oglethorpe University *B*
Paine College *B*
Reinhardt College *B*
Savannah State University *B*
Shorter College *B*
South Georgia College *A*
South University *A, B*
Thomas University *B*
University of Georgia *B, M*
University of West Georgia *B, M*
Valdosta State University *B*
Waycross College *A*
West Georgia Technical College *A*

Hawaii

Brigham Young University-Hawaii *B*
Chaminade University of
 Honolulu *B, M*
Hawaii Business College *C, A*
Hawaii Pacific University *A, B*
Heald College
 Honolulu *A*
University of Hawaii
 Hawaii Community College *A*
 Hilo *B*
 Kapiolani Community College *C, A*
 Kauai Community College *C, A*
 Leeward Community College *A*
 Manoa *B, M*
 Maui Community College *A*
 West Oahu *B*

Idaho

Albertson College of Idaho *B*
Boise State University *B, M*
Brigham Young University-Idaho *B*
College of Southern Idaho *A*
Eastern Idaho Technical College *C, A*
Idaho State University *B*
Northwest Nazarene University *B*
University of Idaho *B, M*

Illinois

Augustana College *B*
Aurora University *B*
Benedictine University *B*
Black Hawk College *A*
Black Hawk College
 East Campus *C, A*
Blackburn College *B*
Bradley University *B, M*
Carl Sandburg College *C, A*
Chicago State University *B*
City Colleges of Chicago
 Harold Washington College *C, A*
 Kennedy-King College *C, A*
 Malcolm X College *C, A*
 Olive-Harvey College *C, A*
 Wright College *C, A*
College of DuPage *C*
College of Lake County *C*
Concordia University *B*
Danville Area Community
 College *C, A*
DePaul University *B, M*
Dominican University *B, M*
Eastern Illinois University *B*
Elgin Community College *C, A*
Elmhurst College *B, M*
Eureka College *B*
Fox College *A*
Governors State University *B, M*
Greenville College *B*
Heartland Community College *C*
Highland Community College *C, A*
Illinois Central College *C, A*
Illinois College *B*
Illinois Eastern Community Colleges
 Olney Central College *A*
Illinois Institute of Technology *M*
Illinois State University *B, M*
Illinois Wesleyan University *B*
John Wood Community College *A*
Joliet Junior College *C, A*
Judson College *B*
Kankakee Community College *C, A*
Kaskaskia College *C, A*
Kishwaukee College *C, A*
Lewis University *B*
Lewis and Clark Community
 College *A*
Lincoln Land Community College *A*
Loyola University of Chicago *B, M*
MacCormac College *A*
MacMurray College *B*
McKendree College *B*
Midstate College *A, B*
Millikin University *B*
Monmouth College *B, T*
Morton College *A*
National-Louis University *C, B*
North Central College *B*
North Park University *B*
Northeastern Illinois University *B, M*
Northern Illinois University *B, M*
Northwestern Business College *A*
Northwestern University *D*
Oakton Community College *C, A*
Olivet Nazarene University *B*
Prairie State College *C*
Quincy University *B*
Richland Community College *A*
Rock Valley College *C, A*
Rockford Business College *A*
Rockford College *B*
Roosevelt University *B, M*
St. Augustine College *C, A*
St. Xavier University *C, B*
Sauk Valley Community College *C, A*
South Suburban College of Cook
 County *C, A*
Southern Illinois University
 Carbondale *B, M*
Southern Illinois University
 Edwardsville *B, M*
Southwestern Illinois College *A*

Taylor Business Institute *C, A*
Trinity Christian College *B*
Trinity International University *B*
Triton College *C, A*
University of Illinois
  Chicago *B, M*
  Springfield *B, M*
  Urbana-Champaign *B, M, D*
University of St. Francis *B*
Waubonsee Community College *C*
Western Illinois University *B, M*
William Rainey Harper College *C, A*

Indiana

Anderson University *B, M*
Ball State University *B, M*
Bethel College *B*
Brown Mackie College: Fort Wayne *A*
Brown Mackie College: Michigan
  City *A*
Butler University *B, M*
Calumet College of St. Joseph *C, A, B*
Franklin College *B*
Goshen College *B*
Grace College *B*
Huntington University *B*
Indiana Business College *C, A*
Indiana Business College
  Anderson *C, A*
  Columbus *C, A*
  Evansville *C, A*
  Fort Wayne *C, A*
  Lafayette *C, A*
  Marion *C, A*
  Muncie *C, A*
  Terre Haute *C, A*
Indiana Institute of Technology *A, B*
Indiana State University *B*
Indiana University
  Bloomington *B, M*
  East *A, B*
  Kokomo *B*
  Northwest *M*
  South Bend *M*
  Southeast *B*
Indiana University-Purdue University
  Fort Wayne *B*
Indiana University-Purdue University
  Indianapolis *B, M*
Indiana Wesleyan University *B*
International Business College *C, A*
Manchester College *A, B, M*
Marian College *A, B*
Martin University *B*
Oakland City University *A, B*
Purdue University *B*
Purdue University
  Calumet *B*
  North Central Campus *A, B*
St. Joseph's College *B*
Saint Mary's College *B*
St. Mary-of-the-Woods College *A, B*
Sawyer College *C, A*
Sawyer College: Merrillville *A*
Taylor University *B*
Tri-State University *A, B*
University of Evansville *B*
University of Indianapolis *B, M*
University of Notre Dame *B, M*
University of St. Francis *A, B*
University of Southern
  Indiana *C, B, M*
Valparaiso University *B, M*
Vincennes University *A*

Iowa

AIB College of Business *A*
Ashford University *B*
Briar Cliff University *B*
Buena Vista University *B*
Central College *B*
Clarke College *B*
Coe College *B*

Des Moines Area Community
  College *A*
Dordt College *B*
Drake University *B, M*
Ellsworth Community College *A*
Graceland University *B*
Grand View College *B*
Hamilton College *C, A, B*
Hamilton College
  Cedar Falls *C, A*
  Cedar Rapids *A*
Hawkeye Community College *C, A*
Iowa Central Community College *A*
Iowa Lakes Community College *A*
Iowa State University *B, M*
Iowa Wesleyan College *B*
Kaplan University *C, A*
Kirkwood Community College *C, A*
Loras College *A*
Luther College *B*
Marshalltown Community
  College *C, A*
Morningside College *B*
Mount Mercy College *B*
Muscatine Community College *A*
North Iowa Area Community
  College *C, A*
Northeast Iowa Community
  College *C, A*
Northwest Iowa Community
  College *A*
Northwestern College *B*
St. Ambrose University *B, M*
Scott Community College *A*
Simpson College *B*
Southeastern Community College
  North Campus *C, A*
Southwestern Community College *A*
University of Dubuque *B*
University of Iowa *B, M, D*
University of Northern Iowa *B, M*
Upper Iowa University *B*
Wartburg College *B*
Western Iowa Tech Community
  College *C, A*
William Penn University *B*

Kansas

Allen County Community College *A*
Baker University *B*
Barton County Community College *A*
Benedictine College *B*
Bethany College *B*
Brown Mackie College *A*
Butler County Community College *A*
Central Christian College of
  Kansas *A, B*
Coffeyville Community College *A*
Colby Community College *A*
Dodge City Community College *C*
Donnelly College *A*
Emporia State University *B*
Fort Hays State University *B*
Friends University *B*
Haskell Indian Nations University *A*
Johnson County Community
  College *A*
Kansas State University *A, B, M*
Kansas Wesleyan University *A, B*
Labette Community College *A*
McPherson College *B*
MidAmerica Nazarene University *B*
Neosho County Community
  College *C, A*
Newman University *B*
Pittsburg State University *B, M*
Pratt Community College *C, A*
Seward County Community
  College *C, A*
Southwestern College *B*
Tabor College *M*
University of Kansas *B, M*
University of St. Mary *B*
Washburn University of Topeka *B, M*

Wichita State University *B, M*

Kentucky

Asbury College *B*
Ashland Community and Technical
  College *A*
Bellarmine University *B*
Big Sandy Community and Technical
  College *A*
Brescia University *B*
Brown Mackie College:
  Hopkinsville *C, A*
Campbellsville University *A, B*
Eastern Kentucky University *B*
Georgetown College *B*
Kentucky State University *B*
Kentucky Wesleyan College *B*
Madisonville Community College *A*
Maysville Community College *C, A*
Morehead State University *B*
Murray State University *B, M*
National College of Business &
  Technology
  Danville *C, A*
  Florence *C, A*
  Lexington *C, A*
  Louisville *C, A*
  Pikeville *C, A*
  Richmond *C, A*
Northern Kentucky University *B, M*
Owensboro Community College *A*
Paducah Technical College *C*
Spalding University *B*
Spencerian College *A*
Sullivan University *C, A, B*
Thomas More College *C, A, B*
Transylvania University *B*
Union College *B*
University of Kentucky *B, M*
University of Louisville *B, M*
University of the Cumberlands *B*
West Kentucky Community and
  Technical College *A*
Western Kentucky University *B*

Louisiana

Centenary College of Louisiana *B*
Delgado Community College *A*
Dillard University *B*
Grambling State University *B*
Louisiana State University
  Shreveport *B*
Louisiana State University and
  Agricultural and Mechanical
  College *B, M, D*
Louisiana Tech University *B, M*
Loyola University New Orleans *B*
Nicholls State University *B*
Northwestern State University *B*
Nunez Community College *C, A*
Our Lady of Holy Cross College *B*
Southeastern Louisiana University *B*
Southern University
  New Orleans *B*
  Shreveport *A*
Southern University and Agricultural
  and Mechanical College *B*
Tulane University *B, M*
University of Louisiana at Lafayette *B*
University of Louisiana at Monroe *B*
University of New Orleans *B, M*
Xavier University of Louisiana *B*

Maine

Andover College *A*
Beal College *A*
Central Maine Community College *A*
Husson College *A, B*
Northern Maine Community
  College *A*
St. Joseph's College *B*
Thomas College *A, B*
University of Maine *C, B*

University of Maine
  Augusta *B*
  Machias *B*
  Presque Isle *B*
University of Southern Maine *B, M*
York County Community College *A*

Maryland

Allegany College of Maryland *A*
Anne Arundel Community
  College *C, A*
Baltimore City Community College *A*
Bowie State University *B*
Carroll Community College *C, A*
Cecil Community College *A*
Chesapeake College *C, A*
Columbia Union College *A, B*
Community College of Baltimore
  County *A*
Frederick Community College *A*
Frostburg State University *B*
Hagerstown Business College *C, A*
Harford Community College *C, A*
Loyola College in Maryland *B*
Montgomery College *A*
Morgan State University *B*
Mount St. Mary's University *B*
Prince George's Community
  College *C, A*
Salisbury University *B*
Towson University *B*
University of Baltimore *B, M*
University of Maryland
  College Park *B*
  Eastern Shore *B*
  University College *C, B, M*
Villa Julie College *B*

Massachusetts

American International College *B, M*
Anna Maria College *B*
Assumption College *B*
Atlantic Union College *A, B*
Babson College *B*
Bay State College *A*
Becker College *A, B*
Bentley College *B, M*
Boston College *B, M*
Boston University *B*
Bridgewater State College *C, B, M*
Bristol Community College *A*
Bunker Hill Community College *C, A*
Cape Cod Community College *A*
College of the Holy Cross *B*
Elms College *B*
Fitchburg State College *B, M*
Gordon College *B*
Greenfield Community College *C, A*
Lasell College *B*
Marian Court College *C, A*
Massachusetts Bay Community
  College *C, A*
Massachusetts College of Liberal
  Arts *B*
Massasoit Community College *C, A*
Middlesex Community College *A*
Mount Ida College *A*
Newbury College *C, A, B*
Nichols College *B*
Northeastern University *B, M*
Northern Essex Community
  College *C, A*
Quinsigamond Community College *C*
Roxbury Community College *C, A*
Salem State College *B*
Springfield Technical Community
  College *A*
Stonehill College *C, B, M*
Suffolk University *C, B, M*
University of Massachusetts
  Amherst *B, M*
  Dartmouth *B*
Western New England College *B, M*
Westfield State College *B*

Michigan

Adrian College *B*
Albion College *B*
Alma College *B*
Alpena Community College *A*
Andrews University *B*
Aquinas College *B, T*
Baker College
  of Auburn Hills *A, B*
  of Cadillac *C, A, B*
  of Clinton Township *C, A, B*
  of Flint *C, A, B*
  of Jackson *C, A, B*
  of Muskegon *C, A, B*
  of Owosso *A, B*
  of Port Huron *C, A, B*
Bay de Noc Community College *C, A*
Calvin College *B*
Central Michigan University *B*
Cleary University *A, B*
Cornerstone University *B*
Davenport University *A, B, M*
Delta College *C, A*
Eastern Michigan University *B, M*
Ferris State University *B*
Finlandia University *B*
Glen Oaks Community College *C*
Gogebic Community College *A*
Grace Bible College *B*
Grand Rapids Community College *A*
Grand Valley State University *B, M*
Henry Ford Community College *A*
Hillsdale College *B*
Hope College *B*
Jackson Community College *C, A*
Kalamazoo Valley Community
  College *C, A*
Kellogg Community College *C, A*
Kettering University *B*
Kuyper College *B*
Lake Michigan College *A*
Lake Superior State University *A, B*
Lansing Community College *A*
Macomb Community College *C, A*
Madonna University *B, M*
Marygrove College *C, A, B*
Michigan State University *B, M, D*
Mid Michigan Community College *A*
Monroe County Community
  College *C, A*
Montcalm Community College *A*
Muskegon Community College *A*
North Central Michigan College *C, A*
Northern Michigan University *B*
Northwestern Michigan College *A*
Northwood University *A, B*
Oakland Community College *C, A*
Oakland University *B, M*
Olivet College *B*
Rochester College *B*
Saginaw Valley State University *B*
St. Clair County Community
  College *A*
Schoolcraft College *C, A*
Siena Heights University *A, B*
Spring Arbor University *B*
University of Detroit Mercy *B*
University of Michigan *M*
University of Michigan
  Flint *B*
Walsh College of Accountancy and
  Business Administration *B, M*
Washtenaw Community College *C, A*
Wayne State University *B, M*
West Shore Community College *A*
Western Michigan University *B, M*

Minnesota

Academy College *C, A, B*
Alexandria Technical College *A*
Anoka Technical College *C*
Anoka-Ramsey Community College *A*
Augsburg College *B*
Bemidji State University *B*

Central Lakes College *A*
Century Community and Technical
  College *C, A*
College of St. Benedict *B*
College of St. Catherine *B*
College of St. Scholastica *B*
Concordia College: Moorhead *B*
Concordia University: St. Paul *B*
Dakota County Technical College *C, A*
Dunwoody College of Technology *A*
Globe College *C, A, B*
Gustavus Adolphus College *B*
Hennepin Technical College *C, A*
Inver Hills Community College *A*
Itasca Community College *A*
Lake Superior College *C, A*
Metropolitan State University *B*
Minneapolis Business College *A*
Minneapolis Community and
  Technical College *A*
Minnesota School of Business *C, A, B*
Minnesota School of Business:
  Brooklyn Center *B*
Minnesota State College - Southeast
  Technical *C, A*
Minnesota State Community and
  Technical College - Fergus
  Falls *C, A*
Minnesota State University
  Mankato *B*
  Moorhead *B*
National American University
  St. Paul *B*
North Central University *B*
North Hennepin Community
  College *A*
Northland Community & Technical
  College *C, A*
Northwest Technical College *C, A*
Northwestern College *B*
Pillsbury Baptist Bible College *B*
Pine Technical College *C, A*
Rasmussen College
  Mankato *C, A*
  Minnetonka *C, A*
  St. Cloud *C, A*
Ridgewater College *C, A*
Riverland Community College *A*
Rochester Community and Technical
  College *A*
St. Cloud State University *B*
St. Cloud Technical College *C, A*
St. John's University *B*
St. Mary's University of Minnesota *B*
St. Paul College *A*
South Central College *A*
Southwest Minnesota State
  University *A, B*
University of Minnesota
  Crookston *A, B*
  Duluth *B*
  Twin Cities *C, B*
University of St. Thomas *C, B, M*
Vermilion Community College *A*
Winona State University *B*

Mississippi

Alcorn State University *B*
Antonelli College
  Jackson *A*
Belhaven College *C, B*
Coahoma Community College *A*
Copiah-Lincoln Community College *A*
Delta State University *B, M*
Itawamba Community College *A*
Jackson State University *B, M*
Millsaps College *B, M*
Mississippi College *B, M*
Mississippi Delta Community
  College *A*
Mississippi Gulf Coast Community
  College
  Jefferson Davis Campus *A*
Mississippi State University *B, M*

Mississippi Valley State University *B*
University of Mississippi *B, M, D*
University of Southern
  Mississippi *B, M*

Missouri

Avila University *B*
Central Methodist University *A, B*
Central Missouri State University *B, M*
College of the Ozarks *B*
Columbia College *B*
Culver-Stockton College *B*
DeVry University
  Kansas City *M*
Drury University *B*
Evangel University *A, B*
Everest College: Springfield *A*
Hannibal-LaGrange College *B*
Harris-Stowe State University *B*
Hickey College *C, A*
Lincoln University *B*
Lindenwood University *B, M*
Longview Community College *C, A*
Maryville University of Saint
  Louis *B, M*
Mineral Area College *A*
Missouri Baptist University *B*
Missouri Southern State
  University *A, B*
Missouri State University *B, M*
Missouri State University: West
  Plains *C*
Missouri Valley College *B*
Missouri Western State University *B*
National American University
  Kansas City *A, B*
North Central Missouri College *C, A*
Northwest Missouri State
  University *B, M*
Ozarks Technical Community
  College *A*
Park University *B*
Penn Valley Community College *C, A*
St. Charles Community College *C, A*
St. Louis Community College
  St. Louis Community College at
    Florissant Valley *C*
  St. Louis Community College at
    Meramec *C, A*
St. Louis University *M*
Southeast Missouri State
  University *B, M*
Southwest Baptist University *A, B*
State Fair Community College *A*
Stephens College *B*
Three Rivers Community College *A*
Truman State University *B, M*
University of Missouri
  Columbia *B, M, D*
  Kansas City *B, M*
  St. Louis *B, M*
Washington University in St.
  Louis *B, M*
Webster University *C, B*
Westminster College *B*
William Jewell College *B*
William Woods University *B*

Montana

Carroll College *B*
Flathead Valley Community
  College *C, A*
Fort Peck Community College *C*
Helena College of Technology of the
  University of Montana *A*
Montana State University
  Bozeman *M*
  College of Technology-Great
    Falls *C, A*
Montana Tech of the University of
  Montana *A, B*
Rocky Mountain College *B, M*
University of Great Falls *B*

University of Montana:
  Missoula *A, M, D*

Nebraska

Bellevue University *B, M*
Chadron State College *B*
College of Saint Mary *A*
Concordia University *B*
Creighton University *B*
Dana College *B*
Hamilton College: Lincoln *A*
Hastings College *B*
Metropolitan Community
  College *C, A*
Midland Lutheran College *A, B*
Nebraska Wesleyan University *B*
Northeast Community College *A*
Southeast Community College
  Lincoln Campus *A*
Union College *A, B*
University of Nebraska
  Lincoln *B, M*
  Omaha *B, M*
Vatterott College: Spring Valley *A*
Western Nebraska Community
  College *C, A*
York College *B*

Nevada

Community College of Southern
  Nevada *A*
Great Basin College *C, A*
Morrison University *A, B*
Truckee Meadows Community
  College *A*
University of Nevada
  Las Vegas *B, M*
  Reno *B, M*
Western Nevada Community
  College *A*

New Hampshire

Franklin Pierce College *B*
McIntosh College *A*
New England College *B*
New Hampshire Community
  Technical College
  Berlin *A*
  Claremont *A*
  Manchester *C, A*
  Nashua *C, A*
  Stratham *C, A*
New Hampshire Technical
  Institute *C, A*
Plymouth State University *B*
St. Anselm College *B*
Southern New Hampshire
  University *C, A, B, M*
University of New Hampshire *B, M*

New Jersey

Atlantic Cape Community College *A*
Berkeley College *A, B*
Bloomfield College *C, B*
Brookdale Community College *A*
Burlington County College *A*
Caldwell College *B, M*
Camden County College *A*
Centenary College *B, M*
The College of New Jersey *B*
College of St. Elizabeth *C*
Cumberland County College *C, A*
Essex County College *C, A*
Fairleigh Dickinson University
  College at Florham *B, M*
  Metropolitan Campus *B, M*
Felician College *B*
Georgian Court University *C, B*
Gloucester County College *C, A*
Hudson County Community
  College *A*
Kean University *B, M*
Mercer County Community College *A*

Middlesex County College *A*
Monmouth University *B*
New Jersey City University *M*
Ocean County College *C*
Passaic County Community College *A*
Ramapo College of New Jersey *B*
Raritan Valley Community College *A*
Rider University *B, M*
Rowan University *B*
Rutgers, The State University of New
    Jersey
    Camden Regional Campus *B, M*
    New Brunswick/Piscataway
        Campus *B, M*
    Newark Regional Campus *B, M*
St. Peter's College *B, M*
Salem Community College *A*
Seton Hall University *B, M*
Sussex County Community
    College *C, A*
Thomas Edison State College *C, A, B*
Warren County Community
    College *C, A*
William Paterson University of New
    Jersey *B*

New Mexico

Albuquerque Technical-Vocational
    Institute *C, A*
Clovis Community College *A*
College of Santa Fe *B*
College of the Southwest *B*
Eastern New Mexico University *B*
Eastern New Mexico University:
    Roswell Campus *C, A*
International Institute of the
    Americas *C, A*
Luna Community College *A*
National American University *C, A, B*
New Mexico Highlands University *B*
New Mexico Junior College *A*
New Mexico State University *B, M*
New Mexico State University
    Carlsbad *C*
Northern New Mexico College *C, A*
Santa Fe Community College *A*
University of New Mexico *M*
Western New Mexico University *B*

New York

Adelphi University *B, M*
Adirondack Community College *A*
Alfred University *B*
Berkeley College *A, B*
Berkeley College of New York
    City *A, B*
Bramson ORT College *A*
Briarcliffe College *C, A, B*
Bryant & Stratton Business Institute
    Bryant & Stratton College: Albany *A*
    Bryant & Stratton College:
        Rochester *A*
    Bryant & Stratton College:
        Syracuse *C, A*
Bryant & Stratton College: Henrietta *A*
Bryant & Stratton College: Syracuse
    North *A*
Canisius College *B, M*
Cayuga County Community
    College *C, A*
Cazenovia College *B*
City University of New York
    Baruch College *B, M, D*
    Borough of Manhattan Community
        College *A*
    Bronx Community College *A*
    Brooklyn College *C, B, M*
    College of Staten Island *B*
    Hostos Community College *A*
    Hunter College *B*
    Kingsborough Community
        College *A*
    LaGuardia Community College *A*
    Lehman College *B, M*

Medgar Evers College *B*
New York City College of
    Technology *A*
Queens College *B, M*
Queensborough Community
    College *A*
York College *B*
Clinton Community College *A*
College of Saint Rose *B, M*
College of Westchester *C, A*
Columbia-Greene Community
    College *C, A*
Concordia College *B*
Cornell University *M, D*
Corning Community College *C, A*
D'Youville College *B*
Daemen College *C, B, M*
Dominican College of Blauvelt *B*
Dowling College *B*
Dutchess Community College *A*
Elmira Business Institute *C, A*
Elmira College *B*
Excelsior College *B*
Finger Lakes Community College *A*
Five Towns College *A*
Fordham University *B, M*
Globe Institute of Technology *C, A, B*
Hartwick College *B*
Herkimer County Community
    College *A*
Hilbert College *A, B*
Hofstra University *B, M*
Houghton College *B*
Hudson Valley Community
    College *C, A*
Iona College *B*
Ithaca College *B, M*
Jamestown Business College *A*
Jefferson Community College *C, A*
Keuka College *B*
Le Moyne College *B*
Long Island Business Institute *A*
Long Island University
    Brooklyn Campus *B, M*
    C.W. Post Campus *B, M*
Manhattan College *B*
Maria College *A*
Marist College *B*
Marymount Manhattan College *B*
Mercy College *B, M*
Mildred Elley *C*
Molloy College *B, M*
Monroe College *A, B*
Monroe Community College *A*
Mount St. Mary College *C, B*
Nassau Community College *A*
Nazareth College of Rochester *B*
New York Institute of
    Technology *A, B*
New York University *A, B, M, D*
Niagara County Community
    College *C, A*
Niagara University *B*
Nyack College *B, M*
Olean Business Institute *A*
Onondaga Community College *A*
Orange County Community College *A*
Pace University *C, B, M*
Plaza College *A*
Roberts Wesleyan College *B*
Rochester Business Institute *C, A*
Rochester Institute of
    Technology *C, A, B, M*
Rockland Community College *A*
Sage College of Albany *B*
St. Bonaventure University *B, M*
St. Francis College *B*
St. John Fisher College *B*
St. John's University *B, M*
St. Joseph's College *B*
St. Joseph's College: Suffolk
    Campus *B*
St. Thomas Aquinas College *B*
Siena College *C, B, T*

State University of New York
    Albany *B, M*
    Binghamton *B, M*
    Buffalo *M*
    College at Brockport *B*
    College at Fredonia *B, M*
    College at Geneseo *B*
    College at Old Westbury *B, M*
    College at Oneonta *B*
    College at Plattsburgh *B*
    College of Agriculture and
        Technology at Cobleskill *A*
    College of Agriculture and
        Technology at Morrisville *A*
    College of Technology at Alfred *A*
    College of Technology at Canton *A*
    College of Technology at Delhi *A*
    Farmingdale *C*
    Institute of Technology at
        Utica/Rome *B, M*
    New Paltz *B, M*
    Oswego *B, M*
Suffolk County Community College *A*
Sullivan County Community
    College *C, A*
Syracuse University *B, M*
Technical Career Institutes *A*
Touro College *C, A, B, M*
Ulster County Community College *A*
Utica College *B*
Utica School of Commerce *C, A*
Wagner College *B, M*
Westchester Community College *C, A*
Wood Tobe-Coburn School *A*
Yeshiva University *B*

North Carolina

Alamance Community College *C, A*
Appalachian State University *B, M*
Asheville-Buncombe Technical
    Community College *A*
Barton College *B*
Beaufort County Community
    College *C, A*
Belmont Abbey College *B*
Bennett College *B*
Caldwell Community College and
    Technical Institute *A*
Campbell University *B*
Catawba College *B*
Catawba Valley Community
    College *C, A*
Central Carolina Community
    College *A*
Cleveland Community College *A*
Craven Community College *A*
Davidson County Community
    College *C, A*
Durham Technical Community
    College *A*
East Carolina University *B, M*
Edgecombe Community College *A*
Elizabeth City State University *B*
Elon University *B*
Fayetteville State University *B*
Fayetteville Technical Community
    College *A*
Forsyth Technical Community
    College *A*
Gardner-Webb University *B*
Gaston College *A*
Greensboro College *B*
Guilford College *C, B*
Halifax Community College *A*
Haywood Community College *C, A*
High Point University *B*
James Sprunt Community
    College *C, A*
Johnson & Wales University *A*
Johnston Community College *A*
King's College *C, A*
Lenoir Community College *A*
Lenoir-Rhyne College *B*
Livingstone College *B*

Mars Hill College *B*
Mayland Community College *A*
McDowell Technical Community
    College *A*
Meredith College *B*
Methodist College *B*
Miller-Motte Technical College *C, A*
Mitchell Community College *A*
Montgomery Community College *A*
Mount Olive College *A, B*
Nash Community College *A*
North Carolina Agricultural and
    Technical State University *B*
North Carolina Central University *B*
North Carolina State University *B, M*
North Carolina Wesleyan College *B*
Pamlico Community College *A*
Pfeiffer University *B*
Piedmont Community College *A*
Pitt Community College *C, A*
Randolph Community College *A*
Richmond Community College *C, A*
Roanoke-Chowan Community
    College *C*
Rockingham Community College *A*
Rowan-Cabarrus Community
    College *C, A*
St. Augustine's College *B*
Salem College *B*
Sampson Community College *A*
Sandhills Community College *C, A*
South College *A*
South Piedmont Community
    College *C, A*
Southwestern Community
    College *C, A*
Stanly Community College *C, A*
Surry Community College *C, A*
Tri-County Community College *A*
University of North Carolina
    Asheville *B*
    Chapel Hill *M*
    Charlotte *B, M*
    Greensboro *B, M*
    Pembroke *B*
    Wilmington *B, M*
Vance-Granville Community
    College *A*
Wake Forest University *B, M*
Wake Technical Community
    College *A*
Wayne Community College *A*
Western Carolina University *B, M*
Western Piedmont Community
    College *C, A*
Wilkes Community College *C, A*
Wilson Technical Community
    College *A*
Wingate University *B*
Winston-Salem State University *B*

North Dakota

Aakers College: Fargo *C, A*
Dickinson State University *B*
Jamestown College *B*
Lake Region State College *A*
Minot State University *B*
North Dakota State University *B*
University of Mary *A, B*
University of North Dakota *B*

Ohio

AEC Southern Ohio College
    Brown Mackie College: Akron *C, A*
Ashland University *B*
Baldwin-Wallace College *B, M*
Belmont Technical College *A*
Bluffton University *B*
Bowling Green State University *B, M*
Bowling Green State University:
    Firelands College *C, A*
Bradford School *C, A*

Bryant & Stratton College
  Parma *A*
  Willoughby Hills *A*
Capital University *B*
Case Western Reserve
  University *B, M, D*
Cedarville University *B*
Central Ohio Technical College *A*
Central State University *B*
Cincinnati State Technical and
  Community College *C, A*
Circleville Bible College *A, B*
Clark State Community College *C, A*
Cleveland State University *B, M*
College of Mount St. Joseph *A, B*
Columbus State Community
  College *C, A*
Cuyahoga Community College
  Metropolitan Campus *A*
David N. Myers University *B*
Davis College *A*
DeVry University
  Columbus *M*
Defiance College *A, B*
Edison State Community College *C, A*
Franciscan University of
  Steubenville *A, B*
Franklin University *A, B*
Gallipolis Career College *A*
Heidelberg College *B*
James A. Rhodes State College *C, A*
Jefferson Community College *A*
John Carroll University *B*
Kent State University *B, M, D*
Lake Erie College *B*
Lakeland Community College *C, A*
Malone College *B*
Marietta College *B*
Marion Technical College *A*
Miami University
  Hamilton Campus *C, A*
  Oxford Campus *B, M*
Mount Union College *B*
Mount Vernon Nazarene University *B*
Muskingum College *B*
Ohio Business College: Sandusky *C, A*
Ohio Dominican University *B*
Ohio Northern University *B*
Ohio State University
  Columbus Campus *B, M, D*
Ohio University *B, M*
Ohio Valley College of Technology *A*
Ohio Wesleyan University *B*
Otterbein College *B*
Owens Community College
  Toledo *C*
Shawnee State University *A*
Sinclair Community College *A*
Southeastern Business College *A*
Southeastern Business College:
  Lancaster *A*
Southeastern Business College: New
  Boston *A*
Stark State College of Technology *A*
Tiffin University *A, B*
Trumbull Business College *A*
University of Akron *B, M*
University of Akron: Wayne College *A*
University of Cincinnati *B, D*
University of Dayton *B*
University of Findlay *A, B*
University of Northwestern Ohio *A, B*
University of Rio Grande *A, B*
University of Toledo *A, B, M*
Urbana University *B*
Ursuline College *B*
Walsh University *A, B*
Washington State Community
  College *A*
Wilmington College *B*
Wright State University *B, M*
Xavier University *B, M*
Youngstown State University *A, B, M*
Zane State College *C, A*

Oklahoma

Bacone College *A*
Cameron University *B*
Carl Albert State College *C, A*
Connors State College *A*
East Central University *B*
Eastern Oklahoma State College *A*
Northeastern Oklahoma Agricultural
  and Mechanical College *C, A*
Northeastern State University *B*
Northwestern Oklahoma State
  University *B*
Oklahoma Baptist University *B*
Oklahoma Christian University *B*
Oklahoma City University *B, M*
Oklahoma Panhandle State
  University *B*
Oklahoma State University *B, M*
Oklahoma State University
  Oklahoma City *A*
  Okmulgee *A*
Oklahoma Wesleyan University *B*
Oral Roberts University *B*
Rogers State University *A*
St. Gregory's University *A, B*
Southeastern Oklahoma State
  University *B*
Southern Nazarene University *B*
Southwestern Oklahoma State
  University *B*
Tulsa Community College *A*
University of Central Oklahoma *B*
University of Oklahoma *B, M*
University of Tulsa *B*

Oregon

Central Oregon Community
  College *A*
Chemeketa Community College *A*
Clackamas Community College *C, A*
Clatsop Community College *A*
Corban College *B*
Eastern Oregon University *B*
Everest College: Portland *A*
George Fox University *B*
Lane Community College *C, A*
Linfield College *B*
Mount Hood Community College *C, A*
Northwest Christian College *B*
Oregon Institute of Technology *B*
Pioneer Pacific College *A*
Pioneer Pacific College: Springfield *A*
Portland Community College *C, A*
Portland State University *C, B*
Southern Oregon University *B*
Southwestern Oregon Community
  College *C, A*
Umpqua Community College *A*
University of Oregon *B, M, D*
University of Portland *B*

Pennsylvania

Academy of Medical Arts and
  Business *C, A*
Albright College *B*
Alvernia College *A, B*
Arcadia University *B*
Berean Institute *A*
Berks Technical Institute *A*
Bloomsburg University of
  Pennsylvania *B*
Bucknell University *B*
Bucks County Community College *A*
Business Institute of Pennsylvania *A*
Business Institute of Pennsylvania
  Meadville *A*
Cabrini College *C, B*
California University of
  Pennsylvania *B*
Cambria-Rowe Business College *C, A*
Cambria-Rowe Business College:
  Indiana *A*
Carlow University *B*
Carnegie Mellon University *D*

Cedar Crest College *C, B*
Central Pennsylvania College *A*
Chatham College *B*
Chestnut Hill College *A, B*
Cheyney University of Pennsylvania *B*
Clarion University of
  Pennsylvania *C, B*
College Misericordia *B*
Commonwealth Technical Institute *A*
Community College of Philadelphia *A*
Consolidated School of Business
  Lancaster *A*
  York *A*
DeSales University *B*
Delaware Valley College *B*
Drexel University *B, M*
DuBois Business College *C, A*
DuBois Business College
  Huntingdon *A*
  Oil City *A*
Duquesne University *B, M*
Eastern University *B*
Edinboro University of
  Pennsylvania *B*
Elizabethtown College *C, A, B*
Erie Business Center *A*
Erie Business Center South *A*
Gannon University *B*
Geneva College *B*
Grove City College *B*
Gwynedd-Mercy College *A, B*
Holy Family University *B*
ICM School of Business & Medical
  Careers *A*
Immaculata University *C, A, B*
Indiana University of Pennsylvania *B*
Juniata College *B*
Keystone College *A, B*
King's College *B*
Kutztown University of
  Pennsylvania *B*
La Roche College *B*
La Salle University *A, B*
Lackawanna College *A*
Lansdale School of Business *C, A*
Laurel Business Institute *A*
Lebanon Valley College *C, A, B*
Lehigh Carbon Community College *C*
Lehigh University *B, M*
Lehigh Valley College *A*
Lincoln Technical Institute *C*
Lincoln University *B*
Lock Haven University of
  Pennsylvania *B*
Luzerne County Community
  College *A*
Lycoming College *B*
Manor College *A*
Mansfield University of
  Pennsylvania *A, B*
Marywood University *B*
McCann School of Business
  Pottsville *A*
Mercyhurst College *B*
Messiah College *B*
Montgomery County Community
  College *C, A*
Moravian College *B*
Mount Aloysius College *A, B*
Muhlenberg College *C, A, B*
Neumann College *C, B*
Newport Business Institute *A*
PJA School *C, A*
Penn State
  Abington *B*
  Altoona *B*
  Beaver *B*
  Delaware County *B*
  Dubois *B*
  Erie, The Behrend College *B*
  Fayette *B*
  Harrisburg *B*
  Hazleton *B*
  Lehigh Valley *B*

  McKeesport *B*
  Mont Alto *B*
  New Kensington *B*
  Schuylkill - Capital College *B*
  Shenango *B*
  University Park *B*
  Wilkes-Barre *B*
  Worthington Scranton *B*
  York *B*
Pennsylvania College of Technology *B*
Pennsylvania Highlands Community
  College *A*
Philadelphia University *C, A, B, M*
Pittsburgh Technical Institute *A*
Point Park University *C, A, B*
Reading Area Community
  College *C, A*
Robert Morris University *C, B, M*
Rosemont College *B*
St. Francis University *B*
St. Joseph's University *A, B, M*
St. Vincent College *C, B, M*
Schuylkill Institute of Business &
  Technology *A*
Seton Hill University *B*
Shippensburg University of
  Pennsylvania *B*
South Hills School of Business &
  Technology *C, A*
Susquehanna University *B*
Temple University *B, M*
Thiel College *A, B*
Tri-State Business Institute *A*
University of Pennsylvania *B, M, D*
University of Pittsburgh *B*
University of Pittsburgh
  Greensburg *B*
  Johnstown *B*
  Titusville *C, A*
University of Scranton *B, M*
Villanova University *B, M*
Washington and Jefferson College *B*
Waynesburg College *B*
West Chester University of
  Pennsylvania *B*
Westminster College *B*
Westmoreland County Community
  College *A*
Widener University *B, M*
Wilkes University *B*
Wilson College *A, B*
York College of Pennsylvania *B*
York Technical Institute *A*
Yorktowne Business Institute *A*

Puerto Rico

American University of Puerto
  Rico *A, B*
Atlantic College *A, B*
Bayamon Central University *B, M*
Columbia College *A*
Inter American University of Puerto
  Rico
  Aguadilla Campus *A, B*
  Arecibo Campus *A, B*
  Barranquitas Campus *A, B*
  Bayamon Campus *C, A, B*
  Fajardo Campus *A, B*
  Guayama Campus *A, B*
  Ponce Campus *A, B, M*
  San German Campus *A, B, M*
National College of Business &
  Technology: Bayamon *A*
Pontifical Catholic University of
  Puerto Rico *B, M*
Turabo University *A, B, M*
Universidad Metropolitana *B, M*
Universidad del Este *A, B*
University College of San Juan *C, A, B*
University of Puerto Rico
  Aguadilla *B*
  Arecibo *B*
  Bayamon University College *B*
  Cayey University College *B*

Humacao *A, B*
Mayaguez *B*
Ponce *B*
Rio Piedras *B, M*
Utuado *B*
University of the Sacred Heart *B*

Rhode Island

Bryant University *B, M*
Community College of Rhode
Island *C, A*
Johnson & Wales University *A, B, M*
Providence College *B*
Rhode Island College *B*
Roger Williams University *B*
Salve Regina University *B*
University of Rhode Island *B, M*

South Carolina

Aiken Technical College *C, A*
Anderson University *B*
Benedict College *B*
Central Carolina Technical College *A*
Charleston Southern University *B, M*
Clemson University *B, M*
Coastal Carolina University *B*
College of Charleston *B, M*
Columbia College *B*
Converse College *B*
Florence-Darlington Technical
College *A*
Forrest Junior College *A*
Francis Marion University *B*
Furman University *B*
Greenville Technical College *C, A*
Horry-Georgetown Technical
College *A*
Limestone College *B*
Midlands Technical College *C, A*
North Greenville College *B*
Northeastern Technical College *A*
Orangeburg-Calhoun Technical
College *C, A*
Piedmont Technical College *C*
Presbyterian College *B*
South Carolina State University *B*
South University *A*
Southern Wesleyan University *B*
Spartanburg Technical College *C, A*
Technical College of the
Lowcountry *C, A*
Tri-County Technical College *A*
Trident Technical College *A*
University of South Carolina *B, M*
University of South Carolina
Aiken *B*
Voorhees College *B*
Wofford College *B*
York Technical College *C, A*

South Dakota

Augustana College *B*
Black Hills State University *B*
Dakota Wesleyan University *B*
Kilian Community College *A*
Lake Area Technical Institute *A*
Mount Marty College *A, B*
Northern State University *B*
Oglala Lakota College *A*
Sisseton Wahpeton College *A*
Southeast Technical Institute *A*
University of Sioux Falls *B*
University of South Dakota *B, M*
Western Dakota Technical Institute *A*

Tennessee

Belmont University *B, M*
Bethel College *B*
Carson-Newman College *B*
Chattanooga State Technical
Community College *A*
Columbia State Community College *A*
Cumberland University *B*

East Tennessee State University *B, M*
Freed-Hardeman University *B*
Hiwassee College *A*
Jackson State Community College *A*
Lambuth University *B*
Lee University *B*
Lincoln Memorial University *B*
Lipscomb University *B, M*
Martin Methodist College *B*
Middle Tennessee State University *B*
Miller-Motte Technical College *A*
Milligan College *B*
Nashville State Community College *A*
National College of Business &
Technology
Tennessee *C, A*
Northeast State Technical Community
College *C*
Rhodes College *M*
South College *A*
Southern Adventist University *A, B, M*
Southwest Tennessee Community
College *C, A*
Tennessee State University *A, B*
Tennessee Technological University *B*
Tennessee Wesleyan College *B*
Trevecca Nazarene University *B*
Tusculum College *B*
Union University *B, T*
University of Memphis *B, M*
University of Tennessee
Chattanooga *M*
Knoxville *B, M*
Martin *B, M*
Walters State Community College *A*

Texas

Abilene Christian University *B, M*
Amarillo College *C, A*
Amberton University *B*
Angelina College *A*
Angelo State University *B, M*
Austin Community College *C, A*
Baylor University *B, M*
Blinn College *A*
Brazosport College *A*
Brookhaven College *C, A*
Cisco Junior College *A*
Clarendon College *A*
Coastal Bend College *A*
College of the Mainland *A*
Dallas Baptist University *B, M*
Del Mar College *A*
East Texas Baptist University *B*
Eastfield College *C, A*
El Centro College *C, A*
El Paso Community College *C, A*
Frank Phillips College *C, A*
Galveston College *C, A*
Grayson County College *C, A*
Hardin-Simmons University *B*
Houston Baptist University *B, M*
Houston Community College
System *C, A*
Howard College *C, A*
Howard Payne University *B*
Huston-Tillotson College *B*
Kilgore College *C, A*
Lamar State College at Orange *C*
Lamar State College at Port
Arthur *C, A*
Lamar University *B*
Laredo Community College *C, A*
LeTourneau University *B*
Lee College *C, A*
Lon Morris College *A*
Lubbock Christian University *B*
MTI College of Business and
Technology *A*
McLennan Community College *C, A*
McMurry University *B*
Midland College *C, A*
Midwestern State University *B*
Mountain View College *C, A*

Navarro College *C, A*
North Harris Montgomery
Community College District *C, A*
North Lake College *A*
Northeast Texas Community
College *C, A*
Northwood University: Texas
Campus *A, B*
Our Lady of the Lake University of San
Antonio *B, M*
Palo Alto College *A*
Paris Junior College *A*
Prairie View A&M University *B, M*
Richland College *A*
St. Edward's University *B*
St. Mary's University *B, M*
St. Philip's College *A*
Sam Houston State University *B*
San Antonio College *C, A*
San Jacinto College
Central Campus *C*
North *C, A*
Schreiner University *B*
South Plains College *A*
South Texas College *C, A*
Southern Methodist University *B, M*
Southwestern Adventist University *B*
Southwestern Assemblies of God
University *B*
Southwestern University *B*
Stephen F. Austin State University *B, M*
Sul Ross State University *B*
Tarleton State University *B*
Tarrant County College *A*
Texas A&M University *B, M, D*
Texas A&M University
Commerce *B, M*
Kingsville *B, M*
Texarkana *B, M*
Texas Christian University *B, M*
Texas Lutheran University *B*
Texas Southern University *B, M*
Texas Southmost College *C, A*
Texas State University: San
Marcos *B, M*
Texas Tech University *B, M*
Texas Wesleyan University *B, M*
Texas Woman's University *B*
Trinity University *B, M*
Trinity Valley Community College *C, A*
University of Dallas *M*
University of Houston *B, M, D*
University of Houston
Clear Lake *B, M*
Downtown *B*
Victoria *B*
University of Mary Hardin-Baylor *B*
University of North Texas *B, M, D*
University of St. Thomas *B, M*
University of Texas
Arlington *B, M, D*
Austin *B, M, D*
Brownsville *B*
Dallas *B, M*
El Paso *B, M*
Pan American *B, M*
San Antonio *B, M, D*
Tyler *B*
of the Permian Basin *B, M*
Vernon College *A*
Weatherford College *C, A*
West Texas A&M University *B, M*
Western Texas College *C, A*
Wiley College *B*

Utah

Brigham Young University *B, M*
College of Eastern Utah *C*
Dixie State College of Utah *A, B*
Everest College: Salt Lake City *C, A*
LDS Business College *C, A*
Provo College *A*
Snow College *A*
Southern Utah University *B, M*

Stevens-Henager College *B*
Stevens-Henager College of
Business *C, A, B*
University of Utah *B, M*
Utah State University *B, M*
Utah Valley State College *C, A, B*
Weber State University *B, M*
Westminster College *B*

Vermont

Castleton State College *B*
Champlain College *C, A, B*
College of St. Joseph in Vermont *A, B*
Lyndon State College *B*
Norwich University *B*
St. Michael's College *B*
Vermont Technical College *A*

Virginia

Averett University *B*
Blue Ridge Community College *A*
Bluefield College *B*
Bryant & Stratton College: Virginia
Beach *A*
Central Virginia Community
College *C, A*
Christopher Newport University *B*
College of William and Mary *M*
Danville Community College *A*
DeVry University
Arlington *M*
ECPI College of Technology *C, A*
Eastern Mennonite University *B*
Ferrum College *B*
George Mason University *B, M*
Germanna Community College *C*
Hampton University *B*
J. Sargeant Reynolds Community
College *C, A*
James Madison University *B, M*
Liberty University *B*
Longwood University *B*
Lord Fairfax Community College *A*
Lynchburg College *B*
Marymount University *C, B*
Mountain Empire Community
College *A*
National College of Business &
Technology
Bluefield *C, A*
Charlottesville *A*
Danville *C, A*
Harrisonburg *C, A*
Lynchburg *C, A*
Martinsville *C, A*
Salem *C, A, B, M*
New River Community College *A*
Norfolk State University *B*
Northern Virginia Community
College *A*
Old Dominion University *B, M*
Patrick Henry Community College *A*
Radford University *B*
Randolph-Macon College *B*
Rappahannock Community
College *C, A*
St. Paul's College *B*
Southwest Virginia Community
College *A*
Thomas Nelson Community
College *A*
Tidewater Community College *C, A*
University of Northern Virginia *M*
University of Richmond *B*
University of Virginia *M*
University of Virginia's College at
Wise *B*
Virginia Commonwealth
University *B, M*
Virginia Highlands Community
College *C, A*
Virginia Polytechnic Institute and
State University *B, M*
Virginia State University *B*

Virginia Union University *B*
Virginia Western Community College *A*
Washington and Lee University *B*
Wytheville Community College *A*

Washington

Bellevue Community College *C, A*
Bellingham Technical College *C, A*
Central Washington University *B, M*
Centralia College *C, A*
City University *C, B, M*
Columbia Basin College *A*
Eastern Washington University *B*
Edmonds Community College *C, A*
Everett Community College *C, A*
Gonzaga University *B, M*
Green River Community College *C, A*
Heritage University *B*
Highline Community College *C, A*
Lake Washington Technical College *C, A*
Lower Columbia College *C, A*
Peninsula College *A*
Pierce College *C, A*
Renton Technical College *C, A*
Saint Martin's University *B*
Seattle Central Community College *C, A*
Seattle Pacific University *B*
Seattle University *B*
Skagit Valley College *C, A*
South Puget Sound Community College *C, A*
South Seattle Community College *C, A*
Spokane Community College *A*
Spokane Falls Community College *A*
Tacoma Community College *C*
University of Washington *B, M*
Walla Walla College *B*
Washington State University *B, M*
Western Washington University *B*
Whatcom Community College *C, A*
Whitworth College *B*
Yakima Valley Community College *C, A*

West Virginia

Alderson-Broaddus College *B*
Bethany College *B*
Bluefield State College *B*
Concord University *B*
Davis and Elkins College *A, B*
Huntington Junior College *A*
Marshall University *B*
Mountain State College *A*
Mountain State University *C, A, B*
Ohio Valley University *B*
Potomac State College of West Virginia University *A*
Salem International University *M*
Shepherd University *B*
Southern West Virginia Community and Technical College *A*
University of Charleston *A, B*
Valley College of Technology *C*
West Liberty State College *B*
West Virginia Business College *A*
West Virginia Northern Community College *C, A*
West Virginia State University *B*
West Virginia University *B, M*
West Virginia Wesleyan College *B*
Wheeling Jesuit University *B, M*

Wisconsin

Blackhawk Technical College *A*
Bryant & Stratton College: Milwaukee *A*
Cardinal Stritch University *B*
Carroll College *B*
Carthage College *B*
Chippewa Valley Technical College *A*
College of Menominee Nation *A*
Concordia University Wisconsin *B*
Edgewood College *B, M*
Fox Valley Technical College *C, A*
Gateway Technical College *C*
Lakeland College *B*
Lakeshore Technical College *A*
Madison Area Technical College *C, A*
Marian College of Fond du Lac *B*
Marquette University *B*
Mid-State Technical College *A*
Milwaukee Area Technical College *A*
Moraine Park Technical College *C, A*
Mount Mary College *B*
Nicolet Area Technical College *A*
Northcentral Technical College *A*
Northeast Wisconsin Technical College *A*
St. Norbert College *B*
Silver Lake College *B*
Southwest Wisconsin Technical College *C, A*
University of Wisconsin
   Eau Claire *B*
   Green Bay *B*
   La Crosse *B*
   Madison *B, M*
   Milwaukee *B*
   Oshkosh *B*
   Parkside *B*
   Platteville *B*
   River Falls *B*
   Stevens Point *B*
   Superior *B*
   Whitewater *B, M*
Viterbo University *B*
Waukesha County Technical College *A*
Western Wisconsin Technical College *A*
Wisconsin Indianhead Technical College *A*

Wyoming

Casper College *A*
Central Wyoming College *A*
Eastern Wyoming College *A*
Laramie County Community College *C, A*
Sheridan College *A*
University of Wyoming *B, M*
Western Wyoming Community College *C, A*

Accounting/business management

California
CEI College
   Maric College: Panorama City *A*
Claremont McKenna College *B*
Westwood College of Technology Inland Empire *B*

Colorado
CollegeAmerica-Denver *A, B*
IntelliTec College: Grand Junction *A*

Illinois
Kaskaskia College *C*
University of Illinois Urbana-Champaign *B*

Indiana
Sawyer College: Merrillville *A*

Iowa
AIB College of Business *A*
Dordt College *B*

Kansas
Central Christian College of Kansas *A, B*
Ottawa University *B*
Tabor College *B*

Louisiana
Centenary College of Louisiana *B*

Maine
Husson College *B, M*

Maryland
DeVry University: Bethesda *M*

Massachusetts
Babson College *B*
Cape Cod Community College *A*
Lasell College *B*

Michigan
Baker College of Muskegon *B*

Minnesota
Augsburg College *B*

Missouri
Park University *A, B*

Montana
University of Great Falls *B*

Nebraska
Hamilton College: Lincoln *B*

New Hampshire
McIntosh College *A*

New York
City University of New York Brooklyn College *M*
DeVry Institute of Technology New York *M*
Five Towns College *A*
Globe Institute of Technology *C, A, B*
Olean Business Institute *C, A*
Rochester Institute of Technology *B, M*
State University of New York College of Agriculture and Technology at Morrisville
Utica College *M*

North Carolina
Chowan College *B*
East Carolina University *B*

Ohio
Circleville Bible College *A, B*
Stark State College of Technology *A*

Oregon
Corban College *B*
DeVry University: Portland *M*

Pennsylvania
Business Institute of Pennsylvania *A*
Business Institute of Pennsylvania Meadville *A*
Chestnut Hill College *C, A, B*
DeVry University Ft. Washington *M*
Harrisburg Area Community College *A*
Keystone College *B*
Mount Aloysius College *A, B*
Newport Business Institute *A*
Peirce College *A*

South Hills School of Business & Technology *A*

South Carolina
Miller-Motte Technical College *A*

Tennessee
Lambuth University *B*

Texas
Cedar Valley College *C, A*

Vermont
Champlain College *A, B*

Virginia
Rappahannock Community College *C, A*

Wisconsin
Maranatha Baptist Bible College *B*
Marquette University *M*

Accounting/computer science

California
California State University Chico *B*
San Jose State University *B*

Iowa
Coe College *B*

Kansas
Central Christian College of Kansas *A, B*

Maine
Central Maine Community College *A*
Northern Maine Community College *B, M*
Southern Maine Community College *B, M*
York County Community College *B, M*

Massachusetts
American International College *B, M*

Michigan
Kuyper College *B*

Missouri
State Fair Community College *A*

New York
Rochester Business Institute *A*
Schenectady County Community College *A*

South Carolina
North Greenville College *B*
University of South Carolina Upstate *B*

Texas
Houston Baptist University *B*
Schreiner University *B*

Washington
Western Washington University *B*

West Virginia
Mountain State University *A, B*

Accounting/finance

California
DeVry University
Fremont *M*
Long Beach *M*
Pomona *M*
West Hills *M*
Westwood College *B*

Colorado
DeVry University: Colorado Springs *M*

Florida
Palm Beach Atlantic University *B*

Illinois
Judson College *B*

Indiana
Huntington University *B*

Iowa
AIB College of Business *A*
Maharishi University of
Management *M*

Kansas
Central Christian College of Kansas *A*

Louisiana
Centenary College of Louisiana *B*

Maine
University of Southern Maine *B*

Massachusetts
Babson College *B*
Lasell College *B*
Massasoit Community College *C*

Michigan
Ferris State University *B*
Kettering University *B*
Olivet College *B*

Missouri
Webster University *B*

New Hampshire
Franklin Pierce College *B*
McIntosh College *A*

New York
Globe Institute of Technology *C, A, B*
Rochester Institute of Technology *M*
State University of New York
College of Agriculture and
Technology at Morrisville *A*

North Carolina
DeVry University: Charlotte *M*

North Dakota
University of North Dakota *B*

Ohio
Hiram College *B*
Lourdes College *B*
Stark State College of Technology *A*

Oklahoma
Northeastern State University *M*
Oklahoma State University
Oklahoma City *A*

Oregon
Corban College *B*

South Carolina
Voorhees College *B*

Vermont
Champlain College *A, B*

Washington
DeVry University
Federal Way *M*
Seattle University *M*

Wisconsin
Alverno College *B*
DeVry University: Milwaukee *M*

Accounting technology/bookkeeping

Alabama
Gadsden State Community College *A*
Jefferson State Community
College *C, A*
Northwest-Shoals Community
College *C, A*
Trenholm State Technical College *C, A*

Alaska
University of Alaska
Fairbanks *C, A*

Arizona
Glendale Community College *A*

Arkansas
Arkansas State University: Newport *C*
Black River Technical College *C*
University of Arkansas
Community College at Hope *C*
Cossatot Community College of the
C

California
CEI College
Maric College: Panorama City *A*
Empire College *C*
Foothill College *C*
Santa Barbara City College *C, A*
Southwestern College *C*

Colorado
Arapahoe Community College *C, A*
Pikes Peak Community College *C, A*
Red Rocks Community College *C, A*

Connecticut
Asnuntuck Community College *C, A*
Naugatuck Valley Community
College *C, A*

Florida
Central Florida Community College *A*
St. Johns River Community College *A*
St. Petersburg College *C, A*
University of Miami *C*
Valencia Community College *C, A*

Georgia
Albany Technical College *C*
Athens Technical College *C, A*
Brown Mackie College: Atlanta *C*
Central Georgia Technical
College *C, A*
Georgia Southwestern State
University *A*
Northwestern Technical College *C*
Savannah Technical College *C*
Southwest Georgia Technical
College *C, A*

Idaho
Lewis-Clark State College *C, A, B*

Illinois
Black Hawk College *C, A*
College of DuPage *C, A*
College of Lake County *C, A*
Illinois Eastern Community Colleges
Wabash Valley College *A*
John A. Logan College *C, A*
John Wood Community College *C, A*
McHenry County College *C, A*
Moraine Valley Community College *C*
Parkland College *C, A*
Robert Morris College: Chicago *C, A*
Waubonsee Community College *C, A*

Indiana
Indiana University
Southeast *A, B*
Ivy Tech State College
Ivy Tech Community College:
Bloomington *A*
Ivy Tech Community College:
Central Indiana *A*
Ivy Tech Community College:
Columbus *C, A*
Ivy Tech Community College: East
Central *C, A*
Ivy Tech Community College:
Kokomo *C, A*
Ivy Tech Community College:
Lafayette *A*
Ivy Tech Community College: North
Central *C, A*
Ivy Tech Community College:
Northeast *C, A*
Ivy Tech Community College:
Northwest *A*
Ivy Tech Community College: South
Central *C, A*
Ivy Tech Community College:
Southeast *C, A*
Ivy Tech Community College:
Southwest *C, A*
Ivy Tech Community College:
Wabash Valley *C, A*
Ivy Tech Community College:
Whitewater *C, A*
Sawyer College: Merrillville *C*

Iowa
Des Moines Area Community
College *C, A*
Hamilton College
Cedar Rapids *C*
Indian Hills Community College *C*
North Iowa Area Community
College *C*

Kentucky
Jefferson Community College *C, A*
Somerset Community College *C*
Southern Ohio College
Brown Mackie College: North
Kentucky *A*

Maryland
Allegany College of Maryland *C, A*
College of Southern Maryland *C, A*
Hagerstown Community College *A*
Wor-Wic Community College *C, A*

Massachusetts
Bunker Hill Community College *C*
Holyoke Community College *C, A*
Mount Wachusett Community
College *C*
North Shore Community College *A*

Michigan
Baker College
of Muskegon *C*
of Port Huron *C*
Ferris State University *A*
Kirtland Community College *A*
Mott Community College *A*
Northwestern Michigan College *A*
Southwestern Michigan College *A*
Wayne County Community College *A*

Minnesota
Central Lakes College *C*
Dakota County Technical College *C*
Hennepin Technical College *C, A*
Minneapolis Community and
Technical College *A*
Minnesota State Community and
Technical College - Fergus Falls *C*
Normandale Community College *A*
Northwest Technical College *C*
Pine Technical College *C*
Ridgewater College *C*
Rochester Community and Technical
College *C*
St. Cloud Technical College *C*
St. Paul College *C*

Missouri
East Central College *C, A*
Maryville University of Saint Louis *B*
Moberly Area Community College *A*

Montana
Montana State University
Billings *C, A*

Nevada
Western Nevada Community
College *C*

New Jersey
Bergen Community College *A*
Burlington County College *C, A*
Essex County College *A*
Union County College *A*

New Mexico
Albuquerque Technical-Vocational
Institute *C*
San Juan College *A*
Southwestern Indian Polytechnic
Institute *C, A*

New York
Broome Community College *A*
Canisius College *B*
Dutchess Community College *C*
Fulton-Montgomery Community
College *A*
Genesee Community College *C, A*
Globe Institute of Technology *C, A, B*
Jamestown Community College *A*
Mercy College *C, A*
Mohawk Valley Community
College *C, A*
Onondaga Community College *C*
Pace University *M*
Rockland Community College *A*
State University of New York
College of Agriculture and
Technology at Morrisville *A*
Taylor Business Institute *A*
Tompkins-Cortland Community
College *C, A*

North Carolina
Cape Fear Community College *A*
Central Piedmont Community
College *C, A*
Coastal Carolina Community
College *A*

Fayetteville Technical Community
 College *A*
Guilford Technical Community
 College *C, A*
Martin Community College *C, A*

North Dakota
Lake Region State College *C, A*
Minot State University: Bottineau
 Campus *A*
Williston State College *A*

Ohio
Davis College *A*
Hocking College *C, A*
Kent State University
 Ashtabula Regional Campus *A*
 East Liverpool Regional Campus *A*
 Trumbull Campus *A*
 Tuscarawas Campus *A*
Marion Technical College *A*
Miami University
 Oxford Campus *C, A*
Ohio University *A*
Owens Community College
 Toledo *C, A*
Southern State Community College *A*
Stark State College of Technology *A*
Stautzenberger College *A*
University of Akron *C, A*
University of Cincinnati
 Clermont College *C, A*
 Raymond Walters College *C, A*
Wright State University *A*
Youngstown State University *A*

Oklahoma
Rose State College *A*

Oregon
Blue Mountain Community
 College *C, A*
Linn-Benton Community College *A*
Treasure Valley Community College *C*

Pennsylvania
Business Institute of Pennsylvania *A*
Business Institute of Pennsylvania
 Meadville *A*
Butler County Community
 College *C, A*
Central Pennsylvania College *A*
Community College of Allegheny
 County *C, A*
Community College of Beaver
 County *A*
Consolidated School of Business
 Lancaster *A*
 York *A*
Delaware County Community
 College *C, A*
Douglas Education Center *C*
Gannon University *A*
Harrisburg Area Community
 College *C, A*
Lehigh Carbon Community
 College *C, A*
Luzerne County Community
 College *C, A*
Montgomery County Community
 College *C, A*
Newport Business Institute *A*
Northampton County Area
 Community College *C, A*
Peirce College *A*
Pennsylvania College of Technology *A*
Pittsburgh Technical Institute *C*
University of Pittsburgh
 Titusville *C*

Rhode Island
Bryant University *B*

South Carolina
Aiken Technical College *C*
Greenville Technical College *C*
York Technical College *C*

South Dakota
Southeast Technical Institute *C*

Tennessee
Pellissippi State Technical Community
 College *A*

Texas
Del Mar College *C*
Lamar State College at Orange *A*
North Harris Montgomery
 Community College District *C*
St. Edward's University *B*
St. Philip's College *C, A*
San Antonio College *C, A*
Texas State Technical College
 Harlingen *C*
Tyler Junior College *C, A*

Utah
Salt Lake Community College *C, A*

Virginia
Southwest Virginia Community
 College *C*

Washington
Bates Technical College *A*
Bellevue Community College *C, A*
Big Bend Community College *C, A*
Clark College *C, A*
Clover Park Technical College *C, A*
Edmonds Community College *C, A*
Grays Harbor College *C, A*
Heritage University *C*
Lower Columbia College *C, A*
Olympic College *C, A*
Peninsula College *C, A*
Shoreline Community College *C, A*
Walla Walla Community College *C, A*
Washington State University *B*
Wenatchee Valley College *C, A*

Wisconsin
Marquette University *C, B, M*
Milwaukee Area Technical College *C*
Wisconsin Indianhead Technical
 College *C*

Wyoming
Casper College *C, A*
Central Wyoming College *C, A*

Acoustics

District of Columbia
American University *B*

Minnesota
Minneapolis Community and
 Technical College *A*

Pennsylvania
Penn State
 University Park *M, D*

Acting

California
American Academy of Dramatic Arts:
 West *C, A*
California Institute of the Arts *C, B, M*
California State University
 Fullerton *B, M*
College of the Desert *A*
Grossmont Community College *C*

Monterey Peninsula College *C, A*
University of Southern
 California *B, M*

Connecticut
University of Connecticut *B*
University of Hartford *B*

Florida
Florida State University *B, M*
Palm Beach Atlantic University *B*
University of Miami *B*

Illinois
Bradley University *B*
Illinois Wesleyan University *B*

Iowa
Coe College *B*
Drake University *B*
University of Northern Iowa *B*

Kansas
Central Christian College of
 Kansas *A, B*

Maine
University of Southern Maine *B*

Maryland
University of Maryland
 Baltimore County *B*

Massachusetts
Boston University *B, M*
Brandeis University *M*
Emerson College *B*
Salem State College *B*
Simon's Rock College of Bard *B*
Suffolk University *B*

Michigan
University of Michigan
 Flint *B*
Western Michigan University *B*

Minnesota
St. Cloud State University *B*

Missouri
College of the Ozarks *B*
Lindenwood University *B*
Webster University *B*

New Hampshire
Franklin Pierce College *B*

New Mexico
College of Santa Fe *B*

New York
American Academy of Dramatic
 Arts *A*
Bard College *B*
City University of New York
 Brooklyn College *B, M*
Five Towns College *B*
Hofstra University *B*
Ithaca College *B*
Marymount Manhattan College *B*
New York University *M*
Syracuse University *B, M*

North Carolina
East Carolina University *B*

Ohio
Bowling Green State University *B*
Ohio University *B, M*
Otterbein College *B*

Youngstown State University *B*

Oklahoma
Oral Roberts University *B*

Pennsylvania
Arcadia University *B*
Northampton County Area
 Community College *A*
Penn State
 Abington *B*
 Altoona *B*
 Beaver *B*
 Berks *B*
 Delaware County *B*
 Dubois *B*
 Fayette *B*
 Hazleton *B*
 Lehigh Valley *B*
 McKeesport *B*
 Mont Alto *B*
 New Kensington *B*
 Shenango *B*
 York *B*
Point Park University *M*
Seton Hill University *B*
Temple University *B, M*

South Carolina
Coker College *B*

Tennessee
Freed-Hardeman University *B*

Texas
Baylor University *B*
Texas Tech University *B, M*

Utah
Brigham Young University *B*

Vermont
Bennington College *B*

Virginia
Old Dominion University *B*
Shenandoah University *B*

Washington
Cornish College of the Arts *B*

Wyoming
Central Wyoming College *A*

Actuarial science

California
Master's College *B*

Connecticut
University of Connecticut *B*

Florida
Florida State University *B*
University of Central Florida *B*

Georgia
Georgia State University *B, M*

Illinois
Bradley University *B*
North Central College *B*
Roosevelt University *B*
St. Xavier University *B*
University of Illinois
 Urbana-Champaign *B, M, D*
University of St. Francis *B*

Indiana
Ball State University *B, M*

Butler University *B*
Indiana University
  Northwest *B*
  South Bend *B*
Valparaiso University *B*

Iowa
Drake University *B*
Northwestern College *B*
University of Iowa *B, M*
University of Northern Iowa *B*

Kansas
Pittsburg State University *B*

Kentucky
Bellarmine University *B*

Massachusetts
Boston University *M*

Michigan
Central Michigan University *B*
Eastern Michigan University *B*
University of Michigan
  Flint *B*

Minnesota
University of Minnesota
  Twin Cities *B*

Missouri
Central Missouri State University *B*
Maryville University of Saint Louis *B*

Nebraska
University of Nebraska
  Kearney *B*
  Lincoln *B, M*

New Jersey
Rider University *B*
St. Peter's College *B, M*

New York
City University of New York
  Baruch College *B*
  Queens College *B*
Hofstra University *B*
New York University *B*
St. John's University *B*

North Dakota
North Dakota State University *B*

Ohio
Ohio State University
  Columbus Campus *B*
Ohio University *B*

Oklahoma
University of Central Oklahoma *B*

Pennsylvania
Elizabethtown College *B*
Lebanon Valley College *B*
Lincoln University *B*
Lycoming College *B*
Mansfield University of
  Pennsylvania *B*
Penn State
  Abington *B*
  Altoona *B*
  Beaver *B*
  Berks *B*
  Delaware County *B*
  Dubois *B*
  Fayette *B*
  Hazleton *B*
  Lehigh Valley *B*
  McKeesport *B*

Mont Alto *B*
New Kensington *B*
Schuylkill - Capital College *B*
Shenango *B*
University Park *B*
Wilkes-Barre *B*
Worthington Scranton *B*
York *B*
Robert Morris University *B*
St. Joseph's University *B*
Temple University *B, M*
Thiel College *B*
University of Pennsylvania *B*

Rhode Island
Bryant University *B*

Tennessee
Southern Adventist University *B*

Texas
University of Texas
  San Antonio *B*

Utah
Brigham Young University *B*

Wisconsin
Carroll College *B*
University of Wisconsin
  Madison *B, M*

Acupuncture

Connecticut
University of Bridgeport *M*

Florida
Florida College of Natural Health *C*

Nevada
Community College of Southern
  Nevada *A*

New York
Swedish Institute *M*

Washington
Bastyr University *B, M*

Administrative/ secretarial services

Alabama
Alabama Southern Community
  College *A*
Bishop State Community College *A*
Central Alabama Community
  College *C, A*
Chattahoochee Valley Community
  College *A*
Enterprise-Ozark Community
  College *C, A*
Faulkner State Community
  College *C, A*
Faulkner University *A*
Gadsden State Community
  College *C, A*
George C. Wallace State Community
  College
    George C. Wallace Community
      College at Dothan *C, A*
    Selma *C, A*
J. F. Drake State Technical College *C, A*
Jefferson State Community
  College *C, A*
Lawson State Community College *A*
Northeast Alabama Community
  College *A*
Northwest-Shoals Community
  College *C, A*

Shelton State Community
  College *C, A*
Snead State Community College *C, A*
Trenholm State Technical College *C, A*

Alaska
University of Alaska
  Fairbanks *C, A*
  Southeast *A*

Arizona
Arizona Western College *C, A*
Central Arizona College *C, A*
Chaparral College *A*
Cochise College *C, A*
Dine College *C, A*
Eastern Arizona College *C, A*
Everest College *C, A*
Gateway Community College *C, A*
Glendale Community College *C, A*
Lamson College *C*
Mohave Community College *C, A*
Northland Pioneer College *C, A*
Paradise Valley Community
  College *C, A*
Pima Community College *C, A*
Scottsdale Community College *A*
South Mountain Community
  College *A*
Tohono O'odham Community
  College *C*
Yavapai College *C, A*

Arkansas
Arkansas Northeastern College *A*
Arkansas State University *C, A*
Arkansas State University
  Beebe *C, A*
  Mountain Home *C, A*
Arkansas Tech University *C, A*
Black River Technical College *C*
East Arkansas Community
  College *C, A*
Henderson State University *A*
National Park Community College *C*
North Arkansas College *C, A*
Northwest Arkansas Community
  College *A*
Philander Smith College *B*
Rich Mountain Community
  College *C, A*
South Arkansas Community
  College *C, A*
Southeast Arkansas College *C*
University of Arkansas
  Community College at Batesville *A*
  Cossatot Community College of the
    C
  Fort Smith *C, A*
  Monticello *B*
University of Central Arkansas *A, B*

California
Allan Hancock College *C, A*
American River College *C, A*
Antelope Valley College *C, A*
Bakersfield College *A*
Barstow College *C, A*
Butte College *C, A*
CEI College
  Maric College: Panorama City *C*
Canada College *C, A*
Cerritos Community College *A*
Cerro Coso Community College *C, A*
Chabot College *C, A*
Chaffey College *C, A*
Citrus College *C*
City College of San Francisco *C, A*
Coastline Community College *C*
College of Alameda *C, A*
College of the Canyons *C, A*
College of the Redwoods *A*
College of the Sequoias *C, A*

College of the Siskiyous *C, A*
Columbia College *C, A*
Contra Costa College *C, A*
Crafton Hills College *C, A*
Cypress College *C, A*
De Anza College *C, A*
Diablo Valley College *C*
East Los Angeles College *A*
El Camino College *C, A*
Empire College *C, A*
Evergreen Valley College *C, A*
Fresno City College *C, A*
Fullerton College *A*
Glendale Community College *C, A*
Golden West College *C, A*
Grossmont Community College *C, A*
Heald College
  Salinas *A*
Humphreys College *C, A, B*
Imperial Valley College *C, A*
Lake Tahoe Community College *C, A*
Laney College *C, A*
Lassen College *A*
Long Beach City College *C, A*
Los Angeles City College *C, A*
Los Angeles Harbor College *C, A*
Los Angeles Mission College *A*
Los Angeles Southwest College *A*
Los Angeles Trade and Technical
  College *C, A*
Los Angeles Valley College *C, A*
MTI College *C*
Mendocino College *C, A*
Merced College *C, A*
MiraCosta College *C, A*
Mission College *A*
Modesto Junior College *C, A*
Moorpark College *C, A*
Mount San Antonio College *C, A*
Napa Valley College *C, A*
Ohlone College *C, A*
Orange Coast College *C, A*
Pacific Union College *A*
Palomar College *C, A*
Pasadena City College *C, A*
Porterville College *A*
Rio Hondo College *A*
Riverside Community College *C, A*
Sacramento City College *C, A*
Saddleback College *C, A*
San Bernardino Valley College *C*
San Diego City College *C, A*
San Diego Miramar College *C, A*
San Joaquin Delta College *A*
San Joaquin Valley College Inc. *A*
San Jose City College *A*
Santa Barbara City College *C, A*
Santa Rosa Junior College *C*
Shasta College *C, A*
Sierra College *C, A*
Skyline College *C, A*
Solano Community College *C, A*
Taft College *A*
Ventura College *C, A*
Victor Valley College *C, A*
West Hills Community College *C, A*
West Los Angeles College *C, A*
West Valley College *C, A*
Yuba Community College
  District *C, A*

Colorado
Aims Community College *C, A*
Arapahoe Community College *C, A*
Community College of Aurora *A*
Community College of Denver *C, A*
Northeastern Junior College *A*
Otero Junior College *A*
Pueblo Community College *C, A*
Red Rocks Community College *A*

Connecticut
Asnuntuck Community College *C, A*
Briarwood College *C, A*

Capital Community College *C, A*
Gateway Community College *C, A*
Gibbs College *C, A*
Goodwin College *C*
Housatonic Community College *C, A*
Manchester Community College *C, A*
Middlesex Community College *A*
Naugatuck Valley Community
   College *C, A*
Northwestern Connecticut
   Community College *C, A*
Quinebaug Valley Community
   College *C, A*
Tunxis Community College *C, A*

Delaware
Delaware Technical and Community
   College
   Owens Campus *C, A*
   Stanton/Wilmington Campus *C, A*
   Terry Campus *C, A*

District of Columbia
University of the District of
   Columbia *A*

Florida
Brevard Community College *A*
Broward Community College *C*
Clearwater Christian College *A*
Florida Community College at
   Jacksonville *C, A*
Hobe Sound Bible College *A*
Indian River Community College *A*
Lake City Community College *C, A*
Manatee Community College *C, A*
Miami Dade College *C, A*
New England Institute of
   Technology *A*
Pensacola Junior College *A*
Polk Community College *A*
St. Johns River Community College *A*
Santa Fe Community College *A*
Seminole Community College *A*
South Florida Community
   College *C, A*
Tallahassee Community College *C, A*
Valencia Community College *C, A*

Georgia
Albany State University *B*
Albany Technical College *C*
Athens Technical College *C, A*
Augusta Technical Institute *A*
Bainbridge College *C, A*
Central Georgia Technical
   College *C, A*
Chattahoochee Technical College *A*
Clayton State University *A*
Coastal Georgia Community
   College *C, A*
Columbus Technical College *C, A*
Dalton State College *C, A*
Darton College *C, A*
DeKalb Technical College *C*
Gainesville State College *A*
Georgia Highlands College *A*
Georgia Southwestern State
   University *A*
Gordon College *A*
Griffin Technical College *A*
Gwinnett College *C*
Gwinnett Technical College *A*
Savannah Technical College *A*
South Georgia College *A*
Southwest Georgia Technical
   College *C, A*
Valdosta State University *B*
West Georgia Technical College *A*

Hawaii
University of Hawaii
   Hawaii Community College *C, A*

Idaho
Boise State University *A*
Eastern Idaho Technical College *C, A*
Idaho State University *C, A*
Lewis-Clark State College *C, A, B*
North Idaho College *A*
University of Idaho *B*

Illinois
Black Hawk College *C, A*
Black Hawk College
   East Campus *C, A*
Career Colleges of Chicago *C*
Carl Sandburg College *C, A*
City Colleges of Chicago
   Harold Washington College *C, A*
   Kennedy-King College *C, A*
   Malcolm X College *C, A*
   Olive-Harvey College *C, A*
   Wright College *C, A*
College of DuPage *C, A*
College of Lake County *C, A*
Danville Area Community
   College *C, A*
East-West University *A*
Elgin Community College *C, A*
Fox College *A*
Heartland Community College *C*
Illinois Central College *C, A*
Illinois Eastern Community Colleges
   Frontier Community College *C, A*
   Lincoln Trail College *C, A*
   Olney Central College *C, A*
   Wabash Valley College *C, A*
John Wood Community College *C, A*
Joliet Junior College *C, A*
Kankakee Community College *C, A*
Kaskaskia College *C*
Lake Land College *A*
Lincoln Land Community College *A*
MacCormac College *A*
McHenry County College *C, A*
Midstate College *A*
Moraine Valley Community
   College *C, A*
Morton College *C, A*
Northwestern Business College *A*
Oakton Community College *C*
Parkland College *C*
Prairie State College *C, A*
Rend Lake College *C, A*
Robert Morris College: Chicago *C, A*
Rock Valley College *C, A*
St. Augustine College *C, A*
Sauk Valley Community College *C, A*
South Suburban College of Cook
   County *C, A*
Southeastern Illinois College *C, A*
Spoon River College *C, A*
Triton College *C, A*
Waubonsee Community College *C, A*
William Rainey Harper College *C, A*

Indiana
Ball State University *B*
Bethel College *A*
Grace College *B*
Indiana Business College *A*
Indiana Business College
   Anderson *A*
   Columbus *C, A*
   Evansville *C, A*
   Fort Wayne *C, A*
   Lafayette *C, A*
   Marion *C, A*
   Muncie *C, A*
   Terre Haute *A*
International Business College *C, A*
Ivy Tech State College
Ivy Tech Community College:
   Northeast *A*
Ivy Tech Community College:
   Northwest *A*
Professional Careers Institute *A*

Sawyer College *C, A*
Sawyer College: Merrillville *C, A*
Vincennes University *A*

Iowa
AIB College of Business *A*
Clinton Community College *C, A*
Dordt College *A*
Ellsworth Community College *A*
Faith Baptist Bible College and
   Theological Seminary *A*
Hamilton College *A*
Hamilton College
   Cedar Falls *A*
   Cedar Rapids *A*
Hawkeye Community College *A*
Indian Hills Community College *C*
Iowa Central Community College *A*
Iowa Lakes Community College *C*
Iowa Western Community College *A*
Kirkwood Community College *C, A*
Marshalltown Community College *A*
Muscatine Community College *C, A*
North Iowa Area Community
   College *C, A*
Northeast Iowa Community
   College *C*
Northwest Iowa Community
   College *C*
Scott Community College *C, A*
Southeastern Community College
   North Campus *C, A*
Southwestern Community
   College *C, A*
Western Iowa Tech Community
   College *C*

Kansas
Allen County Community College *A*
Barton County Community
   College *C, A*
Central Christian College of Kansas *A*
Coffeyville Community College *A*
Fort Hays State University *A*
Fort Scott Community College *C, A*
Garden City Community College *C*
Haskell Indian Nations University *A*
Hutchinson Community College *C, A*
Johnson County Community
   College *C, A*
Kansas City Kansas Community
   College *C, A*
Neosho County Community
   College *C, A*
Seward County Community
   College *C, A*
Tabor College *A, B*

Kentucky
Big Sandy Community and Technical
   College *A*
Bluegrass Community and Technical
   College *A*
Daymar College *C, A*
Draughons Junior College *A*
Eastern Kentucky University *A*
Henderson Community College *A*
Hopkinsville Community College *C, A*
Kentucky State University *A*
Madisonville Community College *A*
Murray State University *A*
National College of Business &
   Technology
   Danville *C, A*
   Florence *C, A*
   Lexington *C, A*
   Louisville *A*
   Pikeville *C, A*
   Richmond *C, A*
Owensboro Community College *A*
Paducah Technical College *C*
St. Catharine College *C, A*
Somerset Community College *C*

Southeast Kentucky Community and
   Technical College *A*
Sullivan University *C, A*
West Kentucky Community and
   Technical College *A*

Louisiana
Delgado Community College *C, A*
ITI Technical College *A*
Northwestern State University *A*
Southeastern Louisiana University *A*

Maine
Andover College *C, A*
Beal College *C, A*
Eastern Maine Community College *A*
Northern Maine Community
   College *A*

Maryland
Allegany College of Maryland *C, A*
Baltimore City Community College *A*
Carroll Community College *C, A*
Cecil Community College *A*
Chesapeake College *C, A*
Community College of Baltimore
   County *C, A*
Hagerstown Business College *A*
Harford Community College *C, A*
Prince George's Community
   College *C, A*
Wor-Wic Community College *C, A*

Massachusetts
Bay State College *A*
Benjamin Franklin Institute of
   Technology *C*
Bristol Community College *A*
Cape Cod Community College *C, A*
Gibbs College *A*
Greenfield Community College *C, A*
Holyoke Community College *C, A*
Marian Court College *C, A*
Massasoit Community College *A*
Middlesex Community College *C, A*
Northern Essex Community
   College *A*
Quinsigamond Community College *A*
Roxbury Community College *A*

Michigan
Baker College
   of Auburn Hills *C, A*
   of Cadillac *A*
   of Clinton Township *C, A, B*
   of Flint *C, A*
   of Jackson *C, A*
   of Muskegon *C, A, B*
   of Owosso *A, B*
   of Port Huron *C, A, B*
Bay Mills Community College *C*
Bay de Noc Community College *A*
Cleary University *A*
Delta College *C, A*
Glen Oaks Community College *C*
Gogebic Community College *A*
Grand Rapids Community College *C*
Kalamazoo Valley Community
   College *C, A*
Kellogg Community College *C, A*
Kirtland Community College *C, A*
Kuyper College *A*
Lake Michigan College *C, A*
Lansing Community College *A*
Macomb Community College *C, A*
Mid Michigan Community College *A*
Monroe County Community
   College *C, A*
Montcalm Community College *A*
Mott Community College *C, A*
Muskegon Community College *C, A*
North Central Michigan College *A*
Northern Michigan University *C, A, B*

Northwestern Michigan College *C*
St. Clair County Community
College *C, A*
Schoolcraft College *C, A*
Southwestern Michigan College *C, A*
Washtenaw Community College *C, A*
Wayne County Community College *A*
West Shore Community College *A*

Minnesota

Alexandria Technical College *C*
Anoka Technical College *C*
Anoka-Ramsey Community College *A*
Central Lakes College *A*
Century Community and Technical
College *C, A*
Dakota County Technical College *C*
Fond du Lac Tribal and Community
College *A*
Globe College *C, A*
Hibbing Community College *A*
Lake Superior College *C*
Mesabi Range Community and
Technical College *A*
Minneapolis Business College *A*
Minneapolis Community and
Technical College *C, A*
Minnesota School of Business *C*
Minnesota State College - Southeast
Technical *C, A*
Minnesota State Community and
Technical College - Fergus
Falls *C, A*
North Hennepin Community
College *A*
Northland Community & Technical
College *C, A*
Northwest Technical College *C, A*
Rasmussen College
Mankato *C*
Minnetonka *C, A*
St. Cloud *C*
Ridgewater College *C*
Riverland Community College *C, A*
Rochester Community and Technical
College *C, A*
St. Paul College *C, A*
South Central College *A*
Winona State University *B, T*

Mississippi

Alcorn State University *B*
Copiah-Lincoln Community College *A*
Hinds Community College *A*
Holmes Community College *C, A*
Itawamba Community College *A*
Meridian Community College *A*
Mississippi Delta Community
College *C, A*
Mississippi Gulf Coast Community
College
Jefferson Davis Campus *C, A*

Missouri

Baptist Bible College *A, B*
Central Missouri State University *A*
Crowder College *C, A*
Everest College: Springfield *A*
Hickey College *C, A*
Jefferson College *A*
Lincoln University *A, B*
Longview Community College *C, A*
Maple Woods Community
College *C, A*
Mineral Area College *C, A*
Patricia Stevens College *C*
Penn Valley Community College *C, A*
St. Charles Community College *C, A*
St. Louis Community College
St. Louis Community College at
Florissant Valley *C, A*
St. Louis Community College at
Meramec *C, A*

Southeast Missouri State
University *C, B*
State Fair Community College *C, A*
Three Rivers Community College *A*
Vatterott College: Springfield *C*

Montana

Dawson Community College *C, A*
Flathead Valley Community College *C*
Fort Peck Community College *C, A*
Helena College of Technology of the
University of Montana *C, A*
Little Big Horn College *C*
Miles Community College *A*
Montana State University
Billings *A*
College of Technology-Great Falls *A*
Montana Tech of the University of
Montana *A*
Salish Kootenai College *A, B*
University of Montana: Missoula *C, A*
University of Montana: Western *A*

Nebraska

Central Community College *C, A*
Hamilton College: Lincoln *A*
Metropolitan Community
College *C, A*
Midland Lutheran College *A*
Northeast Community College *A*
Western Nebraska Community
College *A*

Nevada

Community College of Southern
Nevada *A*
Great Basin College *C, A*
Las Vegas College *A*
Truckee Meadows Community
College *A*

New Hampshire

McIntosh College *A*
New Hampshire Community
Technical College
Berlin *A*
Manchester *C, A*
Stratham *C, A*

New Jersey

Bergen Community College *C, A*
Berkeley College *C*
Brookdale Community College *C, A*
Camden County College *C*
County College of Morris *A*
Cumberland County College *C, A*
Essex County College *A*
Gloucester County College *C, A*
Hudson County Community
College *C, A*
Mercer County Community
College *C, A*
Ocean County College *C*
Passaic County Community
College *C, A*
Salem Community College *C*
Sussex County Community College *C*
Thomas Edison State College *A*
Union County College *C, A*
Warren County Community College *C*

New Mexico

Albuquerque Technical-Vocational
Institute *C, A*
Clovis Community College *C, A*
Dona Ana Branch Community College
of New Mexico State
University *C, A*
Eastern New Mexico University:
Roswell Campus *C, A*
New Mexico Junior College *C, A*

New Mexico State University
Alamogordo *C, A*
Carlsbad *C, A*
Northern New Mexico College *C, A*
San Juan College *C, A*
Santa Fe Community College *C, A*
Western New Mexico University *C, A*

New York

Adirondack Community College *C, A*
Berkeley College *C*
Berkeley College of New York City *C*
Bramson ORT College *A*
Briarcliffe College *C, A*
Broome Community College *C*
Bryant & Stratton Business Institute
Bryant & Stratton College:
Albany *C, A*
Bryant & Stratton College:
Buffalo *C, A*
Bryant & Stratton College:
Rochester *C, A*
Bryant & Stratton College:
Syracuse *C, A*
Bryant & Stratton College: Henrietta *A*
Bryant & Stratton College: Syracuse
North *A*
City University of New York
Borough of Manhattan Community
College *A*
Bronx Community College *A*
Hostos Community College *A*
LaGuardia Community College *A*
Queensborough Community
College *A*
Clinton Community College *C, A*
College of Westchester *C, A*
Columbia-Greene Community
College *C, A*
Concordia College *A*
Corning Community College *C, A*
Dutchess Community College *A*
Erie Community College
City Campus *A*
Finger Lakes Community College *C, A*
Fulton-Montgomery Community
College *A*
Genesee Community College *C, A*
Globe Institute of Technology *C*
Herkimer County Community
College *A*
Hudson Valley Community College *A*
Interboro Institute *A*
Jamestown Business College *C, A*
Jamestown Community College *C*
Katharine Gibbs School
New York *A*
Long Island Business Institute *C, A*
Mildred Elley *C*
Mohawk Valley Community College *A*
Monroe College *A*
Monroe Community College *C, A*
Nassau Community College *C, A*
Niagara County Community
College *C, A*
Olean Business Institute *C, A*
Onondaga Community College *C, A*
Orange County Community
College *C, A*
Rochester Business Institute *C, A*
Rockland Community College *A*
State University of New York
College of Agriculture and
Technology at Morrisville *A*
College of Technology at Alfred *A*
College of Technology at Canton *A*
College of Technology at Delhi *A*
Farmingdale *A*
Suffolk County Community
College *A*
Taylor Business Institute *A*
Technical Career Institutes *C, A*
Tompkins-Cortland Community
College *C, A*

Trocaire College *A*
Utica School of Commerce *C, A*
Westchester Community College *C, A*
Wood Tobe-Coburn School *C, A*

North Carolina

Alamance Community College *A*
Asheville-Buncombe Technical
Community College *A*
Beaufort County Community
College *C, A*
Blue Ridge Community College *C, A*
Brunswick Community College *A*
Caldwell Community College and
Technical Institute *C, A*
Cape Fear Community College *A*
Carteret Community College *A*
Catawba Valley Community
College *C, A*
Central Carolina Community
College *A*
Central Piedmont Community
College *C, A*
Cleveland Community College *C, A*
Coastal Carolina Community
College *C, A*
College of the Albemarle *A*
Craven Community College *C*
Durham Technical Community
College *C, A*
Edgecombe Community College *A*
Fayetteville State University *A*
Fayetteville Technical Community
College *A*
Gaston College *A*
Haywood Community College *C, A*
James Sprunt Community
College *C, A*
Johnston Community College *A*
King's College *C, A*
Lenoir Community College *A*
Mayland Community College *A*
Mitchell Community College *C, A*
Nash Community College *A*
Piedmont Community College *A*
Randolph Community College *A*
Richmond Community College *C, A*
Roanoke-Chowan Community
College *A*
Sampson Community College *A*
Sandhills Community College *A*
South College *C, A*
South Piedmont Community
College *C, A*
Southwestern Community
College *C, A*
Tri-County Community College *A*
Vance-Granville Community
College *A*
Wake Technical Community
College *A*
Wayne Community College *A*
Western Piedmont Community
College *C, A*

North Dakota

Bismarck State College *C, A*
Dickinson State University *A, B*
Lake Region State College *C, A*
Mayville State University *A*
Minot State University: Bottineau
Campus *A*
North Dakota State College of
Science *A*
Trinity Bible College *A, B*
Williston State College *C, A*

Ohio

Bowling Green State University:
Firelands College *A*
Bryant & Stratton College
Parma *A*
Willoughby Hills *A*

Bryant & Stratton College:
  Cleveland *A*
Cedarville University *B*
Central Ohio Technical College *C, A*
Cincinnati State Technical and
  Community College *C, A*
Clark State Community College *C, A*
Columbus State Community
  College *C, A*
Cuyahoga Community College
  Metropolitan Campus *A, B*
David N. Myers University *A, B*
Davis College *A*
Edison State Community College *C, A*
Gallipolis Career College *A*
God's Bible School and College *A*
Hocking College *A*
James A. Rhodes State College *A*
Jefferson Community College *C, A*
Kent State University
  Ashtabula Regional Campus *A*
  Salem Regional Campus *A*
  Trumbull Campus *A*
  Tuscarawas Campus *A*
Lakeland Community College *C, A*
Marion Technical College *C, A*
Miami University
  Oxford Campus *C*
Ohio Business College: Sandusky *C, A*
Ohio University *A*
Ohio University
  Chillicothe Campus *A*
Ohio Valley College of Technology *A*
Sinclair Community College *C, A*
Southeastern Business College *A*
Southeastern Business College: New
  Boston *A*
Southern State Community College *A*
Stark State College of Technology *A*
University of Akron *C, A*
University of Akron: Wayne
  College *A*
University of Cincinnati
  Clermont College *C, A*
  Raymond Walters College *A*
University of Northwestern Ohio *A*
University of Rio Grande *C*
Wright State University *A*
Zane State College *C, A*

Oklahoma

Carl Albert State College *A*
East Central University *B*
Eastern Oklahoma State College *A*
Murray State College *A*
Northeastern Oklahoma Agricultural
  and Mechanical College *C, A*
Oklahoma State University
  Okmulgee *A*
Oklahoma Wesleyan University *A*
Tulsa Community College *C, A*
Western Oklahoma State College *A*

Oregon

Blue Mountain Community
  College *C, A*
Central Oregon Community
  College *C, A*
Chemeketa Community College *A*
Clackamas Community College *C*
Lane Community College *A*
Linn-Benton Community College *A*
Mount Hood Community College *C, A*
Oregon Institute of Technology *A*
Portland Community College *C, A*
Southwestern Oregon Community
  College *A*
Umpqua Community College *C, A*

Pennsylvania

Academy of Medical Arts and
  Business *C, A*
Baptist Bible College of
  Pennsylvania *A, B*

Bucks County Community College *A*
Business Institute of Pennsylvania *A*
Business Institute of Pennsylvania
  Meadville *A*
Butler County Community College *A*
Cambria-Rowe Business College *C, A*
Cambria-Rowe Business College:
  Indiana *A*
Career Training Academy:
  Monroeville *C*
Central Pennsylvania College *A*
Community College of Allegheny
  County *C, A*
Community College of Philadelphia *A*
Consolidated School of Business
  Lancaster *C, A*
  York *C, A*
Delaware County Community
  College *C*
Douglas Education Center *C*
DuBois Business College *C, A*
DuBois Business College
  Oil City *A*
Erie Business Center *A*
Harrisburg Area Community
  College *C, A*
ICM School of Business & Medical
  Careers *A*
Lackawanna College *A*
Lancaster Bible College *A*
Laurel Business Institute *A*
Lehigh Carbon Community
  College *C, A*
Lehigh Valley College *A*
Luzerne County Community
  College *C, A*
McCann School of Business
  Pottsville *A*
Montgomery County Community
  College *C, A*
Newport Business Institute *A*
Northampton County Area
  Community College *A*
Pennsylvania College of Technology *A*
Pennsylvania Highlands Community
  College *A*
Pennsylvania Institute of
  Technology *A*
Reading Area Community
  College *C, A*
Schuylkill Institute of Business &
  Technology *C, A*
South Hills School of Business &
  Technology *C, A*
West Virginia Career Institute *A*
Westmoreland County Community
  College *C, A*
Yorktowne Business Institute *A*

Puerto Rico

American University of Puerto
  Rico *A, B*
Atlantic College *A, B*
Bayamon Central University *A, B*
Columbia College *A*
Electronic Data Processing College:
  San Sebastian *A*
Humacao Community College *A*
Inter American University of Puerto
  Rico
  Aguadilla Campus *A, B*
  Arecibo Campus *A, B*
  Barranquitas Campus *A, B*
  Bayamon Campus *A, B*
  Fajardo Campus *A, B*
  Ponce Campus *A, B*
  San German Campus *A, B*
National College of Business &
  Technology: Arecibo *A*
National College of Business &
  Technology: Bayamon *A, B*
Pontifical Catholic University of
  Puerto Rico *A, B*
Turabo University *A, B*

Universidad Adventista de las
  Antillas *A, B*
Universidad del Este *B*
University College of San Juan *C, A*
University of Puerto Rico
  Arecibo *B*
  Bayamon University College *A, B*
  Carolina Regional College *A, B*
  Cayey University College *A, B*
  Humacao *A, B*
  Mayaguez *B*
  Ponce *A, B*
  Rio Piedras *B*
University of the Sacred Heart *B*

Rhode Island

Community College of Rhode
  Island *A*
New England Institute of
  Technology *A*

South Carolina

Aiken Technical College *C, A*
Central Carolina Technical
  College *C, A*
Denmark Technical College *C*
Florence-Darlington Technical
  College *C, A*
Forrest Junior College *A*
Greenville Technical College *C, A*
Horry-Georgetown Technical
  College *C, A*
Midlands Technical College *C, A*
Northeastern Technical College *C, A*
Orangeburg-Calhoun Technical
  College *A*
Piedmont Technical College *C, A*
Spartanburg Technical College *C, A*
Technical College of the
  Lowcountry *C, A*
Tri-County Technical College *C, A*
Trident Technical College *A*
University of South Carolina
  Lancaster *A*
Williamsburg Technical College *C, A*
York Technical College *C, A*

South Dakota

Black Hills State University *A*
Kilian Community College *A*
Northern State University *A*
Southeast Technical Institute *C*
Western Dakota Technical Institute *C*

Tennessee

Cleveland State Community
  College *C, A*
Columbia State Community College *A*
National College of Business &
  Technology
  Tennessee *C, A*
Northeast State Technical Community
  College *C, A*
Pellissippi State Technical Community
  College *A*
Roane State Community College *C*
South College *C*
Southwest Tennessee Community
  College *A*
Tennessee State University *A, B*
Tennessee Temple University *A, B*
Volunteer State Community College *C*
Walters State Community College *A*

Texas

Amarillo College *C, A*
Angelina College *C, A*
Austin Community College *C, A*
Blinn College *C*
Brazosport College *C, A*
Cedar Valley College *C, A*
Central Texas College *C, A*
Coastal Bend College *C, A*

College of the Mainland *C, A*
Del Mar College *C, A*
Eastfield College *C, A*
El Centro College *C*
El Paso Community College *C, A*
Frank Phillips College *C, A*
Galveston College *C, A*
Grayson County College *C, A*
Hill College *C, A*
Houston Community College
  System *C, A*
Lamar State College at Orange *C, A*
Lamar State College at Port
  Arthur *C, A*
Laredo Community College *A*
Lee College *C, A*
MTI College of Business and
  Technology *C, A*
MTI College of Business and
  Technology *A*
McLennan Community College *C*
Midland College *C, A*
Mountain View College *C*
Navarro College *C, A*
North Central Texas College *A*
North Harris Montgomery
  Community College District *C, A*
North Lake College *A*
Northeast Texas Community
  College *C, A*
Odessa College *C, A*
Palo Alto College *C, A*
Panola College *C, A*
Paris Junior College *A*
Ranger College *C, A*
Richland College *A*
St. Philip's College *C, A*
San Antonio College *C, A*
San Jacinto College
  Central Campus *C, A*
  North *C, A*
South Plains College *A*
Southwest Texas Junior College *A*
Southwestern Adventist
  University *A, B*
Sul Ross State University *B*
Tarleton State University *T*
Tarrant County College *A*
Temple College *C*
Texarkana College *C, A*
Texas State Technical College
  Harlingen *C, A*
Texas Woman's University *B*
Trinity Valley Community College *C, A*
Tyler Junior College *C, A*
Vernon College *A*
Victoria College *C, A*
Weatherford College *C, A*
Western Texas College *C, A*

Utah

College of Eastern Utah *C, A*
Everest College: Salt Lake City *C, A*
LDS Business College *C, A*
Provo College *A*
Stevens-Henager College of
  Business *A*
Utah State University *A, B*
Weber State University *A, B*

Vermont

Vermont Technical College *A*

Virginia

Blue Ridge Community College *C, A*
Bryant & Stratton College: Virginia
  Beach *A*
Central Virginia Community
  College *A*
Dabney S. Lancaster Community
  College *A*
Danville Community College *A*
ECPI College of Technology *C, A*

J. Sargeant Reynolds Community
   College *C, A*
John Tyler Community College *C, A*
Liberty University *A*
Lord Fairfax Community College *A*
National College of Business &
   Technology
   Bluefield *C, A*
   Charlottesville *C, A*
   Danville *C, A*
   Harrisonburg *C, A*
   Lynchburg *C, A*
   Martinsville *C, A*
   Salem *C, A*
New River Community College *A*
Northern Virginia Community
   College *C*
Paul D. Camp Community College *A*
Piedmont Virginia Community
   College *C, A*
St. Paul's College *B*
Southside Virginia Community
   College *A*
Southwest Virginia Community
   College *C, A*
Tidewater Community College *A*
Virginia Highlands Community
   College *A*
Virginia Western Community
   College *A*
Wytheville Community College *A*

Washington

Bellevue Community College *C, A*
Clover Park Technical College *C*
Columbia Basin College *C, A*
Edmonds Community College *C*
Everett Community College *C, A*
Highline Community College *C, A*
Lake Washington Technical
   College *C, A*
Lower Columbia College *C, A*
North Seattle Community
   College *C, A*
Olympic College *C, A*
Peninsula College *C, A*
Pierce College *C, A*
Renton Technical College *C, A*
Seattle Central Community
   College *C, A*
Skagit Valley College *C, A*
South Puget Sound Community
   College *C, A*
South Seattle Community
   College *C, A*
Spokane Community College *C, A*
Spokane Falls Community College *A*
Tacoma Community College *C*
Whatcom Community College *C*
Yakima Valley Community
   College *C, A*

West Virginia

Concord University *A*
Eastern West Virginia Community and
   Technical College *C, A*
Huntington Junior College *C, A*
Mountain State College *A*
Mountain State University *C, A*
Potomac State College of West Virginia
   University *A*
Southern West Virginia Community
   and Technical College *C, A*
Valley College of Technology *C*
West Virginia Business College *A*
West Virginia Business College *A*
West Virginia Northern Community
   College *C, A*

Wisconsin

Blackhawk Technical College *C, A*
Bryant & Stratton College:
   Milwaukee *A*
Chippewa Valley Technical College *A*

College of Menominee Nation *A*
Fox Valley Technical College *A*
Gateway Technical College *C, A*
Lakeshore Technical College *A*
Madison Area Technical College *A*
Maranatha Baptist Bible College *A*
Mid-State Technical College *C, A*
Milwaukee Area Technical College *A*
Moraine Park Technical College *C, A*
Nicolet Area Technical College *A*
Northcentral Technical College *A*
Northeast Wisconsin Technical
   College *A*
Southwest Wisconsin Technical
   College *C, A*
Western Wisconsin Technical
   College *A*
Wisconsin Indianhead Technical
   College *A*

Wyoming

Eastern Wyoming College *A*
Laramie County Community
   College *C, A*
Northwest College *C, A*
Sheridan College *C, A*
Western Wyoming Community
   College *C, A*

Adult/continuing education

Alabama

Auburn University *B*
University of West Alabama *M*

Arizona

University of Phoenix *M*

Arkansas

University of Arkansas *M, D*
University of Arkansas
   Little Rock *M*

California

College of the Sequoias *A*
Patten University *B*
San Diego State University *M*
San Francisco State University *M*
Whittier College *T*

Delaware

Delaware State University *M*

District of Columbia

George Washington University *M*

Florida

Florida Agricultural and Mechanical
   University *M*
Florida International University *M, D*
University of South Florida *M*

Georgia

University of Georgia *M, D*

Idaho

University of Idaho *M*

Illinois

National-Louis University *M, D*
Spoon River College *A*
University of Illinois
   Urbana-Champaign *M*

Indiana

Ball State University *M, D*
Indiana University-Purdue University
   Indianapolis *M*
Martin University *B*

Iowa

Loras College *M*
University of Iowa *M, D*

Kansas

Kansas State University *M, D*

Kentucky

Morehead State University *M*
University of Louisville *M*

Louisiana

Louisiana State University and
   Agricultural and Mechanical
   College *B, M, D*
Northwestern State University *M*

Maine

University of Southern Maine *M*

Massachusetts

Boston University *M, T*
Suffolk University *M*

Michigan

Michigan State University *M, D*
Northern Michigan University *B, M*

Minnesota

Capella University *M, D*
Ridgewater College *A*
University of Minnesota
   Twin Cities *M*

Missouri

Central Missouri State University *M, T*
University of Missouri
   Kansas City *M*
   St. Louis *M*

Nebraska

University of Nebraska
   Lincoln *M*

Nevada

University of Nevada
   Las Vegas *B, M*

New York

Cornell University *B, M, D*
Elmira College *M*
State University of New York
   College at Buffalo *M*
Syracuse University *M, D*

North Carolina

North Carolina Agricultural and
   Technical State University *M*

Ohio

Cleveland State University *M, D*

Oklahoma

Oklahoma State University *M, D*
University of Central Oklahoma *M*
University of Oklahoma *M, D*

Oregon

Oregon State University *M*
Portland State University *D*

Pennsylvania

Cheyney University of
   Pennsylvania *M*
Indiana University of Pennsylvania *M*
Penn State
   Lehigh Valley *B*
   University Park *M, D*
Temple University *M*

South Carolina

University of South Carolina *M*

Tennessee

University of Memphis *D*

Texas

Texas A&M University *B, M, D*
Texas A&M University
   Commerce *M*
   Texarkana *M*
Texas State University: San Marcos *M*
University of North Texas *M, D*
University of Texas
   Tyler *M*

Virginia

James Madison University *M*
Virginia Commonwealth University *M*

Washington

Eastern Washington University *M*
Seattle University *M*
Western Washington University *M*

Wisconsin

Alverno College *M*
University of Wisconsin
   Madison *M, D*

Adult/continuing education administration

Alaska

University of Alaska
   Anchorage *M*

Arizona

University of Phoenix *M*

Arkansas

University of Arkansas *D*

California

San Francisco State University *M*

Florida

Florida State University *M, D*
Nova Southeastern University *D*

Georgia

Valdosta State University *D*

Illinois

Bradley University *M*
DePaul University *M*
Northern Illinois University *M, D*
University of Illinois
   Urbana-Champaign *M, D*

Indiana

Ball State University *M, T*
Purdue University
   Calumet *T*

Iowa

Drake University *M*
Iowa State University *M, D*

Kansas

Newman University *M*

Maine

University of Southern Maine *M*

Maryland

Coppin State University *M*

Massachusetts
Harvard College *M, D*
Lesley University *M*

Michigan
Grand Valley State University *M*
Marygrove College *M*
Michigan State University *M, D*

Mississippi
University of Southern Mississippi *M*

Missouri
University of Missouri
Columbia *M, D*

New York
City University of New York
Lehman College *M, T*
Fordham University *M, D*
State University of New York
College at Buffalo *M*

North Carolina
Appalachian State University *M*
East Carolina University *M*
North Carolina Agricultural and
Technical State University *M*
North Carolina State University *M, D*

Ohio
Ohio State University
Columbus Campus *M*

Oregon
Oregon State University *M*

Pennsylvania
Penn State
University Park *M, D*
Widener University *M*

South Carolina
University of South Carolina *M*

South Dakota
University of South Dakota *M, D*

Tennessee
Tusculum College *M*
University of Memphis *D*

Texas
Texas A&M University
Kingsville *M*
Texas State University: San Marcos *D*

Wisconsin
Carroll College *M*

Adult development/aging

Colorado
University of Northern Colorado *B, M*

Connecticut
Gateway Community College *C, A*

Georgia
Southwest Georgia Technical
College *C*

Indiana
St. Mary-of-the-Woods College *A, B*
Valparaiso University *M*

Maryland
College of Notre Dame of
Maryland *M*

Massachusetts
North Shore Community College *C, A*

Michigan
Eastern Michigan University *M*
Madonna University *C, A, B*
Oakland Community College *C, A*
Wayne County Community College *A*

New Jersey
Georgian Court University *C*

Ohio
Bowling Green State University *B*
Stark State College of Technology *A*
University of Cincinnati
Clermont College *C*
University of Toledo *A*

Oklahoma
University of Central Oklahoma *B*

Pennsylvania
Chestnut Hill College *C, A, B*
Gwynedd-Mercy College *B*
Harrisburg Area Community
College *C*
Lehigh Carbon Community
College *C, A*
Penn State
Wilkes-Barre *B*
St. Joseph's University *M*
York College of Pennsylvania *B*

Rhode Island
Community College of Rhode
Island *A*

Texas
San Antonio College *C, A*

Virginia
Liberty University *B*
Virginia Commonwealth University *M*

Adult health nursing

California
University of San Diego *M*

Connecticut
Western Connecticut State
University *M*

Illinois
Loyola University of Chicago *M*
Saint Anthony College of Nursing *B*

Indiana
Indiana University-Purdue University
Indianapolis *M*

Iowa
Allen College *M*
University of Iowa *M*

Louisiana
Louisiana State University Health
Sciences Center *M*

Michigan
Madonna University *M*
Oakland University *M*
Wayne State University *M*

Minnesota
College of St. Scholastica *M*

Missouri
Jewish Hospital College of Nursing
and Allied Health *M*
Maryville University of Saint Louis *M*

New York
Adelphi University *M*
City University of New York
College of Staten Island *M*
Hunter College *B, M*
Lehman College *M*
College of New Rochelle *M*
Columbia University
School of Nursing *M*
Daemen College *M*
Long Island University
Brooklyn Campus *M*
Mount St. Mary College *M*
Pace University *M*
State University of New York
Buffalo *M*
Stony Brook *M*

Ohio
Case Western Reserve University *M*
Wright State University *B*
Youngstown State University *M*

Oklahoma
University of Oklahoma *M*

Pennsylvania
Pennsylvania College of
Technology *M*
University of Pennsylvania *M*

South Carolina
Medical University of South
Carolina *M*

Virginia
James Madison University *M*

Wisconsin
Marquette University *M*

Adult literacy instruction

Minnesota
Bethel University *M*

Advertising

Alabama
University of Alabama *B, M*

Arizona
Northern Arizona University *B*

Arkansas
Harding University *B*
University of Arkansas
Little Rock *B*

California
Academy of Art University *C, A, B, M*
Art Center College of Design *B*
Art Institute
of California: San Diego *B*
California Lutheran University *B*
California State University
East Bay *B*
Fullerton *B, M*
Chapman University *B*
College of San Mateo *A*
Cosumnes River College *A*

Fullerton College *C*
Irvine Valley College *A*
Long Beach City College *C, A*
Los Angeles City College *A*
Los Angeles Southwest College *A*
Mount San Antonio College *A*
Orange Coast College *A*
Palomar College *C, A*
Pepperdine University *B*
San Diego State University *B, M*
San Jose State University *B*
Santa Ana College *C, A*

Colorado
Adams State College *B*
Johnson & Wales University *A*
Trinidad State Junior College *A*
University of Denver *M*

Connecticut
Middlesex Community College *C*
Quinnipiac University *B*
University of Bridgeport *B*

Delaware
Delaware Technical and Community
College
Terry Campus *A*

District of Columbia
University of the District of
Columbia *A*

Florida
Barry University *B*
Florida Southern College *B*
Florida State University *B*
Gulf Coast Community College *A*
Manatee Community College *A*
Northwood University
Florida Campus *A, B*
University of Central Florida *B*
University of Florida *B*
University of Miami *B*

Georgia
Clark Atlanta University *B*
University of Georgia *B*
Wesleyan College *B*

Hawaii
Hawaii Pacific University *B*

Idaho
Brigham Young University-Idaho *B*

Illinois
American Academy of Art *B*
Bradley University *B*
Columbia College Chicago *B*
Concordia University *B*
Danville Area Community College *A*
Illinois Institute of Art-Schaumburg *B*
North Park University *B*
Oakton Community College *C*
University of Illinois
Urbana-Champaign *B, M*
University of St. Francis *B*

Indiana
Indiana University-Purdue University
Indianapolis *B*
University of Southern Indiana *B*
Vincennes University *A*

Iowa
Drake University *B*
Iowa State University *B*
Morningside College *B*
St. Ambrose University *B*

Kansas

Pittsburg State University *B*

Kentucky

Murray State University *B*
University of Kentucky *B*
Western Kentucky University *B*

Maine

New England School of
    Communications *A, B*
St. Joseph's College *B*

Maryland

Montgomery College *C, A*

Massachusetts

American International College *B*
Babson College *B*
Boston University *B, M*
Eastern Nazarene College *B*
Emerson College *B, M*
Mount Ida College *A*
Salem State College *B*
Suffolk University *B*
Western New England College *B*

Michigan

Bay de Noc Community College *C*
Central Michigan University *B*
Ferris State University *C, B*
Grand Valley State University *B*
Lansing Community College *A*
Michigan State University *B, M*
North Central Michigan College *C*
Northwood University *A, B*
Schoolcraft College *A*

Minnesota

Art Institutes International
    Minnesota *B*
College of St. Scholastica *B*
Concordia College: Moorhead *B*
Hennepin Technical College *C, A*
Metropolitan State University *B*
St. Cloud State University *B*
St. Cloud Technical College *C, A*
Winona State University *B*

Mississippi

Mississippi Delta Community
    College *A*
University of Southern Mississippi *B*

Missouri

Drury University *B*
Fontbonne University *B*
Lindenwood University *B*
St. Louis Community College
    St. Louis Community College at
        Florissant Valley *A*
Stephens College *B*
University of Missouri
    Columbia *B*
Washington University in St. Louis *B*
Webster University *B, M*
Westminster College *B*
William Woods University *B*

Nebraska

Hastings College *B*
University of Nebraska
    Kearney *B*
    Lincoln *B*

New Hampshire

Franklin Pierce College *B*
New England College *B*
Southern New Hampshire
    University *B*

New Jersey

Rider University *B*
Rowan University *B*
Thomas Edison State College *B*
Union County College *C*

New York

City University of New York
    Baruch College *B, M*
    City College *B*
Fashion Institute of Technology *A, B*
Iona College *B*
Long Island University
    C.W. Post Campus *B*
Marist College *B*
Mohawk Valley Community
    College *C, A*
Monroe Community College *A*
New York Institute of Technology *B*
Onondaga Community College *A*
Pace University *B*
Rochester Institute of Technology *B*
St. John's University *B*
School of Visual Arts *B*
Syracuse University *B, M*
Tompkins-Cortland Community
    College *A*

North Carolina

Alamance Community College *C*
Appalachian State University *B*
Campbell University *B*
Halifax Community College *A*

North Dakota

Minot State University: Bottineau
    Campus *C, A*

Ohio

Cleveland State University *C*
Columbus College of Art and
    Design *B*
Kent State University *B*
Marietta College *B*
School of Advertising Art *C, A*
Xavier University *A, B*
Youngstown State University *B*

Oklahoma

Oklahoma Christian University *B*
Oklahoma City University *B*
Southeastern Oklahoma State
    University *B*
University of Central Oklahoma *B*
University of Oklahoma *B*

Oregon

University of Oregon *B, M*

Pennsylvania

Elizabethtown College *B*
Gannon University *B*
Keystone College *A*
Marywood University *B*
Oakbridge Academy of Arts *A*
Penn State
    Abington *B*
    Altoona *B*
    Beaver *B*
    Berks *B*
    Delaware County *B*
    Dubois *B*
    Fayette *B*
    Hazleton *B*
    Lehigh Valley *B*
    McKeesport *B*
    Mont Alto *B*
    New Kensington *B*
    Schuylkill - Capital College *B*
    Shenango *B*
    University Park *B*

Wilkes-Barre *B*
Worthington Scranton *B*
Point Park University *B*
Temple University *B*
Waynesburg College *B*

Puerto Rico

University of Puerto Rico
    Carolina Regional College *A, B*
University of the Sacred Heart *B, M*

Rhode Island

Johnson & Wales University *A*

South Carolina

University of South Carolina *B*

South Dakota

Southeast Technical Institute *A*

Tennessee

Chattanooga State Technical
    Community College *A*
Southern Adventist University *B*
Union University *B*
University of Tennessee
    Knoxville *B*

Texas

Amarillo College *A*
Lamar University *B*
Northwood University: Texas
    Campus *A, B*
Palo Alto College *A*
Sam Houston State University *B*
Southern Methodist University *B*
Texas A&M University
    Commerce *B*
Texas Christian University *B, M*
Texas State University: San Marcos *B*
Texas Tech University *B*
University of North Texas *B*
University of Texas
    Arlington *B*
    Austin *B, M, D*
    El Paso *B*
West Texas A&M University *B*

Utah

Southern Utah University *B*

Virginia

Art Institute
    of Washington *B*
Hampton University *B*
Liberty University *B*

Washington

Everett Community College *C, A*
Seattle Central Community
    College *C, A*

West Virginia

Bethany College *B*
Concord University *B*
West Virginia University *B*

Wisconsin

Marquette University *B, M*

Aeronautical/aerospace engineering

Alabama

Auburn University *B, M, D*
Tuskegee University *B*
University of Alabama *B, M*

Arizona

Arizona State University *B, M, D*

Embry-Riddle Aeronautical University:
    Prescott Campus *B*
Gateway Community College *A*
University of Arizona *B, M, D*

California

Allan Hancock College *A*
California Institute of
    Technology *B, M, D*
California Polytechnic State
    University: San Luis Obispo *B, M*
California State Polytechnic
    University: Pomona *B*
California State University
    Long Beach *B, M*
    Northridge *M*
Merced College *A*
San Diego State University *B, M*
San Jose State University *B, M*
Stanford University *M, D*
University of California
    Davis *B*
    Irvine *B*
    Los Angeles *B, M, D*
    San Diego *B, M, D*
University of Southern
    California *B, M, D*

Colorado

United States Air Force Academy *B*
University of Colorado
    Boulder *B, M, D*
    Colorado Springs *M*

Delaware

University of Delaware *B*

District of Columbia

George Washington University *M, D*

Florida

Embry-Riddle Aeronautical
    University *B, M*
Florida Institute of
    Technology *B, M, D*
University of Central Florida *B, M*
University of Florida *B, M*
University of Miami *B*

Georgia

Georgia Institute of
    Technology *B, M, D*

Hawaii

University of Hawaii
    Honolulu Community College *A*

Illinois

Illinois Institute of Technology *B*
University of Illinois
    Urbana-Champaign *B, M, D*

Indiana

Purdue University *B, M, D*
University of Notre Dame *B, M, D*

Iowa

Iowa State University *B, M, D*

Kansas

University of Kansas *B, M, D*
Wichita State University *B, M, D*

Maryland

Prince George's Community
    College *A*
United States Naval Academy *B*
University of Maryland
    College Park *B, M, D*

Massachusetts
Boston University *B, M, D*
Massachusetts Institute of
Technology *B, M, D*
Worcester Polytechnic Institute *B*

Michigan
University of Michigan *B, M, D*
Western Michigan University *B*

Minnesota
St. Cloud State University *B*
University of Minnesota
Twin Cities *B, M, D*

Mississippi
Mississippi State University *B, M*

Missouri
St. Louis University *B, M*
University of Missouri
Rolla *B, M, D*
Washington University in St.
Louis *B, M, D*

New Hampshire
Daniel Webster College *B*

New York
Clarkson University *B*
Cornell University *B, M, D*
Rensselaer Polytechnic
Institute *B, M, D*
Rochester Institute of Technology *B*
State University of New York
Buffalo *B, M, D*
Syracuse University *B, M, D*
United States Military Academy *B*

North Carolina
North Carolina State
University *B, M, D*

North Dakota
North Dakota State University *B*

Ohio
Case Western Reserve
University *B, M, D*
Ohio State University
Columbus Campus *B, M, D*
University of Cincinnati *B, M, D*
University of Dayton *M, D*

Oklahoma
Oklahoma State University *B*
Southeastern Oklahoma State
University *B*
University of Oklahoma *B, M, D*

Pennsylvania
Gettysburg College *B*
Penn State
Abington *B*
Altoona *B*
Beaver *B*
Berks *B*
Delaware County *B*
Dubois *B*
Fayette *B*
Hazleton *B*
Lehigh Valley *B*
McKeesport *B*
Mont Alto *B*
New Kensington *B*
Schuylkill - Capital College *B*
Shenango *B*
University Park *B, M, D*
Wilkes-Barre *B*
Worthington Scranton *B*
York *B*

Tennessee
University of Tennessee
Knoxville *B, M, D*

Texas
Laredo Community College *A*
Rice University *M, D*
Texas A&M University *B, M, D*
University of Houston *M, D*
University of Texas
Arlington *B, M, D*
Austin *B, M, D*

Utah
Utah State University *B*

Virginia
Old Dominion University *M, D*
University of Virginia *B, M, D*
Virginia Polytechnic Institute and
State University *B, M, D*

Washington
University of Washington *B, M, D*

West Virginia
West Virginia University *B, M, D*

Aeronautical/aerospace engineering technology

Alabama
Calhoun Community College *A*

Arizona
Gateway Community College *A*

California
Antelope Valley College *C, A*
Bakersfield College *A*
Solano Community College *A*
University of California
San Diego *B*

Florida
Embry-Riddle Aeronautical
University *B*

Georgia
Middle Georgia College *A*

Indiana
Purdue University *A*

Maryland
Capitol College *B*

Michigan
Andrews University *B*
Western Michigan University *B*

Missouri
Central Missouri State University *B*
East Central College *A*
St. Louis University *B*

New York
New York Institute of Technology *B*

Ohio
Cincinnati State Technical and
Community College *C, A*

Pennsylvania
Community College of Beaver
County *A*

Texas
LeTourneau University *B*

Vermont
Vermont Technical College *A*

Aeronautics and aviation science

Alabama
Community College of the Air
Force *A*

Alaska
University of Alaska
Anchorage *A, B*

Arizona
Chandler-Gilbert Community College
Pecos *A*
Cochise College *A*
Embry-Riddle Aeronautical University:
Prescott Campus *B, M*

Arkansas
Northwest Arkansas Community
College *A*

California
Chabot College *A*
City College of San Francisco *C, A*
College of San Mateo *C, A*
Cypress College *C, A*
Glendale Community College *C*
Long Beach City College *C, A*
Mount San Antonio College *A*
Orange Coast College *C, A*
Pacific Union College *B*
Palomar College *C, A*
San Diego Mesa College *C*
San Jose State University *B*
Santa Rosa Junior College *C*

Colorado
Aims Community College *C, A*
Colorado Northwestern Community
College *A*
Metropolitan State College of
Denver *B*

Connecticut
Naugatuck Valley Community
College *A*
Three Rivers Community College *A*

Delaware
Delaware State University *B*
Wilmington College *B*

District of Columbia
University of the District of
Columbia *A, B*

Florida
Broward Community College *A*
Embry-Riddle Aeronautical
University *B*
Embry-Riddle Aeronautical University:
Extended Campus *A, B*
Everglades University *B, M*
Florida Community College at
Jacksonville *A*
Florida Institute of Technology *B*
Florida Memorial University *B*
Miami Dade College *A*
Palm Beach Community College *A*

Illinois
Lewis University *A, B*
Quincy University *A*
Springfield College in Illinois *A*

Indiana
Indiana State University *A*

Purdue University *A, B*

Iowa
Iowa Central Community College *A*
Iowa Lakes Community College *A*
University of Dubuque *B*

Kansas
Central Christian College of Kansas *A*
Cloud County Community College *A*
Hesston College *A*

Kentucky
Eastern Kentucky University *B*

Louisiana
Louisiana Tech University *B*

Maryland
Community College of Baltimore
County *C, A*
University of Maryland
Eastern Shore *B*

Michigan
Andrews University *A, B*
Delta College *C, A*
Lansing Community College *A*
Northwestern Michigan College *A*

Minnesota
Academy College *A*
Anoka Technical College *C, A*
Vermilion Community College *A*

Mississippi
Delta State University *B*

Missouri
College of the Ozarks *B*
St. Louis Community College
St. Louis Community College at
Meramec *C*

Nebraska
University of Nebraska
Kearney *B*
Omaha *B*

New Hampshire
Daniel Webster College *A, B*

New Jersey
County College of Morris *A*
Mercer County Community College *A*
Raritan Valley Community College *A*
Thomas Edison State College *A, B*

New Mexico
Clovis Community College *A*
Eastern New Mexico University:
Roswell Campus *A*

New York
Dowling College *B*
St. Francis College *B*
Schenectady County Community
College *A*

North Carolina
Elizabeth City State University *B*

North Dakota
North Dakota State University *M*
University of North Dakota *B, M*

Ohio
Kent State University *B*
Ohio State University
Columbus Campus *B*

Ohio University *A, B*
University of Cincinnati
Clermont College *A*

Oklahoma

National Education Center
Spartan School of Aeronautics *C, A*
Oklahoma City Community College *A*
Oklahoma State University *B*
Rose State College *A*
Southeastern Oklahoma State
University *B*
University of Oklahoma *B*
Western Oklahoma State College *A*

Oregon

Lane Community College *A*
Mount Hood Community College *A*

Pennsylvania

Geneva College *A*

Puerto Rico

Inter American University of Puerto
Rico
Bayamon Campus *C, B*

Tennessee

Middle Tennessee State University *B*

Texas

LeTourneau University *B*
Navarro College *C, A*
Palo Alto College *A*
Texas Southern University *B*
Texas State Technical College
Waco *C, A*

Utah

Utah State University *A*
Westminster College *B*

Virginia

Liberty University *B*
Northern Virginia Community
College *A*

Washington

Central Washington University *B*
Green River Community College *A*
Highline Community College *C, A*

Wisconsin

Gateway Technical College *A*

Aesthetician/skin care

Alabama

Gadsden State Community College *C*

California

San Jose City College *C*

Florida

Indian River Community College *C*

Massachusetts

North Shore Community College *C*

Michigan

Kirtland Community College *C, A*

Minnesota

Minnesota State College - Southeast
Technical *C*
Minnesota State Community and
Technical College - Fergus Falls *C*
Ridgewater College *C*
St. Paul College *C, A*

North Carolina

Brunswick Community College *C*
Carteret Community College *C*
Davidson County Community
College *C*
Isothermal Community College *C*
Southeastern Community College *C*
Stanly Community College *C*

Texas

Lamar State College at Port Arthur *C*
Panola College *C*

Washington

Clover Park Technical College *C*
Olympic College *C*
Renton Technical College *C*

Wyoming

Eastern Wyoming College *C*

African-American studies

Alabama

Talladega College *B*
University of Alabama
Birmingham *B*

Arizona

Arizona State University *B*

California

California State University
Dominguez Hills *B*
East Bay *B*
Fresno *B*
Fullerton *B*
Long Beach *B*
Los Angeles *B*
Northridge *B*
San Bernardino *B*
City College of San Francisco *A*
Claremont McKenna College *B*
College of Alameda *A*
Contra Costa College *A*
De Anza College *A*
East Los Angeles College *A*
El Camino College *A*
Fresno City College *A*
Laney College *A*
Los Angeles City College *A*
Los Angeles Southwest College *A*
Loyola Marymount University *B*
Merritt College *A*
Pitzer College *B*
Pomona College *B*
San Diego City College *A*
San Diego Mesa College *A*
San Diego State University *B*
San Francisco State University *B*
San Jose State University *B*
Santa Ana College *A*
Santa Barbara City College *A*
Scripps College *B*
Solano Community College *A*
Sonoma State University *B*
Southwestern College *A*
Stanford University *B*
University of California
Berkeley *B, D*
Davis *B*
Irvine *B*
Los Angeles *B, M*
Riverside *B*
Santa Barbara *B*
University of Southern California *B*
Ventura College *A*

Colorado

Metropolitan State College of
Denver *B*

University of Northern Colorado *B*

Connecticut

Trinity College *B*
Wesleyan University *B*
Yale University *B, M, D*

District of Columbia

Howard University *B*

Florida

Florida Agricultural and Mechanical
University *B*
Florida International University *M*
Manatee Community College *A*
University of Miami *B*
University of South Florida *B*

Georgia

Atlanta Metropolitan College *A*
Clark Atlanta University *M*
Emory University *B*
Georgia State University *B*
Mercer University *B*
Morehouse College *B*
University of Georgia *B*

Illinois

Chicago State University *B*
City Colleges of Chicago
Kennedy-King College *A*
Olive-Harvey College *A*
DePaul University *B*
Dominican University *B*
Eastern Illinois University *B*
Knox College *B*
Northwestern University *B*
Roosevelt University *B*
University of Chicago *B*
University of Illinois
Chicago *B*
Western Illinois University *B*

Indiana

DePauw University *B*
Earlham College *B*
Indiana State University *B*
Indiana University
Bloomington *B, M*
Northwest *B*
Martin University *B*
Purdue University *B*

Iowa

Coe College *B*
Grinnell College *B*
Luther College *B*
University of Iowa *B, M*

Kansas

University of Kansas *B*

Kentucky

University of Louisville *B, M*

Maine

Bates College *B*
Bowdoin College *B*
Colby College *B*

Maryland

Johns Hopkins University *B*
Morgan State University *B, M, D*
Prince George's Community
College *A*
University of Maryland
Baltimore County *B*
College Park *B*
Eastern Shore *B*

Massachusetts

Amherst College *B*
Boston University *M*
Brandeis University *B*
Hampshire College *B*
Harvard College *B, D*
Mount Holyoke College *B*
Simmons College *B*
Simon's Rock College of Bard *B*
Smith College *B*
Suffolk University *B*
Tufts University *B*
University of Massachusetts
Amherst *B, M, D*
Boston *B*
Wellesley College *B*

Michigan

Eastern Michigan University *B*
Michigan State University *B*
University of Michigan *B*
University of Michigan
Flint *B*
Wayne State University *B*

Minnesota

Carleton College *B*
University of Minnesota
Twin Cities *B*

Mississippi

University of Mississippi *B*

Missouri

University of Missouri
Columbia *B*
Washington University in St. Louis *B*

Nebraska

University of Nebraska
Omaha *B*

New Hampshire

Dartmouth College *B*

New Jersey

Rowan University *B*
Rutgers, The State University of New
Jersey
Camden Regional Campus *B*
New Brunswick/Piscataway
Campus *B*
Newark Regional Campus *B*
Seton Hall University *B*
William Paterson University of New
Jersey *B*

New Mexico

University of New Mexico *B*

New York

Bard College *B*
City University of New York
Brooklyn College *B*
City College *B*
College of Staten Island *B*
Hunter College *B*
Lehman College *B*
York College *B*
Colgate University *B*
Columbia University
Columbia College *B*
School of General Studies *B*
Cornell University *B, M, D*
Eugene Lang College The New School
for Liberal Arts *B*
Fordham University *B*
Hamilton College *B*
Hobart and William Smith Colleges *B*
Metropolitan College of New
York *A, B*
New York University *B, M*

Sarah Lawrence College *B*
State University of New York
   Albany *B, M*
   Binghamton *B*
   Buffalo *B*
   College at Brockport *B*
   College at Cortland *B*
   College at Geneseo *B*
   College at Oneonta *B*
   New Paltz *B*
   Stony Brook *B*
Syracuse University *B*
University of Rochester *B*
Wells College *B*

North Carolina
Duke University *B*
Guilford College *B*
St. Augustine's College *B*
University of North Carolina
   Chapel Hill *B*
   Charlotte *B*

Ohio
Antioch College *B*
College of Wooster *B*
Denison University *B*
Kent State University *B*
Miami University
   Oxford Campus *B*
Oberlin College *B*
Ohio State University
   Columbus Campus *B, M*
Ohio University *B*
Ohio Wesleyan University *B*
Owens Community College
   Toledo *B*
Sinclair Community College *A*
University of Cincinnati *B*
University of Toledo *B*
Wright State University *B*
Youngstown State University *B*

Oklahoma
University of Oklahoma *B*

Pennsylvania
Franklin & Marshall College *B*
Gettysburg College *B*
Lehigh University *B*
Lincoln University *B*
Penn State
   Abington *B*
   Altoona *B*
   Beaver *B*
   Berks *B*
   Delaware County *B*
   Dubois *B*
   Erie, The Behrend College *B*
   Fayette *B*
   Hazleton *B*
   Lehigh Valley *B*
   McKeesport *B*
   Mont Alto *B*
   New Kensington *B*
   Schuylkill - Capital College *B*
   Shenango *B*
   University Park *B*
   Wilkes-Barre *B*
   Worthington Scranton *B*
   York *B*
Temple University *B, M, D*
University of Pennsylvania *B*
University of Pittsburgh *B*

Rhode Island
Brown University *B*
Rhode Island College *B*
University of Rhode Island *B*

South Carolina
Claflin University *B*
University of South Carolina *B*

Tennessee
American Baptist College of ABT
   Seminary *A, B*
University of Memphis *B*
University of Tennessee
   Knoxville *B*
Vanderbilt University *B*

Texas
Southern Methodist University *B*
Texas Southern University *B*

Utah
University of Utah *M*
Weber State University *B*

Vermont
Goddard College *B*

Virginia
College of William and Mary *B*
University of Virginia *B*
Virginia Commonwealth University *B*

Washington
University of Washington *B*

Wisconsin
Marquette University *B*
University of Wisconsin
   Madison *B, M*

African languages

California
University of California
   Los Angeles *B*

Indiana
Indiana University
   Bloomington *B*

Wisconsin
University of Wisconsin
   Madison *M, D*

African studies

California
San Diego City College *A*
San Diego Mesa College *A*
San Francisco State University *B*
Stanford University *B*
University of California
   Los Angeles *M*

Connecticut
Connecticut College *B*
Trinity College *B*
Yale University *B, M*

District of Columbia
Howard University *B, M, D*

Florida
Manatee Community College *A*

Georgia
Clark Atlanta University *M, D*
Emory University *B*

Illinois
Illinois Wesleyan University *B*
University of Chicago *B*
University of Illinois
   Urbana-Champaign *M*

Indiana
Martin University *B*

Iowa
University of Iowa *B*

Kansas
University of Kansas *B*

Louisiana
Dillard University *B*
Tulane University *B*

Maine
Bowdoin College *B*

Maryland
Washington College *B*

Massachusetts
Amherst College *B*
Brandeis University *B*
Harvard College *B*
Simon's Rock College of Bard *B*
Tufts University *M*
Wellesley College *B*

Michigan
Lansing Community College *A*
Oakland University *B*
University of Michigan *B*
Western Michigan University *B*

Minnesota
Carleton College *B*
Macalester College *B*
University of Minnesota
   Twin Cities *B*

Missouri
Washington University in St. Louis *B*

New Hampshire
Dartmouth College *B*

New Jersey
Drew University *B*
Rutgers, The State University of New
   Jersey
   New Brunswick/Piscataway
      Campus *B*
   Newark Regional Campus *B*
William Paterson University of New
   Jersey *B*

New York
Bard College *B*
Barnard College *B*
City University of New York
   Queens College *B, T*
Colgate University *B*
Columbia University
   Columbia College *B*
   School of General Studies *B*
Fordham University *B*
Hobart and William Smith Colleges *B*
Hofstra University *B*
Nassau Community College *A*
St. Lawrence University *B*
Sarah Lawrence College *B*
State University of New York
   Binghamton *B*
   College at Brockport *B*
Vassar College *B*

Ohio
Antioch College *B*
Bowling Green State University *B*
College of Wooster *B*
Oberlin College *B*
Ohio State University
   Columbus Campus *B, M*
Ohio University *B, M*

Oregon
Portland State University *B*

Pennsylvania
Bryn Mawr College *B*
Franklin & Marshall College *B*
University of Pennsylvania *B*

Rhode Island
Brown University *B*

Tennessee
Vanderbilt University *B*
Walters State Community College *A*

Virginia
College of William and Mary *B*

Washington
University of Washington *B*

Wisconsin
University of Wisconsin
   Milwaukee *B*

Agribusiness operations

Alabama
Alabama Agricultural and Mechanical
   University *M*
Wallace State Community College at
   Hanceville *C, A*

Arizona
Eastern Arizona College *A*
Mesa Community College *A*

Arkansas
Arkansas State University *B, M*
Arkansas Tech University *B*
University of Arkansas *B*

California
Allan Hancock College *C, A*
Bakersfield College *A*
College of the Redwoods *A*
College of the Sequoias *C, A*
San Joaquin Delta College *C, A*
Santa Rosa Junior College *C, A*
Shasta College *C, A*
Ventura College *C, A*

Colorado
Colorado State University *B*

Delaware
Delaware Technical and Community
   College
   Owens Campus *C, A*
University of Delaware *B*

Florida
Florida Agricultural and Mechanical
   University *B*
Miami Dade College *A*
South Florida Community College *A*

Georgia
Coastal Georgia Community
   College *A*
South Georgia College *A*
University of Georgia *B*

Hawaii
University of Hawaii
   Hilo *B*

Idaho
Brigham Young University-Idaho *A*

Illinois
Danville Area Community College *A*
Illinois State University *B, M*
Kishwaukee College *A*

Indiana
Purdue University *M*
Vincennes University *A*

Iowa
Dordt College *B*
Iowa State University *B*
Iowa Western Community College *A*
North Iowa Area Community
College *A*

Kansas
Colby Community College *A*
Cowley County Community
College *C, A*
Dodge City Community College *C, A*
McPherson College *B*

Kentucky
Berea College *B*
Morehead State University *A*

Minnesota
Ridgewater College *A*
Southwest Minnesota State
University *B*
University of Minnesota
Crookston *B*

Mississippi
Hinds Community College *A*
Mississippi State University *B*

Missouri
College of the Ozarks *B*
Crowder College *A*
North Central Missouri College *C, A*
Southeast Missouri State University *B*

Nebraska
Nebraska College of Technical
Agriculture *A*
Northeast Community College *A*

New Mexico
Eastern New Mexico University *A, B*
New Mexico State University *B*
Southwestern Indian Polytechnic
Institute *A*

New York
Cornell University *B*
State University of New York
College of Agriculture and
Technology at Morrisville *A*

North Carolina
North Carolina State University *B*
Wayne Community College *A*

North Dakota
Bismarck State College *A*
Dickinson State University *A*
North Dakota State College of
Science *A*
North Dakota State University *B*
Sitting Bull College *A*

Ohio
Clark State Community College *A*
Wilmington College *B*

Oklahoma
Oklahoma Panhandle State
University *B*

Oregon
Chemeketa Community College *A*

Pennsylvania
Delaware Valley College *B, M*
Harrisburg Area Community
College *C, A*
Penn State
Abington *B*
Altoona *B*
Beaver *B*
Berks *B*
Delaware County *B*
Dubois *B*
Erie, The Behrend College *B*
Fayette *B*
Hazleton *B*
Lehigh Valley *B*
McKeesport *B*
Mont Alto *B*
New Kensington *B*
Schuylkill - Capital College *B*
Shenango *B*
University Park *B*
Worthington Scranton *B*
York *B*

Puerto Rico
Universidad del Este *B*
University of Puerto Rico
Mayaguez *B*

South Carolina
Clemson University *B*
South Carolina State University *B, M*

South Dakota
Lake Area Technical Institute *A*
South Dakota State University *B*
Western Dakota Technical Institute *A*

Tennessee
Middle Tennessee State University *B*
Tennessee Technological University *B*

Texas
Abilene Christian University *B*
Palo Alto College *C, A*
Sam Houston State University *B, M*
Southwest Texas Junior College *A*
Stephen F. Austin State University *B*
Sul Ross State University *B, M*
Tarleton State University *B*
Texas A&M University *B, M*
Texas A&M University
Kingsville *B*
Texas State University: San Marcos *B*
West Texas A&M University *B, M*

Utah
Snow College *C, A*
Utah State University *M*

Vermont
Vermont Technical College *A*

Washington
Columbia Basin College *A*

Wisconsin
Fox Valley Technical College *A*
Southwest Wisconsin Technical
College *A*
University of Wisconsin
Platteville *B*

Wyoming
Eastern Wyoming College *A*
Laramie County Community
College *A*
University of Wyoming *B*

Agricultural and biological engineering

Alabama
Auburn University *B*

Arizona
University of Arizona *B, M, D*

Arkansas
University of Arkansas *B, M*

California
Imperial Valley College *A*
University of California
Davis *B, M, D*
Los Angeles *B*

Delaware
University of Delaware *B*

Florida
Florida Agricultural and Mechanical
University *B*
Florida Gulf Coast University *B*
University of Florida *A, B, M*

Georgia
Abraham Baldwin Agricultural
College *A*
Darton College *A*
Fort Valley State University *A, B*
University of Georgia *B, M*

Hawaii
University of Hawaii
Manoa *B, M, D*

Idaho
University of Idaho *B, M, D*

Illinois
Illinois Central College *A*
University of Illinois
Urbana-Champaign *B, M, D*

Indiana
Purdue University *B, M, D*

Iowa
Dordt College *B*
Indian Hills Community College *A*
Iowa Lakes Community College *A*
Iowa State University *B, M, D*

Kansas
Kansas State University *B, M, D*

Kentucky
University of Kentucky *B, M, D*

Louisiana
Louisiana State University and
Agricultural and Mechanical
College *M*

Maine
University of Maine *B, M*

Maryland
University of Maryland
College Park *B, M, D*

Michigan
Michigan State University *B, M, D*

Minnesota
University of Minnesota
Twin Cities *B, M, D*

Mississippi
Mississippi State University *B*

Missouri
University of Missouri
Columbia *B, M, D*

Nebraska
University of Nebraska
Lincoln *B, M*

New York
Cornell University *B, M, D*
State University of New York
College of Agriculture and
Technology at Cobleskill *A, B*

North Carolina
North Carolina Agricultural and
Technical State University *B*
North Carolina State
University *B, M, D*

North Dakota
North Dakota State University *B, M*

Ohio
Ohio State University
Columbus Campus *B, M, D*

Oklahoma
Oklahoma State University *B, M, D*

Oregon
Oregon State University *M, D*

Pennsylvania
Penn State
Abington *B*
Altoona *B*
Beaver *B*
Berks *B*
Delaware County *B*
Dubois *B*
Fayette *B*
Hazleton *B*
Lehigh Valley *B*
McKeesport *B*
Mont Alto *B*
New Kensington *B*
Schuylkill - Capital College *B*
Shenango *B*
University Park *B, M, D*
Worthington Scranton *B*
York *B*

South Carolina
Clemson University *B, M, D*

South Dakota
South Dakota State University *B*

Tennessee
University of Tennessee
Knoxville *B, M, D*

Texas
Laredo Community College *A*
Texas A&M University *B*

Utah
Utah State University *B, M, D*

Virginia
Virginia Polytechnic Institute and
State University *B, M, D*

Washington
Washington State University *B*

Wisconsin

University of Wisconsin
Madison *B, M, D*

Agricultural business

Alabama

Central Alabama Community
College *A*
Enterprise-Ozark Community
College *A*
Faulkner State Community College *A*
Jefferson State Community
College *C, A*
Northeast Alabama Community
College *A*
Northwest-Shoals Community
College *C*

Arizona

Arizona Western College *A*
Central Arizona College *C, A*
Yavapai College *C, A*

Arkansas

Arkansas Northeastern College *C*
Arkansas State University
Beebe *A*
North Arkansas College *C, A*
Southern Arkansas University *B*

California

Butte College *C, A*
California Polytechnic State
University: San Luis Obispo *B*
California State Polytechnic
University: Pomona *B*
California State University
Chico *B*
Fresno *B*
College of the Desert *A*
College of the Redwoods *C*
Cosumnes River College *A*
Imperial Valley College *C, A*
Los Angeles Pierce College *C, A*
Merced College *A*
MiraCosta College *C, A*
Modesto Junior College *A*
Mount San Antonio College *A*
Reedley College *C, A*
San Joaquin Delta College *A*
Santa Rosa Junior College *C*
Shasta College *A*
University of California
Davis *B*
West Hills Community College *A*
Yuba Community College
District *C, A*

Colorado

Adams State College *B*
Fort Lewis College *B*
Northeastern Junior College *C*

Delaware

Delaware State University *B*
University of Delaware *B*

Florida

Florida Southern College *B*
Hillsborough Community
College *C, A*

Georgia

Abraham Baldwin Agricultural
College *A*
Gainesville State College *A*
South Georgia College *A*

Idaho

College of Southern Idaho *C, A*
University of Idaho *B*

Illinois

Black Hawk College *A*
Black Hawk College
East Campus *C, A*
Carl Sandburg College *A*
Highland Community College *A*
Illinois Central College *A*
Illinois Eastern Community Colleges
Wabash Valley College *C, A*
John A. Logan College *A*
John Wood Community College *C, A*
Kishwaukee College *C, A*
Lake Land College *C*
Lewis and Clark Community
College *C*
Parkland College *C, A*
Rend Lake College *A*
Richland Community College *A*
Spoon River College *A*
University of Illinois
Urbana-Champaign *B, M, D*

Indiana

Purdue University *M*
Vincennes University *A*

Iowa

Dordt College *B*
Ellsworth Community College *C, A*
Iowa Western Community College *A*
Marshalltown Community College *A*
North Iowa Area Community
College *A*
Northeast Iowa Community
College *A*
Northwestern College *B*
Southeastern Community College
North Campus *A*
Southwestern Community College *A*

Kansas

Central Christian College of Kansas *A*
Coffeyville Community College *A*
Cowley County Community
College *C, A*
Dodge City Community College *A*
Fort Hays State University *B*
Fort Scott Community College *A*
Garden City Community College *A*
Kansas State University *B, M*
Pratt Community College *C, A*
Seward County Community College *A*

Kentucky

Henderson Community College *C*
Owensboro Community College *A*

Louisiana

Louisiana State University and
Agricultural and Mechanical
College *B*
Louisiana Tech University *B*
Nicholls State University *B*
University of Louisiana at Monroe *B*

Maine

Northern Maine Community
College *A*
University of Maine *B*

Maryland

Community College of Baltimore
County *A*
Garrett College *C, A*
University of Maryland
Eastern Shore *B*

Michigan

Andrews University *A, B*
Delta College *A*
Michigan State University *C, B*

Minnesota

Northland Community & Technical
College *A*
Ridgewater College *C, A*
University of Minnesota
Crookston *B*
Twin Cities *B*

Mississippi

Alcorn State University *B*
Itawamba Community College *A*
Mississippi Delta Community
College *A*
Mississippi State University *M*

Missouri

Central Missouri State University *B*
College of the Ozarks *B*
Lincoln University *B*
Lindenwood University *B*
Missouri State University *B*
Missouri State University: West
Plains *A*
Northwest Missouri State
University *B*
Southeast Missouri State University *B*
State Fair Community College *A*
Three Rivers Community College *A*
University of Missouri
Columbia *B*

Montana

Dawson Community College *C, A*
Miles Community College *A*
Montana State University
Bozeman *B*
Rocky Mountain College *B*

Nebraska

Central Community College *C, A*
Nebraska College of Technical
Agriculture *A*
Northeast Community College *A*
University of Nebraska
Kearney *B*
Lincoln *B*

Nevada

Great Basin College *B*

New Hampshire

University of New Hampshire *B*

New Jersey

County College of Morris *A*

New Mexico

San Juan College *A*

New York

Cornell University *B, M, D*
State University of New York
College of Agriculture and
Technology at Cobleskill *A, B*
College of Agriculture and
Technology at Morrisville *A*
College of Technology at Alfred *A*

North Carolina

James Sprunt Community College *A*
North Carolina Agricultural and
Technical State University *B*
North Carolina State University *A*
Surry Community College *C, A*

North Dakota

Dickinson State University *A, B*
Lake Region State College *C, A*
North Dakota State College of
Science *A*

Ohio

Ohio State University
Agricultural Technical Institute *A*
Columbus Campus *A, B*
Owens Community College
Toledo *A*
University of Northwestern Ohio *C, A*
Wilmington College *B*

Oklahoma

Eastern Oklahoma State College *A*
Northwestern Oklahoma State
University *B*
Oklahoma Panhandle State
University *B*
Oklahoma State University *B*

Oregon

Blue Mountain Community College *A*
Chemeketa Community College *C*
Eastern Oregon University *B*
Linn-Benton Community College *A*
Oregon State University *B*
Treasure Valley Community College *A*

Pennsylvania

Penn State
Abington *A*
Altoona *A*
Beaver *A*
Berks *A*
Delaware County *A*
Dubois *A*
Erie, The Behrend College *A*
Fayette *A*
Hazleton *A*
Lehigh Valley *A*
McKeesport *A*
Mont Alto *A*
New Kensington *A*
Schuylkill - Capital College *A*
Shenango *A*
University Park *C, A*
Wilkes-Barre *A, B*
Worthington Scranton *A*
York *A*

Puerto Rico

University of Puerto Rico
Mayaguez *B*

South Dakota

Oglala Lakota College *A*
Western Dakota Technical Institute *A*

Tennessee

Columbia State Community College *A*
Hiwassee College *A*
Jackson State Community College *A*
University of Tennessee
Martin *M*

Texas

Cisco Junior College *A*
Clarendon College *A*
Del Mar College *A*
Frank Phillips College *C*
Hardin-Simmons University *B*
Hill College *A*
Howard College *A*
Lubbock Christian University *B*
Navarro College *A*
South Plains College *A*
Southwest Texas Junior College *A*
Tarleton State University *B*
Texas A&M University *B, M*
Texas A&M University
Commerce *M*
Kingsville *B, M*
Texas State Technical College
Harlingen *C*
Texas Tech University *B*

Trinity Valley Community College *A*
Weatherford College *C, A*
West Texas A&M University *B, M*

Utah

Snow College *A*
Southern Utah University *B*
Utah State University *B*

Vermont

Sterling College *B*
Vermont Technical College *A*

Virginia

Ferrum College *B*
Lord Fairfax Community College *A*

Washington

Columbia Basin College *A*
Skagit Valley College *A*
Spokane Community College *A*
Walla Walla Community College *C, A*
Washington State University *B, M*
Wenatchee Valley College *C*
Yakima Valley Community
    College *C, A*

West Virginia

West Virginia University *B*

Wisconsin

Fox Valley Technical College *A*
Mid-State Technical College *C*
Moraine Park Technical College *C*
Northcentral Technical College *C*
Northeast Wisconsin Technical
    College *A*
Southwest Wisconsin Technical
    College *A*
University of Wisconsin
    Madison *B*
    River Falls *B*

Wyoming

Casper College *A*
Central Wyoming College *A*
Laramie County Community
    College *A*
Northwest College *A*
Sheridan College *C, A*

Agricultural business technology

Florida

Indian River Community College *A*

Kentucky

Henderson Community College *A*

New York

State University of New York
    College of Agriculture and
        Technology at Morrisville *A*

Texas

Texas State Technical College
    Harlingen *A*

Virginia

Tidewater Community College *A*

Washington

Edmonds Community College *C, A*

Wisconsin

Western Wisconsin Technical
    College *A*

Wyoming

Laramie County Community
    College *A*

Agricultural communications

Georgia

University of Georgia *B*

Illinois

University of Illinois
    Urbana-Champaign *B*

Kansas

Kansas State University *B*

Kentucky

University of Kentucky *B*

Michigan

Michigan State University *B*

Missouri

University of Missouri
    Columbia *B*

Nebraska

University of Nebraska
    Lincoln *B*

Ohio

Ohio State University
    Agricultural Technical Institute *A*
    Columbus Campus *B*

Oklahoma

Oklahoma State University *B*

Texas

Texas A&M University
    Commerce *B*
Texas Tech University *B*

Vermont

Sterling College *B*

Washington

Washington State University *B*

Wisconsin

University of Wisconsin
    Madison *B, M*

Wyoming

University of Wyoming *B*

Agricultural economics

Alabama

Alabama Agricultural and Mechanical
    University *B*
Auburn University *B, M*
Tuskegee University *M*

Arizona

University of Arizona *B, M*

Arkansas

University of Arkansas *M*

California

San Joaquin Delta College *A*
University of California
    Berkeley *D*
    Davis *B, M, D*

Colorado

Colorado State University *B, M, D*

Connecticut

University of Connecticut *B, M, D*

Delaware

University of Delaware *B, M*

Florida

University of Florida *B, M, D*

Georgia

Fort Valley State University *B*
University of Georgia *B, M, D*

Idaho

University of Idaho *B, M*

Illinois

Southern Illinois University
    Carbondale *B, M*
University of Illinois
    Urbana-Champaign *B, M, D*

Indiana

Purdue University *B, M, D*

Iowa

Iowa State University *M, D*

Kansas

Garden City Community College *A*
Kansas State University *B, M, D*
Seward County Community College *A*

Kentucky

University of Kentucky *B, M, D*

Louisiana

Louisiana State University and
    Agricultural and Mechanical
        College *M, D*
Southern University and Agricultural
    and Mechanical College *B*

Maine

University of Maine *B, M*

Maryland

University of Maryland
    College Park *B, M, D*

Massachusetts

Bristol Community College *C*

Michigan

Michigan State University *B, M, D*

Minnesota

Northland Community & Technical
    College *A*
Ridgewater College *A*
University of Minnesota
    Twin Cities *B, M, D*

Mississippi

Alcorn State University *B*
Mississippi Delta Community
    College *A*
Mississippi State University *B, M, D*

Missouri

Central Missouri State University *B*
Truman State University *B*
University of Missouri
    Columbia *B, M, D*

Nebraska

University of Nebraska
    Lincoln *B, M, D*

Nevada

University of Nevada
    Reno *B, M*

New Jersey

Rutgers, The State University of New
    Jersey
    New Brunswick/Piscataway
        Campus *M*

New Mexico

New Mexico State University *M*

New York

Cornell University *B, M, D*

North Carolina

North Carolina Agricultural and
    Technical State University *B, M*
North Carolina State University *M*

North Dakota

North Dakota State University *B, M*

Ohio

Ohio State University
    Columbus Campus *B, M, D*

Oklahoma

Oklahoma State University *B, M, D*

Oregon

Eastern Oregon University *B*
Oregon State University *B, M, D*
Treasure Valley Community College *A*

Pennsylvania

Penn State
    University Park *B, M*

Puerto Rico

University of Puerto Rico
    Mayaguez *B, M*

South Carolina

Clemson University *B, M*

South Dakota

South Dakota State University *B*

Tennessee

Hiwassee College *A*
University of Tennessee
    Knoxville *M, D*

Texas

Clarendon College *A*
Prairie View A&M University *M*
Tarleton State University *B*
Texas A&M University *B, M, D*
Texas A&M University
    Commerce *B, M*
Texas Tech University *B, M, D*

Utah

Utah State University *B, M*

Vermont

University of Vermont *B, M*

Virginia

Virginia Polytechnic Institute and
    State University *B, M*

Washington

Washington State University *B, M, D*

West Virginia

West Virginia University *B, M, D*

Wisconsin

University of Wisconsin
  Madison *B, M, D*
  Platteville *B*

Wyoming

Eastern Wyoming College *A*
University of Wyoming *M*

Agricultural education services

Georgia

University of Georgia *M*

Illinois

University of Illinois
  Urbana-Champaign *B, M, T*

Iowa

Iowa State University *B*

Kentucky

University of Kentucky *B*

New York

Cornell University *B, M, D*

North Carolina

North Carolina State
  University *B, M, D*

Pennsylvania

Penn State
  Abington *B*
  Beaver *B*
  Berks *B*
  Delaware County *B*
  Dubois *B*
  Erie, The Behrend College *B*
  Fayette *B*
  Hazleton *B*
  Lehigh Valley *B*
  McKeesport *B*
  Mont Alto *B*
  New Kensington *B*
  Schuylkill - Capital College *B*
  Shenango *B*
  University Park *C, B, M, D*
  Worthington Scranton *B*
  York *B*

Puerto Rico

University of Puerto Rico
  Mayaguez *B, M*

Washington

Washington State University *B*

Agricultural equipment technology

Georgia

Southwest Georgia Technical
  College *A*

Kansas

North Central Kansas Technical
  College *A*

Michigan

Michigan State University *M, D*

New York

State University of New York
  College of Agriculture and
    Technology at Cobleskill *B*
  College of Agriculture and
    Technology at Morrisville *A*

Ohio

Ohio State University
  Agricultural Technical Institute *A*

Pennsylvania

Penn State
  Abington *B*
  Altoona *B*
  Beaver *B*
  Berks *B*
  Delaware County *B*
  Dubois *B*
  Erie, The Behrend College *B*
  Fayette *B*
  Hazleton *B*
  Lehigh Valley *B*
  McKeesport *B*
  Mont Alto *B*
  New Kensington *B*
  Schuylkill - Capital College *B*
  Shenango *B*
  University Park *B*
  Wilkes-Barre *B*
  Worthington Scranton *B*
  York *B*

Utah

Utah State University *B, M*

Washington

Walla Walla Community College *C, A*

Wisconsin

University of Wisconsin
  River Falls *B*
Wisconsin Indianhead Technical
  College *C*

Agricultural/food products processing

Indiana

Vincennes University *A*

Kansas

Kansas State University *M, D*

New York

State University of New York
  College of Agriculture and
    Technology at Cobleskill *A*

North Dakota

North Dakota State University *M, D*

Oklahoma

Eastern Oklahoma State College *A*

Pennsylvania

Penn State
  Wilkes-Barre *B*

Vermont

Sterling College *A, B*

Washington

Wenatchee Valley College *A*

Agricultural mechanization

California

California Polytechnic State
  University: San Luis Obispo *B*
Yuba Community College District *A*

Illinois

Black Hawk College *C, A*
Kaskaskia College *C*
Parkland College *C, A*

Rend Lake College *C, A*
University of Illinois
  Urbana-Champaign *B, M, D*

Indiana

Purdue University *B*

Iowa

Iowa State University *B*

Minnesota

Ridgewater College *C*

Nebraska

Northeast Community College *A*
University of Nebraska
  Lincoln *B, M*

New York

State University of New York
  College of Agriculture and
    Technology at Morrisville *A*

North Carolina

Beaufort County Community
  College *C, A*
North Carolina State University *B*

North Dakota

North Dakota State University *B*

Ohio

Owens Community College
  Toledo *A*

South Dakota

South Dakota State University *B*

Texas

Sam Houston State University *B, M*
Stephen F. Austin State University *B*
Tarleton State University *B*

Washington

Walla Walla Community College *A*
Washington State University *B*

Agricultural power machinery operation

Georgia

Southwest Georgia Technical
  College *A*

Illinois

Black Hawk College
  East Campus *C*

Iowa

Hawkeye Community College *A*
Iowa Lakes Community College *A*

Kansas

Hutchinson Community College *C, A*

Minnesota

University of Minnesota
  Crookston *B*

Montana

Dawson Community College *C, A*

New York

State University of New York
  College of Agriculture and
    Technology at Cobleskill *A*
  College of Agriculture and
    Technology at Morrisville *A*

North Dakota

North Dakota State College of
  Science *A*

Ohio

Ohio State University
  Agricultural Technical Institute *A*

Agricultural production

Arizona

Arizona Western College *A*

Arkansas

University of Arkansas *M*

Illinois

Black Hawk College *A*
Illinois Eastern Community Colleges
  Wabash Valley College *A*
John Wood Community College *C*
Lincoln Land Community College *A*
Rend Lake College *C, A*

Iowa

Indian Hills Community College *A*
Iowa Lakes Community College *A*
North Iowa Area Community
  College *A*

Kansas

Barton County Community
  College *C, A*
Cloud County Community College *A*

Kentucky

Owensboro Community College *C*
Western Kentucky University *A*

Minnesota

Ridgewater College *C, A*

Missouri

Crowder College *A*
Mineral Area College *A*

Nebraska

Northeast Community College *A*

Ohio

Wilmington College *B*

Oregon

Blue Mountain Community College *A*

Puerto Rico

University of Puerto Rico
  Utuado *A*

Texas

Stephen F. Austin State University *B*
Texas A&M University *B*

Virginia

Virginia Polytechnic Institute and
  State University *A*

Washington

Big Bend Community College *A*
Walla Walla Community College *C, A*
Wenatchee Valley College *C, A*

Agricultural supplies

Arizona

Glendale Community College *A*

California

Modesto Junior College *A*

Colorado

Aims Community College *C, A*

Illinois

Carl Sandburg College *C*
John Wood Community College *C*
Joliet Junior College *C, A*
Kishwaukee College *A*

Iowa

Des Moines Area Community
    College *C, A*
Hawkeye Community College *A*
Iowa Lakes Community College *A*
Kirkwood Community College *C, A*
Muscatine Community College *A*
North Iowa Area Community
    College *A*
Southeastern Community College
    North Campus *A*
Western Iowa Tech Community
    College *C*

Kansas

Coffeyville Community College *A*

Michigan

St. Clair County Community
    College *C, A*

North Dakota

North Dakota State College of
    Science *A*

Texas

Sul Ross State University *C, A*
Tarleton State University *B*

Washington

Yakima Valley Community College *A*

Wisconsin

Fox Valley Technical College *A*
Madison Area Technical College *C*

Agricultural teacher education

Arizona

Prescott College *T*
University of Arizona *B, M*

Arkansas

Arkansas State University *B, M, T*
Southern Arkansas University *B, T*
University of Arkansas *B, M*
University of Arkansas
    Pine Bluff *B, T*

California

California Polytechnic State
    University: San Luis Obispo *B, T*
California State Polytechnic
    University: Pomona *T*
California State University
    Chico *B, T*
    Fresno *M*
University of California
    Davis *T*

Colorado

Colorado State University *B, T*
Northeastern Junior College *A*

Connecticut

University of Connecticut *B, T*

Delaware

University of Delaware *B, T*

Florida

University of Florida *A, B, M*

Georgia

Fort Valley State University *B, T*
University of Georgia *B*

Idaho

University of Idaho *B, M, T*

Illinois

Elmhurst College *B*
University of Illinois
    Urbana-Champaign *B, M, T*

Indiana

Purdue University *B*

Iowa

Ellsworth Community College *A*
Iowa State University *B, M, D, T*

Kansas

Colby Community College *A*
Kansas State University *B*

Kentucky

Western Kentucky University *M, T*

Louisiana

Southern University and Agricultural
    and Mechanical College *B*
University of Louisiana at Lafayette *B*

Maryland

University of Maryland
    Eastern Shore *B, M*

Minnesota

University of Minnesota
    Crookston *B*
    Twin Cities *B, M, T*

Mississippi

Mississippi State University *B, M, T*

Missouri

Central Missouri State University *B, T*
Missouri State University *B*
Northwest Missouri State
    University *B, M, T*
University of Missouri
    Columbia *B, M, D*

Montana

Montana State University
    Bozeman *B, M*

Nebraska

University of Nebraska
    Lincoln *B, M*

Nevada

Great Basin College *B*
University of Nevada
    Reno *B*

New Mexico

Eastern New Mexico University *B*
New Mexico State University *B, M*

New York

Cornell University *M, T*
State University of New York
    Oswego *B*

North Carolina

North Carolina Agricultural and
    Technical State University *B, M, T*

North Carolina State
    University *B, M, T*

North Dakota

North Dakota State University *B, M, T*

Ohio

Ohio State University
    Agricultural Technical Institute *A*
    Columbus Campus *B, M, D*
Wilmington College *B*

Oklahoma

East Central University *B*
Eastern Oklahoma State College *A*
Oklahoma Panhandle State
    University *B*
Oklahoma State University *B, M, D*

Oregon

Oregon State University *M*

Pennsylvania

Penn State
    University Park *B, M, D*

Puerto Rico

University of Puerto Rico
    Mayaguez *B, M*

South Carolina

Clemson University *B, M*

South Dakota

South Dakota State University *B, T*

Tennessee

Tennessee Technological
    University *B, T*
University of Tennessee
    Knoxville *B, M, T*

Texas

Laredo Community College *A*
Lubbock Christian University *B*
Prairie View A&M University *M*
Sam Houston State University *M, T*
Stephen F. Austin State University *T*
Tarleton State University *M, T*
Texas A&M University *M, D*
Texas A&M University
    Commerce *M, T*
    Kingsville *B, M*
Texas State University: San
    Marcos *M, T*
Texas Tech University *M, D*
West Texas A&M University *T*

Utah

Utah State University *B*

Vermont

Sterling College *B*

Washington

Washington State University *B, T*

West Virginia

West Virginia University *B, M, T*

Wisconsin

University of Wisconsin
    Madison *B*
    Platteville *B, T*
    River Falls *B, M, T*

Wyoming

Eastern Wyoming College *A*
Northwest College *A*
University of Wyoming *B*

Agriculture, general

Alabama

Faulkner State Community College *A*
Gadsden State Community College *A*

Arizona

Arizona Western College *C, A*

Arkansas

Arkansas State University *B, M*
East Arkansas Community College *A*
North Arkansas College *A*
Rich Mountain Community College *A*
University of Arkansas
    Community College at Hope *A*

California

California State Polytechnic
    University: Pomona *M*
California State University
    Fresno *B*
    Stanislaus *B*
Fresno City College *C, A*
Napa Valley College *C, A*
Palo Verde College *A*
Shasta College *A*
Sierra College *C, A*
West Hills Community College *A*

Colorado

Aims Community College *C, A*
Colorado School of Trades *C*
Fort Lewis College *A*
Northeastern Junior College *C*

Delaware

University of Delaware *A*

Florida

Florida Southern College *B*
Pensacola Junior College *A*
South Florida Community College *A*

Georgia

Andrew College *A*
Dalton State College *A*
Darton College *A*
East Georgia College *A*
Gainesville State College *A*
Middle Georgia College *A*
South Georgia College *C, A*
University of Georgia *B*

Hawaii

University of Hawaii
    Hawaii Community College *C, A*
    Maui Community College *A*

Illinois

Highland Community College *C, A*
Illinois Valley Community College *A*
John Wood Community College *A*
Joliet Junior College *C, A*
Kaskaskia College *C, A*
Lake Land College *A*
Parkland College *A*
Southern Illinois University
    Carbondale *B*
Western Illinois University *A*

Indiana

Purdue University *A, B*
Vincennes University *A*

Iowa

Iowa Western Community
    College *C, A*
Maharishi University of
    Management *B*

North Iowa Area Community
    College *A*
Southeastern Community College
    North Campus *A*

Kansas

Barton County Community College *A*
Coffeyville Community College *A*
Cowley County Community
    College *C, A*
Garden City Community College *A*
Hutchinson Community College *A*
Pratt Community College *C, A*
Seward County Community College *A*

Kentucky

Berea College *B*
Hopkinsville Community College *C, A*
Morehead State University *B*
Murray State University *A, B, M, T*
Western Kentucky University *B, M, T*

Louisiana

Louisiana State University and
    Agricultural and Mechanical
    College *M*
University of Louisiana at Lafayette *B*

Maryland

University of Maryland
    College Park *B*
    Eastern Shore *B*

Massachusetts

North Shore Community College *C*

Minnesota

Minnesota West Community and
    Technical College: Worthington
    Campus *A*
Northland Community & Technical
    College *C*
Ridgewater College *C, A*
South Central College *A*
University of Minnesota
    Crookston *A*

Mississippi

Alcorn State University *B, M*
Hinds Community College *A*
Mississippi Gulf Coast Community
    College
    Jefferson Davis Campus *C, A*

Missouri

Central Missouri State University *B, M*
Lincoln University *B*
University of Missouri
    Columbia *B*

Nebraska

Nebraska College of Technical
    Agriculture *A*
Northeast Community College *A*
University of Nebraska
    Lincoln *B, M*

Nevada

Great Basin College *A*

New Jersey

Cumberland County College *C, A*

New Mexico

Mesalands Community College *C, A*
New Mexico State University *B, M*
Western New Mexico University *A*

New York

State University of New York
    College of Agriculture and
        Technology at Cobleskill *A*
    College of Agriculture and
        Technology at Morrisville *A*

North Carolina

North Carolina State University *A*

North Dakota

Cankdeska Cikana Community
    College *A*
North Dakota State University *B*
Turtle Mountain Community
    College *C*

Ohio

Ohio State University
    Agricultural Technical Institute *C, A*
Southern State Community College *A*

Oklahoma

Cameron University *B*
Eastern Oklahoma State College *A*
Northeastern Oklahoma Agricultural
    and Mechanical College *A*
Northwestern Oklahoma State
    University *B*
Oklahoma Panhandle State
    University *A*
Oklahoma State University *M*
Redlands Community College *A*

Oregon

Linn-Benton Community College *A*
Oregon State University *B, M*
Treasure Valley Community College *C*

Puerto Rico

University of Puerto Rico
    Utuado *A*

South Dakota

Lake Area Technical Institute *A*
South Dakota State University *A, B*
Western Dakota Technical Institute *A*

Tennessee

Roane State Community College *A*
University of Tennessee
    Martin *B*

Texas

Brazosport College *A*
Clarendon College *A*
Howard College *A*
Kilgore College *A*
Laredo Community College *A*
Lubbock Christian University *A, B*
Northeast Texas Community
    College *A*
Prairie View A&M University *B*
Sam Houston State University *B, M*
Southwest Texas Junior College *A*
Stephen F. Austin State University *B, M*
Tarleton State University *B, M*
Texarkana College *A*
Texas State University: San Marcos *B*
Texas Tech University *B, M*
Tyler Junior College *C, A*
West Texas A&M University *B, M, D*
Wharton County Junior College *A*

Vermont

Sterling College *A, B*
University of Vermont *B, M*

Virginia

Virginia Polytechnic Institute and
    State University *B*

Virginia State University *B*

Washington

Washington State University *B, M*
Yakima Valley Community College *A*

West Virginia

Potomac State College of West Virginia
    University *A*
West Virginia University *M, D*

Wisconsin

Chippewa Valley Technical College *A*
Madison Area Technical College *A*
University of Wisconsin
    Platteville *M*
    River Falls *B*

Wyoming

Casper College *A*
Eastern Wyoming College *A*
Laramie County Community
    College *A*
Northwest College *A*
Sheridan College *A*

Agronomy and crop science

Arizona

Prescott College *B, M*

Arkansas

University of Arkansas *B, M, D*

California

Butte College *C, A*
California State Polytechnic
    University: Pomona *B*
California State University
    Chico *B*
    Fresno *B, M*
Merced College *A*
Modesto Junior College *A*
San Joaquin Delta College *A*
University of California
    Davis *B, M*
Ventura College *C, A*

Colorado

Colorado State University *B, M, D*

Connecticut

University of Connecticut *B*

Delaware

University of Delaware *B*

Florida

Florida Agricultural and Mechanical
    University *B*
University of Florida *M, D*

Georgia

University of Georgia *M, D*

Hawaii

University of Hawaii
    Hilo *B*

Idaho

Brigham Young University-Idaho *B*
University of Idaho *B*

Illinois

University of Illinois
    Urbana-Champaign *B, M, D*

Indiana

Purdue University *B, M, D*

Iowa

Iowa State University *B, M*

Kansas

Colby Community College *A*
Garden City Community College *A*
Kansas State University *B, M, D*
McPherson College *B*

Kentucky

University of Kentucky *B, M, D*

Louisiana

Louisiana State University and
    Agricultural and Mechanical
    College *M, D*

Minnesota

Ridgewater College *C, A*
Southwest Minnesota State
    University *B*
University of Minnesota
    Crookston *B*
    Twin Cities *M, D*

Mississippi

Mississippi State University *B, M, D*

Missouri

College of the Ozarks *B*
Missouri State University *B*
Northwest Missouri State
    University *B*
Truman State University *B*
University of Missouri
    Columbia *M, D*

Nebraska

Northeast Community College *A*
University of Nebraska
    Lincoln *B, M, D*

New Hampshire

University of New Hampshire *B*

New Mexico

New Mexico State University *B, M, D*
Southwestern Indian Polytechnic
    Institute *A*

New York

Cornell University *B, M, D*
State University of New York
    College of Agriculture and
        Technology at Cobleskill *A*
    College of Technology at Alfred *A*

North Carolina

North Carolina State
    University *B, M, D*

North Dakota

North Dakota State University *M, D*

Ohio

Ohio State University
    Agricultural Technical Institute *A*
    Columbus Campus *B*
Wilmington College *B*

Oklahoma

Cameron University *B*
Eastern Oklahoma State College *A*
Oklahoma Panhandle State
    University *B*
Oklahoma State University *D*

Oregon

Eastern Oregon University *B*
Oregon State University *B, M, D*

Treasure Valley Community College *A*

Pennsylvania

Delaware Valley College *B*
Penn State
  Abington *B*
  Altoona *B*
  Beaver *B*
  Berks *B*
  Delaware County *B*
  Dubois *B*
  Erie, The Behrend College *B*
  Fayette *B*
  Hazleton *B*
  Lehigh Valley *B*
  McKeesport *B*
  Mont Alto *B*
  New Kensington *B*
  Schuylkill - Capital College *B*
  Shenango *B*
  University Park *C, B, M, D*
  Wilkes-Barre *B*
  Worthington Scranton *B*
  York *B*

Puerto Rico

University of Puerto Rico
  Mayaguez *B, M*

South Carolina

Clemson University *M, D*

South Dakota

South Dakota State University *B, M, D*

Tennessee

Tennessee Technological University *B*

Texas

Clarendon College *A*
Hardin-Simmons University *B*
Stephen F. Austin State University *B*
Tarleton State University *B*
Texas A&M University *B, M, D*
Texas A&M University
  Commerce *M*
  Kingsville *M*
Texas Tech University *B, D*

Utah

Utah State University *B*

Vermont

Sterling College *B*

Virginia

Virginia Polytechnic Institute and
  State University *B, M, D*

Washington

Washington State University *B, M, D*

West Virginia

Potomac State College of West Virginia
  University *A*
West Virginia University *B, M*

Wisconsin

Chippewa Valley Technical College *A*
University of Wisconsin
  Madison *B, M, D*
  Platteville *B*
  River Falls *B*

Wyoming

University of Wyoming *M, D*

Air traffic control

Alabama

Community College of the Air
  Force *A*

Alaska

University of Alaska
  Anchorage *A, B*

California

Mount San Antonio College *A*

Colorado

Metropolitan State College of
  Denver *B*

Connecticut

Gateway Community College *A*

Florida

Embry-Riddle Aeronautical
  University *B*
Florida Community College at
  Jacksonville *A*

Minnesota

Anoka Technical College *C, A*
Inver Hills Community College *A*
Minneapolis Community and
  Technical College *C*
St. Cloud State University *B*

Missouri

St. Louis Community College
  St. Louis Community College at
    Meramec *A*

New Hampshire

Daniel Webster College *B*

New Jersey

Thomas Edison State College *A, B*

North Dakota

University of North Dakota *B*

Pennsylvania

Community College of Beaver
  County *C, A*
Geneva College *A*

Puerto Rico

Inter American University of Puerto
  Rico
  Bayamon Campus *B*

Texas

Mountain View College *C, A*

Aircraft maintenance/ technology

Alabama

Community College of the Air
  Force *A*
Enterprise-Ozark Community
  College *C, A*

Alaska

University of Alaska
  Anchorage *C, A, B*
  Fairbanks *C, A*

Arizona

Chandler-Gilbert Community College
  Pecos *A*
  Williams Campus *C*
Cochise College *A*

Pima Community College *C, A*

Arkansas

Northwest Arkansas Community
  College *A*
Pulaski Technical College *A*
Southern Arkansas University Tech *C*

California

Antelope Valley College *C, A*
Chaffey College *A*
City College of San Francisco *C, A*
College of Alameda *C, A*
College of San Mateo *C, A*
Cypress College *C, A*
Foothill College *C, A*
Gavilan Community College *C, A*
Glendale Community College *C, A*
Mount San Antonio College *A*
Orange Coast College *C, A*
Reedley College *C*
Sacramento City College *C, A*
San Bernardino Valley College *C*
San Diego Miramar College *C, A*
San Joaquin Valley College Inc. *A*
Shasta College *C, A*
Solano Community College *C, A*
West Los Angeles College *C, A*

Colorado

Colorado Northwestern Community
  College *C, A*

Connecticut

Housatonic Community College *A*
Quinebaug Valley Community
  College *A*

Florida

Florida Community College at
  Jacksonville *C*

Georgia

Central Georgia Technical College *C*
Clayton State University *C, A*
Georgia Southwestern State
  University *A*
Middle Georgia College *A*

Hawaii

University of Hawaii
  Honolulu Community College *C, A*

Illinois

Lewis University *C, A, B*
Lincoln Land Community College *C, A*
Moody Bible Institute *B*
Rock Valley College *A*
Southwestern Illinois College *C, A*

Indiana

Ivy Tech State College
  Ivy Tech Community College:
    Wabash Valley *C, A*
Vincennes University *A*

Iowa

Iowa Western Community College *A*

Kansas

Central Christian College of Kansas *A*
Cowley County Community
  College *C, A*
Kansas State University *A, B*

Maryland

Chesapeake College *C, A*

Massachusetts

Middlesex Community College *A*

Michigan

Andrews University *B*
Lansing Community College *A*
Northern Michigan University *A*
Wayne County Community College *A*

Minnesota

Minneapolis Community and
  Technical College *C, A*
Minnesota State College - Southeast
  Technical *C, A*
Northland Community & Technical
  College *C, A*

Mississippi

Hinds Community College *C*

Montana

Helena College of Technology of the
  University of Montana *A*

Nebraska

Western Nebraska Community
  College *C, A*

New Hampshire

New Hampshire Community
  Technical College
  Nashua *A*

New Jersey

Cumberland County College *A*
Mercer County Community College *A*
Thomas Edison State College *A, B*

New York

Mohawk Valley Community College *A*
State University of New York
  Farmingdale *C, A*
Vaughn College of Aeronautics and
  Technology *A, B*

North Carolina

Wayne Community College *A*

Ohio

Cincinnati State Technical and
  Community College *C, A*
Columbus State Community
  College *C, A*
Sinclair Community College *C*

Oklahoma

Southeastern Oklahoma State
  University *B*

Oregon

Lane Community College *C, A*
Portland Community College *C, A*

Pennsylvania

Pittsburgh Institute of Aeronautics *A*

South Carolina

Trident Technical College *A*

South Dakota

Lake Area Technical Institute *A*

Texas

Amarillo College *C, A*
Del Mar College *C, A*
Hallmark Institute of Aeronautics *A*
Houston Community College
  System *C*
LeTourneau University *B*
Midland College *C*
North Harris Montgomery
  Community College District *C, A*
St. Philip's College *C, A*

Tarrant County College *C, A*
Texas State Technical College
  Harlingen *C, A*
  Waco *C, A*
  West Texas *C, A*

Utah
Utah State University *A, B*

Virginia
Hampton University *A*
Northern Virginia Community
  College *A*

Washington
Big Bend Community College *C, A*
South Seattle Community
  College *C, A*
Spokane Community College *A*

Wisconsin
Blackhawk Technical College *C*
Fox Valley Technical College *C*
Gateway Technical College *C*
Milwaukee Area Technical College *C*

Aircraft powerplant technology

Arizona
Chandler-Gilbert Community College
  Williams Campus *C*

Arkansas
Southern Arkansas University
  Tech *C, A*

California
Antelope Valley College *C*
Long Beach City College *C, A*

Florida
Embry-Riddle Aeronautical
  University *A, B*
Embry-Riddle Aeronautical University:
  Extended Campus *B*

Georgia
Clayton State University *C, A*
Georgia Military College *A*
Georgia Southwestern State
  University *A*

Idaho
Idaho State University *C, A*

Illinois
Lincoln Land Community College *C*

Kansas
Kansas State University *C*

Kentucky
Somerset Community College *C, A*

Michigan
Northern Michigan University *C, A*
Wayne County Community College *A*

Minnesota
Minneapolis Community and
  Technical College *C, A*

Nebraska
Western Nebraska Community
  College *C, A*

New York
Vaughn College of Aeronautics and
  Technology *C, A, B*

Ohio
Sinclair Community College *C*

Oregon
Portland Community College *C, A*

Pennsylvania
Pennsylvania College of
  Technology *C, A*

South Dakota
Lake Area Technical Institute *A*

Texas
Del Mar College *C, A*
Hallmark Institute of Aeronautics *A*
LeTourneau University *B*
Midland College *C*
St. Philip's College *C, A*
Texas State Technical College
  West Texas *C*

Washington
Clover Park Technical College *C, A*
Everett Community College *A*
South Seattle Community
  College *C, A*

Wisconsin
Fox Valley Technical College *A*
Milwaukee Area Technical College *C*

Airline/commercial pilot

Alaska
University of Alaska
  Fairbanks *A*

Arizona
Cochise College *A*
Embry-Riddle Aeronautical University:
  Prescott Campus *B*

Arkansas
Henderson State University *B*

California
College of San Mateo *C, A*
Cypress College *C, A*

Florida
Embry-Riddle Aeronautical
  University *A, B, M*
Embry-Riddle Aeronautical University:
  Extended Campus *M*
Jacksonville University *B*

Hawaii
University of Hawaii
  Honolulu Community College *A*

Illinois
Lewis University *B*
Quincy University *B*
Southern Illinois University
  Carbondale *B*
University of Illinois
  Urbana-Champaign *C, B*
Waubonsee Community College *A*

Indiana
Indiana State University *B*
Vincennes University *A*

Iowa
Indian Hills Community College *A*

Kansas
Kansas State University *A, B*

Louisiana
University of Louisiana at Monroe *B*

Massachusetts
Bridgewater State College *B*
North Shore Community College *A*

Michigan
Baker College
  of Muskegon *A*
Cornerstone University *B*
Eastern Michigan University *B*
Northwestern Michigan College *A*
Western Michigan University *B*

Minnesota
Academy College *A*
Inver Hills Community College *A*
Lake Superior College *A*
St. Cloud State University *B*

Mississippi
Delta State University *B*

Missouri
St. Louis University *B*

Montana
Rocky Mountain College *B*

New Jersey
Ocean County College *A*
Thomas Edison State College *A, B*

New Mexico
Albuquerque Technical-Vocational
  Institute *C, A*
San Juan College *C, A*

New York
Jamestown Community College *A*
State University of New York
  Farmingdale *A*
Vaughn College of Aeronautics and
  Technology *A, B*

North Carolina
Guilford Technical Community
  College *A*
Lenoir Community College *C, A*

North Dakota
University of North Dakota *B*
Williston State College *A*

Oklahoma
Southeastern Oklahoma State
  University *B*

Oregon
Central Oregon Community
  College *A*
Portland Community College *C*

Pennsylvania
Community College of Allegheny
  County *A*
Lehigh Carbon Community College *A*
Luzerne County Community
  College *A*

Puerto Rico
Inter American University of Puerto
  Rico
  Bayamon Campus *B*

Texas
Baylor University *B*
LeTourneau University *B*
Midland College *A*

Mountain View College *C, A*
Tarleton State University *B*
Texas State Technical College
  West Texas *A*

Utah
Salt Lake Community College *A*
Utah Valley State College *B*

Virginia
Averett University *B*

Washington
Big Bend Community College *A*
Clover Park Technical College *A*
Northwest Aviation College *C, A*

Wisconsin
Fox Valley Technical College *A*
Gateway Technical College *A*

Wyoming
Casper College *A*

Algebra/number theory

New York
City University of New York
  Brooklyn College *B*

Wisconsin
Marquette University *D*

Alternative fuel vehicle technology

California
College of the Desert *C*
Long Beach City College *C, A*

Illinois
Morton College *C*

American government/ politics

Arizona
Northern Arizona University *B*

California
Chapman University *B*
Master's College *B*
University of California
  San Diego *B*

District of Columbia
Catholic University of America *M*

Florida
Florida State University *M*

Massachusetts
Bridgewater State College *B*
Harvard College *D*
Suffolk University *B, M*

Michigan
Western Michigan University *B*

New York
Cornell University *B, M, D*
United States Military Academy *B*
Wells College *B*

North Carolina
Meredith College *B*

Ohio
Ohio Wesleyan University *B*

University of Akron *B*

Pennsylvania

Gettysburg College *B*
La Salle University *B*

South Carolina

Wofford College *B*

Texas

Texas A&M University *D*

Utah

University of Utah *C*

Vermont

Bennington College *B*

Wisconsin

Marquette University *M*

American history (U.S.)

California

Chapman University *B*
Pitzer College *B*

Colorado

Fort Lewis College *B*

Iowa

Morningside College *B*
William Penn University *B*

Kansas

Central Christian College of Kansas *A*

Massachusetts

Brandeis University *M, D*
Harvard College *B, D*
Salem State College *B*
Simon's Rock College of Bard *B*
Suffolk University *B*

Michigan

Calvin College *B*

New York

Bard College *B*
Sarah Lawrence College *B*
Syracuse University *B*

Pennsylvania

Gettysburg College *B*
La Salle University *B*

Rhode Island

Salve Regina University *B*

Texas

Baylor University *M*

Vermont

Bennington College *B*

Wisconsin

Marquette University *D*

American literature

California

California State University
  Bakersfield *B, M*
  East Bay *B*
College of the Desert *A*
San Joaquin Delta College *A*
University of California
  Los Angeles *B*

San Diego *B, M, D*
Santa Cruz *B*
University of Southern California *B*
Whittier College *B*

Colorado

Fort Lewis College *B*

District of Columbia

George Washington University *M, D*

Florida

Miami Dade College *A*

Idaho

Boise State University *B*

Illinois

Illinois Valley Community College *A*
Richland Community College *A*

Indiana

Purdue University
  Calumet *B*

Kansas

Central Christian College of Kansas *A*

Maine

University of Maine
  Fort Kent *B*

Maryland

Johns Hopkins University *D*

Massachusetts

Brandeis University *B, M, D*
Hampshire College *B*
Simmons College *B*
Tufts University *B, M, D*

Michigan

Lansing Community College *A*

Minnesota

Concordia College: Moorhead *B*
St. Cloud State University *B*

Missouri

University of Missouri
  St. Louis *M*
Washington University in St.
  Louis *B, M, D*

Montana

Miles Community College *A*

New Jersey

Rowan University *B*

New York

Bard College *B*
City University of New York
  Baruch College *B*
Columbia University
  Columbia College *B*
Eugene Lang College The New School
  for Liberal Arts *B*
New York University *B, M, D*
St. Lawrence University *B*
Sarah Lawrence College *B*
State University of New York
  Purchase *B*
United States Military Academy *B*

Ohio

College of Wooster *B*
Miami University
  Oxford Campus *B*
Ohio Wesleyan University *B*

Pennsylvania

Gettysburg College *B*
Holy Family University *B, T*
La Salle University *B*
Penn State
  Harrisburg *B*
University of Pittsburgh
  Johnstown *B*
West Chester University of
  Pennsylvania *B, M, T*
Westminster College *B, T*

Rhode Island

Brown University *B, M, D*

Texas

Texas A&M University
  Commerce *B*
University of North Texas *D*

Vermont

Bennington College *B*
Castleton State College *B*
Marlboro College *B*
Middlebury College *B*

Washington

Everett Community College *A*

Wisconsin

Lawrence University *B*
Marquette University *M, D*

American Sign Language (ASL)

California

Antelope Valley College *A*
Ohlone College *A*
San Diego Mesa College *A*
Sierra College *A*

District of Columbia

Gallaudet University *B*

Idaho

Idaho State University *A*

Indiana

Goshen College *B*
Indiana University-Purdue University
  Indianapolis *B*
Vincennes University *A*

Massachusetts

Bristol Community College *A*

Michigan

Madonna University *A, B*

Missouri

William Woods University *B*

New Jersey

Union County College *A*

New York

Keuka College *B*
Rochester Institute of
  Technology *A, B*

North Carolina

Gardner-Webb University *B*

South Dakota

Augustana College *T*

Tennessee

Maryville College *B*

Virginia

Tidewater Community College *A*

American studies

Alabama

Faulkner University *B*
Gadsden State Community College *A*
Huntingdon College *B*
University of Alabama *B, M*

Arizona

Arizona State University West *B*
Northern Arizona University *B*

Arkansas

Harding University *B*
University of Arkansas *B*

California

California State University
  Chico *B*
  Fullerton *B, M*
  San Bernardino *B*
Claremont McKenna College *B*
Cosumnes River College *A*
El Camino College *A*
Foothill College *A*
Los Angeles Valley College *A*
Mills College *B*
Mount St. Mary's College *B*
Occidental College *B*
Pepperdine University *M*
Pitzer College *B*
Pomona College *B*
San Diego State University *B*
San Francisco State University *B*
Scripps College *B*
Southwestern College *A*
Stanford University *B*
University of California
  Berkeley *B*
  Davis *B*
  Santa Cruz *B*
University of Southern California *B, D*

Colorado

Fort Lewis College *B*

Connecticut

Connecticut College *B*
Fairfield University *B, M*
St. Joseph College *B*
Trinity College *B, M*
University of Connecticut *B*
Wesleyan University *B*
Western Connecticut State
  University *B*
Yale University *B, M, D*

Delaware

Wesley College *B*

District of Columbia

American University *B*
George Washington
  University *B, M, D*
Georgetown University *B*
Trinity University *B*

Florida

Eckerd College *B*
Florida State University *B, M*
Manatee Community College *A*
Miami Dade College *A*
Stetson University *B*
University of Miami *B*
University of South Florida *B, M*

Georgia

Oglethorpe University *B*

Wesleyan College *B*

Hawaii

University of Hawaii
  Manoa *B, M, D*

Idaho

Idaho State University *B*
University of Idaho *B*

Illinois

DePaul University *B*
Dominican University *B*
Elmhurst College *B*
Illinois Wesleyan University *B*
Knox College *B*
Lake Forest College *B*
Lewis University *B*
Millikin University *B*
Northwestern University *B*
Roosevelt University *B*

Indiana

Franklin College *B*
Indiana University
  Bloomington *D*
University of Notre Dame *B*
Valparaiso University *B*
Vincennes University *A*

Iowa

Coe College *B*
Grinnell College *B*
University of Iowa *B, M, D*
University of Northern Iowa *B*
Upper Iowa University *B*

Kansas

University of Kansas *B, M, D*

Kentucky

Georgetown College *B*
Lindsey Wilson College *B*

Louisiana

Tulane University *B*

Maine

Bates College *B*
Colby College *B*
University of New England *B*
University of Southern Maine *M*

Maryland

Goucher College *B*
Howard Community College *A*
Prince George's Community
  College *A*
University of Maryland
  Baltimore County *B*
  College Park *B, M, D*
Washington College *B*

Massachusetts

Amherst College *B*
Boston College *M*
Boston University *B, M, D*
Brandeis University *B*
Elms College *B*
Emmanuel College *B*
Hampshire College *B*
Harvard College *B*
Lesley University *B, M*
Mount Holyoke College *B*
Smith College *B*
Stonehill College *B*
Tufts University *B, M*
University of Massachusetts
  Boston *B, M*
  Lowell *B*
Wellesley College *B*
Wheaton College *B*

Williams College *B*

Michigan

Albion College *B*
Hillsdale College *B*
Michigan State University *B, M, D*
Siena Heights University *B*
University of Michigan *B, M, D, T*
University of Michigan
  Dearborn *B*
Wayne State University *B*

Minnesota

Carleton College *B*
Macalester College *B*
Minnesota State University
  Moorhead *B*
St. Cloud State University *B*
St. Olaf College *B*
University of Minnesota
  Twin Cities *B, M, D*

Mississippi

Mississippi Delta Community
  College *A*
University of Southern Mississippi *B*

Missouri

Columbia College *B*
Lindenwood University *B*
St. Louis University *B, M, D*
University of Missouri
  Kansas City *B*
Washington University in St.
  Louis *B, M*
Webster University *B*

Nebraska

Creighton University *B*
Midland Lutheran College *B*

New Hampshire

Franklin Pierce College *B*
Keene State College *B*
Southern New Hampshire
  University *B*

New Jersey

Bergen Community College *A*
College of St. Elizabeth *B*
Ramapo College of New Jersey *B*
Rider University *B*
Rowan University *B*
Rutgers, The State University of New
  Jersey
  New Brunswick/Piscataway
    Campus *B*
  Newark Regional Campus *B*
St. Peter's College *B*

New Mexico

New Mexico Highlands University *M*
University of New Mexico *B, M, D*

New York

Bard College *B*
Barnard College *B*
City University of New York
  Brooklyn College *B*
  College of Staten Island *B*
  Lehman College *B*
  Queens College *B, T*
College of New Rochelle *B*
College of Saint Rose *B*
Columbia University
  Columbia College *B*
  School of General Studies *B*
Cornell University *B, M, D*
Elmira College *B*
Eugene Lang College The New School
  for Liberal Arts *B*
Fordham University *B*

Hamilton College *B*
Hobart and William Smith Colleges *B*
Hofstra University *B*
Manhattanville College *B*
Marist College *B*
Nazareth College of Rochester *B*
New York University *M, D*
St. John Fisher College *B*
Sarah Lawrence College *B*
Siena College *B, T*
Skidmore College *B*
State University of New York
  Buffalo *B, M, D*
  College at Fredonia *B*
  College at Geneseo *B*
  College at Old Westbury *B*
  Oswego *B*
  Stony Brook *B*
Syracuse University *B*
Union College *B*
Vassar College *B*
Wells College *B*

North Carolina

High Point University *B*
Meredith College *B*
Montreat College *B*
Queens University of Charlotte *B*
Salem College *B*
University of North Carolina
  Chapel Hill *B*
  Pembroke *B*
Wingate University *B*

Ohio

Antioch College *B*
Ashland University *B*
Bowling Green State
  University *B, M, D*
Case Western Reserve University *B*
Cedarville University *B*
Kent State University *B*
Kenyon College *B*
Miami University
  Oxford Campus *B*
Mount Union College *B*
Mount Vernon Nazarene University *B*
Oberlin College *B*
University of Dayton *B*
University of Rio Grande *B*
University of Toledo *B*
Ursuline College *B*
Wittenberg University *B*
Youngstown State University *B, M*

Oklahoma

Northeastern State University *M*
Oklahoma City University *B*
Oklahoma State University *B*
Southern Nazarene University *B*

Oregon

Oregon State University *B*
Reed College *B*
Warner Pacific College *B*
Willamette University *B*

Pennsylvania

Albright College *B*
Bucks County Community College *A*
Cabrini College *B*
Dickinson College *B*
Franklin & Marshall College *B*
Gettysburg College *B*
Lafayette College *B*
Lebanon Valley College *B*
Lehigh University *B, M*
Lycoming College *B*
Muhlenberg College *B*
Penn State
  Abington *B*
  Altoona *B*
  Beaver *B*

Berks *B*
Delaware County *B*
Dubois *B*
Erie, The Behrend College *B*
Fayette *B*
Harrisburg *B, M*
Hazleton *B*
Lehigh Valley *B*
McKeesport *B*
Mont Alto *B*
New Kensington *B*
Schuylkill - Capital College *B*
Shenango *B*
University Park *B*
Wilkes-Barre *B*
Worthington Scranton *B*
York *B*
St. Francis University *B*
Temple University *B*
University of Pennsylvania *B, M, D*
University of Pittsburgh
  Bradford *B*
  Greensburg *B*
  Johnstown *B*
Ursinus College *B*
West Chester University of
  Pennsylvania *B*

Rhode Island

Brown University *B, M, D*
Providence College *B*
Roger Williams University *B*
Salve Regina University *B*

South Carolina

Claflin University *B*
Erskine College *B*

Tennessee

Cumberland University *B*
King College *B, T*
Lincoln Memorial University *B*
Lipscomb University *B*
Tennessee Wesleyan College *B*
University of Tennessee
  Knoxville *B*
University of the South *B*
Vanderbilt University *B*

Texas

Austin College *B*
Baylor University *B, M*
Southwestern University *B*
Texas A&M University *B*
Texas State University: San Marcos *B*
University of Dallas *M*
University of Texas
  Austin *B, M, D*
  Dallas *B*
  Pan American *B*
  San Antonio *B*

Utah

Brigham Young University *B*
Utah State University *B, M*

Vermont

Bennington College *B*
Goddard College *B*
Marlboro College *B*
Middlebury College *B*
St. Michael's College *B*

Virginia

College of William and Mary *B, M, D*
Randolph-Macon Woman's College *B*
Shenandoah University *B*
University of Mary Washington *B*
University of Richmond *B*
Virginia Wesleyan College *B*

Washington

Heritage University *B*
Washington State University *B, M, D*
Western Washington University *B*
Whitworth College *B*

Wisconsin

Edgewood College *B, T*

Wyoming

University of Wyoming *B, M*

Analysis/functional analysis

Maryland

University of Maryland
College Park *M*

Massachusetts

Simon's Rock College of Bard *B*

Analytical chemistry

Florida

Florida Institute of Technology *B*
Florida State University *M, D*

Georgia

Clark Atlanta University *M, D*

Illinois

Governors State University *M*
Illinois Institute of Technology *M*

Iowa

Iowa State University *M, D*

Massachusetts

Massachusetts College of Pharmacy
and Health Sciences *M, D*
Tufts University *M, D*

Montana

University of Montana: Missoula *M, D*

New York

Sarah Lawrence College *B*
State University of New York
College of Environmental Science
and Forestry *M, D*

Pennsylvania

West Chester University of
Pennsylvania *B*

Texas

University of North Texas *M, D*

Wisconsin

Marquette University *M, D*
University of Wisconsin
Madison *M*

Anatomy

Alabama

Auburn University *M*

Arizona

University of Arizona *M, D*

Arkansas

University of Arkansas
for Medical Sciences *M, D*

California

California State University
Fresno *B*

Loma Linda University *M, D*
University of California
Irvine *M, D*
Los Angeles *M, D*

District of Columbia

Georgetown University *D*
Howard University *M, D*

Florida

Barry University *M*

Georgia

Medical College of Georgia *M, D*

Illinois

Rosalind Franklin University of
Medicine and Science *M, D*
Rush University *M, D*
University of Illinois
Chicago *M, D*

Indiana

Indiana University
Bloomington *M, D*
Indiana University-Purdue University
Indianapolis *M, D*

Iowa

University of Iowa *M, D*

Kansas

Central Christian College of Kansas *A*
University of Kansas Medical
Center *M, D*

Kentucky

University of Kentucky: College of
Medicine *D*
University of Louisville *M, D*

Louisiana

Louisiana State University Health
Sciences Center *M, D*
Tulane University *M, D*

Maryland

University of Maryland
Baltimore *M, D*

Massachusetts

Boston University *M, D*
Harvard College *D*
Tufts University *D*

Michigan

Michigan State University *M, D*
University of Michigan *M, D*
Wayne State University *M, D*

Minnesota

Minnesota State University
Mankato *B*
University of Minnesota
Twin Cities *M*

Mississippi

University of Mississippi Medical
Center *M, D*

Missouri

St. Louis University *M, D*

Nebraska

Creighton University *M*

Nevada

Community College of Southern
Nevada *A*

New York

State University of New York
Buffalo *M, D*
Stony Brook *D*
Upstate Medical University *M, D*
University of Rochester *M*
Yeshiva University *M, D*

North Carolina

Duke University *B, M, D*

North Dakota

University of North Dakota *M, D*

Ohio

Case Western Reserve University *M, D*
Kent State University *D*
Ohio State University
Columbus Campus *M, D*
University of Cincinnati *D*
Wright State University *B*

Oregon

Oregon Health & Science
University *M, D*

Pennsylvania

Temple University *D*

South Dakota

University of South Dakota *M, D*

Tennessee

University of Tennessee
Knoxville *M, D*

Texas

Texas A&M University *M, D*
University of Texas
Health Science Center at
Houston *M, D*
Medical Branch at Galveston *M, D*

Utah

University of Utah *M, D*

Vermont

University of Vermont *M, D*

Virginia

Virginia Commonwealth
University *M, D*

Washington

Eastern Washington University *B*

West Virginia

West Virginia University *M, D*

Ancient Greek

Alabama

Samford University *B*

California

Loyola Marymount University *B*
Santa Clara University *B*
University of California
Berkeley *B, M*
Los Angeles *B, M*
Santa Cruz *B*

Connecticut

Yale University *B*

District of Columbia

Howard University *B*

Florida

Florida State University *B, M*

Georgia

University of Georgia *B, M*

Illinois

Augustana College *B*
Concordia University *B*
Loyola University of Chicago *B*
Monmouth College *B*
Moody Bible Institute *B*
Rockford College *B*
Trinity International University *M*
University of Chicago *B, D*

Indiana

DePauw University *B*
Indiana University
Bloomington *B, M, D*
University of Notre Dame *B*
Wabash College *B*

Iowa

Luther College *B*
University of Iowa *B, M*

Kentucky

Asbury College *B*

Louisiana

Loyola University New Orleans *B*

Maryland

Washington Bible College *M*

Massachusetts

Amherst College *B*
Boston College *B, M*
Boston University *B*
Brandeis University *B*
Harvard College *B, D*
Mount Holyoke College *B*
Smith College *B*
Tufts University *B*
Wellesley College *B*

Michigan

Calvin College *B*
Concordia University *B*
Grand Valley State University *B*
University of Michigan *B, M*

Minnesota

Carleton College *B*
St. Olaf College *B*
University of Minnesota
Twin Cities *B, M, D*
University of St. Thomas *B*

Missouri

Washington University in St.
Louis *B, M*

Nebraska

Creighton University *B*
University of Nebraska
Lincoln *B*

New Hampshire

University of New Hampshire *B*

New York

Bard College *B*
Barnard College *B*
City University of New York
Hunter College *B*
Lehman College *B*
Queens College *B*
Columbia University
Columbia College *B*

Elmira College *B*
Fordham University *B, M, D*
Hamilton College *B*
New York University *B*
Syracuse University *M*
Vassar College *B*

North Carolina
Duke University *B*
Wake Forest University *B*

Ohio
John Carroll University *B*
Kenyon College *B*
Miami University
   Oxford Campus *B*
Oberlin College *B*
Ohio State University
   Columbus Campus *M, D*
Ohio University *B*

Oregon
Multnomah Bible College *B*
University of Oregon *B*

Pennsylvania
Bryn Mawr College *B, M, D*
Duquesne University *B*
Franklin & Marshall College *B*
Haverford College *B*
Swarthmore College *B*
University of Scranton *B*

Rhode Island
Brown University *B*

South Carolina
Furman University *B*

Tennessee
University of Tennessee
   Knoxville *B*
University of the South *B*

Texas
Baylor University *B*
Rice University *B*
University of Dallas *B*
University of Texas
   Austin *B*

Utah
Brigham Young University *B*

Vermont
University of Vermont *B, M*

Virginia
College of William and Mary *B*
Hampden-Sydney College *B*
Randolph-Macon College *B*
Randolph-Macon Woman's College *B*
University of Richmond *B*

Washington
University of Washington *B*

Wisconsin
Lawrence University *B, T*
University of Wisconsin
   Madison *B, M*

Ancient Near Eastern/ Biblical languages

California
Master's College *B*

Connecticut
Yale University *B, M, D*

Delaware
University of Delaware *B*

District of Columbia
Catholic University of America *M, D*

Illinois
University of Chicago *B, M, D*

Iowa
Luther College *B*

Kentucky
Asbury College *B*

Massachusetts
Brandeis University *B, M*

Michigan
Calvin College *B*
Concordia University *B*
Cornerstone University *B*
Hope College *B*
University of Michigan *B*

Montana
Carroll College *B*

New York
Columbia University
   Columbia College *B*
State University of New York
   Binghamton *B*

Ohio
Ohio Wesleyan University *B*

Pennsylvania
La Salle University *B*

South Carolina
Columbia International University *B*

Texas
Baylor University *B*
Howard Payne University *B*

Utah
Brigham Young University *B*

Washington
University of Washington *M*

Wisconsin
Lawrence University *B*

Ancient studies

California
Loyola Marymount University *B*
Santa Clara University *B*
University of California
   Riverside *B*

Connecticut
Wesleyan University *B*
Yale University *B*

Iowa
University of Iowa *B*

Kansas
University of Kansas *B*

Maine
Bates College *B*

Maryland
University of Maryland
   Baltimore County *B*

Massachusetts
Mount Holyoke College *B*
Smith College *B*

Michigan
University of Michigan *B, M, D*

Minnesota
St. Olaf College *B*
University of St. Thomas *B*

Missouri
Missouri State University *B*
Washington University in St. Louis *B*

New Hampshire
Dartmouth College *B*

New York
Barnard College *B*
Columbia University
   Columbia College *B*
Vassar College *B*

Ohio
Ohio State University
   Columbus Campus *B*
Ohio Wesleyan University *B*

Rhode Island
Brown University *B*

Texas
University of Texas
   Austin *B*

Anesthesiologist assistant

Ohio
Case Western Reserve University *M*

Wisconsin
Milwaukee Area Technical College *A*

Animal behavior/ ethology

Arizona
Northern Arizona University *B*

California
University of California
   Davis *D*

Pennsylvania
Bucknell University *M*

Wisconsin
Carroll College *B*
Lawrence University *B*

Animal breeding

California
Modesto Junior College *A*

Illinois
Kishwaukee College *C, A*

Iowa
Iowa State University *M, D*

Mississippi
Hinds Community College *A*

New York
Cornell University *M, D*

Ohio
Lake Erie College *B*

Oklahoma
Oklahoma State University *M, D*

Texas
Texas A&M University *M, D*

Vermont
Sterling College *A, B*

Animal genetics

Connecticut
University of Connecticut *M, D*

New York
Cornell University *B, M, D*

Texas
University of Texas
   Medical Branch at Galveston *M, D*

Washington
Washington State University *B, M, D*

Animal health

California
California State University
   Fresno *B*
Los Angeles Pierce College *A*
San Diego Mesa College *A*

Colorado
Colorado Mountain College
   Spring Valley Campus *A*

Nebraska
Nebraska College of Technical
   Agriculture *A*
University of Nebraska
   Lincoln *M*

Texas
Sul Ross State University *A, B*

Vermont
Sterling College *A, B*

Animal husbandry

California
Santa Rosa Junior College *C*
Sierra College *C, A*

Connecticut
University of Connecticut *A*

Illinois
Black Hawk College *C, A*
Black Hawk College
   East Campus *C*
John Wood Community College *C, A*
Parkland College *C, A*
University of Illinois
   Urbana-Champaign *B, M, D*

Indiana
St. Mary-of-the-Woods College *A, B*

Iowa

Ellsworth Community College C
Hawkeye Community College C, A
Iowa State University M

New York

Niagara County Community
College A
State University of New York
College of Agriculture and
Technology at Morrisville A, B

North Carolina

James Sprunt Community College A
North Carolina State University A

Ohio

Ohio State University
Agricultural Technical Institute A

Oregon

Blue Mountain Community College A

Puerto Rico

University of Puerto Rico
Utuado A

Texas

Angelo State University B
Tarleton State University B
Texas A&M University B

Utah

Utah State University C

Vermont

Sterling College A, B

Animal nutrition

Georgia

University of Georgia D

Illinois

Joliet Junior College C

Iowa

Iowa State University M, D

Oklahoma

Oklahoma State University D

Texas

Texas A&M University M, D

Vermont

Sterling College A, B

Animal physiology

California

University of California
San Diego B

Colorado

Colorado State University M, D

Connecticut

University of Connecticut B, M, D

Indiana

Ball State University M

Iowa

Iowa State University M, D

New York

Cornell University B, M, D

Ohio

Kent State University M, D
Ohio State University
Columbus Campus M, D
University of Akron B

Texas

Texas State University: San Marcos B

Animal sciences

Alabama

Auburn University B, M, D
Northeast Alabama Community
College A
Tuskegee University B, M

Arizona

University of Arizona B, M, D

Arkansas

Arkansas State University B
University of Arkansas B, M, D

California

Bakersfield College A
Butte College C, A
California Polytechnic State
University: San Luis Obispo B
California State Polytechnic
University: Pomona B, M
California State University
Chico B
Fresno B, M
College of the Redwoods C, A
College of the Sequoias A
College of the Siskiyous A
Cosumnes River College A
Los Angeles Pierce College C, A
Merced College A
Modesto Junior College A
Moorpark College C, A
Mount San Antonio College C, A
Reedley College C
San Joaquin Delta College C, A
Santa Rosa Junior College C
University of California
Davis B, M, D
Ventura College C, A
West Hills Community College C, A
Yuba Community College District C

Colorado

Colorado State University B, M, D
University of Denver B

Connecticut

University of Connecticut B, M, D

Delaware

University of Delaware B, M, D

Florida

Florida Agricultural and Mechanical
University B
University of Florida B, M, D

Georgia

Abraham Baldwin Agricultural
College A
Berry College B
Fort Valley State University B, M
University of Georgia B, M, D

Hawaii

University of Hawaii
Hilo B
Manoa B, M

Idaho

Brigham Young University-Idaho A, B

University of Idaho B, M

Illinois

Black Hawk College
East Campus C
John Wood Community College A
Southern Illinois University
Carbondale B, M
University of Illinois
Urbana-Champaign B, M, D

Indiana

Purdue University B, M, D

Iowa

Dordt College B
Iowa State University B, M, D

Kansas

Butler County Community College A
Central Christian College of Kansas A
Colby Community College A
Fort Scott Community College A
Garden City Community College A
Kansas State University B, M, D
McPherson College B
Pratt Community College A
Seward County Community College A

Kentucky

University of Kentucky B, M, D

Louisiana

Louisiana State University and
Agricultural and Mechanical
College B, M, D
Louisiana Tech University B
Southern University and Agricultural
and Mechanical College B

Maine

University of Maine B, M

Maryland

University of Maryland
College Park B, M, D

Massachusetts

Hampshire College B
Mount Ida College A, B
University of Massachusetts
Amherst B, M, D

Michigan

Andrews University B
Michigan State University C, B, M, D

Minnesota

Globe College A
South Central College A
University of Minnesota
Crookston A
Twin Cities B, M, D

Mississippi

Alcorn State University B
Mississippi State University B

Missouri

College of the Ozarks B
Missouri State University B
Northwest Missouri State
University B
Truman State University B
University of Missouri
Columbia B, M, D

Montana

Montana State University
Bozeman B, M

Nebraska

Northeast Community College A
University of Nebraska
Lincoln B, M, D

Nevada

University of Nevada
Reno B, M

New Hampshire

University of New
Hampshire A, B, M, D

New Jersey

Rutgers, The State University of New
Jersey
New Brunswick/Piscataway
Campus B, M, D

New Mexico

New Mexico State University B, M, D

New York

Cornell University B, M, D
Mercy College B
State University of New York
College of Agriculture and
Technology at Cobleskill A, B
College of Agriculture and
Technology at Morrisville A, B
College of Environmental Science
and Forestry B, M, D
College of Technology at Alfred A
College of Technology at Delhi A

North Carolina

James Sprunt Community College A
North Carolina Agricultural and
Technical State University B, M
North Carolina State
University B, M, D
Sampson Community College C

North Dakota

North Dakota State University B, M, D

Ohio

Ohio State University
Columbus Campus B, M, D
Wilmington College B

Oklahoma

Cameron University B
Eastern Oklahoma State College A
Oklahoma Panhandle State
University B
Oklahoma State University B, M

Oregon

Linn-Benton Community College A
Oregon State University B, M, D
Treasure Valley Community College A

Pennsylvania

Delaware Valley College B
Harcum College A
Penn State
Abington B
Altoona B
Beaver B
Berks B
Delaware County B
Dubois B
Erie, The Behrend College B
Fayette B
Hazleton B
Lehigh Valley B
McKeesport B
Mont Alto B
New Kensington B
Schuylkill - Capital College B

Shenango *B*
University Park *C, B, M, D*
Wilkes-Barre *B*
Worthington Scranton *B*
York *B*

Puerto Rico

University of Puerto Rico
Arecibo *A*
Mayaguez *B, M*

Rhode Island

University of Rhode Island *B, M*

South Carolina

Clemson University *B*

South Dakota

South Dakota State University *B, M, D*

Tennessee

Hiwassee College *A*
Middle Tennessee State University *B*
Tennessee State University *B, M*
Tennessee Technological University *B*
University of Tennessee
Knoxville *B, M, D*

Texas

Abilene Christian University *B*
Angelo State University *B, M*
Central Texas College *C*
Cisco Junior College *A*
Clarendon College *A*
Hardin-Simmons University *B*
Lubbock Christian University *B*
Palo Alto College *C, A*
Prairie View A&M University *M*
Sam Houston State University *B*
Stephen F. Austin State University *B*
Sul Ross State University *B, M*
Tarleton State University *B*
Texas A&M University *B, M, D*
Texas A&M University
Commerce *B, M*
Kingsville *B, M*
Texas State University: San Marcos *B*
Texas Tech University *B, M, D*
West Texas A&M University *B, M*
Western Texas College *A*

Utah

Snow College *A*
Utah State University *B, M, D*

Vermont

Sterling College *A, B*
University of Vermont *B, M, D*

Virginia

Blue Ridge Community College *C, A*
Virginia Polytechnic Institute and
State University *B, M, D*

Washington

Everett Community College *A*
Pierce College *A*
Washington State University *B, M, D*
Yakima Valley Community College *C*

West Virginia

Potomac State College of West Virginia
University *A*
West Virginia University *B, M*

Wisconsin

Chippewa Valley Technical College *A*
Madison Area Technical College *A*
University of Wisconsin
Madison *B, M, D*
Platteville *B*

River Falls *B*

Wyoming

Casper College *A*
Eastern Wyoming College *A*
Northwest College *A*
Sheridan College *A*

Animal training

Massachusetts

Becker College *C, A*

Animation

Arizona

Art Center Design College *B*
Collins College *A, B*

California

Art Center College of Design *B, M*
Art Institute
of California: Los Angeles *B*
of California: Orange County *B*
Art Institute of California: San
Francisco *B*
California Institute of the Arts *C, B, M*
Cogswell Polytechnical College *B*
Long Beach City College *C*
Loyola Marymount University *B*
Otis College of Art and Design *B*
Platt College
Ontario *B*
Santa Monica College *C*
Santa Rosa Junior College *C*
Silicon Valley College
Western Career College:
Emeryville *C, A, B*
Westwood College of Technology
Inland Empire *B*
Westwood College: Long Beach *B*
Woodbury University *B*

Colorado

Art Institute
of Colorado *C, A, B*
Rocky Mountain College of Art &
Design *B*
Westwood College of Technology
South *B*

Delaware

Delaware College of Art and Design *A*

District of Columbia

American University *B*

Florida

Miami Dade College *A*
Miami International University of Art
and Design *B, M*
Ringling School of Art and Design *B*

Georgia

Central Georgia Technical College *C*
Savannah College of Art and
Design *C, B, M*
Southwest Georgia Technical
College *C*

Illinois

Bradley University *B*
City Colleges of Chicago
Kennedy-King College *C*
International Academy of Design and
Technology: Chicago *A, B*
International Academy of Design and
Technology: Schaumburg *A, B*
Moraine Valley Community College *C*
Oakton Community College *C*

University of Illinois
Chicago *M*
Waubonsee Community College *C*
Westwood College - Chicago Loop *B*
Westwood College of Technology
O'Hare *B*

Kentucky

Louisville Technical Institute *A*

Maryland

Hagerstown Community College *C, A*

Massachusetts

School of the Museum of Fine
Arts *B, M*
Springfield Technical Community
College *A*

Michigan

College for Creative Studies *B*
Ferris State University *A, B*

Minnesota

Academy College *C, A*
Art Institutes International
Minnesota *B*
Minneapolis College of Art and
Design *B*
Minneapolis Community and
Technical College *C*
St. Paul College *A*

Nebraska

Dana College *B*

Nevada

Community College of Southern
Nevada *C, A*

New Jersey

Burlington County College *A*

New Mexico

Art Center Design College *B*
Eastern New Mexico University:
Roswell Campus *C, A*

New York

Art Institute
of New York City *A*
Fashion Institute of Technology *B*
Rochester Institute of
Technology *B, M*
School of Visual Arts *B*
State University of New York
College at Oneonta *B*

North Carolina

East Carolina University *B*

Ohio

University of Cincinnati
Raymond Walters College *C*
Washington State Community
College *A*

Oregon

Art Institute of Portland *A, B*

Pennsylvania

Art Institute
of Philadelphia *A, B*
of Pittsburgh *A, B*
Bradley Academy for the Visual Arts *A*
Bucks County Community
College *C, A*
Carnegie Mellon University *M*
Douglas Education Center *A*
Keystone College *A*

Northampton County Area
Community College *C*
Philadelphia University *B, M*

Rhode Island

New England Institute of
Technology *A*
Salve Regina University *B*

Tennessee

East Tennessee State University *B*

Texas

Collin County Community College
District *C, A*

Utah

Brigham Young University *B*
Salt Lake Community College *A*
University of Utah *M*

Vermont

Bennington College *B*
Burlington College *B*
Champlain College *A, B*

Virginia

Art Institute
of Washington *B*

Washington

Olympic College *A*

Wisconsin

Herzing College *A, B*

Anthropology

Alabama

Auburn University *B*
University of Alabama *B, M, D*
University of Alabama
Birmingham *B, M*
University of South Alabama *B*

Alaska

University of Alaska
Anchorage *B, M*
Fairbanks *B, M, D*

Arizona

Arizona State University *B, M, D*
Cochise College *A*
Eastern Arizona College *A*
Northern Arizona University *B, M*
Pima Community College *A*
Prescott College *A*
University of Arizona *B, M, D*

Arkansas

Hendrix College *A*
University of Arkansas *B, M*

California

Bakersfield College *A*
Biola University *B*
Cabrillo College *A*
California Institute of Integral
Studies *M, D*
California State Polytechnic
University: Pomona *B*
California State University
Bakersfield *B*
Chico *C, B, M*
Dominguez Hills *B*
East Bay *B, M*
Fresno *B*
Fullerton *B, M*
Long Beach *B, M*
Los Angeles *B, M*
Monterey Bay *B*

Northridge *B*
Sacramento *B, M*
San Bernardino *B*
Stanislaus *B*
Canada College *A*
Cerritos Community College *A*
Chaffey College *A*
College of Alameda *A*
College of the Desert *A*
Copper Mountain College *A*
Crafton Hills College *A*
Cypress College *A*
De Anza College *A*
East Los Angeles College *A*
El Camino College *A*
Foothill College *A*
Fresno City College *A*
Fullerton College *A*
Gavilan Community College *A*
Glendale Community College *A*
Golden West College *A*
Humboldt State University *B*
Imperial Valley College *A*
Irvine Valley College *A*
Los Angeles Pierce College *C*
Los Medanos College *A*
Merced College *A*
Mills College *B*
Monterey Peninsula College *A*
Occidental College *B*
Ohlone College *C*
Orange Coast College *A*
Pitzer College *B*
Pomona College *B*
Saddleback College *A*
St. Mary's College of California *B*
San Diego City College *A*
San Diego Mesa College *A*
San Diego Miramar College *A*
San Diego State University *B, M*
San Francisco State University *B, M*
San Joaquin Delta College *A*
San Jose State University *B*
Santa Ana College *A*
Santa Barbara City College *A*
Santa Clara University *B*
Santa Rosa Junior College *A*
Santiago Canyon College *A*
Scripps College *B*
Sonoma State University *B, M*
Southwestern College *A*
Stanford University *B, M, D*
University of California
    Berkeley *B, D*
    Davis *B, M, D*
    Irvine *B, M, D*
    Los Angeles *B, M, D*
    Riverside *B, M, D*
    San Diego *B, D*
    Santa Barbara *B, M, D*
    Santa Cruz *B, D*
University of La Verne *B*
University of Redlands *B*
University of San Diego *B*
University of Southern
    California *B, M, D*
Vanguard University of Southern
    California *B*
Ventura College *A*
West Los Angeles College *C, A*
Westmont College *B*
Whittier College *B*

Colorado

Colorado College *B*
Colorado State University *B, M*
Fort Lewis College *B*
Metropolitan State College of
    Denver *B, T*
University of Colorado
    Boulder *B, M, D*
    Colorado Springs *B*
    Denver and Health Sciences
        Center *B, M*

University of Denver *B, M*
University of Northern Colorado *B*
Western State College of Colorado *B*

Connecticut

Central Connecticut State
    University *B*
Connecticut College *B*
Trinity College *B*
University of Connecticut *B, M, D*
Wesleyan University *B, M*
Western Connecticut State
    University *B*
Yale University *B, M, D*

Delaware

University of Delaware *B*

District of Columbia

American University *B, M, D*
Catholic University of
    America *B, M, D*
George Washington University *B, M*
Georgetown University *B*
Howard University *B*
University of the District of
    Columbia *B*

Florida

Broward Community College *A*
Eckerd College *B*
Florida Atlantic University *B, M*
Florida State University *B, M, D*
Gulf Coast Community College *A*
Indian River Community College *A*
Miami Dade College *A*
New College of Florida *B*
Palm Beach Community College *A*
Rollins College *B*
Santa Fe Community College *A*
University of Central Florida *B, M*
University of Florida *B, M, D*
University of Miami *B*
University of North Florida *B*
University of South Florida *B, M, D*
University of West Florida *B, M*

Georgia

Agnes Scott College *B*
Berry College *B*
Darton College *A*
East Georgia College *A*
Emory University *B, D*
Gainesville State College *A*
Georgia Perimeter College *A*
Georgia Southern University *B*
Georgia State University *B, M*
Thomas University *B*
University of Georgia *B, M, D*
University of West Georgia *B*

Hawaii

Hawaii Pacific University *C, B*
University of Hawaii
    Hilo *B*
    Manoa *B, M, D*
    West Oahu *B*

Idaho

Albertson College of Idaho *B*
Boise State University *B*
College of Southern Idaho *A*
Idaho State University *B, M*
North Idaho College *A*
University of Idaho *B, M*

Illinois

Black Hawk College
    East Campus *A*
Chicago State University *B*
Illinois State University *B*
Illinois Wesleyan University *B*

Judson College *B*
Knox College *B*
Lake Forest College *B*
Loyola University of Chicago *B*
National-Louis University *B*
North Central College *B*
North Park University *B*
Northeastern Illinois University *B*
Northern Illinois University *B, M*
Northwestern University *B, M, D*
Principia College *B*
Richland Community College *A*
Rockford College *B*
South Suburban College of Cook
    County *A*
Southern Illinois University
    Carbondale *B, M, D*
Southern Illinois University
    Edwardsville *B*
Southwestern Illinois College *A*
Triton College *A*
University of Chicago *B, D*
University of Illinois
    Chicago *B, M, D*
    Urbana-Champaign *B, M, D*
Wheaton College *B*

Indiana

Ball State University *B, M*
Butler University *B*
DePauw University *B*
Earlham College *B*
Goshen College *B*
Hanover College *B*
Indiana State University *B*
Indiana University
    Bloomington *B, M, D*
Indiana University-Purdue University
    Fort Wayne *B*
Indiana University-Purdue University
    Indianapolis *B*
University of Indianapolis *B*
University of Notre Dame *B*
Vincennes University *A*

Iowa

Central College *B*
Drake University *B*
Grinnell College *B*
Iowa State University *B, M*
Luther College *B*
University of Iowa *B, M, D, T*
University of Northern Iowa *B*

Kansas

Barton County Community College *A*
Kansas State University *B*
University of Kansas *B, M, D*
Washburn University of Topeka *B*
Wichita State University *B, M*

Kentucky

Centre College *B*
Eastern Kentucky University *B*
Northern Kentucky University *B*
Transylvania University *B*
University of Kentucky *B, M, D*
University of Louisville *B*
Western Kentucky University *B*

Louisiana

Louisiana State University and
    Agricultural and Mechanical
    College *B, M*
Loyola University New Orleans *B*
Northwestern State University *B*
Tulane University *B, M, D*
University of Louisiana at Lafayette *B*
University of New Orleans *B*

Maine

Bates College *B*
Bowdoin College *B*

Colby College *B*
University of Maine *B*
University of Maine
    Farmington *B*
University of Southern Maine *B*

Maryland

Community College of Baltimore
    County *A*
Goucher College *B*
Howard Community College *A*
Johns Hopkins University *B, M, D*
St. Mary's College of Maryland *B*
University of Maryland
    Baltimore County *B*
    College Park *B*
Washington College *B*

Massachusetts

Amherst College *B*
Boston University *B, M, D*
Brandeis University *B, M, D*
College of the Holy Cross *B*
Hampshire College *B*
Harvard College *B, M, D*
Massachusetts Institute of
    Technology *B*
Mount Holyoke College *B*
Northeastern University *B, M*
Simon's Rock College of Bard *B*
Smith College *B*
Tufts University *B*
University of Massachusetts
    Amherst *B, M, D*
    Boston *B*
Wellesley College *B*
Wheaton College *B*
Williams College *B*

Michigan

Albion College *B*
Alma College *B, T*
Andrews University *B*
Central Michigan University *B, T*
Eastern Michigan University *B*
Grand Valley State University *B*
Kalamazoo College *B, T*
Kellogg Community College *A*
Lansing Community College *A*
Michigan State University *B, M, D*
Oakland University *B*
Olivet College *B*
University of Michigan *B, M, D, T*
University of Michigan
    Dearborn *B*
    Flint *B*
Wayne State University *B, M, D*
Western Michigan University *B, M*

Minnesota

Carleton College *B*
Gustavus Adolphus College *B*
Hamline University *B*
Macalester College *B*
Minnesota State University
    Mankato *B*
    Moorhead *B*
St. Cloud State University *B*
University of Minnesota
    Duluth *B*
    Morris *B*
    Twin Cities *B, M, D*
University of St. Thomas *B*

Mississippi

Millsaps College *B*
Mississippi State University *B, M*
University of Mississippi *B, M*
University of Southern
    Mississippi *B, M*

Missouri

Missouri State University *B*

Southeast Missouri State University *B*
University of Missouri
 Columbia *B, M, D*
 St. Louis *B*
Washington University in St.
 Louis *B, M, D*
Webster University *B*
Westminster College *B*

Montana

Montana State University
 Bozeman *B*
University of Montana: Missoula *B, M*

Nebraska

Creighton University *B*
University of Nebraska
 Lincoln *B, M*
Western Nebraska Community
 College *A*

Nevada

Great Basin College *A*
Truckee Meadows Community
 College *C, A*
University of Nevada
 Las Vegas *B, M, D*
 Reno *B, M, D*

New Hampshire

Dartmouth College *B*
Franklin Pierce College *B*
University of New Hampshire *B*

New Jersey

Drew University *B*
Monmouth University *B*
Montclair State University *B, M*
Princeton University *B, M, D*
Rowan University *B*
Rutgers, The State University of New
 Jersey
 New Brunswick/Piscataway
  Campus *B, M, D*
 Newark Regional Campus *B*
Seton Hall University *B*
Thomas Edison State College *B*
William Paterson University of New
 Jersey *B*

New Mexico

Eastern New Mexico University *B, M*
New Mexico State University *B, M*
San Juan College *A*
University of New Mexico *B, M, D*

New York

Adelphi University *B*
Bard College *B*
Barnard College *B*
Canisius College *B*
City University of New York
 Brooklyn College *B*
 City College *B, M*
 Hunter College *B, M*
 Lehman College *B*
 Queens College *B, T*
 York College *B*
Colgate University *B*
Columbia University
 Columbia College *B*
Cornell University *B, M, D*
Dowling College *B*
Elmira College *B*
Eugene Lang College The New School
 for Liberal Arts *B*
Fordham University *B*
Hamilton College *B*
Hartwick College *B*
Hobart and William Smith Colleges *B*
Hofstra University *B*
Ithaca College *B*
Nazareth College of Rochester *B*

New York University *B, M, D*
St. John Fisher College *B*
St. John's University *B*
St. Lawrence University *B*
Sarah Lawrence College *B*
Skidmore College *B*
State University of New York
 Albany *B, M, D*
 Binghamton *B, M, D*
 Buffalo *B, M, D*
 College at Brockport *B*
 College at Buffalo *B*
 College at Cortland *B*
 College at Geneseo *B, T*
 College at Oneonta *B*
 College at Plattsburgh *B*
 College at Potsdam *B*
 New Paltz *B*
 Oswego *B*
 Purchase *B*
 Stony Brook *B, M, D*
Syracuse University *B, M, D*
Union College *B*
University of Rochester *B*
Vassar College *B*
Wagner College *B*
Wells College *B*

North Carolina

Appalachian State University *B*
Davidson College *B*
Duke University *B, M, D*
East Carolina University *B, M*
Elon University *B*
North Carolina State University *B*
North Carolina Wesleyan College *B*
University of North Carolina
 Chapel Hill *B, M, D*
 Charlotte *B*
 Greensboro *B*
 Wilmington *B*
Wake Forest University *B, M*
Warren Wilson College *B*
Western Carolina University *B*

North Dakota

North Dakota State University *B*
University of North Dakota *B*

Ohio

Case Western Reserve
 University *B, M, D*
Cleveland State University *B, M*
College of Wooster *B*
Denison University *B*
Franciscan University of
 Steubenville *B*
Heidelberg College *B*
Kent State University *B, M*
Kenyon College *B*
Miami University
 Oxford Campus *B*
Oberlin College *B*
Ohio State University
 Columbus Campus *B, M, D*
Ohio University *B*
Ohio Wesleyan University *B*
University of Cincinnati *B, M*
University of Toledo *B*
Wright State University *B*
Youngstown State University *B*

Oklahoma

Oklahoma Baptist University *B*
University of Oklahoma *B, M, D*
University of Tulsa *B, M*

Oregon

Central Oregon Community
 College *A*
Chemeketa Community College *A*
Eastern Oregon University *B, T*
Lewis & Clark College *B*

Linfield College *B, T*
Linn-Benton Community College *A*
Oregon State University *B, M*
Portland State University *B, M, D*
Reed College *B*
Southern Oregon University *B*
University of Oregon *B, M, D*
Western Oregon University *B*
Willamette University *B*

Pennsylvania

Albright College *B*
Bloomsburg University of
 Pennsylvania *B*
Bryn Mawr College *B*
Bucknell University *B*
Clarion University of Pennsylvania *B*
Delaware County Community
 College *B*
Dickinson College *B*
Drexel University *B*
Edinboro University of
 Pennsylvania *B*
Elizabethtown College *B*
Franklin & Marshall College *B*
Gettysburg College *B*
Haverford College *B, T*
Indiana University of Pennsylvania *B*
Juniata College *B*
Kutztown University of
 Pennsylvania *B*
Lafayette College *B*
Lehigh University *B*
Lycoming College *B*
Mansfield University of
 Pennsylvania *B, T*
Mercyhurst College *B*
Millersville University of
 Pennsylvania *B*
Muhlenberg College *C, B*
Penn State
 Abington *B*
 Altoona *B*
 Beaver *B*
 Berks *B*
 Delaware County *B*
 Dubois *B*
 Fayette *B*
 Hazleton *B*
 Lehigh Valley *B*
 McKeesport *B*
 Mont Alto *B*
 New Kensington *B*
 Schuylkill - Capital College *B*
 Shenango *B*
 University Park *B, M, D*
 Wilkes-Barre *B*
 Worthington Scranton *B*
 York *B*
St. Vincent College *B*
Swarthmore College *B*
Temple University *B, M, D*
University of Pennsylvania *A, B, M, D*
University of Pittsburgh *B, M, D*
University of Pittsburgh
 Greensburg *B*
Ursinus College *B*
West Chester University of
 Pennsylvania *B*
Widener University *B*

Puerto Rico

University of Puerto Rico
 Rio Piedras *B*

Rhode Island

Brown University *B, M, D*
Rhode Island College *B*
Roger Williams University *B*
Salve Regina University *B*
University of Rhode Island *B*

South Carolina

College of Charleston *B*
University of South Carolina *B, M*

South Dakota

University of South Dakota *B*

Tennessee

Middle Tennessee State University *B*
Rhodes College *B*
University of Memphis *B, M*
University of Tennessee
 Knoxville *B, M, D*
University of the South *B*
Vanderbilt University *B, M, D*

Texas

Austin Community College *A*
Baylor University *B*
Galveston College *A*
Palo Alto College *A*
Rice University *B, M, D*
Southern Methodist
 University *B, M, D*
Southwestern University *B*
Texas A&M University *B, M, D*
Texas A&M University
 Commerce *B*
 Kingsville *B*
Texas Christian University *B*
Texas State University: San
 Marcos *B, M*
Texas Tech University *B, M*
Trinity University *B*
University of Houston *B, M*
University of Houston
 Clear Lake *B*
University of North Texas *B*
University of Texas
 Arlington *B, M*
 Austin *B, M, D*
 El Paso *B*
 Pan American *B*
 San Antonio *B, M*

Utah

Brigham Young University *B*
Snow College *A*
University of Utah *B, M, D*
Utah State University *B*

Vermont

Bennington College *B*
Green Mountain College *B*
Johnson State College *B*
Marlboro College *B*
St. Michael's College *B*
University of Vermont *B*

Virginia

College of William and Mary *B, M, D*
Emory & Henry College *B*
George Mason University *B*
James Madison University *B*
Longwood University *B, T*
Old Dominion University *B*
Radford University *B*
Sweet Briar College *B*
University of Mary Washington *B*
University of Virginia *B, M, D*
Virginia Commonwealth University *B*
Washington and Lee University *B*

Washington

Central Washington University *B*
Centralia College *A*
Eastern Washington University *B*
Everett Community College *A*
Highline Community College *A*
Olympic College *A*
Pacific Lutheran University *B*
University of Washington *B, M, D*

Washington State University *B, M, D*
Western Washington University *B, M*
Whitman College *B*

Wisconsin

Beloit College *B*
Lawrence University *B, T*
Marquette University *B, T*
Ripon College *B*
University of Wisconsin
  Madison *B, M, D*
  Milwaukee *B, M, D*
  Oshkosh *B*
  Parkside *T*
  River Falls *T*

Wyoming

Casper College *A*
Laramie County Community
  College *A*
University of Wyoming *B, M, D*
Western Wyoming Community
  College *A*

Apparel/accessories marketing

Georgia

Gwinnett Technical College *C*

Iowa

Des Moines Area Community
  College *C, A*

New Hampshire

McIntosh College *A*

New York

Fashion Institute of Technology *M*
Laboratory Institute of
  Merchandising *B*

Ohio

Youngstown State University *B*

Oklahoma

University of Central Oklahoma *B*

Pennsylvania

Philadelphia University *B*

Rhode Island

University of Rhode Island *B*

Wisconsin

Milwaukee Area Technical College *A*

Apparel/textile manufacture

Alabama

Lawson State Community College *C*
Trenholm State Technical College *C*

California

Fashion Institute of Design and
  Merchandising *A*
Fashion Institute of Design and
  Merchandising
  San Diego *A*
  San Francisco *A*

Iowa

Iowa State University *B*

Minnesota

Minneapolis Community and
  Technical College *C*

New York

Fashion Institute of Technology *A, B*

Apparel/textile marketing

Alabama

Auburn University *B, M*

California

California State University
  Sacramento *B*
Fashion Institute of Design and
  Merchandising *A*
Fashion Institute of Design and
  Merchandising
  San Diego *A*
  San Francisco *A*

Colorado

Colorado State University *B, M*

Iowa

Iowa State University *B*

New York

Fashion Institute of Technology *A, B*

North Carolina

North Carolina State University *B*

North Dakota

North Dakota State University *M*

Pennsylvania

Philadelphia University *B, M*

South Dakota

South Dakota State University *B*

Appliance installation and repair

California

Solano Community College *C, A*

Florida

South Florida Community College *C*

Kentucky

Elizabethtown Community and
  Technical College *C, A*
Somerset Community College *C*

Minnesota

St. Paul College *C*

New York

Mohawk Valley Community College *C*

Texas

Del Mar College *C, A*

Applied economics

Alaska

University of Alaska
  Fairbanks *M*

Florida

Florida State University *B*

Iowa

University of Northern Iowa *B*

Louisiana

Centenary College of Louisiana *B*

Massachusetts

University of Massachusetts
  Amherst *B, M, D*

Michigan

Michigan State University *B*
Michigan Technological University *M*
University of Michigan *M*
Western Michigan University *M, D*

Minnesota

Augsburg College *B*
College of St. Scholastica *B*
University of Minnesota
  Twin Cities *B*

Nevada

University of Nevada
  Reno *B*

New Hampshire

Plymouth State University *B*

New York

Ithaca College *B*

North Carolina

East Carolina University *M*

Ohio

Cleveland State University *C*

Oklahoma

University of Central Oklahoma *B*

Pennsylvania

Allegheny College *B*
Penn State
  Schuylkill - Capital College *B*
  University Park *B*
  Wilkes-Barre *B*
  Worthington Scranton *B*
  York *B*

Rhode Island

University of Rhode Island *M, D*

Texas

Southern Methodist University *B, M*
University of Texas
  Dallas *M*

Wisconsin

Marquette University *M*

Applied mathematics

Alabama

Auburn University *B, M*
Oakwood College *B*
University of Alabama *D*
University of Alabama
  Birmingham *D*
  Huntsville *D*

Alaska

University of Alaska
  Fairbanks *B, M*

Arizona

Arizona State University *B*
University of Arizona *M, D*

Arkansas

University of Arkansas
  Little Rock *B, M*
  Pine Bluff *B*

California

California Institute of
  Technology *B, D*
California State University
  Chico *B*
  East Bay *B, M*
  Fullerton *B, M*
  Long Beach *B, M, D*
  Northridge *B, M*
Fresno Pacific University *B*
Harvey Mudd College *B*
Loyola Marymount University *B*
Master's College *B*
Mount St. Mary's College *B*
San Diego City College *A*
San Diego Miramar College *A*
San Diego State University *B, M*
San Francisco State University *B*
San Jose State University *B*
Santa Clara University *M*
University of California
  Berkeley *B, D*
  Davis *M, D*
  Los Angeles *B*
  Riverside *B, M*
  San Diego *B, M*
  Santa Barbara *M*
  Santa Cruz *B, M, D*
University of Southern
  California *M, D*
University of the Pacific *B*

Colorado

Colorado School of Mines *B*
Fort Lewis College *B*
University of Colorado
  Boulder *B, M, D*
  Colorado Springs *M*
  Denver and Health Sciences
    Center *M, D*

Connecticut

University of Connecticut *B*
University of New Haven *B*
Yale University *B, M, D*

District of Columbia

American University *B*
George Washington University *B, M*

Florida

Florida Atlantic University *M*
Florida Institute of
  Technology *B, M, D*
Florida International University *B, M*
Florida State University *B, M, D*
University of Central Florida *M, D*
University of Miami *M*
University of North Florida *M*

Georgia

Armstrong Atlantic State
  University *B, T*
Georgia Institute of
  Technology *B, M, D*
Georgia State University *B, M, D*
University of Georgia *M*
Valdosta State University *B*

Hawaii

Hawaii Pacific University *B*

Idaho

Albertson College of Idaho *B*
Boise State University *B*
University of Idaho *B*

Illinois

Elgin Community College *A*
Illinois Valley Community College *A*
Knox College *B*
Millikin University *B, T*

National-Louis University *B*
North Central College *B*
North Park University *B*
Northern Illinois University *B*
Northwestern University *B, M, D*
University of Chicago *B*
University of Illinois
   Urbana-Champaign *M*

Indiana
Goshen College *B*
Indiana University
   South Bend *B*
Indiana University-Purdue University
   Fort Wayne *M*
Oakland City University *B*
Purdue University
   Calumet *B, M*
Saint Mary's College *B, T*
University of Notre Dame *M*

Iowa
Grand View College *B*
Iowa State University *M, D*
University of Iowa *B, D*
University of Northern Iowa *B*

Kentucky
Brescia University *B*
Paducah Technical College *A*
University of Kentucky *M*
University of Louisville *D*

Louisiana
Tulane University *M, D*

Maryland
Loyola College in Maryland *B*
Towson University *M*
University of Maryland
   Baltimore County *M, D*
   College Park *M, D*

Massachusetts
Harvard College *B, D*
Tufts University *B, M*
University of Massachusetts
   Amherst *M*
   Lowell *A, B*
Worcester Polytechnic Institute *B, M*

Michigan
Ferris State University *B*
Kettering University *B*
Lansing Community College *A*
Michigan State University *B, M, D*
Northern Michigan University *B*
Oakland University *M, D*
Saginaw Valley State University *B*
University of Detroit Mercy *B*
University of Michigan *B, M, D*
Wayne State University *M*
Western Michigan University *B, M*

Minnesota
Concordia College: Moorhead *B*
Metropolitan State University *B*
University of Minnesota
   Duluth *M*
Winona State University *B*

Mississippi
Mississippi State University *D*

Missouri
Central Methodist University *A*
Maryville University of Saint Louis *B*
St. Louis University *B*
Truman State University *B*
University of Missouri
   Columbia *M*

Rolla *B, M*
St. Louis *B, D*
Washington University in St. Louis *B*

Montana
Montana Tech of the University of
   Montana *B*
University of Montana: Western *B*

Nebraska
Creighton University *B*

Nevada
University of Nevada
   Las Vegas *B, M, D*

New Hampshire
Keene State College *B*
University of New Hampshire *B, M*

New Jersey
Bloomfield College *B*
New Jersey Institute of
   Technology *B, M*
Princeton University *M, D*
Rutgers, The State University of New
   Jersey
   Newark Regional Campus *B*
Stevens Institute of Technology *B, M*

New Mexico
New Mexico Institute of Mining and
   Technology *B, M, D*

New York
Barnard College *B*
City University of New York
   Baruch College *M*
   Hunter College *M*
   New York City College of
     Technology *B*
Clarkson University *B*
Columbia University
   Columbia College *B*
   Fu Foundation School of
     Engineering and Applied
     Science *B, M, D*
   School of General Studies *B*
Cornell University *B, M, D*
Hofstra University *B, M*
Iona College *B*
Long Island University
   C. W. Post Campus *B, M*
New York University *B, M*
Rensselaer Polytechnic Institute *M*
Rochester Institute of
   Technology *A, B, M*
St. Thomas Aquinas College *B*
Siena College *B*
State University of New York
   Albany *B*
   Farmingdale *B*
   Institute of Technology at
     Utica/Rome *B*
   Oswego *B*
   Stony Brook *B, M, D*
University of Rochester *B, M*

North Carolina
Johnson C. Smith University *B*
North Carolina Agricultural and
   Technical State University *M*
North Carolina State
   University *B, M, D*
University of North Carolina
   Chapel Hill *B*
   Charlotte *D*
Western Carolina University *M*

North Dakota
Jamestown College *B*

Ohio
Bowling Green State University *B*
Case Western Reserve
   University *B, M, D*
Kent State University *B, M, D*
Ohio State University
   Columbus Campus *M, D*
Ohio University *B*
University of Dayton *M*
Wright State University *B, M*

Oklahoma
East Central University *B*
University of Central Oklahoma *B, M*
University of Tulsa *B, M*

Pennsylvania
Carnegie Mellon University *B*
Elizabethtown College *B*
Geneva College *B*
Indiana University of Pennsylvania *B*
La Salle University *B, T*
Lehigh University *M, D*
Penn State
   Harrisburg *B*
Robert Morris University *B*
University of Pittsburgh *B, M*
University of Pittsburgh
   Bradford *B*
   Greensburg *B*

Puerto Rico
Inter American University of Puerto
   Rico
   Bayamon Campus *B*
University of Puerto Rico
   Mayaguez *M*

Rhode Island
Brown University *B, M, D*
University of Rhode Island *D*

South Carolina
Charleston Southern University *B*
Coastal Carolina University *B*
University of South Carolina *M*
University of South Carolina
   Aiken *B*
   Upstate *B*

South Dakota
University of Sioux Falls *B*

Tennessee
Bethel College *B*
University of Tennessee
   Chattanooga *B*

Texas
Baylor University *B*
Lamar University *B, M*
Rice University *B, M, D*
Southern Methodist University *M, D*
Southwestern Adventist University *B*
Texas A&M University *B*
Texas State University: San
   Marcos *B, M*
University of Houston *B, M*
University of Houston
   Downtown *B*
University of Texas
   Arlington *D*
   Austin *M, D*
   Dallas *B, M, D*
   El Paso *B*
   San Antonio *M*

Utah
Utah State University *D*
Weber State University *B*

Virginia
Hampden-Sydney College *B*
Hampton University *M*
Mary Baldwin College *B*
Old Dominion University *M, D*
University of Virginia *B, M, D*

Washington
University of Washington *B, M, D*
Washington State University *B, M, D*
Western Washington University *B*
Whitworth College *B*

West Virginia
Alderson-Broaddus College *B*
West Virginia State University *B*

Wisconsin
Carroll College *B*
University of Wisconsin
   Madison *B*
   Milwaukee *B*
   Stout *B*

Aquaculture

Alabama
Auburn University *B, M, D*
Gadsden State Community College *C*

Alaska
Sheldon Jackson College *B*

Idaho
College of Southern Idaho *C, A*

Maine
Unity College *B*
University of New England *B*

Mississippi
Mississippi Gulf Coast Community
   College
   Jefferson Davis Campus *C*

New Jersey
Cumberland County College *C, A*

New York
State University of New York
   College of Agriculture and
     Technology at Morrisville *A*

North Carolina
Brunswick Community College *C, A*

Texas
Texas A&M University *B*
Texas A&M University
   Galveston *B*

Washington
Grays Harbor College *C*

West Virginia
Bluefield State College *A*

Wyoming
Sheridan College *C*

Aquatic biology/ limnology

Arizona
Northern Arizona University *B*

California
University of California
   Santa Barbara *B*

Florida

Florida Institute of Technology *B*
Stetson University *B*

Kentucky

Murray State University *M*

New York

State University of New York
College at Brockport *B*

Rhode Island

Brown University *B*

Texas

Baylor University *M*
Texas A&M University
Galveston *B*
Texas State University: San
Marcos *B, M*

Wisconsin

Lawrence University *B*
University of Wisconsin
Superior *B*

Arabic

California

Grossmont Community College *A*
University of California
Los Angeles *B*

District of Columbia

Catholic University of America *M, D*
George Washington University *B*
Georgetown University *B, M, D*

Illinois

University of Chicago *B*

Indiana

University of Notre Dame *B*

Maine

University of Southern Maine *B*

Massachusetts

Brandeis University *B*
Simon's Rock College of Bard *B*

Michigan

University of Michigan *B, M*

Minnesota

North Central University *B*
University of Minnesota
Twin Cities *M*

Missouri

Washington University in St.
Louis *B, M*

New Hampshire

Dartmouth College *B*

New York

State University of New York
Binghamton *B*

Ohio

Ohio State University
Columbus Campus *B*

Texas

University of Texas
Austin *B, M, D*

Utah

Brigham Young University *M*

Vermont

Middlebury College *M, D*

Washington

University of Washington *B*

Archaeology

Arizona

Pima Community College *C*

California

California State University
East Bay *B*
Fresno City College *C*
Imperial Valley College *C*
Merced College *A*
Palomar College *C, A*
St. Mary's College of California *B*
Stanford University *B*
University of California
Los Angeles *M, D*
San Diego *B*
Santa Cruz *D*

Connecticut

Norwalk Community College *C*
Wesleyan University *B*
Yale University *B, M*

District of Columbia

George Washington University *B*

Florida

Gulf Coast Community College *A*

Illinois

Illinois State University *M*
Richland Community College *A*
Southwestern Illinois College *A*
Wheaton College *B*

Indiana

Indiana University
Bloomington *D*
University of Evansville *B*
University of Indianapolis *B*

Maine

Bowdoin College *B*

Massachusetts

Boston University *B, M, D*
Bridgewater State College *B*
Harvard College *B, D*
Tufts University *B*
Wellesley College *B*

Michigan

Michigan Technological
University *M, D*
University of Michigan *M, D*

Minnesota

University of Minnesota
Twin Cities *M, D*

Missouri

University of Missouri
Columbia *B, M, D*
Washington University in St.
Louis *B, M, D*

New Hampshire

Franklin Pierce College *B*

New Mexico

San Juan College *A*

New York

Bard College *B*
City University of New York
Hunter College *B*
Columbia University
Columbia College *B*
Cornell University *B, M, D*
Hamilton College *B*
State University of New York
College at Potsdam *B*

Ohio

College of Wooster *B*
University of Akron *C*
University of Cincinnati *M, D*

Pennsylvania

Bryn Mawr College *B, M, D*
Dickinson College *B*
Haverford College *B*
Lycoming College *B*
University of Pennsylvania *M, D*

Rhode Island

Brown University *B, M, D*

Tennessee

Southern Adventist University *B*

Texas

Baylor University *B*
Texas A&M University *D*
University of Texas
Austin *B*

Utah

Brigham Young University *B*
Weber State University *C, A*

Virginia

Washington and Lee University *B*

Washington

Western Washington University *B*

Wisconsin

University of Wisconsin
La Crosse *B*

Wyoming

Western Wyoming Community
College *A*

Architectural drafting/CAD/CADD

Arizona

Glendale Community College *A*

California

College of the Desert *C, A*
Long Beach City College *C, A*
Santa Rosa Junior College *C*
Shasta College *C, A*
Sierra College *C, A*
Silicon Valley College
Western Career College: San Jose *A*
Southwestern College *C*
Westwood College of Technology
Inland Empire *A*
Westwood College: Long Beach *A*

Colorado

IntelliTec College: Grand Junction *A*
Pikes Peak Community College *C*

Florida

Indian River Community College *A*
New England Institute of
Technology *A*
Palm Beach Community College *C*
St. Petersburg College *A*

Georgia

Albany Technical College *C*
Central Georgia Technical College *C*
Northwestern Technical College *C*
Southwest Georgia Technical
College *C*

Illinois

Kaskaskia College *C, A*
Lincoln Land Community College *C, A*
Moraine Valley Community College *C*
Westwood College of Technology
O'Hare *A*

Indiana

Vincennes University *A*

Iowa

Des Moines Area Community
College *C, A*
Hawkeye Community College *A*

Kentucky

Louisville Technical Institute *C, A*
Western Kentucky University *A*

Maryland

Hagerstown Community College *C*
Wor-Wic Community College *C*

Massachusetts

Springfield Technical Community
College *C*

Michigan

Baker College
of Muskegon *A*
Lawrence Technological University *B*
Northern Michigan University *A*
St. Clair County Community
College *C, A*

Minnesota

Dakota County Technical College *C, A*
Hennepin Technical College *C, A*
Minnesota State Community and
Technical College - Fergus Falls *A*
Northwest Technical Institute *A*
Rochester Community and Technical
College *C*
St. Cloud Technical College *C, A*
St. Paul College *A*

Missouri

Jefferson College *C, A*
Southeast Missouri State University *C*

Nebraska

Northeast Community College *A*

Nevada

Community College of Southern
Nevada *C*

New Jersey

Thomas Edison State College *A, B*

New Mexico

Albuquerque Technical-Vocational
Institute *C, A*

New York

Mohawk Valley Community College *C*

State University of New York
College of Agriculture and
Technology at Morrisville *A*

North Carolina
Gaston College *C*

North Dakota
North Dakota State College of
Science *A*

Ohio
Central Ohio Technical College *A*
Marion Technical College *C*
Owens Community College
Toledo *A*

Oklahoma
Platt College
Tulsa *C*

Pennsylvania
Butler County Community College *A*
Delaware County Community
College *C, A*
Luzerne County Community
College *C, A*
South Hills School of Business &
Technology *C*
Triangle Tech
DuBois *A*
Erie *A*
Greensburg *A*

Puerto Rico
Turabo University *A, B*
Universidad del Este *C*

South Carolina
Spartanburg Technical College *C*

Texas
Westwood College: Ft. Worth *A*

Utah
Salt Lake Community College *C, A*

Washington
North Seattle Community
College *C, A*

Architectural engineering

Alabama
Auburn University *B, M*

Alaska
University of Alaska
Anchorage *A*

California
East Los Angeles College *A*
San Joaquin Delta College *A*
University of Southern California *M*

Colorado
University of Colorado
Boulder *B*

Connecticut
Norwalk Community College *A*

District of Columbia
University of the District of
Columbia *A*

Florida
Miami Dade College *A*
University of Miami *B, M*

Hawaii
University of Hawaii
Honolulu Community College *A*

Illinois
City Colleges of Chicago
Olive-Harvey College *A*
Dominican University *B*
Illinois Institute of Technology *B*
University of Illinois
Urbana-Champaign *B*
Westwood College of Technology
O'Hare *A*

Kansas
Kansas State University *B, M*
University of Kansas *B, M*

Kentucky
Louisville Technical Institute *A*

Massachusetts
Tufts University *B*

Michigan
Delta College *A*

Mississippi
Holmes Community College *A*

Missouri
University of Missouri
Rolla *B*

Nebraska
University of Nebraska
Lincoln *B, M*
Omaha *B*

New York
State University of New York
College of Agriculture and
Technology at Morrisville *A*

North Carolina
North Carolina Agricultural and
Technical State University *B, M*

North Dakota
University of North Dakota *M*

Ohio
Stark State College of Technology *A*

Oklahoma
Oklahoma State University *B, M*
Oklahoma State University
Oklahoma City *A*
University of Oklahoma *B*

Pennsylvania
Drexel University *B*
Penn State
Abington *B*
Altoona *B*
Beaver *B*
Berks *B*
Delaware County *B*
Dubois *B*
Fayette *B*
Hazleton *B*
Lehigh Valley *B*
McKeesport *B*
Mont Alto *B*
New Kensington *B*
Schuylkill - Capital College *B*
Shenango *B*
University Park *B, M, D*
Wilkes-Barre *B*
Worthington Scranton *B*
York *B*

Rhode Island
New England Institute of
Technology *B*

Tennessee
Tennessee State University *B*

Texas
Laredo Community College *A*
University of Texas
Austin *B, M*

Vermont
Vermont Technical College *A*

Virginia
John Tyler Community College *A*

Wisconsin
Milwaukee School of Engineering *B*

Wyoming
University of Wyoming *B*

Architectural engineering technology

Alabama
Lawson State Community
College *C, A*

Alaska
University of Alaska
Anchorage *A*

Arizona
Mesa Community College *A*

California
Allan Hancock College *A*
Chabot College *A*
Chaffey College *C, A*
City College of San Francisco *A*
College of the Desert *C, A*
College of the Sequoias *A*
Contra Costa College *A*
Cuyamaca College *A*
Diablo Valley College *C*
East Los Angeles College *A*
El Camino College *C, A*
Fullerton College *C*
Golden West College *C, A*
Laney College *C, A*
Long Beach City College *C, A*
Los Angeles Harbor College *C, A*
Los Angeles Trade and Technical
College *C, A*
Modesto Junior College *C, A*
Mount San Antonio College *C, A*
Orange Coast College *C, A*
San Joaquin Delta College *C, A*
Santa Monica College *C, A*
Ventura College *A*

Colorado
Arapahoe Community College *C, A*
Front Range Community College *C, A*
Pikes Peak Community College *C, A*
Pueblo Community College *C, A*
Westwood College of Technology *A*

Connecticut
Capital Community College *A*
Norwalk Community College *A*
Three Rivers Community College *C, A*
University of Hartford *B*

Delaware
Delaware Technical and Community
College
Owens Campus *A*
Stanton/Wilmington Campus *A*
Terry Campus *A*

Florida
Daytona Beach Community College *A*
Florida Community College at
Jacksonville *A*
Gulf Coast Community College *A*
Hillsborough Community College *A*
Miami Dade College *A*
Seminole Community College *A*
Valencia Community College *C*

Georgia
Northwestern Technical College *C, A*

Hawaii
University of Hawaii
Hawaii Community College *C*

Idaho
Brigham Young University-Idaho *A*

Illinois
Joliet Junior College *C, A*
Morrison Institute of Technology *A*
Oakton Community College *A*
William Rainey Harper College *C, A*

Indiana
Indiana State University *A, B*
Indiana University-Purdue University
Fort Wayne *A*
Indiana University-Purdue University
Indianapolis *A*
Purdue University *A, B*
Purdue University
North Central Campus *A*

Iowa
Iowa Western Community College *A*
Western Iowa Tech Community
College *A*

Kentucky
Bluegrass Community and Technical
College *A*
Eastern Kentucky University *B*
Louisville Technical Institute *A*
Northern Kentucky University *A, B*

Louisiana
Delgado Community College *A*

Maryland
Montgomery College *A*

Massachusetts
Benjamin Franklin Institute of
Technology *A*
Fitchburg State College *B*
Massasoit Community College *A*
Wentworth Institute of
Technology *A, B*

Michigan
Baker College
of Auburn Hills *A*
of Flint *A*
of Muskegon *A*
of Owosso *A*
Ferris State University *A*
Monroe County Community
College *C, A*
Mott Community College *C, A*
Oakland Community College *A*
Wayne County Community College *A*

Minnesota
Anoka-Ramsey Community College *A*
Lake Superior College *C, A*
Northwest Technical Institute *A*

Mississippi
Mississippi Delta Community
College *A*
University of Southern Mississippi *B*

Missouri
Central Missouri State University *A, B*
St. Charles Community College *C, A*
St. Louis Community College
St. Louis Community College at
Meramec *A*
Washington University in St. Louis *B*

Nebraska
Southeast Community College
Lincoln Campus *A*

Nevada
Truckee Meadows Community
College *C, A*

New Hampshire
New Hampshire Technical Institute *A*

New Jersey
Essex County College *A*
Mercer County Community
College *C, A*

New Mexico
Eastern New Mexico University:
Roswell Campus *A*

New York
City University of New York
New York City College of
Technology *A, B*
Dutchess Community College *A*
Erie Community College
South Campus *A*
Finger Lakes Community College *A*
Institute of Design and
Construction *A*
New York Institute of
Technology *A, B*
Orange County Community College *A*
State University of New York
College of Agriculture and
Technology at Morrisville *A*
College of Technology at
Alfred *A, B*
College of Technology at Delhi *A*
Farmingdale *A, B*
Suffolk County Community College *A*

North Carolina
Cape Fear Community College *A*
Catawba Valley Community College *A*
Central Carolina Community
College *A*
Central Piedmont Community
College *C, A*
Coastal Carolina Community
College *A*
Durham Technical Community
College *C, A*
Fayetteville Technical Community
College *A*
Forsyth Technical Community
College *A*
Gaston College *C, A*
Guilford Technical Community
College *C, A*
Nash Community College *A*
Pitt Community College *A*
Sandhills Community College *A*

Wake Technical Community
College *C, A*
Wilkes Community College *C, A*

North Dakota
North Dakota State College of
Science *A*

Ohio
Cincinnati State Technical and
Community College *A*
Columbus State Community
College *C, A*
Cuyahoga Community College
Metropolitan Campus *A*
James A. Rhodes State College *C*
Lakeland Community College *C*
Marion Technical College *C*
Owens Community College
Toledo *C, A*
Sinclair Community College *A*
Stark State College of Technology *A*

Oklahoma
Oklahoma State University
Oklahoma City *A*

Oregon
Mount Hood Community College *C, A*

Pennsylvania
Community College of Philadelphia *A*
Delaware County Community
College *A*
Harrisburg Area Community
College *C, A*
Northampton County Area
Community College *A*
Penn State
Fayette *A*
Worthington Scranton *A*
Pennsylvania College of
Technology *A, B*
Pennsylvania Highlands Community
College *A*
Pennsylvania Institute of
Technology *A*

South Carolina
Greenville Technical College *C, A*
Midlands Technical College *C, A*
Trident Technical College *C, A*

South Dakota
Southeast Technical Institute *A*

Tennessee
Middle Tennessee State University *B*
Nashville State Community College *A*
Southwest Tennessee Community
College *A*

Texas
Del Mar College *A*
San Antonio College *C, A*
Tarrant County College *C, A*
Texas Tech University *B*
University of Houston *B*

Vermont
Vermont Technical College *A, B*

Virginia
Central Virginia Community
College *A*
J. Sargeant Reynolds Community
College *C, A*
John Tyler Community College *C, A*
New River Community College *A*
Norfolk State University *A*
Northern Virginia Community
College *A*

Virginia Western Community
College *C, A*

Washington
Clover Park Technical College *A*
Lake Washington Technical
College *C, A*
Spokane Community College *A*
Spokane Falls Community
College *C, A*

West Virginia
Bluefield State College *A, B*

Wisconsin
Madison Area Technical College *A*
Milwaukee Area Technical College *A*
Northeast Wisconsin Technical
College *A*
Waukesha County Technical
College *A*
Wisconsin Indianhead Technical
College *A*

Architectural history/ criticism

Georgia
Savannah College of Art and
Design *B, M*

Illinois
University of Illinois
Urbana-Champaign *D*

Kansas
University of Kansas *B*

New York
Barnard College *B*
Cornell University *B, M, D*

Ohio
Kent State University *C*

Pennsylvania
Carnegie Mellon University *B, M*

Rhode Island
Brown University *B, M, D*
Roger Williams University *B*

Texas
University of Texas
Austin *M*

Virginia
University of Virginia *B, M, D*

Architectural technology

California
College of the Desert *C, A*
Diablo Valley College *C*
Southwestern College *C, A*

Colorado
Arapahoe Community College *C, A*
Westwood College of Technology
South *A*

Georgia
Northwestern Technical College *C, A*

Illinois
Rend Lake College *C, A*
University of Illinois
Urbana-Champaign *D*

Maine
University of Maine
Augusta *A, B*

Massachusetts
Benjamin Franklin Institute of
Technology *C, A*
Roxbury Community College *A*

Michigan
Delta College *C, A*
Grand Rapids Community College *A*
Washtenaw Community College *C, A*

Minnesota
Dunwoody College of Technology *A*
Lake Superior College *C, A*
Northland Community & Technical
College *C, A*
Northwest Technical Institute *A*

Missouri
Washington University in St. Louis *B*

New Hampshire
Keene State College *B*

New Jersey
Mercer County Community
College *C, A*

New York
New York Institute of Technology *B*
State University of New York
College of Agriculture and
Technology at Morrisville *A*
College of Technology at Delhi *A*

North Carolina
Catawba Valley Community College *A*
College of the Albemarle *C, A*
Gaston College *C, A*
Nash Community College *A*
Roanoke-Chowan Community
College *A*
Sandhills Community College *A*

North Dakota
North Dakota State College of
Science *A*

Ohio
Marion Technical College *C*
Sinclair Community College *A*

Oklahoma
Oklahoma State University
Oklahoma City *A*

Pennsylvania
Carnegie Mellon University *B, M*

South Dakota
Mitchell Technical Institute *A*

Tennessee
Southern Adventist University *A*

Texas
Abilene Christian University *A*
North Harris Montgomery
Community College District *C, A*
South Texas College *C, A*

West Virginia
Bluefield State College *A*

Wisconsin
Western Wisconsin Technical
College *A*

Architecture

Alabama
Auburn University *B*
Tuskegee University *B*

Arizona
Arizona State University *B, M, D*
University of Arizona *B, M*

Arkansas
University of Arkansas *B*

California
Academy of Art University *M*
California College of the Arts *B, M*
California Polytechnic State
University: San Luis Obispo *B, M*
California State Polytechnic
University: Pomona *B, M*
NewSchool of Architecture &
Design *B, M*
Southern California Institute of
Architecture *B, M*
University of California
Berkeley *B, M, D*
Los Angeles *M, D*
University of Southern
California *B, M*
Woodbury University *B, M*

Colorado
University of Colorado
Denver and Health Sciences
Center *M*

Connecticut
Connecticut College *B*
University of Hartford *M*
Yale University *B, M*

District of Columbia
Catholic University of America *B, M*
Howard University *B*
University of the District of
Columbia *B*

Florida
Florida Agricultural and Mechanical
University *B, M*
Florida Atlantic University *B*
Florida International University *B, M*
University of Florida *B, D*
University of Miami *B, M*
University of South Florida *M*

Georgia
Georgia Institute of
Technology *B, M, D*
Savannah College of Art and
Design *B, M*
Southern Polytechnic State
University *B*

Hawaii
University of Hawaii
Manoa *D*

Idaho
University of Idaho *B, M*

Illinois
Illinois Institute of
Technology *B, M, D*
Judson College *B, M*
Southern Illinois University
Carbondale *B*
University of Illinois
Chicago *M*
Urbana-Champaign *B, M, D*

Indiana
Ball State University *B, M*
University of Notre Dame *B, M*

Iowa
Iowa State University *B, M*

Kansas
Kansas State University *B, M*
University of Kansas *B, M*

Kentucky
University of Kentucky *B*

Louisiana
Louisiana State University and
Agricultural and Mechanical
College *B, M*
Louisiana Tech University *B*
Southern University and Agricultural
and Mechanical College *B*
Tulane University *B, M*
University of Louisiana at
Lafayette *B, M*

Maryland
Morgan State University *M*
University of Maryland
College Park *B, M*
Eastern Shore *B*

Massachusetts
Boston Architectural Center *B, M*
Harvard College *M, D*
Massachusetts Institute of
Technology *B, M, D*
Mount Holyoke College *B*
Northeastern University *B, M*
University of Massachusetts
Amherst *M*
Wellesley College *B*
Wentworth Institute of Technology *B*

Michigan
Andrews University *B, M*
Lawrence Technological
University *B, M*
University of Detroit Mercy *B, M*
University of Michigan *B, M, D*

Minnesota
University of Minnesota
Twin Cities *B, M*

Mississippi
Mississippi State University *B, M*

Missouri
Drury University *B*
Washington University in St.
Louis *B, M*

Montana
Montana State University
Bozeman *M*

Nebraska
University of Nebraska
Lincoln *B, M*

Nevada
University of Nevada
Las Vegas *B, M*

New Jersey
New Jersey Institute of
Technology *B, M*
Princeton University *B, M, D*

New Mexico
University of New Mexico *B, M*

New York
Barnard College *B*
City University of New York
City College *B*
Columbia University
Columbia College *B*
School of General Studies *B*
Cooper Union for the Advancement of
Science and Art *B*
Cornell University *B, M, D*
Hobart and William Smith Colleges *B*
New York Institute of
Technology *B, M*
Parsons The New School for
Design *B, M*
Pratt Institute *B, M*
Rensselaer Polytechnic
Institute *B, M, D*
State University of New York
Buffalo *B, M*
College of Technology at Alfred *B*
College of Technology at Delhi *B*
Syracuse University *B, M*

North Carolina
North Carolina State University *B, M*
University of North Carolina
Charlotte *B, M*

North Dakota
North Dakota State University *B*

Ohio
Kent State University *B, M*
Miami University
Oxford Campus *M*
Ohio State University
Columbus Campus *B, M*
University of Cincinnati *B, M*

Oklahoma
Oklahoma State University *B, M*
University of Oklahoma *B, M*

Oregon
Portland State University *B*
University of Oregon *B, M*

Pennsylvania
Carnegie Mellon University *B, M*
Drexel University *B, M*
Lehigh University *B*
Penn State
University Park *B, M*
Philadelphia University *B*
Temple University *B*
University of Pennsylvania *B, M, D*

Puerto Rico
Inter American University of Puerto
Rico
San German Campus *B*
Universidad Politecnica de Puerto
Rico *B*
University of Puerto Rico
Rio Piedras *M*

Rhode Island
Rhode Island School of Design *B, M*
Roger Williams University *B, M*

South Carolina
Clemson University *B, M*

Tennessee
Tennessee State University *B*
University of Memphis *B*

University of Tennessee
Knoxville *B, M*

Texas
Baylor University *B*
Prairie View A&M University *B, M*
Rice University *B, M, D*
Texas A&M University *M, D*
Texas Tech University *B, M*
University of Houston *B, M*
University of Texas
Arlington *B, M*
Austin *B, M*
San Antonio *B, M*

Utah
University of Utah *B, M*

Vermont
Bennington College *B*
Norwich University *M*

Virginia
Hampton University *B*
University of Virginia *B, M*
Virginia Polytechnic Institute and
State University *B, M*

Washington
University of Washington *B, M*
Washington State University *B, M*

Wisconsin
University of Wisconsin
Milwaukee *B, M, D*

Art

Alabama
Alabama Agricultural and Mechanical
University *B*
Alabama State University *B*
Athens State University *B*
Auburn University at Montgomery *B*
Birmingham-Southern College *B, T*
Faulkner State Community College *A*
Gadsden State Community College *A*
Huntingdon College *B, T*
Jacksonville State University *B*
Judson College *B*
Northeast Alabama Community
College *A*
Samford University *B*
Stillman College *B*
Troy University *B*
University of Alabama
Birmingham *B*
Huntsville *B*
University of Mobile *B, T*
University of Montevallo *B, T*
University of South Alabama *B*
Wallace State Community College at
Hanceville *A*

Alaska
University of Alaska
Anchorage *B*
Fairbanks *B, M*
Southeast *C, B*

Arizona
Arizona State University *B, M*
Central Arizona College *A*
Eastern Arizona College *A*
Grand Canyon University *B*
Northern Arizona University *B*
Phoenix College *A*
Pima Community College *A*
South Mountain Community
College *A*
University of Arizona *M*

Arkansas

Arkansas State University *B, M*
Arkansas Tech University *B*
Black River Technical College *A*
Harding University *B*
Henderson State University *B*
Hendrix College *B*
Lyon College *B*
Southern Arkansas University *B*
University of Arkansas *B, M*
University of Arkansas
    Little Rock *B, M*
    Monticello *B*
    Pine Bluff *B*
University of Central Arkansas *B*
University of the Ozarks *B*

California

Allan Hancock College *A*
Azusa Pacific University *B*
Cabrillo College *A*
California Baptist University *B*
California College of the Arts *B*
California Institute of the Arts *C, B, M*
California Lutheran University *B*
California State Polytechnic
    University: Pomona *B*
California State University
    Bakersfield *B*
    Chico *B, M*
    East Bay *B*
    Fresno *B, M*
    Fullerton *B, M*
    Long Beach *B, M*
    Los Angeles *B, M*
    Monterey Bay *B*
    Northridge *B, M*
    Sacramento *B, M*
    San Bernardino *B, M*
    Stanislaus *B*
Canada College *A*
Cerritos Community College *A*
Cerro Coso Community College *A*
Chabot College *A*
Chaffey College *A*
Chapman University *B*
Citrus College *A*
Claremont McKenna College *B*
College of the Desert *A*
College of the Sequoias *A*
Columbia College *A*
Concordia University *B*
Copper Mountain College *A*
Cosumnes River College *A*
Crafton Hills College *A*
Cypress College *A*
De Anza College *A*
Dominican University of California *B*
East Los Angeles College *A*
El Camino College *A*
Feather River College *A*
Foothill College *C, A*
Fresno City College *A*
Fresno Pacific University *B*
Fullerton College *A*
Gavilan Community College *A*
Golden West College *A*
Humboldt State University *B*
Imperial Valley College *A*
Irvine Valley College *A*
La Sierra University *B*
Lake Tahoe Community College *C, A*
Laney College *A*
Lassen College *A*
Long Beach City College *A*
Los Angeles City College *A*
Los Angeles Harbor College *A*
Los Angeles Mission College *A*
Los Angeles Southwest College *A*
Los Angeles Valley College *A*
Loyola Marymount University *B*
Mendocino College *C, A*
Mills College *B*
MiraCosta College *A*

Mission College *C, A*
Modesto Junior College *A*
Monterey Peninsula College *C, A*
Mount San Jacinto College *A*
Notre Dame de Namur University *B*
Occidental College *B*
Orange Coast College *A*
Palomar College *C, A*
Pepperdine University *B*
Pitzer College *B*
Platt College
    Cerritos *C, A*
Point Loma Nazarene University *B*
Pomona College *B*
Reedley College *A*
Saddleback College *A*
St. Mary's College of California *B*
San Diego Mesa College *C, A*
San Diego Miramar College *A*
San Diego State University *B, M*
San Francisco Art Institute *B, M*
San Francisco State University *B*
San Jose City College *C*
San Jose State University *B, M*
Santa Barbara City College *A*
Santa Rosa Junior College *C, A*
Scripps College *B*
Shasta College *A*
Sierra College *C, A*
Skyline College *A*
Southwestern College *A*
Stanford University *B, M, D*
Taft College *C, A*
University of California
    Berkeley *B, M*
    Davis *M*
    Irvine *B*
    Los Angeles *B, M*
    Riverside *B*
    Santa Barbara *B*
    Santa Cruz *B*
University of La Verne *B*
University of Redlands *B*
University of San Francisco *B*
University of Southern California *B*
University of the Pacific *B*
Victor Valley College *A*
Vista Community College *A*
West Hills Community College *A*
West Los Angeles College *C, A*
West Valley College *A*
Westmont College *B*
Whittier College *B*
Yuba Community College District *A*

Colorado

Adams State College *B, M*
Colorado Mountain College
    Alpine Campus *A*
    Spring Valley Campus *A*
    Timberline Campus *A*
Fort Lewis College *B*
Mesa State College *B*
Metropolitan State College of
    Denver *B*
Morgan Community College *A*
Red Rocks Community College *A*
University of Denver *B*
Western State College of Colorado *B*

Connecticut

Albertus Magnus College *B*
Central Connecticut State
    University *B*
Naugatuck Valley Community
    College *C, A*
Norwalk Community College *A*
Sacred Heart University *B*
Southern Connecticut State
    University *B, M*
Trinity College *B*
University of Hartford *M*
Western Connecticut State
    University *B*

Yale University *B*

Delaware

Delaware State University *B*
University of Delaware *B*

District of Columbia

American University *B*
Catholic University of America *B, M, T*
Corcoran College of Art and Design *B*
Georgetown University *B*
Howard University *B, M*

Florida

Barry University *B*
Broward Community College *A*
Florida Atlantic University *B*
Florida Southern College *B*
Gulf Coast Community College *A*
Hillsborough Community College *A*
Indian River Community College *A*
Jacksonville University *B*
Manatee Community College *A*
New College of Florida *B*
Okaloosa-Walton College *A*
Pensacola Junior College *A*
Rollins College *B*
Stetson University *B*
University of Central Florida *B*
University of Miami *B, M*
University of North Florida *B*
University of South Florida *B*
University of Tampa *B*
University of West Florida *B*
Valencia Community College *A*

Georgia

Agnes Scott College *B*
Armstrong Atlantic State University *B*
Atlanta Metropolitan College *A*
Berry College *B*
Clark Atlanta University *B*
Coastal Georgia Community
    College *A*
Columbus State University *B*
Covenant College *B*
Darton College *A*
East Georgia College *A*
Georgia College and State
    University *B*
Georgia Perimeter College *A*
Georgia Southern University *B*
Georgia Southwestern State
    University *B, T*
Georgia State University *B, M*
Gordon College *A*
Kennesaw State University *B*
Macon State College *A*
Mercer University *B*
Middle Georgia College *A*
Oglethorpe University *B*
Piedmont College *B, T*
Reinhardt College *A*
University of Georgia *B, M, D*
University of West Georgia *B*
Valdosta State University *B*
Young Harris College *A*

Hawaii

Brigham Young University-Hawaii *B*
University of Hawaii
    Hilo *B*
    Manoa *B, M*

Idaho

Albertson College of Idaho *B*
Boise State University *B, M*
Brigham Young University-Idaho *B*
College of Southern Idaho *A*
Idaho State University *A, B, M, T*
University of Idaho *B*

Illinois

Augustana College *B*
Black Hawk College
    East Campus *A*
Blackburn College *B, T*
Bradley University *B, M*
Chicago State University *B*
City Colleges of Chicago
    Harold Washington College *A*
College of DuPage *A*
College of Lake County *A*
Columbia College Chicago *B*
Concordia University *B, T*
Dominican University *B*
Eastern Illinois University *B, M, T*
Elgin Community College *A*
Elmhurst College *B, T*
Eureka College *B*
Governors State University *B, M*
Greenville College *B*
Highland Community College *A*
Illinois College *B*
Illinois Institute of Art-Schaumburg *B*
Illinois State University *B, M, T*
Illinois Valley Community College *A*
Illinois Wesleyan University *B*
John A. Logan College *A*
John Wood Community College *A*
Joliet Junior College *A*
Judson College *B*
Kankakee Community College *A*
Kishwaukee College *A*
Lake Forest College *B*
Lewis University *B, T*
MacMurray College *B*
McHenry County College *A*
Monmouth College *B, T*
North Central College *B*
North Park University *B*
Northeastern Illinois University *B*
Northern Illinois University *B, M*
Northwestern University *B, M*
Olivet Nazarene University *B, T*
Parkland College *A*
Quincy University *B*
Rend Lake College *A*
Richland Community College *A*
Rockford College *B*
Sauk Valley Community College *A*
South Suburban College of Cook
    County *C*
Southern Illinois University
    Carbondale *B*
Southern Illinois University
    Edwardsville *B, T*
Southwestern Illinois College *A*
Spoon River College *A*
Springfield College in Illinois *A*
Trinity Christian College *B*
Triton College *A*
Western Illinois University *B*
Wheaton College *B*
William Rainey Harper College *A*

Indiana

Ball State University *B, M*
Bethel College *B*
Earlham College *B*
Goshen College *B*
Huntington University *B*
Indiana State University *B, M*
Indiana University
    Northwest *B*
    South Bend *B*
    Southeast *B*
Indiana University-Purdue University
    Indianapolis *B*
Manchester College *A, B, T*
Marian College *A, B, T*
Oakland City University *B*
Purdue University *B, M*
Saint Mary's College *B*
St. Mary-of-the-Woods College *B*
Taylor University *B*

University of Evansville *B*
University of Indianapolis *B, M*
University of St. Francis *B*
University of Southern Indiana *B, T*
Valparaiso University *B*
Vincennes University *A*
Wabash College *B*

Iowa

Briar Cliff University *B*
Buena Vista University *B, T*
Central College *B, T*
Clarke College *A, B, T*
Coe College *B*
Cornell College *B, T*
Dordt College *B*
Drake University *B*
Ellsworth Community College *A*
Grinnell College *B*
Iowa State University *B*
Luther College *B*
Maharishi University of
    Management *B*
Mount Mercy College *B*
Northwestern College *B, T*
Simpson College *B*
University of Iowa *B, M, T*
University of Northern Iowa *B, M*
Upper Iowa University *B*
Wartburg College *B, T*

Kansas

Allen County Community College *A*
Barton County Community College *A*
Bethany College *B, T*
Butler County Community College *A*
Central Christian College of Kansas *A*
Coffeyville Community College *A*
Cowley County Community
    College *A*
Dodge City Community College *A*
Emporia State University *B, T*
Fort Hays State University *B*
Friends University *B*
Garden City Community College *A*
McPherson College *B, T*
Neosho County Community
    College *A*
Newman University *B*
Ottawa University *B, T*
Pittsburg State University *B, M*
Seward County Community College *A*
Sterling College *B, T*
University of St. Mary *B*
Washburn University of Topeka *B*
Wichita State University *B, M, T*

Kentucky

Bellarmine University *B, T*
Berea College *B, T*
Brescia University *B*
Campbellsville University *B*
Centre College *B*
Eastern Kentucky University *B*
Kentucky Wesleyan College *B, T*
Pikeville College *B*
University of Louisville *M*

Louisiana

Centenary College of Louisiana *B, T*
Delgado Community College *A*
Dillard University *B*
Grambling State University *B*
Louisiana State University
    Shreveport *B*
Louisiana Tech University *B, M*
Loyola University New Orleans *B*
Nicholls State University *B*
Northwestern State University *M*
Southeastern Louisiana University *B*
Tulane University *B, M*
University of Louisiana at Lafayette *B*
Xavier University of Louisiana *B*

Maine

Bates College *B*
Colby College *B*
Maine College of Art *B*
University of Maine
    Farmington *B*
    Presque Isle *B*
University of Southern Maine *B*

Maryland

Allegany College of Maryland *A*
Baltimore City Community College *A*
College of Notre Dame of Maryland *B*
Coppin State University *B*
Frederick Community College *A*
Goucher College *B*
Hood College *B*
Howard Community College *A*
Loyola College in Maryland *B*
McDaniel College *B*
St. Mary's College of Maryland *B*
Towson University *B*
Washington College *B*

Massachusetts

Anna Maria College *B*
Brandeis University *B*
Bristol Community College *A*
Bunker Hill Community College *A*
Clark University *B*
Framingham State College *B*
Gordon College *B*
Hampshire College *B*
Harvard College *B, D*
Holyoke Community College *A*
Lesley University *B, M*
Massachusetts Bay Community
    College *C*
Montserrat College of Art *B*
Mount Holyoke College *B*
Mount Ida College *A, B*
Mount Wachusett Community
    College *A*
Northeastern University *B*
Regis College *B*
Salem State College *B*
School of the Museum of Fine
    Arts *B, M, T*
Simon's Rock College of Bard *B*
Smith College *B, M*
Springfield College *B*
Suffolk University *C, B*
University of Massachusetts
    Boston *B*
Westfield State College *B*

Michigan

Adrian College *A, B, T*
Albion College *B*
Alma College *B, T*
Andrews University *B*
Aquinas College *B*
Calvin College *B, T*
Central Michigan University *B, M, T*
Concordia University *B*
Delta College *A*
Eastern Michigan University *B*
Finlandia University *B*
Gogebic Community College *A*
Grand Valley State University *B*
Henry Ford Community College *A*
Hillsdale College *B*
Kalamazoo College *B, T*
Kellogg Community College *C, A*
Lake Michigan College *A*
Lansing Community College *A*
Madonna University *C, A, B*
Marygrove College *B, T*
Michigan State University *B, M*
Northern Michigan University *B, T*
Northwestern Michigan College *A*
Oakland Community College *A*
Olivet College *B, T*

Saginaw Valley State University *B, T*
Siena Heights University *A, B*
Spring Arbor University *B, T*
University of Michigan *M*
Wayne State University *B, M*
Western Michigan University *B, M*

Minnesota

Bemidji State University *B*
Bethel University *B*
College of St. Benedict *B*
Concordia College: Moorhead *B*
Concordia University: St. Paul *B*
Gustavus Adolphus College *B*
Minneapolis College of Art and
    Design *M*
Minnesota State University
    Mankato *B, M, T*
    Moorhead *B*
Normandale Community College *A*
Northland Community & Technical
    College *A*
Ridgewater College *A*
St. Cloud State University *B, M*
St. John's University *B*
St. Olaf College *B*
Southwest Minnesota State
    University *B, T*
University of Minnesota
    Duluth *B, M*
    Twin Cities *M, D*
Winona State University *B*

Mississippi

Belhaven College *B*
Hinds Community College *A*
Itawamba Community College *A*
Millsaps College *B, T*
Mississippi College *B, M, T*
Mississippi Gulf Coast Community
    College
    Jefferson Davis Campus *A*
Tougaloo College *B*
William Carey College *B*

Missouri

Central Missouri State University *B, M*
College of the Ozarks *B*
Columbia College *B*
Crowder College *A*
Culver-Stockton College *B, T*
Drury University *B, T*
Fontbonne University *B, M, T*
Hannibal-LaGrange College *A, B*
Lindenwood University *B, M*
Missouri State University *B*
Missouri Valley College *B*
Missouri Western State University *B*
Northwest Missouri State
    University *B*
Southeast Missouri State University *B*
Southwest Baptist University *B*
Truman State University *B*
University of Missouri
    Columbia *B, M*
    Kansas City *B, M*
Washington University in St. Louis *B*
Webster University *B, M*
William Jewell College *B*
William Woods University *B, T*

Montana

Carroll College *A*
Miles Community College *A*
Montana State University
    Billings *A*
    Bozeman *B*
Rocky Mountain College *B*
University of Great Falls *B*
University of Montana: Missoula *B, M*
University of Montana: Western *B, T*

Nebraska

Bellevue University *B*
Chadron State College *B*
Creighton University *B*
Dana College *B*
Doane College *B*
Hastings College *B, T*
Midland Lutheran College *B, T*
Nebraska Wesleyan University *B*
Northeast Community College *A*
Peru State College *B*
Union College *A*
University of Nebraska
    Kearney *B, M, T*
    Omaha *B*
Wayne State College *B, T*
Western Nebraska Community
    College *A*

Nevada

Community College of Southern
    Nevada *A*
Great Basin College *A*
University of Nevada
    Las Vegas *B, M*
    Reno *B*

New Hampshire

Chester College of New England *B*
Colby-Sawyer College *B*
Franklin Pierce College *B*
Keene State College *B*
McIntosh College *A*
New England College *B*
Plymouth State University *B*
St. Anselm College *B*

New Jersey

Brookdale Community College *A*
Caldwell College *B*
The College of New Jersey *B*
College of St. Elizabeth *B, T*
Cumberland County College *A*
Drew University *B*
Essex County College *A*
Felician College *B*
Georgian Court University *B*
Gloucester County College *A*
Kean University *B, T*
Monmouth University *B*
Montclair State University *B, M, T*
New Jersey City University *B, T*
Ocean County College *A*
Rowan University *B, T*
Rutgers, The State University of New
    Jersey
    Camden Regional Campus *B, T*
    New Brunswick/Piscataway
        Campus *B, T*
    Newark Regional Campus *B, T*
Sussex County Community College *A*
Thomas Edison State College *B*
William Paterson University of New
    Jersey *B*

New Mexico

Eastern New Mexico University *A, B*
New Mexico State University
    Alamogordo *A*
    Grants *A*
Northern New Mexico College *A*
San Juan College *A*
Santa Fe Community College *A*
Southwestern Indian Polytechnic
    Institute *C*
University of New Mexico *B, M*

New York

Adirondack Community College *A*
Alfred University *B*
Bard College *B, M, D*
Cayuga County Community College *A*

City University of New York
  Brooklyn College *B*
  City College *B*
  Lehman College *B, M*
  Queensborough Community
    College *A*
Colgate University *B*
Cornell University *B, M, D*
Daemen College *B*
Dowling College *B, T*
Elmira College *B*
Fashion Institute of Technology *A*
Fordham University *B*
Fulton-Montgomery Community
  College *A*
Genesee Community College *A*
Hartwick College *B, T*
Herkimer County Community
  College *A*
Houghton College *B*
Ithaca College *B*
Marist College *B*
Marymount Manhattan College *B*
Mohawk Valley Community College *A*
Molloy College *B*
Nazareth College of Rochester *B, T*
Onondaga Community College *A*
Pace University *B*
Parsons The New School for
  Design *C, A, B, T*
Pratt Institute *B, M*
St. Thomas Aquinas College *B, T*
Sarah Lawrence College *B*
School of Visual Arts *B, M*
State University of New York
  Binghamton *B*
  Buffalo *B*
  College at Brockport *B, M*
  College at Fredonia *B*
  College at Old Westbury *B*
  College at Plattsburgh *B*
  College at Potsdam *B*
  New Paltz *B*
  Oswego *B*
Vassar College *B*
Wells College *B*

North Carolina

Appalachian State University *B*
Brevard College *B*
Caldwell Community College and
  Technical Institute *A*
College of the Albemarle *A*
Davidson College *B*
East Carolina University *B, M*
Elon University *B*
Gardner-Webb University *B*
Guilford College *B*
High Point University *B*
Louisburg College *A*
Mars Hill College *B, T*
Meredith College *B*
Methodist College *B*
North Carolina Agricultural and
  Technical State University *B, T*
North Carolina Central University *B*
St. Andrews Presbyterian College *B*
St. Augustine's College *B*
Sandhills Community College *A*
Southeastern Community College *A*
University of North Carolina
  Asheville *B, T*
  Charlotte *B*
  Greensboro *B*
Warren Wilson College *B*
Western Carolina University *B*
Wingate University *B*
Winston-Salem State University *B*

North Dakota

Dickinson State University *B, T*
Minot State University *B*
North Dakota State University *B*
University of North Dakota *B, M*

Valley City State University *B*

Ohio

Ashland University *A*
Baldwin-Wallace College *B*
Bluffton University *B*
Bowling Green State University *B, M*
Capital University *B*
Central State University *B*
Cleveland State University *B, T*
College of Mount St. Joseph *A, B*
Defiance College *A, B, T*
Edison State Community College *A*
Hocking College *A*
Kenyon College *B*
Lourdes College *A, B*
Miami University
  Oxford Campus *B, M, T*
Mount Union College *B*
Mount Vernon Nazarene University *B*
Muskingum College *B*
Ohio Dominican University *B, T*
Ohio Northern University *B*
Ohio State University
  Columbus Campus *B, M*
Ohio University *B, M*
Otterbein College *B*
Shawnee State University *A*
University of Akron *B*
University of Findlay *B*
University of Rio Grande *A, B, T*
University of Toledo *B*
Wilmington College *B*
Wittenberg University *B*
Wright State University *B*
Youngstown State University *B*

Oklahoma

Bacone College *A*
Cameron University *B*
Carl Albert State College *A*
Connors State College *A*
East Central University *B, T*
Northeastern Oklahoma Agricultural
  and Mechanical College *A*
Northeastern State University *B*
Oklahoma Baptist University *B, T*
Oklahoma Christian University *B*
Oklahoma City University *B*
Oklahoma Panhandle State
  University *A*
Oklahoma State University *B*
Oral Roberts University *B*
Redlands Community College *A*
Rose State College *A*
Seminole State College *A*
Southeastern Oklahoma State
  University *B*
University of Central Oklahoma *B*
University of Science and Arts of
  Oklahoma *B, T*
University of Tulsa *B, M*
Western Oklahoma State College *A*

Oregon

Chemeketa Community College *A*
George Fox University *B*
Lewis & Clark College *B*
Linfield College *B, T*
Linn-Benton Community College *A*
Marylhurst University *C, B*
Oregon State University *B*
Pacific University *B*
Portland State University *B*
Southern Oregon University *B, T*
Treasure Valley Community College *A*
University of Oregon *B, M*
Western Oregon University *B*

Pennsylvania

Allegheny College *B*
Bucknell University *B*

California University of
  Pennsylvania *B*
Carlow University *B*
Carnegie Mellon University *B, M*
Cedar Crest College *B*
Cheyney University of Pennsylvania *B*
Clarion University of Pennsylvania *B*
Community College of Allegheny
  County *A*
Community College of Philadelphia *A*
Edinboro University of
  Pennsylvania *M*
Elizabethtown College *B*
Gettysburg College *B*
Harrisburg Area Community
  College *B*
Holy Family University *B*
Immaculata University *C*
Indiana University of Pennsylvania *B*
Keystone College *A, B*
Kutztown University of
  Pennsylvania *B, M, T*
Lehigh Carbon Community
  College *C, A*
Lehigh University *B*
Lock Haven University of
  Pennsylvania *B*
Lycoming College *B*
Mansfield University of
  Pennsylvania *B, T*
Marywood University *C*
Millersville University of
  Pennsylvania *B, M, T*
Montgomery County Community
  College *A*
Moravian College *B, T*
Muhlenberg College *C, B*
Penn State
  Abington *B*
  Altoona *B*
  Beaver *B*
  Berks *B*
  Delaware County *B*
  Dubois *B*
  Fayette *B*
  Hazleton *B*
  Lehigh Valley *B*
  McKeesport *B*
  Mont Alto *B*
  New Kensington *B*
  Shenango *B*
  University Park *B, M*
  Wilkes-Barre *B*
  Worthington Scranton *B*
  York *B*
Shippensburg University of
  Pennsylvania *B, T*
Slippery Rock University of
  Pennsylvania *B*
Susquehanna University *B*
Temple University *B*
Thiel College *B*
Ursinus College *B*
Washington and Jefferson College *B*
Waynesburg College *B*
Westminster College *B*
Wilson College *B*

Puerto Rico

University of Puerto Rico
  Rio Piedras *B*

Rhode Island

Community College of Rhode
  Island *A*
Providence College *B*

South Carolina

Anderson University *B*
Benedict College *B*
Claflin University *B*
Coker College *B*
Columbia College *B*
Erskine College *B*

Francis Marion University *B*
Furman University *B, T*
Lander University *B*
Newberry College *B*
North Greenville College *A*
Presbyterian College *B*
University of South Carolina
  Lancaster *A*
Winthrop University *B*

South Dakota

Augustana College *B*
Black Hills State University *B*
Dakota Wesleyan University *B*
Northern State University *B*
Oglala Lakota College *A*
University of Sioux Falls *B*
University of South Dakota *B, M*

Tennessee

Austin Peay State University *B*
Belmont University *B, T*
Carson-Newman College *B, T*
Columbia State Community College *A*
East Tennessee State
  University *B, M, T*
Fisk University *B*
Freed-Hardeman University *B, T*
Jackson State Community College *A*
Lambuth University *B*
LeMoyne-Owen College *B*
Lincoln Memorial University *B, T*
Maryville College *B*
Memphis College of Art *B, M*
Middle Tennessee State University *B*
Rhodes College *B*
Roane State Community College *A*
Southern Adventist University *B*
Tennessee Technological University *T*
Union University *B, T*
University of Memphis *B, M*
University of Tennessee
  Chattanooga *B, T*
  Knoxville *B, M*
Walters State Community College *A*

Texas

Abilene Christian University *B*
Alvin Community College *A*
Amarillo College *A*
Angelina College *A*
Angelo State University *B, T*
Austin College *B*
Austin Community College *A*
Brazosport College *A*
Central Texas College *A*
Cisco Junior College *A*
Clarendon College *A*
Dallas Baptist University *B*
Del Mar College *A*
El Paso Community College *A*
Galveston College *A*
Grayson County College *A*
Hill College *A*
Howard College *A*
Howard Payne University *B, T*
Kilgore College *A*
Lamar University *B*
Laredo Community College *A*
Lon Morris College *A*
Lubbock Christian University *T*
McMurry University *B, T*
Midland College *A*
Midwestern State University *B*
Navarro College *C, A*
Northeast Texas Community
  College *A*
Odessa College *A*
Our Lady of the Lake University of San
  Antonio *B*
Palo Alto College *A*
Rice University *B*
St. Edward's University *B*
St. Philip's College *A*

Sam Houston State University *B, M*
San Jacinto College
   North *A*
Southern Methodist University *B*
Southwestern University *B, T*
Stephen F. Austin State
   University *B, M, T*
Sul Ross State University *B, M*
Temple College *A*
Texarkana College *A*
Texas A&M University
   Commerce *B, M*
Texas Lutheran University *B*
Texas Southern University *B, M*
Texas State University: San
   Marcos *B, T*
Texas Tech University *B, M, D*
Texas Wesleyan University *B*
Texas Woman's University *B, M*
Trinity University *B*
Trinity Valley Community College *A*
Tyler Junior College *A*
University of Houston *B*
University of Houston
   Clear Lake *B*
University of Texas
   Arlington *B*
   Austin *B*
   Brownsville *B*
   El Paso *B*
   San Antonio *B, M*
   Tyler *B*
   of the Permian Basin *B*
University of the Incarnate Word *B*
Wayland Baptist University *B, T*
West Texas A&M University *B, M*
Western Texas College *A*
Wharton County Junior College *A*

Utah

Brigham Young University *B, M*
Dixie State College of Utah *A*
Snow College *A*
Southern Utah University *B, T*
University of Utah *B, M*
Utah State University *B, M*
Weber State University *B*
Westminster College *B*

Vermont

Castleton State College *B*
Green Mountain College *B*
Johnson State College *B*
Marlboro College *B*
St. Michael's College *B*

Virginia

Averett University *B*
Bluefield College *B*
College of William and Mary *B*
Eastern Mennonite University *B*
Emory & Henry College *B, T*
Ferrum College *B*
George Mason University *B*
Hampton University *B*
James Madison University *B, M, T*
Longwood University *B, T*
Lynchburg College *B*
Mary Baldwin College *B*
Norfolk State University *B*
Old Dominion University *B, T*
Radford University *B*
Roanoke College *B, T*
University of Virginia *B*
University of Virginia's College at
   Wise *B, T*
Virginia Intermont College *B*
Virginia Polytechnic Institute and
   State University *B*
Virginia Union University *B*
Virginia Wesleyan College *B*

Washington

Central Washington University *B, M*
Centralia College *A*
Cornish College of the Arts *B*
Eastern Washington University *B, M, T*
Everett Community College *A*
Evergreen State College *B*
Highline Community College *A*
North Seattle Community
   College *C, A*
Olympic College *A*
Pacific Lutheran University *B*
Seattle Pacific University *B*
University of Puget Sound *B, T*
University of Washington *B, M*
Walla Walla College *B*
Washington State University *B, M*
Western Washington University *B*
Whitworth College *B, T*

West Virginia

Bethany College *B*
Concord University *B*
Davis and Elkins College *B*
Marshall University *B*
Shepherd University *B*
University of Charleston *B*
West Virginia University *B, M, T*
West Virginia Wesleyan College *B*

Wisconsin

Alverno College *B*
Cardinal Stritch University *B*
Carroll College *B*
Carthage College *B*
Concordia University Wisconsin *B*
Edgewood College *B*
Lakeland College *B*
Lawrence University *B*
Mount Mary College *B*
Northland College *B, T*
Ripon College *B, T*
St. Norbert College *B*
Silver Lake College *B*
University of Wisconsin
   Eau Claire *B*
   Green Bay *B, T*
   La Crosse *B, T*
   Madison *B, M*
   Milwaukee *B, M, D*
   Oshkosh *B*
   Parkside *B, T*
   Platteville *B*
   River Falls *B*
   Stevens Point *B*
   Superior *B*
   Whitewater *A, B, T*
Viterbo University *B, T*
Wisconsin Lutheran College *B*

Wyoming

Casper College *A*
Central Wyoming College *C, A*
Eastern Wyoming College *A*
Sheridan College *A*
University of Wyoming *B*
Western Wyoming Community
   College *A*

Art history

Alabama

Birmingham-Southern College *B*
Chattahoochee Valley Community
   College *A*
University of Alabama *B, M*
University of Alabama
   Birmingham *M*

Arizona

Arizona State University *D*
Northern Arizona University *B*
University of Arizona *B, M, D*

Arkansas

University of Arkansas
   Little Rock *B*

California

Art Center College of Design *M*
California College of the Arts *M*
California State University
   Chico *B*
   Dominguez Hills *B*
   East Bay *B*
   Fullerton *B, M*
   Long Beach *B, M*
   Northridge *B, M*
   San Bernardino *B*
Chapman University *B*
College of the Desert *A*
Cosumnes River College *A*
De Anza College *C, A*
Dominican University of California *B*
Foothill College *C, A*
Gavilan Community College *A*
Grossmont Community College *A*
Los Angeles Southwest College *A*
Los Angeles Valley College *A*
Loyola Marymount University *B*
Mills College *B*
MiraCosta College *A*
Monterey Peninsula College *A*
Occidental College *B*
Ohlone College *C*
Pitzer College *B*
Platt College
   Cerritos *C, A*
Pomona College *B*
San Diego City College *A*
San Diego State University *B, M*
San Francisco Art Institute *B, M*
San Francisco State University *M*
San Jose State University *B, M*
Santa Barbara City College *A*
Santa Clara University *B*
Scripps College *B*
Sonoma State University *B*
University of California
   Berkeley *B, D*
   Davis *B, M*
   Irvine *B*
   Los Angeles *B, M, D*
   Riverside *B, M*
   San Diego *B*
   Santa Barbara *B, M, D*
University of La Verne *B*
University of Redlands *B*
University of San Diego *B*
University of San Francisco *B*
University of Southern
   California *B, M, D*
Whittier College *B*

Colorado

Colorado College *B*
University of Denver *B, M*

Connecticut

Albertus Magnus College *B*
Connecticut College *B*
Fairfield University *B*
St. Joseph College *B*
Southern Connecticut State
   University *B, M*
Trinity College *B*
University of Connecticut *B*
University of Hartford *B*
Wesleyan University *B*
Yale University *B, M, D*

Delaware

University of Delaware *B, M, D*

District of Columbia

American University *B, M*
Catholic University of America *B*

Corcoran College of Art and Design *M*
Gallaudet University *B*
George Washington
   University *B, M, D*
Georgetown University *B*
Howard University *B, M*
Trinity University *B*

Florida

Florida International University *B*
Florida State University *B, M, D*
Jacksonville University *B*
Manatee Community College *A*
New College of Florida *B*
Palm Beach Community College *A*
Rollins College *B*
University of Florida *B, M*
University of Miami *C, B, M*
University of South Florida *B, M*

Georgia

Emory University *B, D*
Georgia State University *M*
Savannah College of Art and
   Design *B, M*
University of Georgia *B, M*
Wesleyan College *B*

Hawaii

University of Hawaii
   Manoa *M*

Illinois

Augustana College *B*
Bradley University *B*
DePaul University *B*
Dominican University *B*
Governors State University *B, M*
Illinois Valley Community College *A*
Knox College *B*
North Park University *B*
Northern Illinois University *B*
Northwestern University *B, M, D*
Principia College *B*
Richland Community College *A*
Rockford College *B*
Roosevelt University *B*
Sauk Valley Community College *A*
School of the Art Institute of
   Chicago *B, M*
University of Chicago *B, D*
University of Illinois
   Chicago *B, M, D*
   Urbana-Champaign *B, M, D*

Indiana

DePauw University *B*
Hanover College *B*
Indiana University
   Bloomington *B, M, D*
Indiana University-Purdue University
   Indianapolis *B*
Indiana Wesleyan University *B*
Marian College *B, T*
University of Evansville *B*
University of Notre Dame *B, M*

Iowa

Clarke College *A, B, T*
Drake University *B*
University of Iowa *B, M, D*
University of Northern Iowa *B*

Kansas

Baker University *B*
University of Kansas *B, M, D*
Washburn University of Topeka *B*
Wichita State University *B*

Kentucky

Thomas More College *A*
University of Kentucky *B, M*

University of Louisville B, D

Louisiana

Grambling State University B
Louisiana State University and
    Agricultural and Mechanical
    College M
Tulane University B
University of New Orleans B

Maine

Bowdoin College B
Colby College B
University of Maine B
University of Southern Maine B

Maryland

College of Notre Dame of Maryland B
Johns Hopkins University B, M, D
Maryland Institute College of Art B
McDaniel College B
Montgomery College A
University of Maryland
    College Park B, M, D

Massachusetts

Boston College B
Boston University B, M, D
Bridgewater State College B
Clark University B
College of the Holy Cross B
Hampshire College B
Massachusetts College of Art B
Massachusetts College of Liberal
    Arts B
Northeastern University B
Salem State College B
Simmons College B
Simon's Rock College of Bard B
Smith College B
Suffolk University B
Tufts University B, M
University of Massachusetts
    Amherst B, M
    Dartmouth B
Wellesley College B
Wheaton College B
Williams College B, M

Michigan

Albion College B
Alma College B
Andrews University B
Aquinas College B
Calvin College B
Eastern Michigan University B
Ferris State University B
Hope College B
Kalamazoo College B
Kendall College of Art and Design of
    Ferris State University B
Madonna University C
Michigan State University B
Oakland University B
University of Michigan B, M, D
Wayne State University B, M
Western Michigan University B

Minnesota

Augsburg College B
Carleton College B
College of St. Benedict B
College of St. Catherine B
Concordia College: Moorhead B
Gustavus Adolphus College B
Hamline University B
Macalester College B
Minnesota State University
    Mankato B
St. Cloud State University B
St. John's University B
St. Olaf College B

University of Minnesota
    Duluth B
    Morris B
    Twin Cities B, M, D
University of St. Thomas B, M

Mississippi

University of Mississippi B, M, T

Missouri

Drury University B
Kansas City Art Institute B
Lindenwood University B
St. Louis University B
Truman State University B
University of Missouri
    Kansas City B, M, D
    St. Louis B
Washington University in St.
    Louis B, M, D
Webster University B

Montana

University of Montana: Missoula B, M

Nebraska

Bellevue University B
Hastings College B
University of Nebraska
    Kearney B
    Lincoln B
    Omaha B

Nevada

University of Nevada
    Reno B

New Hampshire

Dartmouth College B
Franklin Pierce College B
New England College B
University of New Hampshire B

New Jersey

Drew University B
Georgian Court University B
Kean University B
Princeton University B, M, D
Rowan University B
Rutgers, The State University of New
    Jersey
    New Brunswick/Piscataway
      Campus B, M, D
Seton Hall University B

New Mexico

College of Santa Fe B
University of New Mexico B, M, D

New York

Adelphi University B
Bard College B, M, D
Barnard College B
Canisius College B
City University of New York
    Brooklyn College B, M
    City College B, M
    Hunter College B, M
    Lehman College B, M
    Queens College B, M
    York College B
Colgate University B
College of New Rochelle B, T
Columbia University
    Columbia College B
    School of General Studies B
Cornell University B, M, D
Fordham University B
Hamilton College B
Hartwick College B
Hobart and William Smith Colleges B
Hofstra University B

Ithaca College B
Long Island University
    C.W. Post Campus B
Manhattanville College B
Marist College B
Nazareth College of Rochester B
New York University M, D
Pace University B
Parsons The New School for
    Design M
Pratt Institute B, M
Sarah Lawrence College B
Skidmore College B
State University of New York
    Albany B
    Binghamton B, M, D
    Buffalo B, M
    College at Buffalo B, M
    College at Fredonia B
    College at Geneseo B
    College at Oneonta B
    College at Plattsburgh B
    College at Potsdam B
    New Paltz B
    Purchase B, M
    Stony Brook B, M, D
Syracuse University B, M
University of Rochester B, M
Wells College B

North Carolina

Duke University B, D
East Carolina University B
Queens University of Charlotte B
Salem College B
University of North Carolina
    Chapel Hill B, M, D
    Wilmington B
Wake Forest University B

Ohio

Art Academy of Cincinnati B
Baldwin-Wallace College B
Bowling Green State University B, M
Case Western Reserve
    University B, M, D
College of Wooster B
Denison University B
Hiram College B
John Carroll University B
Kent State University B, M
Kenyon College B
Lourdes College B
Miami University
    Oxford Campus B
Oberlin College B
Ohio State University
    Columbus Campus B, M, D
Ohio University B, M
Ohio Wesleyan University B
University of Akron B
University of Cincinnati C, B, M
University of Dayton B
University of Toledo B
Ursuline College B
Wright State University B
Youngstown State University B

Oklahoma

Oklahoma City University B, M
St. Gregory's University A
University of Central Oklahoma B
University of Oklahoma B, M
University of Tulsa B

Oregon

Portland State University B
Reed College B
University of Oregon B, M, D
Willamette University B

Pennsylvania

Allegheny College B

Arcadia University B
Bloomsburg University of
    Pennsylvania B, M
Bryn Mawr College B, M, D
Bucknell University B
Carlow University B
Chatham College B
Duquesne University B
Eastern University B
Edinboro University of
    Pennsylvania B
Franklin & Marshall College B
Gettysburg College B
Haverford College B
Juniata College B
La Salle University B
Lebanon Valley College B
Lehigh University B
Lycoming College B
Mansfield University of
    Pennsylvania B
Marywood University B
Messiah College B
Moore College of Art and Design B
Moravian College B
Penn State
    Abington B
    Altoona B
    Beaver B
    Berks B
    Delaware County B
    Dubois B
    Fayette B
    Hazleton B
    Lehigh Valley B
    McKeesport B
    Mont Alto B
    New Kensington B
    Schuylkill - Capital College B
    Shenango B
    University Park B, M, D
    Wilkes-Barre B
    Worthington Scranton B
    York B
Rosemont College B
St. Vincent College B
Seton Hill University B
Susquehanna University B
Swarthmore College B
Temple University B, M, D
University of Pennsylvania B, M, D
University of Pittsburgh B, M, D
Ursinus College B
Villanova University B

Puerto Rico

University of Puerto Rico
    Mayaguez B
    Rio Piedras B

Rhode Island

Brown University B, M, D
Providence College B
Rhode Island College B
Roger Williams University B
Salve Regina University B
University of Rhode Island B

South Carolina

College of Charleston B
Converse College B
Furman University B
University of South Carolina B, M
Winthrop University B
Wofford College B

Tennessee

Lambuth University B
Middle Tennessee State University B
Tennessee State University B
University of Memphis B, M
University of Tennessee
    Knoxville B

University of the South *B*

Texas

Baylor University *B*
Lamar University *M*
Lon Morris College *A*
Rice University *B*
Southern Methodist University *B, M*
Southwestern University *B*
Stephen F. Austin State University *B*
Texas A&M University
    Commerce *M, D*
Texas Christian University *B, M*
Texas Tech University *B*
Trinity University *B*
University of Dallas *B*
University of Houston *B*
University of North Texas *B, M*
University of Texas
    Arlington *B*
    Austin *B, M, D*
    San Antonio *B, M*

Utah

Brigham Young University *B, M*
Dixie State College of Utah *A*
University of Utah *B, M*

Vermont

Marlboro College *B*
Middlebury College *B*
University of Vermont *B*

Virginia

College of William and Mary *B*
George Mason University *B*
Hollins University *B*
James Madison University *B*
Longwood University *B*
Old Dominion University *B*
Randolph-Macon College *B*
Randolph-Macon Woman's College *B*
Roanoke College *B*
Sweet Briar College *B*
University of Mary Washington *B*
University of Richmond *B*
University of Virginia *M, D*
Virginia Commonwealth
    University *B, M, D*
Washington and Lee University *B*

Washington

Eastern Washington University *B*
Seattle University *B*
University of Washington *B, M, D*
Western Washington University *B*
Whitman College *B*

Wisconsin

Beloit College *B*
Lawrence University *B, T*
Ripon College *B*
University of Wisconsin
    Madison *B, M, D*
    Milwaukee *B, M*
    Superior *B, M*
    Whitewater *B, T*

Art teacher education

Alabama

Alabama Agricultural and Mechanical
    University *M*
Birmingham-Southern College *B, T*
Huntingdon College *B, T*
University of Alabama
    Birmingham *M*

Arizona

Arizona State University *B, T*
Eastern Arizona College *A*
Grand Canyon University *B*

Northern Arizona University *B, T*
Prescott College *B, M, T*
University of Arizona *B, M*

Arkansas

Arkansas State University *B, T*
Arkansas Tech University *B*
Harding University *B, M, T*
Henderson State University *B, M, T*
Ouachita Baptist University *B, T*
Southern Arkansas University *B, T*
University of Arkansas
    Monticello *B*
    Pine Bluff *B, T*
University of Central Arkansas *T*
University of the Ozarks *T*
Williams Baptist College *B*

California

Azusa Pacific University *B, T*
California Baptist University *T*
California Lutheran University *B, T*
California State University
    Chico *B, T*
    Dominguez Hills *T*
    Long Beach *B, T*
    Northridge *B, T*
    San Bernardino *T*
Cuesta College *A*
Humboldt State University *T*
Mount St. Mary's College *T*
Point Loma Nazarene University *B*
San Diego State University *B, T*
San Francisco State University *B, T*
Sonoma State University *T*
University of San Francisco *M*
University of the Pacific *T*
Vista Community College *T*
Westmont College *T*

Colorado

Adams State College *B, M, T*
Colorado State University *T*
Colorado State University
    Pueblo *T*
Fort Lewis College *B*
Metropolitan State College of
    Denver *B, T*
Northeastern Junior College *A*
Rocky Mountain College of Art &
    Design *B*
University of Denver *B*
Western State College of Colorado *T*

Connecticut

Albertus Magnus College *B, T*
Central Connecticut State
    University *B, M, T*
St. Joseph College *B*
Southern Connecticut State
    University *B, M, T*

Delaware

Delaware State University *B*

District of Columbia

Corcoran College of Art and
    Design *B, M*
Gallaudet University *B, T*
George Washington University *M, T*
Howard University *B*
Trinity University *M*
University of the District of
    Columbia *B*

Florida

Flagler College *B*
Florida Agricultural and Mechanical
    University *B, M*
Florida Atlantic University *M*
Florida International
    University *B, M, T*
Florida Southern College *B, M*

Florida State University *B, M, D, T*
Palm Beach Atlantic University *B, T*
Palm Beach Community College *A*
Pensacola Junior College *A*
University of Central Florida *B, M*
University of Florida *A, B*
University of North Florida *B*
University of South Florida *B, M*
University of Tampa *T*
University of West Florida *B*

Georgia

Armstrong Atlantic State
    University *B, M, T*
Brenau University *B*
Clark Atlanta University *B*
Columbus State University *B, M*
Darton College *A*
Gainesville State College *A*
Georgia Southern University *B, M*
Georgia State University *B, M*
Kennesaw State University *B*
North Georgia College & State
    University *B, M*
Piedmont College *M, T*
Shorter College *B*
University of Georgia *M, D*
University of West Georgia *M*
Valdosta State University *B, M*
Young Harris College *A*

Hawaii

Brigham Young University-Hawaii *B, T*

Idaho

Boise State University *B, M, T*
Brigham Young University-Idaho *T*
Northwest Nazarene University *B*
University of Idaho *B, T*

Illinois

Augustana College *B, T*
Blackburn College *B, T*
Bradley University *B, M*
Chicago State University *B*
City Colleges of Chicago
    Olive-Harvey College *A*
Columbia College Chicago *M*
Dominican University *T*
Elmhurst College *B*
Illinois College *T*
John A. Logan College *A*
Kankakee Community College *A*
Knox College *T*
Lewis University *T*
McKendree College *B*
Monmouth College *B, T*
North Central College *B, T*
North Park University *T*
Northern Illinois University *B, M, T*
Olivet Nazarene University *B, T*
Parkland College *A*
Rockford College *T*
St. Xavier University *B*
Sauk Valley Community College *A*
School of the Art Institute of
    Chicago *B, M*
Trinity Christian College *B, T*
University of Illinois
    Chicago *B*
    Urbana-Champaign *B, M, D, T*
Waubonsee Community College *A*

Indiana

Anderson University *B, T*
Ball State University *B, T*
Calumet College of St. Joseph *T*
Goshen College *B*
Grace College *B*
Huntington University *B*
Indiana State University *T*
Indiana University
    Bloomington *B, M*

Indiana University-Purdue University
    Fort Wayne *B*
Indiana University-Purdue University
    Indianapolis *B, M, T*
Indiana Wesleyan University *B, T*
Oakland City University *B*
St. Joseph's College *B*
Saint Mary's College *T*
St. Mary-of-the-Woods College *B, T*
Taylor University *B, T*
University of Evansville *B, T*
University of Indianapolis *B, M, T*
University of St. Francis *B, T*
Valparaiso University *B*
Vincennes University *A*

Iowa

Briar Cliff University *B*
Buena Vista University *B, T*
Central College *T*
Clarke College *B, T*
Coe College *B*
Cornell College *B, T*
Dordt College *B*
Drake University *T*
Graceland University *T*
Iowa State University *T*
Iowa Wesleyan College *B*
Loras College *B*
Maharishi University of
    Management *T*
Morningside College *B*
Mount Mercy College *T*
Northwestern College *T*
St. Ambrose University *B, T*
Simpson College *B, T*
University of Iowa *M, D, T*
Upper Iowa University *T*
Wartburg College *B, T*

Kansas

Baker University *B, T*
Bethany College *B*
Bethel College *T*
Colby Community College *A*
Emporia State University *T*
Friends University *B*
Garden City Community College *A*
Kansas State University *B*
Kansas Wesleyan University *B, T*
McPherson College *B, T*
Ottawa University *B, T*
Pittsburg State University *B, M, T*
Sterling College *T*
University of Kansas *B, M, T*
Wichita State University *B, M, T*

Kentucky

Asbury College *B, T*
Bellarmine University *B, T*
Berea College *B, T*
Brescia University *B, T*
Campbellsville University *B*
Eastern Kentucky University *B*
Kentucky State University *B*
Kentucky Wesleyan College *B, T*
Lindsey Wilson College *B, T*
Morehead State University *M*
Murray State University *B, T*
Spalding University *B*
Thomas More College *B*
University of Kentucky *B, M*
University of Louisville *M*
University of the Cumberlands *B, T*
Western Kentucky University *B, M, T*

Louisiana

Centenary College of Louisiana *B, T*
Grambling State University *B*
Louisiana State University
    Shreveport *B*
Louisiana Tech University *B*
Nicholls State University *B*

Southeastern Louisiana University *B*
Southern University
  New Orleans *B*
University of Louisiana at Lafayette *B*
University of Louisiana at Monroe *B*
Xavier University of Louisiana *B*

Maine

Maine College of Art *T*
University of Maine *B*
University of Maine
  Presque Isle *B*
University of New England *B*
University of Southern Maine *B, T*

Maryland

College of Notre Dame of Maryland *T*
Community College of Baltimore
  County *A*
Maryland Institute College of
  Art *B, M, T*
Mount St. Mary's University *T*
St. Mary's College of Maryland *T*
Salisbury University *T*
Towson University *B, M, T*
University of Maryland
  College Park *B*
  Eastern Shore *B*

Massachusetts

Anna Maria College *B, M, T*
Art Institute of Boston at Lesley
  University *B, M*
Assumption College *T*
Boston University *B, M*
Bridgewater State College *B, M, T*
Fitchburg State College *M*
Framingham State College *M*
Harvard College *M, D*
Lesley University *B, M*
Massachusetts College of Art *B, M*
Montserrat College of Art *T*
Northeastern University *B*
School of the Museum of Fine
  Arts *B, M, T*
Springfield College *B*
Tufts University *M, T*
University of Massachusetts
  Dartmouth *B, M, T*
Westfield State College *B, T*

Michigan

Adrian College *B, T*
Albion College *B, T*
Alma College *T*
Andrews University *M*
Aquinas College *B, T*
Calvin College *B*
Concordia University *B, T*
Delta College *A*
Eastern Michigan University *B, M, T*
Grand Valley State University *T*
Hope College *T*
Kellogg Community College *A*
Kendall College of Art and Design of
  Ferris State University *B*
Lansing Community College *A*
Madonna University *B, T*
Michigan State University *B*
Northern Michigan University *B, M, T*
Olivet College *B, T*
Spring Arbor University *B, T*
University of Michigan *B*
University of Michigan
  Dearborn *B*
  Flint *B, T*
Wayne State University *B, M, T*
Western Michigan University *B, M, T*

Minnesota

Augsburg College *T*
Bemidji State University *T*
Bethel University *B*

College of St. Benedict *B, T*
College of St. Catherine *B, M, T*
Concordia College: Moorhead *B, T*
Concordia University: St. Paul *B, T*
Gustavus Adolphus College *T*
Hamline University *B*
Minnesota State University
  Mankato *B, M, T*
  Moorhead *B*
Northwestern College *B*
Pillsbury Baptist Bible College *T*
Ridgewater College *A*
St. Cloud State University *B*
St. John's University *B, T*
Southwest Minnesota State
  University *B, T*
University of Minnesota
  Duluth *B*
  Morris *T*
  Twin Cities *B, M, T*
Vermilion Community College *A*
Winona State University *B, T*

Mississippi

Coahoma Community College *A*
Delta State University *T*
Itawamba Community College *A*
Mississippi College *B, M*
Mississippi Delta Community
  College *A*
Mississippi Gulf Coast Community
  College
  Jefferson Davis Campus *A*
University of Mississippi *M, T*
University of Southern Mississippi *M*
William Carey College *B, M*

Missouri

Central Missouri State University *B, T*
College of the Ozarks *B, T*
Columbia College *T*
Culver-Stockton College *B, T*
Evangel University *B, T*
Hannibal-LaGrange College *B*
Lincoln University *B, T*
Lindenwood University *B, M*
Maryville University of Saint
  Louis *B, M, T*
Missouri Southern State
  University *B, T*
Missouri State University *B*
Missouri Western State University *B*
Northwest Missouri State
  University *B, M, T*
Park University *T*
Southeast Missouri State
  University *B, T*
Southwest Baptist University *B, T*
Truman State University *M, T*
University of Missouri
  Columbia *B, M, D*
Washington University in St.
  Louis *B, M, T*
William Jewell College *T*
William Woods University *B, T*

Montana

Montana State University
  Billings *B, T*
Rocky Mountain College *B, T*
University of Great Falls *B*
University of Montana: Missoula *B, T*
University of Montana: Western *B, T*

Nebraska

Chadron State College *B*
Concordia University *B, T*
Creighton University *T*
Dana College *B*
Hastings College *B, M, T*
Midland Lutheran College *B, T*
Nebraska Wesleyan University *T*
Peru State College *B, T*

Union College *T*
University of Nebraska
  Kearney *B, M, T*
  Lincoln *B*
Wayne State College *B, T*
Western Nebraska Community
  College *A*
York College *B, T*

Nevada

University of Nevada
  Reno *B*

New Hampshire

Chester College of New England *T*
Colby-Sawyer College *B, T*
New England College *B, T*
Plymouth State University *B, T*
University of New Hampshire *B, T*

New Jersey

Caldwell College *T*
The College of New Jersey *B, T*
College of St. Elizabeth *T*
Cumberland County College *A*
Georgian Court University *T*
Kean University *M*
New Jersey City University *M, T*
Rowan University *B, M*
Seton Hall University *T*
William Paterson University of New
  Jersey *T*

New Mexico

University of New Mexico *B, M*
Western New Mexico University *B*

New York

Adelphi University *B, M, T*
Alfred University *M, T*
City University of New York
  Brooklyn College *B, M*
  City College *B, M, T*
  Hunter College *B*
  Lehman College *M*
  Queens College *B, M, T*
College of New Rochelle *B, M, T*
College of Saint Rose *B, M, T*
Daemen College *B, T*
Dowling College *B*
Elmira College *B, T*
Fordham University *T*
Hofstra University *B, M, T*
Ithaca College *B, T*
Long Island University
  Brooklyn Campus *B, T*
  C. W. Post Campus *B, M, T*
Manhattanville College *M, T*
Marymount Manhattan College *T*
Molloy College *B*
Nazareth College of Rochester *B, M, T*
New York Institute of Technology *B, T*
New York University *B, M, D*
Pace University *M, T*
Pratt Institute *B, M*
Roberts Wesleyan College *B*
Rochester Institute of Technology *M*
St. Lawrence University *T*
St. Thomas Aquinas College *B, T*
School of Visual Arts *M*
State University of New York
  College at Buffalo *B, M, T*
  New Paltz *B, M, T*
  Oswego *M*
Syracuse University *B, M, T*

North Carolina

Appalachian State University *B, T*
Barton College *B, T*
Brevard College *B*
East Carolina University *B, M*
Elizabeth City State University *B, T*
Greensboro College *B, T*

High Point University *B, T*
Lenoir Community College *A*
Lenoir-Rhyne College *B, T*
Mars Hill College *B, T*
Meredith College *B, T*
Methodist College *B, T*
North Carolina Central University *B, T*
University of North Carolina
  Charlotte *B*
  Greensboro *B*
  Pembroke *B, M*
Western Carolina University *B, T*
Wingate University *B, T*
Winston-Salem State University *B*

North Dakota

Dickinson State University *B, T*
Minot State University *B*
University of North Dakota *B, T*
Valley City State University *B, T*

Ohio

Art Academy of Cincinnati *M*
Ashland University *B, T*
Bluffton University *B*
Bowling Green State University *B, T*
Capital University *T*
Case Western Reserve University *B, M*
Central State University *B*
College of Mount St. Joseph *B, T*
Defiance College *B, T*
Hiram College *T*
Kent State University *B, M*
Malone College *B*
Miami University
  Oxford Campus *B, M, T*
Mount Union College *T*
Mount Vernon Nazarene
  University *B, M, T*
Ohio Dominican University *B, T*
Ohio Northern University *T*
Ohio State University
  Columbus Campus *B, M, D*
Ohio University *B, T*
Ohio Wesleyan University *B*
Otterbein College *T*
University of Akron *B*
University of Cincinnati *B, M, T*
University of Dayton *B, M, T*
University of Findlay *B, M, T*
University of Rio Grande *B, T*
University of Toledo *B, M, T*
Ursuline College *B, M, T*
Wright State University *B, M, T*
Youngstown State University *B, M*

Oklahoma

Cameron University *B, T*
Eastern Oklahoma State College *A*
Northeastern State University *B*
Oklahoma Baptist University *B, T*
Oklahoma Christian University *B, T*
Oklahoma City University *B*
Oral Roberts University *B, T*
Southeastern Oklahoma State
  University *B, T*
Southwestern Oklahoma State
  University *B, M, T*
University of Central Oklahoma *B*

Oregon

Linfield College *T*
Portland State University *T*
Southern Oregon University *T*

Pennsylvania

Albright College *B, T*
Arcadia University *B, M, T*
Carlow University *B, M, T*
Indiana University of
  Pennsylvania *B, T*
Keystone College *B, T*
Lincoln University *T*

Lycoming College T
Mansfield University of
  Pennsylvania B, M, T
Marywood University B, M
Mercyhurst College B, T
Messiah College B, T
Millersville University of
  Pennsylvania B, M, T
Moore College of Art and Design B, T
Moravian College T
Penn State
  Abington B
  Altoona B
  Beaver B
  Berks B
  Delaware County B
  Dubois B
  Fayette B
  Hazleton B
  Lehigh Valley B
  McKeesport B
  Mont Alto B
  New Kensington B
  Schuylkill - Capital College B
  Shenango B
  University Park B, M, D
  Wilkes-Barre B
  Worthington Scranton B
  York B
Rosemont College T
St. Vincent College B
Seton Hill University B, T
Temple University B, M
University of the Arts M
Washington and Jefferson
  College B, T

Puerto Rico
Inter American University of Puerto
  Rico
  San German Campus B
Pontifical Catholic University of
  Puerto Rico B, T
Turabo University M

Rhode Island
Rhode Island College B, M
Rhode Island School of Design M, T

South Carolina
Anderson University B, T
Claflin University B
Coker College B, T
Converse College T
Francis Marion University B, T
Furman University T
Limestone College B
South Carolina State University B, T
University of South Carolina B, M
Winthrop University M, T

South Dakota
Augustana College B, T
Black Hills State University B
Dakota State University B, T
Dakota Wesleyan University B, T
Northern State University B, T
University of Sioux Falls B
University of South Dakota T

Tennessee
Belmont University B, M, T
Bethel College B
Freed-Hardeman University B, T
Lambuth University B, T
Lincoln Memorial University B, T
Lipscomb University B, T
Middle Tennessee State University B
Southern Adventist University B
Tennessee Technological University T
Tusculum College B, T
Union University B, T
University of Memphis T

University of Tennessee
  Chattanooga B
  Knoxville B, T

Texas
Abilene Christian University B, T
Austin College M
Baylor University B, T
Del Mar College A
Hardin-Simmons University B, T
Houston Baptist University B, M
Howard Payne University B, T
Kilgore College A
Lamar University B, M, T
Laredo Community College A
Lubbock Christian University B
McMurry University B, T
St. Edward's University B, T
Southwestern University T
Tarleton State University T
Texas A&M University
  Commerce T
  Kingsville B, M
Texas Christian University B
Texas College B, T
Texas State University: San Marcos T
Texas Tech University M
Texas Wesleyan University T
University of Dallas T
University of Houston M, T
University of Houston
  Clear Lake T
University of Mary Hardin-Baylor T
University of North Texas B, M, D, T
University of Texas
  Arlington T
  Austin M
  El Paso M
  San Antonio T
University of the Incarnate Word T
West Texas A&M University T

Utah
Southern Utah University B, T
University of Utah B
Weber State University B

Vermont
Castleton State College B, T
Goddard College B
Green Mountain College B, T
Johnson State College B
St. Michael's College B, M, T
University of Vermont B

Virginia
Averett University B, M, T
Bluefield College T
Bridgewater College T
Eastern Mennonite University T
Hollins University T
Longwood University B, T
Northern Virginia Community
  College A
Old Dominion University B, T
Radford University T
Virginia Commonwealth
  University B, M
Virginia Intermont College B, T
Virginia Wesleyan College B, T

Washington
Central Washington University B, T
Eastern Washington University B, T
Heritage University M
Seattle Pacific University B, T
Western Washington University B, M
Whitworth College B, T

West Virginia
Bethany College B
Concord University B, T
Shepherd University T

West Liberty State College B
West Virginia State University B
West Virginia University T
West Virginia Wesleyan College B

Wisconsin
Alverno College B, T
Beloit College B, T
Carroll College B, T
Concordia University Wisconsin B, M
Edgewood College B, T
Lawrence University T
Marian College of Fond du Lac B, T
Mount Mary College B, T
Silver Lake College B, T
University of Wisconsin
  Green Bay B
  Madison B, M
  Milwaukee B, M
  Parkside T
  Platteville B
  River Falls B, T
  Stout B, T
  Superior B, T
  Whitewater B
Viterbo University B, T

Art therapy

Alabama
Spring Hill College B

Arkansas
Harding University B
University of Central Arkansas B

California
California Institute of Integral
  Studies M
Loyola Marymount University B
Notre Dame de Namur University M

Colorado
Naropa University M

Connecticut
Albertus Magnus College B, M

District of Columbia
George Washington University M

Florida
University of Tampa C

Illinois
Millikin University B
School of the Art Institute of
  Chicago M
Southern Illinois University
  Edwardsville M

Indiana
St. Mary-of-the-Woods College M
University of Indianapolis B

Iowa
Grand View College C

Kansas
Emporia State University M

Kentucky
University of Louisville M

Massachusetts
Anna Maria College B
Emmanuel College B
Endicott College B
Lesley University B, M, D
Springfield College B, M

Michigan
Marygrove College B
Michigan State University D

Missouri
Webster University C

New Mexico
College of Santa Fe B

New York
College of New Rochelle B, M, T
Herkimer County Community
  College A
Hofstra University M
Long Island University
  C. W. Post Campus B, M
Nazareth College of Rochester M
New York University M
Pratt Institute M
Russell Sage College M
St. Thomas Aquinas College B

Ohio
Capital University B
Ursuline College M

Oregon
Marylhurst University M

Pennsylvania
Arcadia University B
Cedar Crest College B
Drexel University M
Marywood University C, A, B, M
Mercyhurst College B
Seton Hill University B, M

South Carolina
Converse College B

Tennessee
Southern Adventist University B

Vermont
Burlington College B
Norwich University M

Wisconsin
Alverno College B
Edgewood College B
Marian College of Fond du Lac B
Mount Mary College B, M
University of Wisconsin
  Superior B, M

Artificial intelligence/ robotics

California
University of Southern California M

Georgia
University of Georgia M

New York
Globe Institute of Technology A, B
Rochester Institute of Technology M

Pennsylvania
Carnegie Mellon University M, D
York Technical Institute A

Texas
Texas State Technical College:
  Marshall A

Arts management

Alabama
Spring Hill College *B*

Arizona
Northern Arizona University *B*

California
California State University
  Dominguez Hills *M*
  East Bay *B*
Santa Rosa Junior College *C*
University of San Francisco *B*

Colorado
Fort Lewis College *B*

Delaware
Delaware State University *B*

District of Columbia
American University *M*
Howard University *B*

Florida
Florida State University *M*

Georgia
Brenau University *B*

Illinois
Benedictine University *B*
Columbia College Chicago *B, M*
Eureka College *B*
Millikin University *B*
Roosevelt University *B, M*
School of the Art Institute of
  Chicago *M*

Indiana
Butler University *B*
Indiana University
  Bloomington *M*

Iowa
Buena Vista University *B*
University of Iowa *B*
Upper Iowa University *B*
Waldorf College *B*

Kansas
Kansas Wesleyan University *B*

Kentucky
Bellarmine University *B*
University of Kentucky *B*

Louisiana
Dillard University *B*
Southeastern Louisiana University *B*
University of New Orleans *M*

Maine
University of Southern Maine *B*

Maryland
Goucher College *M*

Massachusetts
Simmons College *B*
Suffolk University *B*

Michigan
Adrian College *B*
Aquinas College *B*
Bay de Noc Community College *C*
Eastern Michigan University *B*

Minnesota
St. Mary's University of Minnesota *M*

Missouri
Culver-Stockton College *B*
Drury University *B*
Lindenwood University *B, M*
Webster University *M*

Nebraska
Bellevue University *B*
Creighton University *B*

New Hampshire
Franklin Pierce College *B*

New Mexico
College of Santa Fe *B*

New York
City University of New York
  Baruch College *B*
Fashion Institute of Technology *M*
Herkimer County Community
  College *A*
Ithaca College *B*
Long Island University
  C.W. Post Campus *B*
New York University *M*
Pratt Institute *M*
State University of New York
  Purchase *C, B*
Wagner College *B*

North Carolina
Appalachian State University *B*
Bennett College *B*
Catawba College *B*
North Carolina State University *B*
Pfeiffer University *B*
Salem College *B*
University of North Carolina
  Charlotte *M*

Ohio
Baldwin-Wallace College *B*
Cleveland State University *C*
Owens Community College
  Toledo *A*
Tiffin University *B*
University of Cincinnati *M*
Wright State University *B*

Oklahoma
Oklahoma City University *B, M*
Oklahoma State University *M*
University of Tulsa *B*

Oregon
Art Institute of Portland *B*
University of Oregon *M*

Pennsylvania
Carnegie Mellon University *M*
Chatham College *B*
Drexel University *M*
Marywood University *B*
Seton Hill University *B*
Waynesburg College *B*

Puerto Rico
Turabo University *M*

South Carolina
College of Charleston *B*

South Dakota
University of South Dakota *B*

Texas
El Paso Community College *C*
Southern Methodist University *M*
Texas A&M University
  Commerce *B*

Utah
Southern Utah University *M*

Vermont
Green Mountain College *B*

Virginia
Mary Baldwin College *B*
Randolph-Macon College *B*
Shenandoah University *B, M*

West Virginia
West Virginia Wesleyan College *B*

Wisconsin
University of Wisconsin
  Madison *M*
  Stevens Point *B*
Viterbo University *B*

Asian-American studies

California
California State University
  East Bay *B*
  Fullerton *B*
Claremont McKenna College *B*
De Anza College *A*
El Camino College *A*
Los Angeles City College *A*
Pitzer College *B*
Pomona College *B*
San Francisco State University *B, M*
Scripps College *B*
Solano Community College *A*
Southwestern College *A*
Stanford University *B*
University of California
  Berkeley *B*
  Davis *B*
  Irvine *B*
  Los Angeles *B, M*
  Riverside *B*
University of Southern California *B*

Colorado
University of Denver *B*

Massachusetts
Hampshire College *B*
Harvard College *B*

New York
Columbia University
  Columbia College *B*
Sarah Lawrence College *B*
State University of New York
  Binghamton *B*

Pennsylvania
Gettysburg College *B*

Washington
University of Washington *B*

Asian bodywork therapy

New York
Swedish Institute *A*

Pennsylvania
Academy of Medical Arts and
  Business *C, A*

Asian history

Massachusetts
Simon's Rock College of Bard *B*

New York
Bard College *B*
Sarah Lawrence College *B*

Pennsylvania
Gettysburg College *B*

Asian studies

Alabama
Samford University *B*
University of Alabama *B*

California
Cabrillo College *A*
California Institute of Integral
  Studies *M, D*
California State University
  Chico *B*
  Long Beach *M*
  Sacramento *B*
Claremont McKenna College *B*
Cypress College *A*
Laney College *A*
Loyola Marymount University *B*
Occidental College *B*
Pitzer College *B*
Pomona College *B*
San Diego State University *B, M*
San Francisco State University *B, M*
Scripps College *B*
University of California
  Berkeley *B, M, D*
  Los Angeles *B*
  Riverside *B*
  Santa Barbara *B, M*
University of Redlands *B*
University of San Francisco *M*

Colorado
Colorado College *B*
Fort Lewis College *B*
University of Colorado
  Boulder *B*

Connecticut
Trinity College *B*

Florida
Florida International University *B*
Florida State University *B, M*
Miami Dade College *A*
University of Florida *A*

Georgia
Emory University *B*

Hawaii
University of Hawaii
  Manoa *B, M*

Illinois
Augustana College *B*
Illinois Wesleyan University *B*
Lake Forest College *B*
Northwestern University *B*
University of Illinois
  Urbana-Champaign *M*

Indiana
Earlham College *B*
Indiana University
  Bloomington *M, D*

Iowa
Coe College *B*

University of Iowa *B, M*
University of Northern Iowa *B*

Louisiana

Tulane University *B*

Maine

Bowdoin College *B*

Maryland

University of Maryland
University College *B*

Massachusetts

Amherst College *B*
College of the Holy Cross *B*
Hampshire College *B*
Harvard College *B*
Mount Holyoke College *B*
Simon's Rock College of Bard *B*
Smith College *B*
Tufts University *B*
Wellesley College *B*
Wheaton College *B*
Williams College *B*

Michigan

Calvin College *B*
Michigan State University *D*
University of Michigan *B, M*
Wayne State University *B*
Western Michigan University *B*

Minnesota

Carleton College *B*
Hamline University *B*
Macalester College *B*
St. Olaf College *B*

Missouri

Washington University in St. Louis *B*

Montana

University of Montana: Missoula *B*

Nevada

University of Nevada
Las Vegas *B*

New Hampshire

Dartmouth College *B*

New Jersey

Seton Hall University *B, M*

New Mexico

University of New Mexico *B*

New York

Bard College *B*
Barnard College *B*
City University of New York
City College *B*
Colgate University *B*
Columbia University
Columbia College *B*
School of General Studies *B*
Cornell University *B, M, D*
Hamilton College *B*
Hobart and William Smith Colleges *B*
Hofstra University *B*
Manhattanville College *B*
St. John's University *B, M*
St. Lawrence University *B*
Sarah Lawrence College *B*
Skidmore College *B*
State University of New York
Albany *B*
Buffalo *B*
New Paltz *B*
Vassar College *B*

North Carolina

Duke University *B*
St. Andrews Presbyterian College *B*
University of North Carolina
Chapel Hill *B*

Ohio

Antioch College *B*
Bowling Green State University *B*
Case Western Reserve University *B*
Ohio University *B*
University of Cincinnati *B*
University of Toledo *B*

Oregon

University of Oregon *B, M*

Pennsylvania

Gettysburg College *B*
Lehigh University *B*
Rosemont College *B*
Swarthmore College *B*
Temple University *B*

Rhode Island

Brown University *B*

South Carolina

Furman University *B*

Tennessee

University of Tennessee
Knoxville *B*
University of the South *B*

Texas

Baylor University *B*
Rice University *B*
Texas State University: San Marcos *B*
Trinity University *B*
University of Texas
Austin *B, M*

Utah

Brigham Young University *B*
University of Utah *B*
Utah State University *B*

Vermont

Bennington College *B*
Marlboro College *B*
University of Vermont *B*

Virginia

Mary Baldwin College *B*
Old Dominion University *B*

Washington

Central Washington University *B*
Everett Community College *A*
Gonzaga University *B*
South Seattle Community College *A*
University of Puget Sound *B*
University of Washington *B, M, D*
Washington State University *B*
Whitman College *B*

Wisconsin

Lawrence University *B*
University of Wisconsin
Madison *B*

Astronomy

Arizona

Northern Arizona University *B*
University of Arizona *B, M, D*

California

California Institute of
Technology *B, D*
De Anza College *A*
El Camino College *A*
Fullerton College *A*
Gavilan Community College *A*
Golden West College *A*
Orange Coast College *A*
Palomar College *C, A*
Pomona College *B*
Saddleback College *A*
San Bernardino Valley College *A*
San Diego State University *B*
San Francisco State University *B*
San Joaquin Delta College *A*
Southwestern College *A*
University of California
Los Angeles *M, D*
Santa Cruz *D*
University of Southern
California *B, M, D*

Colorado

University of Colorado
Boulder *B*

Connecticut

Wesleyan University *B, M*
Yale University *B, M, D*

Delaware

University of Delaware *B*

District of Columbia

Howard University *M, D*

Florida

Florida Institute of Technology *B*
Santa Fe Community College *A*
University of Florida *B, M, D*

Georgia

Emory University *B*
Georgia State University *D*
Gordon College *A*
University of Georgia *B*
Valdosta State University *B*
Young Harris College *A*

Hawaii

University of Hawaii
Hilo *B*
Manoa *M, D*

Idaho

North Idaho College *A*

Illinois

Illinois Valley Community College *A*
Kishwaukee College *A*
Northwestern University *M, D*
South Suburban College of Cook
County *A*
Southwestern Illinois College *A*
University of Chicago *D*
University of Illinois
Urbana-Champaign *B, M, D*

Indiana

Indiana University
Bloomington *B, M, D*

Iowa

Drake University *B*
University of Iowa *B, M*

Kansas

Benedictine College *B*
Central Christian College of Kansas *A*
University of Kansas *B*

Maryland

Johns Hopkins University *B, D*
University of Maryland
College Park *B, M, D*

Massachusetts

Amherst College *B*
Boston University *B, M, D*
Harvard College *B, D*
Mount Holyoke College *B*
Smith College *B*
Tufts University *B*
University of Massachusetts
Amherst *B, M, D*
Wellesley College *B*
Wheaton College *B*
Williams College *B*

Michigan

Bay de Noc Community College *A*
Central Michigan University *B*
University of Michigan *B, M, D*

Minnesota

Minnesota State University
Mankato *B*
University of Minnesota
Twin Cities *B*
Vermilion Community College *A*

New Hampshire

Dartmouth College *B*

New Mexico

New Mexico State University *M, D*

New York

Barnard College *B*
Colgate University *B*
Columbia University
Columbia College *B*
School of General Studies *B*
Cornell University *B, M, D*
Sarah Lawrence College *B*
State University of New York
Stony Brook *B*
Suffolk County Community College *A*
Union College *B*
University of Rochester *B, M, D*
Vassar College *B*

Ohio

Case Western Reserve
University *B, M, D*
Mount Union College *B*
Ohio Northern University *B*
Ohio State University
Columbus Campus *B, M, D*
Ohio Wesleyan University *B*
University of Toledo *B*
Wilmington College *B*
Youngstown State University *B*

Oklahoma

Tulsa Community College *A*
University of Oklahoma *B*

Pennsylvania

Bryn Mawr College *B*
Eastern University *B*
Franklin & Marshall College *B*
Gettysburg College *B*
Haverford College *B*
Lehigh University *B*
Lycoming College *B*
Penn State
Abington *B*
Altoona *B*
Beaver *B*
Berks *B*
Delaware County *B*
Dubois *B*

Fayette *B*
Hazleton *B*
Lehigh Valley *B*
McKeesport *B*
Mont Alto *B*
New Kensington *B*
Schuylkill - Capital College *B*
Shenango *B*
University Park *B, M, D*
Wilkes-Barre *B*
Worthington Scranton *B*
York *B*
Swarthmore College *B*
Villanova University *B*

Tennessee

Vanderbilt University *M*

Texas

Austin Community College *A*
Lon Morris College *A*
Rice University *B, M, D*
University of Texas
Austin *B, M, D*

Utah

Brigham Young University *B, D*
Snow College *A*

Vermont

Bennington College *B*
Marlboro College *B*

Virginia

University of Virginia *B, M, D*

Washington

Everett Community College *A*
Highline Community College *A*
University of Washington *B, M, D*
Whitman College *B*

Wisconsin

University of Wisconsin
Madison *B, M, D*

Astrophysics

Arizona

Northern Arizona University *B*

California

San Francisco State University *B*
University of California
Berkeley *B, D*
Los Angeles *B*
Santa Cruz *B, D*

Colorado

University of Colorado
Boulder *M, D*

Connecticut

Connecticut College *B*
Yale University *B*

Florida

Florida Institute of Technology *B*

Georgia

Agnes Scott College *B*

Illinois

University of Chicago *D*

Indiana

Indiana University
Bloomington *B*

Iowa

Iowa State University *M, D*

Massachusetts

Boston University *B*
Smith College *B*
Tufts University *M, D*
Williams College *B*

Michigan

Michigan State University *B, M, D*

Minnesota

University of Minnesota
Twin Cities *B, M, D*

New Jersey

Princeton University *B, M, D*

New Mexico

New Mexico Institute of Mining and
Technology *B, M, D*
University of New Mexico *B*

New York

Barnard College *B*
Colgate University *B*
Columbia University
Columbia College *B*
School of General Studies *B*

Ohio

Ohio University *B*

Oklahoma

University of Oklahoma *B*

Pennsylvania

Carnegie Mellon University *B*
Franklin & Marshall College *B*
Lehigh University *B*
Penn State
Schuylkill - Capital College *B*
University Park *B, M, D*
Swarthmore College *B*
Villanova University *B*

Texas

Rice University *B, M, D*
Texas Christian University *D*
University of North Texas *M*

Washington

University of Washington *B*

Wisconsin

University of Wisconsin
Madison *B, M, D*

Athletic training

Alabama

Huntingdon College *C, B*
Samford University *B*
Troy University *B*
University of Alabama *B*
University of Mobile *B*
University of West Alabama *B*
Virginia College *A*
Wallace State Community College at
Hanceville *A*

Arizona

Grand Canyon University *B*
Northern Arizona University *B*

Arkansas

Arkansas State University *B*
Harding University *B*
Henderson State University *B*

John Brown University *B*
Ouachita Baptist University *B*
Southern Arkansas University *B*
University of Arkansas
Monticello *B*

California

California Lutheran University *B*
California State University
East Bay *B*
Northridge *M*
Sacramento *B*
Chapman University *B*
Diablo Valley College *C, A*
Foothill College *C, A*
Fresno Pacific University *B*
Grossmont Community College *C, A*
Hope International University *B*
Orange Coast College *C, A*
Pepperdine University *B*
Point Loma Nazarene University *B*
San Bernardino Valley College *C*
San Diego Christian College *B*
San Francisco State University *B*
Santa Barbara City College *C, A*
Santa Rosa Junior College *C*
University of La Verne *B*
Whittier College *B*

Colorado

Adams State College *B*
Fort Lewis College *B*

Connecticut

Central Connecticut State
University *B*
Mitchell College *A*
Quinnipiac University *B*
Sacred Heart University *B*

Delaware

University of Delaware *B*

Florida

Barry University *B, M*
Broward Community College *A*
Florida Gulf Coast University *B*
Florida Southern College *B*
Florida State University *B*
Nova Southeastern University *B*
Palm Beach Atlantic University *B*
University of Miami *B*
University of North Florida *B*
University of South Florida *B*
University of Tampa *B*

Georgia

Abraham Baldwin Agricultural
College *A*
Darton College *C*
Georgia Southern University *B*
North Georgia College & State
University *B*
Valdosta State University *B*

Hawaii

University of Hawaii
Manoa *B, M*

Idaho

Boise State University *B, M*
University of Idaho *B*

Illinois

Illinois State University *B*
Illinois Valley Community College *A*
Lewis University *B*
McKendree College *B*
Millikin University *B*
North Central College *B*
Olivet Nazarene University *B*
St. Xavier University *C*

Sauk Valley Community College *A*
Trinity International University *B*
Triton College *C*
University of Illinois
Urbana-Champaign *B, M*

Indiana

Anderson University *B*
DePauw University *B*
Franklin College *B*
Indiana State University *B, M*
Indiana Wesleyan University *B*
University of Evansville *B*
University of Indianapolis *B*
Vincennes University *A*

Iowa

Buena Vista University *B*
Coe College *B*
Dordt College *B*
Ellsworth Community College *A*
Graceland University *B*
Loras College *B*
Northwestern College *B*
Simpson College *B*
University of Iowa *B, M*
University of Northern Iowa *B, M*
Upper Iowa University *B*

Kansas

Barton County Community College *A*
Benedictine College *B*
Bethel College *B*
Central Christian College of Kansas *A*
Coffeyville Community College *A*
Dodge City Community College *A*
Emporia State University *B*
Garden City Community College *A*
Kansas State University *B*
MidAmerica Nazarene University *B*
Neosho County Community
College *A*
Seward County Community College *A*
Southwestern College *B*
Sterling College *B*
Tabor College *B*
University of Kansas *B*
Washburn University of Topeka *B*
Wichita State University *B*

Kentucky

Campbellsville University *B*
Eastern Kentucky University *M*
Georgetown College *B*
Northern Kentucky University *B*

Louisiana

Nicholls State University *B*
Southeastern Louisiana University *B*
University of Louisiana at Lafayette *B*

Maine

University of Maine
Presque Isle *B*
University of New England *B*
University of Southern Maine *B*

Maryland

Community College of Baltimore
County *A*
Howard Community College *C, A*
Salisbury University *B*
Towson University *B*

Massachusetts

Boston University *B*
Bridgewater State College *B, M*
Dean College *A*
Endicott College *B*
Lasell College *B*
Merrimack College *B*

Mount Wachusett Community
  College C
Northeastern University B
Salem State College B
Springfield College B, M
Westfield State College B

Michigan

Aquinas College B
Calvin College B
Central Michigan University B
Eastern Michigan University B
Hope College B
Northern Michigan University B
Olivet College B
Saginaw Valley State University B
University of Michigan B, D
Western Michigan University M

Minnesota

Bethel University B
Gustavus Adolphus College B
Hamline University B
Minnesota State University
  Mankato B
  Moorhead B
Northland Community & Technical
  College A
Ridgewater College A
Winona State University B

Mississippi

Belhaven College B
Delta State University B

Missouri

Central Methodist University B
Culver-Stockton College B
Lindenwood University B
Missouri Baptist University B
Missouri State University B
Missouri Valley College B
Park University B
Southwest Baptist University B
Westminster College B
William Woods University B

Montana

Montana State University
  Billings B, M
Rocky Mountain College B
University of Montana: Missoula B

Nebraska

Midland Lutheran College B
Nebraska Wesleyan University B
University of Nebraska
  Lincoln B
Wayne State College B
Western Nebraska Community
  College A

Nevada

University of Nevada
  Las Vegas B

New Hampshire

Colby-Sawyer College B
Keene State College B
Plymouth State University B
University of New Hampshire B

New Jersey

Rowan University B

New Mexico

New Mexico Junior College A
New Mexico State University B

New York

Alfred University B
Canisius College B

Dominican College of Blauvelt B
Finger Lakes Community College A
Hofstra University B
Ithaca College B
Marist College B
Russell Sage College B
State University of New York
  College at Brockport B
Swedish Institute C

North Carolina

Appalachian State University B
Barton College B
Campbell University B
Catawba College B
Chowan College B
East Carolina University B
Elon University B
Gardner-Webb University B
Greensboro College B
Guilford College B
High Point University B
Lenoir-Rhyne College B
Louisburg College A
Mars Hill College B
Methodist College B
North Carolina Central University B
Pfeiffer University B
St.Andrews Presbyterian College B
Shaw University B
University of North Carolina
  Charlotte B
  Pembroke B
  Wilmington B
Wingate University B

North Dakota

Mayville State University B
North Dakota State University B
University of Mary B

Ohio

Ashland University B
Baldwin-Wallace College B
Bowling Green State University B
Capital University B
Cedarville University B
Cincinnati State Technical and
  Community College C
College of Mount St. Joseph B
Defiance College C, B
Heidelberg College B
Kent State University B
Marietta College B
Miami University
  Oxford Campus B
Mount Union College B
Ohio Northern University B
Ohio University B, M
Otterbein College B
Shawnee State University B
University of Akron C, B, M
University of Findlay B, M
Urbana University B
Xavier University B
Youngstown State University B

Oklahoma

East Central University B
Northeastern Oklahoma Agricultural
  and Mechanical College A
Northeastern State University B
Oklahoma Baptist University B
Oklahoma City University B
Oklahoma State University B
Rose State College A
Southern Nazarene University B
Southwestern Oklahoma State
  University B
University of Tulsa B

Oregon

Concordia University B

George Fox University B
Linfield College B
Southern Oregon University B
Treasure Valley Community College A

Pennsylvania

Alvernia College C, B
California University of
  Pennsylvania B, M
Carlow University B
Duquesne University B
East Stroudsburg University of
  Pennsylvania B
Gannon University B
King's College B
Marywood University B
Messiah College B
Slippery Rock University of
  Pennsylvania B
University of Pittsburgh
  Bradford B
Waynesburg College B
West Chester University of
  Pennsylvania C, B

Puerto Rico

Turabo University M
University of Puerto Rico
  Mayaguez B
  Ponce B

South Carolina

Anderson University B
Charleston Southern University C
College of Charleston B
Erskine College B
Lander University B
Limestone College B

South Dakota

Augustana College B
Dakota Wesleyan University B
South Dakota State University B

Tennessee

Bryan College B
Carson-Newman College B
Lambuth University B
Lincoln Memorial University B
Lipscomb University B
Middle Tennessee State University B
Tusculum College B
Union University B
University of Tennessee
  Chattanooga M

Texas

Angelo State University B, T
Baylor University B
East Texas Baptist University B
Hardin-Simmons University B
Howard College A
Howard Payne University B
Lubbock Christian University B
Midwestern State University B
South Plains College A
Southwestern University B
Stephen F.Austin State University M
Texas A&M University
  Commerce B
Texas Lutheran University B
Texas State University: San
  Marcos B, T
Texas Tech University M
Texas Tech University Health Sciences
  Center M
Texas Wesleyan University B
Texas Woman's University M
University of Mary Hardin-Baylor B
University of Texas
  Arlington B
  Austin B
University of the Incarnate Word B

West Texas A&M University B

Utah

Brigham Young University B, M
Utah Career College A
Weber State University B

Vermont

Castleton State College B
Johnson State College B
Lyndon State College B
Norwich University B

Virginia

Averett University B
Bluefield College B
Bridgewater College B
Emory & Henry College B
James Madison University B
Liberty University B
Longwood University B
Lynchburg College B
Roanoke College B
Shenandoah University M

Washington

Centralia College A
Eastern Washington University B
Spokane Falls Community College A
Washington State University B
Whitworth College B

West Virginia

Alderson-Broaddus College B
Concord University B
University of Charleston B
West Virginia University B, T
West Virginia Wesleyan College B

Wisconsin

Carroll College B
Carthage College B
Concordia University Wisconsin B
Marquette University B
University of Wisconsin
  Eau Claire B
  La Crosse B
  Stevens Point B

Atmospheric physics/ dynamics

New Mexico

New Mexico Institute of Mining and
  Technology B, M, D

Pennsylvania

Drexel University B, M, D

Washington

Cascadia Community College A

Atmospheric science

Alabama

Community College of the Air
  Force A
University of Alabama
  Huntsville M, D
University of South Alabama B

Alaska

University of Alaska
  Fairbanks M, D

Arizona

University of Arizona B, M, D

California

San Jose State University M

University of California
Berkeley *B*
Davis *B, M, D*
Los Angeles *B, M, D*

Colorado
Colorado State University *M, D*
Metropolitan State College of
Denver *B*
United States Air Force Academy *B*

Connecticut
Western Connecticut State
University *B*

Delaware
University of Delaware *D*

District of Columbia
Howard University *M, D*

Florida
Embry-Riddle Aeronautical
University *B*
Florida State University *C, B, M, D*
Gulf Coast Community College *A*
Manatee Community College *A*
Miami Dade College *A*
University of Miami *B*

Illinois
Northern Illinois University *B*
University of Illinois
Urbana-Champaign *M, D*

Indiana
Valparaiso University *B*

Kansas
University of Kansas *B*

Louisiana
University of Louisiana at Monroe *B*

Maryland
University of Maryland
College Park *M, D*

Massachusetts
Massachusetts Institute of
Technology *M, D*

Michigan
University of Michigan *B, M, D*

Minnesota
St. Cloud State University *B*

Mississippi
Jackson State University *B*

Missouri
St. Louis University *B, M, D*
University of Missouri
Columbia *B, M, D*

Nebraska
Creighton University *B, M*
University of Nebraska
Lincoln *B*

Nevada
University of Nevada
Reno *M, D*

New Hampshire
Plymouth State University *B, M*

New Jersey
Princeton University *M, D*

Rutgers, The State University of New
Jersey
New Brunswick/Piscataway
Campus *B*

New York
Cornell University *B, M, D*
State University of New York
Albany *B, M, D*
College at Brockport *B*
College at Oneonta *B*
Maritime College *B*

North Carolina
North Carolina State
University *B, M, D*
University of North Carolina
Asheville *B*

North Dakota
University of North Dakota *B, M*

Ohio
Ohio State University
Columbus Campus *M, D*
Ohio University *B*
Shawnee State University *B*

Oregon
Oregon State University *M, D*

Pennsylvania
Millersville University of
Pennsylvania *B*
Penn State
Abington *B*
Altoona *B*
Beaver *B*
Berks *B*
Delaware County *B*
Dubois *B*
Fayette *B*
Hazleton *B*
Lehigh Valley *B*
McKeesport *B*
Mont Alto *B*
New Kensington *B*
Shenango *B*
University Park *B, M, D*
Worthington Scranton *B*
York *B*

South Dakota
South Dakota School of Mines and
Technology *M, D*

Texas
Texas A&M University *B, M, D*
Texas Tech University *M*

Vermont
Lyndon State College *B*

Washington
Everett Community College *A*
University of Washington *B, M, D*

Wisconsin
Northland College *B*
University of Wisconsin
Madison *B, M, D*

Wyoming
University of Wyoming *M, D*

Atomic/molecular physics

California
San Diego State University *B*

University of California
San Diego *B*

District of Columbia
Catholic University of America *B*

Florida
Florida State University *M, D*

Massachusetts
Harvard College *B, D*

Minnesota
St. Mary's University of Minnesota *B*
University of Minnesota
Twin Cities *M, D*

Mississippi
Mississippi College *B*

Nevada
University of Nevada
Reno *D*

Ohio
College of Wooster *B*
Ohio State University
Columbus Campus *M, D*

Texas
Rice University *M, D*
University of North Texas *M, D*

Utah
University of Utah *B, D*

Virginia
Norfolk State University *M*

Wisconsin
University of Wisconsin
Madison *M, D*

Auctioneering

Pennsylvania
Harrisburg Area Community
College *C*

Audiology/hearing sciences

Alabama
University of Alabama *M*
University of Montevallo *B*

California
San Diego State University *M*

Colorado
University of Northern
Colorado *B, M, D*

Connecticut
University of Connecticut *D*

District of Columbia
Gallaudet University *D*

Florida
Nova Southeastern University *D*
University of Florida *B, D*
University of South Florida *D*

Idaho
Idaho State University *D*

Illinois
Northwestern University *M, D*

Rush University *D*
University of Illinois
Urbana-Champaign *B, M, D*

Indiana
Ball State University *M*
Indiana University
Bloomington *B*
Indiana University-Purdue University
Fort Wayne *B*

Iowa
University of Iowa *B*

Kansas
University of Kansas *D*
University of Kansas Medical
Center *M, D*

Kentucky
University of Louisville *D*

Louisiana
Louisiana State University Health
Sciences Center *M, D*

Maryland
University of Maryland
College Park *D*

Massachusetts
Boston University *M, D*
Emerson College *B, M*
Northeastern University *M*

Michigan
Central Michigan University *D*
Wayne State University *M, D*

Mississippi
University of Southern Mississippi *B*

Missouri
Washington University in St.
Louis *M, D*

Nebraska
University of Nebraska
Lincoln *D*

New Jersey
Seton Hall University *D*

New York
City University of New York
Brooklyn College *M*
Hunter College *M*
Lehman College *M*
Hofstra University *M, D*
State University of New York
Buffalo *D*
College at Plattsburgh *B, M*
New Paltz *B, M*
Syracuse University *M, D*

North Carolina
University of North Carolina
Chapel Hill *M, D*

Ohio
Cleveland State University *B, M*
Ohio State University
Columbus Campus *B, M, D*

Oklahoma
University of Oklahoma *D*

Oregon
Portland State University *B, M*

Pennsylvania

Bloomsburg University of
Pennsylvania *D*
La Salle University *B, M*
University of Pittsburgh *D*

Rhode Island

University of Rhode Island *M*

South Dakota

Northern State University *B, T*

Tennessee

East Tennessee State University *D*
University of Memphis *D*
University of Tennessee
Knoxville *B, M, D*

Texas

Lamar University *M, D*
Stephen F. Austin State University *B, T*
Texas Tech University Health Sciences
Center *D*
University of Houston *M*
University of North Texas *M*
University of Texas
Dallas *D*

Utah

University of Utah *B, M, D*

Virginia

James Madison University *D*

Washington

University of Washington *M, D*

West Virginia

West Virginia University *D*

Wyoming

University of Wyoming *M*

Audiology/speech pathology

Alabama

Auburn University *B, M*
University of Alabama *B*
University of South Alabama *B, M, D*

Arizona

Arizona State University *M, D*

Arkansas

Arkansas State University *B*
Ouachita Baptist University *B*
University of Arkansas *B, M*
University of Arkansas
Little Rock *B, M*
for Medical Sciences *M*
University of Central Arkansas *B, M*

California

California State University
East Bay *B, M*
Fullerton *B, M*
Northridge *M*
Sacramento *B, M*
Loma Linda University *B*
San Francisco State University *B, M*
University of California
Santa Barbara *B, M, D*
University of Redlands *B, M*

Colorado

University of Northern Colorado *B*

Connecticut

Southern Connecticut State
University *M*
University of Connecticut *M, D*

District of Columbia

Gallaudet University *M*
George Washington University *B, M*
University of the District of
Columbia *M*

Florida

Florida Atlantic University *M*
Florida International University *M*
Florida State University *B, M, D, T*
University of Central Florida *B, M*
University of Florida *B, D*
University of South Florida *B, M, D*

Hawaii

University of Hawaii
Manoa *B, M*

Idaho

Idaho State University *B*

Illinois

Augustana College *B*
Illinois State University *B, M, T*
Northwestern University *D*
Southern Illinois University
Edwardsville *B, M*
University of Illinois
Urbana-Champaign *B, M, D*

Indiana

Ball State University *B*
Indiana State University *M, T*
Indiana University
Bloomington *B, M, D*
Purdue University *B, M, D*

Iowa

University of Iowa *M, D*

Kansas

Fort Hays State University *M*
Wichita State University *B, M, D*

Kentucky

Brescia University *B*
Murray State University *B, M, T*
University of Kentucky *B, M*
University of Louisville *M*
Western Kentucky University *M, T*

Louisiana

Louisiana State University
Shreveport *B*
Louisiana State University Health
Sciences Center *M*
Louisiana State University and
Agricultural and Mechanical
College *B, M, D*
Louisiana Tech University *B, M*
Nicholls State University *B*
Southern University and Agricultural
and Mechanical College *B*
University of Louisiana at
Lafayette *B, M*
University of Louisiana at
Monroe *B, M*

Maine

University of Maine *B, M*

Maryland

Loyola College in Maryland *M*
Towson University *B, M, D*

Massachusetts

Boston University *M, D*
Elms College *B*
Emerson College *B*
Northeastern University *B*

Michigan

Andrews University *B*
Calvin College *B*
Central Michigan University *B, M, T*
Michigan State University *B, M, D*
Western Michigan University *B, M, D*

Minnesota

Minnesota State University
Moorhead *B*
St. Cloud State University *B*
University of Minnesota
Twin Cities *B*

Mississippi

Delta State University *B*
University of Mississippi *B, M*
University of Southern
Mississippi *B, M*

Missouri

Central Missouri State University *M*
Missouri State University *B, M*
St. Louis University *B, M*
University of Missouri
Columbia *B, M*
Washington University in St.
Louis *M, D*

Nebraska

University of Nebraska
Lincoln *M*

Nevada

University of Nevada
Reno *B, M*

New Hampshire

University of New Hampshire *M*

New Jersey

Richard Stockton College of New
Jersey *B*
William Paterson University of New
Jersey *M*

New Mexico

Eastern New Mexico University *B, M*
University of New Mexico *B, M*

New York

Adelphi University *B, M, D*
City University of New York
Brooklyn College *B*
Lehman College *B*
Queens College *M*
College of Saint Rose *B, M, T*
Elmira College *B*
Hofstra University *B*
Iona College *B*
Ithaca College *B, T*
Long Island University
Brooklyn Campus *B*
C.W. Post Campus *B, M*
Marymount Manhattan College *B*
Mercy College *B*
Molloy College *B*
New York University *M, D*
St. John's University *B, M, D*
State University of New York
Buffalo *B, M, D*
College at Cortland *B*
College at Fredonia *B, M, T*
College at Plattsburgh *B, M*
New Paltz *B, M*
Syracuse University *B, M, D*

Yeshiva University *B*

North Carolina

East Carolina University *B, M, D*
Shaw University *B*
University of North Carolina
Chapel Hill *M, D*
Greensboro *B, M*

North Dakota

University of North Dakota *B, D*

Ohio

College of Wooster *B*
Kent State University *B, M, D*
Miami University
Oxford Campus *B, M, T*
Ohio State University
Columbus Campus *B, M, D*
Ohio University *B, M, D*
University of Akron *B, M*
University of Cincinnati *B, M, D*

Oklahoma

Northeastern State University *B, M*
University of Central Oklahoma *B*
University of Oklahoma *M, D*
University of Tulsa *B, M*

Pennsylvania

Bloomsburg University of
Pennsylvania *B*
Clarion University of
Pennsylvania *B*
East Stroudsburg University of
Pennsylvania *B, M, T*
Indiana University of Pennsylvania *M*
La Salle University *B, M*
Penn State
University Park *B, M*
Temple University *B, M, D*
Thiel College *B*
University of Pittsburgh *B*
West Chester University of
Pennsylvania *B, M*

Puerto Rico

Inter American University of Puerto
Rico
Barranquitas Campus *B*

South Carolina

South Carolina State University *B, M*
University of South Carolina *D*

South Dakota

Augustana College *B*
Northern State University *B, T*

Tennessee

East Tennessee State University *M*
Lambuth University *B*
Tennessee State University *B*
University of Memphis *M, D*
Vanderbilt University *M, D*

Texas

Hardin-Simmons University *B*
Lamar University *B*
Stephen F. Austin State University *B*
Texas State University: San
Marcos *B, M*
Texas Tech University Health Sciences
Center *M*
Texas Woman's University *B*
University of Houston *B, M*
University of North Texas *B, M*
University of Texas
Dallas *B, M*
El Paso *B, M*
Pan American *B, M*

Utah

Brigham Young University *B, M*
University of Utah *B, M, D*
Utah State University *B, M, D*

Vermont

University of Vermont *M*

Virginia

Hampton University *B, M*
Old Dominion University *B, M*
Radford University *M*
University of Virginia *B, M*

Washington

Eastern Washington University *B, T*
University of Washington *B, M, D*
Washington State University *B, M*
Western Washington University *B, M*

West Virginia

Marshall University *M*
West Virginia University *B*

Wisconsin

Marquette University *B*
University of Wisconsin
   Madison *B, M, D*
   Stevens Point *B, M, T*
   Whitewater *M*

Wyoming

University of Wyoming *B, M*

Auditing

Illinois

University of Illinois
   Urbana-Champaign *B*

Massachusetts

Babson College *B*

Ohio

Bowling Green State University *B*

Australian/Oceanic/ Pacific languages

Hawaii

University of Hawaii
   Hilo *M*

Auto body repair

Alabama

Alabama Southern Community
   College *A*
Bevill State Community College *A*
Bishop State Community College *C*
Gadsden State Community College *C*
George C. Wallace State Community
   College
   George C. Wallace Community
     College at Dothan *C*
Lawson State Community
   College *C, A*
Northwest-Shoals Community
   College *C*
Shelton State Community College *C*
Trenholm State Technical College *C*
Virginia College Technical *C, A*
Wallace State Community College at
   Hanceville *C, A*

Arizona

Arizona Western College *C*
Central Arizona College *C*
Mesa Community College *C*

Arkansas

Arkansas Tech University *C*
North Arkansas College *C*
Pulaski Technical College *C*
University of Arkansas
   Cossatot Community College of the
     C

California

Allan Hancock College *C, A*
Antelope Valley College *C, A*
Cerritos Community College *A*
Cerro Coso Community College *C, A*
Chabot College *A*
Chaffey College *A*
College of Marin: Kentfield *C, A*
Columbia College *C*
Contra Costa College *C, A*
Cuesta College *C, A*
Cypress College *C, A*
East Los Angeles College *C*
El Camino College *C, A*
Fresno City College *C, A*
Fullerton College *C, A*
Gavilan Community College *C*
Golden West College *C, A*
Imperial Valley College *C, A*
Lassen College *C, A*
Long Beach City College *C, A*
Los Angeles Pierce College *C, A*
Los Angeles Trade and Technical
   College *C, A*
Mendocino College *C, A*
Merced College *C, A*
MiraCosta College *C, A*
Modesto Junior College *C, A*
Mount San Jacinto College *C*
Palomar College *C, A*
Pasadena City College *C, A*
Porterville College *C, A*
Riverside Community College *C, A*
Santa Monica College *C, A*
Santa Rosa Junior College *C*
Solano Community College *C, A*
Yuba Community College District *C*

Colorado

Aims Community College *C, A*
Mesa State College *C, A*
Morgan Community College *A*
Pikes Peak Community College *C, A*
Pueblo Community College *C, A*
Red Rocks Community College *C, A*
Trinidad State Junior College *C, A*

Florida

Central Florida Community College *C*
Daytona Beach Community College *C*
Florida Community College at
   Jacksonville *C*
Hillsborough Community College *C*
Palm Beach Community College *C*
South Florida Community College *C*

Georgia

Albany Technical College *C*
Athens Technical College *C*
Central Georgia Technical College *C*
Coastal Georgia Community
   College *C*
Columbus Technical College *C*
Georgia Highlands College *A*
Georgia Southwestern State
   University *A*
Middle Georgia College *A*
Savannah Technical College *C, A*

Hawaii

University of Hawaii
   Hawaii Community College *C, A*
   Honolulu Community College *A*
   Kauai Community College *C, A*
   Maui Community College *A*

Idaho

Boise State University *C, A*
College of Southern Idaho *C, A*
Idaho State University *C, A*
Lewis-Clark State College *C, A, B*
North Idaho College *C, A*

Illinois

Black Hawk College *C, A*
Carl Sandburg College *C, A*
City Colleges of Chicago
   Kennedy-King College *C*
College of Lake County *C*
Highland Community College *C, A*
Illinois Eastern Community Colleges
   Olney Central College *A*
John A. Logan College *C, A*
Joliet Junior College *C, A*
Kaskaskia College *C, A*
Kishwaukee College *C, A*
Lake Land College *C*
Lincoln Land Community College *C, A*
Parkland College *C, A*
Prairie State College *C*
Waubonsee Community College *C, A*

Indiana

Vincennes University *A*

Iowa

Des Moines Area Community
   College *C, A*
Hawkeye Community College *C, A*
Indian Hills Community College *A*
Iowa Lakes Community College *C*
Kirkwood Community College *C*
Northeast Iowa Community
   College *C*
Northwest Iowa Community
   College *C, A*
Scott Community College *A*
Southeastern Community College
   North Campus *C*
Southwestern Community College *C*
Western Iowa Tech Community
   College *C, A*

Kansas

Butler County Community
   College *C, A*
Coffeyville Community College *C*
Hutchinson Community College *C, A*
Manhattan Area Technical
   College *C, A*

Kentucky

Big Sandy Community and Technical
   College *C*
Maysville Community College *C, A*
Somerset Community College *C, A*

Louisiana

Gretna Career College *A*

Maine

Northern Maine Community
   College *C, A*

Maryland

Harford Community College *C*

Michigan

Alpena Community College *C*
Bay de Noc Community College *C*
Ferris State University *A*
Kirtland Community College *C*
Mott Community College *A*
Northern Michigan University *C*
Oakland Community College *C*
Washtenaw Community College *C, A*
Wayne County Community College *A*

Minnesota

Century Community and Technical
   College *C, A*
Dakota County Technical College *C, A*
Dunwoody College of
   Technology *C, A*
Hennepin Technical College *C, A*
Lake Superior College *C*
Minnesota State College - Southeast
   Technical *C, A*
Minnesota State Community and
   Technical College - Fergus
   Falls *C, A*
Northland Community & Technical
   College *C, A*
Ridgewater College *C, A*
Riverland Community College *C*
St. Cloud Technical College *C, A*
St. Paul College *C*
South Central College *A*

Mississippi

Coahoma Community College *C*
East Central Community College *C*
Hinds Community College *C*
Itawamba Community College *C*
Mississippi Gulf Coast Community
   College
   Jefferson Davis Campus *C*
Pearl River Community College *C, A*

Missouri

Crowder College *C*
Longview Community College *C, A*
Mineral Area College *C, A*
North Central Missouri College *A*
Ozarks Technical Community
   College *C, A*
Ranken Technical College *A*

Montana

Montana State University
   Billings *C, A*
   College of Technology-Great Falls *C*
Montana Tech of the University of
   Montana *A*

Nebraska

Central Community College *C, A*
Metropolitan Community
   College *C, A*
Mid-Plains Community College
   Area *C, A*
Northeast Community College *A*
Western Nebraska Community
   College *C, A*

New Hampshire

New Hampshire Community
   Technical College
   Nashua *A*

New Mexico

Eastern New Mexico University:
   Roswell Campus *C*
San Juan College *C, A*

New York

Erie Community College
   South Campus *A*
State University of New York
   College of Agriculture and
     Technology at Morrisville *A*
   College of Technology at Alfred *A*

North Carolina

Blue Ridge Community College *C*
Caldwell Community College and
   Technical Institute *C*
Cape Fear Community College *C*
Central Piedmont Community
   College *C*

Cleveland Community College *C*
Coastal Carolina Community
College *C*
Craven Community College *C*
Edgecombe Community College *C*
Fayetteville Technical Community
College *C, D*
Forsyth Technical Community
College *C*
Guilford Technical Community
College *C*
Haywood Community College *C*
Isothermal Community College *C, A*
Mayland Community College *C*
McDowell Technical Community
College *C*
Montgomery Community College *C*
Randolph Community College *C*
Sandhills Community College *C*
South Piedmont Community
College *C*
Surry Community College *C*
Tri-County Community College *C*
Wilkes Community College *C*

North Dakota

Bismarck State College *C, A*
North Dakota State College of
Science *C, A*

Oklahoma

Oklahoma State University
Okmulgee *C*
Rose State College *A*
Western Oklahoma State College *A*

Oregon

Clackamas Community College *C, A*
Lane Community College *C, A*
Linn-Benton Community College *C*
Portland Community College *C, A*

Pennsylvania

Commonwealth Technical Institute *C*
Delaware County Community
College *C*
Pennco Tech *A*
Pennsylvania College of
Technology *C, A*
Thaddeus Stevens College of
Technology *C*

Rhode Island

New England Institute of
Technology *A*

South Carolina

Greenville Technical College *C*

South Dakota

Southeast Technical Institute *A*
Western Dakota Technical Institute *C*

Tennessee

Chattanooga State Technical
Community College *C*

Texas

Amarillo College *C*
Central Texas College *C, A*
Del Mar College *C*
Eastfield College *C, A*
Grayson County College *C, A*
Hill College *C, A*
Houston Community College
System *C*
Howard College *C*
Kilgore College *C, A*
St. Philip's College *C, A*
San Jacinto College
North *C, A*
South Plains College *C, A*

Tarrant County College *C, A*
Texarkana College *C*
Texas Southmost College *C*
Texas State Technical College
Harlingen *C, A*
Waco *C, A*
West Texas *C*
Trinity Valley Community College *C*
University of Texas
Brownsville *C*

Utah

Salt Lake Community College *C, A*
Utah Valley State College *C, A*
Weber State University *C, A*

Virginia

Danville Community College *C*
Northern Virginia Community
College *C*

Washington

Bellingham Technical College *A*
Clover Park Technical College *C*
Columbia Basin College *A*
Green River Community College *C, A*
Lake Washington Technical
College *C, A*
Lower Columbia College *A*
Renton Technical College *C, A*
South Seattle Community
College *C, A*
Spokane Community College *A*
Walla Walla Community College *C, A*

Wisconsin

Chippewa Valley Technical College *C*
Fox Valley Technical College *C*
Lakeshore Technical College *C*
Madison Area Technical College *C*
Milwaukee Area Technical College *C*
Moraine Park Technical College *C*
Northcentral Technical College *A*
Northeast Wisconsin Technical
College *C*
Southwest Wisconsin Technical
College *C*
Waukesha County Technical
College *C*
Wisconsin Indianhead Technical
College *C*

Wyoming

Laramie County Community
College *C, A*
Wyoming Technical Institute *C, A*

Automotive
engineering technology

Alabama

Enterprise-Ozark Community
College *C, A*
Lawson State Community
College *C, A*
Trenholm State Technical College *C, A*

California

Santa Barbara City College *C, A*
Taft College *C, A*

Colorado

Colorado State University
Pueblo *B*

Florida

Manatee Community College *A*

Georgia

Middle Georgia Technical College *C*

Illinois

Southern Illinois University
Carbondale *B*

Indiana

Indiana State University *B*

Massachusetts

Benjamin Franklin Institute of
Technology *A, B*
Massachusetts Bay Community
College *A*
Springfield Technical Community
College *A*

Michigan

Andrews University *A, B*
Central Michigan University *B*
Ferris State University *B*
Gogebic Community College *C, A*
Grand Rapids Community College *A*
Kirtland Community College *C, A*
Western Michigan University *B*

Minnesota

Hennepin Technical College *C, A*
Minnesota State University
Mankato *B*

Missouri

Central Missouri State University *A*

New Jersey

Burlington County College *C, A*
Sussex County Community
College *C, A*

New Mexico

Santa Fe Community College *C*

New York

State University of New York
College of Agriculture and
Technology at
Morrisville *C, A, B*
College of Technology at
Canton *C, A*
Farmingdale *A, B*

North Dakota

North Dakota State College of
Science *A*

Ohio

Cincinnati State Technical and
Community College *C, A*
Owens Community College
Toledo *C, A*
Sinclair Community College *C, A*

Pennsylvania

Community College of Allegheny
County *C, A*
Luzerne County Community
College *A*
Montgomery County Community
College *C, A*
Pennsylvania College of
Technology *C, A, B*

Puerto Rico

University of Puerto Rico
Carolina Regional College *A*

Texas

Brookhaven College *C*

Wisconsin

Mid-State Technical College *C*

Automotive technology

Alabama

Bishop State Community College *C*
Gadsden State Community College *C*
J. F. Drake State Technical College *C*
Northwest-Shoals Community
College *C*
Shelton State Community College *C*
Virginia College Technical *C, A*
Wallace State Community College at
Hanceville *C, A*

Alaska

University of Alaska
Anchorage *C, A*
Fairbanks *C*
Southeast *C, A*

Arizona

Arizona Western College *A*
Central Arizona College *C, A*
Eastern Arizona College *C, A*
Gateway Community College *C, A*
Glendale Community College *C, A*
Mohave Community College *A*
Pima Community College *C, A*
Universal Technical Institute *A*
Yavapai College *C, A*

Arkansas

Arkansas Northeastern College *C*
Arkansas State University *A*
Arkansas Tech University *C*
North Arkansas College *C, A*
Ouachita Technical College *C*
Ozarka College *C, A*
South Arkansas Community College *A*
Southern Arkansas University Tech *C*
University of Arkansas
Cossatot Community College of the
C, A
Fort Smith *C*
University of Arkansas Community
College at Morrilton *C*

California

Allan Hancock College *C, A*
American River College *A*
Antelope Valley College *C, A*
Bakersfield College *A*
Butte College *C, A*
Chabot College *C, A*
Chaffey College *C, A*
Citrus College *C, A*
College of the Desert *C*
Columbia College *A*
Copper Mountain College *C, A*
Cypress College *C, A*
East Los Angeles College *C, A*
El Camino College *C, A*
Fresno City College *C, A*
Golden West College *C, A*
Lassen College *A*
Long Beach City College *C, A*
Los Angeles Harbor College *C, A*
Los Angeles Pierce College *C, A*
MiraCosta College *C, A*
Modesto Junior College *C, A*
Mount San Jacinto College *C, A*
Palo Verde College *C, A*
Rio Hondo College *C, A*
Riverside Community College *C, A*
Saddleback College *C*
San Bernardino Valley College *C, A*
Santa Ana College *C, A*
Santa Barbara City College *C, A*
Santa Rosa Junior College *C*
Santiago Canyon College *A*
Shasta College *C, A*
Sierra College *C, A*
Skyline College *C, A*
Southwestern College *C, A*

Taft College *C, A*
Ventura College *C, A*
Victor Valley College *C, A*
Yuba Community College
   District *C, A*

Colorado

Arapahoe Community College *C, A*
Denver Automotive & Diesel
   College *A*
Front Range Community College *C, A*
IntelliTec College: Grand Junction *A*
Mesa State College *C, A*
Morgan Community College *C, A*
Northeastern Junior College *C, A*
Otero Junior College *C*
Pikes Peak Community College *C, A*
Pueblo Community College *C, A*
Red Rocks Community College *C, A*
Trinidad State Junior College *C, A*
Westwood College of Technology *C, A*

Connecticut

Gateway Community College *A*
Naugatuck Valley Community
   College *C, A*

Florida

Brevard Community College *C*
Broward Community College *A*
Central Florida Community
   College *C, A*
Florida Community College at
   Jacksonville *C, A*
Indian River Community College *C, A*
New England Institute of
   Technology *A*
Palm Beach Community College *C, A*
Pensacola Junior College *A*
St. Petersburg College *A*
Seminole Community College *C, A*
South Florida Community College *C*

Georgia

Albany Technical College *C*
Athens Technical College *C*
Central Georgia Technical College *C*
Chattahoochee Technical College *C, A*
Coastal Georgia Community
   College *C*
Columbus Technical College *C, A*
Dalton State College *C*
DeKalb Technical College *A*
Georgia Southwestern State
   University *A*
Gwinnett Technical College *C, A*
Middle Georgia College *A*
Savannah Technical College *C, A*
Southwest Georgia Technical
   College *C*
Waycross College *A*
West Georgia Technical College *C*

Hawaii

University of Hawaii
   Hawaii Community College *C, A*
   Honolulu Community College *A*
   Kauai Community College *C, A*
   Maui Community College *A*

Idaho

Boise State University *C, A*
Brigham Young University-Idaho *A*
College of Southern Idaho *C, A*
Eastern Idaho Technical College *C, A*
Idaho State University *C, A*
Lewis-Clark State College *C, A, B*
North Idaho College *C, A*

Illinois

Black Hawk College *C, A*
Black Hawk College
   East Campus *C, A*
City Colleges of Chicago
   Kennedy-King College *C, A*
College of DuPage *C, A*
College of Lake County *C, A*
Elgin Community College *C, A*
Highland Community College *C, A*
Illinois Eastern Community Colleges
   Frontier Community College *C*
John A. Logan College *C, A*
Kankakee Community College *C, A*
Kaskaskia College *C, A*
Kishwaukee College *C, A*
Lewis and Clark Community
   College *A*
Lincoln Land Community College *C, A*
McHenry County College *C, A*
Moraine Valley Community
   College *C, A*
Morton College *C, A*
Oakton Community College *C, A*
Parkland College *C, A*
Prairie State College *C, A*
Rend Lake College *C, A*
Richland Community College *A*
Rock Valley College *C, A*
Spoon River College *A*
Triton College *C, A*
Waubonsee Community College *C, A*

Indiana

Ivy Tech State College
   Ivy Tech Community College:
      Central Indiana *C, A*
   Ivy Tech Community College:
      Columbus *A*
   Ivy Tech Community College: East
      Central *C, A*
   Ivy Tech Community College:
      Kokomo *C, A*
   Ivy Tech Community College:
      Lafayette *C, A*
   Ivy Tech Community College: North
      Central *A*
   Ivy Tech Community College:
      Northeast *A*
   Ivy Tech Community College:
      Northwest *C, A*
   Ivy Tech Community College: South
      Central *C, A*
   Ivy Tech Community College:
      Southwest *A*
   Ivy Tech Community College:
      Wabash Valley *C, A*
   Ivy Tech Community College:
      Whitewater *C, A*
Vincennes University *A*

Iowa

Des Moines Area Community
   College *C, A*
Hawkeye Community College *A*
Indian Hills Community College *A*
Iowa Central Community College *A*
Iowa Lakes Community College *C*
Kirkwood Community College *C, A*
North Iowa Area Community
   College *C, A*
Northeast Iowa Community
   College *C, A*
Northwest Iowa Community
   College *C, A*
Scott Community College *A*
Western Iowa Tech Community
   College *C, A*

Kansas

Barton County Community
   College *C, A*
Butler County Community
   College *C, A*
Coffeyville Community College *C*
Cowley County Community
   College *C, A*
Hutchinson Community College *C, A*
Johnson County Community
   College *C, A*
Manhattan Area Technical
   College *C, A*
McPherson College *B*
North Central Kansas Technical
   College *A*
Pittsburg State University *C, A, B*
Pratt Community College *A*

Kentucky

Big Sandy Community and Technical
   College *C, A*
Elizabethtown Community and
   Technical College *C, A*
Hazard Community College *A*
Jefferson Community College *C, A*
Maysville Community College *C, A*
Owensboro Community College *C*
Somerset Community College *C, A*

Louisiana

Delgado Community College *C, A*

Maine

Central Maine Community College *A*
Eastern Maine Community
   College *C, A*
Northern Maine Community
   College *C, A*
Washington County Community
   College *C*

Maryland

Allegany College of Maryland *C, A*
Community College of Baltimore
   County *C, A*
Harford Community College *C*
Montgomery College *C, A*

Massachusetts

Benjamin Franklin Institute of
   Technology *A, B*
Middlesex Community College *A*
Mount Wachusett Community
   College *C, A*
Quinsigamond Community
   College *C, A*

Michigan

Alpena Community College *C, A*
Baker College
   of Clinton Township *A*
   of Flint *A*
   of Owosso *C, A*
Bay de Noc Community College *C, A*
Delta College *A*
Ferris State University *A*
Glen Oaks Community College *C*
Gogebic Community College *C, A*
Grand Rapids Community College *C*
Henry Ford Community College *C, A*
Jackson Community College *C, A*
Kalamazoo Valley Community
   College *C, A*
Kirtland Community College *C, A*
Macomb Community College *C, A*
Mid Michigan Community College *C*
Mott Community College *C, A*
Northern Michigan University *C, A*
Northwestern Michigan College *C, A*
Oakland Community College *C, A*
Southwestern Michigan College *C, A*
Washtenaw Community College *C, A*
Wayne County Community College *A*

Minnesota

Anoka Technical College *C, A*
Anoka-Ramsey Community College *A*
Central Lakes College *C, A*
Century Community and Technical
   College *C, A*
Dakota County Technical College *C, A*
Dunwoody College of
   Technology *C, A*
Hennepin Technical College *C, A*
Hibbing Community College *C*
Lake Superior College *C, A*
Mesabi Range Community and
   Technical College *C, A*
Minneapolis Community and
   Technical College *M*
Minnesota State College - Southeast
   Technical *C*
Minnesota State Community and
   Technical College - Fergus
   Falls *C, A*
Minnesota State University
   Mankato *B*
North Hennepin Community
   College *A*
Northland Community & Technical
   College *C, A*
Northwest Technical College *C*
Pine Technical College *C, A*
Ridgewater College *C, A*
Riverland Community College *C*
Rochester Community and Technical
   College *C*
St. Cloud Technical College *C, A*
St. Paul College *C*
South Central College *A*

Mississippi

Copiah-Lincoln Community College *A*
Itawamba Community College *A*

Missouri

Central Missouri State University *A*
Crowder College *C, A*
East Central College *C, A*
Jefferson College *C, A*
Longview Community College *C, A*
Mineral Area College *C, A*
Ozarks Technical Community
   College *C, A*
Ranken Technical College *A*
State Fair Community College *C, A*

Montana

Dawson Community College *A*
Fort Peck Community College *C, A*
Helena College of Technology of the
   University of Montana *A*
Montana State University
   Billings *C, A*
Montana Tech of the University of
   Montana *A*

Nebraska

Central Community College *C, A*
Metropolitan Community
   College *C, A*
Mid-Plains Community College
   Area *C, A*
Northeast Community College *A*
Western Nebraska Community
   College *C, A*

Nevada

Community College of Southern
   Nevada *A*
Truckee Meadows Community
   College *A*
Western Nevada Community
   College *C, A*

New Hampshire

New Hampshire Community
   Technical College
   Berlin *C, A*
   Manchester *C, A*
   Nashua *A*
   Stratham *C, A*

New Jersey

Brookdale Community College C
Burlington County College C, A
Gloucester County College A
Mercer County Community
College C, A
Middlesex County College A
Sussex County Community
College C, A

New Mexico

Albuquerque Technical-Vocational
Institute C
Clovis Community College C, A
Dona Ana Branch Community College
of New Mexico State
University C, A
Eastern New Mexico University:
Roswell Campus C, A
New Mexico Junior College C, A
New Mexico State University
Grants A
San Juan College C, A
Western New Mexico University C, A

New York

Columbia-Greene Community
College A
Corning Community College C, A
Erie Community College
South Campus A
Fulton-Montgomery Community
College C, A
Monroe Community College A
Onondaga Community College A
Rockland Community College A
State University of New York
College of Agriculture and
Technology at Morrisville A
College of Technology at Alfred A
College of Technology at
Canton C, A
College of Technology at Delhi C, A
Farmingdale A
Suffolk County Community College A
Westchester Community College A

North Carolina

Asheville-Buncombe Technical
Community College C, A
Beaufort County Community
College C, A
Bladen Community College C
Blue Ridge Community College C
Caldwell Community College and
Technical Institute C
Cape Fear Community College A
Catawba Valley Community
College C, A
Central Carolina Community
College A
Central Piedmont Community
College C, A
Coastal Carolina Community
College C
Craven Community College C, A
Davidson County Community
College C, A
Durham Technical Community
College A
Fayetteville Technical Community
College C, A
Guilford Technical Community
College C, A
Halifax Community College C
Haywood Community College C, A
Lenoir Community College C, A
Martin Community College C, A
Pitt Community College C, A
Randolph Community College A
Rowan-Cabarrus Community
College C
Sandhills Community College C, A

Southwestern Community
College C, A
Surry Community College A
Tri-County Community College A
Wilkes Community College C, A
Wilson Technical Community
College C

North Dakota

Bismarck State College C, A
Cankdeska Cikana Community
College C, A
Lake Region State College C, A
North Dakota State College of
Science C, A
Williston State College A

Ohio

Cincinnati State Technical and
Community College C, A
Columbus State Community
College C, A
Cuyahoga Community College
Metropolitan Campus A
Sinclair Community College C, A
Stark State College of Technology A
University of Cincinnati
Raymond Walters College C, A
University of Northwestern Ohio C, A
Washington State Community
College A
Zane State College A

Oklahoma

Oklahoma State University
Okmulgee A
Rose State College A
Western Oklahoma State College A

Oregon

Central Oregon Community
College C
Chemeketa Community College A
Clackamas Community College A
Clatsop Community College C
Lane Community College C, A
Linn-Benton Community College C, A
Mount Hood Community College A
Portland Community College C, A
Rogue Community College C, A
Umpqua Community College C, A

Pennsylvania

Delaware County Community
College C
Harrisburg Area Community
College C, A
Johnson College A
Luzerne County Community
College A
New Castle School of Trades A
Northampton County Area
Community College C, A
Pennco Tech A

Puerto Rico

Electronic Data Processing College:
San Sebastian A

South Carolina

Aiken Technical College C
Florence-Darlington Technical
College C, A
Greenville Technical College C, A
Midlands Technical College C, A
Orangeburg-Calhoun Technical
College A
Piedmont Technical College A
Spartanburg Technical College C, A
Trident Technical College C, A
Williamsburg Technical College C
York Technical College A

South Dakota

Lake Area Technical Institute A
Southeast Technical Institute A
Western Dakota Technical
Institute C, A

Tennessee

Nashville State Community College A
Northeast State Technical Community
College C, A
Southern Adventist University C, A
Southwest Tennessee Community
College A

Texas

Alvin Community College C
Amarillo College C, A
Angelina College C
Austin Community College C, A
Brazosport College C, A
Central Texas College C, A
Del Mar College A
Eastfield College C, A
El Paso Community College C
Houston Community College
System C, A
Kilgore College C, A
Lamar State College at Port
Arthur C, A
Laredo Community College C
Midland College C, A
North Harris Montgomery
Community College District C, A
Odessa College C, A
Ranger College C, A
St. Philip's College C, A
South Plains College C, A
South Texas College C, A
Tarrant County College C, A
Texarkana College C
Texas State Technical College
Harlingen C
Waco A
West Texas C, A
Trinity Valley Community College C
Tyler Junior College C, A
Universal Technical Institute C
University of Texas
Brownsville C
Western Technical Institute: Diana
Drive A

Utah

Dixie State College of Utah C, A
Salt Lake Community College A
Utah Valley State College C, A
Weber State University C, A

Vermont

Vermont Technical College A

Virginia

Blue Ridge Community College C
Danville Community College C
J. Sargeant Reynolds Community
College C, A
John Tyler Community College C
New River Community College A
Northern Virginia Community
College C, A
Southside Virginia Community
College C
Southwest Virginia Community
College C
Thomas Nelson Community
College C, A
Tidewater Community College A

Washington

Bellingham Technical College A
Big Bend Community College C, A
Clark College C, A
Clover Park Technical College C, A

Columbia Basin College A
Grays Harbor College C, A
Lake Washington Technical
College C, A
Lower Columbia College A
Olympic College C, A
Peninsula College C, A
Renton Technical College C, A
Shoreline Community College C, A
Skagit Valley College C, A
South Seattle Community
College C, A
Spokane Falls Community
College C, A
Walla Walla College B
Walla Walla Community College C, A
Wenatchee Valley College C, A
Yakima Valley Community College C

Wisconsin

Fox Valley Technical College A
Gateway Technical College C
Lakeshore Technical College C
Mid-State Technical College C
Milwaukee Area Technical
College C, A
Moraine Park Technical College C
Nicolet Area Technical College C, A
Northcentral Technical College A
Northeast Wisconsin Technical
College C
Southwest Wisconsin Technical
College C
Waukesha County Technical
College A
Western Wisconsin Technical
College A
Wisconsin Indianhead Technical
College C

Wyoming

Casper College C, A
Central Wyoming College C, A
Western Wyoming Community
College C, A
Wyoming Technical Institute C, A

Aviation management

Alabama

Auburn University B
Community College of the Air
Force A
Enterprise-Ozark Community
College C

Alaska

University of Alaska
Anchorage A, B

Arizona

Western International University B

California

College of Alameda C, A
Cypress College A
San Bernardino Valley College A

Colorado

Metropolitan State College of
Denver B

Delaware

Delaware State University B
Wilmington College B

Florida

Broward Community College A
Embry-Riddle Aeronautical
University A, B
Embry-Riddle Aeronautical University:
Extended Campus B, M

Everglades University *B*
Florida Community College at
   Jacksonville *A*
Florida Institute of Technology *B, M*
Jacksonville University *B*
Lynn University *B*
Miami Dade College *C, A*
St. Petersburg College *A*

Hawaii
University of Hawaii
   Honolulu Community College *A*

Illinois
Lewis University *C, B, M*
Lincoln Land Community College *A*
Quincy University *B*
Southern Illinois University
   Carbondale *B*
University of Illinois
   Urbana-Champaign *B*

Indiana
Indiana State University *B*
Vincennes University *A*

Iowa
University of Dubuque *B*

Kansas
Central Christian College of Kansas *A*
Kansas State University *B*

Kentucky
Northern Kentucky University *A*

Louisiana
Louisiana Tech University *B*
Southern University
   Shreveport *C, A*

Maryland
Community College of Baltimore
   County *C, A*

Massachusetts
Bridgewater State College *B*
Salem State College *B*

Michigan
Baker College
   of Flint *A, B*
   of Muskegon *A, B*
Eastern Michigan University *B*
Northern Michigan University *A*
Western Michigan University *B*

Minnesota
Academy College *A*
Anoka Technical College *C, A*
Dakota County Technical College *A*
Inver Hills Community College *A*
Minnesota State University
   Mankato *B*
Northland Community & Technical
   College *C, A*
St. Cloud State University *B*
University of Minnesota
   Crookston *B*
Vermilion Community College *A*
Winona State University *A*

Mississippi
Delta State University *M*

Missouri
Central Missouri State University *M*
Park University *A, B*
St. Louis University *B, M*

Montana
Rocky Mountain College *B*

Nebraska
University of Nebraska
   Omaha *B*

New Hampshire
Daniel Webster College *A, B*

New Jersey
Mercer County Community College *A*

New Mexico
Eastern New Mexico University:
   Roswell Campus *C, A*

New York
Dowling College *B, M*
Schenectady County Community
   College *A*
State University of New York
   Farmingdale *B*
Vaughn College of Aeronautics and
   Technology *A, B*

North Carolina
Caldwell Community College and
   Technical Institute *A*
Lenoir Community College *A*

North Dakota
North Dakota State University *B*
University of North Dakota *B*

Ohio
Bowling Green State University *B*
Ohio University *B*
Sinclair Community College *A*

Oklahoma
National Education Center
   Spartan School of Aeronautics *A, B*
Southern Nazarene University *B*
Tulsa Community College *A*
Western Oklahoma State College *A*

Pennsylvania
Community College of Allegheny
   County *A*
Community College of Beaver
   County *A*
Lehigh Carbon Community College *A*
Luzerne County Community
   College *A*
Marywood University *B*
Robert Morris University *B*

Puerto Rico
Inter American University of Puerto
   Rico
   Bayamon Campus *B*

Tennessee
Middle Tennessee State University *M*

Texas
Mountain View College *A*
Tarleton State University *B*
Texas Southern University *B*

Utah
Utah Valley State College *A*
Westminster College *B*

Virginia
Averett University *B*
Hampton University *B*

West Virginia
Mountain State University *A, B*

Avionics maintenance/technology

Alabama
Bevill State Community College *C*
Enterprise-Ozark Community
   College *A*

Arizona
Chandler-Gilbert Community College
   Pecos *A*
Cochise College *A*

Connecticut
Gateway Community College *C*

Georgia
Georgia Southwestern State
   University *A*

Illinois
Lewis University *B*
Southern Illinois University
   Carbondale *B*

Iowa
Hawkeye Community College *A*
Indian Hills Community College *A*

Michigan
Lansing Community College *A*
Western Michigan University *B*

Minnesota
Northland Community & Technical
   College *A*

Missouri
College of the Ozarks *B*

New Mexico
Eastern New Mexico University:
   Roswell Campus *C, A*

New York
Excelsior College *A*
Tompkins-Cortland Community
   College *A*
Vaughn College of Aeronautics and
   Technology *A, B*

North Carolina
Guilford Technical Community
   College *C, A*

North Dakota
Lake Region State College *A*

Oklahoma
National Education Center
   Spartan School of Aeronautics *C, A*
Tulsa Community College *A*

Pennsylvania
Lehigh Carbon Community College *A*
Pennsylvania College of
   Technology *A, B*

Texas
Hallmark Institute of Aeronautics *A*
Texas State Technical College
   Waco *A*

Utah
Salt Lake Community College *C, A*

Washington
Clover Park Technical College *C, A*
Northwest Aviation College *A*
South Seattle Community
   College *C, A*

Wisconsin
Fox Valley Technical College *A*

Bacteriology

Alabama
Auburn University *B, M, D*

Arizona
Arizona State University *B, M, D*
Northern Arizona University *B*
University of Arizona *B, M, D*

Arkansas
University of Arkansas *B*
University of Arkansas
   for Medical Sciences *M, D*

California
Bakersfield College *A*
California Polytechnic State
   University: San Luis Obispo *B*
California State University
   Dominguez Hills *B*
   Fresno *B, M*
   Long Beach *B, M*
   Northridge *B*
Cerritos Community College *A*
Crafton Hills College *A*
Fullerton College *A*
Loma Linda University *M, D*
Oxnard College *A*
San Diego State University *B, M*
San Francisco State University *B, M*
Stanford University *M, D*
University of California
   Irvine *M, D*
   Los Angeles *B, M, D*
   San Diego *B*
   Santa Barbara *B*

Colorado
Adams State College *B*

Connecticut
Southern Connecticut State
   University *B*
University of Connecticut *M, D*
Yale University *M, D*

District of Columbia
George Washington University *M, D*
Georgetown University *D*

Florida
Manatee Community College *A*
University of Central Florida *B, M*
University of Florida *A, B, M*
University of Miami *B, D*
University of South Florida *B, M*

Hawaii
University of Hawaii
   Manoa *M, D*

Idaho
University of Idaho *B, M, D*

Illinois
Chicago State University *B*
Rosalind Franklin University of
   Medicine and Science *M, D*
University of Illinois
   Chicago *M, D*

Indiana

Indiana University
Bloomington *B, M, D*
Indiana University-Purdue University
Indianapolis *M, D*

Kansas

Central Christian College of Kansas *A*
University of Kansas Medical
Center *M, D*

Kentucky

Eastern Kentucky University *B*
University of Kentucky: College of
Medicine *D*
University of Louisville *M, D*

Louisiana

Louisiana State University Health
Sciences Center *M, D*
Tulane University *M, D*

Maine

University of Maine *B, M, D*

Maryland

University of Maryland
Baltimore *M, D*

Massachusetts

Boston University *M, D*
Tufts University *M, D*

Michigan

Central Michigan University *B*
Michigan State University *B, M, D*
Northern Michigan University *B*
University of Michigan *D*
University of Michigan
Dearborn *B*

Minnesota

Minnesota State University
Mankato *B, M, T*
St. Cloud State University *B*
University of Minnesota
Duluth *M*
Twin Cities *B, M, D*

Mississippi

Mississippi State University *B*
University of Mississippi Medical
Center *M, D*

Missouri

Missouri Southern State University *B*
University of Missouri
Columbia *M, D*
Washington University in St. Louis *D*

Montana

Montana State University
Bozeman *B, M, D*
University of Montana:
Missoula *B, M, D*

Nebraska

Creighton University *M, D*

New Hampshire

University of New Hampshire *B, M, D*

New Jersey

Rowan University *B*
Rutgers, The State University of New
Jersey
New Brunswick/Piscataway
Campus *B, M, D*
Seton Hall University *M*

New Mexico

New Mexico State University *B*

New York

Cornell University *B, M, D*
New York University *M, D*
State University of New York
Buffalo *M, D*
College of Environmental Science
and Forestry *B, M, D*
Upstate Medical University *M, D*
University of Rochester *B, M, D*
Wagner College *B, M*
Yeshiva University *M, D*

North Carolina

Duke University *M, D*
East Carolina University *D*
University of North Carolina
Chapel Hill *M, D*
Wake Forest University *B*

North Dakota

University of North Dakota *M, D*

Ohio

Bowling Green State University *B*
Case Western Reserve University *D*
Miami University
Oxford Campus *B, M, D*
Ohio State University
Columbus Campus *M, D*
Ohio Wesleyan University *B*
University of Akron *B*
University of Cincinnati *M, D*
Wilmington College *B*

Oklahoma

Eastern Oklahoma State College *A*
University of Oklahoma *M, D*

Oregon

Oregon Health & Science
University *M, D*
Oregon State University *B, M, D*

Pennsylvania

Drexel University *M, D*
Keystone College *A*
Penn State
Abington *B*
Altoona *B*
Beaver *B*
Berks *B*
Delaware County *B*
Dubois *B*
Fayette *B*
Hazleton *B*
McKeesport *B*
Mont Alto *B*
New Kensington *B*
Schuylkill - Capital College *B*
Shenango *B*
University Park *B*
Wilkes-Barre *B*
Worthington Scranton *B*
York *B*
Temple University *M, D*
University of Pittsburgh *M, D*
University of the Sciences in
Philadelphia *B*

Puerto Rico

Inter American University of Puerto
Rico
Arecibo Campus *B*
University of Puerto Rico
Arecibo *B*

South Carolina

Clemson University *B, M, D*

Medical University of South
Carolina *M, D*

Tennessee

University of Tennessee
Knoxville *B, M, D*
Vanderbilt University *M, D*

Texas

Laredo Community College *A*
Texas A&M University *B, M, D*
Texas Tech University Health Sciences
Center *M, D*
University of North Texas *M, D*
University of Texas
Health Science Center at
Houston *M, D*
Health Science Center at San
Antonio *M, D*

Utah

Snow College *A*
Weber State University *B*

Vermont

University of Vermont *B, M, D*

Virginia

University of Virginia *D*
Virginia Commonwealth
University *M, D*

Washington

Eastern Washington University *B*
University of Washington *B, D*
Washington State University *B, M, D*

West Virginia

West Liberty State College *B*

Wisconsin

University of Wisconsin
Madison *B, M*
Oshkosh *B, M*

Baking/pastry arts

Alaska

University of Alaska
Fairbanks *C*

California

California Culinary Academy *C*
California School of Culinary Arts *C*
Grossmont Community College *C, A*
Long Beach City College *C, A*
Santa Rosa Junior College *C*

Colorado

Johnson & Wales University *A*

Florida

Johnson & Wales University *A*
New England Institute of
Technology *C, A*
Orlando Culinary Academy *A*
Valencia Community College *C*

Georgia

Savannah Technical College *C*

Illinois

Kendall College *C, A*
Lincoln Land Community College *C*
Moraine Valley Community College *C*
William Rainey Harper College *C*

Indiana

Vincennes University *C*

Maryland

Anne Arundel Community
College *C, A*
Baltimore International College *A*

Massachusetts

Bristol Community College *C*
Massasoit Community College *C*
Newbury College *C*

Michigan

Baker College
of Muskegon *C*
Grand Rapids Community College *C*
Mott Community College *C*
Oakland Community College *C*
Washtenaw Community College *C*

Minnesota

Art Institutes International
Minnesota *C, A*
St. Paul College *C*

Nevada

Art Institute
of Las Vegas *C, A*

New Hampshire

Southern New Hampshire
University *C, A*

New Jersey

Burlington County College *C*
Hudson County Community
College *C*

New Mexico

Albuquerque Technical-Vocational
Institute *C*

New York

Art Institute
of New York City *C*
Culinary Institute of America *C, A, B*
Erie Community College
City Campus *C*
Niagara County Community
College *C*
Paul Smith's College *C, A*

North Carolina

Johnson & Wales University *A*
Wilkes Community College *A*

North Dakota

North Dakota State College of
Science *A*

Pennsylvania

Bucks County Community
College *C, A*
Montgomery County Community
College *A*
Pennsylvania College of Technology *A*

Rhode Island

Johnson & Wales University *A, B*

Texas

Art Institute
of Houston *A*
Del Mar College *C*
El Centro College *C, A*
Houston Community College
System *C*

Virginia

Virginia Intermont College *B*

Washington

Art Institute of Seattle *C*
Clark College *C, A*
Renton Technical College *C*
Seattle Central Community
    College *C, A*
South Seattle Community
    College *C, A*

Wisconsin

Fox Valley Technical College *A*
Milwaukee Area Technical College *C*

Ballet

Mississippi

Belhaven College *C*

Texas

Texas Christian University *B, M*

Utah

Brigham Young University *B*
University of Utah *B, M*

Banking/financial services

Alabama

Alabama Southern Community
    College *A*
George C. Wallace State Community
    College
    Selma *C*
Jefferson State Community
    College *C, A*
Northeast Alabama Community
    College *A*
Wallace State Community College at
    Hanceville *A*

Arizona

Gateway Community College *A*
Phoenix College *A*
Pima Community College *C, A*
Rio Salado College *A*

Arkansas

Northwest Arkansas Community
    College *A*

California

Cabrillo College *A*
California State University
    Dominguez Hills *B*
    Northridge *B*
Canada College *A*
Cerritos Community College *A*
Chabot College *A*
Fresno City College *C, A*
Imperial Valley College *C, A*
Laney College *C, A*
Los Angeles City College *C, A*
Los Angeles Pierce College *C*
Los Angeles Southwest College *A*
Los Angeles Valley College *C*
Merced College *A*
Mission College *A*
Mount San Antonio College *C, A*
Palomar College *C, A*
Pasadena City College *C, A*
Porterville College *C, A*
San Francisco State University *B*
San Joaquin Delta College *C*
San Jose City College *A*
Santa Barbara City College *A*
Shasta College *C*
Solano Community College *C, A*

Colorado

Arapahoe Community College *C, A*
Community College of Aurora *C, A*
Johnson & Wales University *B*
Pueblo Community College *C, A*

Connecticut

Housatonic Community College *C*
Naugatuck Valley Community
    College *C, A*
Sacred Heart University *A*

Delaware

Delaware Technical and Community
    College
    Owens Campus *A*
    Stanton/Wilmington Campus *A*
    Terry Campus *C, A*

District of Columbia

Southeastern University *A, B, M*

Florida

Daytona Beach Community College *A*
Florida Community College at
    Jacksonville *C, A*
Gulf Coast Community College *A*
Johnson & Wales University *A*
Miami Dade College *C, A*
Northwood University
    Florida Campus *A, B*
Okaloosa-Walton College *A*
Pensacola Junior College *A*
Polk Community College *A*
Santa Fe Community College *A*
Schiller International University *B*
Seminole Community College *A*
Tallahassee Community College *A*
University of North Florida *B*

Georgia

Central Georgia Technical College *C*
Darton College *C*
Gwinnett Technical College *C*
South Georgia College *A*

Hawaii

Hawaii Pacific University *B*

Illinois

Black Hawk College *C, A*
Carl Sandburg College *A*
City Colleges of Chicago
    Harold Washington College *C, A*
DePaul University *B*
Illinois Central College *C, A*
Illinois Eastern Community Colleges
    Lincoln Trail College *C, A*
Lewis and Clark Community
    College *A*
Prairie State College *C*
Sauk Valley Community College *C*
Southwestern Illinois College *A*
University of Illinois
    Urbana-Champaign *B, M*
Waubonsee Community College *C, A*
William Rainey Harper College *C, A*

Indiana

Manchester College *B*
University of Evansville *A*
University of Indianapolis *A*
Vincennes University *A*

Iowa

AIB College of Business *A*
Buena Vista University *B*
Northeast Iowa Community
    College *A*

Kansas

Central Christian College of Kansas *A*
Dodge City Community College *C, A*
Neosho County Community
    College *A*
Seward County Community College *C*
Washburn University of Topeka *A*

Kentucky

Ashland Community and Technical
    College *A*
Midway College *B*
Southeast Kentucky Community and
    Technical College *A*
West Kentucky Community and
    Technical College *A*

Louisiana

Southern University
    Shreveport *A*

Maine

Eastern Maine Community College *A*
Husson College *B*

Maryland

Baltimore City Community College *C*
Frederick Community College *C, A*
Garrett College *C*
Hagerstown Community College *A*

Massachusetts

Bristol Community College *A*
Massachusetts Bay Community
    College *C*
New England College of Finance *C, A*

Michigan

Bay de Noc Community College *C*
Delta College *C*
Mid Michigan Community College *A*
Monroe County Community
    College *C, A*
Northwood University *A, B*

Minnesota

Alexandria Technical College *C, A*
Fond du Lac Tribal and Community
    College *C*
Minnesota State Community and
    Technical College - Fergus Falls *A*
Minnesota State University
    Mankato *B*
St. Cloud Technical College *C, A*
University of Minnesota
    Twin Cities *C*

Mississippi

Jackson State University *B*
Mississippi Gulf Coast Community
    College
    Jefferson Davis Campus *A*

Missouri

Mineral Area College *A*
St. Louis Community College
    St. Louis Community College at
        Florissant Valley *A*
    St. Louis Community College at
        Meramec *A*
State Fair Community College *A*
University of Missouri
    Columbia *B*

Nebraska

Northeast Community College *A*
University of Nebraska
    Omaha *B*

Nevada

Community College of Southern
    Nevada *A*

New Jersey

Bergen Community College *A*
Camden County College *A*
St. Peter's College *B*
Thomas Edison State College *A, B*

New Mexico

Albuquerque Technical-Vocational
    Institute *C, A*
Clovis Community College *A*
New Mexico Junior College *A*
New Mexico State University
    Alamogordo *A*
    Carlsbad *C*

New York

Adirondack Community College *A*
Erie Community College
    City Campus *C*
Finger Lakes Community College *A*
Fordham University *M*
Globe Institute of Technology *C, A, B*
Hilbert College *A*
Jamestown Community College *A*
Mercy College *A*
Mohawk Valley Community
    College *C, A*
New York University *C*
Onondaga Community College *C, A*
Suffolk County Community College *C*

North Carolina

Alamance Community College *A*
Fayetteville Technical Community
    College *A*
Isothermal Community College *A*
Southeastern Community College *A*

North Dakota

North Dakota State College of
    Science *A*

Ohio

Defiance College *B*
Jefferson Community College *A*
Shawnee State University *A*
Sinclair Community College *C, A*
Youngstown State University *B, M*

Oklahoma

Northeastern Oklahoma Agricultural
    and Mechanical College *C*
Oklahoma City Community College *C*

Oregon

Southwestern Oregon Community
    College *C, A*

Pennsylvania

Bucks County Community
    College *C, A*
Central Pennsylvania College *A*
Community College of Allegheny
    County *C, A*
Delaware County Community
    College *C, A*
Harrisburg Area Community
    College *C, A*
La Salle University *A, B*
Lackawanna College *A*
Lebanon Valley College *C*
Luzerne County Community
    College *A*
Penn State
    Delaware County *B*
Reading Area Community
    College *C, A*
Westmoreland County Community
    College *A*

Puerto Rico

Universidad Metropolitana *C*

Universidad del Este C
University of Puerto Rico
   Rio Piedras B

Rhode Island
Community College of Rhode
   Island A

South Carolina
Trident Technical College C

South Dakota
Lake Area Technical Institute A
Southeast Technical Institute A

Texas
College of the Mainland A
Houston Community College
   System C, A
Northeast Texas Community
   College C, A
Northwood University: Texas
   Campus A, B
Palo Alto College A
Sam Houston State University B
San Antonio College C, A
South Texas College C, A
Texas Southern University B
University of North Texas B, M, D
University of Texas
   Arlington B, D

Utah
Utah Valley State College C, A

Virginia
Dabney S. Lancaster Community
   College C
Hampton University B
Lord Fairfax Community College C
Southwest Virginia Community
   College C
Tidewater Community College A
University of Richmond C
Virginia Western Community
   College A

Washington
Clover Park Technical College C
Gonzaga University B
Renton Technical College C
Spokane Community College C, A
Spokane Falls Community
   College C, A
Walla Walla Community College C, A

West Virginia
Mountain State University A
West Liberty State College B
West Virginia State University B

Wisconsin
Fox Valley Technical College A
Gateway Technical College A
Mid-State Technical College C
Milwaukee Area Technical College A
University of Wisconsin
   Whitewater M

Wyoming
Sheridan College A

Barbering

Alabama
Calhoun Community College C
Lawson State Community College C
Shelton State Community College C

Florida
Central Florida Community College C

Indian River Community College C
Pensacola Junior College C

Georgia
Central Georgia Technical College C

Minnesota
Minneapolis Community and
   Technical College C

Mississippi
Coahoma Community College C

New Mexico
Northern New Mexico College C
San Juan College C

North Carolina
Central Carolina Community
   College C

Oklahoma
Heritage College Hair Design C, A

Utah
Snow College C, A

Washington
Olympic College C, A
Renton Technical College C

Wisconsin
Fox Valley Technical College C

Bartending

Puerto Rico
Universidad del Este C

Behavioral sciences

Alabama
Athens State University B

Arizona
Northern Arizona University B
Prescott College B, M

California
California Baptist University B
California Institute of Integral
   Studies M, D
California State Polytechnic
   University: Pomona B
California State University
   Bakersfield M
   Monterey Bay B
Concordia University B
La Sierra University B
MiraCosta College A
Mount San Jacinto College A
Notre Dame de Namur University B
San Diego City College A
San Jose State University B
University of California
   San Diego B
University of La Verne B

Colorado
Metropolitan State College of
   Denver B
United States Air Force Academy B
University of Colorado
   Denver and Health Sciences
      Center D

Connecticut
Northwestern Connecticut
   Community College A

Delaware
Wilmington College B

Florida
Lynn University B

Hawaii
Chaminade University of Honolulu B
Hawaii Pacific University B

Idaho
Lewis-Clark State College A

Illinois
National-Louis University B
Southeastern Illinois College A

Indiana
Ancilla College A
Indiana University
   Kokomo B

Iowa
Ellsworth Community College A

Kansas
Garden City Community College A
Sterling College B
University of Kansas B, M, D

Kentucky
Kentucky Christian University B

Maine
University of Maine
   Machias B
   Presque Isle B
University of Southern Maine B

Maryland
Garrett College A
Johns Hopkins University B

Massachusetts
Cape Cod Community College A
Hampshire College B
Simon's Rock College of Bard B

Michigan
Albion College B
Grand Valley State University B
University of Michigan
   Dearborn B

Minnesota
St. Cloud State University B

Missouri
Evangel University M
University of Missouri
   Columbia B

Nebraska
Concordia University B
Northeast Community College A

New Hampshire
Granite State College A, B

New Jersey
Drew University B

New York
Concordia College B
Polytechnic University M
State University of New York
   Downstate Medical Center D
United States Military Academy B

North Dakota
Dickinson State University B, T

Ohio
Mount Union College B
Wright State University M

Oklahoma
Mid-America Christian University B
Murray State College A
Oklahoma Wesleyan University A, B
St. Gregory's University B
Seminole State College A
Southern Nazarene University B

Pennsylvania
Carnegie Mellon University B, D
Franklin & Marshall College B
Gettysburg College B
Mount Aloysius College A, B
Penn State
   Berks B
Point Park University B
Wilson College B
York College of Pennsylvania B

South Dakota
Dakota Wesleyan University B
Mount Marty College B

Tennessee
King College B, T
LeMoyne-Owen College B
Tennessee Wesleyan College B
Trevecca Nazarene University B

Texas
Northwest Vista College A
South Plains College A
University of Houston
   Clear Lake B, M

Utah
Southern Utah University B

West Virginia
Mountain State University B

Wisconsin
Beloit College B
Mount Mary College B
University of Wisconsin
   Madison B

Bible studies

Alabama
Faulkner University B, M
Heritage Christian University A, B, M
Huntsville Bible College C, A, B
Oakwood College A
Southeastern Bible College A, B, T
Southern Christian University B, M

Alaska
Alaska Bible College C, A, B

Arizona
Grand Canyon University B
Southwestern College C, A, B

Arkansas
Central Baptist College B
Ecclesia College A, B
Harding University B, M
Ouachita Baptist University A, B
Williams Baptist College B

California
Azusa Pacific University B, M

Bethesda Christian University *B, M*
Biola University *B, M*
California Baptist University *B*
Fresno Pacific University *B*
Hope International University *C, A, B*
King's College and Seminary *C, B*
LIFE Pacific College *A, B*
Master's College *C, B*
Pacific Union College *B*
Patten University *C, A*
Point Loma Nazarene University *B*
San Diego Christian College *B*
Simpson University *C, A, B*
Vanguard University of Southern
    California *B, M*
William Jessup University *C, A, B*

Colorado
Colorado Christian University *B*
Nazarene Bible College *A, B*

District of Columbia
Catholic University of America *M, D*

Florida
Baptist College of Florida *B*
Clearwater Christian College *B*
Florida Christian College *A, B*
Florida College *B*
Hobe Sound Bible College *C, A, B*
Palm Beach Atlantic University *B*
Southeastern College of the
    Assemblies of God *B*
Trinity College of Florida *C, A, B*
Universidad FLET *C, A, B, M*
Warner Southern College *B*

Georgia
Atlanta Christian College *B*
Beulah Heights Bible College *C, A, B*
Covenant College *A, B*
Emmanuel College *B*
Toccoa Falls College *C, B*

Idaho
Boise Bible College *C, A, B*

Illinois
Judson College *B*
Lincoln Christian College and
    Seminary *A, B, M*
Moody Bible Institute *B, M*
North Park University *B*
Olivet Nazarene University *B*
Trinity International
    University *B, M, D*
Wheaton College *B*

Indiana
Anderson University *B, M*
Bethel College *A, B*
Grace College *A, B*
Huntington University *B*
Indiana Wesleyan University *A, B*
Taylor University *B*
Taylor University: Fort Wayne *B*
University of Evansville *B*

Iowa
Emmaus Bible College *C, A, B*
Faith Baptist Bible College and
    Theological Seminary *C, A, B, M*

Kansas
Barclay College *C, A, B*
Central Christian College of
    Kansas *A, B*
Manhattan Christian College *C, A, B*
Tabor College *B*

Kentucky
Asbury College *B*

Campbellsville University *B*
Clear Creek Baptist Bible
    College *C, A, B*
Kentucky Christian University *B*
Mid-Continent University *C, B*
St. Catharine College *C, A*

Louisiana
New Orleans Baptist Theological
    Seminary: Leavell
    College *A, B, M, D*
New Orleans School of Urban
    Missions *A*

Maryland
Washington Bible College *C, A, B, M, T*

Massachusetts
Boston College *M, D*
Boston University *M, D*

Michigan
Andrews University *M, D*
Calvin College *B*
Cornerstone University *C, A, B, M*
Grace Bible College *A, B*
Great Lakes Christian College *C, A, B*
Kuyper College *A, B*
Rochester College *B*

Minnesota
Bethel University *B*
Concordia University: St. Paul *B*
Crossroads College *A*
Crown College *C, A, B*
North Central University *C, A, B*
Northwestern College *C, B*
Oak Hills Christian College *C, B*
Pillsbury Baptist Bible College *C, A, B*

Mississippi
Belhaven College *C, B*
Blue Mountain College *B*
Magnolia Bible College *B*
Wesley College *B*
William Carey College *B*

Missouri
Calvary Bible College and Theological
    Seminary *C, A, B, M*
Central Bible College *A, B*
Central Christian College of the
    Bible *C, A*
Evangel University *B*
Global University *A, B, M*
Hannibal-LaGrange College *B*
Ozark Christian College *C, A, B*
St. Louis Christian College *B*
Southwest Baptist University *B*

Nebraska
Grace University *C, A, B, M*
Nebraska Christian College *B*
York College *B*

New Jersey
Drew University *M, D*
Somerset Christian College *A*

New York
Davis College *C, A*
Houghton College *B*

North Carolina
Montreat College *B*
Piedmont Baptist College *A, B, M*
Roanoke Bible College *A, B*

North Dakota
Trinity Bible College *C, A, B*

Ohio
Ashland University *B*
Cedarville University *C*
Cincinnati Christian University *B, M*
God's Bible School and College *A*
Laura and Alvin Siegal College of
    Judaic Studies *B*
Malone College *B*
Pontifical College Josephinum *M*
Rosedale Bible College *C, A*

Oklahoma
Mid-America Christian University *B*
Oklahoma Baptist University *B*
Oklahoma Christian University *B*
Oklahoma City University *B*
Oklahoma Wesleyan University *A, B*
Oral Roberts University *B, M*
Southwestern Christian University *B*

Oregon
Corban College *B*
Eugene Bible College *C, B*
George Fox University *B, M*
Mount Angel Seminary *M*
Multnomah Bible College *B, M*
Northwest Christian College *B*

Pennsylvania
Baptist Bible College of
    Pennsylvania *C, D*
Eastern University *B*
Geneva College *A, B*
Lancaster Bible College *C, A, B, M*
Messiah College *B*
Philadelphia Biblical
    University *C, B, M*
Valley Forge Christian College *C, A, B*

Puerto Rico
Bayamon Central University *M*

Rhode Island
Providence College *M*
Zion Bible Institute *C, B*

South Carolina
Charleston Southern University *B*
Columbia International
    University *C, A, B, M*
Erskine College *M*

Tennessee
American Baptist College of ABT
    Seminary *A, B*
Bryan College *B*
Crichton College *C, B*
Free Will Baptist Bible College *A, B*
Freed-Hardeman University *B, M*
Hiwassee College *A*
Johnson Bible College *C, A, B, M*
King College *B*
Lee University *B*
Lipscomb University *B, M*
Milligan College *B*
Southern Adventist University *A*
Tennessee Temple University *A, B*
Trevecca Nazarene University *M*
Union University *C, A, B*
University of the South *M, D*

Texas
Abilene Christian University *B, M*
Arlington Baptist College *C, B*
Austin Graduate School of Theology *B*
Baptist University of the Americas *B*
College of Biblical
    Studies-Houston *C, A, B*
Criswell College *B, M*
Dallas Baptist University *A, B*
Dallas Christian College *B*
East Texas Baptist University *B*

Hardin-Simmons University *B*
Howard Payne University *B*
LeTourneau University *B*
Lubbock Christian University *B, M*
San Jacinto College
    Central Campus *A*
Southwestern Assemblies of God
    University *A, B, M*
Southwestern Christian College *A, B*
Texas Christian University *D*
University of Mary Hardin-Baylor *B*

Virginia
Bluefield College *B*
Eastern Mennonite University *C, A, B*
Liberty University *C, B, M*

Washington
Northwest University *C, B*
Puget Sound Christian College *C, A, B*
Trinity Lutheran College *A, B*

West Virginia
Appalachian Bible College *C, A, B*
Ohio Valley University *A, B*

Wisconsin
Concordia University Wisconsin *B*
Maranatha Baptist Bible College *B, M*
Marquette University *M, D*

Bilingual/bicultural education

Arizona
Northern Arizona University *M, T*
Prescott College *B, M*
University of Arizona *M*
University of Phoenix *M*

California
Butte College *A*
California Lutheran University *M*
California State University
    Chico *M*
    East Bay *T*
    Fullerton *M*
    Long Beach *T*
    Monterey Bay *M*
    Northridge *M*
    Sacramento *B, M, T*
    San Bernardino *M*
    San Marcos *T*
Cerritos Community College *A*
Contra Costa College *A*
Fresno City College *A*
Fresno Pacific University *M, T*
Imperial Valley College *A*
Loyola Marymount University *M*
National University *M, T*
Sacramento City College *A*
San Diego City College *A*
San Diego State University *M*
San Francisco State University *M, T*
University of California
    Riverside *T*
    San Diego *M*
    Santa Cruz *M*
University of La Verne *T*
University of San Francisco *M, D, T*
University of Southern California *T*
University of the Pacific *T*
Ventura College *A*

Colorado
Colorado Mountain College
    Spring Valley Campus *A*
    Timberline Campus *A*
Fort Lewis College *B*

Connecticut
Fairfield University *M, T*

Southern Connecticut State
  University *M*

Delaware
University of Delaware *M*

Florida
Florida State University *B, M, D*

Idaho
Boise State University *B, T*
College of Southern Idaho *A*

Illinois
Chicago State University *M, T*
Columbia College Chicago *M*
Loyola University of Chicago *B*
Monmouth College *T*
North Park University *M*
Northeastern Illinois University *B*
Sauk Valley Community College *A*
University of Illinois
  Urbana-Champaign *M, D*
Western Illinois University *B*

Kansas
Emporia State University *T*

Massachusetts
Boston University *B, M, T*
Eastern Nazarene College *M, T*
Elms College *B, M, T*
Salem State College *M*
University of Massachusetts
  Boston *M*

Michigan
Calvin College *B, T*
Saginaw Valley State University *T*
Wayne State University *M, T*

Minnesota
College of St. Scholastica *T*
Concordia University: St. Paul *B*
University of Minnesota
  Twin Cities *M*
Winona State University *B, T*

Missouri
Rockhurst University *T*

New Jersey
Fairleigh Dickinson University
  Metropolitan Campus *M*
Georgian Court University *T*
Montclair State University *T*
New Jersey City University *T*
Seton Hall University *M*
William Paterson University of New
  Jersey *T*

New Mexico
College of the Southwest *B*
Western New Mexico University *T*

New York
Adelphi University *M, T*
City University of New York
  Brooklyn College *B, M*
  City College *B, M, T*
  Hunter College *M, T*
  LaGuardia Community College *A*
  Lehman College *M, T*
  Queens College *M, T*
  York College *T*
Hofstra University *M, T*
New York University *M, D*
St. John's University *M*
State University of New York
  Albany *M*
  Buffalo *M, T*

College at Brockport *M, T*
College at Buffalo *M*
College at Old Westbury *B, T*
New Paltz *M, T*

North Carolina
Greensboro College *M*

Ohio
University of Findlay *B, M, T*

Oregon
Chemeketa Community College *A*
Eastern Oregon University *T*
Treasure Valley Community College *A*
University of Oregon *T*
Western Oregon University *T*

Pennsylvania
Immaculata University *M, T*
La Salle University *B, M*

Puerto Rico
Turabo University *M*
Universidad del Este *M*
University of the Sacred Heart *B*

Rhode Island
Rhode Island College *B*

Texas
Del Mar College *A*
Houston Baptist University *M*
Laredo Community College *A*
McMurry University *T*
Midwestern State University *B*
Richland College *A*
San Jacinto College
  North *A*
Southern Methodist University *M*
Sul Ross State University *M*
Texas A&M University
  Commerce *B*
  Kingsville *B, M, D*
Texas Christian University *B*
Texas Southern University *M*
Texas State University: San
  Marcos *M, T*
Texas Tech University *M*
Texas Wesleyan University *B, M, T*
University of Houston *M, T*
University of Houston
  Clear Lake *T*
  Downtown *M*
University of North Texas *M*
University of Texas
  Arlington *T*
  Brownsville *M*
  Pan American *M*
  San Antonio *M*
  of the Permian Basin *M*
West Texas A&M University *T*

Utah
Brigham Young University *D*
University of Utah *M*
Weber State University *B*

Washington
Central Washington University *M, T*
Heritage University *B, M*
University of Washington *M*
Washington State University *B, M, T*

Wisconsin
Marquette University *M*
Mount Mary College *B*

Biochemistry

Alabama
Auburn University *B*
Oakwood College *B*
Samford University *B*
Spring Hill College *B*

Arizona
Arizona State University *B*
Grand Canyon University *B*
University of Arizona *B, M, D*

Arkansas
Harding University *B*
John Brown University *B*
University of Arkansas
  for Medical Sciences *M, D*

California
Azusa Pacific University *B*
Biola University *B*
California Institute of Technology *D*
California Lutheran University *B*
California Polytechnic State
  University: San Luis Obispo *B*
California State University
  Chico *B*
  East Bay *B, M*
  Fullerton *B*
  Long Beach *B, M*
  Los Angeles *B*
  Northridge *B*
  San Bernardino *B*
Chapman University *B*
Claremont McKenna College *B*
La Sierra University *B*
Loma Linda University *M, D*
Loyola Marymount University *B*
Mills College *B*
Mount St. Mary's College *B*
Notre Dame de Namur University *B*
Occidental College *B*
Pacific Union College *B*
Pepperdine University *B*
Pitzer College *B*
Point Loma Nazarene University *B*
St. Mary's College of California *B*
San Francisco State University *B, M*
San Jose State University *B*
Scripps College *B*
Stanford University *D*
University of California
  Berkeley *M, D*
  Irvine *M, D*
  Los Angeles *B, M, D*
  Riverside *B, M, D*
  San Diego *B, D*
  Santa Barbara *B, M, D*
  Santa Cruz *B*
University of Redlands *B*
University of Southern
  California *B, M, D*
University of the Pacific *B*

Colorado
Colorado College *B*
Colorado State University *B, M, D*
Fort Lewis College *B*
Regis University *B*
University of Colorado
  Boulder *B*
  Denver and Health Sciences
    Center *D*
University of Denver *B*

Connecticut
Connecticut College *B*
Eastern Connecticut State
  University *B*
Quinnipiac University *B*
Sacred Heart University *B*
St. Joseph College *B, M, T*

Trinity College *B*
University of Connecticut *M, D*
Wesleyan University *B, D*
Yale University *B, M, D*

Delaware
University of Delaware *B, M, D*

District of Columbia
American University *B*
Catholic University of America *B*
George Washington University *M, D*
Georgetown University *B, D*
Howard University *M, D*
Trinity University *B*

Florida
Eckerd College *B*
Florida Institute of Technology *B*
Florida State University *B, M, D*
Pensacola Junior College *A*
Stetson University *B*
University of Florida *B, M*
University of Miami *B, M, D*
University of Tampa *B*

Georgia
Agnes Scott College *B*
Berry College *B*
Kennesaw State University *B*
LaGrange College *B*
Medical College of Georgia *M, D*
Mercer University *B*
Spelman College *B*
University of Georgia *B, M, D*

Hawaii
Brigham Young University-Hawaii *B*

Idaho
Idaho State University *B*

Illinois
Benedictine University *B*
Bradley University *B, T*
Chicago State University *B*
Dominican University *B*
Illinois State University *B*
Knox College *B*
Lewis University *B*
Loyola University of Chicago *M*
Monmouth College *B*
North Central College *B*
Rockford College *B*
Rosalind Franklin University of
  Medicine and Science *M, D*
Rush University *D*
University of Chicago *B, D*
University of Illinois
  Chicago *B, M, D*
  Urbana-Champaign *B, M, D*

Indiana
Anderson University *B*
DePauw University *B*
Earlham College *B*
Indiana University
  Bloomington *B, M, D*
Indiana University-Purdue University
  Indianapolis *M, D*
Manchester College *B*
Purdue University *B, M, D*
St. Joseph's College *A, B*
University of Evansville *B*
University of Notre Dame *B, M, D*
Valparaiso University *B*

Iowa
Coe College *B*
Drake University *B*
Grinnell College *B*
Iowa State University *B, M, D*

Loras College *B*
Simpson College *B*
University of Iowa *B, M, D*
University of Northern Iowa *B*
Wartburg College *B*

Kansas

Benedictine College *B*
Emporia State University *B*
Kansas State University *B, M, D*
Pittsburg State University *B*
Southwestern College *B*
Tabor College *B*
University of Kansas Medical
    Center *M, D*

Kentucky

Asbury College *B*
Centre College *B*
University of Louisville *M, D*
Western Kentucky University *B*

Louisiana

Centenary College of Louisiana *B*
Louisiana State University
    Shreveport *B*
Louisiana State University Health
    Sciences Center *M, D*
Louisiana State University and
    Agricultural and Mechanical
    College *B, M, D*
Tulane University *B, M, D*
Xavier University of Louisiana *B*

Maine

Bates College *B*
Bowdoin College *B*
Colby College *B*
University of Maine *B, M, D*
University of New England *B*

Maryland

Columbia Union College *B*
Hood College *B*
McDaniel College *B*
Mount St. Mary's University *B*
St. Mary's College of Maryland *B*
University of Maryland
    Baltimore *M, D*
    Baltimore County *M, D*
    College Park *B, M, D*

Massachusetts

American International College *B*
Boston College *B, M, D*
Boston University *B, M, D*
Brandeis University *B, M, D*
Bridgewater State College *B*
Clark University *B*
Eastern Nazarene College *B*
Emmanuel College *B*
Harvard College *B, D*
Merrimack College *B*
Mount Holyoke College *B*
Northeastern University *B*
Regis College *B*
Salem State College *B*
Simmons College *B*
Smith College *B*
Stonehill College *B*
Suffolk University *B*
Tufts University *D*
University of Massachusetts
    Boston *B*
Wellesley College *B*
Wheaton College *B*
Worcester Polytechnic Institute *B, M*

Michigan

Albion College *B*
Alma College *B*
Andrews University *B*
Calvin College *B*

Eastern Michigan University *B*
Ferris State University *B*
Grand Valley State University *B*
Hope College *B*
Kettering University *B*
Lawrence Technological University *B*
Madonna University *B*
Michigan State University *B*
Northern Michigan University *B, M*
Oakland University *B*
Olivet College *B, T*
Saginaw Valley State University *B*
Spring Arbor University *B*
University of Detroit Mercy *B*
University of Michigan *B, M, D*
University of Michigan
    Dearborn *B*
Wayne State University *M, D*
Western Michigan University *B*

Minnesota

College of St. Benedict *B*
College of St. Catherine *B*
College of St. Scholastica *B*
Gustavus Adolphus College *B*
Hamline University *B*
Minnesota State University
    Mankato *B*
St. John's University *B*
University of Minnesota
    Duluth *B*
    Twin Cities *B, M, D*
University of St. Thomas *B*

Mississippi

Mississippi College *B*
Mississippi State University *B, M*
University of Mississippi Medical
    Center *M, D*

Missouri

Missouri Southern State University *B*
Missouri Western State University *B*
Rockhurst University *B*
St. Louis University *B*
University of Missouri
    Columbia *B, M, D*
    Rolla *B*
Washington University in St.
    Louis *B, D*
William Jewell College *B*

Montana

Montana State University
    Bozeman *B*
University of Montana: Missoula *M, D*

Nebraska

Nebraska Wesleyan University *B*
Union College *B*
University of Nebraska
    Lincoln *B, M, D*

Nevada

University of Nevada
    Reno *B, M, D*

New Hampshire

Dartmouth College *B, M, D*
St. Anselm College *B*
University of New Hampshire *B, M, D*

New Jersey

College of St. Elizabeth *B*
Drew University *B*
Fairleigh Dickinson University
    Metropolitan Campus *B*
Georgian Court University *B*
Montclair State University *B*
Ramapo College of New Jersey *B*
Richard Stockton College of New
    Jersey *B*

Rider University *B*
Rowan University *B*
Rutgers, The State University of New
    Jersey
    New Brunswick/Piscataway
        Campus *B, M, D*
St. Peter's College *B*
Seton Hall University *B*
Stevens Institute of
    Technology *B, M, D*

New Mexico

New Mexico Institute of Mining and
    Technology *B, M*
New Mexico State University *B*
University of New Mexico *B*

New York

Adelphi University *B*
Bard College *B*
Barnard College *B*
Canisius College *B*
City University of New York
    City College *B, M, D*
    College of Staten Island *B*
    Hunter College *M*
    Lehman College *B*
    Queens College *B, M*
Colgate University *B*
College of Mount St. Vincent *B*
College of Saint Rose *B*
Columbia University
    Columbia College *B*
Cornell University *B, M, D*
Daemen College *B*
Elmira College *B*
Hamilton College *B*
Hartwick College *B*
Hobart and William Smith Colleges *B*
Hofstra University *B*
Iona College *B*
Ithaca College *B*
Keuka College *B*
Le Moyne College *B*
Long Island University
    Brooklyn Campus *B*
Manhattan College *B, T*
Manhattanville College *B*
Marist College *B*
Nazareth College of Rochester *B*
New York University *B, M, D*
Niagara University *B*
Pace University *B*
Rensselaer Polytechnic
    Institute *B, M, D*
Roberts Wesleyan College *B*
Rochester Institute of Technology *B*
Russell Sage College *B*
St. Bonaventure University *B*
St. Lawrence University *B*
Sarah Lawrence College *B*
Siena College *B*
Skidmore College *B*
State University of New York
    Albany *B, M, D*
    Binghamton *B*
    Buffalo *B, M, D*
    College at Brockport *B*
    College at Fredonia *B*
    College at Geneseo *B*
    College at Old Westbury *B*
    College at Oneonta *B*
    College at Plattsburgh *B*
    College at Potsdam *B*
    College of Environmental Science
        and Forestry *B, M, D*
    Downstate Medical Center *D*
    Stony Brook *B*
    Upstate Medical University *M, D*
Syracuse University *B*
Union College *B*
University of Rochester *B, M, D*
Vassar College *B*
Wells College *B*

Yeshiva University *M, D*

North Carolina

Campbell University *B*
Duke University *M, D*
East Carolina University *B, D*
North Carolina State
    University *B, M, D*
Queens University of Charlotte *B*
University of North Carolina
    Chapel Hill *M, D*
    Greensboro *B*
Wake Forest University *D*

North Dakota

Jamestown College *B*
North Dakota State University *M, D*
University of North Dakota *M, D*

Ohio

Capital University *B*
Case Western Reserve
    University *B, M, D*
College of Mount St. Joseph *B*
College of Wooster *B*
Denison University *B*
Hiram College *B*
Kenyon College *B*
Marietta College *B*
Miami University
    Oxford Campus *B*
Mount Union College *B*
Oberlin College *B*
Ohio Northern University *B*
Ohio State University
    Columbus Campus *B, M, D*
Ohio Wesleyan University *B*
Otterbein College *B*
University of Cincinnati *D*
University of Dayton *B*
Wilmington College *B*
Wittenberg University *B*
Wright State University *B, M*

Oklahoma

Oklahoma Baptist University *B*
Oklahoma Christian University *B*
Oklahoma City University *B*
Oklahoma State University *B, M, D*
Oral Roberts University *B*
Southern Nazarene University *B*
University of Oklahoma *B, M, D*
University of Tulsa *B*

Oregon

Lewis & Clark College *B*
Oregon Health & Science
    University *M, D*
Oregon State University *B, M, D*
Portland State University *B*
Reed College *B*
University of Oregon *B*

Pennsylvania

Albright College *B*
Allegheny College *B*
Alvernia College *B*
Cedar Crest College *B*
Chatham College *B*
Chestnut Hill College *B*
College Misericordia *B*
Dickinson College *B*
Drexel University *M, D*
Duquesne University *B*
East Stroudsburg University of
    Pennsylvania *B*
Eastern University *B*
Elizabethtown College *B*
Franklin & Marshall College *B*
Gettysburg College *B*
Grove City College *B*
Holy Family University *B*
Indiana University of Pennsylvania *B*

Juniata College *B*
Keystone College *B*
La Salle University *B*
Lafayette College *B*
Lebanon Valley College *B*
Lehigh University *B, D*
Mansfield University of
Pennsylvania *B*
Mercyhurst College *B*
Messiah College *B*
Moravian College *B*
Muhlenberg College *B*
Penn State
Abington *B*
Altoona *B*
Beaver *B*
Berks *B*
Delaware County *B*
Dubois *B*
Fayette *B*
Hazleton *B*
Lehigh Valley *B*
McKeesport *B*
Mont Alto *B*
New Kensington *B*
Schuylkill - Capital College *B*
Shenango *B*
University Park *B, M, D*
Wilkes-Barre *B*
Worthington Scranton *B*
York *B*
Philadelphia University *B*
Rosemont College *B*
St. Joseph's University *B*
St. Vincent College *B*
Seton Hill University *B*
Susquehanna University *B*
Swarthmore College *B*
Temple University *B, M, D*
University of Pennsylvania *B*
University of Pittsburgh *M, D*
University of Scranton *B, M*
University of the Sciences in
Philadelphia *B, M, D*
Washington and Jefferson College *B*
West Chester University of
Pennsylvania *B, M*
Westminster College *B*
Widener University *B*
Wilkes University *B*

Rhode Island

Brown University *B, M, D*
Providence College *B*
University of Rhode Island *M, D*

South Carolina

Claflin University *B*
Clemson University *B, M, D*
College of Charleston *B*
Converse College *B*
Medical University of South
Carolina *M, D*

South Dakota

University of South Dakota *M, D*

Tennessee

Freed-Hardeman University *B*
King College *B*
Lee University *B*
Lipscomb University *B*
Maryville College *B*
Southern Adventist University *B*
Tennessee State University *B*
Tennessee Technological University *B*
University of Tennessee
Knoxville *B, M, D*
Vanderbilt University *D*

Texas

Abilene Christian University *B*
Angelo State University *B*

Austin College *B*
Baylor University *B*
McMurry University *B*
Rice University *B, M, D*
St. Edward's University *B*
St. Mary's University *B*
Schreiner University *B*
Southern Methodist University *B*
Texas A&M University *B, M, D*
Texas Christian University *B*
Texas State University: San
Marcos *B, M*
Texas Tech University *B*
Texas Tech University Health Sciences
Center *M, D*
Texas Wesleyan University *B*
Trinity University *B*
University of Dallas *B*
University of Houston *B, M, D*
University of North Texas *B, M, D*
University of Texas
Arlington *B*
Austin *B, M, D*
Dallas *B*
Health Science Center at
Houston *M, D*
Health Science Center at San
Antonio *M, D*
Southwestern Medical Center at
Dallas *M, D*

Utah

Brigham Young University *B, M, D*
University of Utah *B, M, D*
Utah State University *M, D*

Vermont

Marlboro College *B*
Middlebury College *B*
Norwich University *B*
St. Michael's College *B*
University of Vermont *B, M, D*

Virginia

Eastern Mennonite University *B*
Hampden-Sydney College *B*
Liberty University *B*
Mary Baldwin College *B*
Old Dominion University *B*
Roanoke College *B*
Sweet Briar College *B*
University of Richmond *B*
University of Virginia *D*
Virginia Commonwealth
University *M, D*
Virginia Polytechnic Institute and
State University *B*

Washington

Eastern Washington University *B*
Gonzaga University *B*
Seattle Pacific University *B*
Seattle University *B*
University of Washington *B, M, D*
Walla Walla College *B*
Washington State University *B, M, D*
Western Washington University *B*

West Virginia

Bethany College *B*
West Virginia University *B, M, D*

Wisconsin

Beloit College *B*
Carroll College *B*
Lakeland College *B*
Lawrence University *B, T*
Marquette University *B, M*
Ripon College *B*
University of Wisconsin
La Crosse *B*
Madison *B, M, D*
Viterbo University *B*

Wisconsin Lutheran College *B*

Biochemistry/
biophysics and
molecular biology

California

University of California
Irvine *B*
Riverside *M, D*

Connecticut

Connecticut College *B*
Yale University *B, M, D*

Florida

Florida State University *D*
Rollins College *B*
University of Central Florida *D*

Illinois

Illinois Institute of Technology *B, M*
Northwestern University *D*
Rosalind Franklin University of
Medicine and Science *M, D*

Iowa

Cornell College *B*

Kansas

University of Kansas *B, M, D*

Maryland

University of Maryland
Baltimore County *D*

Massachusetts

University of Massachusetts
Amherst *B, M, D*

Michigan

Michigan State University *B, M, D*
Western Michigan University *B*

Minnesota

Bethel University *B*

Nebraska

Nebraska Wesleyan University *B*
University of Nebraska
Medical Center *M, D*

New Hampshire

Dartmouth College *B*

North Dakota

North Dakota State University *B*

Ohio

College of Wooster *B*

Pennsylvania

Lebanon Valley College *B*
University of Pennsylvania *M, D*

Tennessee

Rhodes College *B*

Texas

Hardin-Simmons University *B*

Washington

Whitman College *B*

West Virginia

West Virginia University *D*

Wisconsin

Lawrence University *B*

Marquette University *M, D*

Bioethics/medical ethics

California

Loma Linda University *M*
Loyola Marymount University *M*
University of Judaism *B*

Florida

University of South Florida *M*

New Jersey

Drew University *M*

Ohio

Case Western Reserve University *M, D*

Pennsylvania

Duquesne University *M, D*
University of Pennsylvania *M*
University of Pittsburgh *M*

Texas

University of Texas
Medical Branch at Galveston *M, D*

Bioinformatics

Arkansas

University of Arkansas
Little Rock *M, D*

California

DeVry University
Fremont *B*
Long Beach *B*
Foothill College *A*
Stanford University *M, D*
University of California
San Diego *B*
Santa Cruz *B*
University of Southern California *D*

Colorado

University of Denver *B*

Florida

University of South Florida *M*

Georgia

Georgia Institute of Technology *M, D*

Illinois

Loyola University of Chicago *B*
Northwestern University *M*
University of Illinois
Urbana-Champaign *M, D*

Indiana

Indiana University-Purdue University
Indianapolis *M*

Iowa

Iowa State University *M, D*
University of Northern Iowa *B*

Maryland

Morgan State University *M*
University of Maryland
Baltimore County *B*

Massachusetts

Clark University *B*
Massachusetts Institute of
Technology *M, D*

Michigan

Eastern Michigan University *M*
Michigan Technological University *B*

University of Michigan *M, D*

Mississippi
Mississippi Valley State University *M*

Missouri
DeVry University
   Kansas City *B*
Rockhurst University *B*

New Jersey
New Jersey Institute of Technology *M*
Ramapo College of New Jersey *B*
University of Medicine and Dentistry
   of New Jersey
   School of Health Related
     Professions *A, M, D*

New York
Bard College *B*
Canisius College *B*
Polytechnic University *M*
Rochester Institute of
   Technology *B, M*
State University of New York
   Buffalo *B*

North Carolina
North Carolina State University *M, D*

Pennsylvania
Gannon University *B*
St. Vincent College *B*
University of Pennsylvania *B*
University of Pittsburgh *M, D*
University of the Sciences in
   Philadelphia *M*

Puerto Rico
Inter American University of Puerto
   Rico
   Bayamon Campus *B*

South Carolina
Claflin University *B*
Medical University of South
   Carolina *M, D*

Tennessee
University of Memphis *M*

Texas
Baylor University *B*
DeVry University
   Irving *B*
St. Edward's University *B*
Texas Tech University *M*
University of St. Thomas *B*
University of Texas
   Dallas *M*
   El Paso *M*

Utah
Brigham Young University *B*

Virginia
Virginia Commonwealth
   University *B, M*
Virginia Polytechnic Institute and
   State University *D*

Wisconsin
Marquette University *M, D*

Biological immunology

California
Stanford University *M, D*
University of California
   Davis *M, D*
   Los Angeles *M, D*

Connecticut
Yale University *M, D*

Illinois
Loyola University of Chicago *D*
Rosalind Franklin University of
   Medicine and Science *M, D*
Rush University *D*
University of Chicago *D*

Iowa
University of Iowa *D*

Maine
University of Southern Maine *M*

Massachusetts
Harvard College *D*

Michigan
University of Michigan *D*

Missouri
Washington University in St. Louis *D*

New Mexico
Art Center Design College *B*

New York
Cornell University *M, D*
State University of New York
   Downstate Medical Center *D*
Yeshiva University *M, D*

North Carolina
North Carolina State University *M, D*

Ohio
Ohio State University
   Columbus Campus *M, D*

Pennsylvania
University of Pennsylvania *M, D*
University of Pittsburgh *M, D*

Texas
University of North Texas *M*
University of Texas
   Southwestern Medical Center at
     Dallas *M, D*

Washington
University of Washington *M, D*

Biological/physical sciences

Alabama
Faulkner University *B*
University of Alabama *B*
University of Alabama
   Birmingham *B*
University of South Alabama *M, D*

Alaska
University of Alaska
   Anchorage *B*
   Fairbanks *B, M*

Arizona
Central Arizona College *A*
Northern Arizona University *B, M*
Northland Pioneer College *A*
Prescott College *B, M*

Arkansas
Southern Arkansas University *B*
University of Arkansas
   Little Rock *B*

University of Central Arkansas *B*

California
American River College *A*
California Lutheran University *B*
California State University
   Fullerton *M*
Cerro Coso Community College *A*
Citrus College *A*
College of the Canyons *A*
College of the Desert *A*
College of the Sequoias *A*
College of the Siskiyous *A*
Fresno City College *A*
Glendale Community College *A*
Golden West College *A*
Harvey Mudd College *B*
Laney College *A*
Lassen College *A*
Master's College *B*
National University *B*
Ohlone College *A*
Pitzer College *B*
Porterville College *A*
Scripps College *B*
Solano Community College *A*
University of California
   Santa Barbara *B*
University of La Verne *B*
University of the Pacific *B*
Vanguard University of Southern
   California *B*

Colorado
Colorado Christian University *B*
Colorado Mountain College
   Alpine Campus *A*
   Spring Valley Campus *A*
   Timberline Campus *A*
Morgan Community College *A*
University of Colorado
   Denver and Health Sciences
     Center *M*
University of Denver *B*

District of Columbia
American University *B, M*
Trinity University *B*

Florida
Florida Gulf Coast University *B*
Florida Institute of Technology *B*
Florida Southern College *B*
Palm Beach Community College *A*
University of North Florida *B*
University of South Florida *B*
University of West Florida *B*

Georgia
Spelman College *B*
University of Georgia *B*
Young Harris College *A*

Idaho
Northwest Nazarene University *B*

Illinois
Black Hawk College *A*
College of DuPage *A*
College of Lake County *A*
Heartland Community College *A*
Illinois Eastern Community Colleges
   Lincoln Trail College *A*
John A. Logan College *A*
John Wood Community College *A*
Kankakee Community College *A*
Kaskaskia College *A*
Kishwaukee College *A*
Lincoln Land Community College *A*
McHenry County College *A*
Moraine Valley Community College *A*
Morton College *A*
National-Louis University *B*

North Central College *B, T*
Northwestern University *B*
Olivet Nazarene University *B, T*
Parkland College *A*
Prairie State College *A*
Rend Lake College *A*
Rosalind Franklin University of
   Medicine and Science *D*
St. Xavier University *B*
Triton College *A*
Waubonsee Community College *A*

Indiana
Ball State University *M, D, T*
Indiana University
   Bloomington *M*
   East *A, B*
   Kokomo *B*
Purdue University *B*
St. Mary-of-the-Woods College *B*
Taylor University *B*
University of Southern Indiana *B, T*
Valparaiso University *A*

Iowa
Briar Cliff University *B*
Buena Vista University *B, T*
Clarke College *B*
Coe College *B*
Grinnell College *B*
St. Ambrose University *B*
University of Northern Iowa *B, M*
William Penn University *B*

Kansas
Central Christian College of Kansas *A*
Fort Hays State University *B*
Pratt Community College *A*
Seward County Community College *A*
Tabor College *B*
University of Kansas Medical
   Center *M, D*

Kentucky
Alice Lloyd College *B*
Berea College *T*
Brescia University *B*
St. Catharine College *A*

Louisiana
Delgado Community College *A*
Louisiana State University and
   Agricultural and Mechanical
     College *M*
Our Lady of Holy Cross College *B*

Maine
Colby College *B*
University of Maine *B, M*

Maryland
Baltimore City Community College *A*
College of Southern Maryland *A*
Montgomery College *A*
St. Mary's College of Maryland *B*
Towson University *B*
University of Maryland
   College Park *M, D*
Villa Julie College *B*
Washington College *B*

Massachusetts
American International College *B*
Anna Maria College *B*
Eastern Nazarene College *B*
Elms College *B*
Hampshire College *B*
Springfield College *B*
University of Massachusetts
   Amherst *B*
   Dartmouth *D*
Wellesley College *B*

Wheaton College *B*
Worcester Polytechnic
    Institute *B, M, D*
Worcester State College *B*

Michigan

Albion College *B*
Alma College *B*
Andrews University *B, M*
Calvin College *B*
Concordia University *B*
Eastern Michigan University *B, M*
Ferris State University *A*
Grand Valley State University *B*
Hope College *B*
Lake Michigan College *A*
Lansing Community College *A*
Madonna University *A, B*
Michigan State University *B, M*
Northern Michigan University *B, T*
Olivet College *B*
Rochester College *A*

Minnesota

College of St. Benedict *B*
Concordia University: St. Paul *B*
Minnesota State University
    Mankato *B*
St. John's University *B*
University of Minnesota
    Twin Cities *B*
Winona State University *B, T*

Mississippi

Delta State University *B, M*
Mississippi State University *B*

Missouri

Avila University *B*
Maryville University of Saint Louis *B*
Missouri State University *M*
Missouri Valley College *B*
St. Louis Community College
    St. Louis Community College at
        Meramec *A*
Southeast Missouri State University *M*
Washington University in St.
    Louis *B, M, D*

Montana

Carroll College *B*
Montana Tech of the University of
    Montana *B*
Stone Child College *A*

New Hampshire

Keene State College *B*
St. Anselm College *B*

New Jersey

Cumberland County College *A*
Fairleigh Dickinson University
    Metropolitan Campus *B, M*
Gloucester County College *A*
Ramapo College of New Jersey *B*
Rutgers, The State University of New
    Jersey
    Camden Regional Campus *B*
St. Peter's College *B*
Sussex County Community College *A*

New Mexico

Northern New Mexico College *A*

New York

Alfred University *B*
City University of New York
    Baruch College *B*
    Brooklyn College *B, M*
    Lehman College *B*
Colgate University *B*
College of New Rochelle *B, T*

Corning Community College *A*
Le Moyne College *B*
North Country Community College *A*
Paul Smith's College *A*
Rensselaer Polytechnic Institute *B*
Roberts Wesleyan College *B*
St. Thomas Aquinas College *B, T*
Sarah Lawrence College *B*
State University of New York
    College at Potsdam *B*
    College of Agriculture and
        Technology at Cobleskill *A*
    College of Environmental Science
        and Forestry *B, M, D*
    College of Technology at Alfred *A*
    Empire State College *A, B*
Touro College *B*
Union College *B*
University of Rochester *B*

North Carolina

Brevard College *B*
East Carolina University *M, D*
Johnson C. Smith University *B*
Mars Hill College *B*
Southeastern Community College *A*
Wayne Community College *A*

Ohio

Bowling Green State University:
    Firelands College *A*
Clark State Community College *A*
Defiance College *B, T*
Heidelberg College *B*
Jefferson Community College *A*
Urbana University *B*
Walsh University *B*
Wittenberg University *B*
Wright State University *D*

Oklahoma

Bacone College *A*
Cameron University *B*
Eastern Oklahoma State College *A*
Northeastern Oklahoma Agricultural
    and Mechanical College *A*
Oklahoma City University *B*
Oklahoma Panhandle State
    University *B*

Oregon

Linn-Benton Community College *A*
Oregon State University *B*
Portland State University *B, M*
Reed College *B*
Southern Oregon University *B*
University of Oregon *B*
Western Oregon University *B*

Pennsylvania

Arcadia University *B*
Cheyney University of
    Pennsylvania *B, T*
Clarion University of
    Pennsylvania *B, T*
Community College of Beaver
    County *A*
Delaware County Community
    College *A*
Drexel University *B*
East Stroudsburg University of
    Pennsylvania *B, M, T*
Edinboro University of
    Pennsylvania *B*
Gettysburg College *B*
Immaculata University *B*
Indiana University of Pennsylvania *B*
Keystone College *B*
King's College *B, T*
Kutztown University of
    Pennsylvania *B, T*
La Salle University *B*
Lehigh University *B*

Lock Haven University of
    Pennsylvania *B*
Luzerne County Community
    College *A*
Penn State
    Abington *A, B*
    Altoona *A, B*
    Beaver *A, B*
    Berks *B*
    Delaware County *B*
    Dubois *A, B*
    Fayette *B*
    Hazleton *B*
    Lehigh Valley *B*
    McKeesport *A, B*
    Mont Alto *B*
    New Kensington *A, B*
    Schuylkill - Capital College *A, B*
    Shenango *A, B*
    University Park *B*
    Wilkes-Barre *B*
    Worthington Scranton *B*
    York *B*
Ursinus College *B*
Villanova University *A, B*
West Chester University of
    Pennsylvania *T*

Puerto Rico

Bayamon Central University *B*
University of Puerto Rico
    Carolina Regional College *A*

Rhode Island

Brown University *B*
Community College of Rhode
    Island *A*

South Carolina

Charleston Southern University *B*

Tennessee

Bethel College *B*
Christian Brothers University *B*
Middle Tennessee State University *B*
Tennessee State University *B*

Texas

Central Texas College *A*
College of the Mainland *A*
Galveston College *A*
Hill College *A*
McMurry University *B*
Navarro College *A*
North Central Texas College *A*
Palo Alto College *A*
Stephen F. Austin State University *M*
Texas A&M University *B*
Texas A&M University
    Commerce *B, M*
    Galveston *B*
Texas Tech University *B*
University of Houston
    Downtown *B*
University of Texas
    Arlington *M*
    Austin *M, D*
    Dallas *M, T*
    El Paso *B*
    Health Science Center at
        Houston *M, D*
    Medical Branch at Galveston *M*
    Pan American *B, M*
    San Antonio *B*
Wayland Baptist University *M*

Utah

Brigham Young University *B, M*
Snow College *A*

Vermont

Castleton State College *B*
Lyndon State College *B*

Marlboro College *B*
Sterling College *A, B*

Virginia

Averett University *B*
College of William and Mary *M, D*
Danville Community College *A*
J. Sargeant Reynolds Community
    College *A*
Jefferson College of Health
    Sciences *B*
Lord Fairfax Community College *A*
New River Community College *A*
Northern Virginia Community
    College *A*
Paul D. Camp Community College *A*
Piedmont Virginia Community
    College *A*
Southside Virginia Community
    College *A*
Tidewater Community College *A*
University of Virginia *M*
Virginia Commonwealth University *B*
Virginia Highlands Community
    College *A*
Virginia Western Community
    College *A*
Wytheville Community College *A*

Washington

Centralia College *A*
Columbia Basin College *A*
Evergreen State College *B*
University of Washington *M, D*
Washington State University *B, M*
Western Washington University *B, M*

West Virginia

Bluefield State College *A, B*
Mountain State University *B*

Wisconsin

Lawrence University *B, T*
Madison Area Technical College *A*
Marquette University *M*
Mount Mary College *B*
Northland College *B, T*
St. Norbert College *B*
University of Wisconsin
    Green Bay *B*
    Madison *M*
    River Falls *B, T*
    Stevens Point *B, T*
    Superior *B*

Wyoming

Laramie County Community
    College *A*
Northwest College *A*
Sheridan College *A*

Biology

Alabama

Alabama Agricultural and Mechanical
    University *B, M*
Alabama State University *B, M*
Athens State University *B*
Auburn University *B*
Auburn University at Montgomery *B*
Birmingham-Southern College *B, T*
Chattahoochee Valley Community
    College *A*
Faulkner State Community College *A*
Faulkner University *B*
Gadsden State Community College *A*
Huntingdon College *B, T*
Jacksonville State University *B, M*
Judson College *B*
Lawson State Community College *A*
Miles College *B*
Northeast Alabama Community
    College *A*

Oakwood College *B*
Samford University *B*
Southern Union State Community
    College *A*
Spring Hill College *B, T*
Stillman College *B*
Talladega College *B*
Troy University *B*
Tuskegee University *B, M, T*
University of Alabama *B, M, D*
University of Alabama
    Birmingham *B, M, D*
    Huntsville *B, M*
University of Mobile *B, T*
University of Montevallo *B, T*
University of North Alabama *B*
University of South Alabama *B, M*
University of West Alabama *B, T*

Alaska

University of Alaska
    Anchorage *B, M*
    Fairbanks *B, M, D*
    Southeast *B*

Arizona

Arizona State University *B, M, D*
Arizona State University West *B*
Arizona Western College *A*
Central Arizona College *A*
Cochise College *A*
Dine College *A*
Eastern Arizona College *A*
Grand Canyon University *B*
Northern Arizona
    University *B, M, D, T*
Prescott College *B, M*
South Mountain Community
    College *A*
University of Arizona *B*

Arkansas

Arkansas State University *B, M*
Arkansas State University
    Beebe *A*
Arkansas Tech University *B*
Harding University *B*
Henderson State University *B*
Hendrix College *B*
John Brown University *B*
Lyon College *B*
Ouachita Baptist University *B*
Philander Smith College *B*
Phillips Community College of the
    University of Arkansas *A*
Southern Arkansas University *B*
University of Arkansas *B, M, D*
University of Arkansas
    Fort Smith *B*
    Little Rock *B, M*
    Monticello *B*
    Pine Bluff *B*
University of Central Arkansas *B, M*
University of the Ozarks *B*
Williams Baptist College *B*

California

Allan Hancock College *A*
Antelope Valley College *A*
Azusa Pacific University *B*
Bakersfield College *A*
Barstow College *A*
Biola University *B*
Cabrillo College *A*
California Baptist University *B*
California Institute of
    Technology *B, D*
California Lutheran University *B*
California Polytechnic State
    University: San Luis Obispo *B, M*
California State Polytechnic
    University: Pomona *B, M*

California State University
    Bakersfield *B*
    Chico *B, M*
    Dominguez Hills *B, M*
    East Bay *B, M*
    Fresno *B, M*
    Fullerton *B, M*
    Long Beach *B, M*
    Los Angeles *B, M*
    Northridge *B, M*
    Sacramento *B, M*
    San Bernardino *B, M*
    San Marcos *B*
    Stanislaus *B*
Canada College *A*
Cerritos Community College *A*
Chabot College *A*
Chaffey College *A*
Chapman University *B*
City College of San Francisco *A*
Claremont McKenna College *B*
College of Alameda *A*
College of Marin: Kentfield *A*
College of San Mateo *A*
College of the Desert *A*
College of the Siskiyous *A*
Columbia College *A*
Concordia University *B*
Contra Costa College *A*
Crafton Hills College *A*
Cuesta College *A*
De Anza College *A*
Dominican University of California *B*
El Camino College *A*
Feather River College *A*
Foothill College *A*
Fresno Pacific University *B*
Fullerton College *A*
Gavilan Community College *A*
Glendale Community College *A*
Golden West College *A*
Grossmont Community College *A*
Harvey Mudd College *B*
Holy Names University *B*
Humboldt State University *B, M*
Irvine Valley College *A*
La Sierra University *B*
Las Positas College *A*
Loma Linda University *M, D*
Long Beach City College *A*
Los Angeles City College *A*
Los Angeles Southwest College *A*
Los Angeles Valley College *A*
Los Medanos College *A*
Loyola Marymount University *B*
Master's College *B*
Mendocino College *A*
Merced College *A*
Mills College *B*
MiraCosta College *A*
Mission College *A*
Monterey Peninsula College *A*
Moorpark College *A*
Mount St. Mary's College *B*
Mount San Antonio College *A*
Notre Dame de Namur University *B*
Occidental College *B, M*
Ohlone College *A*
Orange Coast College *A*
Pacific Union College *B*
Palomar College *A*
Pasadena City College *A*
Pepperdine University *B*
Pitzer College *B*
Point Loma Nazarene University *B*
Pomona College *B*
Porterville College *A*
Reedley College *A*
Saddleback College *A*
St. Mary's College of California *B*
San Bernardino Valley College *A*
San Diego Christian College *B*
San Diego City College *A*
San Diego Mesa College *A*

San Diego Miramar College *A*
San Diego State University *B, M, D*
San Francisco State University *B, M*
San Joaquin Delta College *A*
San Jose State University *B, M*
Santa Ana College *A*
Santa Barbara City College *A*
Santa Clara University *B*
Santiago Canyon College *A*
Scripps College *B*
Sierra College *A*
Solano Community College *A*
Sonoma State University *B, M*
Southwestern College *A*
Stanford University *B, M, D*
University of California
    Berkeley *B, D*
    Davis *B*
    Irvine *B*
    Los Angeles *B, M, D*
    Riverside *B, M, D*
    San Diego *B*
    Santa Barbara *B, M, D*
    Santa Cruz *B, D*
University of California: Merced *B*
University of La Verne *B*
University of Redlands *B*
University of San Diego *B*
University of San Francisco *B, M*
University of Southern
    California *B, M, D*
University of the Pacific *B, M*
Vanguard University of Southern
    California *B*
Ventura College *A*
West Los Angeles College *A*
West Valley College *A*
Westmont College *B*
Whittier College *B, M*

Colorado

Adams State College *B*
Colorado Christian University *B*
Colorado College *B*
Colorado Mountain College
    Alpine Campus *A*
    Spring Valley Campus *A*
    Timberline Campus *A*
Colorado State University *B*
Colorado State University
    Pueblo *B*
Fort Lewis College *B*
Mesa State College *B*
Metropolitan State College of
    Denver *B, T*
Northeastern Junior College *A*
Otero Junior College *A*
Red Rocks Community College *A*
Regis University *B*
Trinidad State Junior College *A*
United States Air Force Academy *B*
University of Colorado
    Boulder *B, M*
    Colorado Springs *B, M*
    Denver and Health Sciences
        Center *B, M*
University of Denver *B, M, D*
University of Northern
    Colorado *B, M, D, T*
Western State College of Colorado *B*

Connecticut

Albertus Magnus College *B*
Central Connecticut State
    University *B, M, T*
Connecticut College *B*
Eastern Connecticut State
    University *B*
Fairfield University *B*
Post University *B*
Quinnipiac University *B*
Sacred Heart University *B*
St. Joseph College *B, M, T*

Southern Connecticut State
    University *B, M, T*
Trinity College *B*
University of Bridgeport *B*
University of Connecticut *B, M*
University of Hartford *B, M*
University of New Haven *B*
Wesleyan University *B, D*
Western Connecticut State
    University *B, M*
Yale University *B*

Delaware

Delaware State University *B, M*
University of Delaware *B, M, D*
Wesley College *B*

District of Columbia

American University *B, M*
Catholic University of America *B, T*
Gallaudet University *B*
George Washington
    University *B, M, D*
Georgetown University *B, M, D*
Howard University *B, M, D*
Trinity University *B*
University of the District of
    Columbia *B, T*

Florida

Barry University *B, M, T*
Bethune-Cookman College *B*
Broward Community College *A*
Chipola College *A, B*
Clearwater Christian College *B*
Eckerd College *B*
Edward Waters College *B*
Florida Agricultural and Mechanical
    University *B, M*
Florida Atlantic University *B, M*
Florida Gulf Coast University *B*
Florida Institute of Technology *B, D*
Florida International
    University *B, M, D*
Florida Memorial University *B*
Florida Southern College *B*
Florida State University *B, M, D*
Gulf Coast Community College *A*
Indian River Community College *A*
Jacksonville University *B*
Lynn University *B*
Manatee Community College *A*
Miami Dade College *A*
New College of Florida *B*
Nova Southeastern University *B*
Okaloosa-Walton College *A*
Palm Beach Atlantic University *B*
Palm Beach Community College *A*
Pensacola Junior College *A*
Rollins College *B*
St. Leo University *B*
St. Thomas University *B*
Southeastern College of the
    Assemblies of God *B*
Stetson University *B*
University of Central Florida *B, M*
University of Miami *B, M, D*
University of North Florida *B, M*
University of South Florida *B, M, D*
University of Tampa *A, B, T*
University of West Florida *B, M*
Valencia Community College *A*
Warner Southern College *B*

Georgia

Abraham Baldwin Agricultural
    College *A*
Agnes Scott College *B*
Albany State University *B*
Armstrong Atlantic State
    University *B, T*
Atlanta Metropolitan College *A*
Augusta State University *B*

Berry College *B*
Brenau University *B*
Brewton-Parker College *B*
Clark Atlanta University *B, M, D*
Clayton State University *B*
Coastal Georgia Community
   College *A*
Columbus State University *B*
Covenant College *B*
Darton College *A*
East Georgia College *A*
Emmanuel College *B*
Emory University *B, D*
Fort Valley State University *B*
Georgia College and State
   University *B, M*
Georgia Highlands College *A*
Georgia Institute of
   Technology *B, M, D*
Georgia Perimeter College *A*
Georgia Southern University *B, M*
Georgia Southwestern State
   University *B, T*
Georgia State University *B, M, D*
Gordon College *A*
Kennesaw State University *B*
LaGrange College *B*
Life University *B*
Macon State College *A*
Mercer University *B*
Middle Georgia College *A*
Morehouse College *B*
North Georgia College & State
   University *B*
Oglethorpe University *B*
Paine College *B*
Piedmont College *B*
Reinhardt College *B*
Savannah State University *B*
Shorter College *B*
South Georgia College *A*
Southern Polytechnic State
   University *B*
Spelman College *B*
Thomas University *B*
Toccoa Falls College *B*
University of Georgia *B*
University of West Georgia *B, M*
Valdosta State University *B, M*
Waycross College *A*
Wesleyan College *B*
Young Harris College *A*

Hawaii

Brigham Young University-Hawaii *B*
Chaminade University of Honolulu *B*
Hawaii Pacific University *B*
University of Hawaii
   Hilo *B*
   Manoa *B*

Idaho

Albertson College of Idaho *B*
Boise State University *B, M, T*
Brigham Young University-Idaho *A, B*
College of Southern Idaho *A*
Idaho State University *A, B, M, D*
Lewis-Clark State College *B*
North Idaho College *A*
Northwest Nazarene University *B*
University of Idaho *B, M*

Illinois

Augustana College *B*
Aurora University *B*
Benedictine University *B, T*
Black Hawk College
   East Campus *A*
Blackburn College *B*
Bradley University *B, M, T*
Chicago State University *B, T*
City Colleges of Chicago
   Harold Washington College *A*

Malcolm X College *A*
Olive-Harvey College *A*
Concordia University *B, T*
Danville Area Community College *A*
DePaul University *B, M, T*
Dominican University *B*
Eastern Illinois University *B, M, T*
Elmhurst College *B, T*
Eureka College *B, T*
Governors State University *B, T*
Greenville College *B, T*
Highland Community College *A*
Illinois College *B*
Illinois Institute of
   Technology *B, M, D*
Illinois State University *B, M, D, T*
Illinois Valley Community College *A*
Illinois Wesleyan University *B*
John A. Logan College *A*
John Wood Community College *A*
Joliet Junior College *A*
Judson College *B*
Kankakee Community College *A*
Knox College *B*
Lake Forest College *B*
Lewis University *B, T*
Loyola University of Chicago *B, M*
MacMurray College *B, T*
McKendree College *B, T*
Millikin University *B, T*
Monmouth College *B, T*
National-Louis University *B*
North Central College *B, T*
North Park University *B*
Northeastern Illinois University *B, M*
Northern Illinois University *B, M, D, T*
Northwestern University *B, M, D*
Olivet Nazarene University *B, T*
Principia College *B*
Quincy University *B, T*
Richland Community College *A*
Rockford College *B*
Roosevelt University *B, M*
St. Xavier University *B*
Sauk Valley Community College *A*
South Suburban College of Cook
   County *A*
Southern Illinois University
   Carbondale *B, M*
Southern Illinois University
   Edwardsville *B, M, T*
Southwestern Illinois College *A*
Trinity Christian College *B, T*
Trinity International University *B*
Triton College *A*
University of Chicago *B*
University of Illinois
   Chicago *B, M, D*
   Springfield *B, M*
   Urbana-Champaign *B, M, D*
University of St. Francis *B*
Western Illinois University *B, M*
Wheaton College *B, T*

Indiana

Ancilla College *A*
Anderson University *B*
Ball State University *B, M*
Bethel College *A, B*
Butler University *B*
DePauw University *B*
Earlham College *B*
Franklin College *B*
Goshen College *B*
Grace College *B*
Hanover College *B*
Huntington University *B*
Indiana State University *B, M, D, T*
Indiana University
   Bloomington *B, M*
   East *A, B*
   Kokomo *B*
   Northwest *B*

South Bend *A, B*
Southeast *B*
Indiana University-Purdue University
   Fort Wayne *A, B, M, T*
Indiana University-Purdue University
   Indianapolis *B, M, D*
Indiana Wesleyan University *A, B*
Manchester College *B, T*
Marian College *B, T*
Martin University *B*
Oakland City University *B*
Purdue University *B, M, D*
Purdue University
   Calumet *B, M*
   North Central Campus *A, B*
Rose-Hulman Institute of
   Technology *B*
St. Joseph's College *B*
Saint Mary's College *B, T*
St. Mary-of-the-Woods College *B*
Taylor University *B*
Tri-State University *B*
University of Evansville *B*
University of Indianapolis *B, M*
University of Notre Dame *B, M, D*
University of Southern Indiana *B, T*
Valparaiso University *B*
Vincennes University *A*
Wabash College *B*

Iowa

Ashford University *B*
Briar Cliff University *B*
Buena Vista University *B, T*
Central College *B, T*
Clarke College *B, T*
Coe College *B*
Cornell College *B, T*
Dordt College *B*
Drake University *B*
Ellsworth Community College *A*
Graceland University *B, T*
Grand View College *B*
Grinnell College *B*
Iowa State University *B*
Iowa Wesleyan College *B*
Iowa Western Community College *A*
Loras College *B*
Luther College *B*
Maharishi University of
   Management *B*
Marshalltown Community College *A*
Morningside College *B*
Mount Mercy College *B, T*
Northwestern College *B, T*
St.Ambrose University *B*
Simpson College *B*
University of Dubuque *B*
University of Iowa *B, M, D, T*
University of Northern Iowa *B, M*
Upper Iowa University *B*
Waldorf College *B*
Wartburg College *B, T*
William Penn University *B*

Kansas

Allen County Community College *A*
Baker University *B, T*
Barton County Community College *A*
Benedictine College *B*
Bethany College *B, T*
Bethel College *B*
Central Christian College of
   Kansas *A, B*
Cloud County Community College *A*
Coffeyville Community College *A*
Colby Community College *A*
Dodge City Community College *A*
Donnelly College *A*
Emporia State University *B, M, T*
Fort Hays State University *B, M*
Friends University *B*
Garden City Community College *A*
Hutchinson Community College *A*

Kansas State University *B, M, D*
Kansas Wesleyan University *B, T*
Labette Community College *A*
McPherson College *B, T*
MidAmerica Nazarene University *B*
Neosho County Community
   College *A*
Newman University *B*
Ottawa University *B*
Pittsburg State University *B, M*
Pratt Community College *A*
Seward County Community College *A*
Southwestern College *B*
Sterling College *B, T*
Tabor College *B*
University of Kansas *B, M, D*
University of St. Mary *B*
Washburn University of Topeka *B*
Wichita State University *B, M*

Kentucky

Alice Lloyd College *B*
Asbury College *B, T*
Bellarmine University *B, T*
Berea College *B, T*
Brescia University *A, B*
Campbellsville University *B*
Centre College *B*
Eastern Kentucky University *B, M*
Georgetown College *B*
Kentucky State University *B*
Kentucky Wesleyan College *B, T*
Lindsey Wilson College *A, B, T*
Midway College *B*
Morehead State University *B, M, T*
Murray State University *B, M, T*
Northern Kentucky University *B*
Pikeville College *B, T*
Spalding University *B*
Thomas More College *A, B*
Transylvania University *B*
Union College *B*
University of Kentucky *B, M, D*
University of Louisville *B, M, D*
University of the Cumberlands *B*
Western Kentucky University *B, M, T*

Louisiana

Centenary College of Louisiana *B, T*
Dillard University *B*
Grambling State University *B*
Louisiana State University
   Alexandria *B*
Louisiana State University and
   Agricultural and Mechanical
   College *B, M, D*
Louisiana Tech University *B, M*
Loyola University New Orleans *B*
Nicholls State University *B*
Northwestern State University *B*
Our Lady of Holy Cross College *B, T*
Our Lady of the Lake College *B*
Southeastern Louisiana
   University *B, M*
Southern University
   New Orleans *B*
   Shreveport *A*
Southern University and Agricultural
   and Mechanical College *B, M*
Tulane University *B, M, D*
University of Louisiana at
   Lafayette *B, M*
University of Louisiana at
   Monroe *B, M*
University of New Orleans *B, M*
Xavier University of Louisiana *B*

Maine

Bates College *B, T*
Bowdoin College *B*
Colby College *B*
Husson College *B*
Maine Maritime Academy *T*
St. Joseph's College *B*

University of Maine *B, M, D*
University of Maine
 Augusta *B*
 Farmington *B*
 Fort Kent *B*
 Machias *B, T*
 Presque Isle *B*
University of New England *B*
University of Southern Maine *B*

Maryland

Allegany College of Maryland *A*
Bowie State University *B*
Cecil Community College *A*
College of Notre Dame of Maryland *B*
College of Southern Maryland *A*
Columbia Union College *B*
Coppin State University *B*
Frederick Community College *A*
Frostburg State University *B, T*
Goucher College *B*
Harford Community College *A*
Hood College *B, T*
Johns Hopkins University *B, M, D*
Loyola College in Maryland *B*
McDaniel College *B*
Morgan State University *B*
Mount St. Mary's University *B*
Prince George's Community
 College *A*
St. Mary's College of Maryland *B*
Salisbury University *B, T*
Towson University *B, M, T*
University of Maryland
 Baltimore County *B, M, D*
 College Park *B, M, D*
 Eastern Shore *B*
Villa Julie College *B*
Washington College *B, T*

Massachusetts

American International College *B*
Amherst College *B*
Anna Maria College *B, M*
Assumption College *B*
Atlantic Union College *B*
Bay Path College *B*
Becker College *B*
Boston College *B, M, D*
Boston University *B, M, D*
Brandeis University *B*
Bridgewater State College *B*
Bunker Hill Community College *A*
Clark University *B, M, D*
College of the Holy Cross *B*
Curry College *B*
Eastern Nazarene College *B*
Elms College *B*
Emmanuel College *B*
Fitchburg State College *B, M*
Framingham State College *B*
Gordon College *B*
Hampshire College *B*
Harvard College *B*
Lesley University *B*
Massachusetts College of Liberal
 Arts *B*
Massachusetts Institute of
 Technology *B, D*
Merrimack College *B*
Mount Holyoke College *B*
Northeastern University *B, M, D*
Pine Manor College *A, B*
Regis College *B*
Roxbury Community College *A*
Salem State College *B, M*
Simmons College *B*
Simon's Rock College of Bard *B*
Smith College *B, M, D*
Springfield College *B*
Springfield Technical Community
 College *A*
Stonehill College *B*
Suffolk University *B*

Tufts University *B, M, D*
University of Massachusetts
 Amherst *B, M, D*
 Boston *B, M*
 Dartmouth *B, M*
 Lowell *B, M*
Wellesley College *B*
Western New England College *B*
Westfield State College *B*
Wheaton College *B*
Williams College *B*
Worcester Polytechnic Institute *B, M*
Worcester State College *B*

Michigan

Adrian College *A, B, T*
Albion College *B, T*
Alma College *B, T*
Andrews University *B, M*
Aquinas College *B, T*
Calvin College *B, T*
Central Michigan University *B, M, T*
Concordia University *B*
Cornerstone University *B, T*
Delta College *A*
Eastern Michigan University *B, M*
Ferris State University *B*
Gogebic Community College *A*
Grand Valley State University *B, M*
Hillsdale College *B*
Hope College *B*
Kalamazoo College *B, T*
Kellogg Community College *A*
Lake Michigan College *A*
Lake Superior State University *B, T*
Lansing Community College *A*
Macomb Community College *A*
Madonna University *B, T*
Marygrove College *B, T*
Michigan State University *B, M*
Michigan Technological
 University *B, M, D, T*
Mid Michigan Community College *A*
Northern Michigan University *B, M*
Northwestern Michigan College *A*
Oakland University *B, M, T*
Olivet College *B, T*
Saginaw Valley State University *B, T*
Siena Heights University *A, B*
Spring Arbor University *B, T*
University of Detroit Mercy *B*
University of Michigan *B, M, D*
University of Michigan
 Dearborn *B*
 Flint *B, M, T*
Wayne State University *B, M, D*
Western Michigan University *B, M, D*

Minnesota

Augsburg College *B*
Bemidji State University *B, M*
Bethel University *B*
Carleton College *B*
College of St. Benedict *B*
College of St. Catherine *B*
College of St. Scholastica *B*
Concordia College: Moorhead *B*
Concordia University: St. Paul *B*
Crown College *B*
Gustavus Adolphus College *B*
Hamline University *B*
Macalester College *B, T*
Mesabi Range Community and
 Technical College *A*
Metropolitan State University *B*
Minnesota State University
 Mankato *B, M, T*
 Moorhead *B*
Northland Community & Technical
 College *A*
Northwestern College *B*
Ridgewater College *A*
St. Cloud State University *B, M*
St. John's University *B*

St. Mary's University of Minnesota *B*
St. Olaf College *B*
Southwest Minnesota State
 University *B, T*
University of Minnesota
 Duluth *B, M*
 Morris *B*
 Twin Cities *B*
University of St. Thomas *B*
Vermilion Community College *A*
Winona State University *B, T*

Mississippi

Alcorn State University *B, M*
Belhaven College *B, T*
Blue Mountain College *B*
Coahoma Community College *A*
Delta State University *B, T*
East Central Community College *A*
Hinds Community College *A*
Jackson State University *B, M*
Millsaps College *B, T*
Mississippi College *B, M, D*
Mississippi Delta Community
 College *A*
Mississippi Gulf Coast Community
 College
 Jefferson Davis Campus *A*
Mississippi State University *B, M, D*
Mississippi Valley State University *B*
Rust College *B*
Tougaloo College *B*
University of Mississippi *B, M, D, T*
University of Southern
 Mississippi *B, M, D*
William Carey College *B*

Missouri

Avila University *B*
Central Methodist University *B*
Central Missouri State University *B, M*
College of the Ozarks *B*
Columbia College *B*
Crowder College *A*
Culver-Stockton College *B, T*
Drury University *B*
Evangel University *B*
Fontbonne University *B*
Hannibal-LaGrange College *B*
Lincoln University *B*
Lindenwood University *B*
Maryville University of Saint Louis *B*
Missouri Baptist University *B, T*
Missouri Southern State
 University *B, T*
Missouri State University *B, M*
Missouri Valley College *B*
Missouri Western State University *B, T*
Northwest Missouri State
 University *B, M*
Park University *B*
Rockhurst University *B*
St. Louis Community College
 St. Louis Community College at
 Florissant Valley *A*
St. Louis University *B, M, D*
Southeast Missouri State University *B*
Southwest Baptist University *B, T*
Stephens College *B*
Three Rivers Community College *A*
Truman State University *B, M*
University of Missouri
 Columbia *B, M, D*
 Kansas City *B, M*
 Rolla *B*
 St. Louis *B, M, D*
Washington University in St.
 Louis *B, M, D*
Webster University *B*
Westminster College *B*
William Jewell College *B, T*
William Woods University *B, T*

Montana

Carroll College *B, T*
Little Big Horn College *A*
Miles Community College *A*
Montana State University
 Billings *B*
 Bozeman *B, M, D*
Montana Tech of the University of
 Montana *B*
Rocky Mountain College *B, T*
University of Great Falls *B*
University of Montana:
 Missoula *B, M, D*
University of Montana: Western *B*

Nebraska

Bellevue University *B*
Chadron State College *B*
College of Saint Mary *B, T*
Concordia University *B, T*
Creighton University *B*
Dana College *B*
Doane College *B*
Hastings College *B*
Midland Lutheran College *B, T*
Nebraska Wesleyan University *B*
Northeast Community College *A*
Union College *B*
University of Nebraska
 Kearney *B, M, T*
 Lincoln *B, M, D*
 Omaha *B, M*
Wayne State College *B, T*
Western Nebraska Community
 College *A*
York College *B*

Nevada

Community College of Southern
 Nevada *A*
Sierra Nevada College *B*
University of Nevada
 Las Vegas *B, M, D*
 Reno *B, M*

New Hampshire

Colby-Sawyer College *B*
Dartmouth College *B, M, D, T*
Franklin Pierce College *B*
Keene State College *B, T*
New England College *B, T*
Plymouth State University *B*
Rivier College *B, M, T*
St. Anselm College *B, T*
Thomas More College of Liberal
 Arts *B*
University of New Hampshire *B, M, D*
University of New Hampshire at
 Manchester *A*

New Jersey

Atlantic Cape Community College *A*
Bloomfield College *B*
Caldwell College *B*
Centenary College *B*
The College of New Jersey *B, T*
College of St. Elizabeth *B, T*
Drew University *B*
Essex County College *A*
Fairleigh Dickinson University
 College at Florham *B, M*
 Metropolitan Campus *B, M*
Felician College *B*
Georgian Court University *B, M*
Gloucester County College *A*
Kean University *B, T*
Mercer County Community College *A*
Monmouth University *B*
Montclair State University *B, M, T*
New Jersey City University *B*
New Jersey Institute of
 Technology *B, M, D*
Ramapo College of New Jersey *B*

Raritan Valley Community College *A*
Richard Stockton College of New
　Jersey *B*
Rider University *B*
Rowan University *B*
Rutgers, The State University of New
　Jersey
　Camden Regional Campus *B, M, T*
　New Brunswick/Piscataway
　　Campus *B, T*
　Newark Regional
　　Campus *B, M, D, T*
　St. Peter's College *B*
Salem Community College *A*
Seton Hall University *B, M*
Sussex County Community College *A*
Thomas Edison State College *A, B*
Union County College *A*
Warren County Community College *A*
William Paterson University of New
　Jersey *B, M*

New Mexico

College of the Southwest *B*
Eastern New Mexico University *B, M*
New Mexico Highlands
　University *B, M*
New Mexico Institute of Mining and
　Technology *B, M*
New Mexico Junior College *A*
New Mexico State University *B, M, D*
San Juan College *A*
Santa Fe Community College *A*
University of New Mexico *B, M, D*
Western New Mexico University *B*

New York

Adelphi University *B, M*
Adirondack Community College *A*
Alfred University *B*
Bard College *B*
Barnard College *B*
Canisius College *B*
Cayuga County Community College *A*
City University of New York
　Baruch College *B*
　Brooklyn College *B, M*
　City College *B, M, D*
　College of Staten Island *B, M*
　Hunter College *B, M*
　Kingsborough Community
　　College *A*
　Lehman College *B, M*
　Medgar Evers College *A, B*
　Queens College *B, M*
　Queensborough Community
　　College *A*
　York College *B*
Clarkson University *B*
Colgate University *B*
College of Mount St. Vincent *B, T*
College of New Rochelle *B, T*
College of Saint Rose *B*
Columbia University
　Columbia College *B*
　School of General Studies *B*
Columbia-Greene Community
　College *A*
Concordia College *B, T*
Cornell University *B, M, D*
D'Youville College *B*
Daemen College *B*
Dominican College of Blauvelt *B*
Dowling College *B, T*
Elmira College *B, T*
Excelsior College *B*
Fordham University *B, M, D*
Hamilton College *B*
Hartwick College *B, T*
Herkimer County Community
　College *A*
Hobart and William Smith Colleges *B*
Hofstra University *B, M*
Houghton College *B*

Iona College *B*
Ithaca College *B, T*
Keuka College *B*
Le Moyne College *B*
Long Island University
　Brooklyn Campus *B, M*
　C.W. Post Campus *B, M*
Manhattan College *B*
Manhattanville College *B*
Marist College *B*
Marymount Manhattan College *B*
Medaille College *B*
Mercy College *B*
Molloy College *B*
Monroe Community College *A*
Mount St. Mary College *B, T*
Nazareth College of Rochester *B*
New York Institute of Technology *B*
New York University *B, M, D*
Niagara University *B*
Pace University *B*
Paul Smith's College *B*
Rensselaer Polytechnic
　Institute *B, M, D*
Roberts Wesleyan College *B*
Rochester Institute of
　Technology *A, B*
Russell Sage College *B*
St. Bonaventure University *B, T*
St. Francis College *B*
St. John Fisher College *B*
St. John's University *B, M, D*
St. Joseph's College *B*
St. Joseph's College: Suffolk
　Campus *B, T*
St. Lawrence University *B, T*
St. Thomas Aquinas College *B, T*
Sarah Lawrence College *B*
Siena College *B, T*
Skidmore College *B*
State University of New York
　Albany *B, M, D*
　Binghamton *B, M, D*
　Buffalo *B, M, D*
　College at Brockport *B, M, T*
　College at Buffalo *B, M*
　College at Cortland *B*
　College at Fredonia *B, M, T*
　College at Geneseo *B, T*
　College at Old Westbury *B, T*
　College at Oneonta *B*
　College at Plattsburgh *B, M*
　College at Potsdam *B*
　College of Agriculture and
　　Technology at Morrisville *A*
　College of Environmental Science
　　and Forestry *B, M, D*
　College of Technology at Alfred *A*
　College of Technology at Canton *A*
　Farmingdale *B*
　New Paltz *B, M, T*
　Oswego *B*
　Purchase *B*
　Stony Brook *B, M*
Suffolk County Community College *A*
Syracuse University *B, M, D*
Touro College *B*
Union College *B*
University of Rochester *B, M, D*
Utica College *B*
Vassar College *B*
Wagner College *B, T*
Wells College *B*
Yeshiva University *B*

North Carolina

Appalachian State University *B, M*
Barton College *B*
Belmont Abbey College *B*
Bennett College *B*
Cabarrus College of Health
　Sciences *A*
Campbell University *B, T*
Catawba College *B, T*

Chowan College *B*
Davidson College *B*
Duke University *B*
East Carolina University *B, M*
Elizabeth City State University *B, M*
Elon University *B*
Fayetteville State University *B*
Gardner-Webb University *B*
Greensboro College *B, T*
Guilford College *B*
High Point University *B*
Johnson C. Smith University *B*
Lees-McRae College *B*
Lenoir-Rhyne College *B*
Livingstone College *B*
Louisburg College *A*
Mars Hill College *B, T*
Meredith College *B*
Methodist College *A, B, T*
Montreat College *B*
Mount Olive College *A, B*
North Carolina Agricultural and
　Technical State University *B, M*
North Carolina Central
　University *B, M*
North Carolina State University *B*
North Carolina Wesleyan College *B*
Peace College *A, B*
Pfeiffer University *B*
Queens University of Charlotte *B*
St. Andrews Presbyterian College *B*
St. Augustine's College *B*
Salem College *B*
Sandhills Community College *A*
Shaw University *B*
University of North Carolina
　Asheville *B, T*
　Chapel Hill *B, M, D*
　Charlotte *B, M, D*
　Greensboro *B, M, T*
　Pembroke *B*
　Wilmington *B, M*
Wake Forest University *B, M, D*
Warren Wilson College *B*
Western Carolina University *B, M*
Wingate University *B*
Winston-Salem State University *B*

North Dakota

Dickinson State University *B, T*
Jamestown College *B*
Mayville State University *B, T*
Minot State University *B*
Minot State University: Bottineau
　Campus *A*
North Dakota State University *B, M*
University of Mary *B*
University of North Dakota *B, M, D, T*
Valley City State University *B*

Ohio

Antioch College *B*
Ashland University *B*
Baldwin-Wallace College *B, T*
Bluffton University *B*
Bowling Green State
　University *B, M, D*
Capital University *B*
Case Western Reserve
　University *B, M, D*
Cedarville University *B, T*
Central State University *B*
College of Mount St. Joseph *B, T*
College of Wooster *B*
Defiance College *B, T*
Denison University *B*
Franciscan University of
　Steubenville *B*
Heidelberg College *B*
Hiram College *B*
Jefferson Community College *A*
John Carroll University *B, M*
Kent State University *B, M, T*

Kent State University
　Trumbull Campus *A*
Kenyon College *B*
Lake Erie College *B*
Lourdes College *B*
Malone College *B*
Marietta College *B*
Miami University
　Oxford Campus *B, T*
Mount Union College *B*
Mount Vernon Nazarene University *B*
Muskingum College *B*
Oberlin College *B*
Ohio Dominican University *B, T*
Ohio Northern University *B*
Ohio State University
　Columbus Campus *B*
　Lima Campus *B*
Ohio University *B, M, D*
Ohio Wesleyan University *B*
Otterbein College *B*
Owens Community College
　Toledo *B*
Shawnee State University *B*
Sinclair Community College *A*
Union Institute & University *B*
University of Akron *B, M*
University of Cincinnati *B, M, D, T*
University of Cincinnati
　Clermont College *A*
　Raymond Walters College *A*
University of Dayton *B, M, D*
University of Findlay *B*
University of Rio Grande *A, B, T*
University of Toledo *A, B, M, D*
Ursuline College *B*
Walsh University *B*
Wilmington College *B*
Wittenberg University *B*
Wright State University *A, B, M*
Wright State University: Lake
　Campus *A*
Xavier University *B*
Youngstown State University *B, M*

Oklahoma

Bacone College *A*
Cameron University *B*
Carl Albert State College *A*
Connors State College *A*
East Central University *B*
Eastern Oklahoma State College *A*
Northeastern Oklahoma Agricultural
　and Mechanical College *A*
Northeastern State University *B*
Northwestern Oklahoma State
　University *B*
Oklahoma Baptist University *B, T*
Oklahoma Christian University *B*
Oklahoma City Community College *A*
Oklahoma City University *B*
Oklahoma Panhandle State
　University *B*
Oklahoma State University *B*
Oklahoma Wesleyan University *A, B*
Oral Roberts University *B*
Rogers State University *A, B*
Rose State College *A*
St. Gregory's University *A, B*
Southeastern Oklahoma State
　University *B*
Southern Nazarene University *B*
Southwestern Oklahoma State
　University *B*
University of Central Oklahoma *B, M*
University of Science and Arts of
　Oklahoma *B*
University of Tulsa *B, M, D*
Western Oklahoma State College *A*

Oregon

Central Oregon Community
　College *A*
Chemeketa Community College *A*

Concordia University B, T
Eastern Oregon University B, T
George Fox University B
Lewis & Clark College B
Linfield College B, T
Linn-Benton Community College A
Oregon State University B
Pacific University B
Portland State University B, M
Reed College B
Southern Oregon University B, T
Treasure Valley Community College A
University of Oregon B, M, D
University of Portland B, T
Warner Pacific College B, T
Western Oregon University B
Willamette University B

Pennsylvania

Albright College B, T
Allegheny College B
Alvernia College B
Arcadia University B
Bloomsburg University of
    Pennsylvania B, M, T
Bryn Athyn College of the New
    Church B
Bryn Mawr College B, M, D
Bucknell University B, M
Bucks County Community College A
Butler County Community College A
Cabrini College B
California University of
    Pennsylvania B, M
Carlow University B, T
Carnegie Mellon University B, M, D
Cedar Crest College B
Chatham College B, M
Chestnut Hill College A, B
Cheyney University of
    Pennsylvania B, M, T
Clarion University of
    Pennsylvania B, M, T
College Misericordia B
Community College of Allegheny
    County A
DeSales University B, T
Delaware Valley College B
Dickinson College B
Drexel University B, M, D
Duquesne University B, M, D
East Stroudsburg University of
    Pennsylvania B, M
Eastern University B
Edinboro University of
    Pennsylvania B, M, T
Elizabethtown College B
Franklin & Marshall College B
Gannon University B
Geneva College B, T
Gettysburg College B
Grove City College B
Gwynedd-Mercy College B
Harrisburg Area Community
    College A
Haverford College B, T
Holy Family University B, T
Immaculata University A, B
Indiana University of
    Pennsylvania B, M, T
Juniata College B
Keystone College A, B
King's College B, T
Kutztown University of
    Pennsylvania B, M, T
La Roche College B
La Salle University B, T
Lafayette College B
Lebanon Valley College B, T
Lehigh Carbon Community College A
Lehigh University B
Lincoln University B
Lock Haven University of
    Pennsylvania B, T

Lycoming College B
Mansfield University of
    Pennsylvania B, T
Marywood University B
Mercyhurst College B
Messiah College B
Millersville University of
    Pennsylvania B, M, T
Montgomery County Community
    College A
Moravian College B, T
Muhlenberg College B
Neumann College B
Northampton County Area
    Community College A
Penn State
    Abington B
    Altoona B
    Beaver B
    Berks B
    Delaware County B
    Dubois B
    Erie, The Behrend College B
    Fayette B
    Hazleton B
    Lehigh Valley B
    McKeesport B
    Mont Alto B
    New Kensington B
    Schuylkill - Capital College B
    Shenango B
    University Park B, M, D
    Wilkes-Barre B
    Worthington Scranton B
    York B
Philadelphia University B
Point Park University B
Reading Area Community College A
Rosemont College B
St. Francis University B
St. Joseph's University A, B, M
St. Vincent College B
Seton Hill University B, T
Shippensburg University of
    Pennsylvania B, M, T
Slippery Rock University of
    Pennsylvania B
Susquehanna University B, T
Swarthmore College B
Temple University B, M, D
Thiel College B
University of Pennsylvania B, M, D
University of Pittsburgh B, M, D
University of Pittsburgh
    Bradford B
    Greensburg B
    Johnstown B
University of Scranton B, T
University of the Sciences in
    Philadelphia B
Ursinus College B, T
Villanova University B, M
Washington and Jefferson College B
Waynesburg College B
West Chester University of
    Pennsylvania B, M, T
Westminster College B
Widener University B, T
Wilkes University B
Wilson College B
York College of Pennsylvania A, B, T

Puerto Rico

Bayamon Central University B
Inter American University of Puerto
    Rico
    Aguadilla Campus B
    Arecibo Campus B
    Barranquitas Campus B
    Bayamon Campus B
    Guayama Campus B
    Ponce Campus B
    San German Campus B

Pontifical Catholic University of
    Puerto Rico B
Turabo University B
Universidad Adventista de las
    Antillas B
Universidad Metropolitana B
Universidad del Este B
University of Puerto Rico
    Aguadilla A, B
    Bayamon University College B
    Cayey University College B
    Humacao B
    Mayaguez B, M
    Ponce A
    Rio Piedras B, M, D
University of the Sacred Heart B

Rhode Island

Brown University B, M, D
Providence College B
Rhode Island College B, M
Roger Williams University B
Salve Regina University B
University of Rhode Island B

South Carolina

Allen University B
Anderson University B
Benedict College B
Charleston Southern University B
The Citadel B, M
Claflin University B
Clemson University B
Coastal Carolina University B
Coker College B
College of Charleston B, T
Columbia College B
Converse College B
Erskine College B, T
Francis Marion University B
Furman University B, T
Lander University B
Limestone College B
Morris College B
Newberry College B, T
Presbyterian College B, T
South Carolina State University B
Southern Wesleyan University B, T
University of South Carolina B, M, D
University of South Carolina
    Aiken B
    Beaufort B
    Upstate B
Voorhees College B
Winthrop University B, M
Wofford College B, T

South Dakota

Augustana College B, T
Black Hills State University B
Dakota State University B
Dakota Wesleyan University B
Mount Marty College B
Northern State University B
Presentation College A
South Dakota State
    University B, M, D, T
University of Sioux Falls B
University of South Dakota B, M, D

Tennessee

Austin Peay State University B, M
Belmont University B, T
Bethel College B, T
Bryan College B, T
Carson-Newman College B, T
Christian Brothers University B
Columbia State Community College A
Crichton College B
Cumberland University B
Dyersburg State Community
    College A

East Tennessee State
    University B, M, T
Fisk University B, M
Freed-Hardeman University B, T
Hiwassee College A
Jackson State Community College A
King College B, T
Lambuth University B
LeMoyne-Owen College B
Lincoln Memorial University B, T
Lipscomb University B
Martin Methodist College B
Maryville College B, T
Middle Tennessee State
    University B, M
Milligan College B, T
Rhodes College B
Roane State Community College A
Southern Adventist University B
Tennessee State University B, M
Tennessee Technological
    University B, M, T
Tennessee Temple University B
Tennessee Wesleyan College B, T
Trevecca Nazarene University B
Tusculum College B
Union University B, T
University of Memphis B, M, D
University of Tennessee
    Chattanooga B
    Knoxville B
    Martin B
University of the South B
Walters State Community College A

Texas

Abilene Christian University B
Alvin Community College A
Amarillo College A
Angelina College A
Angelo State University B, M, T
Austin College B
Austin Community College A
Baylor University B, M, D
Blinn College A
Brazosport College A
Central Texas College A
Cisco Junior College A
Clarendon College A
Coastal Bend College A
College of the Mainland A
Concordia University at Austin B
Dallas Baptist University B
Del Mar College A
East Texas Baptist University B
El Paso Community College A
Frank Phillips College A
Galveston College A
Grayson County College A
Hardin-Simmons University B
Hill College A
Houston Baptist University B
Howard College A
Howard Payne University B, T
Huston-Tillotson College B
Jarvis Christian College B, T
Kilgore College A
Lamar University B, M
Laredo Community College A
LeTourneau University B
Lon Morris College A
Lubbock Christian University B, T
McMurry University B, T
Midland College A
Midwestern State University B, M
Navarro College A
Northeast Texas Community
    College A
Northwest Vista College A
Odessa College A
Our Lady of the Lake University of San
    Antonio B
Palo Alto College A
Paris Junior College A

Paul Quinn College *B*
Prairie View A&M University *B, M*
Rice University *B, M, D*
St. Edward's University *B*
St. Mary's University *B*
St. Philip's College *A*
Sam Houston State University *B, M*
San Jacinto College
   North *A*
Schreiner University *B*
South Plains College *A*
South Texas College *A*
Southern Methodist
   University *B, M, D*
Southwestern Adventist
   University *B, T*
Southwestern University *B, T*
Stephen F. Austin State
   University *B, M, T*
Sul Ross State University *B, M, T*
Tarleton State University *B, M*
Temple College *A*
Texarkana College *A*
Texas A&M University *B, M, D*
Texas A&M University
   Commerce *B, M*
   Galveston *B*
   Kingsville *B, M*
   Texarkana *B, T*
Texas Christian University *B, M*
Texas College *B*
Texas Lutheran University *B*
Texas Southern University *B, M*
Texas State University: San
   Marcos *B, M, T*
Texas Tech University *B, M, D*
Texas Wesleyan University *B*
Texas Woman's University *B, M*
Trinity University *B*
Trinity Valley Community College *A*
Tyler Junior College *A*
University of Dallas *B*
University of Houston *B, M, D*
University of Houston
   Clear Lake *B, M*
   Downtown *B*
   Victoria *B*
University of North Texas *B, M, D*
University of St. Thomas *B*
University of Texas
   Arlington *B, M*
   Austin *B, M, D*
   Brownsville *B, M*
   Dallas *B*
   El Paso *B, M, D*
   Pan American *B, M*
   San Antonio *B, M*
   Tyler *B, M*
   of the Permian Basin *B, M*
University of the Incarnate Word *B, M*
Wayland Baptist University *B, T*
West Texas A&M University *B, M*
Western Texas College *A*
Wharton County Junior College *A*
Wiley College *B*

Utah

Brigham Young University *B*
Dixie State College of Utah *A*
Salt Lake Community College *A*
Snow College *A*
Southern Utah University *B, T*
University of Utah *B, M, D*
Utah State University *B, M, D*
Utah Valley State College *A, B*
Westminster College *B*

Vermont

Bennington College *B*
Castleton State College *B*
Goddard College *B*
Green Mountain College *B*
Johnson State College *B*
Marlboro College *B*

Middlebury College *B*
Norwich University *B*
St. Michael's College *B*
University of Vermont *B, M, D*
Vermont Technical College *A*

Virginia

Averett University *B*
Bluefield College *B*
Bridgewater College *B*
Christopher Newport University *B*
College of William and Mary *B, M*
Eastern Mennonite University *B*
Emory & Henry College *B, T*
Ferrum College *B*
George Mason University *B, M*
Germanna Community College *A*
Hampden-Sydney College *B*
Hampton University *B, M*
Hollins University *B*
James Madison University *B, M, T*
Liberty University *B, T*
Longwood University *B, T*
Lynchburg College *B*
Mary Baldwin College *B*
Marymount University *B*
Mountain Empire Community
   College *A*
Norfolk State University *B*
Old Dominion University *B, M, T*
Radford University *B*
Randolph-Macon College *B*
Randolph-Macon Woman's College *B*
Roanoke College *B, T*
St. Paul's College *B*
Shenandoah University *B*
Sweet Briar College *B*
University of Mary Washington *B*
University of Richmond *B, M, T*
University of Virginia *B, M, D*
University of Virginia's College at
   Wise *B, T*
Virginia Commonwealth
   University *B, M*
Virginia Intermont College *B*
Virginia Military Institute *B*
Virginia Polytechnic Institute and
   State University *B, M, D*
Virginia State University *B, M*
Virginia Union University *B*
Virginia Wesleyan College *B*
Washington and Lee University *B*

Washington

Cascadia Community College *A*
Central Washington University *B, M*
Centralia College *A*
Eastern Washington University *B, M, T*
Everett Community College *A*
Evergreen State College *B*
Gonzaga University *B*
Heritage University *B*
Northwest University *T*
Pacific Lutheran University *B*
Saint Martin's University *B*
Seattle Pacific University *B*
Seattle University *B*
University of Puget Sound *B, T*
University of Washington *B*
Walla Walla College *B, M*
Washington State University *B, M*
Western Washington University *B, M*
Whitman College *B*
Whitworth College *B, T*

West Virginia

Alderson-Broaddus College *B*
Bethany College *B*
Concord University *B*
Davis and Elkins College *B*
Glenville State College *B*
Marshall University *B, M, D*
Potomac State College of West Virginia
   University *A*

Salem International University *B*
Shepherd University *B, T*
University of Charleston *B*
West Liberty State College *B*
West Virginia State University *B*
West Virginia University *B, M, D, T*
West Virginia University Institute of
   Technology *B*
West Virginia Wesleyan College *B*
Wheeling Jesuit University *B*

Wisconsin

Alverno College *B*
Beloit College *B, T*
Cardinal Stritch University *B*
Carroll College *B*
Carthage College *B, T*
Concordia University Wisconsin *B*
Edgewood College *B*
Lakeland College *B*
Lawrence University *B, T*
Maranatha Baptist Bible College *B*
Marian College of Fond du Lac *B*
Marquette University *B, M, D*
Mount Mary College *B*
Northland College *B*
Ripon College *B*
St. Norbert College *B, T*
Silver Lake College *B, T*
University of Wisconsin
   Green Bay *B*
   La Crosse *B, T*
   Madison *B*
   Milwaukee *B, M, D*
   Oshkosh *B*
   Parkside *B*
   Platteville *B, T*
   River Falls *B*
   Stevens Point *B, M*
   Superior *B*
   Whitewater *B, T*
Viterbo University *B, T*
Wisconsin Lutheran College *B*

Wyoming

Casper College *A*
Central Wyoming College *A*
Eastern Wyoming College *A*
Laramie County Community
   College *A*
Northwest College *A*
Sheridan College *A*
University of Wyoming *B*
Western Wyoming Community
   College *A*

Biology lab technology

Alabama

Auburn University *B*

California

California Lutheran University *B*
De Anza College *C, A*
Foothill College *C, A*
MiraCosta College *C, A*
San Diego City College *A*
Santa Barbara City College *A*
Skyline College *A*
Solano Community College *C, A*

Colorado

Community College of Aurora *C*

Connecticut

Quinnipiac University *B*
University of New Haven *B*

Delaware

Delaware Technical and Community
   College
   Stanton/Wilmington Campus *A*

Georgia

Athens Technical College *A*

Hawaii

Brigham Young University-Hawaii *B*

Indiana

Ball State University *D*

Iowa

Ellsworth Community College *A*
Indian Hills Community College *A*

Maryland

Frederick Community College *A*
Villa Julie College *C, B*

Massachusetts

Massachusetts Bay Community
   College *A*
Middlesex Community College *C, A*
North Shore Community College *A*

Michigan

Delta College *A*

Minnesota

St. Cloud State University *B*

Missouri

Jefferson College *C, A*

Montana

Montana State University
   College of Technology-Great Falls *A*

New Jersey

County College of Morris *A*
Mercer County Community College *A*
Middlesex County College *A*
Ocean County College *A*
Rutgers, The State University of New
   Jersey
   New Brunswick/Piscataway
     Campus *B*
University of Medicine and Dentistry
   of New Jersey
   School of Health Related
     Professions *C, D, T*

New York

Finger Lakes Community College *A*
Manhattan College *M*
Maria College *A*
Monroe Community College *A*
Niagara University *B*
State University of New York
   College at Brockport *B*
   College of Agriculture and
     Technology at Cobleskill *A*
   College of Technology at Alfred *A*

North Carolina

Beaufort County Community
   College *A*
Central Carolina Community
   College *A*
Fayetteville Technical Community
   College *A*
Pitt Community College *A*

Ohio

Lakeland Community College *A*
University of Cincinnati
   Raymond Walters College *A*
Washington State Community
   College *A*

Pennsylvania

Gannon University *B*
Marywood University *B*

Penn State
    Abington *B*
    Altoona *B*
    Beaver *B*
    Berks *B*
    Delaware County *B*
    Dubois *B*
    Fayette *B*
    Hazleton *B*
    Lehigh Valley *B*
    McKeesport *B*
    Mont Alto *B*
    New Kensington *B*
    Schuylkill - Capital College *B*
    Shenango *B*
    University Park *B*
    Wilkes-Barre *B*
    Worthington Scranton *B*
    York *B*
Thomas Jefferson University: College
    of Health Professions *B*

Texas

Austin Community College *C, A*
Collin County Community College
    District *C, A*
El Centro College *C, A*
Houston Community College
    System *C, A*
Mountain View College *C, A*
North Harris Montgomery
    Community College District *A*
Northwest Vista College *A*
Texas State Technical College
    West Texas *A*

Utah

Salt Lake Community College *A*
Weber State University *C, A*

Vermont

Vermont Technical College *A*

Virginia

Piedmont Virginia Community
    College *A*

Washington

Shoreline Community College *C, A*

Wisconsin

Madison Area Technical College *A*

Biology teacher education

Alabama

Athens State University *B*
Birmingham-Southern College *T*
Faulkner University *B*
Oakwood College *B*
Samford University *B*
Talladega College *B*
Tuskegee University *B*
University of Mobile *B, T*

Arizona

Arizona State University *B, T*
Grand Canyon University *B*
Northern Arizona University *B, M, T*
Prescott College *B, M, T*
University of Arizona *B, M*

Arkansas

Arkansas State University *B, M, T*
Arkansas Tech University *B*
Harding University *B, M, T*
Henderson State University *B, M, T*
John Brown University *B, T*
Ouachita Baptist University *B, T*
Philander Smith College *B*
Southern Arkansas University *B, T*

University of Arkansas
    Fort Smith *B*
University of Central Arkansas *T*
University of the Ozarks *B, T*

California

California State University
    Chico *B, T*
    Long Beach *T*
    San Bernardino *T*
Fresno Pacific University *B*
Humboldt State University *T*
Loyola Marymount University *M*
Master's College *T*
Pacific Union College *T*
San Diego State University *B, T*
San Francisco State University *B, T*
Stanford University *M, T*
University of the Pacific *T*
Vanguard University of Southern
    California *T*

Colorado

Adams State College *B, T*
Colorado State University *T*
Colorado State University
    Pueblo *T*
Fort Lewis College *B*
Regis University *B, T*

Connecticut

Albertus Magnus College *B, T*
Fairfield University *T*
Quinnipiac University *B, M*
Sacred Heart University *T*
St. Joseph College *T*
Southern Connecticut State
    University *B, M, T*
University of New Haven *T*

Delaware

Delaware State University *B, M*
University of Delaware *B, T*

District of Columbia

Catholic University of America *B*

Florida

Barry University *T*
Bethune-Cookman College *B, T*
Clearwater Christian College *B*
Florida Agricultural and Mechanical
    University *T*
Florida Institute of Technology *B*
Gulf Coast Community College *A*
Manatee Community College *A*
Palm Beach Atlantic University *B, T*
St. Petersburg College *B*
Southeastern College of the
    Assemblies of God *B, T*
Stetson University *B*
University of Tampa *T*

Georgia

Agnes Scott College *T*
Armstrong Atlantic State University *T*
Brewton-Parker College *B*
Covenant College *B*
Georgia College and State
    University *M, T*
Georgia Southern University *B*
Kennesaw State University *B*
Paine College *B*
Reinhardt College *B*
University of West Georgia *B, M*

Hawaii

Brigham Young University-Hawaii *B, T*

Idaho

Boise State University *T*
Brigham Young University-Idaho *T*

Northwest Nazarene University *B*
University of Idaho *T*

Illinois

Augustana College *B, T*
Benedictine University *T*
Blackburn College *B, T*
Bradley University *B*
Chicago State University *B, T*
Concordia University *B, T*
Dominican University *T*
Eastern Illinois University *B, M, T*
Elmhurst College *B*
Eureka College *T*
Governors State University *B, T*
Greenville College *B, T*
Illinois College *T*
Illinois Wesleyan University *B*
Knox College *T*
Lake Land College *A*
Lewis University *T*
MacMurray College *B, T*
North Park University *T*
Olivet Nazarene University *B, T*
Quincy University *T*
Rockford College *T*
Roosevelt University *B*
St. Xavier University *B*
Sauk Valley Community College *A*
Trinity Christian College *B, T*
Trinity International University *B, T*
University of Illinois
    Urbana-Champaign *B, M, T*
Wheaton College *T*

Indiana

Butler University *T*
Franklin College *B, T*
Goshen College *B*
Huntington University *B, M*
Indiana University
    Bloomington *B, T*
    South Bend *B, T*
    Southeast *B*
Indiana University-Purdue University
    Fort Wayne *B, T*
Indiana University-Purdue University
    Indianapolis *B*
Indiana Wesleyan University *T*
Manchester College *B, T*
Oakland City University *B*
Purdue University
    Calumet *B*
Saint Mary's College *T*
St. Mary-of-the-Woods College *B, T*
Taylor University *B, T*
University of Evansville *B, T*
University of Indianapolis *B, T*
Valparaiso University *T*
Vincennes University *A*

Iowa

Ashford University *B, D*
Briar Cliff University *B*
Buena Vista University *B, T*
Central College *T*
Clarke College *B, T*
Cornell College *B, T*
Dordt College *B*
Drake University *M*
Ellsworth Community College *A*
Graceland University *T*
Iowa State University *T*
Iowa Wesleyan College *B*
Loras College *T*
Maharishi University of
    Management *T*
Morningside College *B*
Mount Mercy College *T*
Northwestern College *T*
St. Ambrose University *B, T*
Simpson College *T*
University of Iowa *T*
Upper Iowa University *B, T*

Wartburg College *T*
William Penn University *B*

Kansas

Baker University *T*
Bethany College *B*
Bethel College *T*
Central Christian College of Kansas *A*
Colby Community College *A*
Emporia State University *T*
McPherson College *B, T*
MidAmerica Nazarene University *B, T*
Newman University *T*
Ottawa University *T*
Pittsburg State University *B, T*
Sterling College *T*
Tabor College *B, T*
University of Kansas *B, T*
University of St. Mary *T*

Kentucky

Alice Lloyd College *B*
Bellarmine University *B, M, T*
Campbellsville University *B*
Eastern Kentucky University *B*
Kentucky State University *B*
Kentucky Wesleyan College *B, T*
Lindsey Wilson College *B, T*
Thomas More College *B*
University of the Cumberlands *T*

Louisiana

Centenary College of Louisiana *B, T*
Louisiana State University
    Shreveport *B*
Northwestern State University *B*
Southern University
    New Orleans *B*
Southern University and Agricultural
    and Mechanical College *B*
University of Louisiana at Lafayette *B*
University of Louisiana at Monroe *B*
Xavier University of Louisiana *B*

Maine

College of the Atlantic *B, T*
Husson College *B, T*
St. Joseph's College *B*
University of Maine *B*
University of Maine
    Farmington *B, T*
    Machias *T*
University of Southern Maine *T*

Maryland

College of Notre Dame of Maryland *T*
Coppin State University *B, T*
Mount St. Mary's University *T*
St. Mary's College of Maryland *T*
Salisbury University *T*
Washington College *T*

Massachusetts

Assumption College *T*
Bridgewater State College *B, M, T*
Eastern Nazarene College *B*
Elms College *T*
Fitchburg State College *B, M, T*
Framingham State College *B, M*
Merrimack College *T*
Northeastern University *M*
Salem State College *M*
Tufts University *T*
University of Massachusetts
    Dartmouth *T*
Western New England College *T*
Westfield State College *B, M, T*
Worcester State College *T*

Michigan

Albion College *B, T*
Alma College *T*
Andrews University *M*

Calvin College *B*
Concordia University *B, T*
Cornerstone University *B, T*
Eastern Michigan University *B, M, T*
Ferris State University *B*
Grand Valley State University *M, T*
Hope College *B*
Michigan Technological University *T*
Northern Michigan University *B, T*
Olivet College *B, T*
University of Detroit Mercy *B, M, T*
University of Michigan
 Flint *T*
Western Michigan University *B, T*

Minnesota

Augsburg College *B, T*
Bemidji State University *T*
Bethel University *B*
College of St. Catherine *T*
College of St. Scholastica *T*
Concordia College: Moorhead *B, T*
Concordia University: St. Paul *B, T*
Gustavus Adolphus College *T*
Minnesota State University
 Mankato *B, M, T*
 Moorhead *B*
Northland Community & Technical
 College *A*
St. Cloud State University *B, T*
St. Mary's University of Minnesota *B*
Southwest Minnesota State
 University *B, T*
University of Minnesota
 Morris *B*
University of St. Thomas *B, T*
Vermilion Community College *A*
Winona State University *B, T*

Mississippi

Blue Mountain College *B*
Itawamba Community College *A*
Mississippi College *B, M*
Mississippi State University *T*
Mississippi Valley State University *B, T*
Rust College *B*
University of Mississippi *B, T*
William Carey College *B*

Missouri

Central Methodist University *B*
Central Missouri State University *B, T*
College of the Ozarks *B, T*
Harris-Stowe State University *T*
Lincoln University *B, T*
Lindenwood University *B*
Maryville University of Saint
 Louis *B, M, T*
Missouri Baptist University *T*
Missouri Southern State
 University *B, T*
Missouri State University *B*
Missouri Valley College *T*
Northwest Missouri State
 University *B, T*
Southwest Baptist University *B, T*
Truman State University *M, T*
University of Missouri
 Columbia *B*
 St. Louis *T*
Washington University in St.
 Louis *B, M, T*
William Woods University *T*

Montana

Montana State University
 Billings *B, T*
Rocky Mountain College *B, T*
University of Great Falls *B*
University of Montana:
 Missoula *B, M, T*
University of Montana: Western *B, T*

Nebraska

Bellevue University *B*
Chadron State College *B*
College of Saint Mary *B, T*
Concordia University *B, T*
Creighton University *T*
Dana College *B*
Hastings College *B, M, T*
Midland Lutheran College *B, T*
Nebraska Wesleyan University *T*
Peru State College *B, T*
Union College *T*
University of Nebraska
 Kearney *B*
 Lincoln *B*
Wayne State College *B, T*
York College *B, T*

Nevada

Great Basin College *B*
University of Nevada
 Reno *B*

New Hampshire

Franklin Pierce College *T*
New England College *B, T*
Rivier College *B, T*
St. Anselm College *T*
University of New Hampshire *T*

New Jersey

Caldwell College *T*
The College of New Jersey *B, T*
Georgian Court University *T*
Rowan University *T*
St. Peter's College *T*
William Paterson University of New
 Jersey *T*

New Mexico

New Mexico Institute of Mining and
 Technology *M*
Western New Mexico University *B*

New York

Adelphi University *M, T*
Alfred University *M, T*
City University of New York
 Brooklyn College *B, M*
 City College *B*
 College of Staten Island *B, M*
 Hunter College *B, M, T*
 Lehman College *M*
 Queens College *M, T*
Colgate University *M*
College of Mount St. Vincent *T*
College of Saint Rose *B, T*
D'Youville College *B, M, T*
Daemen College *B, M, T*
Dominican College of Blauvelt *B, T*
Dowling College *B*
Dutchess Community College *A*
Elmira College *B, T*
Fordham University *M, T*
Hobart and William Smith Colleges *T*
Hofstra University *B, M*
Houghton College *B, T*
Iona College *B, M, T*
Ithaca College *B, T*
Keuka College *B, T*
Le Moyne College *T*
Long Island University
 Brooklyn Campus *B, M, T*
 C. W. Post Campus *B, M, T*
Manhattan College *B, T*
Marist College *B*
Marymount Manhattan College *T*
Molloy College *B*
Nazareth College of Rochester *T*
New York Institute of Technology *B, T*
New York University *B, M, T*
Niagara University *B, M, T*
Pace University *B, M, T*

Roberts Wesleyan College *B, M*
St. Francis College *B*
St. John Fisher College *B, T*
St. John's University *M*
St. Joseph's College: Suffolk
 Campus *B, T*
St. Lawrence University *T*
St. Thomas Aquinas College *B, M, T*
State University of New York
 Albany *B, T*
 Binghamton *M*
 Buffalo *M, T*
 College at Brockport *M, T*
 College at Buffalo *B, M*
 College at Cortland *B, M*
 College at Fredonia *B, M, T*
 College at Geneseo *B, M, T*
 College at Old Westbury *B, T*
 College at Oneonta *B, T*
 College at Plattsburgh *B, M*
 College at Potsdam *B, M*
 College of Environmental Science
 and Forestry *B, T*
 New Paltz *B, M, T*
 Oswego *B, M*
 Stony Brook *T*
Syracuse University *B, M, T*
Utica College *B*
Vassar College *T*
Wagner College *T*
Wells College *T*

North Carolina

Appalachian State University *B*
Campbell University *B, T*
Elizabeth City State University *T*
Gardner-Webb University *B*
Greensboro College *B, T*
Lenoir Community College *A*
Louisburg College *A*
Mars Hill College *T*
Meredith College *T*
Methodist College *A, B, T*
North Carolina Agricultural and
 Technical State University *B, T*
North Carolina Central
 University *B, M, T*
Queens University of Charlotte *T*
St. Augustine's College *B*
Sandhills Community College *A*
University of North Carolina
 Greensboro *B*
 Pembroke *B*
 Wilmington *B*
Wake Forest University *T*
Western Carolina University *M, T*
Wingate University *B, T*

North Dakota

Dickinson State University *B, T*
Jamestown College *B*
Mayville State University *B, T*
Minot State University *B*
North Dakota State University *B, T*
University of Mary *B, T*
Valley City State University *B, T*

Ohio

Ashland University *B*
Baldwin-Wallace College *T*
Bluffton University *T*
Bowling Green State
 University *B, M, T*
Case Western Reserve University *T*
Cedarville University *B, T*
Defiance College *B, T*
Hiram College *T*
John Carroll University *T*
Miami University
 Oxford Campus *B, M, T*
Mount Union College *T*
Mount Vernon Nazarene
 University *B, M, T*
Ohio Dominican University *B, T*

Ohio Northern University *B*
Ohio Wesleyan University *B*
Otterbein College *B*
Shawnee State University *B*
University of Findlay *B, M, T*
University of Rio Grande *B, T*
University of Toledo *M, T*
Urbana University *B*
Wilmington College *B*
Xavier University *B, M*
Youngstown State University *B, M*

Oklahoma

Cameron University *B*
East Central University *T*
Eastern Oklahoma State College *A*
Northeastern State University *B*
Oklahoma Baptist University *B, T*
Southern Nazarene University *B*
University of Central Oklahoma *B*
University of Tulsa *T*

Oregon

Concordia University *B, M, T*
Corban College *B*
George Fox University *T*
Linfield College *T*
Oregon State University *M*
Portland State University *T*
Southern Oregon University *T*
Western Oregon University *T*

Pennsylvania

Albright College *T*
Alvernia College *B*
Arcadia University *B, M, T*
Bryn Athyn College of the New
 Church *T*
Cabrini College *T*
Carlow University *T*
Chatham College *T*
College Misericordia *T*
DeSales University *T*
Dickinson College *T*
Duquesne University *M, T*
Elizabethtown College *B*
Gannon University *T*
Geneva College *B, T*
Gettysburg College *T*
Grove City College *B, T*
Gwynedd-Mercy College *T*
Holy Family University *B, M, T*
Juniata College *B, T*
King's College *T*
La Roche College *B*
La Salle University *B, T*
Lebanon Valley College *T*
Lycoming College *T*
Mansfield University of
 Pennsylvania *B, T*
Marywood University *B*
Mercyhurst College *B, T*
Messiah College *B, T*
Moravian College *T*
Point Park University *B*
St. Francis University *B, T*
St. Vincent College *T*
Seton Hill University *B, T*
Susquehanna University *T*
Thiel College *B*
University of Pittsburgh
 Johnstown *B, T*
Villanova University *T*
Washington and Jefferson College *T*
Waynesburg College *B, T*
Westminster College *T*
Widener University *T*
Wilkes University *M, T*
Wilson College *T*
York College of Pennsylvania *B, T*

Puerto Rico

Inter American University of Puerto
  Rico
  Arecibo Campus *B*
  Barranquitas Campus *B*
  Fajardo Campus *B, T*
  Ponce Campus *B, T*
  San German Campus *B*
Pontifical Catholic University of
  Puerto Rico *B, T*
Turabo University *B*
Universidad Metropolitana *B*

Rhode Island

Rhode Island College *B*
Salve Regina University *B*

South Carolina

Anderson University *B, T*
The Citadel *M*
Coker College *B, T*
Furman University *T*
Limestone College *B*
Morris College *B, T*
South Carolina State University *B, T*
Southern Wesleyan University *B, T*
Wofford College *T*

South Dakota

Augustana College *B, T*
Black Hills State University *B*
Dakota State University *B, T*
Dakota Wesleyan University *B, T*
Mount Marty College *B*
University of Sioux Falls *T*
University of South Dakota *B, M, D, T*

Tennessee

Belmont University *B, M, T*
Bryan College *T*
Christian Brothers University *B, M, T*
Crichton College *B*
Cumberland University *B, T*
Freed-Hardeman University *B, T*
King College *T*
Lambuth University *B, T*
Lincoln Memorial University *B, T*
Lipscomb University *B, T*
Maryville College *B, T*
Middle Tennessee State
  University *M, T*
Southern Adventist University *B*
Tennessee Technological University *T*
Tennessee Temple University *B*
Tennessee Wesleyan College *B, T*
Trevecca Nazarene University *B, T*
Union University *B, T*
University of Memphis *T*
University of Tennessee
  Martin *B*

Texas

Abilene Christian University *B, T*
Del Mar College *A*
East Texas Baptist University *B*
Houston Baptist University *T*
Howard Payne University *B, T*
Jarvis Christian College *B, T*
Kilgore College *A*
Lamar University *T*
Laredo Community College *A*
Lubbock Christian University *B*
McMurry University *T*
St. Edward's University *B, T*
St. Mary's University *T*
Schreiner University *B*
Tarleton State University *T*
Texas A&M University
  Commerce *B*
  Galveston *B*
  Kingsville *T*
Texas College *B, T*

Texas State University: San
  Marcos *M, T*
Texas Wesleyan University *B, T*
University of Dallas *T*
University of Houston *T*
University of Houston
  Clear Lake *T*
University of Mary Hardin-Baylor *T*
University of Texas
  San Antonio *T*
West Texas A&M University *T*

Utah

Southern Utah University *B, T*
University of Utah *B*
Utah State University *B*
Utah Valley State College *B*
Weber State University *B*

Vermont

Castleton State College *B, T*
Johnson State College *B*
St. Michael's College *T*

Virginia

Averett University *B, M, T*
Bluefield College *T*
Bridgewater College *T*
Eastern Mennonite University *T*
Hampton University *M*
Hollins University *T*
Liberty University *B, M, T*
Longwood University *B, T*
Old Dominion University *B, M, T*
Radford University *T*
St. Paul's College *T*
University of Virginia's College at
  Wise *T*
Virginia Intermont College *B, T*

Washington

Central Washington University *B, T*
Heritage University *B, M*
Northwest University *T*
Seattle Pacific University *B*
University of Washington *M, T*
Washington State University *B, M, T*
Western Washington University *B*
Whitworth College *B, T*

West Virginia

Alderson-Broaddus College *T*
Bethany College *B*
Concord University *B, M, T*
Shepherd University *T*
University of Charleston *B*
West Liberty State College *B*
West Virginia Wesleyan College *B*

Wisconsin

Carroll College *B, T*
Carthage College *T*
Concordia University Wisconsin *B*
Edgewood College *B*
Lakeland College *T*
Lawrence University *T*
Marian College of Fond du Lac *B, T*
Mount Mary College *B, T*
Northland College *T*
St. Norbert College *T*
Silver Lake College *T*
University of Wisconsin
  Green Bay *T*
  Parkside *T*
  Platteville *B*
  River Falls *T*
  Superior *B, T*
  Whitewater *B*
Viterbo University *B, T*

Biomedical engineering

Alabama

University of Alabama
  Birmingham *B, M, D*

Arizona

Arizona State University *B, M, D*
University of Arizona *M, D*

Arkansas

University of Arkansas
  for Medical Sciences *A*

California

California Lutheran University *B*
California Polytechnic State
  University: San Luis Obispo *B*
California State University
  Long Beach *B*
Stanford University *M, D*
University of California
  Berkeley *B, D*
  Davis *B, M, D*
  Irvine *B, M, D*
  Los Angeles *M*
  Riverside *B*
  San Diego *B, M, D*
University of California: Merced *B*
University of Southern
  California *B, M, D*

Colorado

University of Denver *M*

Connecticut

Trinity College *B*
University of Connecticut *B, M, D*
Yale University *B, M, D*

Delaware

University of Delaware *B, M, D*

District of Columbia

Catholic University of
  America *B, M, D*
George Washington University *B*

Florida

Florida Community College at
  Jacksonville *A*
Florida International University *B, M*
Florida State University *B, M, D*
University of Florida *B, M*
University of Miami *B, M, D*
University of South Florida *M, D*

Georgia

Emory University *D*
Georgia Institute of
  Technology *B, M, D*
Mercer University *M*

Idaho

University of Idaho *B, M, D*

Illinois

Northwestern University *B, M, D*
University of Illinois
  Chicago *B, M, D*
  Urbana-Champaign *B, M, D*

Indiana

Indiana Institute of Technology *B*
Indiana University-Purdue University
  Indianapolis *B, M, D*
Purdue University *B, M, D*
Rose-Hulman Institute of
  Technology *B, M*

Iowa

Dordt College *B*
University of Iowa *B, M, D*

Kentucky

University of Kentucky *M, D*

Louisiana

Louisiana State University and
  Agricultural and Mechanical
  College *B*
Louisiana Tech University *B, D*
Tulane University *B, M, D*

Maryland

Johns Hopkins University *B, M, D*
University of Maryland
  College Park *M, D*

Massachusetts

Boston University *B, M, D*
Massachusetts Institute of
  Technology *M, D*
Smith College *B*
Tufts University *B, M*
Western New England College *B*
Worcester Polytechnic
  Institute *B, M, D*

Michigan

Baker College
  of Flint *A*
Lawrence Technological University *B*
Michigan State University *B*
Michigan Technological
  University *B, D, T*
Schoolcraft College *A*
University of Michigan *B, M, D*
Wayne State University *M, D*

Minnesota

St. Cloud State University *B*
University of Minnesota
  Twin Cities *M, D*

Mississippi

Mississippi State University *B, M, D*

Missouri

St. Louis University *B*
University of Missouri
  Columbia *B, M, D*
Washington University in St.
  Louis *B, M, D*

Nebraska

University of Nebraska
  Lincoln *B*

Nevada

University of Nevada
  Reno *M, D*

New Hampshire

Dartmouth College *B*

New Jersey

New Jersey Institute of
  Technology *B, M, D*
Rutgers, The State University of New
  Jersey
  Camden Regional Campus *B*
  New Brunswick/Piscataway
    Campus *B, M, D*
  Newark Regional Campus *B*
Stevens Institute of Technology *B, M*

New York

City University of New York
  City College *B, M, D*

Columbia University
Fu Foundation School of
Engineering and Applied
Science *B, M, D*
Cornell University *B, M, D*
Hofstra University *B*
New York Institute of Technology *B*
Polytechnic University *M*
Rensselaer Polytechnic
Institute *B, M, D*
Rochester Institute of Technology *B*
State University of New York
Binghamton *B*
Stony Brook *B, M, D*
Syracuse University *B, M, D*
University of Rochester *B, M, D*

North Carolina
Duke University *B, M, D*
North Carolina State
University *B, M, D*
University of North Carolina
Chapel Hill *M, D*

Ohio
Case Western Reserve
University *B, M, D*
Ohio State University
Columbus Campus *M, D*
University of Akron *B, M*
University of Toledo *B, M*
Wright State University *B, M*

Oklahoma
Oral Roberts University *B*
University of Central Oklahoma *B*
University of Oklahoma *M, D*

Oregon
Oregon State University *B*

Pennsylvania
Bucknell University *B*
Carnegie Mellon University *B, M, D*
Cedar Crest College *B*
Drexel University *M, D*
Gettysburg College *B*
Lehigh University *B*
Penn State
Abington *B*
Altoona *B*
Beaver *B*
Berks *B*
Delaware County *B*
Dubois *B*
Fayette *B*
Hazleton *B*
Lehigh Valley *B*
McKeesport *B*
Mont Alto *B*
New Kensington *B*
Schuylkill - Capital College *B*
Shenango *B*
University Park *B, M, D*
Wilkes-Barre *B*
Worthington Scranton *B*
York *B*
Temple University *M*
University of Pennsylvania *B, M, D*
University of Pittsburgh *B, M, D*

Rhode Island
Brown University *B, M*
University of Rhode Island *B*

South Carolina
Clemson University *B, M, D*

Tennessee
University of Memphis *B, M, D*
Vanderbilt University *B, M, D*

Texas
Baylor University *M*
LeTourneau University *B*
Rice University *B, M, D*
Texas A&M University *B, M, D*
University of Houston *M, D*
University of Texas
Arlington *M, D*
Austin *B, M, D*
San Antonio *M, D*
Southwestern Medical Center at
Dallas *M, D*

Utah
University of Utah *B, M, D*

Vermont
University of Vermont *M*

Virginia
University of Virginia *M, D*
Virginia Commonwealth
University *B, M, D*
Virginia Polytechnic Institute and
State University *M, D*

Washington
University of Washington *B, M, D*
Walla Walla College *B*

Wisconsin
Marquette University *B, M, D*
Milwaukee School of Engineering *B*
University of Wisconsin
Madison *B, M, D*

Biomedical sciences

Alabama
University of Alabama
Birmingham *M*
University of South Alabama *B*

Arkansas
North Arkansas College *A*

California
California State University
East Bay *B*
Cerritos Community College *A*
Charles R. Drew University of
Medicine and Science *B*
College of San Mateo *A*
San Diego Miramar College *A*
San Francisco State University *M*
University of California
Riverside *M, D*
San Diego *M, D*

Colorado
Colorado State University *B*
Community College of Denver *A*
University of Colorado
Denver and Health Sciences
Center *B, M*

Connecticut
Quinnipiac University *B*
University of Connecticut *M, D*

District of Columbia
George Washington University *B*

Florida
Barry University *M*
Florida Atlantic University *M*
Florida Community College at
Jacksonville *A*
Florida Institute of Technology *B*
Florida State University *D*
Hillsborough Community College *A*

Nova Southeastern University *M, D*
University of South Florida *B*

Georgia
Columbus State University *B*
Dalton State College *A*
Emory University *D*

Hawaii
University of Hawaii
Manoa *M, D*

Idaho
University of Idaho *B*

Illinois
Chicago State University *M*
Rosalind Franklin University of
Medicine and Science *M*
South Suburban College of Cook
County *A*
University of Illinois
Urbana-Champaign *B, M, D*

Indiana
Indiana University-Purdue University
Indianapolis *M, D*

Iowa
University of Iowa *D*
University of Northern Iowa *B*

Louisiana
Our Lady of the Lake College *B*

Maine
Kennebec Valley Community
College *A*
University of Maine *B*

Maryland
Hood College *M*
Howard Community College *A*

Massachusetts
Benjamin Franklin Institute of
Technology *A*
Bridgewater State College *B*
Suffolk University *B*
University of Massachusetts
Boston *M, D*
Lowell *D, T*
Worcester Polytechnic Institute *M, D*

Michigan
University of Michigan
Flint *B*
Western Michigan University *B*

Minnesota
Bethany Lutheran College *B*
Rochester Community and Technical
College *A*

Missouri
Maryville University of Saint Louis *B*
St. Louis University *D*
Washington University in St. Louis *M*

Montana
Fort Peck Community College *A*

Nebraska
Creighton University *M, D*
University of Nebraska
Lincoln *D*

New Jersey
Rutgers, The State University of New
Jersey
Camden Regional Campus *B*
University of Medicine and Dentistry
of New Jersey
School of Health Related
Professions *M, D*

New York
Long Island University
C.W. Post Campus *B*
Marist College *B*
Rochester Institute of Technology *B*
St. Francis College *B*
State University of New York
Albany *M, D*
Buffalo *D*

North Carolina
Guilford College *B*
St. Augustine's College *B*

Ohio
Antioch College *B*
DeVry University
Columbus *B*
Hiram College *B*
Ursuline College *B*

Oklahoma
Oklahoma State University *B, M*

Pennsylvania
Delaware County Community
College *A*
Drexel University *M, D*
Keystone College *B*
University of Pennsylvania *B, M, D*

Puerto Rico
Inter American University of Puerto
Rico
Bayamon Campus *B*

South Carolina
Medical University of South
Carolina *M*
University of South Carolina *M, D*

South Dakota
Southeast Technical Institute *A*

Tennessee
East Tennessee State University *M, D*

Texas
Baylor University *M, D*
St. Philip's College *A*
Texas A&M University *B*
Texas A&M University
Baylor College of Dentistry *M, D*
Galveston *B*
University of Mary Hardin-Baylor *B, T*

Vermont
Norwich University *B*

Virginia
Jefferson College of Health
Sciences *A, B*
Old Dominion University *D*

West Virginia
Ohio Valley University *A*

Wisconsin
University of Wisconsin
Eau Claire *B, M*

Biomedical technology

Alabama
Jefferson State Community
College *C, A*
Northwest-Shoals Community
College *C*

Arkansas
North Arkansas College *A*
Phillips Community College of the
University of Arkansas *C, A*

California
DeVry University
Fremont *B*
Pomona *B*
West Hills *B*
Los Angeles City College *C, A*
Napa Valley College *C, A*
Santa Barbara City College *C, A*

Florida
Hillsborough Community College *A*
South Florida Community College *A*

Indiana
Indiana University-Purdue University
Indianapolis *A*

Iowa
Western Iowa Tech Community
College *A*

Louisiana
Delgado Community College *A*

Maryland
Howard Community College *C, A*
Montgomery College *A*

Massachusetts
Benjamin Franklin Institute of
Technology *A*
Northern Essex Community
College *C, A*
Quinsigamond Community College *C*
Suffolk University *B*

Minnesota
Anoka-Ramsey Community College *C*
Dakota County Technical College *C*
Normandale Community College *C, A*

Missouri
DeVry University
Kansas City *B*
Washington University in St. Louis *B*

New Jersey
Thomas Edison State College *A, B*

New York
Albany College of Pharmacy *B*
DeVry Institute of Technology
New York *B*
State University of New York
Farmingdale *A*

North Carolina
Gaston College *C, A*
Rowan-Cabarrus Community
College *A*
Stanly Community College *A*

Ohio
Cincinnati State Technical and
Community College *A*
DeVry University
Columbus *B*

Kettering College of Medical Arts *A*
Owens Community College
Toledo *C, A*
Wright State University *B*

Pennsylvania
Delaware County Community
College *C*
Edinboro University of
Pennsylvania *A*
Lehigh Carbon Community College *A*
Penn State
Altoona *A*
Beaver *A*
Berks *A*
Dubois *A*
Fayette *A*
Hazleton *A*
New Kensington *A*
Schuylkill - Capital College *A*
Shenango *A*
Wilkes-Barre *C*
York *A*

South Carolina
York Technical College *C*

South Dakota
Southeast Technical Institute *A*

Texas
DeVry University
Irving *B*
St. Philip's College *A*
Texas Southern University *B*
Texas State Technical College
Harlingen *A*

Virginia
ECPI College of Technology *C, A*

Washington
North Seattle Community College *A*

Wisconsin
Milwaukee Area Technical College *A*
Western Wisconsin Technical
College *A*

Biometrics

California
University of California
Santa Cruz *B*

Colorado
University of Colorado
Denver and Health Sciences
Center *M, D*

Louisiana
Louisiana State University Health
Sciences Center *M, D*

Nebraska
University of Nebraska
Lincoln *M*

New Jersey
Rutgers, The State University of New
Jersey
New Brunswick/Piscataway
Campus *B*

New York
Cornell University *B, M, D*
State University of New York
Albany *M, D*
College of Environmental Science
and Forestry *M, D*

North Carolina
Duke University *M*
East Carolina University *D*
North Carolina State University *M, D*

Pennsylvania
Temple University *M, D*

South Carolina
Medical University of South
Carolina *M, D*

Texas
University of Texas
Arlington *D*
Health Science Center at
Houston *M, D*

Wisconsin
University of Wisconsin
Madison *M*

Biophysics

California
California Institute of Technology *D*
La Sierra University *B*
Pacific Union College *B*
Pitzer College *B*
Stanford University *M, D*
University of California
Berkeley *D*
Davis *D*
Los Angeles *B, M, D*
San Diego *B, M, D*
University of Southern California *B*

Colorado
University of Colorado
Denver and Health Sciences
Center *M, D*

Connecticut
University of Connecticut *B, M, D*

District of Columbia
George Washington University *B*

Florida
Florida State University *B*
University of Miami *B*

Illinois
Illinois Institute of
Technology *B, M, D*
Rosalind Franklin University of
Medicine and Science *M, D*
University of Illinois
Chicago *M, D*
Urbana-Champaign *B, M, D*

Indiana
Indiana University-Purdue University
Indianapolis *M, D*
University of Notre Dame *M*
University of Southern Indiana *B, T*

Iowa
Iowa State University *B, M, D*

Louisiana
Centenary College of Louisiana *B*

Maryland
Johns Hopkins University *B, M, D*
University of Maryland
Baltimore *M, D*

Massachusetts
Boston University *M, D*

Brandeis University *M, D*
Harvard College *M, D*
Suffolk University *B*
Tufts University *D*

Michigan
Andrews University *B*
Oakland University *B, D*
University of Michigan *B, M, D*

Minnesota
Minnesota State University
Mankato *M*
St. Mary's University of Minnesota *B*
University of Minnesota
Twin Cities *M, D*

Missouri
University of Missouri
Rolla *B*
Washington University in St.
Louis *B, D*

Nevada
Western Nevada Community
College *A*

New York
Barnard College *B*
Columbia University
Columbia College *B*
Rensselaer Polytechnic
Institute *B, M, D*
St. Lawrence University *B*
State University of New York
Albany *D*
Buffalo *B, M, D*
College at Geneseo *B*
Syracuse University *D*
University of Rochester *M, D*
Yeshiva University *M, D*

North Carolina
East Carolina University *D*

Ohio
Case Western Reserve University *D*
Ohio State University
Columbus Campus *M, D*

Oklahoma
Oklahoma City University *B*
Southeastern Oklahoma State
University *B*
Southwestern Oklahoma State
University *B*

Oregon
Oregon State University *B, M, D*

Pennsylvania
Carnegie Mellon University *B*
Temple University *B*
University of Pennsylvania *B, D*
University of Scranton *B*
Westminster College *B*

Rhode Island
Brown University *B, M, D*

Tennessee
King College *B*
Southern Adventist University *B*
Vanderbilt University *D*

Texas
St. Mary's University *B*
Texas A&M University *M*
University of Houston *B*

University of Texas
Health Science Center at
Houston *M, D*
Southwestern Medical Center at
Dallas *M, D*

Utah

Brigham Young University *B*

Virginia

Hampden-Sydney College *B*
University of Virginia *D*

Washington

University of Washington *M, D*
Walla Walla College *B*

Wisconsin

University of Wisconsin
Madison *D*

Biopsychology

California

Chapman University *B*
Holy Names University *B*
St. Mary's College of California *B*
University of California
Santa Barbara *B*
Santa Cruz *B*
University of Southern California *B*

Connecticut

Quinnipiac University *B*
University of Connecticut *M, D*

Illinois

Monmouth College *B*
University of Chicago *D*

Indiana

Earlham College *B*

Iowa

Morningside College *B*

Maine

University of New England *B*

Maryland

College of Notre Dame of Maryland *B*

Massachusetts

Hampshire College *B*
Simmons College *B*

Michigan

Grand Valley State University *B*
University of Michigan *B*

Missouri

Northwest Missouri State
University *B*
Washington University in St. Louis *B*

Nebraska

Hastings College *B*
Nebraska Wesleyan University *B*

New Jersey

Rider University *B*

New York

Barnard College *B*
Hamilton College *B*
Medaille College *B*
Rochester Institute of Technology *B*
Russell Sage College *B*
State University of New York
Albany *D*

New Paltz *B*

Ohio

Wittenberg University *B*

Pennsylvania

Bucknell University *B, M*
Carnegie Mellon University *B*
Franklin & Marshall College *B*
Immaculata University *B*
Lehigh University *B, D*
Messiah College *B*
Philadelphia University *B*
Westminster College *B*
Wilson College *B*

Texas

University of North Texas *M*

Virginia

College of William and Mary *B*
Northern Virginia Community
College *A*

Wisconsin

Ripon College *B*

Biostatistics

Alabama

University of Alabama
Birmingham *M, D*

California

Loma Linda University *M*
University of California
Berkeley *M, D*
Davis *M, D*
Los Angeles *M, D*
University of Southern
California *M, D*

Connecticut

Yale University *M*

District of Columbia

George Washington University *D*
Georgetown University *M*

Florida

Florida State University *M*

Georgia

Emory University *D*

Iowa

University of Iowa *M, D*

Kentucky

University of Louisville *M, D*

Louisiana

Tulane University *M, D*

Massachusetts

Boston University *M, D*
Emmanuel College *B*
Harvard College *M, D*

Michigan

University of Michigan *M, D*

Minnesota

University of Minnesota
Twin Cities *B, M, D*

New York

State University of New York
Albany *M, D*
Buffalo *B, M, D*

College of Environmental Science
and Forestry *M, D*

North Carolina

University of North Carolina
Chapel Hill *B, M, D*

Ohio

Case Western Reserve University *M, D*
Ohio State University
Columbus Campus *D*

Oklahoma

University of Oklahoma *M, D*

Pennsylvania

University of Pennsylvania *M, D*
University of Pittsburgh *M, D*

South Carolina

Medical University of South
Carolina *M, D*
University of South Carolina *M, D*

Texas

Southwestern Adventist University *B*
University of Texas
Southwestern Medical Center at
Dallas *M*

Utah

Brigham Young University *B*
University of Utah *M*

Vermont

University of Vermont *M*

Virginia

Virginia Commonwealth
University *M, D*

Washington

University of Washington *M, D*

Biotechnology

Alabama

University of Alabama
Huntsville *D*

Arizona

University of Arizona *M*

Arkansas

Southeast Arkansas College *A*

California

California State Polytechnic
University: Pomona *B*
Foothill College *A*
San Francisco State University *B*
Southwestern College *A*
University of California
Davis *B*
Irvine *M, D*
Los Angeles *B*
San Diego *B*
Vista Community College *A*

Colorado

Red Rocks Community College *A*

Connecticut

Quinnipiac University *B*
University of Connecticut *M*

Delaware

Delaware State University *B*
University of Delaware *B*

Florida

Florida Gulf Coast University *B*
Florida Institute of Technology *B*

Georgia

Gwinnett Technical College *A*
Kennesaw State University *B*
University of Georgia *B*

Illinois

Northwestern University *M*
University of Illinois
Urbana-Champaign *B, M, D*

Indiana

Ivy Tech State College
Ivy Tech Community College:
Bloomington *B*
Ivy Tech Community College:
Central Indiana *A*
Ivy Tech Community College:
Lafayette *A*
Ivy Tech Community College: North
Central *B*
Ivy Tech Community College:
Southwest *A*
Ivy Tech Community College:
Wabash Valley *A*

Iowa

Des Moines Area Community
College *A*
Ellsworth Community College *A*
Kirkwood Community College *A*
University of Northern Iowa *B*

Maine

University of Southern Maine *B*

Maryland

Baltimore City Community College *A*
University of Maryland
University College *M*

Massachusetts

Bay Path College *B*
Middlesex Community College *A*
Springfield Technical Community
College *A*
Worcester Polytechnic
Institute *B, M, D*
Worcester State College *B, M*

Michigan

Calvin College *B*
Delta College *A*
Ferris State University *B*
Michigan State University *D*
Mid Michigan Community College *A*

Minnesota

Minnesota State University
Mankato *B*
St. Cloud State University *B*

Mississippi

Alcorn State University *M*
Mississippi Gulf Coast Community
College
Jefferson Davis Campus *A*

Missouri

Fontbonne University *B*
Missouri Southern State University *B*
Washington University in St. Louis *M*

Montana

Montana State University
Bozeman *B*
College of Technology-Great Falls *A*

Nebraska

University of Nebraska
  Omaha *B*

Nevada

University of Nevada
  Reno *B, M*

New Hampshire

New Hampshire Community
  Technical College
  Stratham *A*
Plymouth State University *B*

New Jersey

Burlington County College *A*
Kean University *M*
Union County College *A*
William Paterson University of New
  Jersey *B, M*

New Mexico

Albuquerque Technical-Vocational
  Institute *A*

New York

City University of New York
  York College *B*
Finger Lakes Community College *A*
Manhattan College *M*
Rochester Institute of Technology *B*
State University of New York
  Buffalo *B, M*
  College at Brockport *B*
  College at Fredonia *B*
  College at Plattsburgh *B*
  College of Environmental Science
    and Forestry *B, M, D*
Suffolk County Community College *A*
Tompkins-Cortland Community
  College *A*

North Carolina

Alamance Community College *A*
Bladen Community College *A*
North Carolina State University *M*
University of North Carolina
  Pembroke *M*
Winston-Salem State University *B*

North Dakota

North Dakota State University *B*

Ohio

Kent State University *B*
Lakeland Community College *A*
Owens Community College
  Toledo *A*
Sinclair Community College *A*
Ursuline College *B*

Oklahoma

Oklahoma City Community College *A*
Southeastern Oklahoma State
  University *B*

Oregon

Oregon State University *B*

Pennsylvania

Cabrini College *B*
East Stroudsburg University of
  Pennsylvania *B*
Elizabethtown College *B*
Lackawanna College *A*
Lehigh Carbon Community College *A*
Marywood University *B*
Montgomery County Community
  College *A*
Northampton County Area
  Community College *A*

Penn State

University Park *M*
Point Park University *B*
Thomas Jefferson University: College
  of Health Professions *B*
University of Pennsylvania *M*

Puerto Rico

Inter American University of Puerto
  Rico
  Bayamon Campus *B*
University of Puerto Rico
  Mayaguez *B*

South Carolina

Claflin University *B, M*

Texas

North Harris Montgomery
  Community College District *A*
Stephen F. Austin State University *M*
Texas Tech University *M*
Texas Tech University Health Sciences
  Center *M*
University of Texas
  Dallas *M*
  San Antonio *D*
West Texas A&M University *B*

Utah

Brigham Young University *B, M*

Virginia

James Madison University *B*
Piedmont Virginia Community
  College *A*

Washington

Seattle Central Community College *A*
Shoreline Community College *A*
Washington State University *B, M*

West Virginia

West Liberty State College *B*
West Virginia State University *M*

Wisconsin

University of Wisconsin
  Madison *M*
  River Falls *B*

Boilermaking

Indiana

Ivy Tech State College
  Ivy Tech Community College:
    Southwest *C, A*

Botany

Alabama

Auburn University *B, M, D*

Alaska

University of Alaska
  Fairbanks *M*

Arizona

Arizona State University *B, M, D*
Northern Arizona University *B*

Arkansas

Arkansas State University
  Beebe *A*

California

California State Polytechnic
  University: Pomona *B*

California State University
  Chico *M*
  Long Beach *B*
Cerritos Community College *A*
Citrus College *A*
El Camino College *A*
Humboldt State University *B*
San Francisco State University *B*
San Joaquin Delta College *A*
Santa Ana College *A*
University of California
  Berkeley *B, D*
  Davis *B, M, D*
  Irvine *B*
  Los Angeles *B*
  Riverside *B, M, D*
Ventura College *A*

Colorado

Adams State College *B*
Colorado State University *B, M, D*
Northeastern Junior College *A*

Connecticut

Connecticut College *B, M*
Southern Connecticut State
  University *B*
University of Connecticut *M, D*

District of Columbia

George Washington University *M, D*

Florida

Pensacola Junior College *A*
Santa Fe Community College *A*
University of Florida *A, B, M*

Georgia

University of Georgia *B, M, D*

Hawaii

University of Hawaii
  Manoa *B, M, D*

Idaho

College of Southern Idaho *A*
Idaho State University *B*
North Idaho College *A*
University of Idaho *B, M, D*

Illinois

St. Xavier University *B*
Southern Illinois University
  Carbondale *B, M, D*
University of Illinois
  Urbana-Champaign *B, M, D*

Indiana

Indiana University
  Bloomington *M, D*
Purdue University *B, M, D*
Vincennes University *A*

Iowa

Iowa State University *M, D*
Marshalltown Community College *A*

Kansas

Central Christian College of Kansas *A*
Pratt Community College *A*
University of Kansas *M, D*

Maine

College of the Atlantic *B*
University of Maine *B, M, D*

Massachusetts

Simon's Rock College of Bard *B*
University of Massachusetts
  Amherst *M, D*

Michigan

Andrews University *B*
Michigan State University *B, M, D*
Northern Michigan University *B*
University of Michigan *B, M, D*

Minnesota

Minnesota State University
  Mankato *B*
St. Cloud State University *B*

Missouri

Northwest Missouri State
  University *B*
Washington University in St. Louis *D*

Montana

University of Great Falls *B*
University of Montana: Missoula *B*

New Hampshire

University of New Hampshire *M, D*

New Jersey

Rowan University *B*
Rutgers, The State University of New
  Jersey
  Newark Regional Campus *B*

New Mexico

Western New Mexico University *B*

New York

Cornell University *B, M, D*
State University of New York
  College of Environmental Science
    and Forestry *B, M, D*

North Carolina

Duke University *M, D*
Mars Hill College *B*
North Carolina State
  University *B, M, D*

North Dakota

North Dakota State University *B, M, D*

Ohio

Kent State University *B, M, D*
Miami University
  Oxford Campus *B, M, D*
Ohio State University
  Columbus Campus *B, M, D*
Ohio University *B, M, D*
Ohio Wesleyan University *B*
University of Akron *B*

Oklahoma

Oklahoma State University *B, M, D*
University of Oklahoma *B, M, D*

Oregon

Oregon State University *B*

Pennsylvania

Juniata College *B*

South Carolina

Clemson University *M*

Tennessee

University of Tennessee
  Knoxville *B, M, D*

Texas

Hill College *A*
Laredo Community College *A*
Texas A&M University *B, M, D*
Texas A&M University
  Galveston *B*

Texas State University: San Marcos *B*
University of North Texas *M*
University of Texas
  Austin *B, M, D*

Utah

Brigham Young University *B*
Snow College *A*
Southern Utah University *B*
Utah State University *B, M*
Weber State University *B*

Vermont

Bennington College *B*
Marlboro College *B*
University of Vermont *B, M, D*

Washington

Centralia College *A*
Eastern Washington University *B*
University of Washington *B, M, D*
Washington State University *M, D*
Western Washington University *B*

Wisconsin

Lawrence University *B*
University of Wisconsin
  Madison *B, M, D*
  Superior *B*

Wyoming

University of Wyoming *B, M, D*

Broadcast journalism

Arizona

Arizona Western College *A*
Grand Canyon University *B*
Northern Arizona University *B*
University of Arizona *B, M*

Arkansas

Harding University *B*
John Brown University *A, B*
University of Arkansas
  Little Rock *B*

California

Azusa Pacific University *B*
Bakersfield College *A*
Biola University *B*
Butte College *C, A*
California Lutheran University *B*
California State University
  East Bay *A*
  Long Beach *B*
  Northridge *B, M*
Chabot College *A*
Chaffey College *C, A*
Chapman University *B*
City College of San Francisco *C, A*
College of Marin: Kentfield *A*
College of San Mateo *A*
College of the Canyons *C, A*
Columbia College: Hollywood *A, B*
Cosumnes River College *A*
Cuesta College *C, A*
Foothill College *C, A*
Fullerton College *A*
Glendale Community College *A*
Golden West College *C, A*
Grossmont Community College *C, A*
Laney College *C, A*
Long Beach City College *C, A*
Los Angeles City College *C, A*
Los Angeles Valley College *C, A*
Modesto Junior College *C, A*
Moorpark College *C, A*
Mount San Antonio College *C, A*
Ohlone College *C, A*
Orange Coast College *C, A*
Pasadena City College *C, A*

Pepperdine University *B*
Point Loma Nazarene University *B*
Saddleback College *C, A*
San Diego City College *A*
San Diego State University *B, M*
San Francisco State University *B, M*
San Joaquin Delta College *A*
Santa Ana College *C, A*
Santa Rosa Junior College *C*
Southwestern College *C, A*
University of Southern
  California *B, M*
Vanguard University of Southern
  California *B*
Westmont College *B*

Colorado

Metropolitan State College of
  Denver *B*
Northeastern Junior College *A*
Pueblo Community College *C, A*

Connecticut

Briarwood College *A*
Middlesex Community College *C, A*
Quinnipiac University *B*

Delaware

Delaware State University *B*

District of Columbia

Gallaudet University *B*
Howard University *B*

Florida

Brevard Community College *A*
Broward Community College *A*
City College *A*
Florida Agricultural and Mechanical
  University *B*
Gulf Coast Community College *A*
Hillsborough Community College *A*
Lynn University *B*
Manatee Community College *A*
Miami Dade College *A*
Palm Beach Atlantic University *B*
Palm Beach Community College *A*
University of Miami *B*

Georgia

Clark Atlanta University *B*
Paine College *B*
University of Georgia *B*

Hawaii

Chaminade University of Honolulu *B*
University of Hawaii
  Leeward Community College *C, A*

Idaho

Brigham Young University-Idaho *B*

Illinois

Chicago State University *B*
City Colleges of Chicago
  Kennedy-King College *C, A*
Columbia College Chicago *B, M*
Governors State University *B, M*
Illinois Central College *A*
Illinois Eastern Community Colleges
  Wabash Valley College *A*
Lake Land College *A*
Lewis University *B*
Northwestern University *B, M*
Olivet Nazarene University *B*
Quincy University *B*
University of Illinois
  Urbana-Champaign *B*
University of St. Francis *B*

Indiana

Huntington University *B*

Manchester College *A, B*
Purdue University
  Calumet *B*
Taylor University *B*
Vincennes University *A*

Iowa

Dordt College *B*
Drake University *B*
Grand View College *B*
Iowa Central Community College *A*
Iowa Lakes Community College *C, A*
Iowa Wesleyan College *B*
Morningside College *B*
St. Ambrose University *B*
Waldorf College *B*
Wartburg College *B*

Kansas

Central Christian College of
  Kansas *A, B*
Coffeyville Community College *A*
Colby Community College *A*
Dodge City Community College *C, A*

Kentucky

Campbellsville University *B*
Eastern Kentucky University *B*

Maine

New England School of
  Communications *C, A, B*
University of Southern Maine *B*

Maryland

Columbia Union College *B*
Frederick Community College *C*
Montgomery College *A*
Morgan State University *B*

Massachusetts

American International College *B*
Boston University *B, M*
Emerson College *B*
Massachusetts College of Liberal
  Arts *B*
New England Institute of Art *A*
Newbury College *A*
Northeastern University *B*
Suffolk University *B*
Westfield State College *B*

Michigan

Bay de Noc Community College *C*
Cornerstone University *A*
Grand Valley State University *B*
Henry Ford Community College *A*
Lansing Community College *A*
Macomb Community College *C, A*
Northern Michigan University *B*
St. Clair County Community
  College *A*
Schoolcraft College *A*
University of Detroit Mercy *B*
University of Michigan *M*
Wayne State University *B*

Minnesota

Brown College *A*
Concordia College: Moorhead *B*
Northland Community & Technical
  College *C, A*
St. Cloud State University *B*
Southwest Minnesota State
  University *B*
University of St. Thomas *B*
Winona State University *B*

Mississippi

Coahoma Community College *A*
Itawamba Community College *A*
Meridian Community College *A*

Rust College *B*
University of Southern Mississippi *B*

Missouri

Calvary Bible College and Theological
  Seminary *B*
Central Missouri State University *B*
College of the Ozarks *B*
Drury University *B*
Evangel University *A, B*
Missouri State University *B*
Northwest Missouri State
  University *B*
St. Louis Community College
  St. Louis Community College at
    Florissant Valley *A*
Stephens College *B*
University of Missouri
  Columbia *B*
Webster University *B*
William Jewell College *B*
William Woods University *B*

Montana

University of Montana: Missoula *B, M*

Nebraska

Grace University *B*
Hastings College *B*
University of Nebraska
  Kearney *B*
  Lincoln *B*
  Omaha *B*

New Hampshire

Franklin Pierce College *B*
Rivier College *B*

New Jersey

Felician College *B*
Montclair State University *B*
Rowan University *B*

New Mexico

Eastern New Mexico University *B*

New York

Adirondack Community College *C, A*
Cayuga County Community College *A*
City University of New York
  Brooklyn College *B*
  Kingsborough Community
    College *A*
College of New Rochelle *B*
Finger Lakes Community College *A*
Five Towns College *B*
Herkimer County Community
  College *C, A*
Hofstra University *B*
Ithaca College *B*
Manhattan College *B*
Nassau Community College *A*
New York Institute of Technology *B*
Onondaga Community College *A*
St. John Fisher College *B*
St. Thomas Aquinas College *B*
State University of New York
  College at Brockport *B*
  College at Buffalo *B*
  College at Cortland *B*
  College at Fredonia *B*
  New Paltz *B*
  Oswego *B*
Suffolk County Community College *A*
Sullivan County Community
  College *A*
Syracuse University *B, M*
Tompkins-Cortland Community
  College *A*

North Carolina

Campbell University *B*

Central Carolina Community
    College A
East Carolina University B
Elon University B
Gardner-Webb University B
Gaston College B
North Carolina Agricultural and
    Technical State University B
Wingate University B

North Dakota

Minot State University B

Ohio

Bowling Green State University B
Capital University B
Central State University B
Kent State University B
Marietta College B
Mount Vernon Nazarene University B
Ohio Northern University B
Ohio University B
Ohio Wesleyan University B
Otterbein College B
University of Cincinnati M, T
Washington State Community
    College A

Oklahoma

Cameron University B
East Central University B
Northeastern Oklahoma Agricultural
    and Mechanical College A
Northwestern Oklahoma State
    University B
Oklahoma Baptist University B
Oklahoma Christian University B
Oklahoma City Community College A
Oklahoma City University B
Rogers State University A
Rose State College A
Southeastern Oklahoma State
    University B
University of Central Oklahoma B
University of Oklahoma B

Oregon

Lane Community College C, A
Mount Hood Community College A

Pennsylvania

Bucks County Community College C
Chatham College B
Edinboro University of
    Pennsylvania B
Keystone College A
La Salle University B
Mansfield University of
    Pennsylvania B
Marywood University B
Pennsylvania College of Technology A
Point Park University B
Susquehanna University B
Waynesburg College B
Westminster College B

Rhode Island

New England Institute of
    Technology A

South Carolina

Morris College B
North Greenville College B
Tri-County Technical College A
Trident Technical College A
University of South Carolina B
Voorhees College B

Tennessee

Belmont University B
Lincoln Memorial University B
Southern Adventist University B

Union University B
University of Tennessee
    Knoxville B

Texas

Amarillo College A
Austin Community College C, A
Central Texas College C, A
Del Mar College A
Hardin-Simmons University B
Laredo Community College A
Midland College A
Navarro College A
Our Lady of the Lake University of San
    Antonio B
South Plains College A
Southwestern Adventist University B
Texas A&M University
    Commerce B
Texas Christian University B
Texas Southern University B
University of North Texas B, M
West Texas A&M University B

Utah

Dixie State College of Utah A
Weber State University B

Virginia

Hampton University B
Liberty University B
Regent University M
Southwest Virginia Community
    College C

Washington

Centralia College A
Columbia Basin College C
Eastern Washington University B
Gonzaga University B
Green River Community College C
Shoreline Community College A

West Virginia

Bethany College B
Concord University B
West Virginia University B

Wisconsin

Concordia University Wisconsin B
Marquette University B, M
University of Wisconsin
    Oshkosh B
    Superior B
    Whitewater B

Buddhist studies

California

California Institute of Integral
    Studies M, D
University of California
    Berkeley D

Colorado

Naropa University M

Massachusetts

Simon's Rock College of Bard B

Missouri

Webster University C

Wisconsin

University of Wisconsin
    Madison D

Building inspection

Alabama

Trenholm State Technical College C, A

California

Coastline Community College C
College of the Desert C
Southwestern College C, A

Colorado

Arapahoe Community College A

Illinois

McHenry County College C, A
William Rainey Harper College C

Kentucky

Jefferson Community College C

Michigan

Delta College C

Minnesota

Inver Hills Community College C, A

New York

State University of New York
    College of Agriculture and
        Technology at Morrisville A

Oregon

Chemeketa Community College C, A
Portland Community College C, A

Pennsylvania

Harrisburg Area Community
    College C

Utah

Utah Valley State College C, A

Washington

Edmonds Community College C

Building/property maintenance

Alabama

Shelton State Community College C

Arizona

Eastern Arizona College C
Gateway Community College C, A
Northland Pioneer College C
Pima Community College C, A
Yavapai College C, A

California

Allan Hancock College C
Butte College C, A
California Polytechnic State
    University: San Luis Obispo B
California State University
    Fresno B
Chabot College A
City College of San Francisco A
College of San Mateo C
College of the Redwoods C, A
College of the Sequoias C, A
Cosumnes River College C, A
Diablo Valley College C
El Camino College C, A
Feather River College C, A
Fresno City College C, A
Fullerton College A
Laney College C, A
Lassen College A
Los Angeles Trade and Technical
    College C, A
Modesto Junior College C, A
Orange Coast College C, A
Palomar College C, A
Pasadena City College C, A
Porterville College C

Riverside Community College C, A
Saddleback College C
San Francisco State University C
San Joaquin Delta College C, A
Santa Monica College A
Sierra College A
Southwestern College C, A
Ventura College C, A
West Valley College C, A

Colorado

Pikes Peak Community College C, A

Delaware

Delaware Technical and Community
    College
    Terry Campus A

Florida

Brevard Community College C, A
Florida Community College at
    Jacksonville A
Miami Dade College A
Palm Beach Community College C, A
Pensacola Junior College A
Santa Fe Community College A
South Florida Community College C
Tallahassee Community College A

Georgia

DeKalb Technical College C
Savannah Technical College C

Illinois

College of DuPage A
Lincoln Land Community College C, A
Oakton Community College A
Parkland College C
Rend Lake College C
South Suburban College of Cook
    County A
Southwestern Illinois College C, A
Triton College C, A
Waubonsee Community College C

Indiana

Ivy Tech State College
    Ivy Tech Community College:
        Bloomington C, A
    Ivy Tech Community College:
        Central Indiana C, A
    Ivy Tech Community College:
        Columbus C, A
    Ivy Tech Community College: East
        Central C, A
    Ivy Tech Community College:
        Kokomo C, A
    Ivy Tech Community College:
        Lafayette C, A
    Ivy Tech Community College: North
        Central C, A
    Ivy Tech Community College:
        Northeast C, A
    Ivy Tech Community College:
        Northwest C, A
    Ivy Tech Community College: South
        Central C, A
    Ivy Tech Community College:
        Southwest C, A
    Ivy Tech Community College:
        Wabash Valley C, A
    Ivy Tech Community College:
        Whitewater C, A
Vincennes University A

Iowa

Kirkwood Community College C, A
Southeastern Community College
    North Campus A

Kansas

Coffeyville Community College C

Louisiana
Delgado Community College *A*

Maine
Central Maine Community
College *C, A*
Southern Maine Community
College *A*

Maryland
Garrett College *C*
Hagerstown Community College *C*
Montgomery College *A*
University of Maryland
Eastern Shore *B*

Massachusetts
Cape Cod Community College *C*
Wentworth Institute of
Technology *A, B*

Michigan
Delta College *C, A*
Lansing Community College *C, A*
Macomb Community College *C*
Northern Michigan University *C, A, B*
Washtenaw Community College *C, A*

Minnesota
Hennepin Technical College *C, A*
Minnesota State University
Mankato *B*
Rochester Community and Technical
College *C*
University of Minnesota
Twin Cities *B*

Mississippi
Mississippi Delta Community
College *A*

Missouri
North Central Missouri College *C, A*
Park University *A*

Montana
Miles Community College *A*
University of Montana: Missoula *C, A*

Nebraska
Metropolitan Community
College *C, A*
Mid-Plains Community College
Area *C, A*

Nevada
Truckee Meadows Community
College *A*

New Hampshire
New Hampshire Community
Technical College
Manchester *A*

New Jersey
Raritan Valley Community College *A*

New Mexico
Dona Ana Branch Community College
of New Mexico State
University *A*
Northern New Mexico College *C, A*

New York
City University of New York
New York City College of
Technology *C, B*
Erie Community College
City Campus *A*
Hudson Valley Community College *A*

Institute of Design and
Construction *A*
Mohawk Valley Community College *A*
Orange County Community College *C*
State University of New York
College of Agriculture and
Technology at Morrisville *A*
College of Environmental Science
and Forestry *B*
College of Technology at Alfred *A*
College of Technology at Canton *C*
Farmingdale *B*
Suffolk County Community College *A*

North Carolina
Blue Ridge Community College *C*
Guilford Technical Community
College *A*
Haywood Community College *C, A*
Western Piedmont Community
College *C, A*

North Dakota
North Dakota State College of
Science *A*

Ohio
Columbus State Community
College *C, A*
Jefferson Community College *A*

Oklahoma
Oklahoma State University
Okmulgee *A*

Oregon
Chemeketa Community College *C, A*
Lane Community College *C, A*

Pennsylvania
Community College of Allegheny
County *C, A*
Dean Institute of Technology *C*
Delaware County Community
College *C, A*
Johnson College *A*
Luzerne County Community
College *C, A*
Penn State
University Park *C*
Pennsylvania College of Technology *C*
Triangle Tech
Pittsburgh *C*
Westmoreland County Community
College *C*
Williamson Free School of Mechanical
Trades *A*

Puerto Rico
University College of San Juan *C*

South Carolina
Aiken Technical College *C*
Denmark Technical College *C*
Technical College of the
Lowcountry *C*
Trident Technical College *C*

Tennessee
Southwest Tennessee Community
College *A*

Texas
Del Mar College *C, A*
Houston Community College
System *C*
Laredo Community College *C*
North Lake College *C*
Odessa College *C, A*
St. Philip's College *A*
San Jacinto College
North *C, A*

Texas A&M University
Commerce *B*
Texas State Technical College
Waco *A*
Tyler Junior College *A*

Utah
Salt Lake Community College *A*
Southern Utah University *B*
Utah Valley State College *A*
Weber State University *A, B*

Vermont
Vermont Technical College *A*

Virginia
John Tyler Community College *C*

Washington
Bellingham Technical College *C, A*
Spokane Falls Community College *C*

Wisconsin
Gateway Technical College *C*
University of Wisconsin
Platteville *B*

Business administration and management

Alabama
Alabama Agricultural and Mechanical
University *B, M*
Alabama State University *B*
Andrew Jackson University *M*
Athens State University *B*
Auburn University *B, M, D*
Auburn University at Montgomery *B*
Bevill State Community College *A*
Birmingham-Southern College *M*
Bishop State Community College *A*
Calhoun Community College *C, A*
Central Alabama Community
College *A*
Chattahoochee Valley Community
College *A*
Columbia Southern University *B, M*
Concordia College *B*
Enterprise-Ozark Community
College *A*
Faulkner State Community College *A*
Faulkner University *A, B*
Gadsden State Community College *A*
George C. Wallace State Community
College
Selma *A*
Huntingdon College *B*
Jacksonville State University *B, M*
Judson College *B*
Lawson State Community College *A*
Miles College *B*
Northeast Alabama Community
College *A*
Northwest-Shoals Community
College *C*
Oakwood College *B*
Remington College
Mobile *A*
Samford University *B, M*
Snead State Community College *A*
South University *A, B*
Spring Hill College *A, B, M*
Stillman College *B*
Talladega College *B*
Troy University *B, M*
Tuskegee University *B*
University of Alabama *B, M, D*
University of Alabama
Birmingham *B, M*
Huntsville *B, M*
University of Mobile *B*
University of Montevallo *B*

University of North Alabama *B, M*
University of South Alabama *B, M*
University of West Alabama *B*
Virginia College *C, A, B, M*
Virginia College at Huntsville *C, A*

Alaska
Alaska Pacific University *A, B, M*
Charter College *C, A, B*
Sheldon Jackson College *B*
University of Alaska
Anchorage *C, A, B, M*
Fairbanks *C, A, B, M*
Southeast *A, M*

Arizona
Arizona Institute of Business and
Technology
International Institute of the
Americas: Mesa *C, A, B*
Arizona State University *B, M, D*
Arizona State University West *M*
Arizona Western College *A*
Central Arizona College *C, A*
Chaparral College *A, B*
Cochise College *A*
DeVry University
Phoenix *B, M*
Dine College *A*
Eastern Arizona College *A*
Estrella Mountain Community
College *A*
Everest College *C, A*
Glendale Community College *A*
Grand Canyon University *B, M*
International Institute of the Americas
Phoenix *C, A, B*
Tucson *C, A, B*
International Institute of the
Americas: West Valley *C, A, B*
Lamson College *A*
Mesa Community College *A*
Mohave Community College *C, A*
Northcentral University *B, M, D*
Northern Arizona University *B, M*
Northland Pioneer College *C, A*
Phoenix College *C, A*
Pima Community College *C, A*
Prescott College *B, M*
Rio Salado College *C, A*
South Mountain Community
College *C, A*
Southwestern College *A*
Tohono O'odham Community
College *A*
University of Arizona *M, D*
University of Phoenix *B, M, D*
Western International University *B, M*
Yavapai College *C, A*

Arkansas
Arkansas Baptist College *B*
Arkansas State University *B, M*
Arkansas State University
Beebe *A*
Arkansas Tech University *B*
Black River Technical College *A*
Central Baptist College *A*
East Arkansas Community College *A*
Harding University *B, M*
John Brown University *B, M*
Lyon College *B*
Mid-South Community College *A*
Northwest Arkansas Community
College *A*
Ouachita Baptist University *B*
Ouachita Technical College *C, A*
Ozarka College *A*
Philander Smith College *B*
Phillips Community College of the
University of Arkansas *A*
Rich Mountain Community College *A*
South Arkansas Community College *A*
Southeast Arkansas College *C*

Southern Arkansas University *B*
University of Arkansas *B, M, D*
University of Arkansas
  Community College at Batesville *A*
  Fort Smith *C, A, B*
  Little Rock *B, M*
  Monticello *B*
  Pine Bluff *B*
University of Central Arkansas *B, M*
University of the Ozarks *B*
Williams Baptist College *B*

California

Allan Hancock College *C, A*
Alliant International
  University *B, M, D*
Antelope Valley College *C, A*
Azusa Pacific University *B, M*
Bakersfield College *A*
Barstow College *C, A*
Biola University *B, M*
Butte College *A*
CEI College
  Maric College: Panorama City *A*
Cabrillo College *A*
California Baptist University *B, M*
California Lutheran University *B, M*
California Maritime Academy *B*
California National University for
  Advanced Studies *B, M*
California Polytechnic State
  University: San Luis Obispo *B*
California State Polytechnic
  University: Pomona *B, M*
California State University
  Bakersfield *B, M*
  Chico *B, M*
  Dominguez Hills *B, M*
  East Bay *B, M*
  Fresno *B, M*
  Fullerton *B, M*
  Long Beach *M*
  Los Angeles *B, M*
  Monterey Bay *B*
  Northridge *B, M*
  Sacramento *B, M*
  San Bernardino *B, M*
  San Marcos *B*
  Stanislaus *B, M*
Canada College *C, A*
Cerritos Community College *A*
Cerro Coso Community College *C, A*
Chaffey College *C, A*
Chapman University *B, M*
Citrus College *C*
City College of San Francisco *A*
Coastline Community College *C, A*
Coleman College *B, M*
College of Alameda *A*
College of the Canyons *C, A*
College of the Desert *A*
College of the Siskiyous *C, A*
Columbia College *C, A*
Concordia University *B, M*
Copper Mountain College *A*
Cosumnes River College *A*
Crafton Hills College *C, A*
Cuyamaca College *C, A*
Cypress College *A*
De Anza College *C, A*
DeVry University
  Long Beach *B, M*
Diablo Valley College *C*
Dominican University of
  California *B, M*
East Los Angeles College *A*
El Camino College *A*
Evergreen Valley College *C*
Feather River College *C, A*
Foothill College *C, A*
Fresno City College *A*
Fresno Pacific University *B*
Fullerton College *A*
Golden Gate University *C, A, B, M, D*

Golden West College *C, A*
Grossmont Community College *C, A*
Heald College
  Fresno *C, A*
  Roseville *A*
  San Jose *C, A*
Holy Names University *B, M*
Hope International University *B, M*
Humboldt State University *B, M*
Humphreys College *A, B*
Imperial Valley College *A*
Institute of Computer
  Technology *C, A, B*
International Technological
  University *M*
Irvine Valley College *C, A*
John F. Kennedy University *B, M*
La Sierra University *B, M*
Lassen College *A*
Lincoln University *B, M*
Long Beach City College *C, A*
Los Angeles City College *C, A*
Los Angeles Harbor College *C, A*
Los Angeles Mission College *A*
Los Angeles Pierce College *C, A*
Los Angeles Southwest College *A*
Los Angeles Trade and Technical
  College *A*
Loyola Marymount University *C, B, M*
MTI College *C, A*
Maric College: Anaheim *A*
Master's College *B*
Mendocino College *C, A*
Menlo College *B*
Merced College *A*
Mills College *M*
MiraCosta College *C, A*
Mission College *A*
Modesto Junior College *A*
Monterey Peninsula College *A*
Moorpark College *C, A*
Mount St. Mary's College *B*
Mount San Antonio College *C, A*
Mount San Jacinto College *C, A*
National Hispanic University *B*
National Institute of Technology *C*
National University *B, M*
Northwestern Polytechnic
  University *M*
Notre Dame de Namur
  University *B, M*
Ohlone College *C, A*
Pacific States University *B, M*
Pacific Union College *B*
Palo Verde College *C, A*
Palomar College *A*
Patten University *B, M*
Pepperdine University *B, M*
Point Loma Nazarene University *B, M*
Porterville College *A*
Remington College
  San Diego *B, M*
Riverside Community College *C, A*
Saddleback College *C, A*
St. Mary's College of California *B, M*
San Bernardino Valley College *C, A*
San Diego Christian College *B*
San Diego City College *A*
San Diego Mesa College *C, A*
San Diego Miramar College *A*
San Diego State University *B, M*
San Francisco State University *M*
San Joaquin Delta College *C, A*
San Joaquin Valley College Inc. *A*
San Jose City College *C*
San Jose State University *B, M*
Santa Ana College *A*
Santa Barbara Business College:
  Ventura *C, A*
Santa Barbara City College *C, A*
Santa Clara University *M*
Santa Monica College *C, A*
Santa Rosa Junior College *A*
Santiago Canyon College *A*

Shasta College *A*
Sierra College *A*
Silicon Valley College
  Western Career College:
    Emeryville *C*
Simpson University *B*
Skyline College *C, A*
Solano Community College *C, A*
Sonoma State University *B, M*
Southern California Institute of
  Technology *A, B, M*
Southwestern College *A*
Stanford University *M, D*
Taft College *A*
University of California
  Berkeley *B, M, D*
  Davis *M*
  Irvine *M, D*
  Los Angeles *M, D*
  Riverside *B, M*
  Santa Cruz *B*
University of La Verne *B, M*
University of Redlands *B, M*
University of San Diego *B, M*
University of San Francisco *B, M*
University of Southern
  California *B, M, D*
University of the Pacific *B, M*
Vanguard University of Southern
  California *B, M*
Ventura College *A*
Victor Valley College *C, A*
Vista Community College *C, A*
West Hills Community College *C, A*
West Los Angeles College *C, A*
West Valley College *A*
Westwood College *B*
William Jessup University *B*
Woodbury University *B, M*
Yuba Community College
  District *C, A*

Colorado

Adams State College *B*
Blair College *A*
CollegeAmerica-Denver *A, B*
Colorado Christian University *B, M*
Colorado Mountain College
  Alpine Campus *A*
  Spring Valley Campus *C, A*
  Timberline Campus *A*
Colorado Northwestern Community
  College *C*
Colorado State University *B, M*
Colorado Technical University *B, M, D*
Community College of Aurora *C, A*
Community College of Denver *C, A*
DeVry University
  Westminster *B, M*
Fort Lewis College *B*
Front Range Community College *A*
Institute of Business & Medical
  Careers *C, A*
Johnson & Wales University *A, B*
Jones International University *B, M*
Mesa State College *B, M*
Metropolitan State College of
  Denver *B*
National American University
  Denver *A, B*
Northeastern Junior College *A*
Otero Junior College *A*
Parks College *A*
Parks College: Aurora *A*
Pikes Peak Community College *C, A*
Pueblo Community College *C, A*
Red Rocks Community College *C, A*
Regis University *B*
Trinidad State Junior College *A*
University of Colorado
  Boulder *B, M, D*
  Colorado Springs *B, M*
University of Denver *M*
University of Northern Colorado *B*

Western State College of Colorado *B*
Westwood College of Technology *B*

Connecticut

Albertus Magnus College *C, A, B, M*
Asnuntuck Community College *C, A*
Briarwood College *A*
Capital Community College *C, A*
Central Connecticut State
  University *B*
Eastern Connecticut State
  University *B*
Fairfield University *B, M*
Gateway Community College *A*
Housatonic Community College *A*
Manchester Community College *A*
Middlesex Community College *A*
Mitchell College *A, B*
Naugatuck Valley Community
  College *C, A*
Northwestern Connecticut
  Community College *A*
Norwalk Community College *A*
Post University *A, B*
Quinebaug Valley Community
  College *C, A*
Quinnipiac University *B, M*
St. Joseph College *B*
Southern Connecticut State
  University *B, M*
Three Rivers Community College *C, A*
Tunxis Community College *A*
United States Coast Guard Academy *B*
University of Bridgeport *A, M*
University of Connecticut *B*
University of Hartford *B, M*
University of New Haven *A, B, M*
Western Connecticut State
  University *B*
Yale University *M, D*

Delaware

Delaware State University *M*
Delaware Technical and Community
  College
  Owens Campus *C, A*
  Terry Campus *C, A*
Goldey-Beacom College *A, B, M*
University of Delaware *B, M*
Wesley College *A, B, M*
Wilmington College *M*

District of Columbia

American University *B, M*
Gallaudet University *B*
George Washington
  University *B, M, D*
Georgetown University *B, M*
Howard University *B, M*
Southeastern University *A, B, M*
Strayer University *C, A, B, M*
Trinity University *B, M*
University of the District of
  Columbia *B, M*

Florida

Barry University *B, M*
Bethune-Cookman College *B*
Brevard Community College *A*
Broward Community College *C, A*
Carlos Albizu University *M*
Central Florida Community
  College *C, A*
Chipola College *A*
City College *A, B*
City College: Casselberry *A*
Clearwater Christian College *B*
Daytona Beach Community College *A*
DeVry University
  Miramar *B, M*
  Orlando *B, M*
Eckerd College *B*
Edison College *A*

Edward Waters College *B*
Embry-Riddle Aeronautical
University *A, B, M*
Embry-Riddle Aeronautical University:
Extended Campus *A, B, M*
Everglades University *B, M*
Flagler College *B*
Florida Agricultural and Mechanical
University *B, M*
Florida Atlantic University *B, M, D*
Florida Community College at
Jacksonville *A*
Florida Gulf Coast University *B, M*
Florida Institute of Technology *B, M*
Florida International
University *B, M, D*
Florida Keys Community College *A*
Florida Memorial University *B*
Florida Metropolitan University
Melbourne Campus *A, B, M*
Orlando College North *A, B, M*
Orlando College South *A, B, M*
Pinellas *A, B, M*
Pompano Beach *A, B, M*
Tampa College *A, B, M*
Tampa College Lakeland *B, M*
Florida Metropolitan University:
Jacksonville *A, B, M*
Florida Metropolitan University:
Orange Park *A, B*
Florida National College *A*
Florida Southern College *B*
Florida State University *M, D*
Florida Technical College
Deland *A*
Gulf Coast Community College *A*
Herzing College
Orlando *A, B*
Hillsborough Community
College *C, A*
Indian River Community College *A*
International College *A, B, M*
Jacksonville University *B, M*
Johnson & Wales University *A, B*
Jones College *A, B*
Lake City Community College *A*
Lake-Sumter Community College *C, A*
Lynn University *B, M, D*
Manatee Community College *A*
Miami Dade College *C, A*
Northwood University
Florida Campus *A, B*
Nova Southeastern University *B, M, D*
Okaloosa-Walton College *C, A*
Palm Beach Atlantic University *B, M*
Palm Beach Community College *A*
Pasco-Hernando Community
College *C, A*
Pensacola Junior College *A*
Polk Community College *A*
Remington College: Tampa *A*
Rollins College *A*
St. Johns River Community
College *C, A*
St. Leo University *B*
St. Petersburg College *C, A*
St. Thomas University *B, M*
Santa Fe Community College *A*
Schiller International
University *A, B, M*
South Florida Community
College *C, A*
South University: West Palm Beach
Campus *A, B*
Southeastern College of the
Assemblies of God *B*
Southwest Florida College *A*
Stetson University *B, M*
Tallahassee Community College *A*
University of Central Florida *B, M, D*
University of Miami *C, B, M*
University of North Florida *B, M*
University of South Florida *B, M, D*
University of Tampa *B, M*

University of West Florida *B, M*
Valencia Community College *C, A*
Warner Southern College *B, M*
Webber International
University *A, B, M*
Webster College *C, A, B*
Webster College: Holiday *A, B*

Georgia
Abraham Baldwin Agricultural
College *A*
Albany State University *B, M*
Atlanta Christian College *B*
Atlanta Metropolitan College *A*
Augusta State University *B, M*
Bauder College *A, B*
Berry College *B, M*
Brenau University *B*
Brewton-Parker College *B*
Brown Mackie College: Atlanta *A*
Central Georgia Technical College *C*
Clark Atlanta University *B, M, D*
Clayton State University *B*
Columbus State University *B, M*
Columbus Technical College *C, A*
Dalton State College *A*
Darton College *A*
DeKalb Technical College *A*
DeVry University
Alpharetta *B, M*
Decatur *B, M*
East Georgia College *A*
Emmanuel College *A, B*
Emory University *B*
Fort Valley State University *B*
Gainesville State College *A*
Georgia College and State
University *B*
Georgia Institute of
Technology *B, M, D*
Georgia Military College *A*
Georgia Perimeter College *A*
Georgia Southwestern State
University *B, M*
Georgia State University *B, M, D*
Gordon College *A*
Griffin Technical College *A*
Gwinnett College *C, A*
Kennesaw State University *B, M*
LaGrange College *B*
Life University *B*
Macon State College *C, A, B*
Middle Georgia College *A*
Morehouse College *B*
North Georgia College & State
University *B*
Northwestern Technical College *C, A*
Oglethorpe University *M*
Paine College *B*
Piedmont College *B, M*
Reinhardt College *A, B*
Shorter College *B*
South Georgia College *A*
South University *A, B, M*
Southwest Georgia Technical
College *C, A*
Toccoa Falls College *B*
University of Georgia *B, M, D*
University of West Georgia *B, M*
Valdosta State University *B, M*
Waycross College *A*
Wesleyan College *B, M*
West Georgia Technical College *A*

Hawaii
Chaminade University of
Honolulu *A, B, M*
Hawaii Business College *C, A*
Hawaii Pacific University *A, B, M*
Heald College
Honolulu *A*
University of Hawaii
Hilo *B*
Manoa *B, M*

West Oahu *B*

Idaho
Albertson College of Idaho *B*
Boise State University *M*
Brigham Young University-Idaho *B*
Idaho State University *B, M*
Lewis-Clark State College *B*
North Idaho College *A*
Northwest Nazarene University *B, M*

Illinois
Augustana College *B*
Aurora University *M*
Benedictine University *A, M*
Black Hawk College *A*
Blackburn College *B*
Bradley University *B, M*
Carl Sandburg College *A*
Chicago State University *B*
City Colleges of Chicago
Harold Washington College *A*
Harry S. Truman College *A*
Kennedy-King College *A*
Malcolm X College *A*
Olive-Harvey College *A*
Wright College *C, A*
College of DuPage *C, A*
College of Lake County *C, A*
Columbia College Chicago *B*
Concordia University *B*
DePaul University *B, M*
DeVry University
Addison *A*
Chicago *B*
Tinley Park *B, M*
Dominican University *B, M*
East-West University *B*
Eastern Illinois University *B, M*
Elgin Community College *C, A*
Elmhurst College *C, B*
Eureka College *B*
Governors State University *B, M*
Greenville College *B*
Highland Community College *A*
Illinois Central College *A*
Illinois Institute of Technology *M*
Illinois State University *B, M*
Illinois Wesleyan University *B*
John A. Logan College *A*
John Wood Community College *C, A*
Joliet Junior College *A*
Judson College *B*
Kankakee Community College *C, A*
Kaskaskia College *C*
Kendall College *B*
Lewis University *B, M*
Lewis and Clark Community
College *A*
Lexington College *A, B*
Lincoln Christian College and
Seminary *B*
Lincoln Land Community College *C*
Loyola University of Chicago *M*
MacCormac College *A*
MacMurray College *A, B*
McHenry County College *C, A*
McKendree College *B, M*
Midstate College *A, B*
Millikin University *B, M*
Monmouth College *B, T*
Moraine Valley Community College *A*
Morton College *A*
National-Louis University *C, B, M*
North Central College *M*
North Park University *C, B, M*
Northeastern Illinois University *B, M*
Northern Illinois University *M*
Northwestern Business College *A*
Northwestern University *M, D*
Oakton Community College *A*
Olivet Nazarene University *B, M*
Parkland College *A*
Principia College *B*

Quincy University *B, M*
Rend Lake College *C, A*
Robert Morris College:
Chicago *C, A, B*
Rock Valley College *C, A*
Rockford Business College *A*
Rockford College *B, M*
Roosevelt University *B, M*
St. Augustine College *A*
St. Xavier University *M*
Sauk Valley Community College *C, A*
Southeastern Illinois College *A*
Southern Illinois University
Carbondale *B, M, D*
Southern Illinois University
Edwardsville *B, M*
Southwestern Illinois College *A*
Springfield College in Illinois *A*
Triton College *C, A*
University of Chicago *M*
University of Illinois
Chicago *M, D*
Springfield *B, M*
Urbana-Champaign *B, M*
University of St. Francis *B*
Waubonsee Community College *C, A*
Western Illinois University *B, M*

Indiana
Ancilla College *A*
Anderson University *B, M*
Ball State University *B, M*
Bethel College *B, M*
Brown Mackie College: Fort Wayne *A*
Brown Mackie College: Michigan
City *A*
Butler University *M*
Calumet College of St. Joseph *C, A, B*
Earlham College *B*
Goshen College *B*
Grace College *B*
Hanover College *B*
Huntington University *A, B*
Indiana Business College *C, A*
Indiana Business College
Anderson *A*
Columbus *C, A*
Evansville *A*
Fort Wayne *A*
Lafayette *A*
Marion *A*
Muncie *A*
Terre Haute *C, A*
Indiana Institute of Technology *A, B*
Indiana State University *B, M*
Indiana University
Bloomington *B, M, D*
East *A, B*
Kokomo *A, B, M*
South Bend *B, M*
Indiana University-Purdue University
Fort Wayne *A, B, M*
Indiana University-Purdue University
Indianapolis *M*
Indiana Wesleyan University *A, B, M*
International Business College:
Indianapolis *C, A*
Ivy Tech State College
Ivy Tech Community College:
Central Indiana *A*
Ivy Tech Community College:
Columbus *A*
Ivy Tech Community College: East
Central *C, A*
Ivy Tech Community College:
Kokomo *C, A*
Ivy Tech Community College:
Lafayette *A*
Ivy Tech Community College: North
Central *C, A*
Ivy Tech Community College:
Northeast *C, A*
Ivy Tech Community College:
Northwest *C, A*

Ivy Tech Community College: South
Central *C, A*
Ivy Tech Community College:
Southeast *C, A*
Ivy Tech Community College:
Southwest *A*
Ivy Tech Community College:
Wabash Valley *A*
Ivy Tech Community College:
Whitewater *A*
Manchester College *A, B*
Oakland City University *A, B*
Professional Careers Institute *C, A*
Purdue University *B, M, D*
Purdue University
Calumet *B, M*
Saint Mary's College *B*
St. Mary-of-the-Woods College *B*
Sawyer College: Merrillville *C, A*
Taylor University *A, B*
Taylor University: Fort Wayne *A, B*
Tri-State University *A, B*
University of Evansville *B*
University of Indianapolis *A, B*
University of Notre Dame *M*
University of St. Francis *B, M*
University of Southern Indiana *B*
Valparaiso University *M*
Vincennes University *A*

Iowa

AIB College of Business *A*
Ashford University *B*
Briar Cliff University *B*
Central College *B, T*
Clarke College *A, B, M*
Coe College *B*
Des Moines Area Community
College *C, A*
Drake University *M*
Graceland University *B*
Hamilton College *C, A, B*
Hamilton College
Cedar Falls *A*
Cedar Rapids *A, B*
Iowa Central Community College *A*
Iowa Lakes Community College *A*
Iowa State University *M*
Iowa Wesleyan College *B*
Kaplan University *C, A, B, M*
Kirkwood Community College *C, A*
Loras College *B*
Luther College *B*
Maharishi University of
Management *B*
Marshalltown Community College *A*
Morningside College *B*
Mount Mercy College *B*
North Iowa Area Community
College *C, A*
Northeast Iowa Community
College *A*
Northwest Iowa Community
College *A*
Northwestern College *B*
St. Ambrose University *B, M, D*
Simpson College *B*
Southeastern Community College
North Campus *A*
University of Dubuque *B, M*
University of Iowa *B, M*
University of Northern Iowa *B, M*
Upper Iowa University *A, B, M*
Waldorf College *B*
Wartburg College *B*
Western Iowa Tech Community
College *A*
William Penn University *B*

Kansas

Allen County Community College *A*
Barclay College *B*
Benedictine College *B, M*
Bethany College *B*

Brown Mackie College *A*
Butler County Community
College *C, A*
Central Christian College of
Kansas *A, B*
Cloud County Community
College *C, A*
Coffeyville Community College *A*
Cowley County Community
College *A*
Emporia State University *B, M*
Fort Hays State University *B, M*
Fort Scott Community College *C, A*
Friends University *B, M*
Haskell Indian Nations
University *A, B*
Johnson County Community
College *A*
Kansas City Kansas Community
College *A*
Kansas State University *B, M*
Labette Community College *A*
Manhattan Christian College *B*
McPherson College *B*
MidAmerica Nazarene
University *B, M*
Neosho County Community
College *C, A*
Newman University *A, B, M*
Ottawa University *B*
Pittsburg State University *B, M*
Pratt Community College *C, A*
Seward County Community College *A*
Southwestern College *B, M*
Sterling College *B*
Tabor College *B*
University of Kansas *M*
University of St. Mary *B, M*
Washburn University of Topeka *B, M*
Wichita State University *B, M*

Kentucky

Alice Lloyd College *B*
Ashland Community and Technical
College *C, A*
Beckfield College *A, B*
Bellarmine University *B, M*
Bluegrass Community and Technical
College *A*
Brescia University *A, B, M*
Brown Mackie College:
Hopkinsville *C, A*
Campbellsville University *A, B, M*
Daymar College *C, A*
Daymar College
Louisville *C*
Draughons Junior College *A*
Eastern Kentucky University *B*
Elizabethtown Community and
Technical College *C, A*
Georgetown College *B*
Henderson Community College *A*
Hopkinsville Community College *A*
Jefferson Community College *C, A*
Kentucky Christian University *B*
Kentucky State University *B*
Kentucky Wesleyan College *B*
Lindsey Wilson College *A, B*
Madisonville Community College *A*
Maysville Community College *C, A*
Mid-Continent University *B*
Midway College *A, B*
Morehead State University *B*
Murray State University *B*
National College of Business &
Technology
Danville *C, A*
Florence *A*
Lexington *C, A*
Louisville *C, A*
Pikeville *C, A*
Richmond *C, A*
Northern Kentucky University *B*
Owensboro Community College *A*

Pikeville College *A, B*
St. Catharine College *A, B*
Somerset Community College *A*
Southeast Kentucky Community and
Technical College *A*
Southern Ohio College
Brown Mackie College: North
Kentucky *A*
Spencerian College *A*
Sullivan University *C, A, B, M*
Thomas More College *A*
Union College *B*
University of Louisville *B*
West Kentucky Community and
Technical College *A*
Western Kentucky University *A, B*

Louisiana

Centenary College of Louisiana *B, M*
Delgado Community College *C, A*
Dillard University *B*
ITI Technical College *A*
Louisiana State University
Shreveport *B, M*
Louisiana State University and
Agricultural and Mechanical
College *B, M, D*
Louisiana Tech University *B, M, D*
Loyola University New Orleans *B, M*
Nicholls State University *B, M*
Northwestern State University *B*
Nunez Community College *A*
Our Lady of Holy Cross College *B*
Remington College
Lafayette *A*
Southeastern Louisiana
University *B, M*
Southern University
New Orleans *B*
Shreveport *B*
Southern University and Agricultural
and Mechanical College *B*
Southwest University *M*
Tulane University *B, M, D*
University of Louisiana at
Lafayette *B, M*
University of Louisiana at
Monroe *B, M*
University of New Orleans *B, M*
Xavier University of Louisiana *B*

Maine

Andover College *A*
Beal College *C, A*
Central Maine Community
College *C, A*
Eastern Maine Community College *A*
Husson College *A, B, M*
Kennebec Valley Community
College *A*
Maine Maritime Academy *B*
Northern Maine Community
College *A*
St. Joseph's College *B*
Southern Maine Community
College *A*
Thomas College *B, M*
University of Maine *C, B, M*
University of Maine
Augusta *A, B*
Fort Kent *A, B*
Machias *B*
Presque Isle *B*
University of New England *B*
University of Southern Maine *C, B, M*
York County Community College *C, A*

Maryland

Allegany College of Maryland *C, A*
Baltimore City Community College *A*
Bowie State University *B, M*
Capitol College *B*
Cecil Community College *A*
Chesapeake College *C*

College of Southern Maryland *C, A*
Columbia Union College *B*
Community College of Baltimore
County *C, A*
DeVry University: Bethesda *B, M*
Frederick Community College *A*
Frostburg State University *B, M*
Garrett College *C, A*
Goucher College *B*
Hagerstown Business College *A*
Hagerstown Community College *C, A*
Harford Community College *C, A*
Hood College *B, M*
Howard Community College *C, A*
Loyola College in Maryland *M*
McDaniel College *B*
Montgomery College *C, A*
Morgan State University *B, M*
Mount St. Mary's University *M, T*
Prince George's Community
College *C, A*
Salisbury University *B, M*
Sojourner-Douglass College *B*
Towson University *B*
University of Baltimore *B, M*
University of Maryland
College Park *M*
Eastern Shore *B*
University College *C, B, M*
Villa Julie College *C, B*
Wor-Wic Community College *C, A*

Massachusetts

American International
College *A, B, M*
Anna Maria College *A, B, M*
Assumption College *B, M*
Atlantic Union College *B*
Babson College *B, M*
Bay Path College *B*
Bay State College *A, B*
Becker College *A, B*
Bentley College *A, B, M*
Berkshire Community College *A*
Boston College *B, M*
Boston University *B, M, D*
Bridgewater State College *B*
Bristol Community College *A*
Bunker Hill Community College *A*
Cape Cod Community College *A*
Clark University *B, M*
Curry College *B*
Dean College *A*
Eastern Nazarene College *A, B, M*
Elms College *B*
Emmanuel College *B*
Endicott College *B, M*
Fisher College *C, A, B*
Fitchburg State College *B, M*
Gibbs College *A*
Gordon College *B*
Greenfield Community College *A*
Holyoke Community College *C, A*
Lasell College *B*
Lesley University *B*
Marian Court College *C, A*
Massachusetts Bay Community
College *C, A*
Massachusetts College of Liberal
Arts *B*
Massasoit Community College *A*
Merrimack College *A, B*
Middlesex Community College *A*
Mount Ida College *A, B*
Mount Wachusett Community
College *C, A*
New England College of Finance *A*
Newbury College *A, B*
Nichols College *A, B, M*
North Shore Community College *A*
Northern Essex Community
College *A*
Pine Manor College *B*
Quinsigamond Community College *A*

Regis College *M*
Roxbury Community College *A*
Salem State College *B, M*
Simmons College *B, M*
Springfield College *B*
Springfield Technical Community
　　College *A*
Stonehill College *C, B*
Suffolk University *B, M*
University of Massachusetts
　　Amherst *B, M, D*
　　Boston *B, M*
　　Dartmouth *B, M*
　　Lowell *B, M*
Urban College of Boston *C*
Western New England College *B, M*
Westfield State College *B*
Worcester Polytechnic Institute *B, M*
Worcester State College *B*

Michigan

Adrian College *A, B, T*
Albion College *B*
Alma College *B*
Alpena Community College *A*
Andrews University *B, M*
Aquinas College *B, M, T*
Baker College
　　of Auburn Hills *A, B*
　　of Cadillac *A, B*
　　of Clinton Township *A, B, M*
　　of Flint *A, B, M*
　　of Jackson *A*
　　of Muskegon *A, B*
　　of Owosso *A, B*
　　of Port Huron *A, B*
Bay Mills Community College *A*
Bay de Noc Community College *C, A*
Calvin College *B*
Central Michigan University *B, M*
Cleary University *A, B, M*
Concordia University *B*
Cornerstone University *B, M*
Davenport University *A, B, M*
Delta College *A*
Eastern Michigan University *B, M*
Ferris State University *A, B*
Finlandia University *B*
Glen Oaks Community College *C*
Gogebic Community College *A*
Grace Bible College *B*
Grand Rapids Community College *A*
Grand Valley State University *B, M*
Hillsdale College *B*
Hope College *B*
Jackson Community College *C, A*
Kalamazoo Valley Community
　　College *C, A*
Kellogg Community College *C, A*
Kettering University *B*
Kirtland Community College *C, A*
Kuyper College *B*
Lake Michigan College *A*
Lake Superior State University *A, B, M*
Lansing Community College *A*
Lawrence Technological
　　University *B, M, D*
Lewis College of Business *C, A*
Macomb Community College *C, A*
Madonna University *C, A, B, M*
Marygrove College *B*
Michigan Jewish Institute *A, B*
Michigan State University *B, M, D*
Michigan Technological
　　University *B, M, T*
Mid Michigan Community College *A*
Monroe County Community
　　College *C, A*
Montcalm Community College *A*
Mott Community College *C, A*
North Central Michigan College *C, A*
Northern Michigan University *B*
Northwestern Michigan College *A*
Northwood University *A, B, M*

Oakland Community College *A*
Oakland University *M*
Olivet College *B*
Rochester College *B*
Saginaw Chippewa Tribal College *A*
Saginaw Valley State University *B, M*
St. Clair County Community
　　College *A*
Schoolcraft College *A*
Southwestern Michigan College *C, A*
Spring Arbor University *B*
University of Detroit Mercy *B, M*
University of Michigan *B, M, D*
University of Michigan
　　Dearborn *B, M*
　　Flint *B, M*
Walsh College of Accountancy and
　　Business Administration *B*
Washtenaw Community College *C, A*
Wayne County Community College *A*
Western Michigan University *B, M*

Minnesota

Academy College *C, A, B*
Alexandria Technical College *A*
Anoka-Ramsey Community College *A*
Augsburg College *B, M*
Bemidji State University *B*
Bethany Lutheran College *B*
Bethel University *B*
Capella University *M*
Central Lakes College *A*
Century Community and Technical
　　College *A*
College of St. Benedict *B*
College of St. Catherine *B, M*
College of St. Scholastica *B, M*
Concordia College: Moorhead *B*
Concordia University: St. Paul *B*
Crown College *A, B*
Dakota County Technical College *C, A*
Duluth Business University *A*
Globe College *C, A, B, M*
Hamline University *B, M*
Hibbing Community College *A*
Inver Hills Community College *C, A*
Itasca Community College *A*
Lake Superior College *A*
Leech Lake Tribal College *A*
Metropolitan State University *B, M*
Minneapolis Community and
　　Technical College *A*
Minnesota School of
　　Business *C, A, B, M*
Minnesota School of Business:
　　Brooklyn Center *C, A, B*
Minnesota State College - Southeast
　　Technical *C, A*
Minnesota State Community and
　　Technical College - Fergus
　　Falls *C, A*
Minnesota State University
　　Mankato *B, M*
　　Moorhead *B*
National American University
　　St. Paul *B*
North Central University *A, B*
North Hennepin Community
　　College *A*
Northwest Technical College *C, A*
Northwestern College *B, M*
Pillsbury Baptist Bible College *B*
Pine Technical College *A*
Rasmussen College
　　Eagan *A*
　　Mankato *C, A*
　　Minnetonka *C, A*
　　St. Cloud *B*
Rochester Community and Technical
　　College *C, A*
St. Cloud State University *B, M*
St. Cloud Technical College *C, A*
St. John's University *B*

St. Mary's University of
　　Minnesota *B, M*
Southwest Minnesota State
　　University *A, B, M*
University of Minnesota
　　Crookston *A, B*
　　Duluth *B, M*
　　Twin Cities *C, B, M, D*
University of St. Thomas *B, M*
Vermilion Community College *A*
Walden University *B, M*
Winona State University *B, M*

Mississippi

Alcorn State University *B, M*
Belhaven College *C, B, M*
Blue Mountain College *B*
Copiah-Lincoln Community College *A*
Delta State University *B, M*
Holmes Community College *A*
Jackson State University *B, M, D*
Millsaps College *B, M, T*
Mississippi College *B, M, T*
Mississippi Gulf Coast Community
　　College
　　Jefferson Davis Campus *A*
Mississippi State University *B, M, D*
Mississippi Valley State University *B*
Pearl River Community College *A*
Rust College *B*
University of Mississippi *B, M, D*
University of Southern
　　Mississippi *B, M*
William Carey College *B, M*

Missouri

Avila University *B, M*
Blue River Community College *A*
Central Methodist University *B*
Central Missouri State University *B, M*
College of the Ozarks *B*
Columbia College *A, B, M*
Culver-Stockton College *B*
DeVry University
　　Kansas City *B, M*
Drury University *B, M*
Evangel University *B*
Everest College: Springfield *A, B*
Fontbonne University *B, M*
Grantham University *A, B, M*
Hannibal-LaGrange College *B*
Harris-Stowe State University *B*
Lincoln University *B, M*
Lindenwood University *B, M*
Longview Community College *A*
Maple Woods Community
　　College *C, A*
Maryville University of Saint
　　Louis *B, M*
Metro Business College
　　Jefferson City *C, A*
Mineral Area College *A*
Missouri Baptist University *C, A, B, M*
Missouri College *C*
Missouri State University *B, M*
Missouri Valley College *B*
Missouri Western State
　　University *A, B*
National American University
　　Kansas City *A, B*
North Central Missouri College *C, A*
Northwest Missouri State
　　University *M*
Ozarks Technical Community
　　College *C, A*
Park University *A, B, M*
Penn Valley Community College *C, A*
Rockhurst University *B, M*
St. Charles Community College *A*
St. Louis Community College
　　St. Louis Community College at
　　Florissant Valley *A*
St. Louis University *B, M, D*

Southeast Missouri State
　　University *B, M*
Southwest Baptist University *B, M*
State Fair Community College *A*
Stephens College *B, M*
Truman State University *B*
University of Missouri
　　Columbia *B*
　　Rolla *B*
　　St. Louis *B, M*
Washington University in St.
　　Louis *B, M, D*
Webster University *B, M, D*
Westminster College *B*
William Jewell College *B*
William Woods University *B, M*

Montana

Blackfeet Community College *A*
Carroll College *B*
Fort Peck Community College *C, A*
Little Big Horn College *A*
Miles Community College *A*
Montana State University
　　College of Technology-Great Falls *A*
Montana Tech of the University of
　　Montana *A, B*
Rocky Mountain College *B*
University of Great Falls *B*
University of Montana: Missoula *B, M*
University of Montana: Western *A*

Nebraska

Bellevue University *B, M*
Central Community College *C, A*
Chadron State College *B, M*
Clarkson College *B, M*
College of Saint Mary *C, A, B, M*
Concordia University *B, T*
Dana College *B*
Doane College *M*
Hamilton College: Lincoln *A*
Hastings College *B*
Metropolitan Community College *A*
Mid-Plains Community College
　　Area *C, A*
Midland Lutheran College *B*
Nebraska Indian Community
　　College *A*
Nebraska Wesleyan University *B*
Northeast Community College *A*
Peru State College *B*
Southeast Community College
　　Lincoln Campus *A*
Union College *B*
University of Nebraska
　　Kearney *B, M*
　　Lincoln *B, M*
　　Omaha *M*
Wayne State College *B, M, T*
Western Nebraska Community
　　College *C, A*
York College *B*

Nevada

Career College of Northern
　　Nevada *C, A*
Community College of Southern
　　Nevada *C, A*
Great Basin College *C, A, B*
Heritage College *C*
Las Vegas College *A*
Morrison University *A, B, M*
Sierra Nevada College *B*
Truckee Meadows Community
　　College *A*
University of Nevada
　　Las Vegas *M*
　　Reno *M*
Western Nevada Community
　　College *C, A*

New Hampshire

Colby-Sawyer College *B*
Daniel Webster College *M*
Dartmouth College *M*
Franklin Pierce College *B, M*
McIntosh College *A*
New England College *B*
New Hampshire Community
    Technical College
    Berlin *C, A*
    Manchester *C, A*
    Nashua *A*
    Stratham *C, A*
New Hampshire Technical Institute *A*
Plymouth State University *B, M*
Rivier College *A, B, M*
Southern New Hampshire
    University *A, B, M*
University of New Hampshire *A, B, M*
University of New Hampshire at
    Manchester *A, B*

New Jersey

Atlantic Cape Community College *A*
Berkeley College *A, B*
Bloomfield College *C, B*
Brookdale Community College *A*
Burlington County College *A*
Caldwell College *B, M*
Camden County College *A*
Centenary College *B, M*
The College of New Jersey *B*
College of St. Elizabeth *C, B, M*
County College of Morris *A*
Cumberland County College *A*
Essex County College *C, A*
Fairleigh Dickinson University
    College at Florham *B, M*
    Metropolitan Campus *B, M*
Felician College *B*
Georgian Court University *B, M*
Gloucester County College *A*
Hudson County Community
    College *A*
Kean University *B*
Mercer County Community
    College *A*
Middlesex County College *A*
Monmouth University *B, M*
Montclair State University *B, M*
New Jersey City University *B*
New Jersey Institute of
    Technology *B, M*
Ocean County College *A*
Passaic County Community College *C*
Ramapo College of New Jersey *B*
Raritan Valley Community College *C*
Richard Stockton College of New
    Jersey *M*
Rider University *A, B, M*
Rowan University *M*
Rutgers, The State University of New
    Jersey
    Camden Regional Campus *B, M*
    New Brunswick/Piscataway
        Campus *B, M, D*
    Newark Regional Campus *B, M, D*
St. Peter's College *A, B, M*
Salem Community College *A*
Seton Hall University *B, M*
Stevens Institute of Technology *B, M*
Sussex County Community College *A*
Thomas Edison State College *A, B, M*
Union County College *A*
William Paterson University of New
    Jersey *B, M*

New Mexico

Albuquerque Technical-Vocational
    Institute *C, A*
Clovis Community College *A*
College of the Southwest *B*

Dona Ana Branch Community College
    of New Mexico State
    University *C, A*
Eastern New Mexico University *B, M*
International Institute of the
    Americas *C, A, B*
Luna Community College *A*
Mesalands Community College *A*
Metropolitan College of Court
    Reporting *B*
National American University *A, B*
New Mexico Highlands
    University *B, M*
New Mexico Institute of Mining and
    Technology *A*
New Mexico Junior College *A*
New Mexico State
    University *A, B, M, D*
Northern New Mexico College *C, A*
San Juan College *A*
Santa Fe Community College *C, A*
Southwestern Indian Polytechnic
    Institute *C, A*
University of New Mexico *B, M*
Western New Mexico University *B, M*

New York

ASA Institute of Business and
    Computer Technology *A*
Adelphi University *B, M*
Adirondack Community College *A*
Alfred University *B, M*
Berkeley College *A, B*
Berkeley College of New York
    City *A, B*
Boricua College *B*
Bramson ORT College *A*
Briarcliffe College *A, B*
Broome Community College *A*
Bryant & Stratton Business Institute
    Bryant & Stratton College: Albany *A*
    Bryant & Stratton College:
        Lackawanna *C, A*
    Bryant & Stratton College:
        Rochester *A*
    Bryant & Stratton College:
        Syracuse *C, A*
Canisius College *M*
Cayuga County Community College *A*
Cazenovia College *C, A, B*
City University of New York
    Baruch College *B, M*
    Borough of Manhattan Community
        College *A*
    Brooklyn College *B*
    Hostos Community College *A*
    Kingsborough Community
        College *A*
    LaGuardia Community College *A*
    Lehman College *B*
    Queensborough Community
        College *A*
    York College *B*
Clarkson University *B, M*
Clinton Community College *A*
College of Mount St. Vincent *B*
College of Saint Rose *B, M*
College of Westchester *C, A*
Columbia-Greene Community
    College *A*
Concordia College *A, B*
Cornell University *M, D*
Corning Community College *A*
D'Youville College *B*
Daemen College *B*
Dominican College of Blauvelt *B*
Dowling College *C, B, M*
Dutchess Community College *A*
Elmira College *A, B*
Erie Community College
    City Campus *A*
    North Campus *A*
    South Campus *A*
Excelsior College *A, B*

Finger Lakes Community College *A*
Five Towns College *A, B*
Fordham University *B, M*
Fulton-Montgomery Community
    College *A*
Genesee Community College *A*
Globe Institute of Technology *C, A, B*
Hartwick College *B*
Herkimer County Community
    College *A*
Hilbert College *A, B*
Hofstra University *B, M*
Houghton College *B*
Hudson Valley Community College *A*
Iona College *B, M*
Ithaca College *B, M*
Jamestown Business College *A*
Jamestown Community College *A*
Jefferson Community College *C, A*
Katharine Gibbs School
    New York *A*
Keuka College *B*
King's College *B*
Le Moyne College *B, M*
Long Island Business Institute *A*
Long Island University
    Brooklyn Campus *A, B, M*
    C.W. Post Campus *B, M*
Manhattan College *M*
Manhattanville College *B*
Maria College *A*
Marist College *B, M*
Marymount Manhattan College *B*
Medaille College *B, M*
Mercy College *A, B, M*
Metropolitan College of New
    York *B, M*
Mildred Elley *C, A*
Mohawk Valley Community College *A*
Molloy College *B, M*
Monroe College *A, B, M*
Mount St. Mary College *C, B, M*
Nassau Community College *C, A*
New York Institute of
    Technology *C, A, B, M*
New York University *C, B, M, D*
Niagara County Community
    College *C, A*
Niagara University *M*
North Country Community College *A*
Nyack College *A, B, M*
Olean Business Institute *C, A*
Orange County Community College *A*
Pace University *B, M, D*
Paul Smith's College *A, B*
Plaza College *A*
Polytechnic University *M, D*
Rensselaer Polytechnic
    Institute *B, M, D*
Roberts Wesleyan College *B*
Rochester Business Institute *C, A*
Rochester Institute of
    Technology *A, B, M*
Rockland Community College *A*
Russell Sage College *B*
Sage College of Albany *A, B, M*
St. Bonaventure University *M*
St. Francis College *A, B*
St. John Fisher College *B, M*
St. John's University *C, A, B, M*
St. Joseph's College *B*
St. Joseph's College: Suffolk
    Campus *B*
St. Thomas Aquinas College *B, M*
State University of New York
    Albany *B, M*
    Binghamton *M*
    Buffalo *B, M, D*
    College at Brockport *B*
    College at Buffalo *B*
    College at Fredonia *B*
    College at Geneseo *B*
    College at Old Westbury *B*
    College at Plattsburgh *B*

    College at Potsdam *B*
College of Agriculture and
    Technology at Cobleskill *A*
College of Agriculture and
    Technology at Morrisville *A*
College of Technology at
    Alfred *A*
College of Technology at
    Canton *A, B*
College of Technology at Delhi *A, B*
Empire State College *M*
Farmingdale *C, A, B*
Institute of Technology at
    Utica/Rome *B, M*
Maritime College *B*
New Paltz *B, M*
Oswego *B, M*
Stony Brook *B, M*
Suffolk County Community College *A*
Sullivan County Community
    College *A*
Syracuse University *B, M, D*
Taylor Business Institute *A*
Tompkins-Cortland Community
    College *C, A*
Touro College *A, B, D*
Trocaire College *A*
Ulster County Community College *A*
United States Military Academy *B*
University of Rochester *M, D*
Utica College *B*
Utica School of Commerce *A*
Villa Maria College of Buffalo *A*
Wagner College *B, M*
Westchester Community College *A*
Yeshiva University *B*

North Carolina

Alamance Community College *C, A*
Appalachian State University *B, M*
Asheville-Buncombe Technical
    Community College *A*
Barton College *B*
Beaufort County Community
    College *C, A*
Belmont Abbey College *B*
Bennett College *B*
Bladen Community College *C, A*
Brevard College *B*
Brunswick Community College *A*
Caldwell Community College and
    Technical Institute *A*
Campbell University *B, M*
Cape Fear Community College *C, A*
Catawba College *B*
Catawba Valley Community
    College *C, A*
Central Carolina Community
    College *A*
Central Piedmont Community
    College *C, A*
Chowan College *B*
Cleveland Community College *C, A*
Coastal Carolina Community
    College *A*
College of the Albemarle *A*
Craven Community College *A*
Davidson County Community
    College *C, A*
DeVry University: Charlotte *B, M*
Duke University *M, D*
Durham Technical Community
    College *A*
East Carolina University *B, M*
Edgecombe Community College *A*
Elizabeth City State University *B*
Elon University *B, M*
Fayetteville State University *B, M*
Fayetteville Technical Community
    College *C, A*
Forsyth Technical Community
    College *A*
Gardner-Webb University *B, M*
Gaston College *A*

Guilford College *C, B*
Guilford Technical Community
 College *C, A*
Halifax Community College *A*
Haywood Community College *C, A*
High Point University *B, M*
Isothermal Community College *C, A*
James Sprunt Community College *A*
John Wesley College *B*
Johnson & Wales University *A*
Johnson C. Smith University *B*
Johnston Community College *A*
Lees-McRae College *B*
Lenoir Community College *C, A*
Livingstone College *B*
Louisburg College *A*
Mars Hill College *B*
Martin Community College *C, A*
Mayland Community College *A*
Meredith College *B, M*
Methodist College *A, B*
Miller-Motte Technical College *C, A, B*
Mitchell Community College *A*
Montgomery Community College *C, A*
Montreat College *A, B, M*
Mount Olive College *A, B*
Nash Community College *A*
North Carolina Agricultural and
 Technical State University *B*
North Carolina Central
 University *B, M*
North Carolina State University *B, M*
North Carolina Wesleyan College *B*
Pamlico Community College *A*
Peace College *A, B*
Pfeiffer University *B, M*
Piedmont Community College *A*
Pitt Community College *C, A*
Queens University of Charlotte *B, M*
Randolph Community College *A*
Richmond Community College *C, A*
Roanoke-Chowan Community
 College *A*
Robeson Community College *A*
Rockingham Community College *A*
Rowan-Cabarrus Community
 College *C, A*
St. Andrews Presbyterian College *B*
St. Augustine's College *B*
Salem College *B*
Sampson Community College *A*
Sandhills Community College *A*
Shaw University *A, B*
South College *A*
South Piedmont Community
 College *C, A*
Southeastern Community College *A*
Southwestern Community
 College *C, A*
Stanly Community College *C, A*
Surry Community College *C, A*
Tri-County Community College *A*
University of North Carolina
 Asheville *B*
 Chapel Hill *B, M, D*
 Charlotte *B, M*
 Greensboro *B, M*
 Pembroke *B, M*
 Wilmington *B, M*
Vance-Granville Community
 College *A*
Wake Forest University *M*
Warren Wilson College *B*
Wayne Community College *A*
Western Carolina University *B, M*
Western Piedmont Community
 College *C, A*
Wilkes Community College *C, A*
Wilson Technical Community
 College *C, A*
Wingate University *B, M*
Winston-Salem State University *B, M*

North Dakota

Aakers College: Fargo *C, A*
Dickinson State University *B*
Jamestown College *B*
Lake Region State College *C, A*
Mayville State University *B*
Minot State University *B*
North Dakota State College of
 Science *A*
North Dakota State University *B, M*
Sitting Bull College *A*
Turtle Mountain Community
 College *A*
University of Mary *A, B, M*
University of North Dakota *M*
Valley City State University *B*

Ohio

AEC Southern Ohio College
 Brown Mackie College: Akron *C, A*
Antioch College *B*
Ashland University *C, B, M*
Baldwin-Wallace College *B, M*
Bluffton University *B, M*
Bowling Green State University *M*
Bowling Green State University:
 Firelands College *C, A*
Bryant & Stratton College
 Parma *B*
Capital University *B, M*
Case Western Reserve
 University *B, M, D*
Cedarville University *B*
Central Ohio Technical College *A*
Chatfield College *A*
Cincinnati State Technical and
 Community College *C, A*
Circleville Bible College *B*
Cleveland State University *M, D*
College of Mount St. Joseph *A, B, M*
Columbus State Community
 College *C, A*
Cuyahoga Community College
 Metropolitan Campus *A*
David N. Myers University *B, M*
Davis College *A*
DeVry University
 Columbus *B, M*
Defiance College *A, B, M*
Edison State Community College *A*
Franciscan University of
 Steubenville *A, B, M*
Gallipolis Career College *A*
Heidelberg College *B, M*
Hiram College *B*
James A. Rhodes State College *C, A*
Jefferson Community College *C, A*
John Carroll University *B, M*
Kent State University *B, M*
Lake Erie College *B, M*
Lakeland Community College *C, A*
Lourdes College *B*
Malone College *B, M*
Marion Technical College *C, A*
Miami University
 Hamilton Campus *A*
 Oxford Campus *C, A, B, M*
Mount Union College *B*
Mount Vernon Nazarene
 University *A, B, M*
Ohio Business College: Sandusky *A*
Ohio Dominican University *C, A, B, M*
Ohio Northern University *B*
Ohio State University
 Agricultural Technical Institute *A*
 Columbus Campus *M, D*
 Mansfield Campus *B*
 Marion Campus *B*
 Newark Campus *B*
Ohio University *A, B, M*
Ohio University
 Chillicothe Campus *A, B, M*
 Southern Campus at Ironton *A, B*
 Zanesville Campus *M*

Otterbein College *B*
Owens Community College
 Toledo *A*
Shawnee State University *A, B*
Sinclair Community College *A*
Southeastern Business College *A*
Southeastern Business College:
 Lancaster *A*
Southeastern Business College: New
 Boston *A*
Southern State Community College *A*
Southwestern College of Business
 Southwestern College: Franklin *A*
Stark State College of Technology *A*
Tiffin University *A, B, M*
Trumbull Business College *C, A*
Union Institute & University *B*
University of Akron *C, A*
University of Akron: Wayne College *A*
University of Cincinnati *C, A, B, M, D*
University of Cincinnati
 Clermont College *A*
 Raymond Walters College *A*
University of Dayton *B, M*
University of Findlay *B, M*
University of Northwestern Ohio *A, B*
University of Rio Grande *A, B*
University of Toledo *A, B, M, D*
Ursuline College *B*
Walsh University *A, B, M*
Washington State Community
 College *A*
Wilmington College *B*
Wittenberg University *B*
Wright State University *B, M*
Wright State University: Lake
 Campus *A*
Xavier University *A, B, M*
Youngstown State University *A, B, M*
Zane State College *C, A*

Oklahoma

Bacone College *A, B*
Cameron University *B, M*
Carl Albert State College *A*
Connors State College *A*
East Central University *B*
Eastern Oklahoma State College *A*
Mid-America Christian University *B*
Murray State College *A*
Northeastern Oklahoma Agricultural
 and Mechanical College *A*
Northeastern State University *B, M*
Northwestern Oklahoma State
 University *B*
Oklahoma Baptist University *B*
Oklahoma Christian University *B, M*
Oklahoma City University *B, M*
Oklahoma Panhandle State
 University *A, B*
Oklahoma State University *B, M, D*
Oklahoma State University
 Oklahoma City *A*
 Okmulgee *A*
Oklahoma Wesleyan University *B*
Oral Roberts University *B, M*
Redlands Community College *A*
Rogers State University *A, B*
Rose State College *C, A*
St. Gregory's University *A, B*
Seminole State College *A*
Southeastern Oklahoma State
 University *B, M*
Southern Nazarene University *A, B, M*
Southwestern Christian University *B*
Southwestern Oklahoma State
 University *B, M*
Tulsa Community College *A*
University of Central Oklahoma *B, M*
University of Oklahoma *B, M, D*
University of Science and Arts of
 Oklahoma *B, T*
University of Tulsa *B, M*
Western Oklahoma State College *A*

Oregon

Blue Mountain Community College *A*
Central Oregon Community
 College *A*
Chemeketa Community College *A*
Clatsop Community College *A*
Concordia University *B*
Corban College *A, B*
DeVry University: Portland *B, M*
Eastern Oregon University *B, M*
Everest College: Portland *C, A*
George Fox University *B, M*
Lane Community College *C*
Linn-Benton Community College *A*
Marylhurst University *B, M*
Northwest Christian College *B, M*
Oregon Institute of Technology *B*
Oregon State University *B, M*
Pacific University *B*
Pioneer Pacific College *A, B*
Pioneer Pacific College: Springfield *A*
Portland Community College *A*
Portland State University *B, D*
Rogue Community College *C, A*
Southern Oregon University *B, M*
Southwestern Oregon Community
 College *A*
Treasure Valley Community College *A*
University of Oregon *M, D*
University of Portland *B, M*
Warner Pacific College *B*
Willamette University *M*

Pennsylvania

Academy of Medical Arts and
 Business *C, A*
Albright College *B*
Alvernia College *B*
Arcadia University *C, B, M*
Berean Institute *A*
Berks Technical Institute *A*
Bloomsburg University of
 Pennsylvania *B, M*
Bucknell University *B*
Bucks County Community
 College *C, A*
Business Institute of Pennsylvania *A*
Business Institute of Pennsylvania
 Meadville *A*
Butler County Community College *A*
Cabrini College *C, B*
California University of
 Pennsylvania *B*
Cambria-Rowe Business College *A*
Carlow University *B*
Carnegie Mellon University *B, M*
Cedar Crest College *B*
Central Pennsylvania College *A, B*
Chatham College *B, M*
Chestnut Hill College *C, A, B*
Cheyney University of Pennsylvania *B*
Clarion University of
 Pennsylvania *A, B, M*
College Misericordia *B*
Community College of Allegheny
 County *C, A*
Community College of Beaver
 County *A*
Community College of
 Philadelphia *C, A*
Consolidated School of Business
 Lancaster *A*
 York *A*
DeSales University *B, M*
Delaware County Community
 College *A*
Delaware Valley College *B*
Douglas Education Center *A*
Drexel University *B, M, D*
DuBois Business College *A*
Duquesne University *M*
East Stroudsburg University of
 Pennsylvania *B*
Eastern University *B, M*

Edinboro University of
   Pennsylvania A, B
Elizabethtown College C, A, B
Erie Business Center South A
Franklin & Marshall College B
Gannon University B, M
Geneva College A, B, M
Gettysburg College B
Grove City College B
Gwynedd-Mercy College A, B
Harcum College A
Harrisburg Area Community
   College C, A
Holy Family University C, B
ICM School of Business & Medical
   Careers A
Immaculata University C, A, B, M
Indiana University of
   Pennsylvania A, B, M
Juniata College B
Keystone College A, B
King's College A, B
Kutztown University of
   Pennsylvania B, M
La Salle University A, B, M
Lackawanna College A
Lebanon Valley College C, A, B, M
Lehigh Carbon Community
   College C, A
Lehigh University M
Lehigh Valley College A
Lincoln University B
Lock Haven University of
   Pennsylvania A, B
Luzerne County Community
   College A
Lycoming College B
Manor College A
Mansfield University of
   Pennsylvania A, B
Marywood University B, M
McCann School of Business
   Pottsville A
Mercyhurst College A, B
Messiah College B
Metropolitan Career Center C, A
Millersville University of
   Pennsylvania B, M
Montgomery County Community
   College C, A
Moravian College B, M
Mount Aloysius College A, B
Muhlenberg College C, A, B
Neumann College C, B
Newport Business Institute A
Newport Business Institute A
Northampton County Area
   Community College A
Orleans Technical Institute - Center
   City Campus A
Peirce College C, A, B
Penn State
   Abington B
   Altoona B
   Beaver B
   Berks B
   Delaware County B
   Dubois B
   Erie, The Behrend College B, M
   Fayette B
   Harrisburg B, M
   Hazleton B
   Lehigh Valley B
   McKeesport B
   Mont Alto B
   New Kensington A, B
   Schuylkill - Capital College A, B
   University Park C, B, M, D
   Wilkes-Barre A, B
   Worthington Scranton B
   York B
Pennsylvania College of
   Technology A, B

Pennsylvania Highlands Community
   College A
Pennsylvania Institute of
   Technology A
Pennsylvania School of Business C, A
Philadelphia Biblical University B
Philadelphia University A, B, M
Pittsburgh Technical Institute A
Point Park University C, A, B, M
Reading Area Community College A
Restaurant School A
Robert Morris University C, B, M
Rosemont College B, M
St. Francis University A, B, M
St. Joseph's University C, A, B, M
St. Vincent College C, B
Seton Hill University B, M
Shippensburg University of
   Pennsylvania B, M
Slippery Rock University of
   Pennsylvania C, B
South Hills School of Business &
   Technology C, A
Susquehanna University B
Temple University B, M, D
Thiel College B
Thompson Institute A
Tri-State Business Institute A
University of Pennsylvania B, M, D
University of Pittsburgh B, M, D
University of Pittsburgh
   Greensburg B
University of Scranton A, B, M
University of the Sciences in
   Philadelphia M
Valley Forge Christian College B
Villanova University B, M
Waynesburg College B, M
West Chester University of
   Pennsylvania B, M
Western School of Health and
   Business Careers C, A
Western School of Health and
   Business Careers
   Monroeville A
Westminster College B
Westmoreland County Community
   College C, A
Widener University A, B, M
Wilkes University B, M
Wilson College A, B
York College of Pennsylvania B, M
York Technical Institute A
Yorktowne Business Institute A

Puerto Rico

American University of Puerto Rico B
Atlantic College A, B
Bayamon Central University B, M
Columbia College A, B, M
Electronic Data Processing College:
   San Sebastian A
Humacao Community College A
Inter American University of Puerto
   Rico
   Aguadilla Campus A, B
   Arecibo Campus A, B
   Barranquitas Campus A, B
   Bayamon Campus A, B
   Fajardo Campus B
   Guayama Campus A, B
   Ponce Campus A, B
   San German Campus A, B, M
National College of Business &
   Technology: Arecibo A
Pontifical Catholic University of
   Puerto Rico B, M, D
Turabo University A, B, M
Universidad Metropolitana B, M
Universidad Politecnica de Puerto
   Rico B, M
Universidad del Este A, B, M
University of Puerto Rico
   Arecibo B

Bayamon University College A
Carolina Regional College B
Cayey University College B
Humacao A, B
Mayaguez B, M
Ponce A, B
Rio Piedras B, M
Utuado A
University of the Sacred Heart B

Rhode Island

Bryant University B, M
Community College of Rhode
   Island A
Johnson & Wales University A, B
Providence College C, A, B, M
Rhode Island College B, M
Roger Williams University B
Salve Regina University A, B, M
University of Rhode Island B, M, D

South Carolina

Aiken Technical College C, A
Allen University B
Anderson University B
Benedict College B
Charleston Southern University B, M
The Citadel B, M
Claflin University B, M
Clemson University B, M
Coastal Carolina University B, M
Coker College B
College of Charleston B
Columbia College B
Erskine College B
Florence-Darlington Technical
   College C
Forrest Junior College A
Francis Marion University B, M
Furman University B
Greenville Technical College C, A
Lander University C, B
Limestone College A, B
Midlands Technical College A
Miller-Motte Technical College A
Morris College B
Newberry College B
North Greenville College B
Northeastern Technical College A
Piedmont Technical College C
Presbyterian College B
South Carolina State University B
South University A, M
Southern Wesleyan University B, M
Spartanburg Technical College A
Technical College of the
   Lowcountry C
Tri-County Technical College C, A
Trident Technical College A
University of South Carolina B, M, D
University of South Carolina
   Aiken B
   Beaufort B
   Lancaster A
   Sumter B
   Upstate B
Voorhees College B
Winthrop University B, M
York Technical College A

South Dakota

Augustana College B
Black Hills State University B, M
Dakota State University A, B, T
Kilian Community College A
Lake Area Technical Institute A
Mount Marty College C, A, B, M
Northern State University A, B
Oglala Lakota College A, B
Presentation College A, B
Sisseton Wahpeton College C, A
Southeast Technical Institute A
University of Sioux Falls A, B
University of South Dakota B, M

Tennessee

American Baptist College of ABT
   Seminary A, B
Aquinas College A, B
Austin Peay State University A, M
Belmont University M
Bethel College B
Bryan College B
Carson-Newman College B
Christian Brothers University B, M
Cleveland State Community College A
Columbia State Community College C
Crichton College B
Dyersburg State Community
   College A
East Tennessee State University B, M
Fisk University B
Free Will Baptist Bible College B
Freed-Hardeman University B, M
Hiwassee College A
Jackson State Community College A
King College B
Lambuth University B
LeMoyne-Owen College B
Lee University B
Lincoln Memorial University B, M
Lipscomb University B, M
Maryville College B
Middle Tennessee State
   University C, B, M
Miller-Motte Technical College A
Milligan College B
Motlow State Community College A
Nashville State Community College A
National College of Business &
   Technology
   Tennessee C, A
Northeast State Technical Community
   College A
Pellissippi State Technical Community
   College A
Rhodes College B
Roane State Community College A
South College B
Southern Adventist University B, M
Southwest Tennessee Community
   College A
Tennessee State University B, M
Tennessee Temple University A, B
Tennessee Wesleyan College B
Trevecca Nazarene University B, M
Tusculum College B, M
Union University B, M
University of Memphis B, M, D
University of Tennessee
   Chattanooga B, M
   Knoxville B, M, D
   Martin B, M
Vanderbilt University D
Volunteer State Community College A

Texas

Abilene Christian University B
Alvin Community College C, A
Amberton University B, M
Angelina College C, A
Angelo State University B, M
Austin Business College C, A
Austin Community College C, A
Baylor University B, M
Brazosport College C, A
Brookhaven College A
Cedar Valley College A
Central Texas College C, A
Coastal Bend College A
College of the Mainland A
Collin County Community College
   District C, A
Concordia University at Austin B
Dallas Baptist University A, B, M
Dallas Christian College B
Del Mar College A
Eastfield College A
El Centro College C, A

El Paso Community College *C, A*
Frank Phillips College *A*
Galveston College *C, A*
Hardin-Simmons University *B, M*
Hill College *A*
Houston Baptist University *B, M*
Houston Community College
　System *C, A*
Howard Payne University *B*
Huston-Tillotson College *B*
Jarvis Christian College *B, T*
Kilgore College *C, A*
Lamar State College at Orange *C, A*
Lamar State College at Port Arthur *A*
Lamar University *B, M*
LeTourneau University *B, M*
Lee College *C, A*
Lubbock Christian University *B, T*
MTI College of Business and
　Technology *C, A*
McMurry University *B, T*
Midland College *A*
Midwestern State University *B, M*
Mountain View College *C, A*
Navarro College *C, A*
North Harris Montgomery
　Community College District *C, A*
North Lake College *A*
Northeast Texas Community
　College *C, A*
Northwest Vista College *A*
Northwood University: Texas
　Campus *A, B*
Odessa College *C, A*
Our Lady of the Lake University of San
　Antonio *B, M*
Palo Alto College *A*
Paris Junior College *A*
Prairie View A&M University *B, M*
Remington College
　Dallas *C, A*
Rice University *B, M*
Richland College *A*
St. Edward's University *B, M*
St. Mary's University *M*
St. Philip's College *C, A*
Sam Houston State University *B, M*
San Antonio College *C, A*
San Jacinto College
　North *C, A*
South Plains College *A*
South Texas College *C, A*
Southern Methodist University *B, M*
Southwestern Adventist
　University *B, M*
Southwestern Assemblies of God
　University *A, B*
Stephen F. Austin State University *B, M*
Sul Ross State University *B, M*
Tarleton State University *B, M*
Tarrant County College *C, A*
Texarkana College *C, A*
Texas A&M University *M, D*
Texas A&M University
　Commerce *B, M*
　Galveston *B*
　Kingsville *M*
　Texarkana *B, M*
Texas Christian University *M*
Texas College *B*
Texas Lutheran University *B*
Texas Southern University *M*
Texas Southmost College *A*
Texas State University: San
　Marcos *B, M*
Texas Tech University *B, M, D*
Texas Wesleyan University *B, M*
Texas Woman's University *B, M*
Trinity University *B*
Trinity Valley Community College *A*
Tyler Junior College *C, A*
University of Dallas *B, M*
University of Houston *M, D*

University of Houston
　Clear Lake *B, M*
　Downtown *B*
　Victoria *B, T*
University of Mary
　Hardin-Baylor *B, M, T*
University of North Texas *B, M*
University of St. Thomas *B, M*
University of Texas
　Arlington *B, M, D*
　Austin *B, D*
　Brownsville *B, M*
　Dallas *M, D*
　El Paso *B, M*
　Pan American *B, M*
　San Antonio *B, M*
　Tyler *B, M*
　of the Permian Basin *B, M*
University of the Incarnate Word *B, M*
Victoria College *C, A*
Wayland Baptist University *A, B, M*
West Texas A&M University *B, M*
Western Texas College *A*
Wharton County Junior College *A*
Wiley College *B*

Utah

Brigham Young University *B, M*
College of Eastern Utah *A*
Dixie State College of Utah *A, B*
Everest College: Salt Lake City *C, A*
LDS Business College *A*
Neumont University *M*
Provo College *A*
Salt Lake Community College *C, A*
Snow College *A*
Southern Utah University *B, M*
Stevens-Henager College *A, B*
Stevens-Henager College of
　Business *C, A, B, M*
University of Utah *B, M, D*
Utah Career College *A*
Utah State University *B, M*
Utah Valley State College *C, A, B*
Weber State University *B, M*
Westminster College *B, M*

Vermont

Castleton State College *B*
Champlain College *C, A, B*
College of St. Joseph in Vermont *A, B*
Goddard College *B*
Green Mountain College *B, M*
Johnson State College *A, B*
Landmark College *A*
Lyndon State College *A, B*
Norwich University *B, M*
St. Michael's College *B, M*
Southern Vermont College *B*
University of Vermont *B, M*
Vermont Technical College *A*

Virginia

Averett University *A, B, M*
Blue Ridge Community College *A*
Bluefield College *B*
Bridgewater College *B*
Bryant & Stratton College: Virginia
　Beach *A, B*
Central Virginia Community
　College *A*
Christopher Newport University *B*
College of William and Mary *B, M*
Dabney S. Lancaster Community
　College *A*
Danville Community College *A*
DeVry University
　Arlington *B, M*
Eastern Mennonite University *B, M*
Eastern Shore Community College *A*
Emory & Henry College *B*
Ferrum College *B*
George Mason University *B, M*
Germanna Community College *A*

Hampton University *B, M*
J. Sargeant Reynolds Community
　College *C, A*
James Madison University *B, M*
Liberty University *B, M*
Longwood University *B*
Lord Fairfax Community College *A*
Lynchburg College *B, M*
Mary Baldwin College *B*
Marymount University *C, B, M*
Mountain Empire Community
　College *A*
National College of Business &
　Technology
　Bluefield *C, A*
　Charlottesville *C, A*
　Danville *C, A*
　Harrisonburg *C, A*
　Lynchburg *C, A*
　Martinsville *C, A*
　Salem *C, A, B, M*
New River Community College *A*
Northern Virginia Community
　College *A*
Old Dominion University *B, M, D*
Patrick Henry Community College *A*
Paul D. Camp Community College *A*
Piedmont Virginia Community
　College *A*
Potomac College *B*
Radford University *B, M*
Rappahannock Community College *A*
Regent University *B, M*
Roanoke College *B*
St. Paul's College *B*
Shenandoah University *B, M*
Southside Virginia Community
　College *A*
Southwest Virginia Community
　College *A*
Thomas Nelson Community
　College *A*
Tidewater Community College *A*
University of Mary Washington *B*
University of Northern
　Virginia *B, M, D*
University of Richmond *B, M*
University of Virginia *M, D*
University of Virginia's College at
　Wise *B*
Virginia Commonwealth
　University *B, M, D*
Virginia Highlands Community
　College *A*
Virginia Intermont College *B*
Virginia Polytechnic Institute and
　State University *B, M*
Virginia State University *B*
Virginia Union University *B*
Virginia Wesleyan College *B*
Virginia Western Community
　College *A*
Washington and Lee University *B*
Wytheville Community College *A*

Washington

Antioch University Seattle *M*
Bellevue Community College *C, A*
Central Washington University *B*
Centralia College *A*
City University *C, A, B, M*
Clark College *C, A*
Crown College *A, B*
Eastern Washington University *B, M*
Edmonds Community College *C, A*
Everett Community College *C, A*
Evergreen State College *B*
Gonzaga University *B, M*
Grays Harbor College *C, A*
Henry Cogswell College *B*
Heritage University *C, B*
Highline Community College *C, A*
Lower Columbia College *A*
Northwest University *B, M*

Olympic College *C, A*
Pacific Lutheran University *B, M*
Peninsula College *C, A*
Pierce College *C, A*
Saint Martin's University *B, M*
Seattle Pacific University *B, M*
Seattle University *B, M*
Shoreline Community College *A*
Skagit Valley College *C, A*
Spokane Community College *C, A*
Spokane Falls Community
　College *C, A*
University of Puget Sound *B*
University of Washington *B, M, D*
Walla Walla College *B*
Walla Walla Community College *C, A*
Washington State University *B, M, D*
Wenatchee Valley College *C, A*
Western Washington University *B, M*
Whatcom Community College *C*
Whitworth College *B, M*
Yakima Valley Community College *A*

West Virginia

Alderson-Broaddus College *A, B*
Bluefield State College *B*
Concord University *B*
Davis and Elkins College *A, B*
Eastern West Virginia Community and
　Technical College *C, A*
Glenville State College *B*
Marshall University *B*
Mountain State University *C, A, B*
Ohio Valley University *B*
Potomac State College of West Virginia
　University *A*
Salem International University *A, B*
Shepherd University *B, M*
Southern West Virginia Community
　and Technical College *A*
University of Charleston *A, B, M*
Valley College of Technology *A*
West Liberty State College *B*
West Virginia Business College *A*
West Virginia Business College *A*
West Virginia Northern Community
　College *A*
West Virginia State University *B*
West Virginia University *B*
West Virginia University Institute of
　Technology *A, B*
West Virginia University at
　Parkersburg *B*
West Virginia Wesleyan College *B, M*
Wheeling Jesuit University *B, M*

Wisconsin

Alverno College *B*
Beloit College *B*
Cardinal Stritch University *B, M*
Carroll College *B*
Carthage College *B*
College of Menominee Nation *A*
Concordia University Wisconsin *B, M*
DeVry University: Milwaukee *B, M*
Edgewood College *B, M*
Herzing College *A, B*
Lakeland College *B, M*
Madison Area Technical College *A*
Maranatha Baptist Bible College *B*
Marian College of Fond du Lac *B, M*
Marquette University *B, M*
Mid-State Technical College *A*
Milwaukee Area Technical College *A*
Milwaukee School of
　Engineering *B, M*
Mount Mary College *B*
Nicolet Area Technical College *A*
Northeast Wisconsin Technical
　College *A*
Northland College *B*
Ripon College *B*
Silver Lake College *B*

University of Wisconsin
Eau Claire B, M
Green Bay B
La Crosse B, M
Madison B, M
Milwaukee M
Oshkosh B
Parkside B, M
Platteville C, B
River Falls B
Stevens Point B
Stout B
Superior B
Whitewater B, M
Viterbo University B, M
Western Wisconsin Technical
College A

Wyoming

Casper College C, A
Central Wyoming College A
Eastern Wyoming College A
Laramie County Community
College A
Northwest College A
Sheridan College A
University of Wyoming B, M
Western Wyoming Community
College A

Business/commerce

Alabama

Alabama Agricultural and Mechanical
University B
Alabama Southern Community
College A
Andrew Jackson University C, A, B
Auburn University at
Montgomery B, M
Birmingham-Southern College B
Central Alabama Community
College C, A
Enterprise-Ozark Community
College A
Faulkner University B
Huntingdon College B
Jefferson State Community
College C, A
Judson College B
Northeast Alabama Community
College A
Troy University B
University of Mobile B, M
University of South Alabama B
Wallace State Community College at
Hanceville A

Alaska

University of Alaska
Anchorage C, A
Southeast B

Arizona

American Indian College of the
Assemblies of God A
Arizona Western College A
Central Arizona College A
Chandler-Gilbert Community College
Pecos A
Gateway Community College A
Glendale Community College A
Northland Pioneer College A
Paradise Valley Community
College C, A
Phoenix College A
Prescott College B, M
Rio Salado College C, A
Scottsdale Community College C, A
University of Arizona B
Western International University B

Arkansas

Arkansas Northeastern College C, A
Arkansas State University
Beebe A
Arkansas State University: Newport A
Henderson State University B, M
North Arkansas College A
Ouachita Technical College A
Phillips Community College of the
University of Arkansas A
Pulaski Technical College A
South Arkansas Community College A
Southeast Arkansas College C, A
Southern Arkansas University A
University of Arkansas B
University of Arkansas
Community College at
Batesville C, A
Community College at Hope A
Cossatot Community College of the
C, A
Little Rock B
Monticello B
University of Arkansas Community
College at Morrilton A
University of Central Arkansas B

California

Allan Hancock College A
Antelope Valley College C, A
Azusa Pacific University B
Barstow College C, A
Bethany University B
Butte College C, A
Cabrillo College C, A
California Lutheran University B
California Polytechnic State
University: San Luis Obispo M
California State University
Dominguez Hills B
East Bay B
Fresno B, M
Fullerton B, M
Long Beach B
Monterey Bay B
Sacramento B, M
Canada College C, A
Cerritos Community College A
Cerro Coso Community College A
Chabot College A
Citrus College A
Coastline Community College C, A
College of Alameda C, A
College of Marin: Kentfield A
College of San Mateo C, A
College of the Redwoods A
College of the Sequoias A
Columbia College A
Cosumnes River College A
Cuesta College C, A
Cypress College A
DeVry University
Fremont B, M
Pomona B, M
West Hills B, M
Dominican University of California B
El Camino College C, A
Fresno City College C, A
Fresno Pacific University B
Gavilan Community College C, A
Glendale Community College A
Golden West College C, A
Grossmont Community College C, A
Heald College
Salinas A
Humboldt State University B
Humphreys College A, B
Irvine Valley College A
John F. Kennedy University C
Lake Tahoe Community College A
Laney College C, A
Lassen College A
Lincoln University B, M
Long Beach City College C, A

Los Angeles Harbor College C, A
Los Angeles Pierce College C, A
Los Angeles Southwest College A
Los Angeles Trade and Technical
College A
Los Angeles Valley College C, A
Loyola Marymount University B, M
Mendocino College A
Merced College A
Merritt College C, A
Mills College B
Mission College C, A
Modesto Junior College A
Monterey Peninsula College A
Mount St. Mary's College B
Mount San Antonio College A
Napa Valley College A
National University B, M
Notre Dame de Namur University B
Ohlone College A
Orange Coast College C, A
Pacific Union College B
Palomar College A
Pasadena City College A
Platt College
Cerritos C, A
Porterville College A
Rio Hondo College C
Riverside Community College C, A
Sacramento City College A
Saddleback College A
St. Mary's College of California B, M
San Diego City College C, A
San Diego Mesa College C, A
San Joaquin Delta College C, A
San Jose City College C
Santa Ana College A
Santa Barbara Business College C, A
Santa Barbara Business College
Bakersfield C, A
Santa Maria C, A
Santa Barbara City College C, A
Santa Monica College C, A
Shasta College A
Sierra College C, A
Taft College A
University of Judaism B
University of Redlands B
University of San Francisco B
Vanguard University of Southern
California B
Ventura College C, A
Victor Valley College A
West Hills Community College C, A
West Los Angeles College C, A
West Valley College A
Westmont College B
Whittier College B

Colorado

Adams State College B
Arapahoe Community College C
Colorado Mountain College
Alpine Campus C, A
Spring Valley Campus C, A
Timberline Campus C, A
Colorado State University
Pueblo B, M
Community College of Aurora C, A
DeVry University: Colorado
Springs B, M
Jones International University C, B, M
Morgan Community College A
Red Rocks Community College A
Regis University B
Trinidad State Junior College A
University of Colorado
Denver and Health Sciences
Center B, M
University of Denver B, M
Westwood College of Technology B

Connecticut

Briarwood College A

Gibbs College C, A
Goodwin College A
Housatonic Community College C, A
Post University A, B
Quinnipiac University B, M
Sacred Heart University A, B, M
University of Bridgeport B, M
University of Connecticut B, M, D
Western Connecticut State
University M

Delaware

Delaware Technical and Community
College
Owens Campus C, A
Stanton/Wilmington Campus C, A
Terry Campus C, A
Goldey-Beacom College M

District of Columbia

Catholic University of America B
Gallaudet University B
Southeastern University A, B

Florida

Broward Community College A
Carlos Albizu University B
Florida Metropolitan University
Brandon Campus A, B, M
Orlando College North A, B
Pompano Beach A, B
Tampa College A, B
Florida Southern College B, M
Herzing College
Orlando A, B
Hillsborough Community College A
Jacksonville University B
Lake City Community College A
Manatee Community College A
New England Institute of
Technology A
Okaloosa-Walton College A
Palm Beach Community College A
Pensacola Junior College A
Remington College
Jacksonville A
St. Leo University A, M
St. Petersburg College A
St. Thomas University M
Schiller International University B
Tallahassee Community College A
University of Central Florida B, M
University of Florida B, M, D
University of South Florida B, M
Webber International University B

Georgia

Agnes Scott College B
Andrew College A
Atlanta Christian College A, B
Bainbridge College A
Brown Mackie College: Atlanta C
Chattahoochee Technical College A
Clayton State University B
Columbus State University B, M
Covenant College B
Dalton State College A
Darton College C, A
Emory University B, M, D
Fort Valley State University B
Gainesville State College A
Georgia College and State
University B, M
Georgia Highlands College A
Georgia Southern University B, M
Georgia Southwestern State
University B
LaGrange College B
Life University B
Macon State College C, A
Mercer University B, M
Reinhardt College B
South Georgia College C, A

Thomas University A, B, M
Truett-McConnell College A
University of Georgia B
Waycross College C
Young Harris College A

Hawaii

Hawaii Pacific University A, B
University of Hawaii
  Hilo B
  Kapiolani Community College A
  Manoa B
  Maui Community College C, A
  Windward Community College C

Idaho

College of Southern Idaho A
Idaho State University A, B

Illinois

Augustana College B
Aurora University B
Black Hawk College
  East Campus A
City Colleges of Chicago
  Malcolm X College A
  Olive-Harvey College C, A
  Richard J. Daley College C, A
Concordia University B
DePaul University B, M
DeVry University
  Chicago B
Eureka College B
Highland Community College C, A
Illinois Central College A
Illinois College B
Illinois Institute of
  Technology B, M, D
John Wood Community College A
Judson College B
Kaskaskia College A
Kishwaukee College A
Lake Forest College B
Lake Land College A
Lewis University B
Lewis and Clark Community
  College A
Lincoln Land Community College A
MacCormac College A
Midstate College A
Moraine Valley Community
  College C, A
North Central College B
North Park University B, M
Northeastern Illinois University B
Northern Illinois University B
Northwestern University C, M
Olivet Nazarene University A, B
Parkland College A
Richland Community College A
Rock Valley College C, A
Rockford Business College A
Rockford College B
Roosevelt University B, M
St. Augustine College A
St. Xavier University B
Sauk Valley Community College A
South Suburban College of Cook
  County A
Southwestern Illinois College A
Spoon River College A
Springfield College in Illinois A
Trinity Christian College B
Trinity International University B
University of Chicago M, D
University of Illinois
  Urbana-Champaign B, M, D
University of St. Francis M
William Rainey Harper College C, A

Indiana

Anderson University A
Ball State University B, M

Bethel College A
Brown Mackie College: Fort Wayne C
Calumet College of St. Joseph B
Franklin College B
Goshen College C, B
Grace College B
Huntington University B
Indiana Institute of
  Technology A, B, M
Indiana University
  Bloomington C, B, M, D
  Kokomo A, B, M
  Northwest A, B, M
  South Bend A, B, M
  Southeast A, B, M
Indiana University-Purdue University
  Indianapolis C, B, M
International Business College B
Ivy Tech State College
  Ivy Tech Community College:
    Bloomington A
Manchester College A, B
Marian College A, B
Martin University B
Oakland City University A, B
Purdue University
  Calumet A, B
  North Central Campus C, A, B
St. Joseph's College B
St. Mary-of-the-Woods College A, B
University of Evansville B
University of Notre Dame B
University of Southern Indiana B, M
Vincennes University A

Iowa

AIB College of Business A
Ashford University B
Dordt College A, B
Drake University B
Ellsworth Community College A
Grand View College B
Hawkeye Community College A
Iowa State University B
Iowa Wesleyan College B
Kaplan University B
Loras College B
Marshalltown Community College A
Mount Mercy College B
Northeast Iowa Community
  College A
St. Ambrose University B
Southeastern Community College
  North Campus A
Southwestern Community College A
Upper Iowa University A, B
Waldorf College B

Kansas

Baker University B, T
Barclay College B
Barton County Community College A
Bethel College B
Central Christian College of
  Kansas A, B
Cloud County Community College A
Coffeyville Community College A
Colby Community College A
Cowley County Community
  College A
Dodge City Community College A
Donnelly College A
Fort Hays State University B
Fort Scott Community College A
Garden City Community College A
Haskell Indian Nations University A
Hesston College A
Highland Community College A
Hutchinson Community College A
Kansas State University C, B
Kansas Wesleyan University A, B, M
McPherson College T
MidAmerica Nazarene
  University A, B, M

Seward County Community
  College C, A
University of Kansas B, M, D
University of St. Mary B
Washburn University of Topeka B

Kentucky

Asbury College B
Berea College B
Brescia University A, B
Campbellsville University A, B
Eastern Kentucky University B, M
Georgetown College B
Kentucky State University B
Kentucky Wesleyan College B
Maysville Community College C, A
Morehead State University M
Murray State University A, B, M
Northern Kentucky
  University A, B, M
Owensboro Community College A
St. Catharine College A
Spalding University A, B
Thomas More College C, A, B, M
Transylvania University B
University of Kentucky B, M, D
University of Louisville M
University of the Cumberlands B
Western Kentucky University M, T

Louisiana

Baton Rouge Community College C, A
Bossier Parish Community College A
Loyola University New Orleans M
Nicholls State University A
Northwestern State University A
Tulane University C, A, B, M, D

Maine

Eastern Maine Community College A
Husson College B, M
Maine Maritime Academy B, M
Thomas College A
University of Maine B
University of Maine
  Fort Kent A, B
  Machias B
University of Southern Maine B, M

Maryland

Allegany College of Maryland C, A
Anne Arundel Community
  College A
Baltimore City Community College A
Bowie State University B
Carroll Community College A
Cecil Community College A
Chesapeake College A
College of Notre Dame of Maryland B
College of Southern Maryland A
Community College of Baltimore
  County C, A
Garrett College A
Hagerstown Community College A
Harford Community College A
Loyola College in Maryland B
Morgan State University B
Mount St. Mary's University B
University of Baltimore B, M
University of Maryland
  College Park B, M, D
  Eastern Shore B
  University College M, D
Washington College B
Wor-Wic Community College A

Massachusetts

American International College B, M
Babson College B
Bay Path College B
Bentley College B, M
Berkshire Community College A
Clark University B, M

Dean College A
Eastern Nazarene College B
Endicott College A
Fitchburg State College C
Framingham State College B, M
Greenfield Community College A
Hampshire College B
Harvard College B, M
Massachusetts Institute of
  Technology B, M, D
New England College of Finance A
Nichols College M, T
Northeastern University B, M
Northern Essex Community
  College A
Quincy College C, A
Regis College B
Springfield Technical Community
  College A
Suffolk University B
University of Massachusetts
  Lowell A
Western New England College B
Westfield State College B

Michigan

Albion College B
Andrews University A
Baker College
  of Auburn Hills B
  of Cadillac A
  of Flint A
  of Jackson B
  of Muskegon A
  of Owosso A
  of Port Huron A, B
Bay de Noc Community College C
Calvin College B
Central Michigan University B
Davenport University A, B
Delta College A
Eastern Michigan University B
Finlandia University B
Glen Oaks Community College A
Gogebic Community College C, A
Grace Bible College A, B
Grand Rapids Community
  College C, A
Henry Ford Community College A
Hillsdale College B
Jackson Community College C, A
Kettering University B
Lake Superior State University A, B
Lansing Community College A
Macomb Community College C, A
Marygrove College A, B
Mott Community College A
North Central Michigan College C, A
Northern Michigan University A, B, T
Northwestern Michigan College A
Oakland University B
Olivet College B
Saginaw Valley State University B
St. Clair County Community
  College C, A
Schoolcraft College C, A
Siena Heights University A, B
Southwestern Michigan College C, A
University of Detroit Mercy B
Walsh College of Accountancy and
  Business Administration B
Wayne State University B, M
West Shore Community College A
Western Michigan University B

Minnesota

Brown College B
Capella University B, M, D
Concordia College: Moorhead B
Crown College A, B
Gustavus Adolphus College B
Lakeland Academy Division of Herzing
  College C, A

Mesabi Range Community and
Technical College *A*
Minnesota State University
Mankato *B*
Minnesota West Community and
Technical College: Worthington
Campus *A*
National American University
St. Paul *A, B*
Normandale Community College *C, A*
Northland Community & Technical
College *A*
Rasmussen College
Mankato *A*
Ridgewater College *A*
St. Cloud State University *B*
St. Paul College *C, A*
Vermilion Community College *A*
Winona State University *B, M*

Mississippi

Belhaven College *M*
Blue Mountain College *B*
Coahoma Community College *A*
Delta State University *B*
East Central Community College *A*
Itawamba Community College *A*
Mississippi Gulf Coast Community
College
Jefferson Davis Campus *A*

Missouri

Avila University *B*
Blue River Community College *A*
Central Methodist University *A*
Crowder College *C, A*
DeVry University
Kansas City *B*
Drury University *B*
Evangel University *B*
Hannibal-LaGrange College *B*
Harris-Stowe State University *B*
Jefferson College *C, A*
Lindenwood University *B, M*
Longview Community College *A*
Maple Woods Community College *A*
Maryville University of Saint
Louis *B, M*
Mineral Area College *C, A*
Missouri Southern State
University *A, B*
Missouri State University *B*
Missouri State University: West
Plains *A*
Northwest Missouri State
University *B*
Penn Valley Community College *A*
St. Louis Community College
St. Louis Community College at
Meramec *C, A*
Southwest Baptist University *A*
University of Missouri
Columbia *B, M, D*
Kansas City *B, M*
Rolla *B*
Washington University in St. Louis *B*
Webster University *B, M*

Montana

Carroll College *A*
Dawson Community College *A*
Flathead Valley Community
College *C, A*
Fort Belknap College *A*
Fort Peck Community College *A*
Little Big Horn College *A*
Montana State University
Billings *C, A, B*
Bozeman *B*
Montana Tech of the University of
Montana *A, B*
Stone Child College *A*
University of Montana: Missoula *B, M*

University of Montana:
Western *A, B, T*

Nebraska

Bellevue University *B, M*
Clarkson College *B, M*
Creighton University *M*
Little Priest Tribal College *A*
Metropolitan Community College *A*
Midland Lutheran College *B, T*
University of Nebraska
Omaha *B*
Western Nebraska Community
College *C, A*

Nevada

Community College of Southern
Nevada *A*
Great Basin College *A*
Truckee Meadows Community
College *C, A*
University of Nevada
Reno *B*

New Hampshire

Daniel Webster College *B*
Franklin Pierce College *B*
Granite State College *A*
Keene State College *B*
McIntosh College *A*
New Hampshire Community
Technical College
Claremont *A*
Stratham *C, A*
Plymouth State University *B*
St. Anselm College *B*
Southern New Hampshire
University *B*
University of New Hampshire *B, M*

New Jersey

Berkeley College *B*
Brookdale Community College *A*
Burlington County College *A*
The College of New Jersey *B*
DeVry University: North
Brunswick *A, B*
Gloucester County College *A*
Mercer County Community
College *C, A*
Ocean County College *A*
Passaic County Community
College *C, A*
Raritan Valley Community College *C*
Rowan University *B, T*
St. Peter's College *C*
Union County College *A*
Warren County Community
College *C, A*

New Mexico

Clovis Community College *A*
College of Santa Fe *A, B, M*
Eastern New Mexico University:
Roswell Campus *C, A*
Luna Community College *A*
New Mexico Junior College *A*
New Mexico State University *B*
New Mexico State University
Alamogordo *A*
Carlsbad *A*
Grants *A*
Northern New Mexico College *A*
Santa Fe Community College *A*
Southwestern Indian Polytechnic
Institute *C, A*
Western New Mexico
University *C, A, B, M*

New York

Adirondack Community College *A*
Berkeley College *B*
Berkeley College of New York City *B*

Broome Community College *C*
Bryant & Stratton Business Institute
Bryant & Stratton College:
Buffalo *C, A*
Bryant & Stratton College: Syracuse
North *A*
Cayuga County Community
College *C, A*
City University of New York
Baruch College *B, M*
Bronx Community College *A*
City College *B*
College of Staten Island *A, B*
Hostos Community College *A*
Medgar Evers College *A, B*
Queensborough Community
College *A*
College of Mount St. Vincent *A, B*
College of New Rochelle *B, T*
Concordia College *B*
Cornell University *B, M, D*
D'Youville College *B*
DeVry Institute of Technology
New York *B, M*
Finger Lakes Community College *A*
Fordham University *B, M*
Fulton-Montgomery Community
College *A*
Globe Institute of Technology *C, A, B*
Herkimer County Community
College *C, A*
Hofstra University *B*
Houghton College *B*
Hudson Valley Community College *A*
Interboro Institute *A*
Ithaca College *B, M*
Le Moyne College *B*
Manhattan College *B*
Maria College *A*
Medaille College *B*
Mercy College *C*
Metropolitan College of New
York *B, M*
Monroe Community College *A*
Nazareth College of Rochester *B, M*
New York University *A, B, M, D*
Niagara University *A, B*
North Country Community College *A*
Olean Business Institute *C, A*
Onondaga Community College *A*
Orange County Community College *A*
Pace University *B*
Paul Smith's College *A*
Roberts Wesleyan College *B*
Rochester Institute of
Technology *A, B, M*
Rockland Community College *A*
St. Joseph's College *C, B*
St. Joseph's College: Suffolk Campus *C*
St. Thomas Aquinas College *B*
Schenectady County Community
College *A*
Skidmore College *B*
State University of New York
Albany *M*
College at Buffalo *B*
College at Cortland *B*
College at Geneseo *B*
College at Plattsburgh *B*
College of Agriculture and
Technology at Cobleskill *A*
College of Agriculture and
Technology at Morrisville *A*
Empire State College *A, B*
Institute of Technology at
Utica/Rome *B, M*
Maritime College *B*
Purchase *C*
Suffolk County Community College *A*
Sullivan County Community
College *A*
Touro College *A, B*
Ulster County Community
College *C, A*

Utica School of Commerce *A*
Vaughn College of Aeronautics and
Technology *C, B*
Wells College *B*
Westchester Community College *C*

North Carolina

Alamance Community College *C, A*
Blue Ridge Community College *A*
Campbell University *A, B, M*
Carteret Community College *A*
Gardner-Webb University *B, M*
Lenoir-Rhyne College *B, M*
Louisburg College *A*
Mars Hill College *B*
McDowell Technical Community
College *A*
North Carolina Agricultural and
Technical State University *B*
Pfeiffer University *B*
Piedmont Community College *A*
St. Andrews Presbyterian College *B*
Wake Forest University *B*
Wake Technical Community
College *A*
Wayne Community College *A*

North Dakota

Bismarck State College *A*
Cankdeska Cikana Community
College *C, A*
Dickinson State University *B*
Mayville State University *A*
North Dakota State College of
Science *A*
Trinity Bible College *A, B*
University of North Dakota *B*

Ohio

Ashland University *A, B, M*
Belmont Technical College *A*
Bowling Green State University *B*
Bowling Green State University:
Firelands College *A*
Bryant & Stratton College
Parma *A*
Willoughby Hills *A*
Bryant & Stratton College:
Cleveland *A*
Capital University *B*
Central State University *B*
Cincinnati State Technical and
Community College *C*
Circleville Bible College *A, B*
Clark State Community College *A*
Cuyahoga Community College
Metropolitan Campus *A*
David N. Myers University *B*
Davis College *C, A*
Defiance College *A, B, T*
Edison State Community College *C, A*
Franklin University *A, B, M*
Hocking College *A*
James A. Rhodes State College *A*
Jefferson Community College *C, A*
Kent State University *C*
Kent State University
Ashtabula Regional Campus *C, A*
East Liverpool Regional
Campus *C, A*
Salem Regional Campus *C, A*
Trumbull Campus *C, A*
Tuscarawas Campus *C, A*
Lourdes College *A*
Marion Technical College *C, A*
Miami University
Oxford Campus *B*
Muskingum College *B*
Ohio State University
Columbus Campus *B, M, D*
Lima Campus *B*
Ohio University *B, M*

Ohio University
  Lancaster Campus *A*
  Zanesville Campus *B*
Ohio Valley College of Technology *A*
Otterbein College *B*
Owens Community College
  Toledo *A*
Remington College
  Cleveland *A*
Sinclair Community College *C, A*
Southern State Community College *A*
Southwestern College of Business
  Southwestern College: Vine Street
    Campus *A*
Stark State College of Technology *A*
Union Institute & University *B*
University of Akron *B*
University of Akron: Wayne College *A*
University of Cincinnati
  Clermont College *C, A*
  Raymond Walters College *C, A*
University of Dayton *B*
University of Findlay *A, B*
University of Toledo *A, B*
Urbana University *A, B*
Walsh University *A, B*
Washington State Community
  College *A*
Wittenberg University *B*
Wright State University *M*
Wright State University: Lake
  Campus *C, A*
Xavier University *A, B*
Youngstown State University *A, B, M*

Oklahoma

Bacone College *A*
Carl Albert State College *A*
Connors State College *A*
East Central University *B*
Eastern Oklahoma State College *A*
Northeastern Oklahoma Agricultural
  and Mechanical College *A*
Oklahoma Baptist University *B*
Oklahoma Christian University *B, M*
Oklahoma City Community College *A*
Oklahoma City University *B, M*
Oklahoma State University
  Okmulgee *A*
Oklahoma Wesleyan University *B*
Rose State College *C, A*
St. Gregory's University *A, B*
Southern Nazarene University *B, M*
Southwestern Oklahoma State
  University *A, B, M*
Tulsa Community College *A*
Western Oklahoma State College *A*

Oregon

Concordia University *B*
Corban College *B*
Eastern Oregon University *B, T*
George Fox University *B*
Linfield College *B*
Marylhurst University *B, M*
Mount Hood Community College *C, A*
Portland Community College *A*
Portland State University *B, M*
Rogue Community College *C, A*
Southern Oregon University *B*
Treasure Valley Community College *A*
Umpqua Community College *A*
University of Oregon *B*
Western Oregon University *B*

Pennsylvania

Academy of Medical Arts and
  Business *C, A*
Allied Medical and Technical
  Institute *C, A*
Arcadia University *B*
Bucks County Community College *A*
Butler County Community College *C*
Cambria-Rowe Business College *A*

Career Training Academy *C*
Carlow University *B*
Community College of Philadelphia *A*
DeSales University *B, M*
Delaware Valley College *A*
Drexel University *B*
DuBois Business College *A*
DuBois Business College
  Huntingdon *A*
Duquesne University *B*
Gannon University *C, A*
Harcum College *A*
Harrisburg Area Community
  College *C, A*
Indiana University of Pennsylvania *M*
Juniata College *B*
Keystone College *A, B*
La Salle University *B*
Lackawanna College *A*
Lebanon Valley College *C*
Manor College *A*
Montgomery County Community
  College *A*
Northampton County Area
  Community College *A*
PJA School *A*
Penn Commercial Business and
  Technical School *A*
Penn State
  Abington *A, B*
  Altoona *A, B*
  Beaver *A, B*
  Berks *A, B*
  Delaware County *A, B*
  Dubois *A, B*
  Erie, The Behrend College *A*
  Fayette *A, B*
  Harrisburg *A*
  Hazleton *A, B*
  Lehigh Valley *A, B*
  McKeesport *A, B*
  Mont Alto *A, B*
  New Kensington *B*
  Schuylkill - Capital College *A, B*
  Shenango *A, B*
  University Park *C, A*
  Worthington Scranton *A, B*
  York *A, B*
Reading Area Community
  College *C, A*
Rosemont College *B*
St. Joseph's University *M*
Shippensburg University of
  Pennsylvania *T*
Susquehanna University *B*
Temple University *B, M*
University of Pittsburgh
  Bradford *B*
  Johnstown *C, B*
  Titusville *B*
Valley Forge Military College *A*
Washington and Jefferson College *B*
Waynesburg College *A, B*
West Chester University of
  Pennsylvania *B*
West Virginia Career Institute *A*
Western School of Health and
  Business Careers
  Monroeville *C*
York College of Pennsylvania *A, B*

Puerto Rico

American University of Puerto Rico *B*
Bayamon Central University *A, B, M*
Inter American University of Puerto
  Rico
  Barranquitas Campus *B*
  Fajardo Campus *A, B*
Pontifical Catholic University of
  Puerto Rico *B, M*
Universidad Adventista de las
  Antillas *A, B*
Universidad Politecnica de Puerto
  Rico *B*

University of Puerto Rico
  Cayey University College *B*
  Humacao *B*
  Mayaguez *M*
  Rio Piedras *B, M*

Rhode Island

Bryant University *M*
Community College of Rhode
  Island *A*
New England Institute of
  Technology *B*
Rhode Island College *B*
University of Rhode Island *B*

South Carolina

Charleston Southern University *B, M*
Converse College *B*
Denmark Technical College *A*
Forrest Junior College *A*
Horry-Georgetown Technical
  College *C, A*
Midlands Technical College *C*
North Greenville College *A*
Orangeburg-Calhoun Technical
  College *A*
Piedmont Technical College *C, A*
Southern Wesleyan University *A*
Technical College of the
  Lowcountry *C, A*
Trident Technical College *A*
University of South Carolina
  Aiken *B*
Voorhees College *B*
Williamsburg Technical College *A*
York Technical College *A*

South Dakota

Augustana College *B*
Dakota State University *A, B*
Dakota Wesleyan University *A, B*
Northern State University *B*
University of Sioux Falls *M*

Tennessee

Austin Peay State University *B*
Belmont University *B*
Bryan College *A, B*
Carson-Newman College *B, T*
Christian Brothers University *B*
Columbia State Community College *A*
Cumberland University *A, B, M*
Free Will Baptist Bible College *A*
Hiwassee College *A*
Lambuth University *B*
Lee University *B*
Lincoln Memorial University *B, M, T*
Martin Methodist College *B*
Southwest Tennessee Community
  College *A*
Tennessee Technological
  University *B, M*
Tennessee Temple University *B*
University of Tennessee
  Knoxville *B*
Walters State Community College *A*

Texas

Alvin Community College *A*
Amarillo College *C, A*
Amberton University *B, M*
Angelina College *C, A*
Austin College *B*
Austin Community College *A*
Baylor University *B*
Blinn College *A*
Brazosport College *A*
Central Texas College *C, A*
Cisco Junior College *C, A*
Clarendon College *A*
Coastal Bend College *A*
College of the Mainland *A*
Concordia University at Austin *B*

Dallas Baptist University *B*
DeVry University
  Irving *B, M*
East Texas Baptist University *B*
Eastfield College *A*
El Paso Community College *C, A*
Frank Phillips College *C, A*
Grayson County College *C, A*
Houston Baptist University *B*
Howard College *C, A*
Howard Payne University *B*
Kilgore College *C, A*
Lamar University *B, M*
Laredo Community College *A*
LeTourneau University *B*
Lon Morris College *A*
McLennan Community College *C, A*
McMurry University *B*
Midland College *A*
Midwestern State University *B*
Mountain View College *A*
Navarro College *A*
North Central Texas College *A*
North Harris Montgomery
  Community College District *A*
Odessa College *A*
Our Lady of the Lake University of San
  Antonio *M*
Panola College *C, A*
Paris Junior College *A*
St. Mary's University *B*
Sam Houston State University *B*
San Antonio College *C, A*
San Jacinto College
  Central Campus *C, A*
  North *C*
Schreiner University *B*
South Plains College *C*
Southwestern Assemblies of God
  University *A, B*
Southwestern University *B*
Stephen F. Austin State University *B*
Sul Ross State University *B*
Tarleton State University *B, T*
Tarrant County College *A*
Temple College *C, A*
Texarkana College *A*
Texas A&M University
  Commerce *B, M*
  Kingsville *B*
  Texarkana *B*
Texas Lutheran University *B*
Texas Southern University *B*
Texas Southmost College *C, A*
Texas Tech University *B*
Tyler Junior College *A*
University of Houston *M, D*
University of Houston
  Clear Lake *B*
  Downtown *B*
  Victoria *M*
University of Mary Hardin-Baylor *B*
University of North Texas *B, M, D*
University of Texas
  Austin *B, M, D*
  Brownsville *B*
  Dallas *B*
  El Paso *B, M*
  San Antonio *B*
University of the Incarnate Word *A*
Vernon College *C, A*
Weatherford College *C, A*
West Texas A&M University *B*
Western Texas College *A*

Utah

Brigham Young University *B*
Dixie State College of Utah *A*
LDS Business College *A*
Salt Lake Community College *A*
Snow College *C, A*
University of Utah *B, M*
Utah State University *B*
Western Governors University *A*

Westminster College *B*

Vermont

Castleton State College *A, B*
Champlain College *C, A, B*
College of St. Joseph in Vermont *B*
Community College of Vermont *C, A*
Johnson State College *B*
Southern Vermont College *A*
Vermont Technical College *A*

Virginia

Averett University *B*
Blue Ridge Community College *C*
Bluefield College *B*
Central Virginia Community
    College *A*
Danville Community College *A*
George Mason University *B*
Germanna Community College *A*
Hollins University *B*
J. Sargeant Reynolds Community
    College *A*
John Tyler Community College *A*
Liberty University *B, T*
Longwood University *B*
Lord Fairfax Community College *C, A*
Mountain Empire Community
    College *A*
Norfolk State University *B*
Parks College: Arlington *A*
Piedmont Virginia Community
    College *A*
Richard Bland College *A*
Shenandoah University *C*
Southwest Virginia Community
    College *A*
Sweet Briar College *B*
Tidewater Tech *A*
University of Virginia *B*
Virginia Commonwealth University *M*
Virginia Polytechnic Institute and
    State University *D*
Virginia Western Community
    College *A*

Washington

Bellingham Technical College *A*
Centralia College *A*
DeVry University
    Federal Way *B, M*
Everett Community College *C, A*
Henry Cogswell College *B*
Heritage University *A, B*
Highline Community College *C, A*
North Seattle Community College *A*
Olympic College *A*
Pierce College *C, A*
Seattle University *B*
South Puget Sound Community
    College *C, A*
South Seattle Community College *A*
Spokane Community College *C, A*
Spokane Falls Community
    College *C, A*
Tacoma Community College *C*
Walla Walla College *A*
Washington State University *B*
Whatcom Community College *A*
Yakima Valley Community College *A*

West Virginia

Alderson-Broaddus College *A*
Bethany College *B*
Bluefield State College *A*
Concord University *B*
Davis and Elkins College *A, B*
Glenville State College *A*
Huntington Junior College *A*
Marshall University *M*
Mountain State College *A, B*
Potomac State College of West Virginia
    University *A*

Southern West Virginia Community
    and Technical College *A*
Valley College of Technology *A*
West Liberty State College *B*
West Virginia Northern Community
    College *A*
West Virginia State University *B*
West Virginia University *M*
West Virginia University Institute of
    Technology *B*

Wisconsin

Bryant & Stratton College:
    Milwaukee *A, B*
Cardinal Stritch University *A, B*
Chippewa Valley Technical College *A*
Concordia University Wisconsin *B*
Edgewood College *B, M*
Fox Valley Technical College *A*
Marian College of Fond du Lac *B, M*
Marquette University *M*
Milwaukee School of Engineering *B*
Northeast Wisconsin Technical
    College *A*
Northland College *B*
St. Norbert College *B*
University of Wisconsin
    Madison *B, M, D*
    Parkside *B*
    Platteville *B*
    Richland *C*
    Superior *B*
    Whitewater *B*

Wyoming

Laramie County Community
    College *A*
Northwest College *A*
Sheridan College *C, A*

Business communications

Alabama

Auburn University *B*

Arkansas

Harding University *B*

California

Foothill College *C*
Holy Names University *B*
Ohlone College *C*
Point Loma Nazarene University *B*
Saddleback College *C*

Colorado

Jones International University *C, B, M*

Connecticut

Quinnipiac University *B*

District of Columbia

University of the District of
    Columbia *A*

Florida

Barry University *M*
Florida Community College at
    Jacksonville *C*
Gulf Coast Community College *A*
Schiller International University *M*

Georgia

South Georgia College *A*

Hawaii

Hawaii Pacific University *B*

Illinois

Dominican University *B*

Roosevelt University *B, M*
Trinity Christian College *B*
Waubonsee Community College *C*

Indiana

St. Mary-of-the-Woods College *B*

Iowa

Ashford University *B*
Morningside College *B*

Kansas

MidAmerica Nazarene University *B*
Southwestern College *B*

Kentucky

Spalding University *M*

Maine

University of Maine
    Presque Isle *B*

Maryland

Cecil Community College *A*
Villa Julie College *B*

Massachusetts

American International College *B*
Babson College *B*
Bentley College *B, M*
Emerson College *B, M*
Massachusetts College of Liberal
    Arts *B*
Nichols College *B*
Suffolk University *M*

Michigan

Aquinas College *B*
Calvin College *B*
Macomb Community College *C*

Mississippi

Mississippi College *B*

Missouri

Lindenwood University *B, M*
Rockhurst University *B*

Montana

University of Montana: Western *B*

Nebraska

Creighton University *B*

New Hampshire

McIntosh College *A*

New Jersey

College of St. Elizabeth *C*

New York

City University of New York
    Baruch College *B*
Globe Institute of Technology *C*
Metropolitan College of New York *B*
St. Bonaventure University *M*
State University of New York
    College at Fredonia *B*

North Carolina

Campbell University *B*

North Dakota

University of Mary *B*

Ohio

Edison State Community College *A*
Marietta College *B*
Ohio Dominican University *B*
Stark State College of Technology *A*

Urbana University *B*

Oregon

Corban College *B*
Marylhurst University *B, M*

Pennsylvania

Carlow University *B*
Chestnut Hill College *C, A, B*
Community College of Beaver
    County *C*
Duquesne University *B*
Grove City College *B*
La Salle University *B*
Marywood University *C, M*
Montgomery County Community
    College *C, A*
Rosemont College *B*
Thiel College *B*

Puerto Rico

Pontifical Catholic University of
    Puerto Rico *B*

South Carolina

Forrest Junior College *A*

South Dakota

Augustana College *B*

Texas

Houston Community College
    System *C, A*
San Antonio College *C*
Southwestern Adventist University *B*
University of Houston *B*

Vermont

Champlain College *A, B*

Virginia

Dabney S. Lancaster Community
    College *A*
Thomas Nelson Community
    College *C*

Wisconsin

Madison Area Technical College *C, A*

Business machine repair

California

Yuba Community College District *C*

Georgia

Athens Technical College *C*

Idaho

Idaho State University *C, A*

Michigan

Bay de Noc Community College *C*
Mott Community College *C*

Pennsylvania

Community College of Allegheny
    County *A*

Washington

Clover Park Technical College *C, A*

Business/managerial economics

Alabama

Auburn University *B, M*
Auburn University at Montgomery *B*
Huntingdon College *B*
Jacksonville State University *B*
Talladega College *B*

University of Alabama *B, M, D*
University of Alabama
Birmingham *B*
University of North Alabama *B*

Alaska

University of Alaska
Fairbanks *B*

Arizona

Northern Arizona University *C, B*
University of Arizona *B*

Arkansas

Arkansas State University *B*
Hendrix College *B*
University of Arkansas *B*
University of Arkansas
Little Rock *B*
University of Central Arkansas *B*

California

Barstow College *A*
California Institute of Technology *B*
California Lutheran University *B*
California Polytechnic State
University: San Luis Obispo *B, M*
California State University
East Bay *B, M*
Fullerton *B, M*
Long Beach *B*
Northridge *B*
San Bernardino *B*
Chapman University *B*
Claremont McKenna College *B*
College of the Desert *A*
College of the Redwoods *A*
East Los Angeles College *A*
Mills College *B*
San Joaquin Delta College *A*
Santa Clara University *B*
Santiago Canyon College *A*
University of California
Los Angeles *B*
Riverside *B*
Santa Barbara *B, M, D*
Santa Cruz *B*
University of La Verne *B*
University of Redlands *B*
University of San Diego *B*
Ventura College *A*

Colorado

Colorado State University
Pueblo *B*
Fort Lewis College *B*
University of Denver *B*

Connecticut

Albertus Magnus College *B*
Quinnipiac University *B*
Southern Connecticut State
University *B*
University of New Haven *B*

Delaware

University of Delaware *M, D*

Florida

Barry University *B*
Florida Agricultural and Mechanical
University *B*
Stetson University *B*
University of Central Florida *B, M*
University of Miami *B, M, D*
University of North Florida *B*
University of South Florida *B, M*
University of West Florida *B*

Georgia

Clark Atlanta University *B*

Georgia College and State
University *B*
Georgia Institute of Technology *B, M*
Georgia Southern University *B*
Georgia State University *B, M*
Kennesaw State University *B*
Morehouse College *B*
Oglethorpe University *B*
Shorter College *B*
South Georgia College *A*
University of Georgia *B, M, D*
University of West Georgia *B*
Valdosta State University *B*

Hawaii

Hawaii Pacific University *A, B*

Idaho

Boise State University *B*
University of Idaho *B*

Illinois

Benedictine University *B, T*
Bradley University *B*
DePaul University *B, M*
Lewis University *B*
Loyola University of Chicago *B*
Millikin University *B*
Monmouth College *B, T*
Northwestern University *M, D*
Rockford College *B*
Roosevelt University *B*
Southern Illinois University
Carbondale *B*
Southern Illinois University
Edwardsville *B*
University of Chicago *M, D*
Western Illinois University *B*
Wheaton College *B*

Indiana

Anderson University *B*
Ball State University *B*
Huntington University *B*
Indiana University-Purdue University
Fort Wayne *B*
Indiana Wesleyan University *B*
Taylor University *B*
University of Evansville *B*
University of Indianapolis *B*

Iowa

Buena Vista University *B*
Drake University *B*
Northwestern College *B*
Simpson College *B*
University of Iowa *B*

Kansas

Bethany College *B*
Central Christian College of
Kansas *A, B*
Pittsburg State University *B*
Washburn University of Topeka *B*

Kentucky

Eastern Kentucky University *B*
Kentucky State University *B*
Midway College *B*
Morehead State University *B*
Northern Kentucky University *B*
University of Kentucky *B*
University of Louisville *B*
Western Kentucky University *B*

Louisiana

Centenary College of Louisiana *B*
Grambling State University *B*
Louisiana State University
Shreveport *B*

Louisiana State University and
Agricultural and Mechanical
College *B*
Louisiana Tech University *B*
Loyola University New Orleans *B*
Southern University
New Orleans *B*
Southern University and Agricultural
and Mechanical College *B*
University of Louisiana at Lafayette *B*
University of Louisiana at Monroe *B*
University of New Orleans *B, D*

Maine

Husson College *B*
University of Maine *B*
University of Maine
Farmington *B*

Maryland

Allegany College of Maryland *C, A*
University of Baltimore *B*

Massachusetts

American International College *B*
Babson College *B*
Bentley College *B, M*
Boston College *B*
Harvard College *B, M, D*
Nichols College *B*
Salem State College *B*

Michigan

Andrews University *B, M*
Eastern Michigan University *B*
Grand Valley State University *B*
Lake Superior State University *B*
Northwood University *A, B*
Oakland University *B*
Olivet College *B*
Saginaw Valley State University *B*
Spring Arbor University *B*

Minnesota

Winona State University *B*

Mississippi

Mississippi State University *B, M, D*
University of Mississippi *B, M, D*
University of Southern
Mississippi *B, M*

Missouri

College of the Ozarks *B*
Lincoln University *B*
Northwest Missouri State
University *B*
Park University *B*
St. Louis University *D*
Washington University in St. Louis *B*
Webster University *B*
William Jewell College *B*
William Woods University *B*

Montana

Carroll College *B*
Montana State University
Billings *T*

Nebraska

University of Nebraska
Lincoln *B*
Omaha *B, M*

Nevada

University of Nevada
Las Vegas *B, M*
Reno *B, M*

New Hampshire

McIntosh College *A*
St. Anselm College *B*

Southern New Hampshire
University *B*

New Jersey

Fairleigh Dickinson University
College at Florham
Metropolitan Campus *B*
Monmouth University *B*
Rider University *B*
St. Peter's College *B*
Seton Hall University *B*
William Paterson University of New
Jersey *B*

New Mexico

Eastern New Mexico University *B*
Western New Mexico University *B*

New York

City University of New York
Baruch College *B*
Elmira College *B*
Fordham University *B, M*
Hofstra University *B*
Ithaca College *B*
Le Moyne College *B*
Manhattan College *B*
Metropolitan College of New York *B*
New York University *B, M, D*
Pace University *M*
State University of New York
College at Oneonta
College at Potsdam *B*
Touro College *B*
Utica College *B*
Wagner College *B*
Wells College *B*

North Carolina

Barton College *B*
Greensboro College *B*
North Carolina Agricultural and
Technical State University *B*
North Carolina State University *B*
University of North Carolina
Charlotte *B, M*
Greensboro *B, M, D*
Wilmington *B*
Winston-Salem State University *B*

North Dakota

Jamestown College *B*
University of North Dakota *B*

Ohio

Bowling Green State University *B, M*
Cleveland State University *B*
College of Wooster *B*
David N. Myers University *B*
Kent State University *B, M, D*
Miami University
Oxford Campus *B*
Muskingum College *B*
Ohio State University
Columbus Campus *B*
Ohio University *B*
Ohio Wesleyan University *B*
Otterbein College *B*
University of Dayton *B*
University of Rio Grande *B*
Wittenberg University *B*
Wright State University *B, M*
Xavier University *B, M*
Youngstown State University *B*

Oklahoma

East Central University *B*
Oklahoma City University *B, M*
Oklahoma State University *B, M, D*
Tulsa Community College *A*
University of Central Oklahoma *B*
University of Oklahoma *B*

Oregon
Eastern Oregon University *B*
George Fox University *B*

Pennsylvania
Allegheny College *B*
Bloomsburg University of
 Pennsylvania *B*
Carnegie Mellon University *B, D*
Chatham College *B*
Clarion University of Pennsylvania *B*
Drexel University *B*
Duquesne University *B*
Elizabethtown College *B*
Grove City College *B*
La Salle University *B*
Lehigh University *B, M, D*
Messiah College *B*
Penn State
 Abington *B*
 Altoona *B*
 Beaver *B*
 Berks *B*
 Delaware County *B*
 Dubois *B*
 Erie, The Behrend College *B*
 Fayette *B*
 Hazleton *B*
 Lehigh Valley *B*
 McKeesport *B*
 Mont Alto *B*
 New Kensington *B*
 Schuylkill - Capital College *B*
 Shenango *B*
 University Park *C, B*
 Wilkes-Barre *B*
 Worthington Scranton *B*
 York *B*
Robert Morris University *B*
Rosemont College *B*
University of Pittsburgh
 Johnstown *B*
Villanova University *B*
West Chester University of
 Pennsylvania *B*
Westminster College *B*
Widener University *B*
Wilson College *B*
York College of Pennsylvania *B*

Puerto Rico
Inter American University of Puerto
 Rico
 Bayamon Campus *B*
Pontifical Catholic University of
 Puerto Rico *B*
Universidad Metropolitana *B*
University of Puerto Rico
 Rio Piedras *B, M*

Rhode Island
Providence College *B*
Rhode Island College *B*

South Carolina
Coastal Carolina University *B*
Forrest Junior College *A*
Francis Marion University *B*
Limestone College *B*
South Carolina State University *B*
University of South Carolina *B*
University of South Carolina
 Aiken *B*
Wofford College *B*

South Dakota
Northern State University *A*
University of South Dakota *B*

Tennessee
Belmont University *B, M*
Carson-Newman College *B*
East Tennessee State University *B*

Hiwassee College *A*
Lambuth University *B*
Lincoln Memorial University *B*
Lipscomb University *B*
Middle Tennessee State University *B*
Rhodes College *B*
Tennessee State University *B*
Tennessee Technological University *B*
Union University *B*
University of Memphis *B*
University of Tennessee
 Knoxville *M, D*
 Martin *B*

Texas
Baylor University *B, M*
Dallas Baptist University *B*
Houston Baptist University *B*
Lamar University *B*
Midland College *A*
Sam Houston State University *B*
Stephen F. Austin State University *B*
Texas A&M University
 Commerce *B*
 Kingsville *B*
Texas State University: San Marcos *B*
Tyler Junior College *A*
University of Houston *B*
University of North Texas *B*
University of Texas
 Arlington *B, D*
 El Paso *B, M*
 San Antonio *B, M*
 Tyler *B*
 of the Permian Basin *B*
West Texas A&M University *B*

Utah
Snow College *A*
Southern Utah University *B*
Weber State University *B*

Virginia
Christopher Newport University *B*
Hampden-Sydney College *B*
Hampton University *B*
James Madison University *B*
Old Dominion University *B*
Randolph-Macon College *B*
Southwest Virginia Community
 College *A*
Virginia Commonwealth
 University *B, M*
Virginia Polytechnic Institute and
 State University *B*
Virginia State University *B, M*
Wytheville Community College *A*

Washington
Gonzaga University *B*
Seattle Pacific University *B*
Seattle University *B*
Washington State University *B*

West Virginia
Concord University *B*
Marshall University *B*
Potomac State College of West Virginia
 University *A*
West Liberty State College *B*
West Virginia University *B, M, D*
West Virginia Wesleyan College *B*

Wisconsin
Beloit College *B*
Marian College of Fond du Lac *B*
Marquette University *B*
University of Wisconsin
 Whitewater *B*
Wisconsin Lutheran College *B*

Wyoming
Northwest College *A*

University of Wyoming *B, M, D*

Business statistics

Colorado
University of Denver *B*

District of Columbia
Southeastern University *B*

Georgia
South Georgia College *A*

Iowa
Iowa State University *B*

Massachusetts
Babson College *B*
Bentley College *M*

Michigan
Olivet College *B*

Minnesota
Winona State University *A*

New York
Globe Institute of Technology *C*
Manhattan College *B*
Rochester Institute of
 Technology *B, M*

Ohio
Bowling Green State University *M*
Cleveland State University *B*
Wright State University *B*

Oregon
University of Oregon *M, D*

Pennsylvania
La Salle University *B*
Temple University *M, D*

Puerto Rico
University of Puerto Rico
 Rio Piedras *B*

Tennessee
University of Tennessee
 Knoxville *B, M*

Texas
University of Houston *B, M, D*
University of Texas
 Arlington *D*

Utah
Brigham Young University *B*

Business teacher education

Alabama
Alabama Agricultural and Mechanical
 University *B, M*
Chattahoochee Valley Community
 College *A*
Faulkner State Community College *A*
Oakwood College *B*

Arizona
Arizona State University *B, T*
Eastern Arizona College *A*
Everest College *A*
Prescott College *T*

Arkansas
Arkansas State University *B, M, T*

Arkansas Tech University *B*
Henderson State University *B, T*
Ouachita Baptist University *B, T*
Philander Smith College *B*
Southern Arkansas University *B, T*
University of Arkansas
 Monticello *B*
 Pine Bluff *B, T*
University of Central Arkansas *B, M, T*
University of the Ozarks *B, T*

California
Azusa Pacific University *B, T*
California Baptist University *T*
California State University
 Dominguez Hills *T*
 Northridge *B, T*
Fresno Pacific University *B, T*
Fullerton College *A*
Humboldt State University *T*
Merritt College *A*
Mount St. Mary's College *T*

Colorado
Adams State College *B, T*
Colorado State University *T*
Johnson & Wales University *B*
Northeastern Junior College *A*

Connecticut
Albertus Magnus College *B, T*
Central Connecticut State
 University *M, T*
Sacred Heart University *T*

Delaware
Delaware State University *B*

District of Columbia
University of the District of
 Columbia *B*

Florida
Bethune-Cookman College *B, T*
Florida Agricultural and Mechanical
 University *B, M*
St. Petersburg College *B*
University of Central Florida *M*
University of South Florida *B, M*
Warner Southern College *B*

Georgia
Albany State University *M*
Armstrong Atlantic State
 University *B, T*
Atlanta Christian College *A, B*
Clark Atlanta University *B*
Darton College *A*
East Georgia College *A*
Emmanuel College *B*
Georgia Southern University *B, M*
South Georgia College *A*
University of Georgia *A*
University of West Georgia *B, M*
Valdosta State University *B, M*

Hawaii
Brigham Young University-Hawaii *B, T*

Idaho
Boise State University *B*
North Idaho College *A*
University of Idaho *B, M, T*

Illinois
Benedictine University *T*
Chicago State University *B*
Eastern Illinois University *T*
Illinois State University *B, T*
McKendree College *B*
Northern Illinois University *M*
Trinity Christian College *B, T*

Indiana

Ball State University *B, M, T*
Bethel College *B*
Calumet College of St. Joseph *T*
Goshen College *B*
Grace College *B*
Huntington University *B*
Indiana State University *T*
Indiana Wesleyan University *B*
Oakland City University *B*
Saint Mary's College *B*
University of Indianapolis *B, T*
University of St. Francis *B, T*
University of Southern Indiana *B*

Iowa

Buena Vista University *B, T*
Central College *T*
Dordt College *B*
Drake University *M, T*
Ellsworth Community College *A*
Maharishi University of
    Management *T*
Mount Mercy College *T*
Northwestern College *T*
St. Ambrose University *B, T*
Simpson College *T*
University of Northern Iowa *B*
Upper Iowa University *T*
William Penn University *B*

Kansas

Baker University *T*
Bethany College *B*
Butler County Community College *A*
Central Christian College of Kansas *A*
Colby Community College *A*
Emporia State University *M, T*
Fort Hays State University *B, T*
Garden City Community College *A*
Labette Community College *A*
McPherson College *B, T*
MidAmerica Nazarene University *B, T*
Tabor College *B, T*
Washburn University of Topeka *B*

Kentucky

Eastern Kentucky University *B*
Morehead State University *B*
Northern Kentucky University *B*
Spalding University *B*
Thomas More College *B*
University of the Cumberlands *B, T*
Western Kentucky University *B, M, T*

Louisiana

Grambling State University *B*
Nicholls State University *B*
Northwestern State University *B*
Our Lady of Holy Cross College *B*
University of Louisiana at Lafayette *B*

Maine

University of Maine
    Fort Kent *B*
    Machias *B*

Maryland

Morgan State University *B, M*
Mount St. Mary's University *T*
Prince George's Community
    College *A*
University of Maryland
    Eastern Shore *B*

Massachusetts

Bristol Community College *A*
Northern Essex Community
    College *A*
University of Massachusetts
    Dartmouth *T*
Western New England College *T*

Westfield State College *B, T*

Michigan

Central Michigan University *B, T*
Delta College *A*
Eastern Michigan University *B, M, T*
Ferris State University *B*
Michigan Technological University *T*
Northern Michigan University *B, T*
Olivet College *B, T*
Siena Heights University *B, T*
University of Michigan
    Dearborn *B*
Western Michigan University *T*

Minnesota

Bethel University *B*
College of St. Catherine *B*
Concordia College: Moorhead *B, T*
Minnesota State University
    Mankato *B, M, T*
Northland Community & Technical
    College *A*
Ridgewater College *A*
University of Minnesota
    Twin Cities *B, M, T*
Vermilion Community College *A*
Winona State University *B, M, T*

Mississippi

Coahoma Community College *A*
Delta State University *B, T*
Hinds Community College *A*
Itawamba Community College *A*
Jackson State University *B*
Mississippi College *B, M*
Mississippi Delta Community
    College *A*
Mississippi Gulf Coast Community
    College
    Jefferson Davis Campus *A*
Mississippi State University *B, T*
Rust College *B*
University of Southern Mississippi *B*

Missouri

Central Missouri State
    University *B, M, T*
College of the Ozarks *B, T*
Columbia College *T*
Evangel University *B, T*
Hannibal-LaGrange College *B*
Lincoln University *B, T*
Lindenwood University *B, M*
Missouri Baptist University *B, T*
Missouri Southern State
    University *B, T*
Missouri State University *B*
Northwest Missouri State
    University *B, M, T*
Southeast Missouri State
    University *B, T*
University of Missouri
    Columbia *B*
    St. Louis *T*

Montana

University of Montana: Missoula *B, T*
University of Montana: Western *B, T*

Nebraska

Chadron State College *B, M*
Concordia University *B, T*
Dana College *B*
Hastings College *B, M, T*
Midland Lutheran College *B, T*
Union College *T*
University of Nebraska
    Kearney *B, M, T*
    Lincoln *B*
Wayne State College *B, T*
York College *B, T*

Nevada

University of Nevada
    Reno *B*

New Hampshire

Southern New Hampshire
    University *B, M*

New Jersey

Montclair State University *B, M, T*
Rider University *B, M*
Rowan University *T*
St. Peter's College *T*

New Mexico

Eastern New Mexico University *B*
Western New Mexico University *B*

New York

Alfred University *M, T*
Canisius College *M, T*
City University of New York
    Lehman College *B, M, T*
D'Youville College *B, M, T*
Dowling College *B*
Hofstra University *B, M*
Molloy College *B*
Nazareth College of Rochester *B, M, T*
New York Institute of Technology *B, T*
New York University *B, M, D, T*
Niagara University *B, M, T*
Pace University *B, M, T*
St. Bonaventure University *T*
State University of New York
    College at Buffalo *B, M, T*
    Oswego *B*
Utica College *B*

North Carolina

Appalachian State University *B, T*
East Carolina University *B*
Elizabeth City State University *B, T*
Fayetteville State University *B, T*
Lenoir-Rhyne College *B, T*
North Carolina Agricultural and
    Technical State University *B, T*
St. Augustine's College *B*

North Dakota

Dickinson State University *B, T*
Mayville State University *B, T*
Minot State University *B*
University of North Dakota *B, T*
Valley City State University *B, T*

Ohio

Ashland University *B, M, T*
Baldwin-Wallace College *T*
Bluffton University *B*
Bowling Green State
    University *B, M, T*
Capital University *T*
Defiance College *B, T*
Kent State University *B*
Mount Vernon Nazarene
    University *B, M, T*
University of Akron *B*
University of Rio Grande *B, T*
University of Toledo *B, M, T*
Wright State University *B, M, T*
Youngstown State University *B, M*

Oklahoma

East Central University *B*
Eastern Oklahoma State College *A*
Northwestern Oklahoma State
    University *B, T*
Oklahoma City University *B*
Oklahoma Panhandle State
    University *B*
Oklahoma Wesleyan University *B*
Oral Roberts University *B, T*

Southern Nazarene University *B*
Southwestern Oklahoma State
    University *T*
University of Central Oklahoma *B*

Oregon

Concordia University *B, M, T*
Corban College *B*
Oregon State University *M*
Portland State University *T*

Pennsylvania

Bloomsburg University of
    Pennsylvania *B, M, T*
Community College of Philadelphia *A*
Gannon University *B, T*
Gwynedd-Mercy College *B, T*
Immaculata University *B*
Indiana University of
    Pennsylvania *B, M, T*
Mercyhurst College *B, T*
Reading Area Community College *A*
Robert Morris University *B, M*
St. Vincent College *B*
Seton Hill University *T*
Temple University *B*

Puerto Rico

American University of Puerto
    Rico *B, T*
Inter American University of Puerto
    Rico
    San German Campus *M*
Pontifical Catholic University of
    Puerto Rico *B, T*
University of Puerto Rico
    Mayaguez *T*

Rhode Island

Johnson & Wales University *T*

South Carolina

Coker College *B*
South Carolina State University *B, T*
University of South Carolina *M*

South Dakota

Black Hills State University *B*
Dakota State University *B, T*
Dakota Wesleyan University *B, T*
Northern State University *B, T*
Oglala Lakota College *B*

Tennessee

Lambuth University *B, T*
Lee University *B*
Lincoln Memorial University *B, T*
Middle Tennessee State
    University *B, M, T*
Union University *B, T*
University of Memphis *T*
University of Tennessee
    Knoxville *B, T*
    Martin *B*

Texas

Hardin-Simmons University *B, T*
Howard Payne University *B, T*
Jarvis Christian College *B, T*
Lamar University *T*
Laredo Community College *A*
LeTourneau University *B, T*
Lubbock Christian University *B*
McMurry University *T*
St. Mary's University *B*
Southwestern Adventist University *B*
Tarleton State University *T*
Texas A&M University
    Commerce *T*
    Kingsville *T*
Texas State University: San Marcos *T*
Texas Wesleyan University *B, T*

University of Mary Hardin-Baylor *T*
University of North Texas *M, T*
West Texas A&M University *T*

Utah

Snow College *A*
Southern Utah University *B, T*
Utah State University *B, M, D*
Utah Valley State College *B*
Weber State University *B*

Virginia

Bluefield College *B, T*
James Madison University *B, T*
Liberty University *B, T*
Longwood University *B*
Norfolk State University *B*
St. Paul's College *B*
University of Virginia's College at
    Wise *T*
Virginia State University *B*

Washington

Central Washington University *B, M, T*
Eastern Washington University *B, M, T*
Pierce College *A*
Renton Technical College *A*
Walla Walla College *B*

West Virginia

Concord University *B, T*

Wisconsin

Concordia University Wisconsin *B, T*
Edgewood College *B, T*
Lakeland College *T*
Maranatha Baptist Bible College *B*
Mount Mary College *B, T*
Northland College *T*
University of Wisconsin
    Whitewater *B, M, T*
Viterbo University *B, T*

Wyoming

Eastern Wyoming College *A*

Cabinetmaking/ millwright

Alabama

Lawson State Community College *C*
Northwest-Shoals Community
    College *C*
Trenholm State Technical College *C*

California

Long Beach City College *C, A*

Florida

Palm Beach Community College *C*

Georgia

Central Georgia Technical College *C*
Columbus Technical College *C*
Savannah Technical College *C*

Indiana

Ivy Tech State College
    Ivy Tech Community College:
        Bloomington *C, A*
    Ivy Tech Community College:
        Central Indiana *C, A*
    Ivy Tech Community College:
        Columbus *C, A*
    Ivy Tech Community College: East
        Central *C, A*
    Ivy Tech Community College:
        Kokomo *C, A*
    Ivy Tech Community College:
        Lafayette *C, A*

Ivy Tech Community College: North
    Central *C, A*
Ivy Tech Community College:
    Northeast *C, A*
Ivy Tech Community College:
    Northwest *C, A*
Ivy Tech Community College: South
    Central *C, A*
Ivy Tech Community College:
    Southwest *C, A*
Ivy Tech Community College:
    Wabash Valley *C, A*
Ivy Tech Community College:
    Whitewater *C, A*

Iowa

Des Moines Area Community
    College *C*

Kentucky

Jefferson Community College *C*

Minnesota

Minneapolis Community and
    Technical College *C, A*
Minnesota State College - Southeast
    Technical *C*
St. Cloud Technical College *C*
St. Paul College *C*

North Carolina

Tri-County Community College *C*

Pennsylvania

Harrisburg Area Community
    College *C*
Pennsylvania College of Technology *C*

Utah

Salt Lake Community College *A*
Utah Valley State College *C, A*

Washington

Grays Harbor College *C*

Wisconsin

Milwaukee Area Technical College *C*

CAD/CADD drafting/ design technology

Alabama

Northeast Alabama Community
    College *C, A*
Northwest-Shoals Community
    College *A*

Alaska

University of Alaska
    Fairbanks *C*

Arizona

Coconino County Community
    College *A*

Arkansas

Arkansas Northeastern College *C*
University of Arkansas
    Fort Smith *C, A*

California

Ohlone College *A*
Southwestern College *C, A*
Taft College *A*

Colorado

Pikes Peak Community College *C*

Connecticut

Naugatuck Valley Community
    College *C, A*

Georgia

Central Georgia Technical College *C*
Northwestern Technical College *C*
Southwest Georgia Technical
    College *C*

Illinois

Black Hawk College *C*
Heartland Community College *C, A*
Kaskaskia College *C*
Lincoln Land Community College *C*
Moraine Valley Community
    College *C, A*
Morton College *C, A*
Waubonsee Community College *C*

Indiana

Indiana University-Purdue University
    Indianapolis *A*

Iowa

Hamilton Technical College *A*

Kansas

Brown Mackie College *A*
Manhattan Area Technical College *A*

Kentucky

Hopkinsville Community College *C*
Louisville Technical Institute *C, A*

Louisiana

Bossier Parish Community
    College *C, A*

Maryland

College of Southern Maryland *C*
Community College of Baltimore
    County *C, A*
Howard Community College *C, A*

Massachusetts

Roxbury Community College *A*

Michigan

Baker College
    of Muskegon *A*
Eastern Michigan University *B*
Ferris State University *A*
Gogebic Community College *A*
Northern Michigan University *A*
West Shore Community College *A*

Minnesota

Alexandria Technical College *C*
Lake Superior College *C, A*
Minnesota State College - Southeast
    Technical *C*
Ridgewater College *C, A*
Rochester Community and Technical
    College *C, A*
St. Cloud Technical College *C, A*

Mississippi

Mississippi Gulf Coast Community
    College
    Jefferson Davis Campus *A*

Missouri

Mineral Area College *C, A*
Missouri Southern State
    University *C, A, B*
Ozarks Technical Community
    College *C, A*
State Fair Community College *A*
Vatterott College: Springfield *C, A*

Nebraska

Vatterott College: Spring Valley *C*

Nevada

Community College of Southern
    Nevada *C, A*

New Hampshire

University of New Hampshire *A*

New Jersey

Burlington County College *A*
Thomas Edison State College *C*

New York

Jamestown Community College *C*
Niagara County Community
    College *C, A*
State University of New York
    College of Agriculture and
        Technology at Morrisville *A*
    College of Technology at Canton *C*
Vaughn College of Aeronautics and
    Technology *A, B*
Westchester Community College *C*

North Carolina

Edgecombe Community College *C*
Gaston College *C*

Ohio

Bryant & Stratton College:
    Cleveland *A*
Central Ohio Technical College *C, A*
Edison State Community College *C*
James A. Rhodes State College *C*
Marion Technical College *C*
Miami University
    Hamilton Campus *C*
Shawnee State University *C, A*
Sinclair Community College *C, A*
University of Cincinnati
    Clermont College *C, A*

Oklahoma

Northeastern Oklahoma Agricultural
    and Mechanical College *C, A*
Platt College
    Tulsa *C*

Pennsylvania

Delaware County Community
    College *C, A*
Harrisburg Area Community
    College *C*
Northampton County Area
    Community College *A*
South Hills School of Business &
    Technology *C*

South Carolina

York Technical College *A*

Tennessee

Pellissippi State Technical Community
    College *A*

Texas

Eastfield College *C, A*
San Antonio College *C, A*

Utah

Salt Lake Community College *C*

Virginia

Mountain Empire Community
    College *A*
Norfolk State University *B*
Thomas Nelson Community
    College *A*
Tidewater Community College *A*

Washington
Clark College *C*
Everett Community College *C, A*
Grays Harbor College *C*
North Seattle Community
College *C, A*
Olympic College *C*
Renton Technical College *C*
Shoreline Community College *C, A*

Canadian government/politics

Vermont
Sterling College *B*

Canadian history

Vermont
Sterling College *B*

Canadian literature

Indiana
Bethel College *C*

Canadian studies

Indiana
Franklin College *B*

Kentucky
Eastern Kentucky University *B*

Maine
University of Maine
Fort Kent *B*

New York
St. Lawrence University *B*
State University of New York
College at Plattsburgh *B*

Ohio
Owens Community College
Toledo *A*

Vermont
Sterling College *B*
University of Vermont *B*

Washington
University of Washington *B, M*
Western Washington University *B*

Cardiopulmonary technology

Louisiana
Nicholls State University *A*

North Carolina
Johnston Community College *C, A*

Cardiovascular science

South Carolina
Medical University of South
Carolina *D*

Cardiovascular technology

Alabama
Community College of the Air
Force *A*

Arkansas
University of Arkansas
for Medical Sciences *A*

California
Butte College *A*
Grossmont Community College *C, A*
Orange Coast College *C, A*

Connecticut
St. Vincent's College *A*

Florida
Barry University *B*
Broward Community College *A*
Edison College *A*
Hillsborough Community College *C*
Ultrasound Diagnostic School
Sanford-Brown Institute:
Jacksonville *C, A*
Valencia Community College *A*

Georgia
Augusta Technical Institute *A*
Columbus Technical College *C, A*
Darton College *A*
Northwestern Technical College *A*

Illinois
Benedictine University *M*
William Rainey Harper College *A*

Louisiana
Louisiana State University Health
Sciences Center *B*

Maine
Southern Maine Community
College *A*

Maryland
Howard Community College *C, A*

Massachusetts
Bunker Hill Community College *A*

Minnesota
Globe College *A*
Minneapolis Community and
Technical College *C*
Northland Community & Technical
College *A*
Rochester Community and Technical
College *A*
St. Cloud Technical College *A*

Nebraska
Nebraska Methodist College of
Nursing and Allied Health *A, B*

New York
Molloy College *A*

North Carolina
Caldwell Community College and
Technical Institute *C, A*
Central Piedmont Community
College *A*
Stanly Community College *C*

Ohio
University of Toledo *A*

Pennsylvania
Community College of Allegheny
County *A*
Gwynedd-Mercy College *A, B*
Harrisburg Area Community
College *C, A*
Lackawanna College *A*

Pennsylvania College of Technology *B*
Thomas Jefferson University: College
of Health Professions *B*

South Carolina
University of South Carolina *B*

South Dakota
Southeast Technical Institute *A*

Tennessee
Northeast State Technical Community
College *A*

Texas
Alvin Community College *C, A*
El Centro College *A*

Virginia
Northern Virginia Community
College *C*

Washington
Spokane Community College *A*

Wisconsin
Milwaukee Area Technical College *A*

Caribbean studies

California
Pitzer College *B*

Florida
Florida State University *B*

Georgia
Emory University *B*

Illinois
University of Chicago *M*
University of Illinois
Urbana-Champaign *M*

Michigan
University of Michigan *B*

New Hampshire
Dartmouth College *B*

New Jersey
Rutgers, The State University of New
Jersey
New Brunswick/Piscataway
Campus *B*
Newark Regional Campus *B*
William Paterson University of New
Jersey *B*

New York
City University of New York
Brooklyn College *B*
City College *B*
Hofstra University *B*
New York University *M*
State University of New York
Albany *B, M*
Binghamton *B*

Carpentry

Alabama
Alabama Southern Community
College *A*
Bishop State Community College *C*
Central Alabama Community
College *C*
Gadsden State Community College *C*
Lawson State Community College *C*

Northwest-Shoals Community
College *C*
Shelton State Community College *C*
Southern Union State Community
College *A*
Trenholm State Technical College *C*

Arizona
Central Arizona College *C*
Coconino County Community
College *A*
Eastern Arizona College *C*
Gateway Community College *C, A*
Mohave Community College *C*
Northland Pioneer College *C, A*
Tohono O'odham Community
College *C, A*

Arkansas
North Arkansas College *C*
University of Arkansas
Cossatot Community College of the
A

California
Bakersfield College *A*
College of the Sequoias *C, A*
Feather River College *C, A*
Fresno City College *C, A*
Fullerton College *A*
Laney College *C, A*
Long Beach City College *C, A*
Los Angeles Trade and Technical
College *C, A*
Palomar College *C, A*
Pasadena City College *C, A*
Porterville College *C, A*
San Joaquin Delta College *C, A*
Santa Ana College *C, A*
Santa Rosa Junior College *C*
Santiago Canyon College *A*
Shasta College *A*
Sierra College *C, A*
Victor Valley College *A*

Colorado
Community College of Aurora *A*
Red Rocks Community College *C, A*
Trinidad State Junior College *C*

Florida
Brevard Community College *C*
Florida Community College at
Jacksonville *C*
Indian River Community College *C*
Palm Beach Community College *C*

Georgia
Albany Technical College *C, A*
Central Georgia Technical College *C*
Columbus Technical College *C*
Gwinnett Technical College *C*
Savannah Technical College *C*
West Georgia Technical College *C*

Hawaii
University of Hawaii
Hawaii Community College *C, A*
Honolulu Community College *C, A*
Kauai Community College *C, A*
Maui Community College *A*

Idaho
Idaho State University *C, A*
North Idaho College *C, A*

Illinois
Black Hawk College *C, A*
John A. Logan College *A*
Kaskaskia College *C, A*
Southwestern Illinois College *C, A*
Triton College *C, A*

Indiana

Ivy Tech State College
Ivy Tech Community College:
Central Indiana *C, A*
Ivy Tech Community College: East
Central *C, A*
Ivy Tech Community College:
Lafayette *C, A*
Ivy Tech Community College: North
Central *C, A*
Ivy Tech Community College:
Northwest *C, A*
Ivy Tech Community College: South
Central *C, A*
Ivy Tech Community College:
Southwest *C, A*
Ivy Tech Community College:
Wabash Valley *C, A*
Vincennes University *A*

Iowa

Des Moines Area Community
College *A*
Ellsworth Community College *C, A*
Iowa Central Community College *C*
Iowa Lakes Community College *C*
Kirkwood Community College *C*
North Iowa Area Community
College *C*
Northeast Iowa Community
College *C*
Northwest Iowa Community
College *C, A*
Southeastern Community College
North Campus *C, A*
Southwestern Community College *C*
Western Iowa Tech Community
College *C*

Kansas

Coffeyville Community College *C*
Hutchinson Community College *C, A*
Manhattan Area Technical
College *C, A*

Kentucky

Elizabethtown Community and
Technical College *C*
Jefferson Community College *C*
Maysville Community College *C, A*
Somerset Community College *C, A*

Louisiana

Delgado Community College *C*
Nunez Community College *C*

Maine

Eastern Maine Community College *A*
Northern Maine Community
College *C, A*
Southern Maine Community
College *A*

Michigan

Bay de Noc Community College *C*
Delta College *A*
Gogebic Community College *A*
Kirtland Community College *C, A*
Lansing Community College *C, A*
Mott Community College *C*
Northern Michigan University *C*
Oakland Community College *C, A*

Minnesota

Alexandria Technical College *C*
Hennepin Technical College *C, A*
Lake Superior College *C, A*
Leech Lake Tribal College *C*
Mesabi Range Community and
Technical College *A*
Minneapolis Community and
Technical College *C*

Minnesota State College - Southeast
Technical *C, A*
Minnesota State Community and
Technical College - Fergus
Falls *C, A*
Northland Community & Technical
College *C*
Northwest Technical College *C*
Ridgewater College *C, A*
Riverland Community College *C*
Rochester Community and Technical
College *C*
St. Cloud Technical College *C, A*
St. Paul College *C*

Mississippi

Coahoma Community College *C*
Hinds Community College *C*
Mississippi Gulf Coast Community
College
Jefferson Davis Campus *C*
Pearl River Community College *C, A*
Southwest Mississippi Community
College *C*

Missouri

Ranken Technical College *A*

Montana

Helena College of Technology of the
University of Montana *C*
Little Big Horn College *C*
Miles Community College *A*
Salish Kootenai College *C*

Nebraska

Nebraska Indian Community
College *C, A*
Northeast Community College *A*

Nevada

Truckee Meadows Community
College *C, A*

New Mexico

Albuquerque Technical-Vocational
Institute *C*
San Juan College *C, A*

New York

Hudson Valley Community College *A*
Mohawk Valley Community College *C*
State University of New York
College of Agriculture and
Technology at Morrisville *A*
College of Technology at Alfred *A*
College of Technology at Delhi *C, A*

North Carolina

Alamance Community College *C*
Asheville-Buncombe Technical
Community College *C*
Bladen Community College *C*
Blue Ridge Community College *C*
Cape Fear Community College *C*
Cleveland Community College *C*
College of the Albemarle *C*
Davidson County Community
College *C*
Fayetteville Technical Community
College *C*
Forsyth Technical Community
College *C*
Guilford Technical Community
College *C*
McDowell Technical Community
College *C*
Piedmont Community College *C*
Rowan-Cabarrus Community
College *C*
Vance-Granville Community
College *C*

North Dakota

Bismarck State College *C, A*
North Dakota State College of
Science *A*
Sitting Bull College *C, A*

Oklahoma

Rose State College *A*

Oregon

Clackamas Community College *C*
Linn-Benton Community College *A*

Pennsylvania

Community College of Allegheny
County *C*
Delaware County Community
College *C*
Johnson College *A*
Pennsylvania College of Technology *C*
Thaddeus Stevens College of
Technology *C*
Triangle Tech
DuBois *A*
Erie *A*
Greensburg *A*
Pittsburgh *A*
Williamson Free School of Mechanical
Trades *C*

Puerto Rico

Inter American University of Puerto
Rico
San German Campus *C*

Rhode Island

New England Institute of
Technology *A*

South Carolina

Greenville Technical College *C*
Technical College of the
Lowcountry *C*

South Dakota

Lake Area Technical Institute *C*
Oglala Lakota College *A*
Western Dakota Technical Institute *C*

Texas

Austin Community College *C*
Houston Community College
System *C*
Howard College *C*
Laredo Community College *C*
North Lake College *A*
Odessa College *C, A*
Paris Junior College *A*
St. Philip's College *A*

Utah

College of Eastern Utah *C, A*
Salt Lake Community College *C, A*
Southern Utah University *A*

Virginia

Piedmont Virginia Community
College *A*

Washington

Columbia Basin College *A*
Edmonds Community College *C*
Grays Harbor College *A*
Green River Community College *A*
Peninsula College *C*
Renton Technical College *C, A*
Seattle Central Community
College *C, A*
Spokane Community College *C, A*
Walla Walla Community College *C, A*
Wenatchee Valley College *C*

Wisconsin

Chippewa Valley Technical College *C*
College of Menominee Nation *C*
Gateway Technical College *C*
Milwaukee Area Technical College *C*
Waukesha County Technical
College *C*
Western Wisconsin Technical
College *C*

Cartography

Alabama

Samford University *B*

Arizona

Northern Arizona University *B*

Arkansas

University of Arkansas
Fort Smith *C, A*

California

California State University
Chico *C*
Riverside Community College *C, A*

Georgia

Kennesaw State University *B*

Idaho

University of Idaho *B*

Iowa

Iowa Lakes Community College *A*

Kentucky

Western Kentucky University *C*

Maryland

Montgomery College *C*

Massachusetts

Salem State College *B*

Michigan

Northern Michigan University *C*

Minnesota

Alexandria Technical College *C*
Fond du Lac Tribal and Community
College *C, A*

Missouri

Missouri State University *B*

Montana

University of Montana: Missoula *B, M*

Nebraska

University of Nebraska
Omaha *C*

New Mexico

Southwestern Indian Polytechnic
Institute *C, A*

New York

Cayuga County Community College *A*

Ohio

Ohio University *B*
University of Akron *C, B*

Oklahoma

East Central University *B*
Oklahoma State University *C*

Oregon
Central Oregon Community
College *A*

Pennsylvania
Penn State
Schuylkill - Capital College *B*

South Carolina
Greenville Technical College *C, A*
Midlands Technical College *C*

Tennessee
Pellissippi State Technical Community
College *A*
Roane State Community College *C, A*

Texas
Houston Community College
System *C, A*
North Harris Montgomery
Community College District *C, A*
Temple College *C, A*
Texas A&M University *B*
Texas State University: San
Marcos *B, M, D*

Utah
Brigham Young University *B, M*

Wisconsin
University of Wisconsin
Madison *B, M*

Cell biology and histology

Alabama
Huntingdon College *B*
University of Alabama
Birmingham *D*

Arizona
Northern Arizona University *B*
University of Arizona *B*

Arkansas
University of Arkansas *M, D*

California
California Institute of Technology *D*
California State University
Fresno *B*
Long Beach *B*
Northridge *B*
San Francisco State University *B, M*
Stanford University *M, D*
University of California
Davis *B, M, D*
Irvine *B, M, D*
San Diego *B*
Santa Barbara *B, M, D*
Santa Cruz *B*
University of Southern
California *M, D*

Colorado
University of Colorado
Boulder *B, M, D*

Connecticut
Connecticut College *B*
Quinnipiac University *M*
University of Connecticut *M, D*
University of New Haven *M*
Yale University *M, D*

District of Columbia
Catholic University of America *M, D*
Georgetown University *D*

Florida
University of Miami *D*

Georgia
Medical College of Georgia *M, D*
University of Georgia *B, M, D*

Illinois
Rosalind Franklin University of
Medicine and Science *M, D*
University of Chicago *D*
University of Illinois
Urbana-Champaign *B, D*

Indiana
University of Indianapolis *B*

Iowa
Iowa State University *M, D*

Louisiana
Tulane University *B, M, D*

Maine
Colby College *B*
University of Maine *B, M, D*

Maryland
Johns Hopkins University *B, M, D*
University of Maryland
Baltimore *M, D*
Baltimore County *D*

Massachusetts
Boston University *D*
Harvard College *B, D*
Simon's Rock College of Bard *B*
Tufts University *D*

Minnesota
Southwest Minnesota State
University *B*
University of Minnesota
Duluth *B*
Twin Cities *B, M, D*
Winona State University *B*

Missouri
Missouri State University *B, M*
University of Missouri
Kansas City *M*
Washington University in St. Louis *D*

New Hampshire
Dartmouth College *B*

New Jersey
Rowan University *B*
Rutgers, The State University of New
Jersey
New Brunswick/Piscataway
Campus *B, M, D*

New York
Bard College *B*
College of Saint Rose *B*
Long Island University
C.W. Post Campus *B*
New York University *D*
State University of New York
Albany *M, D*
College at Plattsburgh *B*
College of Environmental Science
and Forestry *B, M, D*
University of Rochester *B*
Yeshiva University *M, D*

North Carolina
Duke University *M, D*
East Carolina University *D*
Methodist College *A, B*

University of North Carolina
Chapel Hill *M, D*

Ohio
Case Western Reserve University *D*
Kent State University *M, D*
Ohio State University
Columbus Campus *M, D*

Oklahoma
Northeastern State University *B*
University of Oklahoma *M, D*

Oregon
Oregon Health & Science
University *M, D*

Pennsylvania
Juniata College *B*
Mansfield University of
Pennsylvania *B*
Temple University *M*
University of Pittsburgh *M, D*
University of the Sciences in
Philadelphia *M*

Rhode Island
Brown University *B, M, D*

South Carolina
Medical University of South
Carolina *M, D*

Tennessee
Vanderbilt University *M, D*

Texas
Texas A&M University *B*
Texas A&M University
Commerce *B*
University of Texas
Health Science Center at
Houston *M, D*
Health Science Center at San
Antonio *M, D*
Medical Branch at Galveston *M, D*

Utah
University of Utah *B*

Vermont
Johnson State College *B*
Marlboro College *B*
University of Vermont *M, D*

Virginia
University of Virginia *D*

Washington
University of Washington *M, D*
Western Washington University *B*

Wisconsin
Beloit College *B*
Marquette University *M, D*
University of Wisconsin
Superior *B*

Cell physiology

Ohio
Case Western Reserve University *D*

West Virginia
West Virginia University *D*

Cellular/anatomical biology

California
University of Southern
California *M, D*

Illinois
Loyola University of Chicago *M, D*
Rosalind Franklin University of
Medicine and Science *M, D*

Iowa
University of Iowa *M, D*

Nebraska
University of Nebraska
Medical Center *M, D*

Puerto Rico
Universidad Metropolitana *B*

Texas
University of Texas
Health Science Center at
Houston *M, D*

Wisconsin
Lawrence University *B*
Marquette University *M, D*

Cellular/molecular biology

Arizona
Arizona State University *M, D*
Northern Arizona University *B*

California
California State University
Sacramento *B, M*
University of California
Berkeley *B, M, D*
Los Angeles *B, M, D*
Riverside *M, D*
University of Southern
California *M, D*

Colorado
Fort Lewis College *B*
University of Colorado
Boulder *B, D*
Denver and Health Sciences
Center *D*

Connecticut
Connecticut College *B*
University of Connecticut *B*
Yale University *M, D*

Florida
Florida Institute of Technology *B*
University of Florida *B, M*

Hawaii
University of Hawaii
Manoa *M, D*

Illinois
Bradley University *B*
Rosalind Franklin University of
Medicine and Science *D*
University of Illinois
Urbana-Champaign *B, M, D*

Indiana
Indiana University
Bloomington *D*

Iowa

Drake University *B*

Kansas

Pittsburg State University *B*

Maryland

University of Maryland
  Baltimore County *M*
  College Park *M, D*

Massachusetts

Bridgewater State College *B*
Harvard College *D*
University of Massachusetts
  Amherst *M, D*

Michigan

Eastern Michigan University *M*
Grand Valley State University *B*
Michigan State University *M, D*
University of Michigan *B, M, D*

Missouri

Washington University in St. Louis *D*

Montana

University of Montana: Missoula *B*

Nevada

University of Nevada
  Reno *M, D*

New York

State University of New York
  College at Brockport *B*
  Stony Brook *D*

North Carolina

Wake Forest University *M, D*

North Dakota

North Dakota State University *D*

Ohio

Ohio University *B, D*

Oregon

Oregon State University *D*

Pennsylvania

Bucknell University *B*
Drexel University *M, D*
University of Pennsylvania *M, D*

Texas

Texas A&M University *B*
Texas Tech University *B*
University of Texas
  Austin *M, D*
  Dallas *M, D*
  Health Science Center at
    Houston *M, D*
  Medical Branch at Galveston *M, D*
  San Antonio *M, D*
  Southwestern Medical Center at
    Dallas *M, D*

Utah

University of Utah *B, D*

Vermont

Bennington College *B*
University of Vermont *M, D*

Virginia

Marymount University *B*

Washington

Western Washington University *B*

Wisconsin

Beloit College *B*
Marquette University *M, D*

Wyoming

University of Wyoming *D*

Celtic languages

California

University of California
  Berkeley *B*

Massachusetts

Boston College *M*
Harvard College *B, M, D*

Central Asian studies

Massachusetts

Harvard College *B, M, D*

Central/Middle/Eastern European studies

California

California State University
  Fullerton *B*

Connecticut

Wesleyan University *B*

Florida

Florida State University *B, M*

Georgia

Emory University *B*

Illinois

Illinois Wesleyan University *B*

Maine

Bowdoin College *B*

Massachusetts

Amherst College *B*
Harvard College *B*
Simon's Rock College of Bard *B*
Tufts University *B, M*
Wellesley College *B*

Michigan

University of Michigan *B*

Minnesota

Augsburg College *B*
Macalester College *B*

New Jersey

Rutgers, The State University of New
  Jersey
  New Brunswick/Piscataway
    Campus *B*

New York

Bard College *B*
Columbia University
  Columbia College *B*
State University of New York
  Albany *B*

Ohio

Ohio State University
  Columbus Campus *B, M*

Oregon

Portland State University *B*

Pennsylvania

La Salle University *B, M*

Vermont

Marlboro College *B*
Middlebury College *B*
University of Vermont *B*

Washington

University of Washington *B, M*

Ceramic sciences/ engineering

Illinois

University of Illinois
  Urbana-Champaign *B, M, D*

Missouri

East Central College *A*
University of Missouri
  Rolla *B, M, D*

New Jersey

Rutgers, The State University of New
  Jersey
  Camden Regional Campus *B*
  New Brunswick/Piscataway
    Campus *B, M, D*
  Newark Regional Campus *B*

New York

Alfred University *B, M, D*

Ohio

Ohio State University
  Columbus Campus *B*

South Carolina

Clemson University *B, M, D*

Washington

University of Washington *B*

Ceramics

Arizona

Northern Arizona University *C, B*

California

Butte College *C, A*
California College of the Arts *B, M*
California State University
  East Bay *B*
  Fullerton *B, M*
  Long Beach *B, M*
  Northridge *B, M*
Chabot College *A*
De Anza College *C, A*
Glendale Community College *C*
Grossmont Community College *A*
Laney College *A*
Monterey Peninsula College *C, A*
Ohlone College *C*
Palomar College *A*
Pasadena City College *C, A*
San Francisco Art Institute *B, M*
Santa Rosa Junior College *C*
Ventura College *A*
West Los Angeles College *C, A*

Colorado

Adams State College *B*

Connecticut

University of Hartford *B*

District of Columbia

George Washington University *M*

Florida

University of Miami *B*

Illinois

Bradley University *B*
Judson College *B*
Richland Community College *A*
Rockford College *B*
School of the Art Institute of
  Chicago *B, M*

Indiana

Indiana University-Purdue University
  Indianapolis *B*
Vincennes University *A*

Iowa

Coe College *B*
University of Iowa *B, M*

Kansas

Allen County Community College *A*
Pittsburg State University *B*
Pratt Community College *A*
Seward County Community College *A*
University of Kansas *B, M*

Kentucky

Eastern Kentucky University *B*

Maine

Maine College of Art *B*

Maryland

Maryland Institute College of Art *B*

Massachusetts

Massachusetts College of Art *B, M*
School of the Museum of Fine
  Arts *B, M*
Simon's Rock College of Bard *B*
University of Massachusetts
  Dartmouth *B, M*

Michigan

Andrews University *B*
College for Creative Studies *B*
Finlandia University *B*
Grand Valley State University *B*
Henry Ford Community College *A*
Northern Michigan University *B*
Oakland Community College *C, A*
Siena Heights University *B*
University of Michigan *B*
University of Michigan
  Flint *B*

Minnesota

Minnesota State University
  Mankato *B*
St. Cloud State University *B*

Missouri

Columbia College *B*
Kansas City Art Institute *B*
Washington University in St.
  Louis *B, M*

Nevada

Sierra Nevada College *B*

New Jersey

Cumberland County College *C, A*
Rowan University *B*

New York

Alfred University *M*
Hofstra University *B*
Parsons The New School for
  Design *C, A, B, T*
Pratt Institute *B, M*

Rochester Institute of
Technology *A, B, M*
State University of New York
College at Fredonia *B*
New Paltz *B, M*
Syracuse University *B, M*

North Carolina

East Carolina University *B*
Haywood Community College *A*

Ohio

Cleveland Institute of Art *B*
Ohio State University
Columbus Campus *B, M*
Ohio University *B, M*
Shawnee State University *B*
Sinclair Community College *C*
University of Akron *B*

Oregon

University of Oregon *B, M*

Pennsylvania

Arcadia University *B*
Edinboro University of
Pennsylvania *B*
Keystone College *A, B*
Marywood University *C, B, M*
Seton Hill University *B*
Temple University *B, M*
University of the Arts *M*

Puerto Rico

Inter American University of Puerto
Rico
San German Campus *B, M*

Rhode Island

Rhode Island College *B*
Rhode Island School of Design *B, M*
Salve Regina University *B*

South Carolina

Anderson University *B*

Tennessee

Memphis College of Art *B, M*
Tennessee Technological University *B*

Texas

McMurry University *B*
Sam Houston State University *M*
Texas A&M University
Commerce *B, M*
University of Dallas *B, M*
University of Houston *B, M*
University of North Texas *B, M*
University of Texas
El Paso *B, M*
Western Texas College *A*

Utah

Brigham Young University *M*
Dixie State College of Utah *A*

Vermont

Bennington College *B*
Marlboro College *B*

Virginia

Lord Fairfax Community College *C*

Washington

University of Washington *B, M*
Western Washington University *B*

West Virginia

West Virginia State University *B*
West Virginia Wesleyan College *B*

Wisconsin

University of Wisconsin
Madison *B*

Wyoming

Western Wyoming Community
College *A*

Chemical engineering

Alabama

Auburn University *B, M, D*
Tuskegee University *B*
University of Alabama *B, M, D*
University of Alabama
Huntsville *B, M*
University of South Alabama *B, M*

Arizona

Arizona State University *B, M, D*
University of Arizona *B, M, D*

Arkansas

University of Arkansas *B, M*

California

California Institute of
Technology *B, M, D*
California State Polytechnic
University: Pomona *B*
California State University
Long Beach *B*
Northridge *B, M*
San Jose State University *B, M*
Stanford University *B, M, D*
University of California
Berkeley *B, M, D*
Davis *B, M, D*
Irvine *B, M, D*
Los Angeles *B, M, D*
Riverside *B, M, D*
San Diego *B, M, D*
Santa Barbara *B, M, D*
University of Southern
California *B, M, D*

Colorado

Colorado School of Mines *B, M, D*
Colorado State University *B, M, D*
University of Colorado
Boulder *B, M, D*

Connecticut

Fairfield University *B*
University of Connecticut *B, M, D*
University of New Haven *B*
Yale University *B, M, D*

Delaware

University of Delaware *B, M, D*

District of Columbia

Howard University *B, M*

Florida

Florida Agricultural and Mechanical
University *B, M, D*
Florida Institute of
Technology *B, M, D*
Florida International University *B*
Florida State University *B, M, D*
University of Florida *B, M*
University of South Florida *B, M, D*

Georgia

Georgia Institute of
Technology *B, M, D*
University of Georgia *B, M*

Idaho

North Idaho College *A*

University of Idaho *B, M, D*

Illinois

Dominican University *B*
Illinois Institute of
Technology *B, M, D*
Northwestern University *B, M, D*
University of Illinois
Chicago *B, M, D*
Urbana-Champaign *B, M, D*

Indiana

Purdue University *B, M, D*
Rose-Hulman Institute of
Technology *B, M*
Tri-State University *B*
University of Notre Dame *B, M, D*
Vincennes University *A*

Iowa

Iowa State University *B, M, D*
University of Iowa *B, M, D*

Kansas

Kansas State University *B, M, D*
University of Kansas *B, M, D*

Kentucky

University of Kentucky *B, M, D*
University of Louisville *B, M, D*

Louisiana

Louisiana State University and
Agricultural and Mechanical
College *B, M, D*
Louisiana Tech University *B*
Tulane University *B, M, D*
University of Louisiana at
Lafayette *B, M*

Maine

University of Maine *B, M, D*

Maryland

Johns Hopkins University *B, M, D*
University of Maryland
Baltimore County *B, M, D*
College Park *B, M, D*

Massachusetts

Eastern Nazarene College *B*
Massachusetts Institute of
Technology *B, M, D*
Northeastern University *B, M, D*
Smith College *B*
Tufts University *B, M, D*
University of Massachusetts
Amherst *B, M, D*
Lowell *B, M*
Worcester Polytechnic
Institute *B, M, D*

Michigan

Calvin College *B*
Michigan State University *B, M, D*
Michigan Technological
University *B, M, D, T*
University of Michigan *B, M, D*
Wayne State University *B, M, D*
Western Michigan University *B*

Minnesota

St. Cloud State University *B*
University of Minnesota
Duluth *B*
Twin Cities *B, M, D*
Winona State University *B*

Mississippi

Mississippi State University *B, M*
University of Mississippi *B*

Missouri

University of Missouri
Columbia *B, M, D*
Rolla *B, M, D*
Washington University in St.
Louis *B, M, D*

Montana

Montana State University
Bozeman *B, M*

Nebraska

University of Nebraska
Lincoln *B, M*
Omaha *B*

Nevada

University of Nevada
Reno *B, M, D*

New Hampshire

University of New Hampshire *B, M, D*

New Jersey

New Jersey Institute of
Technology *B, M, D*
Princeton University *B, M, D*
Rowan University *B*
Rutgers, The State University of New
Jersey
Camden Regional Campus *B*
New Brunswick/Piscataway
Campus *B, M, D*
Newark Regional Campus *B*
Stevens Institute of
Technology *B, M, D*

New Mexico

New Mexico Institute of Mining and
Technology *B*
New Mexico State University *B, M*
University of New Mexico *B, M*

New York

City University of New York
City College *B, M, D*
Clarkson University *B, M, D*
Columbia University
Fu Foundation School of
Engineering and Applied
Science *B, M, D*
Cooper Union for the Advancement of
Science and Art *B, M*
Cornell University *B, M, D*
Manhattan College *B, M*
Polytechnic University *B, M, D*
Rensselaer Polytechnic
Institute *B, M, D*
State University of New York
Buffalo *B, M, D*
College of Environmental Science
and Forestry *B, M, D*
Syracuse University *B, M, D*
United States Military Academy *B*
University of Rochester *B, M*

North Carolina

Elon University *B*
North Carolina Agricultural and
Technical State University *B*
North Carolina State
University *B, M, D*

North Dakota

University of North Dakota *B, M*

Ohio

Case Western Reserve
University *B, M, D*
Cleveland State University *B, M, D*
Miami University
Oxford Campus *B*

Ohio State University
Columbus Campus B, M, D
Ohio University B, M, D
University of Akron B, M
University of Cincinnati B, M, D
University of Dayton B, M
University of Toledo B, M
Youngstown State University B, M

Oklahoma
Oklahoma State University B, M, D
University of Oklahoma B, M, D
University of Tulsa B, M, D

Oregon
Oregon State University B, M, D

Pennsylvania
Bucknell University B, M
Carnegie Mellon University B, M, D
Drexel University B, M, D
Gannon University B
Geneva College B
Gettysburg College B
Lafayette College B
Lehigh University B, M, D
Penn State
Abington B
Altoona B
Beaver B
Berks B
Delaware County B
Dubois B
Fayette B
Hazleton B
Lehigh Valley B
McKeesport B
Mont Alto B
New Kensington B
Schuylkill - Capital College B
Shenango B
University Park B, M, D
Wilkes-Barre B
Worthington Scranton B
York B
University of Pennsylvania B, M, D
University of Pittsburgh B, M, D
Villanova University B, M
Widener University B, M

Puerto Rico
University of Puerto Rico
Mayaguez B, M, D
Ponce A

Rhode Island
Brown University B, M, D
University of Rhode Island B, M, D

South Carolina
Clemson University B, M, D
University of South Carolina B, M, D

South Dakota
South Dakota School of Mines and
Technology B, M

Tennessee
Christian Brothers University B
Tennessee Technological
University B, M, D
University of Tennessee
Knoxville B, M, D
Vanderbilt University B, M, D

Texas
Kilgore College A
Lamar University B, M
Prairie View A&M University B
Rice University B, M, D
Texas A&M University B, M, D

Texas A&M University
Kingsville B, M
Texas Tech University B, M, D
University of Houston B, M, D
University of Texas
Austin B, M, D

Utah
Brigham Young University B, M, D
University of Utah B

Virginia
Hampton University B
University of Virginia B, M, D
Virginia Commonwealth University B
Virginia Polytechnic Institute and
State University B, M, D
Washington and Lee University B

Washington
University of Washington B, M, D
Washington State University B, M, D

West Virginia
West Virginia University B, M, D
West Virginia University Institute of
Technology B

Wisconsin
University of Wisconsin
Madison B, M, D

Wyoming
University of Wyoming B, M, D

Chemical physics

California
University of California
San Diego B
University of Southern California D

Colorado
Adams State College B
University of Colorado
Boulder D

Florida
Florida State University M, D

Illinois
University of Illinois
Urbana-Champaign M, D

Indiana
University of Notre Dame M

Kentucky
Centre College B

Maine
Bowdoin College B

Michigan
Michigan State University B, M, D
Saginaw Valley State University B

Nevada
University of Nevada
Reno D

New Hampshire
Keene State College B

New York
Barnard College B
Columbia University
Columbia College B

Ohio
College of Wooster B

Pennsylvania
Carnegie Mellon University B
Swarthmore College B

Rhode Island
Brown University B

Tennessee
Maryville College B
Union University B

Texas
Rice University B

Wisconsin
Marquette University M, D

Chemical technology

Alabama
Northwest-Shoals Community
College C

California
Ohlone College C

Delaware
Delaware Technical and Community
College
Stanton/Wilmington Campus A

Florida
Pensacola Junior College A

Indiana
Ball State University A
Indiana University-Purdue University
Fort Wayne A

Maryland
Community College of Baltimore
County A

Massachusetts
Massachusetts Bay Community
College A

Michigan
Delta College C, A
Ferris State University A
Grand Rapids Community College A
Lawrence Technological University A
Southwestern Michigan College A

Minnesota
St. Paul College A

New Jersey
Burlington County College A
Essex County College C, A

New York
City University of New York
New York City College of
Technology A
Corning Community College A
Excelsior College A
Mohawk Valley Community College A

North Carolina
Guilford Technical Community
College A

Ohio
University of Cincinnati
Raymond Walters College A

Pennsylvania
Bidwell Training Center A
Community College of Allegheny
County A
Delaware County Community
College C
Lehigh Carbon Community College C
Millersville University of
Pennsylvania A
Northampton County Area
Community College A

Puerto Rico
Inter American University of Puerto
Rico
Bayamon Campus B
University of Puerto Rico
Humacao A

Rhode Island
Community College of Rhode
Island C, A

South Carolina
Midlands Technical College C

Texas
Alvin Community College C, A
Del Mar College C, A
Houston Community College
System C, A
Lamar State College at Orange C
Texas State Technical College
Harlingen A

Utah
Salt Lake Community College A

Washington
Big Bend Community College C
Edmonds Community College A

Wisconsin
Milwaukee Area Technical College A

Chemistry

Alabama
Alabama Agricultural and Mechanical
University B
Alabama State University B
Athens State University B
Auburn University B, M, D
Birmingham-Southern College B, T
Chattahoochee Valley Community
College A
Faulkner State Community College A
Gadsden State Community College A
Huntingdon College B, T
Jacksonville State University B
Judson College B
Miles College B
Northeast Alabama Community
College A
Oakwood College B
Samford University B
Southern Union State Community
College A
Spring Hill College B, T
Talladega College B
Troy University B
Tuskegee University B, M
University of Alabama B, M, D
University of Alabama
Birmingham B, M, D
Huntsville B, M
University of Montevallo B, T
University of North Alabama B
University of South Alabama B
University of West Alabama B, T

Alaska

University of Alaska
  Anchorage *B*
  Fairbanks *B, M*

Arizona

Arizona State University *B, M, D*
Arizona Western College *A*
Central Arizona College *A*
Cochise College *A*
Eastern Arizona College *A*
Grand Canyon University *B*
Northern Arizona University *B, M, T*
Phoenix College *A*
South Mountain Community
    College *A*
University of Arizona *B, M, D*

Arkansas

Arkansas State University *B, M*
Arkansas Tech University *B*
Harding University *B*
Henderson State University *B*
Hendrix College *B*
John Brown University *B*
Lyon College *B*
Ouachita Baptist University *B*
Philander Smith College *B*
Phillips Community College of the
    University of Arkansas *A*
Southern Arkansas University *B*
University of Arkansas *B, M, D*
University of Arkansas
  Fort Smith *B*
  Little Rock *B, M*
  Monticello *B*
  Pine Bluff *B*
University of Central Arkansas *B*
University of the Ozarks *B*

California

Allan Hancock College *A*
Azusa Pacific University *B*
Bakersfield College *A*
Cabrillo College *A*
California Institute of
    Technology *B, D*
California Lutheran University *B*
California Polytechnic State
    University: San Luis Obispo *B, M*
California State Polytechnic
    University: Pomona *B, M*
California State University
  Bakersfield *B*
  Chico *C, B*
  Dominguez Hills *B*
  East Bay *B, M*
  Fresno *B, M*
  Fullerton *B, M*
  Long Beach *B, M*
  Los Angeles *B, M*
  Northridge *B, M*
  Sacramento *B, M*
  San Bernardino *B*
  San Marcos *B*
  Stanislaus *B*
Canada College *A*
Cerritos Community College *A*
Chaffey College *A*
Chapman University *B*
Citrus College *A*
City College of San Francisco *A*
Claremont McKenna College *B*
College of San Mateo *A*
College of the Desert *A*
College of the Siskiyous *A*
Columbia College *A*
Concordia University *B*
Contra Costa College *A*
Crafton Hills College *A*
Cuesta College *C, A*
Cypress College *A*
De Anza College *A*

East Los Angeles College *A*
El Camino College *A*
Foothill College *A*
Fresno City College *A*
Fresno Pacific University *B*
Fullerton College *A*
Gavilan Community College *A*
Glendale Community College *A*
Golden West College *A*
Grossmont Community College *C, A*
Harvey Mudd College *B*
Humboldt State University *B*
Irvine Valley College *A*
La Sierra University *B*
Las Positas College *A*
Los Angeles City College *A*
Los Angeles Southwest College *A*
Los Angeles Valley College *A*
Los Medanos College *A*
Loyola Marymount University *B*
Merced College *A*
Mills College *B*
MiraCosta College *A*
Mission College *B*
Monterey Peninsula College *A*
Moorpark College *A*
Mount St. Mary's College *B*
Occidental College *B*
Orange Coast College *A*
Pacific Union College *B*
Palomar College *C, A*
Pepperdine University *B*
Pitzer College *B*
Point Loma Nazarene University *B*
Pomona College *B*
Porterville College *A*
Saddleback College *A*
St. Mary's College of California *B*
San Bernardino Valley College *A*
San Diego City College *A*
San Diego Mesa College *C, A*
San Diego Miramar College *A*
San Diego State University *B, M, D*
San Francisco State University *B, M*
San Joaquin Delta College *A*
San Jose State University *B, M*
Santa Ana College *A*
Santa Barbara City College *A*
Santa Clara University *B*
Santa Monica College *A*
Santa Rosa Junior College *A*
Santiago Canyon College *A*
Scripps College *B*
Sierra College *A*
Solano Community College *A*
Sonoma State University *B*
Southwestern College *A*
Stanford University *B, M, D*
University of California
  Berkeley *B, M, D*
  Davis *B, M, D*
  Irvine *B, M, D*
  Los Angeles *B, M, D*
  Riverside *B, M, D*
  San Diego *B, D*
  Santa Barbara *B, M, D*
  Santa Cruz *B, M, D*
University of California: Merced *B*
University of La Verne *B*
University of Redlands *B*
University of San Diego *B*
University of San Francisco *B, M*
University of Southern
    California *B, M, D*
University of the Pacific *B, M, D*
Vanguard University of Southern
    California *B*
Ventura College *A*
West Hills Community College *A*
West Los Angeles College *C, A*
West Valley College *A*
Westmont College *B*
Whittier College *B*

Colorado

Adams State College *B*
Colorado College *B*
Colorado Mountain College
    Spring Valley Campus *A*
Colorado School of Mines *B, M, D*
Colorado State University *B, M, D*
Colorado State University
    Pueblo *B*
Fort Lewis College *B*
Metropolitan State College of
    Denver *B*
Otero Junior College *A*
Red Rocks Community College *A*
Regis University *B*
Trinidad State Junior College *A*
United States Air Force Academy *B*
University of Colorado
  Boulder *B, D*
  Colorado Springs *B*
  Denver and Health Sciences
    Center *B, M*
University of Denver *B, M, D*
University of Northern
    Colorado *B, M, D, T*
Western State College of Colorado *B*

Connecticut

Albertus Magnus College *B*
Central Connecticut State
    University *B*
Connecticut College *B*
Fairfield University *B*
Quinnipiac University *B*
Sacred Heart University *B, M*
St. Joseph College *B, M, T*
Southern Connecticut State
    University *B, M*
Trinity College *B*
University of Connecticut *B, M, D*
University of Hartford *B*
University of New Haven *A, B*
Wesleyan University *B, M, D*
Western Connecticut State
    University *B*
Yale University *B, M, D*

Delaware

Delaware State University *B, M*
University of Delaware *B, M, D*

District of Columbia

American University *B, M*
Catholic University of
    America *B, M, D, T*
Gallaudet University *B*
George Washington
    University *B, M, D*
Georgetown University *B, M, D*
Howard University *B, M, D*
Trinity University *B*
University of the District of
    Columbia *B*

Florida

Barry University *B*
Bethune-Cookman College *B*
Broward Community College *A*
Eckerd College *B*
Florida Agricultural and Mechanical
    University *B, M*
Florida Atlantic University *B, M, D*
Florida Gulf Coast University *B*
Florida Institute of
    Technology *B, M, D*
Florida International
    University *B, M, D*
Florida Southern College *B*
Florida State University *B, M, D*
Gulf Coast Community College *A*
Indian River Community College *A*
Jacksonville University *B*
Manatee Community College *A*

Miami Dade College *A*
New College of Florida *B*
Okaloosa-Walton College *A*
Palm Beach Community College *A*
Pensacola Junior College *A*
Rollins College *B*
Santa Fe Community College *A*
Stetson University *B*
University of Central Florida *B, M, D*
University of Florida *B, M, D*
University of Miami *B, M, D*
University of North Florida *B*
University of South Florida *B, M, D*
University of Tampa *A, B, T*
University of West Florida *B*
Valencia Community College *A*

Georgia

Abraham Baldwin Agricultural
    College *A*
Agnes Scott College *B*
Albany State University *B*
Armstrong Atlantic State
    University *B, T*
Atlanta Metropolitan College *A*
Augusta State University *B*
Berry College *B*
Clark Atlanta University *B, M, D*
Coastal Georgia Community
    College *A*
Columbus State University *B*
Covenant College *B*
Dalton State College *A*
Darton College *A*
East Georgia College *A*
Emory University *B, D*
Fort Valley State University *B*
Gainesville State College *A*
Georgia College and State
    University *B*
Georgia Highlands College *A*
Georgia Institute of
    Technology *B, M, D*
Georgia Perimeter College *A*
Georgia Southern University *B*
Georgia Southwestern State
    University *B, T*
Georgia State University *B, M, D*
Gordon College *A*
Kennesaw State University *B*
LaGrange College *B*
Macon State College *A*
Mercer University *B*
Middle Georgia College *A*
Morehouse College *B*
North Georgia College & State
    University *B*
Oglethorpe University *B*
Paine College *B*
Piedmont College *B*
Savannah State University *B*
Shorter College *B*
South Georgia College *A*
Spelman College *B*
University of Georgia *B, M, D*
University of West Georgia *B*
Valdosta State University *B*
Waycross College *A*
Wesleyan College *B*
Young Harris College *A*

Hawaii

University of Hawaii
  Hilo *B*
  Manoa *B, M, D*

Idaho

Albertson College of Idaho *B*
Boise State University *B, T*
Brigham Young University-Idaho *A*
College of Southern Idaho *A*
Idaho State University *A, B, M*
Lewis-Clark State College *B*
North Idaho College *A*

Northwest Nazarene University *B*
University of Idaho *B, M, D*

Illinois

Augustana College *B, T*
Benedictine University *B, T*
Black Hawk College
    East Campus *A*
Blackburn College *B*
Bradley University *B, M, T*
Chicago State University *B, T*
City Colleges of Chicago
    Harold Washington College *A*
    Kennedy-King College *A*
    Olive-Harvey College *A*
Concordia University *B, T*
Danville Area Community College *A*
DePaul University *B, M, T*
Dominican University *B*
Eastern Illinois University *B, M, T*
Elmhurst College *B, T*
Eureka College *B*
Governors State University *B, T*
Greenville College *B, T*
Highland Community College *A*
Illinois Central College *A*
Illinois College *B*
Illinois Institute of
    Technology *B, M, D*
Illinois State University *B, M, T*
Illinois Valley Community College *A*
Illinois Wesleyan University *B*
John A. Logan College *A*
Joliet Junior College *A*
Judson College *B*
Kishwaukee College *A*
Knox College *B*
Lake Forest College *B*
Lewis University *B, T*
Loyola University of Chicago *B, M, D*
MacMurray College *B*
McKendree College *B*
Millikin University *B, T*
Monmouth College *B, T*
North Central College *B, T*
North Park University *B*
Northeastern Illinois University *B, M*
Northern Illinois University *B, M, D, T*
Northwestern University *B, M, D*
Olivet Nazarene University *B, T*
Principia College *B*
Quincy University *B*
Rockford College *B*
Roosevelt University *B*
St. Xavier University *B*
Sauk Valley Community College *A*
South Suburban College of Cook
    County *A*
Southern Illinois University
    Carbondale *B, M, D*
Southern Illinois University
    Edwardsville *B, M, T*
Southwestern Illinois College *A*
Trinity Christian College *B, T*
Trinity International University *B*
Triton College *A*
University of Chicago *B, D*
University of Illinois
    Chicago *B, M, D*
    Springfield *B*
    Urbana-Champaign *B, M, D*
Western Illinois University *B, M*
Wheaton College *B, T*

Indiana

Ancilla College *A*
Anderson University *B*
Ball State University *B, M, T*
Bethel College *A, B*
Butler University *B*
DePauw University *B*
Earlham College *B*
Franklin College *B*
Goshen College *B*

Hanover College *B*
Huntington University *B*
Indiana State University *B, M, T*
Indiana University
    Bloomington *B, M, D*
    Kokomo *B*
    Northwest *B*
    South Bend *A, B*
    Southeast *B*
Indiana University-Purdue University
    Fort Wayne *A, B, T*
Indiana University-Purdue University
    Indianapolis *A, B, M, D*
Indiana Wesleyan University *A, B*
Manchester College *B, T*
Marian College *B, T*
Purdue University *B, M, D*
Purdue University
    Calumet *B*
Rose-Hulman Institute of
    Technology *B*
St. Joseph's College *B*
Saint Mary's College *B, T*
Taylor University *B*
Tri-State University *B*
University of Evansville *B*
University of Indianapolis *A, B*
University of Notre Dame *B, M, D*
University of Southern Indiana *B, T*
Valparaiso University *B*
Vincennes University *A*
Wabash College *B*

Iowa

Ashford University *T*
Briar Cliff University *B*
Buena Vista University *B, T*
Central College *B, T*
Clarke College *B, T*
Coe College *B*
Cornell College *B, T*
Dordt College *B*
Drake University *B*
Ellsworth Community College *A*
Graceland University *B, T*
Grinnell College *B*
Iowa State University *B, M, D*
Iowa Wesleyan College *B*
Loras College *B*
Luther College *B*
Morningside College *B*
Northwestern College *B, T*
St. Ambrose University *B*
Simpson College *B*
University of Iowa *B, M, D, T*
University of Northern Iowa *B, M*
Upper Iowa University *B*
Wartburg College *B, T*

Kansas

Allen County Community College *A*
Baker University *B, T*
Barton County Community College *A*
Benedictine College *B*
Bethany College *B, T*
Bethel College *B*
Butler County Community College *A*
Central Christian College of
    Kansas *A, B*
Coffeyville Community College *A*
Colby Community College *A*
Dodge City Community College *A*
Emporia State University *B, T*
Fort Hays State University *B*
Fort Scott Community College *A*
Friends University *B*
Garden City Community College *A*
Kansas State University *B, M, D*
Kansas Wesleyan University *B, T*
McPherson College *B, T*
MidAmerica Nazarene University *B*
Neosho County Community
    College *A*
Newman University *B*

Pittsburg State University *B, M*
Pratt Community College *A*
Seward County Community College *A*
Southwestern College *B*
Sterling College *B, T*
Tabor College *B*
University of Kansas *B, M, D*
University of St. Mary *B*
Washburn University of Topeka *B*
Wichita State University *B, M, D, T*

Kentucky

Asbury College *B, T*
Bellarmine University *B, T*
Berea College *B, T*
Brescia University *B*
Campbellsville University *B*
Centre College *B*
Eastern Kentucky University *B, M*
Georgetown College *B, T*
Kentucky State University *B*
Kentucky Wesleyan College *B, T*
Lindsey Wilson College *A*
Morehead State University *B*
Murray State University *B, M, T*
Northern Kentucky University *B*
Pikeville College *B, T*
Thomas More College *A, B*
Transylvania University *B*
Union College *B*
University of Kentucky *B, M, D*
University of Louisville *B, M, D*
University of the Cumberlands *B*
Western Kentucky University *B, M*

Louisiana

Centenary College of Louisiana *B, T*
Dillard University *B*
Grambling State University *B*
Louisiana State University
    Shreveport *B*
Louisiana State University and
    Agricultural and Mechanical
    College *B, M, D*
Louisiana Tech University *B, M*
Loyola University New Orleans *B*
Nicholls State University *B*
Northwestern State University *B*
Our Lady of Holy Cross College *T*
Southeastern Louisiana University *B*
Southern University
    New Orleans *B*
    Shreveport *A*
Southern University and Agricultural
    and Mechanical College *B, M*
Tulane University *B, M, D*
University of Louisiana at Lafayette *B*
University of Louisiana at Monroe *B*
University of New Orleans *B, M, D*
Xavier University of Louisiana *B*

Maine

Bates College *B*
Bowdoin College *B*
Colby College *B*
St. Joseph's College *B*
University of Maine *B, M, D*
University of New England *B*
University of Southern Maine *B*

Maryland

Allegany College of Maryland *A*
Cecil Community College *A*
College of Notre Dame of Maryland *B*
Columbia Union College *B*
Community College of Baltimore
    County *A*
Coppin State University *B*
Frederick Community College *A*
Frostburg State University *B, T*
Goucher College *B*
Harford Community College *A*
Hood College *B, T*

Johns Hopkins University *B, M, D*
Loyola College in Maryland *B*
McDaniel College *B*
Morgan State University *B*
Mount St. Mary's University *B*
Prince George's Community
    College *A*
St. Mary's College of Maryland *B*
Salisbury University *B, T*
Towson University *B*
United States Naval Academy *B*
University of Maryland
    Baltimore County *B, M, D*
    College Park *B, M, D*
    Eastern Shore *B*
Villa Julie College *B*
Washington College *B*

Massachusetts

American International College *B*
Amherst College *B*
Assumption College *B*
Boston College *B, M, D*
Boston University *B, M, D*
Brandeis University *B, M, D*
Bridgewater State College *B*
Bunker Hill Community College *A*
Clark University *B, M, D*
College of the Holy Cross *B*
Eastern Nazarene College *B*
Elms College *B*
Emmanuel College *B*
Framingham State College *B*
Gordon College *B*
Hampshire College *B*
Harvard College *B, D*
Massachusetts College of Liberal
    Arts *B*
Massachusetts College of Pharmacy
    and Health Sciences *B, M*
Massachusetts Institute of
    Technology *B, D*
Merrimack College *B*
Mount Holyoke College *B*
Northeastern University *B, M, D*
Salem State College *B*
Simmons College *B*
Simon's Rock College of Bard *B*
Smith College *B*
Springfield Technical Community
    College *A*
Stonehill College *B*
Suffolk University *B*
Tufts University *B*
University of Massachusetts
    Amherst *B, M, D*
    Boston *B, M*
    Dartmouth *B, M*
    Lowell *B, M, D*
Wellesley College *B*
Western New England College *B, T*
Wheaton College *B*
Williams College *B*
Worcester Polytechnic
    Institute *B, M, D*
Worcester State College *B*

Michigan

Adrian College *B, T*
Albion College *B, T*
Alma College *B, T*
Andrews University *B*
Aquinas College *B, T*
Calvin College *B*
Central Michigan University *B, M, T*
Concordia University *B*
Delta College *A*
Eastern Michigan University *B, M*
Ferris State University *B*
Gogebic Community College *A*
Grand Valley State University *B*
Hillsdale College *B*
Hope College *B*
Kalamazoo College *B, T*

Kellogg Community College *A*
Kettering University *B*
Lake Michigan College *A*
Lake Superior State University *A, B*
Lansing Community College *A*
Lawrence Technological University *B*
Macomb Community College *A*
Madonna University *B*
Marygrove College *B, T*
Michigan State University *B, M, D*
Michigan Technological
   University *B, M, D, T*
Mid Michigan Community College *A*
Northern Michigan University *A, B, M*
Oakland University *B, M, T*
Olivet College *B, T*
Saginaw Valley State University *B, T*
Siena Heights University *A, B*
Spring Arbor University *B, T*
University of Detroit Mercy *B, M*
University of Michigan *B, M, D, T*
University of Michigan
   Dearborn *B*
   Flint *B, T*
Wayne State University *B, M, D*
Western Michigan University *B, M, D*

Minnesota
Augsburg College *B*
Bemidji State University *B, M*
Bethany Lutheran College *B*
Bethel University *B*
Carleton College *B*
College of St. Benedict *B*
College of St. Catherine *B*
College of St. Scholastica *B*
Concordia College: Moorhead *B*
Gustavus Adolphus College *B*
Hamline University *B*
Macalester College *B, T*
Minnesota State University
   Mankato *B, M, T*
   Moorhead *B*
Ridgewater College *A*
St. Cloud State University *B*
St. John's University *B*
St. Mary's University of Minnesota *B*
St. Olaf College *B*
Southwest Minnesota State
   University *B*
University of Minnesota
   Duluth *B, M*
   Morris *B*
   Twin Cities *B, M, D*
University of St. Thomas *B*
Vermilion Community College *A*
Winona State University *B*

Mississippi
Alcorn State University *B*
Belhaven College *B*
Blue Mountain College *B*
Coahoma Community College *A*
Delta State University *B*
East Central Community College *A*
Hinds Community College *A*
Itawamba Community College *A*
Jackson State University *B, M*
Millsaps College *B, T*
Mississippi College *B, M*
Mississippi State University *B, M, D*
Mississippi Valley State University *B*
Rust College *B*
Tougaloo College *B*
University of Mississippi *B, M, D, T*
University of Southern
   Mississippi *B, M, D*
William Carey College *B*

Missouri
Avila University *B*
Central Methodist University *A, B*
Central Missouri State University *B*
College of the Ozarks *B*

Columbia College *B*
Crowder College *A*
Drury University *B, T*
Evangel University *B*
Lincoln University *B*
Lindenwood University *B*
Maryville University of Saint Louis *B*
Missouri Baptist University *B, T*
Missouri Southern State
   University *B, T*
Missouri State University *B, M*
Missouri Western State University *B, T*
Northwest Missouri State
   University *B*
Park University *B*
Rockhurst University *B*
St. Louis Community College
   St. Louis Community College at
      Florissant Valley *A*
St. Louis University *B, M*
Southeast Missouri State University *B*
Southwest Baptist University *B, T*
Three Rivers Community College *A*
Truman State University *B*
University of Missouri
   Columbia *B, M, D*
   Kansas City *B, M*
   Rolla *B, M, D, T*
   St. Louis *B, M, D*
Washington University in St.
   Louis *B, M, D*
Westminster College *B*
William Jewell College *B, T*

Montana
Carroll College *B, T*
Montana State University
   Billings *B, T*
   Bozeman *B, M, D*
Montana Tech of the University of
   Montana *B*
Rocky Mountain College *B, T*
University of Great Falls *B*
University of Montana:
   Missoula *B, M, D*
University of Montana: Western *B*

Nebraska
Chadron State College *B*
College of Saint Mary *B, T*
Concordia University *B, T*
Creighton University *B*
Dana College *B*
Doane College *B*
Hastings College *B*
Midland Lutheran College *B, T*
Nebraska Wesleyan University *B*
Northeast Community College *A*
Union College *B*
University of Nebraska
   Kearney *B, T*
   Lincoln *B, M, D*
   Omaha *B*
Wayne State College *B, T*
Western Nebraska Community
   College *A*
York College *B*

Nevada
Great Basin College *A*
University of Nevada
   Las Vegas *B, M*
   Reno *B, M, D*
Western Nevada Community
   College *A*

New Hampshire
Dartmouth College *B, M, D, T*
Keene State College *B*
Plymouth State University *B*
St. Anselm College *B, T*
University of New Hampshire *B, M, D*

New Jersey
Atlantic Cape Community College *A*
Bloomfield College *B*
Caldwell College *B*
The College of New Jersey *B, T*
College of St. Elizabeth *B, T*
Drew University *B*
Essex County College *C, A*
Fairleigh Dickinson University
   College at Florham *B, M*
   Metropolitan Campus *B*
Georgian Court University *B*
Gloucester County College *A*
Hudson County Community
   College *A*
Kean University *B, T*
Middlesex County College *A*
Monmouth University *B*
Montclair State University *B, M*
New Jersey City University *B*
New Jersey Institute of
   Technology *B, M, D*
Princeton University *B, M, D*
Ramapo College of New Jersey *B*
Raritan Valley Community College *A*
Richard Stockton College of New
   Jersey *B*
Rider University *B*
Rowan University *B*
Rutgers, The State University of New
   Jersey
   Camden Regional Campus *B, M, T*
   New Brunswick/Piscataway
      Campus *B, M, D*
   Newark Regional Campus *B, M, D*
St. Peter's College *B*
Salem Community College *A*
Seton Hall University *B, M, D, T*
Stevens Institute of
   Technology *B, M, D*
Sussex County Community College *A*
Thomas Edison State College *A, B*
Union County College *A*
Warren County Community College *A*
William Paterson University of New
   Jersey *B*

New Mexico
Eastern New Mexico University *B, M*
New Mexico Highlands
   University *B, M*
New Mexico Institute of Mining and
   Technology *B, M, D*
New Mexico Junior College *A*
New Mexico State University *B, M, D*
San Juan College *A*
University of New Mexico *B, M, D*
Western New Mexico University *B*

New York
Adelphi University *B*
Adirondack Community College *A*
Alfred University *B*
Bard College *B*
Barnard College *B*
Canisius College *B*
Cayuga County Community College *A*
City University of New York
   Brooklyn College *B, M*
   City College *B, M, D*
   College of Staten Island *B*
   Hunter College *B, M*
   Kingsborough Community
      College *A*
   Lehman College *B*
   Queens College *B, M, T*
   Queensborough Community
      College *A*
   York College *B*
Clarkson University *B, M, D*
Colgate University *B*
College of Mount St. Vincent *B, T*
College of New Rochelle *B, T*
College of Saint Rose *B*

Columbia University
   Columbia College *B*
   School of General Studies *B*
Cornell University *B, M, D*
Elmira College *B, T*
Excelsior College *B*
Finger Lakes Community College *A*
Fordham University *B, M, D*
Hamilton College *B*
Hartwick College *B, T*
Hobart and William Smith Colleges *B*
Hofstra University *B*
Houghton College *B*
Hudson Valley Community College *A*
Iona College *B*
Ithaca College *B, T*
Le Moyne College *B*
Long Island University
   Brooklyn Campus *B, M*
   C. W. Post Campus *B*
Manhattan College *B*
Manhattanville College *B*
Marist College *B*
Monroe Community College *A*
Mount St. Mary College *B, T*
Nazareth College of Rochester *B*
New York Institute of Technology *B*
New York University *B, M, D*
Niagara University *B*
Pace University *B*
Polytechnic University *B, M, D*
Rensselaer Polytechnic
   Institute *B, M, D*
Roberts Wesleyan College *B*
Rochester Institute of
   Technology *A, B, M*
Russell Sage College *B*
St. Bonaventure University *B, T*
St. Francis College *B*
St. John Fisher College *B*
St. John's University *B, M*
St. Joseph's College *B*
St. Lawrence University *B, T*
St. Thomas Aquinas College *B, T*
Sarah Lawrence College *B*
Siena College *B, T*
Skidmore College *B*
State University of New York
   Albany *B, M, D*
   Binghamton *B, M, D*
   Buffalo *B, M, D*
   College at Brockport *B, T*
   College at Buffalo *B, M*
   College at Cortland *B*
   College at Fredonia *B, M, T*
   College at Geneseo *B, T*
   College at Old Westbury *B, T*
   College at Oneonta *B*
   College at Plattsburgh *B*
   College at Potsdam *B*
   College of Agriculture and
      Technology at Morrisville *A*
   College of Environmental Science
      and Forestry *B, M, D*
   College of Technology at Alfred *A*
   New Paltz *B, M, T*
   Oswego *B, M*
   Purchase *B*
   Stony Brook *B, M, D*
Suffolk County Community College *A*
Syracuse University *B, M, D*
Touro College *B*
Union College *B*
United States Military Academy *B*
University of Rochester *B, M, D*
Utica College *B*
Vassar College *B*
Wagner College *B, T*
Wells College *B*
Yeshiva University *B*

North Carolina
Appalachian State University *B*
Barton College *B*

Bennett College B
Campbell University B
Catawba College B, T
Davidson College B
Duke University B, M, D
East Carolina University B, M
Elizabeth City State University B
Elon University B
Fayetteville State University B
Gardner-Webb University B
Greensboro College B
Guilford College B
High Point University B
Johnson C. Smith University B
Lenoir-Rhyne College B
Livingstone College B
Louisburg College A
Mars Hill College B, T
Meredith College B
Methodist College A, B, T
North Carolina Agricultural and
    Technical State University B, M
North Carolina Central
    University B, M
North Carolina State
    University B, M, D
North Carolina Wesleyan College B
Pfeiffer University B
St. Andrews Presbyterian College B
St. Augustine's College B
Salem College B
Shaw University B
University of North Carolina
    Asheville B, T
    Chapel Hill B, M, D
    Charlotte B, M
    Greensboro B, M, T
    Pembroke B
    Wilmington B, M
Wake Forest University B, M, D
Warren Wilson College B
Western Carolina University B, M
Wingate University B
Winston-Salem State University B

North Dakota

Dickinson State University B, T
Jamestown College B
Mayville State University B, T
Minot State University B
North Dakota State
    University B, M, D, T
University of North Dakota B, M, D, T
Valley City State University B

Ohio

Antioch College B
Ashland University B
Baldwin-Wallace College B, T
Bluffton University B
Bowling Green State
    University B, M, D
Capital University B
Case Western Reserve
    University B, M, D
Cedarville University B, T
Central State University B
Cleveland State University B, M, D, T
College of Mount St. Joseph B, T
College of Wooster B
Defiance College B, T
Denison University B
Franciscan University of
    Steubenville B
Heidelberg College B
Hiram College B
Jefferson Community College A
John Carroll University B, M
Kent State University B, M, D
Kenyon College B
Lake Erie College B
Malone College B
Marietta College B

Miami University
    Oxford Campus B, M, D, T
Mount Union College B
Mount Vernon Nazarene University B
Muskingum College B
Oberlin College B
Ohio Dominican University A, B, T
Ohio Northern University B
Ohio State University
    Columbus Campus B, M, D
Ohio University B, M, D
Ohio Wesleyan University B
Otterbein College B
Owens Community College
    Toledo A
Shawnee State University B
Sinclair Community College A
University of Akron B, M, D
University of Cincinnati B, M, D
University of Cincinnati
    Clermont College A
    Raymond Walters College A
University of Dayton B, M
University of Rio Grande A, B, T
University of Toledo B, M, D
Walsh University B
Wilmington College B
Wittenberg University B
Wright State University A, B, M
Wright State University: Lake
    Campus A
Xavier University B
Youngstown State University B, M

Oklahoma

Bacone College A
Cameron University B
Connors State College A
East Central University B, T
Eastern Oklahoma State College A
Northeastern State University B
Northwestern Oklahoma State
    University B
Oklahoma Baptist University B, T
Oklahoma Christian University B
Oklahoma City Community College A
Oklahoma City University B
Oklahoma Panhandle State
    University B
Oklahoma State University B, M, D
Oklahoma Wesleyan University A, B
Oral Roberts University B
Rose State College A
Southeastern Oklahoma State
    University B
Southern Nazarene University B
Southwestern Oklahoma State
    University B
Tulsa Community College A
University of Central Oklahoma B
University of Oklahoma B, M, D
University of Science and Arts of
    Oklahoma B
University of Tulsa B, M

Oregon

Central Oregon Community
    College A
Chemeketa Community College A
Concordia University B
Eastern Oregon University B, T
George Fox University B
Lewis & Clark College B
Linfield College B, T
Linn-Benton Community College A
Oregon State University B, M, D
Pacific University B
Portland State University B, M
Reed College B
Southern Oregon University B
Treasure Valley Community College A
University of Oregon B, M, D
University of Portland B
Western Oregon University B

Willamette University B

Pennsylvania

Albright College B, T
Allegheny College B
Alvernia College B
Arcadia University B
Bloomsburg University of
    Pennsylvania B, T
Bryn Mawr College B, M, D
Bucknell University B, M
Bucks County Community College A
Cabrini College B
California University of
    Pennsylvania B, M
Carlow University B
Carnegie Mellon University B, M, D
Cedar Crest College B
Chatham College B
Chestnut Hill College A, B
Cheyney University of
    Pennsylvania B, T
Clarion University of
    Pennsylvania B, T
College Misericordia B
Community College of Allegheny
    County A
DeSales University B, T
Delaware Valley College B
Dickinson College B
Drexel University B, M, D
Duquesne University B, M, D
East Stroudsburg University of
    Pennsylvania B, T
Eastern University B
Edinboro University of
    Pennsylvania B, T
Elizabethtown College B
Franklin & Marshall College B
Gannon University B
Geneva College B, T
Gettysburg College B
Grove City College B
Harrisburg Area Community
    College A
Haverford College B, T
Holy Family University B, T
Immaculata University A, B
Indiana University of
    Pennsylvania B, M, T
Juniata College B
King's College B, T
Kutztown University of
    Pennsylvania B, T
La Roche College B
La Salle University B
Lafayette College B
Lebanon Valley College B, T
Lehigh University B, M, D
Lincoln University B
Lock Haven University of
    Pennsylvania B, T
Lycoming College B
Mansfield University of
    Pennsylvania B, T
Mercyhurst College B
Messiah College B
Millersville University of
    Pennsylvania B, T
Moravian College B, T
Muhlenberg College C, B
Northampton County Area
    Community College A
Penn State
    Abington B
    Altoona B
    Beaver B
    Berks B
    Delaware County B
    Dubois B
    Erie, The Behrend College B
    Fayette B
    Hazleton B
    Lehigh Valley B

    McKeesport B
    Mont Alto B
    New Kensington B
    Schuylkill - Capital College B
    University Park B, M, D
    Wilkes-Barre B
    Worthington Scranton B
    York B
Philadelphia University B
Reading Area Community College A
Rosemont College B
St. Francis University B
St. Joseph's University A, B
St. Vincent College B
Seton Hill University B, T
Shippensburg University of
    Pennsylvania B, T
Slippery Rock University of
    Pennsylvania B
Susquehanna University B, T
Swarthmore College B
Temple University B, M, D
Thiel College B
University of Pennsylvania B, M, D
University of Pittsburgh B, M, D
University of Pittsburgh
    Bradford B
    Johnstown B
University of Scranton B, M, T
University of the Sciences in
    Philadelphia B, M, D
Ursinus College B, T
Villanova University B, M, D
Washington and Jefferson College B
Waynesburg College B
West Chester University of
    Pennsylvania B, M, T
Westminster College B
Widener University B
Wilkes University B
Wilson College B
York College of Pennsylvania A, B

Puerto Rico

Bayamon Central University B
Inter American University of Puerto
    Rico
    Arecibo Campus B
    Bayamon Campus B
    San German Campus B
Pontifical Catholic University of
    Puerto Rico B, M
Turabo University B
Universidad Adventista de las
    Antillas B
Universidad Metropolitana B
University of Puerto Rico
    Cayey University College B
    Mayaguez B, M, D
    Rio Piedras B, M, D
University of the Sacred Heart B

Rhode Island

Brown University B, M, D
Providence College B
Rhode Island College B
Roger Williams University B
Salve Regina University B
University of Rhode Island B, M, D

South Carolina

Allen University B
Benedict College B
Charleston Southern University B
The Citadel B
Claflin University B
Clemson University B, M, D
Coastal Carolina University B
Coker College B
College of Charleston B, T
Columbia College B
Converse College B
Erskine College B
Francis Marion University B

Furman University *B, M, T*
Lander University *B*
Limestone College *B*
Newberry College *B*
Presbyterian College *B*
South Carolina State University *B*
Southern Wesleyan University *B*
University of South Carolina *B, M, D*
University of South Carolina
   Aiken *B*
   Upstate *B*
Winthrop University *B*
Wofford College *B, T*

South Dakota

Augustana College *B, T*
Black Hills State University *B*
Dakota State University *B*
Mount Marty College *B*
Northern State University *B*
South Dakota School of Mines and
   Technology *B, M*
South Dakota State
   University *B, M, D, T*
University of Sioux Falls *B*
University of South Dakota *B, M*

Tennessee

Austin Peay State University *B*
Belmont University *B, T*
Bethel College *B*
Carson-Newman College *B, T*
Christian Brothers University *B*
Columbia State Community College *A*
Crichton College *B*
East Tennessee State
   University *B, M, T*
Fisk University *B, M*
Freed-Hardeman University *B*
Hiwassee College *A*
Jackson State Community College *A*
King College *B, T*
Lambuth University *B*
LeMoyne-Owen College *B*
Lee University *B*
Lincoln Memorial University *B, T*
Lipscomb University *B*
Maryville College *B, T*
Middle Tennessee State
   University *B, M, D*
Milligan College *B, T*
Rhodes College *B*
Roane State Community College *A*
Southern Adventist University *B*
Tennessee State University *B, M*
Tennessee Technological
   University *B, M, T*
Tennessee Wesleyan College *B, T*
Trevecca Nazarene University *B*
Union University *B, T*
University of Memphis *B, M, D*
University of Tennessee
   Chattanooga *B*
   Knoxville *B, M, D*
   Martin *B*
University of the South *B*
Vanderbilt University *B, M, D*

Texas

Abilene Christian University *B*
Amarillo College *A*
Angelo State University *B*
Austin College *B*
Austin Community College *A*
Baylor University *B, M, D*
Blinn College *A*
Brazosport College *A*
Central Texas College *A*
Cisco Junior College *A*
Clarendon College *A*
Coastal Bend College *A*
College of the Mainland *A*
Del Mar College *A*
East Texas Baptist University *B*

El Paso Community College *A*
Frank Phillips College *A*
Galveston College *A*
Grayson County College *A*
Hardin-Simmons University *B*
Hill College *A*
Houston Baptist University *B*
Howard College *A*
Howard Payne University *B, T*
Huston-Tillotson College *B*
Jarvis Christian College *B, T*
Kilgore College *A*
Lamar University *B, M*
Laredo Community College *A*
LeTourneau University *B*
Lon Morris College *A*
Lubbock Christian University *B, T*
McMurry University *B, T*
Midland College *A*
Midwestern State University *B*
Navarro College *A*
Northeast Texas Community
   College *A*
Northwest Vista College *A*
Odessa College *A*
Our Lady of the Lake University of San
   Antonio *B*
Palo Alto College *A*
Paris Junior College *A*
Prairie View A&M University *B, M*
Rice University *B, M, D*
St. Edward's University *B*
St. Mary's University *B*
St. Philip's College *A*
Sam Houston State University *B, M*
San Jacinto College
   North *A*
Schreiner University *B*
South Plains College *A*
South Texas College *A*
Southern Methodist
   University *B, M, D*
Southwestern Adventist
   University *B*
Southwestern University *B, T*
Stephen F. Austin State
   University *B, M, T*
Sul Ross State University *B*
Tarleton State University *B, T*
Texarkana College *A*
Texas A&M University *B, M, D*
Texas A&M University
   Commerce *B, M*
   Kingsville *B, M*
Texas Christian University *B, M, D*
Texas Lutheran University *B*
Texas Southern University *B, M*
Texas State University: San
   Marcos *B, M, T*
Texas Tech University *B, M, D*
Texas Wesleyan University *B*
Texas Woman's University *B, M*
Trinity University *B*
Trinity Valley Community College *A*
Tyler Junior College *A*
University of Dallas *B*
University of Houston *B, M, D*
University of Houston
   Clear Lake *B, M*
   Downtown *B*
University of Mary Hardin-Baylor *B, T*
University of North Texas *B, M, D*
University of St. Thomas *B*
University of Texas
   Arlington *B, M, D*
   Austin *B, M, D*
   Brownsville *B*
   Dallas *B, M, D*
   El Paso *B, M*
   Pan American *B*
   San Antonio *B, M*
   Tyler *B*
   of the Permian Basin *B*
University of the Incarnate Word *A, B*

Wayland Baptist University *B, T*
West Texas A&M University *B, M*
Western Texas College *A*
Wharton County Junior College *A*
Wiley College *B*

Utah

Brigham Young University *B, M, D*
Dixie State College of Utah *A*
Salt Lake Community College *A*
Snow College *A*
Southern Utah University *B, T*
University of Utah *B, M, D*
Utah State University *B, M, D*
Utah Valley State College *A, B*
Weber State University *B*
Westminster College *B*

Vermont

Bennington College *B*
Castleton State College *A*
Marlboro College *B*
Middlebury College *B*
Norwich University *B*
St. Michael's College *B*
University of Vermont *B, M, D*

Virginia

Averett University *B*
Bluefield College *B*
Bridgewater College *B*
Christopher Newport University *B*
College of William and Mary *B, M*
Eastern Mennonite University *B*
Emory & Henry College *B, T*
Ferrum College *B*
George Mason University *B, M*
Hampden-Sydney College *B*
Hampton University *B, M*
Hollins University *B*
James Madison University *B, T*
Longwood University *B, T*
Lynchburg College *B*
Mary Baldwin College *B*
Norfolk State University *B*
Old Dominion University *B, M, D, T*
Radford University *B*
Randolph-Macon College *B*
Randolph-Macon Woman's College *B*
Roanoke College *B, T*
Shenandoah University *B*
Sweet Briar College *B*
University of Mary Washington *B*
University of Richmond *B, T*
University of Virginia *B, M, D*
University of Virginia's College at
   Wise *B, T*
Virginia Commonwealth
   University *B, M, D*
Virginia Military Institute *B*
Virginia Polytechnic Institute and
   State University *B, M, D*
Virginia State University *B*
Virginia Union University *B*
Virginia Wesleyan College *B*
Washington and Lee University *B*

Washington

Cascadia Community College *A*
Central Washington University *B, M*
Centralia College *A*
Eastern Washington University *B*
Everett Community College *A*
Gonzaga University *B*
Heritage University *B*
Olympic College *A*
Pacific Lutheran University *B*
Saint Martin's University *B*
Seattle Pacific University *B*
Seattle University *B*
University of Puget Sound *B, T*
University of Washington *B, M, D*
Walla Walla College *B*

Washington State University *B, M, D*
Western Washington University *B, M*
Whitman College *B*
Whitworth College *B, T*

West Virginia

Alderson-Broaddus College *B*
Bethany College *B*
Concord University *B*
Davis and Elkins College *B*
Glenville State College *B*
Marshall University *B, M*
Potomac State College of West Virginia
   University *A*
Shepherd University *B*
University of Charleston *B*
West Liberty State College *B*
West Virginia State University *B*
West Virginia University *B, M, D, T*
West Virginia University Institute of
   Technology *B*
West Virginia Wesleyan College *B*
Wheeling Jesuit University *B*

Wisconsin

Alverno College *B*
Beloit College *B*
Cardinal Stritch University *B*
Carroll College *B*
Carthage College *B, T*
Edgewood College *B*
Lakeland College *B*
Lawrence University *B, T*
Marian College of Fond du Lac *B*
Marquette University *B, M, D, T*
Mount Mary College *B*
Northland College *B*
Ripon College *B*
St. Norbert College *B, T*
University of Wisconsin
   Eau Claire *B*
   Green Bay *B*
   La Crosse *B, T*
   Madison *B, M, D*
   Milwaukee *B, M, D*
   Oshkosh *B*
   Parkside *B*
   Platteville *B, T*
   River Falls *B*
   Stevens Point *B, T*
   Superior *B, T*
   Whitewater *B, T*
Viterbo University *B, T*
Wisconsin Lutheran College *B*

Wyoming

Casper College *A*
Laramie County Community
   College *A*
Northwest College *A*
University of Wyoming *B, M, D*
Western Wyoming Community
   College *A*

Chemistry teacher education

Alabama

Athens State University *B*
Birmingham-Southern College *T*
Faulkner University *B*
Huntingdon College *T*
Oakwood College *B*
Talladega College *B*
University of Mobile *B*

Arizona

Arizona State University *B, T*
Grand Canyon University *B*
Northern Arizona University *B*
Prescott College *T*
University of Arizona *B, M*

Arkansas

Arkansas State University *B, M, T*
Arkansas Tech University *B*
Harding University *B, M, T*
John Brown University *B, T*
Ouachita Baptist University *B, T*
Southern Arkansas University *B, T*
University of Arkansas
  Fort Smith *B*
University of Central Arkansas *T*
University of the Ozarks *B, T*

California

Azusa Pacific University *T*
California State University
  Chico *B, T*
  Long Beach *T*
  San Bernardino *T*
San Diego State University *B, T*
San Francisco State University *B, T*
Stanford University *M, T*
University of the Pacific *T*
Vanguard University of Southern
  California *T*

Colorado

Adams State College *B, T*
Colorado State University *T*
Colorado State University
  Pueblo *T*
Fort Lewis College *B*
Regis University *B, T*

Connecticut

Albertus Magnus College *B, T*
Fairfield University *T*
Quinnipiac University *B, M*
Sacred Heart University *T*
St. Joseph College *T*
Southern Connecticut State
  University *B, M, T*
University of New Haven *T*

Delaware

University of Delaware *B, T*

District of Columbia

Catholic University of America *B*

Florida

Bethune-Cookman College *B, T*
Florida Agricultural and Mechanical
  University *T*
Florida Institute of Technology *B*
Gulf Coast Community College *A*
Manatee Community College *A*
Stetson University *B*

Georgia

Agnes Scott College *T*
Armstrong Atlantic State University *T*
Georgia Southern University *B*
Kennesaw State University *B*
University of West Georgia *B*

Hawaii

Brigham Young University-Hawaii *B, T*

Idaho

Boise State University *T*
Brigham Young University-Idaho *T*
Northwest Nazarene University *B*
University of Idaho *T*

Illinois

Augustana College *B, T*
Benedictine University *T*
Bradley University *B*
Chicago State University *B, T*
Concordia University *B, T*
Dominican University *T*
Elmhurst College *B*

Governors State University *B, T*
Greenville College *B, T*
Illinois College *T*
Illinois Wesleyan University *B*
Judson College *B, T*
Knox College *T*
Lewis University *T*
North Park University *T*
Olivet Nazarene University *B, T*
Rockford College *T*
Roosevelt University *B*
Sauk Valley Community College *A*
Trinity Christian College *B, T*
University of Illinois
  Chicago *B*
  Urbana-Champaign *B, M, T*
Wheaton College *T*

Indiana

Butler University *T*
Franklin College *B, T*
Goshen College *B*
Huntington University *B, M*
Indiana University
  Bloomington *B, T*
  South Bend *B, T*
Indiana University-Purdue University
  Fort Wayne *B, T*
Indiana University-Purdue University
  Indianapolis *B, T*
Indiana Wesleyan University *T*
Manchester College *B, T*
Purdue University
  Calumet *B*
Saint Mary's College *T*
Taylor University *B, T*
University of Evansville *B, T*
University of Indianapolis *B, T*
University of St. Francis *B, T*
Valparaiso University *B*
Vincennes University *A*

Iowa

Ashford University *B, D*
Briar Cliff University *B*
Buena Vista University *B, T*
Central College *T*
Clarke College *B, T*
Cornell College *B, T*
Dordt College *B*
Drake University *M, T*
Ellsworth Community College *A*
Graceland University *T*
Iowa State University *T*
Iowa Wesleyan College *B*
Loras College *T*
Maharishi University of
  Management *T*
Morningside College *B*
Northwestern College *T*
St. Ambrose University *B, T*
Simpson College *T*
University of Iowa *T*
Upper Iowa University *B, T*
Wartburg College *T*
William Penn University *B*

Kansas

Baker University *T*
Bethany College *B*
Bethel College *T*
Central Christian College of Kansas *A*
Colby Community College *A*
Emporia State University *T*
Garden City Community College *A*
McPherson College *B, T*
Pittsburg State University *B, T*
Sterling College *T*
Tabor College *B, T*
University of Kansas *B, T*
University of St. Mary *T*

Kentucky

Bellarmine University *B, M, T*
Campbellsville University *B*
Kentucky Wesleyan College *B, T*
Thomas More College *B*
University of the Cumberlands *T*

Louisiana

Centenary College of Louisiana *B, T*
Louisiana State University
  Shreveport *B*
Northwestern State University *B*
Our Lady of Holy Cross College *T*
Southern University
  New Orleans *B*
Southern University and Agricultural
  and Mechanical College *B*
University of Louisiana at Lafayette *B*
University of Louisiana at Monroe *B*
University of New Orleans *B*
Xavier University of Louisiana *B*

Maine

University of Maine *B*
University of Southern Maine *T*

Maryland

College of Notre Dame of Maryland *T*
Coppin State University *B, T*
St. Mary's College of Maryland *T*
Salisbury University *T*

Massachusetts

Assumption College *T*
Boston University *B*
Bridgewater State College *T*
Eastern Nazarene College *B*
Elms College *T*
Framingham State College *B*
Merrimack College *T*
Northeastern University *M*
Salem State College *M*
Tufts University *T*
University of Massachusetts
  Dartmouth *T*
Western New England College *T*
Westfield State College *M, T*
Worcester State College *T*

Michigan

Albion College *B, T*
Alma College *T*
Calvin College *B*
Central Michigan University *M*
Concordia University *B, T*
Eastern Michigan University *B, T*
Ferris State University *B*
Grand Valley State University *M, T*
Hope College *T*
Michigan Technological University *T*
Northern Michigan University *B, T*
Olivet College *B, T*
University of Detroit Mercy *B, M, T*
University of Michigan
  Dearborn *B*
  Flint *T*
Western Michigan University *B, T*

Minnesota

Augsburg College *T*
Bethel University *B*
College of St. Scholastica *T*
Concordia College: Moorhead *B, T*
Concordia University: St. Paul *B, T*
Gustavus Adolphus College *T*
Minnesota State University
  Mankato *B, T*
  Moorhead *B*
St. Cloud State University *B, T*
St. Mary's University of Minnesota *B*
Southwest Minnesota State
  University *B, T*

University of Minnesota
  Morris *T*
University of St. Thomas *B, T*
Vermilion Community College *A*
Winona State University *B, T*

Mississippi

Blue Mountain College *B*
Delta State University *T*
Itawamba Community College *A*
Mississippi College *B, M*
Mississippi State University *T*
University of Mississippi *T*

Missouri

Central Methodist University *B*
Central Missouri State University *B, T*
College of the Ozarks *B, T*
Lincoln University *B, T*
Lindenwood University *B*
Maryville University of Saint
  Louis *B, M, T*
Missouri Baptist University *T*
Missouri Southern State
  University *B, T*
Missouri State University *B*
Northwest Missouri State
  University *B, T*
Southwest Baptist University *B, T*
Truman State University *M, T*
University of Missouri
  Columbia *B*
  St. Louis *T*
Washington University in St.
  Louis *B, M, T*

Montana

Montana State University
  Billings *B*
Montana Tech of the University of
  Montana *T*
University of Great Falls *B*
University of Montana: Missoula *M, T*
University of Montana: Western *B, T*

Nebraska

Chadron State College *B*
College of Saint Mary *B*
Concordia University *B, T*
Creighton University *B, T*
Dana College *B*
Hastings College *B, M, T*
Midland Lutheran College *B, T*
Nebraska Wesleyan University *T*
Peru State College *T*
Union College *T*
University of Nebraska
  Kearney *B*
  Lincoln *B*
Wayne State College *B, T*

Nevada

University of Nevada
  Reno *B*

New Hampshire

St. Anselm College *T*
University of New Hampshire *T*

New Jersey

The College of New Jersey *B, T*
Rowan University *T*
St. Peter's College *T*

New Mexico

New Mexico Institute of Mining and
  Technology *M*
Western New Mexico University *B*

New York

Adelphi University *M, T*
Alfred University *M, T*

City University of New York
  Brooklyn College *B, M*
  City College *B*
  College of Staten Island *B*
  Hunter College *B, M, T*
  Queens College *M, T*
Colgate University *M*
College of Mount St. Vincent *T*
College of Saint Rose *B, T*
Cornell University *M, T*
D'Youville College *M, T*
Dowling College *B*
Dutchess Community College *A*
Elmira College *B, T*
Fordham University *M, T*
Hofstra University *B, M*
Houghton College *B, T*
Ithaca College *B, T*
Le Moyne College *T*
Long Island University
  Brooklyn Campus *B, M, T*
  C. W. Post Campus *B, M, T*
Manhattan College *B, T*
Marist College *B*
Nazareth College of Rochester *T*
New York Institute of Technology *B, T*
New York University *B, M, T*
Niagara University *B, M, T*
Pace University *B, M, T*
Roberts Wesleyan College *B, M*
St. Francis College *B*
St. John Fisher College *B, T*
St. Lawrence University *T*
St. Thomas Aquinas College *B, M, T*
State University of New York
  Albany *B, T*
  Binghamton *M*
  Buffalo *M, T*
  College at Brockport *M, T*
  College at Buffalo *B, M*
  College at Cortland *B, M*
  College at Fredonia *B, M, T*
  College at Geneseo *B, M, T*
  College at Old Westbury *B, T*
  College at Oneonta *B, M*
  College at Plattsburgh *B, M*
  College at Potsdam *B, M*
  College of Environmental Science
    and Forestry *B, T*
  New Paltz *B, M, T*
  Oswego *B, M*
  Stony Brook *T*
Syracuse University *B, M, T*
Utica College *B*
Vassar College *T*
Wagner College *T*
Wells College *T*

North Carolina
Appalachian State University *B*
Catawba College *T*
Elizabeth City State University *B*
Gardner-Webb University *B*
Lenoir Community College *A*
Louisburg College *A*
Mars Hill College *T*
Meredith College *T*
Methodist College *A, B, T*
North Carolina Agricultural and
    Technical State University *B, T*
North Carolina Central
    University *B, M, T*
Sandhills Community College *A*
University of North Carolina
  Charlotte *B*
  Wilmington *B*
Wake Forest University *T*

North Dakota
Dickinson State University *B, T*
Jamestown College *B*
Mayville State University *B, T*
Minot State University *B*
North Dakota State University *B, T*

Valley City State University *B, T*

Ohio
Ashland University *B, T*
Baldwin-Wallace College *T*
Bluffton University *B*
Case Western Reserve University *T*
Defiance College *B, T*
Hiram College *T*
John Carroll University *T*
Kent State University *B*
Miami University
  Oxford Campus *B, T*
Mount Union College *T*
Mount Vernon Nazarene
    University *B, M, T*
Ohio Dominican University *B, T*
Ohio Northern University *B*
Ohio Wesleyan University *B*
Otterbein College *B*
Shawnee State University *T*
University of Findlay *T*
University of Rio Grande *B, T*
University of Toledo *B*
Wilmington College *B*
Xavier University *B, M*
Youngstown State University *B, M*

Oklahoma
Cameron University *B*
East Central University *T*
Eastern Oklahoma State College *A*
Northeastern State University *B*
Oklahoma Baptist University *B, T*
Southern Nazarene University *B*
University of Central Oklahoma *B*
University of Tulsa *B, T*

Oregon
Concordia University *B, M, T*
George Fox University *T*
Linfield College *T*
Oregon State University *M*
Portland State University *T*
Western Oregon University *T*

Pennsylvania
Albright College *T*
Alvernia College *B*
Arcadia University *B, M, T*
Cabrini College *T*
Carlow University *T*
Chatham College *T*
College Misericordia *T*
DeSales University *T*
Dickinson College *T*
Duquesne University *M, T*
Elizabethtown College *B*
Gannon University *T*
Geneva College *B, T*
Gettysburg College *T*
Grove City College *B, T*
Holy Family University *B, M, T*
Juniata College *B, T*
King's College *T*
La Roche College *B*
La Salle University *B, T*
Lebanon Valley College *T*
Lycoming College *T*
Mansfield University of
    Pennsylvania *B, T*
Mercyhurst College *B, T*
Messiah College *B, T*
Moravian College *T*
St. Francis University *B, T*
St. Vincent College *T*
Seton Hill University *B, T*
Susquehanna University *T*
Thiel College *B*
University of Pittsburgh
  Johnstown *B, T*
Villanova University *T*
Washington and Jefferson College *T*

Waynesburg College *B, T*
Westminster College *T*
Widener University *T*
Wilkes University *M, T*
Wilson College *T*

Puerto Rico
Inter American University of Puerto
    Rico
  Arecibo Campus *B*
  San German Campus *B*
Pontifical Catholic University of
    Puerto Rico *B, T*
Turabo University *B*

Rhode Island
Rhode Island College *B*

South Carolina
Coker College *B, T*
Furman University *T*
South Carolina State University *B, T*

South Dakota
Black Hills State University *B*
Dakota State University *B, T*
Mount Marty College *B*
University of Sioux Falls *T*
University of South Dakota *B, M, D, T*

Tennessee
Belmont University *B, M, T*
Christian Brothers University *B, M, T*
Crichton College *B*
King College *T*
Lambuth University *B, T*
Lincoln Memorial University *B, T*
Lipscomb University *B, T*
Maryville College *B, T*
Southern Adventist University *B*
Tennessee Technological University *T*
Tennessee Wesleyan College *B, T*
Trevecca Nazarene University *B, T*
Union University *B, T*
University of Memphis *T*
University of Tennessee
    Martin *B*

Texas
East Texas Baptist University *B*
Houston Baptist University *T*
Howard Payne University *B, T*
Kilgore College *A*
Lamar University *T*
Laredo Community College *A*
Lubbock Christian University *B*
McMurry University *T*
St. Mary's University *T*
Tarleton State University *T*
Texas A&M University
  Commerce *B*
  Kingsville *T*
Texas State University: San Marcos *T*
Texas Wesleyan University *B, T*
University of Dallas *T*
University of Houston *T*
University of Houston
  Clear Lake *T*
University of Mary Hardin-Baylor *B, T*
University of Texas
  San Antonio *T*
West Texas A&M University *T*

Utah
Brigham Young University *B*
Southern Utah University *B, T*
University of Utah *B*
Utah State University *B*
Utah Valley State College *B*
Weber State University *B*

Vermont
Castleton State College *B, T*
St. Michael's College *T*

Virginia
Averett University *B, M, T*
Bluefield College *T*
Bridgewater College *T*
Eastern Mennonite University *T*
Hampton University *M*
Hollins University *T*
Longwood University *B, T*
Old Dominion University *B, M, T*
Radford University *T*
University of Virginia's College at
    Wise *T*

Washington
Central Washington University *B, T*
Heritage University *B*
Washington State University *B, M, T*
Western Washington University *B*
Whitworth College *B, T*

West Virginia
Alderson-Broaddus College *T*
Bethany College *T*
Concord University *B, M, T*
Shepherd University *T*
West Liberty State College *B*
West Virginia Wesleyan College *B*

Wisconsin
Carroll College *B, T*
Carthage College *B*
Edgewood College *B*
Lakeland College *T*
Lawrence University *T*
Marian College of Fond du Lac *B, T*
Mount Mary College *B, T*
Northland College *T*
St. Norbert College *T*
University of Wisconsin
  Green Bay *T*
  Platteville *B*
  River Falls *T*
  Superior *B, T*
Viterbo University *B, T*

Child care management

Alabama
Calhoun Community College *C, A*
Gadsden State Community College *C*
Jefferson State Community
    College *C, A*
Northwest-Shoals Community
    College *C, A*
Shelton State Community College *C*
Snead State Community College *C, A*
Trenholm State Technical College *C, A*
Wallace State Community College at
    Hanceville *A*

Alaska
University of Alaska
  Anchorage *C, A*
  Southeast *C, A*

Arizona
Arizona Western College *C, A*
Glendale Community College *C, A*
Mohave Community College *C, A*
Northland Pioneer College *C, A*
Phoenix College *C, A*
Pima Community College *C*
Scottsdale Community College *A*

Arkansas
Arkansas State University *M*
East Arkansas Community College *A*
Henderson State University *A*

Northwest Arkansas Community
College *C, A*
Ouachita Technical College *A*
Pulaski Technical College *C, A*
South Arkansas Community College *A*
Southeast Arkansas College *A*
University of Arkansas
Community College at Hope *A*
Cossatot Community College of the
A
University of Central Arkansas *A*

California

American River College *C, A*
Antelope Valley College *C, A*
Barstow College *C, A*
Butte College *A*
Cabrillo College *C, A*
California State University
Northridge *B*
Canada College *C, A*
Cerro Coso Community College *C, A*
Chabot College *A*
Chaffey College *C, A*
Citrus College *C*
College of the Canyons *C, A*
College of the Desert *A*
College of the Sequoias *C, A*
College of the Siskiyous *C, A*
Cuyamaca College *C, A*
Diablo Valley College *C*
Feather River College *C, A*
Foothill College *C*
Fresno City College *C, A*
Fullerton College *C, A*
Glendale Community College *A*
Grossmont Community College *C, A*
Imperial Valley College *C, A*
Las Positas College *C, A*
Long Beach City College *C, A*
Los Angeles City College *C, A*
Los Angeles Harbor College *C, A*
Los Angeles Southwest College *C, A*
Los Medanos College *C, A*
Merritt College *C, A*
MiraCosta College *C, A*
Modesto Junior College *C, A*
Moorpark College *C, A*
Ohlone College *C, A*
Orange Coast College *C, A*
Palomar College *C, A*
Porterville College *C, A*
Reedley College *C*
Rio Hondo College *C*
Sacramento City College *C, A*
Saddleback College *C*
San Bernardino Valley College *C*
San Diego City College *C, A*
San Joaquin Delta College *C, A*
Santa Barbara City College *C, A*
Santa Rosa Junior College *A*
Shasta College *A*
Sierra College *A*
Southwestern College *C, A*
University of La Verne *B*
Ventura College *C, A*
West Valley College *C, A*

Colorado

Aims Community College *C, A*
Colorado Northwestern Community
College *C, A*
Community College of Aurora *C, A*
Community College of Denver *C, A*
Front Range Community College *C, A*
Pueblo Community College *A*

Connecticut

Asnuntuck Community College *C, A*
Briarwood College *C, A*
Gateway Community College *C*
Housatonic Community College *C, A*
Mitchell College *A*

Naugatuck Valley Community
College *C, A*

Delaware

Delaware Technical and Community
College
Owens Campus *C, A*
Stanton/Wilmington Campus *C, A*
Terry Campus *C, A*
University of Delaware *B, T*

District of Columbia

Gallaudet University *B*

Florida

Brevard Community College *C*
Broward Community College *A*
Daytona Beach Community
College *C, A*
Hillsborough Community
College *C, A*
Indian River Community College *C*
Miami Dade College *C*
Okaloosa-Walton College *C, A*
Palm Beach Community College *A*
Pensacola Junior College *A*
Polk Community College *A*
Santa Fe Community College *A*
Seminole Community College *A*
South Florida Community College *A*

Georgia

Abraham Baldwin Agricultural
College *A*
Albany Technical College *C*
Augusta Technical Institute *C*
Chattahoochee Technical College *C, A*
Darton College *A*
Fort Valley State University *B*
Gainesville State College *C, A*
Georgia Southwestern State
University *A*
Savannah Technical College *C*
Spelman College *B*
Waycross College *A*

Hawaii

University of Hawaii
Honolulu Community College *C, A*

Idaho

Boise State University *C, A*
Idaho State University *C, A*

Illinois

Carl Sandburg College *A*
City Colleges of Chicago
Harold Washington College *C*
Malcolm X College *C, A*
Olive-Harvey College *C, A*
College of DuPage *C, A*
Elgin Community College *C*
Highland Community College *C, A*
Illinois Central College *A*
Illinois Eastern Community Colleges
Wabash Valley College *A*
Illinois Valley Community
College *C, A*
John Wood Community College *A*
Kishwaukee College *A*
Lake Land College *C, A*
Lewis and Clark Community
College *A*
Moraine Valley Community College *C*
Prairie State College *C, A*
Rock Valley College *C, A*
Sauk Valley Community College *A*
South Suburban College of Cook
County *C*
Southeastern Illinois College *A*
Southwestern Illinois College *C, A*
Triton College *A*
William Rainey Harper College *C, A*

Indiana

Ivy Tech State College
Ivy Tech Community College:
Bloomington *C, A*
Ivy Tech Community College:
Central Indiana *C, A*
Ivy Tech Community College:
Columbus *C, A*
Ivy Tech Community College: East
Central *C, A*
Ivy Tech Community College:
Kokomo *C, A*
Ivy Tech Community College:
Lafayette *C, A*
Ivy Tech Community College: North
Central *C, A*
Ivy Tech Community College:
Northeast *C, A*
Ivy Tech Community College:
Northwest *C, A*
Ivy Tech Community College: South
Central *C, A*
Ivy Tech Community College:
Southeast *C, A*
Ivy Tech Community College:
Southwest *C, A*
Ivy Tech Community College:
Wabash Valley *C, A*
Ivy Tech Community College:
Whitewater *C, A*
Vincennes University *A*

Iowa

Iowa Western Community College *A*
Kirkwood Community College *C, A*
Marshalltown Community
College *A*
Muscatine Community College *C*
Northeast Iowa Community
College *A*
Southeastern Community College
North Campus *A*
Western Iowa Tech Community
College *A*

Kansas

Allen County Community College *C*
Barton County Community
College *C, A*
Butler County Community
College *C, A*
Central Christian College of Kansas *A*
Cloud County Community
College *A*
Colby Community College *A*
Cowley County Community
College *A*
Dodge City Community College *C, A*
Garden City Community College *A*
Hutchinson Community College *C, A*
Johnson County Community
College *C*
Kansas City Kansas Community
College *C, A*

Kentucky

Eastern Kentucky University *A*
Hopkinsville Community College *C, A*
St. Catharine College *C*
Somerset Community College *C, A*
Sullivan University *C, A*

Louisiana

Nicholls State University *A*
University of Louisiana at Monroe *A*

Maine

Andover College *C, A*
Southern Maine Community
College *C, A*

Maryland

Anne Arundel Community College *A*

Carroll Community College *C, A*
Chesapeake College *C, A*
College of Southern Maryland *C, A*
Community College of Baltimore
County *C, A*
Frederick Community College *C, A*
Garrett College *C*
Hagerstown Community College *C, A*
Montgomery College *C, A*
Prince George's Community
College *C, A*
Wor-Wic Community College *C, A*

Massachusetts

Bristol Community College *A*
Holyoke Community College *C, A*
Massachusetts Bay Community
College *C, A*
Massasoit Community College *C, A*
Middlesex Community College *C*
Mount Wachusett Community
College *C, A*
Northern Essex Community
College *A*
Roxbury Community College *A*
Wheelock College *B, M*

Michigan

Baker College
of Muskegon *C*
of Owosso *C, A*
Bay de Noc Community College *A*
Ferris State University *A*
Glen Oaks Community College *C, A*
Gogebic Community College *C*
Grand Rapids Community College *A*
Kellogg Community College *C, A*
Lake Superior State University *A, B*
Lansing Community College *A*
Macomb Community College *A*
Mid Michigan Community
College *C, A*
Monroe County Community
College *A*
Montcalm Community College *C, A*
Northern Michigan University *A*
Oakland Community College *A*
St. Clair County Community
College *A*
Schoolcraft College *C, A*
Southwestern Michigan College *A*
Wayne County Community
College *C, A*

Minnesota

Alexandria Technical College *C, A*
Anoka Technical College *C, A*
Anoka-Ramsey Community College *A*
Central Lakes College *C, A*
Concordia University: St. Paul *C, B, M*
Minneapolis Community and
Technical College *A*
Minnesota State College - Southeast
Technical *A*
Northwest Technical College *A*
Pine Technical College *C, A*
Rasmussen College
St. Cloud *C, A*
Rochester Community and Technical
College *C, A*
St. Cloud Technical College *C, A*
St. Paul College *C, A*

Mississippi

Coahoma Community College *A*
Hinds Community College *A*
Itawamba Community College *A*
Meridian Community College *A*
Rust College *B*

Missouri

Central Missouri State University *A*
College of the Ozarks *B*

Mineral Area College *C*
Missouri State University:West
  Plains *C, A*
Moberly Area Community
  College *C, A*
Northwest Missouri State
  University *C*
Penn Valley Community College *C, A*
St. Louis Community College
  St. Louis Community College at
    Florissant Valley *A*
Southeast Missouri State University *A*
State Fair Community College *A*

Montana
Dawson Community College *C*
Little Big Horn College *A*

Nebraska
Central Community College *C, A*
Metropolitan Community
  College *C, A*
Mid-Plains Community College
  Area *C, A*
Southeast Community College
  Lincoln Campus *A*

Nevada
Truckee Meadows Community
  College *C, A*

New Hampshire
New Hampshire Community
  Technical College
  Claremont *C*
  Nashua *C*
  Stratham *C, A*

New Jersey
Atlantic Cape Community College *A*
County College of Morris *C*
Hudson County Community
  College *C, A*
Ocean County College *A*
Thomas Edison State College *A, B*

New Mexico
Albuquerque Technical-Vocational
  Institute *A*
Dona Ana Branch Community College
  of New Mexico State
  University *C*
Eastern New Mexico University *A*
Eastern New Mexico University:
  Roswell Campus *C, A*

New York
Broome Community College *C, A*
City University of New York
  LaGuardia Community College *A*
Dutchess Community College *C, A*
Erie Community College
  City Campus *A*
Fulton-Montgomery Community
  College *C, A*
Genesee Community College *C*
Hudson Valley Community College *A*
Medaille College *B*
Nassau Community College *A*
Orange County Community College *A*
Rockland Community College *C*
State University of New York
  College at Plattsburgh *B*
  College of Agriculture and
    Technology at Cobleskill *A, B*
Sullivan County Community
  College *C, A*
Tompkins-Cortland Community
  College *A*
Trocaire College *C*
Utica College *B*
Westchester Community College *C, A*

North Carolina
Asheville-Buncombe Technical
  Community College *C, A*
Beaufort County Community
  College *C, A*
Blue Ridge Community College *A*
Cape Fear Community College *C, A*
Carteret Community College *C*
Central Carolina Community
  College *C, A*
Central Piedmont Community
  College *C, A*
Cleveland Community College *C, A*
Craven Community College *C, A*
Edgecombe Community College *C, A*
Fayetteville Technical Community
  College *C, A*
Halifax Community College *C*
Haywood Community College *C, A*
James Sprunt Community
  College *C, A*
Johnston Community College *C, A*
Lenoir Community College *C*
Mayland Community College *C*
Nash Community College *A*
Randolph Community College *A*
Richmond Community College *C, A*
Roanoke Bible College *C, A*
Roanoke-Chowan Community
  College *A*
Sandhills Community College *A*
South Piedmont Community
  College *C, A*
Southeastern Community College *A*
Southwestern Community College *A*
Vance-Granville Community
  College *C, A*
Wayne Community College *A*
Western Piedmont Community
  College *C, A*
Wilson Technical Community
  College *C, A*

North Dakota
Lake Region State College *C, A*
Mayville State University *B*

Ohio
Cincinnati State Technical and
  Community College *C, A*
Cuyahoga Community College
  Metropolitan Campus *A*
Edison State Community College *C, A*
Jefferson Community College *C, A*
Kent State University *T*
Kent State University
  Salem Regional Campus *C*
  Trumbull Campus *C*
  Tuscarawas Campus *C*
Lakeland Community College *A*
Mount Vernon Nazarene University *A*
Sinclair Community College *C, A*
Youngstown State University *C, A*
Zane State College *A*

Oklahoma
Connors State College *C, A*
Eastern Oklahoma State College *A*
Murray State College *A*
Oklahoma City Community
  College *C, A*
Oklahoma State University
  Oklahoma City *A*
Redlands Community College *A*
Rose State College *A*
Tulsa Community College *C, A*
Western Oklahoma State College *A*

Oregon
Central Oregon Community
  College *C*
Chemeketa Community College *A*
Clatsop Community College *C*

Lane Community College *C, A*
Linn-Benton Community College *C, A*
Portland Community College *C, A*
Rogue Community College *C, A*
Southwestern Oregon Community
  College *C, A*

Pennsylvania
Academy of Medical Arts and
  Business *A*
Central Pennsylvania College *A*
Chestnut Hill College *C, A, B*
Community College of Philadelphia *A*
Gannon University *M, T*
Keystone College *C, A, B*
Laurel Business Institute *A*
Montgomery County Community
  College *A*
Northampton County Area
  Community College *C*
Penn State
  University Park *C*
Pennsylvania Highlands Community
  College *C*
Reading Area Community
  College *C, A*
Seton Hill University *C, B*
Western School of Health and
  Business Careers *A*
Westmoreland County Community
  College *C, A*

Puerto Rico
University of Puerto Rico
  Rio Piedras *B*

South Carolina
Denmark Technical College *C*
Florence-Darlington Technical
  College *C*
Forrest Junior College *C, A*
Greenville Technical College *A*
Horry-Georgetown Technical
  College *A*
Midlands Technical College *C*
Northeastern Technical College *C*
Orangeburg-Calhoun Technical
  College *C*
Piedmont Technical College *C*
South Carolina State University *B*
Technical College of the
  Lowcountry *C, A*
Tri-County Technical College *C*
Trident Technical College *C, A*

Tennessee
Belmont University *B*
Northeast State Technical Community
  College *C*
Southwest Tennessee Community
  College *A*
Trevecca Nazarene University *A*
Walters State Community College *C, A*

Texas
Amarillo College *C, A*
Angelina College *C*
Austin Community College *C, A*
Blinn College *C, A*
Brazosport College *C, A*
Central Texas College *C, A*
Coastal Bend College *C, A*
College of the Mainland *A*
Del Mar College *C, A*
El Paso Community College *C, A*
Houston Community College
  System *C, A*
Howard College *C*
Kilgore College *C, A*
Lamar State College at Port
  Arthur *C, A*
Laredo Community College *C, A*
McLennan Community College *C, A*

Midland College *C, A*
Navarro College *A*
North Harris Montgomery
  Community College District *C, A*
Odessa College *C*
St. Philip's College *C, A*
San Antonio College *C, A*
San Jacinto College
  Central Campus *C*
  North *C, A*
South Plains College *C, A*
Tarrant County College *C, A*
Temple College *C, A*
Texas Southmost College *C, A*
Trinity Valley Community College *C, A*
Tyler Junior College *C, A*
University of North Texas *B*
University of the Incarnate Word *B*
Vernon College *C*
Victoria College *C*
Weatherford College *C, A*

Utah
College of Eastern Utah *A*
Dixie State College of Utah *A*
Snow College *A*
Weber State University *A*

Vermont
Southern Vermont College *A*

Virginia
Central Virginia Community
  College *C*
Danville Community College *C*
J. Sargeant Reynolds Community
  College *C, A*
John Tyler Community College *C, A*
Lord Fairfax Community College *C*
Southwest Virginia Community
  College *C*
Thomas Nelson Community
  College *C*
Virginia Western Community
  College *A*
Wytheville Community College *A*

Washington
Centralia College *C, A*
Columbia Basin College *C, A*
Edmonds Community College *C, A*
Highline Community College *C, A*
Lake Washington Technical
  College *C, A*
North Seattle Community
  College *C, A*
Peninsula College *A*
Pierce College *A*
Renton Technical College *C*
Shoreline Community College *C*
Spokane Falls Community College *C*
Walla Walla Community College *C*
Yakima Valley Community
  College *C, A*

West Virginia
West Virginia Northern Community
  College *C, A*

Wisconsin
Blackhawk Technical College *C*
Fox Valley Technical College *A*
Gateway Technical College *A*
Madison Area Technical College *A*
Milwaukee Area Technical College *C*
Moraine Park Technical College *C, A*
Nicolet Area Technical College *C, A*
Northeast Wisconsin Technical
  College *C*
Southwest Wisconsin Technical
  College *C, A*
Waukesha County Technical
  College *A*

Western Wisconsin Technical
College *A*

Wyoming

Central Wyoming College *A*
University of Wyoming *C*

Child care service

Arkansas

Arkansas Northeastern College *C, A*
Ouachita Technical College *C*
Rich Mountain Community College *C*
South Arkansas Community
College *C, A*
University of Arkansas
Community College at Hope *C*

California

Antelope Valley College *C, A*
Foothill College *C*
Monterey Peninsula College *A*
Santa Rosa Junior College *C*
Southwestern College *C, A*
Taft College *C*

Florida

Palm Beach Community College *C*

Georgia

Albany Technical College *C*
Northwestern Technical College *C*
Savannah Technical College *C, A*
Southwest Georgia Technical
College *C, A*

Illinois

Black Hawk College *C, A*
Heartland Community College *C, A*
Kaskaskia College *A*
Lincoln Land Community College *C, A*
McHenry County College *C, A*
Moraine Valley Community College *A*
Morton College *C, A*
Parkland College *C, A*
Waubonsee Community College *C, A*

Indiana

St. Mary-of-the-Woods College *A*

Iowa

Des Moines Area Community
College *C, A*
Hawkeye Community College *C, A*
Indian Hills Community College *C, A*
Iowa Lakes Community College *C, A*

Kentucky

Ashland Community and Technical
College *C*
Elizabethtown Community and
Technical College *C, A*
Hopkinsville Community College *C*
Jefferson Community College *C, A*
Murray State University *A, B*
Owensboro Community College *C*
Somerset Community College *C, A*

Massachusetts

Cape Cod Community College *C*
Massasoit Community College *C*
Mount Wachusett Community
College *C*
North Shore Community College *C, A*
Pine Manor College *A*

Michigan

Baker College
of Muskegon *C*
of Port Huron *C*
Mott Community College *A*

Northern Michigan University *A*

Minnesota

Alexandria Technical College *C*
Central Lakes College *C*
Dakota County Technical College *C, A*
Fond du Lac Tribal and Community
College *C*
Minneapolis Community and
Technical College *C*
Minnesota State Community and
Technical College - Fergus Falls *C*
Northwest Technical College *C, A*
Rasmussen College
St. Cloud *C, A*
Ridgewater College *C*
Rochester Community and Technical
College *C*
St. Cloud Technical College *C*
St. Paul College *C*

Missouri

North Central Missouri College *A*
St. Charles Community College *C, A*

Nebraska

Wayne State College *B*

New Mexico

San Juan College *C*

New York

State University of New York
College of Agriculture and
Technology at Cobleskill *C, A*

North Carolina

Bladen Community College *C, A*
Carteret Community College *C, A*
James Sprunt Community College *C*

North Dakota

Lake Region State College *A*
Mayville State University *A*
Turtle Mountain Community
College *C*

Ohio

Stark State College of Technology *A*
Youngstown State University *C*

Oklahoma

Northeastern Oklahoma Agricultural
and Mechanical College *C*

Pennsylvania

Harrisburg Area Community
College *C*
Keystone College *A*
Lehigh Carbon Community
College *C, A*
Luzerne County Community
College *A*
Montgomery County Community
College *C*
Northampton County Area
Community College *C, A*
Pennsylvania College of Technology *A*

Rhode Island

Community College of Rhode
Island *C*

South Carolina

Aiken Technical College *C*
Greenville Technical College *C*
Horry-Georgetown Technical
College *C*
Midlands Technical College *C*
Spartanburg Technical College *C*
Williamsburg Technical College *C*

Texas

Collin County Community College
District *C*
Del Mar College *C*
San Antonio College *C*
University of Texas
Brownsville *C, A*

Utah

Salt Lake Community College *C, A*

Washington

Centralia College *C, A*
Peninsula College *A*

West Virginia

Eastern West Virginia Community and
Technical College *C, A*

Wisconsin

Fox Valley Technical College *C*
Lakeshore Technical College *C*

Child development

Alabama

Calhoun Community College *A*
Gadsden State Community College *A*
Lawson State Community College *C*

Arizona

Prescott College *B, M*

Arkansas

Arkansas Tech University *A*
Mid-South Community College *C*
University of Arkansas
Cossatot Community College of the
C
Fort Smith *A*

California

Antelope Valley College *A*
California State University
Fresno *B*
Sacramento *B, M*
San Bernardino *B*
Columbia College *C, A*
Foothill College *C, A*
Grossmont Community College *C, A*
Long Beach City College *C, A*
Mills College *B*
Monterey Peninsula College *A*
National University *B*
Point Loma Nazarene University *B*
San Diego Mesa College *C, A*
Santa Barbara City College *C*
Santa Rosa Junior College *C*
Southwestern College *C, A*
Taft College *C*

Colorado

Arapahoe Community College *A*
Pikes Peak Community College *C, A*
Red Rocks Community College *C, A*

Connecticut

St. Joseph College *B*

District of Columbia

Southeastern University *A, B*

Florida

Florida State University *B, M, D*
Gulf Coast Community College *C*
Indian River Community College *C*
Miami Dade College *A*
Nova Southeastern University *M, D*

Georgia

Fort Valley State University *B*

University of Georgia *B, M, D*

Idaho

Lewis-Clark State College *A, B*

Illinois

City Colleges of Chicago
Kennedy-King College *A*
Olive-Harvey College *A*
Rend Lake College *C, A*
University of Illinois
Urbana-Champaign *B, M, D*

Kansas

Central Christian College of Kansas *A*
Kansas State University *B*
Pittsburg State University *B*
University of St. Mary *B*

Maryland

Howard Community College *C, A*

Massachusetts

Lasell College *B, T*
Lesley University *B*
Mount Wachusett Community
College *A*
Wheelock College *B, M*

Michigan

Central Michigan University *B, T*
Delta College *C, A*
Grand Rapids Community College *A*
Kuyper College *A, B*
Madonna University *A, B*
Michigan State University *B, M*
Northern Michigan University *A*
Western Michigan University *B*

Minnesota

Hennepin Technical College *C, A*
South Central College *A*

Mississippi

Alcorn State University *B*
Mississippi Gulf Coast Community
College
Jefferson Davis Campus *C*

Missouri

Central Missouri State University *A, B*
Mineral Area College *C, A*
Ozarks Technical Community
College *C, A*
Park University *B*

Nevada

University of Nevada
Reno *B*

New Hampshire

University of New Hampshire *B*

New York

Sarah Lawrence College *B, M*
State University of New York
College at Oneonta *B*
Oswego *B*

North Carolina

Appalachian State University *B*
Beaufort County Community
College *C, A*
Campbell University *B*
Carteret Community College *A*
East Carolina University *B*
Meredith College *B*
Peace College *B*
University of North Carolina
Greensboro *B*

Ohio

Bowling Green State University *B*
Edison State Community College *C, A*
James A. Rhodes State College *C*
Ohio University *A, B*
University of Akron *B, M*
University of Dayton *M*
Youngstown State University *A*

Oklahoma

Redlands Community College *C*
Rose State College *A*
University of Central Oklahoma *B*
Western Oklahoma State College *C*

Pennsylvania

Community College of Allegheny
  County *C, A*
Keystone College *B*
Seton Hill University *B*

South Carolina

York Technical College *C*

Tennessee

Cleveland State Community College *A*
Dyersburg State Community
  College *C, A*
East Tennessee State University *B*
Northeast State Technical Community
  College *C, A*
Pellissippi State Technical Community
  College *A*
Roane State Community College *A*
Volunteer State Community College *A*

Texas

Alvin Community College *A*
Angelina College *C, A*
Collin County Community College
  District *C, A*
Del Mar College *C, A*
Eastfield College *C, A*
Houston Baptist University *B*
North Harris Montgomery
  Community College District *C, A*
San Antonio College *C*
South Texas College *A*
Texarkana College *C, A*
Texas Tech University *B*
Texas Woman's University *B, M, D*
University of Texas
  Arlington *B*
Victoria College *C*
Wharton County Junior College *C, A*

Virginia

Danville Community College *A*

Washington

Eastern Washington University *B, M*
Lower Columbia College *C, A*
Western Washington University *B*

Chinese

California

Cabrillo College *A*
California State University
  Los Angeles *B*
Claremont McKenna College *B*
Foothill College *A*
Los Angeles City College *A*
Pitzer College *B*
Pomona College *B*
San Francisco State University *B, M*
San Jose State University *B*
Scripps College *B*
Stanford University *B, M, D*
University of California
  Berkeley *B, M, D*
  Davis *B*
  Irvine *B*
  Los Angeles *B*
  Santa Barbara *B*
  Santa Cruz *B*
University of Southern California *M*

Colorado

University of Colorado
  Boulder *B*

Connecticut

Connecticut College *B*
Fairfield University *B*
Trinity College *B*
Yale University *B*

District of Columbia

George Washington University *B*
Georgetown University *B*

Georgia

Emory University *B*

Hawaii

University of Hawaii
  Manoa *B, M, D*

Indiana

Indiana University
  Bloomington *M, D*
University of Notre Dame *B*

Iowa

Grinnell College *B*
University of Iowa *B, T*

Maine

Bates College *B, T*

Maryland

University of Maryland
  College Park *B*

Massachusetts

Brandeis University *B*
Harvard College *B*
Simon's Rock College of Bard *B*
Tufts University *B*
University of Massachusetts
  Amherst *B, M*
Wellesley College *B*
Williams College *B*

Michigan

Albion College *B, T*
University of Michigan *M, D*

Minnesota

North Central University *B*
University of Minnesota
  Twin Cities *B, M, D*

Missouri

Washington University in St.
  Louis *B, M, D*

New Hampshire

Dartmouth College *B*

New Jersey

Drew University *B*
Rutgers, The State University of New
  Jersey
  New Brunswick/Piscataway
    Campus *B*
Seton Hall University *T*

New York

Bard College *B*
City University of New York
  Hunter College *B*
Columbia University
  Columbia College *B*
Hamilton College *B*
Hobart and William Smith Colleges *B*
Vassar College *B*

Ohio

Ohio State University
  Columbus Campus *B*

Oklahoma

University of Oklahoma *B*

Oregon

Pacific University *B*
Portland State University *B*
Reed College *B*
University of Oregon *B*

Pennsylvania

Carnegie Mellon University *B*
Haverford College *T*
Lincoln University *B*
Swarthmore College *B*
University of Pittsburgh *B*

Texas

Trinity University *B*

Utah

Brigham Young University *B, M*
University of Utah *B, M*

Vermont

Bennington College *B*
Middlebury College *B, M, D*

Washington

Central Washington University *B*
Pacific Lutheran University *B*
University of Puget Sound *T*
University of Washington *B*

Wisconsin

Lawrence University *B*
University of Wisconsin
  Madison *B, M, D*

Chinese studies

California

California Institute of Integral
  Studies *M, D*
City College of San Francisco *A*
University of California
  San Diego *B*

Colorado

Fort Lewis College *B*

Connecticut

Connecticut College *B*

Massachusetts

Harvard College *B, D*
Simon's Rock College of Bard *B*

New York

Columbia University
  Columbia College *B*
St. John's University *M*
State University of New York
  Albany *B*

Washington

University of Washington *B, M*

Wisconsin

Lawrence University *B*

Chiropractic (D.C.)

California

Cleveland Chiropractic College of Los
  Angeles *F*
Life Chiropractic College West *F*
Los Angeles College of Chiropractic *F*
Palmer College of
  Chiropractic-West *F*

Connecticut

University of Bridgeport College of
  Chiropractic *F*

Georgia

Life College *F*

Illinois

National University of Health
  Sciences: First Professional *F*

Iowa

Palmer College of Chiropractic *F*

Minnesota

Northwestern College of
  Chiropractic *F*

Missouri

Cleveland Chiropractic College of
  Kansas City *F*
Logan College of Chiropractic *F*

New York

New York Chiropractic College *F*

Oregon

Western States Chiropractic College *F*

South Carolina

Sherman College of Straight
  Chiropractic *F*

Texas

Parker College of Chiropractic *F*
Texas Chiropractic College *F*

Chiropractic assistant

Georgia

Life University *C*

Illinois

National University of Health
  Sciences *C*

Minnesota

Rochester Community and Technical
  College *C*

Nebraska

Northeast Community College *A*

Christian studies

Arkansas

Harding University *B, M*
Ouachita Baptist University *A*

California

California Baptist University *B*
Simpson University *B*
Vanguard University of Southern
  California *B*

Florida

Bethune-Cookman College *B*
Trinity College of Florida *C, A, B*

Georgia

Mercer University *B*
Truett-McConnell College *A*

Illinois

North Park University *B, M*
Trinity International University *C, M*

Indiana

University of Notre Dame *M*

Iowa

Iowa Wesleyan College *B*
St. Ambrose University *C*

Kansas

Bethany College *B*
Southwestern College *B*

Kentucky

Lindsey Wilson College *B*

Massachusetts

Gordon College *B*

Michigan

Hillsdale College *B*
Spring Arbor University *B*

Minnesota

North Central University *B*

Missouri

Hannibal-LaGrange College *B*
Lindenwood University *B*

Nebraska

Creighton University *M*

Ohio

Cincinnati Christian
   University *A, B, M*
Ursuline College *B*

Oregon

Eugene Bible College *C, B*

Pennsylvania

Elizabethtown College *B*

South Carolina

North Greenville College *B*

Texas

Hardin-Simmons University *M*
Houston Baptist University *B*
Southwestern Assemblies of God
   University *A, B, M*
University of Mary Hardin-Baylor *B*
Wayland Baptist University *A, B, M*

Virginia

Bluefield College *B*

Washington

Trinity Lutheran College *A, B*

Wisconsin

Maranatha Baptist Bible College *C*

Cinematography and film/video production

Arizona

Scottsdale Community College *A*

Yavapai College *C*

California

Academy of Art University *C, A, B, M*
Allan Hancock College *C*
Antelope Valley College *C, A*
Art Center College of Design *B, M*
Art Institute
   of California: Los Angeles *A*
Biola University *B*
Brooks Institute of Photography *C, B*
California College of the Arts *B, M*
California Institute of the Arts *C, B, M*
California State University
   Long Beach *B*
Chapman University *B, M*
City College of San Francisco *A*
Cogswell Polytechnical College *B*
College of San Mateo *A*
Columbia College: Hollywood *A, B*
Cosumnes River College *A*
De Anza College *C, A*
Grossmont Community College *C, A*
Los Angeles City College *C, A*
Los Angeles Valley College *C*
Loyola Marymount University *B*
Modesto Junior College *A*
Moorpark College *A*
National University *M*
Orange Coast College *A*
Pacific Union College *B*
Pitzer College *B*
San Francisco Art Institute *B, M*
Scripps College *B*
Southwestern College *A*
University of California
   Santa Barbara *B*
University of Southern California *M*
Vanguard University of Southern
   California *B*

Colorado

Art Institute
   of Colorado *A, B*
Red Rocks Community College *C, A*

Connecticut

University of Hartford *B*

District of Columbia

American University *B, M*

Florida

Art Institute of Fort Lauderdale *A*
Florida Atlantic University *C*
Florida Community College at
   Jacksonville *A*
Florida Metropolitan University
   Melbourne Campus *A*
   Orlando College North *A*
   Pompano Beach *A*
Florida State University *B, M*
Full Sail Real World Education *B*
Miami Dade College *A*
Miami International University of Art
   and Design *B*
Palm Beach Community College *A*
University of Central Florida *B*
University of Miami *B, M*

Georgia

Savannah College of Art and
   Design *B, M*

Illinois

Columbia College Chicago *B, M*
School of the Art Institute of
   Chicago *B, M*
Southern Illinois University
   Carbondale *B*
University of Illinois
   Chicago *M*

Iowa

University of Iowa *B, M*

Louisiana

Centenary College of Louisiana *B*

Maine

New England School of
   Communications *C, A, B*
Southern Maine Community
   College *C, A*
University of Southern Maine *B*

Maryland

Cecil Community College *C*
Howard Community College *A*
Villa Julie College *B*

Massachusetts

Boston University *B, M*
Emerson College *B*
Fitchburg State College *B*
Hampshire College *B*
Massachusetts College of Art *B, M*
School of the Museum of Fine
   Arts *B, M*
Simon's Rock College of Bard *B*

Michigan

College for Creative Studies *B*
Lansing Community College *A*
Northern Michigan University *B*

Minnesota

Minneapolis College of Art and
   Design *B*
Minneapolis Community and
   Technical College *A*

Missouri

Kansas City Art Institute *B*
Webster University *B*

Montana

Montana State University
   Bozeman *B*
University of Montana: Missoula *M*

New Jersey

Cumberland County College *A*
Fairleigh Dickinson University
   College at Florham *B*

New Mexico

New Mexico Highlands University *B*

New York

Bard College *B, M*
City University of New York
   Brooklyn College *C, B*
   City College *B, M*
   College of Staten Island *B, M*
   Hunter College *B*
Five Towns College *A, B*
Ithaca College *B*
Long Island University
   C.W. Post Campus *B*
New York University *B, M*
Pratt Institute *B*
Rochester Institute of
   Technology *A, B, M*
Sarah Lawrence College *B*
School of Visual Arts *B*
State University of New York
   Purchase *B*
Syracuse University *B, M*

North Carolina

Cape Fear Community College *A*
East Carolina University *B*

North Carolina School of the
   Arts *B, M*
St. Augustine's College *B*
University of North Carolina
   Wilmington *B*

Ohio

Antioch College *B*
Bowling Green State University *B*
Cincinnati State Technical and
   Community College *A*
Ohio University *B, M*

Oklahoma

Oklahoma City University *B*

Oregon

Portland Community College *C*

Pennsylvania

Art Institute
   of Philadelphia *A, B*
   of Pittsburgh *A, B*
Bucks County Community
   College *C, A*
Chatham College *M*
Drexel University *B*
La Salle University *B*
Penn State
   Abington *B*
   Altoona *B*
   Beaver *B*
   Berks *B*
   Delaware County *B*
   Dubois *B*
   Fayette *B*
   Hazleton *B*
   Lehigh Valley *B*
   McKeesport *B*
   Mont Alto *B*
   New Kensington *B*
   Schuylkill - Capital College *B*
   Shenango *B*
   University Park *B, M*
   Wilkes-Barre *B*
   Worthington Scranton *B*
   York *B*
Point Park University *B*
University of the Arts *B*

Rhode Island

New England Institute of
   Technology *A*
Rhode Island School of Design *B*

South Carolina

Trident Technical College *C*

Tennessee

Pellissippi State Technical Community
   College *A*
Southern Adventist University *B*

Texas

El Paso Community College *C, A*
North Lake College *A*
South Plains College *A*
Texas State Technical College
   Waco *A*

Vermont

Bennington College *B*
Burlington College *C, B*
Champlain College *C, A, B*
Marlboro College *B*
Middlebury College *B*

Virginia

J. Sargeant Reynolds Community
   College *C*

Washington

Art Institute of Seattle *A*
Cornish College of the Arts *B*
Evergreen State College *B*
Shoreline Community College *A*

Wisconsin

University of Wisconsin
  Madison *B*
  Oshkosh *B*

Civil engineering

Alabama

Alabama Agricultural and Mechanical
  University *B*
Alabama Southern Community
  College *A*
Auburn University *B, M, D*
University of Alabama *B, M, D*
University of Alabama
  Birmingham *B, M, D*
  Huntsville *B, M, D*
University of South Alabama *B*

Alaska

University of Alaska
  Anchorage *B, M*
  Fairbanks *B, M*

Arizona

Arizona State University *B, M, D*
Central Arizona College *A*
Northern Arizona University *B*
University of Arizona *B, M, D*

Arkansas

University of Arkansas *B, M*

California

California Institute of
  Technology *B, M, D*
California Polytechnic State
  University: San Luis Obispo *B*
California State Polytechnic
  University: Pomona *B*
California State University
  Chico *B*
  Fresno *B, M*
  Fullerton *B, M*
  Long Beach *B, M*
  Los Angeles *B, M*
  Northridge *B, M*
  Sacramento *B, M*
City College of San Francisco *A*
East Los Angeles College *A*
Loyola Marymount University *B, M*
San Diego State University *B, M*
San Francisco State University *B*
San Jose State University *B, M*
Santa Ana College *A*
Santa Clara University *B, M*
Shasta College *A*
Stanford University *B, M, D*
University of California
  Berkeley *B, M, D*
  Davis *B*
  Irvine *B, M, D*
  Los Angeles *B, M, D*
University of Southern
  California *B, M, D*
University of the Pacific *B*

Colorado

Colorado State University *B, M, D*
United States Air Force Academy *B*
University of Colorado
  Boulder *B, M, D*
  Denver and Health Sciences
    Center *B, M, D*

Connecticut

United States Coast Guard Academy *B*
University of Connecticut *B, M, D*
University of Hartford *B, M*
University of New Haven *B*

Delaware

University of Delaware *B, M, D*

District of Columbia

Catholic University of
  America *B, M, D*
George Washington
  University *B, M, D*
Howard University *B, M*
University of the District of
  Columbia *A, B*

Florida

Broward Community College *A*
Edison College *A*
Embry-Riddle Aeronautical
  University *B*
Florida Agricultural and Mechanical
  University *B, M*
Florida Atlantic University *B, M*
Florida Community College at
  Jacksonville *A*
Florida Gulf Coast University *B*
Florida Institute of
  Technology *B, M, D*
Florida International
  University *B, M, D*
Florida State University *B, M, D*
Manatee Community College *A*
Miami Dade College *A*
Pensacola Junior College *A*
Tallahassee Community College *A*
University of Central Florida *B, M, D*
University of Florida *A, B, M*
University of Miami *B, M, D*
University of North Florida *B*
University of South Florida *B, M, D*

Georgia

Georgia Institute of
  Technology *B, M, D*
Middle Georgia College *A*

Hawaii

University of Hawaii
  Manoa *B, M, D*

Idaho

Boise State University *B, M*
Brigham Young University-Idaho *A*
College of Southern Idaho *A*
Idaho State University *B, M*
North Idaho College *A*
University of Idaho *B, M, D*

Illinois

Bradley University *B, M*
Dominican University *B*
Illinois Institute of
  Technology *B, M, D*
Lake Land College *A*
Northwestern University *B, M, D*
Sauk Valley Community College *A*
Southern Illinois University
  Carbondale *B, M*
Southern Illinois University
  Edwardsville *B, M*
University of Illinois
  Chicago *B, M, D*
  Urbana-Champaign *B, M, D*

Indiana

Purdue University *B, M, D*
Rose-Hulman Institute of
  Technology *B, M*
Tri-State University *B*

University of Evansville *B*
University of Notre Dame *B, M, D*
Valparaiso University *B*
Vincennes University *A*

Iowa

Dordt College *B*
Iowa State University *B, M, D*
University of Iowa *B, M, D*

Kansas

Kansas State University *B, M, D*
University of Kansas *B, M, D*

Kentucky

University of Kentucky *B, M, D*
University of Louisville *B, M, D*
Western Kentucky University *B*

Louisiana

Louisiana State University and
  Agricultural and Mechanical
  College *B, M, D*
Louisiana Tech University *B*
Southern University and Agricultural
  and Mechanical College *B*
University of Louisiana at
  Lafayette *B, M*
University of New Orleans *B*

Maine

University of Maine *B, M, D*

Maryland

Johns Hopkins University *B, M, D*
Montgomery College *A*
Morgan State University *B*
University of Maryland
  Baltimore County *M, D*
  College Park *B, M, D*

Massachusetts

Massachusetts Institute of
  Technology *B, M, D*
Merrimack College *B*
Northeastern University *B, M, D*
Smith College *B*
Tufts University *B, M*
University of Massachusetts
  Amherst *B, M, D*
  Dartmouth *B, M*
  Lowell *B, M*
Worcester Polytechnic
  Institute *B, M, D*

Michigan

Calvin College *B*
Lawrence Technological
  University *B, M*
Michigan State University *B, M, D*
Michigan Technological
  University *B, M, D, T*
University of Detroit Mercy *B, M, D*
University of Michigan *B, M, D*
Wayne State University *B, M, D*
Western Michigan University *B*

Minnesota

Minnesota State University
  Mankato *B*
St. Cloud State University *B*
University of Minnesota
  Twin Cities *B, M, D*
Vermilion Community College *A*

Mississippi

Jackson State University *B*
Mississippi State University *B, M*
University of Mississippi *B*

Missouri

East Central College *A*

University of Missouri

  Columbia *B, M, D*
  Kansas City *B, M*
  Rolla *B, M, D*
  St. Louis *B*
Washington University in St.
  Louis *B, M, D*

Montana

Carroll College *B*
Montana State University
  Bozeman *B, M, D*
Montana Tech of the University of
  Montana *B*

Nebraska

University of Nebraska
  Lincoln *B, M*
  Omaha *B*

Nevada

University of Nevada
  Las Vegas *B, M, D*
  Reno *B, M, D*

New Hampshire

New England College *B*
University of New Hampshire *B, M, D*

New Jersey

Essex County College *A*
Middlesex County College *A*
New Jersey Institute of
  Technology *B, M, D*
Princeton University *B, M, D*
Rowan University *B*
Rutgers, The State University of New
  Jersey
  Camden Regional Campus *B*
  New Brunswick/Piscataway
    Campus *B, M, D*
  Newark Regional Campus *B*
Stevens Institute of
  Technology *B, M, D*

New Mexico

New Mexico Institute of Mining and
  Technology *B*
New Mexico State University *B, M*
University of New Mexico *B, M*

New York

City University of New York
  City College *B, M, D*
  LaGuardia Community College *A*
Clarkson University *B, M, D*
Columbia University
  Fu Foundation School of
    Engineering and Applied
    Science *B, M, D*
Cooper Union for the Advancement of
  Science and Art *B, M*
Cornell University *B, M, D*
Hofstra University *B*
Manhattan College *B, M*
Polytechnic University *B, M, D*
Rensselaer Polytechnic
  Institute *B, M, D*
State University of New York
  Buffalo *B, M, D*
  College of Environmental Science
    and Forestry *B, M, D*
Syracuse University *B, M, D*
United States Military Academy *B*

North Carolina

Central Carolina Community
  College *A*
Duke University *B, M, D*
Johnston Community College *A*
North Carolina Agricultural and
  Technical State University *B*

North Carolina State
    University *B, M, D*
University of North Carolina
    Charlotte *B, M*
Western Piedmont Community
    College *A*

North Dakota

North Dakota State University *B, M, D*
University of North Dakota *B, M*

Ohio

Belmont Technical College *A*
Case Western Reserve
    University *B, M, D*
Cleveland State University *B, M, D*
Ohio Northern University *B*
Ohio State University
    Columbus Campus *B, M, D*
Ohio University *B, M*
Stark State College of Technology *A*
University of Akron *B, M*
University of Cincinnati *B, M, D*
University of Dayton *B, M*
University of Toledo *B, M*
Youngstown State University *B, M*

Oklahoma

Oklahoma State University *B, M, D*
Oklahoma State University
    Oklahoma City *A*
    Okmulgee *A*
University of Oklahoma *B, M, D*

Oregon

Oregon State University *B, M, D*
Portland State University *B, M, D*
University of Portland *B, M*

Pennsylvania

Bucknell University *B, M*
Carnegie Mellon University *B, M, D*
Drexel University *B, M, D*
Gettysburg College *B*
Lafayette College *B*
Lehigh University *B, M, D*
Penn State
    Abington *B*
    Altoona *B*
    Beaver *B*
    Berks *B*
    Delaware County *B*
    Dubois *B*
    Fayette *B*
    Hazleton *B*
    Lehigh Valley *B*
    McKeesport *B*
    Mont Alto *B*
    New Kensington *B*
    Schuylkill - Capital College *B*
    Shenango *B*
    University Park *B, M, D*
    Wilkes-Barre *B*
    Worthington Scranton *B*
    York *B*
Temple University *B, M*
University of Pittsburgh *B, M, D*
Villanova University *B, M*
Widener University *B, M*

Puerto Rico

Universidad Politecnica de Puerto
    Rico *B, M*
University of Puerto Rico
    Bayamon University College *A*
    Mayaguez *B, M, D*
    Ponce *A*

Rhode Island

Brown University *B*
University of Rhode Island *B, M, D*

South Carolina

The Citadel *B*
Clemson University *B, M, D*
University of South Carolina *B, M, D*

South Dakota

Lake Area Technical Institute *A*
South Dakota School of Mines and
    Technology *B, M*
South Dakota State University *B, D*

Tennessee

Chattanooga State Technical
    Community College *A*
Christian Brothers University *B*
Tennessee State University *B*
Tennessee Technological
    University *B, M, D*
University of Memphis *B, M*
University of Tennessee
    Knoxville *B, M, D*
Vanderbilt University *B, M, D*

Texas

Kilgore College *A*
Lamar University *B, M*
Prairie View A&M University *B*
Rice University *B, M, D*
Southern Methodist University *B, M*
Texas A&M University *B, M, D*
Texas A&M University
    Kingsville *B, M*
Texas Tech University *B, M, D*
University of Houston *B, M, D*
University of Texas
    Arlington *B, M, D*
    Austin *B, M, D*
    El Paso *B, M, D*
    San Antonio *B, M*
    Tyler *B*

Utah

Brigham Young University *B, M, D*
University of Utah *B, M, D*
Utah State University *B, M, D*

Vermont

Norwich University *B*
University of Vermont *B, M, D*
Vermont Technical College *A*

Virginia

George Mason University *B, M*
John Tyler Community College *A*
Northern Virginia Community
    College *A*
Old Dominion University *B, M, D*
University of Virginia *B, M, D*
Virginia Military Institute *B*
Virginia Polytechnic Institute and
    State University *B, M, D*

Washington

Centralia College *A*
Gonzaga University *B*
Saint Martin's University *B, M*
Seattle University *B*
Shoreline Community College *A*
University of Washington *B, M, D*
Walla Walla College *B*
Washington State University *B, M, D*

West Virginia

Potomac State College of West Virginia
    University *A*
West Virginia University *B, M, D*
West Virginia University Institute of
    Technology *B*

Wisconsin

Chippewa Valley Technical College *A*
Marquette University *B, M, D*

Northeast Wisconsin Technical
    College *A*
University of Wisconsin
    Madison *B, M, D*
    Milwaukee *B*
    Platteville *B*

Wyoming

University of Wyoming *B, M, D*

Civil engineering drafting/CAD/CADD

Alabama

Gadsden State Community
    College *C, A*

California

National University *B*
Santa Rosa Junior College *C*

Kentucky

Somerset Community College *C*

New Mexico

San Juan College *A*
Southwestern Indian Polytechnic
    Institute *C*

North Dakota

North Dakota State College of
    Science *A*

Ohio

Central Ohio Technical College *A*

Oklahoma

Platt College
    Tulsa *C*

Texas

Tyler Junior College *C, A*

Utah

Salt Lake Community College *A*

Washington

Centralia College *A*

Civil engineering technology

Alabama

Alabama Agricultural and Mechanical
    University *B*
Bishop State Community College *A*
Gadsden State Community
    College *C, A*

Arizona

Eastern Arizona College *A*
Phoenix College *A*

Arkansas

University of Arkansas
    Little Rock *A, B*

California

Allan Hancock College *A*
Butte College *C, A*
California State University
    Fresno *B*
    Long Beach *B*
Chabot College *A*
City College of San Francisco *C, A*
San Joaquin Delta College *C*
Santa Ana College *C, A*
Santa Rosa Junior College *C, A*
Shasta College *C, A*
Ventura College *A*

Colorado

Arapahoe Community College *C*
Colorado State University
    Pueblo *B*
Metropolitan State College of
    Denver *B*
Pueblo Community College *A*
Trinidad State Junior College *C, A*

Connecticut

Central Connecticut State
    University *B*
Three Rivers Community College *A*

Delaware

Delaware State University *B*
Delaware Technical and Community
    College
    Owens Campus *A*
    Stanton/Wilmington Campus *A*
    Terry Campus *C, A*

Florida

Broward Community College *A*
Daytona Beach Community College *A*
Florida Agricultural and Mechanical
    University *B*
Florida Community College at
    Jacksonville *A*
Gulf Coast Community College *A*
Indian River Community College *A*
Manatee Community College *A*
Miami Dade College *A*
Pensacola Junior College *A*
Tallahassee Community College *A*
Valencia Community College *A*

Georgia

Georgia Southern University *B*
Macon State College *A*
Middle Georgia College *A*
Savannah State University *B*
Southern Polytechnic State
    University *B*

Idaho

Idaho State University *C, A*

Illinois

Black Hawk College *A*
College of Lake County *C, A*
Morrison Institute of Technology *A*

Indiana

Indiana University-Purdue University
    Fort Wayne *A*
Indiana University-Purdue University
    Indianapolis *A*
Purdue University
    North Central Campus *A*
Vincennes University *A*

Iowa

Des Moines Area Community
    College *A*
Hawkeye Community College *A*
Iowa Western Community College *A*

Kansas

Cloud County Community College *A*
Johnson County Community
    College *A*
Washburn University of Topeka *A*

Kentucky

Bluegrass Community and Technical
    College *A*
Murray State University *A, B*
Western Kentucky University *B*

Louisiana

Delgado Community College *A*
Louisiana Tech University *B*

Maine

Central Maine Community College *A*
University of Maine *B*

Maryland

Community College of Baltimore
  County *C, A*
Montgomery College *A*
University of Maryland
  Eastern Shore *B*

Massachusetts

Bristol Community College *A*
Northern Essex Community
  College *C*
Springfield Technical Community
  College *A*
University of Massachusetts
  Lowell *A, B*
Wentworth Institute of
  Technology *A, B*

Michigan

Ferris State University *C, A*
Lansing Community College *A*
Macomb Community College *C, A*
Michigan Technological University *A*

Minnesota

Dunwoody College of Technology *C*
Lake Superior College *C, A*
Minnesota School of Business *C, A*
St. Cloud Technical College *C, A*
South Central College *A*

Mississippi

Hinds Community College *A*

Missouri

Lincoln University *B*
Mineral Area College *A*
St. Louis Community College
  St. Louis Community College at
    Florissant Valley *A*
Three Rivers Community College *A*
Washington University in St. Louis *B*

Montana

Montana Tech of the University of
  Montana *A*

Nebraska

Metropolitan Community
  College *C, A*

New Hampshire

New Hampshire Technical Institute *A*
University of New Hampshire *A*

New Jersey

Burlington County College *A*
Essex County College *A*
Fairleigh Dickinson University
  Metropolitan Campus *B*
Gloucester County College *C, A*
Mercer County Community College *A*
Middlesex County College *A*
Ocean County College *A*
Thomas Edison State College *B*
Union County College *A*

New York

Broome Community College *A*
City University of New York
  Hostos Community College *A*
  New York City College of
    Technology *A*

Erie Community College
  North Campus *A*
Hudson Valley Community College *A*
Mohawk Valley Community College *A*
Monroe Community College *C, A*
Nassau Community College *A*
Rochester Institute of Technology *B*
State University of New York
  College of Technology at Alfred *A*
  College of Technology at Canton *A*
  Institute of Technology at
    Utica/Rome *B*
Westchester Community College *A*

North Carolina

Asheville-Buncombe Technical
  Community College *A*
Central Carolina Community
  College *A*
Central Piedmont Community
  College *C, A*
Fayetteville Technical Community
  College *A*
Gaston College *C, A*
Guilford Technical Community
  College *C, A*
Sandhills Community College *A*
University of North Carolina
  Charlotte *B*
Wake Technical Community
  College *A*

North Dakota

Bismarck State College *A*
North Dakota State College of
  Science *A*

Ohio

Cincinnati State Technical and
  Community College *C, A*
Clark State Community College *A*
Columbus State Community
  College *A*
James A. Rhodes State College *A*
Lakeland Community College *A*
Sinclair Community College *A*
Stark State College of Technology *A*
University of Toledo *C, A, B*
Youngstown State University *A, B*

Oklahoma

Oklahoma State University
  Oklahoma City *A*
  Okmulgee *A*
Tulsa Community College *C, A*

Oregon

Blue Mountain Community College *A*
Chemeketa Community College *A*
Linn-Benton Community College *C*
Mount Hood Community College *A*
Portland Community College *C, A*
Umpqua Community College *A*

Pennsylvania

Butler County Community College *A*
Community College of Allegheny
  County *A*
Harrisburg Area Community
  College *C, A*
Penn State
  Harrisburg *B*
Pennsylvania College of
  Technology *A, B*
Pennsylvania Institute of
  Technology *A*
Point Park University *A, B*
Temple University *B*
University of Pittsburgh
  Johnstown *B*
York Technical Institute *C*

Puerto Rico

University of Puerto Rico
  Bayamon University College *A*
  Ponce *A*

South Carolina

Central Carolina Technical College *A*
Florence-Darlington Technical
  College *A*
Greenville Technical College *C*
Horry-Georgetown Technical
  College *A*
Midlands Technical College *A*
South Carolina State University *B*
Spartanburg Technical College *A*
Trident Technical College *C, A*

South Dakota

Southeast Technical Institute *A*

Tennessee

Nashville State Community College *A*
Pellissippi State Technical Community
  College *A*
Southwest Tennessee Community
  College *A*

Texas

Kilgore College *A*
Laredo Community College *A*
San Antonio College *A*
Texas Southern University *B*
University of Houston *B*
University of Houston
  Downtown *B*

Vermont

Vermont Technical College *A*

Virginia

Central Virginia Community
  College *A*
J. Sargeant Reynolds Community
  College *A*
Lord Fairfax Community College *A*
Northern Virginia Community
  College *A*
Old Dominion University *B*
Tidewater Community College *A*
Virginia Western Community
  College *A*

Washington

Bellingham Technical College *A*
Big Bend Community College *A*
Centralia College *C, A*
Shoreline Community College *A*
South Seattle Community College *A*
Spokane Community College *A*
Walla Walla Community College *C, A*
Yakima Valley Community College *C*

West Virginia

Bluefield State College *A, B*
West Virginia University Institute of
  Technology *A*

Wisconsin

Chippewa Valley Technical College *A*
Gateway Technical College *A*
Madison Area Technical College *A*
Mid-State Technical College *A*
Milwaukee Area Technical College *A*
Moraine Park Technical College *A*
Northeast Wisconsin Technical
  College *A*

Classical/ancient Mediterranean/Near Eastern studies

Alabama

Samford University *B*

California

University of California
  Berkeley *B, M, D*
  Davis *B*
  Irvine *B*
  Los Angeles *B*

Maine

Bowdoin College *B*
Colby College *B*

Massachusetts

Wellesley College *B*

Michigan

Calvin College *B*
University of Michigan *B*

New Hampshire

Dartmouth College *B*

New York

Columbia University
  Columbia College *B*
State University of New York
  Albany *B*

Texas

Rice University *B*

Wisconsin

Carthage College *B*

Classics

Alabama

University of Alabama *B*

Arizona

University of Arizona *B, M*

Arkansas

University of Arkansas *B*

California

California State University
  Long Beach *B*
Claremont McKenna College *B*
Loyola Marymount University *B*
Pitzer College *B*
Pomona College *B*
St. Mary's College of California *B*
San Diego State University *B*
San Francisco State University *B, M*
Santa Clara University *B*
Scripps College *B*
Stanford University *B, M, D*
University of California
  Berkeley *B, M, D*
  Davis *B*
  Irvine *B, M, D*
  Los Angeles *M, D*
  Riverside *B, M, D*
  San Diego *B*
  Santa Barbara *B, M, D*
  Santa Cruz *B*
University of Southern
  California *B, M, D*

Colorado

Colorado College *B*
University of Colorado
  Boulder *B, M, D*

Connecticut

Connecticut College *B*
Trinity College *B*
University of Connecticut *B*
Wesleyan University *B*
Yale University *B, M, D*

Delaware

University of Delaware *B*

District of Columbia

Catholic University of America *B, M*
George Washington University *B*
Georgetown University *B*
Howard University *B*

Florida

Florida State University *B, M, D*
New College of Florida *B*
Rollins College *B*
University of Florida *A, B*
University of South Florida *B, M*

Georgia

Agnes Scott College *B*
Emory University *B*
Georgia State University *B*
Mercer University *B*
University of Georgia *B, M*

Hawaii

University of Hawaii
   Manoa *B, M*

Idaho

University of Idaho *B*

Illinois

Augustana College *B, T*
Illinois Wesleyan University *B*
Knox College *B*
Loyola University of Chicago *B, M, D*
Monmouth College *B, T*
North Central College *B*
Northwestern University *B, M, D*
Rockford College *B*
Southern Illinois University
      Carbondale *B*
University of Chicago *B, M, D*
University of Illinois
   Chicago *B*
   Urbana-Champaign *B, M*
Wheaton College *B*

Indiana

Ball State University *B*
DePauw University *B*
Earlham College *B*
Hanover College *B*
University of Evansville *B*
University of Notre Dame *B*
Valparaiso University *B*
Wabash College *B*

Iowa

Coe College *B*
Cornell College *B*
Grinnell College *B*
Luther College *B*
University of Iowa *B, M, D*

Kansas

University of Kansas *B, M*

Kentucky

Asbury College *B*
Centre College *B*
Transylvania University *B*
University of Kentucky *B, M*

Louisiana

Centenary College of Louisiana *B*
Tulane University *B, M*

Maine

Bowdoin College *B*
Colby College *B*
University of Southern Maine *B*

Maryland

College of Notre Dame of Maryland *B*
Johns Hopkins University *B, M, D*
Loyola College in Maryland *B*
University of Maryland
   College Park *B, M*

Massachusetts

Amherst College *B*
Assumption College *B*
Boston College *B*
Boston University *B, M, D*
Brandeis University *B*
Clark University *B*
College of the Holy Cross *B*
Harvard College *B, D*
Hellenic College/Holy Cross *B*
Mount Holyoke College *B*
Smith College *B*
Tufts University *B, M*
University of Massachusetts
   Amherst *B, M*
   Boston *B*
Wellesley College *B*
Wheaton College *B*
Williams College *B*

Michigan

Calvin College *B*
Grand Valley State University *B*
Hillsdale College *B*
Hope College *B*
Kalamazoo College *B*
University of Michigan *B, M, D*
Wayne State University *B, M*

Minnesota

Carleton College *B*
College of St. Benedict *B*
Concordia College: Moorhead *B*
Gustavus Adolphus College *B*
Macalester College *B*
St. John's University *B*
St. Olaf College *B*
University of Minnesota
   Twin Cities *B, M, D*

Mississippi

Millsaps College *B*
University of Mississippi *B, M*

Missouri

St. Louis University *B*
Truman State University *B*
University of Missouri
   Columbia *B, M, D*
Washington University in St.
   Louis *B, M*

Montana

University of Montana: Missoula *B*

Nebraska

Creighton University *B*
University of Nebraska
   Lincoln *B, M*

New Hampshire

Dartmouth College *B*
St. Anselm College *B*
University of New Hampshire *B*

New Jersey

Drew University *B*
Montclair State University *B*
Princeton University *B, M, D*
Rutgers, The State University of New
   Jersey
   New Brunswick/Piscataway
      Campus *B, M, D*
St. Peter's College *B*
Seton Hall University *B*

New Mexico

University of New Mexico *B*

New York

Bard College *B*
Barnard College *B*
City University of New York
   Brooklyn College *B*
   Hunter College *B*
Colgate University *B*
College of New Rochelle *B, T*
Columbia University
   Columbia College *B*
   School of General Studies *B*
Cornell University *B, M, D*
Elmira College *B*
Fordham University *B, M, D*
Hamilton College *B*
Hobart and William Smith Colleges *B*
Hofstra University *B*
New York University *B, M, D*
St. Bonaventure University *B*
Sarah Lawrence College *B*
Siena College *B*
Skidmore College *B*
State University of New York
   Albany *B, M*
   Binghamton *B*
   Buffalo *B, M, D*
Syracuse University *B, M*
Union College *B*
Yeshiva University *B*

North Carolina

Davidson College *B*
Duke University *B, M, D*
Lenoir-Rhyne College *B*
University of North Carolina
   Asheville *B, T*
   Chapel Hill *B, M, D*
   Greensboro *B*
Wake Forest University *B*

North Dakota

North Dakota State University *B*

Ohio

Bowling Green State University *B*
Case Western Reserve University *B*
College of Wooster *B*
Denison University *B*
Franciscan University of
   Steubenville *B*
Hiram College *B*
Kenyon College *B*
Miami University
   Oxford Campus *B*
Oberlin College *B*
Ohio State University
   Columbus Campus *B, M, D*
Ohio University *B*
Ohio Wesleyan University *B*
University of Akron *B*
University of Cincinnati *B, M, D*
University of Toledo *M*
Wright State University *B*
Xavier University *B*

Oklahoma

University of Oklahoma *B*

Oregon

Reed College *B*
University of Oregon *B, M*
Willamette University *B*

Pennsylvania

Bryn Mawr College *B, M, D*
Bucknell University *B*
Dickinson College *B*
Duquesne University *B*
Franklin & Marshall College *B*
Gettysburg College *B*
Haverford College *B*
La Salle University *B*
Lehigh University *B*
Moravian College *B*
Penn State
   Abington *B*
   Altoona *B*
   Beaver *B*
   Berks *B*
   Delaware County *B*
   Dubois *B*
   Fayette *B*
   Hazleton *B*
   Lehigh Valley *B*
   McKeesport *B*
   Mont Alto *B*
   New Kensington *B*
   Schuylkill - Capital College *B*
   Shenango *B*
   University Park *B*
   Wilkes-Barre *B*
   Worthington Scranton *B*
   York *B*
Swarthmore College *B*
Temple University *B*
University of Pennsylvania *B, M, D*
University of Pittsburgh *B, M, D*
University of Scranton *B*
Ursinus College *B, T*
Villanova University *B, M*
Westminster College *B*

Rhode Island

Brown University *B, M, D*
University of Rhode Island *B*

South Carolina

College of Charleston *B, T*
University of South Carolina *B*

Tennessee

Rhodes College *B, T*
University of Tennessee
   Chattanooga *B*
   Knoxville *B*
Vanderbilt University *B, M, D*

Texas

Austin College *B*
Baylor University *B*
Rice University *B*
Southwestern University *B*
Texas Tech University *B, M*
Trinity University *B*
University of Houston *B*
University of Texas
   Arlington *B*
   Austin *B, M, D*
   San Antonio *B*

Utah

Brigham Young University *B*
University of Utah *B, M*

Vermont

Middlebury College *B*
St. Michael's College *B*
University of Vermont *B, M*

Virginia

Christendom College *B*
College of William and Mary *B*
Hampden-Sydney College *B*
Hollins University *B*
Randolph-Macon College *B*
Randolph-Macon Woman's College *B*
Sweet Briar College *B*
University of Mary Washington *B*
University of Richmond *B, T*
University of Virginia *B, M, D*
Washington and Lee University *B*

Washington

Evergreen State College *B*
Pacific Lutheran University *B*
Seattle Pacific University *B*
University of Puget Sound *B*
University of Washington *B, M, D*
Whitman College *B*

West Virginia

Huntington Junior College *A*

Wisconsin

Beloit College *B*
Lawrence University *B, T*
Marquette University *B*
Ripon College *B*
University of Wisconsin
Madison *B, M, D*
Milwaukee *B*

Clinical child psychology

California

California Institute of Integral
Studies *D*

Kansas

University of Kansas *M, D*

New York

Pace University *M*
St. John's University *D*

Ohio

Case Western Reserve University *D*

Pennsylvania

Marywood University *M*

Texas

Prairie View A&M University *D*

Clinical laboratory science

Alabama

Central Alabama Community
College *A*
Enterprise-Ozark Community
College *A*
Faulkner State Community College *A*
Tuskegee University *B*
University of Alabama
Birmingham *B, M*
University of South Alabama *B*

Arizona

Arizona State University *B*
Phoenix College *A*
University of Arizona *B, M*

Arkansas

Arkansas State University *A, B*
Arkansas Tech University *B*
Harding University *B*
Henderson State University *B*

University of Arkansas
for Medical Sciences *B*

California

California State University
Chico *B*
Dominguez Hills *M*
City College of San Francisco *A*
Fullerton College *A*
Loma Linda University *A, B*
San Francisco State University *B*

Connecticut

University of Connecticut *B*
University of Hartford *B*
Western Connecticut State
University *B*

Delaware

University of Delaware *B*
Wesley College *B*

District of Columbia

Catholic University of America *B*
Howard University *B*

Florida

Barry University *B*
Bethune-Cookman College *B*
Florida Memorial University *B*
Manatee Community College *A*
Okaloosa-Walton College *A*
St. Leo University *B*
Stetson University *B*
University of Central Florida *B*
University of South Florida *B*

Georgia

Armstrong Atlantic State University *B*
Augusta State University *B*
Darton College *A*
Georgia Southern University *B*
Oglethorpe University *B*
Savannah State University *B*

Hawaii

University of Hawaii
Manoa *B*

Idaho

Idaho State University *B, M*

Illinois

Aurora University *B*
Benedictine University *B*
Bradley University *B*
DePaul University *B*
Eastern Illinois University *B*
Illinois College *B*
Illinois State University *B*
McKendree College *B*
National-Louis University *B*
North Park University *B*
Northern Illinois University *B*
Quincy University *B*
Rosalind Franklin University of
Medicine and Science *M*
Rush University *B, M*
Springfield College in Illinois *A*
University of Illinois
Chicago *B, M*
Springfield *B*
University of St. Francis *B*
Western Illinois University *B*

Indiana

Ball State University *B*
Indiana State University *B*
Indiana University
Southeast *B*
Indiana University-Purdue University
Fort Wayne *B*

Indiana University-Purdue University
Indianapolis *B*
Manchester College *B*
Purdue University *B*
Purdue University
Calumet *B*
St. Joseph's College *B*
University of St. Francis *B*

Iowa

Briar Cliff University *B*
Dordt College *B*
Graceland University *B*
Loras College *B*
University of Iowa *B*
Wartburg College *B*

Kansas

Barton County Community College *A*
Pittsburg State University *B*
University of Kansas Medical
Center *B*

Kentucky

Bellarmine University *B, M*
Brescia University *B*
Eastern Kentucky University *B*
Hazard Community College *A*
Kentucky State University *B*
Madisonville Community College *A*
Thomas More College *B*
University of Kentucky *B, M, D*
Western Kentucky University *B*

Louisiana

Louisiana State University
Alexandria *A*
Louisiana State University Health
Sciences Center *B*
Louisiana Tech University *B*
Our Lady of the Lake College *A, B*
University of Louisiana at Monroe *B*
University of New Orleans *B*

Maine

University of Maine *B, M*

Maryland

Salisbury University *B*
University of Maryland
Eastern Shore *B*

Massachusetts

Laboure College *A*
Northeastern University *B*
Salem State College *B*
Springfield College *B*
University of Massachusetts
Amherst *B*
Boston *B*
Dartmouth *B*
Lowell *B, M*

Michigan

Andrews University *B, M*
Central Michigan University *B*
Delta College *A*
Eastern Michigan University *B*
Ferris State University *B*
Gogebic Community College *A*
Grand Valley State University *B*
Lake Superior State University *B*
Lansing Community College *A*
Madonna University *B*
Michigan State University *B, M*
Michigan Technological
University *B, T*
Northern Michigan University *A, B*
Oakland University *B*
Saginaw Valley State University *B*
University of Michigan *B*

University of Michigan
Flint *B*
Wayne State University *B*

Minnesota

Augsburg College *B*
Bemidji State University *B*
College of St. Catherine *B*
Concordia College: Moorhead *B*
Minnesota State University
Mankato *B*
Moorhead *B*
Northland Community & Technical
College *A*
St. Cloud State University *B*
St. Mary's University of Minnesota *B*

Mississippi

Alcorn State University *B*
Coahoma Community College *A*
Copiah-Lincoln Community College *A*
Mississippi Gulf Coast Community
College
Jefferson Davis Campus *A*
Mississippi State University *B*
University of Mississippi *B*
University of Mississippi Medical
Center *B*
University of Southern
Mississippi *B, M*

Missouri

Lincoln University *B*
Lindenwood University *B*
Maryville University of Saint Louis *B*
Missouri State University *B*
Northwest Missouri State
University *B*
Rockhurst University *B*
St. Louis University *B*
Southeast Missouri State University *B*
Southwest Baptist University *B*
University of Missouri
Kansas City *B*
William Jewell College *B*

Montana

University of Montana: Missoula *B*

Nebraska

Northeast Community College *A*
University of Nebraska
Medical Center *B*

Nevada

University of Nevada
Las Vegas *B*

New Hampshire

University of New Hampshire *B*

New Jersey

Bloomfield College *B*
College of St. Elizabeth *B*
Fairleigh Dickinson University
College at Florham *B*
Metropolitan Campus *B, M*
Felician College *A*
Kean University *B*
Monmouth University *B*
Ramapo College of New Jersey *B*
Rutgers, The State University of New
Jersey
Newark Regional Campus *B*
St. Peter's College *B*
Thomas Edison State College *A, B*
University of Medicine and Dentistry
of New Jersey
School of Health Related
Professions *B*

New Mexico

Eastern New Mexico University *B*

New York

Albany College of Pharmacy *B*
Canisius College *B*
City University of New York
   Hunter College *B*
College of Saint Rose *B*
Elmira College *B*
Hartwick College *B*
Hudson Valley Community College *A*
Iona College *B*
Keuka College *B*
Long Island University
   Brooklyn Campus *B*
   C.W. Post Campus *M*
Marist College *B*
Mercy College *B*
Mount St. Mary College *B*
Nassau Community College *A*
Orange County Community College *A*
Pace University *B*
St. Francis College *B*
St. John's University *B, M*
State University of New York
   Buffalo *B*
   College at Plattsburgh *B*
   Stony Brook *B*
   Upstate Medical University *B*

North Carolina

Appalachian State University *B*
Durham Technical Community
   College *A*
East Carolina University *B*
High Point University *B*
Southwestern Community College *A*
University of North Carolina
   Chapel Hill *B*
   Charlotte *B*
   Greensboro *B*
   Wilmington *B*
Wake Forest University *B*
Western Carolina University *B*
Winston-Salem State University *B*

North Dakota

Jamestown College *B*
Minot State University *B*
North Dakota State University *B*
University of Mary *B*
University of North Dakota *B, M*

Ohio

Bowling Green State University *B*
Cedarville University *B*
Kent State University *B*
Malone College *B*
Miami University
   Oxford Campus *B*
Mount Vernon Nazarene University *B*
Ohio State University
   Columbus Campus *B*
Shawnee State University *A*
University of Cincinnati *B*
University of Rio Grande *B*
Walsh University *B*
Wright State University *B*
Xavier University *B*
Youngstown State University *B*

Oklahoma

Oklahoma Christian University *B*
Oklahoma Panhandle State
   University *B*
Oklahoma State University *B*
Oral Roberts University *B*
University of Central Oklahoma *B*

Oregon

Oregon Institute of Technology *B*

Pennsylvania

Alvernia College *B*
Bloomsburg University of
   Pennsylvania *B*
Cabrini College *B*
Cheyney University of Pennsylvania *B*
College Misericordia *B*
DeSales University *B*
Drexel University *A, B*
East Stroudsburg University of
   Pennsylvania *B*
Elizabethtown College *B*
Gannon University *B*
Gwynedd-Mercy College *B*
Indiana University of Pennsylvania *B*
Keystone College *A*
King's College *B*
Kutztown University of
   Pennsylvania *B*
Mansfield University of
   Pennsylvania *B*
Marywood University *B*
Reading Area Community College *A*
Seton Hill University *B*
Thomas Jefferson University: College
   of Health Professions *B*
University of Scranton *B*
Wilkes University *B*

Puerto Rico

Inter American University of Puerto
   Rico
   San German Campus *B*
Pontifical Catholic University of
   Puerto Rico *B*

Rhode Island

Rhode Island College *B*
Salve Regina University *B*
University of Rhode Island *B, M*

South Carolina

Clemson University *B*
Coker College *B*
Medical University of South
   Carolina *M*
Winthrop University *B*

South Dakota

Augustana College *B*
Mount Marty College *B*
Northern State University *B*
South Dakota State University *B*
University of South Dakota *M*

Tennessee

Austin Peay State University *B*
Carson-Newman College *B*
King College *B*
Lincoln Memorial University *B*
Southern Adventist University *B*
Trevecca Nazarene University *B*
Tusculum College *B*
University of Tennessee
   Knoxville *B*

Texas

Abilene Christian University *B*
Amarillo College *A*
Angelo State University *B*
Baylor University *B*
Del Mar College *A*
East Texas Baptist University *B*
Grayson County College *A*
Lamar University *B*
LeTourneau University *B*
Midwestern State University *B*
Odessa College *A*
Prairie View A&M University *B*
St. Mary's University *B*
Sam Houston State University *B*
San Jacinto College
   Central Campus *A*

Stephen F. Austin State University *B*
Tarleton State University *A, B*
Texas Southern University *B*
Texas Southmost College *A*
Texas State Technical College
   Waco *A*
Texas State University: San Marcos *B*
Texas Tech University Health Sciences
   Center *B*
Texas Woman's University *B*
University of Houston *B*
University of Mary Hardin-Baylor *B*
University of North Texas *B*
University of Texas
   Arlington *B*
   Austin *B*
   El Paso *B*
   Health Science Center at San
     Antonio *B*
   Medical Branch at Galveston *B*
   Pan American *B*
   San Antonio *B*
   Southwestern Medical Center at
     Dallas *B*
   Tyler *B*
West Texas A&M University *B*

Utah

Brigham Young University *B*
Snow College *A*
University of Utah *B, M*
Utah State University *B*
Weber State University *B*

Vermont

University of Vermont *B, M*

Virginia

Averett University *B*
Bridgewater College *B*
Eastern Mennonite University *B*
Ferrum College *B*
George Mason University *B*
Mary Baldwin College *B*
Norfolk State University *B*
Old Dominion University *B*
Radford University *B*
Roanoke College *B*
University of Virginia's College at
   Wise *B*
Virginia Commonwealth
   University *B, M*

Washington

Seattle University *B*
University of Washington *B, M*

West Virginia

Concord University *B*
Marshall University *B*
West Liberty State College *B*
West Virginia University *B*

Wisconsin

Carroll College *B*
University of Wisconsin
   La Crosse *B*
   Madison *B*
   Milwaukee *B, M*
   Stevens Point *B*

Clinical/medical laboratory assistant

Alabama

Gadsden State Community College *A*

Alaska

University of Alaska
   Fairbanks *C*

Arizona

Arizona Institute of Business and
   Technology
   International Institute of the
     Americas: Mesa *C*
International Institute of the Americas
   Phoenix *C*
   Tucson *C*
International Institute of the
   Americas: West Valley *C*

California

De Anza College *C*

Delaware

Delaware Technical and Community
   College
   Owens Campus *C, A*

Florida

Broward Community College *A*
Lake City Community College *A*

Idaho

North Idaho College *A*

Illinois

Oakton Community College *A*
Southwestern Illinois College *A*

Indiana

Indiana Business College
   Medical *A*

Iowa

Northeast Iowa Community
   College *A*

Kansas

Seward County Community College *A*

Kentucky

Eastern Kentucky University *B*
Somerset Community College *A*
Southeast Kentucky Community and
   Technical College *A*

Maine

University of Maine
   Augusta *A*

Maryland

University of Maryland
   Eastern Shore *B*

Massachusetts

Bunker Hill Community College *C*
Holyoke Community College *C*
Middlesex Community College *C*
Springfield Technical Community
   College *C*

Michigan

Baker College
   of Owosso *A*
Monroe County Community
   College *C*
Northern Michigan University *C*

Minnesota

College of St. Catherine *C*
Lake Superior College *C*
Minnesota State University
   Mankato *B*
South Central College *A*

Mississippi

Hinds Community College *A*

Nevada
Community College of Southern
Nevada *A*

New Hampshire
McIntosh College *A*

New Mexico
International Institute of the
Americas *C*
New Mexico Junior College *A*
New Mexico State University
Alamogordo *A*

New York
Elmira Business Institute *C, A*
Mohawk Valley Community College *C*
State University of New York
College of Agriculture and
Technology at Cobleskill *A*

North Carolina
Alamance Community College *A*
Central Piedmont Community
College *A*
Fayetteville Technical Community
College *C*
Mars Hill College *B*
Western Piedmont Community
College *A*

Ohio
Cincinnati State Technical and
Community College *C, A*
Columbus State Community
College *A*
James A. Rhodes State College *C*
Jefferson Community College *A*
Stark State College of Technology *A*
Washington State Community
College *A*
Youngstown State University *A*

Oklahoma
Rose State College *A*
Tulsa Community College *A*

Pennsylvania
Penn State
Schuylkill - Capital College *A*
Western School of Health and
Business Careers *A*

South Carolina
Aiken Technical College *C*
Forrest Junior College *C, A*
Orangeburg-Calhoun Technical
College *C, A*
Spartanburg Technical College *C*

Tennessee
Miller-Motte Technical College *C*
Northeast State Technical Community
College *A*

Texas
Austin Community College *A*
Central Texas College *C, A*
El Paso Community College *C*
Tarrant County College *C*
Tyler Junior College *A*

Virginia
Northern Virginia Community
College *A*
Virginia Highlands Community
College *A*

Washington
Clover Park Technical College *A*
North Seattle Community College *C*

Pierce College *A*
Shoreline Community College *C, A*
Wenatchee Valley College *A*

Wisconsin
Chippewa Valley Technical College *A*
Lakeshore Technical College *C*

Clinical/medical laboratory technology

Alabama
Faulkner State Community College *A*
Faulkner University *A*
Gadsden State Community College *A*
Jefferson State Community College *A*
Wallace State Community College at
Hanceville *A*

Alaska
University of Alaska
Anchorage *A*

Arkansas
National Park Community College *A*
North Arkansas College *A*
South Arkansas Community College *A*
University of Central Arkansas *B*

California
California State University
Dominguez Hills *B*
East Bay *B*
Chabot College *A*
Fresno City College *A*
Los Angeles Southwest College *A*
Mount St. Mary's College *B*
Pasadena City College *A*

Colorado
Arapahoe Community College *A*

Connecticut
Housatonic Community College *A*
Manchester Community College *A*

Delaware
Delaware Technical and Community
College
Owens Campus *A*
Stanton/Wilmington Campus *A*
University of Delaware *B*

District of Columbia
George Washington University *A*

Florida
Brevard Community College *A*
Broward Community College *A*
Florida Community College at
Jacksonville *A*
Indian River Community College *A*
Lake City Community College *A*
Manatee Community College *A*
Miami Dade College *A*
Palm Beach Community College *A*
St. Petersburg College *A*
Valencia Community College *A*

Georgia
Augusta Technical Institute *A*
Central Georgia Technical College *A*
Coastal Georgia Community
College *A*
Darton College *A*
Macon State College *A*
Medical College of Georgia *B*
Southwest Georgia Technical
College *A*
Waycross College *A*

Hawaii
University of Hawaii
Kapiolani Community College *A*

Illinois
Blackburn College *B*
City Colleges of Chicago
Malcolm X College *A*
Elgin Community College *A*
Illinois Central College *A*
John A. Logan College *A*
John Wood Community College *A*
Kankakee Community College *A*
Moraine Valley Community College *A*
Rend Lake College *A*
Roosevelt University *B*
Rosalind Franklin University of
Medicine and Science *B*
Southeastern Illinois College *A*
Southwestern Illinois College *A*

Indiana
Indiana University
Northwest *A*
Indiana University-Purdue University
Fort Wayne *B*
Ivy Tech State College
Ivy Tech Community College: North
Central *A*
Ivy Tech Community College:
Wabash Valley *A*
Purdue University
North Central Campus *A*
University of Indianapolis *B*

Iowa
Des Moines Area Community
College *A*
Dordt College *B*
Hawkeye Community College *A*
Indian Hills Community College *A*
Iowa Central Community College *A*
Morningside College *B*
Mount Mercy College *B*
North Iowa Area Community
College *A*
Northeast Iowa Community
College *A*
Northwestern College *B*
Scott Community College *A*
Western Iowa Tech Community
College *A*

Kansas
Barton County Community College *A*
Central Christian College of Kansas *A*
Seward County Community College *A*
Tabor College *B*
Washburn University of Topeka *B*

Kentucky
Eastern Kentucky University *A, B*
Henderson Community College *A*
Madisonville Community College *A*
Somerset Community College *A*

Louisiana
Delgado Community College *A*
Southern University
New Orleans *B*
Shreveport *A*

Maine
Central Maine Community College *A*
University of Maine
Presque Isle *A*
University of New England *B*

Maryland
Allegany College of Maryland *A*
Community College of Baltimore
County *A*

Howard Community College *A*
University of Maryland
Eastern Shore *B*

Massachusetts
Bristol Community College *A*
Massachusetts College of Liberal
Arts *B*
Middlesex Community College *A*
Northeastern University *B*
Springfield College *B*
Springfield Technical Community
College *A*

Michigan
Baker College
of Owosso *A*
of Port Huron *A*
Ferris State University *A*
Kellogg Community College *A*
Madonna University *A, B*
Northern Michigan University *A*

Minnesota
Alexandria Technical College *A*
Hibbing Community College *A*
Minnesota State Community and
Technical College - Fergus Falls *A*
Minnesota State University
Mankato *B*
Northland Community & Technical
College *A*
Northwest Technical College *A*
Rochester Community and Technical
College *A*
St. Paul College *A*
South Central College *A*
Winona State University *B*

Mississippi
Blue Mountain College *B*
Copiah-Lincoln Community College *A*
Hinds Community College *A*
Meridian Community College *A*
Mississippi Delta Community
College *A*
Mississippi Gulf Coast Community
College
Jefferson Davis Campus *A*

Missouri
Evangel University *B*
Jewish Hospital College of Nursing
and Allied Health *B*
Mineral Area College *A*
Missouri Southern State University *A*
Missouri Western State University *B*
Three Rivers Community College *A*

Montana
University of Montana: Missoula *A*

Nebraska
College of Saint Mary *B*
Dana College *B*
Mid-Plains Community College Area *A*
Southeast Community College
Lincoln Campus *A*

Nevada
Community College of Southern
Nevada *A*

New Hampshire
New Hampshire Community
Technical College
Claremont *A*
University of New Hampshire *B*

New Jersey
Bergen Community College *A*
Brookdale Community College *A*

Caldwell College *B*
Camden County College *A*
County College of Morris *A*
Mercer County Community College *A*
Middlesex County College *A*
Ocean County College *A*
Rutgers, The State University of New Jersey
  New Brunswick/Piscataway Campus *B*
  Newark Regional Campus *B*
Sussex County Community College *A*
University of Medicine and Dentistry of New Jersey
  School of Health Related Professions *A*

New Mexico
Albuquerque Technical-Vocational Institute *A*
Luna Community College *A*
New Mexico Junior College *A*
New Mexico State University Alamogordo *A*
University of New Mexico *B*
Western New Mexico University *B*

New York
Alfred University *B*
Broome Community College *A*
City University of New York
  Bronx Community College *A*
  College of Staten Island *A*
  Hunter College *B*
  Queensborough Community College *A*
  York College *B*
Clinton Community College *A*
Dutchess Community College *A*
Erie Community College
  North Campus *A*
Hudson Valley Community College *A*
Jamestown Community College *A*
Orange County Community College *A*
State University of New York
  College at Brockport *B*
  College at Fredonia *B*
  College of Agriculture and Technology at Morrisville *A*
  College of Technology at Alfred *A*
  Farmingdale *A*

North Carolina
Alamance Community College *A*
Asheville-Buncombe Technical Community College *A*
Beaufort County Community College *A*
Bennett College *B*
Coastal Carolina Community College *A*
Davidson County Community College *A*
Guilford Technical Community College *A*
Halifax Community College *A*
Salem College *B*
Sandhills Community College *A*
Southeastern Community College *A*
Southwestern Community College *A*
Wake Technical Community College *A*

North Dakota
Bismarck State College *A*

Ohio
Cincinnati State Technical and Community College *A*
Clark State Community College *A*
Columbus State Community College *A*

Cuyahoga Community College
  Metropolitan Campus *A*
Defiance College *B*
Jefferson Community College *A*
Lakeland Community College *A*
Marion Technical College *A*
Muskingum College *B*
Stark State College of Technology *A*
University of Rio Grande *A*
Youngstown State University *A*
Zane State College *A*

Oklahoma
Cameron University *B*
Northeastern Oklahoma Agricultural and Mechanical College *A*
Northeastern State University *B*
Rose State College *A*
Seminole State College *A*
Southeastern Oklahoma State University *B*
Southern Nazarene University *B*
Southwestern Oklahoma State University *B*
Tulsa Community College *A*

Oregon
Oregon Health & Science University *B*
Oregon State University *B*
Portland Community College *A*

Pennsylvania
Bloomsburg University of Pennsylvania *B*
California University of Pennsylvania *B*
Clarion University of Pennsylvania *B*
Community College of Allegheny County *A*
Community College of Philadelphia *A*
Edinboro University of Pennsylvania *B*
Harcum College *A*
Harrisburg Area Community College *A*
Holy Family University *B*
Mansfield University of Pennsylvania *B*
Montgomery County Community College *A*
Neumann College *B*
Penn State
  Dubois *A*
  Hazleton *A*
  New Kensington *A*
St. Francis University *B*
Slippery Rock University of Pennsylvania *B*
Thiel College *B*
University of the Sciences in Philadelphia *B*
Western School of Health and Business Careers *A*
York College of Pennsylvania *B*

Puerto Rico
University of the Sacred Heart *B*

Rhode Island
Community College of Rhode Island *A*
Rhode Island College *B*

South Carolina
Erskine College *B*
Florence-Darlington Technical College *A*
Forrest Junior College *A*
Greenville Technical College *A*
Midlands Technical College *A*
Orangeburg-Calhoun Technical College *A*

Spartanburg Technical College *A*
Tri-County Technical College *A*
Trident Technical College *A*
York Technical College *A*

South Dakota
Augustana College *B*
Dakota State University *A*
Lake Area Technical Institute *A*
Mitchell Technical Institute *A*
Presentation College *A*

Tennessee
Columbia State Community College *A*
Jackson State Community College *A*
Lincoln Memorial University *B*
Southwest Tennessee Community College *A*
Union University *B*
Volunteer State Community College *A*

Texas
Amarillo College *A*
Angelina College *A*
Austin Community College *A*
Central Texas College *A*
Del Mar College *A*
El Centro College *A*
El Paso Community College *A*
Houston Community College System *A*
Kilgore College *A*
Lamar State College at Orange *A*
Laredo Community College *A*
McLennan Community College *A*
St. Philip's College *A*
Southwestern Adventist University *B*
Temple College *A*
University of Texas
  Brownsville *A*
Victoria College *A*
Wharton County Junior College *A*

Utah
Salt Lake Community College *A*
Weber State University *A*

Virginia
Central Virginia Community College *A*
Emory & Henry College *B*
J. Sargeant Reynolds Community College *A*
Northern Virginia Community College *A*
Southside Virginia Community College *A*
Wytheville Community College *A*

Washington
City University *A*
Columbia Basin College *A*
Spokane Community College *A*
Spokane Falls Community College *A*

West Virginia
Marshall University *A*
Southern West Virginia Community and Technical College *A*

Wisconsin
Chippewa Valley Technical College *A*
Lakeshore Technical College *A*
Madison Area Technical College *A*
Marquette University *B*
Milwaukee Area Technical College *A*
University of Wisconsin
  Oshkosh *B*
Western Wisconsin Technical College *A*

Wyoming
Casper College *A*

Clinical/medical social work

California
California State University
  Fresno *B, M*
Loma Linda University *M*

Maine
University of Southern Maine *M*

Maryland
University of Maryland
  Baltimore *M, D*

Michigan
Michigan State University *M*

Minnesota
University of St. Thomas *B*

Mississippi
University of Southern Mississippi *M*

New Mexico
New Mexico Highlands University *B, M*

Pennsylvania
Clarion University of Pennsylvania *B*
Slippery Rock University of Pennsylvania *B*

South Dakota
University of South Dakota *M, D*

Vermont
College of St. Joseph in Vermont *M*

Wisconsin
Concordia University Wisconsin *B*

Clinical nurse specialist

Georgia
Mercer University *M*

Illinois
Loyola University of Chicago *M*

Michigan
Saginaw Valley State University *M*

Minnesota
College of St. Scholastica *M*

New York
Mount St. Mary College *M*
Pace University *M*
State University of New York
  Upstate Medical University *M*

Ohio
Case Western Reserve University *M*
Ursuline College *M*

Pennsylvania
Duquesne University *M*
Gwynedd-Mercy College *M*
University of Pennsylvania *M*
University of Pittsburgh *M*

South Carolina
University of South Carolina *M*

Texas

Angelo State University *M*
Texas Woman's University *M*
University of Texas
  Arlington *M*
  El Paso *M*
  Medical Branch at Galveston *M*
  Pan American *M*

Utah

Brigham Young University *M*

Clinical nutrition

Alabama

University of Alabama
  Birmingham *M*

Illinois

Loyola University of Chicago *B*

Indiana

Indiana University-Purdue University
  Indianapolis *M*

Kentucky

University of Kentucky *M*

Minnesota

Leech Lake Tribal College *A*

New Hampshire

University of New Hampshire *B*

New Jersey

University of Medicine and Dentistry
  of New Jersey
    School of Health Related
      Professions *M, D*

North Carolina

East Carolina University *B*

Ohio

University of Cincinnati
  Raymond Walters College *A*

Pennsylvania

Immaculata University *M*
Marywood University *B, M*
Messiah College *B*

Tennessee

East Tennessee State University *M*

Clinical pastoral counseling

Maryland

Loyola College in Maryland *M, D*

New York

New York Institute of Technology *M*

Ohio

University of Dayton *M*

Pennsylvania

Chestnut Hill College *M*

Texas

Southwestern Assemblies of God
  University *B, M*

Virginia

Virginia Commonwealth University *M*

Clinical psychology

Alabama

Alabama Agricultural and Mechanical
  University *M*
Auburn University *M, D*

Alaska

University of Alaska
  Anchorage *M*

California

Alliant International University *M, D*
Antioch Southern California
  Antioch University Los Angeles *M*
  Antioch University Santa Barbara *M*
Azusa Pacific University *M, D*
Biola University *M, D*
California Institute of Integral
  Studies *D*
California Lutheran University *M*
California State University
  Bakersfield *M*
  Chico *M*
  East Bay *M*
  Fullerton *M*
Chapman University *M*
John F. Kennedy University *M*
Loma Linda University *D*
Pepperdine University *M*
San Diego State University *M, D*
San Francisco State University *M*
San Jose State University *M*
University of La Verne *D*
University of Southern
  California *M, D*
Vanguard University of Southern
  California *M*

Colorado

University of Denver *M, D*

Connecticut

University of Hartford *M, D*

Delaware

University of Delaware *M, D*

District of Columbia

American University *D*
Catholic University of America *M, D*
Gallaudet University *D*
George Washington University *D*
University of the District of
  Columbia *M*

Florida

Carlos Albizu University *D*
Florida Institute of Technology *D*
Florida State University *M, D*
Nova Southeastern University *D*
University of Central Florida *M*

Georgia

Emory University *D*

Idaho

Idaho State University *D*

Illinois

Argosy University *M, D*
Benedictine University *M*
DePaul University *M, D*
Eastern Illinois University *M*
Loyola University of Chicago *M, D*
Northwestern University *M, D*
Roosevelt University *M, D*
Rosalind Franklin University of
  Medicine and Science *D*
Wheaton College *M, D*

Indiana

Ball State University *M*
Indiana State University *D*
Indiana University
  Bloomington *D*
Indiana University-Purdue University
  Indianapolis *M, D*
University of Indianapolis *M, D*

Iowa

Loras College *M*
University of Iowa *D*

Kansas

Emporia State University *M*
Pittsburg State University *M*
Washburn University of Topeka *M*

Kentucky

Eastern Kentucky University *M*
Morehead State University *M*
Murray State University *M*
Spalding University *M, D*
University of Kentucky *M, D*
University of Louisville *M, D*

Louisiana

Northwestern State University *M*

Maine

University of Maine *D*

Maryland

Bowie State University *M*
Loyola College in Maryland *M, D*

Massachusetts

American International College *M*
Clark University *M, D*
Suffolk University *M, D*
University of Massachusetts
  Boston *D*
  Dartmouth *M*
Westfield State College *M*

Michigan

Central Michigan University *D*
Eastern Michigan University *M, D*
Madonna University *M*
University of Detroit Mercy *M, D*
Western Michigan University *M, D*

Minnesota

Capella University *M, D*
Minnesota State University
  Mankato *M*

Mississippi

Jackson State University *D*

Missouri

Evangel University *M*
University of Missouri
  Columbia *M, D*
Washington University in St.
  Louis *M, D*

New Jersey

Fairleigh Dickinson University
  College at Florham *M*
  Metropolitan Campus *D*
Rutgers, The State University of New
  Jersey
    New Brunswick/Piscataway
      Campus *D*
Seton Hall University *D*

New York

Adelphi University *M, D*

City University of New York

  City College *D*
  Queens College *M*
Fordham University *M, D*
Hofstra University *M, D*
Long Island University
  Brooklyn Campus *D*
  C.W. Post Campus *D*
New York University *M, D*
St. John's University *D*
State University of New York
  Albany *D*
  Binghamton *D*
  Buffalo *D*
  Stony Brook *D*
Syracuse University *M, D*
University of Rochester *D*
Yeshiva University *D*

North Carolina

Appalachian State University *M*
Duke University *D*
East Carolina University *M*
University of North Carolina
  Charlotte *M*
Western Carolina University *M*

Ohio

Bowling Green State University *M, D*
Case Western Reserve University *D*
Kent State University *M, D*
Ohio University *M, D*
Union Institute & University *D*
University of Dayton *M*
Wright State University *D*
Xavier University *D*

Oklahoma

University of Tulsa *M, D*

Oregon

George Fox University *M, D*
Pacific University *D*

Pennsylvania

Bryn Mawr College *M, D*
Chestnut Hill College *M, D*
Duquesne University *D*
Edinboro University of
  Pennsylvania *M*
Immaculata University *D*
Indiana University of Pennsylvania *D*
La Salle University *D*
Mansfield University of
  Pennsylvania *M*
Marywood University *M, D*
Millersville University of
  Pennsylvania *M*
Penn State
  Harrisburg *M*
Temple University *M, D*
West Chester University of
  Pennsylvania *M*
Widener University *D*

Puerto Rico

Pontifical Catholic University of
  Puerto Rico *M, D*
University of Puerto Rico
  Rio Piedras *M, D*

Rhode Island

University of Rhode Island *D*

South Carolina

Francis Marion University *M*
University of South Carolina *M, D*
University of South Carolina
  Aiken *M*

South Dakota

University of South Dakota *D*

Tennessee

Vanderbilt University *M, D*

Texas

Abilene Christian University *M*
Baylor University *M, D*
Houston Baptist University *M*
St. Mary's University *M*
Sam Houston State University *M*
Southern Methodist University *M*
Southwestern Assemblies of God
   University *M*
Texas A&M University *D*
Texas Tech University *D*
University of Houston *M, D*
University of Houston
   Clear Lake *M*
University of North Texas *M, D*
University of Texas
   El Paso *M*
   Pan American *M*
   Southwestern Medical Center at
      Dallas *M, D*
   Tyler *M*
   of the Permian Basin *M*

Utah

Brigham Young University *D*

Vermont

College of St. Joseph in Vermont *M*
St. Michael's College *M*

Virginia

College of William and Mary *D*
Norfolk State University *D*
Old Dominion University *D*
Regent University *M, D*
University of Virginia *D*

Washington

Antioch University Seattle *M*
Eastern Washington University *M*
Seattle Pacific University *D*
University of Washington *D*

West Virginia

Marshall University *D*

Wisconsin

Marquette University *M, D*

Clothing, apparel and textile studies

Alabama

University of Alabama *B*

Arizona

Mesa Community College *A*

Arkansas

University of Arkansas *B*
University of Central Arkansas *B*

California

Antelope Valley College *C, A*
California State Polytechnic
   University: Pomona *B*
California State University
   Long Beach *B*
   Northridge *B*
Cerritos Community College *A*
Chabot College *A*
Chaffey College *C*
El Camino College *C*
Fashion Institute of Design and
   Merchandising *A*

Fashion Institute of Design and
   Merchandising
   San Diego *A*
   San Francisco *A*
Fresno City College *C, A*
Glendale Community College *A*
Los Angeles Mission College *A*
Los Angeles Trade and Technical
   College *C, A*
Mendocino College *C*
Modesto Junior College *A*
Monterey Peninsula College *A*
Mount San Antonio College *A*
Sacramento City College *C, A*
Saddleback College *C*
San Francisco State University *B*
Santa Rosa Junior College *C*
University of California
   Davis *B, M*

Delaware

Delaware State University *B*

Florida

Florida Community College at
   Jacksonville *A*
Florida State University *B, M, D*

Georgia

Georgia Southern University *B*
University of Georgia *M*

Hawaii

University of Hawaii
   Manoa *B*

Idaho

University of Idaho *B*

Illinois

Joliet Junior College *A*
Northern Illinois University *B*
Southern Illinois University
   Carbondale *B*
University of Illinois
   Urbana-Champaign *B, M*

Indiana

Indiana State University *B*
Indiana University
   Bloomington *B, M*
Purdue University *B, M, D*
Vincennes University *A*

Iowa

Ellsworth Community College *A*
Iowa State University *B, M, D*
University of Northern Iowa *B*

Kansas

Kansas State University *B, M*

Kentucky

Kentucky State University *B*
Western Kentucky University *B*

Maryland

Baltimore City Community
   College *C, A*

Massachusetts

Fisher College *A*
Framingham State College *B*

Michigan

Western Michigan University *B*

Minnesota

Concordia College: Moorhead *B*
Minnesota State University
   Mankato *B, M*

University of Minnesota
   Twin Cities *B*
University of St. Thomas *B*

Mississippi

University of Southern Mississippi *B*

Missouri

Central Missouri State University *B*
College of the Ozarks *B*
Fontbonne University *B*
Missouri State University *B*
Stephens College *B*
University of Missouri
   Columbia *B, M*

Nebraska

University of Nebraska
   Kearney *B*
   Lincoln *B, M*

New Mexico

New Mexico State University *B*

New York

Fashion Institute of Technology *A*
State University of New York
   College at Buffalo *B*
   College at Oneonta *B*
Syracuse University *B, M*

North Carolina

Appalachian State University *B*
Bennett College *B*
East Carolina University *B*
North Carolina Agricultural and
   Technical State University *B*
North Carolina State University *B*
University of North Carolina
   Greensboro *B, M, D*

North Dakota

North Dakota State University *B*

Ohio

Bluffton University *B*
Miami University
   Oxford Campus *M*
Ohio State University
   Columbus Campus *B, M, D*
Ohio University *B*
University of Akron *B, M*
Youngstown State University *B*

Oklahoma

East Central University *B*

Oregon

Art Institute of Portland *A, B*
Oregon State University *B*

Pennsylvania

Albright College *B*
Cheyney University of Pennsylvania *B*
Philadelphia University *B, M*

Rhode Island

University of Rhode Island *B, M*

South Carolina

Tri-County Technical College *A*

Tennessee

Carson-Newman College *B*
Hiwassee College *A*
Lambuth University *B*
Lipscomb University *B*
Middle Tennessee State University *B*
Southwest Tennessee Community
   College *C*
Tennessee State University *B*

Tennessee Technological University *B*
University of Tennessee
   Knoxville *B*

Texas

Lamar University *B*
Navarro College *C, A*
Texas A&M University
   Kingsville *B*
Texas Southern University *M*
Texas Tech University *B*
University of North Texas *B, M*
University of Texas
   Austin *B*
Wade College *A*

Utah

Snow College *A*
Utah State University *B*

Virginia

Regent University *D*

Washington

Seattle Pacific University *B*
Washington State University *B, M*

West Virginia

West Virginia University *B*

Wisconsin

University of Wisconsin
   Madison *B*
   Stout *B*

Cognitive psychology/ psycholinguistics

California

University of California
   San Diego *D*
   Santa Cruz *D*
University of Southern
   California *M, D*

Delaware

University of Delaware *M, D*

District of Columbia

George Washington University *D*

Florida

Florida State University *M, D*

Georgia

Emory University *D*

Illinois

Loyola University of Chicago *M*

Massachusetts

Massachusetts Institute of
   Technology *D*
Tufts University *M, D*

Missouri

University of Missouri
   Columbia *M, D*

New Jersey

Kean University *M*

New York

Rensselaer Polytechnic Institute *D*
State University of New York
   Albany *D*
   Binghamton *D*
   Buffalo *D*
University of Rochester *M, D*

Pennsylvania

Temple University *D*

Rhode Island

Brown University *M, D*

Texas

Rice University *M, D*

Cognitive science

California

Occidental College *B*
Pomona College *B*
University of California
    Berkeley *B*
    Los Angeles *B*
    San Diego *B*
University of California: Merced *B*

Colorado

University of Colorado
    Boulder *D*

Connecticut

University of Connecticut *B*
Yale University *B*

Illinois

University of Chicago *D*

Indiana

University of Evansville *B*

Louisiana

University of Louisiana at Lafayette *D*

Maryland

Johns Hopkins University *B, M, D*

Massachusetts

Massachusetts Institute of
    Technology *D*
Simon's Rock College of Bard *B*

New York

State University of New York
    Oswego *B*
Vassar College *B*

Ohio

Case Western Reserve University *B*

Pennsylvania

Carnegie Mellon University *B*
Lehigh University *B*
University of Pennsylvania *B*

Rhode Island

Brown University *B, M, D*

Texas

Rice University *B*
University of Texas
    Dallas *B, M*

Utah

University of Utah *M*

Wisconsin

Lawrence University *B*

College student counseling

Arkansas

Arkansas State University *M*
Arkansas Tech University *M*
University of Central Arkansas *M*

California

University of Southern California *M*

Connecticut

Southern Connecticut State
    University *M*

Delaware

University of Delaware *M*

Florida

University of Florida *B, M*

Illinois

Loyola University of Chicago *M*
University of Illinois
    Urbana-Champaign *M, D*
Western Illinois University *M*

Indiana

Ball State University *M*
Indiana State University *M*
Indiana University
    Bloomington *M*

Iowa

Iowa State University *T*
University of Iowa *M, D*
University of Northern Iowa *M*

Kentucky

Eastern Kentucky University *M*
Western Kentucky University *M*

Louisiana

Northwestern State University *M*

Maine

University of Southern Maine *M*

Massachusetts

Bridgewater State College *M*
Northeastern University *M*
Springfield College *M*

Michigan

Eastern Michigan University *M*
Michigan State University *M*
Western Michigan University *D*

Minnesota

Minnesota State University
    Mankato *M*
St. Cloud State University *M*

Missouri

University of Missouri
    Columbia *M, D*

Nebraska

Wayne State College *M*

New Hampshire

Rivier College *M*

New Jersey

The College of New Jersey *M*

New York

Canisius College *M*
Fordham University *M, D*
St. Bonaventure University *M*
State University of New York
    College at Plattsburgh *M, T*

North Carolina

Appalachian State University *M*
North Carolina Central University *M*
North Carolina State University *M*

University of North Carolina
    Charlotte *M*
    Greensboro *M, D*
    Pembroke *M*
Western Carolina University *M*

Ohio

Bowling Green State University *M*
Miami University
    Oxford Campus *M*
Ohio State University
    Columbus Campus *M, D*
Ohio University *M*
University of Dayton *M*
Youngstown State University *M*

Pennsylvania

Eastern University *M*
Indiana University of Pennsylvania *M*
Kutztown University of
    Pennsylvania *M, T*
Shippensburg University of
    Pennsylvania *M*
Villanova University *M*
Widener University *M, T*

South Carolina

University of South Carolina *M*

Tennessee

Hiwassee College *A*
University of Memphis *M, D*

Utah

Brigham Young University *D*

Vermont

Johnson State College *M*

Virginia

Longwood University *M*

Washington

Seattle University *M*
Walla Walla College *M*
Western Washington University *M*

Wisconsin

Marquette University *M*
University of Wisconsin
    La Crosse *M*

Commercial/advertising art

Alabama

Calhoun Community College *A*
Faulkner State Community
    College *C, A*
Oakwood College *A*
Samford University *B*
Shelton State Community College *C*

Arizona

Art Center Design College *A, B*
Collins College *A, B*
Eastern Arizona College *A*
Glendale Community College *C, A*
Grand Canyon University *B*
Phoenix College *C, A*
Yavapai College *C, A*

Arkansas

Arkansas State University *B*
National Park Community College *A*
Northwest Arkansas Community
    College *A*
South Arkansas Community College *A*
Southern Arkansas University
    Tech *C, A*

California

Academy of Art University *C, A, B, M*
Allan Hancock College *A*
Art Center College of Design *B*
Art Institute
    of California: Los Angeles *A, B*
    of California: Orange County *A, B*
    of California: San Diego *A, B*
Art Institute of California: San
    Francisco *A, B*
Biola University *B*
Brooks College *A*
Butte College *A*
California College of the Arts *B, M*
California Institute of the Arts *C, B, M*
California Lutheran University *B*
California Polytechnic State
    University: San Luis Obispo *B*
California State University
    East Bay *B*
    Fresno *B*
    Fullerton *B, M*
    Long Beach *B*
    Los Angeles *B*
    Northridge *B*
    San Bernardino *B*
Cerro Coso Community College *C*
Chabot College *A*
Chaffey College *C, A*
Citrus College *C*
City College of San Francisco *C, A*
College of San Mateo *C, A*
College of the Canyons *C, A*
College of the Redwoods *C, A*
College of the Sequoias *C, A*
Cypress College *C, A*
De Anza College *C, A*
Evergreen Valley College *A*
Fashion Institute of Design and
    Merchandising
    San Francisco *A*
Foothill College *C, A*
Fullerton College *A*
Glendale Community College *C, A*
Golden West College *C, A*
La Sierra University *B*
Laguna College of Art and Design *C, B*
Laney College *A*
Las Positas College *A*
Long Beach City College *C, A*
Los Angeles City College *A*
Los Angeles Pierce College *C, A*
Los Angeles Southwest College *A*
Los Angeles Trade and Technical
    College *A*
Los Angeles Valley College *C, A*
Los Medanos College *C, A*
Merced College *C, A*
MiraCosta College *C, A*
Mission College *C, A*
Modesto Junior College *C, A*
Moorpark College *C, A*
Ohlone College *C, A*
Orange Coast College *C, A*
Pacific Union College *A, B*
Palomar College *C, A*
Pasadena City College *C, A*
Platt College
    Cerritos *C, A*
    Los Angeles *C, A*
    Newport Beach *C, A*
    Ontario *C, A, B*
    San Diego *C, A, B*
Porterville College *C, A*
Riverside Community College *C, A*
Saddleback College *C, A*
San Bernardino Valley College *C, A*
San Diego City College *C, A*
Santa Ana College *A*
Santa Barbara City College *C, A*
Santa Monica College *A*
Santa Rosa Junior College *C, A*
Santiago Canyon College *A*
Shasta College *A*

Solano Community College *A*
Taft College *C*
University of the Pacific *B*
Ventura College *C*
West Hills Community College *C, A*
Westwood College of Technology
  Inland Empire *A*
Woodbury University *B*

Colorado

Art Institute
  of Colorado *A, B*
Colorado Mountain College
  Spring Valley Campus *C, A*
Community College of Denver *C, A*
Red Rocks Community College *A*
Trinidad State Junior College *C, A*
Westwood College of
  Technology *C, A, B*
Westwood College of Technology
  South *A, B*

Connecticut

Albertus Magnus College *B*
Asnuntuck Community College *C*
Housatonic Community College *C, A*
Manchester Community College *C, A*
Mitchell College *A*
Northwestern Connecticut
  Community College *C, A*
Norwalk Community College *C, A*
Paier College of Art *C, B*
Quinebaug Valley Community
  College *C*
Sacred Heart University *B*
Tunxis Community College *C, A*
University of Hartford *B*
Western Connecticut State
  University *B*

Delaware

University of Delaware *B*

District of Columbia

Gallaudet University *B*
George Washington University *M*

Florida

Art Institute of Fort
  Lauderdale *C, A, B*
Brevard Community College *A*
Daytona Beach Community College *A*
Florida Agricultural and Mechanical
  University *B*
Florida Community College at
  Jacksonville *A*
Florida Keys Community College *A*
Florida Metropolitan University
  Tampa College *A*
Florida Southern College *B*
Indian River Community College *A*
Lake-Sumter Community College *A*
Lynn University *B*
Manatee Community College *A*
Miami Dade College *A*
Miami International University of Art
  and Design *A*
Okaloosa-Walton College *C, A*
Palm Beach Community College *A*
Pensacola Junior College *A*
Ringling School of Art and Design *B*
Santa Fe Community College *A*
University of Florida *B*
University of Tampa *B*
Valencia Community College *A*

Georgia

Bauder College *A*
Darton College *A*
Savannah College of Art and
  Design *B, M*

Hawaii

University of Hawaii
  Honolulu Community College *C, A*

Idaho

Boise State University *B*
College of Southern Idaho *A*
North Idaho College *A*
Northwest Nazarene University *B*

Illinois

American Academy of Art *B*
Chicago State University *B*
City Colleges of Chicago
  Harold Washington College *A*
  Kennedy-King College *C, A*
Columbia College Chicago *B*
Dominican University *B*
Highland Community College *C, A*
Illinois Institute of Art-Schaumburg *B*
International Academy of Design and
  Technology: Chicago *A, B*
Judson College *B*
Lewis University *B*
Millikin University *B*
North Park University *B*
Oakton Community College *A*
Parkland College *A*
Rend Lake College *C, A*
Robert Morris College: Chicago *C, A*
Sauk Valley Community College *A*
Triton College *C, A*
University of Illinois
  Chicago *B, M*

Indiana

Anderson University *B*
Huntington University *B*
Indiana University
  Bloomington *B, M*
Indiana University-Purdue University
  Fort Wayne *A, B*
International Business College *C, A*
Marian College *B*
Oakland City University *B*
University of Indianapolis *B*
University of St. Francis *A, B*
Vincennes University *A*

Iowa

Buena Vista University *B*
Clarke College *B*
Des Moines Area Community
  College *A*
Dordt College *B*
Drake University *B*
Ellsworth Community College *A*
Graceland University *B*
Iowa Lakes Community College *A*
Iowa State University *B, M*
Morningside College *B*
Mount Mercy College *B*
St. Ambrose University *B*
University of Dubuque *B*
Upper Iowa University *B*
Wartburg College *B*

Kansas

Cloud County Community College *A*
Cowley County Community
  College *A*
Haskell Indian Nations University *C*
Johnson County Community
  College *A*
Labette Community College *A*
Pittsburg State University *B*
Pratt Community College *A*
Tabor College *B*
University of Kansas *B*
Wichita State University *B*

Kentucky

Brescia University *B*

Louisville Technical Institute *A*
Northern Kentucky University *B*
Spencerian College: Lexington *A*

Louisiana

Delgado Community College *A*
Louisiana Tech University *B*
Loyola University New Orleans *B*

Maryland

Anne Arundel Community
  College *C, A*
Carroll Community College *C, A*
College of Southern Maryland *C*
Community College of Baltimore
  County *C, A*
Frostburg State University *B*
Hagerstown Community College *C, A*
Howard Community College *C, A*
Montgomery College *A*
Prince George's Community
  College *A*
University of Baltimore *M*
University of Maryland
  Eastern Shore *B*

Massachusetts

Art Institute of Boston at Lesley
  University *B*
Becker College *C, A, B*
Boston University *B, M*
Cape Cod Community College *A*
Greenfield Community College *A*
Holyoke Community College *C*
Massachusetts College of Art *B, M*
Massasoit Community College *A*
Middlesex Community College *C, A*
Montserrat College of Art *B*
Mount Ida College *A, B*
New England Institute of Art *A, B*
Newbury College *A, B*
Northeastern University *B*
Northern Essex Community
  College *C, A*
Quinsigamond Community College *A*
Salem State College *B*
Simmons College *B*
Springfield Technical Community
  College *A*
Suffolk University *A, B*
University of Massachusetts
  Dartmouth *B, M*
Westfield State College *B*

Michigan

Andrews University *B*
Baker College
  of Auburn Hills *A*
  of Clinton Township *A*
  of Flint *A, B*
  of Muskegon *A*
  of Owosso *A*
  of Port Huron *A*
College for Creative Studies *B*
Ferris State University *C, A, B*
Finlandia University *B*
Gogebic Community College *A*
Grand Rapids Community College *A*
Grand Valley State University *B*
Henry Ford Community College *A*
Kalamazoo Valley Community
  College *C, A*
Kellogg Community College *A*
Kendall College of Art and Design of
  Ferris State University *B*
Lansing Community College *A*
Macomb Community College *C, A*
Mid Michigan Community College *A*
Muskegon Community College *C, A*
Northern Michigan University *B*
Northwestern Michigan College *A*
Olivet College *B*

St. Clair County Community
  College *A*
Schoolcraft College *A*
Siena Heights University *B*
University of Michigan *B*

Minnesota

Academy College *C, A*
Alexandria Technical College *C, A*
Art Institutes International
  Minnesota *A, B*
Bemidji State University *B*
Central Lakes College *C, A*
College of Visual Arts *B*
Dakota County Technical College *C, A*
Globe College *C, A*
Mesabi Range Community and
  Technical College *A*
Minneapolis Business College *A*
Minneapolis College of Art and
  Design *B*
Minnesota State University
  Mankato *B, M, T*
  Moorhead *B*
North Hennepin Community
  College *A*
St. Mary's University of Minnesota *B*
South Central College *A*
University of Minnesota
  Duluth *B*
  Twin Cities *C, B*
Winona State University *B*

Mississippi

Hinds Community College *A*
Mississippi College *B*
Mississippi Gulf Coast Community
  College
  Jefferson Davis Campus *A*

Missouri

Central Missouri State University *B*
Drury University *B*
East Central College *C, A*
Hickey College *C*
Penn Valley Community College *A*
St. Charles Community College *A*
St. Louis Community College
  St. Louis Community College at
    Florissant Valley *A*
  St. Louis Community College at
    Meramec *A*
Southwest Baptist University *B*
Stephens College *B*
Truman State University *B*
Washington University in St.
  Louis *B, M*

Montana

University of Montana: Western *A*

Nebraska

Bellevue University *B*
Central Community College *C, A*
Concordia University *B*
Creative Center *A*
Creighton University *B*
Dana College *B*
Doane College *B*
Metropolitan Community College *A*
Midland Lutheran College *B*
Union College *A, B*
University of Nebraska
  Kearney *B*
Vatterott College: Spring Valley *C*

Nevada

Community College of Southern
  Nevada *A*

New Hampshire

Franklin Pierce College *B*
Keene State College *B*

McIntosh College *A*
New Hampshire Community
  Technical College
    Manchester *C, A*
Plymouth State University *B*
Rivier College *B*

New Jersey

Bergen Community College *A*
Centenary College *B*
The College of New Jersey *B*
County College of Morris *A*
Cumberland County College *A*
Essex County College *A*
Gloucester County College *C, A*
Mercer County Community College *A*
Middlesex County College *A*
Ocean County College *C*
Raritan Valley Community College *A*
Rowan University *B*
Seton Hall University *B*
Sussex County Community
  College *C, A*

New Mexico

Art Center Design College *A, B*
Clovis Community College *A*
New Mexico Junior College *C, A*
New Mexico State University
  Alamogordo *C, A*
San Juan College *A*

New York

Briarcliffe College *A*
City University of New York
  Bronx Community College *A*
  City College *B*
  Kingsborough Community
    College *A*
  New York City College of
    Technology *A, B*
College of Saint Rose *B*
College of Westchester *C, A*
Cornell University *B*
Dutchess Community College *A*
Eugene Lang College The New School
  for Liberal Arts *B*
Fashion Institute of Technology *A, B*
Finger Lakes Community College *A*
Fulton-Montgomery Community
  College *A*
Genesee Community College *A*
Long Island University
  Brooklyn Campus *B, M*
  C.W. Post Campus *B*
Mercy College *A, B*
Mohawk Valley Community
  College *C, A*
Monroe Community College *A*
Nassau Community College *A*
New York Institute of Technology *B*
Onondaga Community College *A*
Pace University *A*
Parsons The New School for
  Design *C, A, B, T*
Pratt Institute *A, B, M*
Roberts Wesleyan College *B*
Rochester Institute of
  Technology *A, B, M*
Rockland Community College *C, A*
St. Thomas Aquinas College *B*
School of Visual Arts *B, M*
State University of New York
  College at Buffalo *B*
  College at Fredonia *B*
  College of Agriculture and
    Technology at Cobleskill *A*
  Farmingdale *B*
  New Paltz *B*
  Oswego *B*
  Purchase *B*
Suffolk County Community College *A*
Sullivan County Community
  College *A*

Syracuse University *B, M*
Tompkins-Cortland Community
  College *C, A*
Ulster County Community
  College *C, A*
Villa Maria College of Buffalo *A*
Westchester Community College *C*
Wood Tobe-Coburn School *C*

North Carolina

Campbell University *B*
Catawba Valley Community College *A*
Central Piedmont Community
  College *C, A*
Fayetteville Technical Community
  College *A*
Gaston College *C*
Guilford Technical Community
  College *C, A*
Halifax Community College *A*
Isothermal Community College *A*
James Sprunt Community
  College *C, A*
Johnston Community College *A*
King's College *C, A*
Lenoir Community College *C, A*
McDowell Technical Community
  College *A*
Pitt Community College *A*
Randolph Community College *A*
South Piedmont Community
  College *A*
Southwestern Community College *A*
Surry Community College *A*

North Dakota

Bismarck State College *C, A*

Ohio

Art Academy of Cincinnati *A, B*
Ashland University *B*
Bradford School *C*
Cincinnati State Technical and
  Community College *A*
Clark State Community College *A*
Cleveland Institute of Art *B*
College of Art Advertising *A*
Cuyahoga Community College
  Metropolitan Campus *A*
Davis College *A*
Defiance College *B*
Edison State Community College *A*
Kent State University *B, M*
Lakeland Community College *A*
Marietta College *B*
Miami University
  Oxford Campus *B*
Ohio Northern University *B*
Owens Community College
  Toledo *C, A*
School of Advertising Art *C, A*
Sinclair Community College *A*
University of Cincinnati *B*
University of Findlay *B*
Wilmington College *B*
Youngstown State University *B*

Oklahoma

Northeastern State University *B*
Oklahoma City Community College *A*
Oklahoma State University
  Oklahoma City *A*
  Okmulgee *A*
Oral Roberts University *B*
Rogers State University *A*
Southwestern Oklahoma State
  University *B*
Western College of Southern
  California *C*

Oregon

Art Institute of Portland *B*
Lane Community College *C, A*

Linn-Benton Community College *A*
Mount Hood Community College *A*
Portland Community College *A*
Portland State University *B*

Pennsylvania

Antonelli Institute of Art and
  Photography *A*
Arcadia University *B*
Art Institute
  of Philadelphia *A, B*
  of Pittsburgh *A, B*
Berks Technical Institute *A*
Bradley Academy for the Visual Arts *A*
Bucks County Community College *A*
California University of
  Pennsylvania *A, B*
Carlow University *B*
Central Pennsylvania College *A*
Community College of Allegheny
  County *C, A*
Community College of Philadelphia *A*
Delaware County Community
  College *A*
Douglas Education Center *A*
Drexel University *B*
Hussian School of Art *A*
Keystone College *A*
Kutztown University of
  Pennsylvania *B*
Lehigh Carbon Community College *A*
Luzerne County Community
  College *C, A*
Montgomery County Community
  College *A*
Oakbridge Academy of Arts *A*
Penn State
  University Park *B*
Pennsylvania College of
  Technology *A, B*
Pittsburgh Technical Institute *A*
Seton Hill University *C, B*
University of the Arts *B*
Waynesburg College *B*
Westmoreland County Community
  College *A*

Puerto Rico

Atlantic College *A, B*

South Carolina

Clemson University *B*
Coker College *B*
Greenville Technical College *C*
Midlands Technical College *A*
Piedmont Technical College *C*
Spartanburg Technical College *C*
Trident Technical College *A*
University of South Carolina
  Upstate *B*

South Dakota

Black Hills State University *B*
Northern State University *A*
Southeast Technical Institute *A*

Tennessee

Belmont University *B*
Chattanooga State Technical
  Community College *A*
Jackson State Community College *A*
Lipscomb University *B*
Memphis College of Art *B*
Nashville State Community College *A*
Nossi College of Art *A*
O'More College of Design *B*
Pellissippi State Technical Community
  College *A*
Southern Adventist University *A, B*
Southwest Tennessee Community
  College *A*
University of Tennessee
  Knoxville *B*

Texas

Abilene Christian University *B*
Amarillo College *C, A*
Austin Community College *C, A*
Brookhaven College *A*
Clarendon College *A*
Coastal Bend College *A*
Collin County Community College
  District *C, A*
El Paso Community College *A*
Grayson County College *A*
Hill College *A*
Houston Community College
  System *C, A*
Kilgore College *C, A*
Lamar University *B*
Navarro College *A*
Sam Houston State University *B*
San Antonio College *A*
San Jacinto College
  Central Campus *A*
South Plains College *A*
Stephen F. Austin State University *M*
Texas A&M University
  Commerce *B, M*
Texas State Technical College
  Harlingen *C, A*
  Waco *C, A*
Tyler Junior College *C, A*
University of Houston *B, M*
University of North Texas *B, M*

Utah

Provo College *A*
Southern Utah University *B*
Weber State University *B*

Virginia

Central Virginia Community
  College *A*
Hampton University *B*
Longwood University *B*
Northern Virginia Community
  College *A*
Thomas Nelson Community
  College *A*
Tidewater Community College *A*
Virginia Intermont College *A*
Virginia Western Community
  College *A*

Washington

Art Institute of Seattle *C*
Central Washington University *B*
Centralia College *A*
Columbia Basin College *A*
Cornish College of the Arts *B*
Eastern Washington University *B*
Everett Community College *A*
Henry Cogswell College *B*
Highline Community College *A*
Pierce College *A*
Shoreline Community College *C, A*
Skagit Valley College *C, A*
Spokane Falls Community
  College *C, A*
University of Washington *B, M*
Western Washington University *B*
Whatcom Community College *A*

West Virginia

Concord University *B*
West Liberty State College *B*
West Virginia State University *B*

Wisconsin

Cardinal Stritch University *B*
Carroll College *B*
Carthage College *B*
Concordia University Wisconsin *B*
Edgewood College *B*
Gateway Technical College *A*
Madison Area Technical College *A*

Mount Mary College *B*
St. Norbert College *B*
Silver Lake College *A*
University of Wisconsin
  Madison *B*
  Platteville *B*
  Stout *B*

Wyoming

Casper College *A*
Laramie County Community
  College *A*
Northwest College *A*

Commercial fishing

Texas

Texas A&M University
  Galveston *B*

Commercial photography

California

Academy of Art University *C, A, B, M*
Allan Hancock College *A*
Art Center College of Design *B*
Brooks Institute of Photography *B*
Butte College *A*
California State University
  Fullerton *B, M*
Cosumnes River College *C, A*
East Los Angeles College *C*
Lake Tahoe Community College *C*
Long Beach City College *C, A*
Modesto Junior College *A*
Pasadena City College *C, A*
Sacramento City College *C, A*
Saddleback College *A*
Santa Monica College *A*
Solano Community College *C, A*
Ventura College *C, A*

Colorado

Art Institute
  of Colorado *A, B*
Colorado Mountain College
  Spring Valley Campus *A*
Community College of Denver *C, A*

Connecticut

Paier College of Art *C, A, B*

Florida

Art Institute of Fort Lauderdale *C*

Georgia

Gwinnett Technical College *A*

Illinois

College of DuPage *C, A*
Judson College *B*
Prairie State College *C, A*
Waubonsee Community College *C*

Iowa

Hawkeye Community College *A*

Maryland

Community College of Baltimore
  County *A*
Harford Community College *C*
Montgomery College *A*

Massachusetts

Art Institute of Boston at Lesley
  University *B*

Michigan

College for Creative Studies *B*
Washtenaw Community College *A*

Minnesota

Central Lakes College *C*
Ridgewater College *C, A*

Nebraska

Metropolitan Community College *A*

Nevada

Community College of Southern
  Nevada *A*

New Hampshire

McIntosh College *A*

New Jersey

Middlesex County College *A*

New York

City University of New York
  LaGuardia Community College *C, A*
Fashion Institute of Technology *A*
Mohawk Valley Community College *A*
Parsons The New School for
  Design *C, A, B, T*
Rochester Institute of
  Technology *B, M*
Rockland Community College *A*
School of Visual Arts *B*
Sullivan County Community
  College *A*
Syracuse University *B*

North Carolina

Alamance Community College *C*
McDowell Technical Community
  College *A*
Randolph Community College *A*

Ohio

Ohio Institute of Photography and
  Technology *A*
Ohio University *M*
Owens Community College
  Toledo *A*
Sinclair Community College *C*

Pennsylvania

Antonelli Institute of Art and
  Photography *A*
Community College of Philadelphia *A*
Oakbridge Academy of Arts *A*

Tennessee

Memphis College of Art *B*
Nossi College of Art *A*

Texas

Amarillo College *A*
Austin Community College *C, A*
El Paso Community College *A*
Houston Community College
  System *C, A*
Kilgore College *C, A*
North Central Texas College *A*
Odessa College *C, A*
Texas A&M University
  Commerce *B*

Virginia

Northern Virginia Community
  College *A*

Washington

Art Institute of Seattle *A*
Seattle Central Community College *A*
Spokane Falls Community
  College *C, A*

Wisconsin

Madison Area Technical College *A*
Milwaukee Area Technical College *A*

Wyoming

Northwest College *A*

Communication disorders

Alabama

Auburn University *B, M*

Arizona

Arizona State University *B, D*
University of Arizona *B, M, D*

Arkansas

Harding University *B*
University of Arkansas
  Little Rock *D*

California

Biola University *B*
California State University
  Chico *B, M*
  Fresno *B, M*
  Fullerton *B, M*
  Los Angeles *B, M*
San Diego State University *B, M, D*
San Jose State University *B*

Colorado

University of Colorado
  Boulder *B, M, D*

District of Columbia

Howard University *M, D*

Georgia

Armstrong Atlantic State
  University *B, M*
Georgia State University *M*
University of Georgia *B, M, D*

Illinois

Eastern Illinois University *B, M*
Northern Illinois University *B, M*
Northwestern University *B, M, D*
Southern Illinois University
  Carbondale *B, M*
Western Illinois University *B, M*

Indiana

Butler University *B*

Kansas

Kansas State University *B*
University of Kansas *B*

Louisiana

Nicholls State University *B*

Maine

University of Maine *B, M*

Maryland

University of Maryland
  College Park *B, D*

Massachusetts

Boston University *B, M*
Bridgewater State College *B*
Emerson College *B, M, D*
University of Massachusetts
  Amherst *B, M, D*
Worcester State College *B*

Michigan

Calvin College *B*
Northern Michigan University *B, M*
Wayne State University *B, M, D*

Minnesota

Minnesota State University
  Mankato *B, M*
St. Cloud State University *B, M*
University of Minnesota
  Duluth *B, M*
  Twin Cities *M, D*

Mississippi

Jackson State University *M*

Missouri

Southeast Missouri State
  University *B, M*
Truman State University *B, M*
University of Missouri
  Columbia *M, D*

New Hampshire

University of New Hampshire *B, M*

New Jersey

Montclair State University *M*

New York

City University of New York
  Queens College *B*
Nazareth College of Rochester *B*
Pace University *B*
State University of New York
  College at Fredonia *B*
  College at Geneseo *B*
  New Paltz *B, M*
Syracuse University *B*
Touro College *B*

North Carolina

Appalachian State University *B, M*
North Carolina Central University *M*
Western Carolina University *B, M*

North Dakota

Minot State University *B, M*

Ohio

Baldwin-Wallace College *B*
Bowling Green State
  University *B, M, D*
Case Western Reserve
  University *B, M, D*

Oklahoma

University of Oklahoma *B, M, D*
University of Tulsa *B*

Oregon

University of Oregon *B, M, D*

Pennsylvania

California University of
  Pennsylvania *B, M*
Edinboro University of
  Pennsylvania *B*
Marywood University *B, M*
University of Pittsburgh *M, D*
West Chester University of
  Pennsylvania *B, M*

Rhode Island

University of Rhode Island *B*

South Carolina

Medical University of South
  Carolina *M*
Winthrop University *B*

South Dakota

Augustana College *B*
University of South Dakota *B, M*

Tennessee

Lambuth University *B*

Texas

Baylor University *B, M*
Texas Tech University Health Sciences Center *B, D*
University of Houston *B*
University of Texas
  Austin *B, M, D*
  Dallas *D*
West Texas A&M University *B, M*

Vermont

University of Vermont *B, M*

Virginia

Hampton University *B*
Radford University *B, M*

Washington

Eastern Washington University *B, M*

West Virginia

Marshall University *B*

Wisconsin

Marquette University *M*
University of Wisconsin
  Eau Claire *B, M*
  Madison *B, M, D*
  Milwaukee *B, M*
  River Falls *B, M*
  Whitewater *M*

Communications

Alabama

Alabama State University *B*
Andrew Jackson University *C, A, B*
Auburn University at Montgomery *B*
Enterprise-Ozark Community College *A*
Gadsden State Community College *A*
Huntingdon College *B*
Miles College *B*
Oakwood College *B*
Samford University *B*
Southern Union State Community College *A*
Spring Hill College *B*
University of Alabama *B, M*
University of Alabama Birmingham *B, M*
University of Mobile *B*
University of South Alabama *B, M*

Alaska

University of Alaska
  Fairbanks *B, M*
  Southeast *B*

Arizona

Arizona State University *B, M, D*
Arizona State University West *B, M*
Cochise College *A*
Grand Canyon University *B*
Northern Arizona University *B*
Phoenix College *A*
Prescott College *B, M*
South Mountain Community College *C*
University of Arizona *B, M, D*

Arkansas

Harding University *B*
Southern Arkansas University *B*
University of Arkansas *B, M*
University of Arkansas
  Little Rock *B, M*
  Pine Bluff *B*

University of the Ozarks *B*

California

Azusa Pacific University *B*
Barstow College *A*
Biola University *B*
California Lutheran University *B*
California State Polytechnic University: Pomona *B*
California State University
  Bakersfield *B*
  Chico *M*
  Dominguez Hills *B*
  East Bay *B*
  Fresno *B, M*
  Fullerton *B, M*
  Los Angeles *B, M*
  Monterey Bay *B*
  Northridge *M*
  Sacramento *B, M*
  San Bernardino *B, M*
  San Marcos *B*
  Stanislaus *B*
Chaffey College *A*
Chapman University *B*
College of Marin: Kentfield *A*
College of the Desert *A*
College of the Sequoias *A*
College of the Siskiyous *C, A*
Concordia University *B*
Copper Mountain College *A*
Cuesta College *C, A*
De Anza College *A*
Dominican University of California *B*
Foothill College *C, A*
Fresno City College *A*
Fresno Pacific University *B*
Fullerton College *A*
Gavilan Community College *A*
La Sierra University *B*
Loyola Marymount University *B*
Menlo College *B*
Merced College *A*
Mills College *B*
MiraCosta College *A*
Modesto Junior College *C, A*
Monterey Peninsula College *A*
Moorpark College *A*
Notre Dame de Namur University *B*
Pacific Union College *B*
Pasadena City College *C, A*
Pepperdine University *B, M*
Point Loma Nazarene University *B*
St. Mary's College of California *B*
San Bernardino Valley College *C, A*
San Diego Christian College *B*
San Diego State University *B, M, D*
San Jose State University *M*
Santa Ana College *C, A*
Santa Barbara City College *A*
Santa Clara University *B*
Santa Rosa Junior College *C*
Santiago Canyon College *A*
Shasta College *A*
Simpson University *B*
Solano Community College *A*
Sonoma State University *B*
Southwestern College *A*
Stanford University *B, M, D*
University of California
  San Diego *B, M, D*
  Santa Barbara *B, M, D*
University of La Verne *B*
University of San Diego *B*
University of San Francisco *B*
University of Southern California *B, M, D*
University of the Pacific *B, M*
Vanguard University of Southern California *B*
Ventura College *A*
Westmont College *B*

Colorado

Adams State College *B*
Colorado Christian University *B*
Jones International University *C, B, M*
Metropolitan State College of Denver *B*
Northeastern Junior College *A*
Red Rocks Community College *A*
Regis University *B*
University of Colorado
  Boulder *B, M, D*
  Colorado Springs *B, M*
  Denver and Health Sciences Center *B, M*
University of Denver *B, M, D*
University of Northern Colorado *B, M, T*
Western State College of Colorado *B*
Westwood College of Technology *B*

Connecticut

Albertus Magnus College *B*
Briarwood College *A*
Central Connecticut State University *B*
Eastern Connecticut State University *B*
Fairfield University *B*
Middlesex Community College *A*
Quinnipiac University *B, M*
Sacred Heart University *B*
Southern Connecticut State University *B*
Tunxis Community College *C*
University of Bridgeport *B*
University of Connecticut *B, M, D*
University of Hartford *B, M*
University of New Haven *A, B*
Western Connecticut State University *B*

Delaware

University of Delaware *B, M*
Wesley College *B*

District of Columbia

Catholic University of America *B*
Gallaudet University *B*
George Washington University *B*
Howard University *B, M, D*
Trinity University *B*

Florida

Barry University *B, M*
Chipola College *A*
City College *A*
Clearwater Christian College *B*
Eckerd College *B*
Edward Waters College *B*
Embry-Riddle Aeronautical University *B*
Flagler College *B*
Florida Atlantic University *B*
Florida Gulf Coast University *B*
Florida Institute of Technology *B*
Florida International University *B, M*
Florida Southern College *B*
Florida State University *D*
Gulf Coast Community College *A*
Jacksonville University *B*
Lake City Community College *A*
Manatee Community College *A*
Nova Southeastern University *B*
Palm Beach Atlantic University *B*
Pensacola Junior College *A*
St. Thomas University *B*
Seminole Community College *A*
Southeastern College of the Assemblies of God *B*
Stetson University *B*
University of Florida *M, D*
University of Miami *B, M, D*
University of South Florida *B, M*

University of Tampa *B*
Warner Southern College *B*

Georgia

Abraham Baldwin Agricultural College *A*
Andrew College *A*
Atlanta Metropolitan College *A*
Augusta State University *B*
Bainbridge College *A*
Berry College *B*
Brewton-Parker College *B*
Clark Atlanta University *B*
Clayton State University *B*
Coastal Georgia Community College *A*
Emmanuel College *B*
Georgia Highlands College *A*
Georgia Perimeter College *A*
Georgia Southern University *B*
Georgia State University *B, M, D*
Kennesaw State University *B*
Macon State College *B*
Oglethorpe University *B*
Reinhardt College *B*
Savannah State University *B*
Shorter College *B*
South Georgia College *A*
Southern Polytechnic State University *C, B, M*
Toccoa Falls College *B*
Wesleyan College *B*
Young Harris College *A*

Hawaii

Chaminade University of Honolulu *B*
Hawaii Pacific University *B, M*
University of Hawaii
  Hilo *B*
  Manoa *B, M*

Idaho

Boise State University *B, M, T*
Brigham Young University-Idaho *B*
College of Southern Idaho *A*
Idaho State University *A, B, M*
Lewis-Clark State College *B*
North Idaho College *A*
University of Idaho *B*

Illinois

Augustana College *B*
Aurora University *B*
Benedictine University *B*
Blackburn College *B*
Bradley University *B*
Concordia University *B*
Danville Area Community College *A*
DePaul University *B, M*
Dominican University *B*
Elmhurst College *B*
Eureka College *B*
Governors State University *B, M*
Illinois State University *M*
Illinois Valley Community College *A*
John Wood Community College *A*
Judson College *B*
Kishwaukee College *A*
Lake Forest College *B*
Lewis University *B*
Loyola University of Chicago *B*
McKendree College *B*
Millikin University *B*
Monmouth College *B, T*
Moody Bible Institute *B*
North Central College *B*
North Park University *B*
Northern Illinois University *B*
Northwestern University *B, M, D*
Olivet Nazarene University *B*
Quincy University *B*
Roosevelt University *B*
St. Xavier University *B*

Sauk Valley Community College *A*
Southwestern Illinois College *A*
Trinity Christian College *B*
Trinity International University *B*
University of Illinois
Springfield *B, M*
Urbana-Champaign *B, D*
Waubonsee Community College *A*
Western Illinois University *B*
Wheaton College *B*

Indiana

Bethel College *B*
Butler University *B*
Calumet College of St. Joseph *B*
Goshen College *B*
Grace College *B*
Hanover College *B*
Huntington University *B*
Indiana Institute of Technology *B*
Indiana State University *B, M*
Indiana University
Bloomington *B, M, D*
East *B*
Kokomo *B*
Northwest *B*
Southeast *B*
Indiana University-Purdue University
Fort Wayne *B, M, T*
Indiana University-Purdue University
Indianapolis *B*
Indiana Wesleyan University *C, A, B*
Manchester College *B, T*
Marian College *B*
Martin University *B*
Purdue University *B, M, D*
Purdue University
Calumet *B, M*
North Central Campus *C*
Saint Mary's College *B*
Taylor University *B*
Tri-State University *A, B*
University of Evansville *B*
University of Indianapolis *B*
University of St. Francis *B*
University of Southern Indiana *T*
Vincennes University *A*

Iowa

Ashford University *B*
Buena Vista University *B*
Central College *B*
Clarke College *B*
Coe College *B*
Dordt College *B*
Drake University *B*
Ellsworth Community College *A*
Iowa State University *B*
Iowa Wesleyan College *B*
Mount Mercy College *B*
Northwestern College *B*
St. Ambrose University *B*
Simpson College *B*
University of Dubuque *B, M*
University of Iowa *B, M, D, T*
University of Northern Iowa *B, M*
Upper Iowa University *B*
Wartburg College *B*
William Penn University *B*

Kansas

Baker University *B*
Barton County Community College *A*
Bethany College *B*
Central Christian College of
Kansas *A, B*
Cloud County Community College *A*
Coffeyville Community College *A*
Cowley County Community
College *A*
Emporia State University *B*
Fort Hays State University *B, M*
Fort Scott Community College *A*
Friends University *B*

Garden City Community College *A*
Haskell Indian Nations University *A*
Hutchinson Community College *A*
Kansas State University *B, M*
Kansas Wesleyan University *B, T*
McPherson College *B*
MidAmerica Nazarene University *B, T*
Neosho County Community
College *A*
Ottawa University *B*
Pittsburg State University *B, M*
Pratt Community College *A*
Seward County Community College *A*
Southwestern College *B*
Sterling College *B*
Tabor College *B*
University of St. Mary *B*
Washburn University of Topeka *B*
Wichita State University *B, M*

Kentucky

Bellarmine University *B*
Berea College *B*
Campbellsville University *B*
Eastern Kentucky University *B*
Henderson Community College *A*
Kentucky Mountain Bible College *B*
Kentucky Wesleyan College *B*
Lindsey Wilson College *B*
Morehead State University *B, M*
Murray State University *M*
Pikeville College *B*
Spalding University *B*
Thomas More College *A, B*
Union College *B*
University of Kentucky *B, M, D*
University of Louisville *B*
University of the Cumberlands *B, T*
West Kentucky Community and
Technical College *A*
Western Kentucky University *C, B, M*

Louisiana

Centenary College of Louisiana *B*
Dillard University *B*
Loyola University New Orleans *B, M*
Southeastern Louisiana University *B*
University of Louisiana at
Lafayette *B, M*
University of Louisiana at Monroe *M*
University of New Orleans *B, M*

Maine

New England School of
Communications *C, A, B*
Thomas College *B*
University of Maine *B*
University of Southern Maine *B*

Maryland

Allegany College of Maryland *A*
Bowie State University *M*
College of Notre Dame of
Maryland *B, M*
Columbia Union College *B*
Community College of Baltimore
County *A*
Frederick Community College *A*
Frostburg State University *B*
Hood College *B*
Loyola College in Maryland *B*
McDaniel College *B*
Mount St. Mary's University *B*
Salisbury University *B*
Towson University *B, M*
University of Baltimore *B, D*
University of Maryland
College Park *B, M, D*
Eastern Shore *B*
University College *C, B*

Massachusetts

Boston College *B*

Boston University *B, M*
Bridgewater State College *B*
Bristol Community College *A*
Bunker Hill Community College *A*
Cape Cod Community College *A*
Clark University *B, M*
Curry College *B*
Dean College *A*
Eastern Nazarene College *B*
Elms College *B*
Emerson College *B, M*
Emmanuel College *B*
Endicott College *B*
Fitchburg State College *B, M*
Framingham State College *B*
Gordon College *B*
Hampshire College *B*
Lasell College *B*
Massachusetts Bay Community
College *C, A*
Merrimack College *B*
Middlesex Community College *A*
Mount Ida College *A*
Newbury College *A, B*
Northeastern University *B*
Regis College *B*
Salem State College *B*
Simmons College *B, M*
Stonehill College *B*
Suffolk University *B, M*
University of Massachusetts
Amherst *B, M, D*
Boston *C*
Western New England College *B*
Westfield State College *B*

Michigan

Adrian College *A, B, T*
Albion College *B, T*
Andrews University *B, M*
Aquinas College *B, T*
Baker College
of Jackson *A*
Bay de Noc Community College *C*
Calvin College *B*
Concordia University *B*
Cornerstone University *B*
Ferris State University *B*
Grand Valley State University *B, M*
Henry Ford Community College *A*
Hillsdale College *B*
Hope College *B*
Kuyper College *B*
Lansing Community College *A*
Macomb Community College *C, A*
Michigan State University *B, M, D*
Michigan Technological University *B*
Mid Michigan Community College *A*
Northern Michigan University *B*
Northwestern Michigan College *A*
Oakland University *B*
Olivet College *B*
Rochester College *B*
Saginaw Valley State University *B, T*
Schoolcraft College *A*
Siena Heights University *B*
Spring Arbor University *B, M*
University of Detroit Mercy *B*
University of Michigan *B, M, D*
University of Michigan
Dearborn *B*
Flint *B, T*
Wayne State University *B, M, D*
Western Michigan University *B, M*

Minnesota

Augsburg College *B*
Bethany Lutheran College *B*
Bethel University *B, M*
Brown College *B*
College of St. Catherine *B*
College of St. Scholastica *B*
Concordia College: Moorhead *B*
Gustavus Adolphus College *B*

Hamline University *B*
Macalester College *B*
Metropolitan State University *B*
Minnesota State University
Mankato *B, M*
Northland Community & Technical
College *A*
Northwestern College *B*
Ridgewater College *A*
St. Cloud State University *B, M*
Southwest Minnesota State
University *B*
University of Minnesota
Duluth *B*
Morris *B*
University of St. Thomas *B*
Vermilion Community College *A*
Winona State University *B*

Mississippi

Belhaven College *B*
Meridian Community College *A*
Mississippi College *B, M*
Mississippi Delta Community
College *A*
Mississippi Gulf Coast Community
College
Jefferson Davis Campus *A*
Mississippi State University *B*
Mississippi Valley State University *B*
University of Southern
Mississippi *B, M, D*
William Carey College *B*

Missouri

Avila University *B*
Central Methodist University *B*
Central Missouri State University *B, M*
College of the Ozarks *B*
Drury University *B, M*
Evangel University *A, B*
Fontbonne University *B*
Hannibal-LaGrange College *B*
Lindenwood University *B, M*
Missouri Baptist University *B*
Missouri Southern State University *B*
Missouri State University *B, M*
Missouri Western State University *B*
Northwest Missouri State
University *B*
Park University *B, M*
Rockhurst University *B*
St. Louis Community College
St. Louis Community College at
Florissant Valley *A*
St. Louis Community College at
Meramec *A*
St. Louis University *B, M*
Southeast Missouri State University *B*
Southwest Baptist University *B*
Stephens College *B*
University of Missouri
Columbia *B, M, D*
Kansas City *B, M*
St. Louis *B, M*
Webster University *B, M*
William Jewell College *B*
William Woods University *B*

Montana

Carroll College *A, B, T*
Montana State University
Billings *B*
Montana Tech of the University of
Montana *B, M*
Rocky Mountain College *B*
University of Montana: Missoula *B, M*

Nebraska

Bellevue University *B, M*
Concordia University *B*
Creighton University *B*
Dana College *B*

Doane College *B*
Hastings College *B*
Midland Lutheran College *B*
Nebraska Wesleyan University *B*
University of Nebraska
  Kearney *B*
  Lincoln *B, M, D*
  Omaha *B, M*
Wayne State College *B, T*
York College *B*

Nevada
Community College of Southern
  Nevada *A*
University of Nevada
  Las Vegas *B, M*
  Reno *B, M*

New Hampshire
Franklin Pierce College *B*
Keene State College *B*
New England College *B*
Plymouth State University *B*
Rivier College *B*
Southern New Hampshire
  University *B*
University of New Hampshire *B*
University of New Hampshire at
  Manchester *B*

New Jersey
Bloomfield College *C, B*
Caldwell College *B*
Centenary College *B*
The College of New Jersey *B*
College of St. Elizabeth *B*
Fairleigh Dickinson University
  College at Florham *B*
  Metropolitan Campus *B*
Felician College *B*
Georgian Court University *B*
Gloucester County College *A*
Kean University *B*
Middlesex County College *A*
Monmouth University *B, M*
New Jersey City University *B*
Passaic County Community College *A*
Ramapo College of New Jersey *B*
Richard Stockton College of New
  Jersey *B*
Rider University *B*
Rowan University *B*
Rutgers, The State University of New
  Jersey
  New Brunswick/Piscataway
    Campus *B, M, D*
St. Peter's College *B*
Seton Hall University *B, M*
Thomas Edison State College *A, B*
William Paterson University of New
  Jersey *B, M*

New Mexico
College of Santa Fe *B*
Eastern New Mexico University *B, M*
New Mexico Highlands University *B*
New Mexico Junior College *A*
San Juan College *A*

New York
Alfred University *B*
Broome Community College *A*
Canisius College *B*
Cazenovia College *B*
City University of New York
  Baruch College *B, M*
  Brooklyn College *B*
  City College *B*
  College of Staten Island *B*
  Hunter College *M*
  Lehman College *B*
Clarkson University *B*
College of Mount St. Vincent *B*

Cornell University *B, M, D*
Dutchess Community College *A*
Erie Community College
  South Campus *A*
Excelsior College *B*
Fashion Institute of Technology *A*
Finger Lakes Community College *A*
Five Towns College *A, B*
Fordham University *B*
Fulton-Montgomery Community
  College *A*
Genesee Community College *A*
Hamilton College *B*
Hofstra University *B, M*
Houghton College *B*
Iona College *B*
Ithaca College *B, M*
Keuka College *B*
Le Moyne College *B*
Long Island University
  Brooklyn Campus *B*
Manhattan College *B*
Manhattanville College *B*
Marymount Manhattan College *B*
Metropolitan College of New
  York *A, B*
Molloy College *B*
Monroe Community College *A*
Nassau Community College *A*
Nazareth College of Rochester *B*
New York Institute of Technology *B*
New York University *B, M, D*
Niagara County Community
  College *A* .
Niagara University *B*
Nyack College *B*
Orange County Community College *A*
Pace University *B*
Polytechnic University *C*
Rensselaer Polytechnic
  Institute *B, M, D*
Roberts Wesleyan College *B*
Rochester Institute of Technology *B*
Rockland Community College *A*
St. Francis College *B*
St. John Fisher College *B*
St. John's University *B, M*
St. Joseph's College: Suffolk
  Campus *B*
St. Thomas Aquinas College *B*
State University of New York
  Albany *B, M*
  Buffalo *B, M, D*
  College at Brockport *B, M*
  College at Buffalo *B*
  College at Fredonia *B*
  College at Geneseo *B*
  College at Old Westbury *B*
  College at Oneonta *B*
  College at Plattsburgh *B*
  New Paltz *B*
  Oswego *B*
Suffolk County Community College *A*
Sullivan County Community
  College *A*
Syracuse University *B, M*
Tompkins-Cortland Community
  College *A*
Touro College *B*
Ulster County Community College *A*
Utica College *B*
Westchester Community College *A*

North Carolina
Bennett College *B*
Catawba College *B*
East Carolina University *B*
Elon University *B*
Gardner-Webb University *B*
Greensboro College *B*
High Point University *B*
Lees-McRae College *B*
Lenoir-Rhyne College *B*
Louisburg College *A*

Mars Hill College *B*
Meredith College *B, T*
Methodist College *A, B*
Mount Olive College *B*
North Carolina Agricultural and
  Technical State University *B*
North Carolina State University *B*
Peace College *A, B*
Pfeiffer University *B*
Queens University of Charlotte *B*
St. Augustine's College *B*
Salem College *B*
University of North Carolina
  Chapel Hill *C, B, M, D*
  Charlotte *B, M*
Wake Forest University *B, M*
Western Carolina University *B*
Wingate University *B*

North Dakota
Dickinson State University *B, T*
Jamestown College *B*
North Dakota State University *D*
University of Mary *B*
University of North Dakota *B, M, D*

Ohio
Antioch College *B*
Ashland University *C, B*
Baldwin-Wallace College *B*
Bluffton University *B*
Bowling Green State University *M, D*
Capital University *B*
Cedarville University *B*
Cincinnati Christian University *A*
Cleveland State University *B, M*
College of Mount St. Joseph *A, B, T*
College of Wooster *B*
Defiance College *B*
Denison University *B*
Franciscan University of
  Steubenville *B*
Heidelberg College *B*
Hiram College *B*
International College of
  Broadcasting *C, A*
John Carroll University *B, M*
Lake Erie College *B*
Malone College *B*
Marietta College *B*
Miami University
  Oxford Campus *B, M, T*
Mount Union College *B, T*
Mount Vernon Nazarene University *B*
Ohio Dominican University *C, B*
Ohio Northern University *B*
Ohio State University
  Columbus Campus *B, M, D*
Ohio University *B, M, D*
Ohio University
  Southern Campus at Ironton *A*
Otterbein College *B*
Owens Community College
  Toledo *A*
Shawnee State University *A*
Sinclair Community College *C, A*
Tiffin University *B*
Union Institute & University *B*
University of Akron *M*
University of Cincinnati *B, M, T*
University of Cincinnati
  Raymond Walters College *A*
University of Dayton *B, M*
University of Findlay *B*
University of Rio Grande *A, B*
University of Toledo *B*
Urbana University *B*
Walsh University *A, B*
Wilmington College *B*
Wittenberg University *B*
Wright State University *A, B*
Wright State University: Lake
  Campus *A*
Youngstown State University *B*

Oklahoma
Cameron University *B*
Connors State College *A*
East Central University *B*
Northeastern Oklahoma Agricultural
  and Mechanical College *A*
Northeastern State University *M*
Oklahoma Baptist University *B*
Oklahoma Christian University *B, T*
Oklahoma Wesleyan University *B*
Oral Roberts University *B*
Southeastern Oklahoma State
  University *B*
Southern Nazarene University *A, B*
Southwestern Oklahoma State
  University *B*
University of Central Oklahoma *B*
University of Oklahoma *B, M, D*
University of Science and Arts of
  Oklahoma *B*
University of Tulsa *B*

Oregon
Central Oregon Community
  College *A*
Corban College *B*
George Fox University *B*
Lewis & Clark College *B*
Linfield College *B*
Marylhurst University *B*
Multnomah Bible College *B*
Northwest Christian College *B*
Oregon Institute of Technology *B*
Pacific University *B*
Portland Community College *C*
Southern Oregon University *B*
Treasure Valley Community College *A*
University of Oregon *B*
Western Oregon University *B*

Pennsylvania
Albright College *B*
Allegheny College *B*
Alvernia College *B*
Arcadia University *C, B*
Baptist Bible College of
  Pennsylvania *B*
Bloomsburg University of
  Pennsylvania *B, T*
Bucks County Community College *A*
Cabrini College *B*
California University of
  Pennsylvania *B, M*
Carlow University *B, T*
Carnegie Mellon University *M*
Cedar Crest College *B*
Central Pennsylvania College *A, B*
Chatham College *B*
Cheyney University of Pennsylvania *B*
Clarion University of
  Pennsylvania *B, M*
College Misericordia *B*
DeSales University *B*
Delaware County Community
  College *A*
Drexel University *B*
Duquesne University *B, M*
East Stroudsburg University of
  Pennsylvania *B, T*
Eastern University *B*
Edinboro University of
  Pennsylvania *B, M*
Geneva College *B, T*
Gettysburg College *B*
Grove City College *B*
Holy Family University *B*
Indiana University of Pennsylvania *B*
Juniata College *B*
Keystone College *A, B*
Kutztown University of
  Pennsylvania *B, T*
La Salle University *A, B, M*
Lebanon Valley College *C*
Lehigh Carbon Community College *A*

Lincoln University *B*
Lycoming College *B*
Manor College *A*
Mansfield University of
　Pennsylvania *B*
Mercyhurst College *B*
Messiah College *B*
Millersville University of
　Pennsylvania *B*
Montgomery County Community
　College *A*
Muhlenberg College *C, B*
Neumann College *B*
Northampton County Area
　Community College *A*
Penn State
　Erie, The Behrend College *B*
　Harrisburg *B*
　University Park *B, M, D*
Robert Morris University *B*
Rosemont College *B*
St. Francis University *B*
St. Joseph's University *C, A, B*
St. Vincent College *B*
Seton Hill University *B*
Shippensburg University of
　Pennsylvania *M*
Slippery Rock University of
　Pennsylvania *B*
Susquehanna University *B, T*
Thiel College *B*
University of Pennsylvania *B, M, D*
University of Pittsburgh
　Greensburg *B*
　Johnstown *B*
University of Scranton *B, T*
University of the Arts *B*
Ursinus College *B*
Villanova University *B*
Waynesburg College *B*
West Chester University of
　Pennsylvania *B*
Widener University *B*
Wilkes University *B*
York College of Pennsylvania *B*

Puerto Rico

American University of Puerto
　Rico *A, B*
Pontifical Catholic University of
　Puerto Rico *B*
Turabo University *B*
Universidad Metropolitana *B*
University of Puerto Rico
　Rio Piedras *B, M*
University of the Sacred Heart *B*

Rhode Island

Bryant University *B*
Johnson & Wales University *A*
Rhode Island College *B*
Roger Williams University *B*
University of Rhode Island *B, M*

South Carolina

Anderson University *B*
Clemson University *B, M*
Coastal Carolina University *B*
Coker College *B*
College of Charleston *B*
Columbia College *B*
Columbia International University *B*
Furman University *B*
Newberry College *B*
Southern Wesleyan University *B*
University of South Carolina
　Aiken *B*
　Upstate *B*

South Dakota

Augustana College *B*
Dakota Wesleyan University *B*
Presentation College *B*

University of South Dakota *B*

Tennessee

Belmont University *B*
Bryan College *B*
Carson-Newman College *B*
East Tennessee State University *M*
Freed-Hardeman University *B*
Hiwassee College *A*
Jackson State Community College *A*
Lambuth University *B*
Lee University *B*
Lincoln Memorial University *B*
Milligan College *B*
Roane State Community College *A*
Tennessee State University *B*
Tennessee Technological University *B*
Trevecca Nazarene University *B*
Union University *B, T*
University of Tennessee
　Chattanooga *B*
　Knoxville *M, D*
　Martin *B*
Vanderbilt University *B*

Texas

Amarillo College *A*
Angelina College *A*
Angelo State University *B, M, T*
Austin College *B*
Baylor University *B, M*
Blinn College *A*
Brazosport College *A*
Cisco Junior College *A*
Clarendon College *A*
Coastal Bend College *A*
Concordia University at Austin *B*
Dallas Baptist University *B*
El Paso Community College *A*
Hardin-Simmons University *B*
Hill College *A*
Houston Baptist University *B*
Howard Payne University *B, T*
Kilgore College *A*
Lamar University *B*
Laredo Community College *A*
Lubbock Christian University *B*
McLennan Community College *A*
McMurry University *B*
Midland College *A*
Navarro College *A*
Northwest Vista College *A*
Our Lady of the Lake University of San
　Antonio *B*
Palo Alto College *A*
Prairie View A&M University *B*
St. Mary's University *B, M, T*
South Plains College *A*
Southwestern Adventist University *B*
Southwestern Assemblies of God
　University *A*
Southwestern University *B, T*
Stephen F. Austin State
　University *B, M, T*
Sul Ross State University *B*
Tarleton State University *B*
Texas A&M University
　Commerce *B*
　Kingsville *B*
Texas Christian University *B, M*
Texas Lutheran University *B*
Texas Southern University *B, M*
Texas Wesleyan University *B*
Trinity University *B*
Trinity Valley Community College *A*
University of Houston *B, M*
University of Houston
　Clear Lake *B*
　Victoria *B*
University of Mary Hardin-Baylor *B*
University of North Texas *B, M*
University of St. Thomas *B*
University of Texas
　Arlington *M*

Austin *B*
Brownsville *B*
El Paso *B, M*
Pan American *B, M*
San Antonio *B*
　of the Permian Basin *B*
Weatherford College *A*
West Texas A&M University *M*

Utah

Dixie State College of Utah *A*
Salt Lake Community College *A*
Southern Utah University *B*
University of Utah *B, M, D*
Utah Valley State College *A*
Westminster College *B, M*

Vermont

Green Mountain College *B*
Lyndon State College *A, B*
Norwich University *B*
Southern Vermont College *B*

Virginia

Christopher Newport University *B*
Eastern Mennonite University *B*
Emory & Henry College *B*
Hollins University *B*
James Madison University *B*
Liberty University *B*
Longwood University *B*
Lord Fairfax Community College *A*
Lynchburg College *B*
Mary Baldwin College *B*
Marymount University *B*
Northern Virginia Community
　College *A*
Old Dominion University *B*
Randolph-Macon Woman's College *B*
Regent University *B, M, D*
Shenandoah University *B*
Thomas Nelson Community
　College *C*
University of Virginia's College at
　Wise *B*
Virginia Polytechnic Institute and
　State University *B, M*
Virginia Wesleyan College *B*

Washington

Central Washington University *B*
Eastern Washington University *B, M*
Edmonds Community College *C*
Everett Community College *A*
Green River Community College *C*
Highline Community College *A*
Northwest University *B*
Olympic College *A*
Pacific Lutheran University *B*
Seattle Central Community College *A*
Seattle Pacific University *B*
Skagit Valley College *A*
University of Puget Sound *B*
University of Washington *B, M, D*
Walla Walla College *B*
Washington State University *B, M*
Western Washington University *B*
Whitworth College *B*

West Virginia

Bethany College *B*
Concord University *B*
Davis and Elkins College *B*
Shepherd University *B*
West Liberty State College *B*
West Virginia State University *B, M*
West Virginia Wesleyan College *B*

Wisconsin

Alverno College *B*
Cardinal Stritch University *B*
Carroll College *B*
Carthage College *B*

Concordia University Wisconsin *B*
Marian College of Fond du Lac *B*
Marquette University *B*
Milwaukee School of Engineering *B*
Moraine Park Technical College *A*
Mount Mary College *B*
Ripon College *B*
St. Norbert College *B, T*
University of Wisconsin
　Eau Claire *B*
　Green Bay *B*
　La Crosse *B*
　Madison *B, M, D*
　Milwaukee *B, M*
　Oshkosh *B*
　Parkside *B, T*
　Platteville *B*
　Stevens Point *B, M*
　Superior *B, M*
　Whitewater *B, M*
Wisconsin Lutheran College *B*

Wyoming

Casper College *A*
Eastern Wyoming College *A*
Laramie County Community
　College *A*
Northwest College *A*
Sheridan College *A*
University of Wyoming *B, M*
Western Wyoming Community
　College *A*

Communications systems installation/ repair

Arkansas

North Arkansas College *A*

Georgia

Gwinnett Technical College *C*

Idaho

Idaho State University *C, A*

Illinois

College of DuPage *A*

Iowa

Des Moines Area Community
　College *C, A*
Western Iowa Tech Community
　College *C*

Kentucky

Big Sandy Community and Technical
　College *C*

Michigan

Northern Michigan University *A*

Minnesota

Dakota County Technical College *C, A*
Minnesota State Community and
　Technical College - Fergus Falls *C*
St. Paul College *C*

New York

Broome Community College *A*
Erie Community College
　South Campus *A*
Mohawk Valley Community College *A*
Vaughn College of Aeronautics and
　Technology *A, B*

Pennsylvania

Luzerne County Community
　College *C*

Texas
St. Philip's College C, A

Wisconsin
Milwaukee Area Technical College C
Wisconsin Indianhead Technical
College C, A

Communications technology

Alabama
Alabama Agricultural and Mechanical
University B
Calhoun Community College A
Community College of the Air
Force A
Gadsden State Community College A

Arizona
Northland Pioneer College C, A

California
Bakersfield College A
Barstow College C
Butte College C, A
Chabot College C, A
City College of San Francisco A
College of San Mateo A
College of the Canyons C, A
Columbia College: Hollywood A, B
Cosumnes River College A
Diablo Valley College C
El Camino College A
Laney College C, A
Long Beach City College C, A
Los Angeles City College C, A
Los Angeles Southwest College A
Los Angeles Trade and Technical
College C, A
Los Angeles Valley College C
Moorpark College A
Mount San Antonio College C, A
Napa Valley College C, A
Palomar College C, A
Pasadena City College C, A
Rio Hondo College A
San Diego City College A
San Diego State University M
San Jose City College C, A
Santa Barbara City College C, A
Santa Monica College A
Skyline College C, A
Southwestern College C, A
Ventura College A

Colorado
Arapahoe Community College C, A
Jones International University C, B, M
Mesa State College A
Northeastern Junior College A

Connecticut
Asnuntuck Community College A
Manchester Community College C
Naugatuck Valley Community
College C
Norwalk Community College A
Sacred Heart University B

Florida
Florida State University M
Miami Dade College A
Pensacola Junior College A
Seminole Community College A

Georgia
Clark Atlanta University B

Illinois
College of DuPage C, A

Governors State University M
Lewis University B
Southwestern Illinois College C, A

Indiana
Indiana University-Purdue University
Indianapolis A
Martin University B
St. Mary-of-the-Woods College B

Iowa
Dordt College A
Iowa Central Community College A
Kirkwood Community College A
Marshalltown Community College A
Scott Community College A
Waldorf College B

Kansas
Central Christian College of Kansas A
Coffeyville Community College A
Hutchinson Community College A

Kentucky
Jefferson Community College C, A

Maine
New England School of
Communications A, B

Maryland
Allegany College of Maryland A
Anne Arundel Community College C
Bowie State University B
Frederick Community College A
Harford Community College A
Villa Julie College B

Massachusetts
Becker College A, B
Lesley University B
New England Institute of Art A
Newbury College A
North Shore Community College C
Northern Essex Community
College A
Suffolk University B
Worcester State College B

Michigan
Andrews University B
Delta College A
Eastern Michigan University B
Kalamazoo Valley Community
College C, A
Kellogg Community College A
Lansing Community College A
Lawrence Technological
University B, M
Mott Community College C, A
Saginaw Valley State University M
Schoolcraft College A

Minnesota
Academy College A
Century Community and Technical
College C, A
Hennepin Technical College C, A
Rochester Community and Technical
College C, A
St. Mary's University of
Minnesota B, M
Winona State University B

Mississippi
Hinds Community College A
Jackson State University B
Meridian Community College A

Missouri
Evangel University B
Penn Valley Community College C

Ranken Technical College A

Montana
Montana Tech of the University of
Montana A, B

Nebraska
Hastings College B
University of Nebraska
Lincoln D

New Hampshire
New Hampshire Technical
Institute C, A

New Jersey
Bergen Community College C
Brookdale Community College A
County College of Morris A
Mercer County Community College A
Ocean County College A
Rowan University B

New York
Cayuga County Community College A
City University of New York
Borough of Manhattan Community
College A
Queensborough Community
College A
Five Towns College A, B
Herkimer County Community
College A
Monroe Community College A
New York Institute of
Technology C, A, M
New York University B, M, D
State University of New York
College at Plattsburgh A
Institute of Technology at
Utica/Rome B
Suffolk County Community College A

North Carolina
Cleveland Community College C, A

North Dakota
Minot State University B

Ohio
Bowling Green State University:
Firelands College A
Cedarville University B
Columbus State Community
College A
Cuyahoga Community College
Metropolitan Campus A
Owens Community College
Toledo A

Oklahoma
National Education Center
Spartan School of Aeronautics A
Oklahoma State University
Oklahoma City A
Rogers State University A
Southern Nazarene University B
Tulsa Community College A

Oregon
Lane Community College C, A
Portland Community College C

Pennsylvania
Cheyney University of Pennsylvania B
Community College of Beaver
County A
Delaware County Community
College A
East Stroudsburg University of
Pennsylvania A, B
Philadelphia University M

St. Vincent College B
Westmoreland County Community
College A

Puerto Rico
American University of Puerto Rico B
Inter American University of Puerto
Rico
Bayamon Campus A, B
University of Puerto Rico
Humacao A

South Carolina
Trident Technical College C, A

Tennessee
Nashville State Community College A
Southern Adventist University A, B
Tennessee Technological University B

Texas
Amarillo College A
Art Institute
of Houston A
Coastal Bend College A
Eastfield College C, A
El Paso Community College A
Northwest Vista College C, A
Richland College A
St. Philip's College A
Tarrant County College C, A
Texas A&M University
Commerce M
Texas State Technical College
Waco A
West Texas A
Texas State Technical College:
Marshall C, A

Utah
Dixie State College of Utah A

Vermont
Lyndon State College B

Virginia
ECPI College of Technology C, A
George Mason University M
J. Sargeant Reynolds Community
College C
Virginia Western Community
College A

Washington
Eastern Washington University B
Edmonds Community College A
North Seattle Community
College C, A
Spokane Falls Community College A
University of Washington M
Yakima Valley Community
College C, A

West Virginia
Bluefield State College A
Southern West Virginia Community
and Technical College A

Wisconsin
Gateway Technical College A
Western Wisconsin Technical
College A

Community health/ preventative medicine

Florida
Florida Gulf Coast University B
University of North Florida M

Illinois
Southern Illinois University
Carbondale *M*
University of Illinois
Urbana-Champaign *B, M, D*

Indiana
Indiana University-Purdue University
Indianapolis *M*

Iowa
University of Iowa *M, D*

Maine
University of Maine
Farmington *B*

Michigan
Wayne State University *M*

New York
Hofstra University *B*
Long Island University
Brooklyn Campus *B, M*

Ohio
University of Cincinnati
Raymond Walters College *A*
Youngstown State University *B*

Pennsylvania
Temple University *M*
University of Pittsburgh *M, D*

Texas
University of Texas
Health Science Center at
Houston *M, D*
Medical Branch at Galveston *M, D*

Utah
Utah Valley State College *A, B*

Virginia
Liberty University *B*
Old Dominion University *M*

Wisconsin
University of Wisconsin
La Crosse *B, M*
Madison *M, D*

Community health services

Alabama
South University *M*

Arkansas
University of Arkansas *M*

California
California Institute of Integral
Studies *M*
California State University
Sacramento *B*

Connecticut
Western Connecticut State
University *B*

Florida
Florida State University *M*
Manatee Community College *A*
University of West Florida *B, M*

Georgia
Darton College *A*

Illinois
McHenry County College *C*
Northeastern Illinois University *B*
Roosevelt University *C*
Waubonsee Community College *C*

Indiana
Indiana State University *B*
Indiana University-Purdue University
Fort Wayne *B*
Indiana University-Purdue University
Indianapolis *M*
Indiana Wesleyan University *M*

Kansas
University of Kansas *B*

Kentucky
Northern Kentucky University *M*
University of the Cumberlands *B*
Western Kentucky University *B, T*

Massachusetts
Mount Wachusett Community
College *C*

Michigan
Michigan State University *B, M*
Mott Community College *A*
University of Michigan *M*
Western Michigan University *B*

Minnesota
Bethel University *B*
Minneapolis Community and
Technical College *C*
Minnesota State University
Moorhead *B*

Missouri
Maryville University of Saint Louis *B*

Nebraska
University of Nebraska
Lincoln *B*
Omaha *B*

New York
Adelphi University *M*
City University of New York
Brooklyn College *M*
Kingsborough Community
College *A*
Erie Community College
City Campus *A*
Mount St. Mary College *B*
Sarah Lawrence College *M*

Ohio
Ohio University *B*
University of Dayton *M*
Youngstown State University *B*

Oklahoma
University of Oklahoma *M*

Pennsylvania
Duquesne University *M*
University of Pennsylvania *B*

Rhode Island
Brown University *B*

South Carolina
Morris College *B*

Tennessee
Southern Adventist University *M*

Texas
Texas Woman's University *B, M*
University of Texas
El Paso *B*
Health Science Center at
Houston *M, D*
Tyler *B*

Virginia
James Madison University *B*
Old Dominion University *B*

Washington
Edmonds Community College *C, A*
Western Washington University *B*

West Virginia
West Virginia University *M*

Wisconsin
Marquette University *M*

Community/junior college administration

Arkansas
Arkansas State University *M, T*

California
California Lutheran University *M*
University of Southern California *T*

Illinois
Chicago State University *M*
University of Illinois
Urbana-Champaign *M, D*

Massachusetts
Springfield College *D*

Minnesota
University of Minnesota
Twin Cities *M*

Mississippi
Alcorn State University *M*
Mississippi State University *M, D*

Missouri
Columbia College *M*

New Jersey
Rowan University *M*

North Carolina
North Carolina State University *M, D*
Western Carolina University *M*

Oklahoma
Northeastern State University *M*

South Carolina
Clemson University *M*

Texas
Texas A&M University
Commerce *M, D*

Virginia
Old Dominion University *D*

Washington
University of Washington *M, D*

Community organization/advocacy

Alabama
Samford University *A, B*

Alaska
University of Alaska
Fairbanks *A, B, M*

Arizona
Prescott College *B*

Arkansas
Southern Arkansas University *B*
University of Arkansas *D*
University of Central Arkansas *M*

California
California State University
Dominguez Hills *B*
Fullerton *B*
Foothill College *C*
Humphreys College *B*
Los Angeles Trade and Technical
College *C, A*
Merritt College *C, A*
National University *M*

Connecticut
Manchester Community College *C, A*
University of Bridgeport *B*
University of Hartford *B*

Florida
Lynn University *B*
St. Leo University *B*

Georgia
Mercer University *B*

Hawaii
University of Hawaii
Honolulu Community College *C, A*

Illinois
North Park University *M*
Northwestern University *B*
Triton College *A*
University of Illinois
Urbana-Champaign *M, D*
Westwood College of Technology
O'Hare *B*

Indiana
Martin University *M*

Iowa
Des Moines Area Community
College *C, A*
Iowa Central Community College *A*
Kirkwood Community College *A*
Marshalltown Community College *A*

Kentucky
Henderson Community College *A*
Murray State University *M*

Maryland
College of Notre Dame of Maryland *B*

Massachusetts
Berkshire Community College *A*
Clark University *M*
Holyoke Community College *C*
Springfield College *B, M*
University of Massachusetts
Boston *B*
Worcester State College *M*

Michigan

Aquinas College *B*
Central Michigan University *B*
Madonna University *C*
University of Michigan *D*

Minnesota

Bemidji State University *B*
Capella University *M, D*
Winona State University *B*

Mississippi

Delta State University *M*

Missouri

Rockhurst University *B*

Montana

University of Montana: Missoula *C*

New Hampshire

University of New Hampshire *A*

New Jersey

Salem Community College *A*
Thomas Edison State College *A, B*

New Mexico

New Mexico State University *B*
University of New Mexico *A, B*

New York

Alfred University *M*
City University of New York
　Brooklyn College *B*
　John Jay College of Criminal
　　Justice *B, M*
Cornell University *B, M, D*
Erie Community College
　City Campus *C*
　North Campus *C*
　South Campus *C*
Fulton-Montgomery Community
　College *C, A*
Genesee Community College *A*
Hudson Valley Community College *A*
Mercy College *C*
Metropolitan College of New
　York *A, B*
Mohawk Valley Community College *A*
Mount St. Mary College *B*
Pace University *M*
State University of New York
　Empire State College *A, B*
Suffolk County Community College *A*
Tompkins-Cortland Community
　College *C, A*
Ulster County Community College *A*

North Carolina

University of North Carolina
　Greensboro *M, T*

Ohio

University of Akron *A*
University of Cincinnati *M*
Urbana University *B*

Oklahoma

East Central University *B, M*

Oregon

Chemeketa Community College *A*
Clackamas Community College *A*
Corban College *B*
Lane Community College *A*

Pennsylvania

Marywood University *B*
St. Joseph's University *M*
University of Pennsylvania *M*

Rhode Island

Providence College *B*

South Dakota

Black Hills State University *B*
Northern State University *B*

Tennessee

Cumberland University *M*
Pellissippi State Technical Community
　College *A*
Roane State Community College *A*
University of Tennessee
　Chattanooga *B*
Volunteer State Community College *A*

Texas

Texas A&M University *B*
University of North Texas *M*

Vermont

Goddard College *B, M*
Woodbury College *C, A, B*

Virginia

Emory & Henry College *B*
J. Sargeant Reynolds Community
　College *A*

Wisconsin

Alverno College *B*
Marquette University *M*
Western Wisconsin Technical
　College *A*

Community psychology

Alabama

Troy University *M*

Alaska

University of Alaska
　Fairbanks *M*

California

University of La Verne *D*

Colorado

Adams State College *M*

Connecticut

Southern Connecticut State
　University *M*
University of New Haven *M*

District of Columbia

Catholic University of America *M*
George Washington University *M*

Florida

Florida Agricultural and Mechanical
　University *M*

Illinois

Roosevelt University *M*

Michigan

Andrews University *M*

Minnesota

St. Cloud State University *M*

New Hampshire

New England College *M*

New York

College of New Rochelle *M*
Hofstra University *M, D*
New York University *D*

Ohio

Kent State University *M*
University of Akron *M*

Pennsylvania

Mansfield University of
　Pennsylvania *M*
Penn State
　Harrisburg *M*

Puerto Rico

University of Puerto Rico
　Rio Piedras *M*

South Carolina

Clemson University *M*
Columbia College *M*
Francis Marion University *M*

Tennessee

Southern Adventist University *M*
Vanderbilt University *D*

Texas

Lamar University *M*
St. Mary's University *M, D*

Virginia

Norfolk State University *M*

Wisconsin

Marquette University *M*
Mount Mary College *M*

Comparative/ international education

California

Stanford University *M, D*

District of Columbia

American University *M*
George Washington University *M*
Howard University *M*

Florida

Florida International University *M*
Florida State University *M, D*
Lynn University *D*

Illinois

University of Illinois
　Urbana-Champaign *M, D*

Indiana

Indiana University
　Bloomington *M*

Massachusetts

Boston University *M*
Endicott College *M*
Harvard College *M, D*

New Jersey

The College of New Jersey *M*

New York

New York University *M, D*
State University of New York
　Albany *M, D*

Ohio

Ohio State University
　Columbus Campus *M*

Vermont

Sterling College *B*

Virginia

University of Virginia *M, D*

Comparative literature

Arizona

Prescott College *B, M*

Arkansas

University of Arkansas *M, D*

California

California State University
　Fullerton *B, M*
　Long Beach *B*
　Northridge *B*
Mills College *B, M*
San Francisco State University *B, M*
Stanford University *B, M, D*
University of California
　Berkeley *B, M, D*
　Davis *B, M, D*
　Irvine *B, M, D*
　Los Angeles *B, M, D*
　Riverside *M, D*
　San Diego *M, D*
　Santa Barbara *B, M, D*
　Santa Cruz *B*
University of Judaism *B*
University of La Verne *B*
University of Southern
　California *B, M, D*
Whittier College *B*

Colorado

Colorado College *B*
University of Colorado
　Boulder *M, D*

Connecticut

Trinity College *B*
University of Connecticut *M, D*
Yale University *M, D*

Delaware

University of Delaware *B*

District of Columbia

Catholic University of America *M, D*
Georgetown University *B*

Florida

Eckerd College *B*

Georgia

Emory University *B, D*
University of Georgia *B, M, D*

Hawaii

Hawaii Pacific University *B*

Illinois

Northwestern University *B, M, D*
Roosevelt University *B, M*
University of Chicago *B, D*
University of Illinois
　Urbana-Champaign *B, M, D*

Indiana

Earlham College *B*
Indiana University
　Bloomington *B, M, D*
Manchester College *A*
University of Notre Dame *D*

Iowa

Graceland University *B*
University of Iowa *B, M, D*

Louisiana

Louisiana State University and
Agricultural and Mechanical
College *M, D*

Maine

University of Maine
Fort Kent *B*
University of Southern Maine *B*

Maryland

University of Maryland
College Park *M, D*

Massachusetts

Brandeis University *B*
Clark University *B*
College of the Holy Cross *B*
Hampshire College *B*
Harvard College *B, D*
Massachusetts College of Liberal
Arts *B*
Salem State College *B*
Simmons College *B, M*
Simon's Rock College of Bard *B*
Smith College *B*
Tufts University *B, M, D*
University of Massachusetts
Amherst *B, M, D*
Wellesley College *B*
Williams College *B*

Michigan

Central Michigan University *M*
Hillsdale College *B*
University of Michigan *B, M, D*
Wayne State University *M*

Minnesota

St. Cloud State University *B*
University of Minnesota
Twin Cities *B, M, D*

Missouri

Washington University in St.
Louis *B, M, D*

New Hampshire

Dartmouth College *B, M*
New England College *B*

New Jersey

Princeton University *B, M, D*
Ramapo College of New Jersey *B*
Rutgers, The State University of New
Jersey
New Brunswick/Piscataway
Campus *B, M, D*

New Mexico

University of New Mexico *B, M*

New York

Bard College *B*
Barnard College *B*
City University of New York
Baruch College *B*
Brooklyn College *B*
City College *B*
Hunter College *B*
Lehman College *B*
Queens College *B*
Columbia University
Columbia College *B*
School of General Studies *B*
Cornell University *B, M, D*
Eugene Lang College The New School
for Liberal Arts *B*
Fordham University *B*
Hamilton College *B*
Hobart and William Smith Colleges *B*
Hofstra University *B*

New York University *B, M, D*
Sarah Lawrence College *B*
State University of New York
Binghamton *B, M, D*
Buffalo *M, D*
College at Geneseo *B*
College at Old Westbury *B*
Stony Brook *B*
Syracuse University *B*
University of Rochester *B, M*
Wells College *B*

North Carolina

Duke University *M, D*
University of North Carolina
Chapel Hill *B, M, D*

Ohio

Case Western Reserve University *B, M*
Cleveland State University *T*
College of Wooster *B*
John Carroll University *B*
Miami University
Oxford Campus *B*
Oberlin College *B*
Ohio State University
Columbus Campus *B, M*
Ohio Wesleyan University *B*
University of Cincinnati *B, M, D, T*

Oklahoma

East Central University *B*

Oregon

Reed College *B*
University of Oregon *B, M, D*
Willamette University *B*

Pennsylvania

Bryn Mawr College *B*
Gettysburg College *B*
Haverford College *B, T*
La Salle University *B*
Penn State
Abington *B*
Altoona *B*
Beaver *B*
Berks *B*
Delaware County *B*
Dubois *B*
Fayette *B*
Hazleton *B*
Lehigh Valley *B*
McKeesport *B*
Mont Alto *B*
New Kensington *B*
Schuylkill - Capital College *B*
Shenango *B*
University Park *B, M, D*
Wilkes-Barre *B*
Worthington Scranton *B*
York *B*
Swarthmore College *B*
University of Pennsylvania *B, M, D*
West Chester University of
Pennsylvania *B*

Puerto Rico

University of Puerto Rico
Mayaguez *B*
Rio Piedras *B, M*

Rhode Island

Brown University *B, M, D*
University of Rhode Island *B*

South Carolina

University of South Carolina *M, D*

Tennessee

University of Tennessee
Knoxville *B*

University of the South *B*
Vanderbilt University *M, D*

Texas

Texas A&M University *M*
University of North Texas *B*
University of Texas
Austin *M, D*
Dallas *B*
El Paso *B, M*

Utah

Brigham Young University *B*

Vermont

Burlington College *B*
Johnson State College *B*
Marlboro College *B*

Virginia

Lynchburg College *B*
University of Virginia *B*

Washington

Eastern Washington University *B, M*
Everett Community College *A*
Gonzaga University *B*
University of Washington *B, M, D*

Wisconsin

Beloit College *B*
University of Wisconsin
Madison *B, M, D*
Milwaukee *B*

Comparative
psychology

California

California Institute of Integral
Studies *M, D*

Washington

Western Washington University *M*

Computational
mathematics

California

University of California
Davis *B*
Los Angeles *B*

Florida

Florida State University *B, M, D*

Illinois

Northern Illinois University *B*
University of Illinois
Urbana-Champaign *B*

Indiana

Indiana University-Purdue University
Fort Wayne *B*

Kentucky

Asbury College *B*

Michigan

Hillsdale College *B*
Kettering University *B*
Michigan State University *B*

Missouri

Missouri Southern State University *B*

New York

City University of New York
Brooklyn College *B*

Marist College *B*
Rochester Institute of Technology *B*

Ohio

University of Dayton *M*

Pennsylvania

Carnegie Mellon University *B, D*

Puerto Rico

University of Puerto Rico
Humacao *B*

South Dakota

South Dakota State University *D*

Virginia

Old Dominion University *M, D*

Washington

Seattle Pacific University *B*

Wisconsin

Marquette University *B*

Computer education

Arizona

Northern Arizona University *M*

Arkansas

University of Central Arkansas *T*

California

California Baptist University *M*
California State University
Sacramento *T*
Fresno Pacific University *M*
National University *M*
San Diego State University *B, T*

Connecticut

Western Connecticut State
University *M*

District of Columbia

Trinity University *M*

Florida

Barry University *M*
Florida Institute of Technology *B, M*
St. Petersburg College *B*

Hawaii

Hawaii Pacific University *M*

Illinois

Concordia University *B, M, T*
DePaul University *T*
Illinois Institute of Technology *M*

Indiana

Goshen College *B*
Indiana Wesleyan University *T*
University of Indianapolis *T*
Vincennes University *A*

Iowa

Buena Vista University *B, T*
Loras College *T*
Morningside College *M*

Kansas

Emporia State University *T*
McPherson College *B, T*
University of St. Mary *T*

Kentucky

Bellarmine University *T*

Thomas More College *B*
University of the Cumberlands *B, T*

Louisiana

Southern University and Agricultural
and Mechanical College *B*

Maine

Thomas College *M*

Massachusetts

Lesley University *M*
Worcester State College *T*

Michigan

Alma College *T*
Eastern Michigan University *B, T*
Grand Valley State University *T*
Michigan Technological University *T*
Northern Michigan University *B, T*
Saginaw Valley State University *M*

Minnesota

Minnesota State University
Mankato *B, T*
Vermilion Community College *A*

Mississippi

Mississippi College *B, M*
Mississippi State University *B, M, T*

Missouri

Fontbonne University *B*
Northwest Missouri State
University *M, T*
Webster University *M*

Montana

Montana State University
Billings *T*
Montana Tech of the University of
Montana *T*
University of Montana: Western *T*

Nebraska

College of Saint Mary *B, T*
Concordia University *B, T*
Hastings College *M, T*
Peru State College *B, T*
Union College *T*
University of Nebraska
Lincoln *B*

Nevada

University of Nevada
Las Vegas *B*

New Jersey

Rowan University *T*
St. Peter's College *M, T*

New Mexico

New Mexico Institute of Mining and
Technology *M*

New York

College of Mount St. Vincent *T*
Iona College *M, T*
Long Island University
C.W. Post Campus *M*
Manhattan College *B, T*
Nazareth College of Rochester *M*
State University of New York
College at Buffalo *M*
College at Plattsburgh *B, M*

North Dakota

Dickinson State University *B, T*
North Dakota State University *B, T*

Ohio

Ashland University *M, T*
Baldwin-Wallace College *T*
University of Findlay *M, T*
Youngstown State University *B, M*

Oklahoma

Eastern Oklahoma State College *A*
Southwestern Oklahoma State
University *T*

Oregon

Western Oregon University *T*

Pennsylvania

DeSales University *M, T*
St. Joseph's University *M*

South Dakota

Dakota State University *B, M, D, T*

Texas

Baylor University *B, T*
Hardin-Simmons University *B, T*
Lamar University *T*
Laredo Community College *A*
LeTourneau University *B, T*
Lubbock Christian University *B*
McMurry University *T*
St. Mary's University *T*
Tarleton State University *B, T*
Texas A&M University
Commerce *M, T*
University of Houston *T*
University of Houston
Clear Lake *T*
University of Mary Hardin-Baylor *T*
University of North Texas *M*
University of Texas
San Antonio *T*
West Texas A&M University *T*

Vermont

St. Michael's College *M, T*

Virginia

Bridgewater College *T*
Hollins University *T*
Liberty University *B, T*

Washington

Heritage University *B*
Whitworth College *B, T*

Wisconsin

Cardinal Stritch University *M*
Lawrence University *T*
Northland College *T*
Silver Lake College *T*
University of Wisconsin
Whitewater *B, T*

Computer engineering

Alabama

Auburn University *B, M, D*
University of Alabama
Birmingham *D*
Huntsville *B, M, D*
University of South Alabama *B*

Alaska

University of Alaska
Fairbanks *M*

Arizona

Arizona State University *B*
Embry-Riddle Aeronautical University:
Prescott Campus *B*
Northern Arizona University *B*
University of Arizona *B*

Arkansas

Harding University *B*
University of Arkansas *B, M*

California

California Institute of Technology *B*
California Polytechnic State
University: San Luis Obispo *B*
California State Polytechnic
University: Pomona *B*
California State University
Chico *B, M*
Fresno *B*
Fullerton *B*
Long Beach *B, M*
Northridge *B, M*
Sacramento *B, M*
Coleman College *A, B*
De Anza College *A*
International Technological
University *M*
San Diego State University *B*
San Jose State University *B, M*
Santa Ana College *A*
Santa Barbara City College *A*
Santa Clara University *B, M, D*
Sonoma State University *B, M*
University of California
Davis *B, M, D*
Irvine *B, M, D*
Los Angeles *B*
Riverside *B*
San Diego *B, M, D*
Santa Barbara *M, D*
Santa Cruz *B, M, D*
University of California: Merced *B*
University of Southern
California *B, M, D*
University of the Pacific *B*

Colorado

Colorado State University *B, M, D*
Colorado Technical University *B, M*
DeVry University
Westminster *B*
Jones International University *B*
United States Air Force Academy *B*
University of Colorado
Boulder *B*
Colorado Springs *B*
University of Denver *B, M*
Westwood College of Technology *A*

Connecticut

Fairfield University *B, M*
University of Bridgeport *B, M, D*
University of Connecticut *B, M, D*
University of Hartford *B*
University of New Haven *B*

Delaware

University of Delaware *B*

District of Columbia

Catholic University of America *B*
George Washington
University *B, M, D*
Howard University *B*

Florida

Bethune-Cookman College *B*
Brevard Community College *A*
Broward Community College *A*
Chipola College *A*
Daytona Beach Community College *A*
Embry-Riddle Aeronautical
University *B*
Florida Atlantic University *B, M, D*
Florida Career College: Hialeah *A*
Florida Career College: Miami *A*
Florida Career College: Pembroke
Pines *A*

Florida Career College: West Palm
Beach *A*
Florida Community College at
Jacksonville *A*
Florida Institute of
Technology *B, M, D*
Florida International University *B, M*
Florida State University *B*
Hillsborough Community College *A*
Manatee Community College *A*
Pensacola Junior College *A*
Southwest Florida College *A*
University of Central Florida *B, M, D*
University of Florida *A, B, M*
University of Miami *B*
University of South Florida *B, M, D*
University of West Florida *B*
Valencia Community College *A*

Georgia

DeKalb Technical College *A*
Georgia Institute of Technology *B*
Mercer University *M*
Middle Georgia College *A*
University of Georgia *B*

Hawaii

University of Hawaii
Honolulu Community College *A*

Idaho

Brigham Young University-Idaho *B*
College of Southern Idaho *A*
University of Idaho *B, M*

Illinois

Bradley University *B*
Dominican University *B*
Illinois Institute of Technology *B, M*
Northwestern University *B*
Southern Illinois University
Carbondale *B*
Southern Illinois University
Edwardsville *B*
University of Illinois
Chicago *B, M, D*
Urbana-Champaign *B*

Indiana

Indiana Institute of Technology *B*
Indiana University-Purdue University
Fort Wayne *B*
Indiana University-Purdue University
Indianapolis *B*
Purdue University *B*
Purdue University
Calumet *B*
Rose-Hulman Institute of
Technology *B*
Taylor University *B*
University of Evansville *B*
University of Notre Dame *B, M, D*
Valparaiso University *B*

Iowa

Dordt College *B*
Graceland University *B*
Iowa State University *B, M, D*
University of Iowa *M, D*

Kansas

Kansas State University *B*
University of Kansas *B, M*
Wichita State University *B*

Kentucky

Bellarmine University *B*
University of Louisville *B, M, D*

Louisiana

Louisiana State University and
    Agricultural and Mechanical
    College *B*
University of Louisiana at
    Lafayette *B, M, D*
Xavier University of Louisiana *B*

Maine

Southern Maine Community
    College *A*
University of Maine *B*

Maryland

Capitol College *A, B*
Johns Hopkins University *B*
University of Maryland
    Baltimore County *B, M, D*
    College Park *B*

Massachusetts

Boston University *B, M, D*
Eastern Nazarene College *B*
Merrimack College *B*
Northeastern University *B, M, D*
Smith College *B*
Stonehill College *B*
Suffolk University *B*
Tufts University *B, M, D*
University of Massachusetts
    Amherst *B, M, D*
    Dartmouth *B, M*
    Lowell *M*

Michigan

Eastern Michigan University *B*
Kettering University *B*
Kirtland Community College *A*
Lake Superior State University *B*
Lawrence Technological
    University *B, M*
Michigan State University *B*
Michigan Technological
    University *B, T*
Oakland University *B*
University of Detroit Mercy *B*
University of Michigan *B, M, D*
University of Michigan
    Dearborn *B, M*
Wayne State University *M, D*
Western Michigan University *B, M*

Minnesota

Mesabi Range Community and
    Technical College *A*
Minnesota State University
    Mankato *B*
St. Cloud State University *B, M*
University of Minnesota
    Duluth *B*
    Twin Cities *B, M*

Mississippi

Jackson State University *B*
Mississippi State University *B, M, D*

Missouri

East Central College *A*
Grantham University *A, B*
Missouri Technical School *A, B*
University of Missouri
    Columbia *B, M, D*
    Rolla *B, M, D*
Washington University in St.
    Louis *B, M, D*

Montana

Montana State University
    Bozeman *B*
Montana Tech of the University of
    Montana *B*
Salish Kootenai College *A*

Nebraska

University of Nebraska
    Lincoln *B*
    Omaha *B*

Nevada

University of Nevada
    Las Vegas *B*
    Reno *M, D*

New Hampshire

University of New Hampshire *B, M, D*

New Jersey

The College of New Jersey *B*
Fairleigh Dickinson University
    Metropolitan Campus *M*
New Jersey Institute of
    Technology *B, M, D*
Princeton University *B, M, D*
Stevens Institute of
    Technology *B, M, D*

New Mexico

New Mexico State University
    Alamogordo *A*
University of New Mexico *B, M*

New York

City University of New York
    City College *B, M*
    Queensborough Community
        College *A*
Clarkson University *B*
Columbia University
    Fu Foundation School of
        Engineering and Applied
        Science *B, M, D*
Hofstra University *B*
Manhattan College *M*
New York Institute of Technology *B*
Onondaga Community College *A*
Polytechnic University *B, M*
Rensselaer Polytechnic
    Institute *B, M, D*
Rochester Institute of
    Technology *B, M*
State University of New York
    Binghamton *B, M*
    Buffalo *B*
    College of Agriculture and
        Technology at Morrisville *A*
    College of Technology at Alfred *A*
    New Paltz *B, M*
Syracuse University *B, M, D*
United States Military Academy *B*

North Carolina

Central Carolina Community
    College *A*
College of the Albemarle *A*
Elon University *B*
Haywood Community College *A*
Johnson C. Smith University *B*
North Carolina State
    University *B, M, D*
Southwestern Community College *A*
Surry Community College *A*
University of North Carolina
    Charlotte *B*

North Dakota

North Dakota State University *B*

Ohio

Case Western Reserve
    University *B, M, D*
Miami University
    Oxford Campus *B*
Ohio Northern University *B*
Ohio State University
    Columbus Campus *B*

University of Akron *B*
University of Cincinnati *B, M, D*
University of Dayton *B*
University of Toledo *B*
Wright State University *B, M, D*
Youngstown State University *B*

Oklahoma

Oklahoma Christian University *B*
Oklahoma State University
    Oklahoma City *A*
Oral Roberts University *B*
University of Oklahoma *B*

Oregon

Oregon State University *B, M, D*
Portland State University *B*
University of Portland *B*

Pennsylvania

Bucknell University *B*
Drexel University *B, M*
Elizabethtown College *B*
Gannon University *M*
Gettysburg College *B*
ICM School of Business & Medical
    Careers *A*
Lehigh University *B, M, D*
Penn State
    Abington *B*
    Altoona *B*
    Beaver *B*
    Berks *B*
    Delaware County *B*
    Dubois *B*
    Erie, The Behrend College *B*
    Hazleton *B*
    Lehigh Valley *B*
    McKeesport *B*
    Mont Alto *B*
    New Kensington *B*
    Schuylkill - Capital College *B*
    Shenango *B*
    University Park *B*
    Wilkes-Barre *B*
    Worthington Scranton *B*
    York *B*
University of Pennsylvania *B*
University of Pittsburgh *B, M*
University of Scranton *M*
Villanova University *B, M*
York College of Pennsylvania *B*

Puerto Rico

University of Puerto Rico
    Bayamon University College *A*
    Mayaguez *B, M, D*
    Ponce *A*

Rhode Island

Brown University *B*
New England Institute of
    Technology *A*
Roger Williams University *B*
University of Rhode Island *B*

South Carolina

Aiken Technical College *A*
Clemson University *B, M, D*
University of South Carolina *B, M, D*

South Dakota

South Dakota School of Mines and
    Technology *B, M*

Tennessee

Christian Brothers University *B*
Tennessee Technological
    University *B, M, D*
University of Memphis *B*
Vanderbilt University *B*

Texas

Amarillo College *A*
LeTourneau University *B*
Prairie View A&M University *B*
Rice University *B, M, D*
St. Mary's University *B, M*
Southern Methodist
    University *B, M, D*
Texas A&M University *B, M, D*
Texas A&M University
    Kingsville *B, M*
Texas Tech University *B*
University of Houston *B*
University of Houston
    Clear Lake *B, M*
University of Texas
    Arlington *B, M, D*
    Dallas *M, D*
    El Paso *M, D*
    San Antonio *B*

Utah

Brigham Young University *B*
University of Utah *B*
Utah State University *B*

Vermont

Vermont Technical College *A, B*

Virginia

Christopher Newport University *B*
George Mason University *M*
Hampton University *B*
New River Community College *A*
Old Dominion University *B, M, D*
University of Virginia *B*
Virginia Commonwealth University *B*
Virginia Polytechnic Institute and
    State University *B, M, D*
Virginia State University *B*
Wytheville Community College *A*

Washington

Eastern Washington University *B*
Gonzaga University *B*
Pacific Lutheran University *B*
Seattle Pacific University *B*
University of Washington *B, M*
Walla Walla College *B*
Washington State University *B*

West Virginia

West Virginia University *B, D*

Wisconsin

Marquette University *B, M, D*
Milwaukee School of Engineering *B*
University of Wisconsin
    Madison *B*

Wyoming

University of Wyoming *B*

Computer engineering technology

Arizona

DeVry University
    Phoenix *B*
Eastern Arizona College *C*
Glendale Community College *C, A*

Arkansas

Arkansas State University: Newport *A*

California

Coleman College *C, A, B*
DeVry University
    Fremont *B*
    Long Beach *B*

Pomona *B*
West Hills *B*
Santa Barbara City College *C, A*
Southwestern College *C, A*

Colorado
Arapahoe Community College *A*
DeVry University
Westminster *B*

Connecticut
Central Connecticut State
University *B*
Naugatuck Valley Community
College *C*
University of Hartford *A, B*

Florida
DeVry University
Miramar *B*
St. Petersburg College *C, A*
Southwest Florida College
Tampa *C, A*

Georgia
DeVry University
Alpharetta *B*
Decatur *B*
Georgia Southwestern State
University *B*
Middle Georgia College *A*
Savannah Technical College *A*
Southern Polytechnic State
University *B*

Illinois
DeVry University
Addison *B*
Chicago *B*
Tinley Park *B*
Lincoln Land Community College *C*
Moraine Valley Community College *C*

Indiana
Indiana State University *B*
Indiana University-Purdue University
Fort Wayne *B*
Indiana University-Purdue University
Indianapolis *A, B*
Ivy Tech State College
Ivy Tech Community College:
Northeast *C*
Sawyer College: Merrillville *C, A*

Kansas
Kansas City Kansas Community
College *C, A*

Kentucky
Louisville Technical Institute *A*
Southeast Kentucky Community and
Technical College *A*

Louisiana
Nunez Community College *C, A*

Maryland
Cecil Community College *C*

Massachusetts
Benjamin Franklin Institute of
Technology *A*
Bunker Hill Community College *C*
Massachusetts Bay Community
College *A*
Mount Wachusett Community
College *A*
Northeastern University *B*
Quinsigamond Community College *A*
Springfield Technical Community
College *A*

Wentworth Institute of
Technology *A, B*

Michigan
Andrews University *A*
Central Michigan University *B*
Madonna University *A*
Northern Michigan University *C*
Wayne County Community College *A*

Minnesota
Globe College *C, A, B*
Minnesota State Community and
Technical College - Fergus
Falls *C, A*
Minnesota State University
Mankato *B*
Rochester Community and Technical
College *C*

Missouri
DeVry University
Kansas City *B*
Grantham University *A, B*
Missouri Western State
University *A, B*
Vatterott College *C*

New Hampshire
New Hampshire Technical
Institute *C, A*

New York
Broome Community College *A*
DeVry Institute of Technology
New York *B*
Fulton-Montgomery Community
College *C, A*
Rochester Institute of Technology *B*
State University of New York
Farmingdale *B*
Institute of Technology at
Utica/Rome *B*

North Carolina
Catawba Valley Community College *A*
College of the Albemarle *C*
Davidson County Community
College *C, A*
East Carolina University *B*
Gaston College *A*
Isothermal Community College *A*
Nash Community College *A*
Sandhills Community College *C, A*
Stanly Community College *C, A*
Wilkes Community College *A*

Ohio
Bowling Green State University:
Firelands College *A*
Cincinnati State Technical and
Community College *C, A*
DeVry University
Columbus *B*
Edison State Community College *A*
Owens Community College
Toledo *C, A*
Shawnee State University *C, A, B*
University of Dayton *B*

Oregon
Treasure Valley Community College *A*

Pennsylvania
California University of
Pennsylvania *A, B*
DeVry University
Ft. Washington *B*
Lehigh Carbon Community College *A*
Luzerne County Community
College *C*

Penn State
New Kensington *A*
South Hills School of Business &
Technology *A*

Rhode Island
Community College of Rhode
Island *A*

South Carolina
Aiken Technical College *A*
York Technical College *A*

Tennessee
University of Memphis *B*

Texas
DeVry University
Irving *B*
Houston Community College
System *C, A*
LeTourneau University *B*
Mountain View College *A*
Prairie View A&M University *B*
University of Houston
Downtown *B*

Utah
Salt Lake Community College *A*

Vermont
Vermont Technical College *A*

Virginia
National College of Business &
Technology
Salem *C*
Norfolk State University *B*
Old Dominion University *B*

Washington
DeVry University
Federal Way *B*

West Virginia
Marshall University *B*

Computer graphics

Alabama
Faulkner State Community
College *C, A*
Huntingdon College *B*

Arizona
Arizona Western College *A*
Estrella Mountain Community
College *C*
Northland Pioneer College *C, A*
Phoenix College *A*

Arkansas
National Park Community
College *C, A*
South Arkansas Community College *A*

California
Antelope Valley College *C, A*
Art Institute
of California: Los Angeles *A, B*
of California: Orange County *A, B*
of California: San Diego *B*
Art Institute of California: San
Francisco *B*
California Institute of the Arts *B, M*
California Lutheran University *B*
California State University
Chico *B*
Monterey Bay *B*
Chaffey College *C*
College of the Canyons *C, A*

College of the Siskiyous *C*
Cypress College *C*
Dominican University of California *B*
Fashion Institute of Design and
Merchandising
San Francisco *A*
Foothill College *C, A*
Fullerton College *C*
Gavilan Community College *C, A*
Golden West College *C*
Los Angeles Southwest College *C, A*
MiraCosta College *C, A*
Modesto Junior College *C, A*
Ohlone College *C, A*
Orange Coast College *C, A*
Platt College
Cerritos *C, A*
Los Angeles *C, A*
Newport Beach *C, A*
Ontario *C, A, B*
Saddleback College *C*
Santa Ana College *C*
Santa Barbara City College *C*
Santa Rosa Junior College *C*
Silicon Valley College
Western Career College:
Emeryville *A, B*
Western Career College: San Jose *A*
University of California
Irvine *M, D*
Westwood College *A*
Westwood College of Technology
Westwood College: Los Angeles *A*

Colorado
Art Institute
of Colorado *C, A, B*
CollegeAmerica-Denver *A*
Colorado Technical University *C*
Morgan Community College *C*
Northeastern Junior College *C, A*
Pueblo Community College *A*
Westwood College of
Technology *A, B*
Westwood College of Technology
South *A, B*

Connecticut
Norwalk Community College *C*
Quinnipiac University *B*
Tunxis Community College *C, A*

District of Columbia
American University *B*

Florida
Broward Community College *A*
Florida Community College at
Jacksonville *A*
Herzing College
Orlando *C*
Hillsborough Community College *A*
Indian River Community College *A*
International Academy of Design and
Technology: Orlando *A, B*
Miami International University of Art
and Design *A*
Okaloosa-Walton College *C, A*
Polk Community College *A*
Seminole Community College *A*
Southwest Florida College *A*
Southwest Florida College
Tampa *A*
Tallahassee Community College *A*
University of Miami *B*
University of Tampa *B*

Georgia
Middle Georgia College *C*
Savannah College of Art and
Design *B, M*

Hawaii

University of Hawaii
Honolulu Community College *A*

Idaho

College of Southern Idaho *C, A*

Illinois

American Academy of Art *B*
DePaul University *B, M*
Elgin Community College *C, A*
Illinois Institute of Art-Schaumburg *B*
Lewis University *B*
Lewis and Clark Community
College *A*
Richland Community College *A*
Triton College *C, A*
Westwood College of Technology
O'Hare *A*
River Oaks *A*

Indiana

Indiana Institute of Technology *A*
Indiana University-Purdue University
Indianapolis *C, A, B*
Purdue University
Calumet *C, A, B*
Sawyer College: Merrillville *C, A*
Taylor University *B*
Vincennes University *A*

Iowa

Ellsworth Community College *A*
Southeastern Community College
North Campus *A*
University of Dubuque *B, M*

Kansas

Seward County Community
College *C, A*

Kentucky

Kentucky State University *A, B*
Louisville Technical Institute *A*
Spencerian College: Lexington *A*

Louisiana

Remington College
New Orleans *A*

Maine

Southern Maine Community
College *A*

Maryland

Baltimore City Community
College *C, A*
Carroll Community College *C, A*
Community College of Baltimore
County *A*
Frederick Community College *C*
Hagerstown Business College *A*
Howard Community College *A*
Montgomery College *A*

Massachusetts

Bristol Community College *C*
Hampshire College *B*
Mount Wachusett Community
College *C, A*
Newbury College *A, B*
Northern Essex Community
College *A*
Springfield College *B*

Michigan

Baker College
of Auburn Hills *A*
of Muskegon *A*
of Owosso *A, B*
of Port Huron *C, A*

Jackson Community College *C, A*
Kalamazoo Valley Community
College *A*
Northern Michigan University *B*
Washtenaw Community College *C, A*
Wayne County Community College *C*

Minnesota

Academy College *C, A*
Art Institutes International
Minnesota *A, B*
Capella University *C, B, M*
Globe College *C, A*
Hennepin Technical College *C, A*
Minnesota School of Business *C, A*
Rochester Community and Technical
College *C*
South Central College *A*

Mississippi

Antonelli College
Jackson *A*
Meridian Community College *A*

Missouri

Missouri Technical School *C, B*
St. Charles Community College *C, A*

Montana

Fort Peck Community College *A*
Miles Community College *A*
University of Great Falls *B*

Nebraska

Creative Center *A*

Nevada

Community College of Southern
Nevada *C, A*

New Hampshire

Franklin Pierce College *B*

New Jersey

Bergen Community College *C*
Burlington County College *A*
Camden County College *A*
Cumberland County College *C*
Essex County College *C*
Gloucester County College *C, A*
Middlesex County College *A*
Salem Community College *A*

New Mexico

Clovis Community College *A*
Dona Ana Branch Community College
of New Mexico State
University *A*
New Mexico Junior College *A*
San Juan College *A*

New York

City University of New York
Lehman College *B*
College of Westchester *C, A*
Columbia-Greene Community
College *A*
Corning Community College *C, A*
Globe Institute of Technology *C, A, B*
Island Drafting and Technical
Institute *C, A*
New York Institute of Technology *B*
North Country Community
College *C, A*
Pratt Institute *B, M*
Rochester Institute of
Technology *B, M*
Rockland Community College *A*
State University of New York
College at Oneonta *A*
College of Technology at Alfred *A*
Suffolk County Community College *A*

Syracuse University *B, M*

North Carolina

Alamance Community College *C*
Campbell University *B*
Wake Technical Community
College *A*
Western Piedmont Community
College *C*
Wilkes Community College *A*

Ohio

Art Institute of Cincinnati *A*
Belmont Technical College *A*
Columbus State Community
College *A*
Edison State Community College *C, A*
James A. Rhodes State College *C*
Ohio Northern University *B*
School of Advertising Art *C, A*
Stark State College of Technology *A*
University of Cincinnati
Clermont College *A*
Raymond Walters College *C, A*
Washington State Community
College *A*

Oklahoma

Oklahoma State University
Okmulgee *A*

Pennsylvania

Academy of Medical Arts and
Business *C*
Arcadia University *C*
Berks Technical Institute *A*
Bucks County Community College *A*
CHI Institute: Southampton *C, A*
Douglas Education Center *A*
Erie Business Center *A*
La Salle University *B*
Lansdale School of Business *C*
University of Pennsylvania *B*

South Carolina

Aiken Technical College *C*
York Technical College *C*

South Dakota

Dakota State University *B*

Tennessee

Memphis College of Art *B, M*
Roane State Community College *C, A*

Texas

Amarillo College *C, A*
Central Texas College *C*
Midland College *C, A*
Trinity Valley Community College *C, A*
University of Mary Hardin-Baylor *B*
University of the Incarnate Word *B*
Wade College *A*

Utah

College of Eastern Utah *C, A*
Dixie State College of Utah *C, A, B*
Utah Career College *C, A*

Vermont

Champlain College *C, A, B*

Virginia

Central Virginia Community
College *C*
Lord Fairfax Community College *C*
New River Community College *A*
Thomas Nelson Community
College *A*

Washington

Bellevue Community College *C, A*
Everett Community College *A*
Green River Community College *C*
South Seattle Community
College *C, A, T*
Spokane Falls Community College *A*
Walla Walla College *A, B*

Wisconsin

Herzing College *A, B*
Milwaukee Area Technical College *A*
Mount Mary College *B*

Wyoming

Central Wyoming College *A*

Computer hardware engineering

Indiana

Sawyer College: Merrillville *A*

New York

State University of New York
College of Agriculture and
Technology at Morrisville *A*
Stony Brook *B*

Texas

Abilene Christian University *B*

Computer hardware technology

Arizona

South Mountain Community
College *C*

Arkansas

Rich Mountain Community College *A*

California

Canada College *C, A*

Colorado

IntelliTec College: Grand Junction *A*

Florida

Florida Career College: Hialeah *C*
Florida Career College: Miami *C*
Florida Career College: Pembroke
Pines *C*
Florida National College *A*
South Florida Community College *A*

Indiana

Indiana University-Purdue University
Indianapolis *A, B*
Sawyer College: Merrillville *C, A*

Iowa

Kaplan University *C*
Western Iowa Tech Community
College *A*

Kentucky

Louisville Technical Institute *A*

Massachusetts

Benjamin Franklin Institute of
Technology *A*

Michigan

Baker College
of Muskegon *C*
Oakland Community College *C, A*

Minnesota

Globe College C, A, B

Mississippi

Pearl River Community College C

Missouri

St. Louis Community College
  St. Louis Community College at
    Florissant Valley A

New York

Cayuga County Community College A
State University of New York
  College of Agriculture and
    Technology at Morrisville A
  College of Technology at Canton C
  Farmingdale C

North Dakota

North Dakota State College of
  Science A

Ohio

Lakeland Community College C
Miami University
  Hamilton Campus C

Oregon

Oregon Institute of Technology A, B

Pennsylvania

Bucks County Community College C
South Hills School of Business &
  Technology A

Rhode Island

Community College of Rhode
  Island A

South Carolina

York Technical College C

South Dakota

Southeast Technical Institute C, A

Texas

St. Philip's College C, A

Virginia

ECPI College of Technology C, A
Mountain Empire Community
  College A

Washington

North Seattle Community
  College C, A

Computer/information sciences, general

Alabama

Alabama Agricultural and Mechanical
  University B, M
Alabama Southern Community
  College A
American Sentinel University B, M
Athens State University B
Auburn University B
Bevill State Community College A
Birmingham-Southern College B
Bishop State Community College A
Calhoun Community College C, A
Central Alabama Community
  College C, A
Chattahoochee Valley Community
  College A
Community College of the Air
  Force A

Enterprise-Ozark Community
  College A
Faulkner State Community College A
Faulkner University A
Gadsden State Community
  College C, A
George C. Wallace State Community
  College
  George C. Wallace Community
    College at Dothan C, A
  Selma C, A
Herzing College A, B
Jacksonville State University B, M
Jefferson State Community
  College C, A
Miles College B
Northeast Alabama Community
  College A
Northwest-Shoals Community
  College A
Oakwood College A, B
Remington College
  Mobile A
Snead State Community College A
Southern Union State Community
  College C, A
Spring Hill College C, A, B
Stillman College B
Talladega College B
Trenholm State Technical College A
Troy University B
Tuskegee University B
University of Alabama B, M, D
University of Alabama
  Birmingham B, M, D
  Huntsville B, M, D
University of Mobile B
University of North Alabama B
University of South Alabama B, M
Virginia College A

Alaska

University of Alaska
  Anchorage B
  Southeast C, A

Arizona

Arizona Western College C, A
Central Arizona College C, A
Chandler-Gilbert Community College
  Williams Campus A
Cochise College A
DeVry University
  Phoenix B
Dine College A
Everest College C, A
Gateway Community College C, A
Glendale Community College C
Grand Canyon University B
International Institute of the Americas
  Tucson C, A, B
Mesa Community College A
Mohave Community College A
Northcentral University B, M, D
Northern Arizona University B
Northland Pioneer College C, A
Paradise Valley Community
  College C, A
Phoenix College A
Pima Community College A
Prescott College B, M
Rio Salado College C, A
Scottsdale Community College C, A
South Mountain Community
  College C, A
University of Arizona B, M, D
University of Phoenix C, B
Western International
  University A, B, M
Yavapai College C, A

Arkansas

Arkansas State University B, M

Arkansas State University
  Beebe A
Arkansas Tech University B
Harding University B
Henderson State University B
Mid-South Community College A
National Park Community
  College C, A
North Arkansas College C, A
Northwest Arkansas Community
  College A
Ouachita Technical College C, A
Pulaski Technical College A
Rich Mountain Community College A
South Arkansas Community College A
Southeast Arkansas College C, A
Southern Arkansas University B
University of Arkansas B, M, D
University of Arkansas
  Community College at Batesville A
  Fort Smith C, A, B
  Little Rock B, M
  Pine Bluff B
University of Central Arkansas B
Williams Baptist College B

California

Allan Hancock College C, A
Antelope Valley College C, A
Azusa Pacific University B, M
Barstow College C, A
Butte College C, A
CEI College
  Maric College: Panorama City C
Cabrillo College A
California Lutheran University B
California Polytechnic State
  University: San Luis Obispo B, M
California State University
  Dominguez Hills B, M
  East Bay B, M
  Fresno B, M
  Fullerton B, M
  Long Beach B, M
  Los Angeles B
  Monterey Bay B
  Northridge B, M
  Sacramento B, M
  San Marcos B
Canada College C, A
Cerritos Community College A
Cerro Coso Community College C, A
Chabot College A
Chaffey College C, A
Chapman University B
Citrus College C, A
City College of San Francisco C, A
Coastline Community College C, A
Coleman College C, A, B, M
College of Marin: Kentfield A
College of San Mateo A
College of the Canyons C, A
College of the Desert C, A
College of the Redwoods C, A
College of the Sequoias C
College of the Siskiyous A
Columbia College C, A
Contra Costa College A
Copper Mountain College C, A
Crafton Hills College C, A
Cypress College C, A
De Anza College A
DeVry University
  Pomona B
Diablo Valley College C, A
East Los Angeles College A
El Camino College C, A
Evergreen Valley College A
Foothill College C, A
Fresno City College C, A
Fullerton College A
Gavilan Community College C, A
Glendale Community College C, A
Golden West College A

Grossmont Community College C, A
Harvey Mudd College B
Humboldt State University B
Humphreys College A, B
Imperial Valley College A
Institute of Computer
  Technology C, A, B
International Technological
  University B, M
Irvine Valley College C, A
Lake Tahoe Community College C
Laney College C, A
Las Positas College C, A
Lassen College C, A
Lincoln University B
Los Angeles City College C, A
Los Angeles Harbor College C, A
Los Angeles Mission College A
Los Angeles Pierce College C, A
Los Angeles Southwest College A
Los Angeles Trade and Technical
  College C, A
Los Medanos College C
Loyola Marymount University B, M
Maric College: Anaheim C
Master's College B
Mendocino College C, A
Merced College A
Merritt College C, A
Mills College B, M
MiraCosta College C, A
Mission College C
Modesto Junior College A
Monterey Peninsula College C, A
Moorpark College A
Mount San Jacinto College A
Mt. Sierra College B
Napa Valley College A
National Hispanic University B
National University A, B, M
Notre Dame de Namur University B
Orange Coast College C, A
Oxnard College A
Pacific States University B, M
Palo Verde College C
Palomar College C, A
Platt College
  Los Angeles C, A
  Ontario A
Porterville College A
Reedley College A
Riverside Community College C, A
Sacramento City College C, A
Saddleback College C, A
San Diego City College C, A
San Diego Miramar College A
San Diego State University B, M
San Francisco State University B
San Joaquin Delta College C, A
San Joaquin Valley College Inc. A
San Jose City College A
Santa Ana College C, A
Santa Barbara City College C, A
Santa Monica College C
Shasta College A
Skyline College C, A
Solano Community College A
Southwestern College C, A
Stanford University B, M, D
Taft College A
University of California
  Irvine B, M, D
  Los Angeles B, M, D
  San Diego B, M, D
  Santa Barbara B
  Santa Cruz B, M, D
University of La Verne B
University of Redlands B, M
University of San Francisco B, M
University of the Pacific B
Ventura College C, A
Vista Community College C, A
West Hills Community College C, A
West Valley College C, A

Western Career College: Walnut
Creek *C, A*
Woodbury University *B*
Yuba Community College
District *C, A*

Colorado

Adams State College *B*
Blair College *A*
Cambridge College *A*
Colorado Christian University *B*
Colorado School of Mines *B*
Colorado State University *B, M, D*
Colorado Technical University *B, M, D*
Community College of Aurora *C, A*
DeVry University
Westminster *A*
Fort Lewis College *B*
Heritage College *A*
Jones International University *C, B*
Mesa State College *B*
Metropolitan State College of
Denver *B*
Northeastern Junior College *A*
Otero Junior College *C, A*
Parks College *A*
Parks College: Aurora *A*
Pueblo Community College *C, A*
Red Rocks Community College *C, A*
Regis University *B*
Trinidad State Junior College *A*
University of Colorado
Boulder *B, M*
Denver and Health Sciences
Center *B, M, D*
University of Denver *B, M*
Westwood College of
Technology *A, B*

Connecticut

Capital Community College *A*
Central Connecticut State
University *B, M*
Eastern Connecticut State
University *B*
Fairfield University *B*
Goodwin College *C, A*
Housatonic Community College *C, A*
Mitchell College *A*
Norwalk Community College *A*
Post University *B*
Quinebaug Valley Community
College *C, A*
Quinnipiac University *B, M*
Sacred Heart University *B, M*
Southern Connecticut State
University *B*
Three Rivers Community College *A*
Trinity College *B*
Tunxis Community College *C*
University of Bridgeport *B, M, D*
University of Hartford *B*
University of New Haven *B, M*
Wesleyan University *B, M*
Western Connecticut State
University *B*
Yale University *B, M, D*

Delaware

Delaware State University *B*
Delaware Technical and Community
College
Owens Campus *C, A*
Stanton/Wilmington Campus *A*
Terry Campus *A*
Goldey-Beacom College *A, B*
University of Delaware *B, M, D*
Wilmington College *B*

District of Columbia

American University *B, M*
Catholic University of
America *B, M, D*
Gallaudet University *B*
George Washington University *B, M*
Potomac College *B*
Southeastern University *M*
Strayer University *C*
University of the District of
Columbia *C, A, B*

Florida

Art Institute of Fort Lauderdale *A, B*
Barry University *T*
Broward Community College *C, A*
Chipola College *A*
City College: Casselberry *A*
Daytona Beach Community College *A*
Eckerd College *B*
Edison College *A*
Embry-Riddle Aeronautical
University *A*
Florida Agricultural and Mechanical
University *B, M*
Florida Atlantic University *B, M, D*
Florida Career College: Miami *A*
Florida Career College: West Palm
Beach *A*
Florida Community College at
Jacksonville *A*
Florida Gulf Coast University *B*
Florida International
University *B, M, D*
Florida Memorial University *B*
Florida Metropolitan University
Brandon Campus *A, B*
Melbourne Campus *A, B*
Orlando College North *A, B*
Pinellas *A, B*
Tampa College *A, B*
Tampa College Lakeland *B*
Florida National College *A*
Florida State University *B, M, D*
Florida Technical College
Deland *A*
Gulf Coast Community College *A*
Hillsborough Community College *A*
Indian River Community College *A*
Jacksonville University *B*
Jones College *A, B*
Key College *A*
Lake City Community College *A*
Manatee Community College *A*
Miami Dade College *C, A*
Northwood University
Florida Campus *B*
Nova Southeastern University *B, M, D*
Okaloosa-Walton College *A*
Palm Beach Atlantic University *B*
Palm Beach Community College *A*
Pensacola Junior College *A*
Polk Community College *A*
Remington College: Largo *A, B*
Rollins College *B*
St. Johns River Community College *C*
St. Thomas University *B*
Seminole Community College *A*
South University: West Palm Beach
Campus *A*
Southwest Florida College *C, A*
University of Central Florida *B, M, D*
University of Florida *B, M*
University of North Florida *B, M*
University of South Florida *B*
University of Tampa *A, B, M*
University of West Florida *B, M*
Webber International University *B*
Webster College: Holiday *A*

Georgia

Abraham Baldwin Agricultural
College *A*
Albany State University *B*
Armstrong Atlantic State
University *B, M*
Atlanta Metropolitan College *A*
Augusta State University *B*
Bainbridge College *C, A*
Chattahoochee Technical College *C, A*
Clark Atlanta University *B, M*
Clayton State University *B*
Columbus State University *C, A, B, M*
Covenant College *B*
Dalton State College *A, B*
Darton College *A*
DeKalb Technical College *C, A*
East Georgia College *A*
Emmanuel College *B*
Fort Valley State University *B*
Gainesville State College *C, A*
Georgia College and State
University *B*
Georgia Highlands College *A*
Georgia Institute of
Technology *B, M, D*
Georgia Military College *A*
Georgia Southern University *B*
Georgia Southwestern State
University *B*
Georgia State University *B, M, D*
Griffin Technical College *A*
Kennesaw State University *B*
LaGrange College *B*
Macon State College *A*
Middle Georgia College *A*
Morehouse College *B*
North Georgia College & State
University *B*
Northwestern Technical College *C, A*
Savannah State University *B*
Savannah Technical College *C, A*
Shorter College *A*
South Georgia College *A*
Spelman College *B*
University of West Georgia *B*
Valdosta State University *B*
Waycross College *A*
Wesleyan College *B*
West Georgia Technical College *A*

Hawaii

Chaminade University of
Honolulu *A, B*
Hawaii Business College *C*
Hawaii Pacific University *C, B*
Heald College
Honolulu *A*
Remington College
Honolulu *A*
University of Hawaii
Hilo *B*
Honolulu Community College *A*
Leeward Community College *C, A*
Manoa *B*

Idaho

Brigham Young University-Idaho *A, B*
Idaho State University *B*
Lewis-Clark State College *A, B*
North Idaho College *A*
Northwest Nazarene University *B*
University of Idaho *B, M, D*

Illinois

Aurora University *B*
Black Hawk College
East Campus *A*
Blackburn College *B*
Career Colleges of Chicago *C*
Carl Sandburg College *A*
Chicago State University *B*
City Colleges of Chicago
Harold Washington College *A*
Harry S. Truman College *A*
Kennedy-King College *C, A*
Olive-Harvey College *C, A*
Wright College *C, A*
Concordia University *B*
Danville Area Community College *A*
DePaul University *C, B, M, D*
Dominican University *B*
East-West University *A, B*
Eureka College *B*
Governors State University *B, M*
Highland Community College *A*
Illinois Central College *A*
Illinois College *B*
Illinois Eastern Community Colleges
Frontier Community College *C, A*
Lincoln Trail College *A*
Illinois Institute of
Technology *C, M, D*
Illinois Valley Community College *A*
Illinois Wesleyan University *B*
John A. Logan College *A*
John Wood Community College *A*
Joliet Junior College *C, A*
Judson College *B*
Lake Land College *C*
Lewis University *B*
Lewis and Clark Community
College *A*
Loyola University of Chicago *B*
MacCormac College *A*
MacMurray College *B*
McKendree College *B*
Midstate College *A*
Monmouth College *B*
North Central College *B, M*
North Park University *B*
Northern Illinois University *B, M*
Northwestern Business College *A*
Northwestern University *C, B*
Oakton Community College *A*
Olivet Nazarene University *B*
Principia College *B*
Richland Community College *A*
Rock Valley College *C, A*
Rockford Business College *A*
Rockford College *B*
Roosevelt University *B, M*
St. Augustine College *C, A*
St. Xavier University *B*
Sauk Valley Community College *A*
South Suburban College of Cook
County *C, A*
Southern Illinois University
Edwardsville *B, M*
Southwestern Illinois College *C, A*
Triton College *C, A*
University of Chicago *B*
University of Illinois
Chicago *B, M, D*
Urbana-Champaign *B*
Western Illinois University *B, M*
Westwood College - Chicago Loop *A*
Westwood College of Technology
O'Hare *B*
William Rainey Harper College *A*

Indiana

Ancilla College *A*
Ball State University *B, M*
Bethel College *A*
Brown Mackie College: Fort Wayne *A*
Brown Mackie College: Michigan
City *C, A*
Butler University *B*
Calumet College of St. Joseph *A, B*
Earlham College *B*
Franklin College *B*
Goshen College *B*
Hanover College *B*
Huntington University *B*
Indiana Institute of Technology *A, B*
Indiana State University *B*
Indiana University
Bloomington *B, M, D*
East *A*
Kokomo *B*
South Bend *B*
Southeast *B*
Indiana University-Purdue University
Indianapolis *B, M, D*
Indiana Wesleyan University *A, B*

International Business College *C, A*
International Business College:
    Indianapolis *C, A*
Ivy Tech State College
    Ivy Tech Community College:
        Bloomington *A*
    Ivy Tech Community College:
        Central Indiana *A*
    Ivy Tech Community College:
        Columbus *A*
    Ivy Tech Community College: East
        Central *C, A*
    Ivy Tech Community College:
        Kokomo *C, A*
    Ivy Tech Community College:
        Lafayette *A*
    Ivy Tech Community College: North
        Central *C, A*
    Ivy Tech Community College:
        Northeast *C, A*
    Ivy Tech Community College:
        Northwest *C, A*
    Ivy Tech Community College: South
        Central *C, A*
    Ivy Tech Community College:
        Southeast *C, A*
    Ivy Tech Community College:
        Southwest *A*
    Ivy Tech Community College:
        Wabash Valley *A*
    Ivy Tech Community College:
        Whitewater *C, A*
Manchester College *A, B*
Oakland City University *A, B*
Professional Careers Institute *A*
Purdue University *B, M, D*
Purdue University
    Calumet *B*
St. Joseph's College *B*
St. Mary-of-the-Woods College *B*
Sawyer College *C, A*
Sawyer College: Merrillville *C, A*
Taylor University *B*
Taylor University: Fort Wayne *A*
Tri-State University *B*
University of Evansville *B, M*
University of Indianapolis *B*
University of Notre Dame *B*
University of Southern Indiana *C, B*
Vincennes University *A*

Iowa

Ashford University *B*
Briar Cliff University *B*
Central College *B*
Clarke College *B*
Des Moines Area Community
    College *C, A*
Dordt College *B*
Drake University *B*
Ellsworth Community College *A*
Emmaus Bible College *B*
Graceland University *B*
Grand View College *B*
Hamilton College *A*
Hamilton College
    Cedar Rapids *C, A*
Iowa State University *B, M, D*
Iowa Wesleyan College *B*
Marshalltown Community
    College *C, A*
Mount Mercy College *B*
Northeast Iowa Community
    College *C*
Northwestern College *B*
St. Ambrose University *C, B*
Southwestern Community College *C*
University of Dubuque *B*
University of Iowa *B, M, D*
University of Northern Iowa *B, M*
Waldorf College *B*
Wartburg College *B*
William Penn University *B*

Kansas

Allen County Community College *A*
Butler County Community
    College *C, A*
Central Christian College of Kansas *A*
Cloud County Community College *A*
Coffeyville Community College *A*
Dodge City Community College *A*
Emporia State University *B*
Fort Hays State University *B*
Fort Scott Community College *C, A*
Friends University *B*
Garden City Community College *A*
Hesston College *A*
Hutchinson Community College *A*
Kansas State University *B, M, D*
Kansas Wesleyan University *A, B*
Labette Community College *A*
Manhattan Area Technical College *A*
MidAmerica Nazarene University *B*
Neosho County Community
    College *A*
Pratt Community College *C, A*
Seward County Community
    College *C, A*
Sterling College *B*
University of Kansas *B, M, D*
Washburn University of Topeka *B*
Wichita State University *B, M*

Kentucky

Beckfield College *C, A*
Bellarmine University *B*
Brescia University *B*
Brown Mackie College: Louisville *A*
Campbellsville University *C, A, B*
Daymar College *C, A*
Draughons Junior College *C, A*
Eastern Kentucky University *B*
Elizabethtown Community and
    Technical College *C, A*
Georgetown College *B*
Hazard Community College *A*
Henderson Community College *C*
Jefferson Community College *C, A*
Kentucky State University *B*
Kentucky Wesleyan College *B*
Lindsey Wilson College *A*
Maysville Community College *A*
Midway College *A, B*
Morehead State University *B*
Murray State University *B*
Northern Kentucky University *B*
Owensboro Community College *C*
Pikeville College *B*
St. Catharine College *A*
Somerset Community College *C, A*
Southeast Kentucky Community and
    Technical College *A*
Southern Ohio College
    Brown Mackie College: North
        Kentucky *A*
Southwestern College: Florence *C, A*
Sullivan University *A, B*
Thomas More College *C, A, B*
Transylvania University *B*
University of Kentucky *B, M, D*
University of the Cumberlands *B*
West Kentucky Community and
    Technical College *A*
Western Kentucky University *B, M*

Louisiana

Loyola University New Orleans *B*
Our Lady of Holy Cross College *T*
Remington College
    Lafayette *A*
Southern University
    New Orleans *A, B, M*
    Shreveport *A*
Xavier University of Louisiana *B*

Maine

Andover College *A*
Beal College *A*
St. Joseph's College *B*
Southern Maine Community
    College *A*
Thomas College *A, B*
University of Maine *C, B, M, D*
University of Maine
    Augusta *A, B*
    Fort Kent *B*
University of Southern Maine *B*

Maryland

Allegany College of Maryland *A*
Anne Arundel Community
    College *C, A*
Baltimore City Community College *A*
Bowie State University *B, M*
Carroll Community College *C, A*
Chesapeake College *A*
College of Notre Dame of Maryland *B*
Columbia Union College *B*
Community College of Baltimore
    County *C, A*
DeVry University: Bethesda *B*
Frederick Community College *A*
Frostburg State University *C, B, M*
Hagerstown Community College *A*
Harford Community College *C, A*
Hood College *M*
Johns Hopkins University *B, M, D*
Loyola College in Maryland *B*
McDaniel College *B*
Montgomery College *A*
Morgan State University *B*
Mount St. Mary's University *B*
Prince George's Community
    College *C, A*
St. Mary's College of Maryland *B*
Towson University *B, M*
United States Naval Academy *B*
University of Baltimore *B, M*
University of Maryland
    Baltimore County *B, M, D*
    College Park *B, M, D*
    Eastern Shore *B, M*
    University College *C, B*
Villa Julie College *B*
Wor-Wic Community College *A*

Massachusetts

Anna Maria College *B*
Assumption College *B*
Atlantic Union College *C, A, B*
Babson College *B*
Bay State College *A*
Benjamin Franklin Institute of
    Technology *C, A*
Bentley College *B, M*
Berkshire Community College *A*
Boston College *B*
Boston University *B, M, D*
Brandeis University *B, M, D*
Bristol Community College *A*
Bunker Hill Community College *C*
Cape Cod Community College *A*
Clark University *B*
College of the Holy Cross *B*
Curry College *B*
Dean College *A*
Elms College *C, B*
Endicott College *B*
Fitchburg State College *C, B*
Framingham State College *B*
Greenfield Community College *A*
Hampshire College *B*
Lasell College *B*
Massachusetts Bay Community
    College *A*
Massachusetts College of Liberal
    Arts *B*
Massachusetts Institute of
    Technology *M*

Massasoit Community College *A*
Merrimack College *A*
Mount Wachusett Community
    College *A*
Newbury College *A, B*
North Shore Community College *A*
Northeastern University *B, M, D*
Northern Essex Community
    College *C, A*
Regis College *B*
Roxbury Community College *C, A*
Salem State College *B*
Simmons College *B*
Simon's Rock College of Bard *B*
Springfield College *B*
Suffolk University *B, M*
Tufts University *B*
University of Massachusetts
    Boston *B*
    Dartmouth *B, M*
Urban College of Boston *C*
Wellesley College *B*
Wentworth Institute of Technology *B*
Westfield State College *B*
Wheaton College *B*
Worcester State College *B*

Michigan

Albion College *B, T*
Alpena Community College *C, A*
Andrews University *B*
Aquinas College *B*
Baker College
    of Auburn Hills *A*
    of Cadillac *A*
    of Clinton Township *A, B*
    of Flint *B, M*
    of Jackson *A*
    of Muskegon *B*
    of Owosso *A, B*
    of Port Huron *A, B*
Bay Mills Community College *A*
Calvin College *B*
Central Michigan University *B, M, T*
Concordia University *B*
Cornerstone University *B*
Delta College *C, A*
Eastern Michigan University *B, M*
Gogebic Community College *A*
Grace Bible College *B*
Grand Rapids Community
    College *C, A*
Grand Valley State University *B*
Henry Ford Community College *A*
Hope College *B*
Kalamazoo College *B*
Kuyper College *B*
Lake Superior State University *A*
Lansing Community College *A*
Lewis College of Business *A*
Macomb Community College *C, A*
Madonna University *C, A, B*
Marygrove College *C, B*
Michigan Jewish Institute *B*
Michigan State University *B, M, D*
Michigan Technological
    University *B, M, D, T*
Mid Michigan Community
    College *C, A*
Monroe County Community
    College *C, A*
Montcalm Community College *A*
Muskegon Community College *C, A*
North Central Michigan College *C, A*
Northern Michigan University *A, B, T*
Northwood University *B*
Oakland University *B, M*
Rochester College *B*
Saginaw Valley State University *B, T*
Siena Heights University *A, B*
Southwestern Michigan College *C, A*
University of Detroit Mercy *B, M*
University of Michigan *B, M, D*

University of Michigan
  Dearborn *B*
Walsh College of Accountancy and
  Business Administration *B*
Washtenaw Community College *C, A*
Wayne County Community College *C*
Wayne State University *B, M, D*
Western Michigan University *B*

Minnesota

Academy College *C, A, B*
Alexandria Technical College *A*
Bemidji State University *B, M*
Bethel University *B*
Capella University *B, M*
College of St. Catherine *B*
College of St. Scholastica *B*
Crown College *C, A, B*
Globe College *C, A, B*
Gustavus Adolphus College *B*
Hennepin Technical College *C, A*
Hibbing Community College *A*
Lake Superior College *C*
Macalester College *B*
Mesabi Range Community and
  Technical College *C, A*
Minnesota School of Business *C, A*
Minnesota State University
  Mankato *B, M*
  Moorhead *B*
Minnesota West Community and
  Technical College: Worthington
  Campus *A*
National American University
  St. Paul *A, B*
Normandale Community College *A*
North Hennepin Community
  College *A*
Northland Community & Technical
  College *A*
Rainy River Community College *C, A*
Rasmussen College
  St. Cloud *A*
Ridgewater College *C, A*
Riverland Community College *A*
Rochester Community and Technical
  College *C, A*
St. Cloud State University *B*
Southwest Minnesota State
  University *B*
University of Minnesota
  Twin Cities *M, D*
University of St. Thomas *B*
Winona State University *B*

Mississippi

Alcorn State University *B, M*
Antonelli College
  Hattiesburg *C, A*
Coahoma Community College *A*
East Central Community College *A*
Hinds Community College *A*
Holmes Community College *C, A*
Itawamba Community College *A*
Jackson State University *B, M*
Meridian Community College *A*
Mississippi College *B*
Mississippi Gulf Coast Community
  College
  Jefferson Davis Campus *A*
Mississippi State University *B, M, D*
Mississippi Valley State University *B*
University of Mississippi *B*
University of Southern
  Mississippi *B, M*

Missouri

Avila University *B*
Central Missouri State University *B*
College of the Ozarks *B*
Columbia College *A, B*
Crowder College *A*
DeVry University
  Kansas City *B, M*

Drury University *B*
Evangel University *B*
Everest College: Springfield *A*
Fontbonne University *B*
Grantham University *A, B*
Hannibal-LaGrange College *B*
Harris-Stowe State University *B*
Hickey College *C, A*
Jefferson College *C, A*
Lincoln University *A*
Lindenwood University *B*
Longview Community College *A*
Maple Woods Community College *A*
Missouri Baptist University *B*
Missouri Southern State University *B*
Missouri State University *B*
Missouri State University: West
  Plains *A*
Missouri Valley College *B*
Missouri Western State University *B*
North Central Missouri College *C, A*
Northwest Missouri State
  University *B*
Park University *B*
Penn Valley Community College *C, A*
Ranken Technical College *A*
Rockhurst University *B*
St. Charles Community College *C, A*
St. Louis Community College
  St. Louis Community College at
    Florissant Valley *A*
  St. Louis Community College at
    Meramec *C, A*
St. Louis University *B*
Southeast Missouri State University *B*
Southwest Baptist University *B*
State Fair Community College *A*
Truman State University *B*
University of Missouri
  Columbia *B, M, D*
  Kansas City *B, M, D*
  Rolla *B, M, D*
  St. Louis *B, M, D*
Vatterott College: St. Joseph *A*
Washington University in St.
  Louis *B, M, D*
Webster University *M*
Westminster College *B*
William Jewell College *B*
William Woods University *B*

Montana

Blackfeet Community College *C*
Dawson Community College *A*
Miles Community College *A*
Montana State University
  Billings *A*
  College of Technology-Great
    Falls *C, A*
Montana Tech of the University of
  Montana *B*
Salish Kootenai College *C, A, B*
University of Great Falls *B, M*
University of Montana: Western *A*

Nebraska

Bellevue University *B, M*
Central Community College *C, A*
College of Saint Mary *C, A, B*
Doane College *B*
Hastings College *B*
Little Priest Tribal College *C, A*
Metropolitan Community College *C*
Midland Lutheran College *B*
Nebraska Indian Community
  College *A*
Northeast Community College *A*
Peru State College *B*
University of Nebraska
  Kearney *B*
  Lincoln *B, M, D*
Wayne State College *B*
Western Nebraska Community
  College *C, A*

Nevada

Career College of Northern Nevada *C*
Great Basin College *C, A*
Morrison University *A*
Sierra Nevada College *B*
Truckee Meadows Community
  College *A*
University of Nevada
  Reno *B*
Western Nevada Community
  College *A*

New Hampshire

Daniel Webster College *B*
Franklin Pierce College *B*
Granite State College *C, A, B*
Keene State College *A, B*
New England College *B*
New Hampshire Community
  Technical College
  Berlin *A*
  Manchester *A*
  Nashua *C, A*
New Hampshire Technical
  Institute *C, A*
University of New
  Hampshire *A, B, M, D*
University of New Hampshire at
  Manchester *B*

New Jersey

Atlantic Cape Community College *A*
Bergen Community College *C*
Bloomfield College *B*
Brookdale Community College *A*
Caldwell College *C, B*
Camden County College *C, A*
Centenary College *B*
The College of New Jersey *B*
College of St. Elizabeth *C, B*
Essex County College *C, A*
Fairleigh Dickinson University
  College at Florham *B*
  Metropolitan Campus *B, M*
Felician College *B*
Georgian Court University *B*
Gloucester County College *C, A*
Hudson County Community
  College *C*
Kean University *B*
Mercer County Community College *C*
Middlesex County College *A*
Monmouth University *C, B, M*
Montclair State University *B, M*
New Jersey City University *B*
New Jersey Institute of
  Technology *B, M, D*
Ocean County College *A*
Passaic County Community College *A*
Ramapo College of New Jersey *B*
Raritan Valley Community College *A*
Rider University *B*
Rowan University *B*
St. Peter's College *B*
Seton Hall University *B*
Stevens Institute of
  Technology *B, M, D*
Sussex County Community
  College *C, A*
Thomas Edison State College *A*
Warren County Community
  College *C, A*
William Paterson University of New
  Jersey *B*

New Mexico

Clovis Community College *A*
Eastern New Mexico University *B*
Eastern New Mexico University:
  Roswell Campus *A*
Luna Community College *A*
Mesalands Community College *C, A*
New Mexico Highlands University *B*

New Mexico Institute of Mining and
  Technology *B, M, D*
New Mexico Junior College *C, A*
New Mexico State University *B, M, D*
New Mexico State University
  Carlsbad *A*
Northern New Mexico College *A*
San Juan College *A*
Santa Fe Community College *A*
Southwestern Indian Polytechnic
  Institute *C, A*
University of New Mexico *B, M, D*
Western New Mexico University *B*

New York

Adelphi University *B*
Adirondack Community College *A*
Barnard College *B*
Bramson ORT College *A*
Broome Community College *A*
Bryant & Stratton Business Institute
  Bryant & Stratton College: Albany *A*
  Bryant & Stratton College:
    Buffalo *C, A*
  Bryant & Stratton College:
    Lackawanna *A*
  Bryant & Stratton College:
    Syracuse *C, A*
Cayuga County Community College *A*
City University of New York
  Baruch College *B, M*
  Brooklyn College *B, M*
  College of Staten Island *B, M*
  Hunter College *B*
  John Jay College of Criminal
    Justice *B*
  LaGuardia Community College *A*
  Lehman College *B, M*
  Medgar Evers College *A*
  New York City College of
    Technology *A, B*
  Queensborough Community
    College *A*
Clarkson University *B*
Clinton Community College *A*
Colgate University *B*
College of Mount St. Vincent *B*
College of Saint Rose *C, B, M*
College of Westchester *C, A*
Columbia University
  School of General Studies *B*
Columbia-Greene Community
  College *A*
Cornell University *B, M, D*
Corning Community College *C, A*
Dominican College of Blauvelt *B*
Dowling College *B*
Dutchess Community College *C, A*
Erie Community College
  North Campus *A*
Excelsior College *B*
Finger Lakes Community College *C, A*
Fordham University *B*
Fulton-Montgomery Community
  College *A*
Genesee Community College *A*
Globe Institute of Technology *C, A, B*
Hamilton College *B*
Hartwick College *B*
Herkimer County Community
  College *A*
Hobart and William Smith Colleges *B*
Ithaca College *B*
Jamestown Business College *A*
Jefferson Community College *A*
Long Island Business Institute *C, A*
Long Island University
  Brooklyn Campus *B, M*
Manhattan College *B*
Manhattanville College *B*
Maria College *C, A*
Marist College *B*
Medaille College *B*
Mercy College *B*

Mildred Elley *C, A*
Mohawk Valley Community College *A*
Monroe College *A, B*
Monroe Community College *A*
Mount St. Mary College *C, B, T*
Nassau Community College *A*
New York Institute of
   Technology *B, M*
New York University *B, M, D*
Niagara University *C, B*
Nyack College *B*
Olean Business Institute *A*
Onondaga Community College *A*
Orange County Community College *A*
Pace University *B, D*
Polytechnic University *B, M*
Rensselaer Polytechnic
   Institute *B, M, D*
Roberts Wesleyan College *B*
Rochester Institute of
   Technology *A, B, M*
Sage College of Albany *A, B*
St. Bonaventure University *B*
St. John Fisher College *B*
St. John's University *C, A, B*
St. Thomas Aquinas College *B*
Sarah Lawrence College *A*
Schenectady County Community
   College *A*
Siena College *C, B*
Skidmore College *B*
State University of New York
   Albany *B, M, D*
   Binghamton *B, M*
   Buffalo *M, D*
   College at Brockport *B, M*
   College at Buffalo *B*
   College at Fredonia *B*
   College at Geneseo *B*
   College at Old Westbury *B*
   College at Oneonta *B*
   College at Plattsburgh *B*
   College at Potsdam *B*
   College of Agriculture and
      Technology at Cobleskill *A*
   College of Agriculture and
      Technology at Morrisville *A*
   College of Technology at
      Alfred *A, B*
   College of Technology at
      Canton *A, B*
   Farmingdale *C*
   Institute of Technology at
      Utica/Rome *B, M*
   Purchase *C*
Suffolk County Community
   College *C, A*
Sullivan County Community
   College *A*
Syracuse University *B, M, D*
Technical Career Institutes *A*
Tompkins-Cortland Community
   College *A*
Touro College *B*
Trocaire College *C, A*
Ulster County Community College *A*
Union College *B*
United States Military Academy *B*
University of Rochester *B, M, D*
Utica College *B*
Utica School of Commerce *A*
Vassar College *B*
Villa Maria College of Buffalo *A*
Westchester Community College *A*
Yeshiva University *B*

North Carolina

Barton College *B*
Bennett College *B*
Bladen Community College *C, A*
Carteret Community College *C, A*
Catawba College *B*
College of the Albemarle *A*
DeVry University: Charlotte *B*

Duke University *B, M, D*
Edgecombe Community College *A*
Elon University *B*
Fayetteville State University *B*
Gardner-Webb University *B*
Gaston College *C*
Guilford College *B*
Halifax Community College *C, A*
High Point University *B*
Johnson C. Smith University *B*
King's College *A*
Lenoir-Rhyne College *B*
Livingstone College *B*
Louisburg College *A*
Meredith College *B*
Methodist College *A, B*
Miller-Motte Technical College *C, A*
Montreat College *B*
Mount Olive College *B*
North Carolina Agricultural and
   Technical State University *B, M*
Pfeiffer University *B*
St. Augustine's College *B*
Sampson Community College *A*
Sandhills Community College *C, A*
Shaw University *B*
South College *A*
South Piedmont Community
   College *A*
Southwestern Community
   College *C, A*
Wake Technical Community
   College *C, A*
Wilson Technical Community
   College *A*
Winston-Salem State University *M*

North Dakota

Cankdeska Cikana Community
   College *C, A*
Lake Region State College *C, A*
Mayville State University *B*
Minot State University *B*
University of North Dakota *B, M*
Valley City State University *B*

Ohio

Belmont Technical College *A*
Bowling Green State University *B, M*
Bryant & Stratton College
   Willoughby Hills *A*
Capital University *B*
Case Western Reserve
   University *B, M, D*
Cedarville University *B*
Cincinnati State Technical and
   Community College *A*
Cleveland State University *B, M*
College of Mount St. Joseph *A, B*
College of Wooster *B*
Cuyahoga Community College
   Metropolitan Campus *A*
Defiance College *A, B*
Denison University *B*
Edison State Community College *C, A*
Franciscan University of
   Steubenville *B*
Franklin University *A, B, M*
Gallipolis Career College *A*
Heidelberg College *B*
Hiram College *B*
James A. Rhodes State College *A*
Jefferson Community College *C, A*
John Carroll University *B*
Marietta College *B*
Marion Technical College *A*
Miami University
   Hamilton Campus *A*
   Oxford Campus *C, A*
Mount Union College *B*
Mount Vernon Nazarene University *B*
Muskingum College *B*
Oberlin College *B*

Ohio State University
   Columbus Campus *B, M, D*
Ohio University *B*
Ohio Valley College of Technology *A*
Ohio Wesleyan University *B*
Remington College
   Cleveland *A*
Sinclair Community College *C, A*
Southeastern Business College:
   Lancaster *A*
Southeastern Business College: New
   Boston *A*
Stark State College of Technology *A*
Technology Education College *A*
Trumbull Business College *C, A*
Union Institute & University *B*
University of Akron *C, B, M*
University of Cincinnati *B, M, T*
University of Cincinnati
   Clermont College *C, A*
   Raymond Walters College *C, A*
University of Dayton *B*
University of Findlay *A, B*
University of Northwestern Ohio *B*
University of Rio Grande *A, B*
University of Toledo *A*
Walsh University *A, B*
Wilmington College *B*
Wright State University *B, M, D*
Youngstown State University *A, B*
Zane State College *A*

Oklahoma

Bacone College *A*
Cameron University *A, B*
Connors State College *A*
East Central University *B*
Eastern Oklahoma State College *C, A*
Murray State College *A*
Northeastern Oklahoma Agricultural
   and Mechanical College *A*
Northwestern Oklahoma State
   University *B*
Oklahoma Baptist University *B*
Oklahoma Christian University *B*
Oklahoma City Community College *A*
Oklahoma City University *B, M*
Oklahoma Panhandle State
   University *A, B*
Oklahoma State University *B, M, D*
Oklahoma State University
   Oklahoma City *A*
   Okmulgee *A*
Oklahoma Wesleyan University *A, B*
Oral Roberts University *B*
Redlands Community College *A*
Rogers State University *A*
Rose State College *A*
St. Gregory's University *B*
Southeastern Oklahoma State
   University *B*
Southern Nazarene University *B*
Southwestern Oklahoma State
   University *B*
Tulsa Community College *C, A*
University of Central Oklahoma *B*
University of Tulsa *B*
Vatterott College *C, A*
Western Oklahoma State College *A*

Oregon

Central Oregon Community
   College *A*
Chemeketa Community College *A*
DeVry University: Portland *B*
Eastern Oregon University *B*
Everest College: Portland *C, A*
George Fox University *B*
Linn-Benton Community College *A*
Mount Hood Community College *C, A*
Northwest Christian College *B*
Oregon State University *B, M, D*
Pacific University *B*
Southern Oregon University *B*

Treasure Valley Community College *A*
University of Oregon *B, M, D*
Western Oregon University *B*
Willamette University *B*

Pennsylvania

Academy of Medical Arts and
   Business *C, A*
Albright College *B*
Alvernia College *A, B*
Arcadia University *C, B*
Berean Institute *C, A*
Berks Technical Institute *A*
Bidwell Training Center *C*
Bloomsburg University of
   Pennsylvania *B*
Bucknell University *B*
Bucks County Community College *A*
Business Institute of Pennsylvania *A*
Business Institute of Pennsylvania
   Meadville *A*
Cabrini College *B*
California University of
   Pennsylvania *A, B*
Cedar Crest College *C, B*
Chestnut Hill College *B, M*
Cheyney University of Pennsylvania *B*
Clarion University of Pennsylvania *B*
College Misericordia *B*
Commonwealth Technical Institute *A*
Community College of Philadelphia *A*
DeSales University *B, M*
Delaware County Community
   College *A*
Delaware Valley College *A, B*
Dickinson College *B*
Drexel University *M*
East Stroudsburg University of
   Pennsylvania *B, M*
Edinboro University of
   Pennsylvania *A, B, M*
Elizabethtown College *B*
Erie Business Center South *A*
Gannon University *B, M*
Geneva College *B*
Gettysburg College *B*
Grove City College *B*
Gwynedd-Mercy College *B*
Harrisburg Area Community
   College *C, A*
Haverford College *B*
Holy Family University *C, B*
ICM School of Business & Medical
   Careers *A*
Indiana University of Pennsylvania *B*
International Academy of Design and
   Technology: Pittsburgh *A*
Johnson College *A*
Juniata College *B*
Keystone College *A, B*
King's College *A, B*
La Roche College *B*
La Salle University *B, M*
Lackawanna College *A*
Lafayette College *B*
Lincoln University *B*
Lock Haven University of
   Pennsylvania *B*
Luzerne County Community
   College *A*
Lycoming College *B*
Mansfield University of
   Pennsylvania *A, B*
Marywood University *B, M*
McCann School of Business
   Pottsville *C, A*
Mercyhurst College *C, A, B*
Metropolitan Career Center *C*
Millersville University of
   Pennsylvania *A, B*
Montgomery County Community
   College *A*
Mount Aloysius College *B*
Muhlenberg College *C, A, B*

Neumann College *B*
PJA School *C*
Penn State
  Schuylkill - Capital College *A, B*
  University Park *C, B, M, D*
Pennsylvania Highlands Community
  College *C, A*
Pennsylvania School of Business *C, A*
Rosemont College *M*
St. Francis University *B*
St. Joseph's University *B, M*
St. Vincent College *C, B*
Schuylkill Institute of Business &
  Technology *C, A*
Shippensburg University of
  Pennsylvania *B, M*
Slippery Rock University of
  Pennsylvania *B*
South Hills School of Business &
  Technology *C, A*
Swarthmore College *B*
Temple University *B, M, D*
Thiel College *B*
Thompson Institute *C*
Tri-State Business Institute *A*
University of Pennsylvania *B, M, D*
University of Pittsburgh
  Johnstown *A*
University of Scranton *A, B*
University of the Sciences in
  Philadelphia *B*
Valley Forge Christian College *C*
Villanova University *B, M*
Waynesburg College *B*
West Chester University of
  Pennsylvania *B, M*
Western School of Health and
  Business Careers *C*
Westminster College *B*
Widener University *A, B, M*
Wilkes University *B*
York College of Pennsylvania *B*
York Technical Institute *A*
Yorktowne Business Institute *A*

Puerto Rico

Bayamon Central University *A*
Electronic Data Processing College:
  San Sebastian *A*
Inter American University of Puerto
  Rico
  Arecibo Campus *A, B*
  Barranquitas Campus *A, B*
  Bayamon Campus *C*
  Fajardo Campus *A*
  San German Campus *B, M*
National College of Business &
  Technology: Arecibo *C, A*
Universidad Adventista de las
  Antillas *A, B*
University College of San Juan *C, A, B*
University of Puerto Rico
  Arecibo *A, B*
  Mayaguez *B, M*
  Ponce *A, B*
  Rio Piedras *B*

Rhode Island

Bryant University *B, M*
New England Institute of
  Technology *A, B*
Rhode Island College *B*
Roger Williams University *B*
University of Rhode Island *B, M*

South Carolina

Anderson University *B*
Benedict College *B*
The Citadel *B*
Clemson University *B, M, D*
Coastal Carolina University *B*
College of Charleston *B*
Columbia College *B*
Converse College *B*

Denmark Technical College *C*
Forrest Junior College *C, A*
Francis Marion University *B*
Greenville Technical College *C*
Horry-Georgetown Technical
  College *C*
Lander University *B*
South Carolina State University *B*
South University *A*
Spartanburg Technical College *C, A*
Technical College of the
  Lowcountry *C, A*
Tri-County Technical College *C, A*
University of South Carolina *B, M, D*
University of South Carolina
  Upstate *B*
Voorhees College *B*
Williamsburg Technical College *A*
Winthrop University *B*
Wofford College *B*
York Technical College *C*

South Dakota

Black Hills State University *A*
Dakota State University *B, M*
Lake Area Technical Institute *A*
Mitchell Technical Institute *A*
Northern State University *B, M*
Sisseton Wahpeton College *C, A*
South Dakota State University *B*
Southeast Technical Institute *A*
University of Sioux Falls *B*
University of South Dakota *B, M*

Tennessee

Austin Peay State University *B*
Bethel College *B*
Carson-Newman College *B*
Columbia State Community College *A*
East Tennessee State University *B, M*
Freed-Hardeman University *B*
Hiwassee College *A*
Jackson State Community College *A*
Lambuth University *B*
Lincoln Memorial University *B*
Maryville College *B*
Middle Tennessee State University *B*
Miller-Motte Technical College *C, A*
Milligan College *B*
Nashville State Community College *A*
National College of Business &
  Technology
  Tennessee *A*
Northeast State Technical Community
  College *C, A*
Southwest Tennessee Community
  College *A*
Tennessee State University *B*
Tennessee Technological University *B*
Tennessee Wesleyan College *B*
Union University *B, T*
University of Tennessee
  Chattanooga *C, B, M*
  Knoxville *B, M, D*
University of the South *B*
Vanderbilt University *B, M, D*
Walters State Community College *C, A*

Texas

Amarillo College *C, A*
Angelina College *A*
Angelo State University *B, T*
Austin Community College *A*
Blinn College *A*
Brazosport College *A*
Central Texas College *C, A*
Cisco Junior College *C, A*
Clarendon College *A*
Coastal Bend College *A*
College of the Mainland *A*
Collin County Community College
  District *C, A*
Dallas Baptist University *B*
Del Mar College *A*

East Texas Baptist University *B*
Eastfield College *A*
El Paso Community College *C, A*
Frank Phillips College *C, A*
Galveston College *A*
Grayson County College *C, A*
Hill College *A*
Houston Community College
  System *C, A*
Howard College *C, A*
Huston-Tillotson College *B*
Jarvis Christian College *B*
Kilgore College *A*
Lamar State College at Orange *C, A*
Lamar State College at Port
  Arthur *C, A*
Lamar University *B*
Laredo Community College *A*
LeTourneau University *B*
Lee College *C, A*
McLennan Community College *C, A*
McMurry University *B*
Midland College *A*
Midwestern State University *B, M*
Navarro College *C, A*
North Central Texas College *A*
North Harris Montgomery
  Community College District *C, A*
North Lake College *A*
Northeast Texas Community
  College *C, A*
Northwest Vista College *A*
Northwood University: Texas
  Campus *B*
Our Lady of the Lake University of San
  Antonio *B*
Palo Alto College *C, A*
Panola College *A*
Paul Quinn College *B*
Prairie View A&M University *B, M*
Ranger College *C, A*
Remington College
  Houston *A*
Richland College *A*
St. Edward's University *B*
St. Mary's University *B, M*
Sam Houston State University *B, M*
San Antonio College *C, A*
San Jacinto College
  Central Campus *C*
  North *C, A*
South Plains College *A*
South Texas College *A*
Southern Methodist University *C*
Southwest Texas Junior College *A*
Southwestern Adventist University *B*
Southwestern University *B, T*
Stephen F. Austin State
  University *B, M, T*
Sul Ross State University *B*
Tarleton State University *B, T*
Tarrant County College *C, A*
Temple College *C, A*
Texarkana College *C, A*
Texas A&M University *B, M, D*
Texas A&M University
  Commerce *B*
  Texarkana *B*
Texas Christian University *B*
Texas College *B*
Texas Lutheran University *B*
Texas Southern University *B*
Texas Southmost College *C, A*
Texas State Technical College
  Waco *A*
Texas State University: San
  Marcos *B, M*
Texas Tech University *B, M, D*
Texas Wesleyan University *B*
Texas Woman's University *B, T*
Trinity University *B*
Trinity Valley Community College *C, A*
Tyler Junior College *C, A*
University of Houston *B, M, D*

University of Houston
  Clear Lake *B, M*
  Downtown *B*
  Victoria *B, T*
University of Mary Hardin-Baylor *B*
University of North Texas *B, D*
University of Texas
  Arlington *M, D*
  Austin *B, M, D*
  Brownsville *C, A, B*
  Dallas *B, M, D*
  El Paso *B, M*
  Pan American *B*
  San Antonio *B, M*
  Tyler *B, M*
  of the Permian Basin *B*
Victoria College *C, A*
Weatherford College *C, A*
West Texas A&M University *B*
Western Texas College *A*

Utah

College of Eastern Utah *C*
Provo College *A*
Salt Lake Community College *C, A*
Snow College *A*
Stevens-Henager College *B*
University of Utah *M*
Utah State University *B, M*
Weber State University *A, B*
Western Governors University *B*

Vermont

Castleton State College *B*
Champlain College *A, B*
Lyndon State College *A, B*
Marlboro College *B, M*
Norwich University *B*
University of Vermont *B, M*
Vermont Technical College *A, B*

Virginia

Blue Ridge Community College *C, A*
Bluefield College *B*
Bryant & Stratton College: Virginia
  Beach *A*
Christopher Newport University *B*
College of William and Mary *B, M, D*
Dabney S. Lancaster Community
  College *A*
Danville Community College *A*
ECPI College of Technology *C, A, B*
ECPI Technical College
  Glen Allen *A, B*
Eastern Shore Community
  College *C, A*
Emory & Henry College *B*
George Mason University *B, M, D*
Germanna Community College *A*
Hampton University *B*
J. Sargeant Reynolds Community
  College *A*
James Madison University *B, M*
John Tyler Community College *A*
Liberty University *B, T*
Longwood University *B, T*
Lord Fairfax Community College *A*
Lynchburg College *B*
Mary Baldwin College *B*
Marymount University *C, B*
Miller-Motte Technical College:
  Lynchburg *A*
Mountain Empire Community
  College *A*
National College of Business &
  Technology
  Lynchburg *A*
New River Community College *A*
Norfolk State University *B, M*
Northern Virginia Community
  College *A*
Old Dominion University *B, M, D*
Patrick Henry Community College *A*

Paul D. Camp Community
College C, A
Potomac College B
Randolph-Macon College B
Roanoke College B
St. Paul's College B
Southside Virginia Community
College C, A
Southwest Virginia Community
College A
Thomas Nelson Community
College C, A
Tidewater Community College A
University of Northern Virginia B, M
University of Virginia B, M, D
Virginia Commonwealth
University B, M
Virginia Highlands Community
College A
Virginia Intermont College B, T
Virginia Polytechnic Institute and
State University B, M, D
Virginia Union University B
Virginia Western Community
College C, A
Washington and Lee University B

Washington

Bellevue Community College C, A
Bellingham Technical College A
Big Bend Community College A
Cascadia Community College A
Central Washington University B
Centralia College C, A
City University M
Columbia Basin College A
Edmonds Community College C, A
Everett Community College C, A
Evergreen State College B
Heritage University A, B
Highline Community College A
Lower Columbia College A
North Seattle Community
College C, A
Peninsula College A
Renton Technical College C
Saint Martin's University B
Seattle Central Community
College C, A
Seattle Pacific University B
Shoreline Community College C, A
Skagit Valley College C, A
South Seattle Community
College C, A
Spokane Falls Community
College C, A
Tacoma Community College A
University of Puget Sound B
University of Washington B, M, D
Walla Walla College B
Washington State University B
Western Washington University B, M
Whitworth College B
Yakima Valley Community College A

West Virginia

Bethany College B
Bluefield State College A, B
Concord University B
Huntington Junior College A
Marshall University B
Mountain State College A
Potomac State College of West Virginia
University A
Salem International University A, B
Shepherd University B
Southern West Virginia Community
and Technical College A
University of Charleston A, B
West Virginia University Institute of
Technology A
West Virginia Wesleyan College B

Wisconsin

Alverno College B
Carroll College B
Chippewa Valley Technical College A
College of Menominee Nation A
Concordia University Wisconsin B
DeVry University: Milwaukee B
Edgewood College B
Fox Valley Technical College C
Lawrence University B
Madison Area Technical College A
Nicolet Area Technical College A
Northeast Wisconsin Technical
College C, A
Northland College B
St. Norbert College B
University of Wisconsin
Eau Claire B
La Crosse B, T
Madison B, M, D
Milwaukee M
Parkside M
River Falls B
Stevens Point B
Whitewater B, T
Viterbo University B
Waukesha County Technical
College A
Wisconsin Indianhead Technical
College A

Wyoming

Laramie County Community
College A
Northwest College A
Sheridan College A
Western Wyoming Community
College A

Computer installation and repair

Alaska

University of Alaska
Fairbanks C, A

Arkansas

Mid-South Community College C
Ouachita Technical College C
South Arkansas Community College C
Southern Arkansas University Tech C
University of Arkansas
Fort Smith C

California

College of the Canyons C
Diablo Valley College C
Solano Community College C, A

Florida

Miami Dade College C
Polk Community College A

Georgia

Albany Technical College C
Dalton State College C, A
Gwinnett Technical College C
Savannah Technical College C

Illinois

College of Lake County C, A
Illinois Eastern Community Colleges
Frontier Community College C
Lincoln Trail College C
Olney Central College C
Wabash Valley College C
Morton College C
Waubonsee Community College C
William Rainey Harper College C

Kansas

Coffeyville Community College C

Kentucky

Eastern Kentucky University A
Jefferson Community College C
Louisville Technical Institute A

Louisiana

Delgado Community College C, A

Massachusetts

Cape Cod Community College C

Michigan

Baker College
of Muskegon C
Montcalm Community College C, A

New York

Briarcliffe College C
College of Saint Rose C
Corning Community College A
Onondaga Community College C

Ohio

Cincinnati State Technical and
Community College C, A
University of Akron: Wayne College C
University of Cincinnati
Raymond Walters College C, A
University of Rio Grande A

Oklahoma

Vatterott College
Tulsa C, A

Pennsylvania

Harrisburg Area Community
College C, A
Northampton County Area
Community College C, A

Puerto Rico

Inter American University of Puerto
Rico
Bayamon Campus A, B
Guayama Campus A, B
Turabo University A

South Carolina

Midlands Technical College C
York Technical College C

Texas

MTI College of Business and
Technology C
Temple College C, A
Western Texas College C

Virginia

ECPI College of Technology C, A

Washington

Walla Walla Community College A

Wisconsin

Wisconsin Indianhead Technical
College C, A

Computer networking/ telecommunications

Alabama

Community College of the Air
Force A
Gadsden State Community College A
Herzing College A

Alaska

University of Alaska
Southeast B

Arizona

Chandler-Gilbert Community College
Williams Campus A
Chaparral College C, A
DeVry University
Phoenix B
Gateway Community College C, A
Glendale Community College C, A
Mesa Community College A
Pima Community College C, A
University of Phoenix C, B

Arkansas

Arkansas Northeastern College C
Arkansas State University
Mountain Home C
East Arkansas Community College C
Mid-South Community College C
North Arkansas College C
Remington College
Little Rock A
Southeast Arkansas College C, A
Southern Arkansas University
Tech C, A

California

Butte College C, A
California State University
East Bay C, B, M
Chaffey College C
Coastline Community College C
DeVry University
Fremont B, M
Long Beach A, B, M
Pomona B, M
West Hills B, M
Diablo Valley College C, A
Heald College
Rancho Cordova C, A
Irvine Valley College C, A
Platt College
Ontario A
Remington College
San Diego A
Saddleback College C
San Joaquin Valley College Inc. A
San Jose City College C, A
Sierra College C, A
Southwestern College C, A
University of Southern California M
Westwood College A, B

Colorado

Arapahoe Community College C, A
Blair College C, A
CollegeAmerica-Denver A
Colorado Mountain College
Spring Valley Campus A
Colorado Technical University C
Community College of Denver C
DeVry University: Colorado
Springs A, M
Front Range Community College C
Parks College C, A
Westwood College of
Technology A, B
Westwood College of Technology
South A, B

Connecticut

Gibbs College C
Manchester Community College A

Delaware

Delaware Technical and Community
College
Stanton/Wilmington Campus A

Florida

Edison College C
Florida Community College at
Jacksonville A

Florida Metropolitan University
  Orlando College South *A*
Florida Technical College
  Deland *A*
Hillsborough Community
  College *C, A*
Manatee Community College *A*
New England Institute of
  Technology *C, A*
Pasco-Hernando Community
  College *A*
St. Petersburg College *C, A*
Seminole Community College *C, A*
Tallahassee Community College *C, A*

Georgia

Albany Technical College *C, A*
Athens Technical College *C, A*
Central Georgia Technical
  College *C, A*
Clayton State University *C, A*
Darton College *C, A*
DeVry University
  Alpharetta
  Decatur *B*
Gordon College *A*
Northwestern Technical College *C, A*
Savannah Technical College *C, A*
South Georgia College *C*
Southwest Georgia Technical
  College *C, A*
West Georgia Technical College *C, A*

Hawaii

Hawaii Business College *A*
Remington College
  Honolulu *A*

Idaho

Eastern Idaho Technical College *C, A*

Illinois

Aurora University *B*
Black Hawk College *C*
Career Colleges of Chicago *C*
College of Office Technology *C*
DePaul University *B*
DeVry University
  Addison *B*
  Chicago *B*
  Tinley Park *B*
Elgin Community College *C*
Heartland Community College *C, A*
Illinois State University *B*
Kaskaskia College *C*
Lake Land College *A*
Lincoln Land Community College *C, A*
McHenry County College *C*
Midstate College *C, A*
Moraine Valley Community
  College *C, A*
Morton College *C*
Parkland College *C, A*
Robert Morris College: Chicago *C, A*
Roosevelt University *M*
Sauk Valley Community College *C*
Waubonsee Community College *C*
Westwood College of Technology
  O'Hare *A*

Indiana

Indiana Business College *A*
Indiana Business College
  Muncie *A*
Indiana Institute of Technology *A, B*
Indiana University-Purdue University
  Fort Wayne *C*
Indiana University-Purdue University
  Indianapolis *A*
Purdue University
  Calumet *B*
Sawyer College: Merrillville *C, A*
Vincennes University *A*

Iowa

AIB College of Business *A*
Hawkeye Community College *C, A*
Indian Hills Community College *A*
Iowa Central Community College *A*
Iowa Lakes Community College *A*
Marshalltown Community College *A*
Northeast Iowa Community
  College *A*
Northwest Iowa Community
  College *A*
Southeastern Community College
  North Campus *A*
University of Northern Iowa *B*
Vatterott College *C, A*

Kansas

Brown Mackie College *A*
Cloud County Community College *A*
Coffeyville Community College *C, A*
Cowley County Community
  College *A*
Garden City Community College *A*
Johnson County Community
  College *A*
Kansas State University *B*
Labette Community College *C, A*

Kentucky

Beckfield College *C, A*
Big Sandy Community and Technical
  College *C, A*
Daymar College *A*
Hopkinsville Community College *C, A*

Louisiana

Remington College
  New Orleans *A*

Maryland

Anne Arundel Community College *C*
Carroll Community College *C, A*
DeVry University: Bethesda *M*
Howard Community College *C, A*
Morgan State University *B*
University of Maryland
  University College *M*

Massachusetts

Becker College *C, A, B*
Benjamin Franklin Institute of
  Technology *C*
Bristol Community College *C*
Bunker Hill Community College *C, A*
Cape Cod Community College *C, A*
Gibbs College *A*
Holyoke Community College *C*
Massasoit Community College *C*
Middlesex Community College *C, A*
Mount Wachusett Community
  College *C*
Roxbury Community College *C*

Michigan

Alpena Community College *A*
Baker College
  of Cadillac *A*
  of Clinton Township *A*
  of Muskegon *C, A*
  of Owosso *A*
  of Port Huron *C, A*
Calvin College *B*
Davenport University *A, B*
Delta College *C, A*
Grand Rapids Community College *C*
Kettering University *B*
Lansing Community College *A*
Macomb Community College *C, A*
Michigan Technological University *B*
Mott Community College *A*
Northern Michigan University *B*
Oakland Community College *C*

Walsh College of Accountancy and
  Business Administration *M*
Washtenaw Community College *C, A*

Minnesota

Alexandria Technical College *C, A*
Capella University *M, D*
Central Lakes College *A*
Dakota County Technical College *C, A*
Dunwoody College of
  Technology *C, A*
High-Tech Institute *A*
Inver Hills Community College *C, A*
Minneapolis Community and
  Technical College *C, A*
Minnesota School of Business *C, A*
Minnesota State College - Southeast
  Technical *C, A*
Minnesota State Community and
  Technical College - Fergus
  Falls *C, A*
Ridgewater College *C, A*
Rochester Community and Technical
  College *C*
St. Cloud Technical College *C, A*
University of Minnesota
  Twin Cities *B*

Mississippi

Antonelli College
  Jackson *A*
Copiah-Lincoln Community College *A*

Missouri

DeVry University
  Kansas City *A, B*
East Central College *C, A*
Harris-Stowe State University *B*
Mineral Area College *C, A*
Missouri Southern State University *A*
State Fair Community College *A*

Montana

Montana State University
  Billings *A*
Montana Tech of the University of
  Montana *C, A*
University of Great Falls *B*

Nebraska

University of Nebraska
  Kearney *B*

Nevada

Community College of Southern
  Nevada *C, A*
Great Basin College *A*

New Hampshire

Franklin Pierce College *B*
New Hampshire Community
  Technical College
  Manchester *C*
  Nashua *C, A*

New Jersey

Berkeley College *A*
Bloomfield College *B*
Cumberland County College *C, A*
DeVry University: North
  Brunswick *A, B*
Kean University *B*
Mercer County Community
  College *C, A*
Ocean County College *C*
Stevens Institute of
  Technology *B, M, D*

New Mexico

Clovis Community College *A*

New York

ASA Institute of Business and
  Computer Technology *C, A*
Briarcliffe College *C, A, B*
City University of New York
  Borough of Manhattan Community
    College *A*
DeVry Institute of Technology
  New York *B*
Genesee Community College *A*
Globe Institute of Technology *C, A, B*
Herkimer County Community
  College *A*
Hudson Valley Community College *A*
Iona College *M*
New York Institute of Technology *B*
Niagara County Community
  College *C*
Onondaga Community College *A*
Pace University *M*
Polytechnic University *M*
Rochester Institute of
  Technology *B, M*
State University of New York
  College of Agriculture and
    Technology at Cobleskill *A*
Syracuse University *M*
Wood Tobe-Coburn School *A*

North Carolina

Beaufort County Community
  College *C, A*
Central Carolina Community
  College *A*
Cleveland Community College *C, A*
College of the Albemarle *A*
Craven Community College *A*
Davidson County Community
  College *C, A*
DeVry University: Charlotte *M*
Edgecombe Community College *A*
Haywood Community College *C, A*
Isothermal Community College *C, A*
North Carolina State University *M*
Randolph Community College *A*
Richmond Community College *C, A*
South Piedmont Community
  College *C, A*
Southwestern Community College *A*
University of North Carolina
  Greensboro *B, M, D*

North Dakota

Bismarck State College *A*
Lake Region State College *C, A*

Ohio

AEC Southern Ohio College
  Brown Mackie College: Akron *A*
Baldwin-Wallace College *B*
Cincinnati State Technical and
  Community College *A*
DeVry University
  Columbus *B*
Edison State Community College *A*
Hocking College *A*
James A. Rhodes State College *A*
Kent State University
  Trumbull Campus *C*
Marion Technical College *A*
Remington College
  Cleveland *A*
Stark State College of Technology *A*
University of Akron: Wayne College *A*
University of Cincinnati
  Clermont College *C, A*

Oklahoma

Northeastern State University *B*
Oklahoma State University *B, M, D*
Oklahoma State University
  Okmulgee *A*
Rose State College *A*

Southern Nazarene University *B*
University of Oklahoma *M*

Oregon

Clatsop Community College *A*
Portland Community College *C*

Pennsylvania

Berks Technical Institute *A*
Bucks County Community
    College *C, A*
Community College of Beaver
    County *A*
Community College of Philadelphia *A*
Delaware County Community
    College *A*
Erie Business Center *A*
Harrisburg Area Community
    College *C, A*
Holy Family University *M*
Keystone College *B*
Lehigh Valley College *A*
Luzerne County Community
    College *C*
Northampton County Area
    Community College *A*
Pennsylvania College of
    Technology *A, B*
Reading Area Community College *A*
South Hills School of Business &
    Technology *C, A*
University of Pennsylvania *B, M*
University of Pittsburgh *M*
Waynesburg College *B*
York Technical Institute *C*

Rhode Island

Community College of Rhode
    Island *C, A*

South Carolina

Midlands Technical College *C*
York Technical College *C*

South Dakota

Northern State University *A*
Southeast Technical Institute *A*

Texas

Austin Community College *A*
Brookhaven College *C*
Cedar Valley College *C, A*
Central Texas College *C, A*
Collin County Community College
    District *C, A*
DeVry University
    Irving *A, B*
Eastfield College *C, A*
Hallmark Institute of Technology *A*
Lamar State College at Orange *C*
Mountain View College *C, A*
Northwest Vista College *C, A*
Remington College
    Fort Worth *A*
    Houston *A*
South Texas College *A*
Texas State Technical College
    West Texas *C, A*
Texas State Technical College:
    Marshall *C, A*
Texas Tech University *M*
Victoria College *C, A*
Westwood College: Ft. Worth *A*

Utah

Stevens-Henager College *A*
Utah Valley State College *C*
Weber State University *C, A, B*

Vermont

Champlain College *C, A, B*
Vermont Technical College *A, B*

Virginia

DeVry University
    Arlington *B*
ECPI College of Technology *C, A*
Hampton University *B*
J. Sargeant Reynolds Community
    College *C*
Mountain Empire Community
    College *A*
New River Community College *A*
Thomas Nelson Community
    College *A*
Tidewater Community College *A*

Washington

Bellevue Community College *C, A*
Centralia College *C, A*
Clark College *C, A*
Clover Park Technical College *C, A*
DeVry University
    Federal Way *A, M*
Everett Community College *A*
Grays Harbor College *C*
Lower Columbia College *A*
Olympic College *A*
Peninsula College *A*
Renton Technical College *C, A*
Seattle Pacific University *B*
Shoreline Community College *C, A*
Spokane Falls Community College *C*
Wenatchee Valley College *C, A*
Yakima Valley Community College *A*

West Virginia

Mountain State University *B*

Wisconsin

DeVry University: Milwaukee *M*
Gateway Technical College *A*
Herzing College *A, B*
Lakeshore Technical College *A*
Mid-State Technical College *A*
Milwaukee Area Technical College *A*
Northeast Wisconsin Technical
    College *A*
Southwest Wisconsin Technical
    College *A*
University of Wisconsin
    Stout *B*
Western Wisconsin Technical
    College *A*
Wisconsin Indianhead Technical
    College *A*

Wyoming

Casper College *A*
Eastern Wyoming College *C*

Computer programming, general

Alabama

Calhoun Community College *A*
Enterprise-Ozark Community
    College *C*
Gadsden State Community College *A*
J. F. Drake State Technical College *A*
Northwest-Shoals Community
    College *A*
Wallace State Community College at
    Hanceville *A*

Alaska

University of Alaska
    Southeast *C*

Arizona

Central Arizona College *C, A*
Eastern Arizona College *C*
Gateway Community College *C*
Mohave Community College *C*

South Mountain Community
    College *C*
University of Phoenix *B*

Arkansas

Northwest Arkansas Community
    College *A*
Pulaski Technical College *A*
Rich Mountain Community College *A*
South Arkansas Community College *A*
Southern Arkansas University
    Tech *C, A*
University of Arkansas
    Little Rock *A*

California

Antelope Valley College *C, A*
Barstow College *C, A*
California Lutheran University *B*
Canada College *A*
Cerritos Community College *A*
Chabot College *A*
City College of San Francisco *C, A*
College of Marin: Kentfield *A*
College of the Canyons *A*
College of the Redwoods *C*
College of the Siskiyous *C*
Columbia College *A*
Cosumnes River College *C, A*
Crafton Hills College *C, A*
Cypress College *C*
De Anza College *C, A*
East Los Angeles College *A*
Evergreen Valley College *C*
Foothill College *C, A*
Fresno City College *A*
Gavilan Community College *C*
Grossmont Community College *C, A*
Irvine Valley College *C, A*
Los Angeles Mission College *C*
Los Angeles Pierce College *C*
Los Angeles Southwest College *A*
Merced College *A*
MiraCosta College *C, A*
Modesto Junior College *A*
Monterey Peninsula College *A*
Ohlone College *C, A*
Pasadena City College *C, A*
Riverside Community College *C, A*
Saddleback College *C, A*
San Diego Mesa College *C, A*
San Joaquin Delta College *C, A*
San Joaquin Valley College Inc. *A*
San Jose City College *C, A*
Santa Ana College *C, A*
Santa Barbara City College *C*
Santa Monica College *C, A*
Santa Rosa Junior College *C*
Sierra College *C, A*
Solano Community College *C, A*
Sonoma State University *B*
Southwestern College *C, A*
Ventura College *A*
Victor Valley College *C*
West Valley College *C, A*
Westwood College *A*
Westwood College of Technology
    Westwood College: Los Angeles *A*

Colorado

CollegeAmerica-Denver *A*
Colorado Technical University *C*
Jones International University *C, B*
Northeastern Junior College *A*
Red Rocks Community College *C, A*
Trinidad State Junior College *A*
Westwood College of Technology *A*

Connecticut

Capital Community College *C*
Northwestern Connecticut
    Community College *C, A*
Norwalk Community College *A*

Tunxis Community College *C*
University of New Haven *C*

Delaware

Delaware Technical and Community
    College
    Owens Campus *A*
    Stanton/Wilmington Campus *A*
    Terry Campus *A*
Wilmington College *B*

District of Columbia

Southeastern University *A, B, M*

Florida

Art Institute of Fort Lauderdale *A, B*
Brevard Community College *A*
Broward Community College *C, A*
Daytona Beach Community College *A*
Edison College *A*
Florida Career College: Hialeah *A*
Florida Career College: Pembroke
    Pines *A*
Florida Community College at
    Jacksonville *C, A*
Florida Keys Community College *A*
Florida Metropolitan University
    Tampa College *A, B*
Florida National College *A*
Florida Technical College
    Deland *A*
Gulf Coast Community College *A*
Herzing College
    Orlando *A*
Hillsborough Community College *A*
Indian River Community College *A*
Lake City Community College *A*
Manatee Community College *C, A*
New England Institute of
    Technology *A*
Okaloosa-Walton Community *C, A*
Palm Beach Community College *A*
Pasco-Hernando Community
    College *A*
Pensacola Junior College *A*
Polk Community College *A*
Remington College: Largo *A*
St. Johns River Community College *A*
St. Petersburg College *A*
Santa Fe Community College *A*
Seminole Community College *A*
South Florida Community
    College *C, A*
Tallahassee Community College *C, A*
Valencia Community College *A*

Georgia

Abraham Baldwin Agricultural
    College *C*
Athens Technical College *C, A*
Clayton State University *B*
Darton College *A*
DeKalb Technical College *A*
Gwinnett Technical College *A*
Macon State College *A, B*
Middle Georgia College *A*
Northwestern Technical College *C, A*
Savannah Technical College *A*
South Georgia College *A*
Waycross College *A*

Idaho

North Idaho College *A*

Illinois

Black Hawk College *C, A*
Black Hawk College
    East Campus *A*
Blackburn College *B*
City Colleges of Chicago
    Olive-Harvey College *C, A*
Danville Area Community
    College *C, A*

Heartland Community College *C*
Highland Community College *A*
Illinois Central College *A*
Illinois Valley Community College *C*
Joliet Junior College *A*
Lincoln Land Community College *C, A*
Moraine Valley Community College *C*
Morton College *C*
Northwestern Business College *A*
Olivet Nazarene University *B*
Prairie State College *A*
Richland Community College *A*
Rock Valley College *C*
Sauk Valley Community College *A*
South Suburban College of Cook
County *C*
Southwestern Illinois College *A*
University of Illinois
Urbana-Champaign *B, M, D*
Westwood College of Technology
O'Hare *A*
River Oaks *A*
William Rainey Harper College *C, A*

Indiana

Indiana University
East *A*
South Bend *A*
Southeast *A*
Purdue University
Calumet *B*
Sawyer College: Merrillville *A*
Tri-State University *A*
University of Evansville *B*
Vincennes University *A*

Iowa

AIB College of Business *A*
Ellsworth Community College *A*
Grand View College *B*
Hamilton College *A*
Hamilton College
Cedar Falls *A*
Iowa Western Community College *A*
Maharishi University of
Management *C*
Morningside College *B*
Northeast Iowa Community
College *A*
Southeastern Community College
North Campus *A*
Southwestern Community College *A*
Vatterott College *C, A*

Kansas

Cloud County Community College *A*
Donnelly College *C, A*
Kansas State University *A, M*
Labette Community College *A*
McPherson College *B*
Seward County Community
College *C, A*
Southwestern College *B*

Kentucky

Big Sandy Community and Technical
College *C, A*
Hopkinsville Community College *C, A*
Maysville Community College *C, A*

Maine

Andover College *C, A*
Eastern Maine Community College *C*
Husson College *A, B*
Northern Maine Community
College *A*
University of Maine
Fort Kent *B*
University of Southern Maine *B*

Maryland

Cecil Community College *C*
College of Southern Maryland *C, A*

Community College of Baltimore
County *A*
Hagerstown Business College *A*
Hagerstown Community College *C*
Harford Community College *C*
Montgomery College *C, A*
Prince George's Community
College *C, A*
University of Maryland
University College *C*

Massachusetts

Benjamin Franklin Institute of
Technology *A*
Berkshire Community College *C*
Bristol Community College *C, A*
Bunker Hill Community College *C*
Fitchburg State College *C*
Massachusetts College of Liberal
Arts *B*
Massasoit Community College *A*
Newbury College *C, A*
North Shore Community College *C, A*
Northern Essex Community
College *C, A*
Quinsigamond Community
College *C, A*
Simon's Rock College of Bard *B*
Tufts University *B*
Wentworth Institute of Technology *C*

Michigan

Baker College
of Auburn Hills *A*
of Cadillac *A*
of Clinton Township *A*
of Flint *A*
of Jackson *A*
of Muskegon *A*
of Owosso *A*
of Port Huron *A*
Calvin College *B*
Delta College *A*
Gogebic Community College *A*
Grand Rapids Community College *C*
Grand Valley State University *B*
Jackson Community College *C, A*
Kalamazoo Valley Community
College *A*
Kellogg Community College *C, A*
Lansing Community College *A*
Macomb Community College *C, A*
Monroe County Community
College *A*
Mott Community College *C*
Northern Michigan University *B*
Oakland Community College *C, A*
Schoolcraft College *A*
Southwestern Michigan College *A*
University of Michigan
Dearborn *B*
Washtenaw Community College *C, A*
Wayne County Community College *A*

Minnesota

Academy College *A*
Alexandria Technical College *C, A*
Anoka-Ramsey Community College *C*
Central Lakes College *A*
Dakota County Technical College *C, A*
Globe College *C, A*
Hennepin Technical College *C, A*
Inver Hills Community College *A*
Lake Superior College *C, A*
Mesabi Range Community and
Technical College *C, A*
Minneapolis Community and
Technical College *C, A*
Minnesota School of Business *C, A*
Minnesota State Community and
Technical College - Fergus
Falls *C, A*
National American University
St. Paul *A, B*

Normandale Community College *A*
Pine Technical College *A*
St. Cloud Technical College *C, A*
St. Paul College *A*
South Central College *A*
Winona State University *B*

Mississippi

East Central Community College *A*
Holmes Community College *A*
Itawamba Community College *A*
Meridian Community College *A*
Mississippi Delta Community
College *A*

Missouri

Hickey College *A*
Mineral Area College *A*
Missouri Southern State
University *C, A, B*
Missouri Technical School *C, A, B*
Moberly Area Community
College *C, A*
St. Charles Community College *C, A*
St. Louis Community College
St. Louis Community College at
Florissant Valley *A*
Southeast Missouri State University *B*
State Fair Community College *A*
Vatterott College *C, A*
Vatterott College: Springfield *C*

Montana

Helena College of Technology of the
University of Montana *A*
Montana Tech of the University of
Montana *B*
University of Great Falls *B*

Nebraska

Creighton University *B*
Hamilton College: Lincoln *A*
Metropolitan Community College *A*
Midland Lutheran College *B*
Northeast Community College *A*
Peru State College *B*
Western Nebraska Community
College *A*

Nevada

Community College of Southern
Nevada *A*
Truckee Meadows Community
College *A*

New Hampshire

Daniel Webster College *C*
New Hampshire Community
Technical College
Manchester *C*
Stratham *C, A, D*

New Jersey

Atlantic Cape Community College *A*
Bloomfield College *C*
Essex County College *A*
Fairleigh Dickinson University
Metropolitan Campus *C*
Middlesex County College *A*
Ocean County College *C*
Raritan Valley Community
College *C, A*
St. Peter's College *C, A, B*
Salem Community College *C*
Union County College *C*

New Mexico

Clovis Community College *A*
New Mexico Junior College *A*
New Mexico State University
Grants *A*

New York

ASA Institute of Business and
Computer Technology *C, A*
Adirondack Community College *A*
Bramson ORT College *A*
Briarcliffe College *C, A, B*
Cayuga County Community College *C*
City University of New York
Borough of Manhattan Community
College *A*
Brooklyn College *C*
College of Staten Island *A*
LaGuardia Community College *A*
Queensborough Community
College *C, A*
College of Saint Rose *C*
College of Westchester *C, A*
Corning Community College *A*
Dutchess Community College *C*
Excelsior College *A*
Finger Lakes Community College *A*
Globe Institute of Technology *C, A, B*
Ithaca College *B*
Jamestown Community College *A*
Medaille College *B*
Mohawk Valley Community College *A*
Nassau Community College *A*
Rochester Business Institute *C, A*
Rockland Community College *A*
Schenectady County Community
College *C, A*
State University of New York
College at Buffalo *B*
College of Agriculture and
Technology at Cobleskill *A*
College of Agriculture and
Technology at Morrisville *A*
College of Technology at Canton *B*
Farmingdale *C, A, B*
Utica School of Commerce *A*
Wood Tobe-Coburn School *A*

North Carolina

Alamance Community College *C, A*
Beaufort County Community
College *C, A*
Belmont Abbey College *B*
Bladen Community College *C, A*
Blue Ridge Community College *A*
Brunswick Community College *C, A*
Caldwell Community College and
Technical Institute *A*
Catawba Valley Community College *A*
Central Carolina Community
College *A*
Central Piedmont Community
College *C, A*
Cleveland Community College *C, A*
College of the Albemarle *A*
Davidson County Community
College *C, A*
Durham Technical Community
College *C, A*
Fayetteville Technical Community
College *C, A*
Gaston College *C, A*
Johnston Community College *A*
Lenoir Community College *A*
Mayland Community College *C*
McDowell Technical Community
College *A*
Mitchell Community College *C, A*
Piedmont Community College *A*
Rowan-Cabarrus Community
College *C, A*
Sandhills Community College *C, A*
South Piedmont Community
College *A*
Southwestern Community
College *C, A*
Stanly Community College *C, A*
Wake Technical Community
College *C, A*
Wilkes Community College *C, A*

Wilson Technical Community
College *A*

North Dakota

Aakers College: Fargo *C, A*
Minot State University *C*

Ohio

AEC Southern Ohio College
Brown Mackie College: Akron *C, A*
Belmont Technical College *A*
Bowling Green State University:
Firelands College *A*
Bradford School *C, A*
Cincinnati Christian University *B*
Cleveland Institute of Electronics *C*
Columbus State Community
College *C, A*
Edison State Community College *C, A*
Hocking College *A*
James A. Rhodes State College *C, A*
Lakeland Community College *C, A*
Marion Technical College *A*
Ohio Business College: Sandusky *A*
Southern State Community College *A*
Stark State College of Technology *A*
Technology Education College *A*
Tiffin University *A*
University of Cincinnati
Clermont College *A*
University of Toledo *A*
Washington State Community
College *A*
Youngstown State University *A, B, M*

Oklahoma

Eastern Oklahoma State College *A*
Northeastern Oklahoma Agricultural
and Mechanical College *C, A*
Northwestern Oklahoma State
University *B*
Oklahoma City Community College *A*
Oklahoma State University
Okmulgee *A*
St. Gregory's University *A*
Tulsa Community College *C, A*
Vatterott College *C, A*
Vatterott College
Tulsa *C*
Western Oklahoma State College *A*

Oregon

Chemeketa Community College *A*
Lane Community College *A*
Northwest Christian College *B*
Southern Oregon University *B*

Pennsylvania

Academy of Medical Arts and
Business *C, A*
Arcadia University *B*
Berks Technical Institute *A*
Bucks County Community
College *C, A*
Butler County Community College *A*
CHI Institute: Southampton *C, A*
Delaware Valley College *C, A*
Erie Business Center *A*
Gannon University *B*
Gwynedd-Mercy College *A*
ICM School of Business & Medical
Careers *A*
Keystone College *A*
La Salle University *A, B*
Laurel Business Institute *A*
Metropolitan Career Center Computer
Technology Institute *A*
Montgomery County Community
College *C, A*
Northampton County Area
Community College *C, A*
Pennco Tech *A*

Pennsylvania Highlands Community
College *A*
Pittsburgh Technical Institute *A*
Reading Area Community College *A*
St. Francis University *B*
South Hills School of Business &
Technology *C, A*
Tri-State Business Institute *A*
Westminster College *B*
Westmoreland County Community
College *A*

Puerto Rico

American University of Puerto Rico *A*
Atlantic College *A*
National College of Business &
Technology: Bayamon *A, B*
Pontifical Catholic University of
Puerto Rico *A*
Universidad Metropolitana *C*

Rhode Island

Johnson & Wales University *A*
New England Institute of
Technology *A*

South Carolina

Aiken Technical College *C*
Central Carolina Technical College *A*
Charleston Southern University *B*
Greenville Technical College *C*
Limestone College *A, B*
Midlands Technical College *C*
Orangeburg-Calhoun Technical
College *A*
Piedmont Technical College *C*
Technical College of the
Lowcountry *C, A*
Tri-County Technical College *A*
Trident Technical College *A*
York Technical College *A*

South Dakota

Lake Area Technical Institute *A*
Mount Marty College *B*
Southeast Technical Institute *A*

Tennessee

Chattanooga State Technical
Community College *A*
Northeast State Technical Community
College *C*
Southern Adventist University *B*
Tennessee State University *B*

Texas

Alvin Community College *C, A*
Amarillo College *C, A*
Austin Community College *C, A*
Brazosport College *C, A*
Brookhaven College *C, A*
Cedar Valley College *C, A*
Central Texas College *C, A*
Coastal Bend College *A*
College of the Mainland *A*
Collin County Community College
District *C, A*
Del Mar College *C, A*
Eastfield College *C, A*
El Centro College *C, A*
El Paso Community College *A*
Galveston College *C, A*
Grayson County College *A*
Hardin-Simmons University *B*
Hill College *A*
Houston Community College
System *A*
Kilgore College *A*
Laredo Community College *A*
Lee College *C, A*
McLennan Community College *A*
Midland College *A*
Mountain View College *C, A*

North Lake College *C*
Northeast Texas Community
College *A*
Northwest Vista College *C, A*
Odessa College *C, A*
Palo Alto College *A*
Remington College
Houston *A*
St. Philip's College *C, A*
San Antonio College *C, A*
San Jacinto College
North *C, A*
Tarrant County College *C, A*
Temple College *C, A*
Texas Southmost College *C*
Texas State Technical College
Harlingen *A*
Waco *A*
West Texas *A*
Texas State University: San Marcos *M*
Trinity Valley Community College *C, A*
Victoria College *C, A*
Weatherford College *A*
Western Texas College *A*
Wharton County Junior College *A*

Utah

Everest College: Salt Lake City *A*
Provo College *A*
Stevens-Henager College *A*
Utah Valley State College *C*

Vermont

Champlain College *A*
Vermont Technical College *A, B*

Virginia

Blue Ridge Community College *A*
Danville Community College *A*
ECPI College of Technology *C, A*
J. Sargeant Reynolds Community
College *C, A*
John Tyler Community College *A*
Lord Fairfax Community College *A*
New River Community College *A*
Northern Virginia Community
College *A*
Patrick Henry Community College *A*
Piedmont Virginia Community
College *A*
Thomas Nelson Community
College *C, A*

Washington

Bates Technical College *A*
Bellevue Community College *C, A*
Big Bend Community College *A*
Centralia College *A*
City University *C, B*
Clark College *A*
Clover Park Technical College *C, A*
Columbia Basin College *A*
Edmonds Community College *C, A*
Everett Community College *C, A*
Lower Columbia College *A*
North Seattle Community
College *C, A*
Olympic College *A*
Pierce College *C, A*
Renton Technical College *A*
Seattle Central Community
College *C, A*
Skagit Valley College *A*
South Seattle Community
College *C, A*
Walla Walla College *A*

West Virginia

Huntington Junior College *A*
Potomac State College of West Virginia
University *A*
West Virginia University Institute of
Technology *B*

Wisconsin

Blackhawk Technical College *A*
Chippewa Valley Technical College *A*
Gateway Technical College *A*
Herzing College *A, B*
Lakeshore Technical College *A*
Madison Area Technical College *A*
Mid-State Technical College *A*
Milwaukee Area Technical College *A*
Nicolet Area Technical College *A*
Northcentral Technical College *A*
Northeast Wisconsin Technical
College *A*
Silver Lake College *C*
Southwest Wisconsin Technical
College *A*

Wyoming

Casper College *A*
Laramie County Community
College *A*

Computer programming, specific applications

Alabama

Calhoun Community College *A*
Enterprise-Ozark Community
College *A*
Gadsden State Community College *C*
Northwest-Shoals Community
College *C, A*

Alaska

University of Alaska
Anchorage *A*
Southeast *C*

Arizona

Central Arizona College *A*
Chandler-Gilbert Community College
Williams Campus *A*
Collins College *A*
Estrella Mountain Community
College *C, A*
Gateway Community College *C*
Glendale Community College *C, A*
Mesa Community College *A*
South Mountain Community
College *C*

Arkansas

National Park Community
College *C, A*
North Arkansas College *C*
South Arkansas Community College *A*
University of Arkansas
Fort Smith *C*

California

Bakersfield College *A*
Barstow College *A*
Butte College *C, A*
Canada College *A*
Cerritos Community College *A*
Chabot College *A*
Chaffey College *C, A*
City College of San Francisco *A*
College of the Siskiyous *C, A*
Contra Costa College *A*
De Anza College *C, A*
Evergreen Valley College *A*
Fullerton College *A*
Grossmont Community College *C, A*
Irvine Valley College *C, A*
Lassen College *A*
Long Beach City College *C, A*
Los Angeles City College *A*
Los Angeles Harbor College *C, A*
Los Angeles Pierce College *C, A*
Los Angeles Southwest College *A*

Los Angeles Valley College *C, A*
Merced College *A*
Mission College *A*
Moorpark College *A*
Mount San Antonio College *C*
Pasadena City College *A*
Saddleback College *C*
San Diego City College *C, A*
San Joaquin Valley College Inc. *A*
San Jose City College *C, A*
Shasta College *A*
Southwestern College *C, A*
Ventura College *A*
West Hills Community College *C, A*
Westwood College of Technology
    Inland Empire *A*

Colorado

National American University
    Denver *A, B*
Westwood College of Technology *A*

Connecticut

Asnuntuck Community College *C*
Capital Community College *C*
Norwalk Community College *A*
Quinnipiac University *B*
Three Rivers Community College *A*
Tunxis Community College *C, A*

Florida

Edison College *C*
Florida Community College at
    Jacksonville *A*
Gulf Coast Community College *A*
Hillsborough Community College *C*
Indian River Community College *A*
Miami Dade College *C, A*
Palm Beach Community College *A*
Pasco-Hernando Community
    College *A*
St. Petersburg College *C*
Seminole Community College *A*

Georgia

Abraham Baldwin Agricultural
    College *A*
Athens Technical College *C, A*
Augusta Technical Institute *C, A*
Chattahoochee Technical College *C, A*
Dalton State College *C, A*
Darton College *A*
Georgia Southwestern State
    University *A*
Macon State College *A, B*
Middle Georgia College *A*
South Georgia College *A*

Idaho

Idaho State University *C, A*
North Idaho College *A*

Illinois

Black Hawk College *C*
City Colleges of Chicago
    Wright College *C, A*
College of DuPage *C, A*
Elgin Community College *A*
Illinois Central College *A*
Illinois Valley Community College *A*
John Wood Community College *C, A*
Kankakee Community College *A*
Kishwaukee College *A*
McHenry County College *C, A*
Moraine Valley Community
    College *C, A*
National-Louis University *C*
Northwestern Business College *A*
Parkland College *C, A*
Prairie State College *C, A*
Rend Lake College *C, A*
Robert Morris College: Chicago *A*
Sauk Valley Community College *C, A*

Southwestern Illinois College *C, A*
Triton College *C, A*
Waubonsee Community College *C*
William Rainey Harper College *C, A*

Indiana

Indiana Wesleyan University *A, B*
Professional Careers Institute *A*
Purdue University
    North Central Campus *A*
Vincennes University *A*

Iowa

Des Moines Area Community
    College *C, A*
Indian Hills Community College *A*
Iowa Lakes Community College *A*
Kirkwood Community College *A*
Northeast Iowa Community
    College *A*
Scott Community College *A*
Southeastern Community College
    North Campus *C*
Southwestern Community College *A*

Kansas

Central Christian College of Kansas *A*
Johnson County Community
    College *C, A*
Seward County Community
    College *C, A*

Kentucky

Sullivan University *C, A, B, M*
West Kentucky Community and
    Technical College *A*

Louisiana

Southern University
    New Orleans *A*
    Shreveport *A*

Maine

Husson College *B*
Northern Maine Community
    College *A*
University of Southern Maine *B*

Maryland

Community College of Baltimore
    County *C, A*
Frederick Community College *C, A*
Harford Community College *C*

Massachusetts

Bristol Community College *C*
Bunker Hill Community College *A*
Cape Cod Community College *A*
Holyoke Community College *A*
Roxbury Community College *A*
Springfield Technical Community
    College *C, A*

Michigan

Baker College
    of Cadillac *A*
    of Muskegon *A*
    of Port Huron *A*
Jackson Community College *C, A*
Lansing Community College *A*
Mid Michigan Community College *A*
Monroe County Community
    College *C, A*
Washtenaw Community College *C, A*
Western Michigan University *B*

Minnesota

Dakota County Technical College *C, A*
Dunwoody College of Technology *A*
Globe College *C, A*
Hennepin Technical College *C, A*
Lake Superior College *C, A*

Minneapolis Business College *A*
Minneapolis Community and
    Technical College *C*
Minnesota State College - Southeast
    Technical *C*
Ridgewater College *C*
St. Cloud Technical College *C, A*
St. Paul College *A*
Winona State University *B*

Mississippi

East Central Community College *A*
Pearl River Community College *A*

Missouri

Grantham University *A, B*
Longview Community College *C, A*
Maple Woods Community
    College *C, A*
St. Louis Community College
    St. Louis Community College at
        Florissant Valley *A*
    St. Louis Community College at
        Meramec *C, A*
State Fair Community College *A*

Montana

Montana Tech of the University of
    Montana *B*
University of Great Falls *B*

Nebraska

Hamilton College: Lincoln *A*
Northeast Community College *A*

Nevada

Morrison University *A*

New Hampshire

Daniel Webster College *C*
New Hampshire Community
    Technical College
    Nashua *A*

New Jersey

Bergen Community College *A*
Burlington County College *C*
Camden County College *C*
Middlesex County College *C*
Passaic County Community
    College *C, A*
Sussex County Community College *A*
Union County College *C*

New Mexico

New Mexico Junior College *A*
Northern New Mexico College *C*

New York

Bramson ORT College *A*
College of Westchester *C, A*
Columbia-Greene Community
    College *C, A*
Globe Institute of Technology *C, A, B*
State University of New York
    College of Agriculture and
        Technology at Cobleskill *A*
    College of Agriculture and
        Technology at Morrisville *A*
    Farmingdale *C*

North Carolina

Alamance Community College *A*
Asheville-Buncombe Technical
    Community College *A*
Beaufort County Community
    College *C, A*
Bladen Community College *C, A*
Caldwell Community College and
    Technical Institute *C, A*
Campbell University *A*

Central Carolina Community
    College *A*
Cleveland Community College *C, A*
College of the Albemarle *A*
Craven Community College *A*
Durham Technical Community
    College *C, A*
Forsyth Technical Community
    College *A*
Gaston College *A*
Haywood Community College *C, A*
Isothermal Community College *C, A*
James Sprunt Community
    College *C, A*
King's College *A*
McDowell Technical Community
    College *A*
Piedmont Community College *A*
Pitt Community College *C, A*
Sampson Community College *A*
Sandhills Community College *A*
South Piedmont Community
    College *C, A*
Surry Community College *C, A*
Wake Technical Community
    College *C, A*
Wilson Technical Community
    College *A*

North Dakota

Cankdeska Cikana Community
    College *C, A*
North Dakota State College of
    Science *A*
Sitting Bull College *A*

Ohio

Central Ohio Technical College *A*
Cincinnati State Technical and
    Community College *A*
James A. Rhodes State College *C*
Jefferson Community College *C, A*
Kent State University *C*
Kent State University
    Ashtabula Regional Campus *A*
    East Liverpool Regional Campus *A*
    Salem Regional Campus *A*
    Trumbull Campus *C, A*
    Tuscarawas Campus *A*
Marion Technical College *A*
Owens Community College
    Toledo *C, A*
Sinclair Community College *C, A*
Southern State Community College *A*
Stark State College of Technology *A*
Technology Education College *C, A*
Trumbull Business College *A*
University of Akron: Wayne College *A*
University of Cincinnati
    Clermont College *A*
University of Northwestern Ohio *C, A*

Oklahoma

Northeastern Oklahoma Agricultural
    and Mechanical College *A*
Oklahoma Baptist University *B*
Oklahoma State University
    Oklahoma City *A*
    Okmulgee *A*
St. Gregory's University *A*
Tulsa Community College *A*

Oregon

Chemeketa Community College *A*
Clatsop Community College *A*
George Fox University *B*
Linn-Benton Community College *A*
Southwestern Oregon Community
    College *C, A*

Pennsylvania

Community College of Beaver
    County *A*

Community College of Philadelphia *A*
Delaware County Community
   College *C, A*
Grove City College *B*
ICM School of Business & Medical
   Careers *A*
International Academy of Design and
   Technology: Pittsburgh *A*
La Salle University *B, M*
Lehigh Valley College *A*
Manor College *C, A*
Mount Aloysius College *A*
Peirce College *C, A*
Pennsylvania College of Technology *A*
South Hills School of Business &
   Technology *C, A*

Puerto Rico

Universidad del Este *C, A, B*

Rhode Island

Community College of Rhode
   Island *C, A*

South Carolina

York Technical College *A*

South Dakota

Southeast Technical Institute *A*

Tennessee

Southwest Tennessee Community
   College *C*

Texas

Eastfield College *A*
Hill College *A*
Remington College
   Houston *A*
Richland College *A*
Tyler Junior College *A*

Utah

Everest College: Salt Lake City *C, A*
Southern Utah University *A*
Weber State University *C*

Virginia

ECPI College of Technology *C, A*
Piedmont Virginia Community
   College *A*

Washington

Heritage University *C*
Peninsula College *A*
Renton Technical College *C, A*
Seattle Central Community
   College *C, A*
Skagit Valley College *A*
South Puget Sound Community
   College *C, A*
Spokane Community College *C, A*
Spokane Falls Community College *C*

West Virginia

Davis and Elkins College *B*
Mountain State College *A*
Potomac State College of West Virginia
   University *A*
Shepherd University *B*

Wisconsin

Chippewa Valley Technical College *A*
Fox Valley Technical College *A*
Gateway Technical College *A*
Moraine Park Technical College *A*
Western Wisconsin Technical
   College *A*

Computer science

Alabama

Alabama State University *B*
American Sentinel University *B, M*
Bevill State Community College *A*
Birmingham-Southern College *B*
Gadsden State Community College *A*
Huntingdon College *B*
Lawson State Community
   College *C, A*
Northeast Alabama Community
   College *A*
Oakwood College *B*
Samford University *B*

Alaska

University of Alaska
   Anchorage *B*
   Fairbanks *B, M*

Arizona

Arizona State University *B, M, D*
Chaparral College *B*
Cochise College *A*
Dine College *A*
Gateway Community College *C*
Grand Canyon University *B*
Mesa Community College *A*
Mohave Community College *C*
Northern Arizona University *B*
Paradise Valley Community College *C*

Arkansas

Harding University *B*
Hendrix College *B*
John Brown University *B*
Lyon College *B*
Ouachita Baptist University *B*
Philander Smith College *B*
Phillips Community College of the
   University of Arkansas *A*
Pulaski Technical College *A*
South Arkansas Community
   College *C, A*
Southern Arkansas University
   Tech *C, A*
University of Central Arkansas *B, M*

California

Antelope Valley College *C, A*
Biola University *B*
California Institute of
   Technology *B, M, D*
California Lutheran University *B*
California National University for
   Advanced Studies *B*
California Polytechnic State
   University: San Luis Obispo *B*
California State Polytechnic
   University: Pomona *B, M*
California State University
   Bakersfield *B*
   Chico *B, M*
   East Bay *B, M*
   Fresno *B, M*
   Fullerton *B, M*
   Long Beach *B, M*
   Sacramento *B, M*
   San Bernardino *B, M*
   San Marcos *B, M*
   Stanislaus *B*
Chabot College *A*
Chapman University *B*
Claremont McKenna College *B*
College of the Canyons *C, A*
College of the Desert *A*
College of the Sequoias *C, A*
College of the Siskiyous *A*
Columbia College *C*
Copper Mountain College *C, A*
Cuesta College *C, A*
De Anza College *A*

Diablo Valley College *C, A*
El Camino College *C, A*
Feather River College *A*
Foothill College *A*
Fresno City College *C, A*
Fresno Pacific University *B*
Golden West College *C*
Grossmont Community College *C, A*
La Sierra University *B*
Lake Tahoe Community College *C*
Las Positas College *A*
Los Angeles Pierce College *C, A*
Los Angeles Southwest College *C, A*
Los Angeles Trade and Technical
   College *C, A*
Los Medanos College *C*
Loyola Marymount University *M*
Merced College *A*
MiraCosta College *A*
Mission College *A*
Modesto Junior College *A*
Napa Valley College *C*
National University *B, M*
Notre Dame de Namur University *B*
Pacific States University *B, M*
Pacific Union College *B*
Palomar College *C, A*
Point Loma Nazarene University *B*
Pomona College *B*
Reedley College *A*
Saddleback College *A*
San Bernardino Valley College *C, A*
San Francisco State University *B, M*
San Joaquin Delta College *C, A*
San Jose State University *B, M*
Santa Ana College *C, A*
Santa Barbara City College *C, A*
Santa Monica College *C*
Santa Rosa Junior College *C, A*
Santiago Canyon College *A*
Scripps College *B*
Skyline College *A*
Sonoma State University *B*
Southwestern College *C, A*
Stanford University *B, M, D*
Taft College *A*
University of California
   Berkeley *B, M, D*
   Davis *B*
   Irvine *B*
   Riverside *B, M, D*
   San Diego *B, M, D*
   Santa Cruz *B, M, D*
University of San Diego *B*
University of Southern
   California *B, M, D*
University of the Pacific *B*
Westmont College *B*
Yuba Community College
   District *C, A*

Colorado

CollegeAmerica-Denver *B*
Colorado School of Mines *B*
Colorado Technical University *B, M, D*
Fort Lewis College *B*
Heritage College *C, A*
Jones International University *C, B*
Metropolitan State College of
   Denver *B*
Northeastern Junior College *A*
Regis University *B*
Trinidad State Junior College *A*
United States Air Force Academy *B*
University of Colorado
   Boulder *B, M, D*
   Colorado Springs *B, M, D*
University of Denver *B, M, D*

Connecticut

Connecticut College *B*
Fairfield University *B*
Quinnipiac University *B, M*
Sacred Heart University *B, M*

St. Joseph College *B*
Trinity College *B*
University of Connecticut *B*
University of New Haven *A*

Delaware

Delaware State University *B*
Delaware Technical and Community
   College
   Terry Campus *A*

District of Columbia

American University *B, M*
Gallaudet University *B*
Georgetown University *B*
Howard University *M*
University of the District of
   Columbia *A, B*

Florida

Barry University *B*
Bethune-Cookman College *B*
Broward Community College *A*
Chipola College *A*
Edward Waters College *B*
Embry-Riddle Aeronautical
   University *B*
Florida Institute of
   Technology *B, M, D*
Florida Memorial University *B*
Florida Southern College *B*
Florida State University *B, M, D*
Gulf Coast Community College *A*
Hillsborough Community College *A*
Nova Southeastern University *B, M, D*
Pensacola Junior College *A*
St. Petersburg College *A*
St. Thomas University *B*
Seminole Community College *A*
Stetson University *B*
University of Miami *B, M, D*
Valencia Community College *A*

Georgia

Andrew College *A*
Atlanta Metropolitan College *A*
Berry College *B*
Clark Atlanta University *B, M*
Coastal Georgia Community
   College *A*
Covenant College *B*
Darton College *A*
East Georgia College *A*
Emory University *B*
Georgia Perimeter College *A*
Georgia Southwestern State
   University *B, M*
Georgia State University *B, M, D*
Gordon College *A*
Kennesaw State University *M*
LaGrange College *B*
Macon State College *A*
Mercer University *B*
Middle Georgia College *A*
Savannah State University *B*
Southern Polytechnic State
   University *C, B, M*
University of Georgia *B, M, D*
University of West Georgia *M*

Hawaii

Brigham Young University-Hawaii *B*
Chaminade University of Honolulu *B*
Hawaii Pacific University *B*
University of Hawaii
   Manoa *B, M, D*

Idaho

Boise State University *B, M*
Brigham Young University-Idaho *B*
College of Southern Idaho *A*
Lewis-Clark State College *B*

Illinois

Augustana College *B*
Benedictine University *B*
Bradley University *B, M*
Concordia University *B*
DePaul University *B, M, D*
Dominican University *B*
Elmhurst College *B*
Eureka College *B*
Governors State University *B, M*
Greenville College *B*
Highland Community College *A*
Illinois Institute of Technology *B, M*
Illinois State University *B*
Judson College *B*
Knox College *B*
Lake Forest College *B*
Lewis University *B*
Lewis and Clark Community
    College *A*
Loyola University of Chicago *M*
MacCormac College *C, A*
MacMurray College *B*
McKendree College *B*
Millikin University *B*
Monmouth College *B*
Northeastern Illinois University *B, M*
Northern Illinois University *B, M*
Northwestern University *B, M, D*
Olivet Nazarene University *B*
Principia College *B*
Quincy University *B*
Richland Community College *A*
Rockford College *B*
Roosevelt University *C, B, M*
St. Xavier University *B*
Southern Illinois University
    Carbondale *B, M*
Southern Illinois University
    Edwardsville *B, M*
Southwestern Illinois College *C, A*
Trinity Christian College *B*
Triton College *A*
University of Chicago *M, D*
University of Illinois
    Springfield *B, M*
    Urbana-Champaign *B, M, D*
University of St. Francis *B*
Wheaton College *B*
William Rainey Harper College *A*

Indiana

Anderson University *B*
Bethel College *A*
DePauw University *B*
Franklin College *B*
Goshen College *B*
Huntington University *B*
Indiana Institute of Technology *B*
Indiana University-Purdue University
    Fort Wayne *A, B, M*
Manchester College *A, B*
Marian College *A, B, T*
Oakland City University *A, B*
Purdue University
    Calumet *B*
Rose-Hulman Institute of
    Technology *B*
Taylor University *B*
Taylor University: Fort Wayne *B*
Tri-State University *B*
University of Indianapolis *B*
Valparaiso University *B*
Vincennes University *A*

Iowa

Briar Cliff University *B*
Buena Vista University *B*
Clarke College *B*
Coe College *B*
Cornell College *B*
Dordt College *B*
Drake University *B*
Ellsworth Community College *A*

Graceland University *B*
Grinnell College *B*
Iowa Wesleyan College *B*
Loras College *B*
Luther College *B*
Maharishi University of
    Management *M*
Mount Mercy College *B*
Northwestern College *B*
St. Ambrose University *B*
Simpson College *B*
University of Iowa *B*
University of Northern Iowa *B, M*

Kansas

Allen County Community College *A*
Baker University *B*
Barton County Community College *A*
Benedictine College *B*
Bethel College *B*
Butler County Community College *A*
Dodge City Community College *A*
Garden City Community College *A*
Kansas Wesleyan University *A, B, T*
McPherson College *T*
MidAmerica Nazarene University *B*
Pittsburg State University *B*
Seward County Community College *A*
Southwestern College *B*
Tabor College *B*

Kentucky

Bellarmine University *B*
Centre College *B*
Eastern Kentucky University *B, M*
Kentucky State University *B*
Maysville Community College *C, A*
National College of Business &
    Technology
    Danville *A*
    Florence *A*
    Lexington *A*
    Louisville *A*
    Richmond *A*
Northern Kentucky University *M*

Louisiana

Dillard University *B*
Grambling State University *B*
Louisiana State University
    Shreveport *B*
Louisiana State University and
    Agricultural and Mechanical
    College *B, D*
Louisiana Tech University *B, M*
Nicholls State University *B*
Nunez Community College *A*
Southeastern Louisiana University *B*
Southern University
    Shreveport *A*
Southern University and Agricultural
    and Mechanical College *B, M*
University of Louisiana at
    Lafayette *B, M, D*
University of Louisiana at Monroe *B*
University of New Orleans *B, M*
Xavier University of Louisiana *B*

Maine

Andover College *A*
Bowdoin College *B*
Colby College *B*
Southern Maine Community
    College *A*
Thomas College *B*
University of Maine
    Farmington *B, T*
    Fort Kent *A*
University of Southern Maine *B, M*

Maryland

Allegany College of Maryland *A*
Baltimore City Community College *A*

Bowie State University *B, M*
Capitol College *B, M*
College of Notre Dame of Maryland *B*
Columbia Union College *B*
Community College of Baltimore
    County *A*
Coppin State University *B*
Frederick Community College *A*
Goucher College *B*
Harford Community College *A*
Hood College *B*
Howard Community College *A*
Loyola College in Maryland *M*
Montgomery College *A*
Morgan State University *B*
Prince George's Community
    College *A*
Salisbury University *B*
Towson University *B, M*
University of Maryland
    University College *B*
Washington College *B*

Massachusetts

American International College *B*
Amherst College *B*
Atlantic Union College *B*
Boston College *B*
Brandeis University *B, M, D*
Bridgewater State College *B, M*
Bristol Community College *A*
Bunker Hill Community College *A*
Cape Cod Community College *A*
Clark University *B*
Eastern Nazarene College *B*
Fitchburg State College *B, M*
Gordon College *B*
Hampshire College *B*
Harvard College *B, D*
Lasell College *B*
Massachusetts Bay Community
    College *A*
Massachusetts Institute of
    Technology *B, M, D*
Merrimack College *B*
Middlesex Community College *A*
Mount Holyoke College *B*
Newbury College *A, B*
North Shore Community College *A*
Northeastern University *B, M, D*
Northern Essex Community
    College *C, A*
Quincy College *C, A*
Regis College *B*
Simon's Rock College of Bard *B*
Smith College *B*
Springfield Technical Community
    College *A*
Stonehill College *B*
Suffolk University *B, M*
Tufts University *B*
University of Massachusetts
    Amherst *B, M, D*
    Boston *M, D*
    Lowell *B, M, D*
Wellesley College *B*
Wentworth Institute of Technology *B*
Western New England College *B*
Westfield State College *B*
Wheaton College *B*
Williams College *B*
Worcester Polytechnic
    Institute *B, M, D*

Michigan

Albion College *B*
Alma College *B*
Baker College
    of Cadillac *B*
    of Clinton Township *B*
    of Flint *A*
    of Muskegon *B*
    of Owosso *A, B*
    of Port Huron *A, B*

Bay Mills Community College *A*
Calvin College *B*
Cornerstone University *B*
Delta College *A*
Grand Valley State University *B*
Hillsdale College *B*
Kettering University *B*
Lawrence Technological
    University *B, M*
Madonna University *A, B, T*
Mid Michigan Community College *A*
Mott Community College *C*
Northern Michigan University *B*
Olivet College *B*
Spring Arbor University *B*
University of Detroit Mercy *B, M*
University of Michigan *B, T*
University of Michigan
    Flint *B, M*
Washtenaw Community College *C, A*
Western Michigan University *B, M, D*

Minnesota

Academy College *B*
Augsburg College *B*
Bemidji State University *B*
Carleton College *B*
College of St. Benedict *B*
Concordia College: Moorhead *B*
Gustavus Adolphus College *B*
Inver Hills Community College *A*
Metropolitan State University *B*
Minnesota State University
    Mankato *B, M*
    Moorhead *B*
Normandale Community College *A*
Ridgewater College *A*
Rochester Community and Technical
    College *A*
St. Cloud State University *B, M*
St. John's University *B*
St. Mary's University of Minnesota *B*
St. Olaf College *B*
St. Paul College *A*
University of Minnesota
    Duluth *B, M*
    Morris *B*
    Twin Cities *C, B*
Winona State University *B*

Mississippi

Belhaven College *C, B*
Coahoma Community College *A*
Holmes Community College *A*
Itawamba Community College *A*
Millsaps College *B, T*
Mississippi College *B, M*
Rust College *B*

Missouri

Blue River Community College *A*
Central Methodist University *A, B*
College of the Ozarks *B*
Columbia College *B*
Drury University *B*
Grantham University *A, B*
Lindenwood University *B*
Maryville University of Saint
    Louis *C, B*
Missouri Southern State University *B*
Missouri Technical School *C, B*
Northwest Missouri State
    University *B*
Park University *A, B*
Southwest Baptist University *A, B*
University of Missouri
    Columbia *B, M, D*
    Rolla *B, M, D*
Washington University in St.
    Louis *B, M, D*
Webster University *B*
William Jewell College *B*

Montana

Carroll College *A, T*
Montana State University
 Bozeman *B, M, D*
Montana Tech of the University of
 Montana *B*
Rocky Mountain College *B*
University of Great Falls *B*
University of Montana: Missoula *B, M*

Nebraska

Concordia University *B, T*
Creighton University *A, B*
Dana College *B*
Doane College *B*
Hastings College *B*
Midland Lutheran College *B*
Nebraska Wesleyan University *B*
Northeast Community College *A*
Peru State College *B*
Union College *B*
University of Nebraska
 Omaha *B, M*
Western Nebraska Community
 College *A*

Nevada

Sierra Nevada College *B*
University of Nevada
 Las Vegas *B, M, D*
 Reno *B, M, D*

New Hampshire

Daniel Webster College *B*
Dartmouth College *B, M, D*
Franklin Pierce College *B*
New Hampshire Community
 Technical College
 Nashua *C, A*
Plymouth State University *B*
Rivier College *C, A, B, M*
St. Anselm College *B*
University of New Hampshire *B, M, D*

New Jersey

Burlington County College *A*
Caldwell College *B*
College of St. Elizabeth *B*
Cumberland County College *A*
Drew University *B*
Felician College *B*
Gloucester County College *A*
Hudson County Community
 College *A*
New Jersey Institute of Technology *D*
Ocean County College *A*
Raritan Valley Community College *A*
Rowan University *B*
Rutgers, The State University of New
 Jersey
 Camden Regional Campus *B*
 New Brunswick/Piscataway
  Campus *B*
 Newark Regional Campus *B*
St. Peter's College *B*
Salem Community College *A*
Thomas Edison State College *C, A, B*
Union County College *A*
William Paterson University of New
 Jersey *B*

New Mexico

Clovis Community College *A*
College of Santa Fe *B*
College of the Southwest *B*
Dona Ana Branch Community College
 of New Mexico State
 University *A*
Eastern New Mexico University *B*
New Mexico Institute of Mining and
 Technology *B, M, D*

New Mexico State University
 Alamogordo *C*
 Carlsbad *A*
San Juan College *C*
Southwestern Indian Polytechnic
 Institute *C, A*

New York

Adirondack Community College *A*
Bard College *B*
Barnard College *B*
Canisius College *B*
Cayuga County Community College *A*
City University of New York
 Baruch College *B, M*
 Bronx Community College *A*
 City College *B, M*
 Kingsborough Community
  College *A*
 LaGuardia Community College *A*
 Medgar Evers College *A*
 New York City College of
  Technology *A*
 Queens College *B, M*
Clarkson University *B, M*
Clinton Community College *A*
Colgate University *B*
College of Westchester *C, A*
Columbia University
 Columbia College *B*
 Fu Foundation School of
  Engineering and Applied
  Science *B, M, D*
 School of General Studies *B*
Columbia-Greene Community
 College *A*
Corning Community College *A*
Dowling College *B*
Dutchess Community College *A*
Finger Lakes Community College *A*
Globe Institute of Technology *C, A, B*
Herkimer County Community
 College *A*
Hobart and William Smith Colleges *B*
Hofstra University *B, M*
Houghton College *B*
Iona College *B, M*
Ithaca College *B*
Jefferson Community College *A*
Manhattan College *B*
Marist College *B*
Molloy College *B*
Monroe Community College *A*
Mount St. Mary College *C, B, T*
Nassau Community College *A*
New York Institute of Technology *B*
New York University *B, M, D*
Niagara County Community
 College *A*
Niagara University *C, B*
Onondaga Community College *A*
Pace University *B, M*
Polytechnic University *B, M, D*
Rensselaer Polytechnic
 Institute *B, M, D*
Roberts Wesleyan College *B*
Rochester Institute of
 Technology *A, B, M*
Sage College of Albany *A*
St. Bonaventure University *B*
St. John Fisher College *B*
St. Joseph's College: Suffolk
 Campus *B*
St. Lawrence University *B*
Schenectady County Community
 College *A*
State University of New York
 Binghamton *B, M, D*
 Buffalo *B*
 College at Brockport *B*
 College at Oneonta *B*
 College at Plattsburgh *B*
 College of Agriculture and
  Technology at Cobleskill *A*

College of Agriculture and
 Technology at Morrisville *A*
College of Technology at Alfred *A*
Farmingdale *A*
New Paltz *B, M*
Oswego *B*
Stony Brook *B, M, D*
Suffolk County Community College *A*
Syracuse University *B, M*
United States Military Academy *B*
Wagner College *B*
Wells College *B*
Westchester Community College *A*
Yeshiva University *B*

North Carolina

Appalachian State University *B, M*
Campbell University *B*
East Carolina University *B, M*
Elizabeth City State University *B*
Elon University *B*
High Point University *B*
Lees-McRae College *B*
Mars Hill College *B*
Meredith College *B*
Methodist College *A, B*
North Carolina Central University *B*
North Carolina State
 University *B, M, D*
St. Augustine's College *B*
Sandhills Community College *A*
Shaw University *B*
University of North Carolina
 Asheville *B*
 Chapel Hill *B, M, D*
 Charlotte *B, M*
 Greensboro *B, M*
 Pembroke *B*
 Wilmington *B*
Wake Forest University *B, M*
Western Carolina University *B*
Western Piedmont Community
 College *A*
Wingate University *B*
Winston-Salem State University *B*

North Dakota

Dickinson State University *B, T*
Jamestown College *B*
Lake Region State College *A*
North Dakota State University *B, M, D*
Turtle Mountain Community
 College *C, A*

Ohio

Ashland University *B*
Baldwin-Wallace College *B*
Bluffton University *B*
Capital University *B*
Case Western Reserve University *B*
Cedarville University *B*
Central State University *B*
Defiance College *A, B*
Franciscan University of
 Steubenville *B*
Heidelberg College *B*
Hiram College *B*
Jefferson Community College *A*
John Carroll University *B*
Malone College *B*
Marietta College *B*
Mount Union College *B*
Mount Vernon Nazarene University *B*
Muskingum College *B*
Ohio Dominican University *B*
Ohio State University
 Columbus Campus *B, M, D*
Ohio University *B, M*
Ohio University
 Southern Campus at Ironton *A*
Ohio Wesleyan University *B*
Otterbein College *B*
Stark State College of Technology *A*
University of Dayton *B, M*

University of Findlay *A, B*
University of Rio Grande *A, B*
Wilmington College *B*
Wittenberg University *B*
Wright State University *B*
Xavier University *B*
Youngstown State University *C, B*
Zane State College *C, A*

Oklahoma

Cameron University *B*
Carl Albert State College *A*
Eastern Oklahoma State College *A*
Murray State College *A*
Northeastern State University *B*
Oklahoma Baptist University *B*
Oklahoma Christian University *B*
Oklahoma City Community College *A*
Oklahoma City University *B, M*
Oklahoma Wesleyan University *B*
Oral Roberts University *B*
Seminole State College *A*
Southwestern Oklahoma State
 University *B*
University of Oklahoma *B, M, D*
University of Science and Arts of
 Oklahoma *B*
University of Tulsa *B, M, D*
Western Oklahoma State College *A*

Oregon

Central Oregon Community
 College *A*
Corban College *B*
Eastern Oregon University *B*
George Fox University *B*
Lewis & Clark College *B*
Linfield College *B*
Portland State University *B, M, D*
Southern Oregon University *B*
Southwestern Oregon Community
 College *A*
Treasure Valley Community College *A*
University of Portland *B*

Pennsylvania

Allegheny College *B*
Berks Technical Institute *A*
Bloomsburg University of
 Pennsylvania *B*
Bryn Mawr College *B*
Bucks County Community College *A*
CHI Institute: Southampton *C, A*
Carlow University *B*
Carnegie Mellon University *B, D*
Cedar Crest College *B*
Central Pennsylvania College *C, A, B*
Chestnut Hill College *C, A, B*
DeSales University *B*
Drexel University *B, M, D*
Duquesne University *B*
Edinboro University of
 Pennsylvania *A, B*
Gettysburg College *B*
Harrisburg Area Community
 College *A*
King's College *B*
La Roche College *B*
La Salle University *B, M*
Lebanon Valley College *B*
Lehigh University *B, M, D*
Lock Haven University of
 Pennsylvania *B*
Mansfield University of
 Pennsylvania *B*
Messiah College *B*
Moravian College *B*
Mount Aloysius College *A*
Northampton County Area
 Community College *A*
Penn State
 Abington *B*
 Altoona *B*
 Beaver *B*

Berks *B*
Delaware County *B*
Dubois *B*
Fayette *B*
Harrisburg *B, M*
Hazleton *B*
McKeesport *B*
Mont Alto *B*
New Kensington *B*
Shenango *B*
Wilkes-Barre *B*
Worthington Scranton *B*
York *B*
Pennsylvania Institute of
    Technology *A*
St. Francis University *B*
Seton Hill University *C, B*
South Hills School of Business &
    Technology *C, A*
Susquehanna University *B*
Tri-State Business Institute *A*
University of Pittsburgh *B, M, D*
University of Pittsburgh
    Bradford *B*
Ursinus College *B*
Waynesburg College *A, B*
Westminster College *B, T*
Westmoreland County Community
    College *C, A*
Widener University *B*
York College of Pennsylvania *B*

Puerto Rico

Atlantic College *A*
Inter American University of Puerto
    Rico
    Aguadilla Campus *C, A, B*
    Arecibo Campus *A, B*
    Barranquitas Campus *C, A, B*
    Bayamon Campus *A, B*
    Ponce Campus *A, B*
    San German Campus *A, B*
Universidad Adventista de las
    Antillas *A, B*
Universidad Metropolitana *A, B*
University of Puerto Rico
    Bayamon University College *A, B*
    Mayaguez *B, M*
    Rio Piedras *B*
University of the Sacred Heart *B*

Rhode Island

Brown University *B, M, D*
New England Institute of
    Technology *A, B*
Providence College *B*
Rhode Island College *B*
Roger Williams University *B*

South Carolina

Benedict College *B*
The Citadel *M*
Claflin University *B*
Clemson University *B, M, D*
Coker College *B*
College of Charleston *B*
Furman University *B*
Limestone College *A, B*
Presbyterian College *B*
Southern Wesleyan University *B*
Voorhees College *B*
Wofford College *B*

South Dakota

Augustana College *B*
Dakota State University *B, T*
Mount Marty College *B*
South Dakota School of Mines and
    Technology *B, M*
University of Sioux Falls *B*

Tennessee

Belmont University *B*

Bryan College *B*
Carson-Newman College *B*
Christian Brothers University *B*
Fisk University *B*
King College *B*
LeMoyne-Owen College *B*
Lipscomb University *B*
Middle Tennessee State
    University *B, M*
Motlow State Community College *C*
Pellissippi State Technical Community
    College *A*
Rhodes College *B*
Roane State Community College *A*
Southern Adventist University *B*
Southwest Tennessee Community
    College *A*
Tennessee Technological University *B*
Tennessee Temple University *B*
University of Memphis *B*
University of Tennessee
    Knoxville *B, M, D*
    Martin *B*
University of the South *B*

Texas

Abilene Christian University *B*
Austin College *B*
Austin Community College *A*
Baylor University *B, M*
Central Texas College *C, A*
Coastal Bend College *A*
Concordia University at Austin *B*
Dallas Baptist University *B*
Del Mar College *A*
Eastfield College *C, A*
El Paso Community College *A*
Galveston College *A*
Hill College *C, A*
Huston-Tillotson College *B*
Laredo Community College *A*
LeTourneau University *B*
Lon Morris College *A*
Mountain View College *A*
Northwest Vista College *A*
Odessa College *A*
Palo Alto College *A*
Rice University *B, M, D*
St. Edward's University *B*
St. Mary's University *B*
South Plains College *A*
South Texas College *A*
Southern Methodist
    University *B, M, D*
Southwestern Adventist University *B*
Texas A&M University *B, M, D*
Texas A&M University
    Commerce *B, M*
Texas Lutheran University *B*
Texas Southern University *B*
Texas State Technical College
    Waco *A*
Texas Wesleyan University *B*
University of Houston
    Clear Lake *B, M*
University of Mary Hardin-Baylor *B*
University of Texas
    Arlington *B*
    Pan American *B, M*
    San Antonio *D*
Western Texas College *A*
Wiley College *B*

Utah

Brigham Young University *B, M, D*
Dixie State College of Utah *A, B*
Neumont University *B*
Salt Lake Community College *A*
Snow College *A*
Southern Utah University *B*
University of Utah *B, M, D*
Utah Valley State College *A, B*
Weber State University *B*
Westminster College *B*

Vermont

Bennington College *B*
Champlain College *A*
Lyndon State College *A*
Marlboro College *B, M*
Middlebury College *B*
Norwich University *B*
St. Michael's College *B*
University of Vermont *B, M*

Virginia

Bridgewater College *B*
Christopher Newport University *B, M*
Danville Community College *A*
ECPI College of Technology *C, A*
Eastern Mennonite University *B*
Emory & Henry College *B*
Ferrum College *B*
Hampden-Sydney College *B*
Hampton University *B, M*
J. Sargeant Reynolds Community
    College *A*
Longwood University *B, T*
Mary Baldwin College *B*
Marymount University *C, B, M*
National College of Business &
    Technology
    Bluefield *C, A*
    Charlottesville *C, A*
    Danville *C, A*
    Harrisonburg *C, A*
    Lynchburg *C, A*
    Martinsville *C, A*
Northern Virginia Community
    College *A*
Radford University *B*
Roanoke College *B*
Sweet Briar College *B*
Thomas Nelson Community
    College *A*
University of Mary Washington *B*
University of Richmond *B*
University of Virginia's College at
    Wise *B*
Virginia Military Institute *B*
Virginia State University *B*
Virginia Wesleyan College *B*
Virginia Western Community
    College *A*

Washington

Centralia College *A*
Columbia Basin College *A*
DigiPen Institute of Technology *B, M*
Eastern Washington University *B, M*
Everett Community College *A*
Gonzaga University *B*
Henry Cogswell College *B*
Lower Columbia College *A*
North Seattle Community
    College *C, A*
Olympic College *A*
Pacific Lutheran University *B*
Renton Technical College *C, A*
Saint Martin's University *B*
Seattle University *B*
Spokane Falls Community College *A*
University of Puget Sound *B*
University of Washington *B, M, D*
Walla Walla College *B*
Washington State University *B, M, D*
Whatcom Community College *A*
Whitworth College *B*

West Virginia

Alderson-Broaddus College *C, A, B*
Bethany College *B*
Concord University *B*
Davis and Elkins College *B*
Mountain State University *A, B*
Salem International University *B*
West Virginia State University *B*
West Virginia University *B, M, D*

West Virginia University Institute of
    Technology *B*
West Virginia Wesleyan College *B*
Wheeling Jesuit University *B*

Wisconsin

Beloit College *B*
Cardinal Stritch University *A*
Carthage College *B*
Lakeland College *B*
Marquette University *B, M*
Mid-State Technical College *C*
Mount Mary College *B*
Northland College *B*
Ripon College *B*
Silver Lake College *B, T*
University of Wisconsin
    Green Bay *B*
    Milwaukee *B*
    Oshkosh *B*
    Parkside *B*
    Platteville *B*
    Superior *B*

Wyoming

Central Wyoming College *A*
Laramie County Community
    College *A*
University of Wyoming *B, M, D*
Western Wyoming Community
    College *A*

Computer software technology

Arizona

Coconino County Community
    College *A*
South Mountain Community
    College *C, A*

California

San Joaquin Delta College *C, A*

Colorado

IntelliTec College: Grand Junction *A*

Delaware

Wilmington College *B*

Florida

Palm Beach Community College *C*

Illinois

Moraine Valley Community College *C*

Indiana

Indiana University-Purdue University
    Indianapolis *A, B*
Sawyer College: Merrillville *C, A*

Massachusetts

Bunker Hill Community College *C, A*

Minnesota

Globe College *C, A, B*

Missouri

Blue River Community College *A*
Grantham University *A, B*

Montana

Montana Tech of the University of
    Montana *A*

Nebraska

Metropolitan Community College *A*

North Dakota

North Dakota State College of
Science *C, A*

Oregon

Oregon Institute of Technology *A, B*

Pennsylvania

South Hills School of Business &
Technology *A*

Washington

North Seattle Community College *C*

Computer systems analysis

Alabama

Faulkner State Community
College *C, A*

Arizona

Gateway Community College *C, A*
Mohave Community College *C*
Paradise Valley Community College *C*
Pima Community College *C, A*
South Mountain Community
College *C, A*

Arkansas

Arkansas Tech University *B*
Rich Mountain Community
College *C, A*
University of Arkansas *M*

California

California Polytechnic State
University: San Luis Obispo *B*
California State University
San Bernardino *B*
Cerritos Community College *A*
College of Marin: Kentfield *A*
College of the Canyons *C, A*
De Anza College *C, A*
DeVry University
Fremont *B*
Long Beach *B*
Glendale Community College *C*
Irvine Valley College *C, A*
MTI College *C, A*
Platt College
Ontario *A*
San Bernardino Valley College *C, A*
San Diego City College *A*
University of California
San Diego *B, M, D*
Santa Cruz *B, M, D*

Colorado

Colorado Mountain College
Timberline Campus *A*
Colorado Technical University *B, M, D*
DeVry University: Colorado
Springs *A, B*
Jones International University *C, B*
University of Denver *B*
Westwood College of Technology *A*

Connecticut

Norwalk Community College *A*

Delaware

Delaware Technical and Community
College
Owens Campus *A*
Stanton/Wilmington Campus *A*
Terry Campus *A*

District of Columbia

Howard University *B*
Southeastern University *A, B, M*

Florida

Brevard Community College *A*
Broward Community College *A*
Central Florida Community College *A*
Florida Community College at
Jacksonville *A*
Florida Technical College
Deland *A*
Gulf Coast Community College *A*
Indian River Community College *A*
Manatee Community College *C, A*
Palm Beach Community College *A*
Pasco-Hernando Community
College *A*
St. Johns River Community
College *C, A*
Schiller International University *B*
Seminole Community College *A*
Valencia Community College *C, A*

Georgia

Clayton State University *B*
Darton College *C*

Illinois

DePaul University *M*
Illinois Institute of Technology *M*
Moraine Valley Community College *C*
William Rainey Harper College *A*

Indiana

Sawyer College: Merrillville *A*
Valparaiso University *C*

Iowa

Hamilton College
Cedar Rapids *C*
Marshalltown Community College *A*
Northeast Iowa Community
College *A*
St. Ambrose University *B*

Kansas

Kansas State University *A*
Washburn University of Topeka *A, B*

Kentucky

Daymar College *A*

Louisiana

Southern University
New Orleans *A, B, M*

Maine

Husson College *B*
University of Maine
Fort Kent *B*

Maryland

Baltimore City Community College *A*
Frederick Community College *A*
Prince George's Community
College *A*
University of Maryland
University College *C*
Wor-Wic Community College *C, A*

Massachusetts

Mount Ida College *A*
Nichols College *B*
Northeastern University *M*
Wentworth Institute of Technology *C*

Michigan

Baker College
of Muskegon *B*
Davenport University *A, B*
Kirtland Community College *C, A*
Lansing Community College *A*
Oakland Community College *C, A*
Saginaw Valley State University *B*

University of Detroit Mercy *B*

Minnesota

Hennepin Technical College *C, A*
Mesabi Range Community and
Technical College *A*
Metropolitan State University *B*
Winona State University *B*

Missouri

DeVry University
Kansas City *B*
Grantham University *A, B*
Missouri Southern State University *A*
Missouri Technical School *B*
Rockhurst University *B*
St. Louis Community College
St. Louis Community College at
Florissant Valley *A*

Montana

Montana Tech of the University of
Montana *B*
University of Great Falls *B*

Nebraska

Union College *A, B*

Nevada

Community College of Southern
Nevada *A*

New Jersey

DeVry University: North
Brunswick *A, B*

New Mexico

Albuquerque Technical-Vocational
Institute *C, A*
Clovis Community College *A*

New York

City University of New York
Baruch College *M*
College of Westchester *C, A*
DeVry Institute of Technology
New York *B*
Globe Institute of Technology *C, A, B*
Pace University *B, M*
Rochester Institute of
Technology *B, M*
State University of New York
College of Agriculture and
Technology at Cobleskill *A*

North Carolina

Durham Technical Community
College *C, A*
Mayland Community College *A*
Western Piedmont Community
College *C, A*
Wilson Technical Community
College *C, A*

North Dakota

Williston State College *A*

Ohio

Baldwin-Wallace College *B*
Jefferson Community College *A*
Kent State University *C, B, M, D*
Kent State University
Tuscarawas Campus *C*
Miami University
Oxford Campus *B, M*
Southern State Community College *A*
Stark State College of Technology *A*
University of Akron *C, A, B, M*
University of Cincinnati *M*
University of Findlay *B*

Oklahoma

Eastern Oklahoma State College *A*
Oklahoma Baptist University *B*
Oklahoma City Community College *A*

Oregon

Lane Community College *A*

Pennsylvania

Academy of Medical Arts and
Business *C, A*
CHI Institute: Southampton *C, A*
DeVry University
Ft. Washington *B*
Drexel University *B*
Grove City College *B*
ICM School of Business & Medical
Careers *A*
Keystone College *B*
Laurel Business Institute *A*
Luzerne County Community
College *C*
Pennsylvania College of Technology *B*
Robert Morris University *M*
Shippensburg University of
Pennsylvania *B*
South Hills School of Business &
Technology *C, A*

Puerto Rico

Universidad del Este *A*
University of Puerto Rico
Mayaguez *B*

Rhode Island

New England Institute of
Technology *A, B*

Tennessee

Motlow State Community College *C*

Texas

DeVry University
Irving *B*
El Paso Community College *A*
Kilgore College *C, A*
Remington College
Houston *A*
University of Houston *B*
University of North Texas *M*

Utah

College of Eastern Utah *C, A*

Vermont

Champlain College *C, A, B*

Virginia

Blue Ridge Community College *C, A*
ECPI College of Technology *C, A*
Eastern Mennonite University *B*
John Tyler Community College *A*
Tidewater Community College *A*
Virginia Western Community
College *C*

Washington

DeVry University
Federal Way *A*
North Seattle Community
College *C, A*
Renton Technical College *C*
Whatcom Community College *A*

Wisconsin

Bryant & Stratton College:
Milwaukee *A*
Gateway Technical College *A*
Lakeshore Technical College *A*
Milwaukee Area Technical College *A*
Northcentral Technical College *A*

Southwest Wisconsin Technical
College *A*
University of Wisconsin
Whitewater *B*

Computer/systems security

Arizona
High-Tech Institute *A*
South Mountain Community
College *C, A*
University of Advancing
Technology *A, B, M*

California
College of Oceaneering *C*
Mt. Sierra College *B*
Westwood College *B*
Westwood College: Long Beach *B*

Colorado
Colorado Technical University *M*
Westwood College of Technology *B*
Westwood College of Technology
South *B*

Florida
Florida State University *M*
St. Petersburg College *C*
Southwest Florida College *C, A*
University of Miami *B*

Georgia
Northwestern Technical College *C*

Illinois
DePaul University *M*
Heartland Community College *C*
Lewis University *D*
Loyola University of Chicago *B*
University of Illinois
Urbana-Champaign *B, M, D*
Westwood College - Chicago Loop *B*

Indiana
Indiana Business College *A*

Iowa
Indian Hills Community College *A*
Iowa Lakes Community College *A*
Iowa State University *M*
St. Ambrose University *B*

Kansas
Pittsburg State University *B*

Kentucky
Louisville Technical Institute *A*
Maysville Community College *C, A*

Maryland
Howard Community College *C, A*
Johns Hopkins University *M*

Massachusetts
Springfield Technical Community
College *A*

Michigan
Cleary University *B*
Davenport University *B*
Oakland Community College *C, A*
Washtenaw Community College *C, A*

Minnesota
Capella University *C, B, M*
Fond du Lac Tribal and Community
College *C, A*
Globe College *C, A, B*

Hennepin Technical College *C, A*
Hibbing Community College *C, A*
Metropolitan State University *B*
Minneapolis Community and
Technical College *C, A*
Minnesota State Community and
Technical College - Fergus Falls *A*

Mississippi
Antonelli College
Jackson *A*

Missouri
Jefferson College *C, A*

Montana
University of Great Falls *B*

New Jersey
Stevens Institute of Technology *B, M*

New York
Globe Institute of Technology *C, A, B*
Rochester Institute of
Technology *B, M*

North Carolina
Fayetteville Technical Community
College *A*
High Point University *B*

Ohio
James A. Rhodes State College *C, A*
Stark State College of Technology *A*

Oklahoma
Oklahoma City Community College *A*

Oregon
Southern Oregon University *B*

Pennsylvania
Butler County Community College *A*
Carnegie Mellon University *M*
East Stroudsburg University of
Pennsylvania *B*
Harrisburg Area Community
College *C*
ICM School of Business & Medical
Careers *A*
Northampton County Area
Community College *A*
Peirce College *C, A*
Pennsylvania College of Technology *B*
Pittsburgh Technical Institute *C*
Robert Morris University *M*
York Technical Institute *A*

Puerto Rico
Atlantic College *B*

South Carolina
Limestone College *B*
Southern Wesleyan University *B*
York Technical College *C*

South Dakota
Dakota State University *M*

Texas
San Antonio College *A*
South Texas College *A*
University of Texas
San Antonio *B*

Vermont
Champlain College *A, B*
Vermont Technical College *A, B*

Virginia
ECPI College of Technology *C, A*

Washington
Bellevue Community College *C, A*
Clover Park Technical College *C, A*
Olympic College *C, A*

Wisconsin
Milwaukee Area Technical College *A*

Computer systems technology

Alabama
Gadsden State Community College *A*
Herzing College *A, B*

Arizona
Northern Arizona University *B*

Arkansas
Ouachita Technical College *C*

California
Cuyamaca College *C, A*
Westwood College of Technology
Inland Empire *A*

Colorado
Parks College *A*

Florida
Chipola College *C, A*
DeVry University
Orlando *B*
Florida Career College: West Palm
Beach *C*
University of Central Florida *B*

Georgia
Northwestern Technical College *C, A*

Idaho
College of Southern Idaho *C, A*

Illinois
Heartland Community College *C*
Illinois Central College *C*
Lincoln Land Community College *C*
Morton College *C*
Parkland College *C, A*
Waubonsee Community College *C*

Indiana
Indiana University-Purdue University
Fort Wayne *C*
Indiana University-Purdue University
Indianapolis *A, B*
Sawyer College: Merrillville *C, A*

Iowa
Hamilton College
Cedar Falls *C*

Kansas
Barton County Community
College *C, A*
Southwestern College *B*

Massachusetts
Benjamin Franklin Institute of
Technology *A*
Bristol Community College *A*
Bunker Hill Community College *A*
Newbury College *C, A*

Michigan
Wayne State University *B*

Minnesota
Alexandria Technical College *C, A*
Central Lakes College *C, A*
Globe College *C, A, B*
Lake Superior College *A*
Minnesota State Community and
Technical College - Fergus
Falls *C, A*
Rochester Community and Technical
College *C*
St. Paul College *C*

Missouri
Blue River Community College *C*
Southeast Missouri State University *A*

Nebraska
Vatterott College: Spring Valley *C*

New Hampshire
New Hampshire Community
Technical College
Berlin *C, A*
Claremont *A*

New Jersey
Hudson County Community
College *A*
Thomas Edison State College *A, B*

New York
Cayuga County Community College *C*
Erie Community College
South Campus *A*
Genesee Community College *C, A*
Nassau Community College *C*
State University of New York
College of Agriculture and
Technology at Morrisville *A, B*
Farmingdale *C*

North Carolina
Cape Fear Community College *C, A*

Ohio
Cincinnati State Technical and
Community College *A*
Kent State University *C*
Miami University
Hamilton Campus *A*
Oxford Campus *A*
Ohio Business College: Sandusky *C*
University of Cincinnati
Clermont College *C, A*
University of Rio Grande *A*

Oregon
Portland Community College *A*

Pennsylvania
Butler County Community College *A*
Lehigh Carbon Community College *C*
Luzerne County Community
College *A*
Penn State
University Park *C*
Pennsylvania College of Technology *A*
Pittsburgh Technical Institute *A*
South Hills School of Business &
Technology *A*

Puerto Rico
Turabo University *A, B*

Rhode Island
Community College of Rhode
Island *C*

South Carolina
York Technical College *A*

Texas

Clarendon College *C, A*
Kilgore College *C*
MTI College of Business and
    Technology *A*
Texas State Technical College
    Harlingen *C, A*

Utah

Salt Lake Community College *C, A*

Virginia

ECPI College of Technology *C, A*
National College of Business &
    Technology
    Salem *C, A*

Washington

Edmonds Community College *C, A*

Wisconsin

Mid-State Technical College *A*
Milwaukee Area Technical College *A*
Western Wisconsin Technical
    College *C*
Wisconsin Indianhead Technical
    College *A*

Wyoming

Central Wyoming College *C, A*

Computer typography

California

Santa Barbara City College *A*

Nevada

Community College of Southern
    Nevada *C, A*

New Mexico

Southwestern Indian Polytechnic
    Institute *C*

Pennsylvania

Luzerne County Community
    College *C, A*

Concrete finishing

Indiana

Ivy Tech State College
    Ivy Tech Community College:
        Lafayette *C*

Utah

Salt Lake Community College *A*

Wisconsin

Milwaukee Area Technical College *C*
Waukesha County Technical
    College *C*

Conducting

Alabama

Alabama Agricultural and Mechanical
    University *B*
Troy University *M*

Alaska

University of Alaska
    Fairbanks *M*

Arizona

Grand Canyon University *B*
Northern Arizona University *M*
University of Arizona *M*

California

Azusa Pacific University *M*
Bethesda Christian University *B, M*
California State University
    Long Beach *B, M*
    Sacramento *M*
Chapman University *B*
San Diego State University *M*
San Francisco Conservatory of
    Music *M*
San Francisco State University *M*
University of Southern California *M*

Connecticut

University of Hartford *M*

District of Columbia

Catholic University of America *M, D*
Howard University *B*

Florida

Florida State University *M*
University of Miami *M, D*

Illinois

Northwestern University *M, D*
Roosevelt University *B*
University of Illinois
    Urbana-Champaign *M, D*

Indiana

American Conservatory of
    Music *M, D*
Butler University *M*
Indiana University
    Bloomington *B*
Indiana University-Purdue University
    Fort Wayne *T*

Iowa

University of Northern Iowa *M*

Kansas

Central Christian College of Kansas *A*
University of Kansas *M, D*

Kentucky

Campbellsville University *B*

Maine

University of Maine *M*

Maryland

Johns Hopkins University: Peabody
    Conservatory of Music *M, D*

Massachusetts

Boston Conservatory *M*
New England Conservatory of
    Music *M, D*

Michigan

Calvin College *B*
Central Michigan University *M*
Michigan State University *M, D*
University of Michigan *M*

Minnesota

Concordia College: Moorhead *B*

Mississippi

Mississippi College *M*

Missouri

University of Missouri
    Kansas City *M, D*

New Jersey

Rider University *M*

Westminster Choir College of Rider
    University *M*

New York

Bard College *B*
Eastman School of Music of the
    University of Rochester *M, D*
Ithaca College *M*
Juilliard School *M*
Mannes College The New School for
    Music *B, M*
University of Rochester *M, D*

Ohio

Bowling Green State University *M*
Cleveland Institute of Music *M*
Oberlin College *B, M*
University of Cincinnati *B, M, D*

Oregon

Portland State University *M*
University of Oregon *M*

Pennsylvania

Carnegie Mellon University *M*
Penn State
    University Park *M*
Temple University *M*

South Carolina

University of South Carolina *M, D*

Texas

Baylor University *M*
Concordia University at Austin *B*
Rice University *M*
Sam Houston State University *M*
Southern Methodist University *M*
Stephen F. Austin State University *M*
Texas Christian University *M*
Texas Tech University *D*
University of Houston *D*

Utah

Brigham Young University *M*

Virginia

Shenandoah University *M*

Washington

University of Washington *M, D*

Wisconsin

University of Wisconsin
    Madison *B, M*

Conservation biology

Arizona

Arizona State University *B*

Arkansas

Arkansas Tech University *B, M*

California

California State University
    Sacramento *B, M*
San Jose State University *B, M*

Florida

University of Central Florida *D*

Louisiana

University of Louisiana at Lafayette *B*
University of New Orleans *D*

Maryland

University of Maryland
    College Park *M*

Michigan

Central Michigan University *M*

Minnesota

Ridgewater College *A*

Missouri

Missouri Southern State University *B*
University of Missouri
    Columbia *B, M, D*

Nevada

University of Nevada
    Reno *M*

New Mexico

College of Santa Fe *B*

New York

State University of New York
    Albany *M*
    College of Agriculture and
        Technology at Morrisville *A*
    College of Environmental Science
        and Forestry *B, M, D*

Pennsylvania

Cedar Crest College *B*
Gettysburg College *B*

Rhode Island

University of Rhode Island *M*

Vermont

Sterling College *B*

Wisconsin

University of Wisconsin
    Madison *B*
    Milwaukee *B*

Construction engineering

California

National University *B*
University of Southern
    California *B, M*

Illinois

Bradley University *B*

Indiana

Purdue University *B*
Vincennes University *A*

Iowa

Iowa State University *B*

Massachusetts

Worcester Polytechnic Institute *M*

Michigan

Lawrence Technological University *M*
University of Michigan *M*

Missouri

Washington University in St. Louis *M*

New Jersey

Stevens Institute of Technology *M*

New Mexico

University of New Mexico *M*

New York

State University of New York
    College of Agriculture and
        Technology at Morrisville *A*

College of Environmental Science
and Forestry *B, M, D*

North Carolina
North Carolina State University *B*

North Dakota
North Dakota State University *B*

Oregon
Oregon State University *B*

Texas
Southern Methodist University *M*

Wisconsin
Marquette University *M, D*

Construction management

Alabama
Gadsden State Community College *C*

Arizona
Arizona State University *B, M*
Northern Arizona University *B*

Arkansas
John Brown University *B*

California
Cabrillo College *C, A*
College of the Desert *C, A*
Diablo Valley College *C*
National University *B*
Southwestern College *C, A*

Colorado
University of Denver *B, M*

Connecticut
Central Connecticut State
University *B*

Florida
Everglades University *B*
University of Florida *M*

Georgia
Gwinnett Technical College *A*
Southern Polytechnic State
University *C, B, M*

Idaho
Boise State University *B*

Illinois
Kankakee Community College *C, A*
Waubonsee Community College *A*
Western Illinois University *B*

Iowa
Southeastern Community College
North Campus *A*
University of Northern Iowa *B*

Kansas
Pittsburg State University *B*
University of Kansas *M*

Louisiana
Louisiana State University and
Agricultural and Mechanical
College *B*

Massachusetts
Wentworth Institute of
Technology *A, B*

Michigan
Delta College *A*
Eastern Michigan University *B*
Ferris State University *C, B*
Lawrence Technological University *B*
Michigan State University *B, M*
Michigan Technological University *B*
Oakland Community College *C, A*

Minnesota
Dunwoody College of Technology *A*
Inver Hills Community College *C, A*

Mississippi
Mississippi State University *B*

New York
Erie Community College
North Campus *A*
New York University *M*
Polytechnic University *B, M*
Pratt Institute *B*

North Dakota
North Dakota State University *B*

Ohio
Stark State College of Technology *A*

Oklahoma
Oklahoma State University
Oklahoma City *A*
University of Oklahoma *B, M*

Pennsylvania
Delaware County Community
College *C*

Texas
St. Philip's College *A*

Utah
Brigham Young University *B, M*

Virginia
Virginia Polytechnic Institute and
State University *B, M*

Washington
Central Washington University *B*
University of Washington *B, M*

Wisconsin
Milwaukee School of Engineering *B*

Wyoming
Casper College *A*

Construction site management

California
College of the Sequoias *C*
Diablo Valley College *C*

Georgia
Gwinnett Technical College *A*

Indiana
Ivy Tech State College
Ivy Tech Community College:
Kokomo *A*
Ivy Tech Community College:
Northeast *A*
Ivy Tech Community College:
Northwest *A*
Ivy Tech Community College:
Southwest *A*

Minnesota
Minnesota State Community and
Technical College - Fergus Falls *A*
St. Paul College *A*

Missouri
State Fair Community College *A*

New Hampshire
University of New Hampshire *A*

New Jersey
Cumberland County College *C, A*

New York
Pratt Institute *A, B*

Ohio
Sinclair Community College *C*

Pennsylvania
Harrisburg Area Community
College *C*

Rhode Island
Roger Williams University *B*

Texas
University of Texas
Brownsville *C*

Utah
Salt Lake Community College *A*

Washington
Pierce College *C, A*

Construction technology

Alabama
Community College of the Air
Force *A*
Jefferson State Community
College *C, A*
Lawson State Community
College *C, A*
Tuskegee University *B*

Arizona
Coconino County Community
College *A*
Northern Arizona University *B*

Arkansas
University of Arkansas
Little Rock *B*

California
Antelope Valley College *C, A*
Butte College *C, A*
California State Polytechnic
University: Pomona *B*
California State University
Chico *B*
Fresno *B*
Long Beach *B*
College of the Desert *C*
College of the Redwoods *A*
College of the Sequoias *C, A*
El Camino College *C, A*
Feather River College *C, A*
Los Angeles Pierce College *A*
Riverside Community College *C, A*
Saddleback College *C*
San Bernardino Valley College *C*
San Diego Mesa College *C, A*
San Joaquin Delta College *C*
Santa Rosa Junior College *C*
Shasta College *C, A*

Colorado
Colorado State University *B, M*
Red Rocks Community College *C, A*
Trinidad State Junior College *A*

Connecticut
Norwalk Community College *C, A*

Delaware
Delaware Technical and Community
College
Terry Campus *A*

Florida
Daytona Beach Community College *A*
Florida Agricultural and Mechanical
University *B*
Florida Community College at
Jacksonville *A*
Florida International University *B*
Gulf Coast Community College *A*
Indian River Community College *A*
Manatee Community College *A*
Palm Beach Community College *A*
Pensacola Junior College *A*
Seminole Community College *A*
Tallahassee Community College *A*
University of Florida *B*
University of North Florida *B*
Valencia Community College *C, A*

Georgia
Georgia Southern University *B*

Idaho
Boise State University *B*
Brigham Young University-Idaho *A*

Illinois
College of Lake County *C, A*
Joliet Junior College *C, A*
Lincoln Land Community College *A*
Morrison Institute of Technology *A*
Oakton Community College *A*
Rock Valley College *C, A*
South Suburban College of Cook
County *C, A*
Southern Illinois University
Edwardsville *B*
Southwestern Illinois College *C, A*
Triton College *C, A*

Indiana
Indiana University-Purdue University
Fort Wayne *B*
Indiana University-Purdue University
Indianapolis *B*
Purdue University
Calumet *C, A, B*
Vincennes University *A*

Iowa
Southeastern Community College
North Campus *A*

Kansas
Pittsburg State University *B*

Kentucky
Maysville Community College *C*

Louisiana
Bossier Parish Community College *C*
Grambling State University *B*
University of Louisiana at Monroe *B*

Maine
Eastern Maine Community
College *C, A*
Southern Maine Community
College *A*

Maryland

Community College of Baltimore
County *C, A*

Massachusetts

Cape Cod Community College *C*
Fitchburg State College *B*

Michigan

Alpena Community College *A*
Central Michigan University *B*
Eastern Michigan University *M*
Ferris State University *A*
Gogebic Community College *C, A*
Kalamazoo Valley Community
College *C*
Lake Superior State University *A*
Lawrence Technological University *A*
Macomb Community College *C, A*
Northern Michigan University *C, B*
Washtenaw Community College *A*
Western Michigan University *B, M*

Minnesota

Hennepin Technical College *C, A*
Minnesota State University
Moorhead *B*

Missouri

Central Missouri State University *A, B*
Mineral Area College *C, A*
Missouri State University *B*
Missouri Western State
University *A, B*
Ozarks Technical Community
College *C, A*
Southeast Missouri State University *B*

Montana

Montana State University
Bozeman *B*

Nebraska

University of Nebraska
Lincoln *B*
Omaha *B*

Nevada

University of Nevada
Las Vegas *B*
Reno *B*

New Hampshire

New Hampshire Community
Technical College
Manchester *C, A*
University of New Hampshire *A*

New Jersey

Burlington County College *A*
Cumberland County College *C, A*
Essex County College *A*
Fairleigh Dickinson University
Metropolitan Campus *B*
Ocean County College *C*
Thomas Edison State College *B*

New Mexico

Santa Fe Community College *C, A*
Western New Mexico University *C, A*

New York

City University of New York
New York City College of
Technology *C, A*
Dutchess Community College *A*
Herkimer County Community
College *A*
Monroe Community College *A*
Onondaga Community College *A*

State University of New York
College of Agriculture and
Technology at Morrisville *A*
College of Environmental Science
and Forestry *B*
College of Technology at
Alfred *A, B*
College of Technology at Canton *A*
College of Technology at Delhi *A*
Suffolk County Community College *A*
Technical Career Institutes *A*

North Carolina

College of the Albemarle *C*
East Carolina University *B*
Mitchell Community College *C, A*
Vance-Granville Community
College *C*
Western Carolina University *B*
Western Piedmont Community
College *C, A*

North Dakota

North Dakota State College of
Science *A*

Ohio

Bowling Green State University *B*
Cincinnati State Technical and
Community College *A*
Clark State Community College *A*
Columbus State Community
College *C, A*
Hocking College *A*
Jefferson Community College *A*
Lakeland Community College *C*
Ohio State University
Agricultural Technical Institute *A*
Columbus Campus *C, B*
Owens Community College
Toledo *C, A*
Stark State College of Technology *A*
University of Akron *C, A, B*
Wright State University *A*
Youngstown State University *C*

Oklahoma

Oklahoma State University *B*
Oklahoma State University
Oklahoma City *C, A*
Okmulgee *A*
Western Oklahoma State College *A*

Oregon

Chemeketa Community College *A*
Clackamas Community College *C, A*
Lane Community College *C, A*
Portland Community College *C, A*
Rogue Community College *C, A*

Pennsylvania

Community College of Allegheny
County *C*
Community College of Philadelphia *A*
Delaware County Community
College *A*
Harrisburg Area Community
College *C, A*
Lehigh Carbon Community College *A*
New Castle School of Trades *A*
Penn State
University Park *C*
Pennsylvania College of
Technology *C, A, B*

Puerto Rico

University of Puerto Rico
Bayamon University College *A*

Rhode Island

New England Institute of
Technology *A*

South Carolina

Aiken Technical College *C*
Greenville Technical College *C, A*
Horry-Georgetown Technical
College *A*
Midlands Technical College *C*
Piedmont Technical College *C, A*
Technical College of the
Lowcountry *C, A*
Trident Technical College *C*

South Dakota

South Dakota State University *B*

Tennessee

Nashville State Community College *A*

Texas

Brazosport College *C, A*
Houston Community College
System *C, A*
Howard College *C*
Midland College *C*
Prairie View A&M University *B*
St. Philip's College *C, A*
Sam Houston State University *B*
San Antonio College *C*
San Jacinto College
North *C, A*
Texas A&M University *B*
Texas A&M University
Commerce *B*
Texas State Technical College
Harlingen *C, A*
West Texas *C, A*
Texas State University: San Marcos *B*
University of Houston *B*
University of North Texas *B*

Vermont

Vermont Technical College *A*

Virginia

J. Sargeant Reynolds Community
College *C*
Lord Fairfax Community College *C*
Norfolk State University *B*

Washington

Central Washington University *B*
Clark College *C, A*
Eastern Washington University *B*
Edmonds Community College *C, A*
Spokane Community College *C, A*
Washington State University *B*
Yakima Valley Community College *C*

Wisconsin

Northeast Wisconsin Technical
College *C*
University of Wisconsin
Stout *B*
Waukesha County Technical
College *C*

Construction trades

Alabama

Lawson State Community
College *C, A*

Alaska

University of Alaska
Southeast *A*

Arizona

Mohave Community College *C*
Tohono O'odham Community
College *C*

Arkansas

North Arkansas College *C*
Pulaski Technical College *A*
Southern Arkansas University Tech *C*

California

Diablo Valley College *C*
Foothill College *C*
San Jose City College *C, A*
Sierra College *C*

Colorado

Arapahoe Community College *C, A*
Red Rocks Community College *C, A*

Florida

St. Petersburg College *C*
South Florida Community College *A*

Georgia

Gwinnett Technical College *A*

Illinois

Kaskaskia College *C*
Parkland College *C, A*

Indiana

Ivy Tech State College
Ivy Tech Community College: East
Central *A*
Ivy Tech Community College:
Kokomo *A*
Ivy Tech Community College:
Northeast *C, A*
Ivy Tech Community College:
Northwest *C, A*
Ivy Tech Community College:
Whitewater *C, A*
Vincennes University *A*

Iowa

Indian Hills Community College *C, A*

Kentucky

Maysville Community College *C*

Maryland

Frederick Community College *C, A*

Massachusetts

Springfield Technical Community
College *C*

Michigan

Bay Mills Community College *A*
Delta College *C, A*
Gogebic Community College *A*

Minnesota

Northland Community & Technical
College *C, A*

Missouri

East Central College *C, A*

Montana

Blackfeet Community College *C*
Salish Kootenai College *C*

New York

Fulton-Montgomery Community
College *A*
Monroe Community College *A*
Nassau Community College *C*
State University of New York
College of Agriculture and
Technology at Morrisville *A*
Tompkins-Cortland Community
College *C, A*

North Carolina
Edgecombe Community College *C*
Surry Community College *C, A*
Wilkes Community College *C, A*

North Dakota
North Dakota State College of Science *A*
Turtle Mountain Community College *C, A*

Oregon
Rogue Community College *C, A*

Pennsylvania
Community College of Allegheny County *C, A*
Harrisburg Area Community College *C, A*

South Carolina
Williamsburg Technical College *C*

Texas
Midland College *C*

Utah
Snow College *C, A*
Utah Valley State College *C, A*

Washington
Clover Park Technical College *C*

Wisconsin
Fox Valley Technical College *A*
Waukesha County Technical College *C*

Wyoming
Casper College *C, A*
Sheridan College *C*

Consumer economics

California
Long Beach City College *C, A*

Connecticut
St. Joseph College *B*

Florida
Florida State University *M, D*

Georgia
University of Georgia *B*

Illinois
University of Illinois Urbana-Champaign *B, M, D*

Michigan
Western Michigan University *M*

New York
Cornell University *B, M, D*
Syracuse University *B, M*

Pennsylvania
Indiana University of Pennsylvania *B*

South Dakota
South Dakota State University *B*

Tennessee
University of Memphis *M*

Utah
University of Utah *B*

Wisconsin
University of Wisconsin Madison *B*

Consumer merchandising

California
Fashion Institute of Design and Merchandising *A*
Fashion Institute of Design and Merchandising
San Diego *A*
San Francisco *A*

Florida
Florida State University *B, M, D*

Illinois
Bradley University *B*

Michigan
Madonna University *C, A, B*

Oregon
Oregon State University *B*

Wisconsin
University of Wisconsin Madison *B*

Consumer services/ advocacy

Florida
Pensacola Junior College *A*

Correctional facilities administration

Arizona
Arizona Western College *C*

Connecticut
Asnuntuck Community College *C*

Florida
St. Petersburg College *A, B*

Illinois
Lewis University *B, M*
Westwood College of Technology O'Hare *B*

Massachusetts
Bunker Hill Community College *C*

Michigan
Baker College of Muskegon *C, A*
Kirtland Community College *C, A*
Northern Michigan University *A*

Montana
University of Great Falls *M*

New Hampshire
McIntosh College *A*

Pennsylvania
Bucks County Community College *A*

Virginia
Bluefield College *B*

West Virginia
Potomac State College of West Virginia University *A*

Corrections

Arizona
Central Arizona College *C, A*
Northland Pioneer College *C, A*

California
California State University East Bay *B*
College of the Redwoods *C*
Fresno City College *C, A*
Gavilan Community College *C, A*
Grossmont Community College *C, A*
Imperial Valley College *C, A*
Lassen College *A*
Sacramento City College *C, A*
San Joaquin Valley College Inc. *A*
Santa Ana College *C*
Taft College *C, A*

Colorado
Pueblo Community College *A*

Delaware
Wilmington College *M*

District of Columbia
University of the District of Columbia *A*

Florida
Central Florida Community College *C*
Chipola College *C*
Gulf Coast Community College *C*
Hillsborough Community College *C*
Lake City Community College *C*
Palm Beach Community College *C*
South Florida Community College *C*
Valencia Community College *C*

Idaho
Lewis-Clark State College *B*

Illinois
Bradley University *B*
City Colleges of Chicago Harold Washington College *A*
Elgin Community College *A*
Heartland Community College *C*
John A. Logan College *A*
Moraine Valley Community College *A*
Rend Lake College *C, A*
Triton College *C*
Westwood College of Technology O'Hare *B*

Indiana
Vincennes University *A*

Kansas
Cowley County Community College *A*
Labette Community College *A*
Washburn University of Topeka *B*

Kentucky
Eastern Kentucky University *A, B*
Hopkinsville Community College *C, A*

Maryland
Baltimore City Community College *C, A*
Community College of Baltimore County *C, A*
Hagerstown Community College *C*
University of Baltimore *C*

Massachusetts
Bridgewater State College *M*
Bristol Community College *C*
Bunker Hill Community College *A*
Mount Wachusett Community College *A*

Michigan
Alpena Community College *C, A*
Baker College of Port Huron *C, A*
Delta College *C, A*
Glen Oaks Community College *C*
Gogebic Community College *C*
Grand Rapids Community College *A*
Kellogg Community College *C, A*
Kirtland Community College *C, A*
Lake Michigan College *A*
Northwestern Michigan College *C*
Oakland Community College *C, A*
St. Clair County Community College *C*
Schoolcraft College *A*
Washtenaw Community College *A*
Wayne County Community College *A*

Minnesota
Fond du Lac Tribal and Community College *A*
Lake Superior College *C*
Minnesota State Community and Technical College - Fergus Falls *C*
Minnesota State University Mankato *B*
Northland Community & Technical College *A*
Winona State University *B*

Missouri
College of the Ozarks *B*
Longview Community College *C, A*
Penn Valley Community College *C, A*
St. Louis University *B*
Southeast Missouri State University *B*
Southwest Baptist University *B*

Montana
University of Great Falls *B*

Nebraska
Hastings College *B*
Northeast Community College *A*

Nevada
Community College of Southern Nevada *A*
Truckee Meadows Community College *A*
Western Nevada Community College *C, A*

New Hampshire
McIntosh College *A*

New Jersey
Burlington County College *C*
Middlesex County College *A*
Union County College *C*

New Mexico
New Mexico Junior College *C*
University of New Mexico *B*

New York
Adirondack Community College *A*
Broome Community College *A*
Cayuga County Community College *C, A*
Corning Community College *A*
Herkimer County Community College *C*
Monroe Community College *C, A*
Westchester Community College *A*

North Carolina

Central Piedmont Community
College *A*

Ohio

Clark State Community College *A*
Columbus State Community
College *A*
Cuyahoga Community College
Metropolitan Campus *A*
Hocking College *A*
James A. Rhodes State College *A*
Lakeland Community College *C, A*
Owens Community College
Toledo *A*
Sinclair Community College *C, A*
Southern State Community College *A*
Tiffin University *B*
University of Akron *B*
University of Cincinnati
Clermont College *A*
Washington State Community
College *A*
Youngstown State University *A, B, M*

Oklahoma

Oklahoma City University *B*
Oklahoma Panhandle State
University *A*
University of Central Oklahoma *B*
Western Oklahoma State College *A*

Oregon

Clackamas Community College *C, A*
Clatsop Community College *C*
Treasure Valley Community College *C*
Western Oregon University *B*

Pennsylvania

Bucks County Community College *A*
Butler County Community College *C*
Community College of Allegheny
County *A*
Harrisburg Area Community
College *C*
ICM School of Business & Medical
Careers *A*
Lehigh Carbon Community College *C*
University of Pittsburgh
Bradford *B*
York College of Pennsylvania *A, B*

South Carolina

South University *B*
Trident Technical College *C*

South Dakota

Southeast Technical Institute *A*

Texas

Alvin Community College *C, A*
Amarillo College *A*
Central Texas College *C*
Coastal Bend College *C, A*
El Paso Community College *C, A*
Hardin-Simmons University *B*
Lamar State College at Orange *C*
San Antonio College *A*
Stephen F. Austin State University *B*
Texas Southmost College *B*
Texas State University: San Marcos *B*
University of Texas
Brownsville *B*
Weatherford College *A*
Western Texas College *C, A*

Utah

Weber State University *B*

Virginia

Mountain Empire Community
College *A*

Southwest Virginia Community
College *A*

Washington

Centralia College *C*
Everett Community College *A*
Peninsula College *C, A*
Spokane Community College *C, A*
Tacoma Community College *A*
Walla Walla Community College *C, A*
Yakima Valley Community College *C*

West Virginia

Bluefield State College *A*
Glenville State College *A*

Wisconsin

Mid-State Technical College *A*
Moraine Park Technical College *A*
Wisconsin Indianhead Technical
College *A*

Cosmetic services

Alabama

Alabama Southern Community
College *A*
Bishop State Community College *C*
Calhoun Community College *C*
Gadsden State Community College *C*
George C. Wallace State Community
College
George C. Wallace Community
College at Dothan *C*
J. F. Drake State Technical College *C*
Northwest-Shoals Community
College *C*
Shelton State Community College *C*
Trenholm State Technical College *C*
Wallace State Community College at
Hanceville *C*

Arizona

Eastern Arizona College *A*
Northland Pioneer College *C, A*

Arkansas

Arkansas Tech University *C*
Ouachita Technical College *C*

California

Allan Hancock College *C, A*
Butte College *C, A*
Citrus College *C, A*
College of the Sequoias *C, A*
College of the Siskiyous *C*
Contra Costa College *A*
El Camino College *C, A*
Fullerton College *A*
Gavilan Community College *C, A*
Glendale Community College *A*
Golden West College *C, A*
Laney College *C, A*
Los Medanos College *C*
MiraCosta College *C, A*
Napa Valley College *C*
Riverside Community College *C, A*
Sacramento City College *C, A*
Saddleback College *C*
San Jose City College *C, A*
Santa Ana College *C, A*
Santa Barbara City College *C, A*
Santiago Canyon College *A*
Skyline College *C, A*
Solano Community College *C, A*

Colorado

Colorado Northwestern Community
College *C*
Community College of Denver *C*
Northeastern Junior College *C*
Otero Junior College *C*

Trinidad State Junior College *C, A*

Florida

Brevard Community College *C*
Central Florida Community College *C*
Daytona Beach Community College *C*
Florida College of Natural Health
Maitland *A*
Florida Community College at
Jacksonville *C*
Indian River Community College *C*
Lake City Community College *C*
New England Institute of
Technology *C*
North Florida Community College *C*
Palm Beach Community College *C*
Pensacola Junior College *C*
South Florida Community College *C*

Georgia

Albany Technical College *C*
Athens Technical College *C*
Augusta Technical Institute *C*
Central Georgia Technical College *C*
Chattahoochee Technical College *C*
Columbus Technical College *C*
DeKalb Technical College *C*
Georgia Southwestern State
University *A*
Savannah Technical College *A*
Southwest Georgia Technical
College *C*
Waycross College *A*

Hawaii

University of Hawaii
Honolulu Community College *C, A*

Idaho

Idaho State University *C*

Illinois

College of DuPage *C, A*
Danville Area Community
College *C, A*
Highland Community College *C*
Illinois Eastern Community Colleges
Olney Central College *C*
John A. Logan College *C, A*
Kaskaskia College *C*
Lake Land College *C*
Rend Lake College *C*
Southwestern Illinois College *C*

Indiana

Vincennes University *A*

Iowa

Southeastern Community College
North Campus *C*

Kansas

Cowley County Community
College *C, A*
Garden City Community College *C*
Johnson County Community
College *C*

Kentucky

Jefferson Community College *C*
Owensboro Community College *C*

Massachusetts

Greenfield Community College *C, A*
North Shore Community College *C*
Springfield Technical Community
College *C*

Michigan

Gogebic Community College *C*
Kirtland Community College *C, A*
Lansing Community College *A*

Montcalm Community College *C, A*
Mott Community College *C*
Northern Michigan University *C*
Oakland Community College *A*

Minnesota

Century Community and Technical
College *C*
Minnesota State College - Southeast
Technical *C, A*
Minnesota State Community and
Technical College - Fergus Falls *C*
Northland Community & Technical
College *C*
Ridgewater College *A*
St. Paul College *C, A*

Mississippi

Coahoma Community College *C*
Holmes Community College *C*
Mississippi Gulf Coast Community
College
Jefferson Davis Campus *A*
Pearl River Community College *C*

Montana

University of Montana: Missoula *C*

Nebraska

Vatterott College: Spring Valley *C*
Western Nebraska Community
College *C, A*

New Jersey

Ocean County College *C*

New Mexico

Albuquerque Technical-Vocational
Institute *A*
Clovis Community College *A*
New Mexico Junior College *C, A*
Northern New Mexico College *C, A*
San Juan College *C, A*

New York

Sullivan County Community
College *A*

North Carolina

Alamance Community College *C*
Beaufort County Community
College *C*
Bladen Community College *C, A*
Blue Ridge Community College *C*
Brunswick Community College *C, A*
Caldwell Community College and
Technical Institute *C*
Cape Fear Community College *C, A*
Carteret Community College *C*
Catawba Valley Community College *C*
Central Carolina Community
College *A*
Cleveland Community College *C*
Coastal Carolina Community
College *C*
College of the Albemarle *C*
Craven Community College *C*
Davidson County Community
College *C*
Edgecombe Community College *C*
Fayetteville Technical Community
College *C*
Guilford Technical Community
College *C, A*
Haywood Community College *C, A*
Isothermal Community College *C, A*
James Sprunt Community
College *C, A*
Johnston Community College *C*
Martin Community College *C, A*
Mayland Community College *C, A*
Mitchell Community College *C*

Nash Community College *C*
Piedmont Community College *C, A*
Pitt Community College *C, A*
Roanoke-Chowan Community
    College *C*
Robeson Community College *C*
Rockingham Community College *C*
Sampson Community College *A*
Sandhills Community College *C, A*
Southeastern Community College *C*
Southwestern Community
    College *C, A*
Stanly Community College *C, A*
Surry Community College *A*
Vance-Granville Community
    College *C*
Wayne Community College *C*
Wilson Technical Community
    College *C*

Oregon
Mount Hood Community College *A*
Umpqua Community College *A*

Pennsylvania
Berean Institute *C*
Delaware County Community
    College *C*

South Carolina
Denmark Technical College *C*
Florence-Darlington Technical
    College *C*
Greenville Technical College *C*
Technical College of the
    Lowcountry *C, A*
Trident Technical College *C*
Williamsburg Technical College *C*

Texas
Central Texas College *C*
Del Mar College *C*
Frank Phillips College *C*
Grayson County College *C*
Houston Community College
    System *C, A*
Kilgore College *C*
Lamar State College at Port
    Arthur *C, A*
Lee College *C*
McLennan Community College *C*
North Harris Montgomery
    Community College District *C, A*
Northeast Texas Community
    College *C, A*
Odessa College *C, A*
Panola College *C*
Ranger College *C*
San Jacinto College
    Central Campus *C*
    North *C, A*
Texarkana College *C*
Trinity Valley Community College *C*
Vernon College *C*
Weatherford College *C, A*
Wharton County Junior College *C*

Utah
College of Eastern Utah *A*
Salt Lake Community College *C, A*
Snow College *C, A*

Washington
Clover Park Technical College *C*
Lake Washington Technical College *C*
Olympic College *C*
Renton Technical College *C*
Shoreline Community College *C, A*
South Seattle Community
    College *C, A*
Spokane Community College *C, A*
Walla Walla Community College *C, A*

Wisconsin
Chippewa Valley Technical College *C*
Gateway Technical College *C*
Madison Area Technical College *A*
Mid-State Technical College *C*
Moraine Park Technical College *C*
Nicolet Area Technical College *C*
Southwest Wisconsin Technical
    College *C*

Wyoming
Eastern Wyoming College *A*

Cosmetology

Alabama
Lawson State Community College *C*

California
Yuba Community College
    District *C, A*

Florida
Chipola College *C*

Georgia
Savannah Technical College *C*
West Georgia Technical College *C*

Kansas
Seward County Community
    College *C, A*

Kentucky
Somerset Community College *A*

Michigan
Kirtland Community College *C, A*
Mott Community College *C*

Mississippi
Copiah-Lincoln Community College *C*

North Carolina
Brunswick Community College *C*
Isothermal Community College *C*
Pamlico Community College *C*

Texas
North Harris Montgomery
    Community College District *C, A*

Utah
Snow College *C, A*

Washington
Everett Community College *C, A*
Olympic College *C*
Walla Walla Community College *A*

Counseling psychology

Alabama
Alabama Agricultural and Mechanical
    University *M*
Auburn University *D*
Troy University *M*
University of Alabama *M*
University of North Alabama *M*

Alaska
Alaska Pacific University *M*

Arizona
Northern Arizona University *M*
Prescott College *M*
University of Phoenix *M*

Arkansas
Arkansas State University *M*
John Brown University *M*
University of Central Arkansas *M*

California
Alliant International University *M*
California Baptist University *M*
California Institute of Integral
    Studies *M*
California State University
    Bakersfield *M*
    Chico *T*
    East Bay *M*
    Long Beach *M*
    Sacramento *M*
Dominican University of California *M*
Golden Gate University *M*
Holy Names University *M*
Hope International University *M*
John F. Kennedy University *M*
Loyola Marymount University *M*
Mount St. Mary's College *M*
National University *M, T*
Notre Dame de Namur University *M*
Santa Clara University *M*
University of California
    Santa Barbara *M, D*
University of La Verne *M*

Colorado
Adams State College *M*
Colorado Christian University *M*
Naropa University *M*
University of Denver *M, D*
University of Northern Colorado *M, D*

Connecticut
Southern Connecticut State
    University *M*
University of Hartford *M*

Delaware
Wilmington College *M*

District of Columbia
George Washington University *M*
Howard University *M*

Florida
Barry University *M, D*
Carlos Albizu University *M*
Palm Beach Atlantic University *M*
Rollins College *M*
St. Leo University *M*
St. Thomas University *M*
South University: West Palm Beach
    Campus *M*
University of Florida *D*
University of Miami *M, D*
University of North Florida *M*

Georgia
Clark Atlanta University *M, D*
Georgia State University *D*
Mercer University *M*
Paine College *B*
University of Georgia *D*

Hawaii
Chaminade University of Honolulu *M*

Illinois
Argosy University *M*
Chicago State University *M*
Governors State University *M*
Illinois State University *M*
Lewis University *M*
Loyola University of Chicago *M, D*
McKendree College *M*
Northeastern Illinois University *M*
Northwestern University *M, D*

Olivet Nazarene University *M*
Roosevelt University *M*
St. Xavier University *M*
Trinity International University *M*
University of Illinois
    Springfield *M*

Indiana
Ball State University *M, D*
Grace College *M*
Indiana State University *M*
Indiana Wesleyan University *M*
University of St. Francis *M*
Valparaiso University *M*

Iowa
University of Iowa *D*
University of Northern Iowa *M*

Kansas
MidAmerica Nazarene University *M*
Pittsburg State University *M*
University of Kansas *M, D*

Kentucky
Lindsey Wilson College *M*
Western Kentucky University *M*

Louisiana
Louisiana Tech University *D*
Nicholls State University *M*

Maine
University of Maine *M, D*

Maryland
Bowie State University *M*
Coppin State University *M*
Frostburg State University *M*
Loyola College in Maryland *M*
Towson University *T*
University of Baltimore *M*

Massachusetts
Anna Maria College *M*
Assumption College *M*
Boston University *D*
Cambridge College *M*
Eastern Nazarene College *M*
Framingham State College *M*
Lesley University *M*
Northeastern University *M, D*
Salem State College *M*
Springfield College *M*
Tufts University *M*
Westfield State College *M*

Michigan
Andrews University *D*
Cornerstone University *M*
Spring Arbor University *M*
Western Michigan University *M, D*

Minnesota
Capella University *M, D*
Crossroads College *B*
Minnesota State University
    Mankato *M*
St. Cloud State University *M*
St. Mary's University of Minnesota *M*
University of St. Thomas *M, D*

Mississippi
Mississippi College *M*
University of Southern
    Mississippi *M, D*
William Carey College *M*

Missouri
Avila University *M*
Central Missouri State University *M*

Lindenwood University *M*
Northwest Missouri State
University *M*
University of Missouri
Columbia *M, D*
Kansas City *D*
Webster University *M*

Montana
University of Great Falls *M*

Nebraska
Chadron State College *M*
Doane College *M*

Nevada
University of Nevada
Las Vegas *M*

New Hampshire
Rivier College *M*

New Jersey
Caldwell College *M*
Centenary College *M*
College of St. Elizabeth *M*
Georgian Court University *M*
Monmouth University *M*
New Jersey City University *M*
Rider University *M*
Seton Hall University *D*

New Mexico
College of Santa Fe *B*
New Mexico State University *D*

New York
College of New Rochelle *M*
Fordham University *M, D*
Medaille College *M*
Mercy College *M*
New York University *D*
St. Bonaventure University *M*
State University of New York
Albany *D*
Buffalo *D*
Oswego *M*

North Carolina
Campbell University *M*
Gardner-Webb University *M*

North Dakota
University of North Dakota *D*

Ohio
Franciscan University of
Steubenville *M*
Heidelberg College *M*
John Carroll University *M*
Kent State University *M*
University of Akron *D*
Walsh University *M*
Wright State University *M*

Oklahoma
East Central University *M*
Northeastern State University *M*
Northwestern Oklahoma State
University *M*
Southeastern Oklahoma State
University *M*
Southern Nazarene University *M*
University of Central Oklahoma *M*
University of Oklahoma *D*

Oregon
George Fox University *M*
Lewis & Clark College *M*
Northwest Christian College *M*
Oregon State University *M, D*

Pacific University *M*
University of Oregon *D*

Pennsylvania
Arcadia University *M*
Baptist Bible College of
Pennsylvania *M*
Carlow University *M*
Chatham College *M*
Chestnut Hill College *M*
Gannon University *M, D*
Geneva College *M*
Holy Family University *M*
Immaculata University *M, T*
Indiana University of Pennsylvania *M*
Kutztown University of
Pennsylvania *M*
La Salle University *M*
Lehigh University *D*
Marywood University *M*
Penn State
University Park *D*
Rosemont College *M*
Slippery Rock University of
Pennsylvania *M*
Temple University *M, D*
University of Pennsylvania *M*
University of Scranton *M*
Villanova University *M*
West Chester University of
Pennsylvania *M*

Puerto Rico
Inter American University of Puerto
Rico
San German Campus *M, D*
Turabo University *M*

Rhode Island
Salve Regina University *M*

South Carolina
Columbia International University *M*
South University *M*

South Dakota
South Dakota State University *M*

Tennessee
Freed-Hardeman University *M*
Johnson Bible College *M*
Lee University *M*
Southern Adventist University *M*
Tennessee Technological
University *M*
Trevecca Nazarene University *M*
University of Memphis *D*
University of Tennessee
Knoxville *M*

Texas
Abilene Christian University *M*
Amberton University *M*
Angelo State University *M*
Dallas Baptist University *M*
Lamar University *M*
Midwestern State University *M*
St. Mary's University *M, D*
Sam Houston State University *M*
Southern Methodist University *M*
Southwestern Assemblies of God
University *M*
Stephen F. Austin State University *M*
Tarleton State University *M*
Texas A&M University *D*
Texas A&M University
Commerce *M, D*
Kingsville *M*
Texarkana *M*
Texas State University: San
Marcos *M, T*
Texas Tech University *M, D*
Texas Woman's University *M, D*

University of Houston *D*
University of Houston
Victoria *M*
University of North Texas *M, D*
University of Texas
Pan American *M*
Tyler *M*
West Texas A&M University *M*

Vermont
College of St. Joseph in Vermont *M*
Goddard College *M*
Johnson State College *M*

Virginia
Eastern Mennonite University *M*
Liberty University *M, D*
Marymount University *M*
Regent University *M, D, T*

Washington
Bastyr University *M*
Central Washington University *M*
City University *M*
Eastern Washington University *M*
Gonzaga University *M*
Northwest University *M*
Saint Martin's University *M*
Western Washington University *M*

West Virginia
West Virginia University *D*

Wisconsin
Concordia University Wisconsin *M*
Lakeland College *M*
Marquette University *D*
University of Wisconsin
Madison *M, D*
Stout *M*
Whitewater *M*

Counselor education

Alabama
Alabama Agricultural and Mechanical
University *B, M*
Alabama State University *M*
Auburn University *D, T*
Auburn University at Montgomery *M*
Jacksonville State University *M, T*
Troy University *T*
University of Alabama *M, D*
University of Alabama
Birmingham *M*
University of Montevallo *M*
University of North Alabama *M*
University of South Alabama *M, T*
University of West Alabama *M*

Alaska
University of Alaska
Anchorage *M*
Fairbanks *M*

Arizona
Arizona State University *M, D*
Northern Arizona University *M*
Prescott College *B, M*
University of Arizona *M, D*
University of Phoenix *M*

Arkansas
Arkansas State University *M, T*
Arkansas Tech University *M*
Harding University *B, M*
Henderson State University *M*
John Brown University *M*
Southern Arkansas University *M*
University of Arkansas *M, D, T*
University of Arkansas
Little Rock *M*

University of Central Arkansas *M*

California
Azusa Pacific University *M*
California Lutheran University *M*
California Polytechnic State
University: San Luis Obispo *M*
California State University
Bakersfield *M*
Chico *T*
Dominguez Hills *M*
East Bay *M, T*
Fresno *M*
Fullerton *M*
Long Beach *M*
Los Angeles *M*
Northridge *M*
Sacramento *M, T*
San Bernardino *M*
Chapman University *M, T*
Fresno Pacific University *M, T*
Humboldt State University *T*
La Sierra University *M*
Loyola Marymount University *M*
Mount St. Mary's College *M*
National University *M, T*
St. Mary's College of California *M*
San Diego State University *M*
San Francisco State University *M*
San Jose State University *M*
Sonoma State University *M*
University of California
Santa Barbara *M, D*
University of La Verne *M*
University of Redlands *M, T*
University of San Diego *M, T*
University of San Francisco *T*
University of Southern
California *M, D, T*
Whittier College *M*

Colorado
Adams State College *M*
University of Colorado
Colorado Springs *M*
Denver and Health Sciences
Center *M*
University of Northern Colorado *M, D*

Connecticut
Central Connecticut State
University *M*
Fairfield University *M*
Southern Connecticut State
University *M*
University of Bridgeport *M*
University of Hartford *M, T*
Western Connecticut State
University *M*

Delaware
University of Delaware *M*
Wilmington College *M*

District of Columbia
Catholic University of America *M, D*
Gallaudet University *M*
George Washington University *M, D*
Howard University *M*
Trinity University *M*
University of the District of
Columbia *M*

Florida
Barry University *M*
Carlos Albizu University *M*
Florida Agricultural and Mechanical
University *M*
Florida Atlantic University *M*
Florida Gulf Coast University *M*
Florida International University *M*
Florida State University *M, D, T*
Nova Southeastern University *M*

St. Thomas University M
Stetson University M
University of Central Florida M
University of Florida M
University of North Florida M
University of South Florida M

Georgia
Albany State University M
Augusta State University M
Clark Atlanta University M, D
Columbus State University M
Fort Valley State University M
Georgia Southern University M, T
Georgia State University M, D
University of Georgia M, D
University of West Georgia M
Valdosta State University M

Hawaii
University of Hawaii
  Manoa M

Idaho
Boise State University M
Idaho State University D, T
Northwest Nazarene University M
University of Idaho M

Illinois
Bradley University M
Chicago State University M
Concordia University M
DePaul University M
Eastern Illinois University M
Governors State University M
Loyola University of Chicago M
Northeastern Illinois University M
Northern Illinois University M, D
Roosevelt University M
Western Illinois University M

Indiana
Butler University M
Indiana State University M, D
Indiana University
  Bloomington M, D
  South Bend M
  Southeast M
Indiana University-Purdue University
  Fort Wayne M
Indiana University-Purdue University
  Indianapolis M
Indiana Wesleyan University M
Purdue University
  Calumet M
University of St. Francis M

Iowa
Buena Vista University M
Drake University M
Iowa State University M, T
Loras College M
University of Iowa M, D
University of Northern Iowa M

Kansas
Emporia State University M
Fort Hays State University M
Kansas State University M, D
Pittsburg State University M
Wichita State University M

Kentucky
Eastern Kentucky University M
Morehead State University M
Murray State University M, T
Northern Kentucky University M
Spalding University M
University of Kentucky M, D
University of Louisville M, D
Western Kentucky University M, T

Louisiana
Louisiana State University and
  Agricultural and Mechanical
  College M
Louisiana Tech University M
Loyola University New Orleans M
Nicholls State University M
Our Lady of Holy Cross College M
Southeastern Louisiana University M
Southern University and Agricultural
  and Mechanical College M
University of Louisiana at Lafayette M
University of Louisiana at Monroe M
University of New Orleans M, D
Xavier University of Louisiana M

Maine
University of Maine M, D
University of Southern Maine M

Maryland
Bowie State University M
Frostburg State University M
Loyola College in Maryland M
McDaniel College M
University of Maryland
  College Park M, D
  Eastern Shore M

Massachusetts
Assumption College M
Boston College M, D
Boston University M, D, T
Bridgewater State College M, T
Fitchburg State College M, T
Lesley University M
Northeastern University M
Salem State College M
Springfield College M
Suffolk University M
University of Massachusetts
  Boston M
Westfield State College M

Michigan
Andrews University M, D
Central Michigan University M
Eastern Michigan University M
Michigan State University M
Northern Michigan University B, M
Oakland University M, D
Siena Heights University M
University of Detroit Mercy M
Wayne State University M, D, T
Western Michigan University M, D

Minnesota
Minnesota State University
  Mankato B, M
  Moorhead M
St. Cloud State University M
Winona State University M

Mississippi
Delta State University M
Jackson State University M
Mississippi College M
Mississippi State University M, D, T
University of Mississippi A, B, M, D
University of Southern
  Mississippi B, M

Missouri
Central Missouri State University M
Evangel University M
Lincoln University M
Lindenwood University M
Missouri Baptist University M, T
Missouri State University M
Northwest Missouri State
  University M, T
St. Louis University M, D

Southeast Missouri State University M
Stephens College M
University of Missouri
  Columbia M, D
  Kansas City M
  St. Louis M

Montana
Montana State University
  Billings M
University of Montana: Missoula M, D

Nebraska
Chadron State College M
Creighton University M
University of Nebraska
  Kearney M, T
  Omaha M
Wayne State College M

Nevada
University of Nevada
  Las Vegas M
  Reno M, D

New Hampshire
Keene State College M, T
Plymouth State University M, T
Rivier College M
University of New Hampshire M

New Jersey
Caldwell College M
The College of New Jersey M
Kean University M, T
Monmouth University M
Montclair State University M
Rowan University M
Seton Hall University M
William Paterson University of New
  Jersey M

New Mexico
College of the Southwest M
Eastern New Mexico University M
New Mexico Highlands University M
New Mexico State University M, D
University of New Mexico M, D, T
Western New Mexico University M

New York
Alfred University M
Canisius College M
City University of New York
  Brooklyn College M
  Hunter College M
  Queens College M
College of New Rochelle M
College of Saint Rose M
Cornell University D
Hofstra University M, T
Long Island University
  Brooklyn Campus M
  C. W. Post Campus M
Manhattan College M
Mercy College M, T
New York Institute of Technology M
New York University M, D, T
Niagara University M
Roberts Wesleyan College M
St. John's University M, T
St. Lawrence University M
State University of New York
  Albany M
  Buffalo M, D
  College at Brockport M
  College at Buffalo M
  College at Oneonta M
  College at Plattsburgh M, T
  Oswego M
Syracuse University M, D
University of Rochester M

North Carolina
Appalachian State University M
Campbell University M
East Carolina University M, D
Gardner-Webb University M
Lenoir-Rhyne College M
North Carolina Agricultural and
  Technical State University M
North Carolina Central University M
North Carolina State University M, D
University of North Carolina
  Chapel Hill M
  Charlotte M, D
  Greensboro M, D
  Pembroke M
Wake Forest University M, T
Western Carolina University M

North Dakota
North Dakota State University M
University of North Dakota M

Ohio
Bowling Green State University M, T
Cleveland State University M, D
Heidelberg College M
John Carroll University M
Kent State University M, D
Malone College M
Ohio State University
  Columbus Campus M, D
Ohio University M, D
Ohio University
  Zanesville Campus M
Union Institute & University M
University of Akron M, D
University of Cincinnati M, D
University of Dayton M, T
Wright State University M
Xavier University M
Youngstown State University M

Oklahoma
East Central University M, T
Northeastern State University M, T
Northwestern Oklahoma State
  University M, T
Oklahoma State University M
Southeastern Oklahoma State
  University M, T
Southwestern Oklahoma State
  University M, T
University of Central Oklahoma M
University of Oklahoma M

Oregon
Lewis & Clark College M
Northwest Christian College M
Oregon State University M, D
Portland State University M, D, T

Pennsylvania
Arcadia University M
Bucknell University M
California University of
  Pennsylvania M
Chatham College T
Duquesne University M, D, T
Eastern University M
Edinboro University of
  Pennsylvania M
Gwynedd-Mercy College M
Indiana University of Pennsylvania M
Kutztown University of
  Pennsylvania M, T
Lancaster Bible College M
Lehigh University M
Marywood University M
Millersville University of
  Pennsylvania M
Penn State
  University Park M, D
Philadelphia Biblical University M

Shippensburg University of
Pennsylvania *M*
University of Pennsylvania *M*
University of Scranton *M*
Villanova University *M*
Westminster College *M*
Widener University *M, D, T*

Puerto Rico

Bayamon Central University *M*
Inter American University of Puerto
Rico
San German Campus *M, D*
Pontifical Catholic University of
Puerto Rico *M*
Turabo University *M*
University of Puerto Rico
Rio Piedras *M, D*

Rhode Island

Providence College *M*
Rhode Island College *M*

South Carolina

The Citadel *M*
Clemson University *M*
South Carolina State University *M*
University of South Carolina *M, D*
Winthrop University *M, T*

South Dakota

Northern State University *M*
University of South Dakota *M, D*

Tennessee

Austin Peay State University *M*
Carson-Newman College *M*
East Tennessee State University *M, T*
Freed-Hardeman University *M*
Lincoln Memorial University *M*
Middle Tennessee State University *M*
Tennessee State University *M*
Tennessee Technological
University *M*
University of Memphis *M, D, T*
University of Tennessee
Chattanooga *M*
Knoxville *M*
Martin *M*

Texas

Abilene Christian University *M, T*
Angelo State University *M*
Dallas Baptist University *M*
Hardin-Simmons University *M*
Houston Baptist University *M*
Lamar University *B, M, T*
Midwestern State University *M*
Our Lady of the Lake University of San
Antonio *M*
Prairie View A&M University *M*
Sam Houston State University *M, D*
Sul Ross State University *M*
Tarleton State University *M*
Texas A&M University
Kingsville *M*
Texas Christian University *M*
Texas Southern University *M, D*
Texas State University: San
Marcos *M, T*
Texas Tech University *M, D*
Texas Woman's University *M*
University of Houston *M*
University of Houston
Clear Lake *M*
Victoria *M*
University of Mary Hardin-Baylor *M*
University of North Texas *M, D, T*
University of Texas
Brownsville *M*
El Paso *M*
Pan American *M*

San Antonio *M, D*
of the Permian Basin *M*
West Texas A&M University *M, T*

Utah

Brigham Young University *M*

Vermont

College of St. Joseph in Vermont *M*
Goddard College *M*
Johnson State College *M*
Lyndon State College *M*
University of Vermont *M*

Virginia

College of William and Mary *M, D*
George Mason University *M*
Hampton University *M*
James Madison University *M*
Liberty University *M, T*
Longwood University *M*
Lynchburg College *M*
Marymount University *M*
Old Dominion University *M, D, T*
Radford University *M, T*
University of Virginia *M, D*
Virginia Commonwealth University *M*
Virginia Polytechnic Institute and
State University *M, D*
Virginia State University *M*

Washington

Central Washington University *M, T*
City University *M*
Eastern Washington University *M, T*
Gonzaga University *M*
Heritage University *M*
Saint Martin's University *M, T*
Seattle Pacific University *M*
Seattle University *M*
University of Puget Sound *M*
Washington State University *M, D*
Western Washington University *M*
Whitworth College *B, M, T*

West Virginia

Marshall University *B, M*
West Virginia University *M, T*

Wisconsin

Concordia University Wisconsin *M*
Marquette University *M*
University of Wisconsin
Madison *M, D*
Oshkosh *M*
Platteville *M*
River Falls *M*
Stout *M*
Superior *M*
Whitewater *M*

Court reporting

Alabama

Faulkner State Community College *A*
Gadsden State Community College *A*
Prince Institute of Professional
Studies *A*

Arizona

Gateway Community College *C, A*
Metropolitan College of Court
Reporting *A*
Northland Pioneer College *C, A*

California

Butte College *C, A*
CEI College
Maric College: Panorama City *A*
Cerritos Community College *C, A*
Chabot College *A*
City College of San Francisco *C, A*

College of Marin: Kentfield *C, A*
College of the Redwoods *C*
Cypress College *C, A*
Humphreys College *C, A, B*
Sage College *C, A*
Shasta College *C*
West Valley College *A*

Colorado

Denver Academy of Court
Reporting *A*

Florida

Brevard Community College *A*
Broward Community College *A*
Daytona Beach Community College *A*
Key College *A*
Miami Dade College *A*

Illinois

Career Colleges of Chicago *C, A*
Illinois Central College *C, A*
Illinois Eastern Community Colleges
Wabash Valley College *C*
MacCormac College *A*
Midstate College *A*
South Suburban College of Cook
County *C, A*
Triton College *C, A*

Indiana

College of Court Reporting *A*

Iowa

AIB College of Business *A*
Kaplan University *A*

Michigan

Central Michigan University *B*
Lansing Community College *A*
Oakland Community College *C, A*

Minnesota

Rasmussen College
Mankato *A*
Minnetonka *A*

Mississippi

Mississippi Gulf Coast Community
College
Jefferson Davis Campus *A*

Missouri

Kansas City College of Legal Studies *B*
St. Louis Community College
St. Louis Community College at
Meramec *A*
State Fair Community College *A*

Nevada

Las Vegas College *A*
Truckee Meadows Community
College *C*

New Mexico

Albuquerque Technical-Vocational
Institute *C*

New York

Business Informatics Center *A*
Erie Community College
City Campus *C*
Long Island Business Institute *C, A*
Monroe Community College *C*
New York Career Institute *A*
State University of New York
College of Technology at Alfred *A*

North Carolina

Lenoir Community College *A*

Ohio

Clark State Community College *A*
Cuyahoga Community College
Metropolitan Campus *A*
Stark State College of Technology *A*

Oklahoma

Metropolitan College *B*
Metropolitan College *B*
Rogers State University *A*
Rose State College *A*

Pennsylvania

Luzerne County Community
College *A*
Pennsylvania Highlands Community
College *A*

Puerto Rico

National College of Business &
Technology: Bayamon *A*

South Carolina

Midlands Technical College *C, A*

Tennessee

Chattanooga State Technical
Community College *A*
Southwest Tennessee Community
College *A*

Texas

Amarillo College *C, A*
Court Reporting Institute of Dallas *A*
Del Mar College *C, A*
El Paso Community College *A*
Houston Community College
System *A*
Kilgore College *C, A*
Northwood University: Texas
Campus *A, B*
San Antonio College *C, A*

Washington

Green River Community College *A*

West Virginia

Huntington Junior College *A*

Wisconsin

Gateway Technical College *A*
Lakeshore Technical College *A*
Madison Area Technical College *A*

Crafts/folk art/artisanry

Arizona

Prescott College *B, M*

California

California College of the Arts *B, M*
California State University
Northridge *B*
College of the Siskiyous *A*
Fresno City College *C, A*
Palomar College *A*
Pasadena City College *A*
San Joaquin Delta College *A*
Santa Ana College *C*
Santiago Canyon College *A*

Illinois

University of Illinois
Urbana-Champaign *B, M*

Indiana

Indiana University-Purdue University
Fort Wayne *B*

Kansas
Allen County Community College *A*

Massachusetts
Becker College *A*
Bridgewater State College *B*

Michigan
College for Creative Studies *B*

Montana
Miles Community College *A*

New York
Rochester Institute of
Technology *A, B, M*

North Carolina
Montgomery Community College *C, A*

Ohio
Bowling Green State University *B*
Kent State University *B, M*

Pennsylvania
Harrisburg Area Community
College *A*
Kutztown University of
Pennsylvania *B*
University of the Arts *B*

Tennessee
Memphis College of Art *B*

Texas
University of North Texas *B, M*

Vermont
Goddard College *B*

Virginia
Southwest Virginia Community
College *C*
Virginia Commonwealth University *B*

Creative writing

Alabama
Huntingdon College *B*
University of Alabama *M*

Arizona
Arizona State University *M*
Northern Arizona University *M*
Prescott College *B, M*
University of Arizona *B, M*

Arkansas
Arkansas Tech University *B*
University of Arkansas *M*

California
Antioch Southern California
Antioch University Los Angeles *M*
California College of the Arts *B, M*
California State University
Long Beach *B, M*
Northridge *B*
Sacramento *M*
San Bernardino *B*
Chapman University *B, M*
Dominican University of California *B*
Foothill College *A*
Fresno Pacific University *B*
Grossmont Community College *C*
Loyola Marymount University *M*
Mills College *M*
National University *M*
Otis College of Art and Design *M*
Pitzer College *B*

Pomona College *B*
St. Mary's College of California *M*
San Diego State University *M*
San Francisco State University *M*
San Jose State University *M*
University of California
Irvine *M*
Riverside *B, M*
University of Redlands *B*
University of San Francisco *M*
University of Southern
California *B, M, D*

Colorado
Adams State College *B*
Colorado State University *M*
Naropa University *M*

Connecticut
Albertus Magnus College *B*
University of Bridgeport *B*
Western Connecticut State
University *M*

District of Columbia
American University *M*

Florida
Eckerd College *B*
Florida Atlantic University *M*
Florida International University *M*
Florida State University *B, M, D*
St. Leo University *B*
University of Central Florida *M*
University of Florida *M*
University of Miami *B, M*
University of Tampa *A, B*

Georgia
Emory University *B*
Georgia State University *M*
Kennesaw State University *M*

Idaho
Albertson College of Idaho *B*
Boise State University *M*
Lewis-Clark State College *B*
University of Idaho *M*

Illinois
Columbia College Chicago *B, M*
DePaul University *M*
Eureka College *B*
Knox College *B*
Lewis University *B*
Millikin University *B, T*
North Central College *B*
Northwestern University *B, M*
Roosevelt University *M*
School of the Art Institute of
Chicago *B, M*
Southern Illinois University
Carbondale *M*
University of Illinois
Urbana-Champaign *M*

Indiana
Butler University *B*
Indiana University
Bloomington *M*
Indiana Wesleyan University *B*
Manchester College *A*
St. Joseph's College *B*
Saint Mary's College *B*
St. Mary-of-the-Woods College *B*
University of Evansville *B*
Valparaiso University *B*

Iowa
Briar Cliff University *B*
Coe College *B*
Loras College *B*

University of Iowa *M*
Waldorf College *B*

Kansas
Central Christian College of Kansas *A*
Pittsburg State University *B*
University of Kansas *M*
Wichita State University *M*

Louisiana
Louisiana State University and
Agricultural and Mechanical
College *M*
Loyola University New Orleans *B*
Nicholls State University *B*

Maine
Colby College *B*
University of Maine
Farmington *B*
University of Southern Maine *M*

Maryland
Goucher College *M*
Johns Hopkins University *B, M*
Loyola College in Maryland *B*
University of Maryland
College Park *M*

Massachusetts
Boston University *M*
Brandeis University *B*
Bridgewater State College *B*
Emerson College *B, M*
Lesley University *M*
Massachusetts College of Liberal
Arts *B*
Massachusetts Institute of
Technology *B*
Simon's Rock College of Bard *B*
Suffolk University *B*
University of Massachusetts
Amherst *M*
Western New England College *B*

Michigan
Central Michigan University *B, M*
Cornerstone University *B*
Eastern Michigan University *M*
Grand Valley State University *B*
Northern Michigan University *B, M*
Siena Heights University *B*
University of Detroit Mercy *B*
University of Michigan *B, M*
University of Michigan
Flint *B*
Western Michigan University *B, M*

Minnesota
Concordia College: Moorhead *B*
Hamline University *M*
Minnesota State University
Mankato *B, M*
Moorhead *M*
Northwestern College *B*
Southwest Minnesota State
University *B*
University of Minnesota
Twin Cities *B*
University of St. Thomas *B*

Mississippi
Belhaven College *B*

Missouri
Drury University *B*
Kansas City Art Institute *B*
Lindenwood University *B, M*
Missouri Southern State University *B*
Rockhurst University *C*
Stephens College *B*

University of Missouri
St. Louis *M*
Washington University in St. Louis *M*

Montana
Carroll College *A, B*
University of Montana: Missoula *M*

Nebraska
Hastings College *B*
Union College *B*
University of Nebraska
Omaha *B, M*

Nevada
University of Nevada
Las Vegas *M*

New Hampshire
Chester College of New England *B*
New England College *B, M*
Southern New Hampshire
University *B*
University of New Hampshire *M*

New Jersey
Fairleigh Dickinson University
College at Florham *B, M*

New Mexico
College of Santa Fe *B*
Institute of American Indian Arts *A, B*
New Mexico State University *M*
University of New Mexico *M*

New York
Adelphi University *M*
Bard College *B, M*
City University of New York
Baruch College *B*
Brooklyn College *B, M*
City College *B*
Hunter College *B, M*
Lehman College *M*
Columbia University
Columbia College *B*
School of General Studies *B*
Cornell University *B, M, D*
Eugene Lang College The New School
for Liberal Arts *B*
Hamilton College *B*
Hofstra University *B, M*
Ithaca College *B*
Medaille College *B*
New York University *M*
Pratt Institute *B*
St. Lawrence University *B*
Sarah Lawrence College *B, M*
State University of New York
Albany *D*
College at Brockport *B, M*
Purchase *B*
Syracuse University *M*

North Carolina
North Carolina State University *M*
St. Andrews Presbyterian College *B*
University of North Carolina
Greensboro *M*
Wilmington *B, M*
Warren Wilson College *M*

North Dakota
Dickinson State University *B*

Ohio
Antioch University McGregor *M*
Ashland University *B*
Bowling Green State University *B, M*
Hiram College *B*
Miami University
Oxford Campus *B*

Oberlin College *B*
Ohio Northern University *B*
Ohio University *B*
Ohio Wesleyan University *B*
Otterbein College *B*
Owens Community College
  Toledo *A*
Union Institute & University *M*
University of Akron *M*
University of Cincinnati *M, D*
University of Findlay *B*
Youngstown State University *M*

Oklahoma
Oklahoma Christian University *B*
University of Central Oklahoma *M*
University of Oklahoma *M*

Oregon
Linfield College *B*
Oregon State University *M*
Pacific University *B, M*
Portland State University *M*
Reed College *B*
University of Oregon *M*

Pennsylvania
Allegheny College *B*
Carlow University *B*
Carnegie Mellon University *B*
Chatham College *M*
Eastern University *B*
Franklin & Marshall College *B*
Gettysburg College *B*
Moravian College *B*
Rosemont College *M*
St. Joseph's University *M*
Seton Hill University *B, M*
Susquehanna University *B*
Temple University *M*
University of Pittsburgh *B*
University of Pittsburgh
  Bradford *B*
  Johnstown *B*
Waynesburg College *B*
Westminster College *B, T*
Widener University *B, T*
Wilkes University *M*

Rhode Island
Brown University *M*
Rhode Island College *M*
Roger Williams University *B*

South Carolina
Anderson University *B*
University of South Carolina *M*

Tennessee
University of Memphis *M*

Texas
Austin Community College *A*
Houston Baptist University *B*
McMurry University *B*
Southern Methodist University *B*
Texas State University: San
  Marcos *M, T*
University of Houston *M, D*
University of Texas
  Austin *M*
  El Paso *B, M*

Utah
University of Utah *M*

Vermont
Bennington College *B, M*
Burlington College *B*
Champlain College *B*
Goddard College *B, M*
Green Mountain College *B*

Marlboro College *B*
Norwich University *M*
Southern Vermont College *B*

Virginia
George Mason University *M*
Hollins University *B, M*
Old Dominion University *M*
Randolph-Macon Woman's College *B*
Sweet Briar College *B*
University of Virginia *B*
Virginia Commonwealth University *M*
Virginia Polytechnic Institute and
  State University *M*
Virginia Wesleyan College *B*

Washington
Eastern Washington University *M*
Everett Community College *A*
Pacific Lutheran University *M*
Seattle University *B*
University of Washington *M*
Western Washington University *B*

West Virginia
University of Charleston *B*
West Virginia University *M*
West Virginia Wesleyan College *B*
Wheeling Jesuit University *B*

Wisconsin
Beloit College *B*
Cardinal Stritch University *B*
Carroll College *B*
Marquette University *B*
Northland College *B*
University of Wisconsin
  Madison *M*
  Whitewater *B, T*

Wyoming
University of Wyoming *M*

Credit management

New York
Globe Institute of Technology *C*

Criminal justice and law enforcement

Alabama
Bishop State Community College *A*
Columbia Southern University *B*
Gadsden State Community College *A*
George C. Wallace State Community
  College
  Selma *C*
Jefferson Davis Community College *A*
Judson College *B*
Samford University *B*
Troy University *M*
University of Alabama
  Birmingham *M*
University of North Alabama *B, M*

Alaska
University of Alaska
  Fairbanks *M*
  Southeast *C*

Arizona
Arizona Institute of Business and
  Technology
  International Institute of the
    Americas: Mesa *A*
Arizona State University West *B, M*
Arizona Western College *C*
Eastern Arizona College *A*
High-Tech Institute *A*

International Institute of the Americas
  Tucson *A*
International Institute of the
  Americas: West Valley *A*
Northern Arizona University *B, M*
Pima Community College *C*
Rio Salado College *C, A*
Scottsdale Community College *C, A*
University of Arizona *B*
Yavapai College *C, A*

Arkansas
Arkansas State University *C, A*
Arkansas State University
  Mountain Home *A*
North Arkansas College *C, A*
Northwest Arkansas Community
  College *A*
Ouachita Technical College *C*
Ozarka College *A*
Remington College
  Little Rock *A*
University of Arkansas
  Community College at Hope *C, A*
  Cossatot Community College of the
    C, A
  Fort Smith *C, A, B*

California
California Baptist University *B*
California State University
  East Bay *B*
  Fullerton *B*
  Los Angeles *B, M*
  San Bernardino *B, M*
Citrus College *C, A*
College of the Canyons *C, A*
College of the Desert *C, A*
College of the Redwoods *C, A*
College of the Sequoias *C, A*
Copper Mountain College *C, A*
Cosumnes River College *A*
Crafton Hills College *C, A*
Cuesta College *C, A*
De Anza College *A*
Diablo Valley College *C*
El Camino College *C, A*
Feather River College *A*
Fresno City College *C, A*
Gavilan Community College *C*
Glendale Community College *A*
Golden West College *C, A*
Imperial Valley College *C, A*
Irvine Valley College *C, A*
Lake Tahoe Community College *C, A*
Lassen College *A*
Loma Linda University *M*
Long Beach City College *C, A*
Mendocino College *A*
Modesto Junior College *A*
Monterey Peninsula College *C, A*
National University *B*
Ohlone College *C, A*
Palo Verde College *A*
Palomar College *C, A*
San Bernardino Valley College *C, A*
San Diego Miramar College *C, A*
San Diego State University *B, M*
San Jose City College *A*
Santa Barbara City College *C, A*
Santa Monica College *C, A*
Skyline College *C, A*
Sonoma State University *B*
Southwestern College *C, A*
Victor Valley College *C, A*

Colorado
Aims Community College *A*
Arapahoe Community College *C, A*
Colorado Northwestern Community
  College *C, A*
Community College of Aurora *A*
Johnson & Wales University *A, B*
Mesa State College *A*

Metropolitan State College of
  Denver *B*
Pikes Peak Community College *A*
Pueblo Community College *A*
Red Rocks Community College *C, A*
Trinidad State Junior College *A*
University of Colorado
  Denver and Health Sciences
    Center *M*
Westwood College of Technology *B*
Westwood College of Technology
  South *B*

Connecticut
Northwestern Connecticut
  Community College *A*
Norwalk Community College *A*
Tunxis Community College *C*
University of New Haven *B*
Western Connecticut State
  University *B, M*

Delaware
Delaware Technical and Community
  College
  Stanton/Wilmington Campus *A*

District of Columbia
George Washington University *M*
Trinity University *B*
University of the District of
  Columbia *A*

Florida
Bethune-Cookman College *B*
Central Florida Community College *A*
Chipola College *C, A*
Edison College *A*
Edward Waters College *B*
Florida Atlantic University *M*
Florida Community College at
  Jacksonville *A*
Florida International University *M*
Florida Metropolitan University:
  Jacksonville *A, B, M*
Florida Metropolitan University:
  Orange Park *A, B*
Gulf Coast Community College *A*
Hillsborough Community College *A*
International Community College *M*
Johnson & Wales University *A, B*
Lake City Community College *C*
Lake-Sumter Community College *A*
Lynn University *B, M*
Okaloosa-Walton College *A*
Pasco-Hernando Community
  College *A*
Pensacola Junior College *A*
Remington College: Largo *A*
St. Petersburg College *C, A*
Seminole Community College *C, A*
South Florida Community College *A*
Tallahassee Community College *A*
Valencia Community College *A*

Georgia
Atlanta Metropolitan College *A*
Bainbridge College *A*
Bauder College *A*
Coastal Georgia Community
  College *C, A*
Georgia College and State
  University *B, M*
Georgia Perimeter College *A*
Griffin Technical College *A*
Northwestern Technical College *C, A*
South Georgia College *A*

Hawaii
Chaminade University of Honolulu *M*
Hawaii Pacific University *A, B*
University of Hawaii
  Hawaii Community College *A*

Honolulu Community College *A*
West Oahu *B*

Idaho

Boise State University *A, B, M*
College of Southern Idaho *A*

Illinois

Aurora University *B*
Carl Sandburg College *A*
City Colleges of Chicago
    Harold Washington College *C, A*
Concordia University *B*
Danville Area Community College *A*
Eureka College *B*
Greenville College *B*
Illinois Valley Community
    College *C, A*
Joliet Junior College *C, A*
Kaskaskia College *C, A*
Lewis University *B, M*
Rock Valley College *A*
Sauk Valley Community College *A*
Southeastern Illinois College *C*
Southern Illinois University
    Carbondale *B, M*
Spoon River College *A*
Taylor Business Institute *C*
Triton College *C*
Western Illinois University *B, M*
Westwood College of Technology
    O'Hare *B*

Indiana

Calumet College of St. Joseph *M*
Indiana Business College *A*
Indiana Business College
    Muncie *A*
Indiana University-Purdue University
    Fort Wayne *A, B, M*
Purdue University
    Calumet *B*
Taylor University: Fort Wayne *B*
University of Indianapolis *A, B*
Vincennes University *A*

Iowa

Briar Cliff University *B*
Ellsworth Community College *A*
Marshalltown Community College *A*
Southeastern Community College
    North Campus *A*
Western Iowa Tech Community
    College *A*

Kansas

Brown Mackie College *A*
Central Christian College of
    Kansas *A, B*
Cloud County Community College *A*
Cowley County Community
    College *C, A*
Fort Scott Community College *A*
Garden City Community College *A*
Labette Community College *A*
MidAmerica Nazarene University *B*
Newman University *B*
Seward County Community College *A*
Southwestern College *B*
Washburn University of
    Topeka *A, B, M*

Kentucky

Campbellsville University *B*
Eastern Kentucky University *A*
Elizabethtown Community and
    Technical College *A*
Hopkinsville Community College *C, A*
Somerset Community College *C, A*
Thomas More College *A, B*
Union College *A*
University of Louisville *C, B, M*

Louisiana

Southern University
    New Orleans *B, M*
    Shreveport *A*
Southwest University *A, B, M*

Maine

Andover College *A*
Husson College *A, B, M*
Southern Maine Community
    College *A*
Thomas College *B*
University of Maine
    Augusta *B*
    Fort Kent *A*
    Presque Isle *A, B*

Maryland

Anne Arundel Community
    College *C, A*
Baltimore City Community College *A*
Cecil Community College *C, A*
College of Southern Maryland *A*
Community College of Baltimore
    County *C, A*
Coppin State University *B, M*
Frostburg State University *B*
Hagerstown Business College *A*
Montgomery College *A*
TESST College of Technology:
    Towson *A*
University of Baltimore *C*

Massachusetts

American International College *B, M*
Anna Maria College *B, M*
Boston University *M*
Bridgewater State College *M*
Bunker Hill Community College *A*
Cape Cod Community College *A*
Dean College *A*
Lasell College *B*
Marian Court College *A*
Massachusetts Bay Community
    College *A*
Middlesex Community College *A*
Mount Wachusett Community
    College *C, A*
Newbury College *A, B*
Northeastern University *M*
Roxbury Community College *A*
Salem State College *B*
Springfield College *B*
Suffolk University *B*
University of Massachusetts
    Lowell *B*
Western New England College *M*

Michigan

Alpena Community College *A*
Concordia University *B*
Delta College *A*
Ferris State University *M*
Finlandia University *A*
Gogebic Community College *A*
Grand Valley State University *B, M*
Kalamazoo Valley Community
    College *A*
Kirtland Community College *A*
Lansing Community College *A*
Michigan State University *B, M, D*
Muskegon Community College *A*
Northern Michigan University *A*
Northwestern Michigan College *A*
Oakland Community College *C, A*
Olivet College *B*
St. Clair County Community
    College *C, A*
University of Detroit Mercy *B, M*
University of Michigan
    Flint *B, M*
Washtenaw Community College *A*
Wayne County Community College *A*

West Shore Community College *A*

Minnesota

Capella University *M, D*
Concordia University: St. Paul *B*
Inver Hills Community College *A*
Metropolitan State University *C*
Minnesota State University
    Mankato *B*
Northland Community & Technical
    College *A*
St. Cloud State University *B, M*
St. Mary's University of Minnesota *B*
Southwest Minnesota State
    University *B*
Vermilion Community College *A*
Winona State University *B*

Mississippi

Mississippi College *B, M*
Mississippi Delta Community
    College *A*
Mississippi Valley State University *M*

Missouri

Blue River Community College *A*
Central Missouri State University *B, M*
Columbia College *A, B, M*
Culver-Stockton College *B*
Grantham University *A, B*
Hannibal-LaGrange College *B*
Harris-Stowe State University *B*
Jefferson College *A*
Lincoln University *A, B*
Lindenwood University *M*
Maple Woods Community
    College *C, A*
Missouri Southern State
    University *A, B*
Missouri Valley College *B*
Park University *A, B*
Penn Valley Community College *C, A*
St. Charles Community College *C, A*
St. Louis University *B*
University of Missouri
    Kansas City *B, M*
Webster University *M*

Montana

Flathead Valley Community College *A*
University of Great Falls *M*

Nebraska

Bellevue University *B*
Dana College *B*
Northeast Community College *A*
Peru State College *B*

Nevada

Great Basin College *A*
High-Tech Institute *A*
Truckee Meadows Community
    College *A*

New Hampshire

Granite State College *B*
McIntosh College *A*
New Hampshire Community
    Technical College
    Berlin *A*
New Hampshire Technical Institute *A*

New Jersey

The College of New Jersey *B*
Essex County College *A*
Fairleigh Dickinson University
    College at Florham *C*
Georgian Court University *B*
Kean University *B*
Middlesex County College *A*

Rutgers, The State University of New
    Jersey
    New Brunswick/Piscataway
        Campus *B*
Thomas Edison State College *A, B*
Union County College *C, A*

New Mexico

College of Santa Fe *B*
International Institute of the
    Americas *A*
New Mexico State University
    Grants *A*
Western New Mexico University *C, B*

New York

Adelphi University *B*
Bryant & Stratton College: Henrietta *A*
City University of New York
    John Jay College of Criminal
        Justice *B, M*
College of Saint Rose *B*
Columbia-Greene Community
    College *A*
Corning Community College *A*
Erie Community College
    City Campus *A*
    North Campus *A*
Excelsior College *B*
Genesee Community College *C, A*
Herkimer County Community
    College *A*
Iona College *B, M*
Jefferson Community College *C, A*
Keuka College *B*
Long Island University
    C. W. Post Campus *B, M*
Marist College *B*
Mercy College *B*
Mohawk Valley Community College *A*
Monroe College *B*
Monroe Community College *C*
Nassau Community College *A*
New York Institute of Technology *B*
Niagara County Community
    College *A*
Pace University *B*
Roberts Wesleyan College *B*
Rochester Institute of Technology *B*
Sage College of Albany *B*
St. John's University *C, A, B, M*
State University of New York
    College at Potsdam *B*
    Farmingdale *C, A*
Tompkins-Cortland Community
    College *C*

North Carolina

Alamance Community College *A*
Bladen Community College *A*
Catawba College *B*
Chowan College *B*
College of the Albemarle *A*
Craven Community College *A*
Forsyth Technical Community
    College *A*
Johnson C. Smith University *B*
Johnston Community College *A*
North Carolina Central University *B*
Rockingham Community College *A*
South College *A*
Surry Community College *A*
Wilson Technical Community
    College *C*

Ohio

AEC Southern Ohio College
    Brown Mackie College: Akron *C, A*
Ashland University *A, B*
Cedarville University *B*
Central Ohio Technical College *A*
Clark State Community College *A*
Cleveland State University *C*

Columbus State Community
  College *A*
James A. Rhodes State College *A*
Lake Erie College *B*
Marion Technical College *A*
Ohio Institute of Photography and
  Technology *A*
Ohio Northern University *B*
Owens Community College
  Toledo *A*
Remington College
  Cleveland *A*
Tiffin University *A, B, M*
Union Institute & University *B*
University of Akron *A*
University of Cincinnati
  Clermont College *A*
University of Findlay *B*
Urbana University *A*
Washington State Community
  College *A*
Youngstown State University *A, B, M*

Oklahoma
Eastern Oklahoma State College *A*
Mid-America Christian University *B*
Oklahoma City University *B, M*
Rogers State University *B*
University of Central Oklahoma *M*

Oregon
Central Oregon Community
  College *A*
Chemeketa Community College *A*
Portland State University *B*
Southern Oregon University *B*
Treasure Valley Community College *A*
Western Oregon University *B, M*

Pennsylvania
Alvernia College *B*
Berks Technical Institute *A*
Butler County Community College *A*
Chestnut Hill College *C, A, B*
Delaware Valley College *B*
Gwynedd-Mercy College *B*
Harcum College *A*
Harrisburg Area Community
  College *A*
ICM School of Business & Medical
  Careers *A*
Keystone College *B*
Lehigh Carbon Community
  College *C, A*
Lock Haven University of
  Pennsylvania *A, B*
Mansfield University of
  Pennsylvania *A, B*
Marywood University *B, M*
Mercyhurst College *B*
Penn State
  Abington *B*
  Schuylkill - Capital College *B*
  University Park *B*
Point Park University *A, B*
Reading Area Community College *A*
St. Vincent College *C*
University of Pittsburgh *B*
University of Pittsburgh
  Greensburg *B*
  Titusville *C*
Villanova University *M*
Waynesburg College *B*
Widener University *B, M*
York College of Pennsylvania *B*
York Technical Institute *A*

Puerto Rico
Inter American University of Puerto
  Rico
  Guayama Campus *B*
  Ponce Campus *B, M*
Turabo University *M*

Universidad del Este *B*
University of Puerto Rico
  Carolina Regional College *B*

Rhode Island
Johnson & Wales University *A, B*
Roger Williams University *A, B, M*
Salve Regina University *A, B, M*

South Carolina
Anderson University *B*
Charleston Southern University *B*
The Citadel *B*
Claflin University *B*
Limestone College *B*
Morris College *B*
South Carolina State University *B*
South University *B*
Technical College of the
  Lowcountry *A*
Trident Technical College *C, A*
University of South Carolina *B, M*

South Dakota
Kilian Community College *A*
Oglala Lakota College *A*
Southeast Technical Institute *A*

Tennessee
East Tennessee State University *B, M*
Lambuth University *B*
Middle Tennessee State
  University *B, M*
Tennessee State University *M*
University of Memphis *B, M*
University of Tennessee
  Chattanooga *B, M*
  Martin *B*

Texas
Cedar Valley College *C, A*
Central Texas College *C, A*
Concordia University at Austin *B*
Grayson County College *C, A*
Hill College *C, A*
Howard College *C*
Kilgore College *A*
Lubbock Christian University *B*
McLennan Community College *C, A*
Midland College *A*
Palo Alto College *A*
St. Philip's College *A*
Sam Houston State University *M*
South Plains College *A*
South Texas College *A*
Sul Ross State University *M*
Texarkana College *C, A*
Texas A&M University
  Commerce *B*
Texas Southern University *B, M*
Texas Southmost College *A*
Texas State University: San Marcos *M*
Trinity Valley Community College *C, A*
University of Mary Hardin-Baylor *B*
University of Texas
  Brownsville *B*
  Pan American *B, M*
  of the Permian Basin *M*
West Texas A&M University *B*
Western Texas College *A*
Wharton County Junior College *A*
Wiley College *A*

Utah
Snow College *A*
Utah Valley State College *A, B*

Vermont
Champlain College *A, B*

Virginia
Averett University *B*

Blue Ridge Community College *C*
Bluefield College *B*
Central Virginia Community
  College *A*
Danville Community College *A*
Hampton University *B*
Liberty University *B*
Mountain Empire Community
  College *A*
New River Community College *A*
Northern Virginia Community
  College *C, A*
Parks College: Arlington *A*
Rappahannock Community College *C*
Shenandoah University *B*
Thomas Nelson Community
  College *A*
Virginia Commonwealth
  University *B, M*
Virginia Intermont College *B*
Virginia Wesleyan College *B*

Washington
Bellevue Community College *A*
Centralia College *A*
City University *C, B, M*
Columbia Basin College *A*
Everett Community College *A*
Lower Columbia College *A*
Peninsula College *C, A*
Shoreline Community College *A*
Spokane Community College *A*
Spokane Falls Community
  College *C, A*
Washington State University *B, M, D*

West Virginia
Mountain State University *B*
Potomac State College of West Virginia
  University *A*
West Virginia Wesleyan College *B*

Wisconsin
Lakeland College *B*
Marian College of Fond du Lac *B*
University of Wisconsin
  Platteville *B*

Wyoming
Central Wyoming College *A*
Western Wyoming Community
  College *A*

Criminal justice studies

Alabama
Alabama State University *B*
Andrew Jackson University *C, A, B, M*
Athens State University *B*
Auburn University at
  Montgomery *B, M*
Central Alabama Community
  College *C, A*
Chattahoochee Valley Community
  College *C, A*
Community College of the Air
  Force *A*
Faulkner University *A, B, M*
Jacksonville State University *B, M*
Lawson State Community College *A*
Troy University *B*
University of Alabama *B, M*
University of South Alabama *B*

Alaska
University of Alaska
  Fairbanks *B*

Arizona
Arizona State University *B, M, D*
Arizona Western College *A*
Central Arizona College *A*

Estrella Mountain Community
  College *C, A*
Grand Canyon University *B*
Northern Arizona University *B, M*
Northland Pioneer College *A*
Pima Community College *A*
Scottsdale Community College *A*
University of Phoenix *B*

Arkansas
Arkansas Tech University *A*
Black River Technical College *A*
Harding University *B*
Ouachita Technical College *A*
Southeast Arkansas College *A*
Southern Arkansas University *B*
University of Arkansas *B*
University of Arkansas
  Community College at Batesville *A*
  Little Rock *B*
  Monticello *B*
  Pine Bluff *B*

California
California State University
  Bakersfield *B*
  Chico *B*
  Long Beach *B, M*
  Sacramento *B, M*
  Stanislaus *B, M*
Citrus College *A*
College of the Redwoods *C*
Golden West College *C, A*
Los Angeles Mission College *C, A*
Maric College
  Vista *A*
Modesto Junior College *A*
National University *B, M*
Remington College
  San Diego *A, B*
Saddleback College *C*
San Diego Miramar College *A*
San Francisco State University *B*
San Jose State University *B, M*
Santa Barbara Business College *A*
Santa Barbara Business College
  Bakersfield *A*
  Santa Maria *C, A*
Santa Barbara Business College:
  Ventura *A*
Sierra College *A*
Southwestern College *A*
Taft College *A*
Ventura College *C, A*
West Valley College *A*
Westwood College: Long Beach *B*
Yuba Community College District *A*

Colorado
Blair College *A*
Colorado Mountain College
  Spring Valley Campus *A*
Community College of Aurora *A*
Metropolitan State College of
  Denver *A*
Parks College: Aurora *A*
Red Rocks Community College *A*
Remington College
  Colorado Springs *A, B*
Trinidad State Junior College *A*
University of Northern Colorado *B*
Western State College of Colorado *B*

Connecticut
Albertus Magnus College *B*
Briarwood College *A, B*
Central Connecticut State
  University *M*
Quinnipiac University *B*
Three Rivers Community College *C, A*
University of New Haven *M*

Delaware

Delaware State University *B*
Delaware Technical and Community
College
Owens Campus *A*
Terry Campus *A*
University of Delaware *B*
Wilmington College *B*

District of Columbia

American University *B, M*
George Washington University *B, M*

Florida

Barry University *B*
Broward Community College *A*
Edison College *A*
Florida Agricultural and Mechanical
University *B*
Florida Atlantic University *B*
Florida Community College at
Jacksonville *A*
Florida Gulf Coast University *B*
Florida International University *B*
Florida Metropolitan University
Tampa College *A, B*
Tampa College Lakeland *B*
Florida Metropolitan University:
Orange Park *A, B*
Florida National College *A*
Florida Southern College *B*
Florida State University *B, M, D*
Gulf Coast Community College *A*
Hillsborough Community College *A*
Indian River Community College *A*
International College *A, B*
Lake City Community College *A*
Lynn University *B, M*
Manatee Community College *A*
Miami Dade College *C, A*
Okaloosa-Walton College *A*
Polk Community College *A*
Remington College: Largo *A*
St. Leo University *B, M*
St. Thomas University *C, B*
Southwest Florida College *A*
Southwest Florida College
Tampa *A*
Tallahassee Community College *A*
University of Central Florida *B, M*
University of Florida *B*
University of North Florida *B, M*
University of South Florida *B, M, D*
University of West Florida *B*

Georgia

Albany State University *A, B*
Albany Technical College *C, A*
Augusta State University *A, B*
Central Georgia Technical
College *C, A*
Chattahoochee Technical College *C, A*
Clark Atlanta University *M*
Clayton State University *B*
Columbus State University *C, A, B*
Darton College *A*
East Georgia College *A*
Gainesville State College *A*
Georgia Military College *A*
Georgia Southern University *B*
Georgia Southwestern State
University *A*
Georgia State University *B, M*
Gordon College *A*
Kennesaw State University *B*
Macon State College *A*
Mercer University *B*
Middle Georgia College *C, A*
Piedmont College *B*
Savannah Technical College *A*
South Georgia College *A*
Southwest Georgia Technical
College *C, A*

Thomas University *A, B*
University of Georgia *B*
University of West Georgia *B*
Valdosta State University *B, M*
West Georgia Technical College *C, A*
Young Harris College *A*

Hawaii

Remington College
Honolulu *A, B*
University of Hawaii
Hawaii Community College *A*
Honolulu Community College *A*

Idaho

Idaho State University *A*
Lewis-Clark State College *B*
North Idaho College *A*
University of Idaho *B*

Illinois

Aurora University *B*
Blackburn College *B*
Carl Sandburg College *C*
Concordia University *B*
Governors State University *B, M*
Heartland Community College *A*
Illinois Central College *A*
Illinois State University *B, M*
John A. Logan College *C, A*
Lewis University *B, M*
Lewis and Clark Community
College *A*
Lincoln Land Community College *C*
Loyola University of Chicago *B, M*
Northeastern Illinois University *B*
Olivet Nazarene University *B*
Quincy University *B*
Richland Community College *A*
Roosevelt University *B*
St. Xavier University *B*
Sauk Valley Community College *A*
South Suburban College of Cook
County *C, A*
Southern Illinois University
Edwardsville *B*
University of Illinois
Chicago *B, M, D*
Springfield *B*
Westwood College of Technology
O'Hare *B*

Indiana

Ancilla College *A*
Anderson University *A, B*
Ball State University *A, B*
Butler University *B*
Grace College *B*
Indiana Institute of Technology *A, B*
Indiana University
Bloomington *B, M, D*
East *A, B*
Kokomo *A, B*
Northwest *A, B*
South Bend *A, B*
Indiana University-Purdue University
Indianapolis *A, B, M*
Indiana Wesleyan University *A, B*
Ivy Tech State College
Ivy Tech Community College:
Bloomington *A*
Ivy Tech Community College:
Central Indiana *A*
Ivy Tech Community College: East
Central *A*
Ivy Tech Community College:
Kokomo *A*
Ivy Tech Community College:
Lafayette *A*
Ivy Tech Community College: North
Central *A*
Ivy Tech Community College:
Northeast *A*

Ivy Tech Community College:
Northwest *A*
Ivy Tech Community College:
Southwest *A*
Ivy Tech Community College:
Wabash Valley *A*
Manchester College *A*
Oakland City University *A, B*
St. Joseph's College *B*
Tri-State University *A, B*

Iowa

Buena Vista University *B*
Ellsworth Community College *A*
Graceland University *B*
Grand View College *B*
Hamilton College
Cedar Rapids *A*
Iowa Wesleyan College *B*
Kaplan University *A, B, M*
Loras College *B*
St. Ambrose University *B, M, T*
Simpson College *B*
University of Dubuque *B*
Upper Iowa University *B*
William Penn University *B*

Kansas

Bethany College *B*
Butler County Community College *A*
Central Christian College of Kansas *A*
Fort Hays State University *B*
Kansas Wesleyan University *A, B*
Pittsburg State University *B*
Washburn University of Topeka *A, B*
Wichita State University *C, B, M*

Kentucky

Campbellsville University *A*
Eastern Kentucky University *M*
Hopkinsville Community College *C, A*
Kentucky State University *B*
Kentucky Wesleyan College *B*
Lindsey Wilson College *B*
Murray State University *A, B*
Northern Kentucky University *B*
Pikeville College *A, B*

Louisiana

Bossier Parish Community College *A*
Grambling State University *B, M*
Louisiana State University
Alexandria *A*
Shreveport *A*
Loyola University New Orleans *B, M*
Northwestern State University *B*
Southeastern Louisiana University *B*
Southern University and Agricultural
and Mechanical College *B*
University of Louisiana at Lafayette *B*
University of Louisiana at
Monroe *B, M*

Maine

Andover College *A*
Husson College *A, B*
St. Joseph's College *B*
Thomas College *B*
University of Maine
Augusta *A*
Fort Kent *A*
University of Southern Maine *B*

Maryland

Chesapeake College *A*
Frederick Community College *A*
Hagerstown Business College *A*
Howard Community College *A*
Montgomery College *A*
Mount St. Mary's University *B*
Prince George's Community
College *C, A*
University of Baltimore *B, M*

Massachusetts

American International College *B, M*
Bay Path College *B*
Becker College *A, B*
Berkshire Community College *A*
Bridgewater State College *B, M*
Bristol Community College *A*
Cape Cod Community College *A*
Curry College *B*
Dean College *A*
Endicott College *B*
Fitchburg State College *M*
Holyoke Community College *C, A*
Mount Ida College *A, B*
Mount Wachusett Community
College *A*
Nichols College *B*
North Shore Community College *C, A*
Northeastern University *B*
Northern Essex Community
College *A*
Quincy College *A*
Quinsigamond Community College *A*
Suffolk University *M*
University of Massachusetts
Boston *B*
Lowell *M*
Western New England College *B*
Westfield State College *B, M*
Worcester State College *B*

Michigan

Adrian College *A, B*
Jackson Community College *C, A*
Kirtland Community College *A*
Lansing Community College *A*
Madonna University *C, A, B, M*
Michigan State University *B, M*
Montcalm Community College *C, A*
Northern Michigan University *A, B*
Saginaw Valley State University *B*
Schoolcraft College *A*
Siena Heights University *A, B*
University of Detroit Mercy *B, M*
Wayne State University *B, M*
Western Michigan University *B*

Minnesota

Bemidji State University *A, B*
Brown College *A, B*
Capella University *M, D*
Central Lakes College *C, A*
Century Community and Technical
College *A*
Concordia University: St. Paul *B*
Gustavus Adolphus College *B*
Hamline University *B*
Metropolitan State University *B*
Minneapolis Community and
Technical College *A*
Minnesota State Community and
Technical College - Fergus Falls *A*
Minnesota State University
Moorhead *B*
Normandale Community College *A*
Northland Community & Technical
College *A*
Northwestern College *B*
Ridgewater College *A*
Rochester Community and Technical
College *A*
St. Mary's University of Minnesota *B*
Vermilion Community College *A*
Winona State University *B*

Mississippi

Alcorn State University *B*
Coahoma Community College *A*
Delta State University *B, M*
Hinds Community College *A*
Itawamba Community College *A*
Jackson State University *B, M*

Mississippi Gulf Coast Community
College
Jefferson Davis Campus *A*
Mississippi Valley State University *B*
University of Southern
Mississippi *B, M, D*

Missouri
Central Methodist University *B*
Drury University *M*
Evangel University *B*
Lindenwood University *B*
Longview Community College *A*
Maple Woods Community College *A*
Missouri Baptist University *B*
Missouri State University *B*
Missouri Western State University *B*
Moberly Area Community College *A*
North Central Missouri College *C, A*
Penn Valley Community College *A*
St. Louis Community College
St. Louis Community College at
Meramec *A*
Southeast Missouri State University *M*
Truman State University *B*

Montana
University of Great Falls *A, B*

Nebraska
Central Community College *C, A*
University of Nebraska
Kearney *B*
Omaha *B, M, D*
Wayne State College *B*
Western Nebraska Community
College *A*

Nevada
Community College of Southern
Nevada *C, A*
Truckee Meadows Community
College *C, A*

New Hampshire
Franklin Pierce College *B*
Granite State College *B*
McIntosh College *A*
New England College *B*
Plymouth State University *B*
St. Anselm College *B*

New Jersey
Caldwell College *B*
Centenary College *B*
College of St. Elizabeth *B*
Cumberland County College *A*
Essex County College *A*
Fairleigh Dickinson University
Metropolitan Campus *B*
Hudson County Community
College *A*
Monmouth University *B, M*
New Jersey City University *M*
Rowan University *B*
Rutgers, The State University of New
Jersey
Camden Regional Campus *B*
Newark Regional Campus *B, M, D*
Seton Hall University *B*
Sussex County Community College *A*
Warren County Community College *A*

New Mexico
Albuquerque Technical-Vocational
Institute *A*
Clovis Community College *A*
College of the Southwest *B*
Eastern New Mexico University *B*
Eastern New Mexico University:
Roswell Campus *A*
New Mexico Highlands University *B*
New Mexico Junior College *A*

New Mexico State University *A, B, M*
New Mexico State University
Alamogordo *A*
Northern New Mexico College *A*
Santa Fe Community College *A*
Western New Mexico University *B*

New York
Alfred University *B*
Canisius College *B*
Cayuga County Community
College *C, A*
Cazenovia College *A, B*
Columbia-Greene Community
College *A*
Corning Community College *A*
Dutchess Community College *C, A*
Elmira College *B*
Finger Lakes Community College *C, A*
Fordham University *B, M, D*
Fulton-Montgomery Community
College *C, A*
Herkimer County Community
College *A*
Hilbert College *A, B*
Jamestown Community College *A*
Molloy College *B*
Monroe Community College *A*
Niagara University *B, M*
North Country Community College *A*
Onondaga Community College *A*
Orange County Community College *A*
Rockland Community College *A*
Russell Sage College *B*
St. Francis College *A, B*
Schenectady County Community
College *A*
State University of New York
Albany *B, M, D*
College at Buffalo *B, M*
College at Fredonia *B*
College at Oneonta *B*
College at Plattsburgh *B*
College of Technology at
Canton *C, A, B*
Sullivan County Community
College *A*
Utica College *B, M*

North Carolina
Alamance Community College *A*
Appalachian State University *B*
Barton College *B*
Beaufort County Community
College *C, A*
Belmont Abbey College *B*
Campbell University *B*
Carteret Community College *A*
Catawba Valley Community College *A*
Central Carolina Community
College *A*
Cleveland Community College *C, A*
Davidson County Community
College *A*
East Carolina University *B, M*
Edgecombe Community College *A*
Elizabeth City State University *B*
Elon University *B*
Fayetteville State University *B*
Fayetteville Technical Community
College *A*
Guilford College *B*
Guilford Technical Community
College *A*
Haywood Community College *A*
High Point University *B*
Isothermal Community College *C, A*
Lees-McRae College *B*
Livingstone College *B*
Methodist College *A, B*
Montgomery Community College *A*
Mount Olive College *B*
North Carolina Central University *M*
North Carolina Wesleyan College *B*

Pfeiffer University *B*
Piedmont Community College *A*
Pitt Community College *A*
Roanoke-Chowan Community
College *A*
Robeson Community College *C, A*
Rowan-Cabarrus Community
College *A*
St. Augustine's College *B*
Sandhills Community College *A*
Shaw University *A, B*
South Piedmont Community
College *C, A*
Southwestern Community College *A*
Stanly Community College *C, A*
University of North Carolina
Charlotte *B, M*
Pembroke *B*
Wilmington *B*
Western Carolina University *B*
Western Piedmont Community
College *A*
Wilkes Community College *C, A*
Wilson Technical Community
College *A*
Winston-Salem State University *B*

North Dakota
Bismarck State College *A*
Jamestown College *B*
Minot State University *B, M*
North Dakota State University *B, D*
University of Mary *B*
University of North Dakota *B, D*

Ohio
Baldwin-Wallace College *B*
Bluffton University *B*
Bowling Green State University *B*
Bowling Green State University:
Firelands College *A*
Central Ohio Technical College *A*
Kent State University *B, M*
Kent State University
Ashtabula Regional Campus *A*
East Liverpool Regional Campus *A*
Salem Regional Campus *A*
Stark Campus *A*
Trumbull Campus *A*
Tuscarawas Campus *A*
Lourdes College *A, B*
Mount Vernon Nazarene University *B*
Ohio Dominican University *B*
Ohio Northern University *B*
Ohio University
Chillicothe Campus *B*
Southern Campus at Ironton *B*
Sinclair Community College *A*
Union Institute & University *A*
University of Cincinnati *B, M, D*
University of Cincinnati
Clermont College *A*
Raymond Walters College *A*
University of Dayton *B*
University of Toledo *B, M*
Urbana University *B*
Wilmington College *B*
Xavier University *A, B, M*
Youngstown State University *A, B, M*

Oklahoma
Cameron University *A, B*
Carl Albert State College *A*
East Central University *B*
Eastern Oklahoma State College *A*
Northeastern Oklahoma Agricultural
and Mechanical College *A*
Northeastern State University *B, M*
Southeastern Oklahoma State
University *B*
Southern Nazarene University *B*
Southwestern Oklahoma State
University *B*
Tulsa Community College *A*

University of Central Oklahoma *B*

Oregon
Chemeketa Community College *C, A*
Clatsop Community College *A*
Lane Community College *A*
Linn-Benton Community College *A*
Pioneer Pacific College *A, B*
Pioneer Pacific College: Springfield *A*
Portland Community College *A*
Portland State University *B, M*
Southern Oregon University *B*
Southwestern Oregon Community
College *A*
Treasure Valley Community College *A*

Pennsylvania
Bloomsburg University of
Pennsylvania *B*
Bucks County Community College *A*
CHI Institute: Southampton *A*
California University of
Pennsylvania *A, B*
Central Pennsylvania College *A, B*
DeSales University *B, M, T*
Edinboro University of
Pennsylvania *B*
Elizabethtown College *B*
Gannon University *C, A, B*
ICM School of Business & Medical
Careers *A*
Immaculata University *A, B*
Keystone College *A, B*
King's College *A, B*
Kutztown University of
Pennsylvania *B*
La Roche College *B*
La Salle University *A, B*
Lackawanna College *A*
Lehigh Valley College *A*
Lincoln University *B*
Lycoming College *B*
Marywood University *A*
Mercyhurst College *C, A, B, M*
Messiah College *B*
Moravian College *B*
Mount Aloysius College *A, B, M*
Neumann College *B*
Northampton County Area
Community College *A*
Penn State
Abington *B*
Altoona *A, B*
Beaver *B*
Berks *B*
Delaware County *B*
Dubois *B*
Fayette *B*
Harrisburg *B*
Hazleton *B*
Lehigh Valley *B*
McKeesport *B*
Mont Alto *B*
New Kensington *B*
Schuylkill - Capital College *B*
Shenango *B*
University Park *B, M, D*
Wilkes-Barre *B*
Worthington Scranton *B*
York *B*
Point Park University *A, B, M*
Seton Hill University *B*
Shippensburg University of
Pennsylvania *B, M*
Temple University *B, M, D*
Thiel College *B*
University of Scranton *A*
Valley Forge Military College *A*
West Chester University of
Pennsylvania *B, M*
Westminster College *B*
Wilkes University *B*

Puerto Rico

Inter American University of Puerto Rico
  Aguadilla Campus *B, M*
  Arecibo Campus *B*
  Fajardo Campus *B*
Universidad Metropolitana *B*

Rhode Island

Rhode Island College *B*
Roger Williams University *B, M*

South Carolina

Aiken Technical College *C, A*
Charleston Southern University *B, M*
Florence-Darlington Technical
  College *A*
Greenville Technical College *C, A*
Horry-Georgetown Technical
  College *C, A*
Midlands Technical College *C, A*
Northeastern Technical College *C*
Orangeburg-Calhoun Technical
  College *A*
Piedmont Technical College *A*
Technical College of the
  Lowcountry *A*
University of South Carolina
  Lancaster *A*
  Upstate *B*

South Dakota

Dakota Wesleyan University *A, B*
Mount Marty College *A, B*
University of South Dakota *B*

Tennessee

Cumberland University *A, B*
Hiwassee College *A*
Tennessee State University *B, M*
University of Tennessee
  Knoxville *B*

Texas

Alvin Community College *C, A*
Angelina College *A*
Angelo State University *B*
Blinn College *C, A*
Clarendon College *A*
Coastal Bend College *A*
Dallas Baptist University *B*
Del Mar College *A*
Eastfield College *C, A*
El Paso Community College *A*
Galveston College *C, A*
Hill College *A*
Jarvis Christian College *B*
Kilgore College *C, A*
Lamar State College at Port Arthur *A*
Lamar University *B, M*
Laredo Community College *A*
Lon Morris College *A*
Midwestern State University *B*
Mountain View College *C, A*
Navarro College *A*
North Central Texas College *A*
North Harris Montgomery
  Community College District *C, A*
Paul Quinn College *B*
Prairie View A&M University *B*
St. Edward's University *B*
St. Mary's University *B*
Sam Houston State University *B, M, D*
San Antonio College *A*
San Jacinto College
  North *C, A*
Southwestern Adventist University *B*
Stephen F. Austin State University *B*
Sul Ross State University *B*
Tarleton State University *B, M*
Tarrant County College *A*
Temple College *A*
Texarkana College *A*

Texas A&M University
  Commerce *B*
  Texarkana *B*
Texas Christian University *B*
Texas State University: San Marcos *B*
Texas Woman's University *B*
Tyler Junior College *A*
University of Houston
  Downtown *B, M*
University of North Texas *B*
University of Texas
  Arlington *B, M*
  Brownsville *C, A*
  El Paso *B*
  San Antonio *B, M*
  Tyler *B, M*
Vernon College *C, A*
Wayland Baptist University *B*
West Texas A&M University *M*

Utah

Dixie State College of Utah *A*
Salt Lake Community College *A*
Southern Utah University *A, B*
Weber State University *A, B, M*

Vermont

Castleton State College *A, B*
Champlain College *A, B*
Norwich University *B*

Virginia

Dabney S. Lancaster Community
  College *A*
Ferrum College *B*
J. Sargeant Reynolds Community
  College *A*
Liberty University *B*
Longwood University *B*
Marymount University *B*
Mountain Empire Community
  College *A*
Norfolk State University *M*
Parks College: Arlington *A*
Radford University *B, M*
Rappahannock Community College *A*
Roanoke College *B*
St. Paul's College *B*
University of Richmond *B*
University of Virginia's College at
  Wise *B*
Virginia State University *B*
Virginia Wesleyan College *B*
Virginia Western Community
  College *A*

Washington

Central Washington University *B*
Centralia College *A*
Columbia Basin College *C*
Crown College *A*
Gonzaga University *B*
Pierce College *A*
Saint Martin's University *B*
Seattle University *B*
Tacoma Community College *C*
Walla Walla Community College *A*
Yakima Valley Community College *A*

West Virginia

Bluefield State College *B*
Marshall University *B, M*
Mountain State University *A, B, M*
Potomac State College of West Virginia
  University *C, A*
Salem International University *B*
West Liberty State College *B*
West Virginia State University *B*
West Virginia University at
  Parkersburg *C, A*
Wheeling Jesuit University *B*

Wisconsin

Carroll College *B*
Carthage College *B*
Concordia University Wisconsin *B*
Edgewood College *B*
Fox Valley Technical College *A*
Mount Mary College *B*
Nicolet Area Technical College *A*
University of Wisconsin
  Eau Claire *B*
  Madison *B, M*
  Milwaukee *B, M*
  Parkside *B*
  Superior *B*
Viterbo University *B*

Wyoming

Casper College *A*
Eastern Wyoming College *A*
University of Wyoming *B*

Criminalistics/criminal science

Florida

Florida Gulf Coast University *B*
Remington College: Largo *A*
St. Petersburg College *C, A*

Hawaii

Chaminade University of
  Honolulu *A, B*

Illinois

Westwood College of Technology
  O'Hare *B*

Iowa

St. Ambrose University *B*

Michigan

Oakland Community College *C, A*

Minnesota

Central Lakes College *A*

New Hampshire

McIntosh College *A*

New York

Niagara County Community
  College *A*

Pennsylvania

Gannon University *C*
Harrisburg Area Community
  College *C, A*
Keystone College *A, B*

Washington

Seattle University *B*

West Virginia

West Virginia University *B*

Criminology

Alabama

Auburn University *B*
Enterprise-Ozark Community
  College *C*

Arizona

Central Arizona College *A*

Arkansas

Arkansas State University *B*

California

Bakersfield College *A*
California Lutheran University *B*
California State University
  Bakersfield *B*
  Fresno *B, M*
Chabot College *A*
Feather River College *A*
Fresno City College *C, A*
Porterville College *C, A*
San Diego State University *M*
San Francisco State University *M*
San Jose State University *M*
University of California
  Irvine *B, M, D*
University of La Verne *B*
West Hills Community College *A*

Colorado

Adams State College *B*
Regis University *B*
Trinidad State Junior College *A*
University of Denver *B*

Connecticut

Central Connecticut State
  University *B*
Mitchell College *A, B*
Quinnipiac University *B*
Sacred Heart University *B*

Delaware

University of Delaware *M, D*

District of Columbia

Gallaudet University *B*

Florida

Florida State University *B, M, D*
Gulf Coast Community College *A*
Lake City Community College *A*
University of Miami *B*
University of South Florida *B, M, D*
University of Tampa *B*

Georgia

Clark Atlanta University *B*
Dalton State College *A*
Darton College *A*
East Georgia College *A*
Paine College *B*
South Georgia College *A*
University of West Georgia *B*

Illinois

Blackburn College *B*
Dominican University *B*
Kishwaukee College *A*
Roosevelt University *B*
Westwood College of Technology
  O'Hare *B*

Indiana

Ball State University *B*
Butler University *B*
Indiana State University *A, B, M*
Indiana Wesleyan University *B*
Valparaiso University *B*

Iowa

Ellsworth Community College *A*
North Iowa Area Community
  College *A*
University of Northern Iowa *B*
Upper Iowa University *B*

Kansas

Central Christian College of Kansas *A*
Fort Scott Community College *A*
MidAmerica Nazarene University *B*

Louisiana
Dillard University *B*

Maine
Husson College *B, M*
University of Southern Maine *B*

Maryland
College of Notre Dame of Maryland *B*
Howard Community College *A*
University of Maryland
    College Park *B, M, D*
    Eastern Shore *M*
    University College *B*

Massachusetts
American International College *B, M*
Stonehill College *B*
Suffolk University *B, M*

Michigan
Eastern Michigan University *B, M*

Minnesota
Hamline University *B*
Minnesota State University
    Mankato *B*
Rasmussen College
    St. Cloud *A*
Ridgewater College *A*
St. Cloud State University *B*
University of Minnesota
    Duluth *B*
    Twin Cities *B*
University of St. Thomas *B*
Vermilion Community College *A*
Winona State University *B*

Missouri
Drury University *B*
Evangel University *B*
Maryville University of Saint Louis *B*
University of Missouri
    St. Louis *B, M, D*

Montana
University of Montana: Missoula *B, M*

Nebraska
Midland Lutheran College *B*

Nevada
University of Nevada
    Reno *B*

New Hampshire
University of New Hampshire *B*

New Jersey
The College of New Jersey *B*
Richard Stockton College of New
    Jersey *B, M*
Salem Community College *A*

New York
City University of New York
    John Jay College of Criminal
        Justice *B*
Keuka College *B*
Le Moyne College *B*
Medaille College *B*
Niagara University *B*
St. John's University *M*
St. Joseph's College *C*
St. Joseph's College: Suffolk Campus *C*
State University of New York
    College at Cortland *B*
    College at Old Westbury *B*

North Carolina
Belmont Abbey College *B*

Johnson C. Smith University *B*
North Carolina State University *B*

North Dakota
Aakers College: Fargo *A*

Ohio
Capital University *B*
College of Mount St. Joseph *B*
Defiance College *B*
Ohio State University
    Columbus Campus *B*
Ohio University *B*
Tiffin University *M*
Wright State University *B*

Oklahoma
East Central University *B, M*

Oregon
Southern Oregon University *B*

Pennsylvania
Albright College *B*
Drexel University *B*
Indiana University of
    Pennsylvania *B, M, D*
Juniata College *B*
La Salle University *B*
Marywood University *A, B*
Mount Aloysius College *B*
Reading Area Community College *A*
St. Joseph's University *C, A, B, M*
University of Pennsylvania *M, D*
University of Pittsburgh
    Greensburg *B*

Puerto Rico
Pontifical Catholic University of
    Puerto Rico *B, M*
Turabo University *B*
Universidad del Este *A*

South Carolina
Coker College *B*

Tennessee
Hiwassee College *A*

Texas
Abilene Christian University *B*
North Central Texas College *A*
St. Edward's University *B*
South Plains College *B*
Texas A&M University
    Commerce *B*
University of Houston
    Clear Lake *B, M*
University of Texas
    Dallas *B*
    of the Permian Basin *B*
Wharton County Junior College *A*

Vermont
Castleton State College *B*

Virginia
Longwood University *B*
Marymount University *B*
Old Dominion University *B*
Virginia Wesleyan College *B*

Wisconsin
Marquette University *A, B*

Wyoming
Western Wyoming Community
    College *A*

Critical care nursing

Florida
University of Miami *M*

Illinois
Loyola University of Chicago *M*

New York
Columbia University
    School of Nursing *M*
State University of New York
    Buffalo *M*

Ohio
Case Western Reserve University *M*

Pennsylvania
University of Pennsylvania *M*

Puerto Rico
Universidad del Este *B*

Texas
Angelo State University *M*

Virginia
Marymount University *M*

Crop production

Illinois
Black Hawk College *A*

Iowa
Iowa State University *M, D*

Massachusetts
University of Massachusetts
    Amherst *A*

Michigan
Northwestern Michigan College *A*

Nebraska
Northeast Community College *A*

New York
Cornell University *B, M, D*
State University of New York
    College of Agriculture and
        Technology at Cobleskill *A, B*

North Carolina
North Carolina State University *A*

North Dakota
North Dakota State University *B*

Ohio
Ohio State University
    Agricultural Technical Institute *A*

Oregon
Blue Mountain Community College *A*

Pennsylvania
Delaware Valley College *B*

Utah
Brigham Young University *B, M*

Vermont
Sterling College *A, B*

Washington
Washington State University *B*
Wenatchee Valley College *C*

Yakima Valley Community College *C*

Culinary arts and chef training

Alabama
Shelton State Community College *C*
Trenholm State Technical College *C, A*

Alaska
University of Alaska
    Fairbanks *C, A*

Arizona
Estrella Mountain Community
    College *C, A*
Mohave Community College *C*

California
Art Institute
    of California: Orange County *A*
    of California: San Diego *A*
California School of Culinary Arts *A*
College of the Desert *C*
Diablo Valley College *C*
Lake Tahoe Community College *C*
Santa Rosa Junior College *C*

Colorado
Westwood College of Technology *A*

Connecticut
University of New Haven *C*

Florida
Central Florida Community College *A*
Hillsborough Community College *A*
New England Institute of
    Technology *C, A*
Orlando Culinary Academy *A*
Valencia Community College *A*

Georgia
Albany Technical College *C, A*
Savannah Technical College *A*

Idaho
Idaho State University *C, A*

Illinois
Black Hawk College *C*
City Colleges of Chicago
    Kennedy-King College *C*
College of DuPage *C, A*
College of Lake County *C*
John Wood Community College *C*
Kaskaskia College *C, A*
Rend Lake College *C, A*
Robert Morris College: Chicago *A*

Iowa
Des Moines Area Community
    College *C, A*
Indian Hills Community College *C, A*

Kentucky
Elizabethtown Community and
    Technical College *C*
Jefferson Community College *C, A*

Louisiana
Bossier Parish Community College *C*

Maryland
Allegany College of Maryland *A*
Anne Arundel Community
    College *C, A*

Massachusetts
Berkshire Community College *C*

Bristol Community College *A*
Bunker Hill Community College *C, A*
Holyoke Community College *C*
Massasoit Community College *C, A*
Newbury College *A, B*
North Shore Community College *C, A*

Michigan

Baker College
  of Muskegon *A*
Grand Rapids Community College *A*
Mott Community College *A*
Northwestern Michigan College *A*
Oakland Community College *A*

Minnesota

Art Institutes International
  Minnesota *C, A*
Hennepin Technical College *C, A*
Metropolitan State University *B*
Minneapolis Community and
  Technical College *C, A*
St. Cloud Technical College *C*
St. Paul College *C, A*

Missouri

East Central College *C, A*
Jefferson College *C, A*

Nevada

Art Institute
  of Las Vegas *C, A, B*
Community College of Southern
  Nevada *C, A*
Le Cordon Bleu College of Culinary
  Arts *A*

New Hampshire

New Hampshire Community
  Technical College
  Berlin *C, A*
Southern New Hampshire
  University *C, A*

New Jersey

Bergen Community College *C*
Hudson County Community
  College *A*

New Mexico

Albuquerque Technical-Vocational
  Institute *C, A*
Santa Fe Community College *A*

New York

Culinary Institute of America *C, A*
Erie Community College
  City Campus *A*
  North Campus *A*
Mohawk Valley Community College *C*
Niagara County Community
  College *A*
Paul Smith's College *A, B*
Schenectady County Community
  College *C*
State University of New York
  College of Agriculture and
    Technology at Cobleskill *A, B*

North Carolina

Central Piedmont Community
  College *C, A*
Fayetteville Technical Community
  College *C, A*
Johnson & Wales University *A*
Montgomery Community College *C*
Wilkes Community College *C, A*

Ohio

Cincinnati State Technical and
  Community College *C, A*
Hocking College *A*

University of Akron *C, A*

Oregon

Linn-Benton Community College *A*

Pennsylvania

Academy of Medical Arts and
  Business *C*
Art Institute
  of Pittsburgh *A, B*
Bidwell Training Center *C*
Community College of Allegheny
  County *A*
Community College of Beaver
  County *C, A*
Harrisburg Area Community
  College *A*
Indiana University of Pennsylvania *C*
Keystone College *A*
Lehigh Carbon Community College *A*
Mercyhurst College *C, A*
Montgomery County Community
  College *A*
Pennsylvania College of
  Technology *A, B*

Puerto Rico

Universidad del Este *C, A*

Rhode Island

Johnson & Wales University *A, B*

South Carolina

Horry-Georgetown Technical
  College *C, A*
Spartanburg Technical College *C*

Texas

Austin Community College *C, A*
El Centro College *C, A*
Houston Community College
  System *C*
Odessa College *C, A*
St. Philip's College *C, A*
Texas State Technical College
  West Texas *C, A*

Utah

Salt Lake Community College *A*
Snow College *C, A*
Utah Valley State College *A*

Vermont

New England Culinary Institute *C, A*

Virginia

Virginia Intermont College *A, B*

Washington

Art Institute of Seattle *A*
Clark College *C, A*
Edmonds Community College *C, A*
Olympic College *C, A*
Seattle Central Community
  College *C, A*
South Seattle Community
  College *C, A*
Walla Walla Community College *C, A*

West Virginia

Mountain State University *A, B*

Wisconsin

Fox Valley Technical College *A*
Milwaukee Area Technical College *C*

Culinary arts/related services

Alabama

Bishop State Community College *C, A*

Faulkner State Community
  College *C, A*

Alaska

University of Alaska
  Anchorage *A, B*
  Fairbanks *C, A*

Arizona

Arizona Western College *C*
Central Arizona College *C, A*
Estrella Mountain Community
  College *C, A*
Pima Community College *C, A*
Scottsdale Community College *C, A*

Arkansas

Ozarka College *C, A*

California

Art Institute
  of California: Los Angeles *A, B*
  of California: Orange County *A, B*
Bakersfield College *A*
California Culinary Academy *A*
Chaffey College *C*
Columbia College *A*
Cypress College *C, A*
Diablo Valley College *C*
Glendale Community College *C, A*
Grossmont Community College *C, A*
Lake Tahoe Community College *C, A*
Laney College *C, A*
Long Beach City College *C, A*
Los Angeles Mission College *C, A*
Los Angeles Trade and Technical
  College *C, A*
Modesto Junior College *C*
Orange Coast College *C, A*
Saddleback College *C*
San Diego Mesa College *C, A*
San Francisco State University *B*
San Joaquin Delta College *C, A*
Santa Barbara City College *C, A*
Santa Rosa Junior College *C*
Shasta College *C, A*

Colorado

Art Institute
  of Colorado *A, B*
Colorado Mountain College
  Timberline Campus *A*
Community College of Aurora *A*
Johnson & Wales University *B*
Mesa State College *C, A*
Pikes Peak Community College *C, A*
Pueblo Community College *C, A*

Connecticut

International College of Hospitality
  Management *C, A*
Manchester Community College *C*
Norwalk Community College *C*

Delaware

Delaware Technical and Community
  College
  Stanton/Wilmington Campus *C, A*

District of Columbia

University of the District of
  Columbia *A*

Florida

Art Institute of Fort
  Lauderdale *C, A, B*
Brevard Community College *C*
Chipola College *A*
Florida Community College at
  Jacksonville *A*
Gulf Coast Community College *A*
Hillsborough Community College *A*

Indian River Community College *C*
Lake City Community College *C*
Palm Beach Community College *C*
Pensacola Junior College *C, A*
Valencia Community College *C, A*

Georgia

Chattahoochee Technical College *C, A*
Georgia Southwestern State
  University *A*
Gwinnett Technical College *C, A*
Le Cordon Bleu College of Culinary
  Arts *A*
Savannah Technical College *C*
West Georgia Technical College *C*

Hawaii

University of Hawaii
  Kapiolani Community College *A*
  Kauai Community College *C, A*

Idaho

Boise State University *C, A*
Brigham Young University-Idaho *A*
College of Southern Idaho *C, A*
North Idaho College *C*

Illinois

City Colleges of Chicago
  Malcolm X College *A*
College of DuPage *C, A*
Elgin Community College *C, A*
Joliet Junior College *C, A*
Kendall College *C, A, B*
Southwestern Illinois College *C, A*
Triton College *C, A*
William Rainey Harper College *C, A*

Indiana

Oakland City University *A*
Vincennes University *A*

Iowa

Iowa Western Community College *A*
Kirkwood Community College *C, A*
Scott Community College *A*

Kentucky

Sullivan University *C, A, B*
West Kentucky Community and
  Technical College *A*

Louisiana

Nicholls State University *A, B*
Nunez Community College *C, A*

Maine

Central Maine Community College *C*
Eastern Maine Community
  College *C, A*
Southern Maine Community
  College *A*
Washington County Community
  College *C*
York County Community College *A*

Maryland

Anne Arundel Community
  College *C, A*
Baltimore City Community College *C*
Baltimore International College *C, A*
Frederick Community College *C, A*

Massachusetts

Bristol Community College *C*
Cape Cod Community College *C*
Newbury College *C, A, B*

Michigan

Baker College
  of Muskegon *A, B*

Bay de Noc Community College *C*
Henry Ford Community College *C, A*
Lansing Community College *A*
Macomb Community College *C, A*
Monroe County Community
    College *C, A*
Northern Michigan University *B*
Northwestern Michigan College *A*
Schoolcraft College *C, A*
Washtenaw Community College *C, A*

Minnesota

Anoka Technical College *C*
Art Institutes International
    Minnesota *C, A*
Brown College *A*
Hennepin Technical College *C, A*
Hibbing Community College *A*
Minnesota State Community and
    Technical College - Fergus Falls *C*
South Central College *A*

Mississippi

Hinds Community College *C, A*

Missouri

Jefferson College *C, A*
Ozarks Technical Community
    College *A*
St. Louis Community College
    St. Louis Community College at
      Florissant Valley *A*

Montana

University of Montana: Missoula *C, A*

Nebraska

Metropolitan Community
    College *C, A*
Southeast Community College
    Lincoln Campus *A*

Nevada

University of Nevada
    Las Vegas *B*

New Hampshire

Southern New Hampshire
    University *C, A*
University of New Hampshire *A*

New Jersey

Atlantic Cape Community College *A*
Brookdale Community College *C, A*
Hudson County Community
    College *C, A*
Mercer County Community
    College *C, A*
Middlesex County College *C*

New Mexico

Dona Ana Branch Community College
    of New Mexico State
    University *C*
Southwestern Indian Polytechnic
    Institute *C, A*

New York

Adirondack Community College *C, A*
Art Institute
    of New York City *C, A*
Monroe Community College *C, A*
New York Institute of Technology *A*
Niagara County Community
    College *C*
Onondaga Community College *C, A*
Paul Smith's College *C, A, B*
Rockland Community College *C*
Schenectady County Community
    College *C*

State University of New York
    College of Agriculture and
      Technology at Cobleskill *C, A*
    College of Technology at Alfred *A*
Suffolk County Community College *A*
Westchester Community College *A*

North Carolina

Alamance Community College *C, A*
Art Institute
    of Charlotte *C, A*
Cape Fear Community College *C, A*
College of the Albemarle *C*
Lenoir Community College *C, A*
Nash Community College *A*
Piedmont Community College *C*
Robeson Community College *A*
Sandhills Community College *A*
South Piedmont Community
    College *C*
Southwestern Community College *A*
Wake Technical Community
    College *A*

North Dakota

North Dakota State College of
    Science *C, A*

Ohio

Cincinnati State Technical and
    Community College *C, A*
Columbus State Community
    College *C, A*
Cuyahoga Community College
    Metropolitan Campus *A*
Sinclair Community College *C, A*
Zane State College *A*

Oklahoma

Oklahoma State University
    Okmulgee *A*

Oregon

Central Oregon Community
    College *C*
Lane Community College *C, A*
Portland Community College *C*
Southwestern Oregon Community
    College *A*

Pennsylvania

Academy of Medical Arts and
    Business *C, A*
Art Institute
    of Pittsburgh *C*
Bucks County Community
    College *C, A*
Commonwealth Technical Institute *A*
Community College of Philadelphia *A*
Delaware Valley College *C, A*
Drexel University *B*
International Academy of Design and
    Technology: Pittsburgh *A*
JNA Institute of Culinary Arts *C, A*
Keystone College *A*
Pennsylvania Institute of Culinary
    Arts *A*
Reading Area Community College *A*
Restaurant School *A*
Westmoreland County Community
    College *C, A*
York Technical Institute *A*
Yorktowne Business Institute *A*

Rhode Island

Johnson & Wales University *A, B*

South Carolina

Denmark Technical College *C*
Technical College of the
    Lowcountry *C*
Trident Technical College *C, A*

Tennessee

Nashville State Community College *A*
Walters State Community College *C, A*

Texas

Central Texas College *C, A*
Del Mar College *C, A*
El Paso Community College *C, A*
Galveston College *C, A*
Odessa College *C*
St. Philip's College *C, A*
San Jacinto College
    North *C, A*
Trinity Valley Community College *C*

Utah

Snow College *C, A*

Vermont

New England Culinary Institute *A, B*

Virginia

Art Institute
    of Washington *A*
J. Sargeant Reynolds Community
    College *A*
Northern Virginia Community
    College *C*
Tidewater Community College *C, A*

Washington

Bellingham Technical College *A*
Edmonds Community College *C, A*
Lake Washington Technical
    College *C, A*
Renton Technical College *C, A*
Seattle Central Community
    College *C, A*
Skagit Valley College *C, A*
South Puget Sound Community
    College *C, A*
South Seattle Community
    College *C, A*
Spokane Community College *A*

West Virginia

West Virginia Northern Community
    College *C, A*
West Virginia University Institute of
    Technology *A*

Wisconsin

Blackhawk Technical College *A*
Fox Valley Technical College *A*
Madison Area Technical College *C, A*
Moraine Park Technical College *A*
Nicolet Area Technical College *A*
Southwest Wisconsin Technical
    College *C, A*
Waukesha County Technical
    College *A*

Wyoming

Sheridan College *A*

Cultural resource management

Louisiana

Northwestern State University *B, M*

Michigan

Eastern Michigan University *M*

Nevada

Great Basin College *B*

Vermont

Sterling College *B*

Curriculum/instruction

Alaska

University of Alaska
    Fairbanks *M*

Arizona

Arizona State University *M, D*
Northcentral University *M, D*
Northern Arizona University *M, D*
Prescott College *B, M*
University of Phoenix *M*

Arkansas

Arkansas State University *M, T*
Henderson State University *M*
University of Arkansas *D*

California

Azusa Pacific University *M*
California Lutheran University *M*
California Polytechnic State
    University: San Luis Obispo *M*
California State University
    Chico *M*
    Dominguez Hills *M*
    East Bay *M*
    Fresno *M*
    Fullerton *M*
    Northridge *M*
    Sacramento *M*
    San Bernardino *M*
Chapman University *M*
Dominican University of California *M*
Fresno Pacific University *M*
Holy Names University *M*
La Sierra University *M, D*
National University *M*
Notre Dame de Namur University *M*
St. Mary's College of California *M*
San Diego State University *M*
Sonoma State University *M*
Stanford University *M, D*
University of California
    Riverside *D, T*
    San Diego *M*
    Santa Cruz *M*
University of Redlands *M*
University of San Diego *M, D*
University of San Francisco *D*
University of Southern
    California *M, D*
University of the Pacific *M, D*
Vanguard University of Southern
    California *M*

Colorado

Colorado Christian University *M*
Jones International University *M*
University of Colorado
    Boulder *M, D*
    Colorado Springs *M*
    Denver and Health Sciences
      Center *M*
University of Denver *M, D*

Connecticut

Fairfield University *M*
University of Connecticut *M, D, T*
Western Connecticut State
    University *M*

Delaware

Delaware State University *M*
University of Delaware *M, D*
Wilmington College *M*

District of Columbia

Catholic University of America *D*
George Washington University *M, D*
Howard University *M*
Trinity University *M*

Florida

Barry University *M*
Florida Atlantic University *M, D*
Florida Gulf Coast University *M*
Florida International University *M, D*
University of Central Florida *M*
University of Florida *M*
University of South Florida *M, D*
University of West Florida *M, D, T*
Warner Southern College *M*

Georgia

Armstrong Atlantic State University *M*
Berry College *T*
Clark Atlanta University *M*
Covenant College *M*
Georgia Southern University *D*
Valdosta State University *D*

Hawaii

University of Hawaii
  Manoa *M*

Idaho

Boise State University *M, D*
Northwest Nazarene University *M*
University of Idaho *M*

Illinois

Argosy University *M, D*
Aurora University *D*
Benedictine University *M*
Bradley University *M*
Chicago State University *M, T*
Concordia University *M*
DePaul University *M*
Governors State University *M*
Illinois State University *M, D*
Loyola University of Chicago *M, D*
National-Louis University *M*
North Central College *M*
Northeastern Illinois University *M*
Northern Illinois University *M, D*
Northwestern University *D*
Olivet Nazarene University *M*
St. Xavier University *M*
Southern Illinois University
    Carbondale *M, D*
University of Illinois
    Chicago *D*
    Urbana-Champaign *M, D*
University of St. Francis *M*

Indiana

Anderson University *M*
Ball State University *M, D, T*
Huntington University *M*
Indiana State University *M, D*
Indiana University
    Bloomington *D*
Indiana Wesleyan University *M*
University of Indianapolis *M*
Valparaiso University *M*

Iowa

Dordt College *M*
Drake University *B*
Iowa State University *M, D*
University of Iowa *M, D*
University of Northern Iowa *D*

Kansas

Emporia State University *M*
Kansas State University *D*
Newman University *M*
Southwestern College *M*
University of Kansas *M, D*
University of St. Mary *M*
Washburn University of Topeka *M*
Wichita State University *M*

Kentucky

Brescia University *M*
Campbellsville University *M*
Morehead State University *M*
Spalding University *M*
University of Kentucky *M*
University of Louisville *D*

Louisiana

Grambling State University *D*
Louisiana State University and
    Agricultural and Mechanical
    College *D*
Louisiana Tech University *M, D*
Nicholls State University *M*
Our Lady of Holy Cross College *M*
Southeastern Louisiana University *M*
University of Louisiana at Lafayette *M*
University of Louisiana at Monroe *D*
University of New Orleans *M, D*
Xavier University of Louisiana *M*

Maine

University of Southern Maine *M*

Maryland

Coppin State University *M*
Frostburg State University *M*
Hood College *M*
Loyola College in Maryland *M*
McDaniel College *M*
University of Maryland
    Baltimore County *T*
    College Park *M, D*
    University College *M*

Massachusetts

Atlantic Union College *M*
Boston College *M, D*
Boston University *M, D*
Curry College *M*
Eastern Nazarene College *M, T*
Framingham State College *M*
Gordon College *M*
Harvard College *M, D*
Lesley University *M*
Northeastern University *M*
Tufts University *M*
University of Massachusetts
    Lowell *M*
Wheelock College *M*

Michigan

Andrews University *M, D*
Calvin College *M, T*
Eastern Michigan University *M*
Ferris State University *M*
Oakland University *M*
University of Detroit Mercy *M*
Wayne State University *D*

Minnesota

Bemidji State University *M*
Capella University *M, D*
College of St. Scholastica *M*
Minnesota State University
    Mankato *B, M, T*
    Moorhead *M*
St. Cloud State University *M*
University of Minnesota
    Twin Cities *M*
University of St. Thomas *M, D*
Winona State University *B, M, T*

Mississippi

University of Mississippi *M*
University of Southern Mississippi *M*

Missouri

Central Missouri State University *M, T*
Maryville University of Saint
    Louis *M, T*
Northwest Missouri State
    University *B, T*
University of Missouri
    Columbia *M, D*
    Kansas City *M*
    St. Louis *M*
Washington University in St. Louis *M*
William Woods University *M*

Montana

Montana State University
    Billings *B, M*
University of Great Falls *M*
University of Montana: Missoula *M, D*

Nebraska

Concordia University *M*
Doane College *M*
University of Nebraska
    Kearney *M*
    Lincoln *M, D*
Wayne State College *M*

Nevada

University of Nevada
    Las Vegas *M, D, T*
    Reno *D*

New Hampshire

Keene State College *M, T*
Rivier College *M*
University of New Hampshire *D*

New Jersey

Caldwell College *M*
Rider University *M*
Rowan University *M*
Seton Hall University *M*

New Mexico

College of Santa Fe *M*
College of the Southwest *M*
New Mexico Highlands University *M*
New Mexico State University *D*
University of New Mexico *D, T*

New York

Fordham University *M, D*
Jewish Theological Seminary of
    America *M, D*
Medaille College *M*
St. John's University *D, T*
State University of New York
    Albany *M, D*
    College at Fredonia *M*
Syracuse University *M, D*
University of Rochester *M, D*

North Carolina

Campbell University *M*
Elon University *B, T*
North Carolina Central University *M*
North Carolina State University *M, D*
Shaw University *M*
University of North Carolina
    Chapel Hill *D*
    Charlotte *M, D*
    Greensboro *M, D*
    Wilmington *M*

Ohio

Ashland University *M, T*
Bowling Green State University *M*
Cleveland State University *M*
John Carroll University *M*
Kent State University *M, D*
Lake Erie College *B, M*
Malone College *M*
Miami University
    Oxford Campus *M*
Mount Vernon Nazarene University *M*
Ohio Dominican University *M*

Ohio State University
    Columbus Campus *M, D*
Ohio University *M, D*
Otterbein College *M*
Union Institute & University *M*
University of Cincinnati *M, D*
University of Findlay *B, M*
University of Toledo *M, D*
Urbana University *M*
Wright State University *M*
Youngstown State University *M*

Oklahoma

Northeastern State University *M*
Oklahoma State University *M, D*
Oral Roberts University *M*
Southern Nazarene University *M*
University of Central Oklahoma *B*

Oregon

Concordia University *M*
George Fox University *M*
Portland State University *M, D*
Western Oregon University *M, T*

Pennsylvania

Bloomsburg University of
    Pennsylvania *M*
Bucknell University *M*
Duquesne University *D*
Gannon University *M*
Lock Haven University of
    Pennsylvania *M*
Marywood University *M, D*
Neumann College *M, T*
Penn State
    Harrisburg *M*
    University Park *M, D*
Point Park University *M*
Robert Morris University *M, T*
Rosemont College *T*
St. Vincent College *M*
Shippensburg University of
    Pennsylvania *M*
University of Pennsylvania *M, D*
Westminster College *M*
Widener University *D*

Puerto Rico

Inter American University of Puerto
    Rico
    San German Campus *D*
Pontifical Catholic University of
    Puerto Rico *M*
Turabo University *M*
Universidad Adventista de las
    Antillas *M*
Universidad Metropolitana *M*
Universidad del Este *M*
University of Puerto Rico
    Rio Piedras *M, D*

Rhode Island

Rhode Island College *M*

South Carolina

Clemson University *D*
Columbia International University *M*
University of South Carolina *D*
Winthrop University *T*

South Dakota

Black Hills State University *M*
Dakota Wesleyan University *M*
South Dakota State University *M*
University of South Dakota *M, D, T*

Tennessee

Austin Peay State University *M*
Carson-Newman College *M*
Freed-Hardeman University *B, M, T*
Lincoln Memorial University *M*

Lipscomb University *M, T*
Middle Tennessee State
University *M, T*
Southern Adventist University *M*
Tennessee State University *M, D*
Tennessee Technological
University *M*
Tennessee Temple University *M*
Trevecca Nazarene University *M*
University of Memphis *M, D*
University of Tennessee
Knoxville *M, D*
Vanderbilt University *M, D*

Texas

Angelo State University *M*
Baylor University *M, D*
Houston Baptist University *M*
Midwestern State University *M*
Our Lady of the Lake University of San
Antonio *M*
Prairie View A&M University *M*
Sam Houston State University *M*
Southwestern Assemblies of God
University *M*
Texas A&M University *M, D*
Texas A&M University
Commerce *D*
Texarkana *M*
Texas Southern University *M, D*
Texas Tech University *M, D*
University of Houston *M, D, T*
University of Houston
Clear Lake *M*
Downtown *M*
University of North Texas *D*
University of Texas
Arlington *M*
Austin *M, D*
Brownsville *M*
El Paso *M*
San Antonio *M*
Tyler *M*
Wayland Baptist University *M*
West Texas A&M University *M*

Utah

Brigham Young University *D*
Southern Utah University *M*
Utah State University *M, D*

Vermont

Castleton State College *M, T*
Johnson State College *M*
Lyndon State College *M*
St. Michael's College *M*
Sterling College *B*
University of Vermont *M, D*

Virginia

Averett University *M*
College of William and Mary *M*
Eastern Mennonite University *M*
George Mason University *M*
Liberty University *M*
Longwood University *M*
Lynchburg College *M*
Radford University *M*
Sweet Briar College *M*
University of Virginia *M, D*
Virginia Commonwealth University *M*
Virginia Polytechnic Institute and
State University *M, D*
Virginia State University *M*

Washington

City University *M*
Eastern Washington University *M*
Gonzaga University *M*
Seattle Pacific University *M*
Seattle University *M*
University of Puget Sound *M*
University of Washington *D*

Walla Walla College *M*
Washington State University *M, D*
Western Washington University *M*

West Virginia

Shepherd University *M*
West Virginia University *D*

Wisconsin

Alverno College *M*
Carroll College *M*
Concordia University Wisconsin *M*
Marquette University *M, D*
University of Wisconsin
Madison *M, D*
Milwaukee *M*
Whitewater *M*

Customer service management

Arizona

Northern Arizona University *C*

California

Santa Rosa Junior College *C*

Florida

Hillsborough Community
College *C, A*

Iowa

Maharishi University of
Management *M*

Minnesota

Minnesota School of Business:
Brooklyn Center *B*
Rochester Community and Technical
College *C, A*

Missouri

Penn Valley Community College *C*

New York

Bryant & Stratton Business Institute
Bryant & Stratton College:
Rochester *A*
Globe Institute of Technology *C, A, B*
Trocaire College *C*

North Carolina

Forsyth Technical Community
College *C*

Ohio

Edison State Community College *C*

Pennsylvania

Newport Business Institute *A*

South Carolina

Trident Technical College *C, A*

Wisconsin

University of Wisconsin
Stout *B*

Cytogenetics/clinical genetics technology

Alabama

Calhoun Community College *A*

Cytotechnology

Alabama

Oakwood College *B*

University of Alabama
Birmingham *B*

Arkansas

University of Arkansas
for Medical Sciences *B*

California

California State University
Dominguez Hills *M*
Loma Linda University *B*

Connecticut

University of Connecticut *B*

District of Columbia

George Washington University *B*

Florida

Barry University *B*

Illinois

Illinois College *B*

Indiana

Indiana University
Bloomington *B*
Indiana University-Purdue University
Indianapolis *B*
Saint Mary's College *B*

Iowa

Ashford University *B*

Kansas

University of Kansas Medical
Center *B*

Kentucky

Bellarmine University *B*

Michigan

Northern Michigan University *B*

Minnesota

Minnesota State University
Mankato *B, M*
St. Mary's University of Minnesota *B*
Winona State University *B*

Mississippi

University of Mississippi Medical
Center *B*

Missouri

Jewish Hospital College of Nursing
and Allied Health *B*

New Jersey

College of St. Elizabeth *B*
Felician College *B*
St. Peter's College *B*
Thomas Edison State College *B*
University of Medicine and Dentistry
of New Jersey
School of Health Related
Professions *B*

New York

Albany College of Pharmacy *B*
Long Island University
Brooklyn Campus *B*
Sage College of Albany *B*
State University of New York
College at Plattsburgh *B*
Stony Brook *B*
Upstate Medical University *B*

North Carolina

Central Piedmont Community
College *A*

North Dakota

University of North Dakota *B*

Pennsylvania

Keystone College *A*
Slippery Rock University of
Pennsylvania *B*
Thiel College *B*
Thomas Jefferson University: College
of Health Professions *B*

South Carolina

Anderson University *B*
Medical University of South
Carolina *M*

Texas

University of North Texas *B*

Virginia

Old Dominion University *B*

West Virginia

Marshall University *B*

Wisconsin

Edgewood College *B*
Marian College of Fond du Lac *B*

Czech

Texas

University of Texas
Austin *B*

Dairy husbandry

New Hampshire

University of New Hampshire *B*

New York

State University of New York
College of Agriculture and
Technology at Cobleskill *A, B*
College of Agriculture and
Technology at Morrisville *A, B*

Vermont

Sterling College *A, B*

Wisconsin

Wisconsin Indianhead Technical
College *C*

Dairy science

California

California Polytechnic State
University: San Luis Obispo *B*
California State University
Fresno *B*
College of the Sequoias *C*
Los Angeles Pierce College *C, A*
Modesto Junior College *A*

Florida

University of Florida *M*

Georgia

University of Georgia *B, M*

Idaho

University of Idaho *B*

Iowa

Iowa State University *B*
Northeast Iowa Community
College *C*

Minnesota

Ridgewater College *C, A*

Nebraska

Northeast Community College *C*

New Hampshire

University of New Hampshire *A, B*

New York

State University of New York
College of Agriculture and
Technology at Cobleskill *A*
College of Agriculture and
Technology at Morrisville *A*
College of Technology at Alfred *A*

Ohio

Ohio State University
Agricultural Technical Institute *A*

Oregon

Linn-Benton Community College *A*

Pennsylvania

Delaware Valley College *B*

South Carolina

Clemson University *B, M*

South Dakota

South Dakota State University *B*

Texas

Texas A&M University *B, M, D*

Utah

Utah State University *C, B, M*

Vermont

Sterling College *B*
Vermont Technical College *A*

Virginia

Virginia Polytechnic Institute and
State University *B, M*

Washington

Skagit Valley College *A*

Wisconsin

Lakeshore Technical College *C*
Southwest Wisconsin Technical
College *C*
University of Wisconsin
Madison *B, M, D*
River Falls *B*

Dance

Alabama

Birmingham-Southern College *B*
University of Alabama *B*

Arizona

Arizona State University *B, M*
Prescott College *B, M*
University of Arizona *B*

California

Allan Hancock College *C, A*
Cabrillo College *A*
California Institute of the Arts *C, B, M*

California State Polytechnic
University: Pomona *B*
California State University
East Bay *B*
Fresno *B*
Fullerton *B*
Long Beach *B, M*
Northridge *B*
Sacramento *B, M*
Chabot College *A*
Chaffey College *A*
Chapman University *B*
Claremont McKenna College *B*
College of the Desert *A*
Cypress College *A*
El Camino College *A*
Fresno City College *C, A*
Fullerton College *A*
Glendale Community College *C, A*
Golden West College *A*
Grossmont Community College *C, A*
Irvine Valley College *A*
Lake Tahoe Community College *A*
Laney College *A*
Long Beach City College *A*
Loyola Marymount University *B*
Mills College *B, M*
MiraCosta College *A*
Monterey Peninsula College *A*
Mount San Jacinto College *A*
Orange Coast College *C, A*
Palomar College *C, A*
Pitzer College *B*
Pomona College *B*
Saddleback College *A*
St. Mary's College of California *B*
San Diego State University *B*
San Francisco State University *B*
San Jose State University *B*
Santa Ana College *C, A*
Santa Monica College *A*
Santa Rosa Junior College *C*
Santiago Canyon College *A*
Scripps College *B*
Skyline College *A*
Southwestern College *A*
University of California
Berkeley *B*
Irvine *B, M*
Los Angeles *M*
Riverside *B, M, D*
San Diego *B*
Santa Barbara *B*
Santa Cruz *C, B*
Westmont College *B*

Colorado

Colorado College *B*
University of Colorado
Boulder *B, M*

Connecticut

Connecticut College *B*
Naugatuck Valley Community
College *C, A*
Trinity College *B*
University of Hartford *B*
Wesleyan University *B*

District of Columbia

American University *M*
George Washington University *B*
Howard University *B*

Florida

Florida International University *B*
Florida State University *B, M*
Hillsborough Community College *A*
Indian River Community College *A*
Jacksonville University *B*
Miami Dade College *A*
Okaloosa-Walton College *A*
Palm Beach Atlantic University *B*

Palm Beach Community College *A*
University of Florida *B*
University of South Florida *B*
Valencia Community College *A*

Georgia

Brenau University *B*
Emory University *B*
University of Georgia *B*

Hawaii

University of Hawaii
Manoa *B, M*

Idaho

University of Idaho *B*

Illinois

Columbia College Chicago *B*
Illinois Central College *A*
Northwestern University *B*
Southern Illinois University
Edwardsville *B*
University of Illinois
Urbana-Champaign *B, M*

Indiana

Ball State University *B*
Butler University *B*
Indiana University
Bloomington *B, M*

Iowa

University of Iowa *B, M*

Kansas

Barton County Community College *A*
Friends University *B*
University of Kansas *B*

Louisiana

Centenary College of Louisiana *B, T*
Tulane University *B*

Maryland

Frostburg State University *B*
Goucher College *B*
Howard Community College *A*
Montgomery College *A*
Towson University *B, T*
University of Maryland
Baltimore County *B*
College Park *B, M*

Massachusetts

Amherst College *B*
Boston Conservatory *B, M*
Cape Cod Community College *A*
Dean College *A, B*
Hampshire College *B*
Mount Holyoke College *B*
Simon's Rock College of Bard *B*
Smith College *B, M*
Springfield College *B*
University of Massachusetts
Amherst *B*

Michigan

Alma College *B*
Eastern Michigan University *B*
Hope College *B*
Lansing Community College *A*
Marygrove College *B, T*
University of Michigan *B, M, T*
University of Michigan
Flint *B*
Wayne State University *B, T*
Western Michigan University *B*

Minnesota

Gustavus Adolphus College *B*

St. Olaf College *B*
University of Minnesota
Twin Cities *B*
Winona State University *A*

Mississippi

Belhaven College *C, B*
University of Southern Mississippi *B*

Missouri

Lindenwood University *B*
Missouri State University *B*
Stephens College *B*
University of Missouri
Kansas City *B*
Washington University in St. Louis *B*
Webster University *B*

Montana

University of Montana: Missoula *B*

Nebraska

University of Nebraska
Lincoln *B*

Nevada

University of Nevada
Las Vegas *B*

New Hampshire

Franklin Pierce College *B*
Keene State College *B*

New Jersey

Middlesex County College *A*
Montclair State University *B*
Rowan University *B*
Rutgers, The State University of New
Jersey
New Brunswick/Piscataway
Campus *B*

New Mexico

New Mexico State University *B*
Santa Fe Community College *A*
University of New Mexico *B, M*

New York

Adelphi University *B*
Bard College *B*
Barnard College *B*
City University of New York
Hunter College *B*
Lehman College *B*
Queens College *B*
Queensborough Community
College *A*
Columbia University
Columbia College *B*
School of General Studies *B*
Cornell University *B, M, D*
Fordham University *B*
Hamilton College *B*
Hobart and William Smith Colleges *B*
Hofstra University *B*
Ithaca College *B*
Juilliard School *B*
Long Island University
Brooklyn Campus *B*
C.W. Post Campus *B*
Manhattanville College *B*
Marymount Manhattan College *B*
New York University *B, M, D*
Sarah Lawrence College *B, M*
Skidmore College *B*
State University of New York
Buffalo *B*
College at Brockport *B, M*
College at Potsdam *B*
Purchase *B, M*
Wells College *B*

North Carolina

East Carolina University *B*
Elon University *B*
Louisburg College *A*
Meredith College *B*
North Carolina School of the Arts *B*
University of North Carolina
    Charlotte *B*
    Greensboro *B, M, T*

Ohio

Antioch College *B*
Case Western Reserve University *M*
College of Wooster *B*
Denison University *B*
Kent State University *B*
Kenyon College *B*
Lake Erie College *B*
Oberlin College *B*
Ohio State University
    Columbus Campus *B, M*
Ohio University *B*
Ohio Wesleyan University *B*
Owens Community College
    Toledo *A*
Sinclair Community College *C, A*
University of Akron *B*
University of Cincinnati *B*
Wright State University *B*

Oklahoma

Oklahoma City University *B*
University of Central Oklahoma *B*
University of Oklahoma *B, M*

Oregon

University of Oregon *B, M*
Western Oregon University *B*

Pennsylvania

Cedar Crest College *B*
DeSales University *B*
Franklin & Marshall College *B*
La Roche College *B*
Mercyhurst College *B*
Muhlenberg College *C, B*
Point Park University *B*
Slippery Rock University of
    Pennsylvania *B*
Swarthmore College *B*
Temple University *B, M, D*
University of the Arts *C, B*
Ursinus College *B*

Rhode Island

Roger Williams University *B*

South Carolina

Coker College *B*
Columbia College *B*
University of South Carolina *B*
Winthrop University *B*

Tennessee

Columbia State Community College *C*

Texas

Austin Community College *A*
Kilgore College *A*
Lamar University *B*
Sam Houston State University *B, M*
Southern Methodist University *B, M*
Stephen F. Austin State University *B, T*
Texas State University: San
    Marcos *B, T*
Texas Tech University *B*
Texas Woman's University *B, M, D*
Tyler Junior College *A*
University of Houston *B*
University of North Texas *B*
University of Texas
    Austin *B*

El Paso *B*
    Pan American *B*
West Texas A&M University *B*

Utah

Brigham Young University *B, M*
Dixie State College of Utah *A*
Snow College *A*
Southern Utah University *B, T*
University of Utah *B, M*
Utah State University *B*
Utah Valley State College *A, B*
Weber State University *B*

Vermont

Bennington College *B, M*
Johnson State College *B*
Marlboro College *B*
Middlebury College *B*

Virginia

George Mason University *B, M*
Hollins University *B, M*
Old Dominion University *B, T*
Radford University *B*
Randolph-Macon Woman's College *B*
Shenandoah University *B, M*
Sweet Briar College *B*
Virginia Commonwealth University *B*
Virginia Intermont College *B*

Washington

Cornish College of the Arts *B*
University of Washington *B, M*
Western Washington University *B*

Wisconsin

University of Wisconsin
    Madison *B, M*
    Milwaukee *B*
    Stevens Point *B*
    Whitewater *B, T*

Wyoming

Casper College *A*
Western Wyoming Community
    College *A*

Dance therapy

California

California Institute of Integral
    Studies *M*

Colorado

Naropa University *M*

Illinois

Columbia College Chicago *M*

Massachusetts

Lesley University *M, D*

New York

Pratt Institute *M*

Pennsylvania

Cedar Crest College *B*
Drexel University *M*

South Carolina

Coker College *B*

Danish

Washington

University of Washington *B*

Data entry/applications

Alabama

Gadsden State Community College *C*

Arizona

Estrella Mountain Community
    College *C, A*
Gateway Community College *C*

Arkansas

University of Arkansas
    Fort Smith *C*

California

CEI College
    Maric College: Panorama City *C*
Glendale Community College *C*
Heald College
    Stockton *C, A*
MTI College *C*
Orange Coast College *C, A*
San Diego City College *A*
San Jose City College *C, A*
Santa Ana College *C*
Santa Rosa Junior College *C*
Sierra College *C, A*

Colorado

Arapahoe Community College *A*

Connecticut

Manchester Community College *C, A*

Florida

Florida Career College: Hialeah *C*
Florida Career College: Miami *C*
Florida Career College: Pembroke
    Pines *C*
Florida Career College: West Palm
    Beach *C*
Herzing College
    Orlando *C*
Valencia Community College *C, A*

Georgia

Albany Technical College *C*
Central Georgia Technical College *C*
Gwinnett College *C*
Macon State College *A*
Middle Georgia College *A*
Northwestern Technical College *C, A*
Southwest Georgia Technical
    College *C, A*
West Georgia Technical College *C, A*

Illinois

College of Office Technology *C, A*
Heartland Community College *A*
Richland Community College *A*

Indiana

Professional Careers Institute *A*

Iowa

Hamilton College
    Cedar Falls *C*
Western Iowa Tech Community
    College *A*

Kansas

Central Christian College of Kansas *A*
Seward County Community
    College *C, A*

Maine

Central Maine Community
    College *C, A*

Maryland

Community College of Baltimore
    County *C, A*

Massachusetts

Bristol Community College *C*
Bunker Hill Community College *C, A*
Marian Court College *C, A*
Newbury College *C, A*
Roxbury Community College *C*
Springfield Technical Community
    College *C*

Michigan

Baker College
    of Muskegon *A*
Lake Michigan College *C*
Macomb Community College *C, A*
Mott Community College *C*

Minnesota

Central Lakes College *C*
Fond du Lac Tribal and Community
    College *C*
Normandale Community College *A*
Riverland Community College *C*
Rochester Community and Technical
    College *C*

Mississippi

Antonelli College
    Jackson *C, A*

Missouri

Metro Business College
    Jefferson City *C*
St. Louis Community College
    St. Louis Community College at
        Meramec *C*

Montana

Montana State University
    Billings *A*

Nebraska

Metropolitan Community College *A*
Nebraska Indian Community
    College *C, A*

New Hampshire

New Hampshire Community
    Technical College
    Nashua *A*

New Jersey

Mercer County Community College *C*
Union County College *C*

New York

Globe Institute of Technology *C*
Olean Business Institute *A*
Pace University *M*
Rochester Business Institute *A*
Westchester Community College *C*

North Carolina

Beaufort County Community
    College *C*
Forsyth Technical Community
    College *C, A*

North Dakota

North Dakota State College of
    Science *C, A*

Ohio

Central Ohio Technical College *A*
ETI Technical College of Niles *A*
Marion Technical College *C, A*
Ohio Business College: Sandusky *A*
Sinclair Community College *C*

Stark State College of Technology *A*
Stautzenberger College *A*
University of Cincinnati
    Clermont College *C, A*

Pennsylvania

Academy of Medical Arts and
    Business *C, A*
Business Institute of Pennsylvania *A*
Business Institute of Pennsylvania
    Meadville *A*
Consolidated School of Business
    Lancaster *A*
Delaware County Community
    College *C, A*
Gannon University *C*
Harrisburg Area Community
    College *C*
Newport Business Institute *A*
PJA School *C*
South Hills School of Business &
    Technology *C, A*

South Carolina

Williamsburg Technical College *C*
York Technical College *C*

Tennessee

South College *C, A*

Texas

Palo Alto College *C*
St. Philip's College *C, A*
Temple College *C, A*
Wharton County Junior College *C, A*

Utah

Utah Valley State College *C, A*

Virginia

ECPI College of Technology *C, A*

Washington

Clark College *C, A*
Edmonds Community College *C*
Grays Harbor College *C*
Heritage University *C*
Lower Columbia College *A*
Peninsula College *C*
Walla Walla Community College *C, A*

West Virginia

Valley College of Technology *C*

Wisconsin

Western Wisconsin Technical
    College *A*

Wyoming

Western Wyoming Community
    College *C*

Data processing technology

Alabama

Chattahoochee Valley Community
    College *A*
Gadsden State Community College *C*
J. F. Drake State Technical College *A*
Northwest-Shoals Community
    College *C, A*
Wallace State Community College at
    Hanceville *A*

Arizona

Central Arizona College *A*
Eastern Arizona College *C*
Gateway Community College *C*
Mohave Community College *C*
Northland Pioneer College *C, A*

Tohono O'odham Community
    College *C*

Arkansas

Arkansas State University *B*
Central Baptist College *B*
University of Arkansas *B*
University of Arkansas
    Fort Smith *C*
University of Central Arkansas *B*

California

Antelope Valley College *A*
Bakersfield College *A*
Barstow College *C*
Cabrillo College *A*
Cerritos Community College *A*
Chabot College *C, A*
Citrus College *A*
College of the Canyons *C, A*
College of the Redwoods *C*
Cypress College *C, A*
Fresno City College *C, A*
Fullerton College *C, A*
Gavilan Community College *C*
Heald College
    Fresno *C, A*
Institute of Computer Technology *C*
Long Beach City College *C, A*
Los Angeles Mission College *C*
Los Angeles Valley College *C, A*
Monterey Peninsula College *C, A*
Mount San Antonio College *C, A*
Pasadena City College *C, A*
Porterville College *C*
San Diego City College *C, A*
San Joaquin Delta College *A*
Santa Ana College *C, A*
Santa Barbara City College *C, A*
Santa Monica College *C, A*
Skyline College *C, A*
Taft College *C*
Ventura College *A*
Victor Valley College *C*
Yuba Community College District *C*

Colorado

Colorado Mountain College
    Alpine Campus *C*
    Spring Valley Campus *C*
National American University
    Denver *A*
Northeastern Junior College *C, A*
Red Rocks Community College *C, A*

Connecticut

Norwalk Community College *A*
Three Rivers Community College *C*

Delaware

Delaware Technical and Community
    College
    Owens Campus *C, A*
    Stanton/Wilmington Campus *A*
    Terry Campus *A*

District of Columbia

American University *C*

Florida

Broward Community College *A*
Florida Community College at
    Jacksonville *C, A*
Florida Keys Community College *C*
Florida Metropolitan University
    Orlando College North *A*
Gulf Coast Community College *C*
Hillsborough Community College *C*
Indian River Community College *C*
Miami Dade College *C*
Pasco-Hernando Community
    College *C*
Santa Fe Community College *A*

Seminole Community College *C, A*
Tallahassee Community College *C*

Georgia

Abraham Baldwin Agricultural
    College *A*
Albany Technical College *C, A*
Athens Technical College *C, A*
Central Georgia Technical
    College *C, A*
Clayton State University *B*
Dalton State College *C, A*
Darton College *A*
Northwestern Technical College *C, A*
Savannah Technical College *C, A*
South Georgia College *C*
Southwest Georgia Technical
    College *C, A*

Hawaii

Hawaii Pacific University *A*
University of Hawaii
    Kapiolani Community College *C, A*

Illinois

Black Hawk College *C*
Black Hawk College
    East Campus *A*
Chicago State University *B*
City Colleges of Chicago
    Harold Washington College *C, A*
    Olive-Harvey College *C, A*
College of Office Technology *C*
Highland Community College *A*
Kishwaukee College *C*
Lewis and Clark Community
    College *A*
Midstate College *A*
Moraine Valley Community
    College *C, A*
Oakton Community College *C, A*
Rockford Business College *A*
Sauk Valley Community College *C, A*
Southwestern Illinois College *A*
Spoon River College *C, A*
Triton College *C, A*
William Rainey Harper College *C, A*

Indiana

Indiana University
    Kokomo *C*
    Northwest *C, A, B*
Purdue University
    North Central Campus *A*
Sawyer College: Merrillville *C, A*
Tri-State University *A*
University of Southern Indiana *B*
Vincennes University *A*

Iowa

Dordt College *A*
Ellsworth Community College *A*
Northeast Iowa Community
    College *A*
Southeastern Community College
    North Campus *C, A*

Kansas

Barton County Community
    College *C, A*
Colby Community College *A*
Dodge City Community College *C, A*
Donnelly College *C, A*
Haskell Indian Nations University *A*
Kansas City Kansas Community
    College *A*
Labette Community College *A*
Seward County Community
    College *C, A*

Kentucky

Daymar College *C, A*
Eastern Kentucky University *A*

Henderson Community College *A*
Jefferson Community College *A*
Kentucky State University *A*
Maysville Community College *C, A*
Southeast Kentucky Community and
    Technical College *A*
Thomas More College *A*
Western Kentucky University *A*

Louisiana

Delgado Community College *A*
ITT Technical College *A*
Louisiana State University
    Alexandria *A*

Maine

Andover College *C, A*
Husson College *A*
Northern Maine Community
    College *A*

Maryland

Allegany College of Maryland *C*
Cecil Community College *C, A*
Community College of Baltimore
    County *C, A*
Hagerstown Business College *A*
Hagerstown Community College *C*

Massachusetts

Benjamin Franklin Institute of
    Technology *C*
Bristol Community College *A*
Holyoke Community College *C*
Massasoit Community College *C*
Mount Wachusett Community
    College *A*
Springfield Technical Community
    College *A*

Michigan

Baker College
    of Auburn Hills *A*
    of Clinton Township *A*
    of Flint *A*
    of Jackson *A*
    of Muskegon *A*
    of Port Huron *A*
Bay de Noc Community College *C*
Glen Oaks Community College *C*
Gogebic Community College *A*
Grand Rapids Community College *C*
Jackson Community College *C, A*
Kalamazoo Valley Community
    College *A*
Lansing Community College *A*
Montcalm Community College *A*
Muskegon Community College *C, A*
St. Clair County Community
    College *C, A*
Schoolcraft College *C*
Washtenaw Community College *C, A*
West Shore Community College *C, A*

Minnesota

Central Lakes College *A*
Century Community and Technical
    College *A*
Hennepin Technical College *C, A*
Pine Technical College *C, A*
Winona State University *B*

Mississippi

Copiah-Lincoln Community College *A*
East Central Community College *A*
Hinds Community College *C, A*
Itawamba Community College *A*
Pearl River Community College *A*
Southwest Mississippi Community
    College *A*
University of Southern Mississippi *B*

Missouri

Central Missouri State University B
Everest College: Springfield C, A
Grantham University A, B
Missouri College C
St. Louis Community College
 St. Louis Community College at
  Florissant Valley C, A
 St. Louis Community College at
  Meramec C, A
Washington University in St. Louis B

Montana

Fort Belknap College A
Fort Peck Community College C, A
Little Big Horn College A
Miles Community College A
Montana Tech of the University of
 Montana A
Stone Child College A
University of Great Falls B
University of Montana: Missoula A

Nevada

Community College of Southern
 Nevada A
Truckee Meadows Community
 College A

New Hampshire

New Hampshire Community
 Technical College
 Claremont C
 Nashua C, A

New Jersey

Atlantic Cape Community College A
Burlington County College C, A
Essex County College C
Gloucester County College C, A
Hudson County Community
 College A
Ocean County College C
Rowan University B
St. Peter's College A
Union County College C

New Mexico

Albuquerque Technical-Vocational
 Institute C, A
Dona Ana Branch Community College
 of New Mexico State
 University A
New Mexico State University
 Alamogordo C, A
 Carlsbad C
San Juan College A

New York

Adirondack Community College C, A
Bramson ORT College A
Cayuga County Community
 College C, A
City University of New York
 Borough of Manhattan Community
  College A
 Bronx Community College A
 Brooklyn College C
 Hostos Community College A
 Kingsborough Community
  College A
 LaGuardia Community College A
 New York City College of
  Technology A
 Queensborough Community
  College A
College of Saint Rose C
College of Westchester C, A
Genesee Community College C
Globe Institute of Technology C
Herkimer County Community
 College A

Hudson Valley Community
 College C, A
Jamestown Business College A
Jamestown Community College C, A
New York Institute of Technology C
Niagara County Community
 College A
Olean Business Institute A
Onondaga Community College C
Orange County Community College A
Pace University B
Rochester Business Institute A
Rockland Community College C, A
State University of New York
 College of Agriculture and
  Technology at Cobleskill A
 College of Agriculture and
  Technology at Morrisville C
 College of Technology at Alfred A
 College of Technology at Delhi C
 Farmingdale C, A
 Purchase C
Sullivan County Community
 College C, A
Utica School of Commerce A

North Carolina

Caldwell Community College and
 Technical Institute A
Lenoir Community College C, A
Western Piedmont Community
 College C, A

North Dakota

Lake Region State College C, A
Mayville State University C
Williston State College C, A

Ohio

Belmont Technical College C
Cincinnati Christian University B
Jefferson Community College C, A
Miami University
 Oxford Campus A
Mount Vernon Nazarene University A
Ohio Valley College of Technology A
Stark State College of Technology A
University of Akron: Wayne College A
University of Cincinnati
 Clermont College C, A
Washington State Community
 College A
Wright State University A

Oklahoma

Connors State College A
Oklahoma City Community College A

Oregon

Lane Community College A

Pennsylvania

Academy of Medical Arts and
 Business C, A
Berean Institute C
Bucks County Community College A
Business Institute of Pennsylvania A
Business Institute of Pennsylvania
 Meadville A
CHI Institute: Southampton C
Consolidated School of Business
 Lancaster C, A
 York C, A
Keystone College C, A
Laurel Business Institute A
Newport Business Institute A
Peirce College C, A
Reading Area Community College A
South Hills School of Business &
 Technology C, A
University of Pittsburgh
 Titusville C

Westmoreland County Community
 College C, A
Yorktowne Business Institute A

Puerto Rico

Universidad del Este A, B

South Carolina

Aiken Technical College A
Florence-Darlington Technical
 College A
Greenville Technical College C, A
Horry-Georgetown Technical
 College C, A
Midlands Technical College C, A
Northeastern Technical College C, A
Orangeburg-Calhoun Technical
 College C, A
Piedmont Technical College C, A
Technical College of the
 Lowcountry C, A
Tri-County Technical College A
Trident Technical College C, A

South Dakota

Kilian Community College C
Lake Area Technical Institute A
Southeast Technical Institute C

Texas

Angelina College C, A
Austin Community College C
Cedar Valley College C, A
Central Texas College C, A
Coastal Bend College A
Eastfield College A
El Centro College C, A
El Paso Community College C
Frank Phillips College C
Galveston College C
Hill College C, A
Howard College C
Lee College C, A
McLennan Community College C, A
Midland College A
Mountain View College C, A
North Central Texas College A
North Harris Montgomery
 Community College District C
Paris Junior College C, A
St. Philip's College A
San Jacinto College
 North C, A
South Plains College A
Southwest Texas Junior College A
Stephen F. Austin State University B
Texas State Technical College
 Waco C, A
Texas State University: San Marcos B
Trinity Valley Community College A
Tyler Junior College C
Vernon College C, A
Weatherford College C, A
Western Texas College C, A
Wharton County Junior College A

Utah

Dixie State College of Utah A, B
Southern Utah University A
Utah Valley State College A, B

Virginia

ECPI College of Technology C, A
J. Sargeant Reynolds Community
 College C, A
Lord Fairfax Community College C
Mountain Empire Community
 College C
Virginia Highlands Community
 College A

Washington

Bellevue Community College C

Centralia College A
Clover Park Technical College C
Columbia Basin College A
Edmonds Community College A
Grays Harbor College A
Lake Washington Technical
 College C, A
Lower Columbia College C, A
North Seattle Community
 College C, A
Peninsula College A
Pierce College C, A
Renton Technical College C
Shoreline Community College C, A
South Puget Sound Community
 College C, A
Spokane Community College C, A
Tacoma Community College C
Walla Walla College B
Walla Walla Community College C, A
Whatcom Community College C, A
Yakima Valley Community
 College C, A

West Virginia

Potomac State College of West Virginia
 University A
West Virginia Northern Community
 College C, A

Wisconsin

Fox Valley Technical College A
Moraine Park Technical College A
Northeast Wisconsin Technical
 College A
Southwest Wisconsin Technical
 College C
Western Wisconsin Technical
 College A

Wyoming

Western Wyoming Community
 College C, A

Database design/
management

Arizona

University of Phoenix B

California

Foothill College C, A
Golden Gate University C
San Joaquin Delta College A

Colorado

Colorado Technical University C
Jones International University C, B

Connecticut

Norwalk Community College C

Florida

St. Petersburg College C, A

Indiana

Purdue University
 Calumet B

Kentucky

Maysville Community College C, A

Massachusetts

Bunker Hill Community College A

Michigan

Oakland Community College C

Minnesota

Dakota County Technical College C, A

Minneapolis Community and
Technical College *C*
St. Cloud Technical College *C, A*

Nevada

Community College of Southern
Nevada *C, A*

New Mexico

San Juan College *C*

New York

Genesee Community College *C*
Globe Institute of Technology *C, A, B*
Rochester Institute of
Technology *B, M*
State University of New York
College of Agriculture and
Technology at Morrisville *B*

North Carolina

Central Piedmont Community
College *C, A*
College of the Albemarle *C*

Ohio

Davis College *A*
Stark State College of Technology *A*

Pennsylvania

La Salle University *B, M*
Newport Business Institute *A*
Pittsburgh Technical Institute *C*
South Hills School of Business &
Technology *C*

South Carolina

Limestone College *B*

Texas

South Texas College *A*

Washington

Bellevue Community College *A*
Clark College *C*
Clover Park Technical College *C*
Shoreline Community College *C, A*

West Virginia

Huntington Junior College *A*

Demography/ population studies

California

University of California
Berkeley *M, D*

Colorado

University of Denver *M*

Florida

Florida State University *M*

Massachusetts

Hampshire College *B*

Michigan

University of Michigan *D*

Ohio

Bowling Green State University *M*

Pennsylvania

University of Pennsylvania *M, D*
University of Pittsburgh
Bradford *B*

Wisconsin

University of Wisconsin
Madison *M, D*

Dental assistant

Alabama

Calhoun Community College *C, A*
Community College of the Air
Force *A*
Faulkner State Community
College *C, A*
Trenholm State Technical College *A*
University of Alabama
Birmingham *C*
Wallace State Community College at
Hanceville *C, A*

Alaska

University of Alaska
Anchorage *C, A*
Fairbanks *C, A*

Arizona

Mohave Community College *C*
Phoenix College *A*
Pima Community College *C*
Rio Salado College *C*

Arkansas

Arkansas Northeastern College *C*
Pulaski Technical College *C*

California

Allan Hancock College *C, A*
Bakersfield College *A*
California State University
Dominguez Hills *B*
Cerritos Community College *C, A*
Chaffey College *C, A*
Citrus College *C, A*
City College of San Francisco *C, A*
College of Alameda *A*
College of San Mateo *C, A*
College of the Redwoods *C*
Concorde Career College *C*
Contra Costa College *A*
Cypress College *C, A*
Diablo Valley College *C*
Foothill College *C, A*
Modesto Junior College *A*
Monterey Peninsula College *C, A*
Orange Coast College *C, A*
Palomar College *C, A*
Pasadena City College *C, A*
Reedley College *C, A*
Rio Hondo College *A*
Sacramento City College *C, A*
San Diego Mesa College *C, A*
San Joaquin Valley College Inc. *A*
San Jose City College *C, A*
Santa Rosa Junior College *C, A*
Silicon Valley College
Western Career College: San Jose *A*
Western Career College
Pleasant Hill *A*

Colorado

Concorde Career College *C*
Front Range Community College *C*
IntelliTec College: Grand Junction *C*
Pikes Peak Community College *C, A*
Pueblo Community College *C, A*

Connecticut

Briarwood College *C, A*
Tunxis Community College *C*

Florida

Angley College *C*
Brevard Community College *C*
Broward Community College *C*

Daytona Beach Community College *C*
Edison College *C*
Florida Community College at
Jacksonville *C*
Florida National College *C*
Gulf Coast Community College *C*
Indian River Community College *C*
New England Institute of
Technology *C*
Palm Beach Community College *C*
Pasco-Hernando Community
College *C*
Pensacola Junior College *C*
Santa Fe Community College *C*
South Florida Community College *C*
Tallahassee Community College *C*

Georgia

Albany Technical College *C*
Athens Technical College *A*
Augusta Technical Institute *C*
Clayton State University *B*
Georgia Southwestern State
University *A*
Middle Georgia College *A*
Savannah Technical College *C, A*

Hawaii

University of Hawaii
Kapiolani Community College *C, A*

Idaho

Boise State University *C*
College of Southern Idaho *C*
Eastern Idaho Technical College *C*

Illinois

Black Hawk College *C*
Elgin Community College *C*
Illinois Central College *C*
Illinois Valley Community College *C*
John A. Logan College *C*
Kaskaskia College *C*
Lewis and Clark Community
College *C*
Robert Morris College: Chicago *C, A*
Rock Valley College *C*

Indiana

Indiana University
Northwest *C*
South Bend *C*
Indiana University-Purdue University
Fort Wayne *C*
Indiana University-Purdue University
Indianapolis *C*
Ivy Tech State College
Ivy Tech Community College:
Columbus *C*
Ivy Tech Community College: East
Central *C*
Ivy Tech Community College:
Kokomo *C*
Ivy Tech Community College:
Lafayette *C*
Professional Careers Institute *C, A*
University of Southern Indiana *C, A*

Iowa

Des Moines Area Community
College *C*
Hawkeye Community College *C*
Iowa Western Community College *C*
Kirkwood Community College *C, A*
Marshalltown Community College *C*
Northeast Iowa Community
College *C*
Scott Community College *C*
Vatterott College *C*
Western Iowa Tech Community
College *C*

Kansas

Dodge City Community College *C, A*

Kentucky

Jefferson Community College *C*

Maine

University of Maine
Augusta *C*

Maryland

Anne Arundel Community
College *C, A*

Massachusetts

Massasoit Community College *C*
Middlesex Community College *C, A*
Mount Ida College *C, A*
Northern Essex Community
College *C*
Quinsigamond Community College *C*
Springfield Technical Community
College *C*

Michigan

Bay de Noc Community College *C*
Delta College *C, A*
Grand Rapids Community
College *C, A*
Kirtland Community College *C*
Lake Michigan College *C, A*
Mott Community College *C, A*
Northwestern Michigan College *C, A*
Washtenaw Community College *C*
Wayne County Community College *C*

Minnesota

Central Lakes College *C*
Century Community and Technical
College *C, A*
Dakota County Technical College *C, A*
Hennepin Technical College *C, A*
Hibbing Community College *A*
Minneapolis Community and
Technical College *C*
Minnesota State Community and
Technical College - Fergus Falls *C*
Northwest Technical College *C*
Rochester Community and Technical
College *C, A*
St. Cloud Technical College *C, A*
South Central College *A*

Mississippi

Hinds Community College *C, A*

Missouri

Missouri College *C*
Ozarks Technical Community
College *C*
Penn Valley Community College *C, A*
Vatterott College: Springfield *C*

Montana

Montana State University
College of Technology-Great Falls *C*
Salish Kootenai College *C, A*

Nebraska

Central Community College *C, A*
Metropolitan Community College *C*
Mid-Plains Community College
Area *C, A*
Southeast Community College
Lincoln Campus *C*
Vatterott College: Spring Valley *C*

Nevada

High-Tech Institute *A*
Truckee Meadows Community
College *C, A*

New Hampshire

New Hampshire Technical Institute *C*

New Jersey

Camden County College *C, A*
Essex County College *C*
Union County College *C*
University of Medicine and Dentistry
of New Jersey
School of Health Related
Professions *A*

New Mexico

Albuquerque Technical-Vocational
Institute *C*
Eastern New Mexico University:
Roswell Campus *C*
Santa Fe Community College *C*

New York

Monroe Community College *C*
State University of New York
Farmingdale *A*

North Carolina

Alamance Community College *C*
Asheville-Buncombe Technical
Community College *C*
Brunswick Community College *C*
Cape Fear Community College *C*
Central Piedmont Community
College *C*
Coastal Carolina Community
College *C*
Fayetteville Technical Community
College *C*
Guilford Technical Community
College *C*
Martin Community College *C*
Montgomery Community College *C*
Rowan-Cabarrus Community
College *C*
University of North Carolina
Chapel Hill *C*
Wake Technical Community
College *C*
Western Piedmont Community
College *C*
Wilkes Community College *C*

North Dakota

North Dakota State College of
Science *C*

Ohio

Cuyahoga Community College
Metropolitan Campus *C, A*
James A. Rhodes State College *A*
Jefferson Community College *C, A*
Ohio Valley College of Technology *A*

Oklahoma

Platt College
Tulsa *C*
Rose State College *C, A*
Western College of Southern
California *C*

Oregon

Blue Mountain Community College *C*
Central Oregon Community
College *C*
Chemeketa Community College *C, A*
Lane Community College *C*
Linn-Benton Community College *C*
Portland Community College *C*

Pennsylvania

Academy of Medical Arts and
Business *C, A*
Career Training Academy *C*
Community College of Philadelphia *C*

Harcum College *C, A*
Harrisburg Area Community
College *C*
Luzerne County Community
College *C*
Manor College *A*
Thompson Institute
Philadelphia *C*
Western School of Health and
Business Careers
Monroeville *C*
Westmoreland County Community
College *C*
Yorktowne Business Institute *A*

Puerto Rico

National College of Business &
Technology: Arecibo *A*
National College of Business &
Technology: Bayamon *A*

Rhode Island

Community College of Rhode
Island *C*

South Carolina

Aiken Technical College *C*
Florence-Darlington Technical
College *C*
Greenville Technical College *C*
Horry-Georgetown Technical
College *C*
Midlands Technical College *C, A*
Spartanburg Technical College *C*
Tri-County Technical College *C*
Trident Technical College *C*

South Dakota

Lake Area Technical Institute *C*

Tennessee

Northeast State Technical Community
College *C*
Volunteer State Community College *C*

Texas

Amarillo College *C*
Del Mar College *C, A*
El Paso Community College *C, A*
Grayson County College *C*
Houston Community College
System *C*
Lamar State College at Orange *C*
Lon Morris College *C*
San Antonio College *C, A*
Tarrant County College *C*
Texas State Technical College
Harlingen *C*
Waco *C*

Utah

Provo College *C, A*

Virginia

J. Sargeant Reynolds Community
College *C*
Wytheville Community College *C*

Washington

Bellingham Technical College *C*
Clover Park Technical College *C*
Columbia Basin College *C*
Highline Community College *A*
Lake Washington Technical
College *C, A*
Renton Technical College *C, A*
South Puget Sound Community
College *C*
Spokane Community College *C, A*
Yakima Valley Community College *C*

West Virginia

Huntington Junior College *C, A*

Wisconsin

Blackhawk Technical College *C*
Chippewa Valley Technical College *C*
Fox Valley Technical College *C*
Gateway Technical College *C*
Lakeshore Technical College *C*
Madison Area Technical College *C*
Milwaukee Area Technical College *C*
Moraine Park Technical College *C*
Northeast Wisconsin Technical
College *C*
Waukesha County Technical
College *C*
Western Wisconsin Technical
College *C*

Dental clinical services

California

University of California
Los Angeles *M, D*

Connecticut

University of Connecticut *M*

Indiana

Indiana University-Purdue University
Indianapolis *M, D*

Iowa

University of Iowa *M*

Kentucky

University of Louisville *M*

Louisiana

Louisiana State University Health
Sciences Center *M, D*

Missouri

University of Missouri
Kansas City *M, D*

Nebraska

University of Nebraska
Medical Center *M, D*

North Carolina

University of North Carolina
Chapel Hill *M, D*

Ohio

Case Western Reserve University *M*

Texas

Texas A&M University
Baylor College of Dentistry *M, D*

Virginia

Virginia Commonwealth University *M*

West Virginia

West Virginia University *M*

Dental hygiene

Alabama

Wallace State Community College at
Hanceville *A*

Alaska

University of Alaska
Anchorage *A*

Arizona

Mohave Community College *A*

Northern Arizona University *B*
Phoenix College *A*
Pima Community College *A*
Rio Salado College *A*

Arkansas

University of Arkansas
Fort Smith *A*
for Medical Sciences *A, B*

California

Cabrillo College *C, A*
Cerritos Community College *C, A*
Chabot College *C, A*
Cypress College *C, A*
Diablo Valley College *C*
Foothill College *A*
Fresno City College *A*
Loma Linda University *B*
Pasadena City College *C, A*
Sacramento City College *C, A*
San Joaquin Valley College Inc. *A*
Santa Rosa Junior College *C, A*
Silicon Valley College
Western Career College: San Jose *A*
Southwestern College *A*
Taft College *A*
University of Southern California *B*
University of the Pacific *B*
West Los Angeles College *C, A*

Colorado

Colorado Northwestern Community
College *A*
Community College of Denver *A*
Pueblo Community College *A*
University of Colorado
Denver and Health Sciences
Center *B*

Connecticut

Tunxis Community College *A*
University of Bridgeport *A, B*
University of New Haven *A, B*

Delaware

Delaware Technical and Community
College
Stanton/Wilmington Campus *A*
Terry Campus *A*

District of Columbia

Howard University *C*

Florida

Brevard Community College *A*
Broward Community College *A*
Edison College *A*
Florida Community College at
Jacksonville *A*
Gulf Coast Community College *A*
Hillsborough Community College *A*
Indian River Community College *A*
Manatee Community College *A*
Miami Dade College *A*
Palm Beach Community College *A*
Pasco-Hernando Community
College *A*
Pensacola Junior College *A*
St. Petersburg College *A, B*
Santa Fe Community College *A*
South Florida Community College *A*
Tallahassee Community College *A*
Valencia Community College *A*

Georgia

Abraham Baldwin Agricultural
College *A*
Armstrong Atlantic State
University *A, B*
Athens Technical College *A*
Central Georgia Technical College *A*

Clayton State University *B*
Columbus Technical College *A*
Dalton State College *A*
Darton College *A*
Gainesville State College *A*
Georgia Highlands College *A*
Georgia Perimeter College *A*
Gordon College *A*
Medical College of Georgia *B*
Middle Georgia College *A*
Waycross College *A*

Hawaii

University of Hawaii
 Kapiolani Community College *A*
 Manoa *B*

Idaho

College of Southern Idaho *A*
Idaho State University *B, M*

Illinois

City Colleges of Chicago
 Kennedy-King College *A*
College of DuPage *A*
College of Lake County *A*
Illinois Central College *A*
John A. Logan College *A*
Lake Land College *A*
Lewis and Clark Community
 College *A*
Parkland College *A*
Prairie State College *A*
Southern Illinois University
 Carbondale *B*
William Rainey Harper College *A*

Indiana

Indiana University
 Bloomington *A, B*
 Northwest *A*
 South Bend *A*
Indiana University-Purdue University
 Fort Wayne *A*
Indiana University-Purdue University
 Indianapolis *A, B*
University of Southern Indiana *A, B*
Vincennes University *A*

Iowa

Des Moines Area Community
 College *A*
Hawkeye Community College *A*
Iowa Western Community College *A*
Kirkwood Community College *A*
Western Iowa Tech Community
 College *A*

Kansas

Colby Community College *A*
Johnson County Community
 College *A*
Seward County Community College *A*
Wichita State University *A, B*

Kentucky

Big Sandy Community and Technical
 College *A*
Bluegrass Community and Technical
 College *A*
Elizabethtown Community and
 Technical College *A*
Henderson Community College *C*
University of Louisville *A, B*
Western Kentucky University *A, B*

Louisiana

Delgado Community College *A*
Louisiana State University Health
 Sciences Center *B*
Southern University
 Shreveport *A*

University of Louisiana at Lafayette *B*
University of Louisiana at Monroe *B*

Maine

University of Maine
 Augusta *A, B*
University of New England *A, B*

Maryland

Allegany College of Maryland *A*
Baltimore City Community College *A*
University of Maryland
 Baltimore *B, M*
 Baltimore County *B*
 Eastern Shore *B*

Massachusetts

Bristol Community College *A*
Cape Cod Community College *A*
Massachusetts College of Pharmacy
 and Health Sciences *B*
Middlesex Community College *A*
Mount Wachusett Community
 College *A*
Quinsigamond Community College *A*
Springfield Technical Community
 College *A*

Michigan

Baker College
 of Auburn Hills *A*
 of Port Huron *A*
Delta College *A*
Ferris State University *A*
Grand Rapids Community College *A*
Kalamazoo Valley Community
 College *A*
Kellogg Community College *A*
Lansing Community College *A*
Mott Community College *A*
Oakland Community College *A*
University of Detroit Mercy *B*
University of Michigan *B, M*
Wayne County Community College *A*

Minnesota

Century Community and Technical
 College *A*
Lake Superior College *A*
Minnesota State Community and
 Technical College - Fergus Falls *A*
Minnesota State University
 Mankato *B*
Normandale Community College *A*
Rochester Community and Technical
 College *A*
St. Cloud Technical College *A*
University of Minnesota
 Twin Cities *C, B*

Mississippi

Meridian Community College *A*
Mississippi Delta Community
 College *A*
University of Mississippi Medical
 Center *B*

Missouri

Missouri Southern State University *A*
Ozarks Technical Community
 College *A*
State Fair Community College *A*
University of Missouri
 Kansas City *B, M*

Nebraska

Central Community College *C, A*
University of Nebraska
 Medical Center *B*

Nevada

Community College of Southern
 Nevada *A, B*
Truckee Meadows Community
 College *A*

New Hampshire

New Hampshire Technical Institute *A*

New Jersey

Bergen Community College *A*
Brookdale Community College *A*
Burlington County College *A*
Camden County College *A*
Essex County College *A*
Middlesex County College *A*
Thomas Edison State College *B*
Union County College *A*
University of Medicine and Dentistry
 of New Jersey
 School of Health Related
 Professions *A, B*

New Mexico

San Juan College *A*
University of New Mexico *A, B, M*

New York

Broome Community College *A*
City University of New York
 Hostos Community College *A*
 New York City College of
 Technology *A*
Erie Community College
 North Campus *A*
Hudson Valley Community College *A*
Monroe Community College *A*
New York University *A*
Onondaga Community College *A*
Orange County Community College *A*
State University of New York
 Farmingdale *B*

North Carolina

Asheville-Buncombe Technical
 Community College *A*
Cape Fear Community College *A*
Catawba Valley Community College *A*
Central Piedmont Community
 College *A*
Coastal Carolina Community
 College *A*
Fayetteville Technical Community
 College *A*
Guilford Technical Community
 College *A*
University of North Carolina
 Chapel Hill *C, B, M*
Wake Technical Community
 College *A*
Wayne Community College *A*

North Dakota

North Dakota State College of
 Science *A*

Ohio

Columbus State Community
 College *A*
Cuyahoga Community College
 Metropolitan Campus *A*
Lakeland Community College *A*
Ohio State University
 Columbus Campus *B*
Owens Community College
 Toledo *A*
Shawnee State University *A*
Sinclair Community College *A*
Stark State College of Technology *A*
University of Cincinnati
 Raymond Walters College *A*
Youngstown State University *A*

Oklahoma

Rose State College *A*
Tulsa Community College *A*
University of Oklahoma *B*

Oregon

Lane Community College *A*
Mount Hood Community College *A*
Oregon Health & Science
 University *B*
Oregon Institute of Technology *B*
Portland Community College *A*

Pennsylvania

Community College of Philadelphia *A*
Harcum College *A*
Harrisburg Area Community
 College *A*
Luzerne County Community
 College *A*
Manor College *A*
Montgomery County Community
 College *A*
Northampton County Area
 Community College *A*
Pennsylvania College of
 Technology *A, B*
University of Pittsburgh *B*
Westmoreland County Community
 College *A*

Rhode Island

Community College of Rhode
 Island *A*
University of Rhode Island *B*

South Carolina

Aiken Technical College *C*
Central Carolina Technical College *C*
Florence-Darlington Technical
 College *A*
Greenville Technical College *A*
Horry-Georgetown Technical
 College *C, A*
Midlands Technical College *A*
Orangeburg-Calhoun Technical
 College *C*
Piedmont Technical College *C*
Spartanburg Technical College *C*
Tri-County Technical College *C*
Trident Technical College *C, A*
York Technical College *A*

South Dakota

University of South Dakota *A, B*

Tennessee

Chattanooga State Technical
 Community College *A*
Columbia State Community College *A*
East Tennessee State University *B*
Roane State Community College *A*
Southern Adventist University *A*
Tennessee State University *A, B*
University of Tennessee
 Knoxville *B*

Texas

Amarillo College *A*
Blinn College *C, A*
Coastal Bend College *A*
Collin County Community College
 District *A*
Del Mar College *A*
El Paso Community College *A*
Howard College *A*
Midwestern State University *B*
Northeast Texas Community
 College *A*
Tarrant County College *A*
Temple College *A*

Texas A&M University
Baylor College of Dentistry *B, M*
Texas State Technical College
Harlingen *A*
Texas Woman's University *B*
Tyler Junior College *A*
University of Texas
Health Science Center at
Houston *C, B*
Health Science Center at San
Antonio *B*
Wharton County Junior College *A*

Utah

Dixie State College of Utah *C, A*
Salt Lake Community College *A*
Utah Valley State College *A*
Weber State University *A, B*

Vermont

Vermont Technical College *A*

Virginia

Danville Community College *A*
Germanna Community College *A*
Lord Fairfax Community College *A*
Northern Virginia Community
College *A*
Old Dominion University *B, M*
Virginia Commonwealth University *B*
Virginia Highlands Community
College *A*
Virginia Western Community
College *A*
Wytheville Community College *A*

Washington

Clark College *A*
Columbia Basin College *A*
Eastern Washington University *B*
Everett Community College *A*
Lake Washington Technical College *A*
Pierce College *A*
Shoreline Community College *A*
University of Washington *B*
Yakima Valley Community
College *C, A*

West Virginia

West Liberty State College *A, B*
West Virginia University *B, M*
West Virginia University Institute of
Technology *A*

Wisconsin

Blackhawk Technical College *A*
Chippewa Valley Technical College *A*
Fox Valley Technical College *A*
Gateway Technical College *A*
Madison Area Technical College *A*
Milwaukee Area Technical College *A*
Northcentral Technical College *A*
Northeast Wisconsin Technical
College *A*
Waukesha County Technical
College *A*
Western Wisconsin Technical
College *A*

Wyoming

Laramie County Community
College *A*
Sheridan College *A*
University of Wyoming *B*

Dental laboratory technology

Alabama

Community College of the Air
Force *A*
Trenholm State Technical College *A*

Arizona

Pima Community College *A*

California

City College of San Francisco *C, A*
Cypress College *A*
Diablo Valley College *C*
Los Angeles City College *C, A*
Pasadena City College *C, A*
Riverside Community College *C, A*
San Diego Mesa College *A*

Florida

Florida National College *A*
Indian River Community College *A*

Georgia

Gwinnett Technical College *A*

Idaho

Idaho State University *A*

Illinois

Southern Illinois University
Carbondale *A*

Indiana

Indiana University-Purdue University
Fort Wayne *A*

Iowa

Kirkwood Community College *A*

Kentucky

Bluegrass Community and Technical
College *A*

Louisiana

Delgado Community College *A*
Louisiana State University Health
Sciences Center *A, B*

Massachusetts

Boston University *B*
Middlesex Community College *A*

Michigan

Bay de Noc Community College *C*
Wayne County Community College *C*

New York

City University of New York
New York City College of
Technology *A*
Erie Community College
South Campus *A*

North Carolina

Durham Technical Community
College *C, A*

Ohio

Columbus State Community
College *C, A*
Cuyahoga Community College
Metropolitan Campus *C, A*

Oregon

Portland Community College *C, A*

Pennsylvania

Commonwealth Technical Institute *A*
Delaware County Community
College *C*

Tennessee

Northeast State Technical Community
College *C, A*

Texas

Howard College *C, A*
Texas State Technical College
Harlingen *C, A*
University of Texas
Health Science Center at San
Antonio *B*

Virginia

J. Sargeant Reynolds Community
College *C, A*

Washington

Bates Technical College *A*

Wisconsin

Milwaukee Area Technical College *C*

Dentistry (D.D.S., D.M.D.)

Alabama

University of Alabama at Birmingham:
School of Dentistry *F*

California

Loma Linda University: School of
Dentistry *F*
University of California Los Angeles:
School of Dentistry *F*
University of California San Francisco:
School of Dentistry *F*
University of Southern California:
School of Dentistry *F*
University of the Pacific: School of
Dentistry *F*

Colorado

University of Colorado Health
Sciences Center: School of
Dentistry *F*

Connecticut

University of Connecticut: School of
Dentistry *F*

District of Columbia

Howard University: College of
Dentistry *F*

Florida

University of Florida: College of
Dentistry *F*

Georgia

Medical College of Georgia: School of
Dentistry *F*

Illinois

Northwestern University: Dental
School *F*
Southern Illinois University: School of
Dentistry *F*
University of Illinois at Chicago:
College of Dentistry *F*

Indiana

Indiana University School of
Dentistry *F*

Iowa

University of Iowa College of
Dentistry *F*

Kentucky

University of Kentucky: College of
Dentistry *F*
University of Louisville: School of
Dentistry *F*

Louisiana

Louisiana State University Health
Sciences Center: School of
Dentistry *F*

Maryland

University of Maryland at Baltimore:
School of Dentistry *F*

Massachusetts

Boston University Goldman School of
Dental Medicine *F*
Harvard School of Dental Medicine *F*
Tufts University: School of Dental
Medicine *F*

Michigan

University of Detroit Mercy: School of
Dentistry *F*
University of Michigan: School of
Dentistry *F*

Minnesota

University of Minnesota Twin Cities:
School of Dentistry *F*

Mississippi

University of Mississippi Medical
Center: School of Dentistry *F*

Missouri

University of Missouri Kansas City:
School of Dentistry *F*

Nebraska

Creighton University: School of
Dentistry *F*
University of Nebraska Medical
Center: College of Dentistry *F*

New Jersey

University of Medicine and Dentistry
of New Jersey
New Jersey Dental School *F*

New York

Columbia University
School of Dental and Oral
Surgery *F*
New York University: College of
Dentistry *F*
State University of New York Health
Sciences Center at Stony Brook:
School of Dentistry *F*
State University of New York at
Buffalo: School of Dentistry *F*

North Carolina

University of North Carolina at Chapel
Hill: School of Dentistry *F*

Ohio

Case Western Reserve University:
School of Dentistry *F*
Ohio State University Columbus
Campus: College of Dentistry *F*

Oklahoma

University of Oklahoma Health
Sciences Center: College of
Dentistry *F*

Oregon

Oregon Health Sciences University:
School of Dentistry *F*

Pennsylvania

Temple University: School of
Dentistry *F*
University of Pennsylvania: School of
Dental Medicine *F*

University of Pittsburgh: School of
Dental Medicine *F*

Puerto Rico

University of Puerto Rico Medical
Sciences Campus: School of
Dentistry *F*

South Carolina

Medical University of South Carolina:
College of Dental Medicine *F*

Tennessee

Meharry Medical College: School of
Dentistry *F*
University of Tennessee Memphis:
College of Dentistry *F*

Texas

University of Texas Health Science
Center: Dental School *F*
University of Texas Health Sciences
Center-Dental Branch *F*

Virginia

Virginia Commonwealth University:
School of Dentistry *F*

Washington

University of Washington: School of
Dentistry *F*

West Virginia

West Virginia University: School of
Dentistry *F*

Wisconsin

Marquette University: School of
Dentistry *F*

Design/visual communications

Alabama

Auburn University *B*

Arizona

Collins College *A*
Northern Arizona University *B*
Pima Community College *A*
Yavapai College *C*

California

Academy of Art University *C, A, B, M*
Allan Hancock College *A*
Art Institute
of California: Los Angeles *A, B*
of California: San Diego *A*
Bethesda Christian University *B*
California State University
Chico *B*
Long Beach *B*
Sacramento *B*
Chaffey College *C, A*
Fashion Institute of Design and
Merchandising *A*
Fashion Institute of Design and
Merchandising
San Diego *A*
San Francisco *A*
Fullerton College *A*
Laney College *C, A*
Long Beach City College *A*
Loyola Marymount University *B, M*
Mount San Antonio College *A*
Otis College of Art and Design *B*
Platt College
Ontario *C, A, B*
Saddleback College *C, A*
San Diego State University *B*

University of California
Davis *B*
Los Angeles *B, M*
Santa Cruz *C, B*
Westwood College *A, B*
Westwood College of Technology
Inland Empire *B*

Colorado

Art Institute
of Colorado *A, B*
Colorado Mountain College
Spring Valley Campus *A*
Community College of Denver *C, A*
Front Range Community College *C*
Pueblo Community College *C, A*
Westwood College of Technology *B*
Westwood College of Technology
South *B*

Connecticut

Central Connecticut State
University *B, M*
Northwestern Connecticut
Community College *A*
Paier College of Art *C, B*
Sacred Heart University *B*
University of Hartford *B*

District of Columbia

American University *B*
Howard University *B*

Florida

Florida Community College at
Jacksonville *A*
Jacksonville University *B*
University of Miami *B*

Georgia

DeKalb Technical College *C*

Idaho

University of Idaho *B*

Illinois

American Academy of Art *B*
Black Hawk College *A*
City Colleges of Chicago
Harold Washington College *A*
Wright College *C, A*
College of DuPage *C, A*
Columbia College Chicago *B*
Elgin Community College *C, A*
Heartland Community College *A*
Illinois Institute of Art-Schaumburg *B*
Illinois Institute of Technology *M, D*
Judson College *B*
Moraine Valley Community College *A*
Prairie State College *A*
School of the Art Institute of
Chicago *B, M*
Southern Illinois University
Carbondale *B*
Waubonsee Community College *C, A*
Westwood College - Chicago Loop *B*
Westwood College of Technology
O'Hare *B*

Indiana

Bethel College *A, B*
Indiana University-Purdue University
Indianapolis *B, M*
International Business College *C, A*
Ivy Tech State College
Ivy Tech Community College:
Central Indiana *A*
Ivy Tech Community College:
Columbus *A*
Ivy Tech Community College:
Kokomo *A*

Ivy Tech Community College: North
Central *A*
Ivy Tech Community College: South
Central *A*
Ivy Tech Community College:
Southwest *A*
Ivy Tech Community College:
Wabash Valley *A*
Purdue University *B*
St. Mary-of-the-Woods College *B*
University of Evansville *B*
University of Indianapolis *B*
University of Notre Dame *B, M*
Vincennes University *A*

Iowa

Dordt College *B*
Iowa State University *B, M*
Iowa Wesleyan College *B*

Kansas

Cowley County Community
College *A*
University of Kansas *B, M*

Louisiana

Delgado Community College *A*

Maryland

Cecil Community College *C, A*
Howard Community College *A*
Villa Julie College *B*

Massachusetts

Bunker Hill Community College *A*
Endicott College *B*
Fitchburg State College *B*
Gibbs College *A*
Hampshire College *B*
Massachusetts College of Art *B, M*
Montserrat College of Art *B*
Northeastern University *B*
Northern Essex Community
College *A*
University of Massachusetts
Dartmouth *B, M*

Michigan

Alma College *B*
Andrews University *B*
College for Creative Studies *B*
Ferris State University *B*
Finlandia University *B*
Kendall College of Art and Design of
Ferris State University *B*
Northern Michigan University *B*
Saginaw Valley State University *B*
Spring Arbor University *B*
University of Michigan *B*

Minnesota

Brown College *A, B*
College of Visual Arts *B*
Minneapolis College of Art and
Design *A*
University of Minnesota
Twin Cities *B*
Winona State University *B*

Missouri

Drury University *B*
Missouri State University *B*
Washington University in St.
Louis *B, M*
William Woods University *B*

Nevada

Truckee Meadows Community
College *A*

New Hampshire

Franklin Pierce College *B*

McIntosh College *A*
Rivier College *A, B*

New Jersey

Kean University *B*

New Mexico

New Mexico Highlands University *B*
New Mexico State University
Alamogordo *A*
Northern New Mexico College *A*
Santa Fe Community College *C, A*

New York

Bryant & Stratton Business Institute
Bryant & Stratton College:
Rochester *A*
Cazenovia College *B*
City University of New York
Baruch College *B*
Eugene Lang College The New School
for Liberal Arts *B*
Mohawk Valley Community College *A*
Parsons The New School for
Design *C, A, B, M, T*
Pratt Institute *M*
Rochester Institute of Technology *B*
School of Visual Arts *B, M*

North Carolina

Duke University *B*
Mount Olive College *B*
North Carolina State University *B, M*
Peace College *A, B*

Ohio

Art Institute of Cincinnati *A*
Bowling Green State University *B*
Edison State Community College *C, A*
Mount Union College *B*
Mount Vernon Nazarene University *B*
Ohio State University
Columbus Campus *B, M*
University of Cincinnati *M*
University of Cincinnati
Raymond Walters College *C, A*
University of Dayton *B*

Oklahoma

Oral Roberts University *B*
University of Central Oklahoma *M*

Oregon

Art Institute of Portland *B*
Chemeketa Community College *A*
Portland State University *B*
University of Oregon *B*

Pennsylvania

Antonelli Institute of Art and
Photography *A*
Art Institute
of Philadelphia *A, B*
of Pittsburgh *C, A, B*
Carnegie Mellon University *D*
Drexel University *B*
Harrisburg Area Community
College *A*
La Roche College *B*
Lehigh University *B*
Lehigh Valley College *A*
Marywood University *C, B, M*
Oakbridge Academy of Arts *A*
Robert Morris University *B*

South Carolina

Clemson University *B*
Horry-Georgetown Technical
College *A*
University of South Carolina
Upstate *B*
Winthrop University *M*

Tennessee

Freed-Hardeman University *B*
Lambuth University *B*
Memphis College of Art *B, M*

Texas

Amarillo College *C, A*
Angelina College *C, A*
Cedar Valley College *C, A*
Lubbock Christian University *B*
San Jacinto College
    Central Campus *C*
South Plains College *A*
Texas A&M University
    Commerce *B*
Texas State Technical College
    West Texas *A*
University of Texas
    Austin *B, M*
Wade College *A*

Utah

Brigham Young University *B*
Salt Lake Community College *A*
Utah Valley State College *C, A, B*
Weber State University *B*

Vermont

Bennington College *B*
Champlain College *C, A, B*

Virginia

Radford University *B*
Virginia Commonwealth
    University *B, M*

Washington

Cornish College of the Arts *B*
Northwest College of Art *B*
Shoreline Community College *C, A*
Western Washington University *B*
Yakima Valley Community College *A*

West Virginia

Bethany College *B*

Wisconsin

Madison Area Technical College *A*
University of Wisconsin
    Madison *B*
Viterbo University *B*
Western Wisconsin Technical
    College *A*

Wyoming

Northwest College *A*

Desktop publishing

Arkansas

South Arkansas Community College *A*

California

Antelope Valley College *C*
California State University
    Chico *C*
Long Beach City College *C, A*
Ohlone College *A*
Platt College
    Ontario *A*
Silicon Valley College
    Western Career College:
        Emeryville *C, A, B*

Colorado

Westwood College of Technology
    South *A, B*

Connecticut

Manchester Community College *C*

Florida

Miami International University of Art
    and Design *A*

Illinois

Moraine Valley Community College *C*
Morton College *C*
South Suburban College of Cook
    County *C*

Indiana

Vincennes University *A*

Iowa

Des Moines Area Community
    College *C, A*
Graceland University *B*
Western Iowa Tech Community
    College *A*

Kansas

Kansas City Kansas Community
    College *A*

Kentucky

Louisville Technical Institute *A*
Murray State University *B*

Maryland

Howard Community College *A*
Montgomery College *C, A*

Massachusetts

Bristol Community College *C*
Gibbs College *A*
Middlesex Community College *C, A*
Springfield Technical Community
    College *C, A*

Michigan

Baker College
    of Muskegon *A*
Ferris State University *A*

Minnesota

Dakota County Technical College *C*
Hennepin Technical College *C, A*
Minneapolis Community and
    Technical College *C*
Ridgewater College *C, A*
Riverland Community College *C*
St. Mary's University of Minnesota *B*
St. Paul College *C*

Nebraska

Southeast Community College
    Lincoln Campus *C*

Nevada

Community College of Southern
    Nevada *C*

New Jersey

Bergen Community College *C*

New York

Touro College *A*

Ohio

Central Ohio Technical College *A*
Cincinnati State Technical and
    Community College *C, A*
Davis College *C*
Sinclair Community College *C*
University of Cincinnati
    Raymond Walters College *C*
Wright State University *C*

Oregon

Linn-Benton Community College *C*

Portland Community College *C*

Pennsylvania

Art Institute
    of Pittsburgh *C*
La Salle University *B*
Marywood University *C*

Rhode Island

New England Institute of
    Technology *A*

Tennessee

Volunteer State Community College *C*

Texas

Eastfield College *C, A*
Houston Community College
    System *C*
North Harris Montgomery
    Community College District *C*
Texas State University: San Marcos *B*

Utah

Salt Lake Community College *C*

Washington

Clark College *C*
Henry Cogswell College *B*
Walla Walla Community College *C, A*

Wisconsin

Gateway Technical College *C*
Western Wisconsin Technical
    College *A*

Development economics

Alabama

Alabama Agricultural and Mechanical
    University *M*

California

Hope International University *M*
Point Loma Nazarene University *B*
University of California
    Los Angeles *B*

Colorado

University of Denver *M*

Connecticut

Yale University *M*

Georgia

Covenant College *B*
Georgia Southern University *B*

Massachusetts

Brandeis University *M*
University of Massachusetts
    Lowell *M*

Michigan

Andrews University *B, M*
Calvin College *B*

New Hampshire

Southern New Hampshire
    University *M*

New York

Colgate University *B*

Pennsylvania

University of Pittsburgh *M*

Puerto Rico

Turabo University *A*

Rhode Island

Brown University *B*

Virginia

Eastern Mennonite University *B*

Wisconsin

University of Wisconsin
    Madison *D*

Developmental biology/ embryology

Iowa

University of Iowa *M, D*

Missouri

Washington University in St. Louis *D*

New York

University of Rochester *B*

Ohio

Case Western Reserve University *D*

Wisconsin

Lawrence University *B*
Marquette University *M, D*

Developmental/child psychology

California

California Institute of Integral
    Studies *D*
California State University
    East Bay *M*
    San Bernardino *M*
San Francisco State University *M*
University of California
    Santa Cruz *D*

District of Columbia

Catholic University of America *M, D*
George Washington University *D*

Florida

Florida International University *D*

Georgia

University of Georgia *D*

Illinois

DePaul University *M*
Loyola University of Chicago *M, D*
University of Chicago *D*

Iowa

University of Iowa *D*

Kansas

University of Kansas *M*

Kentucky

Lindsey Wilson College *M*

Maryland

University of Maryland
    Baltimore County *M, D*

Massachusetts

Bridgewater State College *M*
Clark University *M, D*
Northeastern University *M*
Tufts University *M, D*
Wheelock College *M*

Minnesota
St. Mary's University of Minnesota *M*
University of Minnesota
  Twin Cities *M, D*

Missouri
University of Missouri
  Columbia *M, D*

Montana
University of Montana: Missoula *M, D*

New Jersey
Rowan University *M*

New York
Cornell University *M, D*
University of Rochester *D*
Yeshiva University *D*

Ohio
Bowling Green State University *M, D*
Case Western Reserve University *D*
University of Akron *D*

Pennsylvania
Duquesne University *M*
Temple University *M, D*
University of Pennsylvania *M*

Tennessee
Vanderbilt University *M, D*

Texas
University of Houston *M, D*
University of Texas
  Dallas *M*

Washington
Eastern Washington University *M, T*

Wisconsin
Marquette University *M*

Diagnostic medical sonography

Alabama
Community College of the Air
  Force *A*
Virginia College *A*
Wallace State Community College at
  Hanceville *A*

Arizona
Gateway Community College *A*

California
Charles R. Drew University of
  Medicine and Science *B*
Foothill College *A*
Lincoln University *A*
Orange Coast College *A*
Santa Barbara City College *A*

Connecticut
Gateway Community College *A*

Delaware
Delaware Technical and Community
  College
  Stanton/Wilmington Campus *A*

District of Columbia
George Washington University *B*

Florida
Barry University *B*
Broward Community College *A*

Florida Community College at
  Jacksonville *A*
Florida Hospital College of Health
  Sciences *A*
Hillsborough Community College *A*
Pensacola Junior College *A*
Valencia Community College *A*

Georgia
Armstrong Atlantic State University *B*
Athens Technical College *A*
Darton College *A*
Gordon College *A*
Medical College of Georgia *B*

Hawaii
University of Hawaii
  Kapiolani Community College *A*

Illinois
City Colleges of Chicago
  Wright College *A*
John A. Logan College *A*
Triton College *A*

Indiana
Indiana University
  Bloomington *B*

Iowa
Mercy College of Health Sciences *A*

Kansas
Fort Hays State University *B*
Newman University *B*
Washburn University of Topeka *B*

Kentucky
St. Catharine College *B*

Maryland
Montgomery College *A*

Massachusetts
Bunker Hill Community College *A*
Middlesex Community College *A*
Springfield Technical Community
  College *A*

Michigan
Baker College
  of Owosso *A*
  of Port Huron *A*
Delta College *A*
Ferris State University *A*
Jackson Community College *A*
Lansing Community College *A*
Oakland Community College *A*

Minnesota
College of St. Catherine *A*
St. Cloud Technical College *A*

Mississippi
Itawamba Community College *A*

Missouri
University of Missouri
  Columbia *B, M*

Nebraska
Nebraska Methodist College of
  Nursing and Allied Health *A, B*
University of Nebraska
  Medical Center *B*

New Jersey
Bergen Community College *A*
Gloucester County College *A*

University of Medicine and Dentistry
  of New Jersey
  School of Health Related
  Professions *B*

New Mexico
Albuquerque Technical-Vocational
  Institute *A*

New York
Rochester Institute of Technology *B*
State University of New York
  Downstate Medical Center *B*

North Carolina
Caldwell Community College and
  Technical Institute *A*
Cape Fear Community College *A*
Forsyth Technical Community
  College *A*
Pitt Community College *A*
Southwestern Community College *A*

Ohio
Central Ohio Technical College *A*
Cincinnati State Technical and
  Community College *A*
Kettering College of Medical Arts *A*
Owens Community College
  Toledo *A*

Oklahoma
University of Oklahoma *B*

Oregon
Oregon Institute of Technology *B*

Pennsylvania
Community College of Allegheny
  County *A*
Harrisburg Area Community
  College *A*
Keystone College *A*
Northampton County Area
  Community College *A*
South Hills School of Business &
  Technology *A*
Thomas Jefferson University: College
  of Health Professions *B*
Western School of Health and
  Business Careers *A*

Puerto Rico
Universidad del Este *A, B*

South Dakota
Southeast Technical Institute *A*

Texas
Austin Community College *A*
Del Mar College *A*
El Centro College *A*
North Harris Montgomery
  Community College District *A*
Tyler Junior College *A*
University of Texas
  Brownsville *A*

Utah
Weber State University *B*

Washington
Bellevue Community College *A*
Seattle University *B*
Wenatchee Valley College *A*

West Virginia
Mountain State University *A, B*

Wisconsin
Chippewa Valley Technical College *A*

Diesel mechanics

Alabama
Alabama Southern Community
  College *A*
Bishop State Community College *C*
Gadsden State Community College *C*
Lawson State Community College *C*
Shelton State Community College *C*
Trenholm State Technical College *C*
Wallace State Community College at
  Hanceville *C, A*

Alaska
University of Alaska
  Anchorage *C, A*
  Southeast *C, A*

Arizona
Central Arizona College *C, A*
Universal Technical Institute *A*

Arkansas
Arkansas State University: Newport *C*
Mid-South Community College *C*
University of Arkansas
  Community College at Hope *C*

California
Allan Hancock College *C, A*
Cerritos Community College *C*
Citrus College *C, A*
Golden West College *A*
Long Beach City College *C, A*
Los Angeles Trade and Technical
  College *C, A*
Merced College *C, A*
Palomar College *C, A*
San Bernardino Valley College *C, A*
Santa Rosa Junior College *C*
Shasta College *C, A*
West Hills Community College *C, A*
Yuba Community College District *C*

Colorado
Denver Automotive & Diesel
  College *A*
Northeastern Junior College *C, A*
Trinidad State Junior College *C, A*

Florida
Florida Community College at
  Jacksonville *C*

Georgia
Albany Technical College *C*
DeKalb Technical College *C*
Georgia Southwestern State
  University *A*
Gwinnett Technical College *C*

Hawaii
University of Hawaii
  Hawaii Community College *C, A*
  Honolulu Community College *C, A*

Idaho
College of Southern Idaho *C, A*
Eastern Idaho Technical College *C, A*
Idaho State University *C, A*
Lewis-Clark State College *C, A, B*
North Idaho College *C, A*

Illinois
Black Hawk College *C, A*
Black Hawk College
  East Campus *C*
Danville Area Community College *A*
Illinois Eastern Community Colleges
  Wabash Valley College *A*
Kishwaukee College *C, A*

Parkland College *A*
Rend Lake College *C, A*
Sauk Valley Community College *A*
Southeastern Illinois College *C, A*
Spoon River College *A*

Indiana
Oakland City University *A*
Vincennes University *A*

Iowa
Des Moines Area Community
    College *C, A*
Hawkeye Community College *A*
Indian Hills Community College *A*
Kirkwood Community College *C, A*
Northeast Iowa Community
    College *C*
Northwest Iowa Community
    College *A*
Scott Community College *A*
Western Iowa Tech Community
    College *C*

Kansas
North Central Kansas Technical
    College *A*
Pittsburg State University *B*

Kentucky
Big Sandy Community and Technical
    College *C*
Elizabethtown Community and
    Technical College *C, A*
Maysville Community College *C, A*
Owensboro Community College *C*
Somerset Community College *C, A*

Maine
Northern Maine Community
    College *C, A*
Washington County Community
    College *C*

Massachusetts
Massasoit Community College *C, A*

Michigan
Wayne County Community College *A*

Minnesota
Alexandria Technical College *C, A*
Central Lakes College *C*
Hennepin Technical College *C, A*
Hibbing Community College *C*
Minnesota State Community and
    Technical College - Fergus
    Falls *C, A*
Riverland Community College *C*
St. Paul College *C*
South Central College *C*

Mississippi
Copiah-Lincoln Community College *A*
Itawamba Community College *C, A*

Missouri
Crowder College *C, A*
Ozarks Technical Community
    College *C, A*

Montana
Helena College of Technology of the
    University of Montana *C, A*
Montana State University
    Billings *C, A*
University of Montana: Missoula *A*

Nebraska
Central Community College *C, A*

Mid-Plains Community College
    Area *C, A*
Nebraska College of Technical
    Agriculture *A*
Northeast Community College *A*

Nevada
Great Basin College *C, A*
Truckee Meadows Community
    College *A*

New Hampshire
New Hampshire Community
    Technical College
    Berlin *C, A*

New Jersey
Raritan Valley Community College *A*

New Mexico
Albuquerque Technical-Vocational
    Institute *C*
San Juan College *C, A*

New York
State University of New York
    College of Agriculture and
        Technology at Cobleskill *A*
    College of Agriculture and
        Technology at Morrisville *A*
    College of Technology at Alfred *A*

North Carolina
Cape Fear Community College *C*
Central Piedmont Community
    College *C, A*
Forsyth Technical Community
    College *C*
Johnston Community College *C, A*
Wilkes Community College *C, A*
Wilson Technical Community
    College *C*

North Dakota
Lake Region State College *C, A*
North Dakota State College of
    Science *C, A*
Williston State College *A*

Ohio
University of Northwestern Ohio *C, A*
Washington State Community
    College *A*

Oklahoma
Oklahoma State University
    Okmulgee *A*
Western Oklahoma State College *A*

Oregon
Lane Community College *C, A*
Linn-Benton Community College *C, A*
Portland Community College *C, A*
Rogue Community College *C, A*

Pennsylvania
Delaware County Community
    College *C*
Johnson College *A*
Pennsylvania College of
    Technology *C, A*

South Carolina
Greenville Technical College *C*

South Dakota
Lake Area Technical Institute *A*
Southeast Technical Institute *A*
Western Dakota Technical Institute *C*

Texas
Angelina College *C*
Cedar Valley College *C*
Central Texas College *C, A*
College of the Mainland *C, A*
Del Mar College *C, A*
Eastfield College *C, A*
Houston Community College
    System *C*
Kilgore College *C, A*
North Central Texas College *A*
Northeast Texas Community
    College *C, A*
Odessa College *C, A*
St. Philip's College *C, A*
San Jacinto College
    North *C, A*
South Plains College *C, A*
South Texas College *C, A*
Texarkana College *C*
Texas Southmost College *C*
Texas State Technical College
    Waco *C*
    West Texas *C, A*
Universal Technical Institute *C*
University of Texas
    Brownsville *C*

Utah
College of Eastern Utah *A*
Dixie State College of Utah *C, A*
Salt Lake Community College *C, A*
Utah Valley State College *C, A*
Weber State University *A*

Vermont
Vermont Technical College *A*

Virginia
J. Sargeant Reynolds Community
    College *C*
New River Community College *C*
Southside Virginia Community
    College *C*
Southwest Virginia Community
    College *C*

Washington
Bellingham Technical College *A*
Centralia College *A*
Clark College *C, A*
Columbia Basin College *A*
Grays Harbor College *C, A*
Lake Washington Technical
    College *C, A*
Lower Columbia College *A*
Peninsula College *C, A*
Skagit Valley College *C, A*
Spokane Community College *A*
Walla Walla Community College *C*

Wisconsin
Blackhawk Technical College *A*
Chippewa Valley Technical College *C*
Mid-State Technical College *C*
Milwaukee Area Technical College *C*
Northeast Wisconsin Technical
    College *C*
Western Wisconsin Technical
    College *A*

Wyoming
Casper College *C, A*
Sheridan College *C, A*
Western Wyoming Community
    College *C, A*
Wyoming Technical Institute *C, A*

Dietetic technician

California
College of the Desert *A*

Long Beach City College *A*

Massachusetts
North Shore Community College *A*

New Hampshire
University of New Hampshire *A*

North Carolina
Gaston College *A*

Ohio
Cincinnati State Technical and
    Community College *A*
Sinclair Community College *A*
Youngstown State University *A*

Wisconsin
Milwaukee Area Technical College *A*

Dietetics

Alabama
University of Alabama *B*
University of Alabama
    Birmingham *M*

Arkansas
Harding University *B*
Ouachita Baptist University *B*
University of Central Arkansas *B*

California
California State Polytechnic
    University: Pomona *B, M*
California State University
    Chico *B, M*
Loma Linda University *A, B*
Point Loma Nazarene University *B*
San Jose State University *B, M*

Colorado
University of Northern Colorado *B*

Connecticut
Briarwood College *A*
St. Joseph College *B*
University of Connecticut *B*
University of New Haven *B, M*

Florida
Florida State University *B, M, D*
Palm Beach Community College *A*

Georgia
University of Georgia *B*

Idaho
Idaho State University *B*

Illinois
Bradley University *B*
Loyola University of Chicago *M*
University of Illinois
    Chicago *B, M, D*
    Urbana-Champaign *B*

Indiana
Ball State University *B, M*
Indiana University-Purdue University
    Indianapolis *M*

Iowa
Iowa State University *B*

Kansas
Kansas State University *B*

Louisiana
Louisiana State University and
Agricultural and Mechanical
College *B*
University of Louisiana at Lafayette *B*

Maine
Southern Maine Community
College *A*

Maryland
University of Maryland
College Park *B*

Massachusetts
Laboure College *A*

Michigan
Andrews University *B*
Central Michigan University *B, M*
Delta College *A*
Eastern Michigan University *B, M*
Madonna University *B*
Michigan State University *B*
Northern Michigan University *B*

Minnesota
Normandale Community College *A*

Missouri
College of the Ozarks *B*
Fontbonne University *B*
Jewish Hospital College of Nursing
and Allied Health *M*
University of Missouri
Columbia *B*

Nebraska
Northeast Community College *A*

New Hampshire
Keene State College *B*
University of New Hampshire *B*

North Carolina
East Carolina University *B*
Meredith College *B*
Western Carolina University *B*

North Dakota
North Dakota State University *B*

Ohio
Bowling Green State University *B, M*
Case Western Reserve
University *B, M, D*
Hocking College *A*
Miami University
Oxford Campus *B*
Ohio State University
Columbus Campus *B*
Ohio University *B*
Owens Community College
Toledo *A*
University of Akron *B*
University of Cincinnati
Raymond Walters College *A*
University of Dayton *B*
Youngstown State University *B*

Oklahoma
University of Oklahoma *M*

Pennsylvania
Gannon University *B*
Harrisburg Area Community
College *A*
Immaculata University *B*
Marywood University *B*
Seton Hill University *B*
University of Pittsburgh *B*

West Chester University of
Pennsylvania *B*

Rhode Island
University of Rhode Island *B*

Tennessee
Lipscomb University *B*
Southern Adventist University *A*

Texas
Abilene Christian University *B*
El Paso Community College *A*
Texas Christian University *B*
Texas Tech University *B*
Texas Woman's University *B*
University of Texas
Pan American *B*
Southwestern Medical Center at
Dallas *B*

Utah
Brigham Young University *B*

Washington
Shoreline Community College *A*

West Virginia
Marshall University *B, M*

Wisconsin
Mount Mary College *B, M*
University of Wisconsin
Stout *B*
Viterbo University *B*

Dietician assistant

Illinois
Lincoln Land Community College *C*

Indiana
Ball State University *A*
Vincennes University *A*

Iowa
Des Moines Area Community
College *C*

Kansas
Barton County Community
College *C, A*
Coffeyville Community College *C*

Minnesota
Alexandria Technical College *C*

New York
Broome Community College *C*
Erie Community College
North Campus *A*
Genesee Community College *A*

Pennsylvania
Harrisburg Area Community
College *C*
Pennsylvania College of Technology *A*

Digital media

Arizona
Northern Arizona University *B*

Arkansas
Arkansas State University *B*
Harding University *B*
John Brown University *B*
South Arkansas Community College *A*

California
Art Institute
of California: Orange County *A, B*
California Baptist University *B*
Diablo Valley College *C*
Grossmont Community College *C, A*
Long Beach City College *C*
Ohlone College *C, A*
Pacific Union College *B*
Santa Barbara City College *C, A*
Sierra College *C, A*
University of California
San Diego *B*
University of Southern California *M*
Vanguard University of Southern
California *B*
Westwood College of Technology
Inland Empire *A, B*

Colorado
Colorado Technical University *C*
Jones International University *C, B*
University of Denver *B, M*

Connecticut
Manchester Community College *A*
Naugatuck Valley Community
College *A*
Quinnipiac University *B*

Florida
Florida Atlantic University *B*
Hillsborough Community
College *C, A*
Manatee Community College *A*

Georgia
Georgia Institute of Technology *B, D*
Georgia Military College *A*

Illinois
Bradley University *B*
Northwestern University *M, D*
School of the Art Institute of
Chicago *B, M*

Indiana
Huntington University *B*
Indiana University
Bloomington *B, M*
Vincennes University *A*

Iowa
Briar Cliff University *B*
University of Northern Iowa *B*

Kansas
Pittsburg State University *B*
Southwestern College *B*

Louisiana
Centenary College of Louisiana *B*

Maine
New England School of
Communications *A, B*
St. Joseph's College *B*

Maryland
Frederick Community College *C*
Howard Community College *A*

Massachusetts
Gibbs College *A*
Massachusetts Institute of
Technology *D*
New England Institute of Art *B*
Newbury College *A*

Michigan
Calvin College *B*

College for Creative Studies *B*
Cornerstone University *B*
Grace Bible College *B*
Oakland Community College *C*
Saginaw Valley State University *M*

Minnesota
Art Institutes International
Minnesota *A, B*
Hennepin Technical College *C, A*
Minneapolis Community and
Technical College *C, A*
Northwestern College *B*
Ridgewater College *C*
Rochester Community and Technical
College *C, A*

Missouri
Lindenwood University *B*
Ozarks Technical Community
College *A*
Webster University *B*

Nebraska
Central Community College *C, A*

New Hampshire
Southern New Hampshire
University *B*
University of New Hampshire *B*

New Jersey
Felician College *B*
Sussex County Community College *C*
Union County College *C*

New York
Canisius College *B*
Clarkson University *B*
Marist College *B*
New York University *B*
Niagara County Community
College *C, A*
Rensselaer Polytechnic Institute *B*
Rochester Institute of
Technology *B, M*
Sage College of Albany *B*

Ohio
Denison University *B*
Franklin University *B*
Kent State University *B*
Mount Union College *B*
Ohio University *B*
Ohio University
Zanesville Campus *A*
Sinclair Community College *C*
University of Cincinnati
Clermont College *A*
Raymond Walters College *C, A*
University of Dayton *B*

Oklahoma
Rose State College *C, A*

Oregon
University of Oregon *B*

Pennsylvania
Juniata College *B*
Kutztown University of
Pennsylvania *B, M*
La Salle University *B*
Lebanon Valley College *B*
Lehigh Carbon Community College *A*
Marywood University *B, M*
Philadelphia University *B, M*
Waynesburg College *B*
Wilkes University *B*
York College of Pennsylvania *B*

Tennessee

King College *B*
Union University *B*

Texas

Abilene Christian University *B*
Del Mar College *A*
Northwest Vista College *C*
Texas A&M University
　Commerce *B*
University of Texas
　Arlington *B*

Utah

Salt Lake Community College *C, A*
Utah Valley State College *A, B*

Vermont

Castleton State College *B*
Champlain College *A, B*

Virginia

Art Institute
　of Washington *A, B*
Liberty University *M*

Washington

Washington State University *B*

Wisconsin

Concordia University Wisconsin *B*

Directing/theatrical production

California

California Institute of the Arts *M*
California State University
　Fullerton *B, M*
Monterey Peninsula College *C, A*
University of Southern California *M*

Florida

Florida State University *M*
University of Miami *B*

Illinois

Bradley University *B*

Indiana

St. Joseph's College *B*

Iowa

Coe College *B*
Drake University *B*
University of Iowa *M*

Maine

University of Southern Maine *B*

Massachusetts

Boston University *B, M*
Emerson College *B*
Simon's Rock College of Bard *B*

Missouri

Lindenwood University *B*
Webster University *B*

New Mexico

College of Santa Fe *B*

New York

Bard College *B*
City University of New York
　Brooklyn College *M*
Hofstra University *B*

North Carolina

East Carolina University *B*

Ohio

Ohio University *M*

Pennsylvania

Carnegie Mellon University *M*
Marywood University *B*
Penn State
　Abington *B*
　Altoona *B*
　Beaver *B*
　Berks *B*
　Delaware County *B*
　Dubois *B*
　Fayette *B*
　Hazleton *B*
　Lehigh Valley *B*
　McKeesport *B*
　Mont Alto *B*
　New Kensington *B*
　Shenango *B*
　York *B*
Temple University *M*

Texas

Baylor University *M*
Texas Christian University *B*

Vermont

Bennington College *B, M*

Washington

Cornish College of the Arts *B*

Divinity/ministry (B.Div., M.Div.)

Alabama

Beeson Divinity School at Samford
　University *F*
Southern Christian University: First
　Professional *F*

California

American Baptist Seminary of the
　West *F*
Azusa Pacific University: School of
　Theology *F*
Church Divinity School of the
　Pacific *F*
Claremont School of Theology *F*
Dominican School of Philosophy and
　Theology *F*
Franciscan School of Theology *F*
Fuller Theological Seminary *F*
Golden Gate Baptist Theological
　Seminary *F*
International School of Theology *F*
Jesuit School of Theology at Berkeley:
　Professional *F*
Mennonite Brethren Biblical
　Seminary *F*
Pacific Lutheran Theological
　Seminary *F*
Pacific School of Religion *F*
St. John's Seminary *F*
St. Patrick's Seminary *F*
San Francisco Theological Seminary *F*
Starr King School for the Ministry *F*
Talbot School of Theology of Biola
　University *F*
Westminster Theological Seminary in
　California *F*

Colorado

Denver Conservative Baptist
　Seminary *F*
Iliff School of Theology *F*

Connecticut

Holy Apostles College and Seminary *F*
Yale University: Divinity School *F*

District of Columbia

Catholic University of America: School
　of Theology *F*
Dominican House of Studies *F*
Howard University: Divinity School *F*
Washington Theological Union *F*
Wesley Theological Seminary *F*

Florida

St. Vincent De Paul Regional
　Seminary *F*

Georgia

Candler School of Theology *F*
Columbia Theological Seminary *F*
Interdenominational Theological
　Center *F*

Illinois

Bethany Theological Seminary *F*
Catholic Theological Union *F*
Chicago Theological Seminary *F*
Garrett-Evangelical Theological
　Seminary *F*
Lincoln Christian Seminary *F*
Lutheran School of Theology at
　Chicago *F*
McCormick Theological Seminary *F*
Meadville-Lombard Theological
　School *F*
North Park Theological Seminary *F*
Northern Baptist Theological
　Seminary *F*
Seabury-Western Theological
　Seminary *F*
Trinity Evangelical Divinity School *F*
University of Chicago: Divinity
　School *F*
University of St. Mary of the
　Lake–Mundelein Seminary *F*

Indiana

Anderson University: School of
　Theology *F*
Associated Mennonite Biblical
　Seminary *F*
Bethel College *F*
Christian Theological Seminary *F*
Concordia Theological Seminary *F*
Earlham School of Religion *F*
St. Meinrad School of Theology *F*
University of Notre Dame: School of
　Theology *F*

Iowa

Faith Baptist Theological Seminary *F*
University of Dubuque: School of
　Theology *F*
Wartburg Theological Seminary *F*

Kansas

Central Baptist Theological
　Seminary *F*

Kentucky

Asbury Theological Seminary *F*
Lexington Theological Seminary *F*
Louisville Presbyterian Theological
　Seminary *F*
Southern Baptist Theological
　Seminary *F*

Louisiana

New Orleans Baptist Theological
　Seminary *F*
Notre Dame Seminary School of
　Theology *F*

Maine

Bangor Theological Seminary *F*

Maryland

Mount St. Mary's College: Seminary *F*

Massachusetts

Andover Newton Theological
　School *F*
Boston University: School of
　Theology *F*
Episcopal Divinity School *F*
Gordon-Conwell Theological
　Seminary *F*
Harvard University: Divinity School *F*
Holy Cross Greek Orthodox School of
　Theology *F*
Pope John XXIII National Seminary *F*
St. John's Seminary *F*
Weston Jesuit School of Theology *F*

Michigan

Andrews University Seminary *F*
Calvin Theological Seminary *F*
Grand Rapids Baptist Seminary *F*
Sacred Heart Major Seminary *F*
Western Theological Seminary *F*

Minnesota

Bethel Theological Seminary *F*
Luther Seminary: Theological
　Professions *F*
St. John's University: School of
　Theology *F*
University of St. Thomas: School of
　Divinity *F*

Mississippi

Reformed Theological Seminary *F*
Wesley Biblical Seminary *F*

Missouri

Assemblies of God Theological
　Seminary *F*
Concordia Seminary *F*
Eden Theological Seminary *F*
Kenrick-Glennon Seminary *F*
Midwestern Baptist Theological
　Seminary *F*
Nazarene Theological Seminary *F*
St. Paul School of Theology *F*

New Jersey

Drew University: School of
　Theology *F*
Immaculate Conception Seminary of
　Seton Hall University *F*
New Brunswick Theological
　Seminary *F*
Princeton Theological Seminary *F*

New York

Alliance Theological Seminary *F*
Christ The King Seminary *F*
Colgate Rochester Divinity
　School-Bexley Crozer Theological
　Seminary *F*
General Theological Seminary *F*
New York Theological Seminary *F*
St. Bernard's Institute *F*
St. John's University *F*
St. Joseph's Seminary and College *F*
St. Vladimir's Orthodox Theological
　Seminary *F*
Seminary of the Immaculate
　Conception *F*
Union Theological Seminary:
　Theological Professions *F*

North Carolina

Duke University: Divinity School *F*
Hood Theological Seminary *F*

Southeastern Baptist Theological
Seminary: Theological
Professions *F*

Ohio

Ashland Theological Seminary *F*
Athenaeum of Ohio *F*
Methodist Theological School in
Ohio *F*
Pontifical College Josephinum: First
Professional *F*
St. Mary Seminary *F*
Trinity Lutheran Seminary *F*
United Theological Seminary *F*
Winebrenner Seminary *F*

Oklahoma

Phillips Theological Seminary *F*

Oregon

Multnomah Biblical Seminary *F*
Western Conservative Baptist
Seminary *F*

Pennsylvania

Academy of the New Church *F*
Biblical Theological Seminary *F*
Eastern Baptist Theological
Seminary *F*
Lancaster Theological Seminary *F*
Lutheran Theological Seminary at
Gettysburg *F*
Lutheran Theological Seminary at
Philadelphia *F*
Moravian Theological Seminary *F*
Pittsburgh Theological Seminary *F*
Reformed Presbyterian Theological
Seminary *F*
St. Charles Borromeo
Seminary-Overbrook *F*
St. Vincent Seminary *F*
Trinity Episcopal School for
Ministry *F*
Westminster Theological Seminary *F*

Puerto Rico

Evangelical Seminary of Puerto Rico *F*

South Carolina

Columbia Biblical Seminary and
Graduate School of Missions *F*
Erskine Theological Seminary *F*
Lutheran Theological Southern
Seminary *F*

South Dakota

North American Baptist Seminary *F*

Tennessee

Church of God School of Theology *F*
Emmanuel School of Religion *F*
Harding University Graduate School of
Religion *F*
Memphis Theological Seminary *F*
Mid-America Baptist Theological
Seminary *F*
Temple Baptist Seminary: Theological
Professions *F*
University of the South: School of
Theology *F*
Vanderbilt University: The Divinity
School *F*

Texas

Abilene Christian University: College
of Biblical and Family Studies *F*
Austin Presbyterian Theological
Seminary *F*
Baptist Missionary Association
Theological Seminary *F*
Episcopal Theological Seminary of the
Southwest *F*

Houston Graduate School of
Theology *F*
Oblate School of Theology *F*
Southern Methodist University:
Perkins School of Theology *F*
Southwestern Baptist Theological
Seminary: Theological
Professions *F*
Texas Christian University: Brite
Divinity School *F*
University of St. Thomas: School of
Theology *F*

Virginia

Eastern Mennonite Seminary *F*
Liberty Baptist Theological
Seminary *F*
Protestant Episcopal Theological
Seminary in Virginia *F*
Regent University: School of
Divinity *F*
Union Theological Seminary in
Virginia *F*
Virginia Union University: School of
Theology *F*

Washington

Gonzaga University: Department of
Religious Studies *F*
Seattle University: School of Theology
and Ministry *F*

Wisconsin

Sacred Heart School of Theology *F*
St. Francis Seminary *F*

Dog/pet/animal grooming

Massachusetts

North Shore Community College *A*

Drafting and design technology

Alabama

Bevill State Community College *A*
Bishop State Community College *A*
Calhoun Community College *C, A*
Central Alabama Community
College *A*
Faulkner University *A*
Gadsden State Community College *C*
George C. Wallace State Community
College
George C. Wallace Community
College at Dothan *C, A*
Selma *A*
J. F. Drake State Technical College *C, A*
Jefferson Davis Community College *C*
Lawson State Community
College *C, A*
Northwest-Shoals Community
College *C, A*
Remington College
Mobile *A*
Shelton State Community
College *C, A*
Southern Union State Community
College *C, A*
Trenholm State Technical College *C, A*
Virginia College *A*
Wallace State Community College at
Hanceville *C, A*

Alaska

University of Alaska
Anchorage *C, A*

Arizona

Arizona Western College *C, A*
Central Arizona College *C*

Cochise College *A*
Eastern Arizona College *C, A*
High-Tech Institute *A*
Mesa Community College *C*
Northland Pioneer College *C*
Pima Community College *C, A*

Arkansas

Arkansas State University
Beebe *A*
North Arkansas College *C, A*
Northwest Arkansas Community
College *A*
Phillips Community College of the
University of Arkansas *A*
Pulaski Technical College *C, A*
Southeast Arkansas College *C, A*
University of Arkansas
Cossatot Community College of the
C

California

American River College *A*
Antelope Valley College *C, A*
Bakersfield College *A*
Barstow College *C*
Butte College *C, A*
Cabrillo College *C*
Cerritos Community College *A*
Cerro Coso Community College *C, A*
Chabot College *C, A*
Chaffey College *C, A*
Citrus College *C, A*
City College of San Francisco *C, A*
College of San Mateo *C, A*
College of the Canyons *C, A*
College of the Desert *C, A*
College of the Redwoods *C, A*
College of the Sequoias *C, A*
Contra Costa College *C, A*
Cosumnes River College *C, A*
Cuyamaca College *A*
De Anza College *C, A*
Diablo Valley College *C*
East Los Angeles College *C*
El Camino College *C, A*
Evergreen Valley College *A*
Fresno City College *C, A*
Fullerton College *C, A*
Glendale Community College *C, A*
Golden West College *C, A*
Irvine Valley College *C, A*
Las Positas College *C, A*
Long Beach City College *C, A*
Los Angeles City College *A*
Los Angeles Harbor College *C, A*
Los Angeles Pierce College *C, A*
Los Angeles Southwest College *C, A*
Los Angeles Trade and Technical
College *C, A*
Los Angeles Valley College *C*
Merced College *C, A*
MiraCosta College *C, A*
Mission College *C, A*
Modesto Junior College *A*
Monterey Peninsula College *C, A*
Mount San Antonio College *C, A*
Napa Valley College *C, A*
NewSchool of Architecture &
Design *A*
Orange Coast College *C, A*
Palomar College *C, A*
Pasadena City College *C, A*
Porterville College *C*
Rio Hondo College *A*
Riverside Community College *C, A*
Sacramento City College *C, A*
Saddleback College *C, A*
San Diego City College *C, A*
San Joaquin Delta College *A*
San Jose City College *A*
Santa Ana College *C, A*
Santa Barbara City College *C, A*
Santa Monica College *C, A*

Santiago Canyon College *A*
Solano Community College *C, A*
Southwestern College *C, A*
Ventura College *C, A*
West Valley College *C, A*
Westwood College of Technology
Inland Empire *A*

Colorado

Aims Community College *C*
Community College of Aurora *A*
Community College of Denver *C, A*
Front Range Community College *C, A*
Otero Junior College *C*
Pikes Peak Community College *C*
Pueblo Community College *C, A*
Red Rocks Community College *C, A*
Trinidad State Junior College *A*
Westwood College of Technology *A*

Connecticut

Gateway Community College *C*
Gibbs College *C*
Three Rivers Community College *C, A*

Delaware

Delaware Technical and Community
College
Stanton/Wilmington Campus *A*

Florida

Brevard Community College *A*
Daytona Beach Community College *A*
Florida Community College at
Jacksonville *A*
Florida Technical College
Deland *A*
Key College *A*
Manatee Community College *A*
North Florida Community College *C*
Okaloosa-Walton College *C*
Palm Beach Community College *A*
St. Petersburg College *C, A*
Santa Fe Community College *A*
Seminole Community College *C*
South Florida Community
College *C, A*
Southwest Florida College *A*
Southwest Florida College
Tampa *A*
Tallahassee Community College *C, A*
Valencia Community College *C, A*

Georgia

Albany Technical College *C, A*
Athens Technical College *C*
Augusta Technical Institute *C*
Bainbridge College *C, A*
Central Georgia Technical
College *C, A*
Chattahoochee Technical College *C*
Clayton State University *C, A*
Coastal Georgia Community
College *C, A*
Dalton State College *C, A*
Darton College *A*
DeKalb Technical College *C*
Georgia Southwestern State
University *A*
Griffin Technical College *C*
Gwinnett Technical College *A*
Macon State College *A*
Middle Georgia College *A*
Northwestern Technical College *C, A*
Savannah Technical College *A*
Southwest Georgia Technical
College *C*
West Georgia Technical College *C*

Hawaii

University of Hawaii
Hawaii Community College *A*
Honolulu Community College *A*

Maui Community College *A*

Idaho

Boise State University *A*
Brigham Young University-Idaho *A*
College of Southern Idaho *C, A*
Idaho State University *C, A*
Lewis-Clark State College *A, B*
North Idaho College *C, A*

Illinois

Carl Sandburg College *C, A*
City Colleges of Chicago
    Harold Washington College *C*
College of DuPage *C, A*
Danville Area Community College *C*
Heartland Community College *C*
Highland Community College *C*
Illinois Central College *C*
Illinois Eastern Community Colleges
    Lincoln Trail College *A*
Illinois Valley Community College *A*
John A. Logan College *C, A*
Joliet Junior College *C, A*
Kankakee Community College *C, A*
Kishwaukee College *A*
Lake Land College *C*
Lewis and Clark Community
    College *C, A*
Oakton Community College *A*
Prairie State College *C*
Rend Lake College *C*
Richland Community College *A*
Robert Morris College: Chicago *C, A*
Sauk Valley Community College *C, A*
South Suburban College of Cook
    County *C, A*
Southwestern Illinois College *C, A*
Triton College *C, A*
Westwood College of Technology
    O'Hare *A*
    River Oaks *A*
William Rainey Harper College *C*

Indiana

Indiana University-Purdue University
    Indianapolis *A*
Ivy Tech State College
    Ivy Tech Community College:
        Bloomington *C, A*
    Ivy Tech Community College:
        Columbus *A*
    Ivy Tech Community College: East
        Central *C*
    Ivy Tech Community College:
        Kokomo *C, A*
    Ivy Tech Community College:
        Lafayette *C, A*
    Ivy Tech Community College: North
        Central *C*
    Ivy Tech Community College: South
        Central *C, A*
    Ivy Tech Community College:
        Southeast *A*
    Ivy Tech Community College:
        Southwest *A*
    Ivy Tech Community College:
        Wabash Valley *C*
Oakland City University *A*
Tri-State University *A, B*
Vincennes University *A*

Iowa

Clinton Community College *A*
Iowa Central Community College *C, A*
Iowa Lakes Community College *A*
Kirkwood Community College *C, A*
Marshalltown Community College *A*
Southeastern Community College
    North Campus *C, A*
Southwestern Community
    College *C, A*
Vatterott College *C, A*

Kansas

Allen County Community College *A*
Butler County Community
    College *C, A*
Coffeyville Community College *C*
Cowley County Community
    College *C, A*
Garden City Community College *A*
Hutchinson Community College *A*
Johnson County Community
    College *C, A*
Kansas City Kansas Community
    College *A*
Neosho County Community
    College *A*

Kentucky

Eastern Kentucky University *A*
Elizabethtown Community and
    Technical College *C*
Hopkinsville Community College *C*
Kentucky State University *A*
Louisville Technical Institute *C, A*
Madisonville Community College *A*
Murray State University *A, B*
Spencerian College: Lexington *C, A*

Louisiana

Grambling State University *B*
ITI Technical College *C, A*
Nunez Community College *C, A*
Remington College
    New Orleans *A*

Maine

Central Maine Community College *A*
Kennebec Valley Community
    College *C*
Northern Maine Community
    College *A*
Southern Maine Community
    College *C, A*

Maryland

Anne Arundel Community College *A*
Baltimore City Community
    College *C, A*
Carroll Community College *C, A*
Chesapeake College *C, A*
College of Southern Maryland *C*
Community College of Baltimore
    County *A*
Harford Community College *C*
Montgomery College *A*
Prince George's Community
    College *C, A*
Wor-Wic Community College *C, A*

Massachusetts

Benjamin Franklin Institute of
    Technology *C*
Bristol Community College *C*
Greenfield Community College *C*
Massachusetts Bay Community
    College *C*
Middlesex Community College *C, A*
Northern Essex Community
    College *C*
Roxbury Community College *A*

Michigan

Alpena Community College *A*
Baker College
    of Auburn Hills *A*
    of Clinton Township *A*
    of Flint *A*
    of Muskegon *A*
    of Owosso *A*
    of Port Huron *A*
Bay de Noc Community College *A*
Delta College *C, A*
Glen Oaks Community College *C*
Grand Rapids Community College *C*

Henry Ford Community College *A*
Kalamazoo Valley Community
    College *C, A*
Kellogg Community College *A*
Kirtland Community College *C, A*
Lake Michigan College *C, A*
Lake Superior State University *C, A*
Lansing Community College *A*
Macomb Community College *C, A*
Michigan Technological University *C*
Mid Michigan Community College *C*
Monroe County Community
    College *C, A*
Montcalm Community College *C, A*
Mott Community College *C, A*
Muskegon Community College *C, A*
North Central Michigan College *C*
Northern Michigan University *B*
Northwestern Michigan College *A*
Oakland Community College *C*
St. Clair County Community
    College *C, A*
Schoolcraft College *C, A*
Southwestern Michigan College *C, A*
Washtenaw Community College *C, A*

Minnesota

Anoka Technical College *C, A*
Century Community and Technical
    College *C, A*
Hennepin Technical College *C, A*
Minnesota State College - Southeast
    Technical *C, A*
Northland Community & Technical
    College *C, A*
Northwest Technical Institute *A*
Ridgewater College *C, A*
Rochester Community and Technical
    College *C, A*
St. Paul College *C, A*
South Central College *A*

Mississippi

Copiah-Lincoln Community College *A*
East Central Community College *A*
Hinds Community College *C, A*
Holmes Community College *A*
Itawamba Community College *C*
Meridian Community College *A*
Mississippi Gulf Coast Community
    College
    Jefferson Davis Campus *A*
Pearl River Community College *A*

Missouri

Central Missouri State University *A, B*
East Central College *C, A*
Jefferson College *C, A*
Lincoln University *A*
Missouri Southern State
    University *C, A, B*
Missouri State University *B*
Missouri State University: West
    Plains *A*
Moberly Area Community
    College *C, A*
St. Charles Community College *C, A*
St. Louis Community College
    St. Louis Community College at
        Florissant Valley *C, A*
Three Rivers Community College *A*
Vatterott College *C, A*
Vatterott College: St. Joseph *A*

Montana

Montana State University
    Billings *C, A*
Montana Tech of the University of
    Montana *A*

Nebraska

Central Community College *C, A*

Metropolitan Community
    College *C, A*
Southeast Community College
    Lincoln Campus *A*

Nevada

Community College of Southern
    Nevada *C, A*
Truckee Meadows Community
    College *C, A*
Western Nevada Community
    College *C, A*

New Hampshire

New Hampshire Community
    Technical College
    Berlin *C, A*
    Manchester *A*
    Nashua *A*
    Stratham *C, A*
University of New Hampshire *A*

New Jersey

Bergen Community College *C*
Brookdale Community College *C*
Burlington County College *A*
Camden County College *C, A*
County College of Morris *C*
Cumberland County College *C*
Gloucester County College *C, A*
Mercer County Community College *C*
Middlesex County College *C*
Ocean County College *C*

New Mexico

Clovis Community College *A*
Dona Ana Branch Community College
    of New Mexico State
    University *C, A*
Eastern New Mexico University:
    Roswell Campus *C, A*
Luna Community College *A*
New Mexico Junior College *C, A*
New Mexico State University
    Alamogordo *C*
Northern New Mexico College *C, A*
San Juan College *A*
Santa Fe Community College *C, A*
Western New Mexico University *C, A*

New York

Adirondack Community College *C, A*
City University of New York
    New York City College of
        Technology *A*
    Queensborough Community
        College *A*
Corning Community College *C*
Dutchess Community College *C*
Genesee Community College *C, A*
Hudson Valley Community College *A*
Institute of Design and
    Construction *A*
Island Drafting and Technical
    Institute *C, A*
Mohawk Valley Community
    College *C, A*
Onondaga Community College *C*
Orange County Community College *C*
State University of New York
    College of Technology at Alfred *A*
    College of Technology at Canton *C*
    College of Technology at Delhi *C, A*
Suffolk County Community College *A*
Ulster County Community
    College *C, A*

North Carolina

Alamance Community College *C, A*
Appalachian State University *B*
Asheville-Buncombe Technical
    Community College *A*

Beaufort County Community
College *C, A*
Blue Ridge Community College *C, A*
Caldwell Community College and
Technical Institute *C, A*
Central Carolina Community
College *A*
College of the Albemarle *C*
Durham Technical Community
College *C, A*
East Carolina University *B*
Forsyth Technical Community
College *A*
Gaston College *C*
Mitchell Community College *C, A*
Piedmont Community College *C*
Richmond Community College *C*
Rockingham Community College *C*
Rowan-Cabarrus Community
College *A*
Sandhills Community College *C, A*
South Piedmont Community
College *A*
Surry Community College *C, A*
Wake Technical Community
College *C, A*
Wilson Technical Community
College *A*

Ohio

AEC Southern Ohio College
Brown Mackie College: Akron *A*
Belmont Technical College *C*
Clark State Community College *C, A*
Cuyahoga Community College
Metropolitan Campus *C, A*
Hocking College *C, A*
James A. Rhodes State College *C*
Jefferson Community College *A*
Lakeland Community College *C*
Marion Technical College *C*
Miami University
Oxford Campus *C*
Sinclair Community College *C, A*
Southern State Community College *A*
University of Rio Grande *A*
Washington State Community
College *A*
Wright State University *A*
Wright State University: Lake
Campus *C, A*
Youngstown State University *A*
Zane State College *A*

Oklahoma

Oklahoma City Community College *A*
Oklahoma State University
Oklahoma City *C, A*
Okmulgee *A*
Platt College
Tulsa *C*
Rose State College *A*
Tulsa Community College *A*
Western College of Southern
California *C*
Western Oklahoma State College *A*

Oregon

Blue Mountain Community College *A*
Central Oregon Community
College *C*
Chemeketa Community College *A*
Clackamas Community College *A*
Clatsop Community College *C*
Lane Community College *C, A*
Linn-Benton Community College *A*
Portland Community College *A*
Treasure Valley Community
College *A*

Pennsylvania

Berks Technical Institute *A*
Commonwealth Technical Institute *A*

Community College of
Philadelphia *C, A*
Johnson College *A*
Lehigh Carbon Community
College *C, A*
Lincoln Technical Institute *A*
Luzerne County Community
College *C, A*
Montgomery County Community
College *A*
Penn State
University Park *C*
Pittsburgh Technical Institute *A*
Thaddeus Stevens College of
Technology *A*
Triangle Tech
Pittsburgh *A*
Westmoreland County Community
College *A*

Rhode Island

Johnson & Wales University *A, B*
New England Institute of
Technology *A*

South Carolina

Aiken Technical College *C*
Central Carolina Technical College *A*
Florence-Darlington Technical
College *A*
Horry-Georgetown Technical
College *C*
Midlands Technical College *C, A*
Northeastern Technical College *C*
Orangeburg-Calhoun Technical
College *A*
Piedmont Technical College *A*
Technical College of the
Lowcountry *C*
Tri-County Technical College *C, A*
Trident Technical College *C*
Williamsburg Technical College *C, A*
York Technical College *A*

South Dakota

Black Hills State University *A*
Lake Area Technical Institute *A*
Southeast Technical Institute *A*
Western Dakota Technical Institute *A*

Tennessee

Chattanooga State Technical
Community College *C*
Northeast State Technical Community
College *C, A*

Texas

Amarillo College *C, A*
Angelina College *C, A*
Austin Community College *C, A*
Brazosport College *C, A*
Central Texas College *C, A*
Cisco Junior College *C, A*
Coastal Bend College *A*
College of the Mainland *A*
Collin County Community College
District *C, A*
Del Mar College *C, A*
El Paso Community College *C, A*
Grayson County College *C, A*
Hill College *C, A*
Houston Community College
System *C, A*
Howard College *C*
Kilgore College *C, A*
LeTourneau University *A*
Lee College *C, A*
Midland College *A*
Mountain View College *C, A*
Navarro College *C, A*
North Central Texas College *A*
North Harris Montgomery
Community College District *C*

Odessa College *C, A*
Paris Junior College *A*
Prairie View A&M University *B*
St. Philip's College *C, A*
Sam Houston State University *B*
San Antonio College *C*
San Jacinto College
Central Campus *C, A*
North *C, A*
South Plains College *C, A*
South Texas College *C, A*
Tarrant County College *C, A*
Temple College *C, A*
Texarkana College *C, A*
Texas Southern University *B*
Texas Southmost College *C, A*
Texas State Technical College
Harlingen *A*
Waco *C, A*
West Texas *C, A*
Trinity Valley Community College *C, A*
Tyler Junior College *C, A*
University of Texas
Brownsville *C, A*
Vernon College *C, A*
Wharton County Junior College *A*

Utah

College of Eastern Utah *C*
Salt Lake Community College *A*
Snow College *A*
Southern Utah University *A*
Utah State University *A*
Utah Valley State College *A*
Weber State University *A*

Virginia

Blue Ridge Community College *C*
Central Virginia Community
College *C*
Danville Community College *A*
Eastern Shore Community College *C*
J. Sargeant Reynolds Community
College *C*
Lord Fairfax Community College *C*
New River Community College *A*
Northern Virginia Community
College *C, A*
Patrick Henry Community College *A*
Paul D. Camp Community
College *A*
Southside Virginia Community
College *C, A*
Southwest Virginia Community
College *C*
Tidewater Community College *A*
Virginia Highlands Community
College *C, A*
Virginia Western Community
College *C*
Wytheville Community College *C, A*

Washington

Big Bend Community College *C*
Centralia College *C, A*
Columbia Basin College *C*
Green River Community College *A*
Highline Community College *A*
Lake Washington Technical
College *C, A*
North Seattle Community
College *C, A*
Olympic College *C, A*
Renton Technical College *C, A*
Seattle Central Community College *A*
Shoreline Community College *C, A*
South Puget Sound Community
College *C, A*
South Seattle Community
College *C, A*
Spokane Community College *C*
Spokane Falls Community
College *C, A*
Walla Walla Community College *C*

Yakima Valley Community College *C*

West Virginia

Southern West Virginia Community
and Technical College *A*
West Virginia University Institute of
Technology *A*

Wisconsin

Blackhawk Technical College *A*
Chippewa Valley Technical College *A*
Fox Valley Technical College *A*
Gateway Technical College *C*
Herzing College *A, B*
Lakeshore Technical College *A*
Madison Area Technical College *C*
Moraine Park Technical College *C, A*
Northcentral Technical College *A*
Northeast Wisconsin Technical
College *A*
Southwest Wisconsin Technical
College *A*
Waukesha County Technical
College *C, A*

Wyoming

Casper College *A*
Northwest College *A*
Sheridan College *C, A*

Drama and theater arts

Alabama

Alabama State University *B*
Auburn University *B*
Birmingham-Southern College *B*
Chattahoochee Valley Community
College *A*
Huntingdon College *B, T*
Jacksonville State University *B*
Northeast Alabama Community
College *A*
Samford University *B*
Spring Hill College *B*
University of Alabama *B, M*
University of Mobile *B*
University of Montevallo *B, T*
University of South Alabama *B*

Alaska

University of Alaska
Anchorage *B*
Fairbanks *B*

Arizona

Arizona State University *B, M, D*
Arizona Western College *A*
Central Arizona College *A*
Eastern Arizona College *A*
Grand Canyon University *B*
Northern Arizona University *B, T*
Pima Community College *A*
Prescott College *B, M*
University of Arizona *B, M*

Arkansas

Arkansas State University *B*
Harding University *B*
Henderson State University *B*
Hendrix College *B*
Lyon College *B*
Ouachita Baptist University *B*
Southern Arkansas University *B*
University of Arkansas *B, M*
University of Arkansas
Little Rock *B*
University of the Ozarks *B*

California

Allan Hancock College *C*
American River College *A*
Azusa Pacific University *B*

Barstow College *A*
Bethany University *B*
Biola University *B*
California Institute of the Arts *C, B, M*
California Lutheran University *B*
California State Polytechnic
    University: Pomona *B*
California State University
    Bakersfield *B*
    Chico *B*
    Dominguez Hills *B*
    East Bay *B*
    Fresno *B*
    Fullerton *B, M*
    Long Beach *B, M*
    Los Angeles *B, M*
    Monterey Bay *B*
    Northridge *B, M*
    Sacramento *B, M*
    San Bernardino *B*
    Stanislaus *B*
Canada College *A*
Cerritos Community College *A*
Chabot College *A*
Chaffey College *A*
Chapman University *B*
Claremont McKenna College *B*
College of the Desert *A*
College of the Sequoias *A*
College of the Siskiyous *A*
Concordia University *B*
Contra Costa College *A*
Cosumnes River College *A*
Crafton Hills College *A*
Cypress College *C, A*
East Los Angeles College *A*
El Camino College *A*
Foothill College *A*
Fresno City College *A*
Fresno Pacific University *B*
Fullerton College *A*
Gavilan Community College *A*
Glendale Community College *C*
Golden West College *A*
Grossmont Community College *A*
Humboldt State University *B, M*
Irvine Valley College *A*
Lake Tahoe Community College *C, A*
Laney College *C, A*
Las Positas College *A*
Long Beach City College *A*
Los Angeles City College *C, A*
Los Angeles Southwest College *A*
Loyola Marymount University *B*
Mendocino College *A*
Merced College *A*
MiraCosta College *A*
Modesto Junior College *A*
Monterey Peninsula College *C, A*
Moorpark College *A*
Mount San Jacinto College *A*
Notre Dame de Namur University *B*
Occidental College *B*
Orange Coast College *A*
Palomar College *A*
Pepperdine University *B*
Pitzer College *B*
Point Loma Nazarene University *B*
Pomona College *B*
Reedley College *A*
Sacramento City College *A*
Saddleback College *A*
St. Mary's College of California *B*
San Diego City College *A*
San Diego Mesa College *A*
San Diego State University *B*
San Francisco State University *B, M*
San Jose State University *B, M*
Santa Ana College *C, A*
Santa Barbara City College *A*
Santa Clara University *B*
Santa Monica College *A*
Santa Rosa Junior College *C, A*
Scripps College *B*

Shasta College *C, A*
Solano Community College *A*
Sonoma State University *B*
Southwestern College *A*
Stanford University *B, M, D*
University of California
    Berkeley *B, M, D*
    Davis *B, M, D*
    Irvine *B, M, D*
    Los Angeles *B, M, D*
    Riverside *B*
    San Diego *B, M*
    Santa Barbara *B, M, D*
    Santa Cruz *C, B*
University of La Verne *B*
University of Redlands *B*
University of San Diego *B, M*
University of Southern
    California *B, M*
University of the Pacific *B*
Vanguard University of Southern
    California *B*
Ventura College *C, A*
West Valley College *A*
Westmont College *B*
Whittier College *B, M*
Yuba Community College District *A*

Colorado

Adams State College *B*
Colorado College *B*
Colorado Mountain College
    Spring Valley Campus *A*
Colorado State University *B*
Fort Lewis College *B*
Mesa State College *B*
Naropa University *B, M*
Otero Junior College *A*
Red Rocks Community College *A*
University of Colorado
    Boulder *B, M, D*
    Denver and Health Sciences
        Center *B*
University of Denver *B*
University of Northern Colorado *B, T*

Connecticut

Albertus Magnus College *B*
Central Connecticut State
    University *B*
Connecticut College *B*
Fairfield University *B*
Naugatuck Valley Community
    College *A*
Southern Connecticut State
    University *B*
Trinity College *B*
University of Connecticut *B, M*
University of Hartford *B*
Wesleyan University *B*
Western Connecticut State
    University *B*
Yale University *B, M, D*

Delaware

Delaware State University *B*
University of Delaware *M*

District of Columbia

American University *B*
Catholic University of America *B, M, T*
Gallaudet University *B*
George Washington University *B, M*
University of the District of
    Columbia *B*

Florida

Barry University *B*
Broward Community College *A*
Eckerd College *B*
Flagler College *B*
Florida Agricultural and Mechanical
    University *B*

Florida Atlantic University *B, M*
Florida Community College at
    Jacksonville *A*
Florida Gulf Coast University *B*
Florida International University *B*
Florida Southern College *B*
Florida State University *B, M*
Gulf Coast Community College *A*
Indian River Community College *A*
Jacksonville University *B*
Manatee Community College *A*
Miami Dade College *A*
Okaloosa-Walton College *A*
Palm Beach Atlantic University *B*
Palm Beach Community College *A*
Pensacola Junior College *A*
Rollins College *B*
Stetson University *B*
University of Central Florida *B, M*
University of Florida *B, M*
University of Miami *B*
University of South Florida *B*
University of West Florida *B*
Valencia Community College *A*

Georgia

Agnes Scott College *B*
Andrew College *B*
Armstrong Atlantic State University *B*
Brenau University *B*
Clark Atlanta University *B*
Columbus State University *B*
Darton College *A*
Emory University *B*
Gainesville State College *A*
Georgia College and State
    University *B*
Georgia Perimeter College *A*
Georgia Southern University *B*
Georgia Southwestern State
    University *B*
Gordon College *A*
Kennesaw State University *B*
LaGrange College *B*
Macon State College *A*
Mercer University *B*
Middle Georgia College *A*
Morehouse College *B*
Paine College *B*
Piedmont College *B*
Savannah College of Art and
    Design *B, M*
Shorter College *B*
Spelman College *B*
University of Georgia *B, M, D*
University of West Georgia *B*
Wesleyan College *B*
Young Harris College *A*

Hawaii

Brigham Young University-Hawaii *A*
University of Hawaii
    Manoa *B, M, D*

Idaho

Albertson College of Idaho *B*
Boise State University *B*
College of Southern Idaho *A*
Idaho State University *B, M*
University of Idaho *B, M*

Illinois

Augustana College *B*
Bradley University *B, T*
City Colleges of Chicago
    Harold Washington College *A*
    Kennedy-King College *C, A*
Columbia College Chicago *B*
DePaul University *B, M*
Dominican University *B*
Eastern Illinois University *B, T*
Elmhurst College *B*
Eureka College *B*

Greenville College *B*
Illinois Central College *B*
Illinois State University *B, M, T*
Illinois Valley Community College *A*
Illinois Wesleyan University *B*
John A. Logan College *A*
Judson College *B*
Kishwaukee College *A*
Knox College *B*
Lewis University *B, T*
Loyola University of Chicago *B*
MacMurray College *B*
Millikin University *B*
National-Louis University *B*
North Central College *B*
North Park University *B*
Northern Illinois University *B, M*
Northwestern University *B, M, D*
Principia College *B*
Rockford College *B*
Roosevelt University *B, M*
Sauk Valley Community College *A*
South Suburban College of Cook
    County *A*
Southern Illinois University
    Carbondale *B, M*
Southern Illinois University
    Edwardsville *B*
Southwestern Illinois College *A*
Spoon River College *A*
Triton College *B*
University of Illinois
    Chicago *B, M*
    Urbana-Champaign *B, M, D*
Western Illinois University *B, M*

Indiana

Anderson University *B*
Ball State University *B*
Bethel College *B*
Butler University *B*
DePauw University *B*
Earlham College *B*
Franklin College *B*
Goshen College *B*
Hanover College *B*
Huntington University *B*
Indiana State University *B*
Indiana University
    Bloomington *B, M, D*
    Northwest *B*
    South Bend *B*
Indiana University-Purdue University
    Fort Wayne *B, T*
Purdue University *B*
Saint Mary's College *B*
St. Mary-of-the-Woods College *B*
Taylor University *B*
University of Evansville *B*
University of Indianapolis *B*
University of Notre Dame *B*
University of Southern Indiana *B*
Valparaiso University *B*
Vincennes University *A*
Wabash College *B*

Iowa

Briar Cliff University *B*
Central College *B*
Clarke College *A, B, T*
Coe College *B*
Cornell College *B, T*
Dordt College *B*
Drake University *B, T*
Ellsworth Community College *A*
Graceland University *B, T*
Grand View College *B*
Grinnell College *B*
Luther College *B*
Maharishi University of
    Management *B*
Morningside College *B*
St. Ambrose University *B*
Simpson College *B*

University of Iowa *B, M*
University of Northern Iowa *B*
Waldorf College *B*
Wartburg College *B*

Kansas
Baker University *B, T*
Barton County Community College *A*
Benedictine College *B*
Butler County Community College *A*
Central Christian College of
  Kansas *A, B*
Coffeyville Community College *A*
Colby Community College *A*
Emporia State University *B*
Friends University *B*
Garden City Community College *A*
Kansas State University *B*
Kansas Wesleyan University *B, T*
McPherson College *B, T*
Neosho County Community
  College *A*
Ottawa University *B, T*
Pratt Community College *A*
Seward County Community College *A*
Southwestern College *B*
Sterling College *B, T*
University of Kansas *B, M, D*
University of St. Mary *B*
Washburn University of Topeka *B*
Wichita State University *B*

Kentucky
Berea College *B*
Campbellsville University *B*
Centre College *B*
Eastern Kentucky University *B*
Georgetown College *B*
Morehead State University *B*
Murray State University *B*
Northern Kentucky University *B*
Thomas More College *A, B*
Transylvania University *B*
University of Kentucky *B, M*
University of Louisville *B, M*
University of the Cumberlands *B*
Western Kentucky University *B*

Louisiana
Bossier Parish Community College *A*
Centenary College of Louisiana *B*
Dillard University *B*
Grambling State University *B*
Louisiana State University and
  Agricultural and Mechanical
  College *B, M, D*
Loyola University New Orleans *B*
Northwestern State University *B*
Southern University and Agricultural
  and Mechanical College *B*
Tulane University *B, M*
University of New Orleans *M*

Maine
Bates College *B*
Colby College *B*
University of Maine *B, M*
University of Maine
  Farmington *B*
University of Southern Maine *B*

Maryland
Community College of Baltimore
  County *A*
Frederick Community College *A*
Frostburg State University *B*
Goucher College *B*
Howard Community College *A*
McDaniel College *B*
Morgan State University *B*
Prince George's Community
  College *C*
St. Mary's College of Maryland *B*

Salisbury University *B*
Towson University *B, M*
University of Maryland
  Baltimore County *B*
  College Park *B*
Washington College *B*

Massachusetts
Amherst College *B*
Boston College *B*
Brandeis University *B, M*
Bridgewater State College *B*
Bristol Community College *A*
Bunker Hill Community College *A*
Cape Cod Community College *A*
Clark University *B*
College of the Holy Cross *B*
Dean College *A*
Eastern Nazarene College *B*
Emerson College *B, M*
Fitchburg State College *B*
Gordon College *B*
Hampshire College *B*
Massachusetts Bay Community
  College *A*
Massachusetts College of Liberal
  Arts *B*
Massasoit Community College *A*
Middlesex Community College *A*
Mount Holyoke College *B*
Northeastern University *B*
Regis College *B*
Salem State College *B*
Simon's Rock College of Bard *B*
Smith College *B*
Suffolk University *B*
University of Massachusetts
  Amherst *B, M*
  Boston *B*
Wellesley College *B*
Westfield State College *B*
Williams College *B*

Michigan
Adrian College *A, B*
Albion College *B, T*
Alma College *B*
Calvin College *B*
Central Michigan University *B, M*
Delta College *A*
Eastern Michigan University *B, M*
Grand Valley State University *B*
Henry Ford Community College *A*
Hillsdale College *B*
Hope College *B*
Kalamazoo College *B, T*
Kellogg Community College *A*
Lake Michigan College *A*
Lansing Community College *A*
Michigan State University *B, M*
Mid Michigan Community College *A*
Northern Michigan University *B*
Northwestern Michigan College *A*
Saginaw Valley State University *B*
Schoolcraft College *A*
Siena Heights University *B*
University of Detroit Mercy *B*
University of Michigan *B, M, D*
University of Michigan
  Flint *B*
Wayne State University *B, M, D*
Western Michigan University *B*

Minnesota
Augsburg College *B*
Bemidji State University *B*
Bethany Lutheran College *B*
Bethel University *B*
College of St. Benedict *B*
College of St. Catherine *B*
Concordia College: Moorhead *B*
Concordia University: St. Paul *B*
Gustavus Adolphus College *B*
Hamline University *B*

Macalester College *B*
Metropolitan State University *B*
Minnesota State University
  Mankato *B, M*
  Moorhead *B*
North Central University *A, B*
Northwestern College *B*
St. Cloud State University *B*
St. John's University *B*
St. Mary's University of Minnesota *B*
St. Olaf College *B*
Southwest Minnesota State
  University *B*
University of Minnesota
  Duluth *B*
  Morris *B*
  Twin Cities *B, M, D*
University of St. Thomas *B*
Vermilion Community College *A*
Winona State University *B*

Mississippi
Belhaven College *B*
Blue Mountain College *B*
Hinds Community College *A*
Millsaps College *B, T*
University of Mississippi *B, M*
University of Southern
  Mississippi *B, M*
William Carey College *B*

Missouri
Avila University *B*
Central Methodist University *B*
Central Missouri State University *B, M*
College of the Ozarks *B*
Culver-Stockton College *B*
Drury University *B*
Evangel University *A, B*
Fontbonne University *B*
Hannibal-LaGrange College *B*
Lindenwood University *B, M*
Missouri Southern State
  University *B, T*
Missouri State University *B, M*
Missouri Valley College *B*
Northwest Missouri State
  University *B*
Park University *B*
St. Louis Community College
  St. Louis Community College at
    Florissant Valley *A*
St. Louis University *B*
Southeast Missouri State University *B*
Southwest Baptist University *B*
Stephens College *B*
Truman State University *B*
University of Missouri
  Columbia *B, M, D*
  Kansas City *B, M*
Washington University in St.
  Louis *B, M*
Webster University *B*
William Jewell College *B*
William Woods University *B, T*

Montana
Carroll College *B*
Miles Community College *A*
Montana State University
  Billings *B*
Rocky Mountain College *B*
University of Montana: Missoula *B, M*
University of Montana: Western *B*

Nebraska
Chadron State College *B*
Concordia University *B, T*
Creighton University *B*
Doane College *B*
Hastings College *B, T*
Midland Lutheran College *B, T*
Nebraska Wesleyan University *B*

Northeast Community College *A*
University of Nebraska
  Kearney *B, T*
  Lincoln *B, M*
  Omaha *B, M*
Wayne State College *B, T*

Nevada
Truckee Meadows Community
  College *C, A*
University of Nevada
  Las Vegas *B, M*
  Reno *B*

New Hampshire
Dartmouth College *B*
Franklin Pierce College *B*
Keene State College *B*
New England College *B*
Plymouth State University *B*
University of New Hampshire *B*

New Jersey
Centenary College *B*
Cumberland County College *A*
Drew University *B*
Essex County College *A*
Fairleigh Dickinson University
  College at Florham *B*
  Metropolitan Campus *B*
Gloucester County College *A*
Kean University *B*
Middlesex County College *A*
Montclair State University *B, M*
Ocean County College *A*
Ramapo College of New Jersey *B*
Raritan Valley Community College *A*
Rowan University *B*
Rutgers, The State University of New
  Jersey
  Camden Regional Campus *B, T*
  New Brunswick/Piscataway
    Campus *B, M*
  Newark Regional Campus *B*
Thomas Edison State College *B*

New Mexico
College of Santa Fe *B*
College of the Southwest *B*
Eastern New Mexico University *B*
New Mexico State University *B*
San Juan College *A*
University of New Mexico *B, M*

New York
Adelphi University *B*
Adirondack Community College *A*
Alfred University *B*
Bard College *B*
Barnard College *B*
City University of New York
  Brooklyn College *B, M*
  City College *B*
  College of Staten Island *B*
  Hunter College *B, M*
  Lehman College *B*
  Queens College *B*
  Queensborough Community
    College *A*
  York College *B*
Colgate University *B*
Columbia University
  Columbia College *B*
  School of General Studies *B*
Cornell University *B, M, D*
Dowling College *B*
Dutchess Community College *A*
Elmira College *B*
Finger Lakes Community College *A*
Five Towns College *B*
Fordham University *B*
Hamilton College *B*
Hartwick College *B*

Hobart and William Smith Colleges *B*
Hofstra University *B*
Iona College *B*
Ithaca College *B*
Juilliard School *B*
Le Moyne College *B*
Long Island University
   C. W. Post Campus *B, M*
Manhattanville College *B*
Marymount Manhattan College *B*
Mohawk Valley Community College *A*
Nazareth College of Rochester *B*
New York University *B, M, D*
Niagara County Community
   College *A*
Niagara University *B*
Pace University *B*
Rockland Community College *A*
Russell Sage College *B*
St. Lawrence University *B*
Sarah Lawrence College *B, M*
Siena College *C*
Skidmore College *B*
State University of New York
   Albany *B, M*
   Binghamton *B, M*
   Buffalo *B*
   College at Brockport *B*
   College at Buffalo *B*
   College at Fredonia *B*
   College at Geneseo *B*
   College at Oneonta *B*
   College at Plattsburgh *B*
   College at Potsdam *B*
   New Paltz *B*
   Oswego *B*
   Purchase *B*
   Stony Brook *B, M*
Suffolk County Community College *A*
Syracuse University *B, M*
Vassar College *B*
Wagner College *B*
Wells College *B*
Westchester Community College *A*

North Carolina

Appalachian State University *B*
Barton College *B*
Brevard College *B*
Campbell University *B*
Catawba College *B*
College of the Albemarle *A*
Davidson College *B*
Duke University *B*
East Carolina University *B*
Elon University *B*
Fayetteville State University *B*
Greensboro College *B, T*
Guilford College *B*
High Point University *B*
Lees-McRae College *B, T*
Lenoir-Rhyne College *B, T*
Livingstone College *B*
Louisburg College *A*
Meredith College *B*
North Carolina Agricultural and
   Technical State University *B*
North Carolina Central University *B*
North Carolina School of the Arts *B*
North Carolina Wesleyan College *B*
Pfeiffer University *B*
Queens University of Charlotte *B*
Shaw University *B*
University of North Carolina
   Asheville *B, T*
   Chapel Hill *B, M*
   Charlotte *B*
   Greensboro *B, M*
   Pembroke *B*
   Wilmington *B*
Wake Forest University *B*
Western Carolina University *B*

North Dakota

Dickinson State University *B*
Jamestown College *B*
North Dakota State University *B, M*
Trinity Bible College *B*
University of North Dakota *B, M*

Ohio

Antioch College *B*
Ashland University *B*
Bowling Green State
   University *B, M, D*
Case Western Reserve University *B, M*
Cedarville University *B*
Cleveland State University *B*
College of Wooster *B*
Denison University *B*
Edison State Community College *A*
Hiram College *B, T*
Kent State University *C, B, M*
Kenyon College *B*
Malone College *B*
Marietta College *B*
Miami University
   Oxford Campus *B, M*
Mount Union College *B*
Mount Vernon Nazarene University *B*
Muskingum College *B*
Oberlin College *B*
Ohio Northern University *B*
Ohio State University
   Columbus Campus *B, M, D*
Ohio University *B, M*
Ohio Wesleyan University *B*
Otterbein College *B*
Owens Community College
   Toledo *A*
Shawnee State University *A*
Sinclair Community College *A*
University of Cincinnati *B, M*
University of Dayton *B*
University of Findlay *B*
University of Toledo *B*
Wilmington College *B*
Wright State University *B*
Youngstown State University *B*

Oklahoma

Cameron University *B*
Carl Albert State College *A*
East Central University *B*
Eastern Oklahoma State College *A*
Northeastern Oklahoma Agricultural
   and Mechanical College *A*
Northeastern State University *B*
Northwestern Oklahoma State
   University *B*
Oklahoma Baptist University *B, T*
Oklahoma City University *B, M*
Oklahoma State University *B, M*
Oral Roberts University *B*
Rose State College *A*
St. Gregory's University *A, B*
Tulsa Community College *A*
University of Central Oklahoma *B*
University of Oklahoma *B, M*
University of Science and Arts of
   Oklahoma *B, T*
University of Tulsa *B*

Oregon

Eastern Oregon University *B*
George Fox University *B*
Lewis & Clark College *B*
Linfield College *B*
Linn-Benton Community College *A*
Mount Hood Community College *A*
Pacific University *B*
Portland State University *B, M*
Reed College *B*
Southern Oregon University *B, T*
University of Oregon *B, M, D*
University of Portland *B, M*

Western Oregon University *B*
Willamette University *B*

Pennsylvania

Albright College *B*
Allegheny College *B*
Arcadia University *B*
Bloomsburg University of
   Pennsylvania *B*
Bucknell University *B*
Bucks County Community College *A*
California University of
   Pennsylvania *B*
Carnegie Mellon University *B*
Cedar Crest College *B*
Chatham College *B*
Cheyney University of Pennsylvania *B*
Clarion University of Pennsylvania *B*
Community College of Philadelphia *A*
DeSales University *B, T*
Delaware County Community
   College *A*
Dickinson College *B*
Duquesne University *B*
East Stroudsburg University of
   Pennsylvania *B*
Edinboro University of
   Pennsylvania *B*
Franklin & Marshall College *B*
Gannon University *B*
Gettysburg College *B*
Harrisburg Area Community
   College *A*
Indiana University of Pennsylvania *B*
Juniata College *B*
King's College *B*
Kutztown University of
   Pennsylvania *B*
Lackawanna College *A*
Lehigh University *B*
Lock Haven University of
   Pennsylvania *B*
Lycoming College *B*
Mansfield University of
   Pennsylvania *B*
Marywood University *B*
Messiah College *B*
Moravian College *B*
Muhlenberg College *C, B*
Penn State
   Abington *B*
   Altoona *B*
   Beaver *B*
   Berks *B*
   Delaware County *B*
   Dubois *B*
   Fayette *B*
   Hazleton *B*
   Lehigh Valley *B*
   McKeesport *B*
   Mont Alto *B*
   New Kensington *B*
   Schuylkill - Capital College *B*
   Shenango *B*
   University Park *B, M*
   Wilkes-Barre *B*
   Worthington Scranton *B*
Point Park University *B*
Seton Hill University *B*
Slippery Rock University of
   Pennsylvania *B*
Swarthmore College *B*
Temple University *B, M*
University of Pennsylvania *B*
University of Pittsburgh *B, M, D*
University of Pittsburgh
   Johnstown *B*
University of Scranton *C, B*
University of the Arts *B*
Ursinus College *B*
Villanova University *M*
West Chester University of
   Pennsylvania *B*
Westminster College *B, T*

Wilkes University *B*
York College of Pennsylvania *B*

Puerto Rico

University of Puerto Rico
   Rio Piedras *B*
University of the Sacred Heart *B*

Rhode Island

Brown University *B, M, D*
Community College of Rhode
   Island *A*
Rhode Island College *B, M*
Roger Williams University *B*
Salve Regina University *B*
University of Rhode Island *B*

South Carolina

Anderson University *B*
Charleston Southern University *B*
Coastal Carolina University *B*
Coker College *B*
College of Charleston *B*
Converse College *B*
Francis Marion University *B*
Furman University *B, T*
Limestone College *B*
Newberry College *B*
North Greenville College *A*
Presbyterian College *B, T*
South Carolina State University *B*
University of South Carolina *B, M*
Winthrop University *B*

South Dakota

Augustana College *B*
Dakota Wesleyan University *B*
University of Sioux Falls *B*
University of South Dakota *B, M*

Tennessee

Belmont University *B, T*
Bethel College *B*
Freed-Hardeman University *T*
Hiwassee College *A*
Lambuth University *B*
Lipscomb University *B*
Maryville College *B*
Middle Tennessee State University *B*
Milligan College *T*
Rhodes College *B*
Roane State Community College *A*
Tennessee State University *B*
Trevecca Nazarene University *B*
Union University *B, T*
University of Memphis *B, M*
University of Tennessee
   Chattanooga *B*
   Knoxville *B, M*
Vanderbilt University *B*
Walters State Community College *A*

Texas

Abilene Christian University *B*
Alvin Community College *A*
Amarillo College *A*
Angelina College *A*
Angelo State University *B, T*
Austin Community College *A*
Baylor University *B, M*
Brazosport College *A*
Cisco Junior College *A*
Clarendon College *A*
College of the Mainland *A*
Del Mar College *A*
East Texas Baptist University *B*
El Paso Community College *A*
Galveston College *A*
Grayson County College *A*
Hardin-Simmons University *B*
Howard College *A*
Howard Payne University *B, T*
Kilgore College *A*

Lamar University *B, M*
Laredo Community College *A*
Lee College *A*
Lon Morris College *A*
Lubbock Christian University *T*
McMurry University *B, T*
Midland College *A*
Midwestern State University *B*
Navarro College *A*
Northeast Texas Community
College *A*
Our Lady of the Lake University of San
Antonio *B*
Paris Junior College *A*
Prairie View A&M University *B*
St. Edward's University *B*
St. Philip's College *A*
Sam Houston State University *B*
San Antonio College *A*
San Jacinto College
North *A*
Schreiner University *B*
South Plains College *A*
Southern Methodist University *B, M*
Southwestern University *B, T*
Stephen F. Austin State
University *B, M, T*
Sul Ross State University *B*
Tarleton State University *B*
Texarkana College *A*
Texas A&M University *B*
Texas A&M University
Commerce *B, M*
Kingsville *B, T*
Texas Christian University *B*
Texas Lutheran University *B*
Texas Southern University *B*
Texas State University: San
Marcos *B, M, T*
Texas Tech University *B, M, D*
Texas Wesleyan University *B*
Texas Woman's University *B, M*
Trinity University *B*
Trinity Valley Community College *A*
Tyler Junior College *A*
University of Dallas *B, T*
University of Houston *B, M*
University of Mary Hardin-Baylor *B*
University of North Texas *B, M*
University of St. Thomas *B*
University of Texas
Arlington *B*
Austin *B, M, D*
El Paso *B, M*
Pan American *B, M*
University of the Incarnate Word *B*
Wayland Baptist University *B, T*
West Texas A&M University *B*
Western Texas College *A*
Wharton County Junior College *A*

Utah

Brigham Young University *B*
Dixie State College of Utah *A*
Southern Utah University *B, T*
University of Utah *B, M, D*
Utah State University *B, M*
Utah Valley State College *A*
Weber State University *B*

Vermont

Bennington College *B, M*
Castleton State College *B*
Johnson State College *B*
Marlboro College *B*
Middlebury College *B*
St. Michael's College *B*
University of Vermont *B*

Virginia

Averett University *B*
Bluefield College *B*
Christopher Newport University *B*
College of William and Mary *B*

Eastern Mennonite University *B*
Emory & Henry College *B*
Ferrum College *B*
George Mason University *B*
Hampton University *B*
Hollins University *B*
James Madison University *B, T*
Liberty University *B*
Longwood University *B, T*
Lynchburg College *B*
Mary Baldwin College *B, M*
Old Dominion University *B, T*
Radford University *B*
Randolph-Macon College *B*
Randolph-Macon Woman's College *B*
Roanoke College *B, T*
Shenandoah University *B*
Sweet Briar College *B*
University of Mary Washington *B*
University of Richmond *B*
University of Virginia *B, M*
University of Virginia's College at
Wise *B, T*
Virginia Commonwealth
University *B, M*
Virginia Intermont College *B*
Virginia Polytechnic Institute and
State University *B, M*
Virginia Union University *B*
Virginia Wesleyan College *B*
Washington and Lee University *B*

Washington

Central Washington University *B*
Centralia College *A*
Cornish College of the Arts *B*
Eastern Washington University *B*
Everett Community College *A*
Evergreen State College *B*
Gonzaga University *B*
Highline Community College *A*
North Seattle Community
College *C, A*
Northwest University *T*
Saint Martin's University *B*
Seattle Pacific University *B*
Seattle University *B*
University of Puget Sound *B*
University of Washington *B, M, D*
Washington State University *B*
Western Washington University *B, M*
Whitman College *B*

West Virginia

Bethany College *B*
Concord University *B*
Davis and Elkins College *B*
West Virginia University *B, M*
West Virginia Wesleyan College *B*

Wisconsin

Beloit College *B*
Cardinal Stritch University *B*
Carroll College *B*
Carthage College *B, T*
Lawrence University *B, T*
Marquette University *B, T*
Ripon College *B, T*
University of Wisconsin
Eau Claire *B*
Green Bay *B, T*
La Crosse *B*
Madison *B, M, D*
Milwaukee *B*
Oshkosh *B*
Parkside *B, T*
Platteville *B*
Stevens Point *B*
Superior *B, M*
Whitewater *B*
Viterbo University *B, T*
Wisconsin Lutheran College *B*

Wyoming

Casper College *A*
Laramie County Community
College *A*
University of Wyoming *B*
Western Wyoming Community
College *A*

Drama/dance teacher education

Alabama

Birmingham-Southern College *T*
Huntingdon College *T*

Arizona

Grand Canyon University *B*
Northern Arizona University *B, T*
Prescott College *T*
University of Arizona *B*

Arkansas

Ouachita Baptist University *B, T*
University of the Ozarks *B, T*

California

California State University
Long Beach *T*
San Diego State University *B, T*
San Francisco State University *B, T*
University of the Pacific *T*

District of Columbia

Catholic University of America *B*
George Washington University *T*

Florida

Flagler College *B*
Jacksonville University *B*
Palm Beach Atlantic University *B, T*
University of South Florida *B*

Georgia

Brenau University *B*
Columbus State University *B*

Idaho

Brigham Young University-Idaho *T*

Illinois

Bradley University *B*
North Park University *T*
Rockford College *T*

Indiana

Anderson University *B, T*
Indiana University-Purdue University
Fort Wayne *B, T*
University of Evansville *B, T*
Valparaiso University *B*

Iowa

Central College *T*
Dordt College *B*
Drake University *B*
Graceland University *T*
Maharishi University of
Management *T*
Simpson College *T*
University of Iowa *T*
Waldorf College *B*

Kansas

Bethel College *T*
Southwestern College *B, T*
Sterling College *T*
University of St. Mary *T*

Louisiana

Centenary College of Louisiana *B, T*

Maryland

Community College of Baltimore
County *A*
St. Mary's College of Maryland *T*

Massachusetts

Boston University *B, M*
Bridgewater State College *B, T*
Emerson College *B, M*
Tufts University *T*

Michigan

Hope College *T*

Minnesota

Minnesota State University
Mankato *B, T*
St. Cloud State University *B, T*
Southwest Minnesota State
University *B, T*
University of Minnesota
Morris *T*
Winona State University *B, T*

Mississippi

William Carey College *B*

Missouri

Washington University in St.
Louis *B, M, T*
William Jewell College *T*

Montana

Montana State University
Billings *T*
Rocky Mountain College *B, T*
University of Montana: Missoula *T*
University of Montana: Western *T*

Nebraska

Chadron State College *B*
Dana College *B*
Hastings College *B, T*
Wayne State College *B, T*
York College *B, T*

Nevada

University of Nevada
Reno *B*

New Jersey

Rowan University *T*

New York

City University of New York
Hunter College *B, T*
New York University *M, D, T*

North Carolina

Appalachian State University *B*
Brevard College *B*
East Carolina University *B*
Greensboro College *B*
Lees-McRae College *B, T*
Meredith College *B, T*
North Carolina Central
University *B, M, T*
University of North Carolina
Charlotte *A*
Greensboro *B, M, T*

North Dakota

Dickinson State University *B, T*

Ohio

Ashland University *B, T*
Baldwin-Wallace College *T*
Bowling Green State University *B, M*
Miami University
Oxford Campus *T*

Ohio State University
  Columbus Campus *M*
Ohio Wesleyan University *B*
University of Akron *B*
University of Findlay *B, M, T*
Youngstown State University *B*

Oklahoma
East Central University *B, T*
Eastern Oklahoma State College *A*
University of Central Oklahoma *B*

Oregon
Portland State University *T*

Pennsylvania
Marywood University *B*
Point Park University *B*

Rhode Island
Salve Regina University *B*

South Carolina
Columbia College *B, T*
Furman University *T*
South Carolina State University *B, T*

South Dakota
University of Sioux Falls *T*
University of South Dakota *B, M, D, T*

Tennessee
Lipscomb University *B, T*
Trevecca Nazarene University *B, T*

Texas
East Texas Baptist University *B*
Hardin-Simmons University *B, T*
Howard Payne University *B, T*
Lamar University *T*
McMurry University *T*
St. Edward's University *B, T*
Tarleton State University *T*
Texas A&M University
  Commerce *T*
  Kingsville *T*
University of Dallas *T*
University of Houston *T*
West Texas A&M University *T*

Utah
Brigham Young University *B*
Southern Utah University *B, T*
University of Utah *B*
Utah Valley State College *B*
Weber State University *B*

Vermont
Castleton State College *B, T*
Johnson State College *B*
St. Michael's College *T*

Virginia
Averett University *B, T*
Longwood University *T*
Old Dominion University *B, T*
Shenandoah University *B*
Virginia Highlands Community
  College *A*

Washington
Central Washington University *B, M, T*
Western Washington University *B*
Whitworth College *B, T*

Wisconsin
University of Wisconsin
  Green Bay *T*
  Whitewater *B*
Viterbo University *B, T*

Drawing

Alabama
Birmingham-Southern College *B*

California
Academy of Art University *C, A, B, M*
Biola University *B*
California College of the Arts *B, M*
California State University
  East Bay *B*
  Fullerton *B, M*
  Long Beach *B, M*
  Northridge *B, M*
Chabot College *A*
College of the Desert *A*
Grossmont Community College *A*
Laguna College of Art and Design *C, B*
Long Beach City College *A*
Monterey Peninsula College *C, A*
Ohlone College *C*
Pasadena City College *A*
Santa Rosa Junior College *C*
Solano Community College *A*
University of San Francisco *B*

Colorado
Adams State College *B*

Connecticut
University of Hartford *B*

Georgia
Albany State University *B*

Illinois
American Academy of Art *B*
Bradley University *B*
City Colleges of Chicago
  Olive-Harvey College *A*
Judson College *B*
Lewis University *B*
Richland Community College *A*
Rockford College *B*
School of the Art Institute of
  Chicago *B, M*

Indiana
Grace College *B*
Indiana University-Purdue University
  Fort Wayne *B*
Vincennes University *A*

Iowa
Drake University *B*
University of Iowa *B, M*

Kansas
Allen County Community College *A*
Central Christian College of Kansas *A*
Pratt Community College *A*

Kentucky
Eastern Kentucky University *B*
Louisville Technical Institute *A*

Maine
University of Southern Maine *B*

Maryland
Cecil Community College *A*
Maryland Institute College of Art *B*

Massachusetts
Art Institute of Boston at Lesley
  University *B*
Boston University *B*
Hampshire College *B*
Montserrat College of Art *B*
Salem State College *B*

School of the Museum of Fine
  Arts *B, M*
Simon's Rock College of Bard *B*
University of Massachusetts
  Dartmouth *M*

Michigan
College for Creative Studies *B*
Finlandia University *B*
Kendall College of Art and Design of
  Ferris State University *B*
Lansing Community College *A*
Northern Michigan University *B*
Siena Heights University *B*
University of Michigan *B*

Minnesota
College of Visual Arts *B*
Minneapolis College of Art and
  Design *B*
Minnesota State University
  Mankato *B*
St. Cloud State University *B*

Missouri
Columbia College *B*
Washington University in St.
  Louis *B, M*

Nevada
Sierra Nevada College *B*

New Hampshire
McIntosh College *A*
Rivier College *B*

New Jersey
Rowan University *B*

New York
Bard College *B*
Parsons The New School for
  Design *C, A, B, T*
Pratt Institute *A, B, M*
Sarah Lawrence College *B*
School of Visual Arts *B, M*
State University of New York
  College at Fredonia *B*
  Purchase *B*

North Carolina
East Carolina University *B*

Ohio
Art Academy of Cincinnati *B*
Cleveland Institute of Art *B*
Ohio State University
  Columbus Campus *B, M*
Shawnee State University *B*
Sinclair Community College *C*
University of Akron *M*
Wright State University *B*

Oregon
Portland State University *B*

Pennsylvania
Edinboro University of
  Pennsylvania *B*
Keystone College *A, B*
Oakbridge Academy of Arts *A*
Seton Hill University *B*

Puerto Rico
Inter American University of Puerto
  Rico
  San German Campus *B, M*
University of Puerto Rico
  Rio Piedras *B*

Rhode Island
Rhode Island College *B*

South Carolina
Anderson University *B*

Tennessee
Carson-Newman College *B*
Tennessee Technological University *B*

Texas
Sam Houston State University *M*
Stephen F. Austin State University *M*
University of North Texas *B, M*
University of Texas
  El Paso *B, M*
Western Texas College *A*

Utah
Dixie State College of Utah *A*

Vermont
Bennington College *B*
Burlington College *B*
Marlboro College *B*

Washington
Cornish College of the Arts *B*
North Seattle Community College *C*
Western Washington University *B*

West Virginia
Marshall University *M*
West Virginia State University *B*
West Virginia Wesleyan College *B*

Driver/safety education

Iowa
Iowa State University *T*
William Penn University *B*

Kansas
Emporia State University *T*

Minnesota
St. Cloud State University *B*

Mississippi
Mississippi State University *T*

Missouri
Missouri Baptist University *T*
Missouri Western State University *T*

Nebraska
Peru State College *T*

North Carolina
North Carolina Agricultural and
  Technical State University *B, M, T*

Ohio
University of Findlay *B, M, T*

Oklahoma
Northeastern State University *T*
Southeastern Oklahoma State
  University *T*
Southwestern Oklahoma State
  University *T*

South Dakota
Northern State University *T*

Texas
Lamar University *T*
Texas A&M University
  Commerce *B*

Texas State University: San Marcos *T*

Virginia
Bridgewater College *T*
Radford University *T*
University of Virginia's College at
Wise *T*

West Virginia
West Virginia University *T*

Drywall installation

Indiana
Ivy Tech State College
Ivy Tech Community College:
Lafayette *C*

Kentucky
Big Sandy Community and Technical
College *C*

Wisconsin
Milwaukee Area Technical College *C*

Dutch/Flemish

California
University of California
Berkeley *B*

Iowa
Dordt College *B*

Michigan
Calvin College *B*

E-commerce

Alabama
University of South Alabama *B*

Arizona
University of Phoenix *M*

California
California State University
Fullerton *M*
Dominican University of California *B*
Foothill College *C*
National University *M*
San Jose City College *C*
University of La Verne *B*
University of San Diego *M*
University of San Francisco *M*
Westwood College of Technology
Inland Empire *B*

Colorado
Colorado Technical University *C, A, B*
Jones International University *C, B, M*
Red Rocks Community College *C*
Westwood College of Technology *B*
Westwood College of Technology
South *B*

Florida
Barry University *M*
Florida Institute of Technology *M*
Stetson University *B*

Georgia
Central Georgia Technical College *C*
Georgia State University *M*

Illinois
Lewis University *C*
Lincoln Land Community College *C*
Northwestern University *M*

Indiana
St. Mary-of-the-Woods College *B*

Kentucky
Maysville Community College *C, A*

Louisiana
Southern University and Agricultural
and Mechanical College *B*

Maine
University of Maine
Fort Kent *B*

Maryland
Howard Community College *C*
Villa Julie College *M*

Massachusetts
Bunker Hill Community College *C*
Holyoke Community College *C*
Nichols College *B*
North Shore Community College *C*

Michigan
Cleary University *B*
Eastern Michigan University *M*
Ferris State University *B*
Madonna University *C*

Minnesota
Capella University *C, B*

Missouri
Maryville University of Saint
Louis *B, M*

Nebraska
Bellevue University *B*
Creighton University *M*

New Jersey
Bergen Community College *C*
Thomas Edison State College *C*

New York
Berkeley College *A, B*
Clarkson University *B*
College of Westchester *A*
Globe Institute of Technology *C*
Rochester Institute of Technology *C*
Westchester Community College *C*

North Carolina
Brunswick Community College *C*
Carteret Community College *C, A*
Cleveland Community College *A*
Davidson County Community
College *C, A*
Fayetteville Technical Community
College *A*
Isothermal Community College *C, A*
Lenoir Community College *A*
Pitt Community College *A*
Sandhills Community College *A*
Surry Community College *A*

Ohio
Lakeland Community College *C, A*
Marion Technical College *A*
Stark State College of Technology *A*
Washington State Community
College *A*

Oklahoma
Northwestern Oklahoma State
University *B*
Rose State College *A*

Oregon
Portland Community College *C*

Pennsylvania
Bucks County Community College *C*
Carnegie Mellon University *M*
DeSales University *B*
Holy Family University *B*
La Salle University *C*
Marywood University *M*
Messiah College *B*
Temple University *B, M*
University of Pennsylvania *B, M*
University of Pittsburgh
Titusville *C*

Rhode Island
Bryant University *M*

South Carolina
Limestone College *B*
Southern Wesleyan University *B*
Trident Technical College *C, A*

South Dakota
Dakota State University *B*

Tennessee
Pellissippi State Technical Community
College *A*
Trevecca Nazarene University *B*
University of Memphis *M*

Texas
Kilgore College *C, A*
Mountain View College *C, A*
Texas Christian University *B*
Texas State Technical College:
Marshall *C, A*
University of Dallas *M*

Utah
Stevens-Henager College *A*

Vermont
Champlain College *A, B*

Washington
Seattle University *B*
Washington State University *B*
Yakima Valley Community College *A*

West Virginia
Mountain State University *B*

Wisconsin
Marquette University *B, M*
Milwaukee Area Technical College *A*

Early childhood education

Alabama
Alabama Agricultural and Mechanical
University *B, M, T*
Alabama State University *B, M*
Athens State University *B*
Auburn University *B, M, D, T*
Birmingham-Southern College *B, T*
Bishop State Community College *C*
Calhoun Community College *A*
Concordia College *B*
Faulkner State Community College *A*
Gadsden State Community College *A*
Huntingdon College *B, T*
Lawson State Community College *A*
Samford University *M, T*
Shelton State Community College *C*
Spring Hill College *B, M*
Troy University *B, M, T*
Tuskegee University *B, T*

University of Alabama *B, M*
University of Alabama
Birmingham *B, M, D, T*
University of Mobile *B, M, T*
University of Montevallo *B, M, T*
University of South Alabama *B, M, T*
University of West Alabama *B, M, T*

Alaska
University of Alaska
Fairbanks *C, A*
Southeast *C, A, M, T*

Arizona
Arizona State University *B*
Arizona Western College *C, A*
Central Arizona College *C, A*
Coconino County Community
College *A*
Northern Arizona University *M, T*
Pima Community College *C, A*
Prescott College *B, M*
Scottsdale Community College *C, A*
South Mountain Community
College *C, A*
University of Arizona *B, M*
Yavapai College *C, A*

Arkansas
Arkansas State University *B, M, T*
Arkansas Tech University *B*
Black River Technical College *A*
Harding University *B, M, T*
Henderson State University *B*
John Brown University *B, T*
Lyon College *B*
Ouachita Baptist University *B, T*
Ouachita Technical College *A*
Ozarka College *C*
Phillips Community College of the
University of Arkansas *C, A*
Pulaski Technical College *A*
South Arkansas Community
College *C, A*
Southern Arkansas University *B, T*
University of Arkansas
Community College at Batesville *A*
Fort Smith *B*
Little Rock *B, M*
Monticello *B*
Pine Bluff *B*
University of Central Arkansas *M, T*
University of the Ozarks *B, T*
Williams Baptist College *B*

California
Allan Hancock College *C, A*
Bethany University *A, B*
Bethesda Christian University *C, B*
Butte College *C, A*
California Lutheran University *B, M*
California State University
Bakersfield *B*
Chico *B*
Fresno *M*
Long Beach *T*
Northridge *M*
Sacramento *B, M, T*
Stanislaus *B*
Canada College *C, A*
Cerritos Community College *A*
Cerro Coso Community College *C, A*
Chabot College *C, A*
Chaffey College *C, A*
College of the Desert *C*
College of the Redwoods *C, A*
College of the Sequoias *C*
Copper Mountain College *C*
Cosumnes River College *C, A*
Crafton Hills College *C, A*
Cuesta College *C, A*
De Anza College *C, A*
Diablo Valley College *C*

East Los Angeles College *C*
El Camino College *C, A*
Foothill College *C, A*
Fresno City College *C, A*
Gavilan Community College *C*
Glendale Community College *C, A*
Imperial Valley College *C, A*
Irvine Valley College *C, A*
Lake Tahoe Community College *C, A*
Lassen College *A*
Long Beach City College *C*
Los Angeles Southwest College *A*
Merced College *C, A*
Merritt College *C, A*
Mills College *M, T*
MiraCosta College *C, A*
Mount St. Mary's College *A*
Mount San Jacinto College *C, A*
Napa Valley College *C, A*
Ohlone College *C, A*
Orange Coast College *C, A*
Pacific Oaks College *C*
Pacific Union College *A, B*
Palomar College *C, A*
Pasadena City College *C, A*
Patten University *A, B*
Reedley College *C, A*
Riverside Community College *C, A*
Saddleback College *C, A*
St. Mary's College of California *M*
San Diego Christian College *B, T*
San Diego Miramar College *A*
San Francisco State University *T*
San Joaquin Delta College *C*
San Jose City College *C, A*
San Jose State University *B, M*
Santa Ana College *C, A*
Santa Barbara City College *C, A*
Santa Rosa Junior College *C, A*
Shasta College *A*
Sierra College *C, A*
Skyline College *C, A*
Solano Community College *C, A*
Sonoma State University *M, T*
Southwestern College *C, A*
Taft College *C, A*
University of California
  Santa Barbara *M*
University of La Verne *B, M, T*
Vanguard University of Southern
  California *T*
Ventura College *C, A*
West Hills Community College *C, A*
West Valley College *A*
Whittier College *B, T*
Yuba Community College
  District *C, A*

Colorado

Colorado Mountain College
  Alpine Campus *A*
Community College of Aurora *A*
Fort Lewis College *B*
Metropolitan State College of
  Denver *T*
Morgan Community College *C*
Northeastern Junior College *C, A*
Otero Junior College *C, A*
Pueblo Community College *A*
Red Rocks Community College *A*
University of Colorado
  Denver and Health Sciences
    Center *M*
University of Northern Colorado *M, T*

Connecticut

Capital Community College *C, A*
Connecticut College *T*
Eastern Connecticut State
  University *B, M, T*
Gateway Community College *C, A*
Housatonic Community College *A*
Manchester Community College *A*
Middlesex Community College *C, A*

Mitchell College *A, B*
Northwestern Connecticut
  Community College *C, A*
Norwalk Community College *C, A*
Post University *C, A*
Quinebaug Valley Community
  College *A*
Sacred Heart University *T*
St. Joseph College *M, T*
Three Rivers Community College *C, A*
Tunxis Community College *C, A*
University of Hartford *B, M*

Delaware

Delaware State University *B*
Delaware Technical and Community
  College
    Stanton/Wilmington Campus *C, A*
University of Delaware *B, T*
Wilmington College *A, B*

District of Columbia

Catholic University of America *B, M, T*
Gallaudet University *B, T*
George Washington University *M*
Howard University *M*
Trinity University *M, T*
University of the District of
  Columbia *B, T*

Florida

Barry University *B, M, T*
Brevard Community College *A*
Broward Community College *A*
Central Florida Community
  College *C, A*
Florida Agricultural and Mechanical
  University *B*
Florida Atlantic University *M*
Florida Community College at
  Jacksonville *C*
Florida Gulf Coast University *B*
Florida International University *M*
Florida Southern College *B*
Florida State University *B, M, D, T*
Indian River Community College *A*
Lake-Sumter Community College *A*
Lynn University *A, B*
Manatee Community College *A*
Miami Dade College *C, A*
Nova Southeastern University *A, B*
Okaloosa-Walton College *A*
Palm Beach Community College *A*
Pensacola Junior College *A*
Remington College: Largo *A*
St. Petersburg College *A*
Santa Fe Community College *C, A*
Southeastern College of the
  Assemblies of God *B, T*
Southwest Florida College *A*
Southwest Florida College
  Tampa *A*
Tallahassee Community College *A*
University of Central Florida *B, M*
University of Florida *M*
University of South Florida *B, M*
University of West Florida *B, T*

Georgia

Agnes Scott College *T*
Albany State University *B, M, T*
Albany Technical College *C, A*
Armstrong Atlantic State University *B*
Athens Technical College *C, A*
Atlanta Christian College *B*
Augusta State University *B, M*
Bainbridge College *C, A*
Berry College *B, M*
Brewton-Parker College *B*
Central Georgia Technical
  College *C, A*
Clark Atlanta University *B, M, D*
Columbus State University *B, M*

Columbus Technical College *C, A*
Covenant College *B, T*
DeKalb Technical College *C*
Gainesville State College *A*
Georgia College and State
  University *B, M, T*
Georgia Military College *A*
Georgia State University *B, M, D*
LaGrange College *B*
Macon State College *A, B*
Middle Georgia College *A*
Middle Georgia Technical College *C*
North Georgia College & State
  University *B, M*
Northwestern Technical College *A*
Oglethorpe University *B, M, T*
Piedmont College *B, M, T*
Reinhardt College *B*
Savannah State University *B*
Savannah Technical College *C*
Southwest Georgia Technical
  College *C, A*
Spelman College *B, T*
Thomas University *B*
Toccoa Falls College *B, T*
Valdosta State University *B, M*
Wesleyan College *B, M, T*
West Georgia Technical College *C, A*

Hawaii

Chaminade University of
  Honolulu *B, M, T*
University of Hawaii
  Hawaii Community College *C, A*
  Honolulu Community College *C, A*
  Kauai Community College *C, A*

Idaho

Boise State University *M, T*
Brigham Young University-Idaho *A*
College of Southern Idaho *A*
Idaho State University *B*
North Idaho College *A*

Illinois

Bradley University *B, T*
Chicago State University *B, M, T*
City Colleges of Chicago
  Harold Washington College *C, A*
  Kennedy-King College *A*
Columbia College Chicago *B*
Concordia University *B, M, T*
DePaul University *C, B, T*
Dominican University *B, T*
Eastern Illinois University *B*
Elmhurst College *B*
Governors State University *B, M, T*
Greenville College *B, T*
Highland Community College *C, A*
Illinois College *B, T*
Illinois State University *B, T*
John A. Logan College *C, A*
John Wood Community College *A*
Joliet Junior College *A*
Judson College *B, T*
Kankakee Community College *A*
Kendall College *B, M*
Kishwaukee College *A*
Lewis and Clark Community
  College *C, A*
Millikin University *B*
National-Louis University *B, M, T*
North Park University *B, M*
Northeastern Illinois University *B*
Northern Illinois University *M, T*
Oakton Community College *A*
Olivet Nazarene University *B, T*
Roosevelt University *B, M*
St. Augustine College *C, A*
St. Xavier University *M*
South Suburban College of Cook
  County *A*
Southern Illinois University
  Carbondale *B*

Southern Illinois University
  Edwardsville *B, T*
Southwestern Illinois College *A*
Spoon River College *A*
Triton College *C, A*
University of Illinois
  Urbana-Champaign *B, M, D, T*
William Rainey Harper College *C, A*

Indiana

Ancilla College *C, A*
Bethel College *A*
Butler University *B, T*
Indiana State University *M, T*
Indiana University
  Bloomington *B, T*
  Kokomo *C*
  South Bend *A*
Indiana University-Purdue University
  Fort Wayne *A*
Indiana Wesleyan University *T*
Manchester College *A*
Martin University *B*
Purdue University *B*
Purdue University
  Calumet *A, B*
St. Mary-of-the-Woods College *A, B, T*
Taylor University *A, T*
Taylor University: Fort Wayne *A*
University of Southern Indiana *B*
Vincennes University *A*

Iowa

Ashford University *B, T*
Central College *T*
Clarke College *B, T*
Drake University *B, M*
Graceland University *T*
Iowa State University *B, T*
Iowa Wesleyan College *B*
Loras College *B*
Mount Mercy College *T*
North Iowa Area Community
  College *A*
Northeast Iowa Community
  College *C*
Northwestern College *T*
St. Ambrose University *B, T*
Simpson College *B, T*
University of Iowa *M*
Upper Iowa University *B, T*
Wartburg College *T*

Kansas

Butler County Community College *A*
Central Christian College of Kansas *A*
Coffeyville Community College *A*
Donnelly College *C, A*
Friends University *B*
Garden City Community College *A*
Hesston College *A*
Kansas Wesleyan University *A*
Labette Community College *A*
McPherson College *B, T*
Pratt Community College *A*
Southwestern College *B, T*
Washburn University of Topeka *A, B*

Kentucky

Bluegrass Community and Technical
  College *A*
Campbellsville University *B*
Elizabethtown Community and
  Technical College *A*
Hazard Community College *A*
Henderson Community College *A*
Hopkinsville Community College *C, A*
Kentucky State University *B*
Lindsey Wilson College *A*
Madisonville Community College *A*
Maysville Community College *C, A*
Morehead State University *B*
Murray State University *B, T*

Owensboro Community College *A*
St. Catharine College *A*
Spalding University *B, M, T*
University of Kentucky *B*
University of Louisville *M*
Western Kentucky University *A, M, T*

Louisiana

Delgado Community College *A*
Dillard University *B, T*
Grambling State University *B, M*
Louisiana State University
  Alexandria *A*
  Shreveport *B*
Louisiana State University and
  Agricultural and Mechanical
  College *B*
Louisiana Tech University *B*
Nicholls State University *M*
Northwestern State University *B*
Nunez Community College *A*
Southeastern Louisiana University *B*
Southern University
  Shreveport *A*
Southern University and Agricultural
  and Mechanical College *B*
University of Louisiana at Lafayette *B*
University of Louisiana at Monroe *T*
University of New Orleans *B*
Xavier University of Louisiana *B*

Maine

Andover College *C, A*
Beal College *A*
Central Maine Community
  College *C, A*
Eastern Maine Community
  College *C, A*
Northern Maine Community
  College *C, A*
University of Maine
  Farmington *B, T*
Washington County Community
  College *C, A*

Maryland

Allegany College of Maryland *A*
Baltimore City Community
  College *C, A*
Bowie State University *B, T*
Carroll Community College *C, A*
Chesapeake College *C*
College of Notre Dame of Maryland *B*
Columbia Union College *A*
Community College of Baltimore
  County *C, A*
Coppin State University *B*
Frederick Community College *A*
Frostburg State University *B, T*
Hagerstown Community College *A*
Hood College *B*
Howard Community College *C, A*
Montgomery College *C, A*
Prince George's Community
  College *C, A*
St. Mary's College of Maryland *T*
Salisbury University *B, T*
Towson University *B, M, T*
Villa Julie College *B, T*
Wor-Wic Community College *A*

Massachusetts

American International College *B, M*
Anna Maria College *B, M, T*
Atlantic Union College *B*
Bay Path College *B*
Bay State College *B*
Becker College *C, A, B, T*
Berkshire Community College *C*
Boston College *B, M, T*
Boston University *B, M, T*
Bridgewater State College *B, M, T*
Bristol Community College *C, A*

Bunker Hill Community College *C, A*
Cape Cod Community College *C, A*
Curry College *B*
Dean College *A*
Eastern Nazarene College *A, B, M, T*
Elms College *B, M, T*
Endicott College *B*
Fisher College *C, A*
Fitchburg State College *B, M, T*
Framingham State College *B, M*
Gordon College *B*
Greenfield Community College *A*
Hampshire College *B*
Hebrew College *C*
Holyoke Community College *C*
Lasell College *B, T*
Lesley University *B, M*
Massachusetts College of Liberal
  Arts *T*
Middlesex Community College *C, A*
Mount Ida College *A, B, T*
North Shore Community College *A*
Northeastern University *B*
Northern Essex Community
  College *C, A*
Pine Manor College *T*
Quincy College *C, A*
Quinsigamond Community
  College *C, A*
Roxbury Community College *A*
Salem State College *B, M*
Simmons College *B, M*
Springfield College *B, M, T*
Stonehill College *B*
Tufts University *B, M, T*
Urban College of Boston *C, A*
Wellesley College *T*
Westfield State College *B, M, T*
Wheaton College *T*
Wheelock College *B, M*

Michigan

Adrian College *A, T*
Alma College *T*
Baker College
  of Cadillac *A*
  of Clinton Township *A*
  of Muskegon *C, A*
  of Owosso *A*
  of Port Huron *C, A*
Bay Mills Community College *A*
Calvin College *B, T*
Central Michigan University *M*
Concordia University *B, T*
Cornerstone University *B*
Eastern Michigan University *M*
Glen Oaks Community College *C, A*
Gogebic Community College *A*
Grace Bible College *B*
Grand Valley State University *M*
Hillsdale College *B*
Jackson Community College *A*
Madonna University *B, T*
Marygrove College *C, B, M, T*
Monroe County Community
  College *C, A*
Mott Community College *A*
Muskegon Community College *C*
North Central Michigan College *C, A*
Northern Michigan University *B, T*
Oakland University *M, D*
Rochester College *B*
Saginaw Valley State University *M*
Spring Arbor University *T*
University of Detroit Mercy *M*
University of Michigan
  Dearborn *B*
  Flint *T*
Washtenaw Community College *C, A*
Wayne State University *M*
Western Michigan University *M*

Minnesota

Augsburg College *B, T*

Bethel University *B*
College of St. Catherine *B, T*
Concordia University: St. Paul *B, M, T*
Crown College *A, B, T*
Leech Lake Tribal College *A*
Martin Luther College *B*
Minnesota State University
  Mankato *M*
Northwestern College *B*
Rasmussen College
  Eagan *C, A*
  St. Cloud *C, A*
St. Cloud State University *B, T*
St. Mary's University of
  Minnesota *B, M*
Southwest Minnesota State
  University *B, T*
University of Minnesota
  Crookston *B*
  Duluth *B, T*
  Morris *T*
  Twin Cities *B, M*
Winona State University *B, M, T*

Mississippi

Coahoma Community College *A*
Jackson State University *M, D*
Mississippi State University *T*
Mississippi Valley State University *B, T*
Rust College *A*
Tougaloo College *A*

Missouri

Central Methodist University *B*
Central Missouri State University *T*
Culver-Stockton College *T*
Evangel University *A, B, T*
Fontbonne University *B*
Hannibal-LaGrange College *B*
Harris-Stowe State University *B, T*
Jefferson College *C, A*
Lincoln University *A*
Lindenwood University *B*
Maryville University of Saint
  Louis *B, M, T*
Missouri Baptist University *B, T*
Missouri Southern State
  University *B, M, T*
Missouri State University *B*
Missouri Valley College *T*
Northwest Missouri State
  University *B, M, T*
Park University *B*
St. Louis Community College
  St. Louis Community College at
    Florissant Valley *A*
Southeast Missouri State
  University *B, T*
Southwest Baptist University *T*
Stephens College *B, T*
University of Missouri
  Columbia *B, M, D*
  Kansas City *M*
  St. Louis *B, M, T*
Washington University in St. Louis *M*
Webster University *M*
William Jewell College *T*
William Woods University *T*

Montana

Blackfeet Community College *A*
Dawson Community College *C, A*
Fort Belknap College *C*
Montana State University
  Billings *A, M*
University of Great Falls *A, B*
University of Montana: Western *A, B*

Nebraska

College of Saint Mary *A, B, T*
Concordia University *B, M, T*
Hastings College *B, M*
Little Priest Tribal College *C*

Midland Lutheran College *B, T*
Nebraska Indian Community
  College *C, A*
Northeast Community College *C, A*
Peru State College *B, T*
University of Nebraska
  Kearney *B, T*
Wayne State College *B*
Western Nebraska Community
  College *C, A*

Nevada

Community College of Southern
  Nevada *A*
Great Basin College *C, A*
Truckee Meadows Community
  College *C, A*
University of Nevada
  Las Vegas *B*
  Reno *B*
Western Nevada Community
  College *C, A*

New Hampshire

Colby-Sawyer College *B, T*
Granite State College *A, B*
Keene State College *B, T*
New Hampshire Community
  Technical College
  Berlin *C, A*
  Manchester *C, A, T*
  Nashua *C, A*
New Hampshire Technical
  Institute *C, A*
Plymouth State University *B, T*
Rivier College *C, A, B, M, T*
Southern New Hampshire
  University *B*
University of New Hampshire *M*

New Jersey

Bergen Community College *A*
Brookdale Community College *C*
Caldwell College *T*
The College of New Jersey *B, T*
College of St. Elizabeth *T*
County College of Morris *A*
Cumberland County College *C, A*
Felician College *B*
Gloucester County College *A*
Hudson County Community
  College *C, A*
New Jersey City University *B, M*
Passaic County Community College *A*
Raritan Valley Community College *A*
Rowan University *B*
Rutgers, The State University of New
  Jersey
  Camden Regional Campus *T*
  New Brunswick/Piscataway
    Campus *T*
  Newark Regional Campus *T*
Salem Community College *C, A*
Seton Hall University *B, T*
Sussex County Community
  College *C, A*
Warren County Community
  College *C, A*
William Paterson University of New
  Jersey *T*

New Mexico

Clovis Community College *A*
Eastern New Mexico University *B*
Luna Community College *A*
New Mexico State University *B*
New Mexico State University
  Alamogordo *A*
Northern New Mexico College *A*
San Juan College *C, A*
Southwestern Indian Polytechnic
  Institute *C, A*
University of New Mexico *B*

Western New Mexico University C, A

New York
Adelphi University M, T
Adirondack Community College C
Barnard College T
Canisius College B, T
Cayuga County Community
  College C, A
Cazenovia College B
City University of New York
  Borough of Manhattan Community
    College A
  Brooklyn College B, M
  City College B, M, T
  Hostos Community College A
  Hunter College B, M, T
  Kingsborough Community
    College A
  Lehman College M, T
  Medgar Evers College B
  Queens College B, M, T
College of Mount St.Vincent T
College of Saint Rose M, T
Corning Community College C, A
D'Youville College B, M, T
Daemen College B, T
Dutchess Community College C, A
Herkimer County Community
  College A
Hofstra University B, M
Iona College B, M, T
Jamestown Community College C
Jefferson Community College A
Keuka College B, T
Manhattan College B, T
Manhattanville College M, T
Maria College A
Marymount Manhattan College T
Medaille College B
Mercy College B
Monroe Community College C
Mount St.Mary College M
Nassau Community College A
Nazareth College of Rochester M, T
New York University B, M
Niagara University B, T
Onondaga Community College C
Pace University A, B, M, T
St. John's University M
St.Joseph's College B, T
St.Joseph's College: Suffolk
  Campus B, M, T
Sarah Lawrence College M
Schenectady County Community
  College C, A
State University of New York
  College at Brockport M, T
  College at Buffalo B, T
  College at Fredonia B, T
  College at Geneseo T
  College at Old Westbury B, T
  College at Oneonta B, M, T
  College at Plattsburgh B
  College of Agriculture and
    Technology at
      Cobleskill C, A, B
  College of Technology at Canton A
  New Paltz M, T
  Purchase C
Suffolk County Community College A
Sullivan County Community
  College A
Syracuse University B, M, T
Trocaire College A
Utica College B
Vassar College T
Villa Maria College of Buffalo A
Wagner College B, M, T
Westchester Community College C, A

North Carolina
Alamance Community College C, A

Beaufort County Community
  College C, A
Bennett College B
Bladen Community College C
Brunswick Community College C, A
Caldwell Community College and
  Technical Institute A
Campbell University M
Catawba Valley Community
  College C, A
Central Carolina Community
  College C, A
Central Piedmont Community
  College C, A
Coastal Carolina Community
  College C, A
College of the Albemarle C, A
Davidson County Community
  College C, A
Durham Technical Community
  College C, A
East Carolina University B
Edgecombe Community College C, A
Fayetteville Technical Community
  College C, A
Forsyth Technical Community
  College A
Gaston College C, A
Greensboro College B, T
Guilford Technical Community
  College C, A
Halifax Community College A
High Point University B, T
Isothermal Community College C, A
Lenoir Community College C, A
Lenoir-Rhyne College B, M, T
Louisburg College A
Martin Community College C, A
Mayland Community College C, A
Meredith College T
Mitchell Community College A
Montgomery Community College C, A
Nash Community College A
North Carolina Agricultural and
  Technical State University B, T
Pamlico Community College C, A
Piedmont Baptist College A
Pitt Community College A
Roanoke-Chowan Community
  College A
Rockingham Community College C, A
Rowan-Cabarrus Community
  College A
Salem College M
Sampson Community College C, A
Sandhills Community College A
Southeastern Community College A
Southwestern Community
  College C, A
Stanly Community College C, A
Surry Community College C, A
University of North Carolina
  Chapel Hill B
  Greensboro B, M
Vance-Granville Community
  College C, A
Wake Technical Community
  College C, A
Warren Wilson College B, T
Western Piedmont Community
  College C, A
Wilkes Community College C, A
Wilson Technical Community
  College C, A
Winston-Salem State University B

North Dakota
Cankdeska Cikana Community
  College A
Dickinson State University B, T
Jamestown College B
Sitting Bull College A
Turtle Mountain Community
  College A

University of Mary B, M, T

Ohio
Antioch University McGregor M
Ashland University B, M, T
Baldwin-Wallace College B
Belmont Technical College A
Bluffton University B
Capital University B
Cedarville University B, T
Central Ohio Technical College A
Central State University B
Chatfield College A
Cincinnati Christian University B, T
Cincinnati State Technical and
  Community College C, A
Circleville Bible College A, B
Clark State Community College A
Cleveland State University B
College of Mount St. Joseph A, B, T
Columbus State Community
  College C, A
Cuyahoga Community College
  Metropolitan Campus A
Defiance College B
Edison State Community College C, A
Franciscan University of
  Steubenville A
Hiram College T
James A. Rhodes State College C, A
Jefferson Community College C, A
John Carroll University M, T
Kent State University B, M
Kent State University
  Ashtabula Regional Campus A
  Tuscarawas Campus A
Lakeland Community College A
Lourdes College A, B
Malone College B
Marietta College B
Miami University
  Oxford Campus B
Mount Union College B, T
Mount Vernon Nazarene
  University B, M, T
Muskingum College B, T
Ohio Northern University B, T
Ohio State University
  Columbus Campus M, D
Ohio University B
Ohio University
  Chillicothe Campus B
  Zanesville Campus B
Ohio Wesleyan University B
Otterbein College B
Owens Community College
  Toledo A
Shawnee State University B
Southern State Community College A
Stark State College of Technology A
Union Institute & University B
University of Cincinnati B, M, T
University of Cincinnati
  Clermont College A
  Raymond Walters College A
University of Dayton B, M
University of Findlay B, M, T
University of Rio Grande A, B
University of Toledo T
Ursuline College B, M, T
Walsh University B
Wilmington College B
Wright State University B, M, T
Xavier University B, M
Youngstown State University B, M

Oklahoma
Bacone College B
Cameron University A, B
Carl Albert State College C
Connors State College A
East Central University B, T
Northeastern Oklahoma Agricultural
  and Mechanical College C, A

Northeastern State University B, M
Northwestern Oklahoma State
  University B, T
Oklahoma Baptist University B, T
Oklahoma Christian University B, T
Oklahoma State University
  Oklahoma City C, A
Oral Roberts University B, T
Rose State College A
Southeastern Oklahoma State
  University B, T
Southern Nazarene University B, M
Southwestern Oklahoma State
  University B, M, T
University of Central Oklahoma B, M
University of Oklahoma B, T
University of Science and Arts of
  Oklahoma B, T
University of Tulsa B, T

Oregon
Blue Mountain Community College A
Central Oregon Community
  College A
Chemeketa Community College A
Concordia University B, M, T
Eastern Oregon University B, M
Linfield College T
Mount Hood Community College A
Oregon State University M
Portland Community College C, A
Portland State University T
Rogue Community College C, A
Umpqua Community College C, A
University of Oregon T
Warner Pacific College T
Western Oregon University M, T
Willamette University M

Pennsylvania
Albright College B, M, T
Alvernia College B
Arcadia University B, M, T
Baptist Bible College of
  Pennsylvania A, B
Bloomsburg University of
  Pennsylvania B, M, T
Bucknell University B, T
Bucks County Community College A
Cabrini College B, T
Carlow University B, M, T
Cedar Crest College C
Chatham College B, M, T
Chestnut Hill College B, M, T
Cheyney University of
  Pennsylvania B, T
Clarion University of
  Pennsylvania B, T
College Misericordia T
DeSales University C, T
Duquesne University B, M, T
East Stroudsburg University of
  Pennsylvania T
Edinboro University of
  Pennsylvania A, B, T
Elizabethtown College B
Gannon University A, B
Grove City College B
Gwynedd-Mercy College T
Harcum College A
Harrisburg Area Community
  College A
Holy Family University B, T
Indiana University of
  Pennsylvania B, M, T
Juniata College B, T
Keystone College C, A, B, T
King's College B, T
Kutztown University of
  Pennsylvania B, T
La Salle University B, M, T
Lackawanna College A
Lehigh Valley College A
Lincoln University B, M, T

Manor College *A*
Mansfield University of
Pennsylvania *B, T*
Marywood University *B, M*
Mercyhurst College *A, B, T*
Messiah College *B, T*
Millersville University of
Pennsylvania *M, T*
Mount Aloysius College *A, B*
Neumann College *B, T*
Pennsylvania Highlands Community
College *A*
Philadelphia Biblical University *B, T*
Point Park University *C, A, B*
Reading Area Community College *A*
Rosemont College *T*
St. Vincent College *T*
Seton Hill University *T*
Susquehanna University *B, T*
University of Pennsylvania *M*
University of Pittsburgh *T*
University of Scranton *B*
Valley Forge Christian College *A, B*
West Chester University of
Pennsylvania *B, M*
Widener University *B, M, T*
York College of Pennsylvania *C*

Puerto Rico

Bayamon Central University *B, M*
Inter American University of Puerto
Rico
Aguadilla Campus *B*
Arecibo Campus *B*
Barranquitas Campus *B*
Fajardo Campus *B, T*
Ponce Campus *B*
San German Campus *B*
Pontifical Catholic University of
Puerto Rico *B, M*
Turabo University *B*
Universidad del Este *C, B*
University of Puerto Rico
Rio Piedras *M*

Rhode Island

Rhode Island College *B, M*
Salve Regina University *B*

South Carolina

Anderson University *B, T*
Benedict College *B*
Charleston Southern University *M*
Claflin University *B*
Clemson University *B, T*
Coastal Carolina University *B, M, T*
Coker College *B, T*
College of Charleston *M*
Columbia College *B, T*
Columbia International
University *M, T*
Converse College *B, M, T*
Erskine College *B, T*
Forrest Junior College *A*
Francis Marion University *B, M, T*
Furman University *M, T*
Lander University *B, T*
Morris College *B, T*
Newberry College *B, T*
North Greenville College *B, T*
Presbyterian College *B, T*
South Carolina State University *B, M*
Southern Wesleyan University *B, T*
University of South Carolina *B, M, D*
University of South Carolina
Aiken *B*
Beaufort *B*
Upstate *B, M, T*
Williamsburg Technical College *C, A*
Winthrop University *B, M, T*
York Technical College *C, A*

South Dakota

Northern State University *B, T*
Oglala Lakota College *A*
Sisseton Wahpeton College *A*
South Dakota State University *B, T*
University of South Dakota *B*

Tennessee

Austin Peay State University *T*
Belmont University *B, M, T*
Carson-Newman College *B*
Chattanooga State Technical
Community College *A*
Columbia State Community
College *C, A*
Cumberland University *B, T*
East Tennessee State University *M, T*
Free Will Baptist Bible College *A, B*
Freed-Hardeman University *B, T*
Hiwassee College *A*
Jackson State Community College *A*
LeMoyne-Owen College *B*
Lee University *B, T*
Lincoln Memorial University *B, T*
Middle Tennessee State
University *B, T*
Milligan College *B, M, T*
Nashville State Community College *A*
Southwest Tennessee Community
College *A*
Tennessee State University *B*
Tennessee Technological
University *B, M, D, T*
Tennessee Temple University *T*
Tusculum College *B, T*
Union University *B, T*
University of Memphis *T*
University of Tennessee
Knoxville *B, T*
Vanderbilt University *B, M, D, T*
Walters State Community College *A*

Texas

Alvin Community College *C, A*
Arlington Baptist College *T*
Baylor University *B, T*
Brookhaven College *C, A*
Dallas Baptist University *B, M, T*
Del Mar College *A*
Eastfield College *C*
Hardin-Simmons University *B, T*
Houston Baptist University *B, M*
Howard Payne University *T*
Jarvis Christian College *B*
Lamar University *B, M, T*
Laredo Community College *A*
Lubbock Christian University *B*
McMurry University *B, T*
Midwestern State University *B*
Mountain View College *A*
North Harris Montgomery
Community College District *C*
Our Lady of the Lake University of San
Antonio *M*
Sam Houston State University *M*
San Jacinto College
North *A*
Schreiner University *B*
South Texas College *C, A*
Southwestern Assemblies of God
University *A, B, M*
Southwestern University *T*
Stephen F. Austin State University *M*
Tarleton State University *T*
Temple College *C*
Texas A&M University
Commerce *B, M*
Kingsville *M*
Texarkana *T*
Texas Christian University *B*
Texas College *A*
Texas Southern University *M*
Texas State University: San
Marcos *M, T*

Texas Wesleyan University *B, M, T*
Texas Woman's University *M*
Trinity Valley Community College *C, A*
University of Houston *M, T*
University of Houston
Clear Lake *M, T*
University of Mary Hardin-Baylor *T*
University of North Texas *B, M, T*
University of Texas
Arlington *T*
Brownsville *M*
Pan American *M*
San Antonio *T*
Tyler *M*
of the Permian Basin *M*
West Texas A&M University *T*
Western Texas College *C, A*
Wharton County Junior College *C, A*

Utah

Brigham Young University *B*
College of Eastern Utah *A*
Dixie State College of Utah *A*
Snow College *A*
Southern Utah University *T*
Utah State University *B*
Utah Valley State College *A, B*
Weber State University *B*
Westminster College *B*

Vermont

Bennington College *B, M*
Champlain College *A, B*
College of St. Joseph in Vermont *B*
Goddard College *B*
Johnson State College *M*
Lyndon State College *B*
University of Vermont *B*

Virginia

Bluefield College *B*
Dabney S. Lancaster Community
College *C*
Eastern Mennonite University *T*
Eastern Shore Community College *C*
Germanna Community College *C*
Hollins University *T*
J. Sargeant Reynolds Community
College *C, A*
James Madison University *T*
Liberty University *M, T*
Longwood University *B, T*
New River Community College *C, A*
Norfolk State University *B, M*
Northern Virginia Community
College *C, A*
Old Dominion University *M, D, T*
Paul D. Camp Community College *C*
Radford University *T*
Southwest Virginia Community
College *A*
Thomas Nelson Community
College *C, A*
Tidewater Community College *C, A*
University of Northern Virginia *M*
University of Richmond *B, T*
Virginia Western Community
College *C, A*

Washington

Bellevue Community College *C, A*
Central Washington University *B, T*
Centralia College *C, A*
Clark College *C, A*
Clover Park Technical College *C, A*
Columbia Basin College *A*
Eastern Washington University *M, T*
Everett Community College *C, A*
Grays Harbor College *C*
Green River Community College *A*
Heritage University *C, A, B*
North Seattle Community
College *C, A*

Olympic College *C, A*
Peninsula College *A*
Pierce College *C, A*
Renton Technical College *C, A*
Seattle Central Community College *C*
Shoreline Community College *A*
Skagit Valley College *C, A*
South Puget Sound Community
College *C, A*
Spokane Falls Community College *A*
Trinity Lutheran College *B*
Walla Walla College *A*
Walla Walla Community College *C, A*
Washington State University *B, T*
Wenatchee Valley College *C, A*
Whatcom Community College *C, A*
Yakima Valley Community
College *C, A*

West Virginia

Concord University *B, T*
Marshall University *M*
Shepherd University *T*
West Liberty State College *B*
West Virginia State University *B*
West Virginia University *T*

Wisconsin

Beloit College *T*
Carroll College *B*
College of Menominee Nation *A*
Concordia University Wisconsin *B, T*
Edgewood College *B, T*
Gateway Technical College *A*
Lakeshore Technical College *A*
Maranatha Baptist Bible College *A, B*
Marian College of Fond du Lac *B, T*
Mid-State Technical College *A*
Milwaukee Area Technical College *C*
Mount Mary College *B, T*
Nicolet Area Technical College *A*
Ripon College *T*
St. Norbert College *T*
Silver Lake College *B, T*
University of Wisconsin
Green Bay *A*
Oshkosh *M*
Parkside *T*
Platteville *B, T*
River Falls *T*
Stevens Point *B, T*
Stout *B, T*
Whitewater *B, T*
Viterbo University *T*
Wisconsin Indianhead Technical
College *A*

Wyoming

Casper College *A*
Northwest College *A*
Sheridan College *C*
Western Wyoming Community
College *A*

Early childhood special education

Arizona

Tohono O'odham Community
College *A*

Arkansas

Harding University *B, M, T*
Henderson State University *M*

California

University of San Diego *A, T*

Illinois

University of Illinois
Urbana-Champaign *B, M, T*

Iowa

Upper Iowa University *T*

Kansas

Tabor College *B, T*

Louisiana

Dillard University *B*
University of Louisiana at Lafayette *B*

Maine

University of Maine
   Farmington *B, T*

Massachusetts

Lesley University *B, M*

Minnesota

University of St. Thomas *M*

Missouri

Lindenwood University *B*

New Jersey

Felician College *B*
Georgian Court University *T*

New York

Canisius College *B, M, T*
Hofstra University *M, T*
St. John's University *M*
St. Joseph's College: Suffolk
   Campus *M*
State University of New York
   Binghamton *M*
   College at Brockport *M*

North Dakota

University of North Dakota *M*

Ohio

University of Findlay *B, M, T*

Oregon

Portland State University *D*
University of Oregon *M, D, T*

Pennsylvania

Juniata College *B*
La Salle University *B, M, T*
Lock Haven University of
   Pennsylvania *B, T*
Marywood University *B, M*

Puerto Rico

Atlantic College *B*
Inter American University of Puerto
   Rico
   Guayama Campus *B*
University of Puerto Rico
   Cayey University College *B*

Tennessee

Union University *B, T*
University of Memphis *T*

Utah

Salt Lake Community College *A*

Virginia

Radford University *T*

Washington

Trinity Lutheran College *B*

Wisconsin

University of Wisconsin
   Superior *M*

East Asian languages

Arizona

Arizona State University *B, M*

California

University of California
   Irvine *M, D*
   Los Angeles *B, M, D*
University of Southern
   California *B, M, D*

Connecticut

Yale University *M, D*

Illinois

University of Chicago *B, D*
University of Illinois
   Urbana-Champaign *B*

Indiana

Indiana University
   Bloomington *B*

Kansas

University of Kansas *B, M*

Massachusetts

Smith College *B*

Missouri

University of Missouri
   Columbia *B*

New York

Columbia University
   Columbia College *B*
Cornell University *B, M, D*

North Carolina

Wake Forest University *B*

Oregon

University of Oregon *M, D*

Pennsylvania

University of Pennsylvania *B, M, D*

Texas

University of Texas
   Austin *B, M, D*

Washington

University of Washington *B*

Wisconsin

Lawrence University *B*

East Asian studies

Arizona

University of Arizona *B, M, D*

California

Stanford University *B, M*
University of California
   Davis *B*
   Irvine *B*
   Los Angeles *B, M*
   Santa Cruz *B*
University of Southern
   California *B, M*

Colorado

Fort Lewis College *B*

Connecticut

Connecticut College *B*
University of Bridgeport *B*

Wesleyan University *B*
Yale University *B, M*

Florida

Eckerd College *B*

Illinois

DePaul University *B*
North Central College *B*
University of Chicago *M, D*
University of Illinois
   Urbana-Champaign *B, D*

Indiana

DePauw University *B*
Indiana University
   Bloomington *B, M*
Valparaiso University *B, M*

Iowa

Grinnell College *B*

Maine

Bates College *B*
Colby College *B*

Maryland

Johns Hopkins University *B*

Massachusetts

Boston University *B*
Brandeis University *B*
Harvard College *B, M, D*
Simmons College *B*
Simon's Rock College of Bard *B*
Tufts University *B, M*
Wellesley College *B*

Michigan

Oakland University *B*
University of Michigan *B, M*
Wayne State University *B*

Minnesota

Augsburg College *B*
Hamline University *B*
Minnesota State University
   Moorhead *B*
St. Cloud State University *B*
University of Minnesota
   Twin Cities *B, M*
University of St. Thomas *B*

Missouri

University of Missouri
   Columbia *B*
Washington University in St.
   Louis *B, M*

New Jersey

Princeton University *B, M, D*
Rutgers, The State University of New
   Jersey
   New Brunswick/Piscataway
   Campus *B*

New York

City University of New York
   Queens College *B, T*
Columbia University
   Columbia College *B*
   School of General Studies *B*
Hamilton College *B*
New York University *B, M, D*
St. John's University *M*
Sarah Lawrence College *B*
State University of New York
   Albany *B*
United States Military Academy *B*

Ohio

College of Wooster *B*
Denison University *B*
Mount Vernon Nazarene University *B*
Oberlin College *B*
Ohio State University
   Columbus Campus *B, M*
Ohio Wesleyan University *B*
Wittenberg University *B*

Oregon

Lewis & Clark College *B*
Portland State University *B*

Pennsylvania

Bryn Mawr College *B*
Bucknell University *B*
Dickinson College *B*
Gettysburg College *B*
Haverford College *B, T*
Penn State
   Abington *B*
   Altoona *B*
   Beaver *B*
   Berks *B*
   Delaware County *B*
   Dubois *B*
   Erie, The Behrend College *B*
   Fayette *B*
   Hazleton *B*
   Lehigh Valley *B*
   McKeesport *B*
   Mont Alto *B*
   New Kensington *B*
   Schuylkill - Capital College *B*
   Shenango *B*
   University Park *B*
   Wilkes-Barre *B*
   Worthington Scranton *B*
   York *B*
University of Pennsylvania *B, M, D*
University of Pittsburgh *M*
Ursinus College *B*

Rhode Island

Brown University *B*

Tennessee

Vanderbilt University *B*

Vermont

Marlboro College *B*
Middlebury College *B*

Virginia

College of William and Mary *B*
Emory & Henry College *B*
University of Virginia *M*
Washington and Lee University *B*

Washington

University of Washington *M*
Western Washington University *B*

Wisconsin

Lawrence University *B*

Ecology

Alabama

Tuskegee University *B, M*

Alaska

Sheldon Jackson College *B*

Arizona

Northern Arizona University *B*
Prescott College *B, M*
University of Arizona *B, M, D*

California

California Polytechnic State
    University: San Luis Obispo *B*
California State University
    Chico *B*
    Fresno *B*
Gavilan Community College *A*
Irvine Valley College *A*
Orange Coast College *A*
San Diego State University *B, M, D*
San Francisco State University *B, M*
University of California
    Davis *M, D*
    Irvine *B*
    Los Angeles *B*
    San Diego *B*
    Santa Barbara *B, M, D*
    Santa Cruz *B, D*

Colorado

University of Colorado
    Boulder *B, M, D*
University of Denver *B*

Connecticut

University of Connecticut *B, M, D*
University of New Haven *B, M*

Florida

Florida Institute of Technology *B, M*
Florida State University *B*
University of Florida *B, M*
University of Miami *B*

Georgia

University of Georgia *B, M, D*

Idaho

Idaho State University *B*

Illinois

Northwestern University *B*
University of Chicago *D*

Indiana

Indiana University
    Bloomington *M, D*

Iowa

Iowa State University *M, D*
Maharishi University of
    Management *B*
University of Dubuque *B*
University of Northern Iowa *B*

Kentucky

Eastern Kentucky University *B*
Georgetown College *B*
Morehead State University *B*

Louisiana

Tulane University *B, M, D*

Maine

College of the Atlantic *B, M*
Unity College *B*
University of Maine *B, M, D*
University of Maine
    Machias *B*

Maryland

Frostburg State University *M*
Towson University *B*
University of Maryland
    College Park *B*
    Eastern Shore *B*

Massachusetts

Boston University *B*
Salem State College *B*
Simon's Rock College of Bard *B*

Tufts University *B, M*

Michigan

Michigan Technological University *M*
Northern Michigan University *B*
University of Michigan *M, D*
University of Michigan
    Dearborn *B*
    Flint *B*

Minnesota

Minnesota State University
    Mankato *B, M, T*
Southwest Minnesota State
    University *B*
University of Minnesota
    Twin Cities *B, M, D*

Missouri

Missouri Southern State University *B*
Washington University in St. Louis *D*

Montana

University of Montana: Missoula *M, D*

Nebraska

Western Nebraska Community
    College *A*

Nevada

Sierra Nevada College *B*
University of Nevada
    Reno *M*

New Hampshire

Dartmouth College *B*

New Jersey

Princeton University *B, M, D*
Rutgers, The State University of New
    Jersey
    New Brunswick/Piscataway
        Campus *M, D*

New York

Bard College *B*
Columbia University
    Columbia College *B*
Concordia College *B*
Cornell University *B, M, D*
Long Island University
    C. W. Post Campus *M*
New York Institute of Technology *M*
Siena College *B*
State University of New York
    College of Environmental Science
        and Forestry *B, M, D*
    Purchase *B*
    Stony Brook *D*
University of Rochester *B*

North Carolina

Appalachian State University *B*
Brevard College *B*
University of North Carolina
    Chapel Hill *M, D*

Ohio

Kent State University *M, D*
Ohio State University
    Columbus Campus *B, M, D*
University of Akron *B*

Oklahoma

Oklahoma State University *B, M, D*

Pennsylvania

East Stroudsburg University of
    Pennsylvania *B*
Juniata College *B*
Lehigh University *B*

Marywood University *B*
Penn State
    University Park *M, D*
Slippery Rock University of
    Pennsylvania *M*
Susquehanna University *B*
University of Pittsburgh *B*
Westminster College *B*

Rhode Island

University of Rhode Island *M*

South Dakota

Northern State University *B*

Tennessee

University of Tennessee
    Knoxville *M, D*

Texas

Rice University *B, M, D*
Texas State University: San Marcos *M*
University of North Texas *M, D*
University of Texas
    Austin *B*

Utah

Dixie State College of Utah *A*
Utah State University *B, M, D*

Vermont

Bennington College *B*
Goddard College *B*
Marlboro College *B*
Sterling College *A, B*

Virginia

Averett University *B*
Lynchburg College *B*
Old Dominion University *D*

Washington

University of Washington *B, M, D*
Western Washington University *B*

Wisconsin

Lawrence University *B, T*
Northland College *B*
University of Wisconsin
    Superior *B*

Wyoming

University of Wyoming *D*
Western Wyoming Community
    College *A*

Econometrics/
quantitative economics

California

Scripps College *B*

Indiana

Anderson University *B*

Iowa

University of Northern Iowa *B*

Maine

Bowdoin College *B*
Colby College *B*

Maryland

United States Naval Academy *B*

Minnesota

University of Minnesota
    Twin Cities *B*
University of St. Thomas *B*

New York

Hofstra University *B*
State University of New York
    Oswego *B*

North Carolina

Wake Forest University *B*

Ohio

Baldwin-Wallace College *B*
University of Dayton *B*
Youngstown State University *B*

Rhode Island

Providence College *B*
University of Rhode Island *B*

Texas

Southern Methodist University *B*

Utah

University of Utah *M*

Virginia

Hampden-Sydney College *B*

Economics

Alabama

Auburn University *B*
Birmingham-Southern College *B*
Jacksonville State University *B*
Lawson State Community College *A*
Talladega College *B*
Tuskegee University *B*

Alaska

University of Alaska
    Anchorage *B*
    Fairbanks *B*

Arizona

Arizona State University *B, M, D*
Northern Arizona University *B*
University of Arizona *B, M, D*

Arkansas

Arkansas State University *B*
Arkansas Tech University *B*
Black River Technical College *A*
Harding University *B*
Hendrix College *B*
Lyon College *B*
University of Arkansas *B, M, D*
University of Arkansas
    Little Rock *B*
University of Central Arkansas *B*

California

Bakersfield College *A*
Cabrillo College *A*
California Institute of Technology *B*
California Lutheran University *B*
California Polytechnic State
    University: San Luis Obispo *B*
California State Polytechnic
    University: Pomona *B, M*
California State University
    Bakersfield *B*
    Chico *B*
    Dominguez Hills *B*
    East Bay *B, M*
    Fresno *B, M*
    Fullerton *B, M*
    Long Beach *B, M*
    Los Angeles *B, M*
    Northridge *B*
    Sacramento *B, M*
    San Bernardino *B*
    San Marcos *B*
    Stanislaus *B*

Cerritos Community College *A*
Chaffey College *A*
Claremont McKenna College *B*
College of Alameda *A*
College of the Desert *A*
Copper Mountain College *A*
Crafton Hills College *A*
Cypress College *A*
De Anza College *A*
East Los Angeles College *A*
El Camino College *A*
Foothill College *A*
Fullerton College *A*
Gavilan Community College *A*
Glendale Community College *A*
Golden West College *A*
Grossmont Community College *A*
Humboldt State University *B*
Irvine Valley College *A*
Los Angeles Valley College *A*
Loyola Marymount University *B*
Merced College *A*
MiraCosta College *A*
Monterey Peninsula College *A*
National University *B*
Occidental College *B*
Orange Coast College *A*
Palomar College *C, A*
Pepperdine University *B*
Pitzer College *B*
Pomona College *B*
Saddleback College *A*
St. Mary's College of California *B*
San Diego State University *B, M*
San Francisco State University *B, M*
San Jose State University *B, M*
Santa Ana College *A*
Santa Barbara City College *A*
Santa Clara University *B*
Santa Rosa Junior College *A*
Santiago Canyon College *A*
Scripps College *B*
Sonoma State University *B*
Southwestern College *A*
Stanford University *B, M, D*
University of California
　Berkeley *B, D*
　Davis *B, M, D*
　Irvine *B, M, D*
　Los Angeles *B, M, D*
　Riverside *B, M, D*
　San Diego *B, D*
　Santa Barbara *B, M, D*
　Santa Cruz *B, M, D*
University of La Verne *B*
University of Redlands *B*
University of San Diego *B*
University of San Francisco *B, M*
University of Southern
　California *B, M, D*
University of the Pacific *B*
Ventura College *A*
West Los Angeles College *C, A*
Westmont College *B*

Colorado

Adams State College *B*
Colorado College *B*
Colorado School of Mines *B, M, D*
Colorado State University *B, M, D*
Fort Lewis College *B*
Metropolitan State College of
　Denver *B, T*
Red Rocks Community College *A*
Regis University *B*
United States Air Force Academy *B*
University of Colorado
　Boulder *B, D*
　Colorado Springs *B*
　Denver and Health Sciences
　　Center *B, M*
University of Denver *B, M*
University of Northern Colorado *B*
Western State College of Colorado *B*

Connecticut

Albertus Magnus College *B*
Central Connecticut State
　University *B*
Connecticut College *B*
Eastern Connecticut State
　University *B*
Fairfield University *B*
Quinnipiac University *B*
Sacred Heart University *B*
St. Joseph College *B*
Trinity College *B, M*
University of Connecticut *B, M, D*
University of Hartford *B*
Wesleyan University *B, M*
Western Connecticut State
　University *B*
Yale University *B, M, D*

Delaware

University of Delaware *B*
Wesley College *B*

District of Columbia

American University *B, M, D*
Catholic University of
　America *B, M, D*
Gallaudet University *B*
George Washington
　University *B, M, D*
Georgetown University *B, D*
Howard University *B, M, D*
Southeastern University *B, M*
Strayer University *A, B*
Trinity University *B*
University of the District of
　Columbia *B*

Florida

Barry University *B*
Broward Community College *A*
Eckerd College *B*
Florida Agricultural and Mechanical
　University *B*
Florida Atlantic University *B, M*
Florida International
　University *B, M, D*
Florida Southern College *B*
Florida State University *B, M, D*
Gulf Coast Community College *A*
Indian River Community College *A*
Jacksonville University *B*
Manatee Community College *A*
Miami Dade College *A*
New College of Florida *B*
Rollins College *B*
Stetson University *B*
University of Central Florida *B, D*
University of Florida *B, M, D*
University of Miami *B*
University of North Florida *B*
University of South Florida *B*
University of Tampa *A, B*
Valencia Community College *A*

Georgia

Agnes Scott College *B*
Armstrong Atlantic State University *B*
Berry College *B*
Clark Atlanta University *B, M*
Covenant College *B*
Dalton State College *A*
Darton College *A*
Emory University *B, D*
Fort Valley State University *B*
Georgia Southern University *B*
Georgia State University *B, M, D*
Mercer University *B*
Middle Georgia College *A*
Morehouse College *B*
Oglethorpe University *B*
South Georgia College *A*
Spelman College *B*

University of Georgia *B*
University of West Georgia *B*
Wesleyan College *B*

Hawaii

Hawaii Pacific University *B*
University of Hawaii
　Hilo *B*
　Manoa *B, M, D*
　West Oahu *B*

Idaho

Albertson College of Idaho *B*
Boise State University *B, T*
Brigham Young University-Idaho *B*
College of Southern Idaho *A*
Idaho State University *B*
University of Idaho *B, M*

Illinois

Augustana College *B*
Aurora University *B*
Benedictine University *B*
Black Hawk College
　East Campus *A*
Bradley University *B*
Chicago State University *B*
DePaul University *B, M*
Dominican University *B*
Eastern Illinois University *B, M*
Elmhurst College *B*
Illinois College *B*
Illinois State University *B, M*
Illinois Wesleyan University *B*
John A. Logan College *A*
John Wood Community College *A*
Kishwaukee College *A*
Knox College *B*
Lake Forest College *B*
Lake Land College *A*
Lewis University *B*
McKendree College *B*
Monmouth College *B*
National-Louis University *B*
North Central College *B*
North Park University *B*
Northeastern Illinois University *B*
Northern Illinois University *B, M, D*
Northwestern University *B, M, D*
Olivet Nazarene University *B*
Principia College *B*
Richland Community College *A*
Rockford College *B*
Roosevelt University *B, M*
Sauk Valley Community College *A*
South Suburban College of Cook
　County *A*
Southern Illinois University
　Carbondale *B, M, D*
Southern Illinois University
　Edwardsville *B, M*
Southwestern Illinois College *A*
Triton College *A*
University of Chicago *B, D*
University of Illinois
　Chicago *B, M, D*
　Springfield *B*
　Urbana-Champaign *B, M, D*
Western Illinois University *B, M*
Wheaton College *B*

Indiana

Ball State University *B*
Butler University *B*
DePauw University *B*
Franklin College *B*
Hanover College *B*
Indiana State University *B*
Indiana University
　Bloomington *B, M, D*
　Northwest *B*
　South Bend *B*
　Southeast *B*

Indiana University-Purdue University
　Fort Wayne *B*
Indiana University-Purdue University
　Indianapolis *B, M*
Indiana Wesleyan University *A, B*
Manchester College *B*
Marian College *B*
Purdue University *M, D*
Rose-Hulman Institute of
　Technology *B*
St. Joseph's College *B*
Saint Mary's College *B*
Taylor University *B*
University of Evansville *B*
University of Indianapolis *B*
University of Notre Dame *B, M, D*
University of Southern Indiana *B, T*
Valparaiso University *B*
Vincennes University *A*
Wabash College *B*

Iowa

Central College *B, T*
Coe College *B*
Cornell College *B, T*
Drake University *B*
Graceland University *B, T*
Grinnell College *B*
Iowa State University *B, M, D*
Loras College *B*
Luther College *B*
Northwestern College *B*
St. Ambrose University *B, T*
Simpson College *B*
University of Iowa *B, D, T*
University of Northern Iowa *B*
Wartburg College *B, T*

Kansas

Allen County Community College *A*
Baker University *B*
Barton County Community College *A*
Benedictine College *B*
Bethany College *B*
Butler County Community College *A*
Central Christian College of Kansas *A*
Coffeyville Community College *A*
Dodge City Community College *A*
Emporia State University *B, T*
Fort Hays State University *B*
Kansas State University *B, M, D*
Seward County Community College *A*
University of Kansas *B, M, D*
Washburn University of Topeka *B*
Wichita State University *B, M*

Kentucky

Bellarmine University *B*
Berea College *B*
Campbellsville University *B*
Centre College *B*
Eastern Kentucky University *B*
Georgetown College *B*
Murray State University *B, M, T*
Thomas More College *A, B*
Transylvania University *B*
University of Kentucky *B, M, D*
University of Louisville *B*
Western Kentucky University *B*

Louisiana

Centenary College of Louisiana *B*
Dillard University *B*
Louisiana State University and
　Agricultural and Mechanical
　College *B, M, D*
Loyola University New Orleans *B*
Southern University
　New Orleans *B*
Tulane University *B, M*
University of New Orleans *B*

Maine

Bates College *B*
Bowdoin College *B*
Colby College *B*
University of Maine *B, M*
University of Maine
   Farmington *B*
University of Southern Maine *B*

Maryland

Allegany College of Maryland *A*
Bowie State University *B*
College of Notre Dame of Maryland *B*
Community College of Baltimore
   County *A*
Frederick Community College *A*
Frostburg State University *B*
Goucher College *B*
Hood College *B*
Johns Hopkins University *B, D*
Loyola College in Maryland *B*
McDaniel College *B*
Morgan State University *B, M*
Mount St. Mary's University *B*
St. Mary's College of Maryland *B*
Salisbury University *B*
Towson University *B*
United States Naval Academy *B*
University of Maryland
   Baltimore County *B, M*
   College Park *B, M, D*
Washington College *B*

Massachusetts

American International College *B*
Amherst College *B*
Assumption College *B*
Boston College *B, M, D*
Boston University *B, M, D*
Brandeis University *B, M, D*
Bridgewater State College *B*
Clark University *B, M, D*
College of the Holy Cross *B*
Fitchburg State College *B*
Framingham State College *B*
Gordon College *B*
Hampshire College *B*
Harvard College *B, D*
Massachusetts Institute of
   Technology *B, D*
Merrimack College *B*
Mount Holyoke College *B*
Nichols College *B*
Northeastern University *B, M, D*
Salem State College *B*
Simmons College *B*
Simon's Rock College of Bard *B*
Smith College *B*
Stonehill College *B*
Suffolk University *B, M, D*
Tufts University *B, M*
University of Massachusetts
   Amherst *B, M, D*
   Boston *B*
   Dartmouth *B*
   Lowell *B*
Wellesley College *B*
Western New England College *B*
Westfield State College *B*
Wheaton College *B*
Williams College *B, M*
Worcester Polytechnic Institute *B*
Worcester State College *B*

Michigan

Adrian College *A, B, T*
Albion College *B*
Alma College *B, T*
Andrews University *B*
Aquinas College *B, T*
Calvin College *B*
Central Michigan University *B, M, T*
Delta College *A*

Eastern Michigan University *B, M*
Grand Valley State University *B*
Hillsdale College *B*
Hope College *B*
Kalamazoo College *B, T*
Michigan State University *B, M, D*
Michigan Technological
   University *B, T*
Northern Michigan University *B, T*
Oakland University *B*
Olivet College *B*
Saginaw Valley State University *B*
University of Detroit Mercy *B*
University of Michigan *B, M, D, T*
University of Michigan
   Dearborn *B*
   Flint *B*
Wayne State University *B, M, D*
Western Michigan University *B*

Minnesota

Augsburg College *B*
Bemidji State University *B*
Bethel University *B*
Carleton College *B*
College of St. Benedict *B*
College of St. Catherine *B*
Concordia College: Moorhead *B*
Gustavus Adolphus College *B*
Hamline University *B*
Macalester College *B*
Metropolitan State University *B*
Minnesota State University
   Mankato *B, M*
   Moorhead *B*
Ridgewater College *A*
St. Cloud State University *B*
St. John's University *B*
St. Olaf College *B*
University of Minnesota
   Duluth *B*
   Morris *B*
   Twin Cities *B, M, D*
University of St. Thomas *B*
Winona State University *B*

Mississippi

Alcorn State University *B*
Itawamba Community College *A*
Jackson State University *B*
Millsaps College *B*
Mississippi State University *B*
Tougaloo College *B*
University of Mississippi *B*

Missouri

Central Methodist University *B*
Central Missouri State University *B, M*
Drury University *B*
Missouri State University *B*
Missouri Valley College *B*
Missouri Western State University *B*
Northwest Missouri State
   University *B*
Park University *B*
Rockhurst University *B*
St. Louis University *B, M*
Southeast Missouri State University *B*
Three Rivers Community College *A*
Truman State University *B*
University of Missouri
   Columbia *B, M, D*
   Kansas City *B, M, D*
   Rolla *B, T*
   St. Louis *B, M*
Washington University in St.
   Louis *B, M, D*
Webster University *B*
Westminster College *B*

Montana

Miles Community College *A*

Montana State University
   Bozeman *B, M*
Rocky Mountain College *B*
University of Montana: Missoula *B, M*

Nebraska

Creighton University *B*
Doane College *B*
Hastings College *B*
Midland Lutheran College *B*
Nebraska Wesleyan University *B*
University of Nebraska
   Kearney *B*
   Lincoln *B, M, D*
Western Nebraska Community
   College *A*

Nevada

University of Nevada
   Reno *B, M*

New Hampshire

Dartmouth College *B*
Keene State College *B*
St. Anselm College *B*
Southern New Hampshire
   University *B*
University of New Hampshire *B, M, D*

New Jersey

Bloomfield College *B*
The College of New Jersey *B*
College of St. Elizabeth *B*
Drew University *B*
Fairleigh Dickinson University
   College at Florham *B*
   Metropolitan Campus *B*
Kean University *B, T*
Montclair State University *B*
New Jersey City University *B*
Princeton University *B, M, D*
Ramapo College of New Jersey *B*
Richard Stockton College of New
   Jersey *B*
Rider University *B*
Rowan University *B*
Rutgers, The State University of New
   Jersey
   Camden Regional Campus *B*
   New Brunswick/Piscataway
      Campus *B, M, D*
   Newark Regional Campus *B*
St. Peter's College *B*
Seton Hall University *B*
Thomas Edison State College *B*
William Paterson University of New
   Jersey *B*

New Mexico

New Mexico State University *B, M*
San Juan College *A*
University of New Mexico *B, M, D*

New York

Adelphi University *B*
Alfred University *B*
Bard College *B*
Barnard College *B*
Canisius College *B*
City University of New York
   Baruch College *B, M*
   Brooklyn College *B, M*
   City College *B, M*
   College of Staten Island *B*
   Hunter College *B, M*
   Lehman College *B*
   Queens College *B, T*
   York College *B*
Colgate University *B*
College of Mount St. Vincent *B*
College of New Rochelle *B*

Columbia University
   Columbia College *B*
   School of General Studies *B*
Cornell University *B, M, D*
Dowling College *B*
Elmira College *B*
Eugene Lang College The New School
   for Liberal Arts *B*
Excelsior College *B*
Fordham University *B, M, D*
Hamilton College *B*
Hartwick College *B*
Hobart and William Smith Colleges *B*
Hofstra University *B*
Iona College *B*
Ithaca College *B*
Le Moyne College *B*
Long Island University
   Brooklyn Campus *B*
   C. W. Post Campus *B*
Manhattan College *B*
Manhattanville College *B*
Marist College *B*
Nazareth College of Rochester *B*
New York Institute of Technology *B*
New York University *B, M, D*
Pace University *B*
Rensselaer Polytechnic
   Institute *B, M, D*
Rochester Institute of Technology *B*
St. Francis College *B*
St. John Fisher College *B*
St. John's University *B*
St. Joseph's College: Suffolk
   Campus *B*
St. Lawrence University *B*
Sarah Lawrence College *B*
Siena College *B, T*
Skidmore College *B*
State University of New York
   Albany *B, M, D*
   Binghamton *B, M, D*
   Buffalo *B, M, D*
   College at Buffalo *B, M*
   College at Cortland *B*
   College at Fredonia *B*
   College at Geneseo *B*
   College at Oneonta *B*
   College at Plattsburgh *B*
   College at Potsdam *B*
   Empire State College *A, B*
   New Paltz *B*
   Oswego *B*
   Purchase *C, B*
   Stony Brook *B, M, D*
Suffolk County Community College *A*
Syracuse University *B, M, D*
Touro College *B*
Union College *B*
United States Military Academy *B*
University of Rochester *B, M, D*
Utica College *B*
Vassar College *B*
Wells College *B*
Yeshiva University *B*

North Carolina

Appalachian State University *B*
Belmont Abbey College *B*
Campbell University *B*
Davidson College *B*
Duke University *B, M, D*
East Carolina University *B*
Elon University *B*
Guilford College *B*
Johnson C. Smith University *B*
Lenoir-Rhyne College *B, T*
Meredith College *B*
North Carolina State University *M, D*
Pfeiffer University *B*
Salem College *B*
University of North Carolina
   Asheville *B, T*
   Chapel Hill *B, M, D*

Charlotte *B*
Greensboro *B*
Wilmington *B*
Wake Forest University *B*
Warren Wilson College *B*

North Dakota

Minot State University *B*
North Dakota State University *B*
University of North Dakota *B*

Ohio

Antioch College *B*
Ashland University *B*
Baldwin-Wallace College *B*
Bluffton University *B*
Bowling Green State University *B, M*
Capital University *B*
Case Western Reserve University *B*
Central State University *B*
Cleveland State University *B, M*
College of Wooster *B*
Denison University *B*
Franciscan University of
   Steubenville *B*
Heidelberg College *B*
Hiram College *B, T*
John Carroll University *B*
Kent State University *D*
Kenyon College *B*
Marietta College *B*
Miami University
   Oxford Campus *B, M*
Mount Union College *B*
Muskingum College *B*
Oberlin College *B*
Ohio Dominican University *B*
Ohio State University
   Columbus Campus *B, M, D*
Ohio University *B, M*
Ohio Wesleyan University *B*
Otterbein College *B*
University of Akron *B, M*
University of Cincinnati *C, B, M, D, T*
University of Cincinnati
   Raymond Walters College *A*
University of Dayton *B*
University of Findlay *B*
University of Rio Grande *B*
University of Toledo *B, M*
Wilmington College *B*
Wittenberg University *B*
Wright State University *B, M*
Xavier University *B*
Youngstown State University *B, M*

Oklahoma

Oklahoma City University *B*
Oklahoma State University *B*
Tulsa Community College *A*
University of Central Oklahoma *B, M*
University of Oklahoma *B, M, D*
University of Science and Arts of
   Oklahoma *B*
University of Tulsa *B*

Oregon

Central Oregon Community
   College *A*
Chemeketa Community College *A*
Lewis & Clark College *B*
Linfield College *B*
Linn-Benton Community College *A*
Oregon State University *B, M, D*
Pacific University *B*
Portland State University *B, M, D*
Reed College *B*
Southern Oregon University *B*
University of Oregon *B, M, D*
Western Oregon University *B*
Willamette University *B*

Pennsylvania

Albright College *B*
Allegheny College *B*
Bloomsburg University of
   Pennsylvania *B*
Bryn Mawr College *B*
Bucknell University *B*
Carnegie Mellon University *B, M, D*
Chatham College *B*
Cheyney University of Pennsylvania *B*
Clarion University of Pennsylvania *B*
Dickinson College *B*
Duquesne University *B*
East Stroudsburg University of
   Pennsylvania *B*
Eastern University *B*
Edinboro University of
   Pennsylvania *B*
Elizabethtown College *B*
Franklin & Marshall College *B*
Gettysburg College *B*
Grove City College *B*
Haverford College *B, T*
Holy Family University *B*
Immaculata University *A, B*
Indiana University of Pennsylvania *B*
Juniata College *B*
King's College *B*
La Salle University *B*
Lafayette College *B*
Lebanon Valley College *B*
Lincoln University *B*
Lock Haven University of
   Pennsylvania *B*
Lycoming College *B*
Mansfield University of
   Pennsylvania *B, T*
Messiah College *B*
Millersville University of
   Pennsylvania *B, T*
Moravian College *B*
Muhlenberg College *C, B*
Penn State
   Abington *B*
   Altoona *B*
   Beaver *B*
   Berks *B*
   Delaware County *B*
   Dubois *B*
   Erie, The Behrend College *B*
   Fayette *B*
   Hazleton *B*
   Lehigh Valley *B*
   McKeesport *B*
   Mont Alto *B*
   New Kensington *B*
   Schuylkill - Capital College *B*
   Shenango *B*
   University Park *B, M, D*
   Wilkes-Barre *B*
   Worthington Scranton *B*
   York *B*
Robert Morris University *B*
Rosemont College *B*
St. Francis University *B*
St. Joseph's University *B*
St. Vincent College *B*
Seton Hill University *B*
Shippensburg University of
   Pennsylvania *B*
Slippery Rock University of
   Pennsylvania *B*
Susquehanna University *B*
Swarthmore College *B*
Temple University *B, M, D*
University of Pennsylvania *B, M, D*
University of Pittsburgh *B, M, D*
University of Pittsburgh
   Bradford *B*
   Johnstown *B*
University of Scranton *B*
Ursinus College *B*
Villanova University *B*
Washington and Jefferson College *B*

Westminster College *B*
Widener University *B*
York College of Pennsylvania *B*

Puerto Rico

University of Puerto Rico
   Cayey University College *B*
   Mayaguez *B*
   Rio Piedras *B, M*

Rhode Island

Brown University *B, M, D*
Bryant University *B*
Providence College *B*
Rhode Island College *B*
Salve Regina University *B*
University of Rhode Island *B*

South Carolina

Benedict College *B*
Charleston Southern University *B*
Clemson University *B, M*
College of Charleston *B*
Converse College *B*
Francis Marion University *B*
Furman University *B*
Limestone College *B*
Presbyterian College *B*
University of South Carolina *B, M, D*
Wofford College *B*

South Dakota

Augustana College *B, T*
Northern State University *B*
South Dakota State University *B, M*
University of South Dakota *B*

Tennessee

Belmont University *B*
Carson-Newman College *B*
Columbia State Community College *A*
East Tennessee State University *B*
Hiwassee College *A*
Maryville College *B, T*
Middle Tennessee State
   University *B, M, D*
Rhodes College *B*
Roane State Community College *A*
Tennessee Technological University *B*
Union University *B, T*
University of Memphis *B, M*
University of Tennessee
   Chattanooga *B*
   Knoxville *B, M, D*
   Martin *B*
University of the South *B*
Vanderbilt University *B, M, D*

Texas

Austin College *B*
Austin Community College *A*
Brazosport College *A*
Cisco Junior College *A*
Clarendon College *A*
College of the Mainland *A*
Galveston College *A*
Hardin-Simmons University *B*
Houston Baptist University *B*
Lamar University *B*
Laredo Community College *A*
Lon Morris College *A*
Midland College *A*
Midwestern State University *B*
Northwest Vista College *A*
Palo Alto College *A*
Rice University *B, M, D*
St. Edward's University *B*
St. Mary's University *M*
St. Philip's College *A*
Southern Methodist
   University *B, M, D*
Southwestern University *B*
Stephen F. Austin State University *B*

Tarleton State University *B, T*
Texas A&M University *B, M, D*
Texas A&M University
   Commerce *B, M*
Texas Christian University *B, M*
Texas Lutheran University *B*
Texas Southern University *B*
Texas State University: San
   Marcos *B, T*
Texas Tech University *B, M, D*
Trinity University *B*
University of Dallas *B*
University of Houston *B, M, D*
University of North Texas *B, M*
University of St. Thomas *B*
University of Texas
   Arlington *B, M*
   Austin *B, M, D*
   Dallas *B, D*
   Pan American *B*
   San Antonio *M*
West Texas A&M University *B*
Western Texas College *A*

Utah

Brigham Young University *B*
Dixie State College of Utah *A*
Salt Lake Community College *A*
Snow College *A*
Southern Utah University *B*
University of Utah *B, M, D*
Utah State University *B, M, D*
Weber State University *B*

Vermont

Marlboro College *B*
Middlebury College *B*
Norwich University *B*
St. Michael's College *B*
University of Vermont *B*

Virginia

Bridgewater College *B*
College of William and Mary *B*
Eastern Mennonite University *B*
Emory & Henry College *B*
George Mason University *B, M, D*
Hampden-Sydney College *B*
Hollins University *B*
James Madison University *B*
Liberty University *B*
Longwood University *B*
Lynchburg College *B*
Mary Baldwin College *B*
Marymount University *B*
Old Dominion University *B, M*
Radford University *B, M*
Randolph-Macon College *B*
Randolph-Macon Woman's College *B*
Roanoke College *B, T*
Sweet Briar College *B*
University of Mary Washington *B*
University of Richmond *B*
University of Virginia *B, M, D*
University of Virginia's College at
   Wise *B, T*
Virginia Military Institute *B*
Virginia Polytechnic Institute and
   State University *B, M, D*
Virginia Wesleyan College *B*
Washington and Lee University *B*

Washington

Central Washington University *B*
Centralia College *A*
Eastern Washington University *B*
Everett Community College *A*
Gonzaga University *B*
Highline Community College *A*
Pacific Lutheran University *B*
Seattle Pacific University *B*
Seattle University *B*
University of Puget Sound *B*

University of Washington B, M, D
Washington State University B, M, D
Western Washington University B
Whitman College B
Whitworth College B

West Virginia

Bethany College B
Marshall University B
Potomac State College of West Virginia
    University A
Shepherd University B
West Virginia State University B
West Virginia University B
West Virginia Wesleyan College B

Wisconsin

Beloit College B
Carthage College B, T
Concordia University Wisconsin B
Edgewood College B
Lawrence University B, T
Marquette University B, M
Northland College B, T
Ripon College B
St. Norbert College B, T
University of Wisconsin
    Eau Claire B
    Green Bay B, T
    La Crosse B, T
    Madison B, M, D
    Milwaukee B, M, D
    Oshkosh B
    Parkside B, T
    Platteville B
    River Falls B, T
    Stevens Point B, T
    Superior B
    Whitewater B, T

Wyoming

Casper College A
Eastern Wyoming College A
Laramie County Community
    College A
Western Wyoming Community
    College A

Education, general

Alabama

Alabama Agricultural and Mechanical
    University B, M
Athens State University B
Auburn University M
Birmingham-Southern College B
Bishop State Community College A
Calhoun Community College A
Central Alabama Community
    College A
Faulkner University B
Gadsden State Community College A
Jacksonville State University T
Lawson State Community College A
Samford University D
Shelton State Community College A
Spring Hill College A
Troy University M, T
Tuskegee University B, T
University of Alabama
    Birmingham D, T
University of Montevallo M, T
Wallace State Community College at
    Hanceville A

Alaska

Sheldon Jackson College A
University of Alaska
    Fairbanks B, M, T
    Southeast M

Arizona

Central Arizona College A

Chandler-Gilbert Community College
    Williams Campus A
Cochise College A
Dine College A
Estrella Mountain Community
    College A
Gateway Community College A
Grand Canyon University B, M
Mohave Community College A
Northern Arizona University B
Phoenix College A
Prescott College B, M, T
South Mountain Community
    College A
University of Arizona M, D

Arkansas

Arkansas State University
    Beebe A
Central Baptist College A
Ouachita Baptist University B
Ozarka College A
Philander Smith College B
Phillips Community College of the
    University of Arkansas A
Rich Mountain Community College A
South Arkansas Community College A
University of Arkansas M
University of Arkansas
    Pine Bluff B, M, T
University of Central Arkansas M
University of the Ozarks A
Williams Baptist College B

California

Allan Hancock College A
Alliant International University M, D
Antioch Southern California
    Antioch University Santa
        Barbara M, T
Azusa Pacific University B, M, D
Barstow College A
Bethany University M
Biola University B, M, T
Butte College A
California Baptist University B, M
California Lutheran University B, M
California Polytechnic State
    University: San Luis Obispo M
California State Polytechnic
    University: Pomona M
California State University
    Bakersfield M, T
    Chico B
    Dominguez Hills M
    East Bay M
    Fresno B, M
    Fullerton M
    Los Angeles M
    Monterey Bay B, M
    Sacramento M
    San Bernardino M
    San Marcos M
    Stanislaus M
Chaffey College A
College of the Siskiyous A
Concordia University B, M, T
Cypress College A
Dominican University of California M
Feather River College A
Holy Names University M
Humphreys College A
John F. Kennedy University M
Laney College A
Lassen College A
Los Angeles Southwest College A
Loyola Marymount University M
Master's College B
Merced College A
Merritt College A
Mills College B
Napa Valley College A
National Hispanic University T
National University M, T

Pacific Union College M
Patten University M
Pepperdine University B, M
Point Loma Nazarene University M
Porterville College A
St. Mary's College of California M
San Diego Christian College B
San Diego State University M, D, T
Santa Rosa Junior College A
Simpson University T
Sonoma State University M
Southwestern College A
Stanford University M, D
Taft College A
University of California
    Berkeley M, D, T
    Davis M, D, T
    Irvine M, D
    Los Angeles M, D
    Riverside M, D, T
    Santa Barbara M, D
    Santa Cruz M, D
University of La Verne B, M, T
University of Redlands M, T
University of Southern
    California B, M, D
University of the Pacific B
Vanguard University of Southern
    California M, T
Ventura College A
Whittier College B, M, T

Colorado

Adams State College B, M, T
Colorado Mountain College
    Alpine Campus A
    Spring Valley Campus A
    Timberline Campus A
Fort Lewis College B
Jones International University M
Morgan Community College A
Naropa University M
National American University
    Denver A
Otero Junior College A
Regis University B, M, T
Trinidad State Junior College A
University of Colorado
    Colorado Springs M

Connecticut

Albertus Magnus College B, T
Northwestern Connecticut
    Community College A
Sacred Heart University M
St. Joseph College M, T
Southern Connecticut State
    University B, T
Trinity College B, T
University of Connecticut M, T
University of New Haven M
Western Connecticut State
    University M

Delaware

Delaware State University B
University of Delaware B, T
Wesley College B, M
Wilmington College D

District of Columbia

American University M, D
Catholic University of America B, M
Gallaudet University B
Howard University M, D
Trinity University M

Florida

Bethune-Cookman College B
Broward Community College A
Chipola College A
Daytona Beach Community College A
Edward Waters College B

Florida National College A
Florida Southern College B, M, T
Hillsborough Community College A
Indian River Community College A
Jacksonville University B, M, T
Lake City Community College A
Manatee Community College A
Nova Southeastern University M
Okaloosa-Walton College A
Palm Beach Atlantic University B
Pensacola Junior College A
Polk Community College A
Rollins College B, M, T
St. Leo University M
Stetson University B, M
Trinity College of Florida B
University of Central Florida D
University of South Florida B, M, D
University of Tampa B
Valencia Community College A

Georgia

Abraham Baldwin Agricultural
    College A
Albany State University B
Andrew College A
Bainbridge College A
Brewton-Parker College B
Clark Atlanta University B
Coastal Georgia Community
    College A
Dalton State College A
Darton College A
East Georgia College A
Emory University B, M, D
Gainesville State College A
Georgia College and State
    University M
Georgia Highlands College A
Georgia Military College A
Georgia Perimeter College A
Georgia Southern University B
Gordon College A
LaGrange College B, M
Life University B
Macon State College A
Morehouse College B
Reinhardt College A
South Georgia College A
Thomas University M
University of Georgia M
Waycross College A
Young Harris College A

Hawaii

University of Hawaii
    Hilo T
    Manoa D

Idaho

Albertson College of Idaho M, T
Boise State University B, M
Idaho State University M
North Idaho College A
University of Idaho D

Illinois

Augustana College B
Aurora University M
Blackburn College B, T
Chicago State University B
City Colleges of Chicago
    Kennedy-King College A
Columbia College Chicago M
Concordia University B, T
Danville Area Community College A
Dominican University M
Elmhurst College B
Eureka College B
Governors State University M
Highland Community College A
Illinois Valley Community College A
Illinois Wesleyan University B

John Wood Community College *A*
Kankakee Community College *A*
Kishwaukee College *A*
Knox College *B*
Lake Forest College *B*
Lake Land College *A*
Lewis University *B*
Lewis and Clark Community
  College *A*
Lincoln Land Community College *A*
McKendree College *B, M*
Millikin University *B, T*
Monmouth College *B, T*
Moody Bible Institute *B*
National-Louis University *M*
North Central College *B*
North Park University *M*
Northern Illinois University *B*
Northwestern University *B*
Olivet Nazarene University *M*
Quincy University *M*
Richland Community College *A*
Rockford College *B, M*
St. Xavier University *B, M*
Sauk Valley Community College *A*
South Suburban College of Cook
  County *A*
Southeastern Illinois College *A*
Southwestern Illinois College *A*
Trinity Christian College *B, T*
Trinity International University *D*
Triton College *A*
University of Chicago *M, D*
University of Illinois
  Urbana-Champaign *M, D*
Wheaton College *M*
William Rainey Harper College *A*

Indiana

Anderson University *B*
Butler University *M*
Calumet College of St. Joseph *B, T*
Earlham College *M*
Goshen College *B*
Huntington University *B, M*
Indiana University
  Bloomington *B, M, D, T*
  Southeast *B, T*
Manchester College *B, T*
Purdue University *B, M, D, T*
Purdue University
  Calumet *B, T*
St. Mary-of-the-Woods College *B*
University of Evansville *B*
University of Indianapolis *B*
University of Southern Indiana *A*
Valparaiso University *M*
Vincennes University *A*

Iowa

Briar Cliff University *B, M*
Clarke College *B, M, T*
Coe College *B, M*
Cornell College *B, T*
Dordt College *B*
Drake University *B, D*
Ellsworth Community College *A*
Graceland University *M*
Iowa State University *B, M, D*
Iowa Wesleyan College *B*
Iowa Western Community College *A*
Loras College *B, M*
Marshalltown Community College *A*
Morningside College *B, M*
North Iowa Area Community
  College *A*
Northeast Iowa Community
  College *A*
Northwestern College *B, T*
St. Ambrose University *B, M, T*
Simpson College *B*
Southwestern Community College *A*
University of Dubuque *M*
University of Northern Iowa *M, D*

Upper Iowa University *B*
William Penn University *B*

Kansas

Barton County Community College *A*
Bethany College *B, T*
Central Christian College of Kansas *A*
Cloud County Community College *A*
Coffeyville Community College *A*
Colby Community College *A*
Cowley County Community
  College *A*
Dodge City Community College *A*
Fort Scott Community College *A*
Friends University *M*
Garden City Community College *A*
Haskell Indian Nations University *B*
Highland Community College *A*
Hutchinson Community College *A*
Labette Community College *A*
McPherson College *B, T*
MidAmerica Nazarene University *M*
Neosho County Community
  College *A*
Newman University *B*
Pratt Community College *A*
Seward County Community College *A*
Southwestern College *B, M*
Tabor College *B, T*
University of St. Mary *M*
Washburn University of Topeka *B*

Kentucky

Bellarmine University *B, M*
Berea College *B*
Campbellsville University *A, B*
Kentucky State University *B*
Madisonville Community College *A*
Morehead State University *M*
Northern Kentucky University *M*
Somerset Community College *A*
Spalding University *B, M, T*
Thomas More College *B*
Western Kentucky University *M*

Louisiana

Louisiana State University
  Alexandria *B*
  Shreveport *M*
Louisiana State University and
  Agricultural and Mechanical
  College *M*
Northwestern State University *M*
Our Lady of Holy Cross College *M*
University of New Orleans *M*
Xavier University of Louisiana *B*

Maine

University of Maine *B, M*
University of Maine
  Fort Kent *B*
  Presque Isle *B*
University of New England *B, M*
University of Southern Maine *B*

Maryland

Anne Arundel Community College *A*
Baltimore City Community College *A*
Carroll Community College *A*
Chesapeake College *A*
College of Notre Dame of
  Maryland *M*
College of Southern Maryland *A*
Columbia Union College *B*
Community College of Baltimore
  County *A*
Frederick Community College *A*
Frostburg State University *M*
Garrett College *A*
Hagerstown Community College *A*
Harford Community College *A*
McDaniel College *M, T*
Montgomery College *A*

Salisbury University *M*
University of Maryland
  Baltimore County *M, T*
  College Park *B*
  Eastern Shore *B*
Washington College *T*
Wor-Wic Community College *A*

Massachusetts

Boston University *B, M, D, T*
Bristol Community College *A*
Bunker Hill Community College *A*
Cambridge College *M*
Cape Cod Community College *A*
Clark University *M*
Curry College *B*
Eastern Nazarene College *B, M, T*
Elms College *B, M*
Hampshire College *B*
Harvard College *M, D*
Lesley University *B, M, D*
Massachusetts College of Liberal
  Arts *B, M, T*
Mount Holyoke College *B*
Mount Ida College *A, B, T*
Northeastern University *B, M, T*
Salem State College *B, M*
Simmons College *B, M*
Smith College *B, M*
Springfield College *M*
Suffolk University *B, M*
Tufts University *M*
University of Massachusetts
  Amherst *B, M, D*
  Boston *D*
Western New England College *B, T*
Westfield State College *B, M, T*
Worcester State College *M, T*

Michigan

Adrian College *B*
Alma College *B*
Alpena Community College *A*
Aquinas College *B, M*
Baker College
  of Auburn Hills *B*
Calvin College *B, M, T*
Cornerstone University *M*
Gogebic Community College *A*
Grand Valley State University *M, T*
Hillsdale College *B*
Kalamazoo Valley Community
  College *A*
Lake Michigan College *A*
Lansing Community College *A*
Madonna University *B*
Marygrove College *B*
Michigan State University *B, M*
Northern Michigan University *B*
Northwestern Michigan College *A*
Olivet College *B, M, T*
Rochester College *B*
Saginaw Valley State University *M*
St. Clair County Community
  College *A*
Spring Arbor University *M*
University of Detroit Mercy *B, M*
University of Michigan *M, D*
University of Michigan
  Dearborn *B, M, T*
  Flint *B, M*
Wayne County Community College *A*
Wayne State University *T*
West Shore Community College *A*

Minnesota

Augsburg College *B*
Bemidji State University *B, M*
Bethel University *M*
Capella University *M, D*
College of St. Benedict *B*
College of St. Catherine *B*
Concordia College: Moorhead *B, T*
Gustavus Adolphus College *B*

Hamline University *B, M, D*
Itasca Community College *A*
Mesabi Range Community and
  Technical College *A*
Minneapolis Community and
  Technical College *A*
Minnesota State University
  Mankato *B, M*
North Hennepin Community
  College *A*
Northland Community & Technical
  College *A*
Ridgewater College *A*
St. John's University *B*
St. Mary's University of
  Minnesota *M, D*
Southwest Minnesota State
  University *M*
University of Minnesota
  Duluth *M*
  Twin Cities *M, D*
Vermilion Community College *A*
Walden University *M, D*
Winona State University *B, M, T*

Mississippi

Belhaven College *M*
Coahoma Community College *A*
Delta State University *D*
East Central Community College *A*
Mississippi Delta Community
  College *A*
Mississippi Gulf Coast Community
  College
  Jefferson Davis Campus *A*
Mississippi State University *D*
Tougaloo College *B, T*
University of Mississippi *D*
University of Southern Mississippi *D*

Missouri

Central Methodist University *M, T*
Columbia College *M, T*
Culver-Stockton College *B*
Drury University *B, M*
Evangel University *A, B, M*
Fontbonne University *B*
Hannibal-LaGrange College *B*
Lindenwood University *B, M*
Missouri Southern State University *B*
National American University
  Kansas City *A*
Park University *M*
Rockhurst University *M*
St. Louis Christian College *B*
St. Louis Community College
  St. Louis Community College at
    Meramec *A*
St. Louis University *B, M, D*
Southwest Baptist University *M*
Stephens College *B*
Three Rivers Community College *A*
University of Missouri
  Columbia *B*
  Kansas City *B, M, D*
  Rolla *T*
  St. Louis *B, M, D*
Washington University in St.
  Louis *B, M, D, T*
Webster University *B, M, T*
William Woods University *B, T*

Montana

Blackfeet Community College *A*
Fort Peck Community College *A*
Miles Community College *A*
Montana State University
  Billings *B, M, T*
  Bozeman *B, M*
Rocky Mountain College *B, T*
University of Montana:
  Missoula *B, M, D*
University of Montana:
  Western *A, B, T*

Nebraska

Concordia University *B, M, T*
Dana College *B*
Hastings College *B, M, T*
Little Priest Tribal College *A*
Midland Lutheran College *B, T*
Northeast Community College *A*
Peru State College *B, M, T*
Union College *B*
University of Nebraska
   Kearney *B, M, T*
Western Nebraska Community
   College *A*
York College *B, T*

New Hampshire

Franklin Pierce College *B*
Keene State College *B, T*
New Hampshire Technical Institute *A*
Rivier College *A, B, M, T*
University of New Hampshire *M, D*

New Jersey

Atlantic Cape Community College *A*
Bloomfield College *B*
Brookdale Community College *A*
College of St. Elizabeth *M*
Essex County College *A*
Felician College *M*
Georgian Court University *M*
Gloucester County College *A*
Middlesex County College *A*
Monmouth University *B, M*
Montclair State University *M, D*
Richard Stockton College of New
   Jersey *T*
Rowan University *B, M*
Rutgers, The State University of New
   Jersey
   New Brunswick/Piscataway
     Campus *M, D*
St. Peter's College *M*
Salem Community College *A*
Seton Hall University *M*
Warren County Community College *A*
William Paterson University of New
   Jersey *M*

New Mexico

Clovis Community College *A*
Eastern New Mexico University *M*
Eastern New Mexico University:
   Roswell Campus *A*
New Mexico Junior College *A*
New Mexico State University *M*
New Mexico State University
   Alamogordo *A*
   Carlsbad *A*
   Grants *A*
San Juan College *A*
Santa Fe Community College *A*
Western New Mexico University *B, M*

New York

Adelphi University *M*
Barnard College *T*
Canisius College *M*
City University of New York
   Brooklyn College *B*
   Hunter College *B, M, T*
   Medgar Evers College *A*
Colgate University *B, M*
College of New Rochelle *B*
Columbia University
   Columbia College *B*
Concordia College *B, T*
Cornell University *B, M, D*
D'Youville College *B, D, T*
Dominican College of Blauvelt *B*
Dowling College *B*
Fordham University *T*
Houghton College *B*
Iona College *B*

Jewish Theological Seminary of
   America *M, D*
Manhattan College *B*
Manhattanville College *B, M*
Medaille College *B, M, T*
Metropolitan College of New
   York *A, B*
Molloy College *B, M, T*
Nazareth College of Rochester *M, T*
New York Institute of Technology *A*
Niagara University *B, M, T*
Orange County Community College *A*
St. John Fisher College *B, M*
St. Joseph's College *B*
St. Joseph's College: Suffolk
   Campus *B, T*
St. Lawrence University *M*
St. Thomas Aquinas College *B, M, T*
Siena College *B*
Skidmore College *B*
State University of New York
   Buffalo *M*
   College at Brockport *M, T*
   College at Buffalo *B*
   College at Cortland *B*
   College at Fredonia *B, M, T*
   Empire State College *A, B, M*
   Oswego *M*
Syracuse University *D*
Touro College *M*
University of Rochester *M, D*
Villa Maria College of Buffalo *A*
Wagner College *B, M*
Yeshiva University *D*

North Carolina

Appalachian State University *M*
Beaufort County Community
   College *A*
Belmont Abbey College *B*
Bladen Community College *A*
Brevard College *B*
Campbell University *A, B, M, T*
Carteret Community College *A*
Central Carolina Community
   College *A*
Chowan College *B*
College of the Albemarle *A*
East Carolina University *M*
Elon University *B, M*
Fayetteville Technical Community
   College *A*
Gardner-Webb University *B, M*
Greensboro College *B, T*
Guilford Technical Community
   College *A*
Isothermal Community College *A*
James Sprunt Community College *A*
Johnson C. Smith University *B*
Lenoir Community College *A*
Louisburg College *A*
Mars Hill College *B, T*
Martin Community College *A*
Mayland Community College *A*
McDowell Technical Community
   College *A*
Methodist College *A, B*
Montreat College *A*
Mount Olive College *A*
Nash Community College *A*
North Carolina Agricultural and
   Technical State University *B, T*
North Carolina State University *B*
Pamlico Community College *A*
Queens University of Charlotte *B*
Sampson Community College *A*
South Piedmont Community
   College *A*
Southwestern Community College *A*
University of North Carolina
   Asheville *T*
   Chapel Hill *M, D*
Vance-Granville Community
   College *A*

Warren Wilson College *B, T*
Western Carolina University *M*

North Dakota

Minot State University *A*
University of North Dakota *M*

Ohio

Antioch University McGregor *M*
Baldwin-Wallace College *B, M*
Bluffton University *M*
Bowling Green State University *B, M*
Capital University *B*
Cedarville University *M*
Central State University *M*
Circleville Bible College *B*
College of Mount St. Joseph *M, T*
Defiance College *B, M, T*
Denison University *B*
Edison State Community College *A*
Heidelberg College *M*
Hiram College *B*
Kent State University *B, M*
Kettering College of Medical Arts *A*
Lake Erie College *B, M*
Marietta College *B, M*
Mount Vernon Nazarene University *B*
Muskingum College *M*
Ohio Northern University *B, M*
Ohio State University
   Columbus Campus *M, D*
   Lima Campus *B, M, T*
   Newark Campus *B, M, T*
Ohio University
   Eastern Campus *M*
Ohio Wesleyan University *B*
Otterbein College *B*
Owens Community College
   Toledo *A*
Shawnee State University *B*
Tiffin University *B*
Union Institute & University *B, M*
University of Akron *B*
University of Cincinnati
   Raymond Walters College *A*
University of Findlay *B, M*
University of Rio Grande *B, M, T*
University of Toledo *B*
Urbana University *B*
Ursuline College *M*
Walsh University *M*
Washington State Community
   College *A*
Wilmington College *B*
Wittenberg University *B, M*
Wright State University *M*
Xavier University *B*
Youngstown State University *B, M*

Oklahoma

Bacone College *A*
Cameron University *B, M, T*
Connors State College *A*
Northeastern State University *B, M*
Northwestern Oklahoma State
   University *B, M*
Oklahoma City Community College *A*
Oklahoma City University *B, M*
Oklahoma State University *B, M, D, T*
Oklahoma State University
   Oklahoma City *A*
   Okmulgee *A*
Oral Roberts University *M*
Redlands Community College *A*
St. Gregory's University *A, B*
Seminole State College *A*
Southeastern Oklahoma State
   University *B*
Southern Nazarene University *B*
Southwestern Oklahoma State
   University *M, T*
Tulsa Community College *A*
University of Central Oklahoma *B, M*
University of Tulsa *M, T*

Western Oklahoma State College *A*

Oregon

Central Oregon Community
   College *A*
Concordia University *B, M, T*
Corban College *B*
Eastern Oregon University *B*
Lewis & Clark College *M*
Linfield College *T*
Linn-Benton Community College *A*
Oregon State University *M, D*
Pacific University *B, M, T*
Portland State University *M*
Rogue Community College *A*
Southern Oregon University *B, M, T*
Umpqua Community College *A*
University of Oregon *B, T*
University of Portland *M*
Warner Pacific College *T*
Western Oregon University *B, M*

Pennsylvania

Allegheny College *B*
Alvernia College *B, M*
Arcadia University *B, M*
Bryn Athyn College of the New
   Church *B*
Bucknell University *B, M*
Bucks County Community College *A*
Cabrini College *B, M*
California University of
   Pennsylvania *B*
College Misericordia *M*
Community College of Philadelphia *A*
Duquesne University *B*
Elizabethtown College *M*
Geneva College *B, T*
Gratz College *M*
Holy Family University *M*
Juniata College *B*
Keystone College *A, B*
Kutztown University of
   Pennsylvania *B, M*
La Salle University *B, M, T*
Lackawanna College *A*
Lehigh Carbon Community College *A*
Luzerne County Community
   College *A*
Mansfield University of
   Pennsylvania *M*
Marywood University *B*
Moravian College *M*
Neumann College *M, T*
Northampton County Area
   Community College *A*
Philadelphia Biblical University *M*
Reading Area Community College *A*
St. Francis University *B, M*
St. Joseph's University *M*
St. Vincent College *T*
Swarthmore College *B*
University of Pennsylvania *B, M, D*
University of Pittsburgh
   Greensburg *B*
Villanova University *M*
Washington and Jefferson College *B*
Westminster College *B, M*
Widener University *M, D*
York College of Pennsylvania *B*

Puerto Rico

American University of Puerto Rico *B*
Inter American University of Puerto
   Rico
   Barranquitas Campus *B*
   Fajardo Campus *B*
   San German Campus *B*
Pontifical Catholic University of
   Puerto Rico *A, B, M*
Turabo University *B*
University of Puerto Rico
   Bayamon University College *A*

Carolina Regional College *A*
Ponce *A*
University of the Sacred Heart *B*

Rhode Island
Brown University *B, M, T*
Community College of Rhode
Island *A*
Johnson & Wales University *D, T*
Rhode Island College *M*
University of Rhode Island *M, D*

South Carolina
Charleston Southern University *B, M*
The Citadel *T*
Coker College *B*
Converse College *B, T*
Furman University *B*
Limestone College *B*
Newberry College *B*
Northeastern Technical College *A*
Southern Wesleyan University *M*
University of South Carolina *D*
University of South Carolina
Aiken *B*

South Dakota
Dakota State University *B, T*
Dakota Wesleyan University *B, T*
Northern State University *B*
Oglala Lakota College *A*

Tennessee
American Baptist College of ABT
Seminary *B*
Austin Peay State University *M*
Belmont University *B, M*
Bethel College *M*
Bryan College *B*
Carson-Newman College *B, T*
Cumberland University *B, M*
Dyersburg State Community
College *A*
Hiwassee College *A*
Jackson State Community College *A*
Lambuth University *B*
Lee University *B, M*
Lincoln Memorial University *B, T*
Maryville College *B, T*
Milligan College *B, M*
Motlow State Community College *A*
Roane State Community College *A*
Southwest Tennessee Community
College *A*
Tennessee State University *B*
Tennessee Technological University *B*
Tennessee Wesleyan College *T*
Tusculum College *B*
Union University *B, M, T*
University of Tennessee
Knoxville *B, M, D*
Vanderbilt University *B*
Walters State Community College *A*

Texas
Amarillo College *A*
Angelina College *A*
Arlington Baptist College *B*
Baylor University *B, M*
Brazosport College *A*
Central Texas College *A*
Cisco Junior College *A*
Clarendon College *A*
Coastal Bend College *A*
Concordia University at Austin *M*
Dallas Baptist University *B, M, T*
East Texas Baptist University *B*
Frank Phillips College *A*
Grayson County College *A*
Hill College *A*
Howard College *A*
Howard Payne University *B*
Huston-Tillotson College *B*

Jarvis Christian College *B*
Kilgore College *A*
Laredo Community College *A*
Lon Morris College *A*
Navarro College *A*
Northeast Texas Community
College *A*
Northwest Vista College *A*
Odessa College *A*
Our Lady of the Lake University of San
Antonio *M*
Palo Alto College *A*
Panola College *A*
Paris Junior College *A*
St. Philip's College *A*
Schreiner University *B*
South Plains College *A*
Southern Methodist University *M*
Southwest Texas Junior College *A*
Southwestern Assemblies of God
University *A*
Southwestern University *B, T*
Texas A&M University
Commerce *M, D*
Kingsville *B, M*
Texarkana *M*
Texas State University: San
Marcos *M, D, T*
Texas Wesleyan University *B, T*
Texas Woman's University *M*
Trinity Valley Community College *A*
Tyler Junior College *A*
University of Dallas *B, M, T*
University of Houston
Clear Lake *B, M, T*
Victoria *B*
University of Mary Hardin-Baylor *M*
University of St.Thomas *B, M*
University of Texas
Arlington *M, T*
El Paso *B, M*
San Antonio *M*
University of the Incarnate
Word *B, M, D*
Western Texas College *A*

Utah
Snow College *A*
Southern Utah University *B, M*
University of Utah *M*
Westminster College *B, M*

Vermont
Bennington College *B, M*
Castleton State College *M, T*
Champlain College *A, B*
College of St. Joseph in Vermont *M*
Community College of Vermont *A*
Goddard College *B*
Johnson State College *B, M*
Lyndon State College *B, M*
Norwich University *M*
University of Vermont *B, M, D, T*

Virginia
Bluefield College *B*
Central Virginia Community
College *A*
Christopher Newport University *M*
Eastern Mennonite University *T*
Eastern Shore Community College *A*
Ferrum College *B*
George Mason University *D*
Germanna Community College *A*
Hampton University *B*
Hollins University *M, T*
James Madison University *M*
Longwood University *B, T*
Lord Fairfax Community College *A*
Mary Baldwin College *M, T*
Mountain Empire Community
College *A*
New River Community College *A*
Norfolk State University *M*

Old Dominion University *D*
Paul D. Camp Community College *A*
Piedmont Virginia Community
College *A*
Radford University *M*
Randolph-Macon Woman's College *M*
Rappahannock Community College *A*
Regent University *B, M, D*
Shenandoah University *M*
Southside Virginia Community
College *A*
Southwest Virginia Community
College *A*
Tidewater Community College *A*
University of Richmond *T*
University of Virginia *M, D*
Virginia Commonwealth
University *M, D, T*
Virginia Highlands Community
College *A*
Virginia Intermont College *B*
Virginia Western Community
College *A*
Wytheville Community College *A*

Washington
Centralia College *A*
City University *T*
Columbia Basin College *A*
Eastern Washington University *B, T*
Edmonds Community College *A*
Everett Community College *A*
Evergreen State College *B*
Gonzaga University *M*
Heritage University *B, M*
Highline Community College *A*
North Seattle Community College *A*
Olympic College *A*
Saint Martin's University *M*
Seattle Central Community College *A*
Spokane Falls Community College *A*
University of Washington *M, D, T*
Walla Walla College *B*
Washington State
University *B, M, D, T*
Whatcom Community College *A*
Whitworth College *B, M, T*
Yakima Valley Community College *A*

West Virginia
Alderson-Broaddus College *B, T*
Bethany College *B*
Bluefield State College *A*
Concord University *B, M, T*
Davis and Elkins College *B*
Marshall University *M, D*
Ohio Valley University *B*
Potomac State College of West Virginia
University *A*
Salem International University *M*
University of Charleston *B*
West Virginia State University *B*
West Virginia University *D*
West Virginia Wesleyan College *B*

Wisconsin
Alverno College *B, M*
Beloit College *B*
Cardinal Stritch University *B, M*
Carroll College *B, M*
Carthage College *B, M, T*
Concordia University Wisconsin *B*
Edgewood College *B, M, D*
Lakeland College *M*
Maranatha Baptist Bible College *B*
Marian College of Fond du Lac *B, M*
Marquette University *M, D*
Mount Mary College *B*
Ripon College *B*
St. Norbert College *M, T*
Silver Lake College *B, M*
University of Wisconsin
Green Bay *B*
La Crosse *M*

Madison *M, D*
Milwaukee *B*
Platteville *M*
Stevens Point *M*
Stout *M*
Superior *M*
Whitewater *B, M, T*
Viterbo University *M*

Wyoming
Casper College *A*
Laramie County Community
College *A*
Northwest College *A*
Sheridan College *A*
University of Wyoming *M, D*
Western Wyoming Community
College *A*

Education of autistic

Illinois
University of Illinois
Urbana-Champaign *M*

Kansas
University of Kansas *M, D*

Massachusetts
Emerson College *B, M*

Ohio
Youngstown State University *B, M*

Puerto Rico
Bayamon Central University *M*

Virginia
Radford University *T*

Wisconsin
University of Wisconsin
Whitewater *T*

Education of blind/
visually handicapped

Arizona
Prescott College *T*

Arkansas
University of Arkansas *B*
University of Arkansas
Little Rock *M*

California
San Francisco State University *T*

Florida
Florida State University *B, M, T*

Illinois
University of Illinois
Urbana-Champaign *M*

Massachusetts
Boston College *M*

Michigan
Eastern Michigan University *B, M, T*
Western Michigan University *M, T*

New York
City University of New York
Hunter College *M, T*
Dominican College of Blauvelt *M, T*
St. Francis College *B*

North Carolina
North Carolina Central University *M*

North Dakota
University of North Dakota *M*

Ohio
Ohio State University
Columbus Campus *M, D*
University of Toledo *T*

Oklahoma
Northeastern State University *T*

Oregon
Portland State University *T*

Pennsylvania
Kutztown University of
Pennsylvania *B*
University of Pittsburgh *T*

Puerto Rico
Inter American University of Puerto
Rico
Barranquitas Campus *B*

West Virginia
West Virginia University *T*

Wisconsin
Silver Lake College *T*

Education of brain injured

Illinois
University of Illinois
Urbana-Champaign *M*

Louisiana
Dillard University *B*

Education of Deaf/ hearing impaired

Arizona
Prescott College *T*

Arkansas
University of Arkansas
Little Rock *M*

California
California State University
Fresno *B*
Northridge *M*
San Francisco State University *T*
University of Southern California *M, T*

District of Columbia
Gallaudet University *B, M, D*

Florida
Flagler College *B*

Georgia
Georgia State University *M*

Idaho
Idaho State University *M*

Illinois
MacMurray College *B, T*
University of Illinois
Urbana-Champaign *M, D*

Kansas
University of Kansas *M, D*

Kentucky
Eastern Kentucky University *B*

Maryland
McDaniel College *M*

Massachusetts
Boston College *M*
Boston University *B, M, T*
Elms College *B, M, T*
Emerson College *B, M*
Smith College *M*

Michigan
Calvin College *B, T*
Eastern Michigan University *B, M, T*
Grand Valley State University *M, T*
Michigan State University *B*

Mississippi
University of Southern Mississippi *B*

Missouri
Fontbonne University *B*
Washington University in St. Louis *M*

Nebraska
University of Nebraska
Lincoln *B*

Nevada
Community College of Southern
Nevada *A*

New Jersey
The College of New Jersey *B, M, T*
William Paterson University of New
Jersey *M*

New York
Adelphi University *M*
Canisius College *M*
City University of New York
Hunter College *M, T*
Elmira College *B, T*
Ithaca College *B, M, T*
Marymount Manhattan College *T*
Nazareth College of Rochester *T*
New York University *M, D, T*
Pace University *M*
Rochester Institute of Technology *M*
State University of New York
College at Cortland *B, T*
New Paltz *B, M, T*

North Carolina
Barton College *B*
Lenoir-Rhyne College *B, M, T*
University of North Carolina
Greensboro *B*

North Dakota
Minot State University *B*

Ohio
Bowling Green State University *B, T*
Cincinnati State Technical and
Community College *A*
Ohio State University
Columbus Campus *M, D*
University of Cincinnati *M, D*
University of Toledo *T*

Oklahoma
University of Science and Arts of
Oklahoma *B, T*
University of Tulsa *B, T*

Oregon
Lewis & Clark College *M*
Western Oregon University *T*

Pennsylvania
Bloomsburg University of
Pennsylvania *M*
Indiana University of Pennsylvania *B*
Marywood University *B, M*
Rosemont College *T*
University of Pittsburgh *T*

South Carolina
Converse College *B, T*

South Dakota
Augustana College *B, M, T*

Tennessee
Lambuth University *B, T*
Tennessee Temple University *B*
University of Tennessee
Knoxville *B, T*

Texas
Lamar University *B, M, D*
Texas Christian University *B*
Texas Woman's University *M*

Virginia
Hampton University *M*
Longwood University *M*
Radford University *T*

Wisconsin
University of Wisconsin
Milwaukee *T*

Education of developmentally delayed

Illinois
University of Illinois
Urbana-Champaign *M*

Iowa
Upper Iowa University *T*

Kansas
Tabor College *B*

New Jersey
William Paterson University of New
Jersey *T*

New York
College of New Rochelle *M*
St. Joseph's College: Suffolk
Campus *M*
State University of New York
College at Brockport *M*

Ohio
University of Findlay *B, M, T*

Pennsylvania
La Salle University *B, M, T*

Tennessee
Lambuth University *B, T*

Wisconsin
University of Wisconsin
Superior *M*

Education of emotionally handicapped

Arizona
Grand Canyon University *B, T*
Prescott College *T*

Arkansas
Arkansas State University *M, T*

California
California Lutheran University *M*
California State University
Northridge *M*
San Diego State University *M*
Sonoma State University *M*

District of Columbia
George Washington University *M, D*
Trinity University *M*

Florida
Florida International University *B, T*
Florida State University *B, M, T*
University of South Florida *B, M*

Georgia
Columbus State University *B, M*
Georgia College and State
University *M, T*
Georgia Southwestern State
University *M*
University of West Georgia *M*

Illinois
Chicago State University *M*
MacMurray College *B, T*
National-Louis University *M*
University of Illinois
Urbana-Champaign *M, D*

Indiana
University of St. Francis *T*
Valparaiso University *M, T*

Iowa
Loras College *B*
Morningside College *B, M, T*

Kansas
Tabor College *B, T*
University of Kansas *M, D*

Massachusetts
Northeastern University *M*

Michigan
Central Michigan University *B, T*
Eastern Michigan University *B, M, T*
Grand Valley State University *M, T*
Hope College *B, T*
Saginaw Valley State University *T*
University of Detroit Mercy *B, M*
Western Michigan University *B, T*

Minnesota
Augsburg College *B, M*
Minnesota State University
Mankato *M*
University of St. Thomas *M*
Winona State University *B, T*

Mississippi
Mississippi State University *T*

Missouri
Harris-Stowe State University *T*
University of Missouri
Kansas City *M*

New Hampshire
Rivier College M

New York
City University of New York
  City College M, T
  Lehman College M
Fordham University M
Manhattan College M
Nazareth College of Rochester T
New York University M
State University of New York
  College at Buffalo B, M
  New Paltz M

North Carolina
East Carolina University B
Greensboro College B, T
North Carolina Central University M
North Carolina State University M, T
University of North Carolina
  Charlotte M
  Wilmington B

North Dakota
University of Mary M
University of North Dakota M

Ohio
University of Cincinnati M, D
University of Findlay B, M, T
University of Toledo T
Walsh University B
Wright State University M
Youngstown State University B, M

Pennsylvania
La Salle University B, T

Rhode Island
Rhode Island College B, M

South Carolina
Converse College T
Furman University M, T
South Carolina State University B, T
Southern Wesleyan University B, T

South Dakota
Augustana College B, T

Texas
West Texas A&M University T

Virginia
Eastern Mennonite University T
Longwood University M
Radford University T
University of Virginia's College at
  Wise T

Wisconsin
Silver Lake College B, T
University of Wisconsin
  Oshkosh B, M, T

Education of gifted/ talented

Arizona
Grand Canyon University M

Arkansas
Arkansas State University M, T
Arkansas Tech University M
University of Arkansas
  Little Rock M
University of Central Arkansas M

California
California State University
  Northridge M
San Diego State University M

Delaware
Delaware State University B

Florida
University of South Florida M

Georgia
Georgia State University M
University of Georgia D

Illinois
Chicago State University M
Northeastern Illinois University M
Sauk Valley Community College A
University of Illinois
  Urbana-Champaign M, D

Iowa
Morningside College T
University of Northern Iowa M

Kentucky
Western Kentucky University M

Louisiana
University of Louisiana at Lafayette M

Michigan
Grand Valley State University M

Minnesota
Minnesota State University
  Mankato M
University of St. Thomas M

Mississippi
Mississippi State University T
William Carey College M

Missouri
Drury University M
Harris-Stowe State University T
Maryville University of Saint
  Louis M, T
University of Missouri
  Columbia M, D

Montana
University of Great Falls B

Nebraska
University of Nebraska
  Kearney M, T

New York
College of New Rochelle M
Hofstra University T
Manhattanville College M, T
St. Bonaventure University M

North Carolina
Catawba College B, T
University of North Carolina
  Charlotte M

Ohio
Ashland University M, T
Bowling Green State University M, T
University of Toledo D
Wright State University M
Youngstown State University M

Oklahoma
Oklahoma City University M

Pennsylvania
Bloomsburg University of
  Pennsylvania M
Chatham College T

South Carolina
Converse College T

Texas
Hardin-Simmons University M, T
Texas Christian University B
University of Houston M, T
University of Texas
  Pan American M

Vermont
Johnson State College M

Virginia
Liberty University M, T

Washington
Eastern Washington University T
Whitworth College M

West Virginia
West Virginia State University B
West Virginia University T

Wisconsin
Carthage College M

Education of learning disabled

Arizona
Grand Canyon University B, T
Northern Arizona University M
Prescott College T
University of Phoenix M

Arkansas
Harding University B, M, T
University of Central Arkansas M

California
California Lutheran University M
California State University
  Dominguez Hills M, T
  Long Beach T
  Northridge M
Holy Names University M, T
San Jose State University M
Sonoma State University M, T
University of California
  Riverside T
University of San Francisco T

District of Columbia
American University M
Trinity University M

Florida
Bethune-Cookman College B, T
Florida Atlantic University D
Florida International University B, T
Florida Southern College B
Florida State University B, M, T
Lynn University M
Stetson University M
University of Miami D
University of South Florida B, M

Georgia
Armstrong Atlantic State
  University B, M, T
Augusta State University M
Columbus State University B, M
Georgia College and State
  University M, T

Georgia Southwestern State
  University M
Georgia State University M
University of West Georgia M

Illinois
Bradley University B, M
Chicago State University M
MacMurray College B, T
National-Louis University M
Northwestern University B, M, D
Rockford College M
St. Xavier University M
University of Illinois
  Urbana-Champaign M, T

Indiana
Ball State University M, T
University of Indianapolis T
University of St. Francis T
Valparaiso University M, T

Iowa
Iowa State University T
Kaplan University M
Northwestern College T

Kansas
Bethany College T
Tabor College B, T
University of Kansas M, D
Washburn University of Topeka M

Michigan
Aquinas College B
Calvin College M, T
Eastern Michigan University M, T
Grand Valley State University M, T
Hope College B, T
Madonna University B, M, T
Michigan State University B
Northern Michigan University B, M
Saginaw Valley State University M, T
University of Detroit Mercy M

Minnesota
Minnesota State University
  Mankato M
University of Minnesota
  Duluth T
University of St. Thomas M
Winona State University B, M, T

Missouri
Harris-Stowe State University T
Northwest Missouri State
  University B, M, T
University of Missouri
  Columbia M, D
  Kansas City M
William Woods University T

Nebraska
Hastings College T
University of Nebraska
  Kearney B, M, T

New Hampshire
New England College B, T
Rivier College M

New Jersey
Fairleigh Dickinson University
  Metropolitan Campus M
Georgian Court University T
Rowan University M
William Paterson University of New
  Jersey M

New York
City University of New York
  Hunter College M, T

Fordham University *M*
Manhattanville College *M, T*
Nazareth College of Rochester *T*
State University of New York
    College at Geneseo *M*
Syracuse University *M*

North Carolina

Appalachian State University *B*
Barton College *B*
East Carolina University *B, M*
Elizabeth City State University *B, T*
Fayetteville State University *M*
Greensboro College *B, T*
North Carolina Central University *M*
North Carolina State University *M, T*
Salem College *M, T*
University of North Carolina
    Charlotte *M*
    Wilmington *B*

North Dakota

Minot State University *M*
University of Mary *M*
University of North Dakota *M*

Ohio

Ashland University *M, T*
Baldwin-Wallace College *B, M*
Capital University *T*
Hiram College *T*
Malone College *B, M*
University of Cincinnati *M, D*
University of Findlay *B, M, T*
University of Toledo *T*
Wright State University *B, M, T*
Youngstown State University *B, M*

Oklahoma

Northwestern Oklahoma State
    University *B, T*
Oklahoma Baptist University *B, T*
Southwestern Oklahoma State
    University *B*

Oregon

Western Oregon University *T*

Pennsylvania

Immaculata University *T*
Lebanon Valley College *T*

Rhode Island

Rhode Island College *M*

South Carolina

Francis Marion University *M*
Furman University *M, T*
South Carolina State University *B, T*
Southern Wesleyan University *B, T*

South Dakota

Augustana College *B, T*

Texas

University of Texas
    El Paso *M*
West Texas A&M University *T*

Utah

Southern Utah University *B, T*

Vermont

St. Michael's College *M, T*

Virginia

Eastern Mennonite University *T*
Hampton University *M*
Longwood University *M*
Lynchburg College *M*
Marymount University *M*

Radford University *T*
University of Virginia's College at
    Wise *T*
Virginia Wesleyan College *T*

West Virginia

Bethany College *B*
Concord University *B, T*
West Virginia University *T*
West Virginia Wesleyan College *B*

Wisconsin

Carthage College *B, T*
Silver Lake College *B, T*
University of Wisconsin
    Oshkosh *B, M, T*
    Superior *M*
    Whitewater *B, T*

Education of mentally handicapped

Alabama

Tuskegee University *B, T*

Arizona

Prescott College *T*
University of Phoenix *M*

Arkansas

University of Central Arkansas *M*

California

California Lutheran University *M*
California State University
    Northridge *M*
San Francisco State University *T*
Sonoma State University *M*

Colorado

Adams State College *M*

Florida

Edward Waters College *B*
Florida International University *B, T*
Florida State University *B, M, T*
University of South Florida *B, M*
University of West Florida *B*

Georgia

Augusta State University *B, M*
Brenau University *B*
Columbus State University *B, M*
Georgia College and State
    University *M, T*
Georgia Southwestern State
    University *M*
University of West Georgia *B, M*

Illinois

Bradley University *B, T*
Chicago State University *B, M*
University of Illinois
    Urbana-Champaign *M, D*

Indiana

Manchester College *B, T*
Valparaiso University *M, T*

Iowa

Iowa State University *T*
Loras College *B*
Morningside College *B, M, T*
Northwestern College *T*

Kansas

Tabor College *B, T*
University of Kansas *M, D*

Michigan

Calvin College *B, T*
Central Michigan University *B, T*
Eastern Michigan University *B, M, T*
Grand Valley State University *M, T*
Northern Michigan University *B*
University of Detroit Mercy *B, M*
Western Michigan University *B, T*

Minnesota

Minnesota State University
    Mankato *M*
University of St. Thomas *M*
Winona State University *B, T*

Mississippi

Mississippi State University *T*

Missouri

Harris-Stowe State University *T*
Northwest Missouri State
    University *B, M, T*
University of Missouri
    Columbia *M, D*
William Woods University *T*

Nebraska

University of Nebraska
    Kearney *B, M, T*

New Jersey

William Paterson University of New
    Jersey *M*

New York

City University of New York
    City College *M, T*
    Lehman College *M*
Fordham University *M*
Manhattan College *M*
Nazareth College of Rochester *T*
State University of New York
    College at Buffalo *B, M*
    College at Geneseo *M, T*
    New Paltz *M*

North Carolina

East Carolina University *B, M*
Greensboro College *B, T*
North Carolina Central University *M*
North Carolina State University *M, T*
Shaw University *B, T*
University of North Carolina
    Charlotte *B, M*
    Wilmington *B*

North Dakota

Minot State University *B*
University of Mary *B*
University of North Dakota *M*

Ohio

Bluffton University *B*
Hiram College *T*
University of Cincinnati *M, D*
University of Findlay *B, M, T*
University of Toledo *T*
Walsh University *B*
Wright State University *B, M*
Youngstown State University *B*

Oklahoma

East Central University *B, T*
Northwestern Oklahoma State
    University *B, T*
Oklahoma Baptist University *B, T*
Southwestern Oklahoma State
    University *B*

Oregon

Western Oregon University *T*

Pennsylvania

La Salle University *B, T*
University of Pittsburgh *T*

Rhode Island

Rhode Island College *B, M*

South Carolina

Converse College *M, T*
Furman University *M, T*
South Carolina State University *B, T*
Southern Wesleyan University *B, T*

South Dakota

Augustana College *B, T*

Tennessee

Lambuth University *B, T*

Texas

Texas A&M University
    Kingsville *M*
Texas Woman's University *M*
West Texas A&M University *T*

Virginia

Eastern Mennonite University *T*
Longwood University *M*
Lynchburg College *M*
Radford University *T*
University of Virginia's College at
    Wise *T*

West Virginia

Alderson-Broaddus College *T*
Concord University *B, T*
West Liberty State College *B*
West Virginia State University *B*
West Virginia University *T*

Wisconsin

Carthage College *B, T*
Silver Lake College *B, T*
University of Wisconsin
    Oshkosh *B, M, T*
    Stout *B*

Education of multiple handicapped

Alabama

University of Alabama *M*

California

California State University
    Dominguez Hills *T*
    Long Beach *T*
San Francisco State University *T*
Sonoma State University *M*

District of Columbia

Gallaudet University *B, M, T*

Georgia

Georgia State University *M*

Illinois

National-Louis University *M*
University of Illinois
    Urbana-Champaign *B, M, D, T*

Indiana

Ball State University *B, T*

Iowa

Clarke College *B*
Iowa State University *T*
Loras College *B*
Morningside College *B, M, T*
Northwestern College *T*

St. Ambrose University *M, T*

Kansas
Tabor College *B, T*
University of Kansas *M, D*

Maine
University of Maine *M*

Massachusetts
Boston College *M*

Minnesota
Minnesota State University
  Mankato *M*
Winona State University *B, T*

Mississippi
Mississippi State University *T*
William Carey College *M*

Missouri
Missouri Valley College *B, T*
University of Missouri
  Columbia *B*

Nebraska
University of Nebraska
  Kearney *B, M, T*

New York
City University of New York
  Hunter College *M, T*
Dominican College of Blauvelt *B, M, T*
Hofstra University *T*
Nazareth College of Rochester *T*
Roberts Wesleyan College *M*
Syracuse University *M, D*

North Carolina
Greensboro College *B, T*

North Dakota
Minot State University *M*

Ohio
Ashland University *M, T*
Ohio Dominican University *B, T*
Ohio State University
  Columbus Campus *M, D*
Sinclair Community College *A*
University of Findlay *B, M, T*
University of Toledo *T*
Walsh University *B*
Wright State University *B, M, T*
Youngstown State University *B*

Oregon
Portland State University *T*
Western Oregon University *T*

Rhode Island
Rhode Island College *B, M*

Tennessee
Lambuth University *B, T*

Virginia
Norfolk State University *M*

West Virginia
Bethany College *B*
West Virginia University *T*

Education of physically handicapped

Arkansas
University of Central Arkansas *B, M*

California
California State University
  Northridge *M*
  Sacramento *T*
Fresno Pacific University *M, T*
San Francisco State University *T*

Georgia
Georgia State University *M*

Illinois
Sauk Valley Community College *A*
University of Illinois
  Urbana-Champaign *M*

Iowa
Ellsworth Community College *A*

Massachusetts
Springfield College *M, T*

Michigan
Eastern Michigan University *B, M, T*

Minnesota
University of St. Thomas *M*
Winona State University *B, T*

Nebraska
University of Nebraska
  Kearney *B, M, T*

New Jersey
William Paterson University of New
  Jersey *M*

New York
City University of New York
  Hunter College *T*
  Lehman College *M*
State University of New York
  College at Buffalo *B, M*

Ohio
Ohio State University
  Columbus Campus *M, D*
University of Cincinnati *M, D*
University of Toledo *T*
Wright State University *M*

Oklahoma
East Central University *B, T*

Oregon
Western Oregon University *T*

Pennsylvania
Cheyney University of Pennsylvania *T*
Indiana University of Pennsylvania *B*
La Salle University *B, T*
University of Pittsburgh *T*

Puerto Rico
Pontifical Catholic University of
  Puerto Rico *B*
University of Puerto Rico
  Bayamon University College *B*

Rhode Island
Rhode Island College *B*

South Dakota
Augustana College *B, T*

Texas
Texas Woman's University *M*
West Texas A&M University *T*

Education of speech impaired

Alabama
Alabama Agricultural and Mechanical
  University *B*

Arizona
Prescott College *T*

Arkansas
University of Central Arkansas *M*

California
California Baptist University *M*
California State University
  Chico *T*
  Fullerton *M*
  Long Beach *T*
  Northridge *B, M*
San Francisco State University *B, M, T*
University of Redlands *B, M*
University of San Francisco *M*

Georgia
Armstrong Atlantic State
  University *B, M, T*
Georgia State University *M*

Illinois
University of Illinois
  Urbana-Champaign *M, T*

Indiana
Ball State University *T*

Kentucky
Eastern Kentucky University *B, M*
Western Kentucky University *B*

Louisiana
Louisiana Tech University *B*
Southeastern Louisiana University *B*

Massachusetts
Emerson College *B, M, D*

Michigan
Calvin College *B, T*
Eastern Michigan University *B, M, T*
Wayne State University *B, T*

Minnesota
Minnesota State University
  Mankato *B, M*

Missouri
Truman State University *B, M*

Nebraska
University of Nebraska
  Kearney *B, M, T*
  Omaha *B, M, T*

New Jersey
Kean University *M*
William Paterson University of New
  Jersey *M*

New Mexico
New Mexico State University *B*

New York
City University of New York
  Brooklyn College *B*
  Hunter College *M, T*
College of New Rochelle *M*
Elmira College *B, T*
Hofstra University *M, T*
Ithaca College *B, M, T*

Long Island University
  Brooklyn Campus *B, T*
Nazareth College of Rochester *M, T*
New York University *B, M, D, T*
Pace University *B*
State University of New York
  Buffalo *M*
  College at Fredonia *B, M, T*
  College at Geneseo *T*
  New Paltz *B, M, T*
Syracuse University *M*

North Dakota
Minot State University *B, M*

Ohio
University of Toledo *B, M, T*

Oregon
Portland State University *T*

Pennsylvania
Indiana University of Pennsylvania *B*
Kutztown University of
  Pennsylvania *B*
Marywood University *B, M*
West Chester University of
  Pennsylvania *T*

Puerto Rico
Pontifical Catholic University of
  Puerto Rico *B*

South Dakota
Augustana College *B, T*

Tennessee
Lambuth University *B, T*

Texas
Our Lady of the Lake University of San
  Antonio *B, M*

Virginia
Hampton University *M*
Longwood University *B, M*
Radford University *T*

West Virginia
West Virginia University *T*

Wisconsin
University of Wisconsin
  River Falls *B, T*
  Whitewater *M*

Educational assessment/testing

California
California State University
  Northridge *M*
Stanford University *M, D*

Colorado
Jones International University *M*

Delaware
University of Delaware *M, D*

Florida
Florida State University *M, D*

Georgia
Georgia State University *M*

Illinois
University of Illinois
  Urbana-Champaign *M, D*

Indiana
Indiana University
  Bloomington *D*

Iowa
Iowa State University *M*
University of Iowa *M, D*

Maryland
University of Maryland
  College Park *M, D*

Massachusetts
Tufts University *M*

Michigan
Michigan State University *M, D*

New Mexico
College of the Southwest *M*

New York
Fordham University *M, D*
State University of New York
  Albany *M, D*
Syracuse University *M, D*

North Carolina
University of North Carolina
  Greensboro *M, D*

Ohio
Kent State University *M, D*
Ohio State University
  Columbus Campus *M, D*
University of Findlay *B, M*

Pennsylvania
University of Pennsylvania *M*

Texas
Sul Ross State University *M*

Utah
Brigham Young University *M*

Washington
University of Washington *M, D*
Washington State University *M, D*

Educational evaluation/ research

California
California State University
  Fresno *M*
San Diego State University *M*

Colorado
Jones International University *M*
University of Colorado
  Boulder *D*

District of Columbia
Catholic University of America *D*

Florida
Florida State University *M, D*
Lynn University *D*
University of Miami *D*

Georgia
Clark Atlanta University *M*

Illinois
University of Illinois
  Urbana-Champaign *M, D*

Kentucky
University of Kentucky *M, D*

Massachusetts
Boston College *M, D*

Michigan
Michigan State University *M, D*
Wayne State University *M, D*
Western Michigan University *D*

Missouri
University of Missouri
  Columbia *M, D*
  Kansas City *M*

New Jersey
Rowan University *M*

North Carolina
North Carolina State University *D*

North Dakota
North Dakota State University *D*

Ohio
Ohio University *M, D*
University of Findlay *B, M*
Youngstown State University *M*

Pennsylvania
Bucknell University *B, M*
Penn State
  University Park *M*

Puerto Rico
University of Puerto Rico
  Rio Piedras *M*

South Carolina
University of South Carolina *M, D*

South Dakota
University of South Dakota *M, D*

Texas
Texas Tech University *M, D*

Washington
Washington State University *M, D*

Educational leadership/ adminstration

Alabama
Alabama Agricultural and Mechanical
  University *M*
Alabama State University *M, D*
Auburn University *M, D*
Auburn University at Montgomery *M*
Jacksonville State University *M, T*
Samford University *M, T*
Troy University *M, T*
University of Alabama *M, D*
University of Alabama
  Birmingham *M, D, T*
University of Montevallo *M, T*
University of North Alabama *M*
University of South Alabama *M, T*
University of West Alabama *M*

Alaska
University of Alaska
  Anchorage *M, T*
  Fairbanks *T*

Arizona
Arizona State University *M, D*
Arizona State University West *M*
Northcentral University *M, D*

Northern Arizona University *M, D*
University of Arizona *M, D*
University of Phoenix *M, D*

Arkansas
Arkansas State University *M, D, T*
Arkansas Tech University *M*
Harding University *M*
Southern Arkansas University *M*
University of Arkansas *M, D*
University of Arkansas
  Little Rock *M, D*
University of Central Arkansas *M*

California
Alliant International
  University *M, D, T*
Azusa Pacific University *M, D*
Bethany University *M*
California Baptist University *M, T*
California Lutheran University *M*
California Polytechnic State
  University: San Luis Obispo *M*
California State University
  Chico *T*
  Dominguez Hills *M*
  East Bay *M, T*
  Fresno *M, D*
  Fullerton *M*
  Long Beach *M, T*
  Los Angeles *M*
  Northridge *M*
  Sacramento *M*
  San Bernardino *M*
  San Marcos *M*
Chapman University *M, T*
Dominican University of California *M*
Fresno Pacific University *M, T*
La Sierra University *M, D*
Loyola Marymount University *M, D, T*
Mills College *D*
Mount St. Mary's College *M*
National University *M, T*
Pepperdine University *M, D*
Point Loma Nazarene University *M*
St. Mary's College of California *M, D*
San Diego State University *M*
San Francisco State University *T*
San Jose State University *M*
Santa Clara University *M*
Simpson University *M*
Sonoma State University *M*
Stanford University *M, D*
University of California
  Berkeley *T*
  Irvine *M, D*
  Los Angeles *D*
  Riverside *D, T*
University of Judaism *M*
University of La Verne *M, D*
University of Redlands *M, T*
University of San Diego *M, D, T*
University of San Francisco *M, D, T*
University of Southern California *M, T*
University of the Pacific *M, D, T*
Whittier College *T*

Colorado
Jones International University *M*
University of Colorado
  Denver and Health Sciences
    Center *M, D, T*
University of Denver *M, D*
University of Northern
  Colorado *M, D, T*

Connecticut
Central Connecticut State
  University *M, D*
Fairfield University *M*
Sacred Heart University *M, T*
University of Bridgeport *D*
University of Connecticut *M, D*

University of Hartford *M, D, T*
University of New Haven *M*
Western Connecticut State
  University *D*

Delaware
University of Delaware *M, D*
Wilmington College *M*

District of Columbia
American University *M, D*
Catholic University of America *M, D*
Gallaudet University *M*
George Washington University *M*
Howard University *M*
Trinity University *M*
University of the District of
  Columbia *M*

Florida
Barry University *M, D, T*
Florida Agricultural and Mechanical
  University *M, D*
Florida Atlantic University *M, D*
Florida Gulf Coast University *M*
Florida International University *M, D*
Florida State University *M, D, T*
Nova Southeastern University *D*
St. Thomas University *M*
Stetson University *M*
University of Central Florida *M, D*
University of Florida *M, D*
University of North Florida *M, D*
University of South Florida *M, D*
University of West Florida *M, T*

Georgia
Albany State University *M*
Augusta State University *M*
Clark Atlanta University *M, D*
Columbus State University *M*
Covenant College *M*
Georgia College and State
  University *M, T*
Georgia Southern University *M, D, T*
Georgia State University *M, D*
Kennesaw State University *M*
University of Georgia *M, D*
University of West Georgia *M, D*
Valdosta State University *M, D*

Hawaii
University of Hawaii
  Manoa *M*

Idaho
Idaho State University *D, T*
University of Idaho *M*

Illinois
Aurora University *M, D*
Benedictine University *M*
Bradley University *M*
Chicago State University *M*
Concordia University *M*
DePaul University *M*
Dominican University *M*
Eastern Illinois University *M*
Governors State University *M*
Illinois State University *M, D*
Lewis University *M, D*
Loyola University of Chicago *M, D*
National-Louis University *M*
North Central College *M*
Northeastern Illinois University *M*
Northern Illinois University *M, D*
Northwestern University *D*
Roosevelt University *M, D*
St. Xavier University *M*
Southern Illinois University
  Carbondale *M*
Southern Illinois University
  Edwardsville *M*

University of Illinois
Chicago *D*
Springfield *M*
Urbana-Champaign *M, D, T*
University of St. Francis *M*
Western Illinois University *M, D*

Indiana

Anderson University *M*
Ball State University *M, D, T*
Butler University *M*
Indiana State University *M, D*
Indiana University
Bloomington *M, D*
Indiana University-Purdue University
Fort Wayne *M*
Indiana University-Purdue University
Indianapolis *M*
Indiana Wesleyan University *D*
Oakland City University *D*
University of St. Francis *M*

Iowa

Clarke College *M*
Drake University *M, D*
Iowa State University *M, D*
St. Ambrose University *M*
University of Iowa *M, D*
University of Northern Iowa *D*

Kansas

Benedictine College *M*
Emporia State University *M*
Friends University *M*
Kansas State University *M, D*
Newman University *M*
Pittsburg State University *M*
University of Kansas *M*
Washburn University of Topeka *M*
Wichita State University *M, D*

Kentucky

Spalding University *M, D, T*
Western Kentucky University *D*

Louisiana

Centenary College of Louisiana *M*
Grambling State University *D*
Louisiana State University and
Agricultural and Mechanical
College *M*
Louisiana Tech University *D*
Nicholls State University *M*
Northwestern State University *T*
Our Lady of Holy Cross College *M*
Southeastern Louisiana University *M*
Southern University and Agricultural
and Mechanical College *M*
University of Louisiana at Lafayette *M*
University of Louisiana at
Monroe *M, D*
University of New Orleans *M, D*
Xavier University of Louisiana *M*

Maine

University of Maine *M, D*
University of Southern Maine *M*

Maryland

Bowie State University *M, D*
College of Notre Dame of
Maryland *M*
Frostburg State University *M*
Hood College *M*
Loyola College in Maryland *M*
McDaniel College *M*
Morgan State University *M, D*
Salisbury University *M*
University of Maryland
College Park *M, D*
Eastern Shore *D*

Massachusetts

Atlantic Union College *M*
Boston College *M, D*
Boston University *M, D*
Bridgewater State College *M, T*
Eastern Nazarene College *M, T*
Emmanuel College *M*
Fitchburg State College *M*
Framingham State College *M*
Lesley University *M, D*
Salem State College *M*
Springfield College *M*
University of Massachusetts
Boston *M, D*
Lowell *M, D*
Westfield State College *M*
Wheelock College *M*

Michigan

Andrews University *M, D*
Central Michigan University *M, D*
Eastern Michigan University *M, D*
Grand Valley State University *M*
Madonna University *M*
Marygrove College *M*
Michigan State University *M, D*
Northern Michigan University *M*
Oakland University *M, D*
Saginaw Valley State University *M*
University of Detroit Mercy *M*
University of Michigan
Flint *M*
Wayne State University *D*
Western Michigan University *M, D*

Minnesota

Augsburg College *M*
Bemidji State University *M*
Capella University *M, D*
Minnesota State University
Mankato *M*
Moorhead *M*
St. Cloud State University *M, T*
St. Mary's University of Minnesota *M*
University of Minnesota
Twin Cities *M, D*
University of St. Thomas *M, D*
Winona State University *M, T*

Mississippi

Delta State University *M*
Jackson State University *M, D*
Mississippi College *M*
Mississippi State University *M, T*
University of Mississippi *M*
University of Southern Mississippi *M*

Missouri

Central Missouri State University *M*
Lincoln University *M*
Lindenwood University *M*
Maryville University of Saint
Louis *M, T*
Missouri State University *M*
Northwest Missouri State
University *M*
St. Louis University *M, D*
Southeast Missouri State University *M*
Southwest Baptist University *M*
University of Missouri
Columbia *M, D*
Kansas City *M*
St. Louis *M*
Webster University *T*
William Woods University *M*

Montana

University of Great Falls *M*
University of Montana: Missoula *M, D*

Nebraska

Concordia University *M, T*
Doane College *M*

University of Nebraska
Kearney *M*
Lincoln *M, D*
Omaha *M, D*
Wayne State College *M*

Nevada

University of Nevada
Las Vegas *M, D*
Reno *M, D*

New Hampshire

Keene State College *M, T*
New England College *M*
Plymouth State University *M, T*
Rivier College *M*
University of New Hampshire *D*
University of New Hampshire at
Manchester *M*

New Jersey

Caldwell College *M*
Centenary College *M*
The College of New Jersey *M*
College of St. Elizabeth *M*
Fairleigh Dickinson University
College at Florham *M*
Metropolitan Campus *M*
Kean University *M, T*
Montclair State University *M*
New Jersey City University *M*
Rider University *M*
Rowan University *M, D*
St. Peter's College *M*
Seton Hall University *M, D*

New Mexico

College of the Southwest *M*
New Mexico Highlands University *M*
New Mexico State University *M, D*
University of New Mexico *M, D, T*
Western New Mexico University *M*

New York

Adelphi University *M, T*
Canisius College *M*
City University of New York
Baruch College *M*
Brooklyn College *M*
City College *M*
College of New Rochelle *M*
Dowling College *D, T*
Fordham University *M, D*
Hofstra University *M, D, T*
Iona College *M*
Manhattan College *M*
New York Institute of Technology *T*
New York University *M, D, T*
Niagara University *M*
Pace University *M*
St. Bonaventure University *M*
St. John Fisher College *M*
St. John's University *M, D, T*
St. Lawrence University *M*
State University of New York
Albany *M, D*
Binghamton *M, D*
Buffalo *M, D*
College at Brockport *M*
College at Cortland *T*
College at Fredonia *T*
College at Plattsburgh *M, T*
New Paltz *M*
Oswego *M*
Syracuse University *M, D*
Touro College *M*
University of Rochester *M, D*

North Carolina

Appalachian State University *M*
Campbell University *M*
East Carolina University *D, T*
Fayetteville State University *M, D*

Gardner-Webb University *M, D*
High Point University *M*
North Carolina Agricultural and
Technical State University *M*
North Carolina State University *M, D*
University of North Carolina
Chapel Hill *D*
Charlotte *D*
Greensboro *M, D*
Wilmington *M*
Western Carolina University *D*

North Dakota

North Dakota State University *M*
University of North Dakota *M, D*

Ohio

Antioch University McGregor *M*
Ashland University *M, D, T*
Baldwin-Wallace College *M*
Bowling Green State
University *M, D, T*
Cleveland State University *M, D*
Franciscan University of
Steubenville *M*
John Carroll University *M*
Lake Erie College *M*
Laura and Alvin Siegal College of
Judaic Studies *M*
Malone College *M*
Miami University
Oxford Campus *M, D*
Ohio State University
Columbus Campus *M, D*
Ohio University *M, D*
Ohio University
Chillicothe Campus *M*
Zanesville Campus *M*
Union Institute & University *M*
University of Cincinnati *M, D*
University of Dayton *M, D, T*
University of Findlay *M*
University of Toledo *M, D, T*
Ursuline College *M*
Wright State University *M*
Xavier University *M*
Youngstown State University *M, D*

Oklahoma

East Central University *M, T*
Northeastern State University *M, T*
Northwestern Oklahoma State
University *M*
Oklahoma State University *M, D*
Oral Roberts University *M, D*
Southeastern Oklahoma State
University *M*
Southwestern Oklahoma State
University *M, T*
University of Central Oklahoma *M*
University of Oklahoma *M, D, T*

Oregon

Concordia University *M*
George Fox University *M, D, T*
Lewis & Clark College *M, D*
Portland State University *D, T*
University of Oregon *M, D, T*

Pennsylvania

Arcadia University *M*
Bucknell University *M*
California University of
Pennsylvania *M*
Carlow University *M*
Chestnut Hill College *M, T*
Cheyney University of
Pennsylvania *M*
Delaware Valley College *M*
Drexel University *D*
Duquesne University *M, D*
Edinboro University of
Pennsylvania *M*

Gannon University *M*
Gratz College *M*
Immaculata University *M, D, T*
Indiana University of Pennsylvania *D*
Lehigh University *M, D*
Marywood University *M, D*
Millersville University of
Pennsylvania *M*
Penn State
University Park *M, D*
Philadelphia Biblical University *M*
Point Park University *M*
Robert Morris University *M*
St. Francis University *M*
St. Joseph's University *M, D*
St. Vincent College *M*
Shippensburg University of
Pennsylvania *T*
Slippery Rock University of
Pennsylvania *M*
Temple University *M, D*
University of Pennsylvania *M, D*
University of Pittsburgh *M, D*
University of Scranton *M*
Westminster College *M*
Widener University *M, D, T*
York College of Pennsylvania *M*

Puerto Rico

Bayamon Central University *M*
Inter American University of Puerto
Rico
San German Campus *M, D*
Pontifical Catholic University of
Puerto Rico *M*
Turabo University *M, D*
Universidad Adventista de las
Antillas *M*
Universidad Metropolitana *M*
Universidad del Este *M*
University of Puerto Rico
Rio Piedras *M, D*

Rhode Island

Johnson & Wales University *D*
Rhode Island College *M*

South Carolina

Charleston Southern University *M*
The Citadel *M*
Clemson University *D*
Columbia International
University *M, D*
Furman University *M*
South Carolina State University *D*
University of South Carolina *M, D*
Winthrop University *M, T*

South Dakota

Oglala Lakota College *M*
South Dakota State University *M*
University of South Dakota *M, D*

Tennessee

Austin Peay State University *M*
East Tennessee State
University *M, D, T*
Lincoln Memorial University *M*
Lipscomb University *M, T*
Middle Tennessee State
University *M, T*
Southern Adventist University *M*
Tennessee Technological
University *M*
Tennessee Temple University *M*
Trevecca Nazarene University *M*
University of Memphis *M, D, T*
University of Tennessee
Chattanooga *M, D*
Knoxville *M, D*
Martin *M*
Vanderbilt University *M, D*

Texas

Abilene Christian University *M, T*
Angelo State University *M*
Baylor University *M*
Houston Baptist University *M*
Lamar University *M, D, T*
Lubbock Christian University *M*
Midwestern State University *M*
Prairie View A&M University *M, D*
St. Mary's University *M*
Sam Houston State University *M, D*
Schreiner University *M*
Southwestern Assemblies of God
University *M*
Stephen F. Austin State
University *M, D*
Sul Ross State University *M*
Tarleton State University *M, D*
Texas A&M University *M, D*
Texas A&M University
Commerce *M, D*
Kingsville *M*
Texarkana *M*
Texas Christian University *M, D*
Texas Southern University *M, D*
Texas State University: San
Marcos *M, D, T*
Texas Tech University *M, D*
Texas Woman's University *M*
Trinity University *M*
University of Houston *M, D*
University of Houston
Clear Lake *M*
Victoria *M*
University of Mary Hardin-Baylor *M*
University of North Texas *M, D*
University of Texas
Arlington *M, D*
Austin *M, D*
Brownsville *M*
El Paso *M, D*
Pan American *M, D*
San Antonio *M, D*
Tyler *M*
of the Permian Basin *M*
West Texas A&M University *M, T*

Utah

Brigham Young University *M, D*
University of Utah *M, D*

Vermont

Castleton State College *M*
Johnson State College *M*
St. Michael's College *M*
University of Vermont *M, D, T*

Virginia

College of William and Mary *M, D*
George Mason University *M*
Liberty University *M, D*
Longwood University *M*
Lynchburg College *M*
Old Dominion University *M, D*
Radford University *M, T*
Regent University *M, T*
Shenandoah University *D*
University of Virginia *M, D*
Virginia Commonwealth University *M*
Virginia State University *M, D*

Washington

Central Washington University *M, T*
City University *M*
Eastern Washington University *M*
Gonzaga University *M*
Heritage University *M*
Pacific Lutheran University *M*
Seattle University *M, D*
University of Washington *M, D*
Walla Walla College *M*
Washington State University *M, D*
Whitworth College *M*

West Virginia

Concord University *M*
West Virginia University *M, D*

Wisconsin

Alverno College *M*
Concordia University Wisconsin *M*
Edgewood College *M, T*
Marian College of Fond du Lac *M, D*
Marquette University *M, D*
University of Wisconsin
Madison *M, D*
Milwaukee *M, T*
Superior *M*
Whitewater *M*
Viterbo University *M*

Educational psychology

Alabama

University of Alabama *M, D*

Arizona

Arizona State University *M, D*
Northern Arizona University *M, D*
Prescott College *M*
University of Arizona *M, D*

California

Alliant International University *D*
Azusa Pacific University *M*
California Lutheran University *M*
California State University
Dominguez Hills *T*
East Bay *M, T*
Long Beach *M*
Northridge *M*
Chapman University *M, T*
Fresno Pacific University *M, T*
La Sierra University *M*
Loyola Marymount University *M*
St. Mary's College of California *M*
University of California
Santa Barbara *M, D*
University of San Francisco *M, D*
University of Southern California *D, T*
University of the Pacific *M, D, T*

Colorado

University of Colorado
Boulder *M, D*
Denver and Health Sciences
Center *M*
University of Denver *M, D*
University of Northern Colorado *M, D*

Connecticut

University of Connecticut *M, D, T*

Delaware

University of Delaware *M, T*

District of Columbia

Catholic University of America *D*
Howard University *M*

Florida

Florida State University *M, D*
University of Florida *M, D*

Georgia

Georgia State University *M, D*
University of Georgia *M, D*

Hawaii

University of Hawaii
Manoa *M, D*

Idaho

Idaho State University *D*

West Virginia (continued column)

Illinois

Loyola University of Chicago *M, D*
National-Louis University *M, D*
Northern Illinois University *M, D*
Southern Illinois University
Carbondale *M, D*
University of Illinois
Chicago *D*
Urbana-Champaign *M, D*

Indiana

Ball State University *M, D*
Indiana University
Bloomington *M, D*

Iowa

Iowa State University *T*
University of Iowa *M, D*

Kansas

Fort Hays State University *M*
University of Kansas *M, D*
Wichita State University *M*

Kentucky

University of Kentucky *M, D*

Louisiana

Louisiana Tech University *M*

Maryland

University of Maryland
College Park *M, D*

Massachusetts

American International College *M, D*
Boston College *M, D*
Harvard College *M, D*
Northeastern University *M*
Tufts University *M, T*

Michigan

Andrews University *M, D*
Eastern Michigan University *M*
Michigan State University *M*
Wayne State University *M, D*

Minnesota

Capella University *M, D*
University of Minnesota
Duluth *M*
Twin Cities *M, D*

Mississippi

Mississippi State University *M, D*
University of Mississippi *M, D*

Missouri

University of Missouri
Columbia *M, D*

Nebraska

University of Nebraska
Kearney *M*
Lincoln *D*

Nevada

University of Nevada
Las Vegas *M, D*

New Jersey

Kean University *M*
Montclair State University *M*
New Jersey City University *M*
Rowan University *M*
Rutgers, The State University of New
Jersey
New Brunswick/Piscataway
Campus *D*

New Mexico
University of New Mexico *M, D*

New York
College of Saint Rose *M*
Cornell University *M*
Marist College *M*
New York University *M, D*
State University of New York
Albany *D*
Buffalo *M, D*
College at Plattsburgh *M, T*
Syracuse University *M, D*
Touro College *M*

Ohio
Bowling Green State University *M, T*
John Carroll University *M*
Kent State University *M, D*
Miami University
Oxford Campus *M*
Ohio State University
Columbus Campus *M, D*
Union Institute & University *M*

Oklahoma
Northwestern Oklahoma State
University *M*
University of Oklahoma *D*

Pennsylvania
Edinboro University of
Pennsylvania *M*
Indiana University of Pennsylvania *M*
Penn State
University Park *M, D*
Temple University *M, D*
University of Pittsburgh *M, D*
Widener University *M*

Puerto Rico
Pontifical Catholic University of
Puerto Rico *M*

Rhode Island
Rhode Island College *M*

Tennessee
Tennessee State University *D*
Tennessee Technological
University *M, D*
University of Tennessee
Knoxville *M, D*
Vanderbilt University *M, D*

Texas
Baylor University *M, D*
Tarleton State University *M*
Texas A&M University *M, D*
Texas A&M University
Commerce *M, D*
Texas Tech University *M, D*
University of Houston *M, D*
University of Mary Hardin-Baylor *M*
University of North Texas *M, D*
University of Texas
Austin *M, D*
El Paso *M, D*
Tyler *M*

Utah
University of Utah *M, D*

Virginia
College of William and Mary *M, D*
University of Virginia *M, D*

West Virginia
West Virginia University *M, D*

Wisconsin
Marquette University *M*
University of Wisconsin
Eau Claire *M*
Madison *M, D*
Milwaukee *M*
Whitewater *M*

Educational statistics/ research methods

Alabama
University of Alabama *D*

California
Stanford University *M, D*

Colorado
Jones International University *M*
University of Denver *M, D*
University of Northern Colorado *M, D*

Connecticut
University of Connecticut *M*

Florida
Florida State University *M, D*
University of Florida *B, M*
University of Miami *M, D*

Georgia
Georgia State University *M*

Illinois
Loyola University of Chicago *M, D*
University of Illinois
Urbana-Champaign *M, D*

Nebraska
University of Nebraska
Lincoln *M*

New York
Fordham University *M, D*
Hofstra University *M*
State University of New York
Albany *M, D*

Ohio
Ohio State University
Columbus Campus *M, D*
University of Toledo *M*

Pennsylvania
University of Pennsylvania *M*
West Chester University of
Pennsylvania *M*

Tennessee
University of Memphis *M, D*

Texas
University of North Texas *D*

Utah
Brigham Young University *D*

Virginia
Virginia Polytechnic Institute and
State University *D*

Educational superintendency

Illinois
Concordia University *M, D*
Lewis University *D*
University of Illinois
Urbana-Champaign *D, T*

Missouri
Lindenwood University *M*
Southwest Baptist University *M*
University of Missouri
Columbia *M, D*

Nebraska
Wayne State College *M*

Nevada
University of Nevada
Reno *M, D*

New Hampshire
Plymouth State University *T*

New Jersey
William Paterson University of New
Jersey *M*

New York
City University of New York
City College *M, T*
St. Bonaventure University *M*

Ohio
University of Findlay *M, T*
Youngstown State University *D*

Oregon
University of Oregon *T*

Pennsylvania
Gannon University *T*
Marywood University *M*

South Dakota
University of South Dakota *M, D*

Vermont
St. Michael's College *T*

Washington
University of Washington *D, T*
Washington State University *T*

Wisconsin
Edgewood College *M*
University of Wisconsin
Superior *M*
Whitewater *M*

Educational supervision

Alabama
University of Alabama *D*

Alaska
University of Alaska
Anchorage *T*

Arizona
Northcentral University *M, D*

Arkansas
Arkansas State University *M*
University of Central Arkansas *M*

California
California Lutheran University *M*
Dominican University of California *M*
National University *M, T*
St. Mary's College of California *M*

Colorado
Jones International University *M*

Connecticut
Central Connecticut State
University *M*
Fairfield University *M*

Delaware
University of Delaware *M, D*

District of Columbia
George Washington University *M*
Howard University *M*
University of the District of
Columbia *M*

Florida
Stetson University *M*

Georgia
Clark Atlanta University *M, D*
Valdosta State University *M*

Idaho
Northwest Nazarene University *M*

Illinois
Loyola University of Chicago *M*
National-Louis University *D*
University of Illinois
Chicago *M*
Springfield *M*
Urbana-Champaign *M, D*

Indiana
Ball State University *D, T*

Kentucky
Eastern Kentucky University *M*

Louisiana
Centenary College of Louisiana *M*
Nicholls State University *M*

Maine
University of Maine *M*

Maryland
Morgan State University *M, D*

Massachusetts
Eastern Nazarene College *M*
Springfield College *M*

Michigan
Central Michigan University *M*
Northern Michigan University *M*
Wayne State University *M*
Western Michigan University *D*

Minnesota
Minnesota State University
Mankato *M*
Winona State University *M, T*

Montana
University of Great Falls *M*

Nebraska
University of Nebraska
Kearney *M*

New Hampshire
New England College *M*
Plymouth State University *T*
University of New Hampshire *M*

New Jersey
Georgian Court University *M*

New York

City University of New York
  Baruch College *M*
  Brooklyn College *T*
College of Saint Rose *M*
Fordham University *M, D*
Long Island University
  C.W. Post Campus *M*
Mercy College *M*
New York Institute of Technology *T*
State University of New York
  Albany *D*
  New Paltz *M*

North Carolina

East Carolina University *M*
Fayetteville State University *M*
North Carolina Agricultural and
    Technical State University *M*
Western Carolina University *M*

Ohio

John Carroll University *M*
Kent State University *M*
Otterbein College *M*
University of Cincinnati *M, D*
University of Toledo *T*
Wright State University *M*
Youngstown State University *M, D*

Oklahoma

Northeastern State University *M*

Pennsylvania

Carlow University *M*
Marywood University *M*
Penn State
  Schuylkill - Capital College *M*
St. Francis University *M*
St. Joseph's University *D*
Shippensburg University of
    Pennsylvania *T*
Villanova University *M*
Widener University *M, D*

Puerto Rico

Turabo University *D*

South Carolina

Clemson University *M*
Furman University *M*
Winthrop University *T*

Tennessee

Tennessee State University *M*
Tennessee Technological
    University *M*

Texas

Lamar University *M*
Prairie View A&M University *M*
Sam Houston State University *M*
Stephen F. Austin State University *M*
Sul Ross State University *M*
Texas A&M University
  Commerce *D*
  Kingsville *M*
Texas Southern University *M*
Texas Woman's University *M*
University of Houston
  Victoria *M*
University of North Texas *M*
University of Texas
  Brownsville *M*
  El Paso *M*
  Pan American *M*

Vermont

Johnson State College *M*
St. Michael's College *M*

Virginia

Longwood University *M*

Washington

Eastern Washington University *M, T*
Seattle Pacific University *T*
Washington State University *M, D*
Western Washington University *M*

Wisconsin

University of Wisconsin
  Oshkosh *M, T*
  River Falls *M*
  Superior *M*

Electrical and communications engineering

Alabama

Alabama Southern Community
    College *A*
Auburn University *B, M, D*
Lawson State Community College *A*
Remington College
  Mobile *A*
Tuskegee University *B, M*
University of Alabama *B, M, D*
University of Alabama
  Birmingham *B, M, D*
  Huntsville *B, M, D*
University of South Alabama *B, M*
Wallace State Community College at
    Hanceville *A*

Alaska

University of Alaska
  Anchorage *B*
  Fairbanks *B, M*

Arizona

Arizona State University *B, M, D*
Embry-Riddle Aeronautical University:
    Prescott Campus *B*
High-Tech Institute *A*
Northern Arizona University *B, M*
University of Arizona *B, M, D*

Arkansas

Arkansas Tech University *B*
Harding University *B*
University of Arkansas *B, M*

California

California Institute of
    Technology *B, M, D*
California Polytechnic State
    University: San Luis Obispo *B, M*
California State Polytechnic
    University: Pomona *B, M*
California State University
  Chico *B, M*
  Fresno *B, M*
  Fullerton *B, M*
  Long Beach *B, M*
  Los Angeles *B, M*
  Northridge *B, M*
  Sacramento *B, M*
City College of San Francisco *A*
Cogswell Polytechnical College *B*
College of the Redwoods *A*
Cuesta College *A*
De Anza College *A*
East Los Angeles College *A*
International Technological
    University *M*
Los Angeles Harbor College *A*
Los Angeles Southwest College *A*
Loyola Marymount University *B, M*
Merritt College *A*
Modesto Junior College *A*

Northwestern Polytechnic
    University *B, M*
San Diego State University *B, M*
San Francisco State University *B*
San Jose State University *B, M*
Santa Clara University *B, M*
Southern California Institute of
    Technology *A, B*
Stanford University *B, M, D*
University of California
  Berkeley *B, M, D*
  Davis *B, M, D*
  Irvine *B, M, D*
  Los Angeles *B, M, D*
  Riverside *B, M, D*
  San Diego *B, M, D*
  Santa Barbara *B, M, D*
  Santa Cruz *B*
University of San Diego *B*
University of Southern
    California *B, M, D*
University of the Pacific *B*

Colorado

Colorado State University *B, M, D*
Colorado Technical University *B, M*
IntelliTec College: Grand Junction *A*
United States Air Force Academy *B*
University of Colorado
  Boulder *B, M, D*
  Colorado Springs *B, M, D*
  Denver and Health Sciences
      Center *B, M*
University of Denver *B, M*
Westwood College of
    Technology *A, B*

Connecticut

Capital Community College *A*
Central Connecticut State
    University *B*
Fairfield University *B*
Trinity College *B*
United States Coast Guard Academy *B*
University of Bridgeport *M*
University of Connecticut *B, M, D*
University of Hartford *B, M*
University of New Haven *B, M*
Yale University *B, M, D*

Delaware

University of Delaware *B, M, D*

District of Columbia

Catholic University of
    America *B, M, D*
George Washington
    University *B, M, D*
Howard University *B, M, D*
University of the District of
    Columbia *B*

Florida

Broward Community College *A*
Embry-Riddle Aeronautical
    University *B*
Florida Agricultural and Mechanical
    University *B, M, D*
Florida Atlantic University *B, M, D*
Florida Institute of
    Technology *B, M, D*
Florida International
    University *B, M, D*
Florida State University *B, M, D*
Gulf Coast Community College *A*
Hillsborough Community College *A*
Jacksonville University *B*
Miami Dade College *A*
Okaloosa-Walton College *A*
Palm Beach Community College *A*
Pensacola Junior College *A*
Seminole Community College *A*
University of Central Florida *B, M, D*

University of Florida *A, B, M*
University of Miami *B, M, D*
University of North Florida *B*
University of South Florida *B, M, D*
University of West Florida *B*
Valencia Community College *A*

Georgia

DeKalb Technical College *A*
Georgia Institute of
    Technology *B, M, D*
Mercer University *M*
Middle Georgia College *A*

Hawaii

University of Hawaii
  Manoa *B, M, D*

Idaho

Boise State University *B, M*
Brigham Young University-Idaho *A*
College of Southern Idaho *A*
Idaho State University *B*
North Idaho College *A*
University of Idaho *B, M, D*

Illinois

Bradley University *B, M*
City Colleges of Chicago
  Olive-Harvey College *A*
Dominican University *B*
Illinois Central College *A*
Illinois Institute of
    Technology *B, M, D*
Joliet Junior College *A*
Northern Illinois University *B, M*
Northwestern University *B, M, D*
Sauk Valley Community College *A*
Southern Illinois University
    Carbondale *B, M*
Southern Illinois University
    Edwardsville *B, M*
University of Illinois
  Chicago *B, M, D*
  Urbana-Champaign *B, M, D*

Indiana

Indiana Institute of Technology *B*
Indiana University-Purdue University
    Fort Wayne *B*
Indiana University-Purdue University
    Indianapolis *B, M, D*
Purdue University *B, M, D*
Purdue University
    Calumet *B*
Rose-Hulman Institute of
    Technology *B, M*
Tri-State University *B*
University of Evansville *B, M*
University of Notre Dame *B, M, D*
Valparaiso University *B*
Vincennes University *A*

Iowa

Dordt College *B*
Iowa State University *B, M, D*
Loras College *B*
Northeast Iowa Community
    College *A*
Southeastern Community College
    North Campus *A*
University of Iowa *B*

Kansas

Allen County Community College *A*
Kansas State University *B, M, D*
University of Kansas *B, M, D*
Wichita State University *B, M, D*

Kentucky

Murray State University *B*
Paducah Technical College *A*

Spencerian College: Lexington *A*
University of Kentucky *B, M, D*
University of Louisville *B, M, D*
Western Kentucky University *B*

Louisiana

Louisiana State University and
    Agricultural and Mechanical
    College *B, M, D*
Louisiana Tech University *B*
Southern University and Agricultural
    and Mechanical College *B*
University of Louisiana at Lafayette *B*
University of New Orleans *B*

Maine

Kennebec Valley Community
    College *A*
Southern Maine Community
    College *A*
University of Maine *B, M*
University of Southern Maine *B*

Maryland

Capitol College *A, B*
Johns Hopkins University *B, M, D*
Loyola College in Maryland *B*
Morgan State University *B*
United States Naval Academy *B*
University of Maryland
    Baltimore County *M, D*
    College Park *B, M, D*

Massachusetts

Boston University *B, M, D*
Eastern Nazarene College *B*
Fitchburg State College *B*
Franklin W. Olin College of
    Engineering *B*
Massachusetts Institute of
    Technology *B, M, D*
Merrimack College *B*
Northeastern University *B, M, D*
Smith College *B*
Suffolk University *B*
Tufts University *B, M, D*
University of Massachusetts
    Amherst *B*
    Dartmouth *B, M, D*
    Lowell *B, M, D*
Wentworth Institute of Technology *B*
Western New England College *B, M*
Worcester Polytechnic
    Institute *B, M, D*

Michigan

Andrews University *B*
Baker College
    of Muskegon *A*
Calvin College *B*
Central Michigan University *B*
Grand Valley State University *B*
Kettering University *B*
Lake Superior State University *B*
Lawrence Technological University *B*
Michigan State University *B, M, D*
Michigan Technological
    University *B, M, D, T*
Monroe County Community
    College *A*
Oakland University *B, M*
Saginaw Valley State University *B*
University of Detroit Mercy *B, M, D*
University of Michigan *B, M, D*
University of Michigan
    Dearborn *B, M*
Wayne State University *B, M, D*
Western Michigan University *B, M*

Minnesota

Minnesota State University
    Mankato *B, M*

Northland Community & Technical
    College *A*
St. Cloud State University *B, M*
South Central College *A*
University of Minnesota
    Duluth *B*
    Twin Cities *B, M, D*
University of St. Thomas *B*

Mississippi

Holmes Community College *A*
Itawamba Community College *A*
Jackson State University *B*
Mississippi State University *B, M, D*
University of Mississippi *B*

Missouri

East Central College *A*
Grantham University *A, B*
Missouri Technical School *A, B*
Ozarks Technical Community
    College *A*
St. Louis University *B*
University of Missouri
    Columbia *B, M, D*
    Kansas City *B, M*
    Rolla *B, M, D*
    St. Louis *B*
Washington University in St.
    Louis *B, M, D*

Montana

Montana State University
    Bozeman *B, M*
Montana Tech of the University of
    Montana *B*
Salish Kootenai College *A*

Nebraska

University of Nebraska
    Lincoln *B, M*
    Omaha *B*

Nevada

Community College of Southern
    Nevada *A*
University of Nevada
    Las Vegas *B, M, D*
    Reno *B, M, D*

New Hampshire

New Hampshire Community
    Technical College
    Nashua *A*
University of New Hampshire *B, M, D*

New Jersey

The College of New Jersey *B*
Essex County College *A*
Fairleigh Dickinson University
    Metropolitan Campus *B, M*
New Jersey Institute of
    Technology *B, M, D*
Princeton University *B, M, D*
Rowan University *B*
Rutgers, The State University of New
    Jersey
    Camden Regional Campus *B*
    New Brunswick/Piscataway
        Campus *B, M, D*
    Newark Regional Campus *B*
Stevens Institute of
    Technology *B, M, D*

New Mexico

Clovis Community College *A*
Dona Ana Branch Community College
    of New Mexico State
    University *A*
Luna Community College *A*
New Mexico Institute of Mining and
    Technology *B, M*

New Mexico State University *B, M*
University of New Mexico *B, M*

New York

Alfred University *B, M*
Bramson ORT College *A*
City University of New York
    City College *B, M, D*
    LaGuardia Community College *A*
Clarkson University *B, M, D*
Columbia University
    Fu Foundation School of
        Engineering and Applied
        Science *B, M, D*
Cooper Union for the Advancement of
    Science and Art *B, M*
Cornell University *B, M, D*
Dutchess Community College *A*
Finger Lakes Community College *A*
Hofstra University *B*
Island Drafting and Technical
    Institute *A*
Manhattan College *B, M*
New York Institute of
    Technology *B, M*
Onondaga Community College *A*
Polytechnic University *B, M, D*
Rensselaer Polytechnic
    Institute *B, M, D*
Rochester Institute of
    Technology *B, M*
State University of New York
    Binghamton *B, M, D*
    Buffalo *B, M, D*
    College of Agriculture and
        Technology at Morrisville *A*
    College of Technology at
        Alfred *A, B*
    Maritime College *B*
    New Paltz *B, M*
    Stony Brook *B, M, D*
Suffolk County Community College *A*
Syracuse University *B, M, D*
Union College *B*
United States Military Academy *B*
University of Rochester *B, M, D*

North Carolina

Alamance Community College *A*
Blue Ridge Community College *A*
Duke University *B, M, D*
Durham Technical Community
    College *A*
Mayland Community College *A*
Mitchell Community College *A*
Nash Community College *A*
North Carolina Agricultural and
    Technical State
    University *B, M, D*
North Carolina State
    University *B, M, D*
Pamlico Community College *A*
Richmond Community College *A*
Rockingham Community College *A*
Southwestern Community College *A*
Surry Community College *A*
University of North Carolina
    Charlotte *B, M, D*
Vance-Granville Community
    College *A*
Western Carolina University *B*
Western Piedmont Community
    College *A*

North Dakota

Lake Region State College *A*
North Dakota State University *B, M, D*
University of North Dakota *B, M*

Ohio

AEC Southern Ohio College
    Brown Mackie College: Akron *A*
Belmont Technical College *A*

Bowling Green State University:
    Firelands College *A*
Case Western Reserve
    University *B, M, D*
Cedarville University *B*
Cleveland State University *B, M, D*
Edison State Community College *A*
Miami University
    Oxford Campus *B*
Ohio Northern University *B*
Ohio State University
    Columbus Campus *B, M, D*
Ohio University *B, M, D*
Stark State College of Technology *A*
University of Akron *B, M*
University of Cincinnati *B, M, D*
University of Dayton *B, M, D*
University of Toledo *B, M*
Washington State Community
    College *A*
Wright State University *B, M*
Youngstown State University *B, M*

Oklahoma

Oklahoma Christian University *B*
Oklahoma State University *B, M, D*
Oklahoma State University
    Oklahoma City *A*
    Okmulgee *A*
Oral Roberts University *B*
University of Oklahoma *B, M, D*
University of Tulsa *B, M*

Oregon

Chemeketa Community College *A*
George Fox University *B*
Oregon State University *B*
Portland State University *B, M, D*
University of Portland *B, M*

Pennsylvania

Bloomsburg University of
    Pennsylvania *B*
Bucknell University *B, M*
Drexel University *B, M, D*
Elizabethtown College *B*
Gannon University *B, M*
Gettysburg College *B*
Grove City College *B*
Lafayette College *B*
Lehigh University *B, M, D*
Penn State
    Abington *B*
    Altoona *B*
    Berks *B*
    Delaware County *B*
    Dubois *B*
    Erie, The Behrend College *B*
    Harrisburg *B*
    McKeesport *B*
    Mont Alto *B*
    New Kensington *B*
    Schuylkill - Capital College *B*
    Shenango *B*
    University Park *B, M, D*
    Wilkes-Barre *B*
    Worthington Scranton *B*
    York *B*
Pennco Tech *A*
Pittsburgh Institute of Aeronautics *A*
Reading Area Community College *A*
Temple University *B, M*
University of Pennsylvania *B, M, D*
University of Pittsburgh *B, M, D*
University of Scranton *A, B*
Villanova University *B, M*
Widener University *B, M*
Wilkes University *B, M*
York College of Pennsylvania *B*

Puerto Rico

Columbia College *A*

Inter American University of Puerto Rico
Bayamon Campus *B*
Turabo University *B*
Universidad Politecnica de Puerto Rico *B*
University of Puerto Rico
Bayamon University College *A*
Mayaguez *B, M*

Rhode Island

Brown University *B, M, D*
University of Rhode Island *B, M, D*

South Carolina

Aiken Technical College *A*
The Citadel *B*
Clemson University *B, M, D*
Horry-Georgetown Technical College *A*
Technical College of the Lowcountry *A*
University of South Carolina *B, M, D*
Williamsburg Technical College *A*

South Dakota

South Dakota School of Mines and Technology *B, M*
South Dakota State University *B*

Tennessee

Christian Brothers University *B*
Tennessee State University *B*
Tennessee Technological University *B, M, D*
Union University *B*
University of Memphis *B, M*
University of Tennessee
Knoxville *B, M, D*
Vanderbilt University *B, M, D*

Texas

Baylor University *B, M*
Del Mar College *A*
Eastfield College *A*
Lamar University *B, M*
Laredo Community College *A*
LeTourneau University *B*
Prairie View A&M University *B, M, D*
Remington College
Houston *A*
Rice University *B, M, D*
St. Mary's University *B, M*
Southern Methodist University *B, M, D*
Texas A&M University *B, M, D*
Texas A&M University
Kingsville *B, M*
Texas Tech University *B, M, D*
University of Houston *B, M, D*
University of Texas
Arlington *B, M, D*
Austin *B, M, D*
Dallas *B, M, D*
El Paso *B, M*
Pan American *B, M*
San Antonio *B, M, D*
Tyler *B*

Utah

Brigham Young University *B, M, D*
Salt Lake Community College *A*
University of Utah *B, M, D*
Utah State University *B, M, D*

Vermont

Norwich University *B*
University of Vermont *B, M, D*
Vermont Technical College *A*

Virginia

ECPI College of Technology *A*
Eastern Shore Community College *A*
George Mason University *B, M, D*
Hampton University *B*
John Tyler Community College *A*
Mountain Empire Community College *A*
Norfolk State University *B*
Old Dominion University *B, M, D*
Southwest Virginia Community College *A*
Thomas Nelson Community College *A*
University of Virginia *B, M, D*
Virginia Commonwealth University *B*
Virginia Military Institute *B*
Virginia Polytechnic Institute and State University *B, M, D*

Washington

Gonzaga University *B*
Henry Cogswell College *B*
Renton Technical College *A*
Seattle Pacific University *B*
Seattle University *B*
Skagit Valley College *A*
University of Washington *B, M, D*
Walla Walla College *B*
Washington State University *B, M, D*

West Virginia

Potomac State College of West Virginia University *A*
West Virginia University *B, M, D*
West Virginia University Institute of Technology *B*

Wisconsin

Blackhawk Technical College *A*
Marquette University *B, M, D*
Milwaukee School of Engineering *B*
University of Wisconsin
Madison *B, M, D*
Milwaukee *B*
Platteville *B*

Wyoming

University of Wyoming *B, M, D*
Western Wyoming Community College *A*

Electrical drafting/CAD/CADD

Florida

Chipola College *C*
Miami Dade College *C, A*
Palm Beach Community College *C*

Georgia

Northwestern Technical College *C*

Illinois

Kaskaskia College *C*
Oakton Community College *C, A*

Minnesota

Dunwoody College of Technology *A*

New Mexico

Albuquerque Technical-Vocational Institute *A*

New York

Cayuga County Community College *C, A*

Ohio

Lakeland Community College *C, A*

Oklahoma

Platt College
Tulsa *C*

Texas

Collin County Community College District *C, A*

Electrical engineering technology

Alabama

Alabama Southern Community College *A*
Central Alabama Community College *A*
Community College of the Air Force *A*
Faulkner State Community College *C*
Gadsden State Community College *C, A*
Jacksonville State University *B*
Lawson State Community College *C, A*
Northeast Alabama Community College *C, A*
Northwest-Shoals Community College *A*
Troy University *B*

Alaska

Prince William Sound Community College *C, A*
University of Alaska
Anchorage *C, A, B*

Arizona

Central Arizona College *C, A*
Cochise College *A*
DeVry University
Phoenix *A, B*
Glendale Community College *C, A*
Northland Pioneer College *C, A*
Pima Community College *C, A*

Arkansas

Arkansas State University *A*
Arkansas State University
Beebe *A*
Mountain Home *C*
Arkansas Tech University *C, A*
East Arkansas Community College *C*
National Park Community College *A*
North Arkansas College *C, A*
Northwest Arkansas Community College *A*
Phillips Community College of the University of Arkansas *C*
Southern Arkansas University Tech *C*
University of Arkansas
Little Rock *A, B*

California

Allan Hancock College *C, A*
Barstow College *C*
Butte College *C, A*
California Polytechnic State University: San Luis Obispo *B*
California State Polytechnic University: Pomona *B*
California State University
Fresno *B*
Long Beach *B*
Cerritos Community College *C, A*
Cerro Coso Community College *C, A*
Chabot College *A*
City College of San Francisco *C, A*
College of San Mateo *C, A*
College of the Redwoods *C*
College of the Sequoias *C, A*
Cuyamaca College *A*

DeVry University
Fremont *A, B*
Long Beach *A, B*
Pomona *A, B*
West Hills *A, B*
Diablo Valley College *C*
Evergreen Valley College *C*
Foothill College *C, A*
Fullerton College *C, A*
Irvine Valley College *C, A*
Los Angeles City College *C, A*
Los Angeles Harbor College *C, A*
Los Angeles Southwest College *C, A*
Los Angeles Trade and Technical College *C, A*
Los Angeles Valley College *C, A*
Merced College *C, A*
Moorpark College *C, A*
Mount San Antonio College *C, A*
Napa Valley College *C, A*
Ohlone College *A*
Orange Coast College *C, A*
Riverside Community College *C, A*
Saddleback College *C*
San Bernardino Valley College *C, A*
San Diego City College *C, A*
San Joaquin Delta College *C, A*
San Joaquin Valley College Inc. *A*
San Jose City College *C, A*
Santa Barbara City College *C, A*
Santa Monica College *C, A*
Santa Rosa Junior College *C, A*
Shasta College *A*
Solano Community College *C, A*
Taft College *A*
Ventura College *A*
West Valley College *C, A*
Yuba Community College District *C, A*

Colorado

Aims Community College *A*
Arapahoe Community College *C, A*
Colorado State University
Pueblo *A*
Colorado Technical University *A, B*
Community College of Aurora *A*
Community College of Denver *C, A*
DeVry University
Westminster *A, B*
DeVry University: Colorado Springs *A*
Front Range Community College *C, A*
Mesa State College *C, A*
Metropolitan State College of Denver *A*
Pikes Peak Community College *C, A*
Pueblo Community College *C, A*
Red Rocks Community College *C, A*
Westwood College of Technology *A, B*

Connecticut

Gateway Community College *A*
Naugatuck Valley Community College *A*
Northwestern Connecticut Community College *C*
Three Rivers Community College *A*
University of Hartford *A, B*

Delaware

Delaware State University *B*
Delaware Technical and Community College
Owens Campus *A*
Stanton/Wilmington Campus *C, A*
Terry Campus *A*

District of Columbia

University of the District of Columbia *A*

Florida

Brevard Community College *C, A*
Daytona Beach Community College *A*
DeVry University
  Miramar *A, B*
  Orlando *A, B*
Embry-Riddle Aeronautical
  University *B*
Florida Agricultural and Mechanical
  University *B*
Florida Community College at
  Jacksonville *A*
Gulf Coast Community College *A*
Hillsborough Community College *A*
Indian River Community College *A*
Manatee Community College *A*
Miami Dade College *C, A*
Okaloosa-Walton College *C, A*
Palm Beach Community College *A*
Pensacola Junior College *A*
Polk Community College *A*
Remington College: Tampa *A, B*
St. Johns River Community College *A*
St. Petersburg College *C, A*
Santa Fe Community College *A*
Seminole Community College *A*
South Florida Community
  College *C, A*
University of Central Florida *B*
Valencia Community College *A*

Georgia

Augusta Technical Institute *C, A*
Bainbridge College *C, A*
Chattahoochee Technical College *A*
Columbus Technical College *A*
DeKalb Technical College *C, A*
DeVry University
  Alpharetta *A, B*
  Decatur *A, B*
Fort Valley State University *A, B*
Gainesville State College *C, A*
Georgia Military College *A*
Georgia Southern University *B*
Griffin Technical College *A*
Macon State College *A*
Northwestern Technical College *C, A*
Savannah State University *B*
Savannah Technical College *A*
Southern Polytechnic State
  University *B*

Hawaii

Heald College
  Honolulu *A*
University of Hawaii
  Hawaii Community College *A*
  Honolulu Community College *C, A*
  Kauai Community College *C, A*

Idaho

Brigham Young University-Idaho *A*
Eastern Idaho Technical College *C, A*
Idaho State University *C*

Illinois

Bradley University *B*
College of DuPage *C, A*
College of Lake County *C, A*
DeVry University
  Addison *A, B*
  Chicago *A, B*
  Tinley Park *A, B*
East-West University *A, B*
Elgin Community College *C, A*
Heartland Community College *C, A*
Highland Community College *A*
Illinois Eastern Community Colleges
  Wabash Valley College *A*
John A. Logan College *C*
Joliet Junior College *C, A*
Kaskaskia College *C, A*
Kishwaukee College *C, A*

Lincoln Land Community College *C, A*
McHenry County College *C, A*
Moraine Valley Community College *C*
Oakton Community College *C, A*
Parkland College *C*
Prairie State College *C, A*
Rend Lake College *C*
Rock Valley College *C, A*
Roosevelt University *B*
South Suburban College of Cook
  County *C, A*
Spoon River College *C*
Waubonsee Community College *C, A*
William Rainey Harper College *C, A*

Indiana

Indiana State University *A, B, M*
Indiana University-Purdue University
  Fort Wayne *C, A, B*
Indiana University-Purdue University
  Indianapolis *A, B*
Ivy Tech State College
  Ivy Tech Community College:
    Bloomington *A*
  Ivy Tech Community College:
    Central Indiana *A*
  Ivy Tech Community College:
    Columbus *A*
  Ivy Tech Community College: East
    Central *A*
  Ivy Tech Community College:
    Lafayette *A*
  Ivy Tech Community College: North
    Central *A*
  Ivy Tech Community College:
    Northwest *A*
  Ivy Tech Community College: South
    Central *A*
  Ivy Tech Community College:
    Southeast *A*
  Ivy Tech Community College:
    Southwest *A*
  Ivy Tech Community College:
    Wabash Valley *A*
  Ivy Tech Community College:
    Whitewater *A*
Oakland City University *A*
Purdue University *A, B*
Purdue University
  Calumet *C, A, B*
  North Central Campus *A*
Vincennes University *A*

Iowa

Clinton Community College *A*
Des Moines Area Community
  College *C, A*
Hamilton Technical College *A, B*
Hawkeye Community College *C, A*
Indian Hills Community College *A*
Iowa Western Community College *A*
Kirkwood Community College *C, A*
North Iowa Area Community
  College *A*
Northeast Iowa Community
  College *A*
Northwest Iowa Community
  College *A*
Southeastern Community College
  North Campus *A*
Southwestern Community College *A*
Western Iowa Tech Community
  College *A*

Kansas

Allen County Community College *C*
Johnson County Community
  College *A*
North Central Kansas Technical
  College *A*
Pittsburg State University *B*
Washburn University of Topeka *A*

Kentucky

Bluegrass Community and Technical
  College *A*
Brown Mackie College: Louisville *A*
Henderson Community College *A*
Hopkinsville Community College *C*
Kentucky State University *A*
Louisville Technical Institute *A*
Madisonville Community College *A*
Maysville Community College *C, A*
Northern Kentucky University *B*
Owensboro Community College *A*
Paducah Technical College *A*
Spencerian College: Lexington *C, A*

Louisiana

Delgado Community College *A*
Grambling State University *B*
ITI Technical College *C, A*
Louisiana Tech University *B*
Northwestern State University *A, B*
Remington College
  Lafayette *A*
  New Orleans *A*
Southern University
  Shreveport *A*
Southern University and Agricultural
  and Mechanical College *B*

Maine

Eastern Maine Community College *A*
Kennebec Valley Community
  College *C, A*
Northern Maine Community
  College *A*
Southern Maine Community
  College *A*
University of Maine *B*
University of Southern Maine *B*

Maryland

Anne Arundel Community
  College *C, A*
Baltimore City Community
  College *C, A*
Capitol College *A, B*
Cecil Community College *C, A*
Chesapeake College *C*
College of Southern Maryland *C, A*
Community College of Baltimore
  County *C, A*
Harford Community College *C, A*
Howard Community College *C, A*
Montgomery College *A*
Prince George's Community
  College *C, A*
TESST College of Technology
  Baltimore *C, A*
TESST College of Technology:
  Towson *A*
Wor-Wic Community College *C, A*

Massachusetts

Benjamin Franklin Institute of
  Technology *C, A*
Berkshire Community College *A*
Bristol Community College *A*
Fitchburg State College *B*
Massachusetts Bay Community
  College *C, A*
Massasoit Community College *C, A*
Northeastern University *B*
Northern Essex Community
  College *C, A*
Quinsigamond Community College *A*
Springfield Technical Community
  College *C, A*
University of Massachusetts
  Lowell *A, B*
Wentworth Institute of
  Technology *A, B*

Michigan

Andrews University *B*
Baker College
  of Flint *A, B*
  of Muskegon *A*
  of Owosso *A*
  of Port Huron *C*
Bay de Noc Community College *C, A*
Central Michigan University *B*
Davenport University *A*
Delta College *C, A*
Eastern Michigan University *B*
Ferris State University *B*
Glen Oaks Community College *C*
Grand Rapids Community College *A*
Henry Ford Community College *A*
Jackson Community College *C, A*
Kalamazoo Valley Community
  College *C, A*
Kellogg Community College *C, A*
Kirtland Community College *C, A*
Lake Michigan College *A*
Lake Superior State University *A, B*
Lansing Community College *A*
Lawrence Technological University *A*
Macomb Community College *C, A*
Michigan Technological
  University *A, B*
Monroe County Community
  College *A*
Montcalm Community College *C, A*
Mott Community College *A*
Muskegon Community College *C, A*
Northern Michigan University *A, B*
Northwestern Michigan College *C, A*
Oakland Community College *C, A*
St. Clair County Community
  College *C, A*
Schoolcraft College *A*
Southwestern Michigan College *C, A*
Washtenaw Community College *A*
Wayne County Community College *A*
Wayne State University *B*
West Shore Community College *A*

Minnesota

Anoka Technical College *C, A*
Anoka-Ramsey Community College *A*
Dunwoody College of Technology *A*
Hennepin Technical College *C, A*
Lake Superior College *C, A*
Minnesota State College - Southeast
  Technical *C, A*
Minnesota State Community and
  Technical College - Fergus
  Falls *C, A*
Minnesota State University
  Mankato *B*
North Hennepin Community
  College *A*
Ridgewater College *C, A*
Riverland Community College *A*
Rochester Community and Technical
  College *C, A*
St. Cloud State University *B*
St. Cloud Technical College *C, A*
St. Paul College *C, A*
South Central College *A*

Mississippi

Coahoma Community College *A*
Copiah-Lincoln Community
  College *C, A*
East Central Community College *A*
Hinds Community College *A*
Itawamba Community College *A*
Mississippi Delta Community
  College *A*
Mississippi Gulf Coast Community
  College
  Jefferson Davis Campus *T*
Pearl River Community College *C, A*
University of Southern Mississippi *B*

Missouri

Central Missouri State University *A, B*
Crowder College *C, A*
DeVry University
   Kansas City *A, B*
Grantham University *A, B*
Jefferson College *C, A*
Mineral Area College *C, A*
Missouri State University *B*
Missouri Technical School *C, A, B*
Missouri Western State
   University *A, B*
Moberly Area Community
   College *C, A*
North Central Missouri College *A*
Ozarks Technical Community
   College *C, A*
Ranken Technical College *A*
St. Louis Community College
   St. Louis Community College at
     Florissant Valley *A*
   St. Louis Community College at
     Meramec *A*
Southeast Missouri State University *C*
State Fair Community College *A*

Montana

University of Montana: Missoula *A*

Nebraska

Central Community College *C, A*
Metropolitan Community
   College *C, A*
Mid-Plains Community College
   Area *C, A*
Northeast Community College *A*
Southeast Community College
   Lincoln Campus *A*
University of Nebraska
   Lincoln *B*
Western Nebraska Community
   College *C, A*

Nevada

Community College of Southern
   Nevada *A*
Great Basin College *C*
Western Nevada Community
   College *C, A*

New Hampshire

Keene State College *A, B*
New Hampshire Community
   Technical College
   Manchester *A*
   Nashua *A*
New Hampshire Technical
   Institute *C, A*
University of New Hampshire at
   Manchester *B*

New Jersey

Bergen Community College *A*
Brookdale Community College *C, A*
Burlington County College *A*
Camden County College *A*
County College of Morris *A*
Cumberland County College *C, A*
DeVry University: North
   Brunswick *A, B*
Essex County College *A*
Fairleigh Dickinson University
   Metropolitan Campus *B*
Hudson County Community
   College *C, A*
Kean University *B*
Mercer County Community
   College *C, A*
Middlesex County College *A*
Passaic County Community College *A*
Thomas Edison State College *C, A, B*

New Mexico

Albuquerque Technical-Vocational
   Institute *C, A*
Dona Ana Branch Community College
   of New Mexico State
   University *C, A*
New Mexico State University
   Alamogordo *A*
   Carlsbad *A*
   Grants *A*
Northern New Mexico College *A*
San Juan College *A*
Santa Fe Community College *C*
Southwestern Indian Polytechnic
   Institute *C, A*

New York

Adirondack Community College *A*
Briarcliffe College *A*
Broome Community College *A*
Bryant & Stratton Business Institute
Bryant & Stratton College:
   Buffalo *C, A*
Cayuga County Community
   College *C, A*
City University of New York
   Bronx Community College *A*
   Hostos Community College *A*
   New York City College of
     Technology *A*
   Queensborough Community
     College *A*
Corning Community College *A*
DeVry Institute of Technology
   New York *A, B*
Dutchess Community College *A*
Erie Community College
   North Campus *A*
Excelsior College *A*
Fulton-Montgomery Community
   College *C, A*
Genesee Community College *A*
Hudson Valley Community College *A*
Island Drafting and Technical
   Institute *C, A*
Jamestown Community College *A*
Mohawk Valley Community College *A*
Monroe Community College *C, A*
Nassau Community College *A*
New York Institute of
   Technology *C, A, B*
Niagara County Community
   College *A*
Onondaga Community College *A*
Orange County Community College *A*
Rochester Institute of
   Technology *A, B, M*
Rockland Community College *A*
State University of New York
   College at Buffalo *B*
   College of Agriculture and
     Technology at Morrisville *A*
   College of Technology at
     Alfred *A, B*
   College of Technology at Canton *A*
   Farmingdale *B*
   Institute of Technology at
     Utica/Rome *B*
Suffolk County Community College *A*
Technical Career Institutes *A*
Tompkins-Cortland Community
   College *A*
Vaughn College of Aeronautics and
   Technology *A, B*
Westchester Community College *A*

North Carolina

Appalachian State University *B*
Asheville-Buncombe Technical
   Community College *A*
Beaufort County Community
   College *C, A*
Bladen Community College *C, A*
Blue Ridge Community College *C, A*

Brunswick Community College *A*
Caldwell Community College and
   Technical Institute *A*
Cape Fear Community College *C, A*
Catawba Valley Community College *A*
Central Carolina Community
   College *A*
Central Piedmont Community
   College *C, A*
Cleveland Community College *C, A*
College of the Albemarle *C, A*
Craven Community College *C, A*
Davidson County Community
   College *C, A*
Durham Technical Community
   College *C, A*
Edgecombe Community College *C, A*
Fayetteville Technical Community
   College *A*
Forsyth Technical Community
   College *A*
Gaston College *C, A*
Guilford Technical Community
   College *C, A*
Halifax Community College *A*
Haywood Community College *A*
Isothermal Community College *A*
James Sprunt Community College *C*
Lenoir Community College *A*
Mitchell Community College *C, A*
Nash Community College *A*
Pamlico Community College *A*
Pitt Community College *C, A*
Randolph Community College *A*
Richmond Community College *A*
Robeson Community College *A*
Rowan-Cabarrus Community
   College *A*
South Piedmont Community
   College *A*
Southeastern Community College *A*
Southwestern Community College *A*
Stanly Community College *C, A*
Surry Community College *C*
University of North Carolina
   Charlotte *B*
Vance-Granville Community
   College *C, A*
Wake Technical Community
   College *C, A*
Western Carolina University *B*
Wilkes Community College *C, A*
Wilson Technical Community
   College *C, A*

North Dakota

Bismarck State College *C, A*
North Dakota State College of
   Science *A*

Ohio

Bowling Green State University *B*
Bowling Green State University:
   Firelands College *A*
Bryant & Stratton College:
   Cleveland *A, B*
Central Ohio Technical College *A*
Cincinnati State Technical and
   Community College *A*
Clark State Community College *C*
Cleveland Institute of Electronics *C, A*
Cleveland State University *B*
Columbus State Community
   College *A*
Cuyahoga Community College
   Metropolitan Campus *A*
DeVry University
   Columbus *A*
ETI Technical College of Niles *C, A*
Edison State Community College *C, A*
Hocking College *A*
James A. Rhodes State College *A*
Jefferson Community College *C, A*

Kent State University
   Ashtabula Regional Campus *A*
   Trumbull Campus *A*
Lakeland Community College *C, A*
Marion Technical College *A*
Miami University
   Hamilton Campus *A*
   Oxford Campus *A*
Owens Community College
   Toledo *C, A*
Shawnee State University *A, B*
Sinclair Community College *A*
Southern State Community College *A*
Stark State College of Technology *A*
University of Akron *C, A, B*
University of Dayton *B*
University of Toledo *A*
Washington State Community
   College *A*
Wright State University *A*
Youngstown State University *A, B*
Zane State College *A*

Oklahoma

Cameron University *A, B*
Oklahoma City Community College *A*
Oklahoma State University *B*
Oklahoma State University
   Oklahoma City *C*
   Okmulgee *A*
Rogers State University *A*
Rose State College *A*
Southeastern Oklahoma State
   University *B*
Tulsa Community College *C, A*

Oregon

Blue Mountain Community College *A*
Central Oregon Community
   College *C*
Chemeketa Community College *A*
Clackamas Community College *C, A*
Lane Community College *A*
Linn-Benton Community College *A*
Oregon Institute of Technology *A, B*
Portland Community College *A*
Rogue Community College *C, A*

Pennsylvania

Berean Institute *A*
Butler County Community College *A*
CHI Institute: Broomall *A*
CHI Institute: Southampton *C, A*
California University of
   Pennsylvania *A, B*
Community College of Allegheny
   County *A*
Community College of
   Philadelphia *C, A*
DeVry University
   Ft. Washington *A*
Delaware County Community
   College *C, A*
Harrisburg Area Community
   College *C, A*
Lehigh Carbon Community
   College *C, A*
Lincoln Technical Institute *A*
Lock Haven University of
   Pennsylvania *A*
Luzerne County Community
   College *C, A*
New Castle School of Trades *A*
Northampton County Area
   Community College *A*
Penn State
   Altoona *A*
   Beaver *A*
   Berks *A*
   Dubois *A*
   Erie, The Behrend College *A, B*
   Fayette *A*
   Harrisburg *B*
   Hazleton *A*

New Kensington *A*
Schuylkill - Capital College *A*
University Park *C, B*
Wilkes-Barre *A*
York *A, B*
Pennsylvania College of Technology *A*
Pennsylvania Institute of
Technology *A*
Pittsburgh Institute of Aeronautics *A*
Pittsburgh Technical Institute *A*
Reading Area Community College *A*
University of Pittsburgh
Johnstown *B*
Westmoreland County Community
College *A*
York Technical Institute *C*

Puerto Rico

Humacao Community College *C, A*
Inter American University of Puerto
Rico
Aguadilla Campus *B*
Bayamon Campus *B*
San German Campus *B*
National College of Business &
Technology: Arecibo *A*
National College of Business &
Technology: Bayamon *A*
Turabo University *B*
Universidad del Este *A*
University College of San Juan *A*
University of Puerto Rico
Aguadilla *A, B*
Bayamon University College *A*
Humacao *A*

Rhode Island

Community College of Rhode
Island *A*
New England Institute of
Technology *A*

South Carolina

Aiken Technical College *C, A*
Benedict College *B*
Florence-Darlington Technical
College *A*
Greenville Technical College *A*
Horry-Georgetown Technical
College *A*
Midlands Technical College *C, A*
Northeastern Technical College *C, A*
Orangeburg-Calhoun Technical
College *A*
Piedmont Technical College *A*
South Carolina State University *B*
Spartanburg Technical College *A*
Technical College of the
Lowcountry *C*
Tri-County Technical College *A*
Trident Technical College *A*
York Technical College *A*

South Dakota

South Dakota State University *B*
Southeast Technical Institute *A*

Tennessee

Columbia State Community College *A*
Dyersburg State Community
College *C, A*
Nashville State Community College *A*
Northeast State Technical Community
College *C, A*
Pellissippi State Technical Community
College *A*
Southwest Tennessee Community
College *A*
University of Memphis *B*

Texas

Alvin Community College *C, A*
Amarillo College *C, A*

Angelina College *C, A*
Austin Community College *C, A*
Brazosport College *C, A*
Brookhaven College *C, A*
College of the Mainland *A*
Collin County Community College
District *C, A*
DeVry University
Irving *A, B*
Del Mar College *A*
Eastfield College *C, A*
El Paso Community College *C, A*
Grayson County College *C, A*
Hallmark Institute of Technology *A*
Hill College *C, A*
Houston Community College
System *A*
Kilgore College *C, A*
Lamar State College at Port
Arthur *C, A*
LeTourneau University *B*
Lee College *A*
Midland College *C, A*
Mountain View College *A*
North Central Texas College *A*
North Harris Montgomery
Community College District *C, A*
North Lake College *A*
Paris Junior College *A*
Prairie View A&M University *B*
Remington College
Fort Worth *A*
Richland College *A*
St. Philip's College *A*
Sam Houston State University *B*
San Antonio College *C, A*
San Jacinto College
Central Campus *C*
North *C, A*
Tarrant County College *C, A*
Texarkana College *C, A*
Texas A&M University *B*
Texas Southern University *B*
Texas Southmost College *C, A*
Texas State Technical College
Harlingen *A*
Waco *C, A*
West Texas *C, A*
Texas Tech University *B*
Tyler Junior College *A*
University of Houston *B, M*
University of North Texas *B*
University of Texas
Brownsville *C, A, B*
Victoria College *C, A*
Weatherford College *C, A*
Wharton County Junior College *A*

Utah

Salt Lake Community College *C*
Utah State University *B*
Utah Valley State College *C, A*
Weber State University *A, B*

Vermont

Vermont Technical College *A*

Virginia

Blue Ridge Community College *A*
Central Virginia Community
College *A*
Dabney S. Lancaster Community
College *C, A*
Danville Community College *C*
DeVry University
Arlington *A, B*
ECPI College of Technology *C, A*
J. Sargeant Reynolds Community
College *C, A*
John Tyler Community College *A*
Lord Fairfax Community College *A*
Mountain Empire Community
College *A*
New River Community College *A*

Norfolk State University *B*
Northern Virginia Community
College *C, A*
Old Dominion University *B*
Paul D. Camp Community College *A*
Piedmont Virginia Community
College *A*
Rappahannock Community
College *C, A*
Southside Virginia Community
College *C, A*
Thomas Nelson Community
College *A*
Virginia Highlands Community
College *A*
Virginia State University *B*
Virginia Western Community
College *C, A*
World College *B*
Wytheville Community College *A*

Washington

Bellingham Technical College *A*
Central Washington University *B*
Centralia College *C, A*
Clark College *C, A*
Columbia Basin College *A*
DeVry University
Federal Way *A, B*
Eastern Washington University *B*
Edmonds Community College *C, A*
Green River Community College *A*
Lake Washington Technical
College *C, A*
Lower Columbia College *A*
North Seattle Community
College *C, A*
Olympic College *C, A*
Pierce College *C, A*
Renton Technical College *C, A*
Skagit Valley College *A*
South Puget Sound Community
College *C, A*
Spokane Community College *C, A*
Spokane Falls Community
College *C, A*
Western Washington University *B*

West Virginia

Bluefield State College *A, B*
Corinthian Schools: National Institute
of Technology *A*
Potomac State College of West Virginia
University *A*
Southern West Virginia Community
and Technical College *A*
West Virginia University Institute of
Technology *A, B*

Wisconsin

Chippewa Valley Technical College *A*
Fox Valley Technical College *A*
Gateway Technical College *A*
Herzing College *A, B*
Lakeshore Technical College *A*
Mid-State Technical College *A*
Milwaukee Area Technical College *A*
Milwaukee School of Engineering *B*
Moraine Park Technical College *C*
Northcentral Technical College *A*
Northeast Wisconsin Technical
College *A*
Southwest Wisconsin Technical
College *A*
Western Wisconsin Technical
College *A*

Wyoming

Casper College *A*

Electrician

Alabama

Bishop State Community College *C*
Calhoun Community College *A*
George C. Wallace State Community
College
George C. Wallace Community
College at Dothan *C, A*
J. F. Drake State Technical College *C*
Lawson State Community College *C*
Northwest-Shoals Community
College *C*
Shelton State Community
College *C, A*
Trenholm State Technical College *C, A*

Arizona

Gateway Community College *C, A*
Mohave Community College *C*
Refrigeration School *C*
Tohono O'odham Community
College *C, A*

Arkansas

University of Arkansas
Cossatot Community College of the
C

California

Allan Hancock College *C*
Foothill College *C*
Fresno City College *C, A*
Los Angeles Trade and Technical
College *C, A*
Modesto Junior College *C, A*
Santiago Canyon College *A*

Florida

Brevard Community College *C*
City College *A*
Florida Community College at
Jacksonville *C*
Gulf Coast Community College *C*
Indian River Community College *C*
Palm Beach Community College *C*
Seminole Community College *C*
South Florida Community College *C*

Georgia

Albany Technical College *C*
Athens Technical College *C*
Bainbridge College *C, A*
Central Georgia Technical College *C*
Chattahoochee Technical College *C*
Georgia Southwestern State
University *A*
Savannah Technical College *C, A*
Southwest Georgia Technical
College *C*
West Georgia Technical College *C*

Hawaii

University of Hawaii
Honolulu Community College *C, A*
Kauai Community College *C, A*

Idaho

Idaho State University *C*

Illinois

Black Hawk College *C*
College of Lake County *A*
Danville Area Community College *C*
Heartland Community College *A*
John Wood Community College *C, A*
Parkland College *C*
Prairie State College *C, A*
Rend Lake College *C*
Richland Community College *A*
Sauk Valley Community College *C*
Southwestern Illinois College *C, A*

Waubonsee Community College *C, A*

Indiana

Ivy Tech State College
   Ivy Tech Community College:
      Bloomington *C, A*
   Ivy Tech Community College:
      Central Indiana *C, A*
   Ivy Tech Community College:
      Columbus *C, A*
   Ivy Tech Community College: East
      Central *C, A*
   Ivy Tech Community College:
      Kokomo *C, A*
   Ivy Tech Community College:
      Lafayette *C, A*
   Ivy Tech Community College: North
      Central *C, A*
   Ivy Tech Community College:
      Northeast *C, A*
   Ivy Tech Community College:
      Northwest *C, A*
   Ivy Tech Community College: South
      Central *C, A*
   Ivy Tech Community College:
      Southwest *C, A*
   Ivy Tech Community College:
      Wabash Valley *C, A*
   Ivy Tech Community College:
      Whitewater *C, A*

Iowa

Des Moines Area Community
   College *C*
Iowa Central Community College *A*
Western Iowa Tech Community
   College *C*

Kansas

Coffeyville Community College *C*

Kentucky

Big Sandy Community and Technical
   College *C*
Elizabethtown Community and
   Technical College *C, A*
Hazard Community College *C*
Jefferson Community College *C*
Owensboro Community College *C*
Somerset Community College *C, A*

Louisiana

Nunez Community College *C*

Maine

Eastern Maine Community College *C*
Northern Maine Community
   College *C, A*
Washington County Community
   College *C*

Massachusetts

Benjamin Franklin Institute of
   Technology *C, A*

Michigan

Delta College *C, A*
Jackson Community College *C, A*
Kellogg Community College *C, A*
Macomb Community College *C*
Mott Community College *C*
Oakland Community College *A*

Minnesota

Anoka Technical College *C*
Dakota County Technical College *C, A*
Dunwoody College of
   Technology *C, A*
Hennepin Technical College *C, A*
Hibbing Community College *C*
Lake Superior College *C, A*
Leech Lake Tribal College *C*

Minneapolis Community and
   Technical College *C*
Minnesota State Community and
   Technical College - Fergus Falls *C*
Northland Community & Technical
   College *C*
Northwest Technical College *C*
Ridgewater College *C, A*
Riverland Community College *C*
St. Cloud Technical College *C, A*
St. Paul College *C*

Mississippi

Itawamba Community College *A*

Missouri

Vatterott College *A*

Nebraska

Central Community College *C, A*
Mid-Plains Community College
   Area *C, A*
Northeast Community College *A*

Nevada

Great Basin College *C, A*

New Hampshire

New Hampshire Community
   Technical College
   Berlin *A*

New Mexico

Albuquerque Technical-Vocational
   Institute *C*
Dona Ana Branch Community College
   of New Mexico State
   University *A*
Northern New Mexico College *C, A*

New York

State University of New York
   College of Technology at Canton *C*
   College of Technology at Delhi *C, A*

North Carolina

Beaufort County Community
   College *C, A*
Bladen Community College *C*
Blue Ridge Community College *C*
Cape Fear Community College *C, A*
Catawba Valley Community College *C*
Central Piedmont Community
   College *C, A*
Cleveland Community College *C*
Coastal Carolina Community
   College *C*
Davidson County Community
   College *C*
Fayetteville Technical Community
   College *A*
Guilford Technical Community
   College *C, A*
Haywood Community College *C, A*
Isothermal Community College *C, A*
Johnston Community College *C*
Martin Community College *C, A*
Montgomery Community College *C, A*
Pitt Community College *C, A*
Randolph Community College *C, A*
Rockingham Community College *C*
Southeastern Community College *C*
Southwestern Community College *C*
Stanly Community College *C*
Tri-County Community College *A*
Vance-Granville Community
   College *C*
Wilkes Community College *A*
Wilson Technical Community
   College *C*

North Dakota

North Dakota State College of
   Science *A*

Oklahoma

Oklahoma State University
   Okmulgee *A*

Oregon

Central Oregon Community
   College *C*
Chemeketa Community College *C*
Lane Community College *A*
Linn-Benton Community College *A*

Pennsylvania

CHI Institute: Southampton *C*
Community College of Allegheny
   County *A*
Delaware County Community
   College *C*
Harrisburg Area Community
   College *C, A*
Luzerne County Community
   College *A*
Northampton County Area
   Community College *A*
Pennsylvania College of
   Technology *C, A*
Thompson Institute
   Philadelphia *C*
Triangle Tech
   DuBois *C, A*
   Erie *A*
   Greensburg *C, A*
   Pittsburgh *A*

Puerto Rico

Inter American University of Puerto
   Rico
   San German Campus *C*

South Carolina

Aiken Technical College *C*
Greenville Technical College *C*
Technical College of the
   Lowcountry *C*
Trident Technical College *A*

South Dakota

Western Dakota Technical Institute *A*

Tennessee

Northeast State Technical Community
   College *C, A*

Texas

Brazosport College *C, A*
Houston Community College
   System *C*
Laredo Community College *C*
St. Philip's College *C, A*
South Plains College *C*
Texarkana College *C*
Texas State Technical College
   Waco *C*
Tyler Junior College *C, A*

Utah

Dixie State College of Utah *C*
Salt Lake Community College *A*
Southern Utah University *C*

Virginia

Central Virginia Community
   College *C*
J. Sargeant Reynolds Community
   College *C*
Paul D. Camp Community College *C*
Piedmont Virginia Community
   College *A*
Rappahannock Community College *C*

Southside Virginia Community
   College *C*
Thomas Nelson Community
   College *C*
Virginia Highlands Community
   College *C*
Wytheville Community College *A*

Washington

Bellingham Technical College *A*
Big Bend Community College *C, A*
Olympic College *A*
South Seattle Community
   College *C, A*

Wisconsin

Gateway Technical College *C*
Milwaukee Area Technical College *C*
Northeast Wisconsin Technical
   College *C*
Waukesha County Technical
   College *C*
Western Wisconsin Technical
   College *C*

Wyoming

Western Wyoming Community
   College *C*

Electrocardiograph technology

California

De Anza College *C*
East Los Angeles College *A*

Florida

Florida National College *C*

Massachusetts

Middlesex Community College *C*

Michigan

Baker College
   of Auburn Hills *A*
   of Muskegon *C*
   of Port Huron *C*
Monroe County Community
   College *C*

Minnesota

North Hennepin Community
   College *A*

Ohio

Columbus State Community
   College *C*
Lakeland Community College *C*
Sinclair Community College *C*
University of Toledo *C*

South Carolina

Tri-County Technical College *C*

Texas

Austin Community College *C*

Virginia

Southwest Virginia Community
   College *C*

Electroencephalograph technology

Arizona

Phoenix College *C*

California

Orange Coast College *C, A*

Colorado
Community College of Denver *A*

Illinois
Black Hawk College *A*
Parkland College *C*

Iowa
Kirkwood Community College *A*

Maryland
Harford Community College *A*

Minnesota
Rochester Community and Technical
College *A*

Pennsylvania
Community College of Allegheny
County *C*

Texas
Temple College *C*

Wisconsin
Milwaukee Area Technical College *A*
Western Wisconsin Technical
College *A*

Electrolysis

New Jersey
Union County College *C*

Electromechanical technology

Arizona
Refrigeration School *C*

Arkansas
John Brown University *A*
North Arkansas College *C, A*

California
Ohlone College *A*
University of California
Santa Cruz *B, M, D*

Idaho
Idaho State University *C, A*

Illinois
Black Hawk College *C, A*

Iowa
University of Northern Iowa *B*

Kentucky
Hopkinsville Community College *C*
Jefferson Community College *C*
Maysville Community College *C, A*
Murray State University *B*
Owensboro Community College *C*

Maryland
Hagerstown Community College *A*

Massachusetts
Bristol Community College *A*
Quinsigamond Community College *A*
Springfield Technical Community
College *A*
Wentworth Institute of Technology *A*

Michigan
Michigan Technological University *A*
Northern Michigan University *A*
Oakland Community College *A*

Wayne County Community College *A*
Wayne State University *B*

Nebraska
Northeast Community College *A*

New Jersey
Union County College *A*

New York
City University of New York
New York City College of
Technology *A, B*
Excelsior College *A*
Rochester Institute of Technology *B*
State University of New York
College at Buffalo *B*

North Carolina
Cape Fear Community College *C*
Catawba Valley Community College *A*
Guilford Technical Community
College *C*
Wilson Technical Community
College *C*

Ohio
Central Ohio Technical College *A*
Cincinnati State Technical and
Community College *A*
Edison State Community College *C*
Marion Technical College *A*
Owens Community College
Toledo *C, A*
Shawnee State University *A*
Sinclair Community College *A*
University of Rio Grande *A*
University of Toledo *B*
Wright State University *A*

Pennsylvania
Northampton County Area
Community College *A*
Penn State
University Park *C*
Pennsylvania College of Technology *A*

South Carolina
Aiken Technical College *A*

Tennessee
Cleveland State Community College *C*

Texas
Angelina College *C, A*
Texas State Technical College
Harlingen *C, A*

Utah
Utah Valley State College *A*

Virginia
Rappahannock Community
College *C, A*
Tidewater Community College *A*

Wisconsin
Gateway Technical College *A*
Lakeshore Technical College *A*
Western Wisconsin Technical
College *A*

Electronics/electrical equipment repair

Alabama
Alabama Southern Community
College *C, A*
Bevill State Community College *A*
Bishop State Community College *A*

Community College of the Air
Force *A*
Gadsden State Community College *A*
George C. Wallace State Community
College
George C. Wallace Community
College at Dothan *C, A*
J. F. Drake State Technical College *C, A*
Lawson State Community College *C*
Wallace State Community College at
Hanceville *C, A*

Alaska
University of Alaska
Anchorage *C, A*

Arizona
Gateway Community College *A*
Northland Pioneer College *C*
Pima Community College *C, A*

Arkansas
Ouachita Technical College *C*
Pulaski Technical College *C, A*
South Arkansas Community College *C*
Southeast Arkansas College *C, A*
University of Arkansas
Community College at Batesville *A*
Fort Smith *A*

California
Allan Hancock College *C, A*
Antelope Valley College *C, A*
Cerritos Community College *A*
Chabot College *A*
Chaffey College *C, A*
Citrus College *C, A*
Coastline Community College *C, A*
College of the Canyons *C, A*
College of the Redwoods *A*
College of the Sequoias *C, A*
Cypress College *C, A*
East Los Angeles College *C*
El Camino College *C, A*
Fresno City College *C, A*
Las Positas College *C, A*
Long Beach City College *C, A*
Los Angeles City College *A*
Los Angeles Harbor College *C, A*
Los Angeles Mission College *C, A*
Los Angeles Trade and Technical
College *C, A*
Los Medanos College *C, A*
Mendocino College *C, A*
Modesto Junior College *C, A*
Mount San Antonio College *C, A*
Ohlone College *C, A*
Orange Coast College *C, A*
Palomar College *C, A*
Sacramento City College *C, A*
Saddleback College *C*
San Bernardino Valley College *C, A*
San Jose City College *A*
Santa Barbara City College *C, A*
Sierra College *C, A*
Southwestern College *C, A*
Victor Valley College *C, A*
Yuba Community College
District *C, A*

Colorado
Red Rocks Community College *C, A*
Westwood College of
Technology *A, B*

Connecticut
Gateway Community College *C*

Florida
Brevard Community College *C*
Florida Community College at
Jacksonville *C*

Florida Technical College
Deland *A*
Indian River Community College *C*
Seminole Community College *C*

Georgia
Albany Technical College *C, A*
Athens Technical College *C*
Augusta Technical Institute *C*
Central Georgia Technical College *C*
Chattahoochee Technical College *C*
Coastal Georgia Community
College *C, A*
Dalton State College *C, A*
Darton College *A*
DeKalb Technical College *C*
Georgia Southwestern State
University *A*
Middle Georgia College *A*
Southwest Georgia Technical
College *C*
Waycross College *A*
West Georgia Technical College *A*

Hawaii
University of Hawaii
Hawaii Community College *A*
Honolulu Community College *A*

Idaho
Boise State University *C, A*
College of Southern Idaho *C*
Lewis-Clark State College *C, A, B*

Illinois
City Colleges of Chicago
Wright College *C, A*
College of DuPage *C, A*
Danville Area Community College *A*
Elgin Community College *C*
Illinois Eastern Community Colleges
Frontier Community College *C*
Lincoln Trail College *C, A*
Olney Central College *C*
Wabash Valley College *C*
John A. Logan College *C, A*
Joliet Junior College *C*
Kankakee Community College *C, A*
Prairie State College *C*
Richland Community College *A*
Sauk Valley Community College *C*
Southwestern Illinois College *C, A*
Spoon River College *A*
Triton College *C, A*
William Rainey Harper College *C, A*

Indiana
Vincennes University *A*

Iowa
Kirkwood Community College *C, A*
Northeast Iowa Community
College *A*
Southwestern Community
College *C, A*

Kansas
Allen County Community College *A*
Butler County Community College *A*
Dodge City Community College *C, A*
Hutchinson Community College *A*
Johnson County Community
College *C*
North Central Kansas Technical
College *A*
Pittsburg State University *C, A*

Kentucky
Spencerian College: Lexington *C, A*

Louisiana
Delgado Community College *A*

ITI Technical College *C*
Nunez Community College *C*

Maine

Central Maine Community
College *C, A*
Northern Maine Community
College *A*
Southern Maine Community
College *A*

Maryland

Anne Arundel Community
College *C, A*
Howard Community College *C, A*
Montgomery College *A*

Massachusetts

Benjamin Franklin Institute of
Technology *A*
Quinsigamond Community
College *C, A*

Michigan

Baker College
of Cadillac *A*
Bay de Noc Community College *C*
Delta College *C, A*
Glen Oaks Community College *C*
Grand Rapids Community
College *C, A*
Jackson Community College *C, A*
Lansing Community College *A*
Macomb Community College *C, A*
Montcalm Community College *C, A*
Northern Michigan University *A*
Northwestern Michigan College *A*
Schoolcraft College *C*
Washtenaw Community College *A*

Minnesota

Dunwoody College of Technology *C*
Hennepin Technical College *C, A*
Minnesota State College - Southeast
Technical *C, A*
Northland Community & Technical
College *C, A*
Riverland Community College *C*
St. Paul College *C*
South Central College *A*

Mississippi

Copiah-Lincoln Community College *A*
Hinds Community College *C, A*
Itawamba Community College *A*
Meridian Community College *A*
Mississippi Delta Community
College *C*
Mississippi Gulf Coast Community
College
Jefferson Davis Campus *A*
Pearl River Community College *C*

Missouri

North Central Missouri College *A*
Ranken Technical College *A*
State Fair Community College *A*

Montana

Helena College of Technology of the
University of Montana *A*

Nebraska

Metropolitan Community College *C*
Mid-Plains Community College
Area *C, A*
Northeast Community College *A*

New Hampshire

New Hampshire Community
Technical College
Berlin *A*
Manchester *C*
Nashua *A*

New Jersey

Raritan Valley Community College *A*

New Mexico

Clovis Community College *C, A*
Dona Ana Branch Community College
of New Mexico State
University *C, A*
Eastern New Mexico University:
Roswell Campus *C, A*
Western New Mexico University *A*

New York

Hudson Valley Community College *A*
Island Drafting and Technical
Institute *C, A*
Mohawk Valley Community College *A*
State University of New York
College of Agriculture and
Technology at Morrisville *A*
College of Technology at Alfred *A*
College of Technology at Canton *C*
Technical Career Institutes *C, A*

North Carolina

Alamance Community College *A*
Asheville-Buncombe Technical
Community College *C*
Bladen Community College *C, A*
Catawba Valley Community College *C*
Coastal Carolina Community
College *C, A*
College of the Albemarle *C*
Durham Technical Community
College *C, A*
Forsyth Technical Community
College *C*
Gaston College *C*
Johnston Community College *C*
Lenoir Community College *C, A*
McDowell Technical Community
College *A*
Piedmont Community College *C, A*
Pitt Community College *C, A*
Richmond Community College *C*
Rockingham Community College *A*
South Piedmont Community
College *C*
Tri-County Community College *A*
Vance-Granville Community
College *C, A*
Wake Technical Community
College *C, A*
Wilson Technical Community
College *C, A*

North Dakota

Bismarck State College *A*
Lake Region State College *A*
North Dakota State College of
Science *C, A*

Ohio

Cleveland Institute of Electronics *C, A*
Columbus State Community
College *A*
Edison State Community College *A*
Jefferson Community College *A*
Stark State College of Technology *A*

Oklahoma

Oklahoma State University
Oklahoma City *C*
Tulsa Community College *A*
Vatterott College
Tulsa *C, A*
Western Oklahoma State College *A*

Oregon

Central Oregon Community
College *C, A*
Clackamas Community College *C, A*
Lane Community College *A*
Linn-Benton Community College *A*
Mount Hood Community College *A*
Rogue Community College *A*
Umpqua Community College *A*

Pennsylvania

Berean Institute *C*
Johnson College *A*
Pennsylvania College of Technology *B*
Pittsburgh Institute of Aeronautics *A*
Thaddeus Stevens College of
Technology *A*

Puerto Rico

Electronic Data Processing College:
San Sebastian *C*
University College of San Juan *C*

Rhode Island

New England Institute of
Technology *A*

South Carolina

Aiken Technical College *C*
Central Carolina Technical College *C*
Denmark Technical College *A*
Florence-Darlington Technical
College *C*
Midlands Technical College *C*
Northeastern Technical College *C*
Orangeburg-Calhoun Technical
College *A*
Piedmont Technical College *C, A*
Technical College of the
Lowcountry *C*
Tri-County Technical College *C*
Trident Technical College *C*
York Technical College *C, A*

South Dakota

Lake Area Technical Institute *A*
Mitchell Technical Institute *A*
Southeast Technical Institute *A*
Western Dakota Technical Institute *A*

Tennessee

Southwest Tennessee Community
College *A*

Texas

Amarillo College *C, A*
Austin Community College *C*
Central Texas College *C, A*
Collin County Community College
District *C, A*
Del Mar College *C, A*
El Paso Community College *C, A*
Grayson County College *C, A*
Kilgore College *C, A*
Laredo Community College *C, A*
Lee College *C, A*
MTI College of Business and
Technology *C*
Midland College *A*
Odessa College *C, A*
St. Philip's College *C, A*
San Jacinto College
North *C, A*
South Plains College *C, A*
Tarrant County College *C, A*
Temple College *C, A*
Texas State Technical College
Waco *C, A*
Vernon College *C, A*

Utah

College of Eastern Utah *C*
Salt Lake Community College *A*
Southern Utah University *A*

Virginia

Danville Community College *C*
ECPI College of Technology *C, A*
Eastern Shore Community
College *C, A*
Mountain Empire Community
College *A*
Northern Virginia Community
College *C, A*
Paul D. Camp Community College *A*
Southwest Virginia Community
College *C*
Virginia Highlands Community
College *C*

Washington

Bellingham Technical College *A*
Centralia College *C, A*
Edmonds Community College *C*
Lower Columbia College *A*
North Seattle Community College *A*
Peninsula College *C, A*
Renton Technical College *C, A*
Skagit Valley College *C, A*
Spokane Community College *A*

West Virginia

West Virginia Northern Community
College *C, A*

Wisconsin

Blackhawk Technical College *A*
Chippewa Valley Technical
College *C, A*
Gateway Technical College *C*
Herzing College *A, B*
Lakeshore Technical College *C*
Madison Area Technical College *C, A*
Mid-State Technical College *A*
Moraine Park Technical College *C, A*
Southwest Wisconsin Technical
College *A*
Waukesha County Technical
College *C, A*
Western Wisconsin Technical
College *C*

Wyoming

Western Wyoming Community
College *C, A*

Elementary education

Alabama

Alabama Agricultural and Mechanical
University *B, M*
Alabama State University *B*
Athens State University *B*
Auburn University *B*
Auburn University at
Montgomery *B, M*
Birmingham-Southern College *B, T*
Calhoun Community College *A*
Chattahoochee Valley Community
College *A*
Concordia College *B*
Faulkner State Community College *A*
Faulkner University *B, T*
Gadsden State Community College *A*
Huntingdon College *B, T*
Jacksonville State University *B, M, T*
Judson College *B*
Miles College *B*
Northeast Alabama Community
College *A*
Oakwood College *B*
Samford University *M, T*
Southeastern Bible College *B, T*
Spring Hill College *B, M*
Stillman College *B, T*

Troy University *B, M, T*
Tuskegee University *B, T*
University of Alabama *B, M, D*
University of Alabama
   Birmingham *B, M*
   Huntsville *B, T*
University of Mobile *B, M, T*
University of Montevallo *B, M, T*
University of North Alabama *B, M*
University of South Alabama *B, M, T*
University of West Alabama *B, M, T*

Alaska

Alaska Pacific University *A, B, M*
Sheldon Jackson College *B*
University of Alaska
   Anchorage *B, T*
   Fairbanks *M, T*
   Southeast *B, M, T*

Arizona

American Indian College of the
   Assemblies of God *B*
Arizona State University *B*
Arizona State University West *B, M*
Arizona Western College *A*
Central Arizona College *A*
Eastern Arizona College *A*
Estrella Mountain Community
   College *A*
Gateway Community College *A*
Glendale Community College *A*
Grand Canyon University *B, M, T*
Northern Arizona University *B, M*
Prescott College *B, M, T*
Southwestern College *B*
University of Arizona *B, M*
University of Phoenix *B, M*

Arkansas

Arkansas Baptist College *B*
Arkansas State University *M, T*
Arkansas Tech University *M*
Black River Technical College *A*
Harding University *B, M, T*
Henderson State University *B, M, T*
Hendrix College *T*
Ozarka College *A*
Philander Smith College *B*
Phillips Community College of the
   University of Arkansas *A*
South Arkansas Community College *A*
Southern Arkansas University *M, T*
University of Arkansas *B, M, D*
University of Arkansas
   Cossatot Community College of the
      A
   Little Rock *B, M, T*
   Pine Bluff *M*
University of Central Arkansas *M, T*
Williams Baptist College *B*

California

Allan Hancock College *A*
Alliant International University *T*
Azusa Pacific University *B, T*
Barstow College *A*
Biola University *B, T*
California Baptist University *M, T*
California Lutheran University *B, M*
California Polytechnic State
   University: San Luis Obispo *T*
California State University
   Chico *T*
   Dominguez Hills *M, T*
   East Bay *T*
   Fullerton *M, T*
   Long Beach *M, T*
   Los Angeles *M*
   Monterey Bay *B*
   Northridge *M*
   Sacramento *M, T*

San Bernardino *M, T*
San Marcos *T*
Chapman University *M, T*
Cypress College *A*
Dominican University of California *T*
Fresno Pacific University *B, T*
Holy Names University *T*
Hope International University *B, T*
Humboldt State University *B, T*
Imperial Valley College *A*
La Sierra University *T*
Loyola Marymount University *M, T*
Master's College *B, T*
Mills College *T*
Mount St. Mary's College *B*
National University *T*
Notre Dame de Namur
   University *M, T*
Occidental College *T*
Pacific Union College *B*
Patten University *T*
St. Mary's College of California *M*
San Diego Christian College *B*
San Diego State University *M, T*
San Francisco State University *M, T*
San Jose State University *M*
Simpson University *B, T*
Sonoma State University *M, T*
Southwestern College *A*
Stanford University *M, T*
University of California
   Riverside *T*
   Santa Barbara *T*
   Santa Cruz *M*
University of La Verne *B, M, T*
University of Redlands *B, T*
University of San Diego *T*
University of San Francisco *T*
University of Southern California *T*
University of the Pacific *B, T*
Vanguard University of Southern
   California *T*
Westmont College *B, T*
Whittier College *T*
William Jessup University *B*

Colorado

Adams State College *B, M, T*
Colorado College *M*
Colorado State University *T*
Colorado State University
   Pueblo *T*
Fort Lewis College *B*
Metropolitan State College of
   Denver *T*
Northeastern Junior College *A*
Otero Junior College *A*
Regis University *B, T*
University of Colorado
   Boulder *T*
   Colorado Springs *T*
University of Northern
   Colorado *M, D, T*
Western State College of Colorado *T*

Connecticut

Central Connecticut State
   University *B, M, T*
Connecticut College *M, T*
Eastern Connecticut State
   University *B, M, T*
Quinnipiac University *B, M*
Sacred Heart University *M, T*
St. Joseph College *M, T*
Southern Connecticut State
   University *B, M, T*
University of Bridgeport *M, T*
University of Connecticut *B, T*
University of Hartford *B, M*
University of New Haven *T*
Western Connecticut State
   University *B, M*

Delaware

Delaware State University *B*
University of Delaware *B, T*
Wesley College *B*
Wilmington College *B, M*

District of Columbia

American University *B, M, T*
Catholic University of America *B, M, T*
Gallaudet University *B, T*
George Washington University *M*
Trinity University *M, T*
University of the District of
   Columbia *B, T*

Florida

Baptist College of Florida *B*
Barry University *B, M, T*
Bethune-Cookman College *B, T*
Broward Community College *A*
Carlos Albizu University *B, M*
Central Florida Community College *A*
Clearwater Christian College *B*
Flagler College *B*
Florida Agricultural and Mechanical
   University *B, M*
Florida Atlantic University *B, M*
Florida Christian College *B*
Florida College *B*
Florida Community College at
   Jacksonville *A*
Florida Gulf Coast University *B, M*
Florida International
   University *B, M, T*
Florida Memorial University *B, M, T*
Florida Southern College *B, M*
Florida State University *B, M, D, T*
Gulf Coast Community College *A*
Hillsborough Community College *A*
Hobe Sound Bible College *B, T*
Indian River Community College *A*
Jacksonville University *B, M, T*
Jones College *A, B*
Lynn University *B*
Manatee Community College *A*
Miami Dade College *A*
Nova Southeastern University *B*
Okaloosa-Walton College *A*
Palm Beach Atlantic University *M*
Palm Beach Community College *A*
Pensacola Junior College *A*
St. Leo University *B*
St. Petersburg College *B*
St. Thomas University *B, T*
Southeastern College of the
   Assemblies of God *B, T*
Stetson University *B, M*
University of Central Florida *B, M*
University of Florida *A, B*
University of Miami *B, M*
University of North Florida *B, M*
University of South Florida *B, M*
University of Tampa *B, T*
University of West Florida *B, T*
Warner Southern College *B*

Georgia

Agnes Scott College *T*
Armstrong Atlantic State
   University *B, M, T*
Atlanta Christian College *B*
Brenau University *B*
Clark Atlanta University *B*
Coastal Georgia Community
   College *A*
Covenant College *B, T*
Dalton State College *A, B*
Emmanuel College *B*
Fort Valley State University *B, M, T*
Gainesville State College *A*
Georgia Southwestern State
   University *B, M*
Kennesaw State University *B, M*

LaGrange College *B*
Macon State College *A*
Mercer University *B, M, T*
Middle Georgia College *A*
Morehouse College *B*
Oglethorpe University *B, M, T*
Paine College *B*
Reinhardt College *B*
Shorter College *B, T*
Thomas University *B*
University of Georgia *D*
University of West Georgia *B, M*

Hawaii

Brigham Young University-Hawaii *B, T*
Chaminade University of
   Honolulu *B, M, T*
University of Hawaii
   Hilo *T*
   Manoa *B*

Idaho

Boise State University *B, M, T*
Brigham Young University-Idaho *B*
College of Southern Idaho *A*
Idaho State University *B*
Lewis-Clark State College *B, T*
North Idaho College *A*
Northwest Nazarene University *B*
University of Idaho *B, T*

Illinois

Augustana College *B, T*
Aurora University *B*
Benedictine University *B, T*
Black Hawk College
   East Campus *A*
Blackburn College *B, T*
Bradley University *B, T*
Chicago State University *B, M, T*
City Colleges of Chicago
   Harold Washington College *A*
   Kennedy-King College *A*
Columbia College Chicago *M*
Concordia University *B, T*
DePaul University *B, T*
Dominican University *T*
Eastern Illinois University *B, M*
Elmhurst College *B*
Eureka College *B*
Governors State University *B, T*
Greenville College *B, M, T*
Illinois Central College *A*
Illinois College *B, T*
Illinois State University *B, T*
Illinois Wesleyan University *B*
John A. Logan College *A*
Joliet Junior College *A*
Judson College *B, T*
Kankakee Community College *A*
Kishwaukee College *A*
Knox College *T*
Lewis University *B, M*
Loyola University of Chicago *B, M*
MacMurray College *B, T*
McKendree College *B*
Millikin University *B, T*
Monmouth College *B, T*
National-Louis University *B, M, T*
North Central College *B*
North Park University *B, M*
Northeastern Illinois University *B*
Northern Illinois University *B, M, T*
Olivet Nazarene University *B, M, T*
Principia College *B, T*
Quincy University *B, T*
Rockford College *B, M*
Roosevelt University *B, M*
St. Xavier University *M*
Sauk Valley Community College *A*
Southern Illinois University
   Carbondale *B*
Southern Illinois University
   Edwardsville *B, M, T*

Southwestern Illinois College *A*
Springfield College in Illinois *A*
Trinity Christian College *B, T*
Trinity International
    University *B, M, T*
University of Illinois
    Chicago *B*
    Urbana-Champaign *B, M, D, T*
University of St. Francis *B, M, T*
Western Illinois University *B, M*
Wheaton College *B, T*

Indiana

Ancilla College *A*
Anderson University *B, T*
Ball State University *B, M, D, T*
Bethel College *B*
Butler University *B, M*
Calumet College of St. Joseph *B, T*
DePauw University *B*
Franklin College *B, T*
Goshen College *B, T*
Grace College *B*
Huntington University *B, M*
Indiana State University *B, M, T*
Indiana University
    Bloomington *B, M, D, T*
    East *B*
    Kokomo *B, M*
    Northwest *B, M, T*
    South Bend *B, M, T*
    Southeast *B, M*
Indiana University-Purdue University
    Fort Wayne *B, M, T*
Indiana University-Purdue University
    Indianapolis *B, M, D, T*
Indiana Wesleyan University *B, T*
Manchester College *B, T*
Marian College *B*
Oakland City University *B, M*
Purdue University *B, M*
Purdue University
    Calumet *B, M, T*
    North Central Campus *B, M, T*
St. Joseph's College *B*
Saint Mary's College *B, T*
St. Mary-of-the-Woods College *B, T*
Taylor University *B, T*
Taylor University: Fort Wayne *B, T*
Tri-State University *B, T*
University of Evansville *B, T*
University of Indianapolis *B, M, T*
University of St. Francis *B, T*
University of Southern Indiana *B, M*
Valparaiso University *B, M, T*
Vincennes University *A*

Iowa

Ashford University *B, T*
Briar Cliff University *B*
Buena Vista University *B, T*
Central College *B, T*
Clarke College *B, T*
Coe College *B*
Cornell College *B, T*
Dordt College *B, T*
Drake University *B, M*
Ellsworth Community College *A*
Emmaus Bible College *B*
Faith Baptist Bible College and
    Theological Seminary *B, T*
Graceland University *B, T*
Grand View College *B, T*
Grinnell College *T*
Iowa State University *B, M, T*
Iowa Wesleyan College *B*
Kaplan University *M*
Loras College *B*
Luther College *B*
Maharishi University of
    Management *B, M*
Marshalltown Community College *A*
Morningside College *B, M*
Mount Mercy College *B*

Northwestern College *B, T*
St. Ambrose University *B, T*
Simpson College *B, T*
University of Dubuque *B, T*
University of Iowa *B, M, D, T*
University of Northern Iowa *B, T*
Upper Iowa University *B, T*
Vennard College *A*
Waldorf College *B*
Wartburg College *B, T*
William Penn University *B*

Kansas

Baker University *B, T*
Barclay College *B*
Benedictine College *B*
Bethany College *B, T*
Bethel College *B, T*
Butler County Community College *A*
Central Christian College of Kansas *A*
Coffeyville Community College *A*
Colby Community College *A*
Dodge City Community College *A*
Donnelly College *A*
Emporia State University *B, M*
Fort Hays State University *B, M, T*
Friends University *B, T*
Garden City Community College *A*
Haskell Indian Nations
    University *A, B*
Kansas State University *B, M, T*
Kansas Wesleyan University *B, T*
Labette Community College *A*
McPherson College *B, T*
MidAmerica Nazarene University *B, T*
Newman University *B, T*
Ottawa University *B, T*
Pittsburg State University *B, M, T*
Pratt Community College *A*
Southwestern College *B, M, T*
Sterling College *B*
Tabor College *B, T*
University of Kansas *B, T*
University of St. Mary *B, T*
Washburn University of Topeka *B*
Wichita State University *B, M, T*

Kentucky

Alice Lloyd College *B*
Asbury College *B, T*
Bellarmine University *B, M, T*
Berea College *B, T*
Brescia University *B, T*
Campbellsville University *B*
Centre College *B, T*
Eastern Kentucky University *B, M*
Georgetown College *B, M*
Kentucky Christian University *B, T*
Kentucky State University *B*
Kentucky Wesleyan College *B, T*
Lindsey Wilson College *B, T*
Mid-Continent University *B*
Midway College *B*
Morehead State University *B, M, T*
Murray State University *B, M, T*
Northern Kentucky University *B, M*
Pikeville College *B, T*
Spalding University *B, M, T*
Thomas More College *B*
Transylvania University *B, T*
Union College *B, M*
University of Kentucky *B, M*
University of Louisville *B, M*
University of the Cumberlands *B, M, T*
Western Kentucky University *B, M, T*

Louisiana

Centenary College of
    Louisiana *B, M, T*
Dillard University *B, T*
Grambling State University *B, M*
Louisiana State University
    Shreveport *B*

Louisiana State University and
    Agricultural and Mechanical
    College *B*
Louisiana Tech University *B*
Loyola University New Orleans *B, M*
Nicholls State University *B, M*
Northwestern State University *B, M*
Our Lady of Holy Cross College *B*
Southeastern Louisiana
    University *B, M*
Southern University
    New Orleans *B*
Southern University and Agricultural
    and Mechanical College *B, M*
University of Louisiana at Lafayette *B*
University of Louisiana at
    Monroe *B, M, T*
University of New Orleans *B*
Xavier University of Louisiana *B, M*

Maine

College of the Atlantic *B, T*
Husson College *B, T*
St. Joseph's College *B*
Thomas College *B*
University of Maine *B, M*
University of Maine
    Farmington *B, T*
    Fort Kent *B*
    Machias *B*
    Presque Isle *B*
University of New England *B*
University of Southern Maine *B, T*

Maryland

Allegany College of Maryland *A*
Anne Arundel Community College *A*
Bowie State University *B, M, T*
Cecil Community College *A*
Chesapeake College *A*
College of Notre Dame of Maryland *B*
College of Southern Maryland *A*
Columbia Union College *B, T*
Community College of Baltimore
    County *A*
Coppin State University *B*
Frostburg State University *B, M, T*
Garrett College *A*
Goucher College *B, M, T*
Hagerstown Community College *A*
Howard Community College *A*
Loyola College in Maryland *B, T*
McDaniel College *M, T*
Morgan State University *B, M, T*
Mount St. Mary's University *B, M, T*
Prince George's Community
    College *A*
St. Mary's College of Maryland *T*
Salisbury University *B, T*
Towson University *B, M, T*
University of Maryland
    College Park *B*
    Eastern Shore *B*
Villa Julie College *B, T*
Washington Bible College *B, T*
Washington College *T*
Wor-Wic Community College *A*

Massachusetts

American International College *B, M*
Anna Maria College *B, M, T*
Assumption College *T*
Atlantic Union College *B*
Bay Path College *B*
Becker College *A, B, T*
Boston College *B, M, T*
Boston University *B, M, T*
Bridgewater State College *B, M, T*
Bristol Community College *A*
Clark University *M*
Curry College *B*
Eastern Nazarene College *B, M, T*
Elms College *B, M, T*
Emmanuel College *B, M, T*

Endicott College *B, M*
Fitchburg State College *B, M, T*
Framingham State College *B, M*
Gordon College *B*
Hampshire College *B*
Hellenic College/Holy Cross *B*
Lasell College *B, T*
Lesley University *B, M*
Massachusetts College of Liberal
    Arts *T*
Merrimack College *M, T*
Northeastern University *B, M*
Pine Manor College *T*
Regis College *M*
Salem State College *B, M*
Simmons College *B, M*
Smith College *M*
Springfield College *B, M, T*
Springfield Technical Community
    College *A*
Stonehill College *B*
Suffolk University *M*
Tufts University *M*
University of Massachusetts
    Boston *M*
    Dartmouth *T*
Wellesley College *T*
Western New England College *M, T*
Westfield State College *B, M, T*
Wheaton College *T*
Wheelock College *B, M*
Worcester State College *B, M, T*

Michigan

Adrian College *B, T*
Albion College *T*
Alma College *B, T*
Andrews University *B, M*
Aquinas College *B, T*
Baker College
    of Auburn Hills *B*
    of Muskegon *B*
    of Owosso *B*
Calvin College *B, T*
Central Michigan University *M*
Concordia University *B, T*
Cornerstone University *B*
Delta College *A*
Eastern Michigan University *B, M, T*
Ferris State University *A, B*
Finlandia University *B*
Gogebic Community College *A*
Grace Bible College *B*
Grand Valley State University *M, T*
Hillsdale College *B*
Hope College *B, T*
Kellogg Community College *A*
Kuyper College *B*
Lake Superior State University *B*
Lansing Community College *A*
Madonna University *B, T*
Marygrove College *T*
Michigan State University *B*
Mid Michigan Community College *A*
Northern Michigan University *B, M, T*
Oakland University *B*
Olivet College *B, T*
Rochester College *B*
Saginaw Valley State University *B, M*
Schoolcraft College *A*
Siena Heights University *B, M, T*
Spring Arbor University *B, T*
University of Detroit Mercy *B, M, T*
University of Michigan *B*
University of Michigan
    Dearborn *T*
    Flint *B, M*
Washtenaw Community College *A*
Wayne County Community College *A*
Wayne State University *B, M, T*
Western Michigan University *B, M, T*

Minnesota

Augsburg College *B, T*

Bemidji State University *B, M, T*
Bethany Lutheran College *B*
Bethel University *B*
Capella University *M, D*
College of St. Benedict *B*
College of St. Catherine *B, M, T*
College of St. Scholastica *B, T*
Concordia College: Moorhead *B, T*
Concordia University: St. Paul *B, T*
Crown College *B, T*
Fond du Lac Tribal and Community
College *B*
Gustavus Adolphus College *B*
Hamline University *B, T*
Martin Luther College *B*
Minnesota State University
Mankato *B, M, T*
Moorhead *B*
Normandale Community College *A*
North Central University *B*
Northland Community & Technical
College *A*
Northwestern College *B*
Pillsbury Baptist Bible College *B*
Ridgewater College *A*
St. Cloud State University *B, T*
St. John's University *B*
Southwest Minnesota State
University *B, T*
University of Minnesota
Duluth *B, T*
Morris *B*
Twin Cities *B, M, T*
University of St. Thomas *B, M, T*
Vermilion Community College *A*
Winona State University *B, M, T*

Mississippi

Alcorn State University *B, M*
Belhaven College *B, M, T*
Blue Mountain College *B*
Coahoma Community College *A*
Delta State University *B, M*
Hinds Community College *A*
Holmes Community College *A*
Itawamba Community College *A*
Jackson State University *B, M*
Millsaps College *B, T*
Mississippi College *B, M, T*
Mississippi Delta Community
College *A*
Mississippi Gulf Coast Community
College
Jefferson Davis Campus *A*
Mississippi State University *B, M, D, T*
Mississippi Valley State
University *B, M, T*
Rust College *B*
Tougaloo College *B, T*
University of Mississippi *B, T*
University of Southern Mississippi *B*
William Carey College *B, M*

Missouri

Avila University *B, T*
Baptist Bible College *B*
Calvary Bible College and Theological
Seminary *B*
Central Methodist University *B*
Central Missouri State
University *B, M, T*
College of the Ozarks *B, T*
Columbia College *T*
Crowder College *A*
Culver-Stockton College *B, T*
Drury University *B, T*
Evangel University *B, T*
Fontbonne University *B*
Hannibal-LaGrange College *B*
Harris-Stowe State University *B, T*
Lincoln University *B, M, T*
Lindenwood University *B*
Maryville University of Saint
Louis *B, M, T*

Missouri Baptist University *B, T*
Missouri Southern State
University *B, T*
Missouri State University *B, M*
Missouri Valley College *B, T*
Missouri Western State University *B*
Northwest Missouri State
University *B, M, T*
Ozark Christian College *A*
Park University *B*
Rockhurst University *B*
St. Louis Community College
St. Louis Community College at
Meramec *A*
Southeast Missouri State
University *B, M, T*
Southwest Baptist University *B, T*
Stephens College *B, T*
Truman State University *M, T*
University of Missouri
Columbia *B, M, D*
Kansas City *B*
St. Louis *B, M, T*
Washington University in St.
Louis *B, M, T*
Westminster College *B, T*
William Jewell College *B, T*
William Woods University *B, T*

Montana

Carroll College *B*
Fort Belknap College *A*
Montana State University
Billings *B, T*
Bozeman *B*
College of Technology-Great Falls *A*
Rocky Mountain College *B, T*
Salish Kootenai College *A*
Stone Child College *A*
University of Great Falls *B*
University of Montana: Missoula *B, M*
University of Montana: Western *B, T*

Nebraska

Chadron State College *B, M*
College of Saint Mary *B, T*
Concordia University *B, M, T*
Creighton University *B*
Dana College *B*
Doane College *B*
Grace University *A*
Hastings College *B, M, T*
Midland Lutheran College *B, T*
Nebraska Wesleyan University *B*
Northeast Community College *A*
Peru State College *B, T*
Union College *B, T*
University of Nebraska
Kearney *B, M, T*
Lincoln *B*
Omaha *B, M, T*
Wayne State College *B, T*
Western Nebraska Community
College *A*
York College *B, T*

Nevada

Great Basin College *A, B*
Sierra Nevada College *M*
Truckee Meadows Community
College *A*
University of Nevada
Las Vegas *B, T*
Reno *B, M, T*

New Hampshire

Dartmouth College *T*
Franklin Pierce College *T*
Keene State College *B, T*
New England College *B, T*
Plymouth State University *B, M, T*
Rivier College *B, M, T*

Southern New Hampshire
University *B, M*
University of New Hampshire *M, T*
University of New Hampshire at
Manchester *M, T*

New Jersey

Caldwell College *B, T*
Centenary College *T*
The College of New Jersey *B, M, T*
College of St. Elizabeth *B, T*
Essex County College *A*
Felician College *B*
Georgian Court University *B, T*
Kean University *B, M, T*
Monmouth University *M*
New Jersey City University *B, T*
Raritan Valley Community College *A*
Rider University *B*
Rowan University *B, M*
Rutgers, The State University of New
Jersey
Camden Regional Campus *T*
New Brunswick/Piscataway
Campus *T*
Newark Regional Campus *T*
St. Peter's College *B, T*
Seton Hall University *B, M, T*
Sussex County Community College *A*
Westminster Choir College of Rider
University *M*
William Paterson University of New
Jersey *B, M, T*

New Mexico

Albuquerque Technical-Vocational
Institute *A*
College of Santa Fe *B*
College of the Southwest *B, T*
Eastern New Mexico University *B*
New Mexico Highlands
University *B, M, T*
New Mexico Junior College *A*
New Mexico State University *B*
Northern New Mexico College *A*
University of New Mexico *B, M*
Western New Mexico
University *B, M, T*

New York

Adelphi University *M, T*
Alfred University *B, M, T*
Barnard College *T*
Boricua College *B*
Canisius College *B, M, T*
City University of New York
Brooklyn College *B, M*
City College *B, M, T*
College of Staten Island *B, M*
Hunter College *B, M, T*
Kingsborough Community
College *A*
Lehman College *M, T*
Medgar Evers College *B, T*
Queens College *B, M, T*
York College *T*
Colgate University *T*
College of Mount St. Vincent *T*
College of New Rochelle *B, M*
College of Saint Rose *B, M, T*
Columbia University
School of General Studies *T*
Concordia College *B, T*
Corning Community College *A*
D'Youville College *B, M, T*
Daemen College *B, M, T*
Dominican College of Blauvelt *B, T*
Dowling College *B, M, T*
Dutchess Community College *A*
Elmira College *B, M, T*
Five Towns College *B, M, T*
Fordham University *M, T*
Hobart and William Smith Colleges *T*
Hofstra University *B, M*

Houghton College *B, T*
Iona College *B, M, T*
Jefferson Community College *A*
King's College *B*
Le Moyne College *M, T*
Long Island University
Brooklyn Campus *B, M, T*
C.W. Post Campus *B, M, T*
Manhattan College *B, T*
Manhattanville College *M, T*
Marymount Manhattan College *B*
Medaille College *B, M, T*
Mercy College *B, M, T*
Mohawk Valley Community College *A*
Molloy College *B, M, T*
Mount St. Mary College *B, M*
Nazareth College of Rochester *B, M, T*
New York Institute of
Technology *B, M, T*
New York University *B, M, D, T*
Niagara County Community
College *A*
Niagara University *B, M, T*
Nyack College *B, M*
Orange County Community College *A*
Pace University *B, M, T*
Roberts Wesleyan College *B*
Rockland Community College *A*
Russell Sage College *B, T*
St. Bonaventure University *B, M*
St. Francis College *B*
St. John Fisher College *B, M, T*
St. John's University *B, M*
St. Joseph's College *T*
St. Joseph's College: Suffolk
Campus *B, T*
St. Thomas Aquinas College *B, M, T*
Sarah Lawrence College *M*
Skidmore College *B, T*
State University of New York
Binghamton *M*
Buffalo *M, D, T*
College at Brockport *M, T*
College at Buffalo *B, M, T*
College at Cortland *B, M*
College at Fredonia *B, M, T*
College at Geneseo *B, M, T*
College at Old Westbury *B, T*
College at Oneonta *B, M, T*
College at Plattsburgh *B, M*
College at Potsdam *B, M*
New Paltz *B, M, T*
Oswego *B, M, T*
Sullivan County Community
College *A*
Syracuse University *B, M, T*
Ulster County Community College *A*
University of Rochester *M*
Utica College *B, M*
Vassar College *T*
Wagner College *M, T*
Wells College *T*
Yeshiva University *B, M*

North Carolina

Appalachian State University *B, M, T*
Barton College *B*
Belmont Abbey College *B*
Bennett College *B*
Brevard College *B*
Campbell University *B, M, T*
Catawba College *B, M, T*
Chowan College *B, T*
East Carolina University *B, M*
Elizabeth City State University *B, M, T*
Elon University *B, M, T*
Fayetteville State University *M*
Fayetteville Technical Community
College *A*
Gardner-Webb University *B, M*
Greensboro College *B, T*
Guilford College *B, T*
High Point University *B, M, T*
Isothermal Community College *A*

James Sprunt Community College A
John Wesley College B
Johnson C. Smith University B, T
Lees-McRae College B, T
Lenoir Community College A
Lenoir-Rhyne College B, T
Livingstone College B
Louisburg College A
Mars Hill College B, T
Martin Community College A
Meredith College M, T
Methodist College A, B, T
Montreat College B
North Carolina Agricultural and
    Technical State University B, M, T
North Carolina Central
    University B, M, T
North Carolina State University M, T
North Carolina Wesleyan College B
Pfeiffer University B, T
Piedmont Baptist College B
Queens University of
    Charlotte B, M, T
St. Andrews Presbyterian College B, T
St. Augustine's College B
Salem College M, T
Sandhills Community College A
Shaw University B, T
Southeastern Community College A
Stanly Community College A
University of North Carolina
    Asheville T
    Chapel Hill B
    Charlotte B, M
    Greensboro B, M
    Pembroke B, M
    Wilmington B, M
Wake Forest University B, T
Warren Wilson College B, T
Western Carolina University B, T
Wilkes Community College A
Wingate University B, M, T
Winston-Salem State University B, M

North Dakota

Dickinson State University B, T
Jamestown College B
Mayville State University B, T
Minot State University B, M
North Dakota State University B
Sitting Bull College A
Trinity Bible College B, T
Turtle Mountain Community
    College A
University of Mary B, M, T
University of North Dakota B, M, T
Valley City State University B, M, T

Ohio

Bluffton University B
Capital University B
Cincinnati Christian University B
Circleville Bible College B
Cleveland State University B, T
College of Wooster T
Defiance College B, T
Franciscan University of
    Steubenville B, M
God's Bible School and College B
Heidelberg College T
Hiram College B, T
John Carroll University B, M, T
Kent State University M
Kent State University
    Salem Regional Campus A
Lake Erie College B, M
Marietta College B
Miami University
    Oxford Campus B, M
Mount Vernon Nazarene
    University B, M, T
Muskingum College B, M, T
Ohio Dominican University B, T
Ohio Northern University B, T

Ohio State University
    Columbus Campus M, T
    Mansfield Campus B, M, T
    Marion Campus B, M, T
Ohio University B, M, T
Ohio University
    Eastern Campus B
    Lancaster Campus A
    Southern Campus at Ironton B, M
Ohio Wesleyan University B
Otterbein College B
Sinclair Community College A
Union Institute & University B, M
University of Akron B, M, D
University of Akron: Wayne College M
University of Cincinnati B, M, D, T
University of Cincinnati
    Clermont College A
    Raymond Walters College A
University of Rio Grande B, T
University of Toledo M, T
Urbana University B
Walsh University B
Washington State Community
    College A
Wilmington College B
Wittenberg University B
Wright State University B, M, T
Xavier University B, M
Youngstown State University B, M

Oklahoma

Bacone College B
Cameron University B, T
Carl Albert State College A
Connors State College A
East Central University B, M, T
Eastern Oklahoma State College A
Mid-America Christian University B
Murray State College A
Northeastern State University B, T
Northwestern Oklahoma State
    University B, M, T
Oklahoma Baptist University B, T
Oklahoma Christian University B, T
Oklahoma City University B, M
Oklahoma Panhandle State
    University B
Oklahoma State University B, T
Oklahoma Wesleyan University B, T
Oral Roberts University B, T
Rogers State University A
Seminole State College A
Southeastern Oklahoma State
    University B, M, T
Southern Nazarene University B, M
Southwestern Oklahoma State
    University B, M, T
University of Central Oklahoma B, M
University of Oklahoma B, T
University of Science and Arts of
    Oklahoma B
University of Tulsa B, T

Oregon

Chemeketa Community College A
Concordia University B, M, T
Corban College B, M
Eastern Oregon University B, M
George Fox University B, T
Lewis & Clark College M
Linfield College B, T
Linn-Benton Community College A
Oregon State University M
Portland State University T
Southern Oregon University M, T
Treasure Valley Community College A
University of Oregon T
University of Portland B, M, T
Warner Pacific College T
Western Oregon University B, T
Willamette University M

Pennsylvania

Albright College B, M, T
Alvernia College B
Arcadia University B, M, T
Baptist Bible College of
    Pennsylvania B
Bloomsburg University of
    Pennsylvania B, M, T
Bucknell University B, T
Butler County Community College A
Cabrini College B, T
California University of
    Pennsylvania B, M
Carlow University B, T
Cedar Crest College B, M, T
Chatham College B, M, T
Chestnut Hill College B, M, T
Cheyney University of
    Pennsylvania B, M, T
Clarion University of
    Pennsylvania B, T
College Misericordia B, T
Community College of Allegheny
    County A
DeSales University B, M, T
Duquesne University B, M, T
East Stroudsburg University of
    Pennsylvania B, M, T
Eastern University B, T
Edinboro University of
    Pennsylvania B, M, T
Elizabethtown College B
Gannon University B
Geneva College B, T
Gettysburg College T
Grove City College B, T
Gwynedd-Mercy College B, T
Harrisburg Area Community
    College A
Holy Family University B, M, T
Immaculata University B
Indiana University of
    Pennsylvania B, M, D, T
Juniata College B, T
Keystone College B, T
King's College B, T
Kutztown University of
    Pennsylvania B, M, T
La Roche College B
La Salle University B, M, T
Lancaster Bible College B
Lebanon Valley College B, T
Lehigh University M
Lincoln University B, M, T
Lock Haven University of
    Pennsylvania B, T
Lycoming College T
Manor College A
Mansfield University of
    Pennsylvania B, M, T
Marywood University B, M
Mercyhurst College B, T
Messiah College B, T
Millersville University of
    Pennsylvania B, M, T
Montgomery County Community
    College A
Moravian College T
Mount Aloysius College B
Muhlenberg College T
Neumann College B, T
Penn State
    Abington B
    Altoona B
    Beaver B
    Berks B
    Delaware County B
    Dubois B
    Fayette B
    Harrisburg B
    Hazleton B
    Lehigh Valley B
    McKeesport B
    Mont Alto B

    New Kensington B
    Schuylkill - Capital College B
    Shenango B
    University Park B
    Wilkes-Barre B
    Worthington Scranton B
    York B
Philadelphia Biblical University B, T
Point Park University B
Reading Area Community College A
Robert Morris University B, T
Rosemont College T
St. Francis University B, T
St. Joseph's University B, M
St. Vincent College T
Seton Hill University M, T
Shippensburg University of
    Pennsylvania B, T
Slippery Rock University of
    Pennsylvania B, T
Susquehanna University B, T
Temple University B, M, D, T
Thiel College B
University of Pennsylvania B, M, T
University of Pittsburgh T
University of Pittsburgh
    Johnstown B, T
University of Scranton B, M
Valley Forge Christian College B
Villanova University B
Washington and Jefferson College T
Waynesburg College B, T
West Chester University of
    Pennsylvania B, M, T
Westminster College B, M, T
Widener University B, M, T
Wilkes University B, T
Wilson College A, B
York College of Pennsylvania B, T

Puerto Rico

American University of Puerto
    Rico B, T
Bayamon Central University B, M
Inter American University of Puerto
    Rico
    Aguadilla Campus B, M
    Arecibo Campus B
    Barranquitas Campus B
    Fajardo Campus B, T
    Guayama Campus B
    Ponce Campus B, M
    San German Campus B
Pontifical Catholic University of
    Puerto Rico B, T
Turabo University B, M
Universidad Adventista de las
    Antillas B
Universidad Metropolitana B
University of Puerto Rico
    Aguadilla B
    Arecibo A, B
    Cayey University College B
    Humacao B
    Ponce B
    Rio Piedras B, M
    Utuado B
University of the Sacred Heart B

Rhode Island

Rhode Island College B, M, T
Roger Williams University B, M
Salve Regina University B
University of Rhode Island B

South Carolina

Anderson University B, T
Benedict College B
Charleston Southern University B, M
Claflin University B
Clemson University B, M, T
Coastal Carolina University B, M, T
Coker College B, T
College of Charleston B, M, T

Columbia College *B, T*
Columbia International
   University *M, T*
Converse College *B, M, T*
Erskine College *B, T*
Francis Marion University *B, M, T*
Furman University *M, T*
Lander University *B, M, T*
Limestone College *B*
Morris College *B, T*
Newberry College *B, T*
North Greenville College *B, T*
South Carolina State University *B, M*
Southern Wesleyan University *B, T*
University of South Carolina *M, D*
University of South Carolina
   Aiken *B, M, T*
   Sumter *B*
   Upstate *B, M, T*
Winthrop University *B, M, T*

South Dakota

Augustana College *B, M, T*
Black Hills State University *B, T*
Dakota State University *B, T*
Dakota Wesleyan University *B, T*
Mount Marty College *B*
Northern State University *B, M, T*
Oglala Lakota College *B*
University of Sioux Falls *B, T*
University of South Dakota *B, M, T*

Tennessee

Aquinas College *B, T*
Austin Peay State University *M, T*
Belmont University *B, M, T*
Bethel College *B, T*
Bryan College *T*
Carson-Newman College *B, M, T*
Christian Brothers University *B, M, T*
Columbia State Community College *A*
Crichton College *B*
Cumberland University *B, T*
East Tennessee State University *M, T*
Fisk University *T*
Free Will Baptist Bible College *B*
Freed-Hardeman University *B, T*
Hiwassee College *A*
Johnson Bible College *T*
King College *T*
Lambuth University *B, T*
Lee University *B, T*
Lincoln Memorial University *B, T*
Lipscomb University *B, T*
Martin Methodist College *B*
Motlow State Community College *A*
Southern Adventist University *B*
Tennessee State University *M, T*
Tennessee Technological
   University *M, T*
Tennessee Temple University *B, M, T*
Tennessee Wesleyan College *T*
Trevecca Nazarene University *B, M, T*
Tusculum College *B, T*
Union University *B, T*
University of Memphis *B, T*
University of Tennessee
   Chattanooga *M*
   Knoxville *T*
Vanderbilt University *B, M, D, T*

Texas

Abilene Christian University *B, M, T*
Amarillo College *A*
Arlington Baptist College *B, T*
Austin College *M*
Baylor University *B, T*
Brazosport College *A*
Clarendon College *A*
Coastal Bend College *A*
College of the Mainland *A*
Concordia University at Austin *B*
Dallas Baptist University *B, M*
East Texas Baptist University *B*

El Paso Community College *A*
Frank Phillips College *A*
Galveston College *A*
Grayson County College *A*
Howard Payne University *B, T*
Huston-Tillotson College *T*
Jarvis Christian College *B, T*
Lamar University *B, M, T*
Laredo Community College *A*
LeTourneau University *B, T*
Lubbock Christian University *B, M*
McMurry University *B, T*
Midwestern State University *M*
Navarro College *A*
Our Lady of the Lake University of San
   Antonio *A*
Paul Quinn College *B*
Prairie View A&M University *M*
St. Edward's University *T*
St. Mary's University *T*
Sam Houston State University *M*
San Jacinto College
   North *A*
Schreiner University *B*
South Texas College *A*
Southwestern Adventist
   University *B, M*
Southwestern Assemblies of God
   University *B, M*
Southwestern University *B, T*
Stephen F. Austin State University *M, T*
Sul Ross State University *B, M, T*
Temple College *A*
Texas A&M University
   Commerce *B, M, D, T*
   Kingsville *B, M*
   Texarkana *T*
Texas Christian University *B, M*
Texas College *B, T*
Texas Lutheran University *B, T*
Texas State University: San
   Marcos *M, T*
Texas Tech University *M*
Texas Wesleyan University *B, M, T*
Texas Woman's University *M*
Trinity University *B, M*
Trinity Valley Community College *A*
University of Dallas *B, T*
University of Houston *M, T*
University of Houston
   Downtown *M*
   Victoria *M*
University of Mary Hardin-Baylor *B, T*
University of North Texas *B, M, D, T*
University of St. Thomas *B*
University of Texas
   Brownsville *M*
   El Paso *B*
   Pan American *M*
   San Antonio *M, T*
   of the Permian Basin *M*
University of the Incarnate
   Word *B, M, T*
Wayland Baptist University *B, T*
West Texas A&M University *M, T*
Wharton County Junior College *A*
Wiley College *B*

Utah

Brigham Young University *B*
Dixie State College of Utah *A, B*
Snow College *A*
Southern Utah University *B, T*
University of Utah *B*
Utah State University *B, M, D*
Utah Valley State College *B*
Weber State University *B, M*
Westminster College *B*

Vermont

Bennington College *B, M*
Castleton State College *B, M*
Champlain College *B*
College of St. Joseph in Vermont *B, M*

Goddard College *B*
Green Mountain College *B, T*
Johnson State College *B, M*
Lyndon State College *B*
Middlebury College *D, T*
Norwich University *T*
St. Michael's College *B, T*
University of Vermont *B*

Virginia

Averett University *M, T*
Bluefield College *B*
Bridgewater College *T*
College of William and Mary *T*
Hampton University *M*
Hollins University *T*
James Madison University *T*
Liberty University *M, T*
Longwood University *B, T*
Lynchburg College *B*
Mary Baldwin College *T*
Marymount University *M*
Old Dominion University *M, T*
Radford University *T*
Randolph-Macon College *T*
Randolph-Macon Woman's College *T*
St. Paul's College *T*
University of Mary Washington *M*
University of Richmond *T*
University of Virginia's College at
   Wise *T*
Virginia Intermont College *B, T*
Virginia Wesleyan College *T*

Washington

Central Washington University *B, M, T*
Eastern Washington University *B, M, T*
Gonzaga University *T*
Heritage University *B, M*
Lower Columbia College *B*
Northwest University *B*
Pacific Lutheran University *B*
Puget Sound Christian College *A*
Saint Martin's University *B, T*
University of Puget Sound *T*
University of Washington *M, T*
Walla Walla College *B, T*
Washington State
   University *B, M, D, T*
Western Washington University *B, M*
Whitworth College *B, M, T*

West Virginia

Alderson-Broaddus College *B, T*
Bethany College *B*
Bluefield State College *B*
Concord University *B, M, T*
Davis and Elkins College *B*
Glenville State College *B*
Marshall University *B, M*
Mountain State University *A*
Ohio Valley University *B*
Potomac State College of West Virginia
   University *A*
Shepherd University *B, T*
University of Charleston *B*
West Liberty State College *B*
West Virginia State University *B*
West Virginia University *M, T*
West Virginia University at
   Parkersburg *A, B*
West Virginia Wesleyan College *B*

Wisconsin

Alverno College *B, T*
Beloit College *T*
Carroll College *B, T*
Carthage College *B, T*
Concordia University Wisconsin *B, T*
Edgewood College *B, T*
Lakeland College *B*
Lawrence University *T*
Maranatha Baptist Bible College *B*

Marian College of Fond du Lac *B, T*
Marquette University *B*
Mount Mary College *B, T*
Northland College *B, T*
Ripon College *T*
St. Norbert College *B, T*
Silver Lake College *B, T*
University of Wisconsin
   Eau Claire *B, M*
   Green Bay *B, T*
   La Crosse *B, M, T*
   Madison *B*
   Oshkosh *B, M, T*
   Parkside *T*
   Platteville *B, T*
   River Falls *B, M, T*
   Stevens Point *B, M, T*
   Superior *M*
   Whitewater *B, T*
Viterbo University *B, M, T*
Wisconsin Lutheran College *B*

Wyoming

Central Wyoming College *A*
Eastern Wyoming College *A*
Laramie County Community
   College *A*
Northwest College *A*
Sheridan College *A*
University of Wyoming *B*
Western Wyoming Community
   College *A*

Elementary/middle school administration

Alabama

University of Alabama *D*

Arkansas

Arkansas State University *M, T*
Henderson State University *M*

Illinois

Concordia University *M*
Lewis University *D*
University of Illinois
   Urbana-Champaign *M, D, T*

Iowa

University of Northern Iowa *M*

Kentucky

University of the Cumberlands *M*

Louisiana

Xavier University of Louisiana *M*

Massachusetts

Lesley University *M*
Worcester State College *M*

Michigan

Marygrove College *M*
Saginaw Valley State University *M*
Western Michigan University *D*

Minnesota

Bethel University *D*
Capella University *M, D*

Mississippi

Mississippi State University *D*

Missouri

Lincoln University *M*
Lindenwood University *M*
Southeast Missouri State University *M*
Southwest Baptist University *M*
University of Missouri
   Columbia *M, D*

Montana
University of Great Falls *M*

Nebraska
Concordia University *T*
Creighton University *M*
Wayne State College *M*

Nevada
University of Nevada
Reno *M, D*

New Jersey
College of St. Elizabeth *T*
William Paterson University of New
Jersey *M*

New York
St. Bonaventure University *M*
St. John Fisher College *M*

North Carolina
East Carolina University *D*

North Dakota
University of Mary *M*

Ohio
Lake Erie College *M*
University of Akron *M*
University of Findlay *M, T*
Youngstown State University *M*

Oklahoma
University of Oklahoma *T*

Pennsylvania
East Stroudsburg University of
Pennsylvania *T*
Marywood University *M*
St. Francis University *M*
Shippensburg University of
Pennsylvania *M, T*
Widener University *M, T*
Wilkes University *M*

Puerto Rico
Universidad del Este *M*

Rhode Island
Providence College *M*

South Carolina
Charleston Southern University *M*

South Dakota
University of South Dakota *M, D*

Tennessee
University of Memphis *T*

Texas
University of Texas
Arlington *T*

Vermont
Castleton State College *D*
St. Michael's College *T*

Washington
Seattle Pacific University *T*
University of Washington *M, D, T*
Washington State University *M*
Western Washington University *M*

Wisconsin
Cardinal Stritch University *D*
Edgewood College *M*
University of Wisconsin
Superior *M*

Emergency care attendant (EMT ambulance)

Arizona
Mohave Community College *C*

Arkansas
University of Arkansas
Community College at Hope *C*

California
Copper Mountain College *C*
San Jose City College *C*
Santa Rosa Junior College *C*

Florida
Pensacola Junior College *C*
South Florida Community College *C*
Valencia Community College *C, A*

Georgia
Northwestern Technical College *C*

Illinois
Heartland Community College *C*
Kankakee Community College *C*
Lincoln Land Community College *C*
Southeastern Illinois College *C*
Waubonsee Community College *C*

Indiana
Vincennes University *A*

Iowa
Kirkwood Community College *A*

Kansas
Kansas City Kansas Community
College *C*

Louisiana
Our Lady of the Lake College *A*

Michigan
Baker College
of Muskegon *C, A*
Kirtland Community College *C*

Minnesota
Central Lakes College *C*

Missouri
Hannibal-LaGrange College *C*

North Carolina
Carteret Community College *A*
Sandhills Community College *A*

Ohio
Lakeland Community College *C*
University of Cincinnati
Clermont College *C, A*

Oregon
Oregon Institute of Technology *A*

Texas
Howard College *C, A*
Midland College *A*
Tyler Junior College *C, A*

Washington
Clark College *C*

West Virginia
Mountain State University *A*

Wisconsin
Fox Valley Technical College *C*
Mid-State Technical College *C*

Emergency medical technology (EMT paramedic)

Alabama
Alabama Southern Community
College *A*
Bishop State Community College *C*
Calhoun Community College *C, A*
Central Alabama Community
College *A*
Enterprise-Ozark Community
College *A*
Faulkner State Community College *A*
Faulkner University *A*
Gadsden State Community College *A*
George C. Wallace State Community
College
George C. Wallace Community
College at Dothan *C, A*
Lawson State Community College *C*
Lurleen B. Wallace Community
College *C, A*
Northeast Alabama Community
College *C, A*
Northwest-Shoals Community
College *C, A*
Shelton State Community College *C*
Southern Union State Community
College *C, A*
Trenholm State Technical College *A*
University of Alabama
Birmingham *A*
University of South Alabama *C*
Wallace State Community College at
Hanceville *C, A*

Alaska
University of Alaska
Anchorage *A*

Arizona
Arizona Western College *C, A*
Central Arizona College *C, A*
Cochise College *A*
Eastern Arizona College *C, A*
Glendale Community College *C, A*
Northland Pioneer College *A*
Phoenix College *C, A*
Pima Community College *C, A*
Scottsdale Community College *C, A*
Yavapai College *C*

Arkansas
Arkansas Northeastern College *C*
Arkansas State University *A*
Arkansas State University
Mountain Home *C, A*
Arkansas State University: Newport *A*
Arkansas Tech University *C*
East Arkansas Community
College *C, A*
National Park Community
College *C, A*
North Arkansas College *C, A*
Northwest Arkansas Community
College *C, A*
Ozarka College *C*
South Arkansas Community
College *A*
Southeast Arkansas College *C, A*
University of Arkansas
Community College at Batesville *A*
Cossatot Community College of the
C
for Medical Sciences *C, A*

Wisconsin
Fox Valley Technical College *C*
Mid-State Technical College *C*

California
Allan Hancock College *C*
Bakersfield College *A*
Barstow College *C*
Butte College *A*
California State University
Chico *C*
College of the Canyons *C*
College of the Desert *C*
College of the Sequoias *C*
College of the Siskiyous *C, A*
Columbia College *C*
Cosumnes River College *C*
Crafton Hills College *C, A*
East Los Angeles College *C*
Foothill College *C*
Imperial Valley College *C*
Long Beach City College *C*
Los Medanos College *C, A*
Modesto Junior College *C*
Mount San Antonio College *C, A*
Palomar College *C, A*
Saddleback College *C*
San Joaquin Delta College *C, A*
San Joaquin Valley College Inc. *A*
San Jose City College *C*
Santa Barbara City College *C*
Santa Rosa Junior College *C, A*
Skyline College *C*
Southwestern College *C, A*
Ventura College *A*
Victor Valley College *C, A*

Colorado
Aims Community College *C*
Arapahoe Community College *C*
Front Range Community College *C*
Morgan Community College *C*
Northeastern Junior College *C, A*
Pikes Peak Community College *C, A*
Pueblo Community College *C, A*
Red Rocks Community College *C, A*

Connecticut
Capital Community College *C, A*
Norwalk Community College *C*
Three Rivers Community College *C*

Delaware
Delaware Technical and Community
College
Owens Campus *A*
Stanton/Wilmington Campus *A*
Terry Campus *A*

Florida
Brevard Community College *C, A*
Broward Community College *C, A*
Central Florida Community
College *C, A*
City College *A*
Daytona Beach Community
College *C, A*
Edison College *C, A*
Florida Community College at
Jacksonville *C, A*
Florida Keys Community College *C*
Gulf Coast Community College *C, A*
Hillsborough Community College *A*
Indian River Community College *C, A*
Lake City Community College *C, A*
Lake-Sumter Community College *A*
Miami Dade College *C, A*
Palm Beach Community College *C, A*
Pasco-Hernando Community
College *C, A*
Pensacola Junior College *C, A*
Polk Community College *C, A*
St. Johns River Community College *A*
St. Petersburg College *C, A*
Santa Fe Community College *C, A*
Seminole Community College *C, A*

South Florida Community
College *C, A*
Tallahassee Community College *C, A*
Valencia Community College *C, A*

Georgia

Albany Technical College *C*
Athens Technical College *C*
Augusta Technical Institute *C, A*
Bainbridge College *C*
Central Georgia Technical College *C*
Dalton State College *C, A*
Darton College *C, A*
DeKalb Technical College *C*
Gainesville State College *A*
Georgia Highlands College *A*
Gwinnett Technical College *C, A*
Macon State College *A*
Savannah Technical College *C, A*
Southwest Georgia Technical
College *C*
Waycross College *A*
West Georgia Technical College *C*

Hawaii

University of Hawaii
Kapiolani Community College *C, A*

Idaho

Brigham Young University-Idaho *A*
College of Southern Idaho *C, A*
Idaho State University *C, A*

Illinois

Black Hawk College *C*
City Colleges of Chicago
Malcolm X College *C, A*
College of DuPage *C, A*
College of Lake County *C*
Elgin Community College *C*
Heartland Community College *C*
Illinois Central College *C*
Illinois Eastern Community Colleges
Frontier Community College *C*
John A. Logan College *C*
John Wood Community College *A*
Kankakee Community College *C, A*
Kaskaskia College *C, A*
Lincoln Land Community College *C*
McHenry County College *C, A*
Moraine Valley Community College *C*
Parkland College *C*
Prairie State College *C*
Rend Lake College *C, A*
Richland Community College *C, A*
South Suburban College of Cook
County *C*
Southeastern Illinois College *C*
Southwestern Illinois College *C, A*
Waubonsee Community College *C*
William Rainey Harper College *C, A*

Indiana

Ball State University *A*
Indiana University
Bloomington *A*
Indiana University-Purdue University
Indianapolis *A*
Ivy Tech State College
Ivy Tech Community College:
Bloomington *A*
Ivy Tech Community College:
Columbus *A*
Ivy Tech Community College:
Kokomo *A*
Ivy Tech Community College: North
Central *A*
Ivy Tech Community College:
Northeast *A*
Ivy Tech Community College:
Southwest *A*
Ivy Tech Community College:
Wabash Valley *A*

Vincennes University *A*

Iowa

Des Moines Area Community
College *C*
Indian Hills Community College *C, A*
Iowa Central Community College *C, A*
Iowa Lakes Community College *C, A*
Kirkwood Community College *A*
North Iowa Area Community
College *A*
Northeast Iowa Community
College *A*
Northwest Iowa Community
College *A*
Southeastern Community College
North Campus *A*
Southwestern Community College *C*
Western Iowa Tech Community
College *C, A*

Kansas

Allen County Community College *A*
Barton County Community
College *C, A*
Cloud County Community College *C*
Coffeyville Community College *A*
Cowley County Community
College *A*
Dodge City Community College *C*
Hutchinson Community College *A*
Johnson County Community
College *C, A*
Kansas City Kansas Community
College *A*
Neosho County Community
College *C*

Kentucky

Eastern Kentucky University *C, A, B*
Jefferson Community College *C*
Western Kentucky University *C, A*

Louisiana

Bossier Parish Community College *A*
Delgado Community College *A*
Nicholls State University *A*
Nunez Community College *C, A*

Maine

Eastern Maine Community College *C*
Kennebec Valley Community
College *A*

Maryland

Anne Arundel Community
College *C, A*
Baltimore City Community
College *C, A*
Chesapeake College *C*
College of Southern Maryland *C, A*
Community College of Baltimore
County *C, A*
Frederick Community College *C, A*
Hagerstown Community College *C, A*
Howard Community College *C, A*
Prince George's Community
College *C, A*
University of Maryland
Baltimore County *B*
Wor-Wic Community College *C, A*

Massachusetts

Cape Cod Community College *C, A*
Greenfield Community College *C*
Massachusetts Bay Community
College *C*
North Shore Community College *C*
Quinsigamond Community
College *C, A*
Springfield College *B*

Michigan

Baker College
of Cadillac *C*
of Clinton Township *C*
of Muskegon *C, A*
Glen Oaks Community College *C*
Gogebic Community College *A*
Henry Ford Community College *C, A*
Jackson Community College *C, A*
Kalamazoo Valley Community
College *C*
Kellogg Community College *C, A*
Kirtland Community College *C, A*
Lansing Community College *A*
Macomb Community College *C, A*
Mid Michigan Community College *A*
Montcalm Community College *C, A*
Mott Community College *A*
North Central Michigan College *A*
Oakland Community College *C, A*
Schoolcraft College *C*
Southwestern Michigan College *A*
Wayne County Community
College *C, A*
West Shore Community College *A*

Minnesota

Anoka Technical College *C*
Century Community and Technical
College *C, A*
Hennepin Technical College *A*
Inver Hills Community College *C, A*
Mesabi Range Community and
Technical College *C*
Northland Community & Technical
College *A*
Rochester Community and Technical
College *C, A*
St. Cloud Technical College *A*
South Central College *A*
University of Minnesota
Duluth *C*

Mississippi

Copiah-Lincoln Community College *C*
Hinds Community College *C, A*
Itawamba Community College *A*
Mississippi Delta Community
College *A*
Mississippi Gulf Coast Community
College
Jefferson Davis Campus *A*
University of Mississippi Medical
Center *C*

Missouri

Crowder College *C*
East Central College *C, A*
Jefferson College *C, A*
Mineral Area College *C*
Missouri Southern State University *C*
Moberly Area Community College *C*
Ozarks Technical Community
College *A*
Penn Valley Community College *A*
St. Louis Community College
St. Louis Community College at
Meramec *A*
Southwest Baptist University *A*
Three Rivers Community College *C*

Montana

Montana State University
Billings *A*
College of Technology-Great Falls *A*

Nebraska

Creighton University *C, A, B*
Northeast Community College *A*
Western Nebraska Community
College *C*

Nevada

Community College of Southern
Nevada *A*

New Hampshire

New Hampshire Technical Institute *A*

New Jersey

Essex County College *A*
Union County College *C, A*
University of Medicine and Dentistry
of New Jersey
School of Health Related
Professions *C, A*

New Mexico

Dona Ana Branch Community College
of New Mexico State
University *C, A*
Eastern New Mexico University:
Roswell Campus *C, A*
New Mexico Junior College *A*
New Mexico State University
Alamogordo *C*
University of New Mexico *B*

New York

Broome Community College *A*
City University of New York
Borough of Manhattan Community
College *A*
LaGuardia Community College *A*
Corning Community College *A*
Dutchess Community College *C, A*
Erie Community College
South Campus *C*
Finger Lakes Community College *C*
Herkimer County Community
College *A*
Hudson Valley Community College *C*
Jefferson Community College *C, A*
Mohawk Valley Community College *A*
Rockland Community College *A*
Westchester Community College *C, A*

North Carolina

Asheville-Buncombe Technical
Community College *A*
Catawba Valley Community College *A*
Coastal Carolina Community
College *A*
Davidson County Community
College *C, A*
Fayetteville Technical Community
College *C, A*
Gaston College *C, A*
Guilford Technical Community
College *A*
Montgomery Community College *A*
Randolph Community College *A*
Robeson Community College *A*
Rockingham Community College *A*
Sandhills Community College *A*
Southwestern Community College *A*
Stanly Community College *A*
Tri-County Community College *C, A*
Wake Technical Community
College *C, A*
Western Carolina University *B*

North Dakota

Bismarck State College *C, A*
Turtle Mountain Community
College *C*

Ohio

Belmont Technical College *C, A*
Central Ohio Technical College *A*
Cincinnati State Technical and
Community College *C, A*
Clark State Community College *A*

Columbus State Community
College C, A
Cuyahoga Community College
Metropolitan Campus A
Hocking College C, A
James A. Rhodes State College A
Jefferson Community College C, A
Lakeland Community College C
Shawnee State University C, A
Sinclair Community College C, A
Southern State Community
College C, A
Stark State College of Technology C
University of Cincinnati
Clermont College C, A
Raymond Walters College C, A
University of Toledo C, A
Youngstown State University C, A

Oklahoma

Oklahoma City Community
College C, A
Redlands Community College A
Rogers State University A
Rose State College A
Western Oklahoma State College A

Oregon

Central Oregon Community
College A
Chemeketa Community College A
Clackamas Community College C
Clatsop Community College C
Lane Community College C, A
Linn-Benton Community College C
Oregon Health & Science
University C
Portland Community College C, A
Rogue Community College C, A
Southwestern Oregon Community
College C
Treasure Valley Community College C
Umpqua Community College A

Pennsylvania

Delaware County Community
College C
Drexel University A, B
Harrisburg Area Community
College C, A
Lackawanna College C, A
Luzerne County Community
College A
Northampton County Area
Community College C
Pennsylvania College of Technology A
University of Pittsburgh
Johnstown A

Puerto Rico

Electronic Data Processing College:
San Sebastian A
Universidad Metropolitana B

South Carolina

Greenville Technical College C, A
Horry-Georgetown Technical
College A
Piedmont Technical College C

Tennessee

Cleveland State Community College C
Jackson State Community College C
Northeast State Technical Community
College C
Roane State Community College C
Southwest Tennessee Community
College C, A
Volunteer State Community College C
Walters State Community College C, A

Texas

Alvin Community College C, A

Amarillo College C, A
Angelina College C, A
Austin Community College C, A
Blinn College C
Brookhaven College C
Clarendon College C
Collin County Community College
District C, A
Del Mar College C, A
El Centro College C
El Paso Community College C
Galveston College C, A
Grayson County College C, A
Houston Community College
System C, A
Kilgore College C, A
Lamar State College at Orange C, A
Laredo Community College A
Lee College C, A
McLennan Community College A
Midland College C, A
Navarro College A
North Central Texas College A
North Harris Montgomery
Community College District C, A
Odessa College C, A
San Antonio College C, A
San Jacinto College
North C, A
South Plains College C, A
South Texas College C, A
Tarrant County College C, A
Temple College C, A
Texarkana College C, A
Texas Southmost College C, A
Texas State Technical College
Harlingen C, A
West Texas C, A
Trinity Valley Community College C
Tyler Junior College C, A
University of North Texas B
University of Texas
Brownsville C, A
Victoria College C, A
Weatherford College C, A
Western Texas College C, A

Utah

Dixie State College of Utah C, A
Snow College C, A
Utah Valley State College C
Weber State University A

Virginia

Jefferson College of Health
Sciences A
Mountain Empire Community
College C, A
Northern Virginia Community
College A
Piedmont Virginia Community
College A
Southwest Virginia Community
College C, A
Tidewater Community College A

Washington

Bellingham Technical College A
Clark College A
Columbia Basin College A
North Seattle Community College C
Spokane Community College C, A
Spokane Falls Community College C
Tacoma Community College A

West Virginia

Mountain State University A

Wisconsin

Blackhawk Technical College C
Chippewa Valley Technical College C
Fox Valley Technical College C
Gateway Technical College C

Lakeshore Technical College C, A
Madison Area Technical College C, A
Mid-State Technical College C, A
Milwaukee Area Technical College C
Moraine Park Technical College C
Nicolet Area Technical College C
Northcentral Technical College C
Western Wisconsin Technical
College C
Wisconsin Indianhead Technical
College C

Wyoming

Central Wyoming College C
Sheridan College C

Endocrinology

California

University of California
Berkeley M, D
Davis M, D

Wisconsin

University of Wisconsin
Madison M, D

Energy systems technology

Alabama

Northwest-Shoals Community
College C

Arizona

Refrigeration School A

Connecticut

Naugatuck Valley Community
College C, A

Iowa

Iowa Lakes Community College C, A

Massachusetts

Fitchburg State College B
University of Massachusetts
Lowell M

Michigan

Alpena Community College C
Ferris State University A, B
Montcalm Community College C
Mott Community College C

New York

New York Institute of Technology B

Ohio

Hocking College A

Oregon

Oregon Institute of Technology B

Vermont

Sterling College B

Engine machinist

Minnesota

Northwest Technical College C, A
Pine Technical College C

Engineering, general

Alabama

Central Alabama Community
College A

Chattahoochee Valley Community
College A
Gadsden State Community College A
Lawson State Community College A
Northeast Alabama Community
College A
Shelton State Community College A
Snead State Community College A
University of Alabama
Huntsville M
Wallace State Community College at
Hanceville A

Alaska

University of Alaska
Anchorage A
Fairbanks M, D

Arizona

Arizona State University M
Arizona Western College A
Central Arizona College A
Embry-Riddle Aeronautical University:
Prescott Campus B
Gateway Community College A
High-Tech Institute A
Mesa Community College A
Northern Arizona University B, M
Phoenix College A
University of Arizona B

Arkansas

Arkansas State University B
John Brown University D
Phillips Community College of the
University of Arkansas A
University of Arkansas M, D

California

Allan Hancock College A
Antelope Valley College A
Biola University B
California Institute of Technology B
California National University for
Advanced Studies B, M
California Polytechnic State
University: San Luis Obispo M
California State Polytechnic
University: Pomona B, M
California State University
Fullerton B, M
Long Beach M
Los Angeles B
Northridge B, M
Chabot College A
Chaffey College A
Citrus College A
City College of San Francisco A
Claremont McKenna College B
College of San Mateo A
College of the Sequoias A
Contra Costa College A
Cypress College A
De Anza College A
East Los Angeles College A
El Camino College A
Foothill College A
Fresno City College A
Fullerton College A
Harvey Mudd College B
Imperial Valley College A
Long Beach City College A
Los Angeles City College A
Los Angeles Pierce College A
Los Angeles Southwest College A
Los Angeles Trade and Technical
College A
Loyola Marymount University B
Merced College A
Mission College A
Modesto Junior College A
Mount San Antonio College A
National University M

Palomar College *A*
Pepperdine University *B*
Riverside Covenant College *A*
Saddleback College *A*
San Diego City College *A*
San Diego Mesa College *A*
San Francisco State University *M*
San Joaquin Delta College *A*
San Jose State University *B, M*
Santa Ana College *A*
Santa Barbara City College *A*
Santa Clara University *B, M*
Santa Rosa Junior College *A*
Santiago Canyon College *A*
Scripps College *B*
Shasta College *A*
Sierra College *A*
Southwestern College *A*
Stanford University *B, M*
Taft College *A*
University of California
   Davis *M, D*
   Irvine *B, M, D*
   Los Angeles *M*
   Riverside *B*
   Santa Barbara *B, M, D*
University of the Pacific *B*
Ventura College *A*
West Los Angeles College *A*
West Valley College *A*

Colorado

Colorado School of Mines *B*
Trinidad State Junior College *A*
United States Air Force Academy *B*
University of Colorado
   Boulder *M*
   Colorado Springs *B, M*
   Denver and Health Sciences
     Center *M*
University of Denver *B, D*

Connecticut

Fairfield University *B*
Norwalk Community College *A*
Trinity College *B*
University of Connecticut *M*
University of Hartford *B*
University of New Haven *B*

District of Columbia

George Washington
   University *B, M, D*

Florida

Barry University *B*
Brevard Community College *A*
Broward Community College *A*
Chipola College *A*
Daytona Beach Community College *A*
Edison College *A*
Embry-Riddle Aeronautical
   University *B*
Florida Community College at
   Jacksonville *A*
Florida Institute of Technology *B*
Gulf Coast Community College *A*
Hillsborough Community College *A*
Indian River Community College *A*
Manatee Community College *A*
Okaloosa-Walton College *A*
Palm Beach Atlantic University *A*
Palm Beach Community College *A*
Pensacola Junior College *A*
Tallahassee Community College *A*
University of Central Florida *M*
University of South Florida *B, M, D*
Valencia Community College *A*

Georgia

Andrew College *A*
Clark Atlanta University *B*
Coastal Georgia Community
   College *A*
Covenant College *A*
Dalton State College *A*
Darton College *A*
Gainesville State College *A*
Georgia Perimeter College *A*
Mercer University *B*
Middle Georgia College *A*
Morehouse College *B*
Spelman College *B*
University of Georgia *B*
Young Harris College *A*

Idaho

Albertson College of Idaho *B*
Brigham Young University-Idaho *B*
North Idaho College *A*

Illinois

City Colleges of Chicago
   Harold Washington College *A*
   Olive-Harvey College *A*
College of DuPage *A*
College of Lake County *A*
Danville Area Community College *A*
Eureka College *B*
Heartland Community College *A*
Highland Community College *A*
Illinois Central College *A*
Illinois College *B*
Illinois Institute of Technology *M, D*
Illinois Valley Community College *A*
John A. Logan College *A*
John Wood Community College *A*
Kankakee Community College *A*
Kishwaukee College *A*
Lake Land College *A*
Lincoln Land Community College *A*
MacMurray College *B*
McHenry County College *A*
Monmouth College *B*
Northwestern University *B*
Oakton Community College *A*
Olivet Nazarene University *B*
Parkland College *A*
Rend Lake College *A*
Richland Community College *A*
Sauk Valley Community College *A*
South Suburban College of Cook
   County *A*
Southern Illinois University
   Carbondale *D*
Southwestern Illinois College *A*
Triton College *A*
University of Illinois
   Urbana-Champaign *B, M*
Waubonsee Community College *A*
Wheaton College *B*
William Rainey Harper College *A*

Indiana

Ball State University *B*
Bethel College *B*
Indiana University-Purdue University
   Indianapolis *B, M*
Purdue University
   Calumet *B, M*
University of Notre Dame *M*
University of Southern Indiana *B*
Vincennes University *A*

Iowa

Dordt College *B*
Ellsworth Community College *A*
Hamilton College *A*
Iowa State University *B*
Iowa Wesleyan College *B*
Kirkwood Community College *A*
Marshalltown Community College *A*
University of Iowa *B*

Kansas

Barton County Community College *A*
Butler County Community College *A*
Cloud County Community College *A*
Coffeyville Community College *A*
Colby Community College *A*
Cowley County Community
   College *A*
Dodge City Community College *A*
Donnelly College *A*
Garden City Community College *A*
Hutchinson Community College *A*
Pratt Community College *A*
Seward County Community College *A*

Kentucky

University of Louisville *B*

Louisiana

Louisiana Tech University *M, D*
Southern University and Agricultural
   and Mechanical College *M*

Maine

Bates College *B*
University of Maine *B, M*

Maryland

Allegany College of Maryland *A*
Anne Arundel Community College *A*
Baltimore City Community College *A*
College of Notre Dame of Maryland *B*
College of Southern Maryland *A*
Columbia Union College *A*
Community College of Baltimore
   County *A*
Frederick Community College *A*
Hagerstown Community College *A*
Harford Community College *A*
Howard Community College *A*
Johns Hopkins University *B*
Loyola College in Maryland *B, M*
Montgomery College *A*
Morgan State University *M, D*
Prince George's Community
   College *A*
United States Naval Academy *B*
University of Maryland
   Baltimore County *B*
   College Park *B, M*
   Eastern Shore *B*

Massachusetts

Berkshire Community College *A*
Boston University *B, M*
Bristol Community College *A*
Cape Cod Community College *A*
Eastern Nazarene College *B*
Franklin W. Olin College of
   Engineering *B*
Holyoke Community College *A*
Massachusetts Maritime Academy *B*
Merrimack College *B*
Mount Ida College *A*
North Shore Community College *A*
Northeastern University *B, M*
Quinsigamond Community College *A*
Simon's Rock College of Bard *B*
Smith College *B*
Springfield Technical Community
   College *A*
Tufts University *B*
Wellesley College *B*

Michigan

Alpena Community College *A*
Andrews University *B*
Calvin College *B*
Delta College *A*
Ferris State University *A*
Gogebic Community College *A*
Hope College *B*
Kalamazoo Valley Community
   College *A*
Kettering University *B*
Lake Michigan College *A*
Lake Superior State University *A*
Lansing Community College *A*
Michigan State University *B*
Michigan Technological
   University *B, M, T*
Mid Michigan Community College *A*
Northwestern Michigan College *A*
Oakland Community College *A*
St. Clair County Community
   College *A*
Schoolcraft College *A*
University of Detroit Mercy *B, M*
University of Michigan *B, M, D*
University of Michigan
   Dearborn *B*
Washtenaw Community College *A*
Wayne County Community College *A*
Western Michigan University *B*

Minnesota

Anoka-Ramsey Community College *A*
Augsburg College *B*
Central Lakes College *A*
Century Community and Technical
   College *A*
Itasca Community College *A*
Minnesota State University
   Mankato *B, M*
Normandale Community College *A*
Northland Community & Technical
   College *A*
Northwest Technical Institute *A*
Rochester Community and Technical
   College *A*
St. Cloud State University *B, M*
Winona State University *B*

Mississippi

East Central Community College *A*
Hinds Community College *A*
Holmes Community College *A*
Itawamba Community College *A*
Jackson State University *M*
Mississippi Delta Community
   College *A*
Mississippi Gulf Coast Community
   College
   Jefferson Davis Campus *A*
Mississippi State University *D*
Mississippi Valley State University *B*
University of Mississippi *B*

Missouri

Blue River Community College *A*
Crowder College *A*
Jefferson College *A*
Longview Community College *A*
Maple Woods Community College *A*
Missouri Southern State University *A*
Moberly Area Community College *A*
Penn Valley Community College *A*
St. Charles Community College *A*
St. Louis Community College
   St. Louis Community College at
     Florissant Valley *A*
   St. Louis Community College at
     Meramec *A*
University of Missouri
   Columbia *M*
Washington University in St.
   Louis *B, M, D*

Montana

Flathead Valley Community College *A*
Miles Community College *A*
Montana State University
   Bozeman *D*
Montana Tech of the University of
   Montana *A, B, M*

Nebraska

Northeast Community College *A*
Union College *A*
University of Nebraska
    Lincoln *M, D*
Western Nebraska Community
    College *A*

Nevada

Great Basin College *A*
Western Nevada Community
    College *A*

New Hampshire

Dartmouth College *M, D*
St. Anselm College *B*
University of New Hampshire *B*

New Jersey

Brookdale Community College *A*
The College of New Jersey *B*
Cumberland County College *A*
Essex County College *A*
Gloucester County College *A*
New Jersey Institute of Technology *M*
Ocean County College *A*
Rowan University *B, M*
Stevens Institute of
    Technology *B, M, D*
Sussex County Community College *A*
Union County College *A*

New Mexico

Albuquerque Technical-Vocational
    Institute *A*
New Mexico Highlands University *B*
New Mexico Institute of Mining and
    Technology *B*
New Mexico Junior College *A*
New Mexico State University *D*
New Mexico State University
    Alamogordo *A*
    Carlsbad *A*
San Juan College *A*
Santa Fe Community College *A*
University of New Mexico *D*

New York

Adirondack Community College *A*
Broome Community College *A*
City University of New York
    Borough of Manhattan Community
        College *A*
    College of Staten Island *A, B*
    Kingsborough Community
        College *A*
    LaGuardia Community College *A*
Clarkson University *B*
Cooper Union for the Advancement of
    Science and Art *B, M*
Cornell University *B*
Erie Community College
    North Campus *A*
Finger Lakes Community College *A*
Fulton-Montgomery Community
    College *A*
Genesee Community College *A*
Hudson Valley Community College *A*
Jamestown Community College *A*
Mohawk Valley Community College *A*
Nassau Community College *A*
Niagara University *A*
Orange County Community College *A*
Rensselaer Polytechnic
    Institute *B, M, D*
St. Thomas Aquinas College *B*
State University of New York
    Buffalo *B, M*
    College of Agriculture and
        Technology at Morrisville *A*
    College of Technology at Alfred *A*
    Maritime College *B*
    Stony Brook *B*

Sullivan County Community
    College *A*
Syracuse University *B*
Tompkins-Cortland Community
    College *A*
Ulster County Community College *A*
University of Rochester *B*
Westchester Community College *A*
Yeshiva University *B*

North Carolina

Cleveland Community College *A*
Elon University *B*
Johnson C. Smith University *B*
Lenoir Community College *A*
Livingstone College *B*
Louisburg College *A*
North Carolina Agricultural and
    Technical State University *M*
North Carolina State University *B, M*
Pfeiffer University *B*
St. Augustine's College *B*
University of North Carolina
    Asheville *B*
    Charlotte *M*
Western Piedmont Community
    College *A*

North Dakota

North Dakota State University *D*
University of North Dakota *D*

Ohio

Baldwin-Wallace College *B*
Case Western Reserve University *B, M*
Edison State Community College *A*
Jefferson Community College *A*
Kent State University *B, M*
Miami University
    Oxford Campus *B*
Muskingum College *B*
Ohio Northern University *B*
Owens Community College
    Toledo *A*
Sinclair Community College *A*
University of Akron *B, M, D*
University of Cincinnati *B, M, D*
University of Dayton *M*
University of Toledo *B*
Washington State Community
    College *A*
Wright State University *B, M, D*
Youngstown State University *B, M*

Oklahoma

Connors State College *A*
Eastern Oklahoma State College *A*
Oklahoma City Community College *A*
Oklahoma State University
    Oklahoma City *A*
Oral Roberts University *B*
Rose State College *A*
St. Gregory's University *A*
Southwestern Oklahoma State
    University *B*
Tulsa Community College *A*
University of Oklahoma *B, M, D*
Western Oklahoma State College *A*

Oregon

Central Oregon Community
    College *A*
Chemeketa Community College *A*
George Fox University *B*
Linn-Benton Community College *A*
Southwestern Oregon Community
    College *A*
Treasure Valley Community College *A*

Pennsylvania

Arcadia University *B*
Bucks County Community College *A*
Butler County Community College *A*

Chatham College *B*
Community College of Philadelphia *A*
Delaware County Community
    College *A*
Dickinson College *B*
Drexel University *M*
Elizabethtown College *B*
Geneva College *A, B*
Gettysburg College *B*
Harrisburg Area Community
    College *A*
Juniata College *B*
Lafayette College *B*
Lehigh Carbon Community College *A*
Lincoln University *B*
Messiah College *B*
Northampton County Area
    Community College *A*
Philadelphia University *B*
Pittsburgh Institute of Aeronautics *A*
Reading Area Community College *A*
Robert Morris University *D*
St. Francis University *B*
St. Vincent College *B*
Seton Hill University *B*
South Hills School of Business &
    Technology *A*
Swarthmore College *B*
Temple University *D*
Thiel College *B*
Thompson Institute *A*
University of Pittsburgh *B, M*
University of Pittsburgh
    Greensburg *B*
Valley Forge Military College *A*
Westminster College *B*
Widener University *B, M*

Puerto Rico

Inter American University of Puerto
    Rico
    Bayamon Campus *B*
University of Puerto Rico
    Mayaguez *B*
    Ponce *A*

Rhode Island

Community College of Rhode
    Island *A*
Roger Williams University *B*

South Dakota

South Dakota State University *M*

Tennessee

Columbia State Community College *A*
Jackson State Community College *A*
Maryville College *B*
Roane State Community College *A*
Southern Adventist University *A*
Tennessee State University *B, M*
University of Memphis *D*
University of Tennessee
    Chattanooga *B, M, D*
    Martin *B*
Walters State Community College *A*

Texas

Abilene Christian University *B*
Amarillo College *A*
Angelina College *A*
Austin Community College *A*
Baylor University *B, M*
Brazosport College *A*
Central Texas College *A*
Cisco Junior College *A*
Clarendon College *A*
Coastal Bend College *A*
College of the Mainland *A*
Del Mar College *A*
El Paso Community College *A*
Galveston College *A*
Grayson County College *A*

Hill College *A*
Kilgore College *A*
Lamar University *B, M, D*
Laredo Community College *A*
LeTourneau University *B*
Lubbock Christian University *B*
Midwestern State University *B*
Navarro College *A*
Palo Alto College *A*
Prairie View A&M University *M*
St. Mary's University *M*
St. Philip's College *A*
San Antonio College *A*
Schreiner University *B*
South Plains College *A*
South Texas College *A*
Texarkana College *A*
Texas A&M University *M, D*
Texas A&M University
    Kingsville *M*
Texas Christian University *B*
Texas Tech University *B, M*
Trinity Valley Community College *A*
Tyler Junior College *A*
University of Houston *M, D*
University of Texas
    El Paso *B, M*
    Tyler *M*
University of the Incarnate Word *B, D*
Western Texas College *A*
Wharton County Junior College *A*

Utah

Dixie State College of Utah *A*
Snow College *A*
Southern Utah University *A, B*
University of Utah *B*
Utah State University *B*
Utah Valley State College *A*

Vermont

St. Michael's College *B*
University of Vermont *B, M, D*

Virginia

Danville Community College *A*
Hampton University *B*
J. Sargeant Reynolds Community
    College *A*
New River Community College *A*
Old Dominion University *M, D*
Southwest Virginia Community
    College *A*
Thomas Nelson Community
    College *A*
Tidewater Community College *A*
University of Virginia *B*
Virginia Commonwealth
    University *M, D*
Virginia Western Community
    College *A*

Washington

Centralia College *A*
Everett Community College *A*
Gonzaga University *B*
Highline Community College *A*
Lower Columbia College *A*
Olympic College *A*
Shoreline Community College *A*
South Seattle Community College *A*
Spokane Falls Community College *A*
University of Washington *B, M*
Walla Walla College *B*
Whitworth College *B*
Yakima Valley Community College *A*

West Virginia

Marshall University *M*
Mountain State University *A*
Potomac State College of West Virginia
    University *A*
West Virginia University *M, D*

West Virginia University at
Parkersburg *A*

Wisconsin

Beloit College *B*
Marquette University *B*
Milwaukee School of Engineering *M*
University of Wisconsin
Madison *M*
Milwaukee *M, D*

Wyoming

Casper College *A*
Laramie County Community
College *A*
Northwest College *A*
Sheridan College *A*
Western Wyoming Community
College *A*

Engineering/industrial management

Arizona

Central Arizona College *A*
Gateway Community College *C*
University of Arizona *B*

California

California State Polytechnic
University: Pomona *M*
Loyola Marymount University *M*
National University *M*
Santa Clara University *M*
Stanford University *B, M, D*
University of Southern California *M*
University of the Pacific *B*

Colorado

Fort Lewis College *B*
University of Denver *M*

Connecticut

Naugatuck Valley Community
College *A*
University of New Haven *M*

District of Columbia

Catholic University of America *M*
George Washington University *M, D*

Florida

Florida Institute of Technology *M*
Florida International University *M*
Hillsborough Community College *A*
Palm Beach Community College *A*
Tallahassee Community College *A*
University of Miami *M*
University of South Florida *M*

Idaho

University of Idaho *M*

Illinois

Aurora University *B*
Illinois Institute of Technology *B*
Northern Illinois University *M*
Northwestern University *M*
University of Illinois
Chicago *B*

Indiana

Purdue University
Calumet *A, B*
Rose-Hulman Institute of
Technology *M*
Tri-State University *B*
University of Evansville *B*

Kansas

Kansas State University *B, M*

University of Kansas *M*
Wichita State University *M*

Kentucky

University of Louisville *M*

Louisiana

Louisiana Tech University *M*
University of Louisiana at Lafayette *M*
University of New Orleans *M*

Massachusetts

Massachusetts Maritime Academy *B*
University of Massachusetts
Amherst *M*
Wentworth Institute of
Technology *A, B*
Western New England College *M*
Worcester Polytechnic Institute *B*

Michigan

Baker College
of Muskegon *B*
Central Michigan University *M*
Eastern Michigan University *B*
Kettering University *B, M*
Lake Superior State University *B*
Lawrence Technological
University *B, M*
Oakland University *M*
University of Detroit Mercy *M*
University of Michigan
Dearborn *M*
Wayne State University *M*
Western Michigan University *B, M*

Missouri

East Central College *A*
Missouri State University *B*
St. Louis University *B*
University of Missouri
Rolla *B, M, D*
Washington University in St. Louis *M*

Montana

Montana State University
Bozeman *M*

New Jersey

New Jersey Institute of Technology *M*
Stevens Institute of
Technology *B, M, D*

New Mexico

New Mexico Institute of Mining and
Technology *M*

New York

Columbia University
Fu Foundation School of
Engineering and Applied
Science *B*
Hofstra University *M*
Rensselaer Polytechnic
Institute *B, M, D*
Rochester Institute of Technology *M*
Syracuse University *M*
United States Merchant Marine
Academy *B*

North Carolina

Central Piedmont Community
College *C, A*
Haywood Community College *A*
Mitchell Community College *A*
North Carolina Agricultural and
Technical State University *B*
Pitt Community College *C, A*
University of North Carolina
Charlotte *M*

Ohio

Case Western Reserve University *M*
David N. Myers University *B*
Miami University
Hamilton Campus *A*
Oxford Campus *B*
Ohio University
Chillicothe Campus *M*
University of Dayton *M*

Oklahoma

University of Tulsa *M*

Oregon

Portland State University *M*

Pennsylvania

Butler County Community College *A*
Drexel University *M*
Grove City College *B*
Philadelphia University *M*
Point Park University *M*
Robert Morris University *M*
York College of Pennsylvania *B*

Puerto Rico

Inter American University of Puerto
Rico
Bayamon Campus *B*
Turabo University *B*
University of Puerto Rico
Mayaguez *M*

South Dakota

South Dakota School of Mines and
Technology *M*
South Dakota State University *B, M*

Tennessee

Christian Brothers University *M*
Middle Tennessee State University *B*
University of Tennessee
Chattanooga *B, M*
Vanderbilt University *M*

Texas

Lamar University *B, M*
St. Mary's University *M*
Southern Methodist
University *B, M, D*
Texas A&M University
Kingsville *B, M*
University of Houston *B, M*

Vermont

University of Vermont *B*

Virginia

Sweet Briar College *B*

Washington

Saint Martin's University *M*
Washington State University *M*

West Virginia

West Virginia University at
Parkersburg *A, B*

Wisconsin

Marquette University *B, M*
Northeast Wisconsin Technical
College *A*

Engineering mechanics

Alabama

Alabama Southern Community
College *A*
University of Alabama *M, D*

Arizona

Central Arizona College *A*
University of Arizona *M, D*

California

California State University
Northridge *B, M*
City College of San Francisco *A*
East Los Angeles College *A*
Santa Clara University *M*
University of California
San Diego *B, M, D*

Colorado

Colorado School of Mines *M*
United States Air Force Academy *B*

Florida

University of Florida *B, M*

Georgia

Georgia Institute of Technology *M, D*

Illinois

Northwestern University *M, D*
University of Illinois
Urbana-Champaign *B, M, D*

Indiana

Purdue University
Calumet *B*

Iowa

Iowa State University *M, D*
Southeastern Community College
North Campus *A*

Maryland

Johns Hopkins University *B*

Massachusetts

Boston University *M*
Smith College *B*

Michigan

Michigan State University *M, D*
Michigan Technological University *M*
Northern Michigan University *B*
University of Michigan *M, D*
Washtenaw Community College *A*

Minnesota

Winona State University *B*

Missouri

University of Missouri
Rolla *B, M, D*

Nebraska

University of Nebraska
Lincoln *M*

New Mexico

New Mexico Institute of Mining and
Technology *M*

New York

Columbia University
Fu Foundation School of
Engineering and Applied
Science *B, M, D*
Cornell University *B, M, D*
Rensselaer Polytechnic
Institute *B, M, D*
State University of New York
College of Agriculture and
Technology at Morrisville *A*

Ohio

Case Western Reserve University *M, D*

Cleveland State University *M*
Muskingum College *B*
Ohio State University
  Columbus Campus *M, D*
University of Cincinnati *B, M, D*
University of Dayton *M*

Pennsylvania

Elizabethtown College *B*
Gettysburg College *B*
Lehigh University *B*
Penn State
  University Park *M*

South Carolina

Clemson University *M, D*

Tennessee

Lipscomb University *B*

Texas

Texas A&M University *M, D*
University of Texas
  Arlington *M*
  Austin *M, D*

Utah

University of Utah *M*

Virginia

Virginia Polytechnic Institute and
  State University *B, M, D*

Wisconsin

University of Wisconsin
  Madison *B, M, D*
Waukesha County Technical
  College *A*

Engineering physics

Alabama

Samford University *B*

Arizona

Northern Arizona University *B*
University of Arizona *B*

Arkansas

Arkansas Tech University *B*
Ouachita Baptist University *B*

California

California Institute of Technology *B*
Loyola Marymount University *B*
Point Loma Nazarene University *B*
Santa Clara University *M*
University of California
  Berkeley *B*
  San Diego *B, M, D*
University of the Pacific *B*
Westmont College *B*

Colorado

Colorado School of Mines *B, M, D*
Fort Lewis College *B*
University of Colorado
  Boulder *B*

Connecticut

Connecticut College *B*
University of Connecticut *B*
Yale University *B, M, D*

Florida

Embry-Riddle Aeronautical
  University *B, M*
Jacksonville University *B*

Idaho

Northwest Nazarene University *B*

Illinois

Augustana College *B*
Bradley University *B*
Sauk Valley Community College *A*
University of Illinois
  Chicago *B*
  Urbana-Champaign *B, M, D*

Indiana

Butler University *B*
Rose-Hulman Institute of
  Technology *B*
Taylor University *B*
Vincennes University *A*

Iowa

Loras College *B*
Morningside College *B*
St. Ambrose University *B*
University of Northern Iowa *B*

Kansas

Southwestern College *B*
University of Kansas *B*

Kentucky

Murray State University *B, T*

Maine

University of Maine *B*

Maryland

Morgan State University *B*

Massachusetts

Eastern Nazarene College *B*
Tufts University *B*
University of Massachusetts
  Boston *B*
Worcester Polytechnic Institute *B*

Michigan

Hope College *B*
Michigan Technological University *D*
Oakland University *B*
University of Michigan *B*

Minnesota

Bemidji State University *B*
St. Mary's University of Minnesota *B*

Mississippi

Mississippi College *B*

Missouri

Missouri State University *B*
Southeast Missouri State University *B*

Nebraska

University of Nebraska
  Omaha *B*

Nevada

University of Nevada
  Reno *B*

New Hampshire

Dartmouth College *B*
St. Anselm College *B*

New Jersey

Stevens Institute of Technology *B, M*

New Mexico

New Mexico State University *B*

New York

Barnard College *B*
Columbia University
  Fu Foundation School of
    Engineering and Applied
    Science *M, D*
Cornell University *B, M, D*
Rensselaer Polytechnic
  Institute *B, M, D*
State University of New York
  Buffalo *B*
Syracuse University *B*
United States Military Academy *B*

North Carolina

Elon University *B*

North Dakota

North Dakota State University *B*

Ohio

Case Western Reserve University *B*
John Carroll University *B*
Miami University
  Oxford Campus *B*
Ohio State University
  Columbus Campus *B*
Wright State University *B*

Oklahoma

Northeastern State University *B*
Oklahoma Christian University *B*
Oral Roberts University *B*
Southwestern Oklahoma State
  University *B*
University of Central Oklahoma *B, M*
University of Oklahoma *B, M, D*
University of Tulsa *B*

Oregon

Oregon State University *B*

Pennsylvania

Elizabethtown College *B*
Gettysburg College *B*
Juniata College *B*
Lehigh University *B*
University of Pittsburgh *B*

Rhode Island

Brown University *B*
Providence College *B*

South Dakota

Augustana College *B*
South Dakota State University *B*

Tennessee

Christian Brothers University *B*
University of Tennessee
  Knoxville *B*

Texas

Abilene Christian University *B*
Northeast Texas Community
  College *A*
Tarleton State University *B*
Texas A&M University *M*
Texas Tech University *B*
University of Texas
  Brownsville *B*

Utah

Weber State University *B*

Vermont

University of Vermont *M*

Virginia

Randolph-Macon Woman's College *B*
University of Virginia *M, D*

Washington and Lee University *B*

Wisconsin

University of Wisconsin
  Madison *B*
  Platteville *B*

Engineering science

Arizona

Arizona State University *M, D*

California

California Institute of
  Technology *M, D*
California Polytechnic State
  University: San Luis Obispo *B*
California State University
  Fullerton *B*
Humboldt State University *B*
San Diego State University *D*
University of California
  Berkeley *B*
  San Diego *B*

Colorado

Colorado State University *B*

Connecticut

Gateway Community College *A*
Manchester Community College *A*
Naugatuck Valley Community
  College *A*
Norwalk Community College *A*
Tunxis Community College *A*
Yale University *B*

District of Columbia

George Washington University *M, D*

Florida

Manatee Community College *A*
University of Florida *A, B*
University of Miami *B*

Idaho

Idaho State University *D, T*

Illinois

Benedictine University *B*
Northwestern University *B, M*
Principia College *B*
South Suburban College of Cook
  County *A*

Indiana

Manchester College *B*

Iowa

Wartburg College *B*

Kansas

Garden City Community College *A*
University of Kansas *M, D*

Kentucky

Eastern Kentucky University *B*

Louisiana

Louisiana State University and
  Agricultural and Mechanical
  College *M, D*
University of New Orleans *B, M, D*

Massachusetts

Boston University *D*
Bristol Community College *A*
Greenfield Community College *A*
Harvard College *B, M, D*
Merrimack College *A*

Middlesex Community College *A*
Northern Essex Community
College *A*
Smith College *B*
Tufts University *B*

Michigan
Glen Oaks Community College *A*
University of Michigan *B*
University of Michigan
Flint *B*
Washtenaw Community College *A*

Minnesota
Bethel University *B*

Mississippi
University of Mississippi *M, D*

Missouri
Washington University in St.
Louis *B, M, D*

Montana
Montana Tech of the University of
Montana *B, M*

New Hampshire
Daniel Webster College *A*
Dartmouth College *B*

New Jersey
Camden County College *A*
The College of New Jersey *B*
County College of Morris *A*
Gloucester County College *A*
Hudson County Community
College *A*
Middlesex County College *A*
New Jersey Institute of
Technology *B, M*
Passaic County Community College *A*
Raritan Valley Community College *A*
Rutgers, The State University of New
Jersey
Camden Regional Campus *B*
New Brunswick/Piscataway
Campus *B*

New Mexico
University of New Mexico *B*

New York
Adirondack Community College *A*
Broome Community College *A*
City University of New York
Borough of Manhattan Community
College *A*
Clarkson University *M, D*
Columbia-Greene Community
College *A*
Corning Community College *A*
Dutchess Community College *A*
Finger Lakes Community College *A*
Hofstra University *B*
Hudson Valley Community College *A*
Jefferson Community College *A*
Monroe Community College *A*
Onondaga Community College *A*
Rensselaer Polytechnic
Institute *B, M, D*
Rochester Institute of Technology *A*
State University of New York
College of Agriculture and
Technology at Morrisville *A*
College of Technology at Alfred *A*
College of Technology at Canton *A*
College of Technology at Delhi *A*
Suffolk County Community College *A*
Sullivan County Community
College *A*
University of Rochester *B*

Westchester Community College *A*

Ohio
Case Western Reserve
University *B, M, D*
Franciscan University of
Steubenville *B*
Jefferson Community College *A*
University of Cincinnati *M, D*
University of Toledo *M, D*
Wright State University *B, M*

Pennsylvania
Gettysburg College *B*
Montgomery County Community
College *A*
Penn State
Abington *B*
Altoona *B*
Beaver *B*
Berks *B*
Delaware County *B*
Dubois *B*
Fayette *B*
Hazleton *B*
Lehigh Valley *B*
McKeesport *B*
Mont Alto *B*
New Kensington *B*
Schuylkill - Capital College *B*
Shenango *B*
University Park *B, M, D*
Wilkes-Barre *B*
Worthington Scranton *B*
York *B*
Valley Forge Military College *A*

Tennessee
Lipscomb University *B*
University of Tennessee
Knoxville *B, M, D*
Vanderbilt University *B*

Texas
Abilene Christian University *B*
St. Mary's University *B*
Trinity University *B*
University of Houston *M, D*

Virginia
George Mason University *M*
Sweet Briar College *B*

Washington
Pacific Lutheran University *B*
Seattle Pacific University *B*
Washington State University *M, D*

Engineering technology, general

Alabama
Jefferson State Community
College *C, A*
Snead State Community College *A*

Arkansas
Arkansas State University *A, B*
Ozarka College *A*
University of Arkansas Community
College at Morrilton *A*

California
California Maritime Academy *B*
California Polytechnic State
University: San Luis Obispo *B*
California State Polytechnic
University: Pomona *B*
California State University
Sacramento *B*
Cerro Coso Community College *C, A*
College of Oceaneering *A*

Maric College: Anaheim *A*
Ohlone College *C*
Santa Barbara City College *C, A*

Colorado
Arapahoe Community College *C, A*

Connecticut
Central Connecticut State
University *M*
Naugatuck Valley Community
College *C, A*
University of Hartford *B*

Florida
University of Central Florida *B*
University of West Florida *B*

Georgia
Atlanta Metropolitan College *A*
Berry College *B*
Darton College *A*
Southern Polytechnic State
University *C, B, M*
Valdosta State University *B*

Illinois
Southern Illinois University
Carbondale *B*

Indiana
Tri-State University *M*
Vincennes University *A*

Kansas
Kansas State University *A, B*
Pittsburg State University *B, M*

Kentucky
Elizabethtown Community and
Technical College *C, A*
Hopkinsville Community College *C, A*
Jefferson Community College *C, A*
Lindsey Wilson College *A*
Murray State University *M*
Northern Kentucky University *M*

Maryland
University of Maryland
Eastern Shore *B*

Massachusetts
Bristol Community College *A*
Wentworth Institute of
Technology *A, B*

Michigan
Davenport University *C*
Eastern Michigan University *D*
Glen Oaks Community College *C*
Grand Rapids Community College *A*
Lawrence Technological University *B*
Michigan Technological University *A*
Southwestern Michigan College *C, A*
Spring Arbor University *B*

Minnesota
Itasca Community College *A*
Northwest Technical Institute *A*
Ridgewater College *C, A*
St. Cloud State University *B*

Missouri
Lincoln University *A*

Nebraska
Wayne State College *B, T*

Nevada
Community College of Southern
Nevada *A*

New Jersey
Bergen Community College *A*
New Jersey Institute of Technology *B*

New Mexico
Eastern New Mexico University *B*
New Mexico State University *A, B*

New York
Excelsior College *B*
State University of New York
College of Agriculture and
Technology at Morrisville *A*

North Carolina
Cleveland Community College *A*

Ohio
Bowling Green State University:
Firelands College *A*
James A. Rhodes State College *A*
Miami University
Hamilton Campus *B*
Oxford Campus *B*
University of Dayton *B*
Wright State University: Lake
Campus *A*
Youngstown State University *A, B*

Oklahoma
Oklahoma State University
Oklahoma City *A*
Southeastern Oklahoma State
University *B*
University of Central Oklahoma *B*

Oregon
Rogue Community College *C*

Pennsylvania
California University of
Pennsylvania *B, M*
Drexel University *B*
Montgomery County Community
College *A*
South Hills School of Business &
Technology *A*
Temple University *B*

Puerto Rico
University of Puerto Rico
Arecibo *A*

Rhode Island
Community College of Rhode
Island *C*

South Carolina
Spartanburg Technical College *C, A*

Tennessee
Austin Peay State University *B*
East Tennessee State University *B, M*
Middle Tennessee State University *B*
University of Memphis *M*

Texas
San Antonio College *C, A*
Tarleton State University *B*
Texas A&M University *B*
Texas State University: San Marcos *B*
Texas Tech University *B*
University of Texas
Tyler *B*

Virginia
Germanna Community College *C*
Old Dominion University *B*
Piedmont Virginia Community
College *A*
Rappahannock Community College *A*

Virginia State University *B*

Washington
Edmonds Community College *C, A*
Everett Community College *A*

Wisconsin
University of Wisconsin
Stout *B*

Wyoming
Laramie County Community
College *C, A*
Sheridan College *C, A*
Western Wyoming Community
College *A*

English composition

Arizona
Grand Canyon University *B*
Prescott College *B, M*

Arkansas
University of Central Arkansas *A*

California
California State University
Chico *C*
Long Beach *B*
San Bernardino *M*
College of the Desert *A*
Dominican University of California *B*
Glendale Community College *A*
Humboldt State University *B, M*
Irvine Valley College *A*
Platt College
Cerritos *A*
San Diego State University *M*
San Francisco State University *M*
Stanford University *B, M, D*
University of California
San Diego *B*

Colorado
University of Colorado
Denver and Health Sciences
Center *B*

Connecticut
Quinnipiac University *B*
Southern Connecticut State
University *B, M*
Western Connecticut State
University *B*

Florida
Florida Southern College *B*

Idaho
Brigham Young University-Idaho *B*

Illinois
Aurora University *B*
East-West University *B*
Eureka College *B*
Illinois State University *M*
Illinois Valley Community College *A*
Lewis University *B*
National-Louis University *M*
Northwestern University *C*
Richland Community College *A*
Sauk Valley Community College *A*
University of Illinois
Urbana-Champaign *B*

Indiana
DePauw University *B*
Indiana University
Bloomington *B*
South Bend *A, B*

Indiana University-Purdue University
Fort Wayne *B*
Martin University *B*
Purdue University
Calumet *B*
University of Evansville *B*

Iowa
Briar Cliff University *B*
Dordt College *B*
Drake University *B*
Graceland University *B, T*
Waldorf College *B*
Wartburg College *B*

Kansas
Butler County Community College *A*
Central Christian College of Kansas *A*

Kentucky
University of Louisville *D*

Maine
University of Southern Maine *B*

Massachusetts
Eastern Nazarene College *B*
Emerson College *M*
Salem State College *B*
Wheaton College *B*

Michigan
Eastern Michigan University *B, M*
Ferris State University *B*
University of Michigan
Flint *B*
Western Michigan University *B*

Minnesota
Bethel University *B*
Concordia College: Moorhead *B*
Metropolitan State University *B*
St. Cloud State University *B*
Winona State University *B*

Mississippi
East Central Community College *A*

Missouri
William Woods University *B*

New Jersey
Rowan University *B*

New York
Bard College *B*
Ithaca College *B*
Manhattan College *B*
Syracuse University *M, D*

North Carolina
High Point University *B*

North Dakota
Jamestown College *B*

Ohio
Ohio Northern University *B*
Ohio State University
Columbus Campus *B*
Ohio Wesleyan University *B*
Otterbein College *B*

Oklahoma
Oral Roberts University *B*
University of Central Oklahoma *B, M*

Pennsylvania
Geneva College *B*
La Roche College *B*

La Salle University *B*
Penn State
Berks *B*
University of Pittsburgh *C*
University of Pittsburgh
Greensburg *B*

Tennessee
Union University *B, T*
University of Tennessee
Knoxville *B*

Texas
Baylor University *B*
Huston-Tillotson College *B*
St. Edward's University *B*
St. Philip's College *A*
Texas A&M University
Commerce *B*
University of North Texas *B*

Utah
Snow College *A*
University of Utah *M*

Vermont
Bennington College *B*
Burlington College *B*
Champlain College *B*
Marlboro College *B*

Washington
Eastern Washington University *M*
Everett Community College *A*

West Virginia
Concord University *B*

Wisconsin
Lakeland College *B*
Marian College of Fond du Lac *B*

English literature

Alabama
Alabama Agricultural and Mechanical
University *B, M*
Alabama State University *B*
Auburn University at Montgomery *B*
Judson College *B*
Lawson State Community College *A*
Miles College *B*
Northeast Alabama Community
College *A*
Samford University *B*
Spring Hill College *B, T*
Talladega College *B*
Troy University *B*
University of Alabama *B, M, D*
University of Alabama
Birmingham *B, M*
University of Montevallo *B, M, T*
University of North Alabama *B, M*
University of South Alabama *B, M*

Alaska
University of Alaska
Fairbanks *B, M*
Southeast *B*

Arizona
Arizona State University *B, M, D*
Arizona State University West *B*
Eastern Arizona College *A*
Northern Arizona University *B, M*
University of Arizona *B, M, D*

Arkansas
Arkansas State University *B, M*
Arkansas Tech University *B, M*
Henderson State University *B*

Hendrix College *B*
John Brown University *B*
Lyon College *B*
Ouachita Baptist University *B*
University of Arkansas *B, M, D*
University of Arkansas
Fort Smith *B*
University of Central Arkansas *A, B*
University of the Ozarks *T*

California
Azusa Pacific University *B*
California Baptist University *B*
California Polytechnic State
University: San Luis Obispo *B*
California State Polytechnic
University: Pomona *B, M*
California State University
Chico *B, M*
Fullerton *B, M*
Los Angeles *B, M*
Sacramento *B, M*
San Bernardino *B*
Stanislaus *B, M*
Chapman University *B, M*
Claremont McKenna College *B*
College of the Canyons *A*
Concordia University *B*
Dominican University of California *B*
Holy Names University *B*
La Sierra University *B*
Long Beach City College *A*
Loyola Marymount University *B*
Master's College *B*
National University *B, M*
Occidental College *B*
Pepperdine University *B*
Pitzer College *B*
Point Loma Nazarene University *B*
St. Mary's College of California *B*
San Jose State University *B, M*
Santa Barbara City College *A*
Santa Clara University *B*
Scripps College *B*
Simpson University *B*
Southwestern College *A*
University of California
Berkeley *B, D*
Davis *B, M, D*
Irvine *B, M, D*
Los Angeles *B, M, D*
Riverside *B, M, D*
San Diego *B*
University of La Verne *B*
University of Redlands *B*
University of San Diego *B*
University of Southern California *B, D*
University of the Pacific *B*
Vanguard University of Southern
California *B*

Colorado
Adams State College *B*
Colorado Christian University *B*
Colorado State University *B, M*
Colorado State University
Pueblo *B*
Fort Lewis College *B*
Mesa State College *B*
Naropa University *B*
United States Air Force Academy *B*
University of Colorado
Boulder *B, M, D*
Colorado Springs *B*
Denver and Health Sciences
Center *B, M*
University of Denver *B, M, D*
University of Northern
Colorado *B, M, T*

Connecticut
Central Connecticut State
University *B, M*
Sacred Heart University *B*

St. Joseph College *B*
Trinity College *B, M*
University of Connecticut *B, M, D*
University of Hartford *B*
University of New Haven *B*
Yale University *B*

District of Columbia

American University *B*
Georgetown University *B, M*

Florida

Barry University *B*
Bethune-Cookman College *B*
Eckerd College *B*
Florida Atlantic University *B, M*
Florida Gulf Coast University *B, M*
Florida Southern College *B*
Florida State University *B, M, D*
Jacksonville University *B*
Lynn University *B*
Manatee Community College *A*
Miami Dade College *A*
New College of Florida *B*
Nova Southeastern University *B*
Palm Beach Atlantic University *B*
Rollins College *B*
St. Leo University *B*
St. Thomas University *B*
Southeastern College of the
    Assemblies of God *B*
Stetson University *B, M*
University of Central Florida *B, M*
University of Miami *B, M, D*
University of North Florida *B, M*
University of South Florida *B, M, D*
University of Tampa *A, B, T*
University of West Florida *B, M*
Valencia Community College *A*
Warner Southern College *B*

Georgia

Armstrong Atlantic State University *B*
Atlanta Christian College *B*
Bainbridge College *A*
Berry College *B*
Brenau University *B*
Brewton-Parker College *B*
Coastal Georgia Community
    College *A*
Columbus State University *B*
Covenant College *B*
Darton College *A*
Emmanuel College *B*
Emory University *B, D*
Georgia Southern University *B, M*
Georgia Southwestern State
    University *B, T*
Georgia State University *B, M, D*
Kennesaw State University *B*
LaGrange College *B*
Mercer University *B*
Morehouse College *B*
Paine College *B*
Piedmont College *B*
Shorter College *B, T*
Spelman College *B*
Toccoa Falls College *B*
University of Georgia *B, M, D*
University of West Georgia *B, M*
Valdosta State University *B, M*
Wesleyan College *B*

Hawaii

Brigham Young University-Hawaii *B*
Chaminade University of Honolulu *B*
University of Hawaii
    Manoa *B, M, D*

Idaho

Albertson College of Idaho *B*
Idaho State University *A, B, M, D, T*
Lewis-Clark State College *B*

Illinois

Benedictine University *B, T*
Bradley University *B, M, T*
Dominican University *B*
Eastern Illinois University *B, M, T*
Elmhurst College *B*
Eureka College *B*
Greenville College *B, T*
Illinois State University *D*
Illinois Wesleyan University *B*
John A. Logan College *A*
Knox College *B*
Lake Forest College *B*
Loyola University of Chicago *B, M, D*
McKendree College *B*
Millikin University *B, T*
North Central College *B, T*
Northeastern Illinois University *B, M*
Northern Illinois University *B*
Northwestern University *B, M, D*
Principia College *B*
Quincy University *B, T*
South Suburban College of Cook
    County *A*
Southern Illinois University
    Carbondale *B, M, D*
Trinity Christian College *B, T*
University of Illinois
    Springfield *B, M*
    Urbana-Champaign *B, M, D*
University of St. Francis *B*
Western Illinois University *B, M*
Wheaton College *B, T*

Indiana

Ancilla College *A*
Anderson University *B*
Ball State University *B, M, D, T*
Butler University *B, M*
Calumet College of St. Joseph *A, B*
DePauw University *B*
Earlham College *B*
Franklin College *B*
Goshen College *B*
Grace College *B*
Hanover College *B*
Huntington University *B*
Indiana State University *B, M, T*
Indiana University
    East *A, B*
    Kokomo *B*
    Northwest *A, B*
    South Bend *B*
    Southeast *B*
Indiana University-Purdue University
    Fort Wayne *B*
Indiana University-Purdue University
    Indianapolis *B, M*
Marian College *B, T*
Purdue University *B, M, D*
St. Joseph's College *B*
St. Mary-of-the-Woods College *B*
Tri-State University *B*
University of Evansville *B*
University of Indianapolis *B*
University of Notre Dame *B, M, D*
University of St. Francis *B*
University of Southern Indiana *B, T*
Valparaiso University *B, M*

Iowa

Briar Cliff University *B*
Buena Vista University *B, T*
Central College *B, T*
Coe College *B*
Cornell College *B*
Dordt College *B*
Grand View College *B*
Iowa State University *B*
Loras College *B, M*
Luther College *B*
Morningside College *B*
Simpson College *B*
University of Northern Iowa *B, M*

Waldorf College *B*

Kansas

Baker University *B, T*
Barton County Community College *A*
Bethel College *B*
Central Christian College of Kansas *A*
Hutchinson Community College *A*
Kansas State University *C, B, M*
MidAmerica Nazarene University *B*
Newman University *B*
Pittsburg State University *B, M*
Southwestern College *B*
Sterling College *B, T*
University of Kansas *B, M, D*
University of St. Mary *B*

Kentucky

Alice Lloyd College *B*
Asbury College *B, T*
Brescia University *B*
Centre College *B*
Georgetown College *B, T*
Kentucky Wesleyan College *B*
Midway College *B*
Morehead State University *B, M*
Murray State University *B, M, T*
Northern Kentucky University *B*
Pikeville College *B, T*
Thomas More College *A, B*
Union College *B*
University of Louisville *B, M*
University of the Cumberlands *B*
Western Kentucky University *B, M, T*

Louisiana

Centenary College of Louisiana *B, T*
Dillard University *B*
Louisiana State University and
    Agricultural and Mechanical
    College *B, M, D*
Loyola University New Orleans *B*
Nicholls State University *B*
Northwestern State University *B, M*
Southeastern Louisiana
    University *B, M*
Tulane University *B, M*
University of Louisiana at
    Lafayette *M, D, T*
University of Louisiana at
    Monroe *B, M*
University of New Orleans *B, M*
Xavier University of Louisiana *B*

Maine

Bates College *B, T*
Bowdoin College *B*
St. Joseph's College *B*
University of Maine
    Augusta *B*
University of New England *B*

Maryland

College of Notre Dame of
    Maryland *B, M*
Coppin State University *B*
Goucher College *B*
Hood College *B, T*
Johns Hopkins University *B, M, D*
Loyola College in Maryland *B*
McDaniel College *B*
Mount St. Mary's University *B, T*
St. Mary's College of Maryland *B*
United States Naval Academy *B*
University of Maryland
    Baltimore County *B*
    College Park *B, M, D*
    Eastern Shore *B*

Massachusetts

Assumption College *B*
Bentley College *B*
Boston College *B, M, D*

Brandeis University *B, M, D*
Bridgewater State College *B, M*
Bunker Hill Community College *A*
College of the Holy Cross *B*
Eastern Nazarene College *B*
Emmanuel College *B*
Endicott College *B*
Fitchburg State College *B*
Framingham State College *B*
Gordon College *B*
Harvard College *B, D*
Massachusetts Institute of
    Technology *B*
Merrimack College *B*
Pine Manor College *B*
Regis College *B*
Salem State College *B, M*
Simon's Rock College of Bard *B*
Smith College *B*
Stonehill College *B*
Suffolk University *B*
University of Massachusetts
    Amherst *B, M, D*
    Boston *B*
    Dartmouth *B*
Wellesley College *B*
Western New England College *B*

Michigan

Adrian College *A, B, T*
Alma College *B, T*
Aquinas College *B*
Calvin College *B, T*
Central Michigan University *B, T*
Concordia University *B*
Cornerstone University *B*
Eastern Michigan University *B, M*
Hillsdale College *B*
Madonna University *A, B*
Marygrove College *A, M*
Michigan State University *B, M, D*
Northern Michigan University *B, M*
Northwestern Michigan College *A*
Oakland University *B, M, T*
Saginaw Valley State University *B*
Spring Arbor University *B, T*
University of Detroit Mercy *B*
University of Michigan *M, D*
University of Michigan
    Flint *B*
Wayne State University *B, M, D*
Western Michigan University *B, M, D*

Minnesota

Augsburg College *B*
Bethany Lutheran College *B*
Bethel University *B*
College of St. Scholastica *B*
Concordia University: St. Paul *B*
Crown College *B*
Hamline University *B*
Metropolitan State University *B*
Minnesota State University
    Moorhead *B*
North Central University *B*
Northwestern College *B*
St. Cloud State University *B, M*
St. Mary's University of Minnesota *B*
St. Olaf College *B*
University of St. Thomas *B, M*

Mississippi

Alcorn State University *B*
Belhaven College *B*
Delta State University *B*
Millsaps College *B, T*
Mississippi Valley State University *B*
Tougaloo College *B*
University of Mississippi *B, M, D*
William Carey College *B*

Missouri

Avila University *B*

College of the Ozarks *B*
Culver-Stockton College *B, T*
Fontbonne University *B*
Hannibal-LaGrange College *B*
Lincoln University *B*
Lindenwood University *B*
Maryville University of Saint Louis *B*
Missouri Baptist University *B*
Missouri Southern State University *B*
Park University *B*
Rockhurst University *B*
St. Louis University *B, M, D*
Southeast Missouri State
   University *B, M*
Southwest Baptist University *B, T*
University of Missouri
   Columbia *B, M, D*
   Kansas City *B, M*
   St. Louis *B, M*
Washington University in St.
   Louis *B, M, D*
Webster University *B*
Westminster College *B*
William Jewell College *B*

Montana

Miles Community College *A*
Montana State University
   Billings *B, T*
Rocky Mountain College *B, T*

Nebraska

Dana College *B*
Hastings College *B*
Northeast Community College *A*
Union College *B*
University of Nebraska
   Lincoln *B, M, D*
   Omaha *B, M*
Wayne State College *B, T*
Western Nebraska Community
   College *A*
York College *B*

Nevada

Community College of Southern
   Nevada *A*
Sierra Nevada College *B*
University of Nevada
   Reno *B, M, D*

New Hampshire

Colby-Sawyer College *B*
Keene State College *B, T*
New England College *B*
Plymouth State University *B*
Rivier College *M*
St. Anselm College *B, T*
Southern New Hampshire
   University *B*
Thomas More College of Liberal
   Arts *B*
University of New Hampshire *B*

New Jersey

Bloomfield College *B*
Caldwell College *B*
The College of New Jersey *B, M*
Drew University *B*
Fairleigh Dickinson University
   College at Florham *B*
   Metropolitan Campus *B, M*
Georgian Court University *B*
Kean University *B, T*
Monmouth University *B, M*
Princeton University *B, M, D*
Richard Stockton College of New
   Jersey *B*
Rider University *B*
Thomas Edison State College *B*

New Mexico

College of Santa Fe *A, B*

New Mexico Highlands
   University *B, M*
New Mexico State University *B, M*
San Juan College *A*
University of New Mexico *M, D*

New York

Adelphi University *B*
Bard College *B*
Barnard College *B*
Canisius College *B*
City University of New York
   Brooklyn College *B, M*
   College of Staten Island *B, M*
   Hunter College *B, M*
   Medgar Evers College *B*
   Queens College *B, M, T*
College of New Rochelle *B, T*
College of Saint Rose *B, M*
Columbia University
   Columbia College *B*
Cornell University *B, M, D*
Daemen College *B*
Dominican College of Blauvelt *B*
Hartwick College *B*
Hofstra University *B, M*
Houghton College *B*
Iona College *B, M*
Le Moyne College *B*
Long Island University
   Brooklyn Campus *B, M*
   C. W. Post Campus *B, M*
Marist College *B*
Marymount Manhattan College *B*
Medaille College *B*
Mercy College *B*
Mount St. Mary College *B, T*
Nyack College *B*
Pace University *B*
Roberts Wesleyan College *B*
Russell Sage College *B*
St. Francis College *B*
St. John's University *B, M, D*
Sarah Lawrence College *B*
Siena College *B, T*
Skidmore College *B*
State University of New York
   Binghamton *B, M, D*
   Buffalo *B, M, D*
   College at Brockport *B, M*
   College at Buffalo *B, M*
   College at Old Westbury *B*
   College at Potsdam *B, M*
   College of Agriculture and
     Technology at Morrisville *A*
   Oswego *B, M*
   Stony Brook *B, M, D*
Syracuse University *B, M, D*
Union College *B*
Utica College *B*
Vassar College *B*
Wagner College *B*
Wells College *B*

North Carolina

Appalachian State University *B, M*
Barton College *B*
Brevard College *B*
Campbell University *B, T*
Catawba College *B*
Chowan College *B*
Davidson College *B*
East Carolina University *B, M*
Elizabeth City State University *B*
High Point University *B*
Johnson C. Smith University *B*
Livingstone College *B*
Meredith College *B*
Montreat College *B*
North Carolina Central
   University *B, M*
North Carolina State University *B, M*
Peace College *B*
Pfeiffer University *B*

St. Augustine's College *B*
University of North Carolina
   Asheville *B*
   Chapel Hill *B, M, D*
   Charlotte *B, M*
   Greensboro *B, M, D*
   Pembroke *B*
   Wilmington *B, M*
Wake Forest University *B, M*
Western Carolina University *B, M*
Wingate University *B*
Winston-Salem State University *B*

North Dakota

Jamestown College *B*
Mayville State University *B, T*
Minot State University *B*
North Dakota State University *B, M, T*
University of Mary *B*
University of North Dakota *B, M, D*

Ohio

Antioch College *B*
Ashland University *B*
Baldwin-Wallace College *B, T*
Bluffton University *B*
Bowling Green State
   University *B, M, D*
Case Western Reserve
   University *B, M, D*
Cedarville University *B*
Central State University *B*
College of Mount St. Joseph *B, T*
Franciscan University of
   Steubenville *B*
Heidelberg College *B*
Hiram College *B*
Jefferson Community College *A*
John Carroll University *B, M*
Kent State University *B, M, D*
Lourdes College *A, B*
Malone College *B*
Marietta College *B*
Miami University
   Oxford Campus *B, M, D*
Mount Vernon Nazarene University *B*
Ohio Northern University *B*
Ohio University *B, M, D*
Ohio Wesleyan University *B*
Otterbein College *B*
Owens Community College
   Toledo *A*
Pontifical College Josephinum *B*
Tiffin University *B*
University of Akron *C, B, M*
University of Dayton *B, M*
University of Findlay *B*
University of Toledo *C, B, M, D*
Ursuline College *B*
Wittenberg University *B*
Xavier University *A, B, M*
Youngstown State University *B, M*

Oklahoma

Cameron University *B*
Oklahoma City University *B*
Oklahoma Panhandle State
   University *B*
Oklahoma State University *B, M, D*
Redlands Community College *A*
Rogers State University *A*
Southeastern Oklahoma State
   University *B*
University of Central Oklahoma *B, M*
University of Oklahoma *B, M, D*
University of Science and Arts of
   Oklahoma *B, T*
University of Tulsa *B, M, D*

Oregon

Concordia University *B*
George Fox University *B*
University of Oregon *B, M, D*

University of Portland *B*
Willamette University *B*

Pennsylvania

Albright College *B, T*
Allegheny College *B*
Bloomsburg University of
   Pennsylvania *B, T*
Bryn Athyn College of the New
   Church *B*
Bucknell University *B, M*
Butler County Community College *A*
Cabrini College *B*
California University of
   Pennsylvania *B, M*
Carlow University *B*
Carnegie Mellon University *B, M*
Chatham College *B*
Chestnut Hill College *B*
College Misericordia *B*
Delaware Valley College *B*
Dickinson College *B*
Duquesne University *B, M, D*
East Stroudsburg University of
   Pennsylvania *B, T*
Edinboro University of
   Pennsylvania *B, T*
Elizabethtown College *B*
Franklin & Marshall College *B*
Geneva College *B*
Gwynedd-Mercy College *B*
Haverford College *B, T*
Immaculata University *A, B*
Indiana University of
   Pennsylvania *B, M, D*
Juniata College *B*
King's College *B, T*
Kutztown University of
   Pennsylvania *B, M, T*
La Roche College *B*
Lebanon Valley College *B*
Lehigh University *B, M, D*
Lincoln University *B*
Lock Haven University of
   Pennsylvania *B, T*
Lycoming College *B*
Marywood University *B*
Mercyhurst College *B*
Messiah College *B*
Millersville University of
   Pennsylvania *B, M, T*
Moravian College *B*
Muhlenberg College *C, B*
Point Park University *B*
Robert Morris University *B*
St. Francis University *B*
St. Joseph's University *A, B*
St. Vincent College *B*
Seton Hill University *B, T*
Shippensburg University of
   Pennsylvania *B, T*
Slippery Rock University of
   Pennsylvania *B, M, T*
Swarthmore College *B*
Temple University *B, M, D*
University of Pennsylvania *B, M, D*
University of Pittsburgh *M, D*
University of Pittsburgh
   Bradford *B*
Ursinus College *B, T*
Villanova University *B*
Washington and Jefferson College *B*
Waynesburg College *B*
Widener University *B, T*
Wilkes University *B*
Wilson College *B*
York College of Pennsylvania *B*

Puerto Rico

University of Puerto Rico
   Cayey University College *B*
   Mayaguez *B*

Rhode Island

Bryant University *B*
Providence College *B*
Salve Regina University *B*
University of Rhode Island *B, M, D*

South Carolina

Anderson University *B*
Charleston Southern University *B*
The Citadel *B, M*
Claflin University *B*
Coastal Carolina University *B*
Coker College *B*
College of Charleston *B, M*
Columbia College *B, T*
Converse College *B*
Francis Marion University *B*
Lander University *B, T*
Limestone College *B*
Morris College *B*
North Greenville College *B*
Presbyterian College *B, T*
University of South Carolina
    Aiken *B*
    Beaufort *B*
    Upstate *B*
Voorhees College *B*

South Dakota

Augustana College *B, T*
Black Hills State University *B*
Mount Marty College *B*
South Dakota State University *B, M, T*
University of South Dakota *B*

Tennessee

Christian Brothers University *B*
Cumberland University *B*
East Tennessee State
    University *B, M, T*
Freed-Hardeman University *B, T*
Hiwassee College *A*
Jackson State Community College *A*
King College *B*
Lambuth University *B*
LeMoyne-Owen College *B*
Lipscomb University *B*
Maryville College *B, T*
Middle Tennessee State
    University *B, M, D*
Milligan College *B*
Rhodes College *B, T*
Southern Adventist University *B*
Tennessee Temple University *B*
Tennessee Wesleyan College *B, T*
Trevecca Nazarene University *B*
University of Memphis *B, M, D*
University of Tennessee
    Chattanooga *B, M*
    Martin *B*

Texas

Abilene Christian University *B, M*
Angelo State University *B, M, T*
Austin College *B*
Baylor University *B, M, D*
Clarendon College *A*
Dallas Baptist University *B*
East Texas Baptist University *B*
Hardin-Simmons University *B, M*
Houston Baptist University *B*
LeTourneau University *B*
Lee College *A*
McMurry University *B*
Midwestern State University *B, M*
Our Lady of the Lake University of San
    Antonio *B, M*
Prairie View A&M University *B, M*
St. Edward's University *B*
St. Mary's University *B*
Sam Houston State University *B, M*
Schreiner University *B*
South Texas College *A*

Southern Methodist University *B, M*
Southwestern University *B*
Stephen F. Austin State University *B, M*
Tarleton State University *B, M*
Texas A&M University *B, M, D*
Texas A&M University
    Texarkana *B, M*
Texas Christian University *B, M, D*
Texas College *B*
Texas Lutheran University *B, T*
Texas State University: San
    Marcos *B, M, T*
Texas Tech University *B, M, D*
Texas Woman's University *D*
University of Dallas *B, M, D*
University of Houston
    Clear Lake *B, M*
    Downtown *B*
University of Mary Hardin-Baylor *B, T*
University of St. Thomas *B*
University of Texas
    Arlington *B, M, D*
    Austin *B, M, D*
    Brownsville *B, M*
    Pan American *B, M*
    San Antonio *B, M, D*
    Tyler *B, M*
    of the Permian Basin *B, M*
University of the Incarnate Word *B, M*
Wayland Baptist University *B, T*
West Texas A&M University *B, M*
Western Texas College *A*

Utah

Brigham Young University *B, M*
Salt Lake Community College *A*
University of Utah *B, M, D*
Utah Valley State College *A, B*
Westminster College *B*

Vermont

Bennington College *B*
Green Mountain College *B*
Middlebury College *B, M*

Virginia

Averett University *B*
Bridgewater College *B*
Christopher Newport University *B*
Eastern Mennonite University *B*
Ferrum College *B*
Hampden-Sydney College *B*
Hampton University *B*
James Madison University *B, M*
Liberty University *B, T*
Lynchburg College *B*
Mary Baldwin College *B*
Marymount University *B, M*
Old Dominion University *B, M, D, T*
Radford University *B, M*
Randolph-Macon College *B*
St. Paul's College *B*
Shenandoah University *B*
Sweet Briar College *B*
University of Virginia *B, M, D*
University of Virginia's College at
    Wise *B, T*
Virginia Commonwealth
    University *B, M*
Virginia Polytechnic Institute and
    State University *B, M*
Virginia State University *B, M*
Virginia Wesleyan College *B*
Washington and Lee University *B*

Washington

Heritage University *B*
Northwest University *B*
Pacific Lutheran University *B*
Seattle University *B*
University of Puget Sound *B, T*
University of Washington *B*
Washington State University *B, M, D*

Western Washington University *B, M*
Whitman College *B*

West Virginia

Concord University *B*
Davis and Elkins College *B*
Glenville State College *B*
Marshall University *B, M*
Mountain State University *B*
University of Charleston *B*
West Virginia University *B, M, D*
West Virginia Wesleyan College *B*
Wheeling Jesuit University *B*

Wisconsin

Alverno College *B*
Carthage College *B*
Concordia University Wisconsin *B*
Edgewood College *B*
Lawrence University *B*
Marian College of Fond du Lac *B*
Marquette University *B, M, D*
Mount Mary College *B*
St. Norbert College *B, T*
University of Wisconsin
    Eau Claire *B, M*
    La Crosse *B, T*
    Madison *B, M, D*
Viterbo University *B, T*

Wyoming

Casper College *A*
Central Wyoming College *A*
Eastern Wyoming College *A*
Sheridan College *A*
University of Wyoming *B, M*
Western Wyoming Community
    College *A*

English literature (British)

California

California State University
    Dominguez Hills *B, M*
    East Bay *B*
    Northridge *B*
Irvine Valley College *A*
Saddleback College *A*
San Diego State University *M*
Stanford University *B*
University of California
    San Diego *B, M, D*
    Santa Cruz *B*
University of Redlands *B*
Whittier College *B*

Connecticut

Albertus Magnus College *B*

District of Columbia

Gallaudet University *B*
George Washington University *M, D*
Trinity University *B*

Florida

University of Miami *B*

Idaho

Boise State University *B*

Illinois

Blackburn College *B*

Indiana

Indiana University-Purdue University
    Fort Wayne *B*
Saint Mary's College *B, T*

Iowa

Drake University *B*

Waldorf College *B*

Maine

University of Maine
    Fort Kent *B*

Maryland

Johns Hopkins University *D*

Massachusetts

Hampshire College *B*
Northeastern University *B*
Simmons College *B, M*
Simon's Rock College of Bard *B*
Tufts University *B, M, D*

Michigan

Eastern Michigan University *M*
University of Michigan *B*

Minnesota

Concordia College: Moorhead *B*
St. Cloud State University *B*

Mississippi

Jackson State University *B*

Missouri

University of Missouri
    St. Louis *M*
Washington University in St.
    Louis *B, M, D*

New Hampshire

University of New Hampshire *B*

New Jersey

Rowan University *B*

New York

Bard College *B*
City University of New York
    Baruch College *B*
    Hunter College *B*
Columbia University
    Columbia College *B*
    School of General Studies *B*
Cornell University *B, M, D*
Elmira College *B, T*
Eugene Lang College The New School
    for Liberal Arts *B*
Excelsior College *B*
Hamilton College *B*
Hofstra University *B, M*
Mercy College *M*
New York University *B, M, D*
St. Bonaventure University *B, M*
St. Lawrence University *B*
Sarah Lawrence College *B*
State University of New York
    Purchase *B*
Syracuse University *B*
United States Military Academy *B*

North Carolina

Campbell University *B, T*
Duke University *B*
Fayetteville State University *B*

Ohio

College of Wooster *B*
Denison University *B*
Miami University
    Oxford Campus *B*
Mount Union College *B*
Ohio Wesleyan University *B*
University of Cincinnati *B, M, D, T*

Pennsylvania

Eastern University *B*
Gannon University *B, M*

Gettysburg College *B*
Holy Family University *B, T*
La Salle University *B*
University of Pittsburgh *B*
University of Pittsburgh
　Johnstown *B*
University of Scranton *M*
Waynesburg College *B*
Westminster College *B, T*

Rhode Island

Brown University *B, M, D*
Roger Williams University *B*

Texas

Texas A&M University
　Commerce *B*
University of North Texas *D*

Utah

Southern Utah University *B*

Vermont

Bennington College *B*
Marlboro College *B*

Virginia

George Mason University *M*
Randolph-Macon Woman's College *B*

West Virginia

Concord University *B*

Wisconsin

Lawrence University *B*
Marian College of Fond du Lac *B*
Marquette University *M, D*

English teacher education

Alabama

Athens State University *B*
Auburn University *B*
Birmingham-Southern College *T*
Faulkner University *B*
Huntingdon College *T*
Judson College *B*
Miles College *B*
Oakwood College *B*
Samford University *B*
Talladega College *B*
University of Mobile *B, T*

Alaska

University of Alaska
　Anchorage *M*

Arizona

Arizona State University *B, T*
Grand Canyon University *B*
Northern Arizona University *B, M, T*
Prescott College *B, M, T*
University of Arizona *B, M, D*

Arkansas

Arkansas State University *B, M, T*
Arkansas Tech University *B, M*
Harding University *B, M, T*
Henderson State University *B, M, T*
John Brown University *B, T*
Ouachita Baptist University *B, T*
Philander Smith College *B*
Southern Arkansas University *B, T*
University of Arkansas *B*
University of Arkansas
　Fort Smith *B*
　Monticello *B*
　Pine Bluff *B, M, T*
University of Central Arkansas *B, M, T*
University of the Ozarks *T*

Williams Baptist College *B*

California

Azusa Pacific University *T*
California Baptist University *T*
California Lutheran University *B, T*
California Polytechnic State
　University: San Luis Obispo *B, T*
California State University
　Chico *B, T*
　Dominguez Hills *T*
　Long Beach *T*
　Northridge *B, T*
　Sacramento *T*
　San Bernardino *T*
Chapman University *M*
Fresno Pacific University *B, T*
Humboldt State University *T*
Loyola Marymount University *M*
Master's College *T*
Mills College *T*
Mount St. Mary's College *T*
Pacific Union College *B*
San Diego Christian College *B, T*
San Diego State University *B, T*
San Francisco State University *B, T*
Simpson University *B, T*
Sonoma State University *T*
Stanford University *M, T*
University of San Francisco *T*
University of the Pacific *T*
Vanguard University of Southern
　California *T*
Westmont College *T*

Colorado

Adams State College *B, T*
Colorado State University *T*
Colorado State University
　Pueblo *T*
Fort Lewis College *B*
Metropolitan State College of
　Denver *T*
Regis University *B, T*
University of Colorado
　Boulder *T*
　Colorado Springs *T*
Western State College of Colorado *T*

Connecticut

Albertus Magnus College *B, T*
Connecticut College *T*
Fairfield University *T*
Quinnipiac University *B, M*
Sacred Heart University *T*
Southern Connecticut State
　University *B, M, T*

Delaware

Delaware State University *B*
University of Delaware *B, T*

District of Columbia

Catholic University of America *B, M*
George Washington University *M, T*
Howard University *B*
Trinity University *M*

Florida

Barry University *T*
Bethune-Cookman College *B, T*
Clearwater Christian College *B*
Flagler College *B*
Florida Agricultural and Mechanical
　University *B, M*
Florida Atlantic University *B*
Florida International
　University *B, M, T*
Florida State University *B, M, D, T*
Hobe Sound Bible College *B, T*
Palm Beach Atlantic University *B, T*
Southeastern College of the
　Assemblies of God *B, T*

Stetson University *B*
University of Central Florida *B, M*
University of Florida *B*
University of South Florida *B, M*
University of Tampa *T*
University of West Florida *B*
Warner Southern College *B*

Georgia

Agnes Scott College *M, T*
Albany State University *M*
Armstrong Atlantic State
　University *B, M, T*
Brewton-Parker College *B*
Clark Atlanta University *B*
Columbus State University *B, M*
Covenant College *B, T*
Emmanuel College *B*
Fort Valley State University *B, T*
Georgia College and State
　University *M, T*
Georgia Southern University *B, M, T*
Georgia Southwestern State
　University *M*
Georgia State University *M*
Kennesaw State University *B*
North Georgia College & State
　University *M*
Paine College *B*
Piedmont College *M, T*
Reinhardt College *B*
Shorter College *T*
Toccoa Falls College *B, T*
University of Georgia *B, M*
University of West Georgia *M*
Wesleyan College *T*

Hawaii

Brigham Young University-Hawaii *B, T*
Hawaii Pacific University *M*

Idaho

Boise State University *M, T*
Brigham Young University-Idaho *T*
Lewis-Clark State College *B, T*
Northwest Nazarene University *B*

Illinois

Augustana College *B, T*
Benedictine University *T*
Blackburn College *B, T*
Bradley University *B, M*
Chicago State University *B*
Columbia College Chicago *M*
Concordia University *B, T*
Dominican University *T*
Elmhurst College *B*
Eureka College *T*
Governors State University *B, M, T*
Greenville College *B, T*
Illinois College *T*
Illinois Wesleyan University *B*
Judson College *B, T*
Lewis University *T*
MacMurray College *B, T*
National-Louis University *M*
North Park University *T*
Northeastern Illinois University *M*
Olivet Nazarene University *B, T*
Quincy University *T*
Rockford College *T*
Roosevelt University *B*
St. Xavier University *M*
Sauk Valley Community College *A*
Trinity Christian College *B, T*
Trinity International University *B, T*
University of Illinois
　Chicago *B*
　Urbana-Champaign *B, M, T*
University of St. Francis *B, M, T*
Wheaton College *T*

Indiana

Anderson University *B, T*
Bethel College *B*
Butler University *T*
Franklin College *B, T*
Goshen College *B*
Grace College *B*
Huntington University *B, M*
Indiana University
　Bloomington *B, T*
　Kokomo *T*
　Northwest *B*
　Southeast *B*
Indiana University-Purdue University
　Fort Wayne *B, M*
Indiana University-Purdue University
　Indianapolis *B, T*
Indiana Wesleyan University *B, T*
Manchester College *B, T*
Oakland City University *B*
Purdue University
　Calumet *B*
Saint Mary's College *T*
St. Mary-of-the-Woods College *B, T*
Taylor University *B, T*
Tri-State University *B, T*
University of Evansville *B, T*
University of Indianapolis *B, M, T*
University of St. Francis *B, T*
Valparaiso University *B*

Iowa

Ashford University *B, T*
Briar Cliff University *B*
Buena Vista University *B, T*
Central College *T*
Clarke College *B, T*
Cornell College *B, T*
Dordt College *B*
Drake University *T*
Faith Baptist Bible College and
　Theological Seminary *B*
Graceland University *T*
Iowa State University *T*
Iowa Wesleyan College *B*
Loras College *T*
Maharishi University of
　Management *T*
Morningside College *B*
Mount Mercy College *T*
Northwestern College *T*
St. Ambrose University *B, T*
Simpson College *T*
University of Iowa *M, D, T*
Upper Iowa University *T*
Waldorf College *B*
Wartburg College *T*
William Penn University *B*

Kansas

Baker University *T*
Bethany College *B*
Bethel College *T*
Emporia State University *T*
Friends University *B*
Kansas Wesleyan University *B, T*
McPherson College *B, T*
MidAmerica Nazarene University *B, T*
Newman University *T*
Ottawa University *B, T*
Pittsburg State University *B, T*
Southwestern College *B, T*
Sterling College *T*
Tabor College *B, T*
University of Kansas *B, T*
University of St. Mary *T*
Washburn University of Topeka *B*

Kentucky

Alice Lloyd College *B*
Bellarmine University *B, M, T*
Campbellsville University *B*
Kentucky State University *B*

Kentucky Wesleyan College *B, T*
Lindsey Wilson College *B, T*
Thomas More College *B*
University of the Cumberlands *T*

Louisiana

Centenary College of Louisiana *B, T*
Grambling State University *B*
Louisiana State University
   Shreveport *B*
Nicholls State University *B*
Northwestern State University *B*
Our Lady of Holy Cross College *B*
Southeastern Louisiana University *B*
Southern University
   New Orleans *B*
Southern University and Agricultural
   and Mechanical College *B*
University of Louisiana at Lafayette *B*
University of Louisiana at Monroe *B*
University of New Orleans *B, M*
Xavier University of Louisiana *B*

Maine

St. Joseph's College *B*
University of Maine *B, M*
University of Maine
   Farmington *B, T*
   Fort Kent *B*
   Machias *T*
University of Southern Maine *T*

Maryland

Bowie State University *B, T*
College of Notre Dame of Maryland *T*
Columbia Union College *B*
Frostburg State University *B, T*
Mount St. Mary's University *T*
St. Mary's College of Maryland *T*
Salisbury University *T*
University of Maryland
   College Park *B*
   Eastern Shore *B*

Massachusetts

Anna Maria College *B, M, T*
Assumption College *T*
Boston University *B, M, T*
Bridgewater State College *B, M, T*
Eastern Nazarene College *B*
Elms College *B, M, T*
Fitchburg State College *B, M, T*
Framingham State College *B, M*
Lasell College *B, T*
Lesley University *B, M*
Merrimack College *T*
Northeastern University *M*
Smith College *M*
Springfield College *T*
Tufts University *M, T*
University of Massachusetts
   Dartmouth *T*
Western New England College *M, T*
Westfield State College *B, T*
Worcester State College *M, T*

Michigan

Albion College *B, T*
Alma College *T*
Andrews University *M*
Calvin College *B*
Central Michigan University *B, T*
Concordia University *B, T*
Cornerstone University *B*
Eastern Michigan University *B, T*
Ferris State University *B*
Grand Valley State University *M, T*
Hope College *T*
Madonna University *T*
Michigan State University *M*
Michigan Technological University *T*
Northern Michigan University *B, M, T*
Olivet College *B, T*

Rochester College *B*
Siena Heights University *T*
University of Michigan *D*
University of Michigan
   Flint *T*
Wayne State University *B, M, T*
Western Michigan University *B, T*

Minnesota

Augsburg College *T*
Bemidji State University *M, T*
Bethel University *B*
College of St. Benedict *T*
College of St. Catherine *B, T*
College of St. Scholastica *T*
Concordia College: Moorhead *B, T*
Concordia University: St. Paul *B, T*
Crown College *B, T*
Gustavus Adolphus College *T*
Minnesota State University
   Mankato *B, M, T*
   Moorhead *B*
Northwestern College *B*
St. Cloud State University *B, T*
St. John's University *T*
St. Mary's University of Minnesota *B*
University of Minnesota
   Duluth *B*
   Morris *T*
   Twin Cities *T*
University of St. Thomas *B, T*
Winona State University *B, M, T*

Mississippi

Blue Mountain College *B*
Delta State University *B, M, T*
Mississippi College *B, M*
Mississippi State University *T*
Mississippi Valley State University *B, T*
Rust College *B*
University of Mississippi *B, T*
William Carey College *B, M*

Missouri

Central Missouri State
   University *B, M, T*
College of the Ozarks *B, T*
Columbia College *T*
Culver-Stockton College *T*
Evangel University *B, T*
Hannibal-LaGrange College *B*
Harris-Stowe State University *T*
Lincoln University *B, T*
Maryville University of Saint
   Louis *B, M, T*
Missouri Baptist University *T*
Missouri Southern State
   University *B, T*
Missouri State University *B*
Missouri Valley College *T*
Missouri Western State University *B*
Northwest Missouri State
   University *B, M, T*
Park University *T*
Southeast Missouri State
   University *B, T*
Southwest Baptist University *B, T*
Truman State University *M, T*
University of Missouri
   Columbia *B*
   St. Louis *T*
Washington University in St. Louis *B*
William Jewell College *T*
William Woods University *B, T*

Montana

Montana State University
   Billings *B, T*
Rocky Mountain College *B, T*
University of Great Falls *B*
University of Montana: Missoula *B, T*
University of Montana: Western *B, T*

Nebraska

Chadron State College *B, M*
College of Saint Mary *B, T*
Concordia University *B, T*
Creighton University *T*
Dana College *B*
Hastings College *B, M, T*
Midland Lutheran College *B, T*
Nebraska Wesleyan University *B*
Peru State College *B, T*
Union College *T*
University of Nebraska
   Kearney *B, M, T*
   Lincoln *B*
Wayne State College *B, T*
York College *B, T*

Nevada

University of Nevada
   Reno *B, M*

New Hampshire

Colby-Sawyer College *B, T*
Franklin Pierce College *T*
Keene State College *B, T*
New England College *B, T*
Plymouth State University *M, T*
Rivier College *B, M, T*
St. Anselm College *T*
Southern New Hampshire
   University *B*
University of New Hampshire *B, T*
University of New Hampshire at
   Manchester *M*

New Jersey

Caldwell College *T*
Centenary College *T*
The College of New Jersey *B, T*
College of St. Elizabeth *T*
Georgian Court University *T*
Rowan University *B, M*
Rutgers, The State University of New
   Jersey
   New Brunswick/Piscataway
     Campus *T*
St. Peter's College *T*
William Paterson University of New
   Jersey *T*

New Mexico

College of the Southwest *B, T*

New York

Adelphi University *M*
Alfred University *M, T*
Bard College *M*
City University of New York
   Brooklyn College *B, M*
   City College *B, M*
   College of Staten Island *B, M*
   Hunter College *B, M, T*
   Lehman College *M*
   Queens College *M, T*
Colgate University *M*
College of Saint Rose *B, T*
Cornell University *M, T*
D'Youville College *B, M, T*
Daemen College *B, M, T*
Dominican College of Blauvelt *B, T*
Dowling College *B*
Dutchess Community College *A*
Elmira College *B, T*
Fordham University *M, T*
Hobart and William Smith Colleges *T*
Hofstra University *B, M*
Houghton College *B, T*
Iona College *B, M, T*
Ithaca College *B, T*
Keuka College *T*
Le Moyne College *T*

Long Island University
   Brooklyn Campus *B, M, T*
   C. W. Post Campus *B, M, T*
Manhattan College *B, T*
Manhattanville College *M, T*
Marist College *B*
Marymount Manhattan College *T*
Mercy College *B, T*
Molloy College *B*
Nazareth College of Rochester *T*
New York Institute of Technology *B, T*
New York University *B, M, D, T*
Niagara University *B, M, T*
Pace University *B, M, T*
Roberts Wesleyan College *B, M*
St. Bonaventure University *M*
St. Francis College *B*
St. John Fisher College *B, M, T*
St. John's University *B, M*
St. Joseph's College: Suffolk
   Campus *B, T*
St. Lawrence University *T*
St. Thomas Aquinas College *B, T*
State University of New York
   Albany *B, M, T*
   Binghamton *M*
   Buffalo *M, D, T*
   College at Brockport *M, T*
   College at Buffalo *B, M*
   College at Cortland *B, M, T*
   College at Fredonia *B, M, T*
   College at Geneseo *B, M, T*
   College at Oneonta *B, T*
   College at Plattsburgh *B, M*
   College at Potsdam *B, M*
   New Paltz *B, M, T*
   Oswego *B, M*
   Stony Brook *T*
Syracuse University *B, M, D, T*
University of Rochester *M, D*
Utica College *B*
Vassar College *T*
Wells College *T*

North Carolina

Appalachian State University *B, M, T*
Belmont Abbey College *T*
Bennett College *T*
Brevard College *B*
Campbell University *B, T*
Catawba College *T*
Chowan College *B, T*
Davidson College *T*
East Carolina University *B, M*
Elizabeth City State University *B, T*
Fayetteville State University *B, T*
Gardner-Webb University *B, M*
Greensboro College *B, T*
Johnson C. Smith University *B*
Lenoir-Rhyne College *B, T*
Livingstone College *T*
Mars Hill College *B, T*
Meredith College *T*
Methodist College *B, T*
North Carolina Agricultural and
   Technical State University *B, M, T*
North Carolina Central
   University *B, M, T*
North Carolina State
   University *B, M, T*
Piedmont Baptist College *B*
Queens University of Charlotte *T*
St. Augustine's College *B*
Shaw University *B, T*
University of North Carolina
   Charlotte *B, M*
   Greensboro *B, M*
   Pembroke *B, M*
   Wilmington *B*
Wake Forest University *T*
Western Carolina University *B, M, T*
Wingate University *B, T*
Winston-Salem State University *B*

North Dakota

Dickinson State University *B, T*
Jamestown College *B*
Mayville State University *B, T*
Minot State University *B, M*
North Dakota State University *B, T*
University of Mary *B, T*
Valley City State University *B, T*

Ohio

Ashland University *B, T*
Baldwin-Wallace College *T*
Bluffton University *B*
Bowling Green State University *B, T*
Capital University *T*
Case Western Reserve University *T*
Cedarville University *B, T*
Defiance College *B, T*
Hiram College *T*
John Carroll University *T*
Malone College *B*
Miami University
  Oxford Campus *B, M, T*
Mount Union College *T*
Mount Vernon Nazarene
  University *B, M, T*
Ohio Dominican University *B, T*
Ohio Northern University *B, T*
Ohio University *B, D, T*
Otterbein College *B*
University of Akron *B*
University of Findlay *B, M, T*
University of Rio Grande *B, T*
University of Toledo *B, M, T*
Urbana University *B*
Ursuline College *B, M, T*
Walsh University *B*
Wilmington College *B*
Wright State University *B, M, T*
Youngstown State University *B, M*

Oklahoma

Cameron University *B, T*
East Central University *B, T*
Mid-America Christian University *B*
Northeastern State University *B*
Northwestern Oklahoma State
  University *B, T*
Oklahoma Baptist University *B, T*
Oklahoma Christian University *B, T*
Oklahoma City University *B*
Oklahoma Wesleyan University *B*
Oral Roberts University *B, T*
Southeastern Oklahoma State
  University *B, T*
Southern Nazarene University *B, M*
Southwestern Oklahoma State
  University *B, M, T*
University of Oklahoma *B, T*
University of Tulsa *T*

Oregon

Concordia University *B, M, T*
Corban College *B*
George Fox University *T*
Linfield College *T*
Oregon State University *M*
Portland State University *T*
Southern Oregon University *T*
Warner Pacific College *T*

Pennsylvania

Albright College *T*
Alvernia College *B*
Arcadia University *B, M, T*
Bryn Athyn College of the New
  Church *B*
Cabrini College *T*
Carlow University *T*
Chatham College *T*
College Misericordia *T*
DeSales University *M, T*
Dickinson College *T*

Duquesne University *B, T*
Eastern University *B, T*
Elizabethtown College *B*
Gannon University *T*
Geneva College *B, T*
Gettysburg College *T*
Grove City College *B, T*
Gwynedd-Mercy College *T*
Holy Family University *B, T*
Indiana University of
  Pennsylvania *B, M, T*
Juniata College *B, T*
King's College *T*
La Roche College *B*
La Salle University *B, T*
Lebanon Valley College *T*
Lincoln University *B, T*
Lycoming College *T*
Mansfield University of
  Pennsylvania *B, T*
Marywood University *B*
Mercyhurst College *B, T*
Messiah College *B, T*
Millersville University of
  Pennsylvania *B, M, T*
Moravian College *T*
Penn State
  Harrisburg *B*
Philadelphia Biblical University *B, T*
Point Park University *B*
St. Francis University *B, T*
St. Joseph's University *B, M*
St. Vincent College *T*
Seton Hill University *B, T*
Susquehanna University *T*
Temple University *B, M, D*
Thiel College *B*
University of Pennsylvania *M, T*
University of Pittsburgh
  Johnstown *B*
Villanova University *T*
Washington and Jefferson College *T*
Waynesburg College *B, T*
Westminster College *B, T*
Widener University *M, D, T*
Wilkes University *M, T*
Wilson College *T*
York College of Pennsylvania *B, T*

Puerto Rico

Bayamon Central University *B*
Inter American University of Puerto
  Rico
  Barranquitas Campus *B, T*
  San German Campus *B*
Pontifical Catholic University of
  Puerto Rico *B, T*
Turabo University *B*
Universidad Metropolitana *B*
University of Puerto Rico
  Aguadilla *B*
  Mayaguez *M*

Rhode Island

Rhode Island College *B, M*
Salve Regina University *B*

South Carolina

Anderson University *B, T*
Charleston Southern University *M, T*
The Citadel *M*
Claflin University *B*
Coker College *B, T*
Francis Marion University *B, T*
Furman University *T*
Limestone College *B*
Morris College *B, T*
South Carolina State University *B, T*
Southern Wesleyan University *B, T*
University of South Carolina
  Aiken *B, T*
Wofford College *T*

South Dakota

Augustana College *B, T*
Black Hills State University *B*
Dakota State University *B, T*
Dakota Wesleyan University *B, T*
Mount Marty College *B*
Northern State University *B, T*
Presentation College *A*
University of Sioux Falls *T*
University of South Dakota *B, T*

Tennessee

Belmont University *B, M, T*
Bethel College *B, T*
Bryan College *T*
Christian Brothers University *B, M, T*
Crichton College *B*
Cumberland University *B*
Freed-Hardeman University *B, T*
King College *T*
Lambuth University *B, T*
Lee University *B*
Lincoln Memorial University *B, T*
Lipscomb University *B, T*
Maryville College *B, T*
Southern Adventist University *B*
Tennessee Technological
  University *B, T*
Tennessee Temple University *B*
Tennessee Wesleyan College *B, T*
Trevecca Nazarene University *B, T*
Tusculum College *B, T*
Union University *B, T*
University of Memphis *T*
University of Tennessee
  Chattanooga *B, T*
  Knoxville *T*
  Martin *B*
Vanderbilt University *M, D*

Texas

Abilene Christian University *B, T*
Baylor University *B, T*
East Texas Baptist University *B*
Hardin-Simmons University *B, T*
Houston Baptist University *B*
Howard Payne University *B, T*
Jarvis Christian College *B, T*
Lamar University *T*
Laredo Community College *A*
LeTourneau University *B, T*
Lubbock Christian University *B*
McMurry University *T*
Midwestern State University *B*
Prairie View A&M University *M*
St. Mary's University *T*
Schreiner University *B*
Southwestern Assemblies of God
  University *B*
Tarleton State University *T*
Texas A&M University
  Commerce *D, T*
Texas Christian University *B*
Texas Lutheran University *B, T*
Texas State University: San Marcos *T*
Texas Wesleyan University *B, M, T*
University of Dallas *T*
University of Houston *T*
University of Houston
  Clear Lake *T*
University of Mary Hardin-Baylor *B, T*
University of Texas
  Arlington *T*
  El Paso *M*
  San Antonio *M*
West Texas A&M University *T*

Utah

Brigham Young University *B*
Southern Utah University *B, T*
University of Utah *B*
Utah Valley State College *B*
Weber State University *B*

Vermont

Castleton State College *B, T*
College of St. Joseph in Vermont *B, M*
Goddard College *B*
Green Mountain College *B, T*
Johnson State College *B*
Lyndon State College *B*
St. Michael's College *T*
University of Vermont *B*

Virginia

Averett University *B, M, T*
Bluefield College *T*
Bridgewater College *T*
Eastern Mennonite University *T*
Emory & Henry College *M*
Hampton University *M*
Hollins University *T*
Liberty University *B, T*
Longwood University *B, T*
Lynchburg College *M*
Old Dominion University *B, T*
Radford University *T*
St. Paul's College *T*
University of Virginia's College at
  Wise *T*
Virginia Intermont College *B, T*

Washington

Central Washington University *B, M, T*
Heritage University *B, M*
Northwest University *T*
Seattle Pacific University *B, T*
Washington State University *B, M, T*
Western Washington University *B*
Whitworth College *B, M, T*

West Virginia

Alderson-Broaddus College *T*
Bethany College *B*
Concord University *B, M, T*
Ohio Valley University *B*
Shepherd University *T*
West Liberty State College *B*
West Virginia State University *B*
West Virginia University *T*
West Virginia Wesleyan College *B*

Wisconsin

Alverno College *B, T*
Carroll College *B, T*
Carthage College *T*
Concordia University Wisconsin *B*
Edgewood College *B, T*
Lakeland College *T*
Lawrence University *T*
Maranatha Baptist Bible College *B*
Marian College of Fond du Lac *B, T*
Marquette University *B*
Mount Mary College *B, T*
Northland College *T*
St. Norbert College *T*
Silver Lake College *T*
University of Wisconsin
  Green Bay *T*
  Parkside *T*
  Platteville *B, T*
  River Falls *T*
  Superior *B, T*
  Whitewater *B*
Viterbo University *B, T*

Entomology

Alabama

Auburn University *B, M, D*

Arizona

University of Arizona *M, D*

Arkansas

University of Arkansas *M, D*

California
University of California
  Davis B, M, D
  Riverside B, M, D

Colorado
Colorado State University M, D

Connecticut
University of Connecticut M, D

Delaware
University of Delaware B, M

Florida
Florida Agricultural and Mechanical
  University D
University of Florida A, B, M

Georgia
University of Georgia B, M, D

Hawaii
University of Hawaii
  Manoa M, D

Idaho
University of Idaho B, M, D

Illinois
University of Illinois
  Urbana-Champaign B, M, D

Indiana
Purdue University B, M, D

Iowa
Iowa State University B, M, D

Kansas
Kansas State University M, D
University of Kansas M, D

Kentucky
University of Kentucky M, D

Louisiana
Louisiana State University and
  Agricultural and Mechanical
  College M, D

Maine
University of Maine B, M

Maryland
University of Maryland
  College Park M, D

Massachusetts
University of Massachusetts
  Amherst M, D

Michigan
Michigan State University B, M, D

Minnesota
University of Minnesota
  Twin Cities M, D

Mississippi
Mississippi State University M, D

Missouri
University of Missouri
  Columbia M, D

Montana
Montana State University
  Bozeman M

Nebraska
University of Nebraska
  Lincoln M, D

New Jersey
Rutgers, The State University of New
  Jersey
  New Brunswick/Piscataway
  Campus M, D

New York
Cornell University B, M, D
State University of New York
  College of Environmental Science
  and Forestry B, M, D

North Carolina
North Carolina State University M, D

North Dakota
North Dakota State University M, D

Ohio
Ohio State University
  Columbus Campus B, M, D

Oklahoma
Eastern Oklahoma State College A
Oklahoma State University B, M, D

Oregon
Oregon State University B, M, D

Pennsylvania
Penn State
  University Park M, D

South Carolina
Clemson University M, D

Tennessee
University of Tennessee
  Knoxville M, D

Texas
Texas A&M University B, M, D
Texas Tech University M

Utah
Utah State University B, M

Virginia
Virginia Polytechnic Institute and
  State University D

Washington
Washington State University B, M, D

Wisconsin
University of Wisconsin
  Madison B, M, D

Wyoming
University of Wyoming M, D

Entrepreneurial studies

Alaska
University of Alaska
  Anchorage C, A, B

Arizona
Eastern Arizona College C, A
Gateway Community College C
Glendale Community College C
Northern Arizona University C
Northland Pioneer College C
Rio Salado College C
University of Arizona B

California
Azusa Pacific University M
Cabrillo College C, A
California State University
  Dominguez Hills B
  East Bay B, M
  Fullerton B, M
Coastline Community College A
College of Alameda C, A
College of Marin: Kentfield C, A
College of San Mateo C, A
Cosumnes River College A
Diablo Valley College C
Fullerton College C
Lake Tahoe Community College C, A
Los Angeles City College C, A
Los Angeles Trade and Technical
  College A
Los Medanos College C, A
Mendocino College A
Merced College A
Mount San Antonio College C, A
Mount San Jacinto College C
Pasadena City College A
San Diego State University M
San Jose City College C, A
Santa Monica College C, A
Shasta College A
Southwestern College C, A
Yuba Community College
  District C, A

Colorado
Colorado Northwestern Community
  College A
Johnson & Wales University A, B
Northeastern Junior College A

Connecticut
Quinnipiac University B
University of Hartford B

District of Columbia
Gallaudet University B
Trinity University M

Florida
Central Florida Community College C
Florida Keys Community College C
Palm Beach Atlantic University B
St. Johns River Community College C
Stetson University B
University of Miami B
Valencia Community College C

Georgia
Albany Technical College C
Darton College A
Georgia State University M
Gwinnett Technical College C
Southern Polytechnic State
  University B, M

Illinois
Bradley University B
College of Lake County C
DePaul University M
Elgin Community College C
Heartland Community College C
Kaskaskia College C
Kendall College B
Kishwaukee College C
McHenry County College C
Moraine Valley Community College A
Northwestern Business College A
Northwestern University M
Parkland College C
Prairie State College C
University of Illinois
  Chicago B
  Urbana-Champaign B
William Rainey Harper College C, A

Indiana
Huntington University B
Purdue University
  Calumet B
University of Southern Indiana B

Iowa
Buena Vista University B
Maharishi University of
  Management C
North Iowa Area Community
  College C, A

Kansas
Central Christian College of
  Kansas A, B
Coffeyville Community College A
Pratt Community College C, A

Kentucky
St. Catharine College A
University of Louisville D

Louisiana
University of Louisiana at Monroe B

Maine
Husson College B
Maine Maritime Academy A, B

Maryland
Salisbury University B

Massachusetts
Babson College B
Berkshire Community College C
Boston University B
Bridgewater State College C
Middlesex Community College C
Northeastern University B
Salem State College B
Suffolk University B
University of Massachusetts
  Lowell B

Michigan
Andrews University B
Central Michigan University B
Cleary University B
Davenport University A, B
Ferris State University C, B
Gogebic Community College A
Kirtland Community College C
Lansing Community College C
Mid Michigan Community College A
Montcalm Community College C, A
Mott Community College A
North Central Michigan College C
Northern Michigan University B
Northwood University A, B
Oakland Community College A
Schoolcraft College A

Minnesota
Dakota County Technical College C
Fond du Lac Tribal and Community
  College C
Minnesota State Community and
  Technical College - Fergus Falls C
St. Paul College C, A
University of St. Thomas C, B, M

Missouri
Missouri Valley College A
Three Rivers Community College A
Washington University in St. Louis B

Nebraska
Northeast Community College A

New Hampshire

New England College *B*
University of New Hampshire *B*

New Jersey

Bergen Community College *C*
Burlington County College *C*
Mercer County Community College *C*
Thomas Edison State College *A, B*
Warren County Community
  College *C, A*

New Mexico

Santa Fe Community College *C, A*

New York

Canisius College *B*
Erie Community College
  City Campus *C*
  North Campus *C*
  South Campus *C*
Herkimer County Community
  College *C, A*
Hofstra University *B*
Medaille College *C, B, M*
Mohawk Valley Community
  College *C, A*
Pace University *B, M*
Paul Smith's College *B*
State University of New York
  College of Technology at Alfred *C, A*
Syracuse University *B*
Tompkins-Cortland Community
  College *C*

North Carolina

Western Carolina University *M*

North Dakota

Sitting Bull College *A*
Williston State College *C, A*

Ohio

Bowling Green State University:
  Firelands College *C*
Case Western Reserve University *M, D*
Cuyahoga Community College
  Metropolitan Campus *A*
Lakeland Community College *C*
Stautzenberger College *C, A*
University of Akron *C, A*
University of Dayton *B*
University of Findlay *B*
University of Toledo *B*
Xavier University *B, M*
Youngstown State University *C*

Oklahoma

Northeastern State University *B*

Oregon

Oregon Institute of Technology *B*
Portland Community College *C*
Southwestern Oregon Community
  College *A*

Pennsylvania

Bucks County Community College *C*
Carnegie Mellon University *D*
Central Pennsylvania College *A*
Community College of Allegheny
  County *C, A*
Delaware County Community
  College *C, A*
Drexel University *B*
Duquesne University *B*
Grove City College *B*
Juniata College *B*
Messiah College *B*
Northampton County Area
  Community College *C*
Peirce College *A*

Reading Area Community
  College *C, A*
Robert Morris University *B*
Seton Hill University *B*
Temple University *B*
University of Pittsburgh
  Bradford *B*
  Titusville *C*
West Chester University of
  Pennsylvania *B*
Wilkes University *B*
Wilson College *C*

Puerto Rico

Inter American University of Puerto
  Rico
  Bayamon Campus *B*
  San German Campus *D*
National College of Business &
  Technology: Bayamon *A*
University of Puerto Rico
  Rio Piedras *B*

Rhode Island

Community College of Rhode
  Island *C*
Johnson & Wales University *A, B*

South Carolina

Florence-Darlington Technical
  College *A*
Greenville Technical College *C*
Horry-Georgetown Technical
  College *C*
Trident Technical College *C, A*

South Dakota

Black Hills State University *B*

Tennessee

Belmont University *B*
Southern Adventist University *M*
Tusculum College *B*

Texas

Baylor University *B*
Brookhaven College *A*
Galveston College *C, A*
Houston Baptist University *B*
Midland College *C, A*
Northwood University: Texas
  Campus *A, B*
Palo Alto College *A*
Richland College *A*
St. Edward's University *B*
St. Mary's University *B*
Southern Methodist University *M*
Tarrant County College *A*
University of Dallas *M*
University of Houston *B*

Utah

Brigham Young University *B*
LDS Business College *C*
Salt Lake Community College *A*

Vermont

Lyndon State College *A, B*

Virginia

J. Sargeant Reynolds Community
  College *C*
Northern Virginia Community
  College *C*

Washington

Heritage University *B*
Lake Washington Technical College *C*
Washington State University *B*
Yakima Valley Community College *A*

West Virginia

Mountain State University *A, B*
Potomac State College of West Virginia
  University *A*
Southern West Virginia Community
  and Technical College *A*

Wisconsin

Fox Valley Technical College *C*
Gateway Technical College *C*
Madison Area Technical College *C*
Moraine Park Technical College *C*
Northcentral Technical College *A*
University of Wisconsin
  Platteville *B*
  Stout *C*

Environmental biology

California

California State Polytechnic
  University: Pomona *B*
College of Marin: Kentfield *A*
Master's College *B*

Colorado

Fort Lewis College *B*
University of Colorado
  Boulder *B, M, D*

District of Columbia

American University *B*

Florida

Eckerd College *B*

Georgia

Brenau University *B*

Illinois

Chicago State University *B*
Eureka College *B*
Governors State University *M*
Greenville College *B*
Lewis University *B*

Iowa

Maharishi University of
  Management *B*

Louisiana

Nicholls State University *B*
University of Louisiana at Lafayette *D*

Maine

Colby College *B*
Maine Maritime Academy *T*
Unity College *B*

Maryland

Hood College *M*
McDaniel College *B*
Morgan State University *D*

Massachusetts

Bridgewater State College *B*
Suffolk University *B*
University of Massachusetts
  Lowell *M*

Michigan

Cornerstone University *B*
Ferris State University *B*
Michigan State University *B, M, D*

Minnesota

St. Cloud State University *B*
St. Mary's University of Minnesota *B*

Missouri

Lindenwood University *B*

New Hampshire

Plymouth State University *B*

New Jersey

Monmouth University *B*

New York

Bard College *B*
Barnard College *B*
Columbia University
  Columbia College *B*
Houghton College *B*
State University of New York
  Albany *B*
  College at Brockport *B*
  College of Environmental Science
    and Forestry *B, M, D*

North Carolina

Queens University of Charlotte *B*
Wingate University *B*

North Dakota

North Dakota State University *M, D*

Ohio

Heidelberg College *B*
Mount Union College *B*
University of Dayton *B*
Ursuline College *B*
Wilmington College *B*

Pennsylvania

Keystone College *B*
Philadelphia University *B*
University of Pennsylvania *M*
Waynesburg College *B*

Puerto Rico

Inter American University of Puerto
  Rico
  Bayamon Campus *B*

Tennessee

Belmont University *B*

Texas

Baylor University *M*

Vermont

Bennington College *B*
Sterling College *B*

Virginia

Hollins University *B*

West Virginia

University of Charleston *B*

Wisconsin

Beloit College *B*
Lawrence University *B*
University of Wisconsin
  Superior *B*

Wyoming

Eastern Wyoming College *A*

Environmental design

Alabama

Auburn University *B*

Arizona

Scottsdale Community College *C, A*
Yavapai College *C, A*

California
Art Center College of Design *B, M*
City College of San Francisco *A*
Cosumnes River College *C, A*
University of California
Davis *B*
Irvine *B, M, D*

Colorado
University of Colorado
Boulder *B*
Denver and Health Sciences
Center *D*

Connecticut
Yale University *M*

Florida
Florida Community College at
Jacksonville *A*

Georgia
Middle Georgia College *A*

Illinois
Westwood College of Technology
O'Hare *B*

Indiana
Ball State University *B*

Maryland
Morgan State University *B*

Massachusetts
Hampshire College *B*
Massachusetts College of Art *B*
University of Massachusetts
Amherst *B*

Michigan
Lawrence Technological University *B*
Michigan State University *M*
University of Michigan *B*

Minnesota
Northland Community & Technical
College *C, A*
University of Minnesota
Twin Cities *B*

Missouri
Ranken Technical College *A*
Washington University in St. Louis *M*

Montana
Montana State University
Bozeman *B*

New Jersey
Rutgers, The State University of New
Jersey
New Brunswick/Piscataway
Campus *B*

New Mexico
University of New Mexico *B*

New York
Cornell University *B, M, D*
Parsons The New School for Design *B*
State University of New York
Buffalo *B*
College of Environmental Science
and Forestry *B, M*
Suffolk County Community College *A*

North Carolina
North Carolina State University *B, D*

North Dakota
North Dakota State University *B*

Ohio
Bowling Green State University *B*
Ohio State University
Columbus Campus *B*
Stark State College of Technology *A*

Oklahoma
University of Oklahoma *B*

Pennsylvania
University of Pennsylvania *B*

Puerto Rico
University of Puerto Rico
Rio Piedras *B*

Texas
Texas A&M University *B*
University of Houston *B*
University of Texas
Austin *M*

Vermont
Sterling College *B*

Virginia
Virginia Polytechnic Institute and
State University *D*

Environmental engineering

Alabama
University of Alabama *M*
University of Alabama
Birmingham *D*

Alaska
University of Alaska
Anchorage *M*
Fairbanks *M*

Arizona
Northern Arizona University *B, M*
University of Arizona *M, D*

Arkansas
Northwest Arkansas Community
College *A*
University of Arkansas *M*

California
Loyola Marymount University *M*
National University *M*
Stanford University *B*
University of California
Berkeley *B*
Irvine *B, M, D*
Los Angeles *D*
Riverside *B, M, D*
University of California: Merced *B*
University of Southern
California *B, M, D*

Colorado
United States Air Force Academy *B*
University of Colorado
Boulder *B*

Connecticut
University of Connecticut *B, M, D*
University of Hartford *M*
University of New Haven *M*
Yale University *B, M, D*

Delaware
University of Delaware *B*

Florida
Florida Gulf Coast University *B*
Florida International University *M*
Florida State University *B*
Hillsborough Community College *A*
University of Central Florida *B, M, D*
University of Florida *A, B, M*
University of Miami *B, M*
University of South Florida *M*

Georgia
Georgia Institute of Technology *M, D*
University of Georgia *B, M*

Idaho
Idaho State University *M*
University of Idaho *M*

Illinois
Bradley University *B*
Illinois Institute of
Technology *B, M, D*
Moraine Valley Community College *C*
Northwestern University *B*
University of Illinois
Urbana-Champaign *M, D*

Indiana
Rose-Hulman Institute of
Technology *M*
Taylor University *B*
University of Notre Dame *B, M*
Vincennes University *A*

Kansas
University of Kansas *M, D*

Louisiana
Louisiana State University and
Agricultural and Mechanical
College *B*
University of New Orleans *M*

Maine
University of Southern Maine *B*

Maryland
Johns Hopkins University *B, M, D*

Massachusetts
Bristol Community College *A*
Massachusetts Institute of
Technology *B*
Smith College *B*
Suffolk University *B*
Tufts University *B, M*
University of Massachusetts
Amherst *B*
Worcester Polytechnic Institute *B, M*

Michigan
Michigan State University *M, D*
Michigan Technological
University *B, M, D, T*
University of Michigan *B, M, D*
Wayne State University *M*

Missouri
University of Missouri
Rolla *B, M*
Washington University in St. Louis *M*

Montana
Montana State University
Bozeman *M*
Montana Tech of the University of
Montana *B, M*

Nebraska
University of Nebraska
Lincoln *M*

Nevada
University of Nevada
Reno *B, M, D*

New Hampshire
University of New Hampshire *B*

New Jersey
New Jersey Institute of
Technology *B, M, D*
Rutgers, The State University of New
Jersey
New Brunswick/Piscataway
Campus *B, M*
Stevens Institute of
Technology *B, M, D*

New Mexico
Albuquerque Technical-Vocational
Institute *A*
New Mexico Institute of Mining and
Technology *B, M*
New Mexico State University *M*
University of New Mexico *M*

New York
Clarkson University *B*
Columbia University
Fu Foundation School of
Engineering and Applied
Science *B, M, D*
Cornell University *B, M, D*
Hofstra University *B*
Manhattan College *B, M*
Polytechnic University *M*
Rensselaer Polytechnic
Institute *B, M, D*
State University of New York
Buffalo *B*
College of Environmental Science
and Forestry *B, M*
Syracuse University *B, M*

North Carolina
North Carolina State University *B*

North Dakota
North Dakota State University *M*
University of North Dakota *B*

Ohio
Stark State College of Technology *A*

Oklahoma
Northeastern State University *B*
Oklahoma State University *M*
University of Oklahoma *B, M, D*

Oregon
Oregon State University *B*
University of Portland *B*

Pennsylvania
Drexel University *B, M, D*
Gannon University *B*
Gettysburg College *B*
Lehigh University *B, M, D*
Penn State
Abington *B*
Altoona *B*
Beaver *B*
Berks *B*
Delaware County *B*
Dubois *B*
Harrisburg *B*
Hazleton *B*
Lehigh Valley *B*
Mont Alto *B*
New Kensington *B*
Schuylkill - Capital College *B*
Shenango *B*
University Park *B, M, D*

Wilkes-Barre *B*
Worthington Scranton *B*
York *B*
University of Pennsylvania *B*
Villanova University *M*
Wilkes University *B*

South Carolina
Clemson University *M, D*

Tennessee
Vanderbilt University *M, D*

Texas
Lamar University *B, M*
Palo Alto College *A*
Rice University *B, M, D*
Southern Methodist
University *B, M, D*
Tarleton State University *B*
Texas Tech University *B, M*
University of Houston *M, D*
University of Texas
Arlington *M, D*
Austin *M*
El Paso *M, D*
San Antonio *D*

Utah
University of Utah *B, M, D*
Utah State University *B*

Vermont
University of Vermont *B*

Virginia
John Tyler Community College *A*
Old Dominion University *B, M, D*
Virginia Polytechnic Institute and
State University *M*

Washington
University of Washington *B*
Washington State University *M, D*

West Virginia
West Virginia University *M, D*

Wisconsin
Marquette University *B, M, D*
Milwaukee School of Engineering *M*
University of Wisconsin
Madison *M*

Wyoming
University of Wyoming *M*

Environmental engineering technology

Alabama
Northwest-Shoals Community
College *C, A*

Arkansas
East Arkansas Community
College *C, A*
Southern Arkansas University Tech *A*
University of Arkansas
Cossatot Community College of the
A

Connecticut
University of Hartford *B*

Illinois
Black Hawk College *C, A*

Iowa
Iowa Lakes Community College *A*

Kentucky
Western Kentucky University *B*

Maryland
College of Southern Maryland *C, A*

Massachusetts
Bristol Community College *A*
Wentworth Institute of Technology *A*

Michigan
Ferris State University *A, B*
Lake Superior State University *B*
Lansing Community College *A*

Nevada
Community College of Southern
Nevada *A*

New Mexico
Southwestern Indian Polytechnic
Institute *A*

New York
New York Institute of Technology *B*
Rochester Institute of
Technology *B, M*
State University of New York
College of Technology at Canton *A*

North Carolina
East Carolina University *B*
Elon University *B*
North Carolina State University *B*

North Dakota
Minot State University: Bottineau
Campus *A*

Ohio
Cincinnati State Technical and
Community College *A*
James A. Rhodes State College *A*
Ohio University *A*
Ohio University
Chillicothe Campus *A, B*
Owens Community College
Toledo *C, A*
Shawnee State University *B*
Sinclair Community College *A*
University of Toledo *A*
Wright State University *B*

Pennsylvania
Community College of Allegheny
County *A*
Delaware County Community
College *C*
Penn State
University Park *M*
Pennsylvania College of Technology *B*
Pennsylvania Highlands Community
College *A*
Temple University *B*

Puerto Rico
Universidad Metropolitana *C*

South Carolina
Greenville Technical College *C*

Tennessee
Middle Tennessee State University *B*

Texas
Angelina College *C, A*
Austin Community College *C, A*
Lamar State College at Orange *A*
Palo Alto College *C, A*

Utah
Salt Lake Community College *C, A*

Vermont
Sterling College *B*

Virginia
Danville Community College *C*

Washington
Clover Park Technical College *A*

West Virginia
Southern West Virginia Community
and Technical College *A*

Environmental health

Alabama
University of Alabama
Birmingham *D*

Arkansas
University of Arkansas
Little Rock *B*
for Medical Sciences *M*

California
California State University
East Bay *B*
Fresno *B*
San Bernardino *B*
Las Positas College *A*
Loma Linda University *M*
San Diego State University *M*
University of California
Berkeley *M, D*
Los Angeles *M, D*

Colorado
Colorado State University *B, M, D*

Delaware
Delaware State University *B*

Georgia
University of Georgia *B, M*

Idaho
Boise State University *B*

Illinois
Illinois State University *B*
University of Illinois
Urbana-Champaign *B*

Indiana
Indiana State University *B*

Iowa
Iowa Wesleyan College *B*
University of Iowa *M, D*
University of Northern Iowa *M*

Louisiana
Tulane University *M, D*

Maine
University of Southern Maine *B*

Maryland
Salisbury University *B*
University of Maryland
University College *M*

Massachusetts
Anna Maria College *M*
Boston University *M, D*
Harvard College *M, D*

Michigan
Oakland University *B*
University of Michigan *M, D*
Wayne County Community College *A*

Minnesota
University of Minnesota
Twin Cities *M, D*
Vermilion Community College *A*

Mississippi
Mississippi Valley State
University *B, M*

Missouri
Crowder College *A*
Missouri Southern State University *B*

New Mexico
New Mexico State University *B*

New York
City University of New York
Queensborough Community
College *A*
York College *B*
Clarkson University *B*
New York University *M, D*
Polytechnic University *M*
State University of New York
Albany *M, D*
University of Rochester *M*

North Carolina
Durham Technical Community
College *A*
East Carolina University *B, M*
University of North Carolina
Chapel Hill *B*
Western Carolina University *B*

Ohio
Bowling Green State University *B*
Case Western Reserve University *M, D*
Ohio University *B*
University of Akron *A*
University of Akron: Wayne College *A*
University of Findlay *B*
Wright State University *B*

Oklahoma
East Central University *B*
University of Oklahoma *M, D*

Oregon
Oregon State University *B, M*

Pennsylvania
Temple University *M*
University of Pennsylvania *M*
University of Pittsburgh *M, D*

South Carolina
University of South Carolina *M, D*

Tennessee
East Tennessee State University *B, M*
Roane State Community College *A*

Texas
Texas State Technical College:
Marshall *A*

Virginia
Old Dominion University *B*

Washington
University of Washington *B, M*

Wisconsin

University of Wisconsin
  Eau Claire B, M

Environmental psychology

Florida

Embry-Riddle Aeronautical
  University M

Environmental science

Alabama

Auburn University B
Huntingdon College B
Miles College B
Samford University B
Troy University B
University of Alabama B

Alaska

Alaska Pacific University B, M
University of Alaska
  Southeast B

Arizona

Arizona Western College A
Dine College A
Northern Arizona University B

California

California Lutheran University B
Claremont McKenna College B
College of the Desert A
Dominican University of California B
Fresno Pacific University B
Loyola Marymount University M
Pitzer College B
Santa Clara University B
Scripps College B
Stanford University B, M, D
University of California
  Berkeley B
  Los Angeles D
  Riverside B, M, D
  San Diego B
University of La Verne B
University of Redlands B
University of San Francisco B
University of Southern California B

Colorado

Colorado College B
Mesa State College B
University of Colorado
  Denver and Health Sciences
    Center M
University of Denver B

Connecticut

Eastern Connecticut State
  University B
Sacred Heart University B
Trinity College B
University of Connecticut B
Yale University M, D

District of Columbia

American University M

Florida

Barry University B
Broward Community College A
Florida Agricultural and Mechanical
  University B, M, D
Florida Gulf Coast University B, M
Florida Institute of
  Technology B, M, D
Florida State University B
Hillsborough Community College A

Miami Dade College A
Nova Southeastern University B, M
Stetson University B
University of Tampa B
University of West Florida B, M
Valencia Community College A

Georgia

Berry College B
Columbus State University M
Mercer University B
Paine College B
Piedmont College B
Spelman College B
University of West Georgia B
Valdosta State University B
Waycross College A

Hawaii

Hawaii Pacific University B
University of Hawaii
  Manoa B

Illinois

Bradley University B
DePaul University B
Dominican University B
Illinois College B
Loyola University of Chicago B
Monmouth College B
Northwestern University B
University of Illinois
  Springfield M
  Urbana-Champaign B, M, D
University of St. Francis B

Indiana

DePauw University B
Huntington University B
Indiana University
  Bloomington B, M, D
Indiana University-Purdue University
  Indianapolis B
Martin University B
St. Joseph's College B
Taylor University B
University of Evansville B
University of Notre Dame B
Valparaiso University B
Vincennes University A

Iowa

Briar Cliff University B
Coe College B
Drake University B
Iowa State University B, M, D
Simpson College B
University of Iowa B
University of Northern Iowa B, M
Upper Iowa University B

Kentucky

Midway College B
Northern Kentucky University B

Louisiana

Centenary College of Louisiana B
Louisiana State University and
  Agricultural and Mechanical
    College B, M
Tulane University B

Maine

Colby College B
St. Joseph's College B
Unity College B
University of Maine
  Farmington B
  Fort Kent B
University of New England B
University of Southern Maine B

Maryland

McDaniel College B
University of Maryland
  Baltimore County B

Massachusetts

Assumption College B
Berkshire Community College A
Boston University B
Cape Cod Community College C, A
Clark University B, M
Curry College B
Harvard College B
Holyoke Community College A
Merrimack College B
Simmons College B
Simon's Rock College of Bard B
Suffolk University B
University of Massachusetts
  Amherst B
  Boston M, D
  Lowell B

Michigan

Albion College B
Andrews University B
Aquinas College B
Calvin College B
Central Michigan University B
Delta College C, A
Hope College B
Marygrove College B
Michigan State University B
Michigan Technological
  University B, T
Olivet College B
University of Michigan
  Flint B
Wayne State University B
Western Michigan University B

Minnesota

Anoka-Ramsey Community College A
Bethel University B
Concordia University: St. Paul B
Fond du Lac Tribal and Community
  College A
Northland Community & Technical
  College A
St. John's University B

Missouri

Drury University B
Lindenwood University B
Maryville University of Saint Louis B
North Central Missouri College C, A
St. Louis University B
Westminster College B

Montana

Rocky Mountain College B

Nebraska

Bellevue University B
Creighton University B

Nevada

Sierra Nevada College B
University of Nevada
  Reno M, D

New Hampshire

Franklin Pierce College B
Keene State College B
New England College B
St. Anselm College B
University of New Hampshire B

New Jersey

New Jersey Institute of
  Technology B, M, D
Ramapo College of New Jersey B

Rider University B
Thomas Edison State College A, B
William Paterson University of New
  Jersey B

New Mexico

College of Santa Fe B
Southwestern Indian Polytechnic
  Institute C, A
University of New Mexico B

New York

Barnard College B
Canisius College B
City University of New York
  College of Staten Island M
  Medgar Evers College B
  Queens College B, T
Columbia University
  Columbia College B
Columbia-Greene Community
  College A
Cornell University B
Marist College B
Pace University M
Paul Smith's College A, B
Polytechnic University M
Rensselaer Polytechnic Institute B
Skidmore College B
State University of New York
  College at Brockport B
  College at Oneonta B
  College of Agriculture and
    Technology at Morrisville A
  College of Environmental Science
    and Forestry B, M, D
Suffolk County Community College A
University of Rochester B
Wells College B

North Carolina

Barton College B
Beaufort County Community
  College C
Brevard College B
Catawba College B
Lenoir-Rhyne College B
Meredith College B
North Carolina Central University B
North Carolina State University B
Roanoke-Chowan Community
  College A
Southeastern Community College A
University of North Carolina
  Chapel Hill B, M, D
  Pembroke B
  Wilmington B
Western Carolina University B

North Dakota

Sitting Bull College A

Ohio

Ashland University B
Lourdes College B
Marietta College B
Miami University
  Oxford Campus B, M
Ohio State University
  Columbus Campus M, D
Ohio University M
University of Dayton B
Wright State University M
Youngstown State University B, M

Oklahoma

Northeastern State University B
Oklahoma State University B, M, D
Rose State College A
Southeastern Oklahoma State
  University B
University of Oklahoma B, M, D

Oregon

Oregon State University *B, M, D*
University of Oregon *B, D*
University of Portland *B*
Willamette University *B*

Pennsylvania

Albright College *B*
Allegheny College *B*
Bucks County Community College *A*
California University of
    Pennsylvania *B, M*
Carlow University *B*
Chestnut Hill College *B*
DeSales University *B*
Dickinson College *B*
Duquesne University *B, M*
Edinboro University of
    Pennsylvania *B*
Elizabethtown College *B*
Franklin & Marshall College *B*
Gannon University *B*
Gettysburg College *B*
Harrisburg Area Community
    College *A*
Juniata College *B*
Keystone College *A*
King's College *B*
Kutztown University of
    Pennsylvania *B*
La Salle University *B*
Lehigh University *B*
Lincoln University *B*
Marywood University *B*
Messiah College *B*
Moravian College *B*
Muhlenberg College *C, B*
Point Park University *B*
Robert Morris University *B*
Rosemont College *B*
St. Francis University *B*
St. Vincent College *B*
Susquehanna University *B, T*
University of Pennsylvania *M*
University of the Sciences in
    Philadelphia *B*

Puerto Rico

Inter American University of Puerto
    Rico
    Bayamon Campus *B*
    San German Campus *M*
Turabo University *B, D*

Rhode Island

Brown University *B*

South Carolina

Benedict College *B*
Claflin University *B*
Lander University *B*

South Dakota

South Dakota State University *D*

Tennessee

Lambuth University *B*
Lipscomb University *B*

Texas

Abilene Christian University *B*
Baylor University *B, M*
Clarendon College *A*
Hardin-Simmons University *B*
McMurry University *B*
Midland College *A*
Midwestern State University *B*
Palo Alto College *C, A*
Rice University *M*
Sam Houston State University *B*
Southern Methodist University *B*
Stephen F. Austin State University *B, M*

Tarleton State University *M*
Texas A&M University *B*
Texas Christian University *B, M*
Texas State Technical College
    West Texas *A*
Texas State University: San
    Marcos *B, M, T*
University of Houston
    Clear Lake *B, M*
University of Texas
    Arlington *M, D*
    El Paso *B*
    San Antonio *B, M*
University of the Incarnate Word *B*
West Texas A&M University *B, M*

Utah

Dixie State College of Utah *A*
University of Utah *B*

Vermont

Bennington College *B*
Castleton State College *B*
St. Michael's College *B*
University of Vermont *B*

Virginia

Averett University *B*
Bridgewater College *B*
Christopher Newport University *B, M*
Eastern Mennonite University *B*
Ferrum College *B*
Hampton University *B*
Lynchburg College *B*
Marymount University *B*
Mountain Empire Community
    College *A*
Roanoke College *B, T*
Sweet Briar College *B*
University of Virginia *B, M, D*
Virginia Polytechnic Institute and
    State University *B*

Washington

Cascadia Community College *A*
Everett Community College *A*
Heritage University *B*
Northwest University *B*
Pacific Lutheran University *B*
Washington State University *B, M, D*
Western Washington University *B, M*

West Virginia

Marshall University *B, M*
University of Charleston *B*
West Virginia Wesleyan College *B*

Wisconsin

Alverno College *B*
Carthage College *B*
St. Norbert College *B*
University of Wisconsin
    Green Bay *B*

Wyoming

Casper College *A*
Central Wyoming College *A*

Environmental studies

Alabama

Birmingham-Southern College *B*
Northwest-Shoals Community
    College *A*
Samford University *A, B*

Alaska

University of Alaska
    Southeast *C, A*

Arizona

Northern Arizona University *B*

Prescott College *B, M*

Arkansas

Arkansas State University *M, D*
Lyon College *B*
University of Arkansas *B, D*
University of the Ozarks *B*

California

Alliant International University *B*
California State University
    Chico *B, M*
    East Bay *B*
    Fullerton *M*
    Monterey Bay *B*
    Sacramento *B*
    San Bernardino *B*
Chaffey College *A*
Claremont McKenna College *B*
College of the Desert *C, A*
Feather River College *A*
Fresno Pacific University *B*
Humboldt State University *B*
National University *B*
Pitzer College *B*
Pomona College *B*
Saddleback College *A*
San Jose State University *B, M*
Santa Barbara City College *C, A*
Santa Clara University *B*
Santa Rosa Junior College *A*
Scripps College *B*
Sonoma State University *B*
Southwestern College *C, A*
University of California
    Berkeley *B, M, D*
    Davis *B*
    Irvine *M, D*
    San Diego *B*
    Santa Barbara *B*
    Santa Cruz *B, D*
University of Redlands *B*
University of San Diego *B*
University of San Francisco *B, M*
University of Southern
    California *B, M*
University of the Pacific *B*

Colorado

Colorado Mountain College
    Timberline Campus *A*
Metropolitan State College of
    Denver *B*
Naropa University *B*
University of Colorado
    Boulder *B, M, D*
Western State College of Colorado *B*

Connecticut

Connecticut College *B*
Post University *B*
St. Joseph College *B*
Yale University *M*

Delaware

Wesley College *B, M*

District of Columbia

American University *B*
George Washington University *B, M*

Florida

Eckerd College *B*
Florida State University *B*
Indian River Community College *A*
International College *M*
New College of Florida *B*
Nova Southeastern University *B*
Rollins College *B*
St. Leo University *B*

Georgia

Darton College *A*
Emory University *B*
Shorter College *B*
University of Georgia *B*
University of West Georgia *B*

Hawaii

Chaminade University of Honolulu *B*
Hawaii Pacific University *B*

Idaho

Albertson College of Idaho *B*

Illinois

Benedictine University *B*
Dominican University *B*
Illinois Wesleyan University *B*
Knox College *B*
Lake Forest College *B*
Northeastern Illinois University *B*
Northwestern University *B*
Olivet Nazarene University *B*
Roosevelt University *B*
University of Chicago *B*
University of Illinois
    Springfield *M*
Wheaton College *B*

Indiana

Earlham College *B*
Goshen College *B*
Indiana University-Purdue University
    Indianapolis *M*
Manchester College *B*
Marian College *B, T*
St. Mary-of-the-Woods College *M*
University of Evansville *B*
University of St. Francis *A, B*

Iowa

Ashford University *B*
Central College *B*
Cornell College *B*
Dordt College *B*
Iowa Lakes Community College *A*
Iowa State University *B*
Maharishi University of
    Management *B*
University of Dubuque *B*
University of Iowa *B*

Kansas

Friends University *M*
McPherson College *B*
Tabor College *B*
University of Kansas *B*

Kentucky

Bluegrass Community and Technical
    College *A*
Maysville Community College *A*

Louisiana

Tulane University *B*
University of New Orleans *B*

Maine

Bates College *B*
Bowdoin College *B*
Colby College *B*
College of the Atlantic *B, M*
St. Joseph's College *B*
Unity College *B*
University of Maine *B, M, D*
University of Maine
    Machias *B*
    Presque Isle *B*
University of New England *B*
University of Southern Maine *B*

Maryland

Frostburg State University *B*
Hood College *B*
Towson University *B*
University of Maryland
Baltimore County *B*

Massachusetts

Boston University *B, M*
Bristol Community College *A*
Cape Cod Community College *C, A*
Clark University *B, M*
College of the Holy Cross *B*
Emmanuel College *B*
Endicott College *B*
Hampshire College *B*
Lesley University *B, M*
Massachusetts College of Liberal
Arts *B*
Mount Holyoke College *B*
Mount Wachusett Community
College *A*
Northeastern University *B*
Simon's Rock College of Bard *B*
Springfield College *B*
University of Massachusetts
Boston *C*
Wellesley College *B*

Michigan

Albion College *B*
Aquinas College *B*
Central Michigan University *B, T*
Michigan State University *B*
Northern Michigan University *B*
University of Michigan *B*
University of Michigan
Dearborn *B*
Western Michigan University *B*

Minnesota

Bethel University *B*
College of St. Benedict *B*
Concordia College: Moorhead *B*
Gustavus Adolphus College *B*
Hamline University *B*
Macalester College *B*
Minnesota State University
Mankato *B, M*
St. Olaf College *B*
University of Minnesota
Duluth *B*
University of St. Thomas *B*
Vermilion Community College *A*
Winona State University *B*

Missouri

Columbia College *B*
Drury University *B*
Maryville University of Saint
Louis *B, M, T*
Southeast Missouri State University *B*
University of Missouri
Kansas City *B*
Washington University in St. Louis *B*
Westminster College *B*

Montana

Carroll College *B*
Montana State University
Billings *B*
Rocky Mountain College *B*
University of Montana: Western *B*

Nebraska

Dana College *B*
Doane College *B*
University of Nebraska
Lincoln *B*
Omaha *B*

Nevada

Truckee Meadows Community
College *A*
University of Nevada
Las Vegas *B*

New Hampshire

Colby-Sawyer College *B*
Dartmouth College *B*
Franklin Pierce College *B*
Keene State College *B*
New Hampshire Community
Technical College
Berlin *A*
Plymouth State University *B*
University of New Hampshire *B, M, D*

New Jersey

Ramapo College of New Jersey *B*
Richard Stockton College of New
Jersey *B*
Rutgers, The State University of New
Jersey
New Brunswick/Piscataway
Campus *B*
Sussex County Community College *A*
Thomas Edison State College *B*
Warren County Community College *A*

New Mexico

College of the Southwest *B*
New Mexico Highlands University *B*
New Mexico Institute of Mining and
Technology *B*
New Mexico State University *B*

New York

Adelphi University *B, M*
Alfred University *B*
Bard College *M*
Barnard College *B*
Cazenovia College *B*
City University of New York
Brooklyn College *B*
Queens College *B, T*
Clarkson University *B*
Colgate University *B*
College of New Rochelle *B*
College of Saint Rose *B*
Columbia University
School of General Studies *B*
Elmira College *B*
Finger Lakes Community College *A*
Genesee Community College *A*
Hobart and William Smith Colleges *B*
Hofstra University *B*
Hudson Valley Community College *A*
Ithaca College *B*
Molloy College *B*
Niagara County Community
College *A*
Pace University *B*
Rensselaer Polytechnic Institute *M, D*
St. John's University *B*
St. Lawrence University *B*
Sarah Lawrence College *B*
Skidmore College *B*
State University of New York
Binghamton *B*
College at Brockport *B*
College at Fredonia *B*
College of Agriculture and
Technology at Cobleskill *A, B*
College of Agriculture and
Technology at Morrisville *A*
College of Environmental Science
and Forestry *B, M, D*
Maritime College *M*
Stony Brook *B*
Suffolk County Community College *A*
Syracuse University *B*
University of Rochester *B*
Vassar College *B*

Wells College *B*

North Carolina

Brevard College *B*
Catawba College *B*
Elon University *B*
Guilford College *B*
Meredith College *B*
Montreat College *B*
Pfeiffer University *B*
University of North Carolina
Asheville *B*
Chapel Hill *B*
Wilmington *B*

Ohio

Antioch College *B*
Capital University *B*
Case Western Reserve University *B*
Cleveland State University *B*
Columbus State Community
College *C, A*
Defiance College *B*
Hiram College *B*
John Carroll University *B*
Lake Erie College *B*
Marietta College *B*
Miami University
Oxford Campus *B*
Oberlin College *B*
Ohio Northern University *B*
Ohio State University
Agricultural Technical Institute *A*
Ohio Wesleyan University *B*
Otterbein College *B*
Stark State College of Technology *A*
University of Akron *C*
University of Toledo *B*
Ursuline College *B*
Wittenberg University *B*

Oklahoma

Eastern Oklahoma State College *A*
University of Tulsa *B*

Oregon

Lewis & Clark College *B*
Linfield College *B*
Marylhurst University *B*
Southern Oregon University *B, M*
Southwestern Oregon Community
College *A*
University of Oregon *B, M*
University of Portland *B*

Pennsylvania

Albright College *B*
Allegheny College *B*
Arcadia University *B, M*
Bucknell University *B*
Chatham College *B*
Delaware Valley College *C*
Dickinson College *B*
Edinboro University of
Pennsylvania *B*
Franklin & Marshall College *B*
Gannon University *M*
Gettysburg College *B*
Grove City College *T*
Harrisburg Area Community
College *A*
Immaculata University *B*
Juniata College *B*
Keystone College *A*
King's College *B*
Lackawanna College *A*
Mansfield University of
Pennsylvania *B*
Messiah College *B*
Moravian College *B*
Neumann College *B*
Penn State
Altoona *B*

St. Francis University *B*
St. Joseph's University *B*
St. Vincent College *B*
Shippensburg University of
Pennsylvania *B, M*
Temple University *B*
Thiel College *B*
University of Pennsylvania *B, M*
University of Pittsburgh
Johnstown *B*
Ursinus College *B*
Wilson College *B*

Puerto Rico

Pontifical Catholic University of
Puerto Rico *B*
Turabo University *M*
Universidad Metropolitana *B*
Universidad Politecnica de Puerto
Rico *M*

Rhode Island

Brown University *B, M*
University of Rhode Island *B*

South Carolina

Furman University *B*

Tennessee

Maryville College *B*
Tennessee Wesleyan College *B*
Tusculum College *B*
University of the South *B*

Texas

Austin College *B*
Baylor University *B, M*
Concordia University at Austin *B*
Lamar University *B*
Panola College *C*
St. Edward's University *B*
Texas A&M University
Commerce *B*
Texas Southern University *B*
University of Houston
Clear Lake *B, M*
University of St. Thomas *B*
University of Texas
of the Permian Basin *B*

Utah

Utah State University *M*

Vermont

Bennington College *B*
Goddard College *B*
Green Mountain College *B, M*
Johnson State College *B*
Marlboro College *B*
Middlebury College *B*
Southern Vermont College *A, B*
Sterling College *A, B*
University of Vermont *B*

Virginia

College of William and Mary *B*
Emory & Henry College *B*
Hollins University *B*
Randolph-Macon College *B*
Randolph-Macon Woman's College *B*
Southwest Virginia Community
College *A*
Sweet Briar College *B*
Tidewater Community College *A*
University of Virginia's College at
Wise *B*
Virginia Commonwealth
University *B, M*
Virginia Intermont College *B*
Virginia Polytechnic Institute and
State University *B*
Virginia Wesleyan College *B*

Washington
Centralia College *A*
Evergreen State College *B, M*
Western Washington University *B*
Whitman College *B*

West Virginia
Bethany College *B*
Davis and Elkins College *B*
Mountain State University *A, B*
Shepherd University *B*

Wisconsin
Lawrence University *B, T*
Northland College *B*
Ripon College *B*
St. Norbert College *B*
University of Wisconsin
Green Bay *B, T*
Madison *M*
Richland *C*

Wyoming
University of Wyoming *B, M*
Western Wyoming Community
College *A*

Environmental toxicology

California
University of California
Davis *B*
Irvine *M, D*
Riverside *M, D*

Louisiana
Southern University and Agricultural
and Mechanical College *D*

Michigan
Michigan State University *D*

Washington
Eastern Washington University *B*

Wisconsin
University of Wisconsin
Madison *M, D*

Epidemiology

Alabama
University of Alabama
Birmingham *D*

Arizona
University of Arizona *M, D*

California
Loma Linda University *M, D*
San Diego State University *M, D*
Stanford University *M, D*
University of California
Berkeley *M, D*
Davis *M, D*
Los Angeles *M, D*
University of Southern California *D*

District of Columbia
George Washington University *D*

Georgia
Emory University *M, D*

Hawaii
University of Hawaii
Manoa *D*

Iowa
University of Iowa *M, D*

Kentucky
University of Louisville *M, D*

Louisiana
Tulane University *M, D*

Maryland
University of Maryland
Baltimore *M, D*

Massachusetts
Boston University *M, D*

Michigan
Michigan State University *M, D*
University of Michigan *M, D*

Minnesota
University of Minnesota
Twin Cities *M, D*

Missouri
Washington University in St. Louis *M*

New York
State University of New York
Albany *M, D*
Buffalo *M, D*

North Carolina
University of North Carolina
Chapel Hill *M, D*
Wake Forest University *M*

Ohio
Case Western Reserve University *M, D*

Oklahoma
University of Oklahoma *M, D*

Pennsylvania
Drexel University *A*
Temple University *M*
University of Pennsylvania *M, D*
University of Pittsburgh *M, D*

South Carolina
Medical University of South
Carolina *M, D*
University of South Carolina *M, D*

Texas
Texas A&M University *M*
University of Texas
Health Science Center at
Houston *M, D*

Virginia
Virginia Commonwealth University *D*

Washington
University of Washington *M*

Equestrian studies

Arizona
Scottsdale Community College *C, A*

California
Cosumnes River College *A*
Feather River College *C, A*
Los Angeles Pierce College *C, A*
Merced College *A*
Mount San Antonio College *C*
Santa Rosa Junior College *C, A*
Shasta College *C, A*

Sierra College *C, A*

Colorado
Colorado State University *B*
Northeastern Junior College *A*

Connecticut
Post University *C, A, B*

Idaho
College of Southern Idaho *A*

Illinois
Black Hawk College *A*
Black Hawk College
East Campus *C, A*
South Suburban College of Cook
County *C*

Indiana
St. Mary-of-the-Woods College *A, B*

Iowa
Ellsworth Community College *A*
Kirkwood Community College *A*

Kansas
Colby Community College *A*
Dodge City Community College *C, A*

Kentucky
Midway College *A, B*

Maine
University of Maine *C*

Massachusetts
Mount Ida College *A, B*
University of Massachusetts
Amherst *A*

Minnesota
University of Minnesota
Crookston *B*

Missouri
Truman State University *B*
William Woods University *B*

Montana
Dawson Community College *A*
Rocky Mountain College *B*

Nebraska
Nebraska College of Technical
Agriculture *A*

New Hampshire
University of New Hampshire *A, B*

New Jersey
Centenary College *A, B*

New York
Cazenovia College *C*
State University of New York
College of Agriculture and
Technology at Cobleskill *A, B*
College of Agriculture and
Technology at Morrisville *A, B*

North Carolina
Martin Community College *C, A*
St. Andrews Presbyterian College *B*

North Dakota
North Dakota State University *B*

Ohio
Hocking College *C, A*
Lake Erie College *B*
Ohio University *A*
Ohio University
Southern Campus at Ironton *A*
Otterbein College *B*
University of Findlay *A, B*

Oklahoma
Connors State College *C, A*
Northeastern Oklahoma Agricultural
and Mechanical College *A*
Redlands Community College *A*

Oregon
Linn-Benton Community College *A*

Pennsylvania
Delaware Valley College *A, B*
Wilson College *B*

Rhode Island
Johnson & Wales University *A, B*

Texas
Central Texas College *C*
Clarendon College *A*
Frank Phillips College *C, A*
North Central Texas College *A*
Sul Ross State University *B*
Weatherford College *A*
West Texas A&M University *B*

Vermont
Sterling College *B*

Virginia
Averett University *B*
J. Sargeant Reynolds Community
College *C*
Lord Fairfax Community College *C*
Virginia Intermont College *B*

Wyoming
Central Wyoming College *C, A*
Laramie County Community
College *A*
Northwest College *C, A*

ESL teacher education

Alabama
University of Alabama *M*

Alaska
Alaska Bible College *B*

Arizona
Arizona State University *M*
Grand Canyon University *M*
Northern Arizona University *M*
University of Arizona *M, D*

Arkansas
Arkansas Tech University *M*
Henderson State University *T*
University of Arkansas
Little Rock *B*

California
Alliant International
University *B, M, D*
Azusa Pacific University *M*
California State University
Dominguez Hills *M*
East Bay *M*
Fullerton *M*
Long Beach *T*
Los Angeles *M*
Sacramento *B, M, T*

College of Marin: Kentfield *A*
Fresno Pacific University *M*
Holy Names University *M, T*
Loyola Marymount University *M*
Master's College *B*
San Francisco State University *M*
San Jose State University *M*
University of California
   Los Angeles *M*
   San Diego *M*
University of San Diego *M*
University of San Francisco *M*
University of Southern California *M, T*
University of the Pacific *T*

Connecticut

Central Connecticut State
   University *M, T*

Delaware

University of Delaware *B, M, T*

District of Columbia

American University *M*
Catholic University of America *B*
George Washington University *A*
Georgetown University *M*

Florida

Barry University *T*
Carlos Albizu University *D*
University of Central Florida *M*
University of South Florida *D*

Georgia

Georgia State University *M, D*

Hawaii

Brigham Young University-Hawaii *B, T*
Hawaii Pacific University *B, M*
University of Hawaii
   Manoa *M*

Idaho

Boise State University *T*
University of Idaho *M*

Illinois

Moody Bible Institute *B*
Southern Illinois University
   Carbondale *M*
Southern Illinois University
   Edwardsville *M*
Spoon River College *A*
University of Illinois
   Urbana-Champaign *M, T*
Wheaton College *M*

Indiana

Ball State University *M, T*
Goshen College *B*
Indiana State University *M*
Indiana University-Purdue University
   Indianapolis *B*
University of Evansville *T*

Iowa

Iowa State University *M, T*
Morningside College *T*
Northwestern College *T*
University of Iowa *T*
University of Northern Iowa *B, M*
William Penn University *B*

Kansas

Emporia State University *T*
McPherson College *T*
Newman University *M*
Pittsburg State University *M*

Kentucky

Asbury College *M, T*
Murray State University *M*

Maryland

College of Notre Dame of
   Maryland *M*

Massachusetts

Boston University *M, T*
Clark University *T*
Eastern Nazarene College *M, T*
Elms College *B, M, T*
Framingham State College *M*
Salem State College *M*
Simmons College *B, M*
University of Massachusetts
   Boston *M*

Michigan

Andrews University *M*
Central Michigan University *M*
Eastern Michigan University *M*
Madonna University *M, T*
Michigan State University *M*

Minnesota

Bethel University *B*
Concordia University: St. Paul *B, T*
Hamline University *B, M, T*
Minnesota State University
   Mankato *T*
North Central University *B*
Northwestern College *B*
St. Cloud State University *M*
University of Minnesota
   Duluth *T*
   Twin Cities *M, T*

Missouri

Central Missouri State University *M, T*
Missouri Southern State University *B*
Webster University *M*

Montana

Carroll College *B*
University of Montana: Missoula *T*

Nebraska

Concordia University *B, M, T*
Hastings College *T*
University of Nebraska
   Kearney *B, T*
   Lincoln *B*

Nevada

University of Nevada
   Reno *M*

New Hampshire

Southern New Hampshire
   University *B*

New Jersey

The College of New Jersey *M, T*
Georgian Court University *T*
Montclair State University *T*
New Jersey City University *T*
Rutgers, The State University of New
   Jersey
   Camden Regional Campus *T*
Seton Hall University *M*
William Paterson University of New
   Jersey *T*

New Mexico

Western New Mexico University *B*

New York

Adelphi University *M, T*

City University of New York
   Hunter College *M, T*
   Queens College *M, T*
College of New Rochelle *M*
Hofstra University *M, T*
Le Moyne College *T*
Long Island University
   Brooklyn Campus *M, T*
   C. W. Post Campus *M*
Manhattanville College *M*
Mercy College *B, M, T*
Nazareth College of Rochester *M*
New York University *M, D, T*
Nyack College *T*
St. John's University *M, T*
State University of New York
   Albany *M*
   Buffalo *M, T*
   College at Fredonia *M*
   New Paltz *M, T*
   Stony Brook *M, T*
Utica College *B*

North Carolina

Meredith College *M, T*
University of North Carolina
   Charlotte *M*

Ohio

Cedarville University *T*
Kent State University *T*
Ohio Dominican University *B, T*
Ohio State University
   Columbus Campus *M*
Union Institute & University *B, M*
University of Findlay *B, M, T*
University of Toledo *M, T*

Oklahoma

Oklahoma Christian University *B, T*
Oklahoma City University *M*
Oral Roberts University *M*
University of Central Oklahoma *B*

Oregon

Concordia University *M*
Eastern Oregon University *B, T*
Northwest Christian College *T*
Portland State University *M, T*
Southern Oregon University *T*
University of Oregon *T*
Western Oregon University *M, T*

Pennsylvania

Bloomsburg University of
   Pennsylvania *T*
Carnegie Mellon University *B*
DeSales University *T*
Drexel University *T*
Duquesne University *M, T*
Gannon University *T*
King's College *T*
Marywood University *B*
Penn State
   University Park *M*
Temple University *M*
University of Pennsylvania *M*
University of Pittsburgh *T*
West Chester University of
   Pennsylvania *M*
Widener University *T*

Puerto Rico

American University of Puerto
   Rico *B, T*
Inter American University of Puerto
   Rico
   Fajardo Campus *B, T*
   Guayama Campus *B*
   Ponce Campus *B, M, T*
   San German Campus *B, M*
National College of Business &
   Technology: Bayamon *A*

Pontifical Catholic University of
   Puerto Rico *B, M, T*
Turabo University *M*
Universidad Adventista de las
   Antillas *M*
University of Puerto Rico
   Cayey University College *B*
   Humacao *B*

Rhode Island

Rhode Island College *M*

South Carolina

Columbia International University *M*

Tennessee

Carson-Newman College *M*
Maryville College *B, T*
Tennessee Technological University *T*
Trevecca Nazarene University *M, T*
Union University *B, T*
University of Memphis *T*

Texas

Houston Baptist University *T*
Lamar University *T*
McMurry University *T*
Texas A&M University
   Commerce *T*
Texas Wesleyan University *M*
University of Texas
   Arlington *M, T*
   Brownsville *M*
   Pan American *M*
   San Antonio *M, T*
West Texas A&M University *T*

Utah

Brigham Young University *M, T*
Snow College *A*
Utah State University *M*

Vermont

St. Michael's College *T*

Virginia

Bridgewater College *T*
Eastern Mennonite University *M, T*
Liberty University *B, D, T*
Marymount University *M*
Shenandoah University *B*

Washington

Central Washington University *T*
City University *M*
Eastern Washington University *M, T*
Gonzaga University *M*
Heritage University *B, M*
Northwest University *T*
Seattle Pacific University *M*
Seattle University *M*
University of Washington *T*
Washington State University *B, M, T*
Whitworth College *B, M, T*

West Virginia

Salem International University *T*

Wisconsin

St. Norbert College *T*
University of Wisconsin
   Green Bay *T*
   River Falls *B, T*

Ethics

California

University of Southern California *B*

District of Columbia

American University *M*

Florida
University of North Florida *M*

Illinois
Loyola University of Chicago *M*

Indiana
Valparaiso University *M*

Iowa
Drake University *B*

Maryland
University of Maryland
Baltimore County *M*

Massachusetts
Bridgewater State College *B*

Michigan
University of Michigan
Flint *B*

Missouri
Truman State University *B*
Webster University *B*

Nevada
University of Nevada
Las Vegas *M*

New York
Wells College *B*

Oregon
Oregon State University *M*

Pennsylvania
Carnegie Mellon University *B*
Duquesne University *M*
Elizabethtown College *B*

Tennessee
Union University *B*

Wisconsin
Marquette University *D*

European history

California
Chapman University *B*
Pitzer College *B*

Colorado
Fort Lewis College *B*

Massachusetts
Harvard College *B, D*
Salem State College *B*
Suffolk University *B*

Michigan
Calvin College *B*
Central Michigan University *M*

New York
Bard College *B*
Sarah Lawrence College *B*

Pennsylvania
Carnegie Mellon University *B*
Gettysburg College *B*

Rhode Island
Salve Regina University *B*

Vermont
Bennington College *B*

Wisconsin
Marquette University *M, D*

European studies

Alabama
Huntingdon College *B*

California
Claremont McKenna College *B*
Loyola Marymount University *B*
Pitzer College *B*
St. Mary's College of California *B*
San Diego State University *B*
Scripps College *B*
University of California
Irvine *B*
Los Angeles *B*
Westmont College *B*

Connecticut
Yale University *B, M, D*

District of Columbia
George Washington University *B*

Florida
Schiller International University *B*

Illinois
Northwestern University *B*

Iowa
University of Northern Iowa *B*

Kansas
University of Kansas *B*

Kentucky
Georgetown College *B*

Massachusetts
Amherst College *B*
Brandeis University *B*
Harvard College *B*
Mount Holyoke College *B*
Tufts University *B, M*
Wellesley College *B*

Michigan
Central Michigan University *B*
Hillsdale College *B*
Western Michigan University *B*

Minnesota
Hamline University *B*
University of Minnesota
Morris *B*
Twin Cities *B*

Mississippi
Millsaps College *B*

Missouri
University of Missouri
Columbia *B*
Washington University in St.
Louis *B, M*

New Hampshire
University of New Hampshire *B*

New Mexico
University of New Mexico *B*

New York
Bard College *B*
Barnard College *B*
Canisius College *B*

Columbia University
Columbia College *B*
Eugene Lang College The New School
for Liberal Arts *B*
Hobart and William Smith Colleges *B*
New York University *B, M*
Sarah Lawrence College *B*
State University of New York
Stony Brook *B*

North Carolina
Queens University of Charlotte *B*
University of North Carolina
Chapel Hill *B*

Ohio
Ohio University *B*
University of Toledo *B*
Wittenberg University *B*

Oregon
Portland State University *B*

Pennsylvania
Carnegie Mellon University *B*
St. Joseph's University *B*

Rhode Island
Brown University *B*

South Carolina
University of South Carolina *B*

Tennessee
Vanderbilt University *B*

Texas
Texas State University: San Marcos *B*
Trinity University *B*

Vermont
Bennington College *B*
Goddard College *B*
Marlboro College *B*
University of Vermont *B*

Virginia
College of William and Mary *B*
Emory & Henry College *B*

Washington
Gonzaga University *B*
Seattle Pacific University *B*
University of Washington *B, M*

Evolutionary biology

California
San Diego State University *B*
University of California
Davis *B*
Los Angeles *B*
San Diego *B*
University of Southern California *D*

Colorado
University of Colorado
Boulder *B, M, D*

Connecticut
Yale University *M, D*

Illinois
University of Chicago *D*

Indiana
Indiana University
Bloomington *M, D*

Louisiana
Tulane University *B, M, D*

Massachusetts
Harvard College *B, D*
University of Massachusetts
Amherst *M, D*

Missouri
Washington University in St. Louis *D*

Nevada
University of Nevada
Reno *M*

New Hampshire
Dartmouth College *B*

New York
Columbia University
Columbia College *B*
School of General Studies *B*

Ohio
Case Western Reserve University *B*

Oklahoma
University of Oklahoma *D*

Texas
Rice University *B, M, D*

Vermont
Bennington College *B*

Washington
Western Washington University *B*

Wisconsin
Lawrence University *B*

Executive assistant

Arkansas
University of Arkansas
Fort Smith *C, A*

California
Grossmont Community College *C, A*
Shasta College *A*

Florida
Central Florida Community
College *C, A*

Georgia
Northwestern Technical College *C, A*
West Georgia Technical College *A*

Illinois
John A. Logan College *A*
John Wood Community College *A*
Kaskaskia College *A*
Moraine Valley Community College *C*
Parkland College *A*
Robert Morris College: Chicago *C, A*
Waubonsee Community College *C, A*
William Rainey Harper College *C, A*

Indiana
Ivy Tech State College
Ivy Tech Community College:
Bloomington *C, A*
Ivy Tech Community College:
Central Indiana *C, A*
Ivy Tech Community College:
Columbus *C, A*
Ivy Tech Community College: East
Central *C, A*

Ivy Tech Community College:
Kokomo *C, A*
Ivy Tech Community College:
Lafayette *C, A*
Ivy Tech Community College: North
Central *C, A*
Ivy Tech Community College:
Northeast *C, A*
Ivy Tech Community College:
Northwest *C, A*
Ivy Tech Community College: South
Central *C, A*
Ivy Tech Community College:
Southeast *C, A*
Ivy Tech Community College:
Southwest *C, A*
Ivy Tech Community College:
Wabash Valley *C, A*
Ivy Tech Community College:
Whitewater *C, A*
Sawyer College: Merrillville *C, A*

Iowa
Hawkeye Community College *A*
Southeastern Community College
North Campus *A*
Western Iowa Tech Community
College *A*

Kansas
Central Christian College of Kansas *A*
Manhattan Area Technical
College *C, A*

Kentucky
Elizabethtown Community and
Technical College *C, A*
Jefferson Community College *C, A*
Maysville Community College *C, A*
Murray State University *C*
Owensboro Community College *C*
Somerset Community College *A*
Western Kentucky University *A*

Louisiana
ITI Technical College *A*

Maryland
Hagerstown Community College *C*

Massachusetts
Cape Cod Community College *C, A*
Mount Wachusett Community
College *A*
North Shore Community College *A*
Springfield Technical Community
College *A*

Michigan
Davenport University *A*
Grand Rapids Community College *A*
Montcalm Community College *A*
Mott Community College *C, A*
Northwestern Michigan College *C*
Wayne County Community College *A*

Minnesota
Dakota County Technical College *A*
Lake Superior College *A*
St. Cloud Technical College *A*

Missouri
Patricia Stevens College *C*

New York
ASA Institute of Business and
Computer Technology *C*
Broome Community College *A*
Genesee Community College *A*
Globe Institute of Technology *C*
Long Island Business Institute *C*
Rochester Business Institute *C, A*

Utica School of Commerce *A*

North Carolina
Cape Fear Community College *C, A*
Fayetteville Technical Community
College *C, A*
Guilford Technical Community
College *A*
Lenoir Community College *C, A*
Martin Community College *C, A*
Wilson Technical Community
College *A*

North Dakota
Lake Region State College *C, A*
North Dakota State College of
Science *A*

Ohio
Cincinnati State Technical and
Community College *C*
Edison State Community College *A*
Marion Technical College *C, A*
Owens Community College
Toledo *C, A*
Stark State College of Technology *A*
University of Cincinnati
Raymond Walters College *A*

Pennsylvania
Business Institute of Pennsylvania *A*
Business Institute of Pennsylvania
Meadville *A*
Consolidated School of Business
Lancaster *A*
York *A*
Douglas Education Center *A*
Lehigh Carbon Community College *A*
Newport Business Institute *A*
Newport Business Institute *A*

Puerto Rico
Inter American University of Puerto
Rico
Bayamon Campus *B*
Universidad del Este *A*

Texas
Alvin Community College *A*
El Centro College *A*
Kilgore College *C, A*
Mountain View College *C, A*

Utah
LDS Business College *C, A*
Utah Valley State College *A*

Virginia
Danville Community College *A*

Washington
Clark College *C, A*
Walla Walla Community College *C, A*

West Virginia
West Virginia University at
Parkersburg *C, A*

Exercise physiology

California
Chapman University *B*
University of California
Davis *B, M*

Colorado
Adams State College *B*

Georgia
Georgia Institute of Technology *D*

Kansas
Central Christian College of
Kansas *A, B*

Massachusetts
Gordon College *B*
Lasell College *B*

Minnesota
College of St. Scholastica *B, M*

Missouri
University of Missouri
Columbia *M, D*

New York
State University of New York
College at Brockport *B*

North Carolina
East Carolina University *D*

Ohio
Baldwin-Wallace College *B*
Ohio Northern University *B*

Oregon
Northwest Christian College *B*

Texas
Baylor University *B*

Virginia
Lynchburg College *B*
Virginia Commonwealth University *D*

West Virginia
West Virginia University *B, M, D*

Wisconsin
Marquette University *M, D*

Exercise sciences

Alabama
Auburn University *B*
Huntingdon College *B*
Samford University *B*
University of Alabama *D*

Alaska
University of Alaska
Fairbanks *B*

Arizona
Arizona State University *B, M, D*
Arizona Western College *A*
Central Arizona College *C, A*
Glendale Community College *C*
Northern Arizona University *B, M*

Arkansas
Arkansas State University *B, M*
Harding University *B*
Hendrix College *B*
John Brown University *B*
Ouachita Baptist University *B*
Southern Arkansas University *B*
University of Arkansas *M, D*
University of Central Arkansas *B, M*

California
California Baptist University *B, M*
California State University
Chico *B, M*
East Bay *B, M*
Fresno *A, B*
Fullerton *B, M*
Sacramento *B, M*
San Bernardino *B*

Concordia University *B, M*
Diablo Valley College *C*
Grossmont Community College *C, A*
La Sierra University *B*
MiraCosta College *C*
Occidental College *B*
Orange Coast College *C, A*
Point Loma Nazarene University *B*
St. Mary's College of California *B*
Santa Ana College *B*
Santa Barbara City College *A*
Santiago Canyon College *A*
University of Southern
California *B, M, D*
Vanguard University of Southern
California *B*
Westmont College *B*

Colorado
Adams State College *B*
Colorado State University *B, M*
Colorado State University
Pueblo *B*
Fort Lewis College *B*
Metropolitan State College of
Denver *B*
University of Colorado
Boulder *B, M, D*
University of Northern
Colorado *B, M, D, T*
Western State College of
Colorado *B, T*

Connecticut
Manchester Community College *A*
Southern Connecticut State
University *B, M, T*

Delaware
University of Delaware *B, M, D*

District of Columbia
George Washington University *B, M*

Florida
Barry University *B, M*
Florida Atlantic University *B, M*
Florida Gulf Coast University *B*
Florida International University *B, M*
Florida State University *B, M, D*
Jacksonville University *B*
Miami Dade College *A*
New England Institute of
Technology *C, A*
Santa Fe Community College *A*
Stetson University *B*
University of Florida *B, M, D*
University of Miami *B, M, D*
University of Tampa *B*
Warner Southern College *B*

Georgia
Brenau University *B*
Columbus State University *B*
Darton College *A*
East Georgia College *A*
Emmanuel College *B*
Georgia Southern University *B, M*
Georgia State University *B, M, D*
Kennesaw State University *B*
Life University *B*
Valdosta State University *B*

Hawaii
Brigham Young University-Hawaii *B*
University of Hawaii
Manoa *B, M*

Idaho
Albertson College of Idaho *B*
Boise State University *B, M*
Lewis-Clark State College *B*

Illinois

Concordia University *B*
Elmhurst College *B*
Greenville College *B*
Illinois State University *B*
North Central College *B*
Northeastern Illinois University *M*
Olivet Nazarene University *B*
Sauk Valley Community College *A*
Trinity Christian College *B*
University of Illinois
   Chicago *B, M, D*
   Urbana-Champaign *B, M, D*
Waubonsee Community College *C*
Western Illinois University *B, M*
Wheaton College *B*
William Rainey Harper College *A*

Indiana

Anderson University *B*
Ball State University *M*
DePauw University *B*
Hanover College *B*
Huntington University *B*
Indiana University
   Bloomington *D*
Indiana University-Purdue University
   Indianapolis *B*
Indiana Wesleyan University *B*
Taylor University *B*
University of Evansville *B*
University of Indianapolis *B*
University of Southern Indiana *B*
Valparaiso University *B*
Vincennes University *A*

Iowa

Briar Cliff University *B*
Buena Vista University *B*
Central College *B, T*
Clarke College *B*
Dordt College *B*
Iowa Wesleyan College *B*
Loras College *B*
Northwestern College *B*
University of Iowa *B, M, D*

Kansas

Baker University *B*
Barton County Community College *A*
Central Christian College of
   Kansas *A, B*
Kansas State University *B, M*
MidAmerica Nazarene University *B*
Neosho County Community
   College *A*
Seward County Community College *A*
Washburn University of Topeka *B*
Wichita State University *B*

Kentucky

Campbellsville University *B*
Georgetown College *B*
Morehead State University *B*
Murray State University *B*
Thomas More College *A*
Transylvania University *B, T*
University of Louisville *M*

Louisiana

Centenary College of Louisiana *B*
University of Louisiana at Monroe *M*

Maine

St. Joseph's College *B*
University of Maine
   Farmington *C*
University of New England *B*
University of Southern Maine *B*

Maryland

Community College of Baltimore
   County *A*
Frostburg State University *B*
Howard Community College *C, A*
McDaniel College *B, M*
Salisbury University *M*
Towson University *B*
University of Maryland
   College Park *B*
   Eastern Shore *B*

Massachusetts

Becker College *B*
Boston University *B, M*
Bridgewater State College *B*
Fitchburg State College *B*
Lasell College *B*
Mount Ida College *A*
Northeastern University *M*
Salem State College *B*
Smith College *M*
Springfield College *B, M*
University of Massachusetts
   Amherst *B, M, D*
   Lowell *B*
Westfield State College *B*

Michigan

Adrian College *B*
Alma College *B*
Calvin College *B*
Central Michigan University *M*
Cornerstone University *B*
Henry Ford Community College *C, A*
Hope College *B*
Lake Superior State University *B*
Michigan State University *B, M, D*
Northern Michigan University *B, M*
Oakland Community College *C, A*
Oakland University *M*
Saginaw Valley State University *B*
University of Michigan *B, M, D*
Western Michigan University *B*

Minnesota

Concordia College: Moorhead *B*
Concordia University: St. Paul *B*
Dakota County Technical College *A*
Globe College *C, A*
Hamline University *B*
Minnesota State University
   Mankato *B, M, T*
   Moorhead *B*
Northwestern College *B*
St. Cloud State University *B*
St. Olaf College *B*
University of Minnesota
   Duluth *B*
Winona State University *B*

Mississippi

Belhaven College *B*
University of Mississippi *B, M, D*

Missouri

Drury University *B*
Missouri Valley College *B*
St. Louis University *B*
Truman State University *B*
University of Missouri
   Columbia *B, M*

Montana

Rocky Mountain College *B*
University of Montana: Missoula *B, M*

Nebraska

Concordia University *B*
Creighton University *B*
Hastings College *B*
Nebraska Wesleyan University *B*

University of Nebraska
   Lincoln *B*
Wayne State College *B*

Nevada

University of Nevada
   Las Vegas *B, M*

New Hampshire

Colby-Sawyer College *B*
New England College *B*
New Hampshire Community
   Technical College
   Manchester *C, A*
University of New Hampshire *B, M*

New Jersey

Bergen Community College *C*
Gloucester County College *A*
Kean University *M*
Ocean County College *C*
Rutgers, The State University of New
   Jersey
   New Brunswick/Piscataway
     Campus *B*
Thomas Edison State College *C, A*
William Paterson University of New
   Jersey *B, T*

New York

City University of New York
   Brooklyn College *M*
   Kingsborough Community
     College *A*
Dutchess Community College *A*
Ithaca College *B, M*
Long Island University
   Brooklyn Campus *B, M*
Orange County Community College *A*
Skidmore College *B*
State University of New York
   Buffalo *B, M, D*
   College at Cortland *B*
   College of Agriculture and
     Technology at Morrisville *A*
Syracuse University *B, M*

North Carolina

Appalachian State University *B, M*
Brevard College *B*
Campbell University *B, T*
Chowan College *B*
East Carolina University *B, M*
Elon University *B*
Greensboro College *B*
Guilford College *B*
High Point University *B*
Louisburg College *A*
Meredith College *B*
Shaw University *B*
University of North Carolina
   Greensboro *B, M, D, T*
Wake Forest University *B, M*
Winston-Salem State University *B*

North Dakota

University of Mary *B*

Ohio

Cedarville University *B*
Cincinnati State Technical and
   Community College *C*
Malone College *B*
Miami University
   Oxford Campus *B, M*
Mount Union College *B*
Mount Vernon Nazarene University *B*
Ohio Northern University *B*
Ohio State University
   Columbus Campus *B*
Ohio University *B, M*
Sinclair Community College *C*
University of Akron *C, B*

University of Dayton *B, M*
University of Findlay *B*
University of Toledo *B, M, D*
Youngstown State University *B*

Oklahoma

East Central University *B*
Northeastern State University *B, M*
Oklahoma Baptist University *B*
Oklahoma Wesleyan University *B*
Oral Roberts University *B*
Redlands Community College *A*
Southern Nazarene University *B*
University of Central Oklahoma *B, M*
University of Oklahoma *B, M, D*
University of Tulsa *B*

Oregon

Central Oregon Community
   College *A*
Linfield College *B*
Oregon State University *M*
Pacific University *B*
Willamette University *B*

Pennsylvania

Bloomsburg University of
   Pennsylvania *B, M*
Cabrini College *B*
Chatham College *B*
DeSales University *B*
East Stroudsburg University of
   Pennsylvania *B*
Gettysburg College *B*
Immaculata University *B*
Marywood University *B, M*
Messiah College *B*
Penn State
   Abington *B*
   Altoona *B*
   Beaver *A, B*
   Berks *B*
   Delaware County *B*
   Dubois *B*
   Fayette *B*
   Hazleton *B*
   Lehigh Valley *B*
   McKeesport *B*
   Mont Alto *B*
   New Kensington *B*
   Schuylkill - Capital College *B*
   Shenango *B*
   University Park *B*
   Wilkes-Barre *B*
   Worthington Scranton *B*
   York *B*
Shippensburg University of
   Pennsylvania *B*
Waynesburg College *B*
West Chester University of
   Pennsylvania *B, M*
Wilson College *B*

Puerto Rico

Inter American University of Puerto
   Rico
   San German Campus *M*

South Carolina

Anderson University *B*
The Citadel *M*
Coker College *B*
Horry-Georgetown Technical
   College *C*
Lander University *B*
Limestone College *B*
University of South Carolina *B, M, D*
University of South Carolina
   Aiken *B*

South Dakota

Augustana College *B*
Black Hills State University *B*

Dakota Wesleyan University *B*
University of Sioux Falls *B*

Tennessee

Belmont University *B*
Bethel College *B*
Bryan College *B, T*
Free Will Baptist Bible College *B*
Freed-Hardeman University *B*
Lipscomb University *B*
Middle Tennessee State University *M*
Southern Adventist University *B*
Union University *B*
University of Memphis *B, M*
University of Tennessee
   Chattanooga *B, M*
   Knoxville *B*

Texas

Baylor University *D*
Blinn College *A*
Clarendon College *A*
Concordia University at Austin *B*
Hardin-Simmons University *B*
Houston Baptist University *B*
Howard Payne University *B*
LeTourneau University *B*
Lubbock Christian University *B*
Midland College *A*
Midwestern State University *B*
Northwest Vista College *A*
Palo Alto College *A*
Rice University *B*
St. Edward's University *B*
St. Mary's University *B, T*
Schreiner University *B*
Texas Christian University *M*
Texas Lutheran University *B*
Tyler Junior College *A*
University of Houston *B*
University of Texas
   Arlington *M*
   Austin *M, D*
   Tyler *M*

Utah

Brigham Young University *M, D*
University of Utah *M*
Utah Career College *A*
Weber State University *B*

Vermont

Castleton State College *B*
Johnson State College *B*

Virginia

Bluefield College *B*
Bridgewater College *B*
Liberty University *B*
Longwood University *B*
Marymount University *B*
Norfolk State University *B*
Old Dominion University *B, M*

Washington

Centralia College *A*
Eastern Washington University *B*
Seattle Pacific University *B*
University of Puget Sound *B*
Washington State University *B, M*

West Virginia

Davis and Elkins College *B*
Marshall University *M*
West Liberty State College *B*
West Virginia University *B, M*

Wisconsin

Carroll College *B*
Carthage College *B*
Marquette University *B*
Ripon College *B*

University of Wisconsin
   Eau Claire *B*
   La Crosse *B, M*
   Madison *B, M, D*
   Milwaukee *B, M*

Wyoming

University of Wyoming *B, M*
Western Wyoming Community
   College *C, A*

Experimental psychology

California

California State University
   San Bernardino *M*
San Francisco State University *M*
University of California
   Santa Cruz *D*

Connecticut

University of Hartford *M*

District of Columbia

American University *D*
Catholic University of America *M, D*

Florida

Florida Atlantic University *D*

Illinois

DePaul University *M, D*

Iowa

University of Iowa *D*

Kansas

Wichita State University *D*

Kentucky

University of Kentucky *M, D*
University of Louisville *M, D*

Maine

University of Maine *M, D*

Massachusetts

Tufts University *M, D*

Michigan

Central Michigan University *M, D*

Missouri

University of Missouri
   Columbia *M, D*

New York

City University of New York
   Brooklyn College *M*
Fordham University *D*
New York University *D*
St. John's University *M*
State University of New York
   Stony Brook *D*
Syracuse University *M, D*

North Carolina

Duke University *M, D*

Ohio

Bowling Green State University *M, D*
Case Western Reserve University *D*
Kent State University *M, D*
Ohio University *M, D*
University of Dayton *M*

Oklahoma

University of Central Oklahoma *M*

Oregon

Oregon Health & Science
   University *M, D*

Pennsylvania

Mansfield University of
   Pennsylvania *M*
Temple University *D*

Rhode Island

University of Rhode Island *D*

South Carolina

University of South Carolina *M, D*

Texas

Texas Tech University *M, D*
University of Houston *M*
University of North Texas *M, D*
University of Texas
   Arlington *D*
   El Paso *M*
   Pan American *M*

Washington

Central Washington University *M*
Eastern Washington University *M*

Wisconsin

Marquette University *M*
University of Wisconsin
   Madison *M, D*
   Oshkosh *M*

Facial treatment

Florida

Central Florida Community College *C*
Palm Beach Community College *C*

Texas

North Harris Montgomery
   Community College District *C*

Facilities/event planning

California

California State University
   East Bay *C*

Massachusetts

Wentworth Institute of Technology *B*

Michigan

Eastern Michigan University *B*

North Dakota

North Dakota State University *B*

Family and consumer sciences

Alabama

Alabama Agricultural and Mechanical
   University *B, M*
Faulkner State Community College *A*
Jacksonville State University *B*
Northeast Alabama Community
   College *A*
Oakwood College *B*
University of Alabama *B, M*
University of Montevallo *B, T*
University of North Alabama *B*

Arizona

Phoenix College *B*
South Mountain Community
   College *A*

Arkansas

Harding University *B, T*
Henderson State University *B*
University of Arkansas *M*
University of Arkansas
   Pine Bluff *B*
University of Central Arkansas *B, M*

California

Allan Hancock College *A*
American River College *C, A*
Antelope Valley College *A*
Bakersfield College *A*
Butte College *C, A*
Cabrillo College *C, A*
California Polytechnic State
   University: San Luis Obispo *B*
California State University
   Long Beach *B*
   Northridge *B, M*
   Sacramento *B*
Canada College *A*
Cerritos Community College *A*
Chaffey College *C, A*
City College of San Francisco *A*
College of the Sequoias *A*
El Camino College *A*
Fresno City College *A*
Fullerton College *A*
Glendale Community College *A*
Long Beach City College *C, A*
Los Angeles City College *A*
Los Angeles Valley College *A*
Master's College *B*
Merced College *A*
Modesto Junior College *A*
Monterey Peninsula College *A*
Moorpark College *A*
Mount San Antonio College *A*
Orange Coast College *A*
Point Loma Nazarene University *B*
Riverside Community College *C, A*
Sacramento City College *C, A*
Saddleback College *C, A*
San Francisco State University *B, M*
San Joaquin Delta College *A*
Santa Monica College *C, A*
Santiago Canyon College *A*
Shasta College *A*
Sierra College *A*
Skyline College *C, A*
Solano Community College *C, A*
Ventura College *C, A*

Colorado

Colorado State University *B*

Connecticut

St. Joseph College *B, T*

Delaware

University of Delaware *B*

District of Columbia

Gallaudet University *B*
University of the District of
   Columbia *B*

Florida

Florida State University *D*
Gulf Coast Community College *A*
Okaloosa-Walton College *A*
Palm Beach Community College *A*

Georgia

Abraham Baldwin Agricultural
   College *A*
Dalton State College *A*
East Georgia College *A*
Fort Valley State University *B*
Life University *A*
University of Georgia *M*

Hawaii

University of Hawaii
  Manoa B

Idaho

Idaho State University B

Illinois

Bradley University B
Eastern Illinois University B, M, T
Illinois Central College A
Illinois State University B, M, T
Illinois Valley Community College A
Kishwaukee College A
Lake Land College A
Olivet Nazarene University B, T
University of Illinois
  Urbana-Champaign M
Western Illinois University B

Indiana

Ball State University B, M
Indiana State University B, M, T
Purdue University B, M, D
Vincennes University A

Iowa

Ellsworth Community College A
Iowa State University B, M
Marshalltown Community College A
North Iowa Area Community
  College A

Kansas

Cloud County Community College A
Coffeyville Community College A
Colby Community College A
Cowley County Community
  College A
Garden City Community College A
Hutchinson Community College A
Kansas State University B, D
Neosho County Community
  College A
Pittsburg State University B

Kentucky

Berea College B, T
University of Kentucky B

Louisiana

Louisiana State University and
  Agricultural and Mechanical
  College B, M, D
Louisiana Tech University M
Nicholls State University B
Northwestern State University B
Southeastern Louisiana University B
Southern University and Agricultural
  and Mechanical College B
University of Louisiana at Lafayette M
University of Louisiana at Monroe B

Maine

York County Community College A

Maryland

University of Maryland
  College Park B
  Eastern Shore B

Massachusetts

Framingham State College B

Michigan

Lansing Community College A
Madonna University B
Michigan State University B, D
Western Michigan University M

Minnesota

College of St. Catherine B
Concordia College: Moorhead B
Minnesota State University
  Mankato B, M
University of Minnesota
  Twin Cities B, M, D
University of St. Thomas B
Vermilion Community College A

Mississippi

Alcorn State University B
Delta State University B
Hinds Community College A
Itawamba Community College A
Mississippi Delta Community
  College A
Mississippi State University B
University of Mississippi B
University of Southern Mississippi B

Missouri

Central Missouri State University B
College of the Ozarks B
Southeast Missouri State University B
University of Missouri
  Columbia D

Montana

Little Big Horn College A
Miles Community College A
Montana State University
  Bozeman B, M

Nebraska

Central Community College C, A
Chadron State College B
University of Nebraska
  Kearney B
  Lincoln M, D
  Omaha B
Wayne State College B, T

New Jersey

Montclair State University B, M, T

New Mexico

Eastern New Mexico University B
New Mexico State University M
University of New Mexico B, M, D

New York

City University of New York
  Lehman College B
  Queens College B, M, T
Cornell University B, M, D
State University of New York
  Binghamton B
  College at Oneonta B

North Carolina

Bennett College B
Campbell University B
Meredith College B
North Carolina Agricultural and
  Technical State University B, T
North Carolina Central
  University B, M

Ohio

Bluffton University B
Mount Vernon Nazarene
  University A, B
Ohio State University
  Columbus Campus B, M, D
University of Akron B
Youngstown State University B

Oklahoma

Cameron University B
Connors State College A
East Central University B

Northeastern State University B
Oklahoma State University M, D
Rose State College A
University of Central Oklahoma B

Oregon

Chemeketa Community College A
George Fox University B
Linn-Benton Community College A

Pennsylvania

Drexel University M
Indiana University of Pennsylvania B
Keystone College B
Marywood University B
Mercyhurst College B, T
Seton Hill University B
University of Pittsburgh
  Titusville A

Puerto Rico

Pontifical Catholic University of
  Puerto Rico B
University of Puerto Rico
  Rio Piedras B, M

South Carolina

South Carolina State University B

Tennessee

East Tennessee State University B, T
Hiwassee College A
Lambuth University B
Lipscomb University B
Middle Tennessee State University M
Tennessee State University B, M
Tennessee Technological
  University B, T
University of Tennessee
  Chattanooga B
  Knoxville B, M, D
  Martin B, M

Texas

Baylor University B
Brazosport College A
Coastal Bend College A
Lamar State College at Port Arthur A
Lamar University B, M
Laredo Community College A
Prairie View A&M University M
Sam Houston State University B, M
South Plains College A
Stephen F. Austin State University B, M
Tarleton State University B, T
Texas A&M University
  Kingsville B, M
Texas State University: San
  Marcos B, T
Texas Tech University B
Texas Woman's University B
Tyler Junior College A
University of Houston B
University of Texas
  Austin B

Utah

Brigham Young University B, M, D
Snow College A
Southern Utah University B, T
Utah State University M

Vermont

University of Vermont B, M

Virginia

Bridgewater College B
Liberty University B, T

Washington

Central Washington University B, M
Highline Community College A

West Virginia

Marshall University B, M
Shepherd University B
West Virginia University B, M, T

Wisconsin

University of Wisconsin
  Madison B, M, D

Wyoming

University of Wyoming B, M
Western Wyoming Community
  College A

Family/community services

Arkansas

John Brown University B

California

California State University
  Northridge B
Fresno City College C
Merritt College C, A
Modesto Junior College A
Monterey Peninsula College A
Point Loma Nazarene University B
Sacramento City College C, A
Santa Ana College A
Southwestern College C
Yuba Community College
  District C, A

Delaware

University of Delaware B, M, D

Florida

University of Florida B, M

Illinois

Moraine Valley Community College C
Olivet Nazarene University B, T

Iowa

Ellsworth Community College A
Iowa State University B
University of Northern Iowa B

Maine

University of Maine C, B

Maryland

University of Maryland
  College Park B, M, D
Villa Julie College B

Michigan

Michigan State University B, M
Northern Michigan University B

Minnesota

Minnesota State University
  Mankato B, M, T

New Hampshire

University of New Hampshire A, B

New York

Iona College M
State University of New York
  College at Plattsburgh B

North Carolina

North Carolina Agricultural and
  Technical State University B

Ohio

James A. Rhodes State College A

Ohio State University
   Columbus Campus *B, M, D*
Youngstown State University *B*

Oklahoma
Oklahoma Christian University *B*

Oregon
Blue Mountain Community College *A*

Pennsylvania
Messiah College *B*

Tennessee
Carson-Newman College *B, T*
Tennessee Technological University *B*
University of Tennessee
   Knoxville *B, M*

Texas
Lamar University *B*
Our Lady of the Lake University of San
   Antonio *B, M*

Utah
Snow College *C, A*
University of Utah *M*

Vermont
Champlain College *B*
University of Vermont *B, M*

West Virginia
Alderson-Broaddus College *B*
West Virginia University *B*

Wisconsin
University of Wisconsin
   Stevens Point *M*

Family/consumer business sciences

California
California State University
   Northridge *B*
Skyline College *C, A*

Illinois
Northern Illinois University *M*

Nebraska
University of Nebraska
   Kearney *B*

Oklahoma
Connors State College *A*

South Carolina
South Carolina State University *B*

Texas
University of Houston *B*
University of North Texas *B*

Virginia
Virginia Polytechnic Institute and
   State University *B, M, D*

Family/consumer sciences education

Alabama
Northeast Alabama Community
   College *A*
Oakwood College *B*

Arizona
Arizona State University *B, T*

Phoenix College *A*
University of Arizona *B*

Arkansas
Harding University *B, M, T*
University of Arkansas *B*
University of Arkansas
   Pine Bluff *B*
University of Central Arkansas *B, M, T*

California
California State University
   Dominguez Hills *T*
   Long Beach *B, T*
   Northridge *B, T*
   Sacramento *T*
Master's College *T*
Saddleback College *A*
San Francisco State University *B, M, T*

Colorado
Colorado State University *T*
Johnson & Wales University *B*

Connecticut
St. Joseph College *B, T*

Delaware
University of Delaware *B, T*

District of Columbia
Gallaudet University *B, T*

Florida
Florida International
   University *B, M, T*
Florida State University *B, M, D, T*
Gulf Coast Community College *A*

Georgia
Fort Valley State University *B, T*
Georgia Southern University *B*
University of Georgia *B*

Idaho
Brigham Young University-Idaho *T*
University of Idaho *T*

Illinois
Bradley University *B, M*
Northern Illinois University *B*
Olivet Nazarene University *B, T*
Sauk Valley Community College *A*

Indiana
Vincennes University *A*

Iowa
Ellsworth Community College *A*
Iowa State University *B, M, D, T*

Kansas
Colby Community College *A*
Kansas State University *B*
Pittsburg State University *B, T*

Kentucky
Berea College *B, T*
Eastern Kentucky University *B*
Morehead State University *B*
Western Kentucky University *B, T*

Louisiana
Grambling State University *B*
Northwestern State University *B*
University of Louisiana at Lafayette *B*
University of Louisiana at Monroe *B*

Maryland
University of Maryland
   Eastern Shore *B*

Massachusetts
Framingham State College *B*

Michigan
Ferris State University *B*
Madonna University *T*
Michigan State University *B, M*
Northern Michigan University *B*
Western Michigan University *B, T*

Minnesota
College of St. Catherine *B, T*
Minnesota State University
   Mankato *B, M, T*
University of Minnesota
   Twin Cities *M, T*

Mississippi
Mississippi State University *T*

Missouri
Central Missouri State University *B*
College of the Ozarks *B*
Fontbonne University *B*
Missouri State University *B*
Northwest Missouri State
   University *B, T*
Southeast Missouri State
   University *B, M, T*

Nebraska
Chadron State College *B*
Concordia University *B, T*
University of Nebraska
   Kearney *B, T*
Wayne State College *B, T*

Nevada
University of Nevada
   Reno *B*

New Jersey
St. Peter's College *T*

New Mexico
New Mexico State University *B*

New York
City University of New York
   Queens College *B, M, T*
Cornell University *M, T*
State University of New York
   College at Oneonta *B, T*

North Carolina
Appalachian State University *B, M, T*
Campbell University *B, T*
East Carolina University *B*
Guilford Technical Community
   College *A*
Meredith College *T*
North Carolina Agricultural and
   Technical State University *B, T*
North Carolina Central
   University *B, M, T*

North Dakota
North Dakota State University *B, M, T*

Ohio
Ashland University *B, T*
Bluffton University *B*
Miami University
   Oxford Campus *M*
Mount Vernon Nazarene
   University *B, M, T*

Ohio State University
   Columbus Campus *M, D*
Ohio University *B, T*
University of Akron *B*
Youngstown State University *B, M*

Oklahoma
East Central University *B*
Northeastern State University *B*
University of Central Oklahoma *B*

Oregon
George Fox University *T*
Oregon State University *M*

Pennsylvania
Immaculata University *B*
Indiana University of
   Pennsylvania *B, M, T*
Marywood University *B*
Mercyhurst College *B, T*
Messiah College *B, T*
Seton Hill University *B, T*

Puerto Rico
Pontifical Catholic University of
   Puerto Rico *B, T*
University of Puerto Rico
   Rio Piedras *B, M*

South Carolina
South Carolina State University *B, T*

Tennessee
Carson-Newman College *B*
Tennessee Technological University *T*
University of Tennessee
   Knoxville *B, M, T*

Texas
Lamar University *B, M, T*
Laredo Community College *A*
Prairie View A&M University *M*
Sam Houston State University *T*
Texas A&M University
   Kingsville *B*
Texas Tech University *M, D*

Utah
Brigham Young University *B*
Snow College *A*
Southern Utah University *B, T*
Utah State University *B*

Virginia
Bridgewater College *B*
Liberty University *B, T*

Washington
Central Washington University *B, T*
Seattle Pacific University *B*
Washington State University *B, T*

West Virginia
Shepherd University *T*

Wisconsin
Mount Mary College *T*
University of Wisconsin
   Madison *B*
   Stevens Point *B, T*
   Stout *B, M, T*

Family practice nurse/ nurse practitioner

Alabama
University of Mobile *M*

Arizona
Northern Arizona University *M*

California
Azusa Pacific University *B*
Holy Names University *M*
Samuel Merritt College *M*
University of San Francisco *M*

Connecticut
Sacred Heart University *M*

Delaware
Wilmington College *M*

Florida
Barry University *M*
University of Tampa *M*

Georgia
Georgia Southern University *M*
Kennesaw State University *M*
Medical College of Georgia *M*
North Georgia College & State
   University *M*

Illinois
Illinois State University *M*
Loyola University of Chicago *M*
Southern Illinois University
   Edwardsville *M*

Indiana
Indiana University-Purdue University
   Indianapolis *M*
Indiana Wesleyan University *M*
University of St. Francis *M*

Iowa
Allen College *M*

Kansas
Pittsburg State University *M*

Louisiana
Grambling State University *M*
Louisiana State University Health
   Sciences Center *M*
Loyola University New Orleans *M*
Southern University and Agricultural
   and Mechanical College *M*

Maine
Husson College *M*
University of Southern Maine *M*

Michigan
Grand Valley State University *M*
Madonna University *M*
Michigan State University *B, M*
Oakland University *M*
Saginaw Valley State University *M*
University of Detroit Mercy *M*

Minnesota
College of St. Scholastica *M*
Minnesota State University
   Moorhead *B*

Missouri
Research College of Nursing *M*

New Hampshire
Rivier College *M*

New York
City University of New York
   Hunter College *B, M*
   Lehman College *M*
College of New Rochelle *M*

Columbia University
   School of Nursing *M*
Dominican College of Blauvelt *M*
Long Island University
   C.W. Post Campus *M*
Pace University *M*
St. John Fisher College *M*
State University of New York
   Binghamton *M*
   Buffalo *M*
   Downstate Medical Center *M*
   Stony Brook *M*
   Upstate Medical University *M*

North Carolina
University of North Carolina
   Wilmington *M*
Western Carolina University *M*
Winston-Salem State University *M*

North Dakota
University of Mary *M*

Ohio
Case Western Reserve University *M*
Ursuline College *M*

Oklahoma
University of Oklahoma *M*

Pennsylvania
DeSales University *M*
Drexel University *M*
Duquesne University *M*
Gwynedd-Mercy College *M*
Millersville University of
   Pennsylvania *M*
University of Pennsylvania *M*
Widener University *D*

Puerto Rico
Turabo University *M*

South Carolina
Medical University of South
   Carolina *M*

Tennessee
Southern Adventist University *M*

Texas
Abilene Christian University *M*
Baylor University *M*
Hardin-Simmons University *M*
Midwestern State University *M*
Prairie View A&M University *M*
Texas Tech University Health Sciences
   Center *M*
Texas Woman's University *M*
University of Texas
   Arlington *M*
   El Paso *M*
   Medical Branch at Galveston *M*
   Pan American *M*
West Texas A&M University *M*

Utah
Brigham Young University *M*

Virginia
Marymount University *M*

Washington
Seattle Pacific University *M*
Seattle University *B, M*

West Virginia
Mountain State University *M*

Wisconsin
Concordia University Wisconsin *M*

Viterbo University *M*

Family psychology

Arizona
Northcentral University *M, D*

California
California Institute of Integral
   Studies *M, D*
Golden Gate University *M*

Minnesota
Capella University *M, D*

Texas
Hardin-Simmons University *M*
University of Houston
   Clear Lake *M*

Family resource management studies

Alabama
University of Alabama *B*

Arizona
Arizona State University *B, M*

California
Antelope Valley College *C, A*
Long Beach City College *C, A*

Illinois
Black Hawk College *C*
University of Illinois
   Urbana-Champaign *D*

Iowa
Iowa State University *B*

Kansas
Pittsburg State University *B*

Missouri
University of Missouri
   Columbia *B, M*

Nebraska
University of Nebraska
   Omaha *B*

New Mexico
New Mexico State University *M*

New York
Cornell University *B*

Ohio
Ohio State University
   Columbus Campus *B, M, D*
Ohio University *M*
University of Toledo *C*

Oregon
George Fox University *B*
Oregon State University *M, D*

South Dakota
South Dakota State University *B, M, T*

Tennessee
Middle Tennessee State University *B*

Texas
Texas Tech University *D*

Utah
Brigham Young University *B*

University of Utah *B*

Family systems

Arizona
Arizona Western College *C*

California
Azusa Pacific University *D*

Connecticut
University of Connecticut *D*

Florida
Florida State University *M, D*

Indiana
Anderson University *B*

Maryland
Towson University *B*

Michigan
Central Michigan University *B*
Cornerstone University *B*
Michigan State University *M*
Western Michigan University *B*

Ohio
Ashland University *B*
University of Akron *C, B*

Oklahoma
University of Central Oklahoma *B*

Pennsylvania
Keystone College *B*

Tennessee
Lipscomb University *B*
Union University *B*

Texas
Texas Tech University *B*

Farm and ranch management

Arizona
Central Arizona College *C*

Colorado
Colorado Northwestern Community
   College *C*
Colorado State University *B*
Morgan Community College *C*
Northeastern Junior College *C, A*
Otero Junior College *C*
Pueblo Community College *C*
Trinidad State Junior College *C*

Florida
University of Florida *B*

Georgia
Fort Valley State University *B*

Idaho
Boise State University *C*

Illinois
University of Illinois
   Urbana-Champaign *B, M, D*

Iowa
Ellsworth Community College *C, A*
Iowa State University *B*
North Iowa Area Community
   College *A*

Kansas

Allen County Community College *A*
Butler County Community College *A*
Colby Community College *A*
Cowley County Community
   College *C, A*
Dodge City Community College *C, A*
Garden City Community College *A*
Hutchinson Community College *A*
McPherson College *B*
Pratt Community College *C, A*
Seward County Community College *A*

Maryland

Community College of Baltimore
   County *C, A*

Minnesota

Alexandria Technical College *C*
Central Lakes College *C*
Northland Community & Technical
   College *C, A*
Ridgewater College *C, A*
Riverland Community College *A*
St. Cloud Technical College *C*
University of Minnesota
   Crookston *B*

Mississippi

Mississippi Delta Community
   College *A*

Missouri

Crowder College *A*
North Central Missouri College *C, A*
Northwest Missouri State
   University *C, B*

Montana

Dawson Community College *A*

Nebraska

Northeast Community College *A*

Nevada

Great Basin College *A*

New York

State University of New York
   College of Agriculture and
     Technology at Morrisville *A, B*

North Dakota

Dickinson State University *C*

Ohio

Lake Erie College *B*
University of Findlay *B*
Wilmington College *B*

Oklahoma

Eastern Oklahoma State College *A*
Northeastern Oklahoma Agricultural
   and Mechanical College *C, A*
Oklahoma Panhandle State
   University *A, B*

Oregon

Blue Mountain Community College *A*
Chemeketa Community College *C*
Treasure Valley Community College *A*

Pennsylvania

Penn State
   University Park *C*

Rhode Island

Johnson & Wales University *A*

South Carolina

Clemson University *B*

South Dakota

Mitchell Technical Institute *C*
Western Dakota Technical Institute *A*

Texas

Central Texas College *C, A*
Clarendon College *C, A*
Frank Phillips College *A*
Navarro College *A*
North Central Texas College *A*
Northeast Texas Community
   College *C*
Southwest Texas Junior College *C, A*
Texas A&M University *B*
Texas Christian University *C*
Trinity Valley Community College *C, A*
Tyler Junior College *C, A*
Vernon College *C, A*
Weatherford College *C, A*
Wharton County Junior College *A*

Utah

Snow College *A*

Vermont

Sterling College *A, B*
Vermont Technical College *A*

Virginia

Virginia Highlands Community
   College *C, A*

Wisconsin

Chippewa Valley Technical College *C*
Lakeshore Technical College *C*
Moraine Park Technical College *C*
Northeast Wisconsin Technical
   College *C*
Southwest Wisconsin Technical
   College *C*
Western Wisconsin Technical
   College *C*
Wisconsin Indianhead Technical
   College *C*

Wyoming

Eastern Wyoming College *C, A*
Laramie County Community
   College *A*
Sheridan College *A*

Fashion and apparel design

Alabama

Wallace State Community College at
   Hanceville *A*

Arizona

Tucson Design College *A*

Arkansas

Harding University *B*

California

Academy of Art University *C, A, B, M*
Allan Hancock College *C, A*
Art Institute of California: San
   Francisco *A, B*
Bethesda Christian University *B*
Brooks College *A*
Butte College *C, A*
California College of the Arts *B*
California Design College *C, A*
Chaffey College *C, A*
Fashion Careers College *C, A*
Fashion Institute of Design and
   Merchandising *A*

Fashion Institute of Design and
   Merchandising
   San Diego *A*
   San Francisco *A*
Fullerton College *A*
Long Beach City College *C, A*
Los Angeles Southwest College *A*
Los Angeles Trade and Technical
   College *A*
Modesto Junior College *C, A*
Orange Coast College *C, A*
Otis College of Art and Design *B*
Palomar College *A*
Saddleback College *C, A*
San Joaquin Delta College *C, A*
Santa Rosa Junior College *C, A*
Santiago Canyon College *A*
Ventura College *C, A*
West Hills Community College *C*
West Valley College *C, A*
Woodbury University *B*

Delaware

University of Delaware *B*

Florida

Art Institute of Fort Lauderdale *A*
Florida State University *B, M, D*
International Academy of Design and
   Technology: Tampa *A, B*
Lynn University *B*
Manatee Community College *A*
Miami International University of Art
   and Design *A*
Santa Fe Community College *A*

Georgia

Bauder College *A*
Brenau University *B*
Savannah College of Art and
   Design *B, M*

Hawaii

University of Hawaii
   Honolulu Community College *C, A*

Illinois

Columbia College Chicago *B*
Dominican University *B*
International Academy of Design and
   Technology: Chicago *A, B*
International Academy of Design and
   Technology: Schaumburg *A, B*
Sauk Valley Community College *A*
School of the Art Institute of
   Chicago *B*
William Rainey Harper College *C, A*

Indiana

Vincennes University *A*

Iowa

Iowa State University *B*

Maryland

Baltimore City Community
   College *C, A*

Massachusetts

Bay State College *A, B*
Lasell College *B*
Massachusetts College of Art *B*
Mount Ida College *A, B*

Michigan

Finlandia University *B*
Michigan State University *B*

Minnesota

College of St. Catherine *B*
University of Minnesota
   Twin Cities *B*

Missouri

Lindenwood University *B*
Penn Valley Community College *A*
Stephens College *B*
Washington University in St.
   Louis *B, M*

Nevada

International Academy of Design and
   Technology: Henderson *A, B*

New Jersey

Burlington County College *C, A*
Centenary College *B*

New Mexico

Santa Fe Community College *C*

New York

Cazenovia College *B*
Eugene Lang College The New School
   for Liberal Arts *B*
Fashion Institute of Technology *A, B*
Marist College *B*
Parsons The New School for
   Design *A, B, T*
Pratt Institute *B*
State University of New York
   College at Buffalo *B*
Syracuse University *B, M*
Wood Tobe-Coburn School *A*

North Carolina

Mars Hill College *B*
Meredith College *B*

Ohio

Columbus College of Art and
   Design *B*
Kent State University *B*
University of Cincinnati *B*
Ursuline College *B*

Oregon

Art Institute of Portland *A, B*
Oregon State University *B*

Pennsylvania

Art Institute
   of Philadelphia *A*
Drexel University *B, M*
Harcum College *A*
Lehigh Carbon Community College *A*
Moore College of Art and Design *B*
Philadelphia University *B*

Puerto Rico

Pontifical Catholic University of
   Puerto Rico *A*

Rhode Island

Rhode Island School of Design *B*

Texas

Baylor University *B*
El Centro College *C, A*
El Paso Community College *A*
Houston Community College
   System *C, A*
Texas Tech University *B*
Texas Woman's University *B*
University of North Texas *B, M*
University of the Incarnate Word *A, B*
Wade College *A*

Utah

Salt Lake Community College *C*

Virginia

Marymount University *B*
Virginia Commonwealth University *B*

Washington

Art Institute of Seattle *A*

Wisconsin

Mount Mary College *B*
University of Wisconsin
Madison *B, M*
Waukesha County Technical
College *A*

Fashion/fabric consultant

California

Fashion Institute of Design and
Merchandising *A*
Fashion Institute of Design and
Merchandising
San Diego *A*
San Francisco *A*
Monterey Peninsula College *A*

Massachusetts

Lasell College *B*

Fashion merchandising

Alabama

Lawson State Community College *C*
Wallace State Community College at
Hanceville *A*

Arizona

Mesa Community College *A*
Northern Arizona University *B*
Phoenix College *C*
Scottsdale Community College *C, A*

Arkansas

Harding University *B*
University of Central Arkansas *B*

California

American River College *C, A*
Art Institute of California: San
Francisco *A, B*
Brooks College *A*
Butte College *C, A*
California State University
Long Beach *B*
Canada College *C, A*
Chaffey College *C, A*
City College of San Francisco *C, A*
College of Alameda *C, A*
College of San Mateo *C, A*
Evergreen Valley College *A*
Fashion Careers College *C, A*
Fashion Institute of Design and
Merchandising *A*
Fashion Institute of Design and
Merchandising
San Diego *A*
San Francisco *A*
Fresno City College *C, A*
Fullerton College *A*
Las Positas College *C*
Long Beach City College *C, A*
Los Angeles Trade and Technical
College *C, A*
Los Angeles Valley College *C, A*
Modesto Junior College *C, A*
Mount San Antonio College *C, A*
Orange Coast College *C, A*
Palomar College *C, A*
Pasadena City College *C, A*
Saddleback College *A*
San Diego Mesa College *C, A*
San Francisco State University *B*
San Joaquin Delta College *C, A*
Santa Ana College *A*
Santa Rosa Junior College *C*
Shasta College *A*

Ventura College *C, A*
West Valley College *C, A*
Westwood College: Long Beach *B*
Woodbury University *B*

Colorado

Johnson & Wales University *A*
Westwood College of Technology
South *B*

Connecticut

Asnuntuck Community College *A*
Briarwood College *A*
Gateway Community College *A*
Tunxis Community College *C, A*
University of Bridgeport *A, B*

Delaware

University of Delaware *B*

District of Columbia

Howard University *B*
University of the District of
Columbia *A*

Florida

Art Institute of Fort Lauderdale *B*
Brevard Community College *A*
Florida Community College at
Jacksonville *A*
International Academy of Design and
Technology: Orlando *B*
Johnson & Wales University *A*
Lynn University *A, B*
Miami International University of Art
and Design *A*
Okaloosa-Walton College *A*
Santa Fe Community College *A*

Georgia

Abraham Baldwin Agricultural
College *A*
Bauder College *A*
Brenau University *B*
Clark Atlanta University *B*
Gwinnett Technical College *A*
Middle Georgia College *C*
University of Georgia *B*

Hawaii

University of Hawaii
Honolulu Community College *C, A*

Illinois

Chicago State University *B*
College of DuPage *A*
Columbia College Chicago *B*
Dominican University *B*
International Academy of Design and
Technology: Chicago *A, B*
Joliet Junior College *A*
Olivet Nazarene University *B*
South Suburban College of Cook
County *C, A*
Triton College *C*
William Rainey Harper College *C, A*

Indiana

Indiana Business College *A*
Vincennes University *A*

Iowa

Ellsworth Community College *C, A*
Kirkwood Community College *C, A*

Kansas

Pittsburg State University *B*
Seward County Community
College *C, A*

Kentucky

Eastern Kentucky University *B*

Louisiana

Louisiana State University and
Agricultural and Mechanical
College *B*
University of Louisiana at Lafayette *B*

Maryland

Baltimore City Community College *A*

Massachusetts

Bay State College *A*
Fisher College *C, A*
Lasell College *B*
Massasoit Community College *C*
Middlesex Community College *A*
Mount Ida College *A, B*
Newbury College *A*

Michigan

Central Michigan University *B*
Eastern Michigan University *B, M*
Finlandia University *B*
Grand Rapids Community College *A*
Lansing Community College *A*
Madonna University *C*
Northwood University *A, B*

Minnesota

Alexandria Technical College *C, A*
College of St. Catherine *B*
Minnesota State Community and
Technical College - Fergus
Falls *C, A*
Rasmussen College
Mankato *A*
Ridgewater College *C*

Mississippi

Hinds Community College *A*
Holmes Community College *A*
Mississippi Gulf Coast Community
College
Jefferson Davis Campus *A*

Missouri

Central Missouri State University *A*
Patricia Stevens College *C*
Penn Valley Community College *A*
St. Louis Community College
St. Louis Community College at
Florissant Valley *A*
Stephens College *B*

New Hampshire

Southern New Hampshire
University *C, A*

New Jersey

Berkeley College *A, B*
Brookdale Community College *A*
Burlington County College *A*
Middlesex County College *A*

New Mexico

Dona Ana Branch Community College
of New Mexico State
University *A*

New York

Berkeley College *A, B*
Berkeley College of New York
City *A, B*
Cazenovia College *B*
City University of New York
Kingsborough Community
College *A*
New York City College of
Technology *A*

Fashion Institute of Technology *A, B*
Genesee Community College *A*
Herkimer County Community
College *A*
Laboratory Institute of
Merchandising *A, B*
Marist College *B*
Nassau Community College *A*
Parsons The New School for
Design *A, B*
State University of New York
College at Buffalo *B*
College at Oneonta *B*
Wood Tobe-Coburn School *A*

North Carolina

Art Institute
of Charlotte *B*
Johnson & Wales University *A*

North Dakota

Lake Region State College *C, A*

Ohio

Bowling Green State University *B*
Davis College *A*
Kent State University *B*
Ohio State University
Columbus Campus *B*
University of Akron *A*
Ursuline College *B*
Youngstown State University *B*

Oklahoma

Tulsa Community College *C, A*

Oregon

George Fox University *B*

Pennsylvania

Art Institute
of Philadelphia *A*
of Pittsburgh *A, B*
Bradley Academy for the Visual Arts *A*
Community College of
Philadelphia *C, A*
Harcum College *A*
ICM School of Business & Medical
Careers *A*
Immaculata University *A, B*
Marywood University *C*
Philadelphia University *B*
Westmoreland County Community
College *A*

Rhode Island

Community College of Rhode
Island *A*
Johnson & Wales University *A, B*

South Carolina

Midlands Technical College *C*
South Carolina State University *B*

Tennessee

Lambuth University *B*
Lipscomb University *B*
O'More College of Design *A, B*

Texas

Austin Community College *C, A*
Baylor University *B*
Brookhaven College *A*
Del Mar College *A*
El Paso Community College *C, A*
Houston Community College
System *C, A*
Laredo Community College *A*
Northwood University: Texas
Campus *A, B*
Palo Alto College *C, A*
Sam Houston State University *B*

San Jacinto College
    Central Campus C, A
South Plains College A
Stephen F. Austin State University B
Tarrant County College C, A
Texas Christian University B
Texas State University: San Marcos B
Texas Tech University B
Texas Woman's University B
University of North Texas B
University of the Incarnate Word A, B
Wade College A

Utah
Utah State University B
Weber State University A

Virginia
J. Sargeant Reynolds Community
    College A
Liberty University B
Marymount University B

Washington
Art Institute of Seattle A
Central Washington University B
Edmonds Community College C, A
Highline Community College A
Pierce College C
Seattle Central Community College A
Shoreline Community College A
Spokane Falls Community College A

Wisconsin
Madison Area Technical College A
Mount Mary College B
Northeast Wisconsin Technical
    College A

Fiber/textile arts

California
Academy of Art University C, A, B, M
California College of the Arts B, M
California State University
    Long Beach B, M
Fashion Institute of Design and
    Merchandising A
Fashion Institute of Design and
    Merchandising
    San Diego A
University of California
    Davis M

Georgia
Savannah College of Art and
    Design B, M

Illinois
School of the Art Institute of
    Chicago B, M

Indiana
Vincennes University A

Kansas
University of Kansas B, M

Maryland
Maryland Institute College of Art B

Massachusetts
Massachusetts College of Art B, M
University of Massachusetts
    Dartmouth B, M

Michigan
College for Creative Studies B
Finlandia University B
Northern Michigan University B
University of Michigan B

Minnesota
Minnesota State University
    Mankato B

Missouri
Kansas City Art Institute B

New Jersey
Rowan University B

New Mexico
Northern New Mexico College C, A

New York
Cornell University B, M, D
Parsons The New School for
    Design C, A, B, T
State University of New York
    College at Buffalo B
Syracuse University B, M

North Carolina
East Carolina University B
Haywood Community College A

Ohio
Cleveland Institute of Art B

Oregon
University of Oregon B, M

Pennsylvania
Edinboro University of
    Pennsylvania B
Marywood University M
Moore College of Art and Design B
Philadelphia University B, M
Temple University B, M

Rhode Island
Rhode Island College B
Rhode Island School of Design B, M

Tennessee
Memphis College of Art B, M
Tennessee Technological University B

Texas
University of North Texas B, M

Washington
University of Washington B, M
Western Washington University B

West Virginia
West Virginia State University B

Wisconsin
University of Wisconsin
    Madison B

Filipino/Tagalog

Hawaii
University of Hawaii
    Manoa B

Film/cinema studies

Arizona
Arizona State University B

California
Allan Hancock College A
California Institute of the Arts C, B, M
Chapman University B, M
Columbia College: Hollywood B
Long Beach City College A
Los Angeles City College A

Loyola Marymount University B
Orange Coast College A
Palomar College C, A
Pitzer College B
San Francisco Art Institute B, M
San Francisco State University B, M
Santa Barbara City College C, A
University of California
    Berkeley B
    Davis B
    Irvine B
    Los Angeles B, M, D
    Riverside B
    Santa Barbara B, M, D
    Santa Cruz B
University of Southern
    California B, M, D

Colorado
Colorado College B
University of Colorado
    Boulder B

Connecticut
Trinity College B
University of Hartford B
Wesleyan University B
Yale University B, D

District of Columbia
American University B, M
Howard University M

Florida
Tallahassee Community College A
University of Central Florida M
University of Miami B, M

Georgia
Emory University B, M
Georgia State University B
University of Georgia B

Illinois
Columbia College Chicago B
University of Chicago B, D
University of Illinois
    Urbana-Champaign B

Indiana
Huntington University B
Purdue University B

Iowa
University of Iowa B, M, D

Kansas
Southwestern College B

Maryland
Johns Hopkins University B

Massachusetts
Boston College B
Clark University B
Emerson College B
Hampshire College B
Massachusetts College of Art B, M
Simon's Rock College of Bard B
Suffolk University B

Michigan
Calvin College B
Spring Arbor University B
University of Michigan B
Wayne State University B

Minnesota
Augsburg College B
St. Cloud State University B

University of Minnesota
    Twin Cities B

Missouri
Washington University in St. Louis B
Webster University B

Nebraska
University of Nebraska
    Lincoln B

Nevada
University of Nevada
    Las Vegas B

New Hampshire
Dartmouth College B
Keene State College B

New Jersey
Rowan University B

New Mexico
College of Santa Fe B
University of New Mexico B

New York
Bard College B, M
Barnard College B
City University of New York
    Brooklyn College B
    City College B, M
    Hunter College B
    Queens College B
Columbia University
    Columbia College B
    School of General Studies B
Cornell University B, M, D
Five Towns College B
Fordham University B
Ithaca College B
New York University B, M, D
Sarah Lawrence College B
School of Visual Arts B
State University of New York
    Binghamton B
    Buffalo B
University of Rochester B
Vassar College B

Ohio
Baldwin-Wallace College B
Bowling Green State University B
Denison University B
Oberlin College B
University of Toledo B
Wright State University B

Oklahoma
Oklahoma City University B
University of Oklahoma B
University of Tulsa B

Pennsylvania
DeSales University B
Gettysburg College B
La Salle University B
Penn State
    Schuylkill - Capital College B
    University Park B, M
Swarthmore College B
Temple University B, M
University of Pennsylvania B
University of Pittsburgh C, B

Rhode Island
Rhode Island College B

South Carolina
University of South Carolina B

Tennessee

University of Tennessee
  Knoxville B

Texas

Southern Methodist University B

Utah

Brigham Young University B, M, D
University of Utah B, M

Vermont

Bennington College B
Burlington College C, B
Marlboro College B

Washington

Whitman College B

Wisconsin

University of Wisconsin
  Madison B
  Milwaukee B

Finance

Alabama

Alabama Agricultural and Mechanical
  University B
Alabama State University B
Auburn University B
Auburn University at Montgomery B
Birmingham-Southern College B
Faulkner State Community College A
Huntingdon College B
Jacksonville State University B
Oakwood College B
Spring Hill College B
Talladega College B
Troy University B
Tuskegee University B
University of Alabama B, M, D
University of Alabama
  Birmingham B
  Huntsville B
University of Montevallo B
University of North Alabama B
University of South Alabama B

Alaska

University of Alaska
  Anchorage B

Arizona

Arizona State University B
Grand Canyon University B, M
Mohave Community College C
Northcentral University M, D
Northern Arizona University B
Scottsdale Community College C
University of Arizona B
University of Phoenix B
Western International University B, M

Arkansas

Arkansas State University B
East Arkansas Community College A
University of Arkansas B
University of Arkansas
  Little Rock B
University of Central Arkansas B
Williams Baptist College B

California

Azusa Pacific University B, M
California Lutheran University B
California State Polytechnic
  University: Pomona B
California State University
  Chico B
  East Bay B, M

Fresno B
Fullerton B, M
Long Beach B
Northridge M
Sacramento B, M
San Bernardino B, M
Cosumnes River College C, A
Golden Gate University C, B, M
La Sierra University B, M
Lake Tahoe Community College A
Master's College B
Modesto Junior College A
National University M
Pacific Union College B
St. Mary's College of California B
San Diego State University B, M
San Francisco State University B
San Joaquin Delta College C
San Jose State University B
Santa Barbara City College C, A
Santa Clara University B
Southwestern College A
University of San Francisco B
Vanguard University of Southern
  California B

Colorado

Adams State College B
Fort Lewis College B
Jones International University M
Metropolitan State College of
  Denver B
University of Colorado
  Boulder B, M, D
  Colorado Springs B
  Denver and Health Sciences
    Center M
University of Denver B, M

Connecticut

Albertus Magnus College B
Central Connecticut State
  University B
Fairfield University B, M
Norwalk Community College A
Post University B
Quinnipiac University B, M
Sacred Heart University B
Southern Connecticut State
  University B
Tunxis Community College A
University of Bridgeport B, M
University of Connecticut B
University of Hartford B
University of New Haven B
Western Connecticut State
  University B

Delaware

Delaware State University B
University of Delaware B
Wilmington College B

District of Columbia

American University B, M
Catholic University of America B, M
George Washington University B, M
Georgetown University B
Howard University B
University of the District of
  Columbia B

Florida

Barry University C
Broward Community College A
Edison College A
Florida Atlantic University B, M
Florida Gulf Coast University B
Florida Institute of Technology M
Florida International University B, M
Florida Southern College B
Florida State University B, M
Jacksonville University B

Nova Southeastern University B
Palm Beach Community College A
St. Thomas University B
Schiller International University B
South University: West Palm Beach
  Campus B
Southeastern College of the
  Assemblies of God B
Stetson University B
University of Central Florida B
University of Florida B, M
University of Miami B, M
University of North Florida B, M
University of South Florida B
University of Tampa B
University of West Florida B
Warner Southern College B
Webber International University A, B

Georgia

Augusta State University B
Berry College B
Clark Atlanta University M
Columbus State University B
Emory University B
Georgia Southern University B
Georgia Southwestern State
  University B
Georgia State University B, M, D
Kennesaw State University B
North Georgia College & State
  University B
South Georgia College A
University of Georgia B
University of West Georgia B
Valdosta State University B

Hawaii

Hawaii Pacific University A, B
University of Hawaii
  Hilo B
  Manoa B

Idaho

Boise State University B
Idaho State University B
University of Idaho B

Illinois

Augustana College B
Aurora University B
Benedictine University B
Bradley University B
Chicago State University B
Danville Area Community College A
DePaul University B, M
Eastern Illinois University B
Elmhurst College B
Eureka College B
Governors State University B
Illinois College B
Illinois Institute of Technology M
Illinois State University B
Lewis University B
Loyola University of Chicago B
MacMurray College B
Millikin University B
North Central College B
North Park University B
Northeastern Illinois University B
Northern Illinois University B, M
Northwestern University M, D
Olivet Nazarene University B
Quincy University B
Roosevelt University B, M
St. Xavier University M
South Suburban College of Cook
  County C, A
Southern Illinois University
  Carbondale B
University of Illinois
  Chicago B
  Urbana-Champaign B, M, D

University of St. Francis B
Western Illinois University B
William Rainey Harper College C, A

Indiana

Anderson University B
Ball State University B
Butler University B
Grace College B
Indiana State University B
Indiana University
  Bloomington B, M, D
  South Bend A, B
Indiana University-Purdue University
  Fort Wayne B
Indiana University-Purdue University
  Indianapolis B
Indiana Wesleyan University B
Marian College A, B
Purdue University
  Calumet B
Taylor University B
Tri-State University B
University of Evansville B
University of Notre Dame B
University of Southern Indiana B
Valparaiso University B

Iowa

AIB College of Business A
Ashford University B
Clarke College B
Drake University B
Iowa State University B
Kirkwood Community College A
Loras College B
Morningside College B
Northwestern College B
St. Ambrose University B
University of Iowa B, D
University of Northern Iowa B
Waldorf College B
Wartburg College B

Kansas

Central Christian College of Kansas A
Kansas State University B
McPherson College B
Pittsburg State University B
Seward County Community College A
University of Kansas B
University of St. Mary M
Washburn University of Topeka B
Wichita State University B

Kentucky

Beckfield College A
Eastern Kentucky University B
Kentucky Christian University B
Madisonville Community College A
Morehead State University B
Murray State University B
Northern Kentucky University B
Southeast Kentucky Community and
  Technical College A
University of Kentucky B
University of Louisville B
Western Kentucky University B

Louisiana

Centenary College of Louisiana B
Dillard University B
Louisiana State University
  Shreveport B
Louisiana State University and
  Agricultural and Mechanical
  College B, M, D
Louisiana Tech University B
Loyola University New Orleans B
Nicholls State University B
Southeastern Louisiana University B
Southern University and Agricultural
  and Mechanical College B

Tulane University *B, M*
University of Louisiana at Lafayette *B*
University of Louisiana at Monroe *B*
University of New Orleans *B*
Xavier University of Louisiana *B*

Maine

Husson College *B*
St. Joseph's College *B*
Thomas College *B*
University of Maine *B*
University of Southern Maine *B, M*

Maryland

Bowie State University *B*
Cecil Community College *A*
College of Notre Dame of Maryland *B*
Columbia Union College *M*
Loyola College in Maryland *M*
Morgan State University *B, M*
University of Maryland
 College Park *B*

Massachusetts

American International College *B, M*
Babson College *B*
Bentley College *B, M*
Boston College *B, M, D*
Boston University *B, M*
Brandeis University *M*
Bridgewater State College *C, B*
Bunker Hill Community College *A*
Clark University *M*
Fitchburg State College *B*
Gordon College *B*
Lasell College *B*
Massachusetts Bay Community
 College *C*
Massachusetts College of Liberal
 Arts *B*
Newbury College *A, B*
Nichols College *B*
Northeastern University *B, M*
Northern Essex Community
 College *C, A*
Salem State College *B*
Simmons College *B*
Springfield Technical Community
 College *A*
Stonehill College *B*
Suffolk University *B, M*
University of Massachusetts
 Amherst *B*
 Dartmouth *B*
Western New England College *B*
Westfield State College *B*

Michigan

Alma College *B*
Andrews University *B*
Central Michigan University *B*
Davenport University *A, B*
Eastern Michigan University *B, M*
Ferris State University *B*
Glen Oaks Community College *C*
Grand Valley State University *B*
Hillsdale College *B*
Jackson Community College *C, A*
Lake Michigan College *A*
Michigan State University *B, M, D*
Northern Michigan University *B*
Oakland University *B*
Olivet College *B*
Saginaw Valley State University *B*
University of Michigan
 Flint *B*
Walsh College of Accountancy and
 Business Administration *B, M*
Wayne State University *B*
Western Michigan University *B*

Minnesota

Academy College *A*

Augsburg College *B*
Capella University *M*
Concordia University: St. Paul *B*
Fond du Lac Tribal and Community
 College *A*
Metropolitan State University *B*
Minnesota State University
 Mankato *B*
 Moorhead *B*
Northwestern College *B*
St. Cloud State University *B*
Southwest Minnesota State
 University *B*
University of St. Thomas *B*
Winona State University *B*

Mississippi

Delta State University *B*
Hinds Community College *A*
Jackson State University *B*
Mississippi State University *B*
University of Mississippi *B*
University of Southern Mississippi *B*

Missouri

Avila University *B*
Central Missouri State University *B*
Columbia College *B*
Culver-Stockton College *B*
Lindenwood University *B, M*
Missouri Southern State University *B*
Missouri State University *B*
Missouri Western State University *B*
Northwest Missouri State
 University *B*
St. Louis University *M*
Southeast Missouri State University *B*
University of Missouri
 St. Louis *B, M*
Washington University in St.
 Louis *B, M*
Webster University *B, M*

Montana

Carroll College *B*
University of Montana: Missoula *B*

Nebraska

Chadron State College *B*
Creighton University *B*
Union College *B*
University of Nebraska
 Lincoln *B*
 Omaha *B*

Nevada

University of Nevada
 Las Vegas *B*
 Reno *B*

New Hampshire

Franklin Pierce College *B*
McIntosh College *A*
New England College *B*
St. Anselm College *B*
Southern New Hampshire
 University *B, M*
University of New Hampshire *B*

New Jersey

The College of New Jersey *B*
Fairleigh Dickinson University
 College at Florham *M*
 Metropolitan Campus *M*
Gloucester County College *A*
Kean University *B*
Monmouth University *B*
Passaic County Community College *C*
Rider University *B*
Rowan University *B*
Rutgers, The State University of New
 Jersey
 Camden Regional Campus *B*

New Brunswick/Piscataway
 Campus *B*
 Newark Regional Campus *B*
St. Peter's College *A*
Seton Hall University *B*
Thomas Edison State College *C, A, B*
William Paterson University of New
 Jersey *B*

New Mexico

Eastern New Mexico University *B*
New Mexico Highlands University *B*
New Mexico State University *B*

New York

Adelphi University *B, M*
Alfred University *B*
Canisius College *B*
City University of New York
 Baruch College *B, M, D*
 Queens College *B*
Clarkson University *B*
Clinton Community College *C*
Concordia College *B*
Dominican College of Blauvelt *B*
Dowling College *C, B*
Excelsior College *B*
Fordham University *B, M*
Globe Institute of Technology *C, A, B*
Hilbert College *B*
Hofstra University *B, M*
Hudson Valley Community College *A*
Iona College *B, M*
Ithaca College *B*
Le Moyne College *B*
Long Island University
 Brooklyn Campus *B*
Manhattan College *B*
Manhattanville College *B*
Mercy College *M*
New York Institute of
 Technology *C, B, M*
New York University *B, M, D*
Orange County Community College *A*
Pace University *B, M*
Rochester Institute of
 Technology *B, M*
St. Bonaventure University *B, M*
St. John Fisher College *B*
St. John's University *B, M*
St. Thomas Aquinas College *B*
Siena College *B, T*
State University of New York
 Albany *M*
 Buffalo *M*
 College at Brockport *B*
 College at Fredonia *B*
 College at Old Westbury *B*
 College at Plattsburgh *B*
 College of Agriculture and
  Technology at Cobleskill *A, B*
 College of Technology at Alfred *A*
 Institute of Technology at
  Utica/Rome *B*
 New Paltz *B*
 Oswego *B*
Suffolk County Community College *A*
Syracuse University *B, M*
Ulster County Community
 College *C, A*
Wagner College *B*

North Carolina

Appalachian State University *B*
Catawba Valley Community
 College *C, A*
East Carolina University *B*
Elon University *B*
Forsyth Technical Community
 College *A*
Lenoir-Rhyne College *B*
Mars Hill College *B*
North Carolina Agricultural and
 Technical State University *B*

University of North Carolina
 Charlotte *B*
 Greensboro *B*
 Wilmington *B*
Wake Forest University *B*
Western Carolina University *B*
Wingate University *B*

North Dakota

Dickinson State University *B*
Jamestown College *B*
Minot State University *B*
North Dakota State College of
 Science *A*
University of North Dakota *B*

Ohio

Ashland University *B*
Baldwin-Wallace College *B*
Bowling Green State University *B, M*
Case Western Reserve University *M*
Cedarville University *B*
Cincinnati State Technical and
 Community College *A*
Cleveland State University *B, D*
David N. Myers University *B*
Defiance College *B*
Edison State Community College *A*
Franklin University *B*
James A. Rhodes State College *C, A*
Jefferson Community College *C*
John Carroll University *B*
Kent State University *B, D*
Marietta College *B*
Miami University
 Oxford Campus *B, M*
Mount Vernon Nazarene University *B*
Ohio State University
 Columbus Campus *B*
Ohio University *B*
Otterbein College *B*
Shawnee State University *A*
Tiffin University *B*
University of Akron *B, M*
University of Cincinnati *B, M, D*
University of Dayton *B*
University of Findlay *A, B*
University of Rio Grande *B*
University of Toledo *B, M*
Walsh University *A, B*
Wright State University *M*
Xavier University *B, M*
Youngstown State University *A, B, M*

Oklahoma

East Central University *B*
Northeastern State University *B*
Oklahoma Baptist University *B*
Oklahoma City Community
 College *C, A*
Oklahoma City University *B*
Oklahoma State University *B*
Oral Roberts University *B*
Southeastern Oklahoma State
 University *B*
Southern Nazarene University *B*
Tulsa Community College *A*
University of Central Oklahoma *B*
University of Oklahoma *B*
University of Tulsa *B, M*

Oregon

Chemeketa Community College *C*
Corban College *B*
Linfield College *B*
Portland State University *B, M*
University of Oregon *M, D*
University of Portland *B*

Pennsylvania

Albright College *B*
Arcadia University *B*
Cabrini College *B*

Carnegie Mellon University D
Chestnut Hill College C, A, B
DeSales University B
Drexel University B, M
Duquesne University B
Gannon University B
Gettysburg College B
Holy Family University B
Immaculata University B
Indiana University of Pennsylvania B
Juniata College B
King's College B
Kutztown University of
     Pennsylvania B
La Roche College B
La Salle University B
Lehigh University B, M
Lincoln University B
Marywood University M
Mercyhurst College B
Penn State
     Abington B
     Altoona B
     Beaver B
     Berks B
     Dubois B
     Erie, The Behrend College B
     Fayette B
     Harrisburg B
     Hazleton B
     Lehigh Valley B
     McKeesport B
     Mont Alto B
     New Kensington B
     Schuylkill - Capital College B
     Shenango B
     University Park B
     Wilkes-Barre B
     Worthington Scranton B
     York B
Philadelphia University B
Robert Morris University B, M
St. Francis University B
St. Joseph's University C, A, B, M
St. Vincent College B
Seton Hill University B
Shippensburg University of
     Pennsylvania B
Susquehanna University B
Temple University B, M
University of Pennsylvania B, M, D
University of Pittsburgh B
University of Pittsburgh
     Johnstown B
University of Scranton B, M
Villanova University B
Waynesburg College B
West Chester University of
     Pennsylvania B, M
Westminster College B
Widener University B
York College of Pennsylvania B

Puerto Rico

Bayamon Central University B, M
Inter American University of Puerto
     Rico
     Bayamon Campus B
     Ponce Campus B, M
     San German Campus B, M
Pontifical Catholic University of
     Puerto Rico B
University of Puerto Rico
     Aguadilla B
     Arecibo B
     Bayamon University College B
     Carolina Regional College B
     Mayaguez B, M
     Ponce B
     Rio Piedras B, M, D

Rhode Island

Bryant University B, M
Johnson & Wales University A, B

Providence College B
Rhode Island College B
Roger Williams University B
Salve Regina University B
University of Rhode Island B

South Carolina

Anderson University B
Charleston Southern University B, M
Coastal Carolina University B
Converse College B
Francis Marion University B
University of South Carolina B
University of South Carolina
     Aiken B
Wofford College B

South Dakota

Lake Area Technical Institute A
Northern State University B
University of South Dakota B

Tennessee

Belmont University B
Cleveland State Community College C
East Tennessee State University B
Freed-Hardeman University B
Hiwassee College A
Lipscomb University M
Middle Tennessee State University B
Southwest Tennessee Community
     College A
Tennessee Technological University B
Tennessee Wesleyan College B
Union University B
University of Memphis B
University of Tennessee
     Knoxville B

Texas

Abilene Christian University B
Amarillo College A
Angelo State University B
Baylor University B
Brazosport College A
Clarendon College A
Coastal Bend College A
Dallas Baptist University B
Del Mar College C, A
El Paso Community College A
Hardin-Simmons University B
Houston Baptist University B
Howard Payne University B
Lamar University B
Laredo Community College C, A
LeTourneau University B
Lubbock Christian University B
McMurry University B
Midwestern State University B
Our Lady of the Lake University of San
     Antonio M
Prairie View A&M University B
St. Edward's University B
Sam Houston State University B, M
Southern Methodist University B, M
Stephen F. Austin State University B
Sul Ross State University B
Tarleton State University B
Texas A&M University B, M, D
Texas A&M University
     Kingsville B
     Texarkana B
Texas Christian University B
Texas State University: San Marcos B
Texas Tech University B
Texas Wesleyan University B
Trinity University B
University of Houston B, M, D
University of Houston
     Clear Lake B, M
     Downtown B
University of Mary Hardin-Baylor B
University of North Texas B, M, D

University of St. Thomas B
University of Texas
     Austin B, D
     Brownsville B
     El Paso B
     Pan American B
     San Antonio B, M, D
     Tyler B
     of the Permian Basin B
West Texas A&M University B, M

Utah

Brigham Young University B
Salt Lake Community College C, A
Southern Utah University B
University of Utah B, M
Utah State University B
Weber State University B

Virginia

Averett University B
Central Virginia Community
     College A
Christopher Newport University B
Dabney S. Lancaster Community
     College C
George Mason University B
Hampton University B
James Madison University B
Liberty University B
Longwood University B
Marymount University C, B
Old Dominion University B
Radford University B
Virginia Highlands Community
     College C
Virginia Polytechnic Institute and
     State University B
Virginia Union University B

Washington

Seattle University B, M
University of Washington B
Walla Walla College B
Washington State University B
Western Washington University B

West Virginia

Bethany College B
Concord University B
Marshall University B
University of Charleston B
West Virginia University B
West Virginia Wesleyan College B

Wisconsin

Carroll College B
Concordia University Wisconsin B
Edgewood College B, M
Madison Area Technical College A
Marquette University B, M
University of Wisconsin
     Eau Claire B
     La Crosse B
     Madison B, M
     Milwaukee B
     Oshkosh B
     Parkside B
     Platteville B
     Superior B
     Whitewater B
Western Wisconsin Technical
     College A
Wisconsin Indianhead Technical
     College A

Wyoming

University of Wyoming B, M

Financial planning

California

Golden Gate University M
San Diego State University M
Southwestern College C, A
University of San Diego C

Connecticut

Manchester Community College C

Florida

Florida Community College at
     Jacksonville C, A
Schiller International University M

Georgia

Georgia State University M

Illinois

DePaul University M
St. Xavier University M
University of Illinois
     Urbana-Champaign B, M, D

Indiana

Taylor University B

Kentucky

Western Kentucky University C

Maine

University of Maine
     Augusta A, B

Maryland

Howard Community College C, A
Villa Julie College C

Massachusetts

Bentley College M
Merrimack College C
New England College of Finance C

Michigan

Central Michigan University B
Cleary University B
Northern Michigan University B
Western Michigan University B

Minnesota

Minnesota State University
     Mankato B

Missouri

Missouri Southern State University B

New Jersey

Seton Hall University M

New York

Bramson ORT College A
Broome Community College A
Globe Institute of Technology C
Medaille College C, B
Pace University M
State University of New York
     College of Technology at
          Alfred A, B
     College of Technology at Canton B

North Carolina

Campbell University B

North Dakota

Jamestown College B

Ohio

Defiance College B

Ohio State University
Lima Campus *B*
University of Cincinnati
Clermont College *C*
Raymond Walters College *C, A*
Youngstown State University *B*

Oklahoma

Oklahoma State University *C*

Pennsylvania

Marywood University *B*
St. Joseph's University *M*
Widener University *B, M*

Rhode Island

Bryant University *B*
University of Rhode Island *B*

Texas

Baylor University *B*
Southern Methodist University *B, M*
University of Dallas *M*

Utah

Brigham Young University *B*

Washington

City University *M*

West Virginia

Mountain State University *B*
University of Charleston *B*

Wisconsin

Fox Valley Technical College *C*
Waukesha County Technical
College *A*

Fine/studio arts

Alabama

Auburn University *B*
Faulkner State Community College *A*
Faulkner University *B*
Huntingdon College *B*
Spring Hill College *B*
Talladega College *B*
University of Alabama *B, M*
University of North Alabama *B*

Alaska

University of Alaska
Anchorage *B*

Arizona

Arizona Western College *A*
Cochise College *A*
Dine College *A*
Eastern Arizona College *A*
Grand Canyon University *B*
Northern Arizona University *B*
Prescott College *B, M*
University of Arizona *B*

Arkansas

Harding University *B*
Ouachita Baptist University *B, T*
University of Arkansas *B*
University of Central Arkansas *B*
Williams Baptist College *B*

California

Academy of Art University *C, A, B, M*
Art Center College of Design *B, M*
Azusa Pacific University *B*
Barstow College *A*
Biola University *B*
Butte College *A*
Cabrillo College *A*
California College of the Arts *B*

California Institute of the Arts *C, B, M*
California State University
Chico *B, M*
East Bay *B*
Fullerton *B, M*
Long Beach *B, M*
Monterey Bay *B*
San Bernardino *B*
Stanislaus *B*
Chabot College *A*
Chaffey College *A*
Chapman University *B*
Citrus College *A*
City College of San Francisco *A*
College of Alameda *A*
College of Marin: Kentfield *A*
College of San Mateo *A*
College of the Desert *A*
College of the Sequoias *A*
Cosumnes River College *A*
El Camino College *A*
Foothill College *C, A*
Gavilan Community College *A*
Golden West College *A*
Irvine Valley College *A*
John F. Kennedy University *M*
La Sierra University *B*
Lake Tahoe Community College *A*
Las Positas College *A*
Los Angeles Pierce College *A*
Los Medanos College *A*
Loyola Marymount University *B*
Merced College *A*
Mills College *B*
Modesto Junior College *A*
Monterey Peninsula College *C, A*
Moorpark College *A*
Mount St. Mary's College *B*
Notre Dame de Namur University *B*
Ohlone College *A*
Orange Coast College *A*
Otis College of Art and Design *B, M*
Pacific Union College *B*
Pasadena City College *A*
Pepperdine University *B*
Pitzer College *B*
Pomona College *B*
Porterville College *C, A*
Sacramento City College *A*
Saddleback College *A*
San Diego City College *A*
San Diego Mesa College *A*
San Diego Miramar College *A*
San Francisco Art Institute *B, M*
San Francisco State University *M*
San Joaquin Delta College *A*
San Jose City College *A*
San Jose State University *B, M*
Santa Barbara City College *C, A*
Santa Clara University *B*
Santa Monica College *A*
Scripps College *B*
Shasta College *A*
Sierra College *A*
Solano Community College *A*
Sonoma State University *B*
Stanford University *B*
University of California
Davis *B*
Irvine *B, M*
Riverside *B, M*
San Diego *B*
Santa Barbara *B, M*
Santa Cruz *B*
University of San Diego *B*
University of San Francisco *B*
University of Southern
California *B, M*
University of the Pacific *B*
Ventura College *A*
West Hills Community College *A*
Yuba Community College District *A*

Colorado

Adams State College *B*
Colorado Christian University *B*
Colorado College *B*
Colorado Mountain College
Alpine Campus *A*
Colorado State University *B, M*
Colorado State University
Pueblo *B*
Mesa State College *B*
Naropa University *B*
University of Colorado
Boulder *B, M*
Colorado Springs *B*
Denver and Health Sciences
Center *B*
University of Denver *B, M*
University of Northern
Colorado *B, M, T*
Western State College of Colorado *B*

Connecticut

Albertus Magnus College *B*
Capital Community College *C*
Eastern Connecticut State
University *B*
Fairfield University *B*
Gateway Community College *A*
Housatonic Community College *A*
Middlesex Community College *A*
Mitchell College *A*
Naugatuck Valley Community
College *C*
Northwestern Connecticut
Community College *A*
Norwalk Community College *A*
Paier College of Art *C, B*
Quinebaug Valley Community
College *A*
St. Joseph College *B*
Trinity College *B*
University of Connecticut *B, M*
University of New Haven *B*
Wesleyan University *B*
Western Connecticut State
University *M*
Yale University *M*

Delaware

Delaware College of Art and Design *A*
University of Delaware *B, M*

District of Columbia

American University *B*
Corcoran College of Art and
Design *A, B*
Gallaudet University *B*
George Washington University *B*
Georgetown University *B*
University of the District of
Columbia *B*

Florida

Eckerd College *B*
Flagler College *B*
Florida Atlantic University *M*
Florida Gulf Coast University *B*
Florida International University *B, M*
Florida Southern College *B*
Florida State University *B, M*
Jacksonville University *B*
Manatee Community College *A*
Miami Dade College *A*
New College of Florida *B*
Palm Beach Atlantic University *B*
Palm Beach Community College *A*
Ringling School of Art and Design *B*
Stetson University *B*
University of Central Florida *B, M*
University of Florida *M*
University of Miami *B*
University of North Florida *B*
University of South Florida *B, M*

University of West Florida *B*

Georgia

Abraham Baldwin Agricultural
College *A*
Agnes Scott College *B*
Brenau University *B*
Clark Atlanta University *B*
Covenant College *B*
Gainesville State College *A*
Georgia Southern University *M*
Morehouse College *B*
Piedmont College *B*
Reinhardt College *B*
Shorter College *B*
Spelman College *B*
University of Georgia *B*
Wesleyan College *B*
Young Harris College *A*

Hawaii

Brigham Young University-Hawaii *B*

Idaho

North Idaho College *A*
University of Idaho *M*

Illinois

American Academy of Art *B*
Augustana College *B*
Benedictine University *B*
Blackburn College *B, T*
Bradley University *B, M, T*
City Colleges of Chicago
Kennedy-King College *A*
Olive-Harvey College *A*
Columbia College Chicago *B*
Dominican University *B*
Illinois Central College *A*
Illinois State University *B, M*
Illinois Valley Community College *A*
Judson College *B*
Kankakee Community College *A*
Knox College *B*
Lake Land College *A*
Lewis University *B*
Lewis and Clark Community
College *A*
Lincoln Land Community College *A*
Loyola University of Chicago *B*
McKendree College *B*
Millikin University *B, T*
Monmouth College *B*
Morton College *A*
National-Louis University *B*
North Central College *B*
North Park University *B*
Northern Illinois University *B, M*
Principia College *B*
Rockford College *B*
St. Xavier University *B*
Sauk Valley Community College *A*
School of the Art Institute of
Chicago *B, M*
South Suburban College of Cook
County *A*
Southern Illinois University
Carbondale *B, M*
Southern Illinois University
Edwardsville *B, M*
Southwestern Illinois College *A*
Trinity Christian College *B*
University of Illinois
Chicago *B, M*
Springfield *B*
Urbana-Champaign *B, M*
Waubonsee Community College *A*
Western Illinois University *B*
William Rainey Harper College *A*

Indiana

Ancilla College *A*
Anderson University *B*

Calumet College of St. Joseph C, B
DePauw University B
Hanover College B
Huntington University B
Indiana State University B, M
Indiana University
    Bloomington B, M
    South Bend B
    Southeast B
Indiana University-Purdue University
    Fort Wayne B
Indiana University-Purdue University
    Indianapolis B
Indiana Wesleyan University B
Martin University B
Oakland City University A, B
St. Joseph's College B
Saint Mary's College B
University of Notre Dame B, M
Vincennes University A

Iowa

Ashford University B
Clarke College B
Coe College B
Drake University B
Ellsworth Community College A
Graceland University B, T
Grand View College B
Iowa Wesleyan College B
Loras College B
Maharishi University of
    Management B, M
Marshalltown Community College A
Morningside College B
St. Ambrose University B
University of Iowa B
University of Northern Iowa B
Upper Iowa University B

Kansas

Allen County Community College A
Baker University B, T
Bethel College B
Coffeyville Community College A
Fort Hays State University M
Kansas State University B, M
Kansas Wesleyan University B, T
Labette Community College A
Neosho County Community
    College A
Pratt Community College A
Seward County Community College A
University of Kansas B, M
Washburn University of Topeka B
Wichita State University B, M

Kentucky

Asbury College B
Berea College B, T
Campbellsville University B
Eastern Kentucky University B
Georgetown College B, T
Kentucky State University B
Kentucky Wesleyan College B
Lindsey Wilson College A, B, T
Morehead State University B, M
Murray State University B, T
Northern Kentucky University B
St. Catharine College A
Spalding University B
Thomas More College A, B
Transylvania University B, T
University of Louisville B
University of the Cumberlands B
Western Kentucky University B

Louisiana

Centenary College of Louisiana B
Louisiana State University and
    Agricultural and Mechanical
    College B, M
Loyola University New Orleans B

Northwestern State University B
Southern University and Agricultural
    and Mechanical College B
Tulane University B
University of Louisiana at Monroe B
University of New Orleans B, M

Maine

Bowdoin College B
Colby College B
College of the Atlantic B
Maine College of Art B, M
University of Maine B
University of Maine
    Augusta A, B
    Presque Isle B
University of Southern Maine B

Maryland

Bowie State University B
College of Notre Dame of Maryland B
Community College of Baltimore
    County A
Frostburg State University B, T
Goucher College M
Howard Community College A
Montgomery College A
Morgan State University B
Prince George's Community
    College A
Salisbury University B
Towson University B
University of Maryland
    College Park B, M

Massachusetts

Amherst College B
Anna Maria College B
Art Institute of Boston at Lesley
    University C, B, M
Atlantic Union College B
Boston College B
Boston University M
Bridgewater State College B
Bristol Community College C
Clark University B
College of the Holy Cross B
Curry College B
Elms College B
Emmanuel College B
Hampshire College B
Lesley University B, M
Massachusetts College of Art B, M
Massachusetts College of Liberal
    Arts B
Massasoit Community College A
Merrimack College B
Middlesex Community College C, A
Montserrat College of Art B
Northeastern University B
School of the Museum of Fine
    Arts B, M, T
Simon's Rock College of Bard B
Smith College B
Springfield Technical Community
    College A
Stonehill College B
Suffolk University C, B
Tufts University B
University of Massachusetts
    Amherst B, M
    Dartmouth B, M
    Lowell B
Wellesley College B
Westfield State College B
Wheaton College B
Williams College B

Michigan

Albion College B
Alma College B
Andrews University B
Calvin College B

College for Creative Studies B
Eastern Michigan University M
Ferris State University B, M
Finlandia University B
Grand Valley State University B
Hope College B
Kendall College of Art and Design of
    Ferris State University B, M
Lake Superior State University B
Marygrove College B
Monroe County Community
    College A
Northwestern Michigan College A
Oakland University B
Olivet College B
Saginaw Valley State University B
St. Clair County Community
    College A
Schoolcraft College A
Siena Heights University B
University of Michigan B, M
University of Michigan
    Flint B
Western Michigan University M

Minnesota

Augsburg College B
Bethany Lutheran College B
Carleton College B
College of St. Catherine B
College of Visual Arts B
Concordia College: Moorhead B
Concordia University: St. Paul B
Hamline University B, M
Macalester College B
Minneapolis College of Art and
    Design B, M
Minnesota State University
    Mankato B
Northland Community & Technical
    College A
Northwestern College B
Ridgewater College A
St. Cloud State University B
St. Mary's University of Minnesota B
University of Minnesota
    Duluth B
    Morris B
University of St. Thomas B
Winona State University B

Mississippi

East Central Community College A
Mississippi Delta Community
    College A
Mississippi State University M
Mississippi Valley State University B
University of Southern Mississippi M
William Carey College B

Missouri

Avila University B
Central Missouri State University B
College of the Ozarks B
Columbia College B
Drury University B, T
Evangel University B
Fontbonne University B, M, T
Hannibal-LaGrange College B
Lincoln University B
Lindenwood University B, M
Maryville University of Saint Louis B
Missouri Southern State
    University B, T
Park University B
St. Louis Community College
    St. Louis Community College at
        Florissant Valley A
    St. Louis Community College at
        Meramec A
St. Louis University B
Three Rivers Community College A
Truman State University B

University of Missouri
    Kansas City B, M
Washington University in St.
    Louis B, M
Webster University B
William Woods University B, T

Montana

Fort Peck Community College C, A

Nebraska

Bellevue University B
College of Saint Mary B
Metropolitan Community College A
Midland Lutheran College B
Nebraska Wesleyan University B
Union College B
University of Nebraska
    Kearney B, M, T
    Lincoln B, M
    Omaha B

Nevada

Community College of Southern
    Nevada A
Sierra Nevada College B
University of Nevada
    Las Vegas B, M

New Hampshire

Chester College of New England B
Colby-Sawyer College B
Dartmouth College B
Franklin Pierce College B
Keene State College B
Plymouth State University B
Rivier College B
University of New Hampshire B
University of New Hampshire at
    Manchester A

New Jersey

Atlantic Cape Community College A
Brookdale Community College A
Caldwell College B
The College of New Jersey B, T
Cumberland County College A
Essex County College A
Felician College B
Georgian Court University B
Kean University B
Middlesex County College A
Monmouth University B
Montclair State University B, M
New Jersey City University B, M
Raritan Valley Community College A
Rider University B
Rowan University B
Rutgers, The State University of New
    Jersey
    New Brunswick/Piscataway
        Campus M
St. Peter's College B
Sussex County Community College A
Warren County Community College A

New Mexico

Clovis Community College A
College of Santa Fe B
College of the Southwest B
Institute of American Indian Arts A, B
New Mexico Junior College A
New Mexico State University B, M
Northern New Mexico College A
Western New Mexico University B

New York

Adelphi University B, M
Alfred University B
Bard College B, M
Cayuga County Community College A
Cazenovia College B

City University of New York
City College *B*
Hunter College *B*
Kingsborough Community
College *A*
LaGuardia Community College *A*
Lehman College *B, M*
Queens College *B, M, T*
Colgate University *B*
College of New Rochelle *B, M, T*
Columbia University
Columbia College *B*
Columbia-Greene Community
College *A*
Cooper Union for the Advancement of
Science and Art *C, B*
Cornell University *B, M, D*
Daemen College *B*
Eugene Lang College The New School
for Liberal Arts *B*
Fashion Institute of Technology *A*
Finger Lakes Community College *A*
Fordham University *B*
Hamilton College *B*
Herkimer County Community
College *A*
Hobart and William Smith Colleges *B*
Hofstra University *B*
Houghton College *B*
Ithaca College *B*
Jamestown Community College *A*
Long Island University
Brooklyn Campus *B*
C. W. Post Campus *B, M*
Mannes College The New School for
Music *B, M*
Marist College *B*
Marymount Manhattan College *B*
Monroe Community College *A*
Nassau Community College *A*
Nazareth College of Rochester *B, T*
New York Institute of Technology *B*
New York University *B, M*
Niagara County Community
College *A*
Pace University *A*
Parsons The New School for
Design *C, A, B, T*
Pratt Institute *B, M*
Rensselaer Polytechnic Institute *B, M*
Roberts Wesleyan College *B*
Rochester Institute of
Technology *A, B, M*
Rockland Community College *A*
Sage College of Albany *A, B*
St. John's University *B*
St. Lawrence University *B*
St. Thomas Aquinas College *B*
Sarah Lawrence College *B*
School of Visual Arts *B, M*
Skidmore College *B*
State University of New York
Albany *B, M*
Binghamton *B*
Buffalo *B, M*
College at Brockport *B, M*
College at Buffalo *B*
College at Cortland *B*
College at Fredonia *B*
College at Geneseo *B*
College at Oneonta *B*
College at Plattsburgh *B*
Empire State College *A, B*
New Paltz *B*
Oswego *M*
Stony Brook *B, M*
Suffolk County Community College *A*
Syracuse University *B, M*
University of Rochester *B*
Villa Maria College of Buffalo *A*
Wagner College *B*
Wells College *B*

North Carolina
Appalachian State University *B*
Barton College *B*
Campbell University *B*
Chowan College *B*
East Carolina University *B, M*
Elizabeth City State University *B*
Greensboro College *B*
Lenoir Community College *A*
Methodist College *B*
Mitchell Community College *A*
Mount Olive College *A, B*
Queens University of Charlotte *B*
Randolph Community College *A*
Rockingham Community College *A*
Salem College *B*
University of North Carolina
Asheville *B*
Chapel Hill *B, M*
Charlotte *B*
Greensboro *B, M*
Pembroke *B*
Wilmington *B*
Wake Forest University *B*
Western Carolina University *B, M*
Western Piedmont Community
College *A*
Wingate University *B*

North Dakota
Dickinson State University *B*
Jamestown College *B*

Ohio
Antioch College *B*
Art Academy of Cincinnati *B*
Ashland University *B*
Baldwin-Wallace College *B*
Bowling Green State University *M*
Capital University *B*
Cedarville University *B*
College of Mount St. Joseph *B*
College of Wooster *B*
Columbus College of Art and
Design *B*
Denison University *B*
Hiram College *B, T*
Kenyon College *B*
Lake Erie College *B*
Malone College *B*
Marietta College *B*
Oberlin College *B*
Ohio Northern University *B*
Ohio State University
Columbus Campus *B, M*
Ohio Wesleyan University *B*
Shawnee State University *B*
Sinclair Community College *A*
Union Institute & University *M*
University of Akron *B*
University of Cincinnati *C, B, M*
University of Dayton *B*
University of Rio Grande *B*
University of Toledo *B*
Ursuline College *B*
Xavier University *B*
Youngstown State University *B*

Oklahoma
Cameron University *B*
East Central University *B*
Northeastern State University *B*
Oklahoma Baptist University *B*
Oklahoma City Community College *A*
Oklahoma City University *B*
Oral Roberts University *B*
Rogers State University *A*
University of Oklahoma *B, M*
University of Science and Arts of
Oklahoma *B, T*
University of Tulsa *M*

Oregon
Central Oregon Community
College *A*
Eastern Oregon University *B*
Lewis & Clark College *B*
Marylhurst University *B*
Pacific Northwest College of Art *B*
Portland State University *B*
Reed College *B*
University of Oregon *B*
Western Oregon University *B*
Willamette University *B*

Pennsylvania
Albright College *B*
Allegheny College *B*
Arcadia University *B*
Bloomsburg University of
Pennsylvania *B, M*
Bryn Mawr College *B*
Bucknell University *B*
Bucks County Community College *A*
Cabrini College *B*
Cedar Crest College *B*
Chatham College *B*
Community College of Beaver
County *A*
Dickinson College *B*
Duquesne University *B*
Franklin & Marshall College *B*
Gettysburg College *B*
Haverford College *B*
Juniata College *B*
Keystone College *A, B*
Kutztown University of
Pennsylvania *B*
La Salle University *B*
Lafayette College *B*
Lebanon Valley College *B*
Lincoln University *B*
Lock Haven University of
Pennsylvania *B*
Mansfield University of
Pennsylvania *B*
Marywood University *B*
Mercyhurst College *B*
Messiah College *B*
Moore College of Art and Design *B*
Moravian College *B*
Northampton County Area
Community College *A*
St. Vincent College *B*
Seton Hill University *B*
Swarthmore College *B*
University of Pennsylvania *B, M*
University of Pittsburgh *B*
University of the Arts *B, M*
West Chester University of
Pennsylvania *B*
Westminster College *B*
Widener University *B*
York College of Pennsylvania *B*

Puerto Rico
Pontifical Catholic University of
Puerto Rico *B*
University of Puerto Rico
Mayaguez *B*
Rio Piedras *B*

Rhode Island
Brown University *B*
Rhode Island College *B, M*
Rhode Island School of Design *B, M*
Roger Williams University *B*
Salve Regina University *B*
University of Rhode Island *B*

South Carolina
Anderson University *B*
Charleston Southern University *B*
Clemson University *B, M*
Coastal Carolina University *B*

Coker College *B*
College of Charleston *B*
Columbia College *B, T*
Converse College *B*
Furman University *B*
Limestone College *B*
North Greenville College *A*
Presbyterian College *B*
University of South Carolina *B, M*
University of South Carolina
Aiken *B*
Winthrop University *B*

South Dakota
Dakota State University *B*
University of South Dakota *B, M*

Tennessee
Bethel College *B*
Cumberland University *B*
Lambuth University *B*
Lipscomb University *B*
Maryville College *B*
Memphis College of Art *B, M*
Tennessee Technological University *B*
University of Tennessee
Knoxville *B*
University of the South *B*
Vanderbilt University *B*

Texas
Abilene Christian University *B*
Angelo State University *B*
Art Institute
of Dallas *B*
Baylor University *B*
Coastal Bend College *A*
College of the Mainland *A*
El Paso Community College *C*
Hardin-Simmons University *B*
Houston Baptist University *B*
Howard Payne University *B*
Lon Morris College *A*
McMurry University *B*
Midwestern State University *B*
Mountain View College *A*
Palo Alto College *A*
Paris Junior College *A*
Rice University *B, M*
St. Philip's College *A*
Sam Houston State University *B, M*
San Antonio College *A*
South Texas College *A*
Southern Methodist University *B, M*
Southwestern University *B*
Tarleton State University *B*
Texas A&M University
Commerce *M*
Kingsville *B, M, T*
Texas Christian University *B, M*
Texas College *B*
Texas Southern University *B, M*
Texas State University: San
Marcos *B, T*
Texas Tech University *B*
Tyler Junior College *A*
University of Houston *B, M*
University of Mary Hardin-Baylor *B, T*
University of North Texas *B, M, D*
University of St. Thomas *B*
University of Texas
Arlington *B*
Austin *B, M*
Dallas *B, M*
El Paso *B*
Pan American *B, M*
San Antonio *B*
Tyler *M*
West Texas A&M University *B, M*

Utah
Brigham Young University *B, M*
Utah State University *M*

Weber State University *B*

Vermont

Bennington College *B*
Burlington College *B*
Goddard College *B, M*
Green Mountain College *B*
Johnson State College *B, M*
Marlboro College *B*
Middlebury College *B*
St. Michael's College *B*
University of Vermont *B*

Virginia

Blue Ridge Community College *C*
Bridgewater College *B*
Christopher Newport University *B*
College of William and Mary *B*
George Mason University *B*
Germanna Community College *C*
Hampden-Sydney College *B*
Hollins University *B*
John Tyler Community College *C, A*
Longwood University *B, T*
Lord Fairfax Community College *C*
Marymount University *B*
Northern Virginia Community
    College *A*
Old Dominion University *B, T*
Radford University *B, M*
Randolph-Macon College *B*
Randolph-Macon Woman's College *B*
Regent University *M*
Sweet Briar College *B*
Thomas Nelson Community
    College *A*
Tidewater Community College *A*
University of Mary Washington *B*
University of Richmond *B, T*
Virginia Commonwealth University *M*
Virginia Wesleyan College *B*
Virginia Western Community
    College *A*
Washington and Lee University *B*

Washington

Central Washington University *B, M*
Centralia College *A*
Cornish College of the Arts *B*
Eastern Washington University *B*
Everett Community College *A*
Evergreen State College *B*
Gonzaga University *B*
North Seattle Community
    College *C, A*
Northwest College of Art *B*
Pacific Lutheran University *B*
Whitman College *B*

West Virginia

Bethany College *B*
Concord University *B*
West Virginia State University *B*
West Virginia Wesleyan College *B*

Wisconsin

Cardinal Stritch University *B*
Carroll College *B*
Carthage College *B*
Lawrence University *B, T*
Marian College of Fond du Lac *B*
Northland College *B*
University of Wisconsin
    Madison *M*
    Oshkosh *B*
    River Falls *B*
    Stout *B*
    Superior *B, M*
Viterbo University *B*

Wyoming

Casper College *A*

Laramie County Community
    College *A*
Western Wyoming Community
    College *A*

Fire protection and safety technology

Alabama

Community College of the Air
    Force *A*
Lawson State Community College *C*

Alaska

University of Alaska
    Fairbanks *C, A*

Arizona

Cochise College *A*

California

Allan Hancock College *C, A*
American River College *A*
Antelope Valley College *C, A*
Bakersfield College *A*
Barstow College *C, A*
Butte College *C, A*
Cerro Coso Community College *C, A*
City College of San Francisco *C, A*
Cogswell Polytechnical College *B*
College of San Mateo *A*
College of the Canyons *C, A*
College of the Desert *C, A*
College of the Sequoias *C, A*
Columbia College *C, A*
Copper Mountain College *C, A*
Cosumnes River College *C, A*
El Camino College *C, A*
Fresno City College *C*
Glendale Community College *C, A*
Long Beach City College *C, A*
Mission College *C, A*
Monterey Peninsula College *C, A*
Rio Hondo College *A*
Riverside Community College *C, A*
San Joaquin Delta College *C, A*
Santa Ana College *A*
Santa Rosa Junior College *C*
Santiago Canyon College *A*
Shasta College *A*
Sierra College *C, A*
Victor Valley College *C, A*
Yuba Community College
    District *C, A*

Colorado

Aims Community College *A*
Arapahoe Community College *C*
Pikes Peak Community College *A*
Red Rocks Community College *A*

Connecticut

Capital Community College *A*
Norwalk Community College *A*
Three Rivers Community College *A*
University of New Haven *C, A, B*

Delaware

Delaware Technical and Community
    College
    Stanton/Wilmington Campus *A*

Florida

Central Florida Community College *A*
Florida Community College at
    Jacksonville *A*
Gulf Coast Community College *A*
Indian River Community College *A*
St. Johns River Community College *A*
St. Petersburg College *A*
Santa Fe Community College *A*
Valencia Community College *A*

Georgia

Savannah Technical College *A*

Hawaii

University of Hawaii
    Honolulu Community College *C, A*

Idaho

Boise State University *C*
College of Southern Idaho *A*

Illinois

College of DuPage *C, A*
College of Lake County *C, A*
Elgin Community College *C, A*
Illinois Central College *A*
John Wood Community College *A*
Kishwaukee College *C, A*
Lincoln Land Community College *C*
Moraine Valley Community
    College *C, A*
Parkland College *C, A*
Prairie State College *C, A*
Waubonsee Community College *C, A*

Indiana

Vincennes University *A*

Iowa

Des Moines Area Community
    College *C, A*

Kansas

Hutchinson Community College *A*

Kentucky

Eastern Kentucky University *C, A, B*

Louisiana

Delgado Community College *A*

Maine

Southern Maine Community
    College *A*

Maryland

Community College of Baltimore
    County *C, A*
Montgomery College *C, A*

Massachusetts

Bunker Hill Community College *A*
Cape Cod Community College *A*
Massasoit Community College *C*
Middlesex Community College *A*
Mount Wachusett Community
    College *A*
North Shore Community College *A*
Springfield Technical Community
    College *A*

Michigan

Aquinas College *B*
Delta College *A*
Kellogg Community College *C, A*
Lake Superior State University *A, B*
Macomb Community College *C, A*
Mott Community College *A*
Wayne County Community College *A*

Mississippi

Hinds Community College *A*
Mississippi Gulf Coast Community
    College
    Jefferson Davis Campus *A*

Missouri

Jefferson College *C, A*
Ozarks Technical Community
    College *A*

St. Louis Community College
    St. Louis Community College at
        Florissant Valley *A*

Montana

Montana State University
    Billings *A*

Nebraska

Southeast Community College
    Lincoln Campus *A*
University of Nebraska
    Lincoln *A*

Nevada

Community College of Southern
    Nevada *A*

New Hampshire

New Hampshire Community
    Technical College
    Berlin *C, A*

New Jersey

Camden County College *A*
Mercer County Community
    College *C, A*
Ocean County College *C, A*
Thomas Edison State College *A, B*
Union County College *C, A*

New Mexico

Albuquerque Technical-Vocational
    Institute *A*
Eastern New Mexico University:
    Roswell Campus *A*

New York

Corning Community College *A*
Mercy College *C*
Monroe Community College *A*
Onondaga Community College *C, A*
Rockland Community College *A*

North Carolina

Central Piedmont Community
    College *A*
Cleveland Community College *C, A*
Coastal Carolina Community
    College *C, A*
Davidson County Community
    College *C, A*
Fayetteville Technical Community
    College *A*
Gaston College *A*
Guilford Technical Community
    College *A*
Rockingham Community College *A*
Rowan-Cabarrus Community
    College *A*
Wilson Technical Community
    College *A*

Ohio

Cuyahoga Community College
    Metropolitan Campus *A*
Owens Community College
    Toledo *A*
Sinclair Community College *C, A*
University of Akron *C, A*

Oklahoma

Oklahoma State University *B*
Oklahoma State University
    Oklahoma City *C*
Tulsa Community College *A*

Oregon

Chemeketa Community College *A*
Portland Community College *C, A*
Rogue Community College *C, A*

Treasure Valley Community
College C, A

Pennsylvania
Community College of Allegheny
County A
Community College of Philadelphia A
Delaware County Community
College A
Luzerne County Community
College C, A
Montgomery County Community
College C, A
Westmoreland County Community
College C, A

Texas
Amarillo College C, A
College of the Mainland A
Collin County Community College
District C, A
Del Mar College A
El Paso Community College A
Galveston College C, A
Houston Community College
System C, A
Laredo Community College A
Midland College A
Navarro College C, A
Odessa College C, A
San Antonio College C, A
San Jacinto College
Central Campus C, A
South Plains College C, A
Tarrant County College C, A
Tyler Junior College A

Virginia
Northern Virginia Community
College C, A

Washington
Bates Technical College A
Bellevue Community College C, A
Edmonds Community College A
Pierce College A
Spokane Falls Community College C

Wisconsin
Blackhawk Technical College A
Fox Valley Technical College A
Moraine Park Technical College C
Northcentral Technical College C
Northeast Wisconsin Technical
College A
Western Wisconsin Technical
College A

Fire services administration

Alabama
Bishop State Community College A
Calhoun Community College C
Jefferson State Community College A
Northwest-Shoals Community
College C
Shelton State Community College C

Alaska
University of Alaska
Anchorage A

California
California State University
Los Angeles B
Cogswell Polytechnical College B
Fresno City College C
Santa Ana College A

Connecticut
Gateway Community College A

Naugatuck Valley Community
College A
Norwalk Community College A

District of Columbia
University of the District of
Columbia A, B

Florida
Florida Community College at
Jacksonville A
Hillsborough Community College C
Miami Dade College A
Palm Beach Community College A

Georgia
Georgia Perimeter College A

Hawaii
University of Hawaii
Honolulu Community College A

Illinois
Black Hawk College A
College of DuPage C
Lewis University M
Lincoln Land Community College C
Moraine Valley Community College C
Rend Lake College C, A
Southern Illinois University
Carbondale B
Waubonsee Community College C

Iowa
Kirkwood Community College C, A
North Iowa Area Community
College A

Maine
Southern Maine Community
College A

Maryland
University of Maryland
University College C

Massachusetts
Cape Cod Community College C
Salem State College B

Michigan
Delta College A

Minnesota
Lake Superior College A
Southwest Minnesota State
University B

Missouri
Lindenwood University B
Park University B

New York
Broome Community College A
Erie Community College
South Campus A

North Carolina
University of North Carolina
Charlotte B

Ohio
Sinclair Community College C

Oklahoma
Oklahoma State University M

Oregon
Eastern Oregon University B
Western Oregon University B

Pennsylvania
Northampton County Area
Community College C, A

South Carolina
Trident Technical College A

Texas
Hill College C, A
San Antonio College A

Utah
Utah Valley State College B

Virginia
Hampton University B
Northern Virginia Community
College C, A
Thomas Nelson Community
College A

Washington
Bates Technical College A
Bellevue Community College A
Edmonds Community College C, A
Olympic College C, A
South Puget Sound Community
College A
Spokane Community College A
Yakima Valley Community College A

Firefighting/fire science

Alabama
Alabama Southern Community
College C, A
Central Alabama Community
College C, A
Chattahoochee Valley Community
College C, A

Alaska
University of Alaska
Fairbanks C, A

Arizona
Arizona Western College C, A
Central Arizona College C, A
Coconino County Community
College A
Eastern Arizona College C
Glendale Community College C, A
Mohave Community College C, A
Northland Pioneer College C, A
Phoenix College C, A
Pima Community College C, A
Scottsdale Community College C, A
Yavapai College C, A

Arkansas
Northwest Arkansas Community
College A
Southeast Arkansas College A
Southern Arkansas University Tech A

California
Allan Hancock College C
Cabrillo College C, A
Chabot College C, A
College of the Sequoias C
College of the Siskiyous C, A
Crafton Hills College C, A
East Los Angeles College C
El Camino College C
Fresno City College C, A
Imperial Valley College C, A
Lake Tahoe Community College C, A
Las Positas College A
Los Angeles Harbor College C, A
Los Medanos College C, A
Merced College C, A

Modesto Junior College A
Mount San Antonio College C, A
Palo Verde College C, A
Palomar College C, A
Pasadena City College C, A
Porterville College C
Santa Ana College A
Santa Monica College C, A
Santa Rosa Junior College C, A
Sierra College C, A
Solano Community College C, A
Southwestern College C, A
Yuba Community College District C

Colorado
Aims Community College C
Arapahoe Community College C

Connecticut
University of New Haven C, B, M

District of Columbia
University of the District of
Columbia A

Florida
Brevard Community College C, A
Broward Community College A
Chipola College C, A
Daytona Beach Community
College C, A
Edison College A
Florida Community College at
Jacksonville C, A
Gulf Coast Community College C, A
Hillsborough Community
College C, A
Indian River Community College C
Lake-Sumter Community College A
Manatee Community College C, A
Miami Dade College C
Palm Beach Community College C, A
Pasco-Hernando Community
College C
Pensacola Junior College C, A
Polk Community College A
Seminole Community College C, A

Georgia
Albany Technical College C
West Georgia Technical College C, A

Hawaii
University of Hawaii
Honolulu Community College C, A

Idaho
Idaho State University A
Lewis-Clark State College A, B

Illinois
Carl Sandburg College C, A
City Colleges of Chicago
Harold Washington College A
College of DuPage C
Illinois Eastern Community Colleges
Frontier Community College C
Joliet Junior College C
Kishwaukee College C, A
Lewis and Clark Community
College A
Lincoln Land Community College C, A
McHenry County College C, A
Moraine Valley Community College C
Oakton Community College C, A
Rend Lake College C
Richland Community College A
Rock Valley College A
Southeastern Illinois College C
Southwestern Illinois College C, A
Triton College C, A
Waubonsee Community College C

William Rainey Harper College *C, A*

Indiana
Vincennes University *A*

Iowa
Iowa Western Community College *A*
Kirkwood Community College *C, A*
Northeast Iowa Community
　　College *A*

Kansas
Barton County Community
　　College *C, A*
Butler County Community
　　College *C, A*
Cloud County Community College *A*
Dodge City Community College *A*
Garden City Community College *C, A*
Johnson County Community
　　College *A*
Kansas City Kansas Community
　　College *C, A*
Labette Community College *C, A*

Kentucky
Elizabethtown Community and
　　Technical College *C, A*
Jefferson Community College *C, A*
Somerset Community College *C*

Maine
Eastern Maine Community College *A*
Southern Maine Community
　　College *A*

Maryland
College of Southern Maryland *A*
Montgomery College *A*

Massachusetts
Anna Maria College *B, M*
Berkshire Community College *A*
Bristol Community College *A*
Cape Cod Community College *A*
Massasoit Community College *A*
Springfield Technical Community
　　College *C*

Michigan
Delta College *A*
Grand Rapids Community College *A*
Henry Ford Community College *A*
Kalamazoo Valley Community
　　College *C, A*
Kellogg Community College *C*
Lansing Community College *A*
Macomb Community College *C, A*
Madonna University *C, A, B*
Mid Michigan Community College *A*
Oakland Community College *C, A*
Schoolcraft College *C, A*

Minnesota
Itasca Community College *C, A*
Minnesota State Community and
　　Technical College - Fergus Falls *C*

Mississippi
Meridian Community College *A*

Missouri
Blue River Community College *C, A*
East Central College *C, A*
Mineral Area College *C, A*
Missouri Southern State University *C*
State Fair Community College *A*
Three Rivers Community College *C*

Montana
Helena College of Technology of the
　　University of Montana *A*

Nebraska
Mid-Plains Community College
　　Area *C, A*

Nevada
Community College of Southern
　　Nevada *A*
Great Basin College *A*
Truckee Meadows Community
　　College *C, A*

New Hampshire
New Hampshire Community
　　Technical College
　　Berlin *A*

New Jersey
Burlington County College *A*
Essex County College *A*
Middlesex County College *A*
Sussex County Community
　　College *C, A*

New Mexico
Dona Ana Branch Community College
　　of New Mexico State
　　University *A*
New Mexico Junior College *C*
New Mexico State University
　　Alamogordo *A*
　　Carlsbad *C, A*
San Juan College *C, A*

New York
Suffolk County Community College *A*

North Carolina
Alamance Community College *A*
Tri-County Community College *C*

Ohio
Cincinnati State Technical and
　　Community College *C, A*
Columbus State Community
　　College *A*
Hocking College *C, A*
Lakeland Community College *C, A*
Owens Community College
　　Toledo *C, A*
Sinclair Community College *C*
Stark State College of Technology *A*

Oklahoma
Oklahoma State University
　　Oklahoma City *A*
Western Oklahoma State College *A*

Oregon
Central Oregon Community
　　College *A*
Chemeketa Community College *A*
Clackamas Community College *C, A*
Clatsop Community College *A*
Mount Hood Community College *C, A*
Southwestern Oregon Community
　　College *C, A*
Treasure Valley Community College *A*
Umpqua Community College *A*

Pennsylvania
Bucks County Community
　　College *C, A*
Butler County Community College *C*
Harrisburg Area Community
　　College *C, A*

Rhode Island
Community College of Rhode
　　Island *A*

South Carolina
Greenville Technical College *C*
Horry-Georgetown Technical
　　College *C*

South Dakota
Oglala Lakota College *B*

Tennessee
Southwest Tennessee Community
　　College *A*
Volunteer State Community
　　College *C, A*

Texas
Austin Community College *C, A*
Blinn College *C, A*
Collin County Community College
　　District *C*
Del Mar College *C*
Houston Community College
　　System *A*
Midland College *A*
North Harris Montgomery
　　Community College District *C, A*
Odessa College *C, A*
South Plains College *A*
Tarrant County College *C, A*
Temple College *C*
Trinity Valley Community College *C, A*
Vernon College *C*
Victoria College *C*

Utah
Utah Valley State College *C, A*

Virginia
J. Sargeant Reynolds Community
　　College *C, A*
Lord Fairfax Community College *C*
Southside Virginia Community
　　College *C*
Southwest Virginia Community
　　College *C*
Tidewater Community College *A*
Virginia Highlands Community
　　College *C*
Virginia Western Community
　　College *C*

Washington
Bellevue Community College *A*
Columbia Basin College *A*
Everett Community College *C, A*
Olympic College *A*
Skagit Valley College *A*
South Puget Sound Community
　　College *C, A*
Spokane Falls Community
　　College *C, A*
Walla Walla Community College *A*
Wenatchee Valley College *A*
Yakima Valley Community
　　College *C, A*

West Virginia
Mountain State University *A*

Wisconsin
Chippewa Valley Technical College *A*
Gateway Technical College *A*
Mid-State Technical College *A*
Milwaukee Area Technical College *A*
Moraine Park Technical College *C*
Waukesha County Technical
　　College *C*

Wyoming
Casper College *C, A*

Fishing and fisheries

Alaska
Sheldon Jackson College *B*
University of Alaska
　　Fairbanks *B, M, D*
　　Southeast *M*

Arkansas
University of Arkansas
　　Pine Bluff *B, M*

California
College of the Redwoods *C, A*
Feather River College *C, A*
Fullerton College *A*
Humboldt State University *B*
University of California
　　Davis *B*

Colorado
Colorado State University *B, M, D*
Trinidad State Junior College *C, A*

Delaware
Delaware State University *B*

Florida
Hillsborough Community
　　College *C, A*
University of Florida *M, D*

Georgia
University of Georgia *B*

Idaho
North Idaho College *A*
University of Idaho *B, M*

Illinois
Lake Land College *A*

Iowa
Iowa State University *M, D*

Kansas
Pittsburg State University *B*

Kentucky
Kentucky State University *M*

Louisiana
Louisiana State University and
　　Agricultural and Mechanical
　　College *M*

Maine
Unity College *B*

Maryland
Frostburg State University *B, M*
Garrett College *A*

Massachusetts
Bristol Community College *C*

Michigan
Grand Rapids Community College *A*
Lake Superior State University *B*
Mid Michigan Community College *A*

Minnesota
University of Minnesota
　　Twin Cities *B, M, D*
Vermilion Community College *A*

Mississippi

Mississippi Gulf Coast Community College
Jefferson Davis Campus *A*

Missouri

University of Missouri
Columbia *B, M, D*

New York

Paul Smith's College *B*
State University of New York
College of Agriculture and Technology at Cobleskill *A, B*
College of Agriculture and Technology at Morrisville *A*
College of Environmental Science and Forestry *B, M, D*

North Carolina

College of the Albemarle *C, A*
Haywood Community College *A*

Ohio

Hocking College *A*
Ohio State University
Columbus Campus *B*

Oregon

Central Oregon Community College *A*
Mount Hood Community College *A*
Oregon State University *B, M, D*

Pennsylvania

Mansfield University of Pennsylvania *B*

Rhode Island

University of Rhode Island *B, M*

South Carolina

Clemson University *B, M, D*

Tennessee

Lincoln Memorial University *B*
Roane State Community College *A*
Tennessee Technological University *B*
University of Tennessee Knoxville *M*

Texas

Texas A&M University *B*
Texas A&M University Galveston *B*
Texas Tech University *B, M, D*

Vermont

Sterling College *A, B*

Virginia

Virginia Polytechnic Institute and State University *M, D*

Washington

Bellingham Technical College *C, A*
Heritage University *C, A*
Peninsula College *A*
University of Washington *B, M, D*

Wisconsin

Northland College *B*

Flight attendant

California

Chabot College *A*
Cypress College *C, A*
Mount San Antonio College *A*
Orange Coast College *C, A*

San Bernardino Valley College *C*

New Jersey

Mercer County Community College *A*

North Carolina

Asheville-Buncombe Technical Community College *C, A*

Washington

Spokane Falls Community College *C*

Flight instructor

Illinois

University of Illinois Urbana-Champaign *C*

Iowa

University of Dubuque *B*

Kansas

Central Christian College of Kansas *A*

Minnesota

Central Lakes College *C*
St. Cloud State University *B*

Ohio

University of Cincinnati Clermont College *A*

Puerto Rico

Inter American University of Puerto Rico
Bayamon Campus *B*

Floriculture

California

MiraCosta College *C, A*
Santa Rosa Junior College *C*
Southwestern College *C, A*

Georgia

Albany Technical College *C*

Massachusetts

North Shore Community College *A*

Minnesota

Hennepin Technical College *C, A*

Nebraska

University of Nebraska Lincoln *D*

New York

State University of New York
College of Agriculture and Technology at Morrisville *A*

Ohio

Ohio State University
Agricultural Technical Institute *A*

Oklahoma

Oklahoma State University
Oklahoma City *C*

Washington

Clover Park Technical College *C*

Food and nutrition studies

Alabama

Auburn University *B*
Lawson State Community College *C*

Oakwood College *B*
Tuskegee University *B, M*
Wallace State Community College at Hanceville *C, A*

Arizona

Central Arizona College *C*
Glendale Community College *A*
Mesa Community College *A*

Arkansas

University of Arkansas *B*

California

Antelope Valley College *A*
Bakersfield College *A*
California Polytechnic State University: San Luis Obispo *B*
California State University
Fresno *B*
Long Beach *B, M*
Los Angeles *B, M*
Northridge *B*
Sacramento *B*
San Bernardino *B*
City College of San Francisco *C, A*
College of the Desert *A*
College of the Sequoias *C*
Fresno City College *C, A*
Glendale Community College *A*
Los Angeles Mission College *A*
Master's College *B*
Merritt College *C*
Modesto Junior College *A*
Ohlone College *C, A*
Orange Coast College *C, A*
Point Loma Nazarene University *B*
Reedley College *C*
Riverside Community College *C, A*
Saddleback College *C, A*
San Diego State University *B*
San Joaquin Delta College *C, A*
Santa Ana College *A*
Santa Rosa Junior College *C*
University of California
Davis *B, M, D*
Ventura College *A*

Colorado

Art Institute
of Colorado *A, B*
Colorado State University *M, D*
Johnson & Wales University *B*

Connecticut

Gateway Community College *A*
St. Joseph College *B, M*

Delaware

Delaware State University *B*
University of Delaware *B, M*

District of Columbia

Gallaudet University *B*
University of the District of Columbia *B*

Florida

Broward Community College *A*
Florida State University *B, M, D*
Hillsborough Community College *A*
Miami Dade College *A*
Pensacola Junior College *C, A*

Georgia

Fort Valley State University *B*
Georgia Southern University *B*
Georgia State University *B, M*
University of Georgia *B, M, D*

Hawaii

University of Hawaii
Hawaii Community College *C, A*

Idaho

Brigham Young University-Idaho *A*
University of Idaho *B*

Illinois

Benedictine University *T*
Dominican University *B*
Illinois Central College *A*
Northern Illinois University *B, M*
Rosalind Franklin University of Medicine and Science *M*
Rush University *M*
Southern Illinois University Carbondale *B, M*
William Rainey Harper College *A*

Indiana

Ball State University *A, B*
Indiana State University *B*
Purdue University *B, M, D*
Purdue University
North Central Campus *C*
Vincennes University *A*

Iowa

Graceland University *B*
Waldorf College *B*

Kansas

Central Christian College of Kansas *A*

Kentucky

Eastern Kentucky University *B*
Murray State University *B*
University of Kentucky *B, M*

Maine

Southern Maine Community College *A*
University of Maine *B, M, D*
University of Maine Presque Isle *T*
Washington County Community College *A*

Maryland

Morgan State University *B*
University of Maryland College Park *B*

Massachusetts

Framingham State College *B, M*
Hampshire College *B*

Michigan

Andrews University *B, M*
Eastern Michigan University *M*
Madonna University *A, B*
Northern Michigan University *B*
Wayne State University *B, M, D*

Minnesota

College of St. Catherine *B*
Concordia College: Moorhead *B*
Fond du Lac Tribal and Community College *A*
Minnesota State University
Mankato *B, M, T*
University of Minnesota
Crookston *B*
Twin Cities *B*
University of St. Thomas *B*

Mississippi

Alcorn State University *B*
University of Mississippi *M*

University of Southern
    Mississippi *B, M, D*

Missouri

College of the Ozarks *B*
Lincoln University *B*
Northwest Missouri State
    University *B*
St. Louis University *B, M*
University of Missouri
    Columbia *B, M, D*

Nebraska

University of Nebraska
    Kearney *B*
    Lincoln *B, M*
Wayne State College *B*
Western Nebraska Community
    College *A*

Nevada

University of Nevada
    Reno *B, M*

New Hampshire

University of New Hampshire *B, M, D*

New Jersey

College of St. Elizabeth *B, M*

New Mexico

New Mexico State University *B*
University of New Mexico *B, M*

New York

City University of New York
    Brooklyn College *B, M*
    Hunter College *B, M*
    Lehman College *B, M*
Cornell University *B*
New York University *B, M, D, T*
Rochester Institute of Technology *B*
Rockland Community College *A*
State University of New York
    College at Buffalo *B*
    College at Oneonta *B*
    College at Plattsburgh *B*
    College of Agriculture and
        Technology at Morrisville *A*
Suffolk County Community College *A*
Syracuse University *B, M, D*
Westchester Community College *A*

North Carolina

Appalachian State University *B*
East Carolina University *M*
North Carolina Agricultural and
    Technical State University *B, M*
University of North Carolina
    Chapel Hill *B*

North Dakota

North Dakota State University *M*
University of North Dakota *B*

Ohio

Ashland University *B*
Bluffton University *B*
Bowling Green State University *B, M*
Kent State University *B, M*
Kent State University
    East Liverpool Regional Campus *C*
Miami University
    Oxford Campus *B, M*
Ohio State University
    Columbus Campus *B, M, D*
Ohio University *B, M*
Sinclair Community College *C, A*
University of Akron *M*
University of Cincinnati *B, M*
University of Cincinnati
    Raymond Walters College *A*

University of Dayton *B*
Youngstown State University *A, B*

Oklahoma

Eastern Oklahoma State College *C*
Northeastern State University *B*
Oklahoma State University *B, M*
University of Central Oklahoma *B, M*

Oregon

George Fox University *B*
Oregon State University *B, M, D*

Pennsylvania

Cedar Crest College *B*
Indiana University of
    Pennsylvania *B, M*
Marywood University *B, M*
Penn State
    Abington *B*
    Altoona *B*
    Beaver *B*
    Berks *B*
    Dubois *B*
    Fayette *B*
    Hazleton *B*
    Lehigh Valley *B*
    Mont Alto *B*
    New Kensington *B*
    Shenango *B*
    University Park *C, B, M, D*
    Worthington Scranton *B*
    York *B*

Puerto Rico

University of Puerto Rico
    Rio Piedras *B*

Rhode Island

University of Rhode Island *C, B, M, D*

South Carolina

South Carolina State University *B*
Winthrop University *B, M*

South Dakota

Sisseton Wahpeton College *C, A*
South Dakota State University *B*

Tennessee

Carson-Newman College *B*
Hiwassee College *A*
Lambuth University *B*
Middle Tennessee State University *B*
Southwest Tennessee Community
    College *A*
Tennessee State University *B*
Tennessee Technological University *B*
University of Tennessee
    Knoxville *B, M*

Texas

Lamar University *B*
Palo Alto College *C, A*
Prairie View A&M University *B*
Sam Houston State University *B*
Stephen F. Austin State University *B*
Texas A&M University *B*
Texas A&M University
    Kingsville *B*
Texas Southern University *B, M*
Texas State University: San Marcos *B*
Texas Tech University *B, M, D*
Texas Woman's University *B*
University of Houston *B*
University of Texas
    Austin *B*

Utah

Dixie State College of Utah *A*
Snow College *A*
University of Utah *M*

Utah State University *B, M, D*

Vermont

University of Vermont *B, M*

Virginia

Bridgewater College *B*
James Madison University *B*
Radford University *B*
Virginia Polytechnic Institute and
    State University *B, M, D*

Washington

Central Washington University *B*
Highline Community College *A*
Seattle Pacific University *B*
Shoreline Community College *A*
Washington State University *B, M, D*

West Virginia

West Virginia University *B*

Wisconsin

College of Menominee Nation *A*
Madison Area Technical College *A*
Northeast Wisconsin Technical
    College *C*
University of Wisconsin
    Stevens Point *M*

Food preparation

Alabama

Shelton State Community College *C*

California

Diablo Valley College *C*
Long Beach City College *C*
Santa Rosa Junior College *C*

Florida

South Florida Community College *C*

Georgia

Albany Technical College *C*
Savannah Technical College *C*

Illinois

City Colleges of Chicago
    Kennedy-King College *C*
Kaskaskia College *C*

Maryland

Anne Arundel Community College *C*

Massachusetts

Massasoit Community College *C*

Minnesota

Hennepin Technical College *A*
Minneapolis Community and
    Technical College *C*
St. Paul College *C*

Missouri

Jefferson College *C, A*

New Mexico

Eastern New Mexico University:
    Roswell Campus *C*
Southwestern Indian Polytechnic
    Institute *C*

New York

Niagara County Community
    College *C*
Paul Smith's College *A*

Ohio

Cincinnati State Technical and
    Community College *A*

Pennsylvania

Northampton County Area
    Community College *C, A*

Puerto Rico

Inter American University of Puerto
    Rico
    Aguadilla Campus *C*

Texas

South Texas College *C*

Washington

Art Institute of Seattle *C*
South Seattle Community
    College *C, A*

Wisconsin

Western Wisconsin Technical
    College *C*

Food science

Arizona

Prescott College *B, M*

Arkansas

Arkansas Northeastern College *A*
University of Arkansas *B, M, D*

California

California Polytechnic State
    University: San Luis Obispo *B*
California State Polytechnic
    University: Pomona *B*
California State University
    Fresno *B, M*
Fresno City College *C, A*
Mission College *C, A*
Modesto Junior College *C, A*
Reedley College *C*
San Joaquin Delta College *A*
San Jose State University *T*
University of California
    Davis *B, M, D*

Delaware

University of Delaware *B, M*

Florida

Florida Agricultural and Mechanical
    University *B*
University of Florida *B, M, D*

Georgia

University of Georgia *B, M, D*

Hawaii

University of Hawaii
    Manoa *M*

Idaho

College of Southern Idaho *A*
University of Idaho *B, M*

Illinois

City Colleges of Chicago
    Malcolm X College *C, A*
Illinois Institute of Technology *M*
University of Illinois
    Urbana-Champaign *B, M, D*

Indiana

Purdue University *B, M, D*

Iowa
Iowa State University *M, D*

Kansas
Kansas State University *B, M, D*

Kentucky
University of Kentucky *B*

Louisiana
Louisiana State University and
   Agricultural and Mechanical
   College *B, M, D*

Maine
Eastern Maine Community
   College *C, A*
University of Maine *B, M, D*

Maryland
University of Maryland
   College Park *B, M, D*
   Eastern Shore *M, D*

Massachusetts
Framingham State College *B, M*
University of Massachusetts
   Amherst *B, M, D*

Michigan
Michigan State University *B, M, D*

Minnesota
Minnesota State University
   Mankato *B*
University of Minnesota
   Twin Cities *B, M, D*

Mississippi
Hinds Community College *A*
Mississippi Gulf Coast Community
   College
   Jefferson Davis Campus *C, A*
Mississippi State University *B, M, D*

Missouri
University of Missouri
   Columbia *B, M, D*

Nebraska
University of Nebraska
   Lincoln *B, M, D*

New Hampshire
University of New Hampshire *B, M, D*

New Jersey
Rutgers, The State University of New
   Jersey
   New Brunswick/Piscataway
   Campus *B*

New York
Cornell University *B, M, D*

North Carolina
North Carolina State
   University *B, M, D*

North Dakota
North Dakota State University *B*

Ohio
Ohio State University
   Columbus Campus *B, M, D*

Oklahoma
Eastern Oklahoma State College *A*
Oklahoma State University *M, D*

Oregon
Oregon State University *B, M, D*

Pennsylvania
Delaware Valley College *B*
Penn State
   Abington *B*
   Altoona *B*
   Beaver *B*
   Berks *B*
   Delaware County *B*
   Dubois *B*
   Erie, The Behrend College *B*
   Fayette *B*
   Hazleton *B*
   Lehigh Valley *B*
   McKeesport *B*
   Mont Alto *B*
   New Kensington *B*
   Schuylkill - Capital College *B*
   Shenango *B*
   University Park *B, M, D*
   Wilkes-Barre *B*
   Worthington Scranton *B*
   York *B*

Puerto Rico
Inter American University of Puerto
   Rico
   Barranquitas Campus *C*
University of Puerto Rico
   Mayaguez *M*

South Carolina
Clemson University *B, M, D*

Tennessee
Hiwassee College *A*
University of Tennessee
   Knoxville *B, M, D*

Texas
Sul Ross State University *B*
Texas A&M University *B, M, D*
Texas A&M University
   Commerce *B*
   Kingsville *B, M*
Texas Tech University *B, M*

Utah
Brigham Young University *B, M*
Snow College *A*
Utah State University *B, M, D*

Virginia
Virginia Polytechnic Institute and
   State University *B*

Washington
Pierce College *C*
Washington State University *M, D*

Wisconsin
Northeast Wisconsin Technical
   College *A*
University of Wisconsin
   Madison *B, M, D*
   River Falls *B*

Wyoming
University of Wyoming *M*

Food service

California
Diablo Valley College *C*
Santa Rosa Junior College *C*

Illinois
Kaskaskia College *C*

Indiana
Indiana University-Purdue University
   Indianapolis *A*

Maryland
Montgomery College *A*

Massachusetts
Newbury College *A*

Mississippi
Copiah-Lincoln Community
   College *C, A*

Missouri
Jefferson College *C, A*

New Hampshire
University of New Hampshire *A*

New York
Paul Smith's College *A*
Schenectady County Community
   College *A*
State University of New York
   College of Agriculture and
      Technology at Morrisville *A*

Pennsylvania
Penn State
   University Park *C*

Puerto Rico
Inter American University of Puerto
   Rico
   Aguadilla Campus *A*

Rhode Island
Johnson & Wales University *A, B*

Washington
Clark College *C*

Food technology/ processing

Arkansas
Arkansas State University *A*

Illinois
University of Illinois
   Urbana-Champaign *B*

Ohio
Ohio State University
   Columbus Campus *B*

Puerto Rico
Inter American University of Puerto
   Rico
   Barranquitas Campus *C*
University of Puerto Rico
   Utuado *A*

Utah
Brigham Young University *B*

Washington
Yakima Valley Community College *A*

Foreign language teacher education

Alabama
Auburn University *B*
Birmingham-Southern College *T*

Arizona
Arizona State University *B, T*

Northern Arizona University *T*
Prescott College *B, M, T*
University of Arizona *B, M*

Arkansas
Arkansas Tech University *B*
Harding University *B, M, T*
Ouachita Baptist University *B, T*
University of Arkansas *B*
University of Central Arkansas *M, T*

California
Azusa Pacific University *T*
California Baptist University *T*
California Lutheran University *B, T*
California State University
   Chico *M*
   Long Beach *T*
   Northridge *B, T*
   San Bernardino *T*
Humboldt State University *T*
Los Angeles Southwest College *A*
Mount St. Mary's College *T*
San Diego State University *B, T*
San Francisco State University *B, T*
Soka University of America *M*
Sonoma State University *T*
Stanford University *M, T*
University of the Pacific *T*
Vanguard University of Southern
   California *T*

Colorado
Colorado State University *T*
Colorado State University
   Pueblo *T*
Metropolitan State College of
   Denver *T*
University of Colorado
   Boulder *T*
Western State College of Colorado *T*

Connecticut
Central Connecticut State
   University *T*
Fairfield University *T*
Quinnipiac University *B, M*

Delaware
Delaware State University *B*
University of Delaware *B, T*

District of Columbia
George Washington University *M, T*

Florida
Florida International
   University *B, M, T*
Florida State University *B, M, D, T*
Manatee Community College *A*
Stetson University *B*
University of Central Florida *B*
University of Florida *B*
University of South Florida *B, M*

Georgia
Darton College *A*
Fort Valley State University *B, T*
Piedmont College *M, T*
University of Georgia *B, M*

Illinois
Augustana College *B, T*
Dominican University *T*
North Park University *T*
Olivet Nazarene University *B, T*
Rockford College *T*
University of Illinois
   Chicago *B*
   Urbana-Champaign *B, M, T*

Indiana

Butler University *T*
Goshen College *B*
Indiana University
    Bloomington *M, D, T*
Indiana University-Purdue University
    Indianapolis *M*
Manchester College *B, T*
Saint Mary's College *T*
St. Mary-of-the-Woods College *B, T*
University of Indianapolis *B, T*
Valparaiso University *B*
Vincennes University *A*

Iowa

Central College *T*
Dordt College *B*
Graceland University *T*
Iowa State University *T*
Morningside College *B*
St. Ambrose University *B, T*
Simpson College *T*
University of Iowa *D, T*
University of Northern Iowa *B*

Kansas

Emporia State University *T*
McPherson College *B, T*
MidAmerica Nazarene University *B, T*
Southwestern College *B, T*
Washburn University of Topeka *B*

Louisiana

Centenary College of Louisiana *B, T*
University of New Orleans *B*
Xavier University of Louisiana *B*

Maine

University of Maine *B*
University of Southern Maine *T*

Maryland

College of Notre Dame of Maryland *T*
St. Mary's College of Maryland *T*
University of Maryland
    College Park *B*

Massachusetts

Boston University *M, T*
Framingham State College *B*
Northeastern University *B*
Tufts University *M, T*
University of Massachusetts
    Dartmouth *T*

Michigan

Albion College *B, T*
Andrews University *M*
Northern Michigan University *B, T*
University of Michigan
    Dearborn *B*
    Flint *T*
Wayne State University *M, T*
Western Michigan University *B*

Minnesota

College of St. Benedict *T*
College of St. Catherine *B*
Gustavus Adolphus College *T*
Minnesota State University
    Mankato *B, M, T*
St. Cloud State University *B*
St. John's University *T*
St. Mary's University of Minnesota *B*
University of Minnesota
    Morris *T*
    Twin Cities *M*
University of St. Thomas *B, T*
Winona State University *B, T*

Mississippi

Blue Mountain College *B*

Delta State University *T*
Mississippi State University *T*
University of Mississippi *B, T*
University of Southern Mississippi *M*

Missouri

Central Methodist University *B*
Central Missouri State University *B, T*
College of the Ozarks *B, T*
Evangel University *B*
Missouri Southern State
    University *B, T*
Northwest Missouri State
    University *B, T*
Southeast Missouri State
    University *B, T*
Truman State University *M, T*
University of Missouri
    Columbia *B, M, D*
William Jewell College *T*

Montana

Montana State University
    Billings *B, T*
University of Montana: Missoula *T*

Nebraska

Creighton University *T*
Dana College *B*
Hastings College *B, M, T*
Union College *T*
University of Nebraska
    Kearney *B, M, T*
    Lincoln *B*
Wayne State College *B, T*

Nevada

University of Nevada
    Reno *B*

New Hampshire

Keene State College *B, T*
Rivier College *B, M, T*
University of New Hampshire *T*

New Jersey

The College of New Jersey *B, T*
Rowan University *T*
Rutgers, The State University of New
    Jersey
    New Brunswick/Piscataway
        Campus *T*
St. Peter's College *T*

New York

City University of New York
    City College *B, T*
    Hunter College *B, M, T*
    Lehman College *M*
    Queens College *M, T*
College of Mount St. Vincent *T*
D'Youville College *M, T*
Dowling College *B*
Elmira College *B, T*
Fordham University *T*
Hobart and William Smith Colleges *T*
Hofstra University *B, M, T*
Houghton College *B, T*
Ithaca College *B, T*
Le Moyne College *T*
Long Island University
    C.W. Post Campus *B, T*
Manhattan College *B, T*
Manhattanville College *M, T*
Nazareth College of Rochester *T*
New York University *B, M, T*
Pace University *M, T*
St. Bonaventure University *T*
St. John Fisher College *B, T*
St. Lawrence University *T*
St. Thomas Aquinas College *B, T*
State University of New York
    Albany *B, M, T*

Buffalo *M, D, T*
    College at Buffalo *B, T*
    College at Cortland *B, M, T*
    College at Fredonia *B, T*
    College at Old Westbury *B, T*
    College at Oneonta *B, T*
    College at Plattsburgh *B*
    New Paltz *B, M, T*
University of Rochester *M*
Vassar College *T*
Wells College *T*
Yeshiva University *B*

North Carolina

Davidson College *T*
Gardner-Webb University *B*
Lenoir-Rhyne College *B, T*
Meredith College *T*
Methodist College *A, B, T*
North Carolina Agricultural and
    Technical State University *B, T*

North Dakota

Dickinson State University *B, T*
Minot State University *B*

Ohio

Bowling Green State University *B, T*
Hiram College *T*
Mount Union College *T*
Ohio Northern University *B*
Ohio State University
    Columbus Campus *M, D*
Ohio Wesleyan University *B*
Otterbein College *B*
University of Dayton *B*
University of Findlay *B, M, T*
University of Toledo *T*
Wright State University *B, T*
Youngstown State University *B, M*

Oklahoma

Oklahoma Baptist University *B, T*
Oklahoma City University *B, M*
Oral Roberts University *B, T*
Southeastern Oklahoma State
    University *B, T*
University of Oklahoma *B, T*
University of Tulsa *T*

Oregon

Linfield College *T*
Western Oregon University *T*

Pennsylvania

Dickinson College *T*
Gannon University *T*
King's College *T*
La Salle University *B, T*
Lincoln University *T*
Lycoming College *T*
Mansfield University of
    Pennsylvania *B, T*
Marywood University *B*
Mercyhurst College *B, T*
Millersville University of
    Pennsylvania *B, M, T*
Moravian College *T*
Rosemont College *T*
St. Francis University *B, T*
St. Joseph's University *B, M*
St. Vincent College *T*
Seton Hill University *B, T*
Susquehanna University *T*
Temple University *A, B, M, T*
University of Pennsylvania *M, T*
Westminster College *B, T*
Widener University *M*

Rhode Island

Rhode Island College *B, M*

South Carolina

Charleston Southern University *B*
College of Charleston *M*
Converse College *T*
Furman University *T*

South Dakota

Black Hills State University *B*
Northern State University *B, T*
University of South Dakota *B, T*

Tennessee

Lee University *B*
Middle Tennessee State
    University *M, T*
Tennessee Technological University *T*
Union University *B, T*
University of Memphis *T*
University of Tennessee
    Chattanooga *B, T*
    Knoxville *T*

Texas

Baylor University *T*
Lamar University *T*
Laredo Community College *A*
University of Houston *M, T*
University of Texas
    Austin *M, D*
West Texas A&M University *T*

Utah

Southern Utah University *B*
University of Utah *B*

Vermont

Bennington College *M*
Castleton State College *B, T*
St. Michael's College *T*
University of Vermont *B*

Virginia

Longwood University *T*
Old Dominion University *B, T*
Regent University *T*
University of Virginia's College at
    Wise *T*
Virginia Wesleyan College *T*

Washington

Central Washington University *B*
Washington State University *B, M, T*
Western Washington University *M*
Whitworth College *B, T*

West Virginia

Bethany College *B*
West Virginia University *T*

Wisconsin

Carroll College *B, T*
Carthage College *M, T*
Edgewood College *B*
Lawrence University *T*
Marquette University *B, M*
Mount Mary College *B, T*
St. Norbert College *T*
University of Wisconsin
    Parkside *T*

Foreign languages, general

Alabama

Auburn University at Montgomery *B*
Jacksonville State University *B*
Judson College *B*
Samford University *B*
University of Alabama
    Birmingham *B*
    Huntsville *B*

University of Montevallo *B*
University of North Alabama *B*
University of South Alabama *B*

Alaska

University of Alaska
Anchorage *B*
Fairbanks *B*

Arizona

Cochise College *A*
Eastern Arizona College *A*
Northern Arizona University *B*
University of Arizona *B*

Arkansas

Arkansas Tech University *B*

California

Cabrillo College *A*
California Lutheran University *B*
California Polytechnic State
University: San Luis Obispo *B*
California State University
Monterey Bay *B*
College of the Sequoias *A*
Crafton Hills College *A*
Fresno City College *A*
Fullerton College *A*
Glendale Community College *A*
Golden West College *A*
Imperial Valley College *A*
Long Beach City College *A*
Los Angeles Southwest College *A*
MiraCosta College *A*
Modesto Junior College *A*
Monterey Peninsula College *A*
Occidental College *B*
Pitzer College *B*
Pomona College *B*
Reedley College *A*
Saddleback College *A*
St. Mary's College of California *B*
San Diego City College *A*
Santa Ana College *A*
Scripps College *B*
Solano Community College *A*
University of California
Riverside *B*
San Diego *B*
West Valley College *A*
Whittier College *B*

Colorado

Colorado State University *M*
Colorado State University
Pueblo *B*
Metropolitan State College of
Denver *B, T*
University of Northern
Colorado *B, M, T*

Connecticut

Central Connecticut State
University *M*
Southern Connecticut State
University *B, M*
Trinity College *B*
University of Hartford *B*

Delaware

University of Delaware *B, M*

District of Columbia

George Washington University *B*
Howard University *M*

Florida

Broward Community College *A*
Eckerd College *B*
Gulf Coast Community College *A*
Indian River Community College *A*

Miami Dade College *A*
New College of Florida *B*
University of Central Florida *B*
University of Miami *D*
University of Tampa *A*

Georgia

Atlanta Metropolitan College *A*
Bainbridge College *A*
Clark Atlanta University *B, M*
Coastal Georgia Community
College *A*
Dalton State College *A*
Darton College *A*
Georgia Perimeter College *A*
Gordon College *A*
Macon State College *A*
Middle Georgia College *A*
South Georgia College *A*
Young Harris College *A*

Idaho

College of Southern Idaho *A*
North Idaho College *A*
University of Idaho *B*

Illinois

City Colleges of Chicago
Harold Washington College *A*
Kennedy-King College *A*
Olive-Harvey College *A*
DePaul University *T*
Eastern Illinois University *B, T*
Illinois Central College *A*
Illinois State University *M*
Illinois Valley Community College *A*
Kishwaukee College *A*
Knox College *B*
Millikin University *B, T*
Olivet Nazarene University *B*
Principia College *B*
Rockford College *B*
Roosevelt University *B, M*
Sauk Valley Community College *A*
Southern Illinois University
Carbondale *M*
Southern Illinois University
Edwardsville *B*
Southwestern Illinois College *A*
Triton College *A*

Indiana

Goshen College *B*
Grace College *B*
Indiana University
Bloomington *B, M, D*
Manchester College *B, T*
Purdue University *B, M, D*
Purdue University
Calumet *B*
Vincennes University *A*

Iowa

Cornell College *B*
Graceland University *B*
University of Northern Iowa *B, M*

Kansas

Barton County Community College *A*
Butler County Community College *A*
Cloud County Community College *A*
Coffeyville Community College *A*
Cowley County Community
College *A*
Emporia State University *B, T*
Fort Hays State University *B*
Hutchinson Community College *A*
Kansas State University *B, M*
Kansas Wesleyan University *B*
McPherson College *B, T*
Neosho County Community
College *A*

Kentucky

Bellarmine University *B*
Eastern Kentucky University *B*

Louisiana

Centenary College of Louisiana *B, T*
Dillard University *B*
University of Louisiana at Lafayette *B*

Maine

University of Maine *B*
University of Maine
Fort Kent *B*
University of Southern Maine *B*

Maryland

College of Notre Dame of Maryland *B*
Frostburg State University *B*
St. Mary's College of Maryland *B*
University of Maryland
Baltimore County *B, M*
Washington College *B*

Massachusetts

Assumption College *B*
Boston University *B*
Bunker Hill Community College *A*
Cape Cod Community College *A*
Clark University *B*
Framingham State College *B*
Gordon College *B*
Harvard College *B*
Massachusetts Institute of
Technology *B*
Northeastern University *B*
Simon's Rock College of Bard *B*
Stonehill College *B*
Suffolk University *B*
Tufts University *B, M*
University of Massachusetts
Lowell *B*
Wellesley College *B*

Michigan

Albion College *T*
Delta College *A*
Lake Michigan College *A*
Lansing Community College *A*
Oakland University *B*
Wayne State University *M, D*

Minnesota

Minnesota State University
Mankato *B*
Northland Community & Technical
College *A*
University of Minnesota
Twin Cities *B*
Winona State University *B*

Mississippi

Delta State University *B*
Jackson State University *B*
Mississippi College *B*
Mississippi State University *B, M*
University of Southern Mississippi *B*

Missouri

St. Louis University *B*
Three Rivers Community College *A*
University of Missouri
Columbia *D*
Kansas City *M*
Washington University in St.
Louis *B, M, D*
Webster University *B*

Montana

Miles Community College *A*
Montana State University
Bozeman *B*
University of Montana: Missoula *M*

Nebraska

Hastings College *B*
University of Nebraska
Lincoln *M, D*
Wayne State College *B*

Nevada

University of Nevada
Las Vegas *M*
Reno *M*

New Jersey

Monmouth University *B*
Richard Stockton College of New
Jersey *B*
Rowan University *B*
St. Peter's College *B*
Seton Hall University *B*
Thomas Edison State College *B*

New Mexico

New Mexico State University *B*
San Juan College *A*
University of New Mexico *B*

New York

Bard College *B*
City University of New York
City College *B, M*
Hunter College *B*
College of Mount St. Vincent *B*
Elmira College *B, T*
Eugene Lang College The New School
for Liberal Arts *B*
Excelsior College *B*
Hamilton College *B*
Ithaca College *B*
Jewish Theological Seminary of
America *B, M, D*
Long Island University
Brooklyn Campus *B*
C.W. Post Campus *B*
New York University *B, M, D, T*
Orange County Community College *A*
Pace University *B*
St. Joseph's College *B, T*
St. Lawrence University *B, T*
St. Thomas Aquinas College *B, T*
Sarah Lawrence College *B*
State University of New York
College at Brockport *B*
Purchase *B*
Stony Brook *D*
Syracuse University *B, M*
Touro College *B*
Union College *B*
University of Rochester *B*
Wells College *B*

North Carolina

Elon University *B*
Gardner-Webb University *B*
High Point University *B*
Queens University of Charlotte *B*
Warren Wilson College *B*

North Dakota

University of North Dakota *B*

Ohio

Antioch College *B*
College of Wooster *B*
Kenyon College *B*
Lake Erie College *B*
Laura and Alvin Siegal College of
Judaic Studies *B, M*
Owens Community College
Toledo *A*
Wright State University *B*
Youngstown State University *B*

Oklahoma

Cameron University *B*
Oklahoma Baptist University *B, T*
Rose State College *A*

Oregon

Central Oregon Community
College *A*
Chemeketa Community College *A*
Lewis & Clark College *B*
Pacific University *B*
Portland State University *M*
Southern Oregon University *B*
Treasure Valley Community College *A*

Pennsylvania

California University of
Pennsylvania *B*
Carnegie Mellon University *B*
Community College of Allegheny
County *A*
Duquesne University *B*
Gannon University *B*
Juniata College *B*
La Salle University *B, T*
Mercyhurst College *B*
Muhlenberg College *B*
Rosemont College *B*
St. Francis University *B*
Westminster College *B*
York College of Pennsylvania *A*

Puerto Rico

University of Puerto Rico
Rio Piedras *B*

Rhode Island

Roger Williams University *B*

South Carolina

Clemson University *B*
Converse College *B*
Newberry College *B*
University of South Carolina *M*
University of South Carolina
Beaufort *B*
Winthrop University *B*

South Dakota

Augustana College *B*

Tennessee

Austin Peay State University *B*
East Tennessee State University *B, T*
King College *B*
Lambuth University *B*
Lee University *B*
Middle Tennessee State University *B*
Southern Adventist University *B*
University of Memphis *B*
University of Tennessee
Knoxville *M, D*
Vanderbilt University *B, M, D*

Texas

Blinn College *A*
Brazosport College *A*
Central Texas College *A*
Clarendon College *A*
Del Mar College *A*
El Paso Community College *A*
Hill College *A*
Howard College *A*
Laredo Community College *A*
Lee College *A*
Midland College *A*
Northwest Vista College *A*
Odessa College *A*
Palo Alto College *A*
Paris Junior College *A*
St. Philip's College *A*

San Jacinto College
North *A*
Southern Methodist University *B*
Southwestern Assemblies of God
University *A*
Texarkana College *A*
Texas A&M University *M*
Texas Tech University *M*
Tyler Junior College *A*
University of Texas
Arlington *B, M*
Austin *B, M, D*
Tyler *B*
Western Texas College *A*

Utah

Brigham Young University *B*
Snow College *A*
Southern Utah University *B, T*
University of Utah *B, M, D*

Vermont

Bennington College *B*
Marlboro College *B*
St. Michael's College *B*
University of Vermont *B, M*

Virginia

George Mason University *B, M*
James Madison University *B, T*
Old Dominion University *B*
Radford University *B*
Sweet Briar College *B*
University of Virginia's College at
Wise *B*
Virginia Commonwealth University *B*
Virginia Military Institute *B*
Virginia Polytechnic Institute and
State University *B*
Virginia Wesleyan College *B*
Washington and Lee University *B*

Washington

Centralia College *A*
Everett Community College *A*
Highline Community College *A*
Spokane Falls Community College *A*
Washington State University *B, M*
Western Washington University *B*

West Virginia

Davis and Elkins College *B*
Marshall University *B*
West Virginia University *B, M*

Wisconsin

Beloit College *B*
Marian College of Fond du Lac *B*
Marquette University *M*
Ripon College *B, T*
University of Wisconsin
Milwaukee *M*

Wyoming

Casper College *A*
Eastern Wyoming College *A*
Northwest College *A*
Sheridan College *A*

Forensic psychology

California

Alliant International University *D*

Colorado

University of Denver *M*

Maryland

Columbia Union College *M*

Massachusetts

American International College *M*

Ohio

Tiffin University *M*

Texas

Prairie View A&M University *M*
Sam Houston State University *D*

Virginia

Marymount University *M*

Forensic science

Alabama

University of Alabama
Birmingham *M*

Arizona

Scottsdale Community College *C*

Arkansas

Arkansas State University *C, A, B*
North Arkansas College *C, A*
Ouachita Technical College *C, A*
University of Arkansas
Community College at Hope *C, A*
Cossatot Community College of the
C, A
Fort Smith *C, A*

California

California State University
Chico *C*
Grossmont Community College *C, A*
National University *M*
San Jose State University *B*
Southwestern College *C, A*
University of California
Davis *M*

Connecticut

Tunxis Community College *C*
University of New Haven *C, B, M*

Florida

Edison College *A*
Florida International University *M*
Remington College: Largo *A*
St. Petersburg College *C, A*
Santa Fe Community College *A*
University of Central Florida *B, M*

Georgia

Darton College *A*

Hawaii

Chaminade University of Honolulu *B*

Illinois

Lewis University *B*
Loyola University of Chicago *B*
University of Illinois
Chicago *M*
Westwood College of Technology
O'Hare *B*

Indiana

Indiana University
Bloomington *M*
Indiana University-Purdue University
Indianapolis *B*
Tri-State University *B*

Iowa

Iowa Western Community
College *C, A*
Simpson College *B*

Kentucky

Eastern Kentucky University *B*
Thomas More College *B*

Louisiana

Loyola University New Orleans *B*

Maryland

Anne Arundel Community
College *C, A*
Hagerstown Business College *A*
Prince George's Community
College *C, A*
University of Baltimore *B*

Massachusetts

Massachusetts Bay Community
College *A*

Michigan

Macomb Community College *A*
Michigan State University *M*

Minnesota

Fond du Lac Tribal and Community
College *C, A*

Mississippi

University of Mississippi *B*

Missouri

College of the Ozarks *B*
Columbia College *B*
Missouri Southern State University *B*

Montana

University of Great Falls *B*

Nebraska

Nebraska Wesleyan University *M*

New Hampshire

McIntosh College *A*

New Mexico

New Mexico State University
Alamogordo *A*

New York

Herkimer County Community
College *A*
Hudson Valley Community College *A*
Long Island University
C.W. Post Campus *B*
Mohawk Valley Community College *C*
Pace University *B, M*
Russell Sage College *B*
State University of New York
College at Buffalo *B*
Tompkins-Cortland Community
College *A*
Touro College *M*

North Carolina

Fayetteville Technical Community
College *C, A*
Guilford College *B*
St. Augustine's College *B*

North Dakota

University of North Dakota *B*

Ohio

Central Ohio Technical College *A*
Defiance College *B*
Ohio Northern University *B*
University of Cincinnati
Clermont College *C, A*
Youngstown State University *B*

Oklahoma

University of Central Oklahoma *B, M*

Pennsylvania

Alvernia College *B*
Chatham College *B*
Community College of Philadelphia *A*
Duquesne University *M*
Keystone College *A*
Lehigh Carbon Community College *A*
Mercyhurst College *B, M*
Seton Hill University *B*
Waynesburg College *B*
York College of Pennsylvania *B*

Puerto Rico

Inter American University of Puerto
     Rico
     Bayamon Campus *B*
Turabo University *M*
University of Puerto Rico
     Carolina Regional College *B*
     Ponce *B*

South Carolina

Southern Wesleyan University *B*
Trident Technical College *C*

South Dakota

Augustana College *B*
Mount Marty College *B*

Texas

Baylor University *B*
St. Edward's University *B*
Sam Houston State University *M*

Vermont

Champlain College *A, B*

Virginia

New River Community College *A*
Virginia Commonwealth
     University *B, M*

Washington

Bellevue Community College *C*
Centralia College *C*

West Virginia

Marshall University *M*
Mountain State University *B*
Southern West Virginia Community
     and Technical College *C, A*
West Virginia University *B*

Wisconsin

Carroll College *B*

Wyoming

Casper College *A*

Forest engineering

Maine

University of Maine *B*

New York

State University of New York
     College of Environmental Science
     and Forestry *B, M, D*

Oregon

Oregon State University *B, M, D*

Washington

University of Washington *B*

Forest management

California

University of California
     Berkeley *B*

Connecticut

Yale University *M*

Louisiana

Louisiana State University and
     Agricultural and Mechanical
     College *B*

Maine

University of Maine *D*
University of Maine
     Presque Isle *A*

Maryland

Allegany College of Maryland *A*

Michigan

Michigan Technological University *C*

New Hampshire

University of New Hampshire *A*

New York

Paul Smith's College *B*
State University of New York
     College of Agriculture and
     Technology at Morrisville *A*

North Carolina

North Carolina State University *B*
Southeastern Community College *A*

Ohio

Hocking College *A*

Oregon

Oregon State University *B*

Pennsylvania

Elizabethtown College *B*
Keystone College *A*
Penn State
     University Park *M, D*
St. Francis University *B*

Texas

Stephen F. Austin State University *B, M*
Texas A&M University *B*

Vermont

Sterling College *A, B*

West Virginia

Potomac State College of West Virginia
     University *A*
West Virginia University *B*

Forest resources production

Alabama

Alabama Southern Community
     College *C, A*
Lurleen B. Wallace Community
     College *A*
Northwest-Shoals Community
     College *C*

Florida

Pensacola Junior College *A*

Idaho

University of Idaho *B, M*

Louisiana

Louisiana Tech University *B*

Maine

University of Maine *B*

Minnesota

University of Minnesota
     Twin Cities *B*
Vermilion Community College *A*

Mississippi

Mississippi State University *D*

New Hampshire

University of New Hampshire *A*

New York

Paul Smith's College *A, B*
State University of New York
     College of Environmental Science
     and Forestry *B, M, D*

North Carolina

Haywood Community College *C, A*
Wayne Community College *A*

Oregon

Oregon State University *B, M, D*

Pennsylvania

Keystone College *A*
Penn State
     Mont Alto *A*
     University Park *B*

South Carolina

Orangeburg-Calhoun Technical
     College *A*

Tennessee

Hiwassee College *A*

Vermont

Sterling College *A, B*

Virginia

Mountain Empire Community
     College *C*
Virginia Polytechnic Institute and
     State University *M, D*

Washington

Green River Community College *A*
Spokane Community College *A*
University of Washington *B*

West Virginia

Potomac State College of West Virginia
     University *A*

Forest sciences/biology

Alabama

Auburn University *B, M*

Arizona

Northern Arizona University *B, D*

Colorado

Colorado State University *B, M, D*

Florida

Chipola College *A*

Georgia

University of Georgia *M, D*

Illinois

University of Illinois
     Urbana-Champaign *B, M, D*

Kentucky

University of Kentucky *B, M*

Michigan

Michigan Technological University *D*

New York

Paul Smith's College *B*
State University of New York
     College of Agriculture and
     Technology at Morrisville *A*

Oregon

Oregon State University *M, D*

Pennsylvania

Elizabethtown College *B*
Keystone College *A*
Penn State
     Abington *B*
     Altoona *B*
     Beaver *B*
     Berks *B*
     Delaware County *B*
     Dubois *B*
     Erie, The Behrend College *B*
     Fayette *B*
     Hazleton *B*
     Lehigh Valley *B*
     McKeesport *B*
     Mont Alto *B*
     New Kensington *B*
     Schuylkill - Capital College *B*
     Shenango *B*
     University Park *B*
     Wilkes-Barre *B*
     Worthington Scranton *B*
     York *B*

Vermont

Sterling College *A, B*

West Virginia

West Virginia University *D*

Wisconsin

University of Wisconsin
     Madison *B*

Forest technology

California

Feather River College *C, A*

Colorado

Red Rocks Community College *C, A*

Georgia

Georgia Southwestern State
     University *A*

New Hampshire

University of New Hampshire *A*

New York

Paul Smith's College *A*
State University of New York
     College of Agriculture and
     Technology at Morrisville *A*
     College of Environmental Science
     and Forestry *A*

North Carolina

Montgomery Community College *A*

Ohio
Hocking College *C*

Pennsylvania
Keystone College *C*
Pennsylvania College of Technology *A*

South Carolina
Horry-Georgetown Technical
College *A*

West Virginia
Glenville State College *A*
Potomac State College of West Virginia
University *A*

Forestry

Alabama
Alabama Southern Community
College *A*
Chattahoochee Valley Community
College *A*
Faulkner State Community College *A*
Gadsden State Community College *A*
Northeast Alabama Community
College *A*
Northwest-Shoals Community
College *C*
Tuskegee University *B*

Alaska
University of Alaska
Fairbanks *B*

Arizona
Eastern Arizona College *A*
Northern Arizona University *B, M, D*

Arkansas
University of Arkansas
Monticello *B, M*

California
Bakersfield College *A*
Citrus College *C, A*
College of the Redwoods *C, A*
Columbia College *C, A*
Cypress College *A*
Feather River College *C, A*
Fullerton College *A*
Humboldt State University *B*
Modesto Junior College *C, A*
Mount San Antonio College *C, A*
Reedley College *A*
Sierra College *A*
University of California
Berkeley *B, M*

Connecticut
Yale University *M, D*

Florida
Gulf Coast Community College *A*
Lake City Community College *A*
Miami Dade College *A*
Pensacola Junior College *A*
University of Florida *B, M, D*

Georgia
Abraham Baldwin Agricultural
College *A*
Albany Technical College *C, A*
Andrew College *A*
Dalton State College *A*
Darton College *A*
Gainesville State College *A*
Gordon College *A*
Middle Georgia College *A*
University of Georgia *B*
Young Harris College *A*

Idaho
College of Southern Idaho *A*
North Idaho College *A*
University of Idaho *B, M*

Illinois
Illinois College *B*
Joliet Junior College *C*
Southern Illinois University
Carbondale *B, M*

Indiana
Purdue University *B, M, D*
Vincennes University *A*

Iowa
Cornell College *B*
Iowa State University *B, M, D*
Iowa Wesleyan College *B*
Marshalltown Community College *A*
Upper Iowa University *B*

Kansas
Barton County Community College *A*
Colby Community College *A*
Garden City Community College *A*
Seward County Community College *A*

Kentucky
Hazard Community College *A*

Louisiana
Louisiana State University and
Agricultural and Mechanical
College *M, D*
Louisiana Tech University *B*

Maine
Unity College *B*
University of Maine *B, M, D*
University of Maine
Fort Kent *A*

Maryland
University of Maryland
Eastern Shore *B*

Massachusetts
University of Massachusetts
Amherst *B, M, D*

Michigan
Delta College *A*
Gogebic Community College *A*
Grand Rapids Community College *A*
Michigan State University *B, M, D*
Michigan Technological
University *B, M, T*
University of Michigan *M*

Minnesota
Itasca Community College *A*
Northwest Technical College *C*
University of Minnesota
Twin Cities *B, M, D*
Vermilion Community College *A*

Mississippi
Holmes Community College *A*
Itawamba Community College *A*
Mississippi Delta Community
College *A*
Mississippi Gulf Coast Community
College
Jefferson Davis Campus *A*
Mississippi State University *B, M*

Missouri
University of Missouri
Columbia *B, M, D*

Montana
Miles Community College *A*
Salish Kootenai College *A*
University of Montana:
Missoula *B, M, D*

Nebraska
Western Nebraska Community
College *A*

Nevada
University of Nevada
Reno *B*

New Hampshire
New Hampshire Community
Technical College
Berlin *A*
University of New Hampshire *B, M*

New Jersey
Thomas Edison State College *A, B*

New Mexico
Northern New Mexico College *A*

New York
Jamestown Community College *A*
Jefferson Community College *C*
Paul Smith's College *A, B*
State University of New York
College of Agriculture and
Technology at Morrisville *A*
College of Environmental Science
and Forestry *A, B, M, D*
Sullivan County Community
College *A*

North Carolina
Duke University *M, D*
Haywood Community College *C, A*
High Point University *B*
North Carolina State University *M, D*
Wake Forest University *B*

Ohio
Miami University
Oxford Campus *B, M*
Ohio State University
Columbus Campus *B, M*

Oklahoma
Eastern Oklahoma State College *A*
Northeastern Oklahoma Agricultural
and Mechanical College *A*
Oklahoma State University *B, M*

Oregon
Central Oregon Community
College *A*
Chemeketa Community College *A*
Mount Hood Community College *C, A*
Oregon State University *M, D*

Pennsylvania
Gettysburg College *B*
Keystone College *C, A*
St. Francis University *B*

South Carolina
Clemson University *B, M, D*

Tennessee
Hiwassee College *A*
Roane State Community College *A*
University of Tennessee
Knoxville *B, M*
University of the South *B*

Texas
Baylor University *B*

Stephen F. Austin State
University *B, M, D*
Texas A&M University *B, M, D*

Utah
Dixie State College of Utah *A*
Snow College *A*
Utah State University *B, M, D*

Vermont
Sterling College *A, B*
University of Vermont *B, M*

Virginia
Dabney S. Lancaster Community
College *A*
Mountain Empire Community
College *C, A*
Virginia Polytechnic Institute and
State University *B*

Washington
Centralia College *A*
Edmonds Community College *C*
Heritage University *C, A*
Spokane Community College *A*
University of Washington *B, M, D*
Washington State University *B*

West Virginia
Potomac State College of West Virginia
University *A*
West Virginia University *M*

Wisconsin
Beloit College *B*
Northland College *B*
University of Wisconsin
Madison *M, D*
Stevens Point *B*

Wyoming
Northwest College *A*

Franchise operations

Ohio
Ashland University *B*

French

Alabama
Auburn University *B, M*
Birmingham-Southern College *B, T*
Oakwood College *B*
Samford University *B*
Talladega College *B*
University of Alabama *B*

Alaska
University of Alaska
Anchorage *B*

Arizona
Arizona State University *B, M*
Northern Arizona University *B, T*
University of Arizona *B, M, D*

Arkansas
Arkansas State University *B*
Harding University *B*
Hendrix College *B*
Ouachita Baptist University *B*
University of Arkansas *B, M*
University of Arkansas
Little Rock *B*
University of Central Arkansas *B*

California
Cabrillo College *A*
California Lutheran University *B*

California State University
  Chico *B*
  Dominguez Hills *B*
  East Bay *B*
  Fresno *B*
  Fullerton *B, M*
  Long Beach *B, M*
  Los Angeles *B, M*
  Northridge *B*
  Sacramento *B*
  San Bernardino *B*
  Stanislaus *B*
Canada College *A*
Cerritos Community College *A*
Chabot College *A*
Chaffey College *A*
Chapman University *B*
Citrus College *A*
Claremont McKenna College *B*
College of San Mateo *A*
College of the Canyons *A*
College of the Desert *A*
College of the Sequoias *A*
Crafton Hills College *A*
Cypress College *A*
De Anza College *A*
El Camino College *A*
Foothill College *A*
Glendale Community College *A*
Golden West College *A*
Grossmont Community College *A*
Humboldt State University *B*
Imperial Valley College *A*
Irvine Valley College *A*
Los Angeles City College *A*
Los Angeles Pierce College *A*
Los Angeles Southwest College *A*
Los Angeles Valley College *A*
Loyola Marymount University *B*
Mendocino College *A*
Merced College *A*
Merritt College *A*
Mills College *B*
MiraCosta College *A*
Modesto Junior College *A*
Mount St. Mary's College *B*
Occidental College *B*
Orange Coast College *A*
Pacific Union College *B*
Pepperdine University *B*
Pitzer College *B*
Pomona College *B*
St. Mary's College of California *B*
San Diego City College *A*
San Diego Mesa College *A*
San Diego Miramar College *A*
San Diego State University *B, M*
San Francisco State University *B, M*
San Joaquin Delta College *A*
San Jose State University *B, M*
Santa Barbara City College *A*
Santa Clara University *B*
Scripps College *B*
Solano Community College *A*
Sonoma State University *B*
Southwestern College *A*
Stanford University *B, M, D*
University of California
  Berkeley *B, M, D*
  Davis *B, M, D*
  Irvine *B, M, D*
  Los Angeles *B, M, D*
  Riverside *B*
  San Diego *B, M*
  Santa Barbara *B, M, D*
  Santa Cruz *B*
University of La Verne *B*
University of Redlands *B*
University of San Diego *B*
University of San Francisco *B*
University of Southern
  California *B, M, D*
University of the Pacific *B*
Ventura College *A*

West Los Angeles College *A*
Westmont College *B*
Whittier College *B*

Colorado
Red Rocks Community College *A*
Regis University *B*
University of Colorado
  Boulder *B, M, D*
  Denver and Health Sciences
  Center *B*
University of Denver *B*

Connecticut
Central Connecticut State
  University *B*
Connecticut College *B*
Fairfield University *B*
St. Joseph College *B, T*
Southern Connecticut State
  University *B, M*
Trinity College *B*
University of Connecticut *B, M, D*
Wesleyan University *B*
Yale University *B, M, D*

Delaware
Delaware State University *B*
University of Delaware *B, M, T*

District of Columbia
American University *B*
Catholic University of
  America *B, M, D, T*
Gallaudet University *B*
George Washington University *B*
Georgetown University *B*
Howard University *B, M, D*
Trinity University *B*
University of the District of
  Columbia *B*

Florida
Barry University *B*
Eckerd College *B*
Florida Agricultural and Mechanical
  University *B*
Florida Atlantic University *B, M*
Florida International University *B*
Florida State University *B, M, D*
Jacksonville University *B*
Manatee Community College *A*
New College of Florida *B*
Okaloosa-Walton College *A*
Rollins College *B*
Schiller International University *B*
Stetson University *B*
University of Central Florida *B*
University of Florida *A, B*
University of Miami *B, M, D*
University of South Florida *B, M*
University of Tampa *A*
Valencia Community College *A*

Georgia
Agnes Scott College *B*
Albany State University *B*
Augusta State University *B*
Berry College *B*
Clark Atlanta University *B, M*
Columbus State University *B*
Emory University *B, D*
Georgia College and State
  University *B*
Georgia Southern University *B*
Georgia State University *B, M*
Mercer University *B*
Morehouse College *B*
North Georgia College & State
  University *B*
Shorter College *B*
South Georgia College *A*
Spelman College *B*

University of Georgia *B, M*
University of West Georgia *B*
Valdosta State University *B*
Wesleyan College *B*
Young Harris College *A*

Hawaii
University of Hawaii
  Manoa *B, M*

Idaho
Boise State University *B*
Idaho State University *A, B*
University of Idaho *B, M*

Illinois
Augustana College *B, T*
Bradley University *B, T*
City Colleges of Chicago
  Harold Washington College *A*
DePaul University *B*
Dominican University *B*
Elmhurst College *B, T*
Illinois College *B, T*
Illinois State University *B, T*
Illinois Wesleyan University *B*
Kishwaukee College *A*
Knox College *B*
Lake Forest College *B*
Loyola University of Chicago *B*
MacMurray College *B*
Millikin University *B, T*
Monmouth College *B, T*
North Central College *B, T*
North Park University *B*
Northeastern Illinois University *B*
Northern Illinois University *B, M, T*
Northwestern University *B, M, D*
Principia College *B*
Richland Community College *A*
Rockford College *B*
Sauk Valley Community College *A*
Southern Illinois University
  Carbondale *B*
Southern Illinois University
  Edwardsville *T*
Triton College *A*
University of Chicago *B*
University of Illinois
  Chicago *B, M*
  Urbana-Champaign *B, M, D*
Western Illinois University *B*
Wheaton College *B*

Indiana
Anderson University *B*
Ball State University *B, T*
Butler University *B*
DePauw University *B*
Earlham College *B*
Franklin College *B*
Grace College *B*
Hanover College *B*
Indiana State University *B, M, T*
Indiana University
  Bloomington *B, M, D*
  Northwest *A, B*
  South Bend *B*
  Southeast *B*
Indiana University-Purdue University
  Fort Wayne *A, B, T*
Indiana University-Purdue University
  Indianapolis *B*
Manchester College *B, T*
Marian College *B, T*
Purdue University
  Calumet *B*
Saint Mary's College *B, T*
St. Mary-of-the-Woods College *B*
Taylor University *B*
University of Evansville *B*
University of Indianapolis *B*
University of Notre Dame *B, M*

University of Southern Indiana *B, T*
Valparaiso University *B*
Vincennes University *A*
Wabash College *B*

Iowa
Central College *B, T*
Coe College *B*
Cornell College *B, T*
Grinnell College *B*
Iowa State University *B*
Luther College *B*
St. Ambrose University *B, T*
Simpson College *B*
University of Iowa *B, M, D, T*
University of Northern Iowa *B, M*
Wartburg College *B, T*

Kansas
Baker University *B, T*
Benedictine College *B*
Butler County Community College *A*
Pittsburg State University *B*
University of Kansas *B, M, D*
Washburn University of Topeka *B*
Wichita State University *B*

Kentucky
Asbury College *B, T*
Berea College *B, T*
Centre College *B*
Eastern Kentucky University *B*
Georgetown College *B, T*
Morehead State University *B*
Murray State University *B, T*
Northern Kentucky University *B*
Thomas More College *A*
Transylvania University *B, T*
University of Kentucky *B, M*
University of Louisville *B, M*
Western Kentucky University *B, T*

Louisiana
Centenary College of Louisiana *B, T*
Dillard University *B*
Grambling State University *B*
Louisiana State University
  Shreveport *B*
Louisiana State University and
  Agricultural and Mechanical
  College *B, M, D*
Louisiana Tech University *B*
Loyola University New Orleans *B*
Nicholls State University *B*
Southeastern Louisiana University *B*
Southern University
  New Orleans *B*
Southern University and Agricultural
  and Mechanical College *B*
Tulane University *B, M, D*
University of Louisiana at
  Lafayette *M, D*
University of Louisiana at Monroe *B*
University of New Orleans *B*
Xavier University of Louisiana *B*

Maine
Bates College *B, T*
Bowdoin College *B*
Colby College *B*
University of Maine *B, M*
University of Maine
  Fort Kent *B*
University of Southern Maine *B*

Maryland
College of Notre Dame of Maryland *B*
Community College of Baltimore
  County *A*
Frostburg State University *T*
Goucher College *B*
Hood College *B, T*
Johns Hopkins University *B, M, D*

Loyola College in Maryland *B*
McDaniel College *B*
Mount St. Mary's University *B*
Salisbury University *B, T*
Towson University *B, T*
University of Maryland
    College Park *B, M, D*
Washington College *B, T*

Massachusetts

Amherst College *B*
Assumption College *B*
Atlantic Union College *B*
Boston College *B, M, D*
Boston University *B, M, D*
Brandeis University *B*
Clark University *B*
College of the Holy Cross *B*
Gordon College *B*
Merrimack College *B*
Mount Holyoke College *B*
Northeastern University *B*
Roxbury Community College *A*
Simmons College *B, M*
Simon's Rock College of Bard *B*
Smith College *B*
Suffolk University *B*
Tufts University *B, M*
University of Massachusetts
    Amherst *B, M*
    Boston *B*
    Dartmouth *B*
Wellesley College *B*
Wheaton College *B*
Williams College *B*

Michigan

Adrian College *A, B, T*
Albion College *B, T*
Alma College *B, T*
Andrews University *B*
Aquinas College *B, T*
Calvin College *B, T*
Central Michigan University *B, T*
Eastern Michigan University *B, M*
Grand Valley State University *B*
Hillsdale College *B*
Hope College *B*
Kalamazoo College *B, T*
Lansing Community College *A*
Madonna University *B*
Michigan State University *B, M, D*
Northern Michigan University *B, T*
Oakland University *B, T*
Saginaw Valley State University *B, T*
University of Michigan *B, M, D*
University of Michigan
    Dearborn *B*
    Flint *B, T*
Wayne State University *B, M*
Western Michigan University *B*

Minnesota

Augsburg College *B*
Bethel University *B*
Carleton College *B*
College of St. Benedict *B*
College of St. Catherine *B*
Concordia College: Moorhead *B, T*
Gustavus Adolphus College *B*
Hamline University *B*
Macalester College *B, T*
Minnesota State University
    Mankato *B, M, T*
St. Cloud State University *B*
St. John's University *B*
St. Mary's University of Minnesota *B*
St. Olaf College *B*
University of Minnesota
    Duluth *B, T*
    Morris *B*
    Twin Cities *B, M, D*
University of St. Thomas *B*
Winona State University *B*

Mississippi

Itawamba Community College *A*
Millsaps College *B, T*
Mississippi College *B*
University of Mississippi *B, M, T*

Missouri

Central Methodist University *B*
Central Missouri State University *B, T*
College of the Ozarks *B*
Drury University *B, T*
Lindenwood University *B*
Missouri Southern State University *B*
Missouri State University *B*
Missouri Western State University *B, T*
Northwest Missouri State
    University *B*
Rockhurst University *B*
St. Louis University *B, M*
Southeast Missouri State University *B*
Truman State University *B*
University of Missouri
    Columbia *B, M*
    Kansas City *B*
    St. Louis *B*
Washington University in St.
    Louis *B, M, D*
Webster University *B*
Westminster College *B*
William Jewell College *B*

Montana

Carroll College *B, T*
University of Montana: Missoula *B, M*

Nebraska

Creighton University *B*
Doane College *B*
Nebraska Wesleyan University *B*
Union College *B*
University of Nebraska
    Kearney *B, M, T*
    Lincoln *B*
    Omaha *B*
Western Nebraska Community
    College *A*

Nevada

University of Nevada
    Las Vegas *B*
    Reno *B*

New Hampshire

Dartmouth College *B, T*
Keene State College *B, T*
Plymouth State University *B*
St. Anselm College *B, T*
University of New Hampshire *B*

New Jersey

Caldwell College *B*
Drew University *B*
Fairleigh Dickinson University
    College at Florham *B*
    Metropolitan Campus *B*
Montclair State University *B, M, T*
Rider University *B*
Rutgers, The State University of New
    Jersey
    Camden Regional Campus *B, T*
    New Brunswick/Piscataway
        Campus *B, M, D, T*
    Newark Regional Campus *B, T*
Seton Hall University *B, T*
William Paterson University of New
    Jersey *B*

New Mexico

University of New Mexico *B, M, D*

New York

Adelphi University *B*

Alfred University *B*
Bard College *B*
Barnard College *B*
Canisius College *B*
City University of New York
    Brooklyn College *B, M*
    City College *B*
    Hunter College *B, M*
    Lehman College *B*
    Queens College *B, M, T*
    York College *B*
Colgate University *B*
College of Mount St. Vincent *B, T*
College of New Rochelle *B, T*
Columbia University
    Columbia College *B*
    School of General Studies *B*
Cornell University *B, M, D*
Daemen College *B*
Elmira College *B, T*
Fordham University *B, M, D*
Hamilton College *B*
Hartwick College *B, T*
Hobart and William Smith Colleges *B*
Hofstra University *B*
Houghton College *B*
Iona College *B*
Ithaca College *B, T*
Le Moyne College *B*
Long Island University
    C.W. Post Campus *B*
Manhattan College *B*
Marist College *B, T*
Molloy College *B*
Nazareth College of Rochester *B*
New York University *B, M, D*
Niagara University *B*
Orange County Community College *A*
Pace University *B*
St. Bonaventure University *B*
St. John Fisher College *B*
St. John's University *B*
St. Lawrence University *B, T*
St. Thomas Aquinas College *B*
Sarah Lawrence College *B*
Siena College *B, T*
Skidmore College *B*
State University of New York
    Albany *B, M, D*
    Binghamton *B, M*
    Buffalo *B, M, D*
    College at Brockport *B, T*
    College at Buffalo *B*
    College at Cortland *B*
    College at Fredonia *B, T*
    College at Geneseo *B, T*
    College at Oneonta *B*
    College at Plattsburgh *B*
    College at Potsdam *B*
    New Paltz *B, T*
    Oswego *B*
    Stony Brook *B*
Syracuse University *B, M*
United States Military Academy *B*
University of Rochester *B, M*
Vassar College *B*
Wells College *B*
Yeshiva University *B*

North Carolina

Appalachian State University *B*
Campbell University *B*
Catawba College *B*
Davidson College *B*
Duke University *B, M, D*
East Carolina University *B*
Elon University *B*
Gardner-Webb University *B*
Greensboro College *B*
Guilford College *B, T*
High Point University *B*
Johnson C. Smith University *B*
Lenoir-Rhyne College *B*
Meredith College *B*

Methodist College *A, B, T*
North Carolina Agricultural and
    Technical State University *B, T*
North Carolina Central University *B*
North Carolina State University *B, M*
Salem College *B*
University of North Carolina
    Asheville *B, T*
    Charlotte *B*
    Greensboro *B, T*
    Wilmington *B*
Wake Forest University *B*

North Dakota

Jamestown College *B*
Minot State University *B*
North Dakota State University *B, T*
University of North Dakota *B*

Ohio

Antioch College *B*
Ashland University *B*
Baldwin-Wallace College *B, T*
Bowling Green State University *B, M*
Capital University *B*
Case Western Reserve University *B, M*
Cleveland State University *B*
College of Wooster *B*
Denison University *B*
Franciscan University of
    Steubenville *B*
Hiram College *B, T*
John Carroll University *B*
Kent State University *B, M*
Kenyon College *B*
Lake Erie College *B*
Miami University
    Oxford Campus *B, M, T*
Mount Union College *B*
Muskingum College *B*
Oberlin College *B*
Ohio Northern University *B*
Ohio State University
    Columbus Campus *B, M, D*
Ohio University *B, M*
Ohio Wesleyan University *B*
Otterbein College *B*
University of Akron *B*
University of Cincinnati *B, M, D, T*
University of Dayton *B*
University of Toledo *B, M*
Walsh University *B*
Wittenberg University *B*
Wright State University *B*
Xavier University *A, B*
Youngstown State University *B*

Oklahoma

Oklahoma Baptist University *B, T*
Oklahoma City Community College *A*
Oklahoma City University *B*
Oklahoma State University *B*
Oral Roberts University *B*
Tulsa Community College *A*
University of Central Oklahoma *B*
University of Oklahoma *B, M, D*
University of Tulsa *B*

Oregon

Lewis & Clark College *B*
Linfield College *B, T*
Oregon State University *B*
Pacific University *B*
Portland State University *B, M*
Reed College *B*
University of Oregon *B, M*
University of Portland *T*
Western Oregon University *T*
Willamette University *B*

Pennsylvania

Albright College *B, T*
Allegheny College *B*

Bloomsburg University of
Pennsylvania *B, T*
Bryn Mawr College *B, M*
Bucknell University *B*
Cabrini College *B*
California University of
Pennsylvania *B*
Carnegie Mellon University *B*
Chatham College *B*
Chestnut Hill College *A, B*
Cheyney University of
Pennsylvania *B, T*
Clarion University of
Pennsylvania *B, T*
Dickinson College *B*
East Stroudsburg University of
Pennsylvania *B, T*
Eastern University *B*
Elizabethtown College *B*
Franklin & Marshall College *B*
Gettysburg College *B*
Grove City College *B, T*
Haverford College *B, T*
Holy Family University *B, T*
Immaculata University *B, T*
Indiana University of Pennsylvania *B*
Juniata College *B*
King's College *B, T*
Kutztown University of
Pennsylvania *B, M, T*
La Salle University *B, T*
Lafayette College *B*
Lebanon Valley College *B*
Lehigh University *B*
Lincoln University *B*
Lock Haven University of
Pennsylvania *B, T*
Lycoming College *B*
Mansfield University of
Pennsylvania *B, T*
Marywood University *B*
Messiah College *B*
Millersville University of
Pennsylvania *B, M, T*
Moravian College *B, T*
Muhlenberg College *B*
Penn State
Abington *B*
Altoona *B*
Beaver *B*
Berks *B*
Delaware County *B*
Dubois *B*
Fayette *B*
Hazleton *B*
Lehigh Valley *B*
McKeesport *B*
Mont Alto *B*
New Kensington *B*
Schuylkill - Capital College *B*
Shenango *B*
University Park *B, M, D*
Wilkes-Barre *B*
Worthington Scranton *B*
York *B*
Rosemont College *B*
St. Francis University *B*
St. Joseph's University *B*
St. Vincent College *B*
Seton Hill University *T*
Shippensburg University of
Pennsylvania *B, T*
Slippery Rock University of
Pennsylvania *B, T*
Susquehanna University *B, T*
Swarthmore College *B*
Temple University *B*
University of Pennsylvania *B*
University of Pittsburgh *B, M, D*
University of Scranton *B, T*
Ursinus College *B, T*
Villanova University *B*
Washington and Jefferson College *B*

West Chester University of
Pennsylvania *B, M, T*
Westminster College *B*
Widener University *B, T*
Wilkes University *B*
Wilson College *B*

Puerto Rico

Pontifical Catholic University of
Puerto Rico *B*
University of Puerto Rico
Mayaguez *B*
Rio Piedras *B*
University of the Sacred Heart *B*

Rhode Island

Brown University *B, M, D*
Providence College *B*
Rhode Island College *B, M*
Salve Regina University *B*
University of Rhode Island *B*

South Carolina

The Citadel *B*
Clemson University *B*
Coker College *B*
College of Charleston *B, T*
Columbia College *B*
Converse College *B*
Erskine College *B*
Francis Marion University *B*
Furman University *B, T*
Newberry College *B*
Presbyterian College *B*
South Carolina State University *B*
University of South Carolina *B, M*
University of South Carolina
Upstate *B*
Wofford College *B, T*

South Dakota

Augustana College *B, T*
Northern State University *B*
South Dakota State University *B, T*
University of South Dakota *B*

Tennessee

Belmont University *B, T*
Carson-Newman College *B, T*
Hiwassee College *A*
King College *B, T*
Lambuth University *B*
Lee University *B*
Lipscomb University *B*
Milligan College *T*
Rhodes College *B, T*
Southern Adventist University *B*
Tennessee State University *B*
Tennessee Technological
University *B, T*
Union University *B, T*
University of Tennessee
Chattanooga *B*
Knoxville *B, M*
Martin *B*
University of the South *B*
Vanderbilt University *B, M, D*

Texas

Angelo State University *B, T*
Austin College *B*
Austin Community College *A*
Baylor University *B*
Blinn College *A*
Cisco Junior College *A*
Coastal Bend College *A*
Houston Baptist University *B*
Kilgore College *A*
Lamar University *B*
McMurry University *B*
Midland College *A*
Paris Junior College *A*
Rice University *B, M, D*

St. Mary's University *B*
Sam Houston State University *B*
South Plains College *A*
Southern Methodist University *B*
Southwestern University *B, T*
Stephen F. Austin State University *B, T*
Texas A&M University *B*
Texas Christian University *B*
Texas Southern University *B*
Texas State University: San
Marcos *B, T*
Texas Tech University *B, M*
Trinity University *B*
Tyler Junior College *A*
University of Dallas *B*
University of Houston *B, M*
University of North Texas *B, M*
University of St. Thomas *B*
University of Texas
Arlington *B, M*
Austin *B, M, D*
El Paso *B*
San Antonio *B*

Utah

Brigham Young University *B, M*
Snow College *A*
Southern Utah University *B*
University of Utah *B, M*
Utah State University *B*
Weber State University *B*

Vermont

Bennington College *B*
Marlboro College *B*
Middlebury College *B, M, D*
St. Michael's College *B*
University of Vermont *B, M*

Virginia

Bridgewater College *B*
Christopher Newport University *B*
College of William and Mary *B*
Eastern Mennonite University *B*
Emory & Henry College *B, T*
Hampden-Sydney College *B*
Hollins University *B*
Longwood University *B, T*
Lynchburg College *B*
Mary Baldwin College *B*
Old Dominion University *B, T*
Randolph-Macon College *B*
Randolph-Macon Woman's College *B*
Roanoke College *B, T*
Sweet Briar College *B*
University of Mary Washington *B*
University of Richmond *B, T*
University of Virginia *B, M, D*
University of Virginia's College at
Wise *B, T*
Virginia Wesleyan College *B*
Washington and Lee University *B*

Washington

Central Washington University *B*
Centralia College *A*
Eastern Washington University *B, M, T*
Everett Community College *A*
Gonzaga University *B*
Highline Community College *A*
Pacific Lutheran University *B*
Seattle Pacific University *B*
Seattle University *B*
University of Puget Sound *B, T*
University of Washington *B*
Walla Walla College *B*
Washington State University *B*
Western Washington University *B*
Whitman College *B*
Whitworth College *B, T*

West Virginia

Bethany College *B*

Davis and Elkins College *B*
Potomac State College of West Virginia
University *A*
West Virginia University *T*
Wheeling Jesuit University *B*

Wisconsin

Beloit College *B*
Cardinal Stritch University *B*
Carthage College *B, T*
Edgewood College *B*
Lawrence University *B, T*
Marquette University *B*
Mount Mary College *B, T*
Ripon College *B, T*
St. Norbert College *B, T*
University of Wisconsin
Eau Claire *B*
Green Bay *B, T*
La Crosse *B, T*
Madison *B, M, D*
Milwaukee *B*
Oshkosh *B*
Parkside *B, T*
River Falls *B*
Stevens Point *B, T*
Whitewater *B, T*

Wyoming

University of Wyoming *B, M*

French studies

California

Scripps College *B*

Colorado

Colorado College *B*

District of Columbia

American University *B*

Florida

New College of Florida *B*

Georgia

Emory University *B, D*

Iowa

Coe College *B*
Cornell College *B*

Louisiana

University of Louisiana at Lafayette *D*

Maine

University of Southern Maine *B*

Massachusetts

Simon's Rock College of Bard *B*
Suffolk University *B*

Minnesota

Concordia College: Moorhead *B, T*
Minnesota State University
Mankato *B*

New Hampshire

University of New Hampshire *B*

New Jersey

William Paterson University of New
Jersey *B*

New York

Bard College *B*
Barnard College *B*
Columbia University
Columbia College *B*
Manhattanville College *B*

Sarah Lawrence College *B*
Skidmore College *B*

Ohio

Case Western Reserve University *B*
Cleveland State University *B*
University of Cincinnati *B*

Pennsylvania

St. Francis University *B*
St. Joseph's University *B*

Rhode Island

Brown University *B, M, D*

Tennessee

University of the South *B*

Washington

University of Washington *B, M*

Wisconsin

University of Wisconsin
Parkside *B*

French teacher education

Alabama

Birmingham-Southern College *T*
Talladega College *B*

Arizona

Arizona State University *B, T*
Northern Arizona University *B*
Prescott College *T*
University of Arizona *B, M*

Arkansas

Arkansas State University *B, T*
Ouachita Baptist University *B, T*
University of Central Arkansas *T*

California

California State University
Chico *B, T*
Long Beach *T*
San Bernardino *T*
Humboldt State University *T*
Pacific Union College *T*
San Diego State University *B, T*
San Francisco State University *B, T*
Stanford University *M, T*
University of the Pacific *T*

Colorado

Colorado State University *T*

Connecticut

Fairfield University *T*

Delaware

Delaware State University *B*
University of Delaware *B, T*

Florida

Stetson University *B*

Georgia

Fort Valley State University *B, T*
Georgia Southern University *B, M*
University of West Georgia *M*

Idaho

Boise State University *T*

Illinois

Augustana College *B, T*
Bradley University *B*
Dominican University *T*

Elmhurst College *B*
Illinois College *T*
Illinois Wesleyan University *B*
Knox College *T*
North Park University *T*
Rockford College *T*
Roosevelt University *B*
Sauk Valley Community College *A*
University of Illinois
Chicago *B*
Urbana-Champaign *B, M, T*
Wheaton College *T*

Indiana

Anderson University *B, T*
Franklin College *B, T*
Grace College *B*
Indiana University
Bloomington *B, T*
Indiana University-Purdue University
Fort Wayne *B, T*
Indiana University-Purdue University
Indianapolis *B, T*
Indiana Wesleyan University *T*
Manchester College *B, T*
Purdue University
Calumet *B*
Saint Mary's College *T*
Taylor University *B, T*
University of Evansville *B, T*
University of Indianapolis *B, T*
Valparaiso University *B*
Vincennes University *A*

Iowa

Central College *T*
Cornell College *B, T*
Graceland University *T*
Iowa State University *T*
Loras College *T*
Northwestern College *T*
St. Ambrose University *B, T*
Simpson College *T*
University of Iowa *T*
Wartburg College *T*

Kansas

Baker University *T*
Pittsburg State University *B, T*
University of Kansas *B, T*

Louisiana

Centenary College of Louisiana *B, T*
Grambling State University *B*
Louisiana State University
Shreveport *B*
Louisiana Tech University *B*
Nicholls State University *B*
Southeastern Louisiana University *B*
Southern University
New Orleans *B*
Southern University and Agricultural
and Mechanical College *B*
University of Louisiana at Lafayette *B*
University of Louisiana at Monroe *B*
Xavier University of Louisiana *B*

Maine

University of Maine *B*
University of Southern Maine *T*

Maryland

College of Notre Dame of Maryland *T*
Mount St. Mary's University *T*
Salisbury University *T*
Towson University *T*
Washington College *T*

Massachusetts

Assumption College *T*
Elms College *T*
Tufts University *T*

University of Massachusetts
Dartmouth *T*
Worcester State College *T*

Michigan

Albion College *B, T*
Alma College *T*
Calvin College *B*
Eastern Michigan University *B, T*
Grand Valley State University *T*
Hope College *T*
Northern Michigan University *B, T*
University of Michigan
Flint *T*
Western Michigan University *B, T*

Minnesota

Augsburg College *T*
Bemidji State University *T*
Bethel University *B*
College of St. Benedict *T*
College of St. Catherine *T*
Concordia College: Moorhead *B, T*
Gustavus Adolphus College *T*
Minnesota State University
Mankato *B, M, T*
St. Cloud State University *T*
St. John's University *T*
St. Mary's University of Minnesota *B*
University of Minnesota
Duluth *B*
Morris *T*
University of St. Thomas *B, T*
Winona State University *B, T*

Mississippi

Itawamba Community College *A*
Mississippi College *B, T*
Mississippi State University *T*

Missouri

Central Missouri State University *B, T*
College of the Ozarks *B, T*
Lindenwood University *B*
Missouri Southern State
University *B, T*
Missouri State University *B*
Missouri Western State University *B*
Northwest Missouri State
University *B, T*
Truman State University *M, T*
University of Missouri
Columbia *M*
St. Louis *T*
Washington University in St.
Louis *B, M, T*
William Jewell College *T*

Montana

University of Montana: Missoula *T*

Nebraska

Creighton University *T*
Nebraska Wesleyan University *T*
University of Nebraska
Kearney *B*
Lincoln *B*

Nevada

University of Nevada
Reno *B*

New Hampshire

Keene State College *B, T*
St. Anselm College *T*
University of New Hampshire *T*

New Jersey

Caldwell College *T*
Rowan University *T*

New York

Alfred University *M, T*
City University of New York
Brooklyn College *B, M*
City College *B*
Hunter College *B, M, T*
Queens College *M, T*
College of Mount St. Vincent *T*
D'Youville College *M, T*
Daemen College *B, M, T*
Dutchess Community College *A*
Elmira College *B, T*
Fordham University *M, T*
Hobart and William Smith Colleges *T*
Hofstra University *B, M*
Houghton College *B, T*
Iona College *B*
Ithaca College *B, T*
Le Moyne College *T*
Long Island University
C.W. Post Campus *B, M, T*
Manhattan College *B*
Marist College *B*
Molloy College *B*
New York University *B, M, T*
Niagara University *B, M, T*
Pace University *B, M, T*
St. Bonaventure University *T*
St. John Fisher College *B, T*
St. Lawrence University *T*
State University of New York
Albany *B, M, T*
Buffalo *M, T*
College at Brockport *T*
College at Buffalo *B*
College at Cortland *B, M*
College at Fredonia *B, T*
College at Geneseo *B, M, T*
College at Oneonta *B, T*
College at Plattsburgh *B, M*
College at Potsdam *B, M*
New Paltz *B, M, T*
Oswego *B, M*
Stony Brook *T*
Vassar College *T*
Wells College *T*

North Carolina

Appalachian State University *B*
Campbell University *B, T*
Davidson College *T*
East Carolina University *B*
Gardner-Webb University *B*
Meredith College *T*
North Carolina Agricultural and
Technical State University *B, T*
North Carolina Central University *B, T*
North Carolina State University *B, T*
Queens University of Charlotte *T*
Salem College *T*
University of North Carolina
Charlotte *B*
Greensboro *B*
Wilmington *B*
Wake Forest University *T*

North Dakota

Minot State University *B*
North Dakota State University *B, T*

Ohio

Ashland University *B, T*
Baldwin-Wallace College *T*
Case Western Reserve University *T*
Hiram College *T*
Kent State University *T*
Miami University
Oxford Campus *B, M, T*
Mount Union College *T*
Ohio Northern University *B*
Ohio University *B, T*
Ohio Wesleyan University *B*
Otterbein College *B*

University of Akron *B*
University of Dayton *B*
University of Toledo *B, M, T*
Youngstown State University *B, M*

Oklahoma
Oklahoma Baptist University *B, T*
Oklahoma City University *B*
University of Central Oklahoma *B*
University of Tulsa *T*

Oregon
Linfield College *T*
Oregon State University *M*
Portland State University *T*
Western Oregon University *T*

Pennsylvania
Albright College *T*
Cabrini College *T*
Chatham College *T*
Dickinson College *T*
Gettysburg College *T*
Grove City College *B, T*
Holy Family University *B, M, T*
Juniata College *B, T*
King's College *T*
La Salle University *B, T*
Lebanon Valley College *T*
Lycoming College *T*
Mansfield University of
    Pennsylvania *B, T*
Marywood University *B*
Messiah College *B, T*
Moravian College *T*
Rosemont College *T*
St. Francis University *B, T*
St. Vincent College *T*
Seton Hill University *T*
Susquehanna University *T*
Villanova University *T*
Washington and Jefferson College *T*
Westminster College *T*
Widener University *T*

Rhode Island
Rhode Island College *B*
Salve Regina University *B*

South Carolina
Furman University *T*
South Carolina State University *B, T*
Wofford College *T*

South Dakota
Augustana College *B, T*
University of South Dakota *B, M, D, T*

Tennessee
Belmont University *B, M, T*
King College *T*
Lipscomb University *B, T*
Southern Adventist University *B*
Tennessee Technological University *T*
Union University *B, T*
University of Memphis *T*
University of Tennessee
    Martin *B*

Texas
Houston Baptist University *T*
Lamar University *T*
St. Mary's University *T*
Texas A&M University
    Commerce *T*
    Kingsville *T*
Texas State University: San Marcos *T*
University of Dallas *T*
University of Houston *T*
University of Texas
    San Antonio *T*

Utah
Brigham Young University *B*
Southern Utah University *B, T*
University of Utah *B*
Weber State University *B*

Vermont
St. Michael's College *T*

Virginia
Bridgewater College *T*
Eastern Mennonite University *T*
Hollins University *T*
Longwood University *B, T*
Old Dominion University *B, T*
University of Virginia's College at
    Wise *T*

Washington
Central Washington University *B, T*
Eastern Washington University *M, T*
Washington State University *B, M, T*
Whitworth College *B, T*

West Virginia
Bethany College *B*

Wisconsin
Carthage College *T*
Edgewood College *B*
Lawrence University *T*
Mount Mary College *B, T*
St. Norbert College *T*
University of Wisconsin
    Green Bay *T*
    Parkside *T*
    River Falls *T*
    Whitewater *B*

Funeral direction

Indiana
Vincennes University *A*

Mississippi
Mississippi Gulf Coast Community
    College
    Jefferson Davis Campus *A*

Missouri
Lindenwood University *B*

North Carolina
Rowan-Cabarrus Community
    College *C*

Tennessee
John A. Gupton College *A*

Texas
San Antonio College *C*

Funeral services/ mortuary science

Alabama
Bishop State Community College *A*
Jefferson State Community
    College *C, A*

Arkansas
Arkansas State University
    Mountain Home *A*
University of Arkansas
    Community College at Hope *A*

California
Cypress College *C, A*

Colorado
Arapahoe Community College *A*

Connecticut
Briarwood College *A, B*

District of Columbia
University of the District of
    Columbia *A*

Florida
Florida Community College at
    Jacksonville *A*
Miami Dade College *C, A*
St. Petersburg College *A*

Georgia
Gupton Jones College of Funeral
    Service *C, A*

Illinois
Carl Sandburg College *A*
City Colleges of Chicago
    Malcolm X College *A*
Southern Illinois University
    Carbondale *B*

Indiana
Ivy Tech State College
    Ivy Tech Community College:
        Central Indiana *A*
    Ivy Tech Community College:
        Northwest *A*
Mid-America College of Funeral
    Service *C, A*
Vincennes University *A*

Iowa
Des Moines Area Community
    College *C*
Marshalltown Community College *A*
North Iowa Area Community
    College *A*
Upper Iowa University *B*

Kansas
Barton County Community College *A*
Kansas City Kansas Community
    College *A*

Louisiana
Delgado Community College *A*

Maryland
Community College of Baltimore
    County *C, A*

Massachusetts
Bristol Community College *C*
Holyoke Community College *C*
Mount Ida College *A, B*

Michigan
Delta College *A*
Ferris State University *A*
Gogebic Community College *A*
Schoolcraft College *A*
Wayne State University *B*

Minnesota
University of Minnesota
    Twin Cities *B*

Mississippi
University of Southern Mississippi *B*

Missouri
Lindenwood University *B*

New Jersey
Hudson County Community
    College *A*
Mercer County Community
    College *C, A*

New York
American Academy McAllister
    Institute of Funeral Service *A*
City University of New York
    LaGuardia Community College *A*
Hudson Valley Community College *A*
Nassau Community College *A*
St. John's University *B*
State University of New York
    College of Technology at
        Canton *A, B*

North Carolina
Edgecombe Community College *A*
Fayetteville Technical Community
    College *C, A*
Forsyth Technical Community
    College *C*
Pitt Community College *A*

Ohio
Cincinnati College of Mortuary
    Science *A, B*
University of Cincinnati
    Raymond Walters College *A*

Oklahoma
University of Central Oklahoma *C, B*

Oregon
Mount Hood Community College *A*

Pennsylvania
Gannon University *B*
Luzerne County Community
    College *A*
Northampton County Area
    Community College *A*
Pittsburgh Institute of Mortuary
    Science *C, A*
Point Park University *A, B*
Thiel College *B*

South Carolina
Florence-Darlington Technical
    College *A*
Piedmont Technical College *A*

Tennessee
John A. Gupton College *C, A*

Texas
Amarillo College *A*
Commonwealth Institute of Funeral
    Service *C, A*
Dallas Institute of Funeral Service *C, A*
San Antonio College *A*

Virginia
John Tyler Community College *A*
Norfolk State University *C*

Wisconsin
Milwaukee Area Technical College *A*

Furniture design/ manufacturing

Georgia
Savannah College of Art and
    Design *B, M*

Michigan
College for Creative Studies *B*

Ferris State University *B*
Kendall College of Art and Design of
Ferris State University *B*

Minnesota
Dakota County Technical College *C*
Minneapolis College of Art and
Design *B*

New Mexico
Northern New Mexico College *C, A*

New York
Rochester Institute of
Technology *A, B, M*
State University of New York
College of Agriculture and
Technology at Morrisville *A*

North Carolina
Catawba Valley Community
College *C, A*

Gay/lesbian studies

California
City College of San Francisco *A*
Claremont McKenna College *B*

New York
Cornell University *B, M, D*
Hobart and William Smith Colleges *B*
Sarah Lawrence College *B*

Ohio
Denison University *B*

Vermont
Bennington College *B*

Gene therapy

Connecticut
University of Connecticut *B*

Genetic counseling

California
University of California
Irvine *M*

Illinois
Northwestern University *M*

Indiana
Martin University *B*

Maryland
University of Maryland
Baltimore *M*

Michigan
Wayne State University *M*

Ohio
Case Western Reserve University *M*

Oklahoma
University of Oklahoma *M*

Pennsylvania
Arcadia University *M*

South Carolina
University of South Carolina *M*

Utah
University of Utah *M*

Virginia
Virginia Commonwealth University *M*

Genetics

Arizona
University of Arizona *M, D*

California
California Institute of Technology *D*
Stanford University *M, D*
University of California
Davis *B, M, D*
Irvine *B*
Riverside *D*

Connecticut
Yale University *M, D*

District of Columbia
George Washington University *M, D*
Howard University *M, D*

Georgia
University of Georgia *B, M, D*

Illinois
University of Chicago *D*

Indiana
Indiana University
Bloomington *D*

Iowa
Iowa State University *B, M, D*
University of Iowa *D*

Kansas
Kansas State University *M, D*

Louisiana
Tulane University *M, D*

Maryland
University of Maryland
Baltimore *M, D*

Massachusetts
Simon's Rock College of Bard *B*
Tufts University *M, D*

Michigan
Michigan State University *M, D*

Minnesota
Minnesota State University
Mankato *B*
University of Minnesota
Twin Cities *M, D*

Mississippi
Mississippi State University *M*

Missouri
Missouri Southern State University *B*
University of Missouri
Columbia *D*
Washington University in St. Louis *D*

New Hampshire
Dartmouth College *B, M, D*
University of New Hampshire *M, D*

New Jersey
Rutgers, The State University of New
Jersey
New Brunswick/Piscataway
Campus *B*

New York
State University of New York
College of Environmental Science
and Forestry *B, M, D*
Stony Brook *D*
University of Rochester *M, D*
Yeshiva University *M, D*

North Carolina
North Carolina State University *M, D*
University of North Carolina
Chapel Hill *M, D*

North Dakota
North Dakota State University *M, D*

Ohio
Ohio State University
Columbus Campus *B, M, D*
Ohio Wesleyan University *B*

Oregon
Oregon State University *M, D*
University of Oregon *M, D*

Pennsylvania
Cedar Crest College *B*
Penn State
University Park *M, D*

South Carolina
Clemson University *B, M, D*

Texas
Texas A&M University *B, M, D*

Utah
Dixie State College of Utah *A*

Vermont
Marlboro College *B*

Washington
University of Washington *M, D*

West Virginia
Concord University *B*
West Virginia University *M, D*

Wisconsin
Lawrence University *B*
Marquette University *M, D*
University of Wisconsin
Madison *B, M, D*

Geochemistry

Arizona
Northern Arizona University *B*

California
California Institute of
Technology *B, D*
Pomona College *B*
San Diego State University *B*
San Francisco State University *B*
University of California
Los Angeles *B, M, D*

Colorado
Colorado School of Mines *M, D*

Maine
Bowdoin College *B*
University of Maine
Farmington *B*

Massachusetts
Bridgewater State College *B*
Harvard College *B*

Michigan
Grand Valley State University *B*
Hope College *B*
Western Michigan University *B*

Missouri
University of Missouri
Rolla *B, M, D*

Montana
Montana Tech of the University of
Montana *M*

Nevada
University of Nevada
Reno *M, D*

New Mexico
New Mexico Institute of Mining and
Technology *M, D*

New York
Columbia University
Columbia College *B*
School of General Studies *B*
State University of New York
Albany *M, D*
College at Cortland *B*
College at Fredonia *B*
College at Geneseo *B*
Oswego *B*

Rhode Island
Brown University *B*

Utah
Snow College *A*

Geography

Alabama
Auburn University *B*
Jacksonville State University *B*
Samford University *B*
University of Alabama *B, M*
University of North Alabama *B*
University of South Alabama *B*

Alaska
University of Alaska
Fairbanks *B*

Arizona
Arizona State University *B, M, D*
Northern Arizona University *B, M, T*
University of Arizona *B, M, D*

Arkansas
Arkansas State University *B*
University of Arkansas *B, M*
University of Central Arkansas *B*

California
Bakersfield College *A*
Cabrillo College *A*
California State Polytechnic
University: Pomona *B*
California State University
Chico *B, M*
Dominguez Hills *B*
East Bay *B, M*
Fresno *B, M*
Fullerton *B, M*
Long Beach *B, M*
Los Angeles *B, M*
Northridge *B*
Sacramento *B*
San Bernardino *B*
Stanislaus *B*
Canada College *A*
Cerritos Community College *A*

Chabot College *A*
Chaffey College *A*
College of Alameda *A*
College of the Desert *A*
Contra Costa College *A*
Crafton Hills College *A*
Cypress College *A*
De Anza College *A*
East Los Angeles College *A*
El Camino College *A*
Foothill College *A*
Fresno City College *A*
Fullerton College *A*
Gavilan Community College *A*
Grossmont Community College *A*
Humboldt State University *B*
Irvine Valley College *A*
Los Angeles Pierce College *C*
Los Angeles Southwest College *A*
Los Angeles Valley College *A*
Merced College *A*
MiraCosta College *A*
Ohlone College *C*
Orange Coast College *A*
Saddleback College *A*
San Bernardino Valley College *A*
San Diego City College *A*
San Diego Miramar College *A*
San Diego State University *B, M, D*
San Francisco State University *B, M*
San Jose State University *B, M*
Santa Ana College *A*
Santa Barbara City College *A*
Santa Rosa Junior College *A*
Santiago Canyon College *A*
Sonoma State University *B*
Southwestern College *A*
University of California
   Berkeley *B, D*
   Davis *M, D*
   Los Angeles *B, M, D*
   Riverside *B*
   Santa Barbara *B, M, D*
University of Southern
   California *B, M, D*
Ventura College *A*
West Hills Community College *A*
West Los Angeles College *C, A*

Colorado

United States Air Force Academy *B*
University of Colorado
   Boulder *B, M, D*
   Colorado Springs *B, M*
   Denver and Health Sciences
     Center *B*
University of Denver *B, M, D*
University of Northern Colorado *B, T*

Connecticut

Central Connecticut State
   University *B, M*
Southern Connecticut State
   University *B*
University of Connecticut *B, M, D*

Delaware

University of Delaware *B, M*

District of Columbia

George Washington University *B, M*
University of the District of
   Columbia *B*

Florida

Broward Community College *A*
Florida Atlantic University *B, M*
Florida International University *B*
Florida State University *B, M, D*
Jacksonville University *B*
Palm Beach Community College *A*
Stetson University *B*
University of Florida *B, M, D*

University of Miami *B, M*
University of South Florida *B, M*

Georgia

Dalton State College *A*
Darton College *A*
Georgia Southern University *B*
Georgia State University *B, M*
University of Georgia *B, M, D*
University of West Georgia *B, M*

Hawaii

University of Hawaii
   Hilo *B*
   Manoa *B, M, D*

Idaho

College of Southern Idaho *A*
University of Idaho *B, M, D*

Illinois

Augustana College *B, T*
Chicago State University *B, M, T*
Concordia University *B*
DePaul University *B, T*
Eastern Illinois University *B*
Elmhurst College *B, T*
Illinois State University *B, T*
Northeastern Illinois University *B, M*
Northern Illinois University *B, M*
Northwestern University *B*
Richland Community College *A*
Roosevelt University *B*
South Suburban College of Cook
   County *A*
Southern Illinois University
   Carbondale *B, M, D*
Southern Illinois University
   Edwardsville *B, M*
Southwestern Illinois College *A*
Triton College *A*
University of Chicago *B, D*
University of Illinois
   Chicago *M*
   Urbana-Champaign *B, M, D*
Western Illinois University *B, M*

Indiana

Ball State University *B, M*
Indiana State University *B, M, D, T*
Indiana University
   Bloomington *B, M, D*
   Southeast *B*
Indiana University-Purdue University
   Indianapolis *C, B, M*
Taylor University *B*
Valparaiso University *B*
Vincennes University *A*

Iowa

Graceland University *T*
North Iowa Area Community
   College *A*
University of Iowa *B, M, D, T*
University of Northern Iowa *B, M*

Kansas

Allen County Community College *A*
Kansas State University *C, B, M, D*
Pittsburg State University *B*
University of Kansas *B, M, D*

Kentucky

Eastern Kentucky University *B*
Morehead State University *B*
Northern Kentucky University *B*
University of Kentucky *B, M, D*
University of Louisville *B*
Western Kentucky University *B, M*

Louisiana

Louisiana State University
   Shreveport *B*
Louisiana State University and
   Agricultural and Mechanical
   College *B, M, D*
Louisiana Tech University *B*
University of New Orleans *B, M*

Maine

University of Maine
   Farmington *B*
University of Southern Maine *B*

Maryland

Community College of Baltimore
   County *A*
Frostburg State University *B*
Johns Hopkins University *B, M, D*
Salisbury University *B, T*
Towson University *B, M*
University of Maryland
   Baltimore County *B*
   College Park *B, M, D*

Massachusetts

Boston University *B, M, D*
Bridgewater State College *B*
Clark University *B, M, D*
Fitchburg State College *B*
Framingham State College *B*
Holyoke Community College *C, A*
Mount Holyoke College *B*
Salem State College *B, M*
University of Massachusetts
   Amherst *B, M*
   Boston *C, B*
Worcester State College *B*

Michigan

Aquinas College *B, T*
Calvin College *B, T*
Central Michigan University *B, T*
Delta College *A*
Eastern Michigan University *B, M*
Grand Valley State University *B*
Lake Michigan College *A*
Lansing Community College *A*
Michigan State University *B, M, D*
Northern Michigan University *B, T*
Olivet College *B*
University of Michigan *B*
Wayne State University *B, M*
Western Michigan University *B, M*

Minnesota

Bemidji State University *B*
Gustavus Adolphus College *B*
Itasca Community College *A*
Macalester College *B*
Minnesota State University
   Mankato *B, M, T*
St. Cloud State University *B, M*
University of Minnesota
   Duluth *B*
   Twin Cities *B, M, D*
University of St. Thomas *B*
Vermilion Community College *A*
Winona State University *A*

Mississippi

University of Southern
   Mississippi *B, M*

Missouri

Central Missouri State University *B*
Missouri State University *B*
Northwest Missouri State
   University *B*
Park University *B*
Southeast Missouri State University *B*
Three Rivers Community College *A*

University of Missouri
   Columbia *B, M*
   Kansas City *B*

Montana

Montana State University
   Billings *T*
University of Montana: Missoula *B, M*

Nebraska

Concordia University *B, T*
University of Nebraska
   Kearney *B, T*
   Lincoln *B, M, D*
   Omaha *B, M*
Wayne State College *B, T*
Western Nebraska Community
   College *A*

Nevada

University of Nevada
   Reno *B, M*

New Hampshire

Dartmouth College *B*
Keene State College *B*
Plymouth State University *B*
University of New Hampshire *B*

New Jersey

Bergen Community College *C*
Montclair State University *B*
Rowan University *B*
Rutgers, The State University of New
   Jersey
   New Brunswick/Piscataway
     Campus *B, M, D*
William Paterson University of New
   Jersey *B*

New Mexico

New Mexico State University *B, M*
University of New Mexico *B, M*

New York

Barnard College *B*
City University of New York
   Hunter College *B, M*
   Lehman College *B*
Colgate University *B*
Erie Community College
   City Campus *C*
   North Campus *C*
   South Campus *C*
Excelsior College *B*
Hofstra University *B*
Long Island University
   C.W. Post Campus *B*
State University of New York
   Albany *B, M*
   Binghamton *B, M*
   Buffalo *B, M, D*
   College at Buffalo *B*
   College at Cortland *B*
   College at Geneseo *B, T*
   College at Oneonta *B*
   College at Plattsburgh *B*
   New Paltz *B*
Syracuse University *B, M, D*
United States Military Academy *B*
Vassar College *B*

North Carolina

Appalachian State University *B, M*
East Carolina University *B, M*
Fayetteville State University *B*
North Carolina Central University *B*
North Carolina State University *B*
University of North Carolina
   Chapel Hill *B, M, D*
   Charlotte *B, M*

Greensboro *B, M, T*
Wilmington *B*
Western Carolina University *B*

North Dakota

Minot State University *B*
University of North Dakota *B, M, T*

Ohio

Bowling Green State University *B*
Kent State University *B, M, D*
Miami University
Oxford Campus *B, M*
Ohio State University
Columbus Campus *B, M, D*
Ohio University *B, M*
Ohio Wesleyan University *B*
Sinclair Community College *A*
University of Akron *B, M*
University of Cincinnati *B, M, D, T*
University of Toledo *B, M*
Wittenberg University *B*
Wright State University *A, B*
Youngstown State University *B*

Oklahoma

Northeastern State University *B*
Oklahoma State University *B, M, D*
Tulsa Community College *A*
University of Central Oklahoma *B*
University of Oklahoma *B, M, D*

Oregon

Central Oregon Community
College *A*
Chemeketa Community College *A*
Linn-Benton Community College *A*
Oregon State University *B, M, D*
Portland State University *B, M*
Southern Oregon University *B*
University of Oregon *B, M, D*
Western Oregon University *B*

Pennsylvania

Bloomsburg University of
Pennsylvania *B*
Bucknell University *B*
California University of
Pennsylvania *B, M*
Cheyney University of Pennsylvania *B*
Clarion University of Pennsylvania *B*
East Stroudsburg University of
Pennsylvania *B*
Edinboro University of
Pennsylvania *B*
Indiana University of
Pennsylvania *B, M*
Kutztown University of
Pennsylvania *B*
Lock Haven University of
Pennsylvania *B, T*
Mansfield University of
Pennsylvania *A, B, T*
Millersville University of
Pennsylvania *B, T*
Penn State
Abington *B*
Altoona *B*
Beaver *B*
Berks *B*
Delaware County *B*
Dubois *B*
Fayette *B*
Hazleton *B*
Lehigh Valley *B*
McKeesport *B*
Mont Alto *B*
New Kensington *B*
Shenango *B*
University Park *B, M, D*
Wilkes-Barre *B*
Worthington Scranton *B*

Shippensburg University of
Pennsylvania *B, T*
Slippery Rock University of
Pennsylvania *B*
Temple University *B, M*
University of Pittsburgh *C, M*
University of Pittsburgh
Johnstown *B*
Villanova University *B*
West Chester University of
Pennsylvania *C, B, M*

Puerto Rico

University of Puerto Rico
Rio Piedras *B*

Rhode Island

Rhode Island College *B*

South Carolina

University of South Carolina *B, M, D*

South Dakota

South Dakota State University *B, M, T*

Tennessee

Columbia State Community College *A*
East Tennessee State University *B, T*
Southwest Tennessee Community
College *A*
University of Memphis *B*
University of Tennessee
Knoxville *B, M, D*

Texas

Austin Community College *A*
Baylor University *B*
Del Mar College *A*
Galveston College *A*
Sam Houston State University *B*
Stephen F. Austin State University *B, T*
Texas A&M University *B, M, D*
Texas A&M University
Commerce *B, M*
Texas State University: San
Marcos *B, M, D, T*
Texas Tech University *B*
University of Houston
Clear Lake *B*
University of North Texas *B, M*
University of Texas
Austin *B, M, D*
Dallas *B, M, D*
San Antonio *B*
West Texas A&M University *B*
Western Texas College *A*

Utah

Brigham Young University *B, M*
Salt Lake Community College *A*
Snow College *A*
University of Utah *C, B, M, D*
Utah State University *B, M*
Weber State University *B*

Vermont

Middlebury College *B*
University of Vermont *B, M*

Virginia

Emory & Henry College *B*
George Mason University *B, M*
James Madison University *B, T*
Longwood University *T*
Old Dominion University *B, T*
Radford University *B*
University of Mary Washington *B*
Virginia Polytechnic Institute and
State University *B, M*

Washington

Central Washington University *B*

Eastern Washington University *B*
Everett Community College *A*
Highline Community College *A*
University of Washington *B, M, D*
Western Washington University *B, M*

West Virginia

Concord University *B*
Marshall University *B, M*
West Virginia University *B, M, D*

Wisconsin

Carthage College *B, T*
University of Wisconsin
Eau Claire *B*
La Crosse *B, T*
Madison *B, M, D*
Milwaukee *B, M, D*
Oshkosh *B*
Parkside *B, T*
Platteville *B, T*
River Falls *B, T*
Stevens Point *B, T*
Whitewater *B, T*

Wyoming

University of Wyoming *B, M*
Western Wyoming Community
College *A*

Geography teacher education

California

Stanford University *M, T*

Delaware

University of Delaware *B, T*

Illinois

University of Illinois
Urbana-Champaign *M*

Indiana

Valparaiso University *B*

Iowa

University of Iowa *T*

Kentucky

Eastern Kentucky University *B*

Massachusetts

Framingham State College *B*

Michigan

Northern Michigan University *B, T*
Western Michigan University *B, T*

Minnesota

University of Minnesota
Morris *T*
Vermilion Community College *A*

Nebraska

Concordia University *B, T*
Wayne State College *B, T*

New York

City University of New York
Hunter College *B, T*

North Dakota

Mayville State University *B, T*

Ohio

Kent State University *T*
University of Findlay *B, M, T*

Tennessee

University of Tennessee
Martin *B*

Texas

McMurry University *T*
West Texas A&M University *T*

Utah

University of Utah *B*

Virginia

Old Dominion University *B, T*

Wisconsin

Carroll College *B, T*

Geological engineering

Alaska

University of Alaska
Fairbanks *B, M*

Arizona

University of Arizona *B*

California

University of California
Berkeley *B*
Los Angeles *B*

Colorado

Colorado School of Mines *B, M, D*

Idaho

University of Idaho *B, M*

Michigan

Michigan Technological
University *B, M, D, T*
University of Michigan *M*

Minnesota

University of Minnesota
Twin Cities *B, M, D*

Mississippi

University of Mississippi *B*

Missouri

East Central College *A*
University of Missouri
Rolla *B, M, D*

Montana

Montana Tech of the University of
Montana *B, M*

Nevada

University of Nevada
Reno *B, M, D*

New Jersey

New Jersey Institute of Technology *B*

New York

Columbia University
Fu Foundation School of
Engineering and Applied
Science *B, M, D*
Cornell University *M*

Oklahoma

University of Oklahoma *M, D*

Pennsylvania

Drexel University *M*
University of Pennsylvania *M*

South Dakota

South Dakota School of Mines and
    Technology *B, M, D*

Utah

University of Utah *B, M, D*

Wisconsin

University of Wisconsin
    Madison *B, M, D*

Geology/earth science

Alabama

Auburn University *B, M*
University of Alabama *B, M, D*
University of North Alabama *B*
University of South Alabama *B*

Alaska

University of Alaska
    Fairbanks *B, M, D*

Arizona

Arizona State University *B, M, D*
Arizona Western College *A*
Eastern Arizona College *A*
Northern Arizona University *B, M*
Prescott College *B, M*
University of Arizona *B, M, D*

Arkansas

Arkansas Tech University *B*
University of Arkansas *B, M*
University of Arkansas
    Little Rock *B*

California

Bakersfield College *A*
California Institute of
    Technology *B, D*
California Lutheran University *B*
California State Polytechnic
    University: Pomona *B*
California State University
    Bakersfield *B, M*
    Chico *B, M*
    Dominguez Hills *B*
    East Bay *B, M*
    Fresno *B, M*
    Fullerton *B, M*
    Long Beach *B, M*
    Los Angeles *B, M*
    Northridge *B, M*
    Sacramento *B, M*
    San Bernardino *B*
    Stanislaus *B*
Cerritos Community College *A*
Chaffey College *A*
College of San Mateo *A*
College of the Desert *A*
College of the Siskiyous *A*
Crafton Hills College *A*
Cypress College *A*
De Anza College *A*
East Los Angeles College *A*
El Camino College *A*
Foothill College *A*
Fullerton College *A*
Gavilan Community College *A*
Golden West College *A*
Grossmont Community College *A*
Humboldt State University *B, M*
Irvine Valley College *A*
Loma Linda University *B, M*
Los Angeles Southwest College *A*
Los Angeles Valley College *A*
MiraCosta College *A*
Moorpark College *A*
National University *B*
Occidental College *B*
Ohlone College *C*

Orange Coast College *A*
Palomar College *A*
Pomona College *B*
Saddleback College *A*
San Bernardino Valley College *A*
San Diego City College *A*
San Diego State University *B, D*
San Francisco State University *B, M*
San Joaquin Delta College *A*
San Jose State University *B, M*
Santa Ana College *A*
Santa Barbara City College *A*
Santa Monica College *A*
Santiago Canyon College *A*
Scripps College *B*
Sierra College *A*
Sonoma State University *B*
Southwestern College *A*
Stanford University *B, M, D*
University of California
    Berkeley *B, M, D*
    Davis *B, M, D*
    Irvine *B, M, D*
    Los Angeles *B, M, D*
    Riverside *B, M, D*
    Santa Barbara *B, M, D*
    Santa Cruz *B, D*
University of California: Merced *B*
University of Southern
    California *B, M, D*
University of the Pacific *B*
Ventura College *A*
West Hills Community College *A*
West Los Angeles College *C, A*
West Valley College *A*

Colorado

Adams State College *B*
Colorado College *B*
Colorado Mountain College
    Spring Valley Campus *A*
Colorado School of Mines *M, D*
Colorado State University *B, M, D*
Fort Lewis College *B*
Red Rocks Community College *A*
University of Colorado
    Boulder *B, M, D*
University of Northern
    Colorado *B, M, T*
Western State College of
    Colorado *B, T*

Connecticut

Central Connecticut State
    University *B*
University of Connecticut *B, M, D*
Wesleyan University *B*
Yale University *B, M, D*

Delaware

University of Delaware *B, M, D*

District of Columbia

George Washington
    University *B, M, D*

Florida

Florida Atlantic University *B, M*
Florida International
    University *B, M, D*
Florida State University *B, M, D*
Gulf Coast Community College *A*
Miami Dade College *A*
Okaloosa-Walton College *A*
Pensacola Junior College *A*
University of Florida *B, M, D*
University of Miami *B, M*
University of South Florida *B, M, D*

Georgia

Columbus State University *B*
East Georgia College *A*
Gainesville State College *A*

Georgia Institute of
    Technology *B, M, D*
Georgia Perimeter College *A*
Georgia Southern University *B*
Georgia Southwestern State
    University *B*
Georgia State University *B, M*
Middle Georgia College *A*
University of Georgia *B, M, D*
University of West Georgia *B*

Hawaii

University of Hawaii
    Hilo *B*
    Manoa *B, M, D*

Idaho

Boise State University *B, M*
Brigham Young University-Idaho *B*
College of Southern Idaho *A*
Idaho State University *A, B, M*
North Idaho College *A*
University of Idaho *B, M, D*

Illinois

Augustana College *B, T*
Bradley University *B, T*
Eastern Illinois University *B*
Highland Community College *A*
Illinois Central College *A*
Illinois State University *B*
Illinois Valley Community College *A*
Northeastern Illinois University *B*
Northern Illinois University *B, M, D*
Northwestern University *B, M, D*
Olivet Nazarene University *B*
South Suburban College of Cook
    County *A*
Southern Illinois University
    Carbondale *B, M*
Triton College *A*
University of Illinois
    Chicago *B, M, D*
    Urbana-Champaign *B, M, D*
Western Illinois University *B*
Wheaton College *B, T*

Indiana

Ball State University *B, M, T*
DePauw University *B*
Earlham College *B*
Hanover College *B*
Indiana State University *B, M*
Indiana University
    Bloomington *B, M, D*
    Northwest *A, B*
Indiana University-Purdue University
    Fort Wayne *B*
Indiana University-Purdue University
    Indianapolis *B, M*
Purdue University *B, M, D*
University of Indianapolis *B*
University of Notre Dame *B*
University of Southern Indiana *B*
Valparaiso University *B*
Vincennes University *A*

Iowa

Cornell College *B, T*
Iowa State University *B, M, D*
University of Iowa *B, M, D, T*
University of Northern Iowa *B*

Kansas

Emporia State University *B, T*
Fort Hays State University *B, M*
Kansas State University *B, M*
University of Kansas *B, M, D*
Wichita State University *B*

Kentucky

Eastern Kentucky University *B, M*
Morehead State University *B*

Murray State University *B, T*
Northern Kentucky University *B*
University of Kentucky *B, M, D*
Western Kentucky University *B*

Louisiana

Centenary College of Louisiana *B*
Louisiana State University and
    Agricultural and Mechanical
    College *B, M, D*
Louisiana Tech University *B*
Tulane University *B, M, D*
University of Louisiana at
    Lafayette *B, M*
University of Louisiana at Monroe *M*
University of New Orleans *B, M*

Maine

Bates College *B*
Bowdoin College *B*
Colby College *B*
University of Maine *B, M, D*
University of Maine
    Presque Isle *B*
University of Southern Maine *B*

Maryland

Johns Hopkins University *B, M, D*
Salisbury University *B*
Towson University *B*
University of Maryland
    College Park *B, M, D*

Massachusetts

Amherst College *B*
Boston College *B, M*
Boston University *B, M, D*
Bridgewater State College *B*
Hampshire College *B*
Harvard College *B, D*
Massachusetts Institute of
    Technology *B, M, D*
Mount Holyoke College *B*
Northeastern University *B*
Salem State College *B*
Smith College *B*
Tufts University *B*
University of Massachusetts
    Amherst *B, M, D*
Wellesley College *B*
Williams College *B*

Michigan

Albion College *B, T*
Calvin College *B, T*
Central Michigan University *B, M, T*
Delta College *A*
Eastern Michigan University *B*
Grand Valley State University *B*
Hope College *B*
Lake Michigan College *A*
Lake Superior State University *B, T*
Michigan State University *B, M, D*
Michigan Technological
    University *B, M, D, T*
University of Michigan *B, M, D, T*
Wayne State University *B, M*
Western Michigan University *B, M, D*

Minnesota

Bemidji State University *B*
Carleton College *B*
Gustavus Adolphus College *B*
Macalester College *B, T*
Ridgewater College *A*
St. Cloud State University *B*
University of Minnesota
    Duluth *B, M*
    Morris *B*
    Twin Cities *B, M, D*
University of St. Thomas *B*
Vermilion Community College *A*
Winona State University *B*

Mississippi

Hinds Community College *A*
Itawamba Community College *A*
Millsaps College *B*
Mississippi State University *B, M*
University of Mississippi *B*
University of Southern
    Mississippi *B, M*

Missouri

Central Missouri State University *B*
Missouri State University *B*
Northwest Missouri State
    University *B*
St. Louis University *B, M*
Southeast Missouri State University *B*
University of Missouri
    Columbia *B, M, D*
    Kansas City *B, M, D*
    Rolla *B, M, D*
Washington University in St.
    Louis *B, M, D*

Montana

Montana Tech of the University of
    Montana *M*
Rocky Mountain College *B*
University of Montana:
    Missoula *B, M, D*
University of Montana: Western *B*

Nebraska

University of Nebraska
    Lincoln *B, M, D*
    Omaha *B*

Nevada

Great Basin College *A*
University of Nevada
    Las Vegas *B, M, D*
    Reno *B, M, D*

New Hampshire

Dartmouth College *M, D*
Keene State College *B*
University of New Hampshire *B, M, D*

New Jersey

Kean University *B, T*
Montclair State University *B, M, T*
New Jersey City University *B*
Princeton University *B, M, D*
Richard Stockton College of New
    Jersey *B*
Rutgers, The State University of New
    Jersey
    New Brunswick/Piscataway
        Campus *B, M, D*
    Newark Regional Campus *B*

New Mexico

Eastern New Mexico University *B*
New Mexico Highlands University *B*
New Mexico Institute of Mining and
    Technology *B, M, D*
New Mexico State University *B, M*
San Juan College *A*
University of New Mexico *B, M, D*

New York

Adirondack Community College *A*
Alfred University *B*
Barnard College *B*
Cayuga County Community College *A*
City University of New York
    Brooklyn College *B, M*
    City College *B, M, D*
    Lehman College *B*
    Queens College *B, M, T*
    York College *B*
Colgate University *B*

Columbia University
    Columbia College *B*
    School of General Studies *B*
Concordia College *B*
Cornell University *B, M, D*
Excelsior College *B*
Hamilton College *B*
Hartwick College *B*
Hobart and William Smith Colleges *B*
Hofstra University *B*
Long Island University
    C.W. Post Campus *B*
Pace University *B*
Rensselaer Polytechnic
    Institute *B, M, D*
St. Lawrence University *B, T*
Sarah Lawrence College *B*
Skidmore College *B*
State University of New York
    Albany *B, M, D*
    Binghamton *B, M, D*
    Buffalo *B, M, D*
    College at Brockport *B*
    College at Buffalo *B*
    College at Cortland *B*
    College at Fredonia *B, T*
    College at Geneseo *B, T*
    College at Oneonta *B, M*
    College at Plattsburgh *B*
    College at Potsdam *B*
    New Paltz *B, M, T*
    Oswego *B*
    Stony Brook *B, M, D*
Suffolk County Community College *A*
Syracuse University *B, M, D*
Union College *B*
University of Rochester *B, M, D*
Vassar College *B*

North Carolina

Appalachian State University *B*
Duke University *B, M, D*
East Carolina University *B, M*
Elizabeth City State University *B*
Guilford College *B*
North Carolina Central University *M*
North Carolina State University *B*
University of North Carolina
    Chapel Hill *B, M, D*
    Charlotte *B, M*
    Wilmington *B, M*
Western Carolina University *B*

North Dakota

Minot State University *B*
North Dakota State University *B, T*
University of North Dakota *B, M, D, T*

Ohio

Antioch College *B*
Ashland University *B*
Bowling Green State University *B, M*
Case Western Reserve
    University *B, M, D*
Central State University *B*
Cleveland State University *B*
College of Wooster *B*
Denison University *B*
Kent State University *B, M, D*
Marietta College *B*
Miami University
    Oxford Campus *B, M, D*
Mount Union College *B*
Muskingum College *B*
Oberlin College *B*
Ohio State University
    Columbus Campus *B, M, D*
Ohio University *B, M*
Ohio Wesleyan University *B*
Sinclair Community College *A*
University of Akron *B, M*
University of Cincinnati *B, M, D, T*
University of Dayton *B*
University of Toledo *B, M*

Wilmington College *B*
Wittenberg University *B*
Wright State University *B, M*
Youngstown State University *B*

Oklahoma

Oklahoma State University *B, M*
Rose State College *A*
Tulsa Community College *A*
University of Oklahoma *B, M, D*
University of Tulsa *B, M, D*

Oregon

Central Oregon Community
    College *A*
Chemeketa Community College *A*
Oregon State University *B, M, D*
Portland State University *B, M*
Southern Oregon University *B*
Treasure Valley Community College *A*
University of Oregon *B, M, D*
Western Oregon University *B*

Pennsylvania

Allegheny College *B*
Bloomsburg University of
    Pennsylvania *B, T*
Bryn Mawr College *B, M, D*
Bucknell University *B*
California University of
    Pennsylvania *B, M*
Clarion University of Pennsylvania *B*
Dickinson College *B*
East Stroudsburg University of
    Pennsylvania *B, T*
Edinboro University of
    Pennsylvania *B*
Franklin & Marshall College *B*
Haverford College *B*
Indiana University of Pennsylvania *B*
Juniata College *B*
Kutztown University of
    Pennsylvania *B, T*
La Salle University *B*
Lafayette College *B*
Lehigh University *B*
Lock Haven University of
    Pennsylvania *B, T*
Mansfield University of
    Pennsylvania *B*
Mercyhurst College *B*
Millersville University of
    Pennsylvania *B, M, T*
Penn State
    Abington *B*
    Altoona *B*
    Beaver *B*
    Berks *B*
    Delaware County *B*
    Dubois *B*
    Fayette *B*
    Hazleton *B*
    Lehigh Valley *B*
    McKeesport *B*
    Mont Alto *B*
    New Kensington *B*
    Schuylkill - Capital College *B*
    Shenango *B*
    University Park *B, M, D*
    Worthington Scranton *B*
    York *B*
Shippensburg University of
    Pennsylvania *B, T*
Slippery Rock University of
    Pennsylvania *B*
Temple University *B, M*
University of Pennsylvania *B, M, D*
University of Pittsburgh *B, M, D*
University of Pittsburgh
    Johnstown *B*
West Chester University of
    Pennsylvania *B, T*
Wilkes University *B*

Puerto Rico

University of Puerto Rico
    Mayaguez *B, M*

Rhode Island

Brown University *B, M, D*
University of Rhode Island *B*

South Carolina

Charleston Southern University *B*
Clemson University *B, M*
College of Charleston *B*
Furman University *B*
University of South Carolina *B, M, D*

South Dakota

South Dakota School of Mines and
    Technology *B, M, D*
University of South Dakota *B, M*

Tennessee

Austin Peay State University *B*
Middle Tennessee State
    University *C, B*
Tennessee Technological University *B*
University of Memphis *B*
University of Tennessee
    Chattanooga *B*
    Knoxville *B, M, D*
    Martin *B*
University of the South *B*
Vanderbilt University *B, M*

Texas

Amarillo College *A*
Austin Community College *A*
Baylor University *B, M, D*
Central Texas College *A*
Clarendon College *A*
Coastal Bend College *A*
Del Mar College *A*
El Paso Community College *A*
Galveston College *A*
Grayson County College *A*
Hardin-Simmons University *B*
Hill College *A*
Lamar University *B*
Laredo Community College *A*
Midland College *A*
Midwestern State University *B*
Odessa College *A*
Rice University *B, M, D*
St. Mary's University *B, T*
St. Philip's College *A*
Sam Houston State University *B*
San Jacinto College
    North *A*
South Plains College *A*
Southern Methodist
    University *B, M, D*
Stephen F. Austin State University *B, M*
Sul Ross State University *B, M*
Tarleton State University *B*
Texas A&M University *B, M, D*
Texas A&M University
    Commerce *B*
    Galveston *B*
    Kingsville *B, M, T*
Texas Christian University *B, M*
Texas Tech University *B, M, D*
Trinity University *B*
Tyler Junior College *A*
University of Houston *B, M, D*
University of Texas
    Arlington *B, M*
    Austin *B, M, D*
    Dallas *B, M, D*
    El Paso *B, M, D*
    San Antonio *B, M*
    of the Permian Basin *B, M*
West Texas A&M University *B*
Western Texas College *A*

Utah

Brigham Young University *B, M*
Dixie State College of Utah *A*
Salt Lake Community College *A*
Snow College *A*
Southern Utah University *B*
University of Utah *B, M, D*
Utah State University *B, M*
Utah Valley State College *A, B*
Weber State University *B*

Vermont

Castleton State College *B*
Middlebury College *B*
Norwich University *B*
University of Vermont *B, M*

Virginia

College of William and Mary *B*
George Mason University *B*
James Madison University *B*
Old Dominion University *B, M, T*
Radford University *B*
University of Mary Washington *B*
Virginia Polytechnic Institute and
   State University *B, M, D*
Virginia Wesleyan College *B*
Washington and Lee University *B*

Washington

Cascadia Community College *A*
Central Washington University *B, M*
Centralia College *A*
Eastern Washington University *B, T*
Everett Community College *A*
Highline Community College *A*
Olympic College *A*
Pacific Lutheran University *B*
University of Puget Sound *B, T*
University of Washington *B, M, D*
Washington State University *B, M, D*
Western Washington University *B, M*
Whitman College *B*

West Virginia

Concord University *B*
Marshall University *B*
Potomac State College of West Virginia
   University *A*
West Virginia University *B, M, D*

Wisconsin

Beloit College *B*
Lawrence University *B, T*
Northland College *B*
St. Norbert College *B, T*
University of Wisconsin
   Eau Claire *B*
   Madison *B, M, D*
   Milwaukee *B, M, D*
   Oshkosh *B*
   Parkside *B, T*
   River Falls *B*

Wyoming

Casper College *A*
University of Wyoming *B, M, D*
Western Wyoming Community
   College *A*

Geophysics/seismology

Alaska

University of Alaska
   Fairbanks *M, D*

California

California Institute of
   Technology *B, D*
California State University
   Northridge *B*
Occidental College *B*
San Diego State University *B, M*
San Francisco State University *B*
Stanford University *B, M, D*
University of California
   Berkeley *B*
   Los Angeles *B, M, D*
   Riverside *B, M, D*
   Santa Barbara *B, M*
   Santa Cruz *B, D*

Colorado

Colorado School of Mines *M, D*
University of Colorado
   Boulder *D*

Delaware

University of Delaware *B*

Idaho

Boise State University *B, M, D*
Idaho State University *M*
University of Idaho *M*

Illinois

Northwestern University *M, D*
University of Chicago *B, D*

Louisiana

University of New Orleans *B*

Maine

Bowdoin College *B*

Massachusetts

Boston College *B, M*
Boston University *B*
Harvard College *B, D*
Massachusetts Institute of
   Technology *M, D*

Michigan

Eastern Michigan University *B*
Hope College *B*
Michigan State University *B*
Michigan Technological
   University *B, M*
Western Michigan University *B*

Minnesota

University of Minnesota
   Twin Cities *B, M, D*

Missouri

St. Louis University *B, M, D*
University of Missouri
   Rolla *B, M, D*

Montana

Montana Tech of the University of
   Montana *M*

Nevada

University of Nevada
   Reno *B, M, D*

New Mexico

New Mexico Institute of Mining and
   Technology *B, M, D*

New York

Columbia University
   Columbia College *B*
   School of General Studies *B*
St. Lawrence University *B*
State University of New York
   College at Fredonia *B*
   College at Geneseo *B*

Ohio

Ohio State University
   Columbus Campus *B, M, D*
University of Akron *B, M*
Wright State University *M*

Oklahoma

University of Oklahoma *B, M, D*
University of Tulsa *B, M, D*

Oregon

Oregon State University *M, D*

Rhode Island

Brown University *B*

South Carolina

University of South Carolina *B*

Tennessee

University of Memphis *M, D*

Texas

Baylor University *B*
Rice University *B, M*
Southern Methodist
   University *B, M, D*
Texas A&M University *B, M, D*
Texas Tech University *B*
University of Houston *B*
University of Texas
   Austin *B*
   El Paso *B, M*

Utah

Snow College *A*
University of Utah *B, M, D*

Washington

University of Washington *M, D*
Western Washington University *B*

Wisconsin

Lawrence University *B*
University of Wisconsin
   Madison *B, M, D*

Wyoming

University of Wyoming *M, D*

Geotechnical engineering

Alaska

University of Alaska
   Fairbanks *B, M*

California

University of Southern California *M*

Illinois

University of Illinois
   Urbana-Champaign *B, M, D*

New Jersey

Stevens Institute of Technology *M*

German

Alabama

Auburn University *B*
Birmingham-Southern College *B, T*
Samford University *B*
University of Alabama *B, M*

Alaska

University of Alaska
   Anchorage *B*

Arizona

Arizona State University *B, M*
Northern Arizona University *B, T*
University of Arizona *B, M*

Arkansas

Black River Technical College *A*
Hendrix College *B*
University of Arkansas *B, M*
University of Arkansas
   Little Rock *B*
University of Central Arkansas *B*

California

Bakersfield College *A*
Cabrillo College *A*
California Lutheran University *B*
California State University
   Chico *A*
   Fullerton *B, M*
   Long Beach *B, M*
   Northridge *B*
Cerritos Community College *A*
Chabot College *A*
Chaffey College *A*
Citrus College *A*
Claremont McKenna College *B*
College of San Mateo *A*
College of the Canyons *A*
College of the Desert *A*
Cypress College *A*
De Anza College *A*
El Camino College *A*
Golden West College *A*
Grossmont Community College *A*
Humboldt State University *B*
Los Angeles City College *A*
Los Angeles Valley College *A*
Loyola Marymount University *B*
Merced College *A*
Mills College *B*
MiraCosta College *A*
Modesto Junior College *A*
Orange Coast College *A*
Pepperdine University *B*
Pitzer College *B*
Pomona College *B*
St. Mary's College of California *B*
San Diego State University *B*
San Francisco State University *B, M*
San Joaquin Delta College *A*
San Jose State University *B*
Scripps College *B*
Solano Community College *A*
Sonoma State University *B*
Stanford University *B, M, D*
University of California
   Berkeley *B, M, D*
   Davis *B, M, D*
   Irvine *B, M, D*
   Los Angeles *B*
   Riverside *B*
   San Diego *B, M*
   Santa Barbara *B, M, D*
   Santa Cruz *B*
University of La Verne *B*
University of Redlands *B*
University of Southern
   California *B, M, D*
University of the Pacific *B*
Ventura College *A*

Colorado

Colorado College *B*
Red Rocks Community College *A*
University of Colorado
   Boulder *B, M*
University of Denver *B*

Connecticut

Central Connecticut State
   University *B*
Connecticut College *B*
Fairfield University *B*
Southern Connecticut State
   University *B*

Trinity College *B*
University of Connecticut *B, M, D*
Wesleyan University *B*
Yale University *B, M, D*

Delaware

University of Delaware *B, M, T*

District of Columbia

American University *B*
Catholic University of America *B, M, T*
George Washington University *B*
Georgetown University *B, M, D*
Howard University *B*

Florida

Eckerd College *B*
Florida Atlantic University *B, M*
Florida International University *B*
Florida State University *B, M*
Manatee Community College *A*
New College of Florida *B*
Schiller International University *B*
Stetson University *B*
University of Florida *A, B, M*
University of Miami *B*
University of South Florida *B*
Valencia Community College *A*

Georgia

Agnes Scott College *B*
Berry College *B*
Clark Atlanta University *B*
Emory University *B*
Georgia Southern University *B*
Georgia State University *B, M*
Mercer University *B*
Morehouse College *B*
North Georgia College & State
　　University *B*
South Georgia College *A*
University of Georgia *B, M*
University of West Georgia *B*

Hawaii

University of Hawaii
　　Manoa *B, M*

Idaho

Boise State University *B*
Idaho State University *A, B*
University of Idaho *B, M*

Illinois

Augustana College *B, T*
Bradley University *B, T*
City Colleges of Chicago
　　Harold Washington College *A*
DePaul University *B*
Elmhurst College *B, T*
Illinois College *B, T*
Illinois State University *B, T*
Illinois Wesleyan University *B*
Knox College *B*
Loyola University of Chicago *B*
North Central College *B*
Northern Illinois University *B, M, T*
Northwestern University *B, M, D*
Principia College *B*
Richland Community College *A*
Sauk Valley Community College *A*
Southern Illinois University
　　Carbondale *B*
Southern Illinois University
　　Edwardsville *T*
University of Chicago *B*
University of Illinois
　　Chicago *B, M, D*
　　Urbana-Champaign *B, M, D*
Wheaton College *B*

Indiana

Ball State University *B, T*
Butler University *B*
DePauw University *B*
Earlham College *B*
Grace College *B*
Hanover College *B*
Indiana State University *B, T*
Indiana University
　　Bloomington *B, M, D*
　　South Bend *B*
　　Southeast *B*
Indiana University-Purdue University
　　Fort Wayne *A, B, T*
Indiana University-Purdue University
　　Indianapolis *B*
Manchester College *B, T*
University of Evansville *B*
University of Indianapolis *B*
University of Notre Dame *B, M*
University of Southern Indiana *B, T*
Valparaiso University *B*
Vincennes University *A*
Wabash College *B*

Iowa

Central College *B, T*
Coe College *B*
Cornell College *B, T*
Graceland University *B, T*
Grinnell College *B*
Iowa State University *B*
Luther College *B*
St. Ambrose University *B, T*
Simpson College *B*
University of Iowa *B, M, D, T*
University of Northern Iowa *B, M*
Wartburg College *B, T*

Kansas

Baker University *B, T*
Bethel College *B*
Kansas Wesleyan University *B*
Washburn University of Topeka *B*

Kentucky

Berea College *B, T*
Centre College *B*
Eastern Kentucky University *B*
Georgetown College *B, T*
Murray State University *B, T*
University of Kentucky *B, M*
Western Kentucky University *B, T*

Louisiana

Centenary College of Louisiana *B, T*
Dillard University *B*
Louisiana State University and
　　Agricultural and Mechanical
　　College *B*
Loyola University New Orleans *B*
Tulane University *B*

Maine

Bates College *B, T*
Bowdoin College *B*
Colby College *B*
University of Maine *B*

Maryland

Community College of Baltimore
　　County *A*
Hood College *B*
Johns Hopkins University *B, M, D*
Loyola College in Maryland *B*
McDaniel College *B*
Mount St. Mary's University *B*
Towson University *B, T*
University of Maryland
　　College Park *B, M, D*
Washington College *B, T*

Massachusetts

Amherst College *B*
Boston College *B*
Boston University *B*
Brandeis University *B*
College of the Holy Cross *B*
Gordon College *B*
Harvard College *B, M, D*
Northeastern University *B*
Simon's Rock College of Bard *B*
Smith College *B*
Suffolk University *B*
Tufts University *B, M*
University of Massachusetts
　　Amherst *B, M, D*
　　Boston *B*
Wellesley College *B*
Wheaton College *B*
Williams College *B*

Michigan

Adrian College *A, B, T*
Albion College *B, T*
Alma College *B, T*
Aquinas College *B, T*
Calvin College *B, T*
Central Michigan University *B, T*
Eastern Michigan University *B, M*
Grand Valley State University *B*
Hillsdale College *B*
Hope College *B*
Kalamazoo College *B, T*
Lansing Community College *A*
Michigan State University *B, M*
Oakland University *B, T*
University of Michigan *B, M, D*
Wayne State University *B, M*
Western Michigan University *B*

Minnesota

Augsburg College *B*
Bemidji State University *B*
Carleton College *B*
College of St. Benedict *B*
Concordia College: Moorhead *B, T*
Gustavus Adolphus College *B*
Hamline University *B*
Minnesota State University
　　Mankato *B, M, T*
St. Cloud State University *B*
St. John's University *B*
St. Olaf College *B*
University of Minnesota
　　Duluth *B, T*
　　Morris *B*
　　Twin Cities *B, M, D*
University of St. Thomas *B*
Winona State University *B*

Mississippi

Millsaps College *B, T*
University of Mississippi *B, M*

Missouri

Central Missouri State University *B, T*
Drury University *B, T*
Missouri Southern State University *B*
Missouri State University *B*
Missouri Western State University *T*
St. Louis University *B*
Southeast Missouri State University *B*
Truman State University *B*
University of Missouri
　　Columbia *B, M*
　　Kansas City *B*
　　St. Louis *B*
Washington University in St.
　　Louis *B, M, D*
Webster University *B*

Montana

University of Montana: Missoula *B, M*

Nebraska

Creighton University *B*
Dana College *B*
Doane College *B*
Hastings College *B*
Nebraska Wesleyan University *B*
Union College *B*
University of Nebraska
　　Kearney *B, M, T*
　　Lincoln *B*
　　Omaha *B*
Western Nebraska Community
　　College *A*

Nevada

University of Nevada
　　Las Vegas *B*
　　Reno *B*

New Hampshire

Dartmouth College *B*
University of New Hampshire *B*

New Jersey

Drew University *B*
Princeton University *B, M, D*
Rider University *B*
Rutgers, The State University of New
　　Jersey
　　Camden Regional Campus *B, T*
　　New Brunswick/Piscataway
　　　　Campus *B, M, D, T*
Seton Hall University *T*

New Mexico

University of New Mexico *B, M*

New York

Alfred University *B*
Bard College *B*
Barnard College *B*
City University of New York
　　Hunter College *B*
　　Lehman College *B*
　　Queens College *B, T*
Colgate University *B*
Columbia University
　　Columbia College *B*
　　School of General Studies *B*
Cornell University *B, M, D*
Fordham University *B*
Hamilton College *B*
Hartwick College *B, T*
Hofstra University *B*
Ithaca College *B, T*
Nazareth College of Rochester *B*
New York University *B, M, D*
Orange County Community College *A*
Rensselaer Polytechnic Institute *B*
St. Lawrence University *B, T*
Sarah Lawrence College *B*
Skidmore College *B*
State University of New York
　　Binghamton *B*
　　Buffalo *B, M, D*
　　New Paltz *B, T*
　　Oswego *B*
　　Stony Brook *B, M*
Syracuse University *B, M*
United States Military Academy *B*
University of Rochester *B, M*
Vassar College *B*
Wells College *B*

North Carolina

Davidson College *B*
Duke University *B, M*
East Carolina University *B*
Guilford College *B, T*
Lenoir-Rhyne College *B*
Methodist College *A*
Salem College *B*

University of North Carolina
Asheville *B, T*
Chapel Hill *B, M, D*
Charlotte *B*
Greensboro *B, T*
Wake Forest University *B*
Western Carolina University *B*

North Dakota

Jamestown College *B*
Minot State University *B*
University of North Dakota *B, T*

Ohio

Antioch College *B*
Baldwin-Wallace College *B, T*
Bowling Green State University *B, M*
Case Western Reserve University *B*
Cleveland State University *B*
College of Wooster *B*
Denison University *B*
Franciscan University of
    Steubenville *B*
Heidelberg College *B*
Hiram College *B, T*
John Carroll University *B*
Kent State University *B, M*
Kenyon College *B*
Lake Erie College *B*
Miami University
    Oxford Campus *B, T*
Mount Union College *B*
Muskingum College *B*
Oberlin College *B*
Ohio Northern University *B*
Ohio State University
    Columbus Campus *B, M, D*
Ohio University *B, M*
Ohio Wesleyan University *B*
University of Akron *M*
University of Cincinnati *B, T*
University of Dayton *B*
University of Toledo *B, M*
Wittenberg University *B*
Wright State University *B*
Xavier University *A, B*
Youngstown State University *B*

Oklahoma

Oklahoma Baptist University *B, T*
Oklahoma City University *B*
Oklahoma State University *B*
Oral Roberts University *B*
Tulsa Community College *A*
University of Central Oklahoma *B*
University of Tulsa *B*

Oregon

Lewis & Clark College *B*
Linfield College *B, T*
Oregon State University *B*
Pacific University *B*
Portland State University *B, M*
Reed College *B*
University of Oregon *B, M, D*
University of Portland *T*
Western Oregon University *T*
Willamette University *B*

Pennsylvania

Allegheny College *B*
Bloomsburg University of
    Pennsylvania *B, T*
Bryn Mawr College *B*
Bucknell University *B*
California University of
    Pennsylvania *B*
Carnegie Mellon University *B*
Dickinson College *B*
Edinboro University of
    Pennsylvania *B, T*
Elizabethtown College *B*
Franklin & Marshall College *B*

Gettysburg College *B*
Haverford College *B, T*
Indiana University of Pennsylvania *B*
Juniata College *B*
Kutztown University of
    Pennsylvania *B, M, T*
La Salle University *B*
Lafayette College *B*
Lebanon Valley College *B*
Lehigh University *B*
Lock Haven University of
    Pennsylvania *B, T*
Lycoming College *B*
Mansfield University of
    Pennsylvania *B, T*
Messiah College *B*
Millersville University of
    Pennsylvania *B, M, T*
Moravian College *B, T*
Muhlenberg College *B*
Penn State
    Abington *B*
    Altoona *B*
    Beaver *B*
    Berks *B*
    Delaware County *B*
    Dubois *B*
    Fayette *B*
    Hazleton *B*
    Lehigh Valley *B*
    McKeesport *B*
    Mont Alto *B*
    New Kensington *B*
    Schuylkill - Capital College *B*
    Shenango *B*
    University Park *B, M, D*
    Wilkes-Barre *B*
    Worthington Scranton *B*
    York *B*
Rosemont College *B*
St. Joseph's University *B*
Susquehanna University *B, T*
Swarthmore College *B*
Temple University *B*
University of Pennsylvania *B, M, D*
University of Pittsburgh *B, M, D*
University of Scranton *B, T*
Ursinus College *B, T*
Villanova University *B*
Washington and Jefferson College *B*
West Chester University of
    Pennsylvania *B, M, T*
Westminster College *B*

Rhode Island

Brown University *B, M, D*
University of Rhode Island *B*

South Carolina

The Citadel *B*
Clemson University *B*
College of Charleston *B, T*
Francis Marion University *B*
Furman University *B, T*
Newberry College *B*
Presbyterian College *B*
University of South Carolina *B, M*
Wofford College *B*

South Dakota

Augustana College *B, T*
Northern State University *B*
South Dakota State University *B, T*
University of South Dakota *B*

Tennessee

Belmont University *B*
Carson-Newman College *B, T*
Lipscomb University *B*
Rhodes College *B, T*
Tennessee Technological
    University *B, T*

University of Tennessee
    Knoxville *M*
University of the South *B*
Vanderbilt University *B, M, D*

Texas

Angelo State University *B, T*
Austin College *B*
Austin Community College *A*
Baylor University *B*
Blinn College *A*
Coastal Bend College *A*
Kilgore College *A*
McMurry University *B*
Paris Junior College *A*
Rice University *B*
St. Mary's University *B*
Southern Methodist University *B*
Southwestern University *B*
Texas A&M University *B*
Texas A&M University
    Commerce *B*
Texas State University: San
    Marcos *B, T*
Texas Tech University *B, M*
Trinity University *B*
University of Dallas *B*
University of Houston *B, M*
University of North Texas *B*
University of Texas
    Arlington *B*
    Austin *B*
    El Paso *B*
    San Antonio *B*

Utah

Brigham Young University *B, M*
Southern Utah University *B*
University of Utah *B, M*
Utah State University *B*
Weber State University *B*

Vermont

Middlebury College *B, M, D*
University of Vermont *B, M*

Virginia

Christopher Newport University *B*
College of William and Mary *B*
Eastern Mennonite University *B*
Hampden-Sydney College *B*
Hollins University *B*
Longwood University *B, T*
Mary Baldwin College *B*
Old Dominion University *B, T*
Randolph-Macon College *B*
Sweet Briar College *B*
University of Mary Washington *B*
University of Richmond *B*
University of Virginia *B, M, D*
Virginia Wesleyan College *B*
Washington and Lee University *B*

Washington

Central Washington University *B*
Centralia College *A*
Eastern Washington University *B, T*
Everett Community College *A*
Highline Community College *A*
Pacific Lutheran University *B*
Seattle Pacific University *B*
University of Puget Sound *B, T*
University of Washington *B, M, D*
Walla Walla College *B*
Washington State University *B*
Western Washington University *B*
Whitman College *B*

West Virginia

Bethany College *B*
West Virginia University *T*

Wisconsin

Beloit College *B*
Carthage College *B, T*
Concordia University Wisconsin *B*
Lakeland College *B*
Lawrence University *B, T*
Marquette University *B*
Ripon College *B, T*
St. Norbert College *B, T*
University of Wisconsin
    Green Bay *B, T*
    La Crosse *B, T*
    Milwaukee *B*
    Oshkosh *B*
    Parkside *B, T*
    Platteville *B*
    River Falls *B*
    Stevens Point *B, T*
    Whitewater *B, T*

Wyoming

University of Wyoming *B, M*

German studies

California

Pomona College *B*
Scripps College *B*
Stanford University *B, M, D*
University of California
    Irvine *B*
    Riverside *B*
    San Diego *B*
    Santa Cruz *B*

Connecticut

Connecticut College *B*

District of Columbia

American University *B*

Georgia

Emory University *B*

Illinois

University of Chicago *B, D*

Iowa

Coe College *B*

Louisiana

Tulane University *B*

Maine

University of Southern Maine *B*

Massachusetts

College of the Holy Cross *B*
Mount Holyoke College *B*
Simon's Rock College of Bard *B*
Suffolk University *B*

Minnesota

Concordia College: Moorhead *B, T*
Macalester College *B*
Minnesota State University
    Mankato *B*

Missouri

Washington University in St. Louis *B*

New Hampshire

Dartmouth College *B*

New York

Bard College *B*
Barnard College *B*
Columbia University
    Columbia College *B*
Cornell University *B, M, D*

Sarah Lawrence College *B*

Ohio

Case Western Reserve University *B*
Cleveland State University *B*
University of Cincinnati *B*

Pennsylvania

Edinboro University of
    Pennsylvania *B*
Moravian College *B*
Muhlenberg College *B*
Swarthmore College *B*

Rhode Island

Brown University *B, M, D*

Tennessee

University of the South *B*

Texas

Rice University *B*
Southern Methodist University *B*
University of Houston *B*

Virginia

Randolph-Macon Woman's College *B*
Sweet Briar College *B*

Washington

University of Washington *B, M*

Wisconsin

University of Wisconsin
    Parkside *B*

German teacher education

Alabama

Birmingham-Southern College *T*

Arizona

Arizona State University *B, T*
Northern Arizona University *B*
Prescott College *T*
University of Arizona *B, M*

California

California State University
    Chico *B, T*
    Long Beach *T*
Humboldt State University *T*
San Diego State University *B, T*
San Francisco State University *B, T*
Stanford University *M, T*
University of the Pacific *T*

Colorado

Colorado State University *T*

Connecticut

Fairfield University *T*

Delaware

University of Delaware *B, T*

Florida

Stetson University *B*

Georgia

Georgia Southern University *B, M*

Idaho

Boise State University *T*

Illinois

Augustana College *B, T*
Bradley University *B*

Elmhurst College *B*
Illinois College *T*
Knox College *T*
North Park University *T*
Sauk Valley Community College *A*
University of Illinois
    Chicago *B*
    Urbana-Champaign *B, M, T*
Wheaton College *T*

Indiana

Grace College *B*
Indiana University
    Bloomington *B, T*
Indiana University-Purdue University
    Fort Wayne *B, T*
Indiana University-Purdue University
    Indianapolis *B, T*
Manchester College *B, T*
University of Evansville *B, T*
University of Indianapolis *T*
Valparaiso University *B*

Iowa

Central College *T*
Cornell College *B, T*
Graceland University *T*
Iowa State University *T*
Loras College *T*
St. Ambrose University *B, T*
Simpson College *T*
University of Iowa *T*
Wartburg College *T*

Kansas

Baker University *T*
Bethel College *T*
University of Kansas *B, T*

Louisiana

Centenary College of Louisiana *B, T*
University of Louisiana at Lafayette *B*

Maryland

Towson University *T*
Washington College *T*

Massachusetts

Tufts University *T*

Michigan

Albion College *B, T*
Alma College *T*
Calvin College *B*
Eastern Michigan University *B, T*
Grand Valley State University *T*
Hope College *T*
Western Michigan University *B, T*

Minnesota

Augsburg College *T*
Bemidji State University *T*
College of St. Benedict *T*
Concordia College: Moorhead *B, T*
Gustavus Adolphus College *T*
Minnesota State University
    Mankato *B, M, T*
St. Cloud State University *T*
St. John's University *T*
University of Minnesota
    Duluth *B*
    Morris *T*
University of St. Thomas *B, T*
Winona State University *B, T*

Mississippi

Mississippi State University *T*

Missouri

Central Missouri State University *B, T*
College of the Ozarks *B, T*

Missouri Southern State
    University *B, T*
Missouri State University *B*
University of Missouri
    Columbia *M*
    St. Louis *T*
Washington University in St.
    Louis *B, M, T*

Montana

University of Montana: Missoula *T*

Nebraska

Creighton University *T*
Dana College *B*
Hastings College *T*
Midland Lutheran College *B, T*
Nebraska Wesleyan University *T*
University of Nebraska
    Kearney *T*
    Lincoln *B*

Nevada

University of Nevada
    Reno *B*

New Hampshire

University of New Hampshire *T*

New York

City University of New York
    Hunter College *B, T*
Dutchess Community College *A*
Fordham University *M, T*
Hofstra University *B, M*
Ithaca College *B, T*
New York University *B, M, T*
St. John Fisher College *B, T*
St. Lawrence University *T*
State University of New York
    Buffalo *M, T*
    New Paltz *B, T*
    Oswego *B*
    Stony Brook *T*
Vassar College *T*
Wells College *T*

North Carolina

East Carolina University *B*
University of North Carolina
    Charlotte *B*
    Greensboro *B, T*
Wake Forest University *T*
Western Carolina University *B, T*

North Dakota

Minot State University *B*
North Dakota State University *B, T*

Ohio

Baldwin-Wallace College *T*
Hiram College *T*
Kent State University *T*
Miami University
    Oxford Campus *B, T*
Mount Union College *T*
Ohio University *B, T*
Ohio Wesleyan University *B*
University of Dayton *B*
University of Toledo *B, M, T*

Oklahoma

Oklahoma Baptist University *B, T*
Oklahoma City University *B*
University of Central Oklahoma *B*
University of Tulsa *T*

Oregon

Eastern Oregon University *B, T*
Linfield College *T*
Oregon State University *M*
Portland State University *T*

Western Oregon University *T*

Pennsylvania

Dickinson College *T*
Gettysburg College *T*
Juniata College *B, T*
La Salle University *B, T*
Lebanon Valley College *T*
Lycoming College *T*
Mansfield University of
    Pennsylvania *B, T*
Messiah College *B, T*
Moravian College *T*
Susquehanna University *T*
Villanova University *T*
Washington and Jefferson College *T*
Westminster College *T*

South Carolina

Furman University *T*

South Dakota

Augustana College *B, T*
University of South Dakota *B, M, D, T*

Tennessee

Lipscomb University *B, T*
Tennessee Technological University *T*
University of Memphis *T*
University of Tennessee
    Martin *B*

Texas

Texas State University: San Marcos *T*
University of Dallas *T*
University of Houston *T*
University of Texas
    San Antonio *T*

Utah

Brigham Young University *B*
Southern Utah University *B, T*
University of Utah *B*
Weber State University *B*

Vermont

St. Michael's College *T*

Virginia

Eastern Mennonite University *T*
Hollins University *T*
Longwood University *B, T*
Old Dominion University *B, T*

Washington

Central Washington University *B, T*
Washington State University *B, M, T*
Western Washington University *B*
Whitworth College *T*

West Virginia

Bethany College *B*

Wisconsin

Carthage College *T*
Lawrence University *T*
St. Norbert College *T*
University of Wisconsin
    Green Bay *T*
    Madison *M*
    Parkside *T*
    Platteville *B, T*
    River Falls *T*
    Whitewater *B*

Germanic languages

California

University of California
    Los Angeles *M, D*

Colorado
University of Colorado
    Boulder B

Kansas
University of Kansas B, M, D

Massachusetts
Simon's Rock College of Bard B

Michigan
Eastern Michigan University B

Missouri
Washington University in St.
    Louis B, M, D

New York
Canisius College B
Columbia University
    Columbia College B

North Carolina
Guilford College B

Ohio
Ohio Northern University B

Oklahoma
University of Oklahoma B, M

Tennessee
Lambuth University B

Texas
University of Texas
    Austin M, D

Washington
University of Washington B

Wisconsin
University of Wisconsin
    Eau Claire B
    Madison B, M, D

Gerontology

Arizona
University of Arizona M

Arkansas
University of Arkansas
    Little Rock A, M
    Pine Bluff B

California
American River College A
California State University
    Chico B
    Dominguez Hills B
    Fullerton M
    Long Beach M
    Sacramento B, M
Chaffey College A
Cosumnes River College A
MiraCosta College A
San Diego State University B
San Francisco State University M
University of La Verne M
University of Southern
    California B, M, D

Connecticut
Quinnipiac University B

Delaware
Delaware Technical and Community
    College
    Stanton/Wilmington Campus A

Wilmington College M

Florida
Bethune-Cookman College B
Florida State University M
Lynn University B, M
University of South Florida B, M, D

Georgia
Columbus State University M
Georgia State University M
University of West Georgia M

Illinois
City Colleges of Chicago
    Wright College A
Concordia University M
Dominican University B
Eastern Illinois University M
Northeastern Illinois University M
Roosevelt University B, M
Western Illinois University M

Indiana
Indiana University
    Kokomo B
Manchester College A
Purdue University
    Calumet B
St. Mary-of-the-Woods College A
Valparaiso University M
Vincennes University A

Iowa
University of Northern Iowa B

Kansas
Central Christian College of Kansas A
University of Kansas M, D
Washburn University of Topeka A, B
Wichita State University B, M

Kentucky
Thomas More College A
University of Kentucky D

Louisiana
University of Louisiana at Monroe M

Maryland
Sojourner-Douglass College B
Towson University B, M
University of Maryland
    Baltimore M, D
    Baltimore County M, D

Massachusetts
Stonehill College B
University of Massachusetts
    Boston B, M, D

Michigan
Alma College B
Aquinas College A
Lansing Community College A
Madonna University A, B
Siena Heights University A
University of Michigan M, D

Minnesota
College of St. Scholastica C
Minnesota State University
    Mankato M
    Moorhead B
St. Cloud State University B, M
Winona State University A

Mississippi
East Central Community College A

Missouri
Central Missouri State University M
Lindenwood University B, M
Missouri State University B
University of Missouri
    St. Louis B
Webster University M

Nebraska
University of Nebraska
    Omaha B, M

New Hampshire
New Hampshire Community
    Technical College
    Stratham A

New Jersey
Ocean County College A
Thomas Edison State College A, B
Union County College A

New York
Alfred University B
Broome Community College A
City University of New York
    Hostos Community College A
    LaGuardia Community College A
    York College B
College of New Rochelle M
Columbia University
    School of Nursing M
Hofstra University M
Ithaca College B
New York Institute of Technology M
State University of New York
    College at Oneonta B
Touro College M

North Carolina
Appalachian State University M
University of North Carolina
    Charlotte M
    Greensboro M
Winston-Salem State University B

Ohio
Bowling Green State University B
Case Western Reserve University B
John Carroll University B
Miami University
    Oxford Campus M, D
Ohio Dominican University A
University of Akron: Wayne College C

Oregon
Chemeketa Community College A
Marylhurst University M
Portland Community College A

Pennsylvania
California University of
    Pennsylvania B
Reading Area Community College A
Shippensburg University of
    Pennsylvania M
University of Scranton A, B

Puerto Rico
Pontifical Catholic University of
    Puerto Rico A, B

Texas
Abilene Christian University M
McLennan Community College A
Stephen F. Austin State University B
University of North Texas B
University of Texas
    Health Science Center at
    Houston M

Utah
University of Utah A, M
Weber State University B

Virginia
New River Community College A
Northern Virginia Community
    College A

Washington
Central Washington University B
Edmonds Community College A

Wisconsin
Mount Mary College M

Geropsychology

Colorado
University of Colorado
    Colorado Springs D

Glazier

Indiana
Ivy Tech State College
    Ivy Tech Community College:
    Central Indiana C

Michigan
Bay de Noc Community College C

Wisconsin
Milwaukee Area Technical College C

Global studies

Alabama
Huntingdon College B

Arizona
Arizona State University B

Arkansas
Arkansas Tech University B
Harding University B
John Brown University B

California
California Maritime Academy B
California State University
    Monterey Bay B
Concordia University B
National University B
Pepperdine University B
Pitzer College B
Point Loma Nazarene University B
Pomona College B
Skyline College A
Sonoma State University B, M
Stanford University B
University of California
    Berkeley M
    Irvine B
    Los Angeles B
    Santa Barbara B
University of Southern California B

Colorado
Colorado Christian University B
University of Colorado
    Boulder B
    Denver and Health Sciences
    Center B

Connecticut
Central Connecticut State
    University B, M
Connecticut College T
University of Connecticut M

District of Columbia

American University *B, M*

Florida

Eckerd College *B*
New College of Florida *B*
Schiller International University *B, M*

Georgia

Georgia Institute of Technology *B*
Shorter College *B*
Spelman College *B*

Illinois

Knox College *B*
Lewis University *B*
Principia College *B*
University of Illinois
    Urbana-Champaign *B*

Indiana

Manchester College *B*

Iowa

Central College *B*
University of Iowa *B*

Kansas

Baker University *B*
University of Kansas *M*

Louisiana

Louisiana State University and
    Agricultural and Mechanical
    College *B*
University of New Orleans *B*

Maine

University of Southern Maine *B*

Maryland

Howard Community College *A*

Massachusetts

Assumption College *B*
Brandeis University *B*
Cape Cod Community College *A*
Clark University *B*
Emmanuel College *B*
Endicott College *B*
Hampshire College *B*
Lesley University *B*
Northeastern University *B*
Western New England College *B*
Worcester Polytechnic Institute *B*

Michigan

Kuyper College *B*
Michigan State University *B, M, D*
Saginaw Valley State University *B*
Western Michigan University *B*

Minnesota

College of St. Scholastica *B*

Missouri

Rockhurst University *B*

Nebraska

Nebraska Wesleyan University *B*
University of Nebraska
    Omaha *B*

Nevada

Sierra Nevada College *B*

New Hampshire

University of New Hampshire *B*

New Jersey

Ramapo College of New Jersey *B*
Rider University *B*

New York

Adelphi University *B*
Bard College *B*
City University of New York
    City College *B, M*
College of New Rochelle *B*
D'Youville College *B*
Iona College *B*
Russell Sage College *B*
St. Lawrence University *B*
Sarah Lawrence College *B*
State University of New York
    Binghamton *B*
    College at Plattsburgh *M, T*
    Oswego *B*
Wells College *B*

North Carolina

High Point University *B*
Meredith College *B*
North Carolina State University *B*
Roanoke-Chowan Community
    College *A*
Wake Technical Community
    College *A*

North Dakota

North Dakota State University *B*

Ohio

Baldwin-Wallace College *B*
Cedarville University *B*
Mount Union College *B*
University of Dayton *B*
Wittenberg University *B*

Oklahoma

Oklahoma State University *M*
University of Oklahoma *B, M*
University of Tulsa *B*

Oregon

University of Oregon *B, M*
Willamette University *B*

Pennsylvania

Allegheny College *B*
Gettysburg College *B*
Juniata College *B*
Mercyhurst College *B*
Susquehanna University *B*
University of Pennsylvania *B, M*

Rhode Island

Providence College *B*

South Carolina

Newberry College *B*
Piedmont Technical College *A*

South Dakota

Augustana College *B*
South Dakota State University *B*
University of South Dakota *B*

Tennessee

Lambuth University *B*
Tennessee Wesleyan College *B*

Texas

Abilene Christian University *B*
Midwestern State University *B*
San Antonio College *A*
Texas State University: San
    Marcos *B, M*

Utah

Salt Lake Community College *A*
University of Utah *B, M*

Vermont

Bennington College *B*
Marlboro College *B*
Sterling College *B*

Virginia

Ferrum College *B*
Randolph-Macon College *B*
Virginia Commonwealth University *B*
Virginia Military Institute *B*
Virginia Wesleyan College *B*

Washington

Evergreen State College *B*
Pacific Lutheran University *B*
Seattle University *B*

West Virginia

Bethany College *B*
Concord University *B*

Wisconsin

Lawrence University *B*
Marquette University *B*
Northland College *B*
Ripon College *B*
University of Wisconsin
    Madison *B, M*
    River Falls *B*
    Whitewater *B*

Graphic communications

Alabama

Gadsden State Community College *A*
Trenholm State Technical College *C, A*

California

Art Center College of Design *B, M*
Platt College
    Ontario *C, A, B*
Point Loma Nazarene University *B*
Santa Rosa Junior College *C*
Santiago Canyon College *A*
Westwood College: Long Beach *B*

Colorado

Pikes Peak Community College *C, A*
Westwood College of Technology
    South *A, B*

Connecticut

Mitchell College *A*
Paier College of Art *C*

Florida

Miami Dade College *A*

Illinois

City Colleges of Chicago
    Kennedy-King College *C, A*
Heartland Community College *C*

Indiana

St. Mary-of-the-Woods College *B*
Sawyer College: Merrillville *C, A*
Vincennes University *A*

Iowa

Briar Cliff University *B*
Dordt College *B*
Grand View College *B*
Hawkeye Community College *A*
University of Northern Iowa *B*

Kentucky

Louisville Technical Institute *A*
Somerset Community College *C, A*

Maryland

Montgomery College *C, A*

Massachusetts

Gibbs College *A*
New England Institute of Art *B*
Newbury College *A*

Michigan

Baker College
    of Muskegon *A*
    of Owosso *A, B*
Gogebic Community College *A*

Minnesota

Academy College *B*
Art Institutes International
    Minnesota *A, B*
Brown College *A, B*
Hennepin Technical College *C, A*
St. Cloud Technical College *C*

Nebraska

Metropolitan Community
    College *C, A*

Nevada

Western Nevada Community
    College *C, A*

New York

New York University *M*
Rochester Institute of
    Technology *B, M*
State University of New York
    College of Technology at Alfred *A*

North Carolina

Chowan College *B*

Ohio

Mount Vernon Nazarene University *B*
University of Cincinnati
    Raymond Walters College *C, A*

Pennsylvania

Delaware County Community
    College *C*
Keystone College *A*
Philadelphia University *B*

Rhode Island

New England Institute of
    Technology *A*
Roger Williams University *B*

Utah

Snow College *C*

Vermont

Champlain College *A, B*

Washington

Centralia College *A*
Seattle Central Community
    College *C, A*

West Virginia

Bethany College *B*

Wisconsin

Carroll College *B*
Edgewood College *B*
Milwaukee Area Technical College *A*

Graphic design

Alabama
Spring Hill College *B*
Virginia College *A, B*

Arizona
Arizona State University *B*
Eastern Arizona College *C*

Arkansas
Harding University *B*
John Brown University *B*
Ouachita Baptist University *B*
University of Arkansas
   Fort Smith *C, A, B*

California
Academy of Art University *C, A, B, M*
Art Center College of Design *B*
Art Institute
   of California: Orange County *A, B*
   of California: San Diego *A, B*
Art Institute of California: San
   Francisco *A, B*
California Baptist University *B*
California College of the Arts *B*
California Institute of the Arts *C, B, M*
California State Polytechnic
   University: Pomona *B*
California State University
   Chico *B*
   Sacramento *B*
Chaffey College *C, A*
Chapman University *B*
College of the Desert *A*
Fashion Institute of Design and
   Merchandising *A*
Fashion Institute of Design and
   Merchandising
   San Diego *A*
   San Francisco *A*
Institute of Computer Technology *A*
Monterey Peninsula College *C, A*
Ohlone College *C, A*
Platt College
   Ontario *A*
Point Loma Nazarene University *B*
San Jose State University *B*
Santa Barbara City College *C*
Southwestern College *A*
University of San Francisco *B*
Westwood College of Technology
   Inland Empire *A*
Westwood College: Long Beach *A*
Woodbury University *B*

Colorado
Arapahoe Community College *C, A*
Mesa State College *B*
Rocky Mountain College of Art &
   Design *B*
University of Denver *B, M*
Westwood College of
   Technology *A, B*
Westwood College of Technology
   South *A, B*

Connecticut
Gateway Community College *A*
Paier College of Art *C, B*
University of Bridgeport *B*
University of New Haven *C, A, B*

Delaware
Delaware College of Art and Design *A*

District of Columbia
American University *B*
Corcoran College of Art and
   Design *A, B*

Florida
Art Institute of Fort
   Lauderdale *C, A, B*
Palm Beach Atlantic University *B*
St. Petersburg College *C, A*
University of Miami *B*
University of Tampa *B*

Georgia
Brenau University *B*
Darton College *C*
Savannah College of Art and
   Design *C, B, M*

Illinois
Bradley University *B*
International Academy of Design and
   Technology: Chicago *A, B*
Judson College *B*
Kankakee Community College *C, A*
Lewis University *B*
Lincoln Land Community College *A*
Quincy University *B*
Robert Morris College: Chicago *B*
School of the Art Institute of
   Chicago *B, M*
Spoon River College *C*
University of Illinois
   Urbana-Champaign *B, M*
Waubonsee Community College *C, A*
Westwood College - Chicago Loop *A*
Westwood College of Technology
   O'Hare *B*

Indiana
Ancilla College *A*
Grace College *B*
Huntington University *B*
Indiana University-Purdue University
   Fort Wayne *B*
St. Mary-of-the-Woods College *B*
University of Evansville *B*
Vincennes University *A*

Iowa
Ashford University *B*
Briar Cliff University *B*
Grand View College *B*
Iowa State University *B, M*
St. Ambrose University *B*
University of Dubuque *B*

Kansas
Barton County Community
   College *C, A*
University of Kansas *B, M*

Kentucky
Louisville Technical Institute *C, A*

Maine
Maine College of Art *B*

Maryland
Cecil Community College *C*
Maryland Institute College of Art *B, M*

Massachusetts
Anna Maria College *B*
Art Institute of Boston at Lesley
   University *B*
Bridgewater State College *B*
Cape Cod Community College *A*
Emmanuel College *B*
Fitchburg State College *B*
Lasell College *B*
New England Institute of Art *B*
Newbury College *A, B*
North Shore Community College *C, A*
Simmons College *B*
Suffolk University *M*

Michigan
Alma College *B*
Andrews University *B*
Baker College
   of Muskegon *A*
Central Michigan University *B*
College for Creative Studies *B*
Delta College *A*
Ferris State University *B*
Finlandia University *B*
Jackson Community College *C, A*
Kendall College of Art and Design of
   Ferris State University *B*
Kirtland Community College *C, A*
Mott Community College *A*
Oakland Community College *A*
University of Michigan *B*
University of Michigan
   Flint *B*
Western Michigan University *B*

Minnesota
Art Institutes International
   Minnesota *B*
Dakota County Technical College *C, A*
Minnesota State Community and
   Technical College - Fergus
   Falls *C, A*
Northwestern College *B*
Pillsbury Baptist Bible College *B*
Rochester Community and Technical
   College *C, A*
South Central College *A*

Mississippi
Antonelli College
   Jackson *A*

Missouri
Columbia College *M*
Kansas City Art Institute *B*
Maryville University of Saint Louis *B*
Missouri Western State University *B*
Ozarks Technical Community
   College *C, A*
Park University *B*
Penn Valley Community College *C, A*
Washington University in St. Louis *B*
William Woods University *B*

Nebraska
Creative Center *A*
Vatterott College: Spring Valley *A*
Wayne State College *B*

Nevada
International Academy of Design and
   Technology: Henderson *A, B*

New Hampshire
Chester College of New England *B*
Colby-Sawyer College *B*
Keene State College *B*
McIntosh College *A*
New Hampshire Community
   Technical College
   Berlin *C, A*
Southern New Hampshire
   University *B*

New Jersey
Cumberland County College *A*

New York
Art Institute
   of New York City *A*
Bryant & Stratton College: Henrietta *A*
Bryant & Stratton College: Syracuse
   North *A*
City University of New York
   City College *B*

Cooper Union for the Advancement of
   Science and Art *C, B*
Daemen College *B*
Pratt Institute *A, B, M*
Rochester Institute of
   Technology *A, B, M*
Sage College of Albany *A, B*
St. John's University *B*
St. Thomas Aquinas College *B*
School of Visual Arts *B*
State University of New York
   College of Technology at Alfred *A*
   Farmingdale *B*
   Purchase *B*
Syracuse University *B*

North Carolina
Appalachian State University *B*
Art Institute
   of Charlotte *A, B*
Chowan College *B*
East Carolina University *B*
North Carolina State University *B, M*

Ohio
Cedarville University *B*
Cleveland State University *C*
College of Mount St. Joseph *A, B*
Ohio Dominican University *B*
Ohio Institute of Photography and
   Technology *A*
Ohio University *B*
Union Institute & University *M*
University of Cincinnati
   Raymond Walters College *C, A*
Ursuline College *B*

Oklahoma
University of Central Oklahoma *B*

Oregon
Art Institute of Portland *A, B*
Pacific Northwest College of Art *B*

Pennsylvania
Arcadia University *B*
Bucks County Community College *A*
Butler County Community College *A*
Cabrini College *B*
California University of
   Pennsylvania *B*
East Stroudsburg University of
   Pennsylvania *B*
Edinboro University of
   Pennsylvania *B*
Harrisburg Area Community
   College *C, A*
Hussian School of Art *A*
Immaculata University *C*
Keystone College *A*
Marywood University *B, M*
Moore College of Art and Design *B*
Moravian College *B*
Northampton County Area
   Community College *A*
Oakbridge Academy of Arts *A*
Philadelphia University *B*
St. Vincent College *B*
Shippensburg University of
   Pennsylvania *C*
Susquehanna University *B*
Temple University *B, M*
York College of Pennsylvania *B*

Puerto Rico
Atlantic College *M*
Turabo University *B*
Universidad del Este *A*

Rhode Island
Rhode Island School of Design *B, M*
Roger Williams University *B*
Salve Regina University *B*

South Carolina

Anderson University *B*
Limestone College *B*
Trident Technical College *C, A*

South Dakota

Mount Marty College *B*
South Dakota State University *B*

Tennessee

Memphis College of Art *B*
Nossi College of Art *B*

Texas

Art Institute
  of Houston *B*
Hardin-Simmons University *B*
McMurry University *B*
St. Edward's University *B*
San Antonio College *A*
Schreiner University *B*
Texas Christian University *B*
Texas State University: San Marcos *B*
Texas Tech University *B*
University of Houston *B, M*
University of Texas
  El Paso *B*
West Texas A&M University *B*

Utah

Brigham Young University *B*

Vermont

Champlain College *C, A, B*
Lyndon State College *A, B*

Virginia

Art Institute
  of Washington *A, B*
Germanna Community College *C*
Liberty University *B*
Marymount University *B*
Old Dominion University *B*
Tidewater Community College *A*

Washington

Art Institute of Seattle *C, A, B*
Centralia College *A*
Cornish College of the Arts *B*
Western Washington University *B*

West Virginia

Concord University *B*
West Virginia Wesleyan College *B*

Wisconsin

Concordia University Wisconsin *B*
Gateway Technical College *A*
Marian College of Fond du Lac *B*
Milwaukee Area Technical College *A*
Nicolet Area Technical College *A*
Viterbo University *B*
Western Wisconsin Technical
  College *A*

Graphic/printing production

Alabama

Alabama Agricultural and Mechanical
  University *B*
Bishop State Community College *C*
J. F. Drake State Technical College *C, A*
Lawson State Community College *C*

Arkansas

Arkansas State University *B*
Phillips Community College of the
  University of Arkansas *A*

California

Allan Hancock College *A*
American River College *A*
Antelope Valley College *C, A*
Bakersfield College *A*
Butte College *A*
California Polytechnic State
  University: San Luis Obispo *B*
City College of San Francisco *A*
Fresno City College *C, A*
Fullerton College *A*
Laney College *C, A*
Las Positas College *A*
Long Beach City College *A*
Los Angeles Trade and Technical
  College *C, A*
Mission College *C, A*
Modesto Junior College *C, A*
Moorpark College *A*
Palomar College *C, A*
Rio Hondo College *A*
Riverside Community College *C, A*
Sacramento City College *C, A*
Saddleback College *C*
San Joaquin Delta College *A*
Santa Barbara City College *C*
Ventura College *A*

Colorado

Aims Community College *C, A*
Community College of Aurora *A*
Community College of Denver *C, A*
Westwood College of
  Technology *A, B*

Connecticut

Gateway Community College *C*

District of Columbia

University of the District of
  Columbia *A, B*

Florida

Florida Community College at
  Jacksonville *A*
Indian River Community College *A*
Miami Dade College *A*
Palm Beach Community College *A*
Tallahassee Community College *C*

Georgia

Albany Technical College *C*
Augusta Technical Institute *C*
Chattahoochee Technical College *C*
Columbus Technical College *C*
DeKalb Technical College *C*
Georgia Southern University *B*
Georgia Southwestern State
  University *A*
West Georgia Technical College *C*

Hawaii

University of Hawaii
  Honolulu Community College *A*

Idaho

Idaho State University *C, A*
Lewis-Clark State College *A, B*

Illinois

College of DuPage *C, A*
Elgin Community College *C*
Kaskaskia College *C*
Prairie State College *C*
Triton College *C, A*
Western Illinois University *B*

Indiana

Ball State University *A*
Sawyer College: Merrillville *C, A*
Vincennes University *A*

Iowa

Clinton Community College *A*
Iowa Western Community College *A*
Kirkwood Community College *A*

Kansas

Coffeyville Community College *C*
Fort Scott Community College *C, A*

Kentucky

Eastern Kentucky University *A*

Maine

Central Maine Community College *A*

Maryland

Montgomery College *A*

Massachusetts

Massasoit Community College *C*
Northern Essex Community
  College *C*
Springfield Technical Community
  College *C*

Michigan

Alpena Community College *C, A*
Baker College
  of Muskegon *A*
Bay de Noc Community College *C*
Delta College *C, A*
Ferris State University *A, B*
Grand Rapids Community College *A*
Henry Ford Community College *A*
Lansing Community College *A*
Macomb Community College *C, A*
Muskegon Community College *A*
Southwestern Michigan College *A*
Washtenaw Community College *A*

Minnesota

Dunwoody College of
  Technology *C, A*
Globe College *C, A*
Hennepin Technical College *C, A*
Mesabi Range Community and
  Technical College *C, A*
South Central College *A*

Mississippi

Hinds Community College *C, A*
Mississippi Delta Community
  College *C*

Missouri

Central Missouri State University *A, B*
College of the Ozarks *B*
Evangel University *A*
Mineral Area College *C, A*
Moberly Area Community
  College *C, A*
Ozarks Technical Community
  College *C, A*
St. Louis Community College
  St. Louis Community College at
    Florissant Valley *A*
Southeast Missouri State University *C*

Nebraska

Metropolitan Community
  College *C, A*
Southeast Community College
  Lincoln Campus *C*

Nevada

Community College of Southern
  Nevada *C, A*
Truckee Meadows Community
  College *C*

New Hampshire

New Hampshire Community
  Technical College
  Berlin *C, A*

New Jersey

Bergen Community College *C*
Brookdale Community College *C, A*

New Mexico

Southwestern Indian Polytechnic
  Institute *C, A*

New York

City University of New York
  New York City College of
    Technology *C, A, B*
Erie Community College
  South Campus *A*
Fulton-Montgomery Community
  College *A*
Rochester Institute of
  Technology *C, A*

North Carolina

Alamance Community College *C*
Central Piedmont Community
  College *C, A*
Chowan College *A*
Forsyth Technical Community
  College *C*
McDowell Technical Community
  College *A*

Ohio

Columbus State Community
  College *C, A*

Oklahoma

Oklahoma State University
  Okmulgee *A*

Oregon

Chemeketa Community College *A*
Mount Hood Community College *C, A*

Pennsylvania

Bucks County Community College *A*
Commonwealth Technical Institute *C*
Delaware County Community
  College *C*
Pennsylvania College of Technology *B*
Thaddeus Stevens College of
  Technology *A*
Westmoreland County Community
  College *A*

Puerto Rico

University of Puerto Rico
  Carolina Regional College *A, B*

Rhode Island

New England Institute of
  Technology *A*

South Carolina

Midlands Technical College *C*
Trident Technical College *C*

South Dakota

Northern State University *A*
Southeast Technical Institute *A*

Texas

Central Texas College *C, A*
College of the Mainland *C*
Eastfield College *C, A*
Houston Community College
  System *C, A*
Lee College *C, A*
Midland College *A*

Navarro College *A*
North Harris Montgomery
    Community College District *C, A*
San Jacinto College
    Central Campus *A*
South Plains College *A*
Tarrant County College *A*
Texas A&M University
    Commerce *B*
Texas State Technical College
    Waco *C, A*
Tyler Junior College *C, A*

Utah

Dixie State College of Utah *C, A*

Virginia

Dabney S. Lancaster Community
    College *C, A*
Danville Community College *A*
J. Sargeant Reynolds Community
    College *C*
John Tyler Community College *C*
Virginia Intermont College *A*

Washington

Clover Park Technical College *C, A*
Edmonds Community College *C*
Lake Washington Technical College *C*
Seattle Central Community
    College *C, A*
Shoreline Community College *C, A*
Spokane Falls Community College *C*
Walla Walla College *A, B*

West Virginia

West Virginia University Institute of
    Technology *A*

Wisconsin

Fox Valley Technical College *C, A*
Gateway Technical College *C*
Lakeshore Technical College *C*
Madison Area Technical College *C, A*
Milwaukee Area Technical College *A*
Moraine Park Technical College *C, A*
Northcentral Technical College *A*
Northeast Wisconsin Technical
    College *C*
Waukesha County Technical
    College *A*

Wyoming

Northwest College *A*

Greenhouse operations

California

Los Angeles Pierce College *C, A*
Southwestern College *C, A*
Yuba Community College District *C*

Georgia

Albany Technical College *C*

Illinois

College of DuPage *C*
Joliet Junior College *C, A*
Kishwaukee College *C, A*
Southwestern Illinois College *A*
Triton College *C, A*
William Rainey Harper College *C*

Kentucky

Maysville Community College *C*

Maine

Southern Maine Community
    College *C, A*
University of Maine *B*

Michigan

Bay de Noc Community College *C*

Minnesota

Rochester Community and Technical
    College *C, A*
University of Minnesota
    Crookston *B*

Nebraska

Nebraska College of Technical
    Agriculture *A*

New Hampshire

University of New Hampshire *A*

New York

State University of New York
    College of Agriculture and
        Technology at Cobleskill *A*
    College of Agriculture and
        Technology at Morrisville *A*

North Carolina

Alamance Community College *C*
Carteret Community College *C, A*
Johnston Community College *C*
Pitt Community College *C*

North Dakota

Minot State University: Bottineau
    Campus *C, A*

Ohio

Ohio State University
    Agricultural Technical Institute *A*
    Columbus Campus *C*

Pennsylvania

Community College of Allegheny
    County *C*
Westmoreland County Community
    College *A*

South Dakota

Southeast Technical Institute *A*

Tennessee

Walters State Community College *A*

Texas

Western Texas College *C, A*

Vermont

Sterling College *A, B*
Vermont Technical College *A*

Virginia

Lord Fairfax Community College *C*

Washington

Spokane Community College *A*

Wisconsin

Fox Valley Technical College *C*

Gunsmithing

Arizona

Yavapai College *C, A*

California

Lassen College *C*

Minnesota

Pine Technical College *C, A*

North Carolina

Montgomery Community College *C, A*

Piedmont Community College *A*

Hair styling

Alabama

Calhoun Community College *C*

California

San Jose City College *C, A*

North Carolina

Lenoir Community College *C*

Wisconsin

Gateway Technical College *C*
Milwaukee Area Technical College *C*
Wisconsin Indianhead Technical
    College *C*

Hazardous materials technology

Alabama

Central Alabama Community
    College *C*
Faulkner State Community College *A*

Arizona

Gateway Community College *C, A*
Paradise Valley Community
    College *C, A*

California

Cabrillo College *C, A*
Sierra College *C, A*

Connecticut

University of New Haven *C*

Florida

Pensacola Junior College *A*

Kansas

Barton County Community
    College *C, A*
Kansas City Kansas Community
    College *A*

Mississippi

Jackson State University *M*

New Jersey

Burlington County College *C*

New Mexico

New Mexico Junior College *C, A*

Ohio

Ohio University *A*
Ohio University
    Chillicothe Campus *C*
University of Findlay *C, A, B, M*

Washington

Green River Community College *C, A*

Wisconsin

Lakeshore Technical College *A*

Health aide

California

College of Alameda *C, A*
National University *A*

Colorado

Red Rocks Community College *C*

Illinois

McHenry County College *C*

Kansas

Barton County Community College *C*
Coffeyville Community College *C*

Massachusetts

North Shore Community College *C*

Michigan

Delta College *C*

Minnesota

St. Cloud Technical College *C*

New Hampshire

McIntosh College *A*

New York

Genesee Community College *C*
Niagara County Community
    College *C*

Pennsylvania

Community College of Beaver
    County *A*

Washington

Edmonds Community College *C, A*

Health care administration

Alabama

Auburn University *B*
Community College of the Air
    Force *A*
University of Alabama
    Birmingham *M, D*
Virginia College *B*

Alaska

Alaska Pacific University *B, M*
University of Alaska
    Southeast *A*

Arizona

Arizona Institute of Business and
    Technology
    International Institute of the
        Americas: Mesa *A*
Arizona State University *M*
Gateway Community College *C, A*
International Institute of the Americas
    Phoenix *A*
    Tucson *A*
International Institute of the
    Americas: West Valley *A*
Northern Arizona University *B*
University of Arizona *B*
University of Phoenix *B, M*
Western International University *M*

Arkansas

Harding University *B, M*
University of Arkansas
    Little Rock *A*
University of Central Arkansas *A, B*

California

Barstow College *C*
California State University
    Bakersfield *M*
    Chico *M*
    Dominguez Hills *B*
    East Bay *M*
    Fresno *M*
    Los Angeles *M*
    Northridge *M*

Sacramento *B*
San Bernardino *B, M*
Imperial Valley College *C, A*
Loma Linda University *M*
Mount St. Mary's College *B*
National University *C, B, M*
St. Mary's College of California *B*
San Joaquin Valley College Inc. *A*
San Jose State University *B*
University of California
Berkeley *D*
University of La Verne *B, M*
University of San Francisco *B*
University of Southern California *M*
West Coast University *A, B*

Colorado

CollegeAmerica-Denver *B*
Community College of Denver *C*
Metropolitan State College of
Denver *B*
National American University
Denver *B*
University of Colorado
Denver and Health Sciences
Center *M*
University of Northern Colorado *B*

Connecticut

Quinnipiac University *B, M*
Sacred Heart University *M*
St. Vincent's College *C*
University of Connecticut *B*
University of New Haven *M*
Western Connecticut State
University *M*

District of Columbia

George Washington University *M*
Georgetown University *M*
Southeastern University *A, B, M*

Florida

Barry University *C, B, M*
Broward Community College *A*
Florida Agricultural and Mechanical
University *B*
Florida Atlantic University *C, B, M*
Florida Institute of Technology *M*
Florida International University *B, M*
Florida State University *M*
International College *B*
Lynn University *C, B, M*
Manatee Community College *A*
Pensacola Junior College *A*
St. Leo University *B*
St. Thomas University *B*
University of Central Florida *B*
University of Florida *M, D*
University of North Florida *M*
University of South Florida *M*
Valencia Community College *A*

Georgia

Armstrong Atlantic State University *M*
Clayton State University *B*
Georgia Institute of Technology *M*
Georgia Southern University *M*
Georgia State University *M*
Life University *B*
Macon State College *B*

Hawaii

University of Hawaii
Hawaii Community College *C*

Idaho

Idaho State University *B*

Illinois

Benedictine University *B*
Governors State University *B, M*

Illinois Central College *C, A*
Lewis University *M*
National-Louis University *B*
Northwestern University *M*
Roosevelt University *B*
Rosalind Franklin University of
Medicine and Science *M*
Rush University *M, D*
Southern Illinois University
Carbondale *B*
University of St. Francis *B, M*
Western Illinois University *B*

Indiana

Calumet College of St. Joseph *B*
Indiana University
Bloomington *B*
Northwest *B*
South Bend *B*
Indiana University-Purdue University
Fort Wayne *B*
Purdue University
North Central Campus *A*

Iowa

Ashford University *B*
Des Moines Area Community
College *A*
Iowa Lakes Community College *A*
Mercy College of Health Sciences *B*
St. Ambrose University *M*
University of Iowa *M, D*
Upper Iowa University *B*

Kansas

Friends University *B*
Kansas City Kansas Community
College *C*
University of Kansas Medical
Center *M*
Wichita State University *B*

Kentucky

Brescia University *A, B*
Eastern Kentucky University *B*
Midway College *B*
University of Kentucky *B, M*
Western Kentucky University *B, M*

Louisiana

Nicholls State University *B*
Our Lady of the Lake College *B*
Tulane University *M, D*
University of Louisiana at Lafayette *M*
University of New Orleans *M*

Maine

University of Southern Maine *M*

Maryland

Baltimore City Community
College *C, A*
Columbia Union College *B*
Sojourner-Douglass College *B*
Towson University *B*
University of Baltimore *B, M*

Massachusetts

Boston University *M*
Brandeis University *B, M*
Elms College *B*
Framingham State College *M*
Lasell College *B*
Newbury College *B*
Northeastern University *M*
Simmons College *M*
Springfield College *B, M*
Stonehill College *B*
Suffolk University *M*
University of Massachusetts
Lowell *M*

Michigan

Baker College
of Clinton Township *B*
of Flint *B, M*
of Muskegon *B*
of Owosso *B*
of Port Huron *B*
Central Michigan University *M*
Davenport University *B*
Eastern Michigan University *B*
Ferris State University *B*
Lansing Community College *A*
Madonna University *A, B, M*
Oakland Community College *C, A*
Spring Arbor University *B*
University of Detroit Mercy *M*
University of Michigan *M, D*
University of Michigan
Dearborn *B*
Flint *B, M*
Wayne State University *M*
Western Michigan University *C*

Minnesota

Capella University *M, D*
Concordia College: Moorhead *C, B*
High-Tech Institute *A*
Minnesota State University
Mankato *B, M, T*
Moorhead *B*
Ridgewater College *C, A*
St. Mary's University of
Minnesota *B, M*
University of Minnesota
Crookston *B*
Duluth *B*
Twin Cities *M*
University of St. Thomas *M, D*
Winona State University *B*

Mississippi

Jackson State University *B*
Mississippi College *M*

Missouri

Lindenwood University *B, M*
Missouri State University *M*
St. Louis University *M*
University of Missouri
Columbia *M*
Webster University *M*

Montana

Flathead Valley Community College *A*
Montana State University
Billings *B, M*

Nebraska

Bellevue University *B*
Clarkson College *B*
Creighton University *B, M*
Hastings College *B*

Nevada

University of Nevada
Las Vegas *B*

New Hampshire

McIntosh College *A*
New England College *B, M*
Rivier College *M*
Southern New Hampshire
University *C*
University of New Hampshire *B, M*

New Jersey

College of St. Elizabeth *M*
Essex County College *A*
Rider University *C*
Seton Hall University *M*

University of Medicine and Dentistry
of New Jersey
School of Health Related
Professions *D*

New Mexico

International Institute of the
Americas *A*

New York

City University of New York
Baruch College *M*
Borough of Manhattan Community
College *A*
Brooklyn College *M*
Lehman College *B*
Cornell University *M, D*
D'Youville College *B, M*
Globe Institute of Technology *C, A, B*
Herkimer County Community
College *A*
Hofstra University *M*
Iona College *B, M*
New York University *A, B, M*
Roberts Wesleyan College *M*
Rochester Institute of Technology *M*
St. John's University *C, B, M*
St. Joseph's College *C, B*
State University of New York
College at Brockport *B, M*
Institute of Technology at
Utica/Rome *B, M*
Stony Brook *M*
Utica School of Commerce *A*

North Carolina

Appalachian State University *B*
Cabarrus College of Health
Sciences *B*
Duke University *M*
Pfeiffer University *B, M*
University of North Carolina
Chapel Hill *B, M, D*
Charlotte *M*
Greensboro *M*

Ohio

Bowling Green State University *B*
David N. Myers University *C, B*
Franklin University *B*
Heidelberg College *B*
Kent State University
Ashtabula Regional Campus *A*
Salem Regional Campus *A*
Lourdes College *B*
Mercy College of Northwest Ohio *B*
Ohio State University
Columbus Campus *M, D*
Ohio University *B, M*
Owens Community College
Toledo *C, A*
University of Akron: Wayne College *A*
University of Cincinnati *B, M*
University of Findlay *B*
University of Northwestern Ohio *B*
University of Rio Grande *B*
University of Toledo *M*
Ursuline College *B*
Wright State University *M*
Xavier University *M*
Youngstown State University *M*

Oklahoma

Northeastern State University *B*
Oklahoma State University
Oklahoma City *A*
Southwestern Oklahoma State
University *B*
University of Oklahoma *M, D*

Oregon

Chemeketa Community College *C, A*
Concordia University *B*

Oregon State University *B, M*
Pioneer Pacific College *A, B*
Pioneer Pacific College: Springfield *A*
Portland State University *M*

Pennsylvania
Arcadia University *C, B*
Butler County Community College *A*
Carnegie Mellon University *M*
Chatham College *M*
Chestnut Hill College *C, A, B*
Drexel University *B*
Duquesne University *B, M*
Eastern University *M*
Harrisburg Area Community
   College *A*
Immaculata University *B*
King's College *M*
Lebanon Valley College *C, B*
Marywood University *M*
Neumann College *C*
Penn State
   Harrisburg *B, M*
   University Park *B, M, D*
Pennsylvania Highlands Community
   College *A*
Philadelphia University *C, B*
Robert Morris University *B*
St. Joseph's University *M*
Shippensburg University of
   Pennsylvania *B*
University of Pennsylvania *B, M, D*
University of Pittsburgh *M*
University of Scranton *C, A, B, M*
West Chester University of
   Pennsylvania *C, B, M*
York College of Pennsylvania *M*

Puerto Rico
Universidad del Este *B*

Rhode Island
Providence College *C, B*
Roger Williams University *C, B*
Salve Regina University *M*
University of Rhode Island *B*

South Carolina
Anderson University *B*
Clemson University *M*
Medical University of South
   Carolina *B, M*
Tri-County Technical College *C*
University of South Carolina *M*

South Dakota
Presentation College *B*

Tennessee
Carson-Newman College *B*
Freed-Hardeman University *B*
Lipscomb University *M*
Martin Methodist College *B*
Middle Tennessee State University *C*
Southern Adventist University *B, M*
Tennessee State University *B*
University of Tennessee
   Knoxville *D*

Texas
Baylor University *M*
Concordia University at Austin *B*
Dallas Baptist University *B*
Galveston College *A*
Houston Baptist University *M*
LeTourneau University *M*
Midwestern State University *M*
Our Lady of the Lake University of San
   Antonio *M*
Southwestern Adventist University *B*
Texas A&M University
   Commerce *B*
Texas Southern University *B*

Texas State University: San
   Marcos *B, M*
Texas Tech University Health Sciences
   Center *B, M*
Texas Woman's University *M*
Trinity University *M*
University of Houston
   Clear Lake *B, M*
University of North Texas *M*
University of Texas
   Arlington *M*
   Dallas *M*
   Health Science Center at
      Houston *M, D*
   Southwestern Medical Center at
      Dallas *B*

Utah
Stevens-Henager College *B*
Stevens-Henager College of
   Business *M*
Weber State University *B*

Virginia
James Madison University *B*
Mary Baldwin College *B*
Marymount University *M*
Norfolk State University *B*
Shenandoah University *C*
Virginia Commonwealth
   University *M, D*

Washington
Eastern Washington University *B*
Heritage University *B*
Highline Community College *A*
University of Washington *M*
Washington State University *M*

West Virginia
Davis and Elkins College *B*
Marshall University *M*
Mountain State University *B, M*
Wheeling Jesuit University *B*

Wisconsin
Cardinal Stritch University *M*
Marquette University *M*
Northeast Wisconsin Technical
   College *A*
University of Wisconsin
   Eau Claire *B*
   Madison *M*

Health communications

Massachusetts
Emerson College *M*

Michigan
Michigan State University *M*

New York
State University of New York
   College at Cortland *B*

Ohio
Ohio University *B, M, D*
Ohio University
   Zanesville Campus *B*

Pennsylvania
Juniata College *B*

Health management/ clinical assistant

Alaska
University of Alaska
   Southeast *C, A*

California
Ohlone College *C*
Platt College
   Ontario *A*

Georgia
Southwest Georgia Technical
   College *C*

Idaho
Lewis-Clark State College *C, A, B*

Maryland
Hagerstown Community College *C*

Massachusetts
Gibbs College *A*

Michigan
Davenport University *B*
Mott Community College *C*
Oakland Community College *C*

New York
Globe Institute of Technology *C*

North Carolina
Fayetteville Technical Community
   College *C, A*
Pitt Community College *C*

Ohio
Owens Community College
   Toledo *A*

Pennsylvania
Bucks County Community
   College *C, A*
Consolidated School of Business
   Lancaster *A*
   York *A*
Pittsburgh Technical Institute *C, A*

Tennessee
Miller-Motte Technical College *C*

Health/medical psychology

Arizona
Northcentral University *M, D*
Northern Arizona University *M*

Indiana
Indiana University-Purdue University
   Indianapolis *D*

Massachusetts
Bridgewater State College *M*

Minnesota
Capella University *M, D*

New York
State University of New York
   Stony Brook *D*
Yeshiva University *D*

North Carolina
University of North Carolina
   Charlotte *D*

Pennsylvania
University of the Sciences in
   Philadelphia *M*

Texas
Texas State University: San Marcos *M*

University of Texas
   El Paso *D*

Health occupations teacher education

Alabama
Lawson State Community College *A*

California
Crafton Hills College *A*

Florida
Palm Beach Community College *A*

Illinois
North Park University *T*
University of Illinois
   Chicago *M*
   Urbana-Champaign *M*

Indiana
Indiana University-Purdue University
   Indianapolis *B, M*

Massachusetts
Bridgewater State College *B*

Minnesota
Bethel University *M*
Gustavus Adolphus College *T*
Minnesota State University
   Mankato *B*
Winona State University *B, M, T*

New York
New York Institute of
   Technology *A, B, T*
State University of New York
   College at Brockport *M, T*
   College at Buffalo *B, M*
   Oswego *B*

North Carolina
North Carolina State University *B, T*
St. Augustine's College *B*

Ohio
Youngstown State University *B, M*

Oklahoma
University of Central Oklahoma *B*

Tennessee
Belmont University *B, M, T*

Texas
Baylor University *B, T*
Kilgore College *A*
Midwestern State University *M*
Texas A&M University *M, D*
Texas A&M University
   Commerce *M*
Texas State University: San Marcos *T*
University of Houston *M, D*

Health/physical fitness

Alabama
Chattahoochee Valley Community
   College *A*
Gadsden State Community College *A*
Huntingdon College *B, T*
Lawson State Community College *A*
Northeast Alabama Community
   College *A*
Samford University *B*
University of Alabama
   Birmingham *D*
University of Mobile *B, T*

University of Montevallo *B, T*

Arizona

Eastern Arizona College *A*
Grand Canyon University *B*
Northern Arizona University *B, M*
Pima Community College *C*
University of Arizona *M*

Arkansas

Arkansas State University *B*
University of Arkansas *M*

California

Antelope Valley College *A*
California State Polytechnic
   University: Pomona *B, M*
California State University
   Chico *B*
   East Bay *B, M*
   Fresno *A*
   Fullerton *B, M*
   Long Beach *M*
   Sacramento *B, M*
   Stanislaus *B*
Chaffey College *C*
Citrus College *A*
College of the Canyons *A*
Columbia College *A*
Cypress College *C*
Diablo Valley College *C*
East Los Angeles College *A*
El Camino College *A*
Foothill College *C*
Fresno Pacific University *B*
Humboldt State University *B*
Imperial Valley College *A*
Irvine Valley College *C, A*
La Sierra University *B*
Lake Tahoe Community College *A*
Long Beach City College *A*
Master's College *A*
Merced College *A*
Modesto Junior College *A*
Northwestern College *C*
Palomar College *A*
Point Loma Nazarene University *B*
Saddleback College *A*
St. Mary's College of California *B, M*
San Diego City College *C, A*
San Diego Miramar College *A*
San Diego State University *M*
San Jose State University *B, M*
Santa Barbara City College *C, A*
Sierra College *A*
Solano Community College *A*
Southwestern College *A*
University of San Francisco *B*
University of the Pacific *B, M, T*
Vanguard University of Southern
   California *B*
West Los Angeles College *C, A*

Colorado

Adams State College *B, M*
Arapahoe Community College *C, A*
Colorado Christian University *B*
Colorado Mountain College
   Timberline Campus *A*
Community College of Denver *A*
Mesa State College *B*
Trinidad State Junior College *A*

Connecticut

Mitchell College *A*

Delaware

Delaware State University *B*
University of Delaware *B, M*
Wesley College *B, M*

District of Columbia

American University *B*

Florida

Barry University *B*
Florida State University *B, M, D*
Gulf Coast Community College *A*
Palm Beach Community College *A*
University of West Florida *B, M*

Georgia

Armstrong Atlantic State
   University *B, T*
Atlanta Metropolitan College *A*
Brewton-Parker College *B*
Darton College *A*
East Georgia College *A*
Georgia Southern University *B*
Georgia State University *B, M*
Gordon College *A*
Middle Georgia College *A*
Morehouse College *B*
North Georgia College & State
   University *B, M*
South Georgia College *A*
Waycross College *A*
Young Harris College *A*

Hawaii

Brigham Young University-Hawaii *B*
University of Hawaii
   Hilo *B*

Idaho

Albertson College of Idaho *B*
Boise State University *B, M*
College of Southern Idaho *A*
North Idaho College *A*
Northwest Nazarene University *B*

Illinois

Chicago State University *B, M, T*
Elmhurst College *B*
Illinois State University *M*
Illinois Valley Community College *A*
John Wood Community College *A*
Judson College *B, T*
Kishwaukee College *A*
McHenry County College *C*
North Central College *B, T*
Robert Morris College: Chicago *A*
South Suburban College of Cook
   County *A*
Southern Illinois University
   Edwardsville *B, M, T*
Southwestern Illinois College *A*
Trinity Christian College *B*
Trinity International University *B*
University of Illinois
   Urbana-Champaign *M, D*

Indiana

Anderson University *B*
Ball State University *B, M, T*
Goshen College *C, B*
Grace College *B*
Indiana Wesleyan University *B*
Oakland City University *B*
Taylor University *B*
Tri-State University *B*
University of Evansville *B*
Valparaiso University *B*
Vincennes University *A*

Iowa

Briar Cliff University *B*
Coe College *B*
Cornell College *B, T*
Dordt College *B*
Ellsworth Community College *A*
Graceland University *B, T*
Iowa State University *B, M, D*
Iowa Wesleyan College *B*
Loras College *M*
Luther College *B*
Northwestern College *B, T*

St. Ambrose University *B*
Simpson College *B*
University of Northern Iowa *B, M*
Upper Iowa University *B*
William Penn University *B*

Kansas

Baker University *B, T*
Barton County Community College *A*
Bethel College *B*
Central Christian College of Kansas *A*
Coffeyville Community College *A*
Dodge City Community College *A*
Friends University *B*
Garden City Community College *A*
Kansas Wesleyan University *B, T*
McPherson College *B, T*
Ottawa University *B*
Seward County Community College *A*
Southwestern College *B*
Sterling College *B, T*
Tabor College *B*
University of Kansas *B*
Washburn University of Topeka *B*

Kentucky

Asbury College *B*
Campbellsville University *B*
Georgetown College *B*
Lindsey Wilson College *B*
Murray State University *B, T*
University of Kentucky *M, D*
University of Louisville *B*
University of the Cumberlands *B*

Louisiana

Centenary College of Louisiana *B, T*
Louisiana State University
   Shreveport *B*
Louisiana Tech University *B*
Xavier University of Louisiana *B*

Maine

Husson College *B, T*

Maryland

Anne Arundel Community College *A*
Chesapeake College *C*
Columbia Union College *B*
Community College of Baltimore
   County *C, A*
Frostburg State University *B*
Hagerstown Community College *C*
Howard Community College *A*

Massachusetts

Becker College *B*
Bridgewater State College *M*
Cape Cod Community College *A*
Dean College *A*
Eastern Nazarene College *B*
Greenfield Community College *C*
Holyoke Community College *C, A*
Lasell College *B*
Mount Ida College *A*
Northeastern University *B*
Roxbury Community College *C*
Salem State College *B*
Springfield College *B, M*
Westfield State College *B*

Michigan

Adrian College *B, T*
Alma College *T*
Aquinas College *B*
Calvin College *B, T*
Concordia University *B*
Delta College *C, A*
Eastern Michigan University *B*
Grand Valley State University *B*
Henry Ford Community College *C, A*
Lake Michigan College *A*
Lake Superior State University *A*

Michigan State University *D*
Northern Michigan University *B, T*
Olivet College *B*
Spring Arbor University *B, T*

Minnesota

Alexandria Technical College *C, A*
Bemidji State University *B*
Bethel University *B*
Concordia College: Moorhead *B*
Concordia University: St. Paul *B*
Gustavus Adolphus College *B*
Hamline University *B*
Inver Hills Community College *A*
Minnesota State University
   Mankato *B, T*
   Moorhead *B*
Northwestern College *B*
Ridgewater College *A*
St. Cloud State University *B, M*
Southwest Minnesota State
   University *B*
University of St. Thomas *B, M*
Winona State University *B, T*

Mississippi

University of Mississippi *T*
University of Southern Mississippi *B*
William Carey College *B*

Missouri

College of the Ozarks *B*
Culver-Stockton College *T*
Missouri Southern State
   University *B, T*
Missouri State University *M*
Missouri Western State University *B, T*
Southeast Missouri State
   University *B, M*
Southwest Baptist University *B, T*
Three Rivers Community College *A*
Truman State University *B*

Montana

Carroll College *B, T*
Miles Community College *A*
Montana State University
   Billings *B, T*
Rocky Mountain College *B, T*
University of Great Falls *B*
University of Montana: Missoula *B, M*

Nebraska

Concordia University *B, T*
Dana College *B*
Hastings College *B*
Nebraska Wesleyan University *B*
Northeast Community College *A*
Union College *B*
University of Nebraska
   Omaha *M*
Wayne State College *B, T*
Western Nebraska Community
   College *A*

Nevada

University of Nevada
   Las Vegas *B*

New Hampshire

Keene State College *B*
Plymouth State University *B*

New Jersey

Camden County College *C*
County College of Morris *A*
Gloucester County College *A*
Middlesex County College *A*
Rowan University *B*
Salem Community College *A*

New Mexico

Albuquerque Technical-Vocational
  Institute *C*
Eastern New Mexico University *B*
Santa Fe Community College *C, A*

New York

City University of New York
  Brooklyn College *B*
  Lehman College *M*
Corning Community College *A*
Finger Lakes Community College *A*
Fulton-Montgomery Community
  College *A*
Herkimer County Community
  College *A*
Houghton College *B*
Ithaca College *B, M, T*
Monroe Community College *A*
Nassau Community College *A*
State University of New York
  College at Buffalo *B*
  College at Cortland *B*
  College of Agriculture and
    Technology at Morrisville *A*
Suffolk County Community College *A*
Syracuse University *B*

North Carolina

Barton College *B*
Campbell University *B*
Catawba College *B*
Chowan College *B, T*
Greensboro College *B, T*
Guilford College *B*
Johnson C. Smith University *B*
Lenoir-Rhyne College *B, T*
Mars Hill College *B*
North Carolina Agricultural and
  Technical State University *B, T*
North Carolina Central
  University *B, M*
St. Augustine's College *B*
University of North Carolina
  Chapel Hill *B, M*
  Charlotte *B*
  Pembroke *B*
  Wilmington *B*

North Dakota

Dickinson State University *B, T*
Mayville State University *B, T*
Minot State University *B*
Valley City State University *B*

Ohio

Baldwin-Wallace College *B*
Bluffton University *B*
Bowling Green State University *M*
Capital University *B*
Cedarville University *B*
Cincinnati State Technical and
  Community College *C*
Cleveland State University *M*
Defiance College *B, T*
Kent State University *M, D*
Malone College *B*
Miami University
  Oxford Campus *B, T*
Mount Vernon Nazarene
  University *B, T*
Ohio Northern University *B*
Ohio State University
  Columbus Campus *B, M, D*
Ohio University *B, M*
Otterbein College *B*
Shawnee State University *B*
Sinclair Community College *A*
University of Findlay *B, T*
University of Rio Grande *A*
University of Toledo *B, M*
Youngstown State University *B*

Oklahoma

Cameron University *B*
Carl Albert State College *A*
East Central University *B, T*
Eastern Oklahoma State College *A*
Northeastern Oklahoma Agricultural
  and Mechanical College *A*
Northeastern State University *B*
Northwestern Oklahoma State
  University *B*
Oklahoma Baptist University *B, T*
Oklahoma Christian University *B*
Oklahoma City University *B*
Oklahoma Panhandle State
  University *B*
Oklahoma State University *M, D*
Oral Roberts University *B*
Redlands Community College *A*
Rose State College *A*
Seminole State College *A*
University of Science and Arts of
  Oklahoma *B, T*
Western Oklahoma State College *A*

Oregon

Blue Mountain Community College *A*
Central Oregon Community
  College *A*
Concordia University *B*
Corban College *B*
Eastern Oregon University *B*
Lane Community College *C, A*
Linfield College *B, T*
Oregon State University *B, M, D*
Portland Community College *A*
Southern Oregon University *B, T*

Pennsylvania

Baptist Bible College of
  Pennsylvania *B*
Bucks County Community College *A*
Community College of Allegheny
  County *A*
Eastern University *B*
Edinboro University of
  Pennsylvania *B*
Gettysburg College *B*
Indiana University of
  Pennsylvania *B, M*
Lincoln University *B*
Marywood University *B*
Neumann College *B*
Philadelphia Biblical University *B*
Slippery Rock University of
  Pennsylvania *C, B, M, T*
Ursinus College *B, T*
West Chester University of
  Pennsylvania *B, M, T*

Puerto Rico

Inter American University of Puerto
  Rico
  San German Campus *B*
University of Puerto Rico
  Mayaguez *B*
University of the Sacred Heart *B*

South Carolina

Anderson University *B*
Benedict College *B*
Charleston Southern University *B*
Claflin University *B*
Erskine College *B, T*
Furman University *B, T*
Limestone College *B*
Technical College of the
  Lowcountry *C*
Voorhees College *B*

South Dakota

Augustana College *B, T*
Dakota State University *B*
Northern State University *B*

South Dakota State University *B, M, T*

Tennessee

Austin Peay State University *B, M*
Belmont University *B, T*
Carson-Newman College *B, T*
Columbia State Community College *A*
Cumberland University *B*
East Tennessee State
  University *B, M, T*
Hiwassee College *A*
Jackson State Community College *A*
Lambuth University *B*
Lee University *B*
Lincoln Memorial University *B, T*
Maryville College *B, T*
Middle Tennessee State
  University *B, M, D*
Milligan College *B, T*
Tennessee Wesleyan College *B, T*
Trevecca Nazarene University *B*
Tusculum College *B*
University of Tennessee
  Knoxville *B, M, D*
  Martin *B*
Walters State Community College *A*

Texas

Abilene Christian University *B*
Alvin Community College *A*
Amarillo College *A*
Angelo State University *B, M, T*
Austin Community College *C, A*
Baylor University *B*
Clarendon College *A*
Del Mar College *A*
East Texas Baptist University *B*
El Paso Community College *A*
Hardin-Simmons University *B*
Hill College *A*
Houston Baptist University *B*
Houston Community College
  System *C, A*
Howard College *A*
Howard Payne University *B*
Kilgore College *A*
Lamar University *B, M*
Lee College *A*
Lubbock Christian University *B*
Midwestern State University *B, M*
Northeast Texas Community
  College *A*
Northwest Vista College *A*
Prairie View A&M University *B*
St. Philip's College *A*
Sam Houston State University *B*
South Plains College *A*
Southwestern Adventist
  University *A, B, T*
Stephen F. Austin State University *B, T*
Sul Ross State University *B, T*
Tarleton State University *B, D*
Texas A&M University *B, M, D*
Texas A&M University
  Commerce *B*
Texas Christian University *B*
Texas Lutheran University *B, T*
Texas Southern University *B*
Texas State University: San
  Marcos *B, T*
Texas Tech University *B, M*
Texas Wesleyan University *B, M*
Texas Woman's University *B, M, D*
Trinity Valley Community College *A*
Tyler Junior College *A*
University of Houston *B, M*
University of Houston
  Clear Lake *B, M*
University of North Texas *B, M, T*
University of Texas
  Arlington *B*
  Austin *B*
  Brownsville *B*
  El Paso *B, M*

Pan American *B, M*
San Antonio *B*
Tyler *B, M*
  of the Permian Basin *B, M*
University of the Incarnate Word *B, M*
West Texas A&M University *B, M*
Western Texas College *A*

Utah

Brigham Young University *B, M, D*
Snow College *A*
University of Utah *B, D*
Utah Valley State College *A, B*
Weber State University *B*

Vermont

Castleton State College *B*
Johnson State College *B*

Virginia

Averett University *B*
Bridgewater College *B, T*
College of William and Mary *B*
Emory & Henry College *B, T*
Ferrum College *B*
George Mason University *B*
James Madison University *B, M, T*
Liberty University *B*
Longwood University *B, T*
Lynchburg College *B*
Northern Virginia Community
  College *C*
Roanoke College *B*
University of Virginia's College at
  Wise *B*
Virginia Intermont College *B, T*

Washington

Central Washington University *M*
Centralia College *A*
Eastern Washington University *B, M, T*
Highline Community College *A*
Pacific Lutheran University *B*
Seattle Pacific University *M*
University of Puget Sound *T*
Washington State University *B*
Western Washington University *B, M*
Whitworth College *B*

West Virginia

Bethany College *B*
Concord University *B, T*
Shepherd University *T*
West Virginia University *B*
West Virginia Wesleyan College *B*

Wisconsin

Carroll College *B*
University of Wisconsin
  Platteville *B, T*
  Stevens Point *B, T*

Wyoming

Sheridan College *A*

Health physics/
radiologic health

Arkansas

University of Central Arkansas *B*

Florida

Gulf Coast Community College *A*

Georgia

Georgia Institute of Technology *M*

Illinois

Illinois Institute of Technology *M*

Indiana

University of Notre Dame *B*

Kentucky

University of Kentucky *M*

Louisiana

Louisiana State University and
    Agricultural and Mechanical
    College *M*

Massachusetts

Northern Essex Community
    College *A*

Michigan

Delta College *A*
Wayne State University *M*

Nevada

University of Nevada
    Las Vegas *B, M*

New York

Monroe Community College *A*

Oregon

Oregon State University *B, M, D*

Pennsylvania

Bloomsburg University of
    Pennsylvania *B*

Texas

Texas A&M University *B*

Virginia

Central Virginia Community
    College *A*

Health services

Alabama

Central Alabama Community
    College *A*
Community College of the Air
    Force *A*
Remington College
    Mobile *C*
University of Alabama
    Birmingham *B*
Wallace State Community College at
    Hanceville *A*

Arizona

Bryman School *C*
Pima Community College *C*
University of Phoenix *B*

Arkansas

Arkansas State University *B, M*
North Arkansas College *C*
University of Central Arkansas *B*

California

Allan Hancock College *C, A*
American River College *A*
CEI College
    Maric College: Panorama City *C*
California State University
    Chico *B*
    Fullerton *B*
Cypress College *A*
Los Angeles City College *A*
Los Angeles Trade and Technical
    College *A*
Maric College: Anaheim *C*
Mission College *A*
Mount San Antonio College *C, A*
Napa Valley College *C, A*

Platt College
    Ontario *A*
Rio Hondo College *A*
San Jose State University *B*
University of California
    Santa Cruz *B*
Ventura College *A*

Colorado

Adams State College *B*
CollegeAmerica-Denver *A*
Community College of Aurora *C*
National American University
    Denver *A, B*
University of Colorado
    Colorado Springs *B*
University of Northern Colorado *B*

Connecticut

Norwalk Community College *C*
University of Hartford *A*

Florida

City College: Casselberry *A*
Daytona Beach Community College *A*
Florida Atlantic University *B*
Florida College of Natural Health
    Miami *C*
Florida Gulf Coast University *B, M*
Florida Hospital College of Health
    Sciences *A, B*
Gulf Coast Community College *A*
Hillsborough Community
    College *C, A*
Nova Southeastern University *B, M, D*
Palm Beach Community College *A*
St. Petersburg College *A*
Stetson University *B*
University of Central Florida *B, M*
University of Florida *B*
University of North Florida *B, M*

Georgia

Armstrong Atlantic State University *B*
Brewton-Parker College *A*
Central Georgia Technical College *C*
Emory University *M*
Georgia Highlands College *A*
Macon State College *A, B*
Middle Georgia Technical College *C*

Idaho

Idaho State University *B*
North Idaho College *A*

Illinois

City Colleges of Chicago
    Kennedy-King College *A*
National University of Health
    Sciences *D*
Roosevelt University *B*
Rush University *D*
South Suburban College of Cook
    County *C*

Iowa

Dordt College *B*
Grand View College *B*
Marshalltown Community
    College *C, A*

Kansas

Bethel College *C*
Central Christian College of
    Kansas *A, B*
Washburn University of
    Topeka *C, A, B*

Kentucky

Asbury College *B*
Lindsey Wilson College *A*
St. Catharine College *B*

Southern Ohio College
    Brown Mackie College: North
    Kentucky *A*
Spencerian College: Lexington *C, A*

Louisiana

Louisiana State University Health
    Sciences Center *M*
Nicholls State University *A, B*
Our Lady of the Lake College *A*
Southeastern Louisiana University *B*
Southern University
    Shreveport *A*

Maryland

Allegany College of Maryland *A*
Anne Arundel Community
    College *C, A*
Baltimore City Community
    College *C, A*
Community College of Baltimore
    County *C, A*
Harford Community College *A*
University of Maryland
    Baltimore County *B*

Massachusetts

Anna Maria College *A, B*
Berkshire Community College *A*
Emmanuel College *B*
Lasell College *B*
Lesley University *B*
Massachusetts College of Pharmacy
    and Health Sciences *B*
Merrimack College *B*
Middlesex Community College *A*
Roxbury Community College *C*
Worcester State College *B*

Michigan

Cornerstone University *A, B*
Davenport University *C*
Kellogg Community College *A*
Macomb Community College *C, A*
Madonna University *C, A, B, M*
Southwestern Michigan College *C, A*
University of Michigan
    Flint *B*
Western Michigan University *B*

Minnesota

College of St. Scholastica *B*
Northland Community & Technical
    College *C, A*
University of Minnesota
    Crookston *B*
Walden University *D*

Mississippi

Alcorn State University *B*
William Carey College *B*

Missouri

Mineral Area College *A*

Montana

Blackfeet Community College *A*
Flathead Valley Community
    College *C, A*

Nebraska

Little Priest Tribal College *A*
Southeast Community College
    Lincoln Campus *A*

New Hampshire

McIntosh College *A*

New Jersey

Bergen Community College *A*
Essex County College *A*

Fairleigh Dickinson University
    College at Florham *B*
    Metropolitan Campus *B*
Felician College *B*
Georgian Court University *M*
Montclair State University *B*
Ramapo College of New Jersey *B*
Seton Hall University *M, D*
Sussex County Community College *A*
Thomas Edison State College *A, B*
Union County College *A*
University of Medicine and Dentistry
    of New Jersey
    School of Health Related
        Professions *C, B, M, D*
Warren County Community College *A*

New York

Canisius College *M*
City University of New York
    LaGuardia Community College *A*
    Lehman College *B, M*
Daemen College *B*
Dominican College of Blauvelt *B*
Dutchess Community College *A*
Mohawk Valley Community College *C*
New York University *A, B*
North Country Community
    College *C, A*
Orange County Community College *A*
State University of New York
    Farmingdale *C*
Utica College *B*

North Carolina

Brevard College *B*
East Carolina University *B, D*
Miller-Motte Technical College *B*
Pitt Community College *A*
South Piedmont Community
    College *C, A*
Wilkes Community College *C, A*

Ohio

Belmont Technical College *A*
Columbus State Community
    College *C, A*
Cuyahoga Community College
    Metropolitan Campus *A*
DeVry University
    Columbus *A*
Ohio State University
    Lima Campus *B*
Ohio University
    Chillicothe Campus *A*
Sinclair Community College *C, A*
Union Institute & University *B*
University of Cincinnati
    Raymond Walters College *A*
Urbana University *B*
Ursuline College *B*
Zane State College *A*

Oklahoma

Oklahoma State University
    Oklahoma City *A*
Redlands Community College *A*
University of Oklahoma *M, D*

Oregon

Mount Hood Community College *A*
Oregon Institute of Technology *B*
Warner Pacific College *A*

Pennsylvania

Bucks County Community College *A*
Cedar Crest College *C*
Chatham College *M*
Community College of Philadelphia *C*
Edinboro University of
    Pennsylvania *A*
Gettysburg College *B*
Harcum College *A*

Keystone College A
King's College B
La Roche College M
Manor College A
Marywood University B
Mercyhurst College B
Mount Aloysius College B
Penn State
  Abington B
  Altoona A
  Beaver B
  Berks B
  Delaware County B
  Dubois B
  Fayette B
  Harrisburg B, M
  Hazleton B
  Lehigh Valley A
  McKeesport B
  Mont Alto B
  New Kensington B
  Schuylkill - Capital College B
  Shenango B
  Wilkes-Barre B
  Worthington Scranton B
  York B
Reading Area Community College A
St. Joseph's University B
Widener University A, B

Puerto Rico

Pontifical Catholic University of
  Puerto Rico M

Rhode Island

Community College of Rhode
  Island C, A
Roger Williams University C, B

South Carolina

Aiken Technical College C
South University M

Tennessee

East Tennessee State University B
Trevecca Nazarene University B

Texas

Baylor University B
Clarendon College A
Howard Payne University A
Northwest Vista College A
Palo Alto College C, A
Prairie View A&M University B
Sam Houston State University B
South Plains College A
Stephen F. Austin State University B
Texas State University: San Marcos B
Texas Tech University B
Texas Tech University Health Sciences
  Center B
Texas Woman's University B
University of Texas
  Austin B
  Brownsville B
  El Paso B
  Pan American B
  San Antonio B
  Tyler M
Vernon College C

Vermont

Community College of Vermont C, A

Virginia

Blue Ridge Community College A
Ferrum College B
Liberty University B
Old Dominion University B, D
Southwest Virginia Community
  College C, A
Virginia Commonwealth University D

Virginia Western Community
  College A

Washington

Clover Park Technical College C, A
Edmonds Community College C, A
Spokane Falls Community College A

West Virginia

Mountain State College A
Mountain State University B, M
Southern West Virginia Community
  and Technical College C, A

Wisconsin

Concordia University Wisconsin B
Moraine Park Technical College A

Wyoming

University of Wyoming B

Health services administration

California

California Institute of Integral
  Studies M
University of California
  Los Angeles M, D

Colorado

Jones International University M
National American University
  Denver B

Florida

Nova Southeastern University M

Illinois

University of Illinois
  Urbana-Champaign B, M, D

Indiana

Indiana University-Purdue University
  Fort Wayne B
University of Evansville B, M

Iowa

University of Iowa M, D

Louisiana

Our Lady of the Lake College B

Maine

University of New England B

Maryland

Howard Community College A

Massachusetts

Elms College B

Missouri

Harris-Stowe State University B
University of Missouri
  Columbia B
Washington University in St. Louis M

New Jersey

Thomas Edison State College B
University of Medicine and Dentistry
  of New Jersey
  School of Health Related
    Professions D

New York

City University of New York
  New York City College of
    Technology B
Molloy College B

Monroe College B
Rochester Institute of Technology M
State University of New York
  Albany M

North Carolina

Cabarrus College of Health
  Sciences B

Ohio

Ohio University M
Xavier University M

Oregon

Northwest Christian College B

Pennsylvania

Arcadia University B
East Stroudsburg University of
  Pennsylvania B
Harrisburg Area Community
  College A
Marywood University M

South Carolina

Medical University of South
  Carolina M, D

South Dakota

University of South Dakota B

Texas

University of Texas
  Health Science Center at
    Houston M, D

Wisconsin

Marquette University M

Health teacher education

Alabama

Auburn University B
Jacksonville State University B, T
Lawson State Community College A
Stillman College B
University of Alabama
  Birmingham B, M, T
University of South Alabama B, M, T

Arizona

Northern Arizona University B
Prescott College T
University of Arizona B

Arkansas

Arkansas State University B, T
Harding University B, M, T
Ouachita Baptist University B, T
University of Arkansas
  Little Rock B
University of Central Arkansas B, M, T

California

Azusa Pacific University T
California State University
  Chico B, T
  Dominguez Hills T
  Long Beach M, T
  Northridge B, T
  Sacramento T
  San Bernardino M, T
San Francisco State University B, M, T
Vanguard University of Southern
  California T

Connecticut

Southern Connecticut State
  University M, T

Western Connecticut State
  University B

Delaware

Delaware State University B
University of Delaware B, T

District of Columbia

Howard University B
University of the District of
  Columbia B

Florida

Florida International
  University B, M, T
Florida State University B, M, T
Gulf Coast Community College A
Manatee Community College A
Palm Beach Community College A
Tallahassee Community College A

Georgia

Armstrong Atlantic State
  University B, M, T
Augusta State University M
Bainbridge College A
Clark Atlanta University B
Georgia College and State
  University B, M, T
Georgia Perimeter College A
Medical College of Georgia M
Middle Georgia College A
South Georgia College A
University of Georgia B

Idaho

Brigham Young University-Idaho T
Idaho State University B, M
Northwest Nazarene University B
University of Idaho B

Illinois

Chicago State University B
Eastern Illinois University B, T
Eureka College T
Illinois State University B, T
McKendree College B
North Park University T
Northern Illinois University B, T
Olivet Nazarene University B, T
Sauk Valley Community College A
Southern Illinois University
  Carbondale B, M, D
Southern Illinois University
  Edwardsville B, T
Western Illinois University B, M

Indiana

Anderson University B, T
Ball State University B, T
Butler University T
Indiana State University M, T
Indiana University
  Bloomington B, M, D, T
Indiana Wesleyan University T
Manchester College B, T
Tri-State University B, T
University of Indianapolis T
University of St. Francis B, T
Vincennes University A

Iowa

Central College T
Dordt College B
Drake University T
Graceland University T
Iowa State University B, T
Iowa Wesleyan College B
Luther College B
Northwestern College T
St. Ambrose University B, T
Simpson College T

University of Northern Iowa *B, M*
Upper Iowa University *B, T*
Wartburg College *T*
William Penn University *B*

Kansas

Bethany College *B*
Bethel College *T*
Emporia State University *T*
Garden City Community College *A*
McPherson College *T*
MidAmerica Nazarene University *B, T*
Ottawa University *T*
Tabor College *B, T*
Washburn University of Topeka *B*

Kentucky

Campbellsville University *B*
Kentucky Wesleyan College *T*
Morehead State University *B*
Murray State University *B, T*
Union College *B*
University of Kentucky *B*
University of the Cumberlands *B, T*

Louisiana

Centenary College of Louisiana *B, T*

Maine

University of Maine
  Farmington *B, T*
  Presque Isle *B*

Maryland

Allegany College of Maryland *A*
Community College of Baltimore
  County *A*
Morgan State University *B*
Prince George's Community
  College *A*
Salisbury University *B, T*
University of Maryland
  College Park *B, M, D*
  Eastern Shore *B*

Massachusetts

Boston University *M, T*
Bridgewater State College *B*
Curry College *B*
Framingham State College *B*
Northeastern University *B*
Springfield College *B, M, T*
University of Massachusetts
  Lowell *B*
Westfield State College *B, T*
Worcester State College *M, T*

Michigan

Adrian College *B, T*
Alma College *T*
Central Michigan University *B, T*
Ferris State University *B*
Madonna University *T*
Michigan State University *M, D*
Northern Michigan University *B, M, T*
Olivet College *B, T*
Wayne State University *B, M, T*
Western Michigan University *B, T*

Minnesota

Augsburg College *B, T*
Bemidji State University *T*
Bethel University *B*
Concordia College: Moorhead *B, T*
Concordia University: St. Paul *B, T*
Gustavus Adolphus College *T*
Hamline University *B, T*
Minnesota State University
  Mankato *B, M, T*
  Moorhead *B*
Northland Community & Technical
  College *A*

Ridgewater College *A*
Southwest Minnesota State
  University *B, T*
University of Minnesota
  Duluth *B*
University of St. Thomas *B, T*
Vermilion Community College *A*
Winona State University *B, M, T*

Mississippi

Coahoma Community College *A*
Itawamba Community College *A*
Mississippi Delta Community
  College *A*
Mississippi State University *T*
Tougaloo College *B*

Missouri

College of the Ozarks *T*
Culver-Stockton College *T*
Lindenwood University *B*
Missouri Baptist University *B, T*
Missouri Southern State
  University *B, T*
Northwest Missouri State
  University *B, T*
Southwest Baptist University *B, T*
Truman State University *M, T*

Montana

Montana State University
  Billings *B, T*
University of Great Falls *B*
University of Montana: Missoula *T*
University of Montana: Western *B, T*

Nebraska

Concordia University *B, T*
University of Nebraska
  Kearney *B, T*
  Lincoln *B*

Nevada

University of Nevada
  Las Vegas *B*
  Reno *B*

New Hampshire

Plymouth State University *M, T*

New Jersey

Caldwell College *T*
The College of New Jersey *B, M*
Montclair State University *B, M, T*
Rowan University *B, T*
Seton Hall University *B, M, T*
William Paterson University of New
  Jersey *B, T*

New Mexico

University of New Mexico *B, M*
Western New Mexico University *B*

New York

Adelphi University *B, M, T*
City University of New York
  Hunter College *B, T*
  Lehman College *B, M, T*
  York College *B, T*
Corning Community College *A*
Hofstra University *B, M*
Ithaca College *B, T*
Long Island University
  C.W. Post Campus *B, T*
Manhattan College *B, T*
New York University *B, M, D, T*
Niagara County Community
  College *A*
St. Bonaventure University *M*
State University of New York
  Buffalo *M*
  College at Brockport *B, M, T*

College at Cortland *B, M, T*
  Oswego *T*

North Carolina

Appalachian State University *B, T*
East Carolina University *B, M*
Elon University *B, T*
Fayetteville State University *B, T*
Gardner-Webb University *B*
Johnson C. Smith University *B*
Lenoir Community College *A*
North Carolina Central University *B, T*
University of North Carolina
  Greensboro *B, T*

North Dakota

Dickinson State University *B, T*
Mayville State University *B, T*
North Dakota State University *B, T*
Valley City State University *B, T*

Ohio

Ashland University *T*
Baldwin-Wallace College *T*
Bluffton University *B*
Bowling Green State University *B*
Capital University *T*
Cedarville University *B, T*
Central State University *B*
Defiance College *B, T*
Kent State University *B, M, D*
Malone College *B*
Miami University
  Oxford Campus *B, M, T*
Mount Union College *B, T*
Mount Vernon Nazarene
  University *B, M, T*
Ohio Northern University *B, T*
Ohio State University
  Columbus Campus *M, D*
Ohio Wesleyan University *B*
Otterbein College *B*
University of Akron *B*
University of Cincinnati *B, M, T*
University of Findlay *B, M, T*
University of Rio Grande *B, T*
University of Toledo *B, M, T*
Wilmington College *B*
Youngstown State University *B, M*

Oklahoma

Bacone College *B*
East Central University *T*
Eastern Oklahoma State College *A*
Northeastern State University *B*
Northwestern Oklahoma State
  University *B, T*
Oklahoma Baptist University *B, T*
Oklahoma City University *B*
Oral Roberts University *B, T*
Southeastern Oklahoma State
  University *B, M, T*
Southwestern Oklahoma State
  University *B, M, T*

Oregon

Chemeketa Community College *A*
Concordia University *B, M, T*
George Fox University *T*
Linfield College *T*
Oregon State University *M*
Portland State University *B, M, T*
Western Oregon University *B, T*

Pennsylvania

Arcadia University *M*
Bucks County Community College *A*
East Stroudsburg University of
  Pennsylvania *B, M, T*
Gettysburg College *T*
Lincoln University *T*
Marywood University *B*

Penn State
  Harrisburg *M*
St. Joseph's University *M*
Temple University *B, M*
West Chester University of
  Pennsylvania *M, T*

Puerto Rico

Universidad del Este *B*

Rhode Island

Rhode Island College *B, M*
Roger Williams University *B*

South Carolina

South Carolina State University *B, T*
University of South Carolina *M*

South Dakota

Dakota State University *B, T*
Mount Marty College *B*
University of Sioux Falls *B*
University of South Dakota *M*

Tennessee

Austin Peay State University *B, T*
Belmont University *B, M, T*
Bethel College *B*
Lambuth University *B, T*
Lincoln Memorial University *B, T*
Maryville College *B, T*
Middle Tennessee State University *B*
Tennessee Technological
  University *B, M, T*
Union University *T*
University of Tennessee
  Knoxville *M, D, T*
Vanderbilt University *M*

Texas

Angelina College *A*
Austin Community College *A*
Baylor University *M*
Brazosport College *A*
Del Mar College *A*
Kilgore College *A*
Lamar University *B, M, T*
Laredo Community College *A*
Prairie View A&M University *M*
Sam Houston State University *M, T*
Texas A&M University *M, D*
Texas A&M University
  Commerce *M, T*
  Kingsville *B*
Texas Southern University *M*
Texas State University: San
  Marcos *M, T*
University of Houston *B, M*
University of Houston
  Clear Lake *T*
University of Texas
  Austin *M, D*
  El Paso *M*
  San Antonio *T*
  Tyler *M*

Utah

Brigham Young University *B*
Snow College *A*
University of Utah *B*
Utah State University *B*
Utah Valley State College *B*

Virginia

Averett University *B, T*
Bluefield College *T*
Eastern Mennonite University *T*
George Mason University *B, M*
Hampton University *B*
James Madison University *M, T*
Liberty University *B, T*
Longwood University *B, T*

Lynchburg College *B*
Radford University *B, T*
University of Virginia's College at
    Wise *T*
Virginia Commonwealth University *B*

Washington
Central Washington University *B, T*
Eastern Washington University *B, T*
Northwest University *T*
Renton Technical College *A*
Washington State University *B, T*
Whitworth College *B, T*

West Virginia
Concord University *B*
Shepherd University *T*
University of Charleston *B*
West Liberty State College *B*
West Virginia State University *B*
West Virginia University *T*
West Virginia Wesleyan College *B*

Wisconsin
Carroll College *B, T*
Concordia University Wisconsin *B*
Ripon College *T*
University of Wisconsin
    La Crosse *B, M, T*
    Platteville *T*
    River Falls *T*
    Superior *T*

Health unit coordinator

Florida
Pasco-Hernando Community
    College *C*
Pensacola Junior College *C*

Georgia
Southwest Georgia Technical
    College *C*

Iowa
Indian Hills Community College *C*

Kentucky
Jefferson Community College *C*

Michigan
Delta College *C*

Minnesota
Hennepin Technical College *C, A*
Minnesota State College - Southeast
    Technical *C*
Rasmussen College
    Eagan *A*
Rochester Community and Technical
    College *C*
St. Paul College *C*

Missouri
Lester L. Cox College of Nursing and
    Health Sciences *C*

New Mexico
Albuquerque Technical-Vocational
    Institute *C*

New York
Globe Institute of Technology *C*

North Carolina
Pitt Community College *C*
Roanoke-Chowan Community
    College *C*

Ohio
Cincinnati State Technical and
    Community College *C, A*

Oklahoma
Oklahoma State University
    Oklahoma City *C*

Pennsylvania
Bidwell Training Center *C*
Career Training Academy:
    Monroeville *A*
Community College of Allegheny
    County *C*
Consolidated School of Business
    Lancaster *A*
    York *A*
Delaware County Community
    College *C*
Douglas Education Center *C*

South Dakota
Southeast Technical Institute *C*

Utah
Salt Lake Community College *C*

Washington
Clover Park Technical College *C*
Spokane Community College *C, A*

Wisconsin
Gateway Technical College *C*
Lakeshore Technical College *C*
Mid-State Technical College *C*
Milwaukee Area Technical College *C*
Western Wisconsin Technical
    College *C*

Wyoming
Casper College *C*

Health unit manager

Illinois
Southern Illinois University
    Carbondale *M*

Heating/air conditioning/ refrigeration maintenance

Alabama
Bevill State Community College *A*
Calhoun Community College *C, A*
Community College of the Air
    Force *A*
Gadsden State Community
    College *C, A*
J. F. Drake State Technical College *C*
Lawson State Community College *C*
Southern Union State Community
    College *C, A*
Wallace State Community College at
    Hanceville *C, A*

Alaska
University of Alaska
    Anchorage *C, A*

Arizona
Arizona Western College *C, A*
Eastern Arizona College *C*
Gateway Community College *C, A*
Mohave Community College *C, A*

Arkansas
Arkansas Northeastern College *C*
Arkansas Tech University *C*

North Arkansas College *C*
Ouachita Technical College *C*
Pulaski Technical College *A*
Southeast Arkansas College *C*
University of Arkansas
    Community College at Hope *C*

California
Cerro Coso Community College *C, A*
Citrus College *C, A*
College of San Mateo *C, A*
College of the Desert *C, A*
Cypress College *A*
El Camino College *C, A*
Foothill College *C*
Fresno City College *C, A*
Laney College *C, A*
Los Angeles Trade and Technical
    College *C, A*
Modesto Junior College *C, A*
Mount San Antonio College *C, A*
Orange Coast College *C, A*
Riverside Community College *C, A*
Sacramento City College *C, A*
San Bernardino Valley College *C, A*
San Diego City College *C, A*
San Joaquin Valley College Inc. *A*
San Jose City College *C, A*
Santa Rosa Junior College *C*
Shasta College *C, A*
Southwestern College *C*

Colorado
Community College of Aurora *A*
Red Rocks Community College *C, A*
Westwood College of Technology *C, A*

Delaware
Delaware Technical and Community
    College
    Owens Campus *C, A*
    Stanton/Wilmington Campus *A*

District of Columbia
University of the District of
    Columbia *C*

Florida
Brevard Community College *C, A*
Central Florida Community College *C*
Daytona Beach Community College *C*
Florida Community College at
    Jacksonville *C*
Hillsborough Community College *A*
Indian River Community College *C, A*
Lake City Community College *C*
Miami Dade College *C, A*
New England Institute of
    Technology *C, A*
Palm Beach Community College *C*
Santa Fe Community College *C*
Seminole Community College *C*
South Florida Community College *C*

Georgia
Albany Technical College *C*
Athens Technical College *C*
Augusta Technical Institute *C*
Central Georgia Technical College *C*
Chattahoochee Technical College *C*
Coastal Georgia Community
    College *C*
Columbus Technical College *C*
Darton College *A*
DeKalb Technical College *C*
Georgia Southwestern State
    University *A*
Gwinnett Technical College *C*
Middle Georgia College *A*
Savannah Technical College *C, A*
Southwest Georgia Technical
    College *C*
Waycross College *A*

Hawaii
University of Hawaii
    Honolulu Community College *C, A*

Idaho
Boise State University *C, A*
College of Southern Idaho *C, A*
Lewis-Clark State College *C, A, B*
North Idaho College *C, A*

Illinois
Black Hawk College *C, A*
City Colleges of Chicago
    Kennedy-King College *C, A*
College of DuPage *C, A*
College of Lake County *C, A*
Elgin Community College *C, A*
Heartland Community College *C*
Illinois Eastern Community Colleges
    Lincoln Trail College *C, A*
John A. Logan College *C*
Joliet Junior College *C*
Kankakee Community College *C, A*
Kaskaskia College *C*
Lake Land College *C*
Lincoln Land Community College *C*
Moraine Valley Community College *C*
Morton College *C, A*
Oakton Community College *C*
Prairie State College *C*
Rend Lake College *C*
Richland Community College *C, A*
Sauk Valley Community College *C, A*
Southwestern Illinois College *C, A*
Triton College *C, A*
Waubonsee Community College *C, A*
William Rainey Harper College *C, A*

Indiana
Ivy Tech State College
    Ivy Tech Community College:
        Bloomington *C, A*
    Ivy Tech Community College:
        Central Indiana *C, A*
    Ivy Tech Community College:
        Columbus *C, A*
    Ivy Tech Community College: East
        Central *C, A*
    Ivy Tech Community College:
        Kokomo *C, A*
    Ivy Tech Community College:
        Lafayette *C, A*
    Ivy Tech Community College: North
        Central *C, A*
    Ivy Tech Community College:
        Northeast *C, A*
    Ivy Tech Community College:
        Northwest *C, A*
    Ivy Tech Community College: South
        Central *C, A*
    Ivy Tech Community College:
        Southwest *C, A*
    Ivy Tech Community College:
        Wabash Valley *C, A*
    Ivy Tech Community College:
        Whitewater *C, A*
Oakland City University *A*

Iowa
Des Moines Area Community
    College *C, A*
Hawkeye Community College *C*
Indian Hills Community College *C*
Kirkwood Community College *C*
Marshalltown Community College *A*
North Iowa Area Community
    College *C, A*
Northeast Iowa Community
    College *C*
Scott Community College *A*
Western Iowa Tech Community
    College *C*

Kansas

Coffeyville Community College *C*
Manhattan Area Technical
   College *C, A*

Kentucky

Big Sandy Community and Technical
   College *C, A*
Elizabethtown Community and
   Technical College *C*
Jefferson Community College *C*
Owensboro Community College *C*
Somerset Community College *C*

Louisiana

ITI Technical College *C*
Nunez Community College *C, A*

Maine

Eastern Maine Community
   College *C, A*
Northern Maine Community
   College *A*
Southern Maine Community
   College *C, A*
Washington County Community
   College *C*

Maryland

Chesapeake College *C*
Community College of Baltimore
   County *C, A*

Massachusetts

Benjamin Franklin Institute of
   Technology *C*
Springfield Technical Community
   College *C*

Michigan

Baker College
   of Owosso *C*
Delta College *C, A*
Grand Rapids Community
   College *C, A*
Henry Ford Community College *C, A*
Jackson Community College *C, A*
Kellogg Community College *C, A*
Kirtland Community College *C, A*
Lansing Community College *A*
Macomb Community College *C, A*
Mid Michigan Community
   College *C, A*
Mott Community College *C*
Northern Michigan University *C, A*
Washtenaw Community College *A*
Wayne County Community
   College *C, A*

Minnesota

Century Community and Technical
   College *C, A*
Dunwoody College of
   Technology *C, A*
Hennepin Technical College *C, A*
Hibbing Community College *C*
Minneapolis Community and
   Technical College *C, A*
Minnesota State College - Southeast
   Technical *C, A*
Minnesota State Community and
   Technical College - Fergus Falls *C*
Northwest Technical College *C*
St. Cloud Technical College *C, A*
South Central College *C, A*

Mississippi

East Central Community College *C*
Hinds Community College *C*
Holmes Community College *A*
Itawamba Community College *C*

Mississippi Delta Community
   College *A*
Mississippi Gulf Coast Community
   College
   Jefferson Davis Campus *C*
Pearl River Community College *C, A*
Southwest Mississippi Community
   College *C*

Missouri

East Central College *C, A*
Jefferson College *C, A*
Mineral Area College *C, A*
Ozarks Technical Community
   College *C, A*
Penn Valley Community College *C, A*
Ranken Technical College *A*
Vatterott College *C, A, B*

Montana

Montana State University
   Billings *A*

Nebraska

Central Community College *C, A*
Metropolitan Community
   College *C, A*
Mid-Plains Community College
   Area *C, A*
Northeast Community College *A*
Vatterott College: Spring Valley *C, A*

Nevada

Community College of Southern
   Nevada *C, A*
Truckee Meadows Community
   College *C, A*

New Hampshire

New Hampshire Community
   Technical College
   Manchester *C, A*

New Jersey

Raritan Valley Community College *A*

New Mexico

Albuquerque Technical-Vocational
   Institute *C*
Clovis Community College *C, A*
Dona Ana Branch Community College
   of New Mexico State
   University *C, A*

New York

Dutchess Community College *C*
Erie Community College
   North Campus *C*
Hudson Valley Community College *A*
Mohawk Valley Community College *C*
Monroe Community College *C, A*
State University of New York
   College of Technology at Alfred *A*
   College of Technology at Canton *C*
   College of Technology at Delhi *C, A*
Technical Career Institutes *C, A*

North Carolina

Alamance Community College *C, A*
Asheville-Buncombe Technical
   Community College *C, A*
Blue Ridge Community College *C*
Brunswick Community College *C*
Caldwell Community College and
   Technical Institute *C*
Cape Fear Community College *C*
Catawba Valley Community College *C*
Central Piedmont Community
   College *C, A*
Cleveland Community College *C*
Coastal Carolina Community
   College *C*

College of the Albemarle *C*
Craven Community College *C, A*
Davidson County Community
   College *C*
Fayetteville Technical Community
   College *C, A, D*
Forsyth Technical Community
   College *C*
Gaston College *C*
Guilford Technical Community
   College *C, A*
Johnston Community College *C, A*
Martin Community College *C, A*
McDowell Technical Community
   College *C*
Mitchell Community College *C*
Piedmont Community College *C*
Pitt Community College *C, A*
Roanoke-Chowan Community
   College *C*
Rockingham Community College *C*
Rowan-Cabarrus Community
   College *C*
South Piedmont Community
   College *C, A*
Southeastern Community College *C*
Southwestern Community College *C*
Stanly Community College *C*
Surry Community College *C, A*
Tri-County Community College *C*
Vance-Granville Community
   College *C*
Wake Technical Community
   College *C*
Wilson Technical Community
   College *C*

North Dakota

Bismarck State College *C, A*
North Dakota State College of
   Science *C, A*

Ohio

Belmont Technical College *C, A*
Cincinnati State Technical and
   Community College *C*
Columbus State Community
   College *C, A*
ETI Technical College of Niles *C*
Sinclair Community College *C, A*
Stark State College of Technology *A*
University of Northwestern Ohio *C, A*
Washington State Community
   College *A*

Oklahoma

Oklahoma State University
   Okmulgee *A*
Rose State College *A*
Tulsa Community College *A*
Vatterott College *C, A, B*
Vatterott College
   Tulsa *C, A*

Oregon

Lane Community College *C, A*
Linn-Benton Community College *C*
Portland Community College *C, A*

Pennsylvania

CHI Institute: Broomall *C*
CHI Institute: Southampton *C*
Community College of Allegheny
   County *C, A*
Dean Institute of Technology *A*
Delaware County Community
   College *C*
Harrisburg Area Community
   College *C, A*
Lehigh Carbon Community
   College *C, A*
Luzerne County Community
   College *A*

Northampton County Area
   Community College *C, A*
Pennsylvania College of Technology *B*
Pennsylvania Highlands Community
   College *A*
Reading Area Community College *C*
Thaddeus Stevens College of
   Technology *A*
Triangle Tech
   Greensburg *C*
   Pittsburgh *C, A*
Westmoreland County Community
   College *A*

Rhode Island

New England Institute of
   Technology *A*

South Carolina

Aiken Technical College *C*
Central Carolina Technical College *C*
Florence-Darlington Technical
   College *C, A*
Greenville Technical College *C*
Horry-Georgetown Technical
   College *C, A*
Midlands Technical College *C, A*
Piedmont Technical College *C, A*
Spartanburg Technical College *C*
Technical College of the
   Lowcountry *C, A*
Tri-County Technical College *A*
Trident Technical College *C*
Williamsburg Technical College *C, A*
York Technical College *C, A*

South Dakota

Mitchell Technical Institute *A*
Southeast Technical Institute *A*

Tennessee

Chattanooga State Technical
   Community College *C*
Northeast State Technical Community
   College *C*

Texas

Austin Community College *C*
Brazosport College *C, A*
Cedar Valley College *C, A*
Central Texas College *C, A*
Coastal Bend College *C, A*
College of the Mainland *C, A*
Del Mar College *C, A*
Eastfield College *C, A*
El Paso Community College *C, A*
Frank Phillips College *C*
Grayson County College *C, A*
Hill College *C*
Houston Community College
   System *C*
Lamar State College at Port
   Arthur *C, A*
Laredo Community College *C*
Lee College *C, A*
Midland College *C, A*
North Harris Montgomery
   Community College District *C, A*
Odessa College *C, A*
Panola College *C*
Paris Junior College *A*
St. Philip's College *C, A*
San Jacinto College
   North *C, A*
South Plains College *C, A*
South Texas College *C, A*
Tarrant County College *C, A*
Texarkana College *C*
Texas Southmost College *C*
Texas State Technical College
   Harlingen *C, A*
   Waco *C, A*
   West Texas *C*

Trinity Valley Community College *C*
Tyler Junior College *C, A*
Universal Technical Institute *C*
University of Texas
  Brownsville *C*
Western Technical Institute: Diana
  Drive *A*
Western Texas College *C*
Wharton County Junior College *C*

Utah

Salt Lake Community College *C, A*
Utah Valley State College *C, A*

Virginia

Central Virginia Community
  College *C*
Danville Community College *A*
John Tyler Community College *C*
Mountain Empire Community
  College *C*
New River Community College *C*
Northern Virginia Community
  College *C, A*
Patrick Henry Community College *C*
Southside Virginia Community
  College *C*
Southwest Virginia Community
  College *C*
Thomas Nelson Community
  College *C*
Tidewater Community College *C*
Virginia Highlands Community
  College *C*
Virginia Western Community
  College *C, A*

Washington

Bellingham Technical College *A*
Clover Park Technical College *C, A*
Renton Technical College *C, A*
Spokane Community College *A*
Spokane Falls Community College *C*
Walla Walla Community College *C, A*
Wenatchee Valley College *C, A*

West Virginia

West Virginia Northern Community
  College *A*

Wisconsin

Chippewa Valley Technical College *A*
Gateway Technical College *A*
Milwaukee Area Technical College *C*
Moraine Park Technical College *C*
Northeast Wisconsin Technical
  College *A*
Waukesha County Technical
  College *C*
Western Wisconsin Technical
  College *C*

Heating/air conditioning/ refrigeration technology

Alabama

Calhoun Community College *A*
Gadsden State Community
  College *C, A*
Northwest-Shoals Community
  College *C*
Shelton State Community
  College *C, A*
Trenholm State Technical College *C, A*

Arizona

Refrigeration School *C*

California

Citrus College *C*
College of the Desert *C, A*
Long Beach City College *C, A*
San Jose City College *C, A*

Florida

Palm Beach Community College *C*

Illinois

City Colleges of Chicago
  Kennedy-King College *C, A*
Oakton Community College *C*

Massachusetts

Massasoit Community College *C, A*
Springfield Technical Community
  College *A*

Michigan

Delta College *C, A*
Ferris State University *A*
Grand Rapids Community College *A*
Jackson Community College *C, A*
Mott Community College *C, A*
Northern Michigan University *A*
Oakland Community College *C, A*

Minnesota

Dunwoody College of Technology *A*
Hennepin Technical College *C, A*
Hibbing Community College *C*

Nebraska

Northeast Community College *A*

New York

City University of New York
  New York City College of
    Technology *A*
Mohawk Valley Community College *A*
State University of New York
  College of Technology at
    Canton *C, A*
Suffolk County Community College *A*

North Carolina

College of the Albemarle *C, A*
Gaston College *C*
Roanoke-Chowan Community
  College *C*
Robeson Community College *C*

North Dakota

North Dakota State College of
  Science *A*

Ohio

Hocking College *A*
Owens Community College
  Toledo *C*
Sinclair Community College *C*

Oklahoma

Rose State College *A*

Pennsylvania

Delaware County Community
  College *C*
Pennsylvania College of
  Technology *A, B*
Triangle Tech
  Greensburg *A*

Puerto Rico

Humacao Community College *C, A*

South Carolina

York Technical College *C, A*

South Dakota

Southeast Technical Institute *C, A*

Tennessee

Northeast State Technical Community
  College *C*

Texas

Austin Community College *C, A*
St. Philip's College *C, A*

Wisconsin

Gateway Technical College *A*
Milwaukee Area Technical College *A*
Western Wisconsin Technical
  College *A*

Heavy/earthmoving equipment operation

Alabama

Shelton State Community College *C*

Arkansas

North Arkansas College *C*

Florida

Indian River Community College *C*

Indiana

Ivy Tech State College
  Ivy Tech Community College:
    Southwest *C, A*
  Ivy Tech Community College:
    Wabash Valley *C, A*

Iowa

Northwest Iowa Community
  College *C*

Minnesota

Central Lakes College *C*

North Carolina

Wilson Technical Community
  College *C*

Virginia

Southside Virginia Community
  College *C*

Heavy equipment maintenance

California

San Joaquin Delta College *C, A*
Shasta College *C*

Georgia

Albany Technical College *C*
Georgia Southwestern State
  University *A*
Gwinnett Technical College *C*
Southwest Georgia Technical
  College *A*

Illinois

Rend Lake College *C, A*

Michigan

Ferris State University *A, B*

Minnesota

Central Lakes College *A*
Dakota County Technical College *C, A*

New York

State University of New York
  College of Agriculture and
    Technology at Morrisville *A*

North Carolina

Asheville-Buncombe Technical
  Community College *C*
Wilson Technical Community
  College *C*

Oregon

Linn-Benton Community College *A*

Pennsylvania

Pennsylvania College of
  Technology *C, A*

Utah

Salt Lake Community College *A*

Washington

Bates Technical College *A*
Clover Park Technical College *C, A*
Lower Columbia College *A*

Wyoming

Western Wyoming Community
  College *C, A*

Hebrew

California

University of California
  Los Angeles *B*

Connecticut

Fairfield University *B*

District of Columbia

Catholic University of America *M, D*
George Washington University *B*

Illinois

Concordia University *B*
Moody Bible Institute *B*
Trinity International University *M*
University of Chicago *B*
University of Illinois
  Urbana-Champaign *B*

Maryland

Baltimore Hebrew University *B, M, D*
Washington Bible College *M*

Massachusetts

Brandeis University *B*

Michigan

University of Michigan *B*

Minnesota

Carleton College *B*
University of Minnesota
  Twin Cities *B*

Missouri

Washington University in St.
  Louis *B, M*

New Hampshire

Dartmouth College *B*

New York

City University of New York
  Hunter College *B*
  Lehman College *B*
  Queens College *B*
Hofstra University *B*

Jewish Theological Seminary of
America *M, D*
New York University *B, M, D*
State University of New York
Binghamton *B*
Touro College *B*
Yeshiva University *B*

Ohio

Laura and Alvin Siegal College of
Judaic Studies *B, M*
Ohio State University
Columbus Campus *B*

Oregon

Multnomah Bible College *B*

Pennsylvania

Temple University *B*

Texas

University of Texas
Austin *B, M, D*

Washington

University of Washington *B*

Wisconsin

University of Wisconsin
Madison *B, M, D*
Milwaukee *B*

Hematology technology

Pennsylvania

Academy of Medical Arts and
Business *A*

Herbalism

Washington

Bastyr University *B*

Higher education administration

Alabama

University of Alabama *M, D*

Alaska

University of Alaska
Anchorage *M, T*

Arizona

Arizona State University *M, D*
Northcentral University *M, D*
University of Arizona *M, D*

Arkansas

University of Arkansas *M, D*
University of Arkansas
Little Rock *M, D*

California

Azusa Pacific University *M, D*
California State University
Fullerton *M*
San Jose State University *M*
Stanford University *D*
University of Southern
California *M, D*

Colorado

Colorado State University *M*
Jones International University *M*
University of Denver *M, D*
University of Northern Colorado *D*

Connecticut

University of Connecticut *M, D, T*

District of Columbia

George Washington University *M, D*

Florida

Barry University *M*
Florida International University *D*
Florida State University *M, D*
Nova Southeastern University *D*
University of Florida *D*
University of Miami *M*
University of South Florida *M*

Georgia

Georgia Southern University *M*
Georgia State University *M, D*
University of Georgia *D*

Illinois

Benedictine University *D*
Loyola University of Chicago *M, D*
Southern Illinois University
Carbondale *M*
University of Illinois
Urbana-Champaign *M, D*

Indiana

Indiana University
Bloomington *D*
Indiana University-Purdue University
Indianapolis *M*

Iowa

Iowa State University *M, D*
University of Iowa *M, D*

Kansas

University of Kansas *M*

Kentucky

University of Kentucky *M*
University of Louisville *M*

Maine

University of Maine *M, D*
University of Southern Maine *M*

Maryland

Morgan State University *D*

Massachusetts

Boston College *M, D*
Harvard College *M, D*
Salem State College *M*
Springfield College *D*
Suffolk University *M*

Michigan

Eastern Michigan University *M*
Grand Valley State University *M*
Michigan State University *M, D*

Minnesota

Capella University *M, D*
Minnesota State University
Mankato *M*

Mississippi

University of Mississippi *M, D*
University of Southern Mississippi *D*

Missouri

Central Missouri State University *M*
St. Louis University *M, D*
Southeast Missouri State University *M*
University of Missouri
Columbia *D*

Nevada

University of Nevada
Reno *M, D*

New Jersey

Rowan University *M*
Seton Hall University *D*

New York

City University of New York
Baruch College *M*
Fordham University *M, D*
New York University *M, D*
St. Bonaventure University *M*
State University of New York
Albany *M, D*
Buffalo *M, D*
College at Buffalo *M*
Syracuse University *M, D*
University of Rochester *M, D*

North Carolina

Appalachian State University *M*
Fayetteville State University *M*
North Carolina State University *M, D*
University of North Carolina
Greensboro *M*

Ohio

Bowling Green State University *D*
Kent State University *M, D*
Ohio State University
Columbus Campus *M, D*
Ohio University *M, D*
University of Akron *M*
University of Dayton *M*
University of Findlay *M, T*
University of Toledo *M, D, T*
Wright State University *M*
Youngstown State University *M*

Oklahoma

Oklahoma State University *D*

Oregon

Portland State University *D*

Pennsylvania

Drexel University *M*
Geneva College *M*
Marywood University *D*
Penn State
University Park *M, D*
University of Pennsylvania *M, D*
Villanova University *M*
Widener University *M, D*

Puerto Rico

Universidad del Este *M*

South Dakota

University of South Dakota *M, D*

Tennessee

University of Memphis *D*
Vanderbilt University *M, D*

Texas

Dallas Baptist University *M, D*
Texas A&M University
Commerce *M, D*
Kingsville *M, D*
Texas Southern University *D*
University of Houston *M, D*
University of North Texas *D*
University of Texas
San Antonio *M*

Vermont

University of Vermont *M*

Virginia

Old Dominion University *M, D*
University of Virginia *D*

Washington

Seattle University *M*
University of Washington *M, D*
Washington State University *M, D*
Western Washington University *M*

Wisconsin

Concordia University Wisconsin *M*

Hindu studies

California

California Institute of Integral
Studies *M, D*

Hispanic-American/ Latino/Chicano studies

Arizona

Arizona State University *B*
University of Arizona *B, M*

California

California State University
East Bay *B*
Fullerton *B*
Long Beach *B*
Los Angeles *B, M*
Northridge *A, B*
San Bernardino *B*
Cerritos Community College *A*
City College of San Francisco *A*
Claremont McKenna College *B*
Contra Costa College *A*
De Anza College *A*
El Camino College *A*
Fresno City College *A*
Loyola Marymount University *B*
Mills College *B*
Pitzer College *B*
San Diego Mesa College *A*
San Diego State University *B*
San Francisco State University *B*
San Jose State University *M*
Santa Ana College *A*
Santa Barbara City College *A*
Scripps College *B*
Solano Community College *A*
Sonoma State University *B*
Southwestern College *A*
Stanford University *B*
University of California
Berkeley *B*
Davis *B*
Irvine *B*
Los Angeles *B*
Riverside *B*
Santa Barbara *B, M, D*
Santa Cruz *B*
University of Southern California *B*
Ventura College *A*

Colorado

Metropolitan State College of
Denver *B*
University of Northern Colorado *B*

Connecticut

Connecticut College *B*

Illinois

University of Illinois
Chicago *M*

Maine

University of Southern Maine *B*

Massachusetts

Boston College *B*
Hampshire College *B*

Michigan

University of Michigan *B*
Wayne State University *B*

Minnesota

University of Minnesota
  Twin Cities *B*

New Hampshire

Dartmouth College *B*

New Jersey

Rutgers, The State University of New
  Jersey
  New Brunswick/Piscataway
    Campus *B*
  Newark Regional Campus *B*

New Mexico

Western New Mexico University *B*

New York

City University of New York
  Brooklyn College *B*
  Lehman College *B*
Columbia University
  Columbia College *B*
  School of General Studies *B*
Cornell University *B, M, D*
Eugene Lang College The New School
  for Liberal Arts *B*
Hobart and William Smith Colleges *B*
Hofstra University *B*
Sarah Lawrence College *B*
State University of New York
  College at Oneonta *B*

Ohio

Pontifical College Josephinum *B*

Puerto Rico

Pontifical Catholic University of
  Puerto Rico *B, M*
University of Puerto Rico
  Cayey University College *B*

Rhode Island

Brown University *B, M, D*

Texas

Our Lady of the Lake University of San
  Antonio *M*
Palo Alto College *A*
Rice University *B, M*
Southern Methodist University *B*
University of Texas
  Austin *M*
  El Paso *B*
  Pan American *B*
  San Antonio *B, M*

Utah

University of Utah *M*
Weber State University *B*

Washington

University of Washington *B*

Histologic assistant

Alabama

Community College of the Air
  Force *A*

Connecticut

Goodwin College *A*

Delaware

Delaware Technical and Community
  College
  Stanton/Wilmington Campus *A*

Georgia

Darton College *A*

Michigan

Mott Community College *A*

Minnesota

Minnesota State Community and
  Technical College - Fergus Falls *A*

New Jersey

Ocean County College *A*

Ohio

Youngstown State University *A*

Texas

Houston Community College
  System *A*
Tarleton State University *A*

Histologic technology

Florida

Miami Dade College *A*

Michigan

Northern Michigan University *B*
Oakland Community College *A*

Ohio

Lakeland Community College *A*

Historic preservation

California

University of Southern California *M*

Delaware

Delaware State University *B*
University of Delaware *B, M*

District of Columbia

George Washington University *M*

Georgia

Georgia State University *M*
Savannah College of Art and
  Design *B, M*
University of Georgia *M*

Illinois

School of the Art Institute of
  Chicago *M*

Indiana

Ball State University *M*

Kentucky

University of Kentucky *M*

Maryland

Goucher College *B, M, T*
University of Maryland
  College Park *M*

Massachusetts

Boston University *M*

Michigan

Eastern Michigan University *M*

New York

Cornell University *B, M, D*

North Carolina

Randolph Community College *A*

Ohio

Belmont Technical College *A*
Ursuline College *B*

Oregon

University of Oregon *M*

Pennsylvania

University of Pennsylvania *M*

Rhode Island

Roger Williams University *B*
Salve Regina University *B*

South Carolina

College of Charleston *B*

Texas

Texas Tech University *M*
University of Texas
  Austin *M, D*

Vermont

University of Vermont *M*

Virginia

University of Mary Washington *B*

History

Alabama

Alabama State University *B*
Athens State University *B*
Auburn University *B, M, D*
Auburn University at Montgomery *B*
Birmingham-Southern College *B, T*
Community College of the Air
  Force *A*
Faulkner University *B*
Gadsden State Community College *A*
Huntingdon College *B, T*
Jacksonville State University *B, M*
Judson College *B*
Lawson State Community College *A*
Miles College *B*
Northeast Alabama Community
  College *A*
Oakwood College *B*
Samford University *B*
Spring Hill College *B, T*
Stillman College *B*
Talladega College *B*
Troy University *B*
Tuskegee University *B*
University of Alabama *B, M, D*
University of Alabama
  Birmingham *B, M*
  Huntsville *B, M*
University of Mobile *B, T*
University of Montevallo *B, T*
University of North Alabama *B*
University of South Alabama *B, M*
University of West Alabama *B, T*

Alaska

University of Alaska
  Anchorage *B*
  Fairbanks *B*

Arizona

Arizona State University *B, M, D*
Arizona State University West *B*
Arizona Western College *A*
Cochise College *A*
Eastern Arizona College *A*
Grand Canyon University *B*
Northern Arizona
  University *B, M, D, T*

Prescott College *M*
South Mountain Community
  College *A*
University of Arizona *B, M, D*

Arkansas

Arkansas State University *B, M*
Arkansas State University
  Beebe *A*
Arkansas Tech University *B, M*
Harding University *B*
Henderson State University *B*
Hendrix College *B*
John Brown University *B*
Lyon College *B*
Ouachita Baptist University *B*
Southern Arkansas University *B*
University of Arkansas *B, M, D*
University of Arkansas
  Fort Smith *B*
  Little Rock *B, M*
  Monticello *B*
  Pine Bluff *B*
University of Central Arkansas *B, M*
University of the Ozarks *B*
Williams Baptist College *B*

California

Azusa Pacific University *B*
Bakersfield College *A*
Biola University *B*
Cabrillo College *A*
California Baptist University *B*
California Institute of Technology *B*
California Lutheran University *B*
California Polytechnic State
  University: San Luis Obispo *B*
California State Polytechnic
  University: Pomona *B, M*
California State University
  Bakersfield *B, M*
  Chico *B, M*
  Dominguez Hills *B*
  East Bay *B, M*
  Fresno *B, M*
  Fullerton *B, M*
  Long Beach *B, M*
  Los Angeles *B, M*
  Northridge *B*
  Sacramento *B, M, D*
  San Bernardino *B*
  San Marcos *B*
  Stanislaus *B, M*
Canada College *A*
Cerritos Community College *A*
Chabot College *A*
Chaffey College *A*
Claremont McKenna College *B*
College of Alameda *A*
College of the Desert *A*
Concordia University *B*
Contra Costa College *A*
Copper Mountain College *A*
Crafton Hills College *A*
Cypress College *A*
De Anza College *A*
Dominican University of California *B*
East Los Angeles College *A*
El Camino College *A*
Feather River College *A*
Foothill College *A*
Fresno City College *A*
Fresno Pacific University *B*
Fullerton College *A*
Gavilan Community College *A*
Glendale Community College *A*
Golden West College *A*
Grossmont Community College *A*
Holy Names University *B*
Humboldt State University *B*
Irvine Valley College *A*
La Sierra University *B*
Los Angeles Southwest College *A*
Los Angeles Valley College *A*

Loyola Marymount University B, M
Master's College B
Merced College A
Mills College B
MiraCosta College A
Monterey Peninsula College A
Mount St. Mary's College B
National University B
Notre Dame de Namur University B
Occidental College B
Orange Coast College A
Pacific Union College B
Palo Verde College A
Pepperdine University B, M
Pitzer College B
Point Loma Nazarene University B
Pomona College B
Saddleback College A
St. Mary's College of California B
San Diego Christian College B
San Diego City College A
San Diego Miramar College A
San Diego State University B, M
San Francisco State University B, M
San Jose State University B, M
Santa Ana College A
Santa Barbara City College A
Santa Clara University B
Santa Monica College A
Santiago Canyon College A
Scripps College B
Simpson University B
Solano Community College A
Sonoma State University B, M
Southwestern College B
Stanford University B, M, D
University of California
   Berkeley B, M, D
   Davis B, M, D
   Irvine B, M, D
   Los Angeles B, M, D
   Riverside B, M, D
   San Diego B, M, D
   Santa Barbara B, M, D
   Santa Cruz B, D
University of La Verne B
University of Redlands B
University of San Diego B, M
University of San Francisco B
University of Southern
   California B, M, D
University of the Pacific B
Vanguard University of Southern
   California B
Ventura College A
West Los Angeles College C, A
West Valley College A
Westmont College B
Whittier College B
Yuba Community College District A

Colorado

Adams State College B
Colorado Christian University B
Colorado College B
Colorado State University B, M, D
Colorado State University
   Pueblo B
Fort Lewis College B
Mesa State College B
Metropolitan State College of
   Denver B, T
Otero Junior College A
Red Rocks Community College A
Regis University B
United States Air Force Academy B
University of Colorado
   Boulder B, M, D
   Colorado Springs B, M
   Denver and Health Sciences
      Center B, M
University of Denver B, M
University of Northern
   Colorado B, M, T

Western State College of Colorado B

Connecticut

Albertus Magnus College B
Central Connecticut State
   University B, M, T
Connecticut College B
Eastern Connecticut State
   University B
Fairfield University B
Post University B
Quinnipiac University B
Sacred Heart University B
St. Joseph College B, T
Southern Connecticut State
   University B, M
Trinity College B, M
University of Connecticut B, M, D
University of Hartford B
University of New Haven B
Wesleyan University B
Western Connecticut State
   University B, M
Yale University B, M, D

Delaware

Delaware State University B
University of Delaware B, M, D
Wesley College B

District of Columbia

American University B, M, D
Catholic University of
   America B, M, D, T
Gallaudet University B
George Washington
   University B, M, D
Georgetown University B, D
Howard University B, M, D
Trinity University B
University of the District of
   Columbia A, B

Florida

Barry University B
Bethune-Cookman College B
Broward Community College A
Chipola College A
Clearwater Christian College B
Eckerd College B
Edward Waters College B
Flagler College B
Florida Agricultural and Mechanical
   University B
Florida Atlantic University B, M
Florida International
   University B, M, D
Florida Southern College B
Florida State University B, M, D
Gulf Coast Community College A
Indian River Community College A
Jacksonville University B
Lynn University B
Manatee Community College A
Miami Dade College A
New College of Florida B
Nova Southeastern University B
Palm Beach Atlantic University B
Palm Beach Community College A
Pensacola Junior College A
Rollins College B
St. Leo University B
St. Thomas University B
Southeastern College of the
   Assemblies of God B
Stetson University B
University of Central Florida B, M
University of Florida B, M, D
University of Miami B, M, D
University of North Florida B, M
University of South Florida B, M
University of Tampa A, B
University of West Florida B, M

Valencia Community College A
Warner Southern College B

Georgia

Abraham Baldwin Agricultural
   College A
Agnes Scott College B
Albany State University B
Andrew College A
Armstrong Atlantic State
   University B, M, T
Atlanta Metropolitan College A
Augusta State University B
Bainbridge College A
Berry College B
Brenau University B
Brewton-Parker College B
Clark Atlanta University B, M
Clayton State University B
Coastal Georgia Community
   College A
Columbus State University B
Covenant College B
Dalton State College A
Darton College A
East Georgia College A
Emmanuel College B
Emory University B, D
Gainesville State College A
Georgia College and State
   University B, M
Georgia Perimeter College A
Georgia Southern University B, M
Georgia Southwestern State
   University B, T
Georgia State University B, M, D
Gordon College A
Kennesaw State University B
LaGrange College B
Macon State College A
Mercer University B
Middle Georgia College A
Morehouse College B
North Georgia College & State
   University B
Oglethorpe University B
Paine College B
Piedmont College B
Reinhardt College B
Savannah State University B
Shorter College B, T
South Georgia College A
Spelman College B
Thomas University B
University of Georgia B, M, D
University of West Georgia B, M
Valdosta State University B, M
Waycross College A
Wesleyan College B
Young Harris College A

Hawaii

Brigham Young University-Hawaii B
Chaminade University of Honolulu B
Hawaii Pacific University B
University of Hawaii
   Hilo B
   Manoa B, M, D
   West Oahu B

Idaho

Albertson College of Idaho B
Boise State University B, M
Brigham Young University-Idaho B
College of Southern Idaho A
Idaho State University A, B, M
North Idaho College A
Northwest Nazarene University B
University of Idaho B, M, D

Illinois

Augustana College B, T
Aurora University B

Benedictine University B, T
Black Hawk College
   East Campus A
Blackburn College B, T
Bradley University B, T
Chicago State University B, M
City Colleges of Chicago
   Kennedy-King College A
Concordia University B
Danville Area Community College A
DePaul University B, M, T
Dominican University B
Eastern Illinois University B, M, T
Elmhurst College B, T
Eureka College B, T
Highland Community College A
Illinois College B
Illinois State University B, M, T
Illinois Valley Community College A
Illinois Wesleyan University B
John Wood Community College A
Joliet Junior College A
Judson College B
Kishwaukee College A
Knox College B
Lake Forest College B
Lewis University B, T
Loyola University of Chicago B, M, D
MacMurray College B
McKendree College B
Millikin University B, T
Monmouth College B, T
North Central College B, T
North Park University B
Northeastern Illinois University B, M
Northern Illinois University B, M, D
Northwestern University B, M, D
Olivet Nazarene University B, T
Principia College B
Quincy University B, T
Richland Community College A
Rockford College B
Roosevelt University B, M
St. Xavier University B
Sauk Valley Community College A
South Suburban College of Cook
   County A
Southern Illinois University
   Carbondale B, M, D
Southern Illinois University
   Edwardsville B, M, T
Southwestern Illinois College A
Spoon River College A
Trinity Christian College B, T
Trinity International University B
Triton College A
University of Chicago B, D
University of Illinois
   Chicago B, M, D
   Springfield B, M
   Urbana-Champaign B, M, D
University of St. Francis B
Western Illinois University B, M
Wheaton College B, T

Indiana

Ancilla College A
Anderson University B
Ball State University B, M
Bethel College B
Butler University B, M
DePauw University B
Earlham College B
Franklin College B
Goshen College B
Hanover College B
Huntington University B
Indiana State University B, M
Indiana University
   Bloomington B, M, D
   East A
   Northwest A, B
   South Bend A, B
   Southeast B

Indiana University-Purdue University
   Fort Wayne A, B
Indiana University-Purdue University
   Indianapolis B, M
Indiana Wesleyan University A, B
Manchester College B, T
Marian College B, T
Martin University B
Oakland City University A, B
Purdue University B, M, D
Purdue University
   Calumet B
St. Joseph's College B
Saint Mary's College B, T
St. Mary-of-the-Woods College B
Taylor University B
University of Evansville B
University of Indianapolis B, M
University of Notre Dame B, M, D
University of St. Francis B
University of Southern Indiana B
Valparaiso University B, M
Vincennes University A
Wabash College B

Iowa

Ashford University T
Briar Cliff University B
Buena Vista University B, T
Central College B, T
Clarke College A, B, T
Coe College B
Cornell College B, T
Dordt College B
Drake University B
Ellsworth Community College A
Graceland University B, T
Grinnell College B
Iowa State University B, M
Iowa Wesleyan College B
Loras College B
Luther College B
Morningside College B
Mount Mercy College B, T
Northwestern College B, T
St. Ambrose University B, T
Simpson College B
University of Iowa B, M, D, T
University of Northern Iowa B, M
Waldorf College B
Wartburg College B, T
William Penn University B

Kansas

Allen County Community College A
Baker University B, T
Barton County Community College A
Benedictine College B
Bethany College B, T
Bethel College B
Butler County Community College A
Central Christian College of Kansas A
Coffeyville Community College A
Colby Community College A
Emporia State University B, M
Fort Hays State University B, M
Fort Scott Community College A
Friends University B
Kansas State University B, M, D
Kansas Wesleyan University B, T
Labette Community College A
McPherson College B, T
MidAmerica Nazarene University B
Newman University B
Ottawa University B, T
Pittsburg State University B, M
Pratt Community College A
Seward County Community College A
Southwestern College B
Sterling College B, T
Tabor College B
University of Kansas B, M, D
University of St. Mary B
Washburn University of Topeka B

Wichita State University B, M, T

Kentucky

Alice Lloyd College B
Asbury College B
Bellarmine University B, T
Berea College B, T
Brescia University B
Campbellsville University B
Centre College B
Eastern Kentucky University B, M
Georgetown College B, T
Kentucky Christian University B
Kentucky State University B
Kentucky Wesleyan College B
Lindsey Wilson College A, B
Morehead State University B
Murray State University B, M, T
Northern Kentucky University B
Pikeville College B
Thomas More College A, B
Transylvania University B
Union College B
University of Kentucky B, M, D
University of Louisville B, M
University of the Cumberlands B
Western Kentucky University B, M

Louisiana

Centenary College of Louisiana B, T
Dillard University B
Grambling State University B
Louisiana State University
   Shreveport B
Louisiana State University and
   Agricultural and Mechanical
   College B, M, D
Louisiana Tech University B, M
Loyola University New Orleans B
Nicholls State University B
Northwestern State University B
Our Lady of Holy Cross College B
Southeastern Louisiana
   University B, M
Southern University
   New Orleans B
Southern University and Agricultural
   and Mechanical College B
Tulane University B, M, D
University of Louisiana at
   Lafayette B, M
University of Louisiana at
   Monroe B, M
University of New Orleans B, M
Xavier University of Louisiana B

Maine

Bates College B
Bowdoin College B
Colby College B
St. Joseph's College B
University of Maine B, M, D
University of Maine
   Farmington B
   Machias B, T
University of New England B
University of Southern Maine B

Maryland

Allegany College of Maryland A
Bowie State University B
College of Notre Dame of Maryland B
Columbia Union College B
Coppin State University B
Frederick Community College A
Frostburg State University B
Goucher College B
Hood College B, T
Johns Hopkins University B, M, D
Loyola College in Maryland B
McDaniel College B
Morgan State University B, M, D
Mount St. Mary's University B

St. Mary's College of Maryland B
Salisbury University B, M, T
Towson University B
United States Naval Academy B
University of Baltimore B
University of Maryland
   Baltimore County B, M
   College Park B, M, D
   Eastern Shore B
   University College B
Washington College B, M, T

Massachusetts

Amherst College B
Anna Maria College B
Assumption College B
Atlantic Union College B
Bentley College B
Boston College B, M, D
Boston University B, M, D
Brandeis University B, M, D
Bridgewater State College B
Bunker Hill Community College A
Clark University B, M, D
College of the Holy Cross B
Dean College A
Eastern Nazarene College B
Elms College B
Emmanuel College B
Endicott College B
Fitchburg State College B, M
Framingham State College B
Gordon College B
Hampshire College B
Harvard College B, D
Lasell College B
Massachusetts College of Liberal
   Arts B
Massachusetts Institute of
   Technology B
Merrimack College B
Mount Holyoke College B
Nichols College B, T
Northeastern University B, M, D
Pine Manor College B
Regis College B
St. John's Seminary College B
Salem State College B, M
Simmons College B
Smith College B
Springfield College B
Stonehill College B
Suffolk University B
Tufts University B, M, T
University of Massachusetts
   Amherst B, M, D
   Boston B, M
   Dartmouth B
   Lowell B
Wellesley College B
Western New England College B
Westfield State College B, M
Wheaton College B
Williams College B
Worcester State College B

Michigan

Adrian College A, B, T
Albion College B, T
Alma College B, T
Andrews University B, M
Aquinas College B, T
Calvin College B, T
Central Michigan
   University B, M, D, T
Concordia University B
Cornerstone University B, T
Eastern Michigan University B, M
Ferris State University B
Grand Valley State University B
Great Lakes Christian College B
Hillsdale College B
Hope College B
Kalamazoo College B, T

Kellogg Community College A
Lake Michigan College A
Lake Superior State University B, T
Lansing Community College A
Madonna University B
Marygrove College B, T
Michigan State University B, M, D
Michigan Technological University B
Northern Michigan University B, T
Oakland University B, M, T
Olivet College B, T
Rochester College B
Saginaw Valley State University B, T
Siena Heights University B
Spring Arbor University B, T
University of Detroit Mercy B
University of Michigan B, M, D, T
University of Michigan
   Dearborn B
   Flint B, T
Wayne State University B, M, D
Western Michigan University B, M, D

Minnesota

Augsburg College B
Bemidji State University B
Bethany Lutheran College B
Bethel University B
Carleton College B
College of St. Benedict B
College of St. Catherine B
College of St. Scholastica B
Concordia College: Moorhead B
Concordia University: St. Paul B
Crown College B
Gustavus Adolphus College B
Hamline University B
Macalester College B
Metropolitan State University B
Minnesota State University
   Mankato B, M
   Moorhead B
Northwestern College B
Ridgewater College A
St. Cloud State University B, M
St. John's University B
St. Mary's University of Minnesota B
St. Olaf College B
Southwest Minnesota State
   University B
University of Minnesota
   Duluth B
   Morris B
   Twin Cities B, M, D
University of St. Thomas B
Vermilion Community College A
Winona State University B

Mississippi

Alcorn State University B
Belhaven College B, T
Blue Mountain College B
Delta State University B
Hinds Community College A
Itawamba Community College A
Jackson State University B, M, D
Millsaps College B, T
Mississippi College B, M
Mississippi Delta Community
   College A
Mississippi State University B, M, D
Mississippi Valley State University B
Tougaloo College B
University of Mississippi B, M, D, T
University of Southern
   Mississippi B, M, D
William Carey College B

Missouri

Avila University B
Central Methodist University B
Central Missouri State University B, M
College of the Ozarks B
Columbia College B

Crowder College *A*
Culver-Stockton College *B*
Drury University *B, T*
Evangel University *B*
Fontbonne University *B*
Hannibal-LaGrange College *B*
Lincoln University *B, M*
Lindenwood University *B*
Maryville University of Saint Louis *B*
Missouri Baptist University *B, T*
Missouri Southern State
    University *B, T*
Missouri State University *B, M*
Missouri Valley College *B*
Missouri Western State University *B, T*
Northwest Missouri State
    University *B, M*
Park University *B*
Rockhurst University *B*
St. Louis University *B, M, D*
Southeast Missouri State
    University *B, M*
Southwest Baptist University *B*
Three Rivers Community College *A*
Truman State University *B, M*
University of Missouri
    Columbia *B, M, D*
    Kansas City *B, M, D*
    Rolla *B*
    St. Louis *B, M*
Washington University in St.
    Louis *B, M, D*
Webster University *B*
Westminster College *B*
William Jewell College *B*
William Woods University *B*

Montana

Carroll College *B, T*
Montana State University
    Billings *B, T*
    Bozeman *B, M*
Rocky Mountain College *B, T*
University of Great Falls *B*
University of Montana: Missoula *B, M*
University of Montana: Western *T*

Nebraska

Chadron State College *B, M*
Concordia University *B, T*
Creighton University *B*
Dana College *B*
Doane College *B*
Hastings College *B*
Midland Lutheran College *B, T*
Nebraska Wesleyan University *B*
Union College *B*
University of Nebraska
    Kearney *B, M, T*
    Lincoln *B, M, D*
    Omaha *B, M*
Wayne State College *B, T*
Western Nebraska Community
    College *A*
York College *B*

Nevada

Great Basin College *A*
University of Nevada
    Las Vegas *B, M, D*
    Reno *B, M, D*

New Hampshire

Dartmouth College *B*
Franklin Pierce College *B*
Keene State College *B*
New England College *B*
Plymouth State University *B*
Rivier College *B*
St. Anselm College *B, T*
Southern New Hampshire
    University *B*
University of New Hampshire *B, M, D*

University of New Hampshire at
    Manchester *B*

New Jersey

Atlantic Cape Community College *A*
Bloomfield College *B*
Caldwell College *B*
Centenary College *B*
The College of New Jersey *B, T*
College of St. Elizabeth *B*
Drew University *B*
Fairleigh Dickinson University
    College at Florham *B*
    Metropolitan Campus *B, M*
Felician College *B*
Georgian Court University *B*
Gloucester County College *A*
Hudson County Community
    College *A*
Kean University *B, T*
Monmouth University *B, M*
Montclair State University *B*
New Jersey City University *B*
New Jersey Institute of
    Technology *B, M*
Princeton University *B, M, D*
Ramapo College of New Jersey *B*
Richard Stockton College of New
    Jersey *B*
Rider University *B*
Rowan University *B*
Rutgers, The State University of New
    Jersey
    Camden Regional Campus *B*
    New Brunswick/Piscataway
        Campus *B, M, D*
    Newark Regional Campus *B*
St. Peter's College *B*
Salem Community College *A*
Seton Hall University *B, T*
Stevens Institute of Technology *B*
Thomas Edison State College *B*
William Paterson University of New
    Jersey *B*

New Mexico

College of the Southwest *B*
Eastern New Mexico University *B*
New Mexico Highlands
    University *B, M*
New Mexico State University *B, M*
San Juan College *A*
University of New Mexico *B, M, D*
Western New Mexico University *B*

New York

Adelphi University *B*
Adirondack Community College *A*
Alfred University *B*
Bard College *B*
Barnard College *B*
Canisius College *B*
City University of New York
    Baruch College *B*
    Brooklyn College *B, M*
    City College *B, M*
    College of Staten Island *B, M*
    Hunter College *B, M*
    Lehman College *B, M*
    Queens College *B, M*
    Queensborough Community
        College *A*
    York College *B*
Clarkson University *B*
Colgate University *B*
College of Mount St. Vincent *A, B, T*
College of New Rochelle *B, T*
College of Saint Rose *B*
Columbia University
    Columbia College *B*
    School of General Studies *B*
Concordia College *B, T*
Cornell University *B, M, D*
D'Youville College *B*

Daemen College *B*
Dominican College of Blauvelt *B*
Dowling College *B*
Elmira College *B, T*
Eugene Lang College The New School
    for Liberal Arts *B*
Excelsior College *B*
Fordham University *B, M, D*
Hamilton College *B*
Hartwick College *B, T*
Hobart and William Smith Colleges *B*
Hofstra University *B*
Houghton College *B*
Iona College *B, M*
Ithaca College *B*
Jewish Theological Seminary of
    America *M, D*
Le Moyne College *B*
Long Island University
    Brooklyn Campus *B*
    C.W. Post Campus *B, M*
Manhattan College *B*
Manhattanville College *B*
Marist College *B*
Marymount Manhattan College *B*
Mercy College *B*
Molloy College *B*
Monroe Community College *A*
Mount St. Mary College *B, T*
Nazareth College of Rochester *B, T*
New York University *B, M, D*
Niagara University *B*
Nyack College *B*
Pace University *B*
Roberts Wesleyan College *B*
Russell Sage College *B*
St. Bonaventure University *B*
St. Francis College *B*
St. John Fisher College *B*
St. John's University *B, M, D*
St. Joseph's College *B*
St. Joseph's College: Suffolk
    Campus *B, T*
St. Lawrence University *B*
St. Thomas Aquinas College *B, T*
Sarah Lawrence College *B*
Siena College *B, T*
Skidmore College *B*
State University of New York
    Albany *B, M, D*
    Binghamton *B, M, D*
    Buffalo *B, M, D*
    College at Brockport *B, M, T*
    College at Buffalo *B, M*
    College at Cortland *B, M*
    College at Fredonia *B*
    College at Geneseo *B, T*
    College at Oneonta *B*
    College at Plattsburgh *B*
    Empire State College *A, B*
    New Paltz *B, T*
    Oswego *B, M*
    Purchase *B*
    Stony Brook *B, M, D*
Suffolk County Community College *A*
Sullivan County Community
    College *A*
Syracuse University *B*
Touro College *B*
Union College *B*
United States Military Academy *B*
University of Rochester *B, M, D*
Utica College *B*
Vassar College *B*
Wagner College *B*
Wells College *B*
Yeshiva University *B*

North Carolina

Appalachian State University *B, M*
Barton College *B*
Belmont Abbey College *B*
Brevard College *B*
Campbell University *B*

Catawba College *B, T*
Chowan College *B*
Davidson College *B*
Duke University *B, M, D*
East Carolina University *B, M*
Elizabeth City State University *B*
Elon University *B, T*
Fayetteville State University *B*
Gardner-Webb University *B*
Greensboro College *B, T*
Guilford College *B, T*
High Point University *B*
Johnson C. Smith University *B*
Lees-McRae College *B*
Lenoir-Rhyne College *B, T*
Livingstone College *B*
Louisburg College *A*
Mars Hill College *B, T*
Meredith College *B*
Methodist College *A, B*
Montreat College *B*
Mount Olive College *B*
North Carolina Agricultural and
    Technical State University *B, M, T*
North Carolina Central
    University *B, M*
North Carolina State University *B, M*
North Carolina Wesleyan College *B*
Pfeiffer University *B*
Queens University of Charlotte *B*
St. Andrews Presbyterian College *B*
St. Augustine's College *B*
Salem College *B*
University of North Carolina
    Asheville *B, T*
    Chapel Hill *B, M, D*
    Charlotte *B, M*
    Greensboro *B, M, D, T*
    Pembroke *B*
    Wilmington *B, M*
Wake Forest University *B*
Warren Wilson College *B*
Western Carolina University *B, M*
Wingate University *B*
Winston-Salem State University *B*

North Dakota

Dickinson State University *B, T*
Jamestown College *B*
Minot State University *B*
Minot State University: Bottineau
    Campus *A*
North Dakota State
    University *B, M, D, T*
University of North Dakota *B, M, D, T*
Valley City State University *B*

Ohio

Antioch College *B*
Ashland University *B*
Baldwin-Wallace College *B*
Bluffton University *B*
Bowling Green State
    University *B, M, D*
Capital University *B*
Case Western Reserve
    University *B, M, D*
Cedarville University *B*
Central State University *B*
Cleveland State University *B, M, T*
College of Mount St. Joseph *B, T*
College of Wooster *B*
Defiance College *B, T*
Denison University *B*
Franciscan University of
    Steubenville *B*
Heidelberg College *B*
Hiram College *B, T*
John Carroll University *B, M*
Kent State University *B, M, D*
Kenyon College *B*
Lake Erie College *B*
Lourdes College *A, B*
Malone College *B*

Marietta College *B*
Miami University
  Oxford Campus *B, M, D*
Mount Union College *B*
Mount Vernon Nazarene University *B*
Muskingum College *B*
Oberlin College *B*
Ohio Dominican University *B, T*
Ohio Northern University *B*
Ohio State University
  Columbus Campus *B, M, D*
  Lima Campus *B*
  Mansfield Campus *B*
  Marion Campus *B*
Ohio University *B, M, D*
Ohio University
  Southern Campus at Ironton *A*
Ohio Wesleyan University *B*
Otterbein College *B*
Owens Community College
  Toledo *A*
Pontifical College Josephinum *B*
Shawnee State University *B*
Sinclair Community College *A*
Union Institute & University *B*
University of Akron *B, M, D*
University of Cincinnati *B, M, D, T*
University of Dayton *B*
University of Findlay *B, T*
University of Rio Grande *A, B*
University of Toledo *B, M, D*
Urbana University *B*
Ursuline College *B*
Walsh University *B*
Wilmington College *B*
Wittenberg University *B*
Wright State University *A, B*
Wright State University: Lake
  Campus *A*
Xavier University *A, B*
Youngstown State University *B, M*

Oklahoma

Cameron University *B, M*
Connors State College *A*
East Central University *B*
Eastern Oklahoma State College *A*
Murray State College *A*
Northeastern Oklahoma Agricultural
  and Mechanical College *A*
Northeastern State University *B*
Northwestern Oklahoma State
  University *B*
Oklahoma Baptist University *B*
Oklahoma Christian University *B*
Oklahoma City Community College *A*
Oklahoma City University *B*
Oklahoma Panhandle State
  University *B*
Oklahoma State University *B, M, D*
Oklahoma Wesleyan University *B*
Oral Roberts University *B*
Rose State College *A*
St. Gregory's University *A, B*
Southeastern Oklahoma State
  University *B*
Southern Nazarene University *B*
Southwestern Oklahoma State
  University *B*
Tulsa Community College *A*
University of Central Oklahoma *B, M*
University of Oklahoma *B, M, D*
University of Science and Arts of
  Oklahoma *B*
University of Tulsa *B, M*
Western Oklahoma State College *A*

Oregon

Central Oregon Community
  College *A*
Chemeketa Community College *A*
Concordia University *B*
Corban College *B*
Eastern Oregon University *B, T*

George Fox University *B, T*
Lewis & Clark College *B*
Linfield College *B, T*
Linn-Benton Community College *A*
Multnomah Bible College *B*
Oregon State University *B*
Pacific University *B*
Portland State University *B, M*
Reed College *B*
Southern Oregon University *B*
Treasure Valley Community College *A*
University of Oregon *B, M, D*
University of Portland *B*
Warner Pacific College *B*
Western Oregon University *B*
Willamette University *B*

Pennsylvania

Albright College *B, T*
Allegheny College *B*
Alvernia College *B*
Arcadia University *B*
Bloomsburg University of
  Pennsylvania *B*
Bryn Athyn College of the New
  Church *B*
Bryn Mawr College *B*
Bucknell University *B*
Cabrini College *B*
California University of
  Pennsylvania *B*
Carlow University *B*
Carnegie Mellon University *M, D*
Cedar Crest College *B*
Chatham College *B*
Chestnut Hill College *B*
Clarion University of Pennsylvania *B*
College Misericordia *B*
DeSales University *B, T*
Dickinson College *B*
Drexel University *B*
Duquesne University *B, M*
East Stroudsburg University of
  Pennsylvania *B, M*
Eastern University *B*
Edinboro University of
  Pennsylvania *B*
Elizabethtown College *B*
Franklin & Marshall College *B*
Gannon University *B*
Geneva College *B, T*
Gettysburg College *B*
Grove City College *B*
Gwynedd-Mercy College *B*
Haverford College *B, T*
Holy Family University *B, T*
Immaculata University *B*
Indiana University of
  Pennsylvania *B, M*
Juniata College *B*
King's College *B*
Kutztown University of
  Pennsylvania *B*
La Roche College *B*
La Salle University *B, T*
Lafayette College *B*
Lebanon Valley College *B*
Lincoln University *B*
Lock Haven University of
  Pennsylvania *B*
Lycoming College *B*
Mansfield University of
  Pennsylvania *B, T*
Marywood University *B*
Mercyhurst College *B*
Messiah College *B*
Millersville University of
  Pennsylvania *B, M, T*
Moravian College *B, T*
Mount Aloysius College *B*
Muhlenberg College *C, B*
Penn State
  Abington *B*
  Altoona *B*

Beaver *B*
Berks *B*
Delaware County *B*
Dubois *B*
Erie, The Behrend College *B*
Fayette *B*
Hazleton *B*
Lehigh Valley *B*
McKeesport *B*
Mont Alto *B*
New Kensington *B*
Schuylkill - Capital College *B*
Shenango *B*
University Park *B, M, D*
Wilkes-Barre *B*
Worthington Scranton *B*
Point Park University *B*
Rosemont College *B*
St. Francis University *B*
St. Joseph's University *B*
St. Vincent College *B*
Seton Hill University *B, T*
Shippensburg University of
  Pennsylvania *B, M, T*
Slippery Rock University of
  Pennsylvania *B, M, T*
Susquehanna University *B*
Swarthmore College *B*
Temple University *B, M, D*
Thiel College *B*
University of Pennsylvania *A, B, M, D*
University of Pittsburgh *B, M, D*
University of Pittsburgh
  Greensburg *B*
  Johnstown *B*
University of Scranton *B, M*
Ursinus College *B, T*
Villanova University *B, M*
Washington and Jefferson College *B*
Waynesburg College *B*
West Chester University of
  Pennsylvania *C, B, M*
Westminster College *B, M*
Widener University *B, T*
Wilkes University *B*
Wilson College *B*
York College of Pennsylvania *B*

Puerto Rico

Pontifical Catholic University of
  Puerto Rico *B*
Universidad Adventista de las
  Antillas *B*
University of Puerto Rico
  Cayey University College *B*
  Mayaguez *B*
  Rio Piedras *B, M, D*
University of the Sacred Heart *B*

Rhode Island

Brown University *B, M, D*
Bryant University *B*
Providence College *B, M, D*
Rhode Island College *B, M*
Roger Williams University *B*
University of Rhode Island *B, M*

South Carolina

Anderson University *B*
Benedict College *B*
Charleston Southern University *B*
The Citadel *B, M*
Claflin University *B*
Clemson University *B, M*
Coastal Carolina University *B*
Coker College *B*
College of Charleston *B, M, T*
Columbia College *B*
Converse College *B*
Erskine College *B*
Francis Marion University *B*
Furman University *B, T*
Lander University *B, T*
Limestone College *B*

Morris College *B*
Newberry College *B, T*
Presbyterian College *B*
South Carolina State University *B*
Southern Wesleyan University *B*
University of South Carolina *B, M, D*
University of South Carolina
  Aiken *B*
  Beaufort *B*
  Upstate *B*
Winthrop University *B, M*
Wofford College *B*

South Dakota

Augustana College *B, T*
Black Hills State University *B*
Dakota Wesleyan University *B*
Mount Marty College *B*
Northern State University *B*
Oglala Lakota College *B*
South Dakota State University *B, T*
University of Sioux Falls *B*
University of South Dakota *B, M*

Tennessee

Austin Peay State University *B*
Belmont University *B, T*
Bethel College *B*
Bryan College *B, T*
Carson-Newman College *B, T*
Christian Brothers University *B*
Columbia State Community College *A*
Crichton College *B*
Cumberland University *B*
East Tennessee State
  University *B, M, T*
Fisk University *B*
Free Will Baptist Bible College *M*
Freed-Hardeman University *B, T*
Hiwassee College *A*
Jackson State Community College *A*
King College *B, T*
Lambuth University *B*
LeMoyne-Owen College *B*
Lee University *B*
Lincoln Memorial University *B, T*
Lipscomb University *B*
Maryville College *B, T*
Middle Tennessee State
  University *B, M, D*
Milligan College *B, T*
Rhodes College *B*
Southern Adventist University *B*
Tennessee State University *B, M*
Tennessee Technological
  University *B, T*
Tennessee Temple University *B*
Tennessee Wesleyan College *B, T*
Trevecca Nazarene University *B*
Tusculum College *B*
Union University *B, T*
University of Memphis *B, M, D*
University of Tennessee
  Chattanooga *B*
  Knoxville *B, M, D*
  Martin *B*
University of the South *B*
Vanderbilt University *B, M, D*

Texas

Abilene Christian University *B, M*
Angelo State University *B, M, T*
Austin College *B*
Austin Community College *A*
Baylor University *B, M*
Blinn College *A*
Brazosport College *A*
Cisco Junior College *A*
Clarendon College *A*
Coastal Bend College *A*
College of the Mainland *A*
Concordia University at Austin *B*
Dallas Baptist University *B*
Del Mar College *A*

East Texas Baptist University *B*
El Paso Community College *A*
Frank Phillips College *A*
Galveston College *A*
Hardin-Simmons University *B, M*
Houston Baptist University *A*
Howard Payne University *B, T*
Jarvis Christian College *B, T*
Kilgore College *A*
Lamar University *B, M*
Laredo Community College *A*
LeTourneau University *B*
Lon Morris College *A*
Lubbock Christian University *T*
McMurry University *B, T*
Midland College *A*
Midwestern State University *B, M*
Northeast Texas Community
    College *A*
Northwest Vista College *A*
Our Lady of the Lake University of San
    Antonio *B*
Palo Alto College *A*
Paris Junior College *A*
Prairie View A&M University *B*
Rice University *B, M, D*
St. Edward's University *B*
St. Mary's University *B*
St. Philip's College *A*
Sam Houston State University *B, M*
San Jacinto College
    North *A*
Schreiner University *B*
South Plains College *A*
South Texas College *A*
Southern Methodist
    University *B, M, D*
Southwestern Adventist
    University *B, T*
Southwestern Assemblies of God
    University *B*
Southwestern University *B, T*
Stephen F. Austin State
    University *B, M, T*
Sul Ross State University *B, M, T*
Tarleton State University *B, M, T*
Texarkana College *A*
Texas A&M University *B, M, D*
Texas A&M University
    Commerce *B, M*
    Kingsville *B, M*
    Texarkana *B, T*
Texas Christian University *B, M, D*
Texas College *B*
Texas Lutheran University *B, T*
Texas Southern University *B, M*
Texas State University: San
    Marcos *B, M, T*
Texas Tech University *B, M, D*
Texas Wesleyan University *B*
Texas Woman's University *B, M*
Trinity University *B*
Tyler Junior College *A*
University of Dallas *B*
University of Houston *B, M, D*
University of Houston
    Clear Lake *B, M*
    Downtown *B*
    Victoria *B, M*
University of Mary Hardin-Baylor *B, T*
University of North Texas *B, M, D*
University of St. Thomas *B*
University of Texas
    Arlington *B, M*
    Austin *B, M, D*
    Brownsville *B, M*
    Dallas *B, M*
    El Paso *B, M*
    Pan American *B, M*
    San Antonio *B, M*
    Tyler *B, M*
    of the Permian Basin *B, M*
University of the Incarnate Word *B*
Wayland Baptist University *B, T*

West Texas A&M University *B, M*
Western Texas College *A*
Wharton County Junior College *A*
Wiley College *B*

Utah

Brigham Young University *B, M*
Dixie State College of Utah *A*
Salt Lake Community College *A*
Snow College *A*
Southern Utah University *B, T*
University of Utah *B, M, D*
Utah State University *B, M*
Utah Valley State College *A, B*
Weber State University *B*
Westminster College *B*

Vermont

Bennington College *B*
Burlington College *B*
Castleton State College *B*
College of St. Joseph in Vermont *B*
Goddard College *B*
Green Mountain College *B*
Johnson State College *B*
Marlboro College *B*
Middlebury College *B*
Norwich University *B*
St. Michael's College *B*
University of Vermont *B, M*

Virginia

Averett University *B*
Bluefield College *B*
Bridgewater College *B*
Christendom College *B*
Christopher Newport University *B*
College of William and Mary *B, M, D*
Eastern Mennonite University *B*
Emory & Henry College *B, T*
Ferrum College *B*
George Mason University *B, M*
Hampden-Sydney College *B*
Hampton University *B*
Hollins University *B*
James Madison University *B, M, T*
Liberty University *B, T*
Longwood University *B, T*
Lynchburg College *B*
Mary Baldwin College *B*
Marymount University *B*
Norfolk State University *B*
Old Dominion University *B, M, T*
Radford University *B*
Randolph-Macon College *B*
Randolph-Macon Woman's College *B*
Roanoke College *B, T*
Shenandoah University *B*
Sweet Briar College *B*
University of Mary Washington *B*
University of Richmond *B, M, T*
University of Virginia *B, M, D*
University of Virginia's College at
    Wise *B, T*
Virginia Commonwealth
    University *B, M*
Virginia Intermont College *B*
Virginia Military Institute *B*
Virginia Polytechnic Institute and
    State University *B, M*
Virginia State University *B, M*
Virginia Union University *B*
Virginia Wesleyan College *B*
Washington and Lee University *B*

Washington

Central Washington University *B, M*
Centralia College *A*
Eastern Washington University *B, M, T*
Everett Community College *A*
Gonzaga University *B*
Highline Community College *A*
Northwest University *B, T*

Pacific Lutheran University *B*
Saint Martin's University *B*
Seattle Pacific University *B*
Seattle University *B*
University of Puget Sound *B, T*
University of Washington *B, M, D*
Walla Walla College *B*
Washington State University *B, M, D*
Western Washington University *B, M*
Whitman College *B*
Whitworth College *B, T*

West Virginia

Alderson-Broaddus College *B*
Bethany College *B*
Concord University *B*
Davis and Elkins College *B*
Glenville State College *B*
Marshall University *B, M*
Potomac State College of West Virginia
    University *A*
Shepherd University *B*
University of Charleston *B*
West Liberty State College *B*
West Virginia State University *B*
West Virginia University *B, M, D*
West Virginia University Institute of
    Technology *B*
West Virginia Wesleyan College *B*
Wheeling Jesuit University *B*

Wisconsin

Alverno College *B*
Beloit College *B*
Cardinal Stritch University *B*
Carroll College *B*
Carthage College *B, T*
Concordia University Wisconsin *B, T*
Edgewood College *B*
Lakeland College *B*
Lawrence University *B, T*
Marian College of Fond du Lac *B*
Marquette University *B, M, D, T*
Mount Mary College *B*
Northland College *B, T*
Ripon College *B, T*
St. Norbert College *B, T*
Silver Lake College *B, T*
University of Wisconsin
    Eau Claire *B, M*
    Green Bay *B, T*
    La Crosse *B, T*
    Madison *B, M, D*
    Milwaukee *B, M*
    Oshkosh *B*
    Parkside *B, T*
    Platteville *B, T*
    River Falls *B*
    Stevens Point *B, M, T*
    Superior *B, T*
    Whitewater *B, T*
Wisconsin Lutheran College *B*

Wyoming

Casper College *A*
Eastern Wyoming College *A*
Laramie County Community
    College *A*
Northwest College *A*
Sheridan College *A*
University of Wyoming *B, M*
Western Wyoming Community
    College *A*

History of science/
technology

Connecticut

Yale University *B, M, D*

Georgia

Georgia Institute of
    Technology *B, M, D*

Indiana

Indiana University
    Bloomington *M, D*
University of Notre Dame *M, D*

Iowa

Iowa State University *M, D*

Maryland

Johns Hopkins University *B, M, D*

Massachusetts

Harvard College *B, M, D*

New York

Cornell University *B, M, D*
Polytechnic University *M*

Ohio

Case Western Reserve University *B*

Oklahoma

University of Oklahoma *M, D*

Oregon

Oregon State University *M, D*

Pennsylvania

University of Pennsylvania *B, M, D*
University of Pittsburgh *B, M, D*

Wisconsin

University of Wisconsin
    Madison *B, M, D*

History teacher
education

Alabama

Athens State University *B*
Birmingham-Southern College *T*
Faulkner University *B*
Huntingdon College *T*
Oakwood College *B*
Samford University *B*
Talladega College *B*
University of Mobile *B, T*

Arizona

Arizona State University *B, T*
Grand Canyon University *B*
Northern Arizona University *B, T*
Prescott College *T*
University of Arizona *B, M*

Arkansas

Ouachita Baptist University *B, T*
University of Arkansas
    Fort Smith *B*
University of Central Arkansas *T*

California

Azusa Pacific University *T*
California State University
    San Bernardino *M, T*
Loyola Marymount University *M*
Master's College *T*
Pacific Union College *T*
San Diego Christian College *B, T*
Stanford University *M, T*
University of the Pacific *T*
Vanguard University of Southern
    California *T*

Colorado

Adams State College *B, T*
Colorado State University
    Pueblo *T*
Fort Lewis College *B*
Regis University *B, T*

Connecticut

Albertus Magnus College *B, T*
Fairfield University *T*
Quinnipiac University *B, M*
Sacred Heart University *T*
St. Joseph College *T*
Southern Connecticut State
    University *B, M, T*
University of New Haven *T*

Delaware

University of Delaware *B, T*

District of Columbia

Catholic University of America *B*

Florida

Barry University *T*
Flagler College *B*
Florida Agricultural and Mechanical
    University *T*
Palm Beach Atlantic University *B, T*

Georgia

Agnes Scott College *T*
Armstrong Atlantic State
    University *M, T*
Brewton-Parker College *B*
Covenant College *B, T*
Georgia Southern University *B*
Paine College *B*
Shorter College *T*
Toccoa Falls College *B, T*
Wesleyan College *T*

Idaho

Boise State University *T*
Brigham Young University-Idaho *T*
Northwest Nazarene University *B*
University of Idaho *T*

Illinois

Augustana College *B, T*
Blackburn College *B, T*
Bradley University *B*
Chicago State University *B, T*
Concordia University *B, T*
Dominican University *T*
Elmhurst College *B*
Eureka College *T*
Greenville College *B, T*
Illinois College *T*
Illinois Wesleyan University *B*
John A. Logan College *A*
Lewis University *T*
MacMurray College *B, T*
McKendree College *B*
Monmouth College *B, T*
North Park University *T*
Olivet Nazarene University *B, T*
Quincy University *T*
Rockford College *T*
Roosevelt University *B*
St. Xavier University *B*
Sauk Valley Community College *A*
Trinity Christian College *B, T*
Trinity International University *B, T*
University of Illinois
    Chicago *B, M*
    Urbana-Champaign *B, M, T*
Wheaton College *T*

Indiana

Butler University *T*
Goshen College *B*
Indiana University-Purdue University
    Fort Wayne *T*
Manchester College *B, T*
Oakland City University *B*
Taylor University *B, T*
University of Indianapolis *B, M, T*
Valparaiso University *B*

Vincennes University *A*

Iowa

Ashford University *B, T*
Briar Cliff University *B*
Buena Vista University *B, T*
Central University *T*
Clarke College *B, T*
Cornell College *B, T*
Dordt College *B*
Drake University *M, T*
Ellsworth Community College *A*
Graceland University *T*
Iowa State University *T*
Loras College *T*
Morningside College *B*
Mount Mercy College *T*
Northwestern College *T*
St. Ambrose University *B, T*
Simpson College *T*
University of Iowa *T*
Upper Iowa University *B, T*
Waldorf College *B*
Wartburg College *B, T*
William Penn University *B*

Kansas

Baker University *T*
Bethany College *B*
Bethel College *T*
Central Christian College of Kansas *A*
Garden City Community College *A*
McPherson College *B, T*
Ottawa University *T*
Pittsburg State University *B, T*
Sterling College *T*
Tabor College *B, T*
University of Kansas *B, T*
University of St. Mary *T*

Kentucky

Bellarmine University *B, M, T*
Campbellsville University *B*
Kentucky State University *B*

Louisiana

Centenary College of Louisiana *B, T*
University of New Orleans *M*
Xavier University of Louisiana *B*

Maine

St. Joseph's College *B*
University of Maine *B*
University of Maine
    Machias *T*
University of Southern Maine *T*

Maryland

Bowie State University *B, T*
College of Notre Dame of Maryland *T*
Mount St. Mary's University *T*
Salisbury University *T*
Washington College *T*

Massachusetts

Assumption College *T*
Bridgewater State College *M, T*
Eastern Nazarene College *B*
Elms College *M, T*
Fitchburg State College *B, M, T*
Framingham State College *B, M*
Lasell College *B, T*
Merrimack College *T*
Northeastern University *M*
Salem State College *M*
Tufts University *T*
University of Massachusetts
    Dartmouth *T*
Western New England College *T*
Westfield State College *B, M, T*
Worcester State College *M, T*

Michigan

Albion College *B, T*
Alma College *T*
Andrews University *M*
Calvin College *B*
Concordia University *B, T*
Cornerstone University *B, T*
Eastern Michigan University *B, T*
Ferris State University *B*
Grand Valley State University *M, T*
Hope College *T*
Madonna University *T*
Michigan State University *M*
Northern Michigan University *B, T*
Olivet College *B, T*
Rochester College *B*
University of Detroit Mercy *B, M, T*
University of Michigan
    Flint *T*
Western Michigan University *B, T*

Minnesota

Bemidji State University *T*
Concordia College: Moorhead *B, T*
Concordia University: St. Paul *B, T*
Crown College *B, T*
Minnesota State University
    Mankato *B, M, T*
Northland Community & Technical
    College *A*
St. Cloud State University *B, T*
University of Minnesota
    Morris *T*
Vermilion Community College *A*
Winona State University *B, T*

Mississippi

Itawamba Community College *A*
Mississippi College *B, M*

Missouri

College of the Ozarks *B, T*
Culver-Stockton College *T*
Lindenwood University *B*
Maryville University of Saint
    Louis *B, M, T*
Missouri Baptist University *T*
Missouri Southern State
    University *B, T*
Missouri State University *B*
Northwest Missouri State
    University *M, T*
Truman State University *M, T*
Washington University in St.
    Louis *B, M, T*

Montana

Montana State University
    Billings *B, T*
Rocky Mountain College *B, T*
University of Great Falls *B*
University of Montana: Missoula *T*
University of Montana: Western *B, T*

Nebraska

Bellevue University *B*
Chadron State College *B*
Concordia University *B, T*
Creighton University *T*
Dana College *B*
Hastings College *B, M, T*
Midland Lutheran College *B, T*
Nebraska Wesleyan University *T*
Peru State College *B, T*
Union College *T*
University of Nebraska
    Kearney *B*
    Lincoln *B*
Wayne State College *B, T*
York College *B, T*

Nevada

Great Basin College *B*

University of Nevada
    Reno *B*

New Hampshire

Franklin Pierce College *T*
Rivier College *B, T*
St. Anselm College *T*

New Jersey

Caldwell College *T*
The College of New Jersey *B, T*
Rowan University *T*
St. Peter's College *T*

New York

Bard College *M*
City University of New York
    City College *B, M*
    College of Staten Island *M*
    Hunter College *B, T*
    Lehman College *M*
    Queens College *M, T*
College of Mount St. Vincent *T*
D'Youville College *B, M, T*
Elmira College *B, T*
Fordham University *M, T*
Hobart and William Smith Colleges *T*
Ithaca College *B, T*
Manhattan College *B, T*
Marist College *B*
Molloy College *B*
Nazareth College of Rochester *T*
Pace University *B*
Roberts Wesleyan College *B, M*
St. John Fisher College *B, T*
St. Joseph's College: Suffolk
    Campus *B, T*
St. Lawrence University *T*
St. Thomas Aquinas College *B, T*
State University of New York
    College at Brockport *M, T*
    College at Geneseo *B, M, T*
    College at Oneonta *T*
    College at Plattsburgh *B, M*
    New Paltz *B, M, T*
    Oswego *B, M*
Vassar College *T*
Wells College *T*

North Carolina

Appalachian State University *B, M*
Campbell University *B, T*
Chowan College *B*
East Carolina University *M*
Elizabeth City State University *B*
Gardner-Webb University *B*
Greensboro College *B, T*
Lenoir Community College *A*
Louisburg College *A*
Mars Hill College *T*
Meredith College *T*
North Carolina Agricultural and
    Technical State University *B, T*
North Carolina Central
    University *B, M, T*
Queens University of Charlotte *T*
Sandhills Community College *A*
University of North Carolina
    Charlotte *B*
    Greensboro *M, T*
    Wilmington *B*
Wake Forest University *T*

North Dakota

Dickinson State University *B, T*
Jamestown College *B*
Mayville State University *B, T*
Minot State University *B*
North Dakota State University *B, T*
University of Mary *B, T*
Valley City State University *B, T*

Ohio

Baldwin-Wallace College *T*
Bluffton University *B*
Case Western Reserve University *T*
Cedarville University *T*
Defiance College *B, T*
Hiram College *T*
John Carroll University *T*
Kent State University *T*
Miami University
   Oxford Campus *M, T*
Mount Union College *T*
Ohio Northern University *B*
Otterbein College *B*
Shawnee State University *B*
University of Findlay *B, M, T*
University of Rio Grande *B, T*
University of Toledo *M, T*
Wilmington College *B*
Youngstown State University *B, M*

Oklahoma

Cameron University *B*
East Central University *B, T*
Eastern Oklahoma State College *A*
Oklahoma Baptist University *B, T*
Oklahoma City University *B*
Southern Nazarene University *B*
Southwestern Oklahoma State
   University *B, M, T*
University of Central Oklahoma *B*
University of Tulsa *T*

Oregon

Concordia University *B, M, T*
Corban College *B*
Linfield College *T*
Warner Pacific College *T*
Western Oregon University *T*

Pennsylvania

Albright College *T*
Alvernia College *B*
Bryn Athyn College of the New
   Church *B*
College Misericordia *T*
DeSales University *T*
Elizabethtown College *B*
Geneva College *B, T*
Gettysburg College *T*
Grove City College *B, T*
King's College *T*
La Salle University *B, T*
Lycoming College *T*
Mansfield University of
   Pennsylvania *B, T*
Moravian College *T*
Rosemont College *T*
St. Francis University *B, T*
St. Vincent College *T*
Susquehanna University *T*
Thiel College *B*
Villanova University *T*
Washington and Jefferson College *T*
Waynesburg College *B, T*
Westminster College *T*
Widener University *T*
Wilkes University *M, T*
York College of Pennsylvania *B, T*

Puerto Rico

Inter American University of Puerto
   Rico
   San German Campus *B*
Pontifical Catholic University of
   Puerto Rico *B, T*
Turabo University *B*
Universidad Metropolitana *B*
University of Puerto Rico
   Cayey University College *B*

Rhode Island

Rhode Island College *B*

Salve Regina University *B*

South Carolina

Anderson University *B, T*
Coker College *B, T*
Francis Marion University *B, T*
South Carolina State University *B, T*

South Dakota

Augustana College *B, T*
Black Hills State University *B*
Dakota State University *B, T*
Mount Marty College *B*
Northern State University *B, T*
University of Sioux Falls *T*
University of South Dakota *B, T*

Tennessee

American Baptist College of ABT
   Seminary *B*
Belmont University *B, M, T*
Bethel College *B, T*
Bryan College *T*
Christian Brothers University *B, M, T*
Cumberland University *B, T*
Freed-Hardeman University *B, T*
King College *T*
Lambuth University *B, T*
Lee University *B*
Lincoln Memorial University *B, T*
Lipscomb University *B, T*
Maryville College *B, T*
Southern Adventist University *B*
Tennessee Technological University *T*
Tennessee Temple University *B*
Tennessee Wesleyan College *B, T*
Trevecca Nazarene University *B, T*
Tusculum College *B, T*
Union University *B, T*
University of Memphis *T*
University of Tennessee
   Martin *B*

Texas

Abilene Christian University *B, T*
Del Mar College *A*
East Texas Baptist University *B*
Hardin-Simmons University *B, T*
Houston Baptist University *T*
Howard Payne University *B, T*
Jarvis Christian College *B, T*
Kilgore College *A*
Lamar University *T*
Laredo Community College *A*
LeTourneau University *B, T*
Lubbock Christian University *B*
McMurry University *T*
St. Edward's University *B, T*
St. Mary's University *T*
Schreiner University *B*
Tarleton State University *T*
Texas A&M University
   Commerce *T*
   Kingsville *T*
Texas College *B, T*
Texas Lutheran University *B, T*
Texas State University: San
   Marcos *M, T*
Texas Wesleyan University *B, T*
University of Dallas *T*
University of Houston *T*
University of Houston
   Clear Lake *T*
University of Mary Hardin-Baylor *T*
University of Texas
   Arlington *T*
   San Antonio *T*
West Texas A&M University *T*

Utah

Brigham Young University *B*
Southern Utah University *B, T*
University of Utah *B*

Utah Valley State College *B*
Weber State University *B*

Vermont

Castleton State College *B, T*
College of St. Joseph in Vermont *B, M*
Johnson State College *B*

Virginia

Averett University *M, T*
Bluefield College *T*
Bridgewater College *T*
Hampton University *M*
Hollins University *T*
Liberty University *B, M, T*
Longwood University *B*
Old Dominion University *B, T*
University of Virginia's College at
   Wise *T*

Washington

Central Washington University *B, T*
Heritage University *B*
Northwest University *T*
Washington State University *B, M, T*
Western Washington University *B*
Whitworth College *B, T*

West Virginia

Bethany College *B*
West Virginia Wesleyan College *B*

Wisconsin

Carroll College *B, T*
Carthage College *T*
Concordia University Wisconsin *B*
Edgewood College *B*
Lakeland College *T*
Lawrence University *T*
Maranatha Baptist Bible College *B*
Marian College of Fond du Lac *B, T*
Mount Mary College *B, T*
Northland College *T*
University of Wisconsin
   Green Bay *T*
   Parkside *T*
   Platteville *B*
   River Falls *T*
   Superior *B, T*
   Whitewater *B*

Holocaust studies

New Jersey

Richard Stockton College of New
   Jersey *M*

Home furnishings

Alabama

Jefferson State Community College *A*
Trenholm State Technical College *C*

California

Antelope Valley College *A*

Illinois

Black Hawk College *A*
William Rainey Harper College *A*

Michigan

Grand Rapids Community College *A*

Home health attendant

Alabama

Lawson State Community College *C*

Arizona

Eastern Arizona College *C*

California

College of the Desert *C*
Copper Mountain College *C*
Santa Barbara City College *C*

Florida

Central Florida College *C*

Georgia

Albany Technical College *C*
Northwestern Technical College *C*

Kansas

Barton County Community College *C*
Coffeyville Community College *C*

Massachusetts

Cape Cod Community College *C*
Springfield Technical Community
   College *C*

Michigan

Baker College
   of Flint *C*

Minnesota

Inver Hills Community College *C*
Itasca Community College *C*
Pine Technical College *C*
Ridgewater College *C*

New Hampshire

McIntosh College *A*

Ohio

Sinclair Community College *C*

Virginia

Eastern Shore Community College *C*

Horse husbandry/ equine science

California

Los Angeles Pierce College *C, A*
Santa Rosa Junior College *C, A*

Indiana

St. Mary-of-the-Woods College *A, B*

Kentucky

Midway College *B*

Minnesota

Rochester Community and Technical
   College *C, A*
University of Minnesota
   Crookston *B*

Missouri

Stephens College *B*

New York

State University of New York
   College of Agriculture and
    Technology at Morrisville *A, B*

Ohio

Lake Erie College *B*
Ohio State University
   Agricultural Technical Institute *A*
Wilmington College *B*

Oregon

Linn-Benton Community College *A*

Rhode Island

Johnson & Wales University *A, B*

Vermont
Sterling College *B*

Horticultural science

Alabama
Auburn University *B, M*

Arizona
Cochise College *C*
Eastern Arizona College *C*

Arkansas
University of Arkansas *B, M*

California
California State Polytechnic
  University: Pomona *B*
California State University
  Fresno *B*
Cosumnes River College *C, A*
Golden West College *C, A*
Los Angeles Pierce College *C, A*
Merritt College *C, A*
Reedley College *C*
University of California
  Davis *M*

Colorado
Colorado State University *B, M, D*

Connecticut
University of Connecticut *B*

Florida
Florida Agricultural and Mechanical
  University *B*
Florida Southern College *B*
South Florida Community College *A*
University of Florida *B, M, D*
Valencia Community College *A*

Georgia
Columbus Technical College *C, A*
Fort Valley State University *A, B*
Georgia Highlands College *A*
Gordon College *A*

Hawaii
University of Hawaii
  Hilo *B*

Idaho
College of Southern Idaho *C, A*
University of Idaho *B*

Illinois
Black Hawk College
  East Campus *C*
Danville Area Community College *A*
Kishwaukee College *A*
Lake Land College *C*
Richland Community College *A*
University of Illinois
  Urbana-Champaign *B, M, D*
William Rainey Harper College *C, A*

Indiana
Oakland City University *A*
Purdue University *B, M, D*
Vincennes University *A*

Kansas
Kansas State University *B, M, D*

Kentucky
Maysville Community College *C, A*

Louisiana
Louisiana State University and
  Agricultural and Mechanical
  College *M, D*
Southeastern Louisiana University *B*

Maine
University of Maine *C, B, M*

Maryland
Howard Community College *A*

Massachusetts
Cape Cod Community College *C*

Michigan
Michigan State University *B, M, D*
St. Clair County Community
  College *C, A*

Minnesota
Rochester Community and Technical
  College *A*
University of Minnesota
  Crookston *B*
  Twin Cities *M, D*

Mississippi
Mississippi State University *B, M, D*

Missouri
College of the Ozarks *B*
Missouri State University *B*
Northwest Missouri State
  University *B*
St. Louis Community College
  St. Louis Community College at
    Meramec *C, A*
University of Missouri
  Columbia *M, D*

Montana
Montana State University
  Bozeman *B*

Nebraska
Nebraska College of Technical
  Agriculture *C, A*
Northeast Community College *A*
University of Nebraska
  Lincoln *B, M*

New Hampshire
University of New Hampshire *A, B*

New Mexico
New Mexico State University *B, M*

New York
City University of New York
  Bronx Community College *A*
Cornell University *B, M, D*
State University of New York
  College of Agriculture and
    Technology at Cobleskill *A, B*
  College of Agriculture and
    Technology at Morrisville *A*
  College of Technology at Delhi *B*

North Carolina
Alamance Community College *C, A*
Brunswick Community College *C, A*
Carteret Community College *C, A*
Catawba Valley Community
  College *C, A*
Johnston Community College *C*
North Carolina State
  University *B, M, D*
Rockingham Community College *C, A*

North Dakota
North Dakota State University *B, M*

Ohio
Ohio State University
  Agricultural Technical Institute *A*
  Columbus Campus *C*

Oklahoma
Cameron University *B*
Eastern Oklahoma State College *A*
Oklahoma State University *B, M*
Tulsa Community College *A*

Oregon
Central Oregon Community
  College *A*
Chemeketa Community College *A*
Linn-Benton Community College *C, A*
Oregon State University *B, M, D*

Pennsylvania
Bidwell Training Center *C*
Delaware Valley College *B*
Lehigh Carbon Community College *A*
Penn State
  Abington *B*
  Altoona *B*
  Beaver *B*
  Berks *B*
  Delaware County *B*
  Dubois *B*
  Erie, The Behrend College *B*
  Fayette *B*
  Hazleton *B*
  Lehigh Valley *B*
  McKeesport *B*
  Mont Alto *B*
  New Kensington *B*
  Schuylkill - Capital College *B*
  University Park *B, M, D*
  Wilkes-Barre *B*
  Worthington Scranton *B*
  York *B*
Temple University *B*
Westmoreland County Community
  College *A*

Puerto Rico
University of Puerto Rico
  Mayaguez *B, M*

South Carolina
Clemson University *B, M*
Trident Technical College *A*

Tennessee
Hiwassee College *A*
Tennessee Technological University *B*

Texas
Grayson County College *C*
Palo Alto College *C, A*
Richland College *A*
Sam Houston State University *B*
Stephen F. Austin State University *B*
Texas A&M University *B, M, D*

Utah
Utah State University *B, M, D*

Vermont
Sterling College *B*
Vermont Technical College *A*

Virginia
Ferrum College *B*
Northern Virginia Community
  College *A*
Virginia Polytechnic Institute and
  State University *B, M, D*

Virginia Western Community
  College *A*

Washington
Washington State University *B, M, D*

West Virginia
Potomac State College of West Virginia
  University *A*
West Virginia University *B*

Wisconsin
Blackhawk Technical College *C*
Gateway Technical College *A*
University of Wisconsin
  Madison *B, M, D*
  River Falls *B*

Horticulture

Alabama
Calhoun Community College *C*
Faulkner State Community College *C*
Northwest-Shoals Community
  College *C*
Wallace State Community College at
  Hanceville *C*

Arizona
Glendale Community College *C, A*
Mesa Community College *A*

Arkansas
Arkansas Northeastern College *C, A*

California
Bakersfield College *A*
Butte College *C, A*
California Polytechnic State
  University: San Luis Obispo *B*
College of San Mateo *C, A*
Diablo Valley College *C*
Fullerton College *A*
Los Angeles Pierce College *C, A*
Merced College *C, A*
Mount San Antonio College *C, A*
San Joaquin Delta College *A*
Santa Barbara City College *C, A*
Shasta College *C*
Sierra College *C, A*
Ventura College *A*

Colorado
Colorado State University *B*
Front Range Community College *C, A*

Connecticut
Naugatuck Valley Community
  College *C, A*
University of Connecticut *A*

Delaware
Delaware Technical and Community
  College
  Owens Campus *C, A*

Florida
Florida Agricultural and Mechanical
  University *B*

Georgia
Albany Technical College *C*
Augusta Technical Institute *C*
Central Georgia Technical College *C*
Darton College *A*
Georgia Southwestern State
  University *A*
University of Georgia *B, M, D*

Idaho
Boise State University *C, A*

Brigham Young University-Idaho *B*

Illinois

Black Hawk College *C, A*
Black Hawk College
  East Campus *C, A*
College of DuPage *C, A*
Illinois Central College *C, A*
Illinois Eastern Community Colleges
  Lincoln Trail College *C, A*
  Wabash Valley College *A*
John Wood Community College *C, A*
Joliet Junior College *C, A*
Kaskaskia College *C, A*
Kishwaukee College *A*
McHenry County College *C, A*
Rend Lake College *C, A*
Richland Community College *A*
Southwestern Illinois College *C, A*
University of Illinois
  Urbana-Champaign *B, M, D*
William Rainey Harper College *C, A*

Indiana

Vincennes University *A*

Iowa

Des Moines Area Community
  College *A*
Hawkeye Community College *C, A*
Indian Hills Community College *C*
Iowa State University *B, M, D*

Kansas

Coffeyville Community College *A*
Dodge City Community College *A*

Kentucky

Jefferson Community College *C, A*
St. Catharine College *A*

Louisiana

Delgado Community College *C, A*

Maryland

Community College of Baltimore
  County *C, A*

Massachusetts

Cape Cod Community College *C*
North Shore Community College *A*

Michigan

Andrews University *B*

Minnesota

Anoka Technical College *C, A*
Central Lakes College *C, A*
Century Community and Technical
  College *C, A*
Pine Technical College *C*
University of Minnesota
  Crookston *B*

Mississippi

Meridian Community College *A*
Mississippi Delta Community
  College *A*

Missouri

College of the Ozarks *B*
Mineral Area College *C, A*
State Fair Community College *A*

Nebraska

Central Community College *C, A*
Metropolitan Community
  College *C, A*
Nebraska College of Technical
  Agriculture *A*

Nebraska Indian Community
  College *C*
Northeast Community College *A*

New Hampshire

University of New Hampshire *A*

New Jersey

Bergen Community College *A*
Ocean County College *A*
Thomas Edison State College *A, B*

New York

Paul Smith's College *A*
State University of New York
  College of Agriculture and
    Technology at Cobleskill *A, B*
  College of Agriculture and
    Technology at Morrisville *A*
  College of Technology at Delhi *A*
  Farmingdale *B*
Suffolk County Community
  College *C, A*

North Carolina

Alamance Community College *C, A*
Blue Ridge Community College *A*
Carteret Community College *C, A*
Central Piedmont Community
  College *C, A*
Fayetteville Technical Community
  College *C, A*
Forsyth Technical Community
  College *A*
Haywood Community College *C, A*
Johnston Community College *C*
Lenoir Community College *C, A*
Mayland Community College *C, A*
Sampson Community College *A*
Surry Community College *A*
Tri-County Community College *C*
Western Piedmont Community
  College *C, A*
Wilkes Community College *C, A*

Ohio

Clark State Community College *A*
Cuyahoga Community College
  Metropolitan Campus *A*
Kent State University
  Salem Regional Campus *A*
Ohio State University
  Agricultural Technical Institute *A*
  Columbus Campus *M, D*

Oklahoma

Eastern Oklahoma State College *A*
Oklahoma State University
  Oklahoma City *C, A*

Oregon

Mount Hood Community College *C, A*

Pennsylvania

Community College of Allegheny
  County *A*
Delaware County Community
  College *C*
Delaware Valley College *B*
Luzerne County Community
  College *C, A*
Penn State
  University Park *C*
Temple University *A*
Westmoreland County Community
  College *A*
Williamson Free School of Mechanical
  Trades *C, A*

Puerto Rico

University of Puerto Rico
  Mayaguez *M*

Utuado *A*

South Carolina

Clemson University *B, M*
Horry-Georgetown Technical
  College *A*
Piedmont Technical College *C*
Spartanburg Technical College *A*
Technical College of the
  Lowcountry *C, A*
Trident Technical College *C, A*

South Dakota

Mount Marty College *A*
South Dakota State University *B*
Southeast Technical Institute *A*

Tennessee

Jackson State Community College *C*
Southwest Tennessee Community
  College *A*
Tennessee Technological University *B*

Texas

Alvin Community College *C*
Central Texas College *C*
Houston Community College
  System *A*
Richland College *A*
Stephen F. Austin State University *B*
Tarrant County College *C, A*
Texas A&M University *B, M, D*
Texas Tech University *B, M*
Trinity Valley Community College *C, A*
Western Texas College *C, A*

Vermont

Sterling College *A, B*
University of Vermont *B*
Vermont Technical College *A*

Virginia

J. Sargeant Reynolds Community
  College *A*
Lord Fairfax Community College *A*
Tidewater Community College *A*
Virginia Western Community
  College *A*

Washington

Clark College *A*
Edmonds Community College *C*
Heritage University *B*
Lake Washington Technical
  College *C, A*
Skagit Valley College *A*
South Puget Sound Community
  College *C, A*
Spokane Community College *A*

Wisconsin

Fox Valley Technical College *A*
Gateway Technical College *A*
Madison Area Technical College *A*
Northeast Wisconsin Technical
  College *C*

Wyoming

Sheridan College *A*

Hospital/health care facilities administration

Alabama

University of Alabama *B*

California

Loma Linda University *M*

Colorado

Jones International University *M*

National American University
  Denver *B*

Connecticut

Quinnipiac University *M*

Florida

St. Leo University *B*
University of Miami *M*

Georgia

Clayton State University *B*
Mercer University *M*

Iowa

Upper Iowa University *B*

Louisiana

Our Lady of the Lake College *B*

Maine

Husson College *M*

Maryland

University of Maryland
  University College *M*

Massachusetts

Newbury College *B*

Michigan

Central Michigan University *B, D*
Madonna University *M*

Minnesota

Concordia College: Moorhead *B*

Missouri

Avila University *B*
St. Louis University *M, D*
Washington University in St. Louis *M*

New Jersey

Thomas Edison State College *B*
University of Medicine and Dentistry
  of New Jersey
  School of Health Related
    Professions *D*

New York

Globe Institute of Technology *B*
Long Island University
  Brooklyn Campus *M*
  C.W. Post Campus *B, M*
Mercy College *M*
Pace University *M*
St. Joseph's College: Suffolk
  Campus *B*
State University of New York
  College of Technology at Canton *B*
Utica College *B*

Ohio

University of Toledo *B*
Ursuline College *B*
Youngstown State University *B, M*

Pennsylvania

Marywood University *B*
St. Joseph's University *B, M*
Temple University *M*

South Dakota

Black Hills State University *B*

Tennessee

University of Memphis *M*
University of Tennessee
  Knoxville *M*

Texas

Texas State University: San Marcos *B*
University of Houston
  Clear Lake *M*

Wisconsin

Marquette University *M*

Hospitality administration and management

Alabama

Faulkner State Community
  College *C, A*
Jefferson State Community
  College *C, A*
Tuskegee University *B*

Alaska

University of Alaska
  Anchorage *B*

Arizona

Arizona Western College *A*
Coconino County Community
  College *C, A*
Northern Arizona University *C, B*
Pima Community College *A*
Scottsdale Community College *C, A*

Arkansas

Arkansas Tech University *B*
National Park Community
  College *C, A*
Northwest Arkansas Community
  College *C*

California

California State Polytechnic
  University: Pomona *B*
Chaffey College *C*
College of the Redwoods *C, A*
Columbia College *C, A*
Diablo Valley College *C*
Grossmont Community College *C, A*
Heald College
  Rancho Cordova *C, A*
MiraCosta College *C, A*
Monterey Peninsula College *A*
National University *C, A, B, M*
San Francisco State University *B*
San Joaquin Valley College Inc. *A*
San Jose State University *B*
Santa Rosa Junior College *C*
Skyline College *C, A*

Colorado

Arapahoe Community College *A*
Colorado Mountain College
  Alpine Campus *A*
Johnson & Wales University *A, B*
Metropolitan State College of
  Denver *B*
University of Denver *B, M*
Westwood College of Technology *A*

Connecticut

International College of Hospitality
  Management *C, A*
Norwalk Community College *A*
Three Rivers Community College *C, A*
University of New Haven *B*

Delaware

Delaware State University *B*
Delaware Technical and Community
  College
  Owens Campus *A*

District of Columbia

Howard University *B*

Florida

Brevard Community College *A*
Broward Community College *A*
Central Florida Community College *C*
Daytona Beach Community College *A*
Edison College *A*
Florida Atlantic University *B*
Florida Community College at
  Jacksonville *A*
Florida International University *B, M*
Florida Metropolitan University
  Pompano Beach *A, B*
Florida Metropolitan University:
  Jacksonville *A, B*
Florida State University *B*
Indian River Community College *A*
Johnson & Wales University *A, B*
Lynn University *B, M*
Palm Beach Community College *A*
St. Leo University *B*
St. Petersburg College *A*
St. Thomas University *B*
South Florida Community College *A*
University of Central Florida *B, M*
University of South Florida *B*
University of West Florida *B*
Valencia Community College *A*
Webber International University *A, B*

Georgia

Abraham Baldwin Agricultural
  College *A*
Albany Technical College *C*
Clark Atlanta University *B*
Coastal Georgia Community
  College *C*
Georgia Southwestern State
  University *A*
Savannah Technical College *C*
Young Harris College *A*

Hawaii

Brigham Young University-Hawaii *B*
Heald College
  Honolulu *A*
University of Hawaii
  Kauai Community College *C, A*

Idaho

Lewis-Clark State College *C, A, B*

Illinois

City Colleges of Chicago
  Harold Washington College *C, A*
Kendall College *B*
Lincoln Land Community College *A*
MacCormac College *C, A*
Northwestern Business College *A*
Richland Community College *C, A*
Roosevelt University *C, B, M*
Southwestern Illinois College *C, A*
Triton College *C, A*
University of Illinois
  Urbana-Champaign *B*
William Rainey Harper College *C, A*

Indiana

Indiana University-Purdue University
  Fort Wayne *A, B*
International Business College *C, A*
Ivy Tech State College
  Ivy Tech Community College:
    Central Indiana *C*
  Ivy Tech Community College: East
    Central *C, A*
  Ivy Tech Community College: North
    Central *A*
  Ivy Tech Community College:
    Northeast *C, A*

Ivy Tech Community College:
    Northwest *C, A*
Vincennes University *A*

Iowa

Des Moines Area Community
  College *C, A*
Iowa State University *B*
North Iowa Area Community
  College *A*

Kansas

Butler County Community College *A*
Seward County Community
  College *C, A*

Kentucky

University of Kentucky *B*
Western Kentucky University *B*

Louisiana

Delgado Community College *A*
Northwestern State University *B*
Southern University
  Shreveport *A*
University of Louisiana at Lafayette *B*
University of New Orleans *B, M*

Maine

Andover College *C, A*
Central Maine Community College *A*
Husson College *B*
Southern Maine Community
  College *A*
Thomas College *B*
University of Maine
  Machias *B*
York County Community College *A*

Maryland

Allegany College of Maryland *A*
Baltimore City Community College *A*
Community College of Baltimore
  County *A*
Frederick Community College *C, A*
Howard Community College *C, A*
Montgomery College *C, A*
Morgan State University *B*
Sojourner-Douglass College *B*
Wor-Wic Community College *C, A*

Massachusetts

American International College *B*
Becker College *B*
Berkshire Community College *A*
Boston University *B*
Bunker Hill Community College *A*
Endicott College *B*
Fisher College *A*
Gibbs College *A*
Lasell College *B*
Marian Court College *C, A*
Massachusetts Bay Community
  College *C, A*
Massasoit Community College *A*
Middlesex Community College *C, A*
Mount Ida College *A, B*
Newbury College *A, B*
North Shore Community College *A*
Quinsigamond Community College *C*
University of Massachusetts
  Amherst *B, M*

Michigan

Baker College
  of Clinton Township *A*
Central Michigan University *B*
Eastern Michigan University *B, M*
Ferris State University *B*
Lake Michigan College *C, A*
Madonna University *B*
Michigan State University *B, M*

Northern Michigan University *B*

Minnesota

Alexandria Technical College *C*
Central Lakes College *C*
Metropolitan State University *B*
Minneapolis Business College *A*
National American University
  St. Paul *B*
Normandale Community College *C, A*
Rasmussen College
  Mankato *A*
  Minnetonka *A*
Winona State University *B*

Mississippi

Copiah-Lincoln Community College *A*
Delta State University *B*

Missouri

Everest College: Springfield *A*
Harris-Stowe State University *B*
Lindenwood University *B, M*
Ozarks Technical Community
  College *A*

Nevada

Community College of Southern
  Nevada *A*
Sierra Nevada College *B*
University of Nevada
  Las Vegas *B, M, D*

New Hampshire

New Hampshire Community
  Technical College
  Berlin *C, A*
New Hampshire Technical Institute *A*
Southern New Hampshire
  University *B, M*
University of New Hampshire *B*

New Jersey

Atlantic Cape Community College *A*
Bergen Community College *C*
Essex County College *A*
Fairleigh Dickinson University
  College at Florham *B, M*
  Metropolitan Campus *B, M*
Gloucester County College *C, A*
Hudson County Community
  College *C, A*
Ocean County College *C*
Rutgers, The State University of New
  Jersey
  Camden Regional Campus *B*

New Mexico

Albuquerque Technical-Vocational
  Institute *C, A*
Dona Ana Branch Community College
  of New Mexico State
  University *A*
New Mexico State University *B*
Southwestern Indian Polytechnic
  Institute *A*

New York

City University of New York
  New York City College of
    Technology *A, B*
Cornell University *B, M, D*
Globe Institute of Technology *C, A, B*
Monroe College *A*
New York University *B, M*
Niagara County Community
  College *C, A*
Niagara University *B*
Paul Smith's College *A, B*
Rochester Institute of
  Technology *A, B, M*
Rockland Community College *A*

St. John's University *B*
State University of New York
　College at Buffalo *B*
　College of Agriculture and
　　Technology at Cobleskill *A*
　College of Agriculture and
　　Technology at Morrisville *B*
Syracuse University *B*

North Carolina

Appalachian State University *B*
Cape Fear Community College *A*
Central Piedmont Community
　College *C, A, B*
Methodist College *B*
North Carolina Central University *B*
University of North Carolina
　Greensboro *B*
Western Carolina University *B*

North Dakota

Bismarck State College *C, A*
North Dakota State University *B*

Ohio

Ashland University *C*
Bowling Green State University *B*
Cincinnati State Technical and
　Community College *A*
Columbus State Community
　College *C, A*
Cuyahoga Community College
　Metropolitan Campus *A*
Lakeland Community College *C, A*
Ohio State University
　Columbus Campus *B*
　Lima Campus *B*
Sinclair Community College *A*
Stark State College of Technology *A*
Tiffin University *B*
University of Akron *C, A*
University of Findlay *B*
Youngstown State University *A, B*

Oklahoma

Oklahoma State University *B, M*
Tulsa Community College *A*

Oregon

Central Oregon Community
　College *A*
Chemeketa Community College *A*
Mount Hood Community College *C, A*
Southern Oregon University *B*

Pennsylvania

Bucks County Community
　College *C, A*
East Stroudsburg University of
　Pennsylvania *B*
Harrisburg Area Community
　College *A*
Marywood University *C, B*
Mercyhurst College *A, B*
Newport Business Institute *A*
Penn State
　Abington *B*
　Altoona *B*
　Beaver *A, B*
　Berks *A, B*
　Delaware County *B*
　Dubois *B*
　Fayette *B*
　Hazleton *B*
　Lehigh Valley *B*
　McKeesport *B*
　Mont Alto *B*
　New Kensington *B*
　Shenango *B*
　University Park *A, B, M, D*
Pennco Tech *C, A*
Restaurant School *A*
Robert Morris University *B*

Rosemont College *B*
Seton Hill University *B*
Temple University *B, M*
Widener University *B, M, D*
York Technical Institute *C*
Yorktowne Business Institute *A*

Rhode Island

Johnson & Wales University *A, B, M*

South Carolina

College of Charleston *B*
Spartanburg Technical College *A*
Technical College of the
　Lowcountry *C*
Trident Technical College *C, A*
University of South Carolina *B, M*
University of South Carolina
　Beaufort *B*

South Dakota

Sisseton Wahpeton College *C, A*
University of Sioux Falls *B*

Tennessee

Belmont University *B*
Hiwassee College *A*
University of Memphis *B*

Texas

Austin Community College *C, A*
Central Texas College *C, A*
Collin County Community College
　District *C, A*
Galveston College *C*
Lamar State College at Port Arthur *C*
St. Philip's College *A*
Stephen F. Austin State University *B*
Tarrant County College *C, A*
Texas Southmost College *A*
Texas Tech University *D*
University of North Texas *B, M*

Utah

Utah Valley State College *A, B*

Vermont

Champlain College *A, B*
Green Mountain College *B*
Johnson State College *B*

Virginia

J. Sargeant Reynolds Community
　College *A*
James Madison University *B*
Norfolk State University *B*
Southwest Virginia Community
　College *C*
Tidewater Community College *A*
Virginia State University *B*

Washington

South Puget Sound Community
　College *C, A*
South Seattle Community College *A*
Washington State University *B*

West Virginia

Concord University *B*
Davis and Elkins College *B*
Mountain State University *A, B*
Southern West Virginia Community
　and Technical College *A*
West Virginia Northern Community
　College *A*

Wisconsin

Fox Valley Technical College *A*
Madison Area Technical College *A*
University of Wisconsin
　Stout *B, M*

Waukesha County Technical
　College *A*

Wyoming

Casper College *A*

Hospitality/recreation marketing

Arizona

Central Arizona College *A*
Northland Pioneer College *C*

Arkansas

National Park Community
　College *C, A*

California

Alliant International University *B*
American River College *A*
City College of San Francisco *A*
Cypress College *C, A*
Glendale Community College *A*
Los Angeles Trade and Technical
　College *A*
Los Angeles Valley College *A*
Monterey Peninsula College *A*
Orange Coast College *C, A*
Pasadena City College *A*
San Francisco State University *B*
Santa Barbara City College *C, A*

Colorado

Colorado Mountain College
　Alpine Campus *A*
Community College of Aurora *C*
Metropolitan State College of
　Denver *B*
Westwood College of Technology *A*

Connecticut

Manchester Community College *C, A*
Norwalk Community College *A*

District of Columbia

Howard University *B*

Florida

Brevard Community College *A*
City College *A*
Johnson & Wales University *B*
Pensacola Junior College *A*
Southwest Florida College *A*

Georgia

Georgia Highlands College *A*
Savannah State University *B*

Hawaii

University of Hawaii
　Kapiolani Community College *C, A*

Idaho

College of Southern Idaho *A*

Illinois

Moraine Valley Community College *C*
William Rainey Harper College *C, A*

Indiana

Vincennes University *A*

Kansas

Butler County Community
　College *C, A*

Maine

Andover College *C, A*
Husson College *B*

University of Maine
　Machias *B*

Maryland

Allegany College of Maryland *A*
Montgomery College *A*

Massachusetts

American International College *M*
Bay State College *A*
Newbury College *A, B*
Quinsigamond Community College *C*
Roxbury Community College *A*

Michigan

Ferris State University *B*
Kirtland Community College *C*
Lansing Community College *A*
Siena Heights University *A, B*

Minnesota

University of Minnesota
　Crookston *A, B*

Nevada

Community College of Southern
　Nevada *A*

New Hampshire

New Hampshire Technical
　Institute *C, A*

New Jersey

Cumberland County College *A*

New Mexico

Southwestern Indian Polytechnic
　Institute *A*

New York

Finger Lakes Community College *A*
Paul Smith's College *B*
Rochester Institute of Technology *M*
State University of New York
　College at Buffalo *B*
　College of Agriculture and
　　Technology at Cobleskill *A*

North Carolina

Wake Technical Community
　College *A*

Ohio

Columbus State Community
　College *C, A*
Ohio State University
　Columbus Campus *B*
University of Findlay *B*
Youngstown State University *A, B*

Oklahoma

Oklahoma State University
　Okmulgee *A*
St. Gregory's University *B*
Tulsa Community College *A*

Oregon

Central Oregon Community
　College *A*

Pennsylvania

Holy Family University *B*
Lehigh Valley College *A*
Montgomery County Community
　College *A*
Newport Business Institute *A*
York Technical Institute *C*
Yorktowne Business Institute *A*

Rhode Island

Johnson & Wales University *B*

South Carolina

Technical College of the
Lowcountry *C, A*

Tennessee

Hiwassee College *A*

Texas

Central Texas College *C*
El Paso Community College *C, A*
San Jacinto College
Central Campus *A*

Utah

Provo College *A*

Vermont

Champlain College *A, B*
Green Mountain College *B*

Washington

Highline Community College *A*
Lake Washington Technical
College *C, A*
Skagit Valley College *A*

West Virginia

Bluefield State College *A*
Concord University *B*
Mountain State College *A*
Mountain State University *B*

Wisconsin

Chippewa Valley Technical College *A*
Fox Valley Technical College *A*
Madison Area Technical College *A*
Northeast Wisconsin Technical
College *A*

Hotel/motel administration/ management

Arizona

Estrella Mountain Community
College *C, A*
Northern Arizona University *B*

Arkansas

North Arkansas College *C, A*

California

College of the Desert *A*
Long Beach City College *C, A*
San Diego Mesa College *C, A*
University of San Francisco *B*

Connecticut

Naugatuck Valley Community
College *A*
University of New Haven *C, A, B*

Florida

Bethune-Cookman College *B*
Northwood University
Florida Campus *A, B*
Schiller International
University *A, B, M*

Georgia

Georgia Southern University *B*
Georgia State University *B, M*

Hawaii

Brigham Young University-Hawaii *B*

Illinois

Kendall College *B*
Lexington College *A, B*
Lincoln Land Community College *C*

Parkland College *C, A*

Indiana

Indiana University-Purdue University
Indianapolis *C*
Purdue University *B, M, D*
Vincennes University *A*

Maine

Husson College *B*

Maryland

University of Maryland
Eastern Shore *B*

Massachusetts

Berkshire Community College *A*
Cape Cod Community College *A*
Lasell College *B*
North Shore Community College *A*

Michigan

Ferris State University *B*
Kirtland Community College *C*
Northwood University *A, B*
Oakland Community College *A*

Minnesota

Alexandria Technical College *C, A*
University of Minnesota
Crookston *A, B*

Mississippi

Coahoma Community College *A*

Missouri

Central Missouri State University *B*
College of the Ozarks *B*
Ozarks Technical Community
College *A*
University of Missouri
Columbia *B, M*

New Hampshire

University of New Hampshire *B*

New Jersey

Bergen Community College *A*
Thomas Edison State College *A, B*

New York

Broome Community College *A*
Bryant & Stratton Business Institute
Bryant & Stratton College:
Syracuse *A*
Cornell University *B, M, D*
Genesee Community College *A*
Globe Institute of Technology *C, A, B*
Mohawk Valley Community
College *C, A*
Monroe College *A*
New York Institute of Technology *B*
Niagara University *B*
Onondaga Community College *A*
Pace University *B*
Paul Smith's College *A, B*
Rochester Institute of
Technology *A, B, M*
State University of New York
College at Plattsburgh *B*
Tompkins-Cortland Community
College *A*

North Carolina

Cape Fear Community College *C, A*
Carteret Community College *A*
East Carolina University *B*
Fayetteville Technical Community
College *C, A*
Johnson & Wales University *A*
Nash Community College *A*

Sandhills Community College *A*
Southwestern Community College *C*

Ohio

Cincinnati State Technical and
Community College *A*
Hocking College *A*
University of Akron *C, A, B*

Oregon

Central Oregon Community
College *A*

Pennsylvania

Bucks County Community
College *C, A*
Central Pennsylvania College *A*
Erie Business Center *C*
Harrisburg Area Community
College *A*
Keystone College *A*
Lehigh Carbon Community College *A*
Lehigh Valley College *A*
Newport Business Institute *A*
Northampton County Area
Community College *A*
Penn State
Schuylkill - Capital College *B*
Wilkes-Barre *B*
Worthington Scranton *B*
York *B*
Pittsburgh Technical Institute *A*

Puerto Rico

Inter American University of Puerto
Rico
Aguadilla Campus *B*
Ponce Campus *B*
San German Campus *C*
Universidad del Este *A, B*
University of Puerto Rico
Carolina Regional College *B*

South Carolina

Horry-Georgetown Technical
College *A*
Spartanburg Technical College *A*
Trident Technical College *A*

South Dakota

South Dakota State University *B*

Texas

Del Mar College *C, A*
Houston Community College
System *C, A*
Northwood University: Texas
Campus *A, B*
Texas Tech University *B, M*

Vermont

Champlain College *A, B*

Virginia

Virginia Polytechnic Institute and
State University *B, M, D*

Washington

Washington State University *B*

West Virginia

Concord University *B*

Wisconsin

Gateway Technical College *A*
Milwaukee Area Technical College *A*

Housing and human environments

Alabama

Auburn University *B*

Arkansas

University of Arkansas *B*

California

California State University
Northridge *B*
San Francisco State University *B*

Florida

Florida State University *B, M, D*
Okaloosa-Walton College *A*

Georgia

University of Georgia *B, M, D*

Illinois

Olivet Nazarene University *B*

Iowa

Iowa State University *B*

Kentucky

Eastern Kentucky University *B*

Michigan

Michigan State University *M, D*

Minnesota

Minnesota State University
Mankato *B, M, T*
University of Minnesota
Twin Cities *B*

Missouri

Missouri State University *B*
University of Missouri
Columbia *B, M*

Nebraska

University of Nebraska
Kearney *B*
Lincoln *B*

New York

Cornell University *B, M, D*

Ohio

Miami University
Oxford Campus *B*
Ohio University *B*
University of Akron *B*

Oklahoma

Oklahoma State University *B, M*

Oregon

Oregon State University *B*

Tennessee

Tennessee Technological University *B*
University of Tennessee
Knoxville *M*

Texas

Texas Tech University *M*
University of North Texas *B*

Utah

Utah State University *B*

Human development and family studies

Alabama
Oakwood College B
Samford University B
University of Alabama B

Arizona
Central Arizona College C, A
Pima Community College C
University of Arizona B

Arkansas
University of Arkansas B
University of Arkansas
   Little Rock M
   Pine Bluff B

California
Azusa Pacific University M
California Polytechnic State
   University: San Luis Obispo B
California State University
   Dominguez Hills M
   Northridge B, M
   Sacramento B
   San Bernardino B
   San Marcos B
Fullerton College A
Hope International University B
Loma Linda University M
Loyola Marymount University M
Merced College A
Moorpark College A
Pacific Oaks College B, M
San Diego Christian College B
San Diego State University B, M
Solano Community College C
Sonoma State University B
University of California
   Davis B, M, D
   San Diego B
University of La Verne M

Colorado
Colorado State University B, M
Community College of Denver C, A

Connecticut
Connecticut College B
Mitchell College A, B
University of Connecticut B, M

Delaware
University of Delaware B

District of Columbia
University of the District of
   Columbia B

Florida
Eckerd College B
Florida State University B, M, D
University of Florida M, D

Georgia
Fort Valley State University B
Georgia Military College A
Georgia Southern University B
Middle Georgia College A
University of Georgia B

Hawaii
Hawaii Pacific University B

Idaho
University of Idaho B

Illinois
City Colleges of Chicago
   Harold Washington College A
Northern Illinois University B, M
University of Illinois
   Urbana-Champaign B, M, D

Indiana
Indiana State University B
Purdue University B, M, D
St. Mary-of-the-Woods College C, A, B

Iowa
Iowa State University M, D

Kansas
Central Christian College of Kansas A
Friends University M
Kansas State University C, B, M

Kentucky
Eastern Kentucky University B
Kentucky State University B
University of Kentucky M

Louisiana
Grambling State University A
Louisiana Tech University B
University of Louisiana at Lafayette B

Maine
University of Maine M

Massachusetts
Hampshire College B
Hellenic College/Holy Cross B
Lesley University B
Springfield College M

Michigan
Andrews University B
Central Michigan University M
Concordia University B
Kalamazoo College B
Kalamazoo Valley Community
   College C, A
Kellogg Community College C
Northern Michigan University B
Spring Arbor University B, M
Wayne State University B, M

Minnesota
Concordia College: Moorhead B
Crown College T
Minnesota State University
   Mankato B
Ridgewater College A
St. Mary's University of Minnesota M
St. Olaf College B
University of Minnesota
   Duluth T
   Twin Cities B

Mississippi
University of Southern Mississippi B

Missouri
Central Missouri State University B
Missouri Baptist University B
Missouri State University B
Northwest Missouri State
   University B
University of Missouri
   Columbia B, M

Nebraska
Grace University B
University of Nebraska
   Kearney B
   Lincoln M, D

Nevada
University of Nevada
   Reno B, M

New Hampshire
University of New Hampshire B, M

New Jersey
Seton Hall University M, D

New Mexico
New Mexico State University B
University of New Mexico B

New York
Cornell University B, M, D
Mercy College M
New York Institute of Technology M
Nyack College M
State University of New York
   College at Oneonta B
Syracuse University B, M, D

North Carolina
Campbell University B
East Carolina University B, M
North Carolina Agricultural and
   Technical State University B
University of North Carolina
   Charlotte B
   Greensboro B, M, D

North Dakota
North Dakota State University B, M

Ohio
Bowling Green State University B, M
Kent State University B, M
Miami University
   Oxford Campus B, M, T
Ohio State University
   Columbus Campus B, M, D
Ohio University B, M
University of Dayton M
University of Toledo A
Youngstown State University B

Oklahoma
Oklahoma Christian University B
Oklahoma State University B, M
St. Gregory's University A
University of Central Oklahoma M

Oregon
Chemeketa Community College A
Clackamas Community College C
Oregon State University B, M, D
Portland State University B
Southwestern Oregon Community
   College A
Warner Pacific College B

Pennsylvania
Indiana University of Pennsylvania B
Penn State
   Abington B
   Altoona A, B
   Beaver B
   Berks B
   Delaware County A, B
   Dubois A, B
   Fayette A, B
   Hazleton B
   Lehigh Valley B
   McKeesport B
   Mont Alto A, B
   New Kensington A, B
   Schuylkill - Capital College A, B
   Shenango A, B
   University Park C, A, B, M, D
   Worthington Scranton A, B
   York A, B

Waynesburg College B

Rhode Island
University of Rhode Island B, T

South Carolina
Benedict College B
Columbia College B
South Carolina State University M

South Dakota
South Dakota State University B

Tennessee
East Tennessee State University B, T
Freed-Hardeman University B
Lee University B
Northeast State Technical Community
   College C, A
Southern Adventist University B
Southwest Tennessee Community
   College A
Tennessee State University B
University of Tennessee
   Knoxville M
Vanderbilt University B

Texas
Abilene Christian University B, M
Baylor University B
El Paso Community College A
Galveston College A
San Jacinto College
   North C, A
Stephen F. Austin State University B
Texas A&M University
   Kingsville B
Texas State University: San
   Marcos B, M
Texas Tech University B, M, D
Texas Woman's University B, M, D
University of Houston B
University of North Texas B, M
University of Texas
   Austin B, M, D
   of the Permian Basin B

Utah
Brigham Young University B
Salt Lake Community College A
University of Utah B, M
Utah State University B, M, D
Weber State University B

Vermont
Southern Vermont College A, B
University of Vermont B, M

Virginia
Lynchburg College B
Radford University B
Virginia Polytechnic Institute and
   State University B, M, D

Washington
Washington State University B, M

Wisconsin
Edgewood College M
Moraine Park Technical College C, A
University of Wisconsin
   Madison B
   Stout B

Human/medical genetics

Alabama
University of Alabama
   Birmingham D

California

University of California
Los Angeles *M, D*

Louisiana

Louisiana State University Health
Sciences Center *M, D*

Michigan

University of Michigan *M, D*

New York

Sarah Lawrence College *M*
State University of New York
College at Fredonia *B*

North Carolina

University of North Carolina
Greensboro *M*

Ohio

Case Western Reserve University *D*

Pennsylvania

Cedar Crest College *B*
Drexel University *M, D*

South Carolina

University of South Carolina *M*

Texas

University of Texas
Medical Branch at Galveston *M, D*
Southwestern Medical Center at
Dallas *M, D*

Utah

University of Utah *B, M, D*

Virginia

Virginia Commonwealth
University *M, D*

Wisconsin

University of Wisconsin
Madison *M*

Human nutrition

Alabama

Samford University *B*

California

College of the Desert *A*

Colorado

Colorado State University *B*

Connecticut

University of Bridgeport *M*

District of Columbia

Howard University *M, D*

Illinois

Rosalind Franklin University of
Medicine and Science *M*
University of Illinois
Urbana-Champaign *B, M, D*

Iowa

Iowa State University *B, M, D*

Kansas

Kansas State University *B, M, D*

Massachusetts

University of Massachusetts
Amherst *B*

Michigan

Michigan State University *M, D*
Northern Michigan University *B*

Missouri

University of Missouri
Columbia *B, M*

New Hampshire

University of New Hampshire *B, M, D*

New York

Cornell University *M, D*
Rochester Institute of Technology *B*

North Carolina

Meredith College *M*

Ohio

Case Western Reserve
University *B, M, D*

Oregon

Central Oregon Community
College *A*

Tennessee

University of Memphis *M*

Texas

Baylor University *B*

Washington

Washington State University *M*

Wisconsin

University of Wisconsin
Stout *M*

Human resources development

Arizona

Northcentral University *M, D*

California

Chapman University *M*
University of San Francisco *M*

Colorado

Colorado Technical University *C*

Georgia

Gwinnett Technical College *C*
West Georgia Technical College *C*

Illinois

Trinity International University *B*
University of Illinois
Urbana-Champaign *M, D*

Kansas

Central Christian College of Kansas *A*
Pittsburg State University *M*
Southwestern College *B*

Maryland

McDaniel College *M*

Massachusetts

Nichols College *B*

Michigan

Andrews University *B*
Oakland University *B*

Minnesota

Academy College *A*
Dakota County Technical College *C*

Rasmussen College
Eagan *A*
Rochester Community and Technical
College *C*
St. Cloud Technical College *C*

Missouri

Webster University *M*

Montana

Montana State University
Billings *A*

Nebraska

University of Nebraska
Omaha *C*

New York

Medaille College *C, B*

North Carolina

Pitt Community College *C, A*

Ohio

Mount Vernon Nazarene University *M*
Sinclair Community College *C*
Union Institute & University *B*

Pennsylvania

Holy Family University *B, M*

Puerto Rico

Inter American University of Puerto
Rico
Ponce Campus *B*

South Carolina

Limestone College *B*

Texas

Brookhaven College *C*
Concordia University at Austin *B*
Midwestern State University *M*
University of Dallas *M*

Wisconsin

Fox Valley Technical College *A*
University of Wisconsin
Stout *M*

Human resources management

Alabama

Athens State University *B*
Auburn University *B*
Auburn University at Montgomery *B*
Birmingham-Southern College *M*
Community College of the Air
Force *A*
Faulkner University *B, M*
Samford University *B*
Troy University *M*
Tuskegee University *M*

Arizona

DeVry University
Phoenix *B*
Northcentral University *M, D*
University of Arizona *B*
University of Phoenix *M*

Arkansas

Harding University *B*
University of Central Arkansas *B*

California

Antioch Southern California
Antioch University Santa Barbara *M*
Azusa Pacific University *M*

California National University for
Advanced Studies *M*
California State University
Chico *B*
Dominguez Hills *B*
East Bay *B, M*
Fresno *B*
Long Beach *B*
Northridge *B, M*
Sacramento *B, M*
San Bernardino *B, M*
Cerritos Community College *A*
Chapman University *M*
City College of San Francisco *A*
College of Marin: Kentfield *A*
DeVry University
Fremont *M*
Long Beach *M*
Pomona *M*
West Hills *M*
Dominican University of California *B*
Fresno Pacific University *B*
Golden Gate University *B, M*
Holy Names University *B*
La Sierra University *M*
National University *B, M*
San Diego State University *M*
San Francisco State University *B*
San Jose State University *B*
Ventura College *A*
Yuba Community College District *A*

Colorado

Colorado Technical University *B, M*
DeVry University: Colorado Springs *M*
University of Colorado
Boulder *B*
Colorado Springs *B*

Connecticut

Quinnipiac University *B*

Delaware

Delaware Technical and Community
College
Owens Campus *A*
Terry Campus *A*
Wilmington College *B, M*

District of Columbia

American University *M*
Catholic University of America *B, M*
George Washington University *D*
Trinity University *M*

Florida

Barry University *M*
DeVry University
Miramar *M*
Orlando *M*
Florida Atlantic University *B*
Florida Institute of Technology *M*
Florida International University *B*
Florida Southern College *B*
Florida State University *B*
Nova Southeastern University *M*
Rollins College *M*
St. Leo University *B*
St. Thomas University *M*
University of Miami *B*
University of North Florida *M*
Valencia Community College *A*

Georgia

DeVry University
Alpharetta *B*
Decatur *M*
Georgia Southwestern State
University *A, B*
Georgia State University *M, D*
Gwinnett Technical College *A*
Macon State College *A*
Middle Georgia College *A*

Savannah Technical College *A*
University of Georgia *M*

Hawaii
Hawaii Pacific University *B, M*
University of Hawaii
    Manoa *B, M*

Idaho
Boise State University *B*
Idaho State University *B, M*
University of Idaho *B*

Illinois
Black Hawk College *A*
Bradley University *B*
DePaul University *B, M*
DeVry University
    Tinley Park *B*
Governors State University *B*
Illinois Institute of Technology *M*
Kishwaukee College *A*
Lake Land College *A*
Lewis University *B*
Loyola University of Chicago *B, M*
Millikin University *B*
Moraine Valley Community
    College *C, A*
National-Louis University *M*
North Central College *B*
Northwestern University *M*
Rockford College *B*
Roosevelt University *B, M*
St. Xavier University *M*
Trinity International University *B, M*
Triton College *A*
University of Illinois
    Urbana-Champaign *B*
University of St. Francis *B*
Western Illinois University *B*
William Rainey Harper College *A*

Indiana
Bethel College *B*
Indiana Institute of Technology *B, M*
Indiana State University *B, M*
Indiana University-Purdue University
    Indianapolis *B*
Oakland City University *B*
Purdue University
    Calumet *B*
    North Central Campus *A, B*
St. Mary-of-the-Woods College *B*
Taylor University *B*
University of St. Francis *B*

Iowa
Ashford University *B*
Briar Cliff University *B, M*
Loras College *B*
Maharishi University of
    Management *M, D*
Morningside College *B*
University of Iowa *B, D*
Vennard College *B*
Western Iowa Tech Community
    College *A*

Kansas
Barton County Community College *A*
Central Christian College of Kansas *A*
Friends University *B, M*
MidAmerica Nazarene University *B*
Southwestern College *B*
University of St. Mary *M*
Wichita State University *B*

Louisiana
Louisiana Tech University *B*
Nicholls State University *B*

Maine
Thomas College *B*

Maryland
Coppin State University *B*
DeVry University: Bethesda *M*
Towson University *M*
University of Baltimore *B*
University of Maryland
    University College *B*

Massachusetts
American International College *B, M*
Becker College *A, B*
Boston College *B*
Emerson College *M*
Emmanuel College *M*
Fisher College *B*
Fitchburg State College *M*
Framingham State College *M*
Holyoke Community College *A*
Marian Court College *A*
Newbury College *A*
Nichols College *B*
Northeastern University *B*
Salem State College *B*
Springfield College *M*
Suffolk University *M*

Michigan
Baker College
    of Cadillac *A, B*
    of Clinton Township *A, B*
    of Flint *M*
    of Muskegon *A, B*
    of Owosso *A, B*
    of Port Huron *A, B*
Central Michigan University *B, M*
Cleary University *B*
Eastern Michigan University *M*
Ferris State University *B*
Grand Valley State University *B*
Lansing Community College *A*
Madonna University *B, M*
Marygrove College *M*
Michigan State University *B, M, D*
Oakland University *M*
Western Michigan University *B, M*

Minnesota
Capella University *B, M, D*
Metropolitan State University *B*
Minnesota State Community and
    Technical College - Fergus Falls *A*
Minnesota State University
    Mankato *B*
St. Cloud State University *B*
St. Mary's University of
    Minnesota *B, M*
St. Paul College *A*
University of Minnesota
    Twin Cities *B, M, D*
University of St. Thomas *B, M, D*
Winona State University *B*

Mississippi
University of Southern Mississippi *B*

Missouri
Central Missouri State University *B*
DeVry University
    Kansas City *M*
Lindenwood University *B, M*
Northwest Missouri State
    University *B*
St. Louis University *B*
Washington University in St.
    Louis *B, M*
Webster University *M*

Montana
Montana State University
    Billings *A*
Montana Tech of the University of
    Montana *A*
University of Montana: Missoula *A*
University of Montana: Western *A*

Nebraska
Bellevue University *B*
Hastings College *B*
York College *B*

Nevada
University of Nevada
    Las Vegas *B*

New Hampshire
New England College *B*
Rivier College *M*

New Jersey
Bloomfield College *B*
Fairleigh Dickinson University
    College at Florham *M*
    Metropolitan Campus *M*
Rider University *A, B*
Rowan University *B*
Rutgers, The State University of New
    Jersey
    New Brunswick/Piscataway
        Campus *M*
Salem Community College *A*
Seton Hall University *M*
Stevens Institute of Technology *M*
Thomas Edison State College *A, B, M*

New Mexico
Eastern New Mexico University *B*

New York
Adelphi University *M*
Boricua College *M*
Bryant & Stratton Business Institute
    Bryant & Stratton College: Albany *A*
Bryant & Stratton College: Henrietta *A*
City University of New York
    Baruch College *B, M*
Cornell University *B, M, D*
Dominican College of Blauvelt *B*
Excelsior College *B*
Herkimer County Community
    College *A*
Hofstra University *M*
Iona College *M*
Le Moyne College *B*
Long Island University
    Brooklyn Campus *M*
Mercy College *M*
New York Institute of
    Technology *B, M*
Niagara University *B*
Pace University *B*
Roberts Wesleyan College *B, M*
Rochester Institute of
    Technology *A, M*
St. John Fisher College *B, M*
St. Joseph's College *B*
State University of New York
    Albany *M*
    Oswego *B*
Suffolk County Community College *A*

North Carolina
Barton College *B*
Davidson County Community
    College *A*
DeVry University: Charlotte *M*
Fayetteville Technical Community
    College *A*
Guilford Technical Community
    College *A*

High Point University *B*
Mount Olive College *B*
Peace College *B*
Pitt Community College *A*
Stanly Community College *A*
University of North Carolina
    Chapel Hill *B*
Western Carolina University *M*

North Dakota
Valley City State University *B*

Ohio
Baldwin-Wallace College *B*
Bowling Green State University *B*
Central Ohio Technical College *A*
Columbus State Community
    College *A*
David N. Myers University *B*
DeVry University
    Columbus *B*
Defiance College *B*
Edison State Community College *A*
Franklin University *B*
Lourdes College *B*
Marietta College *B*
Marion Technical College *A*
Miami University
    Oxford Campus *B*
Ohio State University
    Columbus Campus *B, M, D*
Ohio University *B*
Tiffin University *B*
University of Akron *B, M*
University of Cincinnati *M*
University of Findlay *B*
University of Rio Grande *B*
University of Toledo *B, M*
Urbana University *B*
Ursuline College *B*
Wright State University *B*
Xavier University *B, M*
Youngstown State University *B*

Oklahoma
Northeastern State University *B*
Rose State College *A*
Southwestern Oklahoma State
    University *B*
Tulsa Community College *A*
University of Central Oklahoma *B*

Oregon
DeVry University: Portland *M*
George Fox University *B*
Portland State University *B*

Pennsylvania
Alvernia College *A, B*
Arcadia University *B*
Butler County Community College *A*
Cabrini College *B*
Carlow University *B*
Chestnut Hill College *A, B*
Community College of Allegheny
    County *A*
Community College of Beaver
    County *A*
DeSales University *B*
DeVry University
    Ft. Washington *M*
Drexel University *B*
Geneva College *B*
Holy Family University *B*
Immaculata University *B*
Indiana University of Pennsylvania *B*
Juniata College *B*
Keystone College *A*
King's College *A, B*
Kutztown University of
    Pennsylvania *B*
La Roche College *M*
La Salle University *B*

Lehigh Carbon Community College *A*
Lincoln University *B*
Manor College *A*
Mansfield University of
　Pennsylvania *B*
Messiah College *B*
Muhlenberg College *B*
Peirce College *A*
Point Park University *B*
Reading Area Community College *A*
Robert Morris University *B, M*
Rosemont College *B*
St. Francis University *M*
St. Joseph's University *M*
Seton Hill University *B*
Susquehanna University *B*
University of Pennsylvania *B, M*
University of Scranton *B, M*
Villanova University *B*
West Chester University of
　Pennsylvania *M*
Widener University *B, M*

Puerto Rico
Bayamon Central University *B*
Inter American University of Puerto
　Rico
　Bayamon Campus *B*
　Guayama Campus *B*
　Ponce Campus *B, M*
　San German Campus *B, M*
Turabo University *M*
Universidad Metropolitana *M*
Universidad del Este *M*
University of Puerto Rico
　Aguadilla *A*
　Humacao *B*
　Mayaguez *B, M*
　Rio Piedras *B*
University of the Sacred Heart *M*

Rhode Island
Rhode Island College *B*
University of Rhode Island *T*

South Carolina
Anderson University *B*
Clemson University *M*
Forrest Junior College *A*
Southern Wesleyan University *B*
University of South Carolina *M*

South Dakota
Black Hills State University *B*

Tennessee
Freed-Hardeman University *B*
Lipscomb University *B*
Tennessee Wesleyan College *B*
University of Tennessee
　Knoxville *M, D*
Vanderbilt University *B, M, D*

Texas
Amberton University *M*
Baylor University *B*
DeVry University
　Irving *M*
Houston Baptist University *M*
Lamar University *B*
LeTourneau University *B*
Our Lady of the Lake University of San
　Antonio *B*
St. Mary's University *B*
Sam Houston State University *B*
Tarleton State University *B, M*
Texas A&M University
　Commerce *B*
　Texarkana *B*
University of Dallas *M*
University of Houston *B*
University of Houston
　Clear Lake *M*

University of North Texas *B, M, D*
University of Texas
　Arlington *M*
　Austin *M*
　San Antonio *B, M*
University of the Incarnate Word *B*
Vernon College *A*
Weatherford College *A*

Utah
University of Utah *M*
Utah State University *B*
Weber State University *B*
Western Governors University *B*

Vermont
Champlain College *A, B*

Virginia
Bluefield College *B*
DeVry University
　Arlington *M*
Marymount University *B, M*

Washington
Clark College *A*
DeVry University
　Federal Way *M*
Eastern Washington University *B*
Edmonds Community College *A*
Heritage University *B*
University of Washington *B*
Walla Walla College *B*
Washington State University *B*
Western Washington University *B*

West Virginia
Concord University *B*
Mountain State University *B*
Ohio Valley University *B*
University of Charleston *M*

Wisconsin
Carroll College *B*
DeVry University: Milwaukee *M*
Fox Valley Technical College *A*
Marian College of Fond du Lac *B*
Marquette University *B, M*
Mid-State Technical College *A*
Silver Lake College *B*
University of Wisconsin
　Milwaukee *B*
　Oshkosh *B*
　Parkside *B*
　Platteville *B*
　Whitewater *B, T*
Western Wisconsin Technical
　College *A*

Human sciences communication

Arizona
Arizona Western College *A*

California
Antelope Valley College *A*
California State University
　Sacramento *B*

Georgia
University of Georgia *B*

Kansas
Kansas State University *B*

Nebraska
University of Nebraska
　Omaha *B*

Virginia
Virginia State University *B*

Washington
Seattle Pacific University *B*

Wisconsin
University of Wisconsin
　Madison *B, M*

Human services

Alaska
Sheldon Jackson College *B*
University of Alaska
　Anchorage *A, B*
　Fairbanks *A*

Arizona
Northland Pioneer College *C*
Prescott College *B, M*

California
Allan Hancock College *C, A*
California State University
　Dominguez Hills *B*
　Monterey Bay *B*
Canada College *A*
College of the Sequoias *C, A*
Columbia College *C*
Cypress College *C, A*
Gavilan Community College *C*
Hope International University *B*
Long Beach City College *C, A*
Modesto Junior College *C, A*
Mount St. Mary's College *B*
Notre Dame de Namur University *B*
Riverside Community College *C, A*
Saddleback College *C*
Santa Rosa Junior College *C*
Shasta College *C, A*
Solano Community College *C, A*

Colorado
Metropolitan State College of
　Denver *B*
University of Northern Colorado *B*

Connecticut
Albertus Magnus College *B*
Housatonic Community College *A*
Middlesex Community College *C, A*
Mitchell College *A*
Northwestern Connecticut
　Community College *A*
Norwalk Community College *A*
Post University *B*
Quinebaug Valley Community
　College *A*
St. Vincent's College *C*
Three Rivers Community College *A*
Tunxis Community College *C, A*

District of Columbia
George Washington University *B, M*

Florida
Beacon College *A, B*
Brevard Community College *A*
Central Florida Community College *A*
Florida Community College at
　Jacksonville *A*
Florida Gulf Coast University *B*
Gulf Coast Community College *A*
Hillsborough Community College *A*
Indian River Community College *A*
Miami Dade College *A*
Palm Beach Community College *A*
Pasco-Hernando Community
　College *A*
St. Petersburg College *C, A*

Georgia
Darton College *A*
Fort Valley State University *B*
Kennesaw State University *B*
Macon State College *B*
Spelman College *B*

Hawaii
Hawaii Pacific University *B*
University of Hawaii
　Honolulu Community College *A*
　Maui Community College *A*

Idaho
College of Southern Idaho *C, A*
North Idaho College *A*

Illinois
Carl Sandburg College *C*
Danville Area Community College *A*
Judson College *B*
Lewis University *B*
Loyola University of Chicago *B*
Millikin University *B*
National-Louis University *B, M*
Oakton Community College *C*
Quincy University *B*
Rock Valley College *C, A*
Roosevelt University *M*
Sauk Valley Community College *C, A*
South Suburban College of Cook
　County *A*
Southeastern Illinois College *A*
University of Illinois
　Springfield *M*
Westwood College of Technology
　O'Hare *B*

Indiana
Bethel College *B*
Calumet College of St. Joseph *B*
Indiana Institute of Technology *B*
Indiana Wesleyan University *C*
St. Mary-of-the-Woods College *B*

Iowa
Ellsworth Community College *C, A*
Graceland University *B*
Grand View College *B*
Iowa Western Community College *A*
Northeast Iowa Community
　College *A*
Upper Iowa University *B*
William Penn University *B*

Kansas
Ottawa University *B*

Kentucky
Big Sandy Community and Technical
　College *A*
Elizabethtown Community and
　Technical College *A*
Hazard Community College *A*
Kentucky Wesleyan College *B*

Louisiana
Southern University
　Shreveport *A*

Maine
University of Maine
　Fort Kent *A*
　Machias *B*

Maryland
Bowie State University *M*
Chesapeake College *C*
Coppin State University *M*
Frederick Community College *A*
McDaniel College *M*
University of Baltimore *B, M*

Massachusetts

Anna Maria College *B*
Becker College *C, B*
Bridgewater State College *M*
Bristol Community College *A*
Bunker Hill Community College *C, A*
Cambridge College *B*
Cape Cod Community College *A*
Fitchburg State College *B*
Framingham State College *M*
Lasell College *B*
Massachusetts Bay Community
   College *C, A*
Massasoit Community College *A*
Mount Ida College *A*
Mount Wachusett Community
   College *C, A*
Quinsigamond Community
   College *C, A*
Simmons College *B*
Springfield College *B, M*
University of Massachusetts
   Boston *B, M*
Urban College of Boston *C, A*

Michigan

Baker College
   of Auburn Hills *A*
   of Cadillac *A, B*
   of Clinton Township *A, B*
   of Jackson *A*
   of Muskegon *A, B*
   of Owosso *A, B*
Bay Mills Community College *C*
Delta College *A*
Finlandia University *B*
Grace Bible College *B*
Lake Superior State University *B*

Minnesota

Capella University *M, D*
Concordia University: St. Paul *B, M*
Fond du Lac Tribal and Community
   College *A*
Itasca Community College *A*
Mesabi Range Community and
   Technical College *A*
Metropolitan State University *B*
Minneapolis Community and
   Technical College *C, A*
Minnesota State University
   Mankato *B, M*
Northland Community & Technical
   College *A*
Pine Technical College *C, A*
Riverland Community College *A*
St. Mary's University of Minnesota *B*
South Central College *A*
Winona State University *B*

Missouri

Central Methodist University *B*
Fontbonne University *B*
Hannibal-LaGrange College *B*
Lindenwood University *B, M*
Missouri Baptist University *B*
Missouri State University *M*
North Central Missouri College *A*
St. Charles Community College *A*
Southwest Baptist University *B*

Montana

Flathead Valley Community College *A*
Fort Belknap College *A*
Fort Peck Community College *A*
Miles Community College *A*
Montana State University
   Billings *B*
Stone Child College *A*
University of Great Falls *M*

Nebraska

Bellevue University *B, M*

College of Saint Mary *B*
Doane College *B*
Hastings College *B*
Midland Lutheran College *B*

New Hampshire

New Hampshire Community
   Technical College
   Berlin *C, A*
   Claremont *A*
   Manchester *C, A*
   Nashua *C, A*
New Hampshire Technical
   Institute *C, A*

New Jersey

Burlington County College *A*
College of St. Elizabeth *M*
Essex County College *A*
Mercer County Community College *A*
Ocean County College *A*
Passaic County Community College *A*
Rider University *C, B, M*
Thomas Edison State College *A, B*

New Mexico

New Mexico State University
   Grants *A*
Northern New Mexico College *A*
Santa Fe Community College *A*

New York

Boricua College *B, M*
Broome Community College *A*
Cazenovia College *A, B*
City University of New York
   Borough of Manhattan Community
     College *A*
   New York City College of
     Technology *A, B*
Clinton Community College *A*
Columbia University
   School of General Studies *B*
Corning Community College *A*
Finger Lakes Community College *A*
Herkimer County Community
   College *A*
Hilbert College *A, B*
Jamestown Community College *A*
Jefferson Community College *A*
Metropolitan College of New
   York *A, B*
Monroe Community College *C, A*
Mount St. Mary College *B*
New York University *A*
Niagara County Community
   College *A*
Onondaga Community College *A*
Rockland Community College *A*
Russell Sage College *B*
St. John's University *B, M*
State University of New York
   College of Technology at Alfred *A*
   Oswego *M*
Suffolk County Community College *A*
Sullivan County Community
   College *A*
Touro College *A*
Westchester Community College *C*

North Carolina

Beaufort County Community
   College *C, A*
Central Carolina Community
   College *A*
Elon University *B*
Halifax Community College *A*
Mitchell Community College *A*
South Piedmont Community
   College *C, A*
Wake Technical Community
   College *A*
Wayne Community College *A*

Wingate University *B*

North Dakota

Sitting Bull College *A*

Ohio

Bowling Green State University:
   Firelands College *A*
Central Ohio Technical College *A*
Chatfield College *A*
Cincinnati State Technical and
   Community College *C*
David N. Myers University *B*
Edison State Community College *A*
James A. Rhodes State College *C, A*
John Carroll University *M*
Lakeland Community College *C, A*
Marion Technical College *A*
Mount Vernon Nazarene University *A*
Ohio University
   Zanesville Campus *B*
Sinclair Community College *C, A*
Southern State Community College *A*
Stark State College of Technology *A*
Washington State Community
   College *A*

Oklahoma

East Central University *B*
Oklahoma State University
   Oklahoma City *A*

Oregon

Blue Mountain Community College *A*
Chemeketa Community College *A*
Northwest Christian College *B*

Pennsylvania

Chestnut Hill College *C, A, B, M*
Harrisburg Area Community
   College *C, A*
La Roche College *B*
Lackawanna College *A*
Lincoln University *B, M*
Seton Hill University *B*
University of Scranton *C, A, B*
Villanova University *B*
Waynesburg College *B*
Westmoreland County Community
   College *A*

Puerto Rico

Turabo University *M*

South Carolina

Aiken Technical College *A*
Anderson University *B*
Denmark Technical College *A*
Trident Technical College *C, A*
Williamsburg Technical College *C*
York Technical College *C*

South Dakota

Oglala Lakota College *B*

Tennessee

Bethel College *B*
Hiwassee College *A*
Martin Methodist College *B*
Milligan College *B*
Tennessee Wesleyan College *B*

Texas

Abilene Christian University *M*
Angelina College *C, A*
Austin Community College *C, A*
Laredo Community College *C, A*
North Harris Montgomery
   Community College District *C, A*
South Plains College *A*
South Texas College *A*
Texas Southern University *B*

Tyler Junior College *C, A*
Wayland Baptist University *A, B*

Vermont

Burlington College *B*
Champlain College *A, B*
College of St. Joseph in Vermont *B*
Lyndon State College *B*
Southern Vermont College *A*
Woodbury College *C, A, B*

Virginia

Blue Ridge Community College *A*
Central Virginia Community
   College *A*
John Tyler Community College *A*
New River Community College *C, A*
Northern Virginia Community
   College *A*
Southside Virginia Community
   College *C, A*
Southwest Virginia Community
   College *C, A*
Thomas Nelson Community
   College *A*
Virginia Wesleyan College *B*
Virginia Western Community
   College *A*

Washington

Central Washington University *B*
Columbia Basin College *A*
Edmonds Community College *C, A*
Everett Community College *A*
Grays Harbor College *C, A*
Highline Community College *A*
Seattle Central Community College *A*
Skagit Valley College *A*
Western Washington University *B*

West Virginia

West Virginia Northern Community
   College *C, A*

Wisconsin

College of Menominee Nation *A*
Fox Valley Technical College *A*
Gateway Technical College *A*
Southwest Wisconsin Technical
   College *A*
University of Wisconsin
   Oshkosh *B*
   Superior *M*
Waukesha County Technical
   College *A*

Wyoming

Central Wyoming College *A*

Humanities

Alabama

Spring Hill College *B*
University of Mobile *B*

Arizona

Arizona State University *B, M*
Central Arizona College *A*
Northern Arizona University *B*

Arkansas

Harding University *B*

California

California Institute of Integral
   Studies *B, M, D*
California State University
   Chico *B*
   Sacramento *B*
   San Bernardino *B*
College of the Siskiyous *A*
Concordia University *B*

Dominican University of
California *B, M*
Glendale Community College *A*
Holy Names University *B*
Loyola Marymount University *B*
Pepperdine University *B*
San Jose State University *B*
Scripps College *B*
Southwestern College *A*
Stanford University *B, M*
University of California
Irvine *B*
Riverside *B*
University of San Diego *B*

Colorado

Fort Lewis College *B*
United States Air Force Academy *B*
University of Colorado
Boulder *B*
Denver and Health Sciences
Center *M*

Connecticut

Holy Apostles College and Seminary *B*
University of Bridgeport *B*
Yale University *B*

Florida

Eckerd College *B*
Florida Institute of Technology *B*
Florida State University *B, M, D*
Jacksonville University *B*
Manatee Community College *A*
New College of Florida *B*
Nova Southeastern University *B*
Stetson University *B*
University of Central Florida *B*
University of South Florida *B*
University of West Florida *B, M*
Valencia Community College *A*

Georgia

Darton College *A*

Illinois

Black Hawk College *C*
Bradley University *B*
College of Lake County *C*
McHenry County College *C*
North Central College *B*
Principia College *B*
Quincy University *B*
Shimer College *B*
Trinity International University *B*
University of Illinois
Urbana-Champaign *B*

Indiana

Indiana University
East *B*
Kokomo *B*
South Bend *A*
Indiana University-Purdue University
Indianapolis *A*
Purdue University *B*
Saint Mary's College *B*
St. Mary-of-the-Woods College *A, B*
Valparaiso University *A*

Iowa

University of Northern Iowa *B*
Waldorf College *B*

Kansas

Kansas State University *B*
Tabor College *B*
University of Kansas *B*
Washburn University of Topeka *A*

Kentucky

Lindsey Wilson College *B*

Spalding University *B*
Thomas More College *A, B*

Louisiana

Our Lady of the Lake College *B*

Maine

University of Southern Maine *B*

Maryland

Hood College *M*
St. John's College *B, M*

Massachusetts

Anna Maria College *B*
Lasell College *B*
Newbury College *A*
Roxbury Community College *A*
Suffolk University *B*
University of Massachusetts
Amherst *B*
Worcester Polytechnic Institute *B*

Michigan

Alma College *B*
Central Michigan University *M*
Kirtland Community College *A*
Lake Michigan College *A*
Lawrence Technological University *B*
Michigan State University *B, M*
Michigan Technological University *B*
Olivet College *B*
University of Michigan *B*

Minnesota

College of St. Benedict *B*
College of St. Scholastica *B*
North Central University *A*
St. John's University *B*
University of Minnesota
Morris *B*

Mississippi

Belhaven College *B*

Missouri

Northwest Missouri State
University *B*
St. Louis University *B*
Southeast Missouri State University *B*
Washington University in St. Louis *B*
Webster University *B*

Montana

Blackfeet Community College *A*
Flathead Valley Community College *A*

Nebraska

University of Nebraska
Lincoln *B*

New Hampshire

Plymouth State University *B*
University of New Hampshire *B*

New Jersey

Fairleigh Dickinson University
College at Florham *B*
Metropolitan Campus *B*
Felician College *B*
Georgian Court University *B*
Salem Community College *A*
Thomas Edison State College *B*

New Mexico

College of Santa Fe *B*
College of the Southwest *B*
University of New Mexico *B*

New York

Adelphi University *B*

Canisius College *B*
Cayuga County Community College *A*
City University of New York
Hunter College *B*
Dominican College of Blauvelt *B*
Dutchess Community College *A*
Erie Community College
City Campus *A*
North Campus *A*
South Campus *A*
Fulton-Montgomery Community
College *A*
Genesee Community College *A*
Hofstra University *B, M*
Houghton College *B*
Jamestown Community College *A*
Long Island University
Brooklyn Campus *B*
Marymount Manhattan College *B*
Mohawk Valley Community College *A*
Niagara County Community
College *A*
Roberts Wesleyan College *B, T*
Sage College of Albany *A*
Sarah Lawrence College *B*
State University of New York
Buffalo *B, M*
College at Buffalo *B*
College at Old Westbury *B*
College at Potsdam *B*
College of Agriculture and
Technology at Morrisville *A*
Stony Brook *B*
Tompkins-Cortland Community
College *A*
Union College *B*
Villa Maria College of Buffalo *A*
Wells College *B*

North Dakota

North Dakota State University *B*

Ohio

Antioch University McGregor *B*
Franciscan University of
Steubenville *B*
John Carroll University *M*
Kent State University *B*
Ohio State University
Columbus Campus *M*
Ohio University *A*
Pontifical College Josephinum *B*
Union Institute & University *B*
University of Akron *B*
University of Toledo *B*
Ursuline College *B*
Wright State University *M*

Oklahoma

Oklahoma City University *B*
Oklahoma Panhandle State
University *B*
University of Oklahoma *B*

Oregon

Corban College *B*
University of Oregon *B*
Willamette University *B*

Pennsylvania

Arcadia University *M*
Bucknell University *B*
Bucks County Community College *A*
Community College of Allegheny
County *A*
Community College of Beaver
County *A*
East Stroudsburg University of
Pennsylvania *B*
Edinboro University of
Pennsylvania *B*
Juniata College *B*
Keystone College *A*

Lackawanna College *A*
Lehigh Carbon Community College *A*
Lock Haven University of
Pennsylvania *B*
Luzerne County Community
College *A*
Messiah College *B*
Montgomery County Community
College *C, A*
Mount Aloysius College *B*
Penn State
Harrisburg *B, M*
Rosemont College *B*
St. Joseph's University *B*
University of Pennsylvania *B*
University of Pittsburgh *B*
York College of Pennsylvania *B*

Puerto Rico

Turabo University *B*
University of Puerto Rico
Bayamon University College *A*
Carolina Regional College *A*
Utuado *A*

Rhode Island

Providence College *B*
Salve Regina University *M, D*

South Carolina

Charleston Southern University *B*
Columbia International University *B*
Lander University *B*

Tennessee

LeMoyne-Owen College *B*
Milligan College *B*
University of Tennessee
Chattanooga *B*

Texas

Baylor University *B*
Lubbock Christian University *B*
Midwestern State University *B*
Schreiner University *B*
Southern Methodist University *B*
Stephen F. Austin State University *B*
Texarkana College *A*
University of Dallas *M*
University of Houston
Clear Lake *B, M*
Downtown *B*
University of Texas
Arlington *M*
Austin *B*
El Paso *D*
San Antonio *B*

Utah

Brigham Young University *B*
Salt Lake Community College *A*
University of Utah *B*
Utah Valley State College *A*

Vermont

Bennington College *B*
Burlington College *A, B*

Virginia

Danville Community College *A*
Hampden-Sydney College *B*
Marymount University *M*
Old Dominion University *M*
Virginia Wesleyan College *B*

Washington

Evergreen State College *B*
Heritage University *A*
Saint Martin's University *B*
Seattle University *B*
Washington State University *B*
Western Washington University *B*

West Virginia

Marshall University *B, M*
Mountain State University *B*

Wisconsin

Concordia University Wisconsin *B*
Maranatha Baptist Bible College *B*
St. Norbert College *B*
University of Wisconsin
  Green Bay *B*

Wyoming

Sheridan College *A*
University of Wyoming *B*

Hydraulics technology

Illinois

Moraine Valley Community College *C*

Kentucky

Hopkinsville Community College *C*

Maryland

Community College of Baltimore
  County *C, A*

Michigan

Lansing Community College *A*

Minnesota

Alexandria Technical College *C, A*
Hennepin Technical College *C, A*

Ohio

Ohio State University
  Agricultural Technical Institute *C, A*
Owens Community College
  Toledo *C, A*

Pennsylvania

Community College of Allegheny
  County *C, A*

Washington

Spokane Community College *A*

Wisconsin

Gateway Technical College *A*
Milwaukee Area Technical College *C*

Hydrology/water resources science

Arizona

Northern Arizona University *B*
University of Arizona *B, M, D*

California

California State University
  Chico *B, M*
Santiago Canyon College *A*
University of California
  Davis *B, M, D*

Florida

Florida Institute of Technology *B*

Illinois

Illinois State University *M*

Kansas

University of Kansas *M*

Michigan

Northern Michigan University *B*
Western Michigan University *B*

Minnesota

St. Cloud State University *B*

Nebraska

University of Nebraska
  Lincoln *B*

Nevada

University of Nevada
  Reno *B, M, D*

New Mexico

New Mexico Institute of Mining and
  Technology *M, D*

New York

Rensselaer Polytechnic Institute *B, M*
State University of New York
  College at Brockport *B*
  College at Oneonta *B*

Pennsylvania

University of Pennsylvania *M*

Texas

Tarleton State University *B*
Texas A&M University
  Galveston *B*
University of Texas
  Austin *B*

Utah

Brigham Young University *B, M*
Utah State University *B, M, D*

Illustration

Arkansas

John Brown University *B*

California

Academy of Art University *C, A, B, M*
Art Center College of Design *B*
California College of the Arts *B*
University of San Francisco *B*

Colorado

Rocky Mountain College of Art &
  Design *B*

Connecticut

Paier College of Art *C, B*
University of Bridgeport *B*

Delaware

Delaware College of Art and Design *A*

Florida

Art Institute of Fort Lauderdale *B*

Georgia

Savannah College of Art and
  Design *B, M*

Illinois

Judson College *B*
Lewis University *B*

Indiana

Grace College *B*

Kansas

University of Kansas *B, M*

Kentucky

Louisville Technical Institute *C, A*

Maine

Maine College of Art *B*

Maryland

Maryland Institute College of Art *B*

Massachusetts

Art Institute of Boston at Lesley
  University *B*
New England Institute of Art *B*
School of the Museum of Fine
  Arts *B, M*

Michigan

College for Creative Studies *B*
Finlandia University *B*
Kendall College of Art and Design of
  Ferris State University *B*
Lawrence Technological University *B*
University of Michigan *B*

Minnesota

College of Visual Arts *B*
Minneapolis College of Art and
  Design *B*

Missouri

Columbia College *M*
Washington University in St. Louis *B*

New Hampshire

McIntosh College *A*

New York

Fashion Institute of Technology *A, B*
Pratt Institute *A, B, M*
Rochester Institute of
  Technology *A, B*
Sage College of Albany *B*
St. John's University *B*
School of Visual Arts *B*
Syracuse University *B, M*

North Carolina

East Carolina University *B*

Ohio

Art Academy of Cincinnati *B*
Cleveland Institute of Art *B*
Columbus College of Art and
  Design *B*

Oregon

Pacific Northwest College of Art *B*

Pennsylvania

Keystone College *A, B*
Marywood University *M*
Moore College of Art and Design *B*

Rhode Island

Rhode Island School of Design *B*

Tennessee

Memphis College of Art *B*

Texas

University of Texas
  Pan American *B*

Utah

Brigham Young University *B*

Washington

Cornish College of the Arts *B*

Wisconsin

Concordia University Wisconsin *B*

Industrial design

Alabama

Auburn University *B, M*

Arizona

Arizona State University *B*
Yavapai College *C, A*

California

Academy of Art University *C, A, B, M*
Art Center College of Design *B, M*
Art Institute
  of California: Orange County *B*
California College of the Arts *B*
California State University
  Long Beach *B, M*
Los Angeles Pierce College *C, A*
San Francisco State University *B*
San Jose State University *B*

Colorado

Art Institute
  of Colorado *B*
Metropolitan State College of
  Denver *B*

Connecticut

University of Bridgeport *B*

Florida

Art Institute of Fort Lauderdale *B*

Georgia

Georgia Institute of Technology *B, M*
Savannah College of Art and
  Design *B, M*

Illinois

University of Illinois
  Chicago *B, M*

Indiana

Oakland City University *A, B*

Kansas

University of Kansas *B, M*

Louisiana

University of Louisiana at Lafayette *B*

Massachusetts

Massachusetts College of Art *B*
Wentworth Institute of
  Technology *A, B*

Michigan

College for Creative Studies *B*
Ferris State University *B*
Henry Ford Community College *A*
Kendall College of Art and Design of
  Ferris State University *B*
Northern Michigan University *A*
University of Michigan *B*
Western Michigan University *B*

New Jersey

Kean University *B*

New York

Fashion Institute of Technology *B*
Pratt Institute *B, M*
Rochester Institute of
  Technology *A, B, M*
Syracuse University *B, M*

North Carolina

Appalachian State University *B*
North Carolina State University *B, M*

Ohio

Cleveland Institute of Art *B*
Columbus College of Art and
  Design *B*

Ohio State University
Columbus Campus B, M
University of Cincinnati B

Pennsylvania
Art Institute
of Philadelphia A, B
of Pittsburgh A, B
Carnegie Mellon University B
Philadelphia University B
University of the Arts B, M

Rhode Island
Rhode Island School of Design B, M

South Carolina
Clemson University B, M

Texas
Texas A&M University
Commerce B
University of Houston B

Utah
Brigham Young University B, M

Virginia
Lord Fairfax Community College C
Virginia Polytechnic Institute and
State University B

Washington
Art Institute of Seattle A
University of Washington B, M
Western Washington University B

Wisconsin
Western Wisconsin Technical
College A

Industrial electronics technology

Alabama
Lawson State Community College C
Shelton State Community
College C, A
Trenholm State Technical College C, A

Arkansas
Arkansas Northeastern College C
North Arkansas College C, A
Southern Arkansas University Tech C
University of Arkansas
Community College at Hope C
Fort Smith C

California
Irvine Valley College C
Victor Valley College A

Georgia
Dalton State College C, A

Idaho
Lewis-Clark State College C, A, B

Illinois
College of DuPage C, A
College of Lake County C, A
John Wood Community College C
Lincoln Land Community College C, A
Parkland College C
William Rainey Harper College C

Indiana
Ivy Tech State College
Ivy Tech Community College:
Central Indiana A

Iowa
Des Moines Area Community
College A
Indian Hills Community College C
North Iowa Area Community
College A
Northwest Iowa Community
College A

Kentucky
Jefferson Community College C
Somerset Community College C, A

Michigan
Ferris State University A
Oakland Community College A

Minnesota
Central Lakes College A
Lake Superior College C
Mesabi Range Community and
Technical College A

Missouri
Crowder College A
State Fair Community College C, A

North Carolina
Cleveland Community College C
Surry Community College C, A

Pennsylvania
Lackawanna College A
Northampton County Area
Community College C, A
Pennsylvania College of Technology B

South Carolina
Aiken Technical College C
Greenville Technical College C
Horry-Georgetown Technical
College C, A
Midlands Technical College C
Piedmont Technical College C, A
Spartanburg Technical College C, A

Utah
Salt Lake Community College C

Virginia
Danville Community College C

Washington
Lower Columbia College A
Wenatchee Valley College C, A

Wisconsin
Gateway Technical College C
Milwaukee Area Technical College C
Western Wisconsin Technical
College C

Wyoming
Western Wyoming Community
College C, A

Industrial engineering

Alabama
University of Alabama B, M

Alaska
University of Alaska
Fairbanks B, M

Arizona
Arizona State University B, M, D

California
California State Polytechnic
University: Pomona B
National University M
San Jose State University B, M
Stanford University M, D
University of San Diego B
University of Southern
California B, M, D

Colorado
Colorado State University
Pueblo B, M

Connecticut
University of Connecticut B
University of New Haven M

Florida
Florida State University B, M, D
University of Central Florida B, M, D
University of Miami B, M, D

Georgia
Georgia Institute of
Technology B, M, D

Illinois
Bradley University B, M
Northern Illinois University B
Northwestern University B, M, D
Southern Illinois University
Edwardsville B
University of Illinois
Urbana-Champaign B, M, D

Indiana
Indiana Institute of Technology B
Indiana University
East A
Purdue University B, M, D

Iowa
Iowa State University B, M, D
St. Ambrose University B
University of Iowa B, M, D

Kansas
Kansas State University B, M, D
Wichita State University B, M, D

Kentucky
Maysville Community College A
University of Louisville B, M, D

Louisiana
Louisiana State University and
Agricultural and Mechanical
College B, M

Maryland
Morgan State University B

Massachusetts
University of Massachusetts
Amherst B, M, D
Western New England College B
Worcester Polytechnic Institute B

Michigan
Andrews University B
Kettering University B
Northern Michigan University B
University of Michigan B, M, D
Wayne State University B, M, D
Western Michigan University B, M

Minnesota
St. Cloud State University B

Mississippi
Mississippi State University B, M

Missouri
Missouri Southern State University B
University of Missouri
Columbia B, M, D

Nebraska
University of Nebraska
Lincoln B, M

New Jersey
New Jersey Institute of
Technology B, M, D

New Mexico
New Mexico State University B, M

New York
Hofstra University B
Polytechnic University M
Rensselaer Polytechnic Institute B, M
Rochester Institute of
Technology B, M
State University of New York
Binghamton B, M
Buffalo B, M, D

North Carolina
North Carolina State
University B, M, D

North Dakota
North Dakota State University B, M, D

Ohio
Kent State University B
Ohio State University
Columbus Campus B, M, D
Ohio University B, M
University of Toledo B, M
Youngstown State University B, M

Oklahoma
Northeastern State University B, M
Oklahoma State University B, M, D
University of Oklahoma B, M, D

Oregon
Oregon State University B, M, D

Pennsylvania
Elizabethtown College B
Gannon University B
Lehigh University B, M, D
Penn State
Abington B
Altoona B
Beaver B
Berks B
Delaware County B
Dubois B
Fayette B
Hazleton B
Lehigh Valley B
McKeesport B
Mont Alto B
New Kensington B
Schuylkill - Capital College B
Shenango B
Wilkes-Barre B
Worthington Scranton B
York B
Philadelphia University B
University of Pittsburgh B, M, D

Puerto Rico
Inter American University of Puerto
Rico
Bayamon Campus B

University of Puerto Rico
  Bayamon University College *A*
  Mayaguez *B, M*

Rhode Island
University of Rhode Island *B, M, D*

South Dakota
South Dakota School of Mines and
  Technology *B*

Texas
Lamar University *B, M*
Texas A&M University *B, M, D*
Texas State University: San Marcos *B*
Texas Tech University *B, M, D*
University of Texas
  Arlington *B, M, D*
  Austin *D, T*
  El Paso *B, M*

Virginia
Tidewater Community College *A*
Virginia Polytechnic Institute and
  State University *B, M, D*

Washington
University of Washington *B*

West Virginia
West Virginia University *B, M*

Wisconsin
Milwaukee School of Engineering *B*
University of Wisconsin
  Madison *B, M, D*

Industrial equipment maintenance/repair

Alabama
Alabama Southern Community
  College *C, A*
Community College of the Air
  Force *A*
Gadsden State Community
  College *C, A*
Lawson State Community College *C*
Northwest-Shoals Community
  College *C, A*
Shelton State Community College *C*
Snead State Community College *C*
Trenholm State Technical College *C, A*
University of West Alabama *A*

Alaska
University of Alaska
  Anchorage *C, A*

Arizona
Central Arizona College *A*

Arkansas
Arkansas Northeastern College *C, A*
Arkansas State University
  Mountain Home *C, A*
Arkansas Tech University *C, A*
East Arkansas Community
  College *C, A*
Mid-South Community College *C*
North Arkansas College *C*
Ouachita Technical College *C*
Phillips Community College of the
  University of Arkansas *A*
Pulaski Technical College *C*
South Arkansas Community
  College *C, A*
Southeast Arkansas College *C, A*
Southern Arkansas University
  Tech *C, A*

University of Arkansas
  Community College at Batesville *A*
  Community College at Hope *C*
  Fort Smith *C*
  Monticello *A*

California
Allan Hancock College *C*
Cabrillo College *C, A*
Fresno City College *C, A*
Merced College *C, A*
Taft College *A*

Colorado
Pueblo Community College *C, A*
Red Rocks Community College *C*

Delaware
Delaware Technical and Community
  College
  Terry Campus *C, A*

Florida
Miami Dade College *A*

Georgia
Albany Technical College *C, A*
Athens Technical College *C*
Augusta Technical Institute *C*
Bainbridge College *C*
Central Georgia Technical College *C*
Chattahoochee Technical College *C*
Coastal Georgia Community
  College *C*
Columbus Technical College *C, A*
Georgia Southwestern State
  University *A*
Middle Georgia College *A*
Savannah Technical College *C, A*
Waycross College *A*
West Georgia Technical College *A*

Idaho
Boise State University *C, A*
North Idaho College *A*

Illinois
Black Hawk College *C*
College of Lake County *C, A*
Danville Area Community College *A*
Heartland Community College *C, A*
Illinois Eastern Community Colleges
  Olney Central College *C, A*
  Wabash Valley College *C, A*
John A. Logan College *A*
John Wood Community College *C, A*
Kankakee Community College *C, A*
Kaskaskia College *C, A*
Lake Land College *C*
Moraine Valley Community College *C*
Prairie State College *C*
Rend Lake College *C, A*
Richland Community College *A*
Southwestern Illinois College *C, A*
Triton College *C*
Waubonsee Community College *C, A*
William Rainey Harper College *C*

Indiana
Ivy Tech State College
  Ivy Tech Community College:
    Central Indiana *A*
Vincennes University *A*

Iowa
Des Moines Area Community
  College *A*
Hawkeye Community College *C*
Marshalltown Community College *A*
Muscatine Community College *A*
Western Iowa Tech Community
  College *A*

Kansas
Haskell Indian Nations University *A*

Kentucky
Big Sandy Community and Technical
  College *C*
Jefferson Community College *C*
Maysville Community College *C, A*
Somerset Community College *C, A*

Louisiana
Bossier Parish Community College *A*

Maine
Northern Maine Community
  College *A*
Washington County Community
  College *C*

Maryland
Community College of Baltimore
  County *C, A*
Garrett College *C*

Michigan
Grand Rapids Community College *C*
Kellogg Community College *C, A*
Kirtland Community College *C, A*
Lake Michigan College *C*
Lansing Community College *A*
Macomb Community College *C*
Mott Community College *C*
Muskegon Community College *C*
Northern Michigan University *A*
Southwestern Michigan College *C, A*

Minnesota
Central Lakes College *C*
Hennepin Technical College *C, A*
Mesabi Range Community and
  Technical College *C*
Minnesota State Community and
  Technical College - Fergus
  Falls *C, A*
Northwest Technical College *C, A*
Riverland Community College *C*
St. Paul College *C*

Mississippi
Coahoma Community College *A*
East Central Community College *C*
Hinds Community College *C*
Meridian Community College *C*
Mississippi Delta Community
  College *C*

Missouri
Jefferson College *A*
Mineral Area College *C, A*
Ozarks Technical Community
  College *C, A*
Ranken Technical College *A*
State Fair Community College *C, A*

Montana
University of Montana: Missoula *C*

Nebraska
Central Community College *C, A*
Metropolitan Community College *A*
Northeast Community College *A*

Nevada
Great Basin College *C, A*

New Hampshire
New Hampshire Community
  Technical College
  Nashua *A*

New Jersey
Cumberland County College *A*

North Carolina
Alamance Community College *C, A*
Bladen Community College *C*
Blue Ridge Community College *C*
Brunswick Community College *C, A*
Caldwell Community College and
  Technical Institute *A*
Central Carolina Community
  College *A*
Craven Community College *A*
Durham Technical Community
  College *C*
Halifax Community College *C, A*
Mayland Community College *C*
McDowell Technical Community
  College *A*
Mitchell Community College *A*
Nash Community College *C*
Richmond Community College *C*
Roanoke-Chowan Community
  College *C*
Rockingham Community College *C*
Rowan-Cabarrus Community
  College *C, A*
Sampson Community College *C, A*
Southeastern Community
  College *C, A*
Surry Community College *A*
Vance-Granville Community
  College *C*
Wake Technical Community
  College *C, A*
Wilson Technical Community
  College *C*

Ohio
Jefferson Community College *A*
Stark State College of Technology *A*

Oregon
Blue Mountain Community College *A*
Chemeketa Community College *A*
Linn-Benton Community College *A*
Rogue Community College *C, A*

Pennsylvania
Harrisburg Area Community
  College *C, A*
Johnson College *A*
Pennsylvania College of Technology *A*
Reading Area Community College *A*
Westmoreland County Community
  College *A*

South Carolina
Aiken Technical College *C, A*
Central Carolina Technical College *C*
Greenville Technical College *C, A*
Midlands Technical College *C*
Spartanburg Technical College *C*
Tri-County Technical College *A*
Trident Technical College *C, A*
York Technical College *A*

South Dakota
Western Dakota Technical Institute *A*

Tennessee
Northeast State Technical Community
  College *C, A*
Southwest Tennessee Community
  College *A*

Texas
Amarillo College *C, A*
Eastfield College *A*
Grayson County College *A*
Houston Community College
  System *C*

Texas State Technical College
Waco *C, A*

Utah

Salt Lake Community College *A*
Weber State University *A*

Virginia

John Tyler Community College *C*
New River Community College *C*
Southside Virginia Community
College *C*
Southwest Virginia Community
College *C*
Thomas Nelson Community
College *C*
Tidewater Community College *A*
Virginia Highlands Community
College *C*

Washington

Bellingham Technical College *A*
Big Bend Community College *C, A*
Lake Washington Technical College *C*
Lower Columbia College *A*
Renton Technical College *C, A*
Spokane Community College *A*

West Virginia

Eastern West Virginia Community and
Technical College *C, A*
West Virginia Northern Community
College *C*

Wisconsin

Chippewa Valley Technical College *A*
Gateway Technical College *C*
Lakeshore Technical College *C*
Madison Area Technical College *C*
Milwaukee Area Technical College *C*
Moraine Park Technical College *C*
Northeast Wisconsin Technical
College *A*
Waukesha County Technical
College *C*
Wisconsin Indianhead Technical
College *C*

Wyoming

Western Wyoming Community
College *C, A*

Industrial/ organizational psychology

Alabama

Alabama Agricultural and Mechanical
University *M*

Arizona

Northcentral University *M, D*

Arkansas

University of Arkansas
Little Rock *M*

California

Alliant International University *M, D*
Antioch Southern California
Antioch University Santa Barbara *M*
California State University
Long Beach *M*
Sacramento *M*
San Bernardino *M*
Golden Gate University *M*
John F. Kennedy University *M*
San Diego State University *M*
San Francisco State University *M*
San Jose State University *M*

Connecticut

University of New Haven *M*

District of Columbia

George Washington University *D*

Florida

Carlos Albizu University *M*
Florida Institute of Technology *M, D*
University of Central Florida *M*

Georgia

Georgia Institute of Technology *M, D*

Illinois

DePaul University *M, D*
Roosevelt University *M*
University of Illinois
Urbana-Champaign *M, D*

Kentucky

Eastern Kentucky University *M*
Northern Kentucky University *M*

Louisiana

Louisiana Tech University *M*

Maryland

University of Baltimore *M*

Massachusetts

Bridgewater State College *M*
Salem State College *M*
Springfield College *M*

Michigan

Central Michigan University *M, D*
University of Detroit Mercy *M*
Wayne State University *M*

Minnesota

Capella University *M, D*
Minnesota State University
Mankato *M*

Mississippi

William Carey College *M*

Nebraska

University of Nebraska
Omaha *M, D*

New Jersey

Fairleigh Dickinson University
College at Florham *M*
Rutgers, The State University of New
Jersey
New Brunswick/Piscataway
Campus *D*

New York

Adelphi University *M*
City University of New York
Baruch College *M*
Brooklyn College *M*
Hofstra University *M, D*
New York University *M, D*
State University of New York
Albany *D*

North Carolina

Appalachian State University *M*
University of North Carolina
Charlotte *M*

Ohio

Bowling Green State University *M, D*
Ohio State University
Columbus Campus *M, D*
Ohio University *M, D*

University of Akron *D*
Wright State University *M, D*

Oklahoma

University of Tulsa *M, D*

Pennsylvania

West Chester University of
Pennsylvania *M*

Puerto Rico

Inter American University of Puerto
Rico
San German Campus *M, D*
University of Puerto Rico
Rio Piedras *M*

South Carolina

Clemson University *D*

Tennessee

University of Tennessee
Knoxville *M, D*

Texas

Angelo State University *M*
Lamar University *M*
Rice University *M, D*
St. Mary's University *M*
Texas A&M University *D*
University of Houston *M, D*
University of North Texas *M*
University of Texas
El Paso *D*

Vermont

Goddard College *M*

Virginia

Old Dominion University *D*

Washington

City University *M*

Wisconsin

University of Wisconsin
Oshkosh *M*

Industrial radiologic technology

Alabama

Northwest-Shoals Community
College *C*

Kansas

Newman University *A*

Michigan

Madonna University *B*

Utah

Salt Lake Community College *A*

Industrial safety technology

New Mexico

Eastern New Mexico University:
Roswell Campus *C*
San Juan College *C*

North Carolina

Nash Community College *A*

Ohio

James A. Rhodes State College *C, A*

Oklahoma

Northeastern State University *B*
University of Central Oklahoma *B*

South Dakota

South Dakota State University *B*

Industrial technology

Alabama

Gadsden State Community
College *C, A*

Alaska

University of Alaska
Fairbanks *A*

Arkansas

Arkansas Tech University *C, A*

California

California State University
Los Angeles *B*
College of the Sequoias *C, A*

Colorado

Colorado State University
Pueblo *B*

Connecticut

Asnuntuck Community College *C, A*
Central Connecticut State
University *B*

Florida

St. Petersburg College *A*

Georgia

Darton College *A*
Georgia Southern University *B*
Macon State College *A*
Northwestern Technical College *C, A*
Southern Polytechnic State
University *C, B*

Illinois

Eastern Illinois University *B, M*
Illinois State University *B, M*
Northern Illinois University *B*
Parkland College *C, A*
Southern Illinois University
Carbondale *B*
Western Illinois University *B*

Indiana

Ball State University *B*
Indiana State University *B, M, D*
Indiana University-Purdue University
Fort Wayne *A, B*
Ivy Tech State College
Ivy Tech Community College:
Bloomington *C, A*
Ivy Tech Community College:
Central Indiana *C, A*
Ivy Tech Community College:
Columbus *C, A*
Ivy Tech Community College: East
Central *C, A*
Ivy Tech Community College:
Kokomo *C, A*
Ivy Tech Community College:
Lafayette *C, A*
Ivy Tech Community College: North
Central *C, A*
Ivy Tech Community College:
Northeast *C, A*
Ivy Tech Community College:
Northwest *C, A*
Ivy Tech Community College: South
Central *C, A*

Ivy Tech Community College:
Southeast *C, A*
Ivy Tech Community College:
Southwest *C, A*
Ivy Tech Community College:
Wabash Valley *C*
Ivy Tech Community College:
Whitewater *C*

Iowa
University of Northern Iowa *B, M, D*

Kansas
Manhattan Area Technical College *A*

Kentucky
Hopkinsville Community College *C, A*
Maysville Community College *C, A*
Northern Kentucky University *B*
Western Kentucky University *A, B, T*

Louisiana
Bossier Parish Community College *A*
Northwestern State University *B*
Southeastern Louisiana
University *A, B*
University of Louisiana at Lafayette *B*

Maryland
Hagerstown Community College *C, A*

Massachusetts
Berkshire Community College *C*
Bristol Community College *C*
University of Massachusetts
Lowell *B*

Michigan
Delta College *A*
Eastern Michigan University *B, M*
Ferris State University *A, B*
Kirtland Community College *C, A*
Lawrence Technological University *B*
Mott Community College *A*
Oakland Community College *C, A*
Western Michigan University *B*

Minnesota
Alexandria Technical College *A*
Hennepin Technical College *C, A*
Minnesota State University
Moorhead *B*
Northwest Technical College *A*
St. Mary's University of Minnesota *B*

Mississippi
Alcorn State University *B*
Jackson State University *B*

Missouri
Central Missouri State University *B, M*
North Central Missouri College *A*
Ozarks Technical Community
College *C, A*
Southeast Missouri State
University *B, M*

Nebraska
University of Nebraska
Lincoln *B*
Omaha *B*

New Mexico
San Juan College *A*

New York
Erie Community College
South Campus *A*
State University of New York
College of Technology at Canton *A*
Farmingdale *B*

Institute of Technology at
Utica/Rome *B*

North Carolina
Appalachian State University *B, M*
Bladen Community College *C, A*
Davidson County Community
College *C*
East Carolina University *B, M*
Elizabeth City State University *B*
Gaston College *C, A*
Roanoke-Chowan Community
College *A*
Rowan-Cabarrus Community
College *A*
Wilkes Community College *C, A*

North Dakota
North Dakota State University *M*

Ohio
Bowling Green State University *B, M*
Central State University *B*
Cincinnati State Technical and
Community College *A*
Edison State Community College *C, A*
James A. Rhodes State College *A*
Kent State University
Salem Regional Campus *A*
Trumbull Campus *A*
Tuscarawas Campus *A*
Ohio Northern University *B*
Ohio University *B*
Owens Community College
Toledo *C, A*
University of Akron *A, B*
University of Dayton *B*
University of Toledo *A*
Wright State University *A*

Oregon
Linn-Benton Community College *C*

Pennsylvania
Delaware County Community
College *C*
Lehigh Carbon Community
College *C, A*
Millersville University of
Pennsylvania *A, B*
Penn State
Dubois *A*
Wilkes-Barre *A*

Puerto Rico
University of Puerto Rico
Bayamon University College *A*

South Dakota
Black Hills State University *B*

Tennessee
Cleveland State Community College *A*
Jackson State Community College *A*
Middle Tennessee State
University *B, M*

Texas
Houston Community College
System *C, A*
Lamar University *B*
North Harris Montgomery
Community College District *C, A*
Panola College *C, A*
Prairie View A&M University *B*
Sam Houston State University *B, M*
Tarleton State University *B*
Texas Southern University *M*
Texas State Technical College:
Marshall *C, A*
Texas State University: San
Marcos *B, M*

University of Houston *B*
University of Texas
Brownsville *C, A, B*
Tyler *B, M*
West Texas A&M University *B, M*

Washington
Central Washington University *B*
Olympic College *C, A*
Shoreline Community College *A*
Western Washington University *B*

Wisconsin
Mid-State Technical College *A*
Milwaukee Area Technical College *A*

Information resources management

Alabama
Athens State University *B*

Arkansas
Ozarka College *A*

California
Golden Gate University *B, M*
University of San Diego *M*

Colorado
Colorado Technical University *B*

Delaware
Wilmington College *B*

Illinois
Loyola University of Chicago *M*

Iowa
Dordt College *B*

Maryland
Mount St. Mary's University *B*

Michigan
Michigan State University *D*
Mott Community College *A*
Western Michigan University *B*

Minnesota
University of Minnesota
Crookston *B*

New York
Clarkson University *B*

North Carolina
Chowan College *B*
Coastal Carolina Community
College *A*
Fayetteville Technical Community
College *A*

Pennsylvania
Carnegie Mellon University *M*
Duquesne University *M*
Juniata College *B*
Penn State
Shenango *B*
Temple University *M*

South Carolina
Williamsburg Technical College *A*

Texas
Houston Baptist University *B*
St. Edward's University *M*
University of Dallas *M*

Utah
Brigham Young University *B, M*

Vermont
Champlain College *M*

Wisconsin
University of Wisconsin
Eau Claire *B*

Information systems

Alabama
Alabama State University *B*
American Sentinel University *B, M*
Faulkner University *B*
Gadsden State Community College *A*
Herzing College *A, B*
Northwest-Shoals Community
College *A*
Oakwood College *B*
Prince Institute of Professional
Studies *A*
Virginia College *C, A*

Alaska
Charter College *C, A, B*
University of Alaska
Anchorage *A*

Arizona
Cochise College *A*
Collins College *A*
DeVry University
Phoenix *B*
Eastern Arizona College *C, A*
Everest College *C, A*
Gateway Community College *C, A*
International Institute of the Americas
Tucson *C, A, B*
Phoenix College *A*
Prescott College *B, M*
Scottsdale Community College *C, A*
South Mountain Community
College *C, A*
Western International University *M*

Arkansas
Arkansas State University
Mountain Home *A*
Ozarka College *A*
Rich Mountain Community
College *C, A*
University of Arkansas
Little Rock *B*
University of Central Arkansas *B*

California
Allan Hancock College *A*
Antelope Valley College *C, A*
Azusa Pacific University *B*
California Lutheran University *B*
California State University
East Bay *B, M*
Fresno *B*
Fullerton *B, M*
Long Beach *B*
Los Angeles *M*
Monterey Bay *B*
Chabot College *A*
Coleman College *M*
College of the Canyons *C, A*
College of the Siskiyous *C*
Cosumnes River College *A*
Cypress College *C, A*
Empire College *C, A*
Fresno City College *C, A*
Humboldt State University *B*
Institute of Computer Technology *C*
La Sierra University *B*
Laney College *A*
Los Angeles Harbor College *A*

Merced College *A*
Mission College *C, A*
Moorpark College *C, A*
National University *B*
Ohlone College *C, A*
Orange Coast College *C, A*
Palomar College *C, A*
Platt College
   Ontario *A*
Reedley College *C, A*
Remington College
   San Diego *A*
San Diego City College *A*
San Diego State University *C, B, M*
San Joaquin Delta College *C*
San Joaquin Valley College Inc. *A*
Santa Monica College *C, A*
Santa Rosa Junior College *C*
Santiago Canyon College *A*
Skyline College *C, A*
Southwestern College *A*
Taft College *C, A*
University of California
   Berkeley *M, D*
   Irvine *B*
   Los Angeles *M*
   Riverside *B*
   San Diego *B*
   Santa Cruz *B*
University of Redlands *M*
University of San Francisco *B*
University of the Pacific *B*
Ventura College *C, A*
West Hills Community College *C*

Colorado

Colorado Mountain College
   Alpine Campus *A*
Colorado State University *B*
Colorado State University
   Pueblo *B*
Colorado Technical University *A, B, M*
Community College of Aurora *C, A*
DeVry University
   Westminster *A, B*
Fort Lewis College *B*
National American University
   Denver *A, B*
Northeastern Junior College *A*
University of Colorado
   Denver and Health Sciences
     Center *M*
University of Denver *M*
Westwood College of
   Technology *A, B*

Connecticut

Albertus Magnus College *C, A, B*
Central Connecticut State
   University *M*
Gateway Community College *C, A*
Manchester Community College *C, A*
Middlesex Community College *C, A*
Northwestern Connecticut
   Community College *A*
Norwalk Community College *C, A*
Sacred Heart University *M*
Three Rivers Community College *A*
University of Hartford *B*
University of New Haven *B*

Delaware

Delaware State University *B*
Delaware Technical and Community
   College
   Owens Campus *A*
   Stanton/Wilmington Campus *A*
   Terry Campus *A*

District of Columbia

American University *M*
Gallaudet University *B*
George Washington University *B, M*

Howard University *B*
Southeastern University *M*
Strayer University *A, B, M*

Florida

Barry University *C, B, M*
Bethune-Cookman College *B*
Broward Community College *A*
Chipola College *A*
Daytona Beach Community College *A*
DeVry University
   Miramar *B*
   Orlando *B*
Florida Community College at
   Jacksonville *A*
Florida Institute of Technology *B, M*
Florida Metropolitan University
   Tampa College *A, B*
Florida State University *B, M, D*
Hillsborough Community College *A*
Lake City Community College *A*
Manatee Community College *A*
Miami Dade College *C, A*
New England Institute of
   Technology *A*
Nova Southeastern University *D*
Palm Beach Community College *A*
Pensacola Junior College *A*
Polk Community College *A*
Remington College
   Jacksonville *C, A, B*
Remington College: Tampa *A*
Seminole Community College *A*
South University: West Palm Beach
   Campus *A*
Southwest Florida College
   Tampa *A*
University of Miami *C, B, M*
University of South Florida *B*

Georgia

Brewton-Parker College *B*
Clayton State University *C, A, B*
Columbus Technical College *C*
Darton College *A*
DeVry University
   Alpharetta *B*
   Decatur *B*
Fort Valley State University *B*
Gordon College *A*
Griffin Technical College *A*
Kennesaw State University *B, M*
Life University *A, B*
Macon State College *B*
Mercer University *B*
Northwestern Technical College *C, A*
Reinhardt College *B*
Savannah State University *B*
Valdosta State University *B*

Hawaii

Brigham Young University-Hawaii *B*
Hawaii Pacific University *M*
University of Hawaii
   Honolulu Community College *A*

Idaho

Boise State University *B, M*
Idaho State University *B, M*

Illinois

Benedictine University *B*
Bradley University *B, M*
Chicago State University *B*
City Colleges of Chicago
   Harold Washington College *C, A*
Danville Area Community College *A*
DePaul University *C, B*
DeVry University
   Addison *B*
   Chicago *B*
   Tinley Park *B*
Dominican University *B, M*

Elmhurst College *B*
Highland Community College *A*
Illinois Valley Community College *A*
Joliet Junior College *A*
Kaskaskia College *A*
Lewis University *B*
MacCormac College *C, A*
McKendree College *B*
Midstate College *B*
National-Louis University *C, B*
Northwestern University *B, M*
Olivet Nazarene University *B*
Quincy University *B*
Rockford Business College *A*
Rockford College *B*
Roosevelt University *C, B, M*
Southeastern Illinois College *A*
Southern Illinois University
   Carbondale *B*
Southwestern Illinois College *A*
Trinity Christian College *B*
William Rainey Harper College *C, A*

Indiana

Anderson University *B*
Bethel College *B*
Butler University *B*
Goshen College *B*
Indiana Institute of Technology *A, B*
Indiana University-Purdue University
   Fort Wayne *A, B*
Indiana University-Purdue University
   Indianapolis *B*
Purdue University
   Calumet *A, B*
Taylor University *A*
University of Indianapolis *A, B*
Vincennes University *A*

Iowa

Central College *B*
Dordt College *B*
Ellsworth Community College *C, A*
Graceland University *B*
Hamilton College *A*
St. Ambrose University *B*
Simpson College *B*
Southwestern Community College *A*
Waldorf College *B*
Wartburg College *B*

Kansas

Baker University *B*
Barton County Community College *A*
Central Christian College of Kansas *A*
Emporia State University *B*
Kansas State University *B*
MidAmerica Nazarene University *B*
Newman University *A, B*

Kentucky

Ashland Community and Technical
   College *A*
Daymar College *A*
Louisville Technical Institute *A*
Madisonville Community College *A*
Maysville Community College *C, A*
Murray State University *A, B, M*
Owensboro Community College *A*

Louisiana

Bossier Parish Community College *A*
Grambling State University *B*
ITI Technical College *A*
Louisiana State University
   Shreveport *M*
Louisiana State University and
   Agricultural and Mechanical
   College *M*
Loyola University New Orleans *B*
Northwestern State University *B*
Nunez Community College *C, A*

Remington College
   New Orleans *A*

Maine

Eastern Maine Community College *C*
Husson College *A*
Thomas College *A, B*
University of Maine *M*

Maryland

Allegany College of Maryland *A*
Baltimore City Community College *A*
Bowie State University *M*
Cecil Community College *C, A*
Chesapeake College *C*
Columbia Union College *A, B*
Community College of Baltimore
   County *A*
Frederick Community College *A*
Frostburg State University *C*
Garrett College *C*
Hood College *B, M*
Montgomery College *A*
Morgan State University *B*
Prince George's Community
   College *C, A*
TESST College of Technology
   Baltimore *C, A*
TESST College of Technology:
   Towson *A*
University of Maryland
   Baltimore County *B, M, D*
   College Park *B, M*
   University College *C, B, M*
Villa Julie College *C, B, M*

Massachusetts

American International College *B*
Babson College *B*
Boston College *B*
Bristol Community College *A*
Cape Cod Community College *A*
Massachusetts Bay Community
   College *C, A*
Massachusetts College of Liberal
   Arts *B*
Mount Wachusett Community
   College *C, A*
North Shore Community College *C*
Northeastern University *M, D*
Northern Essex Community
   College *A*
Regis College *B*
Springfield College *B*
Suffolk University *B*
Tufts University *B*
University of Massachusetts
   Lowell *A, B*
Wentworth Institute of
   Technology *A, B*
Westfield State College *B*

Michigan

Alpena Community College *C, A*
Andrews University *B*
Baker College
   of Auburn Hills *A*
   of Jackson *C*
   of Muskegon *B*
   of Owosso *B*
   of Port Huron *A, B*
Calvin College *B*
Central Michigan University *B, M*
Cornerstone University *B*
Delta College *C, A*
Eastern Michigan University *B*
Grand Valley State University *B, M*
Lake Michigan College *A*
Lawrence Technological University *M*
Michigan State University *B*
Northwestern Michigan College *A*
Schoolcraft College *A*
University of Michigan *M, D*

University of Michigan
  Flint *B*
Washtenaw Community College *C, A*
Wayne State University *B*

Minnesota

Anoka Technical College *C, A*
Anoka-Ramsey Community College *A*
Augsburg College *C*
Brown College *B*
Capella University *B, M*
College of St. Catherine *B*
Crown College *C, A, B*
Hennepin Technical College *C, A*
Metropolitan State University *B*
Minneapolis Community and
  Technical College *C*
Minnesota State University
  Mankato *B, M*
National American University
  St. Paul *A*
Northland Community & Technical
  College *A*
Pine Technical College *A*
Rasmussen College
  St. Cloud *A*
St. Mary's University of Minnesota *B*
University of Minnesota
  Crookston *A, B*
  Twin Cities *C*
Winona State University *B*

Mississippi

Belhaven College *B*

Missouri

Central Missouri State University *M*
Drury University *B*
Grantham University *A, B*
Harris-Stowe State University *B*
Lincoln University *B*
Missouri College *C*
Missouri Southern State
  University *A, B*
Missouri Technical School *B*
Missouri Western State University *B*
National American University
  Kansas City *A, B*
Northwest Missouri State
  University *B*
Rockhurst University *B*
University of Missouri
  Kansas City *B*
  Rolla *B, M*
Washington University in St.
  Louis *B, M*
William Jewell College *B*

Montana

Little Big Horn College *A*
Montana Tech of the University of
  Montana *B*
Stone Child College *A*
University of Great Falls *M*

Nebraska

Bellevue University *B*
Chadron State College *B*
Doane College *B*
Hamilton College: Lincoln *A*
Metropolitan Community College *A*
Nebraska College of Technical
  Agriculture *A*
Nebraska Wesleyan University *B*
Southeast Community College
  Lincoln Campus *C, A*
Union College *A, B*
University of Nebraska
  Kearney *B*
Wayne State College *B*

Nevada

Community College of Southern
  Nevada *A*

New Hampshire

Daniel Webster College *A, B*
Franklin Pierce College *B*
New Hampshire Community
  Technical College
  Nashua *A*
  Stratham *C, A*

New Jersey

Burlington County College *C, A*
Essex County College *C*
Mercer County Community College *C*
New Jersey Institute of
  Technology *B, M, D*
Ocean County College *C*
Ramapo College of New Jersey *B*
Richard Stockton College of New
  Jersey *B*
Rutgers, The State University of New
  Jersey
  Newark Regional Campus *B*
St. Peter's College *C, A, B*
Seton Hall University *M*

New Mexico

Albuquerque Technical-Vocational
  Institute *C, A*
New Mexico Highlands University *B*
New Mexico State University *B*
New Mexico State University
  Alamogordo *A*
  Carlsbad *A*
San Juan College *A*

New York

Adelphi University *B*
Adirondack Community College *A*
Broome Community College *C, A*
Cayuga County Community College *C*
City University of New York
  Baruch College *B*
  Brooklyn College *M*
  College of Staten Island *B*
  Lehman College *B*
  Medgar Evers College *B*
  Queensborough Community
    College *A*
Clarkson University *M*
College of Westchester *C, A*
Columbia University
  Fu Foundation School of
    Engineering and Applied
    Science *M, D*
Erie Community College
  City Campus *A*
  North Campus *A*
  South Campus *A*
Excelsior College *B*
Finger Lakes Community College *C, A*
Fulton-Montgomery Community
  College *A*
Genesee Community College *A*
Globe Institute of Technology *C*
Hartwick College *B*
Island Drafting and Technical
  Institute *C*
Ithaca College *B*
Jefferson Community College *C, A*
Long Island University
  C.W. Post Campus *B, M, D*
Manhattan College *B*
Marist College *B, M*
Mercy College *B*
Mildred Elley *C, A*
Molloy College *B*
Nazareth College of Rochester *B*
New York University *B, M, D*
Niagara County Community
  College *A*

Niagara University *C, B*
Pace University *B*
Plaza College *A*
Sage College of Albany *A*
State University of New York
  Albany *B, M, D*
  Buffalo *M*
  College at Buffalo *B*
  College at Old Westbury *B*
  College of Agriculture and
    Technology at Cobleskill *A*
  Farmingdale *C, A*
  Institute of Technology at
    Utica/Rome *B, M*
  Oswego *B*
  Stony Brook *B*
Suffolk County Community
  College *C, A*
Syracuse University *B, M, D*
Tompkins-Cortland Community
  College *A*
United States Military Academy *B*
Westchester Community College *C, A*

North Carolina

Alamance Community College *A*
Beaufort County Community
  College *C, A*
Blue Ridge Community College *A*
Brunswick Community College *A*
Campbell University *B*
Catawba Valley Community College *A*
Central Carolina Community
  College *C, A*
Cleveland Community College *C, A*
Coastal Carolina Community
  College *A*
College of the Albemarle *C, A*
Durham Technical Community
  College *C, A*
Edgecombe Community College *A*
Elon University *B*
Fayetteville Technical Community
  College *C, A*
Guilford College *B*
Guilford Technical Community
  College *A*
Lees-McRae College *B*
Lenoir-Rhyne College *B*
Martin Community College *C, A*
Mitchell Community College *C, A*
Montgomery Community College *A*
Nash Community College *A*
North Carolina Central
  University *B, M*
North Carolina Wesleyan College *B*
Pitt Community College *C, A*
Queens University of Charlotte *B*
Richmond Community College *C, A*
Roanoke-Chowan Community
  College *A*
Rockingham Community College *C, A*
Rowan-Cabarrus Community
  College *C, A*
Sampson Community College *A*
Sandhills Community College *C, A*
South Piedmont Community
  College *A*
Stanly Community College *C, A*
Surry Community College *C, A*
Tri-County Community College *A*
University of North Carolina
  Chapel Hill *B, M*
Vance-Granville Community
  College *A*
Western Piedmont Community
  College *C, A*
Wilkes Community College *C, A*

North Dakota

North Dakota State College of
  Science *A*
University of Mary *B*

Ohio

Bluffton University *B*
Bryant & Stratton College
  Parma *A*
Case Western Reserve University *M, D*
Clark State Community College *C*
Columbus State Community
  College *A*
David N. Myers University *C, B*
DeVry University
  Columbus *B*
Jefferson Community College *C, A*
Lakeland Community College *C, A*
Marietta College *B*
Ohio Dominican University *B*
Ohio State University
  Columbus Campus *B*
Stark State College of Technology *A*
Tiffin University *B*
Union Institute & University *B*
University of Cincinnati *M, D*
University of Toledo *B, M*
Urbana University *B*
Wright State University *B*
Wright State University: Lake
  Campus *A*
Youngstown State University *A, B*
Zane State College *A*

Oklahoma

Northwestern Oklahoma State
  University *B*
Oklahoma Baptist University *B*
Oklahoma Christian University *B*
Oklahoma City University *M*
Oklahoma Panhandle State
  University *B*
Southeastern Oklahoma State
  University *B*
Southwestern Oklahoma State
  University *B*
University of Oklahoma *B*
Western Oklahoma State College *A*

Oregon

George Fox University *B*
Lane Community College *C*
Oregon Institute of Technology *B*
Pioneer Pacific College *B*
Pioneer Pacific College: Springfield *A*
Southwestern Oregon Community
  College *A*
Umpqua Community College *A*

Pennsylvania

Academy of Medical Arts and
  Business *C, A*
Albright College *B*
Bidwell Training Center *C*
Bucks County Community College *A*
Carlow University *B*
Carnegie Mellon University *B, M*
Cedar Crest College *C, B*
Clarion University of Pennsylvania *B*
Delaware County Community
  College *A*
Drexel University *B, M, D*
DuBois Business College
  Oil City *A*
Elizabethtown College *C, A, B*
Immaculata University *C, A, B*
Keystone College *A, B*
La Salle University *A, B, M*
Lehigh Carbon Community
  College *C, A*
Lehigh University *B, M*
Mansfield University of
  Pennsylvania *A, B*
Marywood University *M*
Messiah College *B*
Montgomery County Community
  College *C, A*
Peirce College *C, A, B*

Penn State
  Abington *B*
  Altoona *A, B*
  Beaver *A, B*
  Berks *A, B*
  Delaware County *B*
  Dubois *A, B*
  Fayette *A, B*
  Harrisburg *B*
  Hazleton *A, B*
  Lehigh Valley *A, B*
  McKeesport *B*
  Mont Alto *A, B*
  New Kensington *A, B*
  Schuylkill - Capital College *A, B*
  Shenango *A, B*
  University Park *C, B*
  Wilkes-Barre *A, B*
  Worthington Scranton *A, B*
  York *A, B*
Robert Morris University *B, D*
St. Francis University *B*
St. Joseph's University *A, B*
Shippensburg University of
    Pennsylvania *M*
Susquehanna University *B*
Thiel College *A, B*
Tri-State Business Institute *A*
University of Pittsburgh *B, M, D*
University of Pittsburgh
  Bradford *A*
  Greensburg *B*
University of Scranton *C, B*
Villanova University *B*
Westmoreland County Community
    College *C*
Widener University *B*
Wilkes University *B*
York College of Pennsylvania *B, M*

Puerto Rico

Humacao Community College *A*
Inter American University of Puerto
    Rico
  Barranquitas Campus *B*
  Bayamon Campus *B*
  Ponce Campus *B*
National College of Business &
    Technology: Bayamon *A, B*
Universidad Adventista de las
    Antillas *B*
University of the Sacred Heart *B*

Rhode Island

Bryant University *M*
Johnson & Wales University *B*
Salve Regina University *B*

South Carolina

Charleston Southern University *B*
Clemson University *B*
College of Charleston *B*
Forrest Junior College *C, A*
Orangeburg-Calhoun Technical
    College *C*
Spartanburg Methodist College *A*
Trident Technical College *A*
University of South Carolina
  Upstate *B*

South Dakota

Dakota State University *A, B, M, D*
Kilian Community College *A*
Southeast Technical Institute *C*

Tennessee

Belmont University *B, M*
Chattanooga State Technical
    Community College *C, A*
Dyersburg State Community
    College *C, A*
Lee University *B*

Pellissippi State Technical Community
    College *A*
University of Tennessee
  Knoxville *M*
Walters State Community College *C, A*

Texas

Amarillo College *C, A*
Brookhaven College *A*
Central Texas College *C, A*
El Centro College *C, A*
El Paso Community College *C, A*
Frank Phillips College *C*
Galveston College *C, A*
Howard Payne University *B*
Lamar University *M*
Laredo Community College *A*
LeTourneau University *B*
Lee College *C, A*
McMurry University *B*
Midland College *C, A*
North Harris Montgomery
    Community College District *C, A*
Odessa College *A*
Palo Alto College *A*
Panola College *C*
Prairie View A&M University *M*
St. Philip's College *A*
Southwestern Adventist
    University *A, B, T*
Tarleton State University *M*
Texas A&M University
    Commerce *B*
Texas Lutheran University *B*
Texas State Technical College
    Waco *C, A*
Texas Wesleyan University *B*
Tyler Junior College *C, A*
University of Houston *B*
University of Houston
    Victoria *B*
University of Mary Hardin-Baylor *B, M*
University of North Texas *M, D*
University of Texas
  Brownsville *B*
  El Paso *M*
  Pan American *M*
  San Antonio *M*
  of the Permian Basin *B*
Victoria College *C, A*

Utah

College of Eastern Utah *C*
Snow College *A*
Southern Utah University *A, B*
Utah State University *B, M*
Weber State University *B*

Vermont

Champlain College *C, A, B*
St. Michael's College *B*
University of Vermont *B*

Virginia

Averett University *B*
Blue Ridge Community College *A*
Central Virginia Community
    College *A*
Danville Community College *C*
DeVry University
  Arlington *A*
ECPI College of Technology *C, A*
Ferrum College *B*
George Mason University *M*
J. Sargeant Reynolds Community
    College *A*
James Madison University *B*
Mary Baldwin College *B*
Marymount University *B, M*
Mountain Empire Community
    College *A*
Radford University *B*
Rappahannock Community College *A*

Roanoke College *B*
Shenandoah University *C*
Thomas Nelson Community
    College *C, A*
University of Richmond *C, A*
Virginia Commonwealth
    University *B, M*
Virginia Polytechnic Institute and
    State University *M*
Wytheville Community College *A*

Washington

Bellingham Technical College *C, A*
Centralia College *A*
City University *C*
Eastern Washington University *B*
Edmonds Community College *C*
Everett Community College *C, A*
Green River Community College *C, A*
North Seattle Community
    College *C, A*
Renton Technical College *C*
Seattle Central Community College *C*
Skagit Valley College *A*
South Puget Sound Community
    College *C, A*
South Seattle Community
    College *C, A*
Spokane Community College *A*
Spokane Falls Community College *A*
University of Washington *B, M, D*
Walla Walla College *B*
Walla Walla Community College *A*
Yakima Valley Community College *A*

West Virginia

Eastern West Virginia Community and
    Technical College *A*
Marshall University *M*
Mountain State University *A, B*
West Liberty State College *B*
West Virginia Northern Community
    College *A*
West Virginia University at
    Parkersburg *A*
West Virginia Wesleyan College *B*

Wisconsin

Bryant & Stratton College:
    Milwaukee *A*
Carroll College *B*
Edgewood College *B*
Fox Valley Technical College *A*
Marquette University *B*
Northland College *B*
Silver Lake College *B*
University of Wisconsin
    Green Bay *B*

Wyoming

Laramie County Community
    College *A*
Northwest College *A*
Western Wyoming Community
    College *A*

Information technology

Alabama

American Sentinel University *B, M*
Gadsden State Community College *A*
Northwest-Shoals Community
    College *A*
South University *A, B*

Arizona

Gateway Community College *C*

Arkansas

Arkansas Tech University *A, M*
Harding University *B*

Phillips Community College of the
    University of Arkansas *A*
South Arkansas Community College *A*

California

Bethesda Christian University *B*
CEI College
    Maric College: Panorama City *A*
California State Polytechnic
    University: Pomona *B*
California State University
  Chico *B*
  Fullerton *B, M*
  Stanislaus *B*
Concordia University *B*
DeVry University
  Long Beach *B*
Foothill College *C, A*
Golden Gate University *C, B, M*
Platt College
  Newport Beach *C, A*
  Ontario *A*
San Joaquin Valley College Inc. *A*
San Jose State University *B*
Sierra College *A*
Silicon Valley College
    Western Career College:
      Emeryville *C, A*
Southwestern College *C, A*

Colorado

Colorado Technical
    University *C, A, B, M*
Jones International University *M*

Connecticut

Sacred Heart University *C*

Florida

Barry University *M*
Central Florida Community
    College *C, A*
Everglades University *B, M*
Florida International University *B*
Florida State University *B, M, D*
Herzing College
    Orlando *C, A, B*
Hillsborough Community College *C*
Indian River Community College *A*
International College *A, B, M*
Lake-Sumter Community College *A*
Miami Dade College *C, A*
Pasco-Hernando Community
    College *A*
Remington College: Largo *B*
St. Petersburg College *C, A*
Schiller International
    University *A, B, M*
University of Central Florida *B*
University of South Florida *B*
University of West Florida *B*
Valencia Community College *A*

Georgia

Armstrong Atlantic State University *B*
Bauder College *A*
East Georgia College *A*
Georgia Perimeter College *A*
Gordon College *A, B*
Gwinnett College *A*
Middle Georgia College *A*
Northwestern Technical College *C, A*
South University *A, B*
Southern Polytechnic State
    University *C, B, M*

Illinois

DeVry University
  Addison *B*
  Chicago *B*
Heartland Community College *A*
Illinois Institute of Technology *B*
Illinois State University *B, M*

International Academy of Design and
    Technology: Chicago *A, B*
Lewis and Clark Community
    College *A*
McKendree College *B*
Moraine Valley Community
    College *C, A*
Morton College *A*
Robert Morris College: Chicago *B*
University of St. Francis *B*
Westwood College of Technology
    O'Hare *B*

Indiana
Grace College *B*
Indiana Business College *C, A*
Indiana Business College
    Columbus *C, A*
    Evansville *C, A*
    Lafayette *C, A*
    Muncie *C, A*
Indiana State University *B*
Professional Careers Institute *A*
St. Mary-of-the-Woods College *B*

Iowa
AIB College of Business *A*
Des Moines Area Community
    College *C, A*
Drake University *B*
Hamilton College *A, B*
Hamilton College
    Cedar Falls *B*
Kaplan University *A, B*

Kansas
Brown Mackie College *A*
Central Christian College of Kansas *A*
Ottawa University *B*
Pittsburg State University *B*
Seward County Community
    College *C, A*
University of St. Mary *B*

Kentucky
Big Sandy Community and Technical
    College *A*
Bluegrass Community and Technical
    College *A*
Louisville Technical Institute *A*
Northern Kentucky University *B*

Maine
Husson College *A*
University of Maine
    Fort Kent *B*

Maryland
College of Southern Maryland *C*
Frederick Community College *C, A*
Howard Community College *C, A*
United States Naval Academy *B*

Massachusetts
Bristol Community College *C*
Cape Cod Community College *C, A*

Michigan
Cleary University *A*
Delta College *A*
Ferris State University *C, A*
Grace Bible College *B*
Lawrence Technological
    University *B, D*
Lewis College of Business *A*
Oakland University *M*
Walsh College of Accountancy and
    Business Administration *B*

Minnesota
Brown College *B*
Capella University *C, B, M*

Crown College *C, A, B*
Dunwoody College of Technology *A*
Fond du Lac Tribal and Community
    College *A*
Globe College *B*
Lake Superior College *C, A*
Minnesota School of Business *C, A, B*
Minnesota School of Business:
    Brooklyn Center *B*
Normandale Community College *A*
Rasmussen College
    St. Cloud *A*
Winona State University *B*

Mississippi
Millsaps College *T*

Missouri
Grantham University *A, B, M*
Lindenwood University *B*
Ozarks Technical Community
    College *C, A*
St. Louis University *B*
University of Missouri
    Rolla *B, M*
Vatterott College: Springfield *C*

Montana
Montana Tech of the University of
    Montana *B*
Rocky Mountain College *B*
University of Montana: Western *A*

Nebraska
Bellevue University *B, M*
Mid-Plains Community College
    Area *C, A*
University of Nebraska
    Lincoln *D*
    Omaha *D*

Nevada
University of Nevada
    Reno *B*

New Hampshire
Franklin Pierce College *B*
Plymouth State University *B*
Southern New Hampshire
    University *C, A, B, M*

New Jersey
Bergen Community College *A*
Fairleigh Dickinson University
    Metropolitan Campus *B*
New Jersey Institute of Technology *B*
Union County College *A*

New Mexico
Clovis Community College *C, A*
College of Santa Fe *B*
New Mexico Institute of Mining and
    Technology *B*
New Mexico State University *B*

New York
Bryant & Stratton Business Institute
Bryant & Stratton College:
    Rochester *A*
Bryant & Stratton College: Henrietta *A*
Bryant & Stratton College: Syracuse
    North *A*
D'Youville College *B*
DeVry Institute of Technology
    New York *B*
Globe Institute of Technology *C, A, B*
Houghton College *B*
Ithaca College *B*
Long Island University
    C.W. Post Campus *B*
Marist College *B*
Mount St. Mary College *B*

Olean Business Institute *A*
Rensselaer Polytechnic Institute *B, M*
Rochester Institute of
    Technology *A, B, M*
St. Francis College *B*
St. Joseph's College: Suffolk
    Campus *B*
State University of New York
    College of Agriculture and
        Technology at Cobleskill *B*
    College of Agriculture and
        Technology at Morrisville *A, B*
Suffolk County Community
    College *C, A*
Syracuse University *B, M, D*

North Carolina
Cape Fear Community College *C, A*
Carteret Community College *C, A*
Catawba Valley Community College *A*
Central Piedmont Community
    College *C, A*
Davidson County Community
    College *C, A*
East Carolina University *B, M*
Fayetteville Technical Community
    College *C, A*
Gaston College *A*
Isothermal Community College *C, A*
Johnson C. Smith University *B*
Montgomery Community College *C, A*
Robeson Community College *A*
Southeastern Community College *A*
Stanly Community College *C, A*
University of North Carolina
    Charlotte *M, D*
Wilkes Community College *C, A*
Winston-Salem State University *B*

Ohio
Bluffton University *B*
Bryant & Stratton College:
    Cleveland *B*
Cincinnati Christian University *B*
DeVry University
    Columbus *B*
ETI Technical College of Niles *A*
Edison State Community College *A*
Marion Technical College *A*
Ohio University *B*
Owens Community College
    Toledo *A*
Stark State College of Technology *A*
University of Cincinnati
    Clermont College *C, A*
    Raymond Walters College *C, A*
Youngstown State University *A, B*

Oklahoma
Northeastern Oklahoma Agricultural
    and Mechanical College *A*
University of Central Oklahoma *B*
University of Tulsa *B*
Vatterott College *C, A*

Oregon
Pioneer Pacific College *B*

Pennsylvania
Business Institute of Pennsylvania *A*
Business Institute of Pennsylvania
    Meadville *A*
Carnegie Mellon University *M*
College Misericordia *B*
Edinboro University of
    Pennsylvania *M*
Erie Business Center *C*
Harrisburg Area Community
    College *C, A*
ICM School of Business & Medical
    Careers *A*
Juniata College *B*
Keystone College *A, B*

Kutztown University of
    Pennsylvania *B, M*
La Roche College *B*
La Salle University *B*
Mount Aloysius College *B*
Penn State
    Delaware County *B*
    University Park *B, D*
    Wilkes-Barre *A, B*
Pennsylvania College of Technology *A*
Point Park University *C, A, B*
Slippery Rock University of
    Pennsylvania *B*
South Hills School of Business &
    Technology *C, A*
Temple University *B*
Washington and Jefferson College *B*
Waynesburg College *A, B*
West Chester University of
    Pennsylvania *M*

Puerto Rico
National College of Business &
    Technology: Arecibo *B*

Rhode Island
Bryant University *B*
New England Institute of
    Technology *A, B*

South Carolina
Limestone College *A*
South University *B*
Southern Wesleyan University *B*

South Dakota
Mount Marty College *B*
Northern State University *C*

Tennessee
Lipscomb University *B*
Trevecca Nazarene University *A, B*

Texas
DeVry University
    Irving *B*
Southern Methodist University *M*
Texas State Technical College
    Harlingen *C, A*
University of the Incarnate Word *B*

Utah
Brigham Young University *B, M*
LDS Business College *C, A*
Utah Valley State College *A*

Vermont
Champlain College *M*
Vermont Technical College *A, B*

Virginia
Mountain Empire Community
    College *A*
Piedmont Virginia Community
    College *C*
Potomac College *B*
University of Northern Virginia *B*
Virginia Polytechnic Institute and
    State University *M*
Virginia State University *B*

Washington
Bates Technical College *A*
Crown College *B*
DeVry University
    Federal Way *B*
Seattle Central Community
    College *C, A*
Shoreline Community College *C*
University of Washington *B, M, D*
Yakima Valley Community College *C*

West Virginia

Mountain State University *A*
Ohio Valley University *B*
Potomac State College of West Virginia
   University *A*
Southern West Virginia Community
   and Technical College *A*
University of Charleston *B*

Wisconsin

Carthage College *B*
Gateway Technical College *A*
Herzing College *A, B*
Marian College of Fond du Lac *B*
University of Wisconsin
   Whitewater *B, M*

Wyoming

Laramie County Community
   College *A*

Inorganic chemistry

Florida

Florida State University *M, D*

Georgia

Clark Atlanta University *M, D*

Iowa

Iowa State University *M, D*

Kansas

Pratt Community College *A*

Massachusetts

Tufts University *M, D*

Montana

University of Montana: Missoula *M, D*

New York

Fordham University *M*
Sarah Lawrence College *B*
State University of New York
   Albany *D*

Texas

University of North Texas *M, D*

Wisconsin

Marquette University *M, D*

Institutional food production

Alabama

Enterprise-Ozark Community
   College *A*
Shelton State Community College *C*
Wallace State Community College at
   Hanceville *C, A*

Arizona

Arizona Western College *C*
Phoenix College *C, A*

Arkansas

Southeast Arkansas College *C*

California

American River College *A*
Bakersfield College *A*
Cerritos Community College *A*
Chaffey College *C*
College of the Redwoods *C*
College of the Sequoias *C*
Contra Costa College *A*
Cypress College *C, A*
Fresno City College *C, A*

Long Beach City College *C, A*
Los Angeles Mission College *A*
Los Angeles Trade and Technical
   College *C, A*
Merced College *A*
Modesto Junior College *C*
Monterey Peninsula College *A*
Ohlone College *C, A*
Orange Coast College *C*
Palomar College *C, A*
San Joaquin Delta College *A*
Santa Barbara City College *C, A*
Santa Rosa Junior College *C*
Shasta College *A*
Sierra College *C, A*

Colorado

Art Institute
   of Colorado *A, B*
Front Range Community College *C, A*
Pueblo Community College *A*

Connecticut

Gateway Community College *C, A*
Manchester Community College *A*
Naugatuck Valley Community
   College *C, A*
University of New Haven *A*

Florida

Brevard Community College *C*
Gulf Coast Community College *A*
Indian River Community College *C*
Pensacola Junior College *A*
Valencia Community College *A*

Georgia

Abraham Baldwin Agricultural
   College *A*
Augusta Technical Institute *C*
Darton College *A*

Hawaii

University of Hawaii
   Honolulu Community College *C, A*
   Kapiolani Community College *C, A*

Illinois

City Colleges of Chicago
   Malcolm X College *A*
Lexington College *A, B*
William Rainey Harper College *C, A*

Indiana

Vincennes University *A*

Iowa

Iowa Western Community College *A*
Kirkwood Community College *C, A*

Kansas

Coffeyville Community College *A*
Johnson County Community
   College *C, A*

Kentucky

Eastern Kentucky University *A*

Louisiana

Delgado Community College *A*
Grambling State University *B*

Maine

Eastern Maine Community College *C*
Southern Maine Community
   College *A*
Washington County Community
   College *C, A*

Maryland

Montgomery College *C, A*

Michigan

Bay de Noc Community College *C*
Central Michigan University *B*
Grand Rapids Community College *A*
Henry Ford Community College *A*
Lansing Community College *A*
Mott Community College *A*
Northern Michigan University *A*
Wayne County Community College *A*
Western Michigan University *B*

Mississippi

Hinds Community College *C, A*
Mississippi Gulf Coast Community
   College
   Jefferson Davis Campus *C*

Missouri

Penn Valley Community College *C*

Nebraska

Metropolitan Community College *A*
Southeast Community College
   Lincoln Campus *A*

Nevada

Truckee Meadows Community
   College *C, A*

New Mexico

Albuquerque Technical-Vocational
   Institute *C*
Southwestern Indian Polytechnic
   Institute *A*

New York

City University of New York
   LaGuardia Community College *A*
Mohawk Valley Community College *A*
Rockland Community College *A*
State University of New York
   College of Technology at Delhi *A*
   Farmingdale *A*
Sullivan County Community
   College *C, A*
Westchester Community College *A*

North Carolina

Asheville-Buncombe Technical
   Community College *A*
Cape Fear Community College *C, A*
James Sprunt Community College *C*
Johnston Community College *C*
University of North Carolina
   Greensboro *B*

North Dakota

North Dakota State College of
   Science *A*

Ohio

Cincinnati State Technical and
   Community College *C, A*
Ohio University *B*
Sinclair Community College *C, A*

Pennsylvania

Bucks County Community
   College *C, A*
Butler County Community
   College *C, A*
Community College of
   Philadelphia *C, A*
Harrisburg Area Community
   College *C, A*
International Academy of Design and
   Technology: Pittsburgh *A*
Penn State
   University Park *A*
Pennsylvania College of Technology *A*
Pennsylvania Highlands Community
   College *A*

Westmoreland County Community
   College *A*

Tennessee

Lipscomb University *B*
Southwest Tennessee Community
   College *A*

Texas

El Paso Community College *A*
Hill College *A*
St. Philip's College *A*
San Jacinto College
   Central Campus *C, A*
   North *C, A*
Tarrant County College *A*
Texas State Technical College
   Waco *C, A*
Texas Woman's University *M*

Virginia

J. Sargeant Reynolds Community
   College *C, A*
Northern Virginia Community
   College *A*

Washington

Bellingham Technical College *C*
Renton Technical College *C*

Wisconsin

Blackhawk Technical College *A*
Fox Valley Technical College *C, A*
Gateway Technical College *A*
Milwaukee Area Technical College *C*
Northeast Wisconsin Technical
   College *C*
Southwest Wisconsin Technical
   College *C, A*
University of Wisconsin
   Stout *B*
Waukesha County Technical
   College *C*
Wisconsin Indianhead Technical
   College *C*

Institutional food service

Arkansas

North Arkansas College *C, A*

California

Santa Barbara City College *C, A*

New York

State University of New York
   College of Agriculture and
      Technology at Cobleskill *A*

Pennsylvania

Luzerne County Community
   College *A*
Montgomery County Community
   College *C*

South Carolina

Greenville Technical College *C, A*
Horry-Georgetown Technical
   College *C*

Texas

Sam Houston State University *B*
Texas State Technical College
   Harlingen *C, A*

Instructional media

Alabama

Alabama State University *M*
Auburn University *M*

Jacksonville State University *M, T*
Miles College *B*
University of South Alabama *M, D, T*

Arizona

Arizona State University *M, D*
University of Phoenix *M*

Arkansas

Arkansas Tech University *M*
Southern Arkansas University *M*
Southern Arkansas University Tech *A*
University of Arkansas *M*
University of Arkansas
    Little Rock *M*

California

California State University
    Chico *B, M*
    Fullerton *M*
    San Bernardino *M*
Dominican University of California *M*
Fresno Pacific University *M, T*
National University *M*
San Diego State University *M*
San Francisco State University *M*
San Jose State University *M*
Stanford University *M, D*
University of San Francisco *M*

Colorado

Jones International University *M*
University of Northern Colorado *M, T*

Connecticut

Central Connecticut State
    University *M*
Fairfield University *M*
University of Connecticut *M, D, T*

Delaware

Wilmington College *M*

District of Columbia

American University *M*
Gallaudet University *M*

Florida

Florida State University *M, D*
Nova Southeastern University *M, D*
University of Central Florida *M*
University of West Florida *D*

Georgia

Columbus State University *M*
Georgia College and State
    University *M, T*
Georgia Southern University *M*
Georgia State University *M, D*
University of Georgia *D, T*
University of West Georgia *M*

Hawaii

University of Hawaii
    Manoa *M*

Idaho

Boise State University *M*
Idaho State University *M*
University of Idaho *B*

Illinois

Illinois State University *M*
National-Louis University *M*
Northern Illinois University *M, D*
Southern Illinois University
    Edwardsville *M*
University of Illinois
    Urbana-Champaign *M, D*
University of St. Francis *M*
Western Illinois University *B, M*

Indiana

Indiana State University *M*
Indiana University
    Bloomington *M, D, T*

Iowa

Iowa State University *T*
University of Northern Iowa *M*

Kansas

Emporia State University *M*

Kentucky

Asbury College *M, T*

Maryland

McDaniel College *M*
Towson University *M*
University of Maryland
    University College *M*

Massachusetts

Boston University *M, T*
Bridgewater State College *M, T*
Lesley University *M*
Salem State College *M*
University of Massachusetts
    Boston *M*

Michigan

Eastern Michigan University *M*
Lawrence Technological University *M*
Michigan State University *M*
Wayne State University *M, D, T*

Minnesota

Capella University *M, D*
Minnesota State University
    Mankato *M*
Ridgewater College *A*
St. Cloud State University *B, M*
University of St. Thomas *M*

Mississippi

Jackson State University *B*
University of Southern Mississippi *M*

Missouri

Missouri State University *M*
Webster University *M*

Nevada

University of Nevada
    Reno *M, D*

New Jersey

Georgian Court University *M, T*
Kean University *M*
Richard Stockton College of New
    Jersey *M*
William Paterson University of New
    Jersey *T*

New York

Long Island University
    C.W. Post Campus *M, T*
Rochester Institute of Technology *M*
State University of New York
    Albany *M*
    Buffalo *M*
    College at Potsdam *M*
Syracuse University *M, D*

North Carolina

Appalachian State University *M*
East Carolina University *M*
North Carolina Agricultural and
    Technical State University *M*
North Carolina Central University *M*
North Carolina State University *M*

University of North Carolina
    Charlotte *M*
    Wilmington *M*
Western Carolina University *M*

North Dakota

University of North Dakota *M*
Valley City State University *B*

Ohio

John Carroll University *M*
Kent State University *M*
Malone College *M*
Miami University
    Oxford Campus *M*
Ohio Dominican University *B, T*
Ohio State University
    Columbus Campus *M, D*
Ohio University *M, D*
University of Toledo *M*

Oklahoma

Northwestern Oklahoma State
    University *M*
University of Central Oklahoma *B, M*
University of Oklahoma *M*

Oregon

Portland State University *M, T*
Western Oregon University *B*

Pennsylvania

Bloomsburg University of
    Pennsylvania *M*
Cabrini College *M*
Carlow University *M*
Chestnut Hill College *M, T*
Duquesne University *M, D, T*
East Stroudsburg University of
    Pennsylvania *M, T*
Gannon University *T*
Kutztown University of
    Pennsylvania *M*
Lehigh University *D*
Marywood University *M*
Penn State
    University Park *B, M*
Philadelphia University *M*
St. Joseph's University *M*
Seton Hill University *M*
University of Pittsburgh *M, D, T*
Widener University *M*

Puerto Rico

Bayamon Central University *B*
University of the Sacred Heart *M*

South Carolina

University of South Carolina
    Aiken *M*

South Dakota

University of South Dakota *M*

Tennessee

East Tennessee State University *M, T*
Lincoln Memorial University *M*
University of Tennessee
    Chattanooga *T*

Texas

Angelo State University *M*
Prairie View A&M University *M*
Texas A&M University *M*
Texas State University: San
    Marcos *M, T*
Texas Tech University *M, D*
University of Houston *M, T*
University of Houston
    Clear Lake *M*
University of North Texas *M*

University of Texas
    Brownsville *M*
    Southwestern Medical Center at
        Dallas *M*
    Tyler *M*
West Texas A&M University *M*

Utah

Brigham Young University *M, D*
Southern Utah University *M, T*
Utah State University *M, D*
Western Governors University *M*

Virginia

Longwood University *M*
Old Dominion University *M, D, T*

Washington

City University *M*
Eastern Washington University *M, T*
Walla Walla College *M*
Washington State University *T*

Wisconsin

University of Wisconsin
    La Crosse *M*

Instrumentation technology

Alabama

Athens State University *B*

Georgia

Central Georgia Technical College *C*
DeKalb Technical College *A*

Idaho

Idaho State University *C, A*

Illinois

Kaskaskia College *C*
Moraine Valley Community
    College *C, A*

Louisiana

ITI Technical College *A*

Minnesota

Dunwoody College of
    Technology *C, A*
Ridgewater College *C, A*
St. Cloud Technical College *C, A*

New Mexico

San Juan College *A*

New York

Excelsior College *A, B*

North Carolina

Cape Fear Community College *A*

North Dakota

Bismarck State College *C, A*

Pennsylvania

Butler County Community College *A*
Pennsylvania College of Technology *A*

Puerto Rico

University College of San Juan *A*
University of Puerto Rico
    Bayamon University College *A*

Rhode Island

Community College of Rhode
    Island *A*

Texas
Lamar State College at Port Arthur *A*
St. Philip's College *A*
Victoria College *C, A*

Utah
Salt Lake Community College *A*

Virginia
New River Community College *A*

Wisconsin
Mid-State Technical College *A*

Wyoming
Western Wyoming Community
    College *C, A*

Insurance

Alabama
Wallace State Community College at
    Hanceville *A*

Arkansas
University of Central Arkansas *B*

California
California State University
    Sacramento *B*
Fresno City College *C, A*
Los Angeles Southwest College *A*
San Francisco State University *B*
Santa Ana College *C, A*

Colorado
Community College of Aurora *C*

Connecticut
University of Connecticut *B*
University of Hartford *B*

District of Columbia
Howard University *B*

Florida
Daytona Beach Community College *C*
Florida Community College at
    Jacksonville *C, A*
Florida International University *B*
Florida State University *B, M, D*
Miami Dade College *C*
Okaloosa-Walton College *A*
University of Florida *B, M*

Georgia
Central Georgia Technical College *C*
Georgia State University *B, M, D*
University of Georgia *B*

Illinois
Bradley University *B*
Heartland Community College *C, A*
Illinois State University *B*
Illinois Wesleyan University *B*
Roosevelt University *B*
University of Illinois
    Urbana-Champaign *B, M, D*
William Rainey Harper College *C, A*

Indiana
Indiana State University *B*
Martin University *B*

Iowa
Ellsworth Community College *A*

Kentucky
Eastern Kentucky University *B*

Louisiana
University of Louisiana at Lafayette *B*
University of Louisiana at Monroe *B*

Michigan
Delta College *C*
Lansing Community College *A*
Olivet College *B*

Minnesota
Fond du Lac Tribal and Community
    College *C*
Minnesota State University
    Mankato *B*
St. Cloud State University *B*
University of Minnesota
    Twin Cities *B*

Mississippi
Delta State University *B*
Mississippi State University *B*
University of Mississippi *B*

Missouri
Missouri State University *B*

New Jersey
Thomas Edison State College *A, B*

New York
Excelsior College *B*
Hudson Valley Community College *A*
Onondaga Community College *A*
St. John's University *B, M*
Suffolk County Community College *A*
Sullivan County Community
    College *A*

North Carolina
Appalachian State University *B*
Isothermal Community College *C*
Pitt Community College *C*

Ohio
Ohio State University
    Columbus Campus *B*
University of Akron *C, B*

Oklahoma
Oklahoma City Community College *C*
Tulsa Community College *C, A*
University of Central Oklahoma *B*

Pennsylvania
Delaware County Community
    College *C*
Gannon University *B*
La Salle University *B*
Penn State
    Abington *B*
    Altoona *B*
    Beaver *B*
    Berks *B*
    Delaware County *B*
    Dubois *B*
    Fayette *B*
    Hazleton *B*
    Lehigh Valley *B*
    McKeesport *B*
    Mont Alto *B*
    New Kensington *B*
    Schuylkill - Capital College *B*
    Shenango *B*
    University Park *B*
    Wilkes-Barre *B*
    Worthington Scranton *B*
    York *B*
Temple University *B*
University of Pennsylvania *B, M, D*

Puerto Rico
Universidad del Este *B*

South Carolina
University of South Carolina *B*

Texas
Baylor University *B*
University of North Texas *B, M, D*

Washington
Washington State University *B*

Wisconsin
Chippewa Valley Technical College *C*
Fox Valley Technical College *A*
Madison Area Technical College *A*
University of Wisconsin
    Madison *B, M*

Intercultural/diversity studies

California
Biola University *B*
California Baptist University *B*
California Institute of Integral
    Studies *M, D*
California State University
    Chico *B*
Foothill College *A*
National University *B*
Pitzer College *B*
Stanford University *B*
University of California
    Berkeley *M*
University of California: Merced *B*
University of San Diego *M*

Colorado
University of Denver *B*

Georgia
Atlanta Christian College *B*

Hawaii
Brigham Young University-Hawaii *B*

Illinois
Trinity International University *D*

Indiana
Anderson University *M*

Iowa
Divine Word College *A, B*

Kentucky
Midway College *B*

Maryland
Goucher College *B*
Howard Community College *A*

Massachusetts
Lesley University *M*

Michigan
Kuyper College *B*

New Jersey
Rider University *B*

New Mexico
College of Santa Fe *B*

New York
Alfred University *B*
Bard College *B*

Columbia University
    Columbia College *B*
Fordham University *B*

Ohio
Antioch University McGregor *M*

Pennsylvania
Chatham College *B*

South Carolina
Columbia International University *B*

Tennessee
Tennessee Wesleyan College *B*
Union University *B, M*

Texas
South Texas College *A*
University of Houston
    Clear Lake *M*
University of Texas
    San Antonio *M*
University of the Incarnate Word *B*

Vermont
Sterling College *B*

Washington
Evergreen State College *B*
Western Washington University *M*

Wisconsin
Lawrence University *B*
Marquette University *B*

Interior architecture

Alabama
Auburn University *B*

Arizona
Arizona State University *B*
Phoenix College *A*

California
California College of the Arts *B*
California State University
    Long Beach *B*
Cosumnes River College *C, A*
Woodbury University *B*

Colorado
Westwood College of Technology *B*
Westwood College of Technology
    South *B*

Connecticut
University of New Haven *A, B*

Florida
Florida Community College at
    Jacksonville *A*
Palm Beach Community College *A*
Seminole Community College *A*

Illinois
Columbia College Chicago *B, M*
Harrington College of Design *C, A, B*
Illinois Central College *A*
Illinois Institute of Art-Schaumburg *B*
School of the Art Institute of
    Chicago *B, M*
Triton College *C, A*
Westwood College of Technology
    O'Hare *B*

Indiana
Indiana State University *B*

Kansas

Kansas State University *B*

Kentucky

Louisville Technical Institute *C, A*

Louisiana

Delgado Community College *A*
Louisiana State University and
    Agricultural and Mechanical
    College *B*
Louisiana Tech University *B*
University of Louisiana at Lafayette *B*

Maryland

Community College of Baltimore
    County *C, A*
Harford Community College *C, A*
Montgomery College *C, A*

Massachusetts

Boston Architectural Center *B, M*
Newbury College *A, B*

Michigan

Central Michigan University *B*
Lansing Community College *A*
Lawrence Technological University *B*
Michigan State University *B*

Minnesota

Northland Community & Technical
    College *C, A*

Mississippi

University of Southern Mississippi *B*

Missouri

St. Louis Community College
    St. Louis Community College at
        Meramec *A*
Washington University in St. Louis *M*

Nebraska

Metropolitan Community College *A*
University of Nebraska
    Lincoln *B*

Nevada

University of Nevada
    Las Vegas *B*

New York

Cornell University *B*
Fashion Institute of Technology *A, B*
Onondaga Community College *A*
Parsons The New School for Design *B*
Suffolk County Community College *A*
Syracuse University *B, M*

Ohio

Bowling Green State University *B*
Miami University
    Oxford Campus *B*
Ohio State University
    Columbus Campus *B*

Oregon

University of Oregon *B, M*

Pennsylvania

Chatham College *M*
Indiana University of Pennsylvania *B*
La Roche College *B*
Lehigh Carbon Community College *A*
Marywood University *M*
Philadelphia University *B*

Rhode Island

Rhode Island School of Design *B, M*

Texas

Lamar University *B*
St. Philip's College *C, A*
Sam Houston State University *B*
Stephen F. Austin State University *B*
Texas A&M University
    Kingsville *B, M*
Texas Tech University *B*
University of Houston *B, M*
University of North Texas *B, M*
University of Texas
    Arlington *B*
    San Antonio *B*

Washington

Spokane Falls Community College *A*
Washington State University *B, M*

Interior design

Alabama

Samford University *B*
University of Alabama *B*
Virginia College *A, B*
Wallace State Community College at
    Hanceville *A*

Arizona

Arizona State University *M*
Art Center Design College *A, B*
Glendale Community College *C*
Mesa Community College *A*
Northern Arizona University *B*
Phoenix College *A*
Scottsdale Community College *A*
Tucson Design College *C, A, B*

Arkansas

Harding University *B*

California

Academy of Art University *C, A, B, M*
Allan Hancock College *A*
American River College *A*
Antelope Valley College *C, A*
Art Center College of Design *B, M*
Art Institute
    of California: Orange County *A, B*
    of California: San Diego *B*
Art Institute of California: San
    Francisco *B*
Bakersfield College *A*
Brooks College *A*
California College of the Arts *B*
California State University
    Chico *B*
    Fresno *B*
    Long Beach *B, M*
    Sacramento *B*
Canada College *C, A*
Cerritos Community College *A*
Chaffey College *C, A*
City College of San Francisco *A*
Contra Costa College *A*
Cosumnes River College *C, A*
Cuesta College *C, A*
Design Institute of San Diego *B*
Fashion Institute of Design and
    Merchandising *A*
Fashion Institute of Design and
    Merchandising
    San Diego *A*
    San Francisco *A*
Las Positas College *C, A*
Long Beach City College *C, A*
Los Angeles Harbor College *A*
Los Angeles Mission College *C, A*
Modesto Junior College *C, A*
Monterey Peninsula College *C, A*
Moorpark College *C, A*
Mount San Antonio College *C, A*
Ohlone College *C, A*
Orange Coast College *C, A*

Palomar College *C, A*
Saddleback College *C, A*
San Diego Mesa College *C, A*
San Diego State University *B*
San Joaquin Delta College *C, A*
San Jose State University *B*
Santa Barbara City College *C, A*
Santa Rosa Junior College *C*
Sierra College *C*
Solano Community College *C, A*
Ventura College *A*
West Valley College *C, A*
Westwood College of Technology
    Inland Empire *B*
Westwood College: Long Beach *B*

Colorado

Arapahoe Community College *C, A*
Art Institute
    of Colorado *B*
Colorado State University *B*
Pikes Peak Community College *A*
Rocky Mountain College of Art &
    Design *B*
Westwood College of Technology
    South *B*

Connecticut

Paier College of Art *C, B*
University of Bridgeport *B*
University of New Haven *C, A, B*

Delaware

Delaware College of Art and Design *A*
Delaware Technical and Community
    College
    Terry Campus *A*

District of Columbia

Corcoran College of Art and Design *M*
George Washington University *B, M*
Howard University *B*

Florida

Art Institute of Fort Lauderdale *C, B*
Broward Community College *A*
Daytona Beach Community College *A*
Florida Community College at
    Jacksonville *A*
Florida International University *B*
Florida State University *B, M*
Indian River Community College *A*
International Academy of Design and
    Technology: Orlando *B*
International Academy of Design and
    Technology: Tampa *A, B*
Miami International University of Art
    and Design *A*
Okaloosa-Walton College *A*
Palm Beach Community College *A*
Ringling School of Art and Design *B*
Seminole Community College *A*
University of Florida *B*

Georgia

Bauder College *A*
Brenau University *B*
Georgia Southern University *B*
Gwinnett Technical College *A*
Savannah College of Art and
    Design *B, M*
Valdosta State University *B*

Hawaii

Chaminade University of
    Honolulu *A, B*

Idaho

Brigham Young University-Idaho *B*
University of Idaho *B*

Illinois

Columbia College Chicago *B, M*
Harrington College of Design *C, A, B*
Illinois Institute of Art-Schaumburg *B*
International Academy of Design and
    Technology: Chicago *B*
International Academy of Design and
    Technology: Schaumburg *A, B*
Joliet Junior College *A*
Judson College *B*
Prairie State College *A*
Robert Morris College: Chicago *C, A*
Southern Illinois University
    Carbondale *B*
Triton College *C, A*
Westwood College - Chicago Loop *A*
Westwood College of Technology
    O'Hare *B*
William Rainey Harper College *A*

Indiana

Indiana University
    Bloomington *B, M*
Indiana University-Purdue University
    Fort Wayne *A*
Indiana University-Purdue University
    Indianapolis *A, B*
Ivy Tech State College
    Ivy Tech Community College: North
        Central *A*
    Ivy Tech Community College:
        Southwest *A*
Vincennes University *A*

Iowa

Hawkeye Community College *A*
Iowa State University *B, M*
University of Northern Iowa *B*

Kansas

Kansas State University *B*
Pittsburg State University *B*
University of Kansas *B, M*

Kentucky

Berea College *B*
Eastern Kentucky University *B*
Louisville Technical Institute *C, A*
University of Kentucky *B*

Maryland

Anne Arundel Community
    College *C, A*
Community College of Baltimore
    County *C, A*
Harford Community College *A*
Maryland Institute College of Art *B*
Montgomery College *A*

Massachusetts

Atlantic Union College *B*
Bay Path College *C*
Becker College *C, A, B*
Endicott College *B*
Massachusetts Bay Community
    College *C*
Mount Ida College *A, B*
Newbury College *A, B*
Suffolk University *C, B, M*
University of Massachusetts
    Amherst *B*
Wentworth Institute of
    Technology *A, B*

Michigan

Adrian College *A, B*
Baker College
    of Auburn Hills *A*
    of Cadillac *A*
    of Clinton Township *A*
    of Flint *A, B*

of Muskegon *A*
of Owosso *A*
Bay de Noc Community College *C*
College for Creative Studies *B*
Delta College *A*
Eastern Michigan University *B, M*
Ferris State University *B*
Finlandia University *B*
Grand Rapids Community College *A*
Henry Ford Community College *A*
Kendall College of Art and Design of
Ferris State University *B*
Lawrence Technological University *M*
Michigan State University *B, M*
Oakland Community College *A*
University of Michigan *B*
Western Michigan University *B*

Minnesota
Alexandria Technical College *C, A*
Art Institutes International
Minnesota *A, B*
Dakota County Technical College *C, A*
Minnesota State University
Mankato *B*
University of Minnesota
Twin Cities *B*

Mississippi
Antonelli College
Jackson *A*
Mississippi College *B*
Mississippi Gulf Coast Community
College
Jefferson Davis Campus *A*

Missouri
Central Missouri State University *B*
Maryville University of Saint Louis *B*
Park University *B*
Patricia Stevens College *C, A*

Montana
Montana State University
College of Technology-Great Falls *A*

Nevada
International Academy of Design and
Technology: Henderson *A, B*
University of Nevada
Reno *B*

New Hampshire
New Hampshire Community
Technical College
Manchester *C, A*

New Jersey
Berkeley College *A*
Brookdale Community College *A*
Kean University *B*

New Mexico
Art Center Design College *A, B*
Santa Fe Community College *C, A*

New York
Art Institute
of New York City *A*
Broome Community College *C*
Cazenovia College *B*
Dowling College *B*
Fashion Institute of Technology *A, B*
Institute of Design and
Construction *A*
Monroe Community College *C, A*
Nassau Community College *C, A*
New York Institute of Technology *B*
New York School of Interior
Design *C, A, B, M*
Onondaga Community College *A*

Parsons The New School for
Design *C, A, B, T*
Pratt Institute *B, M*
Rochester Institute of
Technology *A, B, M*
Sage College of Albany *A, B*
School of Visual Arts *B*
State University of New York
College of Technology at Alfred *A*
Suffolk County Community College *A*
Syracuse University *B, M*
Villa Maria College of Buffalo *A, B*

North Carolina
Appalachian State University *B*
Art Institute
of Charlotte *A, B*
Cape Fear Community College *A*
Carteret Community College *A*
Central Piedmont Community
College *C, A*
East Carolina University *B*
Halifax Community College *C, A*
High Point University *B*
Meredith College *B*
Randolph Community College *C, A*
Salem College *B*
University of North Carolina
Greensboro *B, M, T*
Western Carolina University *B*
Western Piedmont Community
College *C, A*

North Dakota
North Dakota State University *B*

Ohio
Cleveland Institute of Art *B*
College of Mount St. Joseph *A, B*
Columbus College of Art and
Design *B*
Davis College *A*
Kent State University *B*
Ohio State University
Columbus Campus *B, M*
Owens Community College
Toledo *A*
Sinclair Community College *A*
University of Cincinnati *B*
Ursuline College *B*

Oklahoma
Oklahoma Christian University *B*
Tulsa Community College *C, A*
University of Central Oklahoma *B, M*
University of Oklahoma *B*

Oregon
Art Institute of Portland *A, B*
Marylhurst University *B*
Oregon State University *B*
Portland Community College *C, A*

Pennsylvania
Arcadia University *B*
Art Institute
of Philadelphia *A, B*
of Pittsburgh *C, A, B*
Bradley Academy for the Visual Arts *A*
Drexel University *B, M*
Harcum College *A*
Marywood University *M*
Moore College of Art and Design *C, B*
Northampton County Area
Community College *C, A*
Philadelphia University *B*

Puerto Rico
University of Puerto Rico
Carolina Regional College *A*

Rhode Island
New England Institute of
Technology *A, B*
Rhode Island School of Design *C*

South Carolina
Anderson University *B*
Converse College *B*

South Dakota
South Dakota State University *B*

Tennessee
Carson-Newman College *B*
Freed-Hardeman University *B*
Lambuth University *B*
Middle Tennessee State University *B*
O'More College of Design *B*
Pellissippi State Technical Community
College *A*
University of Tennessee
Knoxville *B, M*

Texas
Abilene Christian University *B*
Amarillo College *C, A*
Art Institute
of Houston *B*
Baylor University *B*
Collin County Community College
District *C, A*
El Centro College *C, A*
El Paso Community College *C, A*
Houston Community College
System *A*
North Harris Montgomery
Community College District *C, A*
St. Philip's College *C*
San Jacinto College
Central Campus *C*
Texas A&M University
Kingsville *B*
Texas Christian University *B*
Texas State University: San Marcos *B*
Tyler Junior College *A*
University of Houston *B*
University of North Texas *B, M*
University of Texas
Austin *B*
University of the Incarnate Word *A, B*
Wade College *A*

Utah
LDS Business College *C, A*
Salt Lake Community College *C*
Utah State University *B*
Weber State University *A*

Virginia
Art Institute
of Washington *B*
J. Sargeant Reynolds Community
College *C*
Lord Fairfax Community College *C*
Marymount University *B, M*
Northern Virginia Community
College *A*
Tidewater Community College *A*
Virginia Commonwealth University *B*
Virginia Polytechnic Institute and
State University *B*

Washington
Art Institute of Seattle *C, A, B*
Bellevue Community College *A*
Clover Park Technical College *A*
Cornish College of the Arts *B*
Spokane Falls Community
College *C, A*

West Virginia
University of Charleston *B*

Wisconsin
Concordia University Wisconsin *B*
Fox Valley Technical College *A*
Gateway Technical College *A*
Madison Area Technical College *A*
Milwaukee Area Technical College *A*
Mount Mary College *B*
University of Wisconsin
Madison *B*
Stevens Point *B*
Waukesha County Technical
College *A*
Western Wisconsin Technical
College *A*

International agriculture

California
University of California
Davis *B, M*

Iowa
Iowa State University *B*

New York
Cornell University *B, M, D*

Vermont
Sterling College *B*

Virginia
Eastern Mennonite University *B*

International business

Alabama
Auburn University *B*
Birmingham-Southern College *B*
Huntingdon College *B*
Samford University *B*
Spring Hill College *B*

Arizona
Arizona State University West *B*
Cochise College *A*
Gateway Community College *A*
Grand Canyon University *B*
Northcentral University *M, D*
Paradise Valley Community College *A*
Pima Community College *A*
Rio Salado College *A*
Scottsdale Community College *A*
South Mountain Community
College *A*
Western International University *B, M*

Arkansas
Arkansas State University *B*
Harding University *B*
John Brown University *B*
University of Arkansas *B*
University of Arkansas
Little Rock *B*
University of Central Arkansas *M*

California
Alliant International
University *B, M, D*
Antioch Southern California
Antioch University Santa Barbara *M*
Azusa Pacific University *M*
Biola University *B*
California State Polytechnic
University: Pomona *B*
California State University
Dominguez Hills *B*
East Bay *M*
Fresno *B*
Fullerton *B, M*
Long Beach *B*
Monterey Bay *B*

Sacramento *B*
San Bernardino *B*
Concordia University *B*
Dominican University of
    California *B, M*
Foothill College *A*
Fresno Pacific University *B*
Fullerton College *A*
Golden Gate University *B, M*
Grossmont Community College *A*
Lincoln University *B, M*
Monterey Peninsula College *A*
Mount St. Mary's College *B*
National University *M*
Orange Coast College *A*
Pacific Union College *B*
Palomar College *A*
Pepperdine University *B, M*
St. Mary's College of California *B*
San Diego State University *B, M*
San Francisco State University *B*
San Jose State University *B*
Santa Barbara City College *A*
Southwestern College *A*
University of La Verne *B*
University of San Diego *M*
University of San Francisco *B*
University of Southern
    California *B, M*
Vanguard University of Southern
    California *B*

Colorado

Arapahoe Community College *A*
Fort Lewis College *B*
Johnson & Wales University *B*
Jones International University *B, M*
Teikyo Loretto Heights
    University *A, B*
University of Colorado
    Boulder *B*
    Denver and Health Sciences
        Center *M*
University of Denver *B, M*

Connecticut

Albertus Magnus College *B*
Central Connecticut State
    University *B, M*
Fairfield University *B*
Post University *B*
Quinnipiac University *B*
University of Bridgeport *B, M*
University of New Haven *B*
Yale University *M*

Delaware

Goldey-Beacom College *B*

District of Columbia

George Washington University *B, M*
Georgetown University *B*
Howard University *B*

Florida

Barry University *B*
Bethune-Cookman College *B*
Brevard Community College *A*
Broward Community College *A*
Eckerd College *B*
Edison College *A*
Florida Atlantic University *B, M*
Florida Institute of Technology *M*
Florida International University *B, M*
Florida Metropolitan University
    Pinellas *A, B*
    Pompano Beach *A, B*
Florida Southern College *B, M*
Florida State University *B*
Jacksonville University *B*
Lynn University *B, M*
Northwood University
    Florida Campus *A, B*

Nova Southeastern University *M, D*
Palm Beach Atlantic University *B*
Rollins College *B*
St. Leo University *B*
St. Petersburg College *B*
St. Thomas University *B, M*
Schiller International
    University *A, B, M*
Stetson University *B*
University of Miami *B*
University of North Florida *B*
University of South Florida *B*
University of Tampa *B*

Georgia

Georgia College and State
    University *B*
Georgia Southern University *B*
Georgia State University *M*
Mercer University *M*
Paine College *B*
Savannah State University *B*
University of Georgia *B*
Wesleyan College *B*

Hawaii

Brigham Young University-Hawaii *B*
Hawaii Pacific University *B*
Remington College
    Honolulu *A*
University of Hawaii
    Manoa *B, D*

Idaho

Albertson College of Idaho *B*
Boise State University *B*

Illinois

Augustana College *B*
Benedictine University *B*
Black Hawk College *A*
Bradley University *B*
City Colleges of Chicago
    Harold Washington College *A*
DePaul University *M*
Dominican University *B*
Elmhurst College *B*
Governors State University *B*
Illinois Central College *A*
Illinois State University *B*
Illinois Wesleyan University *B*
Judson College *B*
Lewis University *B*
Loyola University of Chicago *B*
MacCormac College *A*
Millikin University *B*
Monmouth College *B*
North Central College *B*
North Park University *B*
Northwestern University *M*
Oakton Community College *A*
Olivet Nazarene University *B*
Roosevelt University *B, M*
St. Xavier University *B, M*
Triton College *A*
William Rainey Harper College *A*

Indiana

Butler University *B*
Grace College *B*
Indiana University-Purdue University
    Indianapolis *B*
Taylor University *B*
Taylor University: Fort Wayne *B*
University of Evansville *B*
University of Indianapolis *B*
Valparaiso University *B, M*

Iowa

Buena Vista University *B*
Central College *B*
Clarke College *B*
Drake University *B*

Graceland University *B*
Iowa State University *B*
Loras College *B*
Morningside College *B*
St. Ambrose University *B*
Simpson College *B*
Wartburg College *B*

Kansas

Baker University *B*
Friends University *B*
Kansas City Kansas Community
    College *A*
McPherson College *B*
Pittsburg State University *B*
University of St. Mary *B*
Wichita State University *B*

Kentucky

Murray State University *B*

Louisiana

Louisiana State University and
    Agricultural and Mechanical
    College *B*
Loyola University New Orleans *B*

Maine

Husson College *B*
Maine Maritime Academy *B*
St. Joseph's College *B*
Thomas College *B*

Maryland

College of Notre Dame of Maryland *B*
Frederick Community College *A*
University of Baltimore *B, M*
University of Maryland
    University College *M*

Massachusetts

American International College *B, M*
Assumption College *B*
Babson College *B, M*
Bentley College *M*
Boston University *B*
Brandeis University *M, D*
Bridgewater State College *B*
Bunker Hill Community College *A*
Elms College *B*
Emerson College *M*
Fitchburg State College *B*
Hampshire College *B*
Lasell College *B*
Newbury College *A, B*
Northeastern University *B*
Northern Essex Community
    College *A*
Salem State College *B*
Stonehill College *B*
Suffolk University *B, M*

Michigan

Adrian College *B*
Alma College *B*
Aquinas College *B*
Baker College
    of Flint *M*
    of Port Huron *B*
Central Michigan University *B, M*
Cornerstone University *B*
Davenport University *B*
Delta College *A*
Eastern Michigan University *B, M*
Ferris State University *B*
Finlandia University *B*
Grace Bible College *B*
Grand Valley State University *B*
Lansing Community College *A*
Madonna University *B, M*
Marygrove College *B*
Mott Community College *A*
Muskegon Community College *A*

Northwood University *A, B*
Oakland Community College *A*
Olivet College *B*
Saginaw Valley State University *B*

Minnesota

Augsburg College *B*
Capella University *M, D*
College of St. Catherine *B*
Concordia College: Moorhead *B*
Gustavus Adolphus College *B*
Hamline University *B*
Metropolitan State University *B*
Minnesota State University
    Mankato *B*
    Moorhead *B*
National American University
    St. Paul *B*
Northwestern College *B*
St. Cloud State University *B*
St. Mary's University of
    Minnesota *B, M*
St. Paul College *A*
University of Minnesota
    Twin Cities *B*
University of St. Thomas *B, M*
Winona State University *A*

Mississippi

Belhaven College *B*

Missouri

Avila University *B*
College of the Ozarks *B*
Columbia College *B*
Drury University *B*
Lindenwood University *B, M*
Missouri Southern State University *B*
Northwest Missouri State
    University *B*
St. Louis University *M*
University of Missouri
    Columbia *B*
    St. Louis *B, M*
Washington University in St. Louis *B*
Webster University *B, M*
William Jewell College *B*
William Woods University *B*

Montana

University of Montana: Missoula *B*

Nebraska

Creighton University *B*
Nebraska Wesleyan University *B*
University of Nebraska
    Lincoln *B*

Nevada

University of Nevada
    Reno *B*

New Hampshire

Southern New Hampshire
    University *B, M, D*

New Jersey

Berkeley College *A, B*
Caldwell College *B*
The College of New Jersey *B*
Fairleigh Dickinson University
    College at Florham *M*
    Metropolitan Campus *M*
Monmouth University *B*
Ramapo College of New Jersey *B*
Rider University *B*
St. Peter's College *A, B, M*
Seton Hall University *M*
Thomas Edison State College *A, B*

New Mexico

College of Santa Fe *B*

New Mexico State University B

New York

Berkeley College A, B
Berkeley College of New York
   City A, B
Canisius College B
City University of New York
   Baruch College M
   Queens College B
Concordia College B
D'Youville College B, M
Daemen College M
Dominican College of Blauvelt B
Dowling College B
Elmira College B
Excelsior College B
Fordham University B, M
Herkimer County Community
   College A
Hofstra University B, M
Hudson Valley Community College A
Iona College B
Ithaca College B, T
Manhattan College B
Monroe Community College A
New York Institute of Technology M
New York University B, M, D
Niagara University B
Pace University B, M
Rochester Institute of
   Technology B, M
St. John Fisher College B
St. John's University M
State University of New York
   College at Brockport B
   College at Plattsburgh B
   New Paltz B, M
Tompkins-Cortland Community
   College A
Touro College M
Wagner College B
Westchester Community College A

North Carolina

Appalachian State University B
Belmont Abbey College B
Campbell University B
Central Piedmont Community
   College A
Elon University B
Gardner-Webb University B
High Point University B
Lenoir-Rhyne College B
Mars Hill College B
St. Andrews Presbyterian College B
Salem College B
Shaw University B
University of North Carolina
   Charlotte B
   Greensboro B
Western Carolina University B

North Dakota

Jamestown College B
Minot State University B

Ohio

Baldwin-Wallace College M
Bowling Green State University B
Cedarville University B
Cincinnati State Technical and
   Community College A
Cleveland State University B
Lake Erie College B
Marietta College B
Mount Union College B
Mount Vernon Nazarene University B
Ohio Dominican University B
Ohio Northern University B
Ohio State University
   Columbus Campus B
Ohio University B

Ohio Wesleyan University B
Stark State College of Technology A
Tiffin University B
University of Akron B, M
University of Cincinnati M, D
University of Dayton B
University of Findlay B
University of Rio Grande B
University of Toledo B, M
Wright State University M
Xavier University B, M

Oklahoma

Northeastern State University B
Oklahoma Baptist University B
Oklahoma City University B, M
Oklahoma State University B
Oral Roberts University B
University of Tulsa B

Oregon

Concordia University B
Linfield College B
Portland State University M
University of Portland B
Warner Pacific College B

Pennsylvania

Albright College B
Arcadia University B
Carlow University B
Chatham College B
Chestnut Hill College B
Clarion University of Pennsylvania B
Dickinson College B
Drexel University B
Duquesne University B
Elizabethtown College B
Gannon University B
Gettysburg College B
Grove City College B
Holy Family University B
Indiana University of Pennsylvania B
Juniata College B
King's College B
Kutztown University of
   Pennsylvania B
La Roche College B
La Salle University B
Lehigh University M
Luzerne County Community
   College A
Manor College A
Mansfield University of
   Pennsylvania B
Marywood University B
Mercyhurst College B
Messiah College B
Moravian College B
Neumann College B
Penn State
   Abington B
   Altoona B
   Beaver B
   Berks B
   Delaware County B
   Dubois B
   Erie, The Behrend College B
   Fayette B
   Hazleton B
   Lehigh Valley B
   McKeesport B
   Mont Alto B
   New Kensington B
   Schuylkill - Capital College B
   Shenango B
   University Park B
   Wilkes-Barre B
   Worthington Scranton B
   York B
Philadelphia University B
St. Joseph's University B, M
St. Vincent College B
Seton Hill University B

Temple University B, M
Thiel College B
University of Pennsylvania B, M
University of Pittsburgh M
University of Scranton B, M
Washington and Jefferson College B
Waynesburg College B
Westminster College B
Widener University B
Wilson College B

Puerto Rico

Inter American University of Puerto
   Rico
   Ponce Campus B, M
   San German Campus D
Pontifical Catholic University of
   Puerto Rico B
University of Puerto Rico
   Humacao B
   Rio Piedras M, D

Rhode Island

Bryant University B
Johnson & Wales University B, M
Rhode Island College B
Roger Williams University B
University of Rhode Island B

South Carolina

Clemson University B
College of Charleston B
Converse College B
North Greenville College B
University of South Carolina M
Wofford College B

South Dakota

Northern State University B

Tennessee

Lambuth University B
Maryville College B
Southern Adventist University B
Union University B
University of Memphis B, M

Texas

Angelo State University B
Baylor University B, M
El Paso Community College A
Houston Community College
   System A
LeTourneau University B
Midwestern State University B
Northwood University: Texas
   Campus A, B
Our Lady of the Lake University of San
   Antonio M
St. Edward's University B
St. Mary's University B
Sam Houston State University B
San Jacinto College
   North A
Southwestern Adventist University B
Stephen F. Austin State University B
Sul Ross State University M
Texas A&M University
   Galveston B
   Kingsville B
   Texarkana B
Texas Christian University B
Texas Tech University B, M
Trinity University B
University of Dallas M
University of Houston M
University of Houston
   Downtown B
University of St. Thomas M
University of Texas
   Arlington B, M
   Dallas M, D
   El Paso D

Pan American B, D
San Antonio B, M

Utah

Utah Valley State College A
Westminster College B

Vermont

Champlain College A, B

Virginia

Eastern Mennonite University B
James Madison University B
Lynchburg College B
Marymount University B, M
Northern Virginia Community
   College B
Old Dominion University B
Regent University B
University of Northern Virginia B
Virginia Intermont College B

Washington

City University A
Edmonds Community College A
Gonzaga University B
Highline Community College A
Seattle University B, M
Shoreline Community College A
Spokane Falls Community College A
University of Washington B
Walla Walla College B
Washington State University B
Western Washington University B
Whitworth College B, M

West Virginia

Bethany College B
Davis and Elkins College B
Mountain State University B
Salem International University M
West Virginia Wesleyan College B
Wheeling Jesuit University B

Wisconsin

Alverno College B
Cardinal Stritch University B
Lakeland College B
Marquette University B, M
Milwaukee School of Engineering B
St. Norbert College B
University of Wisconsin
   La Crosse B
   Madison B, M
   Superior B
Waukesha County Technical
   College A

International economics

California

California State University
   Chico B
University of California
   Los Angeles B

Colorado

University of Denver M

Connecticut

University of Hartford B

District of Columbia

American University M
Catholic University of America M

Florida

Schiller International University B

Georgia

University of West Georgia B

Indiana
Valparaiso University *B*

Louisiana
Tulane University *B*

Maryland
Howard Community College *A*

Massachusetts
Brandeis University *M, D*
Suffolk University *B, M*

Michigan
Eastern Michigan University *M*
Madonna University *M*

Ohio
Youngstown State University *B*

Pennsylvania
La Salle University *B*
Penn State
    Shenango *B*

Tennessee
Carson-Newman College *B*

Texas
Austin College *B*
Baylor University *M*
Texas Christian University *B*

Washington
University of Puget Sound *B*

Wisconsin
Carthage College *B*
Marquette University *M*

International finance

California
University of California
    Santa Cruz *B*

Colorado
University of Denver *M*

District of Columbia
Catholic University of America *B*

Hawaii
Hawaii Pacific University *B*

Illinois
Illinois Institute of Technology *M*
University of Illinois
    Urbana-Champaign *M, D*

Massachusetts
Babson College *B*
Bentley College *M*
Boston University *B, M*
Brandeis University *M, D*

Michigan
Madonna University *M*

Missouri
Washington University in St. Louis *B*

Nebraska
Union College *B*

New Jersey
William Paterson University of New
    Jersey *B*

New York
Broome Community College *A*
Pace University *M*

Ohio
University of Akron *M*

Oklahoma
Oklahoma Baptist University *B*

Pennsylvania
Penn State
    University Park *B*
Westminster College *B*

Texas
Texas A&M University
    Galveston *B*
Texas Christian University *B*

West Virginia
Bethany College *B*

Wisconsin
Concordia University Wisconsin *B*
Lawrence University *B*

International marketing

Arizona
Northern Arizona University *C*

Arkansas
University of Central Arkansas *B*

California
Allan Hancock College *C, A*
Antioch Southern California
    Antioch University Santa Barbara *M*
East Los Angeles College *A*
Sacramento City College *C, A*

Connecticut
Quinnipiac University *B, M*

Florida
Brevard Community College *A*
Broward Community College *A*
Schiller International University *B*

Idaho
Northwest Nazarene University *B*

Illinois
DePaul University *M*
Governors State University *B*
MacCormac College *A*
Roosevelt University *M*

Maine
Husson College *B*

Maryland
Montgomery College *A*

Massachusetts
Babson College *B*
Newbury College *A, B*

Michigan
Adrian College *B*
Finlandia University *B*
Hillsdale College *B*

Minnesota
Rasmussen College
    Eagan *A*
    Minnetonka *A*
St. Paul College *C, A*

Missouri
Northwest Missouri State
    University *B*

Nebraska
Northeast Community College *A*

Nevada
University of Nevada
    Las Vegas *B*

New York
Pace University *B*
St. Thomas Aquinas College *B*
State University of New York
    College at Brockport *B*
    Farmingdale *C*

Ohio
Muskingum College *B*
University of Akron *M*

Oklahoma
Oral Roberts University *B*

Pennsylvania
Community College of Philadelphia *A*
Holy Family University *B*
La Salle University *B*
Penn State
    Schuylkill - Capital College *B*
    University Park *B*
Philadelphia University *M*
St. Joseph's University *B, M*
Waynesburg College *B*

Texas
Houston Community College
    System *C*
Texas Christian University *B, M*
Texas Wesleyan University *B*
University of Texas
    Brownsville *C, A*

Washington
City University *M*

Wisconsin
Marquette University *M*
Milwaukee Area Technical College *A*
Northcentral Technical College *C*

International public health

Michigan
University of Michigan *M, D*

Texas
University of Texas
    Health Science Center at
        Houston *M, D*

International relations

Alabama
Samford University *B*
Spring Hill College *B*
Troy University *M*
University of Alabama *B*
University of Alabama
    Birmingham *B*

Arizona
Embry-Riddle Aeronautical University:
    Prescott Campus *B*
Northern Arizona University *B*

Arkansas
Harding University *B*

Hendrix College *B*
University of Arkansas *B*
University of Arkansas
    Little Rock *B*

California
Allan Hancock College *A*
Alliant International University *B, M*
Azusa Pacific University *B*
California Lutheran University *B*
California State University
    Chico *B*
    Fresno *M*
    Sacramento *M*
Chapman University *B*
Claremont McKenna College *B*
Holy Names University *B*
Las Positas College *A*
Mills College *B*
Occidental College *B*
Pitzer College *B*
Pomona College *B*
Saddleback College *A*
San Diego State University *B*
San Francisco State University *B, M*
San Jose State University *B*
Scripps College *B*
Solano Community College *A*
Stanford University *B, M*
University of California
    Davis *B*
    Riverside *B*
    San Diego *D*
University of La Verne *B*
University of Redlands *B*
University of San Diego *B, M*
University of Southern
    California *B, M, D*
University of the Pacific *B*
Whittier College *B*

Colorado
University of Denver *B, M, D*

Connecticut
Connecticut College *B*
Fairfield University *B*
Trinity College *B*
University of Bridgeport *B*
Yale University *M*

Delaware
University of Delaware *B, M*

District of Columbia
American University *B, M, D*
Catholic University of America *M*
George Washington University *B, M*
Georgetown University *B, M*
Trinity University *B*

Florida
Bethune-Cookman College *B*
Eckerd College *B*
Florida International
    University *B, M, D*
Florida State University *B, M*
Lynn University *B*
Miami Dade College *A*
Palm Beach Community College *A*
Rollins College *B*
St. Leo University *B*
Schiller International University *B, M*
Stetson University *B*
University of Florida *M, D*
University of Miami *B, M, D*
University of North Florida *B*
University of South Florida *B*
University of West Florida *B*

Georgia
Agnes Scott College *B*
Berry College *B*

Brenau University *B*
Clark Atlanta University *M, D*
Emory University *B*
Georgia Institute of Technology *B, M*
Georgia Southern University *B*
Kennesaw State University *B*
Mercer University *B*
Morehouse College *B*
Oglethorpe University *B*
Southern Polytechnic State
　University *B*
University of Georgia *B*
University of West Georgia *B*
Wesleyan College *B*

Hawaii

Chaminade University of Honolulu *B*
Hawaii Pacific University *B*

Idaho

Albertson College of Idaho *B*
Brigham Young University-Idaho *A*
Idaho State University *B*
Northwest Nazarene University *B*

Illinois

Bradley University *B*
DePaul University *B, M*
Dominican University *B*
Governors State University *M*
Illinois College *B*
John A. Logan College *A*
Knox College *B*
Lake Forest College *B*
Loyola University of Chicago *B*
MacMurray College *B*
McKendree College *B*
Millikin University *B*
Monmouth College *B*
North Central College *B*
North Park University *B*
Northwestern University *B*
Roosevelt University *B*
St. Xavier University *B*
University of Chicago *B, M*
Wheaton College *B*

Indiana

Bethel College *B*
Butler University *B*
Indiana University
　Southeast *B*
Indiana Wesleyan University *B*
St. Joseph's College *B*
University of Evansville *B*
University of Indianapolis *B*
University of Southern Indiana *B*
Valparaiso University *B*

Iowa

Cornell College *B*
Drake University *B*
Iowa State University *B*
Loras College *B*
Morningside College *B*
Simpson College *B*
Wartburg College *B*

Kansas

Pittsburg State University *B*
University of Kansas *B*

Kentucky

Centre College *B*
Murray State University *B*
Northern Kentucky University *B*
Thomas More College *A, B*

Maine

Colby College *B*
University of Maine *B*

University of Maine
　Farmington *B*
　Presque Isle *B*
University of Southern Maine *B*

Maryland

College of Notre Dame of Maryland *B*
Frostburg State University *C, B*
Goucher College *B*
Johns Hopkins University *B, M, D*
Mount St. Mary's University *B*
Washington College *B*

Massachusetts

American International College *B*
Boston University *B, M*
Bridgewater State College *B*
Clark University *B, M*
Elms College *B*
Gordon College *B*
Mount Holyoke College *C, B*
Northeastern University *B*
Regis College *B*
Simmons College *B*
Stonehill College *B*
Suffolk University *B, M*
Tufts University *B, M, D*
University of Massachusetts
　Boston *C*
Wellesley College *B*
Wheaton College *B*

Michigan

Adrian College *B*
Albion College *B*
Aquinas College *B*
Calvin College *B*
Central Michigan University *B*
Grand Valley State University *B*
Michigan State University *B*
Northern Michigan University *B*
Wayne State University *B*
Western Michigan University *B*

Minnesota

Augsburg College *B*
Bethel University *B*
Carleton College *B*
College of St. Catherine *B*
Concordia College: Moorhead *B*
Hamline University *B*
Macalester College *B*
Minnesota State University
　Mankato *B*
St. Cloud State University *B*
University of Minnesota
　Twin Cities *B*
University of St. Thomas *B*
Winona State University *A*

Mississippi

University of Mississippi *B*

Missouri

Lindenwood University *C, B*
Missouri Southern State University *B*
Missouri State University *M*
Rockhurst University *B*
St. Louis University *B*
Washington University in St.
　Louis *B, M*
Webster University *B, M*
Westminster College *B*
William Jewell College *B*

Montana

Carroll College *B*
University of Montana: Missoula *B*

Nebraska

Creighton University *B, M*
Doane College *B*

Hastings College *B*
University of Nebraska
　Kearney *B*
　Lincoln *B*

Nevada

University of Nevada
　Reno *B*

New Hampshire

St. Anselm College *B*
University of New Hampshire *B*

New Jersey

The College of New Jersey *B*
Fairleigh Dickinson University
　Metropolitan Campus *B, M*
Seton Hall University *B, M*
William Paterson University of New
　Jersey *M*

New York

Bard College *B*
Canisius College *B*
City University of New York
　City College *B, M*
　College of Staten Island *B*
　Hunter College *B*
Colgate University *B*
Cornell University *B, M, D*
Elmira College *B*
Eugene Lang College The New School
　for Liberal Arts *B*
Hamilton College *B*
Hobart and William Smith Colleges *B*
Houghton College *B*
Le Moyne College *B*
Long Island University
　C.W. Post Campus *B*
Marymount Manhattan College *B*
Mount St. Mary College *B*
New York University *B, M*
Rochester Institute of Technology *B*
Sarah Lawrence College *B*
State University of New York
　College at Brockport *B*
　College at Cortland *B*
　College at Geneseo *B*
　New Paltz *B*
Syracuse University *B, M, D*
Utica College *B*
Vassar College *B*
Wells College *B*

North Carolina

Campbell University *B*
Duke University *M*
Elon University *B*
Guilford College *B*
Lees-McRae College *B*
Meredith College *B*
North Carolina State University *M*
Salem College *B*
Shaw University *B*

Ohio

Antioch College *B*
Bowling Green State University *B*
Capital University *B*
Case Western Reserve University *B*
College of Wooster *B*
Kent State University *B*
Kenyon College *B*
Miami University
　Oxford Campus *B*
Mount Union College *B*
Muskingum College *B*
Ohio Northern University *B*
Ohio State University
　Columbus Campus *B*
Ohio University *M*
Ohio Wesleyan University *B*
Otterbein College *B*

Shawnee State University *B*
Tiffin University *B*
University of Akron *C*
University of Cincinnati *B*
University of Toledo *B*
Wright State University *B*
Xavier University *B*

Oklahoma

Oral Roberts University *B*
Rose State College *A*
University of Central Oklahoma *M*

Oregon

George Fox University *B*
Lewis & Clark College *B*
Pacific University *B*
Portland State University *B*

Pennsylvania

Allegheny College *B*
Arcadia University *B*
Bucknell University *B*
Carnegie Mellon University *B*
Chatham College *B*
Dickinson College *B*
Duquesne University *B*
Gettysburg College *B*
Harrisburg Area Community
　College *A*
Immaculata University *C, A, B*
Indiana University of Pennsylvania *B*
Juniata College *B*
La Roche College *B*
La Salle University *B*
Lafayette College *B*
Lehigh University *B*
Lincoln University *B*
Lock Haven University of
　Pennsylvania *B*
Millersville University of
　Pennsylvania *B*
Muhlenberg College *C, B*
Penn State
　Abington *B*
　Altoona *B*
　Beaver *B*
　Berks *B*
　Delaware County *B*
　Dubois *B*
　Fayette *B*
　Hazleton *B*
　Lehigh Valley *B*
　McKeesport *B*
　Mont Alto *B*
　New Kensington *B*
　Schuylkill - Capital College *B*
　University Park *B*
　Wilkes-Barre *B*
　Worthington Scranton *B*
　York *B*
Point Park University *B*
St. Joseph's University *B*
Seton Hill University *B*
University of Pennsylvania *B*
University of Pittsburgh *M*
University of Scranton *B*
Ursinus College *B*
West Chester University of
　Pennsylvania *B*
Westminster College *B*
Widener University *B*
Wilkes University *B*
Wilson College *B*

Rhode Island

Brown University *B*
Bryant University *B*
Salve Regina University *M*

South Carolina

Francis Marion University *B*
Newberry College *B*

University of South Carolina *B, M, D*

Tennessee
Lambuth University *B*
Maryville College *B*
Middle Tennessee State University *B*
Rhodes College *B*
University of Memphis *B*
University of Tennessee
    Martin *B*

Texas
Austin College *B*
Baylor University *B, M*
St. Edward's University *B*
St. Mary's University *B*
Southern Methodist University *B*
Southwestern Adventist University *B*
Southwestern University *B*
Texas A&M University *M, D*
Texas Christian University *B*
Texas State University: San Marcos *B*
University of North Texas *M, D*
University of St. Thomas *B*
Western Texas College *A*

Utah
Brigham Young University *B*
University of Utah *C*

Vermont
Bennington College *B*
Middlebury College *B*
Norwich University *B*

Virginia
Bridgewater College *B*
College of William and Mary *B*
Ferrum College *B*
George Mason University *B, M*
Hampden-Sydney College *B*
James Madison University *B*
Lynchburg College *B*
Mary Baldwin College *B*
Old Dominion University *B, M, D*
Roanoke College *B*
Sweet Briar College *B*
University of Mary Washington *B*
University of Virginia *B, M, D*
Virginia Polytechnic Institute and
    State University *B*
Virginia Wesleyan College *B*

Washington
City University *B*
Eastern Washington University *B*
Gonzaga University *B*
University of Washington *B, M*
Whitworth College *B*

West Virginia
Bethany College *B*
Marshall University *B*
West Virginia Wesleyan College *B*
Wheeling Jesuit University *B*

Wisconsin
Alverno College *B*
Beloit College *B*
Carroll College *B*
Edgewood College *B*
Marquette University *B, M*
Mount Mary College *B*
St. Norbert College *B*
University of Wisconsin
    Madison *M*

Wyoming
Casper College *A*
University of Wyoming *B, M*
Western Wyoming Community
    College *A*

Investments/securities

Arizona
Northern Arizona University *C*

California
Golden Gate University *M*

Colorado
Johnson & Wales University *B*

Florida
Johnson & Wales University *A, B*

Illinois
Illinois Institute of Technology *M*
St. Xavier University *M*

Massachusetts
Babson College *B*

Minnesota
Minnesota State University
    Mankato *B*
University of St. Thomas *M*

Missouri
Lindenwood University *M*

New York
City University of New York
    Baruch College *M*
Globe Institute of Technology *C*
Mercy College *M*
Pace University *M*
State University of New York
    Albany *M*

Pennsylvania
Duquesne University *B*

Rhode Island
Johnson & Wales University *A, B*

Wisconsin
University of Wisconsin
    Platteville *B*

Iranian/Persian languages

Texas
University of Texas
    Austin *B, M, D*

Ironworking

California
Foothill College *C*

Indiana
Ivy Tech State College
    Ivy Tech Community College:
        Central Indiana *C, A*
    Ivy Tech Community College:
        Lafayette *C, A*
    Ivy Tech Community College: North
        Central *C, A*
    Ivy Tech Community College:
        Northeast *C, A*
    Ivy Tech Community College:
        Northwest *C, A*
    Ivy Tech Community College:
        Southwest *C, A*
    Ivy Tech Community College:
        Wabash Valley *C, A*

Minnesota
Hennepin Technical College *C, A*

St. Paul College *C*

Utah
Salt Lake Community College *A*

Islamic studies

California
University of California
    Los Angeles *M, D*

Massachusetts
Brandeis University *B*

Michigan
University of Michigan *B*
Wayne County Community College *A*

Missouri
Washington University in St.
    Louis *B, M*

New York
Sarah Lawrence College *B*

Ohio
Ohio State University
    Columbus Campus *B*

Texas
University of Texas
    Austin *B*

Italian

Arizona
Arizona State University *B*
University of Arizona *B*

California
Cabrillo College *A*
Chabot College *A*
Claremont McKenna College *B*
College of the Desert *A*
Los Angeles City College *A*
Los Angeles Pierce College *A*
Los Angeles Valley College *A*
Orange Coast College *A*
Pitzer College *B*
St. Mary's College of California *B*
San Diego City College *A*
San Francisco State University *B, M*
Santa Clara University *B*
Scripps College *B*
Stanford University *B, M, D*
University of California
    Berkeley *B, M, D*
    Davis *B*
    Los Angeles *B, M, D*
    San Diego *B*
    Santa Barbara *B*
    Santa Cruz *B, D*
University of Southern California *B*

Colorado
University of Colorado
    Boulder *B*
University of Denver *B*

Connecticut
Central Connecticut State
    University *B*
Connecticut College *B*
Fairfield University *B*
Southern Connecticut State
    University *B, M*
Trinity College *B*
University of Connecticut *B, M, D*
Wesleyan University *B*
Yale University *B, M, D*

Delaware
University of Delaware *B, M, T*

District of Columbia
Catholic University of America *M, D*
George Washington University *B*
Georgetown University *B*

Florida
Florida International University *B*
Florida State University *B*
University of Miami *B*
University of South Florida *B*

Georgia
Emory University *B*
University of Georgia *B*

Illinois
DePaul University *B*
Dominican University *B*
Loyola University of Chicago *B*
Northwestern University *B*
Triton College *A*
University of Chicago *B*
University of Illinois
    Chicago *B*
    Urbana-Champaign *B, M, D*

Indiana
Indiana University
    Bloomington *B, M, D*
University of Notre Dame *B, M*

Iowa
University of Iowa *B, T*

Louisiana
Tulane University *B*

Maryland
Johns Hopkins University *B, M, D*
University of Maryland
    College Park *B*

Massachusetts
Boston College *B, M*
Boston University *B*
Brandeis University *B*
College of the Holy Cross *B*
Mount Holyoke College *B*
Northeastern University *B*
Smith College *B, M*
Tufts University *B*
University of Massachusetts
    Amherst *B, M*
    Boston *B*
Wellesley College *B*
Wheaton College *B*

Michigan
University of Michigan *B, M, D*
Wayne State University *B, M*

Minnesota
University of Minnesota
    Twin Cities *B, M*

Missouri
Washington University in St. Louis *B*

New Hampshire
Dartmouth College *B*

New Jersey
Montclair State University *B, T*
Princeton University *B, M, D*
Rutgers, The State University of New
    Jersey
    New Brunswick/Piscataway
        Campus *B, M, D, T*

Seton Hall University *B, T*

New York
Bard College *B*
Barnard College *B*
City University of New York
  Brooklyn College *B*
  Hunter College *B, M*
  Lehman College *B*
  Queens College *B, M, T*
Columbia University
  Columbia College *B*
  School of General Studies *B*
Cornell University *B, M, D*
Fordham University *B*
Hofstra University *B*
Iona College *B*
Ithaca College *B*
Long Island University
  C.W. Post Campus *B*
Nazareth College of Rochester *B*
New York University *B, M, D*
St. John's University *B*
Sarah Lawrence College *B*
State University of New York
  Albany *B*
  Binghamton *B, M*
  Buffalo *B*
  Stony Brook *B*
Syracuse University *B*
Vassar College *B*

North Carolina
Duke University *B*
University of North Carolina
  Greensboro *B*

Ohio
College of Wooster *B*
Lake Erie College *B*
Ohio State University
  Columbus Campus *B, M, D*
University of Akron *M*
Youngstown State University *B*

Oklahoma
Tulsa Community College *A*

Oregon
University of Oregon *B, M*

Pennsylvania
Bryn Mawr College *B*
Dickinson College *B*
Haverford College *B*
La Salle University *B, T*
Penn State
  Abington *B*
  Altoona *B*
  Beaver *B*
  Berks *B*
  Delaware County *B*
  Fayette *B*
  Hazleton *B*
  Lehigh Valley *B*
  McKeesport *B*
  Mont Alto *B*
  New Kensington *B*
  Schuylkill - Capital College *B*
  Shenango *B*
  University Park *B*
  Wilkes-Barre *B*
  Worthington Scranton *B*
  York *B*
Rosemont College *B*
St. Joseph's University *B*
Temple University *B*
University of Pennsylvania *B*
University of Pittsburgh *B, M*
Villanova University *B*

Rhode Island
Brown University *B, M, D*

Providence College *B*
University of Rhode Island *B*

South Carolina
University of South Carolina *B*

Tennessee
University of Tennessee
  Knoxville *B*

Texas
University of Houston *B*
University of Texas
  Austin *B*

Utah
Brigham Young University *B*
University of Utah *D*

Vermont
Bennington College *B*
Middlebury College *B, M, D*

Virginia
University of Virginia *B, M*

Washington
Gonzaga University *B*
University of Washington *B*

Wisconsin
University of Wisconsin
  Madison *B, M, D*
  Milwaukee *B*

Italian studies

California
Scripps College *B*
University of California
  San Diego *B*
  Santa Cruz *B*

Connecticut
Connecticut College *B*

Florida
Florida State University *M*

Georgia
Emory University *B, D*

Massachusetts
Boston University *B*

New York
Bard College *B*
Columbia University
  Columbia College *B*

Ohio
Cleveland State University *B*
Miami University
  Oxford Campus *B*

Pennsylvania
Dickinson College *B*

Rhode Island
Brown University *B, M, D*

Texas
Southern Methodist University *B*

Virginia
Sweet Briar College *B*

Washington
University of Washington *B, M*

Japanese

Alaska
University of Alaska
  Anchorage *B*
  Fairbanks *B*

California
Cabrillo College *A*
California State University
  Fullerton *B*
  Long Beach *B*
  Los Angeles *B*
Citrus College *A*
Claremont McKenna College *B*
El Camino College *A*
Foothill College *A*
Grossmont Community College *A*
Los Angeles City College *A*
MiraCosta College *A*
Orange Coast College *A*
Pitzer College *B*
Pomona College *B*
St. Mary's College of California *B*
San Diego State University *B*
San Francisco State University *B, M*
San Jose State University *B*
Scripps College *B*
Stanford University *B, M, D*
University of California
  Berkeley *B, M, D*
  Davis *B*
  Irvine *B*
  Los Angeles *B*
  San Diego *B*
  Santa Barbara *B*
  Santa Cruz *B*
University of Southern California *M*
University of the Pacific *B*

Colorado
University of Colorado
  Boulder *B*

Connecticut
Connecticut College *B*
Fairfield University *B*
Trinity College *B*
Yale University *B*

District of Columbia
George Washington University *B*
Georgetown University *B*

Georgia
Emory University *B*
University of Georgia *B*

Hawaii
University of Hawaii
  Hilo *B*
  Manoa *B, M, D*

Illinois
City Colleges of Chicago
  Harold Washington College *A*
North Central College *B*

Indiana
Ball State University *B, T*
Indiana University
  Bloomington *M, D*
University of Notre Dame *B*

Iowa
Grinnell College *B*
University of Iowa *B, T*

Kansas
Butler County Community College *A*

Louisiana
Dillard University *B*

Maine
Bates College *B, T*

Maryland
University of Maryland
  College Park *B*

Massachusetts
Brandeis University *B*
Harvard College *B*
Tufts University *B*
University of Massachusetts
  Amherst *B, M*
Wellesley College *B*
Williams College *B*

Michigan
Aquinas College *B*
Eastern Michigan University *B*
University of Michigan *B, M, D*

Minnesota
Gustavus Adolphus College *B*
University of Minnesota
  Twin Cities *B, M, D*
University of St. Thomas *B*
Winona State University *A*

Missouri
Washington University in St.
  Louis *B, M, D*

Montana
University of Montana: Missoula *B*

New Hampshire
Dartmouth College *B*

New Jersey
Seton Hall University *T*

New York
Bard College *B*
Colgate University *B*
Columbia University
  Columbia College *B*
Hamilton College *B*
Hobart and William Smith Colleges *B*
University of Rochester *B*
Vassar College *B*

Ohio
Antioch College *B*
Mount Union College *B*
Ohio State University
  Columbus Campus *B, M, D*
University of Findlay *B*

Oklahoma
Tulsa Community College *A*

Oregon
Linfield College *B*
Pacific University *B*
Portland State University *B, T*
University of Oregon *B*

Pennsylvania
Carnegie Mellon University *B*
Elizabethtown College *B*
Gettysburg College *B*
Lincoln University *B*
Penn State
  Abington *B*
  Altoona *B*
  Beaver *B*
  Berks *B*
  Delaware County *B*

Dubois *B*
Fayette *B*
Hazleton *B*
Lehigh Valley *B*
McKeesport *B*
Mont Alto *B*
New Kensington *B*
Schuylkill - Capital College *B*
Shenango *B*
University Park *B*
Wilkes-Barre *B*
Worthington Scranton *B*
York *B*
University of Pittsburgh *B*
Ursinus College *T*

Texas

Austin Community College *A*

Utah

Brigham Young University *B, M*
Snow College *A*
University of Utah *B, M*

Vermont

Bennington College *B*
Middlebury College *B, M, D*

Washington

Central Washington University *B*
Everett Community College *A*
University of Puget Sound *T*
University of Washington *B*

Wisconsin

Lawrence University *B*
University of Wisconsin
Madison *B, M, D*

Japanese studies

California

University of California
San Diego *B*

Connecticut

Connecticut College *B*

Louisiana

Dillard University *B*

Massachusetts

Harvard College *B, D*

Michigan

Hope College *B*

Minnesota

Gustavus Adolphus College *B*

Missouri

William Jewell College *B*

New York

Columbia University
Columbia College *B*
Sarah Lawrence College *B*
State University of New York
Albany *B*

Ohio

Case Western Reserve University *B*

Oregon

Willamette University *B*

Pennsylvania

Gettysburg College *B*

Washington

University of Washington *B, M*

Wisconsin

Lawrence University *B*

Jazz studies

California

California Institute of the Arts *C, B, M*
California State University
Long Beach *B, M*
University of Southern
California *B, M, D*

Connecticut

University of Hartford *B*

District of Columbia

Howard University *B*

Florida

Florida State University *B, M*
Manatee Community College *A*
Palm Beach Community College *A*
University of Miami *B, M, D*
University of North Florida *B*

Illinois

Augustana College *B*
Columbia College Chicago *B*
North Central College *B*
Northwestern University *B, M*
Roosevelt University *B*

Indiana

American Conservatory of Music *A, B*
Indiana University
Bloomington *B*

Iowa

University of Iowa *B*
University of Northern Iowa *M*

Louisiana

Loyola University New Orleans *B, M*

Maine

University of Southern Maine *B*

Massachusetts

Berklee College of Music *B*
Boston Conservatory *M*
New England Conservatory of
Music *B, M, D*
Simon's Rock College of Bard *B*
Westfield State College *B*

Michigan

Hope College *B*
Michigan State University *B*
University of Michigan *B*
Western Michigan University *B*

Minnesota

St. Cloud State University *B*
University of Minnesota
Duluth *B*

Missouri

Drury University *B*
University of Missouri
Kansas City *B*
Webster University *M*

Nevada

University of Nevada
Las Vegas *B*

New Jersey

Rowan University *B*
Rutgers, The State University of New
Jersey
Newark Regional Campus *M*
William Paterson University of New
Jersey *B*

New York

Bard College *B*
Barnard College *B*
City University of New York
City College *B*
Columbia University
Columbia College *B*
Eastman School of Music of the
University of Rochester *B, M*
Eugene Lang College The New School
for Liberal Arts *B*
Five Towns College *A, B, M*
Hofstra University *B*
Ithaca College *B*
Juilliard School *B, D*
Sarah Lawrence College *B*
State University of New York
New Paltz *B*
University of Rochester *B, M, D*
Villa Maria College of Buffalo *A*

North Carolina

East Carolina University *B*
North Carolina Central University *B*
University of North Carolina
Greensboro *B*

Ohio

Bowling Green State University *B, M*
Capital University *B*
Central State University *B*
Oberlin College *B, M*
Ohio State University
Columbus Campus *B*
University of Cincinnati *B*
Youngstown State University *B, M*

Oregon

University of Oregon *B, M*

Pennsylvania

Temple University *B*
University of the Arts *B, M*

Puerto Rico

Conservatory of Music of Puerto
Rico *B*

Rhode Island

Community College of Rhode
Island *A*

South Carolina

Limestone College *B*
University of South Carolina *M*

Texas

Texas State University: San Marcos *B*
University of North Texas *B, M*

Utah

Brigham Young University *B*

Vermont

Bennington College *B*
Johnson State College *B*

Washington

Cornish College of the Arts *B*
Whitworth College *B*

Wisconsin

Lawrence University *B*

University of Wisconsin
Madison *B, M*

Journalism

Alabama

Alabama Agricultural and Mechanical
University *B*
Auburn University *B*
Faulkner State Community College *A*
Samford University *B*
Spring Hill College *B*
Talladega College *B*
Troy University *B*
University of Alabama *B, M*

Alaska

University of Alaska
Anchorage *B*
Fairbanks *B*

Arizona

Central Arizona College *B*
Cochise College *A*
Grand Canyon University *B*
Mesa Community College *A*
Northern Arizona University *B*
University of Arizona *B, M*

Arkansas

Arkansas State University *B, M*
Arkansas Tech University *B*
Harding University *B*
Henderson State University *B*
John Brown University *A, B*
University of Arkansas *B, M*
University of Arkansas
Little Rock *B, M*
University of Central Arkansas *B*

California

Alliant International University *B*
Azusa Pacific University *B*
Bakersfield College *A*
Butte College *C, A*
Cabrillo College *A*
California Baptist University *B*
California Lutheran University *B*
California Polytechnic State
University: San Luis Obispo *B*
California State University
Chico *B*
Dominguez Hills *B*
East Bay *B*
Fresno *B, M*
Fullerton *B, M*
Long Beach *B*
Northridge *B, M*
Sacramento *B*
Canada College *A*
Cerritos Community College *A*
Chabot College *A*
Chaffey College *C*
City College of San Francisco *A*
College of the Canyons *C, A*
College of the Desert *A*
College of the Redwoods *C, A*
College of the Sequoias *A*
Cosumnes River College *A*
Cuesta College *C, A*
Cypress College *A*
Diablo Valley College *C*
East Los Angeles College *A*
El Camino College *C, A*
Fresno City College *A*
Fullerton College *A*
Gavilan Community College *A*
Glendale Community College *A*
Golden West College *C, A*
Grossmont Community College *C, A*
Humboldt State University *B*
Imperial Valley College *A*
Laney College *A*

Lassen College *C, A*
Long Beach City College *C, A*
Los Angeles City College *A*
Los Angeles Pierce College *C, A*
Los Angeles Southwest College *A*
Los Angeles Trade and Technical
  College *C, A*
Los Angeles Valley College *C, A*
Los Medanos College *A*
Merced College *A*
Modesto Junior College *C, A*
Mount San Antonio College *A*
Ohlone College *C, A*
Pacific Union College *B*
Palomar College *C, A*
Pasadena City College *C, A*
Pepperdine University *B*
Point Loma Nazarene University *B*
Sacramento City College *C, A*
Saddleback College *C, A*
San Diego State University *B*
San Francisco State University *B*
San Joaquin Delta College *A*
San Jose State University *B*
Santa Ana College *C, A*
Santa Monica College *A*
Santa Rosa Junior College *C*
Shasta College *A*
Solano Community College *A*
Southwestern College *A*
Taft College *A*
University of California
  Berkeley *M*
  Irvine *B*
University of La Verne *B*
University of Southern
  California *B, M*
Ventura College *C, A*
Westmont College *B*
Yuba Community College
  District *C, A*

Colorado

Colorado Mountain College
  Alpine Campus *A*
Colorado State University *B, M*
Jones International University *C, B, M*
Mesa State College *B*
Metropolitan State College of
  Denver *B*
Northeastern Junior College *A*
Trinidad State Junior College *A*
University of Colorado
  Boulder *B, M*
University of Denver *B, M*
University of Northern Colorado *B*

Connecticut

Manchester Community College *A*
Norwalk Community College *A*
Quinnipiac University *B, M*
Southern Connecticut State
  University *B*
University of Bridgeport *B*
University of Connecticut *B*
University of New Haven *C*

Delaware

Delaware State University *B*
Delaware Technical and Community
  College
  Owens Campus *A*
University of Delaware *B*

District of Columbia

American University *B, M*
George Washington University *B*
Howard University *B*

Florida

Bethune-Cookman College *B*
Broward Community College *A*
Chipola College *A*

Edward Waters College *B*
Florida Agricultural and Mechanical
  University *B, M*
Florida Southern College *B*
Gulf Coast Community College *A*
Hillsborough Community College *A*
Manatee Community College *A*
Miami Dade College *A*
Palm Beach Atlantic University *B*
Palm Beach Community College *A*
Pensacola Junior College *A*
University of Central Florida *B*
University of Florida *B*
University of Miami *B, M*
Valencia Community College *A*

Georgia

Abraham Baldwin Agricultural
  College *A*
Albany State University *B*
Andrew College *A*
Clark Atlanta University *B*
Dalton State College *A*
Darton College *A*
Emory University *B*
Fort Valley State University *B*
Gainesville State College *A*
Georgia College and State
  University *B*
Georgia Highlands College *A*
Georgia Perimeter College *A*
Georgia Southern University *B*
Georgia State University *B*
Macon State College *A*
Mercer University *B*
Middle Georgia College *A*
Paine College *B*
South Georgia College *A*
University of Georgia *B, M*
University of West Georgia *B*

Hawaii

Hawaii Pacific University *B*
University of Hawaii
  Manoa *B*

Idaho

Boise State University *B, T*
Brigham Young University-Idaho *B*
North Idaho College *A*
Northwest Nazarene University *B*
University of Idaho *B*

Illinois

Black Hawk College
  East Campus *A*
Bradley University *B*
City Colleges of Chicago
  Harold Washington College *A*
  Kennedy-King College *A*
College of DuPage *C*
Columbia College Chicago *B, M*
Danville Area Community College *A*
Dominican University *B*
Eastern Illinois University *B*
Governors State University *B, M*
Illinois Central College *A*
Illinois State University *B*
Illinois Valley Community College *A*
John A. Logan College *A*
Judson College *B*
Kishwaukee College *A*
Lake Land College *A*
Lewis University *B*
Loyola University of Chicago *B*
MacMurray College *B*
North Central College *B*
Northern Illinois University *B*
Northwestern University *B, M*
Olivet Nazarene University *B*
Quincy University *B*
Richland Community College *A*
Roosevelt University *B, M*

Sauk Valley Community College *A*
Southern Illinois University
  Carbondale *A*
Triton College *A*
University of Illinois
  Springfield *M*
  Urbana-Champaign *B, M*
Western Illinois University *B*
William Rainey Harper College *C, A*

Indiana

Anderson University *B*
Ball State University *B, M, T*
Bethel College *A*
Butler University *B*
Franklin College *B*
Grace College *B*
Huntington University *B*
Indiana State University *B*
Indiana University
  Bloomington *B, M, D, T*
  Southeast *A, B*
Indiana University-Purdue University
  Indianapolis *B*
Manchester College *B*
Purdue University
  Calumet *B*
St. Mary-of-the-Woods College *B*
Taylor University *B*
University of Southern Indiana *B*
Valparaiso University *B*
Vincennes University *A*

Iowa

Dordt College *B*
Drake University *B*
Grand View College *B*
Iowa Lakes Community College *C, A*
Iowa State University *B, M*
Iowa Wesleyan College *B*
Loras College *B*
Marshalltown Community College *A*
Morningside College *B*
St. Ambrose University *B*
Simpson College *B*
University of Iowa *B, M, D, T*
Waldorf College *B*
Wartburg College *B, T*
William Penn University *B*

Kansas

Baker University *T*
Barton County Community College *A*
Butler County Community College *A*
Central Christian College of
  Kansas *A, B*
Coffeyville Community College *A*
Colby Community College *A*
Cowley County Community
  College *A*
Dodge City Community College *A*
Emporia State University *T*
Garden City Community College *A*
Haskell Indian Nations University *A*
Kansas State University *B, M*
Labette Community College *A*
Pittsburg State University *B*
Pratt Community College *A*
Seward County Community College *A*
Tabor College *B*
University of Kansas *B, M*

Kentucky

Asbury College *B*
Campbellsville University *B*
Eastern Kentucky University *B*
Lindsey Wilson College *B*
Murray State University *B*
Northern Kentucky University *B*
University of Kentucky *B*
Western Kentucky University *B*

Louisiana

Grambling State University *B, M*
Louisiana State University
  Shreveport *B*
Louisiana Tech University *B*
Nicholls State University *B*
Northwestern State University *B*

Maine

St. Joseph's College *B*
University of Maine *B*
University of Southern Maine *B*

Maryland

Bowie State University *B*
Columbia Union College *B*
Community College of Baltimore
  County *A*
Towson University *B, M*
University of Maryland
  College Park *B, M, D*

Massachusetts

American International College *B*
Boston University *B, M*
Cape Cod Community College *A*
Eastern Nazarene College *B*
Emerson College *B, M*
Hampshire College *B*
Massachusetts College of Liberal
  Arts *B*
Mount Ida College *B*
Newbury College *A*
Northeastern University *B, M*
Salem State College *B*
Suffolk University *B*
University of Massachusetts
  Amherst *B*
Westfield State College *B*

Michigan

Adrian College *B*
Andrews University *B*
Bay de Noc Community College *C*
Central Michigan University *B*
Concordia University *B*
Delta College *A*
Eastern Michigan University *B*
Grand Valley State University *B*
Hillsdale College *B*
Kellogg Community College *A*
Kuyper College *B*
Lake Michigan College *A*
Lansing Community College *A*
Madonna University *A, B*
Michigan State University *B, M*
Northern Michigan University *B*
Oakland University *B*
Olivet College *B*
St. Clair County Community
  College *A*
Schoolcraft College *A*
University of Detroit Mercy *B*
University of Michigan *M, D*
Wayne State University *B*
Western Michigan University *B*

Minnesota

Bemidji State University *B*
Bethel University *B*
Concordia College: Moorhead *B*
Minnesota State University
  Mankato *B*
North Central University *B*
Northland Community & Technical
  College *A*
Northwestern College *B*
Ridgewater College *A*
St. Cloud State University *B*
St. Mary's University of Minnesota *B*
University of Minnesota
  Twin Cities *B, M, D*
University of St. Thomas *B*

Vermilion Community College *A*
Winona State University *B*

Mississippi

Coahoma Community College *A*
Delta State University *B*
Hinds Community College *A*
Itawamba Community College *A*
Mississippi College *B*
Rust College *B*
University of Mississippi *B, M*
University of Southern Mississippi *B*
William Carey College *B*

Missouri

Central Missouri State University *B, M*
College of the Ozarks *B*
Crowder College *A*
Culver-Stockton College *B*
Drury University *B*
Evangel University *A, B*
Lincoln University *B*
Missouri State University *B*
Moberly Area Community College *A*
Northwest Missouri State
    University *B*
Rockhurst University *C*
St. Louis Community College
    St. Louis Community College at
        Florissant Valley *A*
State Fair Community College *A*
Stephens College *B*
Truman State University *B*
University of Missouri
    Columbia *B, M, D*
    Kansas City *B*
Washington University in St. Louis *B*
Webster University *B*
Westminster College *B*
William Woods University *B*

Montana

Miles Community College *A*
University of Montana: Missoula *B, M*

Nebraska

Creighton University *A, B*
Doane College *B*
Grace University *B*
Hastings College *B, T*
Midland Lutheran College *B, T*
Northeast Community College *A*
Union College *B*
University of Nebraska
    Kearney *B*
    Lincoln *B, M*
    Omaha *B*
Wayne State College *B, T*
Western Nebraska Community
    College *A*

Nevada

University of Nevada
    Reno *B, M*

New Hampshire

Franklin Pierce College *B*
Keene State College *B*
Rivier College *B*
University of New Hampshire *B*

New Jersey

The College of New Jersey *B*
Cumberland County College *A*
Essex County College *A*
Felician College *B*
Gloucester County College *A*
Middlesex County College *A*
Ocean County College *A*
Rider University *B*
Rowan University *B*

Rutgers, The State University of New
    Jersey
    New Brunswick/Piscataway
        Campus *B*
    Newark Regional Campus *B*
Salem Community College *A*
Sussex County Community College *A*
Thomas Edison State College *B*

New Mexico

Eastern New Mexico University *B*
New Mexico State University *B*
University of New Mexico *B*

New York

Adelphi University *B*
City University of New York
    Baruch College *B, M*
    Brooklyn College *B*
    City College *B*
    Kingsborough Community
        College *A*
Five Towns College *B*
Fulton-Montgomery Community
    College *C, A*
Hofstra University *B*
Iona College *B, M*
Ithaca College *B*
Long Island University
    Brooklyn Campus *B*
    C.W. Post Campus *B*
Manhattan College *B*
Marist College *B*
New York Institute of Technology *M*
New York University *B, M*
Polytechnic University *B, M*
St. Bonaventure University *B*
St. John Fisher College *B*
St. John's University *B, M*
St. Thomas Aquinas College *B*
State University of New York
    College at Brockport *B*
    College at Buffalo *B*
    College at Cortland *B*
    College at Plattsburgh *B*
    College of Agriculture and
        Technology at Morrisville *A*
    New Paltz *B*
    Oswego *B*
    Purchase *B*
Syracuse University *B, M, D*
Utica College *B*

North Carolina

Appalachian State University *B*
Bennett College *B*
Campbell University *B*
Elon University *B*
Gardner-Webb University *B*
North Carolina Agricultural and
    Technical State University *B*
Queens University of Charlotte *B*
Wingate University *B*

Ohio

Ashland University *B*
Bowling Green State University *B*
Cleveland State University *C*
Defiance College *B*
Kent State University *B, M*
Malone College *B*
Marietta College *B*
Miami University
    Oxford Campus *B*
Mount Vernon Nazarene University *B*
Muskingum College *B*
Ohio Northern University *B*
Ohio State University
    Columbus Campus *B, M*
Ohio University *B, M, D*
Ohio University
    Southern Campus at Ironton *A*
Ohio Wesleyan University *B*

Otterbein College *B*
University of Cincinnati
    Raymond Walters College *C*
University of Dayton *B*
University of Findlay *B*
University of Rio Grande *B*
Wilmington College *B*
Youngstown State University *B*

Oklahoma

Bacone College *A*
Cameron University *B*
Carl Albert State College *A*
Connors State College *A*
East Central University *B*
Eastern Oklahoma State College *A*
Northeastern Oklahoma Agricultural
    and Mechanical College *A*
Northeastern State University *B*
Northwestern Oklahoma State
    University *B*
Oklahoma Baptist University *B*
Oklahoma Christian University *B*
Oklahoma City Community College *A*
Oklahoma City University *B*
Oklahoma State University *B*
Rose State College *A*
St. Gregory's University *A, B*
Southeastern Oklahoma State
    University *B*
Southern Nazarene University *B*
Tulsa Community College *A*
University of Central Oklahoma *B*
University of Oklahoma *B, M*

Oregon

Chemeketa Community College *A*
Corban College *B*
Lane Community College *C, A*
Linn-Benton Community College *A*
Mount Hood Community College *A*
Multnomah Bible College *B*
Pacific University *B*
Southern Oregon University *B*
Umpqua Community College *C*
University of Oregon *B*

Pennsylvania

Allegheny College *B*
Bucks County Community College *A*
Community College of Allegheny
    County *A*
Delaware County Community
    College *A*
Duquesne University *B*
Edinboro University of
    Pennsylvania *B*
Gettysburg College *B*
Indiana University of Pennsylvania *B*
Keystone College *A, B*
La Salle University *B*
Lehigh University *B*
Lincoln University *B*
Lock Haven University of
    Pennsylvania *B*
Luzerne County Community
    College *A*
Mansfield University of
    Pennsylvania *A, B*
Messiah College *B*
Northampton County Area
    Community College *A*
Penn State
    Abington *B*
    Altoona *B*
    Beaver *B*
    Berks *B*
    Delaware County *B*
    Dubois *B*
    Fayette *B*
    Hazleton *B*
    Lehigh Valley *B*
    McKeesport *B*
    Mont Alto *B*

New Kensington *B*
Schuylkill - Capital College *B*
Shenango *B*
University Park *B*
Wilkes-Barre *B*
Worthington Scranton *B*
York *B*
Point Park University *B, M*
Seton Hill University *B*
Shippensburg University of
    Pennsylvania *B*
Susquehanna University *B*
Temple University *B, M*
University of Pittsburgh
    Greensburg *B*
    Johnstown *B*
Waynesburg College *B*

Puerto Rico

Bayamon Central University *B*
Inter American University of Puerto
    Rico
    Ponce Campus *B*
Universidad Metropolitana *B*
University of the Sacred Heart *B, M*

Rhode Island

Roger Williams University *B*
University of Rhode Island *B*

South Carolina

Anderson University *B*
Columbia College *B*
Morris College *B*
North Greenville College *B*
University of South Carolina *B, M, D*
University of South Carolina
    Aiken *B*
Winthrop University *B*

South Dakota

Augustana College *B*
Dakota Wesleyan University *B*
South Dakota State University *B, M*
University of Sioux Falls *B*
University of South Dakota *B, M*

Tennessee

Austin Peay State University *B, M*
Belmont University *B*
Carson-Newman College *B*
Columbia State Community College *A*
Lee University *B*
Lipscomb University *B*
Southern Adventist University *B*
Tennessee State University *B*
Tennessee Technological University *B*
Tusculum College *B*
Union University *B*
University of Memphis *B, M*
University of Tennessee
    Knoxville *B*

Texas

Abilene Christian University *B*
Amarillo College *A*
Angelo State University *B, T*
Austin Community College *A*
Baylor University *B, M, T*
College of the Mainland *A*
Del Mar College *A*
El Paso Community College *A*
Hill College *C, A*
Howard College *A*
Jarvis Christian College *B*
Kilgore College *A*
Midland College *A*
Navarro College *A*
Northeast Texas Community
    College *A*
Northwest Vista College *A*
Our Lady of the Lake University of San
    Antonio *B*

Palo Alto College *A*
Paris Junior College *A*
Sam Houston State University *B*
San Antonio College *A*
San Jacinto College
    North *A*
South Plains College *A*
Southern Methodist University *B*
Southwestern Adventist University *B*
Stephen F. Austin State
    University *B, M, T*
Texarkana College *A*
Texas A&M University *B, M*
Texas A&M University
    Commerce *B*
Texas Christian University *B*
Texas Southern University *B*
Texas State University: San Marcos *B*
Texas Tech University *B, M*
Texas Wesleyan University *B*
Texas Woman's University *B*
Trinity Valley Community College *A*
Tyler Junior College *A*
University of Houston *B, M*
University of North Texas *B, M*
University of Texas
    Arlington *B*
    Austin *B, M, D*
    El Paso *B*
    Pan American *B*
    Tyler *B*
West Texas A&M University *B*
Western Texas College *A*
Wiley College *B*

Utah
Brigham Young University *B*
Dixie State College of Utah *A*
Snow College *A*
Southern Utah University *B*
Utah State University *B, M*
Weber State University *B*

Vermont
Bennington College *B*
Castleton State College *B*
Champlain College *A, B*
Green Mountain College *B*
Johnson State College *B*
Lyndon State College *B*
St. Michael's College *B*

Virginia
Averett University *B*
Bluefield College *B*
Hampton University *B*
Liberty University *B*
Norfolk State University *B*
Radford University *B, M*
Regent University *M*
Southwest Virginia Community
    College *C*
University of Richmond *B*
Virginia Union University *B*
Washington and Lee University *B*

Washington
Central Washington University *B*
Centralia College *A*
City University *B*
Eastern Washington University *B*
Everett Community College *A*
Gonzaga University *B*
Highline Community College *A*
Peninsula College *A*
Seattle University *B*
Spokane Falls Community College *A*
Walla Walla College *B*
Western Washington University *B*
Whitworth College *B*

West Virginia
Bethany College *B*

Concord University *B*
Marshall University *B, M*
Mountain State University *M*
Potomac State College of West Virginia
    University *A*
University of Charleston *B*
West Virginia University *B, M, T*
West Virginia University at
    Parkersburg *A*

Wisconsin
Carroll College *B*
Marquette University *B, M*
University of Wisconsin
    Eau Claire *B*
    Madison *B, M, D*
    Milwaukee *B, M*
    Oshkosh *B*
    River Falls *B, T*
    Superior *B*
    Whitewater *B*

Wyoming
Laramie County Community
    College *A*
Northwest College *A*
University of Wyoming *B*
Western Wyoming Community
    College *A*

Judaic studies

Arizona
University of Arizona *B*

California
California State University
    Chico *B*
Scripps College *B*
University of California
    Berkeley *D*
    Los Angeles *B*
    San Diego *B, M*
University of Judaism *B*
University of Southern California *B*

Colorado
University of Denver *M*

Connecticut
Trinity College *B*
University of Connecticut *M*
University of Hartford *B*
Yale University *B*

District of Columbia
American University *B*
George Washington University *B*

Florida
Florida Atlantic University *B*
University of Florida *B*
University of Miami *B*
Yeshiva Gedolah Rabbinical
    College *B, M*

Georgia
Emory University *B, M*

Illinois
DePaul University *B*
Moody Bible Institute *B*
University of Chicago *B*

Indiana
Indiana University
    Bloomington *B*

Louisiana
Tulane University *B*

Maryland
Baltimore Hebrew University *B, M, D*
University of Maryland
    College Park *B*
Yeshiva College of the Nations
    Capital *B*

Massachusetts
Brandeis University *B, M, D*
Hampshire College *B*
Hebrew College *B, M, T*
University of Massachusetts
    Amherst *B*
Wellesley College *B*

Michigan
Michigan Jewish Institute *B*
University of Michigan *B*

Minnesota
University of Minnesota
    Twin Cities *B*

Missouri
Washington University in St.
    Louis *B, M*

New Jersey
Rabbinical College of America *B*
Rutgers, The State University of New
    Jersey
    New Brunswick/Piscataway
        Campus *B*

New York
Bard College *B*
City University of New York
    Brooklyn College *B, M*
    City College *B*
    Hunter College *B*
    Lehman College *B*
    Queens College *B*
Hofstra University *B*
Jewish Theological Seminary of
    America *B, M, D*
New York University *B, M, D*
Sarah Lawrence College *B*
State University of New York
    Albany *B*
    Binghamton *B*
Touro College *B, M*
Vassar College *B*
Yeshiva Mikdash Melech *B, M*
Yeshiva University *A, B, M, D, T*

Ohio
Laura and Alvin Siegal College of
    Judaic Studies *B, M*
Oberlin College *B*
Ohio State University
    Columbus Campus *B*
University of Cincinnati *B*

Oregon
University of Oregon *B*

Pennsylvania
Dickinson College *B*
Gratz College *B, M*
Penn State
    Abington *B*
    Altoona *B*
    Beaver *B*
    Berks *B*
    Delaware County *B*
    Dubois *B*
    Fayette *B*
    Hazleton *B*
    Lehigh Valley *B*
    McKeesport *B*
    Mont Alto *B*
    New Kensington *B*

    Schuylkill - Capital College *B*
    Shenango *B*
    University Park *B*
    Worthington Scranton *B*
    York *B*
Temple University *B*
University of Pennsylvania *B*
University of Pittsburgh *C*
West Chester University of
    Pennsylvania *C*

Rhode Island
Brown University *B*

Texas
University of Texas
    Austin *B*

Vermont
Goddard College *B*

Washington
University of Washington *B*

Wisconsin
University of Wisconsin
    Madison *M, D*

Juvenile corrections

Arizona
Arizona Western College *C*

California
Santa Rosa Junior College *C*

Illinois
Kaskaskia College *A*
Westwood College of Technology
    O'Hare *B*

Missouri
Harris-Stowe State University *B*

Montana
University of Great Falls *B*

Nevada
Truckee Meadows Community
    College *A*

New Hampshire
McIntosh College *A*

Oklahoma
University of Central Oklahoma *B*

Oregon
Central Oregon Community
    College *C*
Clatsop Community College *C*
Linn-Benton Community College *C*
Rogue Community College *C*

Pennsylvania
Gannon University *C*

South Carolina
South University *B*

Texas
Prairie View A&M University *M, D*

Kindergarten/preschool education

Alabama
Gadsden State Community College *A*
Troy University *B, M, T*

Arkansas

Ozarka College C
South Arkansas Community College A

California

California State University
   Fullerton B
   Los Angeles B, M
Santa Barbara City College C, A
Southwestern College C, A

Colorado

Naropa University B

Connecticut

Central Connecticut State
   University M
Connecticut College T
Mitchell College B
St. Joseph College B

Florida

Manatee Community College C, A
Seminole Community College C, A
University of Miami M

Georgia

Dalton State College C
Darton College A
Georgia Southern University B
University of Georgia B, M, D

Illinois

Columbia College Chicago B
DePaul University B
Elmhurst College B
University of Illinois
   Urbana-Champaign B, M, D, T

Indiana

Ball State University B, T
Butler University B
Indiana University
   South Bend A
Purdue University B
St. Mary-of-the-Woods College B, T

Iowa

Iowa State University B
University of Northern Iowa B, M
Upper Iowa University B

Kansas

Emporia State University M
Tabor College B, T

Kentucky

Northern Kentucky University B, M
Western Kentucky University A, M

Maine

University of Maine
   Farmington B, T

Maryland

University of Maryland
   College Park B

Massachusetts

Bristol Community College A
Cape Cod Community College A
Lesley University B, M
North Shore Community College A
Worcester State College B, M, T

Michigan

Alma College T
Baker College
   of Muskegon B
Delta College A
Western Michigan University M

Minnesota

Bethel University B
Concordia University: St. Paul B, T
Metropolitan State University B
Minnesota State University
   Moorhead B
Vermilion Community College A

Missouri

Southeast Missouri State University B

Montana

University of Great Falls A, B

Nevada

Community College of Southern
   Nevada A

New Jersey

Caldwell College T
Essex County College A
Kean University -B, M, T
William Paterson University of New
   Jersey T

New Mexico

Santa Fe Community College A

New York

Adelphi University M, T
City University of New York
   Brooklyn College B, M
   Hunter College M, T
Dutchess Community College A
Long Island University
   C.W. Post Campus B, M, T
Mercy College M, T
St. Joseph's College: Suffolk
   Campus B, T
Sarah Lawrence College M
Tompkins-Cortland Community
   College A

North Carolina

Appalachian State University B, M
Meredith College T
North Carolina Central University B, T
University of North Carolina
   Chapel Hill M
   Charlotte B, M
   Pembroke B
   Wilmington B
Western Carolina University B

Ohio

Ashland University B, M, T
Bluffton University B
Bowling Green State University B, T
John Carroll University T
Miami University
   Hamilton Campus A
   Oxford Campus B
Ohio Wesleyan University B
Shawnee State University B
University of Cincinnati
   Clermont College A
University of Findlay B, M, T
University of Toledo B
Youngstown State University B

Pennsylvania

Butler County Community College A
California University of
   Pennsylvania A, B
Kutztown University of
   Pennsylvania B
Lock Haven University of
   Pennsylvania A, B, T
Seton Hill University T
Temple University M

Puerto Rico

Inter American University of Puerto
   Rico
   Guayama Campus B, M
National College of Business &
   Technology: Arecibo B
National College of Business &
   Technology: Bayamon B
University of Puerto Rico
   Bayamon University College B

Rhode Island

Community College of Rhode
   Island A

South Dakota

Black Hills State University B
University of South Dakota B

Tennessee

Middle Tennessee State University B

Texas

Mountain View College A
North Harris Montgomery
   Community College District A
North Lake College A
South Texas College C

Utah

Utah Valley State College C, B

Vermont

Champlain College A, B
University of Vermont B

Washington

Washington State University B, T
Yakima Valley Community College C

West Virginia

Glenville State College B
West Virginia Wesleyan College B

Wisconsin

College of Menominee Nation A
Concordia University Wisconsin B
Edgewood College B, T
Lakeland College B

Kinesiotherapy

Massachusetts

Bridgewater State College B, M

Texas

University of Houston B

Knowledge
management

Florida

University of Tampa M

New York

Rochester Institute of Technology D

Ohio

Kent State University M

Oklahoma

University of Oklahoma M

Pennsylvania

Penn State
   York B
York College of Pennsylvania B

Texas

Texas A&M University M, D

Korean

California

University of California
   Los Angeles B

Hawaii

University of Hawaii
   Manoa B, M, D

New York

Columbia University
   Columbia College B

Utah

Brigham Young University B

Washington

University of Washington B

Korean studies

New York

Columbia University
   Columbia College B

Washington

University of Washington B, M

Labor/industrial
relations

Alabama

Wallace State Community College at
   Hanceville A

California

California State University
   Dominguez Hills B
   San Bernardino M
Los Angeles Trade and Technical
   College C, A
Los Medanos College C, A
San Diego City College A
San Francisco State University B

Connecticut

University of Bridgeport B, M
University of New Haven M

Illinois

Loyola University of Chicago M
Northwestern University M
Roosevelt University B
University of Illinois
   Urbana-Champaign M, D

Indiana

Indiana University
   Bloomington C, A, B
   Kokomo C, A, B
   Northwest C, A, B
   South Bend C, A, B
   Southeast A, B
Indiana University-Purdue University
   Indianapolis A, B
Purdue University
   North Central Campus A, B

Iowa

University of Iowa B

Kentucky

Northern Kentucky University B

Maine
University of Maine *B*

Maryland
Community College of Baltimore
County *C, A*
National Labor College *B*

Massachusetts
University of Massachusetts
Amherst *M*
Boston *C, B*

Michigan
Michigan State University *M*
Wayne County Community College *A*
Wayne State University *M*

Minnesota
University of Minnesota
Twin Cities *C, B, M, D*
Winona State University *B*

New Jersey
Rowan University *B*
Rutgers, The State University of New
Jersey
New Brunswick/Piscataway
Campus *B, M, D*
Seton Hall University *B*
Thomas Edison State College *C, B*

New York
City University of New York
Baruch College *B, M*
Cornell University *B, M, D*
Le Moyne College *B*
New York Institute of Technology *M*
Onondaga Community College *A*
State University of New York
College at Old Westbury *B*
College at Potsdam *B*
Empire State College *A, B, M*
Stony Brook *M*
Tompkins-Cortland Community
College *A*

Ohio
Case Western Reserve University *M, D*
Cincinnati State Technical and
Community College *C*
Cleveland State University *B, M, D*
Edison State Community College *C, A*
Sinclair Community College *C, A*
Youngstown State University *A*

Pennsylvania
Clarion University of Pennsylvania *B*
Indiana University of Pennsylvania *M*
La Salle University *B*
Penn State
Abington *B*
Altoona *B*
Beaver *B*
Berks *B*
Delaware County *B*
Dubois *B*
Fayette *B*
Hazleton *B*
Lehigh Valley *B*
McKeesport *B*
Mont Alto *B*
New Kensington *B*
Schuylkill - Capital College *B*
Shenango *B*
University Park *B, M*
Wilkes-Barre *B*
Worthington Scranton *B*
York *B*
St. Francis University *M*
Temple University *B, M*

Puerto Rico
Inter American University of Puerto
Rico
San German Campus *M, D*
University of Puerto Rico
Rio Piedras *B*

Rhode Island
Rhode Island College *B*
University of Rhode Island *M*

Tennessee
Tennessee Technological University *B*

Texas
College of the Mainland *A*
University of North Texas *B, M, D*

West Virginia
Marshall University *M*
West Virginia University *M*

Wisconsin
Marquette University *C*
University of Wisconsin
Milwaukee *M*

Labor studies

California
San Jose City College *C, A*

Indiana
Indiana University
South Bend *C, A, B*
Indiana University-Purdue University
Fort Wayne *C, A, B*
Indiana University-Purdue University
Indianapolis *C, A, B*

Maryland
National Labor College *B*

Michigan
Eastern Michigan University *B*
Michigan State University *D*

New York
City University of New York
Queens College *B*
Hofstra University *B*

Ohio
Sinclair Community College *A*

Rhode Island
University of Rhode Island *C*

Wisconsin
University of Wisconsin
Madison *M*

LAN/WAN management

Alabama
Gadsden State Community College *A*
Herzing College *A, B*

Alaska
University of Alaska
Southeast *C*

Arizona
Arizona Western College *C*
Collins College *A, B*
Estrella Mountain Community
College *C, A*
Gateway Community College *C, A*

Glendale Community College *C, A*
University of Advancing
Technology *A, B*

Arkansas
Northwest Arkansas Community
College *A*
Phillips Community College of the
University of Arkansas *C, A*
Pulaski Technical College *A*
Rich Mountain Community College *A*

California
CEI College
Maric College: Panorama City *A*
DeVry University
Fremont *A*
Pomona *A*
Foothill College *C, A*
Golden Gate University *M*
Grossmont Community College *C, A*
Maric College
Vista *A*
MiraCosta College *C, A*
Monterey Peninsula College *C, A*
Ohlone College *C, A*
Platt College
Ontario *A*
San Diego Mesa College *C*
Santa Barbara Business College
Bakersfield *C, A*
Santa Barbara City College *C*
Santa Rosa Junior College *C*
Southwestern College *C*
Westwood College of Technology
Inland Empire *B*
Westwood College: Long Beach *A, B*

Colorado
Arapahoe Community College *C, A*
Blair College *C, A*
Colorado Technical University *C*
National American University
Denver *B*
Pikes Peak Community College *C, A*
Red Rocks Community College *C*
Westwood College of Technology
South *B*

Florida
Central Florida Community College *A*
DeVry University
Miramar *B*
Orlando *B*
Herzing College
Orlando *C, A*
International Academy of Design and
Technology: Orlando *B*
Remington College: Largo *A, B*
St. Petersburg College *C*
South Florida Community
College *C, A*
Southwest Florida College *C*

Georgia
Bauder College *C*
Northwestern Technical College *C, A*

Idaho
College of Southern Idaho *C, A*

Illinois
Lake Land College *A*
Lewis and Clark Community
College *A*
Moraine Valley Community
College *C, A*
Morrison Institute of Technology *A*
Oakton Community College *C*
Rend Lake College *C, A*
Southeastern Illinois College *A*
Westwood College - Chicago Loop *A*
William Rainey Harper College *C*

Indiana
Indiana University-Purdue University
Indianapolis *A*
International Business College *A*
Vincennes University *A*

Iowa
Dordt College *B*
Ellsworth Community College *C, A*
Hamilton College
Cedar Falls *C*
Kirkwood Community College *C*
St. Ambrose University *B*

Kansas
Labette Community College *C, A*

Kentucky
Hopkinsville Community College *C, A*
Louisville Technical Institute *A*

Maine
Central Maine Community College *A*

Maryland
Hagerstown Business College *A*

Massachusetts
Cape Cod Community College *A*
North Shore Community College *C*

Michigan
Alpena Community College *C, A*
Baker College
of Muskegon *C, A*
Grand Rapids Community College *C*
Kettering University *B*
Oakland Community College *C*
Washtenaw Community College *C, A*

Minnesota
Capella University *C, B*
Globe College *C, A, B*
Rasmussen College
St. Cloud *C, A*
Riverland Community College *A*
University of Minnesota
Crookston *B*

Missouri
Grantham University *A, B*
Missouri Technical School *C, A, B*
Ozarks Technical Community
College *A*
Ranken Technical College *A*
Vatterott College *B*

Montana
Montana State University
Billings *A*
Montana Tech of the University of
Montana *C, A*
University of Great Falls *B*

Nevada
Community College of Southern
Nevada *A*
Great Basin College *A*
Western Nevada Community
College *C, A*

New Hampshire
Daniel Webster College *C*

New Jersey
Gloucester County College *C, A*
Ocean County College *A*

New Mexico
New Mexico State University
Alamogordo *C*

Southwestern Indian Polytechnic
Institute *C, A*

New York

College of Westchester *A*
Columbia-Greene Community
College *A*
DeVry Institute of Technology
New York *A*
Globe Institute of Technology *C, A, B*
Rochester Institute of
Technology *B, M*
State University of New York
College of Agriculture and
Technology at Cobleskill *B*
College of Agriculture and
Technology at Morrisville *B*
Technical Career Institutes *A*
Trocaire College *A*
Westchester Community College *C, A*

North Carolina

Carteret Community College *C, A*
Catawba Valley Community College *A*
Central Piedmont Community
College *C, A*
Fayetteville Technical Community
College *C, A*
Miller-Motte Technical College *C, A*
Stanly Community College *C, A*
Surry Community College *C, A*
Wilkes Community College *C, A*

North Dakota

North Dakota State College of
Science *C, A*

Ohio

Bradford School *A*
Cincinnati Christian University *B*
Clark State Community College *A*
Davis College *A*
James A. Rhodes State College *A*
Lakeland Community College *A*
Marion Technical College *A*
Stautzenberger College *C, A*
University of Akron: Wayne College *C*
Youngstown State University *C*

Oklahoma

Oklahoma State University
Oklahoma City *A*
Rose State College *A*
Vatterott College *C, A*
Vatterott College
Tulsa *A*

Oregon

DeVry University: Portland *M*
Southwestern Oregon Community
College *C*

Pennsylvania

Consolidated School of Business
York *A*
DeVry University
Ft. Washington *A, B, M*
ICM School of Business & Medical
Careers *A*
Keystone College *C, A, B*
Lehigh Valley College *A*
Peirce College *C, A*
South Hills School of Business &
Technology *C, A*

South Carolina

York Technical College *C, A*

South Dakota

Southeast Technical Institute *A*

Tennessee

Northeast State Technical Community
College *C*
Pellissippi State Technical Community
College *C*
South College *A*

Texas

Del Mar College *C, A*
MTI College of Business and
Technology *C*
Mountain View College *C, A*
St. Philip's College *C, A*
San Antonio College *C, A*
Temple College *C, A*
Texas State Technical College:
Marshall *C, A*
Western Texas College *C, A*
Wharton County Junior College *C, A*

Utah

Salt Lake Community College *C*
Stevens-Henager College *A*

Vermont

Champlain College *A, B*
Vermont Technical College *A, B*

Virginia

ECPI College of Technology *C, A*
Piedmont Virginia Community
College *C, A*
Rappahannock Community College *C*

Washington

Centralia College *C, A*
Clover Park Technical College *C, A*
North Seattle Community
College *C, A*
South Seattle Community College *C, A*
Yakima Valley Community College *C*

Wisconsin

Mid-State Technical College *A*
Western Wisconsin Technical
College *A*

Wyoming

Laramie County Community
College *C, A*

Land use planning

California

California State University
Bakersfield *B*
Chico *M*

Colorado

Metropolitan State College of
Denver *B*

Louisiana

University of Louisiana at Lafayette *B*

Maine

University of Maine
Farmington *B*

Michigan

Northern Michigan University *B*

Nevada

University of Nevada
Reno *M*

Pennsylvania

Keystone College *A*

Texas

Texas State University: San Marcos *M*
Texas Tech University *D*

Utah

Brigham Young University *M*

Vermont

Sterling College *B*

Washington

Washington State University *M*

Wisconsin

University of Wisconsin
Madison *M, D*

Landscape architecture

Alabama

Auburn University *B, M*

Arizona

Arizona State University *B*
University of Arizona *M, D*

Arkansas

University of Arkansas *B*
University of Arkansas
Little Rock *A*

California

American River College *A*
California Polytechnic State
University: San Luis Obispo *B*
California State Polytechnic
University: Pomona *B, M*
City College of San Francisco *A*
Cosumnes River College *C, A*
Diablo Valley College *C*
East Los Angeles College *A*
Fullerton College *A*
MiraCosta College *C, A*
Modesto Junior College *A*
San Diego Mesa College *C, A*
San Joaquin Delta College *C, A*
Santa Rosa Junior College *C*
Southwestern College *C, A*
University of California
Berkeley *B, M*
Davis *B*
University of Southern
California *B, M*
West Valley College *A*

Colorado

Colorado State University *B, M, D*
University of Colorado
Denver and Health Sciences
Center *M*

Connecticut

University of Connecticut *B*

Florida

Broward Community College *A*
Florida Agricultural and Mechanical
University *M*
Florida International University *M*
Lake City Community College *A*
University of Florida *B, M*

Georgia

University of Georgia *B, M*

Idaho

University of Idaho *B, M*

Illinois

Kishwaukee College *A*

University of Illinois
Urbana-Champaign *B, D*

Indiana

Ball State University *B, M*
Purdue University *B*

Iowa

Iowa State University *B, M*

Kansas

Kansas State University *B, M*

Kentucky

University of Kentucky *B*

Louisiana

Louisiana State University and
Agricultural and Mechanical
College *B, M*

Maine

University of Maine *B*

Maryland

Community College of Baltimore
County *C, A*
Morgan State University *M*
University of Maryland
College Park *B*

Massachusetts

Harvard College *M*
University of Massachusetts
Amherst *B, M*

Michigan

Bay de Noc Community College *A*
Lansing Community College *A*
Michigan State University *B*
University of Michigan *B, M, D*

Minnesota

University of Minnesota
Twin Cities *B, M*

Mississippi

Mississippi State University *B, M*

Missouri

Washington University in St. Louis *M*

Nevada

Truckee Meadows Community
College *A*
University of Nevada
Las Vegas *B*

New Hampshire

University of New Hampshire *A*

New Jersey

Cumberland County College *C*

New Mexico

University of New Mexico *M*

New York

Bard College *M*
City University of New York
City College *M*
Cornell University *B, M, D*
Monroe Community College *A*
Parsons The New School for Design *B*
State University of New York
College of Agriculture and
Technology at Morrisville *A*
College of Environmental Science
and Forestry *B, M*
College of Technology at Alfred *A*

College of Technology at Delhi *A*

North Carolina

North Carolina Agricultural and
Technical State University *B*
North Carolina State University *B, M*
Wake Technical Community
College *A*

North Dakota

North Dakota State University *B*

Ohio

Columbus State Community
College *A*
Ohio State University
Columbus Campus *B, M*

Oklahoma

Oklahoma State University *B*
University of Oklahoma *M*

Oregon

Central Oregon Community
College *A*
University of Oregon *B, M*

Pennsylvania

Chatham College *M*
Keystone College *A*
Penn State
University Park *B, M*
Philadelphia University *B*
Temple University *B*
University of Pennsylvania *M*

Rhode Island

Rhode Island School of Design *B, M*
University of Rhode Island *B*

South Carolina

Clemson University *B*

Texas

Howard College *C*
Texas A&M University *B, M*
Texas Tech University *B, M*
University of Texas
Arlington *M*
Austin *M*

Utah

Utah State University *B, M*

Virginia

University of Virginia *M*
Virginia Polytechnic Institute and
State University *B, M*

Washington

South Seattle Community
College *C, A*
University of Washington *B, M*
Washington State University *B, M*

West Virginia

West Virginia University *B*

Wisconsin

University of Wisconsin
Madison *M*

Landscaping/ groundskeeping

Alabama

Faulkner State Community
College *C, A*

Arizona

Glendale Community College *C*
Mesa Community College *A*

Arkansas

University of Arkansas
Little Rock *A*

California

Antelope Valley College *C, A*
California State Polytechnic
University: Pomona *B, M*
College of the Redwoods *C*
College of the Sequoias *C, A*
Cosumnes River College *C*
Diablo Valley College *C*
Foothill College *C, A*
Los Angeles Pierce College *C, A*
Merritt College *C, A*
MiraCosta College *C, A*
Modesto Junior College *A*
Mount San Antonio College *C*
San Joaquin Delta College *C*
Santa Barbara City College *C, A*
Santa Rosa Junior College *C*
Solano Community College *C, A*
Southwestern College *C, A*
Victor Valley College *C*
Yuba Community College
District *C, A*

Colorado

Colorado State University *B*
Pikes Peak Community College *A*

Connecticut

Middlesex Community College *C*

Florida

Florida Agricultural and Mechanical
University *B*
Gulf Coast Community College *A*
Lake City Community College *A*
Miami Dade College *A*
Valencia Community College *C*

Georgia

Albany Technical College *C*
Gainesville State College *C*
Georgia Highlands College *A*
University of Georgia *B*
West Georgia Technical College *C*

Idaho

Brigham Young University-Idaho *A*

Illinois

College of DuPage *C*
College of Lake County *C, A*
Joliet Junior College *C, A*
Kishwaukee College *C, A*
Lincoln Land Community College *C, A*
McHenry County College *C*
Parkland College *A*
Southwestern Illinois College *A*
Triton College *C, A*
William Rainey Harper College *C*

Iowa

Iowa Lakes Community College *A*
Northeast Iowa Community
College *A*
Western Iowa Tech Community
College *C*

Kentucky

Maysville Community College *C*

Maine

Southern Maine Community
College *C, A*

University of Maine *C, B*
University of Maine
Augusta *A*

Massachusetts

Springfield Technical Community
College *C, A*
University of Massachusetts
Amherst *A*

Michigan

Bay de Noc Community College *C*
Grand Rapids Community College *A*
Kirtland Community College *A*
Northwestern Michigan College *A*
Oakland Community College *C, A*
Wayne County Community College *A*

Minnesota

Anoka Technical College *C, A*
Anoka-Ramsey Community College *A*
Dakota County Technical College *C, A*
Hennepin Technical College *C, A*

Mississippi

Hinds Community College *A*
Mississippi Gulf Coast Community
College
Jefferson Davis Campus *C, A*
Mississippi State University *B*

Nebraska

Nebraska College of Technical
Agriculture *A*
University of Nebraska
Lincoln *B*

Nevada

Community College of Southern
Nevada *A*

New Hampshire

New Hampshire Technical Institute *C*
University of New Hampshire *A*

New Jersey

Bergen Community College *C*

New Mexico

Albuquerque Technical-Vocational
Institute *C*
Dona Ana Branch Community College
of New Mexico State
University *A*

New York

Finger Lakes Community College *C, A*
State University of New York
College of Agriculture and
Technology at Cobleskill *A*
College of Agriculture and
Technology at Morrisville *A*
College of Technology at Alfred *A*
College of Technology at Delhi *A*
Suffolk County Community
College *C, A*

North Carolina

Alamance Community College *C*
Blue Ridge Community College *C*
Cape Fear Community College *A*
North Carolina Agricultural and
Technical State University *B*
North Carolina State University *A*
Sampson Community College *C*
Sandhills Community College *A*

North Dakota

Minot State University: Bottineau
Campus *A*

Ohio

Cincinnati State Technical and
Community College *C, A*
Clark State Community College *A*
Ohio State University
Agricultural Technical Institute *A*
Columbus Campus *B*
Owens Community College
Toledo *A*

Oregon

Central Oregon Community
College *A*
Portland Community College *C, A*

Pennsylvania

Chatham College *M*
Community College of Allegheny
County *C, A*
Delaware Valley College *C*
Luzerne County Community
College *C, A*
Penn State
Abington *B*
Altoona *B*
Beaver *B*
Berks *B*
Delaware County *B*
Dubois *B*
Erie, The Behrend College *B*
Fayette *B*
Hazleton *B*
Lehigh Valley *B*
McKeesport *B*
Mont Alto *B*
New Kensington *B*
Schuylkill - Capital College *B*
Shenango *B*
University Park *C, B*
Wilkes-Barre *B*
Worthington Scranton *B*
York *B*
Williamson Free School of Mechanical
Trades *C*

South Carolina

Spartanburg Technical College *C*
Technical College of the
Lowcountry *C*
Trident Technical College *C*

South Dakota

South Dakota State University *B*
Southeast Technical Institute *A*

Tennessee

Chattanooga State Technical
Community College *C*
Tennessee Technological University *B*

Texas

Houston Community College
System *C*
Palo Alto College *C, A*
Western Texas College *C, A*

Utah

Brigham Young University *B*
Salt Lake Community College *A*

Vermont

Vermont Technical College *A*

Virginia

J. Sargeant Reynolds Community
College *A*
Lord Fairfax Community College *C*
Mountain Empire Community
College *C*
Virginia Western Community
College *A*

Washington

Clark College *C, A*
Clover Park Technical College *C, A*
Edmonds Community College *A*
Pierce College *A*
South Seattle Community
    College *C, A*

Wisconsin

Milwaukee Area Technical College *A*

Language interpretation/ translation

California

Bethesda Christian University *B, M*
University of California
    Santa Cruz *B*

District of Columbia

American University *C*

Florida

Gulf Coast Community College *A*
Miami Dade College *A*

Georgia

East Georgia College *A*

Illinois

Waubonsee Community College *A*

Massachusetts

Salem State College *B*

Nebraska

University of Nebraska
    Kearney *B*

Nevada

Great Basin College *A*

New Jersey

Union County College *A*

New York

Bard College *B*
State University of New York
    Binghamton *D*

North Carolina

Fayetteville Technical Community
    College *A*
Wilson Technical Community
    College *A*

Ohio

Kent State University *M*

Oklahoma

Oklahoma City Community College *A*

Puerto Rico

University of Puerto Rico
    Rio Piedras *M*

South Carolina

College of Charleston *M*

Utah

Brigham Young University *B*
Dixie State College of Utah *A*

Vermont

Marlboro College *B*

Laser/optical technology

California

San Jose City College *C, A*
Sierra College *C*

Idaho

Idaho State University *C*

Iowa

Indian Hills Community College *A*

Maryland

Howard Community College *C, A*

Massachusetts

Massachusetts Bay Community
    College *A*
Springfield Technical Community
    College *A*

Michigan

Schoolcraft College *A*

New Mexico

Albuquerque Technical-Vocational
    Institute *C, A*

Ohio

Cincinnati State Technical and
    Community College *A*

South Dakota

Southeast Technical Institute *A*

Latin

Alabama

Samford University *B*

California

Loyola Marymount University *B, M*
Santa Clara University *B*
University of California
    Berkeley *B, M*
    Los Angeles *B, M*
    Santa Cruz *B*

Connecticut

Yale University *B*

Delaware

University of Delaware *B, M, T*

District of Columbia

Catholic University of America *B, M, T*
George Washington University *B*

Florida

Florida State University *B, M*
University of Florida *B*

Georgia

Emory University *B*
Mercer University *B*
University of Georgia *B, M*

Idaho

Idaho State University *A*
University of Idaho *B*

Illinois

Augustana College *B, T*
Concordia University *B*
Loyola University of Chicago *B*
Monmouth College *B*
Rockford College *B*
University of Chicago *B, M*

Indiana

Ball State University *B, T*
Butler University *B*
DePauw University *B*
Indiana University
    Bloomington *B, M, D*
University of Notre Dame *B*
Wabash College *B*

Iowa

Cornell College *B, T*
Luther College *B*
University of Iowa *B, M, T*

Kansas

Wichita State University *B*

Kentucky

Asbury College *B, T*
Berea College *B, T*

Louisiana

Centenary College of Louisiana *B*
Louisiana State University and
    Agricultural and Mechanical
    College *B*

Maine

University of Maine *B*

Maryland

Loyola College in Maryland *B*

Massachusetts

Amherst College *B*
Boston College *B, M*
Boston University *B*
Brandeis University *B*
Harvard College *B, D*
Mount Holyoke College *B*
Simon's Rock College of Bard *B*
Smith College *B*
Tufts University *B*
Wellesley College *B*
Wheaton College *B*

Michigan

Albion College *T*
Calvin College *B, T*
Grand Valley State University *B*
Hope College *B*
University of Michigan *B, M*
Western Michigan University *B*

Minnesota

Carleton College *B*
Concordia College: Moorhead *B*
St. Olaf College *B*
University of Minnesota
    Twin Cities *B, M, D*
University of St. Thomas *B*

Missouri

Missouri State University *B*
Washington University in St.
    Louis *B, M*

Montana

University of Montana: Missoula *B*

Nebraska

Creighton University *B*
University of Nebraska
    Lincoln *B*

New Hampshire

St. Anselm College *T*
University of New Hampshire *B*

New Jersey

Montclair State University *B, T*

Seton Hall University *T*

New York

Bard College *B*
Barnard College *B*
City University of New York
    Hunter College *B*
    Lehman College *B*
    Queens College *B*
Colgate University *B*
College of New Rochelle *B, T*
Columbia University
    Columbia College *B*
Elmira College *B*
Fordham University *B, M, D*
Hamilton College *B*
Hobart and William Smith Colleges *B*
Hofstra University *B*
New York University *B, M*
St. Bonaventure University *B*
Sarah Lawrence College *B*
State University of New York
    Binghamton *B*
Vassar College *B*

North Carolina

Duke University *B*
Wake Forest University *B*

Ohio

College of Wooster *B*
John Carroll University *B*
Kent State University *B, M*
Kenyon College *B*
Miami University
    Oxford Campus *B, T*
Oberlin College *B*
Ohio State University
    Columbus Campus *B, M, D*
Ohio University *B, T*
Ohio Wesleyan University *B*
University of Cincinnati *B, T*
Wright State University *B*

Oregon

University of Oregon *B*

Pennsylvania

Bryn Mawr College *B, M, D*
Duquesne University *B*
Franklin & Marshall College *B*
Gettysburg College *B*
Haverford College *B, T*
La Salle University *B*
St. Joseph's University *B*
Swarthmore College *B*
University of Scranton *B, T*
West Chester University of
    Pennsylvania *B, M, T*
Westminster College *B, T*

Puerto Rico

Pontifical Catholic University of
    Puerto Rico *B*

Rhode Island

Brown University *B*

South Carolina

Furman University *B, T*

Tennessee

Rhodes College *T*
University of Tennessee
    Chattanooga *B*
    Knoxville *B*
University of the South *B*
Vanderbilt University *M*

Texas

Austin College *B*
Austin Community College *A*

Baylor University *B*
Rice University *B*
Southwestern University *B, T*
University of Dallas *B, T*
University of Houston *B*
University of North Texas *B*
University of Texas
  Austin *B*

Utah

Brigham Young University *B*

Vermont

St. Michael's College *B*
University of Vermont *B, M*

Virginia

College of William and Mary *B*
Hampden-Sydney College *B*
Randolph-Macon College *B*
Randolph-Macon Woman's College *B*
University of Mary Washington *B*
University of Richmond *B, T*

Washington

Seattle Pacific University *B*
University of Washington *B*

Wisconsin

Lawrence University *B, T*
University of Wisconsin
  Madison *B*

Latin American studies

Alabama

Samford University *B*
University of Alabama *B, M*

Arizona

Prescott College *B, M*
University of Arizona *B, M*

California

Alliant International University *B*
California State University
  Chico *B*
  East Bay *B*
  Fullerton *B*
  Los Angeles *B, M*
  Monterey Bay *B*
Claremont McKenna College *B*
Cypress College *A*
De Anza College *A*
Fullerton College *A*
Laney College *A*
Los Angeles Pierce College *A*
Pitzer College *B*
Pomona College *B*
St. Mary's College of California *B*
San Diego City College *A*
San Diego State University *B, M*
Scripps College *B*
University of California
  Berkeley *B, M, D*
  Los Angeles *B, M*
  Riverside *B*
  San Diego *B, M*
  Santa Barbara *B, M*
  Santa Cruz *B*
University of Redlands *B*
University of San Francisco *M*
Whittier College *B*

Colorado

Fort Lewis College *B*

Connecticut

Connecticut College *B*
Trinity College *B*
University of Connecticut *B*
Wesleyan University *B*

Yale University *B*

Delaware

University of Delaware *B*

District of Columbia

American University *B, M*
George Washington University *B, M*
Georgetown University *M*
Trinity University *B*

Florida

Flagler College *B*
Florida International University *M*
Florida State University *B*
Manatee Community College *A*
Miami Dade College *A*
Rollins College *B*
Stetson University *B*
University of Florida *B*
University of Miami *B, M, D*
University of South Florida *M*

Georgia

Emory University *B*

Idaho

University of Idaho *B*

Illinois

Blackburn College *B*
DePaul University *B*
Illinois Wesleyan University *B*
Lake Forest College *B*
University of Chicago *B, M*
University of Illinois
  Chicago *B*
  Urbana-Champaign *B, M*

Indiana

Earlham College *B*
Hanover College *B*
Indiana University
  Bloomington *M*

Iowa

Cornell College *B*
Grinnell College *B*
University of Northern Iowa *B*

Kansas

University of Kansas *B, M*

Kentucky

University of Kentucky *B*

Louisiana

Tulane University *B*

Maine

Bowdoin College *B*
Colby College *B*

Maryland

Hood College *B*
Johns Hopkins University *B*

Massachusetts

Assumption College *B*
Boston University *B*
Brandeis University *B*
Hampshire College *B*
Harvard College *B*
Mount Holyoke College *B*
Smith College *B*
Tufts University *B, M*
Wellesley College *B*

Michigan

Oakland University *B*
University of Michigan *B*

Western Michigan University *B*

Minnesota

Carleton College *B*
Hamline University *B*
Macalester College *B*
St. Cloud State University *B*
St. Olaf College *B*
University of Minnesota
  Morris *B*
  Twin Cities *B*

Missouri

University of Missouri
  Columbia *B*
Washington University in St. Louis *B*

Nebraska

University of Nebraska
  Lincoln *B*
  Omaha *B*

Nevada

University of Nevada
  Las Vegas *B*

New Hampshire

Dartmouth College *B*

New Jersey

Rutgers, The State University of New
  Jersey
  New Brunswick/Piscataway
    Campus *B*
William Paterson University of New
  Jersey *B*

New Mexico

University of New Mexico *B, M, D*

New York

Adelphi University *B*
Bard College *B*
Barnard College *B*
Boricua College *B*
City University of New York
  Brooklyn College *B*
  City College *B*
  Hunter College *B*
  Lehman College *B*
  Queens College *B, T*
Colgate University *B*
Columbia University
  Columbia College *B*
  School of General Studies *B*
Cornell University *B, M, D*
Fordham University *B*
Hobart and William Smith Colleges *B*
Hofstra University *B*
New York University *B, M*
Sarah Lawrence College *B*
State University of New York
  Albany *B, M*
  Binghamton *B*
  College at Plattsburgh *B*
  New Paltz *B*
Syracuse University *B*
United States Military Academy *B*
Vassar College *B*

North Carolina

University of North Carolina
  Chapel Hill *B*

Ohio

College of Wooster *B*
Denison University *B*
Kent State University *B*
Oberlin College *B*
Ohio State University
  Columbus Campus *B*
Ohio University *B, M*

Pontifical College Josephinum *B*
University of Cincinnati *B*
University of Toledo *B*

Oklahoma

Southeastern Oklahoma State
  University *B*

Oregon

Portland State University *B*
Willamette University *B*

Pennsylvania

Albright College *B*
Bucknell University *B*
Carnegie Mellon University *B*
Edinboro University of
  Pennsylvania *B*
Gettysburg College *B*
Lock Haven University of
  Pennsylvania *B*
Penn State
  Abington *B*
  Altoona *B*
  Beaver *B*
  Berks *B*
  Delaware County *B*
  Dubois *B*
  Erie, The Behrend College *B*
  Fayette *B*
  Hazleton *B*
  Lehigh Valley *B*
  McKeesport *B*
  Mont Alto *B*
  New Kensington *B*
  Schuylkill - Capital College *B*
  Shenango *B*
  University Park *B*
  Wilkes-Barre *B*
  Worthington Scranton *B*
  York *B*
Temple University *B*
University of Pennsylvania *M*

Rhode Island

Brown University *B, M, D*
University of Rhode Island *B*

South Carolina

College of Charleston *B*
University of South Carolina *B*

Tennessee

Rhodes College *B*
University of Tennessee
  Knoxville *B*
Vanderbilt University *B, M*

Texas

Austin College *B*
Baylor University *B*
Palo Alto College *A*
Rice University *B*
St. Edward's University *B*
St. Mary's University *B*
Southern Methodist University *B*
Texas Christian University *B*
Texas Tech University *B*
Trinity University *B*
University of Texas
  Austin *B, M, D*
  El Paso *B*

Utah

Brigham Young University *B*
University of Utah *M*

Vermont

Burlington College *B*
Goddard College *B*
Marlboro College *B*
University of Vermont *B*

Virginia

College of William and Mary *B*
University of Virginia *B*

Washington

Gonzaga University *B*
Seattle Pacific University *B*
University of Washington *B, M*

Wisconsin

Ripon College *B*
University of Wisconsin
Eau Claire *B*
Madison *B, M*

Latin teacher education

Illinois

Knox College *T*
University of Illinois
Urbana-Champaign *B, M, T*

Indiana

Indiana University
Bloomington *B, T*

Iowa

Cornell College *T*
University of Iowa *T*

Kansas

University of Kansas *B, T*

Maryland

Mount St. Mary's University *T*

Michigan

Hope College *B, T*
Western Michigan University *B, T*

Minnesota

Concordia College: Moorhead *B*

Missouri

Missouri State University *B*

Nebraska

Creighton University *B*

New York

City University of New York
Hunter College *B, M, T*
Hobart and William Smith Colleges *T*

Ohio

Kent State University *T*
Miami University
Oxford Campus *B*
Ohio Wesleyan University *B*

Pennsylvania

Albright College *T*
Duquesne University *B, M, T*
Gettysburg College *T*

Tennessee

University of Memphis *T*

Texas

University of Dallas *T*

Utah

Brigham Young University *B*

Vermont

St. Michael's College *T*

Wisconsin

Lawrence University *T*

Law (J.D.)

Alabama

Samford University: Cumberland
School of Law *F*
Thomas Goode Jones School of
Law–Faulkner University *F*
University of Alabama: School of
Law *F*

Arizona

Arizona State University: College of
Law *F*
University of Arizona: College of
Law *F*

Arkansas

University of Arkansas at Little Rock:
School of Law *F*
University of Arkansas: School of
Law *F*

California

California Western School of Law *F*
Golden Gate University: School of
Law *F*
Humphreys College: School of Law *F*
John F. Kennedy University: School of
Law *F*
Loyola Marymount University: School
of Law *F*
McGeorge School of Law: University
of the Pacific *F*
Pepperdine University: School of
Law *F*
Santa Clara University: School of
Law *F*
Southwestern University School of
Law *F*
Stanford University: School of Law *F*
Thomas Jefferson School of Law *F*
University of California
Hastings College of the Law *F*
University of California Berkeley:
School of Law *F*
University of California Davis: School
of Law *F*
University of California Los Angeles:
School of Law *F*
University of La Verne College of Law
at San Fernando Valley *F*
University of La Verne: School of
Law *F*
University of San Diego: School of
Law *F*
University of San Francisco: School of
Law *F*
University of Southern California: Law
School *F*
University of West Los Angeles: School
of Law *F*
Western State University College of
Law *F*
Whittier Law School *F*

Colorado

University of Colorado at Boulder:
School of Law *F*
University of Denver: College of
Law *F*

Connecticut

Quinnipiac College: School of Law *F*
University of Connecticut: School of
Law *F*
Yale Law School *F*

Delaware

Widener University School of Law *F*

District of Columbia

American University: Washington
College of Law *F*
Catholic University of America: School
of Law *F*
George Washington University Law
School *F*
Georgetown University: Law Center *F*
Howard University: School of Law *F*
University of the District of Columbia:
School of Law *F*

Florida

Florida Coastal School of Law *F*
Florida State University: School of
Law *F*
Nova Southeastern University:
Shepard Broad Law Center *F*
St. Thomas University: School of
Law *F*
Stetson University: College of Law *F*
University of Florida: College of Law *F*
University of Miami: School of Law *F*

Georgia

Emory University: School of Law *F*
Georgia State University: College of
Law *F*
Mercer University: Walter F. George
School of Law *F*
University of Georgia: School of
Law *F*

Hawaii

University of Hawaii William S.
Richardson: School of Law *F*

Idaho

University of Idaho: College of Law *F*

Illinois

Chicago-Kent College of Law, Illinois
Institute of Technology *F*
De Paul University: College of Law *F*
Loyola University Chicago: School of
Law *F*
Northern Illinois University: College
of Law *F*
Northwestern University: School of
Law *F*
Southern Illinois University at
Carbondale: School of Law *F*
University of Chicago: School of
Law *F*
University of Illinois at
Urbana-Champaign: College of
Law *F*

Indiana

Indiana University Bloomington:
School of Law *F*
Indiana University Indianapolis:
School of Law *F*
University of Notre Dame: School of
Law *F*
Valparaiso University: School of Law *F*

Iowa

Drake University Law School *F*
University of Iowa: College of Law *F*

Kansas

University of Kansas: School of Law *F*
Washburn University School of Law *F*

Kentucky

Northern Kentucky University:
Salmon P. Chase School of Law *F*
University of Kentucky: College of
Law *F*
University of Louisville: School of
Law *F*

Louisiana

Louisiana State University and
Agricultural and Mechanical
College: School of Law *F*
Loyola University: School of Law *F*
Southern University: Law Center *F*
Tulane University: School of Law *F*

Maine

University of Maine: School of Law *F*

Maryland

University of Baltimore: School of
Law *F*
University of Maryland at Baltimore:
School of Law *F*

Massachusetts

Boston College: Law School *F*
Boston University: School of Law *F*
Harvard University Law School *F*
New England School of Law *F*
Northeastern University: School of
Law *F*
Suffolk University: Law School *F*
Western New England College: School
of Law *F*

Michigan

Detroit College of Law *F*
Thomas M. Cooley Law School *F*
University of Detroit Mercy: School of
Law *F*
University of Michigan: School of
Law *F*
Wayne State University: School of
Law *F*

Minnesota

Hamline University: School of Law *F*
University of Minnesota Twin Cities:
School of Law *F*
William Mitchell College of Law: Law
Professions *F*

Mississippi

Mississippi College: School of Law *F*
University of Mississippi: School of
Law *F*

Missouri

St. Louis University: School of Law *F*
University of Missouri Columbia:
School of Law *F*
University of Missouri Kansas City:
School of Law *F*
Washington University: School of
Law *F*

Montana

University of Montana: School of
Law *F*

Nebraska

Creighton University: School of Law *F*
University of Nebraska Lincoln:
College of Law *F*

New Hampshire

Franklin Pierce Law Center *F*

New Jersey

Rutgers, The State University of New
Jersey
Camden School of Law *F*
Newark School of Law *F*
Seton Hall University: School of Law *F*

New Mexico

University of New Mexico: School of
Law *F*

New York

Albany Law School of Union University *F*
Benjamin N. Cardozo School of Law *F*
Brooklyn Law School *F*
City University of New York School of Law at Queens College *F*
Columbia University School of Law *F*
Cornell University: School of Law *F*
Fordham University: School of Law *F*
Hofstra University: School of Law *F*
New York Law School *F*
New York University: School of Law *F*
Pace University Westchester: School of Law *F*
St. John's University: School of Law *F*
State University of New York at Buffalo: School of Law *F*
Syracuse University: College of Law *F*
Touro College: Jacob D. Fuchsberg Law Center *F*

North Carolina

Campbell University: Norman Adrian Wiggins School of Law *F*
Duke University: School of Law *F*
North Carolina Central University: School of Law *F*
University of North Carolina at Chapel Hill: School of Law *F*
Wake Forest University: School of Law *F*

North Dakota

University of North Dakota: School of Law *F*

Ohio

Capital University: School of Law *F*
Case Western Reserve University: School of Law *F*
Cleveland State University: College of Law *F*
Ohio Northern University: College of Law *F*
Ohio State University: College of Law *F*
University of Akron: School of Law *F*
University of Cincinnati: College of Law *F*
University of Dayton: School of Law *F*
University of Toledo: College of Law *F*

Oklahoma

Oklahoma City University: School of Law *F*
University of Oklahoma: College of Law *F*
University of Tulsa: College of Law *F*

Oregon

Lewis and Clark College: Northwestern School of Law *F*
University of Oregon: School of Law *F*
Willamette University: College of Law *F*

Pennsylvania

Dickinson School of Law *F*
Duquesne University: School of Law *F*
Temple University: School of Law *F*
University of Pennsylvania Law School *F*
University of Pittsburgh: School of Law *F*
Villanova University: School of Law *F*
Widener University School of Law *F*

Puerto Rico

Inter American University of Puerto Rico: School of Law *F*

Pontifical Catholic University of Puerto Rico: School of Law *F*
University of Puerto Rico Rio Piedras Campus: School of Law *F*

South Carolina

University of South Carolina: School of Law *F*

South Dakota

University of South Dakota: School of Law *F*

Tennessee

University of Memphis: School of Law *F*
University of Tennessee College of Law *F*
Vanderbilt University: School of Law *F*

Texas

Baylor University: School of Law *F*
St. Mary's University: School of Law *F*
South Texas College of Law *F*
Southern Methodist University: School of Law *F*
Texas Southern University: Thurgood Marshall School of Law *F*
Texas Tech University: School of Law *F*
University of Houston: Law Center *F*
University of Texas at Austin: School of Law *F*

Utah

Brigham Young University: School of Law *F*
University of Utah: College of Law *F*

Vermont

Vermont Law School *F*

Virginia

College of William and Mary: School of Law *F*
George Mason University: School of Law *F*
Regent University: School of Law *F*
University of Richmond: The T.C. Williams School of Law *F*
University of Virginia: School of Law *F*
Washington and Lee University: School of Law *F*

Washington

Gonzaga University: School of Law *F*
Seattle University: School of Law *F*
University of Washington: School of Law *F*

West Virginia

West Virginia University: College of Law *F*

Wisconsin

Marquette University: School of Law *F*
University of Wisconsin Madison: School of Law *F*

Wyoming

University of Wyoming: College of Law *F*

Legal administrative assistance

Alabama

Faulkner State Community College *A*

George C. Wallace State Community College
George C. Wallace Community College at Dothan *C, A*
Lawson State Community College *A*
Wallace State Community College at Hanceville *A*

Arizona

Central Arizona College *C, A*
Cochise College *A*
Coconino County Community College *C*
Everest College *C, A*
Northland Pioneer College *C, A*
Phoenix College *C, A*
Yavapai College *C, A*

Arkansas

National Park Community College *C*
Pulaski Technical College *C*

California

Allan Hancock College *C, A*
Butte College *C, A*
CEI College
Maric College: Panorama City *C*
Chabot College *A*
Chaffey College *C*
City College of San Francisco *C, A*
Coastline Community College *C*
College of San Mateo *C, A*
College of the Redwoods *C, A*
Columbia College *C*
Cypress College *C, A*
East Los Angeles College *A*
Empire College *C*
Fresno City College *C, A*
Fullerton College *A*
Glendale Community College *C, A*
Golden West College *C, A*
Heald College
Fresno *C, A*
Rancho Cordova *C, A*
San Jose *A*
Humphreys College *C, A, B*
Lake Tahoe Community College *C, A*
Las Positas College *C*
Lassen College *C*
Long Beach City College *C, A*
Los Angeles City College *C, A*
Los Angeles Harbor College *C, A*
MTI College *C*
Merced College *C, A*
Palomar College *C, A*
Pasadena City College *A*
Platt College
Ontario *C, A, B*
Porterville College *C*
Riverside Community College *C, A*
Sacramento City College *C, A*
Saddleback College *C, A*
San Bernardino Valley College *C*
Santa Rosa Junior College *C*
Shasta College *A*
Sierra College *C, A*
Skyline College *C, A*
Solano Community College *C, A*
Southwestern College *C, A*
Ventura College *C, A*

Colorado

Blair College *A*
Community College of Aurora *A*
Northeastern Junior College *A*
Otero Junior College *A*
Pueblo Community College *C, A*
Red Rocks Community College *C, A*

Connecticut

Briarwood College *A*
Gateway Community College *A*
Gibbs College *C*

Middlesex Community College *A*
Naugatuck Valley Community College *A*
Northwestern Connecticut Community College *B*
Norwalk Community College *C, A*
Quinnipiac University *B*
Three Rivers Community College *A*
Tunxis Community College *C, A*

Florida

Brevard Community College *A*
Broward Community College *C, A*
Daytona Beach Community College *A*
Florida Community College at Jacksonville *C, A*
Indian River Community College *A*
Miami Dade College *C, A*
Okaloosa-Walton College *A*
Pensacola Junior College *A*
Santa Fe Community College *A*
Seminole Community College *A*

Georgia

Augusta Technical Institute *C*
Central Georgia Technical College *C*
DeKalb Technical College *C*
Gwinnett College *C*

Hawaii

Hawaii Business College *C*
Heald College
Honolulu *A*
University of Hawaii
Kapiolani Community College *A*

Idaho

Boise State University *A*
Lewis-Clark State College *C, A, B*
North Idaho College *A*

Illinois

Black Hawk College *A*
Career Colleges of Chicago *A*
College of DuPage *C, A*
Elgin Community College *C, A*
John Wood Community College *A*
Joliet Junior College *A*
Kankakee Community College *A*
Kaskaskia College *C*
Kishwaukee College *C*
Lake Land College *A*
Lewis and Clark Community College *A*
Lincoln Land Community College *C, A*
MacCormac College *A*
McHenry County College *C*
Midstate College *C, A*
Moraine Valley Community College *C*
Robert Morris College: Chicago *C, A*
Rockford Business College *A*
Sauk Valley Community College *C, A*
Waubonsee Community College *C*
Westwood College of Technology
O'Hare *B*
William Rainey Harper College *C, A*

Indiana

Indiana Business College *C*
Professional Careers Institute *A*
Sawyer College *C, A*
Sawyer College: Merrillville *A*
Vincennes University *A*

Iowa

Ellsworth Community College *A*
Hamilton College
Cedar Falls *A*
Iowa Western Community College *A*
Kirkwood Community College *C, A*
Northeast Iowa Community College *A*

Southeastern Community College
  North Campus *A*
Western Iowa Tech Community
  College *A*

Kansas

Dodge City Community College *C, A*
Labette Community College *A*
Pratt Community College *C, A*
Seward County Community
  College *C, A*
Washburn University of Topeka *C, A*

Kentucky

Ashland Community and Technical
  College *A*
Daymar College *A*
Draughons Junior College *A*
National College of Business &
  Technology
    Lexington *A*
    Louisville *A*
    Pikeville *A*
Sullivan University *C, A*

Louisiana

Bossier Parish Community College *C*

Maine

Andover College *C, A*
Beal College *A*
Northern Maine Community
  College *A*

Maryland

Allegany College of Maryland *C*
Baltimore City Community College *A*
Community College of Baltimore
  County *A*
Frederick Community College *C, A*
Hagerstown Business College *C*
Howard Community College *C, A*
Prince George's Community
  College *C, A*

Massachusetts

Atlantic Union College *A*
Bay State College *A*
Boston University *B*
Bristol Community College *C*
Cape Cod Community College *C, A*
Gibbs College *A*
Marian Court College *C, A* ˅
Massasoit Community College *A*
North Shore Community College *C, A*
Roxbury Community College *A*

Michigan

Baker College
  of Auburn Hills *A*
  of Cadillac *A*
  of Flint *A*
  of Jackson *A*
  of Owosso *A*
  of Port Huron *A*
Davenport University *A*
Delta College *A*
Grand Rapids Community College *A*
Henry Ford Community College *A*
Kalamazoo Valley Community
  College *C, A*
Kellogg Community College *A*
Kirtland Community College *A*
Lake Michigan College *A*
Lansing Community College *A*
Madonna University *C, A, B*
Mid Michigan Community College *A*
Monroe County Community
  College *C, A*
Mott Community College *C, A*
Muskegon Community College *A*
Northern Michigan University *A*
Northwestern Michigan College *C*

St. Clair County Community
  College *A*

Minnesota

Academy College *C*
Alexandria Technical College *C, A*
Anoka Technical College *C*
Anoka-Ramsey Community College *A*
Globe College *C, A*
Hibbing Community College *A*
Inver Hills Community College *C, A*
Lake Superior College *C, A*
Minneapolis Business College *C, A*
Minnesota School of Business *C*
Minnesota State College - Southeast
  Technical *C, A*
Minnesota State Community and
  Technical College - Fergus
  Falls *C, A*
Rasmussen College
  Mankato *C*
  Minnetonka *C, A*
  St. Cloud *C, A*
Ridgewater College *C, A*
Riverland Community College *C, A*
Rochester Community and Technical
  College *A*
St. Cloud Technical College *C, A*
South Central College *A*
Winona State University *B*

Mississippi

Hinds Community College *A*
Pearl River Community College *C, A*

Missouri

East Central College *C, A*
Everest College: Springfield *A*
Hickey College *C, A*
Penn Valley Community College *C*
St. Louis Community College
  St. Louis Community College at
    Meramec *A*
State Fair Community College *A*

Montana

Flathead Valley Community College *A*
Helena College of Technology of the
  University of Montana *C, A*
Montana State University
  College of Technology-Great Falls *A*
University of Montana: Missoula *A*

Nebraska

Hamilton College: Lincoln *A*
Midland Lutheran College *A*
Northeast Community College *A*

Nevada

Community College of Southern
  Nevada *C, A*
Great Basin College *C*
Truckee Meadows Community
  College *A*

New Hampshire

McIntosh College *A*
New Hampshire Community
  Technical College
    Nashua *C*

New Jersey

Gloucester County College *A*
Warren County Community College *C*

New Mexico

Clovis Community College *A*
Dona Ana Branch Community College
  of New Mexico State
  University *A*
New Mexico Junior College *C, A*
San Juan College *A*

Western New Mexico University *C, A*

New York

Briarcliffe College *A*
Bryant & Stratton Business Institute
  Bryant & Stratton College:
    Rochester *A*
  Bryant & Stratton College:
    Syracuse *A*
City University of New York
  Kingsborough Community
    College *A*
  LaGuardia Community College *A*
Clinton Community College *C*
Dutchess Community College *C, A*
Elmira Business Institute *C, A*
Globe Institute of Technology *C, A, B*
Herkimer County Community
  College *A*
Interboro Institute *A*
Jamestown Business College *A*
Katharine Gibbs School
  New York *A*
Long Island Business Institute *C*
Nassau Community College *A*
New York Career Institute *A*
Olean Business Institute *C*
Rochester Business Institute *C, A*
State University of New York
  College of Technology at Delhi *A*
Trocaire College *A*
Ulster County Community
  College *C, A*
Utica School of Commerce *C, A*

North Carolina

Alamance Community College *C, A*
Carteret Community College *A*
Central Carolina Community
  College *A*
Central Piedmont Community
  College *A*
Cleveland Community College *A*
Craven Community College *C, A*
Gaston College *A*
King's College *C, A*
Nash Community College *A*
Piedmont Community College *A*
Rockingham Community College *A*
South Piedmont Community
  College *C, A*
Wake Technical Community
  College *A*
Wayne Community College *A*
Western Piedmont Community
  College *C, A*

North Dakota

Aakers College: Fargo *C, A*
Bismarck State College *C, A*
Dickinson State University *A*
Lake Region State College *C, A*

Ohio

Bradford School *C, A*
Bryant & Stratton College
  Parma *A*
Cincinnati State Technical and
  Community College *A*
Clark State Community College *A*
Columbus State Community
  College *A*
David N. Myers University *A, B*
Davis College *A*
ETI Technical College of Niles *A*
Edison State Community College *C, A*
James A. Rhodes State College *A*
Jefferson Community College *A*
Ohio Business College: Sandusky *A*
Ohio University
  Chillicothe Campus *A*
Shawnee State University *A*
Sinclair Community College *A*

Stark State College of Technology *A*
Trumbull Business College *A*
University of Akron *C, A*
University of Akron: Wayne
  College *C, A*
University of Cincinnati
  Clermont College *C, A*
  Raymond Walters College *A*
University of Northwestern Ohio *A*
Wright State University *A*

Oklahoma

Eastern Oklahoma State College *A*
Metropolitan College *A*
Northeastern Oklahoma Agricultural
  and Mechanical College *C, A*
Oklahoma State University
  Okmulgee *A*
Tulsa Community College *C, A*

Oregon

Chemeketa Community College *A*
Clatsop Community College *A*
Lane Community College *A*
Linn-Benton Community College *A*
Mount Hood Community College *A*
Portland Community College *A*
Southwestern Oregon Community
  College *C*
Treasure Valley Community College *A*
Umpqua Community College *A*

Pennsylvania

Bucks County Community
  College *C, A*
Business Institute of Pennsylvania *A*
Business Institute of Pennsylvania
  Meadville *A*
Butler County Community College *A*
Cambria-Rowe Business College *A*
Clarion University of Pennsylvania *A*
Consolidated School of Business
  Lancaster *C, A*
  York *C, A*
DuBois Business College *A*
DuBois Business College
  Huntingdon *A*
  Oil City *A*
Erie Business Center *C, A*
ICM School of Business & Medical
  Careers *A*
Laurel Business Institute *A*
Lehigh Carbon Community College *A*
Luzerne County Community
  College *C*
Newport Business Institute *A*
Northampton County Area
  Community College *C, A*
PJA School *C*
Penn State
  University Park *C*
Reading Area Community
  College *C, A*
South Hills School of Business &
  Technology *A*
Westmoreland County Community
  College *A*
Yorktowne Business Institute *A*

Puerto Rico

National College of Business &
  Technology: Arecibo *A*
National College of Business &
  Technology: Bayamon *A*
Universidad del Este *C, A*

Rhode Island

Community College of Rhode
  Island *C, A*

South Carolina

Forrest Junior College *A*
Greenville Technical College *C*

York Technical College *C*

South Dakota
Western Dakota Technical Institute *C*

Tennessee
Nashville State Community College *A*
South College *C*

Texas
Austin Community College *C, A*
Blinn College *C*
Brookhaven College *A*
Del Mar College *A*
Eastfield College *A*
El Centro College *C*
El Paso Community College *C*
Frank Phillips College *C, A*
Kilgore College *A*
Lamar State College at Port Arthur *A*
Laredo Community College *C*
McLennan Community College *A*
Midland College *C, A*
North Central Texas College *A*
North Harris Montgomery
    Community College District *C, A*
Northeast Texas Community
    College *C, A*
Odessa College *C, A*
Richland College *A*
St. Philip's College *A*
San Antonio College *C, A*
San Jacinto College
    North *C*
South Plains College *A*
South Texas College *C, A*
Texas A&M University
    Commerce *B*
Texas Southmost College *C, A*
Texas State Technical College
    Harlingen *A*
Trinity Valley Community College *C, A*
Tyler Junior College *A*
University of Texas
    Brownsville *C, A*

Utah
Everest College: Salt Lake City *C, A*
LDS Business College *A*
Salt Lake Community College *C*
Stevens-Henager College of
    Business *C, A*
Utah Career College *C*

Vermont
Burlington College *C*

Virginia
Blue Ridge Community College *C*
Danville Community College *C*
J. Sargeant Reynolds Community
    College *C*
Lord Fairfax Community College *C*
Mountain Empire Community
    College *A*
New River Community College *C, A*
Rappahannock Community College *C*
Southwest Virginia Community
    College *C, A*
Tidewater Tech *C*
Virginia Highlands Community
    College *C, A*
Virginia Western Community
    College *A*

Washington
Bellingham Technical College *C*
Centralia College *C, A*
Clark College *C, A*
Clover Park Technical College *C, A*
Columbia Basin College *C*
Edmonds Community College *A*
Everett Community College *C*

Green River Community College *A*
Lake Washington Technical
    College *C, A*
Lower Columbia College *A*
North Seattle Community College *C*
Olympic College *C, A*
Pierce College *C, A*
Renton Technical College *C*
South Puget Sound Community
    College *C, A*
Spokane Community College *C, A*
Walla Walla Community College *C, A*
Wenatchee Valley College *C*
Yakima Valley Community College *C*

West Virginia
Bluefield State College *A*
Huntington Junior College *C, A*
Mountain State College *A*
Valley College of Technology *C*
West Virginia Business College *A*
West Virginia University Institute of
    Technology *A*

Wisconsin
Blackhawk Technical College *A*
Bryant & Stratton College:
    Milwaukee *A*
Fox Valley Technical College *A*
Gateway Technical College *A*
Madison Area Technical College *C*
Milwaukee Area Technical College *A*
Moraine Park Technical College *A*
Northcentral Technical College *A*
Southwest Wisconsin Technical
    College *A*

Wyoming
Sheridan College *C, A*
Western Wyoming Community
    College *A*

Legal studies

Alabama
Faulkner University *A*
South University *B*
Virginia College at Huntsville *A*

Alaska
Charter College *C, A*

Arkansas
Harding University *B*
University of Arkansas *M*

California
Chapman University *B*
Claremont McKenna College *B*
Grossmont Community College *C, A*
Maric College: Anaheim *C, A*
Mills College *B*
National University *B*
Pepperdine University *M*
Platt College
    Cerritos *A*
St. Mary's College of California *B*
Santa Barbara City College *A*
Scripps College *B*
Southwestern College *C, A*
Stanford University *M, D*
Thomas Jefferson School of Law *D*
University of California
    Berkeley *B, M, D*
    Los Angeles *M, D*
    Riverside *B*
    Santa Barbara *B*
    Santa Cruz *B*
University of La Verne *B, D*
University of San Diego *M*
University of Southern
    California *M, D*

University of the Pacific *M, D*
Western State University College of
    Law *D*

Colorado
Parks College: Aurora *A*
United States Air Force Academy *B*

Connecticut
Quinnipiac University *B, M*
University of Connecticut *M, D*
University of Hartford *A, B*
University of New Haven *A, B*
Yale University *M, D*

District of Columbia
American University *B, M, D*
Catholic University of America *M, D*
George Washington University *M, D*
Howard University *M*
Southeastern University *A*

Florida
Barry University *B, M, D*
Florida Agricultural and Mechanical
    University *D*
Gulf Coast Community College *A*
Manatee Community College *A*
Nova Southeastern University *B*
Southwest Florida College *A*
University of Miami *B*

Georgia
Emory University *D*
Georgia State University *M, D*
Mercer University *D*
South University *B*

Illinois
City Colleges of Chicago
    Harold Washington College *A*
    Olive-Harvey College *A*
Illinois Institute of Technology *M, D*
Illinois Valley Community College *A*
Northwestern University *B, M*
Roosevelt University *B*
University of Illinois
    Springfield *B, M*
    Urbana-Champaign *M, D*
Westwood College of Technology
    O'Hare *B*

Indiana
Indiana University
    Bloomington *M, D*
Indiana University-Purdue University
    Fort Wayne *B*
St. Mary-of-the-Woods College *C*
University of Evansville *B*

Iowa
Drake University *B*

Kansas
University of Kansas *M, D*

Kentucky
Daymar College
    Louisville *C*

Louisiana
Tulane University *A, B*

Maine
University of Southern Maine *M*

Maryland
Towson University *B*
University of Baltimore *M*

Massachusetts
Amherst College *B*
Anna Maria College *B*
Bay Path College *B*
Becker College *B*
Boston College *D*
Boston University *M*
Bridgewater State College *B*
Elms College *B*
Hampshire College *B*
Lasell College *B*
Mount Ida College *B*
Newbury College *A, B*
Northeastern University *M, D*
Simon's Rock College of Bard *B*
University of Massachusetts
    Amherst *B*
    Boston *B*

Michigan
Grand Rapids Community College *A*
Grand Valley State University *B*
Wayne State University *M, D*

Minnesota
Hamline University *B, M*
Minnesota School of Business:
    Brooklyn Center *A*
Minnesota State University
    Moorhead *B*
Winona State University *B*

Mississippi
Antonelli College
    Jackson *A*

Missouri
Northwest Missouri State
    University *B*
Park University *B*
University of Missouri
    Columbia *M*
    Kansas City *M*
Webster University *B, M*
William Woods University *B*

Nebraska
Chadron State College *B*
University of Nebraska
    Lincoln *B, D*

Nevada
Heritage College *A*
University of Nevada
    Las Vegas *D*

New Hampshire
McIntosh College *A*

New Jersey
Montclair State University *M*
Ramapo College of New Jersey *B*
Warren County Community College *A*

New Mexico
Clovis Community College *A*

New York
Cornell University *M, D*
Hofstra University *M, D*
Ithaca College *B*
Mildred Elley *C, A*
New York Career Institute *C*
New York University *M, D*
Sage College of Albany *A, B*
St. John's University *C, A, B, M*
State University of New York
    College at Fredonia *B*
Touro College *A*
United States Military Academy *B*

North Carolina
Brevard College *B*
Duke University *D*
Livingstone College *B*
North Carolina Wesleyan College *B*
South College *B*

Ohio
Franciscan University of
  Steubenville *B*
Ohio Dominican University *A*
University of Dayton *M*
University of Toledo *C, D*

Oklahoma
Metropolitan College *A, B*
University of Oklahoma: College of
  Law *D*
University of Tulsa *B, D*

Oregon
Everest College: Portland *A*
Lewis & Clark College *M, D*
University of Oregon *D*

Pennsylvania
Arcadia University *B*
California University of
  Pennsylvania *M*
DeSales University *B*
Dickinson College *B*
Drexel University *D*
Peirce College *C*
Point Park University *B*
St. Joseph's University *C, A, B*
University of Pennsylvania *B, M, D*
University of Pittsburgh: School of
  Law *D*
Villanova University *M*
Western School of Health and
  Business Careers *C, A*
Western School of Health and
  Business Careers
  Monroeville *A*
Widener University *M, D*
Widener University School of Law *D*

Puerto Rico
Pontifical Catholic University of
  Puerto Rico *B, M*
University of Puerto Rico
  Rio Piedras *M*

Rhode Island
Community College of Rhode
  Island *C*
Roger Williams University *B*

South Carolina
South University *B*

South Dakota
University of South Dakota *D*

Tennessee
South College *B*
University of Memphis *D*
Vanderbilt University *D*

Texas
Baylor University *D*
Brazosport College *A*
Central Texas College *A*
Southern Methodist University *M, D*
Texas Southern University *D*
University of Houston *M, D*
University of Texas
  Austin *M*

Vermont
Burlington College *B*

Woodbury College *C, B*

Virginia
Bryant & Stratton College: Virginia
  Beach *A*
College of William and Mary *M*
George Mason University *M, D*
Virginia Intermont College *B*

Washington
Edmonds Community College *C, A*
Gonzaga University *M*
Highline Community College *A*
University of Washington *M, D*

West Virginia
Mountain State University *B*
West Virginia University *M*

Wisconsin
University of Wisconsin
  Madison *B, M*
  Superior *B*

Liberal arts and sciences

Alabama
Alabama Southern Community
  College *A*
Athens State University *B*
Auburn University at
  Montgomery *B, M*
Bevill State Community College *A*
Bishop State Community College *A*
Calhoun Community College *A*
Central Alabama Community
  College *A*
Chattahoochee Valley Community
  College *A*
Enterprise-Ozark Community
  College *A*
Faulkner State Community College *A*
Faulkner University *A, B*
Gadsden State Community College *A*
George C. Wallace State Community
  College
  George C. Wallace Community
    College at Dothan *A*
  Selma *A*
Huntingdon College *A, B*
Jacksonville State University *B, M*
Jefferson Davis Community College *A*
Jefferson State Community College *A*
Lawson State Community College *A*
Lurleen B. Wallace Community
  College *A*
Marion Military Institute *A*
Northeast Alabama Community
  College *A*
Northwest-Shoals Community
  College *A*
Oakwood College *B*
Shelton State Community College *A*
Snead State Community College *A*
Spring Hill College *M*
Troy University *A, B*
University of South Alabama *B*
Virginia College *A*
Wallace State Community College at
  Hanceville *A*

Alaska
Alaska Pacific University *B, M*
Prince William Sound Community
  College *A*
Sheldon Jackson College *B*
University of Alaska
  Anchorage *B*
  Fairbanks *A, B*
  Southeast *A, B*

Arizona
Central Arizona College *A*
Chandler-Gilbert Community College
  Williams Campus *A*
Cochise College *A*
Dine College *A*
Eastern Arizona College *A*
Estrella Mountain Community
  College *A*
Gateway Community College *A*
Glendale Community College *A*
Grand Canyon University *B*
Mohave Community College *A*
Northern Arizona University *B, M*
Northland Pioneer College *A*
Paradise Valley Community College *A*
Phoenix College *A*
Pima Community College *C, A*
Prescott College *B, M*
South Mountain Community
  College *A*
Tohono O'odham Community
  College *A*
Western International University *A, B*
Yavapai College *A*

Arkansas
Arkansas Northeastern College *A*
Arkansas State University
  Beebe *A*
  Mountain Home *A*
Arkansas State University: Newport *A*
Arkansas Tech University *M*
Crowley's Ridge College *A*
Henderson State University *M*
Hendrix College *B*
Mid-South Community College *A*
National Park Community College *A*
North Arkansas College *A*
Northwest Arkansas Community
  College *A*
Ouachita Technical College *A*
Ozarka College *A*
Phillips Community College of the
  University of Arkansas *A*
Pulaski Technical College *A*
Rich Mountain Community College *A*
South Arkansas Community College *A*
Southeast Arkansas College *A*
Southern Arkansas University *A*
University of Arkansas
  Community College at Batesville *A*
  Community College at Hope *A*
  Cossatot Community College of the
    A
  Fort Smith *A, B*
  Little Rock *A, B*
  Monticello *A*
  Pine Bluff *B*
University of Arkansas Community
  College at Morrilton *C, A*
University of Central Arkansas *A*

California
Allan Hancock College *A*
American River College *A*
Antelope Valley College *A*
Antioch Southern California
  Antioch University Los Angeles *B*
  Antioch University Santa Barbara *B*
Azusa Pacific University *B*
Bakersfield College *A*
Barstow College *A*
Bethany University *A, B, T*
Biola University *B*
Butte College *A*
Cabrillo College *A*
California Baptist University *B*
California Institute of Integral
  Studies *B, D*
California Institute of Technology *B*
California Lutheran University *B*
California Polytechnic State
  University: San Luis Obispo *B*

California State Polytechnic
  University: Pomona *B*
California State University
  Bakersfield *B*
  Chico *B*
  Dominguez Hills *B, M*
  East Bay *B*
  Fullerton *B*
  Long Beach *B*
  Los Angeles *B*
  Monterey Bay *B*
  Northridge *B*
  Sacramento *B, M*
  San Bernardino *B*
  San Marcos *B*
  Stanislaus *B*
Canada College *A*
Cerritos Community College *A*
Cerro Coso Community College *A*
Chabot College *A*
Chaffey College *A*
Chapman University *B*
Citrus College *A*
City College of San Francisco *A*
Coastline Community College *A*
College of Alameda *A*
College of Marin: Kentfield *A*
College of San Mateo *A*
College of the Canyons *A*
College of the Desert *A*
College of the Redwoods *A*
College of the Sequoias *A*
College of the Siskiyous *A*
Columbia College *A*
Concordia University *B*
Contra Costa College *A*
Copper Mountain College *A*
Cosumnes River College *A*
Crafton Hills College *A*
Cuesta College *A*
Cuyamaca College *A*
Cypress College *A*
De Anza College *A*
Deep Springs College *A*
Diablo Valley College *A*
Dominican University of California *B*
Evergreen Valley College *A*
Feather River College *A*
Foothill College *A*
Fresno City College *A*
Fresno Pacific University *A, B*
Fullerton College *A*
Gavilan Community College *A*
Glendale Community College *A*
Golden West College *A*
Grossmont Community College *A*
Holy Names University *B*
Humboldt State University *B*
Humphreys College *A*
Imperial Valley College *A*
Irvine Valley College *A*
John F. Kennedy University *B*
La Sierra University *B*
Lake Tahoe Community College *A*
Laney College *A*
Las Positas College *A*
Lassen College *A*
Long Beach City College *A*
Los Angeles City College *A*
Los Angeles Harbor College *A*
Los Angeles Mission College *A*
Los Angeles Pierce College *A*
Los Angeles Southwest College *A*
Los Angeles Trade and Technical
  College *A*
Los Angeles Valley College *A*
Los Medanos College *A*
Loyola Marymount University *B*
Marymount College *A*
Master's College *B*
Mendocino College *A*
Menlo College *A*
Merced College *A*
Merritt College *A*

Mills College *B, M*
MiraCosta College *A*
Mission College *A*
Modesto Junior College *A*
Monterey Peninsula College *A*
Moorpark College *A*
Mount St. Mary's College *A*
Mount San Antonio College *A*
Mount San Jacinto College *A*
Napa Valley College *A*
National Hispanic University *A, B*
National University *A, B*
Notre Dame de Namur University *B*
Ohlone College *A*
Orange Coast College *A*
Oxnard College *A*
Palo Verde College *A*
Palomar College *A*
Pasadena City College *C, A*
Patten University *B*
Pepperdine University *B*
Platt College
    Cerritos *C*
Point Loma Nazarene University *B*
Porterville College *A*
Reedley College *A*
Rio Hondo College *A*
Sacramento City College *A*
Saddleback College *A*
St. Mary's College of California *B, M*
San Bernardino Valley College *A*
San Diego City College *A*
San Diego Mesa College *C, A*
San Diego Miramar College *A*
San Diego State University *B, M*
San Francisco State University *B, M*
San Joaquin Delta College *A*
San Jose City College *A*
San Jose State University *B*
Santa Barbara City College *A*
Santa Clara University *B*
Santa Monica College *A*
Santa Rosa Junior College *A*
Santiago Canyon College *A*
Sierra College *A*
Simpson University *B*
Skyline College *A*
Soka University of America *B*
Solano Community College *A*
Sonoma State University *B*
Southwestern College *A*
Stanford University *M*
Taft College *A*
Thomas Aquinas College *B*
University of California
    Los Angeles *B*
    Riverside *B*
University of Judaism *B*
University of La Verne *B*
University of Redlands *B*
University of San Diego *B*
University of San Francisco *B*
University of the Pacific *B*
Vanguard University of Southern
    California *B*
Ventura College *A*
Victor Valley College *A*
West Hills Community College *A*
West Los Angeles College *C, A*
West Valley College *A*
Whittier College *B*
Yuba Community College District *A*

Colorado

Adams State College *A, B*
Aims Community College *A*
Arapahoe Community College *A*
Colorado Christian University *A, B*
Colorado College *B*
Colorado Mountain College
    Alpine Campus *A*
    Spring Valley Campus *A*
    Timberline Campus *A*

Colorado Northwestern Community
    College *A*
Colorado State University *B*
Colorado State University
    Pueblo *B*
Community College of Denver *A*
Front Range Community College *A*
Mesa State College *A, B*
Morgan Community College *A*
Naropa University *M*
Otero Junior College *A*
Pikes Peak Community College *A*
Pueblo Community College *A*
Red Rocks Community College *A*
Regis University *B*
Trinidad State Junior College *A*
University of Denver *M*

Connecticut

Albertus Magnus College *A, B, M*
Asnuntuck Community College *A*
Briarwood College *A*
Capital Community College *A*
Charter Oak State College *A, B*
Gateway Community College *A*
Housatonic Community College *A*
Manchester Community College *A*
Middlesex Community College *A*
Mitchell College *A, B*
Naugatuck Valley Community
    College *A*
Northwestern Connecticut
    Community College *A*
Norwalk Community College *A*
Quinebaug Valley Community
    College *A*
Quinnipiac University *A*
Sacred Heart University *A, B*
St. Joseph College *B*
Southern Connecticut State
    University *B*
Three Rivers Community College *A*
Tunxis Community College *A*
University of Bridgeport *A, B*
University of Hartford *B*
University of New Haven *B*
Wesleyan University *B, M*
Western Connecticut State
    University *A, B*

Delaware

University of Delaware *A, B, M, D*
Wesley College *A, B*
Wilmington College *A, B*

District of Columbia

American University *A, B*
Catholic University of America *B*
George Washington University *B*
Georgetown University *B, M*
Southeastern University *A, B*
Strayer University *A*
Trinity University *B*

Florida

Barry University *B, M*
Beacon College *A, B*
Bethune-Cookman College *B*
Broward Community College *A*
Central Florida Community College *A*
Clearwater Christian College *A, B*
Daytona Beach Community College *A*
Edison College *A*
Edward Waters College *B*
Flagler College *B*
Florida Agricultural and Mechanical
    University *A*
Florida Atlantic University *A, B, M*
Florida College *A, B*
Florida Gulf Coast University *A, B*
Florida International University *B*
Florida Keys Community College *A*
Florida Southern College *B*

Florida State University *A*
Gulf Coast Community College *A*
Hillsborough Community College *A*
Indian River Community College *A*
Jacksonville University *B*
Lake City Community College *A*
Lake-Sumter Community College *A*
Lynn University *A, B*
Manatee Community College *A*
Miami Dade College *A*
New College of Florida *B*
North Florida Community College *A*
Nova Southeastern University *B*
Palm Beach Community College *A*
Pasco-Hernando Community
    College *A*
Pensacola Junior College *A*
Polk Community College *A*
Rollins College *M*
St. Johns River Community College *A*
St. Leo University *A*
St. Petersburg College *A*
St. Thomas University *B*
Santa Fe Community College *A*
Schiller International University *A*
Seminole Community College *A*
South Florida Community College *A*
Tallahassee Community College *A*
University of Central Florida *A, B, M*
University of Florida *A*
University of Miami *M*
University of North Florida *A, B*
University of South Florida *A, B, M*
University of Tampa *B*
University of West Florida *A*
Valencia Community College *A*
Warner Southern College *A*

Georgia

Abraham Baldwin Agricultural
    College *A*
Andrew College *A*
Atlanta Christian College *B*
Augusta State University *A*
Brenau University *B*
Clark Atlanta University *M, D*
Clayton State University *A, B*
Coastal Georgia Community
    College *A*
Columbus State University *A*
Dalton State College *A*
Darton College *A*
East Georgia College *A*
Emmanuel College *A*
Emory University *A, D*
Fort Valley State University *A, B*
Gainesville State College *A*
Georgia College and State
    University *B*
Georgia Highlands College *A*
Gordon College *A*
LaGrange College *A*
Macon State College *A*
Mercer University *B*
Middle Georgia College *A*
Oglethorpe University *B*
Oxford College of Emory
    University *A*
Reinhardt College *A, B*
Shorter College *B*
South Georgia College *A*
Southern Polytechnic State
    University *A*
Thomas University *A, B*
Truett-McConnell College *A*
University of Georgia *B*
Valdosta State University *A, B*
Wesleyan College *B*
Young Harris College *A*

Hawaii

Chaminade University of
    Honolulu *A, B*
Hawaii Pacific University *B*

Hawaii Tokai International College *A*
University of Hawaii
    Hawaii Community College *A*
    Hilo *B*
    Honolulu Community College *A*
    Kapiolani Community College *A*
    Kauai Community College *A*
    Leeward Community College *C, A*
    Manoa *B*
    Maui Community College *A*
    Windward Community College *A*

Idaho

Albertson College of Idaho *B*
Boise State University *B*
Brigham Young University-Idaho *A*
College of Southern Idaho *A*
Lewis-Clark State College *A*
North Idaho College *A*
Northwest Nazarene University *B*
University of Idaho *B*

Illinois

Augustana College *B*
Aurora University *B*
Black Hawk College *A*
Black Hawk College
    East Campus *A*
Bradley University *B, M*
City Colleges of Chicago
    Harold Washington College *A*
    Kennedy-King College *A*
    Malcolm X College *A*
    Olive-Harvey College *A*
    Richard J. Daley College *C, A*
    Wright College *A*
College of DuPage *A*
College of Lake County *A*
Columbia College Chicago *B*
Danville Area Community College *A*
DePaul University *B, M*
East-West University *A, B*
Eastern Illinois University *B*
Elgin Community College *A*
Elmhurst College *B*
Eureka College *B*
Governors State University *B*
Greenville College *B*
Heartland Community College *A*
Highland Community College *A*
Illinois Central College *A*
Illinois Eastern Community Colleges
    Frontier Community College *A*
    Lincoln Trail College *A*
    Olney Central College *A*
    Wabash Valley College *A*
Illinois State University *B*
John A. Logan College *A*
John Wood Community College *A*
Joliet Junior College *A*
Kankakee Community College *A*
Kaskaskia College *A*
Kishwaukee College *A*
Lake Forest College *M*
Lake Land College *A*
Lewis University *B*
Lewis and Clark Community
    College *A*
Lincoln Land Community College *A*
McHenry County College *A*
McKendree College *B*
Monmouth College *B*
Moraine Valley Community College *A*
Morton College *A*
National-Louis University *B*
North Central College *B, M*
North Park University *B*
Northeastern Illinois University *B*
Northern Illinois University *B*
Northwestern University *B, M*
Oakton Community College *A*
Olivet Nazarene University *B*
Parkland College *A*
Prairie State College *A*

Principia College *B*
Rend Lake College *A*
Richland Community College *A*
Rock Valley College *A*
Roosevelt University *B, M*
St. Augustine College *A*
St. Xavier University *B, M*
Sauk Valley Community College *A*
Shimer College *B*
South Suburban College of Cook
County *A*
Southeastern Illinois College *A*
Southern Illinois University
Carbondale *B*
Southern Illinois University
Edwardsville *B*
Southwestern Illinois College *A*
Spoon River College *A*
Springfield College in Illinois *A*
Triton College *A*
University of Chicago *B, M*
University of Illinois
Chicago *B*
Springfield *B, M*
Urbana-Champaign *A*
University of St. Francis *B*
Waubonsee Community College *A*
Western Illinois University *B*
William Rainey Harper College *A*

Indiana

Ancilla College *A*
Ball State University *A, B*
Bethel College *A, B*
Butler University *A, B*
Calumet College of St. Joseph *A, B*
Holy Cross College *A, B*
Indiana State University *A, B*
Indiana University
Bloomington *A, B*
East *A*
Kokomo *A*
Northwest *A*
South Bend *A, M*
Southeast *A, M*
Indiana University-Purdue University
Fort Wayne *M*
Indiana University-Purdue University
Indianapolis *A, B*
Ivy Tech State College
Ivy Tech Community College:
Bloomington *A*
Ivy Tech Community College:
Central Indiana *A*
Ivy Tech Community College:
Columbus *A*
Ivy Tech Community College: East
Central *A*
Ivy Tech Community College:
Kokomo *A*
Ivy Tech Community College:
Lafayette *A*
Ivy Tech Community College: North
Central *A*
Ivy Tech Community College:
Northeast *A*
Ivy Tech Community College:
Northwest *A*
Ivy Tech Community College: South
Central *A*
Ivy Tech Community College:
Southeast *A*
Ivy Tech Community College:
Southwest *A*
Ivy Tech Community College:
Wabash Valley *A*
Ivy Tech Community College:
Whitewater *A*
Manchester College *B*
Marian College *A*
Martin University *B*
Oakland City University *A, B*

Purdue University
Calumet *A*
North Central Campus *B*
St. Mary-of-the-Woods College *A, B*
Taylor University *A*
Taylor University: Fort Wayne *A*
University of Evansville *B*
University of Indianapolis *A*
University of Notre Dame *B*
University of St. Francis *A, B*
University of Southern Indiana *B, M*
Vincennes University *A*
Wabash College *B*

Iowa

Ashford University *A, B*
Briar Cliff University *A*
Clarke College *A*
Clinton Community College *A*
Des Moines Area Community
College *A*
Dordt College *B*
Ellsworth Community College *A*
Graceland University *B*
Grand View College *A, B*
Hawkeye Community College *A*
Indian Hills Community College *A*
Iowa Central Community College *A*
Iowa Lakes Community College *A*
Iowa State University *B*
Iowa Western Community College *A*
Kirkwood Community College *A*
Loras College *A, B*
Marshalltown Community College *A*
Mount Mercy College *B*
Muscatine Community College *A*
North Iowa Area Community
College *A*
Northwest Iowa Community
College *A*
Northwestern College *B*
Simpson College *B, T*
Southeastern Community College
North Campus *A*
Southwestern Community College *A*
University of Iowa *B*
University of Northern Iowa *B*
Upper Iowa University *A*
Waldorf College *A, B*
Western Iowa Tech Community
College *A*
William Penn University *B*

Kansas

Barton County Community College *A*
Benedictine College *B*
Bethany College *B*
Butler County Community College *A*
Central Christian College of
Kansas *A, B*
Cloud County Community College *A*
Coffeyville Community College *A*
Colby Community College *A*
Emporia State University *B*
Fort Scott Community College *A*
Friends University *A, B*
Garden City Community College *A*
Haskell Indian Nations University *A*
Hesston College *A*
Hutchinson Community College *A*
Johnson County Community
College *A*
Kansas City Kansas Community
College *A*
Labette Community College *A*
McPherson College *B*
MidAmerica Nazarene University *A*
Neosho County Community
College *A*
Newman University *A, B*
Pratt Community College *A*
Seward County Community College *A*
Southwestern College *B*
Tabor College *A*

University of Kansas *B, M, D*
University of St. Mary *A, B*
Washburn University of
Topeka *A, B, M*
Wichita State University *A, B, M*

Kentucky

Ashland Community and Technical
College *A*
Bellarmine University *B*
Big Sandy Community and Technical
College *A*
Bluegrass Community and Technical
College *A*
Brescia University *A, B*
Campbellsville University *A*
Eastern Kentucky University *B*
Elizabethtown Community and
Technical College *A*
Georgetown College *B*
Hazard Community College *A*
Henderson Community College *A*
Hopkinsville Community College *A*
Jefferson Community College *A*
Kentucky Christian University *B*
Kentucky State University *A, B*
Madisonville Community College *A*
Maysville Community College *A*
Murray State University *A, B*
Northern Kentucky
University *A, B, M*
Owensboro Community College *A*
St. Catharine College *A*
Somerset Community College *A*
Southeast Kentucky Community and
Technical College *A*
Spalding University *B*
Thomas More College *A, B*
Transylvania University *B*
University of Louisville *B*
West Kentucky Community and
Technical College *A*
Western Kentucky University *C*

Louisiana

Baton Rouge Community College *A*
Bossier Parish Community College *A*
Centenary College of Louisiana *B*
Delgado Community College *A*
Grambling State University *M*
Louisiana State University
Alexandria *A, B*
Shreveport *B, M*
Louisiana State University and
Agricultural and Mechanical
College *B, M*
Louisiana Tech University *A, B*
Loyola University New Orleans *B*
Nicholls State University *A, B*
Northwestern State University *B*
Nunez Community College *A*
Our Lady of Holy Cross College *B*
St. Joseph Seminary College *B*
Southeastern Louisiana University *B*
Southern University
Shreveport *A*

Maine

Central Maine Community College *A*
Eastern Maine Community College *A*
Husson College *B*
Kennebec Valley Community
College *A*
St. Joseph's College *B*
Southern Maine Community
College *A*
Unity College *A, B*
University of Maine *B, M*
University of Maine
Augusta *C, A*
Farmington *B*
Fort Kent *A, B*
Machias *B*
Presque Isle *A, B*

University of New England *B*
University of Southern Maine *A, B*
Washington County Community
College *A*
York County Community College *C*

Maryland

Allegany College of Maryland *A*
Anne Arundel Community College *A*
Baltimore City Community College *A*
Carroll Community College *A*
Cecil Community College *A*
Chesapeake College *A*
College of Notre Dame of
Maryland *B, M*
College of Southern Maryland *A*
Columbia Union College *B*
Community College of Baltimore
County *C, A*
Coppin State University *B*
Frederick Community College *A*
Frostburg State University *B*
Garrett College *A*
Hagerstown Community College *A*
Harford Community College *A*
Howard Community College *A*
Johns Hopkins University *B, M*
Loyola College in Maryland *M*
McDaniel College *M*
Montgomery College *A*
Mount St. Mary's University *M*
Prince George's Community
College *A*
St. John's College *B, M*
Salisbury University *B*
Towson University *M*
University of Baltimore *B*
University of Maryland
Eastern Shore *B*
University College *A, B*
Villa Julie College *B*
Washington College *B*

Massachusetts

American International College *A, B*
Anna Maria College *B*
Atlantic Union College *B*
Bay Path College *B*
Becker College *A, B*
Bentley College *B*
Berkshire Community College *A*
Bristol Community College *A*
Cape Cod Community College *A*
Clark University *B, M*
Curry College *B*
Dean College *A*
Eastern Nazarene College *A, B*
Elms College *B*
Endicott College *B*
Fisher College *A*
Fitchburg State College *B*
Framingham State College *B*
Greenfield Community College *A*
Hampshire College *B*
Harvard College *B*
Hellenic College/Holy Cross *B*
Holyoke Community College *C, A*
Lesley University *A, B, M*
Marian Court College *A*
Massachusetts Bay Community
College *C, A*
Massachusetts College of Liberal
Arts *B*
Massachusetts Institute of
Technology *B*
Massasoit Community College *A*
Merrimack College *A, B*
Middlesex Community College *A*
Mount Holyoke College *C*
Mount Ida College *A, B*
Mount Wachusett Community
College *A*
Newbury College *A*
North Shore Community College *A*

Northeastern University *B*
Northern Essex Community
    College *A*
Pine Manor College *A, B*
Quincy College *A*
Quinsigamond Community College *A*
Roxbury Community College *A*
St. John's Seminary College *B*
Salem State College *B*
Simon's Rock College of Bard *A, B*
Springfield College *B*
Springfield Technical Community
    College *A*
Suffolk University *A, B*
Tufts University *B*
University of Massachusetts
    Dartmouth *B*
    Lowell *B*
Urban College of Boston *C, A*
Western New England College *A, B*
Westfield State College *B*
Wheaton College *B*
Wheelock College *B*

Michigan

Alma College *B*
Alpena Community College *A*
Aquinas College *A, B*
Bay de Noc Community College *A*
Calvin College *B*
Central Michigan University *B, M*
Concordia University *A*
Delta College *A*
Ferris State University *A*
Finlandia University *A, B*
Glen Oaks Community College *A*
Gogebic Community College *A*
Grace Bible College *A, B*
Grand Rapids Community College *A*
Grand Valley State University *B*
Henry Ford Community College *A*
Hillsdale College *B*
Jackson Community College *A*
Kalamazoo Valley Community
    College *A*
Kellogg Community College *A*
Kirtland Community College *A*
Lake Michigan College *A*
Lake Superior State University *A*
Lansing Community College *A*
Lewis College of Business *A*
Macomb Community College *A*
Madonna University *M*
Marygrove College *A, T*
Michigan Technological
    University *B, T*
Mid Michigan Community College *A*
Monroe County Community
    College *A*
Montcalm Community College *A*
Mott Community College *A*
North Central Michigan College *A*
Northern Michigan University *A, B, M*
Northwestern Michigan College *A*
Oakland Community College *A*
Oakland University *B, M*
Olivet College *B*
Rochester College *A*
Sacred Heart Major Seminary *B*
St. Clair County Community
    College *A*
Schoolcraft College *A*
Siena Heights University *A, B*
Southwestern Michigan College *C, A*
Spring Arbor University *A*
University of Detroit Mercy *B, M*
University of Michigan
    Dearborn *B*
    Flint *B, M*
Washtenaw Community College *A*
Wayne County Community College *A*
West Shore Community College *A*

Minnesota

Anoka-Ramsey Community College *A*
Augsburg College *B, M*
Bemidji State University *A, B*
Bethany Lutheran College *B*
Bethel University *A*
Central Lakes College *A*
Century Community and Technical
    College *A*
College of St. Benedict *B*
College of St. Scholastica *B*
Concordia College: Moorhead *B*
Crossroads College *A*
Crown College *A, B*
Fond du Lac Tribal and Community
    College *A*
Hamline University *M*
Hibbing Community College *A*
Inver Hills Community College *A*
Itasca Community College *A*
Lake Superior College *A*
Leech Lake Tribal College *A*
Macalester College *B*
Mesabi Range Community and
    Technical College *A*
Metropolitan State University *B*
Minneapolis Community and
    Technical College *A*
Minnesota State Community and
    Technical College - Fergus Falls *A*
Minnesota State University
    Mankato *A, B*
    Moorhead *A, M*
Minnesota West Community and
    Technical College: Worthington
    Campus *A*
Normandale Community College *A*
North Hennepin Community
    College *A*
Northland Community & Technical
    College *A*
Northwestern College *A*
Oak Hills Christian College *A*
Rainy River Community College *A*
Ridgewater College *A*
Riverland Community College *A*
Rochester Community and Technical
    College *A*
St. Cloud State University *A, B*
St. John's University *B*
St. Olaf College *B*
St. Paul College *A*
Southwest Minnesota State
    University *A*
University of Minnesota
    Duluth *M*
    Twin Cities *C, B*
University of St. Thomas *B*
Winona State University *A, B*

Mississippi

Alcorn State University *B*
Copiah-Lincoln Community College *A*
East Central Community College *A*
Hinds Community College *A*
Holmes Community College *A*
Itawamba Community College *A*
Jones County Junior College *A*
Mississippi Delta Community
    College *A*
Mississippi Gulf Coast Community
    College
    Jefferson Davis Campus *A*
Mississippi State University *B*
Pearl River Community College *A*
Southwest Mississippi Community
    College *A*
Tougaloo College *B*
University of Mississippi *B*
Wesley College *C*

Missouri

Blue River Community College *A*
Columbia College *A, B*

Conception Seminary College *B*
Cottey College *A*
Crowder College *A*
Drury University *B, M*
Evangel University *A*
Fontbonne University *B*
Hannibal-LaGrange College *A, B*
Jefferson College *A*
Lincoln University *B*
Longview Community College *A*
Maple Woods Community College *A*
Maryville University of Saint Louis *B*
Mineral Area College *A*
Missouri State University: West
    Plains *A*
Missouri Valley College *A, B*
Missouri Western State University *B*
Moberly Area Community College *A*
North Central Missouri College *A*
Northwest Missouri State
    University *A*
Ozarks Technical Community
    College *A*
Park University *A, B*
Penn Valley Community College *A*
Rockhurst University *B*
St. Charles Community College *A*
St. Louis Christian College *A*
St. Louis Community College
    St. Louis Community College at
        Florissant Valley *A*
    St. Louis Community College at
        Meramec *A*
State Fair Community College *A*
Stephens College *A, B*
Three Rivers Community College *A*
University of Missouri
    Kansas City *B, M*
    St. Louis *B*
Washington University in St.
    Louis *B, M*
Webster University *B*

Montana

Dawson Community College *A*
Flathead Valley Community College *A*
Fort Belknap College *A*
Helena College of Technology of the
    University of Montana *A*
Little Big Horn College *A*
Miles Community College *A*
Montana State University
    Billings *A, B*
Montana Tech of the University of
    Montana *A*
Rocky Mountain College *A*
Salish Kootenai College *A*
Stone Child College *A*
University of Montana: Missoula *A, B*
University of Montana: Western *A, B*

Nebraska

Bellevue University *B*
Central Community College *A*
Chadron State College *B, M*
College of Saint Mary *A, B*
Creighton University *M*
Dana College *B*
Grace University *B*
Hastings College *B*
Little Priest Tribal College *A*
Metropolitan Community College *A*
Mid-Plains Community College Area *A*
Midland Lutheran College *B*
Nebraska Christian College *B*
Nebraska Indian Community
    College *A*
Northeast Community College *A*
Southeast Community College
    Lincoln Campus *A*
University of Nebraska
    Kearney *B*
    Lincoln *B*

Western Nebraska Community
    College *A*

Nevada

Community College of Southern
    Nevada *A*
Great Basin College *B*
Sierra Nevada College *B*
University of Nevada
    Las Vegas *B, M*
Western Nevada Community
    College *A*

New Hampshire

Chester College of New England *A*
Colby-Sawyer College *A*
Daniel Webster College *A*
Dartmouth College *M*
Franklin Pierce College *A*
Granite State College *A, B*
Magdalen College *A, B*
New England College *A, B*
New Hampshire Community
    Technical College
    Berlin *A*
    Claremont *C, A*
    Manchester *A*
    Nashua *C, A*
New Hampshire Technical Institute *A*
Rivier College *A, B*
St. Anselm College *B*
Southern New Hampshire
    University *A, B*
University of New Hampshire *M*
University of New Hampshire at
    Manchester *A, B*

New Jersey

Assumption College for Sisters *A*
Bergen Community College *A*
Brookdale Community College *A*
Burlington County College *A*
Caldwell College *M*
Camden County College *A*
Centenary College *A*
County College of Morris *A*
Cumberland County College *A*
Essex County College *A*
Fairleigh Dickinson University
    Metropolitan Campus *A*
Felician College *A*
Georgian Court University *B*
Gloucester County College *A*
Hudson County Community
    College *A*
Kean University *B, M*
Mercer County Community College *A*
Monmouth University *A, M*
Montclair State University *B*
Ocean County College *A*
Passaic County Community College *A*
Ramapo College of New Jersey *B, M*
Raritan Valley Community College *A*
Richard Stockton College of New
    Jersey *B*
Rider University *A, B*
Rowan University *B*
Rutgers, The State University of New
    Jersey
    Camden Regional Campus *B, M*
    Newark Regional Campus *M*
Salem Community College *A*
Seton Hall University *B*
Stevens Institute of Technology *B*
Sussex County Community College *A*
Thomas Edison State College *A, B*
Union County College *A*
Warren County Community College *A*

New Mexico

Albuquerque Technical-Vocational
    Institute *A*
College of the Southwest *B*

Eastern New Mexico University *A, B*
Eastern New Mexico University:
  Roswell Campus *A*
New Mexico Junior College *A*
New Mexico Military Institute Junior
  College *A*
New Mexico State University
  Alamogordo *A*
  Carlsbad *A*
Northern New Mexico College *A*
St. John's College *B, M*
San Juan College *A*
Southwestern Indian Polytechnic
  Institute *A*
University of New Mexico *B*
Western New Mexico University *B*

New York

Adelphi University *A*
Adirondack Community College *A*
Alfred University *B*
Bard College *A, B*
Boricua College *B*
Broome Community College *A*
Canisius College *B*
Cayuga County Community College *A*
Cazenovia College *A, B*
City University of New York
  Baruch College *B*
  Borough of Manhattan Community
    College *A*
  Bronx Community College *A*
  Brooklyn College *M*
  College of Staten Island *A, B, M*
  Hostos Community College *A*
  Kingsborough Community
    College *A*
  LaGuardia Community College *A*
  Lehman College *B, M*
  Medgar Evers College *A, B*
  New York City College of
    Technology *A*
  Queens College *M*
  Queensborough Community
    College *A*
  York College *B*
Clarkson University *B*
Clinton Community College *A*
Colgate University *B*
College of Mount St. Vincent *A, B*
College of Saint Rose *B*
Columbia-Greene Community
  College *A*
Concordia College *A, B*
Cornell University *B*
Corning Community College *A*
Dominican College of Blauvelt *A*
Dowling College *B*
Dutchess Community College *A*
Elmira College *A*
Erie Community College
  City Campus *A*
  North Campus *A*
  South Campus *A*
Eugene Lang College The New School
  for Liberal Arts *B*
Excelsior College *A, B, M*
Finger Lakes Community College *A*
Five Towns College *A*
Fulton-Montgomery Community
  College *C, A*
Genesee Community College *A*
Hamilton College *B*
Hartwick College *B*
Herkimer County Community
  College *A*
Hilbert College *A, B*
Hofstra University *B*
Hudson Valley Community College *C*
Iona College *B*
Ithaca College *B*
Jamestown Community College *C, A*
Jefferson Community College *A*
Keuka College *B*

Long Island University
  Brooklyn Campus *A, B*
  C.W. Post Campus *B, M*
Manhattanville College *B, M*
Maria College *A*
Medaille College *A, B*
Mercy College *C, A, B*
Mohawk Valley Community
  College *C, A*
Molloy College *A*
Monroe Community College *A*
Mount St. Mary College *B, T*
Nassau Community College *A*
New York University *A, B, M*
Niagara County Community
  College *A*
Niagara University *A, B, T*
North Country Community College *A*
Nyack College *A, B*
Onondaga Community College *A*
Orange County Community College *A*
Pace University *A, B*
Paul Smith's College *A, B*
Polytechnic University *B*
Rensselaer Polytechnic Institute *B*
Roberts Wesleyan College *B*
Rockland Community College *A*
Sage College of Albany *A, B*
St. Francis College *A, B*
St. John Fisher College *B*
St. John's University *A, B, M*
St. Joseph's College *B*
St. Joseph's College: Suffolk
  Campus *B*
St. Thomas Aquinas College *A, B*
Sarah Lawrence College *B*
Schenectady County Community
  College *C, A*
Skidmore College *B, M*
State University of New York
  Albany *B, M, D*
  Buffalo *A*
  College at Brockport *M*
  College at Old Westbury *B*
  College at Plattsburgh *B, M*
  College at Potsdam *B*
  College of Agriculture and
    Technology at Cobleskill *A*
  College of Agriculture and
    Technology at Morrisville *A*
  College of Technology at Alfred *A*
  College of Technology at Canton *A*
  College of Technology at Delhi *A*
  Empire State College *A, B, M*
  Farmingdale *A*
  Institute of Technology at
    Utica/Rome *B*
  Maritime College *B*
  New Paltz *B*
  Purchase *B*
  Stony Brook *M*
Suffolk County Community College *A*
Sullivan County Community
  College *A*
Syracuse University *D*
Tompkins-Cortland Community
  College *C, A*
Touro College *A, B*
Trocaire College *A*
Ulster County Community College *A*
Union College *B*
Utica College *B, M*
Vassar College *B*
Villa Maria College of Buffalo *A*
Wagner College *B*
Westchester Community College *A*

North Carolina

Alamance Community College *A*
Appalachian State University *B*
Asheville-Buncombe Technical
  Community College *A*
Barton College *B*

Beaufort County Community
  College *A*
Belmont Abbey College *B*
Bennett College *B*
Bladen Community College *A*
Blue Ridge Community College *A*
Brevard College *B*
Brunswick Community College *A*
Caldwell Community College and
  Technical Institute *A*
Cape Fear Community College *A*
Carteret Community College *A*
Catawba Valley Community College *A*
Central Carolina Community
  College *A*
Central Piedmont Community
  College *A*
Chowan College *B*
Cleveland Community College *A*
Coastal Carolina Community
  College *A*
College of the Albemarle *A*
Craven Community College *A*
Davidson County Community
  College *A*
Duke University *M*
Durham Technical Community
  College *A*
East Carolina University *B*
Edgecombe Community College *A*
Fayetteville Technical Community
  College *A*
Forsyth Technical Community
  College *A*
Gaston College *A*
Guilford Technical Community
  College *A*
Halifax Community College *A*
Haywood Community College *A*
Isothermal Community College *A*
James Sprunt Community College *A*
Johnson C. Smith University *B*
Johnston Community College *A*
Lees-McRae College *B*
Lenoir Community College *A*
Lenoir-Rhyne College *B*
Louisburg College *C, A*
Mars Hill College *B*
Martin Community College *A*
Mayland Community College *A*
McDowell Technical Community
  College *A*
Methodist College *A, B*
Mitchell Community College *A*
Montgomery Community College *A*
Mount Olive College *A, B*
Nash Community College *A*
North Carolina School of the Arts *B*
North Carolina State University *B, M*
Peace College *B*
Piedmont Community College *A*
Pitt Community College *C, A*
Randolph Community College *A*
Richmond Community College *A*
Roanoke-Chowan Community
  College *A*
Rockingham Community College *A*
St. Andrews Presbyterian College *B*
Sandhills Community College *A*
Shaw University *B*
South Piedmont Community
  College *A*
Southeastern Community College *A*
Southwestern Community College *A*
Stanly Community College *A*
Surry Community College *A*
Tri-County Community College *C, A*
University of North Carolina
  Asheville *B, M*
  Chapel Hill *B*
  Charlotte *B*
  Greensboro *B, M*
  Wilmington *M*

Vance-Granville Community
  College *A*
Wake Forest University *M*
Wake Technical Community
  College *A*
Warren Wilson College *B*
Wayne Community College *A*
Western Carolina University *B*
Western Piedmont Community
  College *A*
Wilkes Community College *A*
Wilson Technical Community
  College *A*
Wingate University *B*
Winston-Salem State University *B*

North Dakota

Bismarck State College *A*
Dickinson State University *A, B, T*
Lake Region State College *A*
Minot State University *B*
Minot State University: Bottineau
  Campus *A*
North Dakota State College of
  Science *A*
North Dakota State University *B*
Valley City State University *B*
Williston State College *A*

Ohio

Antioch College *B*
Antioch University McGregor *B*
Ashland University *A, B*
Bowling Green State University *B*
Bowling Green State University:
  Firelands College *A*
Capital University *B*
Chatfield College *A*
Cincinnati State Technical and
  Community College *A*
Clark State Community College *A*
Cleveland State University *B*
College of Mount St. Joseph *A, B*
Columbus State Community
  College *A*
Cuyahoga Community College
  Metropolitan Campus *A*
David N. Myers University *B*
Defiance College *B*
Edison State Community College *A*
Jefferson Community College *A*
John Carroll University *B, M*
Kent State University *C, B, M*
Kent State University
  Ashtabula Regional Campus *A*
  East Liverpool Regional Campus *A*
  Salem Regional Campus *A*
  Stark Campus *A*
  Trumbull Campus *A*
  Tuscarawas Campus *C, A*
Lakeland Community College *A*
Lourdes College *A*
Malone College *B*
Marietta College *A, M*
Miami University
  Oxford Campus *A*
Mount Vernon Nazarene University *A*
Ohio Dominican University *B, M*
Ohio Northern University *B*
Ohio State University
  Columbus Campus *B, M*
  Lima Campus *A*
  Mansfield Campus *A*
  Marion Campus *A*
  Newark Campus *A*
Ohio University *A*
Ohio University
  Chillicothe Campus *A*
  Eastern Campus *A, B*
  Zanesville Campus *A*
Ohio Wesleyan University *B*
Pontifical College Josephinum *B*
Sinclair Community College *A*
Southern State Community College *A*

Stark State College of Technology *A*
Tiffin University *B*
Union Institute & University *B*
University of Akron *C, A, B*
University of Akron: Wayne College *A*
University of Cincinnati *B*
University of Cincinnati
 Clermont College *A*
 Raymond Walters College *A*
University of Findlay *A, M*
University of Rio Grande *A*
University of Toledo *B, M*
Urbana University *A, B*
Ursuline College *M*
Walsh University *A*
Washington State Community
 College *A*
Wilmington College *B*
Wittenberg University *B*
Wright State University *B*
Wright State University: Lake
 Campus *A*
Xavier University *A, B*
Youngstown State University *A*

Oklahoma

Bacone College *A*
Connors State College *A*
Mid-America Christian University *A*
Murray State College *A*
Oklahoma Baptist University *B*
Oklahoma Christian University *B*
Oklahoma City Community College *A*
Oklahoma City University *B, M*
Oklahoma State University *B*
Oral Roberts University *B*
Rogers State University *A, B*
Rose State College *A*
St. Gregory's University *A, B*
Seminole State College *A*
Southern Nazarene University *B*
University of Central Oklahoma *B*
University of Oklahoma *B, M*
University of Tulsa *B*
Western Oklahoma State College *A*

Oregon

Blue Mountain Community College *A*
Central Oregon Community
 College *A*
Chemeketa Community College *A*
Clackamas Community College *A*
Clatsop Community College *A*
Concordia University *A, B*
Corban College *B*
Eastern Oregon University *B*
Lane Community College *A*
Lewis & Clark College *B*
Linn-Benton Community College *A*
Marylhurst University *B*
Mount Angel Seminary *B, M*
Oregon State University *B*
Pacific University *B*
Portland Community College *A*
Portland State University *B*
Reed College *M*
Rogue Community College *A*
Southwestern Oregon Community
 College *A*
Treasure Valley Community College *A*
Umpqua Community College *A*
Warner Pacific College *B*
Western Oregon University *A, B*

Pennsylvania

Alvernia College *B, M*
Arcadia University *B*
Baptist Bible College of
 Pennsylvania *A*
Bryn Athyn College of the New
 Church *A*
Bucks County Community College *A*
Cabrini College *B*

California University of
 Pennsylvania *A, B*
Carlow University *B*
Carnegie Mellon University *B*
Cedar Crest College *B*
Clarion University of
 Pennsylvania *A, B*
College Misericordia *B*
Community College of Allegheny
 County *A*
Community College of Beaver
 County *A*
Community College of Philadelphia *A*
DeSales University *B*
Delaware County Community
 College *A*
Drexel University *B*
Duquesne University *M*
East Stroudsburg University of
 Pennsylvania *B*
Eastern University *A*
Edinboro University of
 Pennsylvania *A*
Gannon University *A, B*
Geneva College *B*
Gettysburg College *B*
Gwynedd-Mercy College *A*
Harcum College *A*
Haverford College *B*
Holy Family University *B*
Juniata College *B*
Keystone College *A*
Kutztown University of
 Pennsylvania *B*
La Roche College *B*
La Salle University *A, B*
Lackawanna College *A*
Lebanon Valley College *A, B*
Lehigh Carbon Community College *A*
Lock Haven University of
 Pennsylvania *B, M, T*
Luzerne County Community
 College *A*
Manor College *A*
Mansfield University of
 Pennsylvania *B*
Mercyhurst College *C, A*
Montgomery County Community
 College *A*
Mount Aloysius College *A, B*
Neumann College *A, B*
Northampton County Area
 Community College *A*
Penn State
 Abington *A, B*
 Altoona *A, B*
 Beaver *A, B*
 Berks *A, B*
 Delaware County *A, B*
 Dubois *A, B*
 Erie, The Behrend College *A, B*
 Fayette *A, B*
 Harrisburg *B, M*
 Hazleton *A, B*
 Lehigh Valley *A, B*
 McKeesport *A, B*
 Mont Alto *A, B*
 New Kensington *A, B*
 Schuylkill - Capital College *A, B*
 Shenango *A, B*
 University Park *A, B*
 Wilkes-Barre *A, B*
 Worthington Scranton *A, B*
 York *A, B*
Pennsylvania Highlands Community
 College *A*
Reading Area Community College *A*
Rosemont College *B, M*
St. Joseph's University *A*
St. Vincent College *B*
Temple University *B, M*
Thiel College *A*
University of Pennsylvania *B, M*
University of Pittsburgh *B*

University of Pittsburgh
 Bradford *B*
 Greensburg *B*
 Johnstown *B*
 Titusville *A*
Valley Forge Military College *A*
Villanova University *A, B, M*
Waynesburg College *A*
West Chester University of
 Pennsylvania *B*
Westmoreland County Community
 College *A*
Widener University *A, B, M*
Wilkes University *B*
Wilson College *A*
York College of Pennsylvania *A, B*

Puerto Rico

Pontifical Catholic University of
 Puerto Rico *B*
University of Puerto Rico
 Aguadilla *A*
 Arecibo *A*
 Cayey University College *B*
 Ponce *A*
 Rio Piedras *B*

Rhode Island

Community College of Rhode
 Island *A*
Providence College *A, B*
Rhode Island College *B*
Salve Regina University *A, B*

South Carolina

Aiken Technical College *A*
Anderson University *A*
Central Carolina Technical College *A*
Charleston Southern University *B*
Coastal Carolina University *B*
Columbia College *B*
Converse College *M*
Denmark Technical College *A*
Florence-Darlington Technical
 College *A*
Francis Marion University *B*
Greenville Technical College *C, A*
Horry-Georgetown Technical
 College *A*
Lander University *B*
Limestone College *A, B*
Midlands Technical College *C, A*
Morris College *B*
North Greenville College *A, B*
Northeastern Technical College *A*
Orangeburg-Calhoun Technical
 College *A*
Piedmont Technical College *C, A*
Spartanburg Methodist College *A*
Spartanburg Technical College *A*
Technical College of the
 Lowcountry *A*
Tri-County Technical College *A*
Trident Technical College *A*
University of South Carolina *A, B*
University of South Carolina
 Beaufort *A*
 Lancaster *A*
 Salkehatchie Regional Campus *A*
 Sumter *A*
 Union *A*
 Upstate *B*
Williamsburg Technical College *A*
Winthrop University *M*
Wofford College *B*
York Technical College *A*

South Dakota

Dakota State University *A*
Dakota Wesleyan University *A*
Kilian Community College *A*
Northern State University *A*
Oglala Lakota College *A*

Sisseton Wahpeton College *A*
South Dakota State University *B*
University of Sioux Falls *B*
University of South Dakota *A, B, M*

Tennessee

American Baptist College of ABT
 Seminary *B*
Aquinas College *A, B*
Austin Peay State University *A, B*
Belmont University *B*
Bethel College *B*
Bryan College *A, B*
Carson-Newman College *B*
Chattanooga State Technical
 Community College *A*
Christian Brothers University *B*
Cleveland State Community
 College *C, A*
Columbia State Community College *A*
Crichton College *B*
Cumberland University *B*
Dyersburg State Community
 College *A*
East Tennessee State University *B, M*
Fisk University *B*
Freed-Hardeman University *B, T*
Hiwassee College *A*
Jackson State Community College *A*
Lambuth University *B*
Lee University *B, M*
Lincoln Memorial University *B, T*
Martin Methodist College *A*
Middle Tennessee State University *B*
Motlow State Community College *A*
Nashville State Community College *C*
Northeast State Technical Community
 College *A*
Pellissippi State Technical Community
 College *A*
Roane State Community College *A*
Southern Adventist University *A*
Southwest Tennessee Community
 College *A*
Tennessee State University *B*
Tennessee Temple University *A, B*
Trevecca Nazarene University *A*
University of Memphis *B, M*
University of Tennessee
 Chattanooga *B*
Vanderbilt University *M*
Volunteer State Community College *A*
Walters State Community College *A*

Texas

Abilene Christian University *B, M*
Alvin Community College *A*
Amarillo College *A*
Amberton University *B*
Austin Community College *A*
Blinn College *A*
Brazosport College *A*
Central Texas College *A*
Clarendon College *A*
Coastal Bend College *A*
College of Saint Thomas More *B*
College of the Mainland *A*
Concordia University at Austin *B*
Dallas Baptist University *A, B, M*
Dallas Christian College *B*
Del Mar College *A*
East Texas Baptist University *A, B*
Eastfield College *A*
El Centro College *A*
El Paso Community College *A*
Frank Phillips College *A*
Galveston College *A*
Grayson County College *A*
Hill College *C, A*
Houston Baptist University *M*
Howard College *A*
Howard Payne University *B*
Huston-Tillotson College *B*
Jacksonville College *A*

Kilgore College *A*
Lamar State College at Orange *A*
Lamar University *B*
Laredo Community College *A*
Lee College *A*
Lon Morris College *A*
Mountain View College *A*
Navarro College *A*
North Harris Montgomery
   Community College District *A*
North Lake College *A*
Northeast Texas Community
   College *A*
Northwest Vista College *A*
Odessa College *A*
Our Lady of the Lake University of San
   Antonio *B*
Palo Alto College *A*
Panola College *A*
Paris Junior College *A*
Ranger College *A*
Richland College *A*
St. Edward's University *B*
St. Mary's University *B*
St. Philip's College *A*
San Antonio College *C, A*
San Jacinto College
   North *A*
Schreiner University *A, B*
South Plains College *A*
South Texas College *A*
Southern Methodist University *M*
Southwest Texas Junior College *A*
Stephen F. Austin State University *B*
Tarleton State University *B, M*
Temple College *A*
Texas A&M University *B, M*
Texas A&M University
   Commerce *B*
   Galveston *B*
Texas Christian University *B, M*
Texas College *B*
Texas Southmost College *A*
Texas Tech University *B*
Trinity Valley Community College *A*
Tyler Junior College *A*
University of Houston
   Clear Lake *B, M*
   Downtown *B*
University of North Texas *B*
University of St. Thomas *B, M*
University of Texas
   Austin *B*
   Brownsville *B*
   Dallas *B, M, D*
   El Paso *B*
   of the Permian Basin *B*
Vernon College *A*
Victoria College *A*
Weatherford College *A*
Western Texas College *A*
Wharton County Junior College *A*

Utah

Brigham Young University *A, B*
College of Eastern Utah *A*
Utah State University *A, B, M*
Weber State University *A, B*

Vermont

Bennington College *B*
Burlington College *A, B*
Champlain College *A, B*
College of St. Joseph in Vermont *A, B*
Community College of Vermont *A*
Goddard College *B*
Green Mountain College *B*
Johnson State College *A, B*
Landmark College *A*
Lyndon State College *A, B*
Marlboro College *B*
Middlebury College *B*
Norwich University *B*
Southern Vermont College *A, B*

Sterling College *A, B*
University of Vermont *B*

Virginia

Averett University *A, B*
Blue Ridge Community College *A*
Bluefield College *B*
Bridgewater College *B*
Central Virginia Community
   College *A*
Christendom College *A*
Dabney S. Lancaster Community
   College *A*
Danville Community College *A*
Eastern Mennonite University *B*
Eastern Shore Community College *A*
Ferrum College *B*
George Mason University *B*
Germanna Community College *A*
Hampton University *B*
Hollins University *M*
J. Sargeant Reynolds Community
   College *A*
James Madison University *B*
John Tyler Community College *A*
Longwood University *B, T*
Lord Fairfax Community College *A*
Marymount University *A, B*
Mountain Empire Community
   College *A*
New River Community College *A*
Northern Virginia Community
   College *A*
Patrick Henry Community College *A*
Piedmont Virginia Community
   College *A*
Radford University *B*
Rappahannock Community College *A*
Richard Bland College *A*
Shenandoah University *B*
Southside Virginia Community
   College *A*
Southwest Virginia Community
   College *A*
Sweet Briar College *B*
Thomas Nelson Community
   College *A*
Tidewater Community College *A*
University of Mary Washington *M*
University of Richmond *C, A, M*
University of Virginia *B*
University of Virginia's College at
   Wise *B, T*
Virginia Highlands Community
   College *A*
Virginia Intermont College *A, B*
Virginia Polytechnic Institute and
   State University *B*
Virginia State University *B*
Virginia Wesleyan College *B*
Virginia Western Community
   College *A*
Wytheville Community College *A*

Washington

Antioch University Seattle *B, M*
Bellevue Community College *A*
Big Bend Community College *A*
Centralia College *A*
City University *A, B*
Clark College *A*
Columbia Basin College *A*
Eastern Washington University *B*
Edmonds Community College *A*
Everett Community College *A*
Evergreen State College *B*
Gonzaga University *B*
Grays Harbor College *A*
Green River Community College *A*
Highline Community College *A*
Lower Columbia College *A*
Northwest University *B*
Olympic College *A*
Peninsula College *A*

Pierce College *A*
Seattle Central Community College *A*
Seattle University *B*
Shoreline Community College *C, A*
Skagit Valley College *A*
South Puget Sound Community
   College *A*
South Seattle Community College *A*
Spokane Community College *A*
Spokane Falls Community College *A*
Tacoma Community College *A*
University of Washington *B*
Walla Walla College *B*
Walla Walla Community College *A*
Washington State University *B*
Wenatchee Valley College *A*
Whatcom Community College *A*
Whitworth College *B*
Yakima Valley Community College *A*

West Virginia

Alderson-Broaddus College *A, B*
Bluefield State College *A, B*
Concord University *B*
Eastern West Virginia Community and
   Technical College *A*
Glenville State College *A*
Mountain State University *A, B, M*
Ohio Valley University *A, B*
Potomac State College of West Virginia
   University *A*
Salem International University *A, B*
Southern West Virginia Community
   and Technical College *A*
West Liberty State College *B*
West Virginia Northern Community
   College *A*
West Virginia State University *B*
West Virginia University *B, M*
West Virginia University Institute of
   Technology *A*
West Virginia University at
   Parkersburg *A*
Wheeling Jesuit University *B*

Wisconsin

Alverno College *A, B*
Beloit College *B*
Cardinal Stritch University *A*
College of Menominee Nation *A*
Concordia University Wisconsin *B*
Edgewood College *A, B*
Lakeland College *A*
Lawrence University *B*
Madison Area Technical College *A*
Marian College of Fond du Lac *B*
Milwaukee Area Technical College *A*
Moraine Park Technical College *A*
Nicolet Area Technical College *A*
Northland College *B*
Silver Lake College *A*
University of Wisconsin
   Baraboo/Sauk County *C, A*
   Eau Claire *A*
   Fond du Lac *A*
   Green Bay *A, B*
   Marathon County *A*
   Marinette *A*
   Marshfield/Wood County *A*
   Milwaukee *B*
   Oshkosh *B*
   Parkside *B*
   Platteville *A*
   Richland *A*
   Rock County *A*
   Stevens Point *A, B*
   Superior *A, B*
   Waukesha *A*
   Whitewater *A, B*
Viterbo University *B*

Wyoming

Casper College *A*
Eastern Wyoming College *A*

Laramie County Community
   College *A*
Northwest College *A*
Sheridan College *A*

Library assistance

Arizona

Mesa Community College *A*
Northland Pioneer College *C, A*

California

Barstow College *C*
Chabot College *A*
Citrus College *C, A*
City College of San Francisco *A*
College of the Canyons *C, A*
College of the Sequoias *C*
Cuesta College *C, A*
Foothill College *C, A*
Fullerton College *A*
Imperial Valley College *C*
Pasadena City College *C, A*
Rio Hondo College *A*
Sacramento City College *C, A*
Sierra College *A*

Colorado

Pueblo Community College *C, A*

Connecticut

Capital Community College *A*
Three Rivers Community College *C*

Florida

Hillsborough Community College *C*
Indian River Community College *A*

Illinois

Black Hawk College *C*
City Colleges of Chicago
   Wright College *C, A*
College of DuPage *C, A*
College of Lake County *C, A*
Illinois Central College *A*

Indiana

Ivy Tech State College
   Ivy Tech Community College:
      Bloomington *A*
   Ivy Tech Community College:
      Columbus *A*
   Ivy Tech Community College: East
      Central *A*
   Ivy Tech Community College:
      Kokomo *A*
   Ivy Tech Community College:
      Lafayette *A*
   Ivy Tech Community College: North
      Central *A*
   Ivy Tech Community College:
      Northeast *A*
   Ivy Tech Community College:
      Northwest *A*
   Ivy Tech Community College: South
      Central *A*
   Ivy Tech Community College:
      Southeast *A*
   Ivy Tech Community College:
      Southwest *A*
   Ivy Tech Community College:
      Wabash Valley *A*
   Ivy Tech Community College:
      Whitewater *A*

Kansas

Seward County Community College *A*

Kentucky

Bluegrass Community and Technical
   College *C*

Maine

University of Maine
  Augusta *A*

Michigan

Bay de Noc Community College *C*
Kirtland Community College *C, A*
Oakland Community College *C, A*

Minnesota

Minneapolis Community and
  Technical College *A*

New Mexico

Dona Ana Branch Community College
  of New Mexico State
  University *A*
Northern New Mexico College *C, A*

Ohio

Ohio Dominican University *A*

Oklahoma

Rose State College *C, A*

Oregon

Portland Community College *C*

Pennsylvania

Northampton County Area
  Community College *C*

Utah

Salt Lake Community College *C*

Washington

Highline Community College *A*
Lake Washington Technical College *C*

Library science

Alabama

University of Alabama *M, D*

Arizona

University of Arizona *M, D*

Arkansas

University of Central Arkansas *M*

California

Azusa Pacific University *M*
Cabrillo College *A*
Citrus College *A*
City College of San Francisco *A*
Fresno City College *A*
Los Angeles Harbor College *A*
Palomar College *A*
San Bernardino Valley College *A*
San Jose State University *M*
Santa Ana College *A*
Santiago Canyon College *A*
Sierra College *A*
University of California
  Los Angeles *M, D*

Colorado

Jones International University *C*
University of Colorado
  Denver and Health Sciences
    Center *M*
University of Denver *M*

Connecticut

Southern Connecticut State
  University *B, M*

District of Columbia

Catholic University of America *M*

Florida

Florida State University *M, D, T*
Gulf Coast Community College *A*
University of South Florida *M*

Georgia

Clark Atlanta University *M, D*
Valdosta State University *M*

Hawaii

University of Hawaii
  Manoa *M*

Idaho

College of Southern Idaho *A*

Illinois

Chicago State University *M*
Dominican University *M*
University of Illinois
  Urbana-Champaign *M, D*

Indiana

Ball State University *B*
Indiana University
  Bloomington *M, D*
Indiana University-Purdue University
  Indianapolis *M*

Iowa

Iowa Wesleyan College *B*
University of Iowa *M*
University of Northern Iowa *M*

Kansas

Allen County Community College *A*
Emporia State University *C, M, D*

Kentucky

University of Kentucky *M*
Western Kentucky University *M, T*

Louisiana

Louisiana State University and
  Agricultural and Mechanical
  College *M*

Maine

University of Maine
  Augusta *B*

Maryland

University of Maryland
  College Park *M, D*

Massachusetts

Simmons College *M, D*

Michigan

Central Michigan University *M*
University of Michigan *M*
Wayne State University *M, D, T*

Minnesota

College of St. Catherine *B, M*
Minnesota State University
  Mankato *M*
St. Cloud State University *B, M*

Mississippi

Itawamba Community College *A*
University of Southern
  Mississippi *B, M*

Missouri

Central Missouri State University *M*
Harris-Stowe State University *T*
Lindenwood University *M*
Missouri Baptist University *T*
Three Rivers Community College *A*

University of Missouri
  Columbia *M*

Montana

University of Montana: Western *T*

Nebraska

Chadron State College *B*
University of Nebraska
  Omaha *B*

New Jersey

Rowan University *M*
Rutgers, The State University of New
  Jersey
  New Brunswick/Piscataway
    Campus *M, D*

New York

City University of New York
  Queens College *M*
Long Island University
  C.W. Post Campus *M*
Pratt Institute *M*
St. John's University *M*
State University of New York
  Albany *M*
  Buffalo *M*
Syracuse University *M*

North Carolina

Appalachian State University *M*
East Carolina University *M*
North Carolina Central University *M*
University of North Carolina
  Chapel Hill *M, D*
  Greensboro *M*

Ohio

Kent State University *C, M*
Miami University
  Oxford Campus *T*

Oklahoma

Northeastern State University *M, T*
Northwestern Oklahoma State
  University *M*
Tulsa Community College *A*
University of Oklahoma *M*

Pennsylvania

Arcadia University *M*
Clarion University of
  Pennsylvania *B, M, T*
Drexel University *M*
Kutztown University of
  Pennsylvania *B, M, T*
Lock Haven University of
  Pennsylvania *B, T*
Marywood University *M*
University of Pittsburgh *M, D*

Puerto Rico

Inter American University of Puerto
  Rico
  San German Campus *M*
Turabo University *M*
University of Puerto Rico
  Rio Piedras *M*

Rhode Island

University of Rhode Island *M*

South Carolina

University of South Carolina *M*

Tennessee

Tennessee Technological
  University *M*
Trevecca Nazarene University *M*
Union University *T*

University of Tennessee
  Knoxville *M, T*

Texas

Brazosport College *A*
Our Lady of the Lake University of San
  Antonio *M*
Sam Houston State University *M*
Texas A&M University
  Commerce *B, M*
Texas Woman's University *M, D*
University of Houston
  Clear Lake *M*
University of North Texas *B, M, D*
University of Texas
  Austin *M, D*
  El Paso *M*

Virginia

University of Virginia's College at
  Wise *T*

Washington

University of Washington *M*

West Virginia

Concord University *B, T*
Mountain State University *A, B*

Wisconsin

University of Wisconsin
  Madison *M, D*
  Milwaukee *M*

Licensed midwifery

Florida

Miami Dade College *A*

Indiana

Vincennes University *C*

Pennsylvania

Philadelphia University *C, M*

Licensed practical nursing

Alabama

Alabama Southern Community
  College *A*
Bevill State Community College *C*
Bishop State Community College *C*
Calhoun Community College *C*
Chattahoochee Valley Community
  College *C*
Gadsden State Community College *C*
George C. Wallace State Community
  College
  Selma *C*
J. F. Drake State Technical College *C*
Northwest-Shoals Community
  College *C*
Shelton State Community College *C*
Southern Union State Community
  College *C*
Trenholm State Technical College *A*
Wallace State Community College at
  Hanceville *C*

Arizona

Arizona Western College *C*
Central Arizona College *C*
Gateway Community College *C*
Glendale Community College *C*
Mesa Community College *C*
Mohave Community College *C*
Northland Pioneer College *C*
Phoenix College *C*
Rio Salado College *C*
Scottsdale Community College *C*

Arkansas

Arkansas Northeastern College C
Arkansas State University
    Mountain Home C
Arkansas State University: Newport C
Arkansas Tech University C
North Arkansas College C
Ouachita Technical College C
Ozarka College C, A
Phillips Community College of the
    University of Arkansas C
Pulaski Technical College C
Rich Mountain Community College C
South Arkansas Community College C
Southeast Arkansas College C
Southern Arkansas University Tech C
University of Arkansas
    Community College at Hope C
    Cossatot Community College of the
      C
    Fort Smith C

California

Allan Hancock College C, A
Antelope Valley College C
Bakersfield College A
Butte College A
Cabrillo College A
Cerritos Community College A
Cerro Coso Community College C, A
Citrus College C, A
College of the Canyons A
College of the Desert C, A
College of the Siskiyous C, A
Concorde Career College A
Copper Mountain College A
El Camino College A
Feather River College C, A
Gavilan Community College C
Glendale Community College A
Imperial Valley College C, A
Long Beach City College C, A
Los Angeles Trade and Technical
    College A
Los Medanos College C
Merced College C, A
Merritt College A
MiraCosta College C, A
Mission College A
Modesto Junior College A
Mount San Jacinto College C
Napa Valley College C, A
National University A, B
Pasadena City College C, A
Porterville College C, A
Rio Hondo College A
Riverside Community College C, A
Sacramento City College C, A
San Joaquin Valley College Inc. A
Santa Barbara City College C, A
Santa Rosa Junior College C, A
Shasta College C
Sierra College C, A
Southwestern College C, A
Ventura College A
West Coast University A
Western Career College
    San Leandro C, A

Colorado

Colorado Mountain College
    Spring Valley Campus C
Community College of Denver C
Concorde Career College C
Front Range Community College C
Morgan Community College C
Northeastern Junior College C
Otero Junior College C
Pikes Peak Community College C
Pueblo Community College C

Delaware

Delaware Technical and Community
    College
    Owens Campus C
    Terry Campus C

District of Columbia

George Washington University C

Florida

Brevard Community College C
Central Florida Community
    College C, A
Daytona Beach Community College C
Florida Community College at
    Jacksonville C
Indian River Community College C
Lake City Community College C
Palm Beach Community College C
Pasco-Hernando Community
    College C
Pensacola Junior College C
Santa Fe Community College C
Seminole Community College C
South Florida Community College C

Georgia

Albany Technical College C
Athens Technical College C
Bainbridge College C
Central Georgia Technical College C
Chattahoochee Technical College C
Coastal Georgia Community
    College C
Columbus Technical College C
Dalton State College C
Darton College C
DeKalb Technical College C
Georgia Southwestern State
    University A
Gwinnett Technical College C
Middle Georgia College A
Northwestern Technical College C
Savannah Technical College A
Southwest Georgia Technical
    College C
West Georgia Technical College C

Hawaii

University of Hawaii
    Hawaii Community College C
    Kapiolani Community College C, A
    Kauai Community College C

Idaho

Boise State University C
College of Southern Idaho C
Eastern Idaho Technical College C
Idaho State University C
Lewis-Clark State College A
North Idaho College C

Illinois

Black Hawk College C
Carl Sandburg College C
City Colleges of Chicago
    Kennedy-King College C
    Olive-Harvey College C
    Wright College A
Danville Area Community College C
Elgin Community College C
Heartland Community College C
Illinois Eastern Community Colleges
    Olney Central College C
Illinois Valley Community College C
John A. Logan College C
John Wood Community College C
Joliet Junior College C
Kankakee Community College C
Kaskaskia College C
Kishwaukee College C
Lake Land College C
Lincoln Land Community College C

Morton College C
Parkland College C
Rend Lake College C
Richland Community College C
Sauk Valley Community College C
South Suburban College of Cook
    County C
Southeastern Illinois College C
Spoon River College C
Triton College C
William Rainey Harper College C

Indiana

Ivy Tech State College
    Ivy Tech Community College:
      Bloomington C
    Ivy Tech Community College:
      Central Indiana C
    Ivy Tech Community College:
      Columbus C
    Ivy Tech Community College: East
      Central C
    Ivy Tech Community College:
      Kokomo C
    Ivy Tech Community College:
      Lafayette C
    Ivy Tech Community College: North
      Central C
    Ivy Tech Community College:
      Northeast C
    Ivy Tech Community College:
      Northwest C
    Ivy Tech Community College: South
      Central C
    Ivy Tech Community College:
      Southeast C
    Ivy Tech Community College:
      Southwest C
    Ivy Tech Community College:
      Wabash Valley C
    Ivy Tech Community College:
      Whitewater C
Vincennes University A

Iowa

Clinton Community College C
Des Moines Area Community
    College C
Ellsworth Community College C
Hawkeye Community College C
Indian Hills Community College C
Iowa Central Community College C
Iowa Lakes Community College C
Iowa Western Community College C
Kirkwood Community College C
Marshalltown Community College C
Muscatine Community College C
North Iowa Area Community
    College C
Northeast Iowa Community
    College C
Northwest Iowa Community
    College C
Scott Community College C
Southeastern Community College
    North Campus C
Southwestern Community College C
Western Iowa Tech Community
    College C

Kansas

Barton County Community College C
Butler County Community
    College C, A
Dodge City Community College C, A
Fort Scott Community College A
Garden City Community College C
Hutchinson Community College C
Johnson County Community
    College C
Labette Community College C
Manhattan Area Technical College C
Neosho County Community
    College C, A

Pratt Community College A
Seward County Community College C

Kentucky

Elizabethtown Community and
    Technical College C
Hopkinsville Community College C
Jefferson Community College C
Maysville Community College C, A
Somerset Community College C, A
Spencerian College C

Louisiana

Delgado Community College C
Nunez Community College C
Our Lady of the Lake College C, A

Maine

Eastern Maine Community College C
Northern Maine Community
    College C
Southern Maine Community
    College C

Maryland

Allegany College of Maryland C
Anne Arundel Community College C
Baltimore City Community College A
Cecil Community College C
College of Southern Maryland C, A
Frederick Community College C
Harford Community College C
Howard Community College C, A
Prince George's Community
    College C
Wor-Wic Community College C

Massachusetts

Berkshire Community College C
Greenfield Community College C
Holyoke Community College C
Mount Wachusett Community
    College C
North Shore Community College C
Northern Essex Community
    College C
Quincy College C
Quinsigamond Community College C
Roxbury Community College C

Michigan

Alpena Community College C
Bay de Noc Community College C
Delta College C, A
Glen Oaks Community College C
Gogebic Community College C
Grand Rapids Community
    College C, A
Henry Ford Community College A
Jackson Community College C
Kalamazoo Valley Community
    College A
Kellogg Community College C
Kirtland Community College C
Lansing Community College A
Mid Michigan Community College C
Montcalm Community College C
Mott Community College C
Muskegon Community College A
Northern Michigan University C
Northwestern Michigan College C
Oakland Community College C
St. Clair County Community
    College C
Schoolcraft College C
Southwestern Michigan College C

Minnesota

Alexandria Technical College C
Anoka Technical College A
Central Lakes College C
Dakota County Technical College C
Hennepin Technical College C, A

Itasca Community College *C*
Lake Superior College *C*
Mesabi Range Community and
    Technical College *C*
Minneapolis Community and
    Technical College *C*
Minnesota State College - Southeast
    Technical *C*
Minnesota State Community and
    Technical College - Fergus
    Falls *C, A*
Minnesota State University
    Mankato *B*
Minnesota West Community and
    Technical College: Worthington
    Campus *C*
Northland Community & Technical
    College *C*
Northwest Technical College *C, A*
Pine Technical College *C*
Rainy River Community College *C*
Rasmussen College
    Mankato *C, A*
Ridgewater College *C*
Riverland Community College *C*
Rochester Community and Technical
    College *C*
St. Cloud Technical College *C, A*
St. Paul College *C*
South Central College *A*

Mississippi

Coahoma Community College *C*
Copiah-Lincoln Community College *C*
East Central Community College *C*
Hinds Community College *A*
Itawamba Community College *C*
Meridian Community College *A*
Mississippi Gulf Coast Community
    College
    Jefferson Davis Campus *C*
Pearl River Community College *C, A*
Southwest Mississippi Community
    College *C*

Missouri

Jefferson College *C*
Mineral Area College *C*
Moberly Area Community College *C*
North Central Missouri College *C*
Ozarks Technical Community
    College *C*
Penn Valley Community College *C*
St. Charles Community College *C*
State Fair Community College *C*

Montana

Helena College of Technology of the
    University of Montana *C*
Montana State University
    Billings *A*
    College of Technology-Great Falls *A*
University of Montana: Missoula *A*

Nebraska

Central Community College *C, A*
Metropolitan Community College *C*
Mid-Plains Community College Area *C*
Northeast Community College *C*
Southeast Community College
    Lincoln Campus *C*
Western Nebraska Community
    College *C*

Nevada

Community College of Southern
    Nevada *C*
Western Nevada Community
    College *C*

New Hampshire

New Hampshire Community
    Technical College
    Claremont *C*

New Jersey

Raritan Valley Community College *A*
Salem Community College *C*
Union County College *C*

New Mexico

Albuquerque Technical-Vocational
    Institute *C*
Eastern New Mexico University:
    Roswell Campus *C*
New Mexico Junior College *C*
New Mexico State University
    Carlsbad *C*
Northern New Mexico College *C*
Western New Mexico University *A*

New York

City University of New York
    Hostos Community College *C*
    Medgar Evers College *C*
Maria College *C*
Niagara County Community
    College *C*
State University of New York
    College of Technology at Delhi *C*
    Farmingdale *C*
Westchester Community College *C*

North Carolina

Alamance Community College *C*
Asheville-Buncombe Technical
    Community College *C*
Beaufort County Community
    College *C*
Bladen Community College *C*
Brunswick Community College *C*
Cape Fear Community College *C*
Carteret Community College *C*
Central Carolina Community
    College *A*
Cleveland Community College *C*
Coastal Carolina Community
    College *C*
College of the Albemarle *C*
Craven Community College *C*
Durham Technical Community
    College *C*
Edgecombe Community College *C*
Forsyth Technical Community
    College *A*
Isothermal Community College *C*
James Sprunt Community College *C*
Lenoir Community College *C*
Mayland Community College *C*
McDowell Technical Community
    College *C*
Montgomery Community College *C*
Nash Community College *A*
Rockingham Community College *C*
Sampson Community College *A*
Sandhills Community College *C*
South Piedmont Community
    College *C*
Southeastern Community College *C*
Southwestern Community College *C*
Surry Community College *C*
Vance-Granville Community
    College *C*
Wayne Community College *A*
Wilson Technical Community
    College *C, A*

North Dakota

Bismarck State College *A*
Dickinson State University *A*
Lake Region State College *C, A*
North Dakota State College of
    Science *A*
Sitting Bull College *A*
Williston State College *A*

Ohio

Belmont Technical College *C*
Central Ohio Technical College *C*
Clark State Community College *C*
Good Samaritan College of Nursing
    and Health Science *C*
Hocking College *C*
James A. Rhodes State College *C*
Jefferson Community College *C*
Ohio University *A*
Owens Community College
    Toledo *C*
Sinclair Community College *A*
Southern State Community College *C*

Oklahoma

Platt College
    Tulsa *A*
Western College of Southern
    California *A*

Oregon

Blue Mountain Community College *C*
Central Oregon Community
    College *C*
Chemeketa Community College *C*
Clackamas Community College *C*
Clatsop Community College *C*
Lane Community College *C*
Linn-Benton Community College *C*
Pioneer Pacific College *C*
Rogue Community College *C*
Southwestern Oregon Community
    College *C, A*
Treasure Valley Community College *C*
Umpqua Community College *C*

Pennsylvania

Community College of Allegheny
    County *C*
Community College of Beaver
    County *C*
Harrisburg Area Community
    College *C*
Lehigh Carbon Community College *C*
Mercyhurst College *C*
Northampton County Area
    Community College *C*
Pennsylvania College of Technology *C*
Reading Area Community
    College *C, A*
Westmoreland County Community
    College *C*

Puerto Rico

Inter American University of Puerto
    Rico
    San German Campus *A*

Rhode Island

Community College of Rhode
    Island *C*

South Carolina

Aiken Technical College *C*
Central Carolina Technical College *C*
Florence-Darlington Technical
    College *C*
Greenville Technical College *C*
Horry-Georgetown Technical
    College *C*
Midlands Technical College *C*
Northeastern Technical College *C*
Orangeburg-Calhoun Technical
    College *C*
Piedmont Technical College *C*
Spartanburg Technical College *C*
Tri-County Technical College *C*
Trident Technical College *C*

South Dakota

Lake Area Technical Institute *C*
Southeast Technical Institute *C*
Western Dakota Technical Institute *C*

Tennessee

Chattanooga State Technical
    Community College *C*
Tennessee State University *A*

Texas

Alvin Community College *C*
Amarillo College *C*
Austin Community College *C*
Brazosport College *C*
Central Texas College *C*
Clarendon College *C*
Coastal Bend College *C*
College of the Mainland *A*
El Centro College *C*
El Paso Community College *C*
Frank Phillips College *C*
Galveston College *C*
Grayson County College *C*
Hill College *C, A*
Houston Community College
    System *C*
Howard College *C*
Kilgore College *C*
Lamar State College at Orange *C*
Lamar State College at Port Arthur *C*
McLennan Community College *C*
Midland College *C*
Navarro College *C, A*
North Harris Montgomery
    Community College District *C*
Northeast Texas Community
    College *C*
Odessa College *C*
Panola College *C*
Paris Junior College *A*
St. Philip's College *C*
San Jacinto College
    North *C*
Schreiner University *C*
South Plains College *C*
South Texas College *C*
Southwest Texas Junior College *A*
Sul Ross State University *C*
Temple College *C*
Texarkana College *C*
Texas Southmost College *C*
Texas State Technical College
    West Texas *C*
Trinity Valley Community College *C*
University of Texas
    Brownsville *C*
Vernon College *C*
Victoria College *C*
Weatherford College *C*
Western Texas College *C*
Wharton County Junior College *C*

Utah

Dixie State College of Utah *C*
Snow College *C, A*
Southern Utah University *A*
Utah Career College *A*
Weber State University *C*

Vermont

Vermont Technical College *C*

Virginia

Danville Community College *C*
ECPI College of Technology *C, A*
Germanna Community College *C*
J. Sargeant Reynolds Community
    College *C*
Lord Fairfax Community College *C*
Mountain Empire Community
    College *C*
New River Community College *C*

Piedmont Virginia Community
    College *C, A*
Rappahannock Community College *C*
Southside Virginia Community
    College *C*
Virginia Western Community
    College *C*
Wytheville Community College *C*

Washington
Bates Technical College *A*
Bellingham Technical College *C*
Big Bend Community College *C*
Centralia College *C*
Clover Park Technical College *C*
Columbia Basin College *A*
Everett Community College *C*
Grays Harbor College *C*
Green River Community College *C*
Heritage University *A*
Lake Washington Technical
    College *C, A*
Lower Columbia College *A*
North Seattle Community
    College *C, A*
Olympic College *C, A*
Renton Technical College *C, A*
Skagit Valley College *C, A*
Spokane Community College *C*
Walla Walla Community College *C*
Wenatchee Valley College *C*
Yakima Valley Community College *C*

Wisconsin
Chippewa Valley Technical College *C*
Fox Valley Technical College *C*
Gateway Technical College *C*
Lakeshore Technical College *C*
Madison Area Technical College *C*
Milwaukee Area Technical College *C*
Moraine Park Technical College *C*
Northcentral Technical College *C*
Northeast Wisconsin Technical
    College *C*
Southwest Wisconsin Technical
    College *C*
Waukesha County Technical
    College *C*
Western Wisconsin Technical
    College *C*

Wyoming
Laramie County Community
    College *C*
Sheridan College *C*
Western Wyoming Community
    College *C, A*

Lineworker

Arizona
Chandler-Gilbert Community College
    Williams Campus *C*

California
Santa Rosa Junior College *C*

Florida
South Florida Community College *C*

Indiana
Ivy Tech State College
    Ivy Tech Community College:
    Lafayette *C, A*

Iowa
Northwest Iowa Community
    College *C, A*
Western Iowa Tech Community
    College *A*

Michigan
Alpena Community College *C*

Minnesota
Dakota County Technical College *C, A*
Minnesota State Community and
    Technical College - Fergus Falls *C*

Mississippi
Mississippi Gulf Coast Community
    College
    Jefferson Davis Campus *A*

Nebraska
Northeast Community College *A*
Western Nebraska Community
    College *C, A*

North Carolina
Nash Community College *A*

North Dakota
Bismarck State College *C, A*

Pennsylvania
Lehigh Carbon Community College *A*
Pennsylvania College of Technology *A*

Utah
Utah Valley State College *C, A*

Washington
Clover Park Technical College *C*

Wisconsin
Milwaukee Area Technical College *C*

Linguistics

Alaska
University of Alaska
    Fairbanks *B*

Arizona
Northern Arizona University *M, D*
University of Arizona *B, M, D*

Arkansas
University of Arkansas *M*

California
California State University
    Chico *B*
    Dominguez Hills *B*
    Fresno *B, M*
    Fullerton *B, M*
    Northridge *B, M*
Foothill College *A*
Pitzer College *B*
Pomona College *B*
San Diego State University *B, M*
San Francisco State University *M*
San Jose State University *B, M*
Scripps College *B*
Stanford University *B, M, D*
University of California
    Berkeley *B, M, D*
    Davis *B, M, D*
    Irvine *B, M, D*
    Los Angeles *B, M, D*
    Riverside *B*
    San Diego *B, M, D*
    Santa Barbara *B, M, D*
    Santa Cruz *B, M, D*
University of Southern
    California *B, M, D*

Colorado
University of Colorado
    Boulder *B, M, D*

Connecticut
University of Connecticut *B, M, D*
Yale University *B, M, D*

Delaware
University of Delaware *M, D*

District of Columbia
Gallaudet University *M, D*
Georgetown University *B, M, D*

Florida
Florida Atlantic University *B, M*
Florida International University *M*
University of Florida *A, B, M*
University of South Florida *M*

Georgia
Emory University *B*
Morehouse College *B*
University of Georgia *B, M, D*

Hawaii
University of Hawaii
    Hilo *B*
    Manoa *M, D*

Illinois
Judson College *B*
Moody Bible Institute *B*
Northeastern Illinois University *B, M*
Northwestern University *B, M, D*
Southern Illinois University
    Carbondale *B, M*
University of Chicago *B, D*
University of Illinois
    Chicago *M*
    Urbana-Champaign *B, M, D*

Indiana
Ball State University *M*
Indiana State University *B*
Indiana University
    Bloomington *B, M, D*
Purdue University *M, D*

Iowa
Central College *B*
Iowa State University *B*
University of Iowa *B, M, D*

Kansas
University of Kansas *B, M, D*

Kentucky
University of Kentucky *B*

Louisiana
Louisiana State University and
    Agricultural and Mechanical
    College *M, D*
Tulane University *B*

Maine
University of Southern Maine *B*

Maryland
University of Maryland
    Baltimore County *B, M*
    College Park *B, M, D*

Massachusetts
Boston College *B, M*
Boston University *B*
Brandeis University *B*
Hampshire College *B*
Harvard College *B, D*
Massachusetts Institute of
    Technology *B, D*
Northeastern University *B*
Simon's Rock College of Bard *B*

University of Massachusetts
    Amherst *B, M, D*
Wellesley College *B*

Michigan
Cornerstone University *B, M*
Eastern Michigan University *B, M*
Michigan State University *B, M, D*
Oakland University *B, M*
University of Michigan *B, M, D*
Wayne State University *B, M*

Minnesota
Crown College *B*
Macalester College *B*
St. Cloud State University *B*
University of Minnesota
    Twin Cities *B, M, D*

Mississippi
Jackson State University *B, M*
University of Mississippi *B*

Missouri
Central Missouri State University *M*
University of Missouri
    Columbia *B*

Montana
University of Montana: Missoula *M*

New Hampshire
Dartmouth College *B*
University of New Hampshire *B*

New Jersey
Montclair State University *B, M*
Rutgers, The State University of New
    Jersey
    New Brunswick/Piscataway
    Campus *B, M, D*

New Mexico
University of New Mexico *B, M, D*

New York
Barnard College *B*
City University of New York
    Brooklyn College *B*
    Lehman College *B*
    Queens College *B*
Columbia University
    Columbia College *B*
Cornell University *B, M, D*
Hofstra University *B*
New York University *B, M, D*
State University of New York
    Albany *B*
    Binghamton *B*
    Buffalo *B, M, D*
    Oswego *B*
    Stony Brook *B, M, D*
Syracuse University *B, M*
University of Rochester *B, M*

North Carolina
University of North Carolina
    Chapel Hill *B, M, D*

North Dakota
University of North Dakota *M*

Ohio
Antioch College *B*
Cleveland State University *B*
Miami University
    Oxford Campus *B*
Ohio State University
    Columbus Campus *B, M, D*
Ohio University *B, M*
University of Cincinnati *B*

University of Toledo *B*
Wright State University *B*

Oklahoma
Cameron University *B*
University of Oklahoma *B*

Oregon
Portland State University *B, M*
Reed College *B*
University of Oregon *B, M, D*

Pennsylvania
Penn State
    University Park *D*
Swarthmore College *B*
Temple University *B, M*
University of Pennsylvania *B, M, D*
University of Pittsburgh *B, M, D*

Puerto Rico
University of Puerto Rico
    Rio Piedras *M*

Rhode Island
Brown University *B*

South Carolina
University of South Carolina *M, D*

Tennessee
University of Tennessee
    Knoxville *B*

Texas
Baylor University *B*
Navarro College *A*
Rice University *B, M, D*
Texas Tech University *M*
University of Houston *M*
University of Texas
    Arlington *M, D*
    Austin *B, M, D*
    El Paso *B, M*

Utah
Brigham Young University *B, M*
University of Utah *B, M, D*

Vermont
Marlboro College *B*

Virginia
College of William and Mary *B*
University of Virginia *M*

Washington
Highline Community College *A*
University of Washington *B, M, D*
Washington State University *B*
Western Washington University *B*

Wisconsin
Lawrence University *B*
University of Wisconsin
    Madison *B, M, D*
    Milwaukee *B*

Livestock management

Nebraska
Northeast Community College *A*

New York
State University of New York
    College of Agriculture and
        Technology at Morrisville *A, B*

Texas
Tarleton State University *B*

Vermont
Sterling College *A, B*

Locksmithing

California
San Joaquin Delta College *C, A*

Kentucky
Elizabethtown Community and
    Technical College *C, A*

Minnesota
Pine Technical College *C, A*

Logic

California
University of California
    Berkeley *D*

Missouri
Truman State University *B*

Pennsylvania
Carnegie Mellon University *B, M, D*
University of Pennsylvania *B*

Logistics/materials management

Alabama
Auburn University *B*

Alaska
University of Alaska
    Anchorage *B*

Arizona
South Mountain Community
    College *C, A*

Arkansas
Southern Arkansas University Tech *C*
University of Arkansas *B, M*

California
California Maritime Academy *B*
California State University
    East Bay *M*
Cerritos Community College *A*
Chabot College *A*
College of San Mateo *C, A*
Golden Gate University *M*
San Jose State University *M*
University of San Diego *M*

Colorado
Colorado Technical University *C, B, M*

Connecticut
University of New Haven *C*

Delaware
Wilmington College *M*

Florida
Brevard Community College *A*
Florida Institute of Technology *M*

Georgia
Albany Technical College *C*
Athens Technical College *C*
Central Georgia Technical
    College *C, A*
Georgia College and State
    University *M*
Georgia Institute of Technology *M*
Georgia Military College *A*

Georgia Southern University *B*
Savannah Technical College *C*
Southern Polytechnic State
    University *C*
West Georgia Technical College *C*

Illinois
Elmhurst College *B, M*
Heartland Community College *C*
Kishwaukee College *C*
Prairie State College *C*
Rock Valley College *C, A*
University of Illinois
    Urbana-Champaign *B*
Waubonsee Community College *C, A*
William Rainey Harper College *C, A*

Iowa
Iowa State University *B*

Maine
Maine Maritime Academy *B, M*

Maryland
University of Maryland
    College Park *B*

Massachusetts
Middlesex Community College *C*
Northeastern University *B*
Northern Essex Community
    College *C, A*
Springfield Technical Community
    College *A*

Michigan
Central Michigan University *B*
Eastern Michigan University *M*
Michigan State University *B, M, D*
Wayne State University *B*
Western Michigan University *B*

Minnesota
St. Paul College *C, A*
University of Minnesota
    Twin Cities *B*

Missouri
Park University *A, B*
University of Missouri
    St. Louis *B, M, D*

Nevada
University of Nevada
    Reno *B*

New Jersey
Bloomfield College *C*
Thomas Edison State College *B*

New York
Globe Institute of Technology *C*
Herkimer County Community
    College *A*
Niagara University *B*

North Carolina
South Piedmont Community
    College *A*

Ohio
Bowling Green State University *B*
Columbus State Community
    College *C, A*
Edison State Community College *C, A*
John Carroll University *B*
Ohio State University
    Columbus Campus *B*
Sinclair Community College *A*
Stark State College of Technology *A*
Tiffin University *B*

University of Akron *C, A*
University of Toledo *A, B, M*
Wright State University *M*

Oregon
Portland State University *B*

Pennsylvania
Duquesne University *B*
Lehigh Carbon Community
    College *C, A*
Lehigh University *B, M*
Penn State
    Abington *B*
    Altoona *B*
    Beaver *B*
    Berks *B*
    Delaware County *B*
    Dubois *B*
    Fayette *B*
    Hazleton *B*
    Lehigh Valley *B*
    McKeesport *B*
    Mont Alto *B*
    New Kensington *B*
    Schuylkill - Capital College *B*
    Shenango *B*
    University Park *C, B*
    Wilkes-Barre *B*
    Worthington Scranton *B*
    York *B*
Pennsylvania Highlands Community
    College *A*
Robert Morris University *C, B*

Puerto Rico
Turabo University *B, M*

South Carolina
Trident Technical College *C, A*

Tennessee
University of Memphis *B*
University of Tennessee
    Knoxville *B*
Volunteer State Community College *C*

Texas
Houston Community College
    System *C, A*
Palo Alto College *C, A*
South Texas College *C*
Texas A&M University *M*
University of Dallas *M*
University of Texas
    Arlington *M*

Utah
Brigham Young University *B*
Salt Lake Community College *A*
Weber State University *B*

Virginia
New River Community College *A*

Washington
Shoreline Community College *C, A*

West Virginia
Mountain State University *B*

Wisconsin
Chippewa Valley Technical College *A*
Gateway Technical College *A*
Lakeshore Technical College *A*
Milwaukee Area Technical College *A*
Northeast Wisconsin Technical
    College *A*

Machine shop technology

Arkansas
University of Arkansas
   Fort Smith *C*

California
Long Beach City College *C, A*
Los Angeles Valley College *C*

Colorado
Arapahoe Community College *C*
Pikes Peak Community College *C, A*

Georgia
Athens Technical College *C*
Central Georgia Technical College *C*
Georgia Southwestern State
   University *A*
Savannah Technical College *A*
Southwest Georgia Technical
   College *C*

Illinois
College of Lake County *C, A*
Illinois Eastern Community Colleges
   Wabash Valley College *C, A*
John A. Logan College *A*
McHenry County College *C*
Moraine Valley Community College *C*
Oakton Community College *C, A*
Waubonsee Community College *C, A*

Indiana
Ivy Tech State College
   Ivy Tech Community College:
     Central Indiana *A*

Iowa
North Iowa Area Community
   College *C*
Northwest Iowa Community
   College *C*

Kansas
Cowley County Community
   College *C, A*

Kentucky
Elizabethtown Community and
   Technical College *C, A*
Jefferson Community College *C*
Somerset Community College *C, A*

Louisiana
Delgado Community College *A*
Nunez Community College *C*

Michigan
Grand Rapids Community
   College *C, A*
Montcalm Community College *C*
Mott Community College *C*
Northwestern Michigan College *C*

Minnesota
Central Lakes College *C*
Hennepin Technical College *C, A*
Pine Technical College *C*
St. Paul College *C*

Missouri
Ranken Technical College *A*

New Mexico
Albuquerque Technical-Vocational
   Institute *C*
San Juan College *C, A*

New York
Adirondack Community College *C*
Mohawk Valley Community College *C*

North Carolina
Cape Fear Community College *C, A*
Catawba Valley Community College *C*
Central Piedmont Community
   College *C, A*
College of the Albemarle *A*
Davidson County Community
   College *C*
Fayetteville Technical Community
   College *C, A*
Guilford Technical Community
   College *C, A*
Isothermal Community College *C, A*
Lenoir Community College *C, A*
Mitchell Community College *C, A*
Pitt Community College *C, A*
Rockingham Community College *C*

Pennsylvania
Butler County Community
   College *C, A*
Community College of Allegheny
   County *C*
Delaware County Community
   College *C*
Pennsylvania College of Technology *C*

South Carolina
Piedmont Technical College *C*

South Dakota
Southeast Technical Institute *A*

Texas
Houston Community College
   System *C*
St. Philip's College *C*
University of Texas
   Brownsville *C*

Utah
Salt Lake Community College *C*

Virginia
New River Community College *C, A*

Washington
Renton Technical College *C, A*

West Virginia
West Virginia University at
   Parkersburg *C, A*

Wisconsin
Gateway Technical College *A*
Lakeshore Technical College *C*
Milwaukee Area Technical College *C*
Western Wisconsin Technical
   College *A*
Wisconsin Indianhead Technical
   College *C*

Wyoming
Eastern Wyoming College *C*

Machine tool technology

Alabama
Calhoun Community College *C, A*
J. F. Drake State Technical College *C, A*
Northwest-Shoals Community
   College *C*

Arkansas
North Arkansas College *C, A*

Rich Mountain Community
   College *C, A*

California
Long Beach City College *C, A*
San Jose City College *C, A*

Colorado
Mesa State College *C, A*
Pueblo Community College *C, A*

Georgia
Coastal Georgia Community
   College *C*
West Georgia Technical College *C*

Idaho
Idaho State University *C, A*

Illinois
Black Hawk College *C*
Heartland Community College *C*
John A. Logan College *C*
Kaskaskia College *C*
Spoon River College *C*
Waubonsee Community College *C, A*

Indiana
Ivy Tech State College
   Ivy Tech Community College:
     Bloomington *C, A*
   Ivy Tech Community College:
     Central Indiana *C, A*
   Ivy Tech Community College:
     Columbus *C, A*
   Ivy Tech Community College: East
     Central *C, A*
   Ivy Tech Community College:
     Kokomo *C, A*
   Ivy Tech Community College:
     Lafayette *C, A*
   Ivy Tech Community College: North
     Central *C, A*
   Ivy Tech Community College:
     Northeast *C, A*
   Ivy Tech Community College:
     Northwest *C, A*
   Ivy Tech Community College: South
     Central *C, A*
   Ivy Tech Community College:
     Southwest *C, A*
   Ivy Tech Community College:
     Wabash Valley *C, A*
   Ivy Tech Community College:
     Whitewater *C, A*

Iowa
Des Moines Area Community
   College *A*
Hawkeye Community College *C, A*
Indian Hills Community College *A*
North Iowa Area Community
   College *A*
Southeastern Community College
   North Campus *C, A*
Western Iowa Tech Community
   College *A*

Kansas
Hutchinson Community College *C, A*

Maine
Eastern Maine Community
   College *C, A*
Kennebec Valley Community
   College *C*

Michigan
Delta College *A*
Glen Oaks Community College *C*
Henry Ford Community College *C*
Kirtland Community College *C, A*

Lake Michigan College *C, A*
Northern Michigan University *A*
Oakland Community College *C*
St. Clair County Community
   College *C, A*
Southwestern Michigan College *C, A*
Wayne County Community
   College *C, A*

Minnesota
Alexandria Technical College *C*
Central Lakes College *C*
Dunwoody College of
   Technology *C, A*
Hennepin Technical College *C, A*
Lake Superior College *C, A*
Pine Technical College *C, A*
Ridgewater College *C, A*
St. Cloud Technical College *C, A*
St. Paul College *C*

Mississippi
Copiah-Lincoln Community
   College *C, A*

Missouri
East Central College *C, A*
Jefferson College *C, A*
Mineral Area College *C, A*
Ozarks Technical Community
   College *C, A*
State Fair Community College *C, A*

Nebraska
Central Community College *C, A*

Nevada
Western Nevada Community
   College *C, A*

New York
Corning Community College *C, A*

North Carolina
Rowan-Cabarrus Community
   College *C*
Surry Community College *A*
Tri-County Community College *C*

North Dakota
North Dakota State College of
   Science *C, A*

Ohio
Cincinnati State Technical and
   Community College *A*

Oregon
Central Oregon Community
   College *C, A*
Lane Community College *A*
Linn-Benton Community College *C*

Pennsylvania
Butler County Community College *C*
Delaware County Community
   College *C, A*
South Hills School of Business &
   Technology *A*
Williamson Free School of Mechanical
   Trades *C*

South Carolina
Aiken Technical College *C, A*
Greenville Technical College *C, A*
Horry-Georgetown Technical
   College *A*
Midlands Technical College *C*
Piedmont Technical College *C, A*
Spartanburg Technical College *C, A*
Williamsburg Technical College *C, A*

York Technical College *C, A*

South Dakota

Southeast Technical Institute *A*

Texas

Angelina College *C, A*
Del Mar College *C, A*
Kilgore College *C, A*
Odessa College *C, A*
St. Philip's College *A*
Texas State Technical College
   Harlingen *C*
   West Texas *C, A*

Utah

Salt Lake Community College *A*
Snow College *C*

Virginia

Danville Community College *C*

Washington

Clark College *C, A*
Clover Park Technical College *C, A*
Shoreline Community College *C, A*

Wisconsin

Mid-State Technical College *C*
Milwaukee Area Technical College *C*
Western Wisconsin Technical
   College *C*

Wyoming

Casper College *C, A*
Sheridan College *C, A*

Make-up artist

North Carolina

Carteret Community College *C*
Martin Community College *C*

Management information systems

Alabama

American Sentinel University *B*
Auburn University *M*
Auburn University at Montgomery *B*
Central Alabama Community
   College *C, A*
Community College of the Air
   Force *A*
Enterprise-Ozark Community
   College *A*
Troy University *B*
University of Alabama *B*
University of Alabama
   Birmingham *B*
   Huntsville *B, M*
University of Montevallo *B*
University of North Alabama *B*
University of West Alabama *B*
Virginia College *C, A, B*

Alaska

University of Alaska
   Anchorage *B*
   Southeast *C, A*

Arizona

Arizona State University *B*
Arizona Western College *C, A*
Central Arizona College *A*
Cochise College *A*
DeVry University
   Phoenix *B*
Glendale Community College *C, A*
Northcentral University *M, D*
Northern Arizona University *C, B, M*

Phoenix College *C, A*
Pima Community College *A*
Scottsdale Community College *C, A*
University of Arizona *B, M*
University of Phoenix *B, M*
Western International University *B, M*

Arkansas

Arkansas Northeastern College *A*
Arkansas State University *C, A, M*
Arkansas State University
   Beebe *C*
   Mountain Home *C*
Arkansas State University:
   Newport *C, A*
Arkansas Tech University *C*
Black River Technical College *C, A*
East Arkansas Community
   College *C, A*
Henderson State University *B*
North Arkansas College *A*
Pulaski Technical College *C, A*
Rich Mountain Community
   College *C, A*
Southern Arkansas University Tech *C*
University of Arkansas
   Cossatot Community College of the
      A
   Little Rock *B*
   Monticello *B*
University of Central Arkansas *B*

California

Allan Hancock College *A*
Alliant International University *B*
American River College *A*
Azusa Pacific University *B*
Bakersfield College *A*
Barstow College *A*
Biola University *B*
Butte College *C, A*
California State University
   Chico *C, B*
   Dominguez Hills *B*
   East Bay *B, M*
   Fresno *B*
   Fullerton *B, M*
   Northridge *B*
   Sacramento *B, M*
   San Bernardino *B, M*
Canada College *C, A*
Chabot College *A*
Chaffey College *C*
Citrus College *A*
City College of San Francisco *A*
College of San Mateo *A*
College of the Sequoias *C, A*
College of the Siskiyous *C, A*
Columbia College *C*
Cypress College *C, A*
DeVry University
   Fremont *M*
   Long Beach *M*
   Pomona *M*
   West Hills *M*
Empire College *C*
Evergreen Valley College *A*
Fresno Pacific University *B*
Fullerton College *A*
Gavilan Community College *C*
Heald College
   Fresno *C, A*
Hope International University *C*
Laney College *C, A*
Lassen College *A*
Lincoln University *M*
Los Angeles City College *C, A*
Los Angeles Harbor College *C, A*
Los Angeles Southwest College *A*
Los Angeles Valley College *C, A*
Master's College *B*
Merced College *A*
Mission College *A*
Modesto Junior College *A*

Moorpark College *A*
Northwestern Polytechnic
   University *B*
Notre Dame de Namur University *M*
Orange Coast College *C, A*
Pacific Union College *B*
Pasadena City College *A*
Point Loma Nazarene University *B*
Porterville College *C*
Sacramento City College *C, A*
San Bernardino Valley College *C*
San Diego City College *C, A*
San Joaquin Delta College *A*
Shasta College *A*
Simpson University *B*
Skyline College *C, A*
Taft College *C, A*
University of California
   Santa Cruz *B*
University of La Verne *M*
University of Redlands *B*
University of San Francisco *B*
Ventura College *A*
West Hills Community College *C, A*

Colorado

Adams State College *B*
Aims Community College *A*
Arapahoe Community College *A*
Colorado Christian University *B*
Colorado Mountain College
   Alpine Campus *C, A*
   Spring Valley Campus *A*
   Timberline Campus *C*
Colorado Northwestern Community
   College *A*
Colorado Technical University *B, M*
Community College of Aurora *C, A*
Community College of Denver *C, A*
DeVry University: Colorado Springs *M*
Fort Lewis College *B*
Front Range Community College *C, A*
Jones International University *M*
Mesa State College *B*
National American University
   Denver *B*
Pikes Peak Community College *A*
Red Rocks Community College *C, A*
University of Colorado
   Boulder *M*
University of Denver *M*
Western State College of Colorado *B*
Westwood College of Technology *B*

Connecticut

Albertus Magnus College *C, A, B*
Asnuntuck Community College *C, A*
Central Connecticut State
   University *B*
Eastern Connecticut State
   University *B*
Fairfield University *B*
Manchester Community College *C, A*
Northwestern Connecticut
   Community College *C, A*
Norwalk Community College *A*
Quinnipiac University *B*
Three Rivers Community College *A*
University of Bridgeport *B, M*
University of Connecticut *B*
University of Hartford *B*
Western Connecticut State
   University *B*

Delaware

Delaware Technical and Community
   College
   Terry Campus *A*
Goldey-Beacom College *B*
University of Delaware *B*
Wilmington College *M*

District of Columbia

American University *B, M*
Gallaudet University *B*
George Washington University *B, M*
Howard University *B*
Southeastern University *A, B, M*
University of the District of
   Columbia *A*

Florida

Barry University *C, B*
Brevard Community College *A*
DeVry University
   Miramar *M*
   Orlando *M*
Florida Atlantic University *B*
Florida Community College at
   Jacksonville *A*
Florida Gulf Coast University *B, M*
Florida Institute of Technology *B, M*
Florida International University *B*
Florida Memorial University *B*
Florida Metropolitan University
   Pompano Beach *A, B*
Florida Southern College *B*
Florida State University *B, M, D*
Indian River Community College *A*
Lynn University *B, M*
Northwood University
   Florida Campus *A, B*
Nova Southeastern University *M*
Okaloosa-Walton College *C, A*
Palm Beach Community College *A*
Pensacola Junior College *A*
St. Leo University *B*
Schiller International University *B, M*
Tallahassee Community College *A*
University of Central Florida *B, M*
University of South Florida *B, M*
University of West Florida *B*
Valencia Community College *C*

Georgia

Albany State University *B*
Augusta State University *B*
Bainbridge College *C, A*
Coastal Georgia Community
   College *C, A*
Dalton State College *B*
Darton College *C, A*
DeVry University
   Alpharetta *B*
   Decatur *M*
Georgia College and State
   University *M*
Georgia Southern University *B*
Georgia Southwestern State
   University *A*
Paine College *B*
South Georgia College *C, A*
Thomas University *B*
University of Georgia *B*
University of West Georgia *B*
West Georgia Technical College *C*

Hawaii

Hawaii Pacific University *B*
University of Hawaii
   Manoa *B*

Idaho

Boise State University *B, M*
Northwest Nazarene University *B*
University of Idaho *B*

Illinois

Augustana College *B*
Aurora University *B*
Benedictine University *M*
Blackburn College *B*
Bradley University *B*
Chicago State University *B*

City Colleges of Chicago
Olive-Harvey College *C, A*
Danville Area Community
College *C, A*
DePaul University *M*
DeVry University
Tinley Park *B*
Eastern Illinois University *B*
Eureka College *B*
Governors State University *B, M*
Greenville College *B*
Highland Community College *A*
Illinois College *B*
Joliet Junior College *C*
Judson College *B*
Kishwaukee College *A*
Lewis University *B*
Loyola University of Chicago *B, M*
MacCormac College *C, A*
MacMurray College *B*
Millikin University *B*
Monmouth College *B*
Moraine Valley Community
College *C, A*
North Central College *B, M*
Northern Illinois University *M*
Northwestern University *M*
Richland Community College *A*
Robert Morris College: Chicago *C, A*
Rockford College *B*
Roosevelt University *M*
St. Augustine College *A*
St. Xavier University *M*
Sauk Valley Community College *A*
Southern Illinois University
Edwardsville *B, M*
Southwestern Illinois College *C, A*
Trinity Christian College *B*
Triton College *C, A*
University of Illinois
Chicago *B, M, D*
Springfield *M*
Urbana-Champaign *B, M, D*
Western Illinois University *B*
William Rainey Harper College *C, A*

Indiana

Grace College *B*
Indiana Institute of Technology *A, B*
Indiana State University *B*
Indiana University
East *B*
South Bend *M*
Southeast *M*
Indiana University-Purdue University
Indianapolis *B*
Indiana Wesleyan University *A, B*
Marian College *B*
Oakland City University *B*
St. Joseph's College *A, B*
Saint Mary's College *B*
Tri-State University *B*
University of Indianapolis *B*
University of Notre Dame *B*
Vincennes University *A*

Iowa

Briar Cliff University *B*
Buena Vista University *B*
Clarke College *B*
Drake University *B*
Iowa State University *B, M*
Kaplan University *B*
Loras College *B*
Luther College *B*
Northeast Iowa Community
College *A*
University of Iowa *B*
University of Northern Iowa *B*
Upper Iowa University *B*

Kansas

Central Christian College of Kansas *A*
Coffeyville Community College *A*

Dodge City Community College *C, A*
Fort Scott Community College *C, A*
Friends University *B, M*
Haskell Indian Nations University *A*
Hutchinson Community College *C, A*
Newman University *B*
Ottawa University *B*
Southwestern College *B*
Wichita State University *B*

Kentucky

Ashland Community and Technical
College *A*
Big Sandy Community and Technical
College *A*
Brown Mackie College:
Hopkinsville *C, A*
Eastern Kentucky University *B*
Henderson Community College *A*
Hopkinsville Community College *A*
Madisonville Community College *A*
Morehead State University *A, B, M*
Murray State University *B*
Northern Kentucky University *B, M*
Owensboro Community College *A*
Southeast Kentucky Community and
Technical College *A*
University of Louisville *B*
West Kentucky Community and
Technical College *A*
Western Kentucky University *B*

Louisiana

Louisiana Tech University *B*
Nicholls State University *B*
Tulane University *B*
University of Louisiana at Lafayette *B*
University of Louisiana at Monroe *B*
University of New Orleans *B*

Maine

Husson College *B*
Northern Maine Community
College *A*
Thomas College *B*
University of Maine *B*
University of Maine
Fort Kent *A, B*
University of Southern Maine *B*

Maryland

Allegany College of Maryland *C, A*
Baltimore City Community College *A*
Bowie State University *B, M*
Capitol College *M*
Carroll Community College *C, A*
Chesapeake College *C, A*
College of Southern Maryland *C, A*
DeVry University: Bethesda *M*
Hagerstown Community College *C, A*
Harford Community College *A*
Howard Community College *A*
Salisbury University *B*
Sojourner-Douglass College *B*
University of Baltimore *B, M*
University of Maryland
University College *M*
Villa Julie College *M*

Massachusetts

American International College *B*
Anna Maria College *B*
Babson College *B*
Bentley College *M*
Boston College *B*
Boston University *B, M*
Bridgewater State College *B*
Greenfield Community College *C*
Lasell College *B*
Marian Court College *C, A*
Massasoit Community College *A*
New England College of Finance *C*
Nichols College *B*

Northeastern University *B*
Roxbury Community College *A*
Salem State College *B*
Simmons College *B*
Suffolk University *B*
University of Massachusetts
Dartmouth *B*
Western New England College *B*
Worcester Polytechnic Institute *B, M*

Michigan

Alpena Community College *A*
Baker College
of Flint *A, B*
of Muskegon *A*
of Owosso *B*
of Port Huron *B*
Calvin College *B*
Central Michigan University *B, M*
Cleary University *A, B*
Cornerstone University *B*
Eastern Michigan University *M*
Grand Rapids Community
College *C, A*
Kalamazoo Valley Community
College *A*
Kettering University *B*
Kirtland Community College *A*
Lake Superior State University *A*
Lansing Community College *A*
Madonna University *B*
Montcalm Community College *A*
Mott Community College *A*
Northern Michigan University *A, B*
Northwestern Michigan College *C, A*
Northwood University *A, B*
Oakland University *B, M*
Rochester College *B*
Spring Arbor University *B*
Walsh College of Accountancy and
Business Administration *M*
Wayne State University *B*
West Shore Community College *A*

Minnesota

Augsburg College *B*
Century Community and Technical
College *C, A*
College of St. Catherine *B*
Concordia University: St. Paul *B*
Itasca Community College *A*
Lake Superior College *C, A*
Metropolitan State University *C, B, M*
Minneapolis Business College *A*
Minnesota State College - Southeast
Technical *C, A*
Minnesota State Community and
Technical College - Fergus Falls *A*
Minnesota State University
Mankato *B*
Moorhead *B*
National American University
St. Paul *A, B*
Northwestern College *B*
Ridgewater College *A*
Rochester Community and Technical
College *A*
St. Paul College *C, A*
University of Minnesota
Crookston *A, B*
Twin Cities *B*
University of St. Thomas *M, D*
Winona State University *B*

Mississippi

Delta State University *B*
Hinds Community College *C, A*
Itawamba Community College *A*
Meridian Community College *A*
Mississippi Gulf Coast Community
College
Jefferson Davis Campus *A*
Mississippi State University *B, M*
Pearl River Community College *A*

University of Mississippi *B*
University of Southern Mississippi *B*

Missouri

Central Methodist University *B*
Central Missouri State University *B*
Culver-Stockton College *B*
DeVry University
Kansas City *M*
Drury University *B*
Grantham University *A, B, M*
Lindenwood University *B, M*
Maryville University of Saint
Louis *B, M*
Missouri State University *B, M*
National American University
Kansas City *A, B*
Park University *B*
St. Louis Community College
St. Louis Community College at
Florissant Valley *C, A*
St. Louis Community College at
Meramec *A*
St. Louis University *B*
State Fair Community College *A*
Three Rivers Community College *A*
University of Missouri
Rolla *B*
St. Louis *B, M, D*
Webster University *M*
Westminster College *B*
William Woods University *B*

Montana

Flathead Valley Community
College *C, A*
Little Big Horn College *A*
Stone Child College *A*
University of Montana: Missoula *B*

Nebraska

Bellevue University *B*
Chadron State College *B*
Concordia University *B*
Creighton University *B, M*
Dana College *B*
Metropolitan Community
College *C, A*
Midland Lutheran College *B*
University of Nebraska
Omaha *B, M*

Nevada

Community College of Southern
Nevada *C, A*
Morrison University *A, B*
University of Nevada
Las Vegas *B, M*
Reno *B*

New Hampshire

Daniel Webster College *B*
Franklin Pierce College *B*
New England College *B*
New Hampshire Community
Technical College
Nashua *C*
Rivier College *A, B*
Southern New Hampshire
University *B*

New Jersey

Atlantic Cape Community College *A*
Bergen Community College *C*
Burlington County College *A*
Camden County College *A*
County College of Morris *A*
Cumberland County College *C, A*
Fairleigh Dickinson University
Metropolitan Campus *M*
Hudson County Community
College *C, A*

Mercer County Community
College *C, A*
Passaic County Community
College *C, A*
Raritan Valley Community College *C*
Rowan University *B*
Rutgers, The State University of New
Jersey
New Brunswick/Piscataway
Campus *B*
St. Peter's College *A, B, M*
Salem Community College *A*
Seton Hall University *B*
Stevens Institute of
Technology *B, M, D*

New Mexico

Clovis Community College *A*
College of Santa Fe *B*
College of the Southwest *B*
Eastern New Mexico University *B*
National American University *C, A, B*
New Mexico Highlands University *B*
New Mexico State University
Alamogordo *C, A*
Northern New Mexico College *A*

New York

Bramson ORT College *A*
Canisius College *B*
City University of New York
Baruch College *B, M*
Bronx Community College *A*
York College *B*
Clarkson University *B*
College of Westchester *C, A*
DeVry Institute of Technology
New York *M*
Dominican College of Blauvelt *B*
Dowling College *B*
Elmira College *B*
Excelsior College *B*
Fordham University *B, M*
Globe Institute of Technology *C, A, B*
Hilbert College *A*
Hofstra University *B, M*
Iona College *B, M*
Le Moyne College *B*
Manhattan College *B*
Mohawk Valley Community College *A*
Nassau Community College *A*
New York Institute of
Technology *B, M*
Pace University *M*
Polytechnic University *B, M*
Rochester Institute of
Technology *C, B, M*
St. Bonaventure University *B*
St. John Fisher College *B*
St. John's University *B, M*
St. Thomas Aquinas College *C*
State University of New York
Albany *M*
Buffalo *M*
College at Fredonia *B*
College of Technology at Alfred *A*
College of Technology at Delhi *A*
Sullivan County Community
College *A*
Touro College *B*
Utica School of Commerce *A*

North Carolina

Appalachian State University *B*
Asheville-Buncombe Technical
Community College *A*
Campbell University *A, B*
Catawba Valley Community
College *C, A*
Central Piedmont Community
College *C, A*
Craven Community College *A*
DeVry University: Charlotte *M*
East Carolina University *B*

Elon University *B*
Fayetteville Technical Community
College *A*
Gardner-Webb University *B*
Guilford Technical Community
College *C, A*
High Point University *B*
Lenoir Community College *C, A*
Lenoir-Rhyne College *B*
Martin Community College *C, A*
Methodist College *B*
Mount Olive College *B*
Nash Community College *A*
Queens University of Charlotte *B*
Randolph Community College *A*
Richmond Community College *C, A*
Roanoke-Chowan Community
College *A*
University of North Carolina
Charlotte *B*
Greensboro *D*
Wilmington *B*
Western Carolina University *B*

North Dakota

Dickinson State University *A, B*
Jamestown College *B*
Lake Region State College *C, A*
Minot State University *C, B*
North Dakota State University *B*
University of North Dakota *B*

Ohio

Ashland University *B*
Bluffton University *B*
Bowling Green State University *B, M*
Case Western Reserve University *M, D*
Cedarville University *B*
Cleveland State University *B, D*
Cuyahoga Community College
Metropolitan Campus *A*
David N. Myers University *C, B*
DeVry University
Columbus *B*
Defiance College *B*
Franklin University *B*
James A. Rhodes State College *A*
Jefferson Community College *C, A*
Kent State University *B, M, D*
Kent State University
Trumbull Campus *C*
Tuscarawas Campus *C*
Lakeland Community College *A*
Marietta College *B*
Miami University
Hamilton Campus *C, A*
Oxford Campus *B*
Mount Vernon Nazarene University *B*
Ohio Dominican University *B*
Ohio State University
Columbus Campus *B*
Ohio University *A, B*
Ohio University
Chillicothe Campus *A*
Shawnee State University *B*
Stark State College of Technology *A*
Union Institute & University *B*
University of Akron *C, B, M*
University of Akron: Wayne
College *C, A*
University of Cincinnati *B*
University of Dayton *B*
University of Toledo *B*
Ursuline College *B*
Walsh University *B*
Wright State University *A, B, M*
Wright State University: Lake
Campus *A*
Xavier University *B, M*
Youngstown State University *B*

Oklahoma

Eastern Oklahoma State College *A*
Mid-America Christian University *B*

Northeastern State University *B*
Oklahoma Baptist University *B*
Oklahoma City University *B, M*
Oklahoma State University *B, M*
Oklahoma State University
Okmulgee *A*
Oral Roberts University *B*
Rogers State University *A*
Southwestern Oklahoma State
University *B*
Tulsa Community College *C, A*
University of Central Oklahoma *B*
University of Oklahoma *B, M*
University of Tulsa *B*

Oregon

Central Oregon Community
College *A*
Chemeketa Community College *A*
Clatsop Community College *A*
Corban College *B*
DeVry University: Portland *M*
George Fox University *B*
Northwest Christian College *B*
Oregon Institute of Technology *B*
Portland State University *B*
Southwestern Oregon Community
College *A*
Treasure Valley Community College *A*
University of Oregon *M, D*

Pennsylvania

Arcadia University *C, B*
Cabrini College *B*
Cambria-Rowe Business College:
Indiana *A*
Carlow University *B, M*
Carnegie Mellon University *M, D*
Central Pennsylvania College *A*
College Misericordia *B*
Community College of Allegheny
County *C, A*
Community College of Beaver
County *A*
DeSales University *B, M*
DeVry University
Ft. Washington *M*
Delaware County Community
College *A*
Delaware Valley College *C, B*
Drexel University *B*
Duquesne University *B, M*
Eastern University *B*
Elizabethtown College *B*
Gannon University *B*
Holy Family University *M*
Immaculata University *C*
Indiana University of Pennsylvania *B*
Keystone College *B*
Lackawanna College *A*
Lock Haven University of
Pennsylvania *A*
Luzerne County Community
College *A*
Marywood University *M*
Montgomery County Community
College *A*
Muhlenberg College *C, B*
Peirce College *A*
Penn State
Abington *B*
Altoona *B*
Beaver *B*
Berks *B*
Delaware County *B*
Dubois *B*
Erie, The Behrend College *B*
Fayette *B*
Harrisburg *B, M*
Hazleton *B*
Lehigh Valley *B*
McKeesport *B*
Mont Alto *B*
New Kensington *B*

Schuylkill - Capital College *B*
Shenango *B*
University Park *C, B*
Worthington Scranton *B*
York *B*
Pennsylvania College of Technology *B*
Philadelphia University *B*
Reading Area Community College *A*
Robert Morris University *C, B, M*
St. Francis University *A, B*
St. Joseph's University *A, B, M*
Seton Hill University *B*
Temple University *B, M, D*
Thiel College *A, B*
University of Pennsylvania *B, M*
University of Pittsburgh *M*
University of Pittsburgh
Greensburg *B*
Titusville *A*
Villanova University *B*
West Chester University of
Pennsylvania *M*
Widener University *B, M*
Wilson College *A, B*

Puerto Rico

Bayamon Central University *A, B*
Columbia College *A*
Inter American University of Puerto
Rico
Aguadilla Campus *B*
Bayamon Campus *A, B*
Ponce Campus *B*
San German Campus *B, M*
Pontifical Catholic University of
Puerto Rico *B*
Turabo University *A, B, M, D*
Universidad Metropolitana *B*
Universidad del Este *B*
University of Puerto Rico
Aguadilla *B*
Rio Piedras *B*
University of the Sacred Heart *M*

Rhode Island

Rhode Island College *B, D*
Roger Williams University *B*
University of Rhode Island *B*

South Carolina

Anderson University *B*
Charleston Southern University *B*
Claflin University *B*
Francis Marion University *B*
Furman University *B*
Voorhees College *B*

South Dakota

Augustana College *B*
Dakota State University *B*
Northern State University *B*
Oglala Lakota College *A*

Tennessee

Aquinas College *B*
Belmont University *B*
Bryan College *B*
Crichton College *B*
Freed-Hardeman University *B*
Lambuth University *B*
Middle Tennessee State University *B*
Southern Adventist University *B*
Southwest Tennessee Community
College *A*
Trevecca Nazarene University *B*
University of Memphis *B*
University of Tennessee
Martin *B*

Texas

Baylor University *B, M*
Brookhaven College *A*
Cedar Valley College *C, A*

Dallas Baptist University *B*
DeVry University
   Irving *M*
Del Mar College *C, A*
East Texas Baptist University *B*
Eastfield College *A*
El Centro College *C, A*
Houston Baptist University *B*
Kilgore College *C, A*
Lamar University *B, M*
LeTourneau University *B*
Lubbock Christian University *B, T*
McMurry University *B*
Midland College *A*
Midwestern State University *B*
Navarro College *A*
Northwood University:Texas
   Campus *A, B*
Our Lady of the Lake University of San
   Antonio *B, M*
Panola College *A*
Prairie View A&M University *B*
Richland College *A*
St. Mary's University *M*
Sam Houston State University *B*
San Jacinto College
   Central Campus *A*
   North *C, A*
Schreiner University *B*
Southern Methodist University *B, M*
Southwest Texas Junior College *A*
Southwestern Adventist
   University *C, A, B*
Tarleton State University *B, M*
Texas A&M University *M*
Texas A&M University
   Commerce *B*
   Kingsville *B*
   Texarkana *B*
Texas State Technical College
   West Texas *C, A*
Texas State University:San Marcos *B*
Texas Tech University *B*
University of Dallas *M*
University of Houston *B, M, D*
University of Houston
   Clear Lake *B, M*
   Downtown *B*
University of Mary Hardin-Baylor *B*
University of North Texas *B, M, D*
University of St.Thomas *B, M*
University of Texas
   Arlington *B, M, D*
   Austin *B*
   Dallas *M*
   El Paso *B*
   Pan American *B*
   San Antonio *B, M, D*
West Texas A&M University *B, M*

Utah

Brigham Young University *B*
Southern Utah University *B*
University of Utah *B*
Weber State University *C, A, B*

Vermont

Champlain College *M*

Virginia

Bridgewater College *B*
Central Virginia Community
   College *C, A*
DeVry University
   Arlington *M*
Hampton University *B*
Liberty University *B*
Longwood University *B*
Lord Fairfax Community College *C, A*
Marymount University *M*
Northern Virginia Community
   College *A*
Old Dominion University *B*

Piedmont Virginia Community
   College *A*
Radford University *B*
St. Paul's College *B*
University of Virginia *M*
University of Virginia's College at
   Wise *B*
Virginia Union University *B*
Virginia Western Community
   College *A*

Washington

City University *M*
Columbia Basin College *A*
DeVry University
   Federal Way *M*
Eastern Washington University *B*
Everett Community College *A*
Gonzaga University *B*
Pacific Lutheran University *M*
Seattle Pacific University *M*
Spokane Community College *A*
Spokane Falls Community
   College *C, A*
University of Washington *B*
Washington State University *B*
Western Washington University *B*

West Virginia

Alderson-Broaddus College *B*
Potomac State College of West Virginia
   University *A*
West Virginia University *B*
West Virginia University at
   Parkersburg *A*

Wisconsin

Cardinal Stritch University *C, B, M*
Carroll College *B*
DeVry University: Milwaukee *M*
Edgewood College *B*
Lawrence University *B*
Maranatha Baptist Bible College *B*
Marquette University *B, M*
Milwaukee School of Engineering *B*
University of Wisconsin
   La Crosse *B*
   Madison *B, M*
   Milwaukee *B*
   Oshkosh *B, M*
   Parkside *B*
   Superior *B*
Viterbo University *B*
Waukesha County Technical
   College *A*

Wyoming

Casper College *A*
Central Wyoming College *A*
Eastern Wyoming College *A*
Northwest College *A*
University of Wyoming *B*

Management science

Alabama

Tuskegee University *B*
University of Alabama *B, M, D*

Alaska

University of Alaska
   Anchorage *M*
   Southeast *B*

Arizona

Arizona State University *M*
Northcentral University *M, D*
Phoenix College *A*

Arkansas

University of Arkansas *M*
University of Central Arkansas *B*

California

Allan Hancock College *A*
California State University
   Dominguez Hills *B*
   East Bay *M*
   Fullerton *B, M*
   Long Beach *B*
   Northridge *B, M*
Canada College *A*
Chabot College *A*
Coastline Community College *A*
Cypress College *A*
Grossmont Community College *A*
Lincoln University *B, M*
Los Angeles Mission College *A*
Los Angeles Pierce College *A*
Mission College *A*
Palomar College *A*
Remington College
   San Diego *A*
San Diego City College *A*
San Francisco State University *B*
University of California
   San Diego *B*
Ventura College *A*

Colorado

Colorado Christian University *B*
National American University
   Denver *A, B*
United States Air Force Academy *B*

Connecticut

Quinnipiac University *B*
Southern Connecticut State
   University *B*

Delaware

Goldey-Beacom College *A, B*

District of Columbia

Catholic University of America *B, M*
Potomac College *B*
Southeastern University *A, B*
University of the District of
   Columbia *A*

Florida

Broward Community College *A*
Eckerd College *B*
Florida Institute of Technology *M*
Florida Metropolitan University
   Pompano Beach *A, B*
Florida State University *B, M, D*
Lynn University *B*
Miami Dade College *A*
Pensacola Junior College *A*
St. Leo University *B*
Stetson University *B*
University of Florida *A, B*
University of Miami *B, M*

Georgia

Dalton State College *B*
Emory University *B*
Griffin Technical College *A*
Savannah State University *B*
West Georgia Technical College *A*

Illinois

Eastern Illinois University *B*
Illinois Institute of Technology *D*
Illinois State University *B*
Illinois Valley Community College *A*
Lewis University *B*
McKendree College *B*
Northwestern University *M*
Roosevelt University *B, M*
Southern Illinois University
   Carbondale *B*
Southwestern Illinois College *A*
Trinity International University *B*

University of Illinois
   Urbana-Champaign *B, M, D*
University of St. Francis *M*

Indiana

Goshen College *B*
Indiana Wesleyan University *M*
Oakland City University *M*
Taylor University *B*
Taylor University: Fort Wayne *B*
Valparaiso University *B*

Iowa

Drake University *B*
St.Ambrose University *B*
University of Iowa *B*

Kansas

Southwestern College *B*

Kentucky

Big Sandy Community and Technical
   College *A*
University of Kentucky *B*

Louisiana

Louisiana State University and
   Agricultural and Mechanical
   College *B, M, D*
Louisiana Tech University *B*
Southwest University *M*
Xavier University of Louisiana *B*

Maryland

Cecil Community College *A*
College of Notre Dame of
   Maryland *M*
Coppin State University *B*
Montgomery College *A*
University of Maryland
   College Park *B*

Massachusetts

American International College *B, M*
Babson College *B*
Cambridge College *B, M*
Cape Cod Community College *A*
Massachusetts College of Liberal
   Arts *B*
Northeastern University *B*
Worcester Polytechnic Institute *B, M*

Michigan

Adrian College *B*
Baker College
   of Auburn Hills *A, B*
   of Clinton Township *A, B*
   of Muskegon *A, B*
Cornerstone University *B, M*
Grace Bible College *B*
Grand Valley State University *B*
Henry Ford Community College *A*
Madonna University *B*
Northern Michigan University *B*
University of Michigan
   Dearborn *B*
Western Michigan University *B*

Minnesota

Minnesota State University
   Mankato *B*
Riverland Community College *A*
St. Mary's University of Minnesota *B*
University of Minnesota
   Morris *B*
Winona State University *B*

Missouri

Central Methodist University *B*
Columbia College *B*
Hickey College *B*
Missouri Southern State University *B*

Montana

Rocky Mountain College *B*

Nebraska

Chadron State College *B*
Grace University *B*
Union College *B*
University of Nebraska
  Lincoln *B*

Nevada

Western Nevada Community
  College *A*

New Hampshire

Granite State College *B*
New Hampshire Community
  Technical College
  Manchester *A*
Rivier College *A, B*

New Jersey

Caldwell College *B*
Kean University *M*
Rider University *B*
Rowan University *B*
Rutgers, The State University of New
  Jersey
  New Brunswick/Piscataway
    Campus *B*

New Mexico

New Mexico State University *B*

New York

Canisius College *B*
City University of New York
  Baruch College *D*
Laboratory Institute of
  Merchandising *B*
Le Moyne College *B*
Olean Business Institute *A*
Pace University *B, M*
Polytechnic University *M*
St. Bonaventure University *B*
St. John Fisher College *B*
State University of New York
  Albany *M*
  Binghamton *B, M, D*
  College at Cortland *B*
  College at Fredonia *B*
  New Paltz *B, M*
  Oswego *B*
Suffolk County Community College *A*

North Carolina

Alamance Community College *A*
Johnson & Wales University *A*
St. Augustine's College *B*
Wake Forest University *B*

North Dakota

University of Mary *B, M*

Ohio

Case Western Reserve University *M*
David N. Myers University *A, B*
Franklin University *B*
Heidelberg College *B*
Kent State University *B*
Miami University
  Oxford Campus *B, M*
Ohio Northern University *B*
Ohio University *B*
University of Cincinnati *B, M, D*
University of Dayton *M*
University of Toledo *B*
Wilmington College *B*
Wright State University *B, M*

Oklahoma

Mid-America Christian University *B*

Northeastern State University *B*
Oklahoma Baptist University *B*
Oklahoma Christian University *B*
Oklahoma City University *B*
Oklahoma State University *B*
Oklahoma State University
  Oklahoma City *A*
Oral Roberts University *B, M*
Southeastern Oklahoma State
  University *B*
University of Oklahoma *B*
Western Oklahoma State College *A*

Oregon

Chemeketa Community College *A*

Pennsylvania

California University of
  Pennsylvania *M*
Carnegie Mellon University *D*
College Misericordia *B*
DeSales University *B*
Drexel University *M*
Duquesne University *B*
Gettysburg College *B*
Kutztown University of
  Pennsylvania *B*
La Roche College *B*
La Salle University *B*
Lehigh University *B, M*
Marywood University *B, M*
Penn State
  Abington *B*
  Altoona *B*
  Beaver *B*
  Berks *B*
  Delaware County *B*
  Dubois *B*
  Fayette *B*
  Hazleton *B*
  Lehigh Valley *B*
  McKeesport *B*
  Mont Alto *B*
  New Kensington *B*
  Schuylkill - Capital College *B*
  Shenango *B*
  Worthington Scranton *B*
Rosemont College *B, M*
Shippensburg University of
  Pennsylvania *B, T*
University of Scranton *B*
Westminster College *B*

Puerto Rico

Bayamon Central University *B, M*
Inter American University of Puerto
  Rico
  Arecibo Campus *B*
  Bayamon Campus *B*
  Ponce Campus *B, M*
  San German Campus *B*
University of Puerto Rico
  Bayamon University College *B*

Rhode Island

Salve Regina University *B, M*

South Carolina

Central Carolina Technical College *A*
Charleston Southern University *B, M*
Clemson University *D*
Southern Wesleyan University *M*
University of South Carolina *B*

Tennessee

Belmont University *B*
Chattanooga State Technical
  Community College *A*
Cumberland University *B*
Lincoln Memorial University *B*
Roane State Community College *A*
Southern Adventist University *B*
Tennessee Technological University *B*

Union University *B*
University of Tennessee
  Knoxville *M, D*

Texas

Clarendon College *A*
El Paso Community College *A*
Hardin-Simmons University *B*
Midland College *A*
North Lake College *A*
Southern Methodist University *B*
Southwestern Adventist University *B*
Texas A&M University
  Kingsville *B*
Texas Christian University *B*
Texas Wesleyan University *B*
Trinity University *B*
University of North Texas *M, D*
University of Texas
  San Antonio *B, M*

Vermont

Castleton State College *B*
College of St. Joseph in Vermont *B, M*

Virginia

Averett University *B*
Longwood University *B*
Miller-Motte Technical College:
  Lynchburg *A*
Southside Virginia Community
  College *A*
Thomas Nelson Community
  College *A*
Virginia Polytechnic Institute and
  State University *B*

Washington

Eastern Washington University *B*
Walla Walla College *B*
Washington State University *B*

West Virginia

Mountain State University *A, B, M*

Wisconsin

Northland College *B*
University of Wisconsin
  Green Bay *B*
  Milwaukee *D*
  Stout *M*

Wyoming

University of Wyoming *B*

Manicurist

Alabama

Gadsden State Community College *C*
Lawson State Community College *C*
Shelton State Community College *C*

Arizona

Eastern Arizona College *C*

Florida

Central Florida Community College *C*
Indian River Community College *C*
Palm Beach Community College *C*
Pensacola Junior College *C*

Georgia

Central Georgia Technical College *C*
Savannah Technical College *C*
West Georgia Technical College *C*

Illinois

Kaskaskia College *C*

Michigan

Kirtland Community College *C, A*

Mott Community College *C*

Minnesota

Minnesota State College - Southeast
  Technical *C*
Minnesota State Community and
  Technical College - Fergus Falls *C*
Ridgewater College *C*
St. Paul College *C*

New Mexico

Clovis Community College *C*

North Carolina

Brunswick Community College *C*
Carteret Community College *C*
Davidson County Community
  College *C*
Isothermal Community College *C*
Lenoir Community College *C*
Martin Community College *C*
Roanoke-Chowan Community
  College *C*
Southeastern Community College *C*
Southwestern Community College *C*

Texas

Lamar State College at Port Arthur *C*
North Harris Montgomery
  Community College District *C*

Washington

Clover Park Technical College *C*
Olympic College *C*
Renton Technical College *C*

Wyoming

Eastern Wyoming College *C*

Manufacturing engineering

Alabama

Auburn University *M*

California

California State Polytechnic
  University: Pomona *B*
University of California
  Berkeley *B*
  Los Angeles *B, M*
University of Southern California *M*

Florida

University of Miami *B*
University of South Florida *B, M, D*

Illinois

Bradley University *B, M*
Northwestern University *B, M*
Southern Illinois University
  Edwardsville *B*

Kansas

Kansas State University *B*
Wichita State University *B*

Kentucky

Maysville Community College *A*

Massachusetts

Bristol Community College *A*
University of Massachusetts
  Amherst *M*
Worcester Polytechnic
  Institute *B, M, D*

Michigan

Central Michigan University *B*
Eastern Michigan University *B*

Grand Valley State University *B, M*
Kettering University *B, M*
Lawrence Technological
University *M, D*
University of Detroit Mercy *B*
University of Michigan *M*
University of Michigan
Dearborn *B*
Wayne State University *B, M*

Minnesota
Dunwoody College of Technology *A*
St. Cloud State University *B*

Missouri
University of Missouri
Rolla *M*

Nebraska
University of Nebraska
Lincoln *M*

New Jersey
New Jersey Institute of
Technology *B, M, D*

New Mexico
University of New Mexico *M*

New York
Hofstra University *B*
Long Island University
C.W. Post Campus *M*
Polytechnic University *M*
Rensselaer Polytechnic Institute *M*
Rochester Institute of
Technology *B, M*
State University of New York
College of Technology at
Alfred *A, B*

North Carolina
Edgecombe Community College *A*
North Carolina State University *M*

North Dakota
North Dakota State University *B, M*

Ohio
Central State University *B*
Miami University
Oxford Campus *B*

Oregon
Oregon State University *B, M*
Portland State University *M*

Pennsylvania
Robert Morris University *B*

Rhode Island
Community College of Rhode
Island *A*
New England Institute of
Technology *A, B*

Texas
Southern Methodist University *M*
Texas State University: San Marcos *B*
Texas Tech University *M*
University of Texas
Austin *M*
El Paso *M*
Pan American *B, M*

Utah
Brigham Young University *B, M*
Salt Lake Community College *A*

Virginia
Mountain Empire Community
College *A*
Virginia State University *B*

Washington
Washington State University *B*

Wisconsin
Marquette University *B, M, D*
University of Wisconsin
Stout *B, M*

Manufacturing technologies

Alabama
Jacksonville State University *B*
University of West Alabama *B*

Arizona
Central Arizona College *A*
Gateway Community College *C, A*
Yavapai College *A*

Arkansas
Phillips Community College of the
University of Arkansas *C, A*
University of Arkansas
Fort Smith *B*

California
California State University
Long Beach *B*
Cerritos Community College *C, A*
College of the Sequoias *A*
Irvine Valley College *C, A*
Long Beach City College *C*
San Diego City College *C, A*

Colorado
Arapahoe Community College *C, A*
Mesa State College *C, A*
Pueblo Community College *C, A*
Red Rocks Community College *C, A*

Connecticut
Asnuntuck Community College *C, A*
Central Connecticut State
University *B*
Gateway Community College *A*
Manchester Community College *A*
Naugatuck Valley Community
College *C, A*
Three Rivers Community College *A*
Tunxis Community College *A*

Florida
Pensacola Junior College *A*
St. Petersburg College *C, A*

Georgia
Central Georgia Technical College *C*
Macon State College *A*
Middle Georgia College *A*

Idaho
Brigham Young University-Idaho *A*
Lewis-Clark State College *A, B*

Illinois
Black Hawk College *C, A*
Bradley University *B, M*
Heartland Community College *C, A*
Illinois Eastern Community Colleges
Wabash Valley College *A*
Illinois Institute of Technology *B*
Kankakee Community College *A*
Kishwaukee College *C, A*
Morrison Institute of Technology *A*
Rend Lake College *A*

Rock Valley College *C, A*
Sauk Valley Community College *A*
Southern Illinois University
Carbondale *M*
Western Illinois University *M*
William Rainey Harper College *C, A*

Indiana
Ball State University *A*
Indiana State University *B*
Ivy Tech State College
Ivy Tech Community College:
Whitewater *C*
Vincennes University *A*

Iowa
Hawkeye Community College *A*
Iowa Central Community College *A*
Northwest Iowa Community
College *A*
University of Northern Iowa *B*

Kansas
Hutchinson Community College *C, A*
Pittsburg State University *B*
Southwestern College *B*

Kentucky
Eastern Kentucky University *B, M*
Maysville Community College *C, A*
Morehead State University *A, B, M*
Murray State University *A, B*
St. Catharine College *A*
Western Kentucky University *A*

Louisiana
Nicholls State University *B*

Maine
Kennebec Valley Community
College *A*
University of Southern Maine *B, M*

Maryland
Chesapeake College *A*
College of Southern Maryland *C, A*

Massachusetts
Fitchburg State College *B*
Mount Wachusett Community
College *A*
Quinsigamond Community
College *C, A*
University of Massachusetts
Lowell *M*

Michigan
Alpena Community College *A*
Baker College
of Flint *A*
Central Michigan University *B*
Delta College *A*
Eastern Michigan University *B, M*
Ferris State University *B*
Kirtland Community College *C, A*
Lake Michigan College *C, A*
Lawrence Technological University *A*
Macomb Community College *C, A*
Mid Michigan Community College *A*
Monroe County Community
College *C, A*
Mott Community College *A*
Northern Michigan University *B*
Oakland Community College *C, A*
St. Clair County Community
College *A*
Southwestern Michigan College *C*
Wayne State University *B*

Minnesota
Alexandria Technical College *C, A*
Dakota County Technical College *A*

Hennepin Technical College *C, A*
Minnesota State Community and
Technical College - Fergus
Falls *C, A*
Minnesota State University
Mankato *B, M*
Northwest Technical College *C, A*
Pine Technical College *C, A*
Rochester Community and Technical
College *A*
St. Cloud State University *B*
St. Paul College *A*

Mississippi
Mississippi State University *B*

Missouri
Central Missouri State University *A*
East Central College *A*
Mineral Area College *A*
Missouri Southern State University *C*
Missouri Western State University *A*
Moberly Area Community
College *C, A*
St. Louis Community College
St. Louis Community College at
Florissant Valley *A*

Montana
Montana Tech of the University of
Montana *A*

Nebraska
University of Nebraska
Omaha *B*

New Hampshire
New Hampshire Community
Technical College
Berlin *A*
Claremont *A*
Nashua *A*
New Hampshire Technical Institute *A*

New Jersey
Bergen Community College *C, A*
Essex County College *A*
Kean University *B*
Middlesex County College *A*
Raritan Valley Community College *A*
Thomas Edison State College *A, B*
Union County College *A*

New Mexico
Albuquerque Technical-Vocational
Institute *C, A*
New Mexico State University
Carlsbad *C, A*
Southwestern Indian Polytechnic
Institute *A*

New York
Corning Community College *A*
Dutchess Community College *A*
Excelsior College *A*
Mohawk Valley Community
College *A*
Monroe Community College *A*
New York Institute of Technology *B*
Rochester Institute of
Technology *B, M*
State University of New York
College of Agriculture and
Technology at Morrisville *A*
College of Technology at Canton *A*
Farmingdale *C, B*

North Carolina
Central Carolina Community
College *A*
Craven Community College *A*
East Carolina University *B*

Edgecombe Community College *C, A*
Mitchell Community College *A*
Pitt Community College *C, A*
Randolph Community College *A*
Richmond Community College *A*
Rockingham Community College *C*
South Piedmont Community
   College *A*
Wake Technical Community
   College *A*
Western Carolina University *B, M*

Ohio
Bowling Green State University:
   Firelands College *A*
Cincinnati State Technical and
   Community College *C, A*
Clark State Community College *C, A*
Edison State Community College *C, A*
James A. Rhodes State College *C, A*
Jefferson Community College *C, A*
Kent State University
   Tuscarawas Campus *C*
Lakeland Community College *C, A*
Marion Technical College *C, A*
Owens Community College
   Toledo *A*
Sinclair Community College *A*
Stark State College of Technology *A*
University of Dayton *B*
University of Rio Grande *A*
Wright State University: Lake
   Campus *A*

Oklahoma
Oklahoma City Community College *A*
Oklahoma Panhandle State
   University *A, B*
Oklahoma State University
   Oklahoma City *A*
   Okmulgee *A*
Rogers State University *B*
Southwestern Oklahoma State
   University *B*
Western Oklahoma State College *A*

Oregon
Central Oregon Community
   College *C, A*
Oregon Institute of Technology *B, M*
Portland Community College *C, A*
Rogue Community College *C, A*

Pennsylvania
Butler County Community College *A*
Johnson College *A*
Lehigh Carbon Community College *A*
Penn State
   Fayette *A*
   York *A*
Pennsylvania College of
   Technology *A, B*

Rhode Island
Community College of Rhode
   Island *C, A*
New England Institute of
   Technology *A, B*

South Carolina
Trident Technical College *C, A*
York Technical College *C*

South Dakota
South Dakota State University *B*

Tennessee
Jackson State Community College *C*
Middle Tennessee State University *M*
Tennessee Technological University *B*
University of Memphis *B*
Walters State Community College *C, A*

Texas
Frank Phillips College *C, A*
Midwestern State University *B*
Richland College *A*
Sam Houston State University *B*
Tarleton State University *B*
Texas A&M University *B*
Texas A&M University
   Commerce *B*
Texas State University: San Marcos *B*
University of Houston *B*
University of Texas
   Brownsville *B*

Utah
Salt Lake Community College *A*

Virginia
Danville Community College *A*
John Tyler Community College *A*
Mountain Empire Community
   College *A*
Piedmont Virginia Community
   College *A*
Thomas Nelson Community
   College *C*

Washington
Clark College *A*
Eastern Washington University *B*
Everett Community College *A*
Highline Community College *A*
Shoreline Community College *A*
Wenatchee Valley College *C, A*
Western Washington University *B*

Wisconsin
Gateway Technical College *A*
Mid-State Technical College *A*
Wisconsin Indianhead Technical
   College *A*

Wyoming
Casper College *C, A*
Central Wyoming College *C*

Marine biology

Alabama
Alabama State University *B*
Auburn University *B*
Samford University *B*
Spring Hill College *B*
Troy University *B*
University of Alabama *B, M*
University of Mobile *B*
University of North Alabama *B*
University of South Alabama *M, D*
University of West Alabama *B*

Alaska
Alaska Pacific University *B*
Sheldon Jackson College *B*
University of Alaska
   Fairbanks *M*
   Southeast *B*

California
California State University
   Fresno *M*
   Monterey Bay *B, M*
   Sacramento *M*
   Stanislaus *M*
Mount San Antonio College *A*
Oxnard College *A*
San Diego State University *B*
San Francisco State University *B, M*
San Jose State University *B, M*
University of California
   Los Angeles *B*
   San Diego *D*

Santa Barbara *B, M, D*
   Santa Cruz *B, M*
University of San Diego *B, M*
University of Southern
   California *M, D*

Connecticut
Mitchell College *A*
Southern Connecticut State
   University *B*
University of Connecticut *B*
University of New Haven *B*

Delaware
University of Delaware *M, D*

District of Columbia
American University *B*

Florida
Barry University *B, T*
Eckerd College *B*
Florida Institute of Technology *B, M*
Florida International University *B*
Florida Keys Community College *A*
Florida State University *B, M, D*
Gulf Coast Community College *A*
Jacksonville University *B*
Manatee Community College *A*
Nova Southeastern University *B, M, D*
Okaloosa-Walton College *A*
University of Miami *B, M, D*
University of Tampa *B*
University of West Florida *B*
Valencia Community College *A*

Georgia
Savannah State University *B*
University of Georgia *M, D*

Hawaii
Hawaii Pacific University *B*
University of Hawaii
   Hilo *B*
   Manoa *B*

Kansas
Southwestern College *B*

Louisiana
Nicholls State University *B, M*

Maine
College of the Atlantic *B*
Maine Maritime Academy *B, T*
St. Joseph's College *B*
Southern Maine Community
   College *A*
Unity College *B*
University of Maine *B, M, D*
University of Maine
   Machias *B*
University of New England *B*

Maryland
University of Maryland
   Baltimore *D*
   Baltimore County *M, D*
   Eastern Shore *M, D*

Massachusetts
Boston University *B*
Massachusetts Bay Community
   College *A*
Northeastern University *B*
Salem State College *B*
Suffolk University *B*
University of Massachusetts
   Lowell *M, D*

Minnesota
Bemidji State University *B*
St. Cloud State University *B*

Mississippi
University of Southern
   Mississippi *B, M, D*

Missouri
Missouri Southern State University *B*

New Jersey
Fairleigh Dickinson University
   College at Florham *B*
   Metropolitan Campus *B*
Richard Stockton College of New
   Jersey *B*
Rider University *B*
Rutgers, The State University of New
   Jersey
   New Brunswick/Piscataway
     Campus *B*

New York
Sarah Lawrence College *B*
State University of New York
   College of Agriculture and
     Technology at Morrisville *A*
   College of Environmental Science
     and Forestry *B*
   Maritime College *M*
   Stony Brook *B*

North Carolina
University of North Carolina
   Wilmington *B, M, D*

Oklahoma
Northeastern State University *B*

Oregon
University of Oregon *B*

Pennsylvania
East Stroudsburg University of
   Pennsylvania *B*
Juniata College *B*
Mansfield University of
   Pennsylvania *B*
St. Francis University *B*
Waynesburg College *B*

Puerto Rico
University of Puerto Rico
   Humacao *B*
   Mayaguez *B, M*

Rhode Island
Roger Williams University *B*
University of Rhode Island *B*

South Carolina
Coastal Carolina University *B, M*
College of Charleston *B, M*
University of South Carolina *B, M, D*

Texas
Galveston College *A*
Lamar University *B*
Laredo Community College *A*
Texas A&M University *B*
Texas A&M University
   Galveston *B*
Texas State University: San Marcos *B*

Utah
Utah State University *M, D*

Virginia
College of William and Mary *M, D*
Hampton University *B*

Old Dominion University *B*
St. Paul's College *B*

Washington

University of Washington *B*
Western Washington University *B*

Wisconsin

Lawrence University *B, T*

Marine engineering/ naval architecture

California

California Maritime Academy *B*
Santa Barbara City College *A*

Connecticut

United States Coast Guard Academy *B*

Florida

Gulf Coast Community College *A*

Louisiana

University of New Orleans *B*

Maine

Maine Maritime Academy *B*

Maryland

United States Naval Academy *B*

Michigan

University of Michigan *B, M, D*

New Jersey

Stevens Institute of Technology *M*

New York

State University of New York
Maritime College *B*
United States Merchant Marine
Academy *B*
Webb Institute *B*

Texas

Texas A&M University
Galveston *B*

Virginia

Virginia Polytechnic Institute and
State University *M*

Wisconsin

University of Wisconsin
Madison *B*

Marine maintenance/ fitter/ship repair

Florida

Florida Keys Community College *C, A*
Palm Beach Community College *A*

Georgia

Central Georgia Technical College *C*

Hawaii

University of Hawaii
Honolulu Community College *A*

Iowa

Iowa Lakes Community College *C*

Maine

Washington County Community
College *C*

Massachusetts

Benjamin Franklin Institute of
Technology *C*

Minnesota

Alexandria Technical College *C*
Central Lakes College *C, A*
Hennepin Technical College *C, A*
Minnesota State Community and
Technical College - Fergus
Falls *C, A*
South Central College *A*

Missouri

State Fair Community College *C*

New York

United States Merchant Marine
Academy *B*

North Carolina

Cape Fear Community College *C*
Carteret Community College *A*

Washington

Northwest School of Wooden
Boatbuilding *A*
Olympic College *A*

Wisconsin

Wisconsin Indianhead Technical
College *C*

Marine science/ Merchant Marine

Maine

Maine Maritime Academy *B*

Massachusetts

Massachusetts Maritime Academy *B*

Michigan

Northwestern Michigan College *A*

New York

United States Merchant Marine
Academy *B*

Texas

Texas A&M University
Galveston *B*

Marketing

Alabama

Alabama Agricultural and Mechanical
University *B*
Alabama State University *B*
Auburn University *B*
Auburn University at Montgomery *B*
Birmingham-Southern College *B*
Faulkner University *B*
Huntingdon College *B*
Jacksonville State University *B*
Spring Hill College *B*
Talladega College *B*
Troy University *B*
University of Alabama *B, M, D*
University of Alabama
Birmingham *B*
Huntsville *B*
University of Mobile *B*
University of Montevallo *B*
University of North Alabama *B*
University of South Alabama *B*

Alaska

University of Alaska
Anchorage *B*

Southeast *B*

Arizona

Arizona State University *B*
Grand Canyon University *B*
Mesa Community College *A*
Northcentral University *B*
Northern Arizona University *C, B*
Phoenix College *C, A*
University of Arizona *B*
University of Phoenix *C, B, M*
Western International University *B, M*

Arkansas

Arkansas State University *B*
Harding University *B*
John Brown University *B*
University of Arkansas *B*
University of Arkansas
Little Rock *B*
University of Central Arkansas *B*
University of the Ozarks *B*

California

Azusa Pacific University *B*
Biola University *B*
Butte College *C, A*
California Lutheran University *B*
California State Polytechnic
University: Pomona *B*
California State University
Chico *B*
Fresno *B*
Fullerton *B, M*
Sacramento *B, M*
San Bernardino *B, M*
City College of San Francisco *A*
College of Alameda *C, A*
Crafton Hills College *C*
De Anza College *C, A*
Fashion Institute of Design and
Merchandising *A, B*
Fashion Institute of Design and
Merchandising
San Diego *A*
Fresno Pacific University *B*
Golden Gate University *B, M*
Grossmont Community College *C, A*
Holy Names University *B*
Lake Tahoe Community College *C, A*
Los Angeles Pierce College *C, A*
Modesto Junior College *A*
National University *M*
Ohlone College *C, A*
Pacific Union College *B*
Riverside Community College *C, A*
Saddleback College *C, A*
San Diego Miramar College *A*
San Diego State University *M*
San Jose City College *C, A*
San Jose State University *B*
Santa Barbara City College *C, A*
Santa Clara University *B*
Santiago Canyon College *A*
University of La Verne *B*
University of San Francisco *B*
Vanguard University of Southern
California *B*
Ventura College *A*
Westwood College *B*
Westwood College of Technology
Inland Empire *B*
Woodbury University *B*
Yuba Community College District *C*

Colorado

Adams State College *B*
Aims Community College *C, A*
Arapahoe Community College *C, A*
Community College of Aurora *A*
Fort Lewis College *B*
Metropolitan State College of
Denver *B*

University of Colorado
Boulder *B, M*
Denver and Health Sciences
Center *M*
University of Denver *B, M*
Westwood College of Technology *B*

Connecticut

Asnuntuck Community College *C*
Central Connecticut State
University *B*
Fairfield University *B*
Middlesex Community College *A*
Northwestern Connecticut
Community College *A*
Norwalk Community College *A*
Quinnipiac University *B, M*
Sacred Heart University *C*
Southern Connecticut State
University *B*
University of Bridgeport *B, M*
University of Connecticut *B*
University of Hartford *B*
University of New Haven *B*
Western Connecticut State
University *B*

Delaware

Delaware State University *B*
Delaware Technical and Community
College
Owens Campus *C, A*
Stanton/Wilmington Campus *C, A*
Terry Campus *C, A*
Goldey-Beacom College *B*
Wilmington College *B*

District of Columbia

American University *C*
Georgetown University *B*
Strayer University *A*

Florida

Brevard Community College *A*
City College: Casselberry *A*
Daytona Beach Community
College *C, A*
Edison College *C, A*
Florida Atlantic University *B*
Florida Gulf Coast University *B*
Florida International University *B*
Florida Metropolitan University
Orlando College North *A, B*
Pinellas *A, B*
Pompano Beach *A, B*
Tampa College *A, B*
Florida Metropolitan University:
Jacksonville *A, B*
Florida Southern College *B*
Florida State University *B, M, D*
Gulf Coast Community College *A*
International Academy of Design and
Technology: Orlando *A, B*
Jacksonville University *B*
Johnson & Wales University *A, B*
Lynn University *B, M*
Northwood University
Florida Campus *B*
Okaloosa-Walton College *C, A*
Palm Beach Atlantic University *B*
Palm Beach Community College *A*
Pasco-Hernando Community
College *A*
Polk Community College *A*
St. Leo University *B*
St. Petersburg College *A*
Santa Fe Community College *A*
Schiller International University *B*
Seminole Community College *C*
Southeastern College of the
Assemblies of God *B*
Southwest Florida College
Tampa *A*

Stetson University *B*
University of Central Florida *B*
University of Florida *B, M*
University of Miami *B*
University of North Florida *B*
University of South Florida *B*
University of Tampa *B*
University of West Florida *B*
Warner Southern College *B*
Webber International University *A, B*

Georgia

Albany State University *B*
Augusta State University *B*
Bainbridge College *C, A*
Bauder College *A*
Berry College *B*
Brenau University *B*
Chattahoochee Technical College *C, A*
Clayton State University *B*
Coastal Georgia Community
    College *C, A*
Columbus State University *B*
Dalton State College *C, A, B*
DeKalb Technical College *A*
Emory University *B*
Fort Valley State University *B*
Georgia College and State
    University *B*
Georgia Southern University *B*
Georgia Southwestern State
    University *B*
Georgia State University *B, M, D*
Gwinnett Technical College *C, A*
Kennesaw State University *B*
North Georgia College & State
    University *B*
Paine College *B*
Savannah Technical College *A*
South Georgia College *A*
Thomas University *B*
University of Georgia *B*
University of West Georgia *B*
Valdosta State University *B*

Hawaii

Chaminade University of Honolulu *B*
Hawaii Pacific University *B*
University of Hawaii
    Hawaii Community College *C, A*
    Hilo *B*
    Manoa *B*

Idaho

Boise State University *B*
College of Southern Idaho *A*
Eastern Idaho Technical College *C, A*
Idaho State University *C, A, B*
University of Idaho *B*

Illinois

Augustana College *B*
Aurora University *B*
Benedictine University *B*
Blackburn College *B*
Bradley University *B*
College of DuPage *C*
Columbia College Chicago *B*
Concordia University *B*
DePaul University *M*
Eastern Illinois University *B*
Elmhurst College *B*
Eureka College *B*
Greenville College *B*
Illinois Institute of Technology *M*
Illinois State University *B*
Judson College *B*
Lewis University *B*
Loyola University of Chicago *B*
MacCormac College *A*
McKendree College *B*
Millikin University *B*
Moraine Valley Community College *C*

North Central College *B*
North Park University *B*
Northeastern Illinois University *B*
Northern Illinois University *B*
Northwestern University *M, D*
Olivet Nazarene University *B*
Parkland College *A*
Quincy University *B*
Rock Valley College *C, A*
Rockford Business College *A*
Rockford College *B*
Roosevelt University *B, M*
St. Xavier University *M*
Sauk Valley Community College *C, A*
South Suburban College of Cook
    County *C, A*
Southern Illinois University
    Carbondale *B*
Trinity International University *B*
Triton College *C, A*
University of Illinois
    Chicago *B*
    Urbana-Champaign *B, D*
University of St. Francis *B*
Western Illinois University *B*
Westwood College - Chicago Loop *B*
Westwood College of Technology
    O'Hare *B*
William Rainey Harper College *C, A*

Indiana

Anderson University *B*
Ball State University *B*
Butler University *B*
Grace College *B*
Indiana Institute of Technology *B, M*
Indiana State University *B*
Indiana University
    East *B*
    Kokomo *B*
    South Bend *B*
Indiana University-Purdue University
    Fort Wayne *B*
Indiana Wesleyan University *B*
Manchester College *B, M*
Marian College *B*
Purdue University
    North Central Campus *A*
St. Mary-of-the-Woods College *B*
Taylor University *B*
University of Evansville *B*
University of Indianapolis *B*
University of Notre Dame *B*
University of Southern Indiana *B*
Valparaiso University *B*
Vincennes University *A*

Iowa

AIB College of Business *A*
Ashford University *B*
Buena Vista University *B*
Clarke College *B*
Des Moines Area Community
    College *C, A*
Dordt College *B*
Drake University *B*
Hawkeye Community College *A*
Iowa State University *B*
Loras College *B*
Maharishi University of
    Management *M*
Morningside College *B*
Northeast Iowa Community
    College *A*
Northwestern College *B*
St. Ambrose University *B*
Simpson College *B*
Southwestern Community College *A*
University of Iowa *B*
University of Northern Iowa *B*
Waldorf College *B*
Wartburg College *B*

Kansas

Central Christian College of Kansas *A*
Emporia State University *B*
Fort Hays State University *B*
Newman University *B*
Pittsburg State University *B*
Southwestern College *B*
Tabor College *B*
Washburn University of Topeka *B*
Wichita State University *B*

Kentucky

Campbellsville University *B*
Eastern Kentucky University *B*
Hazard Community College *A*
Kentucky State University *B*
Morehead State University *B*
Murray State University *B*
Northern Kentucky University *B*
University of Kentucky *B*
University of Louisville *B*
Western Kentucky University *B*

Louisiana

Grambling State University *B*
Louisiana State University and
    Agricultural and Mechanical
    College *B, M, D*
Louisiana Tech University *B*
Loyola University New Orleans *B*
Nicholls State University *B*
Southeastern Louisiana University *B*
Southern University and Agricultural
    and Mechanical College *B*
Tulane University *B*
University of Louisiana at Lafayette *B*
University of Louisiana at Monroe *B*
University of New Orleans *B*
Xavier University of Louisiana *B*

Maine

Husson College *B*
St. Joseph's College *B*
Thomas College *B*
University of Maine
    Machias *B*
University of Southern Maine *B, M*

Maryland

Allegany College of Maryland *A*
Baltimore City Community College *A*
Columbia Union College *B*
Morgan State University *B*
Prince George's Community
    College *C, A*
Salisbury University *B*
University of Baltimore *B, M*
University of Maryland
    College Park *B*
    University College *B*

Massachusetts

American International College *B, M*
Assumption College *B*
Babson College *B*
Bay Path College *B*
Becker College *B*
Bentley College *B, M*
Boston University *B*
Bridgewater State College *B, M*
Cape Cod Community College *A*
Emerson College *B, M*
Fitchburg State College *B*
Greenfield Community College *C*
Lasell College *B, M*
Marian Court College *C, A*
Massasoit Community College *C, A*
Newbury College *A, B*
Nichols College *B*
North Shore Community College *A*
Northeastern University *B*
Northern Essex Community
    College *A*

Salem State College *B, M*
Springfield Technical Community
    College *A*
Stonehill College *B*
Suffolk University *B, M*
University of Massachusetts
    Amherst *B*
    Dartmouth *B*
Western New England College *B*
Worcester Polytechnic Institute *M*

Michigan

Adrian College *B*
Alma College *B*
Baker College
    of Cadillac *A*
    of Flint *A*
    of Muskegon *A, B*
    of Owosso *A, B*
    of Port Huron *A, B*
Central Michigan University *B*
Cleary University *B*
Cornerstone University *B*
Davenport University *A, B*
Delta College *A*
Eastern Michigan University *B, M*
Ferris State University *C, B*
Finlandia University *B*
Glen Oaks Community College *C*
Grace Bible College *B*
Grand Rapids Community College *A*
Grand Valley State University *B*
Hillsdale College *B*
Kellogg Community College *C*
Kettering University *B*
Kirtland Community College *A*
Lansing Community College *A*
Macomb Community College *C, A*
Madonna University *B*
Michigan State University *B, M, D*
Mid Michigan Community College *A*
Mott Community College *C, A*
Muskegon Community College *A*
Northern Michigan University *B*
Northwood University *B*
Oakland University *B*
Rochester College *B*
Saginaw Valley State University *B*
University of Detroit Mercy *B*
University of Michigan
    Flint *B*
Wayne State University *B*
West Shore Community College *A*
Western Michigan University *B*

Minnesota

Alexandria Technical College *C, A*
Anoka-Ramsey Community College *A*
Augsburg College *B*
Century Community and Technical
    College *C, A*
College of St. Scholastica *B*
Concordia University: St. Paul *B*
Dakota County Technical College *C, A*
Mesabi Range Community and
    Technical College *C, A*
Metropolitan State University *B*
Minnesota State Community and
    Technical College - Fergus Falls *A*
Minnesota State University
    Moorhead *B*
National American University
    St. Paul *B*
Normandale Community College *C, A*
Northwestern College *B*
Rasmussen College
    Minnetonka *A*
Ridgewater College *A*
Riverland Community College *A*
St. Cloud State University *B*
St. Mary's University of Minnesota *B*
Southwest Minnesota State
    University *A*

University of Minnesota
Crookston B
Twin Cities B
University of St. Thomas B, M
Winona State University B

Mississippi

Delta State University B
Jackson State University B
Mississippi College B
Mississippi Gulf Coast Community
College
Jefferson Davis Campus A
Mississippi State University B
University of Mississippi B
University of Southern
Mississippi B, M

Missouri

Avila University B
Central Missouri State University B
College of the Ozarks B
Columbia College B
Hannibal-LaGrange College B
Harris-Stowe State University B
Lincoln University B
Lindenwood University B, M
Maryville University of Saint
Louis B, M
Missouri Baptist University B
Missouri Southern State University B
Missouri State University B
Missouri Western State University B
Moberly Area Community
College C, A
National American University
Kansas City A, B
Park University B
St. Charles Community College C, A
Southeast Missouri State University B
Stephens College B
Three Rivers Community College A
University of Missouri
Columbia B
St. Louis B, M
Washington University in St.
Louis B, M
Webster University C, B, M

Montana

Flathead Valley Community College A
Montana Tech of the University of
Montana B
University of Montana: Missoula A, B

Nebraska

Bellevue University B
Creighton University B
Hamilton College: Lincoln A
Hastings College B
Northeast Community College A
Southeast Community College
Lincoln Campus A
University of Nebraska
Lincoln B
Omaha B

Nevada

University of Nevada
Las Vegas B
Reno B

New Hampshire

Franklin Pierce College B
McIntosh College A
New England College B
New Hampshire Community
Technical College
Manchester C, A
New Hampshire Technical Institute A
Plymouth State University B
Rivier College M

New Jersey

Bergen Community College A
Berkeley College A, B
Bloomfield College C, B
Brookdale Community College A
Caldwell College B
Camden County College A
The College of New Jersey B
College of St. Elizabeth C
Cumberland County College A
Fairleigh Dickinson University
College at Florham B
Metropolitan Campus B
Felician College B
Gloucester County College A
Kean University B
Monmouth University B
Passaic County Community College A
Rider University B
Rowan University B
Rutgers, The State University of New
Jersey
Camden Regional Campus B
New Brunswick/Piscataway
Campus B
Newark Regional Campus B
Salem Community College A
Seton Hall University B
Thomas Edison State College C, A, B
Union County College A

New Mexico

College of the Southwest B
Eastern New Mexico University B
New Mexico State University B
Western New Mexico University B

New York

Adirondack Community College A
Alfred University B
Berkeley College A, B
Berkeley College of New York
City A, B
Bryant & Stratton Business Institute
Bryant & Stratton College:
Syracuse A
Canisius College B
City University of New York
Kingsborough Community
College A
New York City College of
Technology A
York College B
Clarkson University B
Dominican College of Blauvelt B
Dowling College B
Elmira College B
Excelsior College B
Five Towns College A
Globe Institute of Technology C
Herkimer County Community
College A
Hofstra University B, M
Iona College B, M
Ithaca College B
Jamestown Business College A
Jamestown Community College A
Le Moyne College B
Monroe Community College A
New York Institute of Technology B
Niagara University B
Pace University B, M
Roberts Wesleyan College B
Rochester Institute of
Technology A, B, M
Sage College of Albany A
St. John Fisher College B
St. John's University B, M
St. Thomas Aquinas College B, M
Siena College B, T
State University of New York
Albany M
College at Old Westbury B
College at Plattsburgh B

College of Technology at Alfred A
Farmingdale C
Suffolk County Community
College C, A
Syracuse University B
Touro College B
Wagner College B
Westchester Community College A

North Carolina

Appalachian State University B
Chowan College B
East Carolina University B
Elon University B
Fayetteville Technical Community
College A
Isothermal Community College A
Lenoir-Rhyne College B
Methodist College B
North Carolina Agricultural and
Technical State University B
Pitt Community College C, A
Queens University of Charlotte B
Southwestern Community College A
University of North Carolina
Charlotte B
Wilmington B
Western Carolina University B
Wilkes Community College C, A
Wingate University B

North Dakota

Jamestown College B
Minot State University B
North Dakota State University C
University of North Dakota B
Williston State College C, A

Ohio

Ashland University B
Baldwin-Wallace College B
Bowling Green State University:
Firelands College C
Case Western Reserve University M, D
Cedarville University B
Cincinnati State Technical and
Community College C, A
Cleveland State University B, M
David N. Myers University B
Davis College A
Defiance College B
Edison State Community College C, A
Franklin University B
James A. Rhodes State College A
Kent State University B, D
Lakeland Community College C
Lourdes College B
Marietta College B
Marion Technical College A
Miami University
Hamilton Campus A
Oxford Campus B, M
Mount Vernon Nazarene University B
Ohio State University
Columbus Campus B
Ohio University B
Stark State College of Technology A
Tiffin University B
University of Akron C, B, M
University of Akron: Wayne College A
University of Cincinnati
Clermont College C
University of Dayton B
University of Findlay B
University of Northwestern Ohio A
University of Rio Grande A, B
University of Toledo B, M
Urbana University B
Ursuline College B
Walsh University A, B
Washington State Community
College A
Wilmington College B
Wittenberg University B

Wright State University A, B, M
Xavier University B, M
Youngstown State University A, B, M
Zane State College A

Oklahoma

East Central University B
Northeastern Oklahoma Agricultural
and Mechanical College C, A
Northeastern State University B
Oklahoma Baptist University B
Oklahoma City University B, M
Oklahoma State University B
Oral Roberts University B
Southeastern Oklahoma State
University B
Southern Nazarene University B
University of Central Oklahoma B
University of Oklahoma B
University of Tulsa B

Oregon

Blue Mountain Community College A
Oregon Institute of Technology B
Portland State University B
Southern Oregon University B
University of Oregon M, D
University of Portland B

Pennsylvania

Albright College B
Arcadia University B
Bucks County Community College A
Business Institute of Pennsylvania A
Business Institute of Pennsylvania
Meadville A
Butler County Community College A
Cabrini College C, B
Carnegie Mellon University D
Cedar Crest College C
Central Pennsylvania College A
Chatham College B
Chestnut Hill College C, A, B
Clarion University of Pennsylvania B
College Misericordia B
Community College of Allegheny
County A
Community College of Beaver
County A
DeSales University B
Delaware Valley College B
Drexel University B, M
Duquesne University B
Edinboro University of
Pennsylvania B
Erie Business Center C, A
Erie Business Center South A
Gannon University B
Gettysburg College B
Grove City College B
Holy Family University B
Juniata College B
King's College B
Kutztown University of
Pennsylvania B
La Roche College B
La Salle University B
Lebanon Valley College C
Lehigh University B, M
Manor College A
Mansfield University of
Pennsylvania B
Marywood University B
Messiah College B
Neumann College B
Peirce College A
Penn State
Erie, The Behrend College B
Schuylkill - Capital College B
University Park B
Worthington Scranton B
Philadelphia University B
Robert Morris University C, B
St. Francis University B

St. Joseph's University C, A, B, M
St. Vincent College B
Seton Hill University C, B
Shippensburg University of
   Pennsylvania B
South Hills School of Business &
   Technology A
Susquehanna University B
Temple University B, M
University of Pennsylvania B, M, D
University of Pittsburgh B
University of Scranton B
University of the Sciences in
   Philadelphia B
Villanova University B
York College of Pennsylvania B
York Technical Institute C

Puerto Rico

Bayamon Central University B, M
Inter American University of Puerto
   Rico
   Aguadilla Campus B
   Bayamon Campus B
   Ponce Campus B, M
   San German Campus B, M
Pontifical Catholic University of
   Puerto Rico B
Turabo University B, M
Universidad Metropolitana A, B, M
Universidad del Este A, B
University of Puerto Rico
   Aguadilla B
   Bayamon University College B
   Mayaguez B, M
   Ponce B
University of the Sacred Heart M

Rhode Island

Bryant University B, M
Community College of Rhode
   Island C, A
Johnson & Wales University A, B, M
Providence College B
Roger Williams University B
University of Rhode Island B

South Carolina

Anderson University B
Central Carolina Technical College A
Charleston Southern University B, M
Claflin University B
Coastal Carolina University B
Forrest Junior College A
Francis Marion University B
Limestone College B
Spartanburg Technical College A
Trident Technical College A
University of South Carolina B

South Dakota

Black Hills State University B
Dakota State University B
Northern State University B
Southeast Technical Institute A
Western Dakota Technical Institute A

Tennessee

Belmont University B
East Tennessee State University B
Freed-Hardeman University B
Lambuth University B
Lipscomb University B
Middle Tennessee State University B
Southern Adventist University B
Trevecca Nazarene University B
Union University B
University of Memphis B
University of Tennessee
   Martin B

Texas

Abilene Christian University B

Angelo State University B
Austin Community College C, A
Baylor University B
Brookhaven College A
Cedar Valley College C, A
Clarendon College A
College of the Mainland A
Dallas Baptist University B, M
Galveston College A
Hardin-Simmons University B
Houston Baptist University B
Houston Community College
   System C, A
Howard Payne University B
Huston-Tillotson College B
Lamar University B
Laredo Community College A
LeTourneau University B
Lubbock Christian University B
McMurry University B
Midwestern State University B
North Harris Montgomery
   Community College District C, A
Northwood University: Texas
   Campus B
Our Lady of the Lake University of San
   Antonio B, M
St. Edward's University B
St. Mary's University B
Sam Houston State University B
South Texas College C, A
Southern Methodist University B, M
Southwestern Assemblies of God
   University B
Stephen F. Austin State University B
Sul Ross State University B
Tarleton State University B
Texarkana College C, A
Texas A&M University B, M, D
Texas A&M University
   Commerce B
   Texarkana B
Texas Christian University B
Texas Southern University B
Texas State University: San Marcos B
Texas Tech University B
Texas Woman's University B
Trinity University B
Tyler Junior College C, A
University of Dallas M
University of Houston B, M, D
University of Houston
   Clear Lake B
   Downtown B
   Victoria B
University of Mary Hardin-Baylor B
University of North Texas B, M, D
University of St. Thomas B
University of Texas
   Arlington B, D
   Austin B, D
   Brownsville B
   El Paso B
   Pan American B
   San Antonio B, M
   Tyler B
Vernon College A
Weatherford College C, A
West Texas A&M University B, M

Utah

Brigham Young University B
Salt Lake Community College C, A
Southern Utah University B
University of Utah C, B, M
Utah State University B
Weber State University B

Vermont

Castleton State College B
Champlain College A, B

Virginia

Averett University B

Christopher Newport University B
George Mason University B
Hampton University B
J. Sargeant Reynolds Community
   College A
James Madison University B
Liberty University B
Longwood University B
Lynchburg College B
Marymount University C, B, M
Old Dominion University B
Radford University B
University of Northern Virginia B, M
Virginia Commonwealth University B
Virginia Intermont College B
Virginia Polytechnic Institute and
   State University B
Virginia State University B

Washington

Bellevue Community College C, A
Centralia College C, A
City University C, B, M
Clover Park Technical College C, A
Eastern Washington University B
Edmonds Community College C, A
Green River Community College A
Heritage University B
Peninsula College C, A
Seattle University B
Shoreline Community College C, A
Spokane Community College C, A
Spokane Falls Community
   College C, A
Washington State University B
Western Washington University B
Whitworth College B
Yakima Valley Community
   College C, A

West Virginia

Concord University B
Davis and Elkins College B
Marshall University B
Mountain State University A, B
Southern West Virginia Community
   and Technical College A
University of Charleston B
West Virginia University B
West Virginia Wesleyan College B

Wisconsin

Cardinal Stritch University C
Carroll College B
Carthage College B
Concordia University Wisconsin B
Gateway Technical College A
Lakeland College B
Lakeshore Technical College A
Maranatha Baptist Bible College B
Marian College of Fond du Lac B
Marquette University B
Mid-State Technical College A
Milwaukee Area Technical College A
Moraine Park Technical College A
Mount Mary College B
University of Wisconsin
   Eau Claire B
   La Crosse B
   Madison B, M
   Milwaukee B
   Superior B
   Whitewater B
Viterbo University B
Waukesha County Technical
   College A
Wisconsin Indianhead Technical
   College A

Wyoming

University of Wyoming B
Western Wyoming Community
   College A

Marketing research

California

California State University
   Northridge M
Los Angeles Mission College A
Southwestern College C, A

District of Columbia

Howard University B
Southeastern University A, B

Georgia

University of Georgia M

Hawaii

University of Hawaii
   Hawaii Community College C, A

Idaho

Boise State University B

Illinois

Southern Illinois University
   Edwardsville M
University of Illinois
   Urbana-Champaign B, D

Indiana

Indiana University-Purdue University
   Indianapolis B
Taylor University: Fort Wayne B

Kansas

Fort Hays State University B

Maine

Husson College B

Massachusetts

Boston University B
Mount Ida College A

Minnesota

Winona State University B

Nebraska

University of Nebraska
   Lincoln M, D
   Omaha B

New Hampshire

McIntosh College A

New Jersey

Fairleigh Dickinson University
   College at Florham M
   Metropolitan Campus M

New York

City University of New York
   Baruch College M
Fordham University B, M
Hofstra University M
Ithaca College B
Rochester Institute of Technology B

North Dakota

Lake Region State College C, A

Ohio

Defiance College B
Lourdes College B
Stark State College of Technology A
University of Toledo B
Wright State University M

Oklahoma

Oklahoma Christian University B

Pennsylvania
La Salle University *B*
Penn State
  Abington *B*
  Altoona *B*
  Beaver *B*
  Berks *B*
  Delaware County *B*
  Dubois *B*
  Fayette *B*
  Harrisburg *B*
  Hazleton *B*
  Lehigh Valley *B*
  McKeesport *B*
  Mont Alto *B*
  New Kensington *B*
  Schuylkill - Capital College *B*
  Shenango *B*
  Wilkes-Barre *B*
  York *B*

Puerto Rico
University of Puerto Rico
  Arecibo *B*

Rhode Island
Salve Regina University *B*

Texas
University of Texas
  Arlington *M*

Wisconsin
Edgewood College *B, M*

Marriage/family therapy

Alabama
Auburn University *M*

Arizona
Arizona State University *D*

Arkansas
Harding University *B, M*
John Brown University *M*

California
Azusa Pacific University *M*
California Institute of Integral
  Studies *M*
California State University
  Fresno *M*
  Los Angeles *M*
Chapman University *M*
Dominican University of California *M*
Loma Linda University *M, D*
Mount St. Mary's College *M*
Notre Dame de Namur University *M*
Pacific Oaks College *M*
University of La Verne *M*
University of San Diego *M*
University of Southern
  California *M, D*

Connecticut
Central Connecticut State
  University *M*

Florida
Nova Southeastern University *M, D*
St. Thomas University *M*
Stetson University *M*
University of Central Florida *M*

Georgia
Mercer University *M*
Valdosta State University *M*

Idaho
Idaho State University *M*

Illinois
Northwestern University *M*

Indiana
Indiana State University *M*
Indiana Wesleyan University *M*

Kansas
Central Christian College of Kansas *A*
Friends University *M*

Louisiana
University of Louisiana at
  Monroe *M, D*

Massachusetts
Eastern Nazarene College *M*
Fitchburg State College *M*

Michigan
Michigan State University *B, M*

Minnesota
Capella University *M, D*

New Hampshire
University of New Hampshire *M*

New Jersey
Kean University *M*

New York
City University of New York
  Hunter College *M*
Hofstra University *M*
Long Island University
  C. W. Post Campus *B*
Mercy College *M*

North Carolina
Appalachian State University *M*
East Carolina University *B*

Ohio
University of Akron *M*

Pennsylvania
Duquesne University *M*
Seton Hill University *M*

Tennessee
Trevecca Nazarene University *M*

Texas
Abilene Christian University *M*
Texas Tech University *M, D*
Texas Woman's University *M, D*
University of Houston
  Clear Lake *M*
University of Texas
  Tyler *M*

Utah
Brigham Young University *M, D*

Virginia
Liberty University *M*

Washington
Pacific Lutheran University *M*

Wisconsin
Edgewood College *M*
Marquette University *D*
University of Wisconsin
  Stout *M*

Masonry

Alabama
Bishop State Community College *C*
Central Alabama Community
  College *C*
Gadsden State Community College *C*
Lawson State Community College *C*

Arizona
Central Arizona College *C*
Cochise College *C*
Eastern Arizona College *C*
Gateway Community College *C, A*

California
Bakersfield College *A*
Palomar College *C, A*
Ventura College *A*

Colorado
Red Rocks Community College *C, A*

Florida
Florida Community College at
  Jacksonville *C*
North Florida Community College *C*
Palm Beach Community College *C*
South Florida Community College *C*

Georgia
Albany Technical College *C*
Savannah Technical College *C*

Illinois
Southwestern Illinois College *C, A*

Indiana
Ivy Tech State College
  Ivy Tech Community College:
    Central Indiana *C, A*
  Ivy Tech Community College:
    Columbus *C, A*
  Ivy Tech Community College: East
    Central *C, A*
  Ivy Tech Community College:
    Lafayette *C, A*
  Ivy Tech Community College: North
    Central *C, A*
  Ivy Tech Community College:
    Northeast *C, A*
  Ivy Tech Community College:
    Northwest *C, A*
  Ivy Tech Community College: South
    Central *C, A*
  Ivy Tech Community College:
    Southwest *C, A*
  Ivy Tech Community College:
    Wabash Valley *C, A*

Iowa
Ellsworth Community College *C*
Kirkwood Community College *C*

Kentucky
Big Sandy Community and Technical
  College *C*
Somerset Community College *C, A*

Michigan
Lansing Community College *A*
Mott Community College *C*
Wayne County Community College *A*

Minnesota
Alexandria Technical College *C*
Dakota County Technical College *C, A*
Riverland Community College *C*
St. Paul College *C*

Mississippi
Hinds Community College *C*
Mississippi Delta Community
  College *C*
Pearl River Community College *C, A*

Nevada
Truckee Meadows Community
  College *C, A*

New York
State University of New York
  College of Technology at Alfred *A*
  College of Technology at Delhi *C, A*

North Carolina
Blue Ridge Community College *C*
Davidson County Community
  College *C*
James Sprunt Community College *C*
Johnston Community College *C*
Piedmont Community College *C*
Pitt Community College *C*
Southeastern Community College *C*
Southwestern Community College *C*
Tri-County Community College *C*

Oklahoma
Rose State College *A*

Pennsylvania
Delaware County Community
  College *C*
Pennsylvania College of
  Technology *C, A, B*
Thaddeus Stevens College of
  Technology *C*
Williamson Free School of Mechanical
  Trades *C*

Texas
Howard College *C*
Trinity Valley Community College *C*

Virginia
Piedmont Virginia Community
  College *A*

Wisconsin
Gateway Technical College *C*
Milwaukee Area Technical College *C*
Southwest Wisconsin Technical
  College *C*
Waukesha County Technical
  College *C*
Western Wisconsin Technical
  College *C*
Wisconsin Indianhead Technical
  College *C*

Massage therapy

Alabama
Gadsden State Community College *C*
Trenholm State Technical College *C*

California
Concorde Career College *C*
Institute of Computer Technology *C*
Maric College
  Vista *C*
Northwestern College *C, A*
Santa Barbara City College *C*
Silicon Valley College
  Western Career College: San Jose *A*

Colorado
Boulder College of Massage
  Therapy *C, A*
Cambridge College *C, A*
Colorado School of Healing Arts *C, A*

Heritage College A
IntelliTec College: Grand Junction C
Parks College C
Parks College: Aurora C

Florida

Angley College C
Florida Career College: Hialeah C
Florida Career College: Miami C
Florida Career College: Pembroke
   Pines C
Florida Career College: West Palm
   Beach C
Florida College of Natural Health C
Florida College of Natural Health
   Bradenton A
   Maitland C, A
   Miami A
Florida Metropolitan University:
   Orange Park C
Miami Dade College C
Palm Beach Community College A
Pensacola Junior College C
Remington College: Largo C
Southwest Florida College
   Tampa C

Illinois

Black Hawk College C
Illinois Eastern Community Colleges
   Olney Central College C
Kaskaskia College C
Kishwaukee College C
Morton College C
National University of Health
   Sciences C
Parkland College C
Rend Lake College C
Waubonsee Community College C, A

Indiana

Indiana Business College
   Medical C, A
Ivy Tech State College
   Ivy Tech Community College:
     Northeast C, A
Professional Careers Institute C, A
Sawyer College C, A
Sawyer College: Merrillville C, A

Iowa

Iowa Lakes Community College C

Kentucky

Spencerian College: Lexington C

Louisiana

Delgado Community College C
Our Lady of the Lake College C

Maryland

Allegany College of Maryland A
College of Southern Maryland A
Community College of Baltimore
   County A
Howard Community College A
TESST College of Technology:
   Towson C

Massachusetts

Berkshire Community College C
Mount Wachusett Community
   College C
Springfield Technical Community
   College A

Michigan

Baker College
   of Clinton Township A
   of Muskegon C
   of Port Huron C, A
Kirtland Community College C, A

Muskegon Community College C
Oakland Community College C, A

Minnesota

Lake Superior College C, A
Minnesota School of Business C, A
Minnesota State Community and
   Technical College - Fergus Falls C
Northwest Technical College C
Rasmussen College
   Mankato C, A
Ridgewater College C
St. Paul College C, A

Mississippi

Antonelli College
   Jackson A

Nevada

High-Tech Institute A

New Hampshire

McIntosh College C
New Hampshire Community
   Technical College
   Claremont C
   Nashua C

New York

Columbia-Greene Community
   College A
Finger Lakes Community College A
Mildred Elley C, A
North Country Community College A
State University of New York
   College of Agriculture and
     Technology at Morrisville A
Swedish Institute A
Trocaire College C, A

North Carolina

Carteret Community College C, A
Gaston College C, A
Lenoir Community College C, A
Miller-Motte Technical College C, A
Sandhills Community College C, A
Southwestern Community College C

North Dakota

Bismarck State College C, A
Williston State College C, A

Ohio

Cincinnati State Technical and
   Community College C, A
Hocking College C, A
Lakeland Community College C
Mercy College of Northwest Ohio A
Ohio College of Massotherapy C, A
Sinclair Community College A
Stark State College of Technology C, A
Stautzenberger College C, A

Oklahoma

Heritage College Hair Design C, A

Oregon

Pioneer Pacific College C
Rogue Community College C

Pennsylvania

Academy of Medical Arts and
   Business C, A
Butler County Community College C
Career Training Academy A
Career Training Academy:
   Monroeville C
Laurel Business Institute C
Pittsburgh Technical Institute C
University of Pittsburgh
   Titusville C

Rhode Island

Community College of Rhode
   Island A

South Carolina

Miller-Motte Technical College C, A

Tennessee

Miller-Motte Technical College C, A
Roane State Community College C

Utah

Utah Career College C, A

Virginia

Miller-Motte Technical College:
   Lynchburg A

Washington

Clover Park Technical College A
Peninsula College C
Renton Technical College C, A
Whatcom Community College A

Wisconsin

Wisconsin Indianhead Technical
   College C

Wyoming

Sheridan College C

Materials engineering

Alabama

Auburn University B, M, D
Tuskegee University D
University of Alabama D
University of Alabama
   Birmingham B, M, D

Arizona

Arizona State University B, M

California

California Polytechnic State
   University: San Luis Obispo B
California State Polytechnic
   University: Pomona B
California State University
   Long Beach B
   Northridge B, M
San Jose State University B, M
Stanford University B, M, D
University of California
   Davis B, M, D
   Irvine B, M, D
   Los Angeles B, M, D
   Santa Barbara M, D
University of Southern California M

Colorado

Colorado School of Mines M

Connecticut

University of Connecticut B

Delaware

University of Delaware M, D

District of Columbia

George Washington University M
Howard University M, D

Florida

Florida International University M
Florida State University B
University of Central Florida M, D
University of Florida A, B, M

Georgia

Georgia Institute of
   Technology B, M, D

Illinois

Illinois Institute of
   Technology B, M, D
Northwestern University B, M, D
University of Illinois
   Chicago M, D
   Urbana-Champaign B, M, D

Indiana

Purdue University B, M, D

Iowa

Iowa State University B, M, D

Kentucky

University of Kentucky B, M, D

Maryland

Johns Hopkins University B, M, D
University of Maryland
   College Park B, M, D

Massachusetts

Massachusetts Institute of
   Technology B, M, D
Northeastern University M
Worcester Polytechnic Institute M, D

Michigan

Michigan Technological
   University B, M, D, T
University of Michigan M, D
Wayne State University M, D

Minnesota

University of Minnesota
   Twin Cities B, M, D
Winona State University B

Missouri

Washington University in St.
   Louis M, D

Montana

Montana Tech of the University of
   Montana B, M

Nevada

University of Nevada
   Reno B

New Hampshire

University of New Hampshire B

New Jersey

New Jersey Institute of
   Technology M, D
Rowan University B
Stevens Institute of
   Technology B, M, D

New Mexico

New Mexico Institute of Mining and
   Technology B, M, D

New York

Alfred University B, M
Columbia University
   Fu Foundation School of
     Engineering and Applied
     Science B, M, D
Cornell University B, M, D
Rensselaer Polytechnic
   Institute B, M, D
Rochester Institute of Technology M

State University of New York
Binghamton *M, D*
College of Environmental Science
and Forestry *B, M, D*
Stony Brook *M, D*
Syracuse University *M*

North Carolina
North Carolina Agricultural and
Technical State University *B*
North Carolina State
University *B, M, D*

Ohio
Case Western Reserve
University *B, M, D*
Ohio State University
Columbus Campus *B, M, D*
University of Cincinnati *M, D*
University of Dayton *M, D*
Wright State University *B*
Youngstown State University *B*

Oregon
Oregon State University *M*

Pennsylvania
Drexel University *B, M, D*
Lehigh University *B, M, D*
Penn State
Abington *B*
Altoona *B*
Beaver *B*
Berks *B*
Delaware County *B*
Dubois *B*
Fayette *B*
Hazleton *B*
Lehigh Valley *B*
McKeesport *B*
Mont Alto *B*
New Kensington *A, B*
Shenango *B*
University Park *M, D*
Wilkes-Barre *B*
Worthington Scranton *B*
York *B*
University of Pennsylvania *B, M, D*
University of Pittsburgh *B, M, D*

Puerto Rico
University of Puerto Rico
Bayamon University College *B*

Rhode Island
Brown University *B, M, D*

South Carolina
Clemson University *M, D*

South Dakota
South Dakota School of Mines and
Technology *M, D*

Tennessee
Vanderbilt University *M, D*

Texas
Rice University *B, M, D*
University of Houston *M, D*
University of Texas
Arlington *M, D*
Austin *M, D*
El Paso *M, D*

Utah
Salt Lake Community College *A*
University of Utah *B, M, D*

Virginia
University of Virginia *M, D*

Virginia Polytechnic Institute and
State University *B, M, D*

Washington
University of Washington *B, M, D*
Washington State University *B, M, D*

Wisconsin
Milwaukee Area Technical College *A*
University of Wisconsin
Madison *B, M, D*
Milwaukee *B*

Materials science

Alabama
Tuskegee University *D*
University of Alabama
Birmingham *D*
Huntsville *M, D*

Arizona
Arizona State University *M, D*
University of Arizona *B, M, D*

California
California Institute of
Technology *M, D*
Stanford University *B, M, D*
University of California
Berkeley *B, M, D*
Los Angeles *M*
San Diego *M, D*
University of Southern
California *M, D*

Colorado
Colorado School of Mines *M, D*
University of Denver *M, D*

Connecticut
University of Connecticut *B, M, D*

Idaho
University of Idaho *M, D*

Illinois
Northwestern University *B*
University of Illinois
Urbana-Champaign *B, M, D*

Iowa
Iowa State University *B, M, D*

Maryland
Johns Hopkins University *B, M, D*

Massachusetts
Worcester Polytechnic Institute *M, D*

Michigan
Michigan State University *B, M, D*
University of Michigan *B, M, D*
Wayne State University *M, D*

Minnesota
University of Minnesota
Twin Cities *B, M, D*
Winona State University *B*

Missouri
Missouri State University *M*
Washington University in St.
Louis *M, D*

Montana
Montana Tech of the University of
Montana *B*

New Hampshire
University of New Hampshire *B, M, D*

New Jersey
Stevens Institute of
Technology *B, M, D*

New York
Alfred University *B, M*
Columbia University
Fu Foundation School of
Engineering and Applied
Science *B, M, D*
Cornell University *B, M, D*
Polytechnic University *M*
Rochester Institute of Technology *M*
State University of New York
Binghamton *M, D*
University of Rochester *M, D*

North Carolina
University of North Carolina
Chapel Hill *M, D*

Ohio
Case Western Reserve
University *B, M, D*
Hocking College *A*
Ohio State University
Columbus Campus *B, M, D*
Youngstown State University *M*

Oregon
Oregon State University *M, D*

Pennsylvania
Carnegie Mellon University *B, M, D*
University of Pennsylvania *B*

South Dakota
South Dakota School of Mines and
Technology *D*

Tennessee
University of Tennessee
Knoxville *B*

Texas
Southern Methodist University *M*

Vermont
University of Vermont *M, D*

Washington
University of Washington *B*
Washington State University *D*

Wisconsin
Marquette University *M, D*

Maternal/child health

Indiana
Indiana University-Purdue University
Indianapolis *M*

Michigan
University of Michigan *M, D*

Minnesota
University of Minnesota
Twin Cities *M*

North Carolina
University of North Carolina
Chapel Hill *M, D*

Ohio
Union Institute & University *B*

Maternal/child health nursing

Indiana
Indiana University-Purdue University
Indianapolis *M*

Michigan
University of Michigan *D*
Wayne State University *M*

New Jersey
William Paterson University of New
Jersey *T*

New York
City University of New York
Hunter College *B, M*
Lehman College *M*
Columbia University
School of Nursing *M*
State University of New York
Buffalo *M*
Stony Brook *M*
Upstate Medical University *M*

Ohio
Case Western Reserve University *M*

Pennsylvania
University of Pennsylvania *M*

South Carolina
Medical University of South
Carolina *M*

Texas
Baylor University *M*

Mathematical statistics/ probability

Arizona
Northern Arizona University *B*

Florida
University of Miami *B*

Illinois
Northern Illinois University *B*

New York
Rochester Institute of
Technology *B, M*

Pennsylvania
Carnegie Mellon University *B*

Mathematics

Alabama
Alabama Agricultural and Mechanical
University *B*
Alabama State University *B, M*
Athens State University *B*
Auburn University *B, M, D, T*
Auburn University at Montgomery *B*
Birmingham-Southern College *B, T*
Calhoun Community College *A*
Chattahoochee Valley Community
College *A*
Faulkner State Community College *A*
Faulkner University *B*
Gadsden State Community College *A*
Huntingdon College *B, T*
Jacksonville State University *B, M*
Judson College *B*
Lawson State Community College *A*
Miles College *B*

Northeast Alabama Community
College *A*
Oakwood College *B*
Samford University *B*
Shelton State Community College *A*
Spring Hill College *B, T*
Stillman College *B*
Talladega College *B*
Troy University *B*
Tuskegee University *B, T*
University of Alabama *B, M, D*
University of Alabama
Birmingham *B, M*
Huntsville *B, M*
University of Mobile *B, T*
University of Montevallo *B, T*
University of North Alabama *B*
University of South Alabama *M*
University of West Alabama *B, T*

Alaska

University of Alaska
Anchorage *B*
Fairbanks *B, M, D*
Southeast *B*

Arizona

Arizona State University *B, M, D*
Arizona Western College *A*
Central Arizona College *A*
Eastern Arizona College *A*
Grand Canyon University *B*
Northern Arizona University *B, M, T*
South Mountain Community
College *A*
University of Arizona *B, M, D*

Arkansas

Arkansas State University *B, M*
Arkansas State University
Beebe *A*
Arkansas Tech University *B*
Black River Technical College *A*
Harding University *B*
Henderson State University *B*
Hendrix College *B*
John Brown University *B*
Lyon College *B*
Ouachita Baptist University *B*
Philander Smith College *B*
Phillips Community College of the
University of Arkansas *A*
Southern Arkansas University *B*
University of Arkansas *B, M, D*
University of Arkansas
Fort Smith *B*
Little Rock *B*
Monticello *B*
Pine Bluff *B*
University of Central Arkansas *B, M*
University of the Ozarks *B*

California

Antelope Valley College *A*
Azusa Pacific University *B*
Bakersfield College *A*
Barstow College *A*
Biola University *B*
Butte College *A*
Cabrillo College *A*
California Baptist University *B*
California Institute of
Technology *B, D*
California Lutheran University *B*
California Polytechnic State
University: San Luis Obispo *B, M*
California State Polytechnic
University: Pomona *B, M*
California State University
Bakersfield *B*
Chico *B*
Dominguez Hills *B*
East Bay *B, M*

Fresno *B, M*
Fullerton *B, M*
Long Beach *B, M*
Los Angeles *B, M*
Northridge *B, M*
Sacramento *B, M*
San Bernardino *B, M*
San Marcos *B, M*
Stanislaus *B*
Canada College *A*
Cerritos Community College *A*
Chabot College *A*
Chaffey College *A*
Chapman University *B*
Citrus College *A*
Claremont McKenna College *B*
College of Alameda *A*
College of Marin: Kentfield *A*
College of San Mateo *A*
College of the Canyons *A*
College of the Desert *A*
College of the Sequoias *A*
College of the Siskiyous *A*
Columbia College *A*
Concordia University *B*
Contra Costa College *A*
Copper Mountain College *A*
Crafton Hills College *A*
Cuesta College *A*
Cypress College *A*
De Anza College *A*
El Camino College *A*
Feather River College *A*
Foothill College *A*
Fresno City College *A*
Fresno Pacific University *B*
Fullerton College *A*
Gavilan Community College *A*
Glendale Community College *A*
Golden West College *A*
Grossmont Community College *A*
Harvey Mudd College *B*
Humboldt State University *B*
Imperial Valley College *A*
Irvine Valley College *A*
La Sierra University *B*
Laney College *A*
Lassen College *A*
Long Beach City College *A*
Los Angeles City College *A*
Los Angeles Mission College *A*
Los Angeles Southwest College *A*
Los Angeles Valley College *A*
Los Medanos College *A*
Loyola Marymount University *B, M*
Master's College *B*
Mendocino College *A*
Merced College *A*
Merritt College *A*
Mills College *B*
MiraCosta College *A*
Mission College *A*
Modesto Junior College *A*
Monterey Peninsula College *A*
Moorpark College *A*
Mount St. Mary's College *B*
Mount San Jacinto College *A*
National University *B*
Occidental College *B*
Orange Coast College *A*
Pacific Union College *B*
Palomar College *A*
Pepperdine University *B*
Pitzer College *B*
Point Loma Nazarene University *B*
Pomona College *B*
Porterville College *A*
Reedley College *A*
Sacramento City College *A*
Saddleback College *A*
St. Mary's College of California *B*
San Bernardino Valley College *A*
San Diego Christian College *B*
San Diego City College *A*

San Diego Mesa College *A*
San Diego Miramar College *A*
San Diego State University *B, M*
San Francisco State University *B, M*
San Joaquin Delta College *A*
San Jose State University *B, M*
Santa Ana College *A*
Santa Barbara City College *A*
Santa Clara University *B*
Santa Rosa Junior College *A*
Santiago Canyon College *A*
Scripps College *B*
Sierra College *A*
Simpson University *B*
Skyline College *A*
Solano Community College *A*
Sonoma State University *B*
Southwestern College *A*
Stanford University *B, M, D*
Taft College *A*
University of California
Berkeley *B, M, D*
Davis *B, M, D*
Irvine *B, M, D*
Los Angeles *B, M, D*
Riverside *B, M, D*
San Diego *B, M, D*
Santa Barbara *B, M, D*
Santa Cruz *B, M, D*
University of La Verne *B*
University of Redlands *B*
University of San Diego *B*
University of San Francisco *B*
University of Southern
California *B, M, D*
University of the Pacific *B*
Vanguard University of Southern
California *B*
Ventura College *A*
Victor Valley College *A*
West Valley College *A*
Westmont College *B*
Whittier College *B*
Yuba Community College District *A*

Colorado

Adams State College *B*
Colorado Christian University *B*
Colorado College *B*
Colorado Mountain College
Alpine Campus *A*
Timberline Campus *A*
Colorado School of Mines *M, D*
Colorado State University *B, M, D*
Colorado State University
Pueblo *B*
Fort Lewis College *B*
Mesa State College *B*
Metropolitan State College of
Denver *B, T*
Otero Junior College *A*
Regis University *B*
Trinidad State Junior College *A*
University of Colorado
Boulder *B, M, D*
Colorado Springs *B*
Denver and Health Sciences
Center *B*
University of Denver *B, M, D*
University of Northern
Colorado *B, M, T*
Western State College of Colorado *B*

Connecticut

Albertus Magnus College *B*
Central Connecticut State
University *B, M, T*
Connecticut College *B*
Eastern Connecticut State
University *B*
Fairfield University *B, M*
Manchester Community College *A*
Northwestern Connecticut
Community College *A*

Norwalk Community College *A*
Quinnipiac University *B*
Sacred Heart University *B*
St. Joseph College *B, T*
Southern Connecticut State
University *B, M*
Trinity College *B*
University of Bridgeport *B*
University of Connecticut *B, M, D*
University of Hartford *B*
University of New Haven *B*
Wesleyan University *B, M, D*
Western Connecticut State
University *B, M*
Yale University *B, M, D*

Delaware

Delaware State University *B*
University of Delaware *B, M, D*

District of Columbia

American University *B, M*
Catholic University of America *B, T*
Gallaudet University *B*
George Washington
University *B, M, D*
Georgetown University *B*
Howard University *B, M, D*
Trinity University *B*
University of the District of
Columbia *B*

Florida

Barry University *B*
Bethune-Cookman College *B*
Broward Community College *A*
Chipola College *A, B*
Clearwater Christian College *B*
Eckerd College *B*
Edward Waters College *B*
Florida Agricultural and Mechanical
University *B*
Florida Atlantic University *B, M, D*
Florida Gulf Coast University *B*
Florida Institute of Technology *B*
Florida International University *B*
Florida Memorial University *B*
Florida Southern College *B*
Florida State University *B, M, D*
Gulf Coast Community College *A*
Indian River Community College *A*
Jacksonville University *B*
Lake City Community College *A*
Manatee Community College *A*
Miami Dade College *A*
New College of Florida *B*
Okaloosa-Walton College *A*
Palm Beach Atlantic University *B*
Palm Beach Community College *A*
Pensacola Junior College *A*
Rollins College *B*
St. Leo University *B*
Southeastern College of the
Assemblies of God *B*
Stetson University *B*
University of Central Florida *B*
University of Florida *A, B, M*
University of Miami *B, M, D*
University of North Florida *B*
University of South Florida *B, M, D*
University of Tampa *A, B, T*
University of West Florida *B, M*
Valencia Community College *A*

Georgia

Abraham Baldwin Agricultural
College *A*
Agnes Scott College *B*
Albany State University *B*
Andrew College *A*
Atlanta Metropolitan College *A*
Augusta State University *B*
Bainbridge College *A*

Berry College B
Brewton-Parker College B
Clark Atlanta University B, M
Coastal Georgia Community
    College A
Columbus State University B
Covenant College B
Dalton State College A
Darton College A
East Georgia College B
Emmanuel College B
Emory University B
Fort Valley State University B
Gainesville State College A
Georgia College and State
    University B
Georgia Highlands College A
Georgia Institute of Technology D
Georgia Perimeter College A
Georgia Southern University B, M
Georgia Southwestern State
    University B, T
Georgia State University B, M
Gordon College A
Kennesaw State University B
LaGrange College B
Macon State College A
Mercer University B
Middle Georgia College A
Morehouse College B
North Georgia College & State
    University B
Oglethorpe University B
Paine College B
Piedmont College B
Savannah State University B
Shorter College B, T
South Georgia College A
Southern Polytechnic State
    University B
Spelman College B
University of Georgia B, M, D
University of West Georgia B
Valdosta State University B
Waycross College A
Wesleyan College B, T
Young Harris College A

Hawaii

Brigham Young University-Hawaii B
Hawaii Pacific University A
University of Hawaii
    Hilo B
    Manoa B, M, D

Idaho

Albertson College of Idaho B
Boise State University B, M, T
Brigham Young University-Idaho B
College of Southern Idaho A
Idaho State University A, B, M, D
Lewis-Clark State College B
North Idaho College A
Northwest Nazarene University B
University of Idaho B, M, D

Illinois

Augustana College B, T
Aurora University B
Benedictine University B, T
Black Hawk College
    East Campus A
Blackburn College B, T
Bradley University B, T
Chicago State University B, M, T
City Colleges of Chicago
    Harold Washington College A
    Kennedy-King College A
    Olive-Harvey College A
Concordia University B, T
Danville Area Community College A
DePaul University B, M, T
Dominican University B
East-West University B

Eastern Illinois University B, M, T
Elmhurst College B, T
Eureka College B, T
Governors State University B
Greenville College B, T
Highland Community College A
Illinois Central College A
Illinois College B, T
Illinois State University B, M, T
Illinois Valley Community College A
Illinois Wesleyan University B
John A. Logan College A
John Wood Community College A
Joliet Junior College A
Judson College B
Kankakee Community College A
Kishwaukee College A
Knox College B
Lake Forest College B
Lake Land College A
Lewis University B, T
Loyola University of Chicago B, M
MacMurray College B, T
McKendree College B, T
Millikin University B, D, T
Monmouth College B, T
National-Louis University B
North Central College B, T
North Park University B
Northeastern Illinois University B, M
Northern Illinois University B, M, D, T
Northwestern University B, M, D
Olivet Nazarene University B, T
Principia College B
Quincy University B
Richland Community College A
Rockford College B
Roosevelt University B, M
St. Xavier University B
Sauk Valley Community College A
South Suburban College of Cook
    County A
Southeastern Illinois College A
Southern Illinois University
    Carbondale B, M, D
Southern Illinois University
    Edwardsville B, M, T
Southwestern Illinois College A
Springfield College in Illinois A
Trinity Christian College B, T
Trinity International University B
Triton College A
University of Chicago B, M, D
University of Illinois
    Chicago B, M, D
    Springfield B
    Urbana-Champaign B, M, D
University of St. Francis B
Western Illinois University B, M
Wheaton College B, T
William Rainey Harper College A

Indiana

Ancilla College A
Anderson University B
Ball State University B, M, T
Bethel College B
Butler University B
DePauw University B
Earlham College B
Franklin College B
Goshen College B
Grace College B
Hanover College B
Huntington University B
Indiana State University B, M, T
Indiana University
    Bloomington B, M, D
    East A
    Kokomo B
    Northwest B
    South Bend B
    Southeast B

Indiana University-Purdue University
    Fort Wayne A, B, M, T
Indiana University-Purdue University
    Indianapolis B, M, D
Indiana Wesleyan University B
Manchester College B, T
Marian College B, T
Martin University B
Purdue University B, M, D
Purdue University
    Calumet B, M
Rose-Hulman Institute of
    Technology B
St. Joseph's College B
Saint Mary's College B, T
St. Mary-of-the-Woods College B
Taylor University B
Tri-State University A, B
University of Evansville B
University of Indianapolis B
University of Notre Dame B, M, D
University of Southern Indiana B, T
Valparaiso University B
Vincennes University A
Wabash College B

Iowa

Briar Cliff University B
Buena Vista University B, T
Central College B, T
Clarke College B, T
Coe College B
Cornell College B, T
Dordt College B
Drake University B
Ellsworth Community College A
Graceland University B, T
Grinnell College B
Iowa State University B, M, D
Iowa Wesleyan College B
Iowa Western Community College A
Loras College B
Luther College B
Marshalltown Community College A
Morningside College B
Mount Mercy College B, T
Northwestern College B, T
St. Ambrose University B
Simpson College B
University of Iowa B, M, D, T
University of Northern Iowa B, M
Upper Iowa University B
Wartburg College B, T
William Penn University B

Kansas

Allen County Community College A
Baker University B, T
Barton County Community College A
Benedictine College B
Bethany College B, T
Bethel College B
Butler County Community College A
Central Christian College of
    Kansas A, B
Cloud County Community College A
Coffeyville Community College A
Colby Community College A
Cowley County Community
    College A
Dodge City Community College A
Donnelly College A
Emporia State University B, M, T
Fort Hays State University B, M
Friends University B
Garden City Community College A
Hutchinson Community College A
Kansas State University B, M, D
Kansas Wesleyan University B, T
McPherson College B, T
MidAmerica Nazarene University B
Neosho County Community
    College A
Newman University B

Ottawa University B
Pittsburg State University B, M
Pratt Community College A
Seward County Community College A
Southwestern College B
Sterling College B
Tabor College B
University of Kansas B, M, D
University of St. Mary B
Washburn University of Topeka B
Wichita State University B, M, D

Kentucky

Asbury College B, T
Bellarmine University B, T
Berea College B, T
Campbellsville University B
Centre College B
Eastern Kentucky University B, M
Georgetown College B
Kentucky Christian University B, T
Kentucky State University B
Kentucky Wesleyan College B, T
Lindsey Wilson College A, B, T
Midway College B
Morehead State University B
Murray State University B, M, T
Northern Kentucky University B
Pikeville College B, T
St. Catharine College A
Thomas More College A, B
Transylvania University B
Union College B
University of Kentucky B, M, D
University of Louisville B, M
University of the Cumberlands B
Western Kentucky University B, M, T

Louisiana

Centenary College of Louisiana B, T
Dillard University B
Grambling State University B
Louisiana State University
    Shreveport B
Louisiana State University and
    Agricultural and Mechanical
    College B, M, D
Louisiana Tech University B, M
Loyola University New Orleans B
Nicholls State University B, M
Northwestern State University B
Southeastern Louisiana University B
Southern University
    New Orleans B
Southern University and Agricultural
    and Mechanical College B, M
Tulane University B, M, D
University of Louisiana at
    Lafayette B, M, D
University of Louisiana at Monroe B
University of New Orleans B, M
Xavier University of Louisiana B

Maine

Bates College B, T
Bowdoin College B
Colby College B
St. Joseph's College B
University of Maine B, M
University of Maine
    Farmington B
University of New England B
University of Southern Maine B

Maryland

Allegany College of Maryland A
Anne Arundel Community College A
Bowie State University B, M
Cecil Community College A
College of Notre Dame of Maryland B
College of Southern Maryland A
Columbia Union College B

Community College of Baltimore
County *A*
Coppin State University *B*
Frederick Community College *A*
Frostburg State University *B*
Garrett College *A*
Goucher College *B*
Harford Community College *A*
Hood College *B, T*
Howard Community College *A*
Johns Hopkins University *B, M, D*
McDaniel College *B*
Morgan State University *B, M*
Mount St. Mary's University *B, T*
St. Mary's College of Maryland *B*
Salisbury University *B, T*
Towson University *B, T*
United States Naval Academy *B*
University of Maryland
Baltimore County *B*
College Park *B, M, D*
Eastern Shore *B*

Massachusetts

American International College *B*
Amherst College *B*
Assumption College *B*
Atlantic Union College *B*
Bentley College *B*
Boston College *B, M*
Boston University *B, M, D*
Brandeis University *B, M, D*
Bridgewater State College *B*
Bunker Hill Community College *A*
Cape Cod Community College *A*
Clark University *B*
College of the Holy Cross *B*
Dean College *A*
Eastern Nazarene College *B*
Elms College *B*
Emmanuel College *B*
Fitchburg State College *B*
Framingham State College *B*
Gordon College *B*
Hampshire College *B*
Harvard College *B, D*
Lesley University *B*
Massachusetts College of Liberal
Arts *B*
Massachusetts Institute of
Technology *B, D*
Merrimack College *B*
Mount Holyoke College *B*
Nichols College *B, T*
Northeastern University *B, M, D*
Roxbury Community College *A*
Salem State College *B, M*
Simmons College *B*
Simon's Rock College of Bard *B*
Smith College *B*
Springfield College *B*
Springfield Technical Community
College *A*
Stonehill College *B*
Suffolk University *B*
Tufts University *B, M, D*
University of Massachusetts
Amherst *B, M, D*
Boston *B*
Dartmouth *B*
Lowell *B, M*
Wellesley College *B*
Western New England College *B*
Westfield State College *B*
Wheaton College *B*
Williams College *B*
Worcester Polytechnic
Institute *B, M, D*
Worcester State College *B*

Michigan

Adrian College *A, B, T*
Albion College *B, T*
Alma College *B, T*

Andrews University *B*
Aquinas College *B, T*
Calvin College *B, T*
Central Michigan University *B, M, T*
Concordia University *B*
Cornerstone University *B, T*
Delta College *A*
Eastern Michigan University *B, M*
Ferris State University *B*
Gogebic Community College *A*
Grand Valley State University *B*
Hillsdale College *B*
Hope College *B*
Kalamazoo College *B, T*
Kellogg Community College *A*
Lake Michigan College *A*
Lake Superior State University *B, T*
Lansing Community College *A*
Lawrence Technological University *B*
Macomb Community College *A*
Madonna University *B*
Marygrove College *B, T*
Michigan State University *B, M, D*
Michigan Technological
University *B, M, D, T*
Mid Michigan Community College *A*
Northern Michigan University *B*
Northwestern Michigan College *A*
Oakland University *B, M, T*
Olivet College *B, T*
Saginaw Valley State University *B, T*
Siena Heights University *A, B*
Spring Arbor University *B, T*
University of Detroit Mercy *B*
University of Michigan *B, M, D, T*
University of Michigan
Dearborn *B, M*
Flint *B, T*
Wayne State University *B, M, D*
West Shore Community College *A*
Western Michigan University *B, M, D*

Minnesota

Augsburg College *B*
Bemidji State University *B*
Bethel University *B*
Carleton College *B*
College of St. Benedict *B*
College of St. Catherine *B*
College of St. Scholastica *B*
Concordia College: Moorhead *B*
Concordia University: St. Paul *B*
Gustavus Adolphus College *B*
Hamline University *B*
Macalester College *B, T*
Minnesota State University
Mankato *B, M, T*
Moorhead *B*
Northland Community & Technical
College *A*
Northwestern College *B*
Ridgewater College *A*
St. Cloud State University *B, M*
St. John's University *B*
St. Mary's University of Minnesota *B*
St. Olaf College *B*
Southwest Minnesota State
University *B, T*
University of Minnesota
Duluth *B*
Morris *B*
Twin Cities *B, M, D*
University of St. Thomas *B*
Winona State University *B, T*

Mississippi

Alcorn State University *B*
Belhaven College *B, T*
Blue Mountain College *B*
Coahoma Community College *A*
Delta State University *B*
East Central Community College *A*
Hinds Community College *A*
Holmes Community College *A*

Itawamba Community College *A*
Jackson State University *B*
Millsaps College *B, T*
Mississippi College *B, M, T*
Mississippi Gulf Coast Community
College
Jefferson Davis Campus *A*
Mississippi State University *B, M*
Mississippi Valley State University *B*
Rust College *B*
Tougaloo College *B*
University of Mississippi *B, M, D, T*
University of Southern
Mississippi *B, M*
William Carey College *B*

Missouri

Central Methodist University *B*
Central Missouri State University *B, M*
College of the Ozarks *B*
Columbia College *B*
Crowder College *A*
Culver-Stockton College *B, T*
Drury University *B, T*
Evangel University *B, T*
Fontbonne University *B, T*
Hannibal-LaGrange College *B*
Lincoln University *B*
Lindenwood University *B*
Maryville University of Saint Louis *B*
Missouri Baptist University *B, T*
Missouri Southern State
University *B, T*
Missouri State University *B, M*
Missouri Valley College *B*
Missouri Western State University *B, T*
Northwest Missouri State
University *B*
Park University *B*
Rockhurst University *B*
St. Louis Community College
St. Louis Community College at
Florissant Valley *A*
St. Louis Community College at
Meramec *A*
St. Louis University *B, M, D*
Southeast Missouri State University *B*
Southwest Baptist University *B, T*
Three Rivers Community College *A*
Truman State University *B, M*
University of Missouri
Columbia *B, M, D*
Kansas City *B, M*
Rolla *M, D, T*
St. Louis *B, M*
Washington University in St.
Louis *B, M, D*
Webster University *B*
Westminster College *B*
William Jewell College *B, T*
William Woods University *B, T*

Montana

Carroll College *B, T*
Little Big Horn College *A*
Miles Community College *A*
Montana State University
Billings *B, T*
Bozeman *B, M, D*
Montana Tech of the University of
Montana *B*
Rocky Mountain College *B, T*
University of Great Falls *B*
University of Montana:
Missoula *B, M, D*

Nebraska

Chadron State College *B*
College of Saint Mary *B*
Concordia University *B, T*
Creighton University *A, B*
Dana College *B*
Doane College *B*
Hastings College *B*

Little Priest Tribal College *A*
Midland Lutheran College *B, T*
Nebraska Wesleyan University *B*
Northeast Community College *A*
Peru State College *B*
Union College *B*
University of Nebraska
Kearney *B, M, T*
Lincoln *B, M, D*
Omaha *B, M*
Wayne State College *B, T*
Western Nebraska Community
College *A*
York College *B*

Nevada

Great Basin College *A*
University of Nevada
Las Vegas *B, M, D*
Reno *B, M*
Western Nevada Community
College *A*

New Hampshire

Dartmouth College *B, M, D*
Franklin Pierce College *B*
Keene State College *B, T*
New England College *B*
Plymouth State University *B*
Rivier College *B, M, T*
St. Anselm College *B, T*
University of New Hampshire *B, M, D*

New Jersey

Atlantic Cape Community College *A*
Bloomfield College *B*
Caldwell College *B*
Centenary College *B*
The College of New Jersey *B, T*
College of St. Elizabeth *B, T*
Cumberland County College *A*
Drew University *B*
Essex County College *A*
Fairleigh Dickinson University
College at Florham *B*
Metropolitan Campus *B*
Felician College *B*
Georgian Court University *B, M*
Gloucester County College *A*
Hudson County Community
College *A*
Kean University *B, T*
Mercer County Community College *A*
Monmouth University *B*
Montclair State University *B, M, T*
New Jersey City University *B, M*
New Jersey Institute of Technology *D*
Passaic County Community College *A*
Princeton University *B, M, D*
Ramapo College of New Jersey *B*
Raritan Valley Community College *A*
Richard Stockton College of New
Jersey *B*
Rider University *B*
Rowan University *B, M*
Rutgers, The State University of New
Jersey
Camden Regional Campus *B, T*
New Brunswick/Piscataway
Campus *B, M, D, T*
Newark Regional Campus *B, T*
St. Peter's College *B*
Salem Community College *A*
Seton Hall University *B, T*
Stevens Institute of Technology *M, D*
Sussex County Community College *A*
Thomas Edison State College *A, B*
William Paterson University of New
Jersey *B, T*

New Mexico

Clovis Community College *A*
College of the Southwest *B*

Eastern New Mexico University *B, M*
New Mexico Highlands University *B*
New Mexico Institute of Mining and Technology *B, M*
New Mexico Junior College *A*
New Mexico State University *B, M, D*
San Juan College *A*
University of New Mexico *B, M, D*
Western New Mexico University *B*

New York

Adelphi University *B*
Adirondack Community College *A*
Alfred University *B*
Bard College *B*
Barnard College *B*
Cayuga County Community College *A*
City University of New York
  Baruch College *B*
  Borough of Manhattan Community College *A*
  Brooklyn College *B, M*
  City College *B, M*
  College of Staten Island *B*
  Hunter College *B, M*
  Kingsborough Community College *A*
  Lehman College *B, M*
  Medgar Evers College *B*
  Queens College *B, M, T*
  York College *B*
Clarkson University *B, M, D*
Clinton Community College *A*
Colgate University *B*
College of Mount St. Vincent *B, T*
College of New Rochelle *B, T*
College of Saint Rose *B*
Columbia University
  Columbia College *B*
  School of General Studies *B*
Columbia-Greene Community College *A*
Concordia College *A, B*
Cornell University *B, M, D*
Corning Community College *A*
Daemen College *B*
Dominican College of Blauvelt *B*
Dowling College *B, T*
Dutchess Community College *A*
Elmira College *B, T*
Excelsior College *B*
Fordham University *B, M, D*
Hamilton College *B*
Hartwick College *B, T*
Herkimer County Community College *A*
Hobart and William Smith Colleges *B*
Hofstra University *B, M*
Houghton College *B*
Iona College *B*
Ithaca College *B, T*
Jefferson Community College *A*
Keuka College *B*
Le Moyne College *B*
Long Island University
  Brooklyn Campus *B*
  C.W. Post Campus *B*
Manhattan College *B*
Manhattanville College *B*
Marist College *B*
Mercy College *B*
Molloy College *B*
Monroe Community College *A*
Mount St. Mary College *B, T*
Nassau Community College *A*
Nazareth College of Rochester *B*
New York University *B, M, D*
Niagara University *B*
Nyack College *B*
Orange County Community College *A*
Pace University *B*
Polytechnic University *B, M, D*
Rensselaer Polytechnic Institute *B, M, D*

Roberts Wesleyan College *B*
Russell Sage College *B*
St. Bonaventure University *B, T*
St. Francis College *B*
St. John Fisher College *B*
St. John's University *B, M*
St. Joseph's College *B*
St. Joseph's College: Suffolk Campus *B, T*
St. Lawrence University *B, T*
St. Thomas Aquinas College *B, T*
Sarah Lawrence College *B*
Siena College *B, T*
Skidmore College *B*
State University of New York
  Albany *B, M, D*
  Binghamton *B, M, D*
  Buffalo *B, M, D*
  College at Brockport *B, M, T*
  College at Buffalo *B*
  College at Cortland *B*
  College at Fredonia *B, T*
  College at Geneseo *B, T*
  College at Old Westbury *B, T*
  College at Oneonta *B*
  College at Plattsburgh *B*
  College at Potsdam *B, M*
  College of Agriculture and Technology at Cobleskill *A*
  College of Agriculture and Technology at Morrisville *A*
  College of Technology at Alfred *A*
  New Paltz *B, M, T*
  Oswego *B*
  Purchase *B*
  Stony Brook *B, M, D, T*
Suffolk County Community College *A*
Sullivan County Community College *A*
Syracuse University *B, M, D*
Touro College *B*
Ulster County Community College *A*
Union College *B*
United States Military Academy *B*
University of Rochester *B, M, D*
Utica College *B*
Vassar College *B*
Wagner College *B, T*
Wells College *B*
Yeshiva University *B, T*

North Carolina

Appalachian State University *B, M*
Barton College *B*
Bennett College *B*
Brevard College *B*
Caldwell Community College and Technical Institute *A*
Campbell University *B, T*
Catawba College *B*
Davidson College *B*
Duke University *B*
East Carolina University *B, M*
Elizabeth City State University *B, M*
Elon University *B, T*
Fayetteville State University *B*
Gardner-Webb University *B*
Greensboro College *B, T*
Guilford College *B*
High Point University *B*
Johnson C. Smith University *B*
Lees-McRae College *B*
Lenoir Community College *A*
Lenoir-Rhyne College *B, T*
Livingstone College *B*
Louisburg College *A*
Mars Hill College *B, T*
Meredith College *B*
Methodist College *B*
Mount Olive College *B*
North Carolina Agricultural and Technical State University *B, M, T*
North Carolina Central University *B, M*

North Carolina State University *B, M, D*
North Carolina Wesleyan College *B*
Pfeiffer University *B*
Queens University of Charlotte *B*
St. Andrews Presbyterian College *B*
St. Augustine's College *B*
Salem College *B*
Sandhills Community College *A*
Shaw University *B*
University of North Carolina
  Asheville *B, T*
  Chapel Hill *B, M, D*
  Charlotte *B*
  Greensboro *B, M, T*
  Pembroke *B*
  Wilmington *B, M*
Wake Forest University *B, M*
Warren Wilson College *B*
Western Carolina University *B*
Wingate University *B*
Winston-Salem State University *B*

North Dakota

Dickinson State University *B, T*
Jamestown College *B*
Mayville State University *B, T*
Minot State University *B*
North Dakota State University *B, M, D, T*
University of Mary *B*
University of North Dakota *B, M, T*
Valley City State University *B*

Ohio

Antioch College *B*
Antioch University McGregor *B*
Ashland University *B*
Baldwin-Wallace College *B, T*
Bluffton University *B*
Bowling Green State University *B, M, D*
Capital University *B*
Case Western Reserve University *B, M, D*
Cedarville University *B, T*
Central State University *B*
Cleveland State University *B, M, T*
College of Mount St. Joseph *B, T*
College of Wooster *B*
Defiance College *B, T*
Denison University *B*
Franciscan University of Steubenville *B*
Heidelberg College *B*
Hiram College *B, T*
John Carroll University *B, M, T*
Kent State University *B, M, D*
Kenyon College *B*
Lake Erie College *B*
Malone College *B*
Marietta College *B*
Miami University
  Oxford Campus *B, M, T*
Mount Union College *B*
Mount Vernon Nazarene University *B*
Muskingum College *B*
Oberlin College *B*
Ohio Dominican University *B, T*
Ohio Northern University *B*
Ohio State University
  Columbus Campus *B, M, D*
  Lima Campus *B*
Ohio University *B, M, D*
Ohio Wesleyan University *B*
Otterbein College *B*
Owens Community College
  Toledo *A*
Shawnee State University *B*
Sinclair Community College *A*
Stark State College of Technology *A*
University of Akron *B, M*
University of Cincinnati *B, M, D, T*
University of Dayton *B*

University of Findlay *B, T*
University of Rio Grande *A, B, T*
University of Toledo *B, M, D*
Urbana University *B*
Ursuline College *B*
Walsh University *B*
Washington State Community College *A*
Wilmington College *B*
Wittenberg University *B*
Wright State University *B, M*
Xavier University *B*
Youngstown State University *B, M*

Oklahoma

Bacone College *A*
Cameron University *B*
Carl Albert State College *A*
Connors State College *A*
East Central University *B, T*
Eastern Oklahoma State College *A*
Murray State College *A*
Northeastern Oklahoma Agricultural and Mechanical College *A*
Northeastern State University *B*
Northwestern Oklahoma State University *B*
Oklahoma Baptist University *B, T*
Oklahoma Christian University *B, T*
Oklahoma City Community College *A*
Oklahoma City University *B*
Oklahoma Panhandle State University *B*
Oklahoma State University *B, M, D*
Oklahoma Wesleyan University *A, B*
Oral Roberts University *B*
Redlands Community College *A*
Rose State College *A*
St. Gregory's University *A, B*
Seminole State College *A*
Southeastern Oklahoma State University *B*
Southern Nazarene University *B*
Southwestern Oklahoma State University *B*
Tulsa Community College *A*
University of Central Oklahoma *B, M*
University of Oklahoma *B, M, D*
University of Science and Arts of Oklahoma *B, T*
Western Oklahoma State College *A*

Oregon

Central Oregon Community College *A*
Chemeketa Community College *A*
Corban College *B*
Eastern Oregon University *B, T*
George Fox University *B*
Lewis & Clark College *B*
Linfield College *B, T*
Linn-Benton Community College *A*
Oregon State University *B, M, D*
Pacific University *B*
Portland State University *B, D*
Reed College *B*
Southern Oregon University *B, T*
Treasure Valley Community College *A*
University of Oregon *B, M, D*
University of Portland *B, T*
Warner Pacific College *T*
Western Oregon University *B*
Willamette University *B*

Pennsylvania

Albright College *B, T*
Allegheny College *B*
Alvernia College *B*
Arcadia University *B*
Bloomsburg University of Pennsylvania *B, T*
Bryn Mawr College *B, M, D*
Bucknell University *B, M*
Bucks County Community College *A*

Butler County Community College *A*
Cabrini College *B*
California University of
    Pennsylvania *B, M*
Carlow University *B, T*
Carnegie Mellon University *M, D*
Cedar Crest College *B*
Chatham College *B*
Cheyney University of
    Pennsylvania *B, T*
Clarion University of
    Pennsylvania *B, T*
College Misericordia *B*
Community College of Allegheny
    County *A*
Community College of Philadelphia *A*
DeSales University *B, T*
Delaware Valley College *B*
Dickinson College *B*
Drexel University *B, M, D*
Duquesne University *B*
East Stroudsburg University of
    Pennsylvania *B, T*
Eastern University *B*
Edinboro University of
    Pennsylvania *B, T*
Elizabethtown College *B*
Franklin & Marshall College *B*
Gannon University *B*
Gettysburg College *B*
Grove City College *B*
Gwynedd-Mercy College *B*
Harrisburg Area Community
    College *A*
Haverford College *B, T*
Holy Family University *B, T*
Immaculata University *B*
Indiana University of
    Pennsylvania *B, M*
Juniata College *B*
King's College *B, T*
Kutztown University of
    Pennsylvania *B, M, T*
La Roche College *B*
La Salle University *B, T*
Lafayette College *B*
Lebanon Valley College *B, T*
Lehigh Carbon Community College *A*
Lehigh University *B, M, D*
Lincoln University *B, M*
Lock Haven University of
    Pennsylvania *B, T*
Luzerne County Community
    College *A*
Lycoming College *B*
Mansfield University of
    Pennsylvania *B, T*
Marywood University *B*
Mercyhurst College *B*
Messiah College *B*
Millersville University of
    Pennsylvania *B, M, T*
Montgomery County Community
    College *A*
Moravian College *B, T*
Muhlenberg College *B*
Northampton County Area
    Community College *A*
Penn State
    Abington *B*
    Altoona *B*
    Beaver *B*
    Berks *B*
    Delaware County *B*
    Dubois *B*
    Erie, The Behrend College *B*
    Fayette *B*
    Harrisburg *B*
    Hazleton *B*
    Lehigh Valley *B*
    McKeesport *B*
    Mont Alto *B*
    New Kensington *B*
    Schuylkill - Capital College *B*

    Shenango *B*
    University Park *B, M, D*
    Wilkes-Barre *B*
    Worthington Scranton *B*
    York *B*
Rosemont College *B*
St. Francis University *B*
St. Joseph's University *B*
St. Vincent College *B*
Seton Hill University *B, T*
Shippensburg University of
    Pennsylvania *B, T*
Slippery Rock University of
    Pennsylvania *B, T*
Susquehanna University *B*
Swarthmore College *B*
Temple University *B, M, D*
Thiel College *B*
University of Pennsylvania *B, M, D*
University of Pittsburgh *B, M, D*
University of Pittsburgh
    Johnstown *B*
University of Scranton *A, B, T*
Ursinus College *B, T*
Villanova University *B, M*
Washington and Jefferson College *B*
Waynesburg College *B*
West Chester University of
    Pennsylvania *B, M, T*
Westminster College *B*
Widener University *B, T*
Wilkes University *B, M*
Wilson College *B*
York College of Pennsylvania *B, T*

Puerto Rico

Inter American University of Puerto
    Rico
    Bayamon Campus *B*
    San German Campus *B*
Pontifical Catholic University of
    Puerto Rico *B*
University of Puerto Rico
    Cayey University College *B*
    Mayaguez *B, M*
    Ponce *B*
    Rio Piedras *B, M*
University of the Sacred Heart *B*

Rhode Island

Brown University *B, M, D*
Providence College *B*
Rhode Island College *B, M*
Roger Williams University *B*
Salve Regina University *B*
University of Rhode Island *B, M, D*

South Carolina

Allen University *B*
Anderson University *B*
Benedict College *B*
Charleston Southern University *B*
The Citadel *B*
Claflin University *B*
Clemson University *B, M, D*
Coker College *B*
College of Charleston *B, M, T*
Columbia College *B, T*
Converse College *B*
Erskine College *B, T*
Francis Marion University *B*
Furman University *B, T*
Lander University *B, T*
Limestone College *B*
Morris College *B*
Newberry College *B, T*
Presbyterian College *B, T*
South Carolina State University *B*
Southern Wesleyan University *B, T*
University of South Carolina *B, M, D*
University of South Carolina
    Upstate *B*
Voorhees College *B*
Winthrop University *B, M*

Wofford College *B, T*

South Dakota

Augustana College *B, T*
Black Hills State University *B*
Dakota State University *B*
Dakota Wesleyan University *B*
Mount Marty College *B*
Northern State University *B*
South Dakota School of Mines and
    Technology *B*
South Dakota State University *B, M, T*
University of Sioux Falls *B*
University of South Dakota *B, M*

Tennessee

Austin Peay State University *B*
Belmont University *B, T*
Bethel College *B*
Bryan College *B, T*
Carson-Newman College *B, T*
Christian Brothers University *B*
Columbia State Community College *A*
Cumberland University *B*
Dyersburg State Community
    College *A*
East Tennessee State
    University *B, M, T*
Fisk University *B*
Freed-Hardeman University *B, T*
Hiwassee College *A*
Jackson State Community College *A*
King College *B, T*
Lambuth University *B*
LeMoyne-Owen College *B*
Lee University *B*
Lincoln Memorial University *B, T*
Lipscomb University *B*
Maryville College *B, T*
Middle Tennessee State
    University *B, M*
Milligan College *B, T*
Rhodes College *B*
Roane State Community College *A*
Southern Adventist University *B*
Tennessee State University *B, M*
Tennessee Technological
    University *B, M, T*
Tennessee Temple University *B*
Tennessee Wesleyan College *B, T*
Trevecca Nazarene University *B*
Tusculum College *B*
Union University *B, T*
University of Memphis *B, M, D*
University of Tennessee
    Chattanooga *B, T*
    Knoxville *B, M, D*
    Martin *B*
University of the South *B*
Vanderbilt University *B, M, D*
Walters State Community College *A*

Texas

Abilene Christian University *B*
Alvin Community College *A*
Amarillo College *A*
Angelina College *A*
Angelo State University *B, T*
Austin College *B*
Austin Community College *A*
Baylor University *B, M, D*
Blinn College *A*
Brazosport College *A*
Central Texas College *A*
Cisco Junior College *A*
Clarendon College *A*
Coastal Bend College *A*
College of the Mainland *A*
Concordia University at Austin *B*
Dallas Baptist University *B*
Del Mar College *A*
East Texas Baptist University *B*
El Paso Community College *A*
Frank Phillips College *A*

Galveston College *A*
Grayson County College *A*
Hardin-Simmons University *B*
Hill College *A*
Houston Baptist University *B*
Howard College *A*
Howard Payne University *B, T*
Huston-Tillotson College *B*
Jarvis Christian College *B, T*
Kilgore College *A*
Lamar University *B, M*
Laredo Community College *A*
LeTourneau University *B*
Lee College *A*
Lon Morris College *A*
Lubbock Christian University *B, T*
McMurry University *B, T*
Midland College *A*
Midwestern State University *B*
Mountain View College *A*
Navarro College *A*
North Lake College *A*
Northeast Texas Community
    College *A*
Northwest Vista College *A*
Odessa College *A*
Our Lady of the Lake University of San
    Antonio *B*
Palo Alto College *A*
Paris Junior College *A*
Prairie View A&M University *B, M*
Rice University *B, M, D*
St. Edward's University *B*
St. Mary's University *B*
St. Philip's College *A*
Sam Houston State University *B, M*
San Antonio College *A*
San Jacinto College
    North *A*
Schreiner University *B*
South Plains College *A*
South Texas College *A*
Southern Methodist University *B*
Southwestern Adventist
    University *B, T*
Southwestern University *B, T*
Stephen F. Austin State
    University *B, M, T*
Sul Ross State University *B*
Tarleton State University *B, M, T*
Texarkana College *A*
Texas A&M University *B, M, D*
Texas A&M University
    Commerce *B, M*
    Kingsville *B, M, T*
    Texarkana *A*
Texas Christian University *B, M*
Texas College *B*
Texas Lutheran University *B, T*
Texas Southern University *B, M*
Texas State University: San
    Marcos *B, M, T*
Texas Tech University *B, M, D*
Texas Wesleyan University *B*
Texas Woman's University *B, M*
Trinity University *B*
Trinity Valley Community College *A*
Tyler Junior College *A*
University of Dallas *B*
University of Houston *B, M, D*
University of Houston
    Clear Lake *B, M*
    Victoria *B, T*
University of Mary Hardin-Baylor *B, T*
University of North Texas *B, M, D*
University of St. Thomas *B*
University of Texas
    Arlington *B, M*
    Austin *B, M, D*
    Brownsville *B*
    Dallas *B, M*
    El Paso *B, M*
    Pan American *B, M*
    San Antonio *B, M*

Tyler *B, M*
of the Permian Basin *B*
University of the Incarnate Word *B, M*
Wayland Baptist University *B, T*
West Texas A&M University *B, M*
Western Texas College *A*
Wharton County Junior College *A*
Wiley College *B*

Utah

Brigham Young University *B, M, D*
Dixie State College of Utah *A*
Snow College *A*
Southern Utah University *B, T*
University of Utah *B, M, D*
Utah State University *B, M*
Utah Valley State College *A, B*
Weber State University *B*
Westminster College *B*

Vermont

Bennington College *B*
Castleton State College *B*
Johnson State College *B*
Lyndon State College *B*
Marlboro College *B*
Middlebury College *B*
Norwich University *B*
St. Michael's College *B*
University of Vermont *B, M, D*

Virginia

Averett University *B*
Bluefield College *B*
Bridgewater College *B*
Christopher Newport University *B*
College of William and Mary *B*
Eastern Mennonite University *B*
Emory & Henry College *B, T*
Ferrum College *B*
George Mason University *B, M*
Hampden-Sydney College *B*
Hampton University *B, M*
Hollins University *B*
James Madison University *B, T*
Liberty University *B, T*
Longwood University *B, T*
Lynchburg College *B*
Mary Baldwin College *B*
Marymount University *B*
Mountain Empire Community
College *A*
Norfolk State University *B*
Northern Virginia Community
College *A*
Old Dominion University *B, M, T*
Radford University *B*
Randolph-Macon College *B*
Randolph-Macon Woman's College *B*
Roanoke College *B, T*
St. Paul's College *B*
Shenandoah University *B*
Sweet Briar College *B*
University of Mary Washington *B*
University of Richmond *B, T*
University of Virginia *B, M, D*
University of Virginia's College at
Wise *B, T*
Virginia Commonwealth
University *B, M*
Virginia Military Institute *B*
Virginia Polytechnic Institute and
State University *B, M, D*
Virginia State University *B, M*
Virginia Union University *B*
Virginia Wesleyan College *B*
Washington and Lee University *B*

Washington

Central Washington University *B*
Centralia College *A*
Eastern Washington University *B, M, T*
Everett Community College *A*

Gonzaga University *B*
Heritage University *B*
Highline Community College *A*
Pacific Lutheran University *B*
Saint Martin's University *B*
Seattle Pacific University *B*
Seattle University *B*
Spokane Falls Community College *A*
University of Puget Sound *B, T*
University of Washington *B, M, D*
Walla Walla College *B*
Washington State University *B*
Western Washington University *B, M*
Whitman College *B*
Whitworth College *B, T*

West Virginia

Bethany College *B*
Concord University *B*
Davis and Elkins College *B*
Marshall University *B, M*
Potomac State College of West Virginia
University *A*
Shepherd University *B*
West Liberty State College *B*
West Virginia State University *B*
West Virginia University *B, M, D, T*
West Virginia University Institute of
Technology *B*
West Virginia Wesleyan College *B*
Wheeling Jesuit University *B*

Wisconsin

Alverno College *B*
Beloit College *B*
Cardinal Stritch University *B*
Carroll College *B*
Carthage College *B, T*
Concordia University Wisconsin *B, T*
Edgewood College *B*
Lakeland College *B*
Lawrence University *B, T*
Marian College of Fond du Lac *B*
Marquette University *B, M, D, T*
Mount Mary College *B*
Northland College *B*
Ripon College *B, T*
St. Norbert College *B, T*
Silver Lake College *B, T*
University of Wisconsin
Eau Claire *B*
Green Bay *B*
La Crosse *B, T*
Madison *B, M, D*
Milwaukee *B, M, D*
Oshkosh *B*
Parkside *B, T*
Platteville *B, T*
River Falls *B*
Stevens Point *B, T*
Superior *B, T*
Whitewater *B, T*
Viterbo University *B, T*
Wisconsin Lutheran College *B*

Wyoming

Casper College *A*
Eastern Wyoming College *A*
Laramie County Community
College *A*
Northwest College *A*
Sheridan College *A*
University of Wyoming *B, M, D*
Western Wyoming Community
College *A*

Mathematics/computer science

Alabama

Birmingham-Southern College *B*
Oakwood College *B*

Arkansas

Philander Smith College *B*

California

California Lutheran University *B*
California State University
Chico *B*
Claremont McKenna College *B*
Mills College *B, M*
Pepperdine University *B*
Pomona College *B*
St. Mary's College of California *B*
Santa Clara University *B*
Stanford University *B*
University of California
San Diego *B*
Santa Cruz *B, M*

Colorado

Colorado College *B*
Colorado School of Mines *B*
Metropolitan State College of
Denver *B*
United States Air Force Academy *B*

Connecticut

Quinnipiac University *B*
Western Connecticut State
University *B*
Yale University *B*

Delaware

Delaware State University *B*

Florida

University of Tampa *A, B*

Georgia

Clark Atlanta University *B, M*
Emory University *B, M, D*
Oglethorpe University *B*
Paine College *B*
Piedmont College *B*

Idaho

Albertson College of Idaho *B*

Illinois

Augustana College *B*
Dominican University *B*
Eastern Illinois University *B*
Eureka College *B*
Loyola University of Chicago *B*
Rockford College *B*
Roosevelt University *B*
Sauk Valley Community College *A*
Southeastern Illinois College *A*
University of Illinois
Chicago *B, M*
Urbana-Champaign *B*
University of St. Francis *B*

Indiana

Anderson University *B*
Huntington University *B*
Indiana University
South Bend *M*
Indiana University-Purdue University
Fort Wayne *B*
Manchester College *B*
Purdue University
Calumet *B*
St. Joseph's College *B*
Saint Mary's College *B, T*
Taylor University *B*

Iowa

Ashford University *B*
Central College *B, T*
Coe College *B*

Kansas

Central Christian College of Kansas *A*
Seward County Community College *A*
Tabor College *B*

Kentucky

Berea College *T*
Brescia University *B*

Maine

Bowdoin College *B*
Colby College *B*
University of Maine
Farmington *B, T*
Fort Kent *B*
University of Southern Maine *B*

Maryland

Community College of Baltimore
County *A*
Washington College *B, T*

Massachusetts

American International College *B*
Amherst College *B*
Boston University *B*
Clark University *B*
Hampshire College *B*
Massachusetts Institute of
Technology *B*
Salem State College *B*
Simon's Rock College of Bard *B*
Tufts University *B, M, D*
Wheaton College *B*

Michigan

Albion College *B, T*
Hillsdale College *B*
Lake Superior State University *B*
Lawrence Technological University *B*

Minnesota

Carleton College *B*
College of St. Benedict *B*
Concordia College: Moorhead *B*
Minnesota State University
Mankato *M*
Northland Community & Technical
College *A*
Ridgewater College *A*
St. John's University *B*
St. Mary's University of Minnesota *B*
University of Minnesota
Twin Cities *M, D*
Winona State University *B, T*

Mississippi

Belhaven College *B*
Mississippi College *M*
Tougaloo College *B*

Missouri

Crowder College *A*
Park University *B*
Washington University in St.
Louis *B, M, D*
William Jewell College *B*

Montana

University of Montana: Missoula *B*

New Hampshire

Keene State College *B*
Rivier College *A, B*
St. Anselm College *B*

New Jersey

Cumberland County College *A*
Gloucester County College *A*
Stevens Institute of
Technology *B, M, D*

New York

Adirondack Community College *A*
City University of New York
  Brooklyn College *B*
Colgate University *B*
Hobart and William Smith Colleges *B*
Hofstra University *B*
Onondaga Community College *A*
Rochester Institute of Technology *B*
St. Lawrence University *B*
St. Thomas Aquinas College *B*
Schenectady County Community
  College *A*
State University of New York
  Purchase *B*

North Carolina

Wingate University *B*

Ohio

Antioch College *B*
Defiance College *B, T*
Hiram College *B*
Jefferson Community College *A*
Wittenberg University *B*

Oklahoma

Connors State College *A*
Oklahoma Baptist University *B*
Oklahoma Christian University *B*

Oregon

Lewis & Clark College *B*
Southern Oregon University *B*
University of Oregon *B*
Western Oregon University *B*

Pennsylvania

Chestnut Hill College *B*
Duquesne University *M*
Gettysburg College *B*
Grove City College *B*
Immaculata University *A, B*
La Salle University *B*
Mount Aloysius College *A, B*
St. Francis University *B*
Swarthmore College *B*
Westminster College *B*

Puerto Rico

Inter American University of Puerto
  Rico
  Bayamon Campus *B*
University of Puerto Rico
  Mayaguez *B, M*

Rhode Island

Brown University *B*

South Carolina

Charleston Southern University *B*
Furman University *B*
Newberry College *B*
University of South Carolina
  Aiken *B*

Tennessee

Bryan College *B*
Christian Brothers University *B*
Maryville College *B*
University of the South *B*

Texas

Laredo Community College *A*
LeTourneau University *B*
McMurry University *B*
University of Houston
  Clear Lake *B, M*

Utah

University of Utah *A, B, M*

Vermont

Bennington College *B*
Castleton State College *B*
Marlboro College *B*

Virginia

Averett University *B*
George Mason University *D*
Hampden-Sydney College *B*
University of Richmond *B*
Virginia Wesleyan College *B*

Washington

Columbia Basin College *A*
Heritage University *A, B*

West Virginia

Bethany College *B*
Mountain State University *B*

Wisconsin

Cardinal Stritch University *B*
Lawrence University *B, T*
Marquette University *B, M, D*
University of Wisconsin
  Parkside *B*

Mathematics teacher education

Alabama

Athens State University *B*
Auburn University *B*
Birmingham-Southern College *T*
Faulkner University *B, T*
Gadsden State Community College *A*
Huntingdon College *T*
Judson College *B*
Miles College *B*
Oakwood College *B*
Talladega College *B*
Tuskegee University *B*
University of Mobile *B, T*

Alaska

University of Alaska
  Fairbanks *M*

Arizona

Arizona State University *B, T*
Grand Canyon University *B*
Northern Arizona University *B, M, T*
Prescott College *B, M, T*
University of Arizona *B, M*

Arkansas

Arkansas State University *B, M, T*
Arkansas Tech University *B, M*
Harding University *B, M, T*
Henderson State University *M, T*
John Brown University *B, T*
Ouachita Baptist University *B, T*
Philander Smith College *B*
Southern Arkansas University *B, T*
University of Arkansas *M*
University of Arkansas
  Fort Smith *B*
  Pine Bluff *B, M, T*
University of Central Arkansas *B, M, T*
University of the Ozarks *T*

California

Azusa Pacific University *T*
California Baptist University *T*
California Lutheran University *B, T*
California State University
  Chico *B, M, T*
  Dominguez Hills *M, T*
  East Bay *M, T*
  Fullerton *M*
  Long Beach *T*
  Northridge *B, T*
  Sacramento *T*
  San Bernardino *M, T*
Cuesta College *A*
Fresno Pacific University *B, M, T*
Humboldt State University *T*
Los Angeles Southwest College *A*
Loyola Marymount University *M*
Master's College *T*
Mills College *T*
Mount St. Mary's College *T*
National University *B*
Pacific Union College *B*
Saddleback College *A*
San Diego Christian College *B, T*
San Diego State University *B, M, T*
San Francisco State University *B, M, T*
Simpson University *B, T*
Sonoma State University *T*
Stanford University *M, T*
University of the Pacific *T*
Vanguard University of Southern
  California *T*
Westmont College *T*

Colorado

Adams State College *B, T*
Colorado State University *T*
Colorado State University
  Pueblo *T*
Fort Lewis College *B*
Metropolitan State College of
  Denver *T*
Regis University *B, T*
University of Colorado
  Boulder *T*
  Colorado Springs *T*
Western State College of Colorado *T*

Connecticut

Albertus Magnus College *B, T*
Connecticut College *T*
Fairfield University *T*
Quinnipiac University *B, M*
Sacred Heart University *T*
Southern Connecticut State
  University *B, M, T*
University of New Haven *T*

Delaware

Delaware State University *B*
University of Delaware *B, T*

District of Columbia

Catholic University of America *B*
George Washington University *M, T*
University of the District of
  Columbia *M*

Florida

Barry University *T*
Broward Community College *A*
Chipola College *B*
Clearwater Christian College *B*
Edward Waters College *B*
Florida Agricultural and Mechanical
  University *B, M, T*
Florida Atlantic University *B*
Florida Institute of
  Technology *B, M, D*
Florida International
  University *B, M, T*
Florida State University *B, M, D, T*
Gulf Coast Community College *A*
Hobe Sound Bible College *B, T*
Manatee Community College *A*
Miami Dade College *A, B*
Palm Beach Atlantic University *B, T*
St. Petersburg College *B*
Southeastern College of the
  Assemblies of God *B, T*
Stetson University *B*
University of Central Florida *B, M*

University of Florida *B*
University of Miami *M*
University of North Florida *B, M*
University of South Florida *B, M*
University of Tampa *B*
University of West Florida *B, M*

Georgia

Agnes Scott College *T*
Albany State University *M*
Armstrong Atlantic State
  University *B, M, T*
Berry College *B*
Brewton-Parker College *B*
Clark Atlanta University *B*
Columbus State University *B, M*
Covenant College *B, T*
Darton College *A*
Emmanuel College *B*
Fort Valley State University *B, T*
Gainesville State College *A*
Georgia College and State
  University *M, T*
Georgia Southern University *B, M*
Georgia Southwestern State
  University *M*
Georgia State University *M*
Kennesaw State University *B*
North Georgia College & State
  University *M*
Paine College *B*
Piedmont College *M, T*
Shorter College *B, T*
University of Georgia *B, M, D*
University of West Georgia *M*
Wesleyan College *M, T*

Hawaii

Brigham Young University-Hawaii *B, T*
Hawaii Pacific University *M*

Idaho

Boise State University *M, T*
Brigham Young University-Idaho *T*
Lewis-Clark State College *B, T*
Northwest Nazarene University *B*

Illinois

Augustana College *B, T*
Benedictine University *T*
Black Hawk College *A*
Blackburn College *B, T*
Chicago State University *B*
Concordia University *M*
DePaul University *M*
Dominican University *T*
Elmhurst College *B*
Eureka College *B*
Governors State University *B*
Greenville College *B, T*
Heartland Community College *A*
Illinois College *T*
Illinois State University *D*
Illinois Wesleyan University *B*
John A. Logan College *A*
Judson College *B, T*
Kankakee Community College *A*
Knox College *T*
Lake Land College *A*
Lewis University *T*
Loyola University of Chicago *B*
MacMurray College *B, T*
National-Louis University *M*
North Park University *T*
Northwestern University *B*
Olivet Nazarene University *B, T*
Quincy University *T*
Rockford College *T*
Roosevelt University *B*
St. Xavier University *B, M, T*
Sauk Valley Community College *A*
Trinity Christian College *B, T*
Trinity International University *B, T*

University of Illinois
  Chicago B, M
  Urbana-Champaign B, M, T
University of St. Francis B, M, T
Waubonsee Community College A
Wheaton College T

Indiana

Anderson University B, T
Bethel College B
Butler University T
Franklin College B, T
Goshen College B
Grace College B
Huntington University B, M
Indiana University
  Bloomington B, T
  Northwest B
  South Bend B, T
  Southeast B
Indiana University-Purdue University
  Fort Wayne B
Indiana University-Purdue University
  Indianapolis B, M
Indiana Wesleyan University B, T
Manchester College B, T
Oakland City University B
Saint Mary's College T
St. Mary-of-the-Woods College B, T
Taylor University B, T
Tri-State University B, T
University of Evansville B, T
University of Indianapolis B, T
Valparaiso University B
Vincennes University A

Iowa

Ashford University B, T
Briar Cliff University B
Buena Vista University B, T
Central College T
Clarke College B, T
Cornell College B, T
Dordt College B
Drake University B, M, T
Ellsworth Community College A
Graceland University T
Iowa State University M, T
Iowa Wesleyan College B
Loras College T
Maharishi University of
  Management T
Morningside College B
Mount Mercy College T
Northwestern College T
St. Ambrose University B, T
Simpson College T
University of Iowa M, D, T
Upper Iowa University T
Wartburg College T
William Penn University B

Kansas

Allen County Community College A
Baker University T
Bethany College B
Bethel College T
Colby Community College A
Emporia State University T
Fort Hays State University M
Friends University B
Garden City Community College A
McPherson College B, T
MidAmerica Nazarene University B, T
Newman University T
Ottawa University B, T
Pittsburg State University B, M, T
Southwestern College B, T
Sterling College B
Tabor College B, T
University of Kansas B, T
University of St. Mary B
Washburn University of Topeka B

Kentucky

Alice Lloyd College B
Bellarmine University B, M, T
Campbellsville University B
Eastern Kentucky University B
Kentucky State University B
Kentucky Wesleyan College B, T
Lindsey Wilson College B, T
Thomas More College B
University of Kentucky B
University of the Cumberlands T

Louisiana

Centenary College of Louisiana B, T
Louisiana State University
  Shreveport B
Nicholls State University B
Northwestern State University •B
Our Lady of Holy Cross College B
Southeastern Louisiana University B
Southern University
  New Orleans B
Southern University and Agricultural
  and Mechanical College B
University of Louisiana at Lafayette B
University of Louisiana at Monroe B
University of New Orleans B
Xavier University of Louisiana B

Maine

St. Joseph's College B
University of Maine B
University of Maine
  Farmington B
University of Southern Maine T

Maryland

Bowie State University B, T
College of Notre Dame of Maryland T
Columbia Union College B
Coppin State University B, T
Frostburg State University B, T
Morgan State University D
Mount St. Mary's University T
Prince George's Community
  College A
St. Mary's College of Maryland T
Salisbury University T
Towson University M, T
University of Maryland
  College Park B
  Eastern Shore B

Massachusetts

Assumption College T
Boston University B, M, T
Bridgewater State College M, T
Eastern Nazarene College B
Elms College M, T
Fitchburg State College B, M, T
Framingham State College B, M
Lasell College B, T
Lesley University B, M
Merrimack College T
Northeastern University B, M
Regis College B
Salem State College M
Springfield College T
Tufts University M, T
University of Massachusetts
  Dartmouth T
Western New England College M, T
Westfield State College B, M, T
Worcester Polytechnic Institute M
Worcester State College T

Michigan

Albion College B, T
Alma College T
Andrews University B
Calvin College B
Central Michigan University M, D
Concordia University B, T

Cornerstone University B, T
Eastern Michigan University B, M, T
Ferris State University B
Grand Valley State University M, T
Hope College T
Lansing Community College A
Madonna University B, T
Michigan State University D
Michigan Technological University T
Northern Michigan University B, M
Rochester College B
University of Detroit Mercy B, M, T
University of Michigan
  Dearborn B
  Flint T
Wayne State University B, M, T
Western Michigan
  University B, M, D, T

Minnesota

Augsburg College T
Bemidji State University M, T
Bethel University T
College of St. Benedict T
College of St. Catherine B, T
College of St. Scholastica T
Concordia College: Moorhead B, T
Concordia University: St. Paul B, T
Gustavus Adolphus College T
Minnesota State University
  Mankato B, M, T
  Moorhead T
Northland Community & Technical
  College A
Northwestern College B
Pillsbury Baptist Bible College B, T
Ridgewater College A
St. Cloud State University B, T
St. John's University T
St. Mary's University of Minnesota B
Southwest Minnesota State
  University B, T
University of Minnesota
  Duluth B
  Morris T
  Twin Cities B, M, T
University of St. Thomas B, T
Vermilion Community College A
Winona State University B, T

Mississippi

Blue Mountain College B
Coahoma Community College A
Delta State University B, T
Itawamba Community College A
Jackson State University M
Mississippi College B, M
Mississippi Gulf Coast Community
  College
  Jefferson Davis Campus A
Mississippi State University T
Mississippi Valley State University B, T
Rust College B
University of Mississippi B, T
William Carey College B

Missouri

Central Missouri State
  University B, M, T
College of the Ozarks B, T
Columbia College T
Culver-Stockton College T
Evangel University B, T
Hannibal-LaGrange College B
Harris-Stowe State University T
Lincoln University B, T
Maryville University of Saint
  Louis B, M, T
Missouri Baptist University T
Missouri Southern State
  University B, T
Missouri State University B
Missouri Valley College T

Northwest Missouri State
  University B, M, T
Park University T
Southeast Missouri State
  University B, T
Southwest Baptist University T
Truman State University M, T
University of Missouri
  Columbia B, M, D
  St. Louis T
Washington University in St.
  Louis B, M, T
Webster University M
William Jewell College T
William Woods University B, T

Montana

Montana State University
  Billings B, T
Montana Tech of the University of
  Montana T
Rocky Mountain College B, T
University of Great Falls B
University of Montana:
  Missoula B, M, T
University of Montana: Western B, T

Nebraska

Chadron State College B, M
College of Saint Mary B, T
Concordia University B, T
Creighton University T
Dana College B
Hastings College B, M, T
Midland Lutheran College B, T
Nebraska Wesleyan University T
Peru State College B, T
Union College T
University of Nebraska
  Kearney B, M, T
  Lincoln B, M
  Omaha M
Wayne State College B, T
York College B, T

Nevada

Great Basin College B
University of Nevada
  Reno B, M

New Hampshire

Franklin Pierce College T
Keene State College B, T
New England College B, T
Plymouth State University M, T
Rivier College B, T
St. Anselm College T
University of New Hampshire B, D, T

New Jersey

Caldwell College T
Centenary College T
The College of New Jersey B, T
College of St. Elizabeth T
Felician College B
Georgian Court University T
Kean University M
Montclair State University D
Rowan University M, T
Rutgers, The State University of New
  Jersey
  New Brunswick/Piscataway
    Campus D, T
St. Peter's College T
William Paterson University of New
  Jersey B, T

New Mexico

College of the Southwest B, T
New Mexico Institute of Mining and
  Technology M
Western New Mexico University B

New York

Adelphi University *M, T*
Alfred University *M, T*
Bard College *M*
City University of New York
  Brooklyn College *B, M*
  City College *B, M, T*
  College of Staten Island *B*
  Hunter College *B, M, T*
  Lehman College *B, M*
  Queens College *M, T*
Colgate University *M*
College of Saint Rose *B, T*
Cornell University *M, T*
D'Youville College *M, T*
Daemen College *B, M, T*
Dominican College of Blauvelt *B, T*
Dowling College *B*
Dutchess Community College *A*
Elmira College *B, T*
Fordham University *T*
Hobart and William Smith Colleges *T*
Hofstra University *B, M*
Houghton College *B, T*
Iona College *B, M, T*
Ithaca College *B, T*
Keuka College *B, T*
Le Moyne College *T*
Long Island University
  Brooklyn Campus *B, M, T*
  C.W. Post Campus *B, M, T*
Manhattan College *B, T*
Manhattanville College *M, T*
Marist College *B*
Mercy College *B, T*
Molloy College *B*
Nazareth College of Rochester *T*
New York Institute of Technology *B, T*
New York University *B, M, D, T*
Niagara University *B, M, T*
Pace University *B, M, T*
Rensselaer Polytechnic Institute *B, T*
Roberts Wesleyan College *B, M*
St. Bonaventure University *M*
St. Francis College *B*
St. John Fisher College *B, M, T*
St. John's University *B, M*
St. Joseph's College *B, T*
St. Joseph's College: Suffolk
  Campus *B, T*
St. Lawrence University *T*
St. Thomas Aquinas College *B, T*
State University of New York
  Albany *B, M, T*
  Binghamton *M*
  Buffalo *M, D, T*
  College at Brockport *M*
  College at Buffalo *B, M, T*
  College at Cortland *B, M, T*
  College at Fredonia *B, M, T*
  College at Geneseo *B, M, T*
  College at Old Westbury *B, T*
  College at Oneonta *B, M, T*
  College at Plattsburgh *B, M*
  College at Potsdam *B, M*
  New Paltz *B, M, T*
  Oswego *B, M*
Syracuse University *B, M, D, T*
Utica College *B*
Vassar College *T*
Wells College *T*

North Carolina

Appalachian State University *B, M, T*
Belmont Abbey College *T*
Bennett College *B, T*
Campbell University *B, T*
Catawba College *T*
Chowan College *T*
Davidson College *T*
East Carolina University *B, M*
Elizabeth City State University *B, T*
Elon University *B, T*
Fayetteville State University *B, T*

Gardner-Webb University *B*
Greensboro College *B, T*
Johnson C. Smith University *B*
Lenoir-Rhyne College *B, T*
Livingstone College *T*
Louisburg College *A*
Mars Hill College *T*
Meredith College *T*
Methodist College *A, B, T*
North Carolina Agricultural and
  Technical State University *B, M, T*
North Carolina Central
  University *B, M, T*
North Carolina State
  University *B, M, D, T*
Queens University of Charlotte *T*
St. Augustine's College *B*
Shaw University *B, T*
University of North Carolina
  Charlotte *B, M*
  Greensboro *B, M, T*
  Pembroke *B, M*
  Wilmington *B*
Wake Forest University *T*
Western Carolina University *B, M, T*
Wingate University *B, T*
Winston-Salem State University *B*

North Dakota

Dickinson State University *B, T*
Jamestown College *B*
Mayville State University *B, T*
Minot State University *B, M*
North Dakota State University *B, T*
University of Mary *B, T*
University of North Dakota *B, T*
Valley City State University *B, T*

Ohio

Ashland University *B, T*
Baldwin-Wallace College *T*
Bluffton University *B*
Bowling Green State
  University *B, M, T*
Capital University *T*
Case Western Reserve University *T*
Cedarville University *B, T*
Defiance College *B, T*
Hiram College *T*
John Carroll University *M*
Kent State University *B, M*
Malone College *T*
Miami University
  Oxford Campus *B, M, T*
Mount Union College *T*
Mount Vernon Nazarene
  University *B, M, T*
Ohio Dominican University *B, T*
Ohio Northern University *B, T*
Ohio State University
  Columbus Campus *M, D*
Ohio University *M, D, T*
Ohio Wesleyan University *B*
Otterbein College *B*
Shawnee State University *B*
University of Akron *B*
University of Findlay *B, M, T*
University of Rio Grande *B, T*
University of Toledo *B, M, T*
Urbana University *B*
Ursuline College *B, M, T*
Walsh University *B*
Wilmington College *B*
Wright State University *B, M, T*
Youngstown State University *B, M*

Oklahoma

Cameron University *B, T*
East Central University *B, T*
Eastern Oklahoma State College *A*
Northeastern State University *B, M*
Northwestern Oklahoma State
  University *B, T*
Oklahoma Baptist University *B, T*

Oklahoma Christian University *B, T*
Oklahoma City University *B*
Oklahoma Wesleyan University *B*
Oral Roberts University *B, T*
Southeastern Oklahoma State
  University *B, M, T*
Southern Nazarene University *B*
Southwestern Oklahoma State
  University *B, M, T*
University of Central Oklahoma *B*
University of Oklahoma *B, T*
University of Tulsa *B, T*

Oregon

Concordia University *B, M, T*
Corban College *B*
George Fox University *T*
Linfield College *T*
Oregon State University *M, D*
Portland State University *D, T*
Southern Oregon University *T*
Western Oregon University *T*

Pennsylvania

Albright College *T*
Alvernia College *B*
Arcadia University *B, M, T*
Cabrini College *T*
Carlow University *T*
Chatham College *T*
College Misericordia *T*
DeSales University *M, T*
Dickinson College *T*
Duquesne University *B, M, T*
Elizabethtown College *B*
Gannon University *T*
Geneva College *B, T*
Gettysburg College *T*
Grove City College *B, T*
Gwynedd-Mercy College *T*
Holy Family University *B, M, T*
Immaculata University *M*
Indiana University of
  Pennsylvania *B, M, T*
Juniata College *B, T*
King's College *T*
La Roche College *B*
La Salle University *B, T*
Lebanon Valley College *T*
Lincoln University *B, T*
Lycoming College *T*
Mansfield University of
  Pennsylvania *B, T*
Marywood University *B*
Mercyhurst College *B, T*
Messiah College *B, T*
Millersville University of
  Pennsylvania *B, M, T*
Moravian College *T*
Philadelphia Biblical University *B, T*
Point Park University *B*
Rosemont College *T*
St. Francis University *B, T*
St. Joseph's University *B, M*
St. Vincent College *T*
Seton Hill University *B, T*
Susquehanna University *T*
Temple University *B*
Thiel College *B*
University of Pennsylvania *M, T*
University of Pittsburgh *T*
University of Pittsburgh
  Johnstown *B, T*
Villanova University *T*
Washington and Jefferson College *T*
Waynesburg College *B, T*
West Chester University of
  Pennsylvania *B, T*
Westminster College *T*
Widener University *T*
Wilkes University *M, T*
Wilson College *T*
York College of Pennsylvania *B, T*

Puerto Rico

American University of Puerto
  Rico *B, T*
Bayamon Central University *B*
Inter American University of Puerto
  Rico
  Barranquitas Campus *B*
  San German Campus *B*
Pontifical Catholic University of
  Puerto Rico *B, T*
Turabo University *B*
University of Puerto Rico
  Cayey University College *B*
  Mayaguez *B*

Rhode Island

Providence College *M*
Rhode Island College *B, M*
Salve Regina University *B*

South Carolina

Anderson University *B, T*
Charleston Southern University *B*
The Citadel *M*
Claflin University *B*
Clemson University *B*
Coker College *B, T*
College of Charleston *M*
Francis Marion University *B, T*
Furman University *T*
Limestone College *B*
Morris College *B, T*
South Carolina State University *B, T*
Southern Wesleyan University *B, T*
University of South Carolina
  Aiken *B, T*
Wofford College *T*

South Dakota

Augustana College *B, T*
Black Hills State University *B*
Dakota State University *B, T*
Dakota Wesleyan University *B, T*
Mount Marty College *B*
Northern State University *B, T*
University of Sioux Falls *T*
University of South Dakota *B, M, T*

Tennessee

Belmont University *B, M, T*
Bryan College *T*
Christian Brothers University *B, M, T*
Cumberland University *B, T*
Freed-Hardeman University *B, T*
King College *T*
Lambuth University *B, T*
Lee University *B*
Lincoln Memorial University *B, T*
Lipscomb University *B, T*
Maryville College *B, T*
Middle Tennessee State
  University *M, T*
Southern Adventist University *B*
Tennessee Technological University *T*
Tennessee Temple University *B*
Trevecca Nazarene University *B, T*
Tusculum College *B, T*
Union University *B, T*
University of Memphis *T*
University of Tennessee
  Chattanooga *B, T*
  Martin *B*
Vanderbilt University *M, D*

Texas

Abilene Christian University *B, T*
Baylor University *B, T*
Del Mar College *A*
East Texas Baptist University *B*
Hardin-Simmons University *B, T*
Houston Baptist University *B, T*
Howard Payne University *B, T*
Jarvis Christian College *B, T*

Lamar University B, M, T
Laredo Community College A
LeTourneau University B, T
Lubbock Christian University B
McMurry University T
Prairie View A&M University M
St. Edward's University B, T
St. Mary's University T
Schreiner University B
Stephen F. Austin State University M
Tarleton State University T
Texas A&M University
    Commerce T
    Kingsville T
Texas Christian University B
Texas College B, T
Texas Lutheran University B, T
Texas State University: San
    Marcos M, T
Texas Wesleyan University B, T
University of Dallas T
University of Houston M, T
University of Houston
    Clear Lake T
    Victoria M
University of Mary Hardin-Baylor B, T
University of Texas
    Arlington T
    Austin M, D
    Dallas M, T
    Pan American M
    San Antonio M, T
West Texas A&M University T

Utah
Brigham Young University B, M
Southern Utah University B, T
University of Utah B, M
Utah State University B
Utah Valley State College B
Weber State University B

Vermont
Castleton State College B, T
Johnson State College B
St. Michael's College T
University of Vermont B

Virginia
Averett University B, M, T
Bluefield College T
Bridgewater College T
Eastern Mennonite University T
Hampton University M
Hollins University T
James Madison University M, T
Liberty University B, M, T
Longwood University B, T
Old Dominion University B, T
Radford University T
St. Paul's College T
University of Virginia's College at
    Wise T

Washington
Central Washington University B, M, T
Heritage University B, M
Northwest University T
Seattle Pacific University B, T
Washington State University B, M, T
Western Washington University B
Whitworth College B, T

West Virginia
Alderson-Broaddus College T
Bethany College B
Concord University B, M, T
Ohio Valley University B
Salem International University T
Shepherd University T
West Liberty State College B
West Virginia State University B
West Virginia University T

West Virginia Wesleyan College B

Wisconsin
Carroll College B, T
Carthage College T
Concordia University Wisconsin B
Edgewood College B
Lakeland College T
Lawrence University T
Maranatha Baptist Bible College B
Marian College of Fond du Lac B, T
Marquette University B, M
Mount Mary College B, T
Northland College T
St. Norbert College T
Silver Lake College T
University of Wisconsin
    Green Bay T
    Oshkosh M, T
    Parkside T
    Platteville B
    River Falls T
    Superior B, T
    Whitewater B
Viterbo University B, T

Wyoming
Eastern Wyoming College A

Mechanical drafting/CAD/CADD

Alabama
Gadsden State Community
    College C, A
Lawson State Community
    College C, A

Arkansas
East Arkansas Community
    College C, A

California
Ohlone College C
Sierra College C, A

Colorado
IntelliTec College: Grand Junction A
Westwood College of Technology
    South A

Connecticut
Naugatuck Valley Community
    College C

Florida
New England Institute of
    Technology A
Palm Beach Community College C

Georgia
Albany Technical College C
Northwestern Technical College C, A
Southwest Georgia Technical
    College C

Illinois
City Colleges of Chicago
    Wright College C, A
John Wood Community College A
Kaskaskia College C
Moraine Valley Community College C
Morton College C
Parkland College C

Indiana
Purdue University A, B

Iowa
Des Moines Area Community
    College C, A

Hawkeye Community College A
Indian Hills Community College A
Iowa Lakes Community College A

Kentucky
Louisville Technical Institute C, A

Massachusetts
Benjamin Franklin Institute of
    Technology A
North Shore Community College C
Springfield Technical Community
    College C

Michigan
Baker College
    of Muskegon A
Eastern Michigan University B
Mott Community College A
Oakland Community College C, A

Minnesota
Alexandria Technical College C, A
Central Lakes College C
Minnesota State Community and
    Technical College - Fergus
    Falls C, A
Northwest Technical Institute A
Rochester Community and Technical
    College C
St. Cloud Technical College C, A
St. Paul College C, A

New Jersey
Bergen Community College A

New Mexico
San Juan College A

New York
Cayuga County Community
    College C, A
Erie Community College
    South Campus A
Mohawk Valley Community College C

North Carolina
Central Piedmont Community
    College C
Davidson County Community
    College C
Isothermal Community College C, A
Piedmont Community College C

North Dakota
North Dakota State College of
    Science A

Ohio
Edison State Community College C, A

Oklahoma
Cameron University A, B
Platt College
    Tulsa C

Pennsylvania
Butler County Community College A
Penn State
    University Park C
South Hills School of Business &
    Technology C
Triangle Tech
    DuBois A
    Erie A
    Greensburg A

South Carolina
Aiken Technical College A
Greenville Technical College C, A
Spartanburg Technical College C

York Technical College C, A

South Dakota
Southeast Technical Institute A

Tennessee
Northeast State Technical Community
    College C, A

Texas
San Antonio College C, A

Wisconsin
Fox Valley Technical College A
Gateway Technical College C
Lakeshore Technical College A
Milwaukee Area Technical
    College C, A
Western Wisconsin Technical
    College A
Wisconsin Indianhead Technical
    College A

Mechanical engineering

Alabama
Alabama Agricultural and Mechanical
    University B
Auburn University B, M, D
Tuskegee University B, M
University of Alabama B, M, D
University of Alabama
    Birmingham B, M, D
    Huntsville B, M, D
University of South Alabama B, M

Alaska
University of Alaska
    Fairbanks B, M

Arizona
Arizona State University B, M, D
Central Arizona College A
Northern Arizona University B
University of Arizona B, M, D

Arkansas
Arkansas Tech University B
Harding University B
University of Arkansas B, M

California
California Institute of
    Technology B, M, D
California Maritime Academy B
California Polytechnic State
    University: San Luis Obispo B
California State Polytechnic
    University: Pomona B, M
California State University
    Chico B
    Fresno B, M
    Fullerton B, M
    Long Beach B, M
    Los Angeles B, M
    Northridge B, M
    Sacramento B, M
City College of San Francisco A
De Anza College A
Loyola Marymount University B, M
San Diego State University B, M
San Francisco State University B
San Jose State University B, M
Santa Clara University B, M, D
Stanford University B, M, D
University of California
    Berkeley B, M, D
    Davis B, M, D
    Irvine B, M, D
    Los Angeles B, M, D
    Riverside B, M, D

San Diego *B, M, D*
Santa Barbara *B, M, D*
University of California: Merced *B*
University of San Diego *B*
University of Southern
California *B, M, D*
University of the Pacific *B*

Colorado

Colorado State University *B, M, D*
United States Air Force Academy *B*
University of Colorado
Boulder *B, M, D*
Colorado Springs *B, M*
Denver and Health Sciences
Center *B, M*
University of Denver *B, M*

Connecticut

Fairfield University *B*
Trinity College *B*
United States Coast Guard Academy *B*
University of Bridgeport *M*
University of Connecticut *B, M, D*
University of Hartford *B, M*
University of New Haven *B, M*
Yale University *B, M, D*

Delaware

University of Delaware *B, M, D*

District of Columbia

Catholic University of
America *B, M, D*
George Washington University *B, M*
Howard University *B, M, D*
University of the District of
Columbia *B*

Florida

Embry-Riddle Aeronautical
University *B*
Florida Agricultural and Mechanical
University *B, M, D*
Florida Atlantic University *B, M, D*
Florida Institute of
Technology *B, M, D*
Florida International
University *B, M, D*
Florida State University *B, M, D*
Jacksonville University *B*
University of Central Florida *B, M, D*
University of Florida *A, B, M*
University of Miami *B, M, D*
University of North Florida *B*
University of South Florida *B, M, D*

Georgia

Georgia Institute of
Technology *B, M, D*
Mercer University *M*

Hawaii

University of Hawaii
Manoa *B, M, D*

Idaho

Boise State University *B, M*
Brigham Young University-Idaho *B*
Idaho State University *B, M*
University of Idaho *B, M, D*

Illinois

Bradley University *B, M*
Dominican University *B*
Illinois Institute of
Technology *B, M, D*
Northern Illinois University *B, M*
Northwestern University *B, M, D*
Southern Illinois University
Carbondale *B, M*

Southern Illinois University
Edwardsville *B, M*
University of Illinois
Chicago *B, M, D*
Urbana-Champaign *B, M, D*

Indiana

Indiana Institute of Technology *B*
Indiana University
East *A*
Indiana University-Purdue University
Fort Wayne *B*
Indiana University-Purdue University
Indianapolis *B, M, D*
Purdue University *B, M, D*
Purdue University
Calumet *B*
Rose-Hulman Institute of
Technology *B, M*
Tri-State University *B*
University of Evansville *B*
University of Notre Dame *B, M, D*
Valparaiso University *B*
Vincennes University *A*

Iowa

Dordt College *B*
Iowa State University *B, M, D*
University of Iowa *B, M, D*
William Penn University *B*

Kansas

Kansas State University *B, M, D*
University of Kansas *B, M, D*
Wichita State University *B, M, D*

Kentucky

University of Kentucky *B, M, D*
University of Louisville *B, M, D*
Western Kentucky University *B*

Louisiana

Louisiana State University and
Agricultural and Mechanical
College *B, M, D*
Louisiana Tech University *B*
Southern University and Agricultural
and Mechanical College *B*
University of Louisiana at
Lafayette *B, M*
University of New Orleans *B*

Maine

University of Maine *B, M, D*

Maryland

Johns Hopkins University *B, M, D*
United States Naval Academy *B*
University of Maryland
Baltimore County *B, M, D*
College Park *B, M, D*

Massachusetts

Boston University *B, M, D*
Bristol Community College *A*
Franklin W. Olin College of
Engineering *B*
Massachusetts Institute of
Technology *B, M, D*
Northeastern University *B, M, D*
Smith College *B*
Tufts University *B, M, D*
University of Massachusetts
Amherst *B, M, D*
Dartmouth *B, M*
Lowell *A, B, M, D*
Wentworth Institute of Technology *B*
Western New England College *B*
Worcester Polytechnic
Institute *B, M, D*

Michigan

Andrews University *B*
Baker College
of Flint *B*
Calvin College *B*
Central Michigan University *B*
Delta College *A*
Grand Valley State University *B, M*
Kettering University *B, M*
Lake Superior State University *B*
Lawrence Technological
University *B, M*
Michigan State University *B, M, D*
Michigan Technological
University *B, M, D, T*
Northern Michigan University *B*
Oakland University *B, M, D*
Saginaw Valley State University *B*
University of Detroit Mercy *B, M, D*
University of Michigan *B, M, D*
University of Michigan
Dearborn *B, M*
Wayne State University *B, M, D*
Western Michigan University *B, M, D*

Minnesota

Minnesota State University
Mankato *B*
Northwest Technical Institute *A*
St. Cloud State University *B*
University of Minnesota
Duluth *B*
Twin Cities *B, M, D*
University of St. Thomas *B*
Winona State University *B*

Mississippi

Mississippi State University *B, M*
University of Mississippi *B*

Missouri

East Central College *A*
St. Louis University *B*
University of Missouri
Columbia *B, M, D*
Kansas City *B, M*
Rolla *B, M, D*
St. Louis *B*
Washington University in St.
Louis *B, M, D*

Montana

Montana State University
Bozeman *B, M*
Montana Tech of the University of
Montana *B*

Nebraska

University of Nebraska
Lincoln *B, M*

Nevada

University of Nevada
Las Vegas *B, M, D*
Reno *B, M, D*

New Hampshire

Daniel Webster College *B*
University of New Hampshire *B, M, D*

New Jersey

The College of New Jersey *B*
New Jersey Institute of
Technology *B, M, D*
Princeton University *B, M, D*
Rowan University *B*
Rutgers, The State University of New
Jersey
Camden Regional Campus *B*
New Brunswick/Piscataway
Campus *B, M, D*
Newark Regional Campus *B*

Stevens Institute of
Technology *B, M, D*

New Mexico

New Mexico Institute of Mining and
Technology *B*
New Mexico State University *B, M*
University of New Mexico *B, M*

New York

Alfred University *B, M*
City University of New York
City College *B, M, D*
LaGuardia Community College *A*
Clarkson University *B, M, D*
Columbia University
Fu Foundation School of
Engineering and Applied
Science *B, M, D*
Cooper Union for the Advancement of
Science and Art *B, M*
Cornell University *B, M, D*
Hofstra University *B*
Manhattan College *B, M*
New York Institute of Technology *B*
Polytechnic University *B, M, D*
Rensselaer Polytechnic
Institute *B, M, D*
Rochester Institute of
Technology *B, M*
State University of New York
Binghamton *B, M, D*
Buffalo *B, M, D*
College of Environmental Science
and Forestry *B, M, D*
College of Technology at
Alfred *A, B*
Maritime College *B*
Stony Brook *B, M, D*
Syracuse University *B, M, D*
Union College *B*
United States Military Academy *B*
University of Rochester *B, M, D*

North Carolina

Duke University *B, M, D*
North Carolina Agricultural and
Technical State
University *B, M, D*
North Carolina State
University *B, M, D*
University of North Carolina
Charlotte *B, M, D*
Western Piedmont Community
College *A*

North Dakota

North Dakota State University *B, M, D*
University of North Dakota *B, M*

Ohio

Case Western Reserve
University *B, M, D*
Cedarville University *B*
Cleveland State University *B, M, D*
Miami University
Oxford Campus *B*
Ohio Northern University *B*
Ohio State University
Columbus Campus *B, M, D*
Ohio University *B, M*
University of Akron *B, M*
University of Cincinnati *B, M, D*
University of Dayton *B, M, D*
University of Toledo *B, M*
Wright State University *B*
Youngstown State University *B, M*

Oklahoma

Oklahoma Christian University *B*
Oklahoma State University *B, M, D*
Oral Roberts University *B*
University of Oklahoma *B, M, D*

University of Tulsa *B, M, D*

Oregon

George Fox University *B*
Oregon State University *B, M, D*
Portland State University *B, M, D*
University of Portland *B, M*

Pennsylvania

Bucknell University *B, M*
Carnegie Mellon University *B, M, D*
Drexel University *B, M, D*
Gannon University *B, M*
Gettysburg College *B*
Grove City College *B*
Lafayette College *B*
Lehigh Carbon Community College *A*
Lehigh University *B, M, D*
Penn State
   Abington *B*
   Altoona *B*
   Beaver *B*
   Berks *B*
   Delaware County *B*
   Dubois *B*
   Erie, The Behrend College *B*
   Fayette *B*
   Harrisburg *B*
   Hazleton *B*
   Lehigh Valley *B*
   McKeesport *B*
   Mont Alto *B*
   New Kensington *B*
   Schuylkill - Capital College *B*
   Shenango *B*
   University Park *B, M, D*
   Wilkes-Barre *B*
   Worthington Scranton *B*
   York *B*
Temple University *B, M*
University of Pennsylvania *B, M, D*
University of Pittsburgh *B, M, D*
Villanova University *B, M*
Widener University *B, M*
Wilkes University *B*
York College of Pennsylvania *B*

Puerto Rico

Inter American University of Puerto
   Rico
   Bayamon Campus *B*
Turabo University *B*
Universidad Politecnica de Puerto
   Rico *B*
University of Puerto Rico
   Bayamon University College *A*
   Carolina Regional College *A*
   Mayaguez *B, M*

Rhode Island

Brown University *B, M, D*
New England Institute of
   Technology *A, B*
University of Rhode Island *B, M, D*

South Carolina

Clemson University *B, M, D*
University of South Carolina *B, M, D*

South Dakota

Lake Area Technical Institute *A*
South Dakota School of Mines and
   Technology *B, M*
South Dakota State University *B*

Tennessee

Chattanooga State Technical
   Community College *A*
Christian Brothers University *B*
Tennessee Technological
   University *B, M, D*
Union University *B*
University of Memphis *B, M*

University of Tennessee
   Knoxville *B, M, D*
Vanderbilt University *B, M, D*

Texas

Baylor University *B, M*
Lamar University *B, M*
LeTourneau University *B*
Midwestern State University *B*
Prairie View A&M University *B*
Rice University *B, M, D*
Southern Methodist
   University *B, M, D*
Texas A&M University *B, M, D*
Texas A&M University
   Kingsville *B, M*
Texas Tech University *B, M, D*
University of Houston *B, M, D*
University of Texas
   Arlington *B, M, D*
   Austin *B, M, D*
   El Paso *B, M*
   Pan American *B, M*
   San Antonio *B, M*
   Tyler *B*
West Texas A&M University *B*

Utah

Brigham Young University *B, M, D*
Salt Lake Community College *A*
University of Utah *B, M, D*
Utah State University *B, M, D*

Vermont

Norwich University *B*
University of Vermont *B, M, D*
Vermont Technical College *A*

Virginia

John Tyler Community College *A*
Old Dominion University *B, M, D*
University of Virginia *B, M, D*
Virginia Commonwealth University *B*
Virginia Military Institute *B*
Virginia Polytechnic Institute and
   State University *B, M, D*

Washington

Gonzaga University *B*
Henry Cogswell College *B*
Saint Martin's University *B*
Seattle University *B*
Shoreline Community College *A*
University of Washington *B, M, D*
Walla Walla College *B*
Washington State University *B, M, D*

West Virginia

Potomac State College of West Virginia
   University *A*
West Virginia University *B, M, D*
West Virginia University Institute of
   Technology *B*

Wisconsin

Marquette University *B, M, D*
Milwaukee School of Engineering *B*
University of Wisconsin
   Madison *B, M, D*
   Milwaukee *B*
   Platteville *B*
Waukesha County Technical
   College *A*

Wyoming

University of Wyoming *B, M, D*

Mechanical engineering technology

Alabama

Gadsden State Community
   College *C, A*

California

California State University
   Sacramento *B*
Diablo Valley College *C*

Colorado

Colorado State University
   Pueblo *B*

Connecticut

Central Connecticut State
   University *B*
Naugatuck Valley Community
   College *A*
University of Hartford *B*

Georgia

Georgia Southern University *B*
Macon State College *A*
Southern Polytechnic State
   University *B*

Illinois

College of Lake County *C, A*
McHenry County College *C, A*
Parkland College *C*

Indiana

Indiana State University *B*
Indiana University-Purdue University
   Fort Wayne *A, B*
Indiana University-Purdue University
   Indianapolis *A, B*

Kansas

Pittsburg State University *B*

Maryland

Community College of Baltimore
   County *C, A*
Hagerstown Community College *C, A*

Massachusetts

Benjamin Franklin Institute of
   Technology *A*
Bristol Community College *A*
Northeastern University *B*
Springfield Technical Community
   College *C, A*
Wentworth Institute of
   Technology *A, B*

Michigan

Andrews University *A, B*
Central Michigan University *B*
Eastern Michigan University *B*
Ferris State University *A, B*
Lawrence Technological University *A*
Michigan Technological University *B*
Mott Community College *A*
Wayne State University *B*

Minnesota

Hennepin Technical College *C, A*
Minnesota State University
   Mankato *B*
Northwest Technical Institute *A*
Rochester Community and Technical
   College *A*
St. Cloud State University *B*

Missouri

Lincoln University *B*

St. Louis Community College
   St. Louis Community College at
     Florissant Valley *A*

Nevada

Community College of Southern
   Nevada *C, A*

New Jersey

Fairleigh Dickinson University
   Metropolitan Campus *B*
Raritan Valley Community College *A*
Thomas Edison State College *A, B*
Union County College *A*

New York

Broome Community College *A*
Cayuga County Community College *A*
City University of New York
   New York City College of
     Technology *A*
Erie Community College
   North Campus *A*
Jamestown Community College *A*
Mohawk Valley Community College *A*
New York Institute of Technology *A*
Niagara County Community
   College *A*
Rochester Institute of Technology *B*
State University of New York
   College at Buffalo *B*
   College of Agriculture and
     Technology at Morrisville *A*
   College of Technology at Canton *A*
   Farmingdale *A, B*
   Institute of Technology at
     Utica/Rome *B*
Tompkins-Cortland Community
   College *A*

North Carolina

Cape Fear Community College *C, A*
Catawba Valley Community College *A*
Central Piedmont Community
   College *A*
Edgecombe Community College *C*
Guilford Technical Community
   College *C, A*
Isothermal Community College *A*
Lenoir Community College *C, A*
University of North Carolina
   Charlotte *B*
Wilson Technical Community
   College *A*

Ohio

Bowling Green State University *B*
Cincinnati State Technical and
   Community College *A*
Edison State Community College *C, A*
James A. Rhodes State College *A*
Kent State University
   Ashtabula Regional Campus *A*
   Trumbull Campus *A*
   Tuscarawas Campus *A*
Lakeland Community College *C, A*
Marion Technical College *A*
Miami University
   Hamilton Campus *A*
   Oxford Campus *A*
Owens Community College
   Toledo *A*
Sinclair Community College *C, A*
University of Akron *A, B*
University of Dayton *B*
University of Toledo *C, A, B*
Youngstown State University *A, B*

Oklahoma

Oklahoma Christian University *B*
Oklahoma State University *B*

Oregon

Oregon Institute of Technology *B*

Pennsylvania

Delaware County Community
College *A*
Harrisburg Area Community
College *C, A*
Lehigh Carbon Community College *A*
Luzerne County Community
College *C, A*
Penn State
Altoona *A*
Berks *A*
Dubois *A*
Fayette *A*
Hazleton *A*
New Kensington *A*
Shenango *A*
York *A*
Pennsylvania College of Technology *B*
Point Park University *A, B*
University of Pittsburgh
Johnstown *B*
Williamson Free School of Mechanical
Trades *C*

Puerto Rico

Turabo University *B*

Rhode Island

Community College of Rhode
Island *C, A*

South Carolina

Greenville Technical College *A*
Spartanburg Technical College *A*
York Technical College *A*

South Dakota

Southeast Technical Institute *A*

Tennessee

Pellissippi State Technical Community
College *A*

Texas

LeTourneau University *B*
Palo Alto College *C*
Texas A&M University
Galveston *B*
Texas Tech University *B*
University of Houston
Downtown *B*
University of Texas
Brownsville *B*

Utah

Salt Lake Community College *A*

Virginia

John Tyler Community College *C, A*
Old Dominion University *B*
Piedmont Virginia Community
College *A*
Virginia State University *B*

Washington

Central Washington University *B*
Clover Park Technical College *A*
Shoreline Community College *A*

Wisconsin

Gateway Technical College *A*
Milwaukee School of Engineering *B*
Western Wisconsin Technical
College *A*

Mechanics/repairers, general

Alabama

Central Alabama Community
College *C*
Enterprise-Ozark Community
College *A*
George C. Wallace State Community
College
Selma *A*
Lawson State Community College *C*
Virginia College at Huntsville *C*

Alaska

University of Alaska
Anchorage *C, A*

Arkansas

Pulaski Technical College *C*
Southeast Arkansas College *C*
University of Arkansas
Community College at
Batesville *C, A*

California

Allan Hancock College *C, A*
Cerritos Community College *A*
College of the Canyons *A*
College of the Redwoods *C*
Columbia College *C*
Fresno City College *C, A*
Imperial Valley College *C, A*
Las Positas College *C*
Long Beach City College *C, A*
Modesto Junior College *C, A*
Palomar College *C, A*
Riverside Community College *C, A*
San Jose City College *C*
Shasta College *C, A*
WyoTech Institute: Fremont *C, A*
Yuba Community College
District *C, A*

Colorado

Colorado School of Trades *A*
Denver Automotive & Diesel
College *C, A*
Otero Junior College *C*
Red Rocks Community College *C, A*
Westwood College of Technology *C, A*

Connecticut

Gateway Community College *A*
Three Rivers Community College *A*

Florida

Brevard Community College *C*
Florida Career College: Miami *C, A*
Florida Community College at
Jacksonville *C*
Seminole Community College *C*

Georgia

Columbus Technical College *C*
Southwest Georgia Technical
College *C*
West Georgia Technical College *A*

Hawaii

University of Hawaii
Honolulu Community College *C, A*

Idaho

Boise State University *C*
Eastern Idaho Technical College *C, A*
Idaho State University *A*
Lewis-Clark State College *C, A, B*
North Idaho College *C*

Illinois

Danville Area Community College *A*
Kankakee Community College *C, A*
Richland Community College *A*
Southwestern Illinois College *C, A*
Triton College *C*

Indiana

Ivy Tech State College
Ivy Tech Community College:
Bloomington *C, A*
Ivy Tech Community College:
Central Indiana *C, A*
Ivy Tech Community College:
Columbus *C, A*
Ivy Tech Community College: East
Central *C, A*
Ivy Tech Community College:
Kokomo *C, A*
Ivy Tech Community College:
Lafayette *C, A*
Ivy Tech Community College: North
Central *A*
Ivy Tech Community College:
Northeast *C, A*
Ivy Tech Community College:
Northwest *C, A*
Ivy Tech Community College: South
Central *C, A*
Ivy Tech Community College:
Southwest *C, A*
Ivy Tech Community College:
Wabash Valley *C, A*
Ivy Tech Community College:
Whitewater *C, A*
Lincoln Technical Institute *C, A*
Vincennes University *A*

Iowa

Iowa Western Community College *A*
Southeastern Community College
North Campus *A*

Kansas

Butler County Community
College *C, A*

Kentucky

Maysville Community College *C, A*

Louisiana

Nunez Community College *C*

Maine

Southern Maine Community
College *A*
Washington County Community
College *C, A*

Massachusetts

Benjamin Franklin Institute of
Technology *A*

Michigan

Bay de Noc Community College *C, A*
Glen Oaks Community College *C*
Lansing Community College *A*
Macomb Community College *C*
Muskegon Community College *C, A*
Oakland Community College *C, A*
Southwestern Michigan College *C, A*

Minnesota

Hennepin Technical College *C, A*
Mesabi Range Community and
Technical College *A*

Missouri

North Central Missouri College *A*

Nebraska

Mid-Plains Community College
Area *C, A*
Nebraska College of Technical
Agriculture *A*

New Jersey

Raritan Valley Community College *A*
Thomas Edison State College *A*

New Mexico

Luna Community College *C*
Mesalands Community College *C*

New York

State University of New York
College of Technology at Alfred *A*

North Carolina

Alamance Community College *C*
Forsyth Technical Community
College *C*
James Sprunt Community College *C*
Johnston Community College *C*
Mayland Community College *C*
Rockingham Community College *A*
Sandhills Community College *C*

Oklahoma

Oklahoma City Community College *A*

Oregon

Linn-Benton Community College *A*

Pennsylvania

Delaware County Community
College *C*
Johnson College *A*
Lincoln Technical Institute:
Philadelphia *C, A*
Penn Commercial Business and
Technical School *A*
Rosedale Technical Institute *C, A*

Puerto Rico

Electronic Data Processing College:
San Sebastian *A*

South Carolina

Central Carolina Technical College *C*
Greenville Technical College *C, A*
Tri-County Technical College *C*
Trident Technical College *C, A*
Williamsburg Technical College *C, A*
York Technical College *A*

South Dakota

Lake Area Technical Institute *A*
Southeast Technical Institute *A*

Tennessee

Chattanooga State Technical
Community College *C*
Northeast State Technical Community
College *C, A*
Southwest Tennessee Community
College *A*

Texas

Central Texas College *C, A*
Cisco Junior College *C, A*
Laredo Community College *C*
MTI College of Business and
Technology *C*
Texas Southern University *B*
Texas State Technical College
Waco *C, A*
Western Technical College *C, A*

Utah

Snow College *C, A*

Vermont

Community College of Vermont A

Virginia

ECPI College of Technology C, A
Virginia Highlands Community
College C
Virginia Western Community
College A

Washington

Bates Technical College A
Bellingham Technical College A
Edmonds Community College C, A
Walla Walla Community College C, A

West Virginia

West Virginia University at
Parkersburg A

Wisconsin

Nicolet Area Technical College C

Media studies

Alabama

Talladega College B
University of Alabama D

Arizona

Arizona State University B, M

Arkansas

Arkansas Tech University M
Ouachita Baptist University B

California

California State University
Fullerton B, M
Claremont McKenna College B
College of the Desert A
Foothill College C, A
Master's College B
National University B
Point Loma Nazarene University B
Pomona College B
University of California
Berkeley B
University of San Francisco B
Westmont College B
Woodbury University B
Yuba Community College
District C, A

Colorado

Colorado State University
Pueblo B
University of Denver M

Connecticut

Sacred Heart University B
University of Bridgeport B
University of New Haven C

District of Columbia

American University B

Florida

Florida State University B, M, D
Lynn University B, M
Manatee Community College A
Rollins College M
St. Leo University B
St. Thomas University B
Schiller International University M
University of Central Florida B, M
University of Miami B
University of North Florida B
University of West Florida B, M

Georgia

Brenau University B
Clark Atlanta University B
Georgia State University M, D
Mercer University B
Piedmont College B
Toccoa Falls College B
University of Georgia M, D
Valdosta State University B

Hawaii

Chaminade University of Honolulu B
Hawaii Pacific University M

Idaho

Idaho State University B

Illinois

Eureka College B
Greenville College B
Judson College B
Loyola University of Chicago B
Principia College B
Southern Illinois University
Carbondale M, D
Southern Illinois University
Edwardsville B, M
University of Illinois
Urbana-Champaign B
University of St. Francis B

Indiana

Ancilla College A
Calumet College of St. Joseph C, A, B
DePauw University B
Huntington University B
Indiana University
Bloomington D
South Bend B
Indiana University-Purdue University
Fort Wayne B
St. Joseph's College B
St. Mary-of-the-Woods College B
Taylor University B
University of Evansville B
University of Southern Indiana B
Valparaiso University A, B
Vincennes University A

Iowa

Briar Cliff University B
Buena Vista University B
Drake University B
Grand View College C, B
Loras College B
Luther College B
Morningside College B
St. Ambrose University B
Simpson College B
University of Iowa B
Waldorf College B

Kansas

Baker University B
Benedictine College B
Bethel College B
Central Christian College of
Kansas A, B
Kansas State University B
MidAmerica Nazarene University B
Newman University B
Washburn University of Topeka B

Louisiana

Centenary College of Louisiana B
Louisiana State University and
Agricultural and Mechanical
College B, M
Southern University and Agricultural
and Mechanical College B, M
Tulane University A, B
University of Louisiana at Lafayette B

University of Louisiana at Monroe B
Xavier University of Louisiana B

Maine

University of Southern Maine B

Maryland

Coppin State University B
Goucher College B

Massachusetts

American International College B
Bunker Hill Community College A
Cape Cod Community College A
Emerson College B
Massachusetts Institute of
Technology B, M
Massasoit Community College A
Newbury College A
Pine Manor College B
Salem State College B
Suffolk University B
Western New England College B
Worcester State College B

Michigan

Alma College B
Calvin College B
Cornerstone University A, B
Madonna University A, B
Michigan State University D
Northern Michigan University B
Olivet College B
University of Michigan
Flint B
Western Michigan University B

Minnesota

Augsburg College B
Bethel University B
Concordia College: Moorhead B
Concordia University: St. Paul B
Minnesota State University
Mankato B
Moorhead B
North Central University A, B
Ridgewater College A
St. Cloud State University B, M
Winona State University B

Mississippi

Alcorn State University B
Jackson State University B, M
Tougaloo College B

Missouri

Calvary Bible College and Theological
Seminary B
Lindenwood University B
Maryville University of Saint Louis B
Missouri Southern State University B
Missouri Valley College B
University of Missouri
Kansas City B
Westminster College B

Montana

Montana State University
Billings B

Nebraska

Doane College B
Hastings College B
Wayne State College B, T

New Hampshire

Colby-Sawyer College B
Franklin Pierce College B
University of New Hampshire B

New Jersey

Essex County College A

Union County College A
William Paterson University of New
Jersey M

New York

Adelphi University B
Adirondack Community College C, A
City University of New York
Hunter College B, M
Lehman College B
Queens College B, M
College of New Rochelle B, M
Five Towns College B
Hobart and William Smith Colleges B
Hofstra University B
Iona College B, M
Ithaca College B
Medaille College B
New York University M, D
Russell Sage College B
St. Bonaventure University B, M
State University of New York
Buffalo B, M
College at Brockport B
College at Buffalo B
College at Oneonta B
Purchase B
Syracuse University D
Vassar College B

North Carolina

Barton College B
Bennett College B
Johnson C. Smith University B
Meredith College B
North Carolina Central University B
Shaw University B
University of North Carolina
Asheville B
Chapel Hill B, M, D
Greensboro B
Pembroke B
Winston-Salem State University B

North Dakota

Bismarck State College A
North Dakota State University B, M

Ohio

Baldwin-Wallace College B
Lakeland Community College C
Miami University
Oxford Campus B
Mount Union College B
University of Akron B
University of Cincinnati
Raymond Walters College C
University of Dayton B
Washington State Community
College A
Wilmington College B
Wright State University B

Oklahoma

Northeastern Oklahoma Agricultural
and Mechanical College A
Oklahoma City University B
Oklahoma State University M

Oregon

Linfield College B
University of Oregon B
University of Portland B, M

Pennsylvania

Allegheny College B
Bloomsburg University of
Pennsylvania B
Elizabethtown College B
Harrisburg Area Community
College A
King's College B
La Salle University B

Lackawanna College *A*
Marywood University *M*
Penn State
  Abington *B*
  Altoona *B*
  Beaver *B*
  Berks *B*
  Delaware County *B*
  Dubois *B*
  Fayette *B*
  Hazleton *B*
  Lehigh Valley *B*
  McKeesport *B*
  Mont Alto *B*
  New Kensington *B*
  Schuylkill - Capital College *B*
  Shenango *B*
  University Park *B, M, D*
  Wilkes-Barre *B*
  Worthington Scranton *B*
Pennsylvania College of Technology *A*
Point Park University *B*
Susquehanna University *B*
University of Pittsburgh *B*
University of Pittsburgh
  Bradford *B*
Wilson College *A, B*
York College of Pennsylvania *B*

Rhode Island

Roger Williams University *B*

South Carolina

Aiken Technical College *C*
Anderson University *B*
Claflin University *B*
Francis Marion University *B*
University of South Carolina *B, M*
Voorhees College *B*

South Dakota

Black Hills State University *B*
University of South Dakota *B, M*

Tennessee

Belmont University *B*
East Tennessee State University *B*
Freed-Hardeman University *B*
Lipscomb University *B*
Middle Tennessee State
  University *B, M*
Southern Adventist University *B*
Trevecca Nazarene University *B*
University of Memphis *B, M, D*

Texas

East Texas Baptist University *B*
Hardin-Simmons University *B*
Houston Baptist University *B*
Midwestern State University *B*
Northwest Vista College *A*
St. Edward's University *B*
Southern Methodist University *B*
Texas A&M University
  Texarkana *B*
Texas Christian University *M*
Texas State University: San
  Marcos *B, M, T*
Texas Tech University *D*
Texas Woman's University *B*
University of Texas
  El Paso *B*
  San Antonio *B*
University of the Incarnate Word *B, M*
Wayland Baptist University *B*

Utah

Brigham Young University *M*
University of Utah *B*

Vermont

Castleton State College *B*
Champlain College *A, B*

Virginia

Bridgewater College *B*
Hampton University *B*
Norfolk State University *B, M*
Virginia Commonwealth
  . University *B, M*
Virginia State University *B*

Washington

Seattle University *B*
Trinity Lutheran College *B*
Walla Walla College *B*
Washington State University *B*

West Virginia

Mountain State University *B*
University of Charleston *B*

Wisconsin

Concordia University Wisconsin *B*
Edgewood College *B*
Marquette University *B, M*
University of Wisconsin
  Eau Claire *B*
  Superior *B*
Western Wisconsin Technical
  College *A*

Wyoming

Laramie County Community
  College *A*

Medical administrative assistant

Alabama

Faulkner State Community College *A*
Lawson State Community
  College *C, A*

Alaska

University of Alaska
  Fairbanks *C*

Arizona

Arizona Institute of Business and
  Technology
  International Institute of the
    Americas: Mesa *C*
Central Arizona College *C, A*
Cochise College *A*
Coconino County Community
  College *A*
Gateway Community College *C*
International Institute of the Americas
  Phoenix *C*
  Tucson *C*
International Institute of the
  Americas: West Valley *C*
Yavapai College *C, A*

Arkansas

Arkansas Tech University *C*
National Park Community College *A*

California

Antelope Valley College *C, A*
Barstow College *C*
Butte College *C, A*
Chaffey College *C*
City College of San Francisco *A*
College of the Redwoods *C*
Columbia College *C*
De Anza College *C*
East Los Angeles College *C*
Empire College *C, A*
Fresno City College *C, A*
Gavilan Community College *C*
Glendale Community College *C, A*

Heald College
  Rancho Cordova *C, A*
  Salinas *A*
Humphreys College *C, A, B*
Lake Tahoe Community College *C*
Lassen College *C*
Los Angeles City College *C, A*
Los Angeles Harbor College *C, A*
MTI College *C*
Merced College *C, A*
Mount San Antonio College *C, A*
Palomar College *C, A*
Pasadena City College *C, A*
Riverside Community College *C, A*
Sacramento City College *C, A*
San Joaquin Valley College Inc. *A*
Santa Rosa Junior College *C*
Shasta College *C*
Sierra College *C, A*
Skyline College *C, A*
Solano Community College *C, A*
Ventura College *C, A*
West Hills Community College *C, A*
Western Career College
  San Leandro *C*

Colorado

Blair College *C, A*
Community College of Aurora *A*
National American University
  Denver *A*
Northeastern Junior College *A*
Otero Junior College *A*
Parks College *A*
Pueblo Community College *C, A*
Red Rocks Community College *C, A*

Connecticut

Briarwood College *C, A*
Gateway Community College *A*
Gibbs College *C*
Middlesex Community College *A*
Quinebaug Valley Community
  College *C*
Three Rivers Community College *A*
Tunxis Community College *C, A*

Delaware

Delaware Technical and Community
  College
  Owens Campus *A*
  Stanton/Wilmington Campus *A*

Florida

Broward Community College *C*
Daytona Beach Community College *A*
Florida Community College at
  Jacksonville *C, A*
Florida Technical College
  Deland *A*
Indian River Community College *C*
Miami Dade College *A*
Palm Beach Community College *C*
Pasco-Hernando Community
  College *C*
Santa Fe Community College *A*
Seminole Community College *A*
South Florida Community
  College *C, A*
Southwest Florida College *A*
Tallahassee Community College *C*
Valencia Community College *A*

Georgia

Augusta Technical Institute *C*
Chattahoochee Technical College *C*
Gwinnett College *C, A*

Hawaii

Hawaii Business College *A*
Heald College
  Honolulu *A*

Idaho

Idaho State University *C, A*
North Idaho College *A*

Illinois

Career Colleges of Chicago *A*
Danville Area Community
  College *C, A*
Elgin Community College *A*
Illinois Eastern Community Colleges
  Olney Central College *C, A*
John Wood Community College *A*
Joliet Junior College *A*
Kankakee Community College *A*
Kaskaskia College *C*
Lincoln Land Community College *C*
Midstate College *C, A*
Northwestern Business College *A*
Rockford Business College *A*
Sauk Valley Community College *C, A*
Waubonsee Community College *C*
William Rainey Harper College *C, A*

Indiana

Brown Mackie College: Michigan
  City *C, A*
International Business College *C, A*
Professional Careers Institute *C, A*
Sawyer College *C, A*
Vincennes University *A*

Iowa

Des Moines Area Community
  College *C, A*
Dordt College *A*
Ellsworth Community College *A*
Hawkeye Community College *C, A*
Iowa Lakes Community College *C*
Iowa Western Community College *A*
Kirkwood Community College *C, A*
Mercy College of Health Sciences *C*
Northeast Iowa Community
  College *A*
Southeastern Community College
  North Campus *A*
Western Iowa Tech Community
  College *A*

Kansas

Central Christian College of Kansas *A*
Labette Community College *A*
Pratt Community College *C, A*
Seward County Community
  College *C, A*
Washburn University of Topeka *A*

Kentucky

Ashland Community and Technical
  College *A*
Daymar College *C, A*
Draughons Junior College *A*
Elizabethtown Community and
  Technical College *C, A*
Jefferson Community College *C*
Maysville Community College *C, A*
National College of Business &
  Technology
  Danville *A*
  Florence *A*
  Lexington *A*
  Louisville *A*
  Pikeville *A*
  Richmond *A*
Owensboro Community College *C*
Somerset Community College *C, A*

Louisiana

ITI Technical College *A*
Nunez Community College *C*

Maine

Andover College *C, A*

Beal College *A*
Northern Maine Community
College *A*
Washington County Community
College *C*

Maryland
Allegany College of Maryland *A*
Baltimore City Community College *A*
College of Southern Maryland *C*
Community College of Baltimore
County *A*
Hagerstown Business College *C, A*
Hagerstown Community College *C, A*
Prince George's Community
College *C, A*

Massachusetts
Bay State College *A*
Bristol Community College *A*
Bunker Hill Community College *C, A*
Cape Cod Community College *C, A*
Gibbs College *A*
Holyoke Community College *C*
Marian Court College *C, A*
Mount Wachusett Community
College *C*
North Shore Community College *C, A*
Northern Essex Community
College *A*
Quinsigamond Community College *A*
Roxbury Community College *A*
Springfield Technical Community
College *A*

Michigan
Baker College
of Auburn Hills *C, A*
of Cadillac *A*
of Clinton Township *A*
of Flint *C, A*
of Jackson *C, A*
of Muskegon *C, A*
of Owosso *A*
of Port Huron *C, A*
Davenport University *A*
Delta College *A*
Glen Oaks Community College *C*
Grand Rapids Community College *A*
Kalamazoo Valley Community
College *C, A*
Kellogg Community College *A*
Kirtland Community College *C, A*
Lake Michigan College *A*
Lansing Community College *A*
Macomb Community College *C, A*
Mid Michigan Community College *A*
Monroe County Community
College *C, A*
Montcalm Community College *C, A*
Mott Community College *C, A*
Muskegon Community College *A*
Northern Michigan University *A*
St. Clair County Community
College *A*

Minnesota
Alexandria Technical College *A*
Anoka Technical College *C, A*
Anoka-Ramsey Community College *A*
Central Lakes College *C, A*
Century Community and Technical
College *C, A*
Dakota County Technical College *C, A*
Hennepin Technical College *C, A*
Hibbing Community College *A*
Lake Superior College *C, A*
Minnesota School of Business *C, A*
Minnesota State College - Southeast
Technical *C, A*
Minnesota State Community and
Technical College - Fergus
Falls *C, A*

Northland Community & Technical
College *C, A*
Northwest Technical College *C, A*
Rasmussen College
Mankato *C*
Minnetonka *C, A*
St. Cloud *C*
Ridgewater College *C, A*
Riverland Community College *C, A*
Rochester Community and Technical
College *A*
South Central College *A*

Mississippi
Meridian Community College *A*
Mississippi Gulf Coast Community
College
Jefferson Davis Campus *A*
Pearl River Community College *A*

Missouri
East Central College *C, A*
Everest College: Springfield *C, A*
Jefferson College *A*
Maple Woods Community College *C*
Northwest Missouri State
University *C*
Penn Valley Community College *C*
State Fair Community College *C, A*
Vatterott College: St. Joseph *A*

Montana
Flathead Valley Community College *A*
Helena College of Technology of the
University of Montana *C, A*
Miles Community College *A*
Montana State University
Billings *A*
College of Technology-Great Falls *A*
Montana Tech of the University of
Montana *A*
University of Montana: Missoula *A*

Nebraska
Hamilton College: Lincoln *A*
Vatterott College: Spring Valley *C, A*

Nevada
Truckee Meadows Community
College *A*

New Hampshire
McIntosh College *A*
New Hampshire Community
Technical College
Claremont *C*
Manchester *C, A*

New Jersey
Bergen Community College *C*
Essex County College *A*
Gloucester County College *C, A*
Mercer County Community College *C*

New Mexico
Clovis Community College *A*
Dona Ana Branch Community College
of New Mexico State
University *A*
International Institute of the
Americas *C*
New Mexico State University
Alamogordo *C*
Western New Mexico University *C, A*

New York
Bryant & Stratton Business Institute
Bryant & Stratton College:
Syracuse *A*
Bryant & Stratton College: Henrietta *A*
City University of New York
Hostos Community College *A*

Clinton Community College *C*
Elmira Business Institute *C, A*
Fulton-Montgomery Community
College *C*
Genesee Community College *C*
Globe Institute of Technology *C*
Herkimer County Community
College *A*
Hudson Valley Community College *A*
Interboro Institute *A*
Jamestown Business College *C, A*
Long Island Business Institute *C*
Nassau Community College *C, A*
New York Career Institute *A*
Olean Business Institute *C, A*
Rochester Business Institute *C, A*
Trocaire College *C*
Utica School of Commerce *C, A*

North Carolina
Alamance Community College *C, A*
Asheville-Buncombe Technical
Community College *C*
Beaufort County Community
College *C, A*
Blue Ridge Community College *C*
Caldwell Community College and
Technical Institute *C, A*
Central Carolina Community
College *A*
Cleveland Community College *C, A*
College of the Albemarle *A*
Craven Community College *C, A*
Durham Technical Community
College *A*
Gaston College *A*
Halifax Community College *A*
Johnston Community College *A*
King's College *C, A*
Lenoir Community College *A*
Martin Community College *C, A*
Mayland Community College *A*
Nash Community College *A*
Piedmont Community College *A*
Pitt Community College *C, A*
Rockingham Community College *A*
South Piedmont Community
College *C, A*
Wake Technical Community
College *A*
Wayne Community College *A*

North Dakota
Aakers College: Fargo *A*
Dickinson State University *A*
Lake Region State College *A*
Minot State University: Bottineau
Campus *A*

Ohio
Bowling Green State University:
Firelands College *C*
Bryant & Stratton College
Parma *A*
Columbus State Community
College *A*
Davis College *A*
ETI Technical College of Niles *A*
Edison State Community College *C, A*
Gallipolis Career College *A*
James A. Rhodes State College *A*
Jefferson Community College *A*
Marion Technical College *A*
Ohio Business College: Sandusky *C, A*
Ohio University
Chillicothe Campus *A*
Ohio Valley College of Technology *A*
Owens Community College
Toledo *C, A*
Sinclair Community College *C*
Southeastern Business College *A*
Southeastern Business College:
Lancaster *A*

Southwestern College of Business
Southwestern College: Franklin *A*
Stautzenberger College *C, A*
Trumbull Business College *A*
University of Akron *C, A*
University of Akron: Wayne College *A*
University of Cincinnati
Raymond Walters College *C, A*
University of Northwestern Ohio *A*
Wright State University *A*

Oklahoma
Eastern Oklahoma State College *A*
Northeastern Oklahoma Agricultural
and Mechanical College *C, A*
Oklahoma State University
Okmulgee *A*
Tulsa Community College *C, A*
Western Oklahoma State College *A*

Oregon
Blue Mountain Community College *A*
Chemeketa Community College *A*
Clackamas Community College *C*
Clatsop Community College *A*
Everest College: Portland *A*
Lane Community College *C*
Linn-Benton Community College *C, A*
Portland Community College *C*
Southwestern Oregon Community
College *C*
Treasure Valley Community College *A*
Umpqua Community College *A*

Pennsylvania
Academy of Medical Arts and
Business *C, A*
Berks Technical Institute *A*
Business Institute of Pennsylvania *A*
Business Institute of Pennsylvania
Meadville *A*
CHI Institute: Southampton *C*
Cambria-Rowe Business College *C, A*
Cambria-Rowe Business College:
Indiana *A*
Career Training Academy *C, A*
Central Pennsylvania College *A*
Commonwealth Technical Institute *A*
Community College of Beaver
County *A*
Consolidated School of Business
Lancaster *A*
York *A*
Douglas Education Center *A*
DuBois Business College *A*
DuBois Business College
Huntingdon *A*
Oil City *A*
Erie Business Center *C, A*
ICM School of Business & Medical
Careers *A*
Lackawanna College *A*
Laurel Business Institute *A*
Lehigh Valley College *A*
Mercyhurst College *C, A*
Newport Business Institute *A*
Newport Business Institute *A*
Northampton County Area
Community College *C, A*
Pennsylvania College of Technology *A*
Pennsylvania Institute of
Technology *A*
Reading Area Community
College *C, A*
Schuylkill Institute of Business &
Technology *C, A*
South Hills School of Business &
Technology *A*
University of Pittsburgh
Titusville *A*
West Virginia Career Institute *A*
Western School of Health and
Business Careers
Monroeville *C*

Westmoreland County Community
College *A*
York Technical Institute *C*
Yorktowne Business Institute *A*

Puerto Rico
Humacao Community College *C, A*
National College of Business &
Technology: Arecibo *A*
Turabo University *T*
Universidad del Este *C, A*

Rhode Island
Community College of Rhode
Island *A*
New England Institute of
Technology *A*

South Carolina
Aiken Technical College *C*
Florence-Darlington Technical
College *C*
Forrest Junior College *A*
Greenville Technical College *C*
Orangeburg-Calhoun Technical
College *C*
Spartanburg Technical College *C*
Tri-County Technical College *C*
Trident Technical College *C*
Williamsburg Technical College *C*
York Technical College *C*

South Dakota
Kilian Community College *A*
Lake Area Technical Institute *C*
Southeast Technical Institute *C*
Western Dakota Technical Institute *C*

Tennessee
Nashville State Community College *A*
National College of Business &
Technology
Tennessee *A*

Texas
Austin Community College *A*
Blinn College *C*
Central Texas College *C*
Coastal Bend College *A*
Del Mar College *C, A*
El Centro College *C*
El Paso Community College *C*
Frank Phillips College *A*
Galveston College *C, A*
Grayson County College *C*
Houston Community College
System *C, A*
Kilgore College *C*
Lamar State College at Orange *C, A*
Lamar State College at Port
Arthur *C, A*
Laredo Community College *A*
McLennan Community College *C, A*
North Harris Montgomery
Community College District *C, A*
Northeast Texas Community
College *C, A*
Odessa College *C, A*
St. Philip's College *A*
San Jacinto College
North *C*
South Plains College *A*
Southwestern Adventist University *B*
Tyler Junior College *C, A*
University of Texas
Brownsville *C, A*
Vernon College *C*

Utah
LDS Business College *A*
Provo College *A*
Salt Lake Community College *C*
Southern Utah University *C*

Virginia
Danville Community College *A*
ECPI College of Technology *C, A*
Mountain Empire Community
College *A*
New River Community College *C, A*
Southwest Virginia Community
College *A*
Tidewater Tech *C*
Virginia Western Community
College *A*

Washington
Bellingham Technical College *C*
Centralia College *C, A*
Clark College *A*
Columbia Basin College *C*
Edmonds Community College *C, A*
Everett Community College *C*
Green River Community College *A*
Lower Columbia College *A*
Peninsula College *C, A*
Pierce College *A*
Renton Technical College *C, A*
Shoreline Community College *C*
South Puget Sound Community
College *C, A*
Spokane Community College *C, A*
Walla Walla Community College *C, A*
Wenatchee Valley College *C*
Whatcom Community College *A*
Yakima Valley Community
College *C, A*

West Virginia
Bluefield State College *C, A*
Potomac State College of West Virginia
University *A*
Valley College of Technology *C*
West Virginia Business College *A*
West Virginia Northern Community
College *C*
West Virginia University Institute of
Technology *A*

Wisconsin
Blackhawk Technical College *C, A*
Bryant & Stratton College:
Milwaukee *A*
Chippewa Valley Technical College *C*
Fox Valley Technical College *C*
Lakeshore Technical College *A*
Madison Area Technical College *A*
Milwaukee Area Technical College *A*
Moraine Park Technical College *C, A*
Northcentral Technical College *A*
Northeast Wisconsin Technical
College *A*
Waukesha County Technical
College *C*
Wisconsin Indianhead Technical
College *A*

Wyoming
Western Wyoming Community
College *A*

Medical claims examiner

Indiana
Indiana Business College
Anderson *A*
Columbus *A*
Evansville *A*
Fort Wayne *A*
Lafayette *A*
Medical *A*
Terre Haute *A*

Pennsylvania
Career Training Academy:
Monroeville *C*

Puerto Rico
Inter American University of Puerto
Rico
Ponce Campus *C*

Washington
Clark College *C*

Medical/clinical assistant

Alabama
Central Alabama Community
College *A*
Community College of the Air
Force *A*
Enterprise-Ozark Community
College *A*
Faulkner University *A*
George C. Wallace State Community
College
George C. Wallace Community
College at Dothan *C, A*
South University *A*
Trenholm State Technical College *A*
Virginia College *A*
Wallace State Community College at
Hanceville *A*

Alaska
University of Alaska
Anchorage *A*
Fairbanks *A*

Arizona
Arizona Institute of Business and
Technology
International Institute of the
Americas: Mesa *C*
Central Arizona College *C, A*
Eastern Arizona College *C*
International Institute of the Americas
Phoenix *C*
Tucson *C*
International Institute of the
Americas: West Valley *C*
Lamson College *A*
Northland Pioneer College *C, A*

Arkansas
Arkansas Tech University *A*
National Park Community
College *C, A*
Remington College
Little Rock *C*
Southeast Arkansas College *A*
University of Arkansas
Cossatot Community College of the
A

California
Allan Hancock College *C, A*
Antelope Valley College *C, A*
Barstow College *C*
Butte College *A*
Cabrillo College *C, A*
Cerritos Community College *C, A*
Chabot College *C, A*
Citrus College *C, A*
City College of San Francisco *C, A*
College of San Mateo *C, A*
College of the Canyons *C*
College of the Redwoods *C*
Contra Costa College *A*
Cosumnes River College *C, A*
Cypress College *A*
De Anza College *C, A*
East Los Angeles College *A*

Empire College *C*
Fresno City College *C, A*
Glendale Community College *A*
Lake Tahoe Community College *C, A*
Long Beach City College *C, A*
MTI College *C*
Maric College: Sacramento *C*
Merced College *A*
Modesto Junior College *A*
Monterey Peninsula College *C, A*
Ohlone College *C, A*
Orange Coast College *C, A*
Palomar College *C, A*
Pasadena City College *C, A*
Platt College
Ontario *A*
Riverside Community College *C, A*
Saddleback College *C, A*
San Diego Mesa College *C, A*
San Joaquin Valley College Inc. *A*
Santa Ana College *C, A*
Santa Rosa Junior College *C*
Santiago Canyon College *A*
Shasta College *C*
Silicon Valley College
Western Career College:
Emeryville *C*
Western Career College: San Jose *A*
Victor Valley College *C, A*
West Valley College *C, A*
Western Career College
Pleasant Hill *A*

Colorado
Blair College *C, A*
Cambridge College *C, A*
Concorde Career College *C*
Heritage College *C*
IntelliTec College: Grand Junction *A*
Morgan Community College *C*
National American University
Denver *A*
Parks College *A*
Parks College: Aurora *C*
Remington College
Colorado Springs *C*
Westwood College of Technology *A*

Connecticut
Briarwood College *C, A*
Capital Community College *C, A*
Goodwin College *C, A*
Northwestern Connecticut
Community College *A*
Norwalk Community College *C*
Quinebaug Valley Community
College *A*
St. Vincent's College *C, A*

Delaware
Delaware Technical and Community
College
Owens Campus *C, A*
Stanton/Wilmington Campus *C, A*
Terry Campus *C, A*

Florida
Angley College *C, A*
Brevard Community College *C*
Broward Community College *C*
Central Florida College *A*
Florida Career College: Hialeah *C*
Florida Career College: Miami *C*
Florida Career College: Pembroke
Pines *C*
Florida Career College: West Palm
Beach *C*
Florida Community College at
Jacksonville *C*
Florida Metropolitan University
Brandon Campus *A*
Melbourne Campus *A*
Pinellas *A*

Tampa College A
Tampa College Lakeland A
Florida Metropolitan University:
    Orange Park A
Florida National College A
Florida Technical College
    Deland A
Indian River Community College C
International College A
Jones College A, B
Miami Dade College C, A
New England Institute of
    Technology C
Palm Beach Community College C
Pasco-Hernando Community
    College C
Remington College: Largo C
Seminole Community College C
South University: West Palm Beach
    Campus A
Southwest Florida College A
Southwest Florida College
    Tampa C, A
Ultrasound Diagnostic School
    Sanford-Brown Institute:
    Jacksonville C
Webster College: Holiday A

Georgia

Albany Technical College C
Athens Technical College C
Augusta Technical Institute C
Brown Mackie College: Atlanta C, A
Central Georgia Technical
    College C, A
Chattahoochee Technical College C
Clayton State University C, A
Columbus Technical College C
Darton College A
DeKalb Technical College C
Fort Valley State University A, B
Georgia Southwestern State
    University A
Gwinnett College C, A
High-Tech Institute: Atlanta A
Macon State College A
Middle Georgia College A
Northwestern Technical College A
Savannah Technical College A
South University A
Southwest Georgia Technical
    College C, A
West Georgia Technical College C

Hawaii

Hawaii Business College C
Heald College
    Honolulu A
Remington College
    Honolulu A
University of Hawaii
    Kapiolani Community College C, A

Idaho

College of Southern Idaho C
Eastern Idaho Technical College C, A
Idaho State University A
North Idaho College A

Illinois

College of DuPage C
College of Office Technology C
Fox College A
Illinois Central College C
Midstate College A
Moraine Valley Community College C
Northwestern Business College A
Parkland College C
Robert Morris College: Chicago C, A
Rockford Business College A
South Suburban College of Cook
    County C
Southwestern Illinois College C, A

Waubonsee Community College C
William Rainey Harper College C, A

Indiana

Brown Mackie College: Fort
    Wayne C, A
Indiana Business College A
Indiana Business College
    Anderson A
    Columbus A
    Evansville A
    Fort Wayne A
    Lafayette A
    Marion A
    Medical A
    Muncie A
    Terre Haute A
International Business College C, A
Ivy Tech State College
    Ivy Tech Community College:
        Central Indiana C, A
    Ivy Tech Community College:
        Columbus C, A
    Ivy Tech Community College: East
        Central C, A
    Ivy Tech Community College:
        Kokomo C, A
    Ivy Tech Community College:
        Lafayette C, A
    Ivy Tech Community College: North
        Central C, A
    Ivy Tech Community College:
        Northeast C, A
    Ivy Tech Community College:
        Northwest C, A
    Ivy Tech Community College: South
        Central C, A
    Ivy Tech Community College:
        Southeast C, A
    Ivy Tech Community College:
        Southwest C, A
    Ivy Tech Community College:
        Wabash Valley C, A
    Ivy Tech Community College:
        Whitewater A
Professional Careers Institute C, A
Sawyer College A
Sawyer College: Merrillville A

Iowa

Des Moines Area Community
    College C
Hamilton College C, A
Hamilton Technical College C
Iowa Central Community College C, A
Iowa Lakes Community College C
Iowa Western Community College C
Kaplan University C, A
Kirkwood Community College C, A
Marshalltown Community College C
North Iowa Area Community
    College C
Southeastern Community College
    North Campus A

Kansas

Barton County Community
    College C, A

Kentucky

Brown Mackie College:
    Hopkinsville C, A
Daymar College C, A
Eastern Kentucky University A, B
Jefferson Community College C
National College of Business &
    Technology
    Danville A
    Florence A
    Lexington A
    Louisville A
    Pikeville A
    Richmond A

Somerset Community College C, A
Southwestern College: Florence C, A
Spencerian College A
Spencerian College: Lexington C

Louisiana

Bossier Parish Community College A
Remington College
    Lafayette A

Maine

Andover College A
Beal College A
Kennebec Valley Community
    College A
Southern Maine Community
    College C

Maryland

Allegany College of Maryland C, A
Anne Arundel Community
    College C, A
Hagerstown Business College C, A
TESST College of Technology:
    Towson C

Massachusetts

Bay State College A
Becker College C
Bristol Community College C
Bunker Hill Community College C
Cape Cod Community College C
Gibbs College A
Holyoke Community College C
Massasoit Community College C
Middlesex Community College C, A
Mount Wachusett Community
    College A
Newbury College C, A
North Shore Community College C
Northern Essex Community
    College C
Quinsigamond Community
    College C, A
Springfield Technical Community
    College C, A

Michigan

Alpena Community College A
Baker College
    of Auburn Hills A
    of Cadillac A
    of Clinton Township A
    of Flint A
    of Jackson A
    of Muskegon C, A
    of Owosso A
    of Port Huron A
Bay de Noc Community College C
Davenport University C, A
Delta College A
Glen Oaks Community College C
Henry Ford Community College C
Jackson Community College C, A
Kalamazoo Valley Community
    College A
Kirtland Community College C, A
Lansing Community College A
Macomb Community College C, A
Mid Michigan Community College A
Montcalm Community College C
Muskegon Community College C
North Central Michigan College C
Northwestern Michigan College A
Oakland Community College C, A
Schoolcraft College C
Southwestern Michigan College C

Minnesota

Academy College C
Anoka Technical College C
Century Community and Technical
    College C

Dakota County Technical College C, A
Globe College C, A
High-Tech Institute A
Lake Superior College C
Minneapolis Business College A
Minnesota School of Business C, A
Northland Community & Technical
    College A
Rasmussen College
    Eagan C, A
    Mankato C, A
    Minnetonka C, A
Ridgewater College C, A

Mississippi

Antonelli College
    Jackson A

Missouri

Everest College: Springfield A
National American University
    Kansas City A
Vatterott College: Springfield C, A

Montana

Flathead Valley Community College A
Montana State University
    Billings A
    College of Technology-Great Falls A
University of Montana: Missoula A

Nebraska

Central Community College C, A
Hamilton College: Lincoln A
Nebraska Methodist College of
    Nursing and Allied Health C
Southeast Community College
    Lincoln Campus C
Vatterott College: Spring Valley C, A

Nevada

High-Tech Institute A
Las Vegas College A

New Hampshire

McIntosh College A
New Hampshire Community
    Technical College
    Claremont C
    Manchester C, A

New Jersey

Bergen Community College A
Hudson County Community
    College C, A
Ocean County College A

New Mexico

Eastern New Mexico University:
    Roswell Campus C, A
International Institute of the
    Americas C

New York

Broome Community College A
Bryant & Stratton Business Institute
    Bryant & Stratton College: Albany A
    Bryant & Stratton College:
        Buffalo C, A
    Bryant & Stratton College:
        Syracuse A
Bryant & Stratton College: Henrietta A
City University of New York
    Bronx Community College A
    Queensborough Community
        College C
Elmira Business Institute C, A
Globe Institute of Technology C
Mildred Elley C, A
Mohawk Valley Community
    College C, A

Niagara County Community
College *A*
Plaza College *A*
Rochester Business Institute *A*
Rockland Community College *C, A*
State University of New York
College of Technology at Alfred *A*
Suffolk County Community College *A*
Trocaire College *A*
Wood Tobe-Coburn School *A*

North Carolina
Cabarrus College of Health
Sciences *C, A*
Carteret Community College *C*
Central Carolina Community
College *A*
Central Piedmont Community
College *C, A*
College of the Albemarle *A*
Davidson County Community
College *C, A*
Edgecombe Community College *A*
Forsyth Technical Community
College *A*
Gaston College *A*
Guilford Technical Community
College *A*
Haywood Community College *C, A*
James Sprunt Community College *A*
Johnston Community College *A*
Lenoir Community College *A*
Martin Community College *C, A*
Miller-Motte Technical College *A*
Mitchell Community College *C*
Montgomery Community College *A*
Pamlico Community College *A*
Piedmont Community College *C*
Pitt Community College *A*
Richmond Community College *A*
South College *A*
South Piedmont Community
College *C, A*
Stanly Community College *C, A*
Surry Community College *A*
Tri-County Community College *A*
Vance-Granville Community
College *A*
Wake Technical Community
College *C, A*
Wayne Community College *A*
Western Piedmont Community
College *C, A*
Wilkes Community College *C, A*

North Dakota
Minot State University: Bottineau
Campus *C, A*

Ohio
AEC Southern Ohio College
Brown Mackie College: Akron *C, A*
Belmont Technical College *A*
Bradford School *C*
Bryant & Stratton College
Parma *A*
Cincinnati State Technical and
Community College *C, A*
Columbus State Community
College *C*
Cuyahoga Community College
Metropolitan Campus *C, A*
Davis College *A*
ETI Technical College of Niles *C, A*
Edison State Community College *A*
Hocking College *C, A*
James A. Rhodes State College *A*
Jefferson Community College *C, A*
Lakeland Community College *C*
Marion Technical College *C*
Ohio Institute of Photography and
Technology *C*
Ohio University *A*
Ohio Valley College of Technology *A*

Remington College
Cleveland *C*
Southern State Community College *A*
Stark State College of Technology *A*
Stautzenberger College *C, A*
Technology Education College *C, A*
University of Akron *C, A*
University of Akron: Wayne College *A*
University of Northwestern Ohio *C, A*
Youngstown State University *C, A*
Zane State College *C, A*

Oklahoma
Platt College
Tulsa *C*
Tulsa Community College *A*

Oregon
Central Oregon Community
College *C*
Chemeketa Community College *C*
Clackamas Community College *C*
Clatsop Community College *A*
Linn-Benton Community College *A*
Mount Hood Community College *A*
Pioneer Pacific College *C, A*
Pioneer Pacific College:
Springfield *C, A*
Portland Community College *C*
Southwestern Oregon Community
College *A*

Pennsylvania
Academy of Medical Arts and
Business *C, A*
Berks Technical Institute *A*
Bucks County Community
College *C, A*
Business Institute of Pennsylvania
Meadville *A*
Butler County Community
College *C, A*
CHI Institute: Broomall *C*
CHI Institute: Southampton *C*
Career Training Academy *C, A*
Career Training Academy:
Monroeville *A*
Central Pennsylvania College *A*
Community College of Allegheny
County *C, A*
Community College of Philadelphia *A*
Delaware County Community
College *C, A*
Douglas Education Center *A*
Erie Business Center *A*
Harrisburg Area Community
College *C, A*
ICM School of Business & Medical
Careers *C, A*
Lansdale School of Business *C, A*
Laurel Business Institute *A*
Lehigh Carbon Community College *A*
McCann School of Business
Pottsville *C*
Mount Aloysius College *A*
Schuylkill Institute of Business &
Technology *C, A*
Thompson Institute
Philadelphia *C*
York Technical Institute *A*
Yorktowne Business Institute *A*

Rhode Island
New England Institute of
Technology *A*

South Carolina
Aiken Technical College *C*
Central Carolina Technical College *C*
Forrest Junior College *C, A*
Horry-Georgetown Technical
College *C*
Midlands Technical College *C*

Miller-Motte Technical College *A*
Piedmont Technical College *C*
South University *A*
Spartanburg Technical College *C*
Technical College of the
Lowcountry *C*
Tri-County Technical College *C*
Trident Technical College *C*

South Dakota
Lake Area Technical Institute *C*
Presentation College *A*

Tennessee
Chattanooga State Technical
Community College *C*
Miller-Motte Technical College *A*
National College of Business &
Technology
Tennessee *A*
Northeast State Technical Community
College *A*
South College *A*
Southwest Tennessee Community
College *C*

Texas
El Centro College *C*
El Paso Community College *C, A*
Hallmark Institute of Technology *A*
Houston Community College
System *C*
Howard College *A*
Kilgore College *A*
Laredo Community College *A*
North Harris Montgomery
Community College District *C*
Remington College
Houston *C*
San Antonio College *C, A*
San Jacinto College
Central Campus *A*
Texas State Technical College
Harlingen *C, A*

Utah
Everest College: Salt Lake City *C, A*
LDS Business College *C*
Salt Lake Community College *C*
Stevens-Henager College *A*
Stevens-Henager College of
Business *C, A*
Utah Career College *C, A*

Virginia
Bryant & Stratton College: Virginia
Beach *A*
ECPI College of Technology *C, A*
Miller-Motte Technical College:
Lynchburg *A*
National College of Business &
Technology
Bluefield *A*
Charlottesville *A*
Danville *A*
Harrisonburg *A*
Lynchburg *A*
Salem *C*

Washington
Clark College *C, A*
Clover Park Technical College *C*
Everett Community College *C, A*
Highline Community College *A*
Lake Washington Technical
College *C, A*
Lower Columbia College *A*
North Seattle Community
College *C, A*
Olympic College *C, A*
Peninsula College *C, A*
Renton Technical College *C, A*
Skagit Valley College *A*

South Puget Sound Community
College *C, A*
Spokane Falls Community
College *C, A*
Wenatchee Valley College *C*
Whatcom Community College *C, A*
Yakima Valley Community
College *C, A*

West Virginia
Bluefield State College *A*
Corinthian Schools: National Institute
of Technology *A*
Huntington Junior College *C, A*
Mountain State College *A*
Mountain State University *A*

Wisconsin
Blackhawk Technical College *C*
Bryant & Stratton College:
Milwaukee *A*
Concordia University Wisconsin *C*
Gateway Technical College *C*
Lakeshore Technical College *C*
Madison Area Technical College *A*
Mid-State Technical College *C*
Milwaukee Area Technical College *C*
Nicolet Area Technical College *C, A*
Northeast Wisconsin Technical
College *C*
Southwest Wisconsin Technical
College *C*
Waukesha County Technical
College *C*
Western Wisconsin Technical
College *C*
Wisconsin Indianhead Technical
College *C*

Wyoming
Western Wyoming Community
College *A*

Medical illustrating

California
California State University
Long Beach *B*

Georgia
Clark Atlanta University *B*
Medical College of Georgia *M*

Illinois
University of Illinois
Chicago *M*

Iowa
Iowa State University *B*

Michigan
Alma College *B*
University of Michigan *M*

New York
Rochester Institute of
Technology *B, M*

Ohio
Cleveland Institute of Art *B, M*

Pennsylvania
Arcadia University *B*

Texas
University of Texas
Southwestern Medical Center at
Dallas *M*

Medical informatics

California
University of California
  Davis *M*

Indiana
Indiana University-Purdue University
  Indianapolis *B*

Massachusetts
Massachusetts Bay Community
  College *A*

Montana
Montana Tech of the University of
  Montana *A, B*

New York
State University of New York
  Downstate Medical Center *M*

Texas
Richland College *A*

Wisconsin
Milwaukee School of Engineering *M*

Medical insurance coding specialist

Alabama
Southern Union State Community
  College *A*

Arizona
Bryman School *A*

California
Charles R. Drew University of
  Medicine and Science *C*
Concorde Career College *C*
Empire College *C*
Loma Linda University *C*
Maric College
  Vista *C*
San Joaquin Valley College Inc. *A*
Santa Barbara City College *C*
Santa Rosa Junior College *C*
Southwestern College *C, A*

Colorado
Blair College *C*
Concorde Career College *C*
IntelliTec College: Grand Junction *C*
National American University
  Denver *A*
Parks College: Aurora *C*
Westwood College of Technology *A*

Connecticut
St. Vincent's College *C*

Florida
Florida Career College: Hialeah *C*
Florida Career College: Miami *C*
Florida Career College: Pembroke
  Pines *C*
Florida Career College: West Palm
  Beach *C*
Florida Metropolitan University:
  Orange Park *A*
Herzing College
  Orlando *C, A*
Hillsborough Community College *C*
Miami Dade College *C*
Palm Beach Community College *C*
Pasco-Hernando Community
  College *C*
Remington College: Largo *C*

St. Johns River Community College *C*
Southwest Florida College
  Tampa *C*

Georgia
Albany Technical College *C*
Central Georgia Technical College *C*
Northwestern Technical College *C*
Southwest Georgia Technical
  College *C*

Illinois
Black Hawk College *C*
Kankakee Community College *A, B*
Lincoln Land Community College *C*
Midstate College *C*

Indiana
Indiana Business College
  Terre Haute *A*

Iowa
Mercy College of Health Sciences *C*

Kentucky
Spencerian College: Lexington *C*

Louisiana
ITI Technical College *A*

Maine
Kennebec Valley Community
  College *C*

Maryland
Hagerstown Community College *C*

Massachusetts
Laboure College *C*
North Shore Community College *C*
Springfield Technical Community
  College *C, A*

Michigan
Baker College
  of Clinton Township *A*
  of Muskegon *C*
Davenport University *C, A*
Delta College *C*
Gogebic Community College *A*
Oakland Community College *C*
Schoolcraft College *C*

Minnesota
Academy College *C*
Alexandria Technical College *C*
Minneapolis Community and
  Technical College *A*
Minnesota State Community and
  Technical College - Fergus Falls *C*
Northland Community & Technical
  College *C, A*
Northwest Technical College *C*
Pine Technical College *C, A*
Rasmussen College
  St. Cloud *C, A*
Rochester Community and Technical
  College *C*
St. Paul College *C*
South Central College *A*

Mississippi
Antonelli College
  Jackson *A*

Nevada
High-Tech Institute *A*

New Hampshire
New Hampshire Community
  Technical College
  Claremont *C*

New Mexico
Eastern New Mexico University:
  Roswell Campus *C*
San Juan College *C*

New York
Elmira Business Institute *A*
Globe Institute of Technology *C*
Rochester Business Institute *A*

North Dakota
Aakers College: Fargo *C, A*
North Dakota State College of
  Science *A*
Turtle Mountain Community
  College *A*
Williston State College *C*

Ohio
Davis College *A*
ETI Technical College of Niles *A*
James A. Rhodes State College *A*
Lakeland Community College *C*
Marion Technical College *C*
Mercy College of Northwest Ohio *C*
Remington College
  Cleveland *C*
Sinclair Community College *C*
Southwestern College of Business
  Southwestern College: Franklin *C*
Stark State College of Technology *C*
Stautzenberger College *C, A*
University of Cincinnati
  Clermont College *C*

Pennsylvania
Business Institute of Pennsylvania *A*
Business Institute of Pennsylvania
  Meadville *A*
Butler County Community College *C*
Consolidated School of Business
  Lancaster *A*
  York *A*
Erie Business Center *C*
Mercyhurst College *C*
Newport Business Institute *A*
Northampton County Area
  Community College *A*
Pennsylvania College of Technology *C*
Pittsburgh Technical Institute *C*
South Hills School of Business &
  Technology *A*
University of Pittsburgh
  Titusville *C*

South Dakota
Kilian Community College *C, A*

Tennessee
Roane State Community College *C*

Texas
Richland College *A*
South Texas College *C*

Utah
LDS Business College *C*
Salt Lake Community College *C*

Virginia
Virginia Western Community
  College *C*

Washington
Centralia College *C*
Clark College *C*

Clover Park Technical College *C*
Everett Community College *C*
Renton Technical College *C, A*
Shoreline Community College *C*

West Virginia
Huntington Junior College *C, A*

Medical insurance specialist

Alabama
Virginia College *A*

Arizona
Bryman School *A*
High-Tech Institute *A*
Lamson College *C*

California
Long Beach City College *C*
MTI College *C*
National University *C*
Santa Barbara City College *C*

Colorado
Blair College *C*
National American University
  Denver *A*
Parks College: Aurora *C*
Westwood College of Technology *A*

Florida
Central Florida College *A*
Florida Metropolitan University
  Brandon Campus *A*
Florida Metropolitan University:
  Orange Park *A*
Herzing College
  Orlando *C, A*
New England Institute of
  Technology *C*
Palm Beach Community College *C*
Remington College: Largo *C*

Georgia
Savannah Technical College *C*

Illinois
Black Hawk College *C*
College of Lake County *C*

Kansas
Brown Mackie College *C*

Louisiana
Gretna Career College *C*
ITI Technical College *A*

Michigan
Baker College
  of Flint *C, A*
  of Muskegon *C*
  of Owosso *C, A*
  of Port Huron *C, A*
Delta College *C*
Kirtland Community College *C*

Minnesota
Academy College *C*
Ridgewater College *C*

New York
Elmira Business Institute *C*
Globe Institute of Technology *C*
Rochester Business Institute *A*
Westchester Community College *C*

North Dakota
Williston State College *C*

Ohio

Southwestern College of Business
Southwestern College: Franklin *C*
University of Cincinnati
Raymond Walters College *A*

Oregon

Pioneer Pacific College *C*
Pioneer Pacific College: Springfield *C*

Pennsylvania

Business Institute of Pennsylvania *A*
Business Institute of Pennsylvania
Meadville *A*
Career Training Academy:
Monroeville *C*
Consolidated School of Business
Lancaster *A*
York *A*
Newport Business Institute *A*
South Hills School of Business &
Technology *A*

Puerto Rico

Inter American University of Puerto
Rico
San German Campus *C*

Texas

MTI College of Business and
Technology *C*

Virginia

National College of Business &
Technology
Salem *C*

Washington

Centralia College *C*

Wisconsin

Herzing College *C, A*

Medical office administration

Alabama

Virginia College *A*

Arizona

Mohave Community College *C*

Arkansas

Ouachita Technical College *C*

California

California Institute of Integral
Studies *M*
Dominican University of California *M*
Heald College
San Jose *C, A*
Institute of Computer Technology *C*
MTI College *C*
Santa Barbara Business College
Bakersfield *C*

Colorado

Arapahoe Community College *C, A*
Blair College *C*
Pikes Peak Community College *C, A*
Red Rocks Community College *C, A*

Florida

Florida Career College: Hialeah *A*
Florida Career College: Miami *A*
Florida Career College: Pembroke
Pines *A*
Florida Career College: West Palm
Beach *A*

Florida Technical College
Deland *A*
Herzing College
Orlando *C*
Hillsborough Community College *C*
Southwest Florida College
Tampa *A*
Valencia Community College *A*

Georgia

Dalton State College *A*
Darton College *A*

Illinois

College of Lake County *C, A*

Indiana

Professional Careers Institute *C, A*
Sawyer College: Merrillville *C, A*

Iowa

Western Iowa Tech Community
College *A*

Kansas

Brown Mackie College *A*

Louisiana

ITI Technical College *A*
Nunez Community College *C, A*

Massachusetts

Gibbs College *A*
Holyoke Community College *C*
North Shore Community College *C*

Michigan

Baker College
of Clinton Township *B*
Kirtland Community College *C*

Minnesota

Academy College *C*
Globe College *C, A*
Hennepin Technical College *C, A*
Lake Superior College *C, A*
University of St. Thomas *M*

Missouri

State Fair Community College *C, A*

Montana

Flathead Valley Community College *A*

New Hampshire

McIntosh College *A*

New Mexico

San Juan College *A*

New York

Bryant & Stratton Business Institute
Bryant & Stratton College:
Rochester *A*
College of Westchester *C, A*
Erie Community College
North Campus *C, A*
Fulton-Montgomery Community
College *C, A*
Globe Institute of Technology *C, A, B*
Monroe College *A*
Olean Business Institute *A*

North Carolina

Beaufort County Community
College *C, A*
Carteret Community College *C, A*
Central Piedmont Community
College *C*
College of the Albemarle *A*

Fayetteville Technical Community
College *C, A*
Gaston College *C, A*
Isothermal Community College *C, A*
Pitt Community College *C, A*
Surry Community College *C, A*
Western Piedmont Community
College *A*

North Dakota

North Dakota State College of
Science *A*
Turtle Mountain Community
College *C*

Ohio

Ohio Institute of Photography and
Technology *A*
Southeastern Business College: New
Boston *A*
University of Akron *A*
Youngstown State University *A*

Pennsylvania

Bidwell Training Center *C*
Business Institute of Pennsylvania *A*
Business Institute of Pennsylvania
Meadville *A*
Consolidated School of Business
Lancaster *A*
Douglas Education Center *A*
Harrisburg Area Community
College *C*
Luzerne County Community
College *C, A*
Newport Business Institute *A*
Pennsylvania Institute of
Technology *C*
South Hills School of Business &
Technology *A*
Thompson Institute
Philadelphia *C*

Tennessee

University of Tennessee
Knoxville *B*

Texas

Tyler Junior College *C, A*

Utah

LDS Business College *A*

Washington

Big Bend Community College *C, A*
North Seattle Community College *C*
Peninsula College *C*

Wisconsin

Western Wisconsin Technical
College *C*

Medical office assistant

Arizona

Mohave Community College *C*

California

Antelope Valley College *C, A*
Feather River College *C*
MTI College *C*
Maric College
Vista *C*
Maric College: Sacramento *C*
Ohlone College *C*
Platt College
Ontario *A*
San Joaquin Delta College *C*
San Joaquin Valley College Inc. *A*
Santa Barbara Business College *C, A*

Santa Barbara Business College
Bakersfield *C, A*
Santa Maria *C, A*
Santa Barbara Business College:
Ventura *C, A*
Southwestern College *C*

Colorado

National American University
Denver *A*

Connecticut

Goodwin College *C*

Florida

Angley College *C, A*
Hillsborough Community College *C*
Remington College: Largo *C*

Georgia

Bauder College *C, A*
Dalton State College *C*

Idaho

Lewis-Clark State College *C, A, B*

Illinois

College of Office Technology *C*
Lincoln Land Community College *A*
Southeastern Illinois College *A*
Westwood College of Technology
O'Hare *C*

Indiana

Indiana Business College *C*
Indiana Business College
Anderson *C*
Evansville *C*
Fort Wayne *C*
Lafayette *C*
Marion *C*
Medical *C*
Muncie *C*
Terre Haute *C*

Iowa

Vatterott College *C*

Kentucky

Brown Mackie College:
Hopkinsville *C*
St. Catharine College *A*
Spencerian College: Lexington *C*

Louisiana

Bossier Parish Community College *C*
Gretna Career College *C, A*
ITI Technical College *A*

Massachusetts

Gibbs College *A*

Michigan

Baker College
of Clinton Township *A*
of Muskegon *A*
Delta College *C, A*
Oakland Community College *C*
West Shore Community College *C*

Minnesota

Academy College *C*
Hennepin Technical College *C*
Rasmussen College
St. Cloud *C, A*
Rochester Community and Technical
College *C*
St. Cloud Technical College *C*
St. Paul College *A*

Missouri
Crowder College *A*
Metro Business College
  Jefferson City *C, A*
North Central Missouri College *C, A*
Patricia Stevens College *A*
Vatterott College: Springfield *C*

Montana
Flathead Valley Community College *A*

New Hampshire
McIntosh College *A*

New York
ASA Institute of Business and
  Computer Technology *C, A*
Globe Institute of Technology *C*
Plaza College *C*

North Carolina
Pitt Community College *C*

North Dakota
Aakers College: Fargo *C*
North Dakota State College of
  Science *C, A*

Ohio
James A. Rhodes State College *A*
Lakeland Community College *C*
Marion Technical College *C*
Stark State College of Technology *A*
Technology Education College *C, A*
University of Cincinnati
  Raymond Walters College *A*

Oklahoma
Vatterott College
  Tulsa *C, A*

Oregon
Blue Mountain Community College *C*
Linn-Benton Community College *C, A*

Pennsylvania
Bucks County Community
  College *C, A*
Business Institute of Pennsylvania *A*
Business Institute of Pennsylvania
  Meadville *A*
Consolidated School of Business
  Lancaster *A*
Douglas Education Center *C, A*
Mercyhurst College *C, A*
Newport Business Institute *A*
Pittsburgh Technical Institute *A*
St. Vincent College *B*
South Hills School of Business &
  Technology *A*
York Technical Institute *C*

Rhode Island
New England Institute of
  Technology *A*

South Carolina
Williamsburg Technical College *C*
York Technical College *C*

South Dakota
Mitchell Technical Institute *A*

Texas
South Texas College *C, A*

Utah
LDS Business College *A*

Virginia
Danville Community College *A*
Miller-Motte Technical College:
  Lynchburg *A*

Washington
Centralia College *A*
Clover Park Technical College *C*
North Seattle Community
  College *C, A*
Yakima Valley Community College *C*

Wisconsin
Herzing College *C*

Medical office computer specialist

Arizona
High-Tech Institute *A*

California
MTI College *C*

Colorado
Front Range Community College *C*

Georgia
Northwestern Technical College *C*

Indiana
Sawyer College: Merrillville *A*

Kansas
Central Christian College of Kansas *A*

Louisiana
ITI Technical College *A*

Minnesota
Hennepin Technical College *C*

Mississippi
Antonelli College
  Jackson *C*

Missouri
Mineral Area College *C*

Montana
Flathead Valley Community College *A*

New York
Globe Institute of Technology *C*
Rochester Business Institute *C, A*

Pennsylvania
Business Institute of Pennsylvania *A*
Business Institute of Pennsylvania
  Meadville *A*
Consolidated School of Business
  Lancaster *A*
  York *A*
Newport Business Institute *A*
South Hills School of Business &
  Technology *A*

South Carolina
York Technical College *C*

Medical radiologic technology/radiation therapy

Alabama
Central Alabama Community
  College *A*
Faulkner University *A*
Gadsden State Community College *A*
George C. Wallace State Community
  College
  George C. Wallace Community
    College at Dothan *A*
Jefferson State Community College *A*
University of Alabama
  Birmingham *B*
University of South Alabama *B*
Wallace State Community College at
  Hanceville *A*

Arizona
Arizona Western College *A*
Gateway Community College *A*
Pima Community College *A*
Scottsdale Community College *A*

Arkansas
Arkansas State University *A, B*
East Arkansas Community College *A*
National Park Community College *A*
North Arkansas College *A*
South Arkansas Community College *A*
Southeast Arkansas College *A*
University of Arkansas
  Fort Smith *A*
  for Medical Sciences *A, B*
University of Central Arkansas *B*

California
Bakersfield College *A*
Cabrillo College *A*
California State University
  Long Beach *B*
Canada College *A*
Chaffey College *A*
City College of San Francisco *A*
Crafton Hills College *A*
Cypress College *A*
El Camino College *A*
Foothill College *A*
Fresno City College *A*
Loma Linda University *A, B*
Long Beach City College *A*
Los Angeles City College *A*
Merced College *A*
Merritt College *A*
Moorpark College *A*
Mount San Antonio College *A*
Orange Coast College *A*
Pasadena City College *A*
San Diego Mesa College *A*
San Diego State University *M*
San Joaquin Delta College *A*
Santa Barbara City College *A*
Santa Rosa Junior College *A*
Yuba Community College District *A*

Colorado
Aims Community College *A*
Community College of Denver *A*
Concorde Career College *A*
Mesa State College *A*
Pueblo Community College *A*

Connecticut
Capital Community College *A*
Gateway Community College *A*
Middlesex Community College *A*
Naugatuck Valley Community
  College *A*
University of Hartford *B*

Delaware
Delaware Technical and Community
  College
  Owens Campus *A*
  Stanton/Wilmington Campus *A*

District of Columbia
George Washington University *A*
Georgetown University *M*
Howard University *B*
University of the District of
  Columbia *A*

Florida
Brevard Community College *A*
Broward Community College *A*
Daytona Beach Community College *A*
Edison College *A*
Florida Community College at
  Jacksonville *A*
Gulf Coast Community College *A*
Hillsborough Community College *A*
Indian River Community College *A*
Manatee Community College *A*
Miami Dade College *A*
Palm Beach Community College *A*
Pensacola Junior College *A*
Santa Fe Community College *A*
University of Central Florida *B*
Valencia Community College *A*

Georgia
Armstrong Atlantic State University *B*
Coastal Georgia Community
  College *A*
Darton College *A*
Georgia Highlands College *A*
Georgia Southwestern State
  University *A*
Gwinnett Technical College *A*
Medical College of Georgia *B*
Middle Georgia College *A*
Southwest Georgia Technical
  College *A*
Waycross College *A*

Hawaii
University of Hawaii
  Kapiolani Community College *A*

Idaho
Boise State University *A, B*
Idaho State University *A, B*

Illinois
City Colleges of Chicago
  Malcolm X College *A*
  Wright College *A*
College of DuPage *A*
College of Lake County *A*
Illinois Central College *A*
Illinois Eastern Community Colleges
  Olney Central College *A*
John Wood Community College *A*
Kankakee Community College *A*
Kishwaukee College *A*
Moraine Valley Community College *A*
National-Louis University *B*
North Central College *B*
Sauk Valley Community College *A*
South Suburban College of Cook
  County *A*
Southern Illinois University
  Carbondale *B*
Southwestern Illinois College *A*
Triton College *A*
University of St. Francis *B*

Indiana
Ball State University *A*
Indiana University
  Bloomington *B*
  Kokomo *A*
  South Bend *A*
Indiana University-Purdue University
  Indianapolis *A, B*
Ivy Tech State College
  Ivy Tech Community College:
    Bloomington *A*
  Ivy Tech Community College:
    Central Indiana *A*
  Ivy Tech Community College:
    Columbus *A*

Ivy Tech Community College:
Wabash Valley *A*
University of St. Francis *A*
University of Southern Indiana *A*

Iowa

Briar Cliff University *B*
Iowa Central Community College *A*
Mercy College of Health Sciences *A*
Northeast Iowa Community
College *A*
St. Luke's College *A*
Scott Community College *A*
Southeastern Community College
North Campus *A*

Kansas

Fort Hays State University *A*
Friends University *B*
Hutchinson Community College *A*
Johnson County Community
College *A*
Newman University *A*
Washburn University of Topeka *A*

Kentucky

Bluegrass Community and Technical
College *A*
Elizabethtown Community and
Technical College *A*
Hazard Community College *A*
Madisonville Community College *A*
Morehead State University *A, B*
Northern Kentucky University *A*
Owensboro Community College *A*
St. Catharine College *A*
Southeast Kentucky Community and
Technical College *A*
Spencerian College *A*

Louisiana

Delgado Community College *A*
Our Lady of Holy Cross College *B*
Southern University
Shreveport *A*

Maine

Central Maine Community College *A*
Eastern Maine Community College *A*
Southern Maine Community
College *A*
University of Southern Maine *B*

Maryland

Allegany College of Maryland *A*
Anne Arundel Community College *A*
Chesapeake College *A*
College of Notre Dame of Maryland *B*
Community College of Baltimore
County *A*
Hagerstown Community College *A*
Montgomery College *A*
Prince George's Community
College *A*
University of Maryland
Eastern Shore *B*
Wor-Wic Community College *A*

Massachusetts

Bunker Hill Community College *A*
Holyoke Community College *A*
Laboure College *A*
Massachusetts Bay Community
College *A*
Massachusetts College of Pharmacy
and Health Sciences *B*
Massasoit Community College *A*
Middlesex Community College *A*
Quinsigamond Community College *A*
Regis College *A*

Michigan

Baker College
of Muskegon *A*
of Owosso *A*
Delta College *A*
Ferris State University *A*
Grand Rapids Community College *A*
Kellogg Community College *A*
Lake Michigan College *A*
Lansing Community College *A*
Mid Michigan Community College *A*
Montcalm Community College *A*
Mott Community College *A*
Oakland Community College *A*
University of Michigan
Flint *B*
Washtenaw Community College *A*
Wayne State University *B*

Minnesota

Century Community and Technical
College *A*
High-Tech Institute *A*
Lake Superior College *A*
Normandale Community College *A*
North Hennepin Community
College *A*
Ridgewater College *A*
Riverland Community College *A*

Mississippi

Copiah-Lincoln Community College *A*
Itawamba Community College *A*
Meridian Community College *A*
Mississippi Delta Community
College *A*
Mississippi Gulf Coast Community
College
Jefferson Davis Campus *A*

Missouri

East Central College *A*
Missouri Southern State University *A*
Missouri State University *B*
Penn Valley Community College *A*
University of Missouri
Columbia *B*

Nebraska

Clarkson College *A, B*
Southeast Community College
Lincoln Campus *A*
University of Nebraska
Kearney *B*
Medical Center *B*
Western Nebraska Community
College *A*

Nevada

Truckee Meadows Community
College *A*
University of Nevada
Las Vegas *B*

New Hampshire

New Hampshire Technical Institute *A*

New Jersey

Bergen Community College *A*
Brookdale Community College *A*
Burlington County College *A*
County College of Morris *A*
Cumberland County College *A*
Essex County College *A*
Fairleigh Dickinson University
College at Florham *A, B*
Metropolitan Campus *A, B*
Mercer County Community College *A*
Passaic County Community College *A*
Thomas Edison State College *A, B*
Union County College *A*

University of Medicine and Dentistry
of New Jersey
School of Health Related
Professions *B*

New Mexico

Albuquerque Technical-Vocational
Institute *A*
Clovis Community College *A*
Dona Ana Branch Community College
of New Mexico State
University *A*
New Mexico Junior College *A*
Northern New Mexico College *A*
University of New Mexico *A, B*

New York

Broome Community College *A*
City University of New York
Bronx Community College *A*
Hostos Community College *A*
New York City College of
Technology *A*
Erie Community College
City Campus *A*
Fulton-Montgomery Community
College *A*
Hudson Valley Community College *A*
Long Island University
C.W. Post Campus *B*
Mohawk Valley Community College *A*
Nassau Community College *A*
Niagara County Community
College *A*
North Country Community College *A*
Orange County Community College *A*
St. Francis College *B*
State University of New York
Oswego *B*
Trocaire College *A*
Westchester Community College *A*

North Carolina

Asheville-Buncombe Technical
Community College *A*
Caldwell Community College and
Technical Institute *A*
Cape Fear Community College *A*
Carolinas College of Health
Sciences *A*
Carteret Community College *A*
Catawba Valley Community College *A*
Cleveland Community College *A*
Edgecombe Community College *A*
Fayetteville Technical Community
College *A*
Forsyth Technical Community
College *A*
Johnston Community College *A*
Pitt Community College *A*
Sandhills Community College *A*
Southwestern Community College *A*
University of North Carolina
Chapel Hill *B*
Vance-Granville Community
College *A*
Wake Technical Community
College *A*

North Dakota

Minot State University *B*
University of Mary *A, B*

Ohio

Bowling Green State University:
Firelands College *A*
Central Ohio Technical College *A*
Columbus State Community
College *A*
James A. Rhodes State College *A*
Jefferson Community College *A*
Kent State University
Salem Regional Campus *A, B*

Kettering College of Medical Arts *A*
Lakeland Community College *A*
Marion Technical College *A*
Ohio State University
Columbus Campus *B*
Owens Community College
Toledo *A*
Shawnee State University *A*
Sinclair Community College *A*
University of Akron *A*
University of Akron: Wayne College *A*
University of Cincinnati
Raymond Walters College *A*
Washington State Community
College *A*
Xavier University *A*
Zane State College *A*

Oklahoma

Bacone College *A*
Tulsa Community College *A*
University of Oklahoma *B, M, D*
Western Oklahoma State College *A*

Oregon

Oregon Health & Science
University *B*
Oregon Institute of Technology *B*
Portland Community College *A*

Pennsylvania

Bloomsburg University of
Pennsylvania *B*
Clarion University of Pennsylvania *B*
College Misericordia *B*
Community College of Allegheny
County *A*
Community College of Philadelphia *A*
Drexel University *A*
Gannon University *A*
Gwynedd-Mercy College *A, B*
Holy Family University *A, B*
Keystone College *A*
La Roche College *A, B*
Lock Haven University of
Pennsylvania *A*
Mansfield University of
Pennsylvania *A*
Montgomery County Community
College *A*
Pennsylvania College of Technology *A*
Reading Area Community College *A*

Puerto Rico

Inter American University of Puerto
Rico
Barranquitas Campus *A*
Ponce Campus *A*
San German Campus *A*
Universidad del Este *A, B*

Rhode Island

Rhode Island College *B*

South Carolina

Aiken Technical College *A*
Florence-Darlington Technical
College *A*
Greenville Technical College *A*
Horry-Georgetown Technical
College *A*
Midlands Technical College *A*
Orangeburg-Calhoun Technical
College *A*
Piedmont Technical College *A*
Spartanburg Technical College *A*
Trident Technical College *A*
York Technical College *A*

South Dakota

Mitchell Technical Institute *A*
Mount Marty College *B*
Presentation College *A, B*

Tennessee
Austin Peay State University *B*
Chattanooga State Technical
   Community College *A*
Columbia State Community College *A*
Jackson State Community College *A*
Roane State Community College *A*
Southwest Tennessee Community
   College *A*
University of Tennessee
   Knoxville *B*
Volunteer State Community College *A*

Texas
Amarillo College *A*
Austin Community College *A*
Blinn College *A*
Del Mar College *A*
El Centro College *A*
El Paso Community College *A*
Galveston College *A*
Houston Community College
   System *A*
Kilgore College *A*
Laredo Community College *A*
McLennan Community College *A*
Midland College *A*
Navarro College *A*
North Harris Montgomery
   Community College District *A*
Odessa College *A*
St. Philip's College *A*
San Jacinto College
   Central Campus *A*
South Plains College *A*
Tarrant County College *A*
Texas Southmost College *A*
Texas State University: San Marcos *B*
Tyler Junior College *A*
Wharton County Junior College *A*

Utah
Salt Lake Community College *A*
Weber State University *A, B*

Vermont
University of Vermont *B*

Virginia
Averett University *B*
Northern Virginia Community
   College *A*
Southwest Virginia Community
   College *A*
Tidewater Community College *A*
Virginia Highlands Community
   College *A*
Virginia Western Community
   College *A*

Washington
Bellevue Community College *A*
Yakima Valley Community College *A*

West Virginia
Alderson-Broaddus College *B*
Bluefield State College *A*
Mountain State University *A*
Southern West Virginia Community
   and Technical College *A*
West Virginia Northern Community
   College *A*

Wisconsin
Blackhawk Technical College *A*
Chippewa Valley Technical College *A*
Concordia University Wisconsin *B*
Gateway Technical College *A*
Lakeshore Technical College *A*
Madison Area Technical College *A*
Milwaukee Area Technical College *A*
Northcentral Technical College *A*

Western Wisconsin Technical
   College *A*

Wyoming
Laramie County Community
   College *A*

Medical receptionist

Arizona
Mohave Community College *C*

California
Platt College
   Ontario *A*
Santa Rosa Junior College *C*

Colorado
Morgan Community College *C*
National American University
   Denver *A*
Parks College: Aurora *C*

Georgia
Central Georgia Technical College *C*
Northwestern Technical College *C*
Savannah Technical College *C*

Iowa
Dordt College *A*

Louisiana
ITI Technical College *A*

Massachusetts
Gibbs College *A*

Michigan
Baker College
   of Muskegon *C*
Delta College *C*
Jackson Community College *C*

Minnesota
Academy College *C*
Alexandria Technical College *C*
Dakota County Technical College *C*
Lake Superior College *C*
Rasmussen College
   St. Cloud *C, A*
St. Paul College *C*

Montana
Flathead Valley Community College *A*

New Hampshire
McIntosh College *A*

New York
Globe Institute of Technology *C*
Utica School of Commerce *C*

Ohio
Stautzenberger College *C, A*

Oregon
Linn-Benton Community College *C*

Pennsylvania
Business Institute of Pennsylvania *A*
Business Institute of Pennsylvania
   Meadville *A*
Consolidated School of Business
   Lancaster *C, A*
   York *C, A*
Douglas Education Center *C*
Newport Business Institute *A*
South Hills School of Business &
   Technology *A*

Washington
Centralia College *A*
Clark College *C*
Everett Community College *C*
North Seattle Community College *C*
Olympic College *C*
Peninsula College *C*

Medical records administration

Alabama
Alabama State University *B*
University of Alabama
   Birmingham *B, M*

Arkansas
Arkansas Tech University *B*

California
Allan Hancock College *C, A*
Barstow College *C*
Chabot College *C, A*
Chaffey College *C*
City College of San Francisco *C, A*
Cypress College *C, A*
Lake Tahoe Community College *A*
Loma Linda University *B*
Oxnard College *A*
Palomar College *C, A*
San Bernardino Valley College *C*
San Joaquin Valley College Inc. *A*
Santa Rosa Junior College *C*
Southwestern College *C, A*

Colorado
Blair College *C*
Regis University *B*
Westwood College of Technology *C, A*

Delaware
Delaware Technical and Community
   College
   Stanton/Wilmington Campus *C*

Florida
Broward Community College *A*
Florida Agricultural and Mechanical
   University *B*
Florida International University *B*
Gulf Coast Community College *A*
Indian River Community College *A*
Miami Dade College *A*
Pensacola Junior College *A*
Polk Community College *A*
St. Petersburg College *A*
University of Central Florida *B*

Georgia
Atlanta Metropolitan College *A*
Clark Atlanta University *B*
Dalton State College *A*
Darton College *A*
Georgia Highlands College *A*
Gordon College *A*
Macon State College *B*
Medical College of Georgia *B, M*
Middle Georgia College *A*

Hawaii
Hawaii Business College *C*

Idaho
Boise State University *A, B*

Illinois
Black Hawk College *C*
Chicago State University *B*
Illinois State University *B*
University of Illinois
   Chicago *B, M*

Indiana
Indiana University
   Northwest *B*
Indiana University-Purdue University
   Indianapolis *B*
Vincennes University *A*

Iowa
Northeast Iowa Community
   College *A*

Kansas
Barton County Community College *A*
Labette Community College *C*
Seward County Community College *C*
University of Kansas Medical
   Center *B*

Kentucky
Eastern Kentucky University *C, B*
Spencerian College *A*

Louisiana
ITI Technical College *A*
Louisiana Tech University *B*
University of Louisiana at Lafayette *B*

Maine
Andover College *A*

Maryland
Baltimore City Community College *A*
Prince George's Community
   College *C, A*

Massachusetts
Benjamin Franklin Institute of
   Technology *C*
Northeastern University *B*
Northern Essex Community
   College *C, A*
Springfield College *B*

Michigan
Baker College
   of Auburn Hills *A*
   of Flint *B*
   of Jackson *A*
Ferris State University *C, B*
Washtenaw Community College *A*

Minnesota
College of St. Catherine *A, B*
College of St. Scholastica *B, M*
Globe College *C, A*
Hennepin Technical College *C*
Rasmussen College
   Minnetonka *A*
   St. Cloud *A*

Mississippi
Coahoma Community College *A*
Itawamba Community College *A*
Mississippi Delta Community
   College *A*
Mississippi Gulf Coast Community
   College
   Jefferson Davis Campus *A*
University of Mississippi Medical
   Center *B*

Missouri
Everest College: Springfield *C*
Park University *A*
St. Louis University *B*
Stephens College *B*

Montana
Montana State University
   College of Technology-Great Falls *A*

Nebraska

College of Saint Mary *A, B*

New Jersey

Kean University *B*

New Mexico

Albuquerque Technical-Vocational
    Institute *A*

New York

Elmira Business Institute *C, A*
Globe Institute of Technology *C*
Long Island University
    C.W. Post Campus *B*
Molloy College *A*
Monroe College *A*
New York Career Institute *A*
Olean Business Institute *A*
State University of New York
    Institute of Technology at
    Utica/Rome *B*

North Carolina

Alamance Community College *A*
Durham Technical Community
    College *C, A*
East Carolina University *B*
Sandhills Community College *A*
Western Carolina University *B*

Ohio

Cuyahoga Community College
    Metropolitan Campus *C, A*
Ohio Business College: Sandusky *A*
Ohio State University
    Columbus Campus *B*
University of Akron: Wayne College *C*
University of Toledo *B*

Oklahoma

Metropolitan College *C*
Southwestern Oklahoma State
    University *B*
Western Oklahoma State College *A*

Oregon

Chemeketa Community College *A*
Linn-Benton Community College *C, A*
Mount Hood Community College *A*
Portland Community College *A*

Pennsylvania

Academy of Medical Arts and
    Business *C, A*
Business Institute of Pennsylvania *A*
Business Institute of Pennsylvania
    Meadville *A*
Consolidated School of Business
    Lancaster *A*
Erie Business Center South *A*
Gwynedd-Mercy College *B*
Harrisburg Area Community
    College *A*
Laurel Business Institute *A*
Mercyhurst College *C, A*
Newport Business Institute *A*
Pennsylvania College of Technology *A*
Pennsylvania Highlands Community
    College *C*
South Hills School of Business &
    Technology *A*
Temple University *B*
University of Pittsburgh *B*
Westmoreland County Community
    College *C*

Puerto Rico

Inter American University of Puerto
    Rico
    Aguadilla Campus *C*
Universidad Metropolitana *C*

South Carolina

Forrest Junior College *C, A*

South Dakota

Dakota State University *B*

Tennessee

Chattanooga State Technical
    Community College *A*
Tennessee State University *B*

Texas

El Centro College *A*
Howard College *C, A*
Laredo Community College *C*
MTI College of Business and
    Technology *C*
St. Philip's College *A*
Texas A&M University
    Commerce *B*
Texas Southern University *B*
Texas State University: San Marcos *B*

Utah

LDS Business College *A*

Virginia

ECPI College of Technology *C, A*
Mountain Empire Community
    College *C*
Norfolk State University *B*

Washington

Columbia Basin College *A*
Renton Technical College *A*
Seattle University *B*

Wisconsin

Madison Area Technical College *A*
Northeast Wisconsin Technical
    College *A*
University of Wisconsin
    Milwaukee *B*

Medical records technology

Alabama

Bishop State Community College *A*
Central Alabama Community
    College *A*
Chattahoochee Valley Community
    College *A*
Enterprise-Ozark Community
    College *A*
Faulkner University *A*
Gadsden State Community College *A*
Virginia College *A*
Wallace State Community College at
    Hanceville *A*

Arizona

Phoenix College *A*
Pima Community College *A*

Arkansas

National Park Community
    College *C, A*
North Arkansas College *C*
Ouachita Technical College *C*

California

Allan Hancock College *C, A*
Cerritos Community College *A*
Chabot College *C, A*
City College of San Francisco *C, A*
College of San Mateo *C*
Cosumnes River College *A*
Cypress College *A*
DeVry University
    Fremont *A*

Long Beach *A*
Pomona *A*
West Hills *A*
East Los Angeles College *C*
Fresno City College *C, A*
Los Angeles City College *A*
Orange Coast College *C, A*
Santa Barbara City College *C*
Santa Rosa Junior College *C*
Silicon Valley College
    Western Career College: San Jose *A*
Southwestern College *C, A*
Ventura College *A*

Colorado

Arapahoe Community College *C, A*
Parks College *C, A*

Connecticut

Briarwood College *C, A*
Quinebaug Valley Community
    College *C*

Delaware

Delaware Technical and Community
    College
    Terry Campus *C*
Wilmington College *M*

Florida

Brevard Community College *C*
Central Florida College *A*
Central Florida Community
    College *C, A*
Daytona Beach Community
    College *C, A*
Florida Community College at
    Jacksonville *A*
Indian River Community College *A*
International College *A*
Lake-Sumter Community College *A*
Miami Dade College *C*
Pasco-Hernando Community
    College *C*
Polk Community College *A*
St. Petersburg College *C*
Southwest Florida College *C*
Tallahassee Community College *C*
Valencia Community College *A*

Georgia

Abraham Baldwin Agricultural
    College *A*
Augusta Technical Institute *C*
Bainbridge College *C*
Clark Atlanta University *B*
Darton College *A*
Macon State College *A*
Middle Georgia College *A*
Southwest Georgia Technical
    College *C*
West Georgia Technical College *C, A*

Idaho

Boise State University *A*
Idaho State University *C, A*

Illinois

Black Hawk College *A*
College of DuPage *A*
Illinois Central College *A*
John A. Logan College *A*
Midstate College *A*
Moraine Valley Community
    College *A*
Morton College *C*
Northwestern Business College *A*
Oakton Community College *A*
Rend Lake College *C, A*
Robert Morris College: Chicago *C, A*
Rock Valley College *C, A*
South Suburban College of Cook
    County *C*

Southeastern Illinois College *A*
Southwestern Illinois College *A*

Indiana

Indiana Business College
    Anderson *A*
    Evansville *A*
    Lafayette *A*
    Marion *A*
    Medical *A*
    Muncie *A*
Indiana University
    Bloomington *B*
    Northwest *A*
    Southeast *A*
Ivy Tech State College
    Ivy Tech Community College:
        Lafayette *A*
    Ivy Tech Community College:
        Northeast *A*
Vincennes University *A*

Iowa

Indian Hills Community College *A*
Kirkwood Community College *A*
Northeast Iowa Community
    College *A*
Northwest Iowa Community
    College *A*

Kansas

Central Christian College of Kansas *A*
Dodge City Community College *C, A*
Hutchinson Community College *C, A*
Johnson County Community
    College *A*
Washburn University of Topeka *C, A*

Kentucky

Eastern Kentucky University *A, B*
Henderson Community College *C*
Hopkinsville Community College *C*
Jefferson Community College *C, A*
National College of Business &
    Technology
    Danville *C*
    Florence *C*
    Lexington *C*
    Louisville *C*
    Pikeville *C*
    Richmond *C*
Western Kentucky University *A*

Louisiana

Delgado Community College *A*
ITI Technical College *A*
Louisiana Tech University *A*
Southern University
    Shreveport *A*

Maine

Andover College *A*

Maryland

Baltimore City Community
    College *C, A*
Chesapeake College *A*
College of Southern Maryland *A*
Hagerstown Business College *C, A*
Montgomery College *A*
Prince George's Community
    College *C, A*

Massachusetts

Bristol Community College *A*
Holyoke Community College *C*
Laboure College *C, A*
Massasoit Community College *C*
Northern Essex Community
    College *C*

Michigan

Baker College
  of Auburn Hills *A*
  of Clinton Township *A*
  of Flint *A*
  of Jackson *A*
  of Owosso *A*
  of Port Huron *A*
Bay de Noc Community College *C*
Davenport University *C, A*
Delta College *C*
Ferris State University *A*
Gogebic Community College *C*
Henry Ford Community College *A*
Schoolcraft College *A*
Southwestern Michigan College *A*

Minnesota

College of St. Catherine *C, A*
Hennepin Technical College *C*
Lake Superior College *C*
Minnesota State Community and
  Technical College - Fergus
  Falls *C, A*
Rasmussen College
  Mankato *A*
  Minnetonka *A*
  St. Cloud *A*
Ridgewater College *C, A*
Riverland Community College *A*
Rochester Community and Technical
  College *A*
St. Cloud Technical College *A*

Mississippi

Hinds Community College *A*
Itawamba Community College *A*
Meridian Community College *A*

Missouri

Missouri Western State University *C, A*
Ozarks Technical Community
  College *C, A*
St. Charles Community College *A*

Montana

Flathead Valley Community College *A*

Nebraska

College of Saint Mary *C*
Western Nebraska Community
  College *C, A*

Nevada

Community College of Southern
  Nevada *A*
Truckee Meadows Community
  College *C*

New Hampshire

McIntosh College *A*
New Hampshire Community
  Technical College
  Manchester *C, A*
New Hampshire Technical Institute *C*

New Jersey

Burlington County College *C, A*
Cumberland County College *C*
Hudson County Community
  College *C, A*
Passaic County Community College *C*

New Mexico

Albuquerque Technical-Vocational
  Institute *C*
Eastern New Mexico University:
  Roswell Campus *C, A*
San Juan College *C, A*

New York

Broome Community College *A*
Elmira Business Institute *C, A*
Erie Community College
  North Campus *A*
Fulton-Montgomery Community
  College *C*
Globe Institute of Technology *C*
Mohawk Valley Community College *A*
Molloy College *A*
Monroe Community College *A*
Onondaga Community College *A*
Rockland Community College *A*
State University of New York
  College of Technology at Alfred *A*
Touro College *C, B*
Trocaire College *A*
Utica School of Commerce *A*

North Carolina

Brunswick Community College *A*
Catawba Valley Community
  College *C, A*
Central Piedmont Community
  College *C, A*
Davidson County Community
  College *A*
Edgecombe Community College *A*
Fayetteville Technical Community
  College *A*
Pitt Community College *C, A*
South Piedmont Community
  College *C, A*
Southwestern Community
  College *C, A*
Wake Technical Community
  College *A*

North Dakota

North Dakota State College of
  Science *A*
Williston State College *C, A*

Ohio

Bowling Green State University:
  Firelands College *A*
Cincinnati State Technical and
  Community College *C, A*
Columbus State Community
  College *C, A*
Cuyahoga Community College
  Metropolitan Campus *A*
Hocking College *A*
Mercy College of Northwest Ohio *A*
Owens Community College
  Toledo *C, A*
Sinclair Community College *C, A*
Stark State College of Technology *A*
University of Cincinnati
  Clermont College *C*

Oklahoma

East Central University *B*
Metropolitan College *A*
Rose State College *A*

Oregon

Central Oregon Community
  College *A*
Lane Community College *C*
Linn-Benton Community College *C*

Pennsylvania

Academy of Medical Arts and
  Business *A*
Berean Institute *C*
Bidwell Training Center *C*
Business Institute of Pennsylvania *A*
Business Institute of Pennsylvania
  Meadville *A*
Community College of Allegheny
  County *C, A*
Community College of Philadelphia *A*
DeVry University
  Ft. Washington *A*
Delaware County Community
  College *A*
Gwynedd-Mercy College *A*
Lehigh Carbon Community
  College *C, A*
Mercyhurst College *C, A, B*
South Hills School of Business &
  Technology *A*
Tri-State Business Institute *A*
Western School of Health and
  Business Careers *A*
Yorktowne Business Institute *A*

Puerto Rico

Inter American University of Puerto
  Rico
  Bayamon Campus *C*
  San German Campus *A*
Universidad Adventista de las
  Antillas *A*
Universidad del Este *A*

South Carolina

Aiken Technical College *C*
Florence-Darlington Technical
  College *A*
Forrest Junior College *C, A*
Greenville Technical College *A*
Midlands Technical College *C, A*
Piedmont Technical College *C*
Spartanburg Technical College *C*

South Dakota

Dakota State University *A*
Presentation College *A*

Tennessee

Dyersburg State Community
  College *C, A*
National College of Business &
  Technology
  Tennessee *C*
Roane State Community College *A*
Southern Adventist University *A*
Tennessee State University *A*
Volunteer State Community College *A*
Walters State Community College *C, A*

Texas

Amarillo College *A*
Austin Community College *C*
Central Texas College *C*
Cisco Junior College *C, A*
Coastal Bend College *A*
DeVry University
  Irving *B*
El Centro College *A*
El Paso Community College *C, A*
Galveston College *C, A*
Houston Community College
  System *C, A*
Howard College *C, A*
Lee College *C, A*
McLennan Community College *A*
Midland College *C, A*
Mountain View College *C, A*
North Harris Montgomery
  Community College District *C, A*
Panola College *C, A*
Paris Junior College *A*
Richland College *A*
St. Philip's College *C, A*
San Jacinto College
  North *C, A*
South Plains College *A*
South Texas College *C, A*
Tarrant County College *C, A*
Texas State Technical College
  Harlingen *A*
  West Texas *C, A*
Tyler Junior College *A*
University of the Incarnate Word *M*
Wharton County Junior College *A*

Utah

LDS Business College *C*
Salt Lake Community College *C*
University of Utah *B, M, D*
Weber State University *A*

Virginia

ECPI College of Technology *C, A*
J. Sargeant Reynolds Community
  College *C*
National College of Business &
  Technology
  Bluefield *C*
  Charlottesville *C*
  Danville *C*
  Harrisonburg *C*
  Lynchburg *C*
  Martinsville *C*
Northern Virginia Community
  College *A*
Tidewater Community College *A*
Wytheville Community College *C*

Washington

Centralia College *A*
Clark College *C*
Grays Harbor College *C*
Renton Technical College *A*
Shoreline Community College *A*
Spokane Falls Community
  College *C, A*
Tacoma Community College *C*
Yakima Valley Community College *C*

West Virginia

Bluefield State College *A*
Potomac State College of West Virginia
  University *A*

Wisconsin

Chippewa Valley Technical College *A*
Gateway Technical College *A*
Milwaukee Area Technical College *A*
Moraine Park Technical College *A*
Western Wisconsin Technical
  College *A*

Medical scientist

California

University of California
  Los Angeles *M*

Colorado

University of Colorado
  Denver and Health Sciences
  Center *M, D*

Connecticut

Yale University *D*

Illinois

Northwestern University *M, D*
Rush University *M, D*

Michigan

University of Michigan *M*

Missouri

Washington University in St. Louis *M*

New Mexico

University of New Mexico *M, D*

New York

State University of New York
  Upstate Medical University *D*

Ohio

Case Western Reserve University *M*

North Carolina

Alamance Community College *C*
Carteret Community College *C*
College of the Albemarle *C*
Durham Technical Community
College *C*
Edgecombe Community College *C*
Guilford Technical Community
College *C*
Sandhills Community College *C*
South College *C*
Western Piedmont Community
College *C*

North Dakota

Aakers College: Fargo *C, A*
Minot State University: Bottineau
Campus *C*
North Dakota State College of
Science *C, A*
Williston State College *C, A*

Ohio

Belmont Technical College *C*
Cincinnati State Technical and
Community College *C*
Columbus State Community
College *C*
Davis College *A*
ETI Technical College of Niles *A*
Mercy College of Northwest Ohio *C*
Owens Community College
Toledo *C*
Sinclair Community College *C*
Southern State Community College *C*
Stark State College of Technology *C*
Stautzenberger College *C, A*
University of Akron: Wayne College *C*
University of Cincinnati
Raymond Walters College *C, A*
Washington State Community
College *A*

Oklahoma

Metropolitan College *C*
Metropolitan College *C*
Oklahoma State University
Okmulgee *A*

Oregon

Central Oregon Community
College *C*
Chemeketa Community College *A*
Linn-Benton Community College *C*
Southwestern Oregon Community
College *C*
Treasure Valley Community College *A*

Pennsylvania

Academy of Medical Arts and
Business *C, A*
Bucks County Community College *C*
Business Institute of Pennsylvania *C*
Cambria-Rowe Business College *A*
Consolidated School of Business
Lancaster *A*
York *A*
Delaware County Community
College *C*
Douglas Education Center *C*
Erie Business Center *A*
Erie Business Center South *A*
Laurel Business Institute *A*
Lehigh Carbon Community College *C*
Mercyhurst College *C*
Newport Business Institute *A*
Northampton County Area
Community College *C*
South Hills School of Business &
Technology *A*
Tri-State Business Institute *A*
Westmoreland County Community
College *A*

York College of Pennsylvania *C, A*

Rhode Island

Community College of Rhode
Island *C*

South Carolina

Aiken Technical College *C*
Florence-Darlington Technical
College *C*
Forrest Junior College *C, A*
Tri-County Technical College *C*
York Technical College *C*

South Dakota

Kilian Community College *C, A*
Mitchell Technical Institute *A*
Presentation College *C*
Southeast Technical Institute *A*
Western Dakota Technical Institute *A*

Tennessee

Dyersburg State Community
College *C*
National College of Business &
Technology
Tennessee *C*
Roane State Community College *C*
South College *C*
Southwest Tennessee Community
College *A*
Walters State Community College *C, A*

Texas

Central Texas College *C*
El Centro College *C*
Galveston College *C*
Houston Community College
System *C*
Howard College *C*
Laredo Community College *C*
Lee College *C*
MTI College of Business and
Technology *C*
North Central Texas College *C*
North Harris Montgomery
Community College District *C*
St. Philip's College *C*
San Antonio College *C*
South Plains College *C*
South Texas College *C*
Texas State Technical College
Harlingen *C*
West Texas *C*
Tyler Junior College *C*

Utah

LDS Business College *C*
Southern Utah University *C*

Virginia

ECPI College of Technology *C, A*
J. Sargeant Reynolds Community
College *C*
Lord Fairfax Community College *C*
Mountain Empire Community
College *A*
National College of Business &
Technology
Bluefield *C*
Charlottesville *C*
Danville *C*
Harrisonburg *C*
Lynchburg *C*
Martinsville *C*
Salem *C*
Northern Virginia Community
College *C*
Tidewater Community College *C*
Virginia Western Community
College *C*

Washington

Bellingham Technical College *C*
Clark College *C*
Clover Park Technical College *C*
Columbia Basin College *C, A*
Edmonds Community College *C*
Everett Community College *C*
Green River Community College *C*
Highline Community College *C, A*
Lake Washington Technical College *C*
North Seattle Community College *C*
Peninsula College *C*
Pierce College *C*
Seattle Central Community College *C*
Shoreline Community College *C*
Skagit Valley College *C*
South Puget Sound Community
College *C, A*
Spokane Community College *C*
Tacoma Community College *C*
Yakima Valley Community College *C*

West Virginia

Mountain State College *A*

Wisconsin

Chippewa Valley Technical College *C*
Fox Valley Technical College *C*
Gateway Technical College *C*
Mid-State Technical College *C*
Moraine Park Technical College *C*
Southwest Wisconsin Technical
College *C*
Waukesha County Technical
College *C*

Wyoming

Casper College *A*
Sheridan College *C*

Medication aide

Kansas

Barton County Community College *C*

Kentucky

Maysville Community College *C*
Somerset Community College *C*

Louisiana

Our Lady of the Lake College *C*

Texas

Tyler Junior College *C*

Wisconsin

Mid-State Technical College *C*

Medicinal/
pharmaceutical
chemistry

Arizona

University of Arizona *M, D*

California

Loma Linda University *D*
University of California
San Diego *B*

Colorado

University of Colorado
Denver and Health Sciences
Center *D*

Connecticut

University of Connecticut *M, D*

Georgia

Mercer University *D*

Illinois

University of Illinois
Chicago *M, D*

Iowa

Drake University *B*

Kansas

University of Kansas *M, D*

Maryland

Towson University *B*
University of Maryland
Baltimore *M*

Massachusetts

Massachusetts College of Pharmacy
and Health Sciences *M, D*
Northeastern University *M*

Michigan

Michigan Technological University *B*
University of Michigan *B, M, D*

Minnesota

University of Minnesota
Twin Cities *M, D*

Mississippi

Mississippi College *B*
University of Mississippi *D*

Nebraska

Chadron State College *B*
University of Nebraska
Medical Center *M, D*

New Jersey

Rutgers, The State University of New
Jersey
New Brunswick/Piscataway
Campus *M, D*

New York

State University of New York
Buffalo *B, M, D*

North Carolina

Campbell University *B*
East Carolina University *D*
Livingstone College *B*

Ohio

Ohio Northern University *B*
Ohio State University
Columbus Campus *M, D*

Pennsylvania

Drexel University *M, D*
Duquesne University *M, D*
Temple University *M, D*
University of the Sciences in
Philadelphia *B, M, D*

South Carolina

Medical University of South
Carolina *M, D*

Texas

Texas Tech University Health Sciences
Center *M, D*
University of Houston *M*

Utah

University of Utah *B, M, D*

Washington

University of Washington *M, D*

West Virginia

West Virginia University M, D

Medicine (M.D.)

Alabama

University of Alabama at Birmingham: School of Medicine F
University of South Alabama: School of Medicine F

Arizona

University of Arizona: College of Medicine F

Arkansas

University of Arkansas for Medical Sciences: College of Medicine F

California

Loma Linda University: School of Medicine F
Stanford University: School of Medicine F
University of California Davis: School of Medicine F
University of California Irvine: College of Medicine F
University of California Los Angeles: School of Medicine F
University of California San Diego: School of Medicine F
University of California San Francisco: School of Medicine F
University of Southern California: School of Medicine F

Colorado

University of Colorado Health Sciences Center: School of Medicine F

Connecticut

University of Connecticut Health Center School of Medicine F
Yale University: School of Medicine F

District of Columbia

George Washington University: School of Medicine and Health Sciences F
Georgetown University: School of Medicine F
Howard University: School of Medicine F

Florida

University of Florida: School of Medicine F
University of Miami: School of Medicine F
University of South Florida: College of Medicine F

Georgia

Emory University: School of Medicine F
Medical College of Georgia: School of Medicine F
Mercer University: School of Medicine F
Morehouse School of Medicine F

Hawaii

University of Hawaii at Manoa: John A. Burns School of Medicine F

Illinois

Loyola University Chicago: Stritch School of Medicine F

Northwestern University: School of Medicine F
Rosalind Franklin University of Medicine and Science: First Professional F
Rush University: Rush Medical College F
Southern Illinois University: School of Medicine F
University of Chicago: Pritzker School of Medicine F
University of Illinois at Chicago: College of Medicine F

Indiana

Indiana University: School of Medicine F

Iowa

University of Iowa: College of Medicine F

Kansas

University of Kansas Medical Center: School of Medicine F

Kentucky

University of Kentucky: College of Medicine F
University of Louisville: School of Medicine F

Louisiana

Louisiana State University Health Sciences Center: School of Medicine F
Louisiana State University: School of Medicine F
Tulane University: School of Medicine F

Maryland

Johns Hopkins University: School of Medicine F
Uniformed Services University of the Health Sciences: School of Medicine F
University of Maryland at Baltimore: School of Medicine F

Massachusetts

Boston University: School of Medicine F
Harvard University: Harvard Medical School F
Tufts University: School of Medicine F
University of Massachusetts Medical School F

Michigan

Michigan State University: College of Human Medicine F
University of Michigan: School of Medicine F
Wayne State University: School of Medicine F

Minnesota

Mayo Medical School F
University of Minnesota Medical School F

Mississippi

University of Mississippi Medical Center: School of Medicine F

Missouri

St. Louis University: School of Medicine F
University of Missouri Columbia: School of Medicine F

University of Missouri Kansas City: School of Medicine F
Washington University: School of Medicine F

Nebraska

Creighton University: School of Medicine F
University of Nebraska Medical Center: College of Medicine F

Nevada

University of Nevada: School of Medicine F

New Hampshire

Dartmouth College: School of Medicine F

New Jersey

University of Medicine and Dentistry of New Jersey
New Jersey Medical School F
Robert Wood Johnson Medical School F
Robert Wood Johnson Medical School at Camden F

New Mexico

University of New Mexico: School of Medicine F

New York

Albany Medical College: School of Medicine F
Albert Einstein College of Medicine F
Columbia University
College of Physicians and Surgeons F
Cornell University Medical College F
Mount Sinai School of Medicine of City University of New York F
New York Medical College F
New York University: School of Medicine F
State University of New York Health Science Center at Brooklyn: School of Medicine F
State University of New York Health Science Center at Syracuse: School of Medicine F
State University of New York Health Sciences Center at Stony Brook: School of Medicine F
State University of New York at Buffalo: School of Medicine F
University of Rochester: School of Medicine and Dentistry F

North Carolina

Duke University: School of Medicine F
East Carolina University: School of Medicine F
University of North Carolina at Chapel Hill: School of Medicine F
Wake Forest University: Bowman Gray School of Medicine F

North Dakota

University of North Dakota: School of Medicine F

Ohio

Case Western Reserve University: School of Medicine F
Medical College of Ohio F
Ohio State University Columbus Campus: College of Medicine F
University of Cincinnati: College of Medicine F

Wright State University: School of Medicine F

Oklahoma

University of Oklahoma Health Sciences Center: College of Medicine F

Oregon

Oregon Health Sciences University: School of Medicine F

Pennsylvania

Jefferson Medical College of Thomas Jefferson University F
Medical College of Pennsylvania and Hahnemann University School of Medicine F
Pennsylvania State University College of Medicine F
Temple University: School of Medicine F
University of Pennsylvania: School of Medicine F
University of Pittsburgh: School of Medicine F

Puerto Rico

Ponce School of Medicine F
Universidad Central del Caribe: Medical School F
University of Puerto Rico Medical Sciences Campus: School of Medicine F

Rhode Island

Brown University: School of Medicine F

South Carolina

Medical University of South Carolina F
University of South Carolina: School of Medicine F

South Dakota

University of South Dakota: School of Medicine F

Tennessee

East Tennessee State University: James H. Quillen College of Medicine F
Meharry Medical College: School of Medicine F
University of Tennessee Memphis: College of Medicine F
Vanderbilt University: School of Medicine F

Texas

Baylor College of Medicine F
Texas A&M University: Health Science Center College of Medicine F
Texas Tech University Health Sciences Center: School of Medicine F
University of Texas
Medical Branch at Galveston: School of Medicine F
University of Texas Health Science Center: Medical School F
University of Texas Southwestern Medical Center at Dallas Southwestern Medical School F
University of Texas-Houston Health Science Center F

Utah

University of Utah: School of Medicine F

Vermont

University of Vermont: College of
Medicine *F*

Virginia

Eastern Virginia Medical School of the
Medical College of Hampton
Roads: Medical Professions *F*
University of Virginia: School of
Medicine *F*
Virginia Commonwealth University:
School of Medicine *F*

Washington

University of Washington: School of
Medicine *F*

West Virginia

Marshall University: School of
Medicine *F*
West Virginia University: School of
Medicine *F*

Wisconsin

Medical College of Wisconsin: School
of Medicine *F*
University of Wisconsin Madison:
School of Medicine *F*

Medieval and
Renaissance studies

California

University of California
Davis *B*
Santa Barbara *B*

Connecticut

Connecticut College *B*
University of Connecticut *M, D*
Wesleyan University *B*
Yale University *B, M, D*

District of Columbia

Catholic University of
America *B, M, D*
Georgetown University *B*

Florida

New College of Florida *B*

Georgia

Emory University *B*

Indiana

Hanover College *B*
University of Notre Dame *B, M, D*

Louisiana

Tulane University *B*

Massachusetts

Boston College *D*
College of the Holy Cross *B*
Mount Holyoke College *B*
Smith College *B*
Wellesley College *B*

Michigan

University of Michigan *B*
Western Michigan University *M*

Minnesota

Augsburg College *B*
College of St. Benedict *B*
St. John's University *B*
St. Olaf College *B*

Nebraska

University of Nebraska
Lincoln *B*

New Jersey

Rutgers, The State University of New
Jersey
New Brunswick/Piscataway
Campus *B*

New York

Bard College *B*
Barnard College *B*
Columbia University
Columbia College *B*
Cornell University *B, M, D*
New York University *B*
Sarah Lawrence College *B*
State University of New York
Albany *B*
Binghamton *B*
Syracuse University *B*
Vassar College *B*

North Carolina

Duke University *B*

Ohio

Ohio State University
Columbus Campus *B*
Ohio Wesleyan University *B*
University of Toledo *B*

Pennsylvania

Dickinson College *B*
Gettysburg College *B*
Penn State
Abington *B*
Altoona *B*
Beaver *B*
Berks *B*
Delaware County *B*
Dubois *B*
Fayette *B*
Hazleton *B*
Lehigh Valley *B*
McKeesport *B*
Mont Alto *B*
New Kensington *B*
Schuylkill - Capital College *B*
Shenango *B*
University Park *B*
Wilkes-Barre *B*
Worthington Scranton *B*
York *B*
Swarthmore College *B*

Rhode Island

Brown University *B*

Tennessee

University of Tennessee
Knoxville *B*
University of the South *B*

Texas

Rice University *B*
Southern Methodist University *B, M*
University of Texas
Austin *D*

Virginia

College of William and Mary *B*
Washington and Lee University *B*

Wisconsin

University of Wisconsin
Madison *M, D*

Medium/heavy vehicle
technology

Michigan

Oakland Community College *C, A*

Minnesota

Dakota County Technical College *C, A*
Hennepin Technical College *C, A*
St. Cloud Technical College *C, A*
St. Paul College *C*

Wisconsin

Milwaukee Area Technical College *C*

Mental health
counseling

Arizona

University of Phoenix *M*

California

California Institute of Integral
Studies *M*
Dominican University of California *M*

Florida

Nova Southeastern University *M*
Stetson University *M*

Georgia

Fort Valley State University *M*

Idaho

Idaho State University *M*

Kansas

Emporia State University *M*

Louisiana

Xavier University of Louisiana *M*

Massachusetts

Bridgewater State College *M*
Fitchburg State College *M*
Lesley University *M*
Suffolk University *M*

New York

Medaille College *M*
New York Institute of Technology *M*
St. John Fisher College *M*

North Carolina

Gardner-Webb University *M*

Ohio

Malone College *M*
Xavier University *M*

Pennsylvania

Marywood University *B, M*

Texas

St. Edward's University *M*

Vermont

College of St. Joseph in Vermont *M*

Wisconsin

Marquette University *M*

Mental health services
technology

California

San Joaquin Delta College *A*
Santa Rosa Junior College *C, A*

Colorado

Community College of Denver *C*
Pikes Peak Community College *C, A*
Pueblo Community College *C*

Connecticut

Asnuntuck Community College *C, A*
Capital Community College *A*
Housatonic Community College *C, A*
Naugatuck Valley Community
College *C, A*
Three Rivers Community College *A*

Delaware

Delaware Technical and Community
College
Owens Campus *C, A*
Stanton/Wilmington Campus *C, A*
Terry Campus *C, A*

Georgia

Darton College *C, A*

Idaho

North Idaho College *A*

Illinois

College of DuPage *C*
Elgin Community College *C*
Illinois Eastern Community Colleges
Frontier Community College *A*
Lincoln Trail College *C*
Olney Central College *C*
Wabash Valley College *C*
Moraine Valley Community College *C*
Prairie State College *A*
Roosevelt University *M*
Waubonsee Community College *C*

Indiana

Indiana University-Purdue University
Fort Wayne *B*
Ivy Tech State College
Ivy Tech Community College:
Bloomington *A*
Ivy Tech Community College:
Central Indiana *A*
Ivy Tech Community College:
Columbus *A*
Ivy Tech Community College: East
Central *C, A*
Ivy Tech Community College:
Kokomo *A*
Ivy Tech Community College:
Lafayette *A*
Ivy Tech Community College: North
Central *A*
Ivy Tech Community College:
Northeast *C, A*
Ivy Tech Community College:
Northwest *A*
Ivy Tech Community College: South
Central *C, A*
Ivy Tech Community College:
Southeast *C, A*
Ivy Tech Community College:
Southwest *A*
Ivy Tech Community College:
Wabash Valley *A*
Ivy Tech Community College:
Whitewater *A*

Kentucky

Northern Kentucky University *A, B*

Louisiana

Southern University and Agricultural
and Mechanical College *M*

Maine

University of Maine
Machias *B*

Maryland
Allegany College of Maryland *A*
Chesapeake College *C, A*
Community College of Baltimore
County *C, A*
Hagerstown Community College *A*

Massachusetts
Berkshire Community College *C*
Massasoit Community College *C*
Mount Wachusett Community
College *C, A*
North Shore Community College *C, A*
Northern Essex Community
College *C, A*

Michigan
Wayne County Community College *A*

Minnesota
Rochester Community and Technical
College *C, A*

Missouri
Penn Valley Community College *A*

Nebraska
Vatterott College: Spring Valley *C*

New Hampshire
New Hampshire Technical Institute *A*

New Jersey
Thomas Edison State College *A, B*

New York
City University of New York
Kingsborough Community
College *A*
Dutchess Community College *A*

North Carolina
Central Piedmont Community
College *C, A*
Guilford Technical Community
College *A*
Pitt Community College *A*
Richmond Community College *A*
Roanoke-Chowan Community
College *A*
Southwestern Community College *A*
Wayne Community College *A*

North Dakota
North Dakota State College of
Science *A*

Ohio
Columbus State Community
College *C, A*
Franciscan University of
Steubenville *B*
Sinclair Community College *A*
University of Toledo *A*

Pennsylvania
Community College of Allegheny
County *C, A*
Community College of Philadelphia *A*
Drexel University *B*
Luzerne County Community
College *A*
Montgomery County Community
College *C, A*
Northampton County Area
Community College *C*
Pennsylvania College of Technology *A*
Westmoreland County Community
College *C, A*

Texas
Alvin Community College *A*
Blinn College *C, A*
Del Mar College *C, A*
Eastfield College *C, A*
El Paso Community College *A*
Houston Community College
System *C, A*
Laredo Community College *A*
McLennan Community College *C, A*
North Harris Montgomery
Community College District *C, A*
San Antonio College *C, A*
Tarrant County College *A*
Wharton County Junior College *C, A*

Vermont
College of St. Joseph in Vermont *M*

Virginia
Virginia Western Community
College *A*

Washington
Edmonds Community College *C, A*
Pierce College *C, A*
Seattle Central Community College *A*

West Virginia
Mountain State College *A*

Wisconsin
Madison Area Technical College *A*

Merchandising/buying operations

Connecticut
Naugatuck Valley Community
College *C, A*

Florida
International Academy of Design and
Technology: Tampa *B*

Georgia
Gwinnett Technical College *C*
Middle Georgia College *A*

Maryland
Montgomery College *A*

Michigan
Delta College *A*

New York
Westchester Community College *A*

Ohio
University of Akron *A*
Youngstown State University *A, B, M*

Pennsylvania
Luzerne County Community
College *C*
Marywood University *C*

Texas
University of Houston *B*

Metal building assembly

Michigan
Mott Community College *C*

Wisconsin
Gateway Technical College *C*
Milwaukee Area Technical College *C*

Metal/jewelry arts

Arizona
Mohave Community College *C, A*
Northern Arizona University *B*

California
Bethesda Christian University *B*
California College of the Arts *B, M*
California State University
Fullerton *M*
Long Beach *B, M*
Northridge *B*
El Camino College *C*
Monterey Peninsula College *C, A*
Palomar College *A*
Santa Rosa Junior College *C*
Santiago Canyon College *A*

Colorado
Adams State College *B*
Pueblo Community College *C, A*

Connecticut
Middlesex Community College *A*

Georgia
Savannah College of Art and
Design *B, M*

Iowa
University of Iowa *B, M*

Kansas
Pittsburg State University *B*
University of Kansas *B, M*

Maine
Maine College of Art *B*

Massachusetts
Bristol Community College *C*
Massachusetts College of Art *B, M*
School of the Museum of Fine
Arts *B, M*
University of Massachusetts
Dartmouth *B, M*

Michigan
College for Creative Studies *B*
Ferris State University *B*
Grand Valley State University *B*
Kendall College of Art and Design of
Ferris State University *B*
Northern Michigan University *B*
Siena Heights University *B*
University of Michigan *B*

New Jersey
Rowan University *B*

New York
Fashion Institute of Technology *A*
Hofstra University *B*
Parsons The New School for
Design *C, A, B, T*
Pratt Institute *B*
Rochester Institute of
Technology *A, B, M*
State University of New York
College at Buffalo *B*
New Paltz *B, M*
Syracuse University *B, M*

North Carolina
East Carolina University *B*
Haywood Community College *A*

Ohio
Cleveland Institute of Art *B*
University of Akron *B*

Oregon
University of Oregon *B, M*

Pennsylvania
Arcadia University *B*
Seton Hill University *B*
Temple University *B, M*

Rhode Island
Rhode Island College *B*
Rhode Island School of Design *B, M*

Tennessee
Memphis College of Art *B, M*

Texas
Paris Junior College *A*
Sam Houston State University *M*
Texas A&M University
Commerce *B*
University of Houston *B, M*
University of North Texas *B, M*
University of Texas
El Paso *B, M*
Western Texas College *A*

Washington
University of Washington *B, M*

Wisconsin
Northeast Wisconsin Technical
College *C*
University of Wisconsin
Madison *B*

Metallurgical engineering

Alabama
University of Alabama *B, M*

California
California Polytechnic State
University: San Luis Obispo *B*

Colorado
Colorado School of Mines *B, M, D*

Connecticut
University of Connecticut *M, D*

Idaho
University of Idaho *B, M*

Illinois
Illinois Institute of
Technology *B, M, D*
University of Illinois
Urbana-Champaign *B*

Iowa
Northeast Iowa Community
College *A*

Maine
Southern Maine Community
College *A*

Michigan
University of Michigan *B, M, D*

Missouri
East Central College *A*
University of Missouri
Rolla *B, M, D*

Montana
Montana Tech of the University of
Montana *B, M*

Nevada

University of Nevada
Reno *B, M, D*

New Mexico

New Mexico Institute of Mining and
Technology *B*

New York

Columbia University
Fu Foundation School of
Engineering and Applied
Science *B, M, D*

Ohio

Ohio State University
Columbus Campus *B*
University of Cincinnati *B, M, D*

Pennsylvania

Penn State
Schuylkill - Capital College *B*
University Park *B, M, D*
University of Pittsburgh *M, D*

South Dakota

South Dakota School of Mines and
Technology *B, M*

Tennessee

University of Tennessee
Knoxville *M, D*

Texas

University of Texas
El Paso *B*

Utah

University of Utah *B, M, D*

Washington

University of Washington *B*

Wisconsin

University of Wisconsin
Madison *D*

Metallurgical technology

Arkansas

Arkansas Northeastern College *C, A*

Illinois

Moraine Valley Community College *C*

Michigan

Mott Community College *C*
Wayne County Community College *A*

Minnesota

Ridgewater College *A*

New York

Mohawk Valley Community College *C*

Oregon

Linn-Benton Community College *C*

Pennsylvania

Penn State
Altoona *A*
Schuylkill - Capital College *A*

Texas

Kilgore College *C, A*

Meteorology

Florida

Florida Institute of Technology *B, M*
University of Miami *B*

Hawaii

University of Hawaii
Manoa *B, M, D*

Illinois

Western Illinois University *B*

Iowa

Iowa State University *M, D*

Kentucky

Western Kentucky University *A*

Massachusetts

Massachusetts Institute of
Technology *M, D*

Michigan

Central Michigan University *B*

New York

Cornell University *B, M, D*
State University of New York
College at Brockport *B*
Oswego *B*
Suffolk County Community College *A*

North Carolina

University of North Carolina
Charlotte *B*

Oklahoma

University of Oklahoma *B, M, D*

Pennsylvania

Penn State
Schuylkill - Capital College *B*
University Park *B, M, D*
Wilkes-Barre *B*

Utah

University of Utah *B, M, D*

Microbiology

Alabama

Alabama State University *D*
University of Alabama *B*
University of Alabama
Birmingham *D*

Arizona

Northern Arizona University *B*

California

California Polytechnic State
University: San Luis Obispo *B*
California State Polytechnic
University: Pomona *B*
California State University
Chico *B*
Los Angeles *B*
Sacramento *B*
Pitzer College *B*
San Jose State University *B, M*
University of California
Berkeley *B, D*
Davis *B, M, D*
University of Southern
California *M, D*

Colorado

Colorado State University *B, M, D*

District of Columbia

Howard University *M, D*

Georgia

Medical College of Georgia *M, D*
University of Georgia *B, M, D*

Hawaii

University of Hawaii
Manoa *B, M, D*

Idaho

Idaho State University *B, M*

Illinois

Rosalind Franklin University of
Medicine and Science *M, D*
Southern Illinois University
Carbondale *B, M, D*
University of Illinois
Urbana-Champaign *B, M, D*

Iowa

Iowa State University *B, M, D*
University of Iowa *B, M, D*
University of Northern Iowa *B*

Kansas

Central Christian College of Kansas *A*
Kansas State University *B, D*
University of Kansas *B, M, D*

Louisiana

Louisiana State University and
Agricultural and Mechanical
College *B*
University of Louisiana at Lafayette *B*
Xavier University of Louisiana *B*

Maryland

University of Maryland
College Park *B*

Massachusetts

Simon's Rock College of Bard *B*
University of Massachusetts
Amherst *B, M, D*

Michigan

Central Michigan University *B, T*
Michigan State University *B, M, D*
Northern Michigan University *B*
University of Michigan *B, M, D*

Missouri

St. Louis University *D*
University of Missouri
Columbia *B*

New Hampshire

University of New Hampshire *B, M, D*

New Mexico

New Mexico State University *B*

New York

Bard College *B*
State University of New York
Stony Brook *D*

North Carolina

North Carolina State
University *B, M, D*

North Dakota

North Dakota State University *B, M*

Ohio

Ohio State University
Columbus Campus *B, M, D*

Ohio University *B, M, D*
Ohio Wesleyan University *B*

Oklahoma

Oklahoma State University *B, M, D*
University of Oklahoma *B, M, D*

Pennsylvania

Juniata College *B*
Penn State
Lehigh Valley *B*
University of Pittsburgh *B*

Puerto Rico

Inter American University of Puerto
Rico
Aguadilla Campus *B*
Bayamon Campus *B*
Universidad del Este *B*
University of Puerto Rico
Humacao *B*
Mayaguez *B*

Rhode Island

University of Rhode Island *B, M, D*

South Dakota

South Dakota State University *B*

Texas

Texas State University: San Marcos *B*
Texas Tech University *B, M*
University of Houston
Downtown *B*
University of Texas
Arlington *B*
Austin *B, M, D*
El Paso *B*
Health Science Center at
Houston *M, D*
Medical Branch at Galveston *M, D*
Southwestern Medical Center at
Dallas *M, D*

Utah

Brigham Young University *B, M, D*

Washington

University of Washington *B*
Washington State University *B, M, D*

Wisconsin

Lawrence University *B*
Marquette University *M, D*
University of Wisconsin
La Crosse *B*
Madison *B, M, D*

Wyoming

Sheridan College *A*
University of Wyoming *B*

Middle school education

Alabama

Athens State University *B*
Birmingham-Southern College *T*
Faulkner University *B, T*
Huntingdon College *B*

Alaska

Alaska Pacific University *A, B, M*

Arkansas

Arkansas Northeastern College *A*
Arkansas State University *B, T*
Arkansas State University
Mountain Home *A*
Arkansas State University: Newport *A*
Arkansas Tech University *B*

East Arkansas Community College *A*
Harding University *B, M, T*
Henderson State University *B, M, T*
John Brown University *B, T*
Mid-South Community College *A*
North Arkansas College *A*
Ouachita Baptist University *B, T*
Ozarka College *A*
South Arkansas Community College *A*
Southern Arkansas University *B*
Southern Arkansas University Tech *A*
University of Arkansas *B, M*
University of Arkansas
  Community College at Hope *A*
  Cossatot Community College of the
    A
  Fort Smith *A, B*
  Little Rock *B, M*
  Monticello *B*
  Pine Bluff *B*
University of Central Arkansas *B, M*
University of the Ozarks *B*

California

Alliant International University *T*
Azusa Pacific University *B, T*
California Baptist University *M, T*
California Lutheran University *B, M*
California State University
  East Bay *T*
  Long Beach *T*
  Northridge *M*
  San Bernardino *M, T*
  San Marcos *T*
Master's College *B, T*
Mills College *T*
Mount St. Mary's College *B*
National University *T*
Occidental College *T*
St. Mary's College of California *T*
San Diego Christian College *B, T*
San Francisco State University *T*
Sonoma State University *M*
University of California
  Riverside *T*
University of Redlands *B, T*
University of Southern California *T*
Whittier College *T*

Colorado

Adams State College *B, T*
Fort Lewis College *T*
Northeastern Junior College *A*
Regis University *B, T*

Connecticut

Albertus Magnus College *B, T*
Connecticut College *T*
Eastern Connecticut State
  University *B, T*
Quinnipiac University *B, M*
St. Joseph College *T*
University of New Haven *T*

Delaware

Delaware State University *B*
University of Delaware *B, T*

Florida

Chipola College *B*
St. Leo University *B*
Southeastern College of the
  Assemblies of God *B, T*
University of Florida *A*
University of North Florida *B*
University of West Florida *B*

Georgia

Albany State University *B, M*
Armstrong Atlantic State
  University *B, M, T*
Augusta State University *B, M*
Bainbridge College *A*

Berry College *B, M*
Brenau University *B*
Brewton-Parker College *B*
Clark Atlanta University *B*
Clayton State University *B*
Coastal Georgia Community
  College *A*
Columbus State University *B, M*
Covenant College *B, T*
Dalton State College *A*
Darton College *A*
Emmanuel College *B*
Fort Valley State University *B, M, T*
Georgia College and State
  University *B, M, T*
Georgia Southern University *B, M*
Georgia Southwestern State
  University *B, M*
Georgia State University *B, M*
Kennesaw State University *B, M*
LaGrange College *B, M*
Mercer University *B, M, T*
Middle Georgia College *A*
Morehouse College *B*
North Georgia College & State
  University *B, M*
Oglethorpe University *B, M, T*
Paine College *B*
Piedmont College *B, T*
Reinhardt College *B*
Shorter College *B, T*
Thomas University *B*
Toccoa Falls College *B, T*
University of Georgia *B, M, D*
University of West Georgia *B, M*
Valdosta State University *B, M*
Wesleyan College *B, M, T*

Idaho

Boise State University *T*
Northwest Nazarene University *B*

Illinois

Augustana College *B, T*
City Colleges of Chicago
  Kennedy-King College *A*
Dominican University *T*
Eureka College *B*
Illinois State University *B, T*
Judson College *B, T*
Monmouth College *T*
North Park University *B, M*
Sauk Valley Community College *A*
Southwestern Illinois College *A*
Trinity Christian College *T*

Indiana

Ball State University *M, T*
Butler University *B, M*
Earlham College *M*
Goshen College *B, T*
Huntington University *M*
Indiana University
  Kokomo *T*
  Northwest *T*
Indiana Wesleyan University *B, T*
Manchester College *B, T*
Tri-State University *B, T*
University of Evansville *T*
University of Indianapolis *T*
Valparaiso University *B, M, T*
Vincennes University *A*

Iowa

Ashford University *B, T*
Buena Vista University *T*
Central College *T*
Clarke College *B, T*
Coe College *B*
Cornell College *B, T*
Dordt College *B, T*
Ellsworth Community College *A*

Faith Baptist Bible College and
  Theological Seminary *B, T*
Graceland University *T*
Grinnell College *T*
Iowa Wesleyan College *B*
Morningside College *T*
Mount Mercy College *T*
Northwestern College *T*
Simpson College *B, T*
University of Northern Iowa *B, M*
Upper Iowa University *B, T*
Waldorf College *B*

Kansas

Bethel College *T*
Central Christian College of Kansas *A*
Friends University *B, T*
Garden City Community College *A*
McPherson College *B, T*
MidAmerica Nazarene University *B, T*
Newman University *B, T*
Ottawa University *T*
Tabor College *B, T*
University of Kansas *B, T*

Kentucky

Alice Lloyd College *B*
Asbury College *B, T*
Bellarmine University *B, M, T*
Berea College *B, T*
Brescia University *B, T*
Campbellsville University *B*
Eastern Kentucky University *B, M*
Georgetown College *B, M*
Kentucky Christian University *B, T*
Kentucky Wesleyan College *B, T*
Lindsey Wilson College *B, T*
Morehead State University *B, M, T*
Murray State University *B, M, T*
Northern Kentucky University *B, M*
Pikeville College *B, T*
Spalding University *B, M, T*
Thomas More College *B*
Transylvania University *B, T*
Union College *B, M*
University of Kentucky *B, M*
University of Louisville *M*
University of the Cumberlands *B, M, T*
Western Kentucky University *B, M, T*

Louisiana

Centenary College of Louisiana *B, T*
Nicholls State University *B*
Northwestern State University *B*
Southeastern Louisiana University *B*
Southern University and Agricultural
  and Mechanical College *B*
University of Louisiana at Lafayette *B*
University of New Orleans *B*

Maine

University of Maine
  Farmington *B, T*
  Machias *B*
University of Southern Maine *T*

Maryland

Goucher College *M*
Morgan State University *M*
St. Mary's College of Maryland *T*

Massachusetts

American International College *B, M*
Assumption College *T*
Clark University *M*
Eastern Nazarene College *B, M, T*
Fitchburg State College *B, M, T*
Gordon College *B*
Lesley University *B, M*
Massachusetts College of Liberal
  Arts *T*
Merrimack College *T*
Salem State College *B, M*

Simmons College *B, M*
Tufts University *M, T*
Wellesley College *T*
Westfield State College *B, M, T*
Worcester State College *M, T*

Michigan

Adrian College *T*
Baker College
  of Auburn Hills *B*
  of Muskegon *B*
  of Owosso *B*
Calvin College *B, T*
Central Michigan University *M, T*
Eastern Michigan University *M*
Grand Valley State University *T*
Madonna University *T*
Northern Michigan University *B, T*
Olivet College *B, T*
Rochester College *B*
Saginaw Valley State University *M*
University of Detroit Mercy *B, M, T*
Western Michigan University *M*

Minnesota

Capella University *M, D*
College of St. Catherine *T*
College of St. Scholastica *T*
Concordia University: St. Paul *B, T*
Minnesota State University
  Mankato *B, T*
Northland Community & Technical
  College *A*
Ridgewater College *A*
University of St. Thomas *B, T*
Vermilion Community College *A*
Winona State University *B, M, T*

Mississippi

Blue Mountain College *B*

Missouri

Avila University *B, T*
Central Methodist University *B*
Central Missouri State University *B, T*
College of the Ozarks *T*
Culver-Stockton College *T*
Evangel University *B, T*
Fontbonne University *B*
Harris-Stowe State University *B, T*
Lincoln University *B, T*
Lindenwood University *B*
Maryville University of Saint
  Louis *B, M, T*
Missouri Baptist University *B, T*
Missouri Southern State
  University *B, T*
Missouri State University *B, M*
Missouri Valley College *T*
Missouri Western State University *B*
Northwest Missouri State
  University *B, M, T*
Ozark Christian College *A*
Southeast Missouri State University *B*
Southwest Baptist University *B, T*
Truman State University *M, T*
University of Missouri
  Columbia *B, M, D*
  Kansas City *B*
  St. Louis *T*
Washington University in St.
  Louis *B, M, T*
Westminster College *B, T*
William Woods University *B, T*

Montana

Rocky Mountain College *B, T*
University of Great Falls *B, M*

Nebraska

Chadron State College *B*
College of Saint Mary *B, T*
Concordia University *B, T*

Midland Lutheran College *B, T*
Nebraska Wesleyan University *B*
Peru State College *B, T*
University of Nebraska
   Kearney *B, M, T*
   Lincoln *B*
Wayne State College *B, T*
York College *B, T*

Nevada

Sierra Nevada College *M*

New Hampshire

Franklin Pierce College *T*
Keene State College *B, T*

New Jersey

Caldwell College *T*
Centenary College *T*
The College of New Jersey *B, M, T*
Rowan University *B*
Rutgers, The State University of New
   Jersey
   Camden Regional Campus *T*
   New Brunswick/Piscataway
      Campus *T*
   Newark Regional Campus *T*

New Mexico

New Mexico Junior College *A*
Western New Mexico University *B, M*

New York

Alfred University *T*
Barnard College *T*
City University of New York
   Brooklyn College *M*
   Lehman College *M, T*
   Queens College *M, T*
College of Mount St. Vincent *T*
D'Youville College *B, M*
Dowling College *B, M, T*
Dutchess Community College *A*
Elmira College *B, T*
Hofstra University *T*
Iona College *T*
Long Island University
   C. W. Post Campus *M, T*
Manhattan College *B, T*
Manhattanville College *M, T*
Medaille College *B*
Mercy College *B, M, T*
Mount St. Mary College *M*
Nazareth College of Rochester *T*
New York Institute of Technology *B, T*
St. Joseph's College *B, T*
St. Joseph's College: Suffolk
   Campus *B, T*
State University of New York
   College at Cortland *B, M*
   College at Fredonia *T*
   College at Old Westbury *B, T*
   New Paltz *B, M, T*
Syracuse University *B, M, T*
Vassar College *T*
Wagner College *B, M, T*

North Carolina

Appalachian State University *B, M, T*
Barton College *B*
Bennett College *B*
Campbell University *B, M, T*
Catawba College *B, M, T*
East Carolina University *B, M*
Elizabeth City State University *B, T*
Elon University *B, M*
Fayetteville State University *B, M*
Gardner-Webb University *B*
Greensboro College *B, T*
High Point University *B, T*
Lenoir-Rhyne College *B, T*
Mars Hill College *B, T*
Meredith College *T*

Methodist College *A, B, T*
North Carolina Central
   University *B, M, T*
North Carolina State
   University *B, M, T*
North Carolina Wesleyan College *B*
University of North Carolina
   Asheville *T*
   Chapel Hill *B*
   Charlotte *B*
   Greensboro *B*
   Pembroke *B, M*
   Wilmington *B, M*
Warren Wilson College *B, T*
Western Carolina University *B, T*
Wingate University *B, T*
Winston-Salem State University *B*

North Dakota

Dickinson State University *B, T*
University of North Dakota *B, T*

Ohio

Ashland University *B, T*
Baldwin-Wallace College *B*
Bluffton University *B*
Bowling Green State University *B, T*
Capital University *B*
Cedarville University *B, T*
Central State University *B*
Cincinnati Christian University *B*
College of Mount St. Joseph *B, T*
College of Wooster *T*
Defiance College *B, T*
Hiram College *T*
Kent State University *B*
Lourdes College *B*
Malone College *B*
Marietta College *B*
Miami University
   Oxford Campus *B*
Mount Union College *B, T*
Mount Vernon Nazarene
   University *B, M, T*
Ohio Dominican University *B, T*
Ohio Northern University *B, T*
Ohio State University
   Columbus Campus *M*
Ohio University *B, M, D, T*
Ohio University
   Chillicothe Campus *B*
   Zanesville Campus *B*
Ohio Wesleyan University *B*
Otterbein College *B*
University of Akron *B*
University of Cincinnati
   Clermont College *A*
   Raymond Walters College *A*
University of Dayton *B, M, T*
University of Findlay *B, M, T*
University of Rio Grande *B, T*
Urbana University *B*
Ursuline College *B, M, T*
Walsh University *B*
Wilmington College *B*
Wright State University *M*
Xavier University *B, M*
Youngstown State University *B, M*

Oklahoma

Northwestern Oklahoma State
   University *T*
Oklahoma Christian University *B, T*
Southeastern Oklahoma State
   University *T*
Southwestern Oklahoma State
   University *M, T*

Oregon

Concordia University *B, M, T*
Corban College *B*
Eastern Oregon University *B, M*
Lewis & Clark College *M*

Linfield College *T*
Portland State University *T*
University of Oregon *T*
Warner Pacific College *T*
Western Oregon University *T*
Willamette University *M*

Pennsylvania

Cedar Crest College *B, T*
DeSales University *T*
Gettysburg College *T*
La Salle University *B, T*
Mansfield University of
   Pennsylvania *B, T*
Reading Area Community College *A*
St. Vincent College *T*
Westminster College *B, T*

Rhode Island

Rhode Island College *B, M*

South Carolina

Charleston Southern University *M*
Coastal Carolina University *B*
Presbyterian College *B, T*
University of South Carolina *M*
Winthrop University *B, M*

South Dakota

Black Hills State University *B*
Dakota State University *B, T*
Mount Marty College *B*

Tennessee

Austin Peay State University *T*
Belmont University *B, M, T*
Cumberland University *B, T*
Freed-Hardeman University *B, T*
King College *T*
Lambuth University *B, T*
Lincoln Memorial University *B, T*
Martin Methodist College *B*
Milligan College *M, T*
Tennessee Technological University *T*
Tennessee Wesleyan College *T*
Tusculum College *B, T*
Union University *B, T*
University of Tennessee
   Chattanooga *B*
   Knoxville *T*

Texas

Abilene Christian University *B, T*
Arlington Baptist College *T*
Austin College *B*
Houston Baptist University *B, M*
Howard Payne University *T*
Jarvis Christian College *B, T*
LeTourneau University *B, T*
McMurry University *T*
Mountain View College *A*
North Harris Montgomery
   Community College District *A*
Our Lady of the Lake University of San
   Antonio *M*
St. Edward's University *T*
Schreiner University *B*
South Texas College *A*
Texas A&M University
   Commerce *B*
   Kingsville *M*
Texas College *B, T*
Texas Lutheran University *B, T*
Trinity Valley Community College *A*
University of Dallas *T*
University of Texas
   El Paso *B*
West Texas A&M University *T*

Vermont

Bennington College *B, M*
Castleton State College *B, M, T*
Champlain College *B*

College of St. Joseph in Vermont *B*
Goddard College *B*
Green Mountain College *B, T*
Johnson State College *B, M*
St. Michael's College *T*
University of Vermont *B*

Virginia

Averett University *M, T*
Bluefield College *B*
Hollins University *T*
Longwood University *B, T*
Mary Baldwin College *T*
Radford University *T*
University of Richmond *B, T*
Virginia Wesleyan College *T*

Washington

Central Washington University *M*
Heritage University *B, M*
Northwest University *B*
University of Puget Sound *T*
University of Washington *M, T*
Whitworth College *B, M, T*

West Virginia

Alderson-Broaddus College *B, T*
Bluefield State College *B*
Salem International University *T*
West Virginia State University *B*

Wisconsin

Alverno College *B, T*
Beloit College *T*
Carroll College *B, T*
Carthage College *T*
Concordia University Wisconsin *B, T*
Edgewood College *B, T*
Lakeland College *B*
Marquette University *B*
Northland College *T*
Ripon College *T*
St. Norbert College *B*
Silver Lake College *T*
University of Wisconsin
   Green Bay *T*
   Parkside *T*
   Platteville *T*
   River Falls *T*
   Superior *M*
Viterbo University *B, T*

Military technologies

Alabama

Community College of the Air
   Force *A*

Arizona

University of Phoenix *A*

Colorado

Colorado Mountain College
   Spring Valley Campus *A*

Florida

Florida Community College at
   Jacksonville *A*

Kansas

Barton County Community College *A*
Seward County Community College *A*

Kentucky

Murray State University *A*

Missouri

Missouri State University *B, M*
University of Missouri
   Columbia *B*

Nevada

Truckee Meadows Community
College *A*

New Jersey

Thomas Edison State College *A*

Ohio

Owens Community College
Toledo *A*
University of Akron *A, B*
Wright State University *B*

Utah

University of Utah *M*
Weber State University *B*

Mining and mineral engineering

Alaska

University of Alaska
Fairbanks *B, M*

Arizona

University of Arizona *B, M, D*

Colorado

Colorado School of Mines *B, M, D*

Idaho

University of Idaho *B, M, D*

Illinois

Southern Illinois University
Carbondale *B, M*

Kentucky

University of Kentucky *B, M, D*

Michigan

Michigan Technological
University *M, D*

Missouri

East Central College *A*
University of Missouri
Rolla *B, M, D*

Montana

Montana Tech of the University of
Montana *B, M*

Nevada

University of Nevada
Reno *B, M*

New Mexico

New Mexico Institute of Mining and
Technology *B, M*

New York

Columbia University
Fu Foundation School of
Engineering and Applied
Science *B, M, D*

Oregon

Oregon State University *B*

Pennsylvania

Penn State
Berks *B*
Delaware County *B*
Dubois *B*
Fayette *B*
Lehigh Valley *B*
McKeesport *B*
Mont Alto *B*

New Kensington *B*
Schuylkill - Capital College *B*
Shenango *B*
University Park *B, M, D*
Wilkes-Barre *B*
Worthington Scranton *B*
York *B*
University of Pittsburgh *M*

Utah

University of Utah *B, M, D*

Virginia

Virginia Polytechnic Institute and
State University *B, M, D*

West Virginia

West Virginia University *B, M, D*

Mining technology

Arizona

Eastern Arizona College *A*

Wyoming

Western Wyoming Community
College *C, A*

Missionary studies

Alabama

Southeastern Bible College *A, B, T*

Arizona

Southwestern College *C, A, B*

Arkansas

Harding University *B, M*
John Brown University *B*
Ouachita Baptist University *B*
Williams Baptist College *B*

California

Bethany University *B*
Bethesda Christian University *B*
Biola University *D*
California Baptist University *B*
Hope International University *A, B, M*
Salvation Army Crestmont
College *C, A, B*
San Diego Christian College *B*
Simpson University *B, M*
Vanguard University of Southern
California *B*
William Jessup University *C, B*

Florida

Florida Christian College *B*
Hobe Sound Bible College *C, A, B*
Southeastern College of the
Assemblies of God *B*
Trinity College of Florida *B*

Georgia

Covenant College *B*
Toccoa Falls College *B*

Idaho

Boise Bible College *B*
Northwest Nazarene University *B*

Illinois

Lincoln Christian College and
Seminary *B, M*
Moody Bible Institute *B*
Trinity International University *M*
Wheaton College *M*

Indiana

Huntington University *B*

Taylor University *C*
Taylor University: Fort Wayne *B*

Iowa

Dordt College *B*
Emmaus Bible College *B*
Faith Baptist Bible College and
Theological Seminary *B*
Vennard College *C, B*

Kansas

Barclay College *B*
Central Christian College of
Kansas *A, B*
Manhattan Christian College *A, B*
MidAmerica Nazarene University *B*

Kentucky

Asbury College *B*
Kentucky Mountain Bible College *B*
Mid-Continent University *B*

Michigan

Andrews University *M, D*
Cornerstone University *M*
Grace Bible College *B*
Kuyper College *B*

Minnesota

Concordia University: St. Paul *B*
Crossroads College *B*
Crown College *B, M*
North Central University *A, B*
Northwestern College *B*
Oak Hills Christian College *B*

Mississippi

Magnolia Bible College *B*
Wesley College *B*

Missouri

Baptist Bible College *B, M*
Calvary Bible College and Theological
Seminary *B*
Central Bible College *A, B*
Evangel University *B*
Global University *B*
Ozark Christian College *C, B*
St. Louis Christian College *A, B*
Southwest Baptist University *B*

Nebraska

Grace University *B*
Nebraska Christian College *A, B*

North Carolina

Pfeiffer University *B*
Piedmont Baptist College *B*
Roanoke Bible College *B*

North Dakota

Trinity Bible College *B*

Ohio

Ashland University *B*
Cedarville University *B*
Cincinnati Christian University *B*
Circleville Bible College *A, B*
God's Bible School and College *B*

Oklahoma

Oklahoma Baptist University *B*
Oklahoma Christian University *B*
Oklahoma Wesleyan University *B*
Oral Roberts University *B, M*
Southern Nazarene University *B*
Southwestern Christian University *B*

Oregon

Corban College *B*
Eugene Bible College *B*

George Fox University *B*
Multnomah Bible College *B*

Pennsylvania

Baptist Bible College of
Pennsylvania *B*
Eastern University *B*
Philadelphia Biblical University *B*
Valley Forge Christian College *B*

South Carolina

Columbia International
University *B, M*

Tennessee

Free Will Baptist Bible College *B*
Freed-Hardeman University *B*
Lee University *B*
Lipscomb University *B*
Tennessee Temple University *B*

Texas

Abilene Christian University *B, M*
Arlington Baptist College *B*
Criswell College *B, M*
East Texas Baptist University *B*
Hardin-Simmons University *B*
Lubbock Christian University *B*
Southwestern Assemblies of God
University *B, M*

Virginia

Liberty University *B, M*

Washington

Northwest University *B*
Puget Sound Christian College *B*
Trinity Lutheran College *B*

Wisconsin

Concordia University Wisconsin *B*
Maranatha Baptist Bible College *B, M*

Modern Greek

California

Loyola Marymount University *B*

District of Columbia

Catholic University of
America *B, M, D*
Howard University *B*

Indiana

Butler University *B*

Kansas

Central Christian College of Kansas *A*

Louisiana

Tulane University *B*

Massachusetts

Boston University *B*
Wheaton College *B*

Michigan

Calvin College *B*
University of Michigan *B*

Missouri

St. Louis University *B*

New Hampshire

University of New Hampshire *B*

New York

Barnard College *B*
Colgate University *B*

Columbia University
Columbia College *B*
Fordham University *B*
New York University *B*

Ohio
College of Wooster *B*
Ohio State University
Columbus Campus *B, M, D*
Wright State University *B*

Tennessee
Rhodes College *B*
University of the South *B*

Molecular biochemistry

Alabama
University of Alabama
Birmingham *D*

California
Mills College *B*
University of California
Davis *B, M, D*
Los Angeles *B, M, D*

Illinois
Loyola University of Chicago *D*
Rosalind Franklin University of
Medicine and Science *M, D*
Southern Illinois University
Carbondale *M*

Maine
Colby College *B*

New York
Polytechnic University *B*

Tennessee
Belmont University *B*

Wisconsin
Lawrence University *B*
Marquette University *M, D*
University of Wisconsin
Madison *D*

Molecular biology

Alabama
Auburn University *B*

Arizona
Arizona State University *B*
Northern Arizona University *B*
University of Arizona *M, D*

Arkansas
University of Arkansas *M, D*

California
California Institute of Technology *D*
California Lutheran University *B*
California State University
Fresno *B*
Long Beach *B*
Northridge *B*
Sacramento *B, M*
Chapman University *B*
Loma Linda University *M, D*
Los Angeles Southwest College *A*
Pomona College *B*
San Diego State University *M*
San Francisco State University *M*
San Jose State University *B*
Scripps College *B*
Stanford University *M, D*
University of California
Irvine *M, D*

Los Angeles *D*
San Diego *B*
Santa Barbara *B, M, D*
Santa Cruz *B*
University of Southern
California *M, D*

Colorado
University of Denver *B*

Connecticut
Central Connecticut State
University *B, M*
Connecticut College *B*
Quinnipiac University *M*
University of Connecticut *M, D*
Wesleyan University *B, D*
Yale University *B, M, D*

District of Columbia
Georgetown University *D*

Florida
Florida Institute of Technology *B*
Stetson University *B*

Georgia
Medical College of Georgia *M, D*

Idaho
University of Idaho *B*

Illinois
Benedictine University *B*
Chicago State University *B*
Loyola University of Chicago *D*
Rosalind Franklin University of
Medicine and Science *D*
University of Chicago *D*

Indiana
Goshen College *B*
Indiana University
Bloomington *D*

Iowa
Coe College *B*
Iowa State University *M, D*
University of Iowa *D*

Kansas
Baker University *B*
University of Kansas *B*

Kentucky
Centre College *B*

Louisiana
Tulane University *B, M, D*

Maine
Colby College *B*
University of Maine *B, M, D*
University of Southern Maine *D*

Maryland
Johns Hopkins University *B, M, D*
University of Maryland
Baltimore *M, D*
Baltimore County *M*
College Park *D*

Massachusetts
Boston University *B, M, D*
Brandeis University *M, D*
Clark University *B*
Harvard College *B, D*
Tufts University *M, D*
Western New England College *B*

Michigan
Andrews University *B*
University of Michigan *M, D*
University of Michigan
Flint *B*
Wayne State University *M, D*

Minnesota
University of Minnesota
Duluth *B*
Twin Cities *D*
Winona State University *B*

Mississippi
Mississippi State University *D*

Missouri
Northwest Missouri State
University *B*
St. Louis University *D*
University of Missouri
Kansas City *M*
Washington University in St. Louis *D*
William Jewell College *B*

Montana
Montana State University
Bozeman *M, D*

New Hampshire
Dartmouth College *B*

New Jersey
Montclair State University *B*
Princeton University *B, M, D*
Rutgers, The State University of New
Jersey
New Brunswick/Piscataway
Campus *B*

New Mexico
New Mexico State University *M, D*

New York
Bard College *B*
Clarkson University *B*
Colgate University *B*
Cornell University *B, M, D*
Hamilton College *B*
State University of New York
Albany *B, M, D*
College of Environmental Science
and Forestry *M, D*
Stony Brook *D*
University of Rochester *B*
Wells College *B*
Yeshiva University *M, D*

North Carolina
East Carolina University *M*
Meredith College *B*
Wake Forest University *M, D*
Winston-Salem State University *B*

Ohio
Case Western Reserve University *D*
College of Wooster *B*
Kenyon College *B*
Muskingum College *B*
Ohio Northern University *B*
Ohio State University
Columbus Campus *M, D*
Otterbein College *B*
University of Cincinnati *M, D*
Wittenberg University *B*

Oklahoma
University of Tulsa *D*

Oregon
Oregon Health & Science
University *M, D*
Oregon State University *D*
Reed College *B*

Pennsylvania
Chestnut Hill College *B*
Clarion University of Pennsylvania *B*
Gettysburg College *B*
Grove City College *B*
Juniata College *B*
Lehigh University *B, M, D*
Mansfield University of
Pennsylvania *B*
Temple University *D*
University of Pittsburgh *B*
West Chester University of
Pennsylvania *B*
Westminster College *B*

Rhode Island
Brown University *B, M, D*
University of Rhode Island *M, D*

South Carolina
Medical University of South
Carolina *D*

Tennessee
Belmont University *B*
Vanderbilt University *B, M, D*

Texas
Houston Baptist University *B*
Texas A&M University *B*
Texas Lutheran University *B*
Texas Tech University Health Sciences
Center *M, D*
Texas Woman's University *D*
University of North Texas *M*
University of Texas
Austin *M, D*
Dallas *B*
Health Science Center at
Houston *M, D*

Utah
Brigham Young University *B, M, D*

Vermont
Johnson State College *B*
Marlboro College *B*
Middlebury College *B*
University of Vermont *B, M, D*

Virginia
Hampton University *B*
Sweet Briar College *B*
University of Richmond *B*

Washington
University of Washington *M, D*

Wisconsin
Alverno College *B*
Beloit College *B*
Marquette University *B, M, D*
University of Wisconsin
Eau Claire *B*
Madison *B, M, D*
Parkside *B, M*
Superior *B*

Wyoming
University of Wyoming *B, M, D*

Molecular biophysics

Florida
Florida State University *D*

Missouri
Washington University in St. Louis *D*

Pennsylvania
University of Pittsburgh *M, D*

Wisconsin
Marquette University *M, D*

Molecular genetics

California
University of California
Los Angeles *B, M, D*

Illinois
University of Chicago *D*
University of Illinois
Chicago *D*

Indiana
Indiana University-Purdue University
Indianapolis *M, D*

Kentucky
Western Kentucky University *B*

Michigan
Michigan Technological
University *M, D*

Missouri
Washington University in St. Louis *D*

New York
University of Rochester *B*

North Carolina
Wake Forest University *D*

Ohio
Ohio State University
Columbus Campus *B, M, D*

South Carolina
Medical University of South
Carolina *D*

Texas
University of Texas
Health Science Center at
Houston *M, D*

Washington
Washington State University *B*

Molecular pharmacology

California
University of California
Los Angeles *M, D*

Illinois
Rosalind Franklin University of
Medicine and Science *M, D*

New York
State University of New York
Buffalo *B, M, D*
Stony Brook *D*

Pennsylvania
University of Pittsburgh *M, D*

South Carolina
Medical University of South
Carolina *D*

Molecular physiology

Alabama
University of Alabama
Birmingham *D*

California
University of California
Los Angeles *D*

Illinois
Southern Illinois University
Carbondale *M, D*

Molecular toxicology

California
University of California
Los Angeles *D*

Montessori teacher education

California
St. Mary's College of California *M*

Maryland
Loyola College in Maryland *M*

Massachusetts
Endicott College *M*

Ohio
Xavier University *B, M*

Oklahoma
Oklahoma City University *B*

Pennsylvania
Chestnut Hill College *T*

Mortuary science/ embalming

Iowa
Buena Vista University *B*
Marshalltown Community College *A*

New York
State University of New York
College of Technology at
Canton *A, B*

Motorcycle maintenance

Iowa
Iowa Lakes Community College *C*

Kansas
Pittsburg State University *B*

Minnesota
Hennepin Technical College *C, A*

New York
State University of New York
College of Technology at Canton *C*

Texas
Austin Community College *C*
Cedar Valley College *C*

Movement therapy

California
California Institute of Integral
Studies *M*

Ohlone College *C*

Missouri
Washington University in St. Louis *D*

North Carolina
University of North Carolina
Chapel Hill *M, D*

Pennsylvania
Academy of Medical Arts and
Business *C, A*

Texas
Texas Christian University *B*

Multicultural education

California
California Baptist University *M*

District of Columbia
American University *M*

Florida
Florida State University *B, M, D*

Illinois
Trinity International University *D*

New Mexico
College of Santa Fe *M*

New York
College of New Rochelle *M*
Iona College *M*

Ohio
University of Findlay *B*

Oklahoma
University of Central Oklahoma *M*

South Dakota
Augustana College *B, M*

Texas
University of Houston
Clear Lake *M*

Washington
University of Washington *M, D*

Multimedia

Arizona
Arizona Western College *C, A*

California
Academy of Art University *C, A, B, M*
Antelope Valley College *C, A*
Art Institute
of California: San Diego *B*
Canada College *C, A*
Chaffey College *A*
College of the Canyons *A*
College of the Sequoias *A*
Long Beach City College *A*
National University *B*
Ohlone College *C, A*
Platt College
Ontario *C*
San Francisco Art Institute *B, M*
Santa Barbara City College *A*

Colorado
Art Institute
of Colorado *A, B*

Connecticut
Naugatuck Valley Community
College *A*

District of Columbia
American University *B*

Florida
Art Institute of Fort Lauderdale *A, B*
University of Central Florida *B, M*
University of Miami *B*

Georgia
Augusta State University *B*

Illinois
American Academy of Art *B*
Columbia College Chicago *B*
Illinois Institute of Art-Schaumburg *B*
Robert Morris College: Chicago *C, A*
School of the Art Institute of
Chicago *B, M*

Iowa
St. Ambrose University *B*
University of Iowa *M*

Louisiana
Tulane University *C, B*

Maryland
Maryland Institute College of Art *B*

Massachusetts
Hampshire College *B*
Holyoke Community College *C*
Massachusetts College of Art *B, M*
New England Institute of Art *B*
School of the Museum of Fine
Arts *B, M*
University of Massachusetts
Dartmouth *B, M*

Michigan
Andrews University *B*
College for Creative Studies *B*
Kendall College of Art and Design of
Ferris State University *B*

Minnesota
Art Institutes International
Minnesota *A, B*
Minneapolis College of Art and
Design *B*

Missouri
Lindenwood University *B*

New Jersey
The College of New Jersey *B*
Ramapo College of New Jersey *B*

New Mexico
College of Santa Fe *B*

New York
Bard College *B*
City University of New York
Borough of Manhattan Community
College *A*
Medaille College *C*
Rochester Institute of Technology *B*
State University of New York
College at Oneonta *B*

North Carolina
Art Institute
of Charlotte *A, B*

Ohio

Sinclair Community College *C*

Oregon

Art Institute of Portland *A, B*
Pacific Northwest College of Art *B*
Pacific University *B*
Portland Community College *C*
University of Oregon *B, M*

Pennsylvania

California University of
    Pennsylvania *M*
Eastern University *B*
Indiana University of
    Pennsylvania *B, M*

Puerto Rico

University of Puerto Rico
    Rio Piedras *B*

Rhode Island

Rhode Island School of Design *M*

South Carolina

Benedict College *B*

Tennessee

Memphis College of Art *B, M*

Vermont

Bennington College *B*
Champlain College *A, B*

Virginia

Tidewater Community College *A*

Washington

Art Institute of Seattle *A*
DigiPen Institute of Technology *A*
Evergreen State College *B*
Highline Community College *A*
Western Washington University *B*

Wisconsin

University of Wisconsin
    Milwaukee *B*

Museum studies

California

California State University
    Chico *M*
    San Bernardino *B*
John F. Kennedy University *M*
San Francisco Art Institute *M*
San Francisco State University *M*
University of Southern California *M*

Colorado

University of Colorado
    Boulder *M*

Connecticut

Connecticut College *T*

District of Columbia

George Washington University *M*

Florida

University of Florida *B*

Kansas

University of Kansas *M*

Massachusetts

Regis College *B*

Michigan

University of Michigan *B*

Mississippi

University of Southern Mississippi *B*

Nebraska

University of Nebraska
    Lincoln *M*

New Jersey

Seton Hall University *M*

New Mexico

Institute of American Indian Arts *A, B*

New York

City University of New York
    City College *M*
Fashion Institute of Technology *M*
New York University *M*
State University of New York
    College at Oneonta *M*
Syracuse University *M*

Pennsylvania

Juniata College *B*
Moore College of Art and Design *B*
University of the Arts *M*

Tennessee

Tusculum College *B*

Texas

Baylor University *B, M*
Texas A&M University *B*
Texas Tech University *M*

Virginia

Randolph-Macon Woman's College *B*

Washington

University of Washington *M*

Wisconsin

University of Wisconsin
    Madison *M, D*

Music, general

Arizona

Paradise Valley Community
    College *C, A*
South Mountain Community
    College *C, A*

California

MTI College *C*
Santa Rosa Junior College *C*

Colorado

Colorado Technical University *A*

Georgia

Albany Technical College *C*
Central Georgia Technical College *C*
Southwest Georgia Technical
    College *C*

Maine

University of Maine
    Augusta *C*

Michigan

Bay de Noc Community College *C*
Davenport University *A*
Glen Oaks Community College *C*

Missouri

Penn Valley Community College *A*

New Jersey

Union County College *A*

New York

Globe Institute of Technology *C*
Westchester Community College *C*

North Carolina

Forsyth Technical Community
    College *C*

Pennsylvania

Newport Business Institute *A*

Texas

Northwest Vista College *C*

Washington

Clark College *C*
Clover Park Technical College *C*
Olympic College *C*

Wisconsin

Milwaukee Area Technical College *C*
Western Wisconsin Technical
    College *A*

Music history/literature

Alabama

Birmingham-Southern College *B*

Arizona

Northern Arizona University *B*

Arkansas

Ouachita Baptist University *B*

California

California State University
    East Bay *M*
    Fullerton *B, M*
    Long Beach *B*
    Northridge *B, M*
    Sacramento *M*
    San Bernardino *B*
Foothill College *C*
Mills College *M*
San Diego State University *M*
San Francisco State University *M*
University of California
    Los Angeles *B*
    Santa Barbara *D*
University of Redlands *B*
University of Southern
    California *M, D*
University of the Pacific *B*
Vanguard University of Southern
    California *B*
Whittier College *B*

Colorado

University of Colorado
    Boulder *D*

Connecticut

University of Hartford *B, M*
Yale University *M, D*

District of Columbia

American University *B*
Catholic University of
    America *B, M, D*
Howard University *B*

Florida

Broward Community College *A*

Florida State University *B*

Idaho

University of Idaho *B*

Illinois

Illinois State University *B, T*
Illinois Valley Community College *A*
North Park University *B*
Northwestern University *M*
Rockford College *B*
Roosevelt University *B*
University of Illinois
    Urbana-Champaign *B, M*
Wheaton College *B*

Indiana

American Conservatory of
    Music *B, M, D*
Ball State University *M, D*
Butler University *M*
Earlham College *B*
St. Joseph's College *B*

Iowa

University of Northern Iowa *M*

Kansas

University of Kansas *B, M*

Kentucky

University of Kentucky *B, M, D*
University of Louisville *D*

Louisiana

Loyola University New Orleans *B*

Maryland

Johns Hopkins University: Peabody
    Conservatory of Music *M*

Massachusetts

Atlantic Union College *B*
Boston University *B, M, D*
New England Conservatory of
    Music *B, M*
Northeastern University *B*
Simmons College *B*
Simon's Rock College of Bard *B*
Tufts University *B, M*
Wellesley College *B*

Michigan

Calvin College *B*
Eastern Michigan University *M*
Northern Michigan University *B, T*
University of Michigan *B, M, D*

Minnesota

St. Cloud State University *B*

Missouri

University of Missouri
    Kansas City *M*
Washington University in St.
    Louis *B, M, D*

Nebraska

Hastings College *B*

New Hampshire

Keene State College *B*
University of New Hampshire *B*

New Jersey

Seton Hall University *B*

New York

Bard College *B*

City University of New York
Hunter College *M*
Queensborough Community
College *A*
Eastman School of Music of the
University of Rochester *M, D*
Five Towns College *A, B, M, D*
Hofstra University *B*
Nazareth College of Rochester *B*
Sarah Lawrence College *B*
State University of New York
Buffalo *M*
College at Fredonia *B*
College at Potsdam *M*
New Paltz *B*
University of Rochester *M, D*

North Carolina

Wake Forest University *B*

Ohio

Baldwin-Wallace College *B*
Bowling Green State University *M*
Case Western Reserve University *M*
College of Wooster *B*
Kent State University *M, D*
Oberlin College *B, M*
Ohio State University
Columbus Campus *B, M, D*
Ohio University *B, M*
Otterbein College *B*
Owens Community College
Toledo *A*
Sinclair Community College *A*
University of Akron *B, M*
University of Cincinnati *B, M*
Wright State University *B*
Youngstown State University *B, M*

Oklahoma

Connors State College *A*

Oregon

University of Oregon *M, D*

Pennsylvania

Bucknell University *B*
La Salle University *B*
Lafayette College *B*
Lehigh University *B*
Penn State
University Park *M*
Temple University *B, M*
West Chester University of
Pennsylvania *M*

South Carolina

Converse College *B, M*
Furman University *B*
Newberry College *B*
North Greenville College *A, B*
University of South Carolina *M*

South Dakota

University of South Dakota *M*

Texas

Baylor University *B, M*
Hardin-Simmons University *B*
Lon Morris College *A*
Rice University *B, M*
Sam Houston State University *B*
Southern Methodist University *M*
Southwestern University *B*
Texas A&M University
Commerce *B*
Texas Lutheran University *B*
Texas Tech University *M*
University of Houston *M*
University of North Texas *B*
University of Texas
Austin *B*

Utah

Brigham Young University *B*

Vermont

Bennington College *B, M*
Johnson State College *B*
Marlboro College *B*

Virginia

Bridgewater College *B*
Randolph-Macon Woman's College *B*
University of Mary Washington *B*
University of Richmond *B*

Washington

University of Washington *B*
Western Washington University *B*

Wisconsin

Lawrence University *B, T*
University of Wisconsin
Madison *B, M, D*
Stevens Point *B*

Music management

Arkansas

Central Baptist College *B*

California

Bethesda Christian University *B, M*
Diablo Valley College *C*
Fresno City College *A*
Los Medanos College *C*
Master's College *B*
Sacramento City College *C, A*
University of Southern California *B*
University of the Pacific *B*

Colorado

Western State College of Colorado *B*

Connecticut

University of Hartford *B*
University of New Haven *B*

District of Columbia

Howard University *B*

Florida

Florida Southern College *B*
Jacksonville University *B*

Georgia

Berry College *B*
Georgia State University *B*

Idaho

Boise State University *B*
University of Idaho *B*

Illinois

Bradley University *B*
Columbia College Chicago *B, M*
DePaul University *B*
Elmhurst College *B*
Lewis University *B*
Millikin University *B*
Roosevelt University *B*

Indiana

Anderson University *B*
Butler University *B*
DePauw University *B*
Huntington University *B*
Indiana University-Purdue University
Indianapolis *M*
St. Joseph's College *B*
Taylor University *B*
University of Evansville *B*

Valparaiso University *B*

Iowa

Drake University *B*
University of Iowa *B*
Waldorf College *B*

Kansas

Benedictine College *B*
Central Christian College of Kansas *A*
Labette Community College *A*

Louisiana

Dillard University *B*
Loyola University New Orleans *B*

Massachusetts

Berklee College of Music *B*
Northeastern University *B*

Michigan

Ferris State University *B*
Madonna University *B*
University of Michigan *M*

Minnesota

Augsburg College *B*
Minnesota State University
Mankato *B, M, T*
Moorhead *B*
St. Mary's University of Minnesota *B*
Winona State University *B*

Mississippi

Mississippi Valley State University *B*

Missouri

College of the Ozarks *B*
Drury University *B*

Nebraska

Northeast Community College *A*

New Hampshire

Franklin Pierce College *B*

New Jersey

William Paterson University of New
Jersey *B*

New York

City University of New York
Baruch College *B*
Five Towns College *A, B*
Hofstra University *B*
New York University *B*
State University of New York
College at Fredonia *B*
College at Oneonta *B*
Syracuse University *B*
Villa Maria College of Buffalo *A*

North Carolina

Appalachian State University *B*
Elizabeth City State University *B*
Guilford Technical Community
College *A*
Johnson C. Smith University *B*
Montreat College *B*
Wingate University *B*
Winston-Salem State University *B*

Ohio

Capital University *B*
Heidelberg College *B*
Ohio Northern University *B*
Owens Community College
Toledo *A*
University of Rio Grande *B*

Oklahoma

Oklahoma City University *B*
Southwestern Oklahoma State
University *B*

Oregon

Northwest Christian College *B*
Southern Oregon University *B*

Pennsylvania

Clarion University of Pennsylvania *B*
Drexel University *B*
Geneva College *B*
Grove City College *B*
Harrisburg Area Community
College *A*
Mansfield University of
Pennsylvania *B*
Waynesburg College *B*

South Carolina

South Carolina State University *B*

South Dakota

South Dakota State University *B*

Tennessee

Belmont University *B, M*
Bryan College *B*
Middle Tennessee State University *B*
Trevecca Nazarene University *B*
University of Memphis *B*

Texas

Angelina College *A*
Collin County Community College
District *A*
Hardin-Simmons University *B*
Houston Community College
System *C, A*
University of Texas
San Antonio *B*
University of the Incarnate Word *B*

Vermont

Johnson State College *B*

Washington

Central Washington University *B*
Shoreline Community College *A*
University of Puget Sound *B*

West Virginia

Davis and Elkins College *B*
University of Charleston *B*

Music pedagogy

Alabama

University of Montevallo *B*

California

Holy Names University *B, M*

Florida

University of Miami *M*

Illinois

Trinity International University *B*

Indiana

Butler University *B, M*
Goshen College *C*
Huntington University *B*
Indiana University-Purdue University
Fort Wayne *C*

Iowa

Drake University *B*

Kansas

Central Christian College of Kansas A

Massachusetts

New England Conservatory of
Music M

Michigan

Eastern Michigan University B
Madonna University C
Michigan State University B, M, D

Minnesota

College of St. Catherine T
University of Minnesota
Duluth B

Nebraska

Hastings College B

New York

Ithaca College M

North Carolina

Meredith College B

Ohio

Cedarville University B

Oklahoma

University of Oklahoma B

Pennsylvania

Carnegie Mellon University M
Marywood University C
Temple University B, M

South Carolina

Converse College B

Tennessee

Belmont University B, M
Bryan College B

Texas

Baylor University B
Texas A&M University
Commerce B, M
Texas Tech University M
University of Houston M

Wisconsin

Maranatha Baptist Bible College B
University of Wisconsin
Parkside C
Viterbo University B

Music performance

Alabama

Alabama Agricultural and Mechanical
University B, M
Huntingdon College B
Samford University B

Alaska

University of Alaska
Anchorage B
Fairbanks B, M

Arizona

Arizona State University B, M
Grand Canyon University B
Northern Arizona University B
University of Arizona B, M

Arkansas

Arkansas State University B, M
Harding University B
Henderson State University B

John Brown University B
Ouachita Baptist University B
University of Arkansas B, M
University of Central Arkansas B, M

California

Antelope Valley College C
Azusa Pacific University B
Bethesda Christian University B, M
Biola University B
California Institute of the Arts C, B, M
California State University
Chico B
Dominguez Hills B
East Bay M
Fullerton B, M
Long Beach B, M
Los Angeles B, M
Northridge B, M
Sacramento B, M
San Bernardino B
Stanislaus B
Chabot College A
Chapman University B
Cypress College C, A
Dominican University of California B
Foothill College C
Fresno Pacific University B
Gavilan Community College A
Golden West College C, A
Holy Names University B, M
Los Angeles Valley College C
Los Medanos College C, A
Mills College M
Mount St. Mary's College B
Notre Dame de Namur
University B, M
Pacific Union College B
Point Loma Nazarene University B
San Diego Christian College B
San Diego State University B, M
San Francisco Conservatory of
Music B, M
San Francisco State University B, M
San Jose State University B
Sierra College A
University of California
Irvine B
University of Redlands B
University of Southern
California B, M, D
University of the Pacific B
Vanguard University of Southern
California B

Colorado

Adams State College B
Colorado Christian University B
Fort Lewis College B
Metropolitan State College of
Denver B
University of Colorado
Boulder B, M, D
University of Denver B

Connecticut

University of Connecticut D
University of Hartford B, M, D
Yale University M, D

Delaware

University of Delaware B, M

District of Columbia

American University B
Catholic University of
America B, M, D
George Washington University M

Florida

Bethune-Cookman College B
Florida Agricultural and Mechanical
University B

Florida State University C, B, M, D
Hobe Sound Bible College B
Jacksonville University B
Lynn University B, M
Palm Beach Atlantic University B
Stetson University B
University of Central Florida B
University of Miami B, M, D
University of North Florida B
University of South Florida B, M
University of Tampa A, B
University of West Florida B

Georgia

Augusta State University B
Berry College B
Brenau University B
Brewton-Parker College B
Clayton State University B
Columbus State University B, M
Covenant College B
Gainesville State College A
Georgia College and State
University B
Georgia Southern University B
Georgia State University B, M
Kennesaw State University B
Mercer University B
Savannah State University B
Toccoa Falls College B
University of Georgia B
University of West Georgia B, M
Valdosta State University B

Idaho

Boise State University B, M
Idaho State University B
North Idaho College A
Northwest Nazarene University B
University of Idaho B

Illinois

Augustana College B
Blackburn College B, T
Bradley University B
Columbia College Chicago B
Concordia University B
DePaul University B, M
Eureka College B, T
Illinois State University B
Illinois Valley Community College A
Illinois Wesleyan University B
Judson College B
Millikin University B
Moody Bible Institute B
North Park University B
Northern Illinois University M
Northwestern University B, M, D
Olivet Nazarene University B
Roosevelt University B, M
Sauk Valley Community College A
Trinity Christian College B
Trinity International University B
University of Illinois
Urbana-Champaign B, M, D
University of St. Francis B
Western Illinois University B
Wheaton College B

Indiana

American Conservatory of
Music C, A, B, M, D
Anderson University B
Butler University B, M
DePauw University B
Earlham College B
Goshen College B
Grace College B
Huntington University B
Indiana State University B, M
Indiana University
Bloomington B, M, D
South Bend B, M

Indiana Wesleyan University B, T
Manchester College B
Martin University B
Oakland City University B
St. Mary-of-the-Woods College B
Taylor University B
University of Evansville B
University of Indianapolis B
Valparaiso University B
Vincennes University A

Iowa

Buena Vista University B
Coe College B
Cornell College B
Drake University B
Morningside College B
Simpson College B
Southwestern Community College A
University of Iowa B
University of Northern Iowa B, M
Waldorf College B
Wartburg College B

Kansas

Bethany College B
Central Christian College of
Kansas A, B
Friends University B
Kansas State University B
Kansas Wesleyan University B
McPherson College B
MidAmerica Nazarene University B
Pittsburg State University B
Seward County Community College A
University of Kansas B, M, D
Washburn University of Topeka B

Kentucky

Berea College B, T
Campbellsville University B
Kentucky Christian University B, T
Morehead State University M
Northern Kentucky University C
Transylvania University B
University of Kentucky B, M

Louisiana

Centenary College of Louisiana B, T
Grambling State University B
Louisiana State University and
Agricultural and Mechanical
College B, M, D
Louisiana Tech University B
Loyola University New Orleans B, M
Northwestern State University B, M
Southeastern Louisiana
University B, M
Southern University and Agricultural
and Mechanical College B
Tulane University B
University of Louisiana at
Lafayette B, M
University of Louisiana at
Monroe B, M
University of New Orleans M
Xavier University of Louisiana B

Maine

College of the Atlantic B
University of Maine B, M
University of Southern Maine B

Maryland

Columbia Union College B
Johns Hopkins University: Peabody
Conservatory of Music B, M, D
Salisbury University B
Towson University M
University of Maryland
College Park B
Washington Bible College A, B

Massachusetts

Anna Maria College *B*
Berklee College of Music *B*
Boston Conservatory *B, M*
Boston University *B, M, D*
Eastern Nazarene College *B*
Gordon College *B*
Greenfield Community College *C*
New England Conservatory of
    Music *B, M, D*
Northeastern University *B*
Simmons College *B*
Simon's Rock College of Bard *B*
University of Massachusetts
    Lowell *B, M*
Westfield State College *B*

Michigan

Adrian College *A, B, T*
Albion College *B*
Alma College *B*
Andrews University *B, M*
Aquinas College *A*
Calvin College *B*
Central Michigan University *M, T*
Cornerstone University *B, T*
Eastern Michigan University *B, M*
Hope College *B*
Lansing Community College *A*
Marygrove College *B*
Michigan State University *B, M, D*
Oakland Community College *A*
Oakland University *B*
Olivet College *B*
Rochester College *B*
University of Michigan *B, M, T*
University of Michigan
    Flint *B*
Western Michigan University *B*

Minnesota

Augsburg College *B*
Bethel University *B*
College of St. Catherine *B*
College of St. Scholastica *B*
Concordia College: Moorhead *B*
Crown College *B*
Gustavus Adolphus College *B*
Hamline University *B*
Minnesota State University
    Mankato *B, M, T*
    Moorhead *B*
North Central University *B*
Northwestern College *B*
St. Mary's University of Minnesota *B*
St. Olaf College *B*
University of Minnesota
    Duluth *B, M*
    Morris *B*
    Twin Cities *B, M, D*
University of St. Thomas *B, M*
Winona State University *B*

Mississippi

Alcorn State University *B*
Belhaven College *B*
Jackson State University *B*
Millsaps College *B, T*
Mississippi College *B, M*
University of Southern Mississippi *D*
William Carey College *B*

Missouri

Avila University *B*
Calvary Bible College and Theological
    Seminary *B*
Central Methodist University *B*
Drury University *B*
Evangel University *B*
Hannibal-LaGrange College *A, B*
Lindenwood University *B*
Missouri Baptist University *B*
Missouri State University *B*

Truman State University *B*
University of Missouri
    Kansas City *B, M, D*
Webster University *M*
William Jewell College *B*

Montana

Montana State University
    Billings *B*
Rocky Mountain College *B*
University of Montana: Missoula *B, M*

Nebraska

Hastings College *B, T*
Nebraska Wesleyan University *B*
Northeast Community College *A*
Union College *B*
University of Nebraska
    Kearney *B*
    Omaha *B*

Nevada

University of Nevada
    Reno *B*

New Hampshire

Franklin Pierce College *B*
Keene State College *B*
University of New Hampshire *B*

New Jersey

Middlesex County College *A*
Montclair State University *B*
Rowan University *B*
Seton Hall University *B*
Westminster Choir College of Rider
    University *M*
William Paterson University of New
    Jersey *B*

New Mexico

New Mexico State University *B, M*
University of New Mexico *B, M*

New York

Bard College *B, M*
City University of New York
    Brooklyn College *B, M*
    City College *B, M*
    Hunter College *B, M*
    Lehman College *B*
    Queens College *B, M*
College of Saint Rose *B, M*
Columbia University
    School of General Studies *B*
Dutchess Community College *C*
Eastman School of Music of the
    University of Rochester *B, M, D*
Five Towns College *A, B, M, D*
Hofstra University *B*
Houghton College *B*
Ithaca College *B, M, T*
Jewish Theological Seminary of
    America *B*
Juilliard School *B, M, D*
Long Island University
    Brooklyn Campus *B*
    C. W. Post Campus *B, M*
Manhattan School of Music *B, M, D*
Mannes College The New School for
    Music *B, M*
Mercy College *B*
Monroe Community College *A*
Nassau Community College *A*
Nazareth College of Rochester *B*
New York University *B, M, D*
Nyack College *B*
Sarah Lawrence College *B*
State University of New York
    Albany *B*
    Binghamton *B, M*
    Buffalo *B, M*
    College at Fredonia *B*

College at Geneseo *B*
College at Potsdam *B, M*
New Paltz *B*
Purchase *B, M*
Stony Brook *M, D*
Syracuse University *B, M*
University of Rochester *M, D*
Villa Maria College of Buffalo *A*
Wagner College *B*
Westchester Community College *A*

North Carolina

Appalachian State University *B, M*
Brevard College *B*
Catawba College *B*
Chowan College *B*
Duke University *M*
East Carolina University *B, M*
Elon University *B*
Gardner-Webb University *B*
Greensboro College *B, T*
Lenoir-Rhyne College *B*
Mars Hill College *B*
Meredith College *B, M*
Methodist College *B*
Montreat College *B*
North Carolina School of the
    Arts *B, M*
Peace College *B*
Queens University of Charlotte *B*
St. Augustine's College *B*
Salem College *B*
University of North Carolina
    Chapel Hill *B*
    Charlotte *B*
    Greensboro *B, M, D*
    Pembroke *B*
    Wilmington *B*
Wake Forest University *B*
Western Carolina University *B, M*
Wingate University *B*

North Dakota

Jamestown College *B*
Minot State University *B*
University of Mary *B*
University of North Dakota *B*

Ohio

Ashland University *B*
Baldwin-Wallace College *B*
Bowling Green State University *B, M*
Capital University *B*
Cedarville University *B*
Central State University *B*
Cleveland Institute of Music *B, M, D*
College of Wooster *B*
Heidelberg College *B*
Kent State University *M*
Miami University
    Oxford Campus *B, M*
Mount Union College *B*
Mount Vernon Nazarene University *B*
Ohio Northern University *B*
Ohio State University
    Columbus Campus *B, M, D*
Ohio University *B, M*
Ohio Wesleyan University *B*
Otterbein College *B*
Owens Community College
    Toledo *A*
Sinclair Community College *C, A*
University of Akron *B, M*
University of Cincinnati *B, M, D*
University of Dayton *B*
University of Toledo *M*
Wright State University *B*
Youngstown State University *B, M*

Oklahoma

Mid-America Christian University *B*
Northwestern Oklahoma State
    University *B*

Oklahoma Baptist University *B*
Oklahoma Christian University *B*
Oklahoma City University *B, M*
Oral Roberts University *B*
Southeastern Oklahoma State
    University *B*
Southwestern Christian University *B*
Southwestern Oklahoma State
    University *B*
University of Central Oklahoma *B, M*
University of Oklahoma *D*
University of Tulsa *B*

Oregon

Corban College *B*
Lewis & Clark College *B*
Linfield College *B*
Pacific University *B*
Portland Community College *C, A*
Portland State University *B, M*
University of Oregon *B, M, D*
Willamette University *B*

Pennsylvania

Allegheny College *B*
Bucknell University *B*
Carnegie Mellon University *B, M*
Clarion University of Pennsylvania *B*
Community College of Philadelphia *A*
Curtis Institute of Music *C, B*
Duquesne University *B, M*
Geneva College *B*
Gettysburg College *B*
Grove City College *B*
Immaculata University *B*
Indiana University of Pennsylvania *B*
Lebanon Valley College *B*
Mansfield University of
    Pennsylvania *B*
Marywood University *B*
Mercyhurst College *B*
Moravian College *B*
Penn State
    University Park *B, M*
Philadelphia Biblical University *B*
St. Vincent College *B*
Seton Hill University *B*
Slippery Rock University of
    Pennsylvania *B*
Susquehanna University *B*
Temple University *B, M, D*
University of the Arts *C, B, M*
Valley Forge Christian College *B*
West Chester University of
    Pennsylvania *B, M*
Westminster College *B*
Wilkes University *B*
York College of Pennsylvania *B*

Puerto Rico

Conservatory of Music of Puerto
    Rico *B, T*
Inter American University of Puerto
    Rico
    San German Campus *B*

Rhode Island

Rhode Island College *B*
University of Rhode Island *B*

South Carolina

Anderson University *B*
Charleston Southern University *B*
Coker College *B, T*
Columbia College *B*
Columbia International University *B*
Converse College *B, M*
Furman University *B*
Newberry College *B*
North Greenville College *A, B*
Presbyterian College *B*
University of South Carolina *M, D*

South Dakota

University of South Dakota B, M

Tennessee

Belmont University B, M
Bryan College B
Carson-Newman College B
Hiwassee College A
Lambuth University B
LeMoyne-Owen College B
Lee University B
Lipscomb University B
Maryville College B, T
Southern Adventist University B
Tennessee Technological University B
Union University B
Vanderbilt University B

Texas

Alvin Community College A
Baylor University B, M
Cedar Valley College C, A
Del Mar College A
Hardin-Simmons University B, M
Houston Baptist University B
Houston Community College
   System C, A
Howard Payne University B
Lon Morris College A
Midland College A
Navarro College A
Prairie View A&M University B
Rice University B, M, D
Sam Houston State University B, M
Southern Methodist
   University C, B, M
Southwestern Assemblies of God
   University B
Southwestern University B
Stephen F. Austin State University B, M
Texas A&M University
   Commerce B, M
Texas Christian University C, B, M
Texas Lutheran University B
Texas State University: San Marcos B
Texas Tech University B, M, D
Trinity University B
Tyler Junior College A
University of Houston B, M, D
University of Mary Hardin-Baylor B
University of North Texas B, M, D
University of Texas
   Austin B
   El Paso B, M
   San Antonio B, M
University of the Incarnate Word B
West Texas A&M University B, M

Utah

Brigham Young University B, M
Weber State University B

Vermont

Bennington College B, M
Johnson State College B
University of Vermont B

Virginia

Bluefield College B
George Mason University B, M
Hampton University B
James Madison University B, M, T
Longwood University B
Norfolk State University M
Old Dominion University B
Randolph-Macon Woman's College B
Shenandoah University B, M, D
University of Mary Washington B
University of Richmond B
Virginia Commonwealth
   University B, M
Virginia State University B

Washington

Central Washington University B
Cornish College of the Arts B
Eastern Washington University B, T
Everett Community College A
Gonzaga University B
Shoreline Community College A
University of Puget Sound B, T
University of Washington B, M, D
Walla Walla College B
Washington State University B
Western Washington University B
Whitworth College B, T

West Virginia

Alderson-Broaddus College B

Wisconsin

Cardinal Stritch University B
Carthage College B
Concordia University Wisconsin B
Lawrence University B, T
Maranatha Baptist Bible College B
Milwaukee Area Technical College A
Northland College B, T
University of Wisconsin
   Madison B, M, D
   Parkside T
   Stevens Point B
   Superior B, M
Viterbo University B

Wyoming

Casper College A
University of Wyoming B

Music teacher education

Alabama

Alabama Agricultural and Mechanical
   University B
Alabama State University B
Auburn University B
Birmingham-Southern College B, T
Huntingdon College B, T
Judson College B
Oakwood College B
Samford University B, M
Shelton State Community College A
Talladega College B
University of Alabama B
University of Alabama
   Birmingham T
University of Mobile B, T

Alaska

University of Alaska
   Anchorage B
   Fairbanks B

Arizona

Arizona State University B, M
Grand Canyon University B
Northern Arizona University B, M, T
Prescott College B, M, T
South Mountain Community
   College A
University of Arizona B, M, D

Arkansas

Arkansas State University B, M, T
Arkansas State University
   Beebe A
Arkansas Tech University B
Harding University B, M, T
John Brown University B, T
Ouachita Baptist University B, T
Southern Arkansas University B, T
University of Arkansas M

University of Arkansas
   Fort Smith B
   Monticello B
University of Central Arkansas M, T
Williams Baptist College B

California

Azusa Pacific University T
Biola University B, T
California Baptist University T
California Lutheran University B, T
California State University
   Chico B, T
   Dominguez Hills T
   East Bay M
   Fullerton B, M
   Long Beach M, T
   Northridge B, T
   Sacramento T
   San Bernardino T
Chapman University B
Fresno Pacific University B, T
Holy Names University M, T
Hope International University B
Humboldt State University T
Los Angeles Southwest College A
Master's College B, T
Mount St. Mary's College T
Pacific Union College B
Pepperdine University B
Point Loma Nazarene University B
Saddleback College A
San Diego Christian College B, T
San Francisco State University B, T
Simpson University B, T
Sonoma State University T
University of Redlands B, T
University of Southern
   California B, M, D
University of the Pacific B, T
Vanguard University of Southern
   California T
Westmont College T

Colorado

Adams State College B, T
Colorado Christian University B
Colorado State University T
Colorado State University
   Pueblo T
Fort Lewis College B
Metropolitan State College of
   Denver B, T
University of Colorado
   Boulder B, M, D, T
University of Northern Colorado B, T
Western State College of Colorado T

Connecticut

Central Connecticut State
   University B, M, T
Connecticut College T
St. Joseph College B
University of Connecticut B
University of Hartford B, M, D
Western Connecticut State
   University B, M

Delaware

Delaware State University B
University of Delaware B, T

District of Columbia

Catholic University of America B, T
George Washington University M, T
Howard University B, M

Florida

Baptist College of Florida B
Bethune-Cookman College B, T
Broward Community College A
Clearwater Christian College B

Florida Agricultural and Mechanical
   University B, T
Florida Atlantic University B
Florida International
   University B, M, T
Florida Southern College B
Florida State University B, M, D, T
Hobe Sound Bible College B, T
Jacksonville University B, M, T
Manatee Community College A
Palm Beach Atlantic University B, T
Palm Beach Community College A
Pensacola Junior College A
Southeastern College of the
   Assemblies of God B, T
Stetson University B
University of Central Florida B, M
University of Florida A, B, M
University of Miami B, M, D
University of North Florida B, M
University of South Florida B, M
University of Tampa B, T
Warner Southern College B

Georgia

Albany State University M
Armstrong Atlantic State
   University B, M, T
Augusta State University B, M
Berry College B
Brenau University B
Brewton-Parker College B
Clark Atlanta University B
Clayton State University B
Columbus State University B, M
Darton College A
Emmanuel College B
Fort Valley State University B, T
Gainesville State College A
Georgia College and State
   University B
Georgia Southern University B, M
Kennesaw State University B
Mercer University B
North Georgia College & State
   University B, M
Piedmont College M, T
Reinhardt College B
Shorter College B, T
Thomas University B
Toccoa Falls College B, T
University of Georgia B, M, D
University of West Georgia B, M
Valdosta State University B, M
Young Harris College A

Hawaii

Brigham Young University-Hawaii B, T

Idaho

Boise State University B, M, T
Brigham Young University-Idaho T
Idaho State University B
Northwest Nazarene University B
University of Idaho B

Illinois

Augustana College B, T
Bradley University B, M, T
Chicago State University B
College of Lake County A
Concordia University B, M, T
DePaul University B, M, T
Elmhurst College B
Eureka College T
Greenville College B, T
Illinois College T
Illinois Eastern Community Colleges
   Lincoln Trail College A
   Olney Central College A
Illinois State University B, M, T
Illinois Wesleyan University B
Judson College B, T

Knox College T
MacMurray College B, T
McKendree College B
Millikin University B, T
Monmouth College B, T
North Central College B, T
North Park University T
Northern Illinois University M
Northwestern University B, M, D
Olivet Nazarene University B, T
Parkland College A
Quincy University B, T
Roosevelt University B, M
St. Xavier University B
Sauk Valley Community College A
Trinity Christian College B, T
Trinity International University B
University of Illinois
    Urbana-Champaign B, M, D, T
University of St. Francis B, T
VanderCook College of Music B, M, T
Waubonsee Community College A
Wheaton College B, T

Indiana

Anderson University B, T
Bethel College B
Butler University B, M, T
DePauw University B
Goshen College B
Grace College B
Huntington University B
Indiana University
    Bloomington B, M, D, T
    South Bend B, T
Indiana University-Purdue University
    Fort Wayne B, T
Indiana Wesleyan University B, T
Manchester College B, T
Oakland City University B
Saint Mary's College T
St. Mary-of-the-Woods College B, T
Taylor University B, T
University of Evansville B, T
University of Indianapolis B, T
Valparaiso University B
Vincennes University A

Iowa

Ashford University B, T
Briar Cliff University B
Buena Vista University B, T
Central College B, T
Clarke College B, T
Coe College B
Cornell College B, T
Dordt College B
Drake University B
Faith Baptist Bible College and
    Theological Seminary B
Graceland University T
Iowa State University B, T
Iowa Wesleyan College B
Loras College T
Morningside College B
Mount Mercy College T
Northwestern College T
St. Ambrose University B, T
Simpson College B, T
University of Iowa M, D, T
University of Northern Iowa B, M
Waldorf College B
Wartburg College B, T

Kansas

Allen County Community College A
Baker University B, T
Benedictine College B
Bethany College B
Bethel College T
Central Christian College of Kansas A
Colby Community College A
Emporia State University B, T
Fort Hays State University B

Friends University B
Garden City Community College A
Kansas State University B, M, T
Labette Community College A
McPherson College B, T
MidAmerica Nazarene University B, T
Ottawa University B, T
Pittsburg State University B, M, T
Southwestern College B, T
Sterling College B
Tabor College B, T
University of Kansas B, M, D, T
Washburn University of Topeka B
Wichita State University B, M, T

Kentucky

Asbury College B, T
Bellarmine University B, T
Berea College B, T
Campbellsville University B, M
Eastern Kentucky University B, M
Georgetown College B
Kentucky Christian University B, T
Kentucky State University B
Kentucky Wesleyan College T
Murray State University B, M, T
Transylvania University B, T
University of Kentucky B, M
University of Louisville B, M
University of the Cumberlands B, T
Western Kentucky University M, T

Louisiana

Centenary College of Louisiana B, T
Grambling State University B
Louisiana State University and
    Agricultural and Mechanical
    College B
Louisiana Tech University B
Loyola University New Orleans B, M
Nicholls State University B
Northwestern State University B
Southeastern Louisiana University B
Southern University
    New Orleans B
Southern University and Agricultural
    and Mechanical College B
University of Louisiana at Lafayette B
University of Louisiana at Monroe B
University of New Orleans B
Xavier University of Louisiana B

Maine

University of Maine B
University of Maine
    Fort Kent B
University of Southern Maine B, T

Maryland

College of Notre Dame of Maryland T
Columbia Union College B
Community College of Baltimore
    County A
Frostburg State University B, T
Johns Hopkins University: Peabody
    Conservatory of Music B, M
Mount St. Mary's University T
St. Mary's College of Maryland T
Salisbury University T
Towson University B, M, T
University of Maryland
    College Park B
    Eastern Shore B
Washington Bible College B, T

Massachusetts

Anna Maria College B, T
Berklee College of Music B
Boston Conservatory B, M
Boston University B, M, D
Bridgewater State College B, M, T
Eastern Nazarene College B, M, T
Gordon College B, M

Northeastern University B
Smith College M
Tufts University M
University of Massachusetts
    Dartmouth T
    Lowell B, M
Westfield State College B, M, T

Michigan

Adrian College B, T
Albion College B, T
Alma College T
Andrews University M
Aquinas College B, T
Calvin College B
Central Michigan University B, M, T
Concordia University B, T
Cornerstone University B, T
Delta College A
Eastern Michigan University B, M, T
Grace Bible College B
Grand Valley State University B, T
Hope College B, T
Lansing Community College A
Madonna University B, T
Michigan State University B, M, D
Northern Michigan University B, T
Oakland University B
Olivet College B, T
Rochester College B
University of Michigan B, M, D
University of Michigan
    Flint B, T
Western Michigan University B, M, T

Minnesota

Augsburg College B, T
Bemidji State University T
Bethel University B
College of St. Benedict T
College of St. Catherine B, T
College of St. Scholastica T
Concordia College: Moorhead B, T
Concordia University: St. Paul B, T
Crown College B, T
Gustavus Adolphus College T
Hamline University B, T
Minnesota State University
    Mankato B, M, T
    Moorhead B, M
Northland Community & Technical
    College A
Northwestern College B
Pillsbury Baptist Bible College T
Ridgewater College A
St. Cloud State University B, T
St. John's University T
St. Mary's University of Minnesota B
St. Olaf College B
Southwest Minnesota State
    University B
University of Minnesota
    Duluth B
    Morris T
    Twin Cities B, M
University of St. Thomas B, M, T
Winona State University B, T

Mississippi

Alcorn State University B
Blue Mountain College B
Coahoma Community College A
Delta State University B, T
Itawamba Community College A
Jackson State University M
Mississippi College B, M
Mississippi State University B, T
Mississippi Valley State University B, T
University of Mississippi B
University of Southern
    Mississippi B, M, D
William Carey College B

Missouri

Baptist Bible College B
Calvary Bible College and Theological
    Seminary B
Central Methodist University B
Central Missouri State
    University B, M, T
College of the Ozarks B, T
Culver-Stockton College B, T
Drury University B, T
Evangel University B, T
Hannibal-LaGrange College B
Lincoln University B, T
Maryville University of Saint Louis B
Missouri Baptist University B, T
Missouri Southern State
    University B, T
Missouri State University B
Missouri Western State University B
Northwest Missouri State
    University B, M, T
Southeast Missouri State
    University B, M, T
Southwest Baptist University B, T
Truman State University M, T
University of Missouri
    Columbia B, M, D
    Kansas City B, M
    St. Louis B, M, T
Washington University in St. Louis M
Webster University B, M
William Jewell College B, T

Montana

Montana State University
    Billings B, T
    Bozeman B
Rocky Mountain College B, T
University of Montana:
    Missoula B, M, T
University of Montana: Western B, T

Nebraska

Chadron State College B
Concordia University B, T
Dana College B
Grace University B
Hastings College B, M, T
Midland Lutheran College B, T
Nebraska Wesleyan University B
Peru State College B, T
Union College T
University of Nebraska
    Kearney B, M, T
    Lincoln B
    Omaha B, T
Wayne State College B, T
Western Nebraska Community
    College A
York College B, T

Nevada

University of Nevada
    Reno B

New Hampshire

Keene State College B, T
Plymouth State University B, T
University of New Hampshire B, M, T

New Jersey

Caldwell College T
The College of New Jersey M, T
Essex County College A
Georgian Court University T
Kean University B, T
New Jersey City University M, T
Rider University B
Rowan University B
Westminster Choir College of Rider
    University B, M
William Paterson University of New
    Jersey B, T

New Mexico

Eastern New Mexico University *B*
New Mexico State University *B*
University of New Mexico *B*
Western New Mexico University *B*

New York

City University of New York
  Brooklyn College *B, M, T*
  City College *B, T*
  Hunter College *B, M, T*
  Lehman College *M*
  Queens College *B, M, T*
College of Saint Rose *B, M, T*
Dowling College *B*
Eastman School of Music of the
    University of
    Rochester *B, M, D, T*
Five Towns College *B, M, D, T*
Fordham University *T*
Hartwick College *B, T*
Hobart and William Smith Colleges *T*
Hofstra University *B, M, T*
Houghton College *B, T*
Ithaca College *B, M, T*
Long Island University
  Brooklyn Campus *B, T*
  C.W. Post Campus *B, M, T*
Manhattanville College *M, T*
Molloy College *B*
Monroe Community College *A*
Nazareth College of Rochester *B, M, T*
New York University *B, M, D, T*
Nyack College *B*
Roberts Wesleyan College *B, M*
State University of New York
  Buffalo *B, M, T*
  College at Fredonia *B, M, T*
  College at Potsdam *B, M*
Syracuse University *B, M, T*
University of Rochester *M, D*
Wagner College *T*

North Carolina

Appalachian State University *B, M, T*
Bennett College *B, T*
Brevard College *B*
Campbell University *B, T*
Catawba College *B, T*
Chowan College *B*
East Carolina University *B, M*
Elizabeth City State University *T*
Elon University *B, T*
Fayetteville State University *B, T*
Gardner-Webb University *B*
Greensboro College *B, T*
Lenoir-Rhyne College *B, T*
Livingstone College *T*
Mars Hill College *B*
Meredith College *B, T*
Methodist College *A, B, T*
North Carolina Agricultural and
    Technical State University *B, T*
North Carolina Central University *B, T*
Pfeiffer University *B, T*
Piedmont Baptist College *B*
St. Augustine's College *B*
Salem College *B*
University of North Carolina
  Charlotte *B*
  Greensboro *B, M, D, T*
  Pembroke *B, M*
  Wilmington *B*
Western Carolina University *B, T*
Wingate University *B, T*
Winston-Salem State University *B*

North Dakota

Dickinson State University *B, T*
Jamestown College *B*
Minot State University *B, M*
North Dakota State University *B, T*
University of Mary *B, T*
University of North Dakota *B, T*
Valley City State University *B, T*

Ohio

Ashland University *B, T*
Baldwin-Wallace College *B, T*
Bluffton University *B*
Bowling Green State
    University *B, M, T*
Capital University *B*
Case Western Reserve
    University *B, M, D*
Cedarville University *B, T*
Circleville Bible College *B*
College of Wooster *B*
God's Bible School and College *B*
Heidelberg College *B*
Hiram College *T*
Kent State University *B, M, D*
Malone College *B*
Miami University
  Oxford Campus *B, M, T*
Mount Union College *B, T*
Mount Vernon Nazarene
    University *B, M, T*
Oberlin College *B, M*
Ohio Northern University *B*
Ohio State University
  Columbus Campus *B*
Ohio Wesleyan University *B*
Otterbein College *B*
Sinclair Community College *A*
University of Akron *B, M*
University of Cincinnati *B, M, D, T*
University of Dayton *B, M*
University of Rio Grande *B, T*
University of Toledo *B, M, T*
Wright State University *B, M, T*
Xavier University *B, M*
Youngstown State University *B, M*

Oklahoma

Cameron University *B, T*
East Central University *B*
Eastern Oklahoma State College *A*
Mid-America Christian University *B*
Northeastern State University *B*
Northwestern Oklahoma State
    University *B, T*
Oklahoma Baptist University *B, T*
Oklahoma Christian University *B, T*
Oklahoma City University *B*
Oklahoma Panhandle State
    University *B*
Oklahoma State University *B*
Oklahoma Wesleyan University *B*
Oral Roberts University *B, T*
Southeastern Oklahoma State
    University *B, M, T*
Southern Nazarene University *B*
Southwestern Oklahoma State
    University *B, M, T*
University of Central Oklahoma *B, M*
University of Oklahoma *B, M, D, T*
University of Tulsa *B, T*

Oregon

Corban College *B*
George Fox University *T*
Linfield College *B, T*
Oregon State University *M*
Portland State University *T*
Southern Oregon University *T*
University of Oregon *B, M, D, T*
University of Portland *B, M, T*
Warner Pacific College *B, T*
Willamette University *M*

Pennsylvania

Baptist Bible College of
    Pennsylvania *B*
Bucknell University *B, T*
Clarion University of
    Pennsylvania *B, T*
Duquesne University *B, M, T*
Elizabethtown College *B*
Geneva College *B*
Gettysburg College *B, T*
Gratz College *M*
Grove City College *B, T*
Immaculata University *B*
Indiana University of
    Pennsylvania *B, T*
Lebanon Valley College *B, M, T*
Lincoln University *B, T*
Lycoming College *T*
Mansfield University of
    Pennsylvania *B, M, T*
Marywood University *B, M*
Mercyhurst College *B, T*
Messiah College *B, T*
Millersville University of
    Pennsylvania *B, T*
Moravian College *B, T*
Penn State
  University Park *B, M, D*
Philadelphia Biblical University *B, T*
Seton Hill University *B, T*
Susquehanna University *B, T*
Temple University *M, D*
University of the Arts *M*
Valley Forge Christian College *B*
West Chester University of
    Pennsylvania *B, T*
Westminster College *T*
Wilkes University *B*
York College of Pennsylvania *B, T*

Puerto Rico

Conservatory of Music of Puerto
    Rico *B, T*
Inter American University of Puerto
    Rico
  San German Campus *B, M*
Pontifical Catholic University of
    Puerto Rico *B, T*
Universidad Adventista de las
    Antillas *B*

Rhode Island

Providence College *B*
Rhode Island College *B, M*
Salve Regina University *B*
University of Rhode Island *B, T*

South Carolina

Anderson University *B, T*
Charleston Southern University *B*
Claflin University *B*
Coker College *B, T*
Columbia College *B, T*
Converse College *T*
Erskine College *B, T*
Furman University *B, T*
Lander University *B*
Limestone College *B*
Newberry College *B, T*
North Greenville College *B, T*
Presbyterian College *B, T*
South Carolina State University *B, T*
Southern Wesleyan University *B, T*
University of South Carolina *M, D*
University of South Carolina
  Aiken *B, T*
Winthrop University *B, M, T*

South Dakota

Augustana College *B, T*
Black Hills State University *B*
Dakota State University *B, T*
Dakota Wesleyan University *B, T*
Mount Marty College *B*
Northern State University *B, T*
South Dakota State University *B, T*
University of Sioux Falls *B*
University of South Dakota *B, M, T*

Tennessee

Belmont University *B, M, T*
Bryan College *T*
Carson-Newman College *T*
Cumberland University *B, T*
Free Will Baptist Bible College *B*
Freed-Hardeman University *B, T*
Hiwassee College *A*
Lambuth University *B, T*
Lee University *B*
Lipscomb University *B, T*
Maryville College *B, T*
Milligan College *B, M, T*
Southern Adventist University *B*
Tennessee Technological
    University *B, T*
Tennessee Temple University *B*
Tennessee Wesleyan College *B, T*
Trevecca Nazarene University *B, T*
Union University *B, T*
University of Memphis *T*
University of Tennessee
  Chattanooga *B*
  Knoxville *B, T*

Texas

Abilene Christian University *B, T*
Amarillo College *A*
Arlington Baptist College *B, T*
Austin College *M*
Baylor University *B, M, T*
Dallas Baptist University *B*
Del Mar College *A*
East Texas Baptist University *B*
Hardin-Simmons University *B, M, T*
Houston Baptist University *B, M, T*
Howard Payne University *B, T*
Lamar University *B, M, T*
Laredo Community College *A*
Lubbock Christian University *B*
McMurry University *B, T*
North Lake College *A*
Prairie View A&M University *M*
Sam Houston State University *M, T*
Schreiner University *B*
Southern Methodist
    University *B, M, T*
Southwestern Assemblies of God
    University *B*
Southwestern University *B, T*
Stephen F. Austin State University *M*
Tarleton State University *T*
Texas A&M University
  Commerce *M, T*
  Kingsville *B, M, T*
Texas Christian University *B, M*
Texas College *B, T*
Texas Lutheran University *B, T*
Texas State University: San
    Marcos *M, T*
Texas Tech University *M*
Texas Wesleyan University *M, T*
University of Houston *M, D, T*
University of Mary Hardin-Baylor *B, T*
University of North Texas *M, D*
University of St. Thomas *B*
University of Texas
  Arlington *D, T*
  Austin *M, D*
  El Paso *M*
  San Antonio *M, T*
University of the Incarnate Word *T*
Wayland Baptist University *B, T*
West Texas A&M University *T*

Utah

Brigham Young University *B, M*
Southern Utah University *B, T*
University of Utah *B*
Utah State University *B*
Weber State University *B*

Vermont

Castleton State College B, T
Johnson State College B
University of Vermont B

Virginia

Bluefield College B, T
Bridgewater College T
Eastern Mennonite University T
Hampton University M
Hollins University T
James Madison University T
Liberty University B, T
Longwood University B, T
Old Dominion University B, M, T
Radford University T
Shenandoah University B, M, D
Virginia Wesleyan College T

Washington

Central Washington University B, T
Eastern Washington University B, M, T
Gonzaga University B, T
Northwest University T
Seattle Pacific University B, T
University of Puget Sound B, T
University of Washington B, M, D
Walla Walla College B
Washington State University B, M, T
Western Washington University B
Whitworth College B, T

West Virginia

Alderson-Broaddus College B, T
Concord University B, T
Potomac State College of West Virginia
    University A
Shepherd University T
University of Charleston B
West Liberty State College B
West Virginia State University B
West Virginia University T
West Virginia Wesleyan College B

Wisconsin

Alverno College B
Carroll College B, T
Carthage College B, T
Concordia University Wisconsin B, T
Edgewood College B
Lakeland College T
Lawrence University B, T
Maranatha Baptist Bible College B
Marian College of Fond du Lac B, T
Mount Mary College B, T
Northland College T
St. Norbert College B, T
Silver Lake College B, M, T
University of Wisconsin
    Green Bay T
    Madison B, M
    Milwaukee B, T
    Oshkosh B, T
    Parkside T
    River Falls B, T
    Stevens Point B, M, T
    Superior B, T
    Whitewater B
Viterbo University B, T

Wyoming

Casper College A
Eastern Wyoming College A
University of Wyoming B

Music theory and composition

Alabama

Birmingham-Southern College B
Huntingdon College B
Samford University B

Alaska

University of Alaska
    Fairbanks M

Arizona

Arizona State University B, M
Northern Arizona University M
University of Arizona M, D

Arkansas

Ouachita Baptist University B

California

Azusa Pacific University B, M
Bethesda Christian University B, M
Biola University B
California Institute of the Arts C, B, M
California State University
    Chico B
    Dominguez Hills B
    East Bay M
    Fresno B
    Fullerton B, M
    Long Beach M
    Northridge B, M
    Sacramento B, M
Chapman University B
Foothill College C
Fresno Pacific University B
Golden West College C, A
Mills College M
Mount St. Mary's College B
Ohlone College C
Point Loma Nazarene University B
San Diego State University M
San Francisco Conservatory of
    Music B, M
San Francisco State University M
Solano Community College C
University of Redlands B
University of Southern
    California B, M, D
University of the Pacific B

Colorado

Adams State College B

Connecticut

University of Hartford B, M, D
Western Connecticut State
    University B
Yale University M, D

Delaware

University of Delaware B

District of Columbia

American University B
Catholic University of
    America B, M, D
Howard University B

Florida

Florida Southern College B
Florida State University B, M, D
Jacksonville University B
Manatee Community College A
Palm Beach Atlantic University B
Stetson University B
University of Miami B, M, D
University of Tampa B

Georgia

Clayton State University B
Georgia Southern University B
University of Georgia B
University of West Georgia B

Idaho

Boise State University B
North Idaho College A
Northwest Nazarene University B

University of Idaho B

Illinois

Bradley University B
Concordia University B
DePaul University B, M
Illinois Wesleyan University B
Moody Bible Institute B
Northwestern University B, M, D
Roosevelt University B, M
Trinity International University B
University of Illinois
    Urbana-Champaign B, M, D
Wheaton College B

Indiana

American Conservatory of
    Music B, M, D
Butler University B, M
DePauw University B
Huntington University B
Indiana University
    Bloomington B, M, D
Indiana Wesleyan University B
Valparaiso University B
Vincennes University A

Iowa

Coe College B
University of Iowa B
University of Northern Iowa B, M
Wartburg College B

Kansas

Central Christian College of Kansas A
University of Kansas B, M, D

Kentucky

Campbellsville University B

Louisiana

Centenary College of Louisiana B
Loyola University New Orleans B
Tulane University B

Maine

University of Maine M

Maryland

Johns Hopkins University: Peabody
    Conservatory of Music B, M, D

Massachusetts

Berklee College of Music B
Boston Conservatory B, M
Boston University B, M, D
Brandeis University M, D
Eastern Nazarene College B
Harvard College B, M, D
New England Conservatory of
    Music B, M, D
Simon's Rock College of Bard B
Tufts University B
Westfield State College B

Michigan

Calvin College B
Central Michigan University B, M
Cornerstone University B, T
Lansing Community College A
Marygrove College B
Michigan State University B, M, D
Oakland Community College A
Oakland University B
University of Michigan B, M, D
Western Michigan University B

Minnesota

Hamline University B
Minnesota State University
    Mankato B
Northwestern College B

Rochester Community and Technical
    College C, A
St. Olaf College B

Mississippi

Mississippi College B, M

Missouri

Drury University B
Lindenwood University B
University of Missouri
    Kansas City B, M, D
Washington University in St. Louis B
Webster University B
William Jewell College B

Montana

University of Montana: Missoula B, M

Nebraska

University of Nebraska
    Omaha B

New Hampshire

Franklin Pierce College B
Keene State College B
University of New Hampshire B

New Jersey

Rider University B, M
Rowan University C
Westminster Choir College of Rider
    University B, M

New York

Bard College B, M
City University of New York
    Brooklyn College B, M
    City College B, M
    Hunter College B, M
    Lehman College B
    Queens College B, M
Cornell University B, M, D
Eastman School of Music of the
    University of Rochester B, M, D
Five Towns College A, B, M, D
Hofstra University B
Houghton College B
Ithaca College B, M
Jewish Theological Seminary of
    America B
Juilliard School B, M, D
Manhattan School of Music B, M, D
Mannes College The New School for
    Music B, M
Nazareth College of Rochester B
New York University B, M, D
Nyack College B
Sarah Lawrence College B
State University of New York
    Albany B
    Buffalo M, D
    College at Fredonia B
    College at Potsdam M
    New Paltz B
    Purchase B, M
Syracuse University B, M
University of Rochester B, M, D

North Carolina

Duke University M
East Carolina University B, M
Meredith College B
North Carolina School of the Arts M
University of North Carolina
    Greensboro B, M

Ohio

Ashland University B
Baldwin-Wallace College B
Bowling Green State University B, M
Capital University B

Cedarville University B
Cleveland Institute of Music B, M, D
College of Wooster B
Heidelberg College B
Kent State University M, D
Miami University
    Oxford Campus M
Oberlin College B
Ohio Northern University B
Ohio State University
    Columbus Campus B, M, D
Ohio University B, M
Otterbein College B
University of Akron B, M
University of Cincinnati B, M, D
University of Dayton B
Wright State University B
Youngstown State University B, M

Oklahoma

Oklahoma Baptist University B
Oklahoma City University B
Oral Roberts University B
Southwestern Oklahoma State
    University B
University of Tulsa B

Oregon

Linfield College B
University of Oregon B, M, D
Willamette University B

Pennsylvania

Bucknell University B
Carnegie Mellon University B, M
Curtis Institute of Music C, B
Duquesne University M
Gettysburg College B
Moravian College B
Penn State
    University Park M
Philadelphia Biblical University B
Susquehanna University B
Temple University B, M, D
University of the Arts B, M
West Chester University of
    Pennsylvania B, M
Westminster College B

Rhode Island

University of Rhode Island B

South Carolina

Coker College B, T
Converse College B, M
Furman University B
Newberry College B
North Greenville College A, B
University of South Carolina M, D

Tennessee

Belmont University B, M
Carson-Newman College B
Lipscomb University B
Southern Adventist University B
Union University B
University of Tennessee
    Knoxville B
Vanderbilt University B

Texas

Baylor University B, M
Dallas Baptist University B
Del Mar College A
Hardin-Simmons University B, M
Houston Baptist University B
Houston Community College
    System C, A
Lon Morris College A
Rice University B, M, D
Sam Houston State University B, M
Southern Methodist University B, M

Texas A&M University
    Commerce B, M
Texas Christian University B, M
Texas Tech University B, M, D
Trinity University B
University of Houston B, M, D
University of Mary Hardin-Baylor B
University of North Texas B, M, D
University of Texas
    Austin B
    El Paso B
    San Antonio B
West Texas A&M University B

Utah

Brigham Young University B, M

Vermont

Bennington College B, M
Johnson State College B

Virginia

Randolph-Macon Woman's College B
Shenandoah University B, M
University of Richmond B
Virginia Union University B

Washington

Central Washington University B
Centralia College A
Cornish College of the Arts B
Eastern Washington University B, M
University of Washington B, M
Western Washington University B

Wisconsin

Lawrence University B, T
University of Wisconsin
    Madison B, M
    Whitewater B, T

Wyoming

University of Wyoming B

Music therapy

Arizona

Arizona State University B, M

California

California State University
    Northridge M
Chapman University B
University of the Pacific B, M

Colorado

Colorado State University B
Naropa University M

District of Columbia

Howard University B

Florida

Florida State University B, M
University of Miami B, M

Georgia

Georgia College and State
    University B, M
University of Georgia B

Indiana

Indiana University-Purdue University
    Fort Wayne B
St. Mary-of-the-Woods College B, M
University of Evansville B

Iowa

University of Iowa B
Wartburg College B

Kansas

Central Christian College of Kansas A
University of Kansas B, M

Kentucky

University of Louisville B

Louisiana

Loyola University New Orleans B, M

Maryland

Howard Community College A

Massachusetts

Anna Maria College B
Berklee College of Music B
Lesley University M, D

Michigan

Eastern Michigan University B
Michigan State University B, M
Western Michigan University B

Minnesota

Augsburg College B
University of Minnesota
    Twin Cities B

Mississippi

William Carey College B

Missouri

Maryville University of Saint
    Louis B, M
University of Missouri
    Kansas City B, M

New Jersey

Montclair State University B

New York

Molloy College B
Nazareth College of Rochester B
New York University M, D
State University of New York
    College at Fredonia B
    New Paltz B

North Carolina

Appalachian State University B
East Carolina University B, M
Queens University of Charlotte B

Ohio

Baldwin-Wallace College B
College of Wooster B
Ohio University M
University of Dayton B

Oklahoma

Southwestern Oklahoma State
    University B

Pennsylvania

Drexel University M
Duquesne University B
Elizabethtown College B
Immaculata University B, M
Mansfield University of
    Pennsylvania B
Marywood University C, B, M
Seton Hill University B
Slippery Rock University of
    Pennsylvania B
Temple University B, M, D

South Carolina

Charleston Southern University C, B

Texas

Sam Houston State University B
Southern Methodist University B, M
Texas Woman's University B
University of the Incarnate Word B
West Texas A&M University B

Utah

Utah State University B, M

Virginia

Radford University B
Shenandoah University C, B, M

Wisconsin

Alverno College B
University of Wisconsin
    Eau Claire B

Musical instrument fabrication/repair

Indiana

Indiana University
    Bloomington A

Iowa

Western Iowa Tech Community
    College A

Minnesota

Minnesota State College - Southeast
    Technical C, A

Washington

Renton Technical College C, A

Musicology/ ethnomusicology

Arizona

University of Arizona M

California

California State University
    San Bernardino B
San Diego State University M
University of California
    Los Angeles B, M, D

Colorado

University of Denver B

Connecticut

Wesleyan University D

Florida

Florida State University M, D
University of Miami B, M

Illinois

DePaul University B, M
Northwestern University B, M, D
Roosevelt University M
University of Illinois
    Urbana-Champaign D

Indiana

Indiana University
    Bloomington M, D

Kansas

University of Kansas B, M

Maryland

University of Maryland
    College Park M, D

Massachusetts

Boston University D
Brandeis University M, D
New England Conservatory of
Music B, M
Simon's Rock College of Bard B
Tufts University B

Michigan

Michigan State University M
University of Michigan M

Minnesota

Bethel University M

Missouri

Washington University in St.
Louis M, D

New York

Columbia University
School of General Studies B
Cornell University B, M, D
Eastman School of Music of the
University of Rochester M, D
Sarah Lawrence College B
State University of New York
Buffalo D
University of Rochester M, D

North Carolina

Duke University M, D
University of North Carolina
Chapel Hill M, D

Ohio

Bowling Green State University B, M
Case Western Reserve University D
Ohio State University
Columbus Campus M, D
University of Akron B
University of Cincinnati D

Pennsylvania

Gratz College M
Penn State
University Park M

Rhode Island

Brown University B, M, D

Texas

Rice University M
Sam Houston State University M
Texas A&M University
Commerce B
Texas Christian University M
University of North Texas M, D

Utah

Brigham Young University M
University of Utah M

Vermont

Bennington College B, M

Washington

University of Washington B

Mycology

South Carolina

Medical University of South
Carolina D

Native American
education

Minnesota

College of St. Scholastica T

Native American
languages

Alaska

University of Alaska
Fairbanks A, B

Arizona

Dine College A

Hawaii

University of Hawaii
Manoa B, M

Idaho

Idaho State University A

Native American
studies

Alaska

University of Alaska
Fairbanks B

Arizona

Arizona State University B
Dine College A
Northern Arizona University B
Pima Community College A
Scottsdale Community College A
University of Arizona M, D

California

California State University
East Bay B
De Anza College A
El Camino College A
Fresno City College A
Grossmont Community College A
Humboldt State University B
Santa Barbara City College A
Solano Community College A
Stanford University B
University of California
Berkeley B
Davis B
Los Angeles B, M
Riverside B

Hawaii

University of Hawaii
Hilo B
Manoa B, M

Idaho

North Idaho College A

Kansas

Haskell Indian Nations University B
University of Kansas M

Massachusetts

Simon's Rock College of Bard B

Michigan

Saginaw Chippewa Tribal College A

Minnesota

Augsburg College B
Bemidji State University B
Itasca Community College A
Leech Lake Tribal College A
Rainy River Community College A
University of Minnesota
Duluth B
Twin Cities B

Montana

Fort Belknap College A
Fort Peck Community College A

Little Big Horn College A
Montana State University
Bozeman M
Salish Kootenai College A
Stone Child College A
University of Montana: Missoula B

Nebraska

Creighton University B
Little Priest Tribal College A
Nebraska Indian Community
College A

New Hampshire

Dartmouth College B

New Mexico

Institute of American Indian Arts A
University of New Mexico B

New York

Colgate University B
Sarah Lawrence College B

North Carolina

University of North Carolina
Pembroke B
Western Carolina University M

North Dakota

Sitting Bull College A
University of North Dakota B

Oklahoma

Bacone College A
Northeastern Oklahoma Agricultural
and Mechanical College A
Northeastern State University B
University of Oklahoma B, M
University of Science and Arts of
Oklahoma B

South Dakota

Black Hills State University B
Sisseton Wahpeton College A
University of South Dakota B

Texas

University of the Incarnate Word B

Utah

University of Utah M
Weber State University B

Vermont

Goddard College B

Washington

Evergreen State College B
University of Washington B

Wisconsin

Northland College B
University of Wisconsin
Eau Claire B
Green Bay B

Wyoming

Central Wyoming College A

Natural resource
economics

New Hampshire

University of New Hampshire B

Pennsylvania

Penn State
University Park B

West Virginia

West Virginia University D

Natural resources and
conservation

Alabama

Tuskegee University B, M
University of West Alabama B

Alaska

Alaska Pacific University B
Sheldon Jackson College B
University of Alaska
Fairbanks B, M

Arizona

Prescott College B, M
University of Arizona B, M, D

Arkansas

John Brown University B
South Arkansas Community
College C, A
University of Arkansas B
University of Arkansas
Pine Bluff B
University of Central Arkansas B
University of the Ozarks B

California

California Polytechnic State
University: San Luis Obispo B
California State University
East Bay B
Monterey Bay B
Sacramento B
College of the Desert A
Columbia College A
Feather River College C, A
Fresno City College C, A
Fullerton College A
Humboldt State University B
Irvine Valley College C, A
Mills College B
Modesto Junior College C, A
Mount San Antonio College A
Ohlone College C
Saddleback College A
San Diego State University B
San Francisco State University M
San Joaquin Delta College A
Santa Rosa Junior College C, A
Sonoma State University B
University of California
Berkeley B
Davis B
Santa Barbara B
Santa Cruz B, M, D
Whittier College B

Colorado

Colorado College B
Colorado Mountain College
Timberline Campus A
Colorado State University B
Metropolitan State College of
Denver B
Trinidad State Junior College A

Connecticut

Gateway Community College A
Middlesex Community College A
Post University B
Sacred Heart University B
University of Connecticut B, M, D
University of New Haven B, M
Wesleyan University B, M

Delaware

University of Delaware B

District of Columbia

George Washington University *B*
Trinity University *B*
University of the District of
Columbia *B*

Florida

Florida Atlantic University *M*
Florida International University *B, M*
Florida Southern College *B*
Gulf Coast Community College *A*
Seminole Community College *A*
University of Florida *B*
University of South Florida *B, M*

Georgia

Shorter College *B*
University of Georgia *M*

Hawaii

Hawaii Pacific University *B*

Idaho

College of Southern Idaho *A*
University of Idaho *B, M*

Illinois

Augustana College *B*
Aurora University *B*
DePaul University *B*
Illinois Central College *A*
Lewis University *B*
Monmouth College *B*
Principia College *B*
Southern Illinois University
Edwardsville *M*
University of Illinois
Urbana-Champaign *B, M, D*

Indiana

Ball State University *B, M*
Bethel College *B*
Goshen College *B*
Indiana University
Bloomington *B, M, D*
Manchester College *B*
Purdue University *B, M*
Tri-State University *B*
University of St. Francis *B*
Vincennes University *A*

Iowa

Dordt College *B*
Ellsworth Community College *A*
Kirkwood Community College *A*
Muscatine Community College *A*
Northwestern College *B*
University of Dubuque *B*
Upper Iowa University *B*

Kansas

Fort Scott Community College *C, A*
Haskell Indian Nations
University *A, B*

Kentucky

University of Kentucky *B*

Louisiana

Louisiana State University
Shreveport *B*
Louisiana Tech University *B*
Southern University and Agricultural
and Mechanical College *M*

Maine

College of the Atlantic *B*
Unity College *B*
University of Maine *M, D*
University of Maine
Machias *B, T*

University of Southern Maine *B*

Maryland

Frostburg State University *B, M*
Garrett College *C*
Harford Community College *C, A*
Howard Community College *A*
University of Maryland
College Park *B*
University College *B*

Massachusetts

Anna Maria College *M*
Boston University *B, M*
Cape Cod Community College *C, A*
Quincy College *C, A*
Roxbury Community College *A*
Simmons College *B*
Springfield College *B*
Suffolk University *A*
University of Massachusetts
Lowell *B*
Westfield State College *B*
Wheaton College *B*

Michigan

Adrian College *A, B*
Albion College *B*
Central Michigan University *B, T*
Delta College *A*
Gogebic Community College *A*
Lake Superior State University *A, B*
Lansing Community College *A*
Mid Michigan Community College *A*
Northern Michigan University *A*
Schoolcraft College *A*
University of Michigan *B, M, D*
University of Michigan
Dearborn *B*

Minnesota

Bemidji State University *B, M*
Central Lakes College *A*
Gustavus Adolphus College *B*
Itasca Community College *A*
Minnesota State University
Mankato *B, M*
Rainy River Community College *A*
St. Cloud State University *B, M*
University of Minnesota
Crookston *B*
Twin Cities *B, M, D*
University of St. Thomas *M*
Vermilion Community College *A*
Winona State University *B*

Missouri

Central Methodist University *B*
Missouri Southern State University *B*
Washington University in St. Louis *B*
Westminster College *B*

Montana

Fort Peck Community College *A*
Miles Community College *A*
Montana State University
Bozeman *B, M*
Salish Kootenai College *B*
University of Montana: Missoula *B, M*
University of Montana: Western *B*

Nebraska

Bellevue University *B*
Dana College *B*
Little Priest Tribal College *A*
Midland Lutheran College *B*
Nebraska Indian Community
College *A*
University of Nebraska
Lincoln *B, M, D*

Nevada

Great Basin College *A*
University of Nevada
Las Vegas *B, M, D*
Reno *B, M*
Western Nevada Community
College *A*

New Hampshire

Dartmouth College *B*
Franklin Pierce College *B*
University of New Hampshire *B, M*

New Jersey

Fairleigh Dickinson University
Metropolitan Campus *B, M*
Montclair State University *M*
Ocean County College *A*
Raritan Valley Community College *A*
Rowan University *M*
Rutgers, The State University of New
Jersey
New Brunswick/Piscataway
Campus *B, M, D*
Newark Regional Campus *B, M, D*
William Paterson University of New
Jersey *B*

New Mexico

College of the Southwest *B*
New Mexico Institute of Mining and
Technology *B*
Northern New Mexico College *C, A*
San Juan College *C, A*
Southwestern Indian Polytechnic
Institute *C, A*

New York

Colgate University *B*
Columbia University
Columbia College *B*
School of General Studies *B*
Cornell University *B, M, D*
Elmira College *B*
Finger Lakes Community College *C, A*
Ithaca College *B*
Keuka College *B*
Paul Smith's College *A, B*
St. Bonaventure University *B*
State University of New York
College at Brockport *B*
College at Plattsburgh *B*
College of Agriculture and
Technology at Cobleskill *A*
College of Agriculture and
Technology at Morrisville *A*
College of Environmental Science
and Forestry *B, M, D*
College of Technology at Alfred *A*
College of Technology at Canton *B*
Maritime College *B*
Purchase *B*
Sullivan County Community
College *A*
Syracuse University *B*
Tompkins-Cortland Community
College *A*
Trocaire College *A*
Wells College *B*

North Carolina

Blue Ridge Community College *C, A*
Cape Fear Community College *C, A*
Duke University *B, M, D*
Elon University *B*
North Carolina State University *B, M*
North Carolina Wesleyan College *B*
Pamlico Community College *A*
Shaw University *B*
Wake Technical Community
College *A*
Warren Wilson College *B*

Western Piedmont Community
College *C, A*
Wilson Technical Community
College *A*

North Dakota

Minot State University: Bottineau
Campus *A*

Ohio

Antioch College *B*
Cleveland State University *B*
Defiance College *B*
Denison University *B*
Hocking College *A*
Kent State University *B*
Lake Erie College *B*
Miami University
Oxford Campus *M*
Mount Vernon Nazarene University *B*
Muskingum College *B*
Ohio Northern University *B*
Ohio State University
Agricultural Technical Institute *A*
Columbus Campus *B, M, D*
Otterbein College *B*
University of Cincinnati *M, D*
University of Rio Grande *B*
Youngstown State University *B*

Oklahoma

Eastern Oklahoma State College *A*
St. Gregory's University *A, B*
Southeastern Oklahoma State
University *B*
Southern Nazarene University *B*

Oregon

Eastern Oregon University *B*
Marylhurst University *B*
Oregon Institute of Technology *B*
Oregon State University *B*
Portland State University *B, D*

Pennsylvania

Albright College *B*
Arcadia University *M*
Bryn Mawr College *B*
Clarion University of Pennsylvania *B*
Drexel University *B, M, D*
Eastern University *B*
Edinboro University of
Pennsylvania *B*
Gannon University *M*
Gettysburg College *B*
Keystone College *A, B*
La Salle University *B*
Mansfield University of
Pennsylvania *B*
Marywood University *B*
Penn State
University Park *C, B*
St. Vincent College *B*
Slippery Rock University of
Pennsylvania *B, M, T*
Thiel College *B*
University of Pittsburgh
Greensburg *B*
University of Scranton *B*
Waynesburg College *B*

Puerto Rico

Bayamon Central University *B*
Inter American University of Puerto
Rico
Bayamon Campus *B*
Ponce Campus *B*
Pontifical Catholic University of
Puerto Rico *B*
University of Puerto Rico
Rio Piedras *B*

Rhode Island
Roger Williams University *B*
University of Rhode Island *M, D*

South Carolina
College of Charleston *M*
Furman University *B*

South Dakota
Oglala Lakota College *A*

Tennessee
Lincoln Memorial University *B*
Tennessee Technological
    University *B, D*
Tusculum College *B*
University of Tennessee
    Chattanooga *B, M*

Texas
Coastal Bend College *A*
Lamar University *B, M*
McMurry University *B*
Sul Ross State University *B*
Texas A&M University *B, M*
Texas A&M University
    Commerce *B*
    Galveston *B, M*
Texas State University: San Marcos *D*
Texas Tech University *B*
University of Houston
    Clear Lake *B, M*
University of North Texas *M, D*

Utah
Dixie State College of Utah *A*
Snow College *A*

Vermont
Green Mountain College *B*
Johnson State College *B*
Marlboro College *B*
Norwich University *B*
Sterling College *A, B*
University of Vermont *B*

Virginia
Mountain Empire Community
    College *A*
St. Paul's College *B*
Shenandoah University *B*
University of Mary Washington *B*

Washington
Everett Community College *A*
Grays Harbor College *A*
Heritage University *C, A, B*
Seattle University *B*
Skagit Valley College *A*
University of Washington *B*
Washington State University *B, M*

West Virginia
Alderson-Broaddus College *B*
Davis and Elkins College *B*
Mountain State University *B*
Potomac State College of West Virginia
    University *A*
Shepherd University *B*

Wisconsin
Carroll College *B*
College of Menominee Nation *A*
Fox Valley Technical College *A*
Northland College *B*
University of Wisconsin
    Madison *M, D*
    Platteville *B*
    River Falls *B*
    Stevens Point *B, T*

Wyoming
University of Wyoming *B*
Western Wyoming Community
    College *A*

Natural resources management/policy

Alaska
University of Alaska
    Fairbanks *B, M*

Arizona
Prescott College *B, M*
University of Arizona *M, D*

California
California State Polytechnic
    University: Pomona *M*
California State University
    Chico *C, B*
    Monterey Bay *B*
College of the Redwoods *C*
Columbia College *C, A*
Feather River College *C, A*
Humboldt State University *B, M*
Los Angeles Pierce College *C, A*
San Joaquin Delta College *C*
University of California
    Berkeley *B*
    Davis *B*
University of Redlands *B*

Colorado
Adams State College *B*
Colorado Mountain College
    Timberline Campus *A*
Colorado State University *B*
Naropa University *M*
Pikes Peak Community College *A*
University of Denver *M*

Connecticut
University of Connecticut *D*
Yale University *M*

Delaware
Delaware State University *B*
University of Delaware *B*

Florida
Florida Institute of Technology *M*
Pensacola Junior College *A*
University of Miami *B*

Hawaii
University of Hawaii
    Manoa *B, M, D*

Idaho
University of Idaho *B, M, D*

Illinois
College of Lake County *C, A*
Elmhurst College *B*
Illinois Institute of Technology *M*
Southern Illinois University
    Carbondale *D*
University of Illinois
    Urbana-Champaign *B, M, D*

Iowa
Cornell College *B*
Drake University *B*
Hawkeye Community College *C, A*
Upper Iowa University *B*

Kansas
Garden City Community College *A*
Haskell Indian Nations University *A*
Pittsburg State University *B*

Kentucky
Eastern Kentucky University *B*

Louisiana
Louisiana State University and
    Agricultural and Mechanical
    College *B*
University of Louisiana at Lafayette *B*

Maine
Unity College *B*
University of Maine *B, M, D*
University of Maine
    Farmington *B*
    Fort Kent *B*

Massachusetts
Boston University *B*
Cape Cod Community College *C*
University of Massachusetts
    Amherst *B*

Michigan
Grand Rapids Community College *A*
Grand Valley State University *B*
Lake Superior State University *A, B*
Michigan State University *M, D*
Michigan Technological University *M*
University of Michigan *B, M, D*

Minnesota
Northland Community & Technical
    College *A*
St. Mary's University of Minnesota *M*
University of St. Thomas *M*
Vermilion Community College *A*

Missouri
Missouri Southern State University *B*

Montana
Flathead Valley Community College *A*
Fort Belknap College *A*
Fort Peck Community College *A*
Montana State University
    Bozeman *B, D*
University of Montana: Missoula *M*

Nebraska
Nebraska College of Technical
    Agriculture *C, A*
University of Nebraska
    Lincoln *B*

Nevada
Sierra Nevada College *B*
University of Nevada
    Las Vegas *B, M*
    Reno *B*

New Hampshire
New Hampshire Community
    Technical College
    Berlin *A*

New Jersey
Rutgers, The State University of New
    Jersey
    New Brunswick/Piscataway
    Campus *B*

New Mexico
College of Santa Fe *B*
New Mexico Highlands University *B*
Northern New Mexico College *C, A*
Southwestern Indian Polytechnic
    Institute *C, A*

New York
Bard College *M*
Finger Lakes Community College *A*

Paul Smith's College *B*
Rensselaer Polytechnic Institute *M, D*
State University of New York
    College of Agriculture and
        Technology at Morrisville *A*
    College of Environmental Science
        and Forestry *B, M, D*
    Purchase *C*

North Carolina
North Carolina State University *B, M*
Western Carolina University *B*

North Dakota
North Dakota State University *B, M, D*

Ohio
Bowling Green State University *B*
Heidelberg College *B*
Hocking College *A*
Ohio State University
    Columbus Campus *B, M, D*
Otterbein College *B*
Xavier University *B*
Zane State College *A*

Oklahoma
Bacone College *A*
Northwestern Oklahoma State
    University *B*

Oregon
Mount Hood Community College *A*
Oregon State University *B*
Portland State University *M*
Treasure Valley Community College *A*

Pennsylvania
Carnegie Mellon University *B*
Gettysburg College *B*
Keystone College *B*
Penn State
    Abington *B*
    Altoona *B*
    Beaver *B*
    Berks *B*
    Delaware County *B*
    Dubois *B*
    Erie, The Behrend College *B*
    Fayette *B*
    Hazleton *B*
    Lehigh Valley *B*
    McKeesport *B*
    Mont Alto *B*
    New Kensington *B*
    Schuylkill - Capital College *B*
    Shenango *B*
    University Park *B*
    Wilkes-Barre *B*
    Worthington Scranton *B*
    York *B*
St. Vincent College *B*
University of Pennsylvania *M*

Puerto Rico
Universidad Metropolitana *M*

Rhode Island
University of Rhode Island *B, M*

South Carolina
Central Carolina Technical College *A*

South Dakota
Oglala Lakota College *A*
South Dakota State University *B*

Tennessee
University of Tennessee
    Martin *B*
University of the South *B*

Texas

Angelo State University *B*
Hardin-Simmons University *M*
Sul Ross State University *B*
Texas A&M University *B*

Utah

Dixie State College of Utah *A*
Snow College *A*
Utah State University *M*

Vermont

Green Mountain College *B*
Johnson State College *B*
Sterling College *A, B*
University of Vermont *B, M, D*

Virginia

Lord Fairfax Community College *A*
Roanoke College *B, T*
Virginia Polytechnic Institute and
    State University *M*

Washington

Central Washington University *M*
University of Washington *M, D*

West Virginia

Glenville State College *B*

Wisconsin

Northland College *B*
University of Wisconsin
    Green Bay *M*
    River Falls *B*

Wyoming

Northwest College *A*

Natural sciences

Alabama

Oakwood College *B*
University of Alabama
    Birmingham *B*

Alaska

University of Alaska
    Anchorage *B*

Arizona

Arizona State University *M*
Prescott College *B, M*

California

California State University
    Fresno *B*
    Los Angeles *B*
Columbia College *A*
Lake Tahoe Community College *A*
Loma Linda University *M, D*
Loyola Marymount University *B*
Master's College *B*
Ohlone College *A*
Pacific Union College *B*
Pepperdine University *B*
Pitzer College *B*
Saddleback College *A*
San Joaquin Delta College *A*
San Jose State University *B, M*
Santa Rosa Junior College *A*
University of La Verne *B*

Colorado

Colorado Mountain College
    Timberline Campus *A*
Colorado State University *B*
Colorado State University
    Pueblo *M*

Connecticut

St. Joseph College *B*

Florida

Lynn University *B*
New College of Florida *B*

Georgia

Covenant College *B*
Reinhardt College *A*

Hawaii

University of Hawaii
    Hilo *B*

Idaho

College of Southern Idaho *A*
Lewis-Clark State College *B*

Illinois

Black Hawk College
    East Campus *A*
Concordia University *B, T*
Shimer College *B*
Southeastern Illinois College *A*

Indiana

Huntington University *B*
Indiana University
    East *A, B*
Tri-State University *A*

Iowa

Central College *B, T*
Ellsworth Community College *A*
Northwestern College *T*
St. Ambrose University *B, T*

Kansas

Benedictine College *B*
Bethel College *B*
Central Christian College of
    Kansas *A, B*
Garden City Community College *A*
Neosho County Community
    College *A*
Seward County Community College *A*
Tabor College *B*
Washburn University of Topeka *A*

Maine

University of Maine *B, M, D*
University of Southern Maine *B*

Massachusetts

Cape Cod Community College *A*
Hampshire College *B*
Lesley University *B*
Simon's Rock College of Bard *B*

Michigan

Albion College *B*
Calvin College *B*
Madonna University *A, B*
Marygrove College *A, B, T*
Olivet College *B*
Siena Heights University *A, B*

Minnesota

College of St. Benedict *B*
Rochester Community and Technical
    College *A*
St. Cloud State University *B*
St. John's University *B*

Missouri

Missouri Western State University *B*
Park University *B*

Nebraska

Concordia University *B, T*

Peru State College *B*
University of Nebraska
    Omaha *B*

New Hampshire

University of New Hampshire *B*

New Jersey

Felician College *B*
Georgian Court University *B*
Thomas Edison State College *B*
Warren County Community College *A*

New Mexico

Clovis Community College *A*

New York

Alfred University *B*
Colgate University *B*
Daemen College *B*
Hofstra University *B*
Houghton College *B*
Mount St. Mary College *B*
Rensselaer Polytechnic Institute *M, T*
Roberts Wesleyan College *A*
State University of New York
    College at Geneseo *B*
    College at Plattsburgh *M*
    College of Agriculture and
        Technology at Cobleskill *A*
    College of Environmental Science
        and Forestry *B*

North Carolina

Johnson C. Smith University *B*
Western Piedmont Community
    College *A*

North Dakota

Dickinson State University *B, T*

Ohio

Case Western Reserve University *B*
Cleveland State University *T*
College of Mount St. Joseph *B*
Defiance College *B*
Shawnee State University *A*
Walsh University *B*
Washington State Community
    College *A*
Xavier University *B*

Oklahoma

Bacone College *A*
Cameron University *B*
Oklahoma State University *M*
St. Gregory's University *A, B*
University of Oklahoma *M*
University of Science and Arts of
    Oklahoma *B, T*

Oregon

Marylhurst University *B*
Western Oregon University *B*

Pennsylvania

Gettysburg College *B*
Juniata College *B*
Keystone College *B*
Muhlenberg College *B*
University of Pittsburgh
    Titusville *A*

Puerto Rico

Bayamon Central University *B*
Pontifical Catholic University of
    Puerto Rico *B*
Turabo University *B*
Universidad del Este *A*
University of Puerto Rico
    Ponce *A*

Rio Piedras *B*
Utuado *A*
University of the Sacred Heart *B*

South Carolina

Charleston Southern University *B, M*
University of South Carolina *M*

South Dakota

Sisseton Wahpeton College *A*

Tennessee

Christian Brothers University *B*

Texas

Lee College *A*
McMurry University *B, T*
Mountain View College *A*
Our Lady of the Lake University of San
    Antonio *B*
Tyler Junior College *A*

Utah

Snow College *A*

Vermont

Castleton State College *B*
Sterling College *A, B*

Virginia

J. Sargeant Reynolds Community
    College *A*
Jefferson College of Health
    Sciences *A*
Thomas Nelson Community
    College *A*
Virginia Commonwealth University *D*
Virginia Union University *B*
Virginia Wesleyan College *B*
Virginia Western Community
    College *A*

Washington

Everett Community College *A*
Evergreen State College *B*
Heritage University *B*
University of Puget Sound *B, T*

West Virginia

Alderson-Broaddus College *A, B*

Wisconsin

Edgewood College *B*
Lawrence University *B, T*
Northland College *B*
Silver Lake College *T*

Wyoming

University of Wyoming *M*

Naturopathic medicine

Connecticut

University of Bridgeport *D*

Washington

Bastyr University *D*

Near and Middle Eastern studies

Arizona

University of Arizona *B, M, D*

Arkansas

University of Arkansas *B*

California

University of California
    Berkeley *B, M, D*

Los Angeles *B, M, D*

Connecticut
Trinity College *B*
University of Connecticut *B*

District of Columbia
George Washington University *B*
Georgetown University *M*

Illinois
University of Chicago *B, M*

Maryland
Johns Hopkins University *B, M, D*

Massachusetts
Brandeis University *B, M, D*
Harvard College *B, M, D*
Tufts University *B, M*
University of Massachusetts
    Amherst *B*

Michigan
University of Michigan *B, M*
Wayne State University *B*

Minnesota
University of Minnesota
    Twin Cities *B*

Missouri
Washington University in St.
    Louis *B, M*

New Hampshire
Dartmouth College *B*

New Jersey
Princeton University *B, M, D*
Rutgers, The State University of New
    Jersey
    New Brunswick/Piscataway
        Campus *B*

New York
Barnard College *B*
City University of New York
    Hunter College *B*
Columbia University
    Columbia College *B*
    School of General Studies *B*
Cornell University *B, M, D*
Fordham University *B*
New York University *B, M, D*
Sarah Lawrence College *B*
United States Military Academy *B*

Ohio
College of Wooster *B*
Mount Vernon Nazarene University *B*
Ohio State University
    Columbus Campus *B*
University of Toledo *B*

Oregon
Portland State University *B*

Rhode Island
Brown University *B*

South Carolina
Columbia International University *B*

Texas
Texas State University: San Marcos *B*
University of Texas
    Austin *B, M*

Utah
University of Utah *B, M, D*

Vermont
Goddard College *B*
Marlboro College *B*

Virginia
College of William and Mary *B*
Emory & Henry College *B*

Washington
University of Washington *B, M, D*

Neuroanatomy

North Carolina
Wake Forest University *D*

Neurobiology/ physiology

Alabama
University of Alabama
    Birmingham *D*

California
University of California
    Davis *B*
    Irvine *M, D*
    Los Angeles *M, D*
University of Southern California *D*

Connecticut
Yale University *M, D*

Florida
University of Miami *B*

Illinois
Northwestern University *M*

Indiana
Indiana University-Purdue University
    Indianapolis *M, D*

Iowa
University of Iowa *D*

Maine
Colby College *B*

Massachusetts
Harvard College *D*

Michigan
University of Michigan *M*

New York
St. Lawrence University *B*

North Carolina
University of North Carolina
    Chapel Hill *D*

Oklahoma
University of Oklahoma *M, D*

Pennsylvania
Drexel University *M*
University of Pittsburgh *M, D*

South Carolina
Medical University of South
    Carolina *D*

Tennessee
King College *M*

Utah
University of Utah *B, M, D*

Wisconsin
Marquette University *M, D*

Neuroscience

Alabama
University of Alabama
    Birmingham *D*

Arizona
University of Arizona *M, D*

California
California Institute of Technology *D*
Claremont McKenna College *B*
Pitzer College *B*
Pomona College *B*
Scripps College *B*
Stanford University *M, D*
University of California
    Berkeley *D*
    Davis *D*
    Irvine *B, D*
    Los Angeles *B, D*
    Riverside *B, M, D*
    San Diego *B, M, D*
    Santa Cruz *B*
University of Southern
    California *M, D*
Westmont College *B*

Colorado
Colorado College *B*
Regis University *B*
University of Colorado
    Boulder *D*
    Denver and Health Sciences
        Center *D*

Connecticut
Connecticut College *B*
Trinity College *B*
Wesleyan University *B, M*
Yale University *M, D*

Delaware
University of Delaware *D*

District of Columbia
George Washington University *D*
Georgetown University *D*

Florida
Florida State University *D*
University of Miami *B, D*

Georgia
University of Georgia *D*

Illinois
Loyola University of Chicago *M, D*
Northwestern University *B, M, D*
Rosalind Franklin University of
    Medicine and Science *D*
Rush University *D*
University of Chicago *D*
University of Illinois
    Urbana-Champaign *D*

Indiana
Indiana University
    Bloomington *D*

Iowa
Iowa State University *M, D*
St. Ambrose University *B*

Kansas
University of Kansas *M, D*

Louisiana
Centenary College of Louisiana *B*
Louisiana State University Health
    Sciences Center *M, D*
Tulane University *B, M, D*

Maine
Bates College *B*
Bowdoin College *B*
Colby College *B*

Maryland
Johns Hopkins University *B, M*
University of Maryland
    Baltimore *M, D*
    Baltimore County *M, D*
    College Park *D*
Washington College *B*

Massachusetts
Amherst College *B*
Boston University *B, M, D*
Brandeis University *B, M, D*
Hampshire College *B*
Massachusetts Institute of
    Technology *D*
Mount Holyoke College *B*
Northeastern University *B*
Smith College *B*
Stonehill College *B*
Tufts University *M, D*
University of Massachusetts
    Amherst *M, D*
Wellesley College *B*

Michigan
Albion College *B*
Andrews University *B*
Central Michigan University *B*
Michigan State University *D*
University of Michigan *M, D*

Minnesota
Macalester College *B*
University of Minnesota
    Twin Cities *D*

Missouri
St. Louis University *D*
University of Missouri
    Columbia *M, D*
Washington University in St.
    Louis *B, D*

New Hampshire
Dartmouth College *B*

New Jersey
Rutgers, The State University of New
    Jersey
    Newark Regional Campus *D*

New York
Bard College *B*
City University of New York
    College of Staten Island *M*
Colgate University *B*
Columbia University
    Columbia College *B*
Cornell University *B, M, D*
Hamilton College *B*
Manhattanville College *B*
New York University *B, M, D*
St. Lawrence University *B*
Skidmore College *B*
State University of New York
    Buffalo *M, D*
    Stony Brook *D*
Syracuse University *M, D*

Union College *B*
University of Rochester *M, D*
Vassar College *B*
Yeshiva University *M, D*

North Carolina

Duke University *B, M, D*

Ohio

Baldwin-Wallace College *B*
Bowling Green State University *B*
Case Western Reserve University *D*
Kent State University *M, D*
Kenyon College *B*
Muskingum College *B*
Oberlin College *B*
Ohio State University
    Columbus Campus *M, D*
Ohio Wesleyan University *B*

Oklahoma

University of Oklahoma *M, D*

Pennsylvania

Allegheny College *B*
Bryn Mawr College *M, D*
Cedar Crest College *B*
Dickinson College *B*
Drexel University *B, M*
Franklin & Marshall College *B*
Gettysburg College *B*
King's College *B*
Muhlenberg College *B*
Temple University *D*
University of Pennsylvania *B, M, D*
University of Pittsburgh *B, M, D*
University of Scranton *B*
Ursinus College *B*

Rhode Island

Brown University *B, M, D*

South Carolina

Furman University *M*
Medical University of South
    Carolina *M, D*

Texas

Baylor University *B, M, D*
Texas Christian University *B*
University of Texas
    Austin *M, D*
    Dallas *B, D*
    Health Science Center at
        Houston *M, D*
    Medical Branch at Galveston *D*
    San Antonio *M, D*
    Southwestern Medical Center at
        Dallas *M, D*

Utah

Brigham Young University *B, M, D*

Vermont

Middlebury College *B*

Virginia

College of William and Mary *B*
University of Virginia *D*
Washington and Lee University *B*

Washington

University of Washington *D*
Washington State University *B, M, D*

West Virginia

West Virginia University *D*

Wisconsin

Carthage College *B*
Lawrence University *B, T*

University of Wisconsin
    Madison *M, D*

Wyoming

University of Wyoming *D*

Nonprofit/public organization management

Alabama

Birmingham-Southern College *M*

Arizona

DeVry University
    Phoenix *M*

California

California State University
    San Bernardino *M*
DeVry University
    Fremont *M*
    Long Beach *M*
    Pomona *M*
    West Hills *M*
Fresno Pacific University *B*
Hope International University *M*
University of Judaism *M*

Colorado

DeVry University: Colorado Springs *M*
University of Denver *M*

Connecticut

Quinnipiac University *B, M*

Florida

DeVry University
    Miramar *M*
    Orlando *M*
Florida Atlantic University *M*
Florida Institute of Technology *M*
Palm Beach Atlantic University *B*
University of Central Florida *M*

Georgia

DeVry University
    Alpharetta *M*
    Decatur *M*
University of Georgia *M*

Illinois

DeVry University
    Tinley Park *M*
Kendall College *B*
Northwestern University *M*
Trinity International University *B*

Indiana

Huntington University *B*
Indiana Business College
    Anderson *A*
    Muncie *A*
Indiana University-Purdue University
    Indianapolis *B*
Manchester College *A, B*
St. Mary-of-the-Woods College *B*

Iowa

University of Northern Iowa *M*

Kansas

Central Christian College of Kansas *A*

Maryland

College of Notre Dame of
    Maryland *B, M*

Massachusetts

American International College *M*

Boston University *M*
Suffolk University *M*
Worcester State College *M*

Michigan

Andrews University *B, M*
Cleary University *B*
Eastern Michigan University *M*
University of Michigan
    Flint *M*
Western Michigan University *B*

Minnesota

Capella University *M, D*
Hamline University *M*
St. Mary's University of Minnesota *M*

Missouri

Rockhurst University *B*

New York

City University of New York
    Baruch College *M*
Globe Institute of Technology *A, B*
New York University *M*
Pace University *B, M*
State University of New York
    College at Brockport *M*
Utica School of Commerce *A*

North Carolina

Pfeiffer University *M*

Ohio

Case Western Reserve University *M*
DeVry University
    Columbus *M*
Franklin University *M*
Mount Vernon Nazarene University *M*
Tiffin University *B*

Oklahoma

University of Central Oklahoma *B*

Pennsylvania

Alvernia College *M*
Carlow University *B, M*
College Misericordia *M*
DeVry University
    Ft. Washington *M*
Duquesne University *B, M*
Eastern University *B, M*
Gettysburg College *B*
La Salle University *B*
Philadelphia Biblical University *M*
Robert Morris University *M*
University of Pennsylvania *M*

Puerto Rico

University of the Sacred Heart *M*

Tennessee

Austin Peay State University *B*
Crichton College *B*
East Tennessee State University *M*
Lipscomb University *M*
Southern Adventist University *B, M*
Williamson Christian College *A, B*

Texas

University of Dallas *M*

Virginia

DeVry University
    Arlington *M*

Washington

DeVry University
    Federal Way *M*
Seattle University *M*

West Virginia

Mountain State University *B*
Ohio Valley University *B*

Wisconsin

Lakeland College *B*
Viterbo University *B*

Norwegian

Minnesota

St. Olaf College *B*

Washington

Pacific Lutheran University *B*
University of Washington *B*

Nuclear engineering

Arizona

University of Arizona *B, M, D*

California

University of California
    Berkeley *B, M, D*

Florida

University of Florida *B, M*

Georgia

Georgia Institute of
    Technology *B, M, D*

Idaho

Idaho State University *B, M, D*
University of Idaho *M, D*

Illinois

University of Illinois
    Urbana-Champaign *B, M, D*

Indiana

Purdue University *B, M, D*

Kansas

Kansas State University *M, D*

Maryland

University of Maryland
    College Park *M, D*

Massachusetts

Massachusetts Institute of
    Technology *B, M, D*

Michigan

University of Michigan *B, M, D*

Missouri

East Central College *A*
University of Missouri
    Columbia *M, D*
    Rolla *B, M, D*

New Mexico

University of New Mexico *B, M*

New York

Columbia University
    Fu Foundation School of
        Engineering and Applied
        Science *M, D*
Cornell University *B, M, D*
Rensselaer Polytechnic
    Institute *B, M, D*
United States Military Academy *B*

North Carolina
North Carolina State
University *B, M, D*

Ohio
Ohio State University
Columbus Campus *M, D*
University of Cincinnati *B, M, D*

Oregon
Oregon State University *B, M, D*

Pennsylvania
Gettysburg College *B*
Penn State
Abington *B*
Altoona *B*
Beaver *B*
Berks *B*
Delaware County *B*
Dubois *B*
Fayette *B*
Hazleton *B*
Lehigh Valley *B*
McKeesport *B*
Mont Alto *B*
New Kensington *B*
Schuylkill - Capital College *B*
Shenango *B*
University Park *B, M, D*
Wilkes-Barre *B*
Worthington Scranton *B*
York *B*

South Carolina
South Carolina State University *B*
University of South Carolina *M, D*

Tennessee
University of Tennessee
Knoxville *B, M, D*

Texas
Texas A&M University *B, M, D*

Utah
University of Utah *B, M, D*

Washington
University of Washington *M, D*

Wisconsin
University of Wisconsin
Madison *B, M, D*

Nuclear engineering technology

Arizona
Glendale Community College *A*

Arkansas
Arkansas Tech University *A*

New Jersey
Thomas Edison State College *A, B*

New York
Excelsior College *B*

Ohio
Lakeland Community College *A*

Virginia
Old Dominion University *B*

Nuclear medical technology

Alabama
Community College of the Air
Force *A*
Enterprise-Ozark Community
College *A*
Faulkner University *A*
University of Alabama
Birmingham *B*

Arizona
Gateway Community College *A*

Arkansas
University of Arkansas
for Medical Sciences *B*
University of Central Arkansas *B*

California
California State University
Dominguez Hills *B*
Charles R. Drew University of
Medicine and Science *B*

Connecticut
Gateway Community College *A*
Middlesex Community College *A*

Delaware
Delaware Technical and Community
College
Stanton/Wilmington Campus *A*

District of Columbia
George Washington University *A, B*

Florida
Barry University *B*
Broward Community College *A*
Florida Hospital College of Health
Sciences *A*
Hillsborough Community College *A*
Manatee Community College *A*
Santa Fe Community College *A*

Georgia
Armstrong Atlantic State University *B*
Dalton State College *A*
Darton College *A*
Gordon College *A*

Illinois
Benedictine University *B*
North Central College *B*
Roosevelt University *B*
Triton College *A*
University of St. Francis *B*

Indiana
Ball State University *A*
Indiana University
Bloomington *B*
Indiana University-Purdue University
Indianapolis *B*

Iowa
Loras College *B*
University of Iowa *B*

Kentucky
Bluegrass Community and Technical
College *A*
Jefferson Community College *A*

Maryland
Frederick Community College *A*
Prince George's Community
College *A*

Massachusetts
Laboure College *A*
Massachusetts College of Pharmacy
and Health Sciences *B*
Salem State College *B*
Springfield Technical Community
College *A*

Michigan
Ferris State University *A, B*
Lansing Community College *A*
Oakland Community College *A*

Minnesota
St. Cloud State University *B*
St. Mary's University of Minnesota *B*

Missouri
St. Louis University *B*
University of Missouri
Columbia *B*

Nebraska
University of Nebraska
Medical Center *B*

Nevada
University of Nevada
Las Vegas *B*

New Jersey
Felician College *B*
Gloucester County College *A*
Thomas Edison State College *A, B*
Union County College *A*
University of Medicine and Dentistry
of New Jersey
School of Health Related
Professions *B*

New York
City University of New York
Bronx Community College *A*
Manhattan College *B*
Molloy College *A*
State University of New York
Buffalo *B*

North Carolina
Caldwell Community College and
Technical Institute *A*
Fayetteville Technical Community
College *A*
Forsyth Technical Community
College *A*
Pitt Community College *A*

Ohio
Kent State University
Salem Regional Campus *A*
Kettering College of Medical Arts *A*
Owens Community College
Toledo *A*
University of Cincinnati *B*
University of Cincinnati
Raymond Walters College *A*
University of Findlay *A, B*

Oklahoma
University of Oklahoma *B*

Pennsylvania
Cedar Crest College *B*
Community College of Allegheny
County *A*
Harrisburg Area Community
College *A*
Indiana University of Pennsylvania *B*
York College of Pennsylvania *B*

South Carolina
Midlands Technical College *A*

South Dakota
Southeast Technical Institute *A*

Texas
Amarillo College *A*
Galveston College *A*
Houston Community College
System *A*
University of Houston *B*
University of the Incarnate Word *B*

Utah
Weber State University *B*

Vermont
University of Vermont *B*

Virginia
Old Dominion University *B*

Washington
Bellevue Community College *A*

West Virginia
Wheeling Jesuit University *B*

Wisconsin
University of Wisconsin
La Crosse *B*

Nuclear physics

Illinois
Northwestern University *M, D*

Iowa
Iowa State University *M, D*

Texas
University of North Texas *M, D*

Nuclear power technology

New York
Excelsior College *A*

Ohio
Lakeland Community College *A*

South Carolina
Aiken Technical College *C, A*

Texas
Texas A&M University *M*

Wisconsin
Lakeshore Technical College *A*

Nurse anesthetist

Alabama
University of Alabama
Birmingham *M*

Arkansas
Arkansas State University *M*

California
California State University
Long Beach *M*
Samuel Merritt College *M*
University of Southern California *M*

Connecticut

Central Connecticut State
University *M*

Florida

Barry University *M*
University of Miami *M*

Georgia

Medical College of Georgia *M*
Mercer University *D*

Illinois

Bradley University *M*
Rush University *M*
Southern Illinois University
Edwardsville *M*

Iowa

University of Iowa *M*

Kansas

Newman University *M*
University of Kansas Medical
Center *M*

Louisiana

Louisiana State University Health
Sciences Center *M*
Our Lady of the Lake College *M*

Maine

University of New England *M*

Massachusetts

Northeastern University *M*

Michigan

Oakland University *M*
University of Detroit Mercy *M*
University of Michigan
Flint *M*
Wayne State University *M*

Minnesota

St. Mary's University of Minnesota *M*
University of Minnesota
Twin Cities *B*

Missouri

Jewish Hospital College of Nursing
and Allied Health *M*
Missouri State University *M*
Webster University *M*

New York

Columbia University
School of Nursing *M*
State University of New York
Buffalo *M*
Downstate Medical Center *M*

Ohio

Case Western Reserve University *M*
Ohio State University
Columbus Campus *M*
Youngstown State University *M*

Pennsylvania

Drexel University *M*
Gannon University *M*
St. Joseph's University *M*
University of Pennsylvania *M*
University of Pittsburgh *M*
Villanova University *M*

Puerto Rico

Inter American University of Puerto
Rico
Arecibo Campus *M*

Pontifical Catholic University of
Puerto Rico *M*

South Carolina

Medical University of South
Carolina *M*
University of South Carolina *M*

South Dakota

Mount Marty College *M*

Texas

Texas Wesleyan University *M*
University of Texas
Health Science Center at
Houston *M*

Virginia

Virginia Commonwealth University *M*

Washington

Gonzaga University *M*

West Virginia

Mountain State University *M*

Nurse midwifery

New Jersey

University of Medicine and Dentistry
of New Jersey
School of Health Related
Professions *M*
William Paterson University of New
Jersey *M*

New York

Columbia University
School of Nursing *M*
New York University *M*
State University of New York
Stony Brook *M*

Ohio

Case Western Reserve University *M*

Oregon

Oregon Health & Science
University *M*

Pennsylvania

University of Pennsylvania *M*

South Carolina

Medical University of South
Carolina *M*

Texas

University of Texas
El Paso *M*
Medical Branch at Galveston *M*

Wisconsin

Marquette University *M*

Nursery operations

Arizona

Glendale Community College *C*

California

College of the Redwoods *C*
Cosumnes River College *C*
Foothill College *C, A*
Fullerton College *A*
Los Angeles Pierce College *C*
MiraCosta College *C, A*
Modesto Junior College *C*
Santa Rosa Junior College *C*
Southwestern College *C, A*

Georgia

Albany Technical College *C*

Illinois

College of DuPage *C*
Joliet Junior College *C, A*
Kishwaukee College *C, A*
Southwestern Illinois College *A*
William Rainey Harper College *C*

Iowa

Kirkwood Community College *A*

Kansas

Dodge City Community College *C*

Kentucky

Maysville Community College *C*

Maine

University of Maine *B*

Michigan

Northwestern Michigan College *A*

Minnesota

Anoka Technical College *C, A*
Anoka-Ramsey Community College *A*
Hennepin Technical College *C, A*

Nebraska

Metropolitan Community
College *C, A*
Nebraska College of Technical
Agriculture *A*

New Hampshire

University of New Hampshire *A*

New York

State University of New York
College of Agriculture and
Technology at Cobleskill *A*
College of Agriculture and
Technology at Morrisville *A*

Ohio

Ohio State University
Agricultural Technical Institute *A*

Pennsylvania

Pennsylvania College of Technology *A*

South Dakota

Southeast Technical Institute *A*

Tennessee

Tennessee Technological University *B*

Texas

Western Texas College *C, A*

Washington

Clark College *C*
Edmonds Community College *A*
South Seattle Community
College *C, A*
Spokane Community College *A*

Nursing (RN)

Alabama

Alabama Southern Community
College *A*
Auburn University *B*
Auburn University at Montgomery *B*
Bevill State Community College *A*
Bishop State Community College *A*
Calhoun Community College *A*

Chattahoochee Valley Community
College *A*
Gadsden State Community College *A*
George C. Wallace State Community
College
Selma *A*
Jacksonville State University *B, M*
Jefferson Davis Community College *A*
Jefferson State Community College *A*
Lawson State Community College *A*
Northeast Alabama Community
College *A*
Northwest-Shoals Community
College *A*
Samford University *B, M*
Shelton State Community College *A*
Southern Union State Community
College *A*
Spring Hill College *B*
Troy University *A, B, M*
University of Alabama *B*
University of Alabama
Birmingham *B, M, D*
Huntsville *B, M*
University of Mobile *A, B, M*
University of North Alabama *B*
University of South Alabama *B, M*
University of West Alabama *A*
Wallace State Community College at
Hanceville *A*

Alaska

University of Alaska
Anchorage *A, B, M*

Arizona

Arizona State University *B, M*
Arizona Western College *A*
Central Arizona College *A*
Cochise College *A*
Eastern Arizona College *A*
Gateway Community College *A*
Glendale Community College *A*
Grand Canyon University *B, M*
International Institute of the Americas
Phoenix *A*
Mesa Community College *A*
Mohave Community College *A*
Northern Arizona University *B, M*
Northland Pioneer College *A*
Phoenix College *A*
Pima Community College *A*
Scottsdale Community College *A*
University of Arizona *B*
Yavapai College *A*

Arkansas

Arkansas Northeastern College *A*
Arkansas State University *A, B, M*
Arkansas State University
Mountain Home *A*
Arkansas Tech University *B*
East Arkansas Community College *A*
Harding University *B, M*
Henderson State University *B*
National Park Community College *A*
North Arkansas College *A*
Northwest Arkansas Community
College *A*
Phillips Community College of the
University of Arkansas *A*
South Arkansas Community College *A*
Southeast Arkansas College *A*
Southern Arkansas University *A, B*
University of Arkansas *B*
University of Arkansas
Community College at Batesville *A*
Cossatot Community College of the
A
Fort Smith *B, M*
Little Rock *A*
Monticello *A, B*
Pine Bluff *B*
for Medical Sciences *B, M*

University of Central Arkansas *B, M*

California
Allan Hancock College *A*
American River College *A*
Antelope Valley College *A*
Azusa Pacific University *B, M, D*
Bakersfield College *A*
Biola University *B*
Butte College *A*
Cabrillo College *A*
California Baptist University *M*
California State University
   Bakersfield *B*
   Chico *B, M*
   Dominguez Hills *B*
   Fresno *B*
   Fullerton *B*
   Long Beach *B*
   Los Angeles *B, M*
   Northridge *B*
   Sacramento *B, M*
   San Bernardino *B, M*
   Stanislaus *B*
Cerritos Community College *A*
Chabot College *A*
Chaffey College *A*
College of San Mateo *A*
College of the Canyons *A*
College of the Desert *A*
College of the Sequoias *A*
Contra Costa College *A*
Cuesta College *A*
Cypress College *A*
De Anza College *A*
Dominican University of
   California *B, M*
East Los Angeles College *A*
El Camino College *A*
Evergreen Valley College *A*
Fresno City College *A*
Gavilan Community College *A*
Glendale Community College *A*
Golden West College *A*
Grossmont Community College *A*
Holy Names University *B*
Imperial Valley College *A*
Lassen College *A*
Loma Linda University *A, B*
Long Beach City College *A*
Los Angeles Harbor College *A*
Los Angeles Pierce College *A*
Los Angeles Southwest College *A*
Los Angeles Valley College *A*
Los Medanos College *A*
Merced College *A*
Merritt College *A*
Mission College *A*
Modesto Junior College *A*
Monterey Peninsula College *A*
Moorpark College *A*
Mount St. Mary's College *A, B*
Mount San Antonio College *A*
Mount San Jacinto College *A*
Napa Valley College *A*
Ohlone College *A*
Pacific Union College *A, B*
Palomar College *A*
Pasadena City College *A*
Point Loma Nazarene University *B, M*
Rio Hondo College *A*
Riverside Community College *A*
Sacramento City College *A*
Saddleback College *A*
Samuel Merritt College *B*
San Diego City College *A*
San Diego State University *B, M*
San Joaquin Delta College *A*
San Jose State University *B, M*
Santa Ana College *A*
Santa Barbara City College *A*
Santa Rosa Junior College *A*
Shasta College *A*
Sierra College *A*

Solano Community College *A*
Sonoma State University *B*
Southwestern College *A*
University of San Diego *B, M*
University of San Francisco *B, M*
Ventura College *A*
Victor Valley College *A*
Yuba Community College District *A*

Colorado
Adams State College *B*
Arapahoe Community College *A*
Colorado Mountain College
   Spring Valley Campus *A*
Colorado State University
   Pueblo *B*
Community College of Denver *A*
Concorde Career College *A*
Front Range Community College *A*
Mesa State College *A, B*
Metropolitan State College of
   Denver *B*
Morgan Community College *A*
Northeastern Junior College *A*
Otero Junior College *A*
Pikes Peak Community College *A*
Pueblo Community College *A*
University of Colorado
   Colorado Springs *B, M*
   Denver and Health Sciences
     Center *B*
University of Northern
   Colorado *B, M, D*

Connecticut
Capital Community College *A*
Central Connecticut State
   University *B*
Fairfield University *B, M*
Gateway Community College *A*
Goodwin College *A*
Housatonic Community College *A*
Naugatuck Valley Community
   College *A*
Norwalk Community College *A*
Quinnipiac University *B, M*
Sacred Heart University *B, M*
St. Joseph College *B, M*
St. Vincent's College *A*
Southern Connecticut State
   University *B*
University of Connecticut *B*
University of Hartford *B*
Western Connecticut State
   University *B*
Yale University *M, D*

Delaware
Delaware State University *B*
Delaware Technical and Community
   College
   Owens Campus *A*
   Stanton/Wilmington Campus *A*
   Terry Campus *A*
University of Delaware *B*
Wesley College *B, M*

District of Columbia
Catholic University of America *B*
Georgetown University *B, M*
University of the District of
   Columbia *A, B*

Florida
Barry University *B*
Bethune-Cookman College *B*
Brevard Community College *A*
Broward Community College *A*
Central Florida Community College *A*
Chipola College *A*
Edison College *A*
Florida Agricultural and Mechanical
   University *B, M*

Florida Atlantic University *B, M*
Florida Community College at
   Jacksonville *A*
Florida Gulf Coast University *B, M*
Florida Hospital College of Health
   Sciences *A, B*
Florida International University *B, M*
Florida Keys Community College *A*
Florida Southern College *B, M*
Florida State University *B, M*
Gulf Coast Community College *A*
Hillsborough Community College *A*
Indian River Community College *A*
Jacksonville University *B, M*
Lake City Community College *A*
Lake-Sumter Community College *A*
Manatee Community College *A*
Miami Dade College *A*
Nova Southeastern University *B, M*
Palm Beach Atlantic University *B*
Palm Beach Community College *A*
Pasco-Hernando Community
   College *A*
Pensacola Junior College *A*
Polk Community College *A*
St. Petersburg College *A, B*
Santa Fe Community College *A*
Seminole Community College *A*
South Florida Community College *A*
South University: West Palm Beach
   Campus *B*
Tallahassee Community College *A*
University of Central Florida *B, M*
University of Florida *A, B, M*
University of Miami *B, M, D*
University of North Florida *B, M*
University of South Florida *B, M*
University of Tampa *B*
University of West Florida *B*
Valencia Community College *A*

Georgia
Albany State University *B, M*
Armstrong Atlantic State
   University *B, M*
Athens Technical College *A*
Augusta State University *A*
Bainbridge College *A*
Berry College *B*
Brenau University *B*
Coastal Georgia Community
   College *A*
Columbus State University *B*
Columbus Technical College *A*
Covenant College *B*
Dalton State College *A*
Darton College *A*
Emory University *M*
Georgia College and State
   University *B, M*
Georgia Highlands College *A*
Georgia Perimeter College *A*
Georgia Southern University *B*
Georgia Southwestern State
   University *B*
Georgia State University *B, M, D*
Gordon College *A*
Kennesaw State University *B*
LaGrange College *B*
Macon State College *A, B*
Mercer University *B*
Middle Georgia College *A*
North Georgia College & State
   University *A, B, M*
Northwestern Technical College *A*
Piedmont College *B*
South Georgia College *A*
Southwest Georgia Technical
   College *A*
Thomas University *B*
University of West Georgia *B, M*
Valdosta State University *B, M*

Hawaii
Hawaii Pacific University *B, M*
University of Hawaii
   Hawaii Community College *A*
   Kapiolani Community College *A*
   Kauai Community College *A*
   Manoa *B, M, D*

Idaho
Boise State University *A, B*
Brigham Young University-Idaho *A, B*
College of Southern Idaho *A*
Idaho State University *A, B*
Lewis-Clark State College *B*
North Idaho College *A*
Northwest Nazarene University *B*

Illinois
Aurora University *B*
Benedictine University *B*
Black Hawk College *A*
Blessing-Reiman College of Nursing *B*
Bradley University *B*
Carl Sandburg College *A*
Chicago State University *B*
City Colleges of Chicago
   Harry S. Truman College *A*
   Kennedy-King College *A*
   Malcolm X College *A*
College of DuPage *A*
College of Lake County *A*
Danville Area Community College *A*
DePaul University *B*
Elgin Community College *A*
Elmhurst College *B*
Heartland Community College *A*
Highland Community College *A*
Illinois Eastern Community Colleges
   Olney Central College *A*
Illinois State University *B*
Illinois Valley Community College *A*
Illinois Wesleyan University *B*
John A. Logan College *A*
John Wood Community College *A*
Joliet Junior College *A*
Kankakee Community College *A*
Kaskaskia College *A*
Kishwaukee College *A*
Lake Land College *A*
Lakeview College of Nursing *B*
Lewis University *B*
Lewis and Clark Community
   College *A*
Lincoln Land Community College *A*
Loyola University of Chicago *B*
McKendree College *B*
Millikin University *B*
Moraine Valley Community College *A*
Morton College *A*
North Park University *B*
Northern Illinois University *B*
Oakton Community College *A*
Parkland College *A*
Prairie State College *A*
Quincy University *B*
Rend Lake College *A*
Richland Community College *A*
Rock Valley College *A*
Rockford College *B*
Rush University *B, M, D*
St. Francis Medical Center College of
   Nursing *B, M*
St. Xavier University *B*
Sauk Valley Community College *A*
South Suburban College of Cook
   County *A*
Southeastern Illinois College *A*
Southern Illinois University
   Edwardsville *B*
Southwestern Illinois College *A*
Trinity Christian College *B*
Triton College *A*
University of Illinois
   Chicago *B*

University of St. Francis *B, M*
Waubonsee Community College *A*
West Suburban College of Nursing *B*
William Rainey Harper College *A*

Indiana

Ancilla College *A*
Anderson University *B*
Ball State University *A, B, M*
Bethel College *A, B*
Goshen College *B*
Indiana State University *B, M*
Indiana University
    Bloomington *B*
    East *A, B*
    Kokomo *A, B*
    Northwest *A, B*
    South Bend *A, B*
    Southeast *B*
Indiana University-Purdue University
    Fort Wayne *A, B*
Indiana University-Purdue University
    Indianapolis *A, B*
Indiana Wesleyan University *B*
Ivy Tech State College
    Ivy Tech Community College:
        Bloomington *A*
    Ivy Tech Community College:
        Central Indiana *A*
    Ivy Tech Community College:
        Columbus *A*
    Ivy Tech Community College: East
        Central *A*
    Ivy Tech Community College:
        Kokomo *A*
    Ivy Tech Community College:
        Lafayette *A*
    Ivy Tech Community College: North
        Central *A*
    Ivy Tech Community College:
        Northeast *A*
    Ivy Tech Community College:
        Northwest *A*
    Ivy Tech Community College: South
        Central *A*
    Ivy Tech Community College:
        Southeast *A*
    Ivy Tech Community College:
        Southwest *A*
    Ivy Tech Community College:
        Wabash Valley *A*
    Ivy Tech Community College:
        Whitewater *A*
Marian College *A, B*
Purdue University *B, M*
Purdue University
    Calumet *A, B, M*
St. Joseph's College *B*
Saint Mary's College *B*
University of Evansville *B*
University of Indianapolis *A, B*
University of St. Francis *A, B*
University of Southern
    Indiana *A, B, M*
Valparaiso University *B, M*
Vincennes University *A*

Iowa

Allen College *B, M*
Briar Cliff University *B, M*
Clinton Community College *A*
Coe College *B*
Des Moines Area Community
    College *A*
Dordt College *M*
Ellsworth Community College *A*
Graceland University *B*
Grand View College *B*
Hawkeye Community College *A*
Indian Hills Community College *A*
Iowa Central Community College *A*
Iowa Lakes Community College *A*
Iowa Wesleyan College *B*
Iowa Western Community College *A*

Kirkwood Community College *A*
Luther College *B*
Marshalltown Community College *A*
Morningside College *B*
North Iowa Area Community
    College *A*
Northeast Iowa Community
    College *A*
Northwest Iowa Community
    College *A*
St. Ambrose University *B, M*
St. Luke's College *A*
Scott Community College *A*
Southeastern Community College
    North Campus *A*
Southwestern Community College *A*
University of Dubuque *B*
University of Iowa *B*
Western Iowa Tech Community
    College *A*

Kansas

Barton County Community College *A*
Bethel College *B*
Butler County Community College *A*
Cloud County Community College *A*
Colby Community College *A*
Cowley County Community
    College *A*
Dodge City Community College *A*
Emporia State University *B*
Garden City Community College *A*
Hesston College *A*
Hutchinson Community College *A*
Johnson County Community
    College *A*
Kansas City Kansas Community
    College *A*
Kansas Wesleyan University *A*
Labette Community College *A*
Manhattan Area Technical College *A*
MidAmerica Nazarene University *B*
Newman University *B*
North Central Kansas Technical
    College *A*
Pittsburg State University *B, M*
Pratt Community College *A*
Seward County Community College *A*
Southwestern College *B*
Washburn University of Topeka *B, M*

Kentucky

Ashland Community and Technical
    College *A*
Beckfield College *B*
Bellarmine University *B, M*
Berea College *B*
Big Sandy Community and Technical
    College *A*
Bluegrass Community and Technical
    College *A*
Eastern Kentucky University *A, B*
Elizabethtown Community and
    Technical College *A*
Hazard Community College *A*
Hopkinsville Community College *A*
Jefferson Community College *A*
Kentucky State University *A, B*
Madisonville Community College *A*
Maysville Community College *A*
Midway College *A, B*
Morehead State University *A, B*
Murray State University *B, M*
Northern Kentucky
    University *A, B, M*
Owensboro Community College *A*
Pikeville College *A*
St. Catharine College *A*
Somerset Community College *A*
Southeast Kentucky Community and
    Technical College *A*
Spalding University *B, M*
Spencerian College *A*
Thomas More College *B*

University of Louisville *B, M*
Western Kentucky University *A, B*

Louisiana

Delgado Community College *A*
Dillard University *B*
Grambling State University *B*
Louisiana State University
    Alexandria *A*
Louisiana State University Health
    Sciences Center *B*
Louisiana Tech University *A*
Loyola University New Orleans *B, M*
Nicholls State University *A, B*
Northwestern State University *A, B*
Our Lady of the Lake College *A, B, M*
Southeastern Louisiana University *B*
Southern University and Agricultural
    and Mechanical College *B, M*
University of Louisiana at
    Lafayette *B, M*
University of Louisiana at Monroe *B*

Maine

Central Maine Community College *A*
Central Maine Medical Center School
    of Nursing *A*
Eastern Maine Community College *A*
Husson College *B, M*
Northern Maine Community
    College *A*
St. Joseph's College *B*
Southern Maine Community
    College *A*
University of Maine *B, M*
University of Maine
    Augusta *A*
    Fort Kent *B*
    Presque Isle *T*
University of New England *A, B*
University of Southern Maine *B, M*

Maryland

Allegany College of Maryland *A*
Anne Arundel Community College *A*
Baltimore City Community College *A*
Bowie State University *B, M*
Cecil Community College *A*
Chesapeake College *A*
College of Southern Maryland *A*
Columbia Union College *B*
Community College of Baltimore
    County *A*
Coppin State University *B, M, T*
Frederick Community College *A*
Hagerstown Community College *A*
Harford Community College *A*
Howard Community College *A*
Montgomery College *A*
Prince George's Community
    College *A*
Salisbury University *B, M*
University of Maryland
    Baltimore *B*
    Eastern Shore *B*
Wor-Wic Community College *A*

Massachusetts

American International College *B, M*
Anna Maria College *B*
Atlantic Union College *B*
Becker College *A*
Berkshire Community College *A*
Boston College *B, M*
Bristol Community College *A*
Bunker Hill Community College *A*
Cape Cod Community College *A*
Curry College *B*
Emmanuel College *B*
Endicott College *B*
Fitchburg State College *B*
Framingham State College *B*
Greenfield Community College *A*

Holyoke Community College *A*
Laboure College *A*
Massachusetts Bay Community
    College *A*
Massachusetts College of Pharmacy
    and Health Sciences *B*
Massasoit Community College *A*
Middlesex Community College *A*
Mount Wachusett Community
    College *A*
North Shore Community College *A*
Northeastern University *B, M*
Northern Essex Community
    College *A*
Quincy College *A*
Quinsigamond Community College *A*
Regis College *A, B, M*
Roxbury Community College *A*
Salem State College *B, M*
Simmons College *B, M*
Springfield Technical Community
    College *A*
University of Massachusetts
    Amherst *B*
    Boston *B*
    Dartmouth *B, M*
    Lowell *B, M, D*
Worcester State College *B*

Michigan

Alpena Community College *A*
Andrews University *B*
Baker College
    of Clinton Township *B*
    of Flint *B*
    of Owosso *B*
Bay de Noc Community College *A*
Davenport University *A, B*
Delta College *A*
Eastern Michigan University *B, M*
Ferris State University *A, B*
Finlandia University *B*
Glen Oaks Community College *A*
Gogebic Community College *A*
Grand Rapids Community College *A*
Grand Valley State University *B, M*
Henry Ford Community College *A*
Hope College *B*
Jackson Community College *A*
Kalamazoo Valley Community
    College *A*
Kellogg Community College *A*
Kirtland Community College *A*
Lake Michigan College *A*
Lake Superior State University *B*
Macomb Community College *A*
Madonna University *B, M*
Michigan State University *B, M*
Mid Michigan Community College *A*
Monroe County Community
    College *A*
Montcalm Community College *A*
Mott Community College *A*
Muskegon Community College *A*
North Central Michigan College *A*
Northern Michigan University *B, M*
Northwestern Michigan College *A*
Oakland Community College *A*
Oakland University *B*
Saginaw Valley State University *B*
St. Clair County Community
    College *A*
Schoolcraft College *A*
Southwestern Michigan College *A*
Spring Arbor University *B*
University of Detroit Mercy *B, M*
University of Michigan *B, M, D*
University of Michigan
    Flint *B, M*
Washtenaw Community College *A*
Wayne County Community College *A*
Wayne State University *B, D*
West Shore Community College *A*
Western Michigan University *B, M*

Minnesota

Anoka-Ramsey Community College *A*
Augsburg College *B*
Bethel University *B*
Central Lakes College *A*
Century Community and Technical College *A*
College of St. Benedict *B*
College of St. Catherine *A, B*
College of St. Scholastica *B*
Concordia College: Moorhead *B*
Gustavus Adolphus College *B*
Hibbing Community College *A*
Inver Hills Community College *A*
Lake Superior College *A*
Metropolitan State University *B*
Minneapolis Community and Technical College *A*
Minnesota School of Business *B*
Minnesota State College - Southeast Technical *A*
Minnesota State Community and Technical College - Fergus Falls *A*
Minnesota State University Mankato *B, M*
Minnesota West Community and Technical College: Worthington Campus *A*
Normandale Community College *A*
North Hennepin Community College *A*
Northland Community & Technical College *A*
Ridgewater College *A*
Riverland Community College *A*
Rochester Community and Technical College *A*
St. Cloud State University *B*
St. John's University *B*
St. Olaf College *B*
South Central College *A*
University of Minnesota Twin Cities *B, M, D*
University of St. Thomas *B*
Walden University *M*
Winona State University *B, M*

Mississippi

Alcorn State University *A, B, M*
Coahoma Community College *A*
Copiah-Lincoln Community College *A*
Delta State University *B, M*
Itawamba Community College *A*
Mississippi College *B*
Mississippi Gulf Coast Community College
Jefferson Davis Campus *A*
University of Southern Mississippi *B*
William Carey College *B, M*

Missouri

Avila University *B*
Central Methodist University *B*
Central Missouri State University *B, M*
Crowder College *A*
Culver-Stockton College *B*
Deaconess College of Nursing *A, B*
East Central College *A*
Hannibal-LaGrange College *A, B*
Jefferson College *A*
Jewish Hospital College of Nursing and Allied Health *A, B, M*
Lester L. Cox College of Nursing and Health Sciences *A, B*
Lincoln University *A, B*
Maple Woods Community College *A*
Maryville University of Saint Louis *B, M*
Mineral Area College *A*
Missouri Southern State University *B*
Missouri State University: West Plains *A*
Missouri Western State University *B*
Moberly Area Community College *A*

National American University Kansas City *A, B*
North Central Missouri College *A*
Park University *A*
Penn Valley Community College *A*
Research College of Nursing *B*
Rockhurst University *B*
St. Charles Community College *A*
St. Louis University *B, M, D*
St. Luke's College *B*
Southeast Missouri State University *B, M*
Southwest Baptist University *A, B*
State Fair Community College *A*
Three Rivers Community College *A*
Truman State University *B*
University of Missouri
Columbia *B, M, D*
Kansas City *B, M, D*
Webster University *B, M*
William Jewell College *B*

Montana

Carroll College *B*
Miles Community College *A*
Montana State University Bozeman *B, M*
Montana Tech of the University of Montana *A, B*
Salish Kootenai College *A, B*

Nebraska

Central Community College *A*
Clarkson College *B*
College of Saint Mary *A, B*
Creighton University *B*
Grace University *B*
Metropolitan Community College *A*
Mid-Plains Community College Area *A*
Nebraska Methodist College of Nursing and Allied Health *B, M*
Nebraska Wesleyan University *B*
Northeast Community College *A*
Southeast Community College Lincoln Campus *A*
University of Nebraska Medical Center *B, M*
Western Nebraska Community College *A*

Nevada

Community College of Southern Nevada *A*
Great Basin College *A, B*
Truckee Meadows Community College *A*
University of Nevada
Las Vegas *B, M, D*
Reno *B*
Western Nevada Community College *A*

New Hampshire

Colby-Sawyer College *B*
New Hampshire Community Technical College
Berlin *A*
Claremont *A*
Manchester *A*
Nashua *A*
Stratham *A*
New Hampshire Technical Institute *A*
Rivier College *A, B*
St. Anselm College *B*
University of New Hampshire *B, M*
University of New Hampshire at Manchester *B*

New Jersey

Atlantic Cape Community College *A*
Bergen Community College *A*
Bloomfield College *B*
Brookdale Community College *A*

Burlington County College *A*
Camden County College *A*
The College of New Jersey *B, M*
County College of Morris *A*
Cumberland County College *A*
Essex County College *A*
Fairleigh Dickinson University
College at Florham *B*
Metropolitan Campus *B, M*
Felician College *A, B, M*
Gloucester County College *A*
Mercer County Community College *A*
Middlesex County College *A*
Monmouth University *B*
Ocean County College *A*
Passaic County Community College *A*
Ramapo College of New Jersey *B, M*
Raritan Valley Community College *A*
Richard Stockton College of New Jersey *B, M*
Rutgers, The State University of New Jersey
Camden Regional Campus *B*
New Brunswick/Piscataway Campus *B*
Newark Regional Campus *B*
St. Peter's College *B, M*
Salem Community College *A*
Thomas Edison State College *B*
Union County College *A*
Warren County Community College *A*
William Paterson University of New Jersey *B*

New Mexico

Albuquerque Technical-Vocational Institute *A*
Dona Ana Branch Community College of New Mexico State University *A*
Eastern New Mexico University *B*
New Mexico State University *B, M*
New Mexico State University Carlsbad *A*
San Juan College *A*
Santa Fe Community College *A*
University of New Mexico *B, M*

New York

Adelphi University *B, M*
Adirondack Community College *A*
Broome Community College *A*
Cayuga County Community College *A*
City University of New York
Borough of Manhattan Community College *A*
Bronx Community College *A*
College of Staten Island *A, B*
Hostos Community College *A*
Hunter College *B, M*
Kingsborough Community College *A*
Lehman College *B, M*
Medgar Evers College *A, B*
New York City College of Technology *A*
Queensborough Community College *A*
York College *B*
Clinton Community College *A*
Cochran School of Nursing-St. John's Riverside Hospital *A*
College of New Rochelle *B, M*
Columbia University
School of Nursing *B*
Columbia-Greene Community College *A*
Corning Community College *A*
D'Youville College *B, M*
Daemen College *B, M*
Dominican College of Blauvelt *B*
Dutchess Community College *A*
Elmira College *B*

Erie Community College
City Campus *A*
North Campus *A*
Excelsior College *A, B, M*
Finger Lakes Community College *A*
Fulton-Montgomery Community College *A*
Genesee Community College *A*
Hartwick College *B*
Helene Fuld College of Nursing *A*
Hudson Valley Community College *A*
Jamestown Community College *A*
Jefferson Community College *A*
Keuka College *B*
Le Moyne College *B*
Long Island College Hospital School of Nursing *A*
Long Island University
Brooklyn Campus *B*
C.W. Post Campus *B*
Maria College *A*
Mohawk Valley Community College *A*
Molloy College *B, M*
Monroe Community College *A*
Mount St. Mary College *B, M*
Nassau Community College *A*
New York Institute of Technology *B*
New York University *B, M, D*
Niagara County Community College *A*
North Country Community College *A*
Pace University *B, M*
Phillips Beth Israel School of Nursing *A*
Roberts Wesleyan College *B*
Rockland Community College *A*
Russell Sage College *B*
St. Elizabeth College of Nursing *A*
St. John Fisher College *B*
St. Joseph's College of Nursing *A*
St. Vincent Catholic Medical Centers *A*
State University of New York
Binghamton *B*
Buffalo *B, D*
College at Brockport *B*
College at Plattsburgh *B*
College of Agriculture and Technology at Morrisville *A*
College of Technology at Alfred *A*
College of Technology at Canton *A*
College of Technology at Delhi *A*
Downstate Medical Center *B, M*
Farmingdale *A*
Institute of Technology at Utica/Rome *B, M*
Stony Brook *B*
Upstate Medical University *B, M*
Suffolk County Community College *A*
Sullivan County Community College *A*
Tompkins-Cortland Community College *A*
Trocaire College *A*
Ulster County Community College *A*
Utica College *B*
Wagner College *B, M*
Westchester Community College *A*

North Carolina

Alamance Community College *A*
Appalachian State University *B*
Asheville-Buncombe Technical Community College *A*
Barton College *B*
Beaufort County Community College *A*
Bladen Community College *A*
Blue Ridge Community College *A*
Brunswick Community College *A*
Cabarrus College of Health Sciences *A, B*
Caldwell Community College and Technical Institute *A*

Cape Fear Community College *A*
Catawba Valley Community College *A*
Central Carolina Community
  College *A*
Central Piedmont Community
  College *A*
Cleveland Community College *A*
Coastal Carolina Community
  College *A*
College of the Albemarle *A*
Craven Community College *A*
Davidson County Community
  College *A*
Durham Technical Community
  College *A*
East Carolina University *B, M*
Edgecombe Community College *A*
Fayetteville Technical Community
  College *A*
Forsyth Technical Community
  College *A*
Gardner-Webb University *A, B, M*
Gaston College *A*
Guilford Technical Community
  College *A*
Halifax Community College *A*
Haywood Community College *A*
Isothermal Community College *A*
James Sprunt Community College *A*
Lenoir Community College *A*
Lenoir-Rhyne College *B*
Mayland Community College *A*
McDowell Technical Community
  College *A*
Mitchell Community College *A*
Nash Community College *A*
North Carolina Central University *B*
Piedmont Community College *A*
Pitt Community College *A*
Queens University of Charlotte *A, B*
Randolph Community College *A*
Richmond Community College *A*
Roanoke-Chowan Community
  College *A*
Robeson Community College *A*
Rockingham Community College *A*
Rowan-Cabarrus Community
  College *A*
Sampson Community College *A*
Sandhills Community College *A*
Southeastern Community College *A*
Southwestern Community College *A*
Stanly Community College *A*
Surry Community College *A*
Tri-County Community College *A*
University of North Carolina
  Chapel Hill *B*
  Charlotte *B, M*
  Greensboro *B*
  Pembroke *B*
  Wilmington *B*
Vance-Granville Community
  College *A*
Wake Technical Community
  College *A*
Wayne Community College *A*
Western Carolina University *B*
Western Piedmont Community
  College *A*
Wilkes Community College *A*
Wilson Technical Community
  College *A*
Winston-Salem State University *B*

North Dakota

Dickinson State University *B*
Jamestown College *B*
Medcenter One College of Nursing *B*
Minot State University *B*
North Dakota State University *B, M*
University of Mary *B, M*
University of North Dakota *B, M, D, T*
Williston State College *A*

Ohio

Belmont Technical College *A*
Bowling Green State University *B*
Bowling Green State University:
  Firelands College *A*
Case Western Reserve
  University *B, M, D*
Cedarville University *B*
Central Ohio Technical College *A*
Cincinnati State Technical and
  Community College *A*
Clark State Community College *A*
Cleveland State University *B*
College of Mount St. Joseph *B, M*
Columbus State Community
  College *A*
Cuyahoga Community College
  Metropolitan Campus *A*
Edison State Community College *A*
Franciscan University of
  Steubenville *B, M*
Good Samaritan College of Nursing
  and Health Science *A*
Hocking College *A*
James A. Rhodes State College *A*
Kent State University *B*
Kent State University
  Ashtabula Regional Campus *A*
  East Liverpool Regional
    Campus *A, B*
  Tuscarawas Campus *A, B*
Kettering College of Medical Arts *A*
Lakeland Community College *A*
Lourdes College *B*
Malone College *B, M*
Marion Technical College *A*
MedCentral College of Nursing *B*
Mercy College of Northwest
  Ohio *A, B*
Miami University
  Hamilton Campus *A, B*
  Oxford Campus *B*
Mount Carmel College of Nursing *B*
Ohio University *B, M*
Ohio University
  Chillicothe Campus *A, B*
  Southern Campus at Ironton *B*
  Zanesville Campus *A*
Otterbein College *B*
Owens Community College
  Toledo *A*
Shawnee State University *A, B*
Southern State Community College *A*
Stark State College of Technology *A*
University of Akron *B, M, D*
University of Cincinnati *B*
University of Cincinnati
  Clermont College *A*
  Raymond Walters College *A*
University of Rio Grande *A, B*
University of Toledo *A, B*
Ursuline College *B*
Walsh University *B*
Washington State Community
  College *A*
Wright State University *B, M*
Xavier University *B*
Youngstown State University *B*

Oklahoma

Bacone College *A, B*
Carl Albert State College *A*
Connors State College *A*
Eastern Oklahoma State College *A*
Northeastern Oklahoma Agricultural
  and Mechanical College *A*
Northeastern State University *B*
Northwestern Oklahoma State
  University *B*
Oklahoma Baptist University *B*
Oklahoma City Community College *A*
Oklahoma City University *B*
Oklahoma Panhandle State
  University *B*

Oklahoma State University
  Oklahoma City *A*
Oklahoma Wesleyan University *A*
Oral Roberts University *B*
Redlands Community College *A*
Rogers State University *A*
Rose State College *A*
Seminole State College *A*
Southwestern Oklahoma State
  University *A*
University of Central Oklahoma *B*
University of Oklahoma *B, M*
University of Tulsa *B*
Western Oklahoma State College *A*

Oregon

Blue Mountain Community College *A*
Central Oregon Community
  College *A*
Chemeketa Community College *A*
Clackamas Community College *A*
Clatsop Community College *A*
Concordia University *B*
Eastern Oregon University *B*
Lane Community College *A*
Linfield College *B*
Linn-Benton Community College *A*
Oregon Health & Science
  University *B*
Rogue Community College *A*
Southern Oregon University *B*
Treasure Valley Community College *A*
Umpqua Community College *A*
University of Portland *B, M*

Pennsylvania

Alvernia College *A*
Bloomsburg University of
  Pennsylvania *B, M*
Bucks County Community College *A*
Butler County Community College *A*
California University of
  Pennsylvania *A, B*
Carlow University *B*
Chatham College *B*
Clarion University of
  Pennsylvania *A, B, M*
College Misericordia *B, M*
Community College of Allegheny
  County *A*
Community College of Beaver
  County *A*
Community College of Philadelphia *A*
DeSales University *B*
Delaware County Community
  College *A*
Drexel University *B, M*
Duquesne University *B*
East Stroudsburg University of
  Pennsylvania *B*
Edinboro University of
  Pennsylvania *B, M*
Gannon University *B, M*
Gettysburg College *B*
Gwynedd-Mercy College *A, B*
Harrisburg Area Community
  College *A*
Immaculata University *B*
Indiana University of
  Pennsylvania *B, M*
Kutztown University of
  Pennsylvania *B*
La Roche College *A, B, M*
La Salle University *B*
Lehigh Carbon Community College *A*
Lock Haven University of
  Pennsylvania *A, B*
Luzerne County Community
  College *A*
Marywood University *B*
Mercyhurst College *A*
Messiah College *B*
Millersville University of
  Pennsylvania *B*

Montgomery County Community
  College *A*
Moravian College *B*
Mount Aloysius College *A, B*
Neumann College *B, M*
Northampton County Area
  Community College *A*
Penn State
  Abington *B*
  Altoona *A, B*
  Beaver *B*
  Berks *B*
  Delaware County *B*
  Dubois *B*
  Fayette *A, B*
  Harrisburg *B*
  Hazleton *B*
  Lehigh Valley *B*
  Mont Alto *A, B*
  New Kensington *B*
  Schuylkill - Capital College *B*
  Shenango *B*
  University Park *B, M, D*
  Wilkes-Barre *B*
  Worthington Scranton *A, B*
  York *B*
Pennsylvania College of Technology *A*
Reading Area Community College *A*
Robert Morris University *B, M*
St. Francis University *B*
Seton Hill University *B*
Slippery Rock University of
  Pennsylvania *B, M*
Temple University *B, M*
Thomas Jefferson University: College
  of Health Professions *M*
University of Pennsylvania *B, M, D*
University of Pittsburgh *B*
University of Pittsburgh
  Bradford *A, B*
  Titusville *A*
University of Scranton *M*
Villanova University *B*
Waynesburg College *B, M*
West Chester University of
  Pennsylvania *B, M*
Westmoreland County Community
  College *A*
Widener University *B, M*
Wilkes University *B, M*
York College of Pennsylvania *B, M*

Puerto Rico

Columbia College *A, B*
Inter American University of Puerto
  Rico
  Aguadilla Campus *A, B*
  Arecibo Campus *A, B*
  Barranquitas Campus *A, B*
  Guayama Campus *A, B*
  Ponce Campus *A, B*
National College of Business &
  Technology: Arecibo *A, B*
National College of Business &
  Technology: Bayamon *A, B*
Turabo University *B*
Universidad Metropolitana *A, B*
Universidad del Este *A*
University College of San Juan *A, B*
University of Puerto Rico
  Humacao *A, B*
  Mayaguez *B*
University of the Sacred Heart *A, B*

Rhode Island

Community College of Rhode
  Island *A*
Salve Regina University *B*
University of Rhode Island *B*

South Carolina

Aiken Technical College *A*
Central Carolina Technical College *A*
Charleston Southern University *B*

Florence-Darlington Technical
College *A*
Francis Marion University *B*
Greenville Technical College *A*
Horry-Georgetown Technical
College *A*
Lander University *B*
Medical University of South
Carolina *B, M*
Midlands Technical College *A*
Orangeburg-Calhoun Technical
College *A*
Piedmont Technical College *A*
South Carolina State University *B*
Spartanburg Technical College *A*
Technical College of the
Lowcountry *A*
Tri-County Technical College *A*
Trident Technical College *A*
University of South Carolina *B*
University of South Carolina
Aiken *A*
Lancaster *A*
Upstate *A, B*
York Technical College *A*

South Dakota

Augustana College *B, M*
Dakota Wesleyan University *A*
Lake Area Technical Institute *A*
Mount Marty College *B*
Presentation College *A, B*
Sisseton Wahpeton College *A*
South Dakota State University *B, M*
University of South Dakota *A*

Tennessee

Aquinas College *A, B*
Austin Peay State University *B*
Belmont University *B, M*
Carson-Newman College *B*
Cleveland State Community College *A*
Cumberland University *B*
Dyersburg State Community
College *A*
East Tennessee State University *B, M*
Fisk University *B*
Jackson State Community College *A*
King College *B*
Lincoln Memorial University *A, B*
Lipscomb University *B*
Maryville College *B*
Middle Tennessee State
University *B, M*
Milligan College *B*
Roane State Community College *A*
Southern Adventist University *A, B*
Southwest Tennessee Community
College *A*
Tennessee Technological University *B*
Tennessee Wesleyan College *B*
Trevecca Nazarene University *B*
Union University *B*
University of Memphis *B*
University of Tennessee
Chattanooga *B, M*
Knoxville *B*
Martin *B*
Walters State Community College *A*

Texas

Abilene Christian University *B, M*
Alvin Community College *A*
Amarillo College *A*
Angelina College *A*
Angelo State University *A, B*
Baylor University *B*
Blinn College *A*
Brazosport College *A*
Central Texas College *A*
Clarendon College *A*
Coastal Bend College *A*
Collin County Community College
District *A*

Del Mar College *A*
East Texas Baptist University *B*
El Centro College *A*
El Paso Community College *A*
Galveston College *A*
Grayson County College *A*
Hardin-Simmons University *B, M*
Houston Baptist University *A, B, M*
Houston Community College
System *A*
Howard College *A*
Kilgore College *A*
Lamar State College at Orange *A*
Lamar State College at Port Arthur *A*
Lamar University *A, B, M*
Laredo Community College *A*
Lubbock Christian University *B*
McMurry University *B*
Midland College *A*
Midwestern State University *B*
North Central Texas College *A*
North Harris Montgomery
Community College District *A*
Northeast Texas Community
College *A*
Odessa College *A*
Panola College *A*
Prairie View A&M University *B, M*
St. Philip's College *A*
San Antonio College *A*
San Jacinto College
Central Campus *A*
South Plains College *A*
Southwest Texas Junior College *A*
Southwestern Adventist
University *A, B*
Stephen F. Austin State University *B*
Tarleton State University *B*
Tarrant County College *A*
Temple College *A*
Texarkana College *A*
Texas A&M University
Texarkana *B*
Texas Christian University *B, M*
Texas Southmost College *A*
Texas Tech University Health Sciences
Center *B*
Texas Woman's University *B, M*
Trinity Valley Community College *A*
Tyler Junior College *A*
University of Mary Hardin-Baylor *B*
University of Texas
Arlington *B, M*
Austin *B, M, D*
Brownsville *A, B*
El Paso *B, D*
Health Science Center at
Houston *B*
Health Science Center at San
Antonio *B*
Medical Branch at Galveston *B*
Pan American *B*
Tyler *B*
University of the Incarnate Word *B, M*
Vernon College *A*
Victoria College *A*
West Texas A&M University *B, M*
Wharton County Junior College *A*

Utah

Brigham Young University *B, M*
Dixie State College of Utah *A, B*
Salt Lake Community College *A*
Southern Utah University *B*
University of Utah *B, M, D*
Utah Valley State College *A, B*
Weber State University *A, B*

Vermont

Castleton State College *A*
Southern Vermont College *A, B*
University of Vermont *B, M*
Vermont Technical College *A*

Virginia

Blue Ridge Community College *A*
Eastern Mennonite University *B*
George Mason University *B, M, D*
Germanna Community College *A*
Hampton University *B*
J. Sargeant Reynolds Community
College *A*
James Madison University *B*
Jefferson College of Health
Sciences *A, B, M*
John Tyler Community College *A*
Liberty University *B, M*
Lord Fairfax Community College *A*
Lynchburg College *B*
Marymount University *A, B*
Mountain Empire Community
College *A*
Norfolk State University *A, B*
Old Dominion University *B, M*
Paul D. Camp Community College *A*
Radford University *B*
Rappahannock Community College *A*
Shenandoah University *B, M*
Southside Virginia Community
College *A*
Southwest Virginia Community
College *A*
Tidewater Community College *A*
University of Virginia *B, M, D*
University of Virginia's College at
Wise *B*
Virginia Commonwealth
University *B, M*
Virginia Highlands Community
College *A*
Virginia State University *A*
Virginia Western Community
College *A*

Washington

Bellevue Community College *A*
Big Bend Community College *A*
Centralia College *A*
Clark College *A*
Everett Community College *A*
Grays Harbor College *A*
Highline Community College *A*
Lower Columbia College *A*
North Seattle Community College *A*
Northwest University *B*
Olympic College *A*
Pacific Lutheran University *B, M*
Peninsula College *A*
Seattle Pacific University *B*
Seattle University *B*
Shoreline Community College *A*
Skagit Valley College *A*
Spokane Falls Community College *A*
University of Washington *B*
Walla Walla College *B*
Walla Walla Community College *A*
Washington State University *B, M*
Wenatchee Valley College *A*
Whatcom Community College *A*
Yakima Valley College *A*

West Virginia

Alderson-Broaddus College *B*
Bluefield State College *A*
Davis and Elkins College *A*
Glenville State College *B*
Marshall University *A, B*
Mountain State University *B, M*
Shepherd University *B*
Southern West Virginia Community
and Technical College *A*
University of Charleston *A, B*
West Virginia Northern Community
College *A*
West Virginia University *B, M, D*
West Virginia University at
Parkersburg *A*
Wheeling Jesuit University *M, D*

Wisconsin

Alverno College *A, B, M*
Bellin College of Nursing *B, M*
Beloit College *B*
Blackhawk Technical College *A*
Cardinal Stritch University *A, B*
Carroll College *B*
Chippewa Valley Technical College *A*
Columbia College of Nursing *B*
Concordia University Wisconsin *B, M*
Edgewood College *B*
Fox Valley Technical College *A*
Gateway Technical College *A*
Lakeshore Technical College *A*
Madison Area Technical College *A*
Maranatha Baptist Bible College *B*
Marian College of Fond du Lac *B, M*
Marquette University *B, M, D*
Mid-State Technical College *A*
Milwaukee Area Technical College *A*
Milwaukee School of Engineering *B*
Moraine Park Technical College *A*
Mount Mary College *B*
Nicolet Area Technical College *A*
Northcentral Technical College *A*
Northeast Wisconsin Technical
College *A*
Southwest Wisconsin Technical
College *A*
University of Wisconsin
Eau Claire *B, M*
Green Bay *B*
Madison *B, M, D*
Milwaukee *B, M, D*
Oshkosh *B, M*
Viterbo University *B, M*
Waukesha County Technical
College *A*
Western Wisconsin Technical
College *A*
Wisconsin Indianhead Technical
College *A*

Wyoming

Casper College *A*
Central Wyoming College *A*
Laramie County Community
College *A*
Sheridan College *A*
University of Wyoming *B, M*

Nursing administration

Alabama

University of Mobile *M*

California

California State University
San Bernardino *M*
Holy Names University *M*
Samuel Merritt College *M*
San Diego State University *M*
University of San Francisco *M*

Colorado

University of Colorado
Denver and Health Sciences
Center *M, D*

Connecticut

Sacred Heart University *M*
Southern Connecticut State
University *M*
University of Connecticut *M*
University of Hartford *M*

District of Columbia

George Washington University *M*

Florida

Barry University *B, M, D*
University of Tampa *M*

Georgia

Clayton State University *B*
Georgia College and State
    University *M*

Illinois

Bradley University *M*
Lewis University *D*
Loyola University of Chicago *M*
North Park University *M*
St. Xavier University *M*
Southern Illinois University
    Edwardsville *M*

Indiana

Indiana University-Purdue University
    Fort Wayne *M*
Indiana University-Purdue University
    Indianapolis *M*
Indiana Wesleyan University *M*

Iowa

Allen College *M*
University of Iowa *M, D*

Kentucky

Bellarmine University *M*

Louisiana

Louisiana State University Health
    Sciences Center *M*
Northwestern State University *M*
Our Lady of the Lake College *M*

Maine

Husson College *M*
University of Southern Maine *M*

Maryland

University of Maryland
    Baltimore *M*

Massachusetts

Northeastern University *M*
Regis College *M*
Salem State College *M*
University of Massachusetts
    Boston *M, D*

Michigan

Andrews University *M*
Ferris State University *M*
Madonna University *M*
Northern Michigan University *M*
Saginaw Valley State University *M*
University of Detroit Mercy *M*
University of Michigan *M*
Wayne State University *M*

Minnesota

College of St. Scholastica *M*
Winona State University *M*

Mississippi

University of Southern Mississippi *M*

Missouri

Central Methodist University *B*
Research College of Nursing *M*

Nebraska

Clarkson College *M*
Nebraska Wesleyan University *M*

Nevada

University of Nevada
    Reno *M*

New Hampshire

University of New Hampshire *M*

New Jersey

Felician College *B, M*
Kean University *M*
Seton Hall University *M*

New York

Adelphi University *M*
City University of New York
    Hunter College *M*
    Lehman College *M*
College of Mount St. Vincent *M*
College of New Rochelle *M*
Mount St. Mary College *M*
Roberts Wesleyan College *M*
St. John Fisher College *M*
State University of New York
    Buffalo *M*
    Institute of Technology at
        Utica/Rome *M*
    Upstate Medical University *M*

North Dakota

University of Mary *M*

Ohio

Ashland University *B*
Kent State University *M, D*
Ohio University *M*
Ohio University
    Chillicothe Campus *B*
Otterbein College *M*
Xavier University *M*

Oklahoma

Oklahoma City University *M*

Pennsylvania

Carlow University *M*
DeSales University *M*
Duquesne University *M*
Marywood University *M*
University of Pennsylvania *M*
Villanova University *M*

South Carolina

Medical University of South
    Carolina *M*
University of South Carolina *M*

Tennessee

Southern Adventist University *M*
Union University *M*

Texas

Baylor University *M*
Lubbock Christian University *M*
Midwestern State University *M*
Texas Tech University Health Sciences
    Center *M*
Texas Woman's University *M*
University of Texas
    Arlington *M*
    Brownsville *M*
    El Paso *M*
    Tyler *M*
West Texas A&M University *M*

Virginia

George Mason University *M, D*
Marymount University *M*

Washington

Seattle Pacific University *M*

West Virginia

Mountain State University *M*

Wisconsin

Marquette University *M*
University of Wisconsin
    Oshkosh *M*

Viterbo University *M*

Nursing assistant

Alabama

Alabama Southern Community
    College *A*
Bevill State Community College *C*
Bishop State Community College *C*
Gadsden State Community College *C*
George C. Wallace State Community
    College
    Selma *C*
Lawson State Community College *C*
Northwest-Shoals Community
    College *C*
Shelton State Community College *C*
Trenholm State Technical College *C*

Arizona

Arizona Western College *C*
Eastern Arizona College *C*
Gateway Community College *C*
Glendale Community College *C*
International Institute of the Americas
    Phoenix *C*
    Tucson *C*
International Institute of the
    Americas: West Valley *C*
Mesa Community College *C*
Northland Pioneer College *C*
Phoenix College *C*
Rio Salado College *C, A*
Scottsdale Community College *C*

Arkansas

Arkansas State University
    Mountain Home *C*
Black River Technical College *C*
Ouachita Technical College *C*
South Arkansas Community College *C*
Southeast Arkansas College *C*
Southern Arkansas University Tech *C*

California

Allan Hancock College *C*
Chaffey College *C*
College of the Canyons *C*
College of the Desert *C*
College of the Sequoias *C*
Copper Mountain College *C*
Gavilan Community College *C*
Imperial Valley College *C*
Lassen College *A*
Long Beach City College *C*
Maric College
    Vista *C*
Merritt College *C*
MiraCosta College *C*
Modesto Junior College *A*
Santa Barbara City College *C*
Santa Rosa Junior College *C, A*
Shasta College *C*
Southwestern College *C*
Yuba Community College District *C*

Colorado

Colorado Mountain College
    Alpine Campus *C*
    Spring Valley Campus *C*
    Timberline Campus *C*
Community College of Denver *C*
Front Range Community College *C*
Morgan Community College *C*
Otero Junior College *C*
Pikes Peak Community College *C*
Red Rocks Community College *C*
Trinidad State Junior College *C*

Connecticut

Capital Community College *C*

Florida

Angley College *C*
Brevard Community College *C*
Central Florida College *C*
Chipola College *C*
Daytona Beach Community College *C*
Florida Community College at
    Jacksonville *C*
Florida National College *C*
Indian River Community College *C*
Lake City Community College *C*
North Florida Community College *C*
Okaloosa-Walton College *B*
Palm Beach Community College *C*
Pasco-Hernando Community
    College *C*
Pensacola Junior College *C*
Seminole Community College *C*
South Florida Community College *C*
Tallahassee Community College *C*

Georgia

Albany Technical College *C*
Athens Technical College *C*
Bainbridge College *C*
Central Georgia Technical College *C*
Coastal Georgia Community
    College *C*
Columbus Technical College *C*
Northwestern Technical College *C*
Savannah Technical College *C*
South University *C*
Southwest Georgia Technical
    College *C*
West Georgia Technical College *C*

Hawaii

University of Hawaii
    Hawaii Community College *C*
    Kapiolani Community College *A*
    Kauai Community College *C*

Illinois

Black Hawk College *C*
City Colleges of Chicago
    Harold Washington College *C*
    Kennedy-King College *C*
    Malcolm X College *C*
    Wright College *C*
College of DuPage *C*
College of Lake County *C*
Elgin Community College *C*
Heartland Community College *C*
Highland Community College *C*
Illinois Eastern Community Colleges
    Frontier Community College *C*
    Lincoln Trail College *C*
    Olney Central College *C*
    Wabash Valley College *C*
John A. Logan College *C*
John Wood Community College *C*
Kankakee Community College *C*
Kaskaskia College *C*
Kishwaukee College *C*
Lewis and Clark Community
    College *C*
Lincoln Land Community College *C*
McHenry County College *C*
Morton College *C*
Parkland College *C*
Prairie State College *C*
Rend Lake College *C*
Richland Community College *C*
Rock Valley College *C*
Sauk Valley Community College *C*
South Suburban College of Cook
    County *C*
Southeastern Illinois College *C*
Southwestern Illinois College *C*
Spoon River College *C, A*
Triton College *C*
Waubonsee Community College *C*
William Rainey Harper College *C*

Iowa

Des Moines Area Community
  College C
Indian Hills Community College C
Iowa Lakes Community College C
Mercy College of Health Sciences C
North Iowa Area Community
  College C
Northeast Iowa Community
  College C
Western Iowa Tech Community
  College C

Kansas

Allen County Community College A
Barton County Community College C
Brown Mackie College C
Cloud County Community College C
Coffeyville Community College C
Dodge City Community College C, A
Johnson County Community
  College C
Kansas City Kansas Community
  College C
Neosho County Community
  College C

Kentucky

Hopkinsville Community College C

Louisiana

Gretna Career College C, A
Nunez Community College C

Maine

Central Maine Medical Center School
  of Nursing C
Southern Maine Community
  College C

Maryland

Allegany College of Maryland C
Anne Arundel Community College C
College of Southern Maryland C

Massachusetts

Becker College C
Bunker Hill Community College C
Cape Cod Community College C
Middlesex Community College C

Michigan

Baker College
  of Flint C
Delta College C
Gogebic Community College C
Kellogg Community College C
Montcalm Community College C
West Shore Community College A

Minnesota

Alexandria Technical College C
Anoka Technical College C
Dakota County Technical College C
Inver Hills Community College C
Itasca Community College C
Mesabi Range Community and
  Technical College C
Minneapolis Community and
  Technical College C
Normandale Community College C
Ridgewater College C
Rochester Community and Technical
  College C
St. Paul College C
South Central College C

Mississippi

Copiah-Lincoln Community College C
Hinds Community College A
Itawamba Community College C

Mississippi Gulf Coast Community
  College
  Jefferson Davis Campus C

Missouri

Moberly Area Community College C
State Fair Community College C

Montana

Montana Tech of the University of
  Montana C

Nebraska

Nebraska Methodist College of
  Nursing and Allied Health C

New Mexico

Albuquerque Technical-Vocational
  Institute C
Clovis Community College C
Dona Ana Branch Community College
  of New Mexico State
  University C
Eastern New Mexico University:
  Roswell Campus C
Northern New Mexico College C

New York

St. Joseph's College of Nursing C
Westchester Community College C, A

North Carolina

Beaufort County Community
  College C
Bladen Community College C
Brunswick Community College C
Carteret Community College C
Central Carolina Community
  College C
Coastal Carolina Community
  College C
College of the Albemarle C
Craven Community College C
Edgecombe Community College C
Gaston College C
Halifax Community College C
Haywood Community College C
McDowell Technical Community
  College C
Mitchell Community College C
Nash Community College C
Richmond Community College C
Robeson Community College C
Sampson Community College C
Sandhills Community College C
South Piedmont Community
  College C
Southeastern Community College C
Stanly Community College C
Tri-County Community College C
Vance-Granville Community
  College C

North Dakota

Lake Region State College C

Ohio

Central Ohio Technical College C
Cincinnati State Technical and
  Community College C
Columbus State Community
  College C
Kent State University
  East Liverpool Regional Campus C
  Tuscarawas Campus C
Marion Technical College C
Sinclair Community College C

Oregon

Central Oregon Community
  College C
Chemeketa Community College C

Linn-Benton Community College C
Southwestern Oregon Community
  College C
Umpqua Community College C

Pennsylvania

Community College of Allegheny
  County C
Delaware County Community
  College C
Douglas Education Center C
Erie Business Center C
Laurel Business Institute A
Mercyhurst College C, A

Puerto Rico

Inter American University of Puerto
  Rico
  San German Campus C

South Carolina

Forrest Junior College C
Trident Technical College C
Williamsburg Technical College C
York Technical College C

South Dakota

Western Dakota Technical Institute C

Texas

Cedar Valley College C
El Centro College C
El Paso Community College C
Galveston College C
Howard College C
Midland College C
North Harris Montgomery
  Community College District C
Palo Alto College A
South Plains College C
South Texas College C, A
Tarrant County College C
Texas State Technical College
  Harlingen C

Utah

Dixie State College of Utah C
Salt Lake Community College C
Southern Utah University C

Virginia

J. Sargeant Reynolds Community
  College C
Mountain Empire Community
  College C
Rappahannock Community College C
Southside Virginia Community
  College C
Virginia Western Community
  College C

Washington

Bellingham Technical College C
Big Bend Community College C
Centralia College C
Clark College C
Clover Park Technical College C
Everett Community College C
Lake Washington Technical College C
Lower Columbia College C, A
Olympic College C
Renton Technical College C
South Puget Sound Community
  College C
Wenatchee Valley College C

Wisconsin

Chippewa Valley Technical College C
Fox Valley Technical College C
Gateway Technical College C
Lakeshore Technical College C
Madison Area Technical College C

Mid-State Technical College C
Milwaukee Area Technical College C
Moraine Park Technical College C
Nicolet Area Technical College C
Northcentral Technical College C
Northeast Wisconsin Technical
  College C
Southwest Wisconsin Technical
  College C
Waukesha County Technical
  College C
Western Wisconsin Technical
  College C
Wisconsin Indianhead Technical
  College C

Wyoming

Laramie County Community
  College C
Sheridan College C

Nursing science

Arizona

University of Phoenix B, M, D

California

California State University
  Fullerton M
University of California
  Los Angeles B, M, D
University of San Diego D

Connecticut

University of Connecticut D
Yale University D

Florida

Florida Atlantic University D
University of Central Florida D
University of South Florida D

Georgia

Emory University B, M, D

Hawaii

University of Hawaii
  Manoa D

Illinois

DePaul University M
Lewis University M
Loyola University of Chicago M, D
University of Illinois
  Chicago M, D

Indiana

Indiana University-Purdue University
  Indianapolis D
University of St. Francis M

Iowa

University of Iowa M, D

Kansas

Wichita State University B, M

Kentucky

University of Louisville D

Louisiana

Louisiana State University Health
  Sciences Center D
Our Lady of the Lake College M
Southern University and Agricultural
  and Mechanical College D

Maryland

University of Maryland
  Baltimore M, D

Massachusetts
Salem State College *M*

Michigan
Michigan State University *D*

Minnesota
Metropolitan State University *M*

Nebraska
University of Nebraska
Medical Center *D*

New Jersey
Kean University *B, M, T*
Monmouth University *M*
New Jersey Institute of Technology *M*
University of Medicine and Dentistry
of New Jersey
School of Nursing *B, M, D*
William Paterson University of New
Jersey *M*

New Mexico
University of New Mexico *D*

New York
Columbia University
School of Nursing *D*
State University of New York
Binghamton *M, D*

North Carolina
East Carolina University *D*
University of North Carolina
Chapel Hill *D*
Greensboro *B, M, D, T*

Ohio
Case Western Reserve University *M, D*
Kent State University *D, T*

Oklahoma
Oklahoma City University *M*

Pennsylvania
Drexel University *D*
Immaculata University *M*
Widener University *D*

Rhode Island
University of Rhode Island *M, D*

South Carolina
Medical University of South
Carolina *D*
University of South Carolina *M, D*

South Dakota
South Dakota State University *D*

Tennessee
East Tennessee State University *D*
University of Memphis *M*

Texas
Texas Tech University Health Sciences
Center *D*
Texas Woman's University *D*
University of Texas
Arlington *D*
Medical Branch at Galveston *D*

Virginia
Hampton University *M, D*
Virginia Commonwealth University *D*

Wisconsin
Marquette University *M, D*
Viterbo University *M*

Nutrition sciences

Alabama
Auburn University *M, D*
Community College of the Air
Force *A*
Samford University *B*
University of Alabama
Birmingham *D*

Arizona
University of Arizona *B, M, D*

Arkansas
University of Arkansas
for Medical Sciences *M*

California
Chapman University *B, M*
Loma Linda University *M*
Pepperdine University *B*
University of California
Berkeley *B, M, D*
Davis *B, M, D*

Connecticut
University of Connecticut *B, M, D*
University of New Haven *B, M*

Delaware
University of Delaware *B, M*

District of Columbia
Howard University *B, M, D*

Florida
Florida State University *B, M, D*
Okaloosa-Walton College *A*

Georgia
Clark Atlanta University *B*
Life University *B*

Hawaii
University of Hawaii
Manoa *B, M*

Illinois
Dominican University *B*
Rosalind Franklin University of
Medicine and Science *M*
Rush University *M*
University of Illinois
Urbana-Champaign *M, D*

Kansas
University of Kansas Medical
Center *M*

Kentucky
University of Kentucky *M, D*

Maine
University of Maine *D*

Maryland
University of Maryland
College Park *M, D*

Massachusetts
Boston University *B, M, D*
Hampshire College *B*
Simmons College *B, M*
Tufts University *M, D*
University of Massachusetts
Amherst *M*

Michigan
Michigan State University *B*
University of Michigan *B, M, D*

Minnesota
College of St. Benedict *B*
St. John's University *B*
University of Minnesota
Twin Cities *B, M, D*

Mississippi
Mississippi State University *M, D*
University of Southern Mississippi *M*

Missouri
Southeast Missouri State University *M*
University of Missouri
Columbia *B, M, D*

Nebraska
University of Nebraska
Lincoln *M, D*

Nevada
University of Nevada
Las Vegas *B*

New Jersey
Rutgers, The State University of New
Jersey
New Brunswick/Piscataway
Campus *B, M, D*

New York
City University of New York
Brooklyn College *M*
Cornell University *B, M, D*
Ithaca College *B*
Long Island University
C.W. Post Campus *M*
Mohawk Valley Community College *A*
New York Institute of
Technology *B, M*
Russell Sage College *B*
State University of New York
Buffalo *M*
College of Agriculture and
Technology at Morrisville *A*
Syracuse University *B*

North Carolina
North Carolina State University *M, D*
University of North Carolina
Chapel Hill *M, D*
Greensboro *D*

Ohio
Case Western Reserve
University *B, M, D*
Ohio State University
Columbus Campus *B, M, D*
University of Cincinnati
Raymond Walters College *A*

Oklahoma
University of Central Oklahoma *M*
University of Oklahoma *B, M*

Pennsylvania
Drexel University *B, M, D*
La Salle University *B*

Rhode Island
Johnson & Wales University *B*

South Carolina
Clemson University *B, M*
South Carolina State University *M*

Texas
Texas A&M University *B, M, D*
Texas Woman's University *B, M, D*
University of Texas
Austin *M, D*
University of the Incarnate Word *B, M*

Utah
Brigham Young University *B, M*
Utah State University *M*

Vermont
University of Vermont *B, M*

Washington
Bastyr University *B, M*
University of Washington *M, D*
Washington State University *D*

Wisconsin
University of Wisconsin
Madison *M, D*

Wyoming
Casper College *B*

Occupational/ environmental health nursing

Pennsylvania
University of Pennsylvania *M*

Tennessee
University of Tennessee
Knoxville *B*

Occupational health/ industrial hygiene

Arkansas
University of Arkansas
for Medical Sciences *M*
University of Central Arkansas *B*

California
California State University
Fresno *B*
Sacramento *B*
San Diego Miramar College *A*
San Diego State University *M*

Connecticut
University of New Haven *M*

Hawaii
University of Hawaii
Honolulu Community College *A*

Illinois
Illinois State University *B*

Iowa
University of Iowa *M, D*

Maine
Central Maine Community College *A*

Maryland
Community College of Baltimore
County *A*

Massachusetts
Harvard College *M, D*
University of Massachusetts
Lowell *M, D*

Michigan
Grand Valley State University *B*
Oakland University *B*
University of Michigan *M, D*
Wayne State University *M*

Mississippi
Itawamba Community College *A*

Missouri
Central Missouri State University *M*

Montana
Montana Tech of the University of
Montana *B, M*

New York
Clarkson University *B*

North Carolina
Durham Technical Community
College *A*
East Carolina University *M*
North Carolina Agricultural and
Technical State University *B*
St. Augustine's College *B*

Ohio
Capital University *B*
Ohio University *B*
University of Findlay *B*

Oklahoma
University of Oklahoma *M, D*

Pennsylvania
University of Pittsburgh *M*

Puerto Rico
Bayamon Central University *B*
University of the Sacred Heart *M*

Texas
Laredo Community College *A*
North Central Texas College *A*
University of Texas
Medical Branch at Galveston *M*

Washington
Central Washington University *B*

West Virginia
Mountain State University *B*

Occupational safety/ health technology

Alabama
Jacksonville State University *B*

Arizona
Gateway Community College *C, A*

California
Southwestern College *C, A*

Colorado
Red Rocks Community College *C*

Connecticut
University of Connecticut *M*
University of New Haven *C, A, B, M*

Florida
Embry-Riddle Aeronautical
University *B*

Hawaii
University of Hawaii
Honolulu Community College *C, A*

Indiana
Indiana State University *B*
Ivy Tech State College
Ivy Tech Community College:
Central Indiana *A*
Ivy Tech Community College:
Kokomo *C, A*

Ivy Tech Community College:
Northeast *A*
Ivy Tech Community College:
Northwest *A*
Ivy Tech Community College:
Wabash Valley *C, A*

Iowa
Clinton Community College *A*

Kentucky
Murray State University *B, M*

Louisiana
Delgado Community College *A*
Southeastern Louisiana University *B*

Maryland
Community College of Baltimore
County *C, A*

Massachusetts
Anna Maria College *M*

Michigan
Madonna University *C, B*

Missouri
Mineral Area College *A*
Southwest Baptist University *A, B*

New Hampshire
Keene State College *B*

New Jersey
New Jersey Institute of Technology *M*
Rider University *C*

New Mexico
Eastern New Mexico University:
Roswell Campus *C*

New York
Rochester Institute of
Technology *C, B*

North Carolina
Central Piedmont Community
College *A*
North Carolina Agricultural and
Technical State University *B*

North Dakota
University of North Dakota *B*

Ohio
James A. Rhodes State College *C*
Ohio University
Chillicothe Campus *C*
Owens Community College
Toledo *C*
Wright State University *A*

Oklahoma
Oklahoma State University
Oklahoma City *A*
Southeastern Oklahoma State
University *B*

Pennsylvania
Gannon University *C*
Indiana University of
Pennsylvania *B, M*
Millersville University of
Pennsylvania *B*
Slippery Rock University of
Pennsylvania *B*

Texas
Kilgore College *C, A*

Odessa College *C, A*
San Antonio College *C, A*
University of Houston
Downtown *B*
University of Texas
Tyler *B, M*

Virginia
Tidewater Community College *A*

West Virginia
Marshall University *B, M*

Wisconsin
University of Wisconsin
Stout *M*
Whitewater *B, M*

Occupational therapy

Alabama
Alabama State University *M*
University of Alabama
Birmingham *M*
University of South Alabama *M*

Arkansas
University of Central Arkansas *M*

California
Dominican University of California *M*
Loma Linda University *M*
Samuel Merritt College *M*
San Jose State University *M*
University of Southern
California *M, D*

Colorado
Colorado State University *D*

Connecticut
Quinnipiac University *M*
Sacred Heart University *M*
University of Hartford *M*

Florida
Barry University *M*
Florida Gulf Coast University *M*
Florida International University *M*
Nova Southeastern University *M, D*
University of Florida *M*

Georgia
Brenau University *M*
Medical College of Georgia *M*

Idaho
Idaho State University *M*

Illinois
Governors State University *M*
Rush University *M*
University of Illinois
Chicago *M*

Indiana
Indiana University-Purdue University
Indianapolis *M*
University of Indianapolis *M*

Iowa
St. Ambrose University *M*

Kansas
University of Kansas Medical
Center *M, D*

Kentucky
Eastern Kentucky University *M*
Spalding University *M*

Louisiana
Louisiana State University Health
Sciences Center *M*

Maine
Husson College *M*
University of New England *M*
University of Southern Maine *M*

Maryland
Towson University *M, D*

Massachusetts
American International College *M*
Bay Path College *M*
Boston University *M*
Salem State College *M*
Springfield College *M*
Worcester State College *M*

Michigan
Baker College
of Flint *D*
Calvin College *M*
Eastern Michigan University *M*
Grand Valley State University *M*
Saginaw Valley State University *M*
Wayne State University *M*
Western Michigan University *M*

Minnesota
College of St. Catherine *M*
College of St. Scholastica *M*
University of St. Thomas *M*

Missouri
Maryville University of Saint Louis *M*
Rockhurst University *M*
St. Louis University *M*
University of Missouri
Columbia *M*
Washington University in St.
Louis *M, D*

Nebraska
College of Saint Mary *M*
Creighton University *D*

New Hampshire
University of New Hampshire *M*

New Jersey
Kean University *M*
Richard Stockton College of New
Jersey *M*
Seton Hall University *M*

New Mexico
University of New Mexico *M*

New York
D'Youville College *M*
Dominican College of Blauvelt *M*
Ithaca College *M*
Long Island University
Brooklyn Campus *M*
Mercy College *M*
New York Institute of Technology *M*
New York University *M, D*
State University of New York
Buffalo *M*
Stony Brook *M*
Touro College *M*
Utica College *M*

North Carolina
East Carolina University *M*
University of North Carolina
Chapel Hill *M, D*
Winston-Salem State University *M*

North Dakota

University of Mary *M*
University of North Dakota *M*

Ohio

Ohio State University
 Columbus Campus *M*
University of Findlay *M*
Xavier University *M*

Oklahoma

University of Oklahoma *M*

Oregon

Pacific University *M*

Pennsylvania

Alvernia College *M*
Chatham College *M*
College Misericordia *M*
Duquesne University *M*
Elizabethtown College *M*
Gannon University *M*
Mount Aloysius College *M*
Philadelphia University *M*
St. Francis University *M*
Temple University *M*
Thomas Jefferson University: College
 of Health Professions *M*
University of Pittsburgh *M*
University of Scranton *M*
University of the Sciences in
 Philadelphia *M*

South Carolina

Medical University of South
 Carolina *M*

South Dakota

University of South Dakota *M*

Tennessee

Belmont University *D*
Milligan College *M*

Texas

Texas Tech University Health Sciences
 Center *M*
Texas Woman's University *M, D*
University of Texas
 Pan American *M*

Utah

University of Utah *M*

Virginia

James Madison University *M*
Shenandoah University *M*
Virginia Commonwealth University *M*

Washington

University of Puget Sound *M*

West Virginia

West Virginia University *M*

Wisconsin

Concordia University Wisconsin *M*
Mount Mary College *M*
University of Wisconsin
 La Crosse *M*
 Madison *M*

Occupational therapy assistant

Alabama

Central Alabama Community
 College *A*
Enterprise-Ozark Community
 College *A*
Faulkner University *A*
Wallace State Community College at
 Hanceville *A*

Arkansas

South Arkansas Community College *A*

California

Loma Linda University *A*
Mount St. Mary's College *C, A*
Sacramento City College *C, A*
Santa Ana College *A*

Colorado

Arapahoe Community College *A*
Morgan Community College *A*
Pueblo Community College *A*

Connecticut

Briarwood College *A*
Manchester Community College *A*

Delaware

Delaware Technical and Community
 College
 Owens Campus *A*
 Stanton/Wilmington Campus *A*

Florida

Florida Hospital College of Health
 Sciences *A*
Hillsborough Community College *A*
Manatee Community College *A*
Palm Beach Community College *A*
Polk Community College *A*
Tallahassee Community College *C*

Georgia

Darton College *A*
Middle Georgia College *A*
Northwestern Technical College *A*

Hawaii

University of Hawaii
 Kapiolani Community College *A*

Illinois

City Colleges of Chicago
 Wright College *A*
College of DuPage *A*
Illinois Central College *A*
John A. Logan College *A*
Lewis and Clark Community
 College *A*
Lincoln Land Community College *A*
Parkland College *A*
Rend Lake College *A*
South Suburban College of Cook
 County *A*
Southeastern Illinois College *A*

Indiana

Brown Mackie College: Fort Wayne *A*
University of St. Francis *A*
University of Southern Indiana *A, M*

Iowa

Iowa Central Community College *A*
Iowa Lakes Community College *C*
Kirkwood Community College *A*

Kansas

Johnson County Community
 College *A*

Kentucky

Jefferson Community College *A*
Madisonville Community College *A*

Louisiana

Delgado Community College *A*
University of Louisiana at Monroe *A*

Maine

Kennebec Valley Community
 College *A*

Maryland

Allegany College of Maryland *A*
Community College of Baltimore
 County *A*

Massachusetts

Bay State College *A*
Bristol Community College *A*
Greenfield Community College *A*
Massachusetts Bay Community
 College *A*
North Shore Community College *A*
Quinsigamond Community College *A*
Springfield Technical Community
 College *A*

Michigan

Baker College
 of Cadillac *A*
 of Muskegon *A*
Grand Rapids Community College *A*
Lake Michigan College *A*
Macomb Community College *A*
Mott Community College *A*
Oakland Community College *C*
Schoolcraft College *A*
Wayne County Community College *A*

Minnesota

Anoka Technical College *A*
Anoka-Ramsey Community College *A*
College of St. Catherine *A*
Lake Superior College *A*
Northland Community & Technical
 College *A*
Riverland Community College *A*

Missouri

Ozarks Technical Community
 College *A*
Penn Valley Community College *A*
St. Charles Community College *A*
St. Louis Community College
 St. Louis Community College at
 Meramec *A*

Montana

Montana State University
 College of Technology-Great Falls *A*

Nebraska

Clarkson College *A*

New Hampshire

New Hampshire Community
 Technical College
 Claremont *A*

New Jersey

Atlantic Cape Community College *A*

New Mexico

Eastern New Mexico University:
 Roswell Campus *A*

New York

City University of New York
 LaGuardia Community College *A*
Erie Community College
 North Campus *A*
Genesee Community College *A*
Herkimer County Community
 College *A*
Jamestown Community College *A*
Maria College *A*
Mercy College *A*
Orange County Community College *A*
Rockland Community College *A*
State University of New York
 College of Technology at Canton *A*
Suffolk County Community College *A*
Touro College *A*

North Carolina

Cape Fear Community College *A*
Durham Technical Community
 College *A*
Pitt Community College *A*
Rockingham Community College *A*

North Dakota

North Dakota State College of
 Science *A*

Ohio

Cincinnati State Technical and
 Community College *A*
Cuyahoga Community College
 Metropolitan Campus *A*
James A. Rhodes State College *A*
Kent State University
 East Liverpool Regional Campus *A*
Owens Community College
 Toledo *A*
Shawnee State University *A*
Sinclair Community College *A*
Stark State College of Technology *A*
Zane State College *A*

Oklahoma

Oklahoma City Community College *A*
Tulsa Community College *A*

Oregon

Mount Hood Community College *A*

Pennsylvania

Clarion University of Pennsylvania *A*
Community College of Allegheny
 County *A*
ICM School of Business & Medical
 Careers *A*
Lehigh Carbon Community College *A*
Mount Aloysius College *A*
Penn State
 Berks *A*
 Dubois *A*
 Mont Alto *A*
 Worthington Scranton *A*
Pennsylvania College of Technology *A*

Puerto Rico

Inter American University of Puerto
 Rico
 Ponce Campus *A*
University of Puerto Rico
 Humacao *A*
 Ponce *A*

Rhode Island

Community College of Rhode
 Island *A*
New England Institute of
 Technology *A*

South Carolina

Central Carolina Technical College *C*
Greenville Technical College *A*
Midlands Technical College *C*
Piedmont Technical College *C*
Tri-County Technical College *C*
Trident Technical College *A*

South Dakota

Lake Area Technical Institute *A*

Tennessee
Roane State Community College *A*
South College *A*

Texas
Amarillo College *A*
Austin Community College *A*
Del Mar College *A*
Houston Community College
System *C, A*
Laredo Community College *A*
North Central Texas College *A*
North Harris Montgomery
Community College District *A*
Panola College *A*
St. Philip's College *A*
South Texas College *A*

Utah
Salt Lake Community College *A*

Virginia
J. Sargeant Reynolds Community
College *A*
Jefferson College of Health
Sciences *A*
Southwest Virginia Community
College *C*
Tidewater Community College *A*

Washington
Green River Community College *A*
Spokane Falls Community College *A*

West Virginia
Mountain State University *A*

Wisconsin
Fox Valley Technical College *A*
Madison Area Technical College *A*
Milwaukee Area Technical College *A*
Western Wisconsin Technical
College *A*
Wisconsin Indianhead Technical
College *A*

Wyoming
Casper College *A*

Ocean engineering

California
University of California
San Diego *M, D*
University of Southern California *M*

Connecticut
University of Connecticut *M*

Florida
Florida Atlantic University *B, M, D*
Florida Institute of
Technology *B, M, D*
University of Florida *B, M*

Hawaii
University of Hawaii
Manoa *M, D*

Maryland
United States Naval Academy *B*

Massachusetts
Massachusetts Institute of
Technology *B, M, D*

New Hampshire
University of New Hampshire *B, M, D*

New Jersey
Stevens Institute of Technology *M, D*

Oregon
Oregon State University *M*

Rhode Island
University of Rhode Island *B, M, D*

Texas
Texas A&M University *B, M, D*
Texas A&M University
Galveston *B*

Oceanography

Alaska
University of Alaska
Fairbanks *M, D, T*

California
California State University
Monterey Bay *B*
Humboldt State University *B*
University of California
Berkeley *B*
San Diego *D*
University of Southern
California *M, D*

Connecticut
United States Coast Guard Academy *B*
University of Connecticut *M, D*

Delaware
University of Delaware *M, D*

Florida
Florida Institute of
Technology *B, M, D*
Florida State University *M, D*
Gulf Coast Community College *A*
Nova Southeastern University *D*
University of Miami *B, M, D*
University of South Florida *M, D*
University of West Florida *B*

Hawaii
Hawaii Pacific University *B*
University of Hawaii
Manoa *M, D*

Illinois
Illinois Valley Community College *A*

Louisiana
Louisiana State University and
Agricultural and Mechanical
College *M, D*

Maine
Maine Maritime Academy *B*
Southern Maine Community
College *A*
University of Maine *B, M, D*

Maryland
United States Naval Academy *B*

Massachusetts
Massachusetts Institute of
Technology *M, D*

Michigan
Central Michigan University *B*
University of Michigan *B, M, D*

Mississippi
University of Southern
Mississippi *M, D*

New Hampshire
University of New Hampshire *M, D*

New Jersey
Rider University *B*
Rutgers, The State University of New
Jersey
New Brunswick/Piscataway
Campus *M, D*

New York
Columbia University
School of General Studies *B*
State University of New York
Maritime College *B*
Stony Brook *D*

North Carolina
Cape Fear Community College *A*
Elizabeth City State University *B*
North Carolina State University *B*
University of North Carolina
Chapel Hill *M, D*
Wilmington *M*

Oregon
Oregon State University *M, D*

Pennsylvania
Kutztown University of
Pennsylvania *B*
Millersville University of
Pennsylvania *B*
Penn State
University Park *C*

Rhode Island
University of Rhode Island *M, D*

Texas
Texas A&M University *M, D*
Texas A&M University
Galveston *B*

Virginia
Old Dominion University *B, M, D*

Washington
Everett Community College *A*
Shoreline Community College *A*
University of Washington *B, M, D*

Wisconsin
University of Wisconsin
Madison *M, D*

Office/clerical services

Alabama
Faulkner State Community College *C*
Gadsden State Community College *C*
Lawson State Community College *C*
Trenholm State Technical College *C*
Wallace State Community College at
Hanceville *C, A*

Alaska
University of Alaska
Anchorage *C*
Southeast *A*

Arizona
Cochise College *C, A*
Coconino County Community
College *C*
Dine College *C, A*
Eastern Arizona College *C*
Everest College *C, A*
Mesa Community College *A*
Paradise Valley Community
College *C, A*

Phoenix College *C*

Arkansas
Arkansas State University: Newport *C*
East Arkansas Community College *C*
National Park Community College *C*
North Arkansas College *C*
Ouachita Technical College *C*
Pulaski Technical College *C*
University of Arkansas
Community College at Hope *C*

California
Allan Hancock College *A*
American River College *A*
Bakersfield College *A*
Barstow College *C, A*
CEI College
Maric College: Panorama City *C*
Canada College *C, A*
Cerritos Community College *A*
Cerro Coso Community College *C, A*
Chabot College *A*
Chaffey College *C*
Citrus College *C, A*
City College of San Francisco *A*
Coastline Community College *C*
College of Alameda *A*
College of San Mateo *A*
College of the Redwoods *C*
College of the Sequoias *A*
College of the Siskiyous *C, A*
Columbia College *C*
Contra Costa College *A*
Crafton Hills College *C, A*
Cypress College *C, A*
East Los Angeles College *A*
Empire College *C*
Evergreen Valley College *A*
Feather River College *C, A*
Fresno City College *C, A*
Gavilan Community College *C*
Golden West College *C, A*
Heald College
Fresno *C, A*
Humphreys College *C, A, B*
Imperial Valley College *C, A*
Lake Tahoe Community College *C, A*
Laney College *C, A*
Lassen College *C, A*
Long Beach City College *C, A*
Los Angeles City College *C, A*
Los Angeles Harbor College *C, A*
Los Angeles Mission College *C, A*
Los Angeles Southwest College *A*
Los Angeles Trade and Technical
College *C, A*
Los Angeles Valley College *A*
MTI College *C*
Merced College *C, A*
MiraCosta College *C, A*
Mission College *A*
Modesto Junior College *C*
Monterey Peninsula College *C, A*
Mount St. Mary's College *A*
Mount San Antonio College *C, A*
Mount San Jacinto College *C*
Ohlone College *C, A*
Orange Coast College *C, A*
Palo Verde College *C, A*
Palomar College *C, A*
Pasadena City College *C, A*
Platt College
Cerritos *C, A*
Porterville College *A*
Reedley College *C*
Rio Hondo College *A*
Sacramento City College *C, A*
Saddleback College *C*
San Bernardino Valley College *C*
San Diego City College *C, A*
San Diego Miramar College *A*
San Joaquin Delta College *C, A*
San Jose City College *C, A*

Santa Barbara City College *C*
Santa Monica College *C, A*
Santa Rosa Junior College *C*
Shasta College *A*
Skyline College *C, A*
Southwestern College *C, A*
Taft College *C, A*
Ventura College *C, A*
Vista Community College *C*
West Hills Community College *C, A*
West Valley College *A*
Yuba Community College District *C*

Colorado

Adams State College *B*
Northeastern Junior College *C*
Pueblo Community College *C, A*
Trinidad State Junior College *C*

Connecticut

Briarwood College *C*
Gateway Community College *C, A*
Northwestern Connecticut
    Community College *C*
Quinebaug Valley Community
    College *C*
Tunxis Community College *A*

Delaware

Delaware Technical and Community
    College
    Owens Campus *C, A*
    Stanton/Wilmington Campus *A*

Florida

Brevard Community College *C*
Broward Community College *A*
Gulf Coast Community College *C, A*
Herzing College
    Orlando *C*
Hillsborough Community College *C*
Lake City Community College *C, A*
Miami Dade College *C, A*
Pensacola Junior College *C*
Polk Community College *A*
Santa Fe Community College *A*
Seminole Community College *C*
Valencia Community College *C, A*

Georgia

Abraham Baldwin Agricultural
    College *A*
Augusta Technical Institute *C*
Central Georgia Technical College *C*
Chattahoochee Technical College *C*
Clayton State University *C*
Dalton State College *C, A*
Darton College *C*
Georgia Southwestern State
    University *A*
Gwinnett Technical College *C*
Macon State College *C, A*
Northwestern Technical College *C, A*
South Georgia College *A*
Southwest Georgia Technical
    College *C, A*

Hawaii

University of Hawaii
    Kauai Community College *C, A*
    Leeward Community College *C, A*

Illinois

City Colleges of Chicago
    Kennedy-King College *C*
    Wright College *C*
Elgin Community College *C*
Highland Community College *C*
John A. Logan College *C*
Joliet Junior College *A*
Kankakee Community College *C*
Kaskaskia College *C*
Kishwaukee College *C, A*

Lake Land College *C*
Lewis and Clark Community
    College *A*
Lincoln Land Community College *C*
MacCormac College *C*
Midstate College *C*
Morton College *C*
Rockford Business College *A*
Sauk Valley Community College *C, A*
Southeastern Illinois College *C*
Southwestern Illinois College *C, A*
Waubonsee Community College *C*
William Rainey Harper College *C*

Indiana

Indiana Business College
    Anderson *C*
Purdue University
    North Central Campus *A*
Sawyer College *C*
Vincennes University *A*

Iowa

Des Moines Area Community
    College *C*
Dordt College *A*
Ellsworth Community College *C, A*
Hawkeye Community College *C*
Iowa Lakes Community College *C, A*
Iowa Western Community College *C*
Marshalltown Community College *C*
Northeast Iowa Community
    College *C*
Southeastern Community College
    North Campus *C, A*

Kansas

Allen County Community College *C*
Butler County Community
    College *C, A*
Central Christian College of Kansas *A*
Coffeyville Community College *A*
Colby Community College *C*
Cowley County Community
    College *C, A*
Donnelly College *A*
Labette Community College *A*
Neosho County Community
    College *C*
Pratt Community College *C, A*
Seward County Community
    College *C, A*
Washburn University of Topeka *C, A*

Kentucky

Ashland Community and Technical
    College *A*
Daymar College *C, A*
Kentucky Christian University *A*
National College of Business &
    Technology
    Lexington *A*
Owensboro Community College *A*
Sullivan University *C, A*

Louisiana

Nunez Community College *C*

Maine

Andover College *C, A*
Northern Maine Community
    College *C*
University of Maine
    Machias *B*

Maryland

College of Southern Maryland *C*
Community College of Baltimore
    County *A*
Hagerstown Business College *C*
Hagerstown Community College *C*

Massachusetts

Bristol Community College *C*
Bunker Hill Community College *A*
Cape Cod Community College *C, A*
Holyoke Community College *C*
Massasoit Community College *C*
Middlesex Community College *C*
Northern Essex Community
    College *C*
Quinsigamond Community
    College *C, A*
Springfield Technical Community
    College *C*

Michigan

Baker College
    of Auburn Hills *C*
    of Cadillac *C*
    of Clinton Township *C*
    of Flint *C*
    of Jackson *C*
    of Muskegon *C*
    of Owosso *C, A*
    of Port Huron *C*
Bay Mills Community College *C*
Bay de Noc Community College *C*
Glen Oaks Community College *C*
Grand Rapids Community College *C*
Henry Ford Community College *A*
Kellogg Community College *C*
Kirtland Community College *C*
Lake Michigan College *C, A*
Mid Michigan Community College *C*
Monroe County Community
    College *C, A*
North Central Michigan College *C, A*
St. Clair County Community
    College *C, A*
West Shore Community College *C, A*

Minnesota

Alexandria Technical College *C*
Central Lakes College *C*
Dakota County Technical College *C*
Fond du Lac Tribal and Community
    College *C*
Hennepin Technical College *C, A*
Hibbing Community College *C, A*
Minnesota State College - Southeast
    Technical *C*
Normandale Community College *A*
Northland Community & Technical
    College *C*
Northwest Technical College *C*
Pine Technical College *C*
Rainy River Community College *C*
Rasmussen College
    Minnetonka *C, A*
Ridgewater College *C*
Rochester Community and Technical
    College *C*
St. Cloud Technical College *C*
St. Paul College *C*
Winona State University *B*

Mississippi

Itawamba Community College *C, A*
Southwest Mississippi Community
    College *C, A*

Missouri

Crowder College *C, A*
Jefferson College *C, A*
Longview Community College *C*
Moberly Area Community
    College *C, A*
North Central Missouri College *C, A*
Penn Valley Community College *C*
St. Louis Community College
    St. Louis Community College at
        Meramec *A*
Three Rivers Community College *C*

Montana

Blackfeet Community College *C*
Helena College of Technology of the
    University of Montana *C*
Little Big Horn College *C*
Miles Community College *C, A*
Montana State University
    College of Technology-Great Falls *A*
Montana Tech of the University of
    Montana *A*
Stone Child College *C, A*

Nebraska

Hamilton College: Lincoln *C*
Southeast Community College
    Lincoln Campus *A*
University of Nebraska
    Kearney *B*
Western Nebraska Community
    College *C, A*

New Hampshire

McIntosh College *A*
New Hampshire Community
    Technical College
    Berlin *A*
    Claremont *C*

New Jersey

Essex County College *C*
Gloucester County College *C, A*
Raritan Valley Community College *C*

New Mexico

Dona Ana Branch Community College
    of New Mexico State
    University *C*
New Mexico State University
    Alamogordo *C*
    Carlsbad *C*

New York

Adirondack Community College *C, A*
College of Westchester *C, A*
Corning Community College *C*
Erie Community College
    City Campus *C*
Fulton-Montgomery Community
    College *C*
Globe Institute of Technology *C*
Herkimer County Community
    College *A*
Mohawk Valley Community College *C*
Niagara County Community
    College *C*
North Country Community
    College *C, A*
Olean Business Institute *C*
Onondaga Community College *C, A*
Plaza College *C*
Rochester Business Institute *C, A*
Schenectady County Community
    College *C*
Tompkins-Cortland Community
    College *C*
Trocaire College *C*
Utica School of Commerce *C*
Westchester Community College *C, A*

North Carolina

Asheville-Buncombe Technical
    Community College *C, A*
Bladen Community College *C, A*
Carteret Community College *A*
Central Carolina Community
    College *A*
College of the Albemarle *A*
Forsyth Technical Community
    College *C, A*
Gaston College *C*
Halifax Community College *A*
Johnston Community College *A*
Mayland Community College *C*

McDowell Technical Community
College A
Pamlico Community College A
Rockingham Community College A
Sampson Community College A
South Piedmont Community
College C, A
Southeastern Community College A
Surry Community College C, A
Western Piedmont Community
College C, A
Wilson Technical Community
College C

North Dakota

Lake Region State College C, A
Minot State University: Bottineau
Campus C
North Dakota State College of
Science C, A

Ohio

Belmont Technical College C, A
Bowling Green State University:
Firelands College C
Cincinnati State Technical and
Community College A
Columbus State Community
College C, A
Jefferson Community College C
Kent State University
Trumbull Campus A
Miami University
Hamilton Campus C, A
Ohio Valley College of Technology A
Southern State Community College C
Stark State College of Technology C
University of Cincinnati
Raymond Walters College C, A
University of Northwestern Ohio C
University of Toledo C
Wright State University A

Oklahoma

Carl Albert State College C
Eastern Oklahoma State College A
Northeastern Oklahoma Agricultural
and Mechanical College C
Oklahoma City Community College A
Seminole State College A
Tulsa Community College C
Western Oklahoma State College A

Oregon

Central Oregon Community
College C
Chemeketa Community College C
Clackamas Community College C
Clatsop Community College C
Lane Community College C
Linn-Benton Community College C
Rogue Community College C
Southwestern Oregon Community
College C
Treasure Valley Community College A
Umpqua Community College C

Pennsylvania

Berean Institute C
Bucks County Community
College C, A
Butler County Community College C
Clarion University of Pennsylvania C
Community College of
Philadelphia C, A
Consolidated School of Business
Lancaster C
York C
Laurel Business Institute A
Lehigh Carbon Community College C
Newport Business Institute A
Northampton County Area
Community College C

Reading Area Community
College C, A
South Hills School of Business &
Technology C, A
Thaddeus Stevens College of
Technology A

Puerto Rico

American University of Puerto Rico B
Humacao Community College C
National College of Business &
Technology: Arecibo A
Pontifical Catholic University of
Puerto Rico A
Universidad Adventista de las
Antillas A
University of Puerto Rico
Aguadilla A
Utuado A, B

Rhode Island

Community College of Rhode
Island C

South Carolina

Aiken Technical College C
Florence-Darlington Technical
College C
Forrest Junior College A
Horry-Georgetown Technical
College C
Northeastern Technical College C, A
Orangeburg-Calhoun Technical
College C
Piedmont Technical College C
Spartanburg Technical College C
Technical College of the
Lowcountry C
Tri-County Technical College C
Trident Technical College C
Williamsburg Technical College C
York Technical College C

South Dakota

Northern State University A, B
Western Dakota Technical Institute C

Tennessee

Chattanooga State Technical
Community College A
Lincoln Memorial University A, B

Texas

Alvin Community College C
Amarillo College A
Austin Community College C
Blinn College A
Central Texas College C
Coastal Bend College A
College of the Mainland A
Del Mar College C
El Centro College C
El Paso Community College C, A
Galveston College C, A
Grayson County College C, A
Hill College A
Houston Community College
System C
Howard College C, A
Kilgore College C
Laredo Community College C, A
Lee College C, A
MTI College of Business and
Technology C
MTI College of Business and
Technology C
McLennan Community College C
Midland College C, A
Mountain View College C
North Central Texas College A
Panola College C
San Jacinto College
North C, A

South Plains College C
Tarrant County College C
Texarkana College C
Texas A&M University
Commerce B
Texas Southern University B
Texas Southmost College C
Tyler Junior College C
University of Texas
Brownsville C, A
Vernon College C
Victoria College C
Weatherford College C, A

Utah

Dixie State College of Utah C, A
LDS Business College C
Salt Lake Community College C

Virginia

Central Virginia Community
College C
Dabney S. Lancaster Community
College C, A
ECPI College of Technology C, A
Eastern Shore Community
College C, A
J. Sargeant Reynolds Community
College C
Lord Fairfax Community College C
Mountain Empire Community
College A
Patrick Henry Community College C
Paul D. Camp Community College C
Southside Virginia Community
College C
Tidewater Community College C
Wytheville Community College C

Washington

Bellingham Technical College C
Centralia College C, A
Clark College C
Clover Park Technical College C
Everett Community College C, A
Green River Community College C, A
Highline Community College C, A
Lake Washington Technical College C
Lower Columbia College A
North Seattle Community
College C, A
Peninsula College C
Pierce College C, A
Renton Technical College C, A
Shoreline Community College C
Skagit Valley College C
South Puget Sound Community
College C, A
Spokane Community College C, A
Spokane Falls Community
College C, A
Walla Walla Community College C
Wenatchee Valley College C
Yakima Valley Community College C

West Virginia

Concord University A
Valley College of Technology C

Wisconsin

Blackhawk Technical College A
Chippewa Valley Technical College C
Fox Valley Technical College C
Gateway Technical College C
Lakeshore Technical College C
Madison Area Technical College C
Mid-State Technical College C, A
Milwaukee Area Technical College C
Moraine Park Technical College C
Nicolet Area Technical College C
Southwest Wisconsin Technical
College C

University of Wisconsin
Whitewater C
Western Wisconsin Technical
College C
Wisconsin Indianhead Technical
College C

Wyoming

Eastern Wyoming College C

Office management

Alabama

Alabama Agricultural and Mechanical
University B
Community College of the Air
Force A
Enterprise-Ozark Community
College A
Faulkner University B
Lawson State Community College A
Northeast Alabama Community
College A
Oakwood College B
Southern Union State Community
College A
Virginia College C, A
Wallace State Community College at
Hanceville A

Alaska

Prince William Sound Community
College C, A
University of Alaska
Fairbanks A

Arizona

Central Arizona College A
Cochise College A
Everest College C, A
Gateway Community College A
Glendale Community College C
Mesa Community College A
Mohave Community College C
Rio Salado College C, A
South Mountain Community
College C
Yavapai College C, A

Arkansas

Arkansas State University
Beebe A
East Arkansas Community College C
National Park Community
College C, A
Southern Arkansas University Tech A
University of Central Arkansas A

California

Barstow College C, A
CEI College
Maric College: Panorama City A
Cerritos Community College A
Cerro Coso Community College C, A
Chabot College A
Chaffey College C, A
Citrus College C, A
Coastline Community College C
College of the Desert C, A
De Anza College C
El Camino College C, A
Foothill College C
Glendale Community College A
Golden West College C, A
Heald College
San Jose C, A
Imperial Valley College C, A
Irvine Valley College C, A
Lake Tahoe Community College C, A
Las Positas College A
Los Angeles Harbor College C, A
Los Angeles Mission College C, A
Los Medanos College C, A

Merced College *A*
MiraCosta College *C, A*
Mission College *A*
Modesto Junior College *C*
Moorpark College *A*
Napa Valley College *C*
Ohlone College *C, A*
Porterville College *C*
Saddleback College *C, A*
San Jose City College *C*
Santa Barbara City College *C, A*
Santa Rosa Junior College *C*
Shasta College *C, A*
Skyline College *C*
Solano Community College *C, A*
Southwestern College *C, A*
West Valley College *A*
Yuba Community College District *C*

Colorado
Arapahoe Community College *C, A*
Colorado Northwestern Community
    College *C, A*
Mesa State College *A*
Red Rocks Community College *C*

Connecticut
Gibbs College *C, A*
Norwalk Community College *C, A*
Quinebaug Valley Community
    College *A*
Quinnipiac University *B*

District of Columbia
University of the District of
    Columbia *B*

Florida
Brevard Community College *C, A*
Clearwater Christian College *B*
Daytona Beach Community
    College *C, A*
Florida Community College at
    Jacksonville *C, A*
Herzing College
    Orlando *C*
Hillsborough Community
    College *C, A*
Indian River Community College *A*
Miami Dade College *C, A*
Okaloosa-Walton College *C, A*
Pasco-Hernando Community
    College *C, A*
Pensacola Junior College *C, A*
Polk Community College *A*
Valencia Community College *A*

Georgia
Atlanta Metropolitan College *C, A*
Chattahoochee Technical College *C, A*
Clayton State University *B*
Darton College *C, A*
Emmanuel College *A*
Fort Valley State University *B*
Georgia College and State
    University *B*
Georgia Military College *A*
Gwinnett Technical College *A*
Macon State College *C*
South Georgia College *A*

Hawaii
Hawaii Business College *C*

Idaho
Boise State University *A*

Illinois
Black Hawk College *C, A*
College of DuPage *C, A*
Elgin Community College *C*
Highland Community College *A*

John A. Logan College *C, A*
Joliet Junior College *C, A*
Kaskaskia College *C*
Kishwaukee College *A*
Lincoln Christian College and
    Seminary *A*
MacCormac College *A*
Oakton Community College *C, A*
Sauk Valley Community College *A*
South Suburban College of Cook
    County *C, A*
William Rainey Harper College *C, A*

Indiana
Ball State University *B*
Indiana State University *B*
University of Southern Indiana *B*
Vincennes University *A*

Iowa
AIB College of Business *A*
Des Moines Area Community
    College *C, A*
Iowa Central Community College *C, A*
Iowa Lakes Community College *A*
Northeast Iowa Community
    College *A*
Southeastern Community College
    North Campus *A*

Kansas
Allen County Community College *A*
Central Christian College of
    Kansas *A, B*
Cloud County Community
    College *C, A*
Coffeyville Community College *A*
Dodge City Community College *C, A*
Fort Hays State University *B*
Haskell Indian Nations University *A*
Neosho County Community
    College *A*
Pratt Community College *C, A*
Seward County Community
    College *C, A*
Tabor College *B*
Washburn University of Topeka *A*

Kentucky
Campbellsville University *A, B*
Daymar College *A*
Eastern Kentucky University *B*
Hopkinsville Community College *C*
Maysville Community College *C, A*
National College of Business &
    Technology
    Lexington *A*
Paducah Technical College *C*

Louisiana
ITT Technical College *A*
Nunez Community College *C*

Maine
Andover College *A*
Beal College *A*
Eastern Maine Community College *A*
Kennebec Valley Community
    College *A*
Northern Maine Community
    College *A*
Southern Maine Community
    College *A*
University of Maine
    Machias *B*
Washington County Community
    College *C, A*

Maryland
Baltimore City Community College *A*
Cecil Community College *A*
Community College of Baltimore
    County *A*

Garrett College *C*
Howard Community College *C, A*
Prince George's Community
    College *C, A*

Massachusetts
Babson College *B*
Bay State College *A*
Cape Cod Community College *C, A*
Massasoit Community College *A*
Middlesex Community College *A*
Northern Essex Community
    College *A*
Roxbury Community College *A*
Salem State College *B*

Michigan
Baker College
    of Auburn Hills *A*
    of Cadillac *A, B*
    of Clinton Township *B*
    of Flint *B*
    of Jackson *C, A*
    of Muskegon *B*
    of Owosso *A, B*
    of Port Huron *A, B*
Davenport University *A, B*
Delta College *A*
Eastern Michigan University *B*
Gogebic Community College *A*
Henry Ford Community College *A*
Lake Superior State University *A*
Lansing Community College *A*
Mott Community College *C, A*
Northern Michigan University *C*
Oakland Community College *A*

Minnesota
Academy College *C*
Alexandria Technical College *A*
Concordia College: Moorhead *B*
Fond du Lac Tribal and Community
    College *C*
Minneapolis Business College *A*
Normandale Community College *A*
North Hennepin Community
    College *A*
Rasmussen College
    Minnetonka *C, A*
    St. Cloud *C, A*
St. Paul College *A*
Winona State University *B*

Mississippi
Delta State University *B*
Hinds Community College *A*
Jackson State University *B*
Mississippi Valley State University *B*

Missouri
Central Missouri State University *B*
Evangel University *A*
Fontbonne University *M*
Longview Community College *C, A*
Park University *A*
Penn Valley Community College *C, A*
St. Louis Community College
    St. Louis Community College at
        Florissant Valley *C*
    St. Louis Community College at
        Meramec *C*
Southeast Missouri State University *B*

Montana
Miles Community College *A*
University of Montana: Missoula *A*

Nebraska
Chadron State College *B*
Mid-Plains Community College
    Area *C, A*
Midland Lutheran College *A, B*
Union College *A*

University of Nebraska
    Kearney *B*
    Lincoln *B*

Nevada
Community College of Southern
    Nevada *C, A*
Great Basin College *A*
Morrison University *A, B*
Truckee Meadows Community
    College *A*

New Hampshire
McIntosh College *A*
New Hampshire Community
    Technical College
    Manchester *C, A*

New Jersey
Berkeley College *A, B*
Cumberland County College *C, A*
Gloucester County College *C, A*
Middlesex County College *A*
Raritan Valley Community College *C*
Rider University *A, B*
Thomas Edison State College *C, A, B*
Warren County Community College *C*

New Mexico
Clovis Community College *C, A*
Dona Ana Branch Community College
    of New Mexico State
    University *C, A*
Luna Community College *A*
New Mexico Junior College *C, A*
New Mexico State University
    Grants *A*
Western New Mexico University *C, A*

New York
ASA Institute of Business and
    Computer Technology *C*
Berkeley College *A, B*
Berkeley College of New York
    City *A, B*
Bryant & Stratton Business Institute
Bryant & Stratton College:
    Syracuse *C, A*
City University of New York
    Borough of Manhattan Community
        College *A*
    Kingsborough Community
        College *A*
    Queensborough Community
        College *A*
Clinton Community College *A*
College of Westchester *C, A*
Columbia-Greene Community
    College *A*
Erie Community College
    City Campus *A*
    North Campus *A*
    South Campus *A*
Globe Institute of Technology *C, A, B*
Herkimer County Community
    College *A*
Jamestown Business College *C*
Jamestown Community College *A*
Jefferson Community College *A*
Long Island Business Institute *C, A*
Mohawk Valley Community College *C*
Olean Business Institute *A*
Rochester Business Institute *C, A*
Rockland Community College *C*
St. Joseph's College: Suffolk Campus *C*
State University of New York
    College at Buffalo *B, M*
    College of Agriculture and
        Technology at Cobleskill *A*
    College of Agriculture and
        Technology at Morrisville *A*
    Farmingdale *C*
Suffolk County Community College *A*

Sullivan County Community
College *A*
Trocaire College *A*

North Carolina

Alamance Community College *A*
Fayetteville State University *A, B*
Fayetteville Technical Community
College *C, A*
Halifax Community College *A*
Isothermal Community College *C, A*
Montgomery Community College *C, A*
Pitt Community College *C, A*
Wilkes Community College *C, A*

North Dakota

Dickinson State University *A, B*
Lake Region State College *C, A*
Mayville State University *B*
North Dakota State College of
Science *A*
Valley City State University *B*

Ohio

Bradford School *C, A*
Cincinnati State Technical and
Community College *A*
Columbus State Community
College *A*
David N. Myers University *A, B*
Defiance College *B*
Edison State Community College *A*
James A. Rhodes State College *C, A*
Jefferson Community College *C, A*
Marion Technical College *C, A*
Miami University
Hamilton Campus *C, A*
Oxford Campus *C, A*
Mount Vernon Nazarene
University *A, B*
Ohio University
Chillicothe Campus *A*
Owens Community College
Toledo *A*
Shawnee State University *A*
Stark State College of Technology *A*
University of Akron: Wayne College *A*
University of Cincinnati
Clermont College *C, A*
Youngstown State University *A, B*

Oklahoma

East Central University *B*
Eastern Oklahoma State College *C*
Oklahoma State University
Oklahoma City *C*
Seminole State College *A*

Oregon

Central Oregon Community
College *A*
Chemeketa Community College *C, A*
Clackamas Community College *C, A*
Clatsop Community College *A*
Everest College: Portland *A*
Lane Community College *C, A*
Linn-Benton Community College *C, A*
Portland Community College *C, A*
Southwestern Oregon Community
College *C, A*
Treasure Valley Community College *A*
Umpqua Community College *C*

Pennsylvania

Bucks County Community
College *C, A*
Community College of Beaver
County *C*
Delaware County Community
College *C, A*
Indiana University of Pennsylvania *B*
Lansdale School of Business *C, A*
Lebanon Valley College *C*

Mercyhurst College *A*
Reading Area Community College *A*
South Hills School of Business &
Technology *C, A*

Puerto Rico

Electronic Data Processing College:
San Sebastian *A*
Inter American University of Puerto
Rico
Guayama Campus *A, B*
National College of Business &
Technology: Arecibo *B*
Turabo University *B*
Universidad Metropolitana *A, B*
University of Puerto Rico
Aguadilla *B*
Cayey University College *B*
Mayaguez *B*

South Carolina

Forrest Junior College *A*
Northeastern Technical College *C*
Technical College of the
Lowcountry *C, A*
Trident Technical College *A*
University of South Carolina *B*
Williamsburg Technical College *A*

South Dakota

Black Hills State University *B*
Dakota State University *A*
Oglala Lakota College *A*
Southeast Technical Institute *C*

Tennessee

Lee University *B*
Middle Tennessee State University *B*
Pellissippi State Technical Community
College *C*
Tennessee Temple University *B*
Walters State Community College *A*

Texas

Brookhaven College *A*
Cedar Valley College *C, A*
Central Texas College *C, A*
College of the Mainland *A*
Eastfield College *A*
Grayson County College *C, A*
Hill College *C, A*
Lamar University *B*
Laredo Community College *C, A*
North Lake College *A*
Palo Alto College *C, A*
Paris Junior College *A*
San Antonio College *A*
San Jacinto College
North *C, A*
South Plains College *C, A*
South Texas College *C, A*
Southwestern Adventist
University *A, B*
Stephen F. Austin State University *B*
Sul Ross State University *C, B*
Tarleton State University *B*
Temple College *C, A*
Texas A&M University
Commerce *B*
Texas Southmost College *C, A*
Tyler Junior College *A*
University of Houston
Downtown *B*
University of North Texas *B*

Utah

College of Eastern Utah *C*
Everest College: Salt Lake City *C, A*
LDS Business College *A*
Weber State University *B*

Vermont

Vermont Technical College *A*

Virginia

Blue Ridge Community College *C*
Central Virginia Community
College *C*
Dabney S. Lancaster Community
College *C, A*
Germanna Community College *C*
Lord Fairfax Community College *A*
Mountain Empire Community
College *A*
National College of Business &
Technology
Bluefield *A*
Harrisonburg *A*
Northern Virginia Community
College *A*
Paul D. Camp Community College *A*
Thomas Nelson Community
College *A*
Virginia Highlands Community
College *C, A*

Washington

Bellevue Community College *C, A*
Bellingham Technical College *C, A*
Big Bend Community College *C, A*
Central Washington University *B*
Clover Park Technical College *A*
Columbia Basin College *C, A*
Edmonds Community College *C, A*
Grays Harbor College *C, A*
Peninsula College *A*
Pierce College *A*
Renton Technical College *C, A*
South Seattle Community
College *C, A*
Spokane Community College *A*
Spokane Falls Community College *A*
Wenatchee Valley College *A*
Whatcom Community College *C*

West Virginia

Concord University *A*
Davis and Elkins College *B*
Mountain State University *C, A, B*
West Virginia University Institute of
Technology *A*

Wisconsin

Blackhawk Technical College *A*
Madison Area Technical College *A*
Maranatha Baptist Bible College *B*
Mid-State Technical College *A*
Moraine Park Technical College *A*
Northeast Wisconsin Technical
College *A*

Wyoming

Eastern Wyoming College *A*
Northwest College *A*
Sheridan College *A*

Office technology/data entry

Alabama

Faulkner State Community
College *C, A*
Lawson State Community College *A*

Alaska

University of Alaska
Anchorage *A*

Arizona

Central Arizona College *A*
Chandler-Gilbert Community College
Pecos *A*
Chaparral College *C*
Eastern Arizona College *C, A*
Everest College *C, A*
Gateway Community College *C*

Glendale Community College *C*
Paradise Valley Community
College *C, A*
Phoenix College *C*
Scottsdale Community College *C*
South Mountain Community
College *C, A*
Yavapai College *C, A*

Arkansas

Arkansas State University
Beebe *A*
National Park Community
College *C, A*
Phillips Community College of the
University of Arkansas *A*
Remington College
Little Rock *C*
Southern Arkansas University Tech *C*

California

Allan Hancock College *C, A*
Bakersfield College *A*
Barstow College *C, A*
Butte College *C, A*
CEI College
Maric College: Panorama City *C*
Cabrillo College *C, A*
Canada College *C, A*
Cerro Coso Community College *A*
Chabot College *C, A*
Chaffey College *C*
City College of San Francisco *C, A*
Coastline Community College *A*
College of the Redwoods *C, A*
College of the Sequoias *C*
Columbia College *C*
Cypress College *C, A*
Diablo Valley College *C*
East Los Angeles College *C, A*
Evergreen Valley College *A*
Foothill College *C, A*
Fresno City College *C*
Gavilan Community College *C*
Golden West College *C, A*
Heald College
Fresno *A*
Rancho Cordova *C, A*
Stockton *A*
Humphreys College *C, A, B*
Imperial Valley College *C, A*
Irvine Valley College *C, A*
Laney College *C, A*
Lassen College *C, A*
Long Beach City College *C, A*
Los Angeles City College *C, A*
Los Angeles Harbor College *C, A*
Los Angeles Southwest College *A*
Los Angeles Valley College *C, A*
MTI College *C*
Maric College
Vista *C*
MiraCosta College *C*
Ohlone College *C, A*
Orange Coast College *C, A*
Reedley College *C*
Riverside Community College *C, A*
Saddleback College *C*
San Diego City College *C, A*
San Joaquin Delta College *A*
San Jose City College *A*
Santa Barbara City College *C*
Santa Rosa Junior College *C*
Shasta College *C, A*
West Hills Community College *C, A*
West Valley College *C, A*

Colorado

Community College of Aurora *A*
Community College of Denver *C*
IntelliTec College: Grand Junction *C*
Morgan Community College *C*
Pueblo Community College *C, A*
Red Rocks Community College *C, A*

Connecticut

Briarwood College *C, A*
Gateway Community College *C*
Middlesex Community College *C*
Northwestern Connecticut
    Community College *C*
Norwalk Community College *C, A*
Quinebaug Valley Community
    College *C, A*
Three Rivers Community College *A*
Tunxis Community College *C*

Delaware

Delaware Technical and Community
    College
    Owens Campus *C, A*
    Stanton/Wilmington Campus *C, A*
    Terry Campus *C, A*

District of Columbia

University of the District of
    Columbia *C, A*

Florida

Daytona Beach Community
    College *C, A*
Florida Community College at
    Jacksonville *C, A*
Indian River Community College *C*
Pasco-Hernando Community
    College *C*
Santa Fe Community College *A*
Tallahassee Community College *C*
Valencia Community College *C, A*

Georgia

Abraham Baldwin Agricultural
    College *C, A*
Coastal Georgia Community
    College *C*
Dalton State College *C, A*
DeKalb Technical College *C*
Gwinnett Technical College *A*
Macon State College *C*
Middle Georgia College *A*
Middle Georgia Technical College *A*
Savannah Technical College *C*
South Georgia College *A*
Southwest Georgia Technical
    College *C*
West Georgia Technical College *C*

Hawaii

University of Hawaii
    Kapiolani Community College *C, A*

Idaho

College of Southern Idaho *A*

Illinois

Black Hawk College *C, A*
Black Hawk College
    East Campus *C, A*
City Colleges of Chicago
    Malcolm X College *C, A*
College of Lake County *C, A*
Danville Area Community College *C*
Elgin Community College *C*
Heartland Community College *C*
Illinois Central College *C*
Illinois Eastern Community Colleges
    Frontier Community College *C, A*
    Lincoln Trail College *C, A*
    Olney Central College *C, A*
    Wabash Valley College *C, A*
John Wood Community College *C*
Joliet Junior College *C, A*
Kaskaskia College *C, A*
Kishwaukee College *C*
Lake Land College *C*
Lincoln Land Community College *C, A*
MacCormac College *C*

McHenry County College *C*
Morton College *C*
National-Louis University *C*
Parkland College *C*
Prairie State College *C*
Rend Lake College *C*
Sauk Valley Community College *A*
Southeastern Illinois College *A*
Triton College *C, A*
Waubonsee Community College *C, A*
William Rainey Harper College *C*

Indiana

College of Court Reporting *A*
Grace College *A*
Vincennes University *A*

Iowa

Des Moines Area Community
    College *C*
Ellsworth Community College *C, A*
Kirkwood Community College *A*
Northeast Iowa Community
    College *C*
Southeastern Community College
    North Campus *A*
Western Iowa Tech Community
    College *A*

Kansas

Allen County Community College *C*
Colby Community College *A*
Cowley County Community
    College *C, A*
Pratt Community College *C, A*
Seward County Community
    College *C, A*
Washburn University of Topeka *A*

Kentucky

Brown Mackie College:
    Hopkinsville *C*
Daymar College *C, A*
West Kentucky Community and
    Technical College *A*

Louisiana

Baton Rouge Community College *C, A*
ITI Technical College *A*
Nunez Community College *C, A*

Maine

Andover College *A*
Central Maine Community
    College *C, A*
Kennebec Valley Community
    College *C*
Northern Maine Community
    College *A*
Southern Maine Community
    College *A*

Maryland

Baltimore City Community
    College *C, A*
Community College of Baltimore
    County *C, A*
Garrett College *C*
Hagerstown Business College *C, A*
Montgomery College *C*
Prince George's Community
    College *C, A*

Massachusetts

Benjamin Franklin Institute of
    Technology *C*
Berkshire Community College *A*
Massasoit Community College *C*
Middlesex Community College *C, A*
North Shore Community College *C, A*
Northern Essex Community
    College *A*

Quincy College *A*
Roxbury Community College *A*
Suffolk University *B*

Michigan

Baker College
    of Auburn Hills *A*
    of Flint *A*
    of Muskegon *A*
    of Port Huron *A*
Cornerstone University *A*
Delta College *A*
Glen Oaks Community College *C*
Gogebic Community College *A*
Lake Superior State University *A*
Lansing Community College *A*
Lewis College of Business *A*
Macomb Community College *C, A*
Monroe County Community
    College *C, A*
Montcalm Community College *C, A*
Mott Community College *C, A*
North Central Michigan College *C*
Northwestern Michigan College *A*
Oakland Community College *C, A*
St. Clair County Community
    College *A*
West Shore Community College *A*

Minnesota

Anoka-Ramsey Community College *C*
Dakota County Technical College *C*
Hennepin Technical College *C, A*
Mesabi Range Community and
    Technical College *C, A*
Minneapolis Community and
    Technical College *A*
Minnesota State College - Southeast
    Technical *C*
Minnesota State Community and
    Technical College - Fergus
    Falls *C, A*
Normandale Community College *C*
Northland Community & Technical
    College *C*
Northwest Technical College *C*
Pine Technical College *C*
Rainy River Community College *A*
Riverland Community College *C*
Rochester Community and Technical
    College *C*
St. Paul College *C, A*

Mississippi

Antonelli College
    Jackson *C, A*
Coahoma Community College *A*
Copiah-Lincoln Community College *A*
Itawamba Community College *C*
Mississippi Gulf Coast Community
    College
    Jefferson Davis Campus *A*
Pearl River Community College *A*

Missouri

Baptist Bible College *A*
Longview Community College *C, A*
Maple Woods Community
    College *C, A*
Missouri State University: West
    Plains *C*
North Central Missouri College *C, A*
Ozarks Technical Community
    College *C, A*
Penn Valley Community College *C, A*
St. Louis Community College
    St. Louis Community College at
        Florissant Valley *C, A*
    St. Louis Community College at
        Meramec *C, A*

Montana

Flathead Valley Community College *A*

Helena College of Technology of the
    University of Montana *A*
University of Montana: Western *A*

Nebraska

Peru State College *B*

Nevada

Great Basin College *C, A*
Las Vegas College *C*
Truckee Meadows Community
    College *A*
Western Nevada Community
    College *A*

New Hampshire

New Hampshire Community
    Technical College
    Berlin *C, A*
    Claremont *A*
    Nashua *C*

New Jersey

Berkeley College *C*
Camden County College *C*
County College of Morris *C*
Essex County College *A*
Gloucester County College *A*
Union County College *C*
Warren County Community College *C*

New Mexico

Clovis Community College *A*
New Mexico Junior College *C, A*
New Mexico State University
    Alamogordo *C*
San Juan College *A*
Southwestern Indian Polytechnic
    Institute *C, A*

New York

Berkeley College *C*
Berkeley College of New York City *C*
Bryant & Stratton Business Institute
    Bryant & Stratton College:
        Rochester *A*
Business Informatics Center *A*
City University of New York
    Bronx Community College *A*
    Hostos Community College *C, A*
    Lehman College *C*
    Queensborough Community
        College *C*
Clinton Community College *C, A*
College of Westchester *C, A*
Columbia-Greene Community
    College *C, A*
Dutchess Community College *C, A*
Globe Institute of Technology *C*
Herkimer County Community
    College *C, A*
Hudson Valley Community
    College *C, A*
Jamestown Community College *C*
Jefferson Community College *C, A*
Mercy College *C, A*
Olean Business Institute *A*
Orange County Community
    College *C, A*
Plaza College *C*
Rochester Business Institute *C, A*
St. Joseph's College: Suffolk Campus *C*
State University of New York
    College of Agriculture and
        Technology at Morrisville *C, A*
    College of Technology at Alfred *A*
Suffolk County Community
    College *C, A*
Sullivan County Community
    College *C, A*
Technical Career Institutes *C, A*
Trocaire College *C*
Ulster County Community College *A*

North Carolina

Asheville-Buncombe Technical
Community College *A*
Bladen Community College *A*
Central Piedmont Community
College *C*
East Carolina University *B*
Halifax Community College *A*
Piedmont Community College *A*
Rockingham Community College *A*
Rowan-Cabarrus Community
College *C, A*
South College *C*
Vance-Granville Community
College *A*
Western Piedmont Community
College *C, A*

North Dakota

Bismarck State College *C, A*
Cankdeska Cikana Community
College *C, A*
Minot State University *C*
Sitting Bull College *A*

Ohio

AEC Southern Ohio College
Brown Mackie College: Akron *A*
Ashland University *C, A*
Bowling Green State University:
Firelands College *C*
Columbus State Community
College *C, A*
David N. Myers University *A, B*
Kent State University
Trumbull Campus *A*
Marion Technical College *C, A*
Miami University
Oxford Campus *C, A*
Ohio University
Chillicothe Campus *A*
Remington College
Cleveland *A*
Sinclair Community College *C*
Southern State Community College *C*
Southwestern College of Business
Southwestern College: Franklin *A*
Stark State College of Technology *A*
Stautzenberger College *C, A*
Trumbull Business College *A*
University of Akron *C, A*
University of Akron: Wayne
College *C, A*
University of Cincinnati
Clermont College *C, A*
Raymond Walters College *C*
University of Northwestern Ohio *C, A*
University of Rio Grande *A*
University of Toledo *A*

Oklahoma

Bacone College *A*
Oklahoma State University
Oklahoma City *C*
St. Gregory's University *A*
Tulsa Community College *A*
Western Oklahoma State College *A*

Oregon

Chemeketa Community College *A*
Clatsop Community College *C, A*
Portland Community College *C, A*
Rogue Community College *C*
Treasure Valley Community College *C*

Pennsylvania

Academy of Medical Arts and
Business *C, A*
Bucks County Community College *C*
Business Institute of Pennsylvania *A*
Business Institute of Pennsylvania
Meadville *A*
CHI Institute: Broomall *C*

Community College of Allegheny
County *C*
Consolidated School of Business
Lancaster *A*
York *A*
Newport Business Institute *A*
Pennsylvania College of Technology *A*
Reading Area Community
College *C, A*
South Hills School of Business &
Technology *C*

Puerto Rico

American University of Puerto Rico *B*
Inter American University of Puerto
Rico
Bayamon Campus *B*
Ponce Campus *A, B*
National College of Business &
Technology: Bayamon *A*
Turabo University *C, A*
Universidad del Este *A*

South Carolina

Aiken Technical College *C*
Central Carolina Technical College *C*
Denmark Technical College *C*
Florence-Darlington Technical
College *C*
Forrest Junior College *A*
Northeastern Technical College *C, A*
Orangeburg-Calhoun Technical
College *C*
Tri-County Technical College *C*
Trident Technical College *C*
York Technical College *C*

Tennessee

Austin Peay State University *A*
Chattanooga State Technical
Community College *C*
Southwest Tennessee Community
College *C, A*

Texas

Amarillo College *C*
Brookhaven College *A*
Cedar Valley College *A*
Central Texas College *C*
Clarendon College *C, A*
Coastal Bend College *A*
College of the Mainland *C, A*
Collin County Community College
District *C, A*
Eastfield College *A*
El Centro College *C*
El Paso Community College *C*
Galveston College *C*
Grayson County College *C, A*
Hallmark Institute of Technology *A*
Hill College *C, A*
Laredo Community College *C, A*
McLennan Community College *C, A*
Midland College *A*
Navarro College *A*
North Central Texas College *A*
North Harris Montgomery
Community College District *C, A*
North Lake College *A*
Palo Alto College *A*
Paris Junior College *A*
San Antonio College *C*
San Jacinto College
Central Campus *A*
North *C, A*
Southwest Texas Junior College *A*
Texas Southmost College *A*
Texas Wesleyan University *B*
Trinity Valley Community College *C, A*
Vernon College *A*
Weatherford College *C*

Utah

Salt Lake Community College *C*
Utah Valley State College *A*

Virginia

Blue Ridge Community College *C*
Dabney S. Lancaster Community
College *C*
ECPI College of Technology *C, A*
J. Sargeant Reynolds Community
College *C*
Mountain Empire Community
College *C*
New River Community College *A*
Northern Virginia Community
College *C*
Paul D. Camp Community College *C*
Virginia Western Community
College *A*

Washington

Centralia College *C, A*
Clark College *C, A*
Green River Community College *C, A*
Lower Columbia College *C, A*
North Seattle Community College *A*
Peninsula College *C*
Seattle Central Community College *C*
South Seattle Community College *A*
Spokane Community College *C, A*
Walla Walla Community College *C*

West Virginia

Mountain State University *C*
West Virginia Northern Community
College *C*

Wisconsin

Blackhawk Technical College *C, A*
Chippewa Valley Technical College *A*
Fox Valley Technical College *C, A*
Gateway Technical College *A*
Lakeshore Technical College *A*
Madison Area Technical College *C*
Milwaukee Area Technical College *C*
Moraine Park Technical College *A*
Northcentral Technical College *A*
Northeast Wisconsin Technical
College *C, A*
Southwest Wisconsin Technical
College *C*

Wyoming

Casper College *C, A*
Laramie County Community
College *A*
Western Wyoming Community
College *C, A*

Oncology

Arizona

University of Arizona *M, D*

California

Stanford University *M, D*

District of Columbia

George Washington University *D*
Georgetown University *M, D*

Florida

University of South Florida *D*

Illinois

University of Chicago *D*

Michigan

Wayne State University *M, D*

Nebraska

University of Nebraska
Medical Center *M, D*

North Carolina

Wake Forest University *D*

Texas

University of Texas
Health Science Center at
Houston *M, D*

Utah

University of Utah *B, M, D*

Wisconsin

University of Wisconsin
Madison *M, D*

Operations management

Alabama

Alabama Southern Community
College *A*
Auburn University *B*
Community College of the Air
Force *A*
Lawson State Community College *A*
Remington College
Mobile *B*

Arizona

DeVry University
Phoenix *B*
Eastern Arizona College *C*
Glendale Community College *A*
University of Arizona *B*

Arkansas

East Arkansas Community College *C*
University of Arkansas *B, M*

California

California State Polytechnic
University: Pomona *B*
California State University
East Bay *M*
Long Beach *B*
Sacramento *B*
San Bernardino *B, M*
Citrus College *C*
City College of San Francisco *C, A*
DeVry University
Long Beach *B*
Fashion Institute of Design and
Merchandising *A*
Golden Gate University *C, B, M*
Laney College *C, A*
National University *B*
Palomar College *C, A*
San Diego City College *C, A*
San Diego State University *B, M*

Connecticut

Central Connecticut State
University *M*

Delaware

University of Delaware *B*

District of Columbia

George Washington University *M*
Trinity University *B*

Florida

DeVry University
Miramar *B*
Florida Community College at
Jacksonville *C*
Florida Southern College *B*

Florida State University *B*
Remington College: Largo *B*
St. Leo University *B*

Georgia

Albany Technical College *C*
Central Georgia Technical
   College *C, A*
Clayton State University *B*
Dalton State College *B*
DeVry University
   Alpharetta *B*
   Decatur *B*
Georgia Institute of Technology *B*
Georgia State University *D*
Kennesaw State University *B*
Savannah Technical College *A*
South Georgia College *A*
Southwest Georgia Technical
   College *C, A*

Hawaii

University of Hawaii
   Hawaii Community College *C, A*

Idaho

Boise State University *B*
University of Idaho *B*

Illinois

Aurora University *B*
Carl Sandburg College *A*
DePaul University *B*
DeVry University
   Addison *B*
Illinois Institute of Technology *M*
Kishwaukee College *C, A*
Loyola University of Chicago *B*
McHenry County College *C, A*
Northern Illinois University *B*
Northwestern University *M*
Prairie State College *C, A*
University of Illinois
   Urbana-Champaign *B, D*
Waubonsee Community College *C, A*
William Rainey Harper College *C, A*

Indiana

Ball State University *A*
Indiana Institute of Technology *B*
Indiana State University *B*
Indiana University-Purdue University
   Fort Wayne *C, A, B*
Purdue University *A, B*
Purdue University
   North Central Campus *C, A, B*
Tri-State University *B*
University of Southern Indiana *M*

Iowa

Iowa State University *B*

Kansas

Barton County Community College *A*
Pratt Community College *C, A*

Kentucky

Daymar College *A*

Louisiana

Louisiana Tech University *A, B*
Nicholls State University *B*

Maine

Northern Maine Community
   College *A*

Maryland

University of Maryland
   University College *M*

Massachusetts

Babson College *B*
Bentley College *M*
Boston College *B*
Boston University *B*
Bridgewater State College *M*
Bunker Hill Community College *A*
Massasoit Community College *A*
Northeastern University *B*
Worcester Polytechnic Institute *B, M*

Michigan

Baker College
   of Flint *A, B*
Central Michigan University *M*
Davenport University *B*
Ferris State University *C, B*
Kettering University *B, M*
Lake Michigan College *A*
Lawrence Technological University *M*
Macomb Community College *C, A*
Michigan State University *B, M, D*
Saginaw Valley State University *B*
Spring Arbor University *B, M*
University of Michigan
   Flint *B*

Minnesota

Alexandria Technical College *C, A*
Metropolitan State University *B*
Minnesota State University
   Mankato *B*
Rasmussen College
   Minnetonka *C, A*
University of St. Thomas *B, M*
Winona State University *B*

Mississippi

Hinds Community College *A*
Mississippi State University *B*

Missouri

Missouri Baptist University *B*
Missouri Southern State University *B*
University of Missouri
   St. Louis *B, M*
Washington University in St.
   Louis *B, M*

Nevada

Truckee Meadows Community
   College *C*

New Hampshire

McIntosh College *A*
New Hampshire Community
   Technical College
   Nashua *C*

New Jersey

Cumberland County College *A*
New Jersey Institute of Technology *M*
Thomas Edison State College *C, A, B*
Warren County Community College *C*

New Mexico

Western New Mexico University *B*

New York

City University of New York
   Baruch College *B*
Clarkson University *B*
Excelsior College *B*
Fashion Institute of Technology *A*
Globe Institute of Technology *C, A, B*
Polytechnic University *M*
State University of New York
   Farmingdale *B*

North Carolina

Asheville-Buncombe Technical
   Community College *A*

Central Piedmont Community
   College *C*
Cleveland Community College *A*
Durham Technical Community
   College *C, A*
Fayetteville Technical Community
   College *A*
Isothermal Community College *C, A*
Johnston Community College *A*
Mitchell Community College *A*
Pitt Community College *C, A*
University of North Carolina
   Asheville *B*
   Charlotte *B*
Western Piedmont Community
   College *C, A*
Wilson Technical Community
   College *A*

Ohio

Bowling Green State University *B*
Bowling Green State University:
   Firelands College *C, A*
Case Western Reserve University *M*
DeVry University
   Columbus *B, M*
Edison State Community College *C, A*
Franklin University *B*
Lakeland Community College *C*
Miami University
   Oxford Campus *B*
Ohio State University
   Columbus Campus *B*
Owens Community College
   Toledo *C, A*
Stark State College of Technology *A*
University of Cincinnati *B, M, D*
University of Dayton *B*
University of Toledo *B, M*
Wright State University *M*
Youngstown State University *B*

Oklahoma

East Central University *B*
University of Central Oklahoma *B*

Oregon

Chemeketa Community College *A*
Oregon Institute of Technology *B*

Pennsylvania

Bucks County Community College *A*
Butler County Community College *C*
Carnegie Mellon University *M, D*
Community College of Philadelphia *A*
Delaware County Community
   College *A*
Drexel University *B*
Edinboro University of
   Pennsylvania *B*
Holy Family University *B*
La Salle University *B*
Lehigh Carbon Community College *A*
Penn State
   University Park *C, B*
Reading Area Community College *A*
Robert Morris University *B*
University of Pennsylvania *B, M, D*
University of Scranton *B, M*
Widener University *B*

Puerto Rico

Inter American University of Puerto
   Rico
   Ponce Campus *B*
Turabo University *M*

Rhode Island

Bryant University *M*

South Carolina

Clemson University *B, M, D*
Morris College *B*

Tennessee

Tennessee Technological University *B*

Texas

Baylor University *B*
Del Mar College *C, A*
El Paso Community College *A*
Houston Community College
   System *C, A*
Kilgore College *C, A*
Lamar University *M*
LeTourneau University *B*
Odessa College *C*
Sam Houston State University *B*
San Antonio College *A*
Tarrant County College *A*
Texas A&M University *M*
Texas A&M University
   Commerce *B*
Texas State Technical College
   Waco *A*
University of Dallas *M*
University of Houston *B, M, D*
University of North Texas *B, M, D*
University of Texas
   El Paso *B*
   San Antonio *B, M*
Weatherford College *C, A*
Wiley College *B*

Utah

Utah State University *B*
Utah Valley State College *B*

Vermont

College of St. Joseph in Vermont *B*

Virginia

George Mason University *M*
St. Paul's College *B*

Washington

Bellingham Technical College *A*
City University *M*
Eastern Washington University *B*
Seattle Central Community College *C*
Washington State University *B*
Western Washington University *B*

Wisconsin

Blackhawk Technical College *A*
Chippewa Valley Technical College *A*
Gateway Technical College *A*
Lakeshore Technical College *A*
Marian College of Fond du Lac *B*
Marquette University *M*
Milwaukee Area Technical College *A*
Northcentral Technical College *A*
University of Wisconsin
   Madison *B, M*
   Milwaukee *B*
   Oshkosh *B*
   Stout *B*
   Whitewater *B*
Western Wisconsin Technical
   College *A*
Wisconsin Indianhead Technical
   College *C*

Operations research

Alabama

University of Alabama
   Huntsville *M*

Arkansas

University of Arkansas
   Little Rock *B*

California

San Diego State University *M*

University of California
Berkeley *B, M, D*
University of Southern California *M*

Colorado
United States Air Force Academy *B*

Delaware
University of Delaware *B, M, D*

District of Columbia
George Washington University *M, D*

Florida
Florida Institute of Technology *M, D*

Georgia
Georgia Institute of Technology *M*

Iowa
Iowa State University *M*

Kansas
Kansas State University *M*

Massachusetts
Massachusetts Institute of
Technology *M, D*

Michigan
Michigan State University *M*
Western Michigan University *M*

Missouri
University of Missouri
Rolla *M*

New Jersey
Princeton University *B, M, D*
Rutgers, The State University of New
Jersey
New Brunswick/Piscataway
Campus *M, D*

New York
City University of New York
Baruch College *B, M*
Columbia University
Fu Foundation School of
Engineering and Applied
Science *B, M, D*
Cornell University *B, M, D*
Long Island University
Brooklyn Campus *B*
Rensselaer Polytechnic Institute *D*
United States Military Academy *B*

North Carolina
North Carolina State University *M, D*
University of North Carolina
Chapel Hill *M, D*

Ohio
Case Western Reserve University *M, D*

Oregon
Oregon State University *M*

Pennsylvania
Carnegie Mellon University *B*
University of Pennsylvania *D*

Texas
Southern Methodist University *M, D*
Texas A&M University
Commerce *B*
University of Texas
Austin *M, D*

Utah
Utah State University *M*

Ophthalmic laboratory technology

Alabama
Community College of the Air
Force *A*

California
Canada College *A*

Connecticut
Middlesex Community College *A*

Delaware
Delaware Technical and Community
College
Owens Campus *A*

Florida
Broward Community College *A*

Georgia
Darton College *A*
DeKalb Technical College *A*

Illinois
Triton College *A*

Indiana
Indiana University
Bloomington *A*

New York
Rochester Institute of Technology *A*

Ohio
Lakeland Community College *A*

Oregon
Eastern Oregon University *B*

Puerto Rico
Inter American University of Puerto
Rico
Ponce Campus *A*

Texas
Abilene Christian University *B*
Tyler Junior College *A*

Ophthalmic technology

Louisiana
Louisiana State University Health
Sciences Center *B*

New York
Rochester Institute of Technology *A*

Tennessee
Volunteer State Community College *A*

Virginia
Old Dominion University *B*

Opticianry/ophthalmic dispensing

Arkansas
Arkansas State University
Mountain Home *A*

Colorado
Pueblo Community College *A*

Connecticut
Middlesex Community College *A*

Florida
Gulf Coast Community College *A*
Hillsborough Community College *A*
Miami Dade College *A*

Georgia
DeKalb Technical College *A*

Indiana
Indiana University
Bloomington *A*

Massachusetts
Holyoke Community College *A*
Mount Ida College *A*

Minnesota
Anoka-Ramsey Community College *A*

Mississippi
Mississippi Gulf Coast Community
College
Jefferson Davis Campus *A*

Nevada
Community College of Southern
Nevada *A*

New Jersey
Camden County College *A*
Essex County College *A*
Raritan Valley Community College *A*

New Mexico
Southwestern Indian Polytechnic
Institute *A*

New York
City University of New York
New York City College of
Technology *A*
Erie Community College
North Campus *A*
Interboro Institute *A*
Suffolk County Community College *A*

North Carolina
Durham Technical Community
College *A*

Ohio
Cuyahoga Community College
Metropolitan Campus *A*
Hocking College *A*
Lakeland Community College *A*

Pennsylvania
Western School of Health and
Business Careers *A*
Westmoreland County Community
College *A*

Tennessee
Roane State Community College *A*
University of Tennessee
Knoxville *B, M*

Texas
El Paso Community College *A*
University of Houston *B, D*

Virginia
J. Sargeant Reynolds Community
College *A*
Thomas Nelson Community
College *A*

Washington
Spokane Community College *A*

Optics

Alabama
University of Alabama
Huntsville *B, D*

Arizona
University of Arizona *B, M, D*

California
Yuba Community College District *C*

Indiana
Indiana University
Bloomington *M, D*

Massachusetts
Tufts University *M, D*

Michigan
Saginaw Valley State University *B*

New Mexico
University of New Mexico *M, D*

New York
Corning Community College *A*
Monroe Community College *A*
University of Rochester *B, M, D*

North Carolina
University of North Carolina
Charlotte *M, D*

Ohio
University of Dayton *M, D*

Oklahoma
Oklahoma State University *D*

Pennsylvania
Albright College *B*
University of Pittsburgh *C*

Texas
University of North Texas *M*

Virginia
Norfolk State University *B*

Optometric assistant

District of Columbia
Georgetown University *C*

Iowa
Hawkeye Community College *C*

Michigan
Delta College *A*
Oakland Community College *C*

New Mexico
Southwestern Indian Polytechnic
Institute *C, A*

New York
Excelsior College *A, B*

Pennsylvania
Central Pennsylvania College *A*

Optometry (O.D.)

Alabama
University of Alabama at Birmingham:
School of Optometry *F*

California
Southern California College of
Optometry *F*
University of California Berkeley:
School of Optometry *F*

Florida
Nova Southeastern University Health
Professions Division: College of
Optometry *F*

Illinois
Illinois College of Optometry *F*

Indiana
Indiana University Bloomington:
School of Optometry *F*

Massachusetts
New England College of Optometry *F*

Michigan
Ferris State University: College of
Optometry *F*

Missouri
University of Missouri St. Louis: School
of Optometry *F*

New York
State University of New York College
of Optometry *F*

Ohio
Ohio State University Columbus
Campus: College of Optometry *F*

Oklahoma
Northeastern State University: College
of Optometry *F*

Oregon
Pacific University: School of
Optometry *F*

Pennsylvania
Pennsylvania College of Optometry *F*

Puerto Rico
Inter American University of Puerto
Rico School of Optometry *F*

Tennessee
Southern College of Optometry *F*

Texas
University of Houston: College of
Optometry *F*

Organic chemistry

California
Pitzer College *B*

Florida
Florida State University *M, D*

Georgia
Clark Atlanta University *M, D*

Iowa
Iowa State University *M, D*

Massachusetts
Massachusetts College of Pharmacy
and Health Sciences *M, D*
Simon's Rock College of Bard *B*
Tufts University *M, D*

Michigan
Olivet College *B*

Montana
University of Montana: Missoula *M, D*

New York
Fordham University *M*
Sarah Lawrence College *B*
State University of New York
Albany *D*
College of Environmental Science
and Forestry *M, D*

Texas
Texas A&M University
Commerce *B*
University of North Texas *M, D*

Vermont
Marlboro College *B*

Wisconsin
Marquette University *M, D*
University of Wisconsin
River Falls *B*

Organizational behavior studies

Arizona
Estrella Mountain Community
College *C, A*
Grand Canyon University *B*
Paradise Valley Community
College *C, A*
University of Phoenix *M, D*

Arkansas
Central Baptist College *B*

California
Antioch Southern California
Antioch University Los Angeles *M*
Antioch University Santa Barbara *M*
California Baptist University *B*
California Institute of Integral
Studies *M, D*
California State University
San Bernardino *B*
Chapman University *B*
Fresno Pacific University *B*
National University *B*
Pepperdine University *M*
Pitzer College *B*
St. Mary's College of California *M*
Santa Clara University *B*
Scripps College *B*
Simpson University *B*
University of La Verne *M*
University of San Francisco *B*
Woodbury University *B, M*

Colorado
Colorado Technical University *C*
University of Colorado
Denver and Health Sciences
Center *M*

Connecticut
Central Connecticut State
University *B*
Eastern Connecticut State
University *M*
University of Hartford *M*

Delaware
Wilmington College *M*

District of Columbia
American University *M*
George Washington University *M*

Florida
Palm Beach Atlantic University *M*
St. Thomas University *B*
Warner Southern College *B*

Georgia
Covenant College *B*
Oglethorpe University *B*
Southern Polytechnic State
University *B*

Illinois
Benedictine University *B, M, D*
Greenville College *B*
Loyola University of Chicago *C, M*
North Park University *B*
Northwestern University *B, M, D*
Trinity Christian College *B*
Trinity International University *B, M*
University of Illinois
Urbana-Champaign *B*
University of St. Francis *B*

Indiana
Calumet College of St. Joseph *B*
Indiana University
Bloomington *D*
Oakland City University *B*

Iowa
St. Ambrose University *B*

Kansas
Central Christian College of Kansas *A*

Kentucky
Mid-Continent University *B*
Northern Kentucky University *B*

Maine
University of Southern Maine *B*

Maryland
Columbia Union College *B*

Massachusetts
Boston College *D*
Boston University *B*
Bridgewater State College *M*
Emerson College *M*
Harvard College *D*

Michigan
Central Michigan University *M*
Concordia University *M*
Michigan State University *D*
University of Michigan *B*
University of Michigan
Flint *B*
Wayne State University *B*

Minnesota
Bethel University *M*
Capella University *C, B*
College of St. Scholastica *B*
Concordia University: St. Paul *B, M*

Missouri
Calvary Bible College and Theological
Seminary *B*
Fontbonne University *B*
Hannibal-LaGrange College *B*
Lindenwood University *M*
St. Louis University *B, D*

University of Missouri
St. Louis *B, M*
Washington University in St. Louis *M*

New Jersey
Thomas Edison State College *B*

New York
City University of New York
Baruch College *M, D*
Cornell University *B, M, D*
New York University *B, M, D*
Polytechnic University *M*
State University of New York
Albany *D*

North Carolina
High Point University *B*
Mount Olive College *B*

Ohio
Bluffton University *B, M*
Bowling Green State University *M*
Case Western Reserve University *M, D*
College of Mount St. Joseph *M*
Denison University *B*
Lourdes College *M*
Miami University
Oxford Campus *B*
Union Institute & University *B*
University of Findlay *M*
University of Toledo *B*

Oklahoma
Oral Roberts University *B*
University of Oklahoma *M*

Pennsylvania
Cabrini College *B, M*
Carnegie Mellon University *D*
Geneva College *M*
La Salle University *B*
Neumann College *M*
Penn State
Harrisburg *B*
Robert Morris University *B, M*
Rosemont College *B*
Shippensburg University of
Pennsylvania *M*
Temple University *B*
University of Pennsylvania *M*
Villanova University *M*
Westminster College *B*

Puerto Rico
University of Puerto Rico
Mayaguez *B, M*

Rhode Island
Providence College *B*

South Carolina
Claflin University *B*
Converse College *B*
Voorhees College *B*

South Dakota
University of Sioux Falls *B*

Texas
Southern Methodist University *B*
University of Dallas *M*
University of Houston *B*
University of North Texas *B, D*
University of Texas
San Antonio *D*
University of the Incarnate Word *B*

Vermont
Champlain College *A, B*

Virginia

Eastern Mennonite University *B*
Marymount University *M*
Regent University *B, D, T*

Washington

Central Washington University *M*
Seattle Pacific University *B*
University of Washington *B, M*

West Virginia

Mountain State University *B*

Wisconsin

Carroll College *B*
Silver Lake College *M*
University of Wisconsin
  Platteville *B*

Organizational communication

California

California State University
  Chico *B*
College of the Desert *A*
Ohlone College *C*
Westmont College *B*

Colorado

Colorado State University *M*
Jones International University *C, B, M*

Florida

Florida Institute of Technology *M*
Palm Beach Atlantic University *B*
Schiller International University *M*
University of Miami *B*

Georgia

Northwestern Technical College *C, A*

Illinois

North Central College *B*
University of Illinois
  Urbana-Champaign *B*

Indiana

Indiana State University *B*
Indiana University-Purdue University
  Fort Wayne *B*
Valparaiso University *B*

Iowa

Buena Vista University *B*
University of Northern Iowa *B*

Kansas

Tabor College *B*

Kentucky

Murray State University *B, M*
Western Kentucky University *B*

Louisiana

Southeastern Louisiana University *M*

Maryland

Bowie State University *M*

Massachusetts

Assumption College *B*
Bay Path College *B*
Regis College *M*
Suffolk University *B, M*

Michigan

Concordia University *B*
Cornerstone University *B*
Michigan Technological University *C*

University of Michigan
  Flint *B*

Minnesota

Augsburg College *B*

Missouri

Lindenwood University *B, M*
Rockhurst University *B*
William Jewell College *B*

Nebraska

Creighton University *A, B*
Dana College *B*
Doane College *B*

New Jersey

Fairleigh Dickinson University
  College at Florham *M*
  Metropolitan Campus *M*
Montclair State University *B*

New York

Canisius College *M*
Ithaca College *B*
Marist College *B*
State University of New York
  College at Cortland *B*

North Carolina

North Carolina State University *M*
Queens University of Charlotte *B*

Ohio

Marietta College *B*
Ohio Northern University *B*
Ohio University *B, M, D*
Ohio University
  Chillicothe Campus *B*
  Zanesville Campus *B*
Otterbein College *B*
Wright State University *B*
Xavier University *A, B*

Oregon

University of Portland *B, M*

Pennsylvania

Butler County Community College *A*
Marywood University *C*
Temple University *B, M*

Tennessee

Lipscomb University *B*
Trevecca Nazarene University *B*

Texas

Lubbock Christian University *B*

Vermont

Champlain College *A, B*

Virginia

Liberty University *M*

Washington

Northwest University *B*

Wisconsin

Carroll College *B*
Marian College of Fond du Lac *B*

Ornamental horticulture

Alabama

Trenholm State Technical College *C, A*

Arkansas

University of Arkansas *B*

California

Antelope Valley College *C, A*
Bakersfield College *A*
Butte College *C, A*
Cabrillo College *C, A*
California Polytechnic State
  University: San Luis Obispo *B*
California State Polytechnic
  University: Pomona *B*
Cerritos Community College *A*
City College of San Francisco *C, A*
College of San Mateo *C, A*
College of the Desert *C, A*
College of the Sequoias *C, A*
Cuyamaca College *A*
El Camino College *C, A*
Foothill College *C, A*
Las Positas College *C, A*
Long Beach City College *C, A*
Los Angeles Pierce College *C, A*
Merced College *C, A*
Modesto Junior College *A*
Monterey Peninsula College *C, A*
Mount San Antonio College *C*
Orange Coast College *C, A*
Saddleback College *C, A*
San Joaquin Delta College *C, A*
Santa Barbara City College *C, A*
Santa Rosa Junior College *C*
Shasta College *C, A*
Solano Community College *C, A*
Southwestern College *C, A*
Ventura College *A*
Victor Valley College *C, A*
Yuba Community College
  District *C, A*

Colorado

Northeastern Junior College *C, A*

Delaware

University of Delaware *B, M*

Florida

Central Florida Community
  College *C, A*
Florida Agricultural and Mechanical
  University *B*
Florida Southern College *B*
Gulf Coast Community College *A*
Hillsborough Community
  College *C, A*
Palm Beach Community College *A*
Pensacola Junior College *A*
Santa Fe Community College *A*
South Florida Community
  College *C, A*
Valencia Community College *A*

Georgia

Abraham Baldwin Agricultural
  College *A*
Fort Valley State University *A*

Illinois

College of DuPage *C*
College of Lake County *C, A*
Joliet Junior College *C, A*
Kishwaukee College *C, A*
McHenry County College *C*
Triton College *C, A*
University of Illinois
  Urbana-Champaign *B*
William Rainey Harper College *C*

Iowa

Kirkwood Community College *C*

Kentucky

Eastern Kentucky University *B*

Maine

University of Maine *C, B*

Maryland

Prince George's Community
  College *C*

Massachusetts

University of Massachusetts
  Amherst *A*

Michigan

Ferris State University *A*
Wayne County Community College *C*

Mississippi

Mississippi Gulf Coast Community
  College
  Jefferson Davis Campus *C, A*

Missouri

St. Louis Community College
  St. Louis Community College at
    Meramec *C, A*

Nebraska

Nebraska College of Technical
  Agriculture *A*

Nevada

Community College of Southern
  Nevada *C, A*

New Hampshire

University of New Hampshire *A*

New Jersey

Brookdale Community College *C*
Cumberland County College *C, A*
Mercer County Community
  College *C, A*

New York

Cornell University *B, M, D*
Finger Lakes Community College *C, A*
Niagara County Community
  College *C*
State University of New York
  College of Agriculture and
    Technology at Cobleskill *A, B*
  College of Agriculture and
    Technology at Morrisville *A*
  College of Technology at Delhi *A*
  Farmingdale *C, A*
Suffolk County Community College *A*

North Carolina

Blue Ridge Community College *C*
Sampson Community College *A*

Ohio

Ohio State University
  Agricultural Technical Institute *A*

Oklahoma

Eastern Oklahoma State College *A*

Oregon

Clackamas Community College *C, A*

Pennsylvania

Community College of Allegheny
  County *C*
Delaware Valley College *B*
Penn State
  University Park *C*
Pennsylvania College of Technology *A*

Puerto Rico

Inter American University of Puerto
Rico
Barranquitas Campus *C, A*
San German Campus *C*

Tennessee

University of Tennessee
Knoxville *B, M*
Walters State Community College *A*

Texas

Houston Community College
System *C*
Palo Alto College *A*
Tarleton State University *B*
Texas A&M University *B, M*
Western Texas College *C, A*

Utah

Utah State University *C, A, B*

Vermont

Vermont Technical College *A*

Virginia

Christopher Newport University *B*
J. Sargeant Reynolds Community
College *C, A*
Piedmont Virginia Community
College *C*

Washington

South Puget Sound Community
College *C, A*
South Seattle Community
College *C, A*
Spokane Community College *C*

Wisconsin

Blackhawk Technical College *C*
Fox Valley Technical College *C*

Orthotics/prosthetics

California

California State University
Dominguez Hills *B*

Florida

Florida International University *B*
St. Petersburg College *B*

Georgia

Georgia Institute of Technology *M*

Massachusetts

Boston University *M, D*

Michigan

Baker College
of Flint *A*

Minnesota

Century Community and Technical
College *C, A*

Mississippi

Mississippi Gulf Coast Community
College
Jefferson Davis Campus *A*

Nevada

Community College of Southern
Nevada *A*

Oklahoma

Oklahoma State University
Okmulgee *A*

Pennsylvania

Alvernia College *A*

Texas

University of Texas
Southwestern Medical Center at
Dallas *B*

Washington

Spokane Falls Community College *A*
University of Washington *B*

Osteopathic medicine (D.O.)

California

Western University of Health
Sciences *F*

Florida

Nova Southeastern University Health
Professions Division: College of
Osteopathic Medicine *F*

Illinois

Midwestern University: Chicago
College of Osteopathic
Medicine *F*

Iowa

Des Moines University - Osteopathic
Medical Center *F*

Maine

University of New England: School of
Osteopathic Medicine *F*

Michigan

Michigan State University: College of
Osteopathic Medicine *F*

Missouri

Kirksville College of Osteopathic
Medicine *F*
University of Health Sciences College
of Osteopathic Medicine *F*

New Jersey

UMDNJ-School of Osteopathic
Medicine *F*

New York

New York College of Osteopathic
Medicine of New York Institute of
Technology *F*

Ohio

Ohio University
College of Osteopathic Medicine *F*

Oklahoma

Oklahoma State University: College of
Osteopathic Medicine *F*

Pennsylvania

Lake Erie College of Osteopathic
Medicine *F*
Philadelphia College of Osteopathic
Medicine *F*

Texas

University of North Texas Health
Science Center at Fort Worth:
Osteopathic Medicine *F*

West Virginia

West Virginia School of Osteopathic
Medicine *F*

Pacific area/rim studies

California

Claremont McKenna College *B*
University of California
San Diego *M*

Hawaii

Brigham Young University-Hawaii *B*
University of Hawaii
Manoa *M*
West Oahu *B*

Missouri

Northwest Missouri State
University *B*

Utah

University of Utah *M*

Painting

Alabama

Birmingham-Southern College *B*

Arizona

Northern Arizona University *B*

Arkansas

Harding University *B*

California

Academy of Art University *C, A, B, M*
Art Center College of Design *B, M*
Biola University *B*
California College of the Arts *B, M*
California Institute of the Arts *C, B, M*
California State University
East Bay *B*
Fullerton *B, M*
Long Beach *B, M*
Northridge *B, M*
Chabot College *A*
College of San Mateo *A*
College of the Desert *A*
De Anza College *C, A*
Grossmont Community College *A*
Laguna College of Art and Design *C, B*
Monterey Peninsula College *C, A*
Ohlone College *C*
Palomar College *A*
Pasadena City College *A*
San Diego State University *B*
San Francisco Art Institute *B, M*
Santa Rosa Junior College *C*
Solano Community College *A*
University of San Francisco *B*

Colorado

Adams State College *B*
Rocky Mountain College of Art &
Design *B*

Connecticut

Lyme Academy College of Fine
Arts *C, B*
Paier College of Art *C, B*
Sacred Heart University *B*
University of Hartford *B*

District of Columbia

American University *M*
George Washington University *M*

Florida

University of Miami *B*

Georgia

Savannah College of Art and
Design *B, M*

Idaho

Northwest Nazarene University *B*

Illinois

American Academy of Art *B*
Bradley University *B*
City Colleges of Chicago
Olive-Harvey College *A*
Lewis University *B*
Richland Community College *A*
Rockford College *B*
School of the Art Institute of
Chicago *B, M*
University of Illinois
Urbana-Champaign *B, M*

Indiana

Indiana University-Purdue University
Fort Wayne *B*
Indiana University-Purdue University
Indianapolis *B*
Vincennes University *A*

Iowa

Coe College *B*
Drake University *B*
University of Iowa *B, M*

Kansas

Allen County Community College *A*
Central Christian College of Kansas *A*
Pittsburg State University *B*
Pratt Community College *A*
Seward County Community College *A*
University of Kansas *B, M*

Kentucky

Eastern Kentucky University *B*

Louisiana

Centenary College of Louisiana *B*

Maine

Maine College of Art *B*
University of Southern Maine *B*

Maryland

Maryland Institute College of Art *B, M*

Massachusetts

Art Institute of Boston at Lesley
University *B*
Boston University *B, M*
Emmanuel College *B*
Hampshire College *B*
Massachusetts College of Art *B, M*
Montserrat College of Art *B*
School of the Museum of Fine
Arts *B, M*
Simon's Rock College of Bard *B*
University of Massachusetts
Dartmouth *B, M*

Michigan

Andrews University *B*
College for Creative Studies *B*
Ferris State University *B*
Finlandia University *B*
Grand Valley State University *B*
Kendall College of Art and Design of
Ferris State University *B*
Lansing Community College *A*
Northern Michigan University *B*
Siena Heights University *B*
University of Michigan
Dearborn *B*
Flint *B*

Minnesota

College of Visual Arts *B*

Minneapolis College of Art and
Design *B*
Minnesota State University
Mankato *B*
St. Cloud State University *B*

Missouri

Columbia College *B*
Kansas City Art Institute *B*
Washington University in St.
Louis *B, M*

Nevada

Sierra Nevada College *B*

New Hampshire

Rivier College *B*
University of New Hampshire *M*

New Jersey

Rowan University *B*

New Mexico

College of Santa Fe *B*

New York

Bard College *B, M*
City University of New York
Brooklyn College *M*
Columbia University
School of General Studies *B*
Hofstra University *B*
Parsons The New School for
Design *C, A, B, M, T*
Pratt Institute *A, B, M*
Rochester Institute of
Technology *A, B, M*
Sarah Lawrence College *B*
School of Visual Arts *B, M*
State University of New York
College at Buffalo *B*
College at Fredonia *B*
New Paltz *B, M*
Purchase *B, M*
Syracuse University *B, M*

North Carolina

East Carolina University *B*

Ohio

Art Academy of Cincinnati *B*
Cleveland Institute of Art *B*
Kent State University *B, M*
Ohio State University
Columbus Campus *B, M*
Ohio University *B, M*
Shawnee State University *B*
University of Akron *M*
Youngstown State University *B*

Oregon

Pacific Northwest College of Art *B*
Portland State University *B, M*
University of Oregon *B, M*

Pennsylvania

Arcadia University *B*
Edinboro University of
Pennsylvania *B*
Keystone College *A, B*
Marywood University *M*
Oakbridge Academy of Arts *A*
Seton Hill University *B*
Temple University *B, M*
University of the Arts *B, M*

Puerto Rico

Inter American University of Puerto
Rico
San German Campus *B, M*
University of Puerto Rico
Rio Piedras *B*

Rhode Island

Rhode Island College *B*
Rhode Island School of Design *B, M*
Salve Regina University *B*

South Carolina

Anderson University *B*

Tennessee

Carson-Newman College *B*
Memphis College of Art *B, M*
Tennessee Technological University *B*

Texas

McMurry University *B*
Sam Houston State University *M*
Stephen F. Austin State University *M*
Texas A&M University
Commerce *B, M*
Texas Christian University *B, M*
University of Dallas *B, M*
University of Houston *B, M*
University of North Texas *B, M*
University of Texas
El Paso *B, M*
Western Texas College *A*

Utah

Dixie State College of Utah *A*

Vermont

Bennington College *B*
Burlington College *B*
Marlboro College *B*

Virginia

Virginia Commonwealth University *B*

Washington

Cornish College of the Arts *B*
North Seattle Community College *C*
University of Washington *B, M*
Western Washington University *B*

West Virginia

Alderson-Broaddus College *B*
West Virginia State University *B*
West Virginia Wesleyan College *B*

Wisconsin

University of Wisconsin
Madison *B*

Painting/wall covering

Arizona

Tohono O'odham Community
College *C, A*

California

Allan Hancock College *C*

Illinois

Parkland College *C*

Indiana

Ivy Tech State College
Ivy Tech Community College:
Central Indiana *C, A*
Ivy Tech Community College: East
Central *C, A*
Ivy Tech Community College:
Lafayette *C, A*
Ivy Tech Community College: North
Central *C, A*
Ivy Tech Community College:
Northeast *C, A*
Ivy Tech Community College:
Northwest *C, A*
Ivy Tech Community College:
Southwest *C, A*

Ivy Tech Community College:
Wabash Valley *C, A*

Kentucky

Big Sandy Community and Technical
College *C*

Michigan

Mott Community College *C*

Minnesota

St. Paul College *C*

Oregon

Linn-Benton Community College *A*

Pennsylvania

Community College of Allegheny
County *A*

Wisconsin

Gateway Technical College *C*
Milwaukee Area Technical College *C*

Paleontology

Arizona

Northern Arizona University *B*

Arkansas

University of Arkansas *D*

California

Loma Linda University *M*
San Diego State University *B*

Michigan

University of Michigan *B, M*

Ohio

Ohio State University
Columbus Campus *M, D*

South Dakota

South Dakota School of Mines and
Technology *M*

Paralegal studies

Alabama

Community College of the Air
Force *A*
Enterprise-Ozark Community
College *A*
Faulkner State Community College *A*
Gadsden State Community College *A*
Huntingdon College *A*
Northeast Alabama Community
College *A*
Samford University *C*
Shelton State Community College *C*
South University *A*
Virginia College *C, A*
Wallace State Community College at
Hanceville *A*

Alaska

University of Alaska
Anchorage *C*
Fairbanks *A*
Southeast *A*

Arizona

Arizona Institute of Business and
Technology
International Institute of the
Americas: Mesa *A*
Coconino County Community
College *A*
Everest College *C*

International Institute of the Americas
Phoenix *A*
Tucson *A*
International Institute of the
Americas: West Valley *A*
Lamson College *A*
Metropolitan College of Court
Reporting *A, B*
Northland Pioneer College *A*
Paralegal Institute *A*
Phoenix College *C, A*
Pima Community College *C, A*
Yavapai College *C, A*

Arkansas

Northwest Arkansas Community
College *A*
Pulaski Technical College *A*
Southeast Arkansas College *A*
University of Arkansas
Community College at Hope *A*
Fort Smith *A*

California

American River College *A*
Butte College *C, A*
CEI College
Maric College: Panorama City *C, A*
California State University
Chico *C, B*
East Bay *C*
Canada College *A*
Cerritos Community College *A*
City College of San Francisco *C, A*
Coastline Community College *C*
College of the Redwoods *C, A*
College of the Sequoias *A*
De Anza College *C, A*
El Camino College *C, A*
Empire College *A*
Fresno City College *C, A*
Fullerton College *A*
Glendale Community College *A*
Humphreys College *C, B*
Imperial Valley College *C, A*
Lake Tahoe Community College *C*
Los Angeles City College *A*
Los Angeles Mission College *C, A*
Los Angeles Southwest College *A*
MTI College *C, A*
Maric College
Vista *A*
Maric College: Sacramento *A*
Merritt College *C, A*
Mount San Antonio College *A*
Napa Valley College *C, A*
Palomar College *C, A*
Pasadena City College *C, A*
Platt College
Cerritos *A*
Ontario *C, A, B*
Saddleback College *C, A*
Sage College *C, A*
San Diego City College *A*
San Diego Miramar College *C, A*
San Francisco State University *C*
Santa Barbara Business College *A*
Santa Barbara Business College
Bakersfield *C, A*
Santa Maria *C, A*
Santa Barbara Business College:
Ventura *C, A*
Santiago Canyon College *A*
Shasta College *A*
Skyline College *A*
Southwestern College *C, A*
University of San Diego *C*
West Los Angeles College *C, A*
West Valley College *A*

Colorado

Arapahoe Community College *C, A*
Blair College *A*

Colorado Northwestern Community
    College A
Community College of Aurora C, A
Community College of Denver C, A
Front Range Community College C
Parks College A
Parks College: Aurora A
Pikes Peak Community College A
Pueblo Community College C, A

Connecticut

Briarwood College A
Manchester Community College C, A
Naugatuck Valley Community
    College A
Norwalk Community College C, A
Post University C, A, B
Quinnipiac University B
University of Hartford C
University of New Haven C

Delaware

Delaware Technical and Community
    College
    Owens Campus C, A
Wesley College C, A, B

District of Columbia

George Washington University C
Southeastern University A
University of the District of
    Columbia A

Florida

Brevard Community College A
Broward Community College A
Central Florida Community College A
City College A
Daytona Beach Community College A
Edison College A
Florida Community College at
    Jacksonville A
Florida Gulf Coast University B
Florida Metropolitan University
    Brandon Campus A, B
    Orlando College North A
    Pompano Beach A
    Tampa College A
    Tampa College Lakeland A
Florida National College A
Florida Technical College
    Deland A
Gulf Coast Community College A
Hillsborough Community College A
Indian River Community College A
International College A, B
Jones College A, B
Key College A
Lake-Sumter Community College A
Manatee Community College C, A
Miami Dade College C, A
New England Institute of
    Technology A
Nova Southeastern University B
Okaloosa-Walton College A
Palm Beach Community College A
Pasco-Hernando Community
    College A
Pensacola Junior College A
St. Petersburg College A, B
Santa Fe Community College A
Seminole Community College A
South University: West Palm Beach
    Campus A, B
Southwest Florida College A
Southwest Florida College
    Tampa A
Tallahassee Community College A
University of Central Florida B
University of West Florida B
Valencia Community College A

Georgia

Athens Technical College A
Augusta State University C
Brown Mackie College: Atlanta C, A
Clayton State University C, A
Darton College C, A
Gainesville State College C, A
Georgia Highlands College A
Gwinnett College C, A
South University A
Thomas University A
Valdosta State University B

Hawaii

University of Hawaii
    Kapiolani Community College C, A

Idaho

Eastern Idaho Technical College C, A
Lewis-Clark State College C, A, B

Illinois

Black Hawk College A
Black Hawk College
    East Campus A
Career Colleges of Chicago A
College of Lake County C, A
Elgin Community College C, A
Illinois Central College C, A
MacCormac College C, A
Midstate College A
Northwestern Business College A
Robert Morris College: Chicago C, A
Rock Valley College C, A
Rockford Business College A
Sauk Valley Community College C
South Suburban College of Cook
    County C, A
Southern Illinois University
    Carbondale B
Southwestern Illinois College C, A
William Rainey Harper College A

Indiana

Ball State University A
Brown Mackie College: Fort
    Wayne C, A
Brown Mackie College: Michigan
    City A
Calumet College of St. Joseph C, A, B
Indiana University-Purdue University
    Indianapolis C
International Business College C, A
International Business College:
    Indianapolis A
Ivy Tech State College
    Ivy Tech Community College:
        Bloomington A
    Ivy Tech Community College:
        Central Indiana A
    Ivy Tech Community College:
        Columbus A
    Ivy Tech Community College: East
        Central A
    Ivy Tech Community College:
        Kokomo C
    Ivy Tech Community College: North
        Central A
    Ivy Tech Community College:
        Northwest A
    Ivy Tech Community College: South
        Central A
    Ivy Tech Community College:
        Southeast A
    Ivy Tech Community College:
        Southwest A
    Ivy Tech Community College:
        Wabash Valley C
    Ivy Tech Community College:
        Whitewater A
Professional Careers Institute A
St. Mary-of-the-Woods College C, A, B
Vincennes University A

Iowa

Des Moines Area Community
    College C, A
Hamilton College
    Cedar Falls A
Iowa Lakes Community College A
Iowa Western Community College A
Kaplan University A, B
Kirkwood Community College A
Northeast Iowa Community
    College C

Kansas

Brown Mackie College A
Cloud County Community
    College C, A
Hutchinson Community College A
Johnson County Community
    College C, A
Kansas City Kansas Community
    College A
Washburn University of
    Topeka C, A, B

Kentucky

Beckfield College C, A, B
Brown Mackie College:
    Hopkinsville C
Daymar College A
Eastern Kentucky University A, B
Morehead State University B
Southwestern College: Florence C
Sullivan University A, B
University of Louisville A
Western Kentucky University A

Louisiana

Grambling State University C, A, B
Nicholls State University A
Nunez Community College A
Tulane University C

Maine

Andover College C, A
Beal College C, A
Husson College A, B
University of Maine
    Augusta A

Maryland

Anne Arundel Community
    College C, A
Baltimore City Community
    College C, A
Chesapeake College C, A
College of Southern Maryland A
Community College of Baltimore
    County A
Frederick Community College C, A
Hagerstown Business College A
Hagerstown Community College C
Harford Community College A
Montgomery College A
Prince George's Community
    College C, A
Villa Julie College B

Massachusetts

Anna Maria College A, B
Atlantic Union College C, A
Bay Path College C, A
Bay State College A
Becker College C, A
Bentley College A, B
Boston University B
Bristol Community College A
Bunker Hill Community College C
Cape Cod Community College C
Elms College C, A, B
Marian Court College C, A
Massachusetts Bay Community
    College C, A
Massasoit Community College A

Merrimack College A
Middlesex Community College C, A
Mount Ida College A
Mount Wachusett Community
    College C, A
Newbury College C, A, B
North Shore Community College C, A
Northern Essex Community
    College C, A
Quincy College C, A
Roxbury Community College A
Stonehill College C
Suffolk University A, B

Michigan

Baker College
    of Auburn Hills A
Bay de Noc Community College C
Davenport University A, B
Delta College C, A
Eastern Michigan University B
Ferris State University A
Henry Ford Community College A
Kellogg Community College C, A
Lake Superior State University A, B
Lansing Community College A
Macomb Community College A
North Central Michigan College A
Northern Michigan University A
Northwestern Michigan College C
Oakland Community College C, A
University of Detroit Mercy C, A, B
Wayne County Community College A

Minnesota

Alexandria Technical College A
Globe College C, A, B
Hamline University B
Inver Hills Community College C, A
Lake Superior College C, A
Minnesota School of Business A
Minnesota School of Business:
    Brooklyn Center B
Minnesota State Community and
    Technical College - Fergus Falls A
Minnesota State University
    Moorhead B
North Hennepin Community
    College A
Northland Community & Technical
    College A
Rasmussen College
    Eagan C
Winona State University B

Mississippi

Hinds Community College A
Itawamba Community College A
Mississippi College B
Mississippi Gulf Coast Community
    College
    Jefferson Davis Campus A
University of Mississippi C, B
University of Southern Mississippi B

Missouri

Avila University C, B
East Central College C
Everest College: Springfield A
Hickey College C, A
Kansas City College of Legal Studies A
Maryville University of Saint Louis B
Missouri Southern State University C
Missouri Western State University C, A
National American University
    Kansas City A, B
Patricia Stevens College A
Penn Valley Community College C, A
Rockhurst University C
St. Louis Community College
St. Louis Community College at
    Meramec C, A
Vatterott College: Springfield C, A

Webster University C, B
William Jewell College C
William Woods University A, B

Montana

Helena College of Technology of the
    University of Montana C, A
University of Great Falls A, B
University of Montana: Missoula A

Nebraska

Central Community College C, A
College of Saint Mary C, A, B
Hamilton College: Lincoln A
Metropolitan Community College A
Midland Lutheran College B
Northeast Community College C, A

Nevada

Community College of Southern
    Nevada C, A
Las Vegas College A
Truckee Meadows Community
    College A
Western Nevada Community
    College A

New Hampshire

Granite State College C
McIntosh College A
New Hampshire Community
    Technical College
    Nashua C, A
New Hampshire Technical
    Institute C, A

New Jersey

Atlantic Cape Community College A
Bergen Community College A
Berkeley College A
Brookdale Community College A
Burlington County College A
Cumberland County College A
Essex County College A
Gloucester County College C, A
Hudson County Community
    College A
Mercer County Community
    College C, A
Middlesex County College A
Montclair State University C
Ocean County College C
Raritan Valley Community College A
Rider University C
Sussex County Community
    College C, A
Thomas Edison State College A, B
Union County College A
Warren County Community
    College C, A

New Mexico

Albuquerque Technical-Vocational
    Institute A
Dona Ana Branch Community College
    of New Mexico State
    University A
Eastern New Mexico University:
    Roswell Campus A
International Institute of the
    Americas A
New Mexico Junior College C, A
New Mexico State University
    Alamogordo C, A
    Grants A
Santa Fe Community College C, A

New York

Berkeley College A
Berkeley College of New York City A
Broome Community College A
Bryant & Stratton Business Institute
    Bryant & Stratton College: Albany A

Bryant & Stratton College:
    Rochester A
Bryant & Stratton College: Henrietta A
Bryant & Stratton College: Syracuse
    North A
City University of New York
    Bronx Community College A
    Hostos Community College A
    LaGuardia Community College A
    New York City College of
        Technology A, B
Columbia-Greene Community
    College C
Corning Community College A
Dutchess Community College C, A
Elmira Business Institute C, A
Erie Community College
    City Campus A
Finger Lakes Community College A
Genesee Community College A
Globe Institute of Technology C, A, B
Herkimer County Community
    College A
Hilbert College A, B
Interboro Institute A
Jefferson Community College A
Maria College C, A
Marist College C
Mercy College B
Mildred Elley C, A
Monroe Community College C
Nassau Community College C, A
New York Career Institute A
New York University A
Olean Business Institute C, A
Rochester Business Institute A
Rockland Community College C, A
Sage College of Albany B
Suffolk County Community
    College C, A
Sullivan County Community
    College A
Tompkins-Cortland Community
    College A
Westchester Community College C, A

North Carolina

Caldwell Community College and
    Technical Institute A
Cape Fear Community College A
Carteret Community College A
Central Carolina Community
    College C, A
Central Piedmont Community
    College C, A
Coastal Carolina Community
    College A
Davidson County Community
    College A
Durham Technical Community
    College A
Fayetteville Technical Community
    College A
Forsyth Technical Community
    College A
Gaston College A
Guilford Technical Community
    College C, A
Isothermal Community College A
Johnston Community College A
King's College A
Pitt Community College A
Rockingham Community College A
Rowan-Cabarrus Community
    College A
South College A
South Piedmont Community
    College A
Southwestern Community College A
Surry Community College A
Western Piedmont Community
    College C, A
Wilson Technical Community
    College A

North Dakota

Lake Region State College C, A
Turtle Mountain Community
    College C

Ohio

AEC Southern Ohio College
    Brown Mackie College: Akron C, A
Bradford School A
College of Mount St. Joseph C, A, B
Columbus State Community
    College C, A
Cuyahoga Community College
    Metropolitan Campus C, A
David N. Myers University A, B
ETI Technical College of Niles A
Edison State Community College A
James A. Rhodes State College C, A
Kent State University B
Kent State University
    East Liverpool Regional Campus A
    Trumbull Campus A
Lake Erie College B
Lakeland Community College C, A
Marion Technical College A
Ohio Business College: Sandusky A
Shawnee State University A
Sinclair Community College A
Stautzenberger College C, A
University of Akron C, A
University of Cincinnati
    Clermont College C, A
University of Northwestern Ohio C, A
University of Rio Grande A
University of Toledo C, A, B
Ursuline College B
Zane State College A

Oklahoma

East Central University B
Metropolitan College A
Northeastern State University B
Oklahoma Wesleyan University A
Rogers State University A
Rose State College A
Tulsa Community College A

Oregon

Everest College: Portland A
Linn-Benton Community College A
Pioneer Pacific College A
Portland Community College C, A
Treasure Valley Community College A

Pennsylvania

Academy of Medical Arts and
    Business C, A
Berean Institute C
Berks Technical Institute A
Bucks County Community
    College C, A
Career Training Academy C
Central Pennsylvania College A
Community College of Philadelphia A
Consolidated School of Business
    York A
Delaware County Community
    College C, A
Erie Business Center A
Gannon University C, A, B
Harrisburg Area Community
    College C, A
Immaculata University C
Lackawanna College A
Lehigh Carbon Community
    College C, A
Lehigh Valley College A
Lock Haven University of
    Pennsylvania B
Luzerne County Community
    College A
Manor College C, A
Marywood University C, A, B

McCann School of Business
    Pottsville A
Mount Aloysius College A
Northampton County Area
    Community College A
PJA School C, A
Peirce College C, A, B
Pennsylvania College of
    Technology C, A
Schuylkill Institute of Business &
    Technology A
South Hills School of Business &
    Technology C
Tri-State Business Institute A
Western School of Health and
    Business Careers A
Western School of Health and
    Business Careers
    Monroeville A
Westmoreland County Community
    College C, A
Widener University A
Yorktowne Business Institute A

Puerto Rico

Turabo University C
Universidad Metropolitana C
Universidad del Este A, B

Rhode Island

Community College of Rhode
    Island A
Johnson & Wales University A, B
Roger Williams University C, B

South Carolina

Aiken Technical College C
Central Carolina Technical College A
Florence-Darlington Technical
    College A
Forrest Junior College C, A
Greenville Technical College C, A
Horry-Georgetown Technical
    College C, A
Midlands Technical College C, A
Miller-Motte Technical College A
Orangeburg-Calhoun Technical
    College A
South University C, A
Spartanburg Methodist College C
Technical College of the
    Lowcountry C
Trident Technical College C, A
York Technical College C, A

South Dakota

Western Dakota Technical Institute A

Tennessee

Chattanooga State Technical
    Community College A
Miller-Motte Technical College A
Pellissippi State Technical Community
    College A
Roane State Community College A
South College A
Southwest Tennessee Community
    College A
University of Tennessee
    Chattanooga B
Volunteer State Community College A
Walters State Community College A

Texas

Alvin Community College C, A
Angelina College A
Austin Community College C, A
Blinn College C, A
Brazosport College A
Central Texas College A
Collin County Community College
    District C, A
Del Mar College A

El Centro College *A*
El Paso Community College *C, A*
Houston Community College
　　System *A*
Howard College *A*
Kilgore College *C, A*
Lee College *A*
McLennan Community College *A*
Midland College *C, A*
Navarro College *C*
North Central Texas College *A*
North Harris Montgomery
　　Community College District *C, A*
Odessa College *C, A*
St. Philip's College *A*
San Antonio College *A*
San Jacinto College
　　North *A*
South Plains College *A*
South Texas College *A*
Stephen F. Austin State University *B*
Tarrant County College *A*
Texas A&M University
　　Commerce *B*
Texas State University: San Marcos *M*
Texas Wesleyan University *B*
Texas Woman's University *B*
Trinity Valley Community College *C, A*
Tyler Junior College *A*
University of Texas
　　Brownsville *C, A*
Vernon College *A*
Victoria College *C, A*

Utah

Everest College: Salt Lake City *A*
Salt Lake Community College *A*
Southern Utah University *A*
Utah Career College *A*
Utah Valley State College *A, B*

Vermont

Burlington College *C*
Champlain College *C, A, B*
Woodbury College *C, A, B*

Virginia

Blue Ridge Community College *C*
Central Virginia Community
　　College *C*
Germanna Community College *C*
Hampton University *C, B*
J. Sargeant Reynolds Community
　　College *A*
Marymount University *C, B, M*
Mountain Empire Community
　　College *A*
National College of Business &
　　Technology
　　Salem *A*
New River Community College *C, A*
Northern Virginia Community
　　College *A*
Parks College: Arlington *A*
Patrick Henry Community College *A*
Thomas Nelson Community
　　College *C*
Tidewater Community College *C, A*
Tidewater Tech *A*
University of Richmond *C, A*
Virginia Highlands Community
　　College *C*
Virginia Intermont College *B*
Virginia Western Community
　　College *A*

Washington

City University *C, A*
Clark College *C, A*
Columbia Basin College *C, A*
Crown College *A*
Edmonds Community College *C, A*
Highline Community College *A*

Lake Washington Technical
　　College *C, A*
Lower Columbia College *A*
Pierce College *A*
Renton Technical College *C, A*
Skagit Valley College *C, A*
South Puget Sound Community
　　College *C, A*
Spokane Community College *C, A*
Spokane Falls Community
　　College *C, A*
Whatcom Community College *A*

West Virginia

Bluefield State College *A*
Mountain State College *A*
Mountain State University *A*
West Virginia Business College *A*
West Virginia Business College *A*

Wisconsin

Carthage College *C*
Chippewa Valley Technical College *A*
College of Menominee Nation *A*
Fox Valley Technical College *A*
Lakeshore Technical College *A*
Milwaukee Area Technical College *A*
Northeast Wisconsin Technical
　　College *A*
University of Wisconsin
　　Superior *C*
Western Wisconsin Technical
　　College *A*

Wyoming

Casper College *C, A*
Laramie County Community
　　College *A*

Parasitology

Louisiana

Tulane University *M, D*

New York

New York University *M, D*

Pennsylvania

University of Pennsylvania *D*

Texas

Texas A&M University *M*

Parks, recreation, and leisure studies

Alabama

Community College of the Air
　　Force *A*
Huntingdon College *B*
Jacksonville State University *B*
University of North Alabama *B, M*
University of South Alabama *B*

Alaska

Sheldon Jackson College *B*
University of Alaska
　　Southeast *C*

Arizona

Arizona State University *B, M*
Arizona State University West *B*
Northern Arizona University *C, B*
Prescott College *B, M*

Arkansas

National Park Community College *A*
University of Arkansas *B*
University of Arkansas
　　Pine Bluff *B*

California

Allan Hancock College *A*
American River College *A*
Bakersfield College *A*
California State University
　　Chico *B, M*
　　East Bay *B*
　　Northridge *B, M*
　　Sacramento *B, M*
Cerritos Community College *A*
Chabot College *A*
College of the Desert *A*
Cypress College *A*
Fresno City College *A*
Fullerton College *A*
Glendale Community College *C, A*
Los Angeles Southwest College *A*
Los Angeles Valley College *A*
Merritt College *A*
Modesto Junior College *A*
Mount San Antonio College *A*
Palomar College *C, A*
Pasadena City College *A*
San Diego State University *B*
San Jose State University *B*
Santa Barbara City College *A*
Santa Monica College *C, A*
Santa Rosa Junior College *C, A*
Southwestern College *A*
Taft College *A*

Colorado

Colorado Mountain College
　　Timberline Campus *A*
Community College of Denver *C, A*
Metropolitan State College of
　　Denver *B*
Western State College of Colorado *B*

Connecticut

Northwestern Connecticut
　　Community College *A*
Norwalk Community College *C, A*
Southern Connecticut State
　　University *B, M*

District of Columbia

Gallaudet University *M*
Howard University *B*
University of the District of
　　Columbia *A, B*

Florida

Broward Community College *A*
Chipola College *A*
Gulf Coast Community College *A*
Okaloosa-Walton College *A*
Palm Beach Community College *A*

Georgia

Coastal Georgia Community
　　College *A*
Darton College *A*
East Georgia College *A*
Georgia College and State
　　University *B*
Georgia Southern University *B*
Middle Georgia College *A*
Savannah State University *B*
Shorter College *B*
South Georgia College *A*

Idaho

Brigham Young University-Idaho *B*
University of Idaho *B, M*

Illinois

Aurora University *B*
Greenville College *B*
Southern Illinois University
　　Carbondale *B, M*

University of Illinois
　　Urbana-Champaign *B, M, D*

Indiana

Franklin College *B*
Indiana University
　　Bloomington *B, M, D*
　　Southeast *A*
Vincennes University *A*

Iowa

Dordt College *B*
Graceland University *B*
University of Dubuque *B*
University of Iowa *B, M*
University of Northern Iowa *B, M, D*

Kansas

Central Christian College of Kansas *A*
Emporia State University *B*
Seward County Community College *A*
Tabor College *B*

Kentucky

Alice Lloyd College *B*
Campbellsville University *B*
Eastern Kentucky University *B*

Louisiana

Grambling State University *B*

Maine

University of Maine
　　Machias *B*
　　Presque Isle *A, B*
University of Southern Maine *B*

Maryland

Community College of Baltimore
　　County *C, A*
Frostburg State University *B, M*
Garrett College *C, A*
University of Maryland
　　Eastern Shore *B*

Massachusetts

American International College *B*
Bridgewater State College *B*
Cape Cod Community College *A*
Gordon College *B*
Salem State College *B*
Westfield State College *B*

Michigan

Aquinas College *B*
Calvin College *B*
Central Michigan University *B, T*
Grand Valley State University *B*
Michigan State University *B*
Northern Michigan University *B*
Olivet College *B, T*
Spring Arbor University *B*
University of Michigan *B*
Wayne State University *B, M*
Western Michigan University *B*

Minnesota

Anoka-Ramsey Community College *A*
Minnesota State University
　　Mankato *B*
Northland Community & Technical
　　College *A*
Ridgewater College *A*
University of Minnesota
　　Duluth *B*
　　Twin Cities *B, M*
Vermilion Community College *A*
Winona State University *B*

Mississippi

Alcorn State University *B*

University of Southern
Mississippi *B, M*

Missouri
Blue River Community College *C*
Central Missouri State University *B*
Missouri State University *B*
Northwest Missouri State
University *B*
Southeast Missouri State University *B*
Southwest Baptist University *B*
University of Missouri
Columbia *B, M*

Montana
University of Montana:Western *A*

Nebraska
Chadron State College *B*
University of Nebraska
Omaha *B*

Nevada
University of Nevada
Las Vegas *B*
Reno *B*

New Hampshire
New England College *B*
New Hampshire Community
Technical College
Claremont *A*
University of New Hampshire *B, M*

New Jersey
Thomas Edison State College *A, B*

New Mexico
San Juan College *C*
University of New Mexico *B, M, T*

New York
City University of New York
Kingsborough Community
College *A*
Dutchess Community College *A*
Houghton College *B*
Ithaca College *B, M*
Paul Smith's College *A, B*
St. Joseph's College: Suffolk
Campus *B*
State University of New York
College at Brockport *B, M*
College at Cortland *B*
College of Agriculture and
Technology at Morrisville *B*
Suffolk County Community College *A*
Ulster County Community College *A*

North Carolina
Carteret Community College *A*
Catawba College *B*
Louisburg College *A*
Montreat College *B*
Mount Olive College *A, B*
Shaw University *B*
Southwestern Community College *A*
University of North Carolina
Greensboro *B*
Vance-Granville Community
College *A*
Warren Wilson College *B*

North Dakota
North Dakota State University *B*

Ohio
Ashland University *B*
Bowling Green State University *B, M*
Central State University *B*
Malone College *B*
Ohio University *B*

University of Toledo *B, M*

Oklahoma
East Central University *B*
Oklahoma State University *B*
Southeastern Oklahoma State
University *B*
Southwestern Oklahoma State
University *B*
University of Central Oklahoma *B*

Oregon
Chemeketa Community College *A*
Oregon State University *B*

Pennsylvania
Butler County Community College *A*
Keystone College *B*
Marywood University *B*
Messiah College *B*
Penn State
Abington *B*
Altoona *B*
Beaver *B*
Berks *B*
Delaware County *B*
Dubois *B*
Fayette *B*
Hazleton *B*
Lehigh Valley *B*
McKeesport *B*
Mont Alto *B*
New Kensington *B*
Shenango *B*
University Park *M, D*
Wilkes-Barre *B*
Worthington Scranton *B*
York *B*
Temple University *M*
York College of Pennsylvania *B*

Puerto Rico
University of Puerto Rico
Carolina Regional College *A*

South Carolina
Erskine College *B*
Horry-Georgetown Technical
College *A*
Newberry College *B*
Southern Wesleyan University *B*

South Dakota
Black Hills State University *B*
South Dakota State University *B*
University of South Dakota *B*

Tennessee
Carson-Newman College *B*
Maryville College *B*
University of Tennessee
Knoxville *B, M*

Texas
Clarendon College *A*
Del Mar College *A*
Howard Payne University *B*
Texas A&M University *B, M, D*
Texas A&M University
Galveston *B*
Texas State University: San
Marcos *M, T*
University of Mary Hardin-Baylor *B*
University of North Texas *B, M*

Utah
Brigham Young University *B, M*
Snow College *A*
University of Utah *B, M, D*
Utah State University *B*

Vermont
Green Mountain College *B*
Johnson State College *B*
Sterling College *B*

Virginia
Ferrum College *B*
George Mason University *B*
Hampton University *B*
Radford University *B*
Tidewater Community College *A*
Virginia Commonwealth
University *B, M*
Virginia Wesleyan College *B*

Washington
Bellevue Community College *A*
Central Washington University *B*
Eastern Washington University *B*
Pacific Lutheran University *B*
Western Washington University *B*

West Virginia
Alderson-Broaddus College *B*
Concord University *B*
Shepherd University *B*

Wisconsin
Northland College *B*
University of Wisconsin
Milwaukee *B*
Parkside *C*

Wyoming
Western Wyoming Community
College *A*

Parks/recreational/
leisure facilities
management

Alabama
Alabama State University *B*
Enterprise-Ozark Community
College *A*
Faulkner State Community
College *C, A*
Wallace State Community College at
Hanceville *A*

Alaska
Alaska Pacific University *B, M*

Arizona
Northern Arizona University *B*
Prescott College *B, M*

Arkansas
Arkansas Tech University *B*
Henderson State University *B*
University of Arkansas *M, D*
University of Arkansas
Pine Bluff *B*

California
Butte College *C, A*
California Polytechnic State
University: San Luis Obispo *B*
California State University
Chico *B*
Dominguez Hills *B*
East Bay *B*
Fresno *A, B*
Long Beach *B, M*
Sacramento *B, M*
Cerro Coso Community College *C, A*
College of the Desert *A*
College of the Sequoias *A*
Fresno City College *A*
Humboldt State University *B*
Mount San Antonio College *A*

National University *B*
Palomar College *C, A*
Professional Golfers Career College *A*
San Francisco State University *B, M*
Santa Rosa Junior College *C*
Ventura College *C, A*
West Valley College *C, A*

Colorado
Colorado Mountain College
Alpine Campus *A*
Timberline Campus *A*
Colorado State University *B, M, D*
Colorado State University
Pueblo *B*
University of Northern Colorado *B*

Connecticut
Northwestern Connecticut
Community College *A*
University of Connecticut *B*

Delaware
Delaware State University *B*
University of Delaware *B*

District of Columbia
Gallaudet University *B*

Florida
Edison College *A*
Florida International University *B, M*
Florida State University *B, M*
Lake City Community College *A*
Lynn University *B, M*
Santa Fe Community College *A*
Tallahassee Community College *A*
University of Florida *B, M*
Webber International
University *A, B, M*

Georgia
Abraham Baldwin Agricultural
College *A*
Georgia Southern University *M*
Georgia Southwestern State
University *B*
Georgia State University *B*
South Georgia College *A*
University of West Georgia *B*

Hawaii
University of Hawaii
Hilo *B*

Idaho
Northwest Nazarene University *B*

Illinois
Aurora University *M*
Eastern Illinois University *B*
Illinois State University *B*
Moraine Valley Community College *A*
University of St. Francis *B*
Western Illinois University *B, M*
William Rainey Harper College *C, A*

Indiana
Bethel College *B*
Huntington University *B*
Indiana Institute of Technology *B*
Indiana State University *B*
Indiana University
Bloomington *B, M, D*
Southeast *A*
Indiana Wesleyan University *B*
Vincennes University *A*

Iowa
Iowa Lakes Community College *A*
University of Iowa *B, M*
University of Northern Iowa *M*

Upper Iowa University *B*

Kansas
Bethany College *B*
Central Christian College of
    Kansas *A, B*
Friends University *B*
Kansas State University *B*
Pittsburg State University *B*

Kentucky
Asbury College *B*
Eastern Kentucky University *B, M*
Murray State University *B, M*
Union College *B*
Western Kentucky University *B, M*

Louisiana
Grambling State University *M*

Maine
Husson College *B*
Unity College *B*
University of Maine *B, M*
University of Maine
    Farmington *C*
    Machias *B*

Maryland
Allegany College of Maryland *A*
Community College of Baltimore
    County *C, A*

Massachusetts
Greenfield Community College *C*
Springfield College *B, M*

Michigan
Bay de Noc Community College *C*
Central Michigan University *B, M, T*
Eastern Michigan University *B*
Ferris State University *B*
Gogebic Community College *A*
Lake Superior State University *B*
Lansing Community College *A*
Michigan State University *B, M, D*
Northern Michigan University *B*

Minnesota
Anoka Technical College *C, A*
Minnesota State University
    Mankato *B*
University of Minnesota
    Crookston *B*
Vermilion Community College *A*
Winona State University *B*

Mississippi
University of Mississippi *B, M*

Missouri
Central Methodist University *B*
Central Missouri State University *B*
College of the Ozarks *B*
Culver-Stockton College *B*
Hannibal-LaGrange College *B*
Missouri Valley College *B*
Missouri Western State University *B*

Montana
University of Montana: Missoula *B, M*

Nebraska
Hastings College *B*
University of Nebraska
    Kearney *B*

Nevada
Truckee Meadows Community
    College *A*

New Hampshire
Franklin Pierce College *B*
New England College *B*

New Jersey
Kean University *B*
Montclair State University *B*

New Mexico
New Mexico Highlands University *B*
New Mexico State University *B*

New York
Dutchess Community College *A*
Erie Community College
    South Campus *A*
Mohawk Valley Community College *A*
North Country Community College *A*
Onondaga Community College *A*
Orange County Community College *A*
Paul Smith's College *A, B*
St. Thomas Aquinas College *B*
State University of New York
    College at Brockport *B, M*
    College at Cortland *M*
    College of Agriculture and
        Technology at Cobleskill *A, B*
    College of Agriculture and
        Technology at Morrisville *A*
    College of Environmental Science
        and Forestry *B, M*
    College of Technology at Delhi *A, B*
Sullivan County Community
    College *A*
Tompkins-Cortland Community
    College *A*

North Carolina
Appalachian State University *B*
Brevard College *B*
Campbell University *B*
Central Piedmont Community
    College *A*
East Carolina University *B, M*
Elon University *B*
High Point University *B*
Louisburg College *A*
Mars Hill College *B*
Methodist College *B*
North Carolina Agricultural and
    Technical State University *B*
North Carolina Central
    University *B, M*
North Carolina State
    University *B, M, D*
Pfeiffer University *B*
Southeastern Community College *A*
University of North Carolina
    Chapel Hill *B, M*
    Greensboro *B, M*
    Pembroke *B*
    Wilmington *B*
Wayne Community College *A*
Western Carolina University *B*
Wingate University *B*

North Dakota
University of North Dakota *B*

Ohio
Ashland University *B*
Bluffton University *B*
Columbus State Community
    College *A*
Kent State University *B*
Ohio State University
    Columbus Campus *B*
University of Dayton *B*

Oklahoma
Eastern Oklahoma State College *A*
Oklahoma Baptist University *B*

Oral Roberts University *B*
Southwestern Oklahoma State
    University *B*

Oregon
Central Oregon Community
    College *A*

Pennsylvania
California University of
    Pennsylvania *B*
Cheyney University of Pennsylvania *B*
East Stroudsburg University of
    Pennsylvania *B*
Keystone College *A, B*
Lock Haven University of
    Pennsylvania *B*
Penn State
    Schuylkill - Capital College *B*
    University Park *B*
Slippery Rock University of
    Pennsylvania *B, M*
York College of Pennsylvania *B*

Puerto Rico
Inter American University of Puerto
    Rico
    Aguadilla Campus *B*
Universidad Metropolitana *M*
University of Puerto Rico
    Mayaguez *B*

Rhode Island
Johnson & Wales University *B*

South Carolina
Clemson University *B, M, D*
Horry-Georgetown Technical
    College *A*
Morris College *B*
Technical College of the
    Lowcountry *C*

South Dakota
Mount Marty College *B*
South Dakota State University *B*

Tennessee
Lambuth University *B*
Middle Tennessee State University *B*

Texas
Midwestern State University *B*
Stephen F. Austin State University *B*
Texas A&M University *B*
Texas State University: San
    Marcos *B, M, T*
Texas Wesleyan University *B*
University of North Texas *B, M*
Western Texas College *A*

Utah
Utah State University *B, M, D*

Vermont
Green Mountain College *B*
Lyndon State College *B*
Sterling College *B*

Virginia
Hampton University *B*
Northern Virginia Community
    College *A*
Old Dominion University *B, M*
Tidewater Community College *A*
Virginia Wesleyan College *B*

Washington
Eastern Washington University *B*
Skagit Valley College *C*
Spokane Community College *A*

Walla Walla Community College *C, A*
Washington State University *B*

West Virginia
Concord University *B*
Marshall University *B*
Potomac State College of West Virginia
    University *A*
West Virginia State University *B*
West Virginia University *B, M*

Wisconsin
Carroll College *B*
Fox Valley Technical College *A*
University of Wisconsin
    La Crosse *B, M*
    Madison *B*

Wyoming
Central Wyoming College *A*
Northwest College *A*
University of Wyoming *B*

Particle physics

Massachusetts
Tufts University *M, D*

Wisconsin
University of Wisconsin
    Madison *M, D*

Pastoral counseling

Alabama
Southeastern Bible College *A, B*
Southern Christian University *M, D*
Spring Hill College *M*
University of Mobile *M*

Arkansas
Harding University *M*
Ouachita Baptist University *B*

California
Biola University *M, D*
Holy Names University *M*
Loyola Marymount University *M*
Master's College *B, M*
Simpson University *B, M*
University of San Diego *C, M*
William Jessup University *B*

Colorado
Naropa University *M*
Nazarene Bible College *B*

Florida
Baptist College of Florida *B*
Barry University *M*
Florida Christian College *B*
St. Leo University *M*
Southeastern College of the
    Assemblies of God *B*
Trinity College of Florida *B*
Warner Southern College *C, A, B*

Georgia
Emmanuel College *B*
Emory University *D*
Toccoa Falls College *B*

Hawaii
Chaminade University of Honolulu *M*

Idaho
Boise Bible College *B*

Illinois
Greenville College *B*

Lewis University *M*
Lincoln Christian College and
    Seminary *M*
Loyola University of Chicago *M*
Moody Bible Institute *M*
North Park University *M*
Olivet Nazarene University *M*
Trinity International University *B, M*

Indiana
Huntington University *M*
Martin University *M*
Oakland City University *M*
St. Joseph's College *B*
St. Mary-of-the-Woods College *B, M*

Iowa
Loras College *M*
St. Ambrose University *M*
Vennard College *B*
Wartburg College *B*

Kansas
Barclay College *B*
Central Christian College of
    Kansas *A, B*
Manhattan Christian College *B*
Newman University *B*
Southwestern College *B*
University of St. Mary *B*

Kentucky
Brescia University *A, B*
Kentucky Christian University *B*

Louisiana
New Orleans School of Urban
    Missions *A*

Maryland
Loyola College in Maryland *M, D*
Washington Bible College *B*

Massachusetts
Anna Maria College *B, M*
Boston College *M*

Michigan
Andrews University *M, D*
Cornerstone University *B, M*
Grace Bible College *B*
Madonna University *B, M*
Marygrove College *M*

Minnesota
Crown College *B*
North Central University *B*
Pillsbury Baptist Bible College *B*
St. Mary's University of
    Minnesota *B, M*
University of St. Thomas *M*

Mississippi
Magnolia Bible College *B*
Wesley College *B*

Missouri
Baptist Bible College *B, M*
Calvary Bible College and Theological
    Seminary *B, M*
Central Christian College of the
    Bible *B*
Global University *B*
Lindenwood University *B*
Southwest Baptist University *B*

Montana
Carroll College *B*

Nebraska
Grace University *M*

Union College *B*

New Jersey
Seton Hall University *M*

New York
Iona College *M*
Roberts Wesleyan College *M*

North Carolina
Gardner-Webb University *M*
John Wesley College *B*
Roanoke Bible College *B*

Ohio
Ashland University *M, D*
Cedarville University *B*
Circleville Bible College *A, B*
College of Mount St. Joseph *B*
Malone College *B*
University of Dayton *M*

Oklahoma
Mid-America Christian University *B*
Oral Roberts University *B, M*
Southwestern Christian University *B*

Oregon
Corban College *B*
Eugene Bible College *B*
George Fox University *M*
Multnomah Bible College *B*

Pennsylvania
Duquesne University *M*
La Salle University *M*
Moravian College *M*
Neumann College *M*
Philadelphia Biblical University *B*
Valley Forge Christian College *B*

Puerto Rico
Bayamon Central University *M*

Rhode Island
Providence College *M*

South Carolina
Charleston Southern University *B*
Columbia International
    University *B, M*
Erskine College *M*

South Dakota
Mount Marty College *M*

Tennessee
American Baptist College of ABT
    Seminary *B*
Freed-Hardeman University *M*
Southern Adventist University *B*
Trevecca Nazarene University *M*

Texas
Abilene Christian University *B, M, D*
Arlington Baptist College *B*
Criswell College *B, M*
Dallas Baptist University *B*
East Texas Baptist University *B*
Hardin-Simmons University *M*
Houston Baptist University *B*
St. Mary's University *M*
Southwestern Assemblies of God
    University *B*
Texas Christian University *D*
University of Dallas *M*
University of Mary Hardin-Baylor *B*
University of St. Thomas *B, M*

Vermont
St. Michael's College *M*

Virginia
Liberty University *B, M, D*

Washington
Northwest University *B*
Seattle University *M*
University of Puget Sound *M*

Wisconsin
Concordia University Wisconsin *B*
Maranatha Baptist Bible College *B, M*

Pathology assistant

Connecticut
Quinnipiac University *M*

Illinois
Rosalind Franklin University of
    Medicine and Science *M*

Massachusetts
Boston University *M, D*

Michigan
Wayne State University *B*

New York
St. John's University *B*
State University of New York
    Farmingdale *C*

Pathology, human/ animal

Alabama
Auburn University *M*
University of Alabama
    Birmingham *D*

Arizona
University of Arizona *M, D*

Arkansas
University of Arkansas
    for Medical Sciences *M*

California
University of California
    Davis *M, D*
    Irvine *D*
    Los Angeles *M, D*
University of Southern
    California *M, D*

Colorado
University of Colorado
    Denver and Health Sciences
    Center *D*

Connecticut
University of Connecticut *B, M, D*
Yale University *M, D*

District of Columbia
Georgetown University *D*

Illinois
Rosalind Franklin University of
    Medicine and Science *M, D*
University of Chicago *D*

Indiana
Indiana University
    Bloomington *M, D*
Indiana University-Purdue University
    Indianapolis *M, D*

Kansas
Kansas State University *M, D*
University of Kansas Medical
    Center *M, D*

Louisiana
Louisiana State University Health
    Sciences Center *M, D*

Maine
University of Maine *B, M*

Maryland
University of Maryland
    Baltimore *M, D*

Massachusetts
Boston University *D*
Harvard College *D*
Tufts University *M, D*

Michigan
Michigan State University *M, D*
University of Michigan *M, D*
Wayne State University *D*

Mississippi
University of Mississippi Medical
    Center *M, D*

Missouri
St. Louis University *D*
University of Missouri
    Columbia *M, D*

Nebraska
University of Nebraska
    Medical Center *M, D*

New York
New York University *M, D*
State University of New York
    Buffalo *M, D*
    Stony Brook *D*
University of Rochester *M, D*
Yeshiva University *M, D*

North Carolina
Duke University *M, D*
East Carolina University *D*
University of North Carolina
    Chapel Hill *B, M, D*

North Dakota
North Dakota State University *D*

Ohio
Case Western Reserve University *D*
Ohio State University
    Columbus Campus *M, D*
University of Cincinnati *M, D*

Oklahoma
University of Oklahoma *M, D*

Pennsylvania
Drexel University *D*
Penn State
    University Park *M, D*
Temple University *D*
University of Pennsylvania *D*
University of Pittsburgh *M, D*

South Carolina
Medical University of South
    Carolina *M, D*

Tennessee
University of Tennessee
    Knoxville *M, D*

Vanderbilt University *M, D*

Texas
Texas A&M University *M, D*
University of Texas
El Paso *D*
Health Science Center at
Houston *M, D*
Medical Branch at Galveston *M, D*

Utah
University of Utah *B, M, D*

Vermont
University of Vermont *M*

Virginia
Virginia Commonwealth University *D*

Washington
University of Washington *M, D*

Wisconsin
University of Wisconsin
Madison *M, D*

Peace and conflict studies

Arizona
Prescott College *B, M*

California
California State University
San Bernardino *M*
Chapman University *B*
University of California
Berkeley *B*
University of San Diego *M*

Colorado
University of Denver *M*

District of Columbia
American University *M*
Georgetown University *B*

Florida
Nova Southeastern University *M, D*

Georgia
Kennesaw State University *M*
Middle Georgia College *T*

Indiana
DePauw University *B*
Earlham College *B*
Goshen College *B*
Manchester College *B*
University of Notre Dame *M*

Iowa
Clarke College *A, B*

Maryland
Goucher College *B*
Salisbury University *B*
University of Baltimore *M*

Massachusetts
Hampshire College *B*
Tufts University *B*
University of Massachusetts
Boston *M*
Wellesley College *B*

Michigan
Wayne State University *B, M*

Minnesota
Bethel University *B*
College of St. Benedict *B*
Hamline University *B, M*
St. John's University *B*
University of St. Thomas *B*

Missouri
University of Missouri
Columbia *B*

Nebraska
Creighton University *B*

New Jersey
Montclair State University *B*

New York
Colgate University *B*
Le Moyne College *B*
Manhattan College *B*
Molloy College *B*
Nazareth College of Rochester *B*

North Carolina
Guilford College *B*
University of North Carolina
Chapel Hill *B*

Ohio
Antioch College *B*
Antioch University McGregor *M*
Bluffton University *B*
Kent State University *B*
Ohio State University
Columbus Campus *B*

Oklahoma
Oklahoma Panhandle State
University *B*

Pennsylvania
Arcadia University *M*
Elizabethtown College *B, T*
Gettysburg College *B*
Juniata College *B*
La Salle University *B*

Vermont
Bennington College *B*
Goddard College *B*
Marlboro College *B*
Norwich University *B*
Woodbury College *M*

Virginia
Eastern Mennonite University *B, M*
George Mason University *D*

Washington
University of Washington *B*
Whitworth College *B*

Wisconsin
Northland College *B*

Pediatric nursing

Georgia
Medical College of Georgia *M*

Illinois
Loyola University of Chicago *M*

Indiana
Indiana University-Purdue University
Indianapolis *M*

Iowa
University of Iowa *M*

Maine
University of Southern Maine *B, M*

New York
City University of New York
Hunter College *B, M*
Lehman College *M*
Columbia University
School of Nursing *M*
State University of New York
Upstate Medical University *M*

Ohio
Case Western Reserve University *M*
Youngstown State University *M*

Pennsylvania
University of Pennsylvania *M*

South Carolina
Medical University of South
Carolina *M*

Wisconsin
Marquette University *M*

Perfusion technology

Connecticut
Quinnipiac University *C*

Illinois
Rush University *B*

Massachusetts
Northeastern University *M*

Nebraska
University of Nebraska
Medical Center *M*

New Jersey
Thomas Edison State College *B*

New York
State University of New York
Oswego *B*
Upstate Medical University *B*

Ohio
Ohio State University
Columbus Campus *B*

Pennsylvania
Drexel University *B*

South Carolina
Medical University of South
Carolina *B*

Wisconsin
Milwaukee School of Engineering *M*

Personal/culinary services

Alabama
Alabama Southern Community
College *A*

Arkansas
Northwest Arkansas Community
College *C*

California
Chabot College *A*
College of San Mateo *C, A*
MiraCosta College *C*
National Institute of Technology *C*

Florida
Florida College of Natural Health *C, B*
Florida College of Natural Health
Miami *C*
Florida Community College at
Jacksonville *C*
Hillsborough Community College *A*
Johnson & Wales University *A, B*
Manatee Community College *A*
Orlando Culinary Academy *A*
Palm Beach Community College *C*

Iowa
Northeast Iowa Community
College *A*

Maine
York County Community College *A*

Maryland
Allegany College of Maryland *A*

Michigan
Baker College
of Muskegon *A, B*
Southwestern Michigan College *C*

New Mexico
Northern New Mexico College *C*
Southwestern Indian Polytechnic
Institute *C, A*

North Carolina
Central Carolina Community
College *A*
College of the Albemarle *C*
Piedmont Community College *A*

Oregon
Central Oregon Community
College *C, A*

Pennsylvania
Allied Medical and Technical
Institute *C, A*
Bidwell Training Center *C*
Career Training Academy:
Monroeville *C*
Restaurant School *A*
Thiel College *B*

South Carolina
Denmark Technical College *C*
Forrest Junior College *A*

Texas
Art Institute
of Houston *A*
South Texas College *A*

Washington
Seattle Central Community
College *C, A*

West Virginia
Potomac State College of West Virginia
University *A*

Wyoming
Sheridan College *C, A*

Personal/financial services marketing

Kansas
Hutchinson Community College *A*

Michigan
Kirtland Community College *C*

New York
Mohawk Valley Community College *C*

Texas
University of Houston *B*

Personality psychology

District of Columbia
Catholic University of America *D*

Massachusetts
Clark University *M, D*

New York
State University of New York
   Albany *D*

Petroleum engineering

Alaska
University of Alaska
   Fairbanks *B, M*

California
Stanford University *B, M, D*
University of Southern
   California *B, M, D*

Colorado
Colorado School of Mines *B, M, D*

Kansas
University of Kansas *B, M, D*

Louisiana
Louisiana State University and
   Agricultural and Mechanical
   College *B, M, D*
University of Louisiana at Lafayette *B*

Michigan
Wayne State University *M*

Missouri
East Central College *A*
University of Missouri
   Rolla *B, M, D*

Montana
Montana Tech of the University of
   Montana *B, M*

New Mexico
New Mexico Institute of Mining and
   Technology *B, M, D*

Ohio
Marietta College *B*

Oklahoma
University of Oklahoma *B, M, D*
University of Tulsa *B, M, D*

Pennsylvania
Penn State
   Abington *B*
   Altoona *B*
   Beaver *B*
   Berks *B*
   Delaware County *B*
   Dubois *B*
   Fayette *B*
   Hazleton *B*
   Lehigh Valley *B*
   McKeesport *B*
   Mont Alto *B*
   New Kensington *B*
   Schuylkill - Capital College *B*
   Shenango *B*

   University Park *B, M, D*
   Wilkes-Barre *B*
   Worthington Scranton *B*
   York *B*
University of Pittsburgh *M*

Texas
Laredo Community College *A*
Midland College *A*
Texas A&M University *B, M, D*
Texas A&M University
   Kingsville *B, M*
Texas Tech University *B, M, D*
University of Houston *M*
University of Texas
   Austin *B, M, D*

Utah
University of Utah *B, M, D*

West Virginia
West Virginia University *B, M, D*

Wyoming
University of Wyoming *M, D*

Petroleum technology

California
Taft College *C, A*

Louisiana
Nicholls State University *A, B*

Montana
Montana State University
   Billings *A*

Texas
Odessa College *C, A*

Pharmacology

Alabama
Auburn University *M*

Arizona
University of Arizona *M, D*

Arkansas
University of Arkansas
   for Medical Sciences *M, D*

California
Loma Linda University *M, D*
Stanford University *M, D*
University of California
   Santa Barbara *B*

Colorado
University of Colorado
   Denver and Health Sciences
   Center *D*

Connecticut
Yale University *M, D*

District of Columbia
George Washington
   University *B, M, D*
Georgetown University *D*
Howard University *M, D*

Florida
University of Miami *D*

Georgia
Medical College of Georgia *M, D*

Illinois
Loyola University of Chicago *M, D*
Rush University *M, D*
Southern Illinois University
   Carbondale *M, D*
University of Chicago *D*
University of Illinois
   Chicago *M, D*

Indiana
Indiana University
   Bloomington *M, D*
Indiana University-Purdue University
   Indianapolis *M, D*

Iowa
Drake University *B, M*
University of Iowa *M, D*

Kansas
University of Kansas Medical
   Center *M, D*

Kentucky
University of Kentucky *D*

Louisiana
Louisiana State University Health
   Sciences Center *M, D*
Tulane University *M, D*

Maryland
University of Maryland
   Baltimore *M, D*

Massachusetts
Boston University *M, D*
Harvard College *D*
Massachusetts College of Pharmacy
   and Health Sciences *M, D*
Tufts University *M*

Michigan
University of Michigan *M, D*
Wayne State University *M, D*

Minnesota
University of Minnesota
   Duluth *M*
   Twin Cities *M, D*

Mississippi
University of Mississippi Medical
   Center *M, D*

Missouri
St. Louis University *D*
University of Missouri
   Columbia *M, D*

Montana
University of Montana: Missoula *D*

Nebraska
Creighton University *M, D*
University of Nebraska
   Medical Center *M, D*

Nevada
University of Nevada
   Reno *M, D*

New Hampshire
Dartmouth College *M, D*

New York
City University of New York
   Hunter College *B, M*
Cornell University *M, D*

Long Island University
   Brooklyn Campus *M*
New York University *M, D*
State University of New York
   Buffalo *M, D*
   Downstate Medical Center *D*
   Stony Brook *B*
   Upstate Medical University *D*
University of Rochester *M, D*
Yeshiva University *M, D*

North Carolina
University of North Carolina
   Chapel Hill *M, D*
Wake Forest University *D*

North Dakota
University of North Dakota *M, D*

Ohio
Case Western Reserve University *D*
Kent State University *M, D*
Ohio State University
   Columbus Campus *M, D*
University of Cincinnati *D*

Pennsylvania
Drexel University *M, D*
Temple University *M, D*
University of Pennsylvania *M, D*
University of the Sciences in
   Philadelphia *B, M, D*

South Carolina
Medical University of South
   Carolina *D*

Tennessee
University of Tennessee
   Knoxville *M, D*
Vanderbilt University *D*

Texas
Texas A&M University *M, D*
University of Texas
   Health Science Center at
     Houston *M, D*
   Health Science Center at San
     Antonio *M, D*

Utah
Snow College *A*

Vermont
University of Vermont *M, D*

Virginia
University of Virginia *D*
Virginia Commonwealth
   University *M, D*

Washington
University of Washington *M, D*

Wisconsin
University of Wisconsin
   Madison *D*

Pharmacology/ toxicology

Alabama
University of Alabama
   Birmingham *D*

California
University of California
   Davis *M, D*
   Irvine *M, D*

University of Southern
   California *M, D*

Kansas

University of Kansas *M, D*

Kentucky

University of Louisville *M, D*

Ohio

Wright State University *B*

Pennsylvania

Duquesne University *M, D*

Texas

University of Texas
   Health Science Center at
      Houston *M, D*
   Medical Branch at Galveston *M, D*

West Virginia

West Virginia University *M, D*

Wisconsin

University of Wisconsin
   Madison *B*

Pharmacy

Alabama

Auburn University: School of
   Pharmacy *F*
Samford University: McWhorter
   School of Pharmacy *F*

Arizona

University of Arizona: College of
   Pharmacy *F*

Arkansas

University of Arkansas for Medical
   Sciences: College of Pharmacy *F*

California

University of California San Francisco:
   School of Pharmacy *F*
University of Southern California:
   School of Pharmacy *F*
University of the Pacific: School of
   Pharmacy *F*

Colorado

University of Colorado Health
   Sciences Center: College of
   Pharmacy *F*

Connecticut

University of Connecticut: School of
   Pharmacy *F*

District of Columbia

Howard University: School of
   Pharmacy *F*

Florida

Florida Agricultural and Mechanical
   University: School of Pharmacy *F*
Nova Southeastern University of the
   Health Sciences: College of
   Pharmacy *F*
University of Florida: College of
   Pharmacy *F*

Georgia

Mercer University Southern School of
   Pharmacy *F*
University of Georgia: College of
   Pharmacy *F*

Idaho

Idaho State University: College of
   Pharmacy *F*

Illinois

Midwestern University: Chicago
   College of Pharmacy *F*
University of Illinois at Chicago:
   College of Pharmacy *F*

Indiana

Butler University: College of
   Pharmacy *F*
Purdue University: School of
   Pharmacy *F*

Iowa

Drake University: College of
   Pharmacy *F*
University of Iowa: College of
   Pharmacy *F*

Louisiana

Northeast Louisiana University School
   of Pharmacy *F*
Xavier University of Louisiana: College
   of Pharmacy *F*

Maryland

University of Maryland at Baltimore:
   School of Pharmacy *F*

Massachusetts

Massachusetts College of Pharmacy
   and Allied Health Sciences:
   School of Pharmacy *F*
Northeastern University: Bouve
   College of Pharmacy and Health
   Sciences *F*

Michigan

Ferris State University College of
   Pharmacy *F*
University of Michigan: College of
   Pharmacy *F*
Wayne State University: College of
   Pharmacy and Allied Health *F*

Mississippi

University of Mississippi: School of
   Pharmacy *F*

Missouri

St. Louis College of Pharmacy *F*

Montana

University of Montana School of
   Pharmacy and Allied Health
   Sciences *F*

Nebraska

University of Nebraska Medical
   Center: College of Pharmacy *F*

New Jersey

Rutgers, The State University of New
   Jersey
   College of Pharmacy *F*

New Mexico

University of New Mexico College of
   Pharmacy *F*

New York

Long Island University: Arnold and
   Marie Schwartz College of
   Pharmacy and Health Sciences *F*
St. John's University: College of
   Pharmacy and Allied Health
   Professions *F*

State University of New York at
   Buffalo: School of Pharmacy *F*

North Carolina

Campbell University: School of
   Pharmacy *F*
University of North Carolina at Chapel
   Hill: School of Pharmacy *F*

North Dakota

North Dakota State University: College
   of Pharmacy *F*

Ohio

Ohio Northern University: College of
   Pharmacy *F*
Ohio State University Columbus
   Campus: College of Pharmacy *F*
University of Cincinnati: College of
   Pharmacy *F*
University of Toledo: College of
   Pharmacy *F*

Oklahoma

Southwestern Oklahoma State
   University School of Pharmacy *F*
University of Oklahoma College of
   Pharmacy *F*

Oregon

Oregon State University: College of
   Pharmacy *F*

Pennsylvania

Philadelphia College of Pharmacy and
   Science: School of Pharmacy *F*
Temple University: School of
   Pharmacy *F*
University of Pittsburgh: School of
   Pharmacy *F*

Puerto Rico

University of Puerto Rico Medical
   Sciences Campus: School of
   Pharmacy *F*

Rhode Island

University of Rhode Island: College of
   Pharmacy *F*

South Carolina

Medical University of South Carolina:
   College of Pharmacy *F*
University of South Carolina: School of
   Pharmacy *F*

South Dakota

South Dakota State University: College
   of Pharmacy *F*

Tennessee

University of Tennessee Memphis:
   College of Pharmacy *F*

Texas

Texas Southern University: College of
   Pharmacy and Health Sciences *F*
University of Houston: College of
   Pharmacy *F*
University of Texas at Austin: College
   of Pharmacy *F*

Utah

University of Utah: College of
   Pharmacy *F*

Washington

Washington State University: College
   of Pharmacy *F*

West Virginia

West Virginia University: School of
   Pharmacy *F*

Wisconsin

University of Wisconsin Madison:
   School of Pharmacy *F*

Wyoming

University of Wyoming: School of
   Pharmacy *F*

Pharmacy assistant

Alabama

Community College of the Air
   Force *A*
Virginia College *A*
Virginia College at Huntsville *C, A*

Arizona

Central Arizona College *A*
Eastern Arizona College *C, A*
Pima Community College *C, A*

Arkansas

Remington College
   Little Rock *C*

California

Charles R. Drew University of
   Medicine and Science *A*
Foothill College *C, A*
Imperial Valley College *C*
Maric College
   Vista *C*
National University *C*
San Joaquin Valley College Inc. *A*
Santa Barbara Business College *C, A*
Santa Barbara Business College
   Bakersfield *C, A*
   Santa Maria *C, A*
Santa Barbara Business College:
   Ventura *C, A*
Santa Rosa Junior College *C, A*
Silicon Valley College
   Western Career College:
      Emeryville *A*
   Western Career College: San Jose *A*
Western Career College
   San Leandro *A*

Colorado

Arapahoe Community College *C*
Front Range Community College *C*
Heritage College *C*
Otero Junior College *A*
Pikes Peak Community College *C*
Remington College
   Colorado Springs *C*

Connecticut

Gateway Community College *C, A*
Manchester Community College *A*

Florida

Florida Metropolitan University
   Brandon Campus *A*
Remington College: Largo *C*
Southwest Florida College *A*
Southwest Florida College
   Tampa *A*

Georgia

Albany Technical College *C, A*
Augusta Technical Institute *C, A*
Central Georgia Technical College *C*
Macon State College *A*
Middle Georgia College *A*
Northwestern Technical College *C, A*

Southwest Georgia Technical
    College C, A
West Georgia Technical College C, A

Idaho
College of Southern Idaho A
North Idaho College A

Illinois
City Colleges of Chicago
    Malcolm X College C
Richland Community College C
Rock Valley College C
South Suburban College of Cook
    County C, A

Indiana
Vincennes University A

Iowa
Clinton Community College C
Indian Hills Community College C
Muscatine Community College C
Scott Community College C, A

Kansas
Labette Community College C

Kentucky
Daymar College A
National College of Business &
    Technology
    Florence C
    Richmond C

Louisiana
Bossier Parish Community
    College C, A
Delgado Community College C
Louisiana State University
    Alexandria C

Maryland
Allegany College of Maryland C
Anne Arundel Community College A

Massachusetts
Benjamin Franklin Institute of
    Technology C
Holyoke Community College C, A
Mount Ida College A
North Shore Community College C

Michigan
Baker College
    of Flint C, A
    of Jackson C, A
    of Muskegon C, A
Bay de Noc Community College C
Delta College A
Henry Ford Community College C
Kirtland Community College C
Oakland Community College C, A
St. Clair County Community
    College C
Southwestern Michigan College C
Washtenaw Community College C
Wayne County Community
    College C, A

Minnesota
Century Community and Technical
    College C, A
Minnesota State Community and
    Technical College - Fergus
    Falls C, A
Northland Community & Technical
    College A

Missouri
Vatterott College: Springfield C, A

Montana
University of Montana: Missoula C

Nebraska
Vatterott College: Spring Valley C, A

Nevada
High-Tech Institute A

New Jersey
County College of Morris C
Middlesex County College A

New Mexico
Albuquerque Technical-Vocational
    Institute C
Eastern New Mexico University:
    Roswell Campus C

New York
ASA Institute of Business and
    Computer Technology A

North Carolina
Cape Fear Community College C
Davidson County Community
    College C
Durham Technical Community
    College C
Southeastern Community College C

North Dakota
North Dakota State College of
    Science C, A

Ohio
AEC Southern Ohio College
    Brown Mackie College: Akron A
Cuyahoga Community College
    Metropolitan Campus C, A
Ohio Institute of Photography and
    Technology C
Remington College
    Cleveland C
Sinclair Community College C
Technology Education College C, A
University of Northwestern Ohio C, A

Oklahoma
Platt College
    Tulsa C

Oregon
Everest College: Portland A
Linn-Benton Community College C
Pioneer Pacific College C
Pioneer Pacific College: Springfield C

Pennsylvania
Bidwell Training Center C
Community College of Allegheny
    County C, A
Johnson College A
Western School of Health and
    Business Careers
    Monroeville A

Puerto Rico
Electronic Data Processing College:
    San Sebastian C
Humacao Community College A
Inter American University of Puerto
    Rico
    Aguadilla Campus C, A
    Guayama Campus A
    Ponce Campus C
    San German Campus C
National College of Business &
    Technology: Arecibo A
National College of Business &
    Technology: Bayamon A

Universidad del Este A

South Carolina
Aiken Technical College C
Central Carolina Technical College C
Greenville Technical College C
Horry-Georgetown Technical
    College A
Midlands Technical College C, A
Piedmont Technical College C
Spartanburg Technical College C
Tri-County Technical College C
Trident Technical College C

South Dakota
Western Dakota Technical Institute C

Tennessee
National College of Business &
    Technology
    Tennessee C
Roane State Community College C
Southwest Tennessee Community
    College C
Walters State Community College C

Texas
Amarillo College C
Angelina College C
Austin Community College C
El Paso Community College C
Houston Community College
    System C
Lamar State College at Orange C
North Harris Montgomery
    Community College District C, A
Northwest Vista College C
San Jacinto College
    North C
South Texas College C, A
Tarrant County College C

Utah
Salt Lake Community College C
Utah Career College C, A

Vermont
Vermont Technical College C, A

Virginia
J. Sargeant Reynolds Community
    College C
Miller-Motte Technical College:
    Lynchburg A
Mountain Empire Community
    College C
National College of Business &
    Technology
    Salem C
Southwest Virginia Community
    College C
Virginia Western Community
    College C
Wytheville Community College C

Washington
Clark College C
Clover Park Technical College C
Edmonds Community College C
Grays Harbor College C
North Seattle Community
    College C, A
Renton Technical College C, A
Spokane Community College C, A
Spokane Falls Community College C
Yakima Valley Community College C

Wisconsin
Lakeshore Technical College C
Madison Area Technical College C
Mid-State Technical College C
Milwaukee Area Technical College C

Wyoming
Casper College C, A

Philosophy

Alabama
Auburn University B
Birmingham-Southern College B
Samford University B
Spring Hill College B
University of Alabama B
University of Alabama
    Birmingham B
    Huntsville B
University of South Alabama B

Alaska
University of Alaska
    Fairbanks B

Arizona
Arizona State University B, M, D
Arizona Western College A
Northern Arizona University B
Prescott College M
University of Arizona B, M, D

Arkansas
Arkansas State University B
Hendrix College B
Lyon College B
Ouachita Baptist University B
Philander Smith College B
University of Arkansas B, M, D
University of Arkansas
    Little Rock B
University of Central Arkansas B

California
Azusa Pacific University B
Bakersfield College A
Biola University B, M, D
California Baptist University B
California Institute of Integral
    Studies M, D
California Lutheran University B
California State Polytechnic
    University: Pomona B
California State University
    Bakersfield B
    Chico B
    Dominguez Hills B
    East Bay B
    Fresno B
    Fullerton B
    Long Beach B, M
    Los Angeles B, M
    Northridge B
    Sacramento B
    San Bernardino B
    Stanislaus B
Canada College A
Cerritos Community College A
Chabot College A
Chaffey College A
Chapman University B
Claremont McKenna College B
College of Alameda A
College of the Desert A
Copper Mountain College A
Cypress College A
De Anza College A
Dominican School of Philosophy and
    Theology B, M
East Los Angeles College A
El Camino College A
Foothill College A
Fresno Pacific University B
Fullerton College A
Gavilan Community College A
Glendale Community College A
Golden West College A
Grossmont Community College A

Holy Names University *B*
Humboldt State University *B*
Irvine Valley College *A*
Los Angeles Mission College *A*
Los Angeles Southwest College *A*
Los Angeles Valley College *A*
Loyola Marymount University *B*
Merced College *A*
Mills College *B*
MiraCosta College *A*
Monterey Peninsula College *A*
Mount St. Mary's College *B*
Notre Dame de Namur University *B*
Occidental College *B*
Orange Coast College *A*
Pepperdine University *B*
Pitzer College *B*
Point Loma Nazarene University *B*
Pomona College *B*
Saddleback College *A*
St. Mary's College of California *B*
San Diego City College *B*
San Diego Mesa College *A*
San Diego Miramar College *A*
San Diego State University *B, M*
San Francisco State University *B, M*
San Jose State University *B, M*
Santa Ana College *A*
Santa Barbara City College *A*
Santa Clara University *B*
Santiago Canyon College *A*
Scripps College *B*
Sierra College *A*
Sonoma State University *B*
Southwestern College *A*
Stanford University *B, M, D*
University of California
    Berkeley *B, D*
    Davis *B, M, D*
    Irvine *B, M, D*
    Los Angeles *B, M, D*
    Riverside *B, M, D*
    San Diego *B, M, D*
    Santa Barbara *B, M, D*
    Santa Cruz *B, M, D*
University of La Verne *B*
University of Redlands *B*
University of San Diego *B*
University of San Francisco *B*
University of Southern
    California *B, M, D*
University of the Pacific *B*
Ventura College *A*
West Los Angeles College *A*
Westmont College *B*
Whittier College *B*

Colorado

Colorado College *B*
Colorado State University *B, M*
Fort Lewis College *B*
Metropolitan State College of
    Denver *B*
Regis University *B*
Trinidad State Junior College *A*
University of Colorado
    Boulder *B, M, D*
    Colorado Springs *B*
    Denver and Health Sciences
        Center *B*
University of Denver *B, M*
University of Northern Colorado *B*

Connecticut

Albertus Magnus College *B*
Central Connecticut State
    University *B*
Connecticut College *B*
Fairfield University *B*
Holy Apostles College and
    Seminary *B, M*
Sacred Heart University *B*
St. Joseph College *B, T*

Southern Connecticut State
    University *B*
Trinity College *B*
University of Connecticut *B, M, D*
University of Hartford *B*
Wesleyan University *B*
Yale University *B, M, D*

Delaware

University of Delaware *B*

District of Columbia

American University *B, M*
Catholic University of
    America *B, M, D*
Gallaudet University *B*
George Washington University *B*
Georgetown University *B, M, D*
Howard University *B, M*
University of the District of
    Columbia *A, B*

Florida

Barry University *B*
Eckerd College *B*
Flagler College *B*
Florida Agricultural and Mechanical
    University *B*
Florida Atlantic University *B*
Florida Christian College *B*
Florida International University *B*
Florida Southern College *B*
Florida State University *B, M, D*
Gulf Coast Community College *A*
Indian River Community College *A*
Jacksonville University *B*
Manatee Community College *A*
Miami Dade College *A*
New College of Florida *B*
Palm Beach Atlantic University *B*
Palm Beach Community College *A*
Pensacola Junior College *A*
Rollins College *B*
St. John Vianney College Seminary *B*
Stetson University *B*
University of Central Florida *B*
University of Florida *B, M, D*
University of Miami *B, M, D*
University of North Florida *B*
University of South Florida *B, M, D*
University of Tampa *A*
University of West Florida *B*
Valencia Community College *A*

Georgia

Agnes Scott College *B*
Clark Atlanta University *B*
Covenant College *B*
Dalton State College *A*
Darton College *A*
Emory University *B, D*
Georgia Perimeter College *A*
Georgia Southern University *B*
Georgia State University *B, M*
Mercer University *B*
Morehouse College *B*
Oglethorpe University *B*
Paine College *B*
Piedmont College *B*
South Georgia College *A*
Spelman College *B*
University of Georgia *B, M, D*
University of West Georgia *B*
Valdosta State University *B*
Wesleyan College *B*

Hawaii

University of Hawaii
    Hilo *B*
    Manoa *B, M, D*
    West Oahu *B*

Idaho

Albertson College of Idaho *B*
Boise State University *B*
Idaho State University *B*
North Idaho College *A*
Northwest Nazarene University *B*
University of Idaho *B*

Illinois

Augustana College *B*
Benedictine University *B*
Bradley University *B*
City Colleges of Chicago
    Harold Washington College *A*
    Olive-Harvey College *A*
Concordia University *B*
DePaul University *B, M, D*
Dominican University *B*
Eastern Illinois University *B*
Elmhurst College *B*
Eureka College *B*
Greenville College *B*
Illinois College *B*
Illinois State University *B*
Illinois Wesleyan University *B*
Judson College *B*
Knox College *B*
Lake Forest College *B*
Lewis University *B*
Loyola University of
    Chicago *C, B, M, D*
MacMurray College *B*
McKendree College *B*
Millikin University *B*
North Central College *B*
North Park University *B*
Northeastern Illinois University *B*
Northern Illinois University *B, M*
Northwestern University *B, M, D*
Principia College *B*
Richland Community College *A*
Rockford College *B*
Roosevelt University *B*
St. Xavier University *B*
Sauk Valley Community College *A*
South Suburban College of Cook
    County *A*
Southern Illinois University
    Carbondale *B, M, D*
Southern Illinois University
    Edwardsville *B*
Southwestern Illinois College *A*
Trinity Christian College *B*
Trinity International University *B, M*
Triton College *A*
University of Chicago *B, D*
University of Illinois
    Chicago *B, M, D*
    Springfield *B*
    Urbana-Champaign *B, M, D*
Western Illinois University *B*
Wheaton College *B*
William Rainey Harper College *A*

Indiana

Anderson University *B*
Ball State University *B*
Bethel College *B*
Butler University *B*
DePauw University *B*
Earlham College *B*
Franklin College *B*
Hanover College *B*
Huntington University *B*
Indiana State University *B*
Indiana University
    Bloomington *B, M, D*
    Northwest *B*
    South Bend *B*
    Southeast *B*
Indiana University-Purdue University
    Fort Wayne *B*
Indiana University-Purdue University
    Indianapolis *B, M*

Indiana Wesleyan University *A, B*
Manchester College *B*
Marian College *B*
Purdue University *B, M, D*
Purdue University
    Calumet *B*
St. Joseph's College *B*
Saint Mary's College *B*
Taylor University *B*
University of Evansville *B*
University of Indianapolis *B*
University of Notre Dame *B, M, D*
University of Southern Indiana *B*
Valparaiso University *B*
Vincennes University *A*
Wabash College *B*

Iowa

Central College *B*
Clarke College *A, B*
Coe College *B*
Cornell College *B*
Divine Word College *B*
Dordt College *B*
Drake University *B*
Grinnell College *B*
Iowa State University *B*
Iowa Wesleyan College *B*
Loras College *B*
Luther College *B*
Morningside College *B*
Mount Mercy College *B*
Northwestern College *B*
St. Ambrose University *B*
Simpson College *B*
University of Dubuque *B*
University of Iowa *B, M, D*
University of Northern Iowa *B*
Wartburg College *B*

Kansas

Baker University *B*
Barton County Community College *A*
Benedictine College *B*
Fort Hays State University *B*
Kansas State University *B*
Tabor College *B*
University of Kansas *B, M, D*
Washburn University of Topeka *B*
Wichita State University *B*

Kentucky

Asbury College *B*
Bellarmine University *B*
Berea College *B*
Centre College *B*
Eastern Kentucky University *B*
Georgetown College *B*
Morehead State University *B*
Murray State University *B*
Northern Kentucky University *B*
Thomas More College *A, B*
Transylvania University *B*
University of Kentucky *B, M, D*
University of Louisville *B*
Western Kentucky University *B*

Louisiana

Centenary College of Louisiana *B*
Louisiana State University and
    Agricultural and Mechanical
    College *B, M*
Loyola University New Orleans *B*
Tulane University *B*
University of Louisiana at Lafayette *B*
University of New Orleans *B*
Xavier University of Louisiana *B*

Maine

Bates College *B*
Bowdoin College *B*
Colby College *B*
College of the Atlantic *M*

St. Joseph's College *B*
University of Maine *B*
University of Southern Maine *B*

Maryland
College of Notre Dame of Maryland *B*
College of Southern Maryland *A*
Community College of Baltimore
   County *A*
Frederick Community College *A*
Frostburg State University *B*
Goucher College *B*
Harford Community College *A*
Hood College *B*
Johns Hopkins University *B, M, D*
Loyola College in Maryland *B*
McDaniel College *B*
Mount St. Mary's University *B*
St. Mary's College of Maryland *B*
Salisbury University *B*
University of Maryland
   Baltimore County *B*
   College Park *B, M, D*
Washington College *B*

Massachusetts
American International College *B*
Amherst College *B*
Assumption College *B*
Bentley College *B*
Boston College *B, M, D*
Boston University *B, M, D*
Brandeis University *B*
Bridgewater State College *B*
Cape Cod Community College *A*
Clark University *B*
College of the Holy Cross *B*
Curry College *B*
Gordon College *B*
Hampshire College *B*
Harvard College *B, D*
Massachusetts College of Liberal
   Arts *B*
Massachusetts Institute of
   Technology *B, D*
Merrimack College *B*
Mount Holyoke College *B*
Northeastern University *B*
St. John's Seminary College *B*
Simmons College *B*
Simon's Rock College of Bard *B*
Smith College *B, D*
Stonehill College *B*
Suffolk University *B*
Tufts University *B, M*
University of Massachusetts
   Amherst *B, M, D*
   Boston *B*
   Dartmouth *B*
   Lowell *B*
Wellesley College *B*
Western New England College *B*
Wheaton College *B*
Williams College *B*

Michigan
Adrian College *B*
Albion College *B*
Alma College *B*
Aquinas College *B*
Calvin College *B*
Central Michigan University *B, T*
Concordia University *B*
Cornerstone University *B*
Eastern Michigan University *B*
Grand Valley State University *B*
Hillsdale College *B*
Hope College *B*
Kalamazoo College *B*
Kellogg Community College *A*
Lake Michigan College *A*
Lansing Community College *A*
Madonna University *B*
Michigan State University *B, M, D*

Northern Michigan University *B*
Oakland University *B*
Sacred Heart Major Seminary *B*
Sacred Heart Major Seminary *B*
Siena Heights University *B*
Spring Arbor University *B*
University of Detroit Mercy *B*
University of Michigan *B, M, D*
University of Michigan
   Dearborn *B*
   Flint *B*
Wayne State University *B, M, D*
Western Michigan University *B, M*

Minnesota
Augsburg College *B*
Bemidji State University *B*
Bethel University *B*
Carleton College *B*
College of St. Benedict *B*
College of St. Catherine *B*
Concordia College: Moorhead *B*
Gustavus Adolphus College *B*
Hamline University *B*
Macalester College *B*
Metropolitan State University *B*
Minnesota State University
   Mankato *B*
   Moorhead *B*
St. Cloud State University *B*
St. John's University *B*
St. Mary's University of Minnesota *B*
St. Olaf College *B*
Southwest Minnesota State
   University *B*
University of Minnesota
   Duluth *B*
   Morris *B*
   Twin Cities *B, M, D*
University of St. Thomas *B, M*
Winona State University *A*

Mississippi
Belhaven College *B*
Itawamba Community College *A*
Millsaps College *B*
Mississippi State University *B*
University of Mississippi *B, M*
University of Southern
   Mississippi *B, M*

Missouri
Central Methodist University *B*
College of the Ozarks *B*
Columbia College *B*
Drury University *B*
Lindenwood University *B*
Missouri State University *B*
Northwest Missouri State
   University *B*
Rockhurst University *B*
St. Louis University *B, M, D*
Southeast Missouri State University *B*
Three Rivers Community College *A*
University of Missouri
   Columbia *B, M, D*
   Kansas City *B*
   Rolla *B*
   St. Louis *B, M*
Washington University in St.
   Louis *B, M, D*
Webster University *B*
Westminster College *B*
William Jewell College *B*

Montana
Carroll College *B*
Montana State University
   Bozeman *B*
University of Montana: Missoula *B, M*

Nebraska
Creighton University *B*

Doane College *B*
Hastings College *B*
Nebraska Wesleyan University *B*
University of Nebraska
   Lincoln *B, M, D*
   Omaha *B*

Nevada
University of Nevada
   Las Vegas *B*
   Reno *B, M*

New Hampshire
Dartmouth College *B*
Keene State College *B*
New England College *B*
Plymouth State University *B*
St. Anselm College *B*
Thomas More College of Liberal
   Arts *B*
University of New Hampshire *B*

New Jersey
Bloomfield College *B*
The College of New Jersey *B*
College of St. Elizabeth *B*
Drew University *B*
Fairleigh Dickinson University
   College at Florham *B*
   Metropolitan Campus *B*
Felician College *B*
Montclair State University *B*
New Jersey City University *B*
Princeton University *B, M, D*
Richard Stockton College of New
   Jersey *B*
Rowan University *B*
Rutgers, The State University of New
   Jersey
   Camden Regional Campus *B*
   New Brunswick/Piscataway
     Campus *B, M, D*
   Newark Regional Campus *B*
St. Peter's College *B*
Seton Hall University *B*
Thomas Edison State College *B*
William Paterson University of New
   Jersey *B*

New Mexico
New Mexico State University *B*
San Juan College *A*
University of New Mexico *B, M, D*

New York
Adelphi University *B*
Alfred University *B*
Bard College *B*
Barnard College *B*
Canisius College *B*
City University of New York
   Baruch College *B*
   Brooklyn College *B*
   City College *B*
   College of Staten Island *B*
   Hunter College *B*
   Lehman College *B*
   Queens College *B, M*
   York College *B*
Colgate University *B*
College of Mount St. Vincent *B*
College of New Rochelle *B*
Columbia University
   Columbia College *B*
   School of General Studies *B*
Cornell University *B, M, D*
D'Youville College *B*
Elmira College *B*
Excelsior College *B*
Fordham University *B, M, D*
Hamilton College *B*
Hartwick College *B*
Hobart and William Smith Colleges *B*

Hofstra University *B*
Houghton College *B*
Iona College *B*
Ithaca College *B*
Le Moyne College *B*
Long Island University
   Brooklyn Campus *B*
   C.W. Post Campus *B*
Manhattan College *B*
Manhattanville College *B*
Marist College *B*
Metropolitan College of New
   York *A, B*
Molloy College *B*
Nazareth College of Rochester *B*
New York University *B, M, D*
Niagara University *B*
Nyack College *B*
Rensselaer Polytechnic Institute *B*
St. Bonaventure University *B*
St. Francis College *B*
St. John Fisher College *B*
St. John's University *B*
St. Lawrence University *B*
St. Thomas Aquinas College *B*
Sarah Lawrence College *B*
Siena College *B*
Skidmore College *B*
State University of New York
   Albany *B, M, D*
   Binghamton *B, M, D*
   Buffalo *B, M, D*
   College at Brockport *B*
   College at Buffalo *B*
   College at Cortland *B*
   College at Fredonia *B*
   College at Geneseo *B*
   College at Old Westbury *B*
   College at Oneonta *B*
   College at Plattsburgh *B*
   College at Potsdam *B*
   New Paltz *B*
   Oswego *B*
   Purchase *B*
   Stony Brook *B, M, D*
Sullivan County Community
   College *A*
Syracuse University *B, M, D*
Touro College *B*
Union College *B*
Union Theological Seminary:
   Theological Professions *D*
United States Military Academy *B*
University of Rochester *B, M, D*
Utica College *B*
Vassar College *B*
Wells College *B*
Yeshiva University *B*

North Carolina
Appalachian State University *B*
Belmont Abbey College *B*
Davidson College *B*
Duke University *B, M, D*
East Carolina University *B*
Elon University *B*
Guilford College *B*
High Point University *B*
Lenoir-Rhyne College *B*
Methodist College *A, B*
North Carolina State University *B*
St. Andrews Presbyterian College *B*
Salem College *B*
University of North Carolina
   Asheville *B*
   Chapel Hill *B, M, D*
   Charlotte *B*
   Greensboro *B*
   Wilmington *B*
Wake Forest University *B*
Warren Wilson College *B*
Western Carolina University *B*
Wingate University *B*

North Dakota

North Dakota State University *B*
University of North Dakota *B*

Ohio

Antioch College *B*
Ashland University *B*
Baldwin-Wallace College *B*
Bowling Green State
   University *B, M, D*
Capital University *B*
Case Western Reserve University *B*
Cedarville University *B*
Cleveland State University *B, M*
College of Wooster *B*
Defiance College *B*
Denison University *B*
Franciscan University of
   Steubenville *B, M*
Hiram College *B*
John Carroll University *B*
Kent State University *B, M*
Kenyon College *B*
Malone College *B*
Miami University
   Oxford Campus *B, M*
Mount Union College *B*
Mount Vernon Nazarene University *B*
Muskingum College *B*
Oberlin College *B*
Ohio Dominican University *B*
Ohio Northern University *B*
Ohio State University
   Columbus Campus *B, M, D*
Ohio University *B, M*
Ohio Wesleyan University *B*
Otterbein College *B*
Pontifical College Josephinum *B*
University of Akron *B*
University of Cincinnati *B, M, D*
University of Dayton *B*
University of Findlay *B*
University of Toledo *B, M*
Urbana University *B*
Ursuline College *B*
Walsh University *B*
Wittenberg University *B*
Wright State University *B*
Xavier University *B*
Youngstown State University *B*

Oklahoma

Oklahoma Baptist University *B*
Oklahoma City University *B*
Oklahoma State University *B, M*
Southern Nazarene University *B*
Tulsa Community College *A*
University of Central Oklahoma *B*
University of Oklahoma *B, M, D*
University of Tulsa *B*

Oregon

Chemeketa Community College *A*
Lewis & Clark College *B*
Linfield College *B*
Marylhurst University *B*
Mount Angel Seminary *B, M*
Oregon State University *B*
Pacific University *B*
Portland State University *B*
Reed College *B*
University of Oregon *B, M, D*
University of Portland *B*
Western Oregon University *B*
Willamette University *B*

Pennsylvania

Albright College *B*
Allegheny College *B*
Alvernia College *B*
Arcadia University *B*
Bloomsburg University of
   Pennsylvania *B*
Bryn Mawr College *B*
Bucknell University *B*
Cabrini College *B*
California University of
   Pennsylvania *B*
Carlow University *B*
Carnegie Mellon University *B, M*
Clarion University of Pennsylvania *B*
College Misericordia *B*
DeSales University *B*
Dickinson College *B*
Duquesne University *B, M, D*
East Stroudsburg University of
   Pennsylvania *B*
Eastern University *B*
Edinboro University of
   Pennsylvania *B*
Elizabethtown College *B*
Franklin & Marshall College *B*
Gannon University *B*
Geneva College *B*
Gettysburg College *B*
Grove City College *B*
Haverford College *B*
Holy Family University *B*
Indiana University of Pennsylvania *B*
Juniata College *B*
King's College *B*
Kutztown University of
   Pennsylvania *B*
La Salle University *B*
Lafayette College *B*
Lebanon Valley College *B*
Lehigh University *B*
Lincoln University *B*
Lock Haven University of
   Pennsylvania *B*
Lycoming College *B*
Mansfield University of
   Pennsylvania *B*
Mercyhurst College *B*
Messiah College *B*
Millersville University of
   Pennsylvania *B*
Moravian College *B*
Muhlenberg College *C, B*
Penn State
   Altoona *B*
   Beaver *B*
   Dubois *B*
   Fayette *B*
   Lehigh Valley *B*
   McKeesport *B*
   Mont Alto *B*
   New Kensington *B*
   University Park *B, M, D*
   Worthington Scranton *B*
   York *B*
Rosemont College *B*
St. Charles Borromeo Seminary -
   Overbrook *B*
St. Francis University *B*
St. Joseph's University *B*
St. Vincent College *B*
Slippery Rock University of
   Pennsylvania *B*
Susquehanna University *B*
Swarthmore College *B*
Temple University *B, M, D*
Thiel College *B*
University of Pennsylvania *B, M, D*
University of Pittsburgh *B, M, D*
University of Scranton *B*
Ursinus College *B*
Villanova University *B, M, D*
Washington and Jefferson College *B*
West Chester University of
   Pennsylvania *B, M*
Westminster College *B*
Wilkes University *B*

Puerto Rico

Bayamon Central University *B*
Pontifical Catholic University of
   Puerto Rico *B*
University of Puerto Rico
   Mayaguez *B*
   Rio Piedras *B, M*

Rhode Island

Brown University *B, M, D*
Providence College *B*
Rhode Island College *B*
Roger Williams University *B*
Salve Regina University *B*
University of Rhode Island *B*

South Carolina

Claflin University *B*
Clemson University *B*
Coastal Carolina University *B*
College of Charleston *B*
Erskine College *B*
Furman University *B*
University of South Carolina *B, M, D*
Winthrop University *B*
Wofford College *B*

South Dakota

Augustana College *B*
University of South Dakota *B*

Tennessee

Austin Peay State University *B*
Belmont University *B*
Carson-Newman College *B*
Christian Brothers University *B*
East Tennessee State University *B*
Freed-Hardeman University *B*
Lipscomb University *B*
Middle Tennessee State University *B*
Rhodes College *B*
Union University *B*
University of Memphis *B, M, D*
University of Tennessee
   Knoxville *B, M, D*
   Martin *B*
University of the South *B*
Vanderbilt University *B, M, D*
Walters State Community College *A*

Texas

Austin College *B*
Baylor University *B, M, D*
Blinn College *A*
Criswell College *A, B, M*
Dallas Baptist University *B*
Frank Phillips College *A*
Hardin-Simmons University *B*
Howard Payne University *B*
Laredo Community College *A*
Lon Morris College *A*
McMurry University *B*
Our Lady of the Lake University of San
   Antonio *B*
Palo Alto College *A*
Rice University *B, M, D*
St. Edward's University *B*
St. Mary's University *B*
St. Philip's College *A*
Sam Houston State University *B*
South Texas College *A*
Southern Methodist University *B*
Southwestern Baptist Theological
   Seminary: Theological
   Professions *D*
Southwestern University *B*
Texas A&M University *B, M, D*
Texas Christian University *B*
Texas Lutheran University *B*
Texas State University: San
   Marcos *B, M*
Texas Tech University *B, M*
Trinity University *B*
University of Dallas *B, M, D*
University of Houston *B, M*

University of Houston
   Downtown *B*
University of North Texas *B, M*
University of St. Thomas *B, M, D*
University of Texas
   Arlington *B*
   Austin *B, M, D*
   El Paso *B*
   Pan American *B*
   San Antonio *B*
University of the Incarnate Word *B*
Western Texas College *A*

Utah

Brigham Young University *B*
Dixie State College of Utah *A*
Snow College *A*
Southern Utah University *B*
University of Utah *B, M, D*
Utah State University *B*
Utah Valley State College *A, B*
Westminster College *B*

Vermont

Bennington College *B*
Burlington College *B*
Goddard College *B, M*
Green Mountain College *B*
Marlboro College *B*
Middlebury College *B*
St. Michael's College *B*
University of Vermont *B*

Virginia

Bluefield College *B*
Bridgewater College *B*
Christendom College *B*
Christopher Newport University *B*
College of William and Mary *B*
Emory & Henry College *B*
Ferrum College *B*
George Mason University *B*
Hampden-Sydney College *B*
Hollins University *B*
Liberty University *B*
Lynchburg College *B*
Mary Baldwin College *B*
Marymount University *B*
Old Dominion University *B*
Radford University *B*
Randolph-Macon College *B*
Randolph-Macon Woman's College *B*
Roanoke College *B, T*
St. Paul's College *B*
Sweet Briar College *B*
University of Mary Washington *B*
University of Richmond *B*
University of Virginia *B, M, D*
Virginia Commonwealth University *B*
Virginia Polytechnic Institute and
   State University *B, M*
Virginia Wesleyan College *B*
Washington and Lee University *B*

Washington

Central Washington University *B*
City University *B*
Everett Community College *A*
Gonzaga University *B, M*
Northwest University *B*
Pacific Lutheran University *B*
Seattle Pacific University *B*
Seattle University *B*
University of Puget Sound *B*
University of Washington *B, M, D*
Washington State University *B*
Western Washington University *B*
Whitman College *B*
Whitworth College *B*

West Virginia

Bethany College *B*
Davis and Elkins College *B*

West Virginia University *B*
West Virginia Wesleyan College *B*
Wheeling Jesuit University *B*

Wisconsin
Alverno College *B*
Carthage College *B*
Lawrence University *B, T*
Marquette University *B, M, D, T*
Mount Mary College *B*
Ripon College *B*
St. Norbert College *B*
University of Wisconsin
  Eau Claire *B*
  Green Bay *B*
  La Crosse *B*
  Madison *B, M, D*
  Milwaukee *B, M*
  Oshkosh *B*
  Parkside *B*
  Platteville *B*
  Stevens Point *B, T*

Wyoming
University of Wyoming *B, M*

Phlebotomy

Arkansas
Phillips Community College of the
  University of Arkansas *A*

Georgia
Dalton State College *C*

Illinois
Kankakee Community College *C*
Moraine Valley Community College *C*
Waubonsee Community College *C*

Iowa
Des Moines Area Community
  College *C*

Kentucky
Somerset Community College *C*
Spencerian College: Lexington *C*

Louisiana
Bossier Parish Community College *C*

Michigan
Ferris State University *C*
Oakland Community College *C*

Minnesota
Lake Superior College *C*
Minnesota State Community and
  Technical College - Fergus Falls *C*
Northland Community & Technical
  College *C*

New Mexico
Eastern New Mexico University:
  Roswell Campus *A*

New York
Mohawk Valley Community College *C*

North Carolina
College of the Albemarle *C*
Fayetteville Technical Community
  College *C*
Halifax Community College *A*

Ohio
James A. Rhodes State College *A*
Marion Technical College *C*
Mercy College of Northwest Ohio *C*
Southwestern College of Business
  Southwestern College: Franklin *C*

Pennsylvania
Harrisburg Area Community
  College *C*

Rhode Island
Community College of Rhode
  Island *C*

Tennessee
Miller-Motte Technical College *A*

Virginia
Germanna Community College *C*
Southwest Virginia Community
  College *C*
Wytheville Community College *C*

Washington
Clark College *C*
Yakima Valley Community College *C*

Wisconsin
Mid-State Technical College *C*
Milwaukee Area Technical College *C*

Photographic/film/video technology

Alabama
Calhoun Community College *A*
Lawson State Community College *C*

California
Academy of Art University *C, A, B, M*
Brooks Institute of Photography *B*
Cypress College *C*
Santiago Canyon College *A*

Colorado
Colorado Mountain College
  Timberline Campus *A*

Kansas
Central Christian College of Kansas *A*

Maine
New England School of
  Communications *C, A, B*

Maryland
Frederick Community College *C*

Massachusetts
New England Institute of Art *B*
Simon's Rock College of Bard *B*

Michigan
Bay de Noc Community College *C*
Grace Bible College *B*
Kirtland Community College *C*

Minnesota
Central Lakes College *C, A*
Hennepin Technical College *C, A*
Minneapolis Community and
  Technical College *A*
St. Cloud State University *B*

New Jersey
Ocean County College *A*

New Mexico
New Mexico State University
  Alamogordo *C, A*

New York
Art Institute
  of New York City *A*
Cayuga County Community College *A*

Mohawk Valley Community College *C*
Rochester Institute of Technology *B*
St. John's University *A, B*

North Carolina
Carteret Community College *C, A*
Catawba Valley Community College *A*
Randolph Community College *A*

Ohio
Sinclair Community College *C*

Puerto Rico
Inter American University of Puerto
  Rico
  Bayamon Campus *C*

Utah
Salt Lake Community College *A*

Vermont
Burlington College *B*

Washington
Seattle Central Community
  College *C, A*

Photography

Alabama
Birmingham-Southern College *B*

Arizona
Northern Arizona University *B*
Prescott College *B, M*

California
Academy of Art University *C, A, B, M*
Allan Hancock College *A*
Antelope Valley College *C, A*
Art Center College of Design *B*
Bakersfield College *A*
Brooks Institute of Photography *B, M*
Butte College *A*
California College of the Arts *B, M*
California Institute of the Arts *C, B, M*
California State University
  East Bay *B*
  Fullerton *B, M*
  Long Beach *B*
Cerritos Community College *A*
Chabot College *A*
Chaffey College *C, A*
Citrus College *C, A*
City College of San Francisco *C, A*
College of San Mateo *A*
College of the Canyons *C, A*
College of the Desert *A*
College of the Siskiyous *A*
Columbia College *A*
Cosumnes River College *C, A*
Cypress College *C*
De Anza College *A*
East Los Angeles College *A*
El Camino College *C, A*
Foothill College *C, A*
Fresno City College *C, A*
Glendale Community College *C*
Golden West College *A*
Grossmont Community College *A*
Irvine Valley College *A*
Los Angeles City College *A*
Los Angeles Pierce College *A*
Los Angeles Southwest College *A*
Los Angeles Trade and Technical
  College *C, A*
Merced College *A*
Modesto Junior College *A*
Monterey Peninsula College *C, A*
Moorpark College *A*
Mount San Antonio College *C, A*
Mount San Jacinto College *A*

Ohlone College *C*
Orange Coast College *C, A*
Pacific Union College *A, B*
Palomar College *C, A*
Riverside Community College *C, A*
Saddleback College *A*
San Diego City College *C, A*
San Francisco Art Institute *B, M*
San Joaquin Delta College *A*
Santa Ana College *C, A*
Santa Monica College *A*
Santa Rosa Junior College *C*
Sierra College *A*
Southwestern College *A*
University of California
  Santa Cruz *B*
University of La Verne *C*
Ventura College *C, A*
Yuba Community College
  District *C, A*

Colorado
Adams State College *B*
Art Institute
  of Colorado *A, B*
Colorado Mountain College
  Spring Valley Campus *C, A*

Connecticut
Albertus Magnus College *B*
Paier College of Art *C, A, B*
University of Hartford *B*

Delaware
Delaware College of Art and Design *A*

District of Columbia
Corcoran College of Art and
  Design *A, B*
George Washington University *M*

Florida
Art Institute of Fort Lauderdale *A*
Barry University *C, B, M*
Brevard Community College *A*
Daytona Beach Community College *A*
International Academy of Design and
  Technology: Tampa *A*
Palm Beach Community College *A*
Ringling School of Art and Design *B*
University of Central Florida *B*
University of Miami *B*

Georgia
Gwinnett Technical College *A*
Savannah College of Art and
  Design *B, M*

Idaho
Brigham Young University-Idaho *A*
College of Southern Idaho *A*

Illinois
Bradley University *B*
City Colleges of Chicago
  Olive-Harvey College *A*
Columbia College Chicago *B, M*
Dominican University *B*
Judson College *B*
Prairie State College *C, A*
School of the Art Institute of
  Chicago *B, M*
Southwestern Illinois College *A*
University of Illinois
  Chicago *B, M*
  Urbana-Champaign *B, M*

Indiana
Indiana University-Purdue University
  Fort Wayne *B*
Indiana University-Purdue University
  Indianapolis *B*

Purdue University *B*
St. Mary-of-the-Woods College *B*

Iowa

Coe College *B*
Iowa Lakes Community College *A*
Morningside College *B*
University of Iowa *B, M*

Kentucky

Brescia University *A*

Louisiana

Louisiana Tech University *B*

Maine

Maine College of Art *B*
University of Maine
    Augusta *A*

Maryland

Cecil Community College *C, A*
College of Notre Dame of Maryland *B*
Harford Community College *A*
Howard Community College *A*
Maryland Institute College of Art *B, M*
Montgomery College *A*

Massachusetts

Art Institute of Boston at Lesley
    University *C, B*
Bridgewater State College *B*
Fitchburg State College *B*
Hampshire College *B*
Massachusetts College of Art *B, M*
Massasoit Community College *C*
Montserrat College of Art *B*
Salem State College *B*
School of the Museum of Fine
    Arts *B, M*
Simon's Rock College of Bard *B*
University of Massachusetts
    Dartmouth *B, M*

Michigan

Andrews University *B*
College for Creative Studies *B*
Delta College *A*
Ferris State University *B*
Grand Valley State University *B*
Kendall College of Art and Design of
    Ferris State University *B*
Lansing Community College *A*
Mott Community College *A*
Northern Michigan University *B*
Oakland Community College *C, A*
Siena Heights University *B*
University of Michigan
    Flint *B*
Washtenaw Community College *A*

Minnesota

College of Visual Arts *B*
Dakota County Technical College *C, A*
Minneapolis College of Art and
    Design *B*
Pillsbury Baptist Bible College *C*
Ridgewater College *C, A*
Rochester Community and Technical
    College *C*

Missouri

Central Missouri State University *B*
Columbia College *B*
Kansas City Art Institute *B*
St. Louis Community College
    St. Louis Community College at
    Meramec *A*
Washington University in St.
    Louis *B, M*
Webster University *B*

Montana

Miles Community College *A*

New Hampshire

Chester College of New England *B*
McIntosh College *A*
New England College *B*
Rivier College *B*

New Jersey

Brookdale Community College *A*
Camden County College *A*
Rowan University *B*
Thomas Edison State College *B*

New Mexico

College of Santa Fe *B*
New Mexico State University
    Alamogordo *C*

New York

Adirondack Community College *C, A*
Bard College *B, M*
Briarcliffe College *A*
City University of New York
    Brooklyn College *M*
    Queensborough Community
        College *C, A*
Fordham University *B*
Herkimer County Community
    College *A*
Hofstra University *B*
Ithaca College *B*
Long Island University
    C.W. Post Campus *B*
Monroe Community College *A*
Nassau Community College *C, A*
New York University *B*
Onondaga Community College *A*
Parsons The New School for
    Design *C, A, B, T*
Pratt Institute *B, M*
Rochester Institute of
    Technology *A, B, M*
Rockland Community College *A*
Sage College of Albany *A*
St. John's University *B*
Sarah Lawrence College *B*
School of Visual Arts *B, M*
State University of New York
    College at Buffalo *B*
    College at Plattsburgh *B*
    New Paltz *B, M*
    Purchase *B*
Syracuse University *B, M*
Tompkins-Cortland Community
    College *A*
Villa Maria College of Buffalo *A*

North Carolina

Carteret Community College *A*
East Carolina University *B*
Randolph Community College *A*

Ohio

Antioch College *B*
Art Academy of Cincinnati *B*
Bowling Green State University *B*
Clark State Community College *C*
Cleveland Institute of Art *B*
Columbus College of Art and
    Design *B*
Cuyahoga Community College
    Metropolitan Campus *A*
Ohio Institute of Photography and
    Technology *A*
Ohio State University
    Columbus Campus *B*
Ohio University *B, M*
Shawnee State University *B*
University of Akron *B*
University of Dayton *B*
Wright State University *B*

Youngstown State University *B*

Oklahoma

Oklahoma State University
    Okmulgee *A*

Oregon

Linn-Benton Community College *A*
Pacific Northwest College of Art *B*
University of Oregon *B, M*

Pennsylvania

Antonelli Institute of Art and
    Photography *A*
Arcadia University *B*
Art Institute
    of Philadelphia *A*
    of Pittsburgh *A, B*
Carlow University *B*
Chatham College *B*
Drexel University *B*
Edinboro University of
    Pennsylvania *B*
Harrisburg Area Community
    College *C, A*
Keystone College *A*
Lehigh Valley College *A*
Marywood University *B, M*
Moore College of Art and Design *B*
Oakbridge Academy of Arts *A*
Point Park University *B*
Temple University *B, M*
University of the Arts *B*
Westmoreland County Community
    College *A*

Puerto Rico

Inter American University of Puerto
    Rico
    Bayamon Campus *A*
    San German Campus *B, M*

Rhode Island

Rhode Island School of Design *B, M*
Salve Regina University *B*

South Carolina

Coker College *B*
Trident Technical College *C*

Tennessee

Carson-Newman College *B*
Memphis College of Art *B, M*
Nashville State Community
    College *C, A*
Pellissippi State Technical Community
    College *C*
Southern Adventist University *B*

Texas

Amarillo College *A*
Austin Community College *C, A*
El Paso Community College *A*
St. Edward's University *B*
Sam Houston State University *B*
San Antonio College *A*
Texas A&M University
    Commerce *B*
Texas Christian University *B, M*
Tyler Junior College *C*
University of Houston *B, M*
University of North Texas *B, M*
Western Texas College *A*

Utah

Brigham Young University *B*
Dixie State College of Utah *A*
Salt Lake Community College *A*
Weber State University *B*

Vermont

Bennington College *B*

Burlington College *B*
Marlboro College *B*

Virginia

Central Virginia Community
    College *C*
J. Sargeant Reynolds Community
    College *C*
Northern Virginia Community
    College *A*
Southwest Virginia Community
    College *C*
Thomas Nelson Community
    College *A*
Tidewater Community College *C, A*
Virginia Commonwealth University *B*
Virginia Intermont College *B*

Washington

Cornish College of the Arts *B*
Everett Community College *A*
Shoreline Community College *A*
University of Washington *B, M*
Western Washington University *B*

West Virginia

West Virginia State University *B*

Wisconsin

Cardinal Stritch University *B*
Carroll College *B*
Concordia University Wisconsin *B*

Wyoming

Casper College *A*
Northwest College *A*
Western Wyoming Community
    College *A*

Photojournalism

California

California State University
    Fullerton *B, M*
Long Beach City College *C*

Colorado

Colorado Mountain College
    Timberline Campus *A*

Illinois

Bradley University *B*

Kansas

Central Christian College of Kansas *A*
Pittsburg State University *B*

Maine

New England School of
    Communications *A, B*

Michigan

Central Michigan University *B*

Minnesota

Art Institutes International
    Minnesota *B*
Winona State University *B*

Missouri

University of Missouri
    Columbia *B*

New York

Rochester Institute of Technology *B*

North Carolina

Carteret Community College *A*

Ohio

Kent State University *B*
Ohio University *B*

Oklahoma

University of Central Oklahoma *B*

Pennsylvania

Point Park University *B*

Texas

Texas A&M University
Commerce *B*
Texas Tech University *B*

Physical anthropology

Maryland

University of Maryland
College Park *M*

Massachusetts

Harvard College *D*

Pennsylvania

Mercyhurst College *M*

Physical education

Alabama

Alabama Agricultural and Mechanical
University *B, M*
Alabama State University *B*
Athens State University *B*
Auburn University *B, M, D*
Chattahoochee Valley Community
College *A*
Faulkner State Community College *A*
Faulkner University *B, T*
Huntingdon College *B, T*
Jacksonville State University *B, M, T*
Lawson State Community College *A*
Oakwood College *B*
Samford University *B*
Southern Union State Community
College *A*
Tuskegee University *B*
University of Alabama *B, M*
University of Alabama
Birmingham *B, M, T*
University of Mobile *B, T*
University of South Alabama *B, M, T*
University of West Alabama *B, M, T*

Alaska

University of Alaska
Anchorage *B*
Fairbanks *B*

Arizona

Arizona State University *B, T*
Grand Canyon University *B*
Northern Arizona University *B, T*
Prescott College *B, M*
South Mountain Community
College *A*
University of Arizona *B*

Arkansas

Arkansas State University *B, M, T*
Arkansas Tech University *B, M*
Harding University *B, M, T*
Henderson State University *M, T*
Hendrix College *B*
Ouachita Baptist University *B, T*
Philander Smith College *B*
Southern Arkansas University *B, M, T*
University of Arkansas *M, D*
University of Arkansas
Monticello *B*
Pine Bluff *B, M, T*

University of Central Arkansas *B, M, T*
University of the Ozarks *B, T*
Williams Baptist College *B*

California

Allan Hancock College *A*
Azusa Pacific University *B, M, T*
Biola University *B, T*
Butte College *A*
California Baptist University *B, M, T*
California Lutheran University *B, T*
California State University
Chico *B, M, T*
Dominguez Hills *M, T*
East Bay *B, M, T*
Fresno *B*
Fullerton *B, M*
Long Beach *B, M, T*
Los Angeles *B, M*
Northridge *B, T*
Sacramento *T*
San Bernardino *B, M, T*
Chaffey College *A*
College of the Sequoias *A*
College of the Siskiyous *A*
Cuesta College *A*
Cypress College *A*
Diablo Valley College *A*
Fresno Pacific University *B, T*
Golden West College *A*
Humboldt State University *B, M, T*
Irvine Valley College *A*
Lassen College *A*
Master's College *B, T*
Mount San Jacinto College *A*
Pacific Union College *B*
Pepperdine University *B*
Reedley College *A*
Saddleback College *A*
San Diego Christian College *B, T*
San Diego Mesa College *A*
San Diego State University *B*
San Francisco State University *B, M, T*
Santa Barbara City College *A*
Sonoma State University *M, T*
Southwestern College *A*
Taft College *A*
University of La Verne *B*
University of the Pacific *T*
Vanguard University of Southern
California *T*
Westmont College *T*
Yuba Community College District *A*

Colorado

Adams State College *B, M, T*
Colorado State University
Pueblo *T*
Fort Lewis College *B*
Metropolitan State College of
Denver *T*
Northeastern Junior College *A*
Regis University *B, T*
Trinidad State Junior College *A*
University of Northern
Colorado *M, D, T*
Western State College of Colorado *T*

Connecticut

Central Connecticut State
University *M, T*
Eastern Connecticut State
University *B, M, T*
Mitchell College *A*
Southern Connecticut State
University *B, M, T*
University of Connecticut *B, M, D, T*

Delaware

Delaware State University *B*
University of Delaware *B, M, T*
Wesley College *B*

District of Columbia

Gallaudet University *B, T*
George Washington
University *A, B, M*
Howard University *B, M, T*
University of the District of
Columbia *B*

Florida

Barry University *B*
Bethune-Cookman College *B, T*
Clearwater Christian College *B*
Edward Waters College *B*
Florida Agricultural and Mechanical
University *B, M, T*
Florida International
University *B, M, T*
Florida Memorial University *B, T*
Florida Southern College *B*
Florida State University *B, M, D, T*
Hillsborough Community College *A*
Jacksonville University *B, T*
Miami Dade College *A*
Palm Beach Atlantic University *B, T*
Palm Beach Community College *A*
Pensacola Junior College *A*
University of Central Florida *B, M*
University of North Florida *B*
University of South Florida *B, M*
University of Tampa *T*
Warner Southern College *B*

Georgia

Albany State University *B, M*
Armstrong Atlantic State
University *B, T*
Augusta State University *B, M*
Bainbridge College *A*
Berry College *B*
Brewton-Parker College *B*
Clark Atlanta University *B*
Columbus State University *B*
Darton College *A*
Fort Valley State University *B, T*
Gainesville State College *A*
Georgia College and State
University *M, T*
Georgia Perimeter College *A*
Georgia Southern University *B, M*
Georgia Southwestern State
University *B, M*
Georgia State University *B, M*
Kennesaw State University *B*
Morehouse College *B*
North Georgia College & State
University *B, M*
Reinhardt College *B*
South Georgia College *A*
University of Georgia *B, M, D*
University of West Georgia *B, M*
Valdosta State University *B, M*
Waycross College *A*

Hawaii

Brigham Young University-Hawaii *B, T*

Idaho

Albertson College of Idaho *B*
Boise State University *B, M, T*
College of Southern Idaho *A*
Idaho State University *B, M*
Lewis-Clark State College *B, T*
Northwest Nazarene University *B*
University of Idaho *B, M, T*

Illinois

Augustana College *B, T*
Aurora University *B*
Blackburn College *B, T*
Chicago State University *B, M*
Concordia University *B, T*
DePaul University *B, T*
Eastern Illinois University *B, M, T*

Elmhurst College *B*
Eureka College *T*
Greenville College *B, T*
Illinois Central College *A*
Illinois College *B, T*
Illinois State University *B, M, T*
John A. Logan College *A*
Judson College *B, T*
Kishwaukee College *A*
Lewis University *T*
MacMurray College *B, T*
McKendree College *B*
Millikin University *B, T*
Monmouth College *B, T*
North Central College *B, T*
North Park University *T*
Northeastern Illinois University *B*
Northern Illinois University *B, M, T*
Olivet Nazarene University *B, T*
Quincy University *B, T*
Rockford College *B, T*
Sauk Valley Community College *A*
Southern Illinois University
Carbondale *B, M*
Trinity Christian College *B, T*
Trinity International University *B*
University of Illinois
Urbana-Champaign *B, M, T*

Indiana

Anderson University *B, T*
Ball State University *B, M, T*
Bethel College *B*
Butler University *T*
DePauw University *B*
Franklin College *B, T*
Goshen College *B*
Grace College *B*
Hanover College *B, T*
Huntington University *B*
Indiana State University *B, M, T*
Indiana University
Bloomington *B, M, D, T*
Indiana University-Purdue University
Indianapolis *B, M*
Indiana Wesleyan University *B, T*
Manchester College *B, T*
Marian College *B, T*
Oakland City University *B*
Purdue University *B, M, D*
St. Joseph's College *B*
Taylor University *B*
Tri-State University *B, T*
University of Evansville *B, T*
University of Indianapolis *B, T*
University of Southern Indiana *B*
Valparaiso University *B*
Vincennes University *A*

Iowa

Briar Cliff University *B*
Buena Vista University *B, T*
Central College *T*
Clarke College *B, T*
Coe College *B*
Cornell College *B, T*
Dordt College *B*
Ellsworth Community College *A*
Graceland University *T*
Iowa State University *T*
Iowa Wesleyan College *B*
Loras College *B, M*
Luther College *B*
Marshalltown Community College *A*
North Iowa Area Community
College *A*
Northwestern College *T*
St. Ambrose University *B, T*
Simpson College *B, T*
University of Dubuque *B, T*
University of Northern Iowa *B, M*
Upper Iowa University *B, T*
Wartburg College *B, T*
William Penn University *B*

Kansas

Baker University *T*
Benedictine College *B*
Bethany College *B, T*
Bethel College *T*
Butler County Community College *A*
Central Christian College of Kansas *A*
Coffeyville Community College *A*
Colby Community College *A*
Emporia State University *M, T*
Fort Hays State University *B, M, T*
Friends University *B*
Garden City Community College *A*
McPherson College *B, T*
MidAmerica Nazarene University *B, T*
Ottawa University *B, T*
Pittsburg State University *B, M, T*
Southwestern College *B, T*
Sterling College *T*
Tabor College *B, T*
University of Kansas *B, M, D, T*
Washburn University of Topeka *B*
Wichita State University *B, M, T*

Kentucky

Alice Lloyd College *B*
Asbury College *B, T*
Berea College *B, T*
Campbellsville University *B*
Eastern Kentucky University *B, M*
Kentucky State University *B*
Kentucky Wesleyan College *B, T*
Lindsey Wilson College *B, T*
Morehead State University *B, M*
Northern Kentucky University *B*
St. Catharine College *A*
Transylvania University *B, T*
Union College *B*
University of Kentucky *B*
University of Louisville *M*
University of the Cumberlands *B, T*
Western Kentucky University *B, M, T*

Louisiana

Centenary College of Louisiana *B, T*
Dillard University *B*
Grambling State University *B*
Louisiana State University
  Shreveport *B*
Louisiana State University and
  Agricultural and Mechanical
  College *B, M, D*
Louisiana Tech University *B, M*
Nicholls State University *B*
Northwestern State University *B, M*
Southeastern Louisiana
  University *B, M*
Southern University and Agricultural
  and Mechanical College *B*
University of Louisiana at Lafayette *B*
University of Louisiana at Monroe *B*
University of New Orleans *B, M*
Xavier University of Louisiana *B*

Maine

Husson College *B, T*
St. Joseph's College *B*
University of Maine *B, M*
University of Maine
  Presque Isle *B*

Maryland

Allegany College of Maryland *A*
Columbia Union College *B*
Frederick Community College *A*
Frostburg State University *B, M, T*
Garrett College *A*
Morgan State University *B, M*
Prince George's Community
  College *A*
Salisbury University *B, T*
Towson University *B, T*

University of Maryland
  College Park *B, M, D*
  Eastern Shore *B*

Massachusetts

Boston University *B, M, T*
Bridgewater State College *B, T*
Dean College *A*
Eastern Nazarene College *B, M, T*
Lasell College *B, T*
Northeastern University *B*
Salem State College *B, M*
Springfield College *B, M, D, T*
University of Massachusetts
  Boston *B*
Westfield State College *B, M, T*

Michigan

Adrian College *B, T*
Albion College *B, T*
Alma College *T*
Aquinas College *B, T*
Calvin College *B, T*
Central Michigan University *B, M, T*
Concordia University *B, T*
Cornerstone University *B, T*
Delta College *A*
Eastern Michigan University *B, M, T*
Grand Valley State University *B, T*
Hillsdale College *B*
Hope College *B, T*
Kellogg Community College *A*
Lansing Community College *A*
Michigan State University *B, M, D*
Northern Michigan University *B, T*
Olivet College *B, T*
Saginaw Valley State University *B, T*
Schoolcraft College *A*
University of Michigan *B, M, D*
Wayne State University *B, M, T*
Western Michigan University *B, M, T*

Minnesota

Augsburg College *B, T*
Bemidji State University *M, T*
Bethel University *B*
College of St. Catherine *B, T*
Concordia College: Moorhead *B, T*
Concordia University: St. Paul *B, T*
Gustavus Adolphus College *T*
Hamline University *B, T*
Minnesota State University
  Mankato *B, M, T*
  Moorhead *B*
Northland Community & Technical
  College *A*
Northwestern College *B*
Pillsbury Baptist Bible College *B*
Ridgewater College *A*
St. Cloud State University *B, T*
Southwest Minnesota State
  University *B, T*
University of Minnesota
  Duluth *B, T*
  Twin Cities *B, M, D, T*
University of St. Thomas *B, T*
Winona State University *B, M, T*

Mississippi

Alcorn State University *B*
Coahoma Community College *A*
Delta State University *B, M*
Hinds Community College *A*
Itawamba Community College *A*
Jackson State University *B, M*
Mississippi Delta Community
  College *A*
Mississippi State University *B, M, T*
Mississippi Valley State University *B, T*
University of Southern
  Mississippi *B, M, D*
William Carey College *B*

Missouri

Central Methodist University *B*
Central Missouri State
  University *B, M, T*
College of the Ozarks *B, T*
Crowder College *A*
Culver-Stockton College *B, T*
Drury University *B, T*
Evangel University *B, T*
Hannibal-LaGrange College *B*
Lincoln University *B, T*
Lindenwood University *B*
Missouri Baptist University *B, T*
Missouri Southern State
  University *B, T*
Missouri State University *B*
Missouri Valley College *B*
Northwest Missouri State
  University *B, M, T*
Southeast Missouri State
  University *B, T*
Southwest Baptist University *B, T*
Truman State University *M, T*
University of Missouri
  St. Louis *B, T*
Westminster College *B, T*
William Woods University *B, T*

Montana

Carroll College *B, T*
Montana State University
  Billings *B, T*
Rocky Mountain College *B, T*
University of Great Falls *B*
University of Montana:
  Missoula *B, M, T*
University of Montana: Western *B, T*

Nebraska

Bellevue University *B*
Chadron State College *B, M*
Concordia University *B, T*
Dana College *B*
Doane College *B*
Hastings College *B, M, T*
Midland Lutheran College *B, T*
Nebraska Wesleyan University *B*
Peru State College *B, T*
Union College *T*
University of Nebraska
  Kearney *B, M, T*
  Lincoln *B, M, D*
  Omaha *B, T*
Wayne State College *B, T*
Western Nebraska Community
  College *A*
York College *B, T*

Nevada

University of Nevada
  Las Vegas *B*
  Reno *B*

New Hampshire

Keene State College *B, T*
New England College *B, T*
University of New Hampshire *M, T*

New Jersey

The College of New Jersey *B, M, T*
Essex County College *A*
Gloucester County College *A*
Kean University *B, T*
Montclair State University *B, M, T*
Rowan University *B, M, T*
William Paterson University of New
  Jersey *B, T*

New Mexico

College of the Southwest *B, T*
Eastern New Mexico University *B, M*
New Mexico Highlands
  University *B, M*

New Mexico Junior College *A*
New Mexico State University *B*
University of New Mexico *B, M, D*
Western New Mexico University *B*

New York

Adelphi University *B, M, T*
Canisius College *B, M, T*
City University of New York
  Brooklyn College *B, M*
  Hunter College *B, T*
  Lehman College *B*
  Queens College *B, M, T*
  York College *B, T*
College of Mount St. Vincent *B, T*
Columbia-Greene Community
  College *A*
Corning Community College *A*
Erie Community College
  City Campus *A*
  North Campus *A*
  South Campus *A*
Herkimer County Community
  College *A*
Hofstra University *B, M*
Houghton College *B, T*
Hudson Valley Community College *A*
Ithaca College *B, M, T*
Long Island University
  Brooklyn Campus *B, M, T*
  C.W. Post Campus *B, T*
Manhattan College *B, T*
Sage College of Albany *B*
St. Bonaventure University *B, T*
St. Francis College *B*
State University of New York
  College at Brockport *B, M, T*
  College at Cortland *B, M, T*
  College of Technology at Delhi *A*
Syracuse University *B, M, T*

North Carolina

Appalachian State University *B, M, T*
Barton College *B, T*
Brevard College *B*
Campbell University *B, M, T*
Catawba College *B, T*
Chowan College *B, T*
East Carolina University *B, M*
Elizabeth City State University *B*
Elon University *B, T*
Fayetteville State University *B, T*
Gardner-Webb University *B, M*
Greensboro College *B, T*
Guilford College *B, T*
High Point University *B, T*
Johnson C. Smith University *B*
Lees-McRae College *B, T*
Lenoir Community College *A*
Lenoir-Rhyne College *B, T*
Livingstone College *T*
Louisburg College *A*
Mars Hill College *B, T*
Meredith College *B, T*
Methodist College *A, B, T*
North Carolina Agricultural and
  Technical State University *B, M, T*
North Carolina Central
  University *B, M, T*
North Carolina Wesleyan College *B*
Pfeiffer University *B*
Piedmont Baptist College *B*
St. Andrews Presbyterian College *B, T*
St. Augustine's College *B*
University of North Carolina
  Greensboro *B*
  Pembroke *B, M*
  Wilmington *B*
Western Carolina University *B, M, T*
Wingate University *B, T*
Winston-Salem State University *B*

North Dakota

Dickinson State University *B, T*

Jamestown College B
Mayville State University B, T
Minot State University B
North Dakota State University B, T
University of Mary B, T
University of North Dakota B, M, T
Valley City State University B, T

Ohio

Ashland University B, M, T
Baldwin-Wallace College T
Bluffton University B
Bowling Green State University B, T
Capital University B
Cedarville University B
Cleveland State University B, M, T
Defiance College B, T
Denison University B
Heidelberg College B
John Carroll University B
Kent State University B
Malone College B
Miami University
    Oxford Campus B, T
Mount Union College B, T
Mount Vernon Nazarene
    University B, M, T
Ohio Northern University B, T
Ohio State University
    Columbus Campus B, M, D
Ohio University B, T
Ohio Wesleyan University B
Otterbein College B
Sinclair Community College A
University of Akron B, M
University of Dayton B, M, T
University of Findlay B, M, T
University of Rio Grande A, B, T
University of Toledo B, M, T
Walsh University B
Wilmington College B
Wright State University B, M, T
Xavier University M
Youngstown State University B

Oklahoma

Bacone College B
Cameron University B, T
Connors State College A
East Central University B, T
Eastern Oklahoma State College A
Northeastern State University B
Northwestern Oklahoma State
    University B, T
Oklahoma Baptist University B, T
Oklahoma Christian University B, T
Oklahoma City University B
Oklahoma State University B
Oklahoma Wesleyan University B
Oral Roberts University B, T
Southern Nazarene University B
Southwestern Oklahoma State
    University B, M, T
Tulsa Community College A
University of Central Oklahoma B
Western Oklahoma State College A

Oregon

Chemeketa Community College A
Concordia University B, M, T
Corban College B
George Fox University T
Linfield College T
Linn-Benton Community College A
Oregon State University M
Warner Pacific College B, T
Western Oregon University B, T

Pennsylvania

Baptist Bible College of
    Pennsylvania B
Bucks County Community College A

East Stroudsburg University of
    Pennsylvania B, M, T
Gettysburg College T
Indiana University of
    Pennsylvania B, T
Lancaster Bible College B
Lincoln University T
Marywood University B
Messiah College B, T
Montgomery County Community
    College A
Philadelphia Biblical University B, T
Temple University B, M, D
University of Pittsburgh B, M, D, T

Puerto Rico

American University of Puerto
    Rico B, T
Bayamon Central University B
Inter American University of Puerto
    Rico
    Guayama Campus B
    San German Campus B, M
Pontifical Catholic University of
    Puerto Rico B, T
Turabo University B, M
Universidad Metropolitana B, M
Universidad del Este B
University of Puerto Rico
    Cayey University College B
    Mayaguez B

Rhode Island

Rhode Island College B
University of Rhode Island M, T

South Carolina

Anderson University B, T
Charleston Southern University B
The Citadel B, M, T
Coastal Carolina University B
Coker College B, T
College of Charleston B, T
Erskine College B, T
Furman University T
Lander University B
Limestone College B
Newberry College B, T
South Carolina State University B, T
Southern Wesleyan University B, T
University of South Carolina B, M, D
University of South Carolina
    Upstate B, T
Winthrop University B, M, T

South Dakota

Augustana College B, T
Black Hills State University B
Dakota State University B, T
Dakota Wesleyan University B, T
Mount Marty College B
Northern State University B, T
University of Sioux Falls T
University of South Dakota B, M, T

Tennessee

Belmont University B, M, T
Bethel College B
Bryan College T
Carson-Newman College B
Cumberland University B, T
Free Will Baptist Bible College B
Freed-Hardeman University B, T
Hiwassee College A
Lambuth University B, T
Lee University B, T
Lincoln Memorial University B, T
Lipscomb University B, T
Maryville College B, T
Southern Adventist University B
Tennessee State University B, T
Tennessee Technological
    University B, M, T

Tennessee Wesleyan College B, T
Trevecca Nazarene University B, T
Tusculum College B, T
Union University B, T
University of Memphis B, T
University of Tennessee
    Knoxville M, D

Texas

Abilene Christian University B, T
Alvin Community College A
Amarillo College A
Austin College M
Baylor University B, T
Dallas Baptist University B, T
Del Mar College A
East Texas Baptist University B
El Paso Community College A
Galveston College A
Hardin-Simmons University B, M, T
Houston Baptist University B, M
Howard Payne University B, T
Huston-Tillotson College B
Jarvis Christian College B, T
Lamar University B, M, T
Laredo Community College A
LeTourneau University B, T
Lubbock Christian University B
McMurry University B, T
Midland College A
Navarro College A
Prairie View A&M University M
St. Edward's University B, T
Sam Houston State University M, T
Schreiner University B
Southwestern Adventist University T
Southwestern University B, T
Stephen F. Austin State University M
Sul Ross State University M
Tarleton State University M, T
Texas A&M University M, D
Texas A&M University
    Commerce B, T
    Kingsville B, M
Texas Christian University B
Texas College B, T
Texas Lutheran University B, T
Texas Southern University M
Texas State University: San
    Marcos M, T
Texas Wesleyan University B, M, T
University of Houston B, M, D, T
University of Mary Hardin-Baylor B, T
University of Texas
    Arlington T
    Austin M, D
    San Antonio T
    of the Permian Basin M
University of the Incarnate Word T
Wayland Baptist University B, T
West Texas A&M University T
Wiley College B

Utah

Brigham Young University B, M
Dixie State College of Utah A
Snow College A
Southern Utah University T
Utah State University B
Utah Valley State College B
Weber State University B

Vermont

Castleton State College B, T
Johnson State College B
Lyndon State College B
Norwich University B, T
University of Vermont B

Virginia

Averett University M, T
Bluefield College B, T
Bridgewater College B, T

Eastern Mennonite University B, T
George Mason University B, M
Hampton University B
Liberty University T
Longwood University B
Lynchburg College B
Old Dominion University B, M, D, T
Radford University B, T
Randolph-Macon Woman's College T
Roanoke College B
Shenandoah University B
University of Richmond T
University of Virginia B, M, D
University of Virginia's College at
    Wise T
Virginia Commonwealth University M
Virginia Intermont College B, T
Virginia Polytechnic Institute and
    State University M
Virginia State University B

Washington

Central Washington University B, M, T
Eastern Washington University B, M, T
Gonzaga University B, M, T
Northwest University T
Seattle Pacific University B, T
Walla Walla College B
Washington State University B, T
Western Washington University B
Whitworth College B, T

West Virginia

Alderson-Broaddus College T
Bethany College B
Concord University B, T
Marshall University B, M
Ohio Valley University B
Potomac State College of West Virginia
    University A
Shepherd University T
West Liberty State College B
West Virginia State University B
West Virginia University B, M, D, T
West Virginia University Institute of
    Technology B
West Virginia Wesleyan College B

Wisconsin

Carroll College B, T
Carthage College B, T
Concordia University Wisconsin B, T
Maranatha Baptist Bible College B
Ripon College T
University of Wisconsin
    Oshkosh B, T
    Parkside T
    River Falls B, T
    Stevens Point B, T
    Superior B, T
    Whitewater B, M, T

Wyoming

Casper College A
Eastern Wyoming College A
Laramie County Community
    College A
University of Wyoming B

Physical sciences

Alabama

Auburn University at Montgomery B

Arizona

Chandler-Gilbert Community College
    Williams Campus A
Glendale Community College A
Northern Arizona University B
South Mountain Community
    College A

Arkansas
Arkansas Tech University *B*

California
Azusa Pacific University *B*
California Polytechnic State
 University: San Luis Obispo *B*
California State University
 Sacramento *B*
 Stanislaus *B*
Cerro Coso Community College *C, A*
Humboldt State University *B*
Long Beach City College *A*
Master's College *B*
National University *B*
Ohlone College *C*
Taft College *A*
University of California
 Berkeley *B*
 Riverside *B*
University of Southern California *B*

Colorado
Mesa State College *B*

Connecticut
Three Rivers Community College *A*
University of Bridgeport *B*

Delaware
Delaware Technical and Community
 College
 Stanton/Wilmington Campus *A*

District of Columbia
University of the District of
 Columbia *A*

Georgia
Andrew College *A*
Gordon College *A*

Illinois
John Wood Community College *A*
William Rainey Harper College *A*

Indiana
Grace College *B*
Taylor University *B*
Vincennes University *A*

Iowa
Coe College *B*
Dordt College *B*
Grand View College *B*
Loras College *B*

Kansas
Barton County Community College *A*
Cloud County Community College *A*
Donnelly College *A*
Emporia State University *B, M*
Garden City Community College *A*
Hutchinson Community College *A*
Kansas State University *B*
Washburn University of Topeka *B*

Kentucky
Alice Lloyd College *B*
Asbury College *B*

Maine
Bates College *T*

Maryland
Howard Community College *A*
United States Naval Academy *B*
University of Maryland
 College Park *B*

Massachusetts
Cape Cod Community College *A*
Dean College *A*
Harvard College *B*
Roxbury Community College *A*
Suffolk University *B*
Westfield State College *B*

Michigan
Central Michigan University *B, T*
Delta College *C, A*
Gogebic Community College *A*
Kalamazoo Valley Community
 College *A*
Kellogg Community College *A*
Michigan State University *B, M*
Northwestern Michigan College *A*
Olivet College *B*

Minnesota
Bethany Lutheran College *B*
Crown College *A, B*
St. Cloud State University *B*
Vermilion Community College *A*

Mississippi
Millsaps College *T*

Missouri
Crowder College *A*
Maple Woods Community
 College *C, A*

Montana
Miles Community College *A*

Nebraska
College of Saint Mary *B*
Concordia University *B, T*

New Jersey
Burlington County College *A*
County College of Morris *A*
Gloucester County College *C, A*
Union County College *A*

New Mexico
Northern New Mexico College *A*
San Juan College *A*
Santa Fe Community College *A*

New York
City University of New York
 John Jay College of Criminal
 Justice *B, M*
Corning Community College *A*
Dutchess Community College *A*
Roberts Wesleyan College *A*
St. John's University *B*
Schenectady County Community
 College *A*
Westchester Community College *A*

North Carolina
Chowan College *B*

North Dakota
Mayville State University *B*

Ohio
University of Dayton *B*
Wittenberg University *B*
Youngstown State University *B, M*

Oklahoma
Northeastern Oklahoma Agricultural
 and Mechanical College *A*
Redlands Community College *A*

Oregon
Linfield College *B*

Warner Pacific College *B*

Pennsylvania
Bloomsburg University of
 Pennsylvania *B, T*
Butler County Community College *A*
California University of
 Pennsylvania *B*
Community College of Philadelphia *A*
East Stroudsburg University of
 Pennsylvania *B*
Harrisburg Area Community
 College *A*
Juniata College *B*
Lehigh Carbon Community College *A*
Lincoln University *B*
Montgomery County Community
 College *A*
Muhlenberg College *C, B*
University of Pittsburgh *B*
University of Pittsburgh
 Bradford *B*
West Chester University of
 Pennsylvania *M*

Puerto Rico
University of Puerto Rico
 Mayaguez *B*

South Carolina
Aiken Technical College *C*
Florence-Darlington Technical
 College *A*
Midlands Technical College *C*
Trident Technical College *A*
University of South Carolina *M*

South Dakota
Black Hills State University *B*

Tennessee
Christian Brothers University *B*
Freed-Hardeman University *B*
Jackson State Community College *A*
Southwest Tennessee Community
 College *A*
Tennessee Temple University *B*
Union University *B*

Texas
Alvin Community College *A*
Amarillo College *A*
Angelo State University *T*
Brazosport College *C, A*
Lee College *A*
McMurry University *T*
Midwestern State University *B*
Palo Alto College *A*
Texas A&M University *M*
Texas A&M University
 Galveston *B*
Texas State Technical College
 Waco *A*
University of Texas
 El Paso *B*
Wayland Baptist University *B*

Utah
Utah Valley State College *A*
Weber State University *C, A*

Vermont
Bennington College *B*
St. Michael's College *B*
University of Vermont *M*

Virginia
Germanna Community College *A*
Piedmont Virginia Community
 College *A*
Radford University *B*
Richard Bland College *A*

Washington
Big Bend Community College *A*
Centralia College *A*
Columbia Basin College *A*
Edmonds Community College *A*
Evergreen State College *B*
Heritage University *B*
Seattle University *B*
Shoreline Community College *A*
Washington State University *B*

West Virginia
Marshall University *M*
Mountain State University *B*

Wisconsin
Ripon College *B*
St. Norbert College *T*

Wyoming
Central Wyoming College *A*
Sheridan College *A*

Physical/theoretical chemistry

Florida
Florida State University *M, D*

Iowa
Iowa State University *M, D*

Maryland
University of Maryland
 College Park *M, D*

Montana
University of Montana: Missoula *M, D*

New Jersey
New Jersey Institute of Technology *M*

New York
Fordham University *M*
Sarah Lawrence College *B*
State University of New York
 Albany *D*
 College of Environmental Science
 and Forestry *M, D*

Puerto Rico
University of Puerto Rico
 Rio Piedras *D*

Texas
LeTourneau University *B*
Rice University *B, M, D*
University of North Texas *M, D*

Wisconsin
Marquette University *M, D*

Physical therapy

Alabama
Alabama State University *D*
University of Alabama
 Birmingham *D*
University of South Alabama *M*

Arizona
Northern Arizona University *M, D*

Arkansas
Arkansas State University *M*
University of Central Arkansas *M, D*

California
Azusa Pacific University *D*

California State University
 Long Beach *M*
 Sacramento *M*
Chapman University *D*
Loma Linda University *M, D*
Samuel Merritt College *D*
San Francisco State University *M*
University of Southern
 California *M, D*
University of the Pacific *M, D*

Colorado

University of Colorado
 Denver and Health Sciences
 Center *M*

Connecticut

Quinnipiac University *M, D*
Sacred Heart University *M*
University of Connecticut *M*
University of Hartford *M, D*

Delaware

University of Delaware *D*

District of Columbia

George Washington University *D*
Howard University *M*

Florida

Florida Gulf Coast University *M*
Florida International University *M*
Nova Southeastern University *D*
University of Central Florida *M*
University of Florida *M*
University of Miami *M, D*
University of North Florida *M*
University of South Florida *M, D*

Georgia

Armstrong Atlantic State University *M*
Emory University *D*
Georgia State University *D*
Medical College of Georgia *D*
North Georgia College & State
 University *M*

Idaho

Idaho State University *D*

Illinois

Bradley University *D*
Governors State University *M*
Northern Illinois University *M*
Northwestern University *M*
Rosalind Franklin University of
 Medicine and Science *M, D*
University of Illinois
 Chicago *M, D*

Indiana

Indiana University-Purdue University
 Indianapolis *D*
University of Evansville *M*
University of Indianapolis *M, D*

Iowa

Clarke College *M*
St. Ambrose University *D*
University of Iowa *M, D*

Kansas

University of Kansas Medical
 Center *M, D*
Wichita State University *M, D*

Kentucky

Bellarmine University *M*
University of Kentucky *M*

Louisiana

Louisiana State University Health
 Sciences Center *M*

Maine

Husson College *M*
University of New England *M*

Maryland

University of Maryland
 Baltimore *M, D*
 Eastern Shore *M, D*

Massachusetts

American International College *M, D*
Boston University *M, D*
Northeastern University *M, D*
Simmons College *M, D*
Springfield College *M*
University of Massachusetts
 Lowell *M, D*

Michigan

Andrews University *M, D*
Baker College
 of Flint *M*
Central Michigan University *D*
Grand Valley State University *M*
Oakland University *M, D*
University of Michigan
 Flint *M*
Wayne State University *M, D*

Minnesota

College of St. Catherine *D*
College of St. Scholastica *M, D*
University of Minnesota
 Twin Cities *M*

Missouri

Maryville University of Saint Louis *M*
Missouri State University *M*
Rockhurst University *D*
St. Louis University *M, D*
Southwest Baptist University *D*
University of Missouri
 Columbia *M*
Washington University in St.
 Louis *M, D*

Montana

University of Montana: Missoula *M, D*

Nebraska

Creighton University *D*
University of Nebraska
 Medical Center *D*

Nevada

University of Nevada
 Las Vegas *M, D*

New Jersey

Richard Stockton College of New
 Jersey *M*
Rutgers, The State University of New
 Jersey
 Camden Regional Campus *M*
University of Medicine and Dentistry
 of New Jersey
 School of Health Related
 Professions *M, D*

New Mexico

University of New Mexico *M*

New York

City University of New York
 College of Staten Island *M*
 Hunter College *M*
Clarkson University *M*

D'Youville College *M, D*
Daemen College *D*
Dominican College of Blauvelt *D*
Ithaca College *D*
Long Island University
 Brooklyn Campus *M*
Mercy College *M*
Nazareth College of Rochester *M*
New York Institute of Technology *M*
New York University *M, D*
State University of New York
 Buffalo *M*
 Stony Brook *M, D*
 Upstate Medical University *D*
Touro College *M, D*
Utica College *D*

North Carolina

Duke University *M*
East Carolina University *M*
Elon University *D*
University of North Carolina
 Chapel Hill *M, D*
Western Carolina University *M*
Winston-Salem State University *M*

North Dakota

University of Mary *D*
University of North Dakota *D*

Ohio

Cleveland State University *M*
College of Mount St. Joseph *M, D*
Ohio State University
 Columbus Campus *M*
Ohio University *D*
University of Findlay *M*
Walsh University *M*
Youngstown State University *M*

Oklahoma

University of Oklahoma *M*

Oregon

Pacific University *D*

Pennsylvania

Arcadia University *D*
Chatham College *D*
College Misericordia *M, D*
Drexel University *M, D*
Duquesne University *D*
Gannon University *M, D*
Mount Aloysius College *D*
Neumann College *M, D*
St. Francis University *D*
Slippery Rock University of
 Pennsylvania *D*
Temple University *D*
Thomas Jefferson University: College
 of Health Professions *M*
University of Pittsburgh *D*
University of Scranton *D*
University of the Sciences in
 Philadelphia *M, D*
Widener University *D*

Rhode Island

University of Rhode Island *M*

South Carolina

Medical University of South
 Carolina *M*
University of South Carolina *D*

South Dakota

University of South Dakota *M*

Tennessee

Belmont University *D*
Carson-Newman College *T*
East Tennessee State University *D*

University of Tennessee
 Chattanooga *M, D*

Texas

Angelo State University *M*
Baylor University *D*
Hardin-Simmons University *M, D*
Texas State University: San Marcos *M*
Texas Tech University Health Sciences
 Center *M, D*
Texas Woman's University *M, D*
University of Texas
 El Paso *M*
 Health Science Center at San
 Antonio *M*
 Medical Branch at Galveston *M*
 Southwestern Medical Center at
 Dallas *M*

Utah

University of Utah *M, D*

Vermont

University of Vermont *M*

Virginia

Marymount University *D*
Old Dominion University *D*
Shenandoah University *D*
Virginia Commonwealth University *D*

Washington

Eastern Washington University *M, D*
University of Puget Sound *D*
University of Washington *D*

West Virginia

West Virginia University *M*
Wheeling Jesuit University *D*

Wisconsin

Carroll College *M*
Concordia University Wisconsin *M*
Marquette University *D*
University of Wisconsin
 La Crosse *M, D*
 Madison *M*

Physical therapy assistant

Alabama

Bishop State Community College *A*
Central Alabama Community
 College *A*
Community College of the Air
 Force *A*
Enterprise-Ozark Community
 College *A*
Faulkner University *A*
Jefferson State Community College *A*
South University *A*
Wallace State Community College at
 Hanceville *A*

Arizona

Gateway Community College *C, A*

Arkansas

Arkansas State University *A*
Northwest Arkansas Community
 College *A*
South Arkansas Community College *A*
University of Central Arkansas *A*

California

Allan Hancock College *A*
Cerritos Community College *A*
De Anza College *C*
Loma Linda University *A*
Mount St. Mary's College *C, A*

Ohlone College *A*
Sacramento City College *C, A*
San Diego Mesa College *A*

Colorado

Arapahoe Community College *A*
Morgan Community College *A*
Pueblo Community College *A*

Connecticut

Capital Community College *A*
Housatonic Community College *A*
Manchester Community College *A*
Naugatuck Valley Community
   College *A*
Northwestern Connecticut
   Community College *A*

Delaware

Delaware Technical and Community
   College
   Stanton/Wilmington Campus *A*

District of Columbia

George Washington University *C*

Florida

Brevard Community College *A*
Broward Community College *C, A*
Central Florida Community College *A*
Florida Community College at
   Jacksonville *A*
Gulf Coast Community College *A*
Indian River Community College *A*
Lake City Community College *A*
Manatee Community College *A*
Pensacola Junior College *A*
Polk Community College *A*
St. Petersburg College *A*
Seminole Community College *A*
South University: West Palm Beach
   Campus *A*

Georgia

Athens Technical College *A*
Darton College *A*
Middle Georgia College *A*
South University *A*

Hawaii

University of Hawaii
   Kapiolani Community College *A*

Idaho

Idaho State University *A*
North Idaho College *A*

Illinois

Black Hawk College *A*
College of DuPage *A*
Elgin Community College *A*
Illinois Central College *A*
Kaskaskia College *A*
Lake Land College *A*
Morton College *A*
Oakton Community College *A*
Southern Illinois University
   Carbondale *A*
Southwestern Illinois College *A*

Indiana

Ivy Tech State College
   Ivy Tech Community College: East
      Central *A*
   Ivy Tech Community College:
      Kokomo *A*
   Ivy Tech Community College:
      Northwest *A*
University of Evansville *A*
University of Indianapolis *A*
University of St. Francis *A*
Vincennes University *A*

Iowa

Indian Hills Community College *A*
Iowa Central Community College *A*
Iowa Lakes Community College *C*
Kirkwood Community College *A*
North Iowa Area Community
   College *A*
Upper Iowa University *B*
Western Iowa Tech Community
   College *A*

Kansas

Central Christian College of Kansas *A*
Colby Community College *A*
Fort Hays State University *B*
Johnson County Community
   College *A*
Kansas City Kansas Community
   College *A*
Washburn University of Topeka *A*

Kentucky

Ashland Community and Technical
   College *A*
Hazard Community College *A*
Jefferson Community College *A*
Madisonville Community College *A*
Somerset Community College *A*
Southeast Kentucky Community and
   Technical College *A*
West Kentucky Community and
   Technical College *A*

Louisiana

Bossier Parish Community College *A*
Delgado Community College *A*
Our Lady of the Lake College *A*

Maine

Kennebec Valley Community
   College *A*

Maryland

Allegany College of Maryland *A*
Anne Arundel Community College *A*
Baltimore City Community College *A*
Carroll Community College *A*
Chesapeake College *A*
College of Southern Maryland *C, A*
Howard Community College *A*
Montgomery College *A*

Massachusetts

Bay State College *A*
Becker College *A*
Berkshire Community College *A*
Massachusetts Bay Community
   College *A*
Mount Wachusett Community
   College *A*
North Shore Community College *A*
Springfield Technical Community
   College *A*

Michigan

Baker College
   of Cadillac *A*
   of Flint *A*
   of Muskegon *A*
Bay de Noc Community College *C*
Delta College *A*
Finlandia University *A*
Henry Ford Community College *A*
Kellogg Community College *A*
Kirtland Community College *C*
Macomb Community College *A*
Mott Community College *A*
Oakland Community College *C*

Minnesota

Anoka Technical College *A*
Anoka-Ramsey Community College *A*

College of St. Catherine *A*
Lake Superior College *A*
Riverland Community College *A*

Mississippi

Alcorn State University *B*
Itawamba Community College *A*
Meridian Community College *A*

Missouri

Missouri Western State University *A*
Ozarks Technical Community
   College *A*
Penn Valley Community College *A*
St. Louis Community College
   St. Louis Community College at
      Meramec *A*

Montana

Montana State University
   College of Technology-Great Falls *A*

Nebraska

Clarkson College *A*

Nevada

Community College of Southern
   Nevada *A*

New Hampshire

New Hampshire Community
   Technical College
   Claremont *A*

New Jersey

Atlantic Cape Community College *A*
Bergen Community College *A*
Essex County College *A*
Fairleigh Dickinson University
   College at Florham *A*
Mercer County Community College *A*
Union County College *A*

New Mexico

San Juan College *A*

New York

Broome Community College *A*
City University of New York
   Kingsborough Community
      College *A*
   LaGuardia Community College *A*
Dutchess Community College *A*
Genesee Community College *A*
Herkimer County Community
   College *A*
Nassau Community College *A*
New York University *A*
Niagara County Community
   College *A*
Onondaga Community College *A*
Orange County Community College *A*
State University of New York
   College of Technology at Canton *A*
Suffolk County Community College *A*
Touro College *A*
Villa Maria College of Buffalo *A*

North Carolina

Caldwell Community College and
   Technical Institute *A*
Central Piedmont Community
   College *A*
Fayetteville Technical Community
   College *A*
Guilford Technical Community
   College *A*
Martin Community College *A*
Southwestern Community College *A*

North Dakota

Williston State College *A*

Ohio

Clark State Community College *A*
Cuyahoga Community College
   Metropolitan Campus *A*
Hocking College *A*
James A. Rhodes State College *A*
Kent State University
   Ashtabula Regional Campus *A, B*
   East Liverpool Regional
      Campus *A, B*
Marion Technical College *A*
Owens Community College
   Toledo *A*
Shawnee State University *A*
Sinclair Community College *A*
Stark State College of Technology *A*
Washington State Community
   College *A*
Zane State College *A*

Oklahoma

Carl Albert State College *A*
Northeastern Oklahoma Agricultural
   and Mechanical College *A*
Oklahoma City Community College *A*
Tulsa Community College *A*

Oregon

Mount Hood Community College *A*

Pennsylvania

Academy of Medical Arts and
   Business *C, A*
Alvernia College *A*
Butler County Community College *A*
California University of
   Pennsylvania *A*
Central Pennsylvania College *A*
Community College of Allegheny
   County *A*
Erie Business Center *C*
Harcum College *A*
Lehigh Carbon Community College *A*
Mercyhurst College *A*
Mount Aloysius College *A*
Penn State
   Dubois *A*
   Hazleton *A*
   Mont Alto *A*
   Shenango *A*
University of Pittsburgh
   Titusville *A*

Puerto Rico

Inter American University of Puerto
   Rico
   Ponce Campus *A*
University of Puerto Rico
   Humacao *A*
   Ponce *A*

Rhode Island

Community College of Rhode
   Island *A*

South Carolina

Aiken Technical College *C*
Central Carolina Technical College *C*
Florence-Darlington Technical
   College *A*
Greenville Technical College *C, A*
Horry-Georgetown Technical
   College *C*
Midlands Technical College *C, A*
Orangeburg-Calhoun Technical
   College *C*
Piedmont Technical College *C*
Spartanburg Technical College *C*
Trident Technical College *A*

South Dakota

Lake Area Technical Institute *A*

Tennessee

Chattanooga State Technical
Community College *A*
Jackson State Community College *A*
Roane State Community College *A*
South College *A*
Southwest Tennessee Community
College *A*
Volunteer State Community College *A*
Walters State Community College *A*

Texas

Amarillo College *A*
Austin Community College *A*
Del Mar College *A*
El Paso Community College *A*
Houston Community College
System *A*
Howard College *A*
Kilgore College *A*
Laredo Community College *A*
North Harris Montgomery
Community College District *A*
Odessa College *A*
St. Philip's College *A*
South Texas College *A*
Tarrant County College *A*
Wharton County Junior College *A*

Utah

Provo College *A*
Salt Lake Community College *A*

Virginia

Jefferson College of Health
Sciences *A*
Northern Virginia Community
College *A*
Tidewater Community College *A*
Virginia Highlands Community
College *A*

Washington

Green River Community College *A*
Spokane Falls Community College *A*
Whatcom Community College *A*

West Virginia

Mountain State University *A*

Wisconsin

Blackhawk Technical College *A*
Gateway Technical College *A*
Milwaukee Area Technical College *A*
Northeast Wisconsin Technical
College *A*
Western Wisconsin Technical
College *A*

Physician assistant

Alabama

Oakwood College *A*
University of Alabama
Birmingham *M*

California

California State University
Dominguez Hills *B*
Charles R. Drew University of
Medicine and Science *B*
City College of San Francisco *A*
Foothill College *A*
Loma Linda University *M*
Samuel Merritt College *M*
University of Southern California *B*

Colorado

University of Colorado
Denver and Health Sciences
Center *M*

Connecticut

Quinnipiac University *B, M*
Yale University *M*

District of Columbia

George Washington University *B, M*
Howard University *B*

Florida

Barry University *M*
Nova Southeastern University *M*
University of Florida *A, B*

Georgia

Dalton State College *A*
Darton College *A*
Gordon College *A*
Medical College of Georgia *B*
South University *B*

Hawaii

University of Hawaii
Kapiolani Community College *A*

Idaho

Idaho State University *M*

Illinois

Rosalind Franklin University of
Medicine and Science *M*
Southern Illinois University
Carbondale *B*
University of St. Francis *M*

Indiana

Butler University *B, M*
University of St. Francis *B, M*

Iowa

University of Iowa *M*

Kansas

Central Christian College of Kansas *A*
Wichita State University *B, M*

Kentucky

National College of Business &
Technology
Danville *A*
Lexington *A*
University of Kentucky *M*

Louisiana

Our Lady of the Lake College *M*

Maine

University of New England *M*

Maryland

University of Maryland
Eastern Shore *B*

Massachusetts

Massachusetts College of Pharmacy
and Health Sciences *M*
Northeastern University *M*
Simmons College *M, D*
Springfield College *B*

Michigan

Central Michigan University *M*
Grand Valley State University *M*
Lansing Community College *A*
University of Detroit Mercy *M*
Wayne State University *M*
Western Michigan University *M*

Minnesota

Augsburg College *M*

Missouri

Missouri State University *M*
St. Louis University *M*

Montana

Rocky Mountain College *B, M*

Nebraska

Northeast Community College *A*
Union College *M*
University of Nebraska
Medical Center *M*

New Jersey

Rutgers, The State University of New
Jersey
New Brunswick/Piscataway
Campus *B*
Seton Hall University *M*
University of Medicine and Dentistry
of New Jersey
School of Health Related
Professions *B, M*

New Mexico

University of New Mexico *B*

New York

Albany College of Pharmacy *B*
City University of New York
City College *B*
College of Staten Island *B*
D'Youville College *B*
Daemen College *M*
Hofstra University *B*
Hudson Valley Community College *A*
Long Island University
Brooklyn Campus *B*
Mercy College *M*
New York Institute of Technology *B*
Pace University *B*
Rochester Institute of Technology *B*
St. Francis College *B*
St. John's University *B*
State University of New York
Downstate Medical Center *B*
Stony Brook *B*
Touro College *B*
Wagner College *B, M*

North Carolina

Duke University *M*
East Carolina University *M*
Lenoir-Rhyne College *B*
Mars Hill College *B*
Methodist College *B, M*
Wake Forest University *M*

Ohio

Kettering College of Medical Arts *A, B*
Marietta College *M*
Ohio Northern University *B*
University of Findlay *B*

Oklahoma

University of Oklahoma *M*

Oregon

Pacific University *M*

Pennsylvania

Arcadia University *M*
Carlow University *B*
Chatham College *M*
DeSales University *B, M*
Drexel University *B, M*
Duquesne University *M*
Gannon University *B, M*
King's College *M*
Lock Haven University of
Pennsylvania *M*
Marywood University *M*

Mount Aloysius College *B, M*
Philadelphia University *M*
St. Francis University *B, M*
Seton Hill University *B, M*
University of the Sciences in
Philadelphia *B, M*

South Carolina

Medical University of South
Carolina *M*

South Dakota

University of South Dakota *M*

Tennessee

Bethel College *A, M*
Carson-Newman College *T*
Southern Adventist University *A*
Trevecca Nazarene University *M*

Texas

Texas Tech University Health Sciences
Center *M*
University of Texas
Health Science Center at San
Antonio *B*
Medical Branch at Galveston *M*
Pan American *B*
Southwestern Medical Center at
Dallas *M*

Utah

University of Utah *M*

Virginia

James Madison University *M*
Jefferson College of Health
Sciences *B*
Shenandoah University *M*

Washington

University of Washington *B*

West Virginia

Alderson-Broaddus College *B, M*
Mountain State University *M*

Wisconsin

Marquette University *M*
University of Wisconsin
La Crosse *B, M*
Madison *B*

Physics

Alabama

Alabama Agricultural and Mechanical
University *B, M*
Alabama State University *B*
Athens State University *B*
Auburn University *B, M, D, T*
Birmingham-Southern College *B, T*
Chattahoochee Valley Community
College *A*
Jacksonville State University *B*
Northeast Alabama Community
College *A*
Samford University *B*
Talladega College *B*
Tuskegee University *B*
University of Alabama *B, M, D*
University of Alabama
Birmingham *B, M, D*
Huntsville *B, M, D*
University of North Alabama *B*
University of South Alabama *B*

Alaska

University of Alaska
Fairbanks *B, M, D*

Arizona

Arizona State University B, M, D
Arizona Western College A
Eastern Arizona College A
Embry-Riddle Aeronautical University:
    Prescott Campus A
Northern Arizona University B, M
South Mountain Community
    College A
University of Arizona B, M, D

Arkansas

Arkansas State University B
Harding University B
Henderson State University B
Hendrix College B
Ouachita Baptist University B
Phillips Community College of the
    University of Arkansas A
University of Arkansas B, M, D
University of Arkansas
    Little Rock B
    Pine Bluff B
University of Central Arkansas B
University of the Ozarks B

California

Allan Hancock College A
Azusa Pacific University B
Bakersfield College A
Cabrillo College A
California Institute of
    Technology B, D
California Lutheran University B
California Polytechnic State
    University: San Luis Obispo B
California State Polytechnic
    University: Pomona B
California State University
    Bakersfield B
    Chico B
    Dominguez Hills B
    East Bay B
    Fresno B, M
    Fullerton B, M
    Long Beach B, M
    Los Angeles B, M
    Northridge B, M
    Sacramento B, M
    San Bernardino B
    Stanislaus B
Canada College A
Cerritos Community College A
Chabot College A
Chaffey College A
Citrus College A
Claremont McKenna College B
College of San Mateo A
College of the Desert A
College of the Siskiyous A
Columbia College A
Contra Costa College A
Crafton Hills College A
Cuesta College A
Cypress College A
De Anza College A
East Los Angeles College A
El Camino College A
Foothill College A
Fullerton College A
Glendale Community College A
Grossmont Community College A
Harvey Mudd College B
Humboldt State University B
Las Positas College A
Los Angeles City College A
Los Angeles Southwest College A
Los Angeles Valley College A
Loyola Marymount University B
Merced College A
MiraCosta College A
Mission College A
Monterey Peninsula College A
Moorpark College A

Occidental College B
Ohlone College C
Orange Coast College A
Pacific Union College B
Pitzer College B
Point Loma Nazarene University B
Pomona College B
Saddleback College A
St. Mary's College of California B
San Bernardino Valley College A
San Diego City College A
San Diego Mesa College A
San Diego Miramar College A
San Diego State University B, M
San Francisco State University B, M
San Joaquin Delta College A
San Jose State University B, M
Santa Ana College A
Santa Barbara City College A
Santa Clara University B
Santa Monica College A
Santa Rosa Junior College A
Santiago Canyon College A
Scripps College B
Solano Community College A
Sonoma State University B
Southwestern College A
Stanford University B, M, D
University of California
    Berkeley B, D
    Davis B, M, D
    Irvine B, M, D
    Los Angeles B, M, D
    Riverside B, M, D
    San Diego B, M, D
    Santa Barbara B, M, D
    Santa Cruz B, M, D
University of California: Merced B
University of La Verne B
University of Redlands B
University of San Diego B
University of San Francisco B
University of Southern
    California B, M, D
University of the Pacific B
Ventura College A
West Hills Community College A
West Los Angeles College A
West Valley College A
Westmont College B
Whittier College B

Colorado

Adams State College B
Colorado Christian University B
Colorado College B
Colorado School of Mines M, D
Colorado State University B, M, D
Colorado State University
    Pueblo B
Fort Lewis College B
Metropolitan State College of
    Denver B
Red Rocks Community College A
United States Air Force Academy B
University of Colorado
    Boulder B, M, D
    Colorado Springs B
    Denver and Health Sciences
        Center B
University of Denver B, M, D
University of Northern Colorado B, T

Connecticut

Central Connecticut State
    University B
Connecticut College B
Fairfield University B
Southern Connecticut State
    University B
Trinity College B
University of Connecticut B, M, D
University of Hartford B
Wesleyan University B, M, D

Yale University B, M, D

Delaware

Delaware State University B, M
University of Delaware B, M, D

District of Columbia

American University B
Catholic University of
    America B, M, D
Gallaudet University B
George Washington
    University B, M, D
Georgetown University B, D
Howard University B, M, D
University of the District of
    Columbia B

Florida

Bethune-Cookman College B
Broward Community College A
Eckerd College B
Embry-Riddle Aeronautical
    University B
Florida Agricultural and Mechanical
    University B, M, D
Florida Atlantic University B, M, D
Florida Institute of
    Technology B, M, D
Florida International
    University B, M, D
Florida State University B, M, D
Gulf Coast Community College A
Indian River Community College A
Jacksonville University B
Manatee Community College A
Miami Dade College A
New College of Florida B
Okaloosa-Walton College A
Palm Beach Community College A
Pensacola Junior College A
Rollins College B
Stetson University B
University of Central Florida B, M, D
University of Florida B, M, D
University of Miami B, M, D
University of North Florida B
University of South Florida B, M, D
University of West Florida B

Georgia

Agnes Scott College B
Armstrong Atlantic State University B
Atlanta Metropolitan College A
Augusta State University B
Berry College B
Clark Atlanta University B, M
Coastal Georgia Community
    College A
Covenant College B
Dalton State College A
Darton College A
Emory University B, M, D
Gainesville State College A
Georgia Institute of
    Technology B, M, D
Georgia Perimeter College A
Georgia Southern University B
Georgia State University B, M, D
Gordon College A
Macon State College A
Mercer University B
Middle Georgia College A
Morehouse College B
North Georgia College & State
    University B
Oglethorpe University B
South Georgia College A
Southern Polytechnic State
    University B
Spelman College B
University of Georgia B, M, D
University of West Georgia B

Valdosta State University B
Wesleyan College B
Young Harris College A

Hawaii

University of Hawaii
    Hilo B
    Manoa B, M, D

Idaho

Boise State University B, T
Brigham Young University-Idaho B
College of Southern Idaho A
Idaho State University A, B, M, D
North Idaho College A
Northwest Nazarene University B
University of Idaho B, M, D

Illinois

Augustana College B, T
Benedictine University B, T
Bradley University B, T
Chicago State University B
City Colleges of Chicago
    Harold Washington College A
    Kennedy-King College A
    Olive-Harvey College A
DePaul University B, M, T
Eastern Illinois University B, T
Elmhurst College B, T
Greenville College B, T
Highland Community College A
Illinois Central College A
Illinois College B
Illinois Institute of
    Technology B, M, D
Illinois State University B, T
Illinois Valley Community College A
Illinois Wesleyan University B
John A. Logan College A
John Wood Community College A
Judson College B
Kishwaukee College A
Knox College B
Lake Forest College B
Lewis University B, T
Loyola University of Chicago B
MacMurray College B
Millikin University B
Monmouth College B, T
North Central College B, T
North Park University B
Northeastern Illinois University B
Northern Illinois University B, M, T
Northwestern University B, M, D
Principia College B
Roosevelt University B
Sauk Valley Community College A
South Suburban College of Cook
    County A
Southern Illinois University
    Carbondale B, M
Southern Illinois University
    Edwardsville B, M
Southwestern Illinois College A
Triton College A
University of Chicago B, D
University of Illinois
    Chicago B, M, D
    Urbana-Champaign B, M, D
Western Illinois University B, M
Wheaton College B, T

Indiana

Anderson University B
Ball State University B, M, T
Butler University B
DePauw University B
Earlham College B
Goshen College B
Hanover College B
Indiana State University B, T

Indiana University
  Bloomington *B, M, D*
  South Bend *B*
  Southeast *B*
Indiana University-Purdue University
  Fort Wayne *B, T*
Indiana University-Purdue University
  Indianapolis *B, M, D*
Manchester College *B, T*
Marian College *T*
Purdue University *B, M, D*
Purdue University
  Calumet *B*
Rose-Hulman Institute of
  Technology *B*
Taylor University *B*
University of Evansville *B*
University of Indianapolis *B*
University of Notre Dame *B, M, D*
University of Southern Indiana *T*
Valparaiso University *B*
Vincennes University *A*
Wabash College *B*

Iowa

Buena Vista University *B, T*
Central College *B, T*
Coe College *B*
Cornell College *B, T*
Dordt College *B*
Drake University *B*
Ellsworth Community College *A*
Graceland University *T*
Grinnell College *B*
Iowa State University *B, M, D*
Loras College *B*
Luther College *B*
Maharishi University of
  Management *B*
Morningside College *B*
Northwestern College *T*
St. Ambrose University *B*
Simpson College *B*
University of Iowa *B, M, D, T*
University of Northern Iowa *B, M*
Wartburg College *B, T*

Kansas

Allen County Community College *A*
Baker University *B*
Barton County Community College *A*
Benedictine College *B*
Bethel College *B*
Butler County Community College *A*
Central Christian College of Kansas *A*
Coffeyville Community College *A*
Emporia State University *B*
Fort Hays State University *B*
Fort Scott Community College *A*
Kansas State University *B, M, D*
Kansas Wesleyan University *B, T*
MidAmerica Nazarene University *B*
Pittsburg State University *B, M*
Pratt Community College *A*
Seward County Community College *A*
Southwestern College *B*
University of Kansas *B, M, D*
Washburn University of Topeka *B*
Wichita State University *B, M, T*

Kentucky

Berea College *B, T*
Campbellsville University *B*
Centre College *B*
Eastern Kentucky University *B*
Georgetown College *B*
Kentucky Wesleyan College *B*
Morehead State University *B*
Murray State University *B, T*
Northern Kentucky University *B*
Thomas More College *A, B*
Transylvania University *B*
University of Kentucky *B, M, D*
University of Louisville *B, M, D*

University of the Cumberlands *B*
Western Kentucky University *B*

Louisiana

Centenary College of Louisiana *B, T*
Dillard University *B*
Grambling State University *B*
Louisiana State University
  Shreveport *B*
Louisiana State University and
  Agricultural and Mechanical
  College *B, M, D*
Louisiana Tech University *B, M*
Loyola University New Orleans *B*
Northwestern State University *B*
Southeastern Louisiana University *B*
Southern University
  New Orleans *B*
Southern University and Agricultural
  and Mechanical College *B, M*
Tulane University *B, M, D*
University of Louisiana at
  Lafayette *B, M*
University of New Orleans *B, M*
Xavier University of Louisiana *B*

Maine

Bates College *B*
Bowdoin College *B*
Colby College *B*
University of Maine *B, M, D*
University of Southern Maine *B*

Maryland

Allegany College of Maryland *A*
Cecil Community College *A*
College of Notre Dame of Maryland *B*
Community College of Baltimore
  County *A*
Frostburg State University *B, T*
Goucher College *B*
Harford Community College *A*
Johns Hopkins University *B, D*
Loyola College in Maryland *B*
McDaniel College *B*
Morgan State University *B*
St. Mary's College of Maryland *B*
Salisbury University *B*
Towson University *B*
United States Naval Academy *B*
University of Maryland
  Baltimore County *B, M, D*
  College Park *B, M, D*
Washington College *B*

Massachusetts

Amherst College *B*
Boston College *B, M, D*
Boston University *B, M, D*
Brandeis University *B, M, D*
Bridgewater State College *B*
Bunker Hill Community College *A*
Clark University *B, M, D*
College of the Holy Cross *B*
Eastern Nazarene College *B*
Gordon College *B*
Hampshire College *B*
Harvard College *B, D*
Massachusetts College of Liberal
  Arts *B*
Massachusetts Institute of
  Technology *B, D*
Merrimack College *B*
Mount Holyoke College *B*
Northeastern University *B, M, D*
Simmons College *B*
Simon's Rock College of Bard *B*
Smith College *B*
Springfield Technical Community
  College *A*
Suffolk University *B*
Tufts University *B, M, D*

University of Massachusetts
  Amherst *B, M, D*
  Boston *B, M*
  Dartmouth *B, M*
  Lowell *B, M, D*
Wellesley College *B*
Wheaton College *B*
Williams College *B*
Worcester Polytechnic
  Institute *B, M, D*

Michigan

Adrian College *A, B, T*
Albion College *B, T*
Alma College *B, T*
Andrews University *B*
Aquinas College *B*
Calvin College *B, T*
Central Michigan University *B, M, T*
Concordia University *B*
Eastern Michigan University *B, M*
Gogebic Community College *A*
Grand Valley State University *B*
Hillsdale College *B*
Hope College *B*
Kalamazoo College *B, T*
Kellogg Community College *A*
Kettering University *B*
Lake Michigan College *A*
Lawrence Technological University *B*
Michigan State University *B, M, D*
Michigan Technological
  University *B, M, D, T*
Northern Michigan University *B, T*
Oakland University *B, M, T*
Saginaw Valley State University *B, T*
University of Michigan *B, M, D, T*
University of Michigan
  Dearborn *B*
  Flint *B, T*
Wayne State University *B, M, D*
Western Michigan University *B, M, D*

Minnesota

Augsburg College *B*
Bemidji State University *B*
Bethel University *B*
Carleton College *B*
College of St. Benedict *B*
College of St. Catherine *B*
Concordia College: Moorhead *B*
Gustavus Adolphus College *B*
Hamline University *B*
Macalester College *B, T*
Minnesota State University
  Mankato *B, M, T*
  Moorhead *B*
St. Cloud State University *B*
St. John's University *B*
St. Mary's University of Minnesota *B*
St. Olaf College *B*
University of Minnesota
  Duluth *B, M*
  Morris *B*
  Twin Cities *B, M, D*
University of St. Thomas *B*
Vermilion Community College *A*
Winona State University *B*

Mississippi

Hinds Community College *A*
Itawamba Community College *A*
Jackson State University *B*
Millsaps College *B, T*
Mississippi College *B*
Mississippi State University *B, M*
Tougaloo College *B*
University of Mississippi *B, M, D, T*
University of Southern
  Mississippi *B, M*

Missouri

Central Methodist University *B*

Central Missouri State University *B*
Crowder College *A*
Lincoln University *B*
Missouri Southern State
  University *B, T*
Missouri State University *B*
Northwest Missouri State
  University *B*
Rockhurst University *B*
St. Louis Community College
  St. Louis Community College at
    Florissant Valley *A*
St. Louis University *B*
Southeast Missouri State University *B*
Truman State University *B*
University of Missouri
  Columbia *B, M, D*
  Kansas City *B, M*
  Rolla *B, M, D, T*
  St. Louis *B, M, D*
Washington University in St.
  Louis *B, M, D*
Westminster College *B*
William Jewell College *B*

Montana

Carroll College *B, T*
Montana State University
  Billings *T*
  Bozeman *B, M, D*
University of Montana: Missoula *B, M*

Nebraska

Creighton University *B, M*
Doane College *B*
Hastings College *B*
Nebraska Wesleyan University *B*
Northeast Community College *A*
Union College *B*
University of Nebraska
  Kearney *B*
  Lincoln *B, M, D*
  Omaha *B*
Western Nebraska Community
  College *A*

Nevada

Great Basin College *A*
University of Nevada
  Las Vegas *B, M, D*
  Reno *B, M, D*
Western Nevada Community
  College *A*

New Hampshire

Dartmouth College *B, M, D, T*
St. Anselm College *B*
University of New Hampshire *B, M, D*

New Jersey

The College of New Jersey *B, T*
Drew University *B*
Georgian Court University *B*
Middlesex County College *A*
Montclair State University *B*
New Jersey City University *B*
New Jersey Institute of
  Technology *B, M, D*
Princeton University *B, M, D*
Ramapo College of New Jersey *B*
Richard Stockton College of New
  Jersey *B*
Rider University *B*
Rowan University *B*
Rutgers, The State University of New
  Jersey
  Camden Regional Campus *B, T*
  New Brunswick/Piscataway
    Campus *B, M, D*
  Newark Regional Campus *B*
St. Peter's College *B*
Salem Community College *A*
Seton Hall University *B, T*

Stevens Institute of
Technology *B, M, D*
Thomas Edison State College *A, B*

New Mexico

Eastern New Mexico University *B*
New Mexico Highlands University *B*
New Mexico Institute of Mining and
Technology *B, M, D*
New Mexico Junior College *A*
New Mexico State University *B, M, D*
San Juan College *A*
University of New Mexico *B, M, D*

New York

Adelphi University *B*
Adirondack Community College *A*
Alfred University *B*
Bard College *B*
Barnard College *B*
Canisius College *B*
City University of New York
Brooklyn College *B, M*
City College *B, M, D*
College of Staten Island *B*
Hunter College *B, M*
Kingsborough Community
College *A*
Lehman College *B*
Queens College *B, M, T*
York College *B*
Clarkson University *B, M, D*
Colgate University *B*
College of Mount St. Vincent *B*
Columbia University
Columbia College *B*
School of General Studies *B*
Cornell University *B, M, D*
Excelsior College *B*
Fordham University *B, M, D*
Hamilton College *B*
Hartwick College *B, T*
Hobart and William Smith Colleges *B*
Hofstra University *B*
Houghton College *B*
Iona College *B*
Ithaca College *B, T*
Le Moyne College *B*
Long Island University
C. W. Post Campus *B*
Manhattan College *B*
Manhattanville College *B*
Monroe Community College *A*
New York Institute of Technology *B*
New York University *B, M, D*
Pace University *B, T*
Polytechnic University *B*
Rensselaer Polytechnic
Institute *B, M, D*
Roberts Wesleyan College *B*
Rochester Institute of
Technology *A, B*
St. Bonaventure University *B, T*
St. John Fisher College *B*
St. John's University *B*
St. Lawrence University *B, T*
St. Thomas Aquinas College *B, T*
Sarah Lawrence College *B*
Siena College *B, T*
Skidmore College *B*
State University of New York
Albany *B, M, D*
Binghamton *B, M*
Buffalo *B, M, D*
College at Brockport *B, T*
College at Buffalo *B*
College at Cortland *B*
College at Fredonia *B, T*
College at Geneseo *B, T*
College at Oneonta *B*
College at Plattsburgh *B*
College at Potsdam *B*
College of Agriculture and
Technology at Morrisville *A*

New Paltz *B, T*
Oswego *B*
Stony Brook *B, M, D*
Suffolk County Community College *A*
Syracuse University *B, M, D*
Union College *B*
United States Military Academy *B*
University of Rochester *B, M, D*
Utica College *B*
Vassar College *B*
Wagner College *B, T*
Wells College *B*
Yeshiva University *B*

North Carolina

Appalachian State University *B, M*
Davidson College *B*
Duke University *B, M, D*
East Carolina University *B, M*
Elizabeth City State University *B*
Elon University *B*
Guilford College *B*
Lenoir-Rhyne College *B*
North Carolina Agricultural and
Technical State University *B, M, T*
North Carolina Central University *B*
North Carolina State
University *B, M, D*
Shaw University *B*
University of North Carolina
Asheville *B, T*
Chapel Hill *B, M, D*
Charlotte *B, M*
Greensboro *B*
Pembroke *B*
Wilmington *B*
Wake Forest University *B, M, D*

North Dakota

Dickinson State University *T*
Minot State University *B*
North Dakota State
University *B, M, D, T*
University of North Dakota *B, M, D, T*

Ohio

Antioch College *B*
Ashland University *B*
Baldwin-Wallace College *B, T*
Bluffton University *B*
Bowling Green State
University *B, M, D*
Case Western Reserve
University *B, M, D*
Cedarville University *B, T*
Cleveland State University *B, M, T*
College of Wooster *B*
Denison University *B*
Heidelberg College *B*
Hiram College *B*
Jefferson Community College *A*
John Carroll University *B, M*
Kent State University *B, M, D*
Kenyon College *B*
Marietta College *B*
Miami University
Oxford Campus *B, M, T*
Mount Union College *B*
Mount Vernon Nazarene University *B*
Muskingum College *B*
Oberlin College *B*
Ohio Northern University *B*
Ohio State University
Columbus Campus *B, M, D*
Ohio University *B, M, D*
Ohio Wesleyan University *B*
Otterbein College *B*
Sinclair Community College *A*
University of Akron *B, M*
University of Cincinnati *B, M, D, T*
University of Dayton *B*
University of Rio Grande *B, T*
University of Toledo *B, M, D*
Wittenberg University *B*

Wright State University *B, M*
Xavier University *B*
Youngstown State University *B*

Oklahoma

Cameron University *B*
Connors State College *A*
East Central University *B, T*
Eastern Oklahoma State College *A*
Oklahoma Baptist University *B, T*
Oklahoma City Community College *A*
Oklahoma City University *B*
Oklahoma State University *B, M, D*
Oral Roberts University *B*
Rogers State University *A*
Rose State College *A*
Southern Nazarene University *B*
Southwestern Oklahoma State
University *B*
Tulsa Community College *A*
University of Central Oklahoma *B, M*
University of Oklahoma *B, M, D*
University of Science and Arts of
Oklahoma *B*
University of Tulsa *B*

Oregon

Central Oregon Community
College *A*
Chemeketa Community College *A*
Eastern Oregon University *B, T*
Lewis & Clark College *B*
Linfield College *B, T*
Linn-Benton Community College *A*
Oregon State University *B, M, D*
Pacific University *B*
Portland State University *B, M*
Reed College *B*
Southern Oregon University *B*
Treasure Valley Community College *A*
University of Oregon *B, M, D*
University of Portland *B*
Willamette University *B*

Pennsylvania

Albright College *B, T*
Allegheny College *B*
Bloomsburg University of
Pennsylvania *B, T*
Bryn Mawr College *B, M, D*
Bucknell University *B*
California University of
Pennsylvania *B, M*
Carnegie Mellon University *B, M, D*
Chatham College *B*
Clarion University of
Pennsylvania *B, T*
Community College of Allegheny
County *A*
Dickinson College *B*
Drexel University *B, M, D*
Duquesne University *B*
East Stroudsburg University of
Pennsylvania *B, T*
Edinboro University of
Pennsylvania *B, T*
Elizabethtown College *B*
Franklin & Marshall College *B*
Geneva College *B, T*
Gettysburg College *B*
Grove City College *B*
Haverford College *B, T*
Indiana University of
Pennsylvania *B, M, T*
Juniata College *B*
Kutztown University of
Pennsylvania *B, T*
Lafayette College *B*
Lebanon Valley College *B, T*
Lehigh University *B, M, D*
Lincoln University *B*
Lock Haven University of
Pennsylvania *B, T*
Lycoming College *B*

Mansfield University of
Pennsylvania *B, T*
Messiah College *B*
Millersville University of
Pennsylvania *B, T*
Moravian College *B, T*
Muhlenberg College *C, B*
Northampton County Area
Community College *A*
Penn State
Abington *B*
Altoona *B*
Beaver *B*
Berks *B*
Delaware County *B*
Dubois *B*
Erie, The Behrend College *B*
Fayette *B*
Hazleton *B*
Lehigh Valley *B*
McKeesport *B*
Mont Alto *B*
Schuylkill - Capital College *B*
Shenango *B*
University Park *B, M, D*
Wilkes-Barre *B*
Worthington Scranton *B*
York *B*
St. Joseph's University *B*
St. Vincent College *B*
Seton Hill University *B*
Shippensburg University of
Pennsylvania *B, T*
Slippery Rock University of
Pennsylvania *B, M*
Susquehanna University *B, T*
Swarthmore College *B*
Temple University *B, M, D*
Thiel College *B*
University of Pennsylvania *B, M, D*
University of Pittsburgh *B, M, D*
University of Scranton *B, T*
Ursinus College *B, T*
Villanova University *B*
Washington and Jefferson College *B*
West Chester University of
Pennsylvania *B, T*
Westminster College *B*
Widener University *B*
York College of Pennsylvania *A*

Puerto Rico

Pontifical Catholic University of
Puerto Rico *B*
University of Puerto Rico
Humacao *B*
Mayaguez *B, M*
Ponce *A*
Rio Piedras *B, M*

Rhode Island

Brown University *B, M, D*
Rhode Island College *B*
University of Rhode Island *B, M, D*

South Carolina

Benedict College *B*
Charleston Southern University *B*
The Citadel *B*
Clemson University *B, M, D*
Coastal Carolina University *B*
College of Charleston *B, T*
Erskine College *B*
Francis Marion University *B*
Furman University *B, T*
Presbyterian College *B*
South Carolina State University *B*
University of South Carolina *B, M, D*
Wofford College *B*

South Dakota

Augustana College *B, T*

South Dakota School of Mines and
    Technology *B*
South Dakota State University *B, T*
University of South Dakota *B, M*

Tennessee

Austin Peay State University *B*
Belmont University *B, T*
Christian Brothers University *B*
Columbia State Community College *A*
East Tennessee State University *B, T*
Fisk University *B, M*
Hiwassee College *A*
King College *B, T*
Lipscomb University *B*
Middle Tennessee State University *B*
Rhodes College *B*
Roane State Community College *A*
Southern Adventist University *B*
Tennessee State University *B*
Tennessee Technological
    University *B, T*
Trevecca Nazarene University *B*
Union University *B, T*
University of Memphis *B, M*
University of Tennessee
    Chattanooga *B*
    Knoxville *B, M, D*
University of the South *B*
Vanderbilt University *B, M, D*

Texas

Abilene Christian University *B*
Amarillo College *A*
Angelina College *A*
Angelo State University *B*
Austin College *B*
Austin Community College *A*
Baylor University *B, M, D*
Blinn College *A*
Brazosport College *A*
Central Texas College *A*
Clarendon College *A*
Coastal Bend College *A*
Del Mar College *A*
El Paso Community College *A*
Frank Phillips College *A*
Galveston College *A*
Grayson County College *A*
Hardin-Simmons University *B*
Hill College *A*
Houston Baptist University *B*
Howard College *A*
Kilgore College *A*
Lamar University *B*
Laredo Community College *A*
Lon Morris College *A*
McMurry University *B, T*
Midland College *A*
Midwestern State University *B*
Navarro College *A*
Palo Alto College *A*
Paris Junior College *A*
Prairie View A&M University *B*
Rice University *B, M, D*
St. Mary's University *B*
Sam Houston State University *B, M*
San Jacinto College
    North *A*
South Plains College *A*
South Texas College *A*
Southern Methodist
    University *B, M, D*
Southwestern Adventist
    University *B, T*
Southwestern University *B, T*
Stephen F. Austin State
    University *B, M, T*
Tarleton State University *B*
Texarkana College *A*
Texas A&M University *B, M, D*
Texas A&M University
   Commerce *B, M*
   Kingsville *B, M*

Texas Christian University *B, M, D*
Texas Lutheran University *B*
Texas State University: San
    Marcos *B, M, T*
Texas Tech University *B, M, D*
Trinity University *B*
Trinity Valley Community College *A*
Tyler Junior College *A*
University of Dallas *B*
University of Houston *B, M, D*
University of North Texas *B, M, D*
University of Texas
    Arlington *B, M*
    Austin *B, M, D*
    Brownsville *B, M*
    Dallas *B, M, D*
    El Paso *B, M*
    Pan American *B*
    San Antonio *B*
West Texas A&M University *B*
Western Texas College *A*
Wharton County Junior College *A*

Utah

Brigham Young University *B, M, D*
Dixie State College of Utah *A*
Salt Lake Community College *A*
Snow College *A*
University of Utah *B, M, D*
Utah State University *B, M, D*
Utah Valley State College *A, B*
Weber State University *B*
Westminster College *B*

Vermont

Bennington College *B*
Marlboro College *B*
Middlebury College *B*
Norwich University *B*
St. Michael's College *B*
University of Vermont *B, M*

Virginia

Bridgewater College *B*
Christopher Newport University *B*
College of William and Mary *B, M, D*
Emory & Henry College *B, T*
George Mason University *B*
Hampden-Sydney College *B*
Hampton University *B, M, D*
Hollins University *B*
James Madison University *B*
Longwood University *B, T*
Lynchburg College *B*
Mary Baldwin College *B*
Norfolk State University *B*
Old Dominion University *B, M, D, T*
Randolph-Macon College *B*
Randolph-Macon Woman's College *B*
Roanoke College *B, T*
Sweet Briar College *B*
University of Mary Washington *B*
University of Richmond *B, T*
University of Virginia *B, M, D*
Virginia Commonwealth
    University *B, M*
Virginia Military Institute *B*
Virginia Polytechnic Institute and
    State University *B, M, D*
Virginia State University *B, M*
Washington and Lee University *B*

Washington

Cascadia Community College *A*
Central Washington University *B*
Centralia College *A*
Eastern Washington University *B, T*
Everett Community College *A*
Gonzaga University *B*
Olympic College *A*
Pacific Lutheran University *B*
Seattle Pacific University *B*
Seattle University *B*

University of Puget Sound *B, T*
University of Washington *B, M, D*
Walla Walla College *B*
Washington State University *B, M, D*
Western Washington University *B*
Whitman College *B*
Whitworth College *B, T*

West Virginia

Bethany College *B*
Marshall University *B*
Potomac State College of West Virginia
    University *A*
West Virginia State University *B*
West Virginia University *B, M, D, T*
West Virginia Wesleyan College *B*
Wheeling Jesuit University *B*

Wisconsin

Beloit College *B*
Carthage College *B, T*
Lawrence University *B, T*
Marquette University *B*
Northland College *T*
Ripon College *B*
St. Norbert College *B, T*
University of Wisconsin
    Eau Claire *B*
    Green Bay *B*
    La Crosse *B, T*
    Madison *B, M, D*
    Milwaukee *B, M, D*
    Oshkosh *B, M*
    Parkside *B, T*
    River Falls *B*
    Stevens Point *B, T*
    Whitewater *B, T*

Wyoming

Casper College *A*
Northwest College *A*
University of Wyoming *B, M, D*

Physics teacher education

Alabama

Athens State University *B*
Birmingham-Southern College *T*

Arizona

Arizona State University *B, T*
Grand Canyon University *B*
Northern Arizona University *B, T*
Prescott College *T*
University of Arizona *B, M*

Arkansas

Arkansas State University *B, T*
Ouachita Baptist University *B, T*
Southern Arkansas University *B, T*
University of Central Arkansas *T*

California

Azusa Pacific University *T*
California State University
    Chico *T*
    San Bernardino *T*
San Francisco State University *B, T*
Stanford University *M, T*
University of the Pacific *T*
Vanguard University of Southern
    California *T*

Colorado

Colorado State University *T*
Colorado State University
    Pueblo *T*

Connecticut

Connecticut College *T*

Southern Connecticut State
    University *B, T*
University of New Haven *T*

Delaware

Delaware State University *B, M*
University of Delaware *B, T*

Florida

Bethune-Cookman College *B, T*
Florida Agricultural and Mechanical
    University *T*
Florida Institute of Technology *B*
Florida State University *B, T*
Gulf Coast Community College *A*
Manatee Community College *A*

Georgia

Agnes Scott College *T*
Georgia Southern University *B*
University of West Georgia *B*

Hawaii

Brigham Young University-Hawaii *B, T*

Idaho

Boise State University *T*
Brigham Young University-Idaho *T*
University of Idaho *T*

Illinois

Augustana College *B, T*
Benedictine University *T*
Bradley University *B*
Elmhurst College *B*
Greenville College *B, T*
Illinois College *T*
Illinois Wesleyan University *B*
Judson College *B, T*
Knox College *T*
Lewis University *T*
North Park University *T*
Sauk Valley Community College *A*
University of Illinois
    Chicago *B*
    Urbana-Champaign *B, M, T*
Wheaton College *T*

Indiana

Butler University *T*
Goshen College *B*
Indiana University
    Bloomington *B, T*
    South Bend *B, T*
Indiana University-Purdue University
    Fort Wayne *B, T*
Indiana University-Purdue University
    Indianapolis *B*
Manchester College *B, T*
Purdue University
    Calumet *B*
Taylor University *B, T*
University of Evansville *B, T*
University of Indianapolis *B, T*
University of Notre Dame *B*
Valparaiso University *B*
Vincennes University *A*

Iowa

Buena Vista University *B, T*
Central College *T*
Cornell College *B, T*
Dordt College *B*
Drake University *T*
Ellsworth Community College *A*
Graceland University *T*
Iowa State University *T*
Loras College *T*
Maharishi University of
    Management *T*
Morningside College *B*
Northwestern College *T*

St. Ambrose University *B, T*
Simpson College *T*
University of Iowa *T*
Wartburg College *T*
William Penn University *B*

Kansas

Bethel College *T*
Emporia State University *T*
Garden City Community College *A*
Pittsburg State University *B, T*
University of Kansas *B, T*

Kentucky

Bellarmine University *B, M, T*
Campbellsville University *B*
Thomas More College *B*

Louisiana

Louisiana State University
  Shreveport *B*
Northwestern State University *B*
Southern University and Agricultural
  and Mechanical College *B*
University of Louisiana at Lafayette *B*
University of Louisiana at Monroe *B*
University of New Orleans *B*

Maine

University of Southern Maine *T*

Maryland

St. Mary's College of Maryland *T*

Massachusetts

Bridgewater State College *M, T*
Eastern Nazarene College *B*
Tufts University *T*
University of Massachusetts
  Dartmouth *T*
Worcester State College *T*

Michigan

Albion College *B, T*
Alma College *T*
Calvin College *B*
Eastern Michigan University *B, M, T*
Grand Valley State University *M, T*
Hope College *T*
Michigan Technological University *T*
Northern Michigan University *B, T*
University of Michigan
  Flint *T*
Western Michigan University *B, T*

Minnesota

Augsburg College *T*
Bethel University *B*
College of St. Catherine *T*
Concordia College: Moorhead *B, T*
Gustavus Adolphus College *T*
Minnesota State University
  Mankato *B, M, T*
  Moorhead *B*
St. Cloud State University *B, T*
St. Mary's University of Minnesota *B*
University of Minnesota
  Morris *T*
University of St. Thomas *B, T*
Vermilion Community College *A*
Winona State University *B, T*

Mississippi

Itawamba Community College *A*
Mississippi College *B*
Mississippi State University *T*

Missouri

Central Methodist University *B*
Central Missouri State University *B, T*
Lincoln University *B, T*
Lindenwood University *B*

Missouri Southern State
  University *B, T*
Missouri State University *B*
Northwest Missouri State
  University *B, T*
Truman State University *M, T*
University of Missouri
  Columbia *B*
  St. Louis *T*
Washington University in St.
  Louis *B, M, T*

Montana

Montana State University
  Billings *B, T*
Montana Tech of the University of
  Montana *T*
University of Montana: Missoula *T*

Nebraska

Chadron State College *B*
Concordia University *B, T*
Creighton University *T*
Hastings College *B, M, T*
Nebraska Wesleyan University *T*
Peru State College *B, T*
Union College *T*
University of Nebraska
  Kearney *B*
  Lincoln *B*

Nevada

University of Nevada
  Reno *B*

New Hampshire

University of New Hampshire *T*

New Jersey

The College of New Jersey *B, T*
Georgian Court University *T*
St. Peter's College *T*

New Mexico

New Mexico Institute of Mining and
  Technology *M*

New York

Adelphi University *M, T*
Alfred University *M, T*
Bard College *M*
City University of New York
  Brooklyn College *B, M*
  City College *B, M*
  Hunter College *B, D, T*
  Queens College *M, T*
Colgate University *M*
Cornell University *M, T*
D'Youville College *M, T*
Fordham University *M, T*
Hobart and William Smith Colleges *T*
Hofstra University *B, M*
Houghton College *B, T*
Ithaca College *B, T*
Manhattan College *B, T*
New York Institute of Technology *B, T*
New York University *B, M, T*
Pace University *B, T*
Roberts Wesleyan College *B, M*
St. John Fisher College *B, T*
St. John's University *B*
St. Lawrence University *T*
St. Thomas Aquinas College *B, T*
State University of New York
  Albany *B, M, T*
  Binghamton *M*
  Buffalo *M, T*
  College at Brockport *M, T*
  College at Buffalo *B*
  College at Cortland *B, M*
  College at Fredonia *T*
  College at Geneseo *B, M, T*
  College at Oneonta *B, T*

College at Plattsburgh *B, M*
College at Potsdam *B, M*
New Paltz *B, T*
Oswego *B, M*
Stony Brook *T*
Syracuse University *B, M, T*
Utica College *B*
Vassar College *T*
Wagner College *T*
Wells College *T*

North Carolina

Appalachian State University *B*
North Carolina Agricultural and
  Technical State University *B, T*
North Carolina Central University *B, T*
University of North Carolina
  Wilmington *B*
Wake Forest University *T*

North Dakota

Mayville State University *B, T*
Minot State University *B*
North Dakota State University *B, T*

Ohio

Baldwin-Wallace College *B, T*
Bluffton University *B*
Bowling Green State University *M*
Case Western Reserve University *T*
Cedarville University *B, T*
Hiram College *T*
John Carroll University *T*
Kent State University *T*
Miami University
  Oxford Campus *B, M, T*
Mount Union College *T*
Mount Vernon Nazarene
  University *B, M, T*
Ohio Dominican University *B, T*
Ohio Northern University *B*
Ohio Wesleyan University *B*
Otterbein College *B*
University of Rio Grande *B, T*
University of Toledo *M, T*
Xavier University *T*
Youngstown State University *B, M*

Oklahoma

East Central University *T*
Eastern Oklahoma State College *A*
Northeastern State University *B*
Oklahoma Baptist University *B, T*
University of Central Oklahoma *B*
University of Tulsa *T*

Oregon

Linfield College *T*
Oregon State University *M*
Portland State University *T*

Pennsylvania

Albright College *T*
Alvernia College *B*
Chatham College *T*
Dickinson College *T*
Duquesne University *M, T*
Geneva College *B, T*
Gettysburg College *T*
Grove City College *B, T*
Juniata College *B, T*
Lebanon Valley College *T*
Lycoming College *T*
Mansfield University of
  Pennsylvania *B, T*
Moravian College *T*
St. Vincent College *B, T*
Susquehanna University *T*
Thiel College *B*
Villanova University *T*
Westminster College *T*
Widener University *T*

Puerto Rico

Pontifical Catholic University of
  Puerto Rico *B, T*

Rhode Island

Rhode Island College *B*

South Carolina

Furman University *T*

South Dakota

Augustana College *B, T*
Dakota State University *B, T*
University of South Dakota *B, M, D, T*

Tennessee

Belmont University *B, M, T*
Christian Brothers University *B, M, T*
King College *T*
Lipscomb University *B, T*
Southern Adventist University *B*
Tennessee Technological University *T*
University of Memphis *T*

Texas

Del Mar College *A*
Houston Baptist University *T*
Lamar University *T*
Laredo Community College *A*
McMurry University *T*
St. Mary's University *T*
Tarleton State University *T*
Texas A&M University
  Commerce *T*
  Kingsville *T*
University of Dallas *T*
University of Houston *T*
University of Houston
  Clear Lake *T*
University of Texas
  San Antonio *T*
West Texas A&M University *T*

Utah

Brigham Young University *B*
Utah State University *B*
Weber State University *B*

Vermont

Castleton State College *B, T*

Virginia

Bridgewater College *T*
Hampton University *M*
Hollins University *T*
Longwood University *B, T*
Old Dominion University *B, T*

Washington

Central Washington University *T*
Washington State University *B, M, T*
Whitworth College *B, T*

Wisconsin

Carthage College *T*
Lawrence University *T*
Northland College *T*
St. Norbert College *T*
University of Wisconsin
  Green Bay *T*
  Parkside *T*
  River Falls *T*

Physiology

Arizona

Northern Arizona University *B*

California

San Jose State University *B, M*

University of California
  Irvine *M, D*
  Los Angeles *B, M*
University of Southern
  California *M, D*

Colorado
University of Colorado
  Denver and Health Sciences
  Center *D*

Connecticut
Yale University *M, D*

District of Columbia
Georgetown University *M, D*
Howard University *M, D*

Florida
University of Miami *D*

Georgia
Medical College of Georgia *M, D*

Hawaii
University of Hawaii
  Manoa *M, D*

Illinois
Loyola University of Chicago *M, D*
Rosalind Franklin University of
  Medicine and Science *M, D*
Southern Illinois University
  Carbondale *B*
University of Illinois
  Chicago *M, D*
  Urbana-Champaign *B, M, D*

Indiana
Indiana University
  Bloomington *M, D*
Indiana University-Purdue University
  Indianapolis *M, D*

Iowa
Iowa State University *M, D*
University of Iowa *M, D*

Kansas
University of Kansas Medical
  Center *M, D*

Kentucky
University of Louisville *M, D*

Louisiana
Louisiana State University Health
  Sciences Center *M, D*

Massachusetts
Harvard College *D*

Michigan
Eastern Michigan University *M*
Michigan State University *B, M, D*
Northern Michigan University *B*
University of Michigan *M, D*

Missouri
University of Missouri
  Columbia *M, D*

New York
State University of New York
  Buffalo *M, D*
  Stony Brook *D*

North Carolina
North Carolina State University *M, D*

University of North Carolina
Chapel Hill *M, D*

North Dakota
University of North Dakota *M, D*

Oklahoma
Oklahoma State University *B*
University of Oklahoma *M, D*

Oregon
University of Oregon *B*

Pennsylvania
Penn State
  University Park *M, D*
Temple University *M, D*

Texas
Texas Tech University Health Sciences
  Center *M, D*
University of Texas
  Health Science Center at
    Houston *M, D*
  Southwestern Medical Center at
    Dallas *M, D*

Utah
Brigham Young University *B, M, D*
Snow College *A*
University of Utah *B, M, D*

Virginia
University of Virginia *D*
Virginia Commonwealth
  University *M, D*

West Virginia
West Virginia University *M, D*

Wisconsin
University of Wisconsin
  Madison *M, D*

Piano/organ

Alabama
Birmingham-Southern College *B*
Huntingdon College *B*
Samford University *B*
Talladega College *B*

Arizona
Grand Canyon University *B*

Arkansas
Ouachita Baptist University *B*
University of Central Arkansas *B*

California
Bethesda Christian University *B, M*
California Institute of the Arts *C, B, M*
California State University
  Chico *C, B*
  Fullerton *B, M*
  Long Beach *B, M*
Fresno City College *A*
Master's College *B*
Notre Dame de Namur University *M*
Ohlone College *C*
San Diego State University *M*
San Francisco Conservatory of
  Music *B, M*
San Francisco State University *B*
University of Southern
  California *B, M, D*
University of the Pacific *B*

Delaware
University of Delaware *B*

District of Columbia
Catholic University of
  America *B, M, D*
Howard University *B*

Florida
Florida State University *B, M, D*
Hobe Sound Bible College *B*
Palm Beach Atlantic University *B*
Southeastern College of the
  Assemblies of God *B*
Stetson University *B*
University of Miami *B, M, D*

Georgia
Shorter College *B*

Hawaii
Brigham Young University-Hawaii *B*

Idaho
Brigham Young University-Idaho *A*

Illinois
Augustana College *B*
Illinois Wesleyan University *B*
Judson College *B*
Millikin University *B*
Moody Bible Institute *B*
North Park University *B*
Northwestern University *B, M, D*
Olivet Nazarene University *B*
Roosevelt University *C, B, M*
Trinity International University *B*

Indiana
American Conservatory of
  Music *C, B, M, D*
Ancilla College *C*
Butler University *B, M*
Huntington University *B*
Indiana University
  Bloomington *B*
Indiana University-Purdue University
  Fort Wayne *B*
Martin University *B*
Valparaiso University *B*
Vincennes University *A*

Iowa
Dordt College *B*
Drake University *B*
University of Iowa *B*
University of Northern Iowa *M*
Waldorf College *B*

Kansas
Central Christian College of Kansas *A*
MidAmerica Nazarene University *T*
University of Kansas *B, M, D*

Kentucky
Campbellsville University *B*

Louisiana
Centenary College of Louisiana *B, T*
Loyola University New Orleans *B*
Xavier University of Louisiana *B*

Maine
University of Southern Maine *B*

Maryland
Johns Hopkins University: Peabody
  Conservatory of Music *B, M, D*
Washington Bible College *B*

Massachusetts
Anna Maria College *B*
Berklee College of Music *B*
Boston Conservatory *B, M*

Boston University *B, M, D*
Eastern Nazarene College *B*
New England Conservatory of
  Music *B, M, D*

Michigan
Calvin College *B*
Hope College *B*
Northwestern Michigan College *A*
Oakland University *B*
University of Michigan *M*

Minnesota
Concordia College: Moorhead *B*
Minnesota State University
  Mankato *B, M, T*
Northwestern College *B*
St. Cloud State University *B*

Mississippi
Blue Mountain College *B*
Mississippi College *B*

Missouri
Calvary Bible College and Theological
  Seminary *B*
Drury University *B*
Hannibal-LaGrange College *B*

Nebraska
Concordia University *B, T*
Hastings College *B*
University of Nebraska
  Omaha *B, M*

New Jersey
Rider University *A, B, M*
Westminster Choir College of Rider
  University *B, M*

New York
Bard College *B*
Eastman School of Music of the
  University of Rochester *B, M, D*
Five Towns College *A, B, M, D*
Houghton College *B*
Juilliard School *B, M, D*
Mannes College The New School for
  Music *B, M*
New York University *B*
Roberts Wesleyan College *B*
Sarah Lawrence College *B*
State University of New York
  College at Fredonia *B*
  New Paltz *B, M*
Syracuse University *B, M*
University of Rochester *M, D*

North Carolina
Campbell University *B*
East Carolina University *B*
Gardner-Webb University *B*
Meredith College *B*
Wingate University *B*

Ohio
Baldwin-Wallace College *B*
Bowling Green State University *B, M*
Capital University *B*
Oberlin College *B, M*
Ohio State University
  Columbus Campus *B*
Ohio University *B*
University of Akron *B*
University of Cincinnati *B, M, D*
Youngstown State University *B, M*

Oklahoma
East Central University *B, T*
Northwestern Oklahoma State
  University *B*
Oklahoma Baptist University *B*

Oklahoma Christian University *B*
Oklahoma City University *B*
Oral Roberts University *B*
Southwestern Oklahoma State
University *B*
University of Central Oklahoma *B*
University of Tulsa *B*

Oregon
Corban College *B*
University of Oregon *M*
Willamette University *B*

Pennsylvania
Carnegie Mellon University *B, M*
Gettysburg College *B*
Mansfield University of
Pennsylvania *B*
Penn State
University Park *M*
Susquehanna University *B*
Temple University *M*
West Chester University of
Pennsylvania *B, M*
Westminster College *B*

Puerto Rico
Conservatory of Music of Puerto
Rico *B*

South Carolina
Coker College *B*
Columbia College *B*
Furman University *B*
North Greenville College *B*
South Carolina State University *B*
University of South Carolina *M, D*

Tennessee
Belmont University *B, M*
Bryan College *B*
Hiwassee College *A*
Lambuth University *B*
Lipscomb University *B*
Union University *B*
University of Tennessee
Knoxville *B*

Texas
Abilene Christian University *B*
Angelina College *A*
Baylor University *M*
Concordia University at Austin *B*
Dallas Baptist University *B*
East Texas Baptist University *B*
Hardin-Simmons University *B, M*
Howard Payne University *B*
Lon Morris College *A*
McMurry University *B, T*
Prairie View A&M University *B*
Southern Methodist University *B, M*
Southwestern Assemblies of God
University *B*
Texas A&M University
Commerce *B, M*
Texas Christian University *B, M*
Texas Tech University *D*
University of Texas
El Paso *B*

Utah
Brigham Young University *B*
Weber State University *B*

Vermont
Bennington College *B*
Johnson State College *B*

Virginia
Shenandoah University *B, M*
Virginia Union University *B*

Washington
Central Washington University *B*
Cornish College of the Arts *B*
Eastern Washington University *B*
University of Washington *B, M, D*
Whitworth College *B*

Wisconsin
Carthage College *B*
Concordia University Wisconsin *B*
Lawrence University *B*
Maranatha Baptist Bible College *B*
University of Wisconsin
Madison *B, M*

Pipefitting

Alabama
Bishop State Community College *C*
Lawson State Community College *C*

Arizona
Central Arizona College *C*
Gateway Community College *C, A*

California
Allan Hancock College *C*
Bakersfield College *A*
College of San Mateo *A*
Foothill College *C*
Fresno City College *A*
Los Angeles Trade and Technical
College *C, A*
Modesto Junior College *C, A*
Orange Coast College *C, A*
Palomar College *C, A*
San Diego City College *C, A*
Santa Rosa Junior College *C*
Ventura College *A*

Colorado
Red Rocks Community College *C, A*

Florida
Brevard Community College *C*
Florida Community College at
Jacksonville *C*
Palm Beach Community College *C*
Seminole Community College *C*
Tallahassee Community College *C*

Indiana
Ivy Tech State College
Ivy Tech Community College:
Bloomington *C, A*
Ivy Tech Community College:
Central Indiana *C, A*
Ivy Tech Community College:
Columbus *C, A*
Ivy Tech Community College: East
Central *C, A*
Ivy Tech Community College:
Kokomo *C, A*
Ivy Tech Community College:
Lafayette *C*
Ivy Tech Community College: North
Central *C, A*
Ivy Tech Community College:
Northeast *C, A*
Ivy Tech Community College:
Northwest *C, A*
Ivy Tech Community College: South
Central *C, A*
Ivy Tech Community College:
Southwest *C, A*
Ivy Tech Community College:
Wabash Valley *C, A*

Iowa
Kirkwood Community College *C*
Northeast Iowa Community
College *C*

Kentucky
Somerset Community College *C, A*

Maine
Eastern Maine Community
College *C, A*
Northern Maine Community
College *C, A*
Southern Maine Community
College *C*
Washington County Community
College *C*

Michigan
Bay de Noc Community College *C*
Delta College *A*
Kellogg Community College *C, A*
Lansing Community College *A*
Macomb Community College *C*
Mott Community College *C*
Oakland Community College *C, A*

Minnesota
Dunwoody College of Technology *C*
St. Paul College *C*

Mississippi
Mississippi Gulf Coast Community
College
Jefferson Davis Campus *C, A*

Missouri
Ranken Technical College *C*

Nevada
Truckee Meadows Community
College *C, A*

New Mexico
Albuquerque Technical-Vocational
Institute *C*
New Mexico State University
Grants *C*
Northern New Mexico College *C, A*

New York
State University of New York
College of Technology at Alfred *A*
College of Technology at Canton *C*

North Carolina
Blue Ridge Community College *C*
Cleveland Community College *C*
Forsyth Technical Community
College *C*
Johnston Community College *C*
Southeastern Community College *C*
Tri-County Community College *C*
Wake Technical Community
College *C*

North Dakota
North Dakota State College of
Science *C*

Oklahoma
Oklahoma State University
Okmulgee *A*

Oregon
Central Oregon Community
College *C*
Chemeketa Community College *C*
Linn-Benton Community College *A*

Pennsylvania
Community College of Allegheny
County *C*
Delaware County Community
College *C*

Luzerne County Community
College *C*
Thaddeus Stevens College of
Technology *C*

Rhode Island
New England Institute of
Technology *A*

South Carolina
Denmark Technical College *C*

Texas
Brazosport College *C, A*
Frank Phillips College *C, A*
Howard College *C*
Lee College *C*
North Lake College *C*
St. Philip's College *C*

Utah
Dixie State College of Utah *C*
Salt Lake Community College *A*
Southern Utah University *C*

Virginia
Central Virginia Community
College *C*

Wisconsin
Chippewa Valley Technical College *C*
Gateway Technical College *C*
Milwaukee Area Technical College *C*

Planetary sciences

Alaska
University of Alaska
Fairbanks *B*

Arizona
Northern Arizona University *B, T*
Prescott College *B, M*
University of Arizona *M, D*

Arkansas
University of Arkansas *B*

California
California Institute of
Technology *B, D*
California State University
Dominguez Hills *B*
Monterey Bay *B*
Northridge *B*
Cerritos Community College *A*
Chaffey College *A*
College of the Redwoods *A*
Columbia College *A*
Los Angeles Valley College *A*
Ohlone College *C*
University of California
San Diego *B, D*
Santa Cruz *B, M, D*

Colorado
University of Colorado
Boulder *B, M, D*

Connecticut
Southern Connecticut State
University *B*
Wesleyan University *B, M*
Western Connecticut State
University *B, M*

Delaware
University of Delaware *B, T*

Idaho
Boise State University *B*

University of Idaho *M*

Illinois
Augustana College *B, T*
Black Hawk College
  East Campus *A*
City Colleges of Chicago
  Olive-Harvey College *A*
Illinois Central College *A*
Illinois Valley Community College *A*
Richland Community College *A*

Indiana
Vincennes University *A*

Iowa
Iowa State University *B, M, D*
University of Dubuque *B*

Maryland
Towson University *B*

Massachusetts
Boston University *B*
Massachusetts Institute of
  Technology *M, D*
Tufts University *T*

Michigan
Adrian College *A, B, T*
Northern Michigan University *B, T*

Minnesota
Minnesota State University
  Mankato *M, T*
St. Cloud State University *B*
Winona State University *B, T*

Missouri
Central Missouri State University *B*
Washington University in St.
  Louis *B, M, D*

Montana
Montana State University
  Bozeman *B, M*

Nebraska
Midland Lutheran College *T*
University of Nebraska
  Kearney *B, T*

New Hampshire
Dartmouth College *B, M, D, T*

New Jersey
Rutgers, The State University of New
  Jersey
  Newark Regional Campus *T*
William Paterson University of New
  Jersey *T*

New York
City University of New York
  City College *B*
Columbia University
  Columbia College *B*
Sarah Lawrence College *B*
State University of New York
  Albany *B*
  College at Brockport *B*
  College at Buffalo *B*
  College at Cortland *B*
  College at Fredonia *B*
  College at Geneseo *T*
  New Paltz *T*
Suffolk County Community College *A*

North Dakota
Minot State University *B*

Ohio
Ashland University *B, T*
Muskingum College *B*
Wilmington College *B*
Youngstown State University *B*

Oregon
Western Oregon University *B*

Pennsylvania
Clarion University of
  Pennsylvania *B, T*
Edinboro University of
  Pennsylvania *B, T*
La Salle University *B*
Mansfield University of
  Pennsylvania *T*
Penn State
  Abington *B*
  Altoona *B*
  Beaver *B*
  Berks *B*
  Delaware County *B*
  Dubois *B*
  Fayette *B*
  Hazleton *B*
  Lehigh Valley *B*
  McKeesport *B*
  Mont Alto *B*
  New Kensington *B*
  Schuylkill - Capital College *B*
  Shenango *B*
  University Park *B, M, D*
  Wilkes-Barre *B*
  Worthington Scranton *B*
  York *B*

South Carolina
University of South Carolina *M*

South Dakota
Sisseton Wahpeton College *A*

Texas
Brazosport College *A*
College of the Mainland *A*
Lamar University *B*
Stephen F. Austin State University *T*
Texas A&M University *B*
Texas A&M University
  Commerce *B, M*
University of Houston *B*
University of Texas
  of the Permian Basin *B*

Utah
Southern Utah University *B*

Virginia
George Mason University *B*

Washington
Central Washington University *B*
Centralia College *A*
Eastern Washington University *B*
University of Washington *B*

Wisconsin
Northland College *B, T*
University of Wisconsin
  Madison *B*
  River Falls *B, T*

Plant breeding

Arizona
Prescott College *B, M*

Iowa
Iowa State University *M, D*

Michigan
Kirtland Community College *A*

Minnesota
University of Minnesota
  Twin Cities *M, D*

New York
Cornell University *B, M, D*

Texas
Texas A&M University *B, M, D*
Texas Tech University *M*

Vermont
Sterling College *A, B*

Plant genetics

California
University of California
  Riverside *D*

Michigan
Michigan State University *M, D*

New York
Cornell University *B, M, D*

Washington
Washington State University *B, M, D*

Wisconsin
University of Wisconsin
  Madison *M, D*

Plant molecular biology

Illinois
University of Illinois
  Urbana-Champaign *B, M, D*

New Hampshire
University of New Hampshire *B*

Washington
Washington State University *D*

Plant pathology

Alabama
Auburn University *M, D*

Arkansas
University of Arkansas *M*

California
University of California
  Davis *M, D*
  Riverside *M, D*

Colorado
Colorado State University *M, D*

Delaware
University of Delaware *B*

Florida
University of Florida *B, M*

Georgia
University of Georgia *M, D*

Hawaii
University of Hawaii
  Manoa *M, D*

Illinois
University of Illinois
  Urbana-Champaign *M, D*

Iowa
Iowa State University *M, D*

Kansas
Kansas State University *M, D*

Kentucky
University of Kentucky *M, D*

Louisiana
Louisiana State University and
  Agricultural and Mechanical
  College *M, D*

Michigan
Michigan State University *B, M, D*

Minnesota
University of Minnesota
  Twin Cities *M, D*

Missouri
University of Missouri
  Columbia *M, D*

Montana
Montana State University
  Bozeman *M*

New Mexico
New Mexico State University *B, M*

New York
Cornell University *B, M, D*
State University of New York
  College of Environmental Science
  and Forestry *B, M, D*

North Carolina
North Carolina State University *M, D*

North Dakota
North Dakota State University *M, D*

Ohio
Ohio State University
  Columbus Campus *M, D*

Oklahoma
Oklahoma State University *M, D*

Oregon
Oregon State University *M, D*

Pennsylvania
Penn State
  University Park *M, D*

South Carolina
Clemson University *B, M, D*

Texas
Texas A&M University *M, D*

Virginia
Virginia Polytechnic Institute and
  State University *D*

Washington
Washington State University *M, D*

Wisconsin
University of Wisconsin
  Madison *B, M, D*

Plant physiology

Iowa
Iowa State University *M, D*

Kansas
Pittsburg State University *B*

Kentucky
University of Kentucky *D*

Massachusetts
Simon's Rock College of Bard *B*

Missouri
Washington University in St. Louis *D*

Nebraska
Peru State College *B*

New Hampshire
University of New Hampshire *B*

New York
State University of New York
  College of Environmental Science
    and Forestry *B, M, D*

Oregon
Oregon State University *M, D*

Pennsylvania
Penn State
  University Park *M, D*

South Carolina
Clemson University *D*

Texas
Texas A&M University *M, D*

Vermont
Marlboro College *B*

Washington
Washington State University *M, D*

Plant protection/pest management

Arkansas
University of Arkansas *B*

California
California State Polytechnic
  University: Pomona *B, M*
California State University
  Fresno *B*
College of the Sequoias *C*
San Joaquin Delta College *A*
University of California
  Davis *M*
  Riverside *M*
Ventura College *A*

Florida
Florida Agricultural and Mechanical
  University *B*

Georgia
University of Georgia *M*

Hawaii
University of Hawaii
  Hilo *B*
  Manoa *B*

Idaho
University of Idaho *B*

Iowa
Iowa State University *B*
Southwestern Community College *A*

Michigan
Michigan State University *M*

Mississippi
Mississippi State University *B, M, D*

Nebraska
University of Nebraska
  Lincoln *B*

New York
Cornell University *B, M, D*
State University of New York
  College of Environmental Science
    and Forestry *M, D*

North Carolina
North Carolina State University *A*

North Dakota
North Dakota State University *B*

Ohio
Ohio State University
  Columbus Campus *B*

Puerto Rico
University of Puerto Rico
  Mayaguez *B, M*
  Utuado *A*

South Carolina
Clemson University *M*

Texas
Texas A&M University *B, M*
Texas Tech University *B*
West Texas A&M University *B*

Vermont
Sterling College *A, B*

Washington
Washington State University *B*

Plant sciences

Alabama
Tuskegee University *B, M*

Arizona
Arizona Western College *A*
University of Arizona *B, M, D*

Arkansas
Arkansas State University *B*
University of Arkansas *D*

California
California Polytechnic State
  University: San Luis Obispo *B*
California State University
  Fresno *B, M*
College of the Desert *A*
College of the Redwoods *C, A*
College of the Sequoias *C*
College of the Siskiyous *A*
Cosumnes River College *A*
Mendocino College *C, A*
Modesto Junior College *A*
Reedley College *A*
San Joaquin Delta College *C, A*
Santa Rosa Junior College *C*
University of California
  Davis *B, M, D*

Riverside *M*
  Santa Cruz *B*
Ventura College *A*
Yuba Community College District *C*

Connecticut
University of Connecticut *M, D*

Delaware
Delaware State University *B*
University of Delaware *B, M, D*

Florida
University of Florida *B, D*

Georgia
Abraham Baldwin Agricultural
  College *A*
Fort Valley State University *B*

Idaho
University of Idaho *B, M, D*

Illinois
Southern Illinois University
  Carbondale *B, M*

Iowa
Dordt College *B*
Iowa State University *B*

Louisiana
Louisiana State University and
  Agricultural and Mechanical
  College *B*
Louisiana Tech University *B*

Maine
Southern Maine Community
  College *C, A*
University of Maine *B, M, D*

Massachusetts
University of Massachusetts
  Amherst *B, M, D*

Minnesota
Minnesota State University
  Mankato *B, M, T*

Missouri
Missouri State University *M*
University of Missouri
  Columbia *B*

Montana
Montana State University
  Bozeman *B, M, D*

New Hampshire
University of New Hampshire *B, M, D*

New Jersey
Mercer County Community College *A*
Rutgers, The State University of New
  Jersey
    New Brunswick/Piscataway
      Campus *B*

New York
Cornell University *B, M, D*
State University of New York
  College of Agriculture and
    Technology at Cobleskill *A, B*
  College of Environmental Science
    and Forestry *M, D*

North Carolina
North Carolina Agricultural and
  Technical State University *B*

North Dakota
North Dakota State University *B, M, D*

Ohio
Ohio State University
  Agricultural Technical Institute *A*
  Columbus Campus *B, M*

Oregon
Oregon State University *B, M*

South Carolina
Clemson University *B, M, D*

South Dakota
South Dakota State University *M*

Tennessee
Hiwassee College *A*
Middle Tennessee State University *B*
University of Tennessee
  Knoxville *B, M, D*

Texas
Lubbock Christian University *B*
Texas A&M University *B, M*
Texas A&M University
  Commerce *B*
  Kingsville *B, M*
West Texas A&M University *B, M*

Utah
Utah State University *M, D*

Vermont
Sterling College *B*
University of Vermont *B, M, D*
Vermont Technical College *A*

West Virginia
West Virginia University *B, M*

Plasma/ high-temperature physics

Texas
Rice University *M, D*

Wisconsin
University of Wisconsin
  Madison *M, D*

Plastics engineering technology

California
Cerritos Community College *C, A*

Connecticut
Naugatuck Valley Community
  College *C, A*
Quinebaug Valley Community
  College *A*

Illinois
College of DuPage *C, A*

Kansas
Pittsburg State University *B*

Massachusetts
Mount Wachusett Community
  College *A*

Michigan
Ferris State University *A, B*
Grand Rapids Community
  College *C, A*

Western Michigan University *B*

Minnesota
Hennepin Technical College *C, A*

Mississippi
University of Southern Mississippi *B*

New York
State University of New York
College of Agriculture and
Technology at Morrisville *A*

North Carolina
Davidson County Community
College *C, A*
Edgecombe Community College *C, A*
Guilford Technical Community
College *A*
Isothermal Community College *C, A*

Ohio
Cincinnati State Technical and
Community College *A*
Edison State Community College *C, A*
Kent State University *C*
Kent State University
Trumbull Campus *A*
Tuscarawas Campus *A*
Shawnee State University *C, A, B*
Sinclair Community College *C, A*

Pennsylvania
Pennsylvania College of
Technology *A, B*

Texas
St. Philip's College *C*

Washington
Western Washington University *B*

Wisconsin
Milwaukee Area Technical College *A*

Platemaker/imager

Ohio
Cincinnati State Technical and
Community College *C*

Pennsylvania
Pennsylvania College of Technology *A*

Playwriting/ screenwriting

California
California Institute of the Arts *M*
Chapman University *B, M*
Loyola Marymount University *B*
Otis College of Art and Design *M*
University of Southern
California *B, M*

Florida
Palm Beach Atlantic University *B*
University of South Florida *M*

Illinois
Columbia College Chicago *B*
DePaul University *B*

Iowa
University of Iowa *M*

Kansas
Central Christian College of
Kansas *A, B*

Massachusetts
Emerson College *B, M*
Hampshire College *B*
Simon's Rock College of Bard *B*
Smith College *M*

Michigan
University of Michigan *B*

Minnesota
Metropolitan State University *B*
Minneapolis Community and
Technical College *A*

New Mexico
University of New Mexico *M*

New York
Bard College *B*
City University of New York
Brooklyn College *C, B*
New York University *B, M*
Sarah Lawrence College *B, M*
State University of New York
Purchase *B*

Ohio
Ohio University *B, M*

Pennsylvania
Drexel University *B*
Temple University *M*

Texas
Texas Tech University *M*

Vermont
Bennington College *B, M*
Marlboro College *B*

Virginia
Hollins University *M*

Washington
Cornish College of the Arts *B*

Plumbing

Alabama
Lawson State Community College *C*

Arizona
Mohave Community College *C*
Tohono O'odham Community
College *C, A*

California
Foothill College *C*

Florida
Gulf Coast Community College *C*
Indian River Community College *C*
South Florida Community College *C*

Georgia
Athens Technical College *C*

Indiana
Ivy Tech State College
Ivy Tech Community College:
Bloomington *C, A*
Ivy Tech Community College:
Central Indiana *C, A*
Ivy Tech Community College: East
Central *C, A*
Ivy Tech Community College:
Kokomo *C, A*
Ivy Tech Community College:
Lafayette *C, A*

Ivy Tech Community College: North
Central *C, A*
Ivy Tech Community College:
Northeast *C, A*
Ivy Tech Community College: South
Central *C, A*
Ivy Tech Community College:
Southwest *C, A*
Ivy Tech Community College:
Wabash Valley *C, A*
Ivy Tech Community College:
Whitewater *C, A*

Kentucky
Elizabethtown Community and
Technical College *C*
Jefferson Community College *C*
Somerset Community College *C, A*

Michigan
Delta College *A*

Minnesota
Minnesota State Community and
Technical College - Fergus Falls *C*
Northland Community & Technical
College *C*
Northwest Technical College *C*
St. Cloud Technical College *C, A*
St. Paul College *C*

New York
State University of New York
College of Technology at Canton *C*

North Carolina
Fayetteville Technical Community
College *C, A*
Southwestern Community College *C*

North Dakota
North Dakota State College of
Science *C*

Oklahoma
Rose State College *A*

Pennsylvania
Community College of Allegheny
County *C*
Pennsylvania College of Technology *C*

Utah
Salt Lake Community College *A*

Virginia
Piedmont Virginia Community
College *A*
Wytheville Community College *A*

Washington
Olympic College *A*

Wisconsin
Gateway Technical College *C*
Milwaukee Area Technical College *C*
Waukesha County Technical
College *C*
Western Wisconsin Technical
College *C*

Podiatry

California
California College of Podiatric
Medicine *F*

Florida
Barry University: School of Graduate
Medical Sciences *F*

Illinois
Dr. William M. Scholl College of
Podiatric Medicine *F*

Iowa
University of Osteopathic Medicine
and Health Sciences: College of
Podiatric Medicine and Surgery *F*

New York
New York College of Podiatric
Medicine *F*

Ohio
Ohio College of Podiatric Medicine *F*

Pennsylvania
Pennsylvania College of Podiatric
Medicine *F*

Police science

Alabama
Central Alabama Community
College *C, A*
Enterprise-Ozark Community
College *A*
George C. Wallace State Community
College
George C. Wallace Community
College at Dothan *C*
Jefferson State Community
College *C, A*
Northwest-Shoals Community
College *C, A*
Shelton State Community College *C*
Wallace State Community College at
Hanceville *A*

Arizona
Central Arizona College *C*
Cochise College *A*
Eastern Arizona College *C, A*
Glendale Community College *C, A*
Mohave Community College *C, A*
Northland Pioneer College *C, A*
Phoenix College *A*
Pima Community College *A*
Scottsdale Community College *C*

Arkansas
Arkansas Northeastern College *C, A*
Arkansas State University *A*
East Arkansas Community
College *A*
North Arkansas College *A*
South Arkansas Community College *A*
University of Arkansas
Community College at Hope *A*
Little Rock *A*

California
Allan Hancock College *C*
American River College *A*
Bakersfield College *A*
Barstow College *C, A*
Butte College *C, A*
Cabrillo College *C, A*
California Lutheran University *B*
Cerritos Community College *A*
Cerro Coso Community College *C, A*
Chabot College *A*
Citrus College *C*
City College of San Francisco *C, A*
College of the Redwoods *C*
College of the Siskiyous *A*
Contra Costa College *A*
East Los Angeles College *C, A*
El Camino College *A*
Evergreen Valley College *A*
Fresno City College *C, A*
Fullerton College *A*

Glendale Community College *A*
Grossmont Community College *C, A*
Irvine Valley College *C, A*
Lassen College *A*
Los Angeles City College *C, A*
Los Angeles Harbor College *C, A*
Los Angeles Valley College *C, A*
Merced College *C, A*
MiraCosta College *C, A*
Modesto Junior College *A*
Moorpark College *C, A*
Mount San Antonio College *C, A*
Mount San Jacinto College *C, A*
Napa Valley College *C, A*
Palomar College *C, A*
Pasadena City College *C, A*
Porterville College *C, A*
Rio Hondo College *A*
Sacramento City College *C, A*
San Bernardino Valley College *C*
San Joaquin Delta College *A*
Santa Ana College *C, A*
Santa Monica College *A*
Santa Rosa Junior College *C, A*
Shasta College *A*
Sierra College *A*
Solano Community College *C, A*
Southwestern College *C*
Ventura College *A*
West Hills Community College *A*
Westwood College of Technology
    Inland Empire *B*
Yuba Community College District *A*

Colorado
Aims Community College *C*
Arapahoe Community College *C*
Colorado Mountain College
    Spring Valley Campus *C*
    Timberline Campus *C*
Pueblo Community College *A*
Red Rocks Community College *C*
Trinidad State Junior College *A*
Western State College of Colorado *B*

Connecticut
Asnuntuck Community College *C, A*
Housatonic Community College *C, A*
Naugatuck Valley Community
    College *C, A*
Three Rivers Community College *A*
University of Hartford *B*
University of New Haven *C, A*
Western Connecticut State
    University *B*

District of Columbia
American University *B, M, D*
George Washington University *A, B*
Southeastern University *A, B*

Florida
Brevard Community College *C*
Daytona Beach Community
    College *C, A*
Florida Community College at
    Jacksonville *C*
Florida Metropolitan University
    Brandon Campus *A, B, M*
Florida Metropolitan University:
    Orange Park *A*
Hillsborough Community College *C*
Indian River Community College *C*
Lake City Community College *C*
Miami Dade College *C*
Nova Southeastern University *B, M*
Okaloosa-Walton College *C*
Palm Beach Community College *C*
Pasco-Hernando Community
    College *C*
Polk Community College *C, A*
Remington College: Largo *A*
Santa Fe Community College *C*

Seminole Community College *C*
South Florida Community College *C*
Tallahassee Community College *C*
Valencia Community College *C, A*

Georgia
Abraham Baldwin Agricultural
    College *A*
Armstrong Atlantic State
    University *A, B, M*
Bainbridge College *C*
Dalton State College *A*
Georgia Highlands College *A*
Gwinnett Technical College *A*
Middle Georgia College *C, A*
Northwestern Technical College *C, A*
South Georgia College *A*
Southwest Georgia Technical
    College *C, A*

Hawaii
University of Hawaii
    Honolulu Community College *A*

Idaho
College of Southern Idaho *C, A*
Idaho State University *C, A*
North Idaho College *A*

Illinois
Black Hawk College *C, A*
City Colleges of Chicago
    Harold Washington College *C, A*
    Olive-Harvey College *C*
College of DuPage *C, A*
College of Lake County *C, A*
Concordia University *B*
Elgin Community College *A*
Illinois Eastern Community Colleges
    Frontier Community College *C*
    Olney Central College *A*
Illinois Valley Community College *A*
John Wood Community College *A*
Kankakee Community College *A*
Kishwaukee College *C, A*
Lake Land College *A*
Lewis University *B, M*
Lincoln Land Community College *C, A*
McHenry County College *A*
Moraine Valley Community College *A*
Morton College *A*
Oakton Community College *C, A*
Parkland College *A*
Prairie State College *C, A*
Rend Lake College *C, A*
Richland Community College *A*
Sauk Valley Community College *A*
Southeastern Illinois College *C, A*
Southwestern Illinois College *C, A*
Triton College *A*
Waubonsee Community College *C, A*
Westwood College - Chicago Loop *B*
Westwood College of Technology
    O'Hare *B*
William Rainey Harper College *C, A*

Indiana
Calumet College of St. Joseph *A, B*
Indiana Wesleyan University *A*
Vincennes University *A*

Iowa
Des Moines Area Community
    College *A*
Dordt College *B*
Hawkeye Community College *A*
Indian Hills Community College *A*
Iowa Central Community College *C, A*
Iowa Lakes Community College *A*
Kirkwood Community College *C, A*
Marshalltown Community College *A*
North Iowa Area Community
    College *A*

Kansas
Allen County Community College *A*
Barton County Community
    College *C, A*
Bethany College *B*
Butler County Community
    College *C, A*
Central Christian College of Kansas *A*
Cloud County Community College *A*
Garden City Community College *A*
Hutchinson Community College *C, A*
Johnson County Community
    College *C, A*
Kansas City Kansas Community
    College *C, A*
Seward County Community
    College *C, A*
Washburn University of Topeka *B*

Kentucky
Ashland Community and Technical
    College *A*
Big Sandy Community and Technical
    College *A*
Eastern Kentucky University *B, M*
Kentucky State University *B*
Madisonville Community College *A*
Northern Kentucky University *A*
Owensboro Community College *A*
Somerset Community College *C, A*
Southeast Kentucky Community and
    Technical College *A*
Western Kentucky University *M*

Louisiana
Delgado Community College *A*
Grambling State University *A*
Nicholls State University *A*
Northwestern State University *A*
Southeastern Louisiana University *A*
Southern University and Agricultural
    and Mechanical College *A*
University of Louisiana at Monroe *A*

Maine
Andover College *A*
Beal College *A*
Southern Maine Community
    College *A*

Maryland
Allegany College of Maryland *C, A*
Baltimore City Community College *A*
Chesapeake College *C, A*
College of Southern Maryland *A*
Community College of Baltimore
    County *C, A*
Frostburg State University *B*
Garrett College *C*
Hagerstown Community College *C, A*
Harford Community College *A*
Montgomery College *A*
University of Maryland
    Eastern Shore *B*
Wor-Wic Community College *C, A*

Massachusetts
American International College *B*
Greenfield Community College *A*
Massasoit Community College *A*
Northeastern University *B*
Springfield Technical Community
    College *A*

Michigan
Delta College *C, A*
Ferris State University *A, B*
Grand Rapids Community College *A*
Henry Ford Community College *A*
Kalamazoo Valley Community
    College *C, A*
Kellogg Community College *A*
Kirtland Community College *C, A*

Lake Michigan College *A*
Lansing Community College *A*
Macomb Community College *C, A*
Mid Michigan Community College *A*
Mott Community College *C, A*
North Central Michigan College *C*
Northern Michigan University *C, B*
Northwestern Michigan College *A*
Oakland Community College *C, A*
Olivet College *B*
Schoolcraft College *A*
University of Detroit Mercy *B, M*
Washtenaw Community College *A*

Minnesota
Alexandria Technical College *C, A*
Central Lakes College *A*
Century Community and Technical
    College *A*
Fond du Lac Tribal and Community
    College *C, A*
Hibbing Community College *A*
Inver Hills Community College *A*
Leech Lake Tribal College *A*
Metropolitan State University *C, B*
Minneapolis Community and
    Technical College *C, A*
Minnesota State University
    Mankato *B*
Normandale Community College *C, A*
North Hennepin Community
    College *A*
Northland Community & Technical
    College *A*
Ridgewater College *A*
Riverland Community College *A*
Rochester Community and Technical
    College *A*
St. Mary's University of Minnesota *B*
Vermilion Community College *A*
Winona State University *B*

Mississippi
Southwest Mississippi Community
    College *A*

Missouri
Blue River Community College *C, A*
College of the Ozarks *B*
East Central College *A*
Jefferson College *C, A*
Mineral Area College *C, A*
Missouri Southern State University *C*
Missouri State University: West
    Plains *A*
Missouri Western State University *A*
Moberly Area Community College *C*
St. Louis Community College
    St. Louis Community College at
        Florissant Valley *A*
    St. Louis Community College at
        Meramec *C, A*
Southwest Baptist University *B*
State Fair Community College *A*
Three Rivers Community College *A*

Montana
Dawson Community College *C, A*
University of Great Falls *B*

Nebraska
Metropolitan Community College *A*
Mid-Plains Community College Area *A*
Nebraska Indian Community
    College *A*
University of Nebraska
    Kearney *B*

Nevada
Community College of Southern
    Nevada *C, A*
Great Basin College *A*

Truckee Meadows Community
  College *A*
Western Nevada Community
  College *C, A*

New Hampshire

McIntosh College *A*

New Jersey

Bergen Community College *A*
Brookdale Community College *A*
Burlington County College *C, A*
Camden County College *A*
County College of Morris *A*
Cumberland County College *C, A*
Essex County College *A*
Gloucester County College *A*
Mercer County Community College *A*
Ocean County College *C, A*
Passaic County Community
  College *C, A*
Rowan University *B*

New Mexico

Eastern New Mexico University:
  Roswell Campus *A*
New Mexico Junior College *A*
San Juan College *C, A*

New York

Adirondack Community College *A*
Broome Community College *A*
Cayuga County Community
  College *C, A*
City University of New York
  John Jay College of Criminal
    Justice *C, A*
Erie Community College
  City Campus *C, A*
  North Campus *A*
Jamestown Community College *A*
Medaille College *B*
Mercy College *C*
Monroe College *A*
Monroe Community College *A*
Orange County Community College *A*
Rochester Business Institute *A*
State University of New York
  College at Brockport *B*
  Farmingdale *A*
Sullivan County Community
  College *A*
Tompkins-Cortland Community
  College *A*
Westchester Community College *A*

North Carolina

Asheville-Buncombe Technical
  Community College *C, A*
Bladen Community College *C*
Brunswick Community College *C*
Cape Fear Community College *C, A*
Carteret Community College *A*
Catawba Valley Community College *C*
Central Piedmont Community
  College *C*
Cleveland Community College *C*
Coastal Carolina Community
  College *C, A*
College of the Albemarle *C*
Craven Community College *C*
Davidson County Community
  College *C*
Durham Technical Community
  College *C*
Fayetteville Technical Community
  College *C*
Gaston College *C*
Halifax Community College *C*
Isothermal Community College *C*
James Sprunt Community
  College *C, A*
Johnston Community College *C, A*

Lenoir Community College *C*
Mayland Community College *C*
Mitchell Community College *C, A*
Montgomery Community College *C*
Nash Community College *A*
Pfeiffer University *B*
Pitt Community College *C, A*
Randolph Community College *C, A*
Sampson Community College *C*
Sandhills Community College *C*
Southwestern Community College *C*
Stanly Community College *C*
Vance-Granville Community
  College *C*
Wake Technical Community
  College *A*
Wayne Community College *A*
Western Piedmont Community
  College *C*
Wilkes Community College *C*
Wilson Technical Community
  College *C*

North Dakota

Lake Region State College *C, A*

Ohio

Cincinnati State Technical and
  Community College *C*
Columbus State Community
  College *A*
Cuyahoga Community College
  Metropolitan Campus *A*
Edison State Community College *A*
Hocking College *A*
James A. Rhodes State College *A*
Jefferson Community College *A*
Lakeland Community College *C, A*
Ohio Northern University *B*
Ohio University *A*
Ohio University
  Chillicothe Campus *A*
  Southern Campus at Ironton *A*
  Zanesville Campus *A*
Owens Community College
  Toledo *A*
Remington College
  Cleveland *A*
Sinclair Community College *A*
Southern State Community College *A*
Technology Education College *A*
University of Akron *C, A*
Wright State University *B*
Youngstown State University *C, A*

Oklahoma

Connors State College *A*
East Central University *B*
Northwestern Oklahoma State
  University *B*
Oklahoma City University *B*
Oklahoma State University
  Oklahoma City *A*
Redlands Community College *A*
Rogers State University *A*
Rose State College *A*
Tulsa Community College *A*
University of Central Oklahoma *B*
Western Oklahoma State College *A*

Oregon

Chemeketa Community College *A*
Clackamas Community College *A*
Everest College: Portland *A*
Lane Community College *C*
Linn-Benton Community College *A*
Rogue Community College *A*
Southern Oregon University *B*
Treasure Valley Community College *A*
Umpqua Community College *C*
Western Oregon University *M*

Pennsylvania

Bucks County Community College *A*
Butler County Community College *A*
Community College of Allegheny
  County *A*
Community College of
  Philadelphia *C, A*
Delaware County Community
  College *C, A*
Edinboro University of
  Pennsylvania *A*
Harrisburg Area Community
  College *C, A*
ICM School of Business & Medical
  Careers *A*
Lackawanna College *C, A*
Lehigh Carbon Community College *A*
Luzerne County Community
  College *C, A*
Montgomery County Community
  College *A*
Reading Area Community College *A*
Westmoreland County Community
  College *A*
York College of Pennsylvania *A, B*
York Technical Institute *A*

Puerto Rico

Universidad del Este *C, A*
University College of San Juan *A, B*

Rhode Island

Community College of Rhode
  Island *A*

South Carolina

South University *B*
Spartanburg Methodist College *A*
Williamsburg Technical College *C*

South Dakota

Western Dakota Technical Institute *A*

Tennessee

Cleveland State Community College *C*
Dyersburg State Community
  College *A*
Jackson State Community College *A*
Middle Tennessee State University *A*
Nashville State Community College *A*
Roane State Community College *C, A*
Southwest Tennessee Community
  College *C, A*
Walters State Community College *C, A*

Texas

Amarillo College *C, A*
Austin Community College *C, A*
Brazosport College *C, A*
Central Texas College *C*
Coastal Bend College *A*
College of the Mainland *A*
Collin County Community College
  District *C*
Del Mar College *C, A*
Eastfield College *C*
El Centro College *C*
Grayson County College *A*
Hardin-Simmons University *B*
Hill College *C, A*
Houston Community College
  System *C, A*
Kilgore College *C, A*
Lee College *A*
Midland College *A*
Navarro College *A*
North Central Texas College *A*
Northeast Texas Community
  College *C, A*
Odessa College *C, A*
San Antonio College *C*

San Jacinto College
  Central Campus *C, A*
  North *C, A*
Stephen F. Austin State University *B*
Tarrant County College *C, A*
Temple College *C, A*
Texas Southmost College *A*
Texas State University: San Marcos *B*
Tyler Junior College *C, A*
Vernon College *C*
Weatherford College *C, A*
Western Texas College *A*

Utah

Salt Lake Community College *C*
Weber State University *B*

Virginia

Bluefield College *B*
Dabney S. Lancaster Community
  College *C, A*
George Mason University *B*
Lord Fairfax Community College *C*
Mountain Empire Community
  College *C*
Parks College: Arlington *A*
Paul D. Camp Community College *A*
Piedmont Virginia Community
  College *C, A*
Southside Virginia Community
  College *C, A*
Southwest Virginia Community
  College *C, A*
Virginia Highlands Community
  College *A*
Virginia Western Community
  College *A*
Wytheville Community College *C, A*

Washington

Centralia College *A*
Columbia Basin College *A*
Grays Harbor College *C, A*
Green River Community College *A*
Olympic College *C, A*
Spokane Community College *A*
Whatcom Community College *A*

West Virginia

Bluefield State College *A*
West Virginia State University *B*

Wisconsin

Blackhawk Technical College *A*
Chippewa Valley Technical College *A*
Fox Valley Technical College *A*
Gateway Technical College *A*
Lakeshore Technical College *C, A*
Madison Area Technical College *A*
Mid-State Technical College *A*
Milwaukee Area Technical College *A*
Moraine Park Technical College *A*
Nicolet Area Technical College *A*
Northcentral Technical College *A*
Northeast Wisconsin Technical
  College *A*
University of Wisconsin
  Superior *A*
Waukesha County Technical
  College *A*
Western Wisconsin Technical
  College *A*
Wisconsin Indianhead Technical
  College *C, A*

Wyoming

Eastern Wyoming College *A*
Laramie County Community
  College *A*
Sheridan College *A*

Polish

Illinois
University of Illinois
Chicago B

Michigan
Madonna University B

Pennsylvania
University of Pittsburgh B

Wisconsin
University of Wisconsin
Madison B

Polish studies

New York
Columbia University
Columbia College B

Political communications

California
Westmont College B

District of Columbia
George Washington University B

Kentucky
Western Kentucky University B

Massachusetts
Emerson College B, M
Suffolk University B

Nebraska
Nebraska Wesleyan University B

Tennessee
Bryan College B

Political science

Alabama
Alabama Agricultural and Mechanical
University B
Alabama State University B
Athens State University B
Auburn University B
Auburn University at
Montgomery B, M
Birmingham-Southern College B, T
Huntingdon College B
Jacksonville State University B
Lawson State Community College A
Miles College B
Samford University B
Spring Hill College B
Troy University B
Tuskegee University B
University of Alabama B, M, D
University of Alabama
Birmingham B
Huntsville B
University of Mobile B
University of Montevallo B, T
University of North Alabama B
University of South Alabama B

Alaska
University of Alaska
Anchorage B
Fairbanks B
Southeast B

Arizona
Arizona State University B, M, D

Arizona State University West B
Arizona Western College A
Cochise College A
Eastern Arizona College A
Grand Canyon University B
Northern Arizona University B, M, D
Pima Community College A
South Mountain Community
College A
University of Arizona B, M, D

Arkansas
Arkansas State University B, M
Harding University B
Henderson State University B
Hendrix College B
John Brown University B
Lyon College B
Ouachita Baptist University B
Philander Smith College B
Southern Arkansas University B
University of Arkansas B, M
University of Arkansas
Little Rock B
Monticello B
Pine Bluff B
University of Central Arkansas B
University of the Ozarks B

California
Azusa Pacific University B
Bakersfield College A
Cabrillo College A
California Baptist University B
California Lutheran University B
California Maritime Academy B
California Polytechnic State
University: San Luis Obispo B
California State Polytechnic
University: Pomona B
California State University
Bakersfield B
Chico B, M
Dominguez Hills B
East Bay B
Fresno B
Fullerton B, M
Los Angeles B, M
Northridge B
Sacramento B, M
San Bernardino B, T
San Marcos B
Stanislaus B
Canada College A
Cerritos Community College A
Chabot College A
Chaffey College A
Chapman University B
Claremont McKenna College B
College of Alameda A
College of the Desert A
Concordia University B
Copper Mountain College A
Crafton Hills College A
Cypress College A
De Anza College A
Dominican University of California B
East Los Angeles College A
El Camino College A
Foothill College A
Fresno Pacific University B
Fullerton College A
Gavilan Community College A
Golden West College A
Grossmont Community College A
Humboldt State University B
Irvine Valley College A
Los Angeles Southwest College A
Los Angeles Valley College A
Loyola Marymount University B
Master's College B
Merced College A
Mills College B
MiraCosta College A

Monterey Peninsula College A
Mount St. Mary's College B
Notre Dame de Namur University B
Occidental College B
Orange Coast College A
Pepperdine University B
Pitzer College B
Point Loma Nazarene University B
Pomona College B
Saddleback College A
St. Mary's College of California B
San Diego City College A
San Diego Miramar College A
San Diego State University B, M
San Francisco State University B, M
San Jose State University B
Santa Ana College A
Santa Barbara City College A
Santa Clara University B
Santa Monica College A
Santa Rosa Junior College A
Santiago Canyon College A
Scripps College B
Solano Community College A
Sonoma State University B
Southwestern College A
Stanford University B, M, D
University of California
Berkeley B, D
Davis B, M, D
Irvine B, M, D
Los Angeles B, M, D
Riverside B, M, D
San Diego B, M, D
Santa Barbara B, M, D
Santa Cruz B, D
University of Judaism B
University of La Verne B
University of Redlands B
University of San Diego B
University of San Francisco B
University of Southern
California B, M, D
University of the Pacific B
Vanguard University of Southern
California B
Ventura College A
West Los Angeles College C, A
Westmont College B
Whittier College B, M

Colorado
Colorado College B
Colorado State University B, M, D
Colorado State University
Pueblo B
Fort Lewis College B
Mesa State College B
Metropolitan State College of
Denver B, T
Otero Junior College A
Red Rocks Community College A
Regis University B
United States Air Force Academy B
University of Colorado
Boulder B, M, D
Colorado Springs B
Denver and Health Sciences
Center B, M
University of Denver B
University of Northern Colorado B
Western State College of Colorado B

Connecticut
Albertus Magnus College B
Central Connecticut State
University B
Connecticut College B
Eastern Connecticut State
University B
Fairfield University B
Quinnipiac University B
Sacred Heart University B
St. Joseph College B

Southern Connecticut State
University B, M
Trinity College B
United States Coast Guard Academy B
University of Bridgeport B
University of Connecticut B, M, D
University of Hartford B
University of New Haven B
Wesleyan University B
Western Connecticut State
University B
Yale University B, M, D

Delaware
Delaware State University B
University of Delaware B, M, D
Wesley College B

District of Columbia
American University B, M, D
Catholic University of
America B, M, D
Gallaudet University B
George Washington
University B, M, D
Georgetown University B, M, D
Howard University B, M, D
Trinity University B
University of the District of
Columbia B

Florida
Barry University B
Bethune-Cookman College B
Broward Community College A
Eckerd College B
Flagler College B
Florida Agricultural and Mechanical
University B
Florida Atlantic University B, M
Florida Gulf Coast University B
Florida International
University B, M, D
Florida Southern College B
Florida State University B, M, D
Gulf Coast Community College A
Indian River Community College A
Jacksonville University B
Lynn University B
Miami Dade College A
New College of Florida B
Palm Beach Atlantic University B
Palm Beach Community College A
Rollins College B
St. Leo University B
St. Thomas University B
Stetson University B
University of Central Florida B, M
University of Florida B, M, D
University of Miami B
University of North Florida B
University of South Florida B, M
University of Tampa B
University of West Florida B, M
Valencia Community College A

Georgia
Agnes Scott College B
Albany State University B
Armstrong Atlantic State
University B, T
Atlanta Metropolitan College A
Augusta State University B
Bainbridge College A
Berry College B
Brewton-Parker College B
Clark Atlanta University B, M, D
Columbus State University B
Dalton State College A
Darton College A
East Georgia College A
Emory University B, D
Fort Valley State University B

Gainesville State College *A*
Georgia College and State
    University *A*
Georgia Perimeter College *A*
Georgia Southern University *B, M*
Georgia Southwestern State
    University *B*
Georgia State University *B, M, D*
Gordon College *A*
Kennesaw State University *B*
LaGrange College *B*
Mercer University *B*
Middle Georgia College *A*
Morehouse College *B*
North Georgia College & State
    University *B*
Oglethorpe University *B*
Piedmont College *B*
Savannah State University *B*
South Georgia College *A*
Spelman College *B*
University of Georgia *B, M, D*
University of West Georgia *B*
Valdosta State University *B*
Waycross College *A*

Hawaii
Brigham Young University-Hawaii *B*
Chaminade University of Honolulu *B*
Hawaii Pacific University *B*
University of Hawaii
    Hilo *B*
    Manoa *B, M, D*
    West Oahu *B*

Idaho
Albertson College of Idaho *B*
Boise State University *B, T*
Brigham Young University-Idaho *B*
College of Southern Idaho *A*
Idaho State University *A, B, M, D, T*
North Idaho College *A*
Northwest Nazarene University *B*
University of Idaho *B, M, D*

Illinois
Augustana College *B, T*
Aurora University *B*
Benedictine University *B*
Black Hawk College
    East Campus *A*
Blackburn College *B*
Bradley University *B*
Chicago State University *B*
Concordia University *B*
Danville Area Community College *A*
DePaul University *B*
Dominican University *B*
Eastern Illinois University *B, M*
Elmhurst College *B, T*
Eureka College *B*
Governors State University *M*
Highland Community College *A*
Illinois College *B*
Illinois State University *B, M*
Illinois Valley Community College *A*
Illinois Wesleyan University *B*
John A. Logan College *A*
Joliet Junior College *A*
Judson College *B*
Kishwaukee College *A*
Knox College *B*
Lake Forest College *B*
Lewis University *B*
Loyola University of Chicago *B, M, D*
MacMurray College *B*
McKendree College *B*
Millikin University *B*
Monmouth College *B, T*
North Central College *B*
North Park University *B*
Northeastern Illinois University *B, M*
Northern Illinois University *B, M, D*
Northwestern University *B, M, D*

Olivet Nazarene University *B*
Principia College *B*
Quincy University *B*
Richland Community College *A*
Rockford College *B*
Roosevelt University *B, M*
St. Xavier University *B*
Sauk Valley Community College *A*
South Suburban College of Cook
    County *A*
Southern Illinois University
    Carbondale *B, M, D*
Southern Illinois University
    Edwardsville *B*
Southwestern Illinois College *A*
Trinity Christian College *B*
Triton College *A*
University of Chicago *B, D*
University of Illinois
    Chicago *B, M, D*
    Springfield *B, M*
    Urbana-Champaign *B, M, D*
University of St. Francis *B*
Western Illinois University *B, M*
Wheaton College *B, T*

Indiana
Anderson University *B*
Ball State University *B, M*
Butler University *B*
DePauw University *B*
Franklin College *B*
Hanover College *B*
Indiana State University *B, M*
Indiana University
    Bloomington *B, M, D*
    Northwest *B*
    South Bend *B*
    Southeast *B*
Indiana University-Purdue University
    Fort Wayne *A, B*
Indiana University-Purdue University
    Indianapolis *B*
Indiana Wesleyan University *A, B*
Manchester College *B*
Marian College *B, T*
Martin University *B*
Purdue University *B, M, D*
Purdue University
    Calumet *B*
St. Joseph's College *B*
Saint Mary's College *B*
Taylor University *B*
University of Evansville *B*
University of Indianapolis *B*
University of Notre Dame *B, M, D*
University of Southern Indiana *B*
Valparaiso University *B*
Vincennes University *A*
Wabash College *B*

Iowa
Briar Cliff University *B*
Buena Vista University *B, T*
Central College *B, T*
Clarke College *A, B, T*
Coe College *B*
Cornell College *B, T*
Dordt College *B*
Drake University *B*
Graceland University *T*
Grand View College *B*
Grinnell College *B*
Iowa State University *B, M*
Loras College *B*
Luther College *B*
Morningside College *B*
North Iowa Area Community
    College *A*
Northwestern College *B*
St. Ambrose University *B, T*
Simpson College *B*
University of Iowa *B, M, D, T*
University of Northern Iowa *B*

Waldorf College *B*
Wartburg College *B, T*
William Penn University *B*

Kansas
Baker University *B, T*
Barton County Community College *A*
Benedictine College *B*
Butler County Community College *A*
Central Christian College of Kansas *A*
Coffeyville Community College *A*
Emporia State University *B, T*
Fort Hays State University *B, M*
Friends University *B*
Kansas State University *C, B, M*
Labette Community College *A*
Ottawa University *B*
Pittsburg State University *B*
Pratt Community College *A*
University of Kansas *B, M, D*
University of St. Mary *B*
Washburn University of Topeka *B*
Wichita State University *B*

Kentucky
Bellarmine University *B*
Berea College *B*
Brescia University *B*
Campbellsville University *B*
Centre College *B*
Eastern Kentucky University *B, M*
Georgetown College *B, T*
Kentucky State University *B*
Kentucky Wesleyan College *B, T*
Morehead State University *B*
Murray State University *B, T*
Northern Kentucky University *B*
Thomas More College *A, B*
Transylvania University *B*
University of Kentucky *B, M, D*
University of Louisville *B, M*
University of the Cumberlands *B*
Western Kentucky University *B*

Louisiana
Centenary College of Louisiana *B, T*
Dillard University *B*
Grambling State University *B*
Louisiana State University
    Shreveport *B*
Louisiana State University and
    Agricultural and Mechanical
    College *B, M, D*
Louisiana Tech University *B*
Loyola University New Orleans *B*
Nicholls State University *B*
Northwestern State University *B*
Southeastern Louisiana University *B*
Southern University
    New Orleans *B*
Southern University and Agricultural
    and Mechanical College *B*
Tulane University *B, M*
University of Louisiana at Lafayette *B*
University of Louisiana at Monroe *B*
University of New Orleans *B, M, D*
Xavier University of Louisiana *B*

Maine
Bates College *B*
Bowdoin College *B*
Colby College *B*
Thomas College *B*
University of Maine *B*
University of Maine
    Farmington *B*
    Presque Isle *B*
University of New England *B*
University of Southern Maine *B*

Maryland
Allegany College of Maryland *A*
Bowie State University *B*

College of Notre Dame of Maryland *B*
Columbia Union College *B*
Community College of Baltimore
    County *A*
Coppin State University *B*
Frederick Community College *A*
Frostburg State University *B*
Goucher College *B*
Hood College *B*
Johns Hopkins University *B, M, D*
Loyola College in Maryland *B*
McDaniel College *B*
Morgan State University *B*
Mount St. Mary's University *B*
St. Mary's College of Maryland *B*
Salisbury University *B, T*
Towson University *B*
United States Naval Academy *B*
University of Baltimore *B*
University of Maryland
    Baltimore County *B*
    College Park *B, M, D*
Washington College *B*

Massachusetts
American International College *B*
Amherst College *B*
Assumption College *B*
Boston College *B, M, D*
Boston University *B, M, D*
Brandeis University *B, M, D*
Bridgewater State College *B*
Clark University *B*
College of the Holy Cross *B*
Emmanuel College *B*
Fitchburg State College *B*
Framingham State College *B*
Gordon College *B*
Hampshire College *B*
Harvard College *B, D*
Massachusetts Institute of
    Technology *B, D*
Merrimack College *B*
Mount Holyoke College *B*
Northeastern University *B, M*
Pine Manor College *B*
Regis College *B*
Salem State College *B*
Simmons College *B*
Simon's Rock College of Bard *B*
Smith College *B*
Springfield College *B*
Stonehill College *B*
Suffolk University *B, M*
Tufts University *B*
University of Massachusetts
    Amherst *B, M, D*
    Boston *B*
    Dartmouth *B*
    Lowell *B*
Wellesley College *B*
Western New England College *B*
Westfield State College *B*
Wheaton College *B*
Williams College *B*

Michigan
Adrian College *A, B, T*
Albion College *B, T*
Alma College *B, T*
Andrews University *B*
Aquinas College *B, T*
Calvin College *B, T*
Central Michigan University *B, M, T*
Cornerstone University *B*
Eastern Michigan University *B*
Grand Valley State University *B*
Hillsdale College *B*
Hope College *B*
Kalamazoo College *B, T*
Kellogg Community College *A*
Lake Michigan College *A*
Lake Superior State University *B*
Lansing Community College *A*

Marygrove College B, T
Michigan State University B, M, D
Northern Michigan University B, T
Oakland University B
Saginaw Valley State University B
Spring Arbor University B
University of Detroit Mercy B
University of Michigan B, M, D, T
University of Michigan
    Dearborn B
    Flint B, T
Wayne State University B, M, D
Western Michigan University B, M, D

Minnesota

Augsburg College B
Bemidji State University B
Bethel University B
Carleton College B
College of St. Benedict B
College of St. Catherine B
Concordia College: Moorhead B
Gustavus Adolphus College B
Hamline University B
Macalester College B
Minnesota State University
    Mankato B, M
    Moorhead B
Ridgewater College A
St. Cloud State University B
St. John's University B
St. Mary's University of Minnesota B
St. Olaf College B
Southwest Minnesota State
    University B
University of Minnesota
    Duluth B
    Morris B
    Twin Cities B, M, D
University of St. Thomas B
Vermilion Community College A
Winona State University B

Mississippi

Alcorn State University B
Belhaven College B
Delta State University B
Hinds Community College A
Jackson State University B, M
Millsaps College B
Mississippi College B, M
Mississippi State University B, M
Mississippi Valley State University B
Rust College B
Tougaloo College B
University of Mississippi B, M, D
University of Southern
    Mississippi B, M

Missouri

Avila University B
Central Methodist University B
Central Missouri State University B
College of the Ozarks B
Columbia College B
Drury University B, T
Evangel University B
Lincoln University B
Lindenwood University B
Missouri Southern State
    University B, T
Missouri State University B
Missouri Valley College B
Missouri Western State University B, T
Northwest Missouri State
    University B
Park University B
Rockhurst University B
St. Louis University B
Southeast Missouri State University B
Southwest Baptist University B
Three Rivers Community College A
Truman State University B

University of Missouri
    Columbia B, M, D
    Kansas City B, M, D
    St. Louis B, M, D
Washington University in St.
    Louis B, M, D
Webster University B
Westminster College B
William Jewell College B
William Woods University B

Montana

Carroll College B, T
Miles Community College A
Montana State University
    Billings T
    Bozeman B
Rocky Mountain College B, T
University of Great Falls B
University of Montana: Missoula B, M

Nebraska

Creighton University B
Doane College B
Hastings College B
Nebraska Wesleyan University B
University of Nebraska
    Kearney B, T
    Lincoln B, M, D
    Omaha B
Wayne State College B, T
Western Nebraska Community
    College A

Nevada

University of Nevada
    Las Vegas B, M
    Reno B, M, D

New Hampshire

Dartmouth College B
Franklin Pierce College B
New England College B
Plymouth State University B
Rivier College B
St. Anselm College B, T
Southern New Hampshire
    University B
Thomas More College of Liberal
    Arts B
University of New Hampshire B, M

New Jersey

Bloomfield College B
Caldwell College B
Centenary College B
The College of New Jersey B
Drew University B
Fairleigh Dickinson University
    College at Florham B
    Metropolitan Campus B, M
Gloucester County College A
Kean University B, M, T
Middlesex County College A
Monmouth University B
Montclair State University B
New Jersey City University B
Princeton University B, M, D
Ramapo College of New Jersey B
Richard Stockton College of New
    Jersey B
Rider University B
Rowan University B
Rutgers, The State University of New
    Jersey
    Camden Regional Campus B
    New Brunswick/Piscataway
        Campus B
    Newark Regional Campus B, M
St. Peter's College B
Salem Community College A
Seton Hall University B, T
Thomas Edison State College B

William Paterson University of New
    Jersey B

New Mexico

College of Santa Fe B
Eastern New Mexico University B
New Mexico Highlands University B
New Mexico State University B, M
San Juan College A
University of New Mexico B, M, D

New York

Adelphi University B
Adirondack Community College A
Alfred University B
Bard College B
Barnard College B
Canisius College B
City University of New York
    Baruch College B
    Brooklyn College B, M
    City College B
    College of Staten Island B
    Hunter College B
    John Jay College of Criminal
        Justice B
    Lehman College B
    Queens College B, M, T
    Queensborough Community
        College A
    York College B
Clarkson University B
Colgate University B
College of New Rochelle B
College of Saint Rose B, M
Columbia University
    Columbia College B
    School of General Studies B
Cornell University B, M, D
Daemen College B
Dowling College B
Elmira College B
Eugene Lang College The New School
    for Liberal Arts B
Excelsior College B
Fordham University B, M, D
Hamilton College B
Hartwick College B
Hobart and William Smith Colleges B
Hofstra University B
Houghton College B
Iona College B
Ithaca College B
Le Moyne College B
Long Island University
    Brooklyn Campus B, M
    C.W. Post Campus B, M
Manhattanville College B
Marist College B
Mercy College B
Molloy College B
Monroe Community College A
Mount St. Mary College B
Nazareth College of Rochester B
New York Institute of Technology B
New York University B, M, D
Niagara University B
Pace University B, M
Russell Sage College B
St. Bonaventure University B
St. Francis College B
St. John Fisher College B
St. John's University B, M
St. Joseph's College: Suffolk
    Campus B
St. Lawrence University B
Sarah Lawrence College B
Siena College B, T
Skidmore College B
State University of New York
    Albany B, M, D
    Binghamton B, M, D
    Buffalo B, M, D
    College at Brockport B

    College at Buffalo B
    College at Cortland B
    College at Fredonia B
    College at Geneseo B, T
    College at Oneonta B
    College at Plattsburgh B
    College at Potsdam B
    New Paltz B
    Oswego B
    Purchase B
    Stony Brook B, M, D
Suffolk County Community College A
Syracuse University B, M, D
Touro College B
Union College B
United States Military Academy B
University of Rochester B, M, D
Utica College B
Vassar College B
Wagner College B
Yeshiva University B

North Carolina

Appalachian State University B, M
Barton College B
Belmont Abbey College B
Bennett College B
Campbell University B
Catawba College B
Davidson College B
Duke University B, M, D
East Carolina University B
Elizabeth City State University B
Elon University B
Fayetteville State University B
Gardner-Webb University B
Greensboro College B
Guilford College B
High Point University B
Johnson C. Smith University B
Lenoir-Rhyne College B, T
Livingstone College B
Mars Hill College B
Meredith College B
Methodist College A, B
North Carolina Agricultural and
    Technical State University B
North Carolina Central University B
North Carolina State University B
North Carolina Wesleyan College B
Peace College B
Queens University of Charlotte B
St. Andrews Presbyterian College B
St. Augustine's College B
University of North Carolina
    Asheville B, T
    Chapel Hill B, M, D
    Charlotte B
    Greensboro B, M, T
    Pembroke B
    Wilmington B
Wake Forest University B
Warren Wilson College B
Western Carolina University B
Winston-Salem State University B

North Dakota

Dickinson State University B
Jamestown College B
North Dakota State University B
University of North Dakota B

Ohio

Antioch College B
Ashland University B
Baldwin-Wallace College B
Bowling Green State University B, M
Capital University B
Case Western Reserve
    University B, M, D
Cedarville University B
Central State University B
Cincinnati State Technical and
    Community College C

Cleveland State University *B*
College of Wooster *B*
Denison University *B*
Franciscan University of
    Steubenville *B*
Heidelberg College *B*
Hiram College *B*
John Carroll University *B*
Kent State University *B, M, D*
Kenyon College *B*
Malone College *B*
Marietta College *B*
Miami University
    Oxford Campus *B, M, D*
Mount Union College *B*
Muskingum College *B*
Oberlin College *B*
Ohio Dominican University *B*
Ohio Northern University *B*
Ohio State University
    Columbus Campus *B, M, D*
Ohio University *B, M*
Ohio Wesleyan University *B*
Otterbein College *B*
University of Akron *M*
University of Cincinnati *B, M, D*
University of Dayton *B*
University of Findlay *B*
University of Rio Grande *A*
University of Toledo *B, M*
Urbana University *B*
Walsh University *B*
Wilmington College *B*
Wittenberg University *B*
Wright State University *B*
Xavier University *A, B*
Youngstown State University *B*

Oklahoma

Cameron University *B*
East Central University *B*
Northeastern State University *B*
Northwestern Oklahoma State
    University *B*
Oklahoma Baptist University *B*
Oklahoma Christian University *B*
Oklahoma City University *B*
Oklahoma State University *B, M*
Oklahoma Wesleyan University *B*
Oral Roberts University *B*
Rose State College *A*
St. Gregory's University *A, B*
Southeastern Oklahoma State
    University *B*
Southern Nazarene University *B*
Southwestern Oklahoma State
    University *B*
Tulsa Community College *A*
University of Central Oklahoma *B, M*
University of Oklahoma *B, M, D*
University of Science and Arts of
    Oklahoma *B*
University of Tulsa *B*
Western Oklahoma State College *A*

Oregon

Chemeketa Community College *A*
Eastern Oregon University *B*
George Fox University *B*
Lewis & Clark College *B*
Linfield College *B, T*
Linn-Benton Community College *A*
Oregon State University *B*
Pacific University *B*
Portland State University *B, M*
Reed College *B*
Southern Oregon University *B*
Treasure Valley Community College *A*
University of Oregon *B, M, D*
University of Portland *B*
Western Oregon University *B*
Willamette University *B*

Pennsylvania

Albright College *B*
Allegheny College *B*
Alvernia College *B*
Arcadia University *B*
Bloomsburg University of
    Pennsylvania *B*
Bryn Mawr College *B*
Bucknell University *B*
Cabrini College *B*
California University of
    Pennsylvania *B, M*
Carlow University *B*
Carnegie Mellon University *B*
Cedar Crest College *B*
Chatham College *B*
Chestnut Hill College *B*
Cheyney University of Pennsylvania *B*
Clarion University of Pennsylvania *B*
DeSales University *B, T*
Dickinson College *B*
Duquesne University *B*
East Stroudsburg University of
    Pennsylvania *B, M*
Eastern University *B*
Edinboro University of
    Pennsylvania *B*
Elizabethtown College *B*
Franklin & Marshall College *B*
Gannon University *B*
Geneva College *B*
Gettysburg College *B*
Grove City College *B*
Haverford College *B, T*
Immaculata University *C, A, B*
Indiana University of Pennsylvania *B*
Juniata College *B*
King's College *B*
Kutztown University of
    Pennsylvania *B, M*
La Salle University *B*
Lafayette College *B*
Lebanon Valley College *B*
Lehigh University *B, M*
Lincoln University *B*
Lock Haven University of
    Pennsylvania *B*
Lycoming College *B*
Mansfield University of
    Pennsylvania *B, T*
Mercyhurst College *B*
Messiah College *B*
Millersville University of
    Pennsylvania *B, T*
Moravian College *B*
Mount Aloysius College *B*
Muhlenberg College *C, B*
Neumann College *B, T*
Penn State
    Abington *B*
    Altoona *B*
    Beaver *B*
    Berks *B*
    Delaware County *B*
    Dubois *B*
    Erie, The Behrend College *B*
    Fayette *B*
    Hazleton *B*
    Lehigh Valley *B*
    McKeesport *B*
    Mont Alto *B*
    New Kensington *B*
    Schuylkill - Capital College *B*
    Shenango *B*
    University Park *B, M, D*
    Wilkes-Barre *B*
    Worthington Scranton *B*
    York *B*
Point Park University *B*
Rosemont College *B*
St. Francis University *B*
St. Joseph's University *B*
St. Vincent College *B*
Seton Hill University *B*

Shippensburg University of
    Pennsylvania *B, T*
Slippery Rock University of
    Pennsylvania *B*
Susquehanna University *B*
Swarthmore College *B*
Temple University *B, M, D*
Thiel College *B*
University of Pennsylvania *B, M, D*
University of Pittsburgh *B, M, D*
University of Pittsburgh
    Bradford *B*
    Greensburg *B*
    Johnstown *B*
University of Scranton *A, B*
Ursinus College *B, T*
Villanova University *B, M*
Washington and Jefferson College *B*
Waynesburg College *B*
West Chester University of
    Pennsylvania *C, B*
Westminster College *B, T*
Widener University *B*
Wilkes University *B*
Wilson College *B*
York College of Pennsylvania *B*

Puerto Rico

Inter American University of Puerto
    Rico
    San German Campus *B*
Pontifical Catholic University of
    Puerto Rico *B*
Universidad del Este *B*
University of Puerto Rico
    Mayaguez *B*
    Rio Piedras *B*

Rhode Island

Brown University *B, M, D*
Providence College *B*
Rhode Island College *B*
Roger Williams University *B*
Salve Regina University *B*
University of Rhode Island *B, M*

South Carolina

Benedict College *B*
Charleston Southern University *B*
The Citadel *B*
Clemson University *B*
Coastal Carolina University *B*
Coker College *B*
College of Charleston *B, T*
Columbia College *B*
Converse College *B*
Francis Marion University *B*
Furman University *B*
Lander University *B*
Morris College *B*
Newberry College *B*
Presbyterian College *B*
South Carolina State University *B*
University of South Carolina *B, M, D*
University of South Carolina
    Aiken *B*
    Upstate *B*
Winthrop University *B*

South Dakota

Augustana College *B, T*
Black Hills State University *B*
Northern State University *B*
South Dakota State University *B, T*
University of Sioux Falls *B*
University of South Dakota *B, M*

Tennessee

Austin Peay State University *B*
Belmont University *B, T*
Carson-Newman College *B, T*
Cumberland University *B*
East Tennessee State University *B, T*

Fisk University *B*
Jackson State Community College *A*
King College *B, T*
Lambuth University *B*
LeMoyne-Owen College *B*
Lee University *B*
Lipscomb University *B*
Maryville College *B, T*
Middle Tennessee State University *B*
Rhodes College *B*
Roane State Community College *A*
Tennessee State University *B*
Tennessee Technological University *B*
Tennessee Temple University *B*
Tusculum College *B*
Union University *B, T*
University of Memphis *B, M*
University of Tennessee
    Chattanooga *B*
    Knoxville *B, M, D*
    Martin *B*
University of the South *B*
Vanderbilt University *B, M, D*

Texas

Abilene Christian University *B*
Angelo State University *B, T*
Austin College *B*
Austin Community College *A*
Baylor University *B, M, D*
Brazosport College *A*
Clarendon College *A*
Coastal Bend College *A*
College of the Mainland *A*
Dallas Baptist University *B*
Del Mar College *A*
El Paso Community College *A*
Frank Phillips College *A*
Galveston College *A*
Hardin-Simmons University *B*
Houston Baptist University *B*
Howard Payne University *B*
Huston-Tillotson College *B*
Lamar University *B, M*
Laredo Community College *A*
LeTourneau University *B*
Lon Morris College *A*
McMurry University *B, T*
Midland College *A*
Midwestern State University *B, M*
Northeast Texas Community
    College *A*
Northwest Vista College *A*
Our Lady of the Lake University of San
    Antonio *B*
Palo Alto College *A*
Paris Junior College *A*
Prairie View A&M University *B*
Rice University *B, M, D*
St. Edward's University *B*
St. Mary's University *B, M, T*
St. Philip's College *A*
Sam Houston State University *B, M*
Schreiner University *B*
South Plains College *A*
South Texas College *A*
Southern Methodist University *B*
Southwestern University *B, T*
Stephen F. Austin State University *B, T*
Sul Ross State University *B, M*
Tarleton State University *B, M, T*
Texarkana College *A*
Texas A&M University *B, M, D*
Texas A&M University
    Commerce *B, M*
    Kingsville *B, M, T*
Texas Christian University *B*
Texas College *B*
Texas Lutheran University *B*
Texas Southern University *B*
Texas State University: San
    Marcos *B, M, T*
Texas Tech University *B, M, D*
Texas Wesleyan University *B, T*

Texas Woman's University *B, M*
Trinity University *B*
University of Dallas *B, M, D*
University of Houston *B, M, D*
University of Houston
  Clear Lake *B*
  Downtown *B*
University of Mary Hardin-Baylor *B*
University of North Texas *B, M, D*
University of St. Thomas *B*
University of Texas
  Arlington *B, M*
  Austin *B, M, D*
  Brownsville *B*
  Dallas *B, D*
  El Paso *B, M*
  Pan American *B*
  San Antonio *B, M*
  Tyler *B, M*
  of the Permian Basin *B*
University of the Incarnate Word *B*
Wayland Baptist University *B*
West Texas A&M University *B, M*
Western Texas College *A*

Utah

Brigham Young University *B*
Dixie State College of Utah *A*
Salt Lake Community College *A*
Snow College *A*
Southern Utah University *B*
University of Utah *B, M, D*
Utah State University *B, M*
Utah Valley State College *B*
Weber State University *B*
Westminster College *B*

Vermont

Bennington College *B*
Johnson State College *B*
Marlboro College *B*
Middlebury College *B*
Norwich University *B*
St. Michael's College *B*
University of Vermont *B*

Virginia

Averett University *B*
Bridgewater College *B*
Christendom College *B*
Christopher Newport University *B*
College of William and Mary *B*
Emory & Henry College *B*
Ferrum College *B*
George Mason University *B*
Hampden-Sydney College *B*
Hampton University *B*
Hollins University *B*
James Madison University *B, T*
Liberty University *B*
Longwood University *B, T*
Lynchburg College *B*
Mary Baldwin College *B*
Marymount University *B*
Norfolk State University *B*
Old Dominion University *B, T*
Radford University *B*
Randolph-Macon College *B*
Randolph-Macon Woman's College *B*
Regent University *B*
Roanoke College *B, T*
St. Paul's College *B*
Sweet Briar College *B*
University of Mary Washington *B*
University of Richmond *B*
University of Virginia *B, M, D*
University of Virginia's College at
  Wise *B, T*
Virginia Commonwealth University *B*
Virginia Intermont College *B*
Virginia Polytechnic Institute and
  State University *B, M*
Virginia State University *B*
Virginia Union University *B*

Virginia Wesleyan College *B*
Washington and Lee University *B*

Washington

Central Washington University *B*
City University *B*
Eastern Washington University *B*
Everett Community College *A*
Evergreen State College *B*
Gonzaga University *B*
Northwest University *B*
Olympic College *A*
Pacific Lutheran University *B*
Saint Martin's University *B*
Seattle Pacific University *B*
Seattle University *B*
University of Puget Sound *B, T*
University of Washington *B, M, D*
Washington State University *B, M, D*
Western Washington University *B, M*
Whitman College *B*
Whitworth College *B*

West Virginia

Bethany College *B*
Concord University *B*
Davis and Elkins College *B*
Marshall University *B, M*
Potomac State College of West Virginia
  University *A*
Shepherd University *B*
University of Charleston *B*
West Liberty State College *B*
West Virginia State University *B*
West Virginia University *B, M, D*
West Virginia Wesleyan College *B*
Wheeling Jesuit University *B*

Wisconsin

Alverno College *B*
Beloit College *B*
Cardinal Stritch University *B*
Carroll College *B*
Carthage College *B*
Edgewood College *B*
Lawrence University *B, T*
Marian College of Fond du Lac *B*
Marquette University *B, M*
Ripon College *B*
St. Norbert College *B, T*
University of Wisconsin
  Eau Claire *B*
  Green Bay *B, T*
  La Crosse *B, T*
  Madison *B, M, D*
  Milwaukee *B, M, D*
  Oshkosh *B*
  Parkside *B, T*
  Platteville *B, T*
  River Falls *B, T*
  Stevens Point *B*
  Superior *B*
  Whitewater *B*
Wisconsin Lutheran College *B*

Wyoming

Casper College *A*
Eastern Wyoming College *A*
Laramie County Community
  College *A*
Northwest College *A*
Sheridan College *A*
University of Wyoming *B, M*
Western Wyoming Community
  College *A*

Polymer chemistry

California

California Polytechnic State
  University: San Luis Obispo *M*

Connecticut

University of Connecticut *M, D*

Georgia

Clark Atlanta University *M, D*
Georgia Institute of Technology *B*

Kansas

Pittsburg State University *B*

Massachusetts

University of Massachusetts
  Amherst *M, D*
  Lowell *D*

Michigan

University of Michigan *M*

Minnesota

Winona State University *B*

Mississippi

University of Southern
  Mississippi *B, M, D*

New York

Polytechnic University *D*
Rochester Institute of Technology *B*
State University of New York
  College of Environmental Science
  and Forestry *B, M, D*

North Carolina

North Carolina State
  University *B, M, D*

North Dakota

North Dakota State University *M, D*

Ohio

University of Akron *B, M, D*

Pennsylvania

Carnegie Mellon University *M*

Wisconsin

University of Wisconsin
  River Falls *B*

Polymer/plastics engineering

California

California Polytechnic State
  University: San Luis Obispo *M*
University of Southern California *B*

Connecticut

Quinebaug Valley Community
  College *A*

Georgia

Georgia Institute of Technology *M*

Hawaii

University of Hawaii
  Honolulu Community College *A*

Illinois

University of Illinois
  Urbana-Champaign *B, M, D*

Massachusetts

University of Massachusetts
  Lowell *B, M, D*

Michigan

Eastern Michigan University *B, M*
University of Michigan *M*

Minnesota

Winona State University *B*

Missouri

University of Missouri
  Rolla *B*

New Jersey

Stevens Institute of Technology *M*

New York

Polytechnic University *M*
Rochester Institute of Technology *B*
State University of New York
  College of Agriculture and
  Technology at Morrisville *A*

North Carolina

Wilson Technical Community
  College *A*

Ohio

Case Western Reserve
  University *B, M, D*
University of Akron *B, M, D*

Pennsylvania

Lehigh University *M, D*

Tennessee

University of Tennessee
  Knoxville *M, D*

Texas

Trinity Valley Community College *A*

Virginia

Virginia Polytechnic Institute and
  State University *M, D*

Population biology

California

University of California
  Davis *M, D*

Colorado

University of Colorado
  Boulder *B, M, D*

Missouri

Washington University in St. Louis *D*

Texas

University of Texas
  Austin *M, D*

Portuguese

California

Chabot College *A*
Santa Rosa Junior College *A*
University of California
  Los Angeles *B, M*
  Santa Barbara *B, M*

Connecticut

Yale University *B, M, D*

District of Columbia

George Washington University *B*
Georgetown University *B*

Florida

Florida International University *B*
University of Florida *A*
Valencia Community College *A*

Illinois

University of Chicago *B*
University of Illinois
Urbana-Champaign *B, M, D*

Indiana

Indiana University
Bloomington *B, M, D*

Iowa

University of Iowa *B, T*

Louisiana

Tulane University *B, M*

Massachusetts

Smith College *B*
University of Massachusetts
Amherst *B*
Dartmouth *B, M*

Minnesota

University of Minnesota
Twin Cities *B, M*

New Jersey

Rutgers, The State University of New
Jersey
New Brunswick/Piscataway
Campus *B*

New Mexico

University of New Mexico *B, M*

New York

Columbia University
School of General Studies *B*
New York University *M, D*
United States Military Academy *B*

Ohio

Ohio State University
Columbus Campus *B*

Rhode Island

Brown University *B, M, D*

Tennessee

University of Tennessee
Knoxville *B*
Vanderbilt University *M, D*

Texas

University of Texas
Austin *B, M, D*

Utah

Brigham Young University *B, M*

Wisconsin

University of Wisconsin
Madison *B, M, D*

Poultry science

Alabama

Auburn University *B*
Tuskegee University *B, M*

Arkansas

University of Arkansas *B, M, D*

California

California Polytechnic State
University: San Luis Obispo *B*
Modesto Junior College *A*

Delaware

Delaware Technical and Community
College
Owens Campus *C, A*

Florida

University of Florida *M*

Georgia

Abraham Baldwin Agricultural
College *A*
University of Georgia *B, M, D*

Maryland

University of Maryland
Eastern Shore *B*

Minnesota

Ridgewater College *C*

Mississippi

Mississippi State University *B, M*

Missouri

Crowder College *A*

North Carolina

James Sprunt Community
College *C, A*
North Carolina State University *B, M*
Surry Community College *A*
Wayne Community College *A*

Ohio

Ohio State University
Columbus Campus *M, D*

Oregon

Oregon State University *M, D*

Pennsylvania

Penn State
University Park *C*

Puerto Rico

Inter American University of Puerto
Rico
Barranquitas Campus *C*

South Carolina

Clemson University *B*

Texas

Stephen F. Austin State University *B*
Texas A&M University *B, M, D*

Utah

Snow College *A*

Vermont

Sterling College *B*

Wisconsin

University of Wisconsin
Madison *B, M, D*

Power/electrical transmission

Alabama

Alabama Southern Community
College *C, A*
Bevill State Community College *A*
Enterprise-Ozark Community
College *C, A*
Lawson State Community College *C*

Arizona

Gateway Community College *C, A*

Arkansas

Phillips Community College of the
University of Arkansas *C*

California

Bakersfield College *A*
Chabot College *A*
Coastline Community College *C*
College of the Redwoods *C*
Foothill College *C*
Fresno City College *C, A*
Los Angeles Trade and Technical
College *A*
Orange Coast College *C, A*
Palomar College *C, A*
San Diego City College *C, A*
San Joaquin Delta College *C, A*
San Jose City College *A*
Santa Ana College *C, A*

Colorado

Community College of Aurora *A*
Mesa State College *C*
Red Rocks Community College *C, A*

Florida

Florida Community College at
Jacksonville *C*
Palm Beach Community College *C*
Polk Community College *A*
South Florida Community
College *C, A*

Georgia

Augusta Technical Institute *C*
Chattahoochee Technical College *C*

Hawaii

University of Hawaii
Hawaii Community College *C, A*

Idaho

Boise State University *C*

Illinois

Illinois Eastern Community Colleges
Lincoln Trail College *C*
Kishwaukee College *C*
Sauk Valley Community College *C*
Southwestern Illinois College *C, A*

Indiana

Ivy Tech State College
Ivy Tech Community College:
Columbus *C, A*

Iowa

Kirkwood Community College *A*
Northeast Iowa Community
College *A*

Kansas

Allen County Community College *C*
Johnson County Community
College *C, A*
Manhattan Area Technical
College *C, A*

Maine

Eastern Maine Community College *A*
Northern Maine Community
College *A*
Southern Maine Community
College *A*

Massachusetts

Benjamin Franklin Institute of
Technology *C*

Michigan

Lansing Community College *A*

Macomb Community College *C*

Minnesota

Fond du Lac Tribal and Community
College *A*
St. Paul College *C*

Mississippi

Hinds Community College *C*
Mississippi Delta Community
College *C*
Mississippi Gulf Coast Community
College
Jefferson Davis Campus *C, A*
Pearl River Community College *A*

Montana

Miles Community College *A*

Nebraska

Metropolitan Community
College *C, A*

Nevada

Truckee Meadows Community
College *C, A*

New York

Mohawk Valley Community College *C*

North Carolina

Durham Technical Community
College *C*
James Sprunt Community College *C*
Mayland Community College *C*
Randolph Community College *C*
Richmond Community College *C*
Robeson Community College *C*
Wake Technical Community
College *C, A*

Ohio

Jefferson Community College *A*
Ohio State University
Agricultural Technical Institute *A*

Oklahoma

Oklahoma State University
Okmulgee *A*

Pennsylvania

Community College of Allegheny
County *A*
Dean Institute of Technology *A*
Delaware County Community
College *C*
Thaddeus Stevens College of
Technology *A*
Triangle Tech
Pittsburgh *A*

South Carolina

Aiken Technical College *C*
Technical College of the
Lowcountry *C*

South Dakota

Western Dakota Technical
Institute *C, A*

Tennessee

Northeast State Technical Community
College *A*
Walters State Community College *A*

Texas

Amarillo College *C, A*
Frank Phillips College *C, A*
Houston Community College
System *C*
Laredo Community College *A*

North Lake College *A*
San Jacinto College
North *C, A*
South Plains College *C, A*
Texas State Technical College
Waco *A*

Virginia
Tidewater Community College *C*

Washington
Clark College *C*
Clover Park Technical College *C*
Spokane Community College *A*

Wisconsin
Chippewa Valley Technical College *C*
Milwaukee Area Technical College *C*
Northeast Wisconsin Technical
College *C*
Western Wisconsin Technical
College *C*

Precision production trades, general

Alabama
Shelton State Community
College *C, A*

Arkansas
Ouachita Technical College *A*

California
Yuba Community College
District *C, A*

Iowa
Southeastern Community College
North Campus *C, A*

Michigan
Grand Rapids Community College *A*
Southwestern Michigan College *C*

Minnesota
Ridgewater College *C*

Missouri
Mineral Area College *A*

Nebraska
Central Community College *C, A*

South Carolina
Greenville Technical College *C*

Texas
South Texas College *C, A*

Washington
Clover Park Technical College *C*

Predental

Alabama
Alabama Southern Community
College *A*
Calhoun Community College *A*
Faulkner State Community College *A*
Faulkner University *B*
Gadsden State Community College *A*
Huntingdon College *B*
Northeast Alabama Community
College *A*
Spring Hill College *B*

Arizona
Grand Canyon University *B*

Arkansas
Harding University *B*
Ouachita Baptist University *B*
University of Central Arkansas *B*
University of the Ozarks *B*

California
Azusa Pacific University *B*
Bakersfield College *A*
California Lutheran University *B*
California State University
Chico *B*
Chabot College *A*
Chapman University *B*
City College of San Francisco *A*
College of the Siskiyous *A*
Cypress College *A*
El Camino College *A*
Foothill College *A*
Golden West College *A*
Monterey Peninsula College *A*
Mount St. Mary's College *B*
Notre Dame de Namur University *B*
Ventura College *A*
Westmont College *B*
Whittier College *B*

Colorado
Adams State College *B*
Otero Junior College *A*
Regis University *B*

Connecticut
Quinnipiac University *B*
Southern Connecticut State
University *B*

Delaware
University of Delaware *B*

District of Columbia
American University *B*

Florida
Barry University *B*
Broward Community College *A*
Florida State University *B*
Gulf Coast Community College *A*
Indian River Community College *A*
Jacksonville University *B*
Miami Dade College *A*
Okaloosa-Walton College *A*
Pensacola Junior College *A*
Santa Fe Community College *A*
University of Central Florida *B*
University of Tampa *B*

Georgia
Abraham Baldwin Agricultural
College *A*
Andrew College *A*
Darton College *A*
Georgia Perimeter College *A*
Macon State College *A*
Mercer University *B*
Middle Georgia College *A*
Oglethorpe University *B*
South Georgia College *A*
Young Harris College *A*

Idaho
Boise State University *B*
Brigham Young University-Idaho *B*
College of Southern Idaho *A*
North Idaho College *A*
Northwest Nazarene University *B*
University of Idaho *B*

Illinois
Augustana College *B*
Black Hawk College
East Campus *A*

Blackburn College *B*
City Colleges of Chicago
Harold Washington College *A*
Kennedy-King College *A*
Dominican University *B*
Elmhurst College *B*
Eureka College *B*
Greenville College *B*
Illinois Central College *A*
Judson College *B*
Kankakee Community College *A*
Kishwaukee College *A*
Lewis University *B*
Lewis and Clark Community
College *A*
MacMurray College *B*
Millikin University *B*
North Park University *B*
Rockford College *B*
Roosevelt University *B*
Sauk Valley Community College *A*
Springfield College in Illinois *A*
University of Illinois
Chicago *B*
University of St. Francis *B*

Indiana
Ball State University *B*
Bethel College *B*
Indiana University-Purdue University
Fort Wayne *B*
Indiana University-Purdue University
Indianapolis *B*
Indiana Wesleyan University *B*
Manchester College *B*
St. Joseph's College *B*
St. Mary-of-the-Woods College *B*
University of Evansville *B*
Vincennes University *A*

Iowa
Clarke College *B*
Coe College *B*
Dordt College *M*
Ellsworth Community College *A*
Iowa Wesleyan College *B*
Marshalltown Community College *A*
Morningside College *B*
Northwestern College *B*
Simpson College *B*
University of Iowa *B*
Upper Iowa University *B*

Kansas
Barton County Community College *A*
Coffeyville Community College *A*
McPherson College *B*
Pittsburg State University *B*
Pratt Community College *A*
Seward County Community College *A*
Tabor College *B*
Washburn University of Topeka *B*

Kentucky
Bellarmine University *B*
Campbellsville University *B*
Eastern Kentucky University *B*
Georgetown College *B*
Thomas More College *B*

Louisiana
Centenary College of Louisiana *B*
Nicholls State University *B*
Xavier University of Louisiana *B*

Maine
University of Maine
Fort Kent *B*
University of Southern Maine *B*

Maryland
Columbia Union College *B*

Community College of Baltimore
County *A*
Coppin State University *B*
Frostburg State University *B*
Howard Community College *A*
Montgomery College *A*
Morgan State University *B*
University of Maryland
Baltimore County *B*
Eastern Shore *B*
Villa Julie College *B*

Massachusetts
American International College *B*
Cape Cod Community College *A*
Eastern Nazarene College *B*
Elms College *B*
Hampshire College *B*
Simmons College *B*
Springfield College *B*
University of Massachusetts
Amherst *B*
Worcester Polytechnic Institute *B*

Michigan
Adrian College *B*
Albion College *B*
Alma College *B*
Calvin College *B*
Cornerstone University *B*
Delta College *A*
Gogebic Community College *A*
Grand Valley State University *B*
Hillsdale College *B*
Kalamazoo College *B*
Kirtland Community College *A*
Lansing Community College *A*
Madonna University *B*
Northern Michigan University *B*
Olivet College *B*
Schoolcraft College *A*
Siena Heights University *A, B*
University of Detroit Mercy *B*

Minnesota
College of St. Benedict *B*
College of St. Catherine *B*
Concordia College: Moorhead *B*
Gustavus Adolphus College *B*
Hamline University *B*
Minnesota State University
Mankato *B*
Moorhead *B*
St. Cloud State University *B*
St. John's University *B*
University of Minnesota
Duluth *B*
Twin Cities *B*
University of St. Thomas *B*
Vermilion Community College *A*
Winona State University *B*

Mississippi
Blue Mountain College *B*
Coahoma Community College *A*
East Central Community College *A*
Holmes Community College *A*
Itawamba Community College *A*
Jackson State University *B*
Mississippi Delta Community
College *A*

Missouri
Drury University *B*
Evangel University *B*
Lindenwood University *B*
Maryville University of Saint Louis *B*
Missouri Southern State University *B*
St. Louis Community College
St. Louis Community College at
Florissant Valley *A*
Truman State University *B*

University of Missouri
  Rolla *B*
Washington University in St. Louis *B*

Montana

Carroll College *B*
Montana Tech of the University of
  Montana *B*

Nebraska

College of Saint Mary *B*
Concordia University *B*
Dana College *B*
Hastings College *B*
Midland Lutheran College *B*
Northeast Community College *A*
University of Nebraska
  Lincoln *B*
Western Nebraska Community
  College *A*
York College *A*

New Hampshire

Franklin Pierce College *B*
Rivier College *B*
St. Anselm College *B*

New Jersey

Rowan University *B*
Rutgers, The State University of New
  Jersey
  Camden Regional Campus *B*
  New Brunswick/Piscataway
    Campus *B*
  Newark Regional Campus *B*
Sussex County Community College *A*

New Mexico

New Mexico Junior College *A*

New York

Albany College of Pharmacy *B*
Alfred University *B*
Bard College *B*
Clarkson University *B*
Colgate University *B*
D'Youville College *B*
Elmira College *B*
Fordham University *B*
Hobart and William Smith Colleges *B*
Hofstra University *B*
Houghton College *B*
Ithaca College *B*
Le Moyne College *B*
Manhattan College *B*
Molloy College *B*
New York University *B*
Niagara University *B*
Paul Smith's College *B*
Rensselaer Polytechnic Institute *B*
Rochester Institute of Technology *B*
St. Joseph's College: Suffolk
  Campus *B*
St. Thomas Aquinas College *B*
Sarah Lawrence College *B*
State University of New York
  Albany *B*
  College at Brockport *B*
  College at Plattsburgh *B*
  College of Environmental Science
    and Forestry *B*
  New Paltz *B*
Sullivan County Community
  College *A*
Syracuse University *B*
Touro College *B*
Wagner College *B*
Wells College *B*

North Carolina

Belmont Abbey College *B*
Brevard College *B*
Campbell University *B*

Carteret Community College *A*
Chowan College *B*
Elon University *B*
Lees-McRae College *B*
Livingstone College *B*
Mars Hill College *B*
Meredith College *B*
Methodist College *B*
Mitchell Community College *A*
Pfeiffer University *B*
Queens University of Charlotte *B*
Sandhills Community College *A*
Wingate University *B*

North Dakota

Dickinson State University *B*
Mayville State University *B*
Valley City State University *B*

Ohio

Capital University *B*
Cedarville University *B*
Defiance College *B*
Heidelberg College *B*
John Carroll University *B*
Kent State University *B*
Kettering College of Medical Arts *A*
Miami University
  Oxford Campus *B*
Mount Vernon Nazarene University *B*
Muskingum College *B*
Oberlin College *B*
Ohio Northern University *B*
Ohio Wesleyan University *B*
Otterbein College *B*
University of Cincinnati *B*
University of Cincinnati
  Clermont College *A*
  Raymond Walters College *A*
University of Dayton *B*
University of Toledo *B*
Urbana University *B*
Walsh University *B*
Wright State University *B*
Youngstown State University *B*

Oklahoma

Connors State College *A*
East Central University *B*
Eastern Oklahoma State College *A*
Northeastern Oklahoma Agricultural
  and Mechanical College *A*
Oklahoma Christian University *B*
Oklahoma City University *B*
Rose State College *A*

Oregon

Central Oregon Community
  College *A*
Chemeketa Community College *A*
Corban College *B*
Eastern Oregon University *B*
Linn-Benton Community College *A*
Southern Oregon University *B*
Treasure Valley Community College *A*

Pennsylvania

Albright College *B*
Allegheny College *B*
Alvernia College *B*
Edinboro University of
  Pennsylvania *B*
Elizabethtown College *B*
Gannon University *B*
Gettysburg College *B*
Grove City College *B*
Holy Family University *B*
Juniata College *B*
Keystone College *B*
La Salle University *B*
Lehigh University *B*
Mansfield University of
  Pennsylvania *B*

Reading Area Community College *A*
St. Vincent College *B*
Susquehanna University *B*
University of Pittsburgh
  Greensburg *B*
  Johnstown *B*
Villanova University *B*
Waynesburg College *B*
Westminster College *B*
Widener University *B*
York College of Pennsylvania *B*

Puerto Rico

University of Puerto Rico
  Ponce *A*

Rhode Island

Rhode Island College *B*

South Carolina

Charleston Southern University *B*
College of Charleston *B*
Furman University *B*
Limestone College *B*
North Greenville College *B*
Spartanburg Technical College *A*
Voorhees College *B*

South Dakota

Augustana College *B*
Dakota State University *B*
Dakota Wesleyan University *B*

Tennessee

Carson-Newman College *B*
Columbia State Community College *A*
Cumberland University *B*
Hiwassee College *A*
Lambuth University *B*
Lincoln Memorial University *B*
Lipscomb University *B*
Maryville College *B*
Roane State Community College *A*
Tennessee Technological University *B*
Tennessee Wesleyan College *B*
Union University *B*
University of Tennessee
  Knoxville *B*
Walters State Community College *A*

Texas

Abilene Christian University *B*
Amarillo College *A*
Angelina College *A*
Austin Community College *A*
Baylor University *B*
Clarendon College *A*
Coastal Bend College *A*
Del Mar College *A*
El Paso Community College *A*
Galveston College *A*
Grayson County College *A*
Hardin-Simmons University *B*
Howard College *A*
Laredo Community College *A*
LeTourneau University *B*
Lon Morris College *A*
Lubbock Christian University *B*
Midland College *A*
Midwestern State University *B*
Navarro College *A*
Paris Junior College *A*
St. Philip's College *A*
Schreiner University *B*
South Plains College *A*
Texas A&M University *B*
Texas A&M University
  Commerce *B*
Texas Wesleyan University *B*
Trinity Valley Community College *A*
Tyler Junior College *A*
Western Texas College *A*

Utah

Snow College *A*
Southern Utah University *B*
University of Utah *B*
Utah State University *B*

Vermont

Green Mountain College *B*

Virginia

Eastern Mennonite University *B*
Longwood University *B*
Mountain Empire Community
  College *A*
Virginia Wesleyan College *B*

Washington

Centralia College *A*
Eastern Washington University *B*
Everett Community College *A*
Saint Martin's University *B*
Seattle Pacific University *B*

West Virginia

Concord University *B*
Davis and Elkins College *B*
Potomac State College of West Virginia
  University *A*
West Virginia Wesleyan College *B*

Wisconsin

Carroll College *B*
Lawrence University *B*
Marquette University *B*
Mount Mary College *B*
Northland College *B*
Ripon College *B*
University of Wisconsin
  Milwaukee *B*
  Oshkosh *B*
  Parkside *B*

Wyoming

Casper College *A*
Eastern Wyoming College *A*
Laramie County Community
  College *A*
Northwest College *A*
Western Wyoming Community
  College *A*

Prelaw

Alabama

Alabama Southern Community
  College *A*
Enterprise-Ozark Community
  College *A*
Faulkner University *B*
Gadsden State Community College *A*
Huntingdon College *B*
Lawson State Community College *A*
Talladega College *B*
Wallace State Community College at
  Hanceville *A*

Alaska

Alaska Pacific University *B*
University of Alaska
  Southeast *A*

Arizona

Arizona State University *B*
Eastern Arizona College *A*
Grand Canyon University *B*
Northern Arizona University *B*

Arkansas

Harding University *B*
Ouachita Baptist University *B*

Phillips Community College of the
  University of Arkansas *A*

California

Bakersfield College *A*
Biola University *B*
Butte College *A*
California Lutheran University *B*
California State University
  Dominguez Hills *B*
Chabot College *A*
Claremont McKenna College *B*
College of the Siskiyous *A*
Concordia University *B*
Cypress College *A*
Foothill College *A*
Golden West College *A*
Master's College *B*
MiraCosta College *A*
Mount St. Mary's College *B*
Notre Dame de Namur University *B*
San Diego City College *A*
San Joaquin Delta College *A*
Vanguard University of Southern
  California *B*
Ventura College *A*
Westmont College *B*
Whittier College *B*

Colorado

Adams State College *B*
Colorado Mountain College
  Spring Valley Campus *A*
  Timberline Campus *A*
Otero Junior College *A*
Regis University *B*
Trinidad State Junior College *A*
Western State College of Colorado *B*

Connecticut

Albertus Magnus College *B*
Post University *B*
Quinnipiac University *B*
St. Joseph College *B*
Southern Connecticut State
  University *B*
Trinity College *B*

Delaware

University of Delaware *B*
Wilmington College *B*

District of Columbia

American University *B*

Florida

Barry University *B*
Broward Community College *A*
Chipola College *A*
Clearwater Christian College *B*
Edward Waters College *B*
Florida State University *B*
Gulf Coast Community College *A*
Indian River Community College *A*
Jacksonville University *B*
Lake City Community College *A*
Manatee Community College *A*
Miami Dade College *A*
Nova Southeastern University *B*
Palm Beach Atlantic University *B*
Pensacola Junior College *A*
St. Thomas University *B*
Southeastern College of the
  Assemblies of God *B*
University of Tampa *B*
Webber International University *B*

Georgia

Abraham Baldwin Agricultural
  College *A*
Andrew College *A*
Brenau University *B*
Brewton-Parker College *B*

Coastal Georgia Community
  College *A*
Emmanuel College *B*
Middle Georgia College *A*
Oglethorpe University *B*
South Georgia College *A*
Toccoa Falls College *B*
University of West Georgia *B*
Young Harris College *A*

Idaho

Brigham Young University-Idaho *A*
College of Southern Idaho *A*
North Idaho College *A*
Northwest Nazarene University *B*

Illinois

Augustana College *B*
Aurora University *B*
Black Hawk College
  East Campus *A*
Blackburn College *B*
City Colleges of Chicago
  Harold Washington College *A*
  Kennedy-King College *A*
Danville Area Community College *A*
Elmhurst College *B*
Eureka College *B*
Highland Community College *A*
Illinois Central College *A*
Illinois Institute of Technology *B*
John Wood Community College *A*
Judson College *B*
Kishwaukee College *A*
Lake Land College *A*
Lewis University *B*
Lewis and Clark Community
  College *A*
Millikin University *B*
Monmouth College *B*
Richland Community College *A*
Rockford College *B*
Roosevelt University *B*
St. Xavier University *B*
Sauk Valley Community College *A*
Southeastern Illinois College *A*
Southwestern Illinois College *A*
Spoon River College *A*
Springfield College in Illinois *A*
Trinity International University *B*
University of Illinois
  Urbana-Champaign *B*
Westwood College of Technology
  O'Hare *B*

Indiana

Anderson University *B*
Ball State University *B*
Huntington University *B*
Indiana University-Purdue University
  Indianapolis *B*
Indiana Wesleyan University *B*
Manchester College *B*
Purdue University
  Calumet *B*
St. Joseph's College *B*
St. Mary-of-the-Woods College *B*
Taylor University: Fort Wayne *B*
University of St. Francis *B*
Vincennes University *A*

Iowa

Ashford University *B*
Briar Cliff University *B*
Coe College *B*
Dordt College *B*
Ellsworth Community College *A*
Grand View College *B*
Iowa Central Community College *A*
Iowa Wesleyan College *B*
Loras College *B*
Marshalltown Community College *A*
Mount Mercy College *B*

Simpson College *B*
University of Iowa *B*
Upper Iowa University *B*
Waldorf College *B*
William Penn University *B*

Kansas

Barton County Community College *A*
Butler County Community College *A*
Central Christian College of Kansas *A*
Coffeyville Community College *A*
Colby Community College *A*
Dodge City Community College *A*
Garden City Community College *A*
Labette Community College *A*
McPherson College *B*
Pittsburg State University *B*
Pratt Community College *A*
Seward County Community College *A*
Tabor College *B*
Washburn University of Topeka *B*

Kentucky

Campbellsville University *B*
Lindsey Wilson College *A*
Thomas More College *A*

Louisiana

Centenary College of Louisiana *B*
Grambling State University *B*
University of Louisiana at Lafayette *B*
Xavier University of Louisiana *B*

Maine

Thomas College *B*
University of Maine
  Fort Kent *B*
University of Southern Maine *B*

Maryland

College of Notre Dame of Maryland *B*
Community College of Baltimore
  County *A*
Morgan State University *B*
University of Baltimore *B*
University of Maryland
  Baltimore County *B*
  College Park *B*
  Eastern Shore *B*
Villa Julie College *B*

Massachusetts

American International College *B*
Babson College *B*
Bay Path College *B*
Becker College *B*
Eastern Nazarene College *B*
Elms College *B*
Newbury College *B*
Springfield College *B*
Suffolk University *B*
Worcester Polytechnic Institute *B*
Worcester State College *B*

Michigan

Adrian College *B*
Albion College *B*
Alma College *B*
Aquinas College *B*
Bay de Noc Community College *A*
Calvin College *B*
Concordia University *B*
Cornerstone University *B*
Delta College *A*
Ferris State University *A*
Gogebic Community College *A*
Hillsdale College *B*
Kalamazoo College *B*
Kellogg Community College *A*
Lansing Community College *A*
Madonna University *B*
Michigan State University *B*
Northern Michigan University *B*

Olivet College *B*
Schoolcraft College *A*
Siena Heights University *B*
University of Detroit Mercy *B*
West Shore Community College *A*

Minnesota

College of St. Benedict *B*
College of St. Catherine *B*
Concordia College: Moorhead *B*
Gustavus Adolphus College *B*
Minnesota State University
  Mankato *B*
Northland Community & Technical
  College *A*
Ridgewater College *A*
St. Cloud State University *B*
St. John's University *B*
University of Minnesota
  Duluth *B*
  Twin Cities *B*
Vermilion Community College *A*
Winona State University *B*

Mississippi

Belhaven College *B*
Blue Mountain College *B*
Coahoma Community College *A*
Hinds Community College *A*
Itawamba Community College *A*
Jackson State University *B*
Meridian Community College *A*
Mississippi College *B*
Mississippi Delta Community
  College *A*
Mississippi Gulf Coast Community
  College
  Jefferson Davis Campus *A*

Missouri

College of the Ozarks *B*
Evangel University *B*
Fontbonne University *B*
Lindenwood University *B*
Maryville University of Saint Louis *B*
Stephens College *B*
Three Rivers Community College *A*
Truman State University *B*
University of Missouri
  Rolla *B*
Washington University in St. Louis *B*

Montana

Montana Tech of the University of
  Montana *B*

Nebraska

Bellevue University *B*
Chadron State College *B*
Concordia University *B*
Creighton University *B*
Dana College *B*
Hastings College *B*
Midland Lutheran College *B*
Northeast Community College *A*
Western Nebraska Community
  College *A*

New Hampshire

New England College *B*
Rivier College *B*
St. Anselm College *B*

New Jersey

Rowan University *B*
Rutgers, The State University of New
  Jersey
  Camden Regional Campus *B*
  New Brunswick/Piscataway
    Campus *B*
  Newark Regional Campus *B*
Warren County Community College *A*

New Mexico

New Mexico Junior College *A*

New York

Albany College of Pharmacy *B*
Bard College *B*
City University of New York
    City College *B*
Clarkson University *B*
College of New Rochelle *B*
Concordia College *B*
Cornell University *B*
D'Youville College *B*
Dominican College of Blauvelt *B*
Elmira College *B*
Fordham University *B*
Hofstra University *B*
Ithaca College *B*
Keuka College *B*
Le Moyne College *B*
Manhattan College *B*
Metropolitan College of New
    York *A, B*
Molloy College *B*
Mount St. Mary College *B*
New York University *B*
Niagara University *B*
Rensselaer Polytechnic Institute *B*
Rochester Institute of Technology *B*
St. Thomas Aquinas College *B*
Sarah Lawrence College *B*
State University of New York
    College at Fredonia *B*
    College at Geneseo *B*
    College of Environmental Science
        and Forestry *B*
    New Paltz *B*
    Oswego *B*
Sullivan County Community
    College *A*
Syracuse University *B*
Wells College *B*

North Carolina

Barton College *B*
Belmont Abbey College *B*
Campbell University *B*
Catawba College *B*
College of the Albemarle *A*
Elon University *B*
Gardner-Webb University *B*
Lenoir-Rhyne College *B*
Mars Hill College *B*
Methodist College *B*
Mitchell Community College *A*
Pfeiffer University *B*
Queens University of Charlotte *B*
St. Andrews Presbyterian College *B*
St. Augustine's College *B*
Sandhills Community College *A*
Wingate University *B*

North Dakota

Dickinson State University *B*
Mayville State University *B*
North Dakota State University *B*
Valley City State University *B*

Ohio

Ashland University *B*
Bowling Green State University *B*
Capital University *B*
Cedarville University *B*
Defiance College *B*
Heidelberg College *B*
Hiram College *B*
John Carroll University *B*
Lake Erie College *B*
Miami University
    Oxford Campus *B*
Muskingum College *B*
Oberlin College *B*
Ohio Wesleyan University *B*

Otterbein College *B*
University of Cincinnati
    Clermont College *B*
    Raymond Walters College *A*
University of Dayton *B*
University of Findlay *B*
University of Rio Grande *B*
University of Toledo *B*
Urbana University *B*
Walsh University *B*
Wilmington College *B*
Wright State University *B*
Youngstown State University *B*

Oklahoma

Bacone College *A, B*
Carl Albert State College *A*
Connors State College *A*
East Central University *B*
Eastern Oklahoma State College *A*
Northwestern Oklahoma State
    University *B*
Oklahoma Christian University *B*
Oklahoma City Community College *A*
Oklahoma City University *B*
St. Gregory's University *B*
Southern Nazarene University *B*
University of Tulsa *B*

Oregon

Central Oregon Community
    College *A*
Chemeketa Community College *A*
Corban College *B*
Eastern Oregon University *B*
Linn-Benton Community College *A*
Southern Oregon University *B*
Treasure Valley Community College *A*

Pennsylvania

Allegheny College *B*
Alvernia College *B*
Chatham College *B*
Dickinson College *B*
Gannon University *B*
Gettysburg College *B*
Grove City College *B*
Holy Family University *B*
Immaculata University *A*
Juniata College *B*
Keystone College *B*
La Salle University *B*
Mansfield University of
    Pennsylvania *B*
Marywood University *B*
Mount Aloysius College *B*
Muhlenberg College *B*
Peirce College *A*
Reading Area Community College *A*
St. Vincent College *B*
Seton Hill University *B*
Susquehanna University *B*
University of Pittsburgh
    Johnstown *B*
Waynesburg College *B*
Westminster College *B*
Widener University *B*
York College of Pennsylvania *B*

Puerto Rico

Pontifical Catholic University of
    Puerto Rico *B*
University of Puerto Rico
    Rio Piedras *B*

Rhode Island

Roger Williams University *B*

South Carolina

Clemson University *B*
Furman University *B*
Limestone College *B*
North Greenville College *B*

South Dakota

Dakota State University *B*
Dakota Wesleyan University *B*

Tennessee

Columbia State Community College *A*
Crichton College *B*
Cumberland University *B*
Hiwassee College *A*
Jackson State Community College *A*
Lambuth University *B*
Lincoln Memorial University *B*
Roane State Community College *A*
Tennessee Temple University *B*
Tennessee Wesleyan College *B*
Tusculum College *B*
Union University *B*
University of Tennessee
    Knoxville *B*

Texas

Abilene Christian University *B*
Amarillo College *A*
Angelina College *A*
Central Texas College *A*
Cisco Junior College *A*
Clarendon College *A*
Coastal Bend College *A*
Concordia University at Austin *B*
Galveston College *A*
Hardin-Simmons University *B*
Hill College *A*
Kilgore College *A*
LeTourneau University *B*
Lon Morris College *A*
Lubbock Christian University *B*
Midland College *A*
Midwestern State University *B*
Northwest Vista College *A*
Paris Junior College *A*
St. Philip's College *A*
Schreiner University *B*
Texas A&M University
    Commerce *B*
Texas Wesleyan University *B*
Trinity Valley Community College *A*
Tyler Junior College *A*
University of Houston
    Clear Lake *B*
West Texas A&M University *B*
Western Texas College *A*

Utah

Dixie State College of Utah *A*
Snow College *A*
Southern Utah University *B*
University of Utah *B*
Utah State University *B*

Vermont

Bennington College *B*
Champlain College *B*
Green Mountain College *B*
Marlboro College *B*
Norwich University *B*
Southern Vermont College *B*
Woodbury College *B*

Virginia

Hampton University *B*
Longwood University *B*
Mountain Empire Community
    College *A*
Virginia Intermont College *B*
Virginia Wesleyan College *B*

Washington

Centralia College *A*
Eastern Washington University *B*
Everett Community College *A*
Highline Community College *A*
Seattle Pacific University *B*
Spokane Community College *A*

Washington State University *B*

West Virginia

Concord University *B*
Potomac State College of West Virginia
    University *A*
West Virginia Wesleyan College *B*

Wisconsin

Concordia University Wisconsin *B*
Lawrence University *B*
Marquette University *B*
Mount Mary College *B*
Northland College *B*
Ripon College *B*
University of Wisconsin
    Milwaukee *B*
    Oshkosh *B*
    Parkside *B*
    Superior *B*
    Whitewater *B*

Wyoming

Casper College *A*
Central Wyoming College *A*
Laramie County Community
    College *A*
Northwest College *A*
Western Wyoming Community
    College *A*

Premedicine

Alabama

Alabama Southern Community
    College *A*
Auburn University *B*
Calhoun Community College *A*
Faulkner State Community College *A*
Faulkner University *B*
Gadsden State Community College *A*
Huntingdon College *B*
Northeast Alabama Community
    College *A*
Samford University *B*
Spring Hill College *B*

Arizona

Arizona State University *B*
Eastern Arizona College *A*
Grand Canyon University *B*
Northern Arizona University *B*
Phoenix College *A*

Arkansas

Harding University *B*
Ouachita Baptist University *B*
University of Arkansas *B*
University of Central Arkansas *B*
University of the Ozarks *B*

California

Azusa Pacific University *B*
Bakersfield College *A*
California Lutheran University *B*
California State University
    Chico *B*
    San Bernardino *B*
Chabot College *A*
Chapman University *B*
City College of San Francisco *A*
Claremont McKenna College *B*
College of the Siskiyous *A*
Cypress College *A*
El Camino College *A*
Foothill College *A*
Fresno Pacific University *B*
Golden West College *A*
Master's College *B*
MiraCosta College *A*
Monterey Peninsula College *A*
Mount St. Mary's College *B*

Notre Dame de Namur University *B*
University of California
Riverside *B*
Ventura College *A*
Westmont College *B*
Whittier College *B*

Colorado

Adams State College *B*
Otero Junior College *A*
Regis University *B*

Connecticut

Albertus Magnus College *B*
Quinnipiac University *B*
St. Joseph College *B*
Southern Connecticut State
University *B*
Trinity College *B*

Delaware

University of Delaware *B*

District of Columbia

American University *B*
George Washington University *A*

Florida

Barry University *B*
Broward Community College *A*
Clearwater Christian College *B*
Florida Southern College *B*
Florida State University *B*
Gulf Coast Community College *A*
Hillsborough Community College *A*
Indian River Community College *A*
Jacksonville University *B*
Lynn University *B*
Miami Dade College *A*
Nova Southeastern University *B*
Okaloosa-Walton College *A*
Palm Beach Community College *A*
Pensacola Junior College *A*
St. Thomas University *B*
Santa Fe Community College *A*
University of Central Florida *B*
University of Miami *B*
University of Tampa *B*

Georgia

Abraham Baldwin Agricultural
College *A*
Andrew College *A*
Darton College *A*
Emmanuel College *B*
Georgia Highlands College *A*
Georgia Perimeter College *A*
Macon State College *A*
Mercer University *B*
Middle Georgia College *A*
Oglethorpe University *B*
South Georgia College *A*
University of West Georgia *B*
Young Harris College *A*

Hawaii

Hawaii Pacific University *B*
University of Hawaii
Hilo *B*

Idaho

Boise State University *B*
Brigham Young University-Idaho *B*
College of Southern Idaho *A*
North Idaho College *A*
Northwest Nazarene University *B*
University of Idaho *B*

Illinois

Augustana College *B*
Black Hawk College
East Campus *A*

Blackburn College *B*
City Colleges of Chicago
Harold Washington College *A*
Kennedy-King College *A*
Dominican University *B*
Elmhurst College *B*
Eureka College *B*
Greenville College *B*
Illinois Central College *A*
Illinois Institute of Technology *B*
Judson College *B*
Kankakee Community College *A*
Kishwaukee College *A*
Lake Land College *A*
Lewis and Clark Community
College *A*
MacMurray College *B*
Millikin University *B*
North Park University *B*
Northwestern University *B*
Rockford College *B*
Roosevelt University *B*
Rosalind Franklin University of
Medicine and Science *M*
St. Xavier University *B*
Sauk Valley Community College *A*
Southwestern Illinois College *A*
Springfield College in Illinois *A*
Trinity International University *B*
University of St. Francis *B*

Indiana

Ball State University *B*
Bethel College *B*
Earlham College *B*
Huntington University *B*
Indiana University-Purdue University
Fort Wayne *B*
Indiana University-Purdue University
Indianapolis *B*
Indiana Wesleyan University *B*
Manchester College *B*
Purdue University *B*
Purdue University
Calumet *B*
St. Joseph's College *B*
St. Mary-of-the-Woods College *B*
Tri-State University *B*
University of Evansville *B*
University of Notre Dame *B*
Vincennes University *A*

Iowa

Ashford University *B*
Buena Vista University *B*
Clarke College *B*
Coe College *B*
Dordt College *M*
Ellsworth Community College *A*
Grand View College *B*
Iowa Central Community College *A*
Iowa State University *B*
Iowa Wesleyan College *B*
Marshalltown Community College *A*
Morningside College *B*
Northwestern College *B*
Simpson College *B*
University of Iowa *B*
Upper Iowa University *B*

Kansas

Barton County Community College *A*
Butler County Community College *A*
Central Christian College of Kansas *A*
Coffeyville Community College *A*
Colby Community College *A*
Dodge City Community College *A*
McPherson College *B*
Pittsburg State University *B*
Pratt Community College *A*
Seward County Community College *A*
Tabor College *B*
Washburn University of Topeka *B*

Kentucky

Bellarmine University *B*
Campbellsville University *B*
Eastern Kentucky University *B*
Thomas More College *B*

Louisiana

Centenary College of Louisiana *B*
Dillard University *B*
Nicholls State University *B*
Our Lady of the Lake College *B*
Xavier University of Louisiana *B*

Maine

University of Maine
Fort Kent *B*
University of Southern Maine *B*

Maryland

Columbia Union College *B*
Community College of Baltimore
County *A*
Frostburg State University *B*
Howard Community College *A*
Montgomery College *A*
Morgan State University *B*
Prince George's Community
College *A*
University of Maryland
Baltimore County *B*
Eastern Shore *B*
Villa Julie College *B*

Massachusetts

American International College *B*
Cape Cod Community College *A*
Eastern Nazarene College *B*
Elms College *B*
Hampshire College *B*
Harvard College *B*
Massachusetts College of Pharmacy
and Health Sciences *B*
Simmons College *B*
Springfield Technical Community
College *A*
University of Massachusetts
Amherst *B*
Worcester Polytechnic Institute *B*

Michigan

Adrian College *B*
Albion College *B*
Alma College *B*
Calvin College *B*
Concordia University *B*
Cornerstone University *B*
Delta College *A*
Gogebic Community College *A*
Grand Valley State University *B*
Hillsdale College *B*
Kalamazoo College *B*
Kellogg Community College *A*
Kirtland Community College *A*
Madonna University *B*
Michigan State University *B*
Northern Michigan University *B*
Olivet College *B*
Schoolcraft College *A*
Siena Heights University *B*
University of Detroit Mercy *B*
Washtenaw Community College *A*

Minnesota

College of St. Benedict *B*
College of St. Catherine *B*
Concordia College: Moorhead *B*
Gustavus Adolphus College *B*
Hamline University *B*
Minnesota State University
Mankato *B*
Moorhead *B*
Rochester Community and Technical
College *A*

St. Cloud State University *B*
St. John's University *B*
University of Minnesota
Twin Cities *B*
Vermilion Community College *A*
Winona State University *B*

Mississippi

Blue Mountain College *B*
Coahoma Community College *A*
East Central Community College *A*
Holmes Community College *A*
Itawamba Community College *A*
Jackson State University *B*

Missouri

Drury University *B*
Evangel University *B*
Lindenwood University *B*
Maryville University of Saint Louis *B*
Missouri Southern State University *B*
St. Louis Community College
St. Louis Community College at
Florissant Valley *A*
Three Rivers Community College *A*
Truman State University *B*
University of Missouri
Columbia *B*
Rolla *B*
Washington University in St. Louis *B*

Montana

Carroll College *B*
Montana Tech of the University of
Montana *B*

Nebraska

Bellevue University *B*
College of Saint Mary *B*
Concordia University *B*
Dana College *B*
Hastings College *B*
Midland Lutheran College *B*
Northeast Community College *A*
University of Nebraska
Lincoln *B*
Western Nebraska Community
College *A*
York College *A*

Nevada

Sierra Nevada College *B*
University of Nevada
Reno *B*

New Hampshire

Franklin Pierce College *B*
New England College *B*
Rivier College *B*
St. Anselm College *B*

New Jersey

Essex County College *A*
Rowan University *B*
Rutgers, The State University of New
Jersey
Camden Regional Campus *B*
New Brunswick/Piscataway
Campus *B*
Newark Regional Campus *B*
Sussex County Community College *A*

New Mexico

New Mexico Junior College *A*
San Juan College *A*

New York

Albany College of Pharmacy *B*
Alfred University *B*
Bard College *B*
City University of New York
City College *B*

Clarkson University *B*
Colgate University *B*
Columbia University
  School of General Studies *B*
Concordia College *B*
Cornell University *B*
D'Youville College *B*
Elmira College *B*
Fordham University *B*
Hobart and William Smith Colleges *B*
Hofstra University *B*
Houghton College *B*
Ithaca College *B*
Le Moyne College *B*
Manhattan College *B*
Molloy College *B*
New York Institute of Technology *B*
New York University *B*
Niagara University *B*
Paul Smith's College *B*
Rensselaer Polytechnic Institute *B*
Rochester Institute of Technology *B*
St. Joseph's College: Suffolk
  Campus *B*
St. Thomas Aquinas College *B*
Sarah Lawrence College *B*
State University of New York
  Albany *B*
  College at Brockport *B*
  College at Plattsburgh *B*
  College of Environmental Science
    and Forestry *B*
  New Paltz *B*
Sullivan County Community
  College *A*
Syracuse University *B*
Touro College *B*
Wagner College *B*
Wells College *B*
Yeshiva University *B*

North Carolina

Belmont Abbey College *B*
Brevard College *B*
Campbell University *B*
Carteret Community College *A*
Chowan College *B*
Elon University *B*
Johnson C. Smith University *B*
Lees-McRae College *B*
Lenoir-Rhyne College *B*
Louisburg College *A*
Mars Hill College *B*
Meredith College *B*
Methodist College *B*
Mitchell Community College *A*
North Carolina Wesleyan College *B*
Pfeiffer University *B*
Queens University of Charlotte *B*
St. Andrews Presbyterian College *B*
St. Augustine's College *B*
Sandhills Community College *A*
Warren Wilson College *B*
Wingate University *B*

North Dakota

Dickinson State University *B*
Mayville State University *B*
Valley City State University *B*

Ohio

Bluffton University *B*
Capital University *B*
Cedarville University *B*
Defiance College *B*
Heidelberg College *B*
John Carroll University *B*
Kent State University *B*
Kettering College of Medical Arts *A*
Miami University
  Oxford Campus *B*
Mount Vernon Nazarene University *B*
Muskingum College *B*
Oberlin College *B*

Ohio Northern University *B*
Ohio Wesleyan University *B*
Otterbein College *B*
Shawnee State University *B*
University of Cincinnati *B*
University of Cincinnati
  Clermont College *A*
  Raymond Walters College *A*
University of Dayton *B*
University of Findlay *B*
University of Rio Grande *B*
University of Toledo *A, B*
Urbana University *B*
Walsh University *B*
Wright State University *B*
Youngstown State University *B*

Oklahoma

Carl Albert State College *A*
Connors State College *A*
East Central University *B*
Eastern Oklahoma State College *A*
Northeastern Oklahoma Agricultural
  and Mechanical College *A*
Oklahoma Christian University *B*
Oklahoma City University *B*
Rose State College *A*

Oregon

Central Oregon Community
  College *A*
Chemeketa Community College *A*
Concordia University *B*
Corban College *B*
Eastern Oregon University *B*
Linn-Benton Community College *A*
Southern Oregon University *B*
Treasure Valley Community College *A*

Pennsylvania

Albright College *B*
Allegheny College *B*
Alvernia College *B*
Cabrini College *B*
Chatham College *B*
Duquesne University *B*
Edinboro University of
  Pennsylvania *B*
Elizabethtown College *B*
Gannon University *B*
Gettysburg College *B*
Grove City College *B*
Gwynedd-Mercy College *B*
Holy Family University *B*
Immaculata University *B*
Juniata College *B*
Keystone College *B*
La Salle University *B*
Lehigh University *B*
Mansfield University of
  Pennsylvania *B*
Penn State
  Abington *B*
  Altoona *B*
  Beaver *B*
  Berks *B*
  Delaware County *B*
  Dubois *B*
  Fayette *B*
  Hazleton *B*
  Lehigh Valley *B*
  McKeesport *B*
  Mont Alto *B*
  New Kensington *B*
  Schuylkill - Capital College *B*
  Shenango *B*
  University Park *B*
  Wilkes-Barre *B*
  Worthington Scranton *B*
  York *B*
Philadelphia University *B*
Reading Area Community College *A*
St. Vincent College *B*
Susquehanna University *B*

University of Pittsburgh
  Greensburg *B*
  Johnstown *B*
Villanova University *B*
Waynesburg College *B*
West Chester University of
  Pennsylvania *B*
Westminster College *B*
Widener University *B*
Wilkes University *B*
Wilson College *B*
York College of Pennsylvania *B*

Puerto Rico

University of Puerto Rico
  Mayaguez *B*
  Ponce *A*

Rhode Island

Rhode Island College *B*
Roger Williams University *B*

South Carolina

Charleston Southern University *B*
Clemson University *B*
College of Charleston *B*
Furman University *B*
Limestone College *B*
North Greenville College *B*
Voorhees College *B*

South Dakota

Augustana College *B*
Dakota State University *B*
Dakota Wesleyan University *B*

Tennessee

Carson-Newman College *B*
Columbia State Community College *A*
Cumberland University *B*
Fisk University *B*
Hiwassee College *A*
Jackson State Community College *A*
Lambuth University *B*
Lincoln Memorial University *B*
Lipscomb University *B*
Maryville College *B*
Roane State Community College *A*
Tennessee Technological University *B*
Tennessee Temple University *B*
Tennessee Wesleyan College *B*
Tusculum College *B*
Union University *B*
University of Tennessee
  Knoxville *B*
Walters State Community College *A*

Texas

Abilene Christian University *B*
Amarillo College *A*
Angelina College *A*
Austin Community College *A*
Baylor University *B*
Central Texas College *A*
Clarendon College *A*
Coastal Bend College *A*
Del Mar College *A*
El Paso Community College *A*
Galveston College *A*
Grayson County College *A*
Hardin-Simmons University *B*
Howard College *A*
Howard Payne University *B*
Jarvis Christian College *B*
Laredo Community College *A*
LeTourneau University *B*
Lon Morris College *A*
Lubbock Christian University *B*
Midland College *A*
Midwestern State University *B*
Navarro College *A*
Northeast Texas Community
  College *A*

Paris Junior College *A*
St. Philip's College *A*
South Plains College *A*
Texas A&M University *B*
Texas A&M University
  Commerce *B*
Texas Wesleyan University *B*
Trinity Valley Community College *A*
Tyler Junior College *A*
Western Texas College *A*

Utah

Snow College *A*
Southern Utah University *B*
University of Utah *B*
Utah State University *B*

Vermont

Bennington College *B*
Green Mountain College *B*
Johnson State College *B*

Virginia

Averett University *B*
Eastern Mennonite University *B*
Jefferson College of Health
  Sciences *B*
Longwood University *B*
Mountain Empire Community
  College *A*
Virginia Intermont College *B*
Virginia Wesleyan College *B*

Washington

Centralia College *A*
Eastern Washington University *B*
Everett Community College *A*
Saint Martin's University *B*
Seattle Pacific University *B*
Washington State University *B*

West Virginia

Concord University *B*
Davis and Elkins College *B*
Mountain State University *B*
Potomac State College of West Virginia
  University *A*
West Virginia Wesleyan College *B*

Wisconsin

Carroll College *B*
Lawrence University *B*
Marquette University *B*
Mount Mary College *B*
Northland College *B*
Ripon College *B*
University of Wisconsin
  Madison *M*
  Milwaukee *B*
  Oshkosh *B*
  Parkside *B*

Wyoming

Casper College *A*
Eastern Wyoming College *A*
Laramie County Community
  College *A*
Northwest College *A*
Western Wyoming Community
  College *A*

Preministerial studies

California
Point Loma Nazarene University *B*

Georgia
Wesleyan College *B*

Illinois
Elmhurst College *B*
Judson College *B*

Trinity International University *B*

Louisiana
New Orleans School of Urban
Missions *C*

Massachusetts
St. John's Seminary College *B*

Michigan
Adrian College *B*
Alma College *B*
Concordia University *B*
Cornerstone University *B*
Hillsdale College *B*
Kuyper College *B*

Minnesota
College of St. Benedict *B*
Northwestern College *B*
St. John's University *B*
St. Mary's University of Minnesota *B*

Nebraska
Concordia University *B*

New York
St. John's University *M*

Ohio
Ohio Wesleyan University *B*
University of Rio Grande *B*

Oregon
Corban College *B*
Warner Pacific College *B*

Pennsylvania
Baptist Bible College of
Pennsylvania *B*
Gettysburg College *B*
Juniata College *B*
Susquehanna University *B*

Tennessee
Hiwassee College *A*
Lambuth University *B*
Tennessee Wesleyan College *B*

Texas
College of Biblical Studies-Houston *B*
Hardin-Simmons University *B*
Texas A&M University
Commerce *B*
Texas Lutheran University *B*
University of Dallas *B*

Virginia
Bluefield College *B*
Eastern Mennonite University *B*
Liberty University *M*
Shenandoah University *C*

Wisconsin
Concordia University Wisconsin *B*
Viterbo University *B*

Prenursing

Alabama
Calhoun Community College *A*
Faulkner State Community College *A*
Gadsden State Community College *A*
Northeast Alabama Community
College *A*

Arkansas
Ouachita Baptist University *B*

California
California State University
East Bay *B*
Fullerton College *A*
Southwestern College *A*
Westmont College *B*

Colorado
Adams State College *B*
Red Rocks Community College *A*

District of Columbia
American University *B*

Florida
Broward Community College *A*
Jacksonville University *B*
Pensacola Junior College *A*

Georgia
Andrew College *A*
Covenant College *B*
East Georgia College *A*
Emmanuel College *A*
Georgia Military College *A*
Middle Georgia College *A*
Reinhardt College *A*
Young Harris College *A*

Idaho
Albertson College of Idaho *B*

Illinois
Concordia University *B*
Dominican University *B*
Eureka College *B*
Kishwaukee College *A*
Lewis and Clark Community
College *A*
Sauk Valley Community College *A*
Springfield College in Illinois *A*
Trinity International University *A*

Indiana
Ancilla College *A*
Indiana University-Purdue University
Indianapolis *B*
Manchester College *A*

Iowa
Dordt College *M*
Marshalltown Community College *A*
University of Iowa *B*

Kansas
Barton County Community College *A*
Central Christian College of Kansas *A*
Coffeyville Community College *A*
Colby Community College *A*
Donnelly College *A*
Seward County Community College *A*
Tabor College *A*

Kentucky
Bellarmine University *B*
Campbellsville University *B*

Maryland
Frederick Community College *A*
Frostburg State University *B*
University of Maryland
Baltimore County *B*

Massachusetts
Cape Cod Community College *A*
Roxbury Community College *A*

Michigan
Delta College *A*
Gogebic Community College *A*
Hillsdale College *B*

Kuyper College *B*

Minnesota
Itasca Community College *A*

Mississippi
Coahoma Community College *A*

Missouri
Lindenwood University *B*

Montana
Miles Community College *A*

Nebraska
Bellevue University *B*
Concordia University *B*
Northeast Community College *A*
Western Nebraska Community
College *A*

Nevada
Sierra Nevada College *B*

New York
St. Joseph's College *B*
St. Thomas Aquinas College *B*
State University of New York
College of Agriculture and
Technology at Morrisville *A*

North Carolina
Brevard College *B*
Carteret Community College *A*
Chowan College *B*
Sandhills Community College *A*

North Dakota
Cankdeska Cikana Community
College *A*
Mayville State University *B*
Valley City State University *B*

Ohio
Edison State Community College *A*
Heidelberg College *B*
Mount Vernon Nazarene University *B*
Muskingum College *B*
University of Cincinnati
Clermont College *A*
University of Findlay *B*
Ursuline College *B*

Oklahoma
Eastern Oklahoma State College *A*
Northeastern Oklahoma Agricultural
and Mechanical College *A*
Northeastern State University *B*
Oklahoma Christian University *B*
Rose State College *A*

Oregon
Chemeketa Community College *A*
Corban College *B*
Linn-Benton Community College *A*

Pennsylvania
Allegheny College *B*
Juniata College *B*
Keystone College *A*
Manor College *A*
Marywood University *B*
Mount Aloysius College *A*
Widener University *B*

South Carolina
Furman University *B*
Limestone College *B*
North Greenville College *A*
Voorhees College *B*

Tennessee
Hiwassee College *A*
Jackson State Community College *A*
Lambuth University *B*
Lipscomb University *B*
Maryville College *B*
Roane State Community College *A*
Tennessee Wesleyan College *B*

Texas
Baylor University *B*
Del Mar College *A*
Lon Morris College *A*
Lubbock Christian University *B*
St. Philip's College *A*
South Plains College *A*
Trinity Valley Community College *A*
Tyler Junior College *A*
Western Texas College *A*

Utah
Snow College *A*

Virginia
Jefferson College of Health
Sciences *B*

Washington
Centralia College *A*
Skagit Valley College *A*
Spokane Falls Community College *A*

West Virginia
West Virginia University *B*

Wisconsin
College of Menominee Nation *A*
Ripon College *B*

Wyoming
Sheridan College *A*
Western Wyoming Community
College *A*

Preoperative/surgical nursing

California
Loma Linda University *B, M*
National University *B*
Sonoma State University *M*

Connecticut
Quinnipiac University *M*
Sacred Heart University *B*

Delaware
Wilmington College *B*

Florida
Lynn University *B*

Georgia
Medical College of Georgia *B, M*

Illinois
Governors State University *B*
Lewis University *M*
Rockford College *B*
St. Xavier University *M*
Southern Illinois University
Edwardsville *M*

Indiana
Purdue University
Calumet *B*

Iowa
Graceland University *B*
Hawkeye Community College *A*

Mercy College of Health Sciences B

Kansas
Kansas Wesleyan University B
Tabor College B
University of Kansas Medical
    Center A, B, M

Kentucky
Eastern Kentucky University B, M

Maine
Eastern Maine Community College A
Husson College M
University of Maine M
University of Southern Maine B

Maryland
University of Maryland
    Baltimore B

Massachusetts
Elms College B
Emmanuel College B
Worcester State College B

Michigan
Calvin College B
University of Michigan D
Wayne State University M

Minnesota
Bemidji State University B
Minneapolis Community and
    Technical College A
Minnesota State University
    Mankato B, M
Winona State University B, M

Missouri
Central Methodist University B
Drury University B
Missouri State University B

Nebraska
Clarkson College B, M
Creighton University M
Midland Lutheran College B

New Hampshire
Rivier College B, M

New Jersey
The College of New Jersey B
College of St. Elizabeth B

New York
College of Mount St. Vincent B
Columbia University
    School of Nursing B, M, D
D'Youville College B, M
Molloy College B, M
Nazareth College of Rochester M
Roberts Wesleyan College B
St. John Fisher College B
State University of New York
    New Paltz B, M
    Upstate Medical University M

North Carolina
Queens University of Charlotte B

Ohio
Capital University B
Case Western Reserve University M
Kent State University
    Ashtabula Regional Campus A, B
Ursuline College B

Oregon
Eastern Oregon University B

Oregon Health & Science
    University M, D
Southern Oregon University B

Pennsylvania
Alvernia College B
Holy Family University B, M
La Salle University M
Mansfield University of
    Pennsylvania B
Mount Aloysius College A
Thomas Jefferson University: College
    of Health Professions M
University of Pennsylvania M

South Carolina
Medical University of South
    Carolina M

Tennessee
Union University B
University of Tennessee
    Knoxville B

Texas
South Plains College A
University of Texas
    Health Science Center at
      Houston M, D
    Health Science Center at San
      Antonio M, D

Washington
Gonzaga University B, M
Seattle Central Community College A

Wisconsin
Cardinal Stritch University M

Prepharmacy

Alabama
Alabama Southern Community
    College A
Calhoun Community College A
Faulkner State Community College A
Gadsden State Community College A
Huntingdon College B
Northeast Alabama Community
    College A

Arizona
Eastern Arizona College A
Grand Canyon University B

Arkansas
Harding University B
Ouachita Baptist University B
University of Central Arkansas B

California
Bakersfield College A
California Lutheran University B
California State University
    Chico B
Chabot College A
City College of San Francisco A
College of the Siskiyous A
Cypress College A
El Camino College A
Foothill College A
Golden West College A
Monterey Peninsula College A
Notre Dame de Namur University B
Ventura College A
Westmont College B
Whittier College B

Colorado
Adams State College B
Otero Junior College A

Connecticut
Southern Connecticut State
    University B
University of Connecticut B

Delaware
University of Delaware B

District of Columbia
American University B

Florida
Barry University B
Broward Community College A
Florida State University B
Gulf Coast Community College A
Indian River Community College A
Miami Dade College A
Okaloosa-Walton College A
Pensacola Junior College A
Santa Fe Community College A
University of Central Florida B
University of Miami B

Georgia
Abraham Baldwin Agricultural
    College A
Andrew College A
Dalton State College A
Darton College A
Emmanuel College A
Georgia Highlands College A
Georgia Perimeter College A
Gordon College A
Macon State College A
Middle Georgia College A
Oglethorpe University B
South Georgia College A
University of West Georgia B
Young Harris College A

Idaho
Brigham Young University-Idaho B
College of Southern Idaho A
North Idaho College A

Illinois
Black Hawk College
    East Campus A
City Colleges of Chicago
    Harold Washington College A
    Kennedy-King College A
Dominican University B
Elmhurst College B
Illinois Central College A
Illinois Institute of Technology B
John A. Logan College A
Kankakee Community College A
Kishwaukee College A
Lake Land College A
Lewis and Clark Community
    College A
Millikin University B
North Park University B
Rockford College B
Roosevelt University B
St. Xavier University B
Sauk Valley Community College A
Southwestern Illinois College A
Springfield College in Illinois B

Indiana
Indiana University-Purdue University
    Indianapolis B
Indiana Wesleyan University B
Manchester College B
Purdue University
    Calumet B
St. Mary-of-the-Woods College B
University of Evansville B
University of St. Francis B
Vincennes University A

Iowa
Clarke College B
Dordt College M
Ellsworth Community College A
Grand View College B
Iowa Central Community College A
Iowa Wesleyan College B
Marshalltown Community College A
Morningside College B
Simpson College B
University of Iowa B
Upper Iowa University B

Kansas
Barton County Community College A
Coffeyville Community College A
Colby Community College A
Dodge City Community College A
McPherson College B
Pittsburg State University B
Pratt Community College A
Seward County Community College A
Tabor College B
Washburn University of Topeka B

Kentucky
Bellarmine University B
Campbellsville University B
Eastern Kentucky University B
Georgetown College B
Thomas More College B

Louisiana
Centenary College of Louisiana B
Xavier University of Louisiana B

Maine
University of Maine
    Fort Kent B

Maryland
Allegany College of Maryland A
Columbia Union College B
Community College of Baltimore
    County A
Coppin State University B
Frederick Community College A
Frostburg State University B
Howard Community College A
Montgomery College A
Morgan State University B
Prince George's Community
    College A
University of Maryland
    Baltimore County B
    Eastern Shore B
Villa Julie College B

Massachusetts
Cape Cod Community College A
Eastern Nazarene College B
Simmons College B

Michigan
Adrian College B
Calvin College B
Delta College A
Ferris State University A
Gogebic Community College A
Grand Valley State University B
Hillsdale College B
Kellogg Community College A
Kirtland Community College A
Madonna University B
Mid Michigan Community College A
Northern Michigan University B
Schoolcraft College A
Siena Heights University A, B
West Shore Community College A

Minnesota
College of St. Benedict B

College of St. Catherine *B*
Concordia College: Moorhead *B*
Minnesota State University
  Mankato *B*
  Moorhead *B*
St. Cloud State University *B*
St. John's University *B*
University of Minnesota
  Duluth *B*
  Twin Cities *B*
Winona State University *B*

Mississippi

Blue Mountain College *B*
Coahoma Community College *A*
East Central Community College *A*
Holmes Community College *A*
Itawamba Community College *A*
Mississippi Delta Community
  College *A*
Mississippi Gulf Coast Community
  College
  Jefferson Davis Campus *A*

Missouri

Missouri Southern State University *B*
St. Louis Community College
  St. Louis Community College at
    Florissant Valley *A*
Three Rivers Community College *A*
Truman State University *B*
University of Missouri
  Columbia *B*
Washington University in St. Louis *B*

Montana

Carroll College *B*
Montana Tech of the University of
  Montana *B*

Nebraska

Bellevue University *B*
College of Saint Mary *B*
Concordia University *B*
Dana College *B*
Midland Lutheran College *B*
Northeast Community College *A*
University of Nebraska
  Lincoln *B*
Western Nebraska Community
  College *A*

Nevada

Sierra Nevada College *B*

New Jersey

Rowan University *B*
Sussex County Community College *A*

New Mexico

New Mexico Junior College *A*

New York

Bard College *B*
City University of New York
  City College *B*
D'Youville College *B*
Fordham University *B*
Rochester Institute of Technology *B*
St. Thomas Aquinas College *B*
State University of New York
  Albany *B*
  College at Plattsburgh *B*
  College of Environmental Science
    and Forestry *B*
Sullivan County Community
  College *A*
Touro College *B*

North Carolina

Belmont Abbey College *B*
Campbell University *B*

Carteret Community College *A*
Chowan College *B*
Lenoir-Rhyne College *B*
Livingstone College *B*
Louisburg College *A*
Mars Hill College *B*
Meredith College *B*
Methodist College *B*
Mitchell Community College *A*
Queens University of Charlotte *B*
St. Andrews Presbyterian College *B*
Sandhills Community College *A*
Wingate University *B*

North Dakota

Dickinson State University *A*
Mayville State University *B*
Valley City State University *B*

Ohio

Capital University *B*
Mount Vernon Nazarene University *B*
Otterbein College *B*
Shawnee State University *B*
University of Cincinnati *B*
University of Cincinnati
  Clermont College *B*
  Raymond Walters College *A*
Wright State University *B*
Youngstown State University *B*

Oklahoma

Carl Albert State College *A*
Connors State College *A*
East Central University *B*
Eastern Oklahoma State College *A*
Northeastern Oklahoma Agricultural
  and Mechanical College *A*
Oklahoma Christian University *B*
Oklahoma City University *B*
Rose State College *A*

Oregon

Central Oregon Community
  College *A*
Chemeketa Community College *A*
Corban College *B*
Eastern Oregon University *B*
Linn-Benton Community College *A*
Southern Oregon University *B*

Pennsylvania

Allegheny College *B*
Alvernia College *B*
Gannon University *B*
Gettysburg College *B*
Holy Family University *B*
Juniata College *B*
Keystone College *B*
Luzerne County Community
  College *A*
Mansfield University of
  Pennsylvania *B*
Reading Area Community College *A*
St. Vincent College *B*
University of Pittsburgh
  Greensburg *B*
Westminster College *B*
York College of Pennsylvania *B*

Puerto Rico

University of Puerto Rico
  Ponce *A*

South Carolina

Charleston Southern University *B*
Clemson University *B*
Furman University *B*
Limestone College *B*
North Greenville College *B*

South Dakota

Augustana College *B*
Dakota State University *B*
Dakota Wesleyan University *B*

Tennessee

Carson-Newman College *B*
Columbia State Community College *A*
Cumberland University *B*
Hiwassee College *A*
Lambuth University *B*
Lincoln Memorial University *B*
Lipscomb University *B*
Maryville College *B*
Roane State Community College *A*
Tennessee Technological University *B*
Tennessee Wesleyan College *B*
Tusculum College *B*
Union University *B*
University of Tennessee
  Knoxville *B*
Walters State Community College *A*

Texas

Abilene Christian University *B*
Amarillo College *A*
Angelina College *A*
Austin Community College *A*
Clarendon College *A*
Coastal Bend College *A*
Del Mar College *A*
El Paso Community College *A*
Grayson County College *A*
Laredo Community College *A*
LeTourneau University *B*
Lon Morris College *A*
Lubbock Christian University *B*
Midland College *A*
Midwestern State University *B*
Navarro College *A*
Paris Junior College *A*
South Plains College *A*
Texas A&M University
  Commerce *B*
Texas Southern University *B*
Trinity Valley Community College *A*
Tyler Junior College *A*
University of Houston *B*
Western Texas College *A*

Utah

Snow College *A*
Southern Utah University *B*
University of Utah *B*

Virginia

Jefferson College of Health
  Sciences *B*
Longwood University *B*
Lord Fairfax Community College *A*
Mountain Empire Community
  College *A*
Virginia Wesleyan College *B*

Washington

Centralia College *A*
Eastern Washington University *B*
Everett Community College *A*
Saint Martin's University *B*

West Virginia

Concord University *B*
Davis and Elkins College *B*
Potomac State College of West Virginia
  University *A*
University of Charleston *A*
West Virginia University *B*
West Virginia Wesleyan College *B*

Wisconsin

Carroll College *B*
Lawrence University *B*

Northland College *B*
Ripon College *B*
University of Wisconsin
  Milwaukee *B*
  Oshkosh *B*

Wyoming

Casper College *A*
Eastern Wyoming College *A*
Laramie County Community
  College *A*
Northwest College *A*
Western Wyoming Community
  College *A*

Preveterinary

Alabama

Alabama Southern Community
  College *A*
Calhoun Community College *A*
Faulkner State Community College *A*
Faulkner University *B*
Gadsden State Community College *A*
Huntingdon College *B*
Northeast Alabama Community
  College *A*
Spring Hill College *B*

Arizona

Central Arizona College *A*
Grand Canyon University *B*
Northern Arizona University *B*
University of Arizona *B*

Arkansas

Harding University *B*
Ouachita Baptist University *B*
University of Central Arkansas *B*
University of the Ozarks *B*

California

Bakersfield College *A*
California Lutheran University *B*
California State University
  Chico *B*
Chabot College *A*
Chapman University *B*
College of the Siskiyous *A*
Cypress College *A*
Foothill College *A*
Golden West College *A*
Los Angeles Pierce College *A*
MiraCosta College *A*
Monterey Peninsula College *A*
Mount St. Mary's College *B*
Notre Dame de Namur University *B*
Ventura College *A*
Westmont College *B*
Whittier College *B*

Colorado

Adams State College *B*
Otero Junior College *A*
Regis University *B*

Connecticut

Quinnipiac University *B*
Southern Connecticut State
  University *B*

Delaware

Delaware State University *B*
University of Delaware *B*

District of Columbia

American University *B*

Florida

Barry University *B*
Broward Community College *A*
Florida State University *B*

Gulf Coast Community College *A*
Indian River Community College *A*
Jacksonville University *B*
Miami Dade College *A*
Okaloosa-Walton College *A*
Pensacola Junior College *A*
St. Thomas University *B*
University of Central Florida *B*
University of Miami *B*
University of Tampa *B*

Georgia

Andrew College *A*
Darton College *A*
Georgia Highlands College *A*
Macon State College *A*
Middle Georgia College *A*
Oglethorpe University *B*
Young Harris College *A*

Idaho

Boise State University *B*
Brigham Young University-Idaho *B*
College of Southern Idaho *A*
North Idaho College *A*
Northwest Nazarene University *B*

Illinois

Blackburn College *B*
Dominican University *B*
Elmhurst College *B*
Eureka College *B*
Greenville College *B*
Illinois Central College *A*
Kankakee Community College *A*
Kishwaukee College *A*
Lake Land College *A*
Lewis University *B*
MacMurray College *B*
Millikin University *B*
North Park University *B*
Rockford College *B*
Roosevelt University *B*
St. Xavier University *B*
Sauk Valley Community College *A*
Southwestern Illinois College *A*
Springfield College in Illinois *A*
University of Illinois
    Urbana-Champaign *B*
University of St. Francis *B*

Indiana

Indiana University-Purdue University
    Fort Wayne *B*
Indiana University-Purdue University
    Indianapolis *B*
Indiana Wesleyan University *B*
Manchester College *B*
Purdue University
    Calumet *B*
St. Joseph's College *B*
St. Mary-of-the-Woods College *B*
University of Evansville *B*
Vincennes University *A*

Iowa

Clarke College *B*
Coe College *B*
Dordt College *M*
Ellsworth Community College *A*
Iowa Central Community College *A*
Iowa State University *B*
Iowa Wesleyan College *B*
Marshalltown Community College *A*
Morningside College *B*
Northwestern College *B*
Simpson College *B*
University of Iowa *B*
Upper Iowa University *B*

Kansas

Barton County Community College *A*
Central Christian College of Kansas *A*

Coffeyville Community College *A*
Colby Community College *A*
Dodge City Community College *A*
Kansas State University *B*
McPherson College *B*
Pittsburg State University *B*
Pratt Community College *A*
Seward County Community College *A*
Tabor College *B*
Washburn University of Topeka *B*

Kentucky

Campbellsville University *B*
Georgetown College *B*
Thomas More College *B*

Louisiana

Centenary College of Louisiana *B*
Nicholls State University *B*
Xavier University of Louisiana *B*

Maine

University of Maine
    Fort Kent *B*
University of Southern Maine *B*

Maryland

Columbia Union College *B*
Community College of Baltimore
    County *A*
Frostburg State University *B*
Howard Community College *A*
University of Maryland
    Baltimore County *B*
    Eastern Shore *B*
Villa Julie College *B*

Massachusetts

American International College *B*
Becker College *B*
Eastern Nazarene College *B*
Elms College *B*
Hampshire College *B*
University of Massachusetts
    Amherst *B*
Worcester Polytechnic Institute *B*

Michigan

Adrian College *B*
Albion College *B*
Alma College *B*
Calvin College *B*
Cornerstone University *B*
Delta College *A*
Gogebic Community College *A*
Grand Valley State University *B*
Hillsdale College *B*
Kalamazoo College *B*
Kellogg Community College *A*
Kirtland Community College *A*
Madonna University *B*
Northern Michigan University *B*
Schoolcraft College *A*
Siena Heights University *A*

Minnesota

College of St. Benedict *B*
College of St. Catherine *B*
Concordia College: Moorhead *B*
Gustavus Adolphus College *B*
Hamline University *B*
Minnesota State University
    Mankato *B*
    Moorhead *B*
St. Cloud State University *B*
St. John's University *B*
University of Minnesota
    Duluth *B*
    Twin Cities *B*
University of St. Thomas *B*
Vermilion Community College *A*
Winona State University *B*

Mississippi

Blue Mountain College *B*
Coahoma Community College *A*
East Central Community College *A*
Holmes Community College *A*
Itawamba Community College *A*
Mississippi Delta Community
    College *A*

Missouri

Drury University *B*
Evangel University *B*
Lindenwood University *B*
Missouri Southern State University *B*
Northwest Missouri State
    University *B*
Three Rivers Community College *A*
Truman State University *B*
University of Missouri
    Columbia *B*
Washington University in St. Louis *B*

Montana

Carroll College *B*
Montana Tech of the University of
    Montana *B*
University of Great Falls *B*

Nebraska

College of Saint Mary *B*
Concordia University *B*
Dana College *B*
Hastings College *B*
Midland Lutheran College *B*
Northeast Community College *A*
University of Nebraska
    Lincoln *B*
Western Nebraska Community
    College *A*
York College *A*

Nevada

University of Nevada
    Reno *B*

New Hampshire

Franklin Pierce College *B*
Rivier College *B*

New Jersey

Rowan University *B*

New York

Albany College of Pharmacy *B*
Alfred University *B*
Bard College *B*
City University of New York
    City College *B*
Clarkson University *B*
Colgate University *B*
Cornell University *B*
D'Youville College *B*
Elmira College *B*
Fordham University *B*
Hobart and William Smith Colleges *B*
Hofstra University *B*
Houghton College *B*
Ithaca College *B*
Le Moyne College *B*
Manhattan College *B*
Molloy College *B*
Niagara University *B*
Paul Smith's College *B*
Rochester Institute of Technology *B*
St. Joseph's College: Suffolk
    Campus *B*
St. Thomas Aquinas College *B*
State University of New York
    Albany *B*
    College at Brockport *B*
    College at Plattsburgh *B*

College of Environmental Science
    and Forestry *B*
New Paltz *B*
Sullivan County Community
    College *A*
Syracuse University *B*
Touro College *B*
Wells College *B*

North Carolina

Belmont Abbey College *B*
Brevard College *B*
Campbell University *B*
Carteret Community College *A*
Chowan College *B*
Elon University *B*
Lees-McRae College *B*
Mars Hill College *B*
Meredith College *B*
Methodist College *B*
Mitchell Community College *A*
Pfeiffer University *B*
Queens University of Charlotte *B*
St. Andrews Presbyterian College *B*
Sandhills Community College *A*
Warren Wilson College *B*
Wingate University *B*

North Dakota

Dickinson State University *B*
Mayville State University *B*
North Dakota State University *B*
Valley City State University *B*

Ohio

Cedarville University *B*
Defiance College *B*
Heidelberg College *B*
John Carroll University *B*
Kent State University *B*
Mount Vernon Nazarene University *B*
Muskingum College *B*
Oberlin College *B*
Ohio Northern University *B*
Ohio Wesleyan University *B*
Otterbein College *B*
Shawnee State University *B*
University of Cincinnati *B*
University of Cincinnati
    Clermont College *A*
    Raymond Walters College *A*
University of Findlay *B*
University of Toledo *B*
Walsh University *B*
Wright State University *B*
Youngstown State University *B*

Oklahoma

Carl Albert State College *A*
Connors State College *A*
East Central University *B*
Eastern Oklahoma State College *A*
Murray State College *A*
Northeastern Oklahoma Agricultural
    and Mechanical College *A*
Oklahoma Christian University *B*
Oklahoma City University *B*
Oklahoma State University *B*

Oregon

Corban College *B*
Eastern Oregon University *B*
Linn-Benton Community College *A*
Southern Oregon University *B*
Treasure Valley Community College *A*

Pennsylvania

Albright College *B*
Allegheny College *B*
Alvernia College *B*
Edinboro University of
    Pennsylvania *B*
Elizabethtown College *B*

Gannon University *B*
Gettysburg College *B*
Grove City College *B*
Gwynedd-Mercy College *B*
Holy Family University *B*
Juniata College *B*
Keystone College *B*
La Salle University *B*
Manor College *A*
Mansfield University of
   Pennsylvania *B*
St. Vincent College *B*
Susquehanna University *B*
University of Pittsburgh
   Greensburg *B*
   Johnstown *B*
Waynesburg College *B*
Westminster College *B*
Widener University *B*
Wilson College *B*
York College of Pennsylvania *B*

Rhode Island
Rhode Island College *B*

South Carolina
Clemson University *B*
Furman University *B*
Limestone College *B*

South Dakota
Augustana College *B*
Dakota State University *B*
Dakota Wesleyan University *B*

Tennessee
Cumberland University *B*
Hiwassee College *A*
Lambuth University *B*
Lincoln Memorial University *B*
Lipscomb University *B*
Maryville College *B*
Roane State Community College *A*
Tennessee Technological University *B*
Tennessee Wesleyan College *B*
Union University *B*
University of Tennessee
   Knoxville *B*
Walters State Community College *A*

Texas
Abilene Christian University *B*
Amarillo College *A*
Angelina College *A*
Austin Community College *A*
Clarendon College *A*
Coastal Bend College *A*
Del Mar College *A*
El Paso Community College *A*
Galveston College *A*
Laredo Community College *A*
LeTourneau University *B*
Lon Morris College *A*
Lubbock Christian University *B*
Midwestern State University *B*
Navarro College *A*
Paris Junior College *A*
South Plains College *A*
Sul Ross State University *A*
Texas A&M University *B*
Texas A&M University
   Commerce *B*
Trinity Valley Community College *A*
Tyler Junior College *A*
Western Texas College *A*

Utah
Snow College *A*
Southern Utah University *B*
Utah State University *B, M*

Vermont
Green Mountain College *B*

Virginia
Eastern Mennonite University *B*
Longwood University *B*
Mountain Empire Community
   College *A*
Virginia Intermont College *B*
Virginia Wesleyan College *B*

Washington
Centralia College *A*
Eastern Washington University *B*
Everett Community College *A*
Saint Martin's University *B*

West Virginia
Concord University *B*
Davis and Elkins College *B*
Potomac State College of West Virginia
   University *A*
West Virginia Wesleyan College *B*

Wisconsin
Carroll College *B*
Lawrence University *B*
Mount Mary College *B*
Northland College *B*
Ripon College *B*
University of Wisconsin
   Milwaukee *B*
   Oshkosh *B*
   Parkside *B*

Wyoming
Casper College *A*
Eastern Wyoming College *A*
Laramie County Community
   College *A*
Northwest College *A*
Western Wyoming Community
   College *A*

Printing management

Kansas
Pittsburg State University *M*

Kentucky
Murray State University *B*
Somerset Community College *C, A*

Michigan
Ferris State University *B*

New Jersey
Kean University *B, M*

New York
Rochester Institute of
   Technology *B, M*

Washington
Seattle Central Community
   College *C, A*

Wisconsin
Carroll College *B*
University of Wisconsin
   Stout *B*

Printing press operator

Georgia
Albany Technical College *C*

Illinois
City Colleges of Chicago
   Kennedy-King College *A*

Indiana
Vincennes University *A*

Minnesota
Hennepin Technical College *A*

New Mexico
Southwestern Indian Polytechnic
   Institute *C*

Ohio
Sinclair Community College *C*

Printmaking

Arizona
Northern Arizona University *B*

Arkansas
Phillips Community College of the
   University of Arkansas *C, A*

California
Academy of Art University *C, A, B, M*
California College of the Arts *B, M*
California State University
   East Bay *B*
   Fullerton *B, M*
   Long Beach *B, M*
   Northridge *B, M*
   Stanislaus *C*
City College of San Francisco *C, A*
College of the Desert *A*
De Anza College *C, A*
Fresno City College *C, A*
Long Beach City College *A*
Monterey Peninsula College *C, A*
Ohlone College *C*
Palomar College *A*
Pasadena City College *C, A*
San Francisco Art Institute *B, M*
Santa Rosa Junior College *C*

Colorado
Adams State College *B*

Connecticut
Capital Community College *C*
University of Hartford *B*

District of Columbia
American University *M*
George Washington University *M*

Florida
University of Miami *B*

Illinois
Bradley University *B*
Rockford College *B*
School of the Art Institute of
   Chicago *B, M*

Indiana
Indiana University-Purdue University
   Fort Wayne *B*
Indiana University-Purdue University
   Indianapolis *B*
Vincennes University *A*

Iowa
Drake University *B*
University of Iowa *B, M*

Kansas
University of Kansas *B, M*

Kentucky
Eastern Kentucky University *B*

Maine
Maine College of Art *B*

Maryland
Maryland Institute College of Art *B*

Massachusetts
Emmanuel College *B*
Massachusetts College of Art *B, M*
Montserrat College of Art *B*
Salem State College *B*
School of the Museum of Fine
   Arts *B, M*
Simon's Rock College of Bard *B*
University of Massachusetts
   Dartmouth *M*

Michigan
Andrews University *B*
College for Creative Studies *B*
Grand Valley State University *B*
Kendall College of Art and Design of
   Ferris State University *B*
Northern Michigan University *B*
University of Michigan *B*
University of Michigan
   Flint *B*

Minnesota
College of Visual Arts *B*
Minneapolis College of Art and
   Design *B*
St. Cloud State University *B*

Missouri
Columbia College *B*
Kansas City Art Institute *B*
Washington University in St.
   Louis *B, M*

Nevada
Sierra Nevada College *B*

New Jersey
Rowan University *B*

New York
Bard College *B, M*
Daemen College *B*
Parsons The New School for Design *C*
Pratt Institute *B, M*
Rochester Institute of
   Technology *A, B, M*
Sarah Lawrence College *B*
School of Visual Arts *B, M*
State University of New York
   College at Buffalo *B*
   College at Fredonia *B*
   New Paltz *B, M*
   Purchase *B, M*
Syracuse University *B, M*

North Carolina
East Carolina University *B*

Ohio
Art Academy of Cincinnati *B*
Cleveland Institute of Art *B*
Ohio State University
   Columbus Campus *B, M*
Ohio University *B, M*
University of Akron *B*
Youngstown State University *B*

Oregon
Pacific Northwest College of Art *B*
Portland State University *B*
University of Oregon *B, M*

Pennsylvania
Arcadia University *B*
Edinboro University of
   Pennsylvania *B*
Keystone College *A, B*

Marywood University *M*
Seton Hill University *B*
Temple University *B, M*
University of the Arts *B, M*

Puerto Rico

Inter American University of Puerto
Rico
San German Campus *M*

Rhode Island

Rhode Island School of Design *B, M*

South Carolina

South Carolina State University *B*

Tennessee

Memphis College of Art *B, M*

Texas

Sam Houston State University *M*
Texas A&M University
Commerce *B*
Texas Christian University *B, M*
University of Dallas *B, M*
University of Houston *B, M*
University of North Texas *B, M*
University of Texas
El Paso *B, M*

Utah

Dixie State College of Utah *A*

Vermont

Bennington College *B*

Washington

Cornish College of the Arts *B*
University of Washington *B, M*
Western Washington University *B*

West Virginia

West Virginia State University *B*

Wisconsin

University of Wisconsin
Madison *B*

Psychiatric nursing

Illinois

Southern Illinois University
Edwardsville *M*

Indiana

Indiana University-Purdue University
Indianapolis *M*

Louisiana

Louisiana State University Health
Sciences Center *M*
Southeastern Louisiana University *M*

Maine

Husson College *M*
University of Southern Maine *B, M*

Michigan

University of Michigan *M, D*
Wayne State University *M*

Minnesota

College of St. Scholastica *M*

New Hampshire

Rivier College *M*

New York

City University of New York
Hunter College *B, M*

Columbia University
School of Nursing *M*
Pace University *M*
State University of New York
Buffalo *M*
Stony Brook *M*

Ohio

Case Western Reserve University *M*

Pennsylvania

Drexel University *M*
Duquesne University *M*
University of Pennsylvania *M*

South Carolina

Medical University of South
Carolina *M*

Psychoanalysis

California

California Institute of Integral
Studies *M*

Psychobiology/ physiological psychology

California

San Francisco State University *M*
University of California
Irvine *D*

District of Columbia

American University *D*

Florida

Florida Atlantic University *D*
Florida State University *M, D*

Georgia

Emory University *D*

New York

State University of New York
Albany *D*
Binghamton *D*
Buffalo *D*
Stony Brook *D*

Oklahoma

University of Oklahoma *M, D*

Texas

University of Houston *M, D*
University of Texas
Dallas *M, D*
Tyler *M*

Psychology

Alabama

Alabama Agricultural and Mechanical
University *B*
Alabama State University *B*
Athens State University *B*
Auburn University *B, M, D*
Auburn University at
Montgomery *B, M*
Birmingham-Southern College *B*
Faulkner University *B*
Gadsden State Community College *A*
Huntingdon College *B*
Jacksonville State University *B, M*
Judson College *B*
Lawson State Community College *A*
Northeast Alabama Community
College *A*
Oakwood College *B*

Samford University *B*
Spring Hill College *B*
Talladega College *B*
Troy University *B*
Tuskegee University *B*
University of Alabama *B, M, D*
University of Alabama
Birmingham *B, M, D*
Huntsville *B, M*
University of Mobile *B*
University of Montevallo *B*
University of North Alabama *B*
University of South Alabama *B, M*
University of West Alabama *B*

Alaska

Alaska Pacific University *B*
University of Alaska
Anchorage *B*
Fairbanks *B*

Arizona

Arizona State University *B, M, D*
Arizona State University West *B*
Arizona Western College *A*
Central Arizona College *A*
Chandler-Gilbert Community College
Williams Campus *A*
Cochise College *A*
Dine College *A*
Eastern Arizona College *A*
Estrella Mountain Community
College *A*
Glendale Community College *A*
Grand Canyon University *B*
Northcentral University *B, M, D*
Northern Arizona University *B, M*
Prescott College *B, M*
South Mountain Community
College *A*
University of Arizona *B, M, D*

Arkansas

Arkansas State University *B*
Arkansas Tech University *B*
Harding University *B*
Henderson State University *B*
Hendrix College *B*
John Brown University *B*
Lyon College *B*
Ouachita Baptist University *B*
Philander Smith College *B*
Phillips Community College of the
University of Arkansas *A*
Southern Arkansas University *B*
University of Arkansas *B, M, D*
University of Arkansas
Fort Smith *B*
Little Rock *B*
Monticello *B*
Pine Bluff *B*
University of Central Arkansas *B*
University of the Ozarks *B*
Williams Baptist College *B*

California

Alliant International
University *C, B, M, D*
Antioch Southern California
Antioch University Los Angeles *M*
Antioch University Santa Barbara *M*
Azusa Pacific University *B*
Bakersfield College *A*
Barstow College *A*
Bethany University *B*
Biola University *B, M, D*
Cabrillo College *A*
California Baptist University *B*
California Institute of Integral
Studies *M, D*
California Lutheran University *B*
California Polytechnic State
University: San Luis Obispo *B*

California State Polytechnic
University: Pomona *B, M*
California State University
Bakersfield *B, M*
Chico *B*
Dominguez Hills *B*
East Bay *B*
Fresno *B, M*
Fullerton *B, M*
Long Beach *B, M*
Los Angeles *B, M*
Northridge *B*
Sacramento *B, M*
San Bernardino *B, M*
San Marcos *B, M*
Stanislaus *B, M*
Canada College *A*
Cerritos Community College *A*
Chabot College *A*
Chaffey College *A*
Chapman University *B*
Citrus College *A*
Claremont McKenna College *B*
College of Alameda *A*
College of the Desert *A*
Concordia University *B*
Contra Costa College *A*
Copper Mountain College *A*
Crafton Hills College *A*
Cypress College *A*
De Anza College *A*
Dominican University of California *B*
East Los Angeles College *A*
El Camino College *A*
Foothill College *A*
Fresno City College *A*
Fresno Pacific University *B*
Fullerton College *A*
Gavilan Community College *A*
Glendale Community College *A*
Golden West College *A*
Holy Names University *B*
Hope International University *B*
Humboldt State University *B, M*
Imperial Valley College *A*
Irvine Valley College *A*
John F. Kennedy University *B, D*
La Sierra University *B*
Lake Tahoe Community College *A*
Loma Linda University *M, D*
Los Angeles City College *A*
Los Angeles Harbor College *A*
Los Angeles Mission College *A*
Los Angeles Southwest College *A*
Los Angeles Valley College *A*
Los Medanos College *A*
Loyola Marymount University *B*
Mendocino College *A*
Merced College *A*
Mills College *B*
MiraCosta College *A*
Monterey Peninsula College *A*
Mount St. Mary's College *B*
National University *B*
Notre Dame de Namur University *B*
Occidental College *B*
Orange Coast College *A*
Pacific Union College *B*
Pasadena City College *A*
Patten University *B*
Pepperdine University *B, M, D*
Pitzer College *B*
Platt College
Cerritos *A*
Point Loma Nazarene University *B*
Pomona College *B*
Remington College
San Diego *B, M*
Saddleback College *A*
St. Mary's College of California *B*
San Bernardino Valley College *A*
San Diego Christian College *B*
San Diego City College *A*
San Diego Mesa College *A*

San Diego Miramar College *A*
San Diego State University *B, M*
San Francisco State University *B*
San Joaquin Delta College *A*
San Jose City College *A*
San Jose State University *B, M*
Santa Ana College *A*
Santa Barbara City College *A*
Santa Clara University *B*
Santa Rosa Junior College *A*
Santiago Canyon College *A*
Scripps College *B*
Simpson University *B*
Skyline College *A*
Solano Community College *A*
Sonoma State University *B, M*
Southwestern College *A*
Stanford University *B, M, D*
University of California
    Berkeley *B, D*
    Davis *B, D*
    Irvine *B, M, D*
    Los Angeles *B, M, D*
    Riverside *B, M, D*
    San Diego *B, M, D*
    Santa Barbara *B, M, D*
    Santa Cruz *B, D*
University of Judaism *M*
University of La Verne *B*
University of Redlands *B*
University of San Diego *B*
University of San Francisco *B*
University of Southern
    California *B, M, D*
University of the Pacific *B, M*
Vanguard University of Southern
    California *B*
Ventura College *A*
West Hills Community College *A*
West Los Angeles College *A*
West Valley College *A*
Westmont College *B*
Whittier College *B*
Woodbury University *B*

Colorado

Adams State College *B*
Colorado Christian University *B*
Colorado College *B*
Colorado Mountain College
    Alpine Campus *A*
Colorado State University *B, M, D*
Colorado State University
    Pueblo *B*
Fort Lewis College *B*
Mesa State College *B*
Metropolitan State College of
    Denver *B*
Naropa University *B, M*
Otero Junior College *A*
Red Rocks Community College *A*
Regis University *B*
Trinidad State Junior College *A*
University of Colorado
    Boulder *B, D*
    Colorado Springs *B, M*
    Denver and Health Sciences
        Center *B, M*
University of Denver *B, M, D*
University of Northern Colorado *B, M*
Western State College of Colorado *B*

Connecticut

Albertus Magnus College *B*
Central Connecticut State
    University *B, M*
Connecticut College *B, M*
Eastern Connecticut State
    University *B*
Fairfield University *B*
Mitchell College *B*
Post University *B*
Quinnipiac University *B*
Sacred Heart University *B*

St. Joseph College *B*
Southern Connecticut State
    University *B, M*
Trinity College *B*
University of Bridgeport *B*
University of Connecticut *B, M, D*
University of Hartford *B, M*
University of New Haven *B*
Wesleyan University *B, M*
Western Connecticut State
    University *B*
Yale University *B, M, D*

Delaware

Delaware State University *B*
University of Delaware *B, M, D*
Wesley College *B*
Wilmington College *B*

District of Columbia

American University *B, M*
Catholic University of America *B, M*
Gallaudet University *B*
George Washington
    University *B, M, D*
Georgetown University *B, D*
Howard University *B, M, D*
Trinity University *B*
University of the District of
    Columbia *B*

Florida

Barry University *B, M*
Bethune-Cookman College *B*
Broward Community College *A*
Carlos Albizu University *B, M, D*
Clearwater Christian College *B*
Eckerd College *B*
Edward Waters College *B*
Flagler College *B*
Florida Agricultural and Mechanical
    University *B*
Florida Atlantic University *B, M*
Florida Gulf Coast University *B*
Florida Institute of Technology *B*
Florida International
    University *B, M, D*
Florida Memorial University *B*
Florida Southern College *B*
Florida State University *B, M, D*
Gulf Coast Community College *A*
Indian River Community College *A*
Jacksonville University *B*
Lynn University *B*
Manatee Community College *A*
Miami Dade College *A*
New College of Florida *B*
Nova Southeastern University *B*
Palm Beach Atlantic University *B*
Palm Beach Community College *A*
Pensacola Junior College *A*
Rollins College *B*
St. Leo University *B*
St. Thomas University *B*
Schiller International University *A, B*
Southeastern College of the
    Assemblies of God *B*
Stetson University *B*
University of Central Florida *B, M, D*
University of Florida *B, M, D*
University of Miami *B, M, D*
University of North Florida *B, M*
University of South Florida *B, M, D*
University of Tampa *A, B*
University of West Florida *B, M*
Valencia Community College *A*
Warner Southern College *B*

Georgia

Abraham Baldwin Agricultural
    College *A*
Agnes Scott College *B*
Albany State University *B*

Andrew College *A*
Armstrong Atlantic State University *B*
Atlanta Christian College *B*
Atlanta Metropolitan College *A*
Augusta State University *B, M*
Bainbridge College *A*
Berry College *B*
Brenau University *B*
Brewton-Parker College *B*
Clark Atlanta University *B*
Clayton State University *B*
Coastal Georgia Community
    College *A*
Columbus State University *B*
Covenant College *B*
Dalton State College *A*
Darton College *A*
East Georgia College *A*
Emmanuel College *B*
Emory University *B, D*
Fort Valley State University *B*
Gainesville State College *A*
Georgia College and State
    University *B*
Georgia Highlands College *A*
Georgia Perimeter College *A*
Georgia Southern University *B, M*
Georgia Southwestern State
    University *B*
Georgia State University *B, M, D*
Gordon College *A*
Kennesaw State University *B*
LaGrange College *B*
Macon State College *A*
Mercer University *B*
Middle Georgia College *A*
Morehouse College *B*
North Georgia College & State
    University *B*
Oglethorpe University *B*
Paine College *B*
Piedmont College *B*
Reinhardt College *B*
Shorter College *B*
South Georgia College *A*
Spelman College *B*
Thomas University *B*
Toccoa Falls College *B*
University of Georgia *B, M, D*
University of West Georgia *B, M*
Valdosta State University *B, M*
Waycross College *A*
Wesleyan College *B*
Young Harris College *A*

Hawaii

Brigham Young University-Hawaii *B*
Chaminade University of Honolulu *B*
Hawaii Pacific University *B*
University of Hawaii
    Hilo *B*
    Manoa *B, M, D*
    West Oahu *B*

Idaho

Albertson College of Idaho *B*
Boise State University *B*
Brigham Young University-Idaho *B*
College of Southern Idaho *A*
Idaho State University *B, M*
Lewis-Clark State College *B*
North Idaho College *A*
Northwest Nazarene University *B*
University of Idaho *B, M*

Illinois

Argosy University *B*
Augustana College *B, T*
Aurora University *B*
Benedictine University *B*
Black Hawk College
    East Campus *A*
Blackburn College *B*
Bradley University *B, T*

Chicago State University *B*
City Colleges of Chicago
    Kennedy-King College *A*
Concordia University *B, M*
Danville Area Community College *A*
DePaul University *B, M*
Dominican University *B*
Eastern Illinois University *B, T*
Elmhurst College *B, T*
Eureka College *B*
Governors State University *B, M*
Greenville College *B*
Highland Community College *A*
Illinois College *B*
Illinois Institute of
    Technology *B, M, D*
Illinois State University *B, M*
Illinois Valley Community College *A*
Illinois Wesleyan University *B*
John A. Logan College *A*
John Wood Community College *A*
Joliet Junior College *A*
Judson College *B*
Kankakee Community College *A*
Kishwaukee College *A*
Knox College *B*
Lake Forest College *B*
Lake Land College *A*
Lewis University *B, T*
Loyola University of Chicago *B*
MacMurray College *B*
McKendree College *B*
Millikin University *B*
Monmouth College *B, T*
National-Louis University *B, M*
North Central College *B*
North Park University *B*
Northeastern Illinois University *B*
Northern Illinois University *B, M, D*
Northwestern University *B, M, D*
Olivet Nazarene University *B, M*
Quincy University *B*
Richland Community College *A*
Rockford College *B*
Roosevelt University *B, M*
St. Augustine College *A*
St. Xavier University *B*
Sauk Valley Community College *A*
South Suburban College of Cook
    County *A*
Southern Illinois University
    Carbondale *B, M, D*
Southern Illinois University
    Edwardsville *B, M*
Southwestern Illinois College *A*
Trinity Christian College *B*
Trinity International University *B, M*
Triton College *A*
University of Chicago *B, D*
University of Illinois
    Chicago *B, M, D*
    Springfield *B*
    Urbana-Champaign *B, M, D*
University of St. Francis *B*
Western Illinois University *B, M*
Wheaton College *B*
William Rainey Harper College *A*

Indiana

Anderson University *B*
Ball State University *B, M*
Bethel College *B*
Butler University *B*
Calumet College of St. Joseph *B*
DePauw University *B*
Earlham College *B*
Franklin College *B*
Goshen College *B*
Grace College *B*
Hanover College *B*
Huntington University *B*
Indiana Institute of Technology *B*
Indiana State University *B, M*

Indiana University
- Bloomington *B, M, D*
- East *B*
- Kokomo *B*
- Northwest *B*
- South Bend *B, M*
- Southeast *B*

Indiana University-Purdue University
  Fort Wayne *A, B*
Indiana University-Purdue University
  Indianapolis *B, M*
Indiana Wesleyan University *B, T*
Manchester College *B*
Marian College *B, T*
Martin University *B*
Oakland City University *B*
Purdue University *B, M, D*
Purdue University
  Calumet *B*
St. Joseph's College *B*
Saint Mary's College *B*
St. Mary-of-the-Woods College *B*
Taylor University *B*
Taylor University: Fort Wayne *B*
Tri-State University *B*
University of Evansville *B*
University of Indianapolis *B*
University of Notre Dame *B, M, D*
University of St. Francis *B, M*
University of Southern Indiana *B*
Valparaiso University *B, M*
Vincennes University *A*
Wabash College *B*

Iowa

Ashford University *B, T*
Briar Cliff University *B*
Buena Vista University *B*
Central College *B*
Clarke College *B, T*
Coe College *B*
Cornell College *B, T*
Dordt College *B*
Drake University *B*
Ellsworth Community College *A*
Graceland University *B, T*
Grand View College *B*
Grinnell College *B*
Iowa Central Community College *A*
Iowa State University *B, M, D*
Iowa Wesleyan College *B*
Iowa Western Community College *A*
Loras College *B, M*
Luther College *B*
Marshalltown Community College *A*
Morningside College *B*
Mount Mercy College *B*
Northwestern College *B, T*
St. Ambrose University *B, T*
Simpson College *B*
University of Dubuque *B*
University of Iowa *B, D, T*
University of Northern Iowa *B, M*
Upper Iowa University *B*
Vennard College *B*
Waldorf College *B*
Wartburg College *B, T*
William Penn University *B*

Kansas

Baker University *B, T*
Barclay College *B*
Barton County Community College *A*
Benedictine College *B*
Bethany College *B, T*
Bethel College *B*
Butler County Community College *A*
Central Christian College of
  Kansas *A, B*
Cloud County Community College *A*
Coffeyville Community College *A*
Colby Community College *A*
Donnelly College *A*
Emporia State University *B, M, T*

Fort Hays State University *B, M*
Fort Scott Community College *A*
Friends University *B*
Garden City Community College *A*
Hutchinson Community College *A*
Kansas State University *B, M, D*
Kansas Wesleyan University *B*
Labette Community College *A*
McPherson College *B, T*
MidAmerica Nazarene University *B, T*
Neosho County Community
  College *A*
Newman University *B*
Ottawa University *B*
Pittsburg State University *B, M*
Pratt Community College *A*
Seward County Community College *A*
Southwestern College *B*
Tabor College *B*
University of Kansas *B, M, D*
University of St. Mary *B, M*
Washburn University of Topeka *B*
Wichita State University *B, M, D*

Kentucky

Asbury College *B*
Bellarmine University *B*
Berea College *B*
Brescia University *B*
Campbellsville University *B*
Centre College *B*
Eastern Kentucky University *B, M*
Georgetown College *B, T*
Kentucky Christian University *B*
Kentucky State University *B*
Kentucky Wesleyan College *B*
Lindsey Wilson College *B*
Mid-Continent University *B*
Midway College *B*
Morehead State University *B, M*
Murray State University *B, M*
Northern Kentucky University *B*
Pikeville College *B*
Spalding University *B*
Thomas More College *A, B*
Transylvania University *B*
Union College *B*
University of Kentucky *B*
University of Louisville *B, M*
University of the Cumberlands *B*
Western Kentucky University *B, M*

Louisiana

Centenary College of Louisiana *B, T*
Dillard University *B*
Grambling State University *B*
Louisiana State University
  Shreveport *B*
Louisiana State University and
  Agricultural and Mechanical
  College *B, M, D*
Louisiana Tech University *B*
Loyola University New Orleans *B*
Nicholls State University *B*
Northwestern State University *B*
Our Lady of the Lake College *B*
Southeastern Louisiana
  University *B, M*
Southern University
  New Orleans *B*
Southern University and Agricultural
  and Mechanical College *B*
Tulane University *B, M*
University of Louisiana at
  Lafayette *B, M*
University of Louisiana at
  Monroe *B, M*
University of New Orleans *B, M*
Xavier University of Louisiana *B*

Maine

Bates College *B*
Bowdoin College *B*
Colby College *B*

Husson College *B*
St. Joseph's College *B*
Thomas College *B*
University of Maine *B, M, D*
University of Maine
  Farmington *B*
  Fort Kent *B*
  Machias *B*
  Presque Isle *B*
University of New England *B*
University of Southern Maine *B*

Maryland

Allegany College of Maryland *A*
Bowie State University *B*
Chesapeake College *A*
College of Notre Dame of Maryland *B*
Columbia Union College *B*
Community College of Baltimore
  County *A*
Coppin State University *B, M*
Frederick Community College *A*
Frostburg State University *B*
Garrett College *A*
Goucher College *B*
Hood College *B*
Howard Community College *A*
Johns Hopkins University *B, M, D*
Loyola College in Maryland *B, M*
McDaniel College *B*
Morgan State University *B*
Mount St. Mary's University *B*
Prince George's Community
  College *A*
St. Mary's College of Maryland *B*
Salisbury University *B*
Towson University *B, M*
University of Baltimore *B, M, D*
University of Maryland
  Baltimore County *B, M*
  College Park *B, M, D*
  University College *B*
Villa Julie College *B*
Washington College *B, M*

Massachusetts

American International College *B, M*
Amherst College *B*
Anna Maria College *B, M*
Assumption College *B*
Atlantic Union College *B*
Bay Path College *B*
Becker College *A, B*
Boston College *B, M, D*
Boston University *B, M, D*
Brandeis University *B, M, D*
Bridgewater State College *B, M*
Bunker Hill Community College *A*
Cambridge College *B*
Cape Cod Community College *A*
Clark University *B, M, D*
College of the Holy Cross *B*
Curry College *B*
Dean College *A*
Eastern Nazarene College *B*
Elms College *B*
Emmanuel College *B*
Endicott College *B*
Fisher College *B*
Fitchburg State College *B*
Framingham State College *B*
Gordon College *B*
Hampshire College *B*
Harvard College *B, D*
Hellenic College/Holy Cross *B*
Lasell College *B*
Massachusetts College of Liberal
  Arts *B*
Merrimack College *B*
Mount Holyoke College *B, M*
Newbury College *A, B*
Nichols College *B, T*
Northeastern University *B, M, D*
Pine Manor College *B*

Regis College *B*
St. John's Seminary College *B*
Salem State College *B*
Simmons College *B*
Simon's Rock College of Bard *B*
Smith College *B*
Springfield College *B*
Stonehill College *B*
Suffolk University *B*
Tufts University *B, M, D*
University of Massachusetts
  Amherst *B, M, D*
  Boston *B*
  Dartmouth *B, M*
  Lowell *B*
Wellesley College *B*
Western New England College *B*
Westfield State College *B, M*
Wheaton College *B*
Williams College *B*
Worcester State College *B*

Michigan

Adrian College *A, B, T*
Albion College *B, T*
Alma College *B, T*
Andrews University *B, M, D*
Aquinas College *B, T*
Calvin College *B, T*
Central Michigan University *B, T*
Concordia University *B*
Cornerstone University *B*
Delta College *A*
Eastern Michigan University *B, M*
Ferris State University *A, B*
Gogebic Community College *A*
Grand Valley State University *B, T*
Hillsdale College *B*
Hope College *B*
Kalamazoo College *B, T*
Kellogg Community College *A*
Lake Michigan College *A*
Lake Superior State University *B*
Lansing Community College *A*
Lawrence Technological University *B*
Madonna University *C, B, M*
Marygrove College *B*
Michigan State University *B, M, D*
Michigan Technological University *B*
Mid Michigan Community College *A*
Northern Michigan University *B, M*
Oakland University *B*
Olivet College *B*
Rochester College *B*
Saginaw Valley State University *B*
Siena Heights University *A, B*
Spring Arbor University *B*
University of Detroit Mercy *B, M*
University of Michigan *B, M, D, T*
University of Michigan
  Dearborn *B*
  Flint *B, T*
Wayne State University *B, M, D*
Western Michigan
  University *B, M, D, T*

Minnesota

Augsburg College *B*
Bemidji State University *B*
Bethany Lutheran College *B*
Bethel University *B, M*
Capella University *M, D*
Carleton College *B*
College of St. Benedict *B*
College of St. Catherine *B*
College of St. Scholastica *B*
Concordia College: Moorhead *B*
Concordia University: St. Paul *B*
Crown College *A, B*
Gustavus Adolphus College *B*
Hamline University *B*
Itasca Community College *A*
Macalester College *B*
Metropolitan State University *B, M*

Minnesota State University
Mankato *B, M*
Moorhead *B*
North Central University *B*
Northland Community & Technical
College *A*
Northwestern College *B*
Oak Hills Christian College *B*
Ridgewater College *A*
St. Cloud State University *B*
St. John's University *B*
St. Mary's University of Minnesota *B*
St. Olaf College *B*
Southwest Minnesota State
University *B*
University of Minnesota
Duluth *B*
Morris *B*
Twin Cities *B, M, D*
University of St. Thomas *B*
Vermilion Community College *A*
Walden University *M, D*
Winona State University *B*

Mississippi

Alcorn State University *B*
Belhaven College *B*
Blue Mountain College *B*
Delta State University *B*
East Central Community College *A*
Hinds Community College *A*
Itawamba Community College *A*
Jackson State University *B*
Millsaps College *B, T*
Mississippi College *B*
Mississippi Delta Community
College *A*
Mississippi Gulf Coast Community
College
Jefferson Davis Campus *A*
Mississippi State University *B, M*
Tougaloo College *B*
University of Mississippi *B, M, D*
University of Southern
Mississippi *B, M, D*
William Carey College *B*

Missouri

Avila University *B*
Central Methodist University *B*
Central Missouri State University *B, M*
College of the Ozarks *B*
Columbia College *B*
Crowder College *A*
Culver-Stockton College *B*
Drury University *B*
Evangel University *B, M*
Fontbonne University *B*
Hannibal-LaGrange College *B*
Lincoln University *B*
Lindenwood University *B*
Maryville University of Saint Louis *B*
Missouri Baptist University *B*
Missouri Southern State University *B*
Missouri State University *B, M*
Missouri Valley College *B*
Missouri Western State University *B*
Northwest Missouri State
University *B*
Park University *B*
Rockhurst University *B*
St. Louis Community College
St. Louis Community College at
Florissant Valley *A*
St. Louis University *B, M, D*
Southeast Missouri State University *B*
Southwest Baptist University *B*
Stephens College *B*
Three Rivers Community College *A*
Truman State University *B*
University of Missouri
Columbia *B, M, D*
Kansas City *B, M, D*

Rolla *B, T*
St. Louis *B, M, D*
Washington University in St.
Louis *B, M, D*
Webster University *B*
Westminster College *B*
William Jewell College *B*
William Woods University *B*

Montana

Carroll College *B, T*
Little Big Horn College *A*
Miles Community College *A*
Montana State University
Billings *A, B, M, T*
Bozeman *B, M*
Rocky Mountain College *B, T*
Salish Kootenai College *A*
University of Great Falls *B*
University of Montana:
Missoula *B, M, D*

Nebraska

Bellevue University *B*
Chadron State College *B*
College of Saint Mary *B*
Concordia University *B*
Creighton University *B*
Dana College *B*
Doane College *B*
Hastings College *B, T*
Midland Lutheran College *B*
Nebraska Wesleyan University *B*
Peru State College *B, T*
Union College *B*
University of Nebraska
Kearney *B, T*
Lincoln *B, M, D*
Omaha *B, M*
Wayne State College *B, T*
Western Nebraska Community
College *A*
York College *B*

Nevada

Community College of Southern
Nevada *A*
Great Basin College *A*
Sierra Nevada College *B*
University of Nevada
Las Vegas *B, M, D*
Reno *B, M, D*

New Hampshire

Colby-Sawyer College *B*
Dartmouth College *B, M, D*
Franklin Pierce College *B*
Keene State College *B*
New England College *B*
Plymouth State University *B*
Rivier College *B*
St. Anselm College *B*
Southern New Hampshire
University *B*
University of New Hampshire *B, D*
University of New Hampshire at
Manchester *B*

New Jersey

Atlantic Cape Community College *A*
Bloomfield College *C, B*
Caldwell College *B*
Centenary College *B*
The College of New Jersey *B*
College of St. Elizabeth *B*
Drew University *B*
Fairleigh Dickinson University
College at Florham *B*
Metropolitan Campus *B, M*
Felician College *B*
Georgian Court University *B*
Gloucester County College *A*
Kean University *B*

Monmouth University *B*
Montclair State University *B, M, T*
New Jersey City University *B, M*
Ocean County College *A*
Passaic County Community College *A*
Princeton University *B, M, D*
Ramapo College of New Jersey *B*
Richard Stockton College of New
Jersey *B*
Rider University *B*
Rowan University *B, M*
Rutgers, The State University of New
Jersey
Camden Regional Campus *B*
New Brunswick/Piscataway
Campus *B, M, D*
Newark Regional Campus *B, D*
St. Peter's College *B*
Salem Community College *A*
Seton Hall University *B, M*
Sussex County Community College *A*
Thomas Edison State College *B*
William Paterson University of New
Jersey *B*

New Mexico

Clovis Community College *A*
College of Santa Fe *B*
College of the Southwest *B*
Eastern New Mexico
University *A, B, M*
New Mexico Highlands
University *B, M*
New Mexico Institute of Mining and
Technology *B*
New Mexico Junior College *A*
New Mexico State University *B, M, D*
San Juan College *A*
University of New Mexico *B, M, D*
Western New Mexico University *B*

New York

Adelphi University *B, M*
Adirondack Community College *A*
Alfred University *B*
Bard College *B*
Barnard College *B*
Canisius College *B*
Cazenovia College *B*
City University of New York
Baruch College *B*
Brooklyn College *B*
City College *B, M*
College of Staten Island *B*
Hunter College *B, M*
John Jay College of Criminal
Justice *B, M*
Lehman College *B*
Medgar Evers College *B*
Queens College *B, M*
Queensborough Community
College *A*
York College *B*
Clarkson University *B*
Colgate University *B*
College of Mount St. Vincent *A, B*
College of New Rochelle *B, T*
College of Saint Rose *B*
Columbia University
Columbia College *B*
School of General Studies *B*
Concordia College *B*
Cornell University *B, M, D*
D'Youville College *B*
Daemen College *B*
Dominican College of Blauvelt *B*
Dowling College *B*
Elmira College *B*
Eugene Lang College The New School
for Liberal Arts *B*
Excelsior College *B*
Fordham University *B, M, D*
Hamilton College *B*
Hartwick College *B*

Hilbert College *B*
Hobart and William Smith Colleges *B*
Hofstra University *B*
Houghton College *B*
Iona College *B, M*
Ithaca College *B*
Jamestown Community College *C*
Keuka College *B*
Le Moyne College *B*
Long Island University
Brooklyn Campus *B, M*
C.W. Post Campus *B, M*
Manhattan College *B*
Manhattanville College *B*
Marist College *B, M*
Marymount Manhattan College *B*
Medaille College *B, M*
Mercy College *B, M*
Metropolitan College of New
York *A, B*
Molloy College *B*
Mount St. Mary College *B, T*
Nazareth College of Rochester *B*
New York Institute of Technology *C, B*
New York University *B, M*
Niagara University *B*
Nyack College *B*
Pace University *B, M, D*
Rensselaer Polytechnic Institute *B*
Roberts Wesleyan College *B*
Rochester Institute of Technology *B*
Russell Sage College *B*
Sage College of Albany *B*
St. Bonaventure University *B*
St. Francis College *B*
St. John Fisher College *B*
St. John's University *B, M*
St. Joseph's College *B*
St. Joseph's College: Suffolk
Campus *B*
St. Lawrence University *B*
St. Thomas Aquinas College *B*
Sarah Lawrence College *B*
Siena College *B*
Skidmore College *B*
State University of New York
Albany *B, M, D*
Binghamton *B, M*
Buffalo *B, M*
College at Brockport *B, M*
College at Buffalo *B*
College at Cortland *B, M*
College at Fredonia *B*
College at Geneseo *B, T*
College at Old Westbury *B*
College at Oneonta *B*
College at Plattsburgh *B*
College at Potsdam *B*
College of Agriculture and
Technology at Cobleskill *A*
College of Technology at Canton *A*
Empire State College *A, B*
Institute of Technology at
Utica/Rome *B*
New Paltz *B, M*
Oswego *B*
Purchase *B*
Stony Brook *B, M*
Suffolk County Community College *A*
Sullivan County Community
College *A*
Syracuse University *B, M, D*
Touro College *B*
Union College *B*
United States Military Academy *B*
University of Rochester *B, M*
Utica College *B*
Vassar College *B*
Wagner College *B*
Wells College *B*
Yeshiva University *B, M, D*

North Carolina

Appalachian State University *B, M*

Barton College *B*
Belmont Abbey College *B*
Bennett College *B*
Brevard College *B*
Campbell University *B*
Catawba College *B*
Chowan College *B*
Davidson College *B*
Duke University *B*
East Carolina University *B, M*
Elizabeth City State University *B*
Elon University *B*
Fayetteville State University *B*
Gardner-Webb University *B*
Gaston College *C*
Greensboro College *B*
Guilford College *B*
High Point University *B*
Johnson C. Smith University *B*
Lees-McRae College *B*
Lenoir Community College *A*
Lenoir-Rhyne College *B*
Livingstone College *B*
Louisburg College *A*
Mars Hill College *B*
Meredith College *B*
Methodist College *A, B*
Mount Olive College *B*
North Carolina Agricultural and
    Technical State University *B*
North Carolina Central
    University *B, M*
North Carolina State
    University *B, M, D*
North Carolina Wesleyan College *B*
Peace College *A, B*
Pfeiffer University *B*
Queens University of Charlotte *B*
St. Andrews Presbyterian College *B*
St. Augustine's College *B*
Salem College *B*
Sandhills Community College *A*
Shaw University *B*
University of North Carolina
    Asheville *B, T*
    Chapel Hill *B, M, D*
    Charlotte *B*
    Greensboro *B, M, D, T*
    Pembroke *B*
    Wilmington *B, M*
Wake Forest University *B, M*
Warren Wilson College *B*
Western Carolina University *B*
Wingate University *B*
Winston-Salem State University *B*

North Dakota

Dickinson State University *B*
Jamestown College *B*
Mayville State University *B*
Minot State University *B, T*
North Dakota State University *B, M, D*
University of Mary *B*
University of North Dakota *B, M, D*
Valley City State University *B*

Ohio

Ashland University *B*
Baldwin-Wallace College *B*
Bluffton University *B*
Bowling Green State
    University *B, M, D*
Capital University *B*
Case Western Reserve
    University *B, M, D*
Cedarville University *B*
Central State University *B*
Cincinnati Christian University *A, B*
Circleville Bible College *A, B*
Cleveland State University *B, M*
College of Mount St. Joseph *B*
College of Wooster *B*
Defiance College *B*
Denison University *B*

Franciscan University of
    Steubenville *B*
Heidelberg College *B, M*
Hiram College *B, T*
Jefferson Community College *A*
John Carroll University *B*
Kent State University *B*
Kenyon College *B*
Lake Erie College *B*
Lourdes College *A, B*
Malone College *B*
Marietta College *B, M*
Miami University
    Oxford Campus *B, M, D*
Mount Union College *B*
Mount Vernon Nazarene University *B*
Muskingum College *B*
Oberlin College *B*
Ohio Dominican University *B*
Ohio Northern University *B*
Ohio State University
    Columbus Campus *B, M, D*
    Lima Campus *B*
    Mansfield Campus *B*
    Marion Campus *B*
    Newark Campus *B*
Ohio University *B*
Ohio University
    Southern Campus at Ironton *A*
Ohio Wesleyan University *B*
Otterbein College *B*
Owens Community College
    Toledo *A*
Shawnee State University *B*
Sinclair Community College *A*
Tiffin University *B*
Union Institute & University *B, M*
University of Akron *B, M*
University of Cincinnati *B, M, D*
University of Dayton *B, M*
University of Findlay *B*
University of Rio Grande *A, B*
University of Toledo *B, M, D*
Urbana University *B*
Ursuline College *B*
Walsh University *B*
Wilmington College *B*
Wittenberg University *B*
Wright State University *A, B*
Wright State University: Lake
    Campus *A*
Xavier University *A, B, M*
Youngstown State University *B*

Oklahoma

Bacone College *A*
Cameron University *B, M*
Carl Albert State College *A*
Connors State College *A*
East Central University *B*
Eastern Oklahoma State College *A*
Northeastern Oklahoma Agricultural
    and Mechanical College *A*
Northeastern State University *B*
Northwestern Oklahoma State
    University *B*
Oklahoma Baptist University *B*
Oklahoma Christian University *B*
Oklahoma City Community College *A*
Oklahoma City University *B*
Oklahoma Panhandle State
    University *B*
Oklahoma State University *B, M, D*
Oral Roberts University *B*
Redlands Community College *A*
Rose State College *A*
St. Gregory's University *A, B*
Southeastern Oklahoma State
    University *B*
Southern Nazarene University *B*
Southwestern Oklahoma State
    University *B, M*
Tulsa Community College *A*
University of Central Oklahoma *B*

University of Oklahoma *B, M, D*
University of Science and Arts of
    Oklahoma *B*
University of Tulsa *B*
Western Oklahoma State College *A*

Oregon

Central Oregon Community
    College *A*
Chemeketa Community College *A*
Concordia University *B*
Corban College *B*
Eastern Oregon University *B, T*
George Fox University *B, M*
Lewis & Clark College *B*
Linfield College *B, T*
Linn-Benton Community College *A*
Marylhurst University *B*
Northwest Christian College *B*
Oregon Institute of Technology *B*
Oregon State University *B*
Pacific University *B, M, D*
Portland State University *B, M, D*
Reed College *B*
Southern Oregon University *B, M*
Treasure Valley Community College *A*
University of Oregon *B, M, D*
University of Portland *B*
Warner Pacific College *A, B*
Western Oregon University *B*
Willamette University *B*

Pennsylvania

Albright College *B*
Allegheny College *B*
Alvernia College *B*
Arcadia University *B*
Bloomsburg University of
    Pennsylvania *B*
Bryn Mawr College *B*
Bucknell University *B, M*
Bucks County Community College *A*
Butler County Community College *A*
Cabrini College *B*
California University of
    Pennsylvania *B*
Carlow University *B*
Carnegie Mellon University *B, D*
Cedar Crest College *B*
Chatham College *B*
Chestnut Hill College *A, B*
Cheyney University of Pennsylvania *B*
Clarion University of Pennsylvania *B*
College Misericordia *B*
Community College of Allegheny
    County *A*
DeSales University *B*
Delaware County Community
    College *A*
Dickinson College *B*
Drexel University *B, M, D*
Duquesne University *B*
East Stroudsburg University of
    Pennsylvania *B*
Eastern University *B*
Edinboro University of
    Pennsylvania *B*
Elizabethtown College *B*
Franklin & Marshall College *B*
Gannon University *B*
Geneva College *B*
Gettysburg College *B*
Grove City College *B*
Gwynedd-Mercy College *B*
Harcum College *A*
Harrisburg Area Community
    College *A*
Haverford College *B*
Holy Family University *B*
Immaculata University *B*
Indiana University of Pennsylvania *B*
Juniata College *B*
King's College *B*

Kutztown University of
    Pennsylvania *B*
La Roche College *B*
La Salle University *B, M, D*
Lafayette College *B*
Lebanon Valley College *B*
Lehigh Carbon Community College *A*
Lehigh University *B, M, D*
Lincoln University *B*
Lock Haven University of
    Pennsylvania *B*
Lycoming College *B*
Manor College *A*
Mansfield University of
    Pennsylvania *B, T*
Marywood University *B, M*
Mercyhurst College *B*
Messiah College *B*
Millersville University of
    Pennsylvania *B, M*
Moravian College *B*
Mount Aloysius College *B, M*
Muhlenberg College *C, A, B*
Neumann College *B*
Penn State
    Abington *B*
    Altoona *B*
    Beaver *B*
    Berks *B*
    Delaware County *B*
    Dubois *B*
    Erie, The Behrend College *B*
    Fayette *B*
    Harrisburg *B, M*
    Hazleton *B*
    Lehigh Valley *B*
    McKeesport *B*
    Mont Alto *B*
    New Kensington *B*
    Schuylkill - Capital College *B*
    Shenango *B*
    University Park *B, M, D*
    Wilkes-Barre *B*
    Worthington Scranton *B*
    York *B*
Philadelphia University *B*
Point Park University *B*
Reading Area Community College *A*
Robert Morris University *B*
Rosemont College *B*
St. Francis University *B*
St. Joseph's University *B, M*
St. Vincent College *B*
Seton Hill University *B*
Shippensburg University of
    Pennsylvania *B, M*
Slippery Rock University of
    Pennsylvania *B*
Susquehanna University *B*
Swarthmore College *B*
Temple University *B, M, D*
Thiel College *B*
University of Pennsylvania *A, B, M, D*
University of Pittsburgh *B, M, D*
University of Pittsburgh
    Bradford *B*
    Greensburg *B*
    Johnstown *B*
University of Scranton *B*
University of the Sciences in
    Philadelphia *B, M*
Ursinus College *B*
Villanova University *B, M*
Washington and Jefferson College *B*
Waynesburg College *B*
West Chester University of
    Pennsylvania *B, M*
Westminster College *B*
Widener University *B*
Wilkes University *B*
Wilson College *B*
York College of Pennsylvania *B*

Puerto Rico

Bayamon Central University *B, M*
Inter American University of Puerto Rico
San German Campus *B*
Pontifical Catholic University of Puerto Rico *B*
Turabo University *B*
Universidad Metropolitana *B*
Universidad del Este *B*
University of Puerto Rico
Cayey University College *B*
Mayaguez *B*
Ponce *B*
Rio Piedras *B, M, D*
University of the Sacred Heart *B*

Rhode Island

Brown University *B, M, D*
Bryant University *B*
Providence College *B*
Rhode Island College *B, M*
Roger Williams University *B*
Salve Regina University *C, B, M*
University of Rhode Island *B*

South Carolina

Anderson University *B*
Charleston Southern University *B*
The Citadel *B, M*
Clemson University *B*
Coastal Carolina University *B*
Coker College *B*
College of Charleston *B*
Columbia College *B*
Columbia International University *B*
Converse College *B*
Erskine College *B*
Francis Marion University *B*
Furman University *B*
Lander University *B*
Limestone College *B*
Newberry College *B*
North Greenville College *B*
Presbyterian College *B*
South Carolina State University *B*
Southern Wesleyan University *B*
University of South Carolina
Aiken *B*
Beaufort *B*
Upstate *B*
Winthrop University *B*
Wofford College *B*

South Dakota

Augustana College *B*
Black Hills State University *B*
Dakota Wesleyan University *B*
Mount Marty College *B*
Northern State University *B*
South Dakota State University *B, T*
University of Sioux Falls *B*
University of South Dakota *B, M, D*

Tennessee

Austin Peay State University *B, M*
Belmont University *B, T*
Bethel College *B*
Bryan College *B, T*
Carson-Newman College *B*
Christian Brothers University *B*
Columbia State Community College *A*
Crichton College *B*
Cumberland University *B*
Dyersburg State Community College *A*
East Tennessee State University *B, M, T*
Fisk University *B, M*
Free Will Baptist Bible College *B*
Freed-Hardeman University *B*
Hiwassee College *A*
Jackson State Community College *A*

King College *B*
Lambuth University *B*
Lee University *B*
Lincoln Memorial University *B*
Lipscomb University *B*
Martin Methodist College *B*
Maryville College *B*
Middle Tennessee State University *B, M*
Milligan College *B, T*
Rhodes College *B*
Roane State Community College *A*
Southern Adventist University *B*
Tennessee State University *B, M*
Tennessee Technological University *B*
Tennessee Temple University *B*
Tennessee Wesleyan College *B*
Trevecca Nazarene University *B*
Tusculum College *B*
Union University *B*
University of Memphis *B, M, D*
University of Tennessee
Chattanooga *B, M*
Knoxville *B, M, D*
Martin *B*
University of the South *B*
Vanderbilt University *B, M, D*
Walters State Community College *A*

Texas

Abilene Christian University *B, M*
Amarillo College *A*
Angelo State University *B, M*
Austin College *B*
Austin Community College *A*
Baylor University *B*
Blinn College *A*
Brazosport College *A*
Cisco Junior College *A*
Clarendon College *A*
Coastal Bend College *A*
College of the Mainland *A*
Dallas Baptist University *B*
Dallas Christian College *B*
Del Mar College *A*
East Texas Baptist University *B*
El Paso Community College *A*
Frank Phillips College *A*
Galveston College *A*
Grayson County College *A*
Hardin-Simmons University *B*
Hill College *A*
Houston Baptist University *B*
Howard College *A*
Howard Payne University *B*
Kilgore College *A*
Lamar University *B, M*
Laredo Community College *A*
LeTourneau University *B*
Lon Morris College *A*
Lubbock Christian University *B*
McMurry University *B*
Midland College *A*
Midwestern State University *B, M*
Navarro College *A*
Northeast Texas Community College *A*
Northwest Vista College *A*
Odessa College *A*
Our Lady of the Lake University of San Antonio *B, M, D*
Palo Alto College *A*
Paris Junior College *A*
Prairie View A&M University *B*
Rice University *B, M, D*
St. Edward's University *B*
St. Philip's College *A*
Sam Houston State University *B, M*
San Antonio College *A*
San Jacinto College
North *A*
Schreiner University *B*
South Plains College *A*

Southern Methodist University *B, M, D*
Southwestern Adventist University *B, T*
Southwestern Assemblies of God University *A*
Southwestern University *B, T*
Stephen F. Austin State University *B, M, T*
Sul Ross State University *B*
Tarleton State University *B*
Texas A&M University *B, M, D*
Texas A&M University
Commerce *B, M*
Kingsville *B, M*
Texarkana *B*
Texas Christian University *B, M, D*
Texas Lutheran University *B*
Texas Southern University *B, M*
Texas State University: San Marcos *B, M*
Texas Tech University *B, M, D*
Texas Wesleyan University *B, T*
Texas Woman's University *B*
Trinity University *B*
Trinity Valley Community College *A*
Tyler Junior College *A*
University of Dallas *B, M*
University of Houston *B, M, D*
University of Houston
Clear Lake *B, M*
Downtown *B*
Victoria *B*
University of Mary Hardin-Baylor *B, M*
University of North Texas *B, M, D*
University of St. Thomas *B*
University of Texas
Arlington *B, M*
Austin *B, M, D*
Brownsville *B*
Dallas *B, M, D*
El Paso *B*
Pan American *B*
San Antonio *B, M*
Tyler *B*
of the Permian Basin *B*
University of the Incarnate Word *B*
Wayland Baptist University *B*
West Texas A&M University *B, M*
Western Texas College *A*
Wharton County Junior College *A*

Utah

Brigham Young University *B, M, D*
Dixie State College of Utah *A*
Salt Lake Community College *A*
Snow College *A*
Southern Utah University *B, T*
University of Utah *B, M, D*
Utah State University *B, M, D*
Utah Valley State College *A, B*
Weber State University *B*
Westminster College *B*

Vermont

Bennington College *B*
Burlington College *B*
Castleton State College *B*
Champlain College *B*
College of St. Joseph in Vermont *B, M*
Goddard College *B, M*
Green Mountain College *B*
Johnson State College *B*
Lyndon State College *B*
Marlboro College *B*
Middlebury College *B*
Norwich University *B*
St. Michael's College *B*
Southern Vermont College *B*
University of Vermont *B, M, D*

Virginia

Bluefield College *B*
Bridgewater College *B*

Christopher Newport University *B*
College of William and Mary *B, M*
Eastern Mennonite University *B*
Emory & Henry College *B*
Ferrum College *B*
George Mason University *B, M, D*
Hampden-Sydney College *B*
Hampton University *B*
Hollins University *B*
James Madison University *B, M, D*
Liberty University *B*
Longwood University *B, T*
Lynchburg College *B*
Mary Baldwin College *B*
Marymount University *B*
Norfolk State University *B*
Northern Virginia Community College *A*
Old Dominion University *B, M, D*
Radford University *B, M*
Randolph-Macon College *B*
Randolph-Macon Woman's College *B*
Regent University *B, T*
Roanoke College *B, T*
Shenandoah University *B*
Sweet Briar College *B*
University of Mary Washington *B*
University of Richmond *B, M*
University of Virginia *B, M, D*
University of Virginia's College at Wise *B, T*
Virginia Commonwealth University *B, M, D*
Virginia Intermont College *B*
Virginia Military Institute *B*
Virginia Polytechnic Institute and State University *B, M, D*
Virginia State University *B, M*
Virginia Union University *B*
Virginia Wesleyan College *B*
Washington and Lee University *B*

Washington

Antioch University Seattle *D*
Bastyr University *B*
Central Washington University *B*
Centralia College *A*
City University *B*
Eastern Washington University *B, T*
Everett Community College *A*
Gonzaga University *B*
Heritage University *A, B*
Highline Community College *A*
Northwest University *B*
Pacific Lutheran University *B*
Saint Martin's University *B*
Seattle Pacific University *B*
Seattle University *B, M*
Trinity Lutheran College *B*
University of Puget Sound *B*
University of Washington *B, M, D*
Walla Walla College *B*
Washington State University *B, D*
Western Washington University *B*
Whitman College *B*
Whitworth College *B*

West Virginia

Alderson-Broaddus College *B*
Bethany College *B*
Concord University *B*
Davis and Elkins College *B*
Marshall University *B, M*
Mountain State University *B*
Ohio Valley University *B*
Potomac State College of West Virginia University *A*
Shepherd University *B*
University of Charleston *B*
West Liberty State College *B*
West Virginia State University *B*
West Virginia University *B, M, D*
West Virginia Wesleyan College *B*
Wheeling Jesuit University *B*

Wisconsin

Alverno College *B*
Beloit College *B*
Cardinal Stritch University *B*
Carroll College *B*
Carthage College *B, T*
Concordia University Wisconsin *B*
Edgewood College *B*
Lakeland College *B*
Lawrence University *B, T*
Marian College of Fond du Lac *B*
Marquette University *B, T*
Mount Mary College *B*
Northcentral Technical College *C*
Northland College *B*
Ripon College *B*
St. Norbert College *B, T*
Silver Lake College *B, T*
University of Wisconsin
  Eau Claire *B*
  Green Bay *B*
  La Crosse *B, T*
  Madison *B, M, D*
  Milwaukee *B, M, D*
  Oshkosh *B, M*
  Parkside *B*
  Platteville *B, T*
  River Falls *B, T*
  Stevens Point *B, T*
  Stout *B, M*
  Superior *B*
  Whitewater *B, T*
Viterbo University *B*
Wisconsin Lutheran College *B*

Wyoming

Casper College *A*
Central Wyoming College *A*
Eastern Wyoming College *A*
Laramie County Community
  College *A*
Northwest College *A*
Sheridan College *A*
University of Wyoming *B, M, D*
Western Wyoming Community
  College *A*

Psychology teacher education

Delaware

University of Delaware *B, T*

Illinois

Bradley University *B*

Indiana

Goshen College *B*
Oakland City University *B*
Valparaiso University *B*

Iowa

St. Ambrose University *B*
Simpson College *T*

Kansas

Central Christian College of Kansas *A*
Emporia State University *T*
Pittsburg State University *B, T*

Louisiana

Centenary College of Louisiana *B, T*

Michigan

Alma College *T*
Concordia University *B, T*
University of Michigan
  Flint *T*

Minnesota

St. Cloud State University *B*

University of Minnesota
  Morris *T*

Montana

University of Great Falls *B*

Nebraska

Wayne State College *B, T*

Ohio

University of Findlay *B, M, T*

Pennsylvania

DeSales University *T*
St. Francis University *B, T*
St. Vincent College *B*
Widener University *T*

South Dakota

Augustana College *B, T*

Tennessee

Bryan College *T*

Utah

University of Utah *B*

Wisconsin

Carroll College *B, T*
Lawrence University *T*

Psychometrics/ quantitative psychology

Alabama

Alabama Agricultural and Mechanical
  University *M*

Arizona

University of Phoenix *M*

Utah

University of Utah *M*

Virginia

James Madison University *D*

Psychopharmacology

California

Alliant International University *M*

Florida

Nova Southeastern University *M*

Public administration

Alabama

Andrew Jackson University *M*
Auburn University *B, M, D*
Auburn University at
  Montgomery *M, D*
Huntingdon College *B*
Jacksonville State University *M*
Samford University *B*
Talladega College *B*
Troy University *M*
University of Alabama *M*
University of Alabama
  Birmingham *M*
  Huntsville *M*
University of South Alabama *M*

Alaska

University of Alaska
  Anchorage *M*
  Southeast *M*

Arizona

Arizona State University *M, D*
Northcentral University *B, M, D*
Northern Arizona University *M*
Rio Salado College *C, A*
Scottsdale Community College *C*
University of Arizona *B, M*
Western International University *M*

Arkansas

Arkansas State University *M*
Harding University *B*
Henderson State University *B*
University of Arkansas *B, M*
University of Arkansas
  Little Rock *M*
University of Central Arkansas *B*
University of the Ozarks *B*

California

California Lutheran University *M*
California Polytechnic State
  University: San Luis Obispo *M*
California State Polytechnic
  University: Pomona *M*
California State University
  Bakersfield *B, M*
  Chico *B, M*
  Dominguez Hills *M*
  East Bay *B, M*
  Fresno *B, M*
  Fullerton *B, M*
  Long Beach *M*
  Los Angeles *M*
  Northridge *M*
  Sacramento *M*
  San Bernardino *B, M*
  Stanislaus *M*
Dominican University of California *M*
Fresno City College *C, A*
Golden Gate University *M*
Long Beach City College *C, A*
Loyola Marymount University *B, M*
National University *B, M*
Notre Dame de Namur University *M*
Palomar College *C, A*
San Francisco State University *M*
San Joaquin Delta College *A*
San Jose State University *M*
Santa Barbara City College *A*
Sonoma State University *M*
University of California
  Riverside *B*
University of La Verne *B, M, D*
University of San Francisco *B, M*
University of Southern
  California *B, M, D*

Colorado

Red Rocks Community College *C, A*
University of Colorado
  Colorado Springs *M*
  Denver and Health Sciences
    Center *M, D*
University of Denver *M*

Connecticut

Mitchell College *A*
Three Rivers Community College *A*
University of Connecticut *M*
University of Hartford *M*
University of New Haven *B, M*

Delaware

University of Delaware *M*
Wilmington College *M*

District of Columbia

American University *M, D*
Howard University *M*
Southeastern University *C, A, B, M*
University of the District of
  Columbia *M*

Florida

Barry University *C, B*
Flagler College *B*
Florida Atlantic University *B, M, D*
Florida Gulf Coast University *M*
Florida International
  University *B, M, D*
Florida Memorial University *B*
Florida State University *M, D*
International College *M*
Manatee Community College *A*
Miami Dade College *A*
Nova Southeastern University *M, D*
Tallahassee Community College *A*
University of Central Florida *B, M, D*
University of Miami *M*
University of North Florida *M*
University of South Florida *M*
Valencia Community College *A*

Georgia

Albany State University *M*
Augusta State University *M*
Clark Atlanta University *M, D*
Columbus State University *M*
Darton College *A*
Georgia College and State
  University *A*
Georgia Southern University *M*
Georgia State University *M*
Kennesaw State University *M*
Macon State College *A*
Middle Georgia College *A*
North Georgia College & State
  University *M*
Savannah State University *M*
University of Georgia *M, D*
University of West Georgia *M*
Valdosta State University *M*

Hawaii

Hawaii Pacific University *B*
University of Hawaii
  Hilo *B*
  Manoa *M*
  West Oahu *B*

Idaho

Boise State University *M*
Idaho State University *M*

Illinois

Augustana College *B*
Blackburn College *B*
DePaul University *M*
Governors State University *B, M*
Illinois Institute of Technology *M*
Lewis University *B*
Northern Illinois University *M*
Roosevelt University *M*
Southern Illinois University
  Carbondale *M*
Southern Illinois University
  Edwardsville *M*
University of Illinois
  Chicago *M, D*
  Springfield *M, D*
  Urbana-Champaign *M*
Westwood College of Technology
  O'Hare *B*

Indiana

Ball State University *M*
Indiana State University *M*
Indiana University
  Bloomington *A, B, M, D*
  Kokomo *B*
  Northwest *A, B, M*
  South Bend *A, B, M*
Indiana University-Purdue University
  Fort Wayne *C, A, B, M*
Indiana University-Purdue University
  Indianapolis *A, B, M*

University of Evansville *M*
University of Notre Dame *M*
University of Southern Indiana *M*

Iowa

Buena Vista University *B*
Dordt College *B*
Drake University *M*
Iowa State University *M*
St.Ambrose University *B*
University of Northern Iowa *B*

Kansas

Barton County Community College *A*
Kansas State University *M*
University of Kansas *B, M, D*
Washburn University of Topeka *C, B*
Wichita State University *M*

Kentucky

Eastern Kentucky University *M*
Kentucky State University *B, M*
Murray State University *M*
Northern Kentucky University *M*
University of Kentucky *M, D*
University of Louisville *M*
Western Kentucky University *M*

Louisiana

Grambling State University *B, M*
Louisiana State University and
    Agricultural and Mechanical
    College *M*
Southern University and Agricultural
    and Mechanical College *M*
University of New Orleans *M*

Maine

University of Maine *B, M*
University of Maine
    Augusta *A, B*
University of Southern Maine *M, D*

Maryland

Bowie State University *B, M*
DeVry University: Bethesda *M*
University of Baltimore *M, D*

Massachusetts

American International College *B, M*
Bridgewater State College *M*
Clark University *B, M*
Framingham State College *M*
Harvard College *M, D*
Mount Ida College *A, B*
Northeastern University *M*
Stonehill College *B*
Suffolk University *B, M*
University of Massachusetts
    Boston *B, M*

Michigan

Calvin College *B*
Central Michigan University *M*
Eastern Michigan University *B, M*
Ferris State University *A, B*
Grand Valley State University *B*
Lake Superior State University *M*
Michigan State University *B*
Northern Michigan University *B, M*
Oakland University *B, M*
Saginaw Valley State University *B, M*
University of Michigan *M, D*
University of Michigan
    Dearborn *B, M*
    Flint *B, M*
Wayne State University *B, M*
Western Michigan University *B, M, D*

Minnesota

Metropolitan State University *M*

Minnesota State University
    Mankato *M*
    Moorhead *M*
St. Cloud State University *B*
St. Mary's University of Minnesota *B*
Southwest Minnesota State
    University *B*
University of Minnesota
    Twin Cities *M*
University of St.Thomas *B, M*
Walden University *M*
Winona State University *B*

Mississippi

Belhaven College *C*
Jackson State University *M, D*
Mississippi State University *M, D*
Mississippi Valley State University *B*
University of Mississippi *B*

Missouri

Central Methodist University *A, B*
Harris-Stowe State University *B*
Lincoln University *B*
Lindenwood University *B, M*
Missouri State University *B, M*
Missouri Valley College *B*
Northwest Missouri State
    University *B*
Park University *B, M*
St. Louis University *M*
Southeast Missouri State University *M*
University of Missouri
    Columbia *M*
    Kansas City *M, D*
    St. Louis *B, M*
Webster University *M*

Montana

Carroll College *B*
Miles Community College *A*
Montana State University
    Billings *M*
    Bozeman *M*
University of Montana: Missoula *M*

Nebraska

Bellevue University *B*
Doane College *B*
Hastings College *B*
University of Nebraska
    Omaha *M, D*

Nevada

University of Nevada
    Las Vegas *M*
    Reno *M*

New Hampshire

Plymouth State University *B*
University of New Hampshire *M*

New Jersey

The College of New Jersey *B*
County College of Morris *A*
Fairleigh Dickinson University
    College at Florham *M*
    Metropolitan Campus *M*
Kean University *B, M*
Princeton University *B, M, D*
Rider University *C*
Rutgers,The State University of New
    Jersey
    Camden Regional Campus *M*
    Newark Regional Campus *M, D*
Seton Hall University *M*
Thomas Edison State College *C, A, B*
William Paterson University of New
    Jersey *M*

New Mexico

College of Santa Fe *B*

New Mexico State University *M*
San Juan College *C, A*
University of New Mexico *M*

New York

Alfred University *B*
City University of New York
    Baruch College *B, M*
    Hostos Community College *A*
    John Jay College of Criminal
        Justice *B, M*
    Medgar Evers College *A, B*
Cornell University *M, D*
Dowling College *M*
Fordham University *B, M*
Long Island University
    Brooklyn Campus *M*
    C.W. Post Campus *B, M*
Marist College *M*
Mohawk Valley Community College *A*
New York University *C, B, M, D*
Pace University *M*
St. John's University *B*
State University of New York
    Albany *M, D*
    Binghamton *M*
    College at Brockport *M*
    Stony Brook *M*
Syracuse University *M, D*

North Carolina

Appalachian State University *M*
Campbell University *B*
DeVry University: Charlotte *M*
East Carolina University *M*
Elon University *B*
Fayetteville State University *B*
Fayetteville Technical Community
    College *A*
High Point University *M*
North Carolina Central University *M*
North Carolina State University *M, D*
Shaw University *B*
University of North Carolina
    Chapel Hill *M*
    Charlotte *M*
    Greensboro *M, T*
    Pembroke *M*
    Wilmington *M*
Western Carolina University *B, M*

North Dakota

University of North Dakota *B, M*

Ohio

Bowling Green State University *B, M*
Capital University *B*
Cedarville University *B*
Cleveland State University *M*
David N. Myers University *A, B*
Heidelberg College *B*
Kent State University *M*
Miami University
    Oxford Campus *B*
Ohio State University
    Columbus Campus *M, D*
Ohio University *M*
Owens Community College
    Toledo *A*
Sinclair Community College *A*
Union Institute & University *B*
University of Akron *M*
University of Cincinnati *M*
University of Dayton *M*
University of Toledo *M*
Wright State University *B, M*
Youngstown State University *B*

Oklahoma

Northeastern State University *B*
University of Oklahoma *B, M*

Oregon

Portland State University *M, D*
University of Oregon *B, M*
Western Oregon University *B*

Pennsylvania

Carnegie Mellon University *M*
Gannon University *M*
Indiana University of Pennsylvania *M*
Juniata College *B*
Kutztown University of
    Pennsylvania *B, M*
La Salle University *B*
Lincoln University *B*
Marywood University *B, M*
Penn State
    Harrisburg *M, D*
Point Park University *A, B*
Reading Area Community College *A*
St. Francis University *B*
St. Joseph's University *B*
Shippensburg University of
    Pennsylvania *B, M*
University of Pennsylvania *M*
University of Pittsburgh *C, B, M*
Villanova University *M*
Widener University *M*
York College of Pennsylvania *B*

Puerto Rico

Bayamon Central University *B*
Inter American University of Puerto
    Rico
    Bayamon Campus *B*
    San German Campus *B*
Pontifical Catholic University of
    Puerto Rico *B, M, D*
Turabo University *B, M*
University of Puerto Rico
    Rio Piedras *M*

Rhode Island

Rhode Island College *B, M*
Roger Williams University *B*
University of Rhode Island *M*

South Carolina

College of Charleston *M*
University of South Carolina *M*

South Dakota

University of South Dakota *M*

Tennessee

Austin Peay State University *B*
Cumberland University *B*
Jackson State Community College *A*
Lipscomb University *B*
Tennessee State University *M, D*
University of Memphis *M*
University of Tennessee
    Chattanooga *M*
    Knoxville *B, M*
    Martin *B*

Texas

Angelo State University *M*
Baylor University *B, M*
Brazosport College *A*
College of the Mainland *A*
Del Mar College *A*
Lamar University *M*
Midwestern State University *M*
St. Mary's University *M*
San Antonio College *C, A*
Stephen F.Austin State University *B, M*
Sul Ross State University *M*
Tarrant County College *C, A*
Texas A&M University *M, D*
Texas Southern University *B, M*
Texas State University: San
    Marcos *B, M*

Texas Tech University *M*
University of Houston *M*
University of Houston
Clear Lake *M*
University of North Texas *B, M, D*
University of Texas
Arlington *M, D*
Dallas *B, M, D*
El Paso *M*
Pan American *M*
San Antonio *M*
Tyler *M*
West Texas A&M University *B*

Utah
Brigham Young University *M*
University of Utah *M*

Vermont
University of Vermont *M*

Virginia
George Mason University *B, M, D*
James Madison University *B, M*
Old Dominion University *M, D*
Regent University *M, T*
Shenandoah University *B*
Thomas Nelson Community
College *A*
Tidewater Community College *A*
University of Virginia's College at
Wise *B*
Virginia Commonwealth
University *M, D*
Virginia Intermont College *B*
Virginia Polytechnic Institute and
State University *M, D*
Virginia State University *B*

Washington
City University *M*
Eastern Washington University *M*
Evergreen State College *M*
Seattle University *B, M*
University of Washington *M*
Washington State University *B, M*

West Virginia
Concord University *B*
West Virginia University *M*

Wisconsin
DeVry University: Milwaukee *M*
Silver Lake College *B*
University of Wisconsin
Green Bay *B*
Madison *M*
Milwaukee *M*
Oshkosh *M*
Stevens Point *B*
Superior *B*
Whitewater *B, M*

Wyoming
University of Wyoming *M*

Public finance

Alabama
Alabama Agricultural and Mechanical
University *B*

California
National University *M*

Colorado
Johnson & Wales University *B*

Florida
Johnson & Wales University *A*

Maine
Husson College *B*

Maryland
Morgan State University *B*

Massachusetts
Boston University *M*

Michigan
Cleary University *B, M*

New York
City University of New York
Baruch College *M*

Ohio
Defiance College *B*
Youngstown State University *B*

Rhode Island
Johnson & Wales University *A, B*

Texas
Texas A&M University
Commerce *B*
University of North Texas *B, M*

Washington
Eastern Washington University *B*

Public health

Alabama
University of Alabama
Birmingham *M, D*

Alaska
University of Alaska
Fairbanks *A*

Arizona
University of Arizona *M, D*

Arkansas
University of Central Arkansas *B*

California
California State University
Fresno *M*
Fullerton *M*
Long Beach *M*
Northridge *M*
Loma Linda University *B, M, D*
San Diego State University *M, D*
San Francisco State University *M*
San Jose State University *M*
University of California
Berkeley *M, D*
Davis *M*
Los Angeles *M, D*
University of Southern
California *B, M, D*

Colorado
University of Colorado
Denver and Health Sciences
Center *M*

Connecticut
Southern Connecticut State
University *B, M*
University of Connecticut *M*
Yale University *M, D*

Delaware
Delaware State University *B*

District of Columbia
George Washington University *M, D*

Trinity University *B*

Florida
Florida Agricultural and Mechanical
University *M*
Florida International University *M*
Nova Southeastern University *M*
Palm Beach Community College *A*
University of Florida *B*
University of Miami *M, D*
University of South Florida *M, D*

Georgia
Armstrong Atlantic State University *M*
Emory University *M*
Fort Valley State University *M*
Georgia State University *M*
Mercer University *M*
University of Georgia *M*

Hawaii
University of Hawaii
Manoa *M, D*

Idaho
Boise State University *M*
Idaho State University *M*

Illinois
Benedictine University *M*
Northern Illinois University *M*
Northwestern University *M*
St. Xavier University *M*
University of Illinois
Chicago *M, D*
Springfield *M*
Urbana-Champaign *M, D*

Indiana
Indiana University
Bloomington *B, M*
Indiana University-Purdue University
Indianapolis *B, M*

Iowa
University of Iowa *M*

Kansas
Kansas State University *M*
University of Kansas Medical
Center *M*

Kentucky
University of Kentucky *M*
University of Louisville *M*
Western Kentucky University *M*

Louisiana
Louisiana State University Health
Sciences Center *M*
Tulane University *M, D*

Maine
University of New England *M*
University of Southern Maine *M*

Maryland
Johns Hopkins University *B*
Morgan State University *M, D*

Massachusetts
Boston University *M, D*
Harvard College *M, D*
Springfield College *B, M*
University of Massachusetts
Amherst *M, D*

Michigan
Central Michigan University *B*
University of Michigan *D*

Minnesota
Minnesota State University
Mankato *B, T*
University of Minnesota
Twin Cities *M*
Walden University *M, D*

Mississippi
Jackson State University *M*
University of Southern
Mississippi *B, M*

Missouri
Missouri State University *M*
St. Louis University *M, D*
University of Missouri
Columbia *M*

Nebraska
University of Nebraska
Medical Center *M*
Omaha *M*

Nevada
University of Nevada
Reno *M*

New Hampshire
University of New Hampshire *B*

New Jersey
New Jersey Institute of Technology *M*
Richard Stockton College of New
Jersey *B*
Rutgers, The State University of New
Jersey
New Brunswick/Piscataway
Campus *B*

New Mexico
University of New Mexico *M*

New York
City University of New York
Brooklyn College *M*
New York University *M*
State University of New York
Albany *M, D*
Buffalo *M*
Downstate Medical Center *M*
University of Rochester *M*

North Carolina
East Carolina University *M*
University of North Carolina
Chapel Hill *M*
Charlotte *D*

Ohio
Bowling Green State University *M*
Case Western Reserve University *M*
Ohio State University
Columbus Campus *M*
Youngstown State University *M*

Oklahoma
Southwestern Oklahoma State
University *B*
University of Central Oklahoma *M*
University of Oklahoma *M, D*

Oregon
Oregon Health & Science
University *M*
Oregon State University *M, D*
Portland State University *B, M*

Pennsylvania
Arcadia University *M*
Drexel University *M, D*

East Stroudsburg University of
Pennsylvania *M*
La Salle University *M*
Slippery Rock University of
Pennsylvania *B*
Temple University *B, M*
West Chester University of
Pennsylvania *B, M*

South Carolina
University of South Carolina *M, D*

Tennessee
East Tennessee State University *B, M*
University of Tennessee
Knoxville *M*

Texas
University of Texas
Health Science Center at
Houston *M, D*
Medical Branch at Galveston *M*

Utah
Snow College *A*
University of Utah *B, M, D*
Utah State University *B*

Virginia
James Madison University *M*
Old Dominion University *M*
University of Virginia *M*
Virginia Commonwealth University *M*

Washington
Highline Community College *A*
University of Washington *B, M*

West Virginia
West Virginia University *M*

Public health education

Arizona
Dine College *A*

Arkansas
University of Central Arkansas *B*

California
California Institute of Integral
Studies *M*
California State University
Chico *T*
Long Beach *B, M*
Sacramento *B*
Loma Linda University *B, M, D*
San Diego State University *M*

Colorado
University of Northern Colorado *B, M*

Georgia
Darton College *A*
Georgia Southern University *B, M*
University of Georgia *B, M, D*

Louisiana
Dillard University *B*
Southeastern Louisiana University *B*

Maine
University of Maine
Farmington *B*

Massachusetts
Boston University *M*
Springfield College *M*

Michigan
University of Michigan *M, D*
University of Michigan
Flint *B, M*

Minnesota
Minnesota State University
Mankato *M*
University of St. Thomas *B*
Winona State University *B*

Nebraska
Nebraska Methodist College of
Nursing and Allied Health *M*

New Hampshire
Plymouth State University *B, M*

New Jersey
Thomas Edison State College *B*
University of Medicine and Dentistry
of New Jersey
School of Health Related
Professions *M*

New Mexico
New Mexico State University *B, M*

New York
City University of New York
Hunter College *M*
Ithaca College *B*
State University of New York
Oswego *B*

North Carolina
Appalachian State University *B*
East Carolina University *B, M*
North Carolina Central University *B*
University of North Carolina
Asheville *B*
Chapel Hill *M, D*
Charlotte *M*
Greensboro *B, M*
Pembroke *B*

Ohio
Malone College *B*
University of Toledo *B, M, D*
Youngstown State University *B*

Oklahoma
Oklahoma State University *B*
University of Central Oklahoma *B*
University of Oklahoma *M, D*

Oregon
Oregon State University *B, M*
Portland State University *B, M*

Pennsylvania
Arcadia University *M*
Drexel University *M*
Temple University *B*
University of Pittsburgh *M*

Puerto Rico
Turabo University *M*

South Carolina
Coastal Carolina University *B*
University of South Carolina *M, D*

Tennessee
University of Tennessee
Knoxville *M*

Texas
University of Texas
Austin *M, D*

Utah
University of Utah *B, M, D*

Virginia
Marymount University *M*

Washington
Eastern Washington University *B, T*

West Virginia
Mountain State University *B*

Public health nursing

Arizona
Northern Arizona University *M*

California
California State University
San Bernardino *M*

Connecticut
University of Hartford *M*

Illinois
Northern Illinois University *B*
Southern Illinois University
Edwardsville *M*

Indiana
Indiana University-Purdue University
Indianapolis *M*

Louisiana
Louisiana State University Health
Sciences Center *M*

Michigan
University of Michigan *M, D*
Wayne State University *M*

Minnesota
Augsburg College *M*

Missouri
Central Missouri State University *M*
Washington University in St. Louis *M*

New Jersey
William Paterson University of New
Jersey *B, M*

New York
City University of New York
Hunter College *B, M*
College of New Rochelle *M*

North Carolina
University of North Carolina
Chapel Hill *M*

Ohio
Case Western Reserve University *M*
Kent State University *M*
University of Akron *M*
Wright State University *M*

Pennsylvania
Drexel University *M*

South Carolina
University of South Carolina *M*

Texas
University of Texas
Brownsville *M*
El Paso *M*

Washington
Seattle University *B, M*

Public history/archives

Alabama
Community College of the Air
Force *A*

California
California State University
Chico *C*
Sacramento *D*
Chapman University *B*

Connecticut
Central Connecticut State
University *M*

District of Columbia
American University *M*

Illinois
Loyola University of Chicago *M*

Maryland
Villa Julie College *B*

Massachusetts
Salem State College *B*

Michigan
University of Michigan *M*
Western Michigan University *B*

North Carolina
Appalachian State University *M*
East Carolina University *B*
Meredith College *B*
North Carolina State University *M*

Pennsylvania
Duquesne University *M*

South Carolina
University of South Carolina *M*

Texas
Texas Lutheran University *B*

Virginia
Longwood University *B*

Public policy analysis

Alabama
Huntingdon College *B*

Arizona
Northern Arizona University *B*

Arkansas
University of Arkansas *D*

California
California Polytechnic State
University: San Luis Obispo *M*
California State University
East Bay *B*
Loma Linda University *D*
Mills College *B*
Pomona College *B*
Scripps College *B*
Stanford University *B*
University of California
Berkeley *M, D*
Los Angeles *M*
San Diego *B*

University of Southern
California *M, D*

Colorado
University of Denver *B, M*

Connecticut
Three Rivers Community College *A*
Trinity College *B, M*
University of New Haven *C*

District of Columbia
American University *M*
George Washington
University *B, M, D*
Georgetown University *M*

Florida
New College of Florida *B*

Georgia
Georgia Institute of
Technology *B, M, D*

Illinois
DePaul University *B*
Northwestern University *B, M*
Olivet Nazarene University *B*
University of Chicago *B, D*
Westwood College of Technology
O'Hare *B*

Indiana
Indiana University
Bloomington *D*
Indiana University-Purdue University
Fort Wayne *B*

Iowa
University of Northern Iowa *M*

Kentucky
Morehead State University *M*

Louisiana
Southern University and Agricultural
and Mechanical College *D*

Maine
University of Southern Maine *M, D*

Maryland
Johns Hopkins University *B, M*
St. Mary's College of Maryland *B*
University of Maryland
Baltimore County *M, D*
College Park *M, D*

Massachusetts
Anna Maria College *B*
Bentley College *B*
Brandeis University *M, D*
Harvard College *M, D*
Simmons College *B*
Suffolk University *B*
University of Massachusetts
Amherst *M*
Boston *M, D*
Dartmouth *M*

Michigan
Albion College *B*
Michigan Technological University *M*
University of Michigan *M, D*

Minnesota
St. Cloud State University *B*
Walden University *D*
Winona State University *B*

Mississippi
University of Mississippi *B*

Missouri
St. Louis University *D*

New Hampshire
New England College *M*

New Jersey
Monmouth University *M*
New Jersey Institute of Technology *M*
Rutgers, The State University of New
Jersey
New Brunswick/Piscataway
Campus *M, D*
St. Peter's College *A, B*
Union County College *C*
William Paterson University of New
Jersey *M*

New York
Cornell University *B, M, D*
Hamilton College *B*
Hobart and William Smith Colleges *B*
Rochester Institute of
Technology *B, M*
Sarah Lawrence College *B*
State University of New York
Albany *M*
College of Environmental Science
and Forestry *B, M, D*
Syracuse University *B*
Wagner College *B*
Wells College *B*

North Carolina
Duke University *B, M*
University of North Carolina
Chapel Hill *B, D*
Charlotte *D*

Ohio
Ohio State University
Columbus Campus *M, D*

Oregon
Oregon State University *M*

Pennsylvania
Carlow University *B*
Carnegie Mellon University *B, M*
Chatham College *B*
Dickinson College *B*
Duquesne University *M*
Immaculata University *B*
Penn State
Harrisburg *B*
University Park *B*
St. Vincent College *B*
University of Pennsylvania *B, M, D*
University of Pittsburgh *M*

Rhode Island
Brown University *B*
University of Rhode Island *B, M, D*

South Carolina
Clemson University *D*

Tennessee
Vanderbilt University *M*

Texas
Rice University *B*
Southern Methodist University *B*
University of Houston
Clear Lake *B*
University of Texas
Austin *M, D*
Dallas *D*

Utah
Brigham Young University *M*

Virginia
College of William and Mary *B, M*
George Mason University *D*
Regent University *T*
Virginia Polytechnic Institute and
State University *B*
Washington and Lee University *B*

Washington
Central Washington University *B*
University of Washington *M*
Washington State University *B, M*

Wisconsin
Northland College *B*
University of Wisconsin
Madison *M*
Superior *B*
Whitewater *B, T*

Public relations

Alabama
Auburn University *B*
Community College of the Air
Force *A*
University of Alabama *B*

Arizona
Glendale Community College *A*
Grand Canyon University *B*
Northern Arizona University *B*
Scottsdale Community College *C, A*

Arkansas
Harding University *B*
John Brown University *A, B*

California
California Lutheran University *B*
California State University
Chico *B*
Dominguez Hills *B*
East Bay *B*
Fresno *B*
Fullerton *B, M*
Long Beach *B*
College of Marin: Kentfield *A*
Cosumnes River College *A*
Fullerton College *C*
Golden Gate University *M*
Golden West College *C, A*
Long Beach City College *C, A*
Los Angeles City College *A*
Master's College *B*
Pacific Union College *B*
Pepperdine University *B*
San Diego State University *B*
San Jose State University *B*
University of Southern
California *B, M*

Colorado
Colorado State University *M*
Jones International University *C, B, M*
University of Denver *M*

Connecticut
Manchester Community College *C*
Quinnipiac University *B*
University of Bridgeport *B*

Delaware
Delaware State University *B*

District of Columbia
American University *B, M*

Florida
Barry University *B*
Florida Agricultural and Mechanical
University *B*
Florida Southern College *B*
Florida State University *B*
Gulf Coast Community College *A*
Indian River Community College *A*
Manatee Community College *A*
University of Florida *B*
University of Miami *B, M*
Valencia Community College *A*

Georgia
Clark Atlanta University *B*
Fort Valley State University *B*
Georgia Southern University *B*
Paine College *B*
Shorter College *B*
University of Georgia *B*

Hawaii
Chaminade University of Honolulu *B*
Hawaii Pacific University *B*

Idaho
Brigham Young University-Idaho *B*
North Idaho College *A*

Illinois
Black Hawk College
East Campus *A*
Bradley University *B*
Columbia College Chicago *B*
Eureka College *B*
Greenville College *B*
Illinois State University *B*
Lewis University *B*
Loyola University of Chicago *B*
Monmouth College *B*
Northwestern University *M*
Roosevelt University *B*
Sauk Valley Community College *A*
University of St. Francis *B*

Indiana
Ball State University *M*
Huntington University *B*
Indiana University-Purdue University
Indianapolis *B*
Purdue University
Calumet *B*
St. Mary-of-the-Woods College *B*
Taylor University: Fort Wayne *B*
Valparaiso University *B*
Vincennes University *A*

Iowa
Coe College *B*
Dordt College *B*
Drake University *B*
Loras College *B*
St. Ambrose University *B*
Simpson College *B*
University of Northern Iowa *B*
Wartburg College *B*
William Penn University *B*

Kansas
Fort Scott Community College *A*
Kansas Wesleyan University *B*
MidAmerica Nazarene University *B*
Pittsburg State University *B*
Tabor College *B*

Kentucky
Campbellsville University *B*
Eastern Kentucky University *B*
Murray State University *B*
Northern Kentucky University *B*
Western Kentucky University *B*

Louisiana

University of Louisiana at Lafayette *B*

Maine

New England School of
　　Communications *A, B*
St. Joseph's College *B*
University of Southern Maine *B*

Massachusetts

American International College *B*
Boston University *B, M*
Cape Cod Community College *A*
Eastern Nazarene College *B*
Emerson College *B, M*
Massachusetts College of Liberal
　　Arts *B*
Northeastern University *B*
Regis College *B*
Salem State College *B*
Simmons College *B*
Suffolk University *B, M*

Michigan

Andrews University *B*
Central Michigan University *B*
Cornerstone University *B*
Eastern Michigan University *B*
Ferris State University *C, B*
Grand Valley State University *B*
Kellogg Community College *A*
Macomb Community College *C, A*
Madonna University *A, B*
Michigan State University *M*
Northern Michigan University *B*
University of Detroit Mercy *B*
Wayne State University *B*
Western Michigan University *B*

Minnesota

Concordia College: Moorhead *B*
Minnesota State University
　　Mankato *B*
Northwestern College *B*
St. Cloud State University *B*
St. Mary's University of Minnesota *B*
Southwest Minnesota State
　　University *B*
Winona State University *B*

Mississippi

Itawamba Community College *A*
Mississippi College *B, M*
University of Southern Mississippi *M*

Missouri

Central Missouri State University *B*
College of the Ozarks *B*
Crowder College *A*
Drury University *B*
Northwest Missouri State
　　University *B*
Rockhurst University *B*
St. Louis Community College
　　St. Louis Community College at
　　　Florissant Valley *A*
Stephens College *B*
University of Missouri
　　Columbia *M*
Webster University *B, M*
William Woods University *B*

Montana

Carroll College *B*
Montana State University
　　Billings *B, M*

Nebraska

Bellevue University *B*
Hastings College *B*
Midland Lutheran College *B*
Union College *B*

New Hampshire

New England College *B*
Rivier College *B*

New Jersey

Kean University *M*
Rider University *C*
Rowan University *B, M*

New York

City University of New York
　　City College *B*
Hofstra University *B*
Iona College *B*
Marist College *B*
New York Institute of Technology *M*
Rochester Institute of
　　Technology *C, B*
State University of New York
　　College at Cortland *B*
　　College at Fredonia *B*
　　New Paltz *B*
　　Oswego *B*
Syracuse University *B, M*
Utica College *B*

North Carolina

Appalachian State University *B*
Campbell University *B*
Gardner-Webb University *B*
North Carolina Agricultural and
　　Technical State University *B*
Wingate University *B*

Ohio

Baldwin-Wallace College *B*
Bowling Green State University *B*
Capital University *B*
Columbus College of Art and
　　Design *B*
Defiance College *B*
Heidelberg College *B*
Kent State University *B*
Malone College *B*
Marietta College *B*
Miami University
　　Oxford Campus *B*
Ohio Dominican University *B*
Ohio Northern University *B*
Ohio State University
　　Columbus Campus *B, M*
Otterbein College *B*
University of Dayton *B*
University of Findlay *B*
University of Rio Grande *A, B*
Ursuline College *B*
Wilmington College *B*
Xavier University *A, B*
Youngstown State University *B*

Oklahoma

Cameron University *B*
Northwestern Oklahoma State
　　University *B*
Oklahoma Baptist University *B*
Oklahoma Christian University *B*
Oklahoma City University *B*
Southeastern Oklahoma State
　　University *B*
University of Central Oklahoma *B*

Oregon

George Fox University *B*
Marylhurst University *C*
Southern Oregon University *B*
University of Oregon *B*

Pennsylvania

Chatham College *B*
Duquesne University *B*
Elizabethtown College *B*
Keystone College *A*

La Salle University *B*
Lebanon Valley College *C*
Mansfield University of
　　Pennsylvania *B*
Marywood University *B*
St. Francis University *B*
Susquehanna University *B*
Temple University *B, M*
University of Pittsburgh
　　Bradford *B*
　　Greensburg *B*
Waynesburg College *B*
Westminster College *B*
York College of Pennsylvania *B*

Puerto Rico

Inter American University of Puerto
　　Rico
　　Ponce Campus *B*
University of the Sacred Heart *M*

Rhode Island

University of Rhode Island *B*

South Carolina

Anderson University *B*
University of South Carolina *B*
Winthrop University *B*

Tennessee

Belmont University *B*
Freed-Hardeman University *B*
Lee University *B*
Lipscomb University *B*
Southern Adventist University *B*
Union University *B*

Texas

Hardin-Simmons University *B*
Howard Payne University *B*
Our Lady of the Lake University of San
　　Antonio *B*
Sam Houston State University *B*
Southern Methodist University *B*
Texas A&M University
　　Commerce *B*
Texas State University: San Marcos *B*
Texas Tech University *B*
Texas Wesleyan University *B*
University of Houston *B, M*
University of North Texas *B*
University of Texas
　　Arlington *B*
　　Austin *B*
　　El Paso *B*
　　San Antonio *B*

Utah

Southern Utah University *B*
Weber State University *B*

Vermont

Champlain College *A, B*

Virginia

Hampton University *B*
Liberty University *B*

Washington

Central Washington University *B*
Eastern Washington University *B*
Edmonds Community College *C*
Gonzaga University *B*
Seattle University *B*

West Virginia

Bethany College *B*
Concord University *B*
West Virginia University *B*
West Virginia Wesleyan College *B*

Wisconsin

Cardinal Stritch University *B*
Carroll College *B*
Marquette University *B, M*
Mount Mary College *B*
University of Wisconsin
　　Whitewater *B*

Publishing

California

California State University
　　Chico *C*
Foothill College *C*
Long Beach City College *C, A*

Illinois

Benedictine University *B*

Massachusetts

Emerson College *B, M*

Minnesota

Hennepin Technical College *C, A*
Ridgewater College *C, A*

New York

City University of New York
　　City College *C*
New York University *M*
Pace University *M*

Purchasing/procurement/contracts

Alabama

Athens State University *C*
Community College of the Air
　　Force *A*
Miles College *B*

Arizona

Arizona State University *B*
DeVry University
　　Phoenix *M*

California

California State University
　　East Bay *C, B*
Coastline Community College *C*
De Anza College *C, A*
Fresno City College *C, A*
Fullerton College *A*
San Diego City College *C, A*

Florida

DeVry University
　　Miramar *M*
　　Orlando *M*
Florida Institute of Technology *M*

Georgia

DeVry University
　　Alpharetta *M*
　　Decatur *M*

Illinois

DeVry University
　　Tinley Park *M*
University of Illinois
　　Urbana-Champaign *B*

Iowa

St. Ambrose University *C*

Kansas

Washburn University of Topeka *C, A*

Massachusetts

Middlesex Community College *C*

Northern Essex Community
College *C*

Michigan
Central Michigan University *B, M*

Minnesota
University of St. Thomas *M*

Missouri
Webster University *M*

Nebraska
Southeast Community College
Lincoln Campus *A*

New Jersey
Thomas Edison State College *A, B*

New York
Cazenovia College *C*
College of Westchester *C, A*
Globe Institute of Technology *C*

Ohio
Ashland University *B, M*
Cincinnati State Technical and
Community College *A*
Columbus State Community
College *C, A*
DeVry University
Columbus *M*
Miami University
Oxford Campus *B*
Sinclair Community College *C, A*
Wright State University *M*
Youngstown State University *B*

Pennsylvania
Penn State
University Park *C*
St. Joseph's University *A, B*

Puerto Rico
American University of Puerto Rico *B*

South Carolina
Greenville Technical College *A*

Tennessee
Middle Tennessee State University *B*

Texas
Brazosport College *A*
University of Houston
Downtown *B*

Virginia
Central Virginia Community
College *C*
DeVry University
Arlington *M*
Northern Virginia Community
College *C, A*

Washington
Columbia Basin College *A*

Wisconsin
Northeast Wisconsin Technical
College *C*

Quality control technology

Arkansas
East Arkansas Community College *C*

California
College of the Canyons *C, A*

San Jose State University *B, M*

Connecticut
Naugatuck Valley Community
College *C, A*

Georgia
Southern Polytechnic State
University *M*

Illinois
Heartland Community College *C*
Moraine Valley Community
College *C, A*
Waubonsee Community College *C, A*

Indiana
Indiana University-Purdue University
Fort Wayne *C*
Ivy Tech State College
Ivy Tech Community College:
Lafayette *A*

Kentucky
Elizabethtown Community and
Technical College *A*

Maryland
Community College of Baltimore
County *C*

Massachusetts
Springfield Technical Community
College *C, A*

Michigan
Baker College
of Muskegon *C, A*
Eastern Michigan University *M*
Ferris State University *C, B*
Grand Rapids Community
College *C, A*
Mott Community College *C, A*

Minnesota
Capella University *C, B*

Missouri
Missouri Southern State University *C*

Nebraska
Central Community College *C, A*

New York
Broome Community College *C, A*
Genesee Community College *C, A*

Ohio
Bowling Green State University *B*
Cincinnati State Technical and
Community College *C*
Edison State Community College *C, A*
James A. Rhodes State College *A*
Marion Technical College *C, A*
Owens Community College
Toledo *C, A*

Pennsylvania
Northampton County Area
Community College *C, A*
Penn State
University Park *C*

Puerto Rico
Inter American University of Puerto
Rico
Bayamon Campus *C*
Turabo University *B*

Virginia
Tidewater Community College *A*

Wisconsin
Gateway Technical College *A*
Lakeshore Technical College *A*

Rabbinical studies (M.H.L., Rav.)

California
Hebrew Union College-Jewish
Institute of Religion *F*

Colorado
Yeshiva Toras Chaim Talmudical
Seminary *F*

Connecticut
Beth Benjamin Academy of
Connecticut *F*

Illinois
Brisk Rabbinical College *F*
Hebrew Theological College *F*

Maryland
Ner Israel Rabbinical College *F*

New York
Jewish Theological Seminary of
America: First Professional *F*
Kehilath Yakov Rabbinical Seminary *F*
Kol Yaakov Torah Center *F*
Mesivta Eastern Parkway Rabbinical
Seminary *F*
Mesivta Tifereth Jerusalem of
America *F*
Mirrer Yeshiva Central Institute *F*
Ohr Hameir Theological Seminary *F*
Ohr Somayach Institutions: School of
Theology *F*
Rabbi Isaac Elchanan Theological
Seminary *F*
Rabbinical College Bobover Yeshiva
B'nei Zion *F*
Rabbinical Seminary M'Kor Chaim *F*
Sh'or Yoshuv Rabbinical College *F*
Yeshiva Karlin Stolin Beth Aron
Y'Israel Rabbinical Institute *F*
Yeshiva of Nitra Rabbinical College *F*
Yeshivat Mikdash Melech *F*

Ohio
Hebrew Union College-Jewish
Institute of Religion *F*

Radiation biology

District of Columbia
George Washington University *D*

Florida
Barry University *B*

Illinois
University of Chicago *D*

Iowa
University of Iowa *M, D*

Maine
University of Southern Maine *B*

Massachusetts
Suffolk University *B*
University of Massachusetts
Lowell *M*

Ohio
University of Cincinnati *M*

Pennsylvania
Drexel University *M, D*

Texas
University of Texas
Health Science Center at San
Antonio *D*
Southwestern Medical Center at
Dallas *M, D*

Radiation protection/ health physics technology

Illinois
Rosalind Franklin University of
Medicine and Science *M, D*

New Jersey
Thomas Edison State College *A, B*

Ohio
University of Cincinnati
Raymond Walters College *C, A*

Radio and television

Alabama
Auburn University *B*
Jacksonville State University *B*
Lawson State Community College *C*
Spring Hill College *B*
Troy University *B*
University of Alabama *B, M*
University of Montevallo *B*

Arizona
Northern Arizona University *B*

Arkansas
Arkansas State University *B, M*

California
California State University
Chico *B*
Fullerton *B, M*
Los Angeles *B*
San Bernardino *B*
Foothill College *C, A*
Loyola Marymount University *B, M*
Master's College *B*
San Jose State University *B*
University of La Verne *B*
University of Southern
California *B, M*

District of Columbia
American University *B*
Howard University *B*

Florida
Barry University *B*
Hillsborough Community College *A*
Manatee Community College *A*
Palm Beach Atlantic University *B*
University of Central Florida *B*
University of Miami *B, M*

Georgia
Georgia Southern University *B*

Illinois
Bradley University *B*
Lewis University *B*
Lewis and Clark Community
College *A*
North Central College *B*

Northwestern University *B, M, D*
Parkland College *A*
Southern Illinois University
    Carbondale *B*
University of St. Francis *B*
Western Illinois University *B, M*

Indiana

Butler University *B*
Huntington University *B*
Indiana State University *B, M*
University of Southern Indiana *B, T*
Valparaiso University *B*

Iowa

Drake University *B*
Grand View College *B*
Morningside College *B*
St. Ambrose University *B*
Waldorf College *B*

Kansas

Central Christian College of Kansas *A*
Pittsburg State University *B*

Kentucky

Murray State University *B*
Northern Kentucky University *B*
University of Kentucky *B*
Western Kentucky University *B*

Maine

New England School of
    Communications *C, A, B*

Massachusetts

American International College *B*
Eastern Nazarene College *B*
New England Institute of Art *A*
Newbury College *A*

Michigan

Kuyper College *B*
Lawrence Technological University *A*
Michigan State University *B, M*
Northern Michigan University *B*

Minnesota

Lake Superior College *C*
Northwestern College *A, B*
St. Cloud State University *B*

Missouri

University of Missouri
    Columbia *B*
William Jewell College *B*

Nebraska

Hastings College *B*
Northeast Community College *A*

New Hampshire

Franklin Pierce College *B*

New Jersey

Cumberland County College *A*

New York

Cayuga County Community College *A*
City University of New York
    Brooklyn College *B, M*
Five Towns College *A, B*
Hofstra University *B*
Ithaca College *B*
Marist College *B*
New York Institute of Technology *B*
New York University *B*
Syracuse University *B, M*

North Carolina

Appalachian State University *B*

Campbell University *B*

North Dakota

Minot State University *B*

Ohio

Ashland University *A, B*
Cedarville University *B*
Central State University *B*
Kent State University *B*
Malone College *B*
Marietta College *B*
Ohio University *B, M, D*
Xavier University *A, B*
Youngstown State University *B*

Oklahoma

Northeastern Oklahoma Agricultural
    and Mechanical College *A*
Oklahoma City University *B*

Oregon

George Fox University *B*

Pennsylvania

Drexel University *M*
Keystone College *A*
La Salle University *B*
Messiah College *B*
Temple University *M*

Tennessee

Trevecca Nazarene University *A*

Texas

Alvin Community College *C, A*
Baylor University *B*
Del Mar College *A*
Hardin-Simmons University *B*
Odessa College *A*
Sam Houston State University *B*
San Antonio College *A*
Southern Methodist University *B, M*
Stephen F. Austin State University *B*
Texas Christian University *B*
Texas State University: San Marcos *B*
Texas Tech University *B*
Texas Wesleyan University *B*
University of Houston *B*
University of Texas
    Arlington *B*
    Austin *B, M, D*

Vermont

Lyndon State College *B*

Washington

Centralia College *A*

West Virginia

Bethany College *B*

Wisconsin

Marquette University *M*

Radio/television broadcasting

Alabama

Jefferson State Community
    College *C, A*
Trenholm State Technical College *C*

Arizona

Glendale Community College *A*

Arkansas

Mid-South Community College *C*

California

Chabot College *C, A*
San Bernardino Valley College *C*
Southwestern College *C, A*

Connecticut

Asnuntuck Community College *C, A*

Florida

Manatee Community College *A*

Georgia

Savannah Technical College *C*
University of Georgia *B*

Idaho

Boise State University *A*

Illinois

Black Hawk College *A*
Lewis University *B*
Parkland College *A*
Waubonsee Community College *C*

Indiana

Vincennes University *A*

Kansas

Central Christian College of Kansas *A*

Kentucky

Asbury College *B*

Maine

New England School of
    Communications *A, B*

Massachusetts

Mount Ida College *B*
Mount Wachusett Community
    College *A*
New England Institute of Art *A*
Newbury College *A*
Roxbury Community College *A*
Springfield Technical Community
    College *A*
Suffolk University *B*

Michigan

Eastern Michigan University *B*
Ferris State University *B*
Oakland Community College *A*

New York

City University of New York
    Brooklyn College *B*
Genesee Community College *A*
Long Island University
    C. W. Post Campus *B, M*
Tompkins-Cortland Community
    College *A*

North Carolina

Isothermal Community College *C, A*
Wilkes Community College *C, A*

Ohio

Ohio University *A*

Pennsylvania

Gannon University *B*
La Salle University *B*
Luzerne County Community
    College *A*
Marywood University *B, M*
Northampton County Area
    Community College *A*
Thiel College *B*

Puerto Rico

University of Puerto Rico
    Arecibo *A, B*

Rhode Island

New England Institute of
    Technology *A*

South Carolina

York Technical College *C*

Texas

Houston Community College
    System *C, A*

Utah

Salt Lake Community College *A*

Virginia

Liberty University *B*

Washington

Centralia College *A*
Clover Park Technical College *A*
Yakima Valley Community College *C*

Wisconsin

Gateway Technical College *A*
Milwaukee Area Technical College *A*

Wyoming

Central Wyoming College *A*

Radiologic technology/ medical imaging

Alabama

Community College of the Air
    Force *A*
Southern Union State Community
    College *A*

Arkansas

South Arkansas Community College *A*
University of Arkansas
    Fort Smith *M*

California

Charles R. Drew University of
    Medicine and Science *A, B*
Foothill College *A*

Colorado

Cambridge College *A*
Colorado State University *M, D*
Heritage College *A*
Red Rocks Community College *A*

Connecticut

St. Vincent's College *A*

Florida

Florida Hospital College of Health
    Sciences *A, B*
Hillsborough Community College *A*
Pasco-Hernando Community
    College *A*
St. Petersburg College *A*

Georgia

Athens Technical College *A*
Dalton State College *A*
Gordon College *A*
Griffin Technical College *A*
Southwest Georgia Technical
    College *A*

Idaho

Lewis-Clark State College *A*

Illinois

Black Hawk College *A*
City Colleges of Chicago
   Wright College *A*
Heartland Community College *A*
Kankakee Community College *A*
Kaskaskia College *A*
Lincoln Land Community College *A*
Parkland College *A*
Richland Community College *A*
University of St. Francis *B*

Indiana

Indiana University
   Northwest *A*
Indiana University-Purdue University
   Fort Wayne *A*
Indiana University-Purdue University
   Indianapolis *B*
Ivy Tech State College
   Ivy Tech Community College:
     Northwest *A*

Iowa

Allen College *A*
Indian Hills Community College *A*
Northwest Iowa Community
   College *A*
University of Iowa *B*

Kansas

Labette Community College *A*
Washburn University of Topeka *A*

Louisiana

Louisiana State University
   Alexandria *A*
Northwestern State University *B*
Our Lady of the Lake College *A*
University of Louisiana at Monroe *B*

Maine

Kennebec Valley Community
   College *A*

Maryland

Howard Community College *A*

Massachusetts

Laboure College *A*
Massachusetts College of Pharmacy
   and Health Sciences *B*
North Shore Community College *A*
Springfield Technical Community
   College *A*

Michigan

Baker College
   of Clinton Township *A*
   of Muskegon *A*
Jackson Community College *A*
Madonna University *A*

Minnesota

Lake Superior College *A*
Minnesota State Community and
   Technical College - Fergus Falls *A*
Northland Community & Technical
   College *A*
Rochester Community and Technical
   College *A*

Missouri

Jewish Hospital College of Nursing
   and Allied Health *A, B*
State Fair Community College *A*
University of Missouri
   Columbia *B*

Montana

Montana State University
   Billings *A*

Nebraska

Clarkson College *B*
Nebraska Methodist College of
   Nursing and Allied Health *A, B*
Northeast Community College *A*
University of Nebraska
   Medical Center *B*

Nevada

Truckee Meadows Community
   College *A*

New Jersey

Union County College *A*

North Carolina

Carteret Community College *A*
Fayetteville Technical Community
   College *A*
Johnston Community College *A*
Lenoir Community College *A*
Robeson Community College *A*
Rowan-Cabarrus Community
   College *A*
Stanly Community College *A*

North Dakota

Jamestown College *B*
North Dakota State University *B*

Ohio

James A. Rhodes State College *A*
Mercy College of Northwest Ohio *A*
Sinclair Community College *A*
University of Cincinnati
   Raymond Walters College *A, B*

Oklahoma

Heritage College Hair Design *A*
Rose State College *A*

Oregon

Oregon Institute of Technology *B*

Pennsylvania

Bloomsburg University of
   Pennsylvania *M*
Harcum College *A*
Harrisburg Area Community
   College *A*
Keystone College *A*
Mount Aloysius College *A, B*
Northampton County Area
   Community College *A*
University of Pittsburgh
   Bradford *B*
Widener University *A*

Puerto Rico

Universidad del Este *A, B*

Rhode Island

Community College of Rhode
   Island *A*

South Carolina

York Technical College *A*

Texas

Angelina College *A*
Midwestern State University *A, B, M*
South Texas College *A*
Tyler Junior College *A*
University of Texas
   Brownsville *A*

Vermont

Champlain College *A*
Southern Vermont College *A*

Virginia

Southwest Virginia Community
   College *A*
Virginia Commonwealth University *B*

Washington

North Seattle Community College *A*
Wenatchee Valley College *A*

West Virginia

Mountain State University *A*
University of Charleston *B*

Wisconsin

Marian College of Fond du Lac *B*
Nicolet Area Technical College *A*

Wyoming

Casper College *A*

Range science

California

California State University
   Chico *A*
College of the Redwoods *C*
Humboldt State University *B*
University of California
   Berkeley *M*
   Davis *B*

Colorado

Colorado State University *B, M, D*

Idaho

College of Southern Idaho *A*
University of Idaho *B, M*

Kansas

Pratt Community College *A*

Montana

Montana State University
   Bozeman *B*

Nebraska

Chadron State College *B*
University of Nebraska
   Lincoln *B*

New Mexico

New Mexico State University *B, M, D*

Oklahoma

Southeastern Oklahoma State
   University *B*

Oregon

Eastern Oregon University *B*
Oregon State University *B, M, D*

South Dakota

South Dakota State University *B*

Texas

Frank Phillips College *A*
Sul Ross State University *B, M*
Texas A&M University *B, M, D*
Texas A&M University
   Kingsville *B, M*
Texas Tech University *B, M, D*

Utah

Utah State University *B, M, D*

Vermont

Sterling College *A, B*

Wyoming

Central Wyoming College *A*
Eastern Wyoming College *A*
Northwest College *A*
University of Wyoming *B, M, D*

Reading teacher education

Alabama

Jacksonville State University *M, T*
University of South Alabama *M*

Arizona

Grand Canyon University *M*
University of Arizona *M, D*

Arkansas

Arkansas State University *M, T*
Harding University *B, M, T*
University of Arkansas
   Little Rock *M*
University of Central Arkansas *M*

California

Azusa Pacific University *M, T*
California Baptist University *M*
California Lutheran University *B, T*
California Polytechnic State
   University: San Luis Obispo *M*
California State University
   Chico *M, T*
   Dominguez Hills *M*
   East Bay *M, T*
   Fresno *M*
   Fullerton *M, T*
   Long Beach *T*
   Sacramento *T*
   San Bernardino *M, T*
Chapman University *M*
Fresno Pacific University *M, T*
Loyola Marymount University *M*
National University *M*
St. Mary's College of California *M*
San Francisco State University *M*
Sonoma State University *M, T*
University of La Verne *M*

Colorado

University of Northern Colorado *M, T*

Connecticut

Central Connecticut State
   University *M*
Eastern Connecticut State
   University *M*
Western Connecticut State
   University *M*

District of Columbia

Howard University *M*
Trinity University *M*
University of the District of
   Columbia *M*

Florida

Barry University *M*
Florida Agricultural and Mechanical
   University *T*
Florida Atlantic University *M*
Florida Gulf Coast University *M*
Florida International University *M*
Florida Memorial University *M*
Florida State University *M, D, T*
Palm Beach Atlantic University *M*
Stetson University *M*
University of Central Florida *M*
University of Florida *B*

University of Miami *M*
University of South Florida *M*
University of West Florida *M*

Georgia
Albany State University *M*
Berry College *M*
Clark Atlanta University *B*
Georgia Southern University *M*
Georgia Southwestern State
 University *M*
Georgia State University *M*
Mercer University *M*
University of Georgia *M, D*
University of West Georgia *M*
Valdosta State University *M*

Illinois
Benedictine University *M*
Chicago State University *M, T*
Concordia University *M*
DePaul University *M*
Governors State University *M*
Illinois State University *M, T*
Lewis University *M, T*
National-Louis University *M, D*
North Park University *T*
Northeastern Illinois University *M*
Northern Illinois University *M*
Rockford College *T*
Roosevelt University *M*
St. Xavier University *M*
University of St. Francis *M*
Western Illinois University *M*

Indiana
Butler University *M, T*
Huntington University *M*
University of Indianapolis *T*

Iowa
Ashford University *B, T*
Briar Cliff University *B*
Buena Vista University *B, T*
Central College *T*
Clarke College *M*
Dordt College *B*
Drake University *M, T*
Graceland University *T*
Iowa State University *T*
Iowa Wesleyan College *T*
Morningside College *M*
Mount Mercy College *T*
Northwestern College *T*
St. Ambrose University *T*
Simpson College *T*
University of Iowa *M*
University of Northern Iowa *B, M*
Upper Iowa University *B, T*
Wartburg College *T*

Kansas
Garden City Community College *A*
Pittsburg State University *M*
Washburn University of Topeka *M*

Kentucky
Campbellsville University *B*
Murray State University *M, T*
Spalding University *M*
Union College *M*
University of Louisville *M*
Western Kentucky University *M*

Louisiana
Centenary College of Louisiana *T*
Loyola University New Orleans *M*
Nicholls State University *M*
University of Louisiana at Monroe *M*

Maine
University of Maine *M*

University of Southern Maine *M, T*

Maryland
Bowie State University *M*
Coppin State University *M*
Frostburg State University *M, T*
Loyola College in Maryland *M*
McDaniel College *M*
Mount St. Mary's University *T*
Salisbury University *T*
Towson University *M, T*

Massachusetts
Boston College *M*
Boston University *M, T*
Bridgewater State College *M*
Eastern Nazarene College *M, T*
Elms College *M*
Endicott College *M*
Framingham State College *M*
Lesley University *M*
Northeastern University *M*
Salem State College *M*
Tufts University *M*
University of Massachusetts
 Lowell *M, D*
Westfield State College *M, T*
Worcester State College *M, T*

Michigan
Andrews University *M*
Aquinas College *B, T*
Calvin College *B, M, T*
Central Michigan University *M, T*
Eastern Michigan University *B, M, T*
Madonna University *M, T*
Marygrove College *M*
Michigan State University *M*
Oakland University *M, D*
Saginaw Valley State University *M*
University of Detroit Mercy *B, M, T*
Wayne State University *M, D, T*
Western Michigan University *M*

Minnesota
Minnesota State University
 Moorhead *M*
St. Cloud State University *B, T*
University of St. Thomas *M*
Winona State University *B, M, T*

Mississippi
Mississippi State University *T*

Missouri
Central Missouri State University *M, T*
Evangel University *M*
Harris-Stowe State University *T*
Maryville University of Saint
 Louis *M, T*
Missouri Baptist University *T*
Missouri Southern State
 University *B, T*
Missouri State University *M*
Northwest Missouri State
 University *M, T*
University of Missouri
 Columbia *M, D*
 Kansas City *M*

Montana
Carroll College *T*
Montana State University
 Billings *M, T*
University of Great Falls *B*
University of Montana: Western *T*

Nebraska
Chadron State College *M*
College of Saint Mary *B, T*
Concordia University *M*
Hastings College *M*

University of Nebraska
 Kearney *M, T*
 Lincoln *B*
 Omaha *M*
York College *B, T*

New Hampshire
Plymouth State University *M, T*
Rivier College *M*
University of New Hampshire *M*

New Jersey
The College of New Jersey *M, T*
Georgian Court University *T*
Kean University *M, T*
Monmouth University *M*
Montclair State University *M, T*
New Jersey City University *B*
Rowan University *M*
St. Peter's College *M, T*
William Paterson University of New
 Jersey *T*

New Mexico
Western New Mexico University *M*

New York
Adelphi University *M, T*
Alfred University *M, T*
Canisius College *M, T*
City University of New York
 Brooklyn College *M*
 Lehman College *M*
 Queens College *M, T*
College of New Rochelle *M*
College of Saint Rose *M, T*
Dowling College *M*
Hofstra University *M, D, T*
Long Island University
 Brooklyn Campus *M, T*
 C.W. Post Campus *M, T*
Manhattanville College *M, T*
Medaille College *M, T*
Mercy College *M*
Nazareth College of Rochester *M*
New York University *M*
Pace University *M, T*
St. Bonaventure University *M*
St. John's University *M, T*
St. Thomas Aquinas College *M*
State University of New York
 Albany *M, D*
 Binghamton *M*
 Buffalo *M, D*
 College at Brockport *M*
 College at Buffalo *B, M, T*
 College at Cortland *M*
 College at Fredonia *M*
 College at Geneseo *M, T*
 College at Oneonta *M, T*
 College at Plattsburgh *M*
 College at Potsdam *M*
 New Paltz *M, T*
 Oswego *M*
Syracuse University *M, D, T*

North Carolina
Appalachian State University *M, T*
Catawba College *T*
East Carolina University *M*
Mars Hill College *T*
Meredith College *M*
North Carolina Agricultural and
 Technical State University *M*
North Carolina State University *M, T*
University of North Carolina
 Asheville *T*
 Charlotte *M*
 Pembroke *M*
 Wilmington *M*
Wingate University *B, T*

North Dakota
Dickinson State University *B, T*
University of Mary *T*
University of North Dakota *M*

Ohio
Ashland University *M, T*
Baldwin-Wallace College *M*
Bowling Green State University *M, T*
Hiram College *T*
John Carroll University *M, T*
Kent State University *M*
Lake Erie College *B, M*
Malone College *M*
Miami University
 Oxford Campus *M*
Ohio Northern University *T*
Ohio State University
 Columbus Campus *M, D*
Ohio University *B, M, T*
Otterbein College *M*
University of Akron *M*
University of Cincinnati *M*
University of Dayton *M*
University of Findlay *B, M, T*
University of Rio Grande *B, T*
Ursuline College *T*
Walsh University *B*
Wilmington College *M, T*
Wright State University *M*
Xavier University *M*
Youngstown State University *M*

Oklahoma
Northeastern State University *M, T*
Northwestern Oklahoma State
 University *M*
Southeastern Oklahoma State
 University *M, T*
Southern Nazarene University *M*
University of Central Oklahoma *B, M*
University of Oklahoma *T*

Oregon
Portland State University *T*
Warner Pacific College *T*
Western Oregon University *T*

Pennsylvania
Arcadia University *M*
Bloomsburg University of
 Pennsylvania *M, T*
Bucknell University *M, T*
Cabrini College *T*
California University of
 Pennsylvania *M*
Chestnut Hill College *T*
Clarion University of Pennsylvania *M*
Drexel University *B*
Duquesne University *M, T*
East Stroudsburg University of
 Pennsylvania *M, T*
Edinboro University of
 Pennsylvania *B, M*
Gannon University *M, T*
Gwynedd-Mercy College *M*
Holy Family University *M*
Indiana University of Pennsylvania *M*
King's College *M*
Kutztown University of
 Pennsylvania *B, M, T*
Lincoln University *M, T*
Marywood University *M*
Millersville University of
 Pennsylvania *M, T*
St. Joseph's University *M*
Shippensburg University of
 Pennsylvania *M, T*
University of Pennsylvania *M, D*
University of Scranton *M*
West Chester University of
 Pennsylvania *M, T*
Westminster College *M*

Widener University *M, D*
York College of Pennsylvania *M*

Puerto Rico
Turabo University *M*

Rhode Island
Providence College *M*
Rhode Island College *M*
Roger Williams University *M*

South Carolina
The Citadel *M*
Clemson University *M*
University of South Carolina *M, D*
Winthrop University *M, T*

South Dakota
University of Sioux Falls *M*

Tennessee
Austin Peay State University *M*
East Tennessee State University *M, T*
Middle Tennessee State University *M*
Tennessee Technological
   University *M, D, T*
Trevecca Nazarene University *M, T*
University of Memphis *T*
Vanderbilt University *M, D*

Texas
Abilene Christian University *B, M, T*
Angelo State University *M*
Dallas Baptist University *T*
Del Mar College *A*
Hardin-Simmons University *B, M, T*
Houston Baptist University *M*
Jarvis Christian College *B*
Laredo Community College *A*
McMurry University *T*
Midwestern State University *M*
Prairie View A&M University *M*
St. Mary's University *M, T*
Sam Houston State University *M, T*
San Jacinto College
   North *A*
Southwestern Assemblies of God
   University *B*
Southwestern University *T*
Stephen F. Austin State University *M, T*
Sul Ross State University *M*
Texas A&M University
   Commerce *M, T*
   Kingsville *M, T*
Texas Lutheran University *B, T*
Texas State University: San
   Marcos *M, T*
Texas Tech University *M*
Texas Wesleyan University *B, M, T*
Texas Woman's University *M, D*
University of Dallas *T*
University of Houston *M, T*
University of Houston
   Clear Lake *M, T*
   Victoria *M*
University of Mary Hardin-Baylor *M, T*
University of North Texas *M, D*
University of Texas
   Arlington *T*
   Brownsville *M*
   El Paso *M*
   Pan American *M*
   San Antonio *M, T*
   Tyler *M*
   of the Permian Basin *M*
West Texas A&M University *M, T*

Vermont
College of St. Joseph in Vermont *M*
Johnson State College *M*
St. Michael's College *M, T*
University of Vermont *M*

Virginia
Averett University *M*
James Madison University *T*
Liberty University *M, T*
Longwood University *M, T*
Old Dominion University *M, D, T*
Radford University *M, T*
Virginia Commonwealth University *M*

Washington
Central Washington University *M, T*
City University *M*
Eastern Washington University *B, M, T*
Heritage University *B*
Northwest University *T*
Pacific Lutheran University *M*
Walla Walla College *M*
Washington State
   University *B, M, D, T*
Western Washington University *M*
Whitworth College *B, T*

West Virginia
Marshall University *M*
West Virginia University *M, T*

Wisconsin
Alverno College *M, T*
Cardinal Stritch University *M*
Carthage College *M*
Concordia University Wisconsin *M, T*
Mount Mary College *T*
Silver Lake College *T*
University of Wisconsin
   Eau Claire *M*
   La Crosse *M*
   Oshkosh *M*
   Platteville *T*
   River Falls *M, T*
   Superior *M, T*
   Whitewater *M*

Real estate

Alabama
Enterprise-Ozark Community
   College *A*

Arizona
Paradise Valley Community College *C*
Pima Community College *C, A*
Yavapai College *C*

California
American River College *C, A*
Antelope Valley College *C, A*
Bakersfield College *A*
Barstow College *C, A*
Butte College *C, A*
Cabrillo College *C, A*
California State University
   Dominguez Hills *B*
   East Bay *B*
   Fresno *B*
   Long Beach *B*
   Northridge *B*
   Sacramento *B, M*
   San Bernardino *B*
Cerritos Community College *C, A*
Chabot College *A*
Citrus College *C*
City College of San Francisco *C, A*
Coastline Community College *C, A*
College of Marin: Kentfield *C, A*
College of San Mateo *C, A*
College of the Canyons *C, A*
College of the Redwoods *A*
College of the Sequoias *C, A*
Contra Costa College *C, A*
Cosumnes River College *C, A*
Cuesta College *C, A*
Cuyamaca College *A*

De Anza College *C, A*
Diablo Valley College *C*
East Los Angeles College *C, A*
El Camino College *C, A*
Foothill College *C, A*
Fresno City College *C, A*
Fullerton College *C, A*
Glendale Community College *C, A*
Golden West College *C, A*
Imperial Valley College *C, A*
Irvine Valley College *C, A*
Lake Tahoe Community College *C, A*
Lassen College *A*
Long Beach City College *C, A*
Los Angeles City College *C, A*
Los Angeles Harbor College *A*
Los Angeles Mission College *C, A*
Los Angeles Southwest College *C, A*
Los Angeles Trade and Technical
   College *C, A*
Los Medanos College *C, A*
Merced College *C, A*
Merritt College *C, A*
MiraCosta College *C, A*
Mission College *A*
Modesto Junior College *A*
Monterey Peninsula College *C, A*
Moorpark College *C, A*
Mount San Antonio College *C, A*
Mount San Jacinto College *C, A*
Napa Valley College *C, A*
Ohlone College *C, A*
Pacific States University *M*
Palo Verde College *A*
Palomar College *C, A*
Pasadena City College *C, A*
Porterville College *C, A*
Rio Hondo College *A*
Riverside Community College *C, A*
Sacramento City College *C, A*
Saddleback College *C, A*
San Bernardino Valley College *C, A*
San Diego City College *C, A*
San Diego Mesa College *C, A*
San Diego State University *M*
San Francisco State University *B*
San Joaquin Delta College *C, A*
San Jose City College *C, A*
Santa Ana College *C, A*
Santa Barbara City College *C, A*
Santa Monica College *C, A*
Santa Rosa Junior College *C*
Shasta College *C, A*
Sierra College *C, A*
Solano Community College *C, A*
Southwestern College *C, A*
University of San Diego *M*
University of Southern California *M*
Ventura College *C, A*
Victor Valley College *C, A*
West Los Angeles College *C, A*
West Valley College *C, A*

Colorado
Arapahoe Community College *C*
Colorado Mountain College
   Spring Valley Campus *C, A*
   Timberline Campus *C, A*
University of Colorado
   Boulder *B, M*
University of Denver *B, M*

Connecticut
Manchester Community College *C*
University of Connecticut *B*

District of Columbia
George Washington University *M*

Florida
Brevard Community College *A*
Florida Atlantic University *B*

Florida Community College at
   Jacksonville *C*
Florida International University *B*
Florida State University *B*
Gulf Coast Community College *A*
Miami Dade College *C, A*
Okaloosa-Walton College *A*
Seminole Community College *C*
University of Florida *B, M*

Georgia
Georgia State University *B, M, D*
University of Georgia *B*
University of West Georgia *B*

Idaho
College of Southern Idaho *A*

Illinois
City Colleges of Chicago
   Kennedy-King College *C*
   Olive-Harvey College *C*
College of DuPage *C, A*
Danville Area Community College *C*
Illinois Central College *C, A*
Joliet Junior College *C*
Kishwaukee College *C*
Lewis and Clark Community
   College *C*
Lincoln Land Community College *C*
McHenry County College *C, A*
Northwestern University *M*
Oakton Community College *C, A*
Prairie State College *C*
Sauk Valley Community College *C*
Southeastern Illinois College *C*
Southwestern Illinois College *C*
Triton College *C*
University of Illinois
   Urbana-Champaign *B, M, D*
Waubonsee Community College *C*
William Rainey Harper College *C, A*

Indiana
Vincennes University *C*

Iowa
University of Northern Iowa *B*

Kansas
Dodge City Community College *C*

Kentucky
Ashland Community and Technical
   College *A*
Big Sandy Community and Technical
   College *A*
Elizabethtown Community and
   Technical College *A*
Jefferson Community College *C, A*
Madisonville Community College *A*
Morehead State University *B*
West Kentucky Community and
   Technical College *A*
Western Kentucky University *C*

Louisiana
Southern University
   New Orleans *A*

Maine
University of Southern Maine *C*

Maryland
Community College of Baltimore
   County *C, A*
Harford Community College *C*

Massachusetts
Greenfield Community College *C*
Massachusetts Bay Community
   College *C*

Michigan

Delta College *C*
Henry Ford Community College *A*
Kirtland Community College *A*
Lansing Community College *A*
Western Michigan University *B*

Minnesota

Dakota County Technical College *C, A*
Fond du Lac Tribal and Community
 College *C*
St. Cloud State University *B*
University of St. Thomas *B, M*

Mississippi

Mississippi State University *B*
University of Mississippi *B*

Missouri

St. Louis Community College
 St. Louis Community College at
  Meramec *C, A*
University of Missouri
 Columbia *B*
Webster University *M*

Nebraska

Northeast Community College *A*
University of Nebraska
 Omaha *B*

Nevada

Community College of Southern
 Nevada *C, A*
Truckee Meadows Community
 College *A*
University of Nevada
 Las Vegas *B*
Western Nevada Community
 College *A*

New Hampshire

New Hampshire Community
 Technical College
 Manchester *C*
New Hampshire Technical Institute *A*

New Jersey

Camden County College *C*
Gloucester County College *C*
Ocean County College *C*
Raritan Valley Community
 College *C, A*
Thomas Edison State College *A, B*

New Mexico

New Mexico Junior College *A*
San Juan College *C, A*

New York

City University of New York
 Baruch College *B*
 Lehman College *C*
Cornell University *M*
Hudson Valley Community College *A*
New York University *B, M*
Orange County Community College *A*
Suffolk County Community
 College *C, A*
Utica School of Commerce *C*

North Carolina

Alamance Community College *A*
Asheville-Buncombe Technical
 Community College *C*
Blue Ridge Community College *C*
Cape Fear Community College *C*
Carteret Community College *C*
Central Carolina Community
 College *C*
Central Piedmont Community
 College *C, A*

Cleveland Community College *C*
College of the Albemarle *C*
Craven Community College *C*
Durham Technical Community
 College *C*
Forsyth Technical Community
 College *C*
Haywood Community College *C*
Isothermal Community College *C*
Pitt Community College *C*
Rockingham Community College *C*
St. Augustine's College *B*
Sampson Community College *C*
Southwestern Community College *C*
Surry Community College *C*
Tri-County Community College *C*
Wilson Technical Community
 College *C*

Ohio

Cincinnati State Technical and
 Community College *A*
Columbus State Community
 College *C, A*
Cuyahoga Community College
 Metropolitan Campus *A*
Edison State Community College *C, A*
Hocking College *C*
Lakeland Community College *C*
Marion Technical College *A*
Miami University
 Hamilton Campus *A*
Ohio Business College: Sandusky *C*
Ohio State University
 Columbus Campus *B*
Owens Community College
 Toledo *C*
Shawnee State University *A*
Sinclair Community College *A*
Southern State Community College *A*
University of Akron *C, A*
University of Cincinnati *B, M*
University of Cincinnati
 Raymond Walters College *C, A*
University of Rio Grande *B*

Oklahoma

Oklahoma City Community College *A*
Tulsa Community College *A*

Oregon

Chemeketa Community College *A*
Clackamas Community College *C*
Lane Community College *C, A*
Marylhurst University *C, B*
Portland Community College *A*

Pennsylvania

Clarion University of Pennsylvania *B*
Community College of Philadelphia *A*
Harrisburg Area Community
 College *C, A*
Immaculata University *C*
La Roche College *B*
Lehigh Carbon Community
 College *C, A*
Luzerne County Community
 College *A*
Montgomery County Community
 College *C, A*
Northampton County Area
 Community College *C*
Peirce College *A*
Penn State
 Abington *B*
 Altoona *B*
 Beaver *B*
 Berks *B*
 Delaware County *B*
 Dubois *B*
 Fayette *B*
 Hazleton *B*
 Lehigh Valley *B*

McKeesport *B*
Mont Alto *B*
New Kensington *B*
Schuylkill - Capital College *B*
Shenango *B*
University Park *B*
Wilkes-Barre *B*
Worthington Scranton *B*
York *B*
St. Francis University *A*
Temple University *B*
University of Pennsylvania *B, M, D*
University of Pittsburgh
 Titusville *C*
Westmoreland County Community
 College *C*

Rhode Island

Community College of Rhode
 Island *A*

South Carolina

University of South Carolina *B*

Texas

Amarillo College *C, A*
Angelina College *C*
Angelo State University *B*
Austin Community College *C, A*
Baylor University *B*
Blinn College *C*
Cedar Valley College *C, A*
Central Texas College *C, A*
Coastal Bend College *A*
College of the Mainland *A*
Collin County Community College
 District *C, A*
Del Mar College *C*
El Paso Community College *C, A*
Hill College *A*
Houston Community College
 System *C, A*
Kilgore College *A*
Laredo Community College *C, A*
Lee College *A*
McLennan Community College *C, A*
Navarro College *C, A*
North Lake College *A*
Northeast Texas Community
 College *A*
Paris Junior College *A*
Richland College *A*
San Antonio College *C, A*
San Jacinto College
 Central Campus *C, A*
 North *C, A*
South Plains College *C, A*
Southern Methodist University *B*
Tarrant County College *C, A*
Texarkana College *C*
Texas A&M University *M*
Texas Christian University *B*
Trinity Valley Community College *C*
Tyler Junior College *C*
University of North Texas *B, M*
University of Texas
 Arlington *B, M*

Utah

Salt Lake Community College *C*

Virginia

Eastern Shore Community College *C*
J. Sargeant Reynolds Community
 College *C*
Lord Fairfax Community College *C*
Northern Virginia Community
 College *C, A*
Southwest Virginia Community
 College *C*
Tidewater Community College *A*
Virginia Western Community
 College *C, A*

Washington

Bellevue Community College *C, A*
Green River Community College *C, A*
North Seattle Community
 College *C, A*
Spokane Falls Community College *C*
Washington State University *B*

Wisconsin

Chippewa Valley Technical College *C*
Fox Valley Technical College *C*
Madison Area Technical College *A*
Milwaukee Area Technical College *A*
University of Wisconsin
 Madison *B, M*
 Milwaukee *B*
Waukesha County Technical
 College *A*

Wyoming

University of Wyoming *C*

Receptionist

Arizona

Glendale Community College *C*

California

CEI College
 Maric College: Panorama City *C*
Ohlone College *A*

Illinois

Moraine Valley Community College *C*

Iowa

Hamilton College
 Cedar Rapids *C*
Southeastern Community College
 North Campus *A*

Kansas

Central Christian College of Kansas *A*

Maryland

Hagerstown Community College *C*

Massachusetts

Holyoke Community College *C*

Michigan

Baker College
 of Muskegon *C*

Minnesota

Alexandria Technical College *C*
Lake Superior College *C*
Minnesota State College - Southeast
 Technical *C*
St. Cloud Technical College *C*
South Central College *C*

New York

Globe Institute of Technology *C*
Rochester Business Institute *C, A*

North Carolina

Lenoir Community College *C*

Pennsylvania

Business Institute of Pennsylvania *C*
Consolidated School of Business
 Lancaster *C*
 York *C*
Newport Business Institute *A*

Puerto Rico

Universidad del Este *C*

Texas

Mountain View College *C*

Utah

Salt Lake Community College *C*
Utah Valley State College *C*

Virginia

Danville Community College *A*

Washington

Centralia College *C, A*
Clark College *C*
Peninsula College *C*

West Virginia

Valley College of Technology *C*

Recording arts

California

Loyola Marymount University *B*
Southwestern College *C, A*

District of Columbia

American University *B*

Georgia

Savannah College of Art and
    Design *B, M*

Illinois

Columbia College Chicago *B*
DePaul University *B*
School of the Art Institute of
    Chicago *B*

Indiana

Indiana University
    Bloomington *A, B*

Kansas

Central Christian College of Kansas *A*
Kansas City Kansas Community
    College *A*

Louisiana

Bossier Parish Community
    College *C, A*

Maine

New England School of
    Communications *A, B*

Maryland

Johns Hopkins University: Peabody
    Conservatory of Music *B, M*

Massachusetts

New England Institute of Art *B*

Michigan

Grace Bible College *B*
Michigan Technological University *B*
Schoolcraft College *C*

Minnesota

Hennepin Technical College *C, A*
Minneapolis Community and
    Technical College *A*

Nebraska

Northeast Community College *A*

New York

Cayuga County Community College *A*
City University of New York
    Queensborough Community
        College *A*

Finger Lakes Community College *A*
Five Towns College *A, B*
Ithaca College *B*

North Carolina

Guilford Technical Community
    College *A*

Ohio

Cleveland Institute of Music *B*
Malone College *B*

Pennsylvania

Harrisburg Area Community
    College *C*
Lebanon Valley College *B*
Luzerne County Community
    College *A*

Rhode Island

New England Institute of
    Technology *A*

Texas

Cedar Valley College *C, A*
Texas State University: San Marcos *B*

Recreational therapy

Alabama

Troy University *M*

Arkansas

University of Central Arkansas *B*

California

California State University
    Chico *B*
    East Bay *B*
Santa Barbara City College *A*
Whittier College *B*

Connecticut

Northwestern Connecticut
    Community College *A*
Norwalk Community College *A*

District of Columbia

Gallaudet University *B*
Howard University *B*

Florida

Broward Community College *A*

Illinois

Moraine Valley Community College *A*
University of St. Francis *B*

Indiana

Indiana Institute of Technology *B*
Indiana University-Purdue University
    Fort Wayne *B*
Vincennes University *A*

Iowa

University of Iowa *B*

Louisiana

Southern University and Agricultural
    and Mechanical College *B*

Maine

University of Southern Maine *A, B*

Massachusetts

Northeastern University *B*
Springfield College *B, M*

Michigan

Calvin College *B*

Central Michigan University *B, M, T*
Eastern Michigan University *B*
Lake Superior State University *B*

Minnesota

Minnesota State University
    Mankato *B*
St. Cloud State University *B*
Winona State University *B*

New Hampshire

University of New Hampshire *B*

New York

Genesee Community College *A*
Ithaca College *B*
Onondaga Community College *A*
Russell Sage College *B*
St. Joseph's College: Suffolk
    Campus *B*
Utica College *B*

North Carolina

Carteret Community College *A*
Catawba College *B*
East Carolina University *B, M*
North Carolina Central University *M*
Shaw University *B*
University of North Carolina
    Wilmington *B*
Vance-Granville Community
    College *A*
Western Carolina University *B*
Western Piedmont Community
    College *A*
Winston-Salem State University *B*

Ohio

Ashland University *B*
University of Toledo *B*

Pennsylvania

Keystone College *A*
Lincoln University *B*
Messiah College *B*
Temple University *B, M, D*
York College of Pennsylvania *B*

South Carolina

Coker College *B*

Texas

Austin Community College *A*
Texas State University: San Marcos *M*

Utah

Brigham Young University *B*

Virginia

Longwood University *B*

Washington

Eastern Washington University *B*
Spokane Community College *A*

West Virginia

Alderson-Broaddus College *B*
West Virginia State University *B*

Wisconsin

Northland College *B*
University of Wisconsin
    La Crosse *B*

Regional studies

California

Claremont McKenna College *B*

Colorado

Colorado College *B*
Fort Lewis College *B*

Georgia

Mercer University *B*

Kansas

Central Christian College of Kansas *A*

Maine

University of Southern Maine *M*

Nebraska

University of Nebraska
    Lincoln *B*

New Mexico

College of Santa Fe *B*
Northern New Mexico College *A*
San Juan College *A*
Santa Fe Community College *A*

New York

City University of New York
    Lehman College *B*
Columbia University
    Columbia College *B*

North Carolina

Appalachian State University *M*

Pennsylvania

La Salle University *B*

Texas

Southern Methodist University *B*

Religious education

Alabama

Faulkner University *B*
Oakwood College *B*
Southeastern Bible College *A, B, T*

Arizona

Southwestern College *C, A, B*

Arkansas

Central Baptist College *A, B*
Harding University *B, M, T*
Williams Baptist College *B*

California

Azusa Pacific University *B, M, D*
Bethesda Christian University *B*
Biola University *B, M, D*
California Lutheran University *B*
Loyola Marymount University *M*
Master's College *B*
Mount St. Mary's College *M*
Notre Dame de Namur University *B*
Patten University *B*
University of San Francisco *M*
Vanguard University of Southern
    California *B*
William Jessup University *B*

Colorado

Nazarene Bible College *A, B*

Connecticut

Holy Apostles College and
    Seminary *M*

District of Columbia

Catholic University of America *M, D*

Florida

Baptist College of Florida *A, B*

Clearwater Christian College *B*
Florida Southern College *B*
St. Thomas University *B*
Southeastern College of the
  Assemblies of God *B*
Yeshiva Gedolah Rabbinical
  College *B, M*

Georgia
LaGrange College *B*
Toccoa Falls College *B*

Idaho
Boise Bible College *A, B*
Northwest Nazarene University *B*

Illinois
Concordia University *B, M, T*
Lincoln Christian College and
  Seminary *B, M*
Moody Bible Institute *B, T*
North Park University *M*
Olivet Nazarene University *B*
Trinity Christian College *B*
Trinity International University *B, M*
Wheaton College *B, M*

Indiana
Huntington University *B, M*
Indiana Wesleyan University *A, B*
Marian College *A, B*
Martin University *B*
Taylor University: Fort Wayne *B*

Iowa
Faith Baptist Bible College and
  Theological Seminary *B*
Loras College *M*
Northwestern College *B*
Vennard College *B*
Wartburg College *B, T*

Kansas
Central Christian College of
  Kansas *A, B*
Kansas Wesleyan University *B*
Manhattan Christian College *A, B*
MidAmerica Nazarene University *A, B*
Sterling College *B*

Kentucky
Asbury College *B*
Brescia University *C, A*
Campbellsville University *B, M*
Kentucky Christian University *B*
Kentucky Mountain Bible College *B*
Mid-Continent University *C, B*
Union College *B*
University of the Cumberlands *B*

Louisiana
Loyola University New Orleans *M*
New Orleans Baptist Theological
  Seminary: Leavell College *A, B*

Maryland
Baltimore Hebrew University *M, D*
Columbia Union College *B*
Washington Bible College *B*

Massachusetts
Boston College *M, D*
Eastern Nazarene College *B*
Hebrew College *B, M*

Michigan
Andrews University *B, M, D*
Concordia University *B*
Cornerstone University *A, B*
Grace Bible College *A, B*
Great Lakes Christian College *B*
Kuyper College *A, B*

Minnesota
College of St. Benedict *B*
Concordia University: St. Paul *B*
Crossroads College *B*
Crown College *C, B*
North Central University *B*
Northwestern College *B*
St. John's University *B*
University of St. Thomas *M*

Mississippi
Magnolia Bible College *B*
Wesley College *B*

Missouri
Baptist Bible College *B*
Calvary Bible College and Theological
  Seminary *A, B*
Central Bible College *A, B*
Central Christian College of the
  Bible *B*
Global University *B*
Hannibal-LaGrange College *B*
Missouri Baptist University *B*
Ozark Christian College *B*
St. Louis Christian College *B*
Southwest Baptist University *B*

Nebraska
Concordia University *B, T*
Grace University *B*
Nebraska Christian College *A, B*
Union College *B, T*
York College *B, T*

New Jersey
College of St. Elizabeth *C*
Felician College *M*
Seton Hall University *B, T*

New York
Concordia College *B*
Davis College *B*
Jewish Theological Seminary of
  America *M*
Nyack College *B*
Yeshiva University *D*

North Carolina
Campbell University *M, D*
Duke University *M*
Gardner-Webb University *B*
John Wesley College *B*
Methodist College *A, B, T*
Pfeiffer University *B, M*
Roanoke Bible College *B*
Shaw University *M*

North Dakota
Trinity Bible College *B*

Ohio
Ashland University *B, M, T*
Capital University *B*
Cedarville University *B*
Cincinnati Christian University *B, M*
Circleville Bible College *A, B*
College of Mount St. Joseph *B*
Defiance College *B, T*
Franciscan University of
  Steubenville *B*
God's Bible School and College *B*
Laura and Alvin Siegal College of
  Judaic Studies *B, M*
Mount Vernon Nazarene University *B*
Muskingum College *B*

Oklahoma
Oklahoma Baptist University *B*
Oklahoma Christian University *B*
Oklahoma City University *B, M*
Oral Roberts University *B, M*

St. Gregory's University *A*
Southern Nazarene University *B*
Southwestern Christian University *B*

Oregon
Concordia University *B*
Corban College *B*
Eugene Bible College *B*
George Fox University *B*
Multnomah Bible College *B*
Warner Pacific College *A*

Pennsylvania
Duquesne University *M*
Gratz College *T*
Holy Family University *B*
Immaculata University *C*
La Roche College *B*
La Salle University *B, M*
Manor College *C, A*
Marywood University *B*
Mercyhurst College *A, B*
Messiah College *B*
Philadelphia Biblical University *B, T*
St. Vincent College *B*
Thiel College *B*
Valley Forge Christian College *B*
Westminster College *B, T*

Puerto Rico
Pontifical Catholic University of
  Puerto Rico *M*

Rhode Island
Providence College *M*

South Carolina
Columbia College *B*
Columbia International
  University *B, M*
Erskine College *B, M*
Morris College *B*
Presbyterian College *B*

Tennessee
American Baptist College of ABT
  Seminary *B*
Bryan College *B*
Free Will Baptist Bible College *B*
Lee University *B*
Southern Adventist University *B, M*
Tennessee Temple University *B, M*

Texas
Arlington Baptist College *B*
Concordia University at Austin *B*
Dallas Baptist University *A, B, M*
Dallas Christian College *B*
East Texas Baptist University *B*
Howard Payne University *B*
St. Edward's University *B, T*
Southern Methodist University *M*
Southwestern Assemblies of God
  University *B*
Texas Wesleyan University *B*
University of Dallas *M*
Wayland Baptist University *B*

Utah
Brigham Young University *M*

Virginia
Liberty University *M*

Washington
Northwest University *B*
Puget Sound Christian College *B*
Seattle Pacific University *B*
Seattle University *M*
Trinity Lutheran College *A, B*

West Virginia
West Virginia Wesleyan College *B*
Wheeling Jesuit University *M*

Wisconsin
Concordia University Wisconsin *B*
Edgewood College *B*
Marquette University *D, T*
Mount Mary College *B*
Viterbo University *B*

Religious studies

Alabama
Athens State University *B*
Auburn University *B*
Birmingham-Southern College *B*
Faulkner University *B*
Gadsden State Community College *A*
Huntingdon College *B*
Judson College *B*
Oakwood College *B*
Samford University *B*
University of Alabama *B*
University of Mobile *B, M*
Wallace State Community College at
  Hanceville *C*

Arizona
Arizona State University *B, M, D*
Northern Arizona University *B*
Prescott College *M*
Southwestern College *C, B*
University of Arizona *B*

Arkansas
Crowley's Ridge College *A*
Harding University *B, M*
Hendrix College *B*
Lyon College *B*
Philander Smith College *B*
University of Central Arkansas *B*

California
Azusa Pacific University *B, M*
Bethesda Christian University *B, M*
Biola University *B*
California Institute of Integral
  Studies *M, D*
California Lutheran University *B*
California State University
  Bakersfield *B*
  Chico *B*
  East Bay *B*
  Fresno *B*
  Fullerton *B*
  Long Beach *B, M*
  Northridge *B*
Chaffey College *A*
Chapman University *B*
Claremont McKenna College *B*
Crafton Hills College *C*
Dominican University of California *B*
Holy Names University *B, M*
Hope International University *M*
Humboldt State University *B*
La Sierra University *B, M*
Loma Linda University *M*
Los Angeles Pierce College *A*
Master's College *B*
Mount St. Mary's College *B, M*
Notre Dame de Namur University *B*
Occidental College *B*
Orange Coast College *A*
Pacific Union College *B*
Patten University *A, B*
Pepperdine University *B, M*
Pitzer College *B*
Point Loma Nazarene University *M*
Pomona College *B*
Queen of the Holy Rosary
  College *C, A*
St. Mary's College of California *B*

San Diego State University *B*
San Jose State University *B*
Santa Clara University *B, M*
Scripps College *B*
Simpson University *B*
Stanford University *B, M, D*
University of California
  Berkeley *B*
  Davis *B*
  Los Angeles *B*
  Riverside *B*
  San Diego *B*
  Santa Barbara *B, M, D*
  Santa Cruz *B, M, D*
University of La Verne *B*
University of Redlands *B*
University of San Diego *B*
University of Southern
  California *B, M, D*
University of the Pacific *B*
Vanguard University of Southern
  California *B, M*
Westmont College *B*
Whittier College *B*
William Jessup University *C, B*

Colorado
Colorado College *B*
Naropa University *B, M*
Nazarene Bible College *C, A*
Regis University *B*
University of Colorado
  Boulder *B, M*
University of Denver *B, M*

Connecticut
Albertus Magnus College *B*
Connecticut College *B*
Fairfield University *B*
Holy Apostles College and
  Seminary *C, A, B, M*
Sacred Heart University *B, M*
St. Joseph College *B, T*
Trinity College *B*
University of Bridgeport *B*
Wesleyan University *B*
Yale University *B, M, D*

Delaware
Wesley College *C*

District of Columbia
Catholic University of
  America *B, M, D*
George Washington University *B, M*
Georgetown University *B*
Howard University *M, D*

Florida
Baptist College of Florida *B*
Broward Community College *A*
Eckerd College *B*
Edward Waters College *B*
Florida Agricultural and Mechanical
  University *B*
Florida Christian College *B*
Florida International University *B, M*
Florida Southern College *B*
Florida State University *B, M, D*
Gulf Coast Community College *A*
Hobe Sound Bible College *B*
Manatee Community College *A*
Miami Dade College *A*
New College of Florida *B*
Palm Beach Atlantic University *B*
Pensacola Junior College *A*
Rollins College *B*
St. Thomas University *B*
Southeastern College of the
  Assemblies of God *B*
Stetson University *B*
University of Florida *B, M*
University of Miami *B*

University of South Florida *B, M*

Georgia
Agnes Scott College *B*
Berry College *B*
Brewton-Parker College *B*
Clark Atlanta University *B*
Emory University *B, D*
Georgia Military College *A*
Georgia State University *B*
LaGrange College *B*
Morehouse College *B*
Paine College *B*
Piedmont College *B*
Reinhardt College *B*
Shorter College *B*
Spelman College *B*
Toccoa Falls College *B*
University of Georgia *B, M*
Wesleyan College *B*
Young Harris College *A*

Hawaii
Chaminade University of Honolulu *B*
University of Hawaii
  Hilo *B*
  Manoa *B, M*

Idaho
Albertson College of Idaho *B*
Northwest Nazarene University *B*

Illinois
Augustana College *B*
Bradley University *B*
DePaul University *B*
Eureka College *B*
Greenville College *B*
Illinois College *B*
Illinois Wesleyan University *B*
Judson College *B*
Lewis University *B*
Lincoln Christian College and
  Seminary *C, A, B, M*
MacMurray College *B*
McKendree College *B*
Moody Bible Institute *C, A, B*
North Central College *B*
North Park University *B*
Northwestern University *B, M, D*
Olivet Nazarene University *B, M*
Principia College *B*
St. Xavier University *B*
Springfield College in Illinois *A*
Trinity International University *M*
University of Chicago *B*
University of Illinois
  Urbana-Champaign *B*
Wheaton College *B*

Indiana
Anderson University *B*
Ball State University *B*
Bethel College *B*
Butler University *B*
Calumet College of St. Joseph *C, A, B*
DePauw University *B*
Earlham College *B*
Franklin College *B*
Huntington University *B*
Indiana University
  Bloomington *B, M, D*
Indiana University-Purdue University
  Indianapolis *B*
Indiana Wesleyan University *C, A, B*
Manchester College *B*
Martin University *B*
Oakland City University *C, A, B*
Saint Mary's College *B*
St. Mary-of-the-Woods College *B*
University of Indianapolis *B*
University of St. Francis *B*
Wabash College *B*

Iowa
Ashford University *B*
Briar Cliff University *A, B*
Central College *B*
Clarke College *A, B*
Coe College *B*
Cornell College *B*
Dordt College *B*
Drake University *B*
Faith Baptist Bible College and
  Theological Seminary *M*
Graceland University *B, M*
Grand View College *B*
Grinnell College *B*
Iowa State University *B*
Iowa Wesleyan College *B*
Loras College *B*
Luther College *B*
Morningside College *B*
Mount Mercy College *B*
Northwestern College *B*
Simpson College *B*
University of Dubuque *B, M*
University of Iowa *B, M, D*
University of Northern Iowa *B*
Wartburg College *B*

Kansas
Baker University *B*
Barclay College *B*
Benedictine College *B*
Bethel College *B*
Central Christian College of
  Kansas *A, B*
Kansas Wesleyan University *B*
Manhattan Christian College *B*
MidAmerica Nazarene University *B, T*
Ottawa University *B*
Seward County Community College *A*
Tabor College *B*
University of Kansas *B, M*
Washburn University of Topeka *B*

Kentucky
Berea College *B*
Brescia University *A, B*
Campbellsville University *B*
Centre College *B*
Georgetown College *B*
Kentucky Christian University *B, M*
Kentucky Mountain Bible College *A*
Kentucky Wesleyan College *B*
Lindsey Wilson College *A*
Pikeville College *B*
Spalding University *C*
Thomas More College *C, A, B*
Transylvania University *B*
Union College *B*
Western Kentucky University *B*

Louisiana
Centenary College of Louisiana *B*
Loyola University New Orleans *B, M*

Maine
Bates College *B*
Bowdoin College *B*
Colby College *B*

Maryland
College of Notre Dame of Maryland *B*
Columbia Union College *B*
Goucher College *B*
Hood College *B*
Loyola College in Maryland *B*
McDaniel College *B*
St. Mary's College of Maryland *B*

Massachusetts
Amherst College *B*
Anna Maria College *B*
Atlantic Union College *B*
Boston University *B, M, D*

College of the Holy Cross *B*
Eastern Nazarene College *B*
Elms College *B, M*
Emmanuel College *B*
Hampshire College *B*
Harvard College *B, D*
Merrimack College *A, B*
Mount Holyoke College *B*
Smith College *B, M*
Stonehill College *B*
Tufts University *B*
Wellesley College *B*
Wheaton College *B*
Williams College *B*

Michigan
Adrian College *B, T*
Albion College *B*
Alma College *B*
Andrews University *B, M*
Aquinas College *B*
Calvin College *B, T*
Central Michigan University *B, T*
Concordia University *B*
Cornerstone University *B*
Hillsdale College *B*
Hope College *B*
Kalamazoo College *B*
Lansing Community College *A*
Madonna University *C, A, B*
Marygrove College *B*
Rochester College *B*
Siena Heights University *B*
Spring Arbor University *B*
University of Detroit Mercy *B, M*
University of Michigan *B*
Wayne County Community College *A*
Western Michigan University *B, M*

Minnesota
Augsburg College *B*
Carleton College *B*
College of St. Scholastica *B*
Concordia College: Moorhead *B*
Gustavus Adolphus College *B*
Hamline University *B*
Macalester College *B*
North Central University *A, B*
St. Olaf College *B*
University of Minnesota
  Twin Cities *B*
University of St. Thomas *B*

Mississippi
Belhaven College *C, B*
Millsaps College *B*
Mississippi College *B*
Tougaloo College *A*
Wesley College *B*

Missouri
Avila University *B*
Baptist Bible College *B*
Central Christian College of the
  Bible *B*
Central Methodist University *B*
College of the Ozarks *B*
Columbia College *B*
Culver-Stockton College *B*
Lindenwood University *B*
Missouri Baptist University *A, B*
Missouri State University *B, M*
Rockhurst University *B*
University of Missouri
  Columbia *B, M*
  Kansas City *D*
Washington University in St.
  Louis *B, M*
Webster University *B*
Westminster College *B*
William Jewell College *B*

Montana

University of Great Falls B

Nebraska

Creighton University A
Dana College B
Doane College B
Hastings College B
Midland Lutheran College B
Nebraska Wesleyan University B
Union College B
University of Nebraska
   Omaha B
York College B, T

New Hampshire

Dartmouth College B

New Jersey

Bloomfield College B
Drew University B
Felician College B
Georgian Court University B
Montclair State University B
Princeton University B, M, D
Rabbinical College of America B
Rowan University B
Rutgers, The State University of New
   Jersey
   New Brunswick/Piscataway
     Campus B
St. Peter's College B
Seton Hall University B, M
Thomas Edison State College B

New Mexico

College of Santa Fe B
Eastern New Mexico University B
University of New Mexico B

New York

Bard College B
Barnard College B
Canisius College B
City University of New York
   Brooklyn College B
   Hunter College B
   Queens College B
Colgate University B
College of Mount St. Vincent B
College of New Rochelle B
College of Saint Rose B
Columbia University
   Columbia College B
   School of General Studies B
Concordia College A, B
Cornell University B, M, D
Daemen College B
Elmira College B
Fordham University B, M, D
Hamilton College B
Hartwick College B
Hobart and William Smith Colleges B
Houghton College B
Iona College B
Le Moyne College B
Manhattan College B
Manhattanville College B
Nazareth College of Rochester B
New York University B, M, D, T
Niagara University B
Nyack College B
Roberts Wesleyan College B
St. Francis College B
St. John Fisher College B
St. Lawrence University B
St. Thomas Aquinas College B
Sarah Lawrence College B
Siena College B
Skidmore College B
State University of New York
   Albany B
   Stony Brook B

Syracuse University B, M, D
University of Rochester B
Vassar College B
Wells College B

North Carolina

Appalachian State University B
Belmont Abbey College B
Brevard College B
Campbell University B
Catawba College B
Chowan College B
Davidson College B
Duke University B, M, D
Elon University B
Gardner-Webb University B
Greensboro College B
Guilford College B
High Point University B
Lees-McRae College B
Lenoir-Rhyne College B
Mars Hill College B
Meredith College B
Methodist College A, B, T
Mount Olive College A, B
North Carolina State University B
North Carolina Wesleyan College B
Pfeiffer University B
Queens University of Charlotte B
Roanoke Bible College C, A, B
St. Andrews Presbyterian College B
St. Augustine's College B
Salem College B
Shaw University A, B
University of North Carolina
   Chapel Hill B, M, D
   Charlotte B, M
   Greensboro B
   Wilmington B
Wake Forest University B, M
Warren Wilson College B
Wingate University B

North Dakota

Jamestown College B
Trinity Bible College A, B
University of Mary B
University of North Dakota B

Ohio

Antioch College B
Ashland University B
Baldwin-Wallace College B
Bluffton University B
Capital University B
Case Western Reserve University B
Circleville Bible College A, B
Cleveland State University B
College of Mount St. Joseph B, M
College of Wooster B
Defiance College B
Denison University B
Heidelberg College B
Hiram College B
John Carroll University B, M, T
Kenyon College B
Lourdes College A, B
Miami University
   Oxford Campus B, M
Mount Union College B
Mount Vernon Nazarene
   University B, M
Muskingum College B
Oberlin College B
Ohio Northern University B
Ohio State University
   Columbus Campus B
Ohio Wesleyan University B
Otterbein College B
Pontifical College Josephinum B
University of Akron M
University of Dayton B
University of Findlay A, B
University of Toledo B

Walsh University B
Wittenberg University B
Wright State University B
Youngstown State University B

Oklahoma

Bacone College A
Mid-America Christian University B
Oklahoma Baptist University B
Oklahoma Christian University B
Oklahoma City University B, M
St. Gregory's University A, B
Southern Nazarene University B
Southwestern Christian
   University A, B
University of Oklahoma B
University of Tulsa B

Oregon

Concordia University B
Corban College A, B
Eugene Bible College B
George Fox University B
Lewis & Clark College B
Linfield College B
Marylhurst University B
Reed College B
University of Oregon B, M
Warner Pacific College A, B, M
Willamette University B

Pennsylvania

Albright College B
Allegheny College B
Bryn Athyn College of the New
   Church B, M
Bryn Mawr College B
Bucknell University B
Cabrini College B
Chestnut Hill College C
Dickinson College B
Elizabethtown College B
Franklin & Marshall College B
Gettysburg College B
Gratz College B, M
Grove City College B
Haverford College B
Holy Family University B
Indiana University of Pennsylvania B
Juniata College B
La Roche College B
La Salle University B, M
Lafayette College B
Lebanon Valley College B
Lehigh University B
Lincoln University B
Lycoming College B
Marywood University B
Mercyhurst College B
Messiah College B
Moravian College B
Muhlenberg College C, B
Neumann College B
Penn State
   Abington B
   Altoona B
   Beaver B
   Berks B
   Delaware County B
   Dubois B
   Fayette B
   Hazleton B
   Lehigh Valley B
   McKeesport B
   Mont Alto B
   New Kensington B
   Schuylkill - Capital College B
   Shenango B
   University Park B
   Wilkes-Barre B
   Worthington Scranton B
   York B
Rosemont College B

St. Charles Borromeo Seminary -
   Overbrook C
St. Francis University B
St. Joseph's University B
Seton Hill University C, B
Susquehanna University B
Swarthmore College B
Temple University B, M, D
Thiel College B
University of Pennsylvania B, M, D
University of Pittsburgh B, M, D
University of Scranton B, M
Villanova University B, M
Waynesburg College B
Westminster College B
Wilson College B

Puerto Rico

Bayamon Central University B
Inter American University of Puerto
   Rico
   Guayama Campus A, B
Pontifical Catholic University of
   Puerto Rico M
Universidad Adventista de las
   Antillas A

Rhode Island

Brown University B, M, D
Providence College M
Salve Regina University B

South Carolina

Allen University B
Anderson University B
Charleston Southern University B
Claflin University B
College of Charleston B
Columbia College B
Converse College B
Erskine College B
Furman University B
Presbyterian College B
Southern Wesleyan University B, M
University of South Carolina B, M
Winthrop University B
Wofford College B

South Dakota

Augustana College B
Mount Marty College B
Presentation College A
University of Sioux Falls B

Tennessee

Belmont University B, T
Carson-Newman College B
Christian Brothers University B
Hiwassee College A
King College B
Lambuth University B
Martin Methodist College B
Maryville College B
Rhodes College B
Southern Adventist University B, M
Tennessee Wesleyan College B
Trevecca Nazarene University B
University of Tennessee
   Knoxville B
University of the South B
Vanderbilt University B, M, D
Williamson Christian College B

Texas

Amarillo College A
Arlington Baptist College B
Austin College B
Baptist Missionary Association
   Theological Seminary A, B, M
Baylor University B, M, D
Clarendon College A
Concordia University at Austin B, T
Criswell College C, A, B, M

East Texas Baptist University *B*
Howard Payne University *B*
Jarvis Christian College *B*
Lon Morris College *A*
McMurry University *B*
Our Lady of the Lake University of San
Antonio *B*
Paul Quinn College *B*
Rice University *B, D*
Schreiner University *B*
Southern Methodist
University *B, M, D*
Southwestern Adventist University *B*
Southwestern University *B*
Texas Christian University *B*
Trinity University *B*
University of Mary Hardin-Baylor *B, M*
University of Texas
Austin *B*
University of the Incarnate Word *B, M*

Vermont
Burlington College *B*
Goddard College *B*
Marlboro College *B*
Middlebury College *B*
St. Michael's College *B*
University of Vermont *B*

Virginia
Averett University *B*
Bridgewater College *B*
Christendom College *M*
College of William and Mary *B*
Emory & Henry College *B*
Ferrum College *B*
Hampden-Sydney College *B*
Hollins University *B*
Liberty University *A, B, M, D*
Lynchburg College *B*
Marymount University *B*
Radford University *B*
Randolph-Macon College *B*
Randolph-Macon Woman's College *B*
Regent University *B, M, D*
Roanoke College *B, T*
St. Paul's College *B*
Shenandoah University *B*
Sweet Briar College *B*
University of Mary Washington *B*
University of Richmond *B*
University of Virginia *B, M, D*
Virginia Commonwealth University *B*
Virginia Intermont College *B*
Virginia Union University *B*
Virginia Wesleyan College *B*
Washington and Lee University *B*

Washington
Central Washington University *B*
Gonzaga University *B, M*
Pacific Lutheran University *B*
Saint Martin's University *B*
Seattle University *B*
University of Puget Sound *B*
University of Washington *B, M*
Walla Walla College *B*
Washington State University *B*
Whitman College *B*
Whitworth College *B*

West Virginia
Alderson-Broaddus College *B*
Bethany College *B*
Davis and Elkins College *B*
Ohio Valley University *B*
West Virginia Wesleyan College *B*

Wisconsin
Alverno College *B*
Cardinal Stritch University *B, M*
Carroll College *B*
Carthage College *B*

Concordia University Wisconsin *B*
Edgewood College *B, M*
Lakeland College *B*
Lawrence University *B, T*
Marquette University *B, M, D*
Mount Mary College *B, T*
Northland College *B*
Ripon College *B*
St. Norbert College *B, T*
Silver Lake College *B, T*
University of Wisconsin
Eau Claire *B*
Madison *B, M*
Milwaukee *B*
Oshkosh *B*
Viterbo University *B, T*

Renal/dialysis technology

Illinois
City Colleges of Chicago
Malcolm X College *A*

Reproductive biology

Texas
University of Texas
Health Science Center at
Houston *M, D*

West Virginia
West Virginia University *M, D*

Wisconsin
Marquette University *M, D*

Wyoming
University of Wyoming *M, D*

Resort management

Florida
Florida Gulf Coast University *B*

Minnesota
Central Lakes College *C*
University of Minnesota
Crookston *B*

Nevada
Sierra Nevada College *B*

New York
Globe Institute of Technology *C, A, B*
Paul Smith's College *B*
Rochester Institute of
Technology *A, B, M*
State University of New York
College of Agriculture and
Technology at Morrisville *B*

Oregon
Central Oregon Community
College *A*

Pennsylvania
Keystone College *A*
Newport Business Institute *A*

South Carolina
Coastal Carolina University *B*

Tennessee
University of Memphis *B*

Vermont
College of St. Joseph in Vermont *B*
Green Mountain College *C, B*

West Virginia
Concord University *B*

Wisconsin
Lakeland College *B*

Respiratory therapy

Alabama
Central Alabama Community
College *A*
Enterprise-Ozark Community
College *A*
Faulkner University *A*
George C. Wallace State Community
College
George C. Wallace Community
College at Dothan *A*
Shelton State Community College *A*
University of Alabama
Birmingham *B*
University of South Alabama *B*
Wallace State Community College at
Hanceville *A*

Arizona
Gateway Community College *A*
Long Technical College *A*
Pima Community College *A*

Arkansas
Northwest Arkansas Community
College *A*
Pulaski Technical College *A*
University of Arkansas
Community College at Hope *A*
Fort Smith *A*
for Medical Sciences *A*
University of Central Arkansas *B*

California
American River College *A*
Butte College *A*
Concorde Career College *A*
Crafton Hills College *A*
East Los Angeles College *A*
El Camino College *A*
Foothill College *A*
Fresno City College *A*
Grossmont Community College *A*
Los Angeles Southwest College *A*
Los Angeles Valley College *A*
Modesto Junior College *A*
Mount San Antonio College *A*
Napa Valley College *A*
Ohlone College *A*
Orange Coast College *A*
Rio Hondo College *A*
Skyline College *A*
Victor Valley College *A*

Colorado
Concorde Career College *A*
Front Range Community College *A*
Pueblo Community College *A*

Connecticut
Manchester Community College *A*
Naugatuck Valley Community
College *A*
Norwalk Community College *A*
Quinnipiac University *B*
University of Hartford *B*

Delaware
Delaware Technical and Community
College
Owens Campus *A*
Stanton/Wilmington Campus *A*

District of Columbia
University of the District of
Columbia *A*

Florida
Brevard Community College *A*
Broward Community College *A*
Daytona Beach Community College *A*
Edison College *A*
Florida Agricultural and Mechanical
University *B*
Florida Community College at
Jacksonville *A*
Gulf Coast Community College *A*
Hillsborough Community College *A*
Indian River Community College *A*
Manatee Community College *A*
Miami Dade College *A*
Palm Beach Community College *A*
Polk Community College *A*
St. Petersburg College *A*
Santa Fe Community College *A*
Seminole Community College *A*
Tallahassee Community College *A*
University of Central Florida *B*
Valencia Community College *A*

Georgia
Armstrong Atlantic State University *B*
Athens Technical College *A*
Augusta Technical Institute *A*
Darton College *A*
Georgia Highlands College *A*
Georgia State University *B, M*
Gwinnett Technical College *A*
Macon State College *A*
Medical College of Georgia *B*
Middle Georgia College *A*
Southwest Georgia Technical
College *A*

Hawaii
University of Hawaii
Kapiolani Community College *A*

Idaho
Boise State University *A, B*
College of Southern Idaho *A*

Illinois
City Colleges of Chicago
Malcolm X College *A*
College of DuPage *A*
Illinois Central College *A*
Kankakee Community College *A*
Kaskaskia College *A*
Moraine Valley Community
College *C, A*
National-Louis University *B*
Parkland College *A*
Rock Valley College *A*
St. Augustine College *A*
Southern Illinois University
Carbondale *A*
Southwestern Illinois College *A*
Triton College *A*

Indiana
Ball State University *A, B*
Indiana University
Bloomington *B*
Northwest *A*
Ivy Tech State College
Ivy Tech Community College:
Bloomington *A*
Ivy Tech Community College:
Central Indiana *A*
Ivy Tech Community College:
Lafayette *A*
Ivy Tech Community College:
Northeast *A*
Ivy Tech Community College:
Northwest *A*

Ivy Tech Community College: South
Central *A*
Ivy Tech Community College:
Wabash Valley *A*
University of Indianapolis *B*
University of Southern Indiana *A*

Iowa

Des Moines Area Community
College *A*
Hawkeye Community College *A*
Kirkwood Community College *A*
Northeast Iowa Community
College *A*
St. Luke's College *A*

Kansas

Johnson County Community
College *A*
Kansas City Kansas Community
College *A*
Labette Community College *A*
Newman University *A*
Seward County Community College *A*
University of Kansas Medical
Center *B*
Washburn University of Topeka *A*

Kentucky

Ashland Community and Technical
College *A*
Bellarmine University *B*
Bluegrass Community and Technical
College *A*
Jefferson Community College *A*
Madisonville Community College *A*
Morehead State University *A*
Northern Kentucky University *A*
Southeast Kentucky Community and
Technical College *A*

Louisiana

Bossier Parish Community College *A*
Delgado Community College *A*
Our Lady of Holy Cross College *A, B*
Our Lady of the Lake College *A*
Southern University
Shreveport *A*

Maine

Kennebec Valley Community
College *A*
Southern Maine Community
College *A*

Maryland

Allegany College of Maryland *A*
Baltimore City Community College *A*
Columbia Union College *A*
Community College of Baltimore
County *A*
Frederick Community College *A*
Prince George's Community
College *A*
Salisbury University *B*

Massachusetts

Berkshire Community College *A*
Massachusetts Bay Community
College *A*
Massasoit Community College *A*
North Shore Community College *A*
Northern Essex Community
College *A*
Quinsigamond Community College *A*
Springfield Technical Community
College *A*

Michigan

Delta College *A*
Ferris State University *A*
Henry Ford Community College *A*

Kalamazoo Valley Community
College *A*
Lansing Community College *A*
Macomb Community College *A*
Monroe County Community
College *A*
Mott Community College *A*
Muskegon Community College *A*
Oakland Community College *A*
Washtenaw Community College *A*
Wayne County Community College *A*

Minnesota

College of St. Catherine *B*
Lake Superior College *A*
Northland Community & Technical
College *A*
St. Paul College *A*

Mississippi

Coahoma Community College *A*
Copiah-Lincoln Community College *A*
Hinds Community College *A*
Itawamba Community College *A*
Meridian Community College *A*
Mississippi Gulf Coast Community
College
Jefferson Davis Campus *A*
Pearl River Community College *A*

Missouri

East Central College *A*
Hannibal-LaGrange College *A*
Jewish Hospital College of Nursing
and Allied Health *A*
Mineral Area College *A*
Missouri Southern State University *A*
Missouri State University *B*
Ozarks Technical Community
College *A*
Penn Valley Community College *A*
University of Missouri
Columbia *B*

Montana

Montana State University
College of Technology-Great Falls *A*
University of Montana: Missoula *A*

Nebraska

Metropolitan Community College *A*
Midland Lutheran College *A, B*
Nebraska Methodist College of
Nursing and Allied Health *A, B*
Southeast Community College
Lincoln Campus *A*
University of Nebraska
Kearney *B*

New Hampshire

New Hampshire Community
Technical College
Claremont *A*

New Jersey

Atlantic Cape Community College *A*
Bergen Community College *A*
Brookdale Community College *A*
Camden County College *A*
County College of Morris *A*
Essex County College *A*
Felician College *B*
Gloucester County College *A*
Hudson County Community
College *A*
Mercer County Community College *A*
Middlesex County College *A*
Passaic County Community College *A*
Sussex County Community College *A*
Thomas Edison State College *A, B*
Union County College *A*

University of Medicine and Dentistry
of New Jersey
School of Health Related
Professions *A, B*

New Mexico

Albuquerque Technical-Vocational
Institute *A*
Dona Ana Branch Community College
of New Mexico State
University *A*

New York

City University of New York
Borough of Manhattan Community
College *A*
Erie Community College
North Campus *A*
Genesee Community College *A*
Hudson Valley Community College *A*
Mohawk Valley Community College *A*
Molloy College *A*
Nassau Community College *A*
Onondaga Community College *A*
Rockland Community College *A*
State University of New York
Stony Brook *B*
Upstate Medical University *B*
Westchester Community College *A*

North Carolina

Carteret Community College *A*
Catawba Valley Community College *A*
Central Piedmont Community
College *A*
Durham Technical Community
College *A*
Edgecombe Community College *A*
Fayetteville Technical Community
College *A*
Forsyth Technical Community
College *A*
Pitt Community College *A*
Robeson Community College *A*
Rockingham Community College *A*
Sandhills Community College *A*
Southwestern Community College *A*
Stanly Community College *A*

North Dakota

North Dakota State University *B*
University of Mary *B*

Ohio

Bowling Green State University:
Firelands College *A*
Cincinnati State Technical and
Community College *A*
Columbus State Community
College *A*
Jefferson Community College *A*
Kettering College of Medical Arts *A, B*
Lakeland Community College *A*
Ohio State University
Columbus Campus *B, M*
Shawnee State University *A*
Sinclair Community College *A*
Stark State College of Technology *A*
University of Akron *A*
University of Akron: Wayne College *A*
University of Cincinnati
Clermont College *A*
University of Toledo *B*
Washington State Community
College *A*
Youngstown State University *B*

Oklahoma

Rose State College *A*
Tulsa Community College *A*

Oregon

Lane Community College *A*

Mount Hood Community College *A*

Pennsylvania

Community College of Allegheny
County *A*
Community College of Philadelphia *A*
Delaware County Community
College *A*
Gannon University *A, B*
Gwynedd-Mercy College *A, B*
Harrisburg Area Community
College *A*
Indiana University of Pennsylvania *B*
La Roche College *B*
Lehigh Carbon Community College *A*
Luzerne County Community
College *A*
Mansfield University of
Pennsylvania *A*
Reading Area Community College *A*
University of Pittsburgh
Johnstown *A*
Western School of Health and
Business Careers *A*
York College of Pennsylvania *A, B*

Puerto Rico

Universidad Adventista de las
Antillas *A, B*
Universidad Metropolitana *A, B*

Rhode Island

Community College of Rhode
Island *A*

South Carolina

Florence-Darlington Technical
College *A*
Greenville Technical College *A*
Midlands Technical College *A*
Piedmont Technical College *A*
Spartanburg Technical College *A*
Trident Technical College *A*

South Dakota

Dakota State University *A, B*

Tennessee

Chattanooga State Technical
Community College *A*
Columbia State Community College *A*
Jackson State Community College *A*
Roane State Community College *A*
Southern Adventist University *A*
Volunteer State Community College *A*

Texas

ATI Career Training Center *A*
Alvin Community College *A*
Amarillo College *A*
Angelina College *A*
Collin County Community College
District *A*
Del Mar College *A*
El Centro College *A*
El Paso Community College *A*
Houston Community College
System *A*
Howard College *A*
McLennan Community College *A*
Midland College *A*
Midwestern State University *B*
North Harris Montgomery
Community College District *A*
Odessa College *A*
St. Philip's College *A*
San Jacinto College
Central Campus *A*
South Plains College *A*
Tarrant County College *A*
Temple College *A*
Texas Southern University *B*
Texas Southmost College *A*

Texas State University: San Marcos *B*
Tyler Junior College *A*
University of Texas
    Brownsville *A*
    Health Science Center at San
        Antonio *B*
    Medical Branch at Galveston *B*
Victoria College *A*
Weatherford College *A*

Utah
Stevens-Henager College of
    Business *A*
Weber State University *A, B*

Virginia
J. Sargeant Reynolds Community
    College *A*
Jefferson College of Health
    Sciences *A*
Mountain Empire Community
    College *A*
Northern Virginia Community
    College *A*
Shenandoah University *A, B*
Southside Virginia Community
    College *A*
Tidewater Community College *A*

Washington
Highline Community College *A*
Seattle Central Community College *A*
Spokane Community College *A*

West Virginia
Mountain State University *A, B*
West Virginia Northern Community
    College *A*
West Virginia University Institute of
    Technology *A*
Wheeling Jesuit University *B*

Wisconsin
Madison Area Technical College *A*
Mid-State Technical College *A*
Milwaukee Area Technical College *A*
Northeast Wisconsin Technical
    College *A*
Western Wisconsin Technical
    College *A*

Wyoming
Casper College *A*

Respiratory therapy assistant

California
Foothill College *C, A*
Santa Rosa Junior College *C*

Connecticut
Goodwin College *A*

Georgia
Darton College *A*
Gordon College *A*

Indiana
Indiana University-Purdue University
    Indianapolis *B*

Kansas
Kansas City Kansas Community
    College *A*

Louisiana
Our Lady of the Lake College *A*

Maryland
Howard Community College *A*

Michigan
Baker College
    of Auburn Hills *A*
Delta College *A*

New Jersey
Cumberland County College *A*

New Mexico
Eastern New Mexico University:
    Roswell Campus *A*

North Carolina
Catawba Valley Community College *A*
Pitt Community College *A*
Southwestern Community College *A*

Ohio
James A. Rhodes State College *A*
Sinclair Community College *A*
Stark State College of Technology *A*

Oklahoma
Rose State College *A*

Pennsylvania
Point Park University *A*

Tennessee
Walters State Community College *A*

Texas
Del Mar College *A*

Virginia
Danville Community College *A*
Southwest Virginia Community
    College *A*

West Virginia
Mountain State University *B*

Wisconsin
Mid-State Technical College *A*

Restaurant/catering management

Alabama
Shelton State Community College *C*

Arkansas
North Arkansas College *C*

California
Art Institute
    of California: Orange County *A, B*
    of California: San Diego *A*
California Culinary Academy *A*
California School of Culinary Arts *C*
College of the Desert *C, A*
Diablo Valley College *C*
Grossmont Community College *C, A*
Long Beach City College *C, A*

Colorado
Arapahoe Community College *C*
Johnson & Wales University *A, B*

Florida
Central Florida Community
    College *C, A*
Hillsborough Community College *A*
Indian River Community College *A*
Johnson & Wales University *A, B*
New England Institute of
    Technology *C, A, B*
Orlando Culinary Academy *A*
Pensacola Junior College *C*
St. Petersburg College *C*

Valencia Community College *C, A*

Georgia
Coastal Georgia Community
    College *C*

Illinois
Black Hawk College *A*
College of DuPage *C, A*
College of Lake County *C, A*
John Wood Community College *A*
Kaskaskia College *C*
Lincoln Land Community College *C*
Moraine Valley Community
    College *C, A*
Parkland College *C, A*
Richland Community College *C*
William Rainey Harper College *C, A*

Indiana
Vincennes University *A*

Maryland
Anne Arundel Community
    College *C, A*
Baltimore International College *A, B*

Massachusetts
Massasoit Community College *C*
Newbury College *C, A, B*

Michigan
Baker College
    of Muskegon *B*
Ferris State University *C*
Grand Rapids Community College *A*
Kirtland Community College *C*
Washtenaw Community College *C*

Minnesota
Art Institutes International
    Minnesota *B*
Hennepin Technical College *C, A*
South Central College *A*
University of Minnesota
    Crookston *B*

Missouri
Jefferson College *C, A*

New Hampshire
New Hampshire Community
    Technical College
    Berlin *C, A*
Southern New Hampshire
    University *A*
University of New Hampshire *A, B*

New Jersey
Bergen Community College *C*
Hudson County Community
    College *C*

New York
Art Institute
    of New York City *C*
Erie Community College
    North Campus *A*
Fulton-Montgomery Community
    College *A*
Mohawk Valley Community College *A*
Monroe College *A*
Nassau Community College *A*
Paul Smith's College *A, B*
Rochester Institute of
    Technology *A, B, M*
Schenectady County Community
    College *A*
State University of New York
    College of Agriculture and
        Technology at Cobleskill *A*

Tompkins-Cortland Community
    College *A*
Westchester Community College *A*

North Carolina
Art Institute
    of Charlotte *B*
Carteret Community College *A*

North Dakota
North Dakota State College of
    Science *A*

Ohio
Cincinnati State Technical and
    Community College *A*
Ohio State University
    Agricultural Technical Institute *A*

Oregon
Linn-Benton Community College *A*

Pennsylvania
Art Institute
    of Pittsburgh *B*
Bucks County Community
    College *C, A*
Community College of Allegheny
    County *C, A*
Harrisburg Area Community
    College *C*
Keystone College *A*

Puerto Rico
Universidad del Este *B*

Rhode Island
Johnson & Wales University *A, B*

Texas
Del Mar College *C, A*
St. Philip's College *C, A*
South Texas College *A*

Vermont
Champlain College *A, B*

Virginia
Virginia Intermont College *B*

Washington
Clover Park Technical College *C*
South Seattle Community
    College *C, A*

West Virginia
Concord University *B*

Wisconsin
Gateway Technical College *A*
Milwaukee Area Technical College *A*
Western Wisconsin Technical
    College *A*

Restaurant/food services management

Alabama
University of Alabama *B*

Arizona
South Mountain Community
    College *C*

California
College of the Desert *C, A*
Diablo Valley College *C*
Long Beach City College *C, A*
University of San Francisco *B*

Florida
Central Florida Community
College *C, A*
St. Petersburg College *C*
University of Central Florida *B*

Georgia
Gwinnett Technical College *C, A*

Illinois
Lexington College *A, B*

Indiana
Vincennes University *A*

Massachusetts
Holyoke Community College *A*
Lasell College *B*

Michigan
Baker College
of Muskegon *A, B*
Ferris State University *A*
Oakland Community College *A*

Minnesota
South Central College *A*
University of Minnesota
Crookston *A, B*

Missouri
College of the Ozarks *B*
University of Missouri
Columbia *B, M*

New Hampshire
New Hampshire Community
Technical College
Berlin *C, A*
University of New Hampshire *A*

New Jersey
Burlington County College *C, A*
Union County College *A*

New Mexico
Santa Fe Community College *A*

New York
Cornell University *B, M, D*
Culinary Institute of America *B*
Globe Institute of Technology *C, A, B*
New York Institute of Technology *B*
Niagara University *B*
Paul Smith's College *B*
Rochester Institute of
Technology *A, B, M*
State University of New York
College at Plattsburgh *B*
College of Agriculture and
Technology at Morrisville *A*

North Carolina
Cape Fear Community College *C, A*
Johnson & Wales University *A, B*
Sandhills Community College *A*
Southwestern Community College *C*

North Dakota
North Dakota State College of
Science *A*

Ohio
Cincinnati State Technical and
Community College *A*
Ohio State University
Agricultural Technical Institute *A*
Owens Community College
Toledo *C, A*

Pennsylvania
Bucks County Community
College *C, A*
Harrisburg Area Community
College *A*
Keystone College *A*
Lehigh Carbon Community College *A*
Northampton County Area
Community College *A*
Penn State
Worthington Scranton *B*

South Carolina
Spartanburg Technical College *A*
Trident Technical College *A*

Texas
Del Mar College *C, A*

Utah
Salt Lake Community College *A*

Vermont
Champlain College *A, B*

Washington
South Seattle Community
College *C, A*

West Virginia
Concord University *B*

Wisconsin
Fox Valley Technical College *A*
Viterbo University *B*

Retailing

Arizona
Eastern Arizona College *C*
Scottsdale Community College *C, A*

Georgia
Gwinnett Technical College *C*

Illinois
Kaskaskia College *C*
McHenry County College *C*
Moraine Valley Community College *A*
Waubonsee Community College *C, A*

Indiana
Purdue University
Calumet *B*

Iowa
Des Moines Area Community
College *C*

Kansas
Coffeyville Community College *A*
Hutchinson Community College *C, A*

Maryland
Howard Community College *C, A*

Massachusetts
Holyoke Community College *C, A*

Michigan
Kirtland Community College *C*

Minnesota
Ridgewater College *A*
Rochester Community and Technical
College *C, A*

Missouri
Lindenwood University *B*

Patricia Stevens College *A*

Nebraska
Northeast Community College *A*

New Jersey
Thomas Edison State College *A, B*

New York
Genesee Community College *A*
Niagara County Community
College *A*
Syracuse University *B*
Tompkins-Cortland Community
College *A*
Utica School of Commerce *A*

North Carolina
Central Piedmont Community
College *C, A*

Ohio
Sinclair Community College *A*
University of Akron *M*
Youngstown State University *B*

Oregon
Central Oregon Community
College *C*
Rogue Community College *C*

Pennsylvania
Bucks County Community College *A*
Erie Business Center *C*
Harrisburg Area Community
College *A*
Montgomery County Community
College *C*
Newport Business Institute *A*
University of Pittsburgh
Titusville *C*

Rhode Island
Community College of Rhode
Island *C, A*

South Carolina
University of South Carolina *B*

Utah
Dixie State College of Utah *C, A*

Washington
Clark College *A*
Walla Walla Community College *C, A*

Wisconsin
Wisconsin Indianhead Technical
College *A*

Wyoming
Casper College *C, A*

Robotics technology

California
Cerritos Community College *A*
Long Beach City College *C*
Orange Coast College *C*
University of California
San Diego *M, D*

Colorado
Pikes Peak Community College *A*
Red Rocks Community College *C*

Illinois
Black Hawk College *A*
College of DuPage *C, A*
Illinois Central College *C, A*

Oakton Community College *A*
Waubonsee Community College *C, A*
William Rainey Harper College *C*

Indiana
Ball State University *A*
Indiana State University *B*
Indiana University-Purdue University
Fort Wayne *C*
Indiana University-Purdue University
Indianapolis *A, B*
Ivy Tech State College
Ivy Tech Community College:
Columbus *A*
Ivy Tech Community College: East
Central *A*
Ivy Tech Community College:
Lafayette *A*
Ivy Tech Community College: North
Central *A*
Ivy Tech Community College:
Northeast *A*
Ivy Tech Community College: South
Central *A*
Ivy Tech Community College:
Southeast *A*
Ivy Tech Community College:
Southwest *A*
Ivy Tech Community College:
Wabash Valley *A*
Ivy Tech Community College:
Whitewater *A*
Purdue University *A, B*
Purdue University
North Central Campus *A*
Vincennes University *A*

Iowa
Indian Hills Community College *A*
Southeastern Community College
North Campus *A*

Kentucky
Louisville Technical Institute *A*

Maine
Central Maine Community College *C*

Maryland
Cecil Community College *C*

Massachusetts
Springfield Technical Community
College *C*

Michigan
Oakland Community College *C, A*

Minnesota
Central Lakes College *C, A*
Dunwoody College of Technology *A*
Mesabi Range Community and
Technical College *C, A*

New Hampshire
New Hampshire Community
Technical College
Nashua *A*

New York
State University of New York
College of Technology at Alfred *A*

North Carolina
Central Carolina Community
College *A*
Forsyth Technical Community
College *A*
Wake Technical Community
College *A*

Ohio
James A. Rhodes State College *C*
Jefferson Community College *A*
Sinclair Community College *A*

Pennsylvania
Community College of Allegheny
  County *A*
Delaware County Community
  College *C, A*

Puerto Rico
University of Puerto Rico
  Carolina Regional College *A*

Rhode Island
Johnson & Wales University *A*

South Carolina
Trident Technical College *A*

Texas
Hill College *A*
Texas State Technical College
  West Texas *A*

Washington
Spokane Community College *A*

Wisconsin
Blackhawk Technical College *A*
Chippewa Valley Technical College *A*
Gateway Technical College *A*

Romance languages

Alabama
University of Alabama *M, D*

California
Point Loma Nazarene University *B*
University of California
  Berkeley *D*

Connecticut
Wesleyan University *B*

District of Columbia
George Washington University *B*

Georgia
Kennesaw State University *B*
University of Georgia *B, M, D*

Indiana
DePauw University *B*
University of Notre Dame *B, M*

Louisiana
University of New Orleans *M*

Maine
Bowdoin College *B*

Maryland
University of Maryland
  College Park *B*

Massachusetts
Boston College *M*
Harvard College *B, M, D*
Merrimack College *B*
Mount Holyoke College *B*

Michigan
Eastern Michigan University *B*

Minnesota
Carleton College *B*

Missouri
University of Missouri
  Columbia *D*

New York
Bard College *B*
City University of New York
  Hunter College *B*
Cornell University *B, M, D*
Manhattanville College *B*
State University of New York
  Stony Brook *M*

North Carolina
Appalachian State University *M*

Oregon
University of Oregon *B, M, D*

Tennessee
University of Memphis *M*

Wisconsin
University of Wisconsin
  Madison *B, M, D*

Roofing

Indiana
Ivy Tech State College
  Ivy Tech Community College: North
  Central *A*

Washington
Clover Park Technical College *C*

Wisconsin
Milwaukee Area Technical College *C*

Russian

Alabama
University of Alabama *B*

Alaska
University of Alaska
  Anchorage *B*
  Fairbanks *B, M*

Arizona
Arizona State University *B*
University of Arizona *B, M*

Arkansas
Ouachita Baptist University *B*

California
Claremont McKenna College *B*
Grossmont Community College *A*
Pitzer College *B*
Pomona College *B*
San Diego State University *B*
San Francisco State University *B, M*
Scripps College *B*
Stanford University *M*
University of California
  Davis *B*
  Irvine *B*
  Los Angeles *B*
  Riverside *B*
  San Diego *B*
  Santa Barbara *B*
  Santa Cruz *B*
University of Southern California *B*

Colorado
University of Denver *B*

Connecticut
Fairfield University *B*

Trinity College *B*
Wesleyan University *B*
Yale University *B*

Delaware
University of Delaware *B, T*

District of Columbia
American University *B*
George Washington University *B*
Georgetown University *B*
Howard University *B*

Florida
Florida State University *B*
New College of Florida *B*
University of Florida *A*
University of South Florida *B*

Georgia
Emory University *B*
University of Georgia *B*

Hawaii
University of Hawaii
  Manoa *B, M*

Idaho
Idaho State University *A*

Illinois
Northern Illinois University *B*
Southern Illinois University
  Carbondale *B*
University of Chicago *B, D*
University of Illinois
  Chicago *B*
  Urbana-Champaign *B, T*

Indiana
University of Notre Dame *B*

Iowa
Cornell College *B, T*
Grinnell College *B*
Iowa State University *B*
University of Iowa *B, T*
University of Northern Iowa *B*

Kentucky
University of Kentucky *B*

Louisiana
Loyola University New Orleans *B*
Tulane University *B*

Maine
Bates College *B*
Bowdoin College *B*
Colby College *B*

Maryland
Goucher College *B*
University of Maryland
  College Park *B*

Massachusetts
Amherst College *B*
Boston College *B, M*
Boston University *B*
Brandeis University *B*
College of the Holy Cross *B*
Harvard College *B*
Northeastern University *B*
Smith College *B*
Tufts University *B*
University of Massachusetts
  Boston *B*
Wellesley College *B*
Wheaton College *B*
Williams College *B*

Michigan
Albion College *T*
Michigan State University *B, M*
University of Michigan *B*
Wayne State University *B*

Minnesota
Carleton College *B*
Concordia College: Moorhead *B, T*
Gustavus Adolphus College *B*
Macalester College *B*
St. Olaf College *B*
University of Minnesota
  Twin Cities *B*
University of St. Thomas *B*

Missouri
St. Louis University *B*
Truman State University *B*
University of Missouri
  Columbia *B, M*

Montana
University of Montana: Missoula *B*

Nebraska
University of Nebraska
  Lincoln *B*

New Hampshire
Dartmouth College *B*
University of New Hampshire *B*

New Jersey
Montclair State University *T*
Rider University *B*
Rutgers, The State University of New
  Jersey
  New Brunswick/Piscataway
  Campus *B, T*
Seton Hall University *T*

New Mexico
University of New Mexico *B*

New York
Bard College *B*
Barnard College *B*
City University of New York
  Brooklyn College *B*
  Hunter College *B*
  Lehman College *B*
  Queens College *B*
Colgate University *B*
Columbia University
  Columbia College *B*
  School of General Studies *B*
Cornell University *B*
Fordham University *B, M*
Hamilton College *B*
Hobart and William Smith Colleges *B*
Hofstra University *B*
New York University *B, M*
Sarah Lawrence College *B*
State University of New York
  Albany *B, M*
  Stony Brook *B*
Syracuse University *B*
United States Military Academy *B*
University of Rochester *B*
Vassar College *B*

North Carolina
Duke University *B, M*
Wake Forest University *B*

Ohio
Bowling Green State University *B*
Kent State University *B*
Miami University
  Oxford Campus *B, T*
Oberlin College *B*

Ohio State University
Columbus Campus *B*
Ohio University *B*

Oklahoma

Oklahoma State University *B*
Tulsa Community College *A*
University of Oklahoma *B*

Oregon

Portland State University *B, T*
Reed College *B*

Pennsylvania

Bryn Mawr College *B, M, D*
Bucknell University *B*
California University of
Pennsylvania *B*
Dickinson College *B*
Haverford College *B, T*
Juniata College *B*
Kutztown University of
Pennsylvania *B, M, T*
Lafayette College *B*
Penn State
Abington *B*
Altoona *B*
Beaver *B*
Berks *B*
Delaware County *B*
Dubois *B*
Fayette *B*
Hazleton *B*
Lehigh Valley *B*
McKeesport *B*
Mont Alto *B*
New Kensington *B*
Schuylkill - Capital College *B*
Shenango *B*
University Park *B, M*
Wilkes-Barre *B*
Worthington Scranton *B*
York *B*
Swarthmore College *B*
Temple University *B*
University of Pennsylvania *B, D*
University of Pittsburgh *B*
West Chester University of
Pennsylvania *B*

South Carolina

University of South Carolina *B*

Tennessee

Rhodes College *B*
University of Tennessee
Knoxville *B*
University of the South *B*
Vanderbilt University *B*

Texas

Austin Community College *A*
Baylor University *B*
Southern Methodist University *B*
Texas A&M University *B*
Trinity University *B*
University of Texas
Arlington *B*
Austin *B*

Utah

Brigham Young University *B, M*
University of Utah *B, M*

Vermont

Middlebury College *B, M, D*
Norwich University *M*
University of Vermont *B*

Virginia

Ferrum College *B*

Washington

Central Washington University *B*
Everett Community College *A*
Seattle Pacific University *B*
University of Washington *B, M, D*
Washington State University *B*

West Virginia

West Virginia University *T*

Wisconsin

Beloit College *B, T*
Lawrence University *B, T*
University of Wisconsin
Madison *B*
Milwaukee *B*

Wyoming

University of Wyoming *B*

Russian/Slavic studies

Alaska

University of Alaska
Fairbanks *B*

California

San Diego State University *B*
Stanford University *M*
University of California
Los Angeles *B*
Riverside *B*
San Diego *B*
Santa Cruz *B*

Colorado

Colorado College *B*
University of Colorado
Boulder *B*

Connecticut

Trinity College *B*
Wesleyan University *B*
Yale University *B, M*

District of Columbia

American University *B*
Georgetown University *M*

Florida

Florida State University *B, M*
Stetson University *B*

Georgia

Emory University *B*

Illinois

Illinois Wesleyan University *B*
University of Chicago *B, D*
University of Illinois
Urbana-Champaign *B, M*

Indiana

DePauw University *B*
Indiana University
Bloomington *M*

Iowa

Grinnell College *B*
Iowa State University *B*
University of Iowa *B*
University of Northern Iowa *B*

Kansas

University of Kansas *B, M*

Louisiana

Tulane University *B*

Maine

Colby College *B*
University of Southern Maine *B*

Maryland

University of Maryland
College Park *B*

Massachusetts

Boston College *M*
Boston University *B*
College of the Holy Cross *B*
Harvard University *B*
Mount Holyoke College *B*
Tufts University *B*
University of Massachusetts
Amherst *B*
Wellesley College *B*
Wheaton College *B*

Michigan

Grand Valley State University *B*
University of Michigan *B, M*
Western Michigan University *B*

Minnesota

Carleton College *B*
Concordia College: Moorhead *B*
Gustavus Adolphus College *B*
Macalester College *B*
St. Olaf College *B*
University of Minnesota
Twin Cities *B, M*
University of St. Thomas *B*

Missouri

University of Missouri
Columbia *B*
Washington University in St. Louis *B*

New Hampshire

Dartmouth College *B*

New Jersey

Rutgers, The State University of New
Jersey
New Brunswick/Piscataway
Campus *B*

New Mexico

University of New Mexico *B*

New York

Bard College *B*
Barnard College *B*
City University of New York
Hunter College *M*
Colgate University *B*
Columbia University
Columbia College *B*
School of General Studies *B*
Cornell University *B, M, D*
Fordham University *B*
Hamilton College *B*
Hobart and William Smith Colleges *B*
New York University *M, D*
Sarah Lawrence College *B*
State University of New York
Albany *B, M*
Syracuse University *B*
United States Military Academy *B*
University of Rochester *B*

North Carolina

University of North Carolina
Chapel Hill *B, M*

Ohio

College of Wooster *B*
Kent State University *B*
Mount Vernon Nazarene University *B*

Oberlin College *B*
Ohio State University
Columbus Campus *B, M*
Wittenberg University *B*

Oregon

University of Oregon *B, M*

Pennsylvania

Carnegie Mellon University *B*
Dickinson College *B*
La Salle University *B*
Lehigh University *B*
Muhlenberg College *B*

Tennessee

Rhodes College *B*
University of Tennessee
Knoxville *B*
University of the South *B*

Texas

Southern Methodist University *B*
Texas State University: San Marcos *B*
Texas Tech University *B*
University of Houston *B*
University of Texas
Austin *B, M*

Vermont

Marlboro College *B*
Middlebury College *B*
University of Vermont *B*

Virginia

College of William and Mary *B*
George Mason University *B*
Randolph-Macon Woman's College *B*
Washington and Lee University *B*

Washington

University of Washington *B, M*

Wisconsin

Lawrence University *B*

Sacred music

Alabama

Birmingham-Southern College *B*
Samford University *B, M*
Southeastern Bible College *A, B*

Arizona

Grand Canyon University *B*
Southwestern College *C, A, B*

Arkansas

Central Baptist College *B*
John Brown University *B*
Ouachita Baptist University *B*
Williams Baptist College *B*

California

Azusa Pacific University *B*
Bethesda Christian University *B*
California Baptist University *C*
Hope International University *B, M*
Master's College *B*
Mount St. Mary's College *B*
Patten University *B*
Point Loma Nazarene University *B*
Santa Clara University *M*
University of Southern
California *M, D*
William Jessup University *B*

Colorado

Nazarene Bible College *A, B*

Connecticut

Holy Apostles College and
Seminary *M*

District of Columbia

Catholic University of America *M, D*

Florida

Baptist College of Florida *A, B*
Clearwater Christian College *B*
Florida Christian College *B*
Florida Southern College *B*
Hobe Sound Bible College *C, B*
Jacksonville University *B*
Palm Beach Atlantic University *B*
Southeastern College of the
Assemblies of God *B*
Warner Southern College *B*

Georgia

Andrew College *C*
Emmanuel College *B*
Emory University *M*
Shorter College *B*
Toccoa Falls College *B*

Idaho

Boise Bible College *A, B*
Northwest Nazarene University *B*

Illinois

Concordia University *B, M*
Judson College *B*
Lincoln Christian College and
Seminary *B*
Moody Bible Institute *B*
Northwestern University *M, D*
Olivet Nazarene University *B*
Trinity International University *B*

Indiana

Anderson University *B*
Bethel College *B*
Huntington University *B*
Indiana Wesleyan University *A, B*
Manchester College *B*
Oakland City University *B*
St. Joseph's College *C, B, M*

Iowa

Dordt College *B*
Faith Baptist Bible College and
Theological Seminary *B*
Vennard College *A*
Wartburg College *B*

Kansas

Barclay College *B*
Central Christian College of
Kansas *A, B*
Manhattan Christian College *A*
MidAmerica Nazarene University *A, B*

Kentucky

Campbellsville University *B, M*
Kentucky Christian University *B*
Kentucky Mountain Bible College *B*

Louisiana

Centenary College of Louisiana *B*

Maryland

Washington Bible College *B*

Massachusetts

Boston University *D*
Eastern Nazarene College *B*
Hebrew College *C*

Michigan

Andrews University *B*
Aquinas College *B*
Calvin College *B*
Concordia University *B*
Grace Bible College *B*
Great Lakes Christian College *B*
Marygrove College *C*

Minnesota

Bethany Lutheran College *B*
Bethel University *B*
College of St. Catherine *C*
Concordia University: St. Paul *B*
Crossroads College *B*
Gustavus Adolphus College *B*
North Central University *C, B*
Oak Hills Christian College *B*
St. John's University *M*
St. Olaf College *B*

Mississippi

Belhaven College *B*
Magnolia Bible College *B*
Mississippi College *B*
William Carey College *B*

Missouri

Baptist Bible College *B*
Calvary Bible College and Theological
Seminary *B*
Central Bible College *A, B*
Central Christian College of the
Bible *B*
Evangel University *B*
Hannibal-LaGrange College *B*
Lincoln University *B*
Missouri Baptist University *B*
Ozark Christian College *C, B*
St. Louis Christian College *B*
Southwest Baptist University *B*
William Jewell College *B*

Nebraska

Concordia University *B*
Grace University *B*
Nebraska Christian College *A, B*

New Jersey

Seton Hall University *B*
Westminster Choir College of Rider
University *B, M*

New York

Concordia College *B*
Holy Trinity Orthodox Seminary *C*
Jewish Theological Seminary of
America *B, M, D*
Nyack College *B*

North Carolina

Campbell University *B, T*
East Carolina University *B*
Lenoir-Rhyne College *B*
Pfeiffer University *B*

Ohio

Ashland University *M*
Cedarville University *B*
Cincinnati Christian University *B*
Circleville Bible College *A, B*
God's Bible School and College *B*
Malone College *B*
Mount Vernon Nazarene
University *A, B*

Oklahoma

Mid-America Christian University *B*
Oklahoma Baptist University *B*
Oklahoma City University *B*
Oklahoma Wesleyan University *B*
Oral Roberts University *B, M*
Southern Nazarene University *B*
Southwestern Christian University *B*

Southwestern Oklahoma State
University *B*

Oregon

Corban College *B*
Eugene Bible College *B*
Multnomah Bible College *B*

Pennsylvania

Baptist Bible College of
Pennsylvania *B*
Duquesne University *M*
Gratz College *B*
Immaculata University *C, A*
Marywood University *B, M*
Moravian College *B*
Philadelphia Biblical University *B*
St. Charles Borromeo Seminary -
Overbrook *C*
Seton Hill University *C, B*
Susquehanna University *B*
Valley Forge Christian College *B*

South Carolina

Anderson University *B*
Charleston Southern University *B*
Columbia International University *B*
Erskine College *M*
Newberry College *B*
North Greenville College *B*

South Dakota

Dakota Wesleyan University *B*

Tennessee

Belmont University *B*
Carson-Newman College *B*
Johnson Bible College *B*
Lambuth University *B*
Lee University *B, M*
Tennessee Temple University *B*
Trevecca Nazarene University *B*
Union University *B*

Texas

Arlington Baptist College *B*
Baylor University *B, M*
Concordia University at Austin *B*
Dallas Baptist University *B, M*
Dallas Christian College *B*
East Texas Baptist University *B*
Hardin-Simmons University *B, M*
Houston Baptist University *B*
Howard Payne University *B*
Lubbock Christian University *B*
McMurry University *B*
St. Mary's University *M*
Southern Methodist University *M*
Southwestern Assemblies of God
University *A, B*
Southwestern Baptist Theological
Seminary: Theological
Professions *M*
Southwestern University *B*
University of Mary Hardin-Baylor *B*
Wayland Baptist University *B*

Virginia

Bluefield College *B*
Liberty University *B*

Washington

Northwest University *B*
Puget Sound Christian College *B*
Trinity Lutheran College *B*

Wisconsin

Concordia University Wisconsin *B*
Maranatha Baptist Bible College *B*

Sales/distribution

Alabama

Gadsden State Community College *A*
Wallace State Community College at
Hanceville *A*

Arkansas

Harding University *B*

California

Chabot College *A*
Chaffey College *C, A*
Citrus College *C*
College of the Sequoias *C, A*
Columbia College *C*
Diablo Valley College *C*
El Camino College *C, A*
Fashion Institute of Design and
Merchandising *A*
Golden West College *C, A*
Grossmont Community College *C, A*
Laney College *C, A*
Las Positas College *A*
Long Beach City College *C, A*
Pasadena City College *A*
Santa Barbara City College *C, A*
Shasta College *A*
Sierra College *C, A*
Skyline College *C*

Colorado

Community College of Aurora *C, A*
Community College of Denver *C*
Front Range Community College *C*

Connecticut

Gateway Community College *A*
Middlesex Community College *C*

Delaware

Wesley College *B*

Florida

Florida Community College at
Jacksonville *A*
Indian River Community College *A*
Palm Beach Community College *A*
Tallahassee Community College *A*

Georgia

Albany Technical College *C, A*
Athens Technical College *C, A*
Augusta Technical Institute *C, A*
Clayton State University *C, A*
Middle Georgia College *A*
Savannah Technical College *A*

Hawaii

University of Hawaii
Kapiolani Community College *C, A*

Idaho

College of Southern Idaho *C*

Illinois

City Colleges of Chicago
Wright College *C, A*
College of DuPage *C, A*
Elgin Community College *C, A*
Illinois Eastern Community Colleges
Wabash Valley College *C*
John Wood Community College *C, A*
Joliet Junior College *C*
Kishwaukee College *C*
Southwestern Illinois College *A*
Triton College *C*
University of Illinois
Urbana-Champaign *B*
William Rainey Harper College *C, A*

Indiana

International Business College *C, A*
Vincennes University *A*

Iowa

Des Moines Area Community
College *A*
Iowa Lakes Community College *C, A*
Iowa Western Community College *A*
Kirkwood Community College *C, A*
Muscatine Community College *C*

Kansas

Allen County Community College *A*
Johnson County Community
College *A*
Seward County Community
College *C, A*

Kentucky

Henderson Community College *C*
Madisonville Community College *A*

Maine

Beal College *A*
Husson College *B*

Maryland

Harford Community College *C, A*
Howard Community College *C, A*
Montgomery College *A*

Massachusetts

Babson College *B*
Bay State College *A*
Middlesex Community College *A*
Mount Ida College *B*
Newbury College *A*
Simmons College *B*

Michigan

Bay de Noc Community College *C, A*
Lake Michigan College *A*
Lansing Community College *A*

Minnesota

Academy College *A*
College of St. Catherine *B*
Metropolitan State University *B*
Minnesota State College - Southeast
Technical *C, A*
Minnesota State Community and
Technical College - Fergus
Falls *C, A*
North Hennepin Community
College *A*
Northwest Technical College *C, A*
Rasmussen College
Mankato *A*
Ridgewater College *C, A*
St. Cloud Technical College *C, A*
University of Minnesota
Twin Cities *B*

Mississippi

Hinds Community College *C, A*

Missouri

Lindenwood University *M*
Longview Community College *A*
Maple Woods Community College *A*
Penn Valley Community College *A*

Montana

University of Montana: Missoula *C*

Nevada

Community College of Southern
Nevada *A*

New Hampshire

McIntosh College *A*
Southern New Hampshire
University *A, B*

New Jersey

Bergen Community College *A*
Burlington County College *C, A*
Camden County College *A*
Cumberland County College *C*
Fairleigh Dickinson University
College at Florham *B, M*
Metropolitan Campus *B, M*
Gloucester County College *C, A*
Mercer County Community College *C*
Ocean County College *C*
Passaic County Community College *A*
Raritan Valley Community College *C*

New Mexico

Clovis Community College *A*

New York

Bryant & Stratton Business Institute
Bryant & Stratton College:
Syracuse *A*
City University of New York
Baruch College *B, M*
Dutchess Community College *A*
Finger Lakes Community College *C, A*
Jefferson Community College *C, A*
Keuka College *B*
Long Island University
Brooklyn Campus *B*
Mercy College *M*
Monroe Community College *C, A*
Nassau Community College *A*
New York Institute of Technology *C*
Onondaga Community College *A*
Orange County Community College *A*
Suffolk County Community College *A*
Sullivan County Community
College *A*
Trocaire College *A*
Utica School of Commerce *A*
Westchester Community College *A*

North Carolina

Alamance Community College *C, A*
Asheville-Buncombe Technical
Community College *A*
Blue Ridge Community College *A*
Craven Community College *A*
Pitt Community College *C, A*
Wake Technical Community
College *C*
Wayne Community College *A*
Western Piedmont Community
College *C, A*

North Dakota

Bismarck State College *C, A*
Lake Region State College *C, A*

Ohio

Bryant & Stratton College
Parma *A*
Cincinnati State Technical and
Community College *C*
Columbus State Community
College *C, A*
Edison State Community College *C, A*
Miami University
Oxford Campus *B*
Owens Community College
Toledo *C*
Sinclair Community College *A*
Stark State College of Technology *A*
University of Cincinnati
Raymond Walters College *C, A*
University of Northwestern Ohio *C*
Wilmington College *B*
Youngstown State University *A, B, M*

Zane State College *A*

Oklahoma

East Central University *B*

Oregon

Clackamas Community College *C, A*
Lane Community College *C*
Pioneer Pacific College *A*
Pioneer Pacific College: Springfield *A*
Southwestern Oregon Community
College *C, A*
Umpqua Community College *C*

Pennsylvania

Commonwealth Technical Institute *C*
Community College of
Philadelphia *C, A*
Delaware County Community
College *A*
Harcum College *A*
Harrisburg Area Community
College *C, A*
Lehigh University *M*
Luzerne County Community
College *C*
Marywood University *C*
Montgomery County Community
College *C, A*
Pittsburgh Technical Institute *A*
Seton Hill University *B*
University of Pennsylvania *B, M*
West Chester University of
Pennsylvania *B*
Westmoreland County Community
College *A*

Puerto Rico

Inter American University of Puerto
Rico
San German Campus *A*
University of Puerto Rico
Mayaguez *B*

South Carolina

Aiken Technical College *C, A*
Florence-Darlington Technical
College *C, A*
Greenville Technical College *C, A*
Midlands Technical College *C*

Tennessee

Middle Tennessee State University *B*
University of Memphis *B*

Texas

Baylor University *B*
Collin County Community College
District *C, A*
Lamar University *B*
Laredo Community College *A*
Tarrant County College *C, A*
Texas Southmost College *C, A*
University of Houston *B*
University of Texas
San Antonio *B*
Tyler *B, M*
Wade College *A*

Utah

Weber State University *A*

Virginia

Tidewater Community College *C, A*
Virginia Union University *B*

Washington

Centralia College *C, A*
Columbia Basin College *A*
Highline Community College *A*
Lake Washington Technical College *C*
Pierce College *C*

Shoreline Community College *A*

Wisconsin

Gateway Technical College *A*
Moraine Park Technical College *C, A*
Northeast Wisconsin Technical
College *A*
University of Wisconsin
Madison *M*
Stout *B*
Western Wisconsin Technical
College *A*

Sales/marketing education

Arkansas

University of Central Arkansas *A*

California

San Diego Mesa College *A*
San Diego State University *B, T*

Colorado

Colorado State University *T*

Florida

Gulf Coast Community College *A*
Palm Beach Community College *A*

Georgia

University of Georgia *B*

Idaho

University of Idaho *B*

Illinois

Sauk Valley Community College *A*

Indiana

Vincennes University *A*

Iowa

Simpson College *T*

Michigan

Eastern Michigan University *B, T*
Western Michigan University *B, T*

Minnesota

Northland Community & Technical
College *A*
University of Minnesota
Twin Cities *B, M*

Nebraska

University of Nebraska
Lincoln *B*

New Hampshire

Southern New Hampshire
University *B*

New Mexico

College of the Southwest *B, T*
Eastern New Mexico University *B*

New York

College of Saint Rose *M, T*
Nazareth College of Rochester *T*
New York Institute of Technology *B, T*
State University of New York
Buffalo *M, T*
College at Buffalo *B, M, T*

North Carolina

East Carolina University *B*
North Carolina State University *B, T*

North Dakota
University of North Dakota *B, T*

Ohio
Bowling Green State University *B, T*
Ohio State University
  Columbus Campus *M, D*
Wright State University *M*

Oregon
Oregon State University *M*

Pennsylvania
Temple University *B, T*

South Carolina
Forrest Junior College *A*

South Dakota
Dakota State University *B, T*

Tennessee
Middle Tennessee State University *B*
University of Tennessee
  Knoxville *B, T*

Texas
University of North Texas *M*

Utah
Utah State University *B, M*

Virginia
Old Dominion University *B, T*

Washington
Eastern Washington University *B, M, T*

Wisconsin
University of Wisconsin
  Stout *B, T*
  Whitewater *B, T*

Wyoming
Laramie County Community
  College *A*

Salon management

Michigan
Kirtland Community College *C, A*
Mott Community College *C, A*
Oakland Community College *A*

Sanskrit/classical Indian languages

Iowa
University of Iowa *B*

Massachusetts
Harvard College *B, M, D*

New York
Bard College *B*

Scandinavian languages

California
University of California
  Berkeley *B, M, D*
  Los Angeles *B, M*

Illinois
Augustana College *B*
North Park University *B*
University of Chicago *B*

Minnesota
Augsburg College *B*
Concordia College: Moorhead *B*
Gustavus Adolphus College *B*
University of Minnesota
  Twin Cities *B*

North Dakota
University of North Dakota *B*

Texas
University of Texas
  Austin *B*

Washington
University of Washington *B, M, D*

Scandinavian studies

Iowa
Luther College *B*

Massachusetts
Harvard College *B*

Michigan
University of Michigan *B*

Minnesota
Augsburg College *B*
Concordia College: Moorhead *B*
Gustavus Adolphus College *B*
Minnesota State University
  Mankato *B*
University of Minnesota
  Twin Cities *M, D*

Vermont
Sterling College *B*

Washington
Pacific Lutheran University *B*
University of Washington *B, M*

Wisconsin
University of Wisconsin
  Madison *B, M*

School librarian education

California
California State University
  Chico *T*

Georgia
Georgia State University *M*

Illinois
University of Illinois
  Urbana-Champaign *M, T*

Kentucky
Eastern Kentucky University *M*

Michigan
Central Michigan University *M, T*

Minnesota
College of St. Scholastica *B, M, T*
Minnesota State University
  Mankato *M*

Missouri
Lindenwood University *M*
University of Missouri
  Columbia *M*

Montana
University of Montana: Western *B, T*

New York
City University of New York
  Queens College *M*
Syracuse University *M*

Ohio
Ohio Dominican University *B, T*

Oklahoma
Northeastern State University *T*

Pennsylvania
Arcadia University *M*
St. Vincent College *M*

Puerto Rico
Turabo University *M*

Rhode Island
University of Rhode Island *T*

Tennessee
University of Memphis *T*

Virginia
Longwood University *M*

School psychology

Alabama
Auburn University *M, D*
University of Alabama *D*

Arizona
Northern Arizona University *M, D*

Arkansas
University of Central Arkansas *M, D*

California
Alliant International University *M*
Azusa Pacific University *M*
California State University
  Chico *M, T*
  East Bay *T*
  Long Beach *M*
Chapman University *M, T*
National University *M*
San Diego State University *M*
San Francisco State University *M*
Stanford University *D*
University of the Pacific *T*

Colorado
University of Colorado
  Denver and Health Sciences
    Center *T*
University of Denver *M, D*
University of Northern Colorado *D, T*

Connecticut
Fairfield University *M, T*

District of Columbia
Gallaudet University *M*
Howard University *M*

Florida
Barry University *M*
Carlos Albizu University *M*
Florida Agricultural and Mechanical
  University *M*
Florida International University *M*
Nova Southeastern University *M*
University of Central Florida *M*
University of Florida *M, D*
University of South Florida *M, D*

Georgia
Georgia Southern University *M, T*
Georgia State University *M, D*
University of Georgia *M*

Illinois
Eastern Illinois University *M*
Governors State University *M*
Illinois State University *M, D*
Lewis University *M*
Loyola University of Chicago *M, D*
National-Louis University *M, D*
Western Illinois University *M*

Indiana
Ball State University *M*
Indiana State University *M*
Valparaiso University *M*

Iowa
University of Iowa *D*
University of Northern Iowa *M*

Kansas
Emporia State University *M*
University of Kansas *D*
Wichita State University *M*

Kentucky
Eastern Kentucky University *M*

Louisiana
Nicholls State University *M*

Maine
University of Southern Maine *M*

Massachusetts
American International College *M*
Northeastern University *M, D*
University of Massachusetts
  Amherst *D*
  Boston *M*

Michigan
Andrews University *M*
Central Michigan University *D*
Michigan State University *M, D*
Northern Michigan University *M*
University of Detroit Mercy *M*

Minnesota
Capella University *M, D*
Minnesota State University
  Mankato *M*
  Moorhead *M*

Missouri
Lindenwood University *M*
University of Missouri
  Columbia *M, D*

Montana
University of Great Falls *M*
University of Montana: Missoula *M*

Nebraska
University of Nebraska
  Kearney *M*
  Omaha *M*

Nevada
University of Nevada
  Las Vegas *M*

New Hampshire
Rivier College *M*

New Jersey

Fairleigh Dickinson University
 Metropolitan Campus *M, D*
Kean University *M*
New Jersey City University *M*
Rider University *M, T*
Rowan University *M*
Rutgers, The State University of New
 Jersey
 New Brunswick/Piscataway
 Campus *D*
Seton Hall University *M*

New York

Adelphi University *M*
Alfred University *M, D*
City University of New York
 Brooklyn College *M, T*
 Queens College *M, T*
College of New Rochelle *M*
College of Saint Rose *M*
Hofstra University *M, D*
Iona College *M*
Long Island University
 Brooklyn Campus *M*
Marist College *M*
New York University *D*
Roberts Wesleyan College *M*
Rochester Institute of Technology *M*
St. John's University *M, D*
State University of New York
 College at Plattsburgh *M*
 Oswego *M*
Syracuse University *D*
Yeshiva University *D*

North Carolina

Appalachian State University *M*
East Carolina University *M*
North Carolina State University *M, D*
University of North Carolina
 Chapel Hill *M, D*
Western Carolina University *M*

North Dakota

Minot State University *M*

Ohio

Bowling Green State University *M*
John Carroll University *M*
Kent State University *M, D*
Miami University
 Oxford Campus *M*
University of Cincinnati *M, D*
University of Dayton *M*
University of Toledo *M*

Oklahoma

Northeastern State University *M*
Oklahoma State University *M, D*
University of Central Oklahoma *M*

Oregon

Lewis & Clark College *M*
University of Oregon *M, D*

Pennsylvania

Bucknell University *M*
California University of
 Pennsylvania *M*
Duquesne University *M, D*
Eastern University *M*
Edinboro University of
 Pennsylvania *M*
Immaculata University *D*
Indiana University of Pennsylvania *D*
Lehigh University *D*
Marywood University *M*
Millersville University of
 Pennsylvania *M*
Penn State
 University Park *M, D*

Temple University *M, D*

Puerto Rico

Inter American University of Puerto
 Rico
 San German Campus *M, D*

Rhode Island

Rhode Island College *M*
University of Rhode Island *M, D*

South Carolina

The Citadel *M*
Francis Marion University *M*
University of South Carolina *M, D*
Winthrop University *M, T*

Tennessee

Southern Adventist University *M*
University of Memphis *M*

Texas

Abilene Christian University *M*
Sam Houston State University *M*
Stephen F. Austin State University *M*
Texas A&M University *M*
Texas A&M University
 Texarkana *M*
Texas State University: San Marcos *M*
Texas Woman's University *M, D*
Trinity University *M*
University of Houston
 Clear Lake *M*
University of North Texas *M*
University of Texas
 Tyler *M*

Utah

Brigham Young University *D*

Virginia

College of William and Mary *M*
James Madison University *M, T*

Washington

Central Washington University *M, T*
Eastern Washington University *M*
Seattle University *M*

West Virginia

Marshall University *M*

Wisconsin

Marquette University *M*
University of Wisconsin
 La Crosse *M*
 Madison *M, D*
 River Falls *M*
 Stout *M*
 Whitewater *M*

Science teacher education

Alabama

Athens State University *B*
Auburn University *B*
Birmingham-Southern College *T*
Faulkner University *B*
Huntingdon College *T*
Judson College *B*
Miles College *B*
Oakwood College *B*
Samford University *B*
Tuskegee University *B*
University of Mobile *T*

Alaska

University of Alaska
 Fairbanks *M*

Arizona

Grand Canyon University *B*
Northern Arizona University *M*
Prescott College *B, M*
University of Arizona *B, M*

Arkansas

Arkansas Tech University *B*
Harding University *B, M, T*
Ouachita Baptist University *B, T*
Philander Smith College *B*
Southern Arkansas University *B, T*
University of Arkansas *B*
University of Arkansas
 Pine Bluff *B, M, T*
University of Central Arkansas *B, M, T*
University of the Ozarks *B, T*

California

Azusa Pacific University *T*
California Lutheran University *B, T*
California State University
 Chico *B, T*
 Dominguez Hills *T*
 Fullerton *M*
 Long Beach *T*
 San Bernardino *M*
Fresno Pacific University *B, M, T*
Humboldt State University *T*
Master's College *B, T*
Mills College *T*
Mount St. Mary's College *T*
San Diego State University *B, T*
San Francisco State University *B, T*
Sonoma State University *T*
Stanford University *M, T*
University of the Pacific *T*
Vanguard University of Southern
 California *T*

Colorado

Adams State College *B, T*
Colorado State University *T*
Colorado State University
 Pueblo *T*
Metropolitan State College of
 Denver *T*
Regis University *B, T*
University of Colorado
 Boulder *T*
 Colorado Springs *T*
Western State College of Colorado *T*

Connecticut

Albertus Magnus College *B, T*
Central Connecticut State
 University *T*
Connecticut College *T*
Eastern Connecticut State
 University *M*
Fairfield University *T*
Quinnipiac University *B, M*
Sacred Heart University *T*
St. Joseph College *T*
Southern Connecticut State
 University *B, M, T*
University of New Haven *T*

Delaware

Delaware State University *B, M*
University of Delaware *B, T*

District of Columbia

George Washington University *M, T*

Florida

Broward Community College *A*
Chipola College *B*
Florida Agricultural and Mechanical
 University *B, M, T*
Florida Atlantic University *B*

Florida Institute of
 Technology *B, M, D*
Florida International
 University *B, M, T*
Florida State University *B, M, D, T*
Gulf Coast Community College *A*
Manatee Community College *A*
Miami Dade College *A, B*
Palm Beach Community College *A*
Southeastern College of the
 Assemblies of God *B, T*
University of Central Florida *B, M*
University of Florida *M*
University of Miami *M*
University of North Florida *B, M*
University of South Florida *B, M*
University of West Florida *M*
Warner Southern College *B*

Georgia

Albany State University *B, M*
Armstrong Atlantic State
 University *B, M, T*
Brewton-Parker College *B*
Clark Atlanta University *M*
Columbus State University *B, M*
Covenant College *B, T*
Gainesville State College *A*
Georgia Southern University *M*
Georgia Southwestern State
 University *M*
Georgia State University *M*
North Georgia College & State
 University *M*
Piedmont College *M, T*
Shorter College *T*
University of Georgia *B, M, D*
University of West Georgia *M*
Wesleyan College *M*

Hawaii

Brigham Young University-Hawaii *B, T*
Hawaii Pacific University *M*

Idaho

Boise State University *M, T*
Brigham Young University-Idaho *T*
Lewis-Clark State College *B, T*
Northwest Nazarene University *B*

Illinois

Augustana College *B, T*
Blackburn College *B, T*
Bradley University *B, M*
Chicago State University *T*
Concordia University *B, T*
Eastern Illinois University *B, M*
Eureka College *T*
Judson College *B, T*
Lewis University *T*
McKendree College *B*
Monmouth College *B, T*
National-Louis University *M*
North Park University *T*
Olivet Nazarene University *B, T*
Sauk Valley Community College *A*
Southern Illinois University
 Edwardsville *B, T*
Trinity Christian College *B, T*
University of Illinois
 Urbana-Champaign *M, T*
University of St. Francis *B, M, T*

Indiana

Anderson University *B, T*
Ball State University *B, D, T*
Bethel College *B*
Butler University *T*
Calumet College of St. Joseph *B*
Goshen College *B*
Grace College *B*
Huntington University *B, M*
Indiana State University *M, T*

Indiana University
Bloomington *B, D, T*
Kokomo *T*
South Bend *B, T*
Southeast *B*
Indiana University-Purdue University
Fort Wayne *B*
Indiana Wesleyan University *B, T*
Manchester College *B, T*
Oakland City University *B*
Purdue University
Calumet *B*
Saint Mary's College *T*
St. Mary-of-the-Woods College *B, T*
Taylor University *B, T*
Tri-State University *B, T*
University of Evansville *B*
University of Indianapolis *B, T*
University of Notre Dame *B*
University of St. Francis *B, T*
Valparaiso University *B*
Vincennes University *A*

Iowa
Ashford University *B, T*
Briar Cliff University *B*
Buena Vista University *B, T*
Central College *T*
Clarke College *B, T*
Coe College *B*
Cornell College *B, T*
Dordt College *B*
Drake University *M, T*
Ellsworth Community College *A*
Graceland University *T*
Iowa State University *T*
Loras College *T*
Morningside College *B*
Mount Mercy College *T*
Northwestern College *T*
St. Ambrose University *B, T*
Simpson College *T*
University of Iowa *M, D, T*
University of Northern Iowa *B, T*
Upper Iowa University *B*
Wartburg College *T*
William Penn University *B*

Kansas
Bethany College *T*
Colby Community College *A*
Emporia State University *T*
Friends University *B*
Garden City Community College *A*
Kansas Wesleyan University *T*
McPherson College *B, T*
Newman University *T*
Southwestern College *B, T*
Tabor College *B, T*
University of Kansas *B, T*
Washburn University of Topeka *B*

Kentucky
Alice Lloyd College *B*
Campbellsville University *B*
Eastern Kentucky University *B*
Kentucky Wesleyan College *T*
Murray State University *M*
Northern Kentucky University *T*
Spalding University *B*
Thomas More College *B*
Union College *B*
University of Kentucky *B*

Louisiana
Centenary College of Louisiana *B, T*
Grambling State University *M*
Louisiana State University
Shreveport *B*
Nicholls State University *B*
Our Lady of Holy Cross College *T*
Southeastern Louisiana University *B*

Southern University
New Orleans *B*
Southern University and Agricultural
and Mechanical College *B*
University of Louisiana at Lafayette *B*
University of New Orleans *B, M*
Xavier University of Louisiana *B*

Maine
University of Maine *B, M*
University of Maine
Farmington *B, T*
Fort Kent *B*
University of Southern Maine *T*

Maryland
Bowie State University *B, T*
College of Notre Dame of Maryland *T*
Columbia Union College *B*
Montgomery College *A*
Morgan State University *D*
Prince George's Community
College *A*
Towson University *T*
University of Maryland
College Park *B*
Eastern Shore *B*

Massachusetts
Assumption College *T*
Boston University *B, M, T*
Bridgewater State College *M, T*
Eastern Nazarene College *B*
Fitchburg State College *M, D, T*
Lesley University *B, M*
Merrimack College *T*
Smith College *M*
Tufts University *M, T*
University of Massachusetts
Lowell *D*
Westfield State College *B, M, T*
Worcester State College *T*

Michigan
Albion College *B, T*
Alma College *T*
Andrews University *M*
Aquinas College *B, T*
Calvin College *T*
Central Michigan University *B, T*
Concordia University *B, T*
Cornerstone University *B, T*
Eastern Michigan University *B, T*
Grand Valley State University *B, T*
Hope College *T*
Lansing Community College *A*
Lawrence Technological University *M*
Madonna University *B, T*
Michigan State University *M*
Michigan Technological
University *M, T*
Northern Michigan University *B, T*
Olivet College *B, T*
Rochester College *B*
Saginaw Valley State University *M*
University of Detroit Mercy *B, M, T*
University of Michigan *M*
University of Michigan
Dearborn *B*
Flint *T*
Wayne State University *B, M, T*
Western Michigan
University *B, M, D, T*

Minnesota
Augsburg College *T*
Bemidji State University *T*
College of St. Benedict *T*
College of St. Catherine *T*
College of St. Scholastica *T*
Concordia College: Moorhead *B, T*
Concordia University: St. Paul *B, T*
Gustavus Adolphus College *T*

Hamline University *B, T*
Minnesota State University
Mankato *B, M, T*
Moorhead *B*
Northland Community & Technical
College *A*
Pillsbury Baptist Bible College *T*
Ridgewater College *A*
St. Cloud State University *B, T*
St. John's University *T*
St. Mary's University of Minnesota *B*
Southwest Minnesota State
University *B, T*
University of Minnesota
Duluth *B*
Morris *T*
Twin Cities *M, T*
University of St. Thomas *B, T*
Vermilion Community College *A*
Winona State University *B, M, T*

Mississippi
Blue Mountain College *B*
Coahoma Community College *A*
Delta State University *T*
Itawamba Community College *A*
Jackson State University *M*
Mississippi College *B, M*
Mississippi Gulf Coast Community
College
Jefferson Davis Campus *A*
Mississippi State University *T*
University of Mississippi *B*
University of Southern
Mississippi *M, D*

Missouri
Central Methodist University *B*
Central Missouri State University *B, T*
College of the Ozarks *B, T*
Culver-Stockton College *T*
Evangel University *B*
Hannibal-LaGrange College *B*
Harris-Stowe State University *T*
Lincoln University *T*
Lindenwood University *B*
Missouri Baptist University *B, T*
Missouri Southern State
University *B, T*
Missouri State University *B*
Missouri Valley College *T*
Northwest Missouri State University *T*
Southeast Missouri State
University *B, M, T*
Southwest Baptist University *B, T*
Truman State University *M, T*
University of Missouri
Columbia *B, M, D*
Washington University in St.
Louis *B, M, T*
Webster University *M*
William Jewell College *T*
William Woods University *B*

Montana
Fort Peck Community College *A*
Montana State University
Billings *B, T*
Bozeman *M*
Montana Tech of the University of
Montana *T*
University of Great Falls *B*
University of Montana: Missoula *T*
University of Montana: Western *B, T*

Nebraska
Chadron State College *B, M*
College of Saint Mary *B, T*
Concordia University *B, T*
Dana College *B*
Hastings College *B, M, T*
Midland Lutheran College *T*
Nebraska Wesleyan University *B*

Peru State College *B, T*
University of Nebraska
Kearney *B, M, T*
Lincoln *B*
Wayne State College *T*

Nevada
Great Basin College *B*
University of Nevada
Reno *B*

New Hampshire
Franklin Pierce College *T*
Keene State College *B, T*
New England College *B, T*
Plymouth State University *M, T*
Rivier College *B, T*
St. Anselm College *T*
University of New Hampshire *B, T*

New Jersey
Caldwell College *T*
Centenary College *T*
The College of New Jersey *M, T*
College of St. Elizabeth *T*
Ramapo College of New Jersey *M*
Rowan University *M, T*
Rutgers, The State University of New
Jersey
New Brunswick/Piscataway
Campus *T*
Newark Regional Campus *T*
St. Peter's College *T*
William Paterson University of New
Jersey *T*

New Mexico
College of the Southwest *B, T*
New Mexico Highlands University *B*
New Mexico Institute of Mining and
Technology *M*
Western New Mexico University *B*

New York
Adelphi University *M, T*
Bard College *M*
City University of New York
Brooklyn College *M*
City College *B, M, T*
Lehman College *M*
Queens College *M, T*
College of Mount St. Vincent *T*
D'Youville College *M, T*
Dowling College *B*
Dutchess Community College *A*
Elmira College *B, T*
Fordham University *M, T*
Hofstra University *B, M, T*
Ithaca College *B, T*
Le Moyne College *T*
Manhattan College *B, T*
Manhattanville College *M, T*
Mount St. Mary College *T*
Nazareth College of Rochester *T*
New York Institute of Technology *B, T*
New York University *B, M, T*
Pace University *B, M, T*
Rensselaer Polytechnic Institute *B, T*
Roberts Wesleyan College *B, M*
St. Bonaventure University *T*
St. John Fisher College *B, T*
St. Joseph's College *B, T*
St. Joseph's College: Suffolk
Campus *B, T*
St. Lawrence University *T*
St. Thomas Aquinas College *B, M, T*
State University of New York
Albany *B, M, T*
Buffalo *M, D, T*
College at Brockport *M, T*
College at Buffalo *B, M*
College at Cortland *B, M, T*
College at Geneseo *B, M, T*

College at Old Westbury B, T
College at Oneonta B, T
College at Plattsburgh B, M
College at Potsdam B, M
College of Environmental Science
    and Forestry B, T
New Paltz B, M, T
Oswego B, M
Syracuse University B, M, D, T
Vassar College T
Wagner College T
Wells College T

North Carolina

Belmont Abbey College T
Bennett College B, T
Brevard College B
Catawba College T
East Carolina University B, M
Elon University B, T
Forsyth Technical Community
    College A
Gardner-Webb University B
Lenoir-Rhyne College B, T
Livingstone College T
Louisburg College A
Mars Hill College T
Meredith College T
North Carolina State
    University B, M, D, T
Sandhills Community College A
University of North Carolina
    Pembroke B, M
Wake Forest University T
Western Carolina University B

North Dakota

Dickinson State University B, T
Minot State University B, M
North Dakota State University B, T
University of North Dakota B, T
Valley City State University B, T

Ohio

Ashland University B, T
Baldwin-Wallace College B, T
Bluffton University B
Bowling Green State
    University B, M, T
Capital University T
Cedarville University B, T
Defiance College B, T
Hiram College T
Kent State University B
Malone College B
Miami University
    Oxford Campus B, T
Mount Union College T
Mount Vernon Nazarene
    University B, M, T
Ohio Dominican University B, T
Ohio Northern University B, T
Ohio State University
    Columbus Campus M, D
Ohio University B, D, T
Ohio Wesleyan University B
Otterbein College B
Shawnee State University B
University of Akron B
University of Findlay B, M, T
University of Rio Grande B, T
University of Toledo B
Urbana University B
Ursuline College B, M, T
Walsh University B
Wilmington College B
Wright State University B, M, T
Youngstown State University B, M

Oklahoma

Cameron University B, T
East Central University B
Eastern Oklahoma State College A

Northeastern State University B, M
Northwestern Oklahoma State
    University B, T
Oklahoma Baptist University B, T
Oklahoma Christian University B, T
Oklahoma City University B
Oklahoma Wesleyan University B
Oral Roberts University B, T
Southeastern Oklahoma State
    University B, M, T
Southern Nazarene University B
Southwestern Oklahoma State
    University B, M, T
University of Central Oklahoma B
University of Oklahoma B, T
University of Tulsa T

Oregon

Concordia University B, M, T
Corban College B
Eastern Oregon University B
Linfield College T
Oregon State University M, D
Western Oregon University T

Pennsylvania

Albright College T
Alvernia College B
Arcadia University B, M, T
Baptist Bible College of
    Pennsylvania B
Bloomsburg University of
    Pennsylvania B, T
Carlow University T
Cedar Crest College B, T
Clarion University of Pennsylvania M
DeSales University M, T
Dickinson College T
Elizabethtown College B
Gannon University M, T
Gettysburg College T
Grove City College T
Holy Family University B, T
Indiana University of
    Pennsylvania B, T
Juniata College B, T
La Salle University B, T
Lebanon Valley College M
Lincoln University T
Lycoming College T
Marywood University B
Mercyhurst College B, T
Millersville University of
    Pennsylvania B, T
St. Francis University T
St. Joseph's University B, M
St. Vincent College T
Susquehanna University T
Temple University B, M, T
Thiel College B
University of Pennsylvania M, T
University of Pittsburgh
    Johnstown B, T
University of Scranton T
University of the Sciences in
    Philadelphia T
Villanova University T
Waynesburg College B, T
West Chester University of
    Pennsylvania T
Widener University B, T
York College of Pennsylvania B, T

Puerto Rico

Bayamon Central University B
Inter American University of Puerto
    Rico
    San German Campus M
Pontifical Catholic University of
    Puerto Rico B, T
Turabo University B
Universidad del Este B
University of Puerto Rico
    Cayey University College B

Rhode Island

Rhode Island College B, M, T

South Carolina

Anderson University B, T
Charleston Southern University B, M
Clemson University B
College of Charleston M
Converse College T
Furman University T
University of South Carolina
    Aiken B, T

South Dakota

Black Hills State University B
Dakota State University B, T
Dakota Wesleyan University B, T
Mount Marty College B
Northern State University B, T
University of South Dakota B, M, T

Tennessee

Belmont University B, M, T
Bethel College B
Freed-Hardeman University B, T
King College T
Lee University B
Lincoln Memorial University B, T
Tennessee Technological University T
Tennessee Temple University B
Tennessee Wesleyan College B, T
Tusculum College B, T
Union University B, T
University of Memphis T
University of Tennessee
    Chattanooga B, T
    Knoxville T
Vanderbilt University M, D

Texas

Abilene Christian University B, T
Baylor University B, T
Dallas Baptist University B, T
Del Mar College A
Hardin-Simmons University B, T
Houston Baptist University B, T
Howard Payne University B, T
Lamar University B, M, T
LeTourneau University B, T
Lubbock Christian University B
McMurry University T
Prairie View A&M University M
Stephen F. Austin State University T
Tarleton State University B, T
Texas A&M University
    Commerce T
    Galveston B
    Kingsville T
Texas Christian University B
Texas Tech University M
Texas Woman's University M
University of Dallas T
University of Houston M, T
University of Houston
    Clear Lake T
University of Mary Hardin-Baylor B, T
University of Texas
    Arlington T
    Austin M, D
    San Antonio T
West Texas A&M University T

Utah

Brigham Young University B
Southern Utah University B
University of Utah B, M
Utah State University B
Utah Valley State College B
Weber State University B

Vermont

Castleton State College B, T
Johnson State College B

Lyndon State College B
St. Michael's College T
Sterling College B
University of Vermont B

Virginia

Averett University M
Bluefield College B
Eastern Shore Community College A
Longwood University B, T
University of Virginia's College at
    Wise T

Washington

Central Washington University B, T
Eastern Washington University M, T
Heritage University B, M
Seattle Pacific University B, T
University of Washington M
Washington State University B, M, T
Western Washington University B, M
Whitworth College B, T

West Virginia

Alderson-Broaddus College T
Concord University B, T
Ohio Valley University B
Shepherd University T
University of Charleston B
West Liberty State College B
West Virginia State University B
West Virginia University T
West Virginia Wesleyan College B
Wheeling Jesuit University B

Wisconsin

Alverno College T
Beloit College B
Carroll College B, T
Carthage College M, T
Concordia University Wisconsin B, T
Edgewood College B
Lakeland College T
Lawrence University T
Maranatha Baptist Bible College B
Marian College of Fond du Lac B, T
Marquette University B
Mount Mary College B, T
Northland College T
St. Norbert College T
Silver Lake College T
University of Wisconsin
    Eau Claire B
    Green Bay T
    La Crosse B, T
    Madison M
    Milwaukee M
    Oshkosh B
    Parkside T
    Platteville B, T
    River Falls T
    Superior B, T
    Whitewater B, T

Science, technology, and society

Alabama

Samford University A, B

Arizona

Embry-Riddle Aeronautical University:
    Prescott Campus B

Arkansas

University of Arkansas
    Fort Smith A, B

California

California Institute of Technology B
Chaffey College A
Pitzer College B

Pomona College *B*
Scripps College *B*
Stanford University *B*
University of California
  Davis *B*

Connecticut
Wesleyan University *B*

District of Columbia
George Washington University *M*
Georgetown University *B, M*

Georgia
Georgia Institute of Technology *B*

Illinois
Northwestern University *B*

Indiana
Butler University *B*
Indiana University
  Bloomington *B, M*

Kentucky
Hazard Community College *A*

Louisiana
Southeastern Louisiana University *M*

Maine
Colby College *B*

Maryland
University of Maryland
  College Park *M*

Massachusetts
Clark University *B*
Hampshire College *B*
Massachusetts Institute of
  Technology *B, D*
Wellesley College *B*
Worcester Polytechnic Institute *B*

Michigan
Eastern Michigan University *M*
Michigan State University *B*

Minnesota
University of Minnesota
  Twin Cities *M*

Missouri
Washington University in St.
  Louis *B, M, D*

Montana
Montana Tech of the University of
  Montana *B*

New Jersey
New Jersey Institute of Technology *B*
Rutgers, The State University of New
  Jersey
  Newark Regional Campus *B*

New York
Cornell University *B, M, D*
Eugene Lang College The New School
  for Liberal Arts *B*
Rensselaer Polytechnic
  Institute *B, M, D*
Sarah Lawrence College *B*
State University of New York
  Farmingdale *B*
Union College *B*
Vassar College *B*

North Carolina
North Carolina State University *B*

Oregon
Willamette University *B*

Pennsylvania
Carnegie Mellon University *B, M, D*
Lehigh University *B*
Slippery Rock University of
  Pennsylvania *B*

Texas
Angelina College *A*

Virginia
Danville Community College *A*
James Madison University *B, M*
University of Virginia *M*
Virginia Polytechnic Institute and
  State University *M, D*

Washington
University of Puget Sound *B*

West Virginia
Mountain State University *A*
West Virginia University *M, D*

Sculpture

Alabama
Birmingham-Southern College *B*

Arizona
Northern Arizona University *B*

California
Academy of Art University *C, A, B, M*
Art Center College of Design *B, M*
Biola University *B*
California College of the Arts *B, M*
California Institute of the Arts *C, B, M*
California State University
  East Bay *B*
  Fullerton *B, M*
  Long Beach *B, M*
  Northridge *B, M*
Chabot College *A*
De Anza College *C, A*
Grossmont Community College *A*
Long Beach City College *A*
Monterey Peninsula College *C, A*
Ohlone College *C*
Palomar College *A*
Pasadena City College *A*
San Diego State University *B*
San Francisco Art Institute *B, M*
Santa Rosa Junior College *C*
Solano Community College *A*

Colorado
Adams State College *B*
Rocky Mountain College of Art &
  Design *B*

Connecticut
Lyme Academy College of Fine
  Arts *C, B*
University of Hartford *B*

District of Columbia
American University *M*
George Washington University *M*

Florida
University of Miami *B*

Idaho
Northwest Nazarene University *B*

Illinois
Bradley University *B*
Judson College *B*
Richland Community College *A*
Rockford College *B*
School of the Art Institute of
  Chicago *B, M*
University of Illinois
  Urbana-Champaign *B, M*

Indiana
Indiana University-Purdue University
  Fort Wayne *B*
Indiana University-Purdue University
  Indianapolis *B*
Vincennes University *A*

Iowa
Drake University *B*
University of Iowa *B, M*

Kansas
University of Kansas *B, M*

Kentucky
Eastern Kentucky University *B*

Louisiana
Centenary College of Louisiana *B*

Maine
Maine College of Art *B*
University of Southern Maine *B*

Maryland
Maryland Institute College of Art *B, M*

Massachusetts
Boston University *B, M*
Hampshire College *B*
Massachusetts College of Art *B, M*
Montserrat College of Art *B*
Salem State College *B*
School of the Museum of Fine
  Arts *B, M*
Simon's Rock College of Bard *B*
University of Massachusetts
  Dartmouth *B, M*

Michigan
College for Creative Studies *B*
Ferris State University *B*
Grand Valley State University *B*
Kendall College of Art and Design of
  Ferris State University *B*
Northern Michigan University *B*
Siena Heights University *B*
University of Michigan *B*
University of Michigan
  Flint *B*

Minnesota
College of Visual Arts *B*
Minneapolis College of Art and
  Design *B*
Minnesota State University
  Mankato *B*
St. Cloud State University *B*

Mississippi
Mississippi Gulf Coast Community
  College
  Jefferson Davis Campus *A*

Missouri
Kansas City Art Institute *B*
Washington University in St.
  Louis *B, M*

Nevada
Sierra Nevada College *B*

New Jersey
Rowan University *B*

New Mexico
College of Santa Fe *B*

New York
Bard College *B, M*
City University of New York
  Brooklyn College *M*
Columbia University
  School of General Studies *B*
Parsons The New School for
  Design *C, A, B, M, T*
Pratt Institute *B, M*
Rochester Institute of
  Technology *A, B, M*
Sarah Lawrence College *B*
School of Visual Arts *B, M*
State University of New York
  College at Buffalo *B*
  College at Fredonia *B*
  New Paltz *B, M*
  Purchase *B, M*
Syracuse University *B, M*

North Carolina
East Carolina University *B*

Ohio
Art Academy of Cincinnati *B*
Cleveland Institute of Art *B*
Ohio State University
  Columbus Campus *B, M*
Ohio University *B, M*
University of Akron *B*

Oregon
Pacific Northwest College of Art *B*
Portland State University *B, M*
University of Oregon *B, M*

Pennsylvania
Edinboro University of
  Pennsylvania *B*
Keystone College *A, B*
Marywood University *M*
Seton Hill University *B*
Temple University *B, M*
University of the Arts *B, M*

Puerto Rico
Inter American University of Puerto
  Rico
  San German Campus *B, M*
University of Puerto Rico
  Rio Piedras *B*

Rhode Island
Rhode Island College *B*
Rhode Island School of Design *B, M*

Tennessee
Memphis College of Art *B, M*
Tennessee Technological University *B*
Union University *B*
University of Tennessee
  Knoxville *M*

Texas
Sam Houston State University *M*
Stephen F. Austin State University *M*
Texas A&M University
  Commerce *B, M*
Texas Christian University *B, M*
University of Dallas *B, M*
University of Houston *B, M*
University of North Texas *B, M*
University of Texas
  El Paso *B, M*
Western Texas College *A*

Utah

Brigham Young University *M*
Dixie State College of Utah *A*

Vermont

Bennington College *B*
Marlboro College *B*

Virginia

Virginia Commonwealth University *B*

Washington

Cornish College of the Arts *B*
University of Washington *B, M*
Western Washington University *B*

West Virginia

West Virginia State University *B*

Wisconsin

University of Wisconsin
  Madison *B*

Secondary education

Alabama

Alabama Agricultural and Mechanical
  University *B, M*
Alabama State University *B, M*
Athens State University *B*
Auburn University *M, D, T*
Auburn University at
  Montgomery *B, M*
Birmingham-Southern College *T*
Calhoun Community College *A*
Chattahoochee Valley Community
  College *A*
Faulkner University *B, T*
Huntingdon College *T*
Jacksonville State University *B, M, T*
Judson College *B*
Miles College *B*
Northeast Alabama Community
  College *A*
Samford University *T*
Shelton State Community College *A*
Spring Hill College *B, M*
Talladega College *B*
Troy University *B, M, T*
University of Alabama *B, M, D*
University of Alabama
  Birmingham *B, M*
University of Montevallo *M, T*
University of North Alabama *B, M*
University of South Alabama *B, M, T*
University of West Alabama *B, M*

Alaska

Sheldon Jackson College *B*
University of Alaska
  Anchorage *T*
  Fairbanks *M, T*
  Southeast *M, T*

Arizona

Arizona State University *B*
Arizona State University West *B, M*
Arizona Western College *A*
Eastern Arizona College *A*
Estrella Mountain Community
  College *A*
Grand Canyon University *B, M, T*
Northern Arizona University *M, T*
Prescott College *B, M*
Southwestern College *B*
University of Arizona *B, M*
University of Phoenix *M*

Arkansas

Harding University *B, M, T*
Hendrix College *T*
Ouachita Baptist University *B, T*

Philander Smith College *B*
South Arkansas Community College *A*
Southern Arkansas University *M, T*
University of Arkansas *M, D*
University of Arkansas
  Little Rock *M*
  Monticello *B, M*
University of Central Arkansas *T*
University of the Ozarks *B, T*
Williams Baptist College *B*

California

Alliant International University *T*
Azusa Pacific University *B, T*
Biola University *B, T*
California Baptist University *M, T*
California Lutheran University *B, M*
California State University
  Dominguez Hills *M*
  East Bay *T*
  Fullerton *M, T*
  Long Beach *M, T*
  Los Angeles *M*
  Northridge *M*
  Sacramento *M, T*
  San Bernardino *M, T*
  San Marcos *T*
Chapman University *M, T*
Cypress College *A*
Dominican University of California *T*
Holy Names University *T*
Humboldt State University *T*
La Sierra University *M, T*
Loyola Marymount University *M, T*
Master's College *B, T*
Mills College *T*
Mount St. Mary's College *B*
National University *T*
Notre Dame de Namur
  University *M, T*
Occidental College *T*
Pacific Union College *T*
St. Mary's College of California *M*
San Diego Christian College *B, T*
San Diego State University *M, T*
San Francisco State University *M, T*
San Jose State University *M*
Sonoma State University *M*
Stanford University *M, T*
University of California
  Riverside *T*
  Santa Barbara *T*
  Santa Cruz *M*
University of La Verne *B, M, T*
University of Redlands *B, T*
University of San Diego *M, T*
University of San Francisco *T*
University of Southern California *T*
University of the Pacific *B, T*
Vanguard University of Southern
  California *T*
Westmont College *T*
Whittier College *T*

Colorado

Adams State College *B, M, T*
Colorado College *M*
Colorado State University *T*
Colorado State University
  Pueblo *T*
Fort Lewis College *B*
Metropolitan State College of
  Denver *T*
Northeastern Junior College *A*
Otero Junior College *A*
Regis University *B, T*
University of Colorado
  Boulder *T*
  Colorado Springs *T*

Connecticut

Albertus Magnus College *B, T*
Central Connecticut State
  University *B, T*

Connecticut College *M, T*
Eastern Connecticut State
  University *B, M, T*
Fairfield University *M*
Quinnipiac University *B, M*
Sacred Heart University *M, T*
St. Joseph College *M, T*
Southern Connecticut State
  University *B, M, T*
University of Bridgeport *M, T*
University of Connecticut *T*
University of Hartford *B, M*
University of New Haven *T*
Western Connecticut State
  University *B, M*

Delaware

University of Delaware *B, M, T*

District of Columbia

American University *B, M, T*
Catholic University of America *B, M, T*
Gallaudet University *B, T*
George Washington University *M, T*
Howard University *M*
Trinity University *M*

Florida

Chipola College *B*
Flagler College *B*
Florida Agricultural and Mechanical
  University *M*
Florida Gulf Coast University *M*
Florida Institute of Technology *M, T*
Florida Southern College *B, T*
Hillsborough Community College *A*
Indian River Community College *A*
Jacksonville University *B, M, T*
Lynn University *B*
Manatee Community College *A*
Miami Dade College *A, B*
Okaloosa-Walton College *A*
Palm Beach Community College *A*
St. Thomas University *B, T*
Southeastern College of the
  Assemblies of God *B, T*
Stetson University *B*
University of North Florida *B, M*
University of Tampa *T*

Georgia

Agnes Scott College *T*
Armstrong Atlantic State
  University *B, M, T*
Augusta State University *M*
Bainbridge College *A*
Berry College *M*
Brewton-Parker College *B*
Clark Atlanta University *B*
Coastal Georgia Community
  College *A*
Columbus State University *B, M*
Covenant College *B, T*
Dalton State College *A*
Darton College *A*
Fort Valley State University *B, T*
Gainesville State College *A*
Georgia College and State
  University *M, T*
Georgia Southwestern State
  University *M*
Macon State College *A*
Mercer University *M*
Middle Georgia College *A*
Morehouse College *B*
Oglethorpe University *B, T*
Piedmont College *M, T*
Thomas University *B*
University of West Georgia *B*
Valdosta State University *B, M*

Hawaii

Brigham Young University-Hawaii *B, T*

Chaminade University of
  Honolulu *B, M, T*
Hawaii Pacific University *M*
University of Hawaii
  Hilo *T*
  Manoa *B, T*

Idaho

Boise State University *T*
College of Southern Idaho *A*
Idaho State University *B*
Lewis-Clark State College *T*
North Idaho College *A*
Northwest Nazarene University *B*
University of Idaho *B, T*

Illinois

Augustana College *B, T*
Aurora University *B*
Benedictine University *T*
Black Hawk College
  East Campus *A*
Blackburn College *B, T*
Bradley University *T*
Chicago State University *B, M, T*
City Colleges of Chicago
  Harold Washington College *A*
Columbia College Chicago *M*
Concordia University *B, T*
DePaul University *B, T*
Dominican University *T*
Elmhurst College *B*
Eureka College *B*
Greenville College *M, T*
Illinois Central College *A*
John A. Logan College *A*
Joliet Junior College *A*
Judson College *B, T*
Kankakee Community College *A*
Kishwaukee College *A*
Knox College *T*
Lewis University *T*
Lincoln Christian College and
  Seminary *B*
Loyola University of Chicago *B, M*
MacMurray College *B, T*
Monmouth College *B, T*
National-Louis University *M, T*
North Central College *T*
North Park University *M, T*
Northern Illinois University *M*
Northwestern University *B*
Olivet Nazarene University *B, M, T*
Quincy University *T*
Rockford College *M, T*
Roosevelt University *B, M*
St. Xavier University *B*
Sauk Valley Community College *A*
Southern Illinois University
  Edwardsville *M, T*
Southwestern Illinois College *A*
Springfield College in Illinois *A*
Trinity Christian College *T*
Trinity International
  University *M, T*
University of Illinois
  Urbana-Champaign *B, M, D, T*
University of St. Francis *M, T*
Western Illinois University *M*
Wheaton College *M, T*

Indiana

Ancilla College *A*
Anderson University *T*
Ball State University *M, T*
Butler University *B, M*
Calumet College of St. Joseph *B, T*
Earlham College *M*
Goshen College *B, T*
Hanover College *T*
Huntington University *B*
Indiana University
  Bloomington *B, M, D, T*
  East *B*

Kokomo *M*
Northwest *B, M, T*
South Bend *B, M, T*
Southeast *B, M*
Indiana University-Purdue University
Fort Wayne *B, M, T*
Indiana University-Purdue University
Indianapolis *B, M, T*
Indiana Wesleyan University *B, T*
Manchester College *B, T*
Marian College *T*
Purdue University
Calumet *B, M*
St. Joseph's College *B*
Saint Mary's College *T*
St. Mary-of-the-Woods College *B, T*
Taylor University *T*
University of Evansville *T*
University of Indianapolis *A, B, T*
University of Southern Indiana *M*
Valparaiso University *B, M, T*
Vincennes University *A*
Wabash College *T*

Iowa

Ashford University *B, T*
Briar Cliff University *B*
Buena Vista University *B, T*
Central College *T*
Clarke College *B, T*
Coe College *B*
Cornell College *B, T*
Dordt College *B, T*
Drake University *B, M*
Ellsworth Community College *A*
Faith Baptist Bible College and
Theological Seminary *B*
Graceland University *T*
Grand View College *B, T*
Grinnell College *T*
Iowa State University *T*
Iowa Wesleyan College *B*
Kaplan University *M*
Loras College *B*
Maharishi University of
Management *B, M*
Marshalltown Community College *A*
Morningside College *B*
Mount Mercy College *B*
North Iowa Area Community
College *A*
Northwestern College *T*
St. Ambrose University *B, T*
Simpson College *B, T*
University of Iowa *M, D, T*
Upper Iowa University *B, T*
Vennard College *A*
Waldorf College *B*
Wartburg College *T*
William Penn University *B*

Kansas

Allen County Community College *A*
Baker University *B, T*
Bethany College *B, T*
Bethel College *T*
Butler County Community College *A*
Central Christian College of Kansas *A*
Coffeyville Community College *A*
Colby Community College *A*
Dodge City Community College *A*
Emporia State University *B, M, T*
Fort Hays State University *M*
Friends University *B, T*
Garden City Community College *A*
Kansas State University *B, M, T*
Kansas Wesleyan University *B, T*
Labette Community College *A*
MidAmerica Nazarene University *B, T*
Neosho County Community
College *A*
Newman University *B, T*
Pittsburg State University *M*
Pratt Community College *A*

Southwestern College *B, M, T*
Tabor College *B, T*
University of Kansas *B, T*
Washburn University of Topeka *B*
Wichita State University *B, T*

Kentucky

Alice Lloyd College *B*
Bellarmine University *B, M, T*
Brescia University *B, T*
Campbellsville University *B*
Centre College *T*
Eastern Kentucky University *M*
Georgetown College *M*
Kentucky State University *B*
Kentucky Wesleyan College *T*
Lindsey Wilson College *B, T*
Midway College *B*
Morehead State University *M*
Murray State University *M, T*
Northern Kentucky University *M*
Spalding University *M, T*
Thomas More College *B*
Union College *M*
University of Kentucky *M*
University of Louisville *M*
University of the Cumberlands *M*
Western Kentucky University *M, T*

Louisiana

Centenary College of
Louisiana *B, M, T*
Dillard University *B, T*
Louisiana State University and
Agricultural and Mechanical
College *B*
Louisiana Tech University *B*
Loyola University New Orleans *M*
Nicholls State University *B, M*
Northwestern State University *M*
Our Lady of Holy Cross College *B*
Southeastern Louisiana University *M*
Southern University
New Orleans *B*
Southern University and Agricultural
and Mechanical College *B, M*
University of Louisiana at
Monroe *M, T*
Xavier University of Louisiana *M*

Maine

Bowdoin College *T*
University of Maine *B, M*
University of Maine
Farmington *B, T*
Fort Kent *B*
Machias *T*
Presque Isle *B*
University of Southern Maine *T*

Maryland

Allegany College of Maryland *A*
Anne Arundel Community College *A*
Bowie State University *M*
Cecil Community College *A*
Chesapeake College *A*
College of Notre Dame of
Maryland *B, M*
College of Southern Maryland *A*
Columbia Union College *B, T*
Community College of Baltimore
County *A*
Coppin State University *B, T*
Frostburg State University *M, T*
Garrett College *A*
Goucher College *T*
Harford Community College *A*
Hood College *T*
Howard Community College *A*
McDaniel College *M, T*
Morgan State University *B, T*
Mount St. Mary's University *M, T*

Prince George's Community
College *A*
St. Mary's College of Maryland *T*
Salisbury University *T*
Towson University *M, T*
University of Maryland
Eastern Shore *M*
University College *M*
Washington College *T*

Massachusetts

American International College *B, M*
Amherst College *T*
Anna Maria College *B*
Assumption College *T*
Atlantic Union College *B*
Boston College *B, M, T*
Clark University *M*
Eastern Nazarene College *M, T*
Elms College *B, M, T*
Fitchburg State College *B, M, T*
Framingham State College *B, M*
Gordon College *B*
Hampshire College *B*
Lasell College *B, T*
Lesley University *B, M*
Massachusetts College of Liberal
Arts *T*
Merrimack College *T*
Nichols College *B*
Salem State College *M*
Simmons College *B, M*
Smith College *M*
Springfield College *B, T*
Suffolk University *M*
Tufts University *M, T*
University of Massachusetts
Boston *M*
Dartmouth *T*
Wellesley College *T*
Western New England College *T*
Westfield State College *M, T*
Wheaton College *T*
Worcester State College *M, T*

Michigan

Adrian College *B*
Albion College *T*
Alma College *B, T*
Andrews University *B, M*
Baker College
of Auburn Hills *B*
of Muskegon *B*
of Owosso *B*
Calvin College *B, T*
Central Michigan University *M*
Concordia University *B, T*
Cornerstone University *T*
Delta College *A*
Eastern Michigan University *M, T*
Ferris State University *A, B*
Gogebic Community College *A*
Grace Bible College *B*
Grand Valley State University *M, T*
Hillsdale College *B*
Hope College *B, T*
Kalamazoo College *T*
Kellogg Community College *A*
Kuyper College *B*
Lansing Community College *A*
Madonna University *B, T*
Marygrove College *T*
Michigan Technological University *T*
Mid Michigan Community College *A*
Northern Michigan University *B, M, T*
Oakland University *M*
Olivet College *B, T*
Rochester College *B*
Saginaw Valley State University *M*
Siena Heights University *B, M, T*
Spring Arbor University *B, T*
University of Detroit Mercy *B, M, T*
University of Michigan *B*

University of Michigan
Dearborn *B, T*
Flint *T*
Washtenaw Community College *A*
Wayne County Community College *A*
Wayne State University *M*
Western Michigan University *B*

Minnesota

Augsburg College *B, T*
Capella University *M, D*
College of St. Benedict *T*
College of St. Catherine *B, T*
College of St. Scholastica *T*
Concordia College: Moorhead *B, T*
Concordia University: St. Paul *B, T*
Crown College *B*
Gustavus Adolphus College *B*
Hamline University *B, T*
Minnesota State University
Mankato *B, M, T*
North Central University *B*
Northland Community & Technical
College *A*
Pillsbury Baptist Bible College *B*
Ridgewater College *A*
St. Cloud State University *B, T*
St. John's University *T*
University of Minnesota
Duluth *T*
Morris *T*
University of St. Thomas *B, M, T*
Vermilion Community College *A*
Winona State University *B, M, T*

Mississippi

Alcorn State University *B, M*
Belhaven College *T*
Delta State University *M*
Hinds Community College *A*
Holmes Community College *A*
Itawamba Community College *A*
Jackson State University *M*
Millsaps College *T*
Mississippi College *B, M, T*
Mississippi Delta Community
College *A*
Mississippi Gulf Coast Community
College
Jefferson Davis Campus *A*
Mississippi State University *B, M, D, T*
Tougaloo College *B, T*
University of Southern Mississippi *M*
William Carey College *M*

Missouri

Calvary Bible College and Theological
Seminary *B*
Central Methodist University *B*
Central Missouri State
University *B, M, T*
College of the Ozarks *B, T*
Columbia College *T*
Crowder College *A*
Drury University *B, M, T*
Evangel University *B, T*
Hannibal-LaGrange College *B*
Harris-Stowe State University *B, T*
Lincoln University *M*
Maryville University of Saint
Louis *B, M, T*
Missouri Baptist University *T*
Missouri Southern State
University *B, T*
Missouri State University *M*
Missouri Valley College *B, T*
Ozark Christian College *A*
Park University *T*
Rockhurst University *B*
St. Louis Community College
St. Louis Community College at
Meramec *A*
Southeast Missouri State
University *M, T*

Truman State University *M, T*
University of Missouri
  Columbia *B, M, D*
  Kansas City *B*
  Rolla *T*
  St. Louis *B, M, T*
Washington University in St.
  Louis *B, M, T*
Westminster College *B, T*
William Woods University *B, T*

Montana

Carroll College *B*
Montana State University
  Billings *B, M, T*
  Bozeman *B*
Montana Tech of the University of
  Montana *T*
Rocky Mountain College *B, T*
University of Great Falls *B, M*
University of Montana: Missoula *B, M*
University of Montana: Western *B, T*

Nebraska

Chadron State College *B, M*
College of Saint Mary *B, T*
Concordia University *B, T*
Dana College *B*
Hastings College *B, M, T*
Midland Lutheran College *B, T*
Nebraska Wesleyan University *T*
Northeast Community College *A*
Peru State College *B, T*
Union College *B, T*
University of Nebraska
  Kearney *B, M, T*
  Omaha *B, M, T*
Western Nebraska Community
  College *A*
York College *B, T*

Nevada

Great Basin College *B*
Sierra Nevada College *M*
Truckee Meadows Community
  College *A*
University of Nevada
  Las Vegas *B, T*
  Reno *B, M, T*

New Hampshire

Dartmouth College *T*
Franklin Pierce College *T*
Keene State College *B, T*
New England College *B, T*
Plymouth State University *M, T*
Rivier College *B, M, T*
St. Anselm College *T*
Southern New Hampshire
  University *B, M*
University of New Hampshire *M*
University of New Hampshire at
  Manchester *T*

New Jersey

Caldwell College *T*
Centenary College *T*
The College of New Jersey *M, T*
College of St. Elizabeth *T*
Essex County College *A*
Rowan University *B, M*
Rutgers, The State University of New
  Jersey
  Camden Regional Campus *T*
  New Brunswick/Piscataway
    Campus *T*
  Newark Regional Campus *T*
St. Peter's College *T*
Seton Hall University *B, M*
Sussex County Community College *A*

New Mexico

College of Santa Fe *B*

College of the Southwest *B, T*
New Mexico Junior College *A*
New Mexico State University *B*
University of New Mexico *B, M*
Western New Mexico
  University *B, M, T*

New York

Adelphi University *B, M, T*
Alfred University *M, T*
Bard College *M*
Barnard College *T*
Canisius College *B, M, T*
City University of New York
  City College *B, M, T*
  Hunter College *B, M, T*
  Lehman College *M, T*
  Queens College *M, T*
  York College *T*
Colgate University *M, T*
College of Mount St. Vincent *T*
College of Saint Rose *B, M, T*
Columbia University
  School of General Studies *T*
Cornell University *B, M, T*
D'Youville College *B, M, T*
Dominican College of Blauvelt *B, T*
Dowling College *B, M, T*
Dutchess Community College *A*
Elmira College *B, M, T*
Fordham University *M, T*
Hobart and William Smith Colleges *T*
Hofstra University *B, M, T*
Houghton College *B, T*
Iona College *B, M, T*
Ithaca College *B, M, T*
Le Moyne College *M, T*
Long Island University
  C.W. Post Campus *M, T*
Manhattan College *B, T*
Manhattanville College *M, T*
Marymount Manhattan College *T*
Mercy College *T*
Mohawk Valley Community College *A*
Molloy College *B, M, T*
Mount St. Mary College *B, M*
Nazareth College of Rochester *B, M, T*
New York University *M*
Niagara University *B, M, T*
Pace University *M, T*
St. Bonaventure University *M*
St. John Fisher College *B, M, T*
St. John's University *M*
St. Joseph's College *B, T*
St. Joseph's College: Suffolk
  Campus *B, T*
St. Thomas Aquinas College *B, M, T*
State University of New York
  Albany *B, M, T*
  College at Brockport *M, T*
  College at Buffalo *B, M, T*
  College at Cortland *B, M*
  College at Fredonia *B, M, T*
  College at Geneseo *T*
  College at Old Westbury *B, T*
  College at Plattsburgh *M*
  New Paltz *B, M, T*
  Oswego *B, M, T*
Suffolk County Community College *A*
Syracuse University *B, M, T*
Tompkins-Cortland Community
  College *A*
University of Rochester *T*
Utica College *B, M*
Vassar College *T*
Wagner College *B, M*
Wells College *T*
Yeshiva University *M*

North Carolina

Brevard College *B*
Campbell University *M*
Catawba College *T*
Chowan College *B*

Davidson College *T*
Duke University *M*
Elon University *B, T*
Fayetteville State University *B*
Gardner-Webb University *B, M*
Greensboro College *T*
Guilford College *B, T*
High Point University *B*
James Sprunt Community College *A*
Johnson C. Smith University *B, T*
Louisburg College *A*
Mars Hill College *B, T*
Martin Community College *A*
Meredith College *T*
Methodist College *A, B, T*
North Carolina Wesleyan College *T*
Pfeiffer University *B, T*
St. Augustine's College *B*
Salem College *T*
Sandhills Community College *A*
Southeastern Community College *A*
University of North Carolina
  Asheville *T*
  Wilmington *M*
Wake Forest University *M, T*
Warren Wilson College *B, T*

North Dakota

Dickinson State University *B, T*
Jamestown College *B*
University of Mary *M, T*
Valley City State University *B, T*

Ohio

Bluffton University *B*
Capital University *B*
Cedarville University *T*
Central State University *B*
Cincinnati Christian University *B*
Circleville Bible College *B*
College of Wooster *T*
Defiance College *B, T*
Heidelberg College *T*
Hiram College *T*
John Carroll University *M, T*
Kent State University *M*
Lake Erie College *B, M*
Lourdes College *B*
Malone College *T*
Marietta College *B*
Miami University
  Oxford Campus *M*
Mount Union College *T*
Mount Vernon Nazarene
  University *B, M, T*
Muskingum College *B, M, T*
Ohio Dominican University *B, T*
Ohio Northern University *B, T*
Ohio State University
  Columbus Campus *M*
Ohio University *B, D, T*
Ohio Wesleyan University *B*
Otterbein College *B*
Sinclair Community College *A*
University of Akron *M, D*
University of Cincinnati *B, M, D, T*
University of Cincinnati
  Clermont College *A*
  Raymond Walters College *A*
University of Dayton *B, M, T*
University of Findlay *B, M, T*
University of Rio Grande *B, T*
University of Toledo *B, M, T*
Urbana University *B*
Walsh University *B*
Washington State Community
  College *A*
Wilmington College *B*
Wright State University *M*
Xavier University *M*
Youngstown State University *B, M*

Oklahoma

Cameron University *B, T*

Carl Albert State College *A*
Connors State College *A*
East Central University *M, T*
Eastern Oklahoma State College *A*
Mid-America Christian University *B*
Northeastern State University *B*
Northwestern Oklahoma State
  University *M*
Oklahoma Baptist University *B, T*
Oklahoma Christian University *B, T*
Oklahoma City Community College *A*
Oklahoma City University *B, M*
Oklahoma State University *B, T*
Rogers State University *A*
St. Gregory's University *B*
Southeastern Oklahoma State
  University *B, M, T*
Southern Nazarene University *B*
Southwestern Oklahoma State
  University *M, T*

Oregon

Chemeketa Community College *A*
Concordia University *B, M, T*
Corban College *B, M*
Eastern Oregon University *B, M*
Lewis & Clark College *M*
Linfield College *T*
Linn-Benton Community College *A*
Oregon State University *M*
Portland State University *T*
Southern Oregon University *M, T*
Treasure Valley Community College *A*
University of Portland *B, M, T*
Warner Pacific College *T*
Western Oregon University *B, M, T*
Willamette University *M*

Pennsylvania

Albright College *B, M, T*
Arcadia University *B, M, T*
Baptist Bible College of
  Pennsylvania *B*
Bryn Mawr College *T*
Bucknell University *B, T*
Butler County Community College *A*
California University of
  Pennsylvania *M*
Carlow University *T*
Cedar Crest College *B, M, T*
Chatham College *M, T*
Chestnut Hill College *T*
College Misericordia *T*
DeSales University *M, T*
Delaware Valley College *B, T*
Dickinson College *T*
Duquesne University *B, M, T*
East Stroudsburg University of
  Pennsylvania *M, T*
Eastern University *B, T*
Gannon University *B, M, T*
Gettysburg College *T*
Grove City College *B*
Harrisburg Area Community
  College *A*
Holy Family University *B, M, T*
Juniata College *B, T*
King's College *T*
Kutztown University of
  Pennsylvania *B, M, T*
La Salle University *B, M, T*
Lebanon Valley College *T*
Lehigh University *M*
Lincoln University *B, M, T*
Lycoming College *T*
Mansfield University of
  Pennsylvania *B, T*
Marywood University *B*
Mercyhurst College *B*
Millersville University of
  Pennsylvania *B*
Montgomery County Community
  College *A*
Muhlenberg College *T*

Penn State
 Abington *B*
 Altoona *B*
 Beaver *B*
 Berks *B*
 Delaware County *B*
 Dubois *B*
 Fayette *B*
 Hazleton *B*
 Lehigh Valley *B*
 McKeesport *B*
 Mont Alto *B*
 New Kensington *B*
 Schuylkill - Capital College *B*
 Shenango *B*
 University Park *B*
 Wilkes-Barre *B*
 Worthington Scranton *B*
 York *B*
Reading Area Community College *A*
Robert Morris University *T*
Rosemont College *T*
St. Francis University *B, T*
St. Joseph's University *B, M*
St. Vincent College *T*
Susquehanna University *T*
University of Pennsylvania *M, T*
University of Pittsburgh *T*
University of Pittsburgh
 Johnstown *B, T*
University of Scranton *B, M*
Villanova University *B, M*
Washington and Jefferson College *T*
Waynesburg College *B, T*
West Chester University of
 Pennsylvania *M, T*
Westminster College *B, T*
Widener University *M*
Wilson College *T*
York College of Pennsylvania *B, T*

Puerto Rico

American University of Puerto
 Rico *B, T*
Bayamon Central University *B*
Inter American University of Puerto
 Rico
 Aguadilla Campus *B*
 Arecibo Campus *B*
 Barranquitas Campus *B*
 Fajardo Campus *B, T*
 Ponce Campus *B, M*
 San German Campus *B*
Pontifical Catholic University of
 Puerto Rico *B*
Universidad Adventista de las
 Antillas *B*
University of Puerto Rico
 Cayey University College *B*
 Rio Piedras *B, M*
 Utuado *A*
University of the Sacred Heart *B*

Rhode Island

Providence College *B, M*
Rhode Island College *B, M, T*
Roger Williams University *B*
Salve Regina University *B*
University of Rhode Island *B*

South Carolina

Anderson University *B, T*
Charleston Southern University *B, M*
The Citadel *B, M*
Clemson University *B, M, T*
Coastal Carolina University *M, T*
Converse College *M, T*
Erskine College *B, T*
Francis Marion University *B, M, T*
Furman University *M, T*
Lander University *B, M, T*
Limestone College *B*
Presbyterian College *B, T*
South Carolina State University *M*

University of South Carolina *M, D*
University of South Carolina
 Aiken *B, T*
 Upstate *B, T*
Winthrop University *M, T*
Wofford College *T*

South Dakota

Augustana College *B, M, T*
Black Hills State University *T*
Dakota State University *B, T*
Mount Marty College *B*
University of Sioux Falls *T*
University of South Dakota *M, T*

Tennessee

Austin Peay State University *T*
Belmont University *B, M, T*
Bethel College *B, T*
Bryan College *T*
Carson-Newman College *B*
Christian Brothers University *B, M, T*
Crichton College *B*
Cumberland University *B, T*
East Tennessee State University *M, T*
Fisk University *T*
Free Will Baptist Bible College *B*
Freed-Hardeman University *B, T*
Hiwassee College *A*
King College *T*
Lambuth University *B, T*
Lee University *B, T*
Lincoln Memorial University *B, T*
Martin Methodist College *B*
Motlow State Community College *A*
Rhodes College *T*
Tennessee State University *B, M, T*
Tennessee Technological
 University *B, M, T*
Tennessee Temple University *B, M, T*
Tennessee Wesleyan College *T*
Trevecca Nazarene University *B, T*
Tusculum College *B, T*
Union University *B, T*
University of Memphis *T*
University of Tennessee
 Chattanooga *B, M, T*
 Knoxville *T*
University of the South *T*
Vanderbilt University *B, M, T*

Texas

Abilene Christian University *B, M, T*
Austin College *M*
Baylor University *T*
Brazosport College *A*
Clarendon College *A*
Coastal Bend College *A*
College of the Mainland *A*
Concordia University at Austin *B*
Dallas Baptist University *B, M*
El Paso Community College *A*
Frank Phillips College *A*
Grayson County College *A*
Houston Baptist University *B, M*
Howard Payne University *B, T*
Huston-Tillotson College *T*
Jarvis Christian College *B, T*
Lamar University *B, M, T*
LeTourneau University *B, T*
Lubbock Christian University *B, M*
McMurry University *B, T*
Navarro College *A*
Our Lady of the Lake University of San
 Antonio *M*
Paul Quinn College *B*
Rice University *M, T*
St. Edward's University *T*
Sam Houston State University *T*
Schreiner University *B*
South Texas College *A*
Southwestern Assemblies of God
 University *B*
Southwestern University *T*

Stephen F. Austin State University *M*
Sul Ross State University *M*
Texas A&M University
 Commerce *M, D, T*
 Kingsville *B, M*
 Texarkana *T*
Texas Christian University *B, M*
Texas Lutheran University *T*
Texas State University: San
 Marcos *M*
Texas Tech University *M*
Texas Wesleyan University *B, M, T*
Trinity University *M*
University of Dallas *T*
University of Houston *M, T*
University of Houston
 Downtown *M*
 Victoria *M*
University of Mary Hardin-Baylor *T*
University of North Texas *M, D*
University of St. Thomas *B*
University of Texas
 Brownsville *M*
 Pan American *M*
University of the Incarnate
 Word *B, M, T*
West Texas A&M University *T*
Wiley College *B*

Utah

Dixie State College of Utah *A*
Snow College *A*
Southern Utah University *B*
Utah State University *B, M, D*
Utah Valley State College *A*
Weber State University *B*
Westminster College *B, T*

Vermont

Bennington College *B, M*
Castleton State College *B, M*
Champlain College *B*
College of St. Joseph in Vermont *B*
Goddard College *B*
Green Mountain College *B, T*
Johnson State College *B, M*
Middlebury College *D, T*
Norwich University *T*
St. Michael's College *T*
University of Vermont *B*

Virginia

Bluefield College *B*
College of William and Mary *T*
Eastern Mennonite University *T*
Hampton University *M*
Hollins University *T*
James Madison University *T*
Liberty University *M, T*
Longwood University *T*
Mary Baldwin College *T*
Marymount University *M*
Old Dominion University *M, T*
Radford University *T*
Randolph-Macon College *T*
Randolph-Macon Woman's College *M*
St. Paul's College *T*
University of Mary Washington *T*
University of Richmond *B, T*
University of Virginia's College at
 Wise *T*
Virginia Intermont College *B*
Virginia Polytechnic Institute and
 State University *B*
Virginia Wesleyan College *T*

Washington

Central Washington University *M*
Eastern Washington University *M*
Gonzaga University *T*
Heritage University *B, M*
Northwest University *B*
Pacific Lutheran University *B*

Saint Martin's University *B, T*
Seattle Pacific University *B*
University of Washington *M, T*
Walla Walla College *M, T*
Washington State University *B, M, T*
Western Washington University *M*
Whitworth College *B, M, T*

West Virginia

Alderson-Broaddus College *B, T*
Bethany College *B*
Davis and Elkins College *B*
Glenville State College *B*
Marshall University *B, M*
Mountain State University *A*
Ohio Valley University *B*
Potomac State College of West Virginia
 University *A*
Salem International University *B, T*
Shepherd University *B, T*
University of Charleston *B*
West Liberty State College *B*
West Virginia State University *B*
West Virginia University *M*
West Virginia Wesleyan College *B*

Wisconsin

Alverno College *T*
Beloit College *T*
Carroll College *T*
Carthage College *T*
Concordia University Wisconsin *B, T*
Edgewood College *B, T*
Lakeland College *B*
Lawrence University *T*
Maranatha Baptist Bible College *B*
Marian College of Fond du Lac *B, T*
Marquette University *B*
Mount Mary College *B, T*
Northland College *T*
Ripon College *T*
St. Norbert College *T*
University of Wisconsin
 Green Bay *T*
 Oshkosh *B, T*
 Parkside *T*
 Platteville *T*
 River Falls *T*
 Stevens Point *B, T*
 Superior *M*
 Whitewater *B, T*
Viterbo University *B, M, T*

Wyoming

Central Wyoming College *A*
Eastern Wyoming College *A*
Laramie County Community
 College *A*
Northwest College *A*
Sheridan College *A*
University of Wyoming *B*
Western Wyoming Community
 College *A*

Secondary school administration

Alabama

University of Alabama *D*

Arkansas

Arkansas State University *M, T*

Illinois

Concordia University *M*
Lewis University *D*
University of Illinois
 Urbana-Champaign *M, D, T*

Indiana

Indiana University-Purdue University
 Indianapolis *M*

Oakland City University *M*

Kentucky
Morehead State University *M*
Murray State University *M, T*
University of the Cumberlands *M*

Louisiana
Xavier University of Louisiana *M*

Massachusetts
Lesley University *M*

Michigan
Eastern Michigan University *M*
Saginaw Valley State University *M*

Minnesota
Bethel University *D*
Capella University *M, D*

Missouri
Lincoln University *M*
Lindenwood University *M*
Southwest Baptist University *M*

Montana
University of Great Falls *M*

Nebraska
Concordia University *M, T*
Creighton University *M*
University of Nebraska
Lincoln *D*
Wayne State College *M*

Nevada
University of Nevada
Reno *M, D*

New Jersey
William Paterson University of New
Jersey *M*

New York
St. Bonaventure University *M*
St. John Fisher College *M*

North Carolina
Appalachian State University *M*
North Carolina Central University *M*
University of North Carolina
Chapel Hill *M*
Pembroke *M*

North Dakota
University of Mary *M*

Ohio
Kent State University *M, D*
University of Findlay *M, T*
Youngstown State University *M*

Oklahoma
University of Oklahoma *T*

Pennsylvania
East Stroudsburg University of
Pennsylvania *T*
Gannon University *T*
Marywood University *M*
Widener University *M, T*

Puerto Rico
Universidad del Este *M*

South Carolina
Charleston Southern University *M*

South Dakota
University of South Dakota *M, D*

Tennessee
University of Memphis *T*

Texas
Our Lady of the Lake University of San
Antonio *M*
University of Texas
Arlington *T*

Vermont
Castleton State College *D*
St. Michael's College *T*

Virginia
Marymount University *M*

Washington
Seattle Pacific University *T*
University of Washington *M, D, T*
Washington State University *M*
Western Washington University *M*

Wisconsin
Concordia University Wisconsin *M*
University of Wisconsin
Superior *M*

Security/loss prevention

Arizona
Arizona Institute of Business and
Technology
International Institute of the
Americas: Mesa *C*
International Institute of the Americas
Phoenix *C*
Tucson *C*
International Institute of the
Americas: West Valley *C*

California
De Anza College *C, A*
Grossmont Community College *C, A*
National University *B*
Palomar College *C, A*
Sierra College *A*

Connecticut
University of New Haven *C*

Florida
Broward Community College *A*
Miami Dade College *C*
St. Petersburg College *C, A*

Georgia
Albany Technical College *C*

Illinois
Black Hawk College *C*
Lewis University *B*
Lincoln Land Community College *C*
Moraine Valley Community College *C*
Southwestern Illinois College *C, A*
Waubonsee Community College *C*
Westwood College of Technology
O'Hare *B*
William Rainey Harper College *C*

Indiana
Vincennes University *A*

Kansas
Washburn University of Topeka *B*

Kentucky
Eastern Kentucky University *B, M*
Hopkinsville Community College *C, A*

Maryland
Community College of Baltimore
County *C, A*

Massachusetts
Bristol Community College *C*
Marian Court College *C, A*
Northeastern University *B*

Michigan
Baker College
of Muskegon *C*
Grand Valley State University *B*
Henry Ford Community College *A*
Macomb Community College *C*
Schoolcraft College *C*

Minnesota
Winona State University *B*

Missouri
Central Missouri State University *M*

Nevada
Community College of Southern
Nevada *A*

New Hampshire
McIntosh College *A*

New Jersey
Essex County College *C*
New Jersey City University *B*

New Mexico
International Institute of the
Americas *C*

New York
Dutchess Community College *C*
Interboro Institute *A*
Nassau Community College *A*
Schenectady County Community
College *A*
State University of New York
Farmingdale *B*

Ohio
Lakeland Community College *C, A*
Ohio University *A*
Ohio University
Zanesville Campus *A*
Owens Community College
Toledo *A*
University of Cincinnati
Clermont College *A*
Youngstown State University *B*

Pennsylvania
ICM School of Business & Medical
Careers *A*
Montgomery County Community
College *C, A*
York College of Pennsylvania *B*
York Technical Institute *A*

Texas
Hill College *A*

Vermont
Champlain College *B*

Virginia
Northern Virginia Community
College *C, A*

Washington
Clover Park Technical College *C*
Spokane Community College *A*

Wisconsin
Fox Valley Technical College *A*

Security services management

Florida
City College: Casselberry *A*
Florida Metropolitan University:
Orange Park *A, B*
St. Petersburg College *C, A*

Illinois
Westwood College of Technology
O'Hare *B*

Kansas
Central Christian College of
Kansas *A, B*
Southwestern College *B*

Massachusetts
Bunker Hill Community College *A*

New Hampshire
McIntosh College *A*

New York
State University of New York
College at Brockport *B*
Farmingdale *B*

Pennsylvania
Harrisburg Area Community
College *C*

Texas
University of Houston
Downtown *M*

Vermont
Champlain College *B*

Security system installation/repair/ inspection

Washington
Clover Park Technical College *C*

Selling/sales operations

Arkansas
Harding University *B*

California
Santa Barbara City College *C, A*
Santiago Canyon College *A*

Colorado
Arapahoe Community College *C, A*

Connecticut
Naugatuck Valley Community
College *C, A*

Georgia
Gwinnett Technical College *C*

Illinois
Bradley University *B*
McHenry County College *C, A*
Moraine Valley Community College *A*
Parkland College *A*

Iowa

AIB College of Business *A*
Des Moines Area Community
College *C*

Kansas

Brown Mackie College *A*

Michigan

Madonna University *C, B*

Minnesota

Alexandria Technical College *C*
Dakota County Technical College *C*
Minnesota State Community and
Technical College - Fergus Falls *A*
Northwest Technical College *C, A*

New York

Genesee Community College *C*

Ohio

University of Akron *A*
University of Toledo *A*
Youngstown State University *A, B, M*

Pennsylvania

Harrisburg Area Community
College *C*

Utah

LDS Business College *C*

Washington

Clark College *C, A*
Spokane Community College *A*

Wyoming

Central Wyoming College *C*

Semitic languages

Illinois

Trinity International University *M*

New York

Cornell University *B, M, D*
Yeshiva University *M, D*

Pennsylvania

University of Pennsylvania *B, M, D*

Texas

University of Texas
Austin *B*

Sheet metal technology

California

Foothill College *C*
Yuba Community College
District *C, A*

Illinois

Black Hawk College *C*

Indiana

Ivy Tech State College
Ivy Tech Community College:
Bloomington *C, A*
Ivy Tech Community College:
Central Indiana *C, A*
Ivy Tech Community College:
Columbus *C, A*
Ivy Tech Community College: East
Central *C, A*
Ivy Tech Community College:
Kokomo *C, A*
Ivy Tech Community College:
Lafayette *C, A*

Ivy Tech Community College: North
Central *C, A*
Ivy Tech Community College:
Northeast *C, A*
Ivy Tech Community College:
Northwest *C, A*
Ivy Tech Community College: South
Central *C, A*
Ivy Tech Community College:
Southwest *C, A*
Ivy Tech Community College:
Wabash Valley *C, A*
Ivy Tech Community College:
Whitewater *C, A*

Michigan

Mott Community College *C*

Minnesota

Dunwoody College of Technology *C*
Hennepin Technical College *C, A*
St. Paul College *C*

Montana

Montana State University
Billings *C*

Pennsylvania

Community College of Allegheny
County *C*

Utah

Salt Lake Community College *A*

Washington

Clover Park Technical College *C*

Wisconsin

Western Wisconsin Technical
College *C*

Shoe/leather repair

Oklahoma

Oklahoma State University
Okmulgee *C*

Sign language interpretation

Arizona

Phoenix College *C, A*
Pima Community College *A*

Arkansas

University of Arkansas
Little Rock *A, B*

California

College of the Sequoias *C*
Golden West College *C, A*
Los Angeles Pierce College *C, A*
Mount San Antonio College *C, A*
Palomar College *C, A*
Riverside Community College *C, A*
Saddleback College *C, A*
San Diego City College *C*
Vista Community College *C, A*

Colorado

Front Range Community College *A*
Pikes Peak Community College *A*

Connecticut

Northwestern Connecticut
Community College *C, A*

Delaware

Delaware Technical and Community
College
Stanton/Wilmington Campus *A*

District of Columbia

Gallaudet University *M*

Florida

Florida Community College at
Jacksonville *A*
Hillsborough Community
College *C, A*
Miami Dade College *C, A*
St. Petersburg College *A*

Georgia

Georgia Highlands College *A*
Georgia Perimeter College *C, A*
Valdosta State University *B*

Idaho

College of Southern Idaho *A*
Idaho State University *B*

Illinois

Black Hawk College *A*
Illinois Central College *C*
MacMurray College *A, B*
Waubonsee Community College *C, A*
William Rainey Harper College *C, A*

Indiana

Bethel College *A, B*
Goshen College *B*
Vincennes University *A*

Iowa

Iowa Western Community College *A*
Kirkwood Community College *A*
Scott Community College *A*

Kansas

Cowley County Community
College *A*
Johnson County Community
College *A*

Kentucky

Eastern Kentucky University *A, B*

Louisiana

Delgado Community College *C, A*

Maryland

Community College of Baltimore
County *C, A*
Frederick Community College *C*

Massachusetts

Northeastern University *B*
Northern Essex Community
College *C, A*

Michigan

Lansing Community College *A*
Mott Community College *A*
Oakland Community College *C, A*

Minnesota

College of St. Catherine *B*
North Central University *B*
St. Paul College *C, A*

Mississippi

Hinds Community College *A*
Itawamba Community College *A*

Missouri

Maple Woods Community College *A*

St. Louis Community College
St. Louis Community College at
Florissant Valley *A*

Nebraska

Metropolitan Community
College *C, A*

New Hampshire

New Hampshire Community
Technical College
Nashua *C*
University of New Hampshire at
Manchester *B*

New Jersey

Burlington County College *C, A*
Camden County College *A*
Ocean County College *C*
Union County College *C, A*

New Mexico

Santa Fe Community College *C, A*
University of New Mexico *B*

New York

Rochester Institute of
Technology *A, B*
Suffolk County Community College *A*
Tompkins-Cortland Community
College *C*
University of Rochester *B*

North Carolina

Blue Ridge Community College *A*
Central Piedmont Community
College *C, A*
Gardner-Webb University *B*
Randolph Community College *C, A*
Wilson Technical Community
College *A*

North Dakota

Lake Region State College *C*

Ohio

Cincinnati State Technical and
Community College *A*
Columbus State Community
College *A*
Cuyahoga Community College
Metropolitan Campus *A*
Kent State University *B*
Ohio University
Chillicothe Campus *A*
Shawnee State University *C*
Sinclair Community College *C, A*
University of Akron *C*

Oklahoma

Oklahoma State University
Oklahoma City *C, A*
Tulsa Community College *C, A*

Oregon

Portland Community College *C, A*
Western Oregon University *B*

Pennsylvania

Community College of
Philadelphia *C, A*
Mount Aloysius College *A, B*

South Carolina

Spartanburg Technical College *C*

Tennessee

Maryville College *B*
Nashville State Community College *A*

Texas

Austin Community College *C, A*
Blinn College *A*
Collin County Community College
    District *C, A*
Del Mar College *C, A*
Eastfield College *C, A*
El Paso Community College *C, A*
Houston Community College
    System *C, A*
Howard College *C, A*
McLennan Community College *C, A*
North Harris Montgomery
    Community College District *C, A*
San Antonio College *A*
Tarrant County College *A*
Tyler Junior College *C, A*

Utah

Salt Lake Community College *A*

Virginia

J. Sargeant Reynolds Community
    College *C*
New River Community College *C*

Washington

Seattle Central Community College *A*
Spokane Falls Community College *A*
Wenatchee Valley College *C, A*

Wisconsin

Gateway Technical College *A*
Milwaukee Area Technical College *A*
Northcentral Technical College *A*

Slavic languages

California

Stanford University *B, D*
University of California
    Berkeley *B, M, D*
    Los Angeles *B, M, D*
    Santa Barbara *B*
University of Southern
    California *M, D*

Connecticut

Connecticut College *B*
Yale University *M, D*

Florida

Florida State University *M*

Illinois

Northwestern University *B, M, D*
University of Chicago *B, D*
University of Illinois
    Chicago *M, D*
    Urbana-Champaign *M, D*

Indiana

Indiana University
    Bloomington *B, M, D*

Kansas

University of Kansas *B, M, D*

Massachusetts

Harvard College *B, M, D*

Michigan

Wayne State University *B*

New Jersey

Princeton University *B, M, D*

New York

Columbia University
    Columbia College *B*

Cornell University *B, M, D*

Pennsylvania

University of Pittsburgh *B, M, D*

Rhode Island

Brown University *B, M, D*

Texas

Rice University *B*
University of Texas
    Austin *M, D*

Virginia

University of Virginia *B, M, D*

Wisconsin

University of Wisconsin
    Madison *M, D*

Slavic studies

Connecticut

Connecticut College *B*

Illinois

University of Chicago *B, D*

Michigan

Oakland University *B*

New York

Barnard College *B*
Columbia University
    Columbia College *B*

Rhode Island

Brown University *B, M, D*

Texas

Baylor University *B*
Rice University *B*

Washington

University of Washington *B, M*

Slovak

New York

State University of New York
    Stony Brook *M*

Small business administration/ management

Alaska

University of Alaska
    Southeast *C*

California

Foothill College *C*
Ohlone College *C, A*
Santa Barbara City College *C, A*
Sierra College *C, A*
Vista Community College *C, A*

Colorado

Adams State College *B*
Colorado Technical University *C*
Jones International University *C, B, M*
Red Rocks Community College *C*
University of Colorado
    Boulder *B, M*

Florida

Pasco-Hernando Community
    College *C*
Valencia Community College *C*

Georgia

Athens Technical College *C*
Coastal Georgia Community
    College *C*
Gwinnett Technical College *C*

Idaho

Lewis-Clark State College *C, A, B*

Illinois

Black Hawk College *C, A*
Bradley University *B*
Heartland Community College *C*
North Central College *B*
Waubonsee Community College *C, A*

Indiana

Huntington University *B*
Purdue University
    Calumet *B*

Iowa

Des Moines Area Community
    College *C*

Kansas

Central Christian College of
    Kansas *A, B*

Maine

Husson College *B*
Washington County Community
    College *A*

Massachusetts

Babson College *B*
Springfield Technical Community
    College *A*

Michigan

Baker College
    of Clinton Township *A*
    of Muskegon *C, A*
Delta College *C, A*
Northern Michigan University *B*

Minnesota

Alexandria Technical College *C*
Central Lakes College *C*
Normandale Community College *C*

New York

Columbia-Greene Community
    College *C*
Globe Institute of Technology *C, A, B*

North Carolina

Chowan College *B*

North Dakota

Lake Region State College *A*
Sitting Bull College *A*

Ohio

Baldwin-Wallace College *B*
Lakeland Community College *C, A*
Miami University
    Hamilton Campus *C*

Oklahoma

Rose State College *A*

Oregon

Oregon Institute of Technology *B*

Pennsylvania

Bucks County Community College *A*
DeVry University
    Ft. Washington *B, M*

Harrisburg Area Community
    College *C, A*
Newport Business Institute *A*

Vermont

Champlain College *A, B*

Washington

Clark College *C*
Grays Harbor College *C*
Shoreline Community College *C, A*

West Virginia

Southern West Virginia Community
    and Technical College *A*
Valley College of Technology *A*

Wisconsin

Milwaukee Area Technical College *C*

Small engine mechanics

Alabama

Gadsden State Community College *C*
Shelton State Community College *C*

Arkansas

University of Arkansas
    Cossatot Community College of the
        C

California

College of the Desert *C*
Los Medanos College *C, A*
Southwestern College *C, A*

Georgia

Central Georgia Technical College *C*
Southwest Georgia Technical
    College *C*

Michigan

Kirtland Community College *C, A*

Minnesota

Alexandria Technical College *C*
Hennepin Technical College *C, A*
Minnesota State Community and
    Technical College - Fergus Falls *C*

Nebraska

Southeast Community College
    Lincoln Campus *C*

New York

Jamestown Community College *A*

North Carolina

Haywood Community College *C*

North Dakota

North Dakota State College of
    Science *C, A*

Pennsylvania

Delaware County Community
    College *C*

Texas

Austin Community College *C*
Cedar Valley College *C*
Texarkana College *C*

Utah

Salt Lake Community College *C*

Wisconsin

Nicolet Area Technical College *A*
Wisconsin Indianhead Technical
    College *C*

Social/philosophical foundations of education

Alabama
Troy University *M*

Arizona
Arizona State University *M*
University of Arizona *M, D*

California
California State University
  Long Beach *M*
  Northridge *M*
Hope International University *M*
Stanford University *M, D*

Colorado
University of Colorado
  Boulder *M, D*

Connecticut
Central Connecticut State
    University *M*
University of Connecticut *D, T*

Florida
Florida Atlantic University *M*
Florida State University *M, D*
University of Florida *B, M*

Georgia
Georgia State University *M*
University of Georgia *D*

Hawaii
University of Hawaii
  Manoa *M*

Illinois
Loyola University of Chicago *M, D*
Northern Illinois University *M*
Northwestern University *B, M*
University of Illinois
  Urbana-Champaign *M, D*
Western Illinois University *M*

Indiana
Indiana University
  Bloomington *M, D*

Iowa
Iowa State University *M*
University of Iowa *M, D*
University of Northern Iowa *M*

Kansas
University of Kansas *M*

Kentucky
University of Kentucky *M*

Massachusetts
Tufts University *M*

Michigan
Eastern Michigan University *M*

Minnesota
University of Minnesota
  Twin Cities *B, M*

Missouri
University of Missouri
  Columbia *M, D*
Washington University in St. Louis *B*

New Jersey
Rutgers, The State University of New
  Jersey
  New Brunswick/Piscataway
    Campus *D*

New Mexico
University of New Mexico *M, D*

New York
Eugene Lang College The New School
  for Liberal Arts *B*
Fordham University *M*
Hofstra University *M, T*
New York University *M, D*
State University of New York
  Buffalo *D*
Syracuse University *D*

Ohio
Ohio University *M, D*
University of Akron *M*
University of Cincinnati *M, D*
University of Findlay *B, M*
University of Toledo *M, D*
Youngstown State University *M*

Oklahoma
University of Oklahoma *M, D*

Pennsylvania
Penn State
  University Park *M, D*
University of Pennsylvania *M, D*

South Carolina
University of South Carolina *D*

Texas
Texas Christian University *M*
Texas Southern University *D*
University of Houston *M, D*
University of Texas
  San Antonio *M*

Utah
University of Utah *M, D*

Vermont
Sterling College *B*

Washington
Eastern Washington University *M*
University of Washington *M, D*

Wisconsin
University of Wisconsin
  Madison *M, D*
  Milwaukee *M*
  Whitewater *M*

Social psychology

California
California Institute of Integral
  Studies *D*
San Francisco State University *M*
University of California
  Irvine *M, D*
  Santa Cruz *D*

District of Columbia
George Washington University *D*

Florida
Florida State University *M, D*

Illinois
Loyola University of Chicago *M, D*

University of Illinois
  Urbana-Champaign *M, D*

Indiana
Ball State University *M*

Iowa
University of Iowa *D*

Massachusetts
Clark University *M, D*
Harvard College *D*
Northeastern University *M*
Tufts University *M, D*
University of Massachusetts
  Lowell *M*

Missouri
University of Missouri
  Columbia *M, D*

Nevada
University of Nevada
  Reno *D*

New York
Fordham University *M, D*
New York University *M, D*
State University of New York
  Albany *D*
  Buffalo *D*
Syracuse University *M, D*
University of Rochester *D*

North Carolina
Duke University *M, D*

Ohio
Bowling Green State University *M, D*
Miami University
  Oxford Campus *T*

Pennsylvania
Temple University *M, D*

Texas
University of Houston *M, D*

Social science teacher education

Alabama
Athens State University *B*
Auburn University *B*
Birmingham-Southern College *T*
Huntingdon College *T*
Judson College *B*
Miles College *B*
Oakwood College *B*
Samford University *B*

Alaska
University of Alaska
  Fairbanks *M*

Arizona
Grand Canyon University *B*
Prescott College *B, M, T*
University of Arizona *B, M*

Arkansas
Arkansas State University *B, M, T*
Henderson State University *B, M, T*
University of Arkansas *B*
University of Arkansas
  Pine Bluff *B, T*
University of Central Arkansas *T*

California
Azusa Pacific University *T*

California Baptist University *T*
California Lutheran University *B, T*
California Polytechnic State
    University: San Luis Obispo *B, T*
California State University
  Chico *B, M, T*
  Dominguez Hills *T*
  Long Beach *T*
  Northridge *B, T*
  Sacramento *T*
  San Bernardino *T*
Fresno Pacific University *B, T*
Hope International University *B*
Humboldt State University *T*
Loyola Marymount University *M*
Master's College *T*
Mills College *T*
Mount St. Mary's College *T*
Pacific Union College *T*
Saddleback College *A*
San Diego Christian College *B, T*
San Diego State University *B, T*
San Francisco State University *B, T*
Simpson University *B, T*
Sonoma State University *T*
Stanford University *M, T*
Taft College *A*
University of Redlands *T*
University of the Pacific *T*
Vanguard University of Southern
    California *T*
Westmont College *T*

Colorado
Adams State College *B, T*
Colorado State University
  Pueblo *T*
Metropolitan State College of
  Denver *T*
Western State College of Colorado *T*

Connecticut
St. Joseph College *T*
Southern Connecticut State
    University *B, M, T*

Delaware
University of Delaware *B, T*

District of Columbia
George Washington University *T*

Florida
Flagler College *B*
Florida Agricultural and Mechanical
    University *T*
Florida Atlantic University *B*
Florida International
    University *B, M, T*
Florida State University *B, M, D, T*
Palm Beach Atlantic University *B, T*
Palm Beach Community College *A*
Stetson University *B*
University of Central Florida *B, M*
University of Florida *B*
University of South Florida *B, M*
University of Tampa *T*
Warner Southern College *B*

Georgia
Armstrong Atlantic State
    University *B, M, T*
Clark Atlanta University *B*
Columbus State University *B, M*
Darton College *A*
Emmanuel College *B*
Gainesville State College *A*
Georgia College and State
    University *B, M, T*
Georgia Southern University *M, T*
Georgia Southwestern State
    University *M*

North Georgia College & State
University *M*
Piedmont College *M, T*
Shorter College *T*
University of Georgia *B, M, D*

Hawaii

Brigham Young University-Hawaii *B, T*

Idaho

Boise State University *T*
Brigham Young University-Idaho *T*
Lewis-Clark State College *B, T*
Northwest Nazarene University *B*

Illinois

Augustana College *B, T*
Benedictine University *T*
Blackburn College *B, T*
Concordia University *B, T*
Dominican University *T*
Eastern Illinois University *B, T*
Knox College *B*
Lake Land College *A*
Lewis University *T*
Millikin University *B, T*
North Park University *T*
Olivet Nazarene University *B, T*
Rockford College *T*
Roosevelt University *B*
St. Xavier University *B*
Sauk Valley Community College *A*
University of Illinois
Urbana-Champaign *T*
Wheaton College *T*

Indiana

Butler University *T*
Goshen College *B*
Manchester College *B, T*
Purdue University
Calumet *B*
St. Mary-of-the-Woods College *B, T*
Taylor University *B, T*
University of Evansville *B*
Valparaiso University *B*
Vincennes University *A*

Iowa

Ashford University *B, T*
Briar Cliff University *B*
Buena Vista University *B, T*
Central College *T*
Cornell College *B, T*
Dordt College *B*
Drake University *M, T*
Ellsworth Community College *A*
Iowa State University *T*
Loras College *T*
Morningside College *B*
Mount Mercy College *T*
Northwestern College *T*
St. Ambrose University *B, T*
Simpson College *T*
University of Northern Iowa *B*
Upper Iowa University *B, T*
Wartburg College *T*
William Penn University *B*

Kansas

Bethany College *B*
Central Christian College of Kansas *A*
Emporia State University *M, T*
Friends University *B*
Garden City Community College *A*
Newman University *T*
Tabor College *B, T*
Washburn University of Topeka *B*

Kentucky

Campbellsville University *B*
Lindsey Wilson College *B, T*

Louisiana

Grambling State University *B*
Southern University
New Orleans *B*

Maine

University of Maine
Farmington *B, T*
University of Southern Maine *T*

Maryland

Frostburg State University *B, T*
Washington College *T*

Massachusetts

Bridgewater State College *T*
Framingham State College *B*
Westfield State College *T*
Worcester State College *T*

Michigan

Adrian College *B, T*
Alma College *T*
Andrews University *B, M*
Aquinas College *B, T*
Cornerstone University *B, T*
Eastern Michigan University *B, T*
Grand Valley State University *T*
Lansing Community College *A*
Madonna University *T*
Michigan Technological University *T*
Northern Michigan University *B, T*
Olivet College *B, T*
University of Detroit Mercy *B, M, T*
University of Michigan
Flint *T*
Western Michigan University *B*

Minnesota

Concordia College: Moorhead *B, T*
Gustavus Adolphus College *T*
Minnesota State University
Mankato *B, M, T*
Pillsbury Baptist Bible College *T*
St. Cloud State University *B, T*
St. Mary's University of Minnesota *B*
University of Minnesota
Morris *T*
Winona State University *B, T*

Mississippi

Blue Mountain College *B*
Coahoma Community College *A*
Delta State University *B, M, T*
Jackson State University *B*
Mississippi College *B, M*
Mississippi State University *T*
Mississippi Valley State University *B, T*
Rust College *B*
William Carey College *B*

Missouri

Central Methodist University *B*
Evangel University *T*
Lincoln University *B, T*
Lindenwood University *B*
Missouri Baptist University *T*
Missouri Southern State
University *B, T*
Northwest Missouri State
University *B, T*
Southwest Baptist University *B, T*
University of Missouri
St. Louis *T*
Washington University in St.
Louis *B, M, T*
Webster University *M*
William Woods University *B, T*

Montana

Montana State University
Billings *B, T*

University of Great Falls *B*
University of Montana: Missoula *T*

Nebraska

Chadron State College *B*
College of Saint Mary *B, T*
Concordia University *B, T*
Creighton University *T*
Dana College *B*
Hastings College *B, M, T*
Midland Lutheran College *B, T*
Nebraska Wesleyan University *B*
Peru State College *B, T*
Union College *T*
University of Nebraska
Kearney *B, M, T*
Lincoln *B*
Wayne State College *B, T*
York College *B, T*

Nevada

Great Basin College *B*
University of Nevada
Reno *B*

New Hampshire

New England College *B, T*
New Hampshire Community
Technical College
Stratham *A*
Rivier College *B, T*
St. Anselm College *T*

New Jersey

The College of New Jersey *B, T*
Georgian Court University *T*
Rowan University *M*
St. Peter's College *T*

New Mexico

College of the Southwest *B, T*
Western New Mexico University *B*

New York

Dominican College of Blauvelt *B, T*
Dowling College *B*
Elmira College *B, T*
Fordham University *M, T*
Houghton College *B, T*
Manhattan College *B, T*
Manhattanville College *M, T*
New York Institute of Technology *B, T*
Roberts Wesleyan College *B, M*
St. John Fisher College *B, T*
State University of New York
College at Oneonta *B, T*
College at Plattsburgh *B*
Utica College *B*
Vassar College *T*
Wells College *T*

North Carolina

Appalachian State University *M, T*
Fayetteville State University *B, T*
Gardner-Webb University *B*
Johnson C. Smith University *B*
Lenoir Community College *A*
Mars Hill College *T*
North Carolina Agricultural and
Technical State University *B, M, T*
Pfeiffer University *B*
Sandhills Community College *A*
University of North Carolina
Greensboro *B*

North Dakota

Dickinson State University *B, T*
Mayville State University *B, T*
Minot State University *B*
North Dakota State University *B, T*
University of Mary *B, T*
Valley City State University *B, T*

Ohio

Defiance College *B, T*
Hiram College *T*
Miami University
Oxford Campus *M*
Ohio Wesleyan University *B*
Shawnee State University *B*
University of Findlay *B, M, T*
University of Rio Grande *B, T*
University of Toledo *M*
Walsh University *B*
Wilmington College *B*
Youngstown State University *B, M*

Oklahoma

Eastern Oklahoma State College *A*
Mid-America Christian University *B*
Northwestern Oklahoma State
University *B, T*
Oklahoma Baptist University *B, T*
Southwestern Oklahoma State
University *B, M, T*
University of Tulsa *T*

Oregon

Corban College *B*
Eastern Oregon University *B*
Linfield College *T*

Pennsylvania

Arcadia University *B, M, T*
Elizabethtown College *B*
Grove City College *T*
Holy Family University *B, M, T*
La Salle University *B, T*
Lebanon Valley College *T*
Mercyhurst College *B, T*
St. Francis University *B, T*
St. Vincent College *T*
Susquehanna University *T*
Thiel College *B*
University of Pittsburgh
Johnstown *B, T*
Washington and Jefferson College *T*
West Chester University of
Pennsylvania *B, T*
Wilson College *T*

Puerto Rico

Turabo University *B*

South Carolina

Charleston Southern University *B, M*
The Citadel *M*
Converse College *T*
University of South Carolina
Aiken *B, T*
Wofford College *T*

South Dakota

Black Hills State University *B*
Dakota Wesleyan University *B, T*
Mount Marty College *B*
Northern State University *B, T*
University of Sioux Falls *T*
University of South Dakota *B, M, T*

Tennessee

American Baptist College of ABT
Seminary *B*
Belmont University *B, M, T*
Cumberland University *B, T*
Lincoln Memorial University *B, T*
Maryville College *B, T*

Texas

Del Mar College *A*
Howard Payne University *B, T*
Kilgore College *A*
McMurry University *T*
North Harris Montgomery
Community College District *A*

Stephen F. Austin State University *T*
Texas A&M University
   Commerce *T*
Texas State University: San Marcos *T*
Texas Wesleyan University *B, M, T*
University of Mary Hardin-Baylor *T*
University of Texas
   San Antonio *T*
West Texas A&M University *T*

Utah

Brigham Young University *B*
Southern Utah University *B*
University of Utah *B*
Weber State University *B*

Vermont

Castleton State College *B, T*
Johnson State College *B*
Lyndon State College *B*
University of Vermont *B*

Virginia

Averett University *M, T*
Bridgewater College *T*
Eastern Mennonite University *T*
Liberty University *B, M, T*
Radford University *T*
University of Virginia's College at
   Wise *T*
Virginia Western Community
   College *A*

Washington

Central Washington University *B, T*
Eastern Washington University *B, M, T*
Seattle Pacific University *B, T*
Western Washington University *B*
Whitworth College *B, T*

West Virginia

West Liberty State College *B*

Wisconsin

Carroll College *B, T*
Carthage College *M, T*
Concordia University Wisconsin *B*
Edgewood College *B*
Lawrence University *T*
Marquette University *B*
Northland College *T*
St. Norbert College *T*
Silver Lake College *T*
University of Wisconsin
   Green Bay *T*
   Oshkosh *B, T*
   Parkside *T*
   Platteville *B, T*
   River Falls *T*
   Superior *B, T*
   Whitewater *B, T*

Social sciences

Alabama

Faulkner State Community College *A*
Samford University *A, B*
Southern Union State Community
   College *A*
Spring Hill College *B, T*
Troy University *B*
University of Mobile *B, T*
University of Montevallo *B, T*
Virginia College *A*

Alaska

University of Alaska
   Southeast *B*

Arizona

Arizona State University West *B*
Central Arizona College *A*

Dine College *A*
Grand Canyon University *B*
Northern Arizona University *B, M*
Prescott College *B, M*
Tohono O'odham Community
   College *A*

Arkansas

Arkansas Baptist College *B*
Arkansas State University
   Beebe *A*
Harding University *B*
Ouachita Baptist University *B*
Phillips Community College of the
   University of Arkansas *A*
University of Arkansas
   Monticello *B*
University of Central Arkansas *M*
University of the Ozarks *B*

California

Allan Hancock College *A*
Azusa Pacific University *B, M*
Barstow College *A*
Bethany University *B*
Biola University *B*
Butte College *A*
Cabrillo College *A*
California Institute of
   Technology *B, D*
California Polytechnic State
   University: San Luis Obispo *B*
California State Polytechnic
   University: Pomona *B*
California State University
   Chico *B, M*
   Fullerton *B, M*
   Los Angeles *M*
   Monterey Bay *B*
   Sacramento *B*
   San Bernardino *B, M*
   San Marcos *B*
   Stanislaus *B*
Canada College *A*
Cerro Coso Community College *A*
Chabot College *A*
Chaffey College *A*
Citrus College *A*
College of Alameda *A*
College of San Mateo *A*
College of the Canyons *A*
College of the Desert *A*
College of the Sequoias *A*
College of the Siskiyous *A*
Columbia College *A*
Copper Mountain College *A*
Crafton Hills College *A*
East Los Angeles College *A*
Feather River College *A*
Foothill College *A*
Fresno City College *A*
Fresno Pacific University *B*
Gavilan Community College *A*
Glendale Community College *A*
Golden West College *A*
Hope International University *B*
Humboldt State University *B, M*
Imperial Valley College *A*
Lake Tahoe Community College *A*
Laney College *A*
Las Positas College *A*
Lassen College *A*
Long Beach City College *A*
Mendocino College *A*
Merced College *A*
Merritt College *A*
Mills College *B*
MiraCosta College *A*
Mission College *A*
Modesto Junior College *A*
Moorpark College *A*
Mount St. Mary's College *B*
Mount San Jacinto College *A*
Napa Valley College *A*

Ohlone College *A*
Pacific Union College *B*
Pasadena City College *A*
Pitzer College *B*
Point Loma Nazarene University *B*
Pomona College *B*
Porterville College *A*
Reedley College *A*
Sacramento City College *C, A*
Saddleback College *A*
San Diego Christian College *B*
San Diego City College *A*
San Diego Mesa College *A*
San Diego Miramar College *A*
San Diego State University *B*
San Francisco State University *B, M*
San Joaquin Delta College *A*
San Jose City College *A*
San Jose State University *B, M*
Santa Ana College *A*
Santa Monica College *A*
Santiago Canyon College *A*
Simpson University *B*
Solano Community College *A*
Taft College *A*
University of California
   Irvine *B, M, D*
University of La Verne *B*
University of the Pacific *B, T*
Vanguard University of Southern
   California *B*
Ventura College *A*
West Hills Community College *A*
West Valley College *A*
Westmont College *B*
Yuba Community College District *A*

Colorado

Adams State College *B*
Colorado Christian University *B*
Colorado Mountain College
   Alpine Campus *A*
   Spring Valley Campus *A*
   Timberline Campus *A*
Colorado State University
   Pueblo *B*
Mesa State College *B*
United States Air Force Academy *B*
University of Colorado
   Denver and Health Sciences
   Center *M*
University of Denver *B*
University of Northern
   Colorado *B, M, T*

Connecticut

Albertus Magnus College *B*
Central Connecticut State
   University *B, M*
Holy Apostles College and Seminary *B*
Northwestern Connecticut
   Community College *A*
Quinnipiac University *B*
St. Joseph College *B, T*
Trinity College *B*
University of Bridgeport *B*
Western Connecticut State
   University *B*

Florida

Florida Agricultural and Mechanical
   University *M*
Florida Atlantic University *B*
Florida Gulf Coast University *B*
Florida Southern College *B*
Florida State University *B, M*
Manatee Community College *A*
New College of Florida *B*
Palm Beach Community College *A*
Stetson University *B*
Tallahassee Community College *A*
University of Central Florida *B*
University of South Florida *B*
University of Tampa *B, T*

University of West Florida *B*
Valencia Community College *A*

Georgia

Abraham Baldwin Agricultural
   College *A*
Andrew College *A*
Berry College *B*
Brewton-Parker College *B*
Clark Atlanta University *B*
Columbus State University *M*
Dalton State College *A*
Darton College *A*
Georgia Highlands College *A*
Piedmont College *B*
Shorter College *B, T*
South Georgia College *A*
Thomas University *B*
Wesleyan College *B*
Young Harris College *A*

Hawaii

Chaminade University of Honolulu *B*
Hawaii Pacific University *B*
University of Hawaii
   West Oahu *B*
   Windward Community College *C*

Idaho

Boise State University *A, B, T*
Lewis-Clark State College *B*
North Idaho College *A*
Northwest Nazarene University *B*

Illinois

Benedictine University *B, T*
City Colleges of Chicago
   Harold Washington College *A*
   Kennedy-King College *A*
   Olive-Harvey College *A*
   Richard J. Daley College *C, A*
DePaul University *B, T*
Dominican University *B*
Governors State University *B*
Highland Community College *A*
Illinois College *T*
Illinois Valley Community College *A*
Kankakee Community College *A*
Kishwaukee College *A*
Lake Land College *A*
Lewis University *T*
McKendree College *B*
National-Louis University *B*
North Central College *T*
North Park University *B*
Northeastern Illinois University *B*
Northern Illinois University *T*
Olivet Nazarene University *B, T*
Principia College *B*
Richland Community College *A*
Rockford College *B*
Roosevelt University *B*
St. Augustine College *A*
St. Xavier University *B*
Sauk Valley Community College *A*
Shimer College *B*
Southern Illinois University
   Carbondale *B*
Trinity International University *B*
Triton College *A*
University of Illinois
   Springfield *B*
Wheaton College *T*
William Rainey Harper College *A*

Indiana

Ball State University *M*
Bethel College *A, B*
Calumet College of St. Joseph *B*
Indiana University
   Bloomington *B, M*
   Kokomo *B*
   South Bend *A*

Indiana Wesleyan University *B*
Manchester College *B, T*
Martin University *B*
Oakland City University *A, B*
Purdue University *B, M*
St. Mary-of-the-Woods College *B*
Taylor University *B*
Tri-State University *A, B*
University of Southern Indiana *A, B, T*
Valparaiso University *A, M*
Vincennes University *A*

Iowa

Ashford University *B*
Buena Vista University *B, T*
Central College *B, T*
Dordt College *B*
Drake University *B*
Ellsworth Community College *A*
Graceland University *B*
Grand View College *B*
Marshalltown Community College *A*
Mount Mercy College *T*
North Iowa Area Community
　　College *A*
Northwestern College *T*
Upper Iowa University *B*
Waldorf College *B*
Wartburg College *T*
William Penn University *B*

Kansas

Benedictine College *B*
Bethany College *B, T*
Central Christian College of
　　Kansas *A, B*
Cloud County Community College *A*
Coffeyville Community College *A*
Cowley County Community
　　College *A*
Dodge City Community College *A*
Donnelly College *A*
Emporia State University *B*
Fort Scott Community College *A*
Garden City Community College *A*
Hutchinson Community College *A*
Kansas State University *B*
Labette Community College *A*
McPherson College *T*
MidAmerica Nazarene University *B*
Neosho County Community
　　College *A*
Pratt Community College *A*
Seward County Community College *A*
Tabor College *B*

Kentucky

Alice Lloyd College *B*
Asbury College *B, T*
Brescia University *A, B*
Campbellsville University *A, B, M*
Kentucky State University *B*
Lindsey Wilson College *A, B, T*
Mid-Continent University *B*
Morehead State University *B*
Northern Kentucky University *B*
Pikeville College *B, T*
St. Catharine College *A*
Spalding University *B*
University of Kentucky *B*
Western Kentucky University *C, B, T*

Louisiana

Grambling State University *B, M*
Loyola University New Orleans *B*
Nunez Community College *A*
Our Lady of Holy Cross College *B, T*
Southern University
　　New Orleans *B*
　　Shreveport *B*
Southern University and Agricultural
　　and Mechanical College *M*

Maine

Bates College *T*
College of the Atlantic *B*
Unity College *B*
University of Maine
　　Augusta *B*
　　Farmington *B*
　　Fort Kent *B*
University of Southern Maine *B*

Maryland

Allegany College of Maryland *A*
Chesapeake College *A*
College of Southern Maryland *A*
Coppin State University *B, M*
Frostburg State University *B, T*
Howard Community College *A*
Johns Hopkins University *B, M*
Mount St. Mary's University *B, T*
Salisbury University *T*
Sojourner-Douglass College *B, M*
Towson University *B*
University of Maryland
　　University College *B*

Massachusetts

Boston University *M*
Cape Cod Community College *A*
Hampshire College *B*
Harvard College *B, D*
Lasell College *B*
Lesley University *B*
Massachusetts Bay Community
　　College *A*
Newbury College *A*
Northeastern University *B, M, D*
Roxbury Community College *A*
Simon's Rock College of Bard *B*
Suffolk University *B*
University of Massachusetts
　　Boston *B*
Worcester Polytechnic Institute *B*

Michigan

Adrian College *B, T*
Andrews University *B*
Aquinas College *B*
Calvin College *B*
Central Michigan University *B, T*
Concordia University *B*
Cornerstone University *B*
Eastern Michigan University *B, M*
Gogebic Community College *A*
Grand Valley State University *B*
Hope College *B*
Kalamazoo College *T*
Lake Superior State University *B, T*
Lansing Community College *A*
Marygrove College *B*
Michigan State University *B, M, D*
Michigan Technological
　　University *B, T*
Northern Michigan University *B, T*
Northwestern Michigan College *A*
Oakland University *B*
Olivet College *B*
Siena Heights University *B*
Spring Arbor University *B, T*
University of Michigan *B, T*
University of Michigan
　　Flint *B, M*
Washtenaw Community College *A*
Wayne County Community College *A*
Western Michigan University *B*

Minnesota

Augsburg College *B*
Bemidji State University *B*
Bethany Lutheran College *B*
Bethel University *B*
College of St. Benedict *B*
College of St. Catherine *B*
College of St. Scholastica *B*

Hamline University *B*
Metropolitan State University *B*
Northland Community & Technical
　　College *A*
Northwestern College *B*
Ridgewater College *A*
St. Cloud State University *B*
St. John's University *B*
St. Mary's University of Minnesota *B*
University of St. Thomas *B*
Vermilion Community College *A*
Winona State University *B*

Mississippi

Blue Mountain College *B*
Coahoma Community College *A*
Delta State University *B*
Jackson State University *B*
Millsaps College *T*
Mississippi College *B, M, T*
Mississippi Delta Community
　　College *A*
Rust College *B*
William Carey College *B*

Missouri

Crowder College *A*
Evangel University *A, B*
Lincoln University *M*
Mineral Area College *A*
Missouri Baptist University *B, T*
Missouri Southern State
　　University *B, T*
Rockhurst University *B*
St. Louis Community College
　　St. Louis Community College at
　　　　Florissant Valley *A*
　　St. Louis Community College at
　　　　Meramec *A*
St. Louis University *B, M*
Washington University in St. Louis *B*
Webster University *B*

Montana

Carroll College *B*
Little Big Horn College *A*
Miles Community College *A*
University of Great Falls *B*
University of Montana: Western *B*

Nebraska

Bellevue University *B*
Chadron State College *B*
College of Saint Mary *B*
Concordia University *B, T*
Dana College *B*
Doane College *B*
Midland Lutheran College *B, T*
Northeast Community College *A*
Peru State College *B, T*
Union College *B*
University of Nebraska
　　Kearney *B, M, T*
Wayne State College *B, T*

Nevada

Community College of Southern
　　Nevada *A*
Great Basin College *B*

New Hampshire

Daniel Webster College *B*
Dartmouth College *T*
Franklin Pierce College *B*
Keene State College *B*
New Hampshire Technical Institute *A*
Plymouth State University *B*
Rivier College *B, T*
Southern New Hampshire
　　University *B*

New Jersey

Atlantic Cape Community College *A*

Brookdale Community College *A*
Caldwell College *B*
Essex County College *A*
Monmouth University *B*
Montclair State University *M*
New Jersey Institute of Technology *D*
Raritan Valley Community College *A*
Rowan University *B, M*
St. Peter's College *A, B*
Salem Community College *A*
Sussex County Community College *A*
Thomas Edison State College *B*
Warren County Community College *A*

New Mexico

College of the Southwest *B*
Eastern New Mexico University *B*
New Mexico Junior College *A*
New Mexico State University
　　Carlsbad *A*
Western New Mexico University *B*

New York

Adelphi University *B*
Adirondack Community College *A*
Bard College *B*
Cazenovia College *B*
Clarkson University *B*
Colgate University *B*
Columbia-Greene Community
　　College *A*
Concordia College *B, T*
Corning Community College *A*
Dominican College of Blauvelt *B*
Dowling College *B*
Elmira College *B, T*
Eugene Lang College The New School
　　for Liberal Arts *B*
Finger Lakes Community College *A*
Herkimer County Community
　　College *A*
Hofstra University *B*
Hudson Valley Community College *A*
Ithaca College *B, T*
Jamestown Community College *A*
Keuka College *B*
Long Island University
　　Brooklyn Campus *B, M*
Marymount Manhattan College *A*
Medaille College *B*
Mercy College *B*
Metropolitan College of New
　　York *A, B*
Monroe Community College *A*
Mount St. Mary College *B, T*
Nazareth College of Rochester *B*
New York Institute of
　　Technology *B, M*
New York University *B, M*
Niagara University *B*
Nyack College *B*
Pace University *B*
Roberts Wesleyan College *B*
Rockland Community College *A*
Sage College of Albany *A, B*
St. Bonaventure University *B*
St. John's University *B*
St. Joseph's College *B*
St. Joseph's College: Suffolk
　　Campus *B*
St. Thomas Aquinas College *B, T*
Sarah Lawrence College *B*
Schenectady County Community
　　College *A*
State University of New York
　　Binghamton *M*
　　College at Old Westbury *B*
　　College of Agriculture and
　　　　Technology at Cobleskill *A*
　　College of Agriculture and
　　　　Technology at Morrisville *A*
　　College of Technology at Alfred *A*
　　College of Technology at Canton *A*

College of Technology at Delhi *A*
Empire State College *A, B*
Suffolk County Community College *A*
Sullivan County Community College *A*
Syracuse University *M, D*
Touro College *B*
Ulster County Community College *A*
Union College *B*
United States Military Academy *B*
Westchester Community College *A*

North Carolina

Belmont Abbey College *B*
Elizabeth City State University *B*
Fayetteville State University *B*
Gardner-Webb University *B*
Johnson C. Smith University *B*
Lenoir-Rhyne College *B*
Livingstone College *B*
Louisburg College *A*
North Carolina Agricultural and Technical State University *B, M, T*
Sandhills Community College *A*
Western Carolina University *B*

North Dakota

Dickinson State University *B, T*
Mayville State University *B, T*
Minot State University *B*
North Dakota State University *B, M, T*
University of Mary *B*
University of North Dakota *B, T*
Valley City State University *B*

Ohio

Antioch College *B*
Bluffton University *B*
Bowling Green State University: Firelands College *A*
Cleveland State University *B, M*
Defiance College *B, T*
Heidelberg College *B*
Hiram College *B*
Lake Erie College *B*
Ohio Northern University *B*
Ohio State University Columbus Campus *B, M, D*
Ohio University *M*
Ohio University Chillicothe Campus *M*
Southern Campus at Ironton *A*
Shawnee State University *A, B, T*
Stark State College of Technology *A*
Union Institute & University *B*
University of Akron *B*
University of Findlay *A, B*
University of Rio Grande *A, B, T*
Urbana University *B*
Wilmington College *B*
Wittenberg University *B*
Youngstown State University *B, M*

Oklahoma

Bacone College *A*
Carl Albert State College *A*
Connors State College *A*
East Central University *B*
Eastern Oklahoma State College *A*
Northeastern Oklahoma Agricultural and Mechanical College *A*
Northwestern Oklahoma State University *B*
Oklahoma Baptist University *B, T*
Oklahoma Panhandle State University *B*
Oklahoma Wesleyan University *A, B*
Redlands Community College *A*
Rogers State University *B*
Rose State College *A*
St. Gregory's University *A, B*
Seminole State College *A*
Southern Nazarene University *B*

Tulsa Community College *A*
Western Oklahoma State College *A*

Oregon

Central Oregon Community College *A*
Concordia University *B*
Corban College *B*
Linn-Benton Community College *A*
Marylhurst University *B*
Portland State University *B, M*
Rogue Community College *A*
Southern Oregon University *B, T*
Treasure Valley Community College *A*
University of Oregon *B*
Warner Pacific College *A, B*
Western Oregon University *B*

Pennsylvania

Bucks County Community College *A*
California University of Pennsylvania *B, M*
Carlow University *B*
Cheyney University of Pennsylvania *B, T*
Clarion University of Pennsylvania *B, T*
Community College of Allegheny County *A*
Community College of Beaver County *A*
East Stroudsburg University of Pennsylvania *B, T*
Edinboro University of Pennsylvania *B, M, T*
Gannon University *B*
Harrisburg Area Community College *A*
Juniata College *B*
Keystone College *A*
Kutztown University of Pennsylvania *B, M, T*
La Salle University *B, T*
Lehigh Carbon Community College *A*
Lehigh University *B, M, D*
Lock Haven University of Pennsylvania *B, T*
Luzerne County Community College *A*
Mansfield University of Pennsylvania *B*
Marywood University *B*
Millersville University of Pennsylvania *B, T*
Montgomery County Community College *A*
Mount Aloysius College *B*
Penn State University Park *M, D*
Pennsylvania Highlands Community College *A*
Point Park University *B*
Reading Area Community College *A*
Robert Morris University *B*
Rosemont College *B*
St. Joseph's University *B*
University of Pennsylvania *A, B, D*
University of Pittsburgh *B*
University of Pittsburgh Bradford *B*
Greensburg *B*
Johnstown *B*
University of Scranton *T*
Waynesburg College *B*
Wilson College *B*
York College of Pennsylvania *B*

Puerto Rico

American University of Puerto Rico *B*
Pontifical Catholic University of Puerto Rico *B*
Turabo University *B*
Universidad Metropolitana *B*

University of Puerto Rico
Bayamon University College *A*
Carolina Regional College *A*
Cayey University College *B*
Mayaguez *B*
Ponce *A*
Rio Piedras *B*
Utuado *A*
University of the Sacred Heart *B*

Rhode Island

Providence College *B*
Rhode Island College *B*

South Carolina

Allen University *B*
Charleston Southern University *B*
The Citadel *M*
Columbia College *B*
Southern Wesleyan University *B*
University of South Carolina *M*
University of South Carolina Beaufort *B*
Wofford College *T*

South Dakota

Augustana College *T*
Black Hills State University *B*
Dakota Wesleyan University *B*
Mount Marty College *B*
University of Sioux Falls *A, B*

Tennessee

American Baptist College of ABT Seminary *A, B*
Bethel College *B*
Cumberland University *B*
Dyersburg State Community College *A*
Freed-Hardeman University *B, T*
Hiwassee College *A*
LeMoyne-Owen College *B*
Lee University *B*
Lincoln Memorial University *B, T*
Northeast State Technical Community College *A*
Roane State Community College *A*
Tennessee State University *B*
Trevecca Nazarene University *B*
University of Tennessee Chattanooga *B*

Texas

Amarillo College *A*
Central Texas College *A*
Cisco Junior College *A*
College of the Mainland *A*
Concordia University at Austin *A, B*
East Texas Baptist University *B*
El Paso Community College *A*
Frank Phillips College *A*
Howard College *A*
Howard Payne University *B*
Huston-Tillotson College *B*
Laredo Community College *A*
Lon Morris College *A*
McMurry University *T*
Midland College *A*
Navarro College *A*
Northwest Vista College *A*
Odessa College *A*
Our Lady of the Lake University of San Antonio *B*
Rice University *B*
Sam Houston State University *B, M*
San Antonio College *A*
San Jacinto College North *A*
South Texas College *A*
Southern Methodist University *B*
Southwestern Adventist University *B*
Southwestern Assemblies of God University *A*

Southwestern University *B, T*
Stephen F. Austin State University *B*
Sul Ross State University *B, M, T*
Texarkana College *A*
Texas A&M University Commerce *B, M*
Texas Wesleyan University *B*
Trinity Valley Community College *A*
Tyler Junior College *A*
University of Houston Downtown *B*
University of North Texas *B*
University of Texas Pan American *B*
San Antonio *D*
West Texas A&M University *B*
Western Texas College *A*

Utah

Snow College *A*
Southern Utah University *B, T*
University of Utah *B*
Utah State University *M*
Westminster College *B*

Vermont

Bennington College *B*
Burlington College *B*
Castleton State College *B*
Goddard College *B*
Johnson State College *B*
Lyndon State College *B*
Marlboro College *B*
University of Vermont *B, M*

Virginia

Bluefield College *B*
Eastern Mennonite University *B*
Ferrum College *B*
Hollins University *M*
J. Sargeant Reynolds Community College *A*
James Madison University *B, T*
Liberty University *B, T*
Radford University *B*
St. Paul's College *B*
Thomas Nelson Community College *A*
University of Virginia's College at Wise *T*
Virginia Wesleyan College *B*
Virginia Western Community College *A*

Washington

Central Washington University *B*
Centralia College *A*
Everett Community College *A*
Evergreen State College *B*
Highline Community College *A*
Northwest University *T*
Puget Sound Christian College *B*
University of Puget Sound *T*
University of Washington *B*
Washington State University *B*
Whitworth College *B, T*

West Virginia

Bluefield State College *B*
Marshall University *B*
Mountain State University *M*
West Liberty State College *B*

Wisconsin

Alverno College *B*
Cardinal Stritch University *B*
Carthage College *B, T*
Edgewood College *B*
Marquette University *B*
Mount Mary College *B*
Northland College *B, T*
St. Norbert College *T*
Silver Lake College *B, T*

University of Wisconsin
Milwaukee *B*
Platteville *B*
River Falls *B*
Stevens Point *B, T*
Superior *B*
Whitewater *B*
Viterbo University *B*
Wisconsin Lutheran College *B*

Wyoming

Central Wyoming College *A*
Laramie County Community
College *A*
Northwest College *A*
Sheridan College *A*
University of Wyoming *B*
Western Wyoming Community
College *A*

Social studies teacher education

Alabama

Athens State University *B*
Birmingham-Southern College *T*
Faulkner University *B, T*
Huntingdon College *T*
Judson College *B*
Lawson State Community College *A*
Miles College *B*
University of Mobile *B, T*

Arizona

Arizona State University *B, T*
Prescott College *B, T*
University of Arizona *B, M*

Arkansas

Arkansas Tech University *B, M*
Harding University *B, M, T*
John Brown University *B, T*
Ouachita Baptist University *B, T*
Southern Arkansas University *B, T*
University of Arkansas *B*
University of Arkansas
Monticello *B*
Pine Bluff *B, M, T*
University of Central Arkansas *B, T*
University of the Ozarks *T*
Williams Baptist College *B*

California

Azusa Pacific University *T*
California Lutheran University *B, T*
California State University
Northridge *B, T*
Master's College *T*
Mount St. Mary's College *T*
Stanford University *M, T*
University of San Francisco *T*
University of the Pacific *T*
Vanguard University of Southern
California *T*

Colorado

Adams State College *B, T*
Colorado State University *T*
Colorado State University
Pueblo *T*
Metropolitan State College of
Denver *T*
Trinidad State Junior College *A*
University of Colorado
Boulder *T*
Colorado Springs *T*
Western State College of Colorado *T*

Connecticut

Albertus Magnus College *B, T*
Central Connecticut State
University *T*

Connecticut College *T*
Fairfield University *T*
Quinnipiac University *B, M*
Sacred Heart University *T*
Southern Connecticut State
University *B, M, T*

Delaware

Delaware State University *B*
University of Delaware *T*

District of Columbia

George Washington University *M, T*

Florida

Barry University *T*
Bethune-Cookman College *B, T*
Clearwater Christian College *B*
Flagler College *B*
Florida Agricultural and Mechanical
University *B, M*
Florida International
University *B, M, T*
Gulf Coast Community College *A*
Manatee Community College *A*
St. Thomas University *B, T*
Southeastern College of the
Assemblies of God *B, T*

Georgia

Agnes Scott College *T*
Columbus State University *B*
Darton College *A*
Georgia State University *M*
Kennesaw State University *B*
University of West Georgia *M*

Hawaii

Hawaii Pacific University *M*

Idaho

Boise State University *T*
Brigham Young University-Idaho *T*

Illinois

Blackburn College *B, T*
Chicago State University *T*
Concordia University *B, T*
Eureka College *T*
Illinois College *T*
Illinois State University *B, T*
John A. Logan College *A*
Knox College *T*
Lewis University *T*
Monmouth College *B, T*
North Park University *T*
Olivet Nazarene University *B, T*
Rockford College *T*
Sauk Valley Community College *A*
University of Illinois
Urbana-Champaign *M*
University of St. Francis *B, M, T*

Indiana

Anderson University *B, T*
Bethel College *B*
Butler University *T*
Franklin College *T*
Grace College *B*
Huntington University *B, M*
Indiana State University *B, M, T*
Indiana University
Bloomington *B, M, T*
Kokomo *T*
Northwest *B*
South Bend *B*
Southeast *B*
Indiana University-Purdue University
Fort Wayne *B*
Indiana University-Purdue University
Indianapolis *B, T*
Indiana Wesleyan University *B, T*

Manchester College *B, T*
Oakland City University *B*
Purdue University
Calumet *B*
Saint Mary's College *T*
St. Mary-of-the-Woods College *B, T*
Taylor University *B, T*
Tri-State University *B, T*
University of Evansville *B, T*
University of Indianapolis *B, T*
University of St. Francis *B, T*
Vincennes University *A*

Iowa

Ashford University *B, T*
Clarke College *B, T*
Cornell College *B, T*
Dordt College *B*
Drake University *M, T*
Ellsworth Community College *A*
Graceland University *T*
Mount Mercy College *T*
Northwestern College *T*
St. Ambrose University *T*
University of Iowa *M, D*
Upper Iowa University *B, T*
Waldorf College *B*
Wartburg College *T*
William Penn University *B*

Kansas

Central Christian College of Kansas *A*
Emporia State University *T*
Garden City Community College *A*
Kansas Wesleyan University *T*
McPherson College *B, T*
MidAmerica Nazarene University *B, T*
Tabor College *B, T*
University of Kansas *B, T*
University of St. Mary *T*
Washburn University of Topeka *B*

Kentucky

Alice Lloyd College *B*
Bellarmine University *B, M, T*
Brescia University *B, T*
Campbellsville University *B*
Kentucky State University *B*
Kentucky Wesleyan College *B, T*
Spalding University *B*
Thomas More College *B*
Union College *B*
University of the Cumberlands *B, T*

Louisiana

Centenary College of Louisiana *B, T*
Louisiana State University
Shreveport *B*
Nicholls State University *B*
Northwestern State University *B*
Our Lady of Holy Cross College *B, T*
Southeastern Louisiana University *B*
Southern University and Agricultural
and Mechanical College *B*
University of Louisiana at Lafayette *B*
University of Louisiana at Monroe *B*
University of New Orleans *B*
Xavier University of Louisiana *B*

Maine

Bowdoin College *T*
College of the Atlantic *B, T*
University of Maine *B, M*
University of Maine
Fort Kent *B*
University of Southern Maine *T*

Maryland

College of Notre Dame of Maryland *T*
Mount St. Mary's University *T*
St. Mary's College of Maryland *T*
Salisbury University *T*

University of Maryland
College Park *B*
Eastern Shore *B*

Massachusetts

Boston University *B, M, T*
Eastern Nazarene College *B*
Elms College *T*
Lesley University *B, M*
Merrimack College *T*
Northeastern University *B*
Simmons College *B*
Springfield College *T*
Tufts University *M, T*
University of Massachusetts
Dartmouth *T*
Western New England College *T*
Westfield State College *B, M, T*
Worcester State College *T*

Michigan

Albion College *B, T*
Alma College *T*
Andrews University *B*
Calvin College *B*
Concordia University *B, T*
Cornerstone University *B, T*
Eastern Michigan University *B, T*
Ferris State University *B*
Grand Valley State University *T*
Hope College *T*
Madonna University *B, T*
Michigan Technological University *T*
Northern Michigan University *B, T*
Olivet College *B, T*
University of Detroit Mercy *B, M, T*
University of Michigan
Dearborn *B*
Flint *T*
Wayne State University *B, M, T*

Minnesota

Augsburg College *T*
Bemidji State University *M, T*
Bethel University *T*
College of St. Benedict *T*
College of St. Catherine *T*
College of St. Scholastica *B, T*
Concordia College: Moorhead *B, T*
Concordia University: St. Paul *B, T*
Crown College *B, T*
Gustavus Adolphus College *T*
Minnesota State University
Mankato *B, M, T*
Moorhead *B*
Northland Community & Technical
College *A*
Northwestern College *B*
St. Cloud State University *B, T*
St. John's University *T*
St. Mary's University of Minnesota *B*
St. Olaf College *B*
Southwest Minnesota State
University *T*
University of Minnesota
Duluth *B*
Morris *T*
Twin Cities *M, T*
University of St. Thomas *B, T*
Vermilion Community College *A*
Winona State University *B, T*

Mississippi

Itawamba Community College *A*
Mississippi College *B*
Mississippi State University *T*
University of Mississippi *B, T*

Missouri

Central Missouri State
University *B, M, T*
College of the Ozarks *B, T*
Columbia College *T*

Evangel University *B, T*
Hannibal-LaGrange College *B*
Harris-Stowe State University *T*
Lindenwood University *B*
Missouri Baptist University *T*
Missouri Valley College *B, T*
Park University *T*
Southeast Missouri State
   University *B, M, T*
Truman State University *M, T*
University of Missouri
   Columbia *B, M, D*
Washington University in St.
   Louis *B, M, T*
William Jewell College *T*

Montana

Montana State University
   Billings *B, T*
Rocky Mountain College *B, T*
University of Great Falls *B*
University of Montana: Missoula *T*
University of Montana: Western *B, T*

Nebraska

Creighton University *T*
Dana College *B*
Hastings College *B, M, T*
Midland Lutheran College *B, T*

Nevada

University of Nevada
   Reno *B*

New Hampshire

Colby-Sawyer College *B, T*
Franklin Pierce College *T*
Keene State College *B, T*
New England College *B, T*
Plymouth State University *M, T*
Rivier College *B, T*
Southern New Hampshire
   University *B*
University of New Hampshire *T*
University of New Hampshire at
   Manchester *M*

New Jersey

Caldwell College *T*
Centenary College *T*
The College of New Jersey *B, T*
College of St. Elizabeth *T*
Rowan University *T*
Rutgers, The State University of New
   Jersey
   Camden Regional Campus *T*
   Newark Regional Campus *T*
St. Peter's College *T*
William Paterson University of New
   Jersey *T*

New Mexico

Western New Mexico University *B*

New York

Adelphi University *M, T*
Alfred University *M, T*
Bard College *M*
City University of New York
   Brooklyn College *B, M*
   City College *B, T*
   Hunter College *B, M, T*
   Lehman College *M*
   Queens College *M, T*
Colgate University *M*
College of Mount St. Vincent *T*
College of Saint Rose *B, T*
D'Youville College *B, M, T*
Daemen College *B, M, T*
Dowling College *B*
Dutchess Community College *A*
Elmira College *B, T*
Fordham University *T*

Hobart and William Smith Colleges *T*
Hofstra University *B, M*
Houghton College *B, T*
Iona College *B, M, T*
Ithaca College *B, T*
Keuka College *B, T*
Le Moyne College *T*
Long Island University
   Brooklyn Campus *M, T*
   C.W. Post Campus *B, M, T*
Manhattan College *B, T*
Manhattanville College *M, T*
Marist College *B*
Marymount Manhattan College *T*
Mercy College *B, T*
Molloy College *B*
Mount St. Mary College *B*
Nazareth College of Rochester *T*
New York Institute of Technology *B, T*
New York University *B, M*
Niagara University *B, M, T*
Pace University *B, M, T*
Roberts Wesleyan College *B, M*
St. Bonaventure University *M, T*
St. Francis College *B*
St. John Fisher College *B, M, T*
St. John's University *B, M*
St. Joseph's College *B, T*
St. Joseph's College: Suffolk
   Campus *B, T*
St. Lawrence University *T*
St. Thomas Aquinas College *B, T*
State University of New York
   Albany *B, M, T*
   Binghamton *M*
   Buffalo *M, T*
   College at Brockport *M, T*
   College at Buffalo *B, M, T*
   College at Cortland *B, M, T*
   College at Fredonia *B, T*
   College at Geneseo *B, M, T*
   College at Old Westbury *B, T*
   College at Plattsburgh *B, M*
   College at Potsdam *B, M*
   New Paltz *B, M, T*
   Oswego *B, M*
   Stony Brook *T*
Syracuse University *B, M, T*
Utica College *B*
Wagner College *T*
Wells College *T*

North Carolina

Appalachian State University *B*
Barton College *B, T*
Belmont Abbey College *T*
Brevard College *B*
Campbell University *B, T*
Catawba College *T*
Davidson College *T*
East Carolina University *B*
Greensboro College *B, T*
Lenoir-Rhyne College *B, T*
Livingstone College *T*
Mars Hill College *T*
Meredith College *T*
Methodist College *A, B, T*
North Carolina State
   University *B, M, T*
Queens University of Charlotte *T*
St. Augustine's College *B*
Sandhills Community College *A*
University of North Carolina
   Greensboro *B*
   Pembroke *B, M*
Wake Forest University *B, T*
Western Carolina University *B, T*
Wingate University *B, T*
Winston-Salem State University *B*

North Dakota

North Dakota State University *B, T*

Ohio

Ashland University *B, T*
Baldwin-Wallace College *T*
Bluffton University *B*
Bowling Green State University *B, M*
Capital University *T*
Cedarville University *B, T*
Defiance College *B, T*
Hiram College *T*
John Carroll University *T*
Kent State University *B*
Malone College *B*
Miami University
   Oxford Campus *B, T*
Mount Union College *T*
Mount Vernon Nazarene
   University *B, M, T*
Ohio Dominican University *B, T*
Ohio Northern University *B, T*
Ohio State University
   Columbus Campus *M, D*
Ohio University *B, D, T*
Ohio Wesleyan University *B*
Otterbein College *B*
University of Akron *B*
University of Findlay *B, M, T*
University of Toledo *B, T*
Urbana University *B*
Ursuline College *B, M, T*
Walsh University *B*
Wilmington College *B*
Wright State University *B, T*
Youngstown State University *B, M*

Oklahoma

Cameron University *B, T*
East Central University *B*
Eastern Oklahoma State College *A*
Mid-America Christian University *B*
Northeastern State University *B*
Oklahoma Baptist University *B, T*
Oklahoma Christian University *B, T*
Oklahoma City University *B*
Oklahoma Wesleyan University *B*
Oral Roberts University *B, T*
Southeastern Oklahoma State
   University *B, M, T*
University of Central Oklahoma *B*
University of Oklahoma *B, T*
University of Tulsa *T*
Western Oklahoma State College *A*

Oregon

Concordia University *B, M, T*
Corban College *B*
Eastern Oregon University *B*
George Fox University *T*
Portland State University *T*
Southern Oregon University *T*
Warner Pacific College *T*
Western Oregon University *T*

Pennsylvania

Albright College *T*
Alvernia College *B*
Arcadia University *B, M, T*
Baptist Bible College of
   Pennsylvania *B*
Bloomsburg University of
   Pennsylvania *B, T*
Cabrini College *T*
Carlow University *B, T*
Chatham College *T*
Clarion University of
   Pennsylvania *B, T*
College Misericordia *T*
DeSales University *T*
Dickinson College *T*
Duquesne University *B, M, T*
Edinboro University of
   Pennsylvania *B, M*
Elizabethtown College *B*
Gannon University *B, T*

Geneva College *B, T*
Gettysburg College *T*
Grove City College *B, T*
Gwynedd-Mercy College *T*
Holy Family University *B, M, T*
Indiana University of
   Pennsylvania *B, T*
Juniata College *B, T*
King's College *T*
La Salle University *B, T*
Lebanon Valley College *T*
Lincoln University *T*
Lycoming College *T*
Mansfield University of
   Pennsylvania *B, T*
Messiah College *B, T*
Millersville University of
   Pennsylvania *B, T*
Penn State
   Harrisburg *B*
Philadelphia Biblical University *B, T*
Rosemont College *T*
St. Francis University *B, T*
St. Joseph's University *B, M*
St. Vincent College *T*
Seton Hill University *T*
Susquehanna University *T*
Temple University *B*
Thiel College *B*
University of Pennsylvania *M, T*
University of Pittsburgh
   Johnstown *B, T*
Villanova University *T*
Waynesburg College *B, T*
West Chester University of
   Pennsylvania *T*
Westminster College *B, T*
Widener University *M, T*

Puerto Rico

Inter American University of Puerto
   Rico
   Barranquitas Campus *B, T*
   Fajardo Campus *B, T*
Pontifical Catholic University of
   Puerto Rico *B, T*
University of Puerto Rico
   Cayey University College *B*

Rhode Island

Rhode Island College *B, M*

South Carolina

Anderson University *B, T*
Charleston Southern University *B, M*
Converse College *T*
Erskine College *B, T*
Francis Marion University *B, T*
Furman University *T*
Limestone College *B*
Morris College *B, T*
Presbyterian College *B, T*
South Carolina State University *B, T*
University of South Carolina
   Aiken *B, T*

South Dakota

Augustana College *B, T*
Dakota State University *B, T*
Dakota Wesleyan University *B, T*

Tennessee

Belmont University *B, M, T*
Bryan College *T*
King College *T*
Lincoln Memorial University *B, T*
Maryville College *B, T*
Tennessee Technological University *T*
University of Memphis *T*
University of Tennessee
   Chattanooga *B, T*
   Knoxville *T*
Vanderbilt University *B, M, D*

Texas

Abilene Christian University *B, T*
Baylor University *B, T*
Dallas Baptist University *T*
East Texas Baptist University *B*
Hardin-Simmons University *B, T*
Houston Baptist University *B*
Howard Payne University *T*
Lamar University *B, M, T*
LeTourneau University *B, T*
Lubbock Christian University *B*
McMurry University *T*
St. Edward's University *B, T*
St. Mary's University *T*
Southwestern Assemblies of God
    University *B*
Texas A&M University
    Commerce *T*
    Kingsville *T*
Texas Christian University *B*
Texas Lutheran University *B, T*
Texas Wesleyan University *B*
University of Dallas *T*
University of Houston *M, T*
University of Houston
    Clear Lake *T*
University of Mary Hardin-Baylor *B*
University of Texas
    Arlington *T*
    San Antonio *T*
West Texas A&M University *T*

Utah

University of Utah *B*
Utah State University *B*
Weber State University *B*

Vermont

Castleton State College *B, T*
College of St. Joseph in Vermont *B, M*
Goddard College *B*
Green Mountain College *B, T*
Johnson State College *B*
St. Michael's College *T*

Virginia

Averett University *B, T*
Bluefield College *T*
Hollins University *T*
Longwood University *B, T*
University of Richmond *T*
University of Virginia's College at
    Wise *T*
Virginia Intermont College *B, T*
Virginia Wesleyan College *T*

Washington

Northwest University *T*
Washington State University *B, M, T*
Western Washington University *B*
Whitworth College *B, T*

West Virginia

Alderson-Broaddus College *T*
Bethany College *B*
Concord University *B, M, T*
Ohio Valley University *B*
Shepherd University *T*
University of Charleston *B*
West Virginia State University *B*
West Virginia University *T*
West Virginia Wesleyan College *B*

Wisconsin

Alverno College *T*
Carroll College *B, T*
Carthage College *T*
Concordia University Wisconsin *B, T*
Maranatha Baptist Bible College *B*
Marian College of Fond du Lac *B, T*
Marquette University *B*
Mount Mary College *B, T*
Northland College *T*

St. Norbert College *T*
University of Wisconsin
    Eau Claire *B*
    Green Bay *T*
    La Crosse *B, T*
    Madison *B*
    Platteville *B, T*
    River Falls *T*
Viterbo University *B, T*

Social work

Alabama

Alabama Agricultural and Mechanical
    University *B, M*
Alabama State University *B*
Auburn University *B*
Community College of the Air
    Force *A*
Jacksonville State University *B*
Lawson State Community College *A*
Miles College *B*
Oakwood College *B*
Shelton State Community College *A*
Talladega College *B*
Troy University *B*
Tuskegee University *B*
University of Alabama *B, M, D*
University of Alabama
    Birmingham *B*
University of Montevallo *B*
University of North Alabama *B*

Alaska

Alaska Pacific University *B*
University of Alaska
    Anchorage *B, M*
    Fairbanks *B*

Arizona

Arizona State University *B, M, D*
Arizona State University West *B, M*
Cochise College *A*
Estrella Mountain Community
    College *A*
Glendale Community College *A*
Northern Arizona University *B*

Arkansas

Arkansas State University *B*
Harding University *B*
Henderson State University *B, M*
Philander Smith College *B*
Southern Arkansas University *B*
University of Arkansas *B*
University of Arkansas
    Little Rock *B, M*
    Monticello *B*
    Pine Bluff *B*

California

Azusa Pacific University *B*
California State University
    Chico *B, M*
    East Bay *B*
    Fresno *B, M*
    Long Beach *B, M*
    Los Angeles *B, M*
    Sacramento *B, M*
    San Bernardino *B, M*
    Stanislaus *M*
Chapman University *B*
Fresno City College *A*
Fresno Pacific University *B*
Humboldt State University *B*
La Sierra University *B*
Loma Linda University *M, D*
Merced College *A*
Pacific Union College *B*
Point Loma Nazarene University *B*
San Bernardino Valley College *A*
San Diego State University *B, M*
San Francisco State University *B, M*

San Jose State University *B, M*
Southwestern College *A*
University of California
    Berkeley *B, M, D*
    Los Angeles *M, D*
University of Southern
    California *M, D*
Whittier College *B*

Colorado

Colorado State University *B, M*
Colorado State University
    Pueblo *B*
Metropolitan State College of
    Denver *B*
University of Denver *M, D*

Connecticut

Central Connecticut State
    University *B*
Eastern Connecticut State
    University *B*
Sacred Heart University *B*
St. Joseph College *B*
Southern Connecticut State
    University *B, M*
University of Connecticut *M, D*
Western Connecticut State
    University *B*

Delaware

Delaware State University *B, M*

District of Columbia

Catholic University of
    America *B, M, D*
Gallaudet University *B, M*
Howard University *M, D*
University of the District of
    Columbia *B*

Florida

Barry University *B, M, D*
Broward Community College *A*
Edward Waters College *B*
Florida Agricultural and Mechanical
    University *B, M*
Florida Atlantic University *B, M*
Florida Gulf Coast University *B, M*
Florida International
    University *B, M, D*
Florida State University *B, M, D, T*
Gulf Coast Community College *A*
Manatee Community College *A*
Miami Dade College *A*
Palm Beach Community College *A*
St. Leo University *B*
Southeastern College of the
    Assemblies of God *B*
University of Central Florida *B, M*
University of South Florida *B, M, D*
University of West Florida *B*
Warner Southern College *B*

Georgia

Albany State University *B*
Atlanta Metropolitan College *A*
Augusta State University *B*
Clark Atlanta University *B, M, D*
Dalton State College *A, B*
Darton College *A*
Fort Valley State University *B*
Gainesville State College *A*
Georgia State University *B, M*
Gordon College *A*
Kennesaw State University *M*
LaGrange College *B*
Middle Georgia College *A*
Oglethorpe University *B*
Savannah State University *B, M*
Thomas University *B*
University of Georgia *B, M, D*
Valdosta State University *M*

Hawaii

Brigham Young University-Hawaii *B*
Hawaii Pacific University *B, M*
University of Hawaii
    Honolulu Community College *A*
    Manoa *B, M, D*

Idaho

Boise State University *B, M*
Idaho State University *B*
Lewis-Clark State College *B*
Northwest Nazarene University *B, M*

Illinois

Aurora University *B, M*
Bradley University *B*
City Colleges of Chicago
    Harold Washington College *A*
    Kennedy-King College *A*
College of DuPage *A*
College of Lake County *A*
Concordia University *B*
Dominican University *M*
Elgin Community College *A*
Governors State University *B, M*
Greenville College *B*
Illinois Eastern Community Colleges
    Wabash Valley College *A*
Illinois State University *B, M*
Illinois Valley Community College *A*
John A. Logan College *A*
Kishwaukee College *A*
Lewis University *B*
Loyola University of Chicago *B, M, D*
MacMurray College *B*
Northeastern Illinois University *B*
Olivet Nazarene University *B*
Parkland College *A*
Quincy University *B*
Roosevelt University *B*
St. Augustine College *B*
Sauk Valley Community College *A*
Southern Illinois University
    Carbondale *B, M*
Southern Illinois University
    Edwardsville *B, M*
Springfield College in Illinois *A*
Trinity Christian College *B*
University of Illinois
    Chicago *B, M, D*
    Springfield *B*
    Urbana-Champaign *M, D*
University of St. Francis *B*
Waubonsee Community College *A*
Western Illinois University *B*

Indiana

Anderson University *B*
Ball State University *B*
Goshen College *B*
Grace College *B*
Huntington University *B*
Indiana State University *B*
Indiana University
    East *A, B*
Indiana University-Purdue University
    Indianapolis *B, M, D*
Indiana Wesleyan University *B*
Manchester College *B*
St. Joseph's College *B*
Saint Mary's College *B*
Taylor University *B*
Taylor University: Fort Wayne *B*
University of Indianapolis *B*
University of St. Francis *B*
University of Southern Indiana *B, M*
Valparaiso University *B*
Vincennes University *A*

Iowa

Briar Cliff University *B*
Buena Vista University *B*
Clarke College *B*

Dordt College *B*
Ellsworth Community College *A*
Iowa Western Community College *A*
Loras College *B*
Luther College *B*
Northwestern College *B*
St. Ambrose University *M*
University of Iowa *B, M, D*
University of Northern Iowa *B, M*
Wartburg College *B*

Kansas

Barton County Community College *A*
Bethany College *B*
Bethel College *B*
Butler County Community College *A*
Central Christian College of Kansas *A*
Coffeyville Community College *A*
Colby Community College *A*
Fort Hays State University *B*
Haskell Indian Nations University *A*
Kansas State University *B*
Neosho County Community
  College *A*
Newman University *M*
Pittsburg State University *B*
Seward County Community College *A*
University of Kansas *B, M, D*
Washburn University of Topeka *B, M*
Wichita State University *B*

Kentucky

Asbury College *B*
Brescia University *B*
Campbellsville University *B, M*
Eastern Kentucky University *B*
Elizabethtown Community and
  Technical College *C, A*
Henderson Community College *A*
Jefferson Community College *C, A*
Kentucky Christian University *B*
Kentucky State University *B*
Morehead State University *B*
Murray State University *B*
Northern Kentucky University *B*
Owensboro Community College *A*
St. Catharine College *A*
Spalding University *B, M*
University of Kentucky *B, M, D*
University of Louisville *M, D*
University of the Cumberlands *B*
Western Kentucky University *B, M*

Louisiana

Dillard University *B*
Grambling State University *B, M*
Louisiana State University and
  Agricultural and Mechanical
  College *M, D*
Northwestern State University *B*
Southeastern Louisiana University *B*
Southern University
  New Orleans *B, M*
Southern University and Agricultural
  and Mechanical College *B*
Tulane University *M*
University of Louisiana at Monroe *B*

Maine

University of Maine *B, M*
University of Maine
  Fort Kent *A, B*
  Presque Isle *B*
University of New England *M*
University of Southern Maine *B, M*

Maryland

Allegany College of Maryland *A*
Baltimore City Community College *A*
Bowie State University *B, M*
Coppin State University *B*
Frostburg State University *B*
Hood College *B*

McDaniel College *B*
Salisbury University *B, M*
Sojourner-Douglass College *B*
University of Maryland
  Baltimore *M, D*
  Baltimore County *B*
  Eastern Shore *B*

Massachusetts

Anna Maria College *B*
Atlantic Union College *B*
Boston College *M, D*
Boston University *M, D*
Bridgewater State College *B, M*
Eastern Nazarene College *B*
Elms College *B*
Gordon College *B*
Holyoke Community College *C, A*
Massachusetts College of Liberal
  Arts *B*
Northern Essex Community
  College *A*
Regis College *B*
Salem State College *B, M*
Simmons College *M, D*
Smith College *M, D*
Springfield College *M*
Western New England College *B*
Westfield State College *B*
Wheelock College *B*

Michigan

Adrian College *B*
Andrews University *B, M*
Calvin College *B*
Central Michigan University *B*
Cornerstone University *B*
Delta College *A*
Eastern Michigan University *B, M*
Ferris State University *A, B*
Gogebic Community College *B*
Grand Valley State University *B, M*
Hope College *B*
Kellogg Community College *A*
Kuyper College *A, B*
Lansing Community College *A*
Madonna University *B, M*
Marygrove College *B*
Michigan State University *B, M, D*
Northern Michigan University *B*
Rochester College *B*
Saginaw Valley State University *B*
Schoolcraft College *A*
Siena Heights University *A, B*
Southwestern Michigan College *A*
Spring Arbor University *B*
University of Detroit Mercy *B*
University of Michigan *M, D*
University of Michigan
  Flint *B*
Wayne County Community College *A*
Wayne State University *B, M, D*
Western Michigan University *B, M*

Minnesota

Augsburg College *B, M*
Bemidji State University *B*
Bethel University *B*
Capella University *M, D*
Century Community and Technical
  College *C, A*
College of St. Benedict *B*
College of St. Catherine *B, M*
College of St. Scholastica *B*
Concordia College: Moorhead *B*
Inver Hills Community College *A*
Itasca Community College *A*
Metropolitan State University *B*
Minnesota State University
  Mankato *B*
  Moorhead *B*
Ridgewater College *A*
St. Cloud State University *B*
St. John's University *B*

St. Olaf College *B*
Southwest Minnesota State
  University *B*
University of Minnesota
  Duluth *M*
  Morris *B*
  Twin Cities *M, D*
University of St. Thomas *B, M*
Winona State University *B*

Mississippi

Belhaven College *B*
Coahoma Community College *A*
Delta State University *B*
Itawamba Community College *A*
Jackson State University *B, M, D*
Mississippi College *B*
Mississippi Delta Community
  College *A*
Mississippi Gulf Coast Community
  College
  Jefferson Davis Campus *A*
Mississippi State University *B*
Mississippi Valley State
  University *B, M*
Rust College *B*
University of Mississippi *B*
University of Southern
  Mississippi *B, M*

Missouri

Avila University *B*
Central Missouri State University *B*
College of the Ozarks *B*
Evangel University *A, B*
Lindenwood University *B*
Missouri State University *B, M*
Missouri Western State University *B*
Park University *B*
St. Louis Community College
  St. Louis Community College at
    Meramec *A*
St. Louis University *B, M*
Southeast Missouri State University *B*
University of Missouri
  Columbia *B, M, D*
  Kansas City *M*
  St. Louis *B, M*
Washington University in St.
  Louis *M, D*
William Woods University *B*

Montana

Miles Community College *A*
Salish Kootenai College *B*
University of Montana: Missoula *B, M*

Nebraska

Chadron State College *B*
Creighton University *B*
Dana College *B*
Metropolitan Community College *A*
Nebraska Indian Community
  College *A*
Nebraska Wesleyan University *B*
Union College *B*
University of Nebraska
  Kearney *B*
  Omaha *B, M*
Western Nebraska Community
  College *A*

Nevada

Great Basin College *A*
University of Nevada
  Las Vegas *B, M*
  Reno *B, M*

New Hampshire

Franklin Pierce College *B*
Plymouth State University *B*
University of New Hampshire *B, M*

University of New Hampshire at
  Manchester *M*

New Jersey

Atlantic Cape Community College *A*
Brookdale Community College *A*
Camden County College *A*
Cumberland County College *A*
Essex County College *A*
Georgian Court University *B*
Kean University *B, M*
Monmouth University *B*
Ocean County College *C, A*
Ramapo College of New Jersey *B*
Richard Stockton College of New
  Jersey *B*
Rutgers, The State University of New
  Jersey
  Camden Regional Campus *B, M*
  New Brunswick/Piscataway
    Campus *B, D*
  Newark Regional Campus *B*
Seton Hall University *B*
Sussex County Community College *A*

New Mexico

Eastern New Mexico University *B*
Eastern New Mexico University:
  Roswell Campus *A*
New Mexico State University *B, M*
New Mexico State University
  Alamogordo *C, A*
Northern New Mexico College *A*
San Juan College *C, A*
Santa Fe Community College *A*
Western New Mexico University *B*

New York

Adelphi University *B, M, D*
City University of New York
  College of Staten Island *B*
  Hunter College *M*
  Lehman College *B*
  York College *B*
College of New Rochelle *B*
College of Saint Rose *B*
Columbia-Greene Community
  College *A*
Concordia College *B, D*
Daemen College *B*
Dominican College of Blauvelt *B*
Elmira College *A, B*
Fordham University *B, M, D*
Hudson Valley Community College *A*
Iona College *B*
Keuka College *B*
Long Island University
  Brooklyn Campus *B, M*
  C. W. Post Campus *B, M*
Marist College *B*
Mercy College *B*
Metropolitan College of New
  York *A, B*
Molloy College *B*
Nazareth College of Rochester *B, M*
New York University *B, M, D*
Niagara County Community
  College *C*
Niagara University *B*
Nyack College *B*
Roberts Wesleyan College *B, M*
Siena College *B*
Skidmore College *B*
State University of New York
  Albany *B, M, D*
  Binghamton *M*
  Buffalo *M, D*
  College at Brockport *B, M*
  College at Buffalo *B*
  College at Fredonia *B*
  College at Plattsburgh *B*
  New Paltz *B, M*
  Stony Brook *B, M, D*
Syracuse University *B, M*

Ulster County Community College *A*
Westchester Community College *C, A*
Yeshiva University *M, D*

North Carolina

Appalachian State University *B*
Asheville-Buncombe Technical
    Community College *A*
Barton College *B*
Bennett College *B*
Campbell University *B*
East Carolina University *B, M*
Elizabeth City State University *B*
Gaston College *A*
Halifax Community College *A*
Johnson C. Smith University *B*
Lenoir Community College *A*
Livingstone College *B*
Louisburg College *A*
Mars Hill College *B*
Meredith College *B, T*
Methodist College *A, B*
North Carolina Agricultural and
    Technical State University *B, M*
North Carolina Central University *B*
North Carolina State University *B, M*
Piedmont Community College *A*
Richmond Community College *A*
Sandhills Community College *A*
Shaw University *B*
University of North Carolina
    Chapel Hill *M, D*
    Charlotte *B, M*
    Greensboro *B, M*
    Pembroke *B*
    Wilmington *B, M*
Warren Wilson College *B*
Western Carolina University *B*
Winston-Salem State University *B*

North Dakota

Minot State University *B*
University of Mary *B*
University of North Dakota *B, M*

Ohio

Ashland University *B*
Bluffton University *B*
Bowling Green State University *B*
Capital University *B*
Case Western Reserve University *M, D*
Cedarville University *B*
Central Ohio Technical College *A*
Central State University *B*
Clark State Community College *A*
Cleveland State University *B, M*
College of Mount St. Joseph *B*
College of Wooster *B*
Defiance College *B*
Franciscan University of
    Steubenville *B*
Lourdes College *B*
Malone College *B*
Miami University
    Oxford Campus *B*
Mount Vernon Nazarene University *B*
Ohio Dominican University *B*
Ohio State University
    Columbus Campus *B, M, D*
    Lima Campus *B*
Ohio University *B, M*
Ohio University
    Chillicothe Campus *A*
Owens Community College
    Toledo *A*
Sinclair Community College *C, A*
Union Institute & University *B*
University of Akron *B, M*
University of Akron: Wayne College *A*
University of Cincinnati *B, M*
University of Cincinnati
    Clermont College *A*
    Raymond Walters College *A*
University of Findlay *B*

University of Rio Grande *A, B*
University of Toledo *B*
Ursuline College *B*
Wilmington College *B*
Wright State University *A, B*
Wright State University: Lake
    Campus *A*
Xavier University *B*
Youngstown State University *A, B, M*
Zane State College *A*

Oklahoma

Connors State College *A*
East Central University *B*
Northeastern Oklahoma Agricultural
    and Mechanical College *A*
Northeastern State University *B*
Northwestern Oklahoma State
    University *B*
Oklahoma Baptist University *B*
Oklahoma City University *B*
Oral Roberts University *B*
Rose State College *A*
Southwestern Oklahoma State
    University *B*
University of Oklahoma *B, M*

Oregon

Chemeketa Community College *A*
Concordia University *B*
George Fox University *B*
Pacific University *B*
Portland State University *M, D*
Rogue Community College *A*
Southwestern Oregon Community
    College *A*
Treasure Valley Community College *A*
University of Portland *B*
Warner Pacific College *B*

Pennsylvania

Alvernia College *B*
Bloomsburg University of
    Pennsylvania *B*
Bryn Mawr College *M, D*
Bucks County Community College *A*
Cabrini College *B*
California University of
    Pennsylvania *B, M*
Carlow University *B*
Cedar Crest College *B*
Chatham College *B*
College Misericordia *B*
Community College of Allegheny
    County *A*
Eastern University *B*
Edinboro University of
    Pennsylvania *A, B, M*
Elizabethtown College *B*
Gannon University *B*
Geneva College *B*
Harrisburg Area Community
    College *A*
Holy Family University *B*
Juniata College *B*
Kutztown University of
    Pennsylvania *B, M*
La Salle University *B*
Lehigh Carbon Community
    College *C, A*
Lock Haven University of
    Pennsylvania *B*
Mansfield University of
    Pennsylvania *A, B*
Marywood University *B, M, D*
Mercyhurst College *B*
Messiah College *B*
Millersville University of
    Pennsylvania *B*
Northampton County Area
    Community College *A*
Philadelphia Biblical University *B*
Reading Area Community College *A*
St. Francis University *B*

Seton Hill University *B*
Shippensburg University of
    Pennsylvania *B, M*
Slippery Rock University of
    Pennsylvania *B*
Temple University *B, M*
University of Pennsylvania *M, D*
University of Pittsburgh *B, M, D*
West Chester University of
    Pennsylvania *B, M*
Westminster College *B*
Widener University *B, M*

Puerto Rico

Bayamon Central University *B*
Inter American University of Puerto
    Rico
    Arecibo Campus *B*
Pontifical Catholic University of
    Puerto Rico *B, M, D*
Turabo University *B*
Universidad Metropolitana *B*
Universidad del Este *A, B*
University of Puerto Rico
    Humacao *B*
    Rio Piedras *B, M, D*
University of the Sacred Heart *B*

Rhode Island

Community College of Rhode
    Island *A*
Providence College *B*
Rhode Island College *B, M*
Salve Regina University *B*

South Carolina

Aiken Technical College *A*
Benedict College *B*
Coker College *B*
Columbia College *B*
Florence-Darlington Technical
    College *A*
Greenville Technical College *C, A*
Horry-Georgetown Technical
    College *A*
Limestone College *B*
Midlands Technical College *A*
Piedmont Technical College *A*
South Carolina State University *B*
University of South Carolina *M, D*
Winthrop University *B*

South Dakota

Kilian Community College *A*
Northern State University *B*
Presentation College *B*
University of Sioux Falls *B*
University of South Dakota *B, M*

Tennessee

Austin Peay State University *B*
Belmont University *B, T*
East Tennessee State University *B, M*
Freed-Hardeman University *B*
Jackson State Community College *A*
LeMoyne-Owen College *B*
Lincoln Memorial University *B*
Lipscomb University *B*
Middle Tennessee State University *B*
Southern Adventist University *B*
Tennessee State University *B*
Trevecca Nazarene University *B*
Union University *B, T*
University of Memphis *B*
University of Tennessee
    Chattanooga *B*
    Knoxville *B, M, D*
    Martin *B*

Texas

Abilene Christian University *B*
Amarillo College *A*
Angelina College *A*

Austin Community College *A*
Baylor University *B, M*
Cisco Junior College *A*
Clarendon College *A*
College of the Mainland *A*
Del Mar College *A*
Eastfield College *A*
Galveston College *A*
Hardin-Simmons University *B*
Howard Payne University *B*
Lamar University *B*
Laredo Community College *A*
Lubbock Christian University *B*
Midland College *A*
Midwestern State University *B*
Northwest Vista College *A*
Our Lady of the Lake University of San
    Antonio *B, M*
Palo Alto College *A*
Prairie View A&M University *B*
St. Edward's University *B*
St. Philip's College *A*
Southwestern Adventist University *B*
Stephen F. Austin State University *B, M*
Tarleton State University *B*
Temple College *A*
Texas A&M University
    Commerce *B, M*
Texas Christian University *B*
Texas College *B*
Texas Southern University *B*
Texas State University: San
    Marcos *B, M*
Texas Tech University *B*
Texas Woman's University *B*
University of Houston *M, D*
University of Houston
    Clear Lake *B*
University of Mary Hardin-Baylor *B*
University of North Texas *B*
University of Texas
    Arlington *B, M, D*
    Austin *B, M, D*
    El Paso *B*
    Pan American *B, M*
    San Antonio *M*
West Texas A&M University *B*

Utah

Brigham Young University *B, M*
Dixie State College of Utah *A*
Salt Lake Community College *A*
Snow College *A*
University of Utah *B, M, D*
Utah State University *B*
Weber State University *B*

Vermont

Castleton State College *B*
Champlain College *A, B*
Goddard College *B*
Southern Vermont College *B*
University of Vermont *B, M*

Virginia

Christopher Newport University *B*
Eastern Mennonite University *B*
Ferrum College *B*
George Mason University *B*
James Madison University *B*
Longwood University *B*
Mary Baldwin College *B*
Mountain Empire Community
    College *A*
Norfolk State University *B, M, D*
Radford University *B, M*
Thomas Nelson Community
    College *A*
Virginia Commonwealth
    University *B, M, D*
Virginia Highlands Community
    College *A*
Virginia Intermont College *B*
Virginia State University *B*

Virginia Union University *B*

Washington

Eastern Washington University *B, M*
Edmonds Community College *C*
Heritage University *B*
Pacific Lutheran University *B*
Seattle University *B*
Trinity Lutheran College *B*
University of Washington *B, M, D*
Walla Walla College *B, M*

West Virginia

Bethany College *B*
Concord University *B*
Marshall University *B*
Mountain State University *B*
Potomac State College of West Virginia
University *A*
Shepherd University *B*
West Virginia State University *B*
West Virginia University *B, M*

Wisconsin

Beloit College *B*
Carthage College *B*
Concordia University Wisconsin *B*
Marian College of Fond du Lac *B*
Mount Mary College *B*
University of Wisconsin
Eau Claire *B*
Green Bay *B, M*
Madison *B, M, D*
Milwaukee *B, M*
Oshkosh *B, M*
River Falls *B*
Superior *B*
Whitewater *B, T*
Viterbo University *B*

Wyoming

Casper College *A*
Sheridan College *A*
University of Wyoming *B, M*
Western Wyoming Community
College *A*

Sociology

Alabama

Alabama Agricultural and Mechanical
University *B*
Alabama State University *B*
Athens State University *B*
Auburn University *B, M*
Auburn University at Montgomery *B*
Birmingham-Southern College *B*
Gadsden State Community College *A*
Jacksonville State University *B*
Lawson State Community College *A*
Samford University *B*
Spring Hill College *B*
Talladega College *B*
Troy University *B*
Tuskegee University *B*
University of Alabama *B*
University of Alabama
Birmingham *B, M*
Huntsville *B*
University of Mobile *B*
University of Montevallo *B, T*
University of North Alabama *B*
University of South Alabama *B, M*
University of West Alabama *B*

Alaska

University of Alaska
Anchorage *B*
Fairbanks *B*

Arizona

Arizona State University *B, M, D*

Arizona State University West *B*
Arizona Western College *A*
Eastern Arizona College *A*
Gateway Community College *A*
Grand Canyon University *B*
Northern Arizona University *B, M*
Pima Community College *A*
Prescott College *B, M*
South Mountain Community
College *A*
University of Arizona *B, M, D*

Arkansas

Arkansas State University *B, M*
Arkansas State University
Beebe *A*
Arkansas Tech University *B*
Henderson State University *B*
Hendrix College *B*
Ouachita Baptist University *B*
Philander Smith College *B*
Southern Arkansas University *B*
University of Arkansas *B, M*
University of Arkansas
Little Rock *B*
Pine Bluff *B*
University of Central Arkansas *B, M*
University of the Ozarks *B*

California

Azusa Pacific University *B*
Bakersfield College *A*
Biola University *B*
Cabrillo College *A*
California Baptist University *B*
California Lutheran University *B*
California State Polytechnic
University: Pomona *B*
California State University
Bakersfield *B*
Chico *B*
Dominguez Hills *B*
East Bay *B, M*
Fresno *B*
Fullerton *B, M*
Long Beach *B*
Los Angeles *B, M*
Northridge *B*
Sacramento *B, M*
San Bernardino *B*
San Marcos *B, M*
Stanislaus *B*
Cerritos Community College *A*
Chabot College *A*
Chaffey College *A*
Chapman University *B*
College of Alameda *A*
College of the Desert *A*
Contra Costa College *A*
Cosumnes River College *A*
Crafton Hills College *A*
Cypress College *A*
De Anza College *A*
East Los Angeles College *A*
El Camino College *A*
Foothill College *A*
Fresno City College *A*
Fresno Pacific University *B*
Fullerton College *A*
Gavilan Community College *A*
Glendale Community College *A*
Golden West College *A*
Holy Names University *B*
Humboldt State University *B, M*
Irvine Valley College *A*
La Sierra University *B*
Las Positas College *A*
Los Angeles Southwest College *A*
Los Angeles Valley College *A*
Los Medanos College *A*
Loyola Marymount University *B*
Merced College *A*
Mills College *B*
MiraCosta College *A*

Monterey Peninsula College *A*
Mount St. Mary's College *B*
National University *B*
Notre Dame de Namur University *B*
Occidental College *B*
Ohlone College *C*
Orange Coast College *A*
Pepperdine University *B*
Pitzer College *B*
Point Loma Nazarene University *B*
Pomona College *B*
Saddleback College *A*
St. Mary's College of California *B*
San Diego Mesa College *A*
San Diego Miramar College *A*
San Diego State University *B, M*
San Francisco State University *B*
San Jose State University *B, M*
Santa Ana College *A*
Santa Barbara City College *A*
Santa Clara University *B*
Santa Rosa Junior College *A*
Santiago Canyon College *A*
Scripps College *B*
Sonoma State University *B*
Southwestern College *A*
Stanford University *B, M, D*
University of California
Berkeley *B, D*
Davis *B, D*
Irvine *B, M, D*
Los Angeles *B, M, D*
Riverside *B, M, D*
San Diego *B, M, D*
Santa Barbara *B, M, D*
Santa Cruz *B, D*
University of La Verne *B*
University of Redlands *B*
University of San Diego *B*
University of San Francisco *B*
University of Southern
California *B, M, D*
University of the Pacific *B*
Vanguard University of Southern
California *B*
Ventura College *A*
West Los Angeles College *C, A*
West Valley College *A*
Westmont College *B*
Whittier College *B*

Colorado

Adams State College *B*
Colorado College *B*
Colorado State University *B, M, D*
Colorado State University
Pueblo *B*
Fort Lewis College *B*
Mesa State College *B*
Metropolitan State College of
Denver *B, T*
Red Rocks Community College *A*
Regis University *B*
University of Colorado
Boulder *B, D*
Colorado Springs *B, M*
Denver and Health Sciences
Center *B, M*
University of Denver *B, M*
University of Northern Colorado *B*
Western State College of Colorado *B*

Connecticut

Albertus Magnus College *B*
Central Connecticut State
University *B*
Connecticut College *B*
Eastern Connecticut State
University *B*
Fairfield University *B*
Post University *B*
Quinnipiac University *B*
Sacred Heart University *B*
St. Joseph College *B*

Southern Connecticut State
University *B, M*
Trinity College *B*
University of Bridgeport *B*
University of Connecticut *B, M, D*
University of Hartford *B*
Wesleyan University *B*
Western Connecticut State
University *B*
Yale University *B, M, D*

Delaware

Delaware State University *B*
University of Delaware *B, M, D*

District of Columbia

American University *B, M*
Catholic University of
America *B, M, D*
Gallaudet University *B*
George Washington University *B, M*
Georgetown University *B*
Howard University *B, M, D*
Trinity University *B*
University of the District of
Columbia *B*

Florida

Barry University *B*
Bethune-Cookman College *B*
Broward Community College *A*
Eckerd College *B*
Edward Waters College *B*
Flagler College *B*
Florida Agricultural and Mechanical
University *B*
Florida Atlantic University *B, M*
Florida International
University *B, M, D*
Florida Memorial University *B*
Florida Southern College *B*
Florida State University *B, M, D*
Gulf Coast Community College *A*
Indian River Community College *A*
Jacksonville University *B*
Miami Dade College *A*
New College of Florida *B*
Palm Beach Community College *A*
Pensacola Junior College *A*
Rollins College *B*
St. Leo University *B*
Stetson University *B*
University of Central Florida *B, M, D*
University of Florida *B, M, D*
University of Miami *B, M, D*
University of North Florida *B, M*
University of South Florida *B, M*
University of Tampa *A, B*
University of West Florida *B*
Valencia Community College *A*

Georgia

Abraham Baldwin Agricultural
College *A*
Agnes Scott College *B*
Albany State University *B*
Andrew College *A*
Augusta State University *B*
Berry College *B*
Brewton-Parker College *B*
Clark Atlanta University *B, M*
Coastal Georgia Community
College *A*
Columbus State University *B*
Covenant College *B*
Dalton State College *B*
Darton College *A*
East Georgia College *A*
Emory University *B, D*
Fort Valley State University *B*
Gainesville State College *A*
Georgia College and State
University *B*

Georgia Perimeter College *A*
Georgia Southern University *B, M*
Georgia Southwestern State
  University *B*
Georgia State University *B, M, D*
Gordon College *A*
Kennesaw State University *B*
Macon State College *A*
Mercer University *B*
Middle Georgia College *A*
Morehouse College *B*
North Georgia College & State
  University *B*
Oglethorpe University *B*
Paine College *B*
Piedmont College *B*
Reinhardt College *B*
Savannah State University *B*
Shorter College *B*
South Georgia College *A*
Spelman College *B*
University of Georgia *B, M, D*
University of West Georgia *B, M*
Valdosta State University *B, M*
Waycross College *A*
Wesleyan College *B*

Hawaii

Hawaii Pacific University *B*
University of Hawaii
  Hilo *B*
  Manoa *B, M, D*
  West Oahu *B*

Idaho

Albertson College of Idaho *B*
Boise State University *A, B, T*
Brigham Young University-Idaho *B*
College of Southern Idaho *A*
Idaho State University *B, M*
North Idaho College *A*
University of Idaho *B*

Illinois

Augustana College *B, T*
Aurora University *B*
Benedictine University *B*
Black Hawk College
  East Campus *A*
Bradley University *B*
Chicago State University *B*
Concordia University *B*
Danville Area Community College *A*
DePaul University *B, M*
Dominican University *B*
Eastern Illinois University *B*
Elmhurst College *B, T*
Greenville College *B*
Highland Community College *A*
Illinois College *B*
Illinois State University *B, M*
Illinois Valley Community College *A*
Illinois Wesleyan University *B*
John A. Logan College *A*
John Wood Community College *A*
Joliet Junior College *A*
Judson College *B*
Kishwaukee College *A*
Knox College *B*
Lake Forest College *B*
Lewis University *B, T*
Loyola University of Chicago *B, M, D*
McKendree College *B*
Millikin University *B*
Monmouth College *B, T*
North Central College *B*
North Park University *B*
Northeastern Illinois University *B*
Northern Illinois University *B, M*
Northwestern University *B, M, D*
Olivet Nazarene University *B*
Principia College *B*
Richland Community College *A*
Rockford College *B*

Roosevelt University *B, M*
St. Xavier University *B*
Sauk Valley Community College *A*
South Suburban College of Cook
  County *A*
Southern Illinois University
  Carbondale *B, M, D*
Southern Illinois University
  Edwardsville *B, M*
Southwestern Illinois College *A*
Trinity Christian College *B*
University of Chicago *B, D*
University of Illinois
  Chicago *B, M, D*
  Urbana-Champaign *B, M, D*
Western Illinois University *B, M*
Wheaton College *B*

Indiana

Anderson University *B*
Ball State University *B, M*
Bethel College *B*
Butler University *B*
DePauw University *B*
Earlham College *B*
Franklin College *B*
Goshen College *B*
Grace College *B*
Hanover College *B*
Huntington University *B*
Indiana State University *B*
Indiana University
  Bloomington *B, M, D*
  East *B*
  Kokomo *B*
  Northwest *A, B*
  South Bend *B*
  Southeast *B*
Indiana University-Purdue University
  Fort Wayne *B*
Indiana University-Purdue University
  Indianapolis *B, M*
Manchester College *B*
Marian College *B, T*
Martin University *B*
Purdue University *B, M, D*
Purdue University
  Calumet *B*
St. Joseph's College *B*
Saint Mary's College *B*
Taylor University *B*
University of Evansville *B*
University of Indianapolis *B, M*
University of Notre Dame *B, M, D*
University of Southern Indiana *B*
Valparaiso University *B*
Vincennes University *A*

Iowa

Ashford University *T*
Briar Cliff University *B*
Buena Vista University *B*
Central College *B, T*
Clarke College *A, B*
Coe College *B*
Cornell College *B, T*
Drake University *B*
Ellsworth Community College *A*
Graceland University *B, T*
Grinnell College *B*
Iowa State University *B, M, D*
Iowa Wesleyan College *B*
Loras College *B*
Luther College *B*
Mount Mercy College *B*
North Iowa Area Community
  College *A*
Northwestern College *B, T*
St. Ambrose University *B, T*
Simpson College *B*
University of Dubuque *B, T*
University of Iowa *B, M, D, T*
University of Northern Iowa *B, M*
Upper Iowa University *B*

Wartburg College *B, T*
William Penn University *B*

Kansas

Allen County Community College *A*
Baker University *B*
Barton County Community College *A*
Benedictine College *B*
Bethany College *B*
Central Christian College of Kansas *A*
Coffeyville Community College *A*
Colby Community College *A*
Dodge City Community College *A*
Emporia State University *B, T*
Fort Hays State University *B*
Friends University *B*
Kansas State University *B, M, D*
Kansas Wesleyan University *B*
McPherson College *B, T*
MidAmerica Nazarene University *B*
Newman University *B*
Ottawa University *B*
Pittsburg State University *B*
Pratt Community College *A*
Seward County Community College *A*
Tabor College *B*
University of Kansas *B, M, D*
University of St. Mary *B*
Washburn University of Topeka *B*
Wichita State University *B, M*

Kentucky

Asbury College *B*
Bellarmine University *B*
Berea College *B*
Brescia University *B*
Campbellsville University *B*
Centre College *B*
Eastern Kentucky University *B*
Georgetown College *B, T*
Kentucky State University *B*
Kentucky Wesleyan College *B*
Morehead State University *B, M*
Murray State University *B*
Northern Kentucky University *B*
Pikeville College *B*
Thomas More College *A, B*
Transylvania University *B*
Union College *B*
University of Kentucky *B, M, D*
University of Louisville *B, M*
Western Kentucky University *B, M*

Louisiana

Centenary College of Louisiana *B*
Dillard University *B*
Grambling State University *B*
Louisiana State University
  Shreveport *B*
Louisiana State University and
  Agricultural and Mechanical
  College *B, M, D*
Louisiana Tech University *B*
Loyola University New Orleans *B*
Nicholls State University *B*
Northwestern State University *B*
Southeastern Louisiana
  University *B, M*
Southern University
  New Orleans *B*
  Shreveport *B*
Southern University and Agricultural
  and Mechanical College *B*
Tulane University *B, M*
University of Louisiana at Lafayette *B*
University of Louisiana at Monroe *B*
University of New Orleans *B, M*
Xavier University of Louisiana *B*

Maine

Bates College *B*
Bowdoin College *B*
Colby College *B*

St. Joseph's College *B*
University of Maine *B*
University of Maine
  Fort Kent *B*
  Presque Isle *B*
University of New England *B*
University of Southern Maine *B*

Maryland

Allegany College of Maryland *A*
Bowie State University *B*
Coppin State University *B*
Frederick Community College *A*
Frostburg State University *B*
Goucher College *B*
Harford Community College *A*
Hood College *B*
Johns Hopkins University *B, M, D*
Loyola College in Maryland *B*
McDaniel College *B*
Morgan State University *B, M*
Mount St. Mary's University *B*
St. Mary's College of Maryland *B*
Salisbury University *B*
Towson University *B*
University of Maryland
  Baltimore County *B, M*
  College Park *B, M, D*
  Eastern Shore *B*
Washington College *B*

Massachusetts

American International College *B*
Amherst College *B*
Assumption College *B*
Boston College *B, M, D*
Boston University *B, M, D*
Brandeis University *B, M, D*
Bridgewater State College *B*
Bunker Hill Community College *A*
Cape Cod Community College *A*
Clark University *B*
College of the Holy Cross *B*
Curry College *B*
Eastern Nazarene College *B*
Elms College *B*
Emmanuel College *B*
Fitchburg State College *B*
Framingham State College *B*
Gordon College *B*
Hampshire College *B*
Harvard College *B, D*
Lasell College *B*
Massachusetts College of Liberal
  Arts *B*
Merrimack College *B*
Mount Holyoke College *B*
Newbury College *A*
Northeastern University *B, M, D*
Regis College *B*
St. John's Seminary College *B*
Salem State College *B*
Simmons College *B*
Simon's Rock College of Bard *B*
Smith College *B*
Springfield College *B*
Stonehill College *B*
Suffolk University *B*
Tufts University *B*
University of Massachusetts
  Amherst *B, M, D*
  Boston *B, M*
  Dartmouth *B*
  Lowell *B*
Wellesley College *B*
Western New England College *B*
Westfield State College *B*
Wheaton College *B*
Williams College *B*
Worcester State College *B*

Michigan

Adrian College *B, T*
Albion College *B*

Alma College *B, T*
Andrews University *B*
Aquinas College *B, T*
Calvin College *B*
Central Michigan University *B, M, T*
Cornerstone University *B*
Delta College *A*
Eastern Michigan University *B, M*
Ferris State University *B*
Grand Valley State University *B*
Hillsdale College *B*
Hope College *B*
Kalamazoo College *B, T*
Kellogg Community College *A*
Lake Michigan College *A*
Lake Superior State University *B*
Lansing Community College *A*
Madonna University *B*
Michigan State University *B, M, D*
Mid Michigan Community College *A*
Northern Michigan University *B, T*
Oakland University *B*
Olivet College *B*
Saginaw Valley State University *B*
Spring Arbor University *B*
University of Detroit Mercy *B*
University of Michigan *B, M, D, T*
University of Michigan
 Dearborn *B*
 Flint *B*
Wayne State University *B, M, D*
Western Michigan University *B, M, D*

Minnesota

Augsburg College *B*
Bemidji State University *B*
Carleton College *B*
College of St. Benedict *B*
College of St. Catherine *B*
Concordia College: Moorhead *B*
Concordia University: St. Paul *B*
Gustavus Adolphus College *B*
Hamline University *B*
Macalester College *B*
Minnesota State University
 Mankato *B, M*
 Moorhead *B*
Ridgewater College *A*
St. Cloud State University *B*
St. John's University *B*
St. Mary's University of Minnesota *B*
St. Olaf College *B*
Southwest Minnesota State
 University *B*
University of Minnesota
 Duluth *B*
 Morris *B*
 Twin Cities *B, M, D*
University of St. Thomas *B*
Winona State University *B*

Mississippi

Alcorn State University *B*
Hinds Community College *A*
Itawamba Community College *A*
Jackson State University *B, M*
Millsaps College *B*
Mississippi College *B*
Mississippi Delta Community
 College *A*
Mississippi State University *B, M, D*
Mississippi Valley State University *B*
Rust College *B*
Tougaloo College *B*
University of Mississippi *B, M*
University of Southern Mississippi *B*

Missouri

Avila University *B*
Central Methodist University *B*
Central Missouri State University *B, M*
College of the Ozarks *B*
Columbia College *B*
Drury University *B*

Evangel University *B*
Lincoln University *B, M*
Lindenwood University *B*
Maryville University of Saint Louis *B*
Missouri Southern State
 University *B, T*
Missouri State University *B*
Missouri Valley College *B*
Northwest Missouri State
 University *B*
Park University *B*
Rockhurst University *C, B*
St. Louis University *B*
Southeast Missouri State University *B*
Southwest Baptist University *B*
Three Rivers Community College *A*
Truman State University *B*
University of Missouri
 Columbia *B, M, D*
 Kansas City *B, M, D*
 St. Louis *B, M*
Webster University *B*
Westminster College *B*

Montana

Carroll College *B*
Montana State University
 Billings *B, T*
 Bozeman *B*
Rocky Mountain College *B, T*
University of Great Falls *B*
University of Montana: Missoula *B, M*

Nebraska

Bellevue University *B*
Chadron State College *B*
Creighton University *B*
Dana College *B*
Doane College *B*
Hastings College *B*
Midland Lutheran College *B*
Nebraska Wesleyan University *B*
Peru State College *B, T*
University of Nebraska
 Kearney *B*
 Lincoln *B, M, D*
 Omaha *B*
Wayne State College *B, T*
Western Nebraska Community
 College *A*

Nevada

Great Basin College *A*
University of Nevada
 Las Vegas *B, M, D*
 Reno *B, M*

New Hampshire

Dartmouth College *B*
Franklin Pierce College *B*
Keene State College *B*
New England College *B*
Rivier College *B*
St. Anselm College *B*
University of New Hampshire *B, M, D*

New Jersey

Atlantic Cape Community College *A*
Bloomfield College *B*
Caldwell College *B*
Centenary College *B*
The College of New Jersey *B*
College of St. Elizabeth *B*
Drew University *B*
Fairleigh Dickinson University
 College at Florham *B*
 Metropolitan Campus *B*
Felician College *B*
Georgian Court University *B*
Gloucester County College *A*
Hudson County Community
 College *A*
Kean University *B, T*

Middlesex County College *A*
Montclair State University *B, M*
New Jersey City University *B*
Passaic County Community College *A*
Princeton University *B, M, D*
Ramapo College of New Jersey *B*
Richard Stockton College of New
 Jersey *B*
Rider University *B*
Rowan University *B*
Rutgers, The State University of New
 Jersey
 Camden Regional Campus *B*
 New Brunswick/Piscataway
  Campus *B, M, D*
 Newark Regional Campus *B*
St. Peter's College *B*
Salem Community College *A*
Seton Hall University *B, T*
Thomas Edison State College *B*
William Paterson University of New
 Jersey *B, M*

New Mexico

Eastern New Mexico University *B*
New Mexico State University *B, M*
San Juan College *A*
University of New Mexico *B, M, D*
Western New Mexico University *B*

New York

Adelphi University *B*
Adirondack Community College *A*
Alfred University *B*
Bard College *B*
Barnard College *B*
Canisius College *B*
City University of New York
 Baruch College *B*
 Brooklyn College *B, M*
 City College *B, M*
 Hunter College *B, M*
 Lehman College *B*
 Queens College *B, M, T*
 Queensborough Community
  College *A*
 York College *B*
Clarkson University *B*
Colgate University *B*
College of Mount St. Vincent *B*
College of New Rochelle *B*
College of Saint Rose *B*
Columbia University
 Columbia College *B*
 School of General Studies *B*
Cornell University *B, M, D*
D'Youville College *B*
Dowling College *B*
Elmira College *B*
Eugene Lang College The New School
 for Liberal Arts *B*
Excelsior College *B*
Fordham University *B, M, D*
Hamilton College *B*
Hartwick College *B*
Hobart and William Smith Colleges *B*
Hofstra University *B*
Houghton College *B*
Iona College *B*
Ithaca College *B*
Keuka College *B*
Le Moyne College *B*
Long Island University
 Brooklyn Campus *B, M*
 C. W. Post Campus *B*
Manhattan College *B*
Manhattanville College *B*
Marymount Manhattan College *B*
Mercy College *B*
Metropolitan College of New
 York *A, B*
Molloy College *B*
Mount St. Mary College *B, T*
Nazareth College of Rochester *B*

New York Institute of Technology *B*
New York University *B, M, D*
Niagara University *B*
Roberts Wesleyan College *B*
Russell Sage College *B*
St. Bonaventure University *B*
St. Francis College *B*
St. John Fisher College *B*
St. John's University *B, M*
St. Joseph's College *B*
St. Joseph's College: Suffolk
 Campus *B*
St. Lawrence University *B*
Sarah Lawrence College *B*
Siena College *B, T*
Skidmore College *B*
State University of New York
 Albany *B, M, D*
 Binghamton *B, M, D*
 Buffalo *B, M, D*
 College at Brockport *B*
 College at Buffalo *B*
 College at Cortland *B*
 College at Fredonia *B*
 College at Geneseo *B, T*
 College at Old Westbury *B*
 College at Oneonta *B*
 College at Plattsburgh *B*
 College at Potsdam *B*
 Institute of Technology at
  Utica/Rome *B, M*
 New Paltz *B, M*
 Oswego *B*
 Purchase *B*
 Stony Brook *B, M, D*
Sullivan County Community
 College *A*
Syracuse University *B, M, D*
Touro College *B*
Union College *B*
United States Military Academy *B*
Utica College *B*
Vassar College *B*
Wagner College *B*
Wells College *B*
Yeshiva University *B*

North Carolina

Appalachian State University *B*
Belmont Abbey College *B*
Bennett College *B*
Catawba College *B*
Davidson College *B*
Duke University *B, M, D*
East Carolina University *B, M*
Elizabeth City State University *B*
Elon University *B*
Fayetteville State University *B*
Gardner-Webb University *B*
Greensboro College *B*
Guilford College *B*
High Point University *B*
Johnson C. Smith University *B*
Lees-McRae College *B*
Lenoir-Rhyne College *B*
Livingstone College *B*
Louisburg College *A*
Mars Hill College *B, T*
Meredith College *B*
Methodist College *A, B*
North Carolina Agricultural and
 Technical State University *B*
North Carolina Central
 University *B, M*
North Carolina State
 University *B, M, D*
North Carolina Wesleyan College *B*
Pfeiffer University *B*
Queens University of Charlotte *B*
St. Augustine's College *B*
Salem College *B*
Shaw University *B*
University of North Carolina
 Asheville *B, T*

Chapel Hill *B, M, D*
Charlotte *B, M*
Greensboro *B, M, T*
Pembroke *B*
Wilmington *B*
Wake Forest University *B*
Warren Wilson College *B*
Western Carolina University *B*
Wingate University *B*
Winston-Salem State University *B*

North Dakota

Minot State University *B*
North Dakota State University *B*
University of North Dakota *B, M*

Ohio

Ashland University *B*
Baldwin-Wallace College *B*
Bluffton University *B*
Bowling Green State
    University *B, M, D*
Capital University *B*
Case Western Reserve
    University *B, M, D*
Cedarville University *B*
Central State University *B*
Cleveland State University *B, M*
College of Mount St. Joseph *B*
College of Wooster *B*
Denison University *B*
Franciscan University of
    Steubenville *B*
Hiram College *B*
John Carroll University *B*
Kent State University *B, M, D*
Kenyon College *B*
Lake Erie College *B*
Lourdes College *A, B*
Miami University
    Oxford Campus *B*
Mount Union College *B*
Mount Vernon Nazarene University *B*
Muskingum College *B*
Oberlin College *B*
Ohio Dominican University *B*
Ohio Northern University *B*
Ohio State University
    Columbus Campus *B, M, D*
Ohio University *B, M*
Ohio Wesleyan University *B*
Otterbein College *B*
Owens Community College
    Toledo *A*
Shawnee State University *B*
Sinclair Community College *A*
Union Institute & University *B*
University of Akron *B, M, D*
University of Cincinnati *B, M, D*
University of Dayton *B*
University of Findlay *B*
University of Rio Grande *A*
University of Toledo *B, M*
Urbana University *B*
Ursuline College *B*
Walsh University *B*
Wilmington College *B*
Wittenberg University *B*
Wright State University *A, B*
Wright State University: Lake
    Campus *A*
Xavier University *A, B*
Youngstown State University *B*

Oklahoma

Cameron University *B*
Carl Albert State College *A*
Connors State College *A*
East Central University *B*
Eastern Oklahoma State College *A*
Northeastern Oklahoma Agricultural
    and Mechanical College *A*
Northeastern State University *B*

Northwestern Oklahoma State
    University *B*
Oklahoma Baptist University *B*
Oklahoma City Community College *A*
Oklahoma City University *B*
Oklahoma State University *B, M, D*
Rose State College *A*
Southeastern Oklahoma State
    University *B*
Southern Nazarene University *B*
Southwestern Oklahoma State
    University *B*
Tulsa Community College *A*
University of Central Oklahoma *B*
University of Oklahoma *B, M, D*
University of Science and Arts of
    Oklahoma *B*
University of Tulsa *B*
Western Oklahoma State College *A*

Oregon

Central Oregon Community
    College *A*
Chemeketa Community College *A*
Eastern Oregon University *B, T*
George Fox University *B*
Lewis & Clark College *B*
Linfield College *B, T*
Linn-Benton Community College *A*
Oregon State University *B*
Pacific University *B*
Portland State University *B, M, D*
Reed College *B*
Southern Oregon University *B*
University of Oregon *B, M, D*
University of Portland *B*
Western Oregon University *B*
Willamette University *B*

Pennsylvania

Albright College *B*
Arcadia University *B*
Bloomsburg University of
    Pennsylvania *B*
Bryn Mawr College *B*
Bucknell University *B*
Cabrini College *B*
Carlow University *B, T*
Cedar Crest College *B*
Chestnut Hill College *B*
Cheyney University of Pennsylvania *B*
Clarion University of Pennsylvania *B*
Community College of Allegheny
    County *A*
Delaware County Community
    College *A*
Dickinson College *B*
Drexel University *B*
Duquesne University *B*
East Stroudsburg University of
    Pennsylvania *B*
Eastern University *B*
Edinboro University of
    Pennsylvania *B*
Elizabethtown College *B*
Franklin & Marshall College *B*
Geneva College *B*
Gettysburg College *B*
Grove City College *B*
Gwynedd-Mercy College *B*
Haverford College *B, T*
Holy Family University *B*
Immaculata University *B*
Indiana University of
    Pennsylvania *B, M*
Juniata College *B*
King's College *B*
Kutztown University of
    Pennsylvania *B*
La Roche College *B*
La Salle University *B*
Lafayette College *B*
Lebanon Valley College *B*
Lehigh University *B, M*

Lincoln University *B*
Lock Haven University of
    Pennsylvania *B*
Lycoming College *B*
Mansfield University of
    Pennsylvania *B, T*
Marywood University *B*
Mercyhurst College *B*
Messiah College *B*
Millersville University of
    Pennsylvania *B, T*
Moravian College *B*
Muhlenberg College *C, B*
Penn State
    Abington *B*
    Altoona *B*
    Beaver *B*
    Berks *B*
    Delaware County *B*
    Dubois *B*
    Fayette *B*
    Harrisburg *B*
    Hazleton *B*
    Lehigh Valley *B*
    McKeesport *B*
    Mont Alto *B*
    New Kensington *B*
    Schuylkill - Capital College *B*
    Shenango *B*
    University Park *A, B, M, D*
    Wilkes-Barre *B*
    Worthington Scranton *B*
    York *B*
Rosemont College *B*
St. Francis University *B*
St. Joseph's University *C, A, B*
St. Vincent College *B*
Seton Hill University *B*
Shippensburg University of
    Pennsylvania *B*
Slippery Rock University of
    Pennsylvania *B*
Susquehanna University *B*
Swarthmore College *B*
Temple University *B, M, D*
Thiel College *B*
University of Pennsylvania *A, B, M, D*
University of Pittsburgh *B, M, D*
University of Pittsburgh
    Bradford *B*
    Johnstown *B*
University of Scranton *A, B*
Ursinus College *B*
Villanova University *B*
Washington and Jefferson College *B*
Waynesburg College *B*
West Chester University of
    Pennsylvania *B*
Westminster College *B, T*
Widener University *B*
Wilkes University *B*
Wilson College *B*
York College of Pennsylvania *B*

Puerto Rico

Inter American University of Puerto
    Rico
    San German Campus *B*
Pontifical Catholic University of
    Puerto Rico *B*
University of Puerto Rico
    Cayey University College *B*
    Mayaguez *B*
    Rio Piedras *B, M*

Rhode Island

Brown University *B, M, D*
Providence College *B*
Rhode Island College *B*
Roger Williams University *B*
Salve Regina University *B*
University of Rhode Island *B*

South Carolina

Charleston Southern University *B*
Claflin University *B*
Clemson University *B, M*
Coastal Carolina University *B*
Coker College *B*
College of Charleston *B, T*
Francis Marion University *B*
Furman University *B*
Lander University *B*
Morris College *B*
Newberry College *B*
Presbyterian College *B*
South Carolina State University *B*
University of South Carolina *B, M, D*
University of South Carolina
    Aiken *B*
    Upstate *B*
Voorhees College *B*
Winthrop University *B*
Wofford College *B*

South Dakota

Augustana College *B, T*
Black Hills State University *B*
Dakota Wesleyan University *B*
Northern State University *B*
Oglala Lakota College *B*
South Dakota State
    University *B, M, D, T*
University of Sioux Falls *B*
University of South Dakota *B, M*

Tennessee

Austin Peay State University *B*
Belmont University *B, T*
Carson-Newman College *B*
Columbia State Community College *A*
Cumberland University *B*
East Tennessee State
    University *B, M, T*
Fisk University *B*
Hiwassee College *A*
Jackson State Community College *A*
Lambuth University *B*
LeMoyne-Owen College *B*
Lee University *B*
Maryville College *B*
Middle Tennessee State
    University *B, M*
Milligan College *B, T*
Rhodes College *B*
Roane State Community College *A*
Tennessee State University *B*
Tennessee Technological University *B*
Union University *B, T*
University of Memphis *B, M*
University of Tennessee
    Chattanooga *B*
    Knoxville *B, M, D*
    Martin *B*
Vanderbilt University *B, M, D*

Texas

Abilene Christian University *B*
Angelo State University *B*
Austin College *B*
Austin Community College *A*
Baylor University *B, M, D*
Brazosport College *A*
Cisco Junior College *A*
Clarendon College *A*
Coastal Bend College *A*
College of the Mainland *A*
Dallas Baptist University *B*
Del Mar College *A*
East Texas Baptist University *B*
El Paso Community College *A*
Frank Phillips College *A*
Galveston College *A*
Grayson County College *A*
Hardin-Simmons University *B*
Houston Baptist University *B*

Howard Payne University *B*
Huston-Tillotson College *B*
Jarvis Christian College *B*
Kilgore College *A*
Lamar University *B*
Laredo Community College *A*
Lon Morris College *A*
McMurry University *B*
Midland College *A*
Midwestern State University *B*
Northeast Texas Community
    College *A*
Northwest Vista College *A*
Our Lady of the Lake University of San
    Antonio *B*
Palo Alto College *A*
Paris Junior College *A*
Prairie View A&M University *B, M*
Rice University *B*
St. Edward's University *B*
St. Mary's University *B, T*
St. Philip's College *A*
Sam Houston State University *B, M*
San Jacinto College
    North *A*
South Plains College *A*
Southern Methodist University *B*
Southwestern University *B*
Stephen F. Austin State University *B, T*
Tarleton State University *B*
Texas A&M University *B, M, D*
Texas A&M University
    Commerce *B, M*
    Kingsville *B, M*
Texas Christian University *B*
Texas College *B*
Texas Lutheran University *B*
Texas Southern University *B, M*
Texas State University: San
    Marcos *B, M, T*
Texas Tech University *B, M*
Texas Woman's University *B, M, D*
Trinity University *B*
Trinity Valley Community College *A*
Tyler Junior College *A*
University of Houston *B, M*
University of Houston
    Clear Lake *B, M*
    Downtown *B*
University of Mary Hardin-Baylor *B*
University of North Texas *B, M, D*
University of Texas
    Arlington *B, M*
    Austin *B, M, D*
    Brownsville *B*
    Dallas *B, M*
    El Paso *B, M*
    Pan American *B, M*
    San Antonio *B, M*
    Tyler *B, M*
    of the Permian Basin *B*
University of the Incarnate Word *B*
Wayland Baptist University *B*
Weatherford College *A*
West Texas A&M University *B*
Western Texas College *A*
Wharton County Junior College *A*
Wiley College *B*

Utah

Brigham Young University *B, M, D*
Dixie State College of Utah *A*
Salt Lake Community College *A*
Snow College *A*
Southern Utah University *B*
University of Utah *B, M, D*
Utah State University *B, M, D*
Weber State University *B*
Westminster College *B*

Vermont

Bennington College *B*
Castleton State College *B*
Green Mountain College *B*

Johnson State College *B*
Marlboro College *B*
Middlebury College *B*
St. Michael's College *B*
University of Vermont *B*

Virginia

Averett University *B*
Bridgewater College *B*
Christopher Newport University *B*
College of William and Mary *B*
Eastern Mennonite University *B*
Emory & Henry College *B*
George Mason University *B, M*
Hampton University *B*
Hollins University *B*
James Madison University *B*
Longwood University *B, M, T*
Lynchburg College *B*
Mary Baldwin College *B*
Marymount University *B*
Norfolk State University *B, M*
Old Dominion University *B, M*
Radford University *B*
Randolph-Macon College *B*
Randolph-Macon Woman's College *B*
Roanoke College *B, T*
St. Paul's College *B*
Shenandoah University *B*
Sweet Briar College *B*
University of Mary Washington *B*
University of Richmond *B*
University of Virginia *B, M, D*
University of Virginia's College at
    Wise *B, T*
Virginia Commonwealth
    University *B, M*
Virginia Polytechnic Institute and
    State University *B, M, D*
Virginia State University *B*
Virginia Union University *B*
Virginia Wesleyan College *B*
Washington and Lee University *B*

Washington

Central Washington University *B*
Centralia College *A*
City University *B*
Eastern Washington University *B, T*
Everett Community College *A*
Gonzaga University *B*
Highline Community College *A*
Olympic College *A*
Pacific Lutheran University *B*
Saint Martin's University *B*
Seattle Pacific University *B*
Seattle University *B*
University of Puget Sound *B, T*
University of Washington *B, M, D*
Walla Walla College *B*
Washington State University *B, M, D*
Western Washington University *B, M*
Whitman College *B*
Whitworth College *B*

West Virginia

Concord University *B*
Davis and Elkins College *B*
Marshall University *B, M*
Potomac State College of West Virginia
    University *A*
Shepherd University *B*
West Liberty State College *B*
West Virginia State University *B*
West Virginia University *B, M*
West Virginia Wesleyan College *B*

Wisconsin

Alverno College *B*
Beloit College *B*
Cardinal Stritch University *B*
Carroll College *B*
Carthage College *B, T*

Edgewood College *B*
Lakeland College *B*
Marian College of Fond du Lac *B*
Marquette University *B*
Northland College *B, T*
Ripon College *B*
St. Norbert College *B, T*
University of Wisconsin
    Eau Claire *B*
    Green Bay *B*
    La Crosse *B, T*
    Madison *B, M, D*
    Milwaukee *B, M*
    Oshkosh *B*
    Parkside *B, T*
    Platteville *B*
    River Falls *B, T*
    Stevens Point *B, T*
    Superior *B*
    Whitewater *B, T*
Viterbo University *B*

Wyoming

Casper College *A*
Eastern Wyoming College *A*
Laramie County Community
    College *A*
Northwest College *A*
Sheridan College *A*
University of Wyoming *B, M*
Western Wyoming Community
    College *A*

Software engineering

Alabama

Auburn University *B, M*

Arizona

Embry-Riddle Aeronautical University:
    Prescott Campus *B*
Everest College *A*
Phoenix College *A*
University of Advancing
    Technology *A, B, M*

California

California Polytechnic State
    University: San Luis Obispo *B*
California State University
    East Bay *B*
    Fullerton *M*
Cogswell Polytechnical College *B*
Foothill College *A*
International Technological
    University *B*
Los Angeles City College *A*
National University *M*
Northwestern Polytechnic
    University *B*
Notre Dame de Namur University *B*
San Jose State University *B, M*
Santa Clara University *B*

Colorado

Colorado Technical University *B, M, D*

District of Columbia

Catholic University of America *M*
George Washington University *M*

Florida

Broward Community College *A*
Embry-Riddle Aeronautical
    University *B, M*
Florida Agricultural and Mechanical
    University *M*
Florida Institute of Technology *B, M*
Florida State University *B, M*
Hillsborough Community College *A*
Lake-Sumter Community College *A*
Seminole Community College *A*

Tallahassee Community College *A*

Georgia

Mercer University *M*
Southern Polytechnic State
    University *C, B, M*

Idaho

Boise State University *D*

Illinois

Moraine Valley Community College *C*

Indiana

Purdue University
    Calumet *B*
Rose-Hulman Institute of
    Technology *B*

Kansas

Southwestern College *B*

Maine

Thomas College *B*

Maryland

Capitol College *B*
University of Maryland
    University College *M*

Massachusetts

Northeastern University *M*

Michigan

Andrews University *M*
Baker College
    of Flint *M*
Michigan Technological University *B*
Oakland University *M*
University of Michigan
    Dearborn *M*

Minnesota

Globe College *A*
Riverland Community College *A*
St. Paul College *A*

Mississippi

Mississippi State University *B*
University of Southern Mississippi *D*

Missouri

Grantham University *A, B*
Hickey College *A*
Missouri Technical School *A, B*

Montana

Carroll College *B*
Montana Tech of the University of
    Montana *B*

Nevada

Community College of Southern
    Nevada *A*
University of Nevada
    Las Vegas *B*

New Jersey

Monmouth University *B, M*

New York

Clarkson University *B*
College of Westchester *A*
Rochester Institute of
    Technology *B, M*
State University of New York
    College of Agriculture and
        Technology at Morrisville *A*
Wood Tobe-Coburn School *A*

North Dakota

North Dakota State University *M, D*

Ohio

Ohio Business College: Sandusky *A*
Stark State College of Technology *A*

Oregon

Oregon State University *M*
Portland State University *M*

Pennsylvania

Allegheny College *B*
Carnegie Mellon University *M, D*
Drexel University *M*
Marywood University *A*
Robert Morris University *B*
Widener University *M*

South Carolina

Claflin University *B*

South Dakota

South Dakota State University *B*

Texas

Eastfield College *A*
Remington College
  Houston *A*
Southern Methodist University *M*
Texas Tech University *M*
University of Houston
  Clear Lake *M*
University of Texas
  Arlington *B, M*
  Dallas *B, M, D*

Vermont

Champlain College *A, B*
Vermont Technical College *A, B*

Washington

North Seattle Community College *A*
Seattle University *M*
South Seattle Community College *A*

West Virginia

West Virginia University *M*

Wisconsin

Carroll College *B, M*
Milwaukee School of Engineering *B*
University of Wisconsin
  La Crosse *M*

Soil science

Alabama

Auburn University *B, M, D*
Tuskegee University *B, M*

Arizona

Prescott College *B, M*
University of Arizona *M, D*

California

California Polytechnic State
  University: San Luis Obispo *B*
California State Polytechnic
  University: Pomona *B*
Merced College *A*
Modesto Junior College *A*
San Joaquin Delta College *A*
University of California
  Davis *B, M, D*
  Riverside *M, D*
Ventura College *A*

Colorado

Colorado Mountain College
  Timberline Campus *A*
Colorado State University *M, D*

Delaware

Delaware State University *B*
University of Delaware *B, M, D*

Florida

University of Florida *B, M, D*

Hawaii

University of Hawaii
  Hilo *B*

Idaho

University of Idaho *B, M, D*

Iowa

Iowa State University *M, D*

Kentucky

University of Kentucky *D*

Maine

Southern Maine Community
  College *C, A*
University of Maine *B, M*

Michigan

Michigan State University *B, M, D*

Minnesota

University of Minnesota
  Crookston *B*
  Twin Cities *M, D*

Missouri

University of Missouri
  Columbia *B, M, D*

Nebraska

University of Nebraska
  Lincoln *B*

New Hampshire

University of New Hampshire *M*

New Mexico

New Mexico State University *B*
Southwestern Indian Polytechnic
  Institute *A*

New York

Cornell University *B, M, D*
State University of New York
  College of Agriculture and
    Technology at Cobleskill *A*
  College of Environmental Science
    and Forestry *M, D*

North Carolina

North Carolina State University *M, D*

North Dakota

North Dakota State University *B, M, D*

Ohio

Ohio State University
  Agricultural Technical Institute *A*
  Columbus Campus *D*

Oklahoma

Eastern Oklahoma State College *A*
Oklahoma State University *B, M, D*

Oregon

Eastern Oregon University *B*

Oregon State University *M, D*

Pennsylvania

Penn State
  Abington *B*
  Altoona *B*
  Beaver *B*
  Berks *B*
  Delaware County *B*
  Dubois *B*
  Erie, The Behrend College *B*
  Fayette *B*
  Hazleton *B*
  Lehigh Valley *B*
  McKeesport *B*
  Mont Alto *B*
  New Kensington *B*
  Schuylkill - Capital College *B*
  Shenango *B*
  University Park *B, M, D*
  Wilkes-Barre *B*
  Worthington Scranton *B*
  York *B*

Puerto Rico

University of Puerto Rico
  Mayaguez *B, M*

Rhode Island

University of Rhode Island *B*

South Carolina

Clemson University *B*

Tennessee

Hiwassee College *A*
Middle Tennessee State University *B*
Tennessee Technological University *B*
University of Tennessee
  Knoxville *B, M, D*

Texas

Prairie View A&M University *M*
Texas A&M University *B, M, D*
Texas A&M University
  Commerce *B*
  Kingsville *M*
Texas Tech University *M*

Utah

Brigham Young University *B*
Utah State University *B, M, D*

Vermont

Sterling College *A, B*
University of Vermont *B, M, D*

Virginia

Mountain Empire Community
  College *A*

Washington

Spokane Community College *A*
Washington State University *B, M, D*

West Virginia

West Virginia University *B*

Wisconsin

University of Wisconsin
  Madison *B, M, D*
  River Falls *B*
  Stevens Point *B*

Wyoming

Northwest College *A*
University of Wyoming *M, D*

Solar energy technology

Arizona

Coconino County Community
  College *A*

Arkansas

University of Arkansas *M*

California

Cabrillo College *A*

Illinois

Sauk Valley Community College *A*

Michigan

Henry Ford Community College *C*

Missouri

Crowder College *A*

Nevada

Truckee Meadows Community
  College *C, A*

New Mexico

San Juan College *C, A*

Vermont

Sterling College *B*

Solid-state/ low-temperature physics

Illinois

Northwestern University *M, D*

Massachusetts

Tufts University *M, D*

New York

State University of New York
  Albany *M, D*

Texas

University of North Texas *M, D*

Wisconsin

University of Wisconsin
  Madison *M, D*

Somatic bodywork

California

California Institute of Integral
  Studies *M*

South Asian languages

Illinois

University of Chicago *B, D*

Massachusetts

Harvard College *B, D*

Minnesota

University of Minnesota
  Twin Cities *M, D*

Missouri

University of Missouri
  Columbia *B*

New Hampshire

Dartmouth College *B*

Washington

University of Washington *B*

South Asian studies

Massachusetts

Harvard College *B*

California

Claremont McKenna College *B*
University of California
Santa Cruz *B*

Illinois

University of Chicago *B*

Massachusetts

Harvard College *B*

Michigan

Oakland University *B*
University of Michigan *B, M*

Minnesota

Hamline University *B*
University of Minnesota
Twin Cities *M, D*

Missouri

University of Missouri
Columbia *B*

New York

Sarah Lawrence College *B*

Ohio

College of Wooster *B*

Pennsylvania

University of Pennsylvania *B, M, D*

Rhode Island

Brown University *B*

Vermont

Marlboro College *B*

Washington

University of Washington *B, M*

Wisconsin

University of Wisconsin
Madison *B, M, D*

Southeast Asian languages

Washington

University of Washington *B*

Southeast Asian studies

California

Claremont McKenna College *B*
University of California
Berkeley *B*
Los Angeles *B*
Santa Cruz *B*

Massachusetts

Harvard College *B*

Michigan

University of Michigan *B, M*

Minnesota

Hamline University *B*

Ohio

Ohio State University
Columbus Campus *M*

Ohio University *M*

Vermont

Marlboro College *B*

Washington

University of Washington *B, M*

Wisconsin

University of Wisconsin
Madison *M*

Spanish

Alabama

Auburn University *B, M*
Birmingham-Southern College *B, T*
Huntingdon College *B*
Oakwood College *B*
Samford University *B*
Spring Hill College *B, T*
Talladega College *B*
University of Alabama *B*

Alaska

University of Alaska
Anchorage *B*

Arizona

Arizona State University *B, M, D*
Arizona State University West *B*
Arizona Western College *A*
Cochise College *A*
Northern Arizona University *B, T*
Prescott College *B, M*
University of Arizona *B, M, D*

Arkansas

Arkansas State University *B*
Arkansas Tech University *M*
Harding University *B*
Henderson State University *B*
Hendrix College *B*
John Brown University *B*
Lyon College *B*
Ouachita Baptist University *B*
Southern Arkansas University *B*
University of Arkansas *B, M*
University of Arkansas
Little Rock *B*
University of Central Arkansas *B, M*

California

Allan Hancock College *A*
Azusa Pacific University *B*
Bakersfield College *A*
Biola University *B*
Cabrillo College *A*
California Lutheran University *B*
California State Polytechnic
University: Pomona *B*
California State University
Bakersfield *B*
Chico *B*
Dominguez Hills *B*
East Bay *B*
Fresno *B, M*
Fullerton *B, M*
Long Beach *B, M*
Los Angeles *B, M*
Monterey Bay *B*
Northridge *B, M*
Sacramento *B, M*
San Bernardino *B*
San Marcos *B*
Stanislaus *B*
Canada College *A*
Cerritos Community College *A*
Chabot College *A*
Chaffey College *A*
Chapman University *B*
Citrus College *A*

Claremont McKenna College *B*
College of Alameda *A*
College of San Mateo *A*
College of the Canyons *A*
College of the Desert *A*
College of the Siskiyous *A*
Copper Mountain College *A*
Crafton Hills College *A*
Cypress College *A*
De Anza College *A*
El Camino College *A*
Foothill College *A*
Fresno City College *A*
Fresno Pacific University *B*
Gavilan Community College *A*
Glendale Community College *A*
Golden West College *A*
Grossmont Community College *A*
Holy Names University *B*
Humboldt State University *B*
Imperial Valley College *A*
Irvine Valley College *A*
La Sierra University *B*
Lake Tahoe Community College *A*
Long Beach City College *A*
Los Angeles City College *A*
Los Angeles Mission College *A*
Los Angeles Pierce College *A*
Los Angeles Southwest College *A*
Los Angeles Valley College *A*
Loyola Marymount University *B*
Mendocino College *A*
Merced College *A*
Merritt College *A*
Mills College *B*
MiraCosta College *A*
Modesto Junior College *A*
Mount St. Mary's College *B*
Occidental College *B*
Orange Coast College *A*
Pacific Union College *B*
Pepperdine University *B*
Pitzer College *B*
Point Loma Nazarene University *B*
Pomona College *B*
St. Mary's College of California *B*
San Diego City College *A*
San Diego Mesa College *A*
San Diego Miramar College *A*
San Diego State University *B, M*
San Francisco State University *B, M*
San Joaquin Delta College *A*
San Jose State University *B, M*
Santa Barbara City College *A*
Santa Clara University *B*
Scripps College *B*
Skyline College *A*
Solano Community College *A*
Sonoma State University *B*
Southwestern College *A*
Stanford University *B, M, D*
University of California
Berkeley *B, M, D*
Davis *B, M, D*
Irvine *B, M, D*
Los Angeles *B, M*
Riverside *B*
San Diego *B, M*
Santa Barbara *B, M, D*
Santa Cruz *B, D*
University of La Verne *B*
University of Redlands *B*
University of San Diego *B*
University of San Francisco *B*
University of Southern
California *B, M, D*
University of the Pacific *B*
Vanguard University of Southern
California *B*
Ventura College *A*
West Los Angeles College *A*
Westmont College *B*
Whittier College *B*

Colorado

Adams State College *B*
Colorado College *B*
Fort Lewis College *B*
Mesa State College *B*
Metropolitan State College of
Denver *B, T*
Red Rocks Community College *A*
Regis University *B*
Trinidad State Junior College *A*
University of Colorado
Boulder *B, M, D*
Colorado Springs *B*
Denver and Health Sciences
Center *B, M*
University of Denver *B, M*
University of Northern Colorado *B, T*
Western State College of Colorado *B*

Connecticut

Central Connecticut State
University *B, M*
Connecticut College *B*
Eastern Connecticut State
University *B*
Fairfield University *B*
Quinnipiac University *B*
Sacred Heart University *B*
St. Joseph College *B, T*
Southern Connecticut State
University *B, M*
Trinity College *B*
University of Connecticut *B, M, D*
Wesleyan University *B*
Western Connecticut State
University *B*
Yale University *B, M, D*

Delaware

Delaware State University *B*
University of Delaware *B, M, T*

District of Columbia

American University *B, M*
Catholic University of
America *B, M, D, T*
Gallaudet University *B*
George Washington University *B*
Georgetown University *B, M, D*
Howard University *B, M, D*
Trinity University *B*
University of the District of
Columbia *B*

Florida

Barry University *B*
Eckerd College *B*
Flagler College *B*
Florida Agricultural and Mechanical
University *B*
Florida Atlantic University *B, M*
Florida Gulf Coast University *B*
Florida International
University *B, M, D*
Florida Southern College *B*
Florida State University *B, M, D*
Jacksonville University *B*
Manatee Community College *A*
New College of Florida *B*
Okaloosa-Walton College *A*
Rollins College *B*
Stetson University *B*
University of Central Florida *B, M*
University of Florida *A, B*
University of Miami *B, D*
University of North Florida *B*
University of South Florida *B, M*
University of Tampa *A, B*
Valencia Community College *A*

Georgia

Agnes Scott College *B*
Albany State University *B*

Armstrong Atlantic State
  University *B, T*
Augusta State University *B*
Berry College *B*
Clark Atlanta University *B, M*
Columbus State University *B*
Emory University *B, D*
Georgia College and State
  University *B*
Georgia Southern University *B*
Georgia State University *B, M*
LaGrange College *B*
Mercer University *B*
Morehouse College *B*
North Georgia College & State
  University *B*
Piedmont College *B*
Shorter College *B*
South Georgia College *A*
Southern Polytechnic State
  University *C*
Spelman College *B*
University of Georgia *B, M*
University of West Georgia *B*
Valdosta State University *B*
Wesleyan College *B*
Young Harris College *A*

Hawaii

University of Hawaii
  Manoa *B, M*

Idaho

Albertson College of Idaho *B*
Boise State University *B*
Idaho State University *A, B*
Northwest Nazarene University *B*
University of Idaho *B, M*

Illinois

Augustana College *B, T*
Aurora University *B*
Benedictine University *B, T*
Blackburn College *B*
Bradley University *B, T*
Chicago State University *B*
City Colleges of Chicago
  Harold Washington College *A*
DePaul University *B*
Dominican University *B*
Elmhurst College *B, T*
Greenville College *B*
Illinois College *B, T*
Illinois State University *B, T*
Illinois Wesleyan University *B*
John Wood Community College *A*
Kishwaukee College *A*
Knox College *B*
Lake Forest College *B*
Loyola University of Chicago *B, M*
MacMurray College *B, T*
Millikin University *B, T*
Monmouth College *B, T*
North Central College *B, T*
North Park University *B*
Northeastern Illinois University *B*
Northern Illinois University *B, M, T*
Northwestern University *B*
Olivet Nazarene University *B, T*
Principia College *B*
Richland Community College *A*
Rockford College *B*
Roosevelt University *B, M*
St. Xavier University *B*
Sauk Valley Community College *A*
South Suburban College of Cook
  County *A*
Southern Illinois University
  Carbondale *B*
Southern Illinois University
  Edwardsville *T*
Trinity Christian College *B, T*
Triton College *A*
University of Chicago *B*

University of Illinois
  Chicago *B, D*
  Urbana-Champaign *B, M, D*
Western Illinois University *B*
Wheaton College *B*

Indiana

Anderson University *B*
Ball State University *B, T*
Butler University *B*
DePauw University *B*
Earlham College *B*
Franklin College *B*
Goshen College *B*
Grace College *B*
Hanover College *B*
Indiana State University *B, M, T*
Indiana University
  Bloomington *B, M, D*
  Northwest *A, B*
  South Bend *B*
  Southeast *B*
Indiana University-Purdue University
  Fort Wayne *A, B, T*
Indiana University-Purdue University
  Indianapolis *B*
Indiana Wesleyan University *B*
Manchester College *B, T*
Marian College *B, T*
Martin University *B*
Purdue University
  Calumet *B*
Saint Mary's College *B, T*
St. Mary-of-the-Woods College *B*
Taylor University *B*
University of Evansville *B*
University of Indianapolis *B*
University of Notre Dame *B, M*
University of Southern Indiana *B, T*
Valparaiso University *B*
Vincennes University *A*
Wabash College *B*

Iowa

Briar Cliff University *B*
Buena Vista University *B, T*
Central College *B, T*
Clarke College *B, T*
Coe College *B*
Cornell College *B, T*
Dordt College *B*
Graceland University *B, T*
Grinnell College *B*
Iowa State University *B*
Loras College *B*
Luther College *B*
Marshalltown Community College *A*
Morningside College *B*
Northwestern College *B, T*
St. Ambrose University *B, T*
Simpson College *B*
University of Iowa *B, M, D, T*
University of Northern Iowa *B, M*
Wartburg College *B, T*

Kansas

Baker University *B, T*
Benedictine College *B*
Bethel College *B*
Butler County Community College *A*
Central Christian College of Kansas *A*
Coffeyville Community College *A*
Friends University *B*
Kansas Wesleyan University *B, T*
McPherson College *B, T*
MidAmerica Nazarene University *B*
Pittsburg State University *B*
University of Kansas *B, M, D*
Washburn University of Topeka *B*
Wichita State University *B, M*

Kentucky

Asbury College *B, T*

Berea College *B, T*
Brescia University *B*
Centre College *B*
Eastern Kentucky University *B*
Georgetown College *B, T*
Kentucky Wesleyan College *B*
Morehead State University *B*
Murray State University *B, T*
Northern Kentucky University *B*
Thomas More College *A*
Transylvania University *B, T*
University of Kentucky *B, M, D*
University of Louisville *B, M*
Western Kentucky University *B, T*

Louisiana

Centenary College of Louisiana *B, T*
Dillard University *B*
Grambling State University *B*
Louisiana State University
  Shreveport *B*
Louisiana State University and
  Agricultural and Mechanical
  College *B, M*
Louisiana Tech University *B*
Loyola University New Orleans *B*
Southeastern Louisiana University *B*
Southern University
  New Orleans *B*
Southern University and Agricultural
  and Mechanical College *B*
Tulane University *B, D*
University of Louisiana at Monroe *B*
University of New Orleans *B*
Xavier University of Louisiana *B*

Maine

Bates College *B, T*
Bowdoin College *B*
Colby College *B*
University of Maine *B*

Maryland

Allegany College of Maryland *A*
College of Notre Dame of Maryland *B*
Community College of Baltimore
  County *A*
Frostburg State University *T*
Goucher College *B*
Hood College *B, T*
Johns Hopkins University *B, M, D*
Loyola College in Maryland *B*
McDaniel College *B*
Mount St. Mary's University *B*
Salisbury University *B, T*
Towson University *B, T*
University of Maryland
  College Park *B, M, D*
Washington College *B, T*

Massachusetts

American International College *B*
Amherst College *B*
Anna Maria College *B*
Assumption College *B*
Atlantic Union College *B*
Boston College *B, M, D*
Boston University *B, M, D*
Brandeis University *B*
Bridgewater State College *B*
Clark University *B*
College of the Holy Cross *B*
Elms College *B, M, T*
Emmanuel College *B*
Endicott College *B*
Gordon College *B*
Merrimack College *B*
Mount Holyoke College *B*
Northeastern University *B*
Regis College *B*
Salem State College *B, M*
Simmons College *B, M*
Simon's Rock College of Bard *B*

Smith College *B*
Suffolk University *B*
Tufts University *B*
University of Massachusetts
  Amherst *B, M, D*
  Boston *B*
  Dartmouth *B*
Wellesley College *B*
Wheaton College *B*
Williams College *B*
Worcester State College *B*

Michigan

Adrian College *A, B, T*
Albion College *B, T*
Alma College *B, T*
Andrews University *B*
Aquinas College *B, T*
Calvin College *B, T*
Central Michigan University *B, M, T*
Concordia University *B*
Eastern Michigan University *B, M*
Grand Valley State University *B*
Hillsdale College *B*
Hope College *B*
Kalamazoo College *B, T*
Lansing Community College *A*
Madonna University *B*
Michigan State University *B, M, D*
Northern Michigan University *B, T*
Oakland University *B, T*
Saginaw Valley State University *B, T*
Siena Heights University *B*
Spring Arbor University *B, T*
University of Michigan *B, M, D*
University of Michigan
  Dearborn *B*
  Flint *B, T*
Wayne State University *B, M*
Western Michigan University *B, M, D*

Minnesota

Augsburg College *B*
Bemidji State University *B*
Bethel University *B*
Carleton College *B*
College of St. Benedict *B*
College of St. Catherine *B*
Concordia College: Moorhead *B, T*
Gustavus Adolphus College *B*
Hamline University *B*
Macalester College *B, T*
Minnesota State University
  Mankato *B, M*
  Moorhead *B*
North Central University *B*
Northland Community & Technical
  College *A*
St. Cloud State University *B*
St. John's University *B*
St. Mary's University of Minnesota *B*
St. Olaf College *B*
Southwest Minnesota State
  University *B*
University of Minnesota
  Duluth *B, T*
  Morris *B*
  Twin Cities *B, M, D*
University of St. Thomas *B*
Winona State University *B*

Mississippi

Blue Mountain College *B*
Itawamba Community College *A*
Millsaps College *B, T*
Mississippi College *B*
University of Mississippi *B, M, T*

Missouri

Central Methodist University *B*
Central Missouri State University *B, T*
College of the Ozarks *B*
Crowder College *A*

Drury University *B, T*
Evangel University *B, T*
Lincoln University *B*
Lindenwood University *B*
Missouri Southern State University *B*
Missouri State University *B*
Missouri Western State University *B, T*
Northwest Missouri State
   University *B*
Park University *B*
Rockhurst University *B*
St. Louis University *B, M*
Southeast Missouri State University *B*
Southwest Baptist University *B*
Truman State University *B*
University of Missouri
   Columbia *B, M*
   Kansas City *B*
   St. Louis *B*
Washington University in St.
   Louis *B, M, D*
Webster University *B*
Westminster College *B*
William Jewell College *B*
William Woods University *B*

Montana

Carroll College *B, T*
Montana State University
   Billings *B, T*
University of Montana: Missoula *B, M*

Nebraska

Chadron State College *B*
Concordia University *B, T*
Creighton University *B*
Dana College *B*
Doane College *B*
Hastings College *B*
Midland Lutheran College *B*
Nebraska Wesleyan University *B*
Union College *B*
University of Nebraska
   Kearney *B, M, T*
   Lincoln *B*
   Omaha *B*
Wayne State College *B, T*
Western Nebraska Community
   College *A*

Nevada

University of Nevada
   Las Vegas *B, M*
   Reno *B*

New Hampshire

Dartmouth College *B, T*
Keene State College *B, T*
Plymouth State University *B*
Rivier College *B, M, T*
St. Anselm College *B, T*
University of New Hampshire *B, M*

New Jersey

Caldwell College *B*
The College of New Jersey *B, M*
College of St. Elizabeth *B, T*
Drew University *B*
Fairleigh Dickinson University
   College at Florham *B*
   Metropolitan Campus *B*
Georgian Court University *B*
Kean University *B, T*
Montclair State University *B, M, T*
New Jersey City University *B*
Princeton University *B, M, D*
Ramapo College of New Jersey *B*
Rider University *B*
Rowan University *B*
Rutgers, The State University of New
   Jersey
   Camden Regional Campus *B, T*

New Brunswick/Piscataway
   Campus *B, M, D, T*
   Newark Regional Campus *B, T*
St. Peter's College *B*
Seton Hall University *B, T*
William Paterson University of New
   Jersey *B*

New Mexico

Eastern New Mexico University *B*
New Mexico Highlands University *B*
New Mexico Junior College *A*
New Mexico State University *M*
Santa Fe Community College *A*
University of New Mexico *B, M, D*
Western New Mexico University *B*

New York

Adelphi University *B*
Alfred University *B*
Bard College *B*
Barnard College *B*
Canisius College *B*
City University of New York
   Baruch College *B*
   Brooklyn College *B, M*
   City College *B, M*
   College of Staten Island *B*
   Hunter College *B, M*
   Lehman College *B*
   Queens College *B, M, T*
   York College *B*
Colgate University *B*
College of Mount St. Vincent *B, T*
College of New Rochelle *B, T*
College of Saint Rose *B*
Columbia University
   Columbia College *B*
   School of General Studies *B*
Cornell University *B, M, D*
Daemen College *B*
Dominican College of Blauvelt *B*
Elmira College *B, T*
Fordham University *B, M*
Hamilton College *B*
Hartwick College *B, T*
Hobart and William Smith Colleges *B*
Hofstra University *B, M*
Houghton College *B*
Iona College *B, M*
Ithaca College *B, T*
Le Moyne College *B*
Long Island University
   C.W. Post Campus *B, M*
Manhattan College *B*
Marist College *B, T*
Mercy College *B*
Molloy College *B*
Mount St. Mary College *B*
Nazareth College of Rochester *B*
New York University *B, M, D*
Niagara University *B*
Orange County Community College *A*
Pace University *B*
Russell Sage College *B*
St. Bonaventure University *B*
St. Francis College *B*
St. John Fisher College *B*
St. John's University *B, M*
St. Joseph's College: Suffolk
   Campus *B*
St. Lawrence University *B, T*
St. Thomas Aquinas College *B*
Sarah Lawrence College *B*
Siena College *B, T*
Skidmore College *B*
State University of New York
   Albany *B, M, D*
   Binghamton *B, M*
   Buffalo *B, M, D*
   College at Brockport *B, T*
   College at Buffalo *B*
   College at Cortland *B*
   College at Fredonia *B, T*

   College at Geneseo *B, T*
   College at Old Westbury *B, T*
   College at Oneonta *B*
   College at Plattsburgh *B*
   College at Potsdam *B*
   New Paltz *B, T*
   Oswego *B*
   Stony Brook *B, M, D*
Syracuse University *B, M, D*
United States Military Academy *B*
University of Rochester *B, M*
Vassar College *B*
Wagner College *B*
Wells College *B*

North Carolina

Appalachian State University *B*
Barton College *B, T*
Campbell University *B*
Catawba College *B*
Davidson College *B*
Duke University *B, M, D*
East Carolina University *B*
Elon University *B*
Gardner-Webb University *B*
Greensboro College *B, T*
Guilford College *B, T*
High Point University *B*
Johnson C. Smith University *B*
Lenoir-Rhyne College *B*
Mars Hill College *B*
Meredith College *B*
Methodist College *A, B, T*
North Carolina Central University *B*
North Carolina State University *B, M*
Peace College *B*
Salem College *B*
University of North Carolina
   Asheville *B, T*
   Charlotte *B, M*
   Greensboro *B, T*
   Pembroke *B*
   Wilmington *B*
Wake Forest University *B*
Western Carolina University *B*
Wingate University *B*
Winston-Salem State University *B*

North Dakota

Dickinson State University *B, T*
Jamestown College *B*
Minot State University *B*
North Dakota State University *B, T*
University of North Dakota *B*
Valley City State University *B*

Ohio

Antioch College *B*
Ashland University *B*
Baldwin-Wallace College *B, T*
Bluffton University *B*
Bowling Green State University *B, M*
Capital University *B*
Case Western Reserve University *B*
Cedarville University *B, T*
Cleveland State University *B, M*
College of Wooster *B*
Denison University *B*
Franciscan University of
   Steubenville *B*
Heidelberg College *B*
Hiram College *B, T*
John Carroll University *B*
Kent State University *B, M*
Kenyon College *B*
Lake Erie College *B*
Malone College *B*
Marietta College *B*
Miami University
   Oxford Campus *B, M, T*
Mount Union College *B*
Mount Vernon Nazarene University *B*
Muskingum College *B*
Oberlin College *B*

Ohio Northern University *B*
Ohio State University
   Columbus Campus *B, M, D*
Ohio University *B, M*
Ohio Wesleyan University *B*
Otterbein College *B*
University of Akron *B, M*
University of Cincinnati *B, M, D, T*
University of Dayton *B*
University of Findlay *B, T*
University of Toledo *B, M*
Walsh University *B*
Wilmington College *B*
Wittenberg University *B*
Wright State University *B*
Xavier University *A, B*
Youngstown State University *B*

Oklahoma

Northeastern State University *B*
Oklahoma Baptist University *B, T*
Oklahoma Christian University *B*
Oklahoma City Community College *A*
Oklahoma City University *B*
Oklahoma Panhandle State
   University *B*
Oklahoma State University *B*
Oral Roberts University *B*
Southeastern Oklahoma State
   University *B*
Southern Nazarene University *B*
Tulsa Community College *A*
University of Central Oklahoma *B*
University of Oklahoma *B, M, D*
University of Tulsa *B*
Western Oklahoma State College *A*

Oregon

George Fox University *B*
Lewis & Clark College *B*
Linfield College *B, T*
Linn-Benton Community College *A*
Oregon State University *B*
Pacific University *B*
Portland State University *B, M*
Reed College *B*
Southern Oregon University *B*
University of Oregon *B, M*
University of Portland *B, T*
Western Oregon University *B, T*
Willamette University *B*

Pennsylvania

Albright College *B, T*
Allegheny College *B*
Arcadia University *B*
Bloomsburg University of
   Pennsylvania *B, T*
Bryn Mawr College *B*
Bucknell University *B*
Cabrini College *B*
California University of
   Pennsylvania *B*
Carlow University *B*
Carnegie Mellon University *B*
Cedar Crest College *B*
Chatham College *B*
Chestnut Hill College *A, B*
Cheyney University of
   Pennsylvania *B, T*
Clarion University of
   Pennsylvania *B, T*
DeSales University *B, T*
Dickinson College *B*
Duquesne University *B*
East Stroudsburg University of
   Pennsylvania *B, T*
Eastern University *B*
Edinboro University of
   Pennsylvania *B, T*
Elizabethtown College *B*
Franklin & Marshall College *B*
Geneva College *B*
Gettysburg College *B*

Grove City College *B, T*
Haverford College *B, T*
Holy Family University *B, T*
Immaculata University *A, B, T*
Indiana University of Pennsylvania *B*
Juniata College *B*
King's College *B, T*
Kutztown University of
   Pennsylvania *B, M, T*
La Salle University *B, T*
Lafayette College *B*
Lebanon Valley College *B*
Lehigh University *B*
Lincoln University *B*
Lock Haven University of
   Pennsylvania *B, T*
Lycoming College *B*
Mansfield University of
   Pennsylvania *B, T*
Marywood University *B*
Messiah College *B*
Millersville University of
   Pennsylvania *B, M, T*
Moravian College *B, T*
Muhlenberg College *B*
Penn State
   Abington *B*
   Altoona *B*
   Beaver *B*
   Berks *B*
   Delaware County *B*
   Dubois *B*
   Fayette *B*
   Hazleton *B*
   Lehigh Valley *B*
   McKeesport *B*
   Mont Alto *B*
   New Kensington *B*
   Schuylkill - Capital College *B*
   Shenango *B*
   University Park *B, M, D*
   Wilkes-Barre *B*
   Worthington Scranton *B*
   York *B*
Rosemont College *B*
St. Francis University *B*
St. Joseph's University *B*
St. Vincent College *B*
Seton Hill University *B, T*
Shippensburg University of
   Pennsylvania *B, T*
Slippery Rock University of
   Pennsylvania *B, T*
Susquehanna University *B, T*
Swarthmore College *B*
Temple University *B, M, D*
Thiel College *B*
University of Pennsylvania *B*
University of Pittsburgh *B*
University of Scranton *B, T*
Ursinus College *B, T*
Villanova University *B*
Washington and Jefferson College *B*
West Chester University of
   Pennsylvania *B, M, T*
Westminster College *B*
Widener University *B, T*
Wilkes University *B*
Wilson College *B*
York College of Pennsylvania *B*

Puerto Rico

Bayamon Central University *B*
Pontifical Catholic University of
   Puerto Rico *B, M*
Universidad Adventista de las
   Antillas *B*
University of Puerto Rico
   Cayey University College *B*
   Mayaguez *B, M*
   Rio Piedras *B, M, D*
University of the Sacred Heart *B*

Rhode Island

Brown University *B, M, D*
Providence College *B*
Rhode Island College *B, M*
Salve Regina University *B*
University of Rhode Island *B, M*

South Carolina

Anderson University *B*
Charleston Southern University *B*
The Citadel *B*
Clemson University *B*
Coastal Carolina University *B*
Coker College *B*
College of Charleston *B, T*
Columbia College *B*
Converse College *B*
Erskine College *B*
Francis Marion University *B*
Furman University *B, T*
Lander University *B, T*
Newberry College *B*
Presbyterian College *B, T*
South Carolina State University *B*
University of South Carolina *B, M*
University of South Carolina
   Upstate *B*
Winthrop University *M*
Wofford College *B, T*

South Dakota

Augustana College *B, T*
Black Hills State University *B*
Northern State University *B*
South Dakota State University *B, T*
University of South Dakota *B*

Tennessee

Austin Peay State University *B*
Belmont University *B, T*
Bryan College *B*
Carson-Newman College *B, T*
Fisk University *B*
Hiwassee College *A*
King College *B, T*
Lambuth University *B*
Lee University *B*
Lipscomb University *B*
Maryville College *B, T*
Milligan College *T*
Rhodes College *B, T*
Southern Adventist University *B*
Tennessee State University *B*
Tennessee Technological
   University *B, T*
Union University *B, T*
University of Tennessee
   Chattanooga *B*
   Knoxville *B, M*
   Martin *B*
University of the South *B*
Vanderbilt University *B, M, D*

Texas

Abilene Christian University *B*
Angelo State University *B, T*
Austin College *B*
Austin Community College *A*
Baylor University *B, M, T*
Blinn College *A*
Cisco Junior College *A*
Coastal Bend College *A*
East Texas Baptist University *B*
Galveston College *A*
Hardin-Simmons University *B*
Houston Baptist University *B*
Howard Payne University *B, T*
Kilgore College *A*
Lamar University *B*
Laredo Community College *A*
Lon Morris College *A*
Lubbock Christian University *T*
McMurry University *B, T*

Midland College *A*
Midwestern State University *B*
Northeast Texas Community
   College *A*
Our Lady of the Lake University of San
   Antonio *B*
Paris Junior College *A*
Prairie View A&M University *B*
Rice University *B, M*
St. Edward's University *B*
St. Mary's University *B*
St. Philip's College *A*
Sam Houston State University *B*
San Jacinto College
   North *A*
South Plains College *A*
Southern Methodist University *B*
Southwestern University *B, T*
Stephen F. Austin State University *B, T*
Sul Ross State University *B*
Tarleton State University *B, T*
Texas A&M University *B, M*
Texas A&M University
   Commerce *B, M*
   Kingsville *B, M*
Texas Christian University *B*
Texas Lutheran University *B*
Texas Southern University *B*
Texas State University: San
   Marcos *B, M, T*
Texas Tech University *B, M, D*
Texas Wesleyan University *B*
Trinity University *B*
Trinity Valley Community College *A*
Tyler Junior College *A*
University of Dallas *B*
University of Houston *B, M, D*
University of Houston
   Downtown *B*
University of Mary Hardin-Baylor *B, T*
University of North Texas *B, M*
University of St. Thomas *B*
University of Texas
   Arlington *B, M*
   Austin *B, M, D*
   Brownsville *B, M*
   El Paso *B, M*
   Pan American *B, M*
   San Antonio *B, M*
   Tyler *B*
   of the Permian Basin *B*
University of the Incarnate Word *B*
Wayland Baptist University *B, T*
West Texas A&M University *B*
Wharton County Junior College *A*

Utah

Brigham Young University *B, M*
Snow College *A*
Southern Utah University *B*
University of Utah *B, M*
Utah State University *B*
Utah Valley State College *B*
Weber State University *B*

Vermont

Bennington College *B*
Castleton State College *B*
Marlboro College *B*
Middlebury College *B, M, D*
St. Michael's College *B*
University of Vermont *B*

Virginia

Bridgewater College *B*
Christopher Newport University *B*
College of William and Mary *B*
Eastern Mennonite University *B*
Emory & Henry College *B, T*
Ferrum College *B*
Hampden-Sydney College *B*
Hampton University *B*
Hollins University *B*
Liberty University *B, T*

Longwood University *B, T*
Lynchburg College *B*
Mary Baldwin College *B*
Old Dominion University *B, T*
Randolph-Macon College *B*
Randolph-Macon Woman's College *B*
Roanoke College *B, T*
Shenandoah University *B*
Sweet Briar College *B*
University of Mary Washington *B*
University of Richmond *B, T*
University of Virginia *B, M, D*
University of Virginia's College at
   Wise *B, T*
Virginia Wesleyan College *B*
Washington and Lee University *B*

Washington

Central Washington University *B*
Centralia College *A*
Eastern Washington University *B, T*
Everett Community College *A*
Gonzaga University *B*
Pacific Lutheran University *B*
Seattle Pacific University *B*
Seattle University *B*
University of Puget Sound *B, T*
University of Washington *B*
Walla Walla College *B*
Washington State University *B*
Western Washington University *B*
Whitman College *B*
Whitworth College *B, T*

West Virginia

Bethany College *B*
Davis and Elkins College *B*
Potomac State College of West Virginia
   University *A*
West Virginia University *T*
Wheeling Jesuit University *B*

Wisconsin

Beloit College *B*
Cardinal Stritch University *B*
Carroll College *B*
Carthage College *B, T*
Concordia University Wisconsin *B*
Edgewood College *B*
Lakeland College *B*
Lawrence University *B, T*
Marian College of Fond du Lac *B*
Marquette University *B, M*
Mount Mary College *B, T*
Ripon College *B, T*
St. Norbert College *B, T*
Silver Lake College *T*
University of Wisconsin
   Eau Claire *B*
   Green Bay *B, T*
   La Crosse *B, T*
   Madison *B, M, D*
   Milwaukee *B*
   Oshkosh *B*
   Parkside *B, T*
   Platteville *B*
   River Falls *B*
   Stevens Point *B, T*
   Whitewater *B, T*
Viterbo University *B, T*
Wisconsin Lutheran College *B*

Wyoming

Sheridan College *A*
University of Wyoming *B, M*
Western Wyoming Community
   College *A*

Spanish/Iberian studies

California

Claremont McKenna College *B*
Scripps College *B*

Colorado
Colorado College B

Iowa
Coe College B

Massachusetts
Elms College B
Simon's Rock College of Bard B

Minnesota
Concordia College: Moorhead B, T

Nevada
University of Nevada
Reno D

New Hampshire
Dartmouth College B

New York
Bard College B
Barnard College B
Columbia University
Columbia College B

Ohio
Cleveland State University B, M
University of Cincinnati B

Pennsylvania
Edinboro University of
Pennsylvania B

Spanish teacher education

Alabama
Birmingham-Southern College T

Arizona
Arizona State University B, T
Northern Arizona University B, T
Prescott College B, M, T
University of Arizona B, M

Arkansas
Arkansas State University B, T
Harding University B, M, T
Ouachita Baptist University B, T
Southern Arkansas University B, T
University of Central Arkansas M

California
Azusa Pacific University T
California State University
Chico B, T
Dominguez Hills T
Fullerton M
Long Beach T
San Bernardino M, T
Humboldt State University T
Pacific Union College T
San Francisco State University B, T
Stanford University M, T
University of the Pacific T
Vanguard University of Southern
California T
Vista Community College A

Colorado
Adams State College B, T
Colorado State University T
Colorado State University
Pueblo T
Fort Lewis College B
Metropolitan State College of
Denver T
University of Colorado
Colorado Springs T

Connecticut
Albertus Magnus College B, T
Fairfield University T
Quinnipiac University B, M
Sacred Heart University T
St. Joseph College T
Southern Connecticut State
University B, M, T

Delaware
Delaware State University B
University of Delaware B, T

District of Columbia
Catholic University of America B

Florida
Barry University T
Stetson University B

Georgia
Armstrong Atlantic State University T
Georgia Southern University B, M
Piedmont College M, T
University of West Georgia M

Idaho
Boise State University T
Brigham Young University-Idaho T
Northwest Nazarene University B
University of Idaho T

Illinois
Augustana College B, T
Benedictine University T
Bradley University B
Dominican University B
Elmhurst College B
Greenville College B, T
Illinois College T
Illinois Wesleyan University B
Knox College T
MacMurray College B, T
North Park University T
Olivet Nazarene University B, T
Rockford College T
Roosevelt University B
St. Xavier University B
Sauk Valley Community College A
Trinity Christian College B, T
University of Illinois
Chicago B
Urbana-Champaign B, M, T
Wheaton College T

Indiana
Anderson University B, T
Butler University T
Franklin College B, T
Goshen College B
Grace College B
Indiana University
Bloomington B, T
Northwest B
South Bend B, T
Indiana University-Purdue University
Fort Wayne B, T
Indiana University-Purdue University
Indianapolis B, T
Indiana Wesleyan University T
Manchester College B, T
Saint Mary's College T
St. Mary-of-the-Woods College B, T
Taylor University B, T
University of Evansville B, T
University of Indianapolis B, T
Valparaiso University B
Vincennes University A

Iowa
Buena Vista University B, T
Central College T

Clarke College B, T
Cornell College B, T
Dordt College B
Graceland University T
Iowa State University T
Loras College T
Morningside College B
Northwestern College T
St. Ambrose University B, T
Simpson College T
University of Iowa T
Wartburg College T

Kansas
Baker University T
Bethel College T
Central Christian College of Kansas A
Friends University B
McPherson College B, T
MidAmerica Nazarene University B, T
Pittsburg State University B, T
University of Kansas B, T
University of St. Mary T

Kentucky
Brescia University B, T
Eastern Kentucky University B
Kentucky Wesleyan College B, T

Louisiana
Centenary College of Louisiana B, T
Southeastern Louisiana University B
Southern University
New Orleans B
Southern University and Agricultural
and Mechanical College B
University of Louisiana at Lafayette B
University of Louisiana at Monroe B
Xavier University of Louisiana B

Maine
University of Maine B

Maryland
College of Notre Dame of Maryland T
Mount St. Mary's University T
Salisbury University T
Towson University T
Washington College T

Massachusetts
Assumption College T
Bridgewater State College T
Elms College T
Framingham State College M
Salem State College M
Tufts University T
University of Massachusetts
Dartmouth T
Worcester State College M, T

Michigan
Albion College B, T
Alma College T
Calvin College B
Concordia University B, T
Eastern Michigan University B, T
Grand Valley State University T
Hope College T
Madonna University T
Michigan State University M
Northern Michigan University B, T
University of Michigan
Flint T
Western Michigan University B, T

Minnesota
Augsburg College T
Bemidji State University T
Bethel University B
College of St. Benedict T
College of St. Catherine T

Concordia College: Moorhead B, T
Gustavus Adolphus College T
Minnesota State University
Mankato B, M, T
Moorhead B
St. Cloud State University B, T
St. John's University T
St. Mary's University of Minnesota B
University of Minnesota
Duluth B
Morris T
University of St. Thomas B, T
Winona State University B, T

Mississippi
Blue Mountain College B
Itawamba Community College A
Mississippi College B, T
Mississippi State University T

Missouri
Central Missouri State
University B, M, T
College of the Ozarks B, T
Lindenwood University B
Missouri Southern State
University B, T
Missouri State University B
Missouri Western State University B
Northwest Missouri State
University B, T
Truman State University M, T
University of Missouri
Columbia B
St. Louis T
Washington University in St.
Louis B, M, T
William Jewell College T

Montana
Montana State University
Billings B, T
University of Montana: Missoula T

Nebraska
Chadron State College B
Concordia University B, T
Creighton University T
Dana College B
Hastings College T
Midland Lutheran College B, T
Nebraska Wesleyan University T
University of Nebraska
Lincoln B

Nevada
University of Nevada
Reno B

New Hampshire
Keene State College B, T
Rivier College B, M, T
St. Anselm College T
University of New Hampshire T

New Jersey
Caldwell College T
The College of New Jersey B, T
College of St. Elizabeth T
Georgian Court University T
Rowan University T
St. Peter's College T
William Paterson University of New
Jersey T

New Mexico
Western New Mexico University B

New York
Adelphi University M, T
Alfred University M, T

City University of New York
  Brooklyn College *B, M*
  City College *B, M*
  College of Staten Island *B*
  Hunter College *B, M, T*
  Lehman College *M*
  Queens College *M, T*
College of Mount St. Vincent *T*
College of Saint Rose *B, T*
D'Youville College *M, T*
Daemen College *B, M, T*
Dowling College *B*
Dutchess Community College *A*
Elmira College *B, T*
Fordham University *M, T*
Hobart and William Smith Colleges *T*
Hofstra University *B, M*
Houghton College *B, T*
Iona College *B, M, T*
Ithaca College *B, T*
Le Moyne College *T*
Long Island University
  Brooklyn Campus *B, T*
  C.W. Post Campus *B, M, T*
Manhattan College *B, T*
Marist College *B*
Mercy College *B, T*
Molloy College *B*
New York University *B, M, T*
Niagara University *B, M, T*
Pace University *B, M, T*
St. Bonaventure University *M, T*
St. John Fisher College *B, T*
St. John's University *B, M*
St. Joseph's College: Suffolk
  Campus *B*
St. Lawrence University *T*
St. Thomas Aquinas College *B, T*
State University of New York
  Albany *B, M, T*
  Buffalo *M, T*
  College at Brockport *M, T*
  College at Buffalo *B*
  College at Cortland *B, M*
  College at Fredonia *B, T*
  College at Geneseo *B, M, T*
  College at Oneonta *B, T*
  College at Plattsburgh *B, M*
  College at Potsdam *B, M*
  New Paltz *B, M, T*
  Oswego *B, M*
Vassar College *T*
Wells College *T*

North Carolina

Appalachian State University *B*
Campbell University *B, T*
Davidson College *T*
East Carolina University *B*
Gardner-Webb University *B*
Greensboro College *B, T*
Meredith College *T*
North Carolina Central University *B, T*
North Carolina State University *B, T*
Queens University of Charlotte *T*
Salem College *T*
University of North Carolina
  Charlotte *B*
  Greensboro *B, T*
  Wilmington *B*
Wake Forest University *T*
Western Carolina University *B, T*
Wingate University *B, T*
Winston-Salem State University *B*

North Dakota

Dickinson State University *B, T*
Minot State University *B*
North Dakota State University *B, T*
Valley City State University *B, T*

Ohio

Ashland University *B, T*
Baldwin-Wallace College *T*

Cedarville University *B, T*
Hiram College *T*
Kent State University *T*
Malone College *B*
Miami University
  Oxford Campus *B, T*
Mount Union College *T*
Mount Vernon Nazarene
  University *B, M, T*
Ohio Northern University *B*
Ohio University *B, T*
Ohio Wesleyan University *B*
Otterbein College *B*
University of Akron *B*
University of Dayton *B*
University of Findlay *B, M, T*
University of Toledo *B, M, T*
Youngstown State University *B, M*

Oklahoma

Northeastern State University *B*
Northwestern Oklahoma State
  University *B, T*
Oklahoma Baptist University *B, T*
Oklahoma City University *B*
Oral Roberts University *B, T*
Southeastern Oklahoma State
  University *B, T*
Southern Nazarene University *B*
University of Central Oklahoma *B*
University of Tulsa *T*

Oregon

Eastern Oregon University *B, T*
Linfield College *T*
Oregon State University *M*
Portland State University *T*
Western Oregon University *T*

Pennsylvania

Albright College *T*
Cabrini College *T*
Chatham College *T*
DeSales University *T*
Dickinson College *T*
Duquesne University *B, M, T*
Gettysburg College *T*
Grove City College *B, T*
Holy Family University *B, M, T*
Juniata College *B, T*
King's College *T*
La Roche College *B*
La Salle University *B, T*
Lebanon Valley College *T*
Lycoming College *T*
Mansfield University of
  Pennsylvania *B, T*
Marywood University *B*
Messiah College *B, T*
Moravian College *T*
Rosemont College *T*
St. Francis University *B, T*
St. Vincent College *T*
Seton Hill University *B, T*
Susquehanna University *T*
Thiel College *B*
Villanova University *T*
Washington and Jefferson College *T*
Westminster College *T*
Widener University *T*
Wilson College *T*

Puerto Rico

American University of Puerto
  Rico *B, T*
Bayamon Central University *B*
Inter American University of Puerto
  Rico
  Arecibo Campus *B*
  Barranquitas Campus *B, T*
  Fajardo Campus *B, T*
  San German Campus *B*

Pontifical Catholic University of
  Puerto Rico *B, T*
Turabo University *B*
Universidad Metropolitana *B*
University of Puerto Rico
  Cayey University College *B*

Rhode Island

Rhode Island College *B*
Salve Regina University *B*

South Carolina

Anderson University *B, T*
Charleston Southern University *B*
Furman University *T*
South Carolina State University *B, T*
Wofford College *T*

South Dakota

Augustana College *B, T*
University of South Dakota *B, M, D, T*

Tennessee

Belmont University *B, M, T*
King College *T*
Lee University *B*
Lipscomb University *B, T*
Maryville College *B, T*
Southern Adventist University *B*
Union University *B, T*
University of Memphis *T*
University of Tennessee
  Martin *B*

Texas

Abilene Christian University *B, T*
Baylor University *T*
East Texas Baptist University *B*
Hardin-Simmons University *B, T*
Houston Baptist University *T*
Howard Payne University *B, T*
Lamar University *T*
Laredo Community College *A*
Lubbock Christian University *B*
McMurry University *T*
St. Edward's University *B, T*
St. Mary's University *T*
Texas A&M University
  Commerce *T*
  Kingsville *T*
Texas State University: San Marcos *T*
Texas Wesleyan University *B, T*
University of Dallas *T*
University of Houston *T*
University of Mary Hardin-Baylor *T*
University of Texas
  San Antonio *T*
University of the Incarnate Word *T*
West Texas A&M University *T*

Utah

Southern Utah University *B, T*
University of Utah *B*
Utah Valley State College *B*
Weber State University *B*

Vermont

Castleton State College *B, T*
St. Michael's College *T*

Virginia

Bridgewater College *T*
Eastern Mennonite University *T*
Hollins University *T*
Liberty University *B*
Longwood University *B, T*
Old Dominion University *B, T*
University of Virginia's College at
  Wise *T*

Washington

Central Washington University *B, T*

Heritage University *B*
Washington State University *B, M, T*
Western Washington University *B*
Whitworth College *B, T*

West Virginia

Bethany College *B*

Wisconsin

Carroll College *B, T*
Carthage College *T*
Concordia University Wisconsin *B*
Edgewood College *B*
Lawrence University *T*
Marian College of Fond du Lac *B, T*
Marquette University *M*
Mount Mary College *B, T*
St. Norbert College *T*
University of Wisconsin
  Green Bay *T*
  Parkside *T*
  Platteville *B, T*
  River Falls *T*
  Whitewater *B*
Viterbo University *B, T*

Special education

Alabama

Alabama Agricultural and Mechanical
  University *B, M*
Alabama State University *B, M*
Athens State University *B*
Auburn University *B, M, D, T*
Birmingham-Southern College *B*
Jacksonville State University *B, M, T*
University of Alabama *B, M, D*
University of Alabama
  Birmingham *B, M*
University of North Alabama *M*
University of South Alabama *B, M, T*
University of West Alabama *B, M, T*

Alaska

University of Alaska
  Anchorage *M, T*

Arizona

Arizona State University *B, M*
Arizona State University West *B*
Central Arizona College *A*
Grand Canyon University *B, T*
Northcentral University *M, D*
Northern Arizona University *B, M, T*
Prescott College *B, M, T*
University of Arizona *B, M, D*

Arkansas

Arkansas State University *B, M, T*
Harding University *B, M, T*
Henderson State University *M*
Philander Smith College *B*
University of Arkansas *B, M, D*
University of Arkansas
  Little Rock *M*
  Monticello *B*
  Pine Bluff *B*
University of Central Arkansas *B, M*
University of the Ozarks *B*

California

Azusa Pacific University *M, D*
California Baptist University *M, T*
California Lutheran University *B, M*
California State University
  Chico *M, T*
  Dominguez Hills *M*
  East Bay *M, T*
  Fresno *M*
  Fullerton *M, T*
  Long Beach *M, T*
  Los Angeles *M, D*

Northridge *M*
Sacramento *M*
San Bernardino *M*
San Marcos *T*
Cerritos Community College *A*
Chapman University *M, T*
Cuesta College *A*
Diablo Valley College *A*
Dominican University of California *M*
Fresno Pacific University *M, T*
Holy Names University *M*
La Sierra University *M*
Loyola Marymount University *M*
Mount St. Mary's College *M*
National University *M, T*
Notre Dame de Namur
　University *M, T*
Sacramento City College *A*
St. Mary's College of California *M*
San Diego State University *M*
San Francisco State University *M, D, T*
San Jose State University *M*
Santa Clara University *B*
University of California
　Berkeley *D, T*
　Los Angeles *D*
　Riverside *D, T*
University of La Verne *M, T*
University of San Diego *M, T*
University of San Francisco *M*
University of the Pacific *D, T*

Colorado

Adams State College *M, T*
Metropolitan State College of
　Denver *T*
Northeastern Junior College *A*
Regis University *B, T*
University of Colorado
　Colorado Springs *B, M*
　Denver and Health Sciences
　　Center *M*
University of Denver *M, D*
University of Northern
　Colorado *B, M, D, T*
Western State College of Colorado *T*

Connecticut

Central Connecticut State
　University *M, T*
Fairfield University *M, T*
Gateway Community College *A*
St. Joseph College *B, M, T*
Southern Connecticut State
　University *M*
Three Rivers Community College *A*
University of Connecticut *B, M, D, T*
University of Hartford *B, M*
Western Connecticut State
　University *M*

Delaware

Delaware State University *B, M*
University of Delaware *B, M, T*
Wilmington College *M*

District of Columbia

American University *M*
George Washington University *M*
Howard University *M*
Trinity University *M*
University of the District of
　Columbia *M*

Florida

Barry University *B, M*
Broward Community College *A*
Clearwater Christian College *B*
Edward Waters College *B*
Flagler College *B*
Florida Atlantic University *B, M, D*
Florida Gulf Coast University *B, M*
Florida International University *M, D*

Florida State University *D*
Gulf Coast Community College *A*
Lynn University *B, M*
Miami Dade College *A, B*
Nova Southeastern University *B*
Pensacola Junior College *A*
St. Leo University *M*
St. Petersburg College *B*
St. Thomas University *M*
University of Central Florida *B, M*
University of Florida *A, B, M*
University of Miami *B, M*
University of North Florida *B, M*
University of South Florida *B, M*
University of West Florida *B, M, T*
Warner Southern College *B*

Georgia

Albany State University *B*
Armstrong Atlantic State
　University *B, M, T*
Augusta State University *B, M*
Clark Atlanta University *B, M*
Coastal Georgia Community
　College *A*
Georgia College and State
　University *B, T*
Georgia Southern University *B, M*
Georgia Southwestern State
　University *B, M*
Georgia State University *D*
Kennesaw State University *M*
Middle Georgia College *A*
North Georgia College & State
　University *B, M*
Piedmont College *B, M, T*
University of Georgia *B, M, D*
Valdosta State University *B, M*

Hawaii

Brigham Young University-Hawaii *B, T*
Chaminade University of Honolulu *M*
University of Hawaii
　Manoa *B, M, T*

Idaho

Boise State University *B, T*
Brigham Young University-Idaho *A*
Idaho State University *B, M, D*
Northwest Nazarene University *M*
University of Idaho *B, M, T*

Illinois

Benedictine University *B, T*
Chicago State University *B*
Dominican University *M*
Eastern Illinois University *B, M*
Elmhurst College *B*
Eureka College *B*
Governors State University *M, T*
Greenville College *B, T*
Illinois Central College *A*
Illinois State University *B, M, D, T*
John A. Logan College *A*
Joliet Junior College *A*
Kishwaukee College *A*
Lewis University *B, M*
Loyola University of Chicago *B, M*
MacMurray College *B, T*
National-Louis University *M*
Northeastern Illinois University *B, M*
Northern Illinois University *B, M, D*
Quincy University *B, T*
Sauk Valley Community College *A*
South Suburban College of Cook
　County *A*
Southern Illinois University
　Carbondale *B, M*
Southern Illinois University
　Edwardsville *B, M, T*
Trinity Christian College *B, T*

University of Illinois
　Chicago *M, D*
　Urbana-Champaign *B, M, D, T*
University of St. Francis *B, M, T*
Western Illinois University *B, M*

Indiana

Ball State University *M, D, T*
Butler University *M*
Goshen College *B, T*
Grace College *B*
Huntington University *B*
Indiana State University *B, M, T*
Indiana University
　Bloomington *B, M, D, T*
　South Bend *B, M*
　Southeast *B*
Indiana University-Purdue University
　Indianapolis *M*
Indiana Wesleyan University *A*
Manchester College *B, T*
Marian College *T*
Oakland City University *B*
Purdue University
　Calumet *B*
St. Mary-of-the-Woods College *B, T*
University of Evansville *B, T*
University of St. Francis *B, M, T*
Valparaiso University *M, T*
Vincennes University *A*

Iowa

Buena Vista University *B, T*
Central College *T*
Clarke College *B, T*
Dordt College *B*
Drake University *B, M*
Iowa State University *M, T*
Loras College *B*
Morningside College *B, M*
Mount Mercy College *T*
St. Ambrose University *M, T*
Simpson College *T*
University of Dubuque *T*
University of Iowa *M, D*
University of Northern Iowa *M*
Upper Iowa University *B, T*
Wartburg College *T*
William Penn University *B*

Kansas

Benedictine College *B*
Bethel College *T*
Emporia State University *M, T*
Fort Hays State University *M*
Kansas State University *M, D*
Kansas Wesleyan University *T*
McPherson College *B, T*
Pittsburg State University *M*
Southwestern College *M*
Tabor College *B, T*
University of Kansas *M, D*
University of St. Mary *M*
Washburn University of Topeka *M*
Wichita State University *M*

Kentucky

Asbury College *M, T*
Bellarmine University *B, M, T*
Brescia University *B, T*
Eastern Kentucky University *B, M*
Midway College *B*
Morehead State University *B, M*
Murray State University *B, M, T*
Spalding University *B, M*
Union College *B, M*
University of Kentucky *B, M, D*
University of Louisville *M*
University of the Cumberlands *B, M, T*
Western Kentucky University *B, M, T*

Louisiana

Dillard University *B*

Grambling State University *B*
Louisiana State University
　Shreveport *B*
Louisiana Tech University *B*
Our Lady of Holy Cross College *B, T*
Southeastern Louisiana
　University *B, M*
Southern University and Agricultural
　and Mechanical College *B, M, D*
University of Louisiana at Lafayette *B*
University of Louisiana at
　Monroe *M, T*
University of New Orleans *M, D*
Xavier University of Louisiana *B, M*

Maine

University of Maine *M*
University of Maine
　Farmington *B, T*
University of Southern Maine *M*

Maryland

Bowie State University *M*
College of Notre Dame of Maryland *B*
Community College of Baltimore
　County *A*
Coppin State University *B, M, T*
Goucher College *B*
Hood College *B*
Loyola College in Maryland *M*
McDaniel College *M*
Mount St. Mary's University *T*
Towson University *B, T*
University of Maryland
　College Park *B, M, D*
　Eastern Shore *B, M, T*

Massachusetts

American International College *B, M*
Assumption College *M*
Atlantic Union College *M*
Boston University *B, M, D, T*
Bridgewater State College *B, M, T*
Curry College *B*
Eastern Nazarene College *B, M, T*
Elms College *B, M, T*
Endicott College *M*
Fitchburg State College *B, M, T*
Framingham State College *M*
Gordon College *B*
Lesley University *B, M*
Northeastern University *M*
Regis College *M*
Salem State College *M*
Simmons College *B, M*
Springfield College *B*
University of Massachusetts
　Boston *M*
Westfield State College *B, T*
Wheelock College *B, M*
Worcester State College *M*

Michigan

Andrews University *M*
Aquinas College *B*
Calvin College *B, T*
Central Michigan University *M*
Delta College *A*
Eastern Michigan University *M*
Gogebic Community College *A*
Grand Valley State University *B, M, T*
Kellogg Community College *A*
Lansing Community College *A*
Madonna University *B*
Marygrove College *B, M, T*
Michigan State University *B, M, D*
Northern Michigan University *B*
Oakland University *M*
Saginaw Valley State University *B, T*
Schoolcraft College *A*
Spring Arbor University *B, T*
University of Detroit Mercy *B, M*
Wayne State University *B, M, D, T*

Western Michigan University *M, D*

Minnesota

Bemidji State University *M*
Bethel University *M*
Concordia University: St. Paul *M, T*
Minnesota State University
  Mankato *M*
  Moorhead *B, M*
Normandale Community College *A*
Northland Community & Technical
  College *A*
Ridgewater College *A*
St. Cloud State University *B, M, T*
University of Minnesota
  Duluth *T*
  Twin Cities *M*
University of St. Thomas *M*
Winona State University *B, M, T*

Mississippi

Alcorn State University *B*
Delta State University *B, M*
Itawamba Community College *A*
Jackson State University *B, M*
Millsaps College *T*
Mississippi College *B*
Mississippi Delta Community
  College *A*
Mississippi State University *B, M, T*
Mississippi Valley State University *M*
University of Mississippi *B, T*
University of Southern
  Mississippi *B, M*

Missouri

Avila University *B, T*
Central Missouri State
  University *B, M, T*
Culver-Stockton College *T*
Evangel University *B*
Fontbonne University *B*
Lincoln University *B, T*
Maryville University of Saint
  Louis *M, T*
Missouri Baptist University *T*
Missouri Southern State
  University *B, T*
Missouri State University *B, M*
Missouri Valley College *B*
Northwest Missouri State
  University *B, T*
Southeast Missouri State
  University *B, M, T*
Truman State University *M, T*
University of Missouri
  Columbia *M, D*
  Kansas City *M*
  St. Louis *B, M, T*
Webster University *M*
William Woods University *B*

Montana

Carroll College *T*
Montana State University
  Billings *A, B, M, T*
University of Great Falls *B*
University of Montana: Western *T*

Nebraska

College of Saint Mary *B, T*
Concordia University *B, T*
Dana College *B*
Doane College *B*
Hastings College *B, M, T*
Nebraska Wesleyan University *B*
Peru State College *B, T*
University of Nebraska
  Kearney *B, M, T*
  Omaha *M*
Wayne State College *B, M, T*
York College *B, T*

Nevada

University of Nevada
  Las Vegas *B, M, D, T*
  Reno *B, M, T*

New Hampshire

Granite State College *T*
Keene State College *B, M, T*
New England College *B, T*
Rivier College *T*
University of New Hampshire *M, T*

New Jersey

Bloomfield College *B*
Caldwell College *T*
Centenary College *M*
The College of New Jersey *B, M, T*
College of St. Elizabeth *B, T*
Georgian Court University *B, M, T*
Gloucester County College *A*
Kean University *B, M, T*
Monmouth University *M*
New Jersey City University *B, M*
Rider University *M*
Rowan University *B, M*
Rutgers, The State University of New
  Jersey
  New Brunswick/Piscataway
    Campus *T*
Seton Hall University *B, T*
William Paterson University of New
  Jersey *B, M, T*

New Mexico

College of Santa Fe *M*
College of the Southwest *B, T*
Eastern New Mexico University *B, M*
New Mexico Highlands
  University *B, M*
New Mexico State University *B*
University of New Mexico *B, M, D, T*
Western New Mexico
  University *B, M, T*

New York

Adelphi University *M, T*
Canisius College *M, T*
Cazenovia College *B*
City University of New York
  Brooklyn College *B, M*
  College of Staten Island *M*
  Hunter College *M, T*
  Lehman College *M, T*
  Medgar Evers College *B, T*
  Queens College *M, T*
College of Mount St. Vincent *B, T*
College of New Rochelle *B, M*
College of Saint Rose *M, T*
D'Youville College *B, M, T*
Daemen College *B, M, T*
Dominican College of Blauvelt *B*
Dowling College *B, M, T*
Fordham University *M*
Hobart and William Smith Colleges *T*
Hofstra University *M, T*
Keuka College *B, T*
Le Moyne College *M, T*
Long Island University
  Brooklyn Campus *M, T*
  C.W. Post Campus *M, T*
Manhattan College *B, M, T*
Manhattanville College *M, T*
Marist College *B, M*
Marymount Manhattan College *T*
Medaille College *M, T*
Mercy College *B, M, T*
Molloy College *B, T*
Mount St. Mary College *B, M, T*
Nazareth College of Rochester *B, M, T*
New York University *B, M, T*
Niagara University *B, M, T*
Pace University *M, T*
Roberts Wesleyan College *B, M*

St. Bonaventure University *M*
St. John Fisher College *B, M, T*
St. John's University *B, M*
St. Joseph's College *B, T*
St. Joseph's College: Suffolk
  Campus *B, T*
St. Thomas Aquinas College *B, M, T*
State University of New York
  Albany *M*
  Binghamton *M*
  Buffalo *D*
  College at Brockport *M, T*
  College at Buffalo *M*
  College at Cortland *B*
  College at Geneseo *B, M, T*
  College at Old Westbury *B, T*
  College at Plattsburgh *B, M*
  College at Potsdam *M*
  New Paltz *B, M, T*
  Oswego *M*
Syracuse University *B, M, D, T*
Touro College *B, M*
Utica College *B, M*

North Carolina

Appalachian State University *B, M*
Bennett College *B*
Elizabeth City State University *B, T*
Elon University *B, M, T*
Fayetteville State University *M*
Fayetteville Technical Community
  College *A*
Greensboro College *B, M, T*
High Point University *B*
Methodist College *A, B, T*
North Carolina Agricultural and
  Technical State University *B*
North Carolina Central University *M*
North Carolina State University *M, T*
Pfeiffer University *B*
St. Augustine's College *B*
Shaw University *B, T*
Stanly Community College *A*
University of North Carolina
  Charlotte *M, D*
  Greensboro *B, M, D*
  Pembroke *B*
  Wilmington *M*
Western Carolina University *B*
Winston-Salem State University *B*

North Dakota

Jamestown College *B*
Minot State University *M*
University of North Dakota *M*

Ohio

Antioch University McGregor *M*
Ashland University *B, M, T*
Bluffton University *B*
Bowling Green State
  University *B, M, T*
Cedarville University *B*
Central State University *B*
Cincinnati Christian University *B*
Cleveland State University *B, T*
College of Mount St. Joseph *B, T*
Kent State University *B, M, D*
Miami University
  Oxford Campus *B, M*
Muskingum College *B, T*
Ohio Dominican University *B, T*
Ohio State University
  Columbus Campus *B, M*
Ohio University *B, M, D*
Ohio University
  Southern Campus at Ironton *M*
  Zanesville Campus *M*
Otterbein College *B*
Sinclair Community College *A*
Union Institute & University *M*
University of Akron *M*
University of Cincinnati *M, D*
University of Dayton *B, M, T*

University of Findlay *B, M, T*
University of Rio Grande *B, T*
University of Toledo *M, T*
Urbana University *B*
Ursuline College *B, M, T*
Wilmington College *M*
Wright State University *M*
Xavier University *B, M*
Youngstown State University *B, M*

Oklahoma

East Central University *B, M, T*
Northeastern State University *B, M*
Northwestern Oklahoma State
  University *B*
Oklahoma Baptist University *B, T*
Oral Roberts University *B, T*
Southeastern Oklahoma State
  University *B*
Southwestern Oklahoma State
  University *B, M, T*
University of Central Oklahoma *B, M*
University of Oklahoma *B, M, D*

Oregon

Eastern Oregon University *T*
Portland State University *M, D, T*
Southern Oregon University *T*
University of Oregon *M, D, T*
Western Oregon University *T*

Pennsylvania

Albright College *B, M, T*
Alvernia College *B*
Arcadia University *B, M, D, T*
Bloomsburg University of
  Pennsylvania *B, M, T*
Cabrini College *B, T*
California University of
  Pennsylvania *B, M*
Carlow University *B, T*
Cedar Crest College *B*
Chatham College *T*
Chestnut Hill College *T*
Cheyney University of
  Pennsylvania *B, M, T*
Clarion University of
  Pennsylvania *B, M, T*
College Misericordia *B, T*
DeSales University *M, T*
Duquesne University *M, T*
East Stroudsburg University of
  Pennsylvania *B, M, T*
Edinboro University of
  Pennsylvania *B, M, T*
Gannon University *B*
Geneva College *B, T*
Gwynedd-Mercy College *B, M, T*
Holy Family University *B, T*
Indiana University of
  Pennsylvania *B, M, T*
Juniata College *T*
King's College *B*
Kutztown University of
  Pennsylvania *B*
La Salle University *B, T*
Lebanon Valley College *T*
Lehigh Carbon Community College *A*
Lehigh University *M, D*
Lincoln University *B*
Lock Haven University of
  Pennsylvania *B, T*
Mansfield University of
  Pennsylvania *B, M, T*
Marywood University *B, M*
Mercyhurst College *B, M, T*
Millersville University of
  Pennsylvania *B, M, T*
Penn State
  Abington *B*
  Altoona *B*
  Beaver *B*
  Berks *B*
  Delaware County *B*

Dubois *B*
Fayette *B*
Hazleton *B*
Lehigh Valley *B*
McKeesport *B*
Mont Alto *B*
New Kensington *B*
Schuylkill - Capital College *B*
Shenango *B*
University Park *B, M, D*
Wilkes-Barre *B*
Worthington Scranton *B*
York *B*
Rosemont College *T*
St. Francis University *B*
St. Joseph's University *B, M*
St. Vincent College *M*
Seton Hill University *M, T*
Shippensburg University of Pennsylvania *M, T*
Slippery Rock University of Pennsylvania *B, M, T*
University of Scranton *B*
Waynesburg College *B*
West Chester University of Pennsylvania *B, M, T*
Widener University *B, M, T*
Wilkes University *B, M, T*
York College of Pennsylvania *B*

Puerto Rico

American University of Puerto Rico *B, T*
Bayamon Central University *B, M*
Inter American University of Puerto Rico
Arecibo Campus *B*
Ponce Campus *B, T*
San German Campus *B, M*
Pontifical Catholic University of Puerto Rico *B*
Turabo University *B, M*
Universidad Metropolitana *B, M*
University of Puerto Rico
Cayey University College *B*
Rio Piedras *M*

Rhode Island

Community College of Rhode Island *A*
Providence College *B, M*
Rhode Island College *B, M*
Salve Regina University *B*

South Carolina

Anderson University *B, T*
Clemson University *B, M*
Coastal Carolina University *B*
College of Charleston *B, M, T*
Columbia College *B, T*
Converse College *B, M, T*
Erskine College *B, T*
Francis Marion University *M*
Furman University *M, T*
Lander University *B, T*
South Carolina State University *B, M, T*
Southern Wesleyan University *B, T*
University of South Carolina *M, D*
University of South Carolina
Aiken *B*
Upstate *B, M, T*
Winthrop University *B, M, T*

South Dakota

Augustana College *B, M, T*
Black Hills State University *B*
Dakota State University *B, T*
Dakota Wesleyan University *B, T*
Northern State University *B, T*
University of South Dakota *B, M*

Tennessee

Austin Peay State University *B, T*
Bethel College *B, M, T*
Carson-Newman College *B, T*
Cumberland University *B*
East Tennessee State University *B, M, T*
Fisk University *B*
Freed-Hardeman University *B, T*
Lambuth University *B, T*
LeMoyne-Owen College *B*
Lee University *B*
Middle Tennessee State University *B, M, T*
Southern Adventist University *M*
Tennessee State University *B, M, T*
Tennessee Technological University *B, M, T*
Tusculum College *B, T*
Union University *B, T*
University of Memphis *B, T*
University of Tennessee
Chattanooga *B, M, T*
Knoxville *M, T*
Martin *B*
Vanderbilt University *B, M, D, T*

Texas

Abilene Christian University *B, M, T*
Angelo State University *M*
Baylor University *B, T*
Del Mar College *A*
El Paso Community College *A*
Houston Baptist University *M*
Jarvis Christian College *B, T*
Lamar University *B, M, T*
Laredo Community College *A*
Lubbock Christian University *B*
McMurry University *T*
Midwestern State University *M*
Our Lady of the Lake University of San Antonio *B, M*
Prairie View A&M University *M*
Sam Houston State University *M*
San Jacinto College
North *A*
Southern Methodist University *T*
Southwestern University *T*
Stephen F.Austin State University *M, T*
Sul Ross State University *M*
Texas A&M University
Commerce *B, M, D, T*
Kingsville *M*
Texarkana *M, T*
Texas Christian University *M*
Texas Southern University *M*
Texas State University: San Marcos *M, T*
Texas Tech University *M, D*
Texas Woman's University *M, D, T*
University of Houston *M, D*
University of Houston
Clear Lake *T*
Victoria *M*
University of Mary Hardin-Baylor *B*
University of North Texas *M, D*
University of Texas
Austin *M, D*
Brownsville *M*
El Paso *B, M*
Pan American *M*
San Antonio *M, T*
Tyler *M*
of the Permian Basin *M*
West Texas A&M University *M, T*

Utah

Brigham Young University *B, M*
Snow College *A*
Southern Utah University *B*
University of Utah *B, M, D*
Utah State University *B, M, D*
Westminster College *B, T*

Vermont

Castleton State College *M, T*
College of St. Joseph in Vermont *B, M*
Green Mountain College *B, T*
Johnson State College *M*
Lyndon State College *B, M*
St. Michael's College *M, T*
University of Vermont *M*

Virginia

Averett University *M*
Bridgewater College *T*
George Mason University *M*
Hampton University *B, M*
James Madison University *M, T*
Liberty University *B, M, T*
Longwood University *B, M, T*
Lynchburg College *M*
Norfolk State University *B*
Old Dominion University *M, D, T*
Radford University *M, T*
University of Virginia *M, D*
University of Virginia's College at Wise *T*
Virginia Commonwealth University *M*
Virginia Intermont College *B, T*

Washington

Central Washington University *B, M, T*
City University *M*
Eastern Washington University *M, T*
Gonzaga University *B, M, T*
Heritage University *B, M*
Pacific Lutheran University *M*
Saint Martin's University *B, T*
Seattle Pacific University *B*
Seattle University *M*
Shoreline Community College *A*
Spokane Falls Community College *A*
University of Washington *M, D*
Walla Walla College *B, M*
Washington State University *B, M, T*
Western Washington University *B, M*
Whitworth College *B, M, T*

West Virginia

Alderson-Broaddus College *B, T*
Bethany College *B*
Glenville State College *B*
Marshall University *M*
Mountain State University *M*
Salem International University *T*
West Liberty State College *B*
West Virginia State University *B*
West Virginia University *M, D*
West Virginia Wesleyan College *B*

Wisconsin

Cardinal Stritch University *M*
Carthage College *B, T*
Concordia University Wisconsin *M*
Edgewood College *B, M, D*
University of Wisconsin
Eau Claire *B, M*
La Crosse *M*
Madison *B, M, D*
Milwaukee *M, T*
Oshkosh *B, M, T*
Superior *M*
Whitewater *B, M, T*

Wyoming

Northwest College *A*
University of Wyoming *B*
Western Wyoming Community College *A*

Special education administration

Arizona

Northcentral University *M, D*

California

California Baptist University *M*

District of Columbia

Gallaudet University *D*

Illinois

University of Illinois Urbana-Champaign *M, D*

Missouri

Lincoln University *M*
University of Missouri Columbia *M, D*

New York

Hofstra University *T*

Ohio

Youngstown State University *M, D*

Pennsylvania

Marywood University *M*

Virginia

Virginia Polytechnic Institute and State University *D*

Special products marketing

Michigan

Madonna University *B*

Minnesota

Rochester Community and Technical College *C, A*

Missouri

State Fair Community College *A*

New Jersey

Bergen Community College *A*

New York

Rochester Institute of Technology *B*

Pennsylvania

St. Joseph's University *B, M*

Speech pathology

Alabama

Alabama Agricultural and Mechanical University *M*
University of Alabama *M*
University of Montevallo *B, M, T*

Arizona

Northern Arizona University *M*
University of Arizona *B, M, D*

Arkansas

Arkansas State University *M*
Harding University *B*
University of Central Arkansas *B*

California

California State University
Fresno *M*
Northridge *B*
Loma Linda University *M*
San Diego State University *M*
Stanford University *D*
University of the Pacific *B, M*

Colorado

University of Northern Colorado *B, M*

District of Columbia

University of the District of
    Columbia *B*

Florida

Nova Southeastern University *M, D*

Georgia

University of West Georgia *B, M*
Valdosta State University *M*

Idaho

Idaho State University *M*

Illinois

Elmhurst College *B, T*
Governors State University *B, M, T*
Northwestern University *M, D*
Rush University *M*
St. Xavier University *B, M*

Indiana

Ball State University *M*
Butler University *M*

Iowa

University of Northern Iowa *B, M*

Kansas

University of Kansas *M, D*

Louisiana

Centenary College of Louisiana *B*
Grambling State University *B*
Southeastern Louisiana University *M*
Xavier University of Louisiana *B*

Maryland

Loyola College in Maryland *B*
University of Maryland
    College Park *M*

Massachusetts

Boston University *M, D*
Elms College *B*
Emerson College *B, M*
Northeastern University *B, M*
Worcester State College *M*

Michigan

Calvin College *B*
Eastern Michigan University *M*
Northern Michigan University *B, M*
Wayne State University *B, M, D*

Minnesota

Minnesota State University
    Mankato *M*
    Moorhead *M*

Missouri

Central Missouri State University *B, T*
Fontbonne University *B, M*
Rockhurst University *B, M*

Nebraska

University of Nebraska
    Kearney *B, M, T*
    Lincoln *B*

Nevada

University of Nevada
    Reno *B, M, D*

New Hampshire

University of New Hampshire *B*

New Jersey

The College of New Jersey *M*
Montclair State University *T*

Seton Hall University *M*
William Paterson University of New
    Jersey *B*

New Mexico

University of New Mexico *M*

New York

City University of New York
    Brooklyn College *B, M*
    Hunter College *B, M*
    Lehman College *B, M*
    Queens College *M*
College of New Rochelle *M*
Hofstra University *M*
Ithaca College *M, T*
Nazareth College of Rochester *B, M, T*
New York University *M*
Pace University *B*
State University of New York
    College at Buffalo *B, M*
    College at Fredonia *M*
    College at Geneseo *M*
    College at Plattsburgh *B, M*
    New Paltz *M*
Touro College *M*

North Carolina

University of North Carolina
    Chapel Hill *M*

North Dakota

University of North Dakota *M*

Ohio

Bowling Green State University *M, T*
Case Western Reserve University *M, D*
Miami University
    Oxford Campus *B*
Ohio University *M*
University of Toledo *M*

Oklahoma

Oklahoma State University *B, M*
University of Central Oklahoma *B, M*
University of Oklahoma *M, D*
University of Science and Arts of
    Oklahoma *B*

Oregon

Portland State University *M*
University of Oregon *T*

Pennsylvania

Bloomsburg University of
    Pennsylvania *M, T*
College Misericordia *M*
Duquesne University *M*
Edinboro University of
    Pennsylvania *M*
Geneva College *B*
La Salle University *B, M*
Marywood University *B, M*
University of Pittsburgh *D*

Puerto Rico

Turabo University *B, M*

Rhode Island

University of Rhode Island *M*

South Carolina

Columbia College *B*
University of South Carolina *M*

South Dakota

Northern State University *B, T*

Tennessee

University of Tennessee
    Knoxville *B, M*

Texas

Abilene Christian University *B, M*
Lamar University *M*
Stephen F. Austin State University *M, T*
Texas A&M University
    Kingsville *B*
Texas Christian University *B, M*
Texas Woman's University *M*
University of Houston *M*
University of North Texas *M*

Utah

Brigham Young University *M*
University of Utah *M*

Vermont

University of Vermont *B*

Virginia

James Madison University *B, M, D, T*

Washington

University of Washington *M*
Western Washington University *M*

West Virginia

Marshall University *B*
West Virginia University *M*

Wisconsin

Marquette University *M*
University of Wisconsin
    Whitewater *B, T*

Speech/rhetorical studies

Alabama

Huntingdon College *B, T*
Samford University *B*
Troy University *B*
University of Alabama
    Huntsville *B*
University of Montevallo *B, T*
University of North Alabama *B*

Alaska

University of Alaska
    Fairbanks *B*

Arizona

Northern Arizona University *B, M*

Arkansas

Arkansas State University *B, M*
Arkansas State University
    Beebe *A*
Arkansas Tech University *B*
Henderson State University *B*
Ouachita Baptist University *B*
Phillips Community College of the
    University of Arkansas *A*
University of Arkansas
    Monticello *B*
    Pine Bluff *B*
University of Central Arkansas *B*

California

Cabrillo College *A*
California Lutheran University *B*
California Polytechnic State
    University: San Luis Obispo *B*
California State University
    Chico *B*
    East Bay *B, M*
    Fullerton *B, M*
    Long Beach *B, M*
    Northridge *B, M*
Cerritos Community College *A*
Chabot College *A*
College of San Mateo *A*

College of the Desert *A*
College of the Sequoias *A*
Columbia College *A*
Cypress College *A*
El Camino College *A*
Foothill College *C, A*
Fresno City College *A*
Fullerton College *A*
Golden West College *A*
Grossmont Community College *A*
Humboldt State University *B*
Irvine Valley College *A*
Las Positas College *A*
Long Beach City College *A*
Master's College *B*
Mendocino College *A*
Merced College *A*
Modesto Junior College *C, A*
Ohlone College *C*
Orange Coast College *A*
Palomar College *A*
Pasadena City College *C, A*
Saddleback College *A*
San Diego City College *A*
San Diego Miramar College *A*
San Diego State University *B*
San Francisco State University *B, M*
San Joaquin Delta College *A*
San Jose State University *B*
Santa Barbara City College *A*
Santa Rosa Junior College *C*
Santiago Canyon College *A*
Sierra College *A*
Skyline College *A*
University of California
    Berkeley *B, D*
    Davis *B*
Ventura College *A*
West Los Angeles College *C, A*
West Valley College *A*

Colorado

Colorado State University *B, M*
Metropolitan State College of
    Denver *B*

Delaware

Delaware State University *B*

District of Columbia

Catholic University of America *M, D*

Florida

Bethune-Cookman College *B*
Gulf Coast Community College *A*
Manatee Community College *A*
Miami Dade College *A*
University of Central Florida *B*
University of South Florida *B, M, D*

Georgia

Albany State University *B*
Atlanta Metropolitan College *A*
Clark Atlanta University *B*
Columbus State University *B*
Darton College *A*
Georgia Southern University *B*
Georgia State University *B*
University of Georgia *B, M, D*
Valdosta State University *B*
Young Harris College *A*

Hawaii

University of Hawaii
    Hilo *B*

Idaho

Northwest Nazarene University *B*

Illinois

Augustana College *B*
Chicago State University *B*

City Colleges of Chicago
Harold Washington College *A*
Eastern Illinois University *B, M, T*
Greenville College *B*
Illinois Central College *A*
Illinois College *B*
Illinois State University *B, T*
Illinois Valley Community College *A*
Judson College *B*
Lake Land College *A*
Lewis University *B, T*
McKendree College *B*
Monmouth College *B, T*
North Central College *B*
Northeastern Illinois University *B, M*
Richland Community College *A*
Roosevelt University *B*
Southern Illinois University
Carbondale *B, M, D*
Southern Illinois University
Edwardsville *B, M, T*
Southwestern Illinois College *A*
Triton College *A*
University of Illinois
Chicago *B, M*
Urbana-Champaign *B, M, D*

Indiana

Ball State University *B, M*
Butler University *B*
Huntington University *B*
Indiana University
South Bend *B*
Vincennes University *A*
Wabash College *B*

Iowa

Coe College *B*
Dordt College *B*
Drake University *B*
Graceland University *B, T*
Iowa State University *B, M, D*
Mount Mercy College *B, T*
Northwestern College *B*
St. Ambrose University *B, T*
University of Dubuque *B*
University of Iowa *B*
University of Northern Iowa *B*
Wartburg College *B, T*

Kansas

Bethany College *B*
Butler County Community College *A*
Central Christian College of Kansas *A*
Coffeyville Community College *A*
Donnelly College *A*
Kansas Wesleyan University *B, T*
Pratt Community College *A*
University of Kansas *B, M, D*
Washburn University of Topeka *B*

Kentucky

Asbury College *B*
Eastern Kentucky University *B*
Morehead State University *B*
Northern Kentucky University *B*
Thomas More College *B*
University of the Cumberlands *B*

Louisiana

Louisiana State University
Shreveport *B*
Louisiana State University and
Agricultural and Mechanical
College *B, M, D*
Louisiana Tech University *B, M*
Southern University and Agricultural
and Mechanical College *B*
University of Louisiana at Monroe *B*

Maine

Bates College *B*
University of Maine *B, M*

Maryland

Frederick Community College *A*
Frostburg State University *B, T*
Morgan State University *B*

Massachusetts

Emerson College *B, M*
Northeastern University *B*

Michigan

Albion College *B*
Calvin College *B*
Central Michigan University *B, M, T*
Cornerstone University *B, T*
Eastern Michigan University *B, M*
Ferris State University *A, B*
Hillsdale College *B*
Lake Michigan College *A*
Madonna University *A, B*
Michigan State University *D*
Mid Michigan Community College *A*
Northern Michigan University *B, M, T*
Spring Arbor University *B*
University of Detroit Mercy *B*
University of Michigan *B, M, D*
University of Michigan
Flint *T*

Minnesota

College of St. Benedict *B*
Minnesota State University
Mankato *B, M*
Moorhead *B*
Ridgewater College *A*
St. Cloud State University *B*
St. John's University *B*
Southwest Minnesota State
University *B*
University of Minnesota
Twin Cities *B, M, D*
Winona State University *B*

Mississippi

Blue Mountain College *B*
Hinds Community College *A*
Jackson State University *B*
Mississippi Valley State University *B*

Missouri

Central Missouri State University *B, M*
Evangel University *B*
Missouri Western State University *B, T*
St. Louis Community College
St. Louis Community College at
Florissant Valley *A*
Southeast Missouri State University *B*
Three Rivers Community College *A*
Truman State University *B*
William Jewell College *B*

Montana

Miles Community College *A*
University of Montana: Missoula *B, M*

Nebraska

Chadron State College *B*
Doane College *B*
Hastings College *B, T*
Nebraska Wesleyan University *B*
Northeast Community College *A*
Union College *B*
University of Nebraska
Kearney *B, M, T*
Omaha *B*

New Jersey

The College of New Jersey *B*
Rutgers, The State University of New
Jersey
Camden Regional Campus *T*

New Mexico

Eastern New Mexico University *B*
New Mexico State University *D*
University of New Mexico *B, M, D*

New York

City University of New York
Brooklyn College *B, M*
York College *B*
Ithaca College *B*
Long Island University
Brooklyn Campus *B*
New York University *B, M, T*
Pace University *B*
Rensselaer Polytechnic Institute *M, D*
St. John's University *B*
St. Joseph's College *B*
State University of New York
Albany *B, M*
Binghamton *B*
College at Oneonta *B*
College at Potsdam *B*
Syracuse University *B, M*
Touro College *B*
Yeshiva University *B*

North Carolina

Appalachian State University *B*
Fayetteville State University *B*
Methodist College *A, B*
North Carolina Agricultural and
Technical State University *B*
University of North Carolina
Greensboro *B, M, T*
Wilmington *B*

North Dakota

Minot State University *B*
North Dakota State University *B, M, D*

Ohio

Bowling Green State University *B*
Defiance College *B, T*
Kent State University *B, M, D*
Miami University
Oxford Campus *B, M, T*
Ohio University *M*
University of Akron *B*
Youngstown State University *B*

Oklahoma

Carl Albert State College *A*
Connors State College *A*
East Central University *B*
Northeastern Oklahoma Agricultural
and Mechanical College *A*
Northeastern State University *B*
Northwestern Oklahoma State
University *B*
Oklahoma Baptist University *B, T*
Oklahoma Christian University *B*
Oklahoma City University *B*
Oklahoma Panhandle State
University *B*
Redlands Community College *A*
Southern Nazarene University *B*
Tulsa Community College *A*

Oregon

Chemeketa Community College *A*
Linn-Benton Community College *A*
Oregon State University *B*
Portland State University *B, M*
Southern Oregon University *B, T*
Western Oregon University *B*
Willamette University *B*

Pennsylvania

Bloomsburg University of
Pennsylvania *B*
Carnegie Mellon University *M, D*

Clarion University of
Pennsylvania *B, T*
Community College of Philadelphia *A*
Duquesne University *B, D*
Geneva College *B*
Kutztown University of
Pennsylvania *B, T*
La Salle University *B*
Lock Haven University of
Pennsylvania *B*
Mansfield University of
Pennsylvania *B*
Penn State
Altoona *B*
Beaver *B*
Berks *B*
Delaware County *B*
Dubois *B*
Fayette *B*
Hazleton *B*
Lehigh Valley *B*
McKeesport *B*
Mont Alto *B*
New Kensington *B*
Schuylkill - Capital College *B*
Shenango *B*
University Park *B, M, D*
Wilkes-Barre *B*
Worthington Scranton *B*
York *B*
Shippensburg University of
Pennsylvania *B*
Temple University *B, M*
University of Pittsburgh *C, B, M, D*
West Chester University of
Pennsylvania *B, M*
York College of Pennsylvania *B*

South Carolina

Clemson University *B*

South Dakota

Augustana College *T*
Black Hills State University *B*
Northern State University *A*
South Dakota State University *B, T*
University of Sioux Falls *B*
University of South Dakota *B, M*

Tennessee

Belmont University *B*
Carson-Newman College *B*
East Tennessee State University *B, T*
Fisk University *B*
Lipscomb University *B*
Tennessee Temple University *B*
Union University *B, T*

Texas

Abilene Christian University *B, M*
Amarillo College *A*
Austin Community College *A*
Blinn College *A*
Brazosport College *A*
Clarendon College *A*
Coastal Bend College *A*
Del Mar College *A*
East Texas Baptist University *B*
El Paso Community College *A*
Galveston College *A*
Grayson County College *A*
Hardin-Simmons University *B*
Howard Payne University *B*
Lamar University *B, M*
Lon Morris College *A*
McMurry University *B*
Midland College *A*
Navarro College *A*
Northeast Texas Community
College *A*
Northwest Vista College *A*
St. Philip's College *A*
Sam Houston State University *B*

San Antonio College *A*
San Jacinto College
　North *A*
Stephen F. Austin State University *B, M*
Sul Ross State University *B*
Texas A&M University *B, M, D*
Texas A&M University
　Commerce *B, M*
Texas State University: San
　Marcos *B, M, T*
Texas Tech University *B, M*
Texas Woman's University *D*
Trinity University *B*
Trinity Valley Community College *A*
Tyler Junior College *A*
University of Houston *B, M*
University of Houston
　Downtown *B*
　Victoria *B*
University of North Texas *B, M*
University of Texas
　Arlington *B, D*
　Austin *M, D*
　El Paso *D*
　San Antonio *B*
　Tyler *B*
Weatherford College *A*
West Texas A&M University *B*

Utah
Brigham Young University *B*
Southern Utah University *B*
Utah State University *B, M*

Virginia
George Mason University *B*
Hampton University *B*
Old Dominion University *B*
University of Richmond *B, M*

Washington
Eastern Washington University *T*
Everett Community College *A*
Gonzaga University *B*
University of Washington *B, M, D*

West Virginia
Marshall University *B, M*

Wisconsin
Beloit College *B*
Marquette University *B*
University of Wisconsin
　River Falls *B, M*
　Superior *B, M*
　Whitewater *B*

Wyoming
Laramie County Community
　College *A*

Speech teacher education

Alabama
Huntingdon College *T*
Samford University *B*

Arizona
Grand Canyon University *B*
Northern Arizona University *B*
University of Arizona *B, M*

Arkansas
Arkansas State University *B, T*
Arkansas Tech University *B*
Harding University *B, M, T*
Ouachita Baptist University *B, T*
University of Arkansas
　Monticello *B*

California
California State University
　East Bay *B, M, T*
San Diego Mesa College *A*
San Francisco State University *B, T*

Colorado
Adams State College *B, T*
Colorado State University *T*
Metropolitan State College of
　Denver *T*

Georgia
Darton College *A*

Idaho
Boise State University *T*

Illinois
Augustana College *B, T*
Bradley University *B*
Lewis University *T*
North Park University *T*
Sauk Valley Community College *A*
University of Illinois
　Urbana-Champaign *M*

Indiana
Indiana University
　Bloomington *B, T*
Indiana University-Purdue University
　Fort Wayne *B, T*
Indiana University-Purdue University
　Indianapolis *B, T*
University of Indianapolis *B, T*
Vincennes University *A*

Iowa
Buena Vista University *B, T*
Central College *T*
Dordt College *B*
Graceland University *T*
Loras College *T*
Maharishi University of
　Management *T*
Northwestern College *T*
Simpson College *T*
University of Iowa *T*
University of Northern Iowa *B, T*
Upper Iowa University *T*
Wartburg College *T*

Kansas
Baker University *T*
Bethel College *T*
Coffeyville Community College *A*
Emporia State University *T*
McPherson College *B, T*
Pittsburg State University *B, T*
University of Kansas *B, T*

Louisiana
Northwestern State University *B*
Southeastern Louisiana University *B*
University of Louisiana at Lafayette *B*
University of Louisiana at Monroe *B*

Massachusetts
Emerson College *B, M*
Northeastern University *B*

Michigan
Concordia University *B, T*
Lansing Community College *A*
Madonna University *B*
Michigan State University *D*
Northern Michigan University *B, T*

Minnesota
Augsburg College *T*
Concordia College: Moorhead *B, T*

Minnesota State University
　Mankato *B, M*
　Moorhead *B*
St. Cloud State University *B, T*
Southwest Minnesota State
　University *B, M*
University of Minnesota
　Morris *T*
Winona State University *B, T*

Mississippi
Itawamba Community College *A*
Mississippi College *B*
Mississippi Delta Community
　College *A*
Mississippi State University *T*
William Carey College *B*

Missouri
Central Missouri State
　University *B, M, T*
Culver-Stockton College *B, T*
Missouri Southern State
　University *B, T*
Southeast Missouri State
　University *B, T*
Southwest Baptist University *T*
William Jewell College *T*
William Woods University *T*

Montana
Montana State University
　Billings *T*

Nebraska
Concordia University *B, T*
Creighton University *T*
Dana College *B*
Hastings College *B, T*
Midland Lutheran College *B, T*
Nebraska Wesleyan University *T*
Peru State College *B, T*
University of Nebraska
　Kearney *B, M, T*
Wayne State College *B, T*
York College *B, T*

Nevada
University of Nevada
　Reno *B*

New Jersey
The College of New Jersey *B, M*
Kean University *B*

New York
City University of New York
　Brooklyn College *B*
　Lehman College *M*
Elmira College *B, T*
Marymount Manhattan College *T*
Nazareth College of Rochester *T*
State University of New York
　College at Cortland *B*
　College at Fredonia *B, M, T*
　College at Plattsburgh *M*
　New Paltz *B, M, T*

North Carolina
North Carolina Agricultural and
　Technical State University *B, T*
University of North Carolina
　Greensboro *B, T*

North Dakota
Dickinson State University *B, T*
North Dakota State University *B, T*

Ohio
Baldwin-Wallace College *T*
Defiance College *B, T*
Hiram College *T*

Kent State University *T*
Miami University
　Oxford Campus *B, T*
University of Findlay *B, M, T*
University of Rio Grande *B, T*
Youngstown State University *B, M*

Oklahoma
East Central University *B, T*
Eastern Oklahoma State College *A*
Northeastern State University *B*
Oklahoma Baptist University *B, T*
Oklahoma Christian University *B, T*
Oklahoma City University *B*
Southeastern Oklahoma State
　University *B, M, T*
Southern Nazarene University *B*
Southwestern Oklahoma State
　University *T*

Oregon
Portland State University *T*
Southern Oregon University *T*
Western Oregon University *T*

Pennsylvania
St. Francis University *B, T*

South Dakota
Augustana College *B, T*
Black Hills State University *B*
Northern State University *B, T*
University of Sioux Falls *T*
University of South Dakota *B, M, D, T*

Tennessee
Tennessee Technological University *T*
Tennessee Temple University *B*
Trevecca Nazarene University *B, T*

Texas
East Texas Baptist University *B*
Hardin-Simmons University *B, T*
Howard Payne University *B, T*
Lamar University *T*
Laredo Community College *A*
Lubbock Christian University *B*
McMurry University *T*
Texas A&M University
　Commerce *T*
　Kingsville *T*
University of Mary Hardin-Baylor *T*
West Texas A&M University *T*

Utah
Brigham Young University *B, M*
Southern Utah University *B, T*
University of Utah *B*

Vermont
Johnson State College *M*

Virginia
University of Virginia's College at
　Wise *T*

Washington
Western Washington University *B*
Whitworth College *B, T*

West Virginia
Concord University *B, T*

Wisconsin
Cardinal Stritch University *T*
Maranatha Baptist Bible College *B*
University of Wisconsin
　Green Bay *T*
　Platteville *B, T*
　River Falls *T*
　Whitewater *B, T*

Sports and fitness administration

Alabama
Faulkner University *B*
Huntingdon College *B*
Shelton State Community College *C*
Troy University *B, M*

Arizona
Arizona Western College *C*
Grand Canyon University *B*

Arkansas
Arkansas State University *B*
Harding University *B*
Henderson State University *M*
John Brown University *B*

California
California State University
  Chico *C*
  East Bay *C*
Fresno Pacific University *B*
Mendocino College *A*
National University *B*
St. Mary's College of California *B*
San Francisco State University *B, M*
Solano Community College *A*
Southwestern College *C*
University of San Francisco *M*
University of the Pacific *B*

Colorado
Fort Lewis College *B*
Front Range Community College *C, A*
Johnson & Wales University *B*

Connecticut
Eastern Connecticut State
  University *B*
Mitchell College *A, B*
Sacred Heart University *B*
University of New Haven *B, M*

Delaware
Delaware State University *B*
University of Delaware *B*

District of Columbia
American University *C, B, M*

Florida
Barry University *B, M*
Flagler College *B*
Florida State University *B, M, D*
Johnson & Wales University *B*
Lake-Sumter Community College *A*
Lynn University *B, M*
Manatee Community College *A*
Northwood University
  Florida Campus *A, B*
Nova Southeastern University *B*
St. Leo University *B*
St. Thomas University *B, M*
Stetson University *B*
University of Central Florida *M*
University of Miami *C, B, M*
University of Tampa *B*
Warner Southern College *B*

Georgia
Emmanuel College *B*
Georgia Southern University *B, M*
Georgia State University *M*
Kennesaw State University *B*
Reinhardt College *B*
South Georgia College *A*
University of Georgia *B*

Idaho
Albertson College of Idaho *B*

Illinois
Elmhurst College *B*
Greenville College *B*
Illinois College *B*
Illinois Valley Community College *A*
Judson College *B*
Lewis University *B*
MacMurray College *B*
Millikin University *B*
Moraine Valley Community College *C*
North Central College *B*
Northwestern University *M*
Olivet Nazarene University *B*
Principia College *B*
Quincy University *B*
Sauk Valley Community College *A*
South Suburban College of Cook
  County *C, A*
Western Illinois University *M*

Indiana
Ball State University *M*
Grace College *B*
Huntington University *B*
Indiana Institute of Technology *B*
Indiana State University *M*
Indiana Wesleyan University *B*
Marian College *B*
Taylor University *B*
Tri-State University *B*
University of Indianapolis *B*
Valparaiso University *B, M*
Vincennes University *A*

Iowa
Briar Cliff University *B*
Buena Vista University *B*
Des Moines Area Community
  College *A*
Graceland University *B*
Grand View College *C*
Iowa Wesleyan College *B*
Loras College *M*
Luther College *B*
North Iowa Area Community
  College *A*
St. Ambrose University *B*
Simpson College *B*
University of Iowa *B, M, D*
Wartburg College *B*
William Penn University *B*

Kansas
Barton County Community College *A*
Bethany College *B*
Central Christian College of
  Kansas *A, B*
MidAmerica Nazarene University *B*
Pittsburg State University *B*
Southwestern College *B*
Tabor College *B*
University of St. Mary *B*
Washburn University of Topeka *B*
Wichita State University *B, M*

Kentucky
Asbury College *B*
Kentucky Wesleyan College *B*
Northern Kentucky University *B*
Union College *B*
University of Louisville *B, M*

Louisiana
Grambling State University *M*

Maine
Husson College *B*
St. Joseph's College *B*
Thomas College *B*

University of New England *B*
University of Southern Maine *B*

Maryland
Community College of Baltimore
  County *A*
Coppin State University *B*
Frostburg State University *B*
Mount St. Mary's University *B*
Towson University *B*

Massachusetts
American International College *B*
Becker College *A, B*
Bridgewater State College *B*
Dean College *A*
Endicott College *B*
Fitchburg State College *B*
Holyoke Community College *C, A*
Lasell College *B*
Mount Ida College *A*
Nichols College *B*
North Shore Community College *C*
Northeastern University *M*
Northern Essex Community
  College *A*
Roxbury Community College *C*
Salem State College *B*
Springfield College *B, M*
University of Massachusetts
  Amherst *B, M, D*
Western New England College *B*

Michigan
Aquinas College *B*
Central Michigan University *B, M*
Cornerstone University *B*
Eastern Michigan University *M*
Northern Michigan University *B*
Northwood University *A, B*
Olivet College *B*
Siena Heights University *B*
University of Michigan *B*
Wayne State University *M*

Minnesota
Century Community and Technical
  College *C, A*
Crown College *B*
Minnesota School of Business *C, A*
Minnesota State University
  Mankato *B, M, T*
University of Minnesota
  Crookston *B*
University of St. Thomas *M*
Winona State University *B*

Mississippi
Belhaven College *B*
Coahoma Community College *A*
University of Southern Mississippi *M*

Missouri
Lindenwood University *B, M*
Missouri Baptist University *B*
Southeast Missouri State University *B*
Southwest Baptist University *B*
William Woods University *B*

Montana
Carroll College *B*
Montana State University
  Billings *B, M*
  Bozeman *B*

Nebraska
Bellevue University *B*
Concordia University *B*
Dana College *B*
Hastings College *B*
Nebraska Wesleyan University *B*
Union College *B*

University of Nebraska
  Kearney *B*
Wayne State College *B*

Nevada
University of Nevada
  Las Vegas *M*

New Hampshire
Colby-Sawyer College *B*
Daniel Webster College *B*
Franklin Pierce College *B*
New England College *B*
New Hampshire Technical Institute *A*
Southern New Hampshire
  University *B*

New Jersey
Raritan Valley Community College *C*
Rowan University *B*
Seton Hall University *B*

New York
Canisius College *M*
Elmira College *B*
Finger Lakes Community College *A*
Herkimer County Community
  College *A*
Ithaca College *B, M*
Medaille College *C, B*
New York University *B, M*
St. John Fisher College *B*
St. John's University *C, B*
State University of New York
  College at Brockport *B*
  College of Agriculture and
    Technology at Morrisville *A*
  College of Technology at Alfred *A*
Syracuse University *B*
Tompkins-Cortland Community
  College *A*

North Carolina
Appalachian State University *M*
Barton College *B*
Campbell University *B*
Catawba College *B*
Chowan College *B*
East Carolina University *B*
Elon University *B*
Greensboro College *B*
Guilford College *B*
High Point University *B*
Johnson C. Smith University *B*
Lenoir-Rhyne College *B*
Livingstone College *B*
Meredith College *B*
Methodist College *B*
North Carolina State University *B*
Pfeiffer University *B*
St. Augustine's College *B*
Western Carolina University *B*
Wingate University *B*
Winston-Salem State University *B*

North Dakota
Jamestown College *B*
North Dakota State University *B*

Ohio
Ashland University *B*
Baldwin-Wallace College *B*
Bluffton University *B*
Bowling Green State University *B, M*
Cedarville University *B*
Cincinnati State Technical and
  Community College *C*
Cleveland State University *M*
Columbus State Community
  College *C, A*
Defiance College *B*
Heidelberg College *B*
Hocking College *A*

Miami University
   Oxford Campus *B, M*
Mount Union College *B*
Mount Vernon Nazarene
   University *A, B*
Ohio Northern University *B*
Ohio State University
   Columbus Campus *B*
Ohio University *M*
Otterbein College *B*
Shawnee State University *B*
Tiffin University *B*
University of Akron *C, B*
University of Dayton *B*
University of Findlay *B*
University of Rio Grande *B*
Urbana University *B*
Wilmington College *B*
Xavier University *B, M*
Youngstown State University *B*

Oklahoma

Oklahoma Baptist University *B*

Oregon

Concordia University *B*
Corban College *B*
George Fox University *B*
Portland Community College *C*
Southern Oregon University *B*

Pennsylvania

Bucks County Community College *A*
Butler County Community College *A*
California University of
   Pennsylvania *B, M*
College Misericordia *B*
DeSales University *B*
Drexel University *B*
Edinboro University of
   Pennsylvania *B*
Gettysburg College *B*
Keystone College *A, B*
Lehigh Carbon Community College *A*
Lock Haven University of
   Pennsylvania *B*
Millersville University of
   Pennsylvania *M*
Neumann College *B, M*
Northampton County Area
   Community College *A*
Robert Morris University *B, M*
University of Pittsburgh
   Bradford *B*
Waynesburg College *B*
West Chester University of
   Pennsylvania *M*
York College of Pennsylvania *B*

Rhode Island

Johnson & Wales University *B*

South Carolina

Claflin University *B*
Coastal Carolina University *B*
Coker College *B*
Erskine College *B*
Limestone College *B*
Newberry College *B*
North Greenville College *B*
Southern Wesleyan University *B*
Technical College of the
   Lowcountry *C*
University of South Carolina *B*
Winthrop University *B*

South Dakota

Black Hills State University *B*
Dakota State University *B*
Dakota Wesleyan University *B*
Northern State University *B*

Tennessee

Belmont University *M*
Cumberland University *B*
East Tennessee State University *B*
Lambuth University *B*
Martin Methodist College *B*
Southern Adventist University *B*
Tennessee Wesleyan College *B*
Tusculum College *B*
Union University *B*
University of Memphis *B*
University of Tennessee
   Knoxville *B*

Texas

Abilene Christian University *B*
Hardin-Simmons University *M*
Howard Payne University *B*
LeTourneau University *B*
Lubbock Christian University *B*
Northwood University: Texas
   Campus *A, B*
Texas Lutheran University *B*
Texas State University: San Marcos *B*
University of Houston *B*
University of Mary Hardin-Baylor *B*
University of Texas
   Austin *B*

Utah

Salt Lake Community College *A*
Utah Career College *A*

Vermont

Castleton State College *B*
College of St. Joseph in Vermont *B*
Johnson State College *B*

Virginia

Averett University *B*
Eastern Mennonite University *B*
Ferrum College *B*
Hampton University *B*
Liberty University *B*
Lynchburg College *B*
Old Dominion University *B, M*
Virginia Intermont College *B*
Virginia State University *M*

Washington

Central Washington University *B*
Clark College *A*
Lake Washington Technical College *C*
Spokane Falls Community College *A*
Washington State University *B*

West Virginia

Bethany College *B*
Concord University *B*
Davis and Elkins College *B*
University of Charleston *B*
West Virginia University *B*
West Virginia Wesleyan College *B*

Wisconsin

Marian College of Fond du Lac *B*
University of Wisconsin
   Parkside *B*

Statistics

Alabama

Auburn University *M, T*
University of Alabama *M, D*
University of South Alabama *B*

Alaska

University of Alaska
   Fairbanks *B, M*

Arizona

Arizona State University *M*
Northern Arizona University *M*

Arkansas

University of Arkansas *M*

California

California Polytechnic State
   University: San Luis Obispo *B*
California State University
   Chico *B*
   East Bay *B, M*
   Fullerton *B, M*
   Long Beach *B*
   Northridge *B*
San Diego State University *B, M*
San Francisco State University *B*
Stanford University *M, D*
University of California
   Berkeley *B, M, D*
   Davis *B, M, D*
   Los Angeles *B, M, D*
   Riverside *B, M, D*
   San Diego *M*
   Santa Barbara *B, M, D*
University of Southern California *M*

Colorado

Colorado State University *M, D*
Fort Lewis College *B*
University of Denver *M*

Connecticut

University of Connecticut *B, M, D*
Yale University *M, D*

Delaware

University of Delaware *B, M, D*

District of Columbia

American University *B, M*
George Washington
   University *B, M, D*

Florida

Florida International University *B, M*
Florida State University *B, M, D*
University of Central Florida *B, M*
University of Florida *A, B, M*
University of Miami *M*
University of North Florida *B*

Georgia

Georgia Institute of Technology *M*
University of Georgia *B, M, D*

Idaho

University of Idaho *M*

Illinois

DePaul University *M*
Loyola University of Chicago *B*
Northern Illinois University *M*
Northwestern University *B, M, D*
Roosevelt University *B*
University of Chicago *B, M, D*
University of Illinois
   Chicago *B*
   Urbana-Champaign *B, M, D*

Indiana

Ball State University *M*
Indiana University-Purdue University
   Fort Wayne *B*
Indiana University-Purdue University
   Indianapolis *M*
Purdue University *B, M, D*
Saint Mary's College *B*

Iowa

Iowa State University *B, M, D*
Luther College *B*
University of Iowa *B, M, D*

Kansas

Kansas State University *B, M, D*

Kentucky

Eastern Kentucky University *B*
University of Kentucky *M, D*

Louisiana

Louisiana State University and
   Agricultural and Mechanical
   College *M*
Tulane University *M*
Xavier University of Louisiana *B*

Maine

University of Southern Maine *M*

Maryland

University of Maryland
   Baltimore County *B, M, D*
   College Park *M, D*

Massachusetts

Harvard College *B, M, D*
Mount Holyoke College *B*
Simon's Rock College of Bard *B*
Worcester Polytechnic Institute *M*

Michigan

Central Michigan University *B*
Eastern Michigan University *B, M*
Ferris State University *B*
Grand Valley State University *B*
Kettering University *B*
Michigan State University *B, M, D*
Oakland University *B, M*
University of Michigan *B, M, D*
Wayne State University *M*
Western Michigan University *B, M, D*

Minnesota

Minnesota State University
   Mankato *M*
St. Cloud State University *B, M*
University of Minnesota
   Duluth *B*
   Morris *B*
   Twin Cities *B, M, D*
Winona State University *B*

Mississippi

Mississippi State University *M*

Missouri

Northwest Missouri State
   University *B*
University of Missouri
   Columbia *B, M, D*
   Kansas City *B, M*
   Rolla *D*
Washington University in St.
   Louis *B, M*

Montana

Montana State University
   Bozeman *M, D*
Montana Tech of the University of
   Montana *B*

Nebraska

University of Nebraska
   Kearney *B*
   Lincoln *M, D*

New Jersey

The College of New Jersey *B*

Montclair State University *M*
New Jersey Institute of Technology *M*
Rutgers, The State University of New
  Jersey
  New Brunswick/Piscataway
    Campus *B, M, D*
Stevens Institute of Technology *M*

New Mexico
New Mexico State University *M*
University of New Mexico *B, M, D*

New York
Barnard College *B*
City University of New York
  Baruch College *B, M*
  Hunter College *B, M*
Clarkson University *B*
Columbia University
  Columbia College *B*
  School of General Studies *B*
Cornell University *B, M, D*
New York University *B, M, D*
Rochester Institute of
  Technology *B, M*
State University of New York
  College at Oneonta *B*
Syracuse University *M*
University of Rochester *B, M, D*

North Carolina
Appalachian State University *B*
North Carolina State
  University *B, M, D*
Queens University of Charlotte *B*
University of North Carolina
  Chapel Hill *M, D*
  Wilmington *B*

North Dakota
North Dakota State University *B, M, D*

Ohio
Bowling Green State University *B, M*
Case Western Reserve
  University *B, M, D*
Miami University
  Oxford Campus *B, M*
Ohio Northern University *B*
Ohio State University
  Columbus Campus *M, D*
Ohio Wesleyan University *B*
University of Akron *B, M*
Wright State University *B, M*

Oklahoma
Oklahoma State University *B, M, D*
University of Central Oklahoma *B*

Oregon
Oregon State University *M, D*
Portland State University *M*

Pennsylvania
Carnegie Mellon University *B, M, D*
La Salle University *B*
Lehigh University *B, M*
Penn State
  Abington *B*
  Altoona *B*
  Beaver *B*
  Berks *B*
  Delaware County *B*
  Dubois *B*
  Fayette *B*
  Hazleton *B*
  Lehigh Valley *B*
  McKeesport *B*
  Mont Alto *B*
  New Kensington *B*
  Schuylkill - Capital College *B*
  Shenango *B*

University Park *B, M, D*
  Wilkes-Barre *B*
  Worthington Scranton *B*
  York *B*
University of Pennsylvania *B, M, D*
University of Pittsburgh *B, M, D*
West Chester University of
  Pennsylvania *M*

Puerto Rico
University of Puerto Rico
  Mayaguez *M*

Rhode Island
Brown University *B*
University of Rhode Island *M*

South Carolina
University of South Carolina *B, M, D*

South Dakota
Dakota State University *B*

Texas
Baylor University *B, M, D*
Rice University *B, M, D*
Sam Houston State University *M*
Southern Methodist
  University *B, M, D*
Stephen F. Austin State University *M*
Texas A&M University *M, D*
Texas Tech University *M*
University of Houston
  Clear Lake *M*
University of Texas
  Austin *M*
  Dallas *B, M, D*
  El Paso *B, M*
  San Antonio *B, M*

Utah
Brigham Young University *B, M*
Snow College *A*
Southern Utah University *B*
University of Utah *M*
Utah State University *B, M*

Vermont
Castleton State College *B*
University of Vermont *B, M*

Virginia
University of Virginia *M, D*
Virginia Polytechnic Institute and
  State University *B, M, D*

Washington
University of Washington *M, D*
Washington State University *M*

West Virginia
West Virginia University *M*

Wisconsin
Marquette University *B*
University of Wisconsin
  Madison *B, M, D*

Wyoming
Eastern Wyoming College *A*
University of Wyoming *B, M, D*

Structural biology

California
Stanford University *D*

Massachusetts
Brandeis University *M, D*

New York
State University of New York
  Buffalo *M, D*
  Stony Brook *D*

Structural engineering

California
California State Polytechnic
  University: Pomona *M*
University of California
  San Diego *B, M, D*
University of Southern
  California *B, M*

Illinois
University of Illinois
  Urbana-Champaign *B, M, D*

Massachusetts
Bristol Community College *A*

Michigan
Western Michigan University *B*

Missouri
Washington University in St.
  Louis *M, D*

New Jersey
Stevens Institute of Technology *M*

New York
State University of New York
  Buffalo *B*

Ohio
Youngstown State University *B*

Pennsylvania
Lehigh University *B*
Penn State
  Harrisburg *B*

Wisconsin
Marquette University *M, D*
Milwaukee School of Engineering *M*

Substance abuse counseling

Alabama
Gadsden State Community College *A*
Wallace State Community College at
  Hanceville *A*

Arizona
Pima Community College *C, A*
Rio Salado College *C, A*
Tohono O'odham Community
  College *C*
University of Phoenix *M*

Arkansas
University of Central Arkansas *B*

California
Allan Hancock College *C*
Alliant International University *C*
Bethany University *C, B*
Butte College *C, A*
California Institute of Integral
  Studies *M, D*
California State University
  East Bay *C*
College of San Mateo *C, A*
College of the Redwoods *C*
Cypress College *C*
Diablo Valley College *C*
East Los Angeles College *C*

Fresno City College *C, A*
Glendale Community College *C*
Imperial Valley College *C, A*
Loma Linda University *M*
Loyola Marymount University *M*
Mendocino College *C, A*
Merced College *C, A*
Modesto Junior College *C*
Mount San Jacinto College *C, A*
Saddleback College *C*
San Diego City College *C, A*
San Jose City College *C, A*
Santa Barbara City College *C, A*
Yuba Community College
  District *C, A*

Connecticut
Gateway Community College *C, A*
Housatonic Community College *A*
Manchester Community College *A*
Middlesex Community College *A*
Naugatuck Valley Community
  College *A*
Northwestern Connecticut
  Community College *A*
Norwalk Community College *A*
Three Rivers Community College *A*
Tunxis Community College *A*

Delaware
Delaware Technical and Community
  College
  Stanton/Wilmington Campus *A*
  Terry Campus *A*

Florida
Florida Community College at
  Jacksonville *A*
St. Petersburg College *C, A*

Illinois
City Colleges of Chicago
  Harold Washington College *C, A*
  Kennedy-King College *C*
College of DuPage *C, A*
College of Lake County *C, A*
Dominican University *B*
Elgin Community College *C*
Governors State University *M*
Moraine Valley Community College *C*
National-Louis University *C, B, M*
Oakton Community College *C*
Prairie State College *A*
Roosevelt University *M*
Triton College *C, A*
Waubonsee Community College *C*

Indiana
Indiana University-Purdue University
  Fort Wayne *B*
Indiana Wesleyan University *A, B*
Vincennes University *C*

Iowa
Graceland University *B*
Iowa Western Community College *A*
Southeastern Community College
  North Campus *A*
University of Iowa *M*

Kansas
Dodge City Community College *A*
Kansas City Kansas Community
  College *C, A*
Neosho County Community
  College *C*
Washburn University of Topeka *A, B*

Louisiana
Northwestern State University *B*
University of Louisiana at Monroe *M*

Maine

University of Southern Maine *M*

Maryland

Community College of Baltimore
County *C, A*
Howard Community College *A*
Towson University *B*
Wor-Wic Community College *C, A*

Massachusetts

Massasoit Community College *C*
Middlesex Community College *C*
North Shore Community College *C, A*
Northern Essex Community
College *C*
Quinsigamond Community College *A*
Springfield College *M*
Stonehill College *C*

Michigan

Lake Superior State University *A*
Madonna University *C*
University of Detroit Mercy *A, B*
Washtenaw Community College *A*
Wayne County Community College *C*
Western Michigan University *C*

Minnesota

Century Community and Technical
College *C, A*
Mesabi Range Community and
Technical College *C, A*
Metropolitan State University *B*
Minneapolis Community and
Technical College *C, A*
Ridgewater College *A*
Rochester Community and Technical
College *C*
St. Cloud State University *B, M*
St. Mary's University of Minnesota *M*
University of Minnesota
Twin Cities *C*

Missouri

Missouri Technical School *B*
Missouri Valley College *B*
St. Charles Community College *A*

Montana

Dawson Community College *A*
Flathead Valley Community College *A*
Fort Belknap College *A*
Fort Peck Community College *A*
Little Big Horn College *A*
Stone Child College *A*
University of Great Falls *A, B*

Nebraska

Bellevue University *B*
Little Priest Tribal College *A*
Vatterott College: Spring Valley *A*

Nevada

Truckee Meadows Community
College *C, A*

New Hampshire

Keene State College *A*
New Hampshire Technical Institute *A*

New Jersey

Georgian Court University *T*
Mercer County Community College *C*

New Mexico

Northern New Mexico College *A*

New York

Broome Community College *A*

Columbia University
School of Nursing *C*
Corning Community College *A*
D'Youville College *C*
Dutchess Community College *C*
Erie Community College
City Campus *A*
Finger Lakes Community College *A*
Genesee Community College *A*
Hudson Valley Community College *A*
Medaille College *C*
Mohawk Valley Community College *A*
Niagara County Community
College *C*
Pace University *M*
St. Joseph's College: Suffolk Campus *C*
Suffolk County Community College *A*
Sullivan County Community
College *A*
Tompkins-Cortland Community
College *A*
Ulster County Community College *A*
Westchester Community College *C, A*

North Carolina

Central Piedmont Community
College *C, A*
East Carolina University *M*
Guilford Technical Community
College *C, A*
Roanoke-Chowan Community
College *A*
Sandhills Community College *A*
Southwestern Community
College *C, A*

North Dakota

Minot State University *B*
University of Mary *B*

Ohio

Columbus State Community
College *C, A*
Kent State University *C*
Sinclair Community College *C*
Southern State Community College *A*
Union Institute & University *B*
University of Akron *C, A*

Oklahoma

Oklahoma State University
Oklahoma City *A*

Oregon

Chemeketa Community College *A*
Lane Community College *A*
Oregon Health & Science
University *C*
Portland Community College *C, A*
Rogue Community College *A*
Southwestern Oregon Community
College *A*

Pennsylvania

Alvernia College *C, B*
College Misericordia *C*
Community College of Allegheny
County *C*
Community College of Philadelphia *C*
Drexel University *B*
Marywood University *B*
Montgomery County Community
College *C*
Northampton County Area
Community College *A*
St. Vincent College *C*
University of Scranton *C*

Rhode Island

Community College of Rhode
Island *A*

South Dakota

Kilian Community College *A*
Oglala Lakota College *A*
Sisseton Wahpeton College *A*
University of South Dakota *B*

Tennessee

Southwest Tennessee Community
College *C*

Texas

Alvin Community College *C*
Amarillo College *C, A*
Angelina College *C, A*
Austin Community College *C, A*
Central Texas College *C, A*
Eastfield College *C, A*
El Paso Community College *A*
Grayson County College *C, A*
Howard College *C, A*
Lamar State College at Port
Arthur *C, A*
Lee College *C, A*
McLennan Community College *C, A*
Midland College *A*
North Harris Montgomery
Community College District *C*
Odessa College *A*
St. Mary's University *M*
San Antonio College *C, A*
Texarkana College *C, A*
Texas Southmost College *C, A*
Tyler Junior College *A*
University of Texas
Pan American *B*

Virginia

J. Sargeant Reynolds Community
College *C*
Northern Virginia Community
College *C, A*

Washington

Bellevue Community College *C*
Clark College *C, A*
Edmonds Community College *C, A*
Lower Columbia College *A*
Peninsula College *C, A*
Pierce College *C, A*
Spokane Falls Community
College *C, A*
Tacoma Community College *C*
Wenatchee Valley College *C, A*
Yakima Valley Community College *C*

West Virginia

Mountain State College *A*

Wisconsin

Chippewa Valley Technical College *A*
Fox Valley Technical College *A*
Gateway Technical College *C*
Marquette University *M*
Moraine Park Technical College *A*
Waukesha County Technical
College *A*

Wyoming

Casper College *C, A*

Surgical technology

Alabama

Calhoun Community College *C*
Community College of the Air
Force *A*
Gadsden State Community College *C*
Southern Union State Community
College *C*
Virginia College *A*

Arizona

Gateway Community College *C, A*
Lamson College *C*

Arkansas

North Arkansas College *C, A*
Southeast Arkansas College *C, A*
University of Arkansas
Fort Smith *C, A*
for Medical Sciences *C, A*

California

Concorde Career College *C*
Saddleback College *C, A*
San Joaquin Valley College Inc. *A*
Silicon Valley College
Western Career College: San Jose *A*
Skyline College *C, A*
Southwestern College *C, A*

Colorado

Cambridge College *A*
Community College of Denver *C*
Concorde Career College *C*
Front Range Community College *C*
Pueblo Community College *C, A*

Connecticut

Manchester Community College *A*

Florida

Brevard Community College *C*
Central Florida Community College *C*
Daytona Beach Community College *C*
Florida Community College at
Jacksonville *C*
Florida Metropolitan University
Brandon Campus *A*
Indian River Community College *C*
Palm Beach Community College *C*
Santa Fe Community College *C*
Southwest Florida College *A*
Southwest Florida College
Tampa *A*

Georgia

Albany Technical College *C*
Athens Technical College *C*
Augusta Technical Institute *C*
Central Georgia Technical College *C*
Chattahoochee Technical College *C*
Coastal Georgia Community
College *C*
Columbus Technical College *C, A*
Darton College *A*
DeKalb Technical College *C*
Georgia Southwestern State
University *A*
Macon State College *A*
Middle Georgia College *A*
Northwestern Technical College *C, A*
Savannah Technical College *C, A*
Southwest Georgia Technical
College *C, A*
Waycross College *A*

Idaho

Boise State University *C*
College of Southern Idaho *C*
Eastern Idaho Technical College *A*

Illinois

City Colleges of Chicago
Malcolm X College *C*
College of DuPage *C, A*
College of Lake County *C*
Elgin Community College *C*
Illinois Central College *C*
John A. Logan College *C*
John Wood Community College *C*
Parkland College *C, A*
Prairie State College *C*

Rend Lake College *C*
Richland Community College *C, A*
Southeastern Illinois College *C*
Triton College *C*
Waubonsee Community College *C*

Indiana

Indiana Business College
  Fort Wayne *A*
  Medical *A*
Ivy Tech State College
  Ivy Tech Community College:
    Central Indiana *A*
  Ivy Tech Community College:
    Columbus *A*
  Ivy Tech Community College: East
    Central *A*
  Ivy Tech Community College:
    Kokomo *A*
  Ivy Tech Community College:
    Lafayette *A*
  Ivy Tech Community College:
    Northwest *A*
  Ivy Tech Community College:
    Southwest *A*
  Ivy Tech Community College:
    Wabash Valley *A*
University of St. Francis *A*
Vincennes University *C*

Iowa

Iowa Lakes Community College *C*
Kirkwood Community College *C, A*
Marshalltown Community College *A*
Mercy College of Health Sciences *C, A*
Western Iowa Tech Community
  College *C*

Kansas

Hutchinson Community College *C*
Johnson County Community
  College *A*
Seward County Community College *C*

Kentucky

Jefferson Community College *C*
Maysville Community College *C, A*
Somerset Community College *C*
Spencerian College *C*

Louisiana

Bossier Parish Community College *C*
Delgado Community College *C*
Our Lady of the Lake College *A*
Southern University
  Shreveport *A*

Maine

Southern Maine Community
  College *A*

Maryland

Baltimore City Community College *C*
Chesapeake College *C*
Frederick Community College *C*
Howard Community College *C, A*

Massachusetts

Bunker Hill Community College *C*
Massachusetts Bay Community
  College *C*
North Shore Community College *C*
Quincy College *C*
Quinsigamond Community College *C*
Springfield Technical Community
  College *A*

Michigan

Baker College
  of Cadillac *A*
  of Clinton Township *A*
  of Flint *A*

of Jackson *A*
  of Muskegon *A*
  of Port Huron *A*
Delta College *C, A*
Kalamazoo Valley Community
  College *A*
Lansing Community College *A*
Macomb Community College *C, A*
Northern Michigan University *C*
Oakland Community College *C*
Washtenaw Community College *C*
Wayne County Community College *A*

Minnesota

Anoka Technical College *C*
High-Tech Institute *A*
Lake Superior College *C, A*
Northland Community & Technical
  College *A*
Rochester Community and Technical
  College *A*
St. Cloud Technical College *C, A*
St. Mary's University of Minnesota *C*

Mississippi

Hinds Community College *C, A*
Itawamba Community College *C, A*

Missouri

Ozarks Technical Community
  College *C*
Penn Valley Community College *C*
Three Rivers Community College *C*

Montana

Montana State University
  Billings *A*
University of Montana: Missoula *A*

Nebraska

Metropolitan Community
  College *C, A*
Nebraska Methodist College of
  Nursing and Allied Health *C*
Northeast Community College *A*
Southeast Community College
  Lincoln Campus *C, A*

Nevada

High-Tech Institute *A*

New Hampshire

New Hampshire Community
  Technical College
  Stratham *A*

New Jersey

Bergen Community College *C*
Ocean County College *C*
University of Medicine and Dentistry
  of New Jersey
  School of Health Related
    Professions *C*

New Mexico

Albuquerque Technical-Vocational
  Institute *C*

New York

Nassau Community College *A*
Niagara County Community
  College *A*
Onondaga Community College *C*
Trocaire College *A*

North Carolina

Blue Ridge Community College *C, A*
Cabarrus College of Health
  Sciences *C, A*
Carolinas College of Health
  Sciences *C*
Catawba Valley Community College *C*

Coastal Carolina Community
  College *C, A*
College of the Albemarle *C*
Durham Technical Community
  College *C*
Edgecombe Community College *C*
Fayetteville Technical Community
  College *A, D*
Guilford Technical Community
  College *C, A*
Lenoir Community College *C*
Miller-Motte Technical College *A*
Rockingham Community College *C*
Sandhills Community College *C, A*
Wake Technical Community
  College *A*
Wilson Technical Community
  College *C*

North Dakota

Bismarck State College *A*

Ohio

Central Ohio Technical College *A*
Cincinnati State Technical and
  Community College *A*
Columbus State Community
  College *C, A*
Cuyahoga Community College
  Metropolitan Campus *A*
Lakeland Community College *A*
Mount Carmel College of Nursing *C*
Owens Community College
  Toledo *A*
Sinclair Community College *A*
University of Akron *C, A*
University of Akron: Wayne College *A*
University of Cincinnati
  Clermont College *A*

Oregon

Mount Hood Community College *A*

Pennsylvania

Community College of Allegheny
  County *C, A*
Delaware County Community
  College *C, A*
Harrisburg Area Community
  College *C, A*
International Academy of Design and
  Technology: Pittsburgh *A*
Lock Haven University of
  Pennsylvania *A*
Luzerne County Community
  College *A*
Montgomery County Community
  College *C, A*
Mount Aloysius College *C, A*
Northampton County Area
  Community College *A*
Pennsylvania College of
  Technology *C, A, B*
Pittsburgh Technical Institute *A*
University of Pittsburgh
  Johnstown *A*
Western School of Health and
  Business Careers *A*
Western School of Health and
  Business Careers
  Monroeville *A*
Westmoreland County Community
  College *C*

Rhode Island

New England Institute of
  Technology *A*

South Carolina

Aiken Technical College *C*
Central Carolina Technical College *C*
Florence-Darlington Technical
  College *C*

Greenville Technical College *C*
Horry-Georgetown Technical
  College *C*
Midlands Technical College *C*
Miller-Motte Technical College *A*
Piedmont Technical College *C*
Spartanburg Technical College *C*
Tri-County Technical College *C*

South Dakota

Presentation College *A*
Southeast Technical Institute *C*

Tennessee

Dyersburg State Community
  College *C*
Miller-Motte Technical College *A*
Nashville State Community College *C*
Northeast State Technical Community
  College *C*

Texas

Amarillo College *C, A*
Austin Community College *C, A*
Del Mar College *C, A*
El Centro College *C*
El Paso Community College *A*
Galveston College *C*
Houston Community College
  System *C*
Kilgore College *C, A*
Lamar State College at Port
  Arthur *C, A*
Odessa College *A*
St. Philip's College *C*
San Jacinto College
  Central Campus *C*
South Plains College *C*
Tarrant County College *C*
Temple College *C*
Texas State Technical College
  Harlingen *C, A*
Trinity Valley Community College *C*
Tyler Junior College *C, A*
Wharton County Junior College *C*

Utah

Dixie State College of Utah *C*
Salt Lake Community College *A*
Stevens-Henager College *A*

Virginia

J. Sargeant Reynolds Community
  College *C*
Miller-Motte Technical College:
  Lynchburg *A*
Piedmont Virginia Community
  College *C*
Virginia Western Community
  College *C*

Washington

Bellingham Technical College *A*
Clover Park Technical College *C*
Renton Technical College *A*
Seattle Central Community College *C*
Spokane Community College *A*
Yakima Valley Community College *C*

West Virginia

Mountain State University *A*
West Virginia Northern Community
  College *C, A*
West Virginia University at
  Parkersburg *C*

Wisconsin

Gateway Technical College *C, A*
Lakeshore Technical College *C*
Madison Area Technical College *C*
Mid-State Technical College *C*
Milwaukee Area Technical College *A*

Nicolet Area Technical College *A*
Northcentral Technical College *A*
Northeast Wisconsin Technical
College *C*
Waukesha County Technical
College *A*
Western Wisconsin Technical
College *C*

Wyoming
Central Wyoming College *A*
Laramie County Community
College *A*

Surveying engineering

Indiana
Vincennes University *A*

Iowa
Des Moines Area Community
College *A*

Michigan
Michigan Technological University *B*

Nevada
Great Basin College *B*

New York
Paul Smith's College *A*
State University of New York
College of Technology at
Alfred *A, B*

North Carolina
Southwestern Community College *A*

Oklahoma
Oklahoma State University
Oklahoma City *A*

Surveying technology

Alabama
Troy University *B*

Alaska
University of Alaska
Anchorage *A, B*

Arkansas
University of Arkansas
Monticello *A, B*

California
California State University
Fresno *B*
Chabot College *A*
City College of San Francisco *C*
Coastline Community College *C*
Cuyamaca College *A*
Diablo Valley College *C*
Palomar College *C, A*
Santa Ana College *C, A*
Shasta College *C*

Colorado
Metropolitan State College of
Denver *B*
Westwood College of Technology *A*

Delaware
Delaware Technical and Community
College
Terry Campus *C, A*

Florida
Palm Beach Community College *A*
University of Florida *B*

Georgia
Albany Technical College *C*
Middle Georgia College *A*
Northwestern Technical College *C*
Southern Polytechnic State
University *C, B*

Idaho
Idaho State University *B*

Illinois
Morrison Institute of Technology *A*
Parkland College *A*
Rend Lake College *A*
Waubonsee Community College *C*

Indiana
Purdue University *B*
Vincennes University *A*

Iowa
Kirkwood Community College *A*

Maine
University of Maine *B, M, D*

Maryland
College of Southern Maryland *C*
Community College of Baltimore
County *C, A*

Massachusetts
Wentworth Institute of Technology *C*

Michigan
Ferris State University *C, A, B*
Macomb Community College *C, A*
Montcalm Community College *A*
Mott Community College *A*

Minnesota
St. Cloud State University *B*
St. Paul College *C, A*

Missouri
Longview Community College *A*

Montana
Flathead Valley Community College *A*
Montana Tech of the University of
Montana *A*

Nevada
Community College of Southern
Nevada *A*

New Hampshire
New Hampshire Community
Technical College
Berlin *A*
University of New Hampshire *A*

New Jersey
Essex County College *A*
Gloucester County College *A*
Middlesex County College *A*
Ocean County College *A*
Thomas Edison State College *A, B*

New Mexico
Albuquerque Technical-Vocational
Institute *C, A*
New Mexico State University *B*
San Juan College *A*
Southwestern Indian Polytechnic
Institute *A*

New York
Mohawk Valley Community
College *C, A*

Orange County Community College *C*
Paul Smith's College *A*
State University of New York
College of Environmental Science
and Forestry *A*
College of Technology at
Alfred *A, B*
Sullivan County Community
College *A*

North Carolina
Asheville-Buncombe Technical
Community College *A*
Central Carolina Community
College *A*
Central Piedmont Community
College *C, A*
Fayetteville Technical Community
College *A*
Guilford Technical Community
College *A*
Sandhills Community College *A*
Tri-County Community College *A*
Wake Technical Community
College *A*

Ohio
Cincinnati State Technical and
Community College *C, A*
Columbus State Community
College *C*
James A. Rhodes State College *C*
Lakeland Community College *C*
Ohio State University
Columbus Campus *B*
Owens Community College
Toledo *C, A*
Sinclair Community College *A*
Stark State College of Technology *A*
University of Akron *A*

Oklahoma
Oklahoma State University
Oklahoma City *A*

Oregon
Chemeketa Community College *C*
Oregon Institute of Technology *B*

Pennsylvania
Penn State
University Park *B*
Wilkes-Barre *A, B*
Pennsylvania College of Technology *A*
Temple University *A*

Puerto Rico
Universidad Politecnica de Puerto
Rico *B*
University of Puerto Rico
Mayaguez *B*

South Carolina
Piedmont Technical College *A*
Trident Technical College *C*

South Dakota
Southeast Technical Institute *A*

Tennessee
East Tennessee State University *B*

Texas
Austin Community College *C, A*
Tyler Junior College *C, A*

Utah
Salt Lake Community College *A*

Virginia
J. Sargeant Reynolds Community
College *C*
Virginia Western Community
College *C*

Washington
Bellingham Technical College *C, A*
Centralia College *A*
Peninsula College *A*
Renton Technical College *C, A*
Walla Walla Community College *C*

West Virginia
Glenville State College *A*

Wisconsin
Nicolet Area Technical College *A*

Wyoming
Sheridan College *C, A*
University of Wyoming *C*

Swedish

Washington
University of Washington *B*

System administration

Alabama
American Sentinel University *B*

Alaska
University of Alaska
Southeast *C*

Arizona
Collins College *A, B*
Eastern Arizona College *A*
Gateway Community College *C, A*
Glendale Community College *C*
Paradise Valley Community College *C*
South Mountain Community
College *A*
Tohono O'odham Community
College *A*

Arkansas
East Arkansas Community College *C*

California
CEI College
Maric College: Panorama City *A*
DeVry University
West Hills *A*
Long Beach City College *C*
MTI College *C, A*
Ohlone College *A*
Platt College
Ontario *A*
Sierra College *C, A*
Silicon Valley College
Western Career College:
Emeryville *A*

Colorado
Colorado Technical University *B*
Jones International University *C, B*
National American University
Denver *B*
Remington College
Colorado Springs *B*
Westwood College of Technology
South *A, B*

Florida
Florida National College *A*
Florida State University *M*
New England Institute of
Technology *C, A*

Remington College: Largo *A, B*
Southwest Florida College *C*

Illinois
Heartland Community College *C*
Kaskaskia College *A*
Lincoln Land Community College *C*
Moraine Valley Community College *C*
Morton College *C*
Richland Community College *C*

Indiana
Indiana University-Purdue University
    Indianapolis *A, B*

Iowa
AIB College of Business *A*
Dordt College *B*
Hamilton College
    Cedar Falls *A*
North Iowa Area Community
    College *A*
Northwest Iowa Community
    College *A*

Kansas
Central Christian College of Kansas *A*
Tabor College *B*

Kentucky
Louisville Technical Institute *A*
Maysville Community College *C, A*

Maryland
Frederick Community College *A*
Hagerstown Business College *A*

Massachusetts
Bunker Hill Community College *C, A*
Springfield Technical Community
    College *C, A*

Michigan
Cleary University *A*
Michigan Technological University *B*
Mott Community College *C*
Oakland Community College *C*

Minnesota
Academy College *C, A*
Globe College *C, A, B*
Minnesota School of Business *C, A*
Rasmussen College
    St. Cloud *C, A*
University of Minnesota
    Crookston *B*

Missouri
Crowder College *A*
Vatterott College *A*
Vatterott College: Springfield *A*

Montana
University of Great Falls *B*

Nevada
Community College of Southern
    Nevada *C*

New Hampshire
Daniel Webster College *C*

New York
Globe Institute of Technology *C, A, B*
Rochester Institute of
    Technology *B, M*
Sage College of Albany *A, B*
State University of New York
    College of Agriculture and
      Technology at Morrisville *B*

North Carolina
Brunswick Community College *C*
College of the Albemarle *C*

North Dakota
Williston State College *A*

Ohio
Southeastern Business College *A*
Southeastern Business College:
    Jackson *A*

Oklahoma
Oklahoma State University
    Oklahoma City *C*

Oregon
Linn-Benton Community College *A*

Pennsylvania
Keystone College *C*
Peirce College *C, A*
Pittsburgh Technical Institute *C*
South Hills School of Business &
    Technology *C, A*

South Carolina
Limestone College *B*
York Technical College *C*

Tennessee
Southern Adventist University *B*

Texas
MTI College of Business and
    Technology *C*
San Antonio College *C, A*
Temple College *C, A*
Victoria College *C, A*

Utah
Salt Lake Community College *C*

Vermont
Champlain College *A, B*
Vermont Technical College *A, B*

Virginia
ECPI College of Technology *C, A*

Washington
Heritage University *C*

Systematic biology

Colorado
University of Colorado
    Boulder *B, M, D*

Pennsylvania
Marywood University *B*

Vermont
Sterling College *B*

Systems engineering

Arizona
University of Arizona *B, M, D*

Arkansas
University of Arkansas
    Little Rock *B*

California
California State University
    Fullerton *M*
    Northridge *M*
Loyola Marymount University *M*

National University *B*
Northwestern Polytechnic
    University *B, M*
University of California
    San Diego *B, M, D*
University of Southern
    California *B, M, D*

Colorado
United States Air Force Academy *B*

District of Columbia
Howard University *B, M*

Florida
Florida Atlantic University *M*
Florida Institute of Technology *B, M*
Florida International University *B*
University of Florida *B, M*

Georgia
Southern Polytechnic State
    University *M*

Idaho
University of Idaho *M*

Illinois
University of Illinois
    Urbana-Champaign *M, D*

Indiana
Rose-Hulman Institute of
    Technology *M*

Iowa
Iowa State University *M*

Louisiana
Louisiana Tech University *M*

Maine
Maine Maritime Academy *B*
University of Maine *B*

Maryland
United States Naval Academy *B*
University of Maryland
    College Park *M*

Massachusetts
Massachusetts Institute of
    Technology *M, D*
Worcester Polytechnic Institute *B, M*

Michigan
Oakland University *B, M, D*
University of Michigan *M*

Minnesota
University of St. Thomas *B, M*

Missouri
University of Missouri
    Rolla *M*
Washington University in St.
    Louis *B, M, D*

Nebraska
University of Nebraska
    Lincoln *M*

New Hampshire
University of New Hampshire *D*

New Jersey
Stevens Institute of Technology *M, D*

New York
Cornell University *B, M, D*

Polytechnic University *M*
Rensselaer Polytechnic
    Institute *B, M, D*
Rochester Institute of
    Technology *B, M*
State University of New York
    Binghamton *M, D*
    College of Environmental Science
      and Forestry *M, D*
United States Merchant Marine
    Academy *B*
United States Military Academy *B*

North Carolina
East Carolina University *B*

Ohio
Case Western Reserve
    University *B, M, D*
Jefferson Community College *A*
Ohio State University
    Columbus Campus *B, M, D*
Wright State University *B*

Oregon
Portland State University *M*

Pennsylvania
Lehigh University *M*
University of Pennsylvania *B, M, D*

Puerto Rico
University of Puerto Rico
    Mayaguez *M*

Rhode Island
Johnson & Wales University *B*

Texas
St. Mary's University *M*
Southern Methodist University *M*
Texas A&M University *B*
Texas A&M University
    Galveston *B*
University of Houston *M, D*
University of Texas
    Arlington *M*

Virginia
George Mason University *B, M*
Old Dominion University *M*
University of Virginia *B, M, D*
Virginia Polytechnic Institute and
    State University *M*

Wisconsin
Marquette University *M, D*
University of Wisconsin
    Madison *M*

Systems science/theory

California
Stanford University *B*

Florida
University of Central Florida *M, D*
University of Miami *M*

Idaho
Idaho State University *M*

Indiana
Indiana University
    Bloomington *B, D*

Massachusetts
Worcester Polytechnic Institute *M*

Missouri

Washington University in St. Louis *B, M, D*

Ohio

Kent State University *M*
Wright State University *B*

Oregon

Portland State University *D*

Pennsylvania

Carnegie Mellon University *B*
La Salle University *B*

Rhode Island

Providence College *B*

Vermont

Sterling College *B*

Washington

Bastyr University *M*

West Virginia

Marshall University *B*
West Virginia University at Parkersburg *A*

Talmudic studies

Florida

Yeshiva Gedolah Rabbinical College *B, M*

Illinois

Telshe Yeshiva-Chicago *B, M*

Maryland

Baltimore Hebrew University *B, M, D*
Yeshiva College of the Nations Capital *B*

Michigan

Michigan Jewish Institute *C*
Yeshiva Beth Yehuda-Yeshiva Gedolah of Greater Detroit *B, M, D*

New Jersey

Beth Medrash Govoha *B*

New York

Machzikei Hadath Rabbinical College *B*
Rabbinical Academy Mesivta Rabbi Chaim Berlin *B, M, D*
Rabbinical College Beth Shraga *B*
Yeshiva Derech Chaim *B, D*
Yeshiva Mikdash Melech *B, M*
Yeshiva and Kolel Bais Medrash Elyon *B, M*

Ohio

Rabbinical College of Telshe *B, M, D*

Pennsylvania

Talmudical Yeshiva of Philadelphia *B*
Yeshivath Beth Moshe *B, M*

Taxation

Alabama

University of Alabama *M*

Arizona

Arizona State University *M*

California

California State University
  East Bay *M*
  Fullerton *M*
  Northridge *M*
  Sacramento *B, M*
  San Bernardino *M*
De Anza College *C, A*
Golden Gate University *M*
National University *M*
San Diego State University *M*
San Jose State University *M*
Santa Rosa Junior College *C*
University of Southern California *M*
Yuba Community College District *A*

Colorado

Colorado Technical University *C*
University of Colorado
  Boulder *M*
University of Denver *M*

Connecticut

Manchester Community College *C*
University of New Haven *M*

District of Columbia

American University *M*
Southeastern University *M*

Florida

Florida Atlantic University *M*
Florida International University *M*
Florida State University *M*
Nova Southeastern University *M*
University of Central Florida *M*
University of Miami *M*

Georgia

Georgia State University *M*

Illinois

DePaul University *M*
Northern Illinois University *M*
St. Xavier University *M*
University of Illinois
  Urbana-Champaign *M*

Louisiana

University of New Orleans *M*

Maine

Thomas College *M*

Maryland

University of Baltimore *M*

Massachusetts

American International College *M*
Bentley College *M*
Boston University *M*
Northeastern University *M*
Suffolk University *M*

Michigan

Grand Valley State University *M*
Walsh College of Accountancy and Business Administration *M*
Washtenaw Community College *C*
Wayne State University *M*

Minnesota

University of Minnesota
  Twin Cities *M*

Mississippi

Mississippi State University *M*
University of Mississippi *M*

Missouri

Fontbonne University *M*

New Hampshire

McIntosh College *A*

New Jersey

Fairleigh Dickinson University College at Florham *M*
Rutgers, The State University of New Jersey
  New Brunswick/Piscataway Campus *M*
  Newark Regional Campus *M*
Seton Hall University *M*

New York

City University of New York
  Baruch College *M*
Hofstra University *M*
Long Island University
  Brooklyn Campus *M*
  C.W. Post Campus *M*
Pace University *M*
St. John's University *M*
State University of New York
  Albany *M*

North Carolina

Cape Fear Community College *C*

Ohio

Capital University *M*
Stark State College of Technology *A*
University of Akron *M*
University of Cincinnati
  Clermont College *C*
University of Toledo *M*

Oklahoma

University of Tulsa *M*

Pennsylvania

Drexel University *M*
Duquesne University *M*
Penn State
  University Park *C*
Philadelphia University *M*
Robert Morris University *M*
Temple University *C*
Villanova University *M*
Widener University *M*

Puerto Rico

Turabo University *M*
University of the Sacred Heart *M*

Rhode Island

Bryant University *M*

Texas

Baylor University *M*
Navarro College *A*
Texas A&M University *M*
University of Houston *M*
University of North Texas *M*
University of Texas
  Arlington *M, D*
  San Antonio *M*

Virginia

ECPI College of Technology *C, A*
George Mason University *M*
Virginia Commonwealth University *M*

Taxidermy

New York

Finger Lakes Community College *C*

North Carolina

Montgomery Community College *C*

Teacher assistance

Arizona

Estrella Mountain Community College *A*
Mesa Community College *A*

California

American River College *A*
Antelope Valley College *A*
Barstow College *A*
Cerritos Community College *A*
Chabot College *A*
City College of San Francisco *A*
College of Alameda *A*
Contra Costa College *A*
Long Beach City College *A*
Los Angeles Mission College *A*
Los Angeles Southwest College *A*
Mount St. Mary's College *A*
Shasta College *A*
Sierra College *A*

Colorado

Otero Junior College *A*

Connecticut

Manchester Community College *A*
Sacred Heart University *A*

Florida

South Florida Community College *A*

Georgia

Darton College *A*

Illinois

City Colleges of Chicago
  Harold Washington College *A*
  Malcolm X College *A*
Heartland Community College *A*
Illinois Eastern Community Colleges
  Lincoln Trail College *A*
John A. Logan College *A*
Joliet Junior College *A*
Kaskaskia College *A*
Lewis and Clark Community College *A*
MacCormac College *A*
Moraine Valley Community College *C*
South Suburban College of Cook County *A*
Waubonsee Community College *A*
William Rainey Harper College *A*

Indiana

Valparaiso University *A*

Iowa

Dordt College *A*
Ellsworth Community College *A*

Kansas

Butler County Community College *A*
Seward County Community College *A*

Kentucky

Elizabethtown Community and Technical College *A*
Hopkinsville Community College *A*
Jefferson Community College *A*
Somerset Community College *A*

Maine

Kennebec Valley Community College *A*

Massachusetts

Massasoit Community College *A*
North Shore Community College *A*

Michigan
Baker College
  of Cadillac A
  of Flint A
  of Port Huron A
Gogebic Community College A
Kirtland Community College A
Mid Michigan Community College A
Mott Community College A
Southwestern Michigan College A

Minnesota
Central Lakes College A
Minnesota State Community and
  Technical College - Fergus Falls A
Northwest Technical College A
Ridgewater College A
Rochester Community and Technical
  College A
St. Cloud Technical College A

Missouri
St. Charles Community College A
St. Louis Community College
St. Louis Community College at
  Florissant Valley A

Montana
University of Montana: Western A

New Jersey
Brookdale Community College A
Middlesex County College A

New Mexico
Clovis Community College A
Eastern New Mexico University:
  Roswell Campus A
New Mexico State University A
New Mexico State University
  Alamogordo A
University of New Mexico A

New York
City University of New York
  Bronx Community College A
  Kingsborough Community
    College A
Dutchess Community College A
Herkimer County Community
  College A
Maria College A

North Carolina
Carteret Community College A
Craven Community College A
Durham Technical Community
  College A
Edgecombe Community College A
Halifax Community College A
Lenoir Community College A
Mitchell Community College A
Nash Community College A
Roanoke-Chowan Community
  College A
Sandhills Community College A
Vance-Granville Community
  College A

North Dakota
Minot State University: Bottineau
  Campus A
Williston State College A

Ohio
Hocking College A
Southern State Community College A
Tiffin University A

Oregon
Blue Mountain Community College A
Chemeketa Community College A

Linn-Benton Community College A

Pennsylvania
Bucks County Community College A
Community College of Allegheny
  County A
Community College of Beaver
  County A
Delaware County Community
  College A
Laurel Business Institute A
Montgomery County Community
  College A
Northampton County Area
  Community College A

Puerto Rico
Pontifical Catholic University of
  Puerto Rico A
Turabo University T

South Carolina
Forrest Junior College A
Southern Wesleyan University A
Williamsburg Technical College A

South Dakota
Black Hills State University A
Oglala Lakota College A
University of Sioux Falls A

Tennessee
Johnson Bible College A

Texas
El Centro College A
Midland College A
North Lake College A
Odessa College A
Richland College A
St. Philip's College A
San Antonio College A
Temple College A
Texas State Technical College
  Harlingen A

Virginia
Eastern Mennonite University B
John Tyler Community College A
Tidewater Community College A

Washington
Big Bend Community College A
Clover Park Technical College A
Grays Harbor College A
Highline Community College A
Lower Columbia College A
Pierce College A
Renton Technical College A
Shoreline Community College A
Spokane Falls Community College A
Tacoma Community College A
Walla Walla Community College A
Whatcom Community College A

West Virginia
West Virginia University at
  Parkersburg A

Wisconsin
Alverno College A
Southwest Wisconsin Technical
  College A
Western Wisconsin Technical
  College A

Wyoming
Casper College A
Central Wyoming College A

Teacher education, multiple levels

Alabama
Alabama State University M
Auburn University D, T
Huntingdon College B, T
Lawson State Community College A
Samford University B
Troy University B, M, T
University of North Alabama B, M

Alaska
University of Alaska
  Anchorage M

Arizona
Central Arizona College A
Northcentral University M, D
Prescott College B, M, T

Arkansas
Harding University B, M, T
South Arkansas Community College A
University of the Ozarks T

California
Alliant International University T
Azusa Pacific University B, T
California State University
  Sacramento M, T
Fresno City College A
Glendale Community College A
Hope International University T
Mills College M
National University T
Notre Dame de Namur University M
Occidental College M
Pepperdine University T
Simpson University T
University of California
  Irvine M
University of San Francisco M
University of the Pacific B, T
Vanguard University of Southern
  California T
Whittier College T
William Jessup University B

Colorado
Adams State College B, T
Colorado College M
University of Denver M

Connecticut
Quinnipiac University B, M

District of Columbia
George Washington University M
Howard University M

Florida
Edward Waters College T
Flagler College B
Lynn University B

Georgia
Atlanta Metropolitan College A
Darton College A
East Georgia College A
Georgia Highlands College A
Gordon College A
Macon State College A

Hawaii
Chaminade University of
  Honolulu M, T
University of Hawaii
  Manoa M

Idaho
Boise State University T

Illinois
Blackburn College B, T
Chicago State University B
Concordia University B, M, T
Dominican University M
Eureka College B
Judson College B, M
Kankakee Community College A
Monmouth College B, T
North Park University B, M
Quincy University T
Roosevelt University B
Sauk Valley Community College A
Southern Illinois University
  Carbondale M
University of Illinois
  Urbana-Champaign B, M, D, T
Waubonsee Community College A

Indiana
Earlham College M
Indiana University
  Bloomington B, T
Manchester College B, T
Purdue University
  Calumet B
University of Indianapolis T
University of Notre Dame M
Vincennes University A

Iowa
Buena Vista University B, T
Ellsworth Community College A
Loras College B
Waldorf College B

Kansas
Bethany College T
Bethel College T
Central Christian College of Kansas A
Coffeyville Community College A
Friends University T
Tabor College B, T

Kentucky
Asbury College M, T
Eastern Kentucky University M
Midway College B

Louisiana
Centenary College of Louisiana B, T
Xavier University of Louisiana B, T

Maine
University of Maine
  Farmington B, T
  Fort Kent B
University of New England M
University of Southern Maine T

Maryland
Baltimore City Community College A
Carroll Community College A
Coppin State University M
Frederick Community College A
Goucher College M
Harford Community College A
Morgan State University B, T

Massachusetts
Brandeis University M
Framingham State College M
Lesley University M
Merrimack College T
Northeastern University B
Smith College M
University of Massachusetts
  Dartmouth M

Michigan

Adrian College *B*
Baker College
  of Auburn Hills *B*
  of Muskegon *B*
  of Owosso *B*
Hillsdale College *B*
Hope College *T*
Lake Superior State University *B, T*
Madonna University *T*
Olivet College *B, T*
University of Michigan *B*

Minnesota

Capella University *M, D*
Martin Luther College *B*
Minnesota State University
  Mankato *M*
Ridgewater College *A*
St. Cloud State University *B*
St. Mary's University of Minnesota *M*
Winona State University *B, M, T*

Mississippi

Alcorn State University *M*
Delta State University *M*
Jackson State University *M*
Mississippi Gulf Coast Community
  College
  Jefferson Davis Campus *A*
Pearl River Community College *A*

Missouri

Central Missouri State University *T*
Harris-Stowe State University *B, T*
Missouri Baptist University *M, T*
Missouri Southern State
  University *B, T*
St. Louis University *B, M, D*
Washington University in St. Louis *T*
William Jewell College *T*
William Woods University *T*

Montana

Rocky Mountain College *B, T*
University of Montana: Western *B, T*

Nebraska

Concordia University *B, T*
Dana College *B*
Hastings College *T*
Midland Lutheran College *B*
University of Nebraska
  Lincoln *B*
York College *B, T*

Nevada

Sierra Nevada College *M*

New Hampshire

New Hampshire Community
  Technical College
  Berlin *A*
Plymouth State University *M, T*

New Jersey

Caldwell College *T*
College of St. Elizabeth *T*
Cumberland County College *A*
Fairleigh Dickinson University
  College at Florham *M*
  Metropolitan Campus *M*
Gloucester County College *A*
Richard Stockton College of New
  Jersey *A*
St. Peter's College *M*

New Mexico

New Mexico Institute of Mining and
  Technology *T*
Western New Mexico University *M*

New York

City University of New York
  Medgar Evers College *A*
College of Saint Rose *M, T*
Columbia-Greene Community
  College *A*
D'Youville College *B, M, T*
Dowling College *B, M*
Elmira College *B, M, T*
Hofstra University *B, M*
Iona College *B*
Ithaca College *B, M, T*
Jewish Theological Seminary of
  America *M, D*
Mount St. Mary College *B, M, T*
Pace University *M*
St. Bonaventure University *M*
St. Thomas Aquinas College *B, M, T*
Schenectady County Community
  College *A*
State University of New York
  Buffalo *M, T*
  College at Oneonta *B*
  College at Plattsburgh *B*
  New Paltz *M*
University of Rochester *M*

North Carolina

Brevard College *B*
Gardner-Webb University *B*
Halifax Community College *A*
University of North Carolina
  Asheville *T*
  Charlotte *M*

North Dakota

North Dakota State University *M*
Sitting Bull College *A*

Ohio

Central State University *B*
Defiance College *B*
John Carroll University *M, T*
Marietta College *B*
Mount Union College *T*
Ohio Wesleyan University *B*
Otterbein College *B*
Owens Community College
  Toledo *A*
Shawnee State University *B*
University of Dayton *B, M, T*
University of Findlay *B, M, T*
University of Rio Grande *B, T*
Washington State Community
  College *A*
Wilmington College *B*
Wright State University *M*
Youngstown State University *B, M*

Oklahoma

Oklahoma City Community College *A*
Oral Roberts University *M*
Rose State College *A*
Southeastern Oklahoma State
  University *B, M, T*
Southwestern Oklahoma State
  University *M*

Oregon

Concordia University *B, M, T*
Corban College *B*
George Fox University *M, T*
Lewis & Clark College *M*
Linfield College *T*
Northwest Christian College *B, T*
University of Oregon *B*
Warner Pacific College *T*
Western Oregon University *B, T*

Pennsylvania

Arcadia University *B, M, T*
Baptist Bible College of
  Pennsylvania *B, M*
Chestnut Hill College *B, T*
Delaware County Community
  College *A*
Edinboro University of
  Pennsylvania *M*
Elizabethtown College *B*
Gannon University *B*
Gettysburg College *T*
Juniata College *B*
Keystone College *B, T*
La Salle University *B, T*
Mansfield University of
  Pennsylvania *B, T*
Marywood University *B, M*
Moravian College *T*
Pennsylvania Highlands Community
  College *A*
St. Francis University *B, M, T*
Westminster College *B, T*

Rhode Island

Rhode Island College *B*

South Carolina

Anderson University *B, T*
Columbia International University *B*
Furman University *T*
University of South Carolina *M*
Winthrop University *T*

South Dakota

Dakota State University *B, T*
Northern State University *B, M, T*
University of Sioux Falls *B*

Tennessee

Cumberland University *B, M*
Freed-Hardeman University *B, T*
LeMoyne-Owen College *T*
Southern Adventist University *M*
Tennessee Wesleyan College *T*
Trevecca Nazarene University *M, T*
University of Memphis *B*
University of Tennessee
  Knoxville *M*
  Martin *M*

Texas

Howard Payne University *B, T*
LeTourneau University *B, T*
Lubbock Christian University *B*
St. Edward's University *T*
St. Mary's University *T*
San Antonio College *A*
Tarleton State University *M, T*
Texas A&M University
  Commerce *B*
Texas Lutheran University *B, T*
Texas Wesleyan University *B, T*
University of Mary Hardin-Baylor *T*
University of Texas
  of the Permian Basin *M*
West Texas A&M University *T*

Utah

Brigham Young University *M*
University of Utah *B, M, D*
Utah State University *B*

Vermont

College of St. Joseph in Vermont *B*
Goddard College *M*
Johnson State College *B, M*

Virginia

Averett University *B, T*
Liberty University *B*
Longwood University *B, T*
Virginia Union University *B*

Washington

Antioch University Seattle *M, T*
City University *T*
Evergreen State College *M, T*
Saint Martin's University *M*
Seattle University *M*
University of Puget Sound *M*
University of Washington *M*
Washington State University *B, M*
Whitworth College *B, M, T*

West Virginia

Alderson-Broaddus College *B, T*
Bethany College *B*
Mountain State University *M*
Ohio Valley University *B*
Salem International University *B, T*

Wisconsin

Beloit College *T*
Concordia University Wisconsin *B*
University of Wisconsin
  Green Bay *T*
  Superior *B, M, T*

Wyoming

Western Wyoming Community
  College *A*

Technical and business writing

Alabama

Auburn University *M*

Alaska

University of Alaska
  Fairbanks *M*

Arizona

Northern Arizona University *C*

Arkansas

University of Arkansas
  Fort Smith *B*
  Little Rock *B, M*

California

De Anza College *C, A*
Orange Coast College *A*
San Francisco State University *C, B*

Colorado

University of Colorado
  Denver and Health Sciences
  Center *M*

Connecticut

University of Hartford *B*

District of Columbia

American University *C*

Florida

University of Central Florida *D*

Georgia

Athens Technical College *C*

Idaho

Boise State University *M, D*

Illinois

Black Hawk College *A*
Chicago State University *B*
College of Lake County *C, A*
Dominican University *B*
Illinois Institute of Technology *B, M*

Indiana

Indiana University-Purdue University
  Fort Wayne *B*

Valparaiso University *B*

Iowa

Iowa State University *B*

Kansas

Central Christian College of Kansas *A*
Pittsburg State University *B*

Kentucky

Murray State University *C*

Louisiana

Nicholls State University *B*

Maryland

Montgomery College *C*
Towson University *M*

Massachusetts

Fitchburg State College *B*
Northeastern University *M*
Salem State College *B*
University of Massachusetts
   Boston *C*
   Dartmouth *M*
Worcester Polytechnic Institute *B*

Michigan

Ferris State University *B*
Grand Valley State University *B*
Kellogg Community College *A*
Madonna University *B*
Michigan State University *B, M*
Michigan Technological University *C*
Northern Michigan University *B, M*
University of Detroit Mercy *B*
Washtenaw Community College *A*

Minnesota

Metropolitan State University *B, M*
Minnesota State University
   Mankato *B, M*
Northwestern College *B*
St. Mary's University of Minnesota *B*
University of Minnesota
   Crookston *B*

Missouri

Missouri Southern State University *B*
Missouri State University *B, M*
St. Louis Community College
   St. Louis Community College at
      Florissant Valley *A*
   St. Louis Community College at
      Meramec *C*
University of Missouri
   Rolla *B*
Webster University *C*

Montana

Montana Tech of the University of
   Montana *B, M*
University of Montana: Missoula *M*

New Jersey

New Jersey Institute of
   Technology *B, M*

New Mexico

College of Santa Fe *B*
New Mexico Institute of Mining and
   Technology *B*

New York

Clarkson University *B*
Medaille College *B*
New York Institute of Technology *C, B*
Rensselaer Polytechnic Institute *M*

State University of New York
   College of Agriculture and
      Technology at Morrisville *A*
   Farmingdale *B*

North Carolina

East Carolina University *D*
North Carolina State University *M*

Ohio

Bowling Green State University *B*
Capital University *B*
Cedarville University *B*
Cincinnati State Technical and
   Community College *C, A*
Cleveland State University *C*
Edison State Community College *C, A*
Miami University
   Oxford Campus *B, M*
Mount Union College *B*
Mount Vernon Nazarene University *B*
Ohio Northern University *B*
University of Findlay *C*
Youngstown State University *B*

Oklahoma

East Central University *B*

Oregon

Linn-Benton Community College *A*
Portland Community College *C*
Portland State University *M*

Pennsylvania

Allegheny College *B*
Cabrini College *B*
Carlow University *B*
Carnegie Mellon University *B, M*
Chatham College *M*
Drexel University *B, M*
Elizabethtown College *B*
Kutztown University of
   Pennsylvania *B*
La Salle University *B*
Mansfield University of
   Pennsylvania *A*
Penn State
   Abington *B*
   University Park *C*
Pennsylvania College of Technology *B*
University of the Sciences in
   Philadelphia *M*
York College of Pennsylvania *B*

South Carolina

Coker College *B*
Winthrop University *B*

Tennessee

Chattanooga State Technical
   Community College *A*
Maryville College *B*
Roane State Community College *A*
Tennessee Technological University *B*

Texas

Austin Community College *C, A*
Lee College *A*
Texas State University: San
   Marcos *M, T*
Texas Tech University *M, D*
University of Houston
   Downtown *B, M*
University of Texas
   El Paso *M*
   San Antonio *B*

Utah

Weber State University *B*

Vermont

Champlain College *B*

Virginia

James Madison University *B, M*
Northern Virginia Community
   College *C*
Thomas Nelson Community
   College *C*

Washington

Eastern Washington University *B, M*
Everett Community College *A*
University of Washington *B*

West Virginia

West Virginia State University *B*
West Virginia University *M*

Wisconsin

Gateway Technical College *A*
Milwaukee School of Engineering *B*
Mount Mary College *B*
University of Wisconsin
   Stout *B*

Technology/industrial arts education

Alabama

Community College of the Air
   Force *A*

Alaska

University of Alaska
   Southeast *M*

Arizona

Arizona Western College *A*
Eastern Arizona College *A*
Northern Arizona University *B, M, T*
Prescott College *B, T*

Arkansas

Arkansas State University *A*
University of Arkansas
   Pine Bluff *T*
University of Central Arkansas *A, M*

California

Azusa Pacific University *M*
California Baptist University *M, T*
California State University
   Los Angeles *B, M*
Cypress College *A*
San Francisco State University *B, T*

Colorado

Colorado State University *T*

Connecticut

Central Connecticut State
   University *B, M, T*
University of Hartford *M*

Delaware

Wilmington College *M*

Florida

Hillsborough Community College *A*
Miami Dade College *A*

Georgia

Darton College *A*
Georgia Southern University *B, M*
University of Georgia *B*
Valdosta State University *M*

Hawaii

University of Hawaii
   Honolulu Community College *A*

Idaho

University of Idaho *B, M, T*

Illinois

Chicago State University *B*
Illinois State University *B*
Sauk Valley Community College *A*

Indiana

Ball State University *B, M, T*
Indiana State University *M*
Purdue University *B, M, D*
Vincennes University *A*

Iowa

Iowa State University *B, M, D, T*
Kaplan University *M*
University of Northern Iowa *B*
William Penn University *B*

Kansas

Fort Hays State University *B*
McPherson College *B, T*
Pittsburg State University *B, M, T*

Kentucky

Berea College *B, T*
Eastern Kentucky University *B, M*
Murray State University *M, T*

Louisiana

Grambling State University *B*
University of Louisiana at Lafayette *B*

Maine

University of Southern Maine *B, T*

Maryland

Loyola College in Maryland *M*
University of Maryland
   Eastern Shore *B, M*

Massachusetts

Fitchburg State College *B, M, T*
Westfield State College *B, T*

Michigan

Central Michigan University *B, M, T*
Delta College *A*
Eastern Michigan University *B, T*
Madonna University *T*
Michigan State University *M, D*
Michigan Technological University *T*
Northern Michigan University *B, T*
Wayne State University *M*
Western Michigan University *B, T*

Minnesota

Bemidji State University *M, T*
Minnesota State University
   Mankato *B, M, T*
St. Cloud State University *B*
University of Minnesota
   Twin Cities *B, M, D, T*

Mississippi

Alcorn State University *B*
Jackson State University *M*
Mississippi State University *D, T*
University of Southern Mississippi *B*

Missouri

Central Missouri State
   University *B, M, T*
College of the Ozarks *B*
Lindenwood University *B*
Missouri Southern State
   University *B, M, T*
Missouri State University *B*
Southeast Missouri State
   University *B, T*

Montana

Montana State University
Bozeman *B*
University of Montana: Western *B, T*

Nebraska

Chadron State College *B, M*
Concordia University *B, T*
University of Nebraska
Kearney *B*
Lincoln *B*
Wayne State College *B, T*

Nevada

University of Nevada
Reno *B*

New Hampshire

Keene State College *B, T*

New Jersey

The College of New Jersey *B, T*
Kean University *B, T*
Montclair State University *B, M, T*

New Mexico

University of New Mexico *B*
Western New Mexico University *B*

New York

City University of New York
New York City College of
Technology *B*
Fashion Institute of Technology *B*
New York Institute of Technology *B, T*
Pace University *M, T*
State University of New York
College at Buffalo *B, M, T*
Oswego *B, M, T*

North Carolina

Appalachian State University *B, M, T*
Elizabeth City State University *B*
North Carolina Agricultural and
Technical State University *B, M, T*
North Carolina State
University *B, M, D, T*

North Dakota

Valley City State University *B, T*

Ohio

Kent State University *B*
Ohio Northern University *B, T*
Ohio State University
Columbus Campus *B*
Youngstown State University *M*

Oklahoma

East Central University *B*
Northeastern State University *B*
Northwestern Oklahoma State
University *B, T*
Oklahoma Panhandle State
University *B*
Southwestern Oklahoma State
University *B, M, T*
University of Central Oklahoma *B*

Oregon

Chemeketa Community College *A*
Oregon State University *B, M*

Pennsylvania

Millersville University of
Pennsylvania *B, M, T*
Pittsburgh Institute of Aeronautics *A*

Puerto Rico

National College of Business &
Technology: Arecibo *B*

National College of Business &
Technology: Bayamon *B*

Rhode Island

Rhode Island College *B, M*

South Carolina

Clemson University *B, M*
Coastal Carolina University *M*
South Carolina State University *B, T*

South Dakota

Black Hills State University *B*

Tennessee

Middle Tennessee State University *B*
Trevecca Nazarene University *M, T*
University of Tennessee
Knoxville *M, D, T*

Texas

El Paso Community College *A*
Prairie View A&M University *M*
Sam Houston State University *M, T*
Sul Ross State University *M*
Texas A&M University
Commerce *M, T*
Kingsville *M*
Texas Southern University *M*
Texas State University: San
Marcos *M, T*
University of Texas
Tyler *M*
Wayland Baptist University *B, T*

Utah

Brigham Young University *B*
Southern Utah University *B, T*
Utah State University *B, D*

Virginia

Old Dominion University *B, M, T*

Washington

Central Washington University *B, T*
Eastern Washington University *B, M, T*
Western Washington University *B*

Wisconsin

University of Wisconsin
Platteville *B, T*
Stout *B, M, T*
Viterbo University *B, T*

Wyoming

Casper College *A*
University of Wyoming *B*

Telecommunications technology

Alabama

Gadsden State Community
College *C, A*

California

College of Oceaneering *C*
National University *M*
Southwestern College *C, A*

Colorado

University of Colorado
Boulder *M*
University of Denver *M*

Florida

Palm Beach Community College *C*
St. Petersburg College *C, A*

Georgia

Southern Polytechnic State
University *B*

Illinois

Moraine Valley Community College *C*

Indiana

Ivy Tech State College
Ivy Tech Community College:
Bloomington *C*
Ivy Tech Community College: North
Central *C, A*
Ivy Tech Community College:
Northeast *A*
Ivy Tech Community College:
Northwest *C, A*
Ivy Tech Community College: South
Central *C, A*
Ivy Tech Community College:
Southeast *C*
Ivy Tech Community College:
Southwest *A*

Maine

University of Southern Maine *B*

Maryland

Capitol College *A, B*
Community College of Baltimore
County *C*
Howard Community College *C, A*
TESST College of Technology
Baltimore *C, A*
TESST College of Technology:
Towson *A*

Massachusetts

Massasoit Community College *C, A*
North Shore Community College *A*
Quinsigamond Community
College *C, A*
Springfield Technical Community
College *A*
Wentworth Institute of Technology *A*

Michigan

Ferris State University *B*
Wayne County Community College *A*

Minnesota

Alexandria Technical College *C, A*
Dakota County Technical College *C, A*
Minnesota State Community and
Technical College - Fergus
Falls *C, A*

Nebraska

University of Nebraska
Lincoln *M*

New York

Canisius College *M*
Cayuga County Community College *A*
City University of New York
New York City College of
Technology *A, B*
Rochester Institute of
Technology *B, M*
St. John's University *C, A, B*
Schenectady County Community
College *A*

Ohio

Marion Technical College *C, A*

Oklahoma

Rose State College *A*

Pennsylvania

Penn State
Abington *B*
Altoona *A*
Beaver *A, B*
Berks *A*
Dubois *A*
Fayette *A*
Hazleton *A*
McKeesport *B*
Mont Alto *B*
New Kensington *A, B*
Schuylkill - Capital College *A, B*
Shenango *A, B*
University Park *B, M*
Wilkes-Barre *A, B*
Worthington Scranton *B*
York *A, B*
Pittsburgh Technical Institute *C*

Puerto Rico

Inter American University of Puerto
Rico
Bayamon Campus *A*
Turabo University *M*

Rhode Island

Community College of Rhode
Island *C, A*

South Carolina

York Technical College *C*

Texas

Collin County Community College
District *C, A*
San Antonio College *C, A*
Texas A&M University *B*
Texas State Technical College
Harlingen *C, A*
Texas State Technical College:
Marshall *C, A*

Utah

Salt Lake Community College *C, A*

Virginia

ECPI College of Technology *C, A*

Washington

Clark College *C, A*

Textile science

Alabama

Auburn University *M*

California

Fashion Institute of Design and
Merchandising *A*
Fashion Institute of Design and
Merchandising
San Diego *A*
San Francisco *A*

Georgia

University of Georgia *D*

New York

Cornell University *B, M, D*

Pennsylvania

Philadelphia University *C, B, M*

Textile sciences/ engineering

Alabama

Auburn University *B*

Georgia

Georgia Institute of
Technology *B, M, D*

Massachusetts

University of Massachusetts
Dartmouth *B, M*

North Carolina

North Carolina State
University *B, M, D*

Pennsylvania

Philadelphia University *B, M, D*

South Carolina

Clemson University *B, M, D*

Theater arts management

California

California Baptist University *B*
California Institute of the Arts *C, B, M*
Ohlone College *C*
University of Southern California *B*

District of Columbia

Howard University *B*

Florida

Florida State University *M*
Nova Southeastern University *B*
University of Miami *B*
Valencia Community College *A*

Georgia

Berry College *B*

Illinois

Lewis University *B*

Indiana

Huntington University *B*
University of Evansville *B*

Iowa

St. Ambrose University *B*
Waldorf College *B*

Kansas

Benedictine College *B*
Central Christian College of
Kansas *A, B*

Maine

University of Southern Maine *B*

Massachusetts

Eastern Nazarene College *B*
Emerson College *B*

Michigan

Aquinas College *B*
Concordia University *B*
Eastern Michigan University *M*
Olivet College *B*

Missouri

Crowder College *A*
Lindenwood University *B, M*

New Jersey

Seton Hall University *B*

New Mexico

College of Santa Fe *B*

New York

City University of New York
Brooklyn College *M*
Lehman College *B*
Ithaca College *B*
State University of New York
College at Buffalo *B*

Ohio

Lake Erie College *B*
Ohio University *B*

Oklahoma

Oklahoma City University *B*

Oregon

University of Portland *B*
Western Oregon University *B*

Pennsylvania

Carnegie Mellon University *M*
Elizabethtown College *B*
Gettysburg College *B*
Marywood University *B*
Seton Hill University *B*
Waynesburg College *B*

South Carolina

North Greenville College *B*

Texas

Texas Tech University *M*

Washington

Pacific Lutheran University *B*

West Virginia

West Virginia Wesleyan College *B*

Wisconsin

University of Wisconsin
Whitewater *B*

Theater design and technology

Alaska

University of Alaska
Fairbanks *B*

Arizona

University of Arizona *B*

California

Allan Hancock College *C*
California Institute of the Arts *C, B, M*
California State University
East Bay *B*
Fresno *B*
Fullerton *B, M*
Long Beach *B, M*
San Bernardino *B*
College of the Sequoias *A*
Cypress College *C, A*
Fashion Institute of Design and
Merchandising *A*
Fashion Institute of Design and
Merchandising
San Diego *A*
San Francisco *A*
Foothill College *C, A*
Fresno City College *C, A*
Gavilan Community College *A*
Glendale Community College *A*
Grossmont Community College *C, A*
Humboldt State University *M*
Irvine Valley College *A*
Long Beach City College *A*
MiraCosta College *C, A*
Ohlone College *C, A*
Palomar College *C*

San Diego State University *B, M*
San Francisco State University *M*
Santa Barbara City College *A*
Santa Rosa Junior College *C*
University of California
Santa Cruz *C, B*
University of Southern
California *B, M*

Colorado

Red Rocks Community College *C, A*

Connecticut

University of Connecticut *B*

Delaware

University of Delaware *B*

District of Columbia

Howard University *B*

Florida

Florida Community College at
Jacksonville *A*
Florida Southern College *B*
Florida State University *B*
University of Miami *B*

Illinois

Columbia College Chicago *B*
DePaul University *B, M*
Illinois Wesleyan University *B*
Millikin University *B*
Rockford College *B*

Indiana

Huntington University *B*
Indiana University
Bloomington *A*
Vincennes University *A*

Iowa

Coe College *B*
Drake University *B*
University of Iowa *M*
University of Northern Iowa *B*

Kansas

Central Christian College of
Kansas *A, B*
University of Kansas *B, M*

Louisiana

Centenary College of Louisiana *B*

Maryland

Howard Community College *A*
Montgomery College *A*
University of Maryland
College Park *M*

Massachusetts

Boston University *B, M*
Brandeis University *M*
Emerson College *B*
Fitchburg State College *B*
Salem State College *B*

Michigan

Michigan Technological University *B*
Oakland University *B*
University of Michigan *B*
University of Michigan
Flint *B*
Western Michigan University *B*

Minnesota

Central Lakes College *A*
Minnesota State University
Mankato *B, T*

University of Minnesota
Duluth *B*

Missouri

College of the Ozarks *B*
Lindenwood University *B*
University of Missouri
Kansas City *M*
Webster University *B*

Montana

Rocky Mountain College *B*

New Hampshire

Franklin Pierce College *B*
Keene State College *B*

New Jersey

Essex County College *A*
Rowan University *B*

New Mexico

College of Santa Fe *B*
San Juan College *A*
University of New Mexico *B*

New York

City University of New York
Brooklyn College *M*
New York City College of
Technology *C, B*
Five Towns College *B*
Fordham University *B*
Genesee Community College *A*
Ithaca College *B*
New York University *M*
Sarah Lawrence College *B, M*
State University of New York
College at Fredonia *B*
New Paltz *B*
Purchase *B, M*
Suffolk County Community College *A*
Syracuse University *B, M*
Wagner College *B*

North Carolina

Greensboro College *B*
High Point University *B*
North Carolina School of the
Arts *B, M*

North Dakota

Dickinson State University *B*

Ohio

Bowling Green State University *B*
Clark State Community College *A*
Hocking College *A*
Otterbein College *B*
Owens Community College
Toledo *A*
Sinclair Community College *A*
University of Cincinnati *B, M*
University of Findlay *B*
University of Rio Grande *A*
Wright State University *B*
Youngstown State University *B*

Oklahoma

Oklahoma City Community College *A*
Oral Roberts University *B*
Southeastern Oklahoma State
University *B*

Oregon

Chemeketa Community College *A*

Pennsylvania

Penn State
York *B*
Seton Hill University *B*

Temple University *M*

Rhode Island
Community College of Rhode
 Island *A*
Rhode Island College *B*

South Carolina
Coker College *B*
Wofford College *B*

Tennessee
Freed-Hardeman University *B*

Texas
Baylor University *B*
Lon Morris College *A*
Texas Tech University *B, M*
Trinity University *B*

Utah
Salt Lake Community College *A*

Vermont
Bennington College *B, M*
Johnson State College *A, B*
Marlboro College *B*

Virginia
Shenandoah University *B*

Washington
Cornish College of the Arts *B*
North Seattle Community College *C*
Shoreline Community College *A*

Wisconsin
University of Wisconsin
 Madison *B, M*

Wyoming
Central Wyoming College *A*
Western Wyoming Community
 College *C, A*

Theater history/criticism

California
California State University
 San Bernardino *B*
College of the Desert *A*
Mills College *B*
San Francisco State University *M*
Scripps College *B*
Whittier College *B*

Delaware
University of Delaware *B*

District of Columbia
George Washington University *B*
Howard University *B*

Florida
Hillsborough Community College *A*
Manatee Community College *A*

Illinois
DePaul University *B*
Northwestern University *B*
University of Illinois
 Urbana-Champaign *B*

Iowa
Buena Vista University *B, T*

Louisiana
Tulane University *B, M*

Maine
Bowdoin College *B*

Maryland
University of Maryland
 College Park *M, D*

Massachusetts
Boston University *B*
Emerson College *M*
Salem State College *B*
Simon's Rock College of Bard *B*
Suffolk University *B*
Tufts University *B, M, D*

Michigan
University of Michigan *B*
University of Michigan
 Flint *B*

Minnesota
Augsburg College *B*

Missouri
Washington University in St.
 Louis *B, M*

New Jersey
Rowan University *B*

New York
Bard College *B*
City University of New York
 Brooklyn College *M*
Columbia University
 Columbia College *B*
Eugene Lang College The New School
 for Liberal Arts *B*
Sarah Lawrence College *B, M*
State University of New York
 Purchase *B*

North Carolina
Gardner-Webb University *B*

Ohio
Ohio University *M*

Pennsylvania
Arcadia University *B*
Washington and Jefferson College *B*

Texas
Texas Christian University *B*

Vermont
Bennington College *B, M*
Burlington College *B*
Marlboro College *B*

Virginia
Averett University *B*
Virginia Wesleyan College *B*

Washington
Whitworth College *B, T*

Wisconsin
University of Wisconsin
 Madison *M, D*
 Whitewater *B, T*

Theological studies

Alabama
Faulkner University *B*
Huntsville Bible College *B*
Judson College *B*
Oakwood College *B*
Samford University *M*

Southeastern Bible College *A, B*
Southern Christian University *M, D*
Spring Hill College *C, B, M*
University of Mobile *B, M*

Arizona
American Indian College of the
 Assemblies of God *B*
Grand Canyon University *B*
Southwestern College *C, A, B*

Arkansas
Harding University *B, M*
John Brown University *B*
Ouachita Baptist University *B*
Williams Baptist College *A, B*

California
Azusa Pacific University *B, D*
Bethany University *A, B*
Bethesda Christian University *B*
Biola University *B, M, D*
California Lutheran University *B*
Concordia University *B, M*
Dominican School of Philosophy and
 Theology *M*
Hope International
 University *C, A, B, M*
LIFE Pacific College *B*
Loyola Marymount University *B, M*
Master's College *B*
Pacific Union College *B*
Pepperdine University *M*
Simpson University *B, M*
University of San Diego *M*
Vanguard University of Southern
 California *B, M*

Colorado
University of Denver *M*

Connecticut
Yale University *M*

District of Columbia
Catholic University of America *M, D*
Georgetown University *D*

Florida
Baptist College of Florida *A, B*
Barry University *C, B, M*
Clearwater Christian College *B*
Florida Christian College *B*
Hobe Sound Bible College *B*
Okaloosa-Walton College *A*
Palm Beach Atlantic University *B*
St. Leo University *B*
Southeastern College of the
 Assemblies of God *B*
Universidad FLET *C, A, B, M*

Georgia
Atlanta Christian College *B*
Brewton-Parker College *B*
Emory University *M*
Mercer University *M, D*
Shorter College *B*

Hawaii
Chaminade University of Honolulu *M*

Idaho
Boise Bible College *A, B*
Northwest Nazarene University *B, M*

Illinois
Concordia University *B*
Dominican University *C, B*
Elmhurst College *B*
Lincoln Christian College and
 Seminary *B, M*
Loyola University of Chicago *B, M, D*

Moody Bible Institute *B, M*
North Park University *M, D*
Olivet Nazarene University *B, M*
Quincy University *B*
St. Xavier University *B*
Trinity Christian College *B*
Trinity International University *B, M*
University of St. Francis *B*
Wheaton College *M, D*

Indiana
Anderson University *B, D*
Bethel College *B, M*
Goshen College *B*
Hanover College *B*
Huntington University *M*
Indiana Wesleyan University *B*
Manchester College *A*
Marian College *A, B*
Oakland City University *M, D*
St. Mary-of-the-Woods
 College *C, A, B, M*
Taylor University: Fort Wayne *B*
University of Evansville *B*
University of Notre Dame *B, M, D*
Valparaiso University *B, M*

Iowa
Briar Cliff University *A, B*
Dordt College *B*
Emmaus Bible College *B*
Faith Baptist Bible College and
 Theological Seminary *B, M*
Loras College *M*
St. Ambrose University *M*
University of Dubuque *M, D*
Vennard College *C, A, B*

Kansas
Barclay College *B*
Central Christian College of
 Kansas *A, B*
Hesston College *A*
Manhattan Christian College *A, B*
Tabor College *B*
University of St. Mary *B*

Kentucky
Brescia University *B*
Campbellsville University *M*
Kentucky Christian University *A, B, M*
Kentucky Mountain Bible College *B*

Louisiana
Loyola University New Orleans *M*
Xavier University of Louisiana *B, M*

Maine
St. Joseph's College *B*

Maryland
Columbia Union College *B*
Mount St. Mary's University *B, M*
Washington Bible College *B, M*

Massachusetts
Assumption College *B*
Atlantic Union College *B*
Eastern Nazarene College *B, M*
Harvard College *M, D*
Hellenic College/Holy Cross *B, M*
Merrimack College *A*
St. John's Seminary College *M*

Michigan
Andrews University *B, M, D*
Cornerstone University *M*
Grace Bible College *B*
Kuyper College *A, B*
Madonna University *B, M*
Rochester College *B*
Sacred Heart Major Seminary *C, A, M*

Sacred Heart Major Seminary *C, A, M*

Minnesota
College of St. Benedict *B*
College of St. Catherine *B, M*
Concordia College: Moorhead *B*
Concordia University: St. Paul *B*
Crossroads College *B*
Crown College *B, M*
Martin Luther College *B*
North Central University *B*
St. John's University *B*
St. Mary's University of
 Minnesota *C, B, M*
University of St. Thomas *M, D*

Mississippi
Blue Mountain College *B*
Magnolia Bible College *B*
Wesley College *B*

Missouri
Baptist Bible College *B*
Calvary Bible College and Theological
 Seminary *A, B, M*
Central Bible College *B*
Central Christian College of the
 Bible *B*
Global University *C, A, B, M*
Missouri Baptist University *C, B*
Ozark Christian College *C, B*
St. Louis Christian College *A, B*
St. Louis University *B, M, D*
Southwest Baptist University *C, B*

Nebraska
College of Saint Mary *B, T*
Concordia University *B*
Creighton University *C, A, B, M*
Grace University *B*
Nebraska Christian College *A, B*
Union College *B*

New Hampshire
St. Anselm College *B*

New Jersey
Beth Medrash Govoha *M*
Caldwell College *B, M*
Drew University *M, D*
Georgian Court University *M*
Seton Hall University *M*

New York
Holy Trinity Orthodox Seminary *C, B*
Houghton College *B*
Jewish Theological Seminary of
 America *D*
Nyack College *B, M*
Roberts Wesleyan College *B*
St. Bonaventure University *M*
St. John's University *C, B, M*

North Carolina
Campbell University *M*
Duke University *M, D*
John Wesley College *C, A, B*
Livingstone College *B*
Roanoke Bible College *B*
Shaw University *M*
Southeastern Baptist Theological
 Seminary: Theological
 Professions *D*
Wake Forest University *M*

North Dakota
Trinity Bible College *B*
University of Mary *B*

Ohio
Allegheny Wesleyan College *B*
Ashland University *M, D*

Cedarville University *B*
Cincinnati Christian University *M*
Circleville Bible College *A, B*
Franciscan University of
 Steubenville *B, M*
God's Bible School and College *B*
Malone College *B, M*
Mount Vernon Nazarene University *M*
Muskingum College *B*
Pontifical College Josephinum *M*
University of Dayton *M, D*
University of Findlay *B*
Walsh University *B, M*
Xavier University *A, B, M*

Oklahoma
Mid-America Christian University *B*
Oklahoma Baptist University *C, A, B*
Oklahoma Christian University *B*
Oklahoma Wesleyan University *B*
Oral Roberts University *B, M, D*
Southern Nazarene University *B*
Southwestern Christian
 University *B, M*

Oregon
Concordia University *B*
Corban College *B*
Eugene Bible College *B*
George Fox University *M*
Mount Angel Seminary *B*
Multnomah Bible College *B, M*
University of Portland *B, M*

Pennsylvania
Baptist Bible College of
 Pennsylvania *M*
Bryn Athyn College of the New
 Church *M*
Carlow University *B*
DeSales University *B*
Duquesne University *B, M, D*
Eastern University *B*
Elizabethtown College *B*
Gannon University *B*
Immaculata University *B*
King's College *B*
Philadelphia Biblical University *B*
St. Charles Borromeo Seminary -
 Overbrook *M*
St. Vincent College *B*
Susquehanna University *B*
Valley Forge Christian College *B*
Waynesburg College *B*

Puerto Rico
Bayamon Central University *M*
Pontifical Catholic University of
 Puerto Rico *M*
Universidad Adventista de las
 Antillas *B*

Rhode Island
Providence College *B*

South Carolina
Anderson University *B*
Charleston Southern University *B*
Columbia International
 University *M, D*
Erskine College *D*
Morris College *B*
Southern Wesleyan University *M*

South Dakota
University of Sioux Falls *B*

Tennessee
American Baptist College of ABT
 Seminary *A, B*
Carson-Newman College *A*
Crichton College *C, B*

Free Will Baptist Bible College *B*
Freed-Hardeman University *B, M*
Southern Adventist University *B, M*
Tennessee Temple University *B*
Trevecca Nazarene University *M*
Union University *B*
University of the South *M, D*
Vanderbilt University *D*

Texas
Austin Graduate School of
 Theology *B, M*
Baptist Missionary Association
 Theological Seminary *A, B, M*
Baptist University of the Americas *B*
Baylor University *M, D*
Brazosport College *A*
Criswell College *B, M*
Dallas Christian College *B*
Hardin-Simmons University *B, M*
Houston Baptist University *M*
Howard Payne University *C, A, B*
St. Mary's University *B, M*
Southern Methodist University *M, D*
Southwestern Adventist University *B*
Southwestern Assemblies of God
 University *M*
Southwestern Baptist Theological
 Seminary: Theological
 Professions *M, D*
Texas Christian University *M*
University of Dallas *B, M*
University of Mary Hardin-Baylor *B*
University of St. Thomas *B, M*

Vermont
St. Michael's College *M*

Virginia
Eastern Mennonite University *C, B, M*
Hampton University *B*
Liberty University *M*
Regent University *M, D*
Roanoke College *B*
Virginia Union University *M, D*

Washington
Northwest University *B*
Puget Sound Christian College *B*
Seattle University *M*
Trinity Lutheran College *A, B*
Walla Walla College *B*
Whitworth College *B*

West Virginia
Alderson-Broaddus College *B*
Wheeling Jesuit University *B*

Wisconsin
Concordia University Wisconsin *B*
Maranatha Baptist Bible College *M*
Marquette University *M*
St. Norbert College *M*
Silver Lake College *B*
Wisconsin Lutheran College *B*

Theoretical/ mathematical physics

Alabama
Southern Union State Community
 College *A*

Arizona
Northern Arizona University *B*

Arkansas
University of Arkansas *M*

California
San Diego State University *B*

Florida
University of Miami *B*

Illinois
Northwestern University *M, D*

Indiana
Indiana University
 Bloomington *D*

Michigan
Spring Arbor University *B*

Minnesota
Winona State University *B*

New York
State University of New York
 Buffalo *B*

Texas
Rice University *M, D*
Southwestern Adventist University *B*

Vermont
Marlboro College *B*

Virginia
Sweet Briar College *B*

Wisconsin
Lawrence University *B*
University of Wisconsin
 Madison *M, D*

Tibetan studies

California
California Institute of Integral
 Studies *M, D*

Tool and die technology

Alabama
Calhoun Community College *C, A*
Shelton State Community
 College *C, A*
Trenholm State Technical College *C, A*

Illinois
Black Hawk College *C*
College of DuPage *C*
College of Lake County *C*
John A. Logan College *C, A*

Indiana
Ivy Tech State College
 Ivy Tech Community College:
  Bloomington *C, A*
 Ivy Tech Community College:
  Central Indiana *C, A*
 Ivy Tech Community College:
  Columbus *C, A*
 Ivy Tech Community College: East
  Central *C, A*
 Ivy Tech Community College:
  Kokomo *C, A*
 Ivy Tech Community College:
  Lafayette *C, A*
 Ivy Tech Community College: North
  Central *C, A*
 Ivy Tech Community College:
  Northeast *C, A*
 Ivy Tech Community College:
  Northwest *C, A*
 Ivy Tech Community College: South
  Central *C, A*
 Ivy Tech Community College:
  Southwest *C, A*

Ivy Tech Community College:
Wabash Valley *C, A*
Ivy Tech Community College:
Whitewater *C, A*

Iowa

Des Moines Area Community
College *C, A*
Hawkeye Community College *A*
Marshalltown Community College *C*
North Iowa Area Community
College *C, A*
Northwest Iowa Community
College *C, A*
Southeastern Community College
North Campus *C, A*
Western Iowa Tech Community
College *A*

Michigan

Ferris State University *A*
Montcalm Community College *C*
Mott Community College *C*
Oakland Community College *C, A*
Southwestern Michigan College *C, A*
Wayne County Community College *A*

Minnesota

Hennepin Technical College *C, A*
Ridgewater College *C, A*
St. Paul College *C*

Mississippi

Itawamba Community College *A*

New York

Mohawk Valley Community College *C*

North Carolina

Asheville-Buncombe Technical
Community College *C*
Davidson County Community
College *A*

Ohio

Owens Community College
Toledo *C, A*
Sinclair Community College *C, A*
Zane State College *A*

Pennsylvania

Lehigh Carbon Community College *C*
Pennsylvania College of Technology *A*

South Carolina

York Technical College *A*

South Dakota

Lake Area Technical Institute *A*

Texas

Texas State Technical College
Harlingen *A*

Wisconsin

Milwaukee Area Technical College *C*
Western Wisconsin Technical
College *C, A*

Tourism promotion

Arizona

Phoenix College *C, A*

California

Alliant International University *B*
Butte College *C, A*
City College of San Francisco *A*
Coastline Community College *C*
Cypress College *C, A*
Empire College *C*

Foothill College *C, A*
Fullerton College *C, A*
Grossmont Community College *C, A*
Long Beach City College *C, A*
Los Angeles City College *C, A*
Los Medanos College *C, A*
Palomar College *C, A*
Pasadena City College *C, A*
Saddleback College *C*
San Diego City College *C, A*
San Francisco State University *B*
Santa Ana College *A*
Southwestern College *C, A*

Colorado

Community College of Aurora *C*
Metropolitan State College of
Denver *B*
Pueblo Community College *C, A*
Red Rocks Community College *C, A*

District of Columbia

George Washington University *B, M*

Florida

Florida National College *A*
Lynn University *B*
Miami Dade College *C, A*

Georgia

Gwinnett Technical College *C*

Idaho

College of Southern Idaho *A*

Illinois

College of DuPage *C, A*
Danville Area Community College *A*
Elgin Community College *C*
MacCormac College *C, A*

Indiana

International Business College *C, A*

Iowa

Iowa Lakes Community College *A*
Northeast Iowa Community
College *C*

Kansas

Cloud County Community
College *C, A*

Kentucky

Sullivan University *C, A, B*

Maine

Andover College *C, A*
Beal College *A*
University of Maine
Machias *B*

Maryland

Allegany College of Maryland *C*
Chesapeake College *A*

Massachusetts

Bay State College *A*
Bristol Community College *C*
Massasoit Community College *C*
Mount Ida College *A, B*
Newbury College *A*
Northern Essex Community
College *A*

Michigan

Grand Valley State University *B*
Lansing Community College *A*

Minnesota

Central Lakes College *C*

Rasmussen College
Mankato *C, A*

Mississippi

Hinds Community College *A*

Missouri

Central Missouri State University *B*
Patricia Stevens College *C*

Nebraska

Hamilton College: Lincoln *C, A*
Midland Lutheran College *A*

New Hampshire

New Hampshire Technical
Institute *C, A*

New Jersey

Raritan Valley Community College *C*

New Mexico

New Mexico State University *B*

New York

Adirondack Community College *A*
Bryant & Stratton Business Institute
Bryant & Stratton College:
Syracuse *C, A*
City University of New York
Kingsborough Community
College *A*
LaGuardia Community College *A*
Corning Community College *A*
Dowling College *B*
Dutchess Community College *A*
Finger Lakes Community College *A*
Genesee Community College *C*
Jefferson Community College *C, A*
Mildred Elley *C*
Monroe Community College *A*
Paul Smith's College *B*
Rochester Institute of
Technology *B, M*
Schenectady County Community
College *C, A*
State University of New York
College of Agriculture and
Technology at Cobleskill *A*
College of Agriculture and
Technology at Morrisville *A*
College of Technology at Delhi *A*
Wood Tobe-Coburn School *C*

North Carolina

Blue Ridge Community College *A*

Ohio

Bowling Green State University *B*
Columbus State Community
College *C, A*
Lakeland Community College *C, A*
Sinclair Community College *A*
Youngstown State University *A, B*

Oklahoma

Oklahoma City Community College *A*

Pennsylvania

Butler County Community College *A*
Consolidated School of Business
York *C, A*
Lehigh Valley College *A*
Luzerne County Community
College *C, A*
Mansfield University of
Pennsylvania *A, B*
Pittsburgh Technical Institute *A*
Reading Area Community College *A*
Westmoreland County Community
College *A*
York Technical Institute *C*

Yorktowne Business Institute *A*

Puerto Rico

Universidad del Este *C*
University of Puerto Rico
Carolina Regional College *B*
University of the Sacred Heart *B*

Rhode Island

Community College of Rhode
Island *C*
Johnson & Wales University *A, B*

Texas

Amarillo College *A*
Central Texas College *C, A*
El Paso Community College *C, A*
Texas A&M University *B*

Vermont

Champlain College *A, B*

Washington

Columbia Basin College *C*
Edmonds Community College *C, A*

West Virginia

Bluefield State College *A*
Concord University *B*
Mountain State College *A*
Mountain State University *C, A*
West Liberty State College *B*

Wisconsin

Fox Valley Technical College *A*

Wyoming

Northwest College *A*

Tourism/travel management

Arizona

Arizona Western College *C, A*
Northern Arizona University *C*
Phoenix College *C, A*
Pima Community College *C, A*

California

California State University
Fullerton *B*
Canada College *C, A*
Chabot College *A*
City College of San Francisco *A*
Coastline Community College *C*
College of the Redwoods *C*
Empire College *C*
Grossmont Community College *C, A*
Long Beach City College *C, A*
Los Angeles City College *C, A*
MiraCosta College *C, A*
Mount St. Mary's College *A*
Saddleback College *C, A*
San Diego Mesa College *C, A*
San Diego State University *B*
San Joaquin Delta College *C*
Santiago Canyon College *A*
Southwestern College *C, A*
Vista Community College *C*

Colorado

Fort Lewis College *B*
Mesa State College *A*
Metropolitan State College of
Denver *B*
Northeastern Junior College *C, A*
Parks College *A*
Pueblo Community College *C, A*
University of Colorado
Boulder *B*
University of Denver *B*

Connecticut

Briarwood College *A*
Three Rivers Community College *C, A*
University of New Haven *C*

District of Columbia

Southeastern University *B*

Florida

Broward Community College *A*
Daytona Beach Community College *A*
Edison College *A*
Florida Community College at
    Jacksonville *C, A*
Florida International University *B, M*
Florida National College *A*
Johnson & Wales University *A*
Lynn University *B*
Miami Dade College *C, A*
St. Thomas University *B*
Schiller International University *A, B*
Webster College: Holiday *A*

Georgia

Gwinnett Technical College *C, A*

Hawaii

Brigham Young University-Hawaii *B*
Hawaii Business College *C, A*
Hawaii Pacific University *B*
Heald College
    Honolulu *A*
University of Hawaii
    Manoa *B, M*
    Maui Community College *A*

Illinois

City Colleges of Chicago
    Harold Washington College *C, A*
Danville Area Community College *A*
MacCormac College *C, A*
Midstate College *A*
Moraine Valley Community College *C*
Northwestern Business College *A*
Robert Morris College: Chicago *C, A*
Roosevelt University *B*
Waubonsee Community College *C*

Indiana

Indiana University-Purdue University
    Indianapolis *B*
University of Indianapolis *A, B*

Iowa

AIB College of Business *A*
Hamilton College
    Cedar Falls *C, A*
    Cedar Rapids *C, A*
Kaplan University *A*
Northeast Iowa Community
    College *C*

Maine

Andover College *C, A*
University of Maine
    Machias *B*

Maryland

Allegany College of Maryland *C*

Massachusetts

Becker College *B*
Bunker Hill Community College *C, A*
Fisher College *C, A*
Lasell College *B*
Marian Court College *C, A*
Massasoit Community College *A*
Middlesex Community College *C*
Mount Ida College *A*
Newbury College *C, A*
North Shore Community College *A*

Northern Essex Community
    College *C, A*
Quincy College *A*

Michigan

Baker College
    of Clinton Township *A*
    of Flint *A*
Central Michigan University *M*
Grand Valley State University *B*
Lansing Community College *A*
Northern Michigan University *B*

Minnesota

Central Lakes College *A*
Dakota County Technical College *C*
Minneapolis Business College *A*
Rasmussen College
    Mankato *C, A*
    Minnetonka *C, A*
    St. Cloud *C*
St. Cloud State University *B*

Montana

University of Montana: Western *A, B*

Nebraska

Hamilton College: Lincoln *C, A*
University of Nebraska
    Kearney *B*

New Hampshire

New Hampshire Technical
    Institute *C, A*
Southern New Hampshire
    University *B*
University of New Hampshire *B*

New Jersey

Atlantic Cape Community College *A*
Cumberland County College *C, A*
Essex County College *A*
Mercer County Community College *C*

New Mexico

New Mexico State University *B*

New York

Adirondack Community College *A*
Bryant & Stratton Business Institute
    Bryant & Stratton College:
        Syracuse *A*
City University of New York
    Kingsborough Community
        College *A*
    New York City College of
        Technology *B*
Corning Community College *C, A*
Dowling College *B*
Dutchess Community College *A*
Finger Lakes Community College *A*
Genesee Community College *C*
Globe Institute of Technology *C, A, B*
Herkimer County Community
    College *A*
Jefferson Community College *A*
Mohawk Valley Community College *C*
Monroe Community College *A*
New York Institute of Technology *B*
New York University *M*
Niagara University *B*
Paul Smith's College *A, B*
Rochester Institute of
    Technology *A, B, M*
Rockland Community College *A*
State University of New York
    College at Plattsburgh *B*
    College of Agriculture and
        Technology at Cobleskill *A*
    College of Agriculture and
        Technology at Morrisville *A*
    College of Technology at Delhi *A*

Taylor Business Institute *A*

North Carolina

Blue Ridge Community College *A*
Central Piedmont Community
    College *C, A*
King's College *A*
Methodist College *B*

North Dakota

Aakers College: Fargo *A*

Ohio

Bradford School *C*
Columbus State Community
    College *C, A*
Davis College *A*
Lakeland Community College *C, A*
Ohio University *A*
Ohio University
    Southern Campus at Ironton *A*
Sinclair Community College *A*
University of Akron *C, A*
University of Northwestern Ohio *C, A*
Youngstown State University *A, B*

Oklahoma

Northeastern State University *B*
Oklahoma City Community College *A*
Tulsa Community College *C, A*

Oregon

Blue Mountain Community College *C*
Central Oregon Community
    College *A*
Chemeketa Community College *A*
Everest College: Portland *A*
Mount Hood Community College *C, A*

Pennsylvania

Bucks County Community
    College *C, A*
Consolidated School of Business
    York *C, A*
Erie Business Center *C, A*
Erie Business Center South *A*
Harrisburg Area Community
    College *C, A*
ICM School of Business & Medical
    Careers *A*
Lehigh Valley College *A*
Mansfield University of
    Pennsylvania *A, B*
Newport Business Institute *A*
Pennsylvania College of Technology *A*
South Hills School of Business &
    Technology *C*
Westmoreland County Community
    College *A*
York Technical Institute *C*

Puerto Rico

Inter American University of Puerto
    Rico
    Fajardo Campus *A*
National College of Business &
    Technology: Bayamon *A*
Pontifical Catholic University of
    Puerto Rico *A, B*
Turabo University *C*
Universidad del Este *C, A, B*
University College of San Juan *C*

Rhode Island

Johnson & Wales University *A, B*

South Carolina

Clemson University *B*
Trident Technical College *A*

South Dakota

Black Hills State University *A, B, M*

Texas

Amarillo College *C*
Austin Community College *C, A*
Central Texas College *C*
Del Mar College *C, A*
El Paso Community College *C, A*
Houston Community College
    System *C, A*
Richland College *A*
St. Philip's College *C, A*
Tarrant County College *C, A*
Texas A&M University *B*
Texas A&M University
    Galveston *B*
University of Texas
    San Antonio *B*

Utah

Everest College: Salt Lake City *C, A*

Vermont

Champlain College *A, B*
Johnson State College *B*

Virginia

Northern Virginia Community
    College *C, A*
Virginia Highlands Community
    College *C*

Washington

Highline Community College *C, A*
Spokane Falls Community
    College *C, A*

West Virginia

Concord University *B*
Davis and Elkins College *B*
Mountain State College *A*
Mountain State University *C, A, B*
West Liberty State College *B*

Wisconsin

Madison Area Technical College *A*
Milwaukee Area Technical
    College *C, A*
Northeast Wisconsin Technical
    College *A*

Tourism/travel services

Connecticut

Central Connecticut State
    University *B*

Illinois

Moraine Valley Community
    College *C, A*

Michigan

Western Michigan University *B*

Minnesota

Dakota County Technical College *C, A*

Missouri

University of Missouri
    Columbia *B, M*

New Jersey

Bergen Community College *C, A*

New York

Dutchess Community College *A*
Genesee Community College *A*
Rochester Institute of
    Technology *B, M*
Schenectady County Community
    College *A*

State University of New York
College of Agriculture and
Technology at Morrisville *A*
Tompkins-Cortland Community
College *A*

Pennsylvania

Central Pennsylvania College *A*
Consolidated School of Business
York *A*
Lehigh Carbon Community
College *C, A*
Lehigh Valley College *A*
Montgomery County Community
College *A*
Newport Business Institute *A*

Utah

Dixie State College of Utah *C, A*

Vermont

Champlain College *A, B*

Washington

Edmonds Community College *C, A*

Toxicology

Arizona

University of Arizona *M, D*

Arkansas

University of Arkansas
for Medical Sciences *M, D*

California

University of California
Berkeley *B, M, D*
Santa Cruz *M, D*

Colorado

University of Colorado
Denver and Health Sciences
Center *D*

District of Columbia

American University *B*
George Washington University *M, D*

Georgia

University of Georgia *M, D*

Indiana

Indiana University-Purdue University
Indianapolis *M, D*

Iowa

Iowa State University *M, D*

Kansas

University of Kansas Medical
Center *M, D*

Kentucky

University of Kentucky *M, D*

Louisiana

University of Louisiana at Monroe *B*

Maryland

University of Maryland
Baltimore *M, D*
Baltimore County *M, D*
College Park *M, D*
Eastern Shore *M, D*

Michigan

Eastern Michigan University *B*
University of Michigan *M, D*

Minnesota

Minnesota State University
Mankato *B, M, T*
University of Minnesota
Duluth *M*
Twin Cities *M, D*

Mississippi

Mississippi State University *D*

Nebraska

University of Nebraska
Lincoln *M, D*
Medical Center *M, D*

New Hampshire

Dartmouth College *D*

New Jersey

College of St. Elizabeth *B*
Felician College *B*
Rutgers, The State University of New
Jersey
New Brunswick/Piscataway
Campus *M, D*
St. Peter's College *B*
University of Medicine and Dentistry
of New Jersey
School of Health Related
Professions *B*

New York

Clarkson University *B*
Cornell University *M, D*
St. John's University *B, M*
State University of New York
Albany *M, D*
College of Environmental Science
and Forestry *B, M, D*
University of Rochester *M, D*

North Carolina

North Carolina State University *M, D*
University of North Carolina
Chapel Hill *M, D*

Oregon

Oregon State University *M, D*

Pennsylvania

University of the Sciences in
Philadelphia *B, M, D*

South Carolina

Clemson University *M*
Medical University of South
Carolina *D*

Tennessee

University of Tennessee
Knoxville *M*

Texas

Prairie View A&M University *M*
Texas A&M University *M, D*
Texas Southern University *M, D*
Texas Tech University *M, D*
University of Texas
Health Science Center at
Houston *M, D*

Utah

Utah State University *M, D*

Washington

Washington State University *M, D*

Trade/industrial education

Alabama

Athens State University *B*

Alaska

University of Alaska
Anchorage *M*

Arizona

Northern Arizona University *B, M*

Arkansas

University of Arkansas *B, M, D*
University of Arkansas
Pine Bluff *B, T*
University of Central Arkansas *M*

California

California Polytechnic State
University: San Luis Obispo *M*
California State University
Los Angeles *B*
San Bernardino *B, M*
Fullerton College *A*
Humboldt State University *B, T*
Vanguard University of Southern
California *T*

Colorado

Colorado School of Trades *A*
Colorado State University *T*

Delaware

Delaware State University *B*

Florida

Florida Agricultural and Mechanical
University *B, M*
Florida International
University *B, M, T*
Florida State University *D*
Manatee Community College *A*
University of Central Florida *B, M*
University of North Florida *B*
University of South Florida *B, M*
University of West Florida *B*

Georgia

Darton College *A*
University of Georgia *M, D*
Valdosta State University *B*

Idaho

University of Idaho *B*

Illinois

Chicago State University *M, D*
Southern Illinois University
Carbondale *B, M, D*

Indiana

Indiana State University *A, B, M, T*
Purdue University *A*
Vincennes University *A*

Iowa

Iowa State University *B, T*
William Penn University *B*

Kansas

Fort Hays State University *B, T*

Kentucky

Eastern Kentucky University *B, M*
Murray State University *A, T*
Northern Kentucky University *B, T*
University of Kentucky *M, D*
University of Louisville *B, M*

Western Kentucky University *B, T*

Massachusetts

Fitchburg State College *M, D*

Michigan

Lansing Community College *A*
Madonna University *B, T*
Western Michigan University *M, T*

Minnesota

St. Cloud State University *T*

Mississippi

Hinds Community College *A*
Mississippi Gulf Coast Community
College
Jefferson Davis Campus *A*

Missouri

Lindenwood University *B*

Nebraska

Chadron State College *B*
University of Nebraska
Kearney *B*
Lincoln *B*

Nevada

Great Basin College *B*
University of Nevada
Reno *B*

New Hampshire

Keene State College *B, T*

New York

College of Saint Rose *B, M*
New York Institute of
Technology *A, B, T*
New York University *M, D, T*
State University of New York
College at Buffalo *B, M, T*
Oswego *B, M, T*

North Carolina

North Carolina Agricultural and
Technical State University *B, T*
Southwestern Community College *A*

North Dakota

Valley City State University *B, T*

Ohio

Kent State University *B, M*
Ohio State University
Columbus Campus *B, M*
University of Toledo *B, M*

Oklahoma

East Central University *B*

Pennsylvania

Indiana University of
Pennsylvania *B, T*
Temple University *B*

Puerto Rico

Turabo University *B*

Rhode Island

Rhode Island College *B*

South Carolina

Clemson University *D*
South Carolina State University *B, T*

Tennessee

University of Tennessee
Knoxville *B, T*

Texas

Sam Houston State University *M*
Texas A&M University *D, T*
Texas A&M University
Commerce *M, T*
Texas State University: San
Marcos *M, T*
University of Houston *B, M*
University of North Texas *M, D*
Wayland Baptist University *B, T*

Utah

Southern Utah University *B, T*

Virginia

Norfolk State University *B*
Virginia Polytechnic Institute and
State University *M, D*
Virginia State University *B, M*

Washington

Central Washington University *B, T*
Renton Technical College *A*
South Seattle Community College *A*
Western Washington University *M*

West Virginia

Marshall University *M*

Wisconsin

University of Wisconsin
Stout *M*

Wyoming

University of Wyoming *B*

Traditional Chinese medicine/herbology

Pennsylvania

Academy of Medical Arts and
Business *C, A*

Washington

Bastyr University *B, M, D*

Transportation

Alabama

Community College of the Air
Force *A*

Alaska

University of Alaska
Anchorage *B, M*

Arkansas

University of Arkansas
Community College at Batesville *C*

California

California State University
Dominguez Hills *M*
Fresno City College *C, A*

Delaware

Wilmington College *M*

Florida

Florida Community College at
Jacksonville *C*

Illinois

Richland Community College *C*
Triton College *A*

Iowa

Northeast Iowa Community
College *C*

Maryland

Morgan State University *M*

Michigan

Baker College
of Muskegon *C*
Henry Ford Community College *A*

Montana

Blackfeet Community College *C*

Nebraska

Southeast Community College
Lincoln Campus *C*

Nevada

University of Nevada
Las Vegas *M*

New Mexico

Mesalands Community College *C*

New York

Nassau Community College *A*
New York Institute of Technology *C*
Niagara University *B*
United States Merchant Marine
Academy *B*

North Dakota

Lake Region State College *A*

Ohio

Columbus State Community
College *A*

South Carolina

Trident Technical College *C, A*

Texas

Brookhaven College *A*
Central Texas College *C*
Texas A&M University
Galveston *B*
Texas Southern University *M*

Virginia

Central Virginia Community
College *C*
J. Sargeant Reynolds Community
College *C*
University of Richmond *C, A*

Washington

Green River Community College *C, A*
Highline Community College *A*
Spokane Falls Community College *A*

Wisconsin

Northeast Wisconsin Technical
College *A*
University of Wisconsin
Superior *B*

Transportation/highway engineering

Arkansas

University of Arkansas *M*

California

University of Southern California *M*

Massachusetts

Massachusetts Institute of
Technology *M, D*

Michigan

University of Michigan *M*

Missouri

Washington University in St. Louis *M*

New Jersey

New Jersey Institute of
Technology *M, D*

New York

Polytechnic University *M, D*
Rensselaer Polytechnic Institute *M, D*

Pennsylvania

Villanova University *M*

Wisconsin

Marquette University *M, D*

Transportation management

Arkansas

Arkansas State University *B*

Delaware

Wilmington College *M*

Florida

Florida Institute of Technology *M*
University of North Florida *B*

Illinois

Northwestern University *M*

Iowa

Iowa State University *M*

Massachusetts

Bridgewater State College *B*
Massachusetts Maritime Academy *B*

Michigan

College for Creative Studies *B*

Minnesota

Academy College *C*

New Jersey

Thomas Edison State College *A, B*

North Carolina

North Carolina Agricultural and
Technical State University *B*

North Dakota

Bismarck State College *A*
North Dakota State University *M, D*

Ohio

Ohio State University
Columbus Campus *B, M, D*

Pennsylvania

University of Pennsylvania *B*

South Carolina

Trident Technical College *C, A*

Texas

Texas A&M University
Galveston *B*

Truck/bus/commercial vehicle operation

Alabama

Shelton State Community College *C*
Trenholm State Technical College *C*

Arizona

Glendale Community College *C*

Arkansas

North Arkansas College *C*
Ouachita Technical College *C*

Florida

Central Florida Community College *C*
Gulf Coast Community College *C*
Indian River Community College *C*

Georgia

Albany Technical College *C*
Athens Technical College *C*
Bainbridge College *C*
Georgia Southwestern State
University *A*
Northwestern Technical College *C*
Savannah Technical College *C*

Illinois

Black Hawk College *C*
John Wood Community College *C*
Kaskaskia College *C*
Lincoln Land Community College *C*
Spoon River College *C*

Indiana

Vincennes University *C*

Iowa

Hawkeye Community College *C*
Indian Hills Community College *C*

Kentucky

Big Sandy Community and Technical
College *C*

Maryland

College of Southern Maryland *C*
Hagerstown Community College *C*

Massachusetts

Holyoke Community College *C*

Minnesota

Alexandria Technical College *C*
Dakota County Technical College *C*
Minnesota State College - Southeast
Technical *C*

Mississippi

Copiah-Lincoln Community College *C*
Itawamba Community College *C*

Missouri

Crowder College *C*

Nebraska

Northeast Community College *C*
Southeast Community College
Lincoln Campus *C*

New Mexico

Albuquerque Technical-Vocational
Institute *C*
San Juan College *C*

North Carolina

Cape Fear Community College *C*
Davidson County Community
College *C*

Oregon

Rogue Community College *C*

South Carolina

Greenville Technical College *C*

Texas

Houston Community College
System *C*
North Harris Montgomery
Community College District *C*

Utah

Salt Lake Community College *C*

Virginia

Southside Virginia Community
College *C*
Tidewater Community College *C, A*

Washington

Big Bend Community College *C*
Clover Park Technical College *C*
Walla Walla Community College *C*

Wisconsin

Fox Valley Technical College *C*
Waukesha County Technical
College *C*

Turf management

Arizona

Northland Pioneer College *C, A*

California

Butte College *C*
College of the Desert *C, A*
Los Angeles Pierce College *C*
MiraCosta College *C, A*
Monterey Peninsula College *C*
Mount San Antonio College *C*
Mount San Jacinto College *C, A*
San Joaquin Delta College *C*
Southwestern College *C, A*

Florida

Edison College *C*
Florida Southern College *B*
Indian River Community College *A*
Lake City Community College *C*

Georgia

University of Georgia *B*

Illinois

College of DuPage *C*
College of Lake County *A*
Danville Area Community College *C*
Joliet Junior College *C, A*
Kishwaukee College *C*
McHenry County College *C*
Southwestern Illinois College *A*
William Rainey Harper College *C, A*

Indiana

Vincennes University *C*

Iowa

Kirkwood Community College *A*
Western Iowa Tech Community
College *A*

Kentucky

Eastern Kentucky University *B*

Maine

University of Maine *B*

Massachusetts

University of Massachusetts
Amherst *A*

Michigan

Kirtland Community College *A*
Northwestern Michigan College *A*

Minnesota

Anoka Technical College *C, A*
Anoka-Ramsey Community College *A*
Rochester Community and Technical
College *C, A*
University of Minnesota
Crookston *B*

Mississippi

Mississippi Gulf Coast Community
College
Jefferson Davis Campus *C, A*

Missouri

Longview Community College *A*
Ozarks Technical Community
College *C, A*

Nebraska

Nebraska College of Technical
Agriculture *A*

New York

State University of New York
College of Agriculture and
Technology at Cobleskill *A*
College of Technology at Delhi *A*

North Carolina

Blue Ridge Community College *C*
Brunswick Community College *C, A*
Catawba Valley Community College *A*
Central Piedmont Community
College *C, A*
Guilford Technical Community
College *A*
North Carolina State University *A*
Sandhills Community College *A*
Wayne Community College *A*

North Dakota

Minot State University: Bottineau
Campus *A*
North Dakota State University *B*

Ohio

Cincinnati State Technical and
Community College *C, A*
Clark State Community College *A*
Ohio State University
Agricultural Technical Institute *A*
Columbus Campus *B*

Oklahoma

Oklahoma State University
Oklahoma City *A*

Oregon

Central Oregon Community
College *A*

Pennsylvania

Community College of Allegheny
County *C, A*
Delaware Valley College *B*
Penn State
Abington *B*
Altoona *B*
Beaver *B*
Berks *B*
Delaware County *B*
Dubois *B*
Erie, The Behrend College *B*
Fayette *B*
Hazleton *B*
Lehigh Valley *B*
McKeesport *B*
Mont Alto *B*
New Kensington *B*
Schuylkill - Capital College *B*
Shenango *B*
University Park *B*

Wilkes-Barre *B*
Worthington Scranton *B*
York *B*
Pennsylvania College of Technology *A*
Westmoreland County Community
College *A*
Williamson Free School of Mechanical
Trades *C*

South Carolina

Clemson University *B*
Horry-Georgetown Technical
College *C, A*
Technical College of the
Lowcountry *C*
Trident Technical College *C*

South Dakota

Southeast Technical Institute *A*

Tennessee

Chattanooga State Technical
Community College *C*
Walters State Community College *A*

Texas

Palo Alto College *C, A*
Texas A&M University *B*
Texas State Technical College
Waco *C, A*
Western Texas College *C, A*

Virginia

J. Sargeant Reynolds Community
College *A*
Northern Virginia Community
College *C*

Washington

Spokane Community College *A*
Walla Walla Community College *C, A*

Turkish

Texas

University of Texas
Austin *B*

Washington

University of Washington *B*

Ukrainian

Washington

University of Washington *B*

Underwater diving

California

Santa Barbara City College *C, A*

Upholstery

Alabama

Gadsden State Community College *C*
Northwest-Shoals Community
College *C*

North Carolina

Catawba Valley Community College *C*

Washington

Clover Park Technical College *C*

Urban, community, and regional planning

Alabama

Alabama Agricultural and Mechanical
University *B, M*
Auburn University *M*

Arizona

Arizona State University *B, M*
University of Arizona *B, M*

California

California Polytechnic State
University: San Luis Obispo *B, M*
California State Polytechnic
University: Pomona *B, M*
California State University
Chico *B*
East Los Angeles College *A*
Modesto Junior College *A*
San Diego State University *M*
San Jose State University *M*
University of California
Berkeley *M, D*
Davis *B, M*
Irvine *M, D*
Los Angeles *M, D*
San Diego *B*
University of San Francisco *B*
University of Southern
California *M, D*

Colorado

University of Colorado
Denver and Health Sciences
Center *M*

District of Columbia

University of the District of
Columbia *A, B, M*

Florida

Florida Atlantic University *B, M*
Florida State University *M, D*
University of Florida *M*
University of Miami *M*

Georgia

Georgia Institute of Technology *M*

Hawaii

University of Hawaii
Manoa *M, D*

Illinois

Illinois Institute of Technology *M*
University of Illinois
Chicago *M, D*
Urbana-Champaign *B, M, D*
Westwood College of Technology
O'Hare *B*

Indiana

Ball State University *B, M*
Indiana University-Purdue University
Indianapolis *M*

Iowa

Iowa State University *B, M*
University of Iowa *M*

Kansas

Kansas State University *M*
University of Kansas *M*

Kentucky

University of Louisville *M*

Louisiana
University of New Orleans *M*

Maine
University of Southern Maine *M*

Maryland
Frostburg State University *B*
Morgan State University *M*
University of Maryland
College Park *D*

Massachusetts
Bridgewater State College *B*
Harvard College *B, M, D*
Massachusetts Institute of
Technology *B, M, D*
Tufts University *M*
University of Massachusetts
Amherst *M, D*
Westfield State College *B*

Michigan
Eastern Michigan University *B, M*
Grand Valley State University *B*
Michigan State University *B, M*
University of Michigan *M, D*
Wayne State University *M*

Minnesota
Minnesota State University
Mankato *B, M*
St. Cloud State University *B*

Mississippi
Jackson State University *M, D*
University of Southern Mississippi *B*

Missouri
Missouri State University *B, M*
St. Louis University *M*
University of Missouri
Kansas City *B*
Washington University in St. Louis *M*

Montana
University of Montana: Missoula *B, M*

Nebraska
University of Nebraska
Lincoln *M*

Nevada
University of Nevada
Las Vegas *B*

New Hampshire
Plymouth State University *B*
University of New Hampshire *B*

New Jersey
New Jersey Institute of Technology *M*
Rutgers, The State University of New
Jersey
New Brunswick/Piscataway
Campus *B, M, D*

New Mexico
New Mexico State University *B*
University of New Mexico *M*

New York
City University of New York
Baruch College *B*
City College *M*
Cornell University *B, M, D*
New York Institute of Technology *M*
New York University *M*
Pratt Institute *M*
State University of New York
Albany *M*

Buffalo *M*
College at Buffalo *B*
College of Environmental Science
and Forestry *B, M*

North Carolina
Appalachian State University *B*
East Carolina University *B*
University of North Carolina
Chapel Hill *M, D*

Ohio
Miami University
Oxford Campus *B*
Ohio State University
Columbus Campus *M, D*
Stark State College of Technology *A*
University of Akron *C, B, M*
University of Cincinnati *B, M*
University of Cincinnati
Clermont College *A*

Oklahoma
University of Oklahoma *M*

Oregon
Portland State University *B, M, D*
University of Oregon *M*

Pennsylvania
Bryn Mawr College *B*
Carnegie Mellon University *M*
Haverford College *B*
Indiana University of Pennsylvania *B*
Mansfield University of
Pennsylvania *B*
Penn State
University Park *M, D*
Temple University *B, M*
University of Pennsylvania *M, D*
West Chester University of
Pennsylvania *M*

Puerto Rico
University of Puerto Rico
Rio Piedras *B*

Rhode Island
University of Rhode Island *M*

South Carolina
Clemson University *M*

Tennessee
University of Memphis *M*
University of Tennessee
Knoxville *M*

Texas
Prairie View A&M University *M*
Rice University *M*
Texas A&M University *M, D*
Texas Southern University *B, M, D*
Texas State University: San Marcos *B*
University of North Texas *B*
University of Texas
Arlington *M*
Austin *M, D*

Utah
Utah State University *M*

Virginia
University of Virginia *B, M*
Virginia Polytechnic Institute and
State University *B*

Washington
Eastern Washington University *B, M*
University of Washington *B, M, D*

Wisconsin
Northland College *B*
University of Wisconsin
Madison *M, D*
Milwaukee *M*

Wyoming
University of Wyoming *M*

Urban education

California
Holy Names University *M*

Florida
Florida International University *M*

Illinois
Columbia College Chicago *M*
Concordia University *M*
University of Illinois
Chicago *D*
Urbana-Champaign *M, D*

Maryland
Morgan State University *M, D*

Massachusetts
Harvard College *M, D*

Nebraska
University of Nebraska
Omaha *T*

New Jersey
St. Peter's College *M*

Ohio
Cleveland State University *D*

Pennsylvania
Temple University *M, D*

Tennessee
University of Tennessee
Chattanooga *M*

Virginia
Norfolk State University *M*

Wisconsin
University of Wisconsin
Milwaukee *D*

Urban forestry

California
University of California
Davis *B*

Illinois
University of Illinois
Urbana-Champaign *B, M, D*

Louisiana
Southern University and Agricultural
and Mechanical College *B, M*

Massachusetts
North Shore Community College *A*

New York
Paul Smith's College *A*

North Dakota
Minot State University: Bottineau
Campus *C, A*

Pennsylvania
Keystone College *A*

Wisconsin
Mid-State Technical College *A*

Urban studies

California
California State University
Northridge *B*
San Bernardino *M*
College of Alameda *C, A*
Loyola Marymount University *B*
San Diego State University *B*
San Francisco State University *B*
Stanford University *B*
University of California
Berkeley *B*
San Diego *B*
University of San Diego *B*
Whittier College *B*

Connecticut
Connecticut College *B*
Trinity College *B*
University of Connecticut *B*

Delaware
University of Delaware *M, D*

District of Columbia
University of the District of
Columbia *A, B*

Florida
New College of Florida *B*

Georgia
Georgia Highlands College *A*
Georgia State University *B, M*
Morehouse College *B*
Savannah State University *M*

Illinois
DePaul University *B*
Elmhurst College *B*
Loyola University of Chicago *M*
North Park University *B*
Northwestern University *B*
Rockford College *B*
Roosevelt University *B, M*
University of Illinois
Chicago *M, D*

Indiana
Ball State University *B*
Butler University *B*
Indiana University-Purdue University
Fort Wayne *C*
Indiana Wesleyan University *B*
Martin University *B*

Iowa
Mount Mercy College *B*

Kansas
MidAmerica Nazarene University *B*

Kentucky
University of Louisville *D*

Louisiana
Dillard University *B*
Tulane University *B*
University of New Orleans *B, M, D*

Maryland
Towson University *B*

University of Maryland
College Park *M*

Massachusetts
Boston University *B*
Hampshire College *B*
Tufts University *M*
Worcester State College *B*

Michigan
Aquinas College *B*
Wayne State University *B*

Minnesota
Augsburg College *B*
Macalester College *B*
Minnesota State University
Mankato *B, M*
Ridgewater College *A*
St. Cloud State University *B*
University of Minnesota
Duluth *B*
Twin Cities *B*
Winona State University *B*

Mississippi
Jackson State University *B*

Missouri
Calvary Bible College and Theological
Seminary *B*
Harris-Stowe State University *B*
St. Louis University *B, M*
University of Missouri
Kansas City *B*

Nebraska
University of Nebraska
Omaha *M*

Nevada
University of Nevada
Reno *M*

New Jersey
Rutgers, The State University of New
Jersey
Camden Regional Campus *B*
New Brunswick/Piscataway
Campus *B, M*
St. Peter's College *A, B*

New York
Barnard College *B*
Canisius College *B*
City University of New York
Hunter College *B, M*
Queens College *B, M, T*
College of Mount St. Vincent *B*
Columbia University
Columbia College *B*
School of General Studies *B*
Daemen College *C*
Eugene Lang College The New School
for Liberal Arts *B*
Fordham University *B*
Hobart and William Smith Colleges *B*
Long Island University
Brooklyn Campus *M*
Metropolitan College of New
York *A, B*
New York University *B, M*
Sarah Lawrence College *B*
State University of New York
Albany *B*
College of Environmental Science
and Forestry *B*
Vassar College *B*

Ohio
Cleveland State University *B, M, D*
College of Wooster *B*

Ohio State University
Columbus Campus *B*
Ohio University *B*
Ohio Wesleyan University *B*
Sinclair Community College *A*
University of Akron *M, D*
University of Cincinnati *B*
University of Cincinnati
Clermont College *A*
Raymond Walters College *A*
University of Toledo *B*
Wittenberg University *B*
Wright State University *B*

Oklahoma
University of Central Oklahoma *B, M*

Oregon
Portland State University *B, M, D*

Pennsylvania
Bryn Mawr College *B*
Drexel University *B*
Eastern University *B*
Haverford College *B*
Lehigh University *B*
Penn State
University Park *M*
Temple University *M*
University of Pennsylvania *B*
University of Pittsburgh *B*

Rhode Island
Brown University *B*
Community College of Rhode
Island *A*

South Carolina
College of Charleston *B*
Furman University *B*

Tennessee
Lipscomb University *B*
Rhodes College *B*
University of Tennessee
Knoxville *B*
Vanderbilt University *B*

Texas
St. Philip's College *A*
Trinity University *B*
University of Houston *B*
University of Texas
Arlington *M*
Austin *B*

Utah
University of Utah *B, M*

Virginia
Norfolk State University *M*
Old Dominion University *M*
University of Richmond *B*
Virginia Commonwealth
University *B, M*
Virginia Polytechnic Institute and
State University *M*

Wisconsin
University of Wisconsin
Green Bay *B*
Milwaukee *B, M, D*
Oshkosh *B*

Vehicle emissions inspection/maintenance

California
College of the Desert *C*
Southwestern College *C*

Vehicle parts/ accessories marketing

Florida
Northwood University
Florida Campus *A, B*

Iowa
Iowa Lakes Community College *C*

Michigan
Northwood University *A, B*

Nebraska
Central Community College *C, A*

New York
State University of New York
Farmingdale *B*

Pennsylvania
Pennsylvania College of Technology *A*

Texas
Northwood University: Texas
Campus *A, B*

Washington
Spokane Community College *C, A*

Vendor/product certification

Arizona
Chandler-Gilbert Community College
Pecos *A*
Estrella Mountain Community
College *C, A*
Paradise Valley Community College *C*

Arkansas
University of Arkansas
Cossatot Community College of the
C

California
College of Oceaneering *C*
Foothill College *C*
Heald College
Stockton *C, A*
Long Beach City College *C*
Maric College
Vista *C*
San Jose City College *C*
Santa Rosa Junior College *C*
Southwestern College *C*

Colorado
Colorado Technical University *C*

Florida
Herzing College
Orlando *C*
Hillsborough Community College *C*
Pasco-Hernando Community
College *A*
St. Petersburg College *C*

Hawaii
Heald College
Honolulu *C, A*

Illinois
Moraine Valley Community College *C*
Morton College *C*
Richland Community College *C*

Kansas
Neosho County Community
College *C*

Kentucky
Ashland Community and Technical
College *A*
Hopkinsville Community College *C*
Louisville Technical Institute *A*

Maryland
Hagerstown Community College *C*

Massachusetts
Bristol Community College *C*

Michigan
Baker College
of Port Huron *C, A*
Davenport University *B*
Lansing Community College *A*

Minnesota
Pine Technical College *C*
St. Paul College *C*

Missouri
Moberly Area Community College *C*

Montana
Dawson Community College *A*

New Jersey
Cumberland County College *A*

New York
Globe Institute of Technology *C, A, B*

North Carolina
Beaufort County Community
College *C, A*
Pitt Community College *C, A*

North Dakota
Lake Region State College *C, A*
Williston State College *C, A*

Ohio
Bryant & Stratton College
Willoughby Hills *C*
James A. Rhodes State College *C*
Marion Technical College *A*
University of Cincinnati
Clermont College *C, A*

Pennsylvania
Keystone College *A*
Peirce College *C, A*

Washington
Bellevue Community College *C*
Big Bend Community College *C*
Clover Park Technical College *C*
Peninsula College *A*

Wyoming
Casper College *C, A*

Veterinary medicine (D.V.M.)

Alabama
Auburn University: College of
Veterinary Medicine *F*
Tuskegee University: School of
Veterinary Medicine *F*

California
University of California Davis: School of Veterinary Medicine *F*

Colorado
Colorado State University: College of Veterinary Medicine and Biomedical Sciences *F*

Florida
University of Florida: College of Veterinary Medicine *F*

Georgia
University of Georgia: College of Veterinary Medicine *F*

Illinois
University of Illinois at Urbana-Champaign: College of Veterinary Medicine *F*

Indiana
Purdue University: School of Veterinary Medicine *F*

Iowa
Iowa State University: College of Veterinary Medicine *F*

Kansas
Kansas State University: College of Veterinary Medicine *F*

Louisiana
Louisiana State University and Agricultural and Mechanical College: School of Veterinary Medicine *F*

Massachusetts
Tufts University: School of Veterinary Medicine *F*

Michigan
Michigan State University: School of Veterinary Medicine *F*

Minnesota
University of Minnesota Twin Cities: College of Veterinary Medicine *F*

Mississippi
Mississippi State University: College of Veterinary Medicine *F*

Missouri
University of Missouri Columbia: School of Veterinary Medicine *F*

New York
Cornell University: College of Veterinary Medicine *F*

North Carolina
North Carolina State University: College of Veterinary Medicine *F*

Ohio
Ohio State University Columbus Campus: College of Veterinary Medicine *F*

Oklahoma
Oklahoma State University: College of Veterinary Medicine *F*

Oregon
Oregon State University: College of Veterinary Medicine *F*

Pennsylvania
University of Pennsylvania: School of Veterinary Medicine *F*

Tennessee
University of Tennessee Knoxville: College of Veterinary Medicine *F*

Texas
Texas A&M University: College of Veterinary Medicine *F*

Virginia
Virginia Polytechnic Institute: Virginia-Maryland Regional College of Veterinary Medicine *F*

Washington
Washington State University: School of Veterinary Medicine *F*

Wisconsin
University of Wisconsin Madison: School of Veterinary Medicine *F*

Veterinary technology

Alabama
Jefferson State Community College *A*

Arizona
Pima Community College *A*

California
California State Polytechnic University: Pomona *B*
Foothill College *C, A*
San Joaquin Valley College Inc. *A*
Silicon Valley College
 Western Career College: San Jose *A*
Western Career College San Leandro *A*
Yuba Community College District *A*

Colorado
Bel-Rea Institute of Animal Technology *A*
Colorado Mountain College Spring Valley Campus *A*
Otero Junior College *A*

Connecticut
Northwestern Connecticut Community College *A*
Quinnipiac University *B*

Delaware
Delaware Technical and Community College
 Owens Campus *A*

Florida
Central Florida Community College *A*
Manatee Community College *A*
Miami Dade College *A*
St. Petersburg College *C, A, B*

Georgia
Athens Technical College *A*
Fort Valley State University *A, B*
Gwinnett Technical College *C, A*

Idaho
College of Southern Idaho *A*

Illinois
Joliet Junior College *A*
Parkland College *A*

Indiana
Purdue University *A, B*

Iowa
Des Moines Area Community College *C, A*
Kirkwood Community College *A*

Kansas
Colby Community College *A*
Johnson County Community College *A*

Kentucky
Morehead State University *A*
Murray State University *B*

Louisiana
Northwestern State University *A*

Maine
University of Maine Augusta *A*

Maryland
Community College of Baltimore County *A*

Massachusetts
Becker College *A*
Berkshire Community College *C*
Holyoke Community College *A*
Mount Ida College *A, B*
North Shore Community College *A*

Michigan
Baker College
 of Cadillac *A*
 of Flint *A*
 of Muskegon *A*
 of Port Huron *A*
Bay de Noc Community College *C*
Kirtland Community College *C*
Macomb Community College *A*
Michigan State University *C, B*
Oakland Community College *C*
Wayne County Community College *A*

Minnesota
Globe College *C, A*
Ridgewater College *A*
Rochester Community and Technical College *C, A*

Mississippi
Hinds Community College *A*
Mississippi Gulf Coast Community College
 Jefferson Davis Campus *A*

Missouri
Jefferson College *C, A*
Maple Woods Community College *A*

Nebraska
Nebraska College of Technical Agriculture *A*
Northeast Community College *A*
University of Nebraska Lincoln *B*
Vatterott College: Spring Valley *A*

New Hampshire
New Hampshire Community Technical College Stratham *A*

New Jersey
Bergen Community College *A*
Camden County College *A*
County College of Morris *A*

Sussex County Community College *A*
Thomas Edison State College *A, B*

New Mexico
Albuquerque Technical-Vocational Institute *A*

New York
City University of New York LaGuardia Community College *A*
Medaille College *A, B*
State University of New York
 College of Technology at Alfred *A*
 College of Technology at Canton *A*
 College of Technology at Delhi *A*
Suffolk County Community College *A*

North Carolina
Central Carolina Community College *A*
Gaston College *A*

North Dakota
North Dakota State University *B*

Ohio
Bradford School *A*
Columbus State Community College *A*
Stautzenberger College *A*
University of Cincinnati Raymond Walters College *A*

Oklahoma
Oklahoma State University Oklahoma City *A*
Redlands Community College *A*

Oregon
Linn-Benton Community College *C*
Portland Community College *A*

Pennsylvania
Harcum College *A*
Johnson College *A*
Lehigh Carbon Community College *A*
Manor College *A*
Northampton County Area Community College *A*
Vet Tech Institute *A*
Wilson College *A, B*

South Carolina
Greenville Technical College *C*
Newberry College *B*
Tri-County Technical College *A*

Tennessee
Columbia State Community College *A*
Lincoln Memorial University *A, B*

Texas
Cedar Valley College *C, A*
Houston Community College System *C*
Midland College *A*
North Harris Montgomery Community College District *A*
Sul Ross State University *A*

Utah
Snow College *A*
Utah Career College *A*

Vermont
Vermont Technical College *A*

Virginia
Blue Ridge Community College *C, A*
Northern Virginia Community College *A*

Washington

Bellingham Technical College C
Pierce College A
Yakima Valley Community
College C, A

Wisconsin

Madison Area Technical College A

Wyoming

Eastern Wyoming College A

Violin/viola/guitar/ stringed instruments

California

Bethesda Christian University B, M
California Institute of the Arts C, B, M
California State University
Fullerton B, M
San Francisco Conservatory of
Music B, M
University of Southern
California B, M, D

Florida

Florida State University B, M, D
Stetson University B

Illinois

Illinois Wesleyan University B
Northwestern University B, M, D

Indiana

Butler University B, M

Iowa

Dordt College B
University of Iowa B

Kansas

University of Kansas B, M, D

Louisiana

Xavier University of Louisiana B

Maine

University of Southern Maine B

Massachusetts

New England Conservatory of
Music B, M, D
Simon's Rock College of Bard B

Michigan

Hope College B
University of Michigan M

Minnesota

Northwestern College B
St. Cloud State University B

Nebraska

Hastings College B
University of Nebraska
Omaha B

New York

Bard College B
Five Towns College A, B, M, D
Houghton College B
Juilliard School B, M, D
Mannes College The New School for
Music B
Sarah Lawrence College B

North Carolina

East Carolina University B
Meredith College B

Ohio

Oberlin College B, M
Youngstown State University B, M

Oklahoma

Oklahoma City University B
University of Central Oklahoma B

Pennsylvania

Carnegie Mellon University B, M
Susquehanna University B

Puerto Rico

Conservatory of Music of Puerto
Rico B

Texas

Hardin-Simmons University B, M
Howard Payne University B

Utah

Brigham Young University B

Vermont

Bennington College B

Washington

Central Washington University B
Cornish College of the Arts B
University of Washington B, M, D

Virology

Illinois

University of Chicago D

Massachusetts

Harvard College D

Ohio

Case Western Reserve University D
Ohio State University
Columbus Campus M, D

Texas

University of Texas
Health Science Center at
Houston M, D

Vision science

Alabama

University of Alabama
Birmingham M, D

California

University of California
Berkeley M, D

Visual/performing arts

Alabama

Birmingham-Southern College B
Faulkner State Community College A
Faulkner University B
University of Alabama
Birmingham B
University of Mobile B
Virginia College at Huntsville A

Alaska

University of Alaska
Anchorage B

Arizona

Arizona State University West B
Central Arizona College A
Northern Arizona University B
Prescott College B, M

University of Arizona B

Arkansas

University of Arkansas
Fort Smith A
University of the Ozarks B

California

Antelope Valley College C, A
Cabrillo College A
California Baptist University B
California Institute of the Arts C, B, M
California Lutheran University B
California State University
Bakersfield B
Monterey Bay B
San Marcos B
College of Alameda A
Cypress College C, A
Fashion Institute of Design and
Merchandising
San Francisco A
Fresno City College C, A
Fullerton College A
Glendale Community College A
Irvine Valley College A
Los Angeles City College C
Merced College A
Modesto Junior College C, A
Moorpark College A
Platt College
Cerritos C, A
Los Angeles C, A
Newport Beach C, A
Ontario C, A, B
San Diego C, A, B
Pomona College B
Porterville College A
Sacramento City College A
St. Mary's College of California B
San Diego City College A
San Joaquin Delta College A
San Jose State University B
Skyline College A
Sonoma State University B
University of California
Riverside M
San Diego M
Santa Barbara B, M, D
University of San Francisco B

Colorado

Colorado Mountain College
Alpine Campus A
Spring Valley Campus A
Regis University B

Connecticut

Albertus Magnus College B
Eastern Connecticut State
University B
Fairfield University B
Trinity College B
Tunxis Community College C, A
University of Hartford B

Delaware

University of Delaware M

District of Columbia

American University B
Catholic University of America M, D
Corcoran College of Art and
Design A, B
Gallaudet University B
George Washington University B, M
Howard University B

Florida

Art Institute of Fort Lauderdale A
Flagler College B
Florida Agricultural and Mechanical
University B

Florida Community College at
Jacksonville A
Lynn University B
Manatee Community College A
Miami International University of Art
and Design B
Palm Beach Atlantic University B
Palm Beach Community College A
St. Johns River Community College A
Tallahassee Community College A
University of Miami B
University of Tampa B

Georgia

Abraham Baldwin Agricultural
College A
Andrew College A
Armstrong Atlantic State University B
Darton College A
LaGrange College B
Savannah College of Art and
Design B, M
Valdosta State University B
Young Harris College A

Illinois

American Academy of Art B
City Colleges of Chicago
Kennedy-King College A
Columbia College Chicago B
Highland Community College A
Illinois College B
Illinois Institute of Art-Schaumburg B
Illinois Valley Community College A
Kishwaukee College A
Moraine Valley Community College A
North Central College B
Northwestern University B
Quincy University B
Richland Community College A
Rockford College B
Roosevelt University B, M
School of the Art Institute of
Chicago B, M
University of Chicago B
University of St. Francis B
William Rainey Harper College A

Indiana

Earlham College B
Goshen College B
Indiana University
Bloomington B, M
International Business College:
Indianapolis C
Vincennes University A

Iowa

Graceland University B
Iowa State University B, M
Loras College B
Maharishi University of
Management B, M
Marshalltown Community College A
Waldorf College B
William Penn University B

Kansas

Central Christian College of
Kansas A, B
Cloud County Community College A
Coffeyville Community College A
Colby Community College A
Cowley County Community
College A
Garden City Community College A
Hutchinson Community College A
MidAmerica Nazarene University B, T
Pratt Community College A
Seward County Community College A
Sterling College T
Washburn University of Topeka B
Wichita State University B

Kentucky
Thomas More College *B*
Western Kentucky University *B*

Louisiana
Centenary College of Louisiana *B*
Loyola University New Orleans *B*
Southern University
   New Orleans *B*
University of Louisiana at Lafayette *B*

Maine
College of the Atlantic *B*
University of Maine
   Machias *B*
University of Southern Maine *B*

Maryland
Frostburg State University *C, B*
Garrett College *A*
Montgomery College *A*
Mount St. Mary's University *B, T*
University of Maryland
   Baltimore County *B, M*

Massachusetts
Art Institute of Boston at Lesley
   University *B*
Assumption College *B*
Berkshire Community College *A*
Boston University *B, M*
Cape Cod Community College *A*
Clark University *B*
Emerson College *B, M*
Hampshire College *B*
Harvard College *B, D*
Massachusetts College of Liberal
   Arts *B*
Massasoit Community College *C*
Middlesex Community College *A*
New England Institute of Art *A*
Northeastern University *B*
Pine Manor College *B*
Roxbury Community College *A*
Simon's Rock College of Bard *B*
Suffolk University *B*
Tufts University *M*
University of Massachusetts
   Dartmouth *B, M*
   Lowell *B*
Wheelock College *B*

Michigan
Albion College *B, T*
Alma College *B*
Andrews University *B*
Calvin College *B*
Lansing Community College *A*
Mid Michigan Community College *A*
Oakland University *B*
Olivet College *B, T*

Minnesota
Academy College *C, A*
Hamline University *B*
Minneapolis College of Art and
   Design *B*
Minnesota School of Business:
   Brooklyn Center *C, A*
Minnesota State University
   Mankato *B*
Northland Community & Technical
   College *A*
Winona State University *B*

Mississippi
Coahoma Community College *A*
Delta State University *B*
Jackson State University *B*
Mississippi College *M*
Mississippi State University *B*
University of Mississippi *B, M*

University of Southern Mississippi *B*

Missouri
Drury University *B, T*
Lindenwood University *B*
St. Louis Community College
   St. Louis Community College at
    Florissant Valley *A*
Southeast Missouri State University *B*
Stephens College *B*
Washington University in St.
   Louis *B, M*

Montana
University of Montana: Missoula *B, M*
University of Montana: Western *B*

Nebraska
University of Nebraska
   Kearney *B, M, T*

Nevada
Art Institute
   of Las Vegas *C, A*
Sierra Nevada College *B*

New Hampshire
Franklin Pierce College *B*

New Jersey
Bloomfield College *C, B*
The College of New Jersey *B*
County College of Morris *A*
Fairleigh Dickinson University
   College at Florham *B*
   Metropolitan Campus *B*
Mercer County Community College *A*
Ramapo College of New Jersey *B*
Richard Stockton College of New
   Jersey *B*
Rowan University *B*
Seton Hall University *B, T*
William Paterson University of New
   Jersey *M*

New Mexico
Art Center Design College *C*
New Mexico Highlands University *B*
New Mexico State University *B, M*
Northern New Mexico College *A*

New York
Adirondack Community College *A*
Bard College *B, M*
Barnard College *B*
Briarcliffe College *B*
City University of New York
   City College *B, M*
   Kingsborough Community
    College *A*
   Queensborough Community
    College *A*
College of Saint Rose *C*
Columbia University
   Columbia College *B*
   School of General Studies *B*
Cornell University *B, M, D*
Dowling College *B*
Eugene Lang College The New School
   for Liberal Arts *B*
Five Towns College *A, B, M, D*
Ithaca College *B, M*
Juilliard School *B, M, D*
Long Island University
   Brooklyn Campus *B, M*
Medaille College *B*
New York University *C, B, M, D*
Pratt Institute *B, M*
St. Bonaventure University *B*
Sarah Lawrence College *B*
School of Visual Arts *B, M*
Siena College *B*

State University of New York
   College at Brockport *B, M*
   College at Buffalo *B*
   College at Old Westbury *B*
   College at Potsdam *B*
   New Paltz *B*
Syracuse University *B*
Union College *B*
Wells College *B*
Westchester Community College *A*

North Carolina
Bennett College *B*
Carteret Community College *A*
Fayetteville State University *B*
Methodist College *B*
North Carolina Agricultural and
   Technical State University *B*
St. Andrews Presbyterian College *B*
St. Augustine's College *B*

North Dakota
University of North Dakota *B*

Ohio
Antioch College *B*
International College of
   Broadcasting *C, A*
Lake Erie College *B*
Mount Union College *T*
Ohio University *B, D*
Otterbein College *B*
Shawnee State University *B*
Sinclair Community College *A*
Union Institute & University *B*
University of Rio Grande *B*
Wittenberg University *B*
Youngstown State University *B, M*

Oklahoma
Murray State College *A*
Oklahoma City University *B, M*
Rose State College *A*
St. Gregory's University *A, B*
Southern Nazarene University *B*
University of Oklahoma *B*

Oregon
Central Oregon Community
   College *A*
Oregon State University *B*
Pacific University *B*
Treasure Valley Community College *A*
Western Oregon University *B*

Pennsylvania
Arcadia University *B*
Bucks County Community College *A*
Cedar Crest College *B*
Douglas Education Center *A*
East Stroudsburg University of
   Pennsylvania *B*
Gannon University *B*
Gettysburg College *B*
Harrisburg Area Community
   College *A*
Kutztown University of
   Pennsylvania *B*
Marywood University *B*
Oakbridge Academy of Arts *A*
Penn State
   Abington *B*
   Altoona *B*
   Beaver *B*
   Berks *B*
   Delaware County *B*
   Dubois *B*
   Fayette *B*
   Hazleton *B*
   Lehigh Valley *B*
   McKeesport *B*
   Mont Alto *B*
   New Kensington *B*

   Schuylkill - Capital College *B*
   Shenango *B*
   University Park *B*
   Wilkes-Barre *B*
   Worthington Scranton *B*
   York *B*
St. Joseph's University *B*
University of Pennsylvania *B*
University of Pittsburgh
   Bradford *B*
University of the Arts *B*
York College of Pennsylvania *A, B*

Puerto Rico
Inter American University of Puerto
   Rico
   San German Campus *B, M*
University of Puerto Rico
   Rio Piedras *B*
University of the Sacred Heart *B*

Rhode Island
Brown University *B*
Providence College *B*

South Carolina
Charleston Southern University *B*

South Dakota
South Dakota State University *B, T*

Tennessee
Carson-Newman College *B*
King College *B*
Lambuth University *B*
Lincoln Memorial University *B, T*
Milligan College *B*
Nossi College of Art *A*
Roane State Community College *A*
Tusculum College *B*
University of Tennessee
   Martin *B*
University of the South *B*

Texas
Art Institute
   of Dallas *A*
   of Houston *C, A*
Coastal Bend College *A*
College of the Mainland *A*
Hill College *A*
Howard College *A*
Lon Morris College *A*
Rice University *B, M*
South Texas College *A*
Texas A&M University
   Commerce *B*
Texas Lutheran University *B*
Texas Tech University *D*
Texas Wesleyan University *B, T*
Trinity Valley Community College *A*
Tyler Junior College *A*
University of Texas
   Austin *B*
   Dallas *B*

Utah
Provo College *A*
Snow College *A*
University of Utah *B*
Weber State University *B*

Vermont
Bennington College *B*
Burlington College *A, B*
Castleton State College *B*
Goddard College *B*
Green Mountain College *B*
Johnson State College *B*
Marlboro College *B*
Norwich University *M*
University of Vermont *B*

Virginia

Ferrum College *B*
George Mason University *M*
Longwood University *B, T*
Mary Baldwin College *M*
Norfolk State University *M*
Old Dominion University *M*
Piedmont Virginia Community
College *A*
Regent University *M*
Shenandoah University *B*
Virginia State University *B*

Washington

Art Institute of Seattle *A, B*
Centralia College *A*
Columbia Basin College *A*
Cornish College of the Arts *B*
Eastern Washington University *B, T*
Everett Community College *A*
Evergreen State College *B*
Green River Community College *C, A*
Highline Community College *A*
North Seattle Community
College *C, A*
Olympic College *A*
Seattle Pacific University *B, T*
Seattle University *B*
Western Washington University *B*
Whitworth College *B, T*

West Virginia

Bethany College *B*
West Virginia University *B, M*

Wisconsin

Edgewood College *B*
University of Wisconsin
Green Bay *B*
Milwaukee *M*
Stevens Point *B*
Superior *B, M, T*
Viterbo University *B*

Wyoming

Western Wyoming Community
College *A*

Vocational rehabilitation counseling

Alabama

University of Alabama *M*

Arkansas

University of Arkansas *M, D*
University of Arkansas
Little Rock *M*

California

California State University
Fresno *B, M*
San Bernardino *M*

Colorado

University of Northern Colorado *B, M*

Florida

Florida State University *B, M, D*
University of Florida *B*
University of North Florida *M*
University of South Florida *M*

Georgia

Fort Valley State University *M*
Georgia State University *M*

Illinois

Illinois Institute of Technology *M*

Southern Illinois University
Carbondale *M*
University of Illinois
Urbana-Champaign *B, M, D*

Kansas

Emporia State University *B, M*

Kentucky

University of Kentucky *M*

Louisiana

Louisiana State University Health
Sciences Center *B, M*
Southern University and Agricultural
and Mechanical College *B, M*

Massachusetts

Boston University *M, D*
Springfield College *M*

Michigan

Michigan State University *M*

Mississippi

Jackson State University *M*

Missouri

Maryville University of Saint
Louis *B, M*

Montana

Montana State University
Billings *B, M*

New Jersey

Seton Hall University *M*
Union County College *A*
University of Medicine and Dentistry
of New Jersey
School of Health Related
Professions *M*

New York

Hofstra University *M*
State University of New York
Buffalo *M*

North Carolina

Appalachian State University *M*
East Carolina University *B, M*
University of North Carolina
Chapel Hill *M*
Winston-Salem State University *B, M*

Ohio

Bowling Green State University *M*
University of Cincinnati *M*
University of Cincinnati
Raymond Walters College *A*
Wright State University *B*

Oklahoma

East Central University *B*

Oregon

Western Oregon University *M*

Pennsylvania

Edinboro University of
Pennsylvania *M*

Tennessee

University of Tennessee
Knoxville *M*

Texas

Stephen F. Austin State University *M*
Texas Tech University Health Sciences
Center *D*

University of Texas
Pan American *B, M*
Southwestern Medical Center at
Dallas *B, M*

Virginia

Virginia Commonwealth University *M*

Washington

Edmonds Community College *A*
Spokane Falls Community College *A*
Western Washington University *M*

West Virginia

West Virginia University *M*

Wisconsin

University of Wisconsin
Madison *B, M, D*
Stout *B, M*

Vocational/technical education

Alabama

Auburn University *B, M, D*
Northeast Alabama Community
College *A*
Tuskegee University *B*

Arizona

Northern Arizona University *B*
Prescott College *B*

California

San Diego State University *B*

Connecticut

University of Connecticut *D, T*

Delaware

Wilmington College *M*

Florida

Palm Beach Community College *A*

Georgia

Georgia Southern University *M*

Hawaii

University of Hawaii
Honolulu Community College *A*

Idaho

University of Idaho *B, M, T*

Illinois

City Colleges of Chicago
Kennedy-King College *A*
Eastern Illinois University *B, T*
Sauk Valley Community College *A*
University of Illinois
Urbana-Champaign *M, D*

Indiana

Ball State University *M, T*
Vincennes University *A*

Kansas

Pittsburg State University *B, M*

Kentucky

Eastern Kentucky University *A*
Western Kentucky University *A*

Maine

University of Southern Maine *B, T*

Michigan

Cornerstone University *B, T*
Ferris State University *B, M*
Wayne State University *B, M, T*

Minnesota

Bemidji State University *B*
Minnesota State University
Mankato *B, M, T*
Ridgewater College *A*

Mississippi

Mississippi State University *B, M, T*

Missouri

Mineral Area College *A*
Moberly Area Community College *A*
North Central Missouri College *A*
State Fair Community College *A*
University of Missouri
Columbia *B, M, D*

Nebraska

Chadron State College *M*
Peru State College *B, T*

New Jersey

College of St. Elizabeth *M*

New Mexico

University of New Mexico *M, D, T*
Western New Mexico University *B*

New York

New York Institute of
Technology *A, B, T*
State University of New York
College at Buffalo *B, M, T*
Oswego *B*

North Carolina

East Carolina University *M*

North Dakota

Lake Region State College *A*
Valley City State University *B*

Ohio

Bowling Green State University *B, T*
Ohio State University
Columbus Campus *M, D*
University of Akron *B, M*

Oklahoma

Oklahoma State University *B, T*

Oregon

Oregon State University *M*

Pennsylvania

Pittsburgh Institute of Aeronautics *A*
Temple University *M*

Puerto Rico

Inter American University of Puerto
Rico
San German Campus *B*

Rhode Island

Rhode Island College *B*

South Carolina

Aiken Technical College *A*
Florence-Darlington Technical
College *A*
Horry-Georgetown Technical
College *A*
Piedmont Technical College *A*
Spartanburg Technical College *A*
Trident Technical College *A*

South Dakota
South Dakota State University *B, T*

Tennessee
Middle Tennessee State University *M*

Texas
Texas A&M University *M*
Texas A&M University
 Commerce *T*
Texas Christian University *B*
University of North Texas *M, D*

Utah
Utah State University *B, M*

Washington
Renton Technical College *A*
Walla Walla College *B*

Wisconsin
University of Wisconsin
 Platteville *B, T*
 Stout *B*

Voice/opera

Alabama
Birmingham-Southern College *B*
Huntingdon College *B*
Samford University *B*
Talladega College *B*

Arizona
Grand Canyon University *B*
Northern Arizona University *B, M*

Arkansas
Harding University *B*
Ouachita Baptist University *B*
University of Central Arkansas *B*

California
Bethesda Christian University *B, M*
California Institute of the Arts *C, B, M*
California State University
 Chico *C*
 Fullerton *B, M*
 Long Beach *B*
Chapman University *B*
Fresno City College *A*
Master's College *B*
Notre Dame de Namur University *M*
Ohlone College *C*
San Diego State University *M*
San Francisco Conservatory of
 Music *B, M*
San Francisco State University *B*
Solano Community College *C*
University of Southern
 California *B, M, D*
University of the Pacific *B*

Colorado
Adams State College *B*

Delaware
University of Delaware *B*

District of Columbia
Catholic University of
 America *B, M, D*
Howard University *B*

Florida
Florida State University *B, M, D*
Jacksonville University *B*
Palm Beach Atlantic University *B*
Southeastern College of the
 Assemblies of God *B*
Stetson University *B*

University of Miami *B, M, D*

Georgia
Emory University *M*
Georgia College and State
 University *B*
Shorter College *B*

Hawaii
Brigham Young University-Hawaii *B*

Idaho
University of Idaho *B*

Illinois
Augustana College *B*
Columbia College Chicago *B*
Illinois Wesleyan University *B*
Judson College *B*
Millikin University *B*
Monmouth College *T*
Moody Bible Institute *B*
North Park University *M*
Northwestern University *B, M, D*
Olivet Nazarene University *B*
Quincy University *T*
Roosevelt University *B, M*
St. Xavier University *B*
Sauk Valley Community College *A*
Trinity International University *B*
University of Illinois
 Urbana-Champaign *B, M, D*

Indiana
American Conservatory of
 Music *C, B, M, D*
Butler University *B, M*
Huntington University *B*
Indiana University
 Bloomington *B*
Indiana University-Purdue University
 Fort Wayne *B, T*
Indiana Wesleyan University *T*
Valparaiso University *B*
Vincennes University *A*

Iowa
Dordt College *B*
Drake University *B*
University of Iowa *B*
Waldorf College *B*

Kansas
Allen County Community College *A*
Central Christian College of Kansas *A*
MidAmerica Nazarene University *B, T*
Pittsburg State University *B, M*
Seward County Community College *A*
University of Kansas *B, M, D*

Kentucky
Campbellsville University *B*

Louisiana
Centenary College of Louisiana *B, T*
Xavier University of Louisiana *B*

Maine
University of Southern Maine *B*

Maryland
Johns Hopkins University: Peabody
 Conservatory of Music *B, M, D*
Washington Bible College *B*

Massachusetts
Anna Maria College *B*
Berklee College of Music *B*
Boston Conservatory *B*
Boston University *B, M, D*
Eastern Nazarene College *B*

New England Conservatory of
 Music *B, M, D*

Michigan
Calvin College *B, T*
Eastern Michigan University *B*
Hope College *B*
Northwestern Michigan College *A*
Oakland Community College *A*
Oakland University *B*
Olivet College *B*

Minnesota
Concordia College: Moorhead *B*
Minnesota State University
 Mankato *B, M, T*
Northwestern College *B*
St. Cloud State University *B*
St. Mary's University of Minnesota *B*

Mississippi
Blue Mountain College *B*
Mississippi College *B, M*

Missouri
Calvary Bible College and Theological
 Seminary *B*
Drury University *B*
Hannibal-LaGrange College *B*
Washington University in St.
 Louis *B, M*

Nebraska
Concordia University *B, T*
Hastings College *B*
University of Nebraska
 Omaha *B*
York College *B*

New Jersey
Rider University *B*
Westminster Choir College of Rider
 University *B*

New York
Bard College *B*
Columbia University
 School of General Studies *B*
Eastman School of Music of the
 University of Rochester *B, M, D*
Five Towns College *A, B, M, D*
Houghton College *B*
Mannes College The New School for
 Music *B, M*
New York University *B*
Roberts Wesleyan College *B*
Sarah Lawrence College *B*
State University of New York
 Binghamton *M*
 College at Fredonia *B*
 New Paltz *B*
Syracuse University *B, M*
University of Rochester *M, D*

North Carolina
Campbell University *B*
East Carolina University *B*
Gardner-Webb University *B*
Meredith College *B*
Wingate University *B*

Ohio
Bowling Green State University *B, M*
Capital University *B*
Cleveland Institute of Music *B, M, D*
Oberlin College *B, M*
Ohio State University
 Columbus Campus *B*
Ohio University *B*
University of Akron *B*
University of Cincinnati *B, M, D*
Youngstown State University *B, M*

Oklahoma
East Central University *B, T*
Northwestern Oklahoma State
 University *B*
Oklahoma Baptist University *B*
Oklahoma Christian University *B*
Oklahoma City University *B*
Oral Roberts University *B*
Southwestern Oklahoma State
 University *B*
University of Central Oklahoma *B*
University of Tulsa *B*

Oregon
Corban College *B*
Willamette University *B*

Pennsylvania
Carnegie Mellon University *B, M*
Curtis Institute of Music *M*
Gettysburg College *B*
Gratz College *M*
Mansfield University of
 Pennsylvania *B*
Marywood University *C*
Penn State
 University Park *M*
Susquehanna University *B*
Temple University *B, M, D*
Westminster College *B*

Puerto Rico
Conservatory of Music of Puerto
 Rico *B*

South Carolina
Anderson University *B*
Charleston Southern University *B*
Coker College *B*
Columbia College *B*
Furman University *B*
North Greenville College *B*
South Carolina State University *B*
University of South Carolina *M*

Tennessee
Belmont University *B, M*
Bryan College *B*
Hiwassee College *A*
Lambuth University *B*
Lipscomb University *B*
Union University *B*
University of Tennessee
 Knoxville *B*

Texas
Abilene Christian University *B*
Angelina College *A*
Dallas Baptist University *B*
East Texas Baptist University *B*
Hardin-Simmons University *B, M*
Howard Payne University *B*
Lamar University *B, M*
Lon Morris College *A*
McMurry University *B, T*
Navarro College *A*
Prairie View A&M University *B*
Southern Methodist University *B, M*
Southwestern Assemblies of God
 University *B*
Texas A&M University
 Commerce *B, M*
Texas Christian University *M*
Trinity University *B*
University of Texas
 El Paso *B*

Utah
Brigham Young University *B*
Weber State University *B*

Vermont

Bennington College *B*
Johnson State College *B*

Virginia

Virginia Union University *B*

Washington

Central Washington University *B*
Cornish College of the Arts *B*
Eastern Washington University *B, T*
University of Washington *B, M, D*
Whitworth College *B*

West Virginia

Davis and Elkins College *B*

Wisconsin

Carthage College *B*
Lawrence University *B*
Northland College *B, T*
University of Wisconsin
Madison *B, M*
Parkside *T*

Waldorf/Steiner teacher education

Michigan

University of Detroit Mercy *B*

Vermont

Sterling College *B*

Warehousing/inventory management

Iowa

Iowa Lakes Community College *C*

Washington

Clover Park Technical College *C*

Watch/jewelrymaking

Colorado

Pueblo Community College *A*

Minnesota

Minneapolis Community and
Technical College *C, A*
St. Paul College *C*

Montana

Flathead Valley Community College *A*

Oklahoma

Oklahoma State University
Okmulgee *A*

Pennsylvania

Commonwealth Technical Institute *C*

Texas

Paris Junior College *A*

Washington

North Seattle Community
College *C, A*

Wisconsin

Milwaukee Area Technical College *C*

Water quality/ treatment/recycling technology

Alabama

Gadsden State Community College *C*
Northwest-Shoals Community
College *C*

Arizona

Gateway Community College *C, A*
Rio Salado College *C, A*

California

Citrus College *C*
College of the Canyons *A*
San Diego Mesa College *C, A*
Santa Barbara City College *C*
Shasta College *C*
Solano Community College *C, A*
Yuba Community College
District *C, A*

Colorado

Red Rocks Community College *A*

Connecticut

Three Rivers Community College *C, A*

Kentucky

Eastern Kentucky University *B*
Murray State University *A, B*

Massachusetts

Bristol Community College *A*
Cape Cod Community College *C*
Springfield Technical Community
College *C*

Michigan

Bay de Noc Community College *A*
Grand Rapids Community College *A*
Northern Michigan University *C, A, B*

Minnesota

St. Cloud Technical College *C, A*

Nevada

Community College of Southern
Nevada *C, A*

New Hampshire

New Hampshire Community
Technical College
Berlin *C, A*

North Dakota

Minot State University: Bottineau
Campus *C, A*

Ohio

Wright State University *A*

Oklahoma

Rose State College *C, A*

Oregon

Clackamas Community College *C, A*
Linn-Benton Community College *C, A*

Texas

Angelina College *C*
Houston Community College
System *C, A*

Wisconsin

Milwaukee Area Technical College *A*

Wyoming

Casper College *A*

Water resource engineering

Arizona

Gateway Community College *A*

California

University of Southern
California *B, M*

Nevada

University of Nevada
Reno *B, M, D*

New Jersey

Stevens Institute of Technology *M*

New Mexico

University of New Mexico *M*

Ohio

Central State University *B*

Pennsylvania

Villanova University *M*

Wisconsin

Marquette University *M, D*
University of Wisconsin
Madison *M, D*

Water, wetlands, and marine management

Colorado

Colorado State University *B, M*

Idaho

College of Southern Idaho *C, A*

Michigan

Delta College *C, A*

Minnesota

University of Minnesota
Crookston *B*

New Hampshire

University of New Hampshire *M*

New Mexico

Santa Fe Community College *C*

North Carolina

Lenoir Community College *C, A*

Pennsylvania

Gettysburg College *B*
Keystone College *A, B*

Rhode Island

University of Rhode Island *B*

Texas

Texas State University: San Marcos *B*

Vermont

Sterling College *B*

Washington

Grays Harbor College *C*
Spokane Community College *A*

Wisconsin

University of Wisconsin
Madison *M*
Stevens Point *B*

Wyoming

Western Wyoming Community
College *A*

Web/multimedia management

Alabama

Gadsden State Community College *C*
Shelton State Community College *C*

Arizona

Eastern Arizona College *C*
Paradise Valley Community College *C*
University of Advancing
Technology *A, B*
University of Phoenix *C*

Arkansas

Mid-South Community College *C*
Northwest Arkansas Community
College *A*
Pulaski Technical College *A*
Southeast Arkansas College *C, A*

California

Art Institute
of California: San Diego *B*
Foothill College *C*
Grossmont Community College *C, A*
Santa Rosa Junior College *C*
Sierra College *C, A*
Skyline College *C, A*
Southwestern College *C, A*
Westwood College *B*

Colorado

Colorado Technical University *C*
Westwood College of Technology *B*
Westwood College of Technology
South *B*

District of Columbia

American University *B*

Florida

Florida Career College: Hialeah *A*
Florida Career College: Miami *A*
Florida Career College: Pembroke
Pines *A*
Hillsborough Community
College *C, A*
International Academy of Design and
Technology: Orlando *B*
Lake-Sumter Community College *A*
St. Johns River Community College *C*
St. Petersburg College *C, A*

Georgia

Northwestern Technical College *C, A*

Idaho

Lewis-Clark State College *A, B*

Illinois

Lewis and Clark Community
College *A*
Midstate College *C, A*
Oakton Community College *C*
Rend Lake College *C*
Spoon River College *C*
University of St. Francis *B*

Indiana

Indiana University-Purdue University
Indianapolis *B*

Sawyer College: Merrillville *C, A*
Vincennes University *A*

Iowa
Hamilton College
   Cedar Falls *A*
Southwestern Community
   College *C, A*

Kentucky
Big Sandy Community and Technical
   College *C, A*
Elizabethtown Community and
   Technical College *C*
Hopkinsville Community College *C, A*

Maryland
Community College of Baltimore
   County *A*
Hagerstown Business College *A*

Massachusetts
Cape Cod Community College *A*
Holyoke Community College *C*
Mount Wachusett Community
   College *C*

Michigan
Davenport University *A, B*
Delta College *C, A*
Gogebic Community College *C*
Grand Rapids Community College *A*
Kirtland Community College *C, A*
Northwestern Michigan College *C*
Oakland Community College *C*

Minnesota
Art Institutes International
   Minnesota *A, B*
Dakota County Technical College *C, A*
Globe College *C, A*
Rasmussen College
   St. Cloud *C, A*
Ridgewater College *C, A*
St. Paul College *C*

Mississippi
Antonelli College
   Jackson *A*

Missouri
Missouri Southern State University *A*
Ranken Technical College *A*

Nevada
Community College of Southern
   Nevada *A*
Western Nevada Community
   College *A*

New Hampshire
Daniel Webster College *C*
New Hampshire Community
   Technical College
   Manchester *C*
   Nashua *C, A*

New Jersey
Salem Community College *A*
Union County College *C*

New York
Bryant & Stratton Business Institute
   Bryant & Stratton College:
     Rochester *A*
Columbia-Greene Community
   College *C*
Erie Community College
   North Campus *C*
Globe Institute of Technology *C, A, B*

Mohawk Valley Community
   College *C, A*
Onondaga Community College *C*
Rochester Institute of
   Technology *B, M*
State University of New York
   College of Agriculture and
     Technology at Morrisville *B*
   Farmingdale *C*
Suffolk County Community
   College *C, A*
Tompkins-Cortland Community
   College *A*
Westchester Community College *C*

North Carolina
Carteret Community College *C, A*
Central Piedmont Community
   College *C, A*
College of the Albemarle *C*
Sandhills Community College *C, A*

North Dakota
Minot State University: Bottineau
   Campus *A*

Ohio
Baldwin-Wallace College *B*
James A. Rhodes State College *C*
Marion Technical College *A*
School of Advertising Art *C, A*
Shawnee State University *C*
Sinclair Community College *C, A*
Stark State College of Technology *A*
University of Cincinnati
   Raymond Walters College *C, A*
Youngstown State University *C*

Oklahoma
Rose State College *A*

Oregon
Pioneer Pacific College *A*
Portland Community College *C*
Southwestern Oregon Community
   College *C, A*

Pennsylvania
Cabrini College *C, B*
Consolidated School of Business
   Lancaster *A*
   York *A*
Douglas Education Center *A*
Duquesne University *B*
Gannon University *C*
ICM School of Business & Medical
   Careers *A*
Lehigh Valley College *A*

Rhode Island
Johnson & Wales University *B*

South Carolina
Limestone College *A, B*
Southern Wesleyan University *B*
York Technical College *C*

Tennessee
Northeast State Technical Community
   College *A*

Texas
Mountain View College *C*
St. Philip's College *C, A*
South Texas College *A*
Temple College *C, A*
Victoria College *C, A*

Utah
LDS Business College *A*

Vermont
Castleton State College *B*
Champlain College *A, B*
Vermont Technical College *A*

Virginia
ECPI College of Technology *C, A*

Washington
Clark College *C, A*
Everett Community College *A*
Heritage University *C*
North Seattle Community
   College *C, A*
Peninsula College *C*
Walla Walla Community College *C, A*
Yakima Valley Community College *C*

West Virginia
Mountain State University *B*

Wisconsin
Gateway Technical College *A*
Lakeshore Technical College *A*

Wyoming
Laramie County Community
   College *C, A*
Western Wyoming Community
   College *C*

Web page/multimedia design

Alabama
Gadsden State Community College *C*

Alaska
University of Alaska
   Southeast *C*

Arizona
Collins College *B*
Estrella Mountain Community
   College *C*
Gateway Community College *C*
High-Tech Institute *A*
University of Advancing
   Technology *A, B*

Arkansas
East Arkansas Community
   College *C, A*
Pulaski Technical College *A*
Rich Mountain Community College *C*
Southeast Arkansas College *A*

California
Art Institute
   of California: Los Angeles *A, B*
   of California: Orange County *A, B*
   of California: San Diego *B*
Art Institute of California: San
   Francisco *A, B*
Azusa Pacific University *B*
California State University
   East Bay *M*
College of San Mateo *C, A*
Foothill College *C*
Monterey Peninsula College *A*
Mt. Sierra College *B*
Ohlone College *C*
Platt College
   Ontario *C, B*
San Diego Mesa College *C, A*
San Jose City College *C*
Santiago Canyon College *A*
Sierra College *C, A*
Southwestern College *C, A*
Taft College *C*
Westwood College *B*

Westwood College of Technology
   Inland Empire *B*

Colorado
Arapahoe Community College *C, A*
Colorado Technical University *C*
Westwood College of Technology *B*
Westwood College of Technology
   South *B*

Delaware
Wilmington College *B*

Florida
Florida Career College: Hialeah *C*
Florida Career College: Miami *C*
Florida Career College: Pembroke
   Pines *C*
Florida Career College: West Palm
   Beach *C*
Florida National College *A*
Full Sail Real World Education *A*
Hillsborough Community
   College *C, A*
Indian River Community College *A*
Miami Dade College *C, A*
New England Institute of
   Technology *A*
St. Petersburg College *C, A*
Stetson University *B*

Georgia
Albany Technical College *C*
Central Georgia Technical
   College *C, A*
Northwestern Technical College *C, A*
Southwest Georgia Technical
   College *C*
West Georgia Technical College *C, A*

Hawaii
Hawaii Business College *A*

Illinois
Black Hawk College *C*
Columbia College Chicago *B*
DePaul University *B, M*
Heartland Community College *C*
International Academy of Design and
   Technology: Schaumburg *A, B*
Lake Land College *C*
Lewis and Clark Community
   College *C*
Lincoln Land Community College *C*
Midstate College *C, A*
Moraine Valley Community College *C*
Morton College *C*
Oakton Community College *C*
Robert Morris College: Chicago *A*
Waubonsee Community College *C*
William Rainey Harper College *C, A*

Indiana
Indiana Institute of Technology *A*
Indiana University-Purdue University
   Indianapolis *C, A, B*
Sawyer College: Merrillville *C, A*
Valparaiso University *C*
Vincennes University *A*

Iowa
Hawkeye Community College *A*
Southeastern Community College
   North Campus *A*

Kansas
Central Christian College of Kansas *A*
Kansas City Kansas Community
   College *C, A*

Kentucky
Hopkinsville Community College *C*

Louisville Technical Institute A
Maysville Community College C, A
Thomas More College A

Louisiana
Bossier Parish Community College A

Maine
New England School of
 Communications A, B

Maryland
Community College of Baltimore
 County A
Hagerstown Community College C, A

Massachusetts
Bristol Community College C
Bunker Hill Community College A
Cape Cod Community College A
Marian Court College C, A
Massasoit Community College C
Middlesex Community College C
Mount Wachusett Community
 College C, A
New England Institute of Art B
North Shore Community College C
Quinsigamond Community College C
Springfield Technical Community
 College C, A
Wentworth Institute of Technology C
Worcester Polytechnic Institute B

Michigan
Baker College
 of Jackson C
 of Muskegon A
 of Port Huron C, A
Delta College A
Grace Bible College B
Grand Rapids Community College C
Jackson Community College C, A
Macomb Community College A
Washtenaw Community College C, A

Minnesota
Academy College C, A
Alexandria Technical College C, A
Capella University C, B
Dakota County Technical College A
Globe College C, A, B
Hennepin Technical College C, A
Hibbing Community College A
Lake Superior College C
Minneapolis Community and
 Technical College C, A
Minnesota School of Business C, A
Minnesota State College - Southeast
 Technical C, A
Minnesota State Community and
 Technical College - Fergus
 Falls C, A
Rasmussen College
 St. Cloud C, A
Ridgewater College C, A
Rochester Community and Technical
 College A
St. Cloud Technical College C, A
St. Paul College C
University of Minnesota
 Crookston B

Mississippi
Antonelli College
 Jackson A

Missouri
Ozarks Technical Community
 College A
State Fair Community College A
Vatterott College: Springfield A
Webster University C

Nebraska
Bellevue University B
Dana College B

Nevada
Community College of Southern
 Nevada C

New Hampshire
Chester College of New England B
New Hampshire Community
 Technical College
 Nashua C
 Stratham A

New Jersey
Berkeley College A
Gloucester County College C, A
Raritan Valley Community College A
Salem Community College C

New Mexico
New Mexico State University
 Alamogordo C, A

New York
Cayuga County Community College A
Clinton Community College C
College of Westchester A
Erie Community College
 South Campus A
Genesee Community College C
Globe Institute of Technology C, A, B
Medaille College B
Parsons The New School for Design C
Rochester Institute of
 Technology B, M, D
State University of New York
 College of Agriculture and
  Technology at Cobleskill B
 College of Agriculture and
  Technology at Morrisville B

North Carolina
Art Institute
 of Charlotte C, A, B
Carteret Community College A
College of the Albemarle C
University of North Carolina
 Asheville B

North Dakota
North Dakota State College of
 Science A
Williston State College C, A

Ohio
Central Ohio Technical College A
Davis College A
ETI Technical College of Niles A
Edison State Community College C, A
James A. Rhodes State College C, A
Lakeland Community College C, A
Marion Technical College A
Shawnee State University C
Stark State College of Technology A
Stautzenberger College C, A
University of Cincinnati
 Clermont College A
 Raymond Walters College C, A
Youngstown State University C

Oklahoma
Cameron University A, B
Oklahoma City Community College A
Rose State College C, A
Vatterott College
 Tulsa A

Oregon
Art Institute of Portland A, B
Eastern Oregon University B

Lane Community College C, A

Pennsylvania
Academy of Medical Arts and
 Business C
Art Institute
 of Philadelphia A, B
 of Pittsburgh C, A, B
Bradley Academy for the Visual Arts A
Bucks County Community College C
Butler County Community College A
Central Pennsylvania College A, B
Chestnut Hill College C
Consolidated School of Business
 Lancaster A
 York A
Duquesne University B, M
Harrisburg Area Community
 College C, A
La Salle University B
Lehigh Valley College A
Newport Business Institute A
Northampton County Area
 Community College A
Pennsylvania College of
 Technology A, B
Pittsburgh Technical Institute A
South Hills School of Business &
 Technology C, A

Puerto Rico
Inter American University of Puerto
 Rico
 Bayamon Campus C
Universidad del Este A

Rhode Island
Johnson & Wales University A
New England Institute of
 Technology A

South Carolina
Limestone College B
York Technical College C

South Dakota
Dakota State University B
Dakota Wesleyan University B

Tennessee
Pellissippi State Technical Community
 College C, A
Tennessee Technological University B
Trevecca Nazarene University B

Texas
Collin County Community College
 District C, A
Del Mar College C, A
Eastfield College C
McMurry University B
Mountain View College C, A
South Texas College C, A
Texas State Technical College
 West Texas A
Tyler Junior College A
Victoria College C, A

Utah
LDS Business College C

Vermont
Champlain College A, B
Vermont Technical College A

Virginia
Art Institute
 of Washington A, B
ECPI College of Technology C, A
Marymount University C
Mountain Empire Community
 College C

Piedmont Virginia Community
 College C, A

Washington
Bellevue Community College C, A
Clark College C
Clover Park Technical College C, A
Heritage University C
North Seattle Community College C
Peninsula College C, A
Shoreline Community College C, A
South Seattle Community College A
Spokane Falls Community College A
Walla Walla Community College A
Yakima Valley Community College C

West Virginia
Huntington Junior College A
Mountain State University A

Wisconsin
Mid-State Technical College A
University of Wisconsin
 Parkside C
 Stevens Point B
Wisconsin Indianhead Technical
 College A

Wyoming
Central Wyoming College C, A
Laramie County Community
 College C, A
Western Wyoming Community
 College C

Welding technology

Alabama
Gadsden State Community College C
Northwest-Shoals Community
 College C
Shelton State Community College C
Trenholm State Technical College C
Virginia College Technical C, A

Alaska
University of Alaska
 Anchorage C, A

Arizona
Arizona Western College C, A
Eastern Arizona College C

Arkansas
Arkansas Northeastern College C
Arkansas Tech University C
North Arkansas College C, A
Ouachita Technical College C
University of Arkansas
 Community College at Hope C
 Cossatot Community College of the
  C
 Fort Smith C

California
Antelope Valley College C, A
Barstow College C, A
Butte College A
Chabot College A
College of the Canyons C, A
Long Beach City College C, A
Shasta College C, A
Solano Community College C, A
Ventura College C, A
Victor Valley College C, A

Colorado
Morgan Community College C
Pikes Peak Community College C, A
Pueblo Community College C, A

Florida

Central Florida Community College *C*
Gulf Coast Community College *C*
Palm Beach Community College *C*

Georgia

Albany Technical College *C*
Athens Technical College *C*
Central Georgia Technical College *C*
Coastal Georgia Community
    College *C*
Columbus Technical College *C*
Dalton State College *C*
Georgia Southwestern State
    University *A*
Savannah Technical College *A*
Southwest Georgia Technical
    College *C*
West Georgia Technical College *C*

Idaho

Brigham Young University-Idaho *A*
College of Southern Idaho *C, A*
Eastern Idaho Technical College *C, A*
Idaho State University *C, A*
Lewis-Clark State College *C, A, B*

Illinois

Black Hawk College *C*
College of DuPage *C*
College of Lake County *C*
Heartland Community College *C, A*
John A. Logan College *C, A*
Kaskaskia College *C*
Lincoln Land Community College *C*
Moraine Valley Community College *C*
Rend Lake College *C*
Rock Valley College *C*
Spoon River College *C*
Waubonsee Community College *C*

Indiana

Vincennes University *C*

Iowa

Des Moines Area Community
    College *C, A*
Hawkeye Community College *C*
Indian Hills Community College *C*
Iowa Lakes Community College *C*
North Iowa Area Community
    College *C*
Northwest Iowa Community
    College *C*
Southeastern Community College
    North Campus *C*
Western Iowa Tech Community
    College *C*

Kansas

Coffeyville Community College *C*
Cowley County Community
    College *C, A*
Hutchinson Community College *C, A*
Manhattan Area Technical
    College *C, A*

Kentucky

Elizabethtown Community and
    Technical College *C, A*
Jefferson Community College *C, A*
Somerset Community College *C, A*

Louisiana

Delgado Community College *C*
Nunez Community College *C*

Maine

Eastern Maine Community
    College *C, A*

Michigan

Bay de Noc Community College *C*
Delta College *C, A*
Ferris State University *A, B*
Grand Rapids Community
    College *C, A*
Kirtland Community College *C, A*
Montcalm Community College *C*
Mott Community College *C*
Oakland Community College *C, A*
St. Clair County Community
    College *C, A*
Southwestern Michigan College *C, A*
Wayne County Community College *A*
West Shore Community College *A*

Minnesota

Alexandria Technical College *C*
Central Lakes College *C, A*
Dakota County Technical College *C*
Dunwoody College of Technology *C*
Hennepin Technical College *C, A*
Minneapolis Community and
    Technical College *C*
Northland Community & Technical
    College *C, A*
Ridgewater College *C, A*
St. Cloud Technical College *C*
St. Paul College *C*

Mississippi

Itawamba Community College *C*

Missouri

East Central College *C, A*
Jefferson College *C, A*
Mineral Area College *C, A*
Moberly Area Community
    College *C, A*
Ozarks Technical Community
    College *C, A*
State Fair Community College *C*
Vatterott College *C, A*

Montana

Montana Tech of the University of
    Montana *B*

Nebraska

Central Community College *C, A*
Mid-Plains Community College
    Area *C, A*
Northeast Community College *C*
Southeast Community College
    Lincoln Campus *C, A*
Western Nebraska Community
    College *C, A*

Nevada

Community College of Southern
    Nevada *C, A*
Great Basin College *C, A*
Western Nevada Community
    College *C, A*

New Hampshire

New Hampshire Community
    Technical College
    Manchester *C, A*

New Mexico

Albuquerque Technical-Vocational
    Institute *C*
Eastern New Mexico University:
    Roswell Campus *C, A*
New Mexico State University
    Carlsbad *C, A*
Northern New Mexico College *C, A*
San Juan College *C, A*

New York

Excelsior College *A*

Michigan

Mohawk Valley Community
    College *C, A*
State University of New York
    College of Technology at Alfred *C, A*

North Carolina

Asheville-Buncombe Technical
    Community College *C*
Beaufort County Community
    College *C, A*
Bladen Community College *C, A*
Brunswick Community College *C*
Cape Fear Community College *C, A*
Catawba Valley Community College *C*
Central Piedmont Community
    College *C, A*
Coastal Carolina Community
    College *C*
Davidson County Community
    College *C*
Fayetteville Technical Community
    College *C, D*
Guilford Technical Community
    College *C*
Halifax Community College *A*
Haywood Community College *C*
Isothermal Community College *C, A*
James Sprunt Community College *C*
Lenoir Community College *C, A*
Pitt Community College *C, A*
Robeson Community College *C*
Rowan-Cabarrus Community
    College *C*
South Piedmont Community
    College *C*
Southwestern Community College *C*
Surry Community College *C*
Tri-County Community College *C*
Wilkes Community College *C*
Wilson Technical Community
    College *C*

North Dakota

Bismarck State College *C, A*
North Dakota State College of
    Science *C, A*
Turtle Mountain Community
    College *C*

Ohio

Edison State Community College *A*
Ohio State University
    Columbus Campus *B, M, D*
Owens Community College
    Toledo *C, A*

Oklahoma

Tulsa Welding School *C, A*

Oregon

Central Oregon Community
    College *C, A*
Clatsop Community College *C*
Portland Community College *C*
Rogue Community College *C, A*
Treasure Valley Community
    College *C, A*

Pennsylvania

Community College of Allegheny
    County *C, A*
Dean Institute of Technology *C*
Delaware County Community
    College *C*
Harrisburg Area Community
    College *C*
Lehigh Carbon Community
    College *C, A*
Northampton County Area
    Community College *C*
Pennsylvania College of
    Technology *C, A*

Triangle Tech
    DuBois *A*

South Carolina

Aiken Technical College *C*
Greenville Technical College *C*
Horry-Georgetown Technical
    College *C*
Piedmont Technical College *C, A*
Spartanburg Technical College *C*
Williamsburg Technical College *C*
York Technical College *C, A*

South Dakota

Lake Area Technical Institute *A*

Texas

Alvin Community College *C*
Angelina College *C, A*
Del Mar College *C, A*
Frank Phillips College *C*
Houston Community College
    System *C*
Kilgore College *C*
Midland College *C, A*
Mountain View College *C, A*
North Harris Montgomery
    Community College District *C, A*
Odessa College *C, A*
Paris Junior College *C, A*
Ranger College *C, A*
St. Philip's College *C, A*
Texarkana College *C*
Texas State Technical College
    Harlingen *C*
    West Texas *C*
Victoria College *C*
Western Texas College *C, A*

Utah

Salt Lake Community College *C, A*
Snow College *C*
Utah Valley State College *C, A*

Virginia

Eastern Shore Community College *C*
Mountain Empire Community
    College *C*
New River Community College *C*
Tidewater Community College *C, A*

Washington

Big Bend Community College *C, A*
Centralia College *C, A*
Clark College *C, A*
Clover Park Technical College *C*
Edmonds Community College *C, A*
Grays Harbor College *C, A*
Lower Columbia College *C, A*
Olympic College *C*
South Seattle Community
    College *C, A*
Walla Walla Community College *C, A*

West Virginia

West Virginia University at
    Parkersburg *C, A*

Wisconsin

Gateway Technical College *C*
Lakeshore Technical College *C*
Mid-State Technical College *C*
Milwaukee Area Technical
    College *C, A*
Nicolet Area Technical College *A*
Southwest Wisconsin Technical
    College *C*
Western Wisconsin Technical
    College *C*
Wisconsin Indianhead Technical
    College *C*

Wyoming
Casper College C, A
Central Wyoming College C, A
Eastern Wyoming College A
Sheridan College C, A
Western Wyoming Community
College C, A

Well drilling

New Mexico
San Juan College C, A

Western European studies

California
Claremont McKenna College B

District of Columbia
Georgetown University M

Illinois
Illinois Wesleyan University B

Indiana
Indiana University
Bloomington M

Iowa
Grinnell College B

Maryland
St. John's College B, M

Massachusetts
Amherst College B
Harvard College B
Tufts University B, M

Michigan
University of Michigan B

Nebraska
University of Nebraska
Lincoln B

New Hampshire
University of New Hampshire B

New York
Bard College B
Eugene Lang College The New School
for Liberal Arts B
New York University M, D
United States Military Academy B

Ohio
College of Wooster B
Denison University B
Ohio State University
Columbus Campus B

Vermont
Marlboro College B

Wildlife and wilderness management

Alabama
Auburn University B

Alaska
University of Alaska
Fairbanks B, M

Arizona
Northern Arizona University B
Prescott College B, M

University of Arizona B

Arkansas
Arkansas State University B
University of Arkansas
Monticello B

California
California State University
Chico C
Cerritos Community College A
Feather River College C, A
Humboldt State University B
Modesto Junior College C, A
Napa Valley College C, A
San Joaquin Delta College A
University of California
Davis B

Colorado
Colorado State University M, D

Delaware
Delaware State University B
University of Delaware B

District of Columbia
University of the District of
Columbia A

Florida
University of Florida B, M, D

Georgia
Abraham Baldwin Agricultural
College A
University of Georgia B

Idaho
College of Southern Idaho A
North Idaho College A
University of Idaho B, M

Illinois
Lake Land College A
Southeastern Illinois College A
University of Illinois
Urbana-Champaign B, M, D

Indiana
Purdue University B, M, D

Iowa
Ellsworth Community College A
Iowa State University M, D

Kansas
Colby Community College A
Garden City Community College A
Pittsburg State University B
Pratt Community College A
Seward County Community College A

Kentucky
Eastern Kentucky University B
Murray State University B

Louisiana
Louisiana State University and
Agricultural and Mechanical
College M, D

Maine
Unity College B
University of Maine B, M, D

Maryland
Frostburg State University B, M
Garrett College C, A

Massachusetts
University of Massachusetts
Amherst B, M, D

Michigan
Bay de Noc Community College C
Grand Rapids Community College A
Lake Superior State University B
Michigan State University B, M, D
Michigan Technological
University B, T

Minnesota
St. Cloud State University B
University of Minnesota
Crookston B
Twin Cities B, M, D
Vermilion Community College C, A

Mississippi
Mississippi State University B, M

Missouri
College of the Ozarks B
Missouri State University B
Northwest Missouri State
University B
University of Missouri
Columbia B, M, D

Montana
Miles Community College A
Montana State University
Bozeman M, D
University of Montana:
Missoula B, M, D
University of Montana: Western B

Nevada
University of Nevada
Reno B

New Hampshire
University of New Hampshire B, M

New Jersey
Rowan University B

New Mexico
Eastern New Mexico University B
New Mexico State University B, M
Western New Mexico University B

New York
Paul Smith's College B
State University of New York
College of Agriculture and
Technology at Cobleskill A, B
College of Environmental Science
and Forestry B, M, D

North Carolina
Haywood Community College A

North Dakota
Minot State University: Bottineau
Campus A
Sitting Bull College A

Ohio
Hocking College A
Ohio State University
Columbus Campus B
University of Rio Grande B

Oklahoma
Eastern Oklahoma State College A
Northeastern Oklahoma Agricultural
and Mechanical College A
Western Oklahoma State College A

Oregon
Central Oregon Community
College A
Oregon State University B, M, D
Treasure Valley Community College A

Pennsylvania
Delaware Valley College B
Keystone College A
Penn State
Abington B
Altoona B
Beaver B
Berks B
Delaware County B
Dubois A, B
Erie, The Behrend College B
Fayette B
Hazleton B
Lehigh Valley B
McKeesport B
Mont Alto B
New Kensington B
Schuylkill - Capital College B
Shenango B
University Park C, B, M, D
Wilkes-Barre B
Worthington Scranton B
York B

Puerto Rico
University of Puerto Rico
Humacao B

Rhode Island
University of Rhode Island B

South Dakota
Dakota Wesleyan University B
South Dakota State University B, M

Tennessee
Lincoln Memorial University B
Roane State Community College A
Tennessee Technological University B
University of Tennessee
Knoxville M

Texas
Stephen F. Austin State University B
Sul Ross State University B, M
Tarleton State University B
Texas A&M University B, M, D
Texas A&M University
Commerce B
Kingsville B, M, D
Texas Tech University B, M, D
West Texas A&M University B

Utah
Brigham Young University B, M, D
Dixie State College of Utah A
Snow College A
Utah State University B, M, D

Vermont
Sterling College A, B
University of Vermont B, M

Washington
Grays Harbor College A
Spokane Community College A
University of Washington B
Washington State University B

West Virginia
Potomac State College of West Virginia
University A
West Virginia University B, M

Wisconsin

Northland College B
University of Wisconsin
   Madison B, M
   Stevens Point B

Wyoming

Casper College A
Eastern Wyoming College A
Northwest College A
Western Wyoming Community
   College A

Wildlife biology

Arizona

Eastern Arizona College A
Northern Arizona University B

California

Feather River College A

Kansas

Baker University B
Barton County Community College A
Kansas State University B

Michigan

University of Michigan
   Flint B

New York

State University of New York
   College of Environmental Science
   and Forestry B, M, D

Ohio

Ohio University B

Pennsylvania

Keystone College A

Texas

Texas State University: San Marcos B

Vermont

Sterling College B

Wyoming

Laramie County Community
   College A
Western Wyoming Community
   College A

Women's studies

Alabama

Huntingdon College B
University of Alabama M

Arizona

Arizona State University B
Arizona State University West B
Northern Arizona University B
Prescott College B, M
University of Arizona B, M

California

California Institute of Integral
   Studies M, D
California State University
   Chico B
   Fresno B
   Fullerton B
   Long Beach B
   Monterey Bay B
   San Marcos B
Claremont McKenna College B
Cosumnes River College A
Foothill College A

Fresno City College A
Irvine Valley College A
Loyola Marymount University B
Mills College B
Monterey Peninsula College A
Occidental College B
Pitzer College B
Pomona College B
Sacramento City College A
Saddleback College A
St. Mary's College of California B
San Diego State University B, M
San Francisco State University B, M
Santa Ana College A
Scripps College B
Sonoma State University B
Southwestern College A
Stanford University B
University of California
   Berkeley B
   Davis B
   Irvine B
   Los Angeles B, M, D
   Riverside B
   San Diego B
   Santa Barbara B
   Santa Cruz B
University of Redlands B
University of Southern California B
West Valley College A

Colorado

Colorado College B
Regis University B
University of Colorado
   Boulder B
University of Denver B

Connecticut

Connecticut College B
Manchester Community College A
Southern Connecticut State
   University M
Trinity College B
University of Connecticut B
University of Hartford B
Wesleyan University B
Yale University B

Delaware

University of Delaware B

District of Columbia

American University C, B
George Washington University M
Georgetown University B

Florida

Eckerd College B
Florida Atlantic University M
Florida International University B
Florida State University B
Manatee Community College A
University of Miami B
University of South Florida B, M

Georgia

Agnes Scott College B
Emory University B, D
Georgia State University B, M
Spelman College B
University of Georgia B

Illinois

DePaul University B
Illinois Wesleyan University B
Knox College B
Loyola University of Chicago M
Northeastern Illinois University B
Northwestern University B
Roosevelt University B, M
University of Illinois
   Urbana-Champaign B

Western Illinois University B

Indiana

Ball State University B
DePauw University B
Earlham College B
Indiana University
   Bloomington B
   South Bend B
Indiana University-Purdue University
   Fort Wayne A, B
Manchester College B

Iowa

Cornell College B
Grinnell College B
Iowa State University B
University of Iowa B, D
University of Northern Iowa M

Kansas

University of Kansas B
Wichita State University B

Kentucky

Berea College B
University of Louisville B

Louisiana

Louisiana State University and
   Agricultural and Mechanical
   College B
Tulane University B

Maine

Bates College B
Bowdoin College B
Colby College B
University of Maine B
University of Maine
   Farmington B
University of Southern Maine B

Maryland

Goucher College B
Howard Community College A
Prince George's Community
   College A
Towson University B, M
University of Maryland
   College Park B, M, D

Massachusetts

Amherst College B
Brandeis University B, M
Clark University D
Hampshire College B
Harvard College B
Mount Holyoke College B
Simmons College B
Simon's Rock College of Bard B
Smith College B
Suffolk University B
Tufts University B
University of Massachusetts
   Amherst B
   Boston B
Wellesley College B
Wheaton College B

Michigan

Central Michigan University B
Eastern Michigan University B, M
Henry Ford Community College A
Michigan State University B
Oakland University B
University of Michigan B, M, D
Wayne State University B
Western Michigan University B

Minnesota

Augsburg College B

Carleton College B
College of St. Catherine B
College of St. Scholastica C
Gustavus Adolphus College B
Hamline University B
Macalester College B
Metropolitan State University B
Minnesota State University
   Mankato B, M
St. Olaf College B
University of Minnesota
   Duluth B
   Morris B
   Twin Cities B
University of St. Thomas B
Winona State University A

Missouri

St. Louis University B
University of Missouri
   Columbia B
Washington University in St. Louis B

Montana

University of Montana: Missoula B

Nebraska

Bellevue University M
Nebraska Wesleyan University B
University of Nebraska
   Lincoln B
   Omaha B

Nevada

University of Nevada
   Las Vegas B
   Reno B

New Hampshire

Dartmouth College B
University of New Hampshire B

New Jersey

The College of New Jersey B
Drew University B, M, D
Montclair State University B
Rowan University B
Rutgers, The State University of New
   Jersey
   New Brunswick/Piscataway
     Campus B, M
   Newark Regional Campus B
William Paterson University of New
   Jersey B

New Mexico

University of New Mexico B

New York

Barnard College B
City University of New York
   Brooklyn College B
   College of Staten Island B
   Hunter College B
   Queens College B
Colgate University B
College of New Rochelle B
College of Saint Rose B
Columbia University
   Columbia College B
   School of General Studies B
Cornell University B, M, D
Eugene Lang College The New School
   for Liberal Arts B
Fordham University B
Hamilton College B
Hobart and William Smith Colleges B
New York University B
Pace University B
St. Bonaventure University B
Sarah Lawrence College B, M
Skidmore College B

State University of New York
- Albany *B, M*
- Buffalo *B*
- College at Brockport *B*
- New Paltz *B*
- Oswego *B*
- Purchase *B*
- Stony Brook *B*

Suffolk County Community College *A*
Syracuse University *B*
University of Rochester *B*
Vassar College *B*
Wells College *B*

North Carolina
Duke University *B*
East Carolina University *B*
Guilford College *B*
Meredith College *B*
University of North Carolina
- Asheville *B*
- Chapel Hill *B*
- Greensboro *B*

North Dakota
North Dakota State University *M*

Ohio
Antioch College *B*
Bowling Green State University *B*
Case Western Reserve University *B*
Cleveland State University *B*
College of Wooster *B*
Denison University *B*
Miami University
- Oxford Campus *B*

Oberlin College *B*
Ohio State University
- Columbus Campus *B, M, D*

Ohio University *B*
Ohio Wesleyan University *B*
Owens Community College
- Toledo *A*

University of Toledo *B*
Wright State University *B*

Oklahoma
University of Oklahoma *B*

Oregon
Portland State University *B*
University of Oregon *B*

Pennsylvania
Albright College *B*
Allegheny College *B*
Bucknell University *B*
Chatham College *B*
Community College of Philadelphia *A*
Dickinson College *B*
Gettysburg College *B*
Penn State
- Abington *B*
- Altoona *B*
- Beaver *B*
- Berks *B*
- Delaware County *B*
- Dubois *B*
- Erie, The Behrend College *B*
- Fayette *B*
- Hazleton *B*
- Lehigh Valley *B*
- McKeesport *B*
- Mont Alto *B*
- New Kensington *B*
- Schuylkill - Capital College *B*
- Shenango *B*
- University Park *B*
- Wilkes-Barre *B*
- Worthington Scranton *B*
- York *B*

Rosemont College *B*
Temple University *B*

University of Pennsylvania *A, B*
West Chester University of
- Pennsylvania *B*

Widener University *B*

Rhode Island
Brown University *B*
Rhode Island College *B*
University of Rhode Island *B*

South Carolina
University of South Carolina *B*

Tennessee
University of Memphis *M*
University of Tennessee
- Knoxville *B*

Texas
El Paso Community College *A*
Rice University *B*
Southwestern University *B*
Texas Woman's University *M*
University of Texas
- Austin *M*
- Dallas *B*

Utah
University of Utah *B, M*

Vermont
Bennington College *B*
Burlington College *B*
Goddard College *B*
Middlebury College *B*
University of Vermont *B*

Virginia
College of William and Mary *B*
Hollins University *B*
Old Dominion University *B*
Randolph-Macon College *B*
University of Richmond *B*

Washington
Gonzaga University *B*
Pacific Lutheran University *B*
University of Washington *B, M, D*
Washington State University *B*

Wisconsin
Beloit College *B*
Carthage College *B*
Lawrence University *B*
Marquette University *B*
Ripon College *B*
University of Wisconsin
- Green Bay *B*
- Madison *B, M*
- Marinette *A*
- Whitewater *B*

Wyoming
Casper College *A*
University of Wyoming *B*

Wood science/pulp/ paper technology

Maine
University of Maine *C, B*

Massachusetts
University of Massachusetts
- Amherst *B*

Michigan
Bay de Noc Community College *A*
Mott Community College *C*
Western Michigan University *B*

Mississippi
Copiah-Lincoln Community College
Mississippi State University *B, M*

New York
State University of New York
- College of Agriculture and
  Technology at Morrisville *A*

North Carolina
Halifax Community College *C, A*
Haywood Community College *A*
North Carolina State
- University *B, M, D*

Ohio
Miami University
- Oxford Campus *B, M*

Pennsylvania
Keystone College *A*
Penn State
- Abington *B*
- Altoona *B*
- Beaver *B*
- Berks *B*
- Delaware County *B*
- Dubois *B*
- Erie, The Behrend College *B*
- Fayette *B*
- Hazleton *B*
- Lehigh Valley *B*
- McKeesport *B*
- Mont Alto *B*
- New Kensington *B*
- Schuylkill - Capital College *B*
- Shenango *B*
- University Park *B*
- Worthington Scranton *B*
- York *B*

South Carolina
York Technical College *C*

Vermont
Sterling College *B*

West Virginia
Potomac State College of West Virginia
- University *A*

West Virginia University *B*

Wisconsin
University of Wisconsin
- Stevens Point *B*

Woodworking

Alabama
Gadsden State Community College *C*
Wallace State Community College at
- Hanceville *C, A*

Alaska
University of Alaska
- Anchorage *C, A*

Arkansas
Phillips Community College of the
- University of Arkansas *C*

California
Bakersfield College *A*
College of the Redwoods *C*
Laney College *C, A*
Palomar College *C, A*
San Joaquin Delta College *C, A*
Sierra College *C, A*

Colorado
Red Rocks Community College *C, A*

...essing
: Comm
Arizona
Gateway Comm...
Paradise Vall...
College...
Calif...
CR...

Kan...
Allen C...
Pittsburg...

Maine
Northern Maine Community
- College *A*

Southern Maine Community
- College *A*

Michigan
Bay de Noc Community College *C*

Minnesota
Dakota County Technical College *C*
Hennepin Technical College *C, A*
St. Paul College *C*

Mississippi
East Central Community College *C*

New Mexico
Northern New Mexico College *C, A*
Santa Fe Community College *C*

New York
Rochester Institute of
- Technology *A, B, M*

State University of New York
- College of Agriculture and
  Technology at Morrisville *A*

North Carolina
Haywood Community College *C, A*
Mayland Community College *C*
Rockingham Community College *A*
Tri-County Community College *C*

Ohio
University of Rio Grande *C, A*

Pennsylvania
Bucks County Community College *A*
Johnson College *A*

South Dakota
Western Dakota Technical Institute *C*

Texas
Austin Community College *C*
San Jacinto College
- North *C*

Utah
Southern Utah University *A*

Washington
Peninsula College *C*
Seattle Central Community College *A*

Wisconsin
Fox Valley Technical College *C*
Madison Area Technical College *C*
Northeast Wisconsin Technical
- College *C*

Western Wisconsin Technical
- College *C*

...munity College C
...ey Community
 ...ge C,A

...ornia
...n College
 Maric College: Panorama City C
Long Beach City College C,A
Monterey Peninsula College C,A
Ohlone College C

Colorado
Trinidad State Junior College C,A

Florida
Hillsborough Community College C

Georgia
Darton College C
Northwestern Technical College C,A

Illinois
Lincoln Land Community College C
Southeastern Illinois College C

Indiana
Sawyer College: Merrillville C,A

Maryland
Frederick Community College C
Hagerstown Business College C

Massachusetts
Bunker Hill Community College C

Michigan
Kirtland Community College C,A
Lake Michigan College C,A

Minnesota
Rasmussen College
 St. Cloud C,A
Ridgewater College C

Montana
Montana State University
 Billings A

New York
Corning Community College C
Globe Institute of Technology C
Olean Business Institute A
Rochester Business Institute A
State University of New York
 College of Agriculture and
 Technology at Morrisville C
Utica School of Commerce C,A

North Carolina
Beaufort County Community
 College C
Carteret Community College C
College of the Albemarle C

Ohio
ETI Technical College of Niles A
James A. Rhodes State College C
Marion Technical College C,A
Stark State College of Technology A
University of Cincinnati
 Raymond Walters College C

Pennsylvania
Business Institute of Pennsylvania A

Business Institute of Pennsylvania
 Meadville A
Consolidated School of Business
 Lancaster C,A
 York C,A
Newport Business Institute A
Northampton County Area
 Community College C
South Hills School of Business &
 Technology C

Rhode Island
Community College of Rhode
 Island C

South Carolina
Williamsburg Technical College C
York Technical College C

Texas
Palo Alto College C

Virginia
ECPI College of Technology C,A
Mountain Empire Community
 College A

Washington
Centralia College C
Lower Columbia College C
Spokane Falls Community College C
Yakima Valley Community College C

Wyoming
Western Wyoming Community
 College C

Work/family studies

Arizona
Estrella Mountain Community
 College C

Georgia
Dalton State College A, B

Kentucky
Morehead State University A, B

Michigan
Cornerstone University B

Minnesota
St. Cloud State University B

Mississippi
Belhaven College C

Ohio
Ursuline College B
Youngstown State University B

Texas
Lubbock Christian University B
Texas Tech University B, M

Yoga teacher/therapy

California
California Institute of Integral
 Studies C

Colorado
Naropa University C, B

Youth ministry

Arkansas
Central Baptist College B

Harding University B
John Brown University B
Ouachita Baptist University B
Williams Baptist College B

California
Azusa Pacific University M
Hope International University B
Point Loma Nazarene University B
Simpson University B
Vanguard University of Southern
 California B
William Jessup University B

Colorado
Colorado Christian University B

Florida
Trinity College of Florida B

Georgia
Emmanuel College B
Toccoa Falls College B

Idaho
Boise Bible College B

Illinois
Greenville College B
Judson College B
Lincoln Christian College and
 Seminary B, M
North Park University B, M
Trinity International University B

Indiana
Grace College B
Huntington University B
Taylor University B
Valparaiso University B

Iowa
Dordt College B
Emmaus Bible College B
St. Ambrose University C
Vennard College B

Kansas
Barclay College B
Benedictine College B
Bethel College C
Central Christian College of
 Kansas A, B
Friends University B
MidAmerica Nazarene University B
Tabor College B

Kentucky
Asbury College B

Louisiana
New Orleans School of Urban
 Missions A

Maryland
Washington Bible College B

Massachusetts
Gordon College B

Michigan
Andrews University B, M
Cornerstone University B
Grace Bible College B
Kuyper College B
Spring Arbor University B

Minnesota
Augsburg College B
Bethel University B
Crossroads College B

Ohio
Bluffton University B
Cedarville University B
Circleville Bible College B
God's Bible School and College B
Malone College B
Mount Vernon Nazarene University B

Crown College B
North Central University B
Northwestern College B
Pillsbury Baptist Bible College B

Mississippi
Wesley College B

Missouri
Calvary Bible College and Theological
 Seminary B
Lindenwood University B

Nebraska
Concordia University B

New Jersey
College of St. Elizabeth C

North Carolina
Gardner-Webb University B
Pfeiffer University B
Piedmont Baptist College B
Roanoke Bible College B

Oklahoma
Oklahoma Christian University B
Oklahoma City University B
Southwestern Christian University B

Oregon
Corban College B
Eugene Bible College B
Multnomah Bible College B
Warner Pacific College A

Pennsylvania
Baptist Bible College of
 Pennsylvania B
Eastern University B
Geneva College B

South Carolina
Charleston Southern University B
Columbia International University B

South Dakota
Dakota Wesleyan University B

Tennessee
Freed-Hardeman University B
King College B
Lipscomb University B
Union University B

Texas
Abilene Christian University B, M
Arlington Baptist College B
East Texas Baptist University B
Hardin-Simmons University B
Howard Payne University B
Lubbock Christian University B
Southwestern Assemblies of God
 University B
Texas Lutheran University B

Virginia
Liberty University B, M
Regent University B

Washington
Northwest University B
Trinity Lutheran College B

Wisconsin

Concordia University Wisconsin *B*
Maranatha Baptist Bible College *B*

Youth services

Massachusetts

Brandeis University *M*

Minnesota

Concordia University: St. Paul *B, M*
Crown College *B*

New York

City University of New York
  New York City College of
    Technology *C*
Dutchess Community College *C*
Medaille College *B*

South Carolina

Trident Technical College *C*

Washington

Olympic College *C*

Zoology

Alabama

Auburn University *B, M, D*

Alaska

University of Alaska
  Fairbanks *D*

Arizona

Northern Arizona University *B*

Arkansas

Arkansas State University
  Beebe *A*

California

California State Polytechnic
  University: Pomona *B*
Cerritos Community College *A*
Citrus College *A*
El Camino College *A*
Fullerton College *A*
Humboldt State University *B*
Palomar College *A*
San Diego State University *B, M*
San Francisco State University *B*
San Joaquin Delta College *A*
University of California
  Davis *B*
  Santa Barbara *B*
Ventura College *A*

Colorado

Adams State College *B*
Colorado State University *B, M, D*

Connecticut

Connecticut College *B, M*
Southern Connecticut State
  University *B*
University of Connecticut *M, D*

District of Columbia

George Washington University *M, D*

Florida

Florida State University *B*
Palm Beach Community College *A*
Pensacola Junior College *A*
University of Florida *A, B, M*

Georgia

University of West Georgia *B*

Hawaii

University of Hawaii
  Manoa *B, M, D*

Idaho

Brigham Young University-Idaho *B*
Idaho State University *B*
North Idaho College *A*
University of Idaho *B, M, D*

Illinois

Olivet Nazarene University *B*
Southern Illinois University
  Carbondale *B, M, D*

Indiana

Indiana University
  Bloomington *M, D*

Iowa

Iowa State University *M, D*

Kentucky

Kentucky Wesleyan College *B*

Maine

College of the Atlantic *B*
University of Maine *B, M, D*

Michigan

Andrews University *B*
Michigan State University *B, M, D*
Northern Michigan University *B*
University of Michigan *B, M, D*

Minnesota

Minnesota State University
  Mankato *B, M, T*
University of Minnesota
  Twin Cities *M, D*

Missouri

Northwest Missouri State
  University *B*

Montana

University of Montana:
  Missoula *B, M, D*

New Hampshire

University of New Hampshire *B, M, D*

New Jersey

Rowan University *B*
Rutgers, The State University of New
  Jersey
  Newark Regional Campus *B*

New Mexico

Western New Mexico University *B*

New York

Cornell University *M, D*
State University of New York
  College of Environmental Science
    and Forestry *B, M, D*
  Oswego *B*

North Carolina

Duke University *D*
Mars Hill College *B*
North Carolina State
  University *B, M, D*

North Dakota

North Dakota State University *B, M, D*

Ohio

Kent State University *B, D*

Miami University
  Oxford Campus *B, M, D*
Ohio State University
  Columbus Campus *B*
Ohio University *B, M, D*
Ohio Wesleyan University *B*
University of Akron *B*

Oklahoma

Carl Albert State College *A*
Oklahoma State University *B, M, D*
Southeastern Oklahoma State
  University *B*
University of Oklahoma *B, M, D*

Oregon

Oregon State University *B, M, D*

Pennsylvania

Delaware Valley College *M*
Juniata College *B*

Rhode Island

University of Rhode Island *B, M, D*

South Carolina

Clemson University *M, D*

Tennessee

Bethel College *B*
University of Tennessee
  Knoxville *B, M, D*

Texas

Tarleton State University *B, T*
Texas A&M University *B, M, D*
Texas A&M University
  Galveston *B*
Texas State University: San Marcos *B*
Texas Tech University *B, M, D*
Texas Woman's University *B*
University of Texas
  Austin *B, M, D*

Utah

Snow College *A*
Southern Utah University *B*
Utah State University *B, M*
Weber State University *B*

Vermont

Bennington College *B*
University of Vermont *B*

Washington

Eastern Washington University *B*
University of Washington *B, M, D*
Washington State University *B, M, D*
Western Washington University *B*

Wisconsin

Lawrence University *B*
University of Wisconsin
  Madison *B, M, D*

Wyoming

University of Wyoming *B, M, D*

Special academic programs

Combined bachelor's/graduate program in accounting

Alabama

Alabama State University
Jacksonville State University

Arkansas

Harding University
University of Arkansas
  Cossatot Community College of the
  Monticello
University of Central Arkansas

California

California State University
  Fresno
Pacific States University
Southern California Institute of
  Technology
University of San Diego
University of Southern California

Colorado

University of Colorado
  Boulder
  Colorado Springs

Connecticut

Quinnipiac University
Sacred Heart University

Delaware

Goldey-Beacom College

District of Columbia

Catholic University of America
Gallaudet University

Florida

Edward Waters College
Florida Agricultural and Mechanical
  University
Florida Christian College
Florida Memorial University
Webber International University

Georgia

Clark Atlanta University
Georgia Southern University
South University
University of Georgia

Idaho

Albertson College of Idaho

Illinois

Bradley University
Dominican University
Illinois State University

Indiana

Ivy Tech State College
  Ivy Tech Community College:
    Bloomington
  Ivy Tech Community College:
    Central Indiana
  Ivy Tech Community College:
    Columbus
  Ivy Tech Community College: East
    Central
  Ivy Tech Community College:
    Kokomo
  Ivy Tech Community College:
    Lafayette
  Ivy Tech Community College: North
    Central
  Ivy Tech Community College:
    Northeast
  Ivy Tech Community College:
    Northwest
  Ivy Tech Community College: South
    Central
  Ivy Tech Community College:
    Southeast
  Ivy Tech Community College:
    Southwest
  Ivy Tech Community College:
    Wabash Valley
  Ivy Tech Community College:
    Whitewater
Purdue University
  Calumet

Iowa

Drake University
Iowa Wesleyan College
Southeastern Community College
  North Campus
University of Dubuque
University of Northern Iowa

Kansas

Pittsburg State University

Kentucky

Madisonville Community College
Murray State University
Transylvania University

Louisiana

Louisiana State University
  Shreveport
Tulane University

Maine

Husson College
Thomas College
University of Maine
  Presque Isle
University of Southern Maine

Maryland

Bowie State University
University of Baltimore
Villa Julie College

Massachusetts

American International College
Babson College
Bentley College
Stonehill College

Suffolk University

Michigan

Baker College
  of Clinton Township
  of Flint
  of Muskegon
  of Port Huron
Cleary University
Eastern Michigan University
Grace Bible College
Grand Valley State University
Kuyper College
Northern Michigan University
Rochester College
Saginaw Valley State University

Minnesota

Bemidji State University
Northwest Technical College

Mississippi

Millsaps College
University of Southern Mississippi

Missouri

Drury University
Missouri State University
Stephens College
University of Missouri
  Columbia
Washington University in St. Louis
Webster University

Montana

Rocky Mountain College

Nebraska

Creighton University

Nevada

Morrison University

New Hampshire

McIntosh College

New Jersey

Caldwell College
Fairleigh Dickinson University
  College at Florham

New Mexico

College of the Southwest
New Mexico Highlands University
San Juan College

New York

Canisius College
City University of New York
  Baruch College
  Medgar Evers College
College of Saint Rose
Daemen College
Fordham University
Globe Institute of Technology
Hofstra University
Ithaca College
Long Island University
  C.W. Post Campus
Mercy College

Molloy College
Mount St. Mary College
Pace University
Rochester Institute of Technology
St. John's University
Siena College
State University of New York
  Binghamton
  College at Old Westbury
  College at Oneonta
  Oswego
Wagner College
Yeshiva University

North Carolina

East Carolina University
Guilford College
Meredith College
North Carolina State University
Wake Forest University

North Dakota

Lake Region State College
University of Mary

Ohio

Ashland University
Baldwin-Wallace College
Case Western Reserve University
Hiram College
Mount Vernon Nazarene University
Tiffin University
University of Dayton
University of Rio Grande
Xavier University

Oklahoma

Oklahoma State University
University of Oklahoma

Oregon

Oregon Institute of Technology

Pennsylvania

Elizabethtown College
Lock Haven University of
  Pennsylvania
Moravian College
Mount Aloysius College
Philadelphia University
Robert Morris University
University of Pennsylvania
University of Pittsburgh
  Greensburg
Villanova University
Widener University
York College of Pennsylvania

Puerto Rico

Atlantic College

South Carolina

Aiken Technical College
University of South Carolina
  Lancaster
Voorhees College

South Dakota

University of South Dakota

Tennessee
Freed-Hardeman University
Tennessee Wesleyan College
University of Memphis
University of Tennessee
    Knoxville

Texas
Angelo State University
Baylor University
Houston Baptist University
Prairie View A&M University
Southwestern Adventist University
Stephen F. Austin State University
Texas A&M University
Texas A&M University
    Texarkana
Texas Tech University
Trinity University
University of Houston
    Clear Lake
University of North Texas
University of Texas
    Arlington
    El Paso
    Pan American
West Texas A&M University

Utah
Southern Utah University
University of Utah

Virginia
Randolph-Macon College
University of Northern Virginia
Virginia Commonwealth University
Virginia Polytechnic Institute and
    State University

Washington
Olympic College
Yakima Valley Community College

West Virginia
Davis and Elkins College
University of Charleston
Wheeling Jesuit University

Wisconsin
Lakeshore Technical College
Marquette University
Northland College
Silver Lake College
University of Wisconsin
    Madison
    Whitewater

Combined bachelor's/ graduate program in architecture

Connecticut
Yale University

District of Columbia
Catholic University of America

Florida
Florida Agricultural and Mechanical
    University
University of Miami

Georgia
Agnes Scott College
Georgia Institute of Technology
Morehouse College

Illinois
Judson College
Knox College
Monmouth College

Indiana
Goshen College
Purdue University
    Calumet

Iowa
Central College
Coe College
Cornell College
Southeastern Community College
    North Campus

Louisiana
Tulane University

Maine
University of Maine
    Augusta

Michigan
Adrian College
Lawrence Technological University
University of Detroit Mercy
University of Michigan

Missouri
Ranken Technical College
Washington University in St. Louis
Webster University

Montana
Montana State University
    Bozeman

Nebraska
Nebraska Wesleyan University

New York
Colgate University
Cooper Union for the Advancement of
    Science and Art
Cornell University
Hobart and William Smith Colleges
New York Institute of Technology
State University of New York
    Buffalo

North Carolina
North Carolina State University

North Dakota
North Dakota State University

Ohio
College of Wooster
Kent State University

Pennsylvania
University of Pennsylvania

Rhode Island
Roger Williams University

South Carolina
Aiken Technical College

Tennessee
University of Tennessee
    Knoxville

Texas
Prairie View A&M University

Utah
University of Utah

Vermont
Norwich University

Virginia
Virginia Polytechnic Institute and
    State University

Washington
University of Washington
Washington State University

Combined bachelor's/ graduate program in business administration

Alabama
Jacksonville State University
Spring Hill College
University of Alabama
University of Mobile

Arizona
Grand Canyon University

Arkansas
Harding University
Southern Arkansas University
University of Arkansas
University of Arkansas
    Monticello
University of Central Arkansas

California
California State University
    Fresno
Claremont McKenna College
Harvey Mudd College
John F. Kennedy University
Mills College
Pacific States University
Pitzer College
San Francisco State University
Scripps College
Sonoma State University
Southern California Institute of
    Technology
University of California
    Irvine
University of Judaism

Colorado
Colorado State University
    Pueblo
Jones International University
Mesa State College
Regis University
University of Colorado
    Colorado Springs
    Denver and Health Sciences Center
University of Denver
Western State College of Colorado

Connecticut
Fairfield University
Post University
Quinnipiac University
Sacred Heart University
St. Joseph College
University of Bridgeport

Delaware
Goldey-Beacom College

District of Columbia
Georgetown University

Florida
Florida Agricultural and Mechanical
    University
Florida Metropolitan University
    Melbourne Campus
Florida Southern College
Northwood University
    Florida Campus

Nova Southeastern University
Rollins College
Stetson University
University of Miami
University of South Florida
University of Tampa
Webber International University

Georgia
South University
University of Georgia

Hawaii
Hawaii Pacific University

Idaho
Albertson College of Idaho
Northwest Nazarene University

Illinois
Benedictine University
Dominican University
Illinois Institute of Technology
Lewis University
National-Louis University
North Central College
North Park University
Rockford College
University of Illinois
    Urbana-Champaign
University of St. Francis

Indiana
Indiana Institute of Technology
Indiana University
    Bloomington
Purdue University
    Calumet
Taylor University
Taylor University: Fort Wayne
University of St. Francis

Iowa
Drake University
Southeastern Community College
    North Campus
University of Dubuque
Upper Iowa University

Kansas
Benedictine College
Pittsburg State University

Kentucky
Bellarmine University
Kentucky State University
Madisonville Community College
Murray State University
Thomas More College
University of Kentucky
University of Louisville

Louisiana
Centenary College of Louisiana
Louisiana State University
    Shreveport
Louisiana Tech University
Tulane University
Xavier University of Louisiana

Maine
Husson College
Thomas College
University of Maine
University of Southern Maine

Maryland
Bowie State University
Capitol College
Frostburg State University
Towson University
University of Baltimore

Massachusetts

American International College
Anna Maria College
Assumption College
Babson College
Bentley College
Berkshire Community College
Clark University
Endicott College
Franklin W. Olin College of
Engineering
Massachusetts Maritime Academy
Nichols College
Suffolk University
University of Massachusetts
Boston
Lowell
Western New England College
Wheaton College
Worcester Polytechnic Institute

Michigan

Baker College
of Auburn Hills
of Muskegon
Cleary University
Lake Superior State University
Lawrence Technological University
Northwood University
Spring Arbor University
University of Michigan
Flint
Wayne State University

Minnesota

Capella University

Mississippi

Millsaps College
University of Southern Mississippi

Missouri

Avila University
Drury University
Grantham University
Maryville University of Saint Louis
Missouri Baptist University
Missouri State University
Missouri Valley College
Northwest Missouri State University
Rockhurst University
Stephens College
University of Missouri
Kansas City
Washington University in St. Louis
Webster University
William Woods University

Nebraska

Creighton University
Hastings College

Nevada

Morrison University

New Hampshire

Southern New Hampshire University

New Jersey

Caldwell College
College of St. Elizabeth
Fairleigh Dickinson University
College at Florham
Metropolitan Campus
Georgian Court University
Richard Stockton College of New
Jersey
Rutgers, The State University of New
Jersey
New Brunswick/Piscataway
Campus
Newark Regional Campus

St. Peter's College
Seton Hall University

New Mexico

San Juan College
University of New Mexico

New York

Albany College of Pharmacy
Alfred University
Bard College
Canisius College
Cazenovia College
Clarkson University
College of Saint Rose
Cornell University
Dowling College
Elmira College
Fordham University
Hartwick College
Hilbert College
Hobart and William Smith Colleges
Hofstra University
Iona College
Ithaca College
Laboratory Institute of Merchandising
Marist College
Medaille College
Molloy College
Mount St. Mary College
New York Institute of Technology
Niagara University
Pace University
Paul Smith's College
Rensselaer Polytechnic Institute
Rochester Institute of Technology
Russell Sage College
Sage College of Albany
St. Bonaventure University
St. John's University
St. Joseph's College: Suffolk Campus
St. Lawrence University
St. Thomas Aquinas College
Siena College
Skidmore College
State University of New York
Albany
Binghamton
Buffalo
College at Cortland
College at Fredonia
College at Geneseo
College at Oneonta
College at Plattsburgh
College at Potsdam
Empire State College
Oswego
Stony Brook
Touro College
Union College
University of Rochester
Wells College

North Carolina

Campbell University
Elon University
Fayetteville State University
Gardner-Webb University
North Carolina State University
Pfeiffer University
University of North Carolina
Greensboro

North Dakota

University of Mary
University of North Dakota

Ohio

Ashland University
Baldwin-Wallace College
Case Western Reserve University
Central State University
David N. Myers University

Edison State Community College
Franciscan University of Steubenville
Franklin University
John Carroll University
Kent State University
Mount Vernon Nazarene University
Otterbein College
Tiffin University
University of Dayton
University of Toledo

Oklahoma

Cameron University
Mid-America Christian University
Southern Nazarene University
University of Tulsa

Oregon

Portland State University
Willamette University

Pennsylvania

Carnegie Mellon University
Chatham College
Duquesne University
Elizabethtown College
Gannon University
Geneva College
Keystone College
Lehigh University
Marywood University
Millersville University of Pennsylvania
Moravian College
Penn State
Erie, The Behrend College
University Park
Philadelphia University
St. Francis University
St. Vincent College
University of Pennsylvania
University of Pittsburgh
Greensburg
University of Scranton
University of the Sciences in
Philadelphia
Waynesburg College
Widener University
Wilkes University
York College of Pennsylvania

Puerto Rico

Pontifical Catholic University of
Puerto Rico
Turabo University
Universidad Metropolitana

Rhode Island

Providence College
Salve Regina University

South Carolina

Claflin University
Coastal Carolina University
University of South Carolina
Sumter

South Dakota

University of South Dakota

Tennessee

Cumberland University
Fisk University
Freed-Hardeman University
King College
Vanderbilt University

Texas

Dallas Baptist University
Midwestern State University
Prairie View A&M University
Rice University
Sam Houston State University

Southwestern Adventist University
Texas A&M University
Commerce
Texas Christian University
Texas Tech University
Texas Wesleyan University
University of Dallas
University of Mary Hardin-Baylor
University of St. Thomas
University of Texas
Arlington
Brownsville
Dallas
El Paso

Utah

Brigham Young University
Southern Utah University
University of Utah
Westminster College

Vermont

Castleton State College
Champlain College
College of St. Joseph in Vermont
St. Michael's College
University of Vermont

Virginia

Hampton University
Marymount University
Old Dominion University
Regent University
University of Northern Virginia
Virginia Polytechnic Institute and
State University

Washington

Seattle University
Whitman College

West Virginia

Davis and Elkins College
University of Charleston
West Virginia Wesleyan College
Wheeling Jesuit University

Wisconsin

Lakeland College
Marquette University
University of Wisconsin
River Falls
Whitewater

Combined bachelor's/ graduate program in chemistry

Alabama

Jacksonville State University

Arkansas

University of Arkansas
Monticello
University of Central Arkansas

California

California Polytechnic State
University: San Luis Obispo
California State University
Fresno

Colorado

Colorado School of Mines
University of Colorado
Colorado Springs

Connecticut

Sacred Heart University
Wesleyan University

District of Columbia

American University
Gallaudet University

Florida

Florida Agricultural and Mechanical
University
Florida Atlantic University

Georgia

Clark Atlanta University
Emory University
University of Georgia

Idaho

Idaho State University

Illinois

DePaul University
Northwestern University
University of Illinois
Urbana-Champaign

Indiana

Purdue University
Calumet

Iowa

Iowa Wesleyan College
Southeastern Community College
North Campus
University of Northern Iowa

Kansas

Pittsburg State University

Kentucky

Kentucky State University
Murray State University

Louisiana

Louisiana State University
Shreveport

Maine

University of Maine

Massachusetts

Clark University
University of Massachusetts
Dartmouth

Michigan

Northern Michigan University

Minnesota

Bemidji State University

Missouri

Missouri State University
University of Missouri
Rolla

Montana

Montana State University
Billings

Nebraska

Creighton University

New Jersey

Rutgers, The State University of New
Jersey
Camden Regional Campus

New Mexico

New Mexico Highlands University

New York

City University of New York
Hunter College
Queens College
Cornell University
Rochester Institute of Technology
St. John's University
State University of New York
Binghamton
College at Fredonia
Stony Brook
University of Rochester
Vassar College

North Carolina

Guilford College

North Dakota

University of North Dakota

Ohio

Ashland University
Case Western Reserve University
Mount Vernon Nazarene University
University of Rio Grande
Youngstown State University

Oregon

Southern Oregon University

Pennsylvania

Bryn Mawr College
Bucknell University
Carlow University
Duquesne University
Lock Haven University of
Pennsylvania
University of Pennsylvania
University of Pittsburgh
Greensburg
University of Scranton

South Carolina

Aiken Technical College
University of South Carolina
Lancaster

South Dakota

University of South Dakota

Texas

University of Texas
Arlington

Utah

University of Utah

Virginia

George Mason University
Old Dominion University
Virginia Polytechnic Institute and
State University

Washington

Olympic College

West Virginia

Davis and Elkins College

Combined bachelor's/graduate program in dentistry

California

University of the Pacific

Colorado

Western State College of Colorado

Connecticut

University of Connecticut

District of Columbia

Howard University

Florida

Nova Southeastern University
St. Leo University
University of North Florida

Georgia

Mercer University

Idaho

Idaho State University

Illinois

Southern Illinois University
Edwardsville

Indiana

Purdue University
Calumet

Iowa

Buena Vista University
Iowa Wesleyan College
Southeastern Community College
North Campus
University of Iowa

Kansas

McPherson College
Pittsburg State University

Kentucky

Kentucky State University
Murray State University
University of Louisville

Maryland

Bowie State University
Coppin State University
Salisbury University
University of Maryland
College Park

Massachusetts

Boston University
Tufts University

Michigan

Olivet College
University of Detroit Mercy

Minnesota

College of St. Benedict
St. John's University
University of Minnesota
Twin Cities

Mississippi

Mississippi College

Nebraska

Chadron State College
Creighton University
Hastings College
University of Nebraska
Lincoln
Medical Center
Omaha

New Jersey

Caldwell College
Fairleigh Dickinson University
College at Florham
Metropolitan Campus
Montclair State University

New Jersey Institute of Technology
Ramapo College of New Jersey
Richard Stockton College of New
Jersey
Rutgers, The State University of New
Jersey
Camden Regional Campus
New Brunswick/Piscataway
Campus
Newark Regional Campus
St. Peter's College
Stevens Institute of Technology

New York

Adelphi University
Alfred University
Barnard College
Canisius College
Le Moyne College
Manhattanville College
New York University
St. Bonaventure University
St. Francis College
St. John's University
Siena College
State University of New York
Albany
Buffalo
College at Fredonia
College at Geneseo
Utica College
Wagner College

North Dakota

Valley City State University

Ohio

Case Western Reserve University
College of Wooster
Ohio State University
Columbus Campus

Oregon

Eastern Oregon University
Portland State University

Pennsylvania

Indiana University of Pennsylvania
Juniata College
Lehigh University
Moravian College
Muhlenberg College
Penn State
Erie, The Behrend College
Rosemont College
St. Francis University
Susquehanna University
University of Pennsylvania
University of Pittsburgh
University of Pittsburgh
Greensburg
Villanova University
Widener University
Wilkes University

South Carolina

Furman University

Tennessee

Fisk University
Union University

Texas

McMurry University
Texas A&M University
Baylor College of Dentistry
Commerce
Texas Lutheran University
Texas State University: San Marcos
University of Texas
Arlington
Health Science Center at Houston

Utah
University of Utah

Virginia
Old Dominion University
Virginia Commonwealth University

Wisconsin
Marquette University
University of Wisconsin
 Green Bay

Combined bachelor's/ graduate program in education

Alabama
Alabama State University
Faulkner University
Jacksonville State University

Alaska
University of Alaska
 Southeast

Arizona
Arizona Western College
Gateway Community College
Rio Salado College

Arkansas
Harding University
Ozarka College
Southern Arkansas University
University of Arkansas
 Cossatot Community College of the
 Monticello
University of Central Arkansas

California
Antioch Southern California
 Antioch University Los Angeles
Bethany University
Bethesda Christian University
California State University
 Fresno
Occidental College
Pacific Union College
Pitzer College
Simpson University
University of California
 Santa Cruz
University of San Francisco

Colorado
Adams State College
Colorado College
Jones International University
University of Colorado
 Colorado Springs

Connecticut
Quinnipiac University
Sacred Heart University
University of Bridgeport
University of Connecticut

District of Columbia
American University
Catholic University of America
Corcoran College of Art and Design
Gallaudet University

Florida
Edward Waters College
Florida Agricultural and Mechanical
 University
Florida Atlantic University
Florida Christian College
Florida Memorial University
Florida Southern College

Florida State University
Nova Southeastern University
Pasco-Hernando Community College

Georgia
Piedmont College
Reinhardt College
University of Georgia

Hawaii
Hawaii Pacific University

Idaho
Northwest Nazarene University

Illinois
Dominican University
Lincoln Christian College and
 Seminary
National-Louis University
North Park University
University of Chicago

Indiana
Oakland City University
Purdue University
 Calumet
University of St. Francis
Valparaiso University

Iowa
Emmaus Bible College
Faith Baptist Bible College and
 Theological Seminary
Graceland University
Iowa Wesleyan College
St. Ambrose University
Southeastern Community College
 North Campus
Waldorf College

Kansas
Pittsburg State University

Kentucky
Bellarmine University
Kentucky State University
Madisonville Community College
Murray State University

Maine
University of Maine
University of Southern Maine

Maryland
Anne Arundel Community College
Bowie State University
College of Notre Dame of Maryland
Maryland Institute College of Art
Towson University

Massachusetts
American International College
Anna Maria College
Art Institute of Boston at Lesley
 University
Assumption College
Berkshire Community College
Boston College
Bridgewater State College
Clark University
Hebrew College
Lesley University
Northern Essex Community College
Simmons College
University of Massachusetts
 Lowell
Wheelock College

Michigan
Albion College

Baker College
 of Cadillac
 of Flint
 of Port Huron
Grace Bible College
Kendall College of Art and Design of
 Ferris State University
Kuyper College
Northern Michigan University
Olivet College
Rochester College

Minnesota
Bemidji State University
Capella University
Central Lakes College
Normandale Community College
Northwest Technical College
University of Minnesota
 Twin Cities

Missouri
Avila University
Lindenwood University
Maryville University of Saint Louis
Missouri Baptist University
Missouri Valley College
St. Charles Community College
Truman State University
Washington University in St. Louis
Webster University
William Woods University

Montana
Montana State University
 Billings

Nebraska
Creighton University
Hastings College

Nevada
Sierra Nevada College

New Hampshire
New England College

New Jersey
Caldwell College
The College of New Jersey
Fairleigh Dickinson University
 College at Florham
 Metropolitan Campus
Richard Stockton College of New
 Jersey
Rutgers, The State University of New
 Jersey
 New Brunswick/Piscataway
 Campus

New Mexico
College of the Southwest
New Mexico Highlands University
New Mexico State University
 Alamogordo
San Juan College

New York
Adelphi University
City University of New York
 Hunter College
 Medgar Evers College
Colgate University
College of Mount St. Vincent
College of New Rochelle
Columbia-Greene Community College
Cornell University
D'Youville College
Five Towns College
Fordham University
Hilbert College
Hobart and William Smith Colleges

Iona College
Long Island University
 Brooklyn Campus
 C. W. Post Campus
Manhattan College
Manhattanville College
Nazareth College of Rochester
Pace University
Russell Sage College
Sage College of Albany
St. John's University
State University of New York
 College at Fredonia
 College at Potsdam
Union College
Wells College

North Carolina
Elon University
Gardner-Webb University
Guilford College

North Dakota
University of Mary

Ohio
Ashland University
Circleville Bible College
Edison State Community College
Kenyon College
Mount Vernon Nazarene University
Otterbein College
Tiffin University
University of Rio Grande

Oklahoma
Cameron University
Mid-America Christian University

Oregon
Corban College
Lewis & Clark College
Pacific University
Portland State University
Southern Oregon University

Pennsylvania
Albright College
Allegheny College
Arcadia University
Baptist Bible College of Pennsylvania
Cedar Crest College
Chatham College
Chestnut Hill College
Duquesne University
Gwynedd-Mercy College
Immaculata University
Lehigh University
Lock Haven University of
 Pennsylvania
Marywood University
Mount Aloysius College
Philadelphia Biblical University
St. Francis University
St. Joseph's University
University of Pennsylvania
University of Pittsburgh
 Greensburg
Valley Forge Christian College
Widener University
Wilkes University

Puerto Rico
Atlantic College
Turabo University
Universidad Metropolitana
University of the Sacred Heart

South Carolina
Aiken Technical College
Coastal Carolina University
Columbia International University

University of South Carolina
University of South Carolina
   Lancaster
   Sumter

South Dakota
University of South Dakota

Tennessee
Cumberland University
Johnson Bible College

Texas
Concordia University at Austin
Grayson County College
Hill College
North Harris Montgomery
   Community College District
Prairie View A&M University
Trinity University
University of Texas
   Brownsville

Utah
Southern Utah University
University of Utah
Westminster College

Vermont
Bennington College
College of St. Joseph in Vermont
Lyndon State College
University of Vermont

Virginia
Averett University
Hampton University
Longwood University
Old Dominion University
Regent University
University of Mary Washington
University of Northern Virginia
University of Virginia
Virginia Commonwealth University
Virginia Polytechnic Institute and
   State University

Washington
Olympic College
Puget Sound Christian College
Trinity Lutheran College
Walla Walla College
Washington State University
Whitman College
Yakima Valley Community College

West Virginia
Davis and Elkins College
West Virginia University

Wisconsin
Lakeland College
Silver Lake College
University of Wisconsin
   River Falls
   Superior
   Whitewater

Combined bachelor's/ graduate program in engineering

Alabama
Huntingdon College
Tuskegee University
University of Alabama
   Huntsville

Arkansas
Harding University
Lyon College

California
California Polytechnic State
   University: San Luis Obispo
California State University
   Fresno
Claremont McKenna College
Harvey Mudd College
Mills College
Occidental College
San Francisco State University
Santa Clara University
Scripps College
Southern California Institute of
   Technology
University of California
   Santa Cruz
University of San Francisco
University of Southern California
Whittier College

Colorado
Colorado College
Colorado School of Mines
Regis University
University of Colorado
   Boulder
   Colorado Springs
   Denver and Health Sciences Center
University of Denver
Western State College of Colorado

Connecticut
Fairfield University
Trinity College
University of Bridgeport
Yale University

Florida
Eckerd College
Florida Agricultural and Mechanical
   University
Florida Memorial University
Florida Southern College
Florida State University
Palm Beach Atlantic University
Remington College: Tampa
University of Miami

Georgia
Berry College
Georgia Institute of Technology
Mercer University
Morehouse College
North Georgia College & State
   University
Paine College
University of Georgia

Idaho
Albertson College of Idaho
University of Idaho

Illinois
Augustana College
Illinois College
Illinois Institute of Technology
Illinois Wesleyan University
Knox College
MacMurray College
North Park University
Northwestern University
Southern Illinois University
   Edwardsville
University of Illinois
   Urbana-Champaign
Wheaton College

Indiana
Anderson University
DePauw University
Goshen College
Indiana Institute of Technology

Purdue University
   Calumet
Taylor University
Wabash College

Iowa
Buena Vista University
Central College
Cornell College
Iowa State University
Iowa Wesleyan College
Luther College
Northwestern College
Simpson College
Southeastern Community College
   North Campus
University of Iowa
Waldorf College

Kansas
Benedictine College
Bethany College
Pittsburg State University

Kentucky
Berea College
Brescia University
Murray State University
Transylvania University
University of Kentucky
University of Louisville

Louisiana
Dillard University
Tulane University
Xavier University of Louisiana

Maine
Bates College
Bowdoin College
Colby College
St. Joseph's College
University of Maine

Maryland
Capitol College
Goucher College
Johns Hopkins University
St. Mary's College of Maryland
University of Maryland
   Baltimore County
Washington College

Massachusetts
Berkshire Community College
Clark University
Franklin W. Olin College of
   Engineering
Massachusetts Institute of Technology
Massachusetts Maritime Academy
Mount Holyoke College
Northeastern University
Regis College
Simon's Rock College of Bard
Tufts University
University of Massachusetts
   Boston
   Dartmouth
   Lowell
Wheaton College
Williams College
Worcester Polytechnic Institute

Michigan
Adrian College
Albion College
Alma College
Grand Valley State University
Kettering University
Lawrence Technological University
Northern Michigan University
Spring Arbor University

University of Michigan
Wayne State University

Minnesota
Bethel University
Central Lakes College
Hamline University
Northwestern College

Mississippi
Millsaps College
Mississippi College

Missouri
College of the Ozarks
Drury University
Rockhurst University
St. Charles Community College
University of Missouri
   Rolla
Washington University in St. Louis
Westminster College

Montana
Montana Tech of the University of
   Montana
University of Great Falls

Nebraska
Concordia University
Creighton University
Doane College
Hastings College
Nebraska Wesleyan University

New Hampshire
Dartmouth College

New Jersey
Drew University
Fairleigh Dickinson University
   College at Florham
   Metropolitan Campus
Richard Stockton College of New
   Jersey
Rutgers, The State University of New
   Jersey
   Newark Regional Campus
Stevens Institute of Technology

New York
Adelphi University
Bard College
Barnard College
Clarkson University
Colgate University
Columbia University
   Columbia College
   Fu Foundation School of
      Engineering and Applied
      Science
Cooper Union for the Advancement of
   Science and Art
Cornell University
Fordham University
Hartwick College
Hobart and William Smith Colleges
Ithaca College
Manhattan College
New York Institute of Technology
Polytechnic University
Rochester Institute of Technology
St. Lawrence University
St. Thomas Aquinas College
Sarah Lawrence College
Siena College
Skidmore College
State University of New York
   Albany
   Binghamton
   Buffalo
   College at Geneseo

College at Oneonta
College at Plattsburgh
Stony Brook
Union College
University of Rochester
Vassar College
Wells College

North Carolina

Elon University
Gardner-Webb University
North Carolina State University

North Dakota

Jamestown College
University of North Dakota
Valley City State University

Ohio

Case Western Reserve University
College of Wooster
Edison State Community College
Hiram College
John Carroll University
Mount Vernon Nazarene University
University of Dayton
Wittenberg University

Oklahoma

Oklahoma Baptist University
University of Oklahoma

Oregon

Eastern Oregon University
George Fox University
Oregon Institute of Technology
Pacific University
Portland State University
Reed College
Southern Oregon University
Willamette University

Pennsylvania

Allegheny College
Arcadia University
Bryn Mawr College
Bucknell University
Carlow University
Carnegie Mellon University
Dickinson College
Drexel University
Franklin & Marshall College
Gettysburg College
Indiana University of Pennsylvania
Juniata College
La Roche College
Lehigh University
Lock Haven University of
Pennsylvania
Millersville University of Pennsylvania
Moravian College
Muhlenberg College
Penn State
University Park
Rosemont College
Slippery Rock University of
Pennsylvania
University of Pennsylvania
University of Pittsburgh
Greensburg
Villanova University
Washington and Jefferson College
Waynesburg College
Widener University
Wilkes University

Puerto Rico

Inter American University of Puerto
Rico
Barranquitas Campus

South Carolina

Aiken Technical College
Charleston Southern University
The Citadel
Furman University
Morris College
Presbyterian College
University of South Carolina
University of South Carolina
Lancaster

South Dakota

Augustana College
South Dakota School of Mines and
Technology

Tennessee

King College
Lambuth University
Rhodes College

Texas

Jarvis Christian College
McMurry University
Our Lady of the Lake University of San
Antonio
Paul Quinn College
Prairie View A&M University
Southwestern University
Texas A&M University
Commerce
Texas Lutheran University
Texas State University: San Marcos
Texas Tech University
University of Texas
Arlington
Dallas

Utah

University of Utah
Westminster College

Virginia

College of William and Mary
Emory & Henry College
George Mason University
Hollins University
James Madison University
Longwood University
Norfolk State University
Old Dominion University
Randolph-Macon College
Roanoke College
Sweet Briar College
University of Virginia
Virginia Polytechnic Institute and
State University

Washington

Olympic College
Saint Martin's University
Whitman College

West Virginia

West Virginia University Institute of
Technology
West Virginia Wesleyan College

Wisconsin

Beloit College
Lawrence University
Marquette University
Milwaukee School of Engineering
Northland College
Ripon College
University of Wisconsin
Platteville
River Falls
Superior

Combined bachelor's/ graduate program in environmental studies

Arkansas

University of Central Arkansas

California

California State University
Fresno
San Francisco State University

Colorado

University of Colorado
Colorado Springs
Western State College of Colorado

Connecticut

University of New Haven
Wesleyan University
Yale University

District of Columbia

American University

Florida

Florida Agricultural and Mechanical
University

Georgia

Georgia Institute of Technology
University of Georgia

Illinois

Augustana College
Knox College

Indiana

Taylor University
Taylor University: Fort Wayne

Iowa

Cornell College
Iowa Wesleyan College
Luther College
Southeastern Community College
North Campus
University of Northern Iowa

Kansas

McPherson College
Pittsburg State University

Kentucky

Kentucky State University
Murray State University

Louisiana

Southern University and Agricultural
and Mechanical College

Maine

University of Maine

Massachusetts

Anna Maria College
Berkshire Community College
Clark University
Lesley University

Michigan

Albion College
Northern Michigan University

Minnesota

Bemidji State University
Central Lakes College

Missouri

Drury University

Montana

Montana State University
Billings

Nebraska

Doane College
University of Nebraska
Omaha

New Mexico

College of the Southwest

New York

Adelphi University
Bard College
City University of New York
Medgar Evers College
Cornell University
New York Institute of Technology
Pace University
Rochester Institute of Technology
Siena College
State University of New York
College of Environmental Science
and Forestry

North Carolina

Guilford College
High Point University
Wake Forest University

Ohio

College of Wooster
Miami University
Oxford Campus
Ohio State University
Columbus Campus
University of Rio Grande
Wittenberg University
Xavier University

Oregon

Eastern Oregon University
Pacific University
Portland State University
Reed College
Southern Oregon University

Pennsylvania

Albright College
Arcadia University
Carlow University
Duquesne University
Franklin & Marshall College
Gettysburg College
Lebanon Valley College
Lycoming College
Muhlenberg College
St. Francis University
Susquehanna University
University of Pennsylvania
University of Pittsburgh
Greensburg

South Carolina

Furman University
Presbyterian College

Utah

University of Utah

Vermont

Sterling College

Virginia

College of William and Mary
Old Dominion University
Virginia Commonwealth University

Virginia Polytechnic Institute and
State University

Washington
Whitman College

West Virginia
Davis and Elkins College

Wisconsin
Milwaukee School of Engineering
University of Wisconsin
Platteville

Combined bachelor's/ graduate program in fine arts

California
Academy of Art University
John F. Kennedy University
San Francisco State University
University of California
Santa Cruz

Colorado
Western State College of Colorado

Georgia
University of Georgia

Idaho
University of Idaho

Indiana
University of St. Francis

Maine
Maine College of Art
University of Maine
University of Southern Maine

Maryland
Towson University
University of Maryland
Baltimore County

Massachusetts
Art Institute of Boston at Lesley
University
Lesley University
Suffolk University
Wheaton College

Minnesota
Bemidji State University
Minneapolis College of Art and Design
Minnesota State University
Mankato

Missouri
Northwest Missouri State University
Webster University

New Jersey
Fairleigh Dickinson University
Metropolitan Campus

New York
Cornell University
Pratt Institute
Rochester Institute of Technology
State University of New York
Buffalo

Ohio
Cleveland Institute of Art
Kent State University

Oregon
Pacific University
Portland State University

Pennsylvania
Carlow University
Chatham College
Marywood University

South Dakota
University of South Dakota

Tennessee
Memphis College of Art

Texas
Prairie View A&M University
Rice University

Utah
Southern Utah University
University of Utah

Virginia
Hollins University
Mary Baldwin College
Virginia Polytechnic Institute and
State University

West Virginia
Davis and Elkins College

Combined bachelor's/ graduate program in forestry

Arkansas
University of Arkansas
Monticello

Colorado
Western State College of Colorado

Connecticut
Yale University

Georgia
University of Georgia

Illinois
Augustana College
Illinois Wesleyan University
Knox College

Iowa
Cornell College
Iowa Wesleyan College
Southeastern Community College
North Campus

Kansas
Pittsburg State University

Maine
University of Maine

Michigan
Albion College

Nebraska
Doane College

New Jersey
Drew University

New York
Alfred University
Bard College

State University of New York
College of Environmental Science
and Forestry

North Carolina
Guilford College
High Point University
Lees-McRae College
North Carolina State University
Wake Forest University

Ohio
College of Wooster
Miami University
Oxford Campus
Ohio State University
Columbus Campus
Xavier University

Oregon
Eastern Oregon University
Portland State University
Reed College
Willamette University

Pennsylvania
Albright College
Allegheny College
Franklin & Marshall College
Gettysburg College
Lebanon Valley College
Lycoming College
Moravian College
Muhlenberg College
St. Francis University
Susquehanna University

South Carolina
Aiken Technical College
Furman University
Presbyterian College

Vermont
Sterling College

Virginia
Bridgewater College
College of William and Mary
James Madison University
Randolph-Macon College
Virginia Polytechnic Institute and
State University

Washington
Whitman College

West Virginia
Davis and Elkins College
Marshall University

Wisconsin
Northland College
Ripon College

Combined bachelor's/ graduate program in law

Arkansas
University of Arkansas

California
Claremont McKenna College
Humphreys College
John F. Kennedy University
Occidental College
University of La Verne
University of San Francisco
Whittier College

Colorado
Western State College of Colorado

Connecticut
Quinnipiac University

District of Columbia
Catholic University of America

Florida
Florida Agricultural and Mechanical
University
Nova Southeastern University
St. Thomas University
Stetson University

Idaho
Albertson College of Idaho
University of Idaho

Illinois
Illinois Institute of Technology
Knox College
Loyola University of Chicago
Roosevelt University
University of Illinois
Chicago

Indiana
Valparaiso University
Wabash College

Iowa
Drake University
Grinnell College
Iowa Wesleyan College
Southeastern Community College
North Campus

Kansas
McPherson College
Pittsburg State University

Maine
Bowdoin College
University of Southern Maine

Maryland
Salisbury University
University of Baltimore
University of Maryland
College Park

Massachusetts
Becker College
Newbury College
Northeastern University
Suffolk University
University of Massachusetts
Dartmouth
Western New England College
Worcester Polytechnic Institute

Michigan
Olivet College
Siena Heights University

Minnesota
Hamline University

Mississippi
Mississippi College

Missouri
Central Missouri State University
College of the Ozarks
Drury University
University of Missouri
Kansas City
Washington University in St. Louis

Nebraska
Creighton University
Hastings College
University of Nebraska
  Lincoln
  Omaha

New Jersey
Rutgers, The State University of New
  Jersey
  New Brunswick/Piscataway
    Campus
  Newark Regional Campus
St. Peter's College
Seton Hall University
Stevens Institute of Technology

New York
Adelphi University
Albany College of Pharmacy
Barnard College
College of Saint Rose
Columbia University
  Columbia College
Cornell University
Eugene Lang College The New School
  for Liberal Arts
Fordham University
Hamilton College
Hartwick College
Hofstra University
New York Institute of Technology
Pace University
Rensselaer Polytechnic Institute
Russell Sage College
St. Bonaventure University
St. John's University
Siena College
Skidmore College
State University of New York
  Albany
Union College

North Carolina
Campbell University

North Dakota
Valley City State University

Ohio
College of Wooster
Ohio Northern University
University of Cincinnati
University of Toledo

Oklahoma
University of Tulsa

Oregon
Portland State University
Willamette University

Pennsylvania
Dickinson College
Drexel University
Duquesne University
Edinboro University of Pennsylvania
Gannon University
Juniata College
Kutztown University of Pennsylvania
St. Francis University
St. Vincent College
Seton Hill University
Slippery Rock University of
  Pennsylvania
Temple University
University of Pennsylvania
University of Pittsburgh
  Greensburg
Villanova University
Washington and Jefferson College
Waynesburg College

Widener University

Puerto Rico
Pontifical Catholic University of
  Puerto Rico

Rhode Island
Roger Williams University

Tennessee
Lambuth University
Vanderbilt University

Texas
Texas A&M University
  Commerce

Utah
Brigham Young University
University of Utah

Vermont
University of Vermont

Virginia
James Madison University
Regent University
Virginia Commonwealth University
Virginia Union University
Washington and Lee University

Washington
Whitman College

Wisconsin
Marquette University
University of Wisconsin
  Green Bay

Combined bachelor's/ graduate program in mathematics

Alabama
Alabama State University
Faulkner University
Jacksonville State University
University of Alabama
  Birmingham

Arkansas
University of Arkansas
  Monticello
University of Central Arkansas

California
California State University
  Fresno
Harvey Mudd College
Pitzer College
University of Southern California

Colorado
Colorado School of Mines
University of Colorado
  Boulder
  Colorado Springs

Connecticut
Wesleyan University
Yale University

District of Columbia
American University
Gallaudet University

Florida
Edward Waters College
Florida Christian College
Florida State University

Georgia
Clark Atlanta University
Emory University
University of Georgia

Illinois
DePaul University

Indiana
Purdue University
  Calumet

Iowa
Iowa Wesleyan College
Southeastern Community College
  North Campus

Kansas
Pittsburg State University

Kentucky
Kentucky State University
Murray State University

Maine
University of Maine

Maryland
Bowie State University
Hood College
Johns Hopkins University

Michigan
Northern Michigan University

Minnesota
Bemidji State University

Missouri
Missouri State University
University of Missouri
  Rolla

Montana
Montana State University
  Billings

New Jersey
Rutgers, The State University of New
  Jersey
  Camden Regional Campus

New Mexico
College of the Southwest

New York
City University of New York
  City College
  Hunter College
  Medgar Evers College
Cornell University
Rochester Institute of Technology
St. John's University
St. Joseph's College: Suffolk Campus
State University of New York
  Buffalo
  College at Fredonia
  College at Potsdam
  Stony Brook
University of Rochester

North Carolina
Guilford College

Ohio
Case Western Reserve University
Mount Vernon Nazarene University
University of Rio Grande

Oklahoma
University of Oklahoma

Oregon
Southern Oregon University

Pennsylvania
Bryn Mawr College
Bucknell University
Duquesne University
Lock Haven University of
  Pennsylvania
Mount Aloysius College
University of Pennsylvania
University of Pittsburgh
University of Pittsburgh
  Greensburg
Villanova University
Wilkes University

South Carolina
Aiken Technical College
University of South Carolina
  Lancaster
Voorhees College

South Dakota
South Dakota School of Mines and
  Technology

Tennessee
King College

Texas
Prairie View A&M University

Utah
University of Utah

Virginia
Old Dominion University
Virginia Polytechnic Institute and
  State University

Washington
Olympic College

West Virginia
Davis and Elkins College

Combined bachelor's/ graduate program in medicine

California
University of Southern California

Colorado
Western State College of Colorado

Connecticut
University of Connecticut

District of Columbia
Howard University

Florida
University of Central Florida
University of Miami
University of South Florida

Illinois
Bradley University
Illinois Institute of Technology
Knox College
Loyola University of Chicago
Northwestern University
Rush University
University of Chicago

Indiana
Purdue University
Calumet

Iowa
Iowa Wesleyan College
Southeastern Community College
North Campus

Kansas
McPherson College
Pittsburg State University

Kentucky
Kentucky State University
Murray State University

Louisiana
Louisiana State University
Shreveport

Maryland
University of Maryland
College Park

Massachusetts
Boston University
Tufts University

Michigan
Olivet·College
Wayne State University

Mississippi
Mississippi College

Missouri
Central Missouri State University
Drury University
University of Missouri
Kansas City

Nebraska
Chadron State College
Creighton University
Hastings College
University of Nebraska
Lincoln
Medical Center
Omaha

New Jersey
The College of New Jersey
Drew University
Fairleigh Dickinson University
College at Florham
Metropolitan Campus
Monmouth University
Montclair State University
New Jersey Institute of Technology
Richard Stockton College of New
Jersey
Rutgers, The State University of New
Jersey
Camden Regional Campus
New Brunswick/Piscataway
Campus
Newark Regional Campus
St. Peter's College
Stevens Institute of Technology

New Mexico
University of New Mexico

New York
Albany College of Pharmacy
Canisius College
City University of New York
Brooklyn College
City College
Colgate University

Rensselaer Polytechnic Institute
St. Bonaventure University
Siena College
Union College
University of Rochester
Utica College

North Dakota
Valley City State University

Ohio
College of Wooster
Kent State University
Ohio State University
Columbus Campus
University of Akron
University of Cincinnati

Oregon
Eastern Oregon University
Portland State University

Pennsylvania
Delaware Valley College
Drexel University
Gannon University
Indiana University of Pennsylvania
Juniata College
Lehigh University
Muhlenberg College
Penn State
Erie, The Behrend College
University Park
Rosemont College
St. Francis University
Temple University
Thomas Jefferson University: College
of Health Professions
University of Pittsburgh
University of Pittsburgh
Greensburg
Ursinus College
Villanova University
Washington and Jefferson College
Widener University
Wilkes University

Rhode Island
Brown University

South Carolina
Furman University
Voorhees College

Tennessee
East Tennessee State University
Fisk University
Lambuth University
Union University

Texas
McMurry University
Rice University
Texas A&M University
Commerce
Texas State University: San Marcos
Texas Tech University Health Sciences
Center
University of Texas
Arlington
Health Science Center at Houston

Utah
University of Utah

Virginia
Old Dominion University
Virginia Commonwealth University

West Virginia
Davis and Elkins College

Wisconsin
University of Wisconsin
Green Bay

Combined bachelor's/ graduate program in nursing

Alabama
Birmingham-Southern College
George C. Wallace State Community
College
George C. Wallace Community
College at Dothan
Jacksonville State University
University of Mobile

Arizona
Gateway Community College

Arkansas
University of Arkansas
Monticello
University of Central Arkansas

California
California State University
Fresno
Loma Linda University
Samuel Merritt College
San Francisco State University
University of San Diego

Colorado
University of Colorado
Colorado Springs

Connecticut
Quinnipiac University
Sacred Heart University
St. Joseph College

District of Columbia
Catholic University of America

Florida
Florida Agricultural and Mechanical
University
Florida Christian College
Florida Gulf Coast University
Florida Hospital College of Health
Sciences
Florida Memorial University
Florida Southern College
Jacksonville University
Okaloosa-Walton College
Pasco-Hernando Community College
St. Leo University
University of Central Florida
University of Miami
University of Tampa

Georgia
Agnes Scott College
Berry College
Georgia Southern University
Reinhardt College
South University

Hawaii
Hawaii Pacific University

Idaho
Albertson College of Idaho

Illinois
Blessing-Reiman College of Nursing
Knox College
National-Louis University
North Park University

Rush University
St. Xavier University
Wheaton College

Indiana
Purdue University
Calumet
North Central Campus
University of St. Francis
University of Southern Indiana
Valparaiso University

Iowa
Cornell College
Dordt College
Graceland University
Grand View College
Iowa Wesleyan College
Mercy College of Health Sciences
Northwestern College
St. Luke's College
Southeastern Community College
North Campus
University of Dubuque

Kansas
Pittsburg State University

Kentucky
Bellarmine University
Kentucky State University
Madisonville Community College
Murray State University

Louisiana
Loyola University New Orleans
Our Lady of the Lake College
Southern University and Agricultural
and Mechanical College

Maine
Husson College
St. Joseph's College
University of Maine
University of Southern Maine

Maryland
Salisbury University
Towson University
Washington College

Massachusetts
Berkshire Community College
Mount Holyoke College
Northeastern University
Regis College
Simmons College
University of Massachusetts
Boston
Dartmouth

Michigan
Albion College
Kuyper College
Northern Michigan University
University of Michigan

Minnesota
Bemidji State University
Northwest Technical College

Mississippi
Blue Mountain College
Millsaps College

Missouri
Culver-Stockton College
Jewish Hospital College of Nursing
and Allied Health
Missouri State University
Ozark Christian College

St. Charles Community College
St. Luke's College
University of Missouri
    Kansas City
    Rolla
Webster University

Montana
Fort Belknap College
University of Great Falls

Nebraska
Chadron State College
Clarkson College
Creighton University
University of Nebraska
    Omaha

New Jersey
Fairleigh Dickinson University
    Metropolitan Campus
Felician College
Ocean County College
Ramapo College of New Jersey
Richard Stockton College of New
    Jersey
St. Peter's College

New Mexico
New Mexico State University
    Alamogordo
San Juan College

New York
Adelphi University
City University of New York
    Medgar Evers College
Cochran School of Nursing-St. John's
    Riverside Hospital
Columbia University
    School of Nursing
D'Youville College
Excelsior College
Hobart and William Smith Colleges
Long Island College Hospital School of
    Nursing
Long Island University
    C.W. Post Campus
Molloy College
New York University
Pace University
Russell Sage College
Sage College of Albany
St. Elizabeth College of Nursing
State University of New York
    Buffalo
    Stony Brook

North Carolina
Edgecombe Community College
Gardner-Webb University

North Dakota
Lake Region State College
Valley City State University

Ohio
Bowling Green State University
Circleville Bible College
College of Wooster
Franciscan University of Steubenville
John Carroll University
Kent State University
Mercy College of Northwest Ohio
Mount Vernon Nazarene University
Otterbein College
University of Akron
University of Rio Grande
Ursuline College
Wittenberg University

Oregon
Eastern Oregon University
Oregon Health & Science University
Oregon Institute of Technology
Portland State University
Southern Oregon University

Pennsylvania
Allegheny College
Arcadia University
Carlow University
Drexel University
Duquesne University
Gannon University
Gwynedd-Mercy College
Juniata College
Keystone College
Lock Haven University of
    Pennsylvania
Mount Aloysius College
Neumann College
Northampton County Area
    Community College
Rosemont College
St. Francis University
Susquehanna University
Thomas Jefferson University: College
    of Health Professions
University of Pennsylvania
University of Scranton
Widener University
Wilkes University

South Carolina
Aiken Technical College
Furman University
University of South Carolina
    Lancaster

South Dakota
Augustana College

Tennessee
Bryan College
Fisk University
King College
Lambuth University
Maryville College
Southern Adventist University
Tennessee Wesleyan College
Vanderbilt University

Texas
Baylor University
Grayson County College
Jarvis Christian College
Prairie View A&M University
Texas A&M University
    Commerce
Texas Tech University Health Sciences
    Center
Texas Woman's University
University of Texas
    Health Science Center at Houston
    Health Science Center at San
        Antonio

Utah
University of Utah
Westminster College

Virginia
Bridgewater College
Mary Baldwin College
Old Dominion University
Radford University
Virginia Commonwealth University

Washington
Gonzaga University
Olympic College
Yakima Valley Community College

West Virginia
Davis and Elkins College
Mountain State University
Wheeling Jesuit University

Wisconsin
Beloit College
Columbia College of Nursing
Lakeshore Technical College
Marquette University
Mount Mary College
Northland College
Silver Lake College

Combined bachelor's/ graduate program in occupational therapy

Alabama
Alabama State University
Spring Hill College

Arkansas
University of Central Arkansas

California
Dominican University of California
Loma Linda University

Connecticut
Quinnipiac University
Sacred Heart University

Florida
International College
Nova Southeastern University
St. Leo University

Georgia
Brenau University

Idaho
Albertson College of Idaho

Illinois
Augustana College
Dominican University
Illinois College
Knox College
McKendree College
Rush University

Iowa
St. Ambrose University
Southeastern Community College
    North Campus

Kansas
University of Kansas Medical Center

Maine
Husson College
University of New England
University of Southern Maine

Maryland
Mount St. Mary's University

Massachusetts
American International College
Bay Path College
Boston University
Springfield College
Worcester State College

Michigan
Alma College
Baker College
    of Flint
Calvin College

Grand Valley State University

Minnesota
College of St. Catherine
College of St. Scholastica

Missouri
Avila University
Culver-Stockton College
Drury University
Maryville University of Saint Louis
Rockhurst University
St. Louis University
Stephens College
Washington University in St. Louis

Montana
Rocky Mountain College

Nebraska
Chadron State College
College of Saint Mary
Creighton University
Hastings College
University of Nebraska
    Omaha

New Jersey
Caldwell College
Kean University
Richard Stockton College of New
    Jersey
St. Peter's College
Seton Hall University

New York
D'Youville College
Dominican College of Blauvelt
Ithaca College
Long Island University
    Brooklyn Campus
    C.W. Post Campus
Mercy College
New York Institute of Technology
Pace University
Russell Sage College
Siena College
Touro College
Utica College

North Dakota
University of Mary
Valley City State University

Ohio
Mount Vernon Nazarene University
University of Findlay
Wittenberg University
Xavier University

Oregon
Pacific University
Portland State University

Pennsylvania
Alvernia College
Bloomsburg University of
    Pennsylvania
Carlow University
Chatham College
College Misericordia
Duquesne University
Elizabethtown College
Gannon University
Juniata College
Keystone College
La Roche College
La Salle University
Moravian College
Mount Aloysius College
St. Francis University
St. Vincent College

Susquehanna University
Temple University
Thomas Jefferson University: College
    of Health Professions
University of Pittsburgh
    Greensburg
University of Scranton
University of the Sciences in
    Philadelphia
Villanova University

South Carolina

Aiken Technical College

Tennessee

Belmont University

Texas

Texas Tech University Health Sciences
    Center

Utah

University of Utah

Vermont

Castleton State College

Virginia

Shenandoah University

West Virginia

West Virginia University

Wisconsin

Carthage College
Concordia University Wisconsin
Lawrence University
Mount Mary College
University of Wisconsin
    Green Bay

Combined bachelor's/ graduate program in optometry

Colorado

Western State College of Colorado

Florida

Nova Southeastern University

Illinois

Knox College

Indiana

Indiana University
    Bloomington
Purdue University
    Calumet

Iowa

Iowa Wesleyan College
Southeastern Community College
    North Campus

Kansas

McPherson College
Pittsburg State University

Kentucky

Murray State University

Maine

St. Joseph's College
University of Maine

Maryland

Salisbury University

Massachusetts

Assumption College
Massachusetts College of Pharmacy
    and Health Sciences
Wheaton College

Nebraska

University of Nebraska
    Omaha

New Jersey

Caldwell College
The College of New Jersey
Ramapo College of New Jersey

New York

Adelphi University
Canisius College
City University of New York
    City College
Ithaca College
Le Moyne College
Pace University
St. John's University
Siena College
State University of New York
    Albany
    Binghamton
    College at Fredonia
    College at Geneseo
    College at Oneonta
    College at Plattsburgh
    College at Potsdam
    New Paltz
    Oswego
Utica College

North Dakota

Valley City State University

Ohio

Ohio State University
    Columbus Campus

Oklahoma

Northeastern State University

Oregon

Eastern Oregon University
Pacific University
Portland State University
Southern Oregon University

Pennsylvania

Arcadia University
Gannon University
Gettysburg College
Indiana University of Pennsylvania
Juniata College
Lehigh University
Lycoming College
Millersville University of Pennsylvania
Muhlenberg College
St. Francis University
University of Pittsburgh
    Greensburg
Villanova University
Washington and Jefferson College
Wilkes University

Tennessee

Union University

Texas

Texas A&M University
    Commerce

Virginia

Old Dominion University

Wisconsin

University of Wisconsin
    Green Bay

Combined bachelor's/ graduate program in osteopathic medicine

California

Pitzer College

Florida

Jacksonville University
Nova Southeastern University
St. Leo University

Iowa

Southeastern Community College
    North Campus

Kansas

McPherson College

Kentucky

Kentucky State University

Maine

University of Maine

Missouri

Avila University
Drury University
Missouri Western State University

New Jersey

Caldwell College
Ramapo College of New Jersey
Richard Stockton College of New
    Jersey

New York

Marist College
New York Institute of Technology
Pace University
St. Bonaventure University
Siena College
State University of New York
    College at Geneseo
    New Paltz
Touro College
Utica College

Ohio

Kent State University

Oregon

Portland State University

Pennsylvania

Edinboro University of Pennsylvania
Gannon University
Indiana University of Pennsylvania
Juniata College
Kutztown University of Pennsylvania
Penn State
    Erie, The Behrend College
St. Francis University
University of Pittsburgh
    Greensburg
Widener University
Wilkes University

Texas

University of Texas
    Dallas

Combined bachelor's/ graduate program in pharmacy

Alabama

Samford University

Arizona

University of Arizona

California

University of Southern California
University of the Pacific

Florida

Florida Agricultural and Mechanical
    University
International College
Nova Southeastern University
St. Leo University

Georgia

South University

Hawaii

Hawaii Pacific University

Idaho

Albertson College of Idaho
Idaho State University

Illinois

Lewis University
Loyola University of Chicago
Millikin University

Indiana

Butler University
Purdue University
    Calumet

Iowa

Iowa Wesleyan College
Southeastern Community College
    North Campus

Kansas

McPherson College
Pittsburg State University
University of Kansas

Kentucky

Kentucky State University
Murray State University

Louisiana

University of Louisiana at Monroe

Maine

St. Joseph's College

Maryland

Coppin State University
Salisbury University
University of Baltimore
Villa Julie College
Washington College

Massachusetts

Northeastern University

Michigan

Ferris State University
University of Michigan
Wayne State University

Minnesota

University of Minnesota
    Twin Cities

Montana
University of Montana: Missoula

Nebraska
Chadron State College
Creighton University
Hastings College
University of Nebraska
  Lincoln
  Medical Center
  Omaha

Nevada
Sierra Nevada College

New Jersey
New Jersey Institute of Technology
Rutgers, The State University of New
  Jersey
  Camden Regional Campus
St. Peter's College

New York
Albany College of Pharmacy
Canisius College
Long Island University
  Brooklyn Campus
St. Bonaventure University
St. John's University
St. Thomas Aquinas College

North Carolina
Campbell University
Elizabeth City State University
Wingate University

North Dakota
North Dakota State University
Valley City State University

Ohio
Ohio Northern University
Ohio State University
  Columbus Campus
University of Cincinnati
University of Toledo

Oklahoma
Southwestern Oklahoma State
  University

Oregon
Pacific University
Portland State University

Pennsylvania
Gannon University
Juniata College
Keystone College
Mercyhurst College
Penn State
  Erie, The Behrend College
St. Vincent College
Temple University
Thiel College
University of Pittsburgh
University of Pittsburgh
  Greensburg
  Johnstown
University of the Sciences in
  Philadelphia
Wilkes University

South Carolina
Clemson University
Furman University
University of South Carolina
  Lancaster

South Dakota
South Dakota State University

Tennessee
East Tennessee State University
Fisk University
King College
Lambuth University
Tennessee Wesleyan College
Union University

Texas
El Centro College
Texas A&M University
  Commerce
Texas Tech University Health Sciences
  Center
University of Texas
  Austin
  El Paso

Utah
University of Utah

Virginia
Old Dominion University
Shenandoah University
Virginia Commonwealth University

Washington
University of Washington
Washington State University

West Virginia
Davis and Elkins College
West Virginia University

Wisconsin
University of Wisconsin
  Green Bay
  Madison

Wyoming
University of Wyoming

Combined bachelor's/ graduate program in physical therapy

Alabama
Alabama State University
Spring Hill College

Arizona
Gateway Community College

Arkansas
Harding University
University of Central Arkansas

California
California State University
  Fresno
Loma Linda University
San Francisco State University

Colorado
Western State College of Colorado

Connecticut
Quinnipiac University
Sacred Heart University
University of Connecticut
University of Hartford

Florida
International College
Nova Southeastern University
St. Leo University
University of Miami

Georgia
Armstrong Atlantic State University

South University

Idaho
Albertson College of Idaho

Illinois
Bradley University
Millikin University

Indiana
Purdue University
  Calumet
University of Evansville

Iowa
Clarke College
Iowa Wesleyan College
St. Ambrose University
Southeastern Community College
  North Campus

Kansas
McPherson College
Pittsburg State University

Kentucky
Bellarmine University
Kentucky State University

Maine
Husson College

Maryland
Coppin State University
Mount St. Mary's University
University of Maryland
  College Park
Villa Julie College

Massachusetts
American International College
Boston University
Northeastern University
Simmons College
Springfield College
University of Massachusetts
  Lowell

Michigan
Andrews University
Grand Valley State University

Minnesota
College of St. Catherine
College of St. Scholastica

Missouri
Avila University
Maryville University of Saint Louis
Rockhurst University
St. Louis University
Stephens College
Washington University in St. Louis

Nebraska
Chadron State College
Creighton University
Hastings College
University of Nebraska
  Medical Center
  Omaha

New Jersey
Caldwell College
Kean University
Ramapo College of New Jersey
Richard Stockton College of New
  Jersey
St. Peter's College
Seton Hall University

University of Medicine and Dentistry
  of New Jersey
  School of Health Related
    Professions

New York
Adelphi University
City University of New York
  College of Staten Island
Clarkson University
D'Youville College
Daemen College
Dominican College of Blauvelt
Iona College
Ithaca College
Le Moyne College
Long Island University
  Brooklyn Campus
Manhattanville College
Mercy College
Nazareth College of Rochester
New York Institute of Technology
Pace University
Russell Sage College
St. Thomas Aquinas College
Siena College
State University of New York
  College at Brockport
  College at Geneseo
  College at Oneonta
  Downstate Medical Center
  Oswego
  Upstate Medical University
Touro College
Utica College

North Dakota
University of Mary
University of North Dakota
Valley City State University

Ohio
Bowling Green State University
Mount Vernon Nazarene University
Ohio University
University of Findlay
Walsh University

Oregon
Pacific University
Portland State University

Pennsylvania
Allegheny College
Arcadia University
Bloomsburg University of
  Pennsylvania
Cabrini College
Carlow University
Chatham College
College Misericordia
Drexel University
Duquesne University
Elizabethtown College
Gannon University
Gettysburg College
Indiana University of Pennsylvania
Juniata College
Keystone College
La Roche College
Lebanon Valley College
Moravian College
Mount Aloysius College
Penn State
  Abington
  Delaware County
St. Francis University
St. Vincent College
Temple University
Thomas Jefferson University: College
  of Health Professions
University of Pittsburgh
  Greensburg

University of Scranton
University of the Sciences in
Philadelphia
Villanova University
Waynesburg College
Widener University
Wilkes University

South Carolina
Aiken Technical College
Furman University

Tennessee
Belmont University
King College
Lambuth University
University of Tennessee
Chattanooga
Knoxville

Texas
Texas A&M University
Commerce
Texas Tech University Health Sciences
Center
University of Texas
El Paso

Utah
University of Utah

Vermont
Castleton State College
University of Vermont

Virginia
Bridgewater College
Old Dominion University
Shenandoah University
Virginia Commonwealth University

Washington
University of Puget Sound

West Virginia
Davis and Elkins College
West Virginia University

Wisconsin
Concordia University Wisconsin
Marquette University
University of Wisconsin
Green Bay

Combined bachelor's/ graduate program in podiatry

District of Columbia
Howard University

Florida
Barry University

Maryland
Salisbury University

Massachusetts
Assumption College

New Jersey
Caldwell College
Richard Stockton College of New
Jersey

New York
Canisius College
Le Moyne College
Pace University
St. Francis College

St. Joseph's College: Suffolk Campus
St. Thomas Aquinas College
Siena College
Utica College

Oregon
Portland State University

Pennsylvania
Cabrini College
Chestnut Hill College
Gannon University
Indiana University of Pennsylvania
Juniata College
Lycoming College
Millersville University of Pennsylvania
St. Francis University
St. Vincent College
Washington and Jefferson College
Widener University

Tennessee
Union University

Combined bachelor's/ graduate program in psychology

Alabama
Faulkner University

Arkansas
University of Arkansas
Monticello
University of Central Arkansas

California
California State University
Fresno
Claremont McKenna College
John F. Kennedy University

Colorado
University of Colorado
Boulder
Colorado Springs

Connecticut
St. Joseph College
Wesleyan University
Yale University

District of Columbia
American University
Catholic University of America
Gallaudet University

Florida
Edward Waters College
Nova Southeastern University

Georgia
University of Georgia

Illinois
DePaul University
Illinois Institute of Technology
Lewis University
National-Louis University

Indiana
University of St. Francis
Valparaiso University

Iowa
Iowa State University
Iowa Wesleyan College
Southeastern Community College
North Campus
Waldorf College

Kansas
Pittsburg State University

Kentucky
Kentucky State University
Murray State University

Louisiana
Centenary College of Louisiana
Our Lady of the Lake College

Maine
University of Maine

Maryland
Bowie State University
Johns Hopkins University
Towson University
University of Baltimore

Massachusetts
American International College
Anna Maria College
Lesley University
Suffolk University

Michigan
Central Michigan University
Northern Michigan University
Rochester College

Minnesota
Bemidji State University
Capella University
Oak Hills Christian College

Missouri
Avila University
Stephens College

Montana
Montana State University
Billings
University of Great Falls

New Jersey
Caldwell College
College of St. Elizabeth
Fairleigh Dickinson University
College at Florham
Metropolitan Campus

New Mexico
College of the Southwest
New Mexico Highlands University

New York
City University of New York
City College
John Jay College of Criminal Justice
Medgar Evers College
College of New Rochelle
Cornell University
Iona College
Marist College
Rochester Institute of Technology
St. John's University
St. Thomas Aquinas College
State University of New York
Albany
College at Plattsburgh

North Carolina
Guilford College

Ohio
Case Western Reserve University
Circleville Bible College
Marietta College
Mount Vernon Nazarene University
Tiffin University

Walsh University

Oklahoma
Mid-America Christian University

Oregon
Oregon Institute of Technology
Southern Oregon University

Pennsylvania
Baptist Bible College of Pennsylvania
Bryn Mawr College
Chatham College
Chestnut Hill College
Geneva College
Lock Haven University of
Pennsylvania
Marywood University
Mount Aloysius College
Rosemont College
St. Joseph's University
University of Pittsburgh
Greensburg
University of the Sciences in
Philadelphia
Valley Forge Christian College
Widener University

Rhode Island
Salve Regina University

South Carolina
Aiken Technical College
University of South Carolina
Lancaster

South Dakota
University of South Dakota

Texas
Prairie View A&M University
University of Dallas

Utah
University of Utah

Vermont
Burlington College

Virginia
Old Dominion University
Regent University
Virginia Polytechnic Institute and
State University

Washington
Olympic College
Walla Walla College

West Virginia
Davis and Elkins College

Wisconsin
University of Wisconsin
Whitewater

Combined bachelor's/ graduate program in social work

Alabama
Alabama State University
Jacksonville State University

Arizona
Arizona Western College

Arkansas
University of Arkansas
Monticello

California
California State University
  Fresno
San Francisco State University

District of Columbia
Gallaudet University

Florida
Florida Agricultural and Mechanical
  University
Florida Christian College

Hawaii
Hawaii Pacific University

Idaho
Northwest Nazarene University

Illinois
Lake Forest College
St. Augustine College
University of Chicago

Indiana
Grace College

Iowa
Southeastern Community College
  North Campus

Kansas
Manhattan Christian College
Pittsburg State University

Kentucky
Brescia University
Kentucky State University
Madisonville Community College
Murray State University

Maine
University of Maine
University of Southern Maine

Maryland
Bowie State University
Columbia Union College
Salisbury University
University of Maryland
  Baltimore County

Massachusetts
Berkshire Community College
Boston College
Lesley University
Regis College
Wheelock College

Michigan
Andrews University
Kuyper College
Northern Michigan University

Minnesota
Bemidji State University
Capella University

Missouri
Maryville University of Saint Louis
Washington University in St. Louis
Webster University

Montana
Montana State University
  Billings

Nebraska
Chadron State College

New Mexico
New Mexico Highlands University
San Juan College

New York
Adelphi University
Bard College
Concordia College
Fordham University
Molloy College
Mount St. Mary College
Nazareth College of Rochester
Sarah Lawrence College
Siena College
State University of New York
  Albany
  Buffalo
  New Paltz

North Dakota
Dickinson State University
Valley City State University

Ohio
Ashland University
Baldwin-Wallace College
Circleville Bible College
College of Wooster
Mount Vernon Nazarene University
University of Rio Grande

Oregon
Portland State University

Pennsylvania
Bryn Mawr College
Cedar Crest College
Lock Haven University of
  Pennsylvania
Marywood University
Millersville University of Pennsylvania
University of Pittsburgh
  Greensburg
Widener University

South Carolina
Aiken Technical College

South Dakota
University of South Dakota

Texas
University of Texas
  Health Science Center at Houston

Utah
University of Utah

Washington
Olympic College
Walla Walla College
Yakima Valley Community College

West Virginia
Davis and Elkins College

Wisconsin
University of Wisconsin
  River Falls
  Superior

Combined bachelor's/ graduate program in veterinary medicine

Colorado
Colorado State University
Western State College of Colorado

Iowa
Iowa Wesleyan College
Southeastern Community College
  North Campus

Kansas
McPherson College
Pittsburg State University

Maryland
Salisbury University
University of Maryland
  College Park

Massachusetts
Tufts University
Worcester Polytechnic Institute

Michigan
Olivet College

Mississippi
Mississippi College
Mississippi State University

Nebraska
University of Nebraska
  Omaha

New York
Cornell University
Siena College
Wells College

North Carolina
North Carolina State University

North Dakota
Valley City State University

Ohio
College of Wooster
Kent State University
University of Findlay

Pennsylvania
Delaware Valley College
St. Francis University
University of Pittsburgh
  Greensburg
Widener University

Puerto Rico
Pontifical Catholic University of
  Puerto Rico

Tennessee
Lambuth University
Union University

Texas
Texas A&M University
  Commerce

Vermont
University of Vermont

Virginia
Bridgewater College
Old Dominion University
Virginia Polytechnic Institute and
  State University

Washington
Washington State University

Wisconsin
University of Wisconsin
  Madison

Double major

Alabama

Alabama State University
Athens State University
Auburn University
Auburn University at Montgomery
Birmingham-Southern College
Faulkner State Community College
Faulkner University
George C. Wallace State Community
    College
    Selma
Huntingdon College
Jacksonville State University
Judson College
Lawson State Community College
Miles College
Northeast Alabama Community
    College
Oakwood College
Samford University
Shelton State Community College
South University
Southeastern Bible College
Southern Christian University
Spring Hill College
Stillman College
Talladega College
Troy University
Tuskegee University
University of Alabama
University of Alabama
    Birmingham
    Huntsville
University of Mobile
University of Montevallo
University of North Alabama
University of South Alabama
University of West Alabama
Wallace State Community College at
    Hanceville

Alaska

Alaska Bible College
Alaska Pacific University
Charter College
Prince William Sound Community
    College
Sheldon Jackson College
University of Alaska
    Anchorage
    Fairbanks

Arizona

American Indian College of the
    Assemblies of God
Arizona State University
Arizona State University West
Chandler-Gilbert Community College
    Williams Campus
Chaparral College
Cochise College
Dine College
Eastern Arizona College
Embry-Riddle Aeronautical University:
    Prescott Campus
Gateway Community College
Grand Canyon University
Northern Arizona University
Pima Community College
Prescott College
Rio Salado College
University of Advancing Technology
University of Arizona
Western International University

Arkansas

Arkansas Baptist College
Arkansas Northeastern College
Arkansas State University
Arkansas State University
    Beebe
Arkansas Tech University
Harding University
Hendrix College
John Brown University
Lyon College
National Park Community College
Ouachita Baptist University
Southern Arkansas University
Southern Arkansas University Tech
University of Arkansas
University of Arkansas
    Community College at Hope
    Cossatot Community College of the
        Little Rock
    Monticello
    Pine Bluff
University of Central Arkansas
University of the Ozarks
Williams Baptist College

California

Allan Hancock College
Antelope Valley College
Antioch Southern California
    Antioch University Los Angeles
    Antioch University Santa Barbara
Art Institute
    of California: San Diego
Azusa Pacific University
Bakersfield College
Bethany University
Bethesda Christian University
Biola University
Brooks Institute of Photography
Butte College
California Baptist University
California Institute of Technology
California Lutheran University
California Maritime Academy
California Polytechnic State
    University: San Luis Obispo
California State Polytechnic
    University: Pomona
California State University
    Bakersfield
    Chico
    Dominguez Hills
    East Bay
    Fresno
    Fullerton
    Long Beach
    Los Angeles
    Monterey Bay
    Northridge
    Sacramento
    San Bernardino
    San Marcos
    Stanislaus
Canada College
Cerro Coso Community College
Chabot College
Chapman University
Citrus College
Claremont McKenna College
Coleman College
College of San Mateo
College of the Desert
College of the Redwoods
Columbia College
Concordia University
Cosumnes River College
Cuesta College
Cuyamaca College
Dominican School of Philosophy and
    Theology
Dominican University of California
East Los Angeles College
El Camino College
Empire College
Evergreen Valley College
Feather River College
Fresno City College

Fresno Pacific University
Fullerton College
Golden West College
Grossmont Community College
Harvey Mudd College
Holy Names University
Hope International University
Humboldt State University
Humphreys College
Imperial Valley College
Irvine Valley College
John F. Kennedy University
La Sierra University
Laguna College of Art and Design
Lake Tahoe Community College
Los Angeles Harbor College
Los Angeles Southwest College
Loyola Marymount University
Master's College
Mendocino College
Menlo College
Mills College
MiraCosta College
Modesto Junior College
Monterey Peninsula College
Mount St. Mary's College
Mount San Jacinto College
Napa Valley College
National University
NewSchool of Architecture & Design
Notre Dame de Namur University
Occidental College
Ohlone College
Pacific States University
Pacific Union College
Patten University
Pepperdine University
Pitzer College
Point Loma Nazarene University
Pomona College
Porterville College
Reedley College
Riverside Community College
Sacramento City College
Saddleback College
St. Mary's College of California
San Bernardino Valley College
San Diego Christian College
San Diego City College
San Diego Mesa College
San Diego State University
San Francisco Art Institute
San Francisco State University
San Jose State University
Santa Ana College
Santa Barbara City College
Santa Clara University
Santiago Canyon College
Scripps College
Shasta College
Sierra College
Simpson University
Solano Community College
Sonoma State University
Southwestern College
Stanford University
University of California
    Berkeley
    Davis
    Irvine
    Los Angeles
    Riverside
    San Diego
    Santa Barbara
    Santa Cruz
University of California: Merced
University of La Verne
University of Redlands
University of San Diego
University of San Francisco
University of Southern California
University of the Pacific
Vanguard University of Southern
    California

Victor Valley College
West Valley College
Westmont College
Whittier College
William Jessup University
Woodbury University

Colorado

Adams State College
Aims Community College
Blair College
Colorado Christian University
Colorado College
Colorado School of Mines
Colorado State University
Colorado State University
    Pueblo
Colorado Technical University
Community College of Denver
Fort Lewis College
Front Range Community College
Johnson & Wales University
Mesa State College
Metropolitan State College of Denver
Morgan Community College
Naropa University
National American University
    Denver
Nazarene Bible College
Parks College: Aurora
Pikes Peak Community College
Pueblo Community College
Red Rocks Community College
Regis University
Rocky Mountain College of Art &
    Design
Trinidad State Junior College
University of Colorado
    Boulder
    Colorado Springs
    Denver and Health Sciences Center
University of Denver
University of Northern Colorado
Western State College of Colorado

Connecticut

Albertus Magnus College
Asnuntuck Community College
Briarwood College
Capital Community College
Central Connecticut State University
Connecticut College
Eastern Connecticut State University
Fairfield University
Holy Apostles College and Seminary
Housatonic Community College
Lyme Academy College of Fine Arts
Manchester Community College
Naugatuck Valley Community College
Northwestern Connecticut
    Community College
Norwalk Community College
Post University
Quinebaug Valley Community College
Quinnipiac University
Sacred Heart University
St. Joseph College
Southern Connecticut State University
Three Rivers Community College
Trinity College
Tunxis Community College
United States Coast Guard Academy
University of Bridgeport
University of Connecticut
University of Hartford
University of New Haven
Wesleyan University
Western Connecticut State University
Yale University

Delaware

Delaware State University

Delaware Technical and Community
    College
  Owens Campus
  Stanton/Wilmington Campus
  Terry Campus
Goldey-Beacom College
University of Delaware
Wesley College
Wilmington College

District of Columbia

American University
Catholic University of America
Gallaudet University
George Washington University
Georgetown University
Howard University
Southeastern University
Strayer University
Trinity University
University of the District of Columbia

Florida

Baptist College of Florida
Barry University
Beacon College
Bethune-Cookman College
Brevard Community College
City College
Clearwater Christian College
Eckerd College
Edison College
Edward Waters College
Embry-Riddle Aeronautical University
Flagler College
Florida Agricultural and Mechanical
    University
Florida Atlantic University
Florida Community College at
    Jacksonville
Florida Gulf Coast University
Florida Institute of Technology
Florida International University
Florida Keys Community College
Florida Memorial University
Florida Metropolitan University
  Pinellas
  Pompano Beach
  Tampa College
Florida Southern College
Florida State University
Hillsborough Community College
Hobe Sound Bible College
International College
Jacksonville University
Jones College
Lynn University
New College of Florida
New England Institute of Technology
Northwood University
  Florida Campus
Nova Southeastern University
Palm Beach Atlantic University
Palm Beach Community College
Pasco-Hernando Community College
Pensacola Junior College
Polk Community College
Rollins College
St. Leo University
St. Thomas University
Schiller International University
South Florida Community College
South University: West Palm Beach
    Campus
Southeastern College of the
    Assemblies of God
Southwest Florida College
Southwest Florida College
    Tampa
Stetson University
Tallahassee Community College
Trinity College of Florida
University of Central Florida
University of Florida

University of Miami
University of North Florida
University of South Florida
University of Tampa
University of West Florida
Valencia Community College
Warner Southern College
Webber International University

Georgia

Agnes Scott College
Albany State University
Andrew College
Armstrong Atlantic State University
Atlanta Christian College
Augusta State University
Augusta Technical Institute
Bainbridge College
Bauder College
Berry College
Beulah Heights Bible College
Brenau University
Brewton-Parker College
Clark Atlanta University
Clayton State University
Columbus State University
Covenant College
Dalton State College
Darton College
East Georgia College
Emory University
Fort Valley State University
Georgia College and State University
Georgia Highlands College
Georgia Institute of Technology
Georgia Military College
Georgia Perimeter College
Georgia Southern University
Georgia Southwestern State
    University
Georgia State University
Gwinnett College
Gwinnett Technical College
Kennesaw State University
LaGrange College
Life University
Mercer University
Middle Georgia College
Morehouse College
North Georgia College & State
    University
Northwestern Technical College
Oglethorpe University
Oxford College of Emory University
Piedmont College
Reinhardt College
Savannah College of Art and Design
Savannah State University
Shorter College
South University
Southern Polytechnic State University
Southwest Georgia Technical College
Spelman College
Toccoa Falls College
Truett-McConnell College
University of Georgia
University of West Georgia
Valdosta State University
Wesleyan College

Hawaii

Brigham Young University-Hawaii
Chaminade University of Honolulu
Hawaii Business College
Hawaii Pacific University
University of Hawaii
  Hawaii Community College
  Hilo
  Kapiolani Community College
  Manoa
  Maui Community College
  West Oahu
  Windward Community College

Idaho

Albertson College of Idaho
Boise Bible College
Boise State University
Brigham Young University-Idaho
Idaho State University
Lewis-Clark State College
North Idaho College
Northwest Nazarene University
University of Idaho

Illinois

Augustana College
Aurora University
Benedictine University
Black Hawk College
  East Campus
Blackburn College
Bradley University
Chicago State University
City Colleges of Chicago
  Harold Washington College
College of DuPage
Concordia University
Danville Area Community College
DePaul University
Dominican University
East-West University
Eastern Illinois University
Elgin Community College
Elmhurst College
Eureka College
Greenville College
Heartland Community College
Illinois College
Illinois Eastern Community Colleges
  Frontier Community College
  Lincoln Trail College
  Olney Central College
  Wabash Valley College
Illinois Institute of Technology
Illinois State University
Illinois Wesleyan University
Judson College
Kaskaskia College
Kendall College
Kishwaukee College
Knox College
Lake Forest College
Lewis University
Lewis and Clark Community College
Lincoln Christian College and
    Seminary
Lincoln Land Community College
Loyola University of Chicago
MacMurray College
McKendree College
Midstate College
Millikin University
Monmouth College
Moody Bible Institute
Moraine Valley Community College
Morrison Institute of Technology
Morton College
National-Louis University
North Central College
North Park University
Northeastern Illinois University
Northern Illinois University
Northwestern Business College
Northwestern University
Olivet Nazarene University
Parkland College
Principia College
Quincy University
Rockford College
Roosevelt University
Rosalind Franklin University of
    Medicine and Science
St. Augustine College
School of the Art Institute of Chicago
Shimer College
South Suburban College of Cook
    County

Southeastern Illinois College
Southern Illinois University
    Carbondale
Southern Illinois University
    Edwardsville
Southwestern Illinois College
Springfield College in Illinois
Trinity Christian College
Trinity International University
University of Chicago
University of Illinois
  Chicago
  Springfield
  Urbana-Champaign
University of St. Francis
Western Illinois University
Wheaton College

Indiana

American Conservatory of Music
Ancilla College
Anderson University
Ball State University
Bethel College
Butler University
Calumet College of St. Joseph
DePauw University
Earlham College
Franklin College
Goshen College
Grace College
Hanover College
Huntington University
Indiana Institute of Technology
Indiana State University
Indiana University
  Bloomington
  East
  Kokomo
  Northwest
  South Bend
  Southeast
Indiana University-Purdue University
    Fort Wayne
Indiana University-Purdue University
    Indianapolis
Manchester College
Marian College
Martin University
Oakland City University
Purdue University
Purdue University
  Calumet
Rose-Hulman Institute of Technology
St. Joseph's College
Saint Mary's College
St. Mary-of-the-Woods College
Taylor University
Taylor University: Fort Wayne
Tri-State University
University of Evansville
University of Indianapolis
University of Notre Dame
University of St. Francis
University of Southern Indiana
Valparaiso University
Wabash College

Iowa

AIB College of Business
Ashford University
Briar Cliff University
Buena Vista University
Central College
Clarke College
Clinton Community College
Coe College
Cornell College
Divine Word College
Dordt College
Drake University
Ellsworth Community College
Emmaus Bible College

Faith Baptist Bible College and
    Theological Seminary
Graceland University
Grand View College
Grinnell College
Hamilton College
    Cedar Rapids
Iowa State University
Iowa Wesleyan College
Kaplan University
Loras College
Luther College
Maharishi University of Management
Morningside College
Mount Mercy College
Muscatine Community College
Northeast Iowa Community College
Northwestern College
St. Ambrose University
Scott Community College
Simpson College
Southwestern Community College
University of Dubuque
University of Iowa
University of Northern Iowa
Upper Iowa University
Vennard College
Waldorf College
Wartburg College
Western Iowa Tech Community
    College
William Penn University

Kansas
Allen County Community College
Baker University
Barclay College
Benedictine College
Bethany College
Bethel College
Central Christian College of Kansas
Coffeyville Community College
Cowley County Community College
Dodge City Community College
Emporia State University
Fort Hays State University
Friends University
Highland Community College
Hutchinson Community College
Johnson County Community College
Kansas State University
Kansas Wesleyan University
Manhattan Christian College
McPherson College
MidAmerica Nazarene University
Newman University
Ottawa University
Pittsburg State University
Seward County Community College
Southwestern College
Sterling College
Tabor College
University of Kansas
University of St. Mary
Washburn University of Topeka
Wichita State University

Kentucky
Alice Lloyd College
Asbury College
Bellarmine University
Berea College
Bluegrass Community and Technical
    College
Brescia University
Campbellsville University
Centre College
Clear Creek Baptist Bible College
Daymar College
Draughons Junior College
Eastern Kentucky University
Georgetown College
Henderson Community College
Hopkinsville Community College

Kentucky Christian University
Kentucky State University
Kentucky Wesleyan College
Louisville Technical Institute
Madisonville Community College
Maysville Community College
Mid-Continent University
Midway College
Morehead State University
Murray State University
National College of Business &
    Technology
    Danville
    Florence
    Lexington
    Pikeville
    Richmond
Northern Kentucky University
Owensboro Community College
Pikeville College
Spalding University
Spencerian College: Lexington
Sullivan University
Thomas More College
Transylvania University
Union College
University of Kentucky
University of Louisville
University of the Cumberlands
Western Kentucky University

Louisiana
Bossier Parish Community College
Centenary College of Louisiana
Delgado Community College
Dillard University
Grambling State University
Louisiana State University
    Shreveport
Louisiana State University Health
    Sciences Center
Louisiana State University and
    Agricultural and Mechanical
    College
Louisiana Tech University
Loyola University New Orleans
Northwestern State University
Nunez Community College
Southeastern Louisiana University
Southern University
    New Orleans
Southern University and Agricultural
    and Mechanical College
Tulane University
University of Louisiana at Lafayette
University of Louisiana at Monroe
University of New Orleans
Xavier University of Louisiana

Maine
Andover College
Bates College
Beal College
Bowdoin College
Colby College
Husson College
Maine College of Art
New England School of
    Communications
Northern Maine Community College
St. Joseph's College
Southern Maine Community College
Unity College
University of Maine
University of Maine
    Augusta
    Farmington
    Fort Kent
    Machias
    Presque Isle
University of New England
University of Southern Maine
Washington County Community
    College

Maryland
Allegany College of Maryland
Anne Arundel Community College
Baltimore City Community College
Baltimore Hebrew University
Baltimore International College
Bowie State University
Capitol College
Cecil Community College
College of Notre Dame of Maryland
Columbia Union College
Coppin State University
Frostburg State University
Garrett Community College
Goucher College
Hagerstown Business College
Hagerstown Community College
Harford Community College
Hood College
Johns Hopkins University
Johns Hopkins University: Peabody
    Conservatory of Music
Loyola College in Maryland
Maryland Institute College of Art
McDaniel College
Montgomery College
Morgan State University
Mount St. Mary's University
Prince George's Community College
St. Mary's College of Maryland
Salisbury University
Towson University
United States Naval Academy
University of Maryland
    Baltimore
    Baltimore County
    College Park
    Eastern Shore
    University College
Villa Julie College
Washington Bible College
Washington College
Wor-Wic Community College

Massachusetts
American International College
Amherst College
Anna Maria College
Art Institute of Boston at Lesley
    University
Assumption College
Atlantic Union College
Bay Path College
Bentley College
Berklee College of Music
Berkshire Community College
Boston College
Boston Conservatory
Boston University
Brandeis University
Bridgewater State College
Bunker Hill Community College
Clark University
College of the Holy Cross
Curry College
Eastern Nazarene College
Elms College
Emerson College
Emmanuel College
Fisher College
Fitchburg State College
Framingham State College
Gordon College
Harvard College
Holyoke Community College
Lasell College
Lesley University
Marian Court College
Massachusetts College of Art
Massachusetts College of Liberal Arts
Massachusetts Maritime Academy
Merrimack College
Mount Holyoke College
Mount Wachusett Community College

Newbury College
Nichols College
North Shore Community College
Northeastern University
Northern Essex Community College
Pine Manor College
Quinsigamond Community College
Regis College
Roxbury Community College
St. John's Seminary College
Salem State College
School of the Museum of Fine Arts
Simmons College
Smith College
Springfield College
Stonehill College
Suffolk University
Tufts University
University of Massachusetts
    Amherst
    Boston
    Dartmouth
    Lowell
Wellesley College
Western New England College
Westfield State College
Wheaton College
Wheelock College
Williams College
Worcester Polytechnic Institute
Worcester State College

Michigan
Adrian College
Albion College
Alma College
Alpena Community College
Andrews University
Aquinas College
Baker College
    of Auburn Hills
    of Cadillac
    of Clinton Township
    of Flint
    of Jackson
    of Muskegon
    of Owosso
    of Port Huron
Bay Mills Community College
Calvin College
Central Michigan University
College for Creative Studies
Concordia University
Cornerstone University
Delta College
Eastern Michigan University
Ferris State University
Finlandia University
Glen Oaks Community College
Gogebic Community College
Grace Bible College
Grand Valley State University
Great Lakes Christian College
Hillsdale College
Hope College
Kalamazoo College
Kellogg Community College
Kendall College of Art and Design of
    Ferris State University
Kettering University
Kirtland Community College
Kuyper College
Lake Superior State University
Lansing Community College
Lawrence Technological University
Lewis College of Business
Madonna University
Marygrove College
Michigan Jewish Institute
Michigan State University
Michigan Technological University
Mid Michigan Community College
Mott Community College
Muskegon Community College

Northern Michigan University
Northwood University
Oakland University
Olivet College
Rochester College
Saginaw Valley State University
St. Clair County Community College
Schoolcraft College
Siena Heights University
Southwestern Michigan College
Spring Arbor University
University of Detroit Mercy
University of Michigan
University of Michigan
  Dearborn
  Flint
Walsh College of Accountancy and
  Business Administration
Wayne County Community College
Wayne State University
Western Michigan University

Minnesota

Alexandria Technical College
Augsburg College
Bemidji State University
Bethany Lutheran College
Bethel University
Carleton College
College of St. Benedict
College of St. Catherine
College of St. Scholastica
Concordia College: Moorhead
Concordia University: St. Paul
Crossroads College
Crown College
Dakota County Technical College
Gustavus Adolphus College
Hamline University
Hennepin Technical College
Lake Superior College
Leech Lake Tribal College
Macalester College
Martin Luther College
Metropolitan State University
Minnesota State University
  Mankato
  Moorhead
National American University
  St. Paul
Normandale Community College
North Central University
Northwest Technical College
Northwestern College
Oak Hills Christian College
Pine Technical College
Rasmussen College
  St. Cloud
Riverland Community College
St. Cloud State University
St. Cloud Technical College
St. John's University
St. Mary's University of Minnesota
St. Olaf College
Southwest Minnesota State University
University of Minnesota
  Crookston
  Duluth
  Morris
  Twin Cities
University of St. Thomas
Walden University
Winona State University

Mississippi

Alcorn State University
Belhaven College
Blue Mountain College
Delta State University
Hinds Community College
Itawamba Community College
Jackson State University
Millsaps College
Mississippi College

Mississippi State University
Mississippi Valley State University
Rust College
Tougaloo College
University of Mississippi
University of Southern Mississippi
Wesley College
William Carey College

Missouri

Avila University
Calvary Bible College and Theological
  Seminary
Central Bible College
Central Methodist University
Central Missouri State University
College of the Ozarks
Columbia College
Culver-Stockton College
Drury University
Evangel University
Fontbonne University
Hannibal-LaGrange College
Jefferson College
Kansas City Art Institute
Lincoln University
Lindenwood University
Maryville University of Saint Louis
Missouri Baptist University
Missouri Southern State University
Missouri State University
Missouri Technical School
Missouri Valley College
Missouri Western State University
National American University
  Kansas City
North Central Missouri College
Northwest Missouri State University
Ozark Christian College
Park University
Patricia Stevens College
Research College of Nursing
Rockhurst University
St. Charles Community College
St. Louis University
Southeast Missouri State University
Southwest Baptist University
Stephens College
Truman State University
University of Missouri
  Columbia
  Kansas City
  Rolla
  St. Louis
Washington University in St. Louis
Webster University
Westminster College
William Jewell College
William Woods University

Montana

Carroll College
Chief Dull Knife College
Dawson Community College
Fort Peck Community College
Montana State University
  Billings
  Bozeman
Montana Tech of the University of
  Montana
Rocky Mountain College
Salish Kootenai College
Stone Child College
University of Great Falls
University of Montana: Missoula
University of Montana: Western

Nebraska

Bellevue University
Central Community College
Chadron State College
Clarkson College
College of Saint Mary
Concordia University

Creighton University
Dana College
Doane College
Grace University
Hastings College
Metropolitan Community College
Midland Lutheran College
Nebraska Christian College
Nebraska College of Technical
  Agriculture
Nebraska Indian Community College
Nebraska Wesleyan University
Peru State College
Union College
University of Nebraska
  Kearney
  Lincoln
  Omaha
Wayne State College
Western Nebraska Community
  College
York College

Nevada

Community College of Southern
  Nevada
Morrison University
Sierra Nevada College
University of Nevada
  Las Vegas
  Reno
Western Nevada Community College

New Hampshire

Chester College of New England
Colby-Sawyer College
Daniel Webster College
Dartmouth College
Franklin Pierce College
Granite State College
Keene State College
New England College
New Hampshire Community
  Technical College
  Berlin
  Claremont
  Manchester
  Stratham
New Hampshire Technical Institute
Plymouth State University
Rivier College
Southern New Hampshire University
University of New Hampshire
University of New Hampshire at
  Manchester

New Jersey

Atlantic Cape Community College
Bloomfield College
Burlington County College
Caldwell College
Centenary College
The College of New Jersey
College of St. Elizabeth
County College of Morris
Cumberland County College
Drew University
Essex County College
Fairleigh Dickinson University
  College at Florham
  Metropolitan Campus
Felician College
Georgian Court University
Kean University
Mercer County Community College
Middlesex County College
Monmouth University
Montclair State University
New Jersey City University
New Jersey Institute of Technology
Passaic County Community College
Ramapo College of New Jersey
Raritan Valley Community College

Richard Stockton College of New
  Jersey
Rider University
Rowan University
Rutgers, The State University of New
  Jersey
  Camden Regional Campus
  New Brunswick/Piscataway
    Campus
  Newark Regional Campus
St. Peter's College
Salem Community College
Seton Hall University
Stevens Institute of Technology
Sussex County Community College
University of Medicine and Dentistry
  of New Jersey
  School of Health Related
    Professions
  School of Nursing
Warren County Community College
Westminster Choir College of Rider
  University
William Paterson University of New
  Jersey

New Mexico

Albuquerque Technical-Vocational
  Institute
Clovis Community College
College of Santa Fe
College of the Southwest
Dona Ana Branch Community College
  of New Mexico State University
Eastern New Mexico University
Institute of American Indian Arts
New Mexico Highlands University
New Mexico Institute of Mining and
  Technology
New Mexico State University
New Mexico State University
  Alamogordo
  Carlsbad
  Grants
Southwestern Indian Polytechnic
  Institute
University of New Mexico
Western New Mexico University

New York

Adelphi University
Adirondack Community College
Alfred University
Bard College
Barnard College
Bramson ORT College
Bryant & Stratton Business Institute
  Bryant & Stratton College: Albany
  Bryant & Stratton College:
    Lackawanna
  Bryant & Stratton College:
    Rochester
  Bryant & Stratton College: Syracuse
Canisius College
Cayuga County Community College
City University of New York
  Baruch College
  Brooklyn College
  College of Staten Island
  Hunter College
  Lehman College
  Queens College
  York College
Clarkson University
Colgate University
College of Mount St. Vincent
College of New Rochelle
College of Saint Rose
College of Westchester
Columbia University
  Columbia College
  School of General Studies
  School of Nursing
Concordia College

Cornell University
Corning Community College
D'Youville College
Daemen College
Dowling College
Eastman School of Music of the
 University of Rochester
Elmira College
Erie Community College
 City Campus
 North Campus
 South Campus
Finger Lakes Community College
Fordham University
Fulton-Montgomery Community
 College
Genesee Community College
Hamilton College
Hartwick College
Hobart and William Smith Colleges
Hofstra University
Houghton College
Hudson Valley Community College
Institute of Design and Construction
Iona College
Ithaca College
Jamestown Community College
Jefferson Community College
Jewish Theological Seminary of
 America
Keuka College
Le Moyne College
Long Island University
 Brooklyn Campus
 C.W. Post Campus
Manhattan College
Manhattanville College
Mannes College The New School for
 Music
Marist College
Marymount Manhattan College
Medaille College
Mercy College
Mildred Elley
Mohawk Valley Community College
Molloy College
Mount St. Mary College
Nazareth College of Rochester
New York Institute of Technology
New York University
Niagara County Community College
Niagara University
North Country Community College
Nyack College
Onondaga Community College
Pace University
Paul Smith's College
Polytechnic University
Rensselaer Polytechnic Institute
Roberts Wesleyan College
Rochester Institute of Technology
Rockland Community College
Russell Sage College
Sage College of Albany
St. Bonaventure University
St. Francis College
St. John Fisher College
St. John's University
St. Joseph's College: Suffolk Campus
St. Lawrence University
St. Thomas Aquinas College
Sarah Lawrence College
Siena College
Skidmore College
State University of New York
 Albany
 Binghamton
 Buffalo
 College at Brockport
 College at Buffalo
 College at Cortland
 College at Fredonia
 College at Geneseo
 College at Old Westbury

College at Oneonta
College at Plattsburgh
College at Potsdam
College of Environmental Science
 and Forestry
College of Technology at Delhi
Empire State College
Farmingdale
Institute of Technology at
 Utica/Rome
New Paltz
Oswego
Purchase
Stony Brook
Syracuse University
Ulster County Community College
Union College
United States Military Academy
University of Rochester
Utica College
Vassar College
Vaughn College of Aeronautics and
 Technology
Villa Maria College of Buffalo
Wagner College
Webb Institute
Wells College
Westchester Community College
Yeshiva University

North Carolina

Alamance Community College
Appalachian State University
Asheville-Buncombe Technical
 Community College
Barton College
Belmont Abbey College
Bennett College
Bladen Community College
Blue Ridge Community College
Brevard College
Campbell University
Carteret Community College
Catawba College
Catawba Valley Community College
Central Piedmont Community College
Chowan College
Cleveland Community College
College of the Albemarle
Craven Community College
Davidson College
Duke University
East Carolina University
Edgecombe Community College
Elizabeth City State University
Elon University
Fayetteville State University
Forsyth Technical Community College
Gardner-Webb University
Gaston College
Greensboro College
Guilford College
High Point University
James Sprunt Community College
John Wesley College
Johnson C. Smith University
Johnston Community College
Lees-McRae College
Lenoir-Rhyne College
Livingstone College
Mars Hill College
Martin Community College
Mayland Community College
McDowell Technical Community
 College
Meredith College
Methodist College
Miller-Motte Technical College
Montgomery Community College
Montreat College
Mount Olive College
North Carolina Agricultural and
 Technical State University
North Carolina Central University

North Carolina State University
North Carolina Wesleyan College
Peace College
Pfeiffer University
Piedmont Baptist College
Piedmont Community College
Pitt Community College
Queens University of Charlotte
Randolph Community College
Richmond Community College
Robeson Community College
St. Andrews Presbyterian College
St. Augustine's College
Salem College
Sandhills Community College
Shaw University
South College
Southeastern Community College
Southwestern Community College
Surry Community College
Tri-County Community College
University of North Carolina
 Asheville
 Chapel Hill
 Charlotte
 Greensboro
 Pembroke
 Wilmington
Vance-Granville Community College
Wake Forest University
Wake Technical Community College
Warren Wilson College
Wayne Community College
Western Carolina University
Wilkes Community College
Wilson Technical Community College
Wingate University
Winston-Salem State University

North Dakota

Dickinson State University
Fort Berthold Community College
Jamestown College
Mayville State University
Minot State University
Minot State University: Bottineau
 Campus
North Dakota State University
Trinity Bible College
University of Mary
University of North Dakota
Valley City State University
Williston State College

Ohio

Antioch College
Antioch University McGregor
Ashland University
Baldwin-Wallace College
Belmont Technical College
Bluffton University
Bowling Green State University
Bryant & Stratton College
 Parma
 Willoughby Hills
Bryant & Stratton College: Cleveland
Capital University
Case Western Reserve University
Cedarville University
Central Ohio Technical College
Central State University
Cincinnati Christian University
Cincinnati State Technical and
 Community College
Circleville Bible College
Clark State Community College
Cleveland Institute of Music
Cleveland State University
College of Mount St. Joseph
College of Wooster
Columbus College of Art and Design
Columbus State Community College
David N. Myers University
Defiance College

Denison University
Edison State Community College
Franciscan University of Steubenville
Franklin University
Gallipolis Career College
God's Bible School and College
Heidelberg College
Hiram College
Hocking College
James A. Rhodes State College
Jefferson Community College
John Carroll University
Kent State University
Kent State University
 Ashtabula Regional Campus
 East Liverpool Regional Campus
 Salem Regional Campus
 Stark Campus
 Trumbull Campus
 Tuscarawas Campus
Kenyon College
Lake Erie College
Lourdes College
Malone College
Marietta College
Marion Technical College
Mercy College of Northwest Ohio
Miami University
 Hamilton Campus
 Oxford Campus
Mount Union College
Mount Vernon Nazarene University
Muskingum College
Oberlin College
Ohio Business College: Sandusky
Ohio Dominican University
Ohio Institute of Photography and
 Technology
Ohio Northern University
Ohio State University
 Agricultural Technical Institute
 Columbus Campus
 Lima Campus
 Mansfield Campus
 Marion Campus
 Newark Campus
Ohio University
Ohio University
 Chillicothe Campus
 Eastern Campus
 Lancaster Campus
 Zanesville Campus
Ohio Valley College of Technology
Ohio Wesleyan University
Otterbein College
Owens Community College
 Toledo
Pontifical College Josephinum
Shawnee State University
Stark State College of Technology
Tiffin University
Union Institute & University
University of Akron
University of Cincinnati
University of Cincinnati
 Clermont College
 Raymond Walters College
University of Dayton
University of Findlay
University of Northwestern Ohio
University of Rio Grande
University of Toledo
Urbana University
Ursuline College
Walsh University
Washington State Community College
Wilmington College
Wittenberg University
Wright State University
Wright State University: Lake Campus
Xavier University
Youngstown State University

Oklahoma

Bacone College
Cameron University
East Central University
Mid-America Christian University
Northeastern State University
Northwestern Oklahoma State
    University
Oklahoma Baptist University
Oklahoma Christian University
Oklahoma City Community College
Oklahoma City University
Oklahoma Panhandle State University
Oklahoma State University
Oklahoma State University
    Oklahoma City
    Okmulgee
Oklahoma Wesleyan University
Oral Roberts University
Rogers State University
Rose State College
St. Gregory's University
Southeastern Oklahoma State
    University
Southern Nazarene University
Southwestern Christian University
Southwestern Oklahoma State
    University
University of Central Oklahoma
University of Oklahoma
University of Science and Arts of
    Oklahoma
University of Tulsa

Oregon

Blue Mountain Community College
Central Oregon Community College
Chemeketa Community College
Clackamas Community College
Clatsop Community College
Concordia University
Corban College
Eastern Oregon University
Eugene Bible College
George Fox University
Lane Community College
Lewis & Clark College
Linfield College
Marylhurst University
Mount Angel Seminary
Mount Hood Community College
Multnomah Bible College
Northwest Christian College
Oregon Institute of Technology
Oregon State University
Pacific University
Portland Community College
Portland State University
Reed College
Rogue Community College
Southern Oregon University
Southwestern Oregon Community
    College
Treasure Valley Community College
Umpqua Community College
University of Oregon
University of Portland
Warner Pacific College
Western Oregon University
Willamette University

Pennsylvania

Albright College
Allegheny College
Alvernia College
Arcadia University
Baptist Bible College of Pennsylvania
Bloomsburg University of
    Pennsylvania
Bryn Mawr College
Bucknell University
Cabrini College
California University of Pennsylvania
Carlow University

Carnegie Mellon University
Cedar Crest College
Central Pennsylvania College
Chatham College
Chestnut Hill College
Cheyney University of Pennsylvania
Clarion University of Pennsylvania
College Misericordia
Community College of Beaver County
Curtis Institute of Music
DeSales University
Delaware County Community College
Delaware Valley College
Dickinson College
Douglas Education Center
Drexel University
DuBois Business College
Duquesne University
East Stroudsburg University of
    Pennsylvania
Eastern University
Edinboro University of Pennsylvania
Elizabethtown College
Franklin & Marshall College
Gannon University
Geneva College
Gettysburg College
Gratz College
Grove City College
Gwynedd-Mercy College
Harcum College
Harrisburg Area Community College
Haverford College
ICM School of Business & Medical
    Careers
Immaculata University
Indiana University of Pennsylvania
Juniata College
Keystone College
King's College
Kutztown University of Pennsylvania
La Roche College
La Salle University
Lackawanna College
Lafayette College
Lancaster Bible College
Lansdale School of Business
Laurel Business Institute
Lebanon Valley College
Lehigh University
Lock Haven University of
    Pennsylvania
Lycoming College
Manor College
Mansfield University of Pennsylvania
Marywood University
Mercyhurst College
Messiah College
Millersville University of Pennsylvania
Moore College of Art and Design
Moravian College
Muhlenberg College
Neumann College
Northampton County Area
    Community College
PJA School
Peirce College
Penn State
    Abington
    Altoona
    Beaver
    Delaware County
    Dubois
    Erie, The Behrend College
    Fayette
    Harrisburg
    Hazleton
    McKeesport
    Mont Alto
    New Kensington
    Schuylkill - Capital College
    Shenango
    University Park
    Wilkes-Barre

    Worthington Scranton
    York
Pennsylvania Institute of Technology
Philadelphia Biblical University
Philadelphia University
Point Park University
Rosemont College
St. Francis University
St. Joseph's University
St. Vincent College
Seton Hill University
Shippensburg University of
    Pennsylvania
Slippery Rock University of
    Pennsylvania
South Hills School of Business &
    Technology
Susquehanna University
Swarthmore College
Temple University
Thiel College
University of Pennsylvania
University of Pittsburgh
University of Pittsburgh
    Bradford
    Greensburg
    Johnstown
University of Scranton
University of the Arts
University of the Sciences in
    Philadelphia
Ursinus College
Valley Forge Military College
Villanova University
Washington and Jefferson College
Waynesburg College
West Chester University of
    Pennsylvania
Westminster College
Westmoreland County Community
    College
Widener University
Wilkes University
Wilson College
York College of Pennsylvania
Yorktowne Business Institute

Puerto Rico

Bayamon Central University
Inter American University of Puerto
    Rico
    Fajardo Campus
    San German Campus
Pontifical Catholic University of
    Puerto Rico
Universidad Adventista de las Antillas
University College of San Juan
University of Puerto Rico
    Bayamon University College
    Mayaguez
    Rio Piedras
University of the Sacred Heart

Rhode Island

Brown University
Bryant University
Community College of Rhode Island
New England Institute of Technology
Providence College
Rhode Island College
Roger Williams University
Salve Regina University
University of Rhode Island

South Carolina

Aiken Technical College
Anderson University
Benedict College
Charleston Southern University
The Citadel
Claflin University
Clemson University
Coastal Carolina University
Coker College

College of Charleston
Columbia College
Columbia International University
Converse College
Erskine College
Forrest Junior College
Francis Marion University
Furman University
Horry-Georgetown Technical College
Lander University
Limestone College
Morris College
Newberry College
North Greenville College
Orangeburg-Calhoun Technical
    College
Piedmont Technical College
Presbyterian College
South Carolina State University
South University
Southern Wesleyan University
Spartanburg Technical College
Technical College of the Lowcountry
Trident Technical College
University of South Carolina
University of South Carolina
    Aiken
    Upstate
Winthrop University
Wofford College

South Dakota

Augustana College
Black Hills State University
Dakota State University
Dakota Wesleyan University
Kilian Community College
Mount Marty College
Northern State University
Presentation College
Sisseton Wahpeton College
South Dakota School of Mines and
    Technology
South Dakota State University
Southeast Technical Institute
University of Sioux Falls
University of South Dakota

Tennessee

American Baptist College of ABT
    Seminary
Austin Peay State University
Belmont University
Bethel College
Bryan College
Carson-Newman College
Chattanooga State Technical
    Community College
Christian Brothers University
Cleveland State Community College
Crichton College
Cumberland University
East Tennessee State University
Fisk University
Free Will Baptist Bible College
Freed-Hardeman University
Johnson Bible College
King College
Lambuth University
LeMoyne-Owen College
Lee University
Lincoln Memorial University
Lipscomb University
Maryville College
Memphis College of Art
Middle Tennessee State University
Milligan College
Motlow State Community College
Nashville State Community College
Northeast State Technical Community
    College
Pellissippi State Technical Community
    College
Rhodes College

Roane State Community College
South College
Southern Adventist University
Southwest Tennessee Community
College
Tennessee State University
Tennessee Technological University
Tennessee Temple University
Tennessee Wesleyan College
Trevecca Nazarene University
Tusculum College
Union University
University of Memphis
University of Tennessee
Chattanooga
Knoxville
Martin
University of the South
Vanderbilt University
Volunteer State Community College

Texas

Abilene Christian University
Angelo State University
Arlington Baptist College
Austin College
Baylor University
College of the Mainland
Concordia University at Austin
Criswell College
Dallas Baptist University
Dallas Christian College
East Texas Baptist University
El Centro College
El Paso Community College
Hardin-Simmons University
Houston Baptist University
Howard Payne University
Huston-Tillotson College
Jarvis Christian College
Lamar State College at Port Arthur
Lamar University
LeTourneau University
Lubbock Christian University
McMurry University
Midwestern State University
Mountain View College
Northwood University: Texas Campus
Our Lady of the Lake University of San
Antonio
Prairie View A&M University
Rice University
St. Edward's University
St. Mary's University
St. Philip's College
Sam Houston State University
San Antonio College
Schreiner University
Southern Methodist University
Southwestern Adventist University
Southwestern Assemblies of God
University
Southwestern University
Stephen F. Austin State University
Tarleton State University
Tarrant County College
Texas A&M University
Texas A&M University
Commerce
Galveston
Kingsville
Texas Christian University
Texas College
Texas Lutheran University
Texas Southern University
Texas State University: San Marcos
Texas Tech University
Texas Wesleyan University
Texas Woman's University
University of Dallas
University of Houston
University of Houston
Clear Lake

Downtown
Victoria
University of Mary Hardin-Baylor
University of North Texas
University of St. Thomas
University of Texas
Arlington
Austin
Brownsville
Dallas
El Paso
Pan American
San Antonio
Tyler
of the Permian Basin
University of the Incarnate Word
Wade College
Wayland Baptist University
West Texas A&M University
Wiley College

Utah

Brigham Young University
College of Eastern Utah
Salt Lake Community College
Southern Utah University
University of Utah
Utah State University
Weber State University
Westminster College

Vermont

Bennington College
Burlington College
Castleton State College
Champlain College
College of St. Joseph in Vermont
Community College of Vermont
Green Mountain College
Johnson State College
Lyndon State College
Marlboro College
Middlebury College
Norwich University
St. Michael's College
Southern Vermont College
University of Vermont
Vermont Technical College
Woodbury College

Virginia

Averett University
Blue Ridge Community College
Bluefield College
Bridgewater College
Bryant & Stratton College: Virginia
Beach
Christendom College
Christopher Newport University
College of William and Mary
Dabney S. Lancaster Community
College
Danville Community College
ECPI College of Technology
Eastern Mennonite University
Emory & Henry College
Ferrum College
George Mason University
Germanna Community College
Hampden-Sydney College
Hampton University
Hollins University
J. Sargeant Reynolds Community
College
James Madison University
Liberty University
Longwood University
Lord Fairfax Community College
Lynchburg College
Mary Baldwin College
Marymount University
Mountain Empire Community College

National College of Business &
Technology
Bluefield
Charlottesville
Danville
Harrisonburg
Lynchburg
Martinsville
Salem
Norfolk State University
Northern Virginia Community College
Old Dominion University
Patrick Henry Community College
Radford University
Randolph-Macon College
Randolph-Macon Woman's College
Rappahannock Community College
Regent University
Roanoke College
St. Paul's College
Shenandoah University
Southwest Virginia Community
College
Sweet Briar College
Tidewater Community College
University of Mary Washington
University of Northern Virginia
University of Richmond
University of Virginia
University of Virginia's College at Wise
Virginia Commonwealth University
Virginia Highlands Community
College
Virginia Intermont College
Virginia Military Institute
Virginia Polytechnic Institute and
State University
Virginia State University
Virginia Wesleyan College
Washington and Lee University

Washington

Bastyr University
Central Washington University
Centralia College
City University
Eastern Washington University
Evergreen State College
Gonzaga University
Grays Harbor College
Henry Cogswell College
Heritage University
Highline Community College
Northwest College of Art
Northwest University
Pacific Lutheran University
Peninsula College
Pierce College
Puget Sound Christian College
Saint Martin's University
Seattle Pacific University
Seattle University
University of Puget Sound
University of Washington
Walla Walla College
Washington State University
Wenatchee Valley College
Western Washington University
Whitman College
Whitworth College

West Virginia

Alderson-Broaddus College
Bethany College
Concord University
Davis and Elkins College
Glenville State College
Huntington Junior College
Marshall University
Mountain State College
Mountain State University
Ohio Valley University
Potomac State College of West Virginia
University

Salem International University
Shepherd University
University of Charleston
West Liberty State College
West Virginia Northern Community
College
West Virginia State University
West Virginia University
West Virginia University Institute of
Technology
West Virginia University at
Parkersburg
West Virginia Wesleyan College
Wheeling Jesuit University

Wisconsin

Alverno College
Beloit College
Bryant & Stratton College: Milwaukee
Cardinal Stritch University
Carroll College
Carthage College
Chippewa Valley Technical College
College of Menominee Nation
Columbia College of Nursing
Concordia University Wisconsin
Edgewood College
Fox Valley Technical College
Lakeland College
Lakeshore Technical College
Lawrence University
Maranatha Baptist Bible College
Marian College of Fond du Lac
Marquette University
Mid-State Technical College
Milwaukee Area Technical College
Milwaukee School of Engineering
Moraine Park Technical College
Mount Mary College
Nicolet Area Technical College
Northcentral Technical College
Northeast Wisconsin Technical
College
Northland College
Ripon College
St. Norbert College
Silver Lake College
Southwest Wisconsin Technical
College
University of Wisconsin
Eau Claire
Green Bay
La Crosse
Madison
Oshkosh
Parkside
Platteville
River Falls
Stevens Point
Stout
Superior
Whitewater
Viterbo University
Waukesha County Technical College
Western Wisconsin Technical College
Wisconsin Indianhead Technical
College
Wisconsin Lutheran College

Wyoming

Northwest College
Sheridan College
University of Wyoming
Wyoming Technical Institute

External Degree

Alabama
Troy University
University of Alabama

Alaska
Prince William Sound Community
   College
University of Alaska
   Southeast

Arizona
Northern Arizona University
Prescott College

Arkansas
Arkansas Tech University
Pulaski Technical College
Rich Mountain Community College
University of Arkansas
   Fort Smith

California
Bethany University
California Polytechnic State
   University: San Luis Obispo
California State Polytechnic
   University: Pomona
California State University
   Bakersfield
   Chico
   Northridge
   Stanislaus
Cogswell Polytechnical College
King's College and Seminary
LIFE Pacific College
Oxnard College
Pacific Union College
St. Mary's College of California
Sonoma State University
University of San Francisco
Vanguard University of Southern
   California

Colorado
Colorado State University
   Pueblo
Metropolitan State College of Denver
National American University
   Denver
Pikes Peak Community College
University of Northern Colorado

Connecticut
Charter Oak State College

Florida
Florida Agricultural and Mechanical
   University
Florida Community College at
   Jacksonville
Hobe Sound Bible College
Northwood University
   Florida Campus
South Florida Community College
University of Florida

Georgia
Abraham Baldwin Agricultural College
Brenau University
Brewton-Parker College
Dalton State College
Fort Valley State University
Georgia College and State University
Georgia Military College
Georgia Southern University
North Georgia College & State
   University
Reinhardt College

University of Georgia
University of West Georgia
Valdosta State University

Hawaii
University of Hawaii
   Kapiolani Community College

Illinois
Governors State University
Greenville College
McKendree College
Moody Bible Institute
Rock Valley College
St. Xavier University
University of Illinois
   Springfield
Western Illinois University

Indiana
Indiana Institute of Technology
Indiana University
   Bloomington
   East
   Kokomo
   Northwest
   South Bend
   Southeast
Indiana University-Purdue University
   Indianapolis
Oakland City University
St. Mary-of-the-Woods College
Taylor University: Fort Wayne
University of Evansville
Vincennes University

Iowa
Allen College
Graceland University
Hawkeye Community College
Iowa Central Community College
Iowa State University
Kirkwood Community College
Simpson College
University of Iowa
University of Northern Iowa
Upper Iowa University

Kansas
Fort Hays State University
Friends University
Kansas City Kansas Community
   College
Pittsburg State University
Seward County Community College

Kentucky
Murray State University
Western Kentucky University

Maine
Eastern Maine Community College

Maryland
Columbia Union College
Coppin State University
Howard Community College
Salisbury University
University of Maryland
   College Park
   University College

Massachusetts
Atlantic Union College
Bunker Hill Community College

Michigan
Baker College
   of Cadillac
   of Clinton Township
   of Flint
   of Jackson

   of Muskegon
   of Owosso
   of Port Huron
Central Michigan University
Ferris State University
Northwood University
Schoolcraft College
Siena Heights University

Minnesota
Bemidji State University
College of St. Scholastica
Metropolitan State University
Minnesota State University
   Mankato
   Moorhead
Northwest Technical College
Southwest Minnesota State University
University of Minnesota
   Twin Cities
Winona State University

Missouri
Global University
Lindenwood University
Missouri Valley College
Stephens College
University of Missouri
   Columbia

Montana
Montana State University
   Billings

Nebraska
Clarkson College
Doane College
University of Nebraska
   Lincoln

New Hampshire
New England College
University of New Hampshire at
   Manchester

New Jersey
Caldwell College
County College of Morris
Fairleigh Dickinson University
   College at Florham
Mercer County Community College
Ramapo College of New Jersey
Thomas Edison State College

New Mexico
San Juan College

New York
City University of New York
   Bronx Community College
Excelsior College
Fulton-Montgomery Community
   College
Hofstra University
Manhattanville College
Skidmore College
State University of New York
   Empire State College
   Oswego

North Carolina
Forsyth Technical Community College
Lenoir-Rhyne College
Mount Olive College
North Carolina State University
University of North Carolina
   Pembroke

North Dakota
Minot State University
University of Mary
University of North Dakota

Ohio
David N. Myers University
Jefferson Community College
Kent State University
Ohio State University
   Mansfield Campus
Ohio University
Ohio University
   Chillicothe Campus
   Eastern Campus
Union Institute & University
University of Findlay
University of Toledo
Walsh University

Oklahoma
Mid-America Christian University
Oklahoma City University
Oral Roberts University
Southern Nazarene University
University of Oklahoma

Oregon
Eastern Oregon University
George Fox University
Linfield College
Oregon Institute of Technology

Pennsylvania
Bucks County Community College
Community College of Allegheny
   County
Duquesne University
Elizabethtown College
Gannon University
Lehigh University
Luzerne County Community College
Penn State
   Abington
   New Kensington
   University Park
University of Pittsburgh
University of Pittsburgh
   Bradford
Wilkes University

Puerto Rico
Inter American University of Puerto
   Rico
   Guayama Campus
University of Puerto Rico
   Rio Piedras
University of the Sacred Heart

Rhode Island
Johnson & Wales University
Roger Williams University
University of Rhode Island

South Carolina
Benedict College
Southern Wesleyan University
University of South Carolina

South Dakota
Northern State University
Presentation College
University of South Dakota

Tennessee
Lee University
Tennessee Temple University
University of Memphis

Texas
El Centro College
Huston-Tillotson College
Lamar State College at Port Arthur
Northwood University: Texas Campus
Prairie View A&M University
Southwestern Adventist University

Southwestern Assemblies of God
     University
Texas A&M University
   Commerce
Texas Tech University
University of North Texas
Wayland Baptist University

Utah

Brigham Young University
Weber State University

Vermont

Burlington College
Community College of Vermont
Goddard College
Johnson State College
Norwich University

Virginia

George Mason University
Liberty University
Mary Baldwin College
Virginia Western Community College

Washington

City University
Renton Technical College
Seattle Pacific University
Skagit Valley College
Walla Walla Community College

West Virginia

Alderson-Broaddus College
Davis and Elkins College
Eastern West Virginia Community and
     Technical College
West Liberty State College
West Virginia State University
West Virginia University
West Virginia University Institute of
     Technology

Wisconsin

Blackhawk Technical College
Cardinal Stritch University
Chippewa Valley Technical College
Madison Area Technical College
University of Wisconsin
   Baraboo/Sauk County
   Green Bay
   Platteville
   Stout
   Superior
   Whitewater

Wyoming

University of Wyoming
Western Wyoming Community
     College

Semester at sea

Alabama
Birmingham-Southern College

Alaska
University of Alaska
  Fairbanks

Arizona
University of Arizona

California
California Polytechnic State
  University: San Luis Obispo
California State University
  Monterey Bay
Chapman University
Loyola Marymount University
Point Loma Nazarene University
Sonoma State University
University of California
  San Diego
Victor Valley College
Westmont College
Whittier College

Colorado
Colorado Christian University
Colorado College
Colorado State University
Red Rocks Community College
University of Colorado
  Boulder
University of Denver
University of Northern Colorado
Western State College of Colorado

Connecticut
Fairfield University
Manchester Community College
Quinnipiac University
Trinity College
University of Connecticut
Wesleyan University

Florida
Barry University
Eckerd College
Jacksonville University
Rollins College
Warner Southern College

Georgia
Agnes Scott College
Georgia College and State University
Morehouse College

Hawaii
Chaminade University of Honolulu

Idaho
Albertson College of Idaho
North Idaho College

Illinois
Greenville College
Lake Forest College
McKendree College

Indiana
Franklin College
Indiana University
  Bloomington
Taylor University
University of Evansville
Wabash College

Iowa
Cornell College

Kentucky
Bellarmine University
Murray State University

Maine
Bates College
Bowdoin College
Colby College
College of the Atlantic
Maine Maritime Academy
St. Joseph's College
Unity College
University of Maine
University of Maine
  Farmington
University of Southern Maine

Maryland
Hood College
McDaniel College
University of Maryland
  Baltimore County
  College Park

Massachusetts
Babson College
Boston University
College of the Holy Cross
Eastern Nazarene College
Lasell College
Massachusetts Maritime Academy
Mount Holyoke College
Northeastern University
Pine Manor College
Simmons College
Smith College
Springfield College
Tufts University
Wellesley College

Michigan
Albion College
Central Michigan University
Michigan Technological University

Minnesota
Concordia College: Moorhead
Minnesota State University
  Mankato
University of Minnesota
  Morris

Mississippi
Millsaps College

Missouri
Culver-Stockton College
Maryville University of Saint Louis
Stephens College
Truman State University

Nebraska
Dana College
Nebraska Wesleyan University

New Hampshire
Colby-Sawyer College
Dartmouth College
Keene State College
New England College
University of New Hampshire
University of New Hampshire at
  Manchester

New Jersey
The College of New Jersey
Richard Stockton College of New
  Jersey

Rowan University

New Mexico
College of Santa Fe
University of New Mexico

New York
Alfred University
Colgate University
Cornell University
Hobart and William Smith Colleges
Le Moyne College
Marist College
State University of New York
  Buffalo
  College at Brockport
  Maritime College
United States Merchant Marine
  Academy

North Carolina
Duke University
Lenoir-Rhyne College
University of North Carolina
  Asheville

North Dakota
University of North Dakota

Ohio
Denison University
Heidelberg College
Ohio State University
  Columbus Campus
Otterbein College
University of Dayton
University of Findlay

Oklahoma
Oklahoma State University

Oregon
Eastern Oregon University
Linfield College
University of Oregon
Willamette University

Pennsylvania
Drexel University
Duquesne University
Franklin & Marshall College
Gettysburg College
Immaculata University
Lafayette College
Marywood University
Mercyhurst College
Moravian College
Penn State
  Beaver
  Erie, The Behrend College
St. Francis University
Susquehanna University
Thiel College
University of Pennsylvania
University of Pittsburgh
  Bradford
  Greensburg
University of Scranton
Ursinus College
Westminster College

Puerto Rico
University of the Sacred Heart

Rhode Island
Roger Williams University
Salve Regina University

South Carolina
College of Charleston
Presbyterian College

Tennessee
O'More College of Design
University of the South

Texas
St. Edward's University
Texas A&M University
  Galveston
Texas Christian University
Texas Tech University
Trinity University
University of Houston

Utah
University of Utah
Weber State University
Westminster College

Vermont
Middlebury College
St. Michael's College
Southern Vermont College
Sterling College

Virginia
College of William and Mary
Hampden-Sydney College
Mary Baldwin College
University of Mary Washington

Washington
Gonzaga University

West Virginia
West Virginia University
Wheeling Jesuit University

Wisconsin
Alverno College
Bellin College of Nursing

Student-designed major

Alabama

Birmingham-Southern College
Huntingdon College
Judson College
Lawson State Community College
Snead State Community College
Spring Hill College
Stillman College
University of Alabama
University of Alabama
  Birmingham
University of North Alabama
University of South Alabama

Alaska

Alaska Pacific University
Sheldon Jackson College
University of Alaska
  Anchorage
  Fairbanks

Arizona

Arizona State University West
Central Arizona College
Mohave Community College
Pima Community College
Prescott College
University of Advancing Technology

Arkansas

Arkansas Tech University
Hendrix College
Lyon College
National Park Community College
North Arkansas College
Rich Mountain Community College
University of Arkansas
  Cossatot Community College of the
  Little Rock

California

Academy of Art University
Antioch Southern California
  Antioch University Los Angeles
  Antioch University Santa Barbara
California College of the Arts
California Institute of Technology
California Institute of the Arts
California Lutheran University
California State University
  Bakersfield
  Chico
  Dominguez Hills
  East Bay
  Fresno
  Fullerton
  Long Beach
  Los Angeles
  Monterey Bay
  Northridge
  Sacramento
  San Marcos
  Stanislaus
Chabot College
Chapman University
Claremont McKenna College
College of the Sequoias
College of the Siskiyous
Concordia University
Cuesta College
Dominican University of California
Fresno Pacific University
Grossmont Community College
Harvey Mudd College
Holy Names University
Hope International University
Humboldt State University

John F. Kennedy University
La Sierra University
Las Positas College
Los Angeles Pierce College
Mendocino College
Menlo College
Mills College
MiraCosta College
Mount St. Mary's College
Notre Dame de Namur University
Occidental College
Orange Coast College
Pepperdine University
Pitzer College
Pomona College
Saddleback College
St. Mary's College of California
San Diego City College
San Diego Mesa College
San Diego State University
San Francisco State University
San Jose State University
Santa Clara University
Scripps College
Simpson University
Sonoma State University
Stanford University
University of California
  Berkeley
  Davis
  Los Angeles
  Riverside
  San Diego
  Santa Barbara
  Santa Cruz
University of Judaism
University of La Verne
University of Redlands
University of San Francisco
University of Southern California
University of the Pacific
West Los Angeles College
Westmont College
Whittier College
Woodbury University

Colorado

Arapahoe Community College
Colorado Christian University
Colorado College
Colorado Northwestern Community
  College
Fort Lewis College
Heritage College
Metropolitan State College of Denver
Morgan Community College
Naropa University
Red Rocks Community College
Regis University
University of Colorado
  Boulder
  Colorado Springs
  Denver and Health Sciences Center
University of Denver
University of Northern Colorado

Connecticut

Albertus Magnus College
Central Connecticut State University
Charter Oak State College
Connecticut College
Eastern Connecticut State University
Fairfield University
Manchester Community College
Middlesex Community College
Post University
Quinnipiac University
Sacred Heart University
St. Joseph College
Southern Connecticut State University
Trinity College
University of Bridgeport
University of Connecticut
University of Hartford

Wesleyan University
Western Connecticut State University
Yale University

Delaware

University of Delaware

District of Columbia

American University
Gallaudet University
George Washington University
Georgetown University
Howard University
Trinity University

Florida

Brevard Community College
Eckerd College
Embry-Riddle Aeronautical University
Florida Atlantic University
Florida Christian College
Florida Metropolitan University
  Pompano Beach
Florida National College
Jacksonville University
Jones College
New College of Florida
Okaloosa-Walton College
Rollins College
Stetson University
University of Florida
University of Miami
University of North Florida
Valencia Community College

Georgia

Agnes Scott College
Berry College
Brenau University
Clayton State University
Covenant College
Fort Valley State University
Georgia College and State University
Georgia Institute of Technology
Georgia Southern University
Mercer University
Oglethorpe University
Piedmont College
Shorter College
Spelman College
University of Georgia
Wesleyan College

Hawaii

Brigham Young University-Hawaii
Chaminade University of Honolulu
Hawaii Pacific University
University of Hawaii
  Hilo
  Honolulu Community College
  Manoa
  Windward Community College

Idaho

Albertson College of Idaho
Boise State University
Brigham Young University-Idaho
Idaho State University
Lewis-Clark State College
Northwest Nazarene University
University of Idaho

Illinois

Aurora University
Blackburn College
Bradley University
Carl Sandburg College
Chicago State University
City Colleges of Chicago
  Olive-Harvey College
College of DuPage
College of Lake County
Columbia College Chicago

Eureka College
Governors State University
Greenville College
Highland Community College
Illinois College
Illinois Eastern Community Colleges
  Frontier Community College
  Lincoln Trail College
  Olney Central College
  Wabash Valley College
Illinois State University
Illinois Wesleyan University
John Wood Community College
Kaskaskia College
Kendall College
Knox College
Lake Forest College
Lewis University
Lewis and Clark Community College
McKendree College
Millikin University
Monmouth College
North Central College
North Park University
Northeastern Illinois University
Northern Illinois University
Northwestern University
Olivet Nazarene University
Parkland College
Principia College
Quincy University
Rock Valley College
Roosevelt University
St. Xavier University
School of the Art Institute of Chicago
Southeastern Illinois College
Southern Illinois University
  Carbondale
Southern Illinois University
  Edwardsville
Trinity International University
University of Chicago
University of Illinois
  Chicago
  Springfield
  Urbana-Champaign
University of St. Francis
Western Illinois University
Wheaton College

Indiana

Anderson University
Ball State University
Butler University
Calumet College of St. Joseph
DePauw University
Earlham College
Goshen College
Hanover College
Indiana Institute of Technology
Indiana University
  Bloomington
  Northwest
  Southeast
Indiana University-Purdue University
  Fort Wayne
Indiana University-Purdue University
  Indianapolis
Indiana Wesleyan University
Manchester College
Martin University
St. Joseph's College
Saint Mary's College
St. Mary-of-the-Woods College
Taylor University
Taylor University: Fort Wayne
University of Evansville
University of Indianapolis
University of Notre Dame
Valparaiso University
Vincennes University
Wabash College

Iowa

Ashford University
Briar Cliff University
Buena Vista University
Central College
Clarke College
Coe College
Cornell College
Dordt College
Drake University
Graceland University
Grand View College
Grinnell College
Iowa State University
Iowa Wesleyan College
Kirkwood Community College
Loras College
Luther College
Morningside College
Northeast Iowa Community College
Northwestern College
St. Ambrose University
University of Iowa
University of Northern Iowa
Upper Iowa University
Wartburg College

Kansas

Allen County Community College
Baker University
Benedictine College
Bethany College
Central Christian College of Kansas
Coffeyville Community College
Cowley County Community College
Emporia State University
Fort Hays State University
Friends University
Garden City Community College
Highland Community College
Kansas Wesleyan University
McPherson College
Newman University
Ottawa University
Pittsburg State University
Southwestern College
Sterling College
Tabor College
University of St. Mary
Washburn University of Topeka

Kentucky

Alice Lloyd College
Berea College
Brescia University
Centre College
Georgetown College
Kentucky State University
Lindsey Wilson College
Morehead State University
Thomas More College
Transylvania University
Union College
University of Louisville
University of the Cumberlands
Western Kentucky University

Louisiana

Centenary College of Louisiana
Delgado Community College
Louisiana State University and
    Agricultural and Mechanical
    College
Loyola University New Orleans
Nunez Community College
Tulane University
University of Louisiana at Lafayette
University of New Orleans

Maine

Bates College
Bowdoin College
Colby College
College of the Atlantic
Eastern Maine Community College
Husson College
Maine College of Art
New England School of
    Communications
St. Joseph's College
Unity College
University of Maine
University of Maine
    Augusta
    Farmington
    Fort Kent
    Machias
    Presque Isle
University of New England
University of Southern Maine
Washington County Community
    College

Maryland

Anne Arundel Community College
Chesapeake College
College of Notre Dame of Maryland
Columbia Union College
Goucher College
Hood College
Johns Hopkins University
Maryland Institute College of Art
McDaniel College
Montgomery College
Mount St. Mary's University
St. Mary's College of Maryland
Salisbury University
Towson University
University of Baltimore
University of Maryland
    Baltimore County
    College Park
    University College
Villa Julie College
Washington College

Massachusetts

Amherst College
Anna Maria College
Art Institute of Boston at Lesley
    University
Assumption College
Babson College
Bentley College
Berklee College of Music
Berkshire Community College
Boston College
Boston University
Brandeis University
Bristol Community College
Clark University
College of the Holy Cross
Curry College
Dean College
Emerson College
Emmanuel College
Endicott College
Fitchburg State College
Franklin W. Olin College of
    Engineering
Gordon College
Hampshire College
Harvard College
Hebrew College
Holyoke Community College
Lasell College
Lesley University
Massachusetts College of Art
Massachusetts College of Liberal Arts
Merrimack College
Montserrat College of Art
Mount Holyoke College
Mount Ida College
New England College of Finance
North Shore Community College
Northeastern University
Pine Manor College
Regis College
Salem State College
School of the Museum of Fine Arts
Simmons College
Simon's Rock College of Bard
Smith College
Springfield College
Stonehill College
Tufts University
University of Massachusetts
    Amherst
    Boston
    Dartmouth
Wellesley College
Wentworth Institute of Technology
Western New England College
Westfield State College
Wheaton College
Williams College
Worcester Polytechnic Institute

Michigan

Adrian College
Albion College
Alma College
Andrews University
Aquinas College
Calvin College
Central Michigan University
Concordia University
Davenport University
Delta College
Eastern Michigan University
Finlandia University
Gogebic Community College
Grand Valley State University
Hope College
Lake Superior State University
Madonna University
Marygrove College
Michigan State University
Northern Michigan University
Oakland University
Olivet College
Saginaw Valley State University
Siena Heights University
Spring Arbor University
University of Michigan
University of Michigan
    Dearborn
    Flint
Western Michigan University

Minnesota

Augsburg College
Bethel University
Carleton College
College of St. Benedict
College of St. Catherine
College of St. Scholastica
Crossroads College
Gustavus Adolphus College
Hamline University
Inver Hills Community College
Macalester College
Metropolitan State University
Minnesota State University
    Mankato
    Moorhead
Minnesota West Community and
    Technical College: Worthington
    Campus
North Central University
Northwestern College
Ridgewater College
St. Cloud State University
St. John's University
St. Mary's University of Minnesota
St. Olaf College
Southwest Minnesota State University
University of Minnesota
    Crookston
    Duluth
    Morris
    Twin Cities
University of St. Thomas
Walden University
Winona State University

Mississippi

Belhaven College
Millsaps College
Mississippi State University
Tougaloo College

Missouri

Calvary Bible College and Theological
    Seminary
Central Methodist University
Central Missouri State University
College of the Ozarks
Columbia College
Culver-Stockton College
Drury University
Fontbonne University
Harris-Stowe State University
Lindenwood University
Maryville University of Saint Louis
Missouri Baptist University
Missouri State University
Missouri State University: West Plains
Missouri Valley College
Park University
St. Louis University
Southeast Missouri State University
Stephens College
Truman State University
University of Missouri
    Columbia
    Rolla
    St. Louis
Washington University in St. Louis
Webster University
Westminster College
William Jewell College
William Woods University

Montana

Carroll College
Montana State University
    Bozeman
Montana Tech of the University of
    Montana
Rocky Mountain College

Nebraska

Chadron State College
College of Saint Mary
Dana College
Doane College
Hastings College
Midland Lutheran College
Union College
University of Nebraska
    Lincoln
    Omaha
Wayne State College
Western Nebraska Community
    College

Nevada

Community College of Southern
    Nevada
University of Nevada
    Las Vegas

New Hampshire

Colby-Sawyer College
Dartmouth College
Franklin Pierce College
Granite State College
Keene State College
New England College
New Hampshire Community
    Technical College
    Berlin

Manchester
Nashua
Plymouth State University
University of New Hampshire
University of New Hampshire at
Manchester

New Jersey

Bloomfield College
Caldwell College
Centenary College
The College of New Jersey
College of St. Elizabeth
Drew University
Fairleigh Dickinson University
Metropolitan Campus
Felician College
Monmouth University
Passaic County Community College
Princeton University
Ramapo College of New Jersey
Richard Stockton College of New
Jersey
Rutgers, The State University of New
Jersey
Camden Regional Campus
New Brunswick/Piscataway
Campus
Newark Regional Campus
St. Peter's College

New Mexico

College of Santa Fe
Eastern New Mexico University
New Mexico Institute of Mining and
Technology
New Mexico State University
New Mexico State University
Carlsbad
Grants
University of New Mexico

New York

Adelphi University
Alfred University
Bard College
Barnard College
Broome Community College
Cazenovia College
City University of New York
Baruch College
College of Staten Island
Hunter College
John Jay College of Criminal Justice
LaGuardia Community College
Lehman College
Queens College
Clarkson University
Clinton Community College
Colgate University
College of New Rochelle
Columbia University
Columbia College
School of General Studies
Columbia-Greene Community College
Concordia College
Cooper Union for the Advancement of
Science and Art
Cornell University
Daemen College
Dowling College
Eastman School of Music of the
University of Rochester
Elmira College
Erie Community College
City Campus
North Campus
South Campus
Eugene Lang College The New School
for Liberal Arts
Fordham University
Fulton-Montgomery Community
College
Hamilton College

Hartwick College
Hobart and William Smith Colleges
Hofstra University
Hudson Valley Community College
Ithaca College
Jefferson Community College
Jewish Theological Seminary of
America
Keuka College
Long Island University
Brooklyn Campus
C.W. Post Campus
Manhattanville College
Medaille College
Mercy College
Mohawk Valley Community College
Molloy College
Mount St. Mary College
New York University
North Country Community College
Parsons The New School for Design
Rensselaer Polytechnic Institute
Rochester Institute of Technology
Rockland Community College
Russell Sage College
Sage College of Albany
St. Bonaventure University
St. Francis College
St. John Fisher College
St. Lawrence University
Sarah Lawrence College
Skidmore College
State University of New York
Albany
Binghamton
Buffalo
College at Brockport
College at Cortland
College at Fredonia
College at Plattsburgh
College at Potsdam
College of Agriculture and
Technology at Morrisville
College of Technology at Alfred
College of Technology at Canton
College of Technology at Delhi
Empire State College
New Paltz
Purchase
Stony Brook
Syracuse University
Touro College
Ulster County Community College
Union College
University of Rochester
Vassar College
Wells College
Westchester Community College
Yeshiva University

North Carolina

Appalachian State University
Bennett College
Brevard College
Catawba College
Catawba Valley Community College
Craven Community College
Davidson College
Duke University
East Carolina University
Elon University
Forsyth Technical Community College
Greensboro College
Guilford College
High Point University
John Wesley College
Lees-McRae College
Lenoir-Rhyne College
Mars Hill College
Meredith College
Methodist College
Montreat College
North Carolina State University
Queens University of Charlotte

Richmond Community College
Rockingham Community College
St. Andrews Presbyterian College
Salem College
Shaw University
University of North Carolina
Asheville
Chapel Hill
Greensboro
Warren Wilson College
Western Carolina University

North Dakota

Dickinson State University
Jamestown College
Mayville State University
Minot State University
North Dakota State College of Science
North Dakota State University
University of North Dakota
Valley City State University
Williston State College

Ohio

Antioch College
Antioch University McGregor
Art Academy of Cincinnati
Ashland University
Baldwin-Wallace College
Belmont Technical College
Bluffton University
Bowling Green State University
Bowling Green State University:
Firelands College
Capital University
Case Western Reserve University
Cedarville University
Cincinnati State Technical and
Community College
Circleville Bible College
Clark State Community College
Cleveland State University
College of Wooster
Columbus State Community College
David N. Myers University
Defiance College
Denison University
Edison State Community College
Heidelberg College
Hiram College
Hocking College
James A. Rhodes State College
John Carroll University
Kent State University
Kent State University
Ashtabula Regional Campus
East Liverpool Regional Campus
Salem Regional Campus
Stark Campus
Trumbull Campus
Tuscarawas Campus
Kenyon College
Lake Erie College
Lourdes College
Malone College
Marietta College
Marion Technical College
Miami University
Hamilton Campus
Oxford Campus
Mount Union College
Muskingum College
Oberlin College
Ohio State University
Agricultural Technical Institute
Columbus Campus
Lima Campus
Mansfield Campus
Marion Campus
Newark Campus
Ohio University
Ohio University
Chillicothe Campus
Eastern Campus

Lancaster Campus
Southern Campus at Ironton
Zanesville Campus
Ohio Wesleyan University
Otterbein College
Owens Community College
Toledo
Shawnee State University
Sinclair Community College
Southern State Community College
Stark State College of Technology
Union Institute & University
University of Akron
University of Akron: Wayne College
University of Cincinnati
Clermont College
Raymond Walters College
University of Dayton
University of Findlay
University of Rio Grande
University of Toledo
Urbana University
Washington State Community College
Wilmington College
Wittenberg University
Wright State University
Wright State University: Lake Campus
Youngstown State University
Zane State College

Oklahoma

Northeastern State University
Oklahoma Baptist University
Oklahoma City Community College
Oklahoma City University
Oklahoma State University
Oklahoma Wesleyan University
Oral Roberts University
St. Gregory's University
Southern Nazarene University
Southwestern Oklahoma State
University
University of Oklahoma
University of Science and Arts of
Oklahoma
University of Tulsa

Oregon

Central Oregon Community College
Clatsop Community College
Eastern Oregon University
George Fox University
Lewis & Clark College
Linfield College
Linn-Benton Community College
Marylhurst University
Northwest Christian College
Oregon State University
Pacific Northwest College of Art
Southern Oregon University
Umpqua Community College
University of Oregon
University of Portland
Warner Pacific College
Western Oregon University
Willamette University

Pennsylvania

Albright College
Allegheny College
Alvernia College
Arcadia University
Bryn Athyn College of the New
Church
Bryn Mawr College
Bucknell University
Bucks County Community College
Cabrini College
California University of Pennsylvania
Carlow University
Carnegie Mellon University
Cedar Crest College
Chatham College
Chestnut Hill College

College Misericordia
Delaware County Community College
Dickinson College
Duquesne University
East Stroudsburg University of
    Pennsylvania
Eastern University
Edinboro University of Pennsylvania
Franklin & Marshall College
Geneva College
Gettysburg College
Harrisburg Area Community College
Haverford College
Juniata College
Keystone College
King's College
Kutztown University of Pennsylvania
La Roche College
Lafayette College
Lebanon Valley College
Lock Haven University of
    Pennsylvania
Lycoming College
Mansfield University of Pennsylvania
Marywood University
Mercyhurst College
Messiah College
Montgomery County Community
    College
Moravian College
Mount Aloysius College
Muhlenberg College
Neumann College
Northampton County Area
    Community College
Penn State
    Abington
    Altoona
    Dubois
    Fayette
    Harrisburg
    Hazleton
    Schuylkill - Capital College
    Shenango
    University Park
    Wilkes-Barre
    York
Pennsylvania College of Technology
Point Park University
Reading Area Community College
Rosemont College
St. Francis University
St. Joseph's University
Seton Hill University
Susquehanna University
Swarthmore College
Temple University
University of Pennsylvania
University of Pittsburgh
University of Pittsburgh
    Greensburg
    Johnstown
Ursinus College
Washington and Jefferson College
West Chester University of
    Pennsylvania
Westminster College
Westmoreland County Community
    College
Widener University
Wilkes University
Wilson College
York College of Pennsylvania

Puerto Rico

Atlantic College

Rhode Island

Brown University
New England Institute of Technology
Providence College
Rhode Island College
Roger Williams University

South Carolina

Coastal Carolina University
Coker College
Columbia College
Converse College
Furman University
Lander University
Limestone College
Newberry College
North Greenville College
Southern Wesleyan University
Tri-County Technical College
University of South Carolina
University of South Carolina
    Aiken
    Beaufort
    Salkehatchie Regional Campus
    Sumter
    Union
    Upstate
Williamsburg Technical College
Wofford College

South Dakota

Augustana College
Dakota Wesleyan University
Mount Marty College
Northern State University
South Dakota School of Mines and
    Technology
University of Sioux Falls
University of South Dakota

Tennessee

Belmont University
Bethel College
Carson-Newman College
Chattanooga State Technical
    Community College
Crichton College
Fisk University
Freed-Hardeman University
King College
Lambuth University
LeMoyne-Owen College
Maryville College
Nashville State Community College
Rhodes College
Southwest Tennessee Community
    College
Tennessee Wesleyan College
Tusculum College
University of Memphis
University of Tennessee
    Knoxville
    Martin
University of the South
Vanderbilt University

Texas

Abilene Christian University
Austin College
Baylor University
Cedar Valley College
Clarendon College
Jarvis Christian College
Lubbock Christian University
Rice University
Schreiner University
Southern Methodist University
Southwestern Adventist University
Southwestern University
Stephen F. Austin State University
Texas A&M University
    Texarkana
Texas Tech University
Trinity University
University of Dallas
University of Houston
    Clear Lake
University of Texas
    Arlington
    Austin

Dallas
Tyler
West Texas A&M University

Utah

University of Utah
Utah State University
Utah Valley State College
Weber State University
Westminster College

Vermont

Bennington College
Burlington College
Castleton State College
Community College of Vermont
Goddard College
Green Mountain College
Lyndon State College
Marlboro College
Middlebury College
Norwich University
St. Michael's College
Southern Vermont College
Sterling College
University of Vermont
Woodbury College

Virginia

Averett University
Bluefield College
Christopher Newport University
College of William and Mary
Emory & Henry College
Ferrum College
George Mason University
Hollins University
Liberty University
Mary Baldwin College
Marymount University
Mountain Empire Community College
Northern Virginia Community College
Old Dominion University
Radford University
Randolph-Macon Woman's College
St. Paul's College
Shenandoah University
Sweet Briar College
University of Mary Washington
University of Richmond
University of Virginia
University of Virginia's College at Wise
Virginia Commonwealth University
Virginia Polytechnic Institute and
    State University
Virginia Wesleyan College
Washington and Lee University

Washington

Antioch University Seattle
Central Washington University
Centralia College
City University
Eastern Washington University
Evergreen State College
Heritage University
Highline Community College
Lower Columbia College
Northwest University
Pacific Lutheran University
Pierce College
Renton Technical College
Seattle Pacific University
Seattle University
Spokane Community College
Trinity Lutheran College
University of Puget Sound
University of Washington
Washington State University
Wenatchee Valley College
Western Washington University
Whatcom Community College
Whitman College

Whitworth College

West Virginia

Bethany College
Bluefield State College
Concord University
Davis and Elkins College
Eastern West Virginia Community and
    Technical College
Glenville State College
Mountain State University
Ohio Valley University
Salem International University
University of Charleston
West Liberty State College
West Virginia University
West Virginia University Institute of
    Technology
West Virginia Wesleyan College
Wheeling Jesuit University

Wisconsin

Alverno College
Beloit College
Blackhawk Technical College
Cardinal Stritch University
Carroll College
Carthage College
Chippewa Valley Technical College
Concordia University Wisconsin
Edgewood College
Lakeshore Technical College
Lawrence University
Marian College of Fond du Lac
Mount Mary College
Nicolet Area Technical College
Northcentral Technical College
Northland College
Ripon College
St. Norbert College
Silver Lake College
University of Wisconsin
    Green Bay
    Madison
    Milwaukee
    Oshkosh
    Platteville
    River Falls
    Stevens Point
    Superior
    Whitewater
Viterbo University
Waukesha County Technical College
Western Wisconsin Technical College
Wisconsin Lutheran College

Wyoming

Central Wyoming College
University of Wyoming

Alabama

Alabama Agricultural and Mechanical
  University
Alabama State University
Athens State University
Auburn University
Auburn University at Montgomery
Birmingham-Southern College
Faulkner University
Huntingdon College
Jacksonville State University
Judson College
Oakwood College
Samford University
Southeastern Bible College
Spring Hill College
Stillman College
Talladega College
Troy University
Tuskegee University
University of Alabama
University of Alabama
  Birmingham
  Huntsville
University of Mobile
University of Montevallo
University of North Alabama
University of South Alabama
University of West Alabama

Alaska

Alaska Pacific University
Sheldon Jackson College
University of Alaska
  Anchorage
  Fairbanks
  Southeast

Arizona

American Indian College of the
  Assemblies of God
Arizona State University
Arizona State University West
Arizona Western College
Chandler-Gilbert Community College
  Williams Campus
Cochise College
Gateway Community College
Grand Canyon University
Northern Arizona University
Paradise Valley Community College
Pima Community College
Prescott College
Southwestern College
University of Arizona
University of Phoenix
Yavapai College

Arkansas

Arkansas State University
Arkansas Tech University
Harding University
Henderson State University
Hendrix College
John Brown University
Lyon College
Ouachita Baptist University
Philander Smith College
Southern Arkansas University
University of Arkansas
University of Arkansas
  Fort Smith
  Little Rock
  Monticello
  Pine Bluff
University of Central Arkansas
University of the Ozarks

California

Academy of Art University
Antelope Valley College
Antioch Southern California
  Antioch University Los Angeles
  Antioch University Santa Barbara
Azusa Pacific University
Bethany University
California Baptist University
California Lutheran University
California Polytechnic State
  University: San Luis Obispo
California State Polytechnic
  University: Pomona
California State University
  Bakersfield
  Chico
  Dominguez Hills
  East Bay
  Fresno
  Fullerton
  Long Beach
  Los Angeles
  Monterey Bay
  Northridge
  Sacramento
  San Bernardino
  San Marcos
  Stanislaus
Chapman University
College of the Redwoods
Concordia University
Dominican University of California
Fresno Pacific University
Hope International University
Humboldt State University
John F. Kennedy University
La Sierra University
Loyola Marymount University
Master's College
Mills College
MiraCosta College
Mount St. Mary's College
Mount San Antonio College
National Hispanic University
National University
Notre Dame de Namur University
Pacific Oaks College
Pacific Union College
Patten University
Pepperdine University
Point Loma Nazarene University
St. Mary's College of California
San Diego Christian College
San Diego City College
San Diego Mesa College
San Diego State University
San Francisco State University
San Jose State University
Santa Clara University
Simpson University
Sonoma State University
University of California
  Berkeley
  Davis
  Irvine
  Los Angeles
  Riverside
  San Diego
  Santa Barbara
  Santa Cruz
University of La Verne
University of Redlands
University of San Diego
University of San Francisco
University of Southern California
University of the Pacific
Vanguard University of Southern
  California
West Valley College
Westmont College
Whittier College
William Jessup University

Colorado

Adams State College
Colorado Christian University
Colorado College
Colorado State University
Colorado State University
  Pueblo
Fort Lewis College
Front Range Community College
Johnson & Wales University
Mesa State College
Metropolitan State College of Denver
Morgan Community College
Regis University
University of Colorado
  Boulder
  Colorado Springs
  Denver and Health Sciences Center
University of Denver
University of Northern Colorado
Western State College of Colorado

Connecticut

Albertus Magnus College
Central Connecticut State University
Connecticut College
Eastern Connecticut State University
Fairfield University
Quinnipiac University
Sacred Heart University
St. Joseph College
Southern Connecticut State University
Trinity College
University of Bridgeport
University of Connecticut
University of Hartford
University of New Haven
Western Connecticut State University
Yale University

Delaware

Delaware State University
University of Delaware
Wesley College
Wilmington College

District of Columbia

American University
Catholic University of America
Gallaudet University
Howard University
Trinity University
University of the District of Columbia

Florida

Baptist College of Florida
Barry University
Bethune-Cookman College
Central Florida Community College
Chipola College
Clearwater Christian College
Edward Waters College
Flagler College
Florida Agricultural and Mechanical
  University
Florida Atlantic University
Florida Christian College
Florida College
Florida Gulf Coast University
Florida Institute of Technology
Florida International University
Florida Memorial University
Florida Southern College
Florida State University
Gulf Coast Community College
Hillsborough Community College
Hobe Sound Bible College
Jacksonville University
North Florida Community College
Nova Southeastern University
Palm Beach Atlantic University
Rollins College
St. Leo University

St. Petersburg College
St. Thomas University
Seminole Community College
Southeastern College of the
  Assemblies of God
Stetson University
Trinity College of Florida
University of Central Florida
University of Florida
University of Miami
University of North Florida
University of South Florida
University of Tampa
University of West Florida
Warner Southern College

Georgia

Agnes Scott College
Albany State University
Armstrong Atlantic State University
Atlanta Metropolitan College
Augusta State University
Berry College
Brenau University
Brewton-Parker College
Clark Atlanta University
Clayton State University
Coastal Georgia Community College
Columbus State University
Covenant College
Emmanuel College
Emory University
Fort Valley State University
Georgia College and State University
Georgia Southern University
Georgia Southwestern State
  University
Georgia State University
Kennesaw State University
LaGrange College
Macon State College
Mercer University
North Georgia College & State
  University
Paine College
Piedmont College
Reinhardt College
Shorter College
Spelman College
Thomas University
Toccoa Falls College
University of Georgia
University of West Georgia
Valdosta State University
Wesleyan College

Hawaii

Brigham Young University-Hawaii
Chaminade University of Honolulu
Hawaii Pacific University
University of Hawaii
  Hilo
  Kapiolani Community College
  Manoa

Idaho

Albertson College of Idaho
Boise State University
Brigham Young University-Idaho
Idaho State University
Lewis-Clark State College
Northwest Nazarene University
University of Idaho

Illinois

Augustana College
Aurora University
Benedictine University
Blackburn College
Bradley University
Chicago State University
Columbia College Chicago
Concordia University

DePaul University
Dominican University
Eastern Illinois University
Elmhurst College
Eureka College
Governors State University
Greenville College
Illinois College
Illinois Eastern Community Colleges
    Frontier Community College
Illinois Institute of Technology
Illinois State University
Illinois Wesleyan University
Judson College
Kankakee Community College
Kendall College
Knox College
Lake Forest College
Lewis University
Lincoln Christian College and
    Seminary
Loyola University of Chicago
MacMurray College
McKendree College
Millikin University
Monmouth College
Moody Bible Institute
National-Louis University
North Central College
North Park University
Northeastern Illinois University
Northern Illinois University
Northwestern University
Oakton Community College
Olivet Nazarene University
Principia College
Quincy University
Richland Community College
Rockford College
Roosevelt University
St. Xavier University
School of the Art Institute of Chicago
Southern Illinois University
    Carbondale
Southern Illinois University
    Edwardsville
Trinity Christian College
Trinity International University
Triton College
University of Chicago
University of Illinois
    Chicago
    Springfield
    Urbana-Champaign
University of St. Francis
VanderCook College of Music
Western Illinois University
Wheaton College

Indiana

Anderson University
Ball State University
Bethel College
Butler University
Calumet College of St. Joseph
DePauw University
Franklin College
Goshen College
Grace College
Hanover College
Huntington University
Indiana State University
Indiana University
    Bloomington
    East
    Kokomo
    Northwest
    South Bend
    Southeast
Indiana University-Purdue University
    Fort Wayne
Indiana University-Purdue University
    Indianapolis
Indiana Wesleyan University

Ivy Tech State College
Ivy Tech Community College:
    Bloomington
Ivy Tech Community College:
    Central Indiana
Ivy Tech Community College:
    Columbus
Ivy Tech Community College: East
    Central
Ivy Tech Community College:
    Kokomo
Ivy Tech Community College:
    Lafayette
Ivy Tech Community College: North
    Central
Ivy Tech Community College:
    Northeast
Ivy Tech Community College:
    Northwest
Ivy Tech Community College: South
    Central
Ivy Tech Community College:
    Southeast
Ivy Tech Community College:
    Southwest
Ivy Tech Community College:
    Wabash Valley
Ivy Tech Community College:
    Whitewater
Manchester College
Marian College
Oakland City University
Purdue University
Purdue University
    Calumet
    North Central Campus
St. Joseph's College
Saint Mary's College
St. Mary-of-the-Woods College
Taylor University
Taylor University: Fort Wayne
Tri-State University
University of Evansville
University of Indianapolis
University of Notre Dame
University of St. Francis
University of Southern Indiana
Valparaiso University
Wabash College

Iowa

Ashford University
Briar Cliff University
Buena Vista University
Central College
Clarke College
Coe College
Cornell College
Dordt College
Drake University
Emmaus Bible College
Faith Baptist Bible College and
    Theological Seminary
Graceland University
Grand View College
Grinnell College
Iowa State University
Iowa Wesleyan College
Loras College
Luther College
Maharishi University of Management
Morningside College
Mount Mercy College
Northwestern College
St. Ambrose University
Simpson College
University of Dubuque
University of Iowa
University of Northern Iowa
Upper Iowa University
Vennard College
Waldorf College
Wartburg College
William Penn University

Kansas

Baker University
Barclay College
Benedictine College
Bethany College
Bethel College
Cloud County Community College
Cowley County Community College
Emporia State University
Fort Hays State University
Fort Scott Community College
Friends University
Kansas State University
Kansas Wesleyan University
McPherson College
MidAmerica Nazarene University
Newman University
Ottawa University
Pittsburg State University
Southwestern College
Sterling College
Tabor College
University of Kansas
University of St. Mary
Washburn University of Topeka
Wichita State University

Kentucky

Alice Lloyd College
Asbury College
Bellarmine University
Berea College
Brescia University
Campbellsville University
Centre College
Eastern Kentucky University
Georgetown College
Jefferson Community College
Kentucky Christian University
Kentucky State University
Kentucky Wesleyan College
Lindsey Wilson College
Maysville Community College
Mid-Continent University
Midway College
Morehead State University
Murray State University
Northern Kentucky University
Pikeville College
Spalding University
Thomas More College
Transylvania University
Union College
University of Kentucky
University of Louisville
University of the Cumberlands
Western Kentucky University

Louisiana

Centenary College of Louisiana
Dillard University
Grambling State University
Louisiana State University
    Shreveport
Louisiana State University and
    Agricultural and Mechanical
    College
Louisiana Tech University
Loyola University New Orleans
Nicholls State University
Northwestern State University
Our Lady of Holy Cross College
Southeastern Louisiana University
Southern University
    New Orleans
Southern University and Agricultural
    and Mechanical College
Tulane University
University of Louisiana at Lafayette
University of Louisiana at Monroe
University of New Orleans
Xavier University of Louisiana

Maine

Andover College
Bates College
Bowdoin College
Colby College
College of the Atlantic
Husson College
Maine College of Art
St. Joseph's College
Thomas College
University of Maine
University of Maine
    Farmington
    Fort Kent
    Machias
    Presque Isle
University of New England
University of Southern Maine

Maryland

Baltimore City Community College
Baltimore Hebrew University
Bowie State University
Cecil Community College
Chesapeake College
College of Notre Dame of Maryland
Columbia Union College
Community College of Baltimore
    County
Coppin State University
Frederick Community College
Frostburg State University
Goucher College
Hood College
Howard Community College
Johns Hopkins University: Peabody
    Conservatory of Music
Loyola College in Maryland
Maryland Institute College of Art
McDaniel College
Morgan State University
Mount St. Mary's University
Prince George's Community College
St. Mary's College of Maryland
Salisbury University
Towson University
University of Maryland
    Baltimore County
    College Park
    Eastern Shore
    University College
Villa Julie College
Washington Bible College
Washington College

Massachusetts

American International College
Amherst College
Anna Maria College
Art Institute of Boston at Lesley
    University
Assumption College
Atlantic Union College
Bay Path College
Becker College
Berklee College of Music
Boston College
Boston Conservatory
Boston University
Bridgewater State College
Clark University
College of the Holy Cross
Curry College
Eastern Nazarene College
Elms College
Emerson College
Emmanuel College
Endicott College
Fitchburg State College
Framingham State College
Gordon College
Hampshire College
Harvard College
Hebrew College

Holyoke Community College
Lasell College
Lesley University
Massachusetts College of Liberal Arts
Massachusetts Institute of Technology
Merrimack College
Montserrat College of Art
Mount Holyoke College
Mount Ida College
Nichols College
Northeastern University
Pine Manor College
Regis College
Salem State College
School of the Museum of Fine Arts
Simmons College
Smith College
Springfield College
Stonehill College
Tufts University
University of Massachusetts
  Amherst
  Boston
  Dartmouth
  Lowell
Wellesley College
Western New England College
Westfield State College
Wheaton College
Wheelock College
Williams College
Worcester Polytechnic Institute
Worcester State College

Michigan
Adrian College
Albion College
Alma College
Andrews University
Aquinas College
Baker College
  of Auburn Hills
  of Clinton Township
  of Muskegon
Calvin College
Central Michigan University
College for Creative Studies
Concordia University
Cornerstone University
Eastern Michigan University
Ferris State University
Finlandia University
Grand Valley State University
Hillsdale College
Hope College
Kendall College of Art and Design of
    Ferris State University
Kuyper College
Lake Superior State University
Lansing Community College
Madonna University
Marygrove College
Michigan State University
Michigan Technological University
Northern Michigan University
Oakland University
Olivet College
Rochester College
Saginaw Valley State University
Siena Heights University
Spring Arbor University
University of Detroit Mercy
University of Michigan
University of Michigan
  Dearborn
  Flint
Wayne State University
Western Michigan University

Minnesota
Augsburg College
Bemidji State University
Bethany Lutheran College
Bethel University

Carleton College
College of St. Benedict
College of St. Catherine
College of St. Scholastica
Concordia College: Moorhead
Concordia University: St. Paul
Crown College
Gustavus Adolphus College
Hamline University
Leech Lake Tribal College
Macalester College
Martin Luther College
Minnesota State University
  Mankato
  Moorhead
North Central University
Northwestern College
St. Cloud State University
St. John's University
St. Mary's University of Minnesota
St. Olaf College
Southwest Minnesota State University
University of Minnesota
  Duluth
  Morris
  Twin Cities
University of St. Thomas
Winona State University

Mississippi
Alcorn State University
Belhaven College
Blue Mountain College
Delta State University
Jackson State University
Millsaps College
Mississippi College
Mississippi State University
Mississippi Valley State University
Rust College
Tougaloo College
University of Mississippi
University of Southern Mississippi
William Carey College

Missouri
Avila University
Calvary Bible College and Theological
    Seminary
Central Methodist University
Central Missouri State University
College of the Ozarks
Columbia College
Culver-Stockton College
Drury University
Evangel University
Fontbonne University
Hannibal-LaGrange College
Harris-Stowe State University
Lincoln University
Lindenwood University
Maryville University of Saint Louis
Missouri Baptist University
Missouri Southern State University
Missouri State University
Missouri Valley College
Missouri Western State University
Moberly Area Community College
Northwest Missouri State University
Park University
Rockhurst University
St. Louis Community College
  St. Louis Community College at
    Florissant Valley
St. Louis University
Southeast Missouri State University
Southwest Baptist University
Stephens College
Truman State University
University of Missouri
  Columbia
  Kansas City
  Rolla
  St. Louis

Washington University in St. Louis
Webster University
Westminster College
William Jewell College
William Woods University

Montana
Carroll College
Fort Peck Community College
Montana State University
  Billings
  Bozeman
Montana Tech of the University of
    Montana
Rocky Mountain College
University of Great Falls
University of Montana: Missoula
University of Montana: Western

Nebraska
Chadron State College
College of Saint Mary
Concordia University
Creighton University
Dana College
Doane College
Grace University
Hastings College
Midland Lutheran College
Nebraska Wesleyan University
Peru State College
Union College
University of Nebraska
  Kearney
  Lincoln
  Omaha
Wayne State College
York College

Nevada
Great Basin College
Sierra Nevada College
University of Nevada
  Las Vegas
  Reno

New Hampshire
Chester College of New England
Colby-Sawyer College
Dartmouth College
Franklin Pierce College
Keene State College
New England College
Plymouth State University
Rivier College
St. Anselm College
Southern New Hampshire University
University of New Hampshire
University of New Hampshire at
    Manchester

New Jersey
Bloomfield College
Caldwell College
Centenary College
The College of New Jersey
College of St. Elizabeth
Drew University
Essex County College
Fairleigh Dickinson University
  College at Florham
  Metropolitan Campus
Felician College
Georgian Court University
Kean University
Monmouth University
Montclair State University
New Jersey City University
Princeton University
Ramapo College of New Jersey
Richard Stockton College of New
    Jersey
Rider University

Rowan University
Rutgers, The State University of New
    Jersey
  Camden Regional Campus
  New Brunswick/Piscataway
    Campus
  Newark Regional Campus
St. Peter's College
Salem Community College
Seton Hall University
Sussex County Community College
Westminster Choir College of Rider
    University
William Paterson University of New
    Jersey

New Mexico
College of Santa Fe
College of the Southwest
Eastern New Mexico University
New Mexico Highlands University
New Mexico Institute of Mining and
    Technology
New Mexico State University
Northern New Mexico College
San Juan College
University of New Mexico
Western New Mexico University

New York
Adelphi University
Alfred University
Barnard College
Canisius College
Cazenovia College
City University of New York
  Brooklyn College
  City College
  College of Staten Island
  Hunter College
  Lehman College
  Medgar Evers College
  New York City College of
    Technology
  Queens College
  York College
Colgate University
College of Mount St. Vincent
College of New Rochelle
College of Saint Rose
Columbia University
  Columbia College
  Fu Foundation School of
    Engineering and Applied
    Science
  School of General Studies
Concordia College
Cornell University
D'Youville College
Daemen College
Dominican College of Blauvelt
Dowling College
Eastman School of Music of the
    University of Rochester
Elmira College
Erie Community College
  City Campus
  North Campus
  South Campus
Five Towns College
Fordham University
Hartwick College
Hobart and William Smith Colleges
Hofstra University
Houghton College
Iona College
Ithaca College
Keuka College
Le Moyne College
Long Island University
  Brooklyn Campus
  C.W. Post Campus
Manhattan College
Manhattanville College

Marist College
Marymount Manhattan College
Medaille College
Mercy College
Mohawk Valley Community College
Molloy College
Mount St. Mary College
Nazareth College of Rochester
New York Institute of Technology
New York University
Niagara University
Nyack College
Pace University
Parsons The New School for Design
Pratt Institute
Roberts Wesleyan College
Rochester Institute of Technology
Russell Sage College
St. Bonaventure University
St. Francis College
St. John Fisher College
St. John's University
St. Joseph's College
St. Joseph's College: Suffolk Campus
St. Lawrence University
St. Thomas Aquinas College
Sarah Lawrence College
Schenectady County Community
    College
School of Visual Arts
Siena College
Skidmore College
State University of New York
    Binghamton
    Buffalo
    College at Brockport
    College at Buffalo
    College at Cortland
    College at Fredonia
    College at Geneseo
    College at Old Westbury
    College at Oneonta
    College at Plattsburgh
    College at Potsdam
    College of Environmental Science
        and Forestry
    New Paltz
    Oswego
    Stony Brook
Syracuse University
Touro College
University of Rochester
Utica College
Vassar College
Wagner College
Wells College
Yeshiva University

North Carolina

Appalachian State University
Barton College
Belmont Abbey College
Bennett College
Brevard College
Campbell University
Carteret Community College
Catawba College
Catawba Valley Community College
Chowan College
Davidson College
Duke University
East Carolina University
Elizabeth City State University
Elon University
Fayetteville State University
Gardner-Webb University
Greensboro College
Guilford College
High Point University
Johnson C. Smith University
Lees-McRae College
Lenoir-Rhyne College
Livingstone College
Mars Hill College

Meredith College
Methodist College
Montreat College
Mount Olive College
North Carolina Agricultural and
    Technical State University
North Carolina Central University
North Carolina State University
North Carolina Wesleyan College
Pfeiffer University
Piedmont Baptist College
Queens University of Charlotte
Richmond Community College
Rowan-Cabarrus Community College
St. Andrews Presbyterian College
St. Augustine's College
Salem College
Sandhills Community College
Shaw University
University of North Carolina
    Asheville
    Chapel Hill
    Charlotte
    Greensboro
    Pembroke
    Wilmington
Wake Forest University
Warren Wilson College
Western Carolina University
Wingate University
Winston-Salem State University

North Dakota

Dickinson State University
Jamestown College
Mayville State University
Minot State University
North Dakota State University
Trinity Bible College
University of Mary
University of North Dakota
Valley City State University

Ohio

Ashland University
Baldwin-Wallace College
Bluffton University
Bowling Green State University
Bowling Green State University:
    Firelands College
Capital University
Case Western Reserve University
Cedarville University
Central State University
Cincinnati Christian University
Cleveland Institute of Music
Cleveland State University
College of Mount St. Joseph
College of Wooster
Columbus State Community College
Defiance College
Denison University
Franciscan University of Steubenville
Heidelberg College
Hiram College
John Carroll University
Kent State University
Lake Erie College
Lourdes College
Malone College
Marietta College
Miami University
    Hamilton Campus
    Oxford Campus
Mount Union College
Mount Vernon Nazarene University
Muskingum College
Oberlin College
Ohio Dominican University
Ohio Northern University
Ohio State University
    Columbus Campus
    Lima Campus
    Mansfield Campus

    Marion Campus
    Newark Campus
Ohio University
Ohio University
    Chillicothe Campus
    Eastern Campus
    Southern Campus at Ironton
    Zanesville Campus
Ohio Wesleyan University
Otterbein College
Shawnee State University
Tiffin University
University of Akron
University of Cincinnati
University of Cincinnati
    Raymond Walters College
University of Dayton
University of Findlay
University of Rio Grande
University of Toledo
Urbana University
Ursuline College
Walsh University
Wilmington College
Wittenberg University
Wright State University
Xavier University
Youngstown State University

Oklahoma

Cameron University
East Central University
Mid-America Christian University
Northeastern State University
Northwestern Oklahoma State
    University
Oklahoma Baptist University
Oklahoma Christian University
Oklahoma City University
Oklahoma Panhandle State University
Oklahoma State University
Oklahoma Wesleyan University
Oral Roberts University
St. Gregory's University
Southeastern Oklahoma State
    University
Southern Nazarene University
Southwestern Oklahoma State
    University
University of Central Oklahoma
University of Oklahoma
University of Science and Arts of
    Oklahoma
University of Tulsa

Oregon

Chemeketa Community College
Clatsop Community College
Concordia University
Corban College
Eastern Oregon University
George Fox University
Linfield College
Northwest Christian College
Oregon State University
Pacific University
Portland State University
Southern Oregon University
University of Oregon
University of Portland
Warner Pacific College
Western Oregon University
Willamette University

Pennsylvania

Albright College
Alvernia College
Arcadia University
Baptist Bible College of Pennsylvania
Bloomsburg University of
    Pennsylvania
Bryn Athyn College of the New
    Church
Bryn Mawr College

Bucknell University
Cabrini College
California University of Pennsylvania
Carlow University
Carnegie Mellon University
Cedar Crest College
Chatham College
Chestnut Hill College
Cheyney University of Pennsylvania
Clarion University of Pennsylvania
College Misericordia
DeSales University
Delaware Valley College
Dickinson College
Drexel University
Duquesne University
East Stroudsburg University of
    Pennsylvania
Eastern University
Edinboro University of Pennsylvania
Elizabethtown College
Franklin & Marshall College
Gannon University
Geneva College
Gettysburg College
Gratz College
Grove City College
Gwynedd-Mercy College
Haverford College
Holy Family University
Immaculata University
Indiana University of Pennsylvania
Juniata College
Keystone College
King's College
Kutztown University of Pennsylvania
La Roche College
La Salle University
Lancaster Bible College
Lebanon Valley College
Lincoln University
Lock Haven University of
    Pennsylvania
Lycoming College
Mansfield University of Pennsylvania
Marywood University
Mercyhurst College
Messiah College
Millersville University of Pennsylvania
Montgomery County Community
    College
Moore College of Art and Design
Moravian College
Mount Aloysius College
Muhlenberg College
Neumann College
Northampton County Area
    Community College
Penn State
    Altoona
    Delaware County
    Erie, The Behrend College
    Harrisburg
    University Park
Philadelphia Biblical University
Point Park University
Robert Morris University
Rosemont College
St. Francis University
St. Joseph's University
St. Vincent College
Seton Hill University
Shippensburg University of
    Pennsylvania
Slippery Rock University of
    Pennsylvania
Susquehanna University
Swarthmore College
Temple University
Thiel College
University of Pennsylvania
University of Pittsburgh

University of Pittsburgh
 Bradford
 Johnstown
University of Scranton
University of the Arts
University of the Sciences in
 Philadelphia
Ursinus College
Valley Forge Christian College
Villanova University
Washington and Jefferson College
Waynesburg College
West Chester University of
 Pennsylvania
Westminster College
Widener University
Wilkes University
Wilson College
York College of Pennsylvania

Puerto Rico

Bayamon Central University
Conservatory of Music of Puerto Rico
Inter American University of Puerto
 Rico
 Aguadilla Campus
 Arecibo Campus
 Barranquitas Campus
 Ponce Campus
 San German Campus
National College of Business &
 Technology: Arecibo
National College of Business &
 Technology: Bayamon
Universidad Adventista de las Antillas
Universidad Metropolitana
Universidad del Este
University of Puerto Rico
 Aguadilla
 Arecibo
 Cayey University College
 Humacao
 Mayaguez
 Utuado
University of the Sacred Heart

Rhode Island

Brown University
Providence College
Rhode Island College
Rhode Island School of Design
Roger Williams University
Salve Regina University
University of Rhode Island

South Carolina

Allen University
Anderson University
Benedict College
Charleston Southern University
The Citadel
Claflin University
Clemson University
Coastal Carolina University
Coker College
College of Charleston
Columbia College
Columbia International University
Converse College
Erskine College
Francis Marion University
Furman University
Greenville Technical College
Lander University
Limestone College
Morris College
Newberry College
North Greenville College
Presbyterian College
South Carolina State University
Southern Wesleyan University
University of South Carolina
University of South Carolina
 Aiken

Beaufort
Sumter
Upstate
Winthrop University
Wofford College

South Dakota

Augustana College
Black Hills State University
Dakota State University
Dakota Wesleyan University
Mount Marty College
Northern State University
South Dakota State University
University of Sioux Falls
University of South Dakota

Tennessee

Aquinas College
Austin Peay State University
Belmont University
Bethel College
Bryan College
Carson-Newman College
Christian Brothers University
Crichton College
Cumberland University
East Tennessee State University
Fisk University
Free Will Baptist Bible College
Freed-Hardeman University
Johnson Bible College
King College
Lambuth University
LeMoyne-Owen College
Lee University
Lincoln Memorial University
Lipscomb University
Maryville College
Middle Tennessee State University
Milligan College
Roane State Community College
South College
Southern Adventist University
Tennessee State University
Tennessee Technological University
Tennessee Temple University
Tennessee Wesleyan College
Trevecca Nazarene University
Tusculum College
Union University
University of Memphis
University of Tennessee
 Chattanooga
 Knoxville
University of the South
Vanderbilt University

Texas

Abilene Christian University
Angelo State University
Arlington Baptist College
Austin College
Austin Community College
Baylor University
Blinn College
Collin County Community College
 District
Concordia University at Austin
Dallas Baptist University
Dallas Christian College
East Texas Baptist University
El Centro College
El Paso Community College
Galveston College
Hardin-Simmons University
Houston Baptist University
Howard Payne University
Huston-Tillotson College
Jarvis Christian College
Lamar State College at Orange
Lamar University
Laredo Community College
LeTourneau University

Lubbock Christian University
McMurry University
Midwestern State University
Mountain View College
North Harris Montgomery
 Community College District
Our Lady of the Lake University of San
 Antonio
Paul Quinn College
Prairie View A&M University
Rice University
Richland College
St. Edward's University
St. Mary's University
Sam Houston State University
Schreiner University
Southern Methodist University
Southwestern Adventist University
Southwestern Assemblies of God
 University
Southwestern University
Stephen F. Austin State University
Sul Ross State University
Tarleton State University
Texas A&M University
Texas A&M University
 Commerce
 Galveston
 Kingsville
 Texarkana
Texas Christian University
Texas College
Texas Lutheran University
Texas Southern University
Texas State Technical College
 Harlingen
Texas State University: San Marcos
Texas Tech University
Texas Wesleyan University
Texas Woman's University
Trinity University
University of Dallas
University of Houston
University of Houston
 Clear Lake
 Downtown
 Victoria
University of Mary Hardin-Baylor
University of North Texas
University of St. Thomas
University of Texas
 Arlington
 Austin
 Brownsville
 Dallas
 El Paso
 Pan American
 San Antonio
 Tyler
 of the Permian Basin
University of the Incarnate Word
Wayland Baptist University
Weatherford College
West Texas A&M University
Wharton County Junior College
Wiley College

Utah

Brigham Young University
Southern Utah University
University of Utah
Utah State University
Utah Valley State College
Weber State University
Westminster College

Vermont

Bennington College
Castleton State College
Champlain College
College of St. Joseph in Vermont
Goddard College
Green Mountain College
Johnson State College

Lyndon State College
Middlebury College
Norwich University
St. Michael's College
University of Vermont

Virginia

Averett University
Bluefield College
Bridgewater College
Christopher Newport University
College of William and Mary
Eastern Mennonite University
Emory & Henry College
Ferrum College
George Mason University
Hampton University
Hollins University
James Madison University
Liberty University
Longwood University
Lynchburg College
Mary Baldwin College
Marymount University
New River Community College
Norfolk State University
Old Dominion University
Patrick Henry Community College
Radford University
Randolph-Macon College
Randolph-Macon Woman's College
Regent University
Roanoke College
St. Paul's College
Shenandoah University
Sweet Briar College
University of Mary Washington
University of Northern Virginia
University of Richmond
University of Virginia
University of Virginia's College at Wise
Virginia Commonwealth University
Virginia Intermont College
Virginia Military Institute
Virginia Polytechnic Institute and
 State University
Virginia State University
Virginia Union University
Virginia Wesleyan College
Washington and Lee University

Washington

Antioch University Seattle
Central Washington University
City University
Eastern Washington University
Evergreen State College
Gonzaga University
Heritage University
Northwest University
Pacific Lutheran University
Saint Martin's University
Seattle Pacific University
Seattle University
South Seattle Community College
University of Puget Sound
University of Washington
Walla Walla College
Washington State University
Western Washington University
Whitworth College

West Virginia

Alderson-Broaddus College
Appalachian Bible College
Bethany College
Bluefield State College
Concord University
Davis and Elkins College
Glenville State College
Marshall University
Ohio Valley University
Salem International University
Shepherd University

Southern West Virginia Community
    and Technical College
University of Charleston
West Liberty State College
West Virginia State University
West Virginia University
West Virginia University at
    Parkersburg
West Virginia Wesleyan College
Wheeling Jesuit University

Wisconsin

Alverno College
Beloit College
Cardinal Stritch University
Carroll College
Carthage College
Concordia University Wisconsin
Edgewood College
Lakeland College
Lawrence University
Maranatha Baptist Bible College
Marian College of Fond du Lac
Marquette University
Mount Mary College
Northland College
Ripon College
St. Norbert College
Silver Lake College
University of Wisconsin
    Eau Claire
    Green Bay
    La Crosse
    Madison
    Milwaukee
    Oshkosh
    Parkside
    Platteville
    Richland
    River Falls
    Stevens Point
    Stout
    Superior
    Whitewater
Viterbo University
Wisconsin Lutheran College

Wyoming

Northwest College
University of Wyoming

United Nations semester

Arkansas
University of Arkansas

California
Mount St. Mary's College
Occidental College
Point Loma Nazarene University
Scripps College
Sonoma State University
University of Redlands
University of the Pacific

Connecticut
Sacred Heart University
Trinity College
University of Bridgeport

Florida
Barry University
Eckerd College
Florida Southern College

Georgia
Agnes Scott College

Illinois
Illinois Wesleyan University
Lincoln Land Community College
Millikin University
North Central College

Indiana
Franklin College
Indiana University
    Bloomington
Valparaiso University
Wabash College

Iowa
Morningside College
Simpson College

Kansas
Fort Hays State University

Maryland
McDaniel College

Minnesota
University of Minnesota
    Morris

Mississippi
Millsaps College

Nebraska
Dana College
Nebraska Wesleyan University

New Hampshire
Keene State College
Southern New Hampshire University

New Jersey
College of St. Elizabeth
Drew University

New York
Alfred University
College of New Rochelle
Fordham University
Hobart and William Smith Colleges
Long Island University
    Brooklyn Campus
    C. W. Post Campus

Marist College
State University of New York
    Buffalo
    New Paltz
Utica College
Wagner College

North Carolina
Meredith College
Salem College

Ohio
Baldwin-Wallace College
College of Wooster
Muskingum College
Ohio Wesleyan University

Pennsylvania
Gettysburg College
Lycoming College
Seton Hill University
Susquehanna University
Thiel College
University of Scranton
Ursinus College

South Carolina
Furman University
Winthrop University

Texas
Hardin-Simmons University
Trinity University

Utah
Weber State University

Vermont
Sterling College

Virginia
Randolph-Macon College

West Virginia
Bethany College
Wheeling Jesuit University

Wisconsin
Carroll College
University of Wisconsin
    Milwaukee

Urban semester

Arkansas
John Brown University

California
Azusa Pacific University
California Lutheran University
Laguna College of Art and Design
Pitzer College
San Francisco Art Institute
Scripps College
Sonoma State University
University of Redlands
Westmont College

Colorado
Colorado Christian University
Colorado College

Connecticut
Trinity College
University of Bridgeport
University of Connecticut
Wesleyan University

Florida
Florida Southern College
Ringling School of Art and Design
Warner Southern College

Georgia
Savannah College of Art and Design
Spelman College
University of West Georgia

Idaho
Brigham Young University-Idaho

Illinois
Greenville College
Illinois Wesleyan University
Knox College
Lake Forest College
Millikin University
Monmouth College
North Central College
School of the Art Institute of Chicago
Trinity Christian College
Trinity International University
Wheaton College

Indiana
Anderson University
Bethel College
DePauw University
Earlham College
Goshen College
Manchester College
Taylor University
Valparaiso University
Wabash College

Iowa
Briar Cliff University
Central College
Coe College
Cornell College
Dordt College
Grinnell College
Loras College
University of Dubuque
Wartburg College

Kansas
Bethany College
Bethel College
Central Christian College of Kansas
McPherson College

Southwestern College

Kentucky
Western Kentucky University

Maine
Bates College

Maryland
Maryland Institute College of Art
McDaniel College
University of Maryland
    Eastern Shore

Massachusetts
Art Institute of Boston at Lesley
    University
Eastern Nazarene College
Gordon College
Lesley University
Montserrat College of Art
School of the Museum of Fine Arts
Stonehill College
Williams College
Worcester State College

Michigan
Albion College
Alma College
Calvin College
College for Creative Studies
Cornerstone University
Hope College
Kalamazoo College
Kendall College of Art and Design of
    Ferris State University

Minnesota
Augsburg College
Bethel University
Carleton College
Concordia College: Moorhead
Hamline University
Macalester College
Minneapolis College of Art and Design
St. Mary's University of Minnesota
St. Olaf College
University of Minnesota
    Morris
University of St. Thomas

Mississippi
Millsaps College
Tougaloo College

Missouri
Rockhurst University
Westminster College
William Woods University

Nebraska
Dana College
Hastings College
Nebraska Wesleyan University

New Hampshire
St. Anselm College

New Jersey
Berkeley College
Drew University

New Mexico
College of Santa Fe

New York
Alfred University
Bard College
Berkeley College
City University of New York
    Queens College

Clinton Community College
Colgate University
Cornell University
Eugene Lang College The New School
    for Liberal Arts
Hamilton College
Hartwick College
Hobart and William Smith Colleges
Manhattanville College
Niagara University
Onondaga Community College
State University of New York
    College at Brockport
    College at Buffalo
    College at Oneonta
    New Paltz
    Stony Brook
Vassar College

North Carolina
Duke University
Gardner-Webb University
Meredith College

Ohio
Baldwin-Wallace College
Cleveland Institute of Art
College of Wooster
Columbus College of Art and Design
Denison University
Kenyon College
Oberlin College
Ohio Wesleyan University
Ursuline College
Wittenberg University
Xavier University
Youngstown State University

Oklahoma
Southern Nazarene University

Oregon
Lewis & Clark College
Pacific Northwest College of Art
Willamette University

Pennsylvania
Albright College
East Stroudsburg University of
    Pennsylvania
Franklin & Marshall College
Gettysburg College
Indiana University of Pennsylvania
Juniata College
Lafayette College
Lebanon Valley College
Lehigh University
Mercyhurst College
Messiah College
Seton Hill University
Susquehanna University

South Dakota
Augustana College
South Dakota State University

Tennessee
Memphis College of Art

Texas
Hardin-Simmons University
Southwestern University
Trinity University

Utah
University of Utah
Weber State University

Vermont
Sterling College

Virginia
Virginia Commonwealth University

Washington
Trinity Lutheran College
Whitman College

Wisconsin
Beloit College
Lawrence University
Ripon College
Viterbo University

Alabama

Alabama Agricultural and Mechanical
    University
Birmingham-Southern College
Huntingdon College
Judson College
Spring Hill College
University of Alabama

Arizona

Arizona State University

Arkansas

Hendrix College
John Brown University
Lyon College

California

Azusa Pacific University
Biola University
California Baptist University
California Lutheran University
California State University
    Long Beach
Chapman University
Claremont McKenna College
Dominican School of Philosophy and
    Theology
Fresno Pacific University
Loyola Marymount University
Master's College
Mills College
Mount St. Mary's College
Occidental College
Pepperdine University
Point Loma Nazarene University
Pomona College
Santa Clara University
Scripps College
Simpson University
Sonoma State University
Stanford University
University of California
    Davis
    Irvine
    Los Angeles
    Riverside
    San Diego
    Santa Barbara
    Santa Cruz
University of California: Merced
University of Redlands
University of San Francisco
University of Southern California
University of the Pacific
Vanguard University of Southern
    California
Westmont College
Whittier College

Colorado

Colorado Christian University
Colorado College
Metropolitan State College of Denver
University of Denver

Connecticut

Connecticut College
Fairfield University
Quinnipiac University
Sacred Heart University
Trinity College
University of Bridgeport
University of Hartford
Wesleyan University

Delaware

University of Delaware

District of Columbia

American University
Catholic University of America
Georgetown University
Trinity University

Florida

Barry University
Eckerd College
Florida Gulf Coast University
Florida Southern College
Jacksonville University
Lynn University
Palm Beach Atlantic University
Rollins College
Stetson University
University of Miami
University of North Florida
University of South Florida
University of Tampa
University of West Florida
Warner Southern College

Georgia

Agnes Scott College
Berry College
Clark Atlanta University
Covenant College
Emory University
Georgia College and State University
Oglethorpe University
Oxford College of Emory University
Spelman College
University of Georgia

Illinois

Blackburn College
Bradley University
Dominican University
Elmhurst College
Eureka College
Greenville College
Illinois College
Illinois State University
Illinois Wesleyan University
Judson College
Knox College
Lake Forest College
Loyola University of Chicago
MacMurray College
McKendree College
Millikin University
Monmouth College
North Central College
North Park University
Olivet Nazarene University
Rockford College
Southern Illinois University
    Carbondale
Trinity Christian College
Trinity International University
University of Chicago
University of Illinois
    Urbana-Champaign
University of St. Francis
Wheaton College

Indiana

Ball State University
Bethel College
Butler University
DePauw University
Franklin College
Goshen College
Hanover College
Huntington University
Indiana University
    Bloomington
    Northwest

Indiana University-Purdue University
    Fort Wayne
St. Joseph's College
Saint Mary's College
Taylor University
University of Evansville
University of Notre Dame
Valparaiso University
Wabash College

Iowa

Briar Cliff University
Buena Vista University
Central College
Coe College
Cornell College
Dordt College
Drake University
Grand View College
Grinnell College
Iowa State University
Iowa Wesleyan College
Loras College
Luther College
Morningside College
Northwestern College
Simpson College
University of Iowa
University of Northern Iowa
Wartburg College

Kansas

Bethany College
Bethel College
Central Christian College of Kansas
MidAmerica Nazarene University
Southwestern College
Sterling College
Tabor College
University of Kansas
Wichita State University

Kentucky

Alice Lloyd College
Asbury College
Bellarmine University
Campbellsville University
Centre College
Kentucky Wesleyan College
Morehead State University
Pikeville College
Transylvania University
Western Kentucky University

Louisiana

Centenary College of Louisiana
Louisiana State University
    Shreveport
Loyola University New Orleans
Tulane University
University of Louisiana at Lafayette
University of New Orleans

Maine

Bates College
Bowdoin College
Colby College
St. Joseph's College
Unity College
University of Southern Maine

Maryland

Columbia Union College
Goucher College
Hood College
Johns Hopkins University
McDaniel College
Mount St. Mary's University
Salisbury University
Villa Julie College
Washington College

Massachusetts

Anna Maria College
Assumption College
Bay Path College
Bentley College
Boston College
Boston University
Brandeis University
Bridgewater State College
Clark University
College of the Holy Cross
Eastern Nazarene College
Elms College
Emmanuel College
Framingham State College
Gordon College
Lesley University
Massachusetts College of Liberal Arts
Merrimack College
Mount Holyoke College
Nichols College
Northeastern University
Pine Manor College
Regis College
Simmons College
Smith College
Stonehill College
Suffolk University
Tufts University
University of Massachusetts
    Dartmouth
Wellesley College
Western New England College
Westfield State College
Wheaton College
Wheelock College
Worcester Polytechnic Institute
Worcester State College

Michigan

Adrian College
Albion College
Alma College
Calvin College
Central Michigan University
Cornerstone University
Eastern Michigan University
Grand Valley State University
Hillsdale College
Hope College
Northern Michigan University
Spring Arbor University
University of Detroit Mercy
University of Michigan
University of Michigan
    Dearborn

Minnesota

Bethel University
College of St. Catherine
College of St. Scholastica
Concordia College: Moorhead
Gustavus Adolphus College
Hamline University
Macalester College
Northwestern College
St. Mary's University of Minnesota
St. Olaf College
University of Minnesota
    Morris
University of St. Thomas

Mississippi

Millsaps College
Mississippi State University
Tougaloo College

Missouri

Avila University
Culver-Stockton College
Drury University
Evangel University
Maryville University of Saint Louis

Northwest Missouri State University
Park University
Rockhurst University
Southwest Baptist University
Stephens College
Truman State University
University of Missouri
   Columbia
Washington University in St. Louis
Westminster College
William Woods University

Nebraska

Creighton University
Nebraska Wesleyan University

New Hampshire

Colby-Sawyer College
Daniel Webster College
Dartmouth College
Franklin Pierce College
Keene State College
New England College
St. Anselm College
University of New Hampshire
University of New Hampshire at
   Manchester

New Jersey

Caldwell College
Drew University
Fairleigh Dickinson University
   College at Florham
Kean University
Monmouth University
Montclair State University
New Jersey City University
Richard Stockton College of New
   Jersey
Rutgers, The State University of New
   Jersey
   New Brunswick/Piscataway
      Campus
   Newark Regional Campus
St. Peter's College
Seton Hall University
William Paterson University of New
   Jersey

New Mexico

University of New Mexico

New York

Adelphi University
Alfred University
Bard College
Cazenovia College
City University of New York
   Brooklyn College
   Lehman College
Colgate University
College of New Rochelle
Cornell University
Daemen College
Hamilton College
Hartwick College
Hilbert College
Hobart and William Smith Colleges
Hofstra University
Houghton College
Ithaca College
Jamestown Community College
Keuka College
Le Moyne College
Long Island University
   C. W. Post Campus
Manhattan College
Manhattanville College
Marist College
Nazareth College of Rochester
New York University
Niagara University
Nyack College

Roberts Wesleyan College
St. Bonaventure University
St. Francis College
St. John Fisher College
St. Lawrence University
St. Thomas Aquinas College
Siena College
Skidmore College
State University of New York
   Albany
   Binghamton
   Buffalo
   College at Brockport
   College at Buffalo
   College at Cortland
   College at Fredonia
   College at Geneseo
   College at Oneonta
   Oswego
   Stony Brook
Union College
United States Military Academy
University of Rochester
Utica College
Vassar College
Wagner College
Wells College

North Carolina

Bennett College
Campbell University
Davidson College
Duke University
East Carolina University
Elon University
Gardner-Webb University
Guilford College
Lenoir-Rhyne College
Meredith College
Methodist College
Montreat College
Pfeiffer University
Queens University of Charlotte
St. Andrews Presbyterian College
Salem College
University of North Carolina
   Asheville
   Charlotte
   Greensboro
   Pembroke
Wake Forest University
Warren Wilson College
Winston-Salem State University

Ohio

Ashland University
Baldwin-Wallace College
Bluffton University
Bowling Green State University
Capital University
Case Western Reserve University
Cedarville University
College of Wooster
Denison University
Heidelberg College
Hiram College
John Carroll University
Kent State University
Kenyon College
Malone College
Marietta College
Miami University
   Oxford Campus
Mount Vernon Nazarene University
Muskingum College
Oberlin College
Ohio Dominican University
Ohio Northern University
Ohio State University
   Columbus Campus
Ohio Wesleyan University
Otterbein College
Shawnee State University
Tiffin University

University of Cincinnati
University of Dayton
University of Findlay
Walsh University
Wilmington College
Wittenberg University
Xavier University
Youngstown State University

Oklahoma

Oklahoma City University
Oklahoma State University
Oklahoma Wesleyan University
Oral Roberts University
Southern Nazarene University
University of Oklahoma
University of Tulsa

Oregon

Corban College
George Fox University
Lewis & Clark College
Linfield College
Pacific University
Portland State University
University of Portland
Warner Pacific College
Willamette University

Pennsylvania

Albright College
Allegheny College
Alvernia College
Arcadia University
Bucknell University
Cabrini College
Carnegie Mellon University
Cedar Crest College
Chatham College
Dickinson College
Duquesne University
Eastern University
Elizabethtown College
Franklin & Marshall College
Gannon University
Geneva College
Gettysburg College
Grove City College
Immaculata University
Indiana University of Pennsylvania
Juniata College
King's College
La Roche College
Lafayette College
Lebanon Valley College
Lehigh University
Lycoming College
Mansfield University of Pennsylvania
Mercyhurst College
Messiah College
Moravian College
Muhlenberg College
Rosemont College
St. Francis University
St. Joseph's University
Seton Hill University
Shippensburg University of
   Pennsylvania
Susquehanna University
Thiel College
University of Pennsylvania
University of Pittsburgh
University of Pittsburgh
   Greensburg
University of Scranton
Ursinus College
Villanova University
Washington and Jefferson College
Waynesburg College
Westminster College
Wilson College

Puerto Rico

Inter American University of Puerto
   Rico
   Aguadilla Campus
   Barranquitas Campus
   Fajardo Campus
Universidad Metropolitana
University of Puerto Rico
   Arecibo
   Rio Piedras

Rhode Island

Providence College
Roger Williams University
Salve Regina University

South Carolina

Clemson University
College of Charleston
Columbia College
Francis Marion University
Furman University
Presbyterian College
Southern Wesleyan University
University of South Carolina
   Upstate
Wofford College

South Dakota

Augustana College
Dakota Wesleyan University
Northern State University
University of Sioux Falls

Tennessee

Belmont University
Bryan College
Carson-Newman College
Crichton College
King College
Lambuth University
Lee University
Maryville College
Milligan College
Rhodes College
Tennessee Temple University
Union University
University of the South
Vanderbilt University

Texas

Austin College
Dallas Baptist University
East Texas Baptist University
Hardin-Simmons University
Jarvis Christian College
Midland College
St. Mary's University
Southern Methodist University
Southwestern University
Texas Christian University
Texas Lutheran University
Texas State University: San Marcos
Trinity University
University of Houston
University of Texas
   Austin
   Dallas
West Texas A&M University

Utah

Brigham Young University
University of Utah
Weber State University

Vermont

Middlebury College
St. Michael's College
Sterling College
University of Vermont

Virginia

Averett University
Bridgewater College
College of William and Mary
Eastern Mennonite University
Hampden-Sydney College
Hollins University
James Madison University
Randolph-Macon College
Randolph-Macon Woman's College
Roanoke College
Sweet Briar College
University of Mary Washington
University of Richmond
Virginia Commonwealth University
Virginia Polytechnic Institute and
    State University
Washington and Lee University

Washington

Gonzaga University
Northwest University
Saint Martin's University
Seattle Pacific University
University of Washington
Whitman College
Whitworth College

West Virginia

Bethany College
Davis and Elkins College
Marshall University
Salem International University
Shepherd University
University of Charleston
West Liberty State College
West Virginia University
West Virginia Wesleyan College
Wheeling Jesuit University

Wisconsin

Beloit College
Carroll College
Carthage College
Lawrence University
Marquette University
Ripon College
St. Norbert College
University of Wisconsin
    Milwaukee
Viterbo University

Wyoming

University of Wyoming

Colleges in this book

Alabama

Alabama Agricultural and Mechanical University, www.aamu.edu
Alabama Southern Community College, www.ascc.edu
Alabama State University, www.alasu.edu
American Sentinel University, www.accis.edu
Andrew Jackson University, www.aju.edu
Athens State University, www.athens.edu
Auburn University, www.auburn.edu
Auburn University at Montgomery, www.aum.edu
Auburn University: College of Veterinary Medicine, Auburn 36849
Auburn University: School of Pharmacy, Auburn 36849
Beeson Divinity School at Samford University, Birmingham 35229
Bevill State Community College, www.bscc.edu
Birmingham-Southern College, www.bsc.edu
Bishop State Community College, www.bishop.edu
Calhoun Community College, www.calhoun.edu
Central Alabama Community College, www.cacc.cc.al.us
Chattahoochee Valley Community College, www.cv.edu
Columbia Southern University, www.columbiasouthern.edu
Community College of the Air Force, www.au.af.mil/au/ccaf
Concordia College, www.concordiaselma.edu
Enterprise-Ozark Community College, www.eocc.edu
Faulkner State Community College, www.faulknerstate.edu
Faulkner University, www.faulkner.edu
Gadsden State Community College, www.gadsdenstate.edu
George C. Wallace Community College at Dothan, www.wallace.edu
George C. Wallace State Community College at Selma, wccs.edu
Heritage Christian University, www.hcu.edu
Herzing College, www.herzing.edu
Huntingdon College, www.huntingdon.edu
Huntsville Bible College, www.huntsvillebiblecollege.com/
J. F. Drake State Technical College, www.drakestate.edu
Jacksonville State University, www.jsu.edu
Jefferson Davis Community College, www.jdcc.edu
Jefferson State Community College, www.jeffstateonline.com
Judson College, www.judson.edu
Lawson State Community College, www.lawsonstate.edu
Lurleen B. Wallace Community College, www.lbw.edu
Marion Military Institute, www.marionmilitary.edu
Miles College, www.miles.edu
Northeast Alabama Community College, www.nacc.edu
Northwest-Shoals Community College, www.nwscc.edu
Oakwood College, www.oakwood.edu
Prince Institute of Professional Studies, www.princeinstitute.edu
Remington College: Mobile, www.educationamerica.com
Samford University, www.samford.edu
Samford University: Cumberland School of Law, Birmingham 35229
Samford University: McWhorter School of Pharmacy, Birmingham 35229
Shelton State Community College, www.sheltonstate.edu
Snead State Community College, www.snead.edu
South University, www.southuniversity.edu
Southeastern Bible College, www.sebc.edu
Southern Christian University, www.southernchristian.edu
Southern Christian University: First Professional, Montgomery 36117
Southern Union State Community College, suscc.edu
Spring Hill College, www.shc.edu
Stillman College, www.stillman.edu
Talladega College, www.talladega.edu
Thomas Goode Jones School of Law–Faulkner University, Montgomery 36109
Trenholm State Technical College, www.trenholmtech.cc.al.us
Troy University, www.troy.edu
Tuskegee University, www.tuskegee.edu
Tuskegee University: School of Veterinary Medicine, Tuskegee 36088
University of Alabama, www.ua.edu
University of Alabama at Birmingham, www.uab.edu
University of Alabama at Birmingham: School of Dentistry, Birmingham 35294
University of Alabama at Birmingham: School of Medicine, Birmingham 35294
University of Alabama at Birmingham: School of Optometry, Birmingham 35294
University of Alabama in Huntsville, www.uah.edu
University of Alabama: School of Law, Tuscaloosa 35487
University of Mobile, www.umobile.edu
University of Montevallo, www.montevallo.edu
University of North Alabama, www.una.edu
University of South Alabama, www.southalabama.edu
University of South Alabama: School of Medicine, Mobile 36688
University of West Alabama, www.uwa.edu
Virginia College, www.vc.edu
Virginia College Technical, www.vctechnical.com
Virginia College at Huntsville, www.vc.edu
Wallace State Community College at Hanceville, www.wallacestate.edu

Alaska

Alaska Bible College, www.akbible.edu
Alaska Pacific University, www.alaskapacific.edu
Charter College, www.chartercollege.edu
Prince William Sound Community College, www.pwscc.edu
Sheldon Jackson College, www.sj-alaska.edu
University of Alaska Anchorage, www.uaa.alaska.edu
University of Alaska Fairbanks, www.uaf.edu
University of Alaska Southeast, www.uas.alaska.edu

Arizona

American Indian College of the Assemblies of God, www.aicag.edu
Arizona State University, www.asu.edu
Arizona State University West, www.west.asu.edu
Arizona State University: College of Law, Tempe 85287
Arizona Western College, www.azwestern.edu
Art Center Design College, www.theartcenter.edu
Bryman School, www.hightechschools.com
Central Arizona College, www.centralaz.edu
Chandler-Gilbert Community College: Pecos, www.cgc.maricopa.edu
Chandler-Gilbert Community College: Williams Campus, www.cgc.maricopa.edu
Chaparral College, www.chap-col.edu
Cochise College, www.cochise.edu
Coconino County Community College, www.coconino.edu
Collins College, www.collinscollege.edu
DeVry University: Phoenix, www.devry-phx.edu
Dine College, www.dinecollege.edu
Eastern Arizona College, www.eac.edu
Embry-Riddle Aeronautical University: Prescott Campus, www.embryriddle.edu
Estrella Mountain Community College, www.emc.maricopa.edu
Everest College, www.everest-college.com
Gateway Community College, www.gwc.maricopa.edu
Glendale Community College, www.gc.maricopa.edu
Grand Canyon University, www.gcu.net
High-Tech Institute, www.hightechinstitute.edu
International Institute of the Americas: Mesa, www.iia.edu
International Institute of the Americas: Phoenix, www.iia.edu
International Institute of the Americas: Tucson, www.iia.edu
International Institute of the Americas: West Valley, www.iia.edu
Lamson College, www.lamsoncollege.com
Long Technical College, www.longtechnicalcollege.com
Mesa Community College, www.mc.maricopa.edu
Metropolitan College of Court Reporting, www.metropolitancollege.edu
Mohave Community College, www.mohave.edu
Northcentral University, www.ncu.edu
Northern Arizona University, www.nau.edu
Northland Pioneer College, www.npc.edu
Paradise Valley Community College, www.pvc.maricopa.edu
Paralegal Institute, www.theparalegalinstitute.com
Phoenix College, www.pc.maricopa.edu
Pima Community College, www.pima.edu
Prescott College, www.prescott.edu
Refrigeration School, www.refrigerationschool.com
Rio Salado College, www.riosalado.edu
Scottsdale Community College, www.sc.maricopa.edu
South Mountain Community College, www.smc.maricopa.edu
Southwestern College, www.swcaz.edu
Tohono O'odham Community College, www.tocc.cc.az.us
Tucson Design College, www.tucsondesigncollege.edu
Universal Technical Institute, www.uticorp.com
University of Advancing Technology, www.uat.edu
University of Arizona, www.arizona.edu
University of Arizona: College of Law, Tucson 85721
University of Arizona: College of Medicine, Tucson 85724
University of Arizona: College of Pharmacy, Tucson 85721
University of Phoenix, www.phoenix.edu

Western International University, www.wintu.edu

Yavapai College, www.yc.edu

Arkansas

Arkansas Baptist College, www.arbaptcol.edu

Arkansas Northeastern College, www.anc.edu

Arkansas State University, www.astate.edu

Arkansas State University: Beebe, www.asub.edu

Arkansas State University: Mountain Home, www.asumh.edu

Arkansas State University: Newport, www.asun.edu

Arkansas Tech University, www.atu.edu

Black River Technical College, www.blackrivertech.org

Central Baptist College, www.cbc.edu

Cossatot Community College of the University of Arkansas, http://cccua.edu

Crowley's Ridge College, www.crowleysridgecollege.edu

East Arkansas Community College, www.eacc.edu

Ecclesia College, www.ecollege.edu

Harding University, www.harding.edu

Henderson State University, www.getreddie.com

Hendrix College, www.hendrix.edu

John Brown University, www.jbu.edu

Lyon College, www.lyon.edu

Mid-South Community College, www.midsouthcc.edu

National Park Community College, www.npcc.edu

North Arkansas College, www.northark.edu

Northwest Arkansas Community College, www.nwacc.edu

Ouachita Baptist University, www.obu.edu

Ouachita Technical College, www.otcweb.edu

Ozarka College, www.ozarka.edu

Philander Smith College, www.philander.edu

Phillips Community College of the University of Arkansas, www.pccua.edu

Pulaski Technical College, www.pulaskitech.edu

Remington College: Little Rock, www.remingtoncollege.edu

Rich Mountain Community College, www.rmcc.edu

South Arkansas Community College, www.southark.edu

Southeast Arkansas College, www.seark.edu

Southern Arkansas University, www.saumag.edu

Southern Arkansas University Tech, www.sautech.edu

University of Arkansas, www.uark.edu

University of Arkansas Community College at Morrilton, www.uaccm.edu

University of Arkansas at Fort Smith, www.uafortsmith.edu

University of Arkansas at Little Rock, www.ualr.edu

University of Arkansas at Little Rock: School of Law, Little Rock 72202

University of Arkansas at Monticello, www.uamont.edu

University of Arkansas at Pine Bluff, www.uapb.edu

University of Arkansas for Medical Sciences, www.uams.edu

University of Arkansas for Medical Sciences: College of Medicine, Little Rock 72205

University of Arkansas for Medical Sciences: College of Pharmacy, Little Rock 72205

University of Arkansas: Community College at Batesville, www.uaccb.edu

University of Arkansas: Community College at Hope, www.uacch.edu

University of Arkansas: School of Law, Fayetteville 72701

University of Central Arkansas, www.uca.edu

University of the Ozarks, www.ozarks.edu

Williams Baptist College, www.wbcoll.edu

California

Academy of Art University, www.academyart.edu

Allan Hancock College, www.hancockcollege.edu

Alliant International University, www.alliant.edu

American Academy of Dramatic Arts: West, www.aada.org

American Baptist Seminary of the West, www.absw.edu

American River College, www.arc.losrios.edu

Antelope Valley College, www.avc.edu

Antioch University Los Angeles, www.antiochla.edu

Antioch University Santa Barbara, www.antiochsb.edu

Art Center College of Design, www.artcenter.edu

Art Institute of California: Los Angeles, www.aila.artinstitutes.edu

Art Institute of California: Orange County, www.aicaoc.artinstitutes.edu

Art Institute of California: San Diego, www.aicasd.artinstitutes.edu

Art Institute of California: San Francisco, www.aicasf.aii.edu

Azusa Pacific University, www.apu.edu

Azusa Pacific University: School of Theology, Azusa 91702

Bakersfield College, www.bakersfieldcollege.edu

Barstow College, www.barstow.edu

Bethany University, www.bethany.edu

Bethesda Christian University, www.bcu.edu

Biola University, www.biola.edu

Brooks College, www.brookscollege.edu

Brooks Institute of Photography, www.brooks.edu

Butte College, www.butte.edu

Cabrillo College, www.cabrillo.edu

California Baptist University, www.calbaptist.edu

California College of Podiatric Medicine, San Francisco 94115

California College of the Arts, www.cca.edu

California Culinary Academy, www.caculinary.edu

California Design College, www.cdc.edu

California Institute of Integral Studies, www.ciis.edu

California Institute of Technology, www.caltech.edu

California Institute of the Arts, www.calarts.edu

California Lutheran University, www.clunet.edu

California Maritime Academy, www.csum.edu

California National University for Advanced Studies, www.cnuas.edu

California Polytechnic State University: San Luis Obispo, www.calpoly.edu

California School of Culinary Arts, www.csca.edu

California State Polytechnic University: Pomona, www.csupomona.edu

California State University: Bakersfield, www.csub.edu

California State University: Chico, www.csuchico.edu

California State University: Dominguez Hills, www.csudh.edu

California State University: East Bay, www.csueastbay.edu

California State University: Fresno, www.csufresno.edu

California State University: Fullerton, www.fullerton.edu

California State University: Long Beach, www.csulb.edu

California State University: Los Angeles, www.calstatela.edu

California State University: Monterey Bay, www.csumb.edu

California State University: Northridge, www.csun.edu

California State University: Sacramento, www.csus.edu

California State University: San Bernardino, www.csusb.edu

California State University: San Marcos, www.csusm.edu

California State University: Stanislaus, www.csustan.edu

California Western School of Law, San Diego 92101

Canada College, canadacollege.edu

Cerritos Community College, www.cerritos.edu

Cerro Coso Community College, www.cerrocoso.edu

Chabot College, www.chabotcollege.edu

Chaffey College, www.chaffey.edu

Chapman University, www.chapman.edu

Charles R. Drew University of Medicine and Science, www.cdrewu.edu

Church Divinity School of the Pacific, www.cdsp.edu

Citrus College, www.citruscollege.edu

City College of San Francisco, www.ccsf.edu

Claremont McKenna College, www.claremontmckenna.edu

Claremont School of Theology, Claremont 91711

Cleveland Chiropractic College of Los Angeles, Los Angeles 90004

Coastline Community College, www.coastline.cccd.edu

Cogswell Polytechnical College, www.cogswell.edu

Coleman College, www.coleman.edu

College of Alameda, alameda.peralta.edu

College of Marin: Kentfield, www.marin.cc.ca.us

College of Oceaneering, www.natpoly.edu

College of San Mateo, www.collegeofsanmateo.edu

College of the Canyons, www.canyons.edu

College of the Desert, www.collegeofthedesert.edu

College of the Redwoods, www.redwoods.edu

College of the Sequoias, www.cos.edu

College of the Siskiyous, www.siskiyous.edu

Columbia College, www.gocolumbia.org

Columbia College: Hollywood, www.columbiacollege.edu

Concorde Career College, www.concordecareercolleges.com

Concordia University, www.cui.edu

Contra Costa College, www.contracosta.edu

Copper Mountain College, www.cmccd.edu

Cosumnes River College, www.crc.losrios.edu

Crafton Hills College, www.craftonhills.edu

Cuesta College, www.cuesta.org

Cuyamaca College, www.cuyamaca.net

Cypress College, www.cypress.cc.ca.us

De Anza College, www.deanza.edu

DeVry University: Fremont, www.devry.edu

DeVry University: Long Beach, www.devry.edu

DeVry University: Pomona, www.devry.edu

DeVry University: West Hills, www.devry.edu

Deep Springs College, www.deepsprings.edu

Design Institute of San Diego, www.disd.edu

Diablo Valley College, www.dvc.edu

Dominican School of Philosophy and Theology, Berkeley 94709

Dominican School of Philosophy and Theology, www.dspt.edu

Dominican University of California, www.dominican.edu

East Los Angeles College, www.elac.edu

El Camino College, www.elcamino.edu

Empire College, www.empcol.edu

Evergreen Valley College, www.evc.edu

Fashion Careers College, www.fashioncareerscollege.com

Fashion Institute of Design and Merchandising, www.fidm.edu

Fashion Institute of Design and Merchandising: San Diego, www.fidm.edu

Fashion Institute of Design and Merchandising: San Francisco, www.fidm.com

Feather River College, www.frc.edu

Foothill College, www.foothill.edu

Franciscan School of Theology, Berkeley 94709

Fresno City College, www.fresnocitycollege.edu

Fresno Pacific University, www.fresno.edu

Fuller Theological Seminary, Pasadena 91182

Fullerton College, www.fullcoll.edu

Gavilan Community College, www.gavilan.edu

Glendale Community College, www.glendale.edu

Golden Gate Baptist Theological Seminary, Mill Valley 94941

Golden Gate University, www.ggu.edu

Golden Gate University: School of Law, San Francisco 94105
Golden West College, www.gwc.info
Grossmont Community College, www.grossmont.edu
Harvey Mudd College, www.hmc.edu
Heald College: Fresno, www.heald.edu
Heald College: Rancho Cordova, www.heald.edu
Heald College: Roseville, www.heald.edu
Heald College: Salinas, www.heald.edu
Heald College: San Jose, www.heald.edu
Heald College: Stockton, www.heald.edu
Hebrew Union College-Jewish Institute of Religion, Los Angeles 90007
Holy Names University, www.hnu.edu
Hope International University, www.hiu.edu
Humboldt State University, www.humboldt.edu
Humphreys College, www.humphreys.edu
Humphreys College: School of Law, Stockton 95207
Imperial Valley College, www.imperial.edu
Institute of Computer Technology, www.ictcollege.edu
International School of Theology, San Bernardino 92414
International Technological University, www.itu.edu/
Irvine Valley College, www.ivc.edu
Jesuit School of Theology at Berkeley: Professional, Berkeley 94709
John F. Kennedy University, www.jfku.edu
John F. Kennedy University: School of Law, Orinda 94563
King's College and Seminary, www.kingscollege.edu
LIFE Pacific College, www.lifepacific.edu
La Sierra University, www.lasierra.edu
Laguna College of Art and Design, www.lagunacollege.edu
Lake Tahoe Community College, www.ltcc.edu
Laney College, www.peralta.cc.ca.us
Las Positas College, www.laspositas.cc.ca.us
Lassen College, www.lassencollege.edu
Life Chiropractic College West, San Lorenzo 94580
Lincoln University, www.lincolnuca.edu
Loma Linda University, www.llu.edu
Loma Linda University: School of Dentistry, Loma Linda 92350
Loma Linda University: School of Medicine, Loma Linda 92350
Long Beach City College, www.lbcc.edu
Los Angeles City College, www.lacitycollege.edu
Los Angeles College of Chiropractic, Whittier 90604
Los Angeles Harbor College, www.lahc.edu
Los Angeles Mission College, www.lamission.cc.ca.us
Los Angeles Pierce College, www.piercecollege.edu
Los Angeles Southwest College, www.lasc.cc.ca.us
Los Angeles Trade and Technical College, www.lattc.edu
Los Angeles Valley College, www.lavc.edu

Los Medanos College, www.losmedanos.edu
Loyola Marymount University, www.lmu.edu
Loyola Marymount University: School of Law, Los Angeles 90015
MTI College, www.mticollege.edu
Maric College: Anaheim, www.mariccollege.edu
Maric College: Panorama City, www.mariccollege.edu
Maric College: Sacramento, www.mariccollege.edu
Maric College: Vista, www.mariccollege.edu
Marymount College, www.marymountpv.edu
Master's College, www.masters.edu
McGeorge School of Law: University of the Pacific, Sacramento 95817
Mendocino College, www.mendocino.edu
Menlo College, www.menlo.edu
Mennonite Brethren Biblical Seminary, Fresno 93727
Merced College, www.merced.cc.ca.us
Merritt College, www.merritt.edu
Mills College, www.mills.edu
MiraCosta College, www.miracosta.edu
Mission College, www.missioncollege.org
Modesto Junior College, www.mjc.edu
Monterey Peninsula College, www.mpc.edu
Moorpark College, www.moorpark.net
Mount St. Mary's College, www.msmc.la.edu
Mount San Antonio College, www.mtsac.edu
Mount San Jacinto College, www.msjc.edu
Mt. Sierra College, www.mtsierra.edu
Napa Valley College, www.napavalley.edu
National Hispanic University, www.nhu.edu
National Institute of Technology, www.nitschools.com
National University, www.nu.edu
NewSchool of Architecture & Design, www.newschoolarch.edu
Northwestern College, www.ntcollege.com
Northwestern Polytechnic University, www.npu.edu
Notre Dame de Namur University, www.ndnu.edu
Occidental College, www.oxy.edu
Ohlone College, www.ohlone.cc.ca.us
Orange Coast College, www.orangecoastcollege.edu
Otis College of Art and Design, www.otis.edu
Oxnard College, www.oxnard.cc.ca.us
Pacific Lutheran Theological Seminary, Berkeley 94708
Pacific Oaks College, www.pacificoaks.edu
Pacific School of Religion, Berkeley 94709
Pacific States University, www.psuca.edu
Pacific Union College, www.puc.edu
Palmer College of Chiropractic-West, San Jose 95134
Palo Verde College, www.paloverde.edu
Palomar College, www.palomar.edu
Pasadena City College, www.pasadena.edu

Patten University, www.patten.edu
Pepperdine University, www.pepperdine.edu
Pepperdine University: School of Law, Malibu 90263
Pitzer College, www.pitzer.edu
Platt College: Cerritos, www.westerncollegesocal.com
Platt College: Los Angeles, www.plattcollege.edu
Platt College: Newport Beach, www.plattcollege.edu
Platt College: Ontario, www.plattcollege.edu
Platt College: San Diego, www.platt.edu
Point Loma Nazarene University, www.ptloma.edu
Pomona College, www.pomona.edu
Porterville College, www.portervillecollege.edu
Professional Golfers Career College, www.progolfed.com
Queen of the Holy Rosary College, www.msjdominicans.org/college.html
Reedley College, www.reedleycollege.edu
Remington College: San Diego, www.remingtoncollege.edu
Rio Hondo College, www.riohondo.edu
Riverside Community College, www.rcc.edu
Sacramento City College, www.scc.losrios.edu
Saddleback College, www.saddleback.edu
Sage College, www.sagecollege.edu
St. John's Seminary, Camarillo 93012
St. Mary's College of California, www.stmarys-ca.edu
St. Patrick's Seminary, Menlo Park 94025
Salvation Army Crestmont College, www.crestmont.edu
Samuel Merritt College, www.samuelmerritt.edu
San Bernardino Valley College, www.valleycollege.edu
San Diego Christian College, www.sdcc.edu
San Diego City College, www.sdccd.edu
San Diego Mesa College, www.sandiegomesacollege.net
San Diego Miramar College, www.miramarcollege.net
San Diego State University, www.sdsu.edu
San Francisco Art Institute, www.sfai.edu
San Francisco Conservatory of Music, www.sfcm.edu
San Francisco State University, www.sfsu.edu
San Francisco Theological Seminary, San Anselmo 94960
San Joaquin Delta College, www.deltacollege.edu
San Joaquin Valley College Inc., www.sjvc.edu
San Jose City College, www.sjcc.edu
San Jose State University, www.sjsu.edu
Santa Ana College, www.sac.edu
Santa Barbara Business College, www.sbbcollege.edu
Santa Barbara Business College: Bakersfield, www.sbbcollege.edu
Santa Barbara Business College: Santa Maria, www.sbbcollege.com
Santa Barbara Business College: Ventura, www.sbbcollege.edu

Santa Barbara City College, www.sbcc.edu
Santa Clara University, www.scu.edu
Santa Clara University: School of Law, Santa Clara 95053
Santa Monica College, www.smc.edu
Santa Rosa Junior College, www.santarosa.edu
Santiago Canyon College, www.sccollege.edu
Scripps College, www.scrippscollege.edu
Shasta College, www.shastacollege.edu
Sierra College, www.sierracollege.edu
Simpson University, www.simpsonuniversity.edu
Skyline College, skylinecollege.net
Soka University of America, www.soka.edu/
Solano Community College, www.solano.edu
Sonoma State University, www.sonoma.edu
Southern California College of Optometry, Fullerton 92631
Southern California Institute of Architecture, www.sciarc.edu
Southern California Institute of Technology, www.scit-scu.edu
Southwestern College, www.swc.cc.ca.us
Southwestern University School of Law, Los Angeles 90005
Stanford University, www.stanford.edu
Stanford University: School of Law, Stanford 94305
Stanford University: School of Medicine, Stanford 94304
Starr King School for the Ministry, Berkeley 94709
Taft College, www.taft.cc.ca.us
Talbot School of Theology of Biola University, La Mirada 90639
Thomas Aquinas College, www.thomasaquinas.edu
Thomas Jefferson School of Law, www.jeffersonlaw.edu
University of California Berkeley: School of Law, Berkeley 94720
University of California Berkeley: School of Optometry, Berkeley 94720
University of California Davis: School of Law, Davis 95616
University of California Davis: School of Medicine, Davis 95616
University of California Davis: School of Veterinary Medicine, Davis 95616
University of California Hastings College of the Law, San Francisco 94102
University of California Irvine: College of Medicine, Irvine 92697
University of California Los Angeles: School of Dentistry, Los Angeles 90095
University of California Los Angeles: School of Law, Los Angeles 90095
University of California Los Angeles: School of Medicine, Los Angeles 90095
University of California San Diego: School of Medicine, La Jolla 92093
University of California San Francisco: School of Dentistry, San Francisco 94143
University of California San Francisco: School of Medicine, San Francisco 94143

University of California San Francisco: School of Pharmacy, San Francisco 94143

University of California: Berkeley, www.berkeley.edu

University of California: Davis, www.ucdavis.edu

University of California: Irvine, www.uci.edu

University of California: Los Angeles, www.ucla.edu

University of California: Merced, www.ucmerced.edu

University of California: Riverside, www.ucr.edu

University of California: San Diego, www.ucsd.edu

University of California: Santa Barbara, www.ucsb.edu

University of California: Santa Cruz, www.ucsc.edu

University of Judaism, www.uj.edu

University of La Verne, www.ulv.edu

University of La Verne College of Law at San Fernando Valley, Woodland Hills 91367

University of La Verne: School of Law, La Verne 91750

University of Redlands, www.redlands.edu

University of San Diego, www.sandiego.edu

University of San Diego: School of Law, San Diego 92110

University of San Francisco, www.usfca.edu

University of San Francisco: School of Law, San Francisco 94117

University of Southern California, www.usc.edu

University of Southern California: Law School, Los Angeles 90089

University of Southern California: School of Dentistry, Los Angeles 90089

University of Southern California: School of Medicine, Los Angeles 90033

University of Southern California: School of Pharmacy, Los Angeles 90033

University of West Los Angeles: School of Law, Inglewood 90301

University of the Pacific, www.pacific.edu

University of the Pacific: School of Dentistry, San Francisco 94115

University of the Pacific: School of Pharmacy, Stockton 95211

Vanguard University of Southern California, www.vanguard.edu

Ventura College, www.venturacollege.edu

Victor Valley College, www.vvc.edu

Vista Community College, www.peralta.cc.ca.us

West Coast University, www.westcoastuniversity.com/

West Hills Community College, www.westhillscollege.com

West Los Angeles College, www.wlac.edu

West Valley College, www.westvalley.edu

Western Career College: Emeryville, www.siliconvalley.edu

Western Career College: Pleasant Hill, www.westerncollege.edu

Western Career College: San Jose, www.svcollege.com

Western Career College: San Leandro, www.westerncollege.edu

Western Career College: Walnut Creek, www.westerncollege.edu

Western State University College of Law, www.wsulaw.edu

Western University of Health Sciences, Pomona 91766

Westminster Theological Seminary in California, Escondido 92027

Westmont College, www.westmont.edu

Westwood College, www.westwood.edu

Westwood College of Technology: Inland Empire, www.westwood.edu

Westwood College: Long Beach, Long Beach 90502

Westwood College: Los Angeles, www.westwood.edu

Whittier College, www.whittier.edu

Whittier Law School, Los Angeles 90020

William Jessup University, www.jessup.edu

Woodbury University, www.woodbury.edu

WyoTech Institute: Fremont, www.wyotech.com

Yuba Community College District, www.yccd.edu

Colorado

Adams State College, www.adams.edu

Aims Community College, www.aims.edu

Arapahoe Community College, www.arapahoe.edu

Art Institute of Colorado, www.aic.artinstitutes.edu

Bel-Rea Institute of Animal Technology, www.bel-rea.com

Blair College, www.cci.edu

Boulder College of Massage Therapy, www.bcmt.org

Cambridge College, www.hightechschools.edu

CollegeAmerica-Denver, www.collegeamerica.com

Colorado Christian University, www.ccu.edu

Colorado College, www.coloradocollege.edu

Colorado Mountain College: Alpine Campus, www.coloradomtn.edu

Colorado Mountain College: Spring Valley Campus, www.coloradomtn.edu

Colorado Mountain College: Timberline Campus, www.coloradomtn.edu

Colorado Northwestern Community College, www.cncc.edu

Colorado School of Healing Arts, www.csha.net

Colorado School of Mines, www.mines.edu

Colorado School of Trades, www.schooloftrades.com

Colorado State University, www.colostate.edu

Colorado State University: College of Veterinary Medicine and Biomedical Sciences, Fort Collins 80523

Colorado State University: Pueblo, www.colostate-pueblo.edu

Colorado Technical University, www.coloradotech.edu

Community College of Aurora, www.ccaurora.edu

Community College of Denver, http://ccd.rightchoice.org

Concorde Career College, www.concorde.edu/denver/

DeVry University: Colorado Springs, www.cs.devry.edu

DeVry University: Westminster, www.den.devry.edu

Denver Academy of Court Reporting, www.dacr.org

Denver Automotive & Diesel College, www.dadc.com

Denver Conservative Baptist Seminary, Denver 80250

Fort Lewis College, www.fortlewis.edu

Front Range Community College, www.frcc.cc.co.us

Heritage College, www.heritage-education.com

Iliff School of Theology, Denver 80210

Institute of Business & Medical Careers, www.ibmc.edu

IntelliTec College: Grand Junction, www.intelliteccollege.com

Johnson & Wales University, www.jwu.edu

Jones International University, www.jonesinternational.edu

Mesa State College, www.mesastate.edu

Metropolitan State College of Denver, www.mscd.edu

Morgan Community College, www.morgancc.edu

Naropa University, www.naropa.edu

National American University: Denver, www.national.edu

Nazarene Bible College, www.nbc.edu

Northeastern Junior College, www.njc.edu

Otero Junior College, www.ojc.edu

Parks College, www.cci.edu

Parks College: Aurora, www.cci.edu

Pikes Peak Community College, www.ppcc.edu

Pueblo Community College, www.pueblocc.edu

Red Rocks Community College, www.rrcc.cccoes.edu

Regis University, www.regis.edu

Remington College: Colorado Springs, www.remingtoncollege.com

Rocky Mountain College of Art & Design, www.rmcad.edu

Teikyo Loretto Heights University, www.tlhu.edu

Trinidad State Junior College, www.trinidadstate.edu

United States Air Force Academy, www.usafa.edu

University of Colorado Health Sciences Center: College of Pharmacy, Denver 80262

University of Colorado Health Sciences Center: School of Dentistry, Denver 80262

University of Colorado Health Sciences Center: School of Medicine, Denver 80262

University of Colorado at Boulder, www.colorado.edu

University of Colorado at Boulder: School of Law, Boulder 80309

University of Colorado at Colorado Springs, www.uccs.edu

University of Colorado at Denver and Health Sciences Center, www.ucdhsc.edu

University of Denver, http://www.du.edu/

University of Denver: College of Law, Denver 80220

University of Northern Colorado, www.unco.edu

Western State College of Colorado, www.western.edu

Westwood College of Technology, www.westwood.edu

Westwood College of Technology: South, www.westwood.edu

Yeshiva Toras Chaim Talmudical Seminary, Denver 80204

Connecticut

Albertus Magnus College, www.albertus.edu

Asnuntuck Community College, www.acc.commnet.edu

Beth Benjamin Academy of Connecticut, Stamford 06901

Briarwood College, www.briarwood.edu

Capital Community College, www.ccc.commnet.edu

Central Connecticut State University, www.ccsu.edu

Charter Oak State College, www.charteroak.edu

Connecticut College, www.conncoll.edu

Eastern Connecticut State University, www.easternct.edu

Fairfield University, www.fairfield.edu

Gateway Community College, www.gwcc.commnet.edu

Gibbs College, www.gibbscollege.com

Goodwin College, www.goodwin.edu

Holy Apostles College and Seminary, www.holyapostles.edu

Holy Apostles College and Seminary, Cromwell 06416

Housatonic Community College, www.hcc.commnet.edu

International College of Hospitality Management, www.ichm.edu

Lyme Academy College of Fine Arts, www.lymeacademy.edu

Manchester Community College, www.mcc.commnet.edu

Middlesex Community College, www.mxcc.commnet.edu

Mitchell College, www.mitchell.edu

Naugatuck Valley Community College, www.nvcc.commnet.edu

Northwestern Connecticut Community College, www.nwctc.commnet.edu

Norwalk Community College, www.ncc.commnet.edu

Paier College of Art, www.paiercollegeofart.edu

Post University, www.post.edu

Quinebaug Valley Community College, www.qvcc.commnet.edu

Quinnipiac College: School of Law, Hamden 06518

Quinnipiac University, www.quinnipiac.edu

Sacred Heart University, www.sacredheart.edu

St. Joseph College, www.sjc.edu

St. Vincent's College, www.stvincentscollege.edu

Southern Connecticut State University, www.southernct.edu

Three Rivers Community College, www.trcc.commnet.edu

Trinity College, www.trincoll.edu

Tunxis Community College, www.tunxis.commnet.edu

United States Coast Guard Academy, www.cga.edu

University of Bridgeport, www.bridgeport.edu

University of Bridgeport College of Chiropractic, Bridgeport 06601

University of Connecticut, www.uconn.edu

University of Connecticut Health Center School of Medicine, Farmington 06032
University of Connecticut: School of Dentistry, Farmington 06030
University of Connecticut: School of Law, Hartford 06105
University of Connecticut: School of Pharmacy, Storrs 06269
University of Hartford, www.hartford.edu
University of New Haven, www.newhaven.edu
Wesleyan University, www.wesleyan.edu
Western Connecticut State University, www.wcsu.edu
Yale Law School, New Haven 06520
Yale University, www.yale.edu
Yale University: Divinity School, New Haven 06511
Yale University: School of Medicine, New Haven 06510

Delaware

Delaware College of Art and Design, www.dcad.edu
Delaware State University, www.desu.edu
Delaware Technical and Community College: Owens Campus, www.dtcc.edu
Delaware Technical and Community College: Stanton/Wilmington Campus, www.dtcc.edu
Delaware Technical and Community College: Terry Campus, www.dtcc.edu
Goldey-Beacom College, www.gbc.edu
University of Delaware, www.udel.edu
Wesley College, www.wesley.edu
Widener University School of Law, Wilmington 19803
Wilmington College, www.wilmcoll.edu

District of Columbia

American University, www.american.edu
American University: Washington College of Law, Washington 20016
Catholic University of America, www.cua.edu
Catholic University of America: School of Law, Washington 20064
Catholic University of America: School of Theology, Washington 20064
Corcoran College of Art and Design, www.corcoran.edu
Dominican House of Studies, Washington 20017
Gallaudet University, www.gallaudet.edu
George Washington University, www.gwu.edu
George Washington University Law School, Washington 20052
George Washington University: School of Medicine and Health Sciences, Washington 20037
Georgetown University, www.georgetown.edu
Georgetown University: Law Center, Washington 20001
Georgetown University: School of Medicine, Washington 20007
Howard University, www.howard.edu
Howard University: College of Dentistry, Washington 20059

Howard University: Divinity School, Washington 20017
Howard University: School of Law, Washington 20008
Howard University: School of Medicine, Washington 20059
Howard University: School of Pharmacy, Washington 20059
Potomac College, www.potomac.edu
Southeastern University, www.seu.edu
Strayer University, www.strayer.edu
Trinity University, www.trinitydc.edu
University of the District of Columbia, www.udc.edu
University of the District of Columbia: School of Law, Washington 20008
Washington Theological Union, Washington 20012
Wesley Theological Seminary, Washington 20016

Florida

Angley College, www.angley.edu
Art Institute of Fort Lauderdale, www.artinstitute.edu
Baptist College of Florida, www.baptistcollege.edu
Barry University, www.barry.edu
Barry University: School of Graduate Medical Sciences, Miami Shores 33161
Beacon College, www.beaconcollege.edu
Bethune-Cookman College, www.bethune.cookman.edu
Brevard Community College, www.brevard.cc.fl.us
Broward Community College, www.broward.edu
Carlos Albizu University, www.albizu.edu
Central Florida College, www.centralfloridacollege.edu
Central Florida Community College, www.gocfcc.com
Chipola College, www.chipola.edu
City College, www.citycollege.edu
City College: Casselberry, Casselberry 32707-5353
Clearwater Christian College, www.clearwater.edu
Daytona Beach Community College, www.dbcc.edu
DeVry University: Miramar, www.mir.devry.edu
DeVry University: Orlando, www.orl.devry.edu
Eckerd College, www.eckerd.edu
Edison College, www.edison.edu
Edward Waters College, www.ewc.edu
Embry-Riddle Aeronautical University, www.embryriddle.edu
Embry-Riddle Aeronautical University: Extended Campus, www.embryriddle.edu
Everglades University, www.evergladesuniversity.edu
Flagler College, www.flagler.edu
Florida Agricultural and Mechanical University, www.famu.edu
Florida Agricultural and Mechanical University: School of Pharmacy, Tallahassee 32307
Florida Atlantic University, www.fau.edu
Florida Career College: Hialeah, www.careercollege.edu
Florida Career College: Miami, www.careercollege.edu
Florida Career College: Pembroke Pines, www.careercollege.edu

Florida Career College: West Palm Beach, West Palm Beach 33417
Florida Christian College, www.fcc.edu
Florida Coastal School of Law, www.fcsl.edu
Florida College, www.floridacollege.edu
Florida College of Natural Health, www.fcnh.com
Florida College of Natural Health: Bradenton, www.fcnh.com
Florida College of Natural Health: Maitland, www.fcnh.com
Florida College of Natural Health: Miami, www.fcnh.com
Florida Community College at Jacksonville, www.fccj.org
Florida Gulf Coast University, www.fgcu.edu
Florida Hospital College of Health Sciences, www.fhchs.edu
Florida Institute of Technology, www.fit.edu
Florida International University, www.fiu.edu
Florida Keys Community College, www.fkcc.edu
Florida Memorial University, www.fmuniv.edu
Florida Metropolitan University: Brandon Campus, www.fmu.edu
Florida Metropolitan University: Jacksonville, www.fmu.edu
Florida Metropolitan University: Melbourne Campus, www.cci.edu
Florida Metropolitan University: Orange Park, www.fmu.edu
Florida Metropolitan University: Orlando College North, www.cci.edu
Florida Metropolitan University: Orlando College South, www.fmu.edu
Florida Metropolitan University: Pinellas, www.fmu.edu
Florida Metropolitan University: Pompano Beach, www.fmu.edu
Florida Metropolitan University: Tampa College, www.fmu.edu
Florida Metropolitan University: Tampa College Lakeland, www.cci.edu
Florida National College, www.fnc.edu
Florida Southern College, www.flsouthern.edu
Florida State University, www.fsu.edu
Florida State University: School of Law, Tallahassee 32306
Florida Technical College: Deland, www.flatech.edu
Full Sail Real World Education, www.fullsail.com
Gulf Coast Community College, www.gulfcoast.edu
Herzing College: Orlando, www.herzing.edu
Hillsborough Community College, www.hccfl.edu
Hobe Sound Bible College, www.hsbc.edu
Indian River Community College, www.ircc.edu
International Academy of Design and Technology: Orlando, www.iadt.edu
International Academy of Design and Technology: Tampa, www.academy.edu
International College, www.internationalcollege.edu

Jacksonville University, www.jacksonville.edu
Johnson & Wales University, www.jwu.edu/florida
Jones College, www.jones.edu
Key College, www.keycollege.edu
Lake City Community College, www.lakecitycc.edu
Lake-Sumter Community College, www.lscc.edu
Lynn University, www.lynn.edu
Manatee Community College, www.mccfl.edu
Miami Dade College, www.mdc.edu
Miami International University of Art and Design, www.aimiami.aii.edu
New College of Florida, www.ncf.edu
New England Institute of Technology, www.newenglandtech.com
North Florida Community College, www.nfcc.edu
Northwood University: Florida Campus, www.northwood.edu
Nova Southeastern University, www.nova.edu
Nova Southeastern University Health Professions Division: College of Optometry, Fort Lauderdale 33328
Nova Southeastern University Health Professions Division: College of Osteopathic Medicine, Fort Lauderdale 33314
Nova Southeastern University of the Health Sciences: College of Pharmacy, Fort Lauderdale 33314
Nova Southeastern University: Shepard Broad Law Center, Fort Lauderdale 33314
Okaloosa-Walton College, www.owc.edu
Orlando Culinary Academy, www.orlandoculinary.com
Palm Beach Atlantic University, www.pba.edu
Palm Beach Community College, www.pbcc.edu
Pasco-Hernando Community College, www.phcc.edu
Pensacola Junior College, www.pjc.edu
Polk Community College, www.polk.edu
Remington College: Jacksonville, www.remingtoncollege.edu
Remington College: Largo, www.remingtoncollege.edu/largo
Remington College: Tampa, www.remingtoncollege.edu
Ringling School of Art and Design, www.ringling.edu
Rollins College, www.rollins.edu
St. John Vianney College Seminary, www.sjvcs.edu
St. Johns River Community College, www.sjrcc.cc.fl.us
St. Leo University, www.saintleo.edu
St. Petersburg College, www.spcollege.edu
St. Thomas University, www.stu.edu
St. Thomas University: School of Law, Miami 33054
St. Vincent De Paul Regional Seminary, Boynton Beach 33436
Sanford-Brown Institute: Jacksonville, www.sbjacksonville.com
Santa Fe Community College, www.santafe.sfcc.edu
Schiller International University, www.schiller.edu
Seminole Community College, www.scc-fl.edu

South Florida Community College, www.southflorida.edu

South University: West Palm Beach Campus, www.southuniversity.edu

Southeastern College of the Assemblies of God, www.seuniversity.edu

Southwest Florida College, www.swfc.edu

Southwest Florida College: Tampa, www.swfc.edu

Stetson University, www.stetson.edu

Stetson University: College of Law, St. Petersburg 33707

Tallahassee Community College, www.tcc.fl.edu

Trinity College of Florida, www.trinitycollege.edu

Universidad FLET, www.flet.edu

University of Central Florida, www.ucf.edu

University of Florida, www.ufl.edu

University of Florida: College of Dentistry, Gainesville 32610

University of Florida: College of Law, Gainesville 32611

University of Florida: College of Pharmacy, Gainesville 32610

University of Florida: College of Veterinary Medicine, Gainesville 32610

University of Florida: School of Medicine, Gainesville 32610

University of Miami, www.miami.edu

University of Miami: School of Law, Coral Gables 33124

University of Miami: School of Medicine, Miami 33101

University of North Florida, www.unf.edu

University of South Florida, www.usf.edu

University of South Florida: College of Medicine, Tampa 33612

University of Tampa, www.ut.edu

University of West Florida, www.uwf.edu

Valencia Community College, www.valenciacc.edu

Warner Southern College, www.warner.edu

Webber International University, www.webber.edu

Webster College, www.webstercollege.edu

Webster College: Holiday, www.webstercollege.edu

Yeshiva Gedolah Rabbinical College, Miami Beach 33139

Georgia

Abraham Baldwin Agricultural College, www.abac.edu

Agnes Scott College, www.agnesscott.edu

Albany State University, www.asuweb.asurams.edu

Albany Technical College, www.albanytech.edu

Andrew College, www.andrewcollege.edu

Armstrong Atlantic State University, www.armstrong.edu

Athens Technical College, www.athenstech.edu

Atlanta Christian College, www.acc.edu

Atlanta Metropolitan College, www.atlm.edu

Augusta State University, www.aug.edu

Augusta Technical Institute, www.augustatech.edu

Bainbridge College, www.bainbridge.edu

Bauder College, www.bauder.edu

Berry College, www.berry.edu

Beulah Heights Bible College, www.beulah.org

Brenau University, www.brenau.edu

Brewton-Parker College, www.bpc.edu

Brown Mackie College: Atlanta, Atlanta 30328

Candler School of Theology, Atlanta 30322

Central Georgia Technical College, www.cgtcollege.org

Chattahoochee Technical College, www.chattcollege.com

Clark Atlanta University, www.cau.edu

Clayton State University, www.clayton.edu

Coastal Georgia Community College, www.cgcc.edu

Columbia Theological Seminary, Decatur 30031

Columbus State University, www.colstate.edu

Columbus Technical College, www.columbustech.org

Covenant College, www.covenant.edu

Dalton State College, www.daltonstate.edu

Darton College, www.darton.edu

DeKalb Technical College, www.dekalbtech.edu

DeVry University: Alpharetta, www.atl.devry.edu

DeVry University: Decatur, www.atl.devry.edu

East Georgia College, www.ega.edu

Emmanuel College, www.emmanuelcollege.edu

Emory University, www.emory.edu

Emory University: School of Law, Atlanta 30322

Emory University: School of Medicine, Atlanta 30322

Fort Valley State University, www.fvsu.edu

Gainesville State College, www.gsc.edu

Georgia College and State University, www.gcsu.edu

Georgia Highlands College, www.highlands.edu

Georgia Institute of Technology, www.gatech.edu

Georgia Military College, www.gmc.cc.ga.us

Georgia Perimeter College, www.gpc.edu

Georgia Southern University, www.georgiasouthern.edu

Georgia Southwestern State University, www.gsw.edu

Georgia State University, www.gsu.edu

Georgia State University: College of Law, Atlanta 30303

Gordon College, www.gdn.edu

Griffin Technical College, www.griftec.org

Gupton Jones College of Funeral Service, www.gupton-jones.edu

Gwinnett College, www.gwinnettcollege.edu

Gwinnett Technical College, www.gwinnetttech.edu

High-Tech Institute: Atlanta, www.high-techinstitute.com

Interdenominational Theological Center, Atlanta 30314

Kennesaw State University, www.kennesaw.edu

LaGrange College, www.lagrange.edu

Le Cordon Bleu College of Culinary Arts, www.atlantaculinary.ciom

Life College, Marietta 30060

Life University, www.life.edu

Macon State College, www.maconstate.edu

Medical College of Georgia, www.mcg.edu

Medical College of Georgia: School of Dentistry, Augusta 30912

Medical College of Georgia: School of Medicine, Augusta 30912

Mercer University, www.mercer.edu

Mercer University Southern School of Pharmacy, Atlanta 30341

Mercer University: School of Medicine, Macon 31207

Mercer University: Walter F. George School of Law, Macon 31207

Middle Georgia College, www.mgc.edu

Middle Georgia Technical College, www.mgtc.org

Morehouse College, www.morehouse.edu

Morehouse School of Medicine, Atlanta 30310

North Georgia College & State University, www.ngcsu.edu

Northwestern Technical College, www.nwtcollege.org

Oglethorpe University, www.oglethorpe.edu

Oxford College of Emory University, www.emory.edu/OXFORD

Paine College, www.paine.edu

Piedmont College, www.piedmont.edu

Reinhardt College, www.reinhardt.edu

Savannah College of Art and Design, www.scad.edu

Savannah State University, www.savstate.edu

Savannah Technical College, www.savannahtech.edu

Shorter College, www.shorter.edu

South Georgia College, www.sga.edu

South University, www.southuniversity.edu

Southern Polytechnic State University, www.spsu.edu

Southwest Georgia Technical College, www.southwestgatech.edu

Spelman College, www.spelman.edu

Thomas University, www.thomasu.edu

Toccoa Falls College, www.tfc.edu

Truett-McConnell College, www.truett.edu

University of Georgia, www.uga.edu

University of Georgia: College of Pharmacy, Athens 30602

University of Georgia: College of Veterinary Medicine, Athens 30602

University of Georgia: School of Law, Athens 30602

University of West Georgia, www.westga.edu

Valdosta State University, www.valdosta.edu

Waycross College, www.waycross.edu

Wesleyan College, www.wesleyancollege.edu

West Georgia Technical College, www.westgatech.org

Young Harris College, www.yhc.edu

Hawaii

Brigham Young University-Hawaii, www.byuh.edu

Chaminade University of Honolulu, www.chaminade.edu

Hawaii Business College, www.hbc.edu

Hawaii Pacific University, www.hpu.edu

Hawaii Tokai International College, www.hawaiitokai.edu

Heald College: Honolulu, www.heald.edu

Remington College: Honolulu, www.remingtoncollege.edu

University of Hawaii William S. Richardson: School of Law, Honolulu 96822

University of Hawaii at Hilo, www.uhh.hawaii.edu

University of Hawaii at Manoa, www.manoa.hawaii.edu

University of Hawaii at Manoa: John A. Burns School of Medicine, Honolulu 96822

University of Hawaii: Hawaii Community College, www.hawcc.hawaii.edu

University of Hawaii: Honolulu Community College, www.hcc.hawaii.edu

University of Hawaii: Kapiolani Community College, www.kcc.hawaii.edu

University of Hawaii: Kauai Community College, www.kauai.hawaii.edu

University of Hawaii: Leeward Community College, www.lcc.hawaii.edu

University of Hawaii: Maui Community College, www.maui.hawaii.edu

University of Hawaii: West Oahu, www.uhwo.hawaii.edu

University of Hawaii: Windward Community College, www.wcc.hawaii.edu

Idaho

Albertson College of Idaho, www.albertson.edu

Boise Bible College, www.boisebible.edu

Boise State University, www.boisestate.edu

Brigham Young University-Idaho, www.byui.edu

College of Southern Idaho, www.csi.edu

Eastern Idaho Technical College, www.eitc.edu

Idaho State University, www.isu.edu

Idaho State University: College of Pharmacy, Pocatello 83209

Lewis-Clark State College, www.lcsc.edu

North Idaho College, www.nic.edu

Northwest Nazarene University, www.nnu.edu

University of Idaho, www.uidaho.edu

University of Idaho: College of Law, Moscow 83844

Illinois

American Academy of Art, www.aaart.edu

Argosy University, www.auchicago.net

Augustana College, www.augustana.edu

Aurora University, www.aurora.edu

Benedictine University, www.ben.edu

Bethany Theological Seminary, Richmond 47374

Black Hawk College, www.bhc.edu

Black Hawk College: East Campus, www.bhc.edu

Blackburn College, www.blackburn.edu

Blessing-Reiman College of Nursing, www.brcn.edu

Bradley University, www.bradley.edu

Brisk Rabbinical College, Chicago 60659

Career Colleges of Chicago, www.careerchi.com

Carl Sandburg College, www.sandburg.edu

Catholic Theological Union, Chicago 60615

Chicago State University, www.csu.edu

Chicago Theological Seminary, Chicago 60637

Chicago-Kent College of Law, Illinois Institute of Technology, Chicago 60661

City Colleges of Chicago: Harold Washington College, www.ccc.edu

City Colleges of Chicago: Harry S. Truman College, www.ccc.edu

City Colleges of Chicago: Kennedy-King College, www.ccc.edu

City Colleges of Chicago: Malcolm X College, malcolmx.ccc.edu

City Colleges of Chicago: Olive-Harvey College, www.ccc.edu

City Colleges of Chicago: Richard J. Daley College, daley.ccc.edu

City Colleges of Chicago: Wright College, www.ccc.edu

College of DuPage, www.cod.edu

College of Lake County, www.clcillinois.edu

College of Office Technology, www.cot.edu

Columbia College Chicago, www.colum.edu

Concordia University, www.curf.edu

Danville Area Community College, www.dacc.cc.il.us

De Paul University: College of Law, Chicago 60604

DePaul University, www.depaul.edu

DeVry University: Addison, www.dpg.devry.edu

DeVry University: Chicago, www.chi.devry.edu

DeVry University: Tinley Park, www.tp.devry.edu

Dominican University, www.dom.edu

Dr. William M. Scholl College of Podiatric Medicine, Chicago 60610

East-West University, www.eastwest.edu

Eastern Illinois University, www.eiu.edu

Elgin Community College, www.elgin.edu

Elmhurst College, www.elmhurst.edu

Eureka College, www.eureka.edu

Fox College, www.foxcollege.edu

Garrett-Evangelical Theological Seminary, Evanston 60201

Governors State University, www.govst.edu

Greenville College, www.greenville.edu

Harrington College of Design, www.harringtoncollege.com

Heartland Community College, www.heartland.edu

Hebrew Theological College, Skokie 60077

Highland Community College, www.highland.edu

Illinois Central College, www.icc.edu

Illinois College, www.ic.edu

Illinois College of Optometry, Chicago 60616

Illinois Eastern Community Colleges: Frontier Community College, www.iecc.edu/fcc

Illinois Eastern Community Colleges: Lincoln Trail College, www.iecc.edu/ltc

Illinois Eastern Community Colleges: Olney Central College, www.iecc.edu/occ

Illinois Eastern Community Colleges: Wabash Valley College, www.iecc.edu/wvc

Illinois Institute of Art-Schaumburg, www.ilis.aii.edu

Illinois Institute of Technology, www.iit.edu

Illinois State University, www.ilstu.edu

Illinois Valley Community College, www.ivcc.edu

Illinois Wesleyan University, www.iwu.edu

International Academy of Design and Technology: Chicago, www.iadtchicago.edu

International Academy of Design and Technology: Schaumburg, www.iadtschaumburg.com

John A. Logan College, www.jalc.edu

John Wood Community College, www.jwcc.edu

Joliet Junior College, www.jjc.cc.il.us

Judson College, www.judsoncollege.edu

Kankakee Community College, www.kcc.edu

Kaskaskia College, www.kaskaskia.edu

Kendall College, www.kendall.edu

Kishwaukee College, www.kishwaukeecollege.edu

Knox College, www.knox.edu

Lake Forest College, www.lakeforest.edu

Lake Land College, www.lakelandcollege.edu

Lakeview College of Nursing, www.lakeviewcol.edu

Lewis University, www.lewisu.edu

Lewis and Clark Community College, www.lc.edu

Lexington College, www.lexingtoncollege.edu

Lincoln Christian College and Seminary, www.lccs.edu

Lincoln Christian Seminary, Lincoln 62656

Lincoln Land Community College, www.llcc.edu

Loyola University Chicago: School of Law, Chicago 60611

Loyola University Chicago: Stritch School of Medicine, Maywood 60153

Loyola University of Chicago, www.luc.edu

Lutheran School of Theology at Chicago, Chicago 60615

MacCormac College, www.maccormac.edu

MacMurray College, www.mac.edu

McCormick Theological Seminary, Chicago 60637

McHenry County College, www.mchenry.edu

McKendree College, www.mckendree.edu

Meadville-Lombard Theological School, Chicago 60637

Midstate College, www.midstate.edu

Midwestern University: Chicago College of Osteopathic Medicine, Downers Grove 60515

Midwestern University: Chicago College of Pharmacy, Downers Grove 60515

Millikin University, www.millikin.edu

Monmouth College, www.monm.edu

Moody Bible Institute, www.moody.edu

Moraine Valley Community College, www.morainevalley.edu

Morrison Institute of Technology, www.morrison.tec.il.us

Morton College, www.morton.edu

National University of Health Sciences, www.nuhs.edu

National University of Health Sciences: First Professional, Lombard 60148

National-Louis University, www.nl.edu

North Central College, www.northcentralcollege.edu

North Park Theological Seminary, Chicago 60625

North Park University, www.northpark.edu

Northeastern Illinois University, www.neiu.edu

Northern Baptist Theological Seminary, Lombard 60148

Northern Illinois University, www.niu.edu

Northern Illinois University: College of Law, DeKalb 60115

Northwestern Business College, northwesternbc.edu

Northwestern University, www.northwestern.edu

Northwestern University: Dental School, Chicago 60611

Northwestern University: School of Law, Chicago 60611

Northwestern University: School of Medicine, Chicago 60611

Oakton Community College, www.oakton.edu

Olivet Nazarene University, www.olivet.edu

Parkland College, www.parkland.edu

Prairie State College, www.prairiestate.edu

Principia College, www.prin.edu

Quincy University, www.quincy.edu

Rend Lake College, www.rlc.edu

Richland Community College, www.richland.edu

Robert Morris College: Chicago, www.robertmorris.edu

Rock Valley College, www.rockvalleycollege.edu

Rockford Business College, www.rbcsuccess.com

Rockford College, www.rockford.edu

Roosevelt University, www.roosevelt.edu

Rosalind Franklin University of Medicine and Science, www.rosalindfranklin.edu

Rosalind Franklin University of Medicine and Science: First Professional, North Chicago 60064

Rush University, www.rushu.rush.edu

Rush University: Rush Medical College, Chicago 60612

Saint Anthony College of Nursing, www.sacn.edu

St. Augustine College, www.staugustinecollege.edu

St. Francis Medical Center College of Nursing, www.sfmccon.edu

St. Xavier University, www.sxu.edu

Sauk Valley Community College, www.svcc.edu

School of the Art Institute of Chicago, www.artic.edu/saic

Seabury-Western Theological Seminary, Evanston 60201

Shimer College, www.shimer.edu

South Suburban College of Cook County, www.southsuburbancollege.edu

Southeastern Illinois College, www.sic.edu

Southern Illinois University Carbondale, www.siuc.edu

Southern Illinois University Edwardsville, www.siue.edu

Southern Illinois University at Carbondale: School of Law, Carbondale 62901

Southern Illinois University: School of Dentistry, Alton 62002

Southern Illinois University: School of Medicine, Springfield 62794

Southwestern Illinois College, www.swic.edu

Spoon River College, www.spoonrivercollege.net

Springfield College in Illinois, www.sci.edu

Taylor Business Institute, www.tbiil.org

Telshe Yeshiva-Chicago, Chicago 60625

Trinity Christian College, www.trnty.edu

Trinity Evangelical Divinity School, Deerfield 60015

Trinity International University, www.tiu.edu

Triton College, www.triton.edu

University of Chicago, www.uchicago.edu

University of Chicago: Divinity School, Chicago 60637

University of Chicago: Pritzker School of Medicine, Chicago 60637

University of Chicago: School of Law, Chicago 60637

University of Illinois at Chicago, www.uic.edu

University of Illinois at Chicago: College of Dentistry, Chicago 60612

University of Illinois at Chicago: College of Medicine, Chicago 60612

University of Illinois at Chicago: College of Pharmacy, Chicago 60612

University of Illinois at Urbana-Champaign, www.uiuc.edu

University of Illinois at Urbana-Champaign: College of Law, Champaign 61820

University of Illinois at Urbana-Champaign: College of Veterinary Medicine, Urbana 61801

University of Illinois: Springfield, www.uis.edu

University of St. Francis, www.stfrancis.edu

University of St. Mary of the Lake–Mundelein Seminary, Mundelein 60060

VanderCook College of Music, www.vandercook.edu

Waubonsee Community College, www.waubonsee.edu

West Suburban College of Nursing, www.wscn.edu
Western Illinois University, www.wiu.edu
Westwood College - Chicago Loop, www.westwood.edu
Westwood College of Technology: O'Hare, www.westwood.edu
Westwood College of Technology: River Oaks, www.westwood.edu
Wheaton College, www.wheaton.edu
William Rainey Harper College, www.harpercollege.edu

Indiana

American Conservatory of Music, www.americanconservatory.edu
Ancilla College, www.ancilla.edu
Anderson University, www.anderson.edu
Anderson University: School of Theology, Anderson 46012
Associated Mennonite Biblical Seminary, Elkhart 46517
Ball State University, www.bsu.edu
Bethel College, www.bethelcollege.edu
Bethel College, Mishawaka 46545
Brown Mackie College: Fort Wayne, www.brownmackie.com
Brown Mackie College: Michigan City, www.cbcaec.com
Butler University, www.butler.edu
Butler University: College of Pharmacy, Indianapolis 46208
Calumet College of St. Joseph, www.ccsj.edu
Christian Theological Seminary, Indianapolis 46208
College of Court Reporting, www.ccredu.com
Concordia Theological Seminary, Fort Wayne 46825
DePauw University, www.depauw.edu
Earlham College, www.earlham.edu
Earlham School of Religion, Richmond 47374
Franklin College, www.franklincollege.edu
Goshen College, www.goshen.edu
Grace College, www.grace.edu
Hanover College, www.hanover.edu
Holy Cross College, www.hcc-nd.edu
Huntington University, www.huntington.edu
Indiana Business College, www.ibcschools.edu
Indiana Business College: Anderson, www.ibcschools.edu
Indiana Business College: Columbus, www.ibcschools.edu
Indiana Business College: Evansville, www.ibcschools.edu
Indiana Business College: Fort Wayne, www.ibcschools.edu
Indiana Business College: Lafayette, www.ibcschools.edu
Indiana Business College: Marion, www.ibcschools.edu
Indiana Business College: Medical, www.ibcschools.edu
Indiana Business College: Muncie, www.ibcschools.edu
Indiana Business College: Terre Haute, www.ibcschools.edu
Indiana Institute of Technology, www.indianatech.edu
Indiana State University, www.indstate.edu
Indiana University Bloomington, www.iub.edu

Indiana University Bloomington: School of Law, Bloomington 47405
Indiana University Bloomington: School of Optometry, Bloomington 47405
Indiana University East, www.iue.edu
Indiana University Indianapolis: School of Law, Indianapolis 46202
Indiana University Kokomo, www.iuk.edu
Indiana University Northwest, www.iun.edu
Indiana University School of Dentistry, Indianapolis 46202
Indiana University South Bend, www.iusb.edu
Indiana University Southeast, www.ius.edu
Indiana University-Purdue University Fort Wayne, www.ipfw.edu
Indiana University-Purdue University Indianapolis, www.iupui.edu
Indiana University: School of Medicine, Indianapolis 46202
Indiana Wesleyan University, www.indwes.edu
International Business College, Fort Wayne 46804
International Business College: Indianapolis, www.intlbusinesscollege.com
Ivy Tech Community College: Bloomington, www.ivytech.edu
Ivy Tech Community College: Central Indiana, www.ivytech.edu
Ivy Tech Community College: Columbus, www.ivytech.edu
Ivy Tech Community College: East Central, www.ivytech.edu
Ivy Tech Community College: Kokomo, www.ivytech.edu
Ivy Tech Community College: Lafayette, www.ivytech.edu
Ivy Tech Community College: North Central, www.ivytech.edu
Ivy Tech Community College: Northeast, www.ivytech.edu
Ivy Tech Community College: Northwest, www.ivytech.edu
Ivy Tech Community College: South Central, www.ivytech.edu
Ivy Tech Community College: Southeast, www.ivytech.edu
Ivy Tech Community College: Southwest, www.ivytech.edu
Ivy Tech Community College: Wabash Valley, www.ivytech.edu
Ivy Tech Community College: Whitewater, www.ivytech.edu
Lincoln Technical Institute, www.lincolntech.com
Manchester College, www.manchester.edu
Marian College, www.marian.edu
Martin University, www.martin.edu
Mid-America College of Funeral Service, www.mid-america.edu
Oakland City University, www.oak.edu
Professional Careers Institute, www.pcicareers.com
Purdue University, www.purdue.edu
Purdue University: Calumet, www.calumet.purdue.edu
Purdue University: North Central Campus, www.pnc.edu
Purdue University: School of Pharmacy, West Lafayette 47907
Purdue University: School of Veterinary Medicine, West Lafayette 47907
Rose-Hulman Institute of Technology, www.rose-hulman.edu

St. Joseph's College, www.saintjoe.edu
Saint Mary's College, www.saintmarys.edu
St. Mary-of-the-Woods College, www.smwc.edu
St. Meinrad School of Theology, St. Meinrad 47577
Sawyer College, www.sawyercollege.com
Sawyer College: Merrillville, www.sawyercollege.edu
Taylor University, www.taylor.edu
Taylor University: Fort Wayne, http://fw.taylor.edu
Tri-State University, www.tristate.edu
University of Evansville, www.evansville.edu
University of Indianapolis, www.uindy.edu
University of Notre Dame, www.nd.edu
University of Notre Dame: School of Law, Notre Dame 46556
University of Notre Dame: School of Theology, Notre Dame 46556
University of St. Francis, www.sf.edu
University of Southern Indiana, www.usi.edu
Valparaiso University, www.valpo.edu
Valparaiso University: School of Law, Valparaiso 46383
Vincennes University, www.vinu.edu
Wabash College, www.wabash.edu

Iowa

AIB College of Business, www.aib.edu
Allen College, www.allencollege.edu
Ashford University, www.ashford.edu
Briar Cliff University, www.briarcliff.edu
Buena Vista University, www.bvu.edu
Central College, www.central.edu
Clarke College, www.clarke.edu
Clinton Community College, www.eicc.edu
Coe College, www.coe.edu
Cornell College, www.cornellcollege.edu
Des Moines Area Community College, www.dmacc.edu
Des Moines University - Osteopathic Medical Center, Des Moines 50312
Divine Word College, www.dwci.edu
Dordt College, www.dordt.edu
Drake University, www.drake.edu
Drake University Law School, Des Moines 50311
Drake University: College of Pharmacy, Des Moines 50311
Ellsworth Community College, www.ellsworthcollege.edu
Emmaus Bible College, www.emmaus.edu
Faith Baptist Bible College and Theological Seminary, www.faith.edu
Faith Baptist Theological Seminary, Ankeny 50021
Graceland University, www.graceland.edu
Grand View College, www.gvc.edu
Grinnell College, www.grinnell.edu
Hamilton College, www.hamiltonia.edu
Hamilton College: Cedar Falls, www.hamiltoncf.com
Hamilton College: Cedar Rapids, www.hamiltonia.edu
Hamilton Technical College, www.hamiltontechcollege.com
Hawkeye Community College, www.hawkeyecollege.edu

Indian Hills Community College, www.indianhills.edu
Iowa Central Community College, www.iccc.cc.ia.us
Iowa Lakes Community College, www.iowalakes.edu
Iowa State University, www.iastate.edu
Iowa State University: College of Veterinary Medicine, Ames 50011
Iowa Wesleyan College, www.iwc.edu
Iowa Western Community College, www.iwcc.edu
Kaplan University, www.kaplan.edu/ku
Kirkwood Community College, www.kirkwood.cc.ia.us
Loras College, www.loras.edu
Luther College, www.luther.edu
Maharishi University of Management, www.mum.edu
Marshalltown Community College, www.marshalltowncommunitycollege.com
Mercy College of Health Sciences, www.mchs.edu
Morningside College, www.morningside.edu
Mount Mercy College, www.mtmercy.edu
Muscatine Community College, www.eicc.edu
North Iowa Area Community College, www.niacc.edu
Northeast Iowa Community College, www.nicc.edu
Northwest Iowa Community College, www.nwicc.edu
Northwestern College, www.nwciowa.edu
Palmer College of Chiropractic, Davenport 52803
St. Ambrose University, www.sau.edu
St. Luke's College, www.stlukes.org
Scott Community College, www.eicc.edu
Simpson College, www.simpson.edu
Southeastern Community College: North Campus, www.scciowa.edu
Southwestern Community College, www.swcciowa.edu
University of Dubuque, www.dbq.edu
University of Dubuque: School of Theology, Dubuque 52001
University of Iowa, www.uiowa.edu
University of Iowa College of Dentistry, Iowa City 52242
University of Iowa: College of Law, Iowa City 52242
University of Iowa: College of Medicine, Iowa City 52242
University of Iowa: College of Pharmacy, Iowa City 52242
University of Northern Iowa, www.uni.edu
University of Osteopathic Medicine and Health Sciences: College of Podiatric Medicine and Surgery, Des Moines 50312
Upper Iowa University, www.uiu.edu
Vatterott College, www.vatterott-college.edu
Vennard College, www.vennard.edu
Waldorf College, www.waldorf.edu
Wartburg College, www.wartburg.edu
Wartburg Theological Seminary, Dubuque 52003
Western Iowa Tech Community College, www.witcc.com
William Penn University, www.wmpenn.edu

Kansas

Allen County Community College,
www.allencc.edu
Baker University, www.bakeru.edu
Barclay College,
www.barclaycollege.edu
Barton County Community College,
www.bartonccc.edu
Benedictine College,
www.benedictine.edu
Bethany College, www.bethanylb.edu
Bethel College, www.bethelks.edu
Brown Mackie College,
www.brownmackie.edu/sa
Butler County Community College,
www.butlercc.edu
Central Baptist Theological Seminary,
Kansas City 66102
Central Christian College of Kansas,
www.centralchristian.edu
Cloud County Community College,
www.cloud.edu
Coffeyville Community College,
www.coffeyville.edu
Colby Community College,
www.colbycc.edu
Cowley County Community College,
www.cowley.edu
Dodge City Community College,
www.dccc.cc.ks.us
Donnelly College, www.donnelly.edu
Emporia State University,
www.emporia.edu
Fort Hays State University,
www.fhsu.edu
Fort Scott Community College,
www.ftscott.cc.ks.us
Friends University, www.friends.edu
Garden City Community College,
www.gcc>cks.edu
Haskell Indian Nations University,
www.haskell.edu
Hesston College, www.hesston.edu
Highland Community College,
www.highlandcc.edu
Hutchinson Community College,
www.hutchcc.edu
Johnson County Community College,
www.jccc.edu
Kansas City Kansas Community
College, www.kckcc.edu
Kansas State University, www.ksu.edu
Kansas State University: College of
Veterinary Medicine, Manhattan
66506
Kansas Wesleyan University,
www.kwu.edu
Labette Community College,
www.labette.edu
Manhattan Area Technical College,
www.matc.net
Manhattan Christian College,
www.mccks.edu
McPherson College,
www.mcpherson.edu
MidAmerica Nazarene University,
www.mnu.edu
Neosho County Community College,
www.neosho.cc.ks.us
Newman University,
www.newmanu.edu
North Central Kansas Technical
College, www.ncktc.tec.ks.us
Ottawa University, www.ottawa.edu
Pittsburg State University,
www.pittstate.edu
Pratt Community College,
www.prattcc.edu
Seward County Community College,
www.sccc.edu
Southwestern College,
www.sckans.edu
Sterling College, www.sterling.edu

Tabor College, www.tabor.edu
University of Kansas, www.ku.edu
University of Kansas Medical Center,
www.kumc.edu
University of Kansas Medical Center:
School of Medicine, Kansas City
66160
University of Kansas: School of Law,
Lawrence 66045
University of St. Mary,
www.stmary.edu
Washburn University School of Law,
Topeka 66621
Washburn University of Topeka,
www.washburn.edu
Wichita State University,
www.wichita.edu

Kentucky

Alice Lloyd College, www.alc.edu
Asbury College, www.asbury.edu
Asbury Theological Seminary, Wilmore
40390
Ashland Community and Technical
College, www.ashland.kctcs.edu
Beckfield College, www.beckfield.edu
Bellarmine University,
www.bellarmine.edu
Berea College, www.berea.edu
Big Sandy Community and Technical
College, www.bigsandy.kctcs.edu
Bluegrass Community and Technical
College,
www.bluegrass.kctcs.edu
Brescia University, www.brescia.edu
Brown Mackie College: Hopkinsville,
www.brownmackie.edu
Brown Mackie College: Louisville,
www.brownmackie.edu
Brown Mackie College: North
Kentucky,
www.brownmackie.edu
Campbellsville University,
www.campbellsville.edu
Centre College, www.centre.edu
Clear Creek Baptist Bible College,
www.ccbbc.edu
Daymar College,
www.daymarcollege.edu
Daymar College: Louisville, Louisville
40218
Draughons Junior College,
www.draughons.org
Eastern Kentucky University,
www.eku.edu
Elizabethtown Community and
Technical College,
www.elizabethtown.kctcs.edu
Georgetown College,
www.georgetowncollege.edu
Hazard Community College,
www.hazard.kctcs.edu
Henderson Community College,
www.hencc.kctcs.edu
Hopkinsville Community College,
www.hopkinsville.kctcs.edu
Jefferson Community College,
www.jefferson.kctcs.edu
Kentucky Christian University,
www.kcu.edu
Kentucky Mountain Bible College,
www.kmbc.edu
Kentucky State University,
www.kysu.edu
Kentucky Wesleyan College,
www.kwc.edu
Lexington Theological Seminary,
Lexington 40508
Lindsey Wilson College,
www.lindsey.edu
Louisville Presbyterian Theological
Seminary, Louisville 40205

Louisville Technical Institute,
www.louisvilletech.edu
Madisonville Community College,
www.madisonville.kctcs.edu
Maysville Community College,
www.maysville.kctcs.edu
Mid-Continent University,
www.midcontinent.edu
Midway College, www.midway.edu
Morehead State University,
www.moreheadstate.edu
Murray State University,
www.murraystate.edu
National College of Business &
Technology: Danville,
www.ncbt.edu
National College of Business &
Technology: Florence,
www.ncbt.edu
National College of Business &
Technology: Lexington,
www.ncbt.edu
National College of Business &
Technology: Louisville,
www.ncbt.edu
National College of Business &
Technology: Pikeville,
www.ncbt.edu
National College of Business &
Technology: Richmond,
www.ncbt.edu
Northern Kentucky University,
www.nku.edu
Northern Kentucky University:
Salmon P. Chase School of Law,
Highland Heights 41099
Owensboro Community College,
www.octc.kctcs.edu
Paducah Technical College,
www.paducahtech.edu
Pikeville College, www.pc.edu
St. Catharine College, www.sccky.edu
Somerset Community College,
www.somerset.kctcs.edu
Southeast Kentucky Community and
Technical College,
www.secc.kctcs.net
Southern Baptist Theological
Seminary, Louisville 40280
Southwestern College: Florence,
www.swcollege.net
Spalding University,
www.spalding.edu
Spencerian College,
www.spencerian.edu
Spencerian College: Lexington,
www.spencerian.edu
Sullivan University, www.sullivan.edu
Thomas More College,
www.thomasmore.edu
Transylvania University,
www.transy.edu
Union College, www.unionky.edu
University of Kentucky, www.uky.edu
University of Kentucky: College of
Dentistry, Lexington 40536
University of Kentucky: College of
Law, Lexington 40506
University of Kentucky: College of
Medicine, Lexington 40536
University of Louisville,
www.louisville.edu
University of Louisville: School of
Dentistry, Louisville 40292
University of Louisville: School of Law,
Louisville 40292
University of Louisville: School of
Medicine, Louisville 40202
University of the Cumberlands,
www.ucumberlands.edu
West Kentucky Community and
Technical College,
www.pccky.com

Western Kentucky University,
www.wku.edu

Louisiana

Baton Rouge Community College,
www.mybr.cc
Bossier Parish Community College,
www.bpcc.edu
Centenary College of Louisiana,
www.centenary.edu
Delgado Community College,
www.dcc.edu
Dillard University, www.dillard.edu
Grambling State University,
www.gram.edu
Gretna Career College,
www.gretnacareercollege.edu
ITI Technical College,
www.iticollege.edu
Louisiana State University Health
Sciences Center, www.lsuhsc.edu
Louisiana State University Health
Sciences Center: School of
Dentistry, New Orleans 70119
Louisiana State University Health
Sciences Center: School of
Medicine, New Orleans 70112
Louisiana State University and
Agricultural and Mechanical
College, www.lsu.edu
Louisiana State University and
Agricultural and Mechanical
College: School of Law, Baton
Rouge 70803
Louisiana State University and
Agricultural and Mechanical
College: School of Veterinary
Medicine, Baton Rouge 70803
Louisiana State University at
Alexandria, www.lsua.edu
Louisiana State University in
Shreveport, www.lsus.edu
Louisiana State University: School of
Medicine, Shreveport 71130
Louisiana Tech University,
www.latech.edu
Loyola University New Orleans,
www.loyno.edu
Loyola University: School of Law, New
Orleans 70118
New Orleans Baptist Theological
Seminary, www.nobts.edu
New Orleans Baptist Theological
Seminary: Leavell College,
www.nobts.edu
New Orleans School of Urban
Missions, www.sumonline.org
Nicholls State University,
www.nicholls.edu
Northeast Louisiana University School
of Pharmacy, Monroe 71209
Northwestern State University,
www.nsula.edu
Notre Dame Seminary School of
Theology, New Orleans 70118
Nunez Community College,
www.nunez.edu
Our Lady of Holy Cross College,
www.olhcc.edu
Our Lady of the Lake College,
www.ololcollege.edu
Remington College: Lafayette,
www.educationamerica.com
Remington College: New Orleans,
www.remingtoncollege.edu/
neworleans/index.html
St. Joseph Seminary College,
www.sjasc.edu
Southeastern Louisiana University,
www.selu.edu
Southern University and Agricultural
and Mechanical College,
www.subr.edu

Southern University at New Orleans, www.suno.edu
Southern University at Shreveport, www.susla.edu
Southern University: Law Center, Baton Rouge 70813
Southwest University, www.southwest.edu
Tulane University, www.tulane.edu
Tulane University: School of Law, New Orleans 70118
Tulane University: School of Medicine, New Orleans 70112
University of Louisiana at Lafayette, www.louisiana.edu
University of Louisiana at Monroe, www.ulm.edu
University of New Orleans, www.uno.edu
Xavier University of Louisiana, www.xula.edu
Xavier University of Louisiana: College of Pharmacy, New Orleans 70125

Maine

Andover College, www.andovercollege.edu
Bangor Theological Seminary, Bangor 04401
Bates College, www.bates.edu
Beal College, www.bealcollege.edu
Bowdoin College, www.bowdoin.edu
Central Maine Community College, www.cmcc.edu
Central Maine Medical Center School of Nursing, www.cmmcson.edu
Colby College, www.colby.edu
College of the Atlantic, www.coa.edu
Eastern Maine Community College, www.emcc.edu
Husson College, www.husson.edu
Kennebec Valley Community College, www.kvcc.me.edu
Maine College of Art, www.meca.edu
Maine Maritime Academy, www.mainemaritime.edu
New England School of Communications, www.nescom.edu
Northern Maine Community College, www.nmcc.edu
St. Joseph's College, www.sjcme.edu
Southern Maine Community College, www.smccme.edu
Thomas College, www.thomas.edu
Unity College, www.unity.edu
University of Maine, www.umaine.edu
University of Maine at Augusta, www.uma.maine.edu
University of Maine at Farmington, www.umf.maine.edu
University of Maine at Fort Kent, www.umfk.maine.edu
University of Maine at Machias, www.umm.maine.edu
University of Maine at Presque Isle, www.umpi.maine.edu
University of Maine: School of Law, Portland 04102
University of New England, www.une.edu
University of New England: School of Osteopathic Medicine, Biddeford 04005
University of Southern Maine, www.usm.maine.edu
Washington County Community College, www.wccc.me.edu
York County Community College, www.yccc.edu

Maryland

Allegany College of Maryland, www.allegany.edu
Anne Arundel Community College, www.aacc.edu
Baltimore City Community College, www.bccc.edu
Baltimore Hebrew University, www.bhu.edu
Baltimore International College, www.bic.edu
Bowie State University, www.bowiestate.edu
Capitol College, www.capitol-college.edu
Carroll Community College, www.carrollcc.edu
Cecil Community College, www.cecilcc.edu
Chesapeake College, www.chesapeake.edu
College of Notre Dame of Maryland, www.ndm.edu
College of Southern Maryland, www.csmd.edu
Columbia Union College, www.cuc.edu
Community College of Baltimore County, www.ccbcmd.edu
Coppin State University, www.coppin.edu
DeVry University: Bethesda, Bethesda 20814
Frederick Community College, www.frederick.edu
Frostburg State University, www.frostburg.edu
Garrett College, www.garrettcollege.edu
Goucher College, www.goucher.edu
Hagerstown Business College, www.hagerstownbusinesscol.org
Hagerstown Community College, www.hagerstowncc.edu
Harford Community College, www.harford.cc.md.us
Hood College, www.hood.edu
Howard Community College, www.howardcc.edu
Johns Hopkins University, www.jhu.edu
Johns Hopkins University: Peabody Conservatory of Music, www.peabody.jhu.edu
Johns Hopkins University: School of Medicine, Baltimore 21205
Loyola College in Maryland, www.loyola.edu
Maryland Institute College of Art, www.mica.edu
McDaniel College, www.mcdaniel.edu
Montgomery College, www.montgomerycollege.edu
Morgan State University, www.morgan.edu
Mount St. Mary's College: Seminary, www.msmary.edu
Mount St. Mary's University, www.msmary.edu
National Labor College, www.georgemeany.org/
Ner Israel Rabbinical College, Baltimore 21208
Prince George's Community College, www.pgcc.edu
St. John's College, www.stjohnscollege.edu
St. Mary's College of Maryland, www.smcm.edu
Salisbury University, www.salisbury.edu
Sojourner-Douglass College, www.sdc.edu

TESST College of Technology: Baltimore, www.retstraining.com
TESST College of Technology: Towson, www.tesst.com
Towson University, www.towson.edu
Uniformed Services University of the Health Sciences: School of Medicine, Bethesda 20814
United States Naval Academy, www.usna.edu
University of Baltimore, www.ubalt.edu
University of Baltimore: School of Law, www.law.ubalt.edu
University of Maryland at Baltimore: School of Dentistry, Baltimore 21201
University of Maryland at Baltimore: School of Law, Baltimore 21201
University of Maryland at Baltimore: School of Medicine, Baltimore City 21201
University of Maryland at Baltimore: School of Pharmacy, Baltimore 21201
University of Maryland: Baltimore, www.umaryland.edu
University of Maryland: Baltimore County, www.umbc.edu
University of Maryland: College Park, www.maryland.edu
University of Maryland: Eastern Shore, www.umes.edu
University of Maryland: University College, www.umuc.edu
Villa Julie College, www.vjc.edu
Washington Bible College, www.bible.edu
Washington College, www.washcoll.edu
Wor-Wic Community College, www.worwic.edu
Yeshiva College of the Nations Capital, Silver Spring 20902

Massachusetts

American International College, www.aic.edu
Amherst College, www.amherst.edu
Andover Newton Theological School, Newton Centre 02159
Anna Maria College, www.annamaria.edu
Art Institute of Boston at Lesley University, www.aiboston.edu
Assumption College, www.assumption.edu
Atlantic Union College, www.atlanticuc.edu
Babson College, www.babson.edu
Bay Path College, www.baypath.edu
Bay State College, www.baystate.edu
Becker College, www.beckercollege.edu
Benjamin Franklin Institute of Technology, www.bfit.edu
Bentley College, www.bentley.edu
Berklee College of Music, www.berklee.edu
Berkshire Community College, www.berkshirecc.edu
Boston Architectural Center, www.the-bac.edu
Boston College, www.bc.edu
Boston College: Law School, Newton 02159
Boston Conservatory, www.bostonconservatory.edu
Boston University, www.bu.edu
Boston University Goldman School of Dental Medicine, www.dentalschool.bu.edu

Boston University: School of Law, Boston 02215
Boston University: School of Medicine, Boston 02118
Boston University: School of Theology, Boston 02215
Brandeis University, www.brandeis.edu
Bridgewater State College, www.bridgew.edu
Bristol Community College, www.bristolcommunitycollege.edu
Bunker Hill Community College, www.bhcc.mass.edu
Cambridge College, www.cambridgecollege.edu
Cape Cod Community College, www.capecod.edu
Clark University, www.clarku.edu
College of the Holy Cross, www.holycross.edu
Curry College, www.curry.edu
Dean College, www.dean.edu
Eastern Nazarene College, www.enc.edu
Elms College, www.elms.edu
Emerson College, www.emerson.edu
Emmanuel College, www.emmanuel.edu
Endicott College, www.endicott.edu
Episcopal Divinity School, Cambridge 02138
Fisher College, www.fisher.edu
Fitchburg State College, www.fsc.edu
Framingham State College, www.framingham.edu
Franklin W. Olin College of Engineering, www.olin.edu
Gibbs College, www.gibbsboston.edu
Gordon College, www.gordon.edu
Gordon-Conwell Theological Seminary, South Hamilton 01982
Greenfield Community College, www.gcc.mass.edu
Hampshire College, www.hampshire.edu
Harvard College, www.college.harvard.edu
Harvard School of Dental Medicine, Boston 02115
Harvard University Law School, Cambridge 02138
Harvard University: Divinity School, Cambridge 02138
Harvard University: Harvard Medical School, Boston 02115
Hebrew College, www.hebrewcollege.edu
Hellenic College/Holy Cross, www.hchc.edu
Holy Cross Greek Orthodox School of Theology, Brookline 02146
Holyoke Community College, www.hcc.mass.edu
Laboure College, www.laboure.edu
Lasell College, www.lasell.edu
Lesley University, www.lesley.edu/lc
Marian Court College, www.mariancourt.edu
Massachusetts Bay Community College, www.massbay.edu
Massachusetts College of Art, www.massart.edu
Massachusetts College of Liberal Arts, www.mcla.mass.edu
Massachusetts College of Pharmacy and Allied Health Sciences: School of Pharmacy, Boston 02115
Massachusetts College of Pharmacy and Health Sciences, www.mcphs.edu
Massachusetts Institute of Technology, web.mit.edu

Massachusetts Maritime Academy,
www.maritime.edu
Massasoit Community College,
www.massasoit.mass.edu
Merrimack College,
www.merrimack.edu
Middlesex Community College,
www.middlesex.mass.edu
Montserrat College of Art,
www.montserrat.edu
Mount Holyoke College,
www.mtholyoke.edu
Mount Ida College,
www.mountida.edu
Mount Wachusett Community
College, www.mwcc.mass.edu
New England College of Finance,
www.finance.edu
New England College of Optometry,
Boston 02115
New England Conservatory of Music,
www.newenglandconservatory.edu
New England Institute of Art,
www.neia.aii.edu
New England School of Law, Boston
02116
Newbury College, www.newbury.edu
Nichols College, www.nichols.edu
North Shore Community College,
www.northshore.edu
Northeastern University,
www.northeastern.edu
Northeastern University: Bouve
College of Pharmacy and Health
Sciences, Boston 02115
Northeastern University: School of
Law, Boston 02115
Northern Essex Community College,
www.necc.mass.edu
Pine Manor College, www.pmc.edu
Pope John XXIII National Seminary,
Weston 02193
Quincy College,
www.quincycollege.com
Quinsigamond Community College,
www.qcc.mass.edu
Regis College, www.regiscollege.edu
Roxbury Community College,
www.rcc.mass.edu
St. John's Seminary, Brighton 02135
St. John's Seminary College,
www.sjs.edu
Salem State College,
www.salemstate.edu
School of the Museum of Fine Arts,
www.smfa.edu
Simmons College, www.simmons.edu
Simon's Rock College of Bard,
www.simons-rock.edu
Smith College, www.smith.edu
Springfield College, www.spfldcol.edu
Springfield Technical Community
College, www.stcc.edu
Stonehill College, www.stonehill.edu
Suffolk University, www.suffolk.edu
Suffolk University: Law School, Boston
02114
Tufts University, www.tufts.edu
Tufts University: School of Dental
Medicine, Boston 02111
Tufts University: School of Medicine,
Boston 02111
Tufts University: School of Veterinary
Medicine, North Grafton 01536
University of Massachusetts Amherst,
www.umass.edu
University of Massachusetts Boston,
www.umb.edu
University of Massachusetts
Dartmouth, www.umassd.edu
University of Massachusetts Lowell,
www.uml.edu
University of Massachusetts Medical
School, Worcester 01655

Urban College of Boston,
www.urbancollege.edu
Wellesley College, www.wellesley.edu
Wentworth Institute of Technology,
www.wit.edu
Western New England College,
www.wnec.edu
Western New England College: School
of Law, Springfield 01119
Westfield State College,
www.wsc.ma.edu
Weston Jesuit School of Theology,
Cambridge 02138
Wheaton College,
www.wheatoncollege.edu
Wheelock College,
www.wheelock.edu
Williams College, www.williams.edu
Worcester Polytechnic Institute,
www.wpi.edu
Worcester State College,
www.worcester.edu

Michigan

Adrian College, www.adrian.edu
Albion College, www.albion.edu
Alma College, www.alma.edu
Alpena Community College,
www.alpenacc.edu
Andrews University,
www.andrews.edu
Andrews University Seminary, Berrien
Springs 49104
Aquinas College, www.aquinas.edu
Baker College of Auburn Hills,
www.baker.edu
Baker College of Cadillac,
www.baker.edu
Baker College of Clinton Township,
www.baker.edu
Baker College of Flint, www.baker.edu
Baker College of Jackson,
www.baker.edu
Baker College of Muskegon,
www.baker.edu
Baker College of Owosso,
www.baker.edu
Baker College of Port Huron,
www.baker.edu
Bay Mills Community College,
www.bmcc.edu
Bay de Noc Community College,
www.baycollege.edu
Calvin College, www.calvin.edu
Calvin Theological Seminary, Grand
Rapids 49546
Central Michigan University,
www.cmich.edu
Cleary University, www.cleary.edu
College for Creative Studies,
www.ccscad.edu
Concordia University, www.cuaa.edu
Cornerstone University,
www.cornerstone.edu
Davenport University,
www.davenport.edu
Delta College, www.delta.edu
Detroit College of Law, Detroit 48201
Eastern Michigan University,
www.emich.edu
Ferris State University, www.ferris.edu
Ferris State University College of
Pharmacy, Big Rapids 49307
Ferris State University: College of
Optometry, Big Rapids 49307
Finlandia University,
www.finlandia.edu
Glen Oaks Community College,
www.glenoaks.cc.mi.us
Gogebic Community College,
www.gogebic.edu
Grace Bible College, www.gbcol.edu

Grand Rapids Baptist Seminary, Grand
Rapids 49505
Grand Rapids Community College,
www.grcc.edu
Grand Valley State University,
www.gvsu.edu
Great Lakes Christian College,
www.glcc.edu
Henry Ford Community College,
www.hfcc.edu
Hillsdale College, www.hillsdale.edu
Hope College, www.hope.edu
Jackson Community College,
www.jccmi.edu
Kalamazoo College, www.kzoo.edu
Kalamazoo Valley Community College,
www.kvcc.edu
Kellogg Community College,
www.kellogg.edu
Kendall College of Art and Design of
Ferris State University,
www.kcad.edu
Kettering University,
www.kettering.edu
Kirtland Community College,
www.kirtland.edu
Kuyper College, www.reformed.edu
Lake Michigan College,
www.lakemichigancollege.edu
Lake Superior State University,
www.lssu.edu
Lansing Community College,
www.lansing.cc.mi.us
Lawrence Technological University,
www.ltu.edu
Lewis College of Business,
www.lewiscollege.edu
Macomb Community College,
www.macomb.edu
Madonna University,
www.madonna.edu
Marygrove College,
www.marygrove.edu
Michigan Jewish Institute,
www.mji.edu
Michigan State University,
www.msu.edu
Michigan State University: College of
Human Medicine, East Lansing
48824
Michigan State University: College of
Osteopathic Medicine, East
Lansing 48824
Michigan State University: School of
Veterinary Medicine, East Lansing
48824
Michigan Technological University,
www.mtu.edu
Mid Michigan Community College,
www.midmich.edu
Monroe County Community College,
www.monroeccc.edu
Montcalm Community College,
www.montcalm.edu
Mott Community College,
www.mcc.edu
Muskegon Community College,
www.muskegon.edu
North Central Michigan College,
www.ncmc.cc.mi.us
Northern Michigan University,
www.nmu.edu
Northwestern Michigan College,
www.nmc.edu
Northwood University,
www.northwood.edu
Oakland Community College,
www.oaklandcc.edu
Oakland University, www.oakland.edu
Olivet College, www.olivetcollege.edu
Rochester College, www.rc.edu
Sacred Heart Major Seminary,
www.shmsonline.org

Sacred Heart Major Seminary,
www.shmsonline.org
Saginaw Chippewa Tribal College,
www.sagchip.org/tribalcollege
Saginaw Valley State University,
www.svsu.edu
St. Clair County Community College,
www.sc4.edu
Schoolcraft College,
www.schoolcraft.cc.mi.us
Siena Heights University,
www.sienahts.edu
Southwestern Michigan College,
www.swmich.edu
Spring Arbor University,
www.arbor.edu
Thomas M. Cooley Law School,
Lansing 48901
University of Detroit Mercy,
www.udmercy.edu
University of Detroit Mercy: School of
Dentistry, Detroit 48219-0900
University of Detroit Mercy: School of
Law, Detroit 48226
University of Michigan,
www.umich.edu
University of Michigan: College of
Pharmacy, Ann Arbor 48109
University of Michigan: Dearborn,
www.umd.umich.edu
University of Michigan: Flint,
www.umflint.edu
University of Michigan: School of
Dentistry, Ann Arbor 48109
University of Michigan: School of Law,
Ann Arbor 48109
University of Michigan: School of
Medicine, Ann Arbor 48109
Walsh College of Accountancy and
Business Administration,
www.walshcollege.edu
Washtenaw Community College,
www.wccnet.edu
Wayne County Community College,
www.wccd.edu
Wayne State University,
www.wayne.edu
Wayne State University: College of
Pharmacy and Allied Health,
Detroit 48202
Wayne State University: School of Law,
Detroit 48202
Wayne State University: School of
Medicine, Detroit 48201
West Shore Community College,
www.westshore.edu
Western Michigan University,
www.wmich.edu
Western Theological Seminary,
Holland 49419
Yeshiva Beth Yehuda-Yeshiva Gedolah
of Greater Detroit, Oak Park
48237

Minnesota

Academy College,
www.academycollege.edu
Alexandria Technical College,
www.alextech.edu
Anoka Technical College,
www.anokatech.edu
Anoka-Ramsey Community College,
www.anokaramsey.edu
Art Institutes International Minnesota,
www.aim.artinstitutes.edu
Augsburg College, www.augsburg.edu
Bemidji State University,
www.bemidjistate.edu
Bethany Lutheran College,
www.blc.edu
Bethel Theological Seminary, St. Paul
55112
Bethel University, www.bethel.edu

Brown College, www.browncollege.edu

Capella University, www.capellauniversity.edu

Carleton College, www.carleton.edu

Central Lakes College, www.clcmn.edu

Century Community and Technical College, www.century.edu

College of St. Benedict, www.csbsju.edu

College of St. Catherine, www.stkate.edu

College of St. Scholastica, www.css.edu

College of Visual Arts, www.cva.edu

Concordia College: Moorhead, www.concordiacollege.edu

Concordia University: St. Paul, www.csp.edu

Crossroads College, www.crossroadscollege.edu

Crown College, www.crown.edu

Dakota County Technical College, www.dctc.edu

Duluth Business University, www.dbumn.edu

Dunwoody College of Technology, www.dunwoody.edu

Fond du Lac Tribal and Community College, www.fdltcc.edu

Globe College, www.globecollege.com

Gustavus Adolphus College, www.gustavus.edu

Hamline University, www.hamline.edu

Hamline University: School of Law, St. Paul 55104

Hennepin Technical College, www.htc.mnscu.edu

Hibbing Community College, www.hibbing.edu

High-Tech Institute, www.hightechschools.com

Inver Hills Community College, www.inverhills.edu

Itasca Community College, www.itascacc.edu

Lake Superior College, www.lsc.edu

Lakeland Academy Division of Herzing College, www.herzing.edu

Leech Lake Tribal College, www.lltc.org

Luther Seminary: Theological Professions, St. Paul 55108

Macalester College, www.macalester.edu

Martin Luther College, www.mlc-wels.edu

Mayo Medical School, Rochester 55905

Mesabi Range Community and Technical College, www.mr.mnscu.edu

Metropolitan State University, www.metrostate.edu

Minneapolis Business College, www.mplsbusinesscollege.com

Minneapolis College of Art and Design, www.mcad.edu

Minneapolis Community and Technical College, www.minneapolis.edu

Minnesota School of Business, www.msbcollege.edu

Minnesota School of Business: Brooklyn Center, www.msbcollege.edu

Minnesota State College - Southeast Technical, www.southeastmn.edu

Minnesota State Community and Technical College - Fergus Falls, www.minnesota.edu

Minnesota State University: Mankato, www.mnsu.edu

Minnesota State University: Moorhead, www.mnstate.edu

Minnesota West Community and Technical College: Worthington Campus, www.mnwest.mnscu.edu

National American University: St. Paul, www.national.edu

Normandale Community College, www.normandale.edu

North Central University, www.northcentral.edu

North Hennepin Community College, www.nh.cc.edu

Northland Community & Technical College, www.northlandcollege.edu

Northwest Technical College, www.ntcmn.edu

Northwest Technical Institute, www.nti.edu

Northwestern College, www.nwc.edu

Northwestern College of Chiropractic, Bloomington 55431

Oak Hills Christian College, www.oakhills.edu

Pillsbury Baptist Bible College, www.pillsbury.edu/

Pine Technical College, www.pinetech.edu

Rainy River Community College, www.rrcc.mnscu.edu

Rasmussen College-Eagan, www.rasmussen.edu

Rasmussen College-Mankato, www.rasmussen.edu

Rasmussen College-Minnetonka, www.rasmussen.edu

Rasmussen College-St. Cloud, www.rasmussen.edu

Ridgewater College, www.ridgewater.edu

Riverland Community College, www.riverland.cc.mn.us

Rochester Community and Technical College, www.roch.edu

St. Cloud State University, www.stcloudstate.edu

St. Cloud Technical College, www.sctc.edu

St. John's University, www.csbsju.edu

St. John's University: School of Theology, Collegeville 56321

St. Mary's University of Minnesota, www.smumn.edu

St. Olaf College, www.stolaf.edu

St. Paul College, www.saintpaul.edu

South Central College, www.southcentral.edu

Southwest Minnesota State University, www.southwest.msus.edu

University of Minnesota Medical School, Minneapolis 55455

University of Minnesota Twin Cities: College of Veterinary Medicine, St. Paul 55108

University of Minnesota Twin Cities: School of Dentistry, Minneapolis 55455

University of Minnesota Twin Cities: School of Law, Minneapolis 55455

University of Minnesota: Crookston, www.UMCrookston.edu

University of Minnesota: Duluth, www.d.umn.edu

University of Minnesota: Morris, www.morris.umn.edu

University of Minnesota: Twin Cities, www.umn.edu/tc

University of St. Thomas, www.stthomas.edu

University of St. Thomas: School of Divinity, St. Paul 55105

Vermilion Community College, www.vcc.edu

Walden University, www.waldenu.edu

William Mitchell College of Law: Law Professions, St. Paul 55105

Winona State University, www.winona.edu

Mississippi

Alcorn State University, www.alcorn.edu

Antonelli College: Hattiesburg, www.antonellic.com

Antonelli College: Jackson, www.antonellicollege.edu

Belhaven College, www.belhaven.edu

Blue Mountain College, www.bmc.edu

Coahoma Community College, www.coahomacc.edu

Copiah-Lincoln Community College, www.colin.edu

Delta State University, www.deltastate.edu

East Central Community College, www.eccc.cc.ms.us

Hinds Community College, www.hindscc.edu

Holmes Community College, www.holmes.cc.ms.us

Itawamba Community College, www.iccms.edu

Jackson State University, www.jsums.edu

Jones County Junior College, www.jcjc.cc.ms.us

Magnolia Bible College, www.magnolia.edu

Meridian Community College, www.meridiancc.edu

Millsaps College, www.millsaps.edu

Mississippi College, www.mc.edu

Mississippi College: School of Law, Jackson 39201

Mississippi Delta Community College, www.msdelta.edu

Mississippi Gulf Coast Community College: Jefferson Davis Campus, www.mgccc.edu

Mississippi State University, www.msstate.edu

Mississippi State University: College of Veterinary Medicine, Mississippi University 39762

Mississippi Valley State University, www.mvsu.edu

Pearl River Community College, www.prcc.edu

Reformed Theological Seminary, Jackson 39209

Rust College, www.rustcollege.edu

Southwest Mississippi Community College, www.smcc.edu

Tougaloo College, www.tougaloo.edu

University of Mississippi, www.olemiss.edu

University of Mississippi Medical Center, www.umc.edu

University of Mississippi Medical Center: School of Dentistry, Jackson 39216

University of Mississippi Medical Center: School of Medicine, Jackson 39216

University of Mississippi: School of Law, University 38677

University of Mississippi: School of Pharmacy, University 38677

University of Southern Mississippi, www.usm.edu

Wesley Biblical Seminary, Jackson 39286

Wesley College, www.wesleycollege.edu

William Carey College, www.wmcarey.edu

Missouri

Assemblies of God Theological Seminary, Springfield 65802

Avila University, www.avila.edu

Baptist Bible College, www.baptist.edu

Blue River Community College, www.mcckc.edu

Calvary Bible College and Theological Seminary, www.calvary.edu

Central Bible College, www.cbcag.edu

Central Christian College of the Bible, www.cccb.edu

Central Methodist University, www.centralmethodist.edu

Central Missouri State University, www.cmsu.edu

Cleveland Chiropractic College of Kansas City, Kansas City 64131

College of the Ozarks, www.cofo.edu

Columbia College, www.ccis.edu

Conception Seminary College, www.conceptionabbey.org

Concordia Seminary, Clayton 63105

Cottey College, www.cottey.edu

Crowder College, www.crowder.edu

Culver-Stockton College, www.culver.edu

DeVry University: Kansas City, www.kc.devry.edu

Deaconess College of Nursing, www.deaconess.edu

Drury University, www.drury.edu

East Central College, www.eastcentral.edu

Eden Theological Seminary, Webster Groves 63119

Evangel University, www.evangel.edu

Everest College: Springfield, www.springfield-college.com

Fontbonne University, www.fontbonne.edu

Global University, www.globaluniversity.edu

Grantham University, www.grantham.edu

Hannibal-LaGrange College, www.hlg.edu

Harris-Stowe State University, www.hssu.edu

Hickey College, www.hickeycollege.edu

Jefferson College, www.jeffco.edu

Jewish Hospital College of Nursing and Allied Health, www.barnesjewishcollege.edu

Kansas City Art Institute, www.kcai.edu

Kansas City College of Legal Studies, www.metropolitancollege.edu

Kenrick-Glennon Seminary, St. Louis 63119

Kirksville College of Osteopathic Medicine, Kirksville 63501

Lester L. Cox College of Nursing and Health Sciences, www.coxcollege.edu

Lincoln University, www.lincolnu.edu

Lindenwood University, www.lindenwood.edu

Logan College of Chiropractic, www.logan.edu

Longview Community College, www.mcckc.edu

Maple Woods Community College, www.mcckc.edu

Maryville University of Saint Louis, www.maryville.edu

Metro Business College: Jefferson City, www.metrobusinesscollege.edu

Midwestern Baptist Theological Seminary, Kansas City 64118

Mineral Area College, www.mineralarea.edu

Missouri Baptist University, www.mobap.edu

Missouri College, www.missouricollege.com

Missouri Southern State University, www.mssu.edu

Missouri State University, www.smsu.edu

Missouri State University: West Plains, www.wp.missouristate.edu

Missouri Technical School, www.motech.edu

Missouri Valley College, www.moval.edu

Missouri Western State University, www.missouriwestern.edu

Moberly Area Community College, www.macc.edu

National American University: Kansas City, www.national.edu

Nazarene Theological Seminary, Kansas City 64131

North Central Missouri College, www.ncmissouri.edu

Northwest Missouri State University, www.nwmissouri.edu

Ozark Christian College, www.occ.edu

Ozarks Technical Community College, www.otc.edu

Park University, www.park.edu

Patricia Stevens College, www.patriciastevenscollege.edu

Penn Valley Community College, www.mcckc.edu

Ranken Technical College, www.ranken.edu

Research College of Nursing, www.researchcollege.edu

Rockhurst University, www.rockhurst.edu

St. Charles Community College, www.stchas.edu

St. Louis Christian College, www.slcconline.edu

St. Louis College of Pharmacy, St. Louis 63110

St. Louis Community College at Florissant Valley, www.stlcc.edu

St. Louis Community College at Meramec, www.stlcc.edu

St. Louis University, www.slu.edu

St. Louis University: School of Law, St. Louis 63108

St. Louis University: School of Medicine, St. Louis 63104

St. Luke's College, www.saintlukescollege.edu

St. Paul School of Theology, Kansas City 64127

Southeast Missouri State University, www.semo.edu

Southwest Baptist University, www.sbuniv.edu

State Fair Community College, www.sfccmo.edu

Stephens College, www.stephens.edu

Three Rivers Community College, www.trcc.edu

Truman State University, www.admissions.truman.edu

University of Health Sciences College of Osteopathic Medicine, Kansas City 64124

University of Missouri Columbia: School of Law, Columbia 65211

University of Missouri Columbia: School of Medicine, Columbia 65212

University of Missouri Columbia: School of Veterinary Medicine, Columbia 65211

University of Missouri Kansas City: School of Dentistry, Kansas City 64108

University of Missouri Kansas City: School of Law, Kansas City 64110

University of Missouri Kansas City: School of Medicine, Kansas City 64108

University of Missouri St. Louis: School of Optometry, St. Louis 63121

University of Missouri: Columbia, www.missouri.edu

University of Missouri: Kansas City, www.umkc.edu

University of Missouri: Rolla, www.umr.edu

University of Missouri: St. Louis, www.umsl.edu

Vatterott College, www.vatterott-college.edu

Vatterott College: St. Joseph, www.vatterott-college.edu

Vatterott College: Springfield, www.vatterott-college.edu

Washington University in St. Louis, www.wustl.edu

Washington University: School of Law, St. Louis 63130

Washington University: School of Medicine, St. Louis 63110

Webster University, www.webster.edu

Westminster College, www.westminster-mo.edu

William Jewell College, www.jewell.edu

William Woods University, www.williamwoods.edu

Montana

Blackfeet Community College, www.bfcc.org

Carroll College, www.carroll.edu

Chief Dull Knife College, www.cdkc.edu

Dawson Community College, www.dawson.edu

Flathead Valley Community College, www.fvcc.edu

Fort Belknap College, www.fbcc.edu

Fort Peck Community College, www.fpcc.edu

Helena College of Technology of the University of Montana, www.hct.umontana.edu

Little Big Horn College, www.lbhc.cc.mt.us

Miles Community College, www.milescc.edu

Montana State University College of Technology-Great Falls, www.msugf.edu

Montana State University: Billings, www.msubillings.edu

Montana State University: Bozeman, www.montana.edu

Montana Tech of the University of Montana, www.mtech.edu

Rocky Mountain College, www.rocky.edu

Salish Kootenai College, www.skc.edu

Stone Child College, www.montana.edu/wwwscc/

University of Great Falls, www.ugf.edu

University of Montana School of Pharmacy and Allied Health Sciences, Missoula 59812

University of Montana: Missoula, www.umt.edu

University of Montana: School of Law, Missoula 59812

University of Montana: Western, www.umwestern.edu

Nebraska

Bellevue University, www.bellevue.edu

Central Community College, www.cccneb.edu

Chadron State College, www.csc.edu

Clarkson College, www.clarksoncollege.edu

College of Saint Mary, www.csm.edu

Concordia University, www.cune.edu

Creative Center, www.creativecenter.edu

Creighton University, www.creighton.edu

Creighton University: School of Dentistry, Omaha 68178

Creighton University: School of Law, Omaha 68178

Creighton University: School of Medicine, Omaha 68178

Dana College, www.dana.edu

Doane College, www.doane.edu

Grace University, www.graceu.edu

Hamilton College: Lincoln, www.hamiltonlincoln.edu

Hastings College, www.hastings.edu

Little Priest Tribal College, www.lptc.bia.edu

Metropolitan Community College, www.mccneb.edu

Mid-Plains Community College Area, www.mpcc.edu

Midland Lutheran College, www.mlc.edu

Nebraska Christian College, www.nechristian.edu

Nebraska College of Technical Agriculture, www.ncta.unl.edu

Nebraska Indian Community College, www.thenicc.edu

Nebraska Methodist College of Nursing and Allied Health, www.methodistcollege.edu

Nebraska Wesleyan University, www.nebrwesleyan.edu

Northeast Community College, www.northeastcollege.com

Peru State College, www.peru.edu

Southeast Community College: Lincoln Campus, www.southeast.edu

Union College, www.ucollege.edu

University of Nebraska - Kearney, www.unk.edu

University of Nebraska - Lincoln, www.unl.edu

University of Nebraska - Omaha, www.unomaha.edu

University of Nebraska Lincoln: College of Law, Lincoln 68583

University of Nebraska Medical Center, www.unmc.edu

University of Nebraska Medical Center: College of Dentistry, Lincoln 68583

University of Nebraska Medical Center: College of Medicine, Omaha 68134

University of Nebraska Medical Center: College of Pharmacy, Omaha 68198

Vatterott College: Spring Valley, www.vatterott-college.com

Wayne State College, www.wsc.edu

Western Nebraska Community College, www.wncc.net

York College, www.york.edu

Nevada

Art Institute of Las Vegas, www.ailv.artinstitutes.edu

Career College of Northern Nevada, www.ccnn.edu

Community College of Southern Nevada, www.ccsn.nevada.edu

Great Basin College, www.gbcnv.edu

Heritage College, www.heritagecollege.com

High-Tech Institute, www.hightechinstitute.edu

International Academy of Design and Technology: Henderson, www.iadtvegas.com

Las Vegas College, lasvegas-college.com

Le Cordon Bleu College of Culinary Arts, www.VegasCulinary.com

Morrison University, www.morrison.neumont.edu

Sierra Nevada College, www.sierranevada.edu

Truckee Meadows Community College, www.tmcc.edu

University of Nevada: Las Vegas, www.unlv.edu

University of Nevada: Reno, www.unr.edu

University of Nevada: School of Medicine, Reno 89557

Western Nevada Community College, www.wncc.edu

New Hampshire

Chester College of New England, www.chestercollege.edu

Colby-Sawyer College, www.colby-sawyer.edu

Daniel Webster College, www.dwc.edu

Dartmouth College, www.dartmouth.edu

Dartmouth College: School of Medicine, Hanover 03755

Franklin Pierce College, www.fpc.edu

Franklin Pierce Law Center, Concord 03301

Granite State College, www.granite.edu

Keene State College, www.keene.edu

Magdalen College, www.magdalen.edu

McIntosh College, www.mcintoshcollege.edu

New England College, www.nec.edu

New Hampshire Community Technical College: Berlin, www.berlin.nhctc.edu

New Hampshire Community Technical College: Claremont, www.ncctc.edu

New Hampshire Community Technical College: Manchester, www.manchester.nhctc.edu

New Hampshire Community Technical College: Nashua, www.nashua.nhctc.edu

New Hampshire Community Technical College: Stratham, www.stratham.nhctc.edu

New Hampshire Technical Institute, www.nhti.edu

Plymouth State University, www.plymouth.edu

Rivier College, www.rivier.edu

St. Anselm College, www.anselm.edu

Southern New Hampshire University, www.snhu.edu

Thomas More College of Liberal Arts, www.thomasmorecollege.edu
University of New Hampshire, www.unh.edu
University of New Hampshire at Manchester, www.unhm.unh.edu

New Jersey

Assumption College for Sisters, www.acscollegeforsisters.org
Atlantic Cape Community College, www.atlantic.edu
Bergen Community College, www.bergen.edu
Berkeley College, www.berkeleycollege.edu
Beth Medrash Govoha, Lakewood 08701
Bloomfield College, www.bloomfield.edu
Brookdale Community College, www.brookdalecc.edu
Burlington County College, www.bcc.edu
Caldwell College, www.caldwell.edu
Camden County College, www.camdencc.edu
Centenary College, www.centenarycollege.edu
The College of New Jersey, www.tcnj.edu
College of St. Elizabeth, www.cse.edu
County College of Morris, www.ccm.edu
Cumberland County College, www.cccnj.net
DeVry University: North Brunswick, www.nj.devry.edu
Drew University, www.drew.edu
Drew University: School of Theology, Madison 07940
Essex County College, www.essex.edu
Fairleigh Dickinson University: College at Florham, www.fdu.edu
Fairleigh Dickinson University: Metropolitan Campus, www.fdu.edu
Felician College, www.felician.edu
Georgian Court University, www.georgian.edu
Gloucester County College, www.gccnj.edu
Hudson County Community College, www.hccc.edu
Immaculate Conception Seminary of Seton Hall University, South Orange 07079
Kean University, www.kean.edu
Mercer County Community College, www.mccc.edu
Middlesex County College, www.middlesexcc.edu
Monmouth University, www.monmouth.edu
Montclair State University, www.montclair.edu
New Brunswick Theological Seminary, New Brunswick 08901
New Jersey City University, www.njcu.edu
New Jersey Institute of Technology, www.njit.edu
Ocean County College, www.ocean.edu
Passaic County Community College, www.pccc.cc.nj.us
Princeton Theological Seminary, Princeton 08542
Princeton University, www.princeton.edu
Rabbinical College of America, Morristown 07962

Ramapo College of New Jersey, www.ramapo.edu
Raritan Valley Community College, www.raritanval.edu
Richard Stockton College of New Jersey, www.stockton.edu
Rider University, www.rider.edu
Rowan University, www.rowan.edu
Rutgers, The State University of New Jersey: Camden Regional Campus, www.rutgers.edu
Rutgers, The State University of New Jersey: Camden School of Law, Camden 08102
Rutgers, The State University of New Jersey: College of Pharmacy, New Brunswick 08903
Rutgers, The State University of New Jersey: New Brunswick/Piscataway Campus, www.rutgers.edu
Rutgers, The State University of New Jersey: Newark Regional Campus, www.rutgers.edu
Rutgers, The State University of New Jersey: Newark School of Law, Newark 07102
St. Peter's College, www.spc.edu
Salem Community College, www.salemcc.edu
Seton Hall University, www.shu.edu
Seton Hall University: School of Law, Newark 07102
Somerset Christian College, www.somerset.edu
Stevens Institute of Technology, www.stevens.edu
Sussex County Community College, www.sussex.edu
Thomas Edison State College, www.tesc.edu
UMDNJ-School of Osteopathic Medicine, Stratford 08084
Union County College, www.ucc.edu
University of Medicine and Dentistry of New Jersey: New Jersey Medical School, Newark 07103
University of Medicine and Dentistry of New Jersey: Robert Wood Johnson Medical School at Camden, Camden 08103
University of Medicine and Dentistry of New Jersey: New Jersey Dental School, Newark 07103
University of Medicine and Dentistry of New Jersey: Robert Wood Johnson Medical School, Piscataway 08854
University of Medicine and Dentistry of New Jersey: School of Health Related Professions, www.shrp.umdj.edu
University of Medicine and Dentistry of New Jersey: School of Nursing, Newark 07101
Warren County Community College, www.warren.edu
Westminster Choir College of Rider University, www.rider.edu/284.htm
William Paterson University of New Jersey, www.wpunj.edu

New Mexico

Albuquerque Technical-Vocational Institute, www.tvi.edu
Art Center Design College, www.theartcenter.edu
Clovis Community College, www.clovis.edu
College of Santa Fe, www.csf.edu
College of the Southwest, www.csw.edu

Dona Ana Branch Community College of New Mexico State University, www.nmsu.edu
Eastern New Mexico University, www.enmu.edu
Eastern New Mexico University: Roswell Campus, www.roswell.enmu.edu
Institute of American Indian Arts, www.iaiancad.org
International Institute of the Americas, www.iia.edu
Luna Community College, www.luna.edu
Mesalands Community College, www.mesalands.edu
Metropolitan College of Court Reporting, www.metropolitancollege.edu
National American University, www.national.edu
New Mexico Highlands University, www.nmhu.edu
New Mexico Institute of Mining and Technology, www.nmt.edu
New Mexico Junior College, www.nmjc.cc.nm.us
New Mexico Military Institute Junior College, www.nmmi.edu
New Mexico State University, www.nmsu.edu
New Mexico State University at Alamogordo, www.alamo.nmsu.edu
New Mexico State University at Carlsbad, cavern.nmsu.edu
New Mexico State University at Grants, www.grants.nmsu.edu
Northern New Mexico College, www.nnmcc.edu
St. John's College, www.stjohnscollege.edu
San Juan College, www.sanjuancollege.edu
Santa Fe Community College, www.sfccnm.edu
Southwestern Indian Polytechnic Institute, www.sipi.bia.edu
University of New Mexico, www.unm.edu
University of New Mexico College of Pharmacy, Albuquerque 87131
University of New Mexico: School of Law, Albuquerque 87131
University of New Mexico: School of Medicine, Albuquerque 87131
Western New Mexico University, www.wnmu.edu

New York

ASA Institute of Business and Computer Technology, www.asa.edu
Adelphi University, www.adelphi.edu
Adirondack Community College, www.sunyacc.edu
Albany College of Pharmacy, www.acp.edu
Albany Law School of Union University, Albany 12208
Albany Medical College: School of Medicine, Albany 12208
Albert Einstein College of Medicine, Bronx 10461
Alfred University, www.alfred.edu
Alliance Theological Seminary, Nyack 10960
American Academy McAllister Institute of Funeral Service, www.funeraleducation.org
American Academy of Dramatic Arts, www.aada.org

Art Institute of New York City, www.ainyc.artinstitutes.edu
Bard College, www.bard.edu
Barnard College, www.barnard.edu
Benjamin N. Cardozo School of Law, New York 10003
Berkeley College, www.berkeleycollege.edu
Berkeley College of New York City, www.berkeleycollege.edu
Boricua College, www.boricuacollege.edu
Bramson ORT College, www.bramsonort.org
Briarcliffe College, www.briarcliffe.edu
Brooklyn Law School, Brooklyn 11201
Broome Community College, www.sunybroome.edu
Bryant & Stratton College: Albany, www.bryantstratton.edu
Bryant & Stratton College: Buffalo, www.bryantstratton.edu
Bryant & Stratton College: Henrietta, www.bryantstratton.edu
Bryant & Stratton College: Lackawanna, www.bryantstratton.edu
Bryant & Stratton College: Rochester, www.bryantstratton.edu
Bryant & Stratton College: Syracuse, www.bryantstratton.edu
Bryant & Stratton College: Syracuse North, www.bryantstratton.edu
Business Informatics Center, www.thecollegeforbusiness.com
Canisius College, www.canisius.edu
Cayuga County Community College, www.cayuga-cc.edu
Cazenovia College, www.cazenovia.edu
Christ The King Seminary, East Aurora 14052
City University of New York: Baruch College, www.baruch.cuny.edu
City University of New York: Borough of Manhattan Community College, www.bmcc.cuny.edu
City University of New York: Bronx Community College, www.bcc.cuny.edu
City University of New York: Brooklyn College, www.brooklyn.cuny.edu
City University of New York: City College, www.ccny.cuny.edu
City University of New York: College of Staten Island, www.csi.cuny.edu
City University of New York: Hostos Community College, www.hostos.cuny.edu
City University of New York: Hunter College, www.hunter.cuny.edu
City University of New York: John Jay College of Criminal Justice, www.jjay.cuny.edu
City University of New York: Kingsborough Community College, www.kbcc.cuny.edu
City University of New York: LaGuardia Community College, www.lagcc.cuny.edu
City University of New York: Lehman College, www.lehman.cuny.edu
City University of New York: Medgar Evers College, www.mec.cuny.edu
City University of New York: New York City College of Technology, www.citytech.cuny.edu
City University of New York: Queens College, www.qc.cuny.edu

City University of New York: Queensborough Community College, www.qcc.cuny.edu

City University of New York: School of Law at Queens College, Flushing 11367

City University of New York: York College, www.york.cuny.edu

Clarkson University, www.clarkson.edu

Clinton Community College, www.clinton.edu

Cochran School of Nursing-St. John's Riverside Hospital, www.riversidehealth.org

Colgate Rochester Divinity School-Bexley Crozer Theological Seminary, Rochester 14620

Colgate University, www.colgate.edu

College of Mount St. Vincent, www.mountsaintvincent.edu

College of New Rochelle, www.cnr.edu

College of Saint Rose, www.strose.edu

College of Westchester, www.cw.edu

Columbia University: College of Physicians and Surgeons, New York 10032

Columbia University: Columbia College, www.college.columbia.edu

Columbia University: Fu Foundation School of Engineering and Applied Science, www.engineering.columbia.edu

Columbia University: School of Dental and Oral Surgery, New York 10032

Columbia University: School of General Studies, www.gs.columbia.edu

Columbia University: School of Law, New York 10027

Columbia University: School of Nursing, www.nursing.hs.columbia.edu

Columbia-Greene Community College, www.sunycgcc.edu

Concordia College, www.concordia-ny.edu

Cooper Union for the Advancement of Science and Art, www.cooper.edu

Cornell University, www.cornell.edu

Cornell University Medical College, New York 10021

Cornell University: College of Veterinary Medicine, Ithaca 14853

Cornell University: School of Law, Ithaca 14853

Corning Community College, www.corning-cc.edu

Culinary Institute of America, www.ciachef.edu

D'Youville College, www.dyc.edu

Daemen College, www.daemen.edu

Davis College, www.davisny.edu

DeVry Institute of Technology: New York, http://www.ny.devry.edu/

Dominican College of Blauvelt, www.dc.edu

Dowling College, www.dowling.edu

Dutchess Community College, www.sunydutchess.edu

Eastman School of Music of the University of Rochester, www.rochester.edu/eastman

Elmira Business Institute, www.ebi-college.com

Elmira College, www.elmira.edu

Erie Community College: City Campus, www.ecc.edu

Erie Community College: North Campus, www.ecc.edu

Erie Community College: South Campus, www.ecc.edu

Eugene Lang College The New School for Liberal Arts, www.lang.edu

Excelsior College, www.excelsior.edu

Fashion Institute of Technology, www.fitnyc.edu

Finger Lakes Community College, www.flcc.edu

Five Towns College, www.fivetowns.edu

Fordham University, www.fordham.edu

Fordham University: School of Law, New York 10023

Fulton-Montgomery Community College, www.fmcc.suny.edu

General Theological Seminary, New York 10011

Genesee Community College, www.genesee.edu

Globe Institute of Technology, www.globe.edu

Hamilton College, www.hamilton.edu

Hartwick College, www.hartwick.edu

Helene Fuld College of Nursing, www.helenefuld.edu

Herkimer County Community College, www.hccc.ntcnet.com

Hilbert College, www.hilbert.edu

Hobart and William Smith Colleges, www.hws.edu

Hofstra University, www.hofstra.edu

Hofstra University: School of Law, Hempstead 11550

Holy Trinity Orthodox Seminary, www.hts.edu

Houghton College, www.houghton.edu

Hudson Valley Community College, www.hvcc.edu

Institute of Design and Construction, www.idc.edu

Interboro Institute, www.interboro.edu

Iona College, www.iona.edu

Island Drafting and Technical Institute, www.idti.edu

Ithaca College, www.ithaca.edu

Jamestown Business College, www.jbcny.org

Jamestown Community College, www.sunyjcc.edu

Jefferson Community College, www.sunyjefferson.edu

Jewish Theological Seminary of America, www.jtsa.edu

Jewish Theological Seminary of America: First Professional, New York 10027

Juilliard School, www.juilliard.edu

Katharine Gibbs School: New York, www.gibbsny.com

Kehilath Yakov Rabbinical Seminary, Brooklyn 11211

Keuka College, www.keuka.edu

King's College, www.tkc.edu

Kol Yaakov Torah Center, Monsey 10952

Laboratory Institute of Merchandising, www.limcollege.edu

Le Moyne College, www.lemoyne.edu

Long Island Business Institute, www.libi.edu

Long Island College Hospital School of Nursing, Brooklyn 11231

Long Island University: Brooklyn Campus, www.liu.edu

Long Island University: C.W. Post Campus, www.liu.edu

Long Island University: Arnold and Marie Schwartz College of Pharmacy and Health Sciences, Brooklyn 11201

Machzikei Hadath Rabbinical College, Brooklyn 11204

Manhattan College, www.manhattan.edu

Manhattan School of Music, www.msmnyc.edu

Manhattanville College, www.manhattanville.edu

Mannes College The New School for Music, www.mannes.edu

Maria College, www.mariacollege.edu

Marist College, www.marist.edu

Marymount Manhattan College, www.mmm.edu

Medaille College, www.medaille.edu

Mercy College, www.mercy.edu

Mesivta Eastern Parkway Rabbinical Seminary, Brooklyn 11218

Mesivta Tifereth Jerusalem of America, New York 10002

Metropolitan College of New York, www.metropolitan.edu

Mildred Elley, www.mildred-elley.edu

Mirrer Yeshiva Central Institute, Brooklyn 11223

Mohawk Valley Community College, www.mvcc.edu

Molloy College, www.molloy.edu

Monroe College, www.monroecollege.edu

Monroe Community College, www.monroecc.edu

Mount St. Mary College, www.msmc.edu

Mount Sinai School of Medicine of City University of New York, New York 10029

Nassau Community College, www.ncc.edu

Nazareth College of Rochester, www.naz.edu

New York Career Institute, www.nyci.com

New York Chiropractic College, www.nycc.edu

New York College of Osteopathic Medicine of New York Institute of Technology, Old Westbury 11568

New York College of Podiatric Medicine, New York 10035

New York Institute of Technology, www.nyit.edu

New York Law School, New York 10013

New York Medical College, Valhalla 10595

New York School of Interior Design, www.nysid.edu

New York Theological Seminary, New York 10001

New York University, www.nyu.edu

New York University: College of Dentistry, New York 10010

New York University: School of Law, New York 10012

New York University: School of Medicine, New York 10016

Niagara County Community College, www.niagaracc.suny.edu

Niagara University, www.niagara.edu

North Country Community College, www.nccc.edu

Nyack College, www.nyack.edu

Ohr Hameir Theological Seminary, Peekskill 10566

Ohr Somayach Institutions: School of Theology, Monsey 10952

Olean Business Institute, www.obi.edu

Onondaga Community College, www.sunyocc.edu

Orange County Community College, orange.cc.ny.us

Pace University, www.pace.edu

Pace University Westchester: School of Law, White Plains 10603

Parsons The New School for Design, www.parsons.edu

Paul Smith's College, www.paulsmiths.edu

Phillips Beth Israel School of Nursing, www.futurenursebi.org

Plaza College, www.plazacollege.edu

Polytechnic University, www.poly.edu

Pratt Institute, www.pratt.edu

Rabbi Isaac Elchanan Theological Seminary, New York 10033

Rabbinical Academy Mesivta Rabbi Chaim Berlin, Brooklyn 11230

Rabbinical College Beth Shraga, Monsey 10952

Rabbinical College Bobover Yeshiva B'nei Zion, Brooklyn 11219

Rabbinical Seminary M'Kor Chaim, Brooklyn 11219

Rensselaer Polytechnic Institute, www.rpi.edu

Roberts Wesleyan College, www.roberts.edu

Rochester Business Institute, www.rochester-institute.com

Rochester Institute of Technology, www.rit.edu

Rockland Community College, www.sunyrockland.edu

Russell Sage College, www.sage.edu/rsc

Sage College of Albany, www.sage.edu

St. Bernard's Institute, Rochester 14620

St. Bonaventure University, www.sbu.edu

St. Elizabeth College of Nursing, www.secon.edu

St. Francis College, www.stfranciscollege.edu

St. John Fisher College, www.sjfc.edu

St. John's University, www.stjohns.edu

St. John's University, Jamaica 11439

St. John's University: College of Pharmacy and Allied Health Professions, Jamaica 11439

St. John's University: School of Law, Jamaica 11439

St. Joseph's College, www.sjcny.edu

St. Joseph's College of Nursing, www.sjhsyr.org/nursing

St. Joseph's College: Suffolk Campus, www.sjcny.edu

St. Joseph's Seminary and College, Yonkers 10704

St. Lawrence University, www.stlawu.edu

St. Thomas Aquinas College, www.stac.edu

St. Vincent Catholic Medical Centers, Fresh Meadows 11365

St. Vladimir's Orthodox Theological Seminary, Crestwood 10707

Sarah Lawrence College, www.sarahlawrence.edu

Schenectady County Community College, www.sunysccc.edu

School of Visual Arts, www.schoolofvisualarts.edu

Seminary of the Immaculate Conception, Huntington 11743

Sh'or Yoshuv Rabbinical College, Far Rockaway 11691

Siena College, www.siena.edu

Skidmore College, www.skidmore.edu

State University of New York College at Brockport, www.brockport.edu

State University of New York College at Buffalo, www.buffalostate.edu

State University of New York College at Cortland, www.cortland.edu

State University of New York College at Fredonia, www.fredonia.edu

State University of New York College at Geneseo, www.geneseo.edu

State University of New York College at Old Westbury, www.oldwestbury.edu

State University of New York College at Oneonta, www.oneonta.edu

State University of New York College at Plattsburgh, www.plattsburgh.edu

State University of New York College at Potsdam, www.potsdam.edu

State University of New York College of Agriculture and Technology at Cobleskill, www.cobleskill.edu

State University of New York College of Agriculture and Technology at Morrisville, www.morrisville.edu

State University of New York College of Environmental Science and Forestry, www.esf.edu

State University of New York College of Optometry, New York 10010

State University of New York College of Technology at Alfred, www.alfredstate.edu

State University of New York College of Technology at Canton, www.canton.edu

State University of New York College of Technology at Delhi, www.delhi.edu

State University of New York Downstate Medical Center, www.downstate.edu

State University of New York Empire State College, www.esc.edu

State University of New York Health Science Center at Brooklyn: School of Medicine, Brooklyn 11203

State University of New York Health Science Center at Syracuse: School of Medicine, Syracuse 13210

State University of New York Health Sciences Center at Stony Brook: School of Dentistry, Stony Brook 11794

State University of New York Health Sciences Center at Stony Brook: School of Medicine, Stony Brook 11794

State University of New York Institute of Technology at Utica/Rome, www.sunyit.edu

State University of New York Maritime College, www.sunymaritime.edu

State University of New York Upstate Medical University, www.upstate.edu

State University of New York at Albany, www.albany.edu

State University of New York at Binghamton, www.binghamton.edu

State University of New York at Buffalo, www.buffalo.edu

State University of New York at Buffalo: School of Dentistry, Buffalo 14214

State University of New York at Buffalo: School of Law, Buffalo 14260

State University of New York at Buffalo: School of Medicine, Buffalo 14214

State University of New York at Buffalo: School of Pharmacy, Buffalo 14260

State University of New York at Farmingdale, www.farmingdale.edu

State University of New York at New Paltz, www.newpaltz.edu

State University of New York at Oswego, www.oswego.edu

State University of New York at Purchase, www.purchase.edu

State University of New York at Stony Brook, www.stonybrook.edu

Suffolk County Community College, www.sunysuffolk.edu

Sullivan County Community College, www.sullivan.suny.edu

Swedish Institute, www.swedishinstitute.com

Syracuse University, www.syracuse.edu

Syracuse University: College of Law, Syracuse 13244

Taylor Business Institute, www.tbiglobal.com

Technical Career Institutes, www.tcicollege.net

Tompkins-Cortland Community College, www.tc3.edu

Touro College, www.touro.edu

Touro College: Jacob D. Fuchsberg Law Center, Huntington 11743

Trocaire College, www.trocaire.edu

Ulster County Community College, www.sunyulster.edu

Union College, www.union.edu

Union Theological Seminary: Theological Professions, www.uts.columbia.edu

United States Merchant Marine Academy, www.usmma.edu

United States Military Academy, www.usma.edu

University of Rochester, www.rochester.edu

University of Rochester: School of Medicine and Dentistry, Rochester 14642

Utica College, www.utica.edu

Utica School of Commerce, www.uscny.edu

Vassar College, www.vassar.edu

Vaughn College of Aeronautics and Technology, www.vaughn.edu

Villa Maria College of Buffalo, www.villa.edu

Wagner College, www.wagner.edu

Webb Institute, www.webb-institute.edu

Wells College, www.wells.edu

Westchester Community College, www.sunywcc.edu

Wood Tobe-Coburn School, www.woodtobecoburn.com

Yeshiva Derech Chaim, Brooklyn 11218

Yeshiva Karlin Stolin Beth Aron Y'Israel Rabbinical Institute, Brooklyn 11204

Yeshiva Mikdash Melech, Brooklyn 11230

Yeshiva University, www.yu.edu

Yeshiva and Kolel Bais Medrash Elyon, Monsey 10952

Yeshiva of Nitra Rabbinical College, Mt. Kisco 11211

Yeshivat Mikdash Melech, Brooklyn 11230

North Carolina

Alamance Community College, www.alamancecc.edu

Appalachian State University, www.appstate.edu

Art Institute of Charlotte, www.aich.artinstitutes.edu

Asheville-Buncombe Technical Community College, www.abtech.edu

Barton College, www.barton.edu

Beaufort County Community College, www.beaufortccc.edu

Belmont Abbey College, www.belmontabbeycollege.edu

Bennett College, www.bennett.edu

Bladen Community College, www.bladen.cc.nc.us

Blue Ridge Community College, www.blueridge.edu

Brevard College, www.brevard.edu

Brunswick Community College, www.brunswickcc.edu

Cabarrus College of Health Sciences, www.cabarruscollege.edu

Caldwell Community College and Technical Institute, www.cccti.edu

Campbell University, www.campbell.edu

Campbell University: Norman Adrian Wiggins School of Law, Buies Creek 27506

Campbell University: School of Pharmacy, Buies Creek 27506

Cape Fear Community College, www.cfcc.edu

Carolinas College of Health Sciences, www.carolinascollege.edu

Carteret Community College, www.carteret.cc.nc.us

Catawba College, www.catawba.edu

Catawba Valley Community College, www.cvcc.edu

Central Carolina Community College, www.cccc.edu

Central Piedmont Community College, www.cpcc.edu

Chowan College, www.chowan.edu

Cleveland Community College, www.clevelandcommunitycollege.edu

Coastal Carolina Community College, www.coastal.cc.nc.us

College of the Albemarle, www.albemarle.cc.nc.us

Craven Community College, www.cravencc.edu

Davidson College, www.davidson.edu

Davidson County Community College, www.davidson.cc.nc.us

DeVry University: Charlotte, Charlotte 28211

Duke University, www.duke.edu

Duke University: Divinity School, Durham 27708

Duke University: School of Law, Durham 27708

Duke University: School of Medicine, Durham 27710

Durham Technical Community College, www.durhamtech.edu

East Carolina University, www.ecu.edu

East Carolina University: School of Medicine, Greenville 27858

Edgecombe Community College, www.edgecombe.edu

Elizabeth City State University, www.ecsu.edu

Elon University, www.elon.edu

Fayetteville State University, www.uncfsu.edu

Fayetteville Technical Community College, www.faytechcc.edu

Forsyth Technical Community College, www.forsyth.tec.nc.us

Gardner-Webb University, www.gardner-webb.edu

Gaston College, www.gaston.cc.nc.us

Greensboro College, www.gborocollege.edu

Guilford College, www.guilford.edu

Guilford Technical Community College, www.gtcc.edu

Halifax Community College, www.halifaxcc.edu

Haywood Community College, www.haywood.edu

High Point University, www.highpoint.edu

Hood Theological Seminary, Salisbury 28144

Isothermal Community College, www.isothermal.edu

James Sprunt Community College, www.sprunt.com

John Wesley College, www.johnwesley.edu

Johnson & Wales University, www.jwu.edu/charlotte/

Johnson C. Smith University, www.jcsu.edu

Johnston Community College, www.johnston.cc.nc.us

King's College, www.kingscollegecharlotte.edu

Lees-McRae College, www.lmc.edu

Lenoir Community College, www.lenoir.cc.nc.us

Lenoir-Rhyne College, www.lrc.edu

Livingstone College, www.livingstone.edu

Louisburg College, www.louisburg.edu

Mars Hill College, www.mhc.edu

Martin Community College, www.martincc.edu

Mayland Community College, www.mayland.edu

McDowell Technical Community College, www.mcdowelltech.cc.nc.us

Meredith College, www.meredith.edu

Methodist College, www.methodist.edu

Miller-Motte Technical College, www.miller-motte.com

Mitchell Community College, www.mitchell.cc.nc.us

Montgomery Community College, www.montgomery.edu

Montreat College, www.montreat.edu

Mount Olive College, www.mountolivecollege.edu

Nash Community College, www.nash.cc.nc.us

North Carolina Agricultural and Technical State University, www.ncat.edu

North Carolina Central University, www.nccu.edu

North Carolina Central University: School of Law, Durham 27707

North Carolina School of the Arts, www.ncarts.edu

North Carolina State University, www.ncsu.edu

North Carolina State University: College of Veterinary Medicine, Raleigh 27606

North Carolina Wesleyan College, www.ncwc.edu

Pamlico Community College, www.pamlico.cc.nc.us

Peace College, www.peace.edu

Pfeiffer University, www.pfeiffer.edu

Piedmont Baptist College, www.pbc.edu

Piedmont Community College, www.piedmont.cc.nc.us

Pitt Community College, www.pitt.cc.nc.us

Queens University of Charlotte, www.queens.edu/admissions
Randolph Community College, www.randolph.edu
Richmond Community College, www.richmondcc.edu
Roanoke Bible College, www.roanokebible.edu
Roanoke-Chowan Community College, www.roanokechowan.edu
Robeson Community College, www.robeson.cc.nc.us
Rockingham Community College, www.rcc.cc.nc.us
Rowan-Cabarrus Community College, www.rccc.cc.nc.us
St. Andrews Presbyterian College, www.sapc.edu
St. Augustine's College, www.st-aug.edu
Salem College, www.salem.edu
Sampson Community College, www.sampson.cc.nc.us
Sandhills Community College, www.sandhills.edu
Shaw University, www.shawuniversity.edu
South College, Asheville 28806
South Piedmont Community College, www.spcc.edu
Southeastern Baptist Theological Seminary: Theological Professions, www.sebts.edu
Southeastern Community College, www.sccnc.edu
Southwestern Community College, www.southwest.cc.nc.us
Stanly Community College, www.stanly.edu
Surry Community College, www.surry.edu
Tri-County Community College, www.tricountycc.edu
University of North Carolina at Asheville, www.unca.edu
University of North Carolina at Chapel Hill, www.unc.edu
University of North Carolina at Chapel Hill: School of Dentistry, Chapel Hill 27599
University of North Carolina at Chapel Hill: School of Law, Chapel Hill 27599
University of North Carolina at Chapel Hill: School of Medicine, Chapel Hill 27599
University of North Carolina at Chapel Hill: School of Pharmacy, Chapel Hill 27599
University of North Carolina at Charlotte, www.uncc.edu
University of North Carolina at Greensboro, www.uncg.edu
University of North Carolina at Pembroke, www.uncp.edu
University of North Carolina at Wilmington, www.uncw.edu
Vance-Granville Community College, www.vgcc.edu
Wake Forest University, www.wfu.edu
Wake Forest University: Bowman Gray School of Medicine, Winston-Salem 27157
Wake Forest University: School of Law, Winston-Salem 27109
Wake Technical Community College, www.wake.tec.nc.us
Warren Wilson College, www.warren-wilson.edu
Wayne Community College, www.wayne.cc.nc.us
Western Carolina University, www.wcu.edu

Western Piedmont Community College, www.wpcc.edu
Wilkes Community College, www.wilkescc.edu
Wilson Technical Community College, www.wilsontech.edu
Wingate University, www.wingate.edu
Winston-Salem State University, www.wssu.edu

North Dakota

Aakers College: Fargo, www.aakers.edu
Bismarck State College, www.bismarckstate.edu
Cankdeska Cikana Community College, www.littlehoop.edu
Dickinson State University, www.dsu.nodak.edu
Fort Berthold Community College, New Town 58763
Jamestown College, www.jc.edu
Lake Region State College, www.lrsc.nodak.edu
Mayville State University, www.mayvillestate.edu
Medcenter One College of Nursing, www.medcenterone.com/college/nursing.htm
Minot State University, www.minotstateu.edu
Minot State University: Bottineau Campus, www.misu-b.nodak.edu
North Dakota State College of Science, www.ndscs.nodak.edu
North Dakota State University, www.ndsu.edu
North Dakota State University: College of Pharmacy, Fargo 58105
Sitting Bull College, www.sittingbull.edu
Trinity Bible College, www.trinitybiblecollege.edu
Turtle Mountain Community College, www.tm.edu
University of Mary, www.umary.edu
University of North Dakota, www.und.edu
University of North Dakota: School of Law, Grand Forks 58202
University of North Dakota: School of Medicine, Grand Forks 58202
Valley City State University, www.vcsu.edu
Williston State College, www.wsc.nodak.edu

Ohio

Allegheny Wesleyan College, www.awc.edu
Antioch College, www.antioch-college.edu
Antioch University McGregor, www.mcgregor.edu
Art Academy of Cincinnati, www.artacademy.edu
Art Institute of Cincinnati, www.theartinstituteofcincinnati.com
Ashland Theological Seminary, Ashland 44805
Ashland University, www.ashland.edu
Athenaeum of Ohio, Cincinnati 45230
Baldwin-Wallace College, www.bw.edu
Belmont Technical College, www.btc.edu
Bluffton University, www.bluffton.edu
Bowling Green State University, www.bgsu.edu
Bowling Green State University: Firelands College, www.firelands.bgsu.edu

Bradford School, www.bradfordschoolcolumbus.edu
Brown Mackie College: Akron, www.brownmackie.edu
Bryant & Stratton College: Cleveland, www.bryantstratton.edu
Bryant & Stratton College: Parma, www.bryantstratton.edu
Bryant & Stratton College: Willoughby Hills, www.bryantstratton.edu
Capital University, www.capital.edu
Capital University: School of Law, Columbus 43215
Case Western Reserve University, www.case.edu
Case Western Reserve University: School of Dentistry, Cleveland 44106
Case Western Reserve University: School of Law,
Case Western Reserve University: School of Medicine, Cleveland 44106
Cedarville University, www.cedarville.edu
Central Ohio Technical College, www.cotc.edu
Central State University, www.centralstate.edu
Chatfield College, www.chatfield.edu
Cincinnati Christian University, www.ccuniversity.edu
Cincinnati College of Mortuary Science, www.ccms.edu
Cincinnati State Technical and Community College, www.cincinnatistate.edu
Circleville Bible College, www.biblecollege.edu
Clark State Community College, www.clark.cc.oh.us
Cleveland Institute of Art, www.cia.edu
Cleveland Institute of Electronics, www.cie-wc.edu
Cleveland Institute of Music, www.cim.edu
Cleveland State University, www.csuohio.edu
Cleveland State University: College of Law, Cleveland 44115
College of Art Advertising, Cincinnati 45211-4427
College of Mount St. Joseph, www.msj.edu
College of Wooster, www.wooster.edu
Columbus College of Art and Design, www.ccad.edu
Columbus State Community College, www.cscc.edu
Cuyahoga Community College: Metropolitan Campus, www.tri-c.edu
David N. Myers University, www.myers.edu
Davis College, www.daviscollege.edu
DeVry University: Columbus, www.devrycols.edu
Defiance College, www.defiance.edu
Denison University, www.denison.edu
ETI Technical College of Niles, www.eticollege.edu
Edison State Community College, www.edisonohio.edu
Franciscan University of Steubenville, www.franciscan.edu
Franklin University, www.franklin.edu
Gallipolis Career College, www.gallipoliscareercollege.com
God's Bible School and College, www.gbs.edu
Good Samaritan College of Nursing and Health Science, www.goodsamaritancollege.com

Hebrew Union College-Jewish Institute of Religion, Cincinnati 45220
Heidelberg College, www.heidelberg.edu
Hiram College, www.hiram.edu
Hocking College, www.hocking.edu
International College of Broadcasting, www.icbcollege.com
James A. Rhodes State College, www.rhodesstate.edu
Jefferson Community College, www.jcc.edu
John Carroll University, www.jcu.edu
Kent State University, www.kent.edu
Kent State University: Ashtabula Regional Campus, www.ashtabula.kent.edu
Kent State University: East Liverpool Regional Campus, www.kenteliv.kent.edu
Kent State University: Salem Regional Campus, www.salem.kent.edu
Kent State University: Stark Campus, www.stark.kent.edu
Kent State University: Trumbull Campus, www.trumbull.kent.edu
Kent State University: Tuscarawas Campus, www.tusc.kent.edu
Kenyon College, www.kenyon.edu
Kettering College of Medical Arts, www.kcma.edu
Lake Erie College, www.lec.edu
Lakeland Community College, www.lakelandcc.edu
Laura and Alvin Siegal College of Judaic Studies, www.siegalcollege.edu
Lourdes College, www.lourdes.edu
Malone College, www.malone.edu
Marietta College, www.marietta.edu
Marion Technical College, www.mtc.edu
MedCentral College of Nursing, www.medcentral.edu
Medical College of Ohio, Toledo 43699
Mercy College of Northwest Ohio, www.mercycollege.edu
Methodist Theological School in Ohio, Delaware 43015
Miami University: Hamilton Campus, www.ham.muohio.edu
Miami University: Oxford Campus, www.muohio.edu
Mount Carmel College of Nursing, www.mccn.edu
Mount Union College, www.muc.edu
Mount Vernon Nazarene University, www.mvnu.edu
Muskingum College, www.muskingum.edu
Oberlin College, www.oberlin.edu
Ohio Business College: Sandusky, www.ohiobusinesscollege.edu
Ohio College of Massotherapy, www.ocm.edu
Ohio College of Podiatric Medicine, Cleveland 44106
Ohio Dominican University, www.ohiodominican.edu
Ohio Institute of Photography and Technology, www.oipt.com
Ohio Northern University, www.onu.edu
Ohio Northern University: College of Law, Ada 45810
Ohio Northern University: College of Pharmacy, Ada 45810
Ohio State University Agricultural Technical Institute, www.ati.osu.edu
Ohio State University Columbus Campus: College of Dentistry, Columbus 43210

Ohio State University Columbus Campus: College of Medicine, Columbus 43210

Ohio State University Columbus Campus: College of Optometry, Columbus 43210

Ohio State University Columbus Campus: College of Pharmacy, Columbus 43210

Ohio State University Columbus Campus: College of Veterinary Medicine, Columbus 43210

Ohio State University: College of Law, Columbus 43210

Ohio State University: Columbus Campus, www.osu.edu

Ohio State University: Lima Campus, www.lima.ohio-state.edu

Ohio State University: Mansfield Campus, www.mansfield.ohio-state.edu

Ohio State University: Marion Campus, www.marion.ohio-state.edu

Ohio State University: Newark Campus, www.newark.osu.edu

Ohio University, www.ohio.edu

Ohio University: Chillicothe Campus, http://oucweb.chillicothe.ohiou.edu

Ohio University: College of Osteopathic Medicine, Athens 45701

Ohio University: Eastern Campus, www.eastern.ohiou.edu

Ohio University: Lancaster Campus, www.lancaster.ohiou.edu

Ohio University: Southern Campus at Ironton, www.southern.ohiou.edu

Ohio University: Zanesville Campus, www.zanesville.ohiou.edu

Ohio Valley College of Technology, www.ovct.edu

Ohio Wesleyan University, http://web.owu.edu

Otterbein College, www.otterbein.edu

Owens Community College: Toledo, www.owens.edu

Pontifical College Josephinum, www.pcj.edu

Pontifical College Josephinum: First Professional, Columbus 43235

Rabbinical College of Telshe, Wickliffe 44092

Remington College: Cleveland, www.remingtoncollege.edu

Rosedale Bible College, www.rosedale.edu

St. Mary Seminary, Wickliffe 44092

School of Advertising Art, www.saacollege.com

Shawnee State University, www.shawnee.edu

Sinclair Community College, www.sinclair.edu

Southeastern Business College, www.careersohio.com

Southeastern Business College: Jackson, www.southeasternbusinesscollege.com

Southeastern Business College: Lancaster, www.careersohio.com

Southeastern Business College: New Boston, www.southeasternbusinesscollege.com

Southern State Community College, www.sscc.edu

Southwestern College: Franklin, www.swcollege.net

Southwestern College: Vine Street Campus, www.swcollege.net

Stark State College of Technology, www.starkstate.edu

Stautzenberger College, www.sctoday.edu

Technology Education College, www.teceducation.com

Tiffin University, www.tiffin.edu

Trinity Lutheran Seminary, Columbus 43209

Trumbull Business College, www.tbc-trumbullbusiness.com

Union Institute & University, www.tui.edu

United Theological Seminary, Dayton 45406

University of Akron, www.uakron.edu

University of Akron: School of Law, Akron 44325

University of Akron: Wayne College, www.wayne.uakron.edu

University of Cincinnati, www.uc.edu

University of Cincinnati: Clermont College, www.ucclermont.edu

University of Cincinnati: College of Law, Cincinnati 45221

University of Cincinnati: College of Medicine, Cincinnati 45267

University of Cincinnati: College of Pharmacy, Cincinnati 45267

University of Cincinnati: Raymond Walters College, www.rwc.uc.edu

University of Dayton, www.udayton.edu

University of Dayton: School of Law, Dayton 45469

University of Findlay, www.findlay.edu

University of Northwestern Ohio, www.unoh.edu

University of Rio Grande, www.rio.edu

University of Toledo, www.utoledo.edu

University of Toledo: College of Law, Toledo 43606

University of Toledo: College of Pharmacy, Toledo 43606

Urbana University, www.urbana.edu

Ursuline College, www.ursuline.edu

Walsh University, www.walsh.edu

Washington State Community College, www.wscc.edu

Wilmington College, www.wilmington.edu

Winebrenner Seminary, Findlay 45839

Wittenberg University, www.wittenberg.edu

Wright State University, www.wright.edu

Wright State University: Lake Campus, www.wright.edu/lake

Wright State University: School of Medicine, Dayton 45401

Xavier University, www.xavier.edu

Youngstown State University, www.ysu.edu

Zane State College, www.zanestate.edu

Oklahoma

Bacone College, www.bacone.edu

Cameron University, www.cameron.edu

Carl Albert State College, www.carlalbert.edu

Connors State College, www.connorsstate.edu

East Central University, www.ecok.edu

Eastern Oklahoma State College, www.eosc.edu

Heritage College Hair Design, www.heritage-education.com

Metropolitan College, www.metropolitancollege.edu

Metropolitan College, www.metropolitancollege.edu

Mid-America Christian University, www.macu.edu

Murray State College, www.msc.cc.ok.us

National Education Center: Spartan School of Aeronautics, www.spartan.edu

Northeastern Oklahoma Agricultural and Mechanical College, www.neoam.edu

Northeastern State University, www.nsuok.edu

Northeastern State University: College of Optometry, Tahlequah 74464

Northwestern Oklahoma State University, www.nwalva.edu

Oklahoma Baptist University, www.okbu.edu

Oklahoma Christian University, www.oc.edu

Oklahoma City Community College, www.okccc.edu

Oklahoma City University, www.okcu.edu

Oklahoma City University: School of Law, Oklahoma City 73146

Oklahoma Panhandle State University, www.opsu.edu

Oklahoma State University, www.okstate.edu

Oklahoma State University: College of Osteopathic Medicine, Tulsa 74107

Oklahoma State University: College of Veterinary Medicine, Stillwater 74078

Oklahoma State University: Oklahoma City, www.osuokc.edu

Oklahoma State University: Okmulgee, www.osu-okmulgee.edu

Oklahoma Wesleyan University, www.okwu.edu

Oral Roberts University, www.oru.edu

Phillips Theological Seminary, Enid 73702

Platt College: Tulsa, www.plattcollege.org

Redlands Community College, www.redlandscc.edu

Rogers State University, www.rsu.edu

Rose State College, www.rose.edu

St. Gregory's University, www.stgregorys.edu

Seminole State College, www.ssc.cc.ok.us

Southeastern Oklahoma State University, www.sosu.edu

Southern Nazarene University, www.snu.edu

Southwestern Christian University, www.swcu.edu

Southwestern Oklahoma State University, www.swosu.edu

Southwestern Oklahoma State University School of Pharmacy, Weatherford 73096

Tulsa Community College, www.tulsacc.edu

Tulsa Welding School, www.weldingschool.com

University of Central Oklahoma, www.ucok.edu

University of Oklahoma, www.ou.edu

University of Oklahoma College of Pharmacy, Oklahoma City 73190

University of Oklahoma Health Sciences Center: College of Dentistry, Oklahoma City 73117

University of Oklahoma Health Sciences Center: College of Medicine, Oklahoma City 73104

University of Oklahoma: College of Law, Norman 73019

University of Science and Arts of Oklahoma, www.usao.edu

University of Tulsa, www.utulsa.edu

University of Tulsa: College of Law, Tulsa 74104

Vatterott College, www.vatterott-college.com

Vatterott College: Tulsa, www.vatterott-college.edu

Western College of Southern California, www.platt.org

Western Oklahoma State College, www.wosc.edu

Oregon

Art Institute of Portland, www.aipd.artinstitutes.edu

Blue Mountain Community College, www.bluecc.edu

Central Oregon Community College, www.cocc.edu

Chemeketa Community College, www.chemeketa.edu

Clackamas Community College, www.clackamas.cc.or.us

Clatsop Community College, www.clatsop.cc.or.us

Concordia University, www.cu-portland.edu

Corban College, www.corban.edu

DeVry University: Portland, www.devry.edu

Eastern Oregon University, www.eou.edu

Eugene Bible College, www.ebc.edu

Everest College: Portland, www.everest-college.com

George Fox University, www.georgefox.edu

Lane Community College, www.lanecc.edu

Lewis & Clark College, www.lclark.edu

Lewis and Clark College: Northwestern School of Law, Portland 97219

Linfield College, www.linfield.edu

Linn-Benton Community College, www.linnbenton.edu

Marylhurst University, www.marylhurst.edu

Mount Angel Seminary, www.mtangel.edu/Seminary/Seminary.htm

Mount Hood Community College, www.mhcc.cc.or.us/

Multnomah Bible College, www.multnomah.edu

Multnomah Biblical Seminary, Portland 97220

Northwest Christian College, www.nwcc.edu

Oregon Health & Science University, www.ohsu.edu

Oregon Health Sciences University: School of Dentistry, Portland 97201

Oregon Health Sciences University: School of Medicine, Portland 97201

Oregon Institute of Technology, www.oit.edu

Oregon State University, www.oregonstate.edu

Oregon State University: College of Pharmacy, Corvallis 97331

Oregon State University: College of Veterinary Medicine, Corvallis 97331

Pacific Northwest College of Art, www.pnca.edu

Pacific University, www.pacificu.edu
Pacific University: School of
    Optometry, Forest Grove 97116
Pioneer Pacific College,
    www.pioneerpacific.edu
Pioneer Pacific College: Springfield,
    www.pioneerpacific.edu
Portland Community College,
    www.pcc.edu
Portland State University,
    www.pdx.edu
Reed College, www.reed.edu
Rogue Community College,
    www.roguecc.edu
Southern Oregon University,
    www.sou.edu
Southwestern Oregon Community
    College, www.socc.edu
Treasure Valley Community College,
    www.tvcc.cc
Umpqua Community College,
    www.umpqua.edu
University of Oregon,
    www.uoregon.edu
University of Oregon: School of Law,
    Eugene 97403
University of Portland, www.up.edu
Warner Pacific College,
    www.warnerpacific.edu
Western Conservative Baptist
    Seminary, Portland 97215
Western Oregon University,
    www.wou.edu
Western States Chiropractic College,
    Portland 97230
Willamette University,
    www.willamette.edu
Willamette University: College of Law,
    Salem 97301

Pennsylvania

Academy of Medical Arts and
    Business, www.acadcampus.com
Academy of the New Church, Bryn
    Athyn 19009
Albright College, www.albright.edu
Allegheny College,
    www.allegheny.edu
Allied Medical and Technical Institute,
    www.alliedtech.edu
Alvernia College, www.alvernia.edu
Antonelli Institute of Art and
    Photography, www.antonelli.edu
Arcadia University, www.arcadia.edu
Art Institute of Philadelphia,
    www.aiph.aii.edu
Art Institute of Pittsburgh,
    www.aip.artinstitutes.edu
Baptist Bible College of Pennsylvania,
    www.bbc.edu
Berean Institute,
    www.bereaninstitute.org
Berks Technical Institute,
    www.berks.edu
Biblical Theological Seminary, Hatfield
    19440
Bidwell Training Center,
    www.bidwell-training.org
Bloomsburg University of
    Pennsylvania, www.bloomu.edu
Bradley Academy for the Visual Arts,
    www.aiba.artinstitutes.edu
Bryn Athyn College of the New
    Church, www.brynathyn.edu
Bryn Mawr College,
    www.brynmawr.edu
Bucknell University,
    www.bucknell.edu
Bucks County Community College,
    www.bucks.edu
Business Institute of Pennsylvania,
    www.biop.com

Business Institute of Pennsylvania:
    Meadville, www.biop.edu
Butler County Community College,
    www.bc3.edu
CHI Institute: Broomall,
    www.chitraining.com
CHI Institute: Southampton,
    www.chitraining.com
Cabrini College, www.cabrini.edu
California University of Pennsylvania,
    www.cup.edu
Cambria-Rowe Business College,
    www.crbc.net
Cambria-Rowe Business College:
    Indiana, www.crbc.net
Career Training Academy,
    www.careerta.com
Career Training Academy: Monroeville,
    www.careerta.edu
Carlow University, www.carlow.edu
Carnegie Mellon University,
    www.cmu.edu
Cedar Crest College,
    www.cedarcrest.edu
Central Pennsylvania College,
    www.centralpenn.edu
Chatham College, www.chatham.edu
Chestnut Hill College, www.chc.edu
Cheyney University of Pennsylvania,
    www.cheyney.edu
Clarion University of Pennsylvania,
    www.clarion.edu
College Misericordia,
    www.misericordia.edu
Commonwealth Technical Institute,
    www.hgac.org
Community College of Allegheny
    County, www.ccac.edu
Community College of Beaver County,
    www.ccbc.edu
Community College of Philadelphia,
    www.ccp.edu
Consolidated School of Business:
    Lancaster, www.csb.edu
Consolidated School of Business: York,
    www.csb.edu
Curtis Institute of Music,
    www.curtis.edu
DeSales University, www.desales.edu
DeVry University: Ft. Washington,
    www.devry.edu
Dean Institute of Technology,
    www.deantech.edu
Delaware County Community College,
    www.dccc.edu
Delaware Valley College,
    www.devalcol.edu
Dickinson College,
    www.dickinson.edu
Dickinson School of Law, Carlisle
    17013
Douglas Education Center,
    www.douglas-school.com
Drexel University, www.drexel.edu
DuBois Business College,
    www.dbcollege.com
DuBois Business College: Huntingdon,
    dbcollege.com
DuBois Business College: Oil City,
    www.dbcollege.com
Duquesne University, www.duq.edu
Duquesne University: School of Law,
    Pittsburgh 15282
East Stroudsburg University of
    Pennsylvania, www3.esu.edu
Eastern Baptist Theological Seminary,
    Wynnewood 19096
Eastern University, www.eastern.edu
Edinboro University of Pennsylvania,
    www.edinboro.edu
Elizabethtown College,
    www.etown.edu
Erie Business Center, www.eriebc.edu

Erie Business Center South,
    www.eriebc.edu/newcastle
Franklin & Marshall College,
    www.fandm.edu
Gannon University, www.gannon.edu
Geneva College, www.geneva.edu
Gettysburg College,
    www.gettysburg.edu
Gratz College, www.gratzcollege.edu
Grove City College, www.gcc.edu
Gwynedd-Mercy College,
    www.gmc.edu
Harcum College, www.harcum.edu
Harrisburg Area Community College,
    www.hacc.edu
Haverford College,
    www.haverford.edu
Holy Family University,
    www.holyfamily.edu
Hussian School of Art,
    www.hussianart.edu
ICM School of Business & Medical
    Careers, www.icmschool.com
Immaculata University,
    www.immaculata.edu
Indiana University of Pennsylvania,
    www.iup.edu
International Academy of Design and
    Technology: Pittsburgh,
    www.iadtpitt.edu
JNA Institute of Culinary Arts,
    www.culinaryarts.com
Jefferson Medical College of Thomas
    Jefferson University, Philadelphia
    19107
Johnson College, www.johnson.edu
Juniata College, www.juniata.edu
Keystone College, www.keystone.edu
King's College, www.kings.edu
Kutztown University of Pennsylvania,
    www.kutztown.edu
La Roche College, www.laroche.edu
La Salle University, www.lasalle.edu
Lackawanna College,
    www.lackawanna.edu
Lafayette College, www.lafayette.edu
Lake Erie College of Osteopathic
    Medicine, www.lecom.edu
Lancaster Bible College, www.lbc.edu
Lancaster Theological Seminary,
    Lancaster 17603
Lansdale School of Business,
    www.lsb.edu
Laurel Business Institute,
    www.laurelbusiness.edu
Lebanon Valley College, www.lvc.edu
Lehigh Carbon Community College,
    www.lccc.edu
Lehigh University, www.lehigh.edu
Lehigh Valley College,
    www.lehighvalley.edu
Lincoln Technical Institute,
    www.lincolntech.com
Lincoln Technical Institute:
    Philadelphia,
    www.lincolntech.com
Lincoln University, www.lincoln.edu
Lock Haven University of
    Pennsylvania, www.lhup.edu
Lutheran Theological Seminary at
    Gettysburg, Gettysburg 17325
Lutheran Theological Seminary at
    Philadelphia, www.ltsp.edu
Luzerne County Community College,
    www.luzerne.edu
Lycoming College, www.lycoming.edu
Manor College, www.manor.edu
Mansfield University of Pennsylvania,
    www.mnsfld.edu
Marywood University,
    www.marywood.edu
McCann School of Business: Pottsville,
    www.mccannschool.edu

Medical College of Pennsylvania and
    Hahnemann University School of
    Medicine, Philadelphia 19129
Mercyhurst College,
    www.mercyhurst.edu
Messiah College, www.messiah.edu
Metropolitan Career Center,
    www.mccweb-gt.org
Metropolitan Career Center Computer
    Technology Institute,
    www.mccweb-gt.org
Millersville University of Pennsylvania,
    www.millersville.edu
Montgomery County Community
    College, www.mc3.edu
Moore College of Art and Design,
    www.moore.edu
Moravian College, www.moravian.edu
Moravian Theological Seminary,
    www.moravianseminary.edu
Mount Aloysius College,
    www.mtaloy.edu
Muhlenberg College,
    www.muhlenberg.edu
Neumann College,
    www.neumann.edu
New Castle School of Trades,
    www.ncstrades.com
Newport Business Institute,
    www.newportbusiness.com
Newport Business Institute,
    www.newportbusiness.com
Northampton County Area
    Community College,
    www.northampton.edu
Oakbridge Academy of Arts,
    www.oakbridgeacademy.com
Orleans Technical Institute - Center
    City Campus,
    www.orleanstech.org
PJA School, www.pjaschool.com
Peirce College, www.peirce.edu
Penn Commercial Business and
    Technical School,
    www.penncommercial.net
Penn State Abington,
    www.abington.psu.edu
Penn State Altoona, www.aa.psu.edu
Penn State Beaver, www.br.psu.edu
Penn State Berks, www.bk.psu.edu
Penn State Delaware County,
    www.de.psu.edu
Penn State Dubois, www.ds.psu.edu
Penn State Erie, The Behrend College,
    www.pennstatebehrend.psu.edu
Penn State Fayette, www.fe.psu.edu
Penn State Harrisburg,
    www.hbg.psu.edu
Penn State Hazleton, www.hn.psu.edu
Penn State Lehigh Valley,
    www.lv.psu.edu
Penn State McKeesport,
    www.mk.psu.edu
Penn State Mont Alto,
    www.ma.psu.edu
Penn State New Kensington,
    www.nk.psu.edu
Penn State Schuylkill - Capital College,
    www.sl.psu.edu
Penn State Shenango,
    www.shenango.psu.edu
Penn State University Park,
    www.psu.edu
Penn State Wilkes-Barre,
    www.wb.psu.edu
Penn State Worthington Scranton,
    www.sn.psu.edu
Penn State York, www.yk.psu.edu
Pennco Tech, www.penncotech.com
Pennsylvania College of Optometry,
    Philadelphia 19141
Pennsylvania College of Podiatric
    Medicine, Philadelphia 19107

Pennsylvania College of Technology, www.pct.edu
Pennsylvania Highlands Community College, www.pennhighlands.edu
Pennsylvania Institute of Culinary Arts, www.paculinary.com
Pennsylvania Institute of Technology, www.pit.edu
Pennsylvania School of Business, www.pennschoolofbusiness.edu
Pennsylvania State University College of Medicine, Hershey 17033
Philadelphia Biblical University, www.pbu.edu
Philadelphia College of Osteopathic Medicine, Philadelphia 19131
Philadelphia College of Pharmacy and Science: School of Pharmacy, Philadelphia 19104
Philadelphia University, www.philau.edu
Pittsburgh Institute of Aeronautics, www.pia.edu
Pittsburgh Institute of Mortuary Science, www.p-i-m-s.com
Pittsburgh Technical Institute, www.pti.edu
Pittsburgh Theological Seminary, www.pts.edu
Point Park University, www.pointpark.edu
Reading Area Community College, www.racc.cc.pa.us
Reformed Presbyterian Theological Seminary, Pittsburgh 15208
Restaurant School, www.walnuthillcollege.edu
Robert Morris University, www.rmu.edu
Rosedale Technical Institute, www.rosedaletech.org
Rosemont College, www.rosemont.edu
St. Charles Borromeo Seminary - Overbrook, www.scs.edu
St. Charles Borromeo Seminary-Overbrook, Wynnewood 19096
St. Francis University, www.francis.edu
St. Joseph's University, www.sju.edu
St. Vincent College, www.stvincent.edu
St. Vincent Seminary, Latrobe 15650
Schuylkill Institute of Business & Technology, www.sibt.edu
Seton Hill University, www.setonhill.edu
Shippensburg University of Pennsylvania, www.ship.edu
Slippery Rock University of Pennsylvania, www.sru.edu
South Hills School of Business & Technology, www.southhills.edu
Susquehanna University, www.susqu.edu
Swarthmore College, www.swarthmore.edu
Talmudical Yeshiva of Philadelphia, Philadelphia 19131
Temple University, www.temple.edu
Temple University: School of Dentistry, Philadelphia 19140
Temple University: School of Law, Philadelphia 19122
Temple University: School of Medicine, Philadelphia 19122
Temple University: School of Pharmacy, Philadelphia 19104
Thaddeus Stevens College of Technology, www.stevenstech.org
Thiel College, www.thiel.edu

Thomas Jefferson University: College of Health Professions, www.jefferson.edu/jchp
Thompson Institute, www.thompson.edu
Thompson Institute: Philadelphia, www.thompson.edu
Tri-State Business Institute, www.tsbi.edu
Triangle Tech: DuBois, www.triangle-tech.edu
Triangle Tech: Erie, www.triangle-tech.edu
Triangle Tech: Greensburg, www.triangle-tech.edu
Triangle Tech: Pittsburgh, www.triangle-tech.edu
Trinity Episcopal School for Ministry, www.tesm.edu
University of Pennsylvania, www.upenn.edu
University of Pennsylvania Law School, www.law.upenn.edu
University of Pennsylvania: School of Dental Medicine, Philadelphia 19104
University of Pennsylvania: School of Medicine, Philadelphia 19104
University of Pennsylvania: School of Veterinary Medicine, Philadelphia 19104
University of Pittsburgh, www.pitt.edu
University of Pittsburgh at Bradford, www.upb.pitt.edu
University of Pittsburgh at Greensburg, www.upg.pitt.edu
University of Pittsburgh at Johnstown, www.upj.pitt.edu
University of Pittsburgh at Titusville, www.upt.pitt.edu
University of Pittsburgh: School of Dental Medicine, Pittsburgh 15261
University of Pittsburgh: School of Law, Pittsburgh 15260
University of Pittsburgh: School of Medicine, Pittsburgh 15261
University of Pittsburgh: School of Pharmacy, Pittsburgh 15261
University of Scranton, www.scranton.edu
University of the Arts, www.uarts.edu
University of the Sciences in Philadelphia, www.usip.edu
Ursinus College, www.ursinus.edu
Valley Forge Christian College, www.vfcc.edu
Valley Forge Military College, www.vfmac.edu
Vet Tech Institute, www.vettechinstitute.com
Villanova University, www.villanova.edu
Villanova University: School of Law, www.law.vill.edu
Washington and Jefferson College, www.washjeff.edu
Waynesburg College, www.waynesburg.edu
West Chester University of Pennsylvania, www.wcupa.edu
West Virginia Career Institute, www.wvci.edu
Western School of Health and Business Careers, www.westernschoolpitt.com
Western School of Health and Business Careers: Monroeville, www.wshb-monroeville.com
Westminster College, www.westminster.edu
Westminster Theological Seminary, Philadelphia 19118

Westmoreland County Community College, www.wccc-pa.edu
Widener University, www.widener.edu
Widener University School of Law, www.law.widener.edu
Wilkes University, www.wilkes.edu
Williamson Free School of Mechanical Trades, www.williamson.edu
Wilson College, www.wilson.edu
Yeshivath Beth Moshe, Scranton 18505
York College of Pennsylvania, www.ycp.edu
York Technical Institute, www.yti.edu
Yorktowne Business Institute, www.ybi.edu

Puerto Rico

American University of Puerto Rico, www.aupr.edu
Atlantic College, www.atlanticcollege-pr.com
Bayamon Central University, www.ucb.edu.pr
Columbia College, www.columbiaco.edu
Conservatory of Music of Puerto Rico, www.cmpr.edu
Electronic Data Processing College: San Sebastian, San Sebastian 00685
Evangelical Seminary of Puerto Rico, San Juan 00925
Humacao Community College, www.humacaocommunitycollege.com
Inter American University of Puerto Rico School of Optometry, San Juan 00919
Inter American University of Puerto Rico: Aguadilla Campus, www.aguadilla.inter.edu
Inter American University of Puerto Rico: Arecibo Campus, www.arecibo.inter.edu
Inter American University of Puerto Rico: Barranquitas Campus, www.br.inter.edu
Inter American University of Puerto Rico: Bayamon Campus, www.bc.inter.edu
Inter American University of Puerto Rico: Fajardo Campus, fajardo.inter.edu
Inter American University of Puerto Rico: Guayama Campus, www.inter.edu
Inter American University of Puerto Rico: Ponce Campus, ponce.inter.edu
Inter American University of Puerto Rico: San German Campus, www.sg.inter.edu
Inter American University of Puerto Rico: School of Law, www.derecho.inter.edu
National College of Business & Technology: Arecibo, www.nationalcollegepr.edu
National College of Business & Technology: Bayamon, www.nationalcollegepr.edu
Ponce School of Medicine, Ponce 00732
Pontifical Catholic University of Puerto Rico, www.pucpr.edu
Pontifical Catholic University of Puerto Rico: School of Law, Ponce 00731
Turabo University, www.suagm.edu/ut
Universidad Adventista de las Antillas, www.uaa.edu

Universidad Central del Caribe: Medical School, Bayamon 00960
Universidad Metropolitana, www.suagm.edu/umet
Universidad Politecnica de Puerto Rico, www.pupr.edu
Universidad del Este, www.suagm.edu
University College of San Juan, www.cunisanjuan.edu
University of Puerto Rico Medical Sciences Campus: School of Dentistry, Rio Piedras 00936
University of Puerto Rico Medical Sciences Campus: School of Medicine, Rio Piedras 00936
University of Puerto Rico Medical Sciences Campus: School of Pharmacy, San Juan 00936
University of Puerto Rico Rio Piedras Campus: School of Law, Rio Piedras 00931
University of Puerto Rico: Aguadilla, www.uprag.edu
University of Puerto Rico: Arecibo, www.upra.edu
University of Puerto Rico: Bayamon University College, www.uprb.edu
University of Puerto Rico: Carolina Regional College, www.uprc.edu
University of Puerto Rico: Cayey University College, www.cayey.upr.edu
University of Puerto Rico: Humacao, www.uprh.edu
University of Puerto Rico: Mayaguez, www.uprm.edu
University of Puerto Rico: Ponce, upr-ponce.upr.edu
University of Puerto Rico: Rio Piedras, www.rrp.upr.edu
University of Puerto Rico: Utuado, http://upr-utuado.upr.clu.edu/
University of the Sacred Heart, www.sagrado.edu

Rhode Island

Brown University, www.brown.edu
Brown University: School of Medicine, Providence 02912
Bryant University, www.bryant.edu
Community College of Rhode Island, www.ccri.edu
Johnson & Wales University, www.jwu.edu
New England Institute of Technology, www.neit.edu
Providence College, www.providence.edu
Rhode Island College, www.ric.edu
Rhode Island School of Design, www.risd.edu
Roger Williams University, www.rwu.edu
Salve Regina University, www.salve.edu
University of Rhode Island, www.uri.edu
University of Rhode Island: College of Pharmacy, www.uri.edu/pharmacy/
Zion Bible Institute, www.zbc.edu

South Carolina

Aiken Technical College, www.atc.edu
Allen University, www.allenuniversity.edu
Anderson University, www.ac.edu
Benedict College, www.benedict.edu
Central Carolina Technical College, www.cctech.edu

Charleston Southern University, www.csuniv.edu
The Citadel, www.citadel.edu
Claflin University, www.claflin.edu
Clemson University, www.clemson.edu
Coastal Carolina University, www.coastal.edu
Coker College, www.coker.edu
College of Charleston, www.cofc.edu
Columbia Biblical Seminary and Graduate School of Missions, Columbia 29230
Columbia College, www.columbiacollegesc.edu
Columbia International University, www.ciu.edu
Converse College, www.converse.edu
Denmark Technical College, www.denmarktech.edu
Erskine College, www.erskine.edu
Erskine Theological Seminary, www.erskine.edu/seminary/
Florence-Darlington Technical College, www.fdtc.edu
Forrest Junior College, www.forrestcollege.edu
Francis Marion University, www.fmarion.edu
Furman University, www.furman.edu
Greenville Technical College, www.greenvilletech.com
Horry-Georgetown Technical College, www.hgtc.edu
Lander University, www.lander.edu
Limestone College, www.limestone.edu
Lutheran Theological Southern Seminary, Columbia 29203
Medical University of South Carolina, www.musc.edu
Medical University of South Carolina, Charleston 29425
Medical University of South Carolina: College of Dental Medicine, Charleston 29425
Medical University of South Carolina: College of Pharmacy, Charleston 29425
Midlands Technical College, www.midlandstech.edu
Miller-Motte Technical College, www.miller-motte.net
Morris College, www.morris.edu
Newberry College, www.newberry.edu
North Greenville College, www.ngc.edu
Northeastern Technical College, www.netc.edu
Orangeburg-Calhoun Technical College, www.octech.edu
Piedmont Technical College, www.ptc.edu
Presbyterian College, www.presby.edu
Sherman College of Straight Chiropractic, Spartanburg 29304
South Carolina State University, www.scsu.edu
South University, www.southuniversity.com
Southern Wesleyan University, www.swu.edu
Spartanburg Methodist College, www.smcsc.edu
Spartanburg Technical College, www.stcsc.edu
Technical College of the Lowcountry, www.tcl.edu
Tri-County Technical College, www.tctc.edu
Trident Technical College, www.tridenttech.edu

University of South Carolina, www.sc.edu
University of South Carolina Upstate, www.uscupstate.edu
University of South Carolina at Aiken, www.usca.edu
University of South Carolina at Beaufort, www.uscb.edu
University of South Carolina at Lancaster, www.usclancaster.sc.edu
University of South Carolina at Sumter, www.uscsumter.edu
University of South Carolina at Union, http://uscunion.sc.edu
University of South Carolina: Salkehatchie Regional Campus, www.uscsalkehatchie.sc.edu
University of South Carolina: School of Law, www.law.sc.edu
University of South Carolina: School of Medicine, www.med.sc.edu
University of South Carolina: School of Pharmacy, Columbia 29208
Voorhees College, www.voorhees.edu
Williamsburg Technical College, www.wiltech.edu
Winthrop University, www.winthrop.edu
Wofford College, www.wofford.edu
York Technical College, www.yorktech.com

South Dakota

Augustana College, www.augie.edu
Black Hills State University, www.bhsu.edu
Dakota State University, www.dsu.edu
Dakota Wesleyan University, www.dwu.edu
Kilian Community College, www.kilian.edu
Lake Area Technical Institute, www.lati.tec.sd.us
Mitchell Technical Institute, www.mitchelltech.com
Mount Marty College, www.mtmc.edu
North American Baptist Seminary, www.nabs.edu
Northern State University, www.northern.edu
Oglala Lakota College, www.olc.edu
Presentation College, www.presentation.edu
Sisseton Wahpeton College, www.swc.tc
South Dakota School of Mines and Technology, www.sdsmt.edu
South Dakota State University, www.sdstate.edu
South Dakota State University: College of Pharmacy, Brookings 57007
Southeast Technical Institute, www.southeasttech.com
University of Sioux Falls, www.usiouxfalls.edu
University of South Dakota, www.usd.edu
University of South Dakota: School of Law, www.usd.edu/law/
University of South Dakota: School of Medicine, www.usd.edu/med
Western Dakota Technical Institute, www.westerndakotatech.org

Tennessee

American Baptist College of ABT Seminary, www.abcnash.edu
Aquinas College, www.aquinas-tn.edu
Austin Peay State University, www.apsu.edu

Belmont University, www.belmont.edu
Bethel College, www.bethel-college.edu
Bryan College, www.bryan.edu
Carson-Newman College, www.cn.edu
Chattanooga State Technical Community College, www.chattanoogastate.edu
Christian Brothers University, www.cbu.edu
Church of God School of Theology, Cleveland 37320
Cleveland State Community College, www.clevelandstatecc.edu
Columbia State Community College, www.columbiastate.edu
Crichton College, www.crichton.edu
Cumberland University, www.cumberland.edu
Dyersburg State Community College, www.dscc.edu
East Tennessee State University, www.etsu.edu
East Tennessee State University: James H. Quillen College of Medicine, com.etsu.edu
Emmanuel School of Religion, www.esr.edu
Fisk University, www.fisk.edu
Free Will Baptist Bible College, www.fwbbc.edu
Freed-Hardeman University, www.fhu.edu
Harding University Graduate School of Religion, www.hugsr.edu
Hiwassee College, www.hiwassee.edu
Jackson State Community College, www.jscc.edu
John A. Gupton College, www.guptoncollege.com
Johnson Bible College, www.jbc.edu
King College, www.king.edu
Lambuth University, www.lambuth.edu
LeMoyne-Owen College, www.loc.edu
Lee University, www.leeuniversity.edu
Lincoln Memorial University, www.lmunet.edu
Lipscomb University, www.lipscomb.edu
Martin Methodist College, www.martinmethodist.edu
Maryville College, www.maryvillecollege.edu
Meharry Medical College: School of Dentistry, dentistry.mmc.edu
Meharry Medical College: School of Medicine, medical.mmc.edu
Memphis College of Art, www.mca.edu
Memphis Theological Seminary, www.mtscampus.edu
Mid-America Baptist Theological Seminary, www.mabts.edu
Middle Tennessee State University, www.mtsu.edu
Miller-Motte Technical College, www.miller-motte.com/clarksvillemain.html
Milligan College, www.milligan.edu
Motlow State Community College, www.mscc.cc.tn.us
Nashville State Community College, www.nscc.edu
National College of Business & Technology: Tennessee, www.ncbt.edu
Northeast State Technical Community College, www.NortheastState.edu
Nossi College of Art, www.nossi.com
O'More College of Design, www.omorecollege.edu

Pellissippi State Technical Community College, www.pstcc.edu
Rhodes College, www.rhodes.edu
Roane State Community College, www.roanestate.edu
South College, www.southcollegetn.edu
Southern Adventist University, www.southern.edu
Southern College of Optometry, www.sco.edu
Southwest Tennessee Community College, www.southwest.tn.edu
Temple Baptist Seminary: Theological Professions, www.templebaptistseminary.edu
Tennessee State University, www.tnstate.edu
Tennessee Technological University, www.tntech.edu
Tennessee Temple University, www.tntemple.edu
Tennessee Wesleyan College, www.twcnet.edu
Trevecca Nazarene University, www.trevecca.edu
Tusculum College, www.tusculum.edu
Union University, www.uu.edu
University of Memphis, www.memphis.edu
University of Memphis: School of Law, www.law.memphis.edu
University of Tennessee College of Law, www.law.utk.edu
University of Tennessee Knoxville: College of Veterinary Medicine, www.vet.utk.edu
University of Tennessee Memphis: College of Dentistry, www.utmem.edu/dentistry
University of Tennessee Memphis: College of Medicine, www.utmem.edu/medicine
University of Tennessee Memphis: College of Pharmacy, pharmacy.utmem.edu
University of Tennessee: Chattanooga, www.utc.edu
University of Tennessee: Knoxville, www.tennessee.edu
University of Tennessee: Martin, www.utm.edu
University of the South, www.sewanee.edu
University of the South: School of Theology, theology.sewanee.edu
Vanderbilt University, www.vanderbilt.edu
Vanderbilt University: School of Law, www.law.vanderbilt.edu
Vanderbilt University: School of Medicine, www.mc.vanderbilt.edu/medschool
Vanderbilt University: The Divinity School, divinity.library.vanderbilt.edu/div
Volunteer State Community College, www.volstate.edu
Walters State Community College, www.ws.edu
Williamson Christian College, www.williamsoncc.edu

Texas

ATI Career Training Center, http://ati.edu-search.com/
Abilene Christian University, www.acu.edu
Abilene Christian University: College of Biblical and Family Studies, www.acu.edu/academics/cbs

Alvin Community College,
www.alvincollege.edu
Amarillo College, www.actx.edu
Amberton University,
www.amberu.edu
Angelina College, www.angelina.edu
Angelo State University,
www.angelo.edu
Arlington Baptist College,
www.abconline.edu
Art Institute of Dallas, www.aid.edu
Art Institute of Houston,
www.aih.artinstitutes.edu
Austin Business College,
www.abctx.edu
Austin College,
www.austincollege.edu
Austin Community College,
www.austincc.edu
Austin Graduate School of Theology,
www.austingrad.edu
Austin Presbyterian Theological
Seminary,
www.austinseminary.edu
Baptist Missionary Association
Theological Seminary, bmats.edu
Baptist Missionary Association
Theological Seminary,
www.bmats.edu
Baptist University of the Americas, San
Antonio 78224
Baylor College of Medicine,
www.bcm.edu
Baylor University, www.baylor.edu
Baylor University: School of Law,
law.baylor.edu
Blinn College, www.blinn.edu
Brazosport College,
www.brazosport.edu
Brookhaven College,
www.brookhavencollege.edu
Cedar Valley College,
www.cedarvalleycollege.edu
Central Texas College, www.ctcd.edu
Cisco Junior College,
www.cisco.cc.tx.us
Clarendon College,
www.clarendoncollege.edu
Coastal Bend College,
www.coastalbend.edu
College of Biblical Studies-Houston,
www.cbshouston.edu
College of Saint Thomas More,
www.cstm.edu
College of the Mainland,
www.com.edu
Collin County Community College
District, www.ccccd.edu
Commonwealth Institute of Funeral
Service,
www.commonwealthinst.org
Concordia University at Austin,
www.concordia.edu
Court Reporting Institute of Dallas,
www.crid.com
Criswell College, www.criswell.edu
Dallas Baptist University,
www.dbu.edu
Dallas Christian College,
www.dallas.edu
Dallas Institute of Funeral Service,
www.dallasinstitute.edu
DeVry University: Irving,
www.devry.edu
Del Mar College, www.delmar.edu
East Texas Baptist University,
www.etbu.edu
Eastfield College, www.efc.dcccd.edu
El Centro College,
www.elcentrocollege.edu
El Paso Community College,
www.epcc.edu
Episcopal Theological Seminary of the
Southwest, www.etss.edu

Frank Phillips College, www.fpctx.edu
Galveston College, www.gc.edu
Grayson County College,
www.grayson.edu
Hallmark Institute of Aeronautics,
www.hallmarkinstitute.com
Hallmark Institute of Technology,
www.hallmarkinstitute.com
Hardin-Simmons University,
www.hsutx.edu
Hill College, www.hillcollege.edu
Houston Baptist University,
www.hbu.edu
Houston Community College System,
www.hccs.edu
Houston Graduate School of Theology,
Houston 77004
Howard College,
www.howardcollege.edu
Howard Payne University,
www.hputx.edu
Huston-Tillotson College,
www.htu.edu
Jacksonville College,
www.jacksonville-college.edu
Jarvis Christian College,
www.jarvis.edu
Kilgore College, www.kilgore.edu
Lamar State College at Orange,
www.lsco.edu
Lamar State College at Port Arthur,
www.lamarpa.edu
Lamar University, www.lamar.edu
Laredo Community College,
www.laredo.edu
LeTourneau University, www.letu.edu
Lee College, www.lee.edu
Lon Morris College,
www.lonmorris.edu
Lubbock Christian University,
www.lcu.edu
MTI College of Business and
Technology, www.mti-tex.com
MTI College of Business and
Technology, www.mti.edu
McLennan Community College,
www.mclennan.edu
McMurry University, www.mcm.edu
Midland College, www.midland.edu
Midwestern State University,
www.mwsu.edu
Mountain View College,
www.mvc.dcccd.edu
Navarro College, www.nav.cc.tx.us
North Central Texas College,
www.nctc.edu
North Harris Montgomery
Community College District,
www.nhmccd.edu
North Lake College,
www.northlakecollege.edu
Northeast Texas Community College,
www.ntcc.edu
Northwest Vista College,
www.accd.edu/nvc
Northwood University: Texas Campus,
www.northwood.edu
Oblate School of Theology,
www.ost.edu
Odessa College, www.odessa.edu
Our Lady of the Lake University of San
Antonio, www.ollusa.edu
Palo Alto College, www.accd.edu
Panola College, www.panola.edu
Paris Junior College,
www.paris.cc.tx.us
Parker College of Chiropractic,
www.parkercc.edu
Paul Quinn College, www.pqc.edu
Prairie View A&M University,
www.pvamu.edu
Ranger College, www.ranger.cc.tx.us
Remington College: Dallas,
www.educationamerica.com

Remington College: Fort Worth,
www.remingtoncollege.edu
Remington College: Houston,
www.remingtoncollege.edu
Rice University, www.rice.edu
Richland College, www.rlc.dcccd.edu
St. Edward's University,
www.stedwards.edu
St. Mary's University,
www.stmarytx.edu
St. Mary's University: School of Law,
www.stmarytx.edu/law
St. Philip's College,
www.accd.edu/spc
Sam Houston State University,
www.shsu.edu
San Antonio College,
www.accd.edu/sac
San Jacinto College: Central Campus,
www.sjcd.edu
San Jacinto College: North,
www.sjcd.edu
Schreiner University,
www.schreiner.edu
South Plains College,
www.southplainscollege.edu
South Texas College,
www.southtexascollege.edu
South Texas College of Law,
www.stcl.edu
Southern Methodist University,
www.smu.edu
Southern Methodist University:
Perkins School of Theology,
www.smu.edu/theology
Southern Methodist University: School
of Law, www.law.smu.edu
Southwest Texas Junior College,
www.swtjc.cc.tx.us
Southwestern Adventist University,
www.swau.edu
Southwestern Assemblies of God
University, www.sagu.edu
Southwestern Baptist Theological
Seminary: Theological
Professions, www.swbts.edu
Southwestern Christian College,
www.swcc.edu
Southwestern University,
www.southwestern.edu
Stephen F. Austin State University,
www.sfasu.edu
Sul Ross State University,
www.sulross.edu
Tarleton State University,
www.tarleton.edu
Tarrant County College,
www.tccd.edu
Temple College, www.templejc.edu
Texarkana College,
www.texarkanacollege.edu
Texas A&M University, www.tamu.edu
Texas A&M University-Baylor College
of Dentistry,
www.bcd.tamhsc.edu
Texas A&M University-Commerce,
www.tamu-commerce.edu
Texas A&M University-Galveston,
www.tamug.edu
Texas A&M University-Kingsville,
www.tamuk.edu
Texas A&M University-Texarkana,
www.tamut.edu
Texas A&M University: College of
Veterinary Medicine,
www.cvm.tamu.edu
Texas A&M University: Health Science
Center College of Medicine,
medicine.tamu.edu
Texas Chiropractic College,
www.txchiro.edu
Texas Christian University,
www.tcu.edu

Texas Christian University: Brite
Divinity School,
www.brite.tcu.edu
Texas College, www.texascollege.edu
Texas Lutheran University,
www.tlu.edu
Texas Southern University,
www.tsu.edu
Texas Southern University: College of
Pharmacy and Health Sciences,
www.tsu.edu/academics/
pharmacy
Texas Southern University: Thurgood
Marshall School of Law,
www.tsu.edu/academics/law
Texas Southmost College,
www.utb.edu
Texas State Technical College:
Harlingen,
www.harlingen.tstc.edu
Texas State Technical College:
Marshall, www.marshall.tstc.edu
Texas State Technical College: Waco,
www.waco.tstc.edu
Texas State Technical College: West
Texas, www.westtexas.tstc.edu
Texas State University: San Marcos,
www.txstate.edu
Texas Tech University, www.ttu.edu
Texas Tech University Health Sciences
Center, www.ttuhsc.edu
Texas Tech University Health Sciences
Center: School of Medicine,
www.ttuhsc.edu
Texas Tech University: School of Law,
www.law.ttu.edu
Texas Wesleyan University,
www.txwesleyan.edu
Texas Woman's University,
www.twu.edu
Trinity University, www.trinity.edu
Trinity Valley Community College,
www.tvcc.edu
Tyler Junior College, www.tjc.edu
Universal Technical Institute,
www.uticorp.com
University of Dallas, www.udallas.edu
University of Houston, www.uh.edu
University of Houston: Clear Lake,
www.uhcl.edu
University of Houston: College of
Optometry, www.opt.uh.edu
University of Houston: College of
Pharmacy,
www.uh.edu/pharmacy
University of Houston: Downtown,
www.uhd.edu
University of Houston: Law Center,
www.law.uh.edu
University of Houston: Victoria,
www.uhv.edu
University of Mary Hardin-Baylor,
www.umhb.edu
University of North Texas,
www.unt.edu
University of North Texas Health
Science Center at Fort Worth:
Osteopathic Medicine,
www.hsc.unt.edu/education/
tcom
University of St. Thomas,
www.stthom.edu
University of St. Thomas: School of
Theology, Houston 77024
University of Texas Health Science
Center at Houston,
www.uth.tmc.edu
University of Texas Health Science
Center at San Antonio,
www.uthscsa.edu
University of Texas Health Science
Center: Dental School,
www.dental.uthscsa.edu

University of Texas Health Science Center: Medical School, San Antonio 78284

University of Texas Health Sciences Center-Dental Branch, Houston 77030

University of Texas Medical Branch at Galveston, www.utmb.edu

University of Texas Medical Branch at Galveston: School of Medicine, Galveston 77555

University of Texas Southwestern Medical Center at Dallas, www.utsouthwestern.edu

University of Texas Southwestern Medical Center at Dallas Southwestern Medical School, Dallas 75235

University of Texas at Arlington, www.uta.edu

University of Texas at Austin, www.utexas.edu

University of Texas at Austin: College of Pharmacy, Austin 78712

University of Texas at Austin: School of Law, Austin 78714

University of Texas at Brownsville, www.utb.edu

University of Texas at Dallas, www.utdallas.edu

University of Texas at El Paso, www.utep.edu

University of Texas at San Antonio, www.utsa.edu

University of Texas at Tyler, www.uttyler.edu

University of Texas of the Permian Basin, www.utpb.edu

University of Texas-Houston Health Science Center, Houston 77225

University of Texas: Pan American, www.utpa.edu

University of the Incarnate Word, www.uiw.edu

Vernon College, www.vernoncollege.edu

Victoria College, www.victoriacollege.edu

Wade College, www.wadecollege.com

Wayland Baptist University, www.wbu.edu

Weatherford College, www.wc.edu

West Texas A&M University, www.wtamu.edu

Western Technical College, www.wtc-ep.edu

Western Technical Institute: Diana Drive, www.wtc-ep.edu

Western Texas College, www.wtc.edu

Westwood College: Ft. Worth, Fort Worth 76137

Wharton County Junior College, www.wcjc.edu

Wiley College, www.wileyc.edu

Utah

Brigham Young University, www.byu.edu

Brigham Young University: School of Law, Provo 84602

College of Eastern Utah, www.ceu.edu

Dixie State College of Utah, www.dixie.edu

Everest College: Salt Lake City, www.cci.edu

LDS Business College, www.ldsbc.edu

Neumont University, www.neumont.edu

Provo College, www.provocollege.edu

Salt Lake Community College, www.slcc.edu

Snow College, www.snow.edu

Southern Utah University, www.suu.edu

Stevens-Henager College, www.stevenshenager.edu

Stevens-Henager College of Business, www.stevenshenager.edu

University of Utah, www.utah.edu

University of Utah: College of Law, Salt Lake City 84112

University of Utah: College of Pharmacy, Salt Lake City 84112

University of Utah: School of Medicine, Salt Lake City 84132

Utah Career College, www.utahcollege.edu

Utah State University, www.usu.edu

Utah Valley State College, www.uvsc.edu

Weber State University, www.weber.edu

Western Governors University, www.wgu.edu

Westminster College, www.westminstercollege.edu

Vermont

Bennington College, www.bennington.edu

Burlington College, www.burlingtoncollege.edu

Castleton State College, www.castleton.edu

Champlain College, www.champlain.edu

College of St. Joseph in Vermont, www.csj.edu

Community College of Vermont, www.ccv.edu

Goddard College, www.goddard.edu

Green Mountain College, www.greenmtn.edu

Johnson State College, www.jsc.vsc.edu

Landmark College, www.landmark.edu

Lyndon State College, www.lyndonstate.edu

Marlboro College, www.marlboro.edu

Middlebury College, www.middlebury.edu

New England Culinary Institute, www.neci.edu

Norwich University, www.norwich.edu

St. Michael's College, www.smcvt.edu

Southern Vermont College, www.svc.edu

Sterling College, www.sterlingcollege.edu

University of Vermont, www.uvm.edu

University of Vermont: College of Medicine, Burlington 05405

Vermont Law School, South Royalton 05068

Vermont Technical College, www.vtc.edu

Woodbury College, www.woodbury-college.edu

Virginia

Art Institute of Washington, www.aiw.artinstitutes.edu

Averett University, www.averett.edu

Blue Ridge Community College, www.brcc.edu

Bluefield College, www.bluefield.edu

Bridgewater College, www.bridgewater.edu

Bryant & Stratton College: Virginia Beach, www.bryantstratton.edu

Central Virginia Community College, www.cv.cc.va.us

Christendom College, www.christendom.edu

Christopher Newport University, www.cnu.edu

College of William and Mary, www.wm.edu

College of William and Mary: School of Law, Williamsburg 23187

Dabney S. Lancaster Community College, www.dslcc.edu

Danville Community College, www.dcc.vccs.edu

DeVry University: Arlington, www.crys.devry.edu

ECPI College of Technology, www.ecpi.edu

ECPI Technical College: Glen Allen, www.ecpitech.edu

Eastern Mennonite Seminary, Harrisonburg 22801

Eastern Mennonite University, www.emu.edu

Eastern Shore Community College, www.es.vccs.edu

Eastern Virginia Medical School of the Medical College of Hampton Roads: Medical Professions, Norfolk 23501

Emory & Henry College, www.ehc.edu

Ferrum College, www.ferrum.edu

George Mason University, www.gmu.edu

George Mason University: School of Law, Arlington 22201

Germanna Community College, www.gcc.vccs.edu

Hampden-Sydney College, www.hsc.edu

Hampton University, www.hamptonu.edu

Hollins University, www.hollins.edu

J. Sargeant Reynolds Community College, www.reynolds.edu

James Madison University, www.jmu.edu

Jefferson College of Health Sciences, www.jchs.edu

John Tyler Community College, www.jtcc.edu

Liberty Baptist Theological Seminary, Lynchburg 24502

Liberty University, www.liberty.edu

Longwood University, www.whylongwood.com

Lord Fairfax Community College, www.lfcc.edu

Lynchburg College, www.lynchburg.edu

Mary Baldwin College, www.mbc.edu

Marymount University, www.marymount.edu

Miller-Motte Technical College: Lynchburg, www.miller-motte.com

Mountain Empire Community College, www.me.vccs.edu

National College of Business & Technology: Bluefield, www.ncbt.edu

National College of Business & Technology: Charlottesville, www.ncbt.edu

National College of Business & Technology: Danville, www.ncbt.edu

National College of Business & Technology: Harrisonburg, www.ncbt.edu

National College of Business & Technology: Lynchburg, www.ncbt.edu

National College of Business & Technology: Martinsville, www.ncbt.edu

National College of Business & Technology: Salem, www.ncbt.edu

New River Community College, www.nr.edu

Norfolk State University, www.nsu.edu

Northern Virginia Community College, www.nv.cc.va.us

Old Dominion University, www.odu.edu

Parks College: Arlington, Arlington 22207

Patrick Henry Community College, www.ph.vccs.edu

Paul D. Camp Community College, www.pc.vccs.edu

Piedmont Virginia Community College, www.pvcc.edu

Potomac College, www.potomac.edu

Protestant Episcopal Theological Seminary in Virginia, Alexandria 22304

Radford University, www.radford.edu

Randolph-Macon College, www.rmc.edu

Randolph-Macon Woman's College, www.rmwc.edu

Rappahannock Community College, www.rcc.vccs.edu

Regent University, www.regent.edu

Regent University: School of Divinity, Virginia Beach 23464

Regent University: School of Law, Virginia Beach 23464

Richard Bland College, www.rbc.edu

Roanoke College, www.roanoke.edu

St. Paul's College, www.saintpauls.edu

Shenandoah University, www.su.edu

Southside Virginia Community College, www.sv.vccs.edu

Southwest Virginia Community College, www.sw.edu

Sweet Briar College, www.sbc.edu

Thomas Nelson Community College, www.tncc.edu

Tidewater Community College, www.tcc.vccs.edu

Tidewater Tech, www.tidetech.com

Union Theological Seminary in Virginia, Richmond 23227

University of Mary Washington, www.umw.edu

University of Northern Virginia, www.unva.edu

University of Richmond, www.richmond.edu

University of Richmond: The T.C. Williams School of Law, University of Richmond 23173

University of Virginia, www.virginia.edu

University of Virginia's College at Wise, www.uvawise.edu

University of Virginia: School of Law, Charlottesville 22903

University of Virginia: School of Medicine, Charlottesville 22908

Virginia Commonwealth University, www.vcu.edu

Virginia Commonwealth University: School of Dentistry, Richmond 23298

Virginia Commonwealth University: School of Medicine, Richmond 23298

Virginia Highlands Community College, www.vhcc.edu

Virginia Intermont College, www.vic.edu

Virginia Military Institute, www.vmi.edu

Virginia Polytechnic Institute and State University, www.vt.edu

Virginia Polytechnic Institute: Virginia-Maryland Regional College of Veterinary Medicine, Blacksburg 24061

Virginia State University, www.vsu.edu

Virginia Union University, www.vuu.edu

Virginia Union University: School of Theology, Richmond 23220

Virginia Wesleyan College, www.vwc.edu

Virginia Western Community College, www.virginiawestern.edu

Washington and Lee University, www.wlu.edu

Washington and Lee University: School of Law, Lexington 24450

World College, www.cie-wc.edu

Wytheville Community College, www.wcc.vccs.edu

Washington

Antioch University Seattle, www.antiochsea.edu

Art Institute of Seattle, www.ais.edu

Bastyr University, www.bastyr.edu

Bates Technical College, www.bates.ctc.edu/

Bellevue Community College, www.bcc.ctc.edu

Bellingham Technical College, www.btc.ctc.edu

Big Bend Community College, www.bigbend.edu

Cascadia Community College, www.cascadia.ctc.edu/

Central Washington University, www.cwu.edu

Centralia College, www.centralia.edu

City University, www.cityu.edu

Clark College, www.clark.edu

Clover Park Technical College, www.cptc.edu

Columbia Basin College, www.columbiabasin.edu

Cornish College of the Arts, www.cornish.edu

Crown College, www.crowncollege.edu

DeVry University: Federal Way, www.sea.devry.edu

DigiPen Institute of Technology, www.digipen.edu

Eastern Washington University, www.ewu.edu

Edmonds Community College, www.edcc.edu

Everett Community College, www.everettcc.edu

Evergreen State College, www.evergreen.edu

Gonzaga University, www.gonzaga.edu

Gonzaga University: Department of Religious Studies, Spokane 99258

Gonzaga University: School of Law, Spokane 99220

Grays Harbor College, www.ghc.edu

Green River Community College, www.greenriver.edu

Henry Cogswell College, www.henrycogswell.edu

Heritage University, www.heritage.edu

Highline Community College, www.highline.ctc.edu

Lake Washington Technical College, www.lwtc.ctc.edu

Lower Columbia College, www.lcc.ctc.edu

North Seattle Community College, www.northseattle.edu

Northwest Aviation College, www.afsnac.com

Northwest College of Art, www.nca.edu

Northwest School of Wooden Boatbuilding, www.nwboatschool.org

Northwest University, www.northwestu.edu

Olympic College, www.olympic.edu

Pacific Lutheran University, www.plu.edu

Peninsula College, www.pc.ctc.edu

Pierce College, www.pierce.ctc.edu

Puget Sound Christian College, www.pscc.edu

Renton Technical College, www.RTC.edu

Saint Martin's University, www.stmartin.edu

Seattle Central Community College, www.seattlecentral.org

Seattle Pacific University, www.spu.edu

Seattle University, www.seattleu.edu

Seattle University: School of Law, Tacoma 98402

Seattle University: School of Theology and Ministry, Seattle 98122

Shoreline Community College, www.shoreline.edu

Skagit Valley College, www.skagit.edu

South Puget Sound Community College, www.spscc.ctc.edu

South Seattle Community College, www.southseattle.edu

Spokane Community College, www.scc.spokane.edu

Spokane Falls Community College, www.spokanefalls.edu

Tacoma Community College, www.tacoma.ctc.edu

Trinity Lutheran College, www.tlc.edu

University of Puget Sound, www.ups.edu

University of Washington, www.washington.edu

University of Washington: School of Dentistry, Seattle 98195

University of Washington: School of Law, Seattle 98105

University of Washington: School of Medicine, Seattle 98195

Walla Walla College, www.wwc.edu

Walla Walla Community College, www.wwcc.edu

Washington State University, www.wsu.edu

Washington State University: College of Pharmacy, Pullman 99164

Washington State University: School of Veterinary Medicine, Pullman 99164

Wenatchee Valley College, www.wvc.edu

Western Washington University, www.wwu.edu

Whatcom Community College, www.whatcom.ctc.edu

Whitman College, www.whitman.edu

Whitworth College, www.whitworth.edu

Yakima Valley Community College, www.yvcc.edu

West Virginia

Alderson-Broaddus College, www.ab.edu

Appalachian Bible College, www.abc.edu

Bethany College, www.bethanywv.edu

Bluefield State College, www.bluefieldstate.edu

Concord University, www.concord.edu

Corinthian Schools: National Institute of Technology, www.cci.edu

Davis and Elkins College, www.davisandelkins.edu

Eastern West Virginia Community and Technical College, www.eastern.wvnet.edu

Glenville State College, www.glenville.edu

Huntington Junior College, www.huntingtonjuniorcollege.edu

Marshall University, www.marshall.edu

Marshall University: School of Medicine, Huntington 25704

Mountain State College, www.mountainstate.org

Mountain State University, www.mountainstate.edu

Ohio Valley University, www.ovc.edu

Potomac State College of West Virginia University, www.potomacstatecollege.edu

Salem International University, www.salemiu.edu

Shepherd University, www.shepherd.edu

Southern West Virginia Community and Technical College, www.southern.wvnet.edu

University of Charleston, www.ucwv.edu

Valley College of Technology, www.vct.edu

West Liberty State College, www.wlsc.edu

West Virginia Business College, www.wvbusinesscollege.com

West Virginia Business College, www.wvbusinesscollege.com

West Virginia Northern Community College, www.northern.wvnet.edu

West Virginia School of Osteopathic Medicine, www.wvsom.edu

West Virginia State University, www.wvstateu.edu

West Virginia University, www.wvu.edu

West Virginia University Institute of Technology, www.wvutech.edu

West Virginia University at Parkersburg, www.wvup.edu

West Virginia University: College of Law, Morgantown 26506

West Virginia University: School of Dentistry, Morgantown 26506

West Virginia University: School of Medicine, Morgantown 26506

West Virginia University: School of Pharmacy, Morgantown 26506

West Virginia Wesleyan College, www.wvwc.edu

Wheeling Jesuit University, www.wju.edu

Wisconsin

Alverno College, www.alverno.edu

Bellin College of Nursing, www.bcon.edu

Beloit College, www.beloit.edu

Blackhawk Technical College, www.blackhawk.edu

Bryant & Stratton College: Milwaukee, www.bryantstratton.edu

Cardinal Stritch University, www.stritch.edu

Carroll College, www.cc.edu

Carthage College, www.carthage.edu

Chippewa Valley Technical College, www.cvtc.edu

College of Menominee Nation, www.menominee.edu

Columbia College of Nursing, www.ccon.edu

Concordia University Wisconsin, www.cuw.edu

DeVry University: Milwaukee, Milwaukee 53202

Edgewood College, www.edgewood.edu

Fox Valley Technical College, www.fvtc.edu

Gateway Technical College, www.gtc.edu

Herzing College, www.herzing.edu

Lakeland College, www.lakeland.edu

Lakeshore Technical College, www.gotoltc.edu

Lawrence University, www.lawrence.edu

Madison Area Technical College, www.madison.tec.wi.us

Maranatha Baptist Bible College, www.mbbc.edu

Marian College of Fond du Lac, www.mariancollege.edu

Marquette University, www.marquette.edu

Marquette University: School of Dentistry, Milwaukee 53201

Marquette University: School of Law, Milwaukee 53233

Medical College of Wisconsin: School of Medicine, Milwaukee 53226

Mid-State Technical College, www.mstc.edu

Milwaukee Area Technical College, www.matc.edu

Milwaukee School of Engineering, www.msoe.edu

Moraine Park Technical College, www.morainepark.edu

Mount Mary College, www.mtmary.edu

Nicolet Area Technical College, www.nicoletcollege.edu

Northcentral Technical College, www.ntc.edu

Northeast Wisconsin Technical College, www.nwtc.edu

Northland College, www.northland.edu

Ripon College, www.ripon.edu

Sacred Heart School of Theology, Hales Corners 53130

St. Francis Seminary, St. Francis 53235

St. Norbert College, www.snc.edu

Silver Lake College, www.sl.edu

Southwest Wisconsin Technical College, www.swtc.edu

University of Wisconsin Madison: School of Law, Madison 53706

University of Wisconsin Madison: School of Medicine, Madison 53706

University of Wisconsin Madison: School of Pharmacy, Madison 53706

University of Wisconsin Madison: School of Veterinary Medicine, Madison 53706

University of Wisconsin-Baraboo/Sauk County, www.baraboo.uwc.edu

University of Wisconsin-Eau Claire, www.uwec.edu

University of Wisconsin-Fond du Lac, www.fdl.uwc.edu

University of Wisconsin-Green Bay,
www.uwgb.edu
University of Wisconsin-La Crosse,
www.uwlax.edu
University of Wisconsin-Madison,
www.wisc.edu
University of Wisconsin-Marathon
County, www.uwmc.uwc.edu
University of Wisconsin-Marinette,
www.marinette.uwc.edu
University of
Wisconsin-Marshfield/Wood
County,
www.marshfield.uwc.edu
University of Wisconsin-Milwaukee,
www.uwm.edu
University of Wisconsin-Oshkosh,
www.uwosh.edu
University of Wisconsin-Parkside,
www.uwp.edu
University of Wisconsin-Platteville,
www.uwplatt.edu
University of Wisconsin-Richland,
www.richland.uwc.edu
University of Wisconsin-River Falls,
www.uwrf.edu
University of Wisconsin-Rock County,
www.rock.uwc.edu
University of Wisconsin-Stevens Point,
www.uwsp.edu
University of Wisconsin-Stout,
www.uwstout.edu
University of Wisconsin-Superior,
www.uwsuper.edu
University of Wisconsin-Waukesha,
www.waukesha.uwc.edu
University of Wisconsin-Whitewater,
www.uww.edu
Viterbo University, www.viterbo.edu
Waukesha County Technical College,
www.wctc.edu
Western Wisconsin Technical College,
www.wwtc.edu
Wisconsin Indianhead Technical
College, www.witc.edu
Wisconsin Lutheran College,
www.wlc.edu

Wyoming

Casper College,
www.caspercollege.edu
Central Wyoming College,
www.cwc.edu
Eastern Wyoming College,
www.ewc.wy.edu
Laramie County Community College,
www.lccc.wy.edu
Northwest College,
www.northwestcollege.edu
Sheridan College, www.sheridan.edu
University of Wyoming,
www.uwyo.edu
University of Wyoming: College of
Law, Laramie 82071
University of Wyoming: School of
Pharmacy, Laramie 82071
Western Wyoming Community
College, www.wwcc.wy.edu
Wyoming Technical Institute,
www.wyotech.com

Also Available
from the College Board